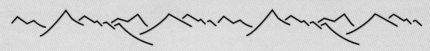

Certified genius.

It's official. The Blended Winglet™ Performance Enhancement System has been certified by the FAA for the Hawker 800 series.

Now you can upgrade your current aircraft with advanced technology Blended Winglets. You'll burn up to 7% in fuel. Boost your range by as much as 180 nautical miles. And dramatically improve second segment climbs.

See what all smart Hawker 800 series owners have been so eagerly anticipating. Call (206) 762-1171 or fly to www.aviationpartners.com.

Aviation Partners, Ir
Leaders in Advanced Winglet Techno

Citation **Sovereign**

Large economy size now available across the Continent.

Try this on for size: True transcontinental range for millions less than anything comparable. Cruise at up to 459 knots (851 km/hr). Operate from runways as short as 1,085 km. And do it in the largest double-club cabin ever created for a traditional midsize aircraft. All told, the Sovereign gives value-conscious business jet enthusiasts far, far more for their money. Size one up for yourself. Contact Trevor Esling, Cessna Aircraft Company,* 17 Thatcham Business Village, Colthrop Lane, Thatcham, Berks RG19 4LW U.K. Tel: +44 (0) 1635 873399. Fax: +44 (0) 1635 873322. Email: tesling@cessna.textron.com. Or visit Sovereign.Cessna.com.

*Incorporated with limited liability in the state of Kansas, U.S.A.

Sure Thing®

Cessna
A **Textron** Company

jp Biz-Jet 2005

& Turboprops

By Brian Gates

38th Edition
ISBN 1-898779-28-7
48 Colour photographs
Published by:
BUCHair (U.K.) Ltd
P.O. Box 89, Reigate, Surrey, RH2 7FG
Tel: +44 (0)1737 224747
Fax: +44 (0)1737 226777
Email: buchair_uk@compuserve.com
Web: www.buchairshop.co.uk

Where to get the products of BUCHair (UK) Ltd, and Bucher & Co Zurich

Australia: Technical Bookshop 295 Swanston Street, Melbourne   VIC 3000, Australia
Phone: (3) 9663 3951   Fax: (3) 9663 2094

Austria: Freytag & Berndt, Reisebuchhandlung, Kohlmarkt 9, A1010 Viena
Phone: (1) 5338685

Canada: Aviation World, 195 Carlingview Drive, Rexdale, Ontario, M9W 5E8
Phone: (416) 674-5959   Fax: (416) 674-5915
Email: avworld@interlog.com   Web www.interlog.com/-avworld

Denmark: Nyboder Boghandel, ApS, 114 Store Kongensgade, DK-1264 Copenhagen K
Phone: 33 32 33 20   Fax: 33 32 33 62

Finland: Aviation Shop, Kajanuksenkatu 12, SF-00250 Helsinki
Phone: (09) 449 801   Fax: (09) 149 6163

France: La Maison Du Livre, 76 Boulevard Malesherbes, F-75008 Paris
Phone: (1) 45 22 74 16   Fax: (1) 42 93 81 23

Ireland: Hughes & Hughes Booksellers, Dublin Airport
Phone: 353 1 844 5808

Italy: La Bancarella Aeronautica S.A.S., Corso Duca Degli Abruzzi 12, I-10128 Torino
Phone: (011) 53 13 41   Fax: (011) 562 93 59

Japan: Nishiyama Yosho Co Ltd, Takin Building 3F, 12 4-7-11 Ginza, Chuo-ku, Tokyo 104
Phone: (03) 3562-0820   Fax: (03) 3562-0828

Netherlands: Boekhandel Venstra B.V., Binnenhof 50, Postbus 77, NL-1180 AB Amstelveen
Phone: (020) 641 98 80   Fax: (020) 640 02 52

Portugal: Ocean Wings, Rua Jose Lins do Rego, 3 - D
1700-262 Lisboa Portugal
Phone: +351 21 793 24 57 email: oceanwings@netcabo.pt

Switzerland: Bucher & Co Publikationen, Postfach 44, CH8058 Zurich Flughafen
Phone: (044)874 1 747   Fax: (044)874 1 757
Email jp@buchair.ch   Web: buchairnet.com
Shop: BUCHairSHOP, Schaffhauserstrasse 76, CH-8152 Glattbrugg
Shop Flughafen: BUCHairSHOP, Terrasse, Terminal B, Zurich Flughafen

South Africa: Mr Karel Zayman, Sky Needs, PO Box 1385, Kempton Park 1620
Phone: (011) 472 32 55   Fax: (011) 792 83 18

Spain: La Aeroteca Libreria Miguel Creus, C/Congost,11 E-08024 Barcelona
Phone: (93) 210 54 07   Fax: (93) 210 59 92

Sweden: Stenvalls, Box 17111, S-20010 Malmo, Sweden

UK: BUCHair UK Ltd, PO Box 89, Reigate, Surrey, RH2 7FG
Phone: 01737 224747   Fax: 01737 226777
Email: buchair_uk@compuserve.com Web: www.buchairshop.co.uk

USA: BUCHair(USA), Inc. PO Box 750515, Forest Hills, NY 11375-0515
Phone: (718) 263 8748   Fax: (718) 275 6190
Email: best_of_flight@buchair.com Web: buchair.com

INTRODUCTION

The following gained their FAA certification during 2004

Cessna 680 Sovereign	2 Jun 04	Cessna 525B CJ-3	15 Oct 04
Cessna Citation XLS	23 Mar 04	Gulfstream G450	12 Aug 04
Raytheon Horizon	27 Dec 04	Global 5000	19 Oct 04
Bombardier Learjet 40	11 Jul 04	Falcon 2000EX EASY	22 Jun 04

IN PRODUCTION

Gulfstream Aerospace	G300/G400, G450 & G550
Bombardier	Global Express, Global 5000
	Challengers 300, 604 & 800
	Learjets 40, 45 & 60
Cessna	Citation CJ-1, CJ-2, CJ-3, Citation X
	Encore, Excel XLS, Bravo & Sovereign
	Mustang
Raytheon	Hawker 400XP, 800XP, Premier 1 & Horizon
Israel Aircraft Industries	Gulfstream G100 & G200
Dassault	Falcons 50EX, 2000, 2000EX EASY, 900C
	& 900EX EASY
Sino Swearingen	SJ30-2
Airbus Industrie & Boeing	Airbus A319CJ, Boeing 737 BBJ & BBJ2
Embraer	EMB-135 Legacy

Raytheon	King Airs C90B, B200 & 350
Pilatus	PC-12/45 & PC-12M
Socata Groupe	TBM 700C
Piaggio	P-180 Avanti
New Piper Aircraft Corp	PA-46-500TP Meridian
IBIS Aerospace	Ae 270

This 38th edition is in the usual format. The Cessna Caravan listing is not included. *against the registration indicates that at the time of going to press it was a reservation only. Mexico & South America continue to present problems with little official data being available. Comments with regard to content, please contact the editor via:
Email: briangatesBizJet @aol.com   15 December 2004

ACKNOWLEDGEMENTS
I am indebted to the following for their invaluable help: Air Britain News, Aviation Letter, Corporate Monthly, Anton Heumann, Pierre Parvaud, Armin Stotter, Warwick Bigsworth, Walter Hager, Jean-Luc Altherr, Paul Suter, Tony Dann, Steve Garner and to many individuals who provided a little but essential data.

Aviation Partners Inc of Seattle provided the front cover of their Hawker 800 Series aircraft illustrating their 'Blended Winglet Performance Enhancement System'.

Biz-Jet Database

If you need more information then call us for a quote.

We can supply a database updated monthly or a simple report.

Data Includes:

Registration
Registration Country
Construction Number
Aircraft Type
Engine Manufacturer
Engine Model
Year of manufacturer
Base of Operation
Operator/Owners Name
Operator/Owners Address
Contact
Telephone Number
Fax Number
Purchase date
History of Aircraft

BUCHair UK Ltd, 78 High Street,
Reigate, Surrey, RH2 9AP
Tele: +44 (0)1737 224747   Fax: +44 (0)1737 226777
Email buchair_uk@compuserve.com

Contents

Business Jets - By Country within Continent   includes Civil And Military

Total Jets	13883

Africa

7T	=	ALGERIA	8
D2	=	ANGOLA	12
A2	=	BOTSWANA	2
XT	=	BURKINA FASO	1
9U	=	BURUNDI	1
TJ	=	CAMEROON	2
TL	=	CENTRAL AFRICAN REPUBLIC	1
TT	=	CHAD	1
TN	=	CONGO BRAZZAVILLE	1
9Q	=	CONGO KINSHASA	4
J2	=	DJIBOUTI	1
SU	=	EGYPT	18
3C	=	EQUATORIAL GUINEA	5
TR	=	GABON	5
9G	=	GHANA	2
TU	=	IVORY COAST	5
5Y	=	KENYA	3
7P	=	LESOTHO	2
5A	=	LIBYA	8
5R	=	MADAGASCAR	4
7Q	=	MALAWI	1
5T	=	MAURITANIA	1
3B	=	MAURITIUS	2
CN	=	MOROCCO	11
V5	=	NAMIBIA	5
5U	=	NIGER	1
5N	=	NIGERIA	39
9X	=	RWANDA	1
S9	=	SAO TOME & PRINCIPE	1
6V	=	SENEGAL	1
ZS	=	SOUTH AFRICA	106
ST	=	SUDAN	4
3D	=	SWAZILAND	3
5H	=	TANZANIA	2
5V	=	TOGO	2
TS	=	TUNISIA	3
5X	=	UGANDA	1
Z	=	ZIMBABWE	1
Total for Continent			**271**

Australasia

VH	=	AUSTRALIA	82
ZK	=	NEW ZEALAND	5
P2	=	PAPUA NEW GUINEA	2

Total for Continent	**89**

Central America

P4	=	ARUBA	38
C6	=	BAHAMAS	3
8P	=	BARBADOS	1
VP-	=	CAYMAN ISLANDS	75
HI	=	DOMINICAN REPUBLIC	1
TG	=	GUATEMALA	4
HR	=	HONDURAS	1
HP	=	PANAMA	3
Total for Continent			**126**

Europe

OE	=	AUSTRIA	96
EW	=	BELARUS	1
OO	=	BELGIUM	27
T9	=	BOSNIA-HERZEGOVINA	1
LZ	=	BULGARIA	2
9A	=	CROATIA	1
5B	=	CYPRUS	7
OK	=	CZECH REPUBLIC / CZECHIA	6
OY	=	DENMARK	45
EI	=	EIRE	8
ES	=	ESTONIA	1
OH	=	FINLAND	15
F	=	FRANCE	175
D	=	GERMANY	241
G	=	GREAT BRITAIN	144
SX	=	GREECE	10
I	=	ITALY	120
YL	=	LATVIA	4
LY	=	LITHUANIA	2
LX	=	LUXEMBOURG	45
Z3	=	MACEDONIA	1
9H	=	MALTA	1
ER	=	MOLDOVA	1
3A	=	MONACO	2
PH	=	NETHERLANDS	20
LN	=	NORWAY	8
SP	=	POLAND	1
CS	=	PORTUGAL	75
YR	=	ROMANIA	1
RA	=	RUSSIA / RUSSIAN FEDERATION	10
S5	=	SLOVENIA	4
EC	=	SPAIN	75

SE	=	SWEDEN	35
HB	=	SWITZERLAND	112
TC	=	TURKEY	34
UR	=	UKRAINE	4
YU	=	YUGOSLAVIA	4

Total for Continent   **1339**

Far East

YA	=	AFGHANISTAN	1
V8	=	BRUNEI	3
XU	=	CAMBODIA	2
B	=	CHINA	37
B-	=	CHINA - HONG KONG	3
B-	=	CHINA - MACAU	2
B	=	CHINA - TAIWAN	3
VT	=	INDIA	33
PK	=	INDONESIA	21
JA	=	JAPAN	77
UN	=	KAZAKHSTAN	2
HL	=	KOREA	19
9M	=	MALAYSIA	11
XY	=	MYANMAR	1
AP	=	PAKISTAN	13
RP	=	PHILIPPINES	17
HS	=	THAILAND	9
EZ	=	TURKMENISTAN	3
UK	=	UZBEKISTAN	1

Total for Continent   **258**

Middle East

A9	=	BAHRAIN	11
EP	=	IRAN	23
YI	=	IRAQ	7
4X	=	ISRAEL	23
JY	=	JORDAN	7
9K	=	KUWAIT	6
OD	=	LEBANON	1
A4	=	OMAN	5
A7	=	QATAR	11
HZ	=	SAUDI ARABIA	71
YK	=	SYRIA	3
A6	=	UNITED ARAB EMIRATES	25
7O	=	YEMEN	2

Total for Continent   **195**

North America

VP-	=	BERMUDA	105
C	=	CANADA	301
XA	=	MEXICO	522
N	=	USA	10208

Total for Continent   **11136**

South America

LV	=	ARGENTINA	59
CP	=	BOLIVIA	4
PP	=	BRAZIL	289
CC	=	CHILE	23
HK	=	COLOMBIA	10
HC	=	ECUADOR	7
ZP	=	PARAGUAY	3
OB	=	PERU	12
YV	=	VENEZUELA	62

Total for Continent   **469**

BizJet Country Index

Country	Code	Page	Country	Code	Page
AFGHANISTAN	YA	210	KOREA	HL	22
ALGERIA	7T	216	KUWAIT	9K	216
ANGOLA	D2	13	LATVIA	YL	210
ARGENTINA	LV	28	LEBANON	OD	184
ARUBA	P4	193	LESOTHO	7P	216
AUSTRALIA	VH	197	LIBYA	5A	214
AUSTRIA	OE	184	LITHUANIA	LY	29
BAHAMAS	C6	9	LUXEMBOURG	LX	29
BAHRAIN	A9C	2	MACEDONIA	Z3	213
BARBADOS	8P	216	MADAGASCAR	5R	215
BELARUS	EW	15	MALAWI	7Q	216
BELGIUM	OO	186	MALAYSIA	9M	216
BERMUDA	VP-B	198	MALTA	9H	216
BOLIVIA	CP	8	MAURITANIA	5T	215
BOSNIA-HERZEGOVINA	T9	196	MAURITIUS	3B	213
BOTSWANA	A2	1	MEXICO	XA	202
BRAZIL	PP	188	MOLDOVA	ER	15
BRUNEI	V8	202	MONACO	3A	213
BULGARIA	LZ	29	MOROCCO	CN	8
BURKINA FASO	XT	210	MYANMAR	XY	210
BURUNDI	9U	217	NAMIBIA	V5	201
CAMBODIA	XU	210	NETHERLANDS	PH	188
CAMEROON	TJ	196	NEW ZEALAND	ZK	211
CANADA	C	3	NIGER	5U	215
CAYMAN ISLANDS	VP-C	200	NIGERIA	5N	215
CENTRAL AFRICAN REPUBLIC	TL	196	NORWAY	LN	27
CHAD	TT	196	OMAN	A4O	1
CHILE	CC	7	PAKISTAN	AP	1
CHINA	B	2	PANAMA	HP	23
CHINA - HONG KONG	B-H	2	PAPUA NEW GUINEA	P2	193
CHINA - MACAU	B-M	2	PARAGUAY	ZP	211
CHINA - TAIWAN	B	3	PERU	OB	184
COLOMBIA	HK	22	PHILIPPINES	RP	194
CONGO BRAZZAVILLE	TN	196	POLAND	SP	194
CONGO KINSHASA	9Q	216	PORTUGAL	CS	8
CROATIA	9A	216	QATAR	A7	1
CYPRUS	5B	214	ROMANIA	YR	210
CZECH REPUBLIC / CZECHIA	OK	186	RUSSIA / RUSSIAN FEDERATION	RA	193
DENMARK	OY	187	RWANDA	9XR	217
DJIBOUTI	J2	27	SAO TOME & PRINCIPE	S9	195
DOMINICAN REPUBLIC	HI	22	SAUDI ARABIA	HZ	23
ECUADOR	HC	22	SENEGAL	6V	215
EGYPT	SU	195	SLOVENIA	S5	195
EIRE	EI	14	SOUTH AFRICA	ZS	212
EQUATORIAL GUINEA	3C	213	SPAIN	EC	13
ESTONIA	ES	15	SUDAN	ST	194
FINLAND	OH	186	SWAZILAND	3D	213
FRANCE	F	15	SWEDEN	SE	194
GABON	TR	196	SWITZERLAND	HB	20
GERMANY	D	9	SYRIA	YK	210
GHANA	9G	216	TANZANIA	5H	215
GREAT BRITAIN	G	18	THAILAND	HS	23
GREECE	SX	195	TOGO	5V	215
GUATEMALA	TG	196	TUNISIA	TS	196
HONDURAS	HR	23	TURKEY	TC	195
INDIA	VT	201	TURKMENISTAN	EZ	15
INDONESIA	PK	188	UGANDA	5X	215
IRAN	EP	15	UKRAINE	UR	197
IRAQ	YI	210	UNITED ARAB EMIRATES	A6	1
ISRAEL	4X	214	USA	N	29
ITALY	I	24	UZBEKISTAN	UK	197
IVORY COAST	TU	196	VENEZUELA	YV	210
JAPAN	JA	26	YEMEN	7O	215
JORDAN	JY	27	YUGOSLAVIA	YU	210
KAZAKHSTAN	UN	197	ZIMBABWE	Z	211
KENYA	5Y	215			

Business Jets - By Country

AP = PAKISTAN   Total   13

Civil

Reg	Yr	Type	c/n	Owner/Operator	Prev Regn
☐ AP-...	98	Citation Excel	560-5004		N504BM
☐ AP-BEH	92	B 737-33A	25504	Government of Pakistan, Karachi.	
☐ AP-BEK	92	Learjet 31A	31A-062	Government of Baluchistan, Quetta.	N25997
☐ AP-BEX	93	Beechjet 400A	RK-80	Government of Punjab, Lahore.	N8180Q
☐ AP-BGI	71	HS 125/400B	25269	Royal Airlines Pvt Ltd. Karachi.	EX-269
☐ AP-BNO	04	Hawker 400XP	RK-392	Government of Punjab, Lahore.	N36792

Military

Reg	Yr	Type	c/n	Owner/Operator	Prev Regn
☐ 0233	93	Citation V	560-0233	Pakistan Army, Qasimaab, Rawalpindi.	N1288A
☐ 1003	01	Citation Bravo	550-1003	Pakistan Army,	N777UU
☐ 68-19635	68	B 707-351C	19635	Pakistan Air Force, Islamabad.	AP-BAA
☐ 68-19866	68	B 707-340C	19866	Pakistan Air Force, Islamabad.	AP-AWY
☐ J 468	82	Falcon 20F	468	Pakistan Air Force, Sargodha. 'Lohdi'	F-WMKG
☐ J 469	82	Falcon 20F	469	Pakistan Air Force, Sargodha. 'Iqbal'	F-WMKI
☐ J 753	72	Falcon 20E	277	Pakistan Air Force, 12 Squadron Chakala, Islamabad.	F-WPXD

A2 = BOTSWANA   Total   2

Civil

Reg	Yr	Type	c/n	Owner/Operator	Prev Regn
☐ A2-MCB	86	Citation S/II	S550-0112	NAC Executive Charter P/L. Gaborone.	N112QS

Military

Reg	Yr	Type	c/n	Owner/Operator	Prev Regn
☐ OK1	91	Gulfstream 4	1173	Government/Botswana Defence Force, Gaborone. 'Puna'	N17587

A4O = OMAN   Total   5

Civil

Reg	Yr	Type	c/n	Owner/Operator	Prev Regn
☐ A4O-AB	91	Gulfstream 4	1168	Government of Oman, Seeb.	N462GA
☐ A4O-AC	92	Gulfstream 4	1196	Government of Oman, Seeb.	N420GA
☐ A4O-OMN	01	B 747-430	32445	Government of Oman, Seeb.	D-ARFO
☐ A4O-SO	79	B 747SP-27	21785	Government of Oman, Seeb.	N351AS
☐ A4O-SP	80	B 747SP-27	21992	Government of Oman, Seeb.	N150UA

A6 = UNITED ARAB EMIRATES   Total   25

Civil

Reg	Yr	Type	c/n	Owner/Operator	Prev Regn
☐ A6-AIN	99	BBJ-7Z5	29268	Government of Abu Dhabi Amiri Flight.	N1786B
☐ A6-AUH	03	BBJ2-8EX	33473	Government of Abu Dhabi Amiri Flight.	N379BC
☐ A6-DAS	00	BBJ-7Z5	29858	Government of Abu Dhabi Amiri Flight.	N1786B
☐ A6-EJA	00	Learjet 60	60-200	Execujet Middle East Ltd. Dubai.	(OY-TCG)
☐ A6-EJB	02	Global Express	9094	Execujet Middle East Ltd. Dubai.	OY-GLA
☐ A6-ELJ	97	Beechjet 400A	RK-140		ZS-OCG
☐ A6-ESH	99	Airbus A319CJ	910	Government of Sharjah.	D-AWFR
☐ A6-HEH	04	BBJ2-8AJ	32825	Dubai Air Wing, Dubai.	N.....
☐ A6-HHH	87	Gulfstream 4	1011	Dubai Air Wing, Dubai.	N17581
☐ A6-HRM	98	B 747-422	26903	Dubai Air Wing, Dubai.	N108UA
☐ A6-HRS	98	BBJ-7EO	29251	Dubai Air Wing, Dubai.	
☐ A6-MMM	98	B 747-422	26906	Dubai Air Wing, Dubai.	N109UA
☐ A6-MRM	01	BBJ2-8EC	32450	Dubai Air Wing, Dubai.	
☐ A6-OME	94	Gulfstream 4SP	1233	Hitech FZE Flight Operations, Dubai.	VP-BFW
☐ A6-RJA	02	Gulfstream G300MPA	1503	The Royal Jet Group, Abu Dhabi.	N403GA
☐ A6-RJB	03	Gulfstream G300MPA	1505	The Royal Jet Group, Abu Dhabi.	N405GA
☐ A6-RJY	99	BBJ-7Z5	29857	The Royal Jet Group, Abu Dhabi.	A6-LIH
☐ A6-RJZ	99	BBJ-7Z5	29269	The Royal Jet Group, Abu Dhabi.	A6-SIR
☐ A6-SMR	79	B 747SP-31	21961	Dubai Air Wing, Dubai.	N58201
☐ A6-SMS	04	Challenger 300	20015	Fujairah Aviation Centre, Fujairah.	N115LJ
☐ A6-UAE		B 747-48E	28551	Dubai Air Wing, Dubai.	V5-NMA
☐ A6-YAS	99	B 747-4F6	28961	Government of Abu Dhabi Amiri Flight.	
☐ A6-ZSN	87	B 747SP-31	23610	Government of Abu Dhabi Amiri Flight.	N60697

Military

Reg	Yr	Type	c/n	Owner/Operator	Prev Regn
☐ 8..	79	Learjet 35A	35A-265	UAE Navy, Naval Aviation Group, Al Bhutein.	G-LEAR
☐ 800	81	Learjet 35A	35A-429	UAE Navy, Naval Aviation Group, Al Bhutein.	G-ZENO

A7 = QATAR   Total   11

Civil

Reg	Yr	Type	c/n	Owner/Operator	Prev Regn
☐ A7-AAF	88	Airbus A310-304	473	Qatari Government Amiri Flight, Doha.	F-ODSV
☐ A7-AAG	98	Airbus A320-232	927	Qatari Government Amiri Flight, Doha.	F-WWBA
☐ A7-AAM	02	Global Express	9126	Qatari Government Amiri Flight, Doha.	C-GZPT

Reg	Yr	Type	c/n	Owner/Operator	Prev Regn

Reg	Yr	Type	c/n	Owner/Operator	Prev Regn
☐ A7-AAN*	05	Challenger 300	20042	Qatari Government Amiri Flight, Doha.	C-G...
☐ A7-CJA	01	Airbus A319-133X	1656	Qatari Government Amiri Flight, Doha.	D-AVYT
☐ A7-CJB	03	Airbus A319-133CJ	2341	Qatari Government Amiri Flight, Doha.	F-W...
☐ A7-GEX	02	Global Express	9134	Qatari Government Amiri Flight, Doha.	C-FZXZ
☐ A7-HHH	03	Airbus A340-541	495	Qatari Government Amiri Flight, Doha.	F-WWTQ
☐ A7-HHJ	00	Airbus A319CJ-133X	1335	Qatari Government Amiri Flight, Doha.	A7-ABZ
☐ A7-HHK	93	Airbus A340-211	026	Qatari Government Amiri Flight, Doha.	F-WWJQ
☐ A7-HJJ	04	Airbus A330-203	487	Qatari Government Amiri Flight, Doha.	F-WWYM

A9C = BAHRAIN — Total 11

Civil

Reg	Yr	Type	c/n	Owner/Operator	Prev Regn
☐ A9C-BA	80	B 727-2M7	21824	Government of Bahrain Amiri Flight. 'Al Bahrain'	N740RW
☐ A9C-BAH	98	Gulfstream 4SP	1353	Government of Bahrain Amiri Flight.	(N555KC)
☐ A9C-BG	77	Gulfstream 2TT	202	Government of Bahrain Amiri Flight.	N17586
☐ A9C-BXA	99	Citation Excel	560-5046	Bexair-Bahrain Executive Air Services, Dubai, UAE.	N966MT
☐ A9C-BXB	00	Challenger 604	5477	Bexair-Bahrain Executive Air Services, Dubai, UAE.	N477AT
☐ A9C-BXC	03	Citation Bravo	550-1050	Bexair-Bahrain Executive Air Services, Dubai, UAE.	N105BX
☐ A9C-BXD	96	Challenger 601-3R	5194	Bexair-Bahrain Executive Air Services, Dubai, UAE.	N601R
☐ A9C-HMH	79	B 747SP-21	21649	Government of Bahrain Amiri Flight. 'Gulf of Bahrain'	A9C-HHH
☐ A9C-HMK	02	B 747-4PB	33684	Government of Bahrain Amiri Flight.	

Military

Reg	Yr	Type	c/n	Owner/Operator	Prev Regn
☐ A9C-BDF	01	BAe 146/RJ-85	E2390	Bahrain Defence Force.	G-3-390
☐ A9C-HWR	97	BAe 146/RJ-85	E2306	Bahrain Defence Force,	EI-CNK

B = CHINA — Total 37

Civil

Reg	Yr	Type	c/n	Owner/Operator	Prev Regn
☐ B-3642	04	Citation Excel XLS	560-5539		N4007J
☐ B-3643	04	Citation Excel XLS	560-5540		N4008S
☐ B-3990	99	Hawker 800XP	8408	DeerJet Aviation Ltd. Beijing.	N30319
☐ B-3991	00	Hawker 800XP	8470	DeerJet Aviation Ltd. Beijing.	N42830
☐ B-3992	00	Hawker 800XP	8501	DeerJet Aviation Ltd. Beijing.	N5001S
☐ B-3993	01	Hawker 800XP	8525	Thai Air Charter, Bangkok.	N4425R
☐ B-3995	01	Hawker 800XP	8526	DeerJet Aviation Ltd. Beijing.	N50626
☐ B-3996	01	Hawker 800XP	8536	DeerJet Aviation Ltd. Beijing.	N51336
☐ B-3997	01	Hawker 800XP	8575	DeerJet Aviation Ltd. Beijing.	N3215M
☐ B-3999	90	Gulfstream 4	1144	Air China Business Jet,	N114GA
☐ B-4005	96	Challenger 800	7138	Government/China United Airlines, Beijing.	C-FZAT
☐ B-4006	96	Challenger 800	7149	Government/China United Airlines, Beijing.	C-FZIS
☐ B-4007	97	Challenger 800	7180	Government/China United Airlines, Beijing.	C-GATM
☐ B-4010	97	Challenger 800	7189	Government/China United Airlines, Beijing.	C-GATY
☐ B-4011	97	Challenger 800	7193	Government/China United Airlines, Beijing.	C-GBFR
☐ B-4018	01	B 737-33A	25502	Government of China, Beijing.	
☐ B-4019	01	B 737-33A	25503	Government of China, Beijing.	
☐ B-4020	95	B 737-34N	28081	Government of China, Beijing.	
☐ B-4021	95	B 737-34N	28082	Government of China, Beijing.	
☐ B-4101	85	Citation S/II	S550-0049	CAAC Special Services Division, Beijing.	N1270K
☐ B-4102	85	Citation S/II	S550-0050	CAAC Special Services Division, Beijing.	N1270S
☐ B-4103	81	Citation II	550-0301	Zhongfei Airlines, Xian.	091
☐ B-4104	82	Citation II	550-0297	Zhongfei Airlines, Xian.	092
☐ B-4105	81	Citation II	550-0305	Zhongfei Airlines, Xian.	090
☐ B-4108	97	CitationJet	525-0204	Broad Air Conditioning/China Southern Airways, Baiyun.	(N323LM)
☐ B-4599	78	Learjet 36A	36A-034		HY-985
☐ B-7019	00	Citation Excel	560-5118	Yuanda Group/China Southern Airways, Balyun.	N1241K
☐ B-7021	01	Citation X	750-0157	CAAC Special Services Division, Beijing.	N52081
☐ B-7022	92	Citation VI	650-0220	CAAC Special Services Division, Beijing.	B-4106
☐ B-7696	01	Challenger 604	5510	Rainbow Jet Co/Shandong Airlines, Jinan.	N511SC
☐ B-7697	01	Challenger 604	5523	Rainbow Jet Co/Shandong Airlines, Jinan.	N552SC
☐ B-8006	03	390 Premier 1	RB-87	DeerJet Aviation Ltd. Beijing.	N6187Q
☐ B-8080	89	Gulfstream 4	1100	DeerJet Aviation Ltd. Beijing.	N100GX
☐ HY-984	85	Learjet 36A	36A-053	Geological Survey, Chinese Government, Beijing.	N39418
☐ HY-986	85	Learjet 35A	35A-601	Geological Survey, Chinese Government, Beijing.	
☐ HY-987	85	Learjet 35A	35A-602	Geological Survey, Chinese Government, Beijing.	
☐ HY-988	85	Learjet 35A	35A-603	Geological Survey, Chinese Government, Beijing.	

B-H = CHINA - HONG KONG — Total 3

Civil

Reg	Yr	Type	c/n	Owner/Operator	Prev Regn
☐ B-HMA	00	Global Express	9063	Jet Aviation, Hong Kong.	N700BD
☐ B-HWB	00	Gulfstream G200	030	HKR International, Hong Kong.	N303MC

Reg	Yr	Type	c/n	Owner/Operator	Prev Regn
☐ B-KMJ	03	Gulfstream G200	090	Metrojet Ltd. Hong Kong.	N790GA

B-M = CHINA - MACAU Total 2

Civil

Reg	Yr	Type	c/n	Owner/Operator	Prev Regn
☐ B-MAC	95	Challenger 601-3R	5178	Jet Asia Ltd. Macau.	CS-MAC
☐ B-MAI	89	Challenger 601-3A	5049	Jet Asia Ltd. Macau.	N888JA

B = CHINA - TAIWAN Total 3

Military

Reg	Yr	Type	c/n	Owner/Operator	Prev Regn
☐ 3701	99	B 737-8AR	30139	Taiwan Air Force, Taipei.	
☐ B-10001	98	B 737-43Q	28492	Taiwan Air Force, Taipei.	B-18675
☐ B-20001	99	Astra-1125SPX	119	AIDC-Aerospace Industrial Development Corp.Taipei.	

C = CANADA Total 301

Civil

Reg	Yr	Type	c/n	Owner/Operator	Prev Regn
☐ C-FABF	86	Citation S/II	S550-0101	Provincial Airlines Ltd. St Johns, NS.	N101QS
☐ C-FACO	90	Citation V	560-0053	Northwestern Utilities Ltd. Edmonton, AB.	C-GCUW
☐ C-FAGU	04	Global Express	9143	Bombardier Inc. Downsview, ON.	
☐ C-FAGV	04	Global Express	9144	Bombardier Inc. Downsview, ON.	
☐ C-FAHN	04	Global Express	9145	Bombardier Inc. Downsview, ON.	
☐ C-FAHQ	04	Global Express	9146	Bombardier Inc. Downsview, ON.	
☐ C-FAHX	04	Global Express	9147	Bombardier Inc. Downsview, ON.	
☐ C-FAIO	04	Global Express	9148	Bombardier Inc. Downsview, ON.	
☐ C-FALI	00	Citation Encore	560-0573	Irving Oil Transport Ltd. Saint John, NB.	N162TF
☐ C-FAMI	01	Citation Encore	560-0566	Image Air Charter Inc. Toronto, ON.	N560BL
☐ C-FAMJ	00	Citation Bravo	550-0931	Omega Air Corp. Vancouver, BC.	N233DW
☐ C-FAUZ	04	Challenger 300	20024	Bombardier Inc. Dorval, PQ.	C-GZDY
☐ C-FAWU	04	Challenger 604	5584	Bombardier Inc. Dorval, PQ.	C-GLXM
☐ C-FBCL	98	Learjet 60	60-133	Aviation CMP Inc. St Georges, PQ.	C-FIDO
☐ C-FBCL	98	Learjet 45	45-024	London Air Services Ltd. Vancouver, BC.'Spirit of London'	N145ST
☐ C-FBCR	93	Challenger 601-3A	5117	Execaire Inc/IMP Group Ltd. Dorval, PQ.	N80BF
☐ C-FBDR	97	Global Express	9003	Skyservice Aviation Inc. Dorval, PQ.	C-FJGX
☐ C-FBEL	84	Challenger 601	3028	Execaire Inc/IMP Group Ltd. Dorval, PQ.	C-GLXB
☐ C-FBFP	75	Learjet 35	35-038	Canada Global Air Ambulance Ltd. Winnipeg, MT.	VH-ELJ
☐ C-FBGX	96	Global Express	9001	ASTOR-Airborne Stand-Off Radar prototype. Ff 3 Aug 01.	
☐ C-FBLJ	96	Learjet 60	60-092	Skyservice Aviation Inc. Dorval, PQ.	N5092R
☐ C-FBLU	02	Learjet 60	60-253	Skyservice Aviation Inc. Dorval, PQ.	C-GIIT
☐ C-FBNS	98	Challenger 604	5364	Bank of Nova Scotia, Toronto, ON.	C-GLXK
☐ C-FBNW	81	Falcon 10	190	Flightexec Corp. London, ON.	N190L
☐ C-FBOC	04	Global 5000	9151	Bombardier Inc. Dorval, PQ.	
☐ C-FBOM	93	Challenger 601-3A	5124	Execaire Inc/IMP Group Ltd-Bank of Montreal, Toronto, ON.	C-GLXD
☐ C-FBPJ	04	Global Express	9153	Bombardier Inc. Dorval, PQ	
☐ C-FBPL	04	Global 5000	9154	Bombardier Inc. Dorval, PQ.	
☐ C-FBPZ	04	Global 5000	9156	Bombardier Inc. Dorval, PQ.	
☐ C-FBQD	04	Global 5000	9157	Bombardier Inc. Dorval, PQ.	
☐ C-FBUR	92	BAe 125/800A	8232	Burmac Corp/Skycharter Ltd. Toronto-Pearson, ON.	N723HH
☐ C-FBVF	81	Falcon 50	48	Skyservice Aviation Inc. Toronto, ON.	N247BC
☐ C-FBYJ	83	Challenger 601	3017	Jim Pattison Industries Ltd. Vancouver, BC.	C-GJPG
☐ C-FCDE	98	Challenger 604	5392	Execaire Inc/IMP Group Ltd. Dorval, PQ.	C-FLPC
☐ C-FCIB	95	Challenger 601-3R	5181	Execaire Inc/IMP Group Ltd. Toronto-Pearson, ON.	N602D
☐ C-FCLJ	85	Learjet 55	55-118	Canada Jet Charters Ltd. Vancouver, BC.	
☐ C-FCNR	99	Learjet 60	60-179	Canadian National Railway Co. Dorval, PQ.	N60LR
☐ C-FCOG	04	Global 5000	9158	Bombardier Inc. Downsview, ON.	
☐ C-FCOI	04	Global Express	9159	Bombardier Inc. Downsview, ON.	
☐ C-FCOJ	04	Global 5000	9160	Bombardier Inc. Downsview, ON.	
☐ C-FCOK	04	Global 5000	9161	Bombardier Inc. Downsview, ON.	
☐ C-FCOZ	04	Global Express	9162	Bombardier Inc. Downsview, ON.	
☐ C-FCPH	04	Global Express	9163	Bombardier Inc. Downsview, ON.	
☐ C-FCRH	92	Citation V	560-0182	Harvard Oil & Gas Inc. Calgary, AB.	N920PM
☐ C-FCSD	04	Challenger 604	5596	Bombardier Inc. Dorval, PQ.	C-GLWR
☐ C-FCSS	83	Citation II	550-0488	Skyservice Aviation Inc. Dorval, PQ.	N84EB
☐ C-FCXJ	04	Challenger 300	20034	Bombardier Inc. Dorval, PQ.	C-GZES
☐ C-FCXL	02	Citation Excel	560-5234	RJM Aviation Ltd/Airsprint, Calgary, AB.	N.....
☐ C-FDAX	91	Astra-1125SP	058	Sobeys Group Inc. Halifax, NS.	N1125E
☐ C-FDBJ	04	Challenger 604	5602	Bombardier Inc. Dorval, PQ.	C-G...
☐ C-FDDD	85	BAe 125/800A	8038	Chartright Air Inc. Toronto-Pearson, ON.	C-GTNT
☐ C-FDIH	04	Challenger 300	20030	Bombardier Inc. Dorval, PQ.	C-GZEM
☐ C-FDIJ	04	Challenger 300	20032	Bombardier Inc. Dorval, PQ.	C-GZEP

Reg	Yr	Type	c/n	Owner/Operator	Prev Regn

Reg	Yr	Type	c/n	Owner/Operator	Prev Regn
C-FDJN	04	Challenger 604	5598	Bombardier Inc. Dorval, PQ.	C-GLWV
C-FDMB	76	Citation	500-0341	M B E Jet Ltd. Red Deer, AB.	C-GVKL
C-FEMA	85	Citation S/II	S550-0040	Manitoba Emergency Aero-Medical Services, Winnipeg, MT.	(N1269D)
C-FEPC	98	Hawker 800XP	8349	Canadian Pacific Railway Co. Calgary, AB.	(N74WF)
C-FETB	61	B 720-023B	18024	Pratt & Whitney Canada Inc. Montreal. PQ. (PW530 testbed).	OD-AFQ
C-FETJ	90	Citation V	560-0082	Canadaian Forest Products Ltd. Vancouver, BC.	N950WA
C-FEXD	76	Falcon 10	78	Flightexec Corp. London, ON.	N199SA
C-FGFI	94	Falcon 900B	138	Grant Forest Products Inc. Mississauga, ON.	VH-FHR
C-FGGH	87	Westwind-1124	431	IMP Group Ltd/Execaire Inc. Toronto-Pearson, ON.	N431AM
C-FGJC	01	Learjet 60	60-210	Aviation CMP Inc. St Georges, PQ.	N700JE
C-FHGC	00	Challenger 604	5453	Jetport Inc. Hamilton, ON.	N453AD
C-FHPM	89	Gulfstream 4	1103	Barrick Gold Corp. Toronto, ON.	N3KN
C-FHRD	99	Hawker 800XP	8460	FHR Real Estate Corp. Toronto, ON.	N810N
C-FHRL	03	Gulfstream G100	150	Jetport Inc. Hamilton, ON.	N750GA
C-FHYL	01	Challenger 604	5506	London Air Services Ltd. Vancouver, 'Spirit of Enterprise'	C-GJFI
C-FICU	79	Learjet 35A	35A-249	Canadian Global Air Ambulance Ltd. Winnipeg, MT.	N300DA
C-FIGD	67	Falcon 20C	109	Government/National Research Council, Ottawa, ON.	117506
C-FIGO	87	BAe 125/800A	8087	Execaire Inc/IMP Group Ltd. Dorval, PQ.	C-GAWH
C-FIMO	84	Citation III	650-0065	AeroPro, Ste Foy, PQ.	N500E
C-FIMP	79	Citation II	550-0113	Services Aeronautiques Saggas International Inc. Dorval, PQ.	C-GDMF
C-FIPE	97	Hawker 800XP	8319	Enbridge Inc. Calgary, AB.	N2291X
C-FJBO	97	Citation Bravo	550-0812	Chartright Air Inc. Toronto-Pearson, ON.	N5223P
C-FJCZ	92	Citation II	550-0700	Department of Transport, Montreal, PQ.	
C-FJGG	94	Learjet 60	60-038	Skyservice Aviation Inc. Toronto, ON.	N638LJ
C-FJJC	91	Challenger 601-3A	5096	Fox Aviation Inc. Dorval, PQ.	C-FNNS
C-FJJG	86	Citation III	650-0116	Fox Aviation Inc. Dorval, PQ.	C-FJJC
C-FJOI	00	Falcon 900EX	69	Future Electronics Inc. Dorval, PQ.	N969EX
C-FJOJ	79	Westwind-1124	271	Fast Air Ltd. Winnipeg, MT.	C-FREE
C-FJWZ	91	Citation II	550-0685	Department of Transport, Ottawa, ON.	(N6778T)
C-FJXN	91	Citation II	550-0684	Department of Transport, Ottawa, ON.	(N6778L)
C-FKCE	91	Citation II	550-0686	Department of Transport, Edmonton, AB.	(N6778V)
C-FKCI	81	Falcon 50	63	Irving Oil Transport Ltd. Saint John, NB.	N48GP
C-FKDX	91	Citation II	550-0687	Department of Transport, Hamilton, ON.	(N6778Y)
C-FKEB	91	Citation II	550-0688	Department of Transport, Ottawa, ON.	(N6779D)
C-FKLB	92	Citation II	550-0699	Department of Transport, Hamilton, ON.	
C-FKMC	73	Citation	500-0073	Klemke Mining Corp. Edmonton, AB.	(N881M)
C-FLPD	80	Citation II	550-0234	AeroPro, Ste Foy, PQ.	N511WC
C-FLZA	92	Citation II	550-0701	Department of Transport, Moncton, NB.	
C-FMCI	97	Citation Bravo	550-0816	Mountain Cabelevision Ltd. Hamilton, ON.	N5225K
C-FMFL	82	Falcon 50	96	McCain Foods Ltd. Florenceville, NB.	N4AC
C-FMFM	92	Citation II	550-0702	Department of Transport, Montreal, PQ.	
C-FMGL	99	Learjet 45	45-088	London Air Services Ltd. Vancouver, BC.'Spirit of Tong'	N454MK
C-FMHL	92	Astra-1125SP	066	Kelowna Flightcraft Air Charter Ltd. Kelowna, BC.	N419MK
C-FNNS	90	Challenger 601-3A	5068	Nortel Networks Ltd. Toronto, ON.	N66NT
C-FNNT	96	Challenger 604	5317	Skyservice Aviation Inc. Toronto, ON.	C-GGPK
C-FNRG	02	Learjet 45	45-223	Hughes Air Corp. Calgary, AB.	(D-CTAN)
C-FONX	70	Falcon 20D	225	Knighthawk Air Express, Hamilton, ON.	N102AD
C-FPCE	00	Hawker 800XP	8500	Sunwest Home Aviation Ltd. Calgary, AB.	C-FPCP
C-FPDO	82	Falcon 50	97	Masonite International Corp. Toronto-Pearson, ON.	N597J
C-FPEL	78	Citation II	550-0042	161768 Canada Inc/Decair, Riviere de Loup, PQ.	N66AT
C-FPRP	81	Learjet 35A	35A-390	Skyservice Aviation Inc. Dorval, PQ.	C-FJEF
C-FPUB	72	Learjet 25B	25B-090	L & C Canada Coastal Aviation Inc. Victoria, BC.	N754CA
C-FPWC	00	Citation Excel	560-5078	Pratt & Whitney Canada Inc. Montreal, PQ.	N5203J
C-FPXD	68	B 727-171C	19859	First Air, Carp, ON.	N1727T
C-FRJZ	97	Astra-1125SPX	087	Jetport Inc. Hamilton, ON.	4X-CUU
C-FROY	87	Westwind-1124	429	Royal Group Technologies Ltd. Toronto, ON.	4X-CUK
C-FRST	01	Citation Bravo	550-1011	Jet-Share Aviation Inc. Toronto, ON.	N51870
C-FSCI	87	BAe 125/800A	NA0406	Shaw Communications Inc. Calgary, AB.	C-FSCY
C-FSDL	04	Learjet 45	45-255	London Air Services Ltd. Vancouver, BC.	N40081
C-FSJR	99	Challenger 604	5413	Shaw Communications Inc. Calgary, AB.	C-GLXM
C-FTDB	99	Astra-1125SPX	117	Partner Jet Inc. Toronto-Pearson, ON.	N528GA
C-FTEN	02	Citation X	750-0188	Telus Communications Ltd. Vancouver, BC.	N5163K
C-FTIL	01	Citation Excel	560-5253	Omega Air Corp. Kelowna, BC.	N73SG
C-FTKX	99	CitationJet CJ-1	525-0364	FlightWx Inc. Waterloo, ON.	N525DE
C-FTMS	81	Citation II	550-0289	Omega Air Corp. Kelowna, BC.	C-FTIL
C-FTOM	81	Citation II	550-0292	Kal Aviation Group Inc. Vernon, BC.	(N63FS)

Reg	Yr	Type	c/n	Owner/Operator	Prev Regn
C-FTOR	96	Citation VII	650-7067	Jet Share Aviation Inc. Toronto, ON.	N502T
C-FUND	95	Challenger 601-3R	5172	ACASS Canada Ltd. Dorval, PQ.	N601FS
C-FURG	86	Challenger 601	3063	Government of Quebec, Sainte-Foy, PQ. (Air Ambulance).	C-GLYH
C-FYMM	95	Citation V Ultra	560-0314	Syncrude Canada Ltd. Fort McMurray, AB.	N314CV
C-FZEI	88	Westwind-Two	441	Chartright Air Inc. Mississauga, ON.	HK-3893X
C-FZOP	75	Falcon 10	44	Air Nunavut Ltd. Iqaluit, NT.	(N90AB)
C-FZQP	78	Learjet 35A	35A-168	Skyservice Aviation Inc. Dorval, PQ.	C-GPDO
C-G...	98	Falcon 50EX	278		N623QW
C-GAAA	82	HS 125/700A	NA0327	LID Brokerage & Realty Co (1977) Ltd. Calgary, AB.	N810SC
C-GAGS	04	Global Express	9141	Bombardier Inc. Downsview, ON.	
C-GAGU	90	BAe 125/800A	NA0450	Agrium Inc. Calgary, AB.	N355WG
C-GAJS	81	Learjet 35A	35A-380	Canadian Global Air Ambulance Ltd. Winnipeg, MT.	N903WJ
C-GAPC	89	Citation V	560-0033	Sunwest Home Aviation Ltd. Calgary, AB.	N4333W
C-GAPT	00	Citation X	750-0131	Centaero Aviation Ltd. Windsor, ON.	N131CX
C-GAPV	91	Citation II	550-0691	Sunwest Home Aviation Ltd. Calgary, AB.	C-GAPD
C-GAWH	03	Challenger 604	5557	Clearwater Fine Foods Inc. Bedford, NS. (600th Challenger).	C-FZSO
C-GAWR	96	Citation V Ultra	560-0351	Execaire Inc/IMP Group Ltd. Winnipeg, MT.	N560DM
C-GAZU	02	Falcon 900C	198	Cathton Holdings Ltd. Edmonton, AB.	N198FJ
C-GBBB	83	Gulfstream 3	368	Chartright Air Inc. Toronto-Pearson, ON.	(N112GS)
C-GBFP	74	Learjet 25B	25B-167	Adlair Aviation (1983) Ltd. Cambridge Bay, NT. 'Ernie Lyall'	
C-GBKB	82	Challenger 600S	1045	Morningstar Air Express, Edmonton. 'Marjorie Morningstar'	N900FC
C-GBLX	03	Global Express	9112	ACASS Canada Ltd. Toronto, ON.	C-GJTP
C-GBNE	78	Citation	500-0378	Province of Manitoba, Winnipeg, MT. (status ?).	N3156M
C-GBNX	90	Citation V	560-0074	Manitoba Provincial Government, Winnipeg, MT.	N593MD
C-GBPM	98	CitationJet	525-0287	Wetcorp Inc. Edmonton, AB.	N73PM
C-GBSW	00	Astra-1125SPX	130	Sobeys Group Inc. Halifax, NS.	N100GA
C-GCDF	00	Challenger 604	5455	Execaire Inc/IMP Group Ltd. Dorval, PQ.	C-GCDS
C-GCFG	84	Challenger 601	3022	NAV Canada, Ottawa, ON.	C-GLXS
C-GCFI	84	Challenger 601	3020	NAV Canada, Ottawa, ON.	C-GLXO
C-GCGS	88	BAe 125/800A	NA0416	Perimeter Aviation Ltd. Winnipeg, MT.	N353WG
C-GCGT	79	Challenger 601	1003	Bombardier Inc. Dorval, PQ. 'Queen of the Fleet'	
C-GCMP	01	Learjet 45	45-153	Aviation CMP Inc. St Georges, PQ.	N30137
C-GCUL	99	Citation X	750-0090	Canadian Utilities Ltd. Edmonton, AB.	N193ZP
C-GCXL	00	Citation Excel	560-5096	Corporate Airlink Ltd. Toronto, ON.	N5202D
C-GDDR	82	Challenger 600S	1048	Pal Air Ltd. Calgary, AB.	C-FSIP
C-GDII	96	Hawker 800XP	8316	Avionair Inc. Dorval, PQ.	N516GP
C-GDJH	80	Learjet 35A	35A-353	Canada Jet Charters Ltd. Vancouver, BC.	N3819G
C-GDKI	93	CitationJet	525-0008	161768 Canada Inc/Decair, Riviere de Loup, PQ.	N1327G
C-GDLR	79	Citation II	550-0062	Sunwest Home Aviation Ltd. Calgary, AB.	(N77SF)
C-GDMI	00	Learjet 45	45-096	Uniform Yankee Juliet Air Inc. Toronto-Pearson, ON.	N5009T
C-GDPF	94	Challenger 601-3R	5145	Power Corp of Canada/Execaire-IMP Group Ltd. Dorval, PQ.	C-GPGD
C-GDSH	03	Citation Encore	560-0647	Derek Stimson Holdings Ltd. Calgary, AB.	N647CE
C-GDSR	80	Westwind-1124	313	Fast Air Ltd. Winnipeg, MT.	N611WW
C-GDWS	95	CitationJet	525-0109	Lindenhome Corp. Edmonton, AB.	N393N
C-GEIV	93	Gulfstream 4SP	1224	Skyservice Aviation Inc. Dorval, PQ.	N124TS
C-GERS	03	Global 5000	9127	Bombardier Inc. Dorval, PQ. (first flight 7 Mar 03).	
C-GESR	83	Challenger 601	3003	Rogers Telecommunications Ltd/Skyservice Aviation, Toronto.	N500TD
C-GFCL	96	Citation V Ultra	560-0346	West Wind Aviation Inc. Saskatoon, SK.	N346CC
C-GFEE	80	Citation 1/SP	501-0169	Jalair S E C, Sherbrooke, PQ.	D-IBWG
C-GGBL	01	Challenger 604	5489	London Air Services Ltd. Vancouver, BC.	N604BD
C-GGFP	91	Falcon 50	227	Grant Executive Jets Inc. Earlton, ON.	(N37LQ)
C-GGMI	01	Falcon 900EX	87	Magna International Inc. Buttonville, ON.	N487MA
C-GGWH	98	Challenger 604	5371	Sunwest Home Aviation Ltd. Calgary, AB.	N371CL
C-GHCY	02	Learjet 45	45-216	Husky Injection Molding Systems Ltd. Toronto, ON.	N5016V
C-GHGC	88	Challenger 601-3A	5019	Sky Service FBO Inc. Toronto, ON.	N575CF
C-GHKY	97	Challenger 604	5343	Husky Injection Molding Systems Ltd. Toronto, ON.	C-GAUK
C-GHML	94	Falcon 900B	141	Flightexec Corp. London, ON.	XA-OVA
C-GHYD	80	Westwind-1124	278	Adler Aviation Ltd. Waterloo Regional, ON.	N10S
C-GIBU	00	Hawker 800XP	8507	Execaire Inc/IMP Group Ltd. Dorval, PQ.	N507BW
C-GIGT	99	Citation X	750-0097	Execaire Inc/IMP Group Ltd. Vancouver, BC.	C-FTEL
C-GINT	94	CitationJet	525-0062	Interforest Ltd. Hanover, ON.	C-FVRE
C-GIOH	89	Challenger 601-3A	5034	Imperial Oil Ltd. Toronto, ON.	C-GLXK
C-GIPX	01	Challenger 300	20003	Bombardier Inc. Dorval, PQ.	
C-GIPZ	03	Challenger 300	20005	Bombardier Inc. Dorval, PQ. (first flight 8 Mar 03).	
C-GIRE	74	Learjet 35	35-004	Skyservice Aviation Inc. Dorval, PQ.	N74MJ
C-GIWO	81	Learjet 35A	35A-407	Skyservice Aviation Inc. Toronto, ON.	C-GIWD
Reg	Yr	Type	c/n	Owner/Operator	Prev Regn

Reg	Yr	Type	c/n	Owner/Operator	Prev Regn
☐ C-GIWZ	98	Citation X	750-0041	Uniform Yankee Juliet Air Inc. Toronto-Pearson, ON.	C-GIWD
☐ C-GJBJ	83	HS 125/700A	NA0335	Skyservice Aviation Inc. Dorval, PQ.	N702E
☐ C-GJCF	01	Challenger 300	20002	Bombardier Inc. Dorval, PQ. (Ff 8 Oct 01).	
☐ C-GJCJ	01	Challenger 300	20001	Bombardier Inc. Dorval, PQ. (Ff 14 Aug 01).	
☐ C-GJCV	02	Challenger 300	20004	Bombardier Inc. Dorval, PQ. (Ff 5 Apr 02).	
☐ C-GJCY	04	Learjet 45	45-239	Skyservice Aviation Inc. Dorval, PQ.	N45LJ
☐ C-GJEI	01	Citation Encore	560-0588	Irving Oil Transport Ltd. Saint John, NB.	N5243K
☐ C-GJKI	02	Hawker 800XP	8605	Irving Oil Transport Ltd. Saint John, NB.	N61805
☐ C-GJPG	92	Falcon 900B	110	Jim Pattison Industries Ltd. Vancouver, BC.	N110FJ
☐ C-GJRB	99	Citation Excel	560-5026	CEC Flight Exec, London, ON.	(N17UG)
☐ C-GKAU	81	Citation II	550-0280	146157 Canada Inc/Jetair, Sept-Iles, PQ.	N7SN
☐ C-GKCI	98	Falcon 50EX	272	Irving Oil Transport Ltd. Saint John, NB.	N272F
☐ C-GKCZ	73	Citation	500-0101	Fox & Assocs Inc/Fox Flight, Toronto, ON.	N15CQ
☐ C-GKGD	90	BAe 125/800A	NA0457	Partner Jet Inc. Toronto-Pearson, ON.	N893EJ
☐ C-GKPE	75	Learjet 35	35-030	Equipe de Voltige Northern Lights, Montreal, PQ.	(N30TK)
☐ C-GKPM	78	HS 125/700A	NA0239	Ledair Inc. Dorval, PQ.	N33BK
☐ C-GKPP	89	BAe 125/800A	NA0439	Ledair Ltd. Dorval, PQ.	N74PQ
☐ C-GKTM	83	Learjet 55	55-076	Samuel Son & Co Ltd/Kim-Tam, Toronto, ON.	N30GL
☐ C-GLBB	00	Challenger 604	5465	Skyservice Aviation Inc. Dorval, PQ.	C-GHIH
☐ C-GLIG	81	HS 125/700A	NA0302	Lignum Ltd. Vancouver, BC.	C-GEPF
☐ C-GLJQ	90	Learjet 35A	35A-660	Aviation CMP Inc. St Georges, PQ.	N660L
☐ C-GLMI	00	Citation Excel	560-5097	Corporate Airlink Ltd. Toronto, ON.	N5226B
☐ C-GLMK	79	Citation II	550-0100	Northwest International Jet, Vancouver (was 551-0143)	N140DA
☐ C-GLRJ	97	Learjet 45	45-019	Bombardier Inc. Dorval, PQ.	C-GCMP
☐ C-GLRM	04	Global 5000	9130	Bombardier Inc. Dorval, PQ. (Ff 8 Jan 04)	
☐ C-GLRP	82	Falcon 50	87	Skyservice Aviation Inc. Toronto, ON.	N55NT
☐ C-GLRS	04	Learjet 45	45-249	Skyservice Aviation Inc. Toronto-Pearson, ON.	N40075
☐ C-GMAJ	75	Citation	500-0247	CitiCapital Ltd. Toronto, ON.	XA-JUA
☐ C-GMII	03	Falcon 50EX	335	Magna International Inc. Buttonville, ON.	N535EX
☐ C-GMKZ	03	Citation Excel	560-5309	Magna International Inc. Buttonville, ON.	N309XL
☐ C-GMLR	93	BAe 125/800A	8239	Millar Western Industries Ltd. Edmonton, AB.	N84CT
☐ C-GMMA	90	Learjet 35A	35A-655	Wal-Mart Stores Inc. Toronto-Pearson, ON.	N785JM
☐ C-GMMI	94	Challenger 601-3R	5151	Image Air Charter Inc. Toronto, ON.	N333MX
☐ C-GMMY	88	Learjet 35A	35A-644	Wal-Mart Canada Corp. Toronto-Pearson, ON.	N54SB
☐ C-GMND	01	Falcon 900C	189	Celtic Tech Jet Ltd. Toronto, ON.	N189FJ
☐ C-GMRO	00	Learjet 45	45-086	Uniform Yankee Juliet Air Inc. Toronto-Pearson, ON.	N386K
☐ C-GMTR	89	BAe 125/800A	NA0435	Sunwest Home Aviation Ltd. Calgary, AB.	N800BA
☐ C-GNCB	00	Global Express	9088	Berkshire Securities Inc. Mount Hope, ON.	C-FDLR
☐ C-GNCR	97	Challenger 604	5339	Canadian National Railway Co. Dorval, PQ.	N604CU
☐ C-GNET	99	Falcon 50EX	281	Ledcor Industries Ltd. Vancouver, BC.	N17AN
☐ C-GNSA	74	Citation	500-0160	Air Spray (1967) Ltd. Edmonton, AB.	N59TS
☐ C-GNWM	82	Citation II	550-0410	Northwest International Jet, Vancouver, BC.	N46MF
☐ C-GOAG	97	Falcon 900EX	15	Sunwest Home Aviation Ltd. Calgary, AB.	N914JL
☐ C-GOGM	81	HS 125/700A	NA0325	Morningstar Air Express, Edmonton, AB.	N26H
☐ C-GOXB	86	Citation III	650-0104	Skyservice Aviation Inc. Dorval, PQ.	C-FLMJ
☐ C-GPDA	99	Astra-1125SPX	120	North Cariboo Flying Service Ltd. Calgary, AB.	N770UP
☐ C-GPDO	92	Learjet 35A	35A-673	Masonite International Corp. Toronto-Pearson, ON.	C-FBDH
☐ C-GPDQ	99	Learjet 45	45-041	Hughes Air Corp. Calgary, AB.	N541LJ
☐ C-GPFC	96	Challenger 604	5310	Power Corp of Canada/Execaire-IMP Group Ltd. Dorval, PQ.	C-GPGD
☐ C-GPGA	97	Citation Bravo	550-0807	Air Georgian Ltd. Vancouver, BC.	C-FANS
☐ C-GPGD	99	Challenger 604	5432	Power Corp of Canada/Execaire-IMP Group Ltd. Dorval, PQ.	C-FDRS
☐ C-GPLN	72	Citation Eagle	500-0016	ACASS Canada Ltd. Dorval, PQ.	N9AX
☐ C-GPOP	84	Citation III	650-0042	Expressair/102662 Canada Inc. Ottawa-Gatineau, PQ.	N342AS
☐ C-GPOT	91	Challenger 601-3A	5088	Potash Corp of Saskatchewan Inc. Saskatoon, SK.	N601HC
☐ C-GPWM	01	CitationJet CJ-1	525-0440	Corporate Airlink Ltd. Toronto, ON.	N5233J
☐ C-GQBQ	89	Challenger 601-3A	5051	Government of Quebec, Sainte-Foy, PQ.	N190SB
☐ C-GQCC	73	Citation	500-0066	Algonquin Airlink Inc. Oakville, ON.	N66CC
☐ C-GQPA	98	Challenger 604	5379	ACASS Canada Ltd. Dorval, PQ.	N604CA
☐ C-GQWI	87	Challenger 601-3A	5016	ACASS Canada Ltd. Dorval, PQ.	N868CE
☐ C-GRCC	94	Citation V Ultra	560-0269	Jet Share Aviation Inc. Mississauga, ON.	N357EC
☐ C-GRDP	76	Westwind-1124	188	McCain Foods Ltd. Florenceville, NB.	N1124G
☐ C-GRFO	77	Learjet 35A	35A-100	Skyservice Aviation Inc. Dorval, PQ.	N558E
☐ C-GRHC	79	Citation II	550-0046	Omega Air Corp. Vancouver, BC.	(N3292M)
☐ C-GRIS	73	Falcon 10	2	Skycharter Ltd. Toronto-Pearson, ON.	N103JM
☐ C-GRPF	94	Challenger 601-3R	5168	1429255 Ontario Ltd/ Royal Group Technologies Ltd. Toronto.	C-GLYC
☐ C-GRPM	84	Falcon 200	500	Celtic Tech Jet Ltd. Ottawa, ON.	C-GMPO

| Reg | Yr | Type | c/n | Owner/Operator | Prev Regn |

Reg	Yr	Type	c/n	Owner/Operator	Prev Regn
☐ C-GRSD	68	Falcon 20C	157	Knighthawk Air Express, Hamilton, ON.	C-GRSD-X
☐ C-GSAP	84	Challenger 601	3034	Skyservice Aviation Inc. Dorval, PQ.	N120MP
☐ C-GSCL	93	BAe 125/800B	8243	Shell Canada Ltd. Calgary, AB.	VH-XMO
☐ C-GSCX	82	Citation II	550-0348	Sunwest Home Aviation Ltd. Calgary, AB.	N550CA
☐ C-GSEC	02	Citation Excel	560-5298	Execaire Inc/IMP Group Ltd. Dorval, PQ.	N5061P
☐ C-GSKL	74	Learjet 25B	25B-179	Skycharter Ltd. Toronto-Pearson, ON.	C-GBQC
☐ C-GSMR	88	Falcon 900B	55	Chartright Air Inc. Mississauga, ON.	(N955FJ)
☐ C-GSRS	82	Falcon 50	130	Sears Canada Inc. Toronto, ON.	N988T
☐ C-GSSS	96	Astra-1125SPX	080	Partner Jet Inc. Toronto-Pearson, ON.	VP-CUT
☐ C-GSUN	97	Citation V Ultra	560-0448	Suncor Energy Inc. Calgary, AB.	N5100J
☐ C-GSUX	02	Citation X	750-0205	Suncor Energy Inc. Calgary, AB.	N4005T
☐ C-GSWP	82	Learjet 55	55-019	Sunwest Home Aviation Ltd. Calgary, AB.	N141SM
☐ C-GTAK	69	Falcon 20D	197	Knighthawk Air Express, Hamilton, ON.	N399SW
☐ C-GTCP	87	Falcon 900B	29	Trans Canada Pipelines Ltd. Calgary, AB.	N421FJ
☐ C-GTDE	76	Learjet 35	35-057	Skyservice Aviation Inc. Dorval, PQ.	N35MR
☐ C-GTDO	03	Gulfstream G100	151	TDL Group Ltd/Jetport Inc. Mount Hope, ON.	N751GA
☐ C-GTJL	77	Learjet 35A	35A-124	Sunwest Home Aviation Ltd. Calgary, AB.	N8LA
☐ C-GTOG	03	Citation Encore	560-0648	Anderson Air Ltd. Richmond, BC.	N820QS
☐ C-GTOR	78	HS 125/700A	NA0221	Partner Jet Inc. Toronto-Pearson, ON.	N705JH
☐ C-GTRG	00	CitationJet CJ-1	525-0376	Visionaire Services Inc. Red Deer, AB.	N802JH
☐ C-GTVO	78	Falcon 10	137	Fraser Papers Inc. Edmundston, NB.	N837F
☐ C-GUAC	80	Learjet 35A	35A-309	All Canada Express Inc. Toronto, ON.	D-CHPD
☐ C-GVIJ	01	Citation Bravo	550-0982	Omega Air Corp. Calgary, AB.	C-GDSH
☐ C-GVVA	74	Learjet 35	35-002	Sunwest Home Aviation Ltd. Calgary, AB.	N35SC
☐ C-GVVZ	98	Learjet 45	45-020	Sunwest Home Aviation Ltd. Calgary, AB.	N45NP
☐ C-GWCR	96	Citation V Ultra	560-0379	Weldwood of Canada Ltd. Vancouver, BC.	N5101J
☐ C-GWFG	91	Learjet 35A	35A-669	West Fraser Air Ltd. Vancouver, BC.	N893CF
☐ C-GWFM	84	BAe 125/800A	8015	Skyservice Aviation Inc. Toronto, ON.	C-FTLA
☐ C-GWII	02	Citation Excel	560-5258	1102734 Ontario Inc. Wingham, ON.	N52334
☐ C-GWLE	83	BAe 125/800B	8007	Execaire Inc/IMP Group Ltd. Winnipeg, MT.	C-GWLL
☐ C-GWLL	01	Challenger 604	5484	Execaire Inc/IMP Group Ltd. Dorval, PQ.	N684TS
☐ C-GWXP	95	Learjet 31A	31A-102	Western Express Air Lines Inc. Vancouver, BC.	N731RA
☐ C-GXCG	98	Citation V Ultra	560-0481	AeroPro, Ste Foy, PQ.	C-GXCO
☐ C-GXCO	01	Citation Excel	560-5200	Exco Technologies Ltd. Toronto-Buttonville, ON.	N5109R
☐ C-GYMM	98	Citation V Ultra	560-0484	Syncrude Canada Inc. Fort McMurray, AB.	N5125J
☐ C-GZEK	97	Challenger 604	5360	Execaire Inc/IMP Group Ltd. Toronto, ON.	N14SR
☐ C-GZPV	04	Global Express	9136	Bombardier Inc. Downsview, ON.	
☐ C-GZPW	04	Global Express	9137	Execaire/IMP Group Ltd. Dorval, PQ.	
☐ C-GZPX	00	Challenger 604	5458	Skyservice Aviation Inc. Toronto-Pearson, ON.	N458MS
☐ C-GZRA	04	Global Express	9138	Bombardier Inc. Downsview, ON.	

Military

☐ 144601	82	Challenger 600S	1040	CC144, DND, 412 (Transport) Squadron, Uplands, ON.	C-GLYM
☐ 144614	85	Challenger 601	3036	CC144, DND, 412 (Transport) Squadron, Uplands, ON.	C-GCUP
☐ 144615	85	Challenger 601	3037	CC144, DND, 412 (Transport) Squadron, Uplands, ON.	C-GCUR
☐ 144616	85	Challenger 601	3038	CC144, DND, 412 (Transport) Squadron, Uplands, ON.	C-GCUT
☐ 144617	02	Challenger 604	5533	DND, 412 (Transport) Squadron, Uplands, ON.	C-GKGR
☐ 144618	02	Challenger 604	5535	DND, 412 (Transport) Squadron, Uplands, ON.	C-GKGS
☐ 15001	87	Airbus A310-304	446	Canadian Armed Forces, 437 Squadron, 8 Wing, Trenton.	C-GBWD
☐ 15002	88	Airbus A310-304	482	Canadian Armed Forces, 437 Squadron, 8 Wing, Trenton.	C-GLWD
☐ 15003	86	Airbus A310-304	425	Canadian Armed Forces, 437 Squadron, 8 Wing, Trenton.	C-FWDX
☐ 15004	87	Airbus A310-304	444	Canadian Armed Forces, 437 Squadron, 8 Wing, Trenton.	F-WQCQ

CC = CHILE   *Total*   23

Civil

☐ CC-CHE	03	CitationJet CJ-2	525A-0171		N271CJ
☐ CC-CPS	94	Citation VII	650-7045	Rimac SA. Santiago.	CC-PGL
☐ CC-CTC	76	Sabre-60	306-112	Aguos Clara Inc. Santiago.	N740RC
☐ CC-CWK	01	Gulfstream G100	141	Cardal AG/Aerocardal Ltda. Santiago.	N106GX
☐ CC-CWW	84	Citation S/II	S550-0002	Cardal AG/Aerocardal Ltda. Santiago.	N211VP
☐ CC-CWZ	79	Citation II/SP	551-0141	Cardal AG/Aerocardal Ltda. Santiago. (was 550-0093).	N388MA
☐ CC-DAC	93	Citation VI	650-0233	Directorate of Civil Aviation, Santiago.	N1303H
☐ CC-DGA	90	Citation II	550-0657	Directorate of Civil Aviation, Santiago.	N3986G
☐ CC-LLM	01	Citation Bravo	550-0996	Club Aero de Cabineros de Chile, Santiago.	N5270P
☐ CC-PVJ	98	CitationJet	525-0243	Binah SA. Santiago.	

Military

☐ 301	80	Citation II	550-0104	Chilean Navy, Santiago.	E-301
☐ 303	87	Citation III	650-0131	Chilean Navy, Santiago.	E-303
Reg	*Yr*	*Type*	*c/n*	*Owner/Operator*	*Prev Regn*

Reg	Yr	Type	c/n	Owner/Operator	Prev Regn
☐ 351	76	Learjet 35	35-050	Fuerza Aerea Chilena, Santiago.	CC-ECO
☐ 352	76	Learjet 35	35-066	Fuerza Aerea Chilena, Santiago.	CC-ECP
☐ 361	01	CitationJet CJ-1	525-0463	Fuerza Aerea Chilena, Grupo Aviacion 5, El Tepual.	N1284D
☐ 362	01	CitationJet CJ-1	525-0464	Fuerza Aerea Chilena, Grupo Aviacion 5, El Tepual.	N1284P
☐ 363	01	CitationJet CJ-1	525-0465	Fuerza Aerea Chilena, Grupo Aviacion 5, El Tepual.	N1285P
☐ 364	03	CitationJet CJ-1	525-0507	Fuerza Aerea Chilena, Grupo Aviacion 5, El Tepual.	N.....
☐ 902	67	B 707-351C	19443	Fuerza Aerea Chilena, Gr 10, Santiago.	CC-CCK
☐ 903	65	B 707-330B	18926	Fuerza Aerea Chilena, Gr 10, Santiago. 'Aguila'	CC-CEA
☐ 904	65	B 707-385C	19000	Fuerza Aerea Chilena, Gr 10, Santiago. 'Condor'	905
☐ 911	89	Gulfstream 4	1089	Fuerza Aerea Chilena, Gr 10, Santiago.	N53MU
☐ 921	70	B 737-58N	28866	Fuerza Aerea Chilena, Gr 10, Santiago.	

CN = MOROCCO   Total   11
Civil

Reg	Yr	Type	c/n	Owner/Operator	Prev Regn
☐ CN-TDE	74	Corvette	5	CASA Air Services, Casablanca.	F-BVPA
☐ CN-TKK	81	Citation II	550-0265	Air Marrakech Services, Marrekech.	(N265QS)

Military

Reg	Yr	Type	c/n	Owner/Operator	Prev Regn
☐ CNA-NL	76	Gulfstream 2TT	182	Government of Morocco, Rabat.	N17589
☐ CNA-NM	69	Falcon 20ECM	165	Ministry of Defence, Kenitra.	CN-MBH
☐ CNA-NN	68	Falcon 20ECM	152	Ministry of Defence, Kenitra.	CN-MBG
☐ CNA-NO	80	Falcon 50	12	Government of Morocco, Rabat.	F-WZHC
☐ CNA-NS	61	B 707-138B	18334	Government of Morocco, Rabat. 'Africa Crown'	N58937
☐ CNA-NU	82	Gulfstream 3	365	Government of Morocco, Rabat.	HZ-AFO
☐ CNA-NV	89	Citation V	560-0025	Government of Morocco, Rabat.	(N12285)
☐ CNA-NW	89	Citation V	560-0039	Government of Morocco, Rabat.	
☐ CNA-NZ	88	Falcon 100	212	Government of Morocco, Rabat.	CN-TNA

CP = BOLIVIA   Total   4
Civil

Reg	Yr	Type	c/n	Owner/Operator	Prev Regn
☐ CP-2317	74	Sabre-40A	282-136	Aerojet SA. Cochabamaba.	N112ML

Military

Reg	Yr	Type	c/n	Owner/Operator	Prev Regn
☐ FAB 001	76	Sabre-60	306-115	President of Bolivia, Esc 810, La Paz.	(XA-LEI)
☐ FAB 008	75	Learjet 25B	25B-192	Fuerza Aerea Boliviana, Esc 810, La Paz. (photo survey)	
☐ FAB 010	76	Learjet 25D	25D-211	Fuerza Aerea Boliviana, Esc 810, La Paz.	

CS = PORTUGAL   Total   75
Civil

Reg	Yr	Type	c/n	Owner/Operator	Prev Regn
☐ CS-AYY	80	Citation 1/SP	501-0183	Airjetsul, Cascais-Tires.	(N8NC)
☐ CS-DCK	74	Falcon 20E	297	Air Luxor Lda. Paris-Le Bourget, France.	(N297AG)
☐ CS-DCT	00	Citation X	750-0134	Air Luxor Lda. Lisbon.	N51780
☐ CS-DDI	94	Falcon 900B	143	Air Luxor Lda. Paris-Le Bourget, France.	VP-BZB
☐ CS-DDV	87	Citation S/II	S550-0147	Airjetsul, Cascais-Tires.	OO-OSA
☐ CS-DDZ	91	Learjet 31	31-034	OMNI Aviacao y Tecnologia Ltda. Cascais-Tires.	N394SA
☐ CS-DFB	91	Falcon 900	94	NTA/European NetJets, Lisbon.	N94WA
☐ CS-DFC	01	Falcon 2000	148	NTA/European NetJets, Lisbon.	F-WWVC
☐ CS-DFD	01	Falcon 2000	174	NTA/European NetJets, Lisbon.	F-WWMA
☐ CS-DFE	03	Falcon 2000	205	NTA/European NetJets, Lisbon.	F-WWVS
☐ CS-DFF	04	Falcon 2000EX EASY	41	NTA/European NetJets, Lisbon.	F-WWGW
☐ CS-DFG	04	Falcon 2000EX EASY	44	NTA/European NetJets, Lisbon.	F-WWGA
☐ CS-DFH	91	Falcon 900	91	NTA/European NetJets, Lisbon.	N991EJ
☐ CS-DFM	02	Citation Excel	560-5257	NTA/European NetJets, Lisbon.	N5196U
☐ CS-DFN	02	Citation Excel	560-5283	NTA/European NetJets, Lisbon.	N.....
☐ CS-DFO	03	Citation Excel	560-5314	NTA/European NetJets, Lisbon.	N5000R
☐ CS-DFP	03	Citation Excel	560-5315	NTA/European NetJets, Lisbon.	N5095N
☐ CS-DFQ	03	Citation Excel	560-5334	NTA/European NetJets, Lisbon.	N5093L
☐ CS-DFR	03	Citation Excel	560-5355	NTA/European NetJets, Lisbon.	N5200Z
☐ CS-DFS	04	Citation Excel	560-5372	NTA/European NetJets, Lisbon.	N5091J
☐ CS-DFT	04	Citation Excel XLS	560-5512	NTA/European NetJets, Lisbon.	N52433
☐ CS-DFU	04	Citation Excel XLS	560-5520	NTA/European NetJets, Lisbon.	N5269A
☐ CS-DFW	03	Hawker 800XP	8664	NTA/European NetJets, Lisbon.	N664XP
☐ CS-DFX	03	Hawker 800XP	8656	NTA/European NetJets, Lisbon.	N656XP
☐ CS-DFY	03	Hawker 800XP	8663	NTA/European NetJets, Lisbon.	N663XP
☐ CS-DFZ	04	Hawker 800XP	8673	NTA/European NetJets, Lisbon.	N673XP
☐ CS-DHA	02	Citation Bravo	550-1005	NTA/European NetJets, Lisbon.	N5247U
☐ CS-DHB	01	Citation Bravo	550-1009	NTA/European NetJets, Lisbon.	N5155G
☐ CS-DHC	02	Citation Bravo	550-1013	NTA/European NetJets, Lisbon.	N5166U
☐ CS-DHD	02	Citation Bravo	550-1017	NTA/European NetJets, Lisbon.	N51666
☐ CS-DHE	02	Citation Bravo	550-1022	NTA/European NetJets, Lisbon.	N5168Y

Reg	Yr	Type	c/n	Owner/Operator	Prev Regn
❑ CS-DHF	02	Citation Bravo	550-1025	NTA/European NetJets, Lisbon.	N5172M
❑ CS-DHG	02	Citation Bravo	550-1034	NTA/European NetJets, Lisbon.	N52086
❑ CS-DHH	02	Citation Bravo	550-1043	NTA/European NetJets, Lisbon.	N52235
❑ CS-DHI	03	Citation Bravo	550-1048	NTA/European NetJets, Lisbon.	N5253S
❑ CS-DHJ	04	Citation Bravo	550-1082	NTA/European NetJets, Lisbon.	N5180C
❑ CS-DHK	04	Citation Bravo	550-1090	NTA/European NetJets, Lisbon.	N51038
❑ CS-DHL	04	Citation Bravo	550-1092	NTA/European NetJets, Lisbon.	N52645
❑ CS-DHM	04	Citation Bravo	550-1093	NTA/European NetJets, Lisbon.	N5263D
❑ CS-DHN	04	Citation Bravo	550-1098	NTA/European NetJets, Lisbon.	N5132T
❑ CS-DHO*	04	Citation Bravo	550-1099	NTA/European NetJets, Lisbon.	N5180C
❑ CS-DIG	03	Citation Encore	560-0637	Air Luxor Lda. Lisbon.	N5073G
❑ CS-DKA	01	Gulfstream 4SP	1480	NTA/European NetJets, Lisbon.	N482QS
❑ CS-DKB	01	Gulfstream V	642	NTA/European NetJets, Lisbon.	N510QS
❑ CS-DMA	04	Hawker 400XP	RK-393	NTA/European NetJets, Lisbon.	N118QS
❑ CS-DNE	98	Citation VII	650-7093	NTA/European NetJets, Lisbon.	N793QS
❑ CS-DNF	97	Citation VII	650-7080	NTA/European NetJets, Lisbon.	N780QS
❑ CS-DNG	97	Citation VII	650-7081	NTA/European NetJets, Lisbon.	N781QS
❑ CS-DNJ	98	Hawker 800XP	8399	NTA/European NetJets, Lisbon.	N899QS
❑ CS-DNK	99	Hawker 800XP	8430	NTA/European NetJets, Lisbon.	N31590
❑ CS-DNL	99	Hawker 800XP	8439	NTA/European NetJets, Lisbon.	N31596
❑ CS-DNM	99	Hawker 800XP	8422	NTA/European NetJets, Lisbon.	N822QS
❑ CS-DNN	99	Hawker 800XP	8435	NTA/European NetJets, Lisbon.	N835QS
❑ CS-DNO	00	Hawker 800XP	8457	NTA/European NetJets, Lisbon.	N41984
❑ CS-DNP	00	Falcon 2000	109	NTA/European NetJets, Lisbon.	N2218
❑ CS-DNQ	00	Falcon 2000	115	NTA/European NetJets, Lisbon.	F-WWVK
❑ CS-DNR	00	Falcon 2000	120	NTA/European NetJets, Lisbon.	F-WWVP
❑ CS-DNS	01	Falcon 2000	139	NTA/European NetJets, Lisbon.	F-WWVR
❑ CS-DNT	00	Hawker 800XP	8468	NTA/European NetJets, Lisbon.	N43436
❑ CS-DNU	00	Hawker 800XP	8479	NTA/European NetJets, Lisbon.	N44779
❑ CS-DNV	00	Hawker 800XP	8499	NTA/European NetJets, Lisbon.	N51099
❑ CS-DNW	02	Citation Excel	560-5221	NTA/European NetJets, Lisbon.	N5094D
❑ CS-DNX	00	Hawker 800XP	8511	NTA/European NetJets, Lisbon.	N5011J
❑ CS-DNY	01	Citation Excel	560-5216	NTA/European NetJets, Lisbon.	N5103J
❑ CS-DNZ	01	Citation Excel	560-5235	NTA/European NetJets, Lisbon.	N5086W
❑ CS-DRA	04	Hawker 800XP	8686	NTA/European NetJets, Lisbon.	N61746
❑ CS-DRB	04	Hawker 800XP	8690	NTA/European NetJets, Lisbon.	N36990
❑ CS-TLP	04	Falcon 2000EX EASY	39	Heliavia Transporte Aereo Ltda. Lisbon.	F-WWGU
❑ CS-TMJ	89	Falcon 50	190	Heliavia Transporte Aereo Ltda. Lisbon.	I-CAFE
❑ CS-TMK	90	Falcon 900B	66	Vinair Aeroservicos SA. Cascais-Tires.	F-GJPM
❑ CS-TMQ	98	Falcon 900B	175	Heliavia Transporte Aereo Ltda. Lisbon.	F-WWFN
Military					
❑ 17103	69	Falcon 20D	217	Portuguese Air Force, Esc 504, Montijo, Lisbon.	8103
❑ 17401	89	Falcon 50	195	Portuguese Air Force, Esc 504, Montijo, Lisbon.	7401
❑ 17402	89	Falcon 50	198	Portuguese Air Force, Esc 504, Montijo, Lisbon.	7402
❑ 17403	91	Falcon 50	221	Portuguese Air Force, Esc 504, Montijo, Lisbon.	7403

C6 = BAHAMAS   Total   3

Civil					
❑ C6-...	03	CitationJet CJ-2	525A-0170		N915RJ
❑ C6-JET	97	Astra-1125SPX	095	Advanced Aviation Ltd, Freeport.	N98AD
❑ C6-MED	68	HS 125/3B-RA	25140	Plane 1 Leasing Co. Naples, Fl. USA.	G-DJLW

D = GERMANY   Total   241

Civil					
❑ D-ABCD	03	Challenger 604	5565	Knorr-Bremse GmbH/Bonair Business Air Charter GmbH. Koeln.	N604KB
❑ D-ACME	92	Airbus A340-211	004	(conversion to flying hospital 2003-2004)	HZ-124
❑ D-ADAM	78	VFW 614	G17	DLR Flugbetrieb, Oberpfaffenhofen.	D-BABP
❑ D-ADNA	99	Airbus A319CJ-133X	1053	Daimler Chrysler AG. Stuttgart.	D-AVYN
❑ D-ADNB	00	Global Express	9071	Daimler Chrysler AG. Stuttgart.	C-GHDQ
❑ D-ADND	99	Challenger 604	5403	Daimler Chrysler AG. Stuttgart.	N604DC
❑ D-ADNE	99	Challenger 604	5422	Daimler Chrysler AG. Stuttgart.	N605DC
❑ D-AETV	99	Challenger 604	5417	Air Independence GmbH. Munich.	N605MP
❑ D-AHEI	00	Challenger 604	5463	Hapag-Lloyd Executive GmbH. Hannover.	N463AG
❑ D-AHLE	00	Challenger 604	5462	Hapag-Lloyd Executive GmbH. Hannover.	N462PG
❑ D-AJAD	00	Falcon 900EX	64	Deutsche Telekom GmbH. Koeln.	N900VM
❑ D-AJAG	02	Challenger 604	5528	Deutsche Telekom AG. Cologne.	N528DT
❑ D-AJGK	01	Gulfstream 4SP	1459	Windrose Air Jetcharter GmbH. Berlin.	(D-AJJJ)

Reg	Yr	Type	c/n	Owner/Operator	Prev Regn

Reg	Yr	Type	c/n	Owner/Operator	Prev Regn
D-AKUE	95	Challenger 601-3R	5173	Ullmann Krockow Esch/Challenge Air GmbH. Cologne.	N181JC
D-ANKE	01	Challenger 604	5494	Jet Connection Business Flight AG. Frankfurt.	N494JC
D-APAA	03	Airbus A319-132LR	1947	PrivatAir SA/Airbus Industrie, Toulouse, France.	D-AVWI
D-APAB	03	Airbus A319-132LR	1955	PrivatAir SA/Airbus Industrie, Toulouse, France.	D-AVWD
D-APAC	03	Airbus A319-132LR	1727	Privatair SA/DLH Shuttle, Dusseldorf.	D-AVWQ
D-APAD	03	Airbus A319-132LR	1880	PrivatAir SA/DLH Shuttle, Dusseldorf.	D-AVYM
D-ASFB	98	Airbus A340-213X	204	Government of Brunei, Bandar Seri Begawan, Brunei.	V8-AC3
D-ASIE	00	Challenger 604	5475	Aero-Dienst GmbH. Nuremberg.	N475AD
D-ASTS	98	Challenger 604	5378	ACM Air Charter GmbH. Baden-Baden.	C-GDBZ
D-AUKE	98	Challenger 604	5389	Ullmann Krockow Esch/Challenge Air GmbH. Cologne.	N604JE
D-AZEM	03	Falcon 900EX EASY	133	Zeman Flugtechnik GmbH. Munich.	F-WQBJ
D-BADC	03	Dornier Do328JET	3216	ADAC Luftrettung GmbH. Munich.	D-BIUU
D-BDNL	00	Falcon 2000	119	EADS, Paris-Le Bourget, France.	F-WQBN
D-BERT	04	Falcon 2000EX EASY	30	Bertlesmann AG. Paderborn.	F-WWGG
D-BEST	97	Falcon 2000	50	Bauhaus GmbH. Mannheim.	F-WWME
D-BILL	04	Falcon 2000EX EASY	33	BASF AG. Speyer.	F-WWGL
D-BIRD	03	Falcon 2000EX	7	Sony Europe GmbH. Berlin.	F-WWGF
D-BKLI	03	Citation X	750-0219	Daimler Chrysler/LIDL Dienstleistung GmbH. Bad Wimpfen.	N5192E
D-BLDI	03	Citation X	750-0218	Daimler Chrysler/LIDL Dienstleistung GmbH. Bad Wimpfen.	N5223X
D-BLUE	00	Citation X	750-0140	ACM Air Charter GmbH. Baden-Baden.	N5112K
D-BOOK	91	Falcon 50	215	Bertelsmann AG. Paderborn.	XA-SIM
D-BSNA	82	Challenger 600S	1066	Fondsprojekt Josef Esch GmbH/Challenge Air GmbH. Cologne.	N51TJ
D-BTEN	99	Citation X	750-0085	ACM Air Charter GmbH. Baden-Baden.	(N985QS)
D-BUSY	82	Challenger 600S	1070	Bonair Business Charter GmbH. Muenchen.	N670CL
D-C...	90	Citation III	650-0190		N260VP
D-CAKE	94	Citation VI	650-0240	Solidair, Eindhoven, Holland.	PH-MFX
D-CALL	98	Citation Bravo	550-0834	ACH Hamburg Flug GmbH. Hamburg.	N834CB
D-CAMS	93	Citation V	560-0243	Triple Alpha GmbH/Club Airways, Geneva, Switzerland.	N39N
D-CAPO	78	Learjet 35A	35A-159	Phoenix Air GmbH. Munich.	(N135CK)
D-CARE	86	Citation III	650-0134	Excellent Air GmbH. Stadtlohn.	N1239L
D-CARL	81	Learjet 35A	35A-387	GFD fuer Flugzieldarstellungen mbH. Hohn.	
D-CASA	00	Citation Encore	560-0544	Adolf Wuerth GmbH. Niederstetten.	N701DK
D-CATL	83	Learjet 55	55-051	FAI rent-a-jet AG. Nuremberg.	N55KD
D-CAUW	01	Citation Encore	560-0578	A W Aerowest GmbH. Hannover.	(D-CSUN)
D-CAVE	81	Learjet 35A	35A-423	Deutsche Rettungsflugwacht, Karlsruhe/Baden-Baden.	(N335GA)
D-CAWU	90	Citation V	560-0042	Adolf Wuerth GmbH. Niederstetten.	N42CV
D-CBEN	94	Citation V Ultra	560-0282	Adolf Wuerth GmbH. Niederstetten.	N51055
D-CBMW	97	Hawker 800XP	8345	BMW GmbH. Munich.	D-CBMV
D-CBPL	87	Citation III	650-0149	Eheim GmbH/SFD-Stuttgarter Flugdienst GmbH. Stuttgart.	(CS-DNE)
D-CBWW	92	BAe 1000B	9028	ADAC Luftrettung GmbH. Munich.	G-5-749
D-CCAA	80	Learjet 35A	35A-315	Deutsche Rettungsflugwacht, Karlsruhe/Baden-Baden.	N662AA
D-CCAB	97	Citation Bravo	550-0827	Albert Berner GmbH. Kuenzelsau.	N51042
D-CCCA	78	Learjet 35A	35A-160	Taunus Air GmbH. Duesseldorf.	
D-CCCB	90	Learjet 35A	35A-663	Maschinenfabrik E Mollers GmbH. Beckum.	N91480
D-CCCF	80	Citation II	550-0189	CCF Manager Airline GmbH. Cologne.	HB-VGP
D-CCGG	02	Learjet 60	60-256	GAS Air Service GmbH. Muenster-Osnabrueck.	OY-LJK
D-CCGN	82	Learjet 55	55-017	Juliane Griesemann/Quick Air Jet Charter GmbH. Cologne.	N760AQ
D-CCHB	76	Learjet 35A	35A-089	Bauhaus GmbH. Mannheim.	N3547F
D-CDEN	01	Learjet 45	45-148	Air Evex GmbH. Duesseldorf.	N40075
D-CDNX	01	Learjet 60	60-231	Daimler Chrysler AG. Stuttgart.	N40012
D-CDNY	99	Learjet 60	60-160	Daimler Chrysler AG. Stuttgart.	
D-CDNZ	99	Learjet 60	60-161	Daimler Chrysler AG. Stuttgart.	
D-CDSF	81	Learjet 35A	35A-421		I-VULC
D-CEFM*	02	Citation Bravo	550-1018		SU-HEC
D-CEIS	90	Beechjet 400A	RK-10	Suedzucker AG/Haberlein Metzer Reise Service, Mannheim.	(D-CLSG)
D-CEMG	98	Citation V Ultra	560-0463	SFD Stuttgarter Flugdienst GmbH. Stuttgart.	N48LQ
D-CEMM	01	Learjet 45	45-144	BASF AG. Speyer.	N5011C
D-CESH	98	Learjet 45	45-017	HDE Air GmbH/Air Evex GmbH. Duesseldorf.	N417LJ
D-CETV	98	Learjet 60	60-148	Air Independence GmbH. Munich.	N80701
D-CEWR	02	Learjet 45	45-213	MAHA Air GmbH. Memmingen AFB.	N50126
D-CFAI	81	Learjet 35A	35A-365	FAI rent-a-jet AG. Nuremberg.	G-GJET
D-CFAN	87	BAe 125/800B	8094	ThyssenKrupp/TS-Transport Services, Duesseldorf.	G-5-576
D-CFCF	81	Learjet 35A	35A-413	Senator Aviation Charter GmbH. Hamburg.	N27KG
D-CFFB	97	Learjet 60	60-107	F & F Burda GmbH. Baden Baden.	N107LJ
D-CFLY	91	Citation V	560-0145	Excellent Air GmbH. Stadtlohn.	N57ML
D-CFTG	78	Learjet 35A	35A-204	Juliane Griesemann/Quick Air Jet Charter GmbH. Cologne.	(N277AM)
Reg	*Yr*	*Type*	*c/n*	*Owner/Operator*	*Prev Regn*

Reg	Yr	Type	c/n	Owner/Operator	Prev Regn
D-CFUX	82	Learjet 55	55-061	Deutsche Rettungsflugwacht, Karlsruhe/Baden-Baden.	N132EL
D-CGBR	85	Learjet 55	55-122	Taunus Air GmbH. Duesseldorf.	OE-GRO
D-CGFA	78	Learjet 35A	35A-179	GFD fuer Flugzieldarstellungen mbH. Hohn.	N801PF
D-CGFB	79	Learjet 35A	35A-268	GFD fuer Flugzieldarstellungen mbH. Hohn.	N2U
D-CGFC	80	Learjet 35A	35A-331	GFD fuer Flugzieldarstellungen mbH. Hohn.	N435JW
D-CGFD	77	Learjet 35A	35A-139	GFD fuer Flugzieldarstellungen mbH. Hohn.	N15SC
D-CGFE	89	Learjet 36A	36A-062	GFD fuer Flugzieldarstellungen mbH. Hohn.	N4291N
D-CGFF	89	Learjet 36A	36A-063	GFD fuer Flugzieldarstellungen mbH. Hohn.	N1048X
D-CGFG	79	Learjet 35A	35A-222	GFD fuer Flugzieldarstellungen mbH. Hohn.	N789KW
D-CGFH	86	Learjet 35A	35A-607	GFD fuer Flugzieldarstellungen mbH. Hohn.	N68MJ
D-CGFI	86	Learjet 35A	35A-612	GFD fuer Flugzieldarstellungen mbH. Hohn.	N36BP
D-CGFJ	88	Learjet 35A	35A-643	GFD fuer Flugzieldarstellungen mbH. Hohn.	N643MJ
D-CGGG	01	Learjet 31A	31A-227	GAS Air Service GmbH. Muenster-Osnabrueck.	N40073
D-CGRC	79	Learjet 35A	35A-223	Taunus Air GmbH. Duesseldorf.	N215JW
D-CHAN	99	Citation Bravo	550-0874	Hapag-Lloyd Executive GmbH. Hannover.	N5194B
D-CHDE	89	Citation V	560-0031	BBP-Kunstoffwerk Marbach Baier GmbH. Marbach.	N1229F
D-CHEF	01	Hawker 800XP	8514	HDE Air GmbH/Air Evex GmbH. Duesseldorf.	N4021Z
D-CHEP	92	Citation II	550-0697	Triple Alpha Luftfahrt GmbH. Duesseldorf.	HB-VMP
D-CHER	95	Learjet 60	60-051	Comfort Air GmbH. Munich.	OY-LJH
D-CHLE	01	Learjet 60	60-211	Hapag-Lloyd Executive GmbH. Hannover.	N5012Z
D-CHSW	94	Beechjet 400A	RK-84	Augusta Air GmbH. Augsburg.	N8138M
D-CHZF	99	Citation Bravo	550-0866	ZF Friedrichshafen AG/Kuri-Flugdienst KG. Friedrichshafen.	N866CB
D-CIFA	80	Citation II	550-0378	FAI rent-a-jet AG. Nuremberg.	OH-CAT
D-CIMM	01	Learjet 60	60-214	Jetalliance Flugbetriebs AG. Vienna, Austria.	N5016Z
D-CITA	95	Learjet 60	60-069	Senator Aviation Charter GmbH. Hamburg.	N60CE
D-CITY	78	Learjet 35A	35A-177	Helmut Idzkowiak/Senator Aviation Charter GmbH.Hamburg.	N174CP
D-CJET	98	Hawker 800XP	8358	ThyssenKrupp/TS Transport Services, Duesseldorf.	N240B
D-CJPG	77	Learjet 35A	35A-108	Juliane Griesemann/Quick Air Jet Charter GmbH. Cologne.	(N86PQ)
D-CKKK	98	Learjet 60	60-144	Windrose Air Jetcharter GmbH. Berlin.	N60144
D-CLBA	91	Beechjet 400A	RK-25	LBA-Luftfahrt Bundesamt, Braunschweig.	(VR-CDA)
D-CLBB	74	Falcon 20E-5	315	Elbe Air Lufttransport AG. Paderborn.	F-GSXF
D-CLBE	73	Falcon 20E	279	Elbe Air Lufttransport AG. Paderborn.	N854GA
D-CLBR	66	Falcon 20C	52	Elbe Air Lufttransport AG. Paderborn.	N852TC
D-CLEO	91	Citation V	560-0159	Comfort Air GmbH. Munich.	N68MA
D-CLUB	02	Learjet 60	60-249	Jet Connection Business Flight AG. Frankfurt.	N4004Q
D-CLUE	89	Citation III	650-0174	GEG Grundstuecksentwicklungs H H Goettsch KG. Cologne.	N674CC
D-CMAD	90	Learjet 55C	55C-143	Quelle Flug GmbH. Nuremberg.	N10871
D-CMEI	91	Citation V	560-0117	Siegfried Meister/Lech Air GmbH Lech AFB.	(N6804F)
D-CMET	75	Falcon 20E-5B	329	Deutsches Zentrum fuer Luft und Raumfahrt GmbH.	F-WRQV
D-CMIC	99	Citation Excel	560-5021	Michael Nixdorf, Paderborn	N5244F
D-CMMM	76	Learjet 24D	24D-328	Taunus Air GmbH/PARI Holding GmbH Krass, Munich.	D-IMMM
D-CMPI	95	Citation VII	650-7055	SFD Stuttgarter Flugdienst GmbH. Stuttgart.	N817MZ
D-CMRM	00	Learjet 31A	31A-213	Aero-Dienst GmbH. Nuremberg.	
D-CMSC	00	Learjet 45	45-097	SAP AG Systeme, Mannheim.	N5017J
D-CNCJ	99	Citation VII	650-7102	ACM Air Charter GmbH. Baden-Baden.	N5223X
D-CNIK	03	Learjet 40	45-2006	Cirrus Airlines Luftfahrt GmbH. Saarbruecken.	N50111
D-COKE	81	Learjet 35A	35A-447	Private Wings Flugcharter GmbH. Berlin-Tempelhof.	N300FN
D-COOL	83	Learjet 55	55-052	Bonair Business Charter GmbH. Muenchen.	N551DB
D-CPPP	98	Citation Bravo	550-0865	Windrose Air Jetcharter GmbH. Berlin.	N505X
D-CRAN*	93	Learjet 60	60-019	Aero-Dienst GmbH. Nuremberg.	HB-VKI
D-CRHR	87	Citation III	650-0142	EFS Flug Service GmbH. Duesseldorf.	(N492BA)
D-CRIS	98	Astra-1125SPX	107	Fondsprojekt Josef Esch GmbH/Challenge Air GmbH. Cologne.	N997GA
D-CROB	02	Learjet 60	60-261	Cirrus Airlines Luftfahrt GmbH. Saarbruecken.	N4003Q
D-CRRR	90	Citation III	650-0187	EFS Flug Service GmbH. Duesseldorf.	LN-AAA
D-CSAP	92	Learjet 31A	31A-057	SAP AG Systeme, Mannheim.	N9147Q
D-CSFD	88	Citation S/II	S550-0148	Eheim GmbH/SFD-Stuttgarter Flugdienst GmbH. Stuttgart.	N170RD
D-CSIE	00	Learjet 31A	31A-207	Aero-Dienst GmbH. Nuremberg.	N50126
D-CSIM	04	Learjet 60	60-274	Aero-Dienst GmbH. Nuremberg.	N4003K
D-CSIX	97	Learjet 60	60-120	Jet Connection Business Flight AG. Frankfurt.	N120LJ
D-CSUN	90	Citation V	560-0078	Excellent Air GmbH. Stadtlohn.	OY-CKT
D-CTLX*	05	Citation	560-5585		N.....
D-CURT	91	Learjet 31A	31A-042	Air Traffic GmbH. Duesseldorf.	D-CGGG
D-CVHI	01	Citation Excel	560-5195	Viessmann Werke GmbH. Allendorf.	N51143
D-CVIP	84	Learjet 55	55-109	WDL Aviation GmbH. Koeln.	N348HM
D-CWAY	84	Learjet 55	55-107	Cirrus Airlines Luftfahrt GmbH. Saarbruecken.	N304AT
D-CWDL	83	Learjet 55	55-084	WDL Aviation GmbH. Koeln.	I-FLYJ

Reg   Yr Type   c/n   Owner/Operator   Prev Regn

Reg	Yr	Type	c/n	Owner/Operator	Prev Regn
D-CWHS	01	Learjet 60	60-246	Cirrus Airlines Luftfahrt GmbH. Saarbruecken.	N5035F
D-CWWW	03	Citation Excel	560-5316	Augusta Air GmbH. Augsburg.	N5096S
D-CZAR	91	Citation V	560-0114	Excellent Air GmbH. Stadtlohn.	OE-GPS
D-IAGG	01	390 Premier 1	RB-35	Vibro Air Flugservice GmbH. Moenchengladbach.	N435K
D-IAJJ	75	Citation	500-0245	Travel Air Flug GmbH. Duesseldorf.	(N245BC)
D-IALL	96	CitationJet	525-0143	Vibro Air Flugservice GmbH. Moenchengladbach.	D-IOMP
D-IAMO	03	CitationJet CJ-2	525A-0166	Windrose/Bizair Flug GmbH. Berlin-Tempelhof.	N5218R
D-IATT	02	390 Premier 1	RB-48	Vibro Air Flugservice GmbH. Moenchengladbach.	N51480
D-IBBA	93	CitationJet	525-0025	Aerocharter L U Bettermann OHG. Menden.	D-IOBO
D-IBBB	03	390 Premier 1	RB-82	Augusta Air GmbH. Augsburg.	N61882
D-IBIT	00	CitationJet CJ-1	525-0393	Air Traffic GmbH. Duesseldorf.	
D-IBMS	99	CitationJet	525-0309	Brose Fahrzeugteile GmbH. Coburg.	
D-ICAC	79	Citation II/SP	551-0010	Oldenburg Kunstoff Technik GmbH. Kassel.	(N460JR)
D-ICCC	75	Citation	500-0269	EFS Flug Service GmbH. Duesseldorf.	(PH-CTW)
D-ICEE	95	CitationJet	525-0096	Krause/Private Flight GmbH. Bayreuth.	(EC-...)
D-ICEY	98	CitationJet	525-0286	Lenoxhandels u Speditions GmbH. Hamburg.	N51666
D-ICIA	73	Citation	500-0086	Cirrus Airlines Luftfahrt GmbH. Saarbruecken.	LX-YKH
D-ICMS	02	CitationJet CJ-2	525A-0108	Brose Fahrzeugteile GmbH. Coburg.	N5136J
D-ICOL	99	CitationJet	525-0353	Colloseum II Handels und Beteilings mbH. Moenchengladbach.	N5211Q
D-ICSS	95	CitationJet	525-0121	EFD-Eisele Flugdienst GmbH. Stuttgart.	TC-EMA
D-ICTA	81	Citation II/SP	551-0051	Flugbereitschaft GmbH. Karlsruhe.	(D-IHAT)
D-ICWB	99	CitationJet	525-0349	BFD-Brandenburger Flugdienst GmbH. Berlin-Schoenefeld.	
D-IDAG	96	CitationJet	525-0144	DAS-Direct Air Service GmbH. Mannheim.	N5200R
D-IDAS	00	CitationJet CJ-1	525-0389	Donau Air Service GmbH. Mengen.	N389CJ
D-IDBW	93	CitationJet	525-0044	DBW Verwaltungs GmbH/Lufttaxi Flug GmbH. Dortmund.	N55DG
D-IDMH	03	CitationJet CJ-2	525A-0174	Herrenknecht AG. Lahr.	N5076K
D-IEAR	79	Citation II/SP	551-0018	Rieker Air Service GmbH. Stuttgart. (was 550-0373).	N387MA
D-IEFD	02	CitationJet CJ-2	525A-0049	EFD-Eisele Flugdienst GmbH. Stuttgart.	N51575
D-IEIR	83	Citation 1/SP	501-0259	Rieker Air Service GmbH. Stuttgart.	(N225WT)
D-IEWS	97	CitationJet	525-0217	Vibro Air Flugservice GmbH. Moenchengladbach.	N5202D
D-IFDH	03	CitationJet CJ-1	525-0517	Flugbetrieb Gesellschaft Dix mbH. Diepholz.	N52626
D-IFIS	01	CitationJet CJ-1	525-0442	Aircharter Flugservice GmbH. Donaueschingen.	N51872
D-IFMC	01	390 Premier 1	RB-27	GEMU Gebr Muller GmbH. Schwaebisch Hall.	N3216P
D-IFUP	97	CitationJet	525-0172	Fox Air/Fuchs und Partners GmbH. Augsburg.	VP-CTA
D-IGAS	97	CitationJet	525-0223	Excellent Air GmbH. Stadtlohn.	
D-IGME	98	CitationJet	525-0279	Charter Service Hetzler GmbH. Frankfurt.	
D-IGRO*	04	CitationJet CJ-2	525A-0230		N.....
D-IHAP	01	CitationJet CJ-2	525A-0026	SFD Stuttgarter Flugdienst GmbH. Stuttgart.	D-IMYA
D-IHEB	94	CitationJet	525-0064	Fortuna-Werbung GmbH/Business Flugservice GmbH. Speyer.	N2649S
D-IJOA	01	CitationJet CJ-2	525A-0034	Air Evex GmbH. Duesseldorf.	N5211F
D-IKAL	03	CitationJet CJ-2	525A-0193	Daimler Chrysler AG. Stuttgart.	N5183U
D-IKJS	01	CitationJet CJ-2	525A-0029	MSR-Flug Charter GmbH. Muenster-Osnabrueck.	N92CJ
D-IKOP	93	CitationJet	525-0016	Triple Alpha Luftfahrt GmbH. Duesseldorf.	N216CJ
D-ILAM	02	CitationJet CJ-2	525A-0070	Liebherr-Aerospace Lindenberg GmbH. Friedrichshafen.	N5157E
D-ILAT	97	CitationJet	525-0209	Liebherr-Aerospace Lindenberg GmbH. Friedrichshafen.	
D-ILCB	97	CitationJet	525-0193	Dieter Eifler Elektro GmbH. Nohfelden.	N193CJ
D-ILCC	81	Citation II/SP	551-0335	ATB-Air Ticket Buero Gmbh. Mannheim. (was 550-0298).	N431DS
D-ILDL	03	CitationJet CJ-2	525A-0167	Diamler Chrysler AG. Stuttgart.	N51806
D-ILLL	03	CitationJet CJ-1	525-0518	Eisele Flugdienst GmbH. Stuttgart.	N.....
D-ILME	01	CitationJet CJ-1	525-0421	Charter Service Hetzler GmbH. Frankfurt.	N.....
D-IMAC	00	CitationJet CJ-1	525-0396	Comfort Air GmbH. Munich.	N51575
D-IMAX	04	CitationJet CJ-2	525A-0195	Silver Cloud GmbH. Speyer.	N51942
D-IMMD	97	CitationJet	525-0211	Makro-Medien-Dienst GmbH. Ostfildern.	
D-IMME	82	Citation II/SP	551-0400	Commander Flugdienst GmbH. Hamburg. (was 550-0359).	N280JS
D-IMMF	87	Citation II/SP	551-0560	Multibeton GmbH/Multiflug GmbH. Troisdorf. (was 550-0560).	N560AJ
D-IMMI	99	CitationJet	525-0303	Dr Schenk Flugbetrieb GmbH. Munich.	N51612
D-IMMP*	99	CitationJet	525-0354	Milhansa Inc. Merzhausen.	N821P
D-IMPC	95	CitationJet	525-0126	Rio Antonio GmbH. Hamburg.	D-IHGW
D-IMRX	85	Citation 1/SP	501-0688	Franz Haslberger KG/Lech Air GmbH. Lech AFB.	
D-INOB	04	CitationJet CJ-2	525A-0196	Atlas Air Service GmbH. Gandersee.	N5166T
D-INOC	02	CitationJet CJ-1	525-0477	Atlas Air Service GmbH. Gandersee.	N.....
D-IOBO	01	CitationJet CJ-2	525A-0032	Aerocharter L U Bettermann OHG. Menden.	D-IOBU
D-IPCS	98	CitationJet	525-0264	MSR-Flug Charter GmbH. Muenster-Osnabrueck.	EC-HBC
D-IPMI	04	CitationJet CJ-1	525-0533	Papier Mettler, Hahn.	(D-IPMM)
D-IPVD	04	CitationJet CJ-2	525A-0218	GIL-Gebaude u Industrieguter Leasing GmbH. Heidelberg.	N.....
D-IRKE	95	CitationJet	525-0123	VHM Schul u Charterflug GmbH. Muelheim.	N5223P
Reg	Yr	Type	c/n	Owner/Operator	Prev Regn

Reg	Yr	Type	c/n	Owner/Operator	Prev Regn
D-IRMA	00	CitationJet CJ-1	525-0366	Comfort Air GmbH. Munich.	N5223Y
D-IRON	96	CitationJet	525-0168	Geisers Stahlbau GmbH. Duesseldorf.	N51522
D-IRWR	95	CitationJet	525-0118	Bizair Flug GmbH. Berlin-Tempelhof.	N118AZ
D-ISCH	02	CitationJet CJ-2	525A-0052	Gerhard Schubert GmbH. Nordlingen.	N51881
D-ISGW	94	CitationJet	525-0070	MSR Flug Charter GmbH. Muenster-Osnabrueck.	N26504
D-ISHW	98	CitationJet	525-0289	Siemag Verwaltungs GmbH. Hilchenbach.	
D-ISJP	01	CitationJet CJ-2	525A-0030	Juergen Persch, Alzenau.	N302DM
D-ISSS	79	Citation	500-0392	Windrose Air Jetcharter GmbH. Berlin.	I-FLYB
D-ISUN	03	CitationJet CJ-2	525A-0143	Sunseeker Germany AG. Bremen.	N.....
D-ISWA	98	CitationJet	525-0236	Herbert Waldmann Lichttechnik GmbH. Villingen-Schwenningen	
D-ISXT	02	390 Premier 1	RB-50	Sixt Autovermietung GmbH. Paderborn.	N390NS
D-ITAN	00	CitationJet CJ-1	525-0399	EFD-Eisele Flugdienst GmbH. Stuttgart.	(VP-CTN)
D-ITSV	94	CitationJet	525-0084	Air Independence GmbH. Munich.	N5092D
D-IUAC	02	CitationJet CJ-2	525A-0106	UAC Air Charter GmbH. Munich.	N5148B
D-IURS	99	CitationJet	525-0343	Excellent Air GmbH. Stadtlohn.	N5244F
D-IWAN*	04	CitationJet CJ-2	525A-0223		N.....
D-IWHL	93	CitationJet	525-0029	ABC Nordflug GmbH. Hamburg.	(N525KT)
D-IWIL	97	CitationJet	525-0221	Charterflug Rademacher GmbH. Rhede.	
D-IWIR	02	CitationJet CJ-2	525A-0102	Wirtgen Beteiligungs GmbH. Koeln-Bonn.	N888KL
D-IWWW	03	390 Premier 1	RB-89	MSR-Flug Charter GmbH. Muenster-Osnabrueck.	N61589

Military

Reg	Yr	Type	c/n	Owner/Operator	Prev Regn
10+21	89	Airbus A310-304	498	Bundesrepublik Deutschland, Cologne. 'Konrad Adenauer'	D-AOAA
10+22	89	Airbus A310-304	499	Bundesrepublik Deutschland, Cologne. 'Theodor Heuss'	D-AOAB
10+23	89	Airbus A310-304	503	Bundesrepublik Deutschland, Cologne. 'Kurt Schumacher'	D-AOAC
10+27	89	Airbus A310-304	523	Luftwaffe, FBS, Cologne. 'August Euler'	D-AIDI
12+02	85	Challenger 601	3040	Luftwaffe, FBS, Cologne.	N608CL
12+03	85	Challenger 601	3043	Luftwaffe, FBS, Cologne.	N609CL
12+04	85	Challenger 601	3049	Luftwaffe, FBS, Cologne.	C-FQYT
12+05	86	Challenger 601	3053	Luftwaffe, FBS, Cologne.	N604CL
12+06	86	Challenger 601	3056	Luftwaffe, FBS, Cologne.	N612CL
12+07	86	Challenger 601	3059	Luftwaffe, FBS, Cologne.	N614CL

D2 = ANGOLA   Total   12

Civil

Reg	Yr	Type	c/n	Owner/Operator	Prev Regn
D2-EBA	99	Citation V Ultra	560-0502	Aeromercado Ltda. Luanda.	N1298X
D2-ECB	85	Gulfstream 3	474	Government of Angola, Luanda. 'Cunene'	N311GA
D2-ECE	02	Citation Bravo	550-1008	Aeromercado Ltda. Luanda.	N40435
D2-EDC	73	Citation	500-0071	MRI Angola, Luanda.	ZS-AMB
D2-EFM	71	HS 125/400B	25260		ZS-JIH
D2-EVD	67	B 727-29C	19403	SONANGOL Aeronautica - Helipetrol, Luanda.	CB-02
D2-EVG	67	B 727-29C	19402	SONANGOL Aeronautica - Helipetrol, Luanda.	N70PA
D2-EXR	70	HS 125/403B	25215	Intertransit, Luanda. (status ?)	ZS-NPV
D2-FEZ	69	HS 125/F3B-RA	25171	Gira Globo Ltda Aeronautica, Luanda.	(N171AV)
D2-FFH	70	HS 125/F400A	25219	Gira Globo Ltda Aeronautica, Luanda.	(ZS-OZU)
D2-MAN	69	B 707-321B	20025	Government of Angola, Luanda.	N707KS
D2-TPR	74	B 707-3J6B	20715	Government of Angola, Luanda.	B-2404

EC = SPAIN   Total   75

Civil

Reg	Yr	Type	c/n	Owner/Operator	Prev Regn
EC-EDC	65	Falcon 20C	6	Audeli SA. Madrid-Torrejon.	N750SS
EC-EDN	77	Citation 1/SP	501-0010	Instituto Cartografic de Catelunya, Barcelona-El Prat.	VH-POZ
EC-EHC	66	Falcon 20DC	46	Audeli SA. Madrid-Torrejon.	N46VG
EC-EQP	68	Falcon 20C	149	Delta Aviation SA. Madrid. (status ?).	EC-263
EC-FES	91	Citation II	550-0678	Industrias Titan SA. Barcelona-Sabadell.	EC-777
EC-FRV	79	Gulfstream 2B	237	Gestair Executive Jet SA. Madrid-Torrejon.	EC-363
EC-FZP	94	CitationJet	525-0065	Gestair Executive Jet SA. Madrid-Torrejon.	EC-704
EC-GIE	96	CitationJet	525-0133	Gestair Executive Jet SA. Madrid-Torrejon.	EC-261
EC-GJF	79	Citation 1/SP	501-0107	Jose Maria Caballe Horta, Alicante.	(N75471)
EC-GNK	96	Falcon 2000	37	Gestair Executive Jet SA. Madrid-Torrejon.	F-WWMH
EC-GOV	97	Citation V Ultra	560-0419	Gestair Executive Jet SA. Madrid-Torrejon.	N5233J
EC-GSL	81	Westwind-Two	353	Gestair Executive Jet SA. Burgos.	C-GRGE
EC-GTS	72	Citation	500-0037	Clipper National Air SA. Barcelona-El Prat.	N407SC
EC-HCX	72	Falcon 20C	184	Audeli SA. Madrid-Torrejon.	OE-GCJ
EC-HFA	74	Citation	500-0209	Clipper National Air SA. Barcleona-El Prat.	N800AV
EC-HGI	88	Citation II	550-0596	Helisureste SA. Alicante.	D-CAWA
EC-HHS	90	Falcon 50	204	Gestair Executive Jet SA. Madrid-Torrejon.	EC-GPN
EC-HHZ	75	Corvette	15	Aerovento SA. Pamplona.	F-GNAF

Reg	Yr	Type	c/n	Owner/Operator	Prev Regn

Reg	Yr	Type	c/n	Owner/Operator	Prev Regn
EC-HIA	75	Corvette	19	Aeropublic SL. Valencia.	F-GEPQ
EC-HIN	97	CitationJet	525-0197	Gestair-Sky Service Aviation SL. Madrid-Torrejon.	N525KH
EC-HNU	00	Falcon 900EX	62	Gestair-Sky Service Aviation SL. Madrid-Torrejon.	F-WWFM
EC-HOB	99	Falcon 900EX	43	Executive Airlines SA. Barcelona-El Prat.	F-WQBK
EC-HPQ	74	Citation	500-0157	Airnor - Aeronaves del Noroeste SL. Ponteareas.	EC-HFY
EC-HRH	73	Citation	500-0116	PRT Aviation, Barcelona-El Prat.	D-IATC
EC-HRO	00	Citation Bravo	550-0938	CIRSA/Executive Airlines SA. Barcelona-El Prat.	N5VN
EC-HRQ	82	HS 125/700B	7166	Audeli SA. Madrid-Torrejon.	F-GRON
EC-HTR	00	Beechjet 400A	RK-293	Marina Aeroservice SA. Pamplona.	N4293K
EC-HVQ	01	CitationJet CJ-1	525-0436	Gestair Executive Jet SA. Madrid-Torrejon.	N5141F
EC-HVV	82	Falcon 100	193	Dominguez Toledo SA/Mayoral Executive Jet, Malaga.	(N30TN)
EC-HYI	01	Falcon 2000	150	Gestair Executive Jet SA. Madrid-Torrejon.	F-WWVH
EC-IAX*	80	Citation II	550-0156	TRAGSA-Empresa de Transformacion Agraria SA. Madrid.	N205SC
EC-IBA	74	Citation	500-0178	Airnor - Aeronaves del Noroeste SL. Ponteareas.	HB-VKK
EC-IBD	01	Global Express	9060	Gestair Executive Jet SA. Madrid-Torrejon.	(EC-FPI)
EC-IEB	02	CitationJet CJ-2	525A-0064	Gestair Exceutive Jet SA. Madrid-Torrejon.	N5135K
EC-IFS	02	Global Express	9089	Gestair Executive Jet SA. Madrid-Torrejon.	C-GHZH
EC-IIC	80	Learjet 35A	35A-346	Gestair-Sky Service Aviation SL. Madrid-Torrejon.	N34LZ
EC-IIR	02	EMB-135BJ Legacy	145540	FADESA/Audeli Air Express, Madrid-Torrejon.	PT-SAI
EC-IKP	90	Gulfstream 4	1109	Telefonica Internacional/Gestair Executive Jet SA. Madrid.	N101GA
EC-ILK	99	Learjet 45	45-064	Mango, Punto Fa SL. Barcelona-El Prat.	N800UA
EC-IMF	82	Citation II	550-0443	Aerodynamics Malaga SL. Malaga.	D-CGAS
EC-INJ	79	Citation 1/SP	501-0086	Clipper National Air SA. Barcelona-El Prat	(N554T)
EC-INS	87	Learjet 55B	55B-133	Gestair-Sky Service Aviation SL. Madrid-Torrejon.	N810V
EC-IOZ	02	390 Premier 1	RB-61	Gestair Executive Jet SA. Madrid-Torrejon.	N61161
EC-IRB	03	CitationJet CJ-1	525-0516	Gestair-Sky Service Aviation SL. Madrid-Torrejon.	N5060K
EC-IRZ	99	Gulfstream V	582	Gestair Executive Jet SA. Madrid-Torrejon.	N271JG
EC-ISP	79	Citation 1/SP	501-0084	Ibiza Flight, Ibiza.	G-CITI
EC-ISQ	03	Citation Excel	560-5353	Industrias Titan SA. Barcelona-Sabadell.	(N678QS)
EC-ISS	00	CitationJet CJ-1	525-0415	MAC Aviation SL. Zaragoza.	N26SW
EC-IUQ	98	Global Express	9007	Iberostar Group. Palma.	N907GX
EC-IVJ	00	CitationJet CJ-1	525-0429	Executive Airlines SA. Palma di Mallorca.	N429PK
EC-J..	01	CitationJet CJ-1	525-0448		N448JC
EC-JBB	98	Falcon 900C	182	Aire Executive SA. Madrid-Torrejon.	N168HT
EC-JBH	87	Falcon 200	511	Mayoral Executive Jet, Malaga.	F-WQBK
EC-JDV	70	Falcon 20E-5	237	SOKO,	HB-VJV
EC-JEG	04	Challenger 300	20025	Banco Bilbao Vizcaya Argentaria SA.	N125LJ
Military					
T 17-1	68	B 707-331B	20060	47 Grupo Mixto, 471 Esc. Torrejon.	N275B
T 17-2	64	B 707-331C	18757	47 Grupo Mixto, 471 Esc. Torrejon.	N792TW
T 17-3	77	B 707-368C	21367	47 Grupo Mixto, 471 Esc. Torrejon.	N7667B
T 18-1	88	Falcon 900	38	45-40, 45 Grupo, 451 Esc. Torrejon.	F-WWFE
T 18-2	91	Falcon 900	90	45-41, 45 Grupo, 451 Esc. Torrejon.	F-WWFG
T 18-3	89	Falcon 900	77	45-42, 45 Grupo, 451 Esc. Torrejon.	N107BK
T 18-4	89	Falcon 900	74	45-43, 45 Grupo, 451 Esc. Torrejon.	N108BK
T 18-5	89	Falcon 900	73	45-44, 45 Grupo, 451 Esc. Torrejon.	N109BK
T 22-1	90	Airbus A310-304	550	45-50, 45 Grupo, 451 Esc. Torrejon.	F-WEMP
T 22-2	90	Airbus A310-304	551	45-51, 45 Grupo, 451 Esc. Torrejon.	F-WEMQ
TM 11-1	71	Falcon 20E	253	47 Grupo Mixto, 471 Esc. Torrejon. (prev code 45-02).	T 11-1
TM 11-2	71	Falcon 20D	222	47 Grupo Mixto, 471 Esc. Torrejon. (prev code 45-03).	EC-BXV
TM 11-3	70	Falcon 20D	219	47 Grupo Mixto, 472 Esc. Torrejon. (prev code 408-11).	EC-BVV
TM 11-4	75	Falcon 20E	332	47 Grupo Mixto, 472 Esc. Torrejon. (prev code 408-12).	EC-CTV
TM 17-4	66	B 707-351C	19164	408-21, Ed1A/45 Grupo, Torrejon.	SX-DBO
TR 20-01	92	Citation V	560-0161	403-11, 403 Esc. Madrid-Cuatro Vientos.	(XA-CYC)
TR 20-02	92	Citation V	560-0193	403-12, 403 Esc. Madrid-Cuatro Vientos.	N1282K
U 20-1	82	Citation II	550-0425	01-405, Armada, 4a Escuadrilla, Rota.	(LN-FOX)
U 20-2	83	Citation II	550-0446	01-406, Armada, 4a Escuadrilla, Rota.	N1248N
U 20-3	88	Citation II	550-0592	01-407, Armada, 4a Escuadrilla, Rota.	N1302N

EI = EIRE   **Total   8**

Civil

Reg	Yr	Type	c/n	Owner/Operator	Prev Regn
EI-CIR	80	Citation II/SP	551-0174	Air Liberte/Semavil SA. Dinard, France. (was 550-0128).	N60AR
EI-IAW	01	Learjet 60	60-218	Voltage Plus Ltd. Shannon.	N8084J
EI-IRE	01	Challenger 604	5515	Starair (Ireland) Ltd. Dublin.	N515DM
EI-MAX	01	Learjet 31A	31A-233	Airlink Airways Ltd. Dublin.	N233BR
EI-WGV	96	Gulfstream V	505	Westair Aviation Ltd. Shannon. 'Born Free'	N505GV
EI-WJN	79	HS 125/700A	7062	Westair Aviation Ltd. Shannon.	N416RD
Reg	Yr	Type	c/n	Owner/Operator	Prev Regn

Reg	Yr	Type	c/n	Owner/Operator	Prev Regn
⊐ 251	91	Gulfstream 4	1160	Irish Air Corps. Casement-Dublin.	N17584
⊐ 258	03	Learjet 45	45-234	Irish Air Corps. Casement-Dublin.	N5009T

EP = IRAN *Total 23*

Civil

⊐ EP-AGA	77	B 737-286	21317	Government of Iran, Teheran.	
⊐ EP-AGY	73	Falcon 20E	286	Iran Asseman Airlines, Teheran.	F-WRQU
⊐ EP-AKC	74	Falcon 20E	301	National Cartographic Centre, Teheran.	F-WNGL
⊐ EP-FIC	75	Falcon 20E	334	Iran Asseman Airlines, Teheran.	F-WRQU
⊐ EP-FID	75	Falcon 20E	338	CAO/Iran Asseman Airlines, Teheran.	F-WMKG
⊐ EP-FIF	75	Falcon 20E	320	Iran Asseman Airlines, Teheran.	YI-AHG
⊐ EP-IPA	71	Falcon 20E	251	Department of Police, Teheran.	EP-FIE
⊐ EP-PAZ	76	F 28-1000	11104	Government of Iran, Teheran.	F-GIAK
⊐ EP-PLN	64	B 727-30	18363	Government of Iran, Teheran. "Palestine"	EP-SHP
⊐ EP-SEA	77	Falcon 20E	367	Iran Asseman Airlines, Teheran.	F-WRQR
⊐ EP-TFA	82	Falcon 50	101	Government of Iran, Teheran.	5-9012
⊐ EP-TFI	83	Falcon 50	120	Government of Iran, Teheran.	5-9011

Military

⊐ 1001	78	B 707-386C	21396	Government of Iran, Teheran.	EP-NHY
⊐ 1003	76	JetStar 2	5203	Government of Iran, Teheran. (status ?).	EP-VLP
⊐ 1004	69	JetStar-8	5137	Government of Iran, Teheran.	EP-VRP
⊐ 15-2233	75	Falcon 20E	318	Ministry of SEPHA L.D. D.A.L. Teheran.	EP-FIG
⊐ 15-2235	75	Falcon 20E	333	Ministry of SEPHA L.D. D.A.L. Teheran.	5-2801
⊐ 5-2802	75	Falcon 20E	336	Iranian Navy, Mehrabad.	F-WRQP
⊐ 5-2803	76	Falcon 20E	340	Iranian Navy, Mehrabad.	F-WRQX
⊐ 5-2804	76	Falcon 20E	346	Iranian Navy, Mehrabad.	F-WRQP
⊐ 5-3021	76	Falcon 20E	350	Iranian Air Army, Mehrabad.	5-4040
⊐ 5-9003	76	Falcon 20F	354	Iranian Air Force, 1st Transport Base, Mehrabad.	F-WRQR
⊐ 5-9013	83	Falcon 50	122	Government of Iran, Teheran.	YI-ALE

ER = MOLDOVA *Total 1*

Civil

⊐ ER-LGA	81	Learjet 35A	35A-406	Nobil Air SRL. Chisinau.	I-KELM

ES = ESTONIA *Total 1*

Civil

⊐ ES-PVS	00	Learjet 60	60-190	Avies Air Co. Tallinn.	EI-IAU

EW = BELARUS *Total 1*

Civil

⊐ EW-001PA	02	BBJ-8EV	33079	Government of Belarus, Minsk.	N375BC

EZ = TURKMENISTAN *Total 3*

Civil

⊐ EZ-A001	93	B 737-341	26855	Government of Turkmenistan, Ashkhabad.	EK-A001
⊐ EZ-A010	94	B 757-23A	25345	Government of Turkmenistan, Ashkhabad.	
⊐ EZ-B021	92	BAe 1000B	9029	National State Aviacompany, Ashkhabad.	G-5-751

F = FRANCE *Total 175*

Civil

⊐ F-BVPG	76	Corvette	25	Betrand Lehouck, Lille-Lesquin.	F-OBZV
⊐ F-BVPK	74	Corvette	7	Aero Stock, Paris-Le Bourget.	N611AC
⊐ F-BVPN	75	Falcon 20E-5B	311	Michelin Air Services, Clermont-Ferrand.	F-WRQS
⊐ F-BVPR	75	Falcon 10	5	AVDEF-Aviation Defense Service, Nimes-Garons.	F-WVPR
⊐ F-BXAS	75	AC 690A-TU	11240	Ste. Turbomeca, Pau.	F-WXAS
⊐ F-GBRF	75	Falcon 10	38	Aero Services Executive, Paris-Le Bourget.	N20ET
⊐ F-GBTM	78	Falcon 20GF	397	Institut National des Sciences de l'Universe du CNRS, Creil.	F-WBTM
⊐ F-GDLR	78	Falcon 10	121	Unijet SA. Paris-Le Bourget.	HB-VFT
⊐ F-GELT	86	Falcon 100	211	CATEX SA. St Etienne.	F-WZGT
⊐ F-GFDH	75	Corvette	13	EADS Airbus SA. Toulouse-Blagnac.	N601AM
⊐ F-GFMD	81	Falcon 10	136	Aero Services Executive, Paris-Le Bourget.	F-WZGS
⊐ F-GFPF	75	Falcon 10	68	Aero Services Executive, Paris-Le Bourget.	N80MP
⊐ F-GGAL	86	Citation III	650-0117	Avialair/Gilbert Gross, Paris-Le Bourget.	N1321N
⊐ F-GGCP	80	Falcon 50	9	Aero Services Executive, Paris-Le Bourget.	(N100WJ)
⊐ F-GGGA	88	Citation II	550-0586	Aero Vision SARL. Toulouse-Blagnac.	N1301N
⊐ F-GGGT	89	Citation II	550-0611	Cie Financiere et de Participations Roullier, Dinard.	(N1242K)
⊐ F-GGVB	79	Falcon 50	11	Bollore SA. Paris-Le Bourget.	N5739
⊐ F-GHDT	69	Falcon 20-5	176	Dassault Aviation, Paris-Le Bourget.	F-WGTM

Reg	Yr	Type	c/n	Owner/Operator	Prev Regn

Reg	Yr	Type	c/n	Owner/Operator	Prev Regn
☐ F-GHDX	79	Falcon 10	140	GIE Flying Bird. Quimper.	N88WL
☐ F-GHPB	88	Falcon 100	215	Mascaralain EURL. Auberviliers.	F-WZGY
☐ F-GILM	76	Corvette	32	Air Entreprise International, Paris-Le Bourget.	EC-DUF
☐ F-GIPH	82	Falcon 100	194	Regourd Aviation/Occitania SA. Paris-Le Bourget.	N61FC
☐ F-GIRH*	75	Corvette	14	Aero Stock, Paris-Le Bourget. (stored at LBG).	SP-FOA
☐ F-GJAP	76	Corvette	31	Airbus France SAS, Toulouse-Blagnac.	EC-DYE
☐ F-GJAS	74	Corvette	8	Aero Vision SARL, Toulouse-Blagnac.	6V-AEA
☐ F-GJBZ	97	Falcon 50EX	269	Air BG, Paris-Le Bourget.	(F-GPBG)
☐ F-GJDB	67	Falcon 20C	76	Jet 2000 Business Jets, Moscow-Vnukovo, Russia.	F-GGFO
☐ F-GJDG	76	Citation	500-0312	Eurojet Italia SRL. Milan, Italy.	N82AT
☐ F-GJLB	78	Corvette	39	Aero Vision SARL. Toulouse-Blagnac.	TL-RCA
☐ F-GJSK	96	Falcon 2000	27	Dassault Aviation, Paris-Le Bourget.	G-JCBI
☐ F-GJXX	89	Citation V	560-0070	Ste J C Decaux, Toussus le Noble.	
☐ F-GJYD	82	Citation II	550-0415	DARTA Aero Charter, Paris-Le Bourget.	N1949M
☐ F-GKBZ	88	Falcon 50	185	Cora SA. Paris-Le Bourget.	N238Y
☐ F-GKDB	73	Falcon 20E	271	Laboratoire de Recherche, Avignon-Caumont.	F-GHPO
☐ F-GKGA	75	Corvette	11	Airbus France SAS. Toulouse-Blagnac.	F-WFPD
☐ F-GKHJ	87	Falcon 900	11	Dassault Aviation, Paris Le-Bourget.	N251SJ
☐ F-GKHL	90	Citation V	560-0059	Penauille + SARI + UPSA/Euralair, Paris.	N2687L
☐ F-GKID	76	Citation	500-0319	Berry Flight, Oostrozelke, Belgium.	N94MA
☐ F-GKIR	77	Citation	500-0361	Soc de Location pour l'Industrie Aerienne-Solid Air, Paris.	N90EB
☐ F-GLEC	76	Corvette	30	Airbus France SAS, Toulouse-Blagnac.	(F-GKGB)
☐ F-GLIM	91	Citation V	560-0119	Ste Limagrain Stelia, Clermont Ferrand.	(N6804N)
☐ F-GLTK	89	Citation II	550-0609	Knauf Trade SNC/Alsair SA. Colmar.	N344A
☐ F-GLYC	92	Citation V	560-0205	SA Lyreco France, Prouvy.	
☐ F-GMCI	79	Citation II	550-0050	Ste Bretonne de Developpement, Brest.	F-ODUT
☐ F-GMOE	93	Falcon 2000	1	Dassault Aviation, Paris-Le Bourget.	(F-GMIR)
☐ F-GMOF	75	Corvette	12	Aero Stock, Paris-Le Bourget.	TJ-AHR
☐ F-GMOT	82	Falcon 50	111	Occitania, Paris-Le Bourget.	N50AH
☐ F-GNCP	78	Citation II	550-0004	Air Taxi SAT. Blois Le Breuil.	N312GA
☐ F-GNDZ	74	Falcon 10	17	Unijet SA. Paris-Le Bourget.	EC-949
☐ F-GNMF	88	Falcon 900	47	AST/Artisona Shipping, Lugano, Switzerland.	(F-GOFC)
☐ F-GOAL	82	Falcon 50	131	SAS Carrefour Mobilier Hypermarches France, Paris-Le Bourget	F-WGTF
☐ F-GOPM	74	Falcon 20E-5B	302	Michelin Air Services, Clermont-Ferrand.	F-WQBM
☐ F-GOYA	96	Falcon 900EX	11	Pinaud SA/SNC Artemis Conseil, Paris-Le Bourget.	F-WWFI
☐ F-GPAA	67	Falcon 20EW	103	AVDEF-Aviation Defense Service, Nimes-Garons.	G-FRAV
☐ F-GPAB	71	Falcon 20EW	254	AVDEF-Aviation Defense Service, Nimes-Garons.	G-FRAC
☐ F-GPAD	73	Falcon 20EW	280	AVDEF-Aviation Defense Service, Nimes-Garons.	(F-GPAE)
☐ F-GPFC	95	CitationJet	525-0101	Promod SA. Marcq en Baroeul.	N5157E
☐ F-GPFD	90	Falcon 100	221	SNC Sporto et Cie. Paris-Le Bourget.	OE-GHA
☐ F-GPLA	76	Corvette	28	Aero Vision SARL. Toulouse-Blagnac.	(OO-TTL)
☐ F-GPLF	98	CitationJet	525-0291	Financiere Pierre Le Foll, Deauville.	N51744
☐ F-GPNJ	99	Falcon 900EX	50	Aero Services Executive, Paris-Le Bourget.	F-WWFS
☐ F-GPPF	81	Falcon 50	65	Laboratoires Pierre Fabre SA/ASE, Paris-Le Bourget.	N1EV
☐ F-GPSA	83	Falcon 50	123	Ste Gefco & Cie/Air Gefco, Paris-Le Bourget.	N211EF
☐ F-GPUJ	03	CitationJet CJ-2	525A-0169	Unijet SA. Paris-Le Bourget.	N5262W
☐ F-GRAX	93	Falcon 900B	120	Dassault Aviation, Paris-Le Bourget.	VP-BNJ
☐ F-GRCH	74	Citation	500-0201	Laval Distributing SA.	(F-GIHU)
☐ F-GSEF	03	Falcon 900EX EASY	121	Dassault Aviation, Paris-Le Bourget.	F-WWFW
☐ F-GSER	78	Falcon 50	2	Occitania, Paris-Le Bourget.	F-BINR
☐ F-GSLZ	86	Falcon 100	208	Toperline, Nancy-Essey.	F-WQBJ
☐ F-GSMC	76	Citation	500-0308	Wing Aviation, Paris-Le Bourget.	F-GMLH
☐ F-GSVU	00	Airbus A319CJ-133X	1256	Aero Services Corporate SA. Paris-Le Bourget.	D-AVYZ
☐ F-GTJF	95	Falcon 50	246	Dassault Aviation, Paris-Le Bourget.	TC-YSR
☐ F-GTMD	98	CitationJet	525-0312	Jose Manuel Diaz, Paris-Le Bourget.	
☐ F-GTOD	80	Falcon 10	155	Olivier Dassault/DARTA Aero Charter, Paris-Le Bourget.	N725PA
☐ F-GTRY	00	CitationJet	525-0359	Air Ailes, Colmar-Houssen.	
☐ F-GUAJ	86	Falcon 50	169	Aero Services Executive, Paris-Le Bourget.	I-SNAB
☐ F-GUTC	05	Falcon 2000EX EASY	42	Dassault Aviation, Paris-Le Bourget.	(D-BMVV)
☐ F-GVAE	90	Falcon 900	86	Eurofly Service SpA. Turin, Italy.	A6-UAE
☐ F-GVML	00	Global Express	9081	LVMH Services, Paris-Le Bourget.	C-GZTZ
☐ F-GYAS	03	Airbus A319-155	1999	Aero Services Corporate SA. Paris-Le Bourget.	
☐ F-GYOL	82	Falcon 50	88	Dassault Aviation, Paris-Le Bourget.	LZ-010
☐ F-GYPB	74	Falcon 20E-5	307	ASE/Berlys Aero SA. Luxembourg/Yves St Laurent. Paris.	F-GKIS
☐ F-GYSL	75	Falcon 20F-5B	341	ASE/Berlys Aero SA. Luxembourg/Yves St Laurent, Paris.	F-OHCJ
☐ F-GZLC	80	Citation II	550-0190	Biotonic, Cannes-Mandelieu.	F-VTEL

Reg	*Yr*	*Type*	*c/n*	*Owner/Operator*	*Prev Regn*

Reg	Yr	Type	c/n	Owner/Operator	Prev Regn
☐ F-GZUJ	04	CitationJet CJ-2	525A-0200	Unijet SA. Paris-Le Bourget.	N5203S
☐ F-HACA	80	Citation II	550-0182	Champagne Airlines, Reims-Champagne.	N107CF
☐ F-HAIR	80	Falcon 50	37	Groupe Jean Claude Darmon, Paris-Le Bourget.	F-GMCU
☐ F-HAJD	03	CitationJet CJ-1	525-0523	Star Service International, Orleans.	N51246
☐ F-HALM	84	Falcon 50	134	Marionnaud Parfumeries SA. Paris-Le Bourget.	(OY-CKH)
☐ F-HAOA	93	CitationJet	525-0024	Occitania, Paris-Le Bourget.	N525DJ
☐ F-HAPP	00	CitationJet CJ-2	525A-0009	Air Taxi SAT, Blois Le Breuil.	N525LC
☐ F-HASC	97	CitationJet	525-0177	Socri Aero SARL. Cannes.	G-OWRC
☐ F-HAXA	97	Falcon 900EX	12	AXA Reassurance SA/Unijet SA. Paris-Le Bourget.	F-WQBL
☐ F-HBBM	80	Falcon 50	16	Bernard Magrez SA. Paris-Le Bourget.	F-WQBL
☐ F-HBFP	04	Hawker 800XP	8689	Unijet SA. Paris Le-Bourget.	N36689
☐ F-HBOL	02	Falcon 900EX	107	Unijet SA. Paris-Le Bourget.	F-WWFE
☐ F-HEOL	04	CitationJet CJ-2	525A-0219	Domair SAS. Paris-Le Bourget.	N5247U
☐ F-HFBW*	05	Falcon 7X	001	Dassault Aviation, Bordeaux. (FBW-Fly By Wire).	F-WFBW
☐ F-HILM*	04	Citation Encore	560-0683	Ste Limagrain Stelia, Clermont-Ferrand.	N.....
☐ F-HRBS*	02	Falcon 900EX	113	The Royal Bank of Scotland plc. Edinburgh, UK.	G-RBSG
☐ F-ODSR	76	Corvette	35	Monique Arimanana, Antananarivo, Malagasy.	5R-MVD
☐ F-OHFO	97	Falcon 50EX	267	Adolf Wuerth GmbH. Niederstetten, Germany.	(D-BETI)
☐ F-ORAV	02	Falcon 2000	171	National Private Air Transport Ltd. Jeddah, Saudi Arabia.	(HZ-KSDD)
☐ F-WNCO	02	Falcon 900EX EASY	97	Dassault Aviation, Bordeaux.	(F-GOEA)
☐ F-WQBK	01	Falcon 2000	133	Dassault Aviation, Paris-Le Bourget.	HZ-KSDB
☐ F-WQBN	98	Falcon 2000	76	Dassault Aviation, Paris-Le Bourget.	OY-CKN
☐ F-WWFF	04	Falcon 900C	202	Dassault Aviation, Bordeaux.	
☐ F-WWFG	04	Falcon 900EX EASY	148	Dassault Aviation, Bordeaux.	
☐ F-WWFV	04	Falcon 900EX EASY	143	Dassault Aviation, Bordeaux.	
☐ F-WWFX	04	Falcon 900EX EASY	145	Dassault Aviation, Bordeaux.	
☐ F-WWFY	04	Falcon 900C	203	Dassault Aviation, Bordeaux.	
☐ F-WWGN	04	Falcon 2000EX EASY	49	Dassault Aviation, Bordeaux.	
☐ F-WWMA	04	Falcon 2000EX EASY	52	Dassault Aviation, Bordeaux.	
☐ F-WXEY	03	Falcon 2000EX	6	Dassault Aviation, Bordeaux.	F-W...

Military

Reg	Yr	Type	c/n	Owner/Operator	Prev Regn
☐ 101	77	Falcon 10MER	101	Marine Nationale, 57S, Landivisiau.	F-WPXJ
☐ 129	79	Falcon 10MER	129	Marine Nationale, 57S, Landivisiau.	F-WZGA
☐ 132	83	Falcon 50 SURMAR	132	Marine Nationale, Flotille 24F, Lanne Bihoue.	I-EDIK
☐ 133	79	Falcon 10MER	133	Marine Nationale, 57S, Landivisiau.	F-ZGTI
☐ 143	80	Falcon 10MER	143	Marine Nationale, 57S, Landivisiau.	F-WZGO
☐ 185	81	Falcon 10MER	185	Marine Nationale, 57S, Landivisiau.	F-WZGQ
☐ 27/F-RAFK	81	Falcon 50	27	A de l'Air, ET 1/60, Villacoublay.	F-WGTG
☐ 30/F-ZVMB	80	Falcon 50 SURMAR	30	Marine Nationale, Flotille 24F, Lanne-Bihoue.	F-WQFZ
☐ 32	75	Falcon 10MER	32	Marine Nationale, 57S, Landivisiau.	F-W...
☐ 36	80	Falcon 50 SURMAR	36	Marine Nationale, Flotille 24F, Lanne Bihoue.	F-ZJTL
☐ 48	82	Gardian	448	Aeronavale, Flotille 25F, BA-190 Tahiti.	F-ZWVF
☐ 65	83	Gardian	465	Aeronavale, Flotille 25F, BA-190 Tahiti.	F-ZJTS
☐ 7	80	Falcon 50 SURMAR	7	Marine Nationale, Flotille 25, Lanne-Bihoue.	F-WQBN
☐ 72	83	Gardian	472	Aeronavale, Flotille 25F, BA-190 Tahiti.	F-Z...
☐ 77	83	Gardian	477	Aeronavale, Flotille 25F, BA-190 Tahiti.	F-Z...
☐ 80	84	Gardian	480	Aeronavale, Flotille 25F, BA-190 Tahiti.	F-ZJSA
☐ F-RADA	87	Airbus A310-304	421	A de l'Air, COTAM, Esterel Squadron, Villacoublay.	F-ODVD
☐ F-RADB	87	Airbus A310-304	422	A de l'Air, COTAM, Esterel Squadron, Villacoublay.	F-ODVE
☐ F-RADC	86	Airbus A310-304	418	A de l'Air, COTAM, Esterel Squadron, Villacoublay.	F-WQIC
☐ F-RAEA	72	Falcon 20E	260	A de l'Air, ET 1/65, Villacoublay.	F-WMKJ
☐ F-RAEB	68	Falcon 20C	167	A de l'Air, ET 1/65, Villacoublay.	F-RAFL
☐ F-RAEC	76	Falcon 20F	342	A de l'Air, ET 1/65, Villacoublay.	F-RAEG
☐ F-RAED	67	Falcon 20C	93	A de l'Air, ET 1/65, Villacoublay.	F-RAEC
☐ F-RAEE	71	Falcon 20C	238	A de l'Air, ET 1/65, Villacoublay.	F-RAFM
☐ F-RAEF	72	Falcon 20E	268	A de l'Air, ET 1/65, Villacoublay.	F-RAFK
☐ F-RAEG	74	Falcon 20E	291	A de l'Air, ET 3/65, Villacoublay.	F-RAEC
☐ F-RAEH	80	Falcon 20F	422	A de l'Air, ET 3/65, Villacoublay.	F-RCAL
☐ F-RAFC	65	DC 8F-55F	45819	A de l'Air, ET 3/60, Roissy.	F-BNLD
☐ F-RAFE	64	DC 8-53	45570	A de l'Air, SARIGUE ELINT, EE/51, Evreaux-Fauville.	F-ZARK
☐ F-RAFF	69	DC 8-72CF	46130	A de l'Air, ET 3/60, Roissy.	OH-LFY
☐ F-RAFG	69	DC 8-72CF	46013	A de l'Air, ET 3/60, Roissy.	OH-LFT
☐ F-RAFI	79	Falcon 50	5	A de l'Air, ETEC 00.065, Villacoublay.	F-WZHB
☐ F-RAFJ	82	Falcon 50	78	A de l'Air, ETEC 00.065, Villacoublay.	F-GEOY
☐ F-RAFL	80	Falcon 50	34	A de l'Air, ETEC 00.065, Villacoublay.	F-WEFS
☐ F-RAFP	85	Falcon 900	2	A de l'Air, ETEC 00.065, Villacoublay.	F-GFJC

Reg	Yr	Type	c/n	Owner/Operator	Prev Regn
☐ F-RAFQ	86	Falcon 900	4	A de l'Air, ETEC 00.065, Villacoublay.	F-WWFA
☐ F-RBFA	01	Airbus A319CJ-115X	1485	A de l'Air, COTAM, Esterel Squadron, Villacoublay.	
☐ F-RBFB	01	Airbus A319CJ-115X	1556	A de l'Air, COTAM, Esterel Squadron, Villacoublay.	
☐ F-UKJA	70	Falcon 20SP	182	A de l'Air, 339-JA, CITAC-339, Luxeuil.	F-BVFV
☐ F-UKJC	81	Falcon 20SNA	451	A de l'Air, 339-JC, CITAC-339, Luxeuil. 'Fil d'Ariane'	F-UGWN
☐ F-UKJE/463	70	Falcon 20SNA	186	Stored at Chateaudun.	F-UGWM/4
☐ F-UKJG	67	Falcon 20SNA	115	Stored at Chateaudun.	F-UGWL/11
☐ F-UKJI	83	Falcon 20F	483	A de l'Air, 339-JI, CITAC-339, Luxeuil. 'L'Oeil des Fees'	F-UGWO
☐ F-ZACA	71	Falcon 20E	252	CEV, Bretigny.	I-GIAZ
☐ F-ZACB	67	Falcon 20C	96	CEV, Cazaux.	F-GERT
☐ F-ZACC	68	Falcon 20C	124	CEV, Bretigny.	F-WJMJ
☐ F-ZACD	68	Falcon 20C	131	CEV, Bretigny.	F-WJMK
☐ F-ZACG	67	Falcon 20C	86	CEV, Cazaux.	F-WRGQ
☐ F-ZACR	68	Falcon 20C	138	CEV, Bretigny.	F-BUIC
☐ F-ZACS	66	Falcon 20C	22	CEV, Istres.	F-BMKK
☐ F-ZACT	67	Falcon 20C	79	CEV, Bretigny.	F-BNRH
☐ F-ZACU	68	Falcon 20C	145	CEV, Bretigny.	F-GCGY
☐ F-ZACV	73	Falcon 20E	288	CEV, Bretigny.	F-BUYE
☐ F-ZACW	67	Falcon 20C	104	CEV, Bretigny.	F-BOXV
☐ F-ZACX	69	Falcon 20C	188	CEV, Bretigny.	F-BRPK
☐ F-ZACY	72	Falcon 20E	263	CEV, Bretigny.	F-BSBU
☐ F-ZACZ	78	Falcon 20F	375	CEV, Bretigny.	F-GBMD
☐ F-ZVMT	69	DC 8-72CF	46043	A de l'Air, SARIGUE ELINT, EE/51, Evreaux-Fauville.	F-RAFD
☐ F-ZVMV	72	Corvette	1	CEV, Bretigny.	F-BUAS
☐ F-ZVMW	73	Corvette	2	CEV, Istres.	F-BNRZ
☐ F-ZVMX	74	Corvette	10	CEV, Istres.	F-GFEJ

G = GREAT BRITAIN   Total   144

Civil

Reg	Yr	Type	c/n	Owner/Operator	Prev Regn
☐ G-BJIR	81	Citation II	550-0296	Aviation Beauport Ltd. Jersey, C.I. (AVB 8IR).	N6888C
☐ G-BLRA	84	BAe 146-100	E1017	BAe Systems (Corporate Air Travel) Ltd. Warton.	N117TR
☐ G-BRNM	97	Leopard	002	Chichester-Miles Consultants Ltd. Cranfield.	
☐ G-BTAB	87	BAe 125/800B	8088	ARAVCO Ltd. Farnborough.	G-BOOA
☐ G-BVCM	93	CitationJet	525-0022	Kenmore Aviation Ltd. Edinburgh.	(N1329N)
☐ G-BYHM	92	BAe 125/800B	8233	Club 328 Ltd. Southampton.	VP-BTM
☐ G-BZNR	90	BAe 125/800B	8180	Executive Jet Charter Ltd. Staverton.	G-XRMC
☐ G-CBHT	99	Falcon 900EX	48	TAG Aviation (UK) Ltd. Farnborough.	G-GPWH
☐ G-CBRG	02	Citation Excel	560-5266	Stadium City Ltd. Humberside.	N5245D
☐ G-CBTU	88	Citation II	550-0601	Thames Aviation Ltd. Fairoaks.	G-OCDB
☐ G-CDCX	02	Citation X	750-0194	Peter Harris, Luton.	N194CX
☐ G-CJAA	93	BAe 125/800B	8240	Club 328 Ltd. Southampton.	(G-OURC)
☐ G-CJAD	01	CitationJet CJ-1	525-0435	Davis Aircraft Operations, Edinburgh.	N525AD
☐ G-CJAE	90	Citation V	560-0046	Club 328 Ltd. Southampton.	(G-OURD)
☐ G-DAEX	01	Falcon 900EX	78	Triair (Bermuda) Ltd. Farnborough.	F-WWFR
☐ G-DEZC	79	HS 125/700B	7070	Club 328 Ltd. Southampton.	(G-JETG)
☐ G-DJAE	76	Citation	500-0339	Source Ltd/XClusive Jet Charter Ltd. Hurn.	G-JEAN
☐ G-DNVT	89	Gulfstream 4	1078	Shell Aircraft Ltd. London.	N17589
☐ G-EJEL	90	Citation II	550-0643	Elliott Brick Co. Leeds-Bradford.	N747CR
☐ G-ELNX	01	Regional Jet	7508	Eurolynx Corp. Farnborough.	VH-KXJ
☐ G-ESTA	80	Citation II	550-0127	Executive Aviation Services Ltd. Staverton.	G-GAUL
☐ G-EVLN	91	Gulfstream 4	1175	Metropix Ltd. London.	N18WF
☐ G-FBFI	94	Challenger 601-3R	5152	GAMA Aviation Ltd. Farnborough.	(HB-JRX)
☐ G-FCDB	01	Citation Bravo	550-0985	Chris de Burgh/Eurojet Aviation Ltd. Birmingham.	N.....
☐ G-FFRA	68	Falcon 20EW	132	F R Aviation Ltd. Hurn.	N902FR
☐ G-FIRM	00	Citation Bravo	550-0940	Marshall Executive Aviation, Cambridge.	N5263S
☐ G-FJET	82	Citation II	550-0419	London Executive Aviation Ltd. Stansted.	G-DCFR
☐ G-FLVU	81	Citation 1/SP	501-0178	A D Aviation Ltd. Hawarden-Chester.	N83ND
☐ G-FRAF	74	Falcon 20EW	295	F R Aviation Ltd. Hurn.	N911FR
☐ G-FRAH	69	Falcon 20EW	223	F R Aviation Ltd. Durham Tees Valley.	G-60-01
☐ G-FRAI	72	Falcon 20EW	270	F R Aviation Ltd. Durham Tees Valley.	N901FR
☐ G-FRAJ	66	Falcon 20EW	20	F R Aviation Ltd. Durham Tees Valley.	N903FR
☐ G-FRAK	69	Falcon 20EW	213	F R Aviation Ltd. Hurn.	(N213FC)
☐ G-FRAL	68	Falcon 20EW	151	F R Aviation Ltd. Durham Tees Valley.	N904FR
☐ G-FRAM	70	Falcon 20EW	224	F R Aviation Ltd. Hurn.	N907FR
☐ G-FRAO	69	Falcon 20EW	214	F R Aviation Ltd. Hurn.	N906FR
☐ G-FRAP	69	Falcon 20EW	207	F R Aviation Ltd. Hurn.	N908FR
☐ G-FRAR	69	Falcon 20EW	209	F R Aviation Ltd. Hurn.	N909FR

Reg	Yr	Type	c/n	Owner/Operator	Prev Regn
☐ G-FRAS	67	Falcon 20EW	82	F R Aviation Ltd. Durham Tees Valley.	117501
☐ G-FRAT	67	Falcon 20EW	87	F R Aviation Ltd. Durham Tees Valley.	117502
☐ G-FRAU	67	Falcon 20EW	97	F R Aviation Ltd. Durham Tees Valley.	117504
☐ G-FRAW	67	Falcon 20EW	114	F R Aviation Ltd. Durham Tees Valley.	117507
☐ G-FRBA	70	Falcon 20EW	178	F R Aviation Ltd. Hurn.	OH-FFA
☐ G-FRYL	03	390 Premier 1	RB-97	Houston Jet Services Ltd/Gregg Air, Oxford-Kidlington.	N6197F
☐ G-FTSL	99	Challenger 604	5416	Farglobe Transport Services Ltd. Farnborough.	N161MD
☐ G-GDEZ	92	BAe 1000B	9026	G De Z Ltd/Aviation Beauport Ltd. Jersey, C.I. (AVB 1EZ).	G-5-743
☐ G-GEDY	03	Falcon 2000	208	Victoria Aviation Ltd. Cairo, Egypt.	F-WWVV
☐ G-GHPG	99	Citation Bravo	550-0897	MCP Aviation (Charters) Ltd/LEA, Stapleford.	EI-GHP
☐ G-GIRA	80	HS 125/700B	7103	E A S Aeroservizi, Venice, Italy.	YL-VIR
☐ G-GMAA	01	Learjet 45	45-167	GAMA Aviation Ltd. Farnborough.	N5012V
☐ G-GMAB	93	BAe 1000B	9034	GAMA Aviation Ltd. Farnborough.	N81HH
☐ G-GRGS	98	Citation V Ultra	560-0457	Houston Jet Services Ltd/Gregg Air, Oxford-Kidlington.	VP-CMS
☐ G-HARF	90	Gulfstream 4	1117	Fayair (Jersey) Ltd. Jersey, C.I.	N1761J
☐ G-HMEI	84	Falcon 900B	1	Executive Jet Group Ltd. Northolt.	F-HOCI
☐ G-HMMV	99	CitationJet	525-0358	Stellar Aviation, Snetterton.	N51564
☐ G-HRDS	03	Gulfstream G550	5032	Fayair (Jersey) Ltd. Stansted.	N932GA
☐ G-IAMS	01	Citation Excel	560-5183	Amsair Ltd/London Executive Aviation, Stansted.	G-CFRA
☐ G-IDAB	00	Citation Bravo	550-0917	Pool Aviation Ltd. Blackpool.	(SE-RBY)
☐ G-IFTE	78	HS 125/700B	7037	Albion Aviation Management Ltd. Biggin Hill.	G-BFVI
☐ G-IKOS	00	Citation Bravo	550-0957	London Executive Aviation Ltd. Biggin Hill.	N957PH
☐ G-IOOX	04	Learjet 45	45-243	100% Aviation Ltd/David Richards BAR Racing, Oxford.	N4004Q
☐ G-IPAL	00	Citation Bravo	550-0935	Pacific Aviation Ltd. Dublin, Ireland.	EI-PAL
☐ G-IPAX	01	Citation Excel	560-5228	Pacific Aviation Ltd. Dublin, Ireland.	EI-PAX
☐ G-IUAN	98	CitationJet	525-0324	RF Celada SpA. Milan, Italy.	N5163C
☐ G-JCBV	03	Gulfstream V	682	JCB Aviation, East Midlands.	(VP-BFD)
☐ G-JETC	81	Citation II	550-0282	Ability Air Ltd/London Executive Aviation, Stansted.	G-JCFR
☐ G-JETI	86	BAe 125/800B	8056	Ford Motor Co. Stansted.	G-5-509
☐ G-JETJ	80	Citation II	550-0154	G-JETJ Ltd. Liverpool.	G-EJET
☐ G-JJMX	02	Falcon 900EX	112	J-MAX Air Services Ltd. Blackpool.	F-WWFK
☐ G-JJSI	86	BAe 125/800B	8058	GAMA Aviation Ltd. Farnborough.	G-OMGG
☐ G-JMAX	99	Hawker 800XP	8456	J-MAX Air Services Ltd. Blackpool.	N41762
☐ G-JMDW	80	Citation II	550-0183	MAS Airways Ltd. Biggin Hill.	HB-VGS
☐ G-JPSX	03	Falcon 900EX EASY	132	Sorven Aviation Ltd/Group 4 Securities, Staverton.	F-WWFJ
☐ G-JTNC	75	Citation	500-0264	Eurojet Aviation Ltd. Birmingham.	G-OEJA
☐ G-KDMA	00	Citation Encore	560-0553	Forest Aviation Ltd. Gamston.	N5145V
☐ G-LAOR	98	Hawker 800XP	8384	Select Plant Hire Co. Southend.	N955MC
☐ G-LCYA	01	Falcon 900EX	105	London City Airport Jet Centre Ltd. London City.	F-WWFC
☐ G-LOBL	99	Global Express	9038	1427 Ltd. Manchester.	G-52-24
☐ G-LOFT	76	Citation	500-0331	Atlantic Express Ltd. Coventry.	LN-NAT
☐ G-LVLV	03	Challenger 604	5372	GAMA Aviation Ltd. Farnborough.	(N413LV)
☐ G-MAAH	78	BAC 1-11/488GH	259	Gazelle Ltd/ARAVCO, Bournemouth-Hurn, UK.	VP-CDA
☐ G-MKSS	82	HS 125/700B	7175	Markoss Aviation Ltd. Biggin Hill.	VP-BEK
☐ G-NETA	02	Citation Excel	560-5230	Houston Jet Services Ltd/Gregg Air, Oxford-Kidlington.	N5085E
☐ G-OBBJ	01	BBJ2-8DR	32777	Multi Flight Jet Charter LLP. Leeds-Bradford.	N379BJ
☐ G-OCBA	67	HS 125/3B	25132	Richard Everett, Bentwaters.	EI-WDC
☐ G-OFOA	83	BAe 146-100	E1006	Formula One Management Ltd. Biggin Hill.	EI-COF
☐ G-OFOM	90	BAe 146-100	E1144	Formula One Management Ltd. Biggin Hill.	N3206T
☐ G-OGRG	99	Citation V Ultra	560-0506	Houston Jet Services Ltd/Gregg Air, Oxford-Kidlington.	G-RIBV
☐ G-OLDC	01	Learjet 45	45-156	Gold Air International Ltd. Biggin Hill.	N3017F
☐ G-OLDD	88	BAe 125/800B	8106	Gold Air International Ltd. Biggin Hill.	N888SS
☐ G-OLDF	99	Learjet 45	45-055	Gold Air International Ltd. Biggin Hill.	G-JRJR
☐ G-OLDJ	01	Learjet 45	45-138	Gold Air International Ltd. Biggin Hill.	N5018G
☐ G-OLDL	01	Learjet 45	45-124	Gold Air International Ltd. Biggin Hill.	N4003Q
☐ G-OLDR	01	Learjet 45	45-161	Gold Air International Ltd. Biggin Hill.	N3000S
☐ G-OMAK	98	Airbus A319-132	913	Twinjet Aircraft Sales Ltd. Luton.	F-WWFI
☐ G-OMJC	03	390 Premier 1	RB-88	Manhattan Jet Charter Ltd. Farnborough.	N4488F
☐ G-ORDB	02	Citation Bravo	550-1042	Houston Jet Services Ltd/Gregg Air, Oxford-Kidlington.	N51869
☐ G-ORHE	74	Citation	500-0220	R H Everett/Thruxton Aviation Services Ltd. Lee on Solent.	(N619EA)
☐ G-OSPG	88	BAe 125/800B	8130	Houston Jet Services Ltd/Gregg Air, Oxford-Kidlington.	D-CPAS
☐ G-OURA	86	BAe 125/800B	8050	Club 328 Ltd. Southampton.	G-CIFR
☐ G-OURB	79	HS 125/700B	7054	Club 328 Ltd. Southampton.	G-NCFR
☐ G-OWDB	78	HS 125/700B	7040	Bizair Ltd. Jersey/Wily de Bruyn, Nice, France.	(G-BYFO)
☐ G-RCEJ	85	BAe 125/800B	8021	Albion Aviation Management Ltd. Biggin Hill.	VR-CEJ
☐ G-RDBS	79	Citation II	550-0094	Albion Aviation Management Ltd. Biggin Hill. 'Carolin'	G-JETA

Reg	Yr	Type	c/n	Owner/Operator	Prev Regn
☐ G-REDS	01	Citation Excel	560-5167	Aviation Beauport Ltd. Jersey, C.I.	N250SM
☐ G-REYS	00	Challenger 604	5467	Greyscape Ltd/TAG Aviation (UK) Ltd. Farnborough.	(VP-CAR)
☐ G-SFCJ	98	CitationJet	525-0245	Sureflight Aviation Ltd. Birmingham.	N33CJ
☐ G-SIRS	01	Citation Excel	560-5185	Amsair Ltd/London Executive Aviation, Stansted.	N51042
☐ G-SPUR	92	Citation II	550-0714	Banecorp Ltd/London Executive Aviation, Stansted.	N593EM
☐ G-TBAE	83	BAe 146-200	E2018	BAe Systems (Corporate Air Travel) Ltd. Warton.	G-JEAR
☐ G-TCAP	88	BAe 125/800B	8115	BAe Systems (Corporate Air Travel) Ltd. Warton.	G-5-599
☐ G-TTFN	99	Citation V Ultra	560-0537	Falcon Jet Centre Ltd. Fairoaks.	N5181U
☐ G-VIPI	92	BAe 125/800B	8222	Executive Jet Charter Ltd. Staverton.	G-5-745
☐ G-VUEA	91	Citation II	550-0671	A D Aviation Ltd. Hawarden-Chester.	G-BWOM
☐ G-WINA	03	Citation Excel	560-5343	Ability Air Ltd/London Executive Aviation, Stansted.	N5145V
☐ G-XLMB	02	Citation Excel	560-5259	Aviation Beauport Ltd. Jersey, C.I.	N52526
☐ G-XPRS	02	Global Express	9133	TAG Aviation Charter UK Ltd. Farnborough.	C-FZXE
☐ G-ZIZI	99	CitationJet	525-0345	Ortac Air Ltd. Guernsey, C.I.	N5185V
☐ G-ZXZX	97	Learjet 45	45-005	GAMA Aviation Ltd. Farnborough.	N455LJ

Military

Reg	Yr	Type	c/n	Owner/Operator	Prev Regn
☐ XS709/M	65	Dominie T1	25011	RAF, 55 (R) Squadron, Cranwell.	
☐ XS711/L	65	Dominie T2	25024	RAF, 55 (R) Squadron, Cranwell.	
☐ XS712/A	65	Dominie T2	25040	RAF, 55 (R) Squadron, Cranwell.	
☐ XS713/C	65	Dominie T1	25041	RAF, 55 (R) Squadron, Cranwell.	
☐ XS727/D	65	Dominie T2	25045	RAF, 55 (R) Squadron, Cranwell.	
☐ XS728/E	65	Dominie T2	25048	RAF, 55 (R) Squadron, Cranwell.	
☐ XS730/H	65	Dominie T2	25050	RAF, 55 (R) Squadron, Cranwell.	
☐ XS731/J	66	Dominie T1	25055	RAF, 55 (R) Squadron, Cranwell.	
☐ XS736/S	66	Dominie T2	25072	RAF, 55 (R) Squadron, Cranwell.	
☐ XS737/K	66	Dominie T2	25076	RAF, 55 (R) Squadron, Cranwell.	
☐ XS739/F	66	Dominie T2	25081	RAF, 55 (R) Squadron, Cranwell.	
☐ ZD620	82	BAe 125/CC3	7181	RAF, 32 (The Royal) Squadron, Northolt.	G-5-16
☐ ZD621	82	BAe 125/CC3	7190	RAF, 32 (The Royal) Squadron, Northolt.	
☐ ZD703	82	BAe 125/CC3	7183	RAF, 32 (The Royal) Squadron, Northolt.	G-5-20
☐ ZD704	82	BAe 125/CC3	7194	RAF, 32 (The Royal) Squadron, Northolt.	G-5-870
☐ ZE395	83	BAe 125/CC3	7205	RAF, 32 (The Royal) Squadron, Northolt.	G-5-19
☐ ZE396	84	BAe 125/CC3	7211	RAF, 32 (The Royal) Squadron, Northolt.	G-5-12
☐ ZE700	86	BAe 146/CC2	E1021	RAF, 32 (The Royal) Squadron, Northolt.	G-6-021
☐ ZE701	86	BAe 146/CC2	E1029	RAF, 32 (The Royal) Squadron, Northolt.	G-5-03
☐ ZH763	80	BAC 1-11/539GL	263	QINETIQ Ltd. Boscome Down.	G-BGKE
☐ ZJ690	01	Sentinel R1	9107	Royal Air Force, 5 Squadron, Waddington.	C-GJRG
☐ ZJ691	02	Sentinel R1	9123	Royal Air Force, 5 Squadron, Waddington.	C-FVZM
☐ ZJ692	02	Sentinel R1	9131	Royal Air Force, 5 Squadron, Waddington.	C-FZWW
☐ ZJ693	02	Sentinel R1	9132	Royal Air Force, 5 Squadron, Waddington.	C-FZXC
☐ ZJ694	02	Sentinel R1	9135	Royal Air Force, 5 Squadron, Waddington.	C-FZYL

HB = SWITZERLAND   *Total* 112

Civil

Reg	Yr	Type	c/n	Owner/Operator	Prev Regn
☐ HB-IAH	98	Falcon 900EX	28	TAG Aviation SA. Geneva.	F-WWFZ
☐ HB-IAJ	02	Falcon 2000EX	3	Altona SA/TAG Aviation SA. Geneva.	F-WWGC
☐ HB-IAQ	98	Falcon 900EX	35	BG Investments Ltd-Bermuda/Swiss Jet AG. Zurich.	(N2BD)
☐ HB-IAU	03	Falcon 2000EX	14	CAT Aviation AG. Zurich.	F-WWGM
☐ HB-IAW	95	Falcon 2000	16	Starjet Establishment for Aviation, Lugano-Agno.	F-WWMB
☐ HB-IAX	96	Falcon 2000	33	Rabbit Air AG. Zurich.	F-WWME
☐ HB-IAZ	96	Falcon 2000	30	TAG Aviation SA. Geneva.	F-WWMB
☐ HB-IBH	96	Falcon 2000	42	TAG Aviation SA. Geneva.	F-WWMG
☐ HB-IBX	93	Gulfstream 4	1183	Jetclub AG. Farnborough, UK.	VR-BDC
☐ HB-IDJ	97	Challenger 800	7136	TAG Aviation SA. Geneva.	VP-CRJ
☐ HB-IEE	89	B 757-23A	24527	PrivatAir SA. Geneva.	HB-IHU
☐ HB-IES	81	Falcon 50	61	Aviatrans Anstalt/Aviatrans Establishment, Rugell.	F-WZHI
☐ HB-IFJ	01	Falcon 900EX	92	B-Jet SA. Geneva/Albinati Aeronautics SA. Geneva.	F-WWFK
☐ HB-IFQ	92	Falcon 900B	121	Malaysian Jet Services, Kuala Lumpur, Malaysia.	9M-BAB
☐ HB-IGH	69	DC 8-72	46067	Al Nassar Ltd/Jet Aviation Business Jets AG. Zurich.	VP-BJR
☐ HB-IGI	00	Falcon 900EX	83	Fast Bird AG/CAT Aviation AG. Zurich.	F-WWFY
☐ HB-IGL	88	Falcon 900B	58	SIMU Trade Consutling GmbH/TAG Aviation SA. Geneva.	OE-ILS
☐ HB-IGM	02	Gulfstream G550	5004	G-5 Executive AG. Zurich.	N904GA
☐ HB-IGP	00	Galaxy-1126	013	Jetclub AG. Zurich.	N160HA
☐ HB-IGQ	03	Falcon 2000EX	9	Alpcom SA/Dasnair SA. Geneva.	(N209EX)
☐ HB-IGR	82	Falcon 50	104	Dasnair SA. Geneva.	F-GUAE
☐ HB-IGX	01	Falcon 900EX	86	Dasnair SA. Geneva.	N986EX
☐ HB-IGY	01	Falcon 900EX	95	Advanced Aviation Services Ltd/CAT Aviation AG. Zurich.	F-WWFO
Reg	*Yr*	*Type*	*c/n*	*Owner/Operator*	*Prev Regn*

Reg	Yr	Type	c/n	Owner/Operator	Prev Regn
❒ HB-IHQ	98	Global Express	9011	Execujet Charter AG. Zurich.	VP-BJJ
❒ HB-IIO	99	BBJ-7AK	29865	PrivatAir SA. Geneva.	N1786B
❒ HB-IIP	99	BBJ-7AK	29866	PrivatAir SA. Geneva.	N1779B
❒ HB-IIQ	99	BBJ-7AK	30752	PrivatAir SA. Geneva.	HB-IIQ
❒ HB-IIS	99	Gulfstream V	572	Jetclub AG. Zurich.	P4-FAZ
❒ HB-IIY	00	Gulfstream V	638	Aviation G-5 Ltd. Zurich.	N638GA
❒ HB-IKR	91	Gulfstream 4	1159	MWM AG/Jetclub AG. Zurich.	N458FA
❒ HB-IKS	89	Challenger 601-3A	5042	Air Charter AG/Kraus und Naimer, Basle.	N28UA
❒ HB-IKZ	00	Global Express	9054	Execujet Charter AG. Zurich. 'Le Tout Coeur II'	N700LA
❒ HB-ILK	84	Challenger 601	3033	Jet Aviation Business Jets AG. Zurich.	N601TJ
❒ HB-IMJ	97	Gulfstream V	517	G-5 Executive AG. Zurich.	N517GA
❒ HB-IMY	89	Gulfstream 4	1084	Sit Set AG. Geneva.	(N448GA)
❒ HB-INJ	01	Global Express	9086	Japat AG/Execujet Charter AG. Zurich.	C-GHZC
❒ HB-ISD	85	Falcon 50	159	Jet Aviation Business Jets AG. Zurich.	VP-CWI
❒ HB-ISF	96	Falcon 2000	26	Servair Private Charter AG. Zurich.	(N112CD)
❒ HB-ITF	93	Gulfstream 4SP	1202	GAMA Aviation SA. Zurich.	N369XL
❒ HB-ITG	99	Global Express	9036	TAG Aviation SA. Geneva.	N777GX
❒ HB-ITK	91	Challenger 601-3A	5090	QAMAR Ltd/TAG Aviation SA. Geneva.	VP-CAM
❒ HB-IUT	99	Galaxy-1126	007	TASair Aviation SA/Private X-Press AG. Altenrhein.	(C-GRJZ)
❒ HB-IUW	95	Falcon 900B	150	Inter Retail AG/Jet Aviation Business Jets AG. Zurich.	N335MC
❒ HB-IUX	99	Falcon 900EX	54	Montres Rolex SA/Corporate Jet Management SA. Geneva.	F-WWFY
❒ HB-IVL	97	Gulfstream V	513	Private Jet Services, Basle.	N513GA
❒ HB-IVM	97	Falcon 2000	55	IBM Euroflight, Paris-Le Bourget, France.	F-WWMM
❒ HB-IVN	98	Falcon 2000	61	IBM Euroflight, Paris-Le Bourget, France.	F-WWME
❒ HB-IVO	98	Falcon 2000	62	Icebird Ltd. Lugano/Jet Aviation Business Jets AG. Zurich.	F-WWMF
❒ HB-IVR	96	Challenger 604	5318	Interline SA/Execujet Charter AG. Zurich.	HB-IKQ
❒ HB-IVS	94	Challenger 601-3R	5166	Becket Holdings Inc/Jetclub AG. Zurich.	N601A
❒ HB-IVZ	99	Gulfstream V	577	Neet-Air AG/Jet Aviation Business Jets AG. Zurich.	N577GA
❒ HB-IWZ	88	Gulfstream 4	1061	Servair Private Charter AG. Zurich.	N429AL
❒ HB-JEA	02	EMB-135BJ Legacy	145555	G-5 Executive AG. Zurich.	PT-...
❒ HB-JEB	01	Gulfstream G200	032	TAG Aviation SA. Geneva.	N406LM
❒ HB-JEC*	04	Challenger 300	20029		N129LJ
❒ HB-JED	03	EMB-135BJ Legacy	145644	DiaMed SA/DiamAir SA. Berne.	PT-SAR
❒ HB-JEE	03	Gulfstream G550	5025	Venturi Enterprises/Aviation 604 AG. Cairo, Egypt.	N925GA
❒ HB-JEG	04	Falcon 2000EX EASY	34	Comlux Aviation AG. Zurich.	F-WWGM
❒ HB-JEN	98	Global Express	9015	Radar 9015 Ltd/ExecuJet Charter AG. Zurich.	N708KS
❒ HB-JEZ	02	Citation X	750-0179	TAG Aviation SA. Geneva.	OE-HFE
❒ HB-JRA	02	Challenger 604	5529	Swiss Air Ambulance, Zurich.	C-GJZB
❒ HB-JRB	02	Challenger 604	5530	Swiss Air Ambulance, Zurich.	C-GJZD
❒ HB-JRC	02	Challenger 604	5540	Swiss Air Ambulance, Zurich.	C-GKMU
❒ HB-JRZ	02	Challenger 604	5553	Air Luther AG/Comlux Aviation AG. Zurich.	C-GZTU
❒ HB-JSY	01	Falcon 900EX	96	Cayley Aviation Ltd/Swiss Jet AG. Zurich.	N900ZA
❒ HB-VAA	02	Citation Excel	560-5269	Federal Air Transport Services, Berne-Belp.	N51160
❒ HB-VCN	80	Sabre-65	465-32	Sonnig AG. Geneva.	N303A
❒ HB-VDO	79	Citation II/SP	551-0133	Sonnig AG. Geneva.	I-JESA
❒ HB-VHV	89	BAe 125/800A	8153	CAT Aviation AG. Zurich.	G-5-627
❒ HB-VIS	82	Citation II	550-0447	Swiss Eagle AG. Bern-Belp.	(N447CJ)
❒ HB-VJB	78	Citation 1/SP	501-0067	AFLAG AG/Sius Electronics SA. Zurich.	VR-BLW
❒ HB-VJI	89	Learjet 31	31-011	Birdy SA. Jouxtens-Mezery/TAG Aviation SA. Geneva.	N3803G
❒ HB-VKW	93	BAe 125/800B	8246	Sky Jet AG. Zurich.	N387H
❒ HB-VLE	76	Citation Eagle	500-0313	GE Lisca AG/ Sky Work AG. Berne-Belp.	N313BA
❒ HB-VLF	94	Hawker 800	8264	Robert Bosch GmbH. Stuttgart, Germany.	G-5-806
❒ HB-VLG	94	Hawker 800	8265	Robert Bosch GmbH. Stuttgart, Germany.	G-5-809
❒ HB-VLQ	81	Citation II	550-0324	Speedwings SA. Geneva.	N23W
❒ HB-VLR	96	Learjet 31A	31A-127	Liebherr-Aerospace Toulouse SA/TAG Aviation SA. Geneva.	N80727
❒ HB-VLZ	98	Citation V Ultra	560-0446	Sky Work AG. Bern-Belp.	N51038
❒ HB-VMB	99	Learjet 45	45-021	TAG Aviation SA. Geneva.	N5009T
❒ HB-VMH	90	Citation II	550-0649	Servair Private Charter AG. Zurich.	N44LQ
❒ HB-VMI	91	BAe 125/800B	8210	G-5 Executive AG. Zurich.	G-RAAR
❒ HB-VMJ	85	Citation S/II	S550-0029	Libra Travel AG. Bern.	N608LB
❒ HB-VML	00	Learjet 45	45-084	Sun Heli Estab. Vaduz/Execujet Charter AG. Zurich.	N5009V
❒ HB-VMN	70	Falcon 20E-5B	240	Ciernes Overseas Inc. Panama/Sonnig AG. Geneva.	N240AT
❒ HB-VMO	99	Citation Excel	560-5061	Fly Away Jet SA/Sky Work AG. Bern-Belp.	N5200R
❒ HB-VMT	98	CitationJet	525-0250	Sky Work AG. Bern-Belp.	N250CJ
❒ HB-VMU	99	Citation Excel	560-5066	Jetclub AG. Zurich.	N134SW
❒ HB-VMV	92	Citation V	560-0166	Sonnig AG. Geneva.	N166JV

Reg	Yr	Type	c/n	Owner/Operator	Prev Regn

Reg	Yr	Type	c/n	Owner/Operator	Prev Regn
☐ HB-VMW	01	Citation Bravo	550-0955	Servair Private Charter AG. Zurich.	N50715
☐ HB-VMX	00	Citation Bravo	550-0946	Jet Aviation Business Jets AG. Zurich.	N52229
☐ HB-VMY	01	Citation Bravo	550-0964	Jet Aviation Business Jets AG. Zurich.	N52234
☐ HB-VNA	95	Citation V Ultra	560-0280	GE Lisca AG/Speedwings SA. Geneva.	PH-MDC
☐ HB-VNB	94	Citation V Ultra	560-0271	Speedwings SA. Geneva.	N49TT
☐ HB-VNC	99	Citation Excel	560-5058	Bex Aviation Ltd/Servair Private Charter AG. Zurich.	N555WE
☐ HB-VND	00	Citation Excel	560-5106	TAG Aviation SA. Geneva.	N506AM
☐ HB-VNE	01	Beechjet 400A	RK-318	Sirius AG. Zurich.	N3185K
☐ HB-VNG	85	Falcon 200	502	Sphinx Wings AG. Solothurn.	N64YR
☐ HB-VNH	01	Citation Excel	560-5172	Burbank Aviation Ltd/Servair Private Charter AG. Zurich.	N5086W
☐ HB-VNI	01	Citation Excel	560-5154	Good Aero Ltd/TAG Aviation SA. Geneva.	N154XL
☐ HB-VNJ	00	Hawker 800XP	8521	Johnson Control Systems AG/JABJ AG. Zurich.	N50521
☐ HB-VNK	98	CitationJet	525-0271	Primjet SA/Albinati Aeronautics SA. Geneva.	N860DB
☐ HB-VNL	00	CitationJet CJ-1	525-0375	Girard-Perregaux SA. Geneva.	N375KH
☐ HB-VNM	80	Falcon 20F-5B	426	Altria Corporate Services SA. Moscow, Russia.	I-BAEL
☐ HB-VNO	01	CitationJet CJ-2	525A-0033	AT Airtaxi AG. Basle.	N163PB
☐ HB-VNP	02	CitationJet CJ-1	525-0499	Mathys Aviation Ltd. Bettlach Grenchen.	N5200Z
☐ HB-VNS	01	Citation Excel	560-5209	Sky Work AG, Bern-Belp.	N501XL
☐ HB-VNU	75	Citation	500-0282	RAMSU Business AG/Jetclub AG. Zurich.	N510RC
☐ HB-VNZ	00	Citation Bravo	550-0906	Jet Aviation Business Jets AG. Zurich.	D-CSSS
☐ HB-VOA	99	Astra-1125SPX	111	GE Lisca AG/Libra Travel AG. Altenrhein.	OE-GAM
Military					
☐ T-781	76	Learjet 35A	35A-068	Swiss Air Force, Berne.	HB-VEM
☐ T-783	81	Falcon 50	67	Swiss Air Force, Berne.	HB-IEP

HI = DOMINICAN REPUBLIC *Total 1*

Civil

☐ HI-766SP	98	Beechjet 400A	RK-208		N890BH

HC = ECUADOR *Total 7*

Civil

☐ HC-BSS	68	Falcon 20C	150	Aero Express del Ecuador, Guayaquil.	TG-RBW
☐ HC-BVX	84	Westwind-1124	411	AFAC Ltda.	N47LR
Military					
☐ FAE-001A	76	Sabre-60	306-117	Aviacion del Ejercito,	N22MY
☐ FAE-043	65	Sabre-40R	282-43	Ministry of National Defence, Quito.	N4469F
☐ FAE-047	72	Sabre-40A	282-109	Ministry of National Defence, Quito.	N77AT
☐ FAE-049	73	Sabre-60	306-68	Ministry of National Defence, Quito.	N265DP
☐ IGM-628	90	Citation II	550-0628	Aviacion del Ejercito,	N183AB

HK = COLOMBIA *Total 10*

Civil

☐ HK-2485W	79	Westwind-Two	239	Ingenio del Cauca SA. Bogota.	HK-2485
☐ HK-4204X	80	Westwind-Two	306	Petroleum Helicopters de Colombia SA. Bogota.	HK-3971X
☐ HK-4250	00	Citation Bravo	550-0961	Central Charter de Colombia SA. Bogota.	HK-4250X
☐ HK-4304	95	Citation V Ultra	560-0355	Central Charter de Colombia SA. Bogota.	N67GU
Military					
☐ FAC-0001	70	F 28-1000	11992	Fuerza Aerea Colombiana, ETE, Bogota-El Dorado.	FAC-001
☐ FAC-001	99	BBJ-74V	29272	Fuerza Aerea Colombiana, ETE, Bogota-El Dorado.	N7378P
☐ FAC-1201	67	B 707-373C	19716	Fuerza Aerea Colombiana, Esc 711, Bogota-El Dorado.	HL7425
☐ FAC-1211	88	Citation II	550-0582	Fuerza Aerea Colombiana, Esc 713, Bogota-El Dorado.	(N1301A)
☐ FAC-5760	95	Citation OT-47B	560-0350	Fuerza Aerea Colombiana, Bogota-El Dorado.	N2500N
☐ FAC-5761	96	Citation OT-47B	560-0374	Fuerza Aerea Colombiana, Bogota-El Dorado.	N1066W

HL = KOREA *Total 19*

Civil

☐ HL7222	92	Gulfstream 4	1188	Korean Air Lines, Seoul.	N482GA
☐ HL7501	95	Citation V Ultra	560-0292	Korean Air Lines, Cheju.	N1295N
☐ HL7502	95	Citation V Ultra	560-0294	Korean Air Lines, Cheju.	N1295Y
☐ HL7503	95	Citation V Ultra	560-0297	Korean Air Lines, Cheju.	N1296N
☐ HL7504	95	Citation V Ultra	560-0300	Korean Air Lines, Cheju.	N1297V
☐ HL7576	99	Global Express	9019	Samsung Aerospace Industries, Seoul.	N600CC
☐ HL7577	95	Challenger 601-3R	5182	Regional Aviation Administration, Seoul.	C-FVZC
☐ HL7770	01	BBJ-7EG	32807	Samsung Aerospace Industries, Seoul.	N375BJ
Military					
☐ 258-342	98	Hawker 800XP	8342	Republic of Korea Air Force,	N2320J
☐ 258-343	97	Hawker 800XP	8343	Republic of Korea Air Force,	N1102U
☐ 258-346	97	Hawker 800XP	8346	Republic of Korea Air Force,	N23204

Reg	Yr	Type	c/n	Owner/Operator	Prev Regn

Reg	Yr	Type	c/n	Owner/Operator	Prev Regn
❏ 258-350	98	Hawker 800XP	8350	Republic of Korea Air Force,	N23207
❏ 258-351	98	Hawker 800XP	8351	Republic of Korea Air Force,	N23208
❏ 258-352	98	Hawker 800XP	8352	Republic of Korea Air Force,	N2321S
❏ 258-353	98	Hawker 800XP	8353	Republic of Korea Air Force,	N2321V
❏ 258-357	98	Hawker 800XP	8357	Republic of Korea Air Force,	N2321Z
❏ 5327	77	Citation	500-0327	Republic of Korea Air Force.	HL7277
❏ 701	99	Challenger 604	5429	Maritime National Police Agency, Seoul.	N604KM
❏ 85101	85	B 737-3Z8	23152	Government of South Korea, Seoul.	

HP = PANAMA Total 3

Civil

Reg	Yr	Type	c/n	Owner/Operator	Prev Regn
❏ HP-....	76	Learjet 24E	24E-346	Agroganaderia Avalos Panama SA. Panama City.	N69AX
❏ HP-1461	02	CitationJet CJ-2	525A-0075	Nose Corp. Panama City.	N51246
❏ HP-1A	69	Gulfstream II SP	78	Government of Panama, Panama City.	N90HH

HR = HONDURAS Total 1

Civil

Reg	Yr	Type	c/n	Owner/Operator	Prev Regn
❏ HR-PHO	81	Westwind-1124	333	Government of Honduras, Tegucigalpa.	HR-CEF

HS = THAILAND Total 9

Civil

Reg	Yr	Type	c/n	Owner/Operator	Prev Regn
❏ 60221	03	Airbus A319-115X	1908	HS-TYR. Royal Thai Air Force, Bangkok.	D-AIJO
❏ HS-DCG	96	Citation VII	650-7071	Aeronautical Radio of Thailand, Bangkok.	N1130N
❏ HS-HRH		B 737-448	24866	Government of Thailand, Bangkok.	EI-BXD
❏ HS-TPD	00	Beechjet 400A	RK-294	Directorate of Civil Aviation, Bangkok.	N5049E

Military

Reg	Yr	Type	c/n	Owner/Operator	Prev Regn
❏ 22-222	83	B 737-2Z6	23059	Royal Thai Air Force, Bangkok.	N45733
❏ 40207	87	Learjet 35A	35A-623	Royal Thai Air Force, 605 Sqn 6 Wing, Bangkok-Don Muang.	60504
❏ 40208	88	Learjet 35A	35A-635	Royal Thai Air Force, 605 Sqn 6 Wing, Bangkok-Don Muang.	60505
❏ 44-444	91	Airbus A310-324	591	HS-TYQ, Royal Thai Air Force, Bangkok.	F-WWCH
❏ 55-555	95	B 737-4Z6	27906	HS-RTA, Royal Thai Air Force, Bangkok.	

HZ = SAUDI ARABIA Total 71

Civil

Reg	Yr	Type	c/n	Owner/Operator	Prev Regn
❏ HZ-AB3	80	B 727-2U5	22362	Al-Anwae Aviation/Sheikh Hassan Enany, Riyadh.	V8-BG1
❏ HZ-ABI	83	TriStar 500	1247	Prince Abdul Aziz Al Ibrahim,	JY-HKJ
❏ HZ-AFA	00	Global Express	9029	JABJ AG/ASASCO Aviation Co. Riyadh.	C-GEZZ
❏ HZ-AFA1	93	MD-11	48533	Saudi Royal Family, Riyadh.	HZ-HM8
❏ HZ-AFA2	96	Challenger 604	5320	JABJ AG/ASASCO Aviation Co. Riyadh.	N605CC
❏ HZ-AFH	75	Gulfstream 2	171	Saudia Special Flight Services, Jeddah. (stored Geneva)	N17586
❏ HZ-AFI	77	Gulfstream 2TT	201	Saudia Special Flight Services, Jeddah.	N17585
❏ HZ-AFJ	77	Gulfstream 2TT	203	Saudia Special Flight Services, Jeddah.	N17587
❏ HZ-AFK	79	Gulfstream 2TT	239	Saudia Special Flight Services, Jeddah.	N17582
❏ HZ-AFN	82	Gulfstream 3	364	Saudia Special Flight Services, Jeddah.	N1761D
❏ HZ-AFR	83	Gulfstream 3	410	Saudia Special Flight Services, Jeddah.	N350GA
❏ HZ-AFT	87	Falcon 900B	21	Saudia Special Flight Services, Jeddah.	(HZ-R4A)
❏ HZ-AFU	87	Gulfstream 4	1031	Saudia Special Flight Services, Jeddah.	N434GA
❏ HZ-AFV	87	Gulfstream 4	1035	Saudia Special Flight Services, Jeddah.	N435GA
❏ HZ-AFW	88	Gulfstream 4	1038	Saudia Special Flight Services, Jeddah.	N438GA
❏ HZ-AFX	90	Gulfstream 4	1143	Saudia Special Flight Services, Jeddah.	N410GA
❏ HZ-AFY	91	Gulfstream 4	1166	Saudia Special Flight Services, Jeddah.	HZ-SAR
❏ HZ-AFZ	89	Falcon 900B	61	Saudia Special Flight Services, Jeddah.	HZ-AB2
❏ HZ-AIJ	82	B 747SP-68	22750	Saudi Royal Family, Riyadh.	
❏ HZ-BL2	88	BAe 125/800A	NA0419	Sheikh Bin Laden, Jeddah.	N564BA
❏ HZ-DG1	66	B 727-51	19124	Dallah Al Baraka, Jeddah.	N604NA
❏ HZ-DG2	80	Gulfstream 3	317	Dallah Al Baraka, Jeddah.	N83D
❏ HZ-FYZ	99	Citation Excel	560-5022	Zahid Tractor & Heavy Machinery Co.	(PT-XGL)
❏ HZ-HA1	78	Gulfstream 2TT	216	Harth Trading Establishment, Jeddah.	HZ-ND1
❏ HZ-HM11	69	DC 8-72	46084	Saudi Armed Forces Medical Services, Riyadh. (stored Dallas)	HZ-MS11
❏ HZ-HM1A	83	B 747-3G1	23070	Saudi Royal Family, Riyadh.	N1784B
❏ HZ-HM1B	78	B 747SP-68	21652	Saudi Royal Family, Riyadh.	HZ-HM1
❏ HZ-HM5	83	TriStar 500	1250	Saudi Royal Family, Riyadh.	7T-VRA
❏ HZ-HM6	83	TriStar 500	1249	Saudi Royal Family, Riyadh.	VR-CZZ
❏ HZ-HM7	93	MD-11	48532	Saudi Royal Family, Riyadh.	N9093P
❏ HZ-HMED	94	B 757-23A	25495	Saudi Armed Forces Medical Services, Riyadh.	
❏ HZ-HR2	82	Gulfstream 3	346	Saudi Oger Ltd. Riyadh.	(N126AH)
❏ HZ-HR3	82	B 727-2Y4	22968	R B Hariri/Saudi Oger Ltd. Riyadh.	HZ-RH3
❏ HZ-KAA	96	Gulfstream 4SP	1294	International Jet Club Ltd. Farnborough, UK.	(HZ-MAL)

Reg	Yr	Type	c/n	Owner/Operator	Prev Regn

Reg	Yr	Type	c/n	Owner/Operator	Prev Regn
☐ HZ-KSDC	01	Falcon 2000	142	NetJets Middle East, Jeddah.	F-WWVV
☐ HZ-KSRC	00	Hawker 800XP	8481	NetJets Middle East, Jeddah.	N43926
☐ HZ-MA1	67	JetStar-8	5105	Sheikh Ashmawi Aviation, Malaga, Spain.	N17005
☐ HZ-MF1	02	BBJ-7FG	33405	Saudi Ministry of Finance & Economy, Riyadh.	N373JM
☐ HZ-MF2	02	BBJ-7FG	33499	Saudi Ministry of Finance & Economy, Riyadh.	
☐ HZ-MF3	03	Gulfstream G300	1520	Saudi Ministry of Finance & Economy, Riyadh.	N520GA
☐ HZ-MF4	03	Gulfstream G300	1525	Saudi Ministry of Finance & Economy, Riyadh.	N425GA
☐ HZ-MF5	03	Gulfstream G400	1532	Saudi Ministry of Finance & Economy, Riyadh.	N532GA
☐ HZ-MFL	90	Gulfstream 4	1128	Saudia Special Flight Services, Jeddah.	N429GA
☐ HZ-MIS	81	B 737-2K5	22600	Sheikh Mustafa Idrees,	D-AHLH
☐ HZ-MS1	82	Learjet 35A	35A-467	Saudi Armed Forces Medical Services, Riyadh.	N3796Q
☐ HZ-MS3	83	Gulfstream 3	385	Saudi Armed Forces Medical Services, Riyadh.	N1761K
☐ HZ-MS4	98	Gulfstream 4SP	1365	Saudi Armed Forces Medical Services, Riyadh.	HZ-MS04
☐ HZ-MS5	99	Gulfstream V	583	Saudi Armed Forces Medical Services, Riyadh.	HZ-MS05
☐ HZ-MS5A	01	Gulfstream V	644	Saudi Armed Forces Medical Services, Riyadh.	N644GA
☐ HZ-NSA	87	Airbus A310-304	431	ARABASCO-Arabian Aircraft Services Co Ltd. Jeddah.	P4-ABU
☐ HZ-OCV	66	B 727-21	19006	Salem bin Zaid Ahmed Al Hassan, Jeddah.	HZ-TFA
☐ HZ-OFC4	98	Falcon 900EX	31	Olayan Finance Co. Dhahran.	F-WQBM
☐ HZ-PCA	76	Gulfstream 2	179	ARABASCO-Arabian Aircraft Services Co Ltd. Jeddah.	HZ-CAD
☐ HZ-RC3	81	Gulfstream 3	331	Saudia Special Flight Services, Jeddah.	N17LB
☐ HZ-SAB2	92	Falcon 900B	113	JABJ AG/SABIC-Saudi Arabian Basic Industries Corp. Riyadh.	F-WWFB
☐ HZ-SJP3	97	Challenger 604	5346	Jounaou & Parskevaides, Farnborough, UK.	N604JP
☐ HZ-TAA	99	BBJ-7P3	29188	JABJ AG/H R H Talal bin Abdul Aziz,	N1779B
☐ HZ-WBT3		B 747-4J6	25880	Kingdom Establishment, Riyadh.	HZ-WBT6
☐ HZ-WBT4	96	Airbus A340-213	151	Kingdom Establishment, Riyadh.	V8-JBB
☐ HZ-WBT5	85	BAe 125/800A	8032	ROTANA, Jeddah.	N526M
☐ HZ-WBT6	93	B 767-3P6ER	27255	Kingdom Establishment, Riyadh.	HZ-WBT3

Military

Reg	Yr	Type	c/n	Owner/Operator	Prev Regn
☐ HZ-101	01	BBJ-7DP	32805	Royal Saudi Air Force, Riyadh.	HZ-102
☐ HZ-102	01	BBJ2-8DP	32451	Royal Saudi Air Force, Riyadh.	HZ-101
☐ HZ-103	88	Gulfstream 4	1037	Royal Saudi Air Force, Riyadh.	HZ-ADC
☐ HZ-105	88	BAe 125/800B	8118	Royal Saudi Air Force, Riyadh.	105
☐ HZ-106	81	Learjet 35A	35A-374	Royal Saudi Air Force, Riyadh.	
☐ HZ-107	81	Learjet 35A	35A-375	Royal Saudi Air Force, Riyadh.	
☐ HZ-109	89	BAe 125/800A	8146	Royal Saudi Air Force, Riyadh.	G-5-825
☐ HZ-110	89	BAe 125/800B	8148	Royal Saudi Air Force, Riyadh.	RSAF-110
☐ HZ-123	59	B 707-138B	17696	RESA, Riyadh. (stored Southend-UK).	N138MJ
☐ HZ-130	89	BAe 125/800B	8164	Royal Saudi Air Force, Riyadh.	130

I   =   ITALY   *Total*   120

Civil

Reg	Yr	Type	c/n	Owner/Operator	Prev Regn
☐ I-....	78	Citation 1/SP	501-0077		(N678JG)
☐ I-....	92	BAe 1000A	9012		N512LR
☐ I-....	79	Citation II	550-0263	(was 551-0009).	N13VP
☐ I-....	73	Citation	500-0095		M950AM
☐ I-....	83	Citation II	550-0469		(OY-ERY)
☐ I-AEAL	72	Citation	500-0053	TAI-Trasporti Aerei Italiani SRL. Pescara.	HB-VGO
☐ I-AIRW	90	Learjet 31	31-025	Soc. Air Vallee SpA. Aosta.	N39399
☐ I-ALHO	01	Hawker 800XP	8561	Soc. ALBA Servizi Trasporti SpA. Milan.	N16300
☐ I-ALKA	82	Citation II	550-0351	Air One SpA. Roma-Fiumicino.	(N167WE)
☐ I-ALPG	81	Citation II/SP	551-0355	Action Air SRL. Milan.	N551AS
☐ I-AMCY	74	Citation	500-0192	Easy Way SRL/Airclub SpA. Ciampino.	(N70WA)
☐ I-ARIF	02	Falcon 2000	203	Soc. Aer Marche SpA. Ancona-Falconara	F-WWVQ
☐ I-AROM	77	Citation 1/SP	501-0042	Aeroitalia SRL. Roma-Ciampino.	N420AM
☐ I-AROO	79	Citation II	550-0081	Aeroitalia SRL. Roma-Ciampino.	N254AM
☐ I-ASER	98	Beechjet 400A	RK-204	Soc. Aliserio SpA. Milan.	N2357K
☐ I-AUNY	81	Citation 1/SP	501-0213	TAI-Trasporti Aerei Italiani SRL. Pescara.	N6785D
☐ I-AVEB	84	Diamond 1A	A087SA	Avioprese Jet Executive SpA. Naples.	N870AM
☐ I-AVGM	84	Citation II	550-0492	ENAV Flight Inspection, Roma-Ciampino.	(N1254G)
☐ I-AVRM	84	Citation II	550-0491	ENAV Flight Inspection, Roma-Ciampino.	(N1254D)
☐ I-AVSS	93	Beechjet 400A	RK-66	SLAM Lavori Aerei SpA. Naples.	N6048F
☐ I-AVVM	85	Citation S/II	S550-0062	ENAV Flight Inspection, Roma-Ciampino.	N12715
☐ I-BEAU	87	Falcon 900	23	Soc. SARAS/Sirio SpA. Milan.	F-WWFK
☐ I-BENN	98	Citation Bravo	550-0859	Soc. Benetton/Benair SpA. Treviso.	(N550KH)
☐ I-BENT	99	Citation Excel	560-5053	Soc. Benetton/Benair SpA. Treviso.	N5231S
☐ I-BLUB	92	Citation VI	650-0216	Vitrociset SpA. Roma.	N68269
☐ I-BMFE	73	Learjet 25C	25C-146	Gruppo Compagnie Aeronautiche SRL. Parma.	N6KJ
Reg	*Yr*	*Type*	*c/n*	*Owner/Operator*	*Prev Regn*

Reg	Yr	Type	c/n	Owner/Operator	Prev Regn
☐ I-BOAT	01	CitationJet CJ-1	525-0450	Ferretti SpA/Sirio SpA.. Milan.	N5156D
☐ I-CAEX	01	Falcon 900EX	91	Soc. CAI, Roma-Ciampino.	F-WQBJ
☐ I-CAFD	88	Falcon 50	183	Eurofly Service SpA. Turin.	F-WWHF
☐ I-CARY	76	Citation	500-0320	Icaro SRL. Forli.	N70WA
☐ I-CIGB	80	Citation 1/SP	501-0163	Jonathan SARL/Datamat,	(I-AGIK)
☐ I-CIGH	83	HS 125/700A	NA0341	Euraviation SRL. Milan.	N2KW
☐ I-CMAL	03	Citation Excel	560-5344	Aliven SRL. Verona.	N51055
☐ I-CMUT	79	Falcon 20F	389	Soc. Aer Marche SpA. Ancona-Falconara.	F-WRQV
☐ I-CREM	80	Falcon 10	161	Interjet SRL. Bologna.	F-WWZK
☐ I-DAGF	99	CitationJet	525-0347	Sirio SpA. Milan.	N1133G
☐ I-DAGS	91	Challenger 601-3A	5085	Finzeta Due SRL/Eurofly Service SpA. Turin.	D-ACTE
☐ I-DDVF	01	Falcon 2000	161	Sirio SpA. Milan.	F-WWVA
☐ I-DEAS	00	Gulfstream V	593	Soc. ALBA Servizi Trasporti SpA. Milan.	(I-MPUT)
☐ I-DEUM	02	CitationJet CJ-2	525A-0095	Ritmo SRL/Eurojet Italia SRL. Milan.	N5221Y
☐ I-DIES	88	Falcon 900	30	Soc. CAI, Roma-Ciampino.	F-WGTH
☐ I-DLOH	99	Hawker 800XP	8450	De Longhi SpA/Soc Nauta SRL. Treviso.	D-CTAN
☐ I-EDEM	96	CitationJet	525-0155	Ritmo SRL/Eurojet Italia SRL. Milan.	N155CJ
☐ I-ELYS	04	Learjet 40	45-2016	Eurojet Italia SRL. Milan.	N40078
☐ I-ERJA	77	Citation 1/SP	501-0006	Eurojet Italia SRL. Milan.	N93TJ
☐ I-ERJD	00	Learjet 45	45-068	Eurojet Italia SRL. Milan.	
☐ I-ERJE	02	Learjet 45	45-226	Eurojet Italia SRL. Milan.	N40085
☐ I-ERJG	04	Learjet 40	45-2015	Eurojet Italia SRL. Milan.	N40077
☐ I-FARN	80	Citation	500-0401	Aliven SRL. Verona.	N2651
☐ I-FEEV	86	Citation III	650-0105	Aviomar SRL. Roma-Ciampino.	N67BG
☐ I-FICV	88	Falcon 900	54	Soc. CAI, Roma-Ciampino.	F-WWFC
☐ I-FJDC	83	Falcon 100	203	Soc. Flynor Jet SpA. Milan.	F-WQBM
☐ I-FJDN	00	Falcon 50EX	295	Soc. Flynor Jet SpA/De Nora, Ciampino.	F-WWHW
☐ I-FJTB	00	Citation Bravo	550-0922	Fly Jet SRL. Turin.	(I-FJTM)
☐ I-FJTC	01	Citation Bravo	550-0988	Fly Jet SRL. Turin.	N32FJ
☐ I-FLYA	79	Citation 1/SP	501-0099	Soc. Alma Fly SRL. Como.	N3170A
☐ I-FLYD	81	Citation II	550-0393	Panair Compagnie Aerea Mediterranea SRL. Palermo.	N12GK
☐ I-FLYP	99	Falcon 2000	103	Eurofly Service SpA. Turin.	F-WWVX
☐ I-FLYV	00	Falcon 2000	108	Eurofly Service SpA. Turin.	F-WWVC
☐ I-FLYW	97	Falcon 900EX	27	Eurofly Service SpA. Turin.	N626CC
☐ I-GASD	84	Citation III	650-0037	Soc. Gretair SRL./Eurofly Service SpA. Turin.	N37VP
☐ I-GIWW	99	Citation Bravo	550-0871	Editoriale Domus SpA/Soc. Ariete 21 SRL. Milan.	N871CB
☐ I-GOBJ	70	Falcon 20C-5B	180	Eurofly Service SpA. Turin.	OY-BDS
☐ I-GOBZ	73	Falcon 20E-5	293	Eurofly Service SpA. Turin.	F-GOBZ
☐ I-GOSF	03	CitationJet CJ-2	525A-0199	Airlegs SpA/Sirio SpA. Milan.	N5152X
☐ I-IMMG	01	CitationJet CJ-2	525A-0038	Aliven SRL. Verona.	N5235G
☐ I-IMMI	00	CitationJet CJ-1	525-0379	Aliven SRL. Verona.	N5188A
☐ I-IPIZ	91	Beechjet 400A	RK-29	Aliparma SRL. Parma.	N15693
☐ I-JAMY	97	Falcon 2000	54	Sirio SpA. Milan.	D-BOND
☐ I-JESO	81	Citation II	550-0255	Icaro SRL. Forli.	N28GA
☐ I-JETX	02	Citation X	750-0184	Delta Aerotaxi SRL. Florence.	N51896
☐ I-KETO	01	Citation X	750-0161	Soc. Barilia Servizi Finanziari SpA. Parma.	N5245L
☐ I-LALL	00	CitationJet CJ-2	525A-0005	Interfly SRL. Brescia.	OY-LLA
☐ I-LIAB	68	Falcon 20C	172	S I S A V SRL. Roma-Ciampino.	F-BRHB
☐ I-LIAC	70	Falcon 20D	234	S I S A V SRL. Roma-Ciampino.	D-COLL
☐ I-LIAD	77	Learjet 35A	35A-111	S I S A V SRL. Roma-Ciampino.	OE-GMA
☐ I-LVNB	02	CitationJet CJ-2	525A-0073	Aliven SRL. Verona.	N5165T
☐ I-LXGR	94	Gulfstream 4SP	1234	Soc. Luxottica SpA/Sirio SpA. Turin.	N924ML
☐ I-MESK	78	Citation II/SP	551-0003	Giorgio Forno, Nairobi. Kenya.	(5Y-GGG)
☐ I-MTVB	99	Citation Bravo	550-0932	Miroglio UK Ltd. London/Fly Jet SRL, Turin.	G-MIRO
☐ I-NATS	03	Falcon 2000EX	11	Natuzzi Trade Service SRL./Sirio SpA. Milan.	F-WWGJ
☐ I-NUMI	91	Falcon 900	89	Soc. CAI, Roma-Ciampino.	F-WWFB
☐ I-OTEL	77	Citation 1/SP	501-0048	Italfy SRL. Caproni-Trento.	(I-DAEP)
☐ I-PABL	04	Citation Bravo	550-1083	Aeroitalia SRL. Roma-Ciampino.	N5201M
☐ I-PEGA	73	Citation	500-0081	Icaro SRL. Forli.	HB-VDA
☐ I-PIAL	69	PD 808	504	Soc. Rinaldo Piaggio, Genoa.	
☐ I-PNCA	81	Citation II	550-0235	Panair SpA. Roma-Ciampino.	N67SG
☐ I-RAGW	76	Citation Eagle	500-0311	Air Umbria SRL. Perugia.	LN-AAF
☐ I-RELT	73	Sabre-40A	282-133	Conair Jet Sales Inc. Fort Lauderdale, Fl. USA. (status ?).	N41NR
☐ I-RONY	00	Hawker 800XP	8506	Soc. ALBA Servizi Trasporti SpA. Milan.	N50166
☐ I-RVRP	00	CitationJet CJ-1	525-0397	Esair SRL. Turin.	N5163C
☐ I-SDFC	03	Challenger 300	20013	Same Deutz-Fahr Group/Sirio SpA. Milan.	N315LJ
Reg	Yr	Type	c/n	Owner/Operator	Prev Regn

Reg	Yr	Type	c/n	Owner/Operator	Prev Regn
☐ I-SEAE	02	Falcon 2000	200	Servizi Aerei SpA. Roma-Ciampino.	F-WWVN
☐ I-SIRF	94	Hawker 800	8267	Sirio SpA. Milan.	N601VC
☐ I-SNAW	95	Falcon 2000	12	Servizi Aerei SpA. Roma-Ciampino.	(F-GLHJ)
☐ I-SNAX	89	Falcon 900	69	Servizi Aerei SpA. Milan.	F-WWFD
☐ I-TAKA	04	Citation Excel XLS	560-5537		N5152X
☐ I-TLCM	90	Falcon 900	81	Servizi Aerei SpA. Roma-Ciampino.	N81GN
☐ I-TOIO	82	Citation 1/SP	501-0252	Soc. Jolly Hotels, Valdagno (Vicenza).	N574CC
☐ I-TOPB	96	Beechjet 400A	RK-133	Euraviation SRL/Sirio SpA. Milan.	N133BP
☐ I-TOPD	97	Beechjet 400A	RK-163	Euraviation SRL/Sirio SpA. Milan.	N163BJ
☐ I-TOPJ	88	Beechjet 400	RJ-44	Euraviation SRL/Sirio SpA. Milan.	N22WJ
☐ I-ULJA	78	Falcon 20F-5B	380	Air One SpA. Roma-Fiumicino.	N3848U
☐ I-UUNY	77	Citation	500-0358	Panair SpA. Roma-Caimpino.	SE-DEP
☐ I-VITH	01	Beechjet 400A	RK-309	Aliparma SRL. Parma.	N3239A
Military					
☐ MM578	68	PD 808-TA	502	AMI, RS-5, RSV=Reparto Sperimentale Volo, Pratica di Mare.	
☐ MM61950	69	PD 808-VIP	508	AMI, 14 Stormo, 8 Gruppo, Pratica di Mare.	
☐ MM61954	69	PD 808-TP	512	AMI, 14 Stormo, 8 Gruppo, Pratica di Mare. (status ?).	
☐ MM61955	69	PD 808-GE2	513	AMI, 14 Stormo, 71 Gruppo, Pratica di Mare. (status ?)	
☐ MM62012	74	DC 9-32	47595	AMI, 306 Grupo, Roma-Ciampino. (ex 31-12). (status ?).	N54635
☐ MM62020	85	Falcon 50	151	AMI, 93 Grupo, Roma-Ciampino.	F-WPXD
☐ MM62021	85	Falcon 50	155	AMI, 93 Grupo, Roma-Ciampino.	F-WPXH
☐ MM62026	89	Falcon 50	193	AMI, 93 Grupo, Roma-Ciampino.	F-WWHH
☐ MM62029	91	Falcon 50	211	AMI, 93 Grupo, Roma-Ciampino.	F-WWHR
☐ MM62171	99	Falcon 900EX	45	AMI, 93 Grupo, Roma-Ciampino.	F-WWFJ
☐ MM62172	99	Falcon 900EX	52	AMI, 93 Grupo, Roma-Ciampino.	F-WWFV
☐ MM62173	99	Airbus A319CJ-115X	1002	AMI, Government of Italy, Roma-Ciampino.	D-AJWF
☐ MM62174	00	Airbus A319CJ-115X	1157	AMI, Government of Italy, Roma-Ciampino.	D-AACI
☐ MM62209	02	Airbus A319-115X	1795	Government of Italy, Rome.	D-AWOR
☐ MM62210	02	Falcon 900EX	116	AMI, 93 Grupo, Roma-Ciampino.	F-WWFO

JA = JAPAN   Total   77

Civil

Reg	Yr	Type	c/n	Owner/Operator	Prev Regn
☐ JA001A	96	Citation V Ultra	560-0349	Aero Asahi Corp. Tokyo-Haneda.	N1127P
☐ JA001G	92	Gulfstream 4	1190	JCAB Flight Inspection, Tokyo-Haneda.	N403GA
☐ JA002A	02	Citation Encore	560-0597	Aero Asahi Corp. Tokyo-Haneda.	N597KC
☐ JA002G	94	Gulfstream 4SP	1244	JCAB Flight Inspection, Tokyo-Haneda.	N404GA
☐ JA005G	99	Global Express	9034	JCAB Flight Inspection, Tokyo-Haneda.	N700HF
☐ JA006G	00	Global Express	9082	JCAB Flight Inspection, Tokyo-Haneda.	N700AY
☐ JA01CP	97	Learjet 31A	31A-144	Chunichi Press, Nagoya.	N144LJ
☐ JA01TM	97	Citation V Ultra	560-0403	Aero Asahi Corp. Tokyo-Haneda.	N1202D
☐ JA02AA	99	Citation V Ultra	560-0518	Aero Asahi Corp. Tokyo-Haneda.	N1295B
☐ JA100C	04	CitationJet CJ-1	525-0534	Sanyomega Co. Tokyo.	N1269B
☐ JA119N	90	Citation V	560-0067	Naha Nikon Air Service Co. Nagoya.	N45BA
☐ JA120N	90	Citation V	560-0072	Kawasho Corp. Tokyo.	(N772KC)
☐ JA30DA	83	Diamond 1	A053SA	Diamond Air Service Co/MHI, Nagoya.	D-CDRB
☐ JA525A	01	CitationJet CJ-1	525-0449	Auto Panther, Kagoshima,	(JA001T)
☐ JA525B	02	CitationJet CJ-2	525A-0156	Auto Panther, Kagoshima.	N256CJ
☐ JA55TH	01	Falcon 900EX	100	Sony Corp. Tokyo-Haneda.	N997EX
☐ JA8248	79	Diamond 1	A002SA	Mitsubishi Heavy Industries, Nagoya.	JQ8003
☐ JA8380	76	Citation 1/SP	501-0027	Konno Kiseki & Partner, Miyagi.	N54DS
☐ JA8420	94	CitationJet	525-0056	Itogumi Construction Co. Sapporo Hokkaido.	N56NZ
☐ JA8431	74	Gulfstream 2	141	Diamond Air Service Co/MHI, Nagoya.	N17584
☐ JA8493	83	Citation 1/SP	501-0324	San-Kei Press Ltd. Haneda.	N2b51J
☐ JA8570	88	Falcon 900	53	JCG-Japanese Coast Guard, Tokyo-Haneda.	N438FJ
☐ JA8571	88	Falcon 900	56	JCG-Japanese Coast Guard, Tokyo-Haneda.	N440FJ
☐ JA8576	90	Citation V	560-0080	Yomiuri Shimbun, Tokyo-Haneda.	N2746E
Military					
☐ 01-5060	96	Beechjet 400T	TX-10	060. JASDF, 41st Flight Training Squadron, Miho AB.	N3221Z
☐ 02-3013	99	BAe U-125A	8370	013, JASDF, Air Rescue Wing, Hyakuri.	N23566
☐ 02-3014	99	BAe U-125A	8381	014, JASDF, Air Rescue Wing, Chitose.	N23566
☐ 05-3255	98	Gulfstream U-4	1359	255, JASDF, Air Defense Command HQ Squadron, Iruma AB.	N359GA
☐ 12-3015	00	BAe U-125A	8407	015, JASDF, Air Rescue Wing, Hyakuri.	N30562
☐ 12-3016	00	BAe U-125A	8427	016, JASDF, Air Rescue Wing, Hyakuri.	N31833
☐ 12-3017	00	BAe U-125A	8445	017, JASDF, Air Rescue Wing,	N40708
☐ 12-3018	00	BAe U-125A	8493	018. JASDF, Air Rescue Wing, Chitose.	N40933
☐ 20-1101	90	B 747-47C	24730	Government of Japan, Tokyo.	JA8091
☐ 20-1102	91	B 747-47C	24731	Government of Japan, Tokyo.	JA8092
Reg	*Yr*	*Type*	*c/n*	*Owner/Operator*	*Prev Regn*

Reg	Yr	Type	c/n	Owner/Operator	Prev Regn
☐ 21-5011	01	Beechjet 400T	TX-11	011, JASDF, 41st Flight Training Squadron, Miho AB.	N50561
☐ 21-5012	01	Beechjet 400T	TX-12	012, JASDF, 41st Flight Training Squadron, Miho AB.	N50512
☐ 22-3019	00	BAe U-125A	8469	019, JASDF, Air Rescue Wing,	N43079
☐ 22-3020	01	BAe U-125A	8513	020, JASDF, Air Rescue Wing,	N50513
☐ 29-3041	92	BAe U-125A	8215	041. JASDF-Japanese Air Self Defence Force, Iruma.	G-JFCX
☐ 32-3021	01	BAe U-125A	8533	021, JASDF, Air Rescue Wing,	N50733
☐ 39-3042	92	BAe U-125A	8227	042. JASDF-Japanese Air Self Defence Force, Iruma.	G-BUUW
☐ 41-5051	93	Beechjet 400T	TX-1	051, JASDF, 41st Flight Training Squadron, Miho AB.	N82884
☐ 41-5052	93	Beechjet 400T	TX-2	052, JASDF, 41st Flight Training Squadron, Miho AB.	N82885
☐ 41-5053	93	Beechjet 400T	TX-3	053, JASDF, 41st Flight Training Squadron, Miho AB.	N82886
☐ 41-5054	94	Beechjet 400T	TX-4	054, JASDF, 41st Flight Training Squadron, Miho AB.	N3195K
☐ 41-5055	94	Beechjet 400T	TX-5	055, JASDF, 41st Flight Training Squadron, Miho AB.	N3195Q
☐ 41-5063	02	Beechjet 400T	TX-13	JASDF, 41st Flight Training Squadron, Miho AB.	N50543
☐ 42-3022	02	BAe U-125A	8610	JASDF,	N61320
☐ 49-3043	94	BAe U-125A	8242	043. JASDF-Japanese Air Self Defence Force, Iruma.	G-BVFE
☐ 51-5056	95	Beechjet 400T	TX-6	056, JASDF, 41st Flight Training Squadron, Miho AB.	N3195X
☐ 51-5057	95	Beechjet 400T	TX-7	057, JASDF, 41st Flight Training Squadron, Miho AB.	N3228M
☐ 51-5058	95	Beechjet 400T	TX-8	058, JASDF, 41st Flight Training Squadron, Miho AB.	N3228V
☐ 52-3001	93	BAe U-125A	8245	001. JASDF, Air Rescue Wing, Komaki.	G-JHSX
☐ 52-3002	94	BAe U-125A	8247	002. JASDF, Air Rescue Wing, Hyakuri.	G-5-813
☐ 52-3003	94	BAe U-125A	8250	003. JASDF, Air Rescue Wing, Komaki.	G-BVRG
☐ 62-3004	95	BAe U-125A	8268	004. JASDF, Air Rescue Wing, Komaki.	N809H
☐ 71-5059	95	Beechjet 400T	TX-9	059, JASDF, 41st Flight Training Squadron, Miho AB.	N1069L
☐ 72-3005	96	BAe U-125A	8288	005. JASDF, Air Rescue Wing, Nyutabaru.	N816H
☐ 72-3006	96	BAe U-125A	8305	006. JASDF, Air Rescue Wing, Hyakuri.	N305XP
☐ 75-3251	95	Gulfstream U-4	1270	251, JASDF, Air Defence Command HQ Squadron, Iruma AB.	N442GA
☐ 75-3252	95	Gulfstream U-4	1271	252, JASDF, Air Defence Command HQ Squadron, Iruma AB.	N452GA
☐ 82-3007	97	BAe U-125A	8306	007, JASDF, Air Rescue Wing, Matsushima.	N1103U
☐ 82-3008	97	BAe U-125A	8325	008, JASDF, Air Rescue Wing, Komatsu.	N1112N
☐ 85-3253	96	Gulfstream U-4	1303	253, JASDF, Air Defence Command HQ Squadron, Iruma AB.	N435GA
☐ 9201	86	Learjet U36A	36A-054	JMSDF, 91 Kokutai, Iwakuni.	N1087Z
☐ 9204	90	Learjet U36A	36A-059	JMSDF, 91 Kokutai, Iwakuni.	N1087Z
☐ 9205	90	Learjet U36A	36A-060	JMSDF, 91 Kokutai, Iwakuni.	N1088A
☐ 9206	93	Learjet U36A	36A-061	JMSDF, 91 Kokutai, Iwakuni.	N2601B
☐ 92-3009	98	BAe U-125A	8333	009, JASDF, Air Rescue Wing, Nyutabaru.	N3261Y
☐ 92-3010	98	BAe U-125A	8341	010, JASDF, Air Rescue Wing, Chitose.	N3251M
☐ 92-3011	98	BAe U-125A	8348	011, JASDF, Air Rescue Wing, Naha.	N2175W
☐ 92-3012	99	BAe U-125A	8360	012, JASDF, Air Rescue Wing, Komatsu.	N3189H
☐ 95-3254	97	Gulfstream U-4	1326	254, JASDF, Air Defence Command HQ Squadron, Iruma AB.	N325GA
☐ JA500A	02	Gulfstream V	683	LAJ 500. Japanese Coast Guard,	N683GA
☐ JA501A	02	Gulfstream V	689	LAJ 501. Japanese Coast Guard,	N689GA
☐ N36685	04	BAe U-125A	8685	JASDF,	
☐ N61729	03	BAe U-125A	8629	JASDF,	

JY = JORDAN   Total   7

Civil

Reg	Yr	Type	c/n	Owner/Operator	Prev Regn
☐ JY-ABH	93	Airbus A340-211	009	Government of Jordan, Amman.	V8-AM1
☐ JY-AFH	77	Sabre-75A	380-57	Arab Wings Ltd. Amman.	HZ-RBH
☐ JY-AFP	78	Sabre-75A	380-62	Arab Wings Ltd. Amman.	
☐ JY-HS1	69	B 727-76	20228	HS Aviation, Paris, France.	VR-CHS
☐ JY-HS2	75	B 727-2L4	21010	HS Aviation, Paris, France. (stored FTW since 8/00).	VR-CCA
☐ JY-ONE	99	Challenger 604	5426	Government of Jordan, Amman.	N604JA
☐ JY-TWO	99	Challenger 604	5443	Government of Jordan, Amman.	N605JA

J2 = DJIBOUTI   Total   1

Civil

Reg	Yr	Type	c/n	Owner/Operator	Prev Regn
☐ J2-KBA	67	B 727-191	19394	Government of Djibouti, Djibouti.	N727X

LN = NORWAY   Total   8

Civil

Reg	Yr	Type	c/n	Owner/Operator	Prev Regn
☐ LN-AAU	90	Citation III	650-0192	Sundt Air A/S. Oslo-Gardermoen.	N15TZ
☐ LN-SUN	01	Challenger 604	5517	Sundt Air A/S. Oslo-Gardermoen.	N517RH
☐ LN-SUS	01	Gulfstream G200	051	Sundt Air A/S. Oslo-Gardermoen.	OY-RAK
☐ LN-SUV	00	Citation Bravo	550-0951	Sundt Air A/S. Oslo-Gardermoen.	N51KR
☐ LN-SUX	02	Citation Excel	560-5271	Sundt Air A/S. Oslo-Gardermoen.	N5103J

Military

Reg	Yr	Type	c/n	Owner/Operator	Prev Regn
☐ 0125	67	Falcon 20-5B	125	RNAF, 335 Squadron, Kjeller.	LN-FOE
☐ 041	66	Falcon 20-5B	41	RNAF, 335 Squadron, Kjeller.	LN-FOI
Reg	Yr	Type	c/n	Owner/Operator	Prev Regn

Reg	Yr	Type	c/n	Owner/Operator	Prev Regn
☐ 053	66	Falcon 20-5B	53	RNAF, 335 Squadron, Kjeller.	LN-FOD

LV = ARGENTINA   *Total*   59

Civil

Reg	Yr	Type	c/n	Owner/Operator	Prev Regn
☐ LQ-MRM	78	Citation	500-0386	Argentine Federal Police, Buenos Aires.	LV-PAX
☐ LV-AHX	90	Citation V	560-0090		N30PQ
☐ LV-AIT	81	Learjet 35A	35A-408	Direccion de Aeronautica, Ushaia, Tierra del Fuego.	LV-POG
☐ LV-AIW	03	Citation Excel	560-5350		N325FN
☐ LV-AMB	94	CitationJet	525-0045	Royal Air SA. Buenos Aires.	N525AP
☐ LV-APL	81	Citation II/SP	551-0361	Banco de Misiones SA. Posadas, Santa Fe. (was 550-0330).	LV-PNB
☐ LV-ARD	03	Learjet 45	45-232	Provincial Government of Salta.	N45XR
☐ LV-AXN	99	CitationJet	525-0327		(N398EB)
☐ LV-AXZ	71	HS 125/400B	25251	SASA-Sudamericana de Aviacion SA. Buenos Aires.	5-T-30-065
☐ LV-JTD	71	B 737-287	20523	Aerolineas Executive Jet SA. Buenos Aires.	LV-PRQ
☐ LV-JTZ	70	Learjet 24D	24D-234	C T Air SA. Buenos Aires.	LV-PRA
☐ LV-LRC	75	Learjet 24D	24D-316	Gobierno Provincia de la Rioja, La Rioja.	T-03
☐ LV-OEL	80	Learjet 25D	25D-307	Macair Jet SA. Buenos Aires.	LV-PEU
☐ LV-RED	91	Citation V	560-0126	Aguila del Sur SA. Buenos Aires.	LV-PFN
☐ LV-WDR	93	Citation V	560-0227	Royal Class SA. Buenos Aires.	LV-PGR
☐ LV-WEJ	93	Citation II	550-0724	Gobierno Provincia de Buenos Aires.	LV-PGU
☐ LV-WES	67	Jet Commander	119	Aerocat SA. Catamarca. (status ?).	N119AC
☐ LV-WGO	94	Citation V	560-0251	Cia Interamericana de Automov. Buenos Aires.	LV-PGZ
☐ LV-WGY	94	Citation V	560-0246	TIA SA. Buenos Aires.	LV-PHD
☐ LV-WJN	87	Citation II	550-0558	Banco del Buen Ayre SA. Buenos Aires.	N558AG
☐ LV-WJO	94	Citation II	550-0728	Gobierno Provincia de Corrientes.	LV-PHN
☐ LV-WLG	81	Learjet 25D	25D-345	Medical Jet SA. Buenos Aires.	LV-PHU
☐ LV-WLR	72	Westwind-1123	183	Charter Jet SRL. Buenos Aires.	N51990
☐ LV-WLS	95	Citation V Ultra	560-0289	Gobierno Provincia de Santa Cruz.	LV-PHY
☐ LV-WMM	66	Falcon 20C	29	Air Service SA. Buenos Aires.	LV-PLD
☐ LV-WMT	95	Citation V Ultra	560-0305	Royal Class SA. Buenos Aires.	LV-PLE
☐ LV-WOC	79	Learjet 25D	25D-269	Heli-Air SA. Buenos Aires.	LV-PLL
☐ LV-WPE	95	Beechjet 400A	RK-104	Gobierno Provincia de Chubut. Rawson, Chubut.	LV-PLT
☐ LV-WRE	81	Learjet 25D	25D-355	Helyjet SA. Buenos Aires.	N355AM
☐ LV-WSS	96	Gulfstream 4SP	1297	Aguila del Sur SA. Buenos Aires. 'Santa Marguerita III'	N420GA
☐ LV-WTN	95	Citation VII	650-7054	Ledesma S A A I, Buenos Aires.	N7243U
☐ LV-WTP	96	Beechjet 400A	RK-118	Gym SA. Buenos Aires.	LV-PMH
☐ LV-WXD	82	Citation II/SP	551-0396	Digital Air Taxi SA. Buenos Aires.	N45GA
☐ LV-WXX	74	Sabre-60	306-91	Patria Cargas Aereas SA. Buenos Aires.	(N45MM)
☐ LV-WXY	82	Learjet 25D	25D-357	Helyjet SA. Buenos Aires.	N27KG
☐ LV-WYL	75	Westwind-1123	182	M G Montoto, Buenos Aires.	(N123SE)
☐ LV-YGC	65	HS 125/1A-522	25046	Aviajet SA. Buenos Aires.	N125AD
☐ LV-YHC	92	Citation II	550-0715	Gobierno Provincia de San Juan.	LV-PNL
☐ LV-YMA	98	Citation V Ultra	560-0458	Viajaire SA. Buenos Aires.	LV-PNR
☐ LV-YMB	93	Learjet 31A	31A-081	Editorial Sarmiento SA. Buenos Aires.	N83WN
☐ LV-YRB	74	Citation	500-0191	Ecodyma Empresa Constructora SA. Buenos Aires.	N701BR
☐ LV-ZSZ	79	Learjet 35A	35A-235	American Jet SA. Buenos Aires.	N166HE
☐ LV-ZTH	71	Learjet 25C	25C-071	Federal Aviation SA. Buenos Aires.	N97AM
☐ LV-ZTR	00	Hawker 800XP	8462	Puyel SA. Buenos Aires.	LV-PIW
☐ LV-ZZF	76	Learjet 35	35-049	Baires Fly SA. Buenos Aires.	N899WA

Military

Reg	Yr	Type	c/n	Owner/Operator	Prev Regn
☐ 5-P-20-0741		F 28-3000C	11145	Armada-Argentina, Buenos Aires. 'Canal de Beagle'	LV-RRA
☐ 5-T-21-0742		F 28-3000M	11150	Armada-Argentina, Buenos Aires. 'Islas Malvinas'	PH-EXX
☐ AE-175	74	Sabre-75A	380-13	Ejercito/Comision Especial de Adquisiciones, Buenos Aires.	N65761
☐ AE-185	77	Citation	500-0356	Ejercito Argentina, Buenos Aires. 'Alvarez de Condarco'	N36848
☐ T-03	70	F 28-1000	11028	FAA=Fuerza Aerea Argentina, Buenos Aires.	T-04
☐ T-10	98	Learjet 60	60-140	FAA=Fuerza Aerea Argentina, Buenos Aires.	N140LJ
☐ T-11	74	Sabre-75A	380-3	FAA=Fuerza Aerea Argentina, Buenos Aires.	T-10
☐ T-21	77	Learjet 35A	35A-115	Grupo 1 de Aerofotografico, II Brigada Aerea, Parana.	
☐ T-22	77	Learjet 35A	35A-136	Grupo 1 de Aerofotografico, II Brigada Aerea, Parana.	
☐ T-23	80	Learjet 35A	35A-319	Grupo 1 de Aerofotografico, II Brigada Aerea, Parana.	
☐ T-24	81	Learjet 35A	35A-369	Escuadron Verificacion Radio Ayudos, Parana.	VR-17
☐ T-25	82	Learjet 35A	35A-484	Escuadron Verificacion Radio Ayudos, Parana.	VR-18
☐ T-50	83	F 28-4000	11203	FAA=Fuerza Aerea Argentina, Buenos Aires.	(T-03)
☐ TP-01	92	B 757-23A	25487	FAA=Fuerza Aerea Argentina, Buenos Aires.	T-01

LX = LUXEMBOURG — Total 45

Civil

Reg	Yr	Type	c/n	Owner/Operator	Prev Regn
❑ LX-AKI	00	Falcon 50EX	306	Kalair Luxembourg/Silver Arrows SA. Luxembourg.	F-WWHH
❑ LX-ARC	99	Hawker 800XP	8444	Arbed SA/Arcelor Group, Luxembourg.	EC-HJL
❑ LX-COS	96	Falcon 900B	159	Soldano Ltd/Silver Arrows SA. Cannes, France.	LX-NAN
❑ LX-DSL	01	Learjet 45	45-158	Diesel Jeans/Skyliner SA. Treviso, Italy.	N3019T
❑ LX-EAR	98	Learjet 31A	31A-160	Silver Arrows SA. Luxembourg.	VP-BMX
❑ LX-FAZ	96	Challenger 604	5307	Silver Arrows SA. Cannes, France.	C-GIDG
❑ LX-FBY	01	Challenger 604	5485	Bouygues Transport Air Service, Paris-Le Bourget, France.	N485CL
❑ LX-FMR	86	Falcon 50	165	Silver Arrows SA. Cannes, France.	HZ-HM3
❑ LX-FOX	97	CitationJet	525-0229	Hub Industries SA/Ameridair SA.	LX-TRA
❑ LX-FTA	03	Falcon 900C	201	Northgas, Moscow, Russia.	N210FJ
❑ LX-GBY	98	Hawker 800XP	8392	Bouygues Transport Air Service, Paris-Le Bourget, France.	G-0504
❑ LX-GCA	98	CitationJet	525-0235	Serlux SA. Luxembourg.	I-ESAI
❑ LX-GDC	86	Challenger 601	3065	Ergo AG. Farnborough, UK.	(N54PA)
❑ LX-GDL	78	Citation II	550-0033	Transrent SA/Luxaviation SA. Luxembourg.	LX-JET
❑ LX-GES	89	Falcon 900B	78	Gedair SA. Luxembourg.	N522KM
❑ LX-GEX	98	Global Express	9013	Global Jet Luxembourg/Silver Arrows SA. Luxembourg.	C-GZSM
❑ LX-GJL	02	Falcon 900C	197	Global Jet Luxembourg/Silver Arrows SA. Luxembourg.	(LX-MAM)
❑ LX-GOL	92	Astra-1125SP	059	Superfund Aviation SA. Cannes, France.	HB-VNF
❑ LX-IIH	00	CitationJet CJ-1	525-0391	Italtrieste International Holding SA. Luxembourg.	N5130J
❑ LX-IMS	00	Learjet 45	45-070	Husky Injection Molding Systems Ltd.	N50163
❑ LX-IMS*	04	Learjet 45	45-261	Husky Injection Molding Systems Ltd.	N5010U
❑ LX-IRE	02	Falcon 50EX	324	Flying Star SA/Silver Arrows SA. Cannes, France.	F-WWHD
❑ LX-JCD	00	Citation Excel	560-5104	Jean Claude Decaux International, Toussus Le Noble, France.	(F-GXXX)
❑ LX-LAR	89	Learjet 35A	35A-653	Luxembourg Air Rescue/Ducair SA. Liege, Belgium.	HB-VJL
❑ LX-LCG	02	390 Premier 1	RB-51	Jetco SA. Milan, Italy.	N4251D
❑ LX-LFA	95	Falcon 900B	154	Lux Flight Executive SA. Luxembourg.	F-GVBF
❑ LX-LFB	88	Falcon 900B	62	Lux Flight Executive SA. Luxembourg.	F-WQBJ
❑ LX-LOU	04	Learjet 60	60-277		N40079
❑ LX-LOV	95	CitationJet	525-0102	Jet Corporate Consulting SA. Luxembourg.	TC-CRO
❑ LX-MEL	92	Falcon 900B	115	Melia SA/Eurofly Service SpA. Turin, Italy.	HB-IBG
❑ LX-MRC	01	CitationJet CJ-1	525-0473	Air Print SA. Cannes, France.	N5201M
❑ LX-OMC	98	Learjet 31A	31A-167	Cerfin Luxembourg SA/Eurojet Italia SRL. Milan, Italy.	D-CGOM
❑ LX-ONE	81	Learjet 35A	35A-417	Ducair SA/Luxair Executive, Luxembourg.	N281CD
❑ LX-PAK	02	Global Express	9115	Jex SARL/Aiglemont, Paris-Le Bourget, France.	(F-GOAK)
❑ LX-PCT	95	Learjet 31A	31A-112	JABJ AG/Powder Coating Technologies International SA.	N5082S
❑ LX-PMR	02	390 Premier 1	RB-64	Premier SA. Luxembourg.	N6164U
❑ LX-PRA	98	Learjet 60	60-145	Prada Co SA. Luxembourg/ALBA Servizi Aerotrasporti, Milan.	N145LJ
❑ LX-PRE	02	390 Premier 1	RB-60	Craft Air SA/Premier Aviation, Blackbushe, UK.	N6160D
❑ LX-PRS	84	Citation II/SP	551-0496	Products Usines Metallurgiques, Reims. (was 550-0496).	N999GH
❑ LX-RPL	01	Learjet 60	60-212	Skyways Luxembourg SA/Eurojet Italia SRL. Milan.	N5012H
❑ LX-SUP	99	CitationJet	525-0351	Superfund Aviation SA. Luxembourg.	VP-BRJ
❑ LX-VAZ	89	Citation II	550-0622	Jani SA/Silver Arrows SA. Luxembourg.	HB-VKP
❑ LX-VIP	00	Global Express	9076	Silver Arrows SA. Luxembourg.	N700XT
❑ LX-YSL	99	CitationJet	525-0322	Berlys Aero SA/Yves St Laurent, Paris-Le Bourget, France.	N52LT
❑ LX-ZAK	02	Falcon 900EX	106	HRH Prince Karim Aga Khan/Aiglemont, Paris-Le Bourget.	F-GSDA

LY = LITHUANIA — Total 2

Civil

Reg	Yr	Type	c/n	Owner/Operator	Prev Regn
❑ LY-BSK	84	HS 125/700A	7212	Aurela Co Ltd. Vilnius.	LY-ASL
❑ LY-LRJ	81	Learjet 55	55-011	Apatas Air, Kaunas.	ES-PVV

LZ = BULGARIA — Total 2

Civil

Reg	Yr	Type	c/n	Owner/Operator	Prev Regn
❑ LZ-AVB	04	Citation Bravo	550-1103		N.....
❑ LZ-OOI	01	Falcon 2000	123	Government of Bulgaria, Avio Detachment 28, Sofia.	F-WWVS

N = USA — Total 10208

Civil

Reg	Yr	Type	c/n	Owner/Operator	Prev Regn
❑ N1	89	Gulfstream 4	1071	FAA, Washington, DC. 'Spirit of America'	N410GA
❑ N1AG	81	Citation 1/SP	501-0174	Gossett Aviation LLC. Memphis, Tn.	N454DQ
❑ N1AP	02	Citation X	750-0176	Arnold Palmer, Youngstown, Pa.	N51806
❑ N1AT	88	Citation II/SP	551-0591	Betaco Inc. Indianapolis, In. (was 550-0591).	N672CA
❑ N1BN	03	Gulfstream G550	5036	Iliad Leasing Inc. West Palm Beach, Fl.	N936GA
❑ N1BS	99	Citation X	750-0081	Bank of Stockton, Portland, Or.	N810X
❑ N1C	96	Falcon 2000	40	Maverick Air LLC/C & S Aviation LLC. Addison, Tx.	F-W...

Reg	Yr	Type	c/n	Owner/Operator	Prev Regn

Reg	Yr	Type	c/n	Owner/Operator	Prev Regn
☐ N1CA*	04	Hawker 800XP	8672	Coin Acceptors Inc. St Louis, Mo.	N672XP
☐ N1CC	79	Gulfstream 2B	257	North American Financial Corp. Minnetonka, Mn.	N56D
☐ N1CF	98	Citation V Ultra	560-0473	Intermet Corp. Pontiac, Mi.	N473SB
☐ N1CG	81	Learjet 55	55-014	ICG LLC. Denver, Co.	N551CG
☐ N1CH	94	Citation V Ultra	560-0283	CMH Homes Inc. Knoxville, Tn.	N560JC
☐ N1DA	75	Citation	500-0288	Donald Anderson, Roswell, NM.	(N502BA)
☐ N1DB	68	JetStar-731	5119	BKR Investments LLC. Chicago, Il.	N500AG
☐ N1DC	01	Gulfstream V	651	Ark-Air Flight Inc. Irving, Tx.	N651GV
☐ N1DE	90	Learjet 31	31-016	Champion Air LLC. Statesville, NC.	N92LJ
☐ N1DG	01	Challenger 604	5516	Ogden Flight Services Group Inc. Bridgeport, Ct.	N516DG
☐ N1DH	00	Citation X	750-0136	Jacob Aviation of Minnesota LLC. Minnneapolis, Mn.	N799TG
☐ N1DM	04	CitationJet CJ-2	525A-0214	MacNeil Aviation LLC. Aurora, Il.	N.....
☐ N1ED	00	Learjet 31A	31A-218	DeBartolo Corp/San Francisco Forty-Niners,Youngstown ,Oh.	N30050
☐ N1EG	02	390 Premier 1	RB-43	Malibu Leasing Corp. Aspen, Co.	
☐ N1FE	01	Global Express	9091	FEDEX, Memphis, Tn.	N700XM
☐ N1GG	75	Citation	500-0249	Gerald Glasauer, Schwabish Hall, Germany.	N501SE
☐ N1GH	80	Citation II	550-0201	Victor X LLC. Newport Beach, Ca.	N566TX
☐ N1GM	76	Sabre-60	306-120	Victory Christian Ministries International, Clinton, Md.	N265SR
☐ N1GN	03	Gulfstream G550	5023	Greg Norman Arcraft Leasing Inc. West Palm Beach, Fl.	N923GA
☐ N1H	86	Citation S/II	S550-0094	Sunrise Leasing Inc. White Plains, NY.	N6LL
☐ N1HA	78	Citation 1/SP	501-0072	Aker Plastics Co. Plymouth, In.	N3110M
☐ N1HC	02	Gulfstream G550	5009	United States Aviation Co. Tulsa, Ok.	N909GA
☐ N1HF	82	Falcon 20F-5	474	Harbison-Fischer Inc. Fort Worth, Tx.	N211HF
☐ N1HP	00	Learjet 45	45-082	Helmerich & Payne Inc. Tulsa, Ok.	N40082
☐ N1HS	03	Citation Excel	560-5351	Erickson Petroleum Corp. Minneapolis-Anoka, Mn.	N53XL
☐ N1HZ	82	Challenger 600S	1056	Herzog Contracting Corp. St Joseph, Mo.	N712HL
☐ N1JB	98	CitationJet	525-0251	Bryan Automotive Group Inc. Winter Park, Fl.	N50ET
☐ N1JC	83	Diamond 1A	A059SA	N1JC Ltd/New Braunfels Aviation Ltd. New Braunfels, Tx.	N126GA
☐ N1JK	81	Gulfstream 3	342	Pegasus North Inc. New Orleans, La.	N1AQ
☐ N1JN	89	Gulfstream 4	1088	Nicklaus Design LLC. Palm Beach International, Fl.	N2600J
☐ N1JX	70	Sabre-60	306-61	Jet Harbor Inc. Fort Lauderdale, Fl.	N1JN
☐ N1KE	99	Gulfstream V	574	Nike Inc/Aero Air LLC. Hillsboro, Or.	N674GA
☐ N1KT	78	Westwind-1124	230	Med Jet/McDonald Group Inc. Birmingham, Al.	N102U
☐ N1LB	00	Gulfstream 4SP	1448	Lehman Brothers/Executive Fliteways Inc. Ronkonkoma, NY.	N448GA
☐ N1LT	77	Sabre-75A	380-59	J & M Air Inc. Westwood, Ks.	N27LT
☐ N1M	90	Astra-1125SP	043	United Aircraft Holdings LLC. Concord, NC.	N90CE
☐ N1MC	99	Astra-1125SPX	112	Jernigan Air LLC. Birmingham, Al.	N633GA
☐ N1MG	99	Learjet 45	45-060	Co-Mar of Dayton Inc. Bowling Green, Ky.	
☐ N1MJ	77	JetStar 2	5217	486MJ Inc. Daphne, Al.	N486MJ
☐ N1MM	81	Citation II	550-0269	Erin Air Inc. Seattle, Wa.	N28RC
☐ N1NA	80	Gulfstream 3	309	NASA, Washington, DC.	N18LB
☐ N1NL	81	Citation II	550-0271	Neil F Lampson Inc. Kennewick, Wa.	N729MJ
☐ N1PB	98	Citation Excel	560-5013	Francis S Baldwin Jr. Longboat Key, Fl.	N1243C
☐ N1PG	99	Gulfstream 4SP	1374	Proctor & Gamble Co. Cincinnati-Lunken, Oh.	N7PG
☐ N1PR	81	Gulfstream 3	341	Paragon Ranch Inc. Broomfield, Co.	N263C
☐ N1QH	71	HS 125/731	NA763	Aspen 1 LLC. Van Nuys, Ca.	N19H
☐ N1RB	01	Learjet 60	60-202	Rooney Brothers Co. Tulsa, Ok.	(N260RB)
☐ N1S	87	Falcon 900	28	Sunoco Inc. Philadelphia, Pa.	N86MC
☐ N1SA	01	Global Express	9100	Stanford Aviation LLC. Houston, Tx.	N700CX
☐ N1SF	99	Gulfstream V	598	Gulf States Toyota Inc. Houston, Tx.	N598GA
☐ N1SL	02	Global Express	9114	Sara Lee Corp. Chicago-Midway, Il.	N11EA
☐ N1SN	00	Gulfstream 4SP	1433	Sky Night LLC. Greeneville, Tn.	N433GA
☐ N1SV	80	Citation II	550-0150	Viersen Air Services LLC. Okmulgee, Ok.	N2668A
☐ N1TF	04	Gulfstream G550	5035	Gulf States Toyota Inc. Houston, Tx.	N935GA
☐ N1TK	97	Global Express	9004	Consolidated Charter Service Inc. Fort Wayne, In.	C-FKGX
☐ N1TM	02	Gulfstream 4SP	1490	Marsico Aviation LLC. Denver, Co.	(N490QS)
☐ N1TS	99	Global Express	9046	Siebel Systems Inc. San Jose, Ca.	N700BV
☐ N1UA	80	Citation II	550-0162	University of Alabama, Tuscaloosa, Al.	N550KP
☐ N1UM	77	Citation 1/SP	501-0011	University of Mississippi, Oxford, Ms.	N650AC
☐ N1UP	92	Citation VI	650-0224	Foresight Management LLC. Wilmington, De.	(N7UL)
☐ N1VA	87	Citation S/II	S550-0143	Department of Aviation, Richmond, Va.	N1430S
☐ N1WB	79	Citation II	550-0068	Ward Burton Aviation Inc. West Columbia, SC.	N402ST
☐ N1WP	87	Gulfstream 4	1030	AMSI/Wm Pennington/WNP Aviation Inc. Reno, Nv.	(N811JK)
☐ N1WS	79	Westwind-1124	252	Spirit Aviation Inc. Van Nuys, Ca.	(N9WW)
☐ N1XH	03	390 Premier 1	RB-76	Thayer Lodging Group Inc. Fort Lauderdale, Fl.	N6076Y
☐ N1XL	81	Learjet 35A	35A-392	Northstar LLC. St Croix, USVI.	N18DY
Reg	*Yr*	*Type*	*c/n*	*Owner/Operator*	*Prev Regn*

Reg	Yr	Type	c/n	Owner/Operator	Prev Regn
N1XT	02	390 Premier 1	RB-36	JB Services Inc. Wilmington, De.	
N1ZC	84	Citation III	650-0031	Zachary Construction Corp. San Antonio, Tx.	N631CC
N2	02	Citation Excel	560-5333	FAA, Oklahoma City, Ok.	N533XL
N2AT	97	Falcon 2000	51	ALLTEL Corp. Little Rock, Ar.	N82AT
N2BA	76	Learjet 35	35-051	Silver Lining Leasing Inc. Pensacola, Fl.	(N123MJ)
N2BD	00	Falcon 900EX	72	Becton-Dickinson & Co. Teterboro, NJ.	F-WWFH
N2BG	02	Gulfstream G200	064	California Hotel & Casino, Las Vegas, Nv.	(N706QS)
N2CC	04	Falcon 2000EX	28	Tonkawa Inc/Carlson Companies Inc. Minneapolis, Mn.	F-GUFM
N2CJ	99	CitationJet CJ-2	708	Cessna Aircraft Co. 525A CJ-2 prototype Ff 27 Apr 99.	
N2DD	76	Learjet 24E	24E-335	N2DD Inc. Newark, De.	N8AE
N2DF	70	Gulfstream 2B	95	Suburban Properties 3 LLC. Detroit, Mi.	N889DF
N2FE	91	Challenger 601-3A	5095	FEDEX, Memphis, Tn.	N95FE
N2FQ	86	Falcon 50	167	SK Aviation LLC/Sweeney Development Co. St Helena, Ca.	N2T
N2FU	90	Learjet 31	31-027	Formula One Management Ltd. Biggin Hill, UK.	N30LJ
N2G	97	Hawker 800XP	8354	CCA Financial LLC. Ashland, Va.	
N2GG	81	Citation II	550-0286	Pro Aviation Inc. Wadsworth, Il.	N78BA
N2HB	03	Citation Excel	560-5222	Hilliard Leasing LLC. Clewiston, Fl.	N.....
N2HL	03	Gulfstream G200	091	Leach Capital LLC. San Francisco, Ca.	N391GA
N2HP	82	HS 125/700A	NA0328	Helmerich & Payne Inc. Tulsa, Ok.	N710BG
N2JR	73	Gulfstream 2B	131	CIT Group, Tempe, Az.	N759A
N2JW	02	Challenger 604	5549	Excel Three LLC. Houston, Tx.	N540JW
N2KZ	89	Learjet 35A	35A-652	K2 Inc. Carlsbad, Ca.	N49AZ
N2N	99	Gulfstream V	586	Steven Jobs/Glass Aviation Inc. San Jose, Ca.	N586GA
N2NL	81	Sabre-65	465-63	Stewart Lubricants & Service Co. Birmingham, Al.	N2N
N2NT	92	Citation VII	650-7013	Northcote Inc. Bend, Or.	(N713VP)
N2PG	99	Gulfstream 4SP	1378	Procter & Gamble Co. Cincinnati-Lunken, Oh.	N378GA
N2QG	91	BAe 125/800A	NA0467	Boyd Atlantic City Inc. Atlantic City, NJ.	(N103BG)
N2RC	95	Citation V Ultra	560-0319	Rico Marketing Corp. Flint-Bishop, Mi.	LV-WOE
N2RM	74	Citation	500-0153	Coastal Atlantic Aviation Investments, Suffolk, Va.	N153JP
N2UP	93	Citation VI	650-0227	Mid-America Aviation LLC. Oklahoma City, Ok.	(N2UX)
N2WC	83	Diamond 1	A047SA	Robert Tanner Aviation, Little Rock, Ar.	N333TS
N2WQ	79	Learjet 35A	35A-277	White Industries Inc. Bates City, Mo.	(N489)
N2ZC	00	Citation Excel	560-5156	Zachary Construction Corp. San Antonio, Tx.	N5155G
N3	03	Citation Excel	560-5341	FAA, Oklahoma City, Ok.	N5061W
N3AS	04	Learjet 45	45-247	Shamrock Foods Co. Scottsdale, Az.	N50154
N3AV	81	Westwind-Two	361	Avjet Corp. Burbank, Ca.	N610HC
N3BL	64	Learjet 23	23-003	Alpha Jet International Inc. Bartow, Fl.	N3BL
N3BM	04	Falcon 2000EX EASY	38	Morris Communications Corp. Augusta, Ga.	F-WWGT
N3CJ	02	CitationJet CJ-3	711	Cessna Aircraft Co. Wichita, Ks.	
N3FA	89	Citation V	560-0023	Truck Body Aviation Inc. Lynchburg, Va.	N345MB
N3FE	89	Challenger 601-3A	5054	FEDEX, Memphis, Tn.	N619FE
N3FW	82	Citation II	550-0337	Sunbelt Leasing Operations LLC/F W Ops Inc. New Castle, De.	N406SS
N3GN	78	Citation 1/SP	501-0090	Esper Petersen/Wisconsin Aviation Inc. Watertown, Wi.	N41JP
N3HB	96	Challenger 604	5313	Hamilton Companies LLC. Englewood, Co.	N906SB
N3MB	81	Learjet 35A	35A-335	Pace American of Indiana/Pair Corp. Middlebury, In.	(N880CH)
N3PC	99	Challenger 604	5411	Trinity Broadcasting of Florida Inc. Pembroke Park, Fl.	N604TS
N3PG	95	Gulfstream 4SP	1260	1260 LLC. Burlingame, Ca.	N461GA
N3RC	80	HS 125/700A	NA0262	Richard Childress Racing Enterprises Inc. Lexington, NC.	N711WM
N3RP	77	Sabre-75A	380-42	N3R LLC. Groton, Ct.	N6YL
N3SA	91	Gulfstream 4	1171	Stanford Aviation 5555 LLC. Miami, Fl.	N686CG
N3ST	01	CitationJet CJ-2	525A-0045	Beehawk Aviation Inc. Smyrna, Ga.	N5214L
N3VF	77	Falcon 20F-5	363	VF Corp. Greensboro-Highpoint, NC.	N363FJ
N3VJ	91	Learjet 31A	31A-035	Bergen Jet LLC/Venture Jets Inc. Lititz, Pa.	N618RF
N3WT	79	Citation 1/SP	501-0088	Eagle Ventures LLC. Mobile, Al.	(N23TZ)
N4AS	99	BBJ-74U	29233	Air Shamrock Inc. Van Nuys, Ca.	N1786B
N4AZ		McDonnell 220	1	Grecoair Inc. El Paso, Tx.	N220N
N4CP	02	Gulfstream G550	5005	Pfizer Inc. Mercer County Airport, NJ.	N805GA
N4CR	66	HS 125/1A-522	25109	Smallville Express LLC. Thousand Oaks, Ca.	N201H
N4CS	80	Sabre-65	465-27	Career Sports Management Inc. Atlanta-Dekalb, Ga.	N39TR
N4EA	82	Learjet 35A	35A-458	Rolex/Woodhill Aviation Corp. Palwaukee, Il.	N86RX
N4ES	70	HS 125/F400A	25243	Aerohawk Leasing & Sales Inc. Dallas, Tx.	VP-CTS
N4FC	94	Citation V Ultra	560-0270	Jack Henry & Associates Inc. Monett, Mo.	(N259JH)
N4FE	99	Learjet 45	45-032	FEDEX, Memphis, Tn.	
N4GA	98	CitationJet	525-0272	Aircraft Owners & Pilots Association, Frederick, Md.	
N4GX	99	Global Express	9048	Sierra Aviation Inc. Kansas City, Mo.	N700BY
N4J	77	Learjet 35A	35A-110	RR Investments Inc/Million Air, Dallas, Tx.	(N12EP)

Reg	Yr	Type	c/n	Owner/Operator	Prev Regn
N4JB	00	Citation Excel	560-5125	Breco International, Harare, Zimbabwe.	N5124K
N4JS	99	Citation Excel	560-5035	John F Scarpa Inc. Pleasantville, NJ.	N35XL
N4LK	82	Diamond 1	A021SA	Reuben Setliff III MD PC. Sioux Falls, SD.	N222Q
N4MB	94	Falcon 900B	146	Mellon Bank NA. Allegheny County, Pa.	N881P
N4MH	78	Westwind-1124	232	Amscray Air LLC. Newark, De.	N773AW
N4MM	91	Citation V	560-0109A	Morgan McClure Motorsports Inc. Abingdon, Va.	(N560RD)
N4NM	82	Citation II/SP	551-0431	OK Doke Aviation Inc. Longmont, Co.	(N20WH)
N4NR	79	Gulfstream 2B	255	Wilmington Aero Ventures Inc. Wilmington, De.	N442A
N4NT	70	Sabre-60	306-48	Sabre Leasing Associates Inc. Swanton, Oh.	N4228A
N4PG	94	Gulfstream 4SP	1259	Procter & Gamble Co. Cincinnati-Lunken, Oh.	N1PG
N4QB	71	HS 125/F400A	25255	River Run Projects LLC. Nashua, NH.	(N255TS)
N4QN	93	Citation VII	650-7031	Blessey Travel LLC. Big Sky, Mt.	N40N
N4RP	02	CitationJet CJ-2	525A-0135	Pratte Transportation Inc. Las Vegas, Nv.	N5211Q
N4RT	68	Gulfstream II SP	26	Hazben Inc. Chicago, Il.	(N711RT)
N4SA	76	HS 125/600A	6065	Stanford Aviation LLC. Houston, Tx.	N125SF
N4SQ	80	Westwind-Two	307	Sunquest Executive Air Charter Inc. Van Nuys, Ca.	N494BP
N4TL	95	Citation V Ultra	560-0334	Toyota-Lexus/Morningstar Aviation Inc. Greenville, SC.	N5109W
N4UC	03	Gulfstream G400	1513	United Aviation Holdings Inc. Key Biscayne, Fl.	N113GA
N4VF	85	Falcon 50	160	V F Corp. Greensboro-Highpoint, NC.	N487F
N4WC	72	HS 125/F400A	NA771	W C Aviation LLC. Vail, Co.	N298NM
N4WG	76	Westwind-1124	200	Owners Jet Services Ltd. DuPage, Il.	N1124X
N4Y	86	Citation III	650-0137	Heartland Aviation Inc. Eau Claire, Wi.	N874G
N5CA	81	Falcon 10	187	ABI LLC. Van Nuys, Ca.	(N600AP)
N5DA	03	Gulfstream G550	5021	Adam Aviation LLP. College Station, Tx.	N921GA
N5DL	78	Gulfstream II SP	226	RELCO Resources, Cincinnati-Lunken, Oh.	N1902L
N5FE	00	Learjet 45	45-079	FEDEX, Memphis, Tn.	
N5FF	02	Citation X	750-0192	Frederick Furth, Healdsburg, Ca.	N51817
N5GF	95	Gulfstream 4SP	1277	685TA Corp/American Home Products, Teterboro, NJ.	N426GA
N5HN	99	Gulfstream V	568	Proctor & Gamble Co. Cincinnati-Lunken, Oh.	HB-INQ
N5HQ	79	Westwind-1124	266	Wild Turkey LLC. Midland, Tx.	N7HM
N5LK	75	Citation	500-0274	Citation Flight LLC. Kirkland, Wa.	N70TF
N5MC	93	Gulfstream 4SP	1218	McCaw Communications Inc. Seattle, Wa.	N418SP
N5NC	00	Learjet 31A	31A-211	Air Operations LLC/Noland Co. Newport News, Va.	N574BA
N5NE	93	Citation II	550-0723	Dubois County Flight Services Inc. Huntingburg, In.	(N888NA)
N5NG	02	Gulfstream 4SP	1485	Northrop Grumman Aviation Inc. Van Nuys, Ca.	N485GA
N5NR	85	Citation III	650-0083	Flying M LLC. Long Beach, Ca.	N2NR
N5PF	93	Beechjet 400A	RK-59	Fleming Investments LLC. Missoula, Mt.	N50KH
N5RD	74	Gulfstream 2	142	RDC Marine Inc. Houston, Tx.	N60CC
N5SA	98	Gulfstream V	527	WEKEL SA. Bogota, Colombia.	N527GA
N5T	99	Citation X	750-0104	Azlon LLC. Austin, Tx.	N51478
N5TQ	80	Citation II/SP	551-0031	MBSW Aviation LLC. Pascagoula, Ms.	N5T
N5TR	81	Citation II	550-0322	Housey Aviation LLC. Southfield, Mi. (was 551-0351).	N322CS
N5UH	98	Gulfstream V	536	United Healthcare Services Inc. St Paul, Mn.	N536GA
N5UU	94	Falcon 900B	133	Southern Aircraft Leasing Inc. Rockville, Md.	N395L
N5VF	86	Falcon 50	166	V F Corp. Greensboro-Highpoint, NC.	N316PA
N5VG	90	Learjet 31	31-014	Wal-Mart Stores Inc. Rogers, Ar.	PT-OFJ
N5VJ	87	Falcon 900B	27	Yet Again Inc. Dulles, Va.	N91EW
N5VP	77	Citation 1/SP	501-0046	Air East Charters of Ashoskie Inc. Aulander, NC.	N405CC
N5VS	00	Gulfstream 4SP	1414	N811BP Inc. Wilmington, De.	(N819JF)
N5WC	85	Citation S/II	S550-0027	Gunslinger Aviation LLC. Telluride, Co.	N27FP
N5WF	78	Citation 1/SP	501-0082	Mociva Inc. Carlsbad-Palomar, Ca.	XB-ERX
N5WM	79	B 737-268	22050	Interlease Aviation Corp. Northfield, Il.	HZ-HM4
N5WT	79	Citation II/SP	551-0149	CCHDDNV Inc. Waco, Tx. (was 550-0107).	(N715PS)
N5XP	01	Learjet 45	45-118	Xpress Air Inc. Chattanooga, Tn.	N50163
N5YD	02	CitationJet CJ-2	525A-0121	Inversiones Chocolido CA. Caracas, Venezuela.	N121YD
N6BB	90	Challenger 601-3A	5082	Blockbuster Inc. Dallas, Tx.	N611GS
N6BX	89	Falcon 900B	79	Baxter Healthcare Corp/Allegiance Healthcare, Waukegan, Il.	N901FJ
N6FE	01	Learjet 45	45-098	FEDEX, Memphis, Tn.	
N6FR	97	Citation Bravo	550-0828	Fall River Group Inc. Fall River, Wi.	N5058J
N6GV	79	Sabre-65	465-9	AG Atlantic Investment Inc. Ocean City, Md.	(N769EG)
N6HF	80	Citation II	550-0260	HCF Realty Inc. St Clair Shores, Mi.	N8CF
N6JB	93	Challenger 601-3A	5131	Fuqua National Corp. Atlanta, Ga.	N602JB
N6JU	81	Citation II	550-0252	Denver Air LLC. Broomfield, Co.	N6JL
N6JW	73	Gulfstream 2	138	Walter Industries Inc. Tampa, Fl.	
N6M	01	CitationJet CJ-2	525A-0051	Mark Martin Enterprises Inc. Daytona Beach, Fl.	N.....
N6MF	01	Beechjet 400A	RK-315	Midwest Flight LLC. Joplin, Mo.	N3215J

Reg	Yr	Type	c/n	Owner/Operator	Prev Regn
N6MW	82	Challenger 600S	1057	M A Inc. Oshkosh, Wi.	N78SR
N6NR	81	Sabre-65	465-68	Jasmine Aviation LLC. Wabasso, Fl.	N930RA
N6NY	97	Citation V Ultra	560-0439	Bob Jones University Inc. Greenville, SC.	VP-CSC
N6QZ	78	JetStar 2	5224	Kuse Enterprises Inc. Atlanta, Ga.	N3QS
N6SS	66	HS 125/1A-522	25100	J-Bird Air Service Corp. Rosedale, NY.	N44TQ
N6TM	03	Citation Bravo	550-1067	Liberty Mutual Insurance Co. Bedford, Ma.	N5085E
N6VF	84	Falcon 20F-5B	486	V F Corp. Greensboro-Highpoint, NC.	F-GEFS
N6VG	75	Falcon 10	62	Vahe Deverian/Variant Investments, Burbank, Ca.	N12LB
N7AB	96	Citation VII	650-7068	Marathon Aircraft Corp 1 & 2, North Platte, Ne.	N111BZ
N7CC	04	CitationJet CJ-3	525B-0007	Intrust Financial Corp. Wichita, Ks.	N5239J
N7CQ	93	CitationJet	525-0004	DNJ Aviation LLC. East Lansing, Mi.	N7CC
N7DJ	79	Westwind-1124	265	Robert Lanphere, Beaverton, Or.	N167J
N7EJ	76	Learjet 24E	24E-343	Fabair LLC. Milwaukee, Wi.	(N602JF)
N7EN	80	Citation 1/SP	501-0302	Omega Industries Inc. Las Vegas, Nv. (was 500-0402).	N801EL
N7FE	99	Learjet 45	45-099	FEDEX, Memphis, Tn.	(N545RS)
N7GF	66	Learjet 23	23-093	Newport/Signal Air Inc. Van Nuys, Ca.	N80775
N7GJ	72	Citation	500-0021	Castores USA LLC. Wilmington, De.	XA-JLV
N7GX	83	Falcon 50	139	Dura Automotive Systems Inc. Rochester Hills, Mi.	N1S
N7GZ	03	CitationJet CJ-2	525A-0145	Duval Asphalt Products Inc. Cincinnati, Oh.	N.....
N7HB	01	Citation Encore	560-0584	Hunt Building Corp. El Paso, Tx.	N5296X
N7HF	87	Citation III	650-0148	Windsong Aviation LLC. St Paul, Mn.	N50EJ
N7HM	81	Westwind-1124	329	Wild Turkey LLC. Midland, Tx.	N711SE
N7JM	80	Challenger 600S	1010	Life in the Word Inc. Fenton, Mo.	N802Q
N7KG	73	Sabre-40A	282-111	ESP Matik Inc. Keene, NH.	(N246GS)
N7MZ	81	Citation 1/SP	501-0217	SMDA LLC. Jefferson City, Mo.	N500TW
N7NE*	04	CitationJet CJ-3	525B-0025	Norfolk Iron & Metal Co/NIM Air LLC. Norfolk, Me.	N.....
N7NN	98	Citation Bravo	550-0851	Knauss Ventures LLC. Las Vegas, Nv.	
N7NR	80	Sabre-65	465-44	Rockwell Automation Inc. Milwaukee, Wi.	
N7PW	82	Diamond 1	A027SA	TCB & Assocs Inc. Marietta, Ga.	N27TJ
N7RX	90	Gulfstream 4	1137	IMS Health Transportation Services Corp. White Plains, NY.	N21CZ
N7SB	02	Citation X	750-0209	OPA LLC/Business Resources International Inc. Winnetka, Il.	N52229
N7SN	01	Learjet 31A	31A-226	Sevenson Enviromental Services Inc. Niagara Falls, NY.	N226LJ
N7SV	81	Citation 1/SP	501-0199	Christian Life Church Inc. Montgomery, Al.	N62RG
N7TK	79	Citation 1/SP	501-0116	Timothy Mellon, Lyme, Ct.	(N90MT)
N7UF	81	Citation 1/SP	501-0260	Eagle Air LLC. Fairfield, Oh.	N500GA
N7WG	79	Gulfstream II SP	248	Hawker Air LP/Jones & Granger, Houston, Tx.	N248TH
N7XE*	00	CitationJet CJ-1	525-0419	Norfolk Iron & Metal Co/NIM Air LLC. Norfolk, Ne.	N7NE
N7YA	99	Citation Bravo	550-0880	Rolling Green Enterprises LLC. Edina, Mn.	N5112K
N7ZU	82	Citation II	550-0433	Air 1st Aviation Companies Inc. Aiken, SC.	N131GA
N8AF	64	Sabre-40	282-24	American Horizons Ltd. Fort Wayne, In.	N40DW
N8BX	91	Falcon 900B	111	Baxter Healthcare Corp/Allegiance Healthcare, Waukegan, Il.	N472FJ
N8DX	76	Citation Eagle	500-0303	Shelter Charter Services Inc. Atlanta, Ga.	C-GDWS
N8HQ	88	Beechjet 400	RJ-50	E-Solutions Research LLC.	N406GJ
N8JC	01	Citation X	750-0154	Jepson Associates Inc. Savannah, Ga.	N5206T
N8JL	83	Gulfstream 3	388	Continental Aviation Services Inc. Fort Myers, Fl.	N561ST
N8JQ	97	Citation X	750-0020	Case Corp. Racine, Wi.	N8JC
N8KG	88	Falcon 50	174	Plum Creek Marketing Inc. Seattle, Wa.	N565A
N8LE	83	Diamond 1A	A042SA	Turbine Aircraft Marketing Inc. San Angelo, Tx.	(N420FA)
N8LT	80	Falcon 10	173	Aviation Enterprises Inc. Atlanta-Hartsfield, Ga.	(N34LT)
N8MC	90	Gulfstream 4	1129	Monaco Coach Corp. Eugene, Or.	N1129X
N8MF	86	Learjet 55B	55B-128	Aviation Partners of America LLC. Las Vegas, Nv.	N717JB
N8QM	96	Falcon 2000	38	Tenet Healthcare Corp. Santa Barbara, Ca.	(N800BG)
N8SP	01	Challenger 604	5518	SPX Corp. Charlotte, NC.	C-GLXM
N8TG	99	Learjet 31A	31A-190	Kitty Hawk Aircraft Services LLC. Hayden, Id.	N316AC
N8TP	67	Falcon 20-5	74	448 Alliance Corp. Fort Worth, Tx.	N522DD
N8UA	77	Learjet 36A	36A-026	Denmark Investments Inc. Murrieta, Ca.	N1U
N8VB	99	Global Express	9021	Viacom Inc. Morristown, NJ.	C-GEYY
N8YM	85	Beechjet 400	RJ-4	FractionAir Inc. Nashville, Tn. (was A1004SA).	(N401TJ)
N9AZ	76	HS 125/600A	6063	Alas Air Leasing Inc. Wilmington, De.	5N-...
N9CH	01	Learjet 45	45-129	C W Hurd Jr. Santa Teresa, NM.	N4003W
N9CN	01	Citation Encore	560-0602	Nearburg Producing Co. Dallas, Tx.	N5206T
N9CR	84	Citation II/SP	551-0500	Cedar Ridge Estates, Macon, Ga.	N501MC
N9CU	96	Learjet 60	60-075	PMG Acquisition/Pediatric Medical Group Inc. Ft Lauderdale.	N675LJ
N9FE	04	Learjet 45	45-240	FEDEX, Memphis, Tn.	N50579
N9GY	88	Citation S/II	S550-0159	Astro-Galaxy Inc. Winston-Salem, NC.	N9GT
N9KL	81	Gulfstream 3	321	SPW LLC/Ozark Management Inc. Jefferson City, Mo.	(N91KL)

Reg	Yr	Type	c/n	Owner/Operator	Prev Regn
☐ N9NG	03	Citation X	750-0213	Northrop Grumman Aviation Inc. Baltimore, Md.	N50715
☐ N9NL	85	Citation III	650-0101	LTH Jet Leasing Inc. Fort Lauderdale, Fl.	XA-LTH
☐ N9PW	90	Beechjet 400A	RK-7	Air Charlotte Inc. Oak Park. Mi.	N401AB
☐ N9QM	79	Learjet 25D	25D-286	First Star Inc. Hollister, Ca.	N850MX
☐ N9RA	66	Learjet 23	23-095	Royal Air Freight Inc. Waterford, Mi.	N5D
☐ N9RD	77	Westwind-1124	220	Share Force One LLC. Orlando, Fl.	N106BC
☐ N9SC	98	Gulfstream V	552	SCI Texas Funeral Services Inc. Houston, Tx.	N652GA
☐ N9SS	80	Citation II/SP	551-0214	Thomas G Somermeier Jr. Santa Monica, Ca. (was 550-0163).	N178HH
☐ N9TE	69	Falcon 20D-5	202	Mountain High Aviation LLC. Indian Harbor Beach, Fl.	N48TJ
☐ N9UP	89	BAe 125/800A	NA0433	W C Leasing LLC. Franklin Lakes, NJ.	N919P
☐ N9VF	90	Citation II	550-0646	Air-Ger LLC. Charlotte, NC.	N1310G
☐ N9WV	02	Falcon 900EX	108	SCB Falcon LLC/JCL Corp. Bentonville, Ar.	G-JCBX
☐ N9WW	97	Beechjet 400A	RK-142	W W Williams Co. Columbus, Oh.	N142BJ
☐ N9ZD	80	Learjet 35A	35A-306	White Industries Inc. Bates City, Mo.	(N63602)
☐ N9ZM	99	Learjet 60	60-151	Zyman Group LLC. Atlanta-Fulton County, Ga.	N234FX
☐ N10AH	90	Learjet 35A	35A-657	Kokomo Aviation Inc. Indianapolis, In.	N1CA
☐ N10AU	99	Citation V Ultra	560-0512	Auburn University, Auburn, Al.	N29WE
☐ N10AZ	78	Falcon 20F-5B	382	The Anshutz Corp. Denver-Centennial, Co.	N382E
☐ N10C	78	HS 125/700A	NA0235	Robert Hewitt, Victoria, Tx.	N700GB
☐ N10CR	90	Learjet 55C	55C-145	NCR Corp. Dayton, Oh.	N66WM
☐ N10D	65	HS 125/1A-522	25029	White Industries Inc. Bates City, Mo.	N391DA
☐ N10EG	79	Citation II	550-0055	Aviation Sales Inc. Miamisburg, Oh.	(N1466K)
☐ N10EH	85	Gulfstream 3	436	Sinclair Oil Corp. Salt Lake City, Ut.	N436GA
☐ N10F	74	Falcon 10	12	King Leasing Corp/Air 88 Inc. San Diego, Ca.	(N76TJ)
☐ N10FE	95	Challenger 601-3R	5188	FEDEX, Memphis, Tn.	N575CF
☐ N10FG	76	Citation Eagle	500-0295	AEGON USA Inc. Cedar Rapids, Ia.	N44HC
☐ N10FL	00	Beechjet 400A	RK-266	Delhaize America Inc. Salisbury, NC.	N41283
☐ N10FN	75	Learjet 36	36-015	Flight Capital LLC. Madison, Ms.	N14CF
☐ N10J	99	Learjet 45	45-063	Sterling Aviation Inc. Wyomissing, Pa.	
☐ N10JP*	95	Falcon 2000	23	JP Air Transportation LLC/Pattco Inc. Louisville, Ky.	N23FJ
☐ N10LR	79	Citation II/SP	551-0122	DJL Properties Inc. Baker, Or. (was 550-0059).	(N2662F)
☐ N10LX	70	Sabre-60	306-59	Lockheed Martin Tactical Defence Systems, Goodyear, Az.	N20GX
☐ N10LY	83	Citation II	550-0466	First Air Leasing Inc. Greenville, SC.	N412MA
☐ N10M	71	Sabre-75	370-2	Addison Aircraft Sales Inc. Holly Lake Ranch, Tx.	N80K
☐ N10MB	74	DC 10/30CF	47907	Minebea Technologies P/L. Singapore.	OO=SLB
☐ N10MV	80	Westwind-Two	300	EFC Enterprises LLC. San Diego, Ca.	(N20NW)
☐ N10MZ	87	Falcon 900B	32	ZWA Inc. Teterboro, NJ.	N500BL
☐ N10NC	80	Falcon 10	172	Hayward Enterprises Inc. Fort Lauderdale, Fl.	N172CP
☐ N10NL	00	Learjet 45	45-128	O'Neal Steel Inc. Birmingham, Al.	
☐ N10R	99	Learjet 45	45-042	Brown Shoe Co. St Louis, Mo.	
☐ N10RQ	78	Gulfstream 2	232	Aircraft Inventory Corp. Roanoke, Va.	N508T
☐ N10RZ	68	Falcon 20C-5	161	Pacific Air Aviation Inc. Las Vegas, Nv.	N10PP
☐ N10SE	01	Learjet 31A	31A-217	Richards Aviation Inc. Memphis, Tn.	N40078
☐ N10ST	01	Learjet 60	60-228	SouthTrust Bank NA. Birmingham, Al.	N255FX
☐ N10TB	91	Citation V	560-0143	Tim-Bar Corp. Harrisburg, Pa.	N744WW
☐ N10TC	84	Citation II	550-0495	Fantasy Air Ltd. Boring, Or.	(N400MC)
☐ N10TD	91	Citation V	560-0096	SBM Cleaning LLC. Corvallis, Or.	(N96JJ)
☐ N10TN	80	HS 125/700A	7085	Cando Air Inc. Bridgewater, Ma.	RP-C1714
☐ N10UC	80	HS 125/700A	NA0284	Blue Hawk LLC. Van Nuys, Ca.	N125AP
☐ N10UF	78	Learjet 35A	35A-166	Horsham Valley Airways Inc. Horsham, Pa.	N719JB
☐ N10UH	76	Citation	500-0304	University Alabama Critical Care Transport, Birmingham, Al.	N70U
☐ N10VG	73	Learjet 25B	25B-125	Vince Granatelli Racing Inc. Phoenix, Az.	(N11MC)
☐ N10VQ	05	Citation Excel XLS	560-5570	Cessna Aircraft Co. Wichita, Ks.	N.....
☐ N10YJ	87	BAe 125/800A	8099	Jones International Aviation Inc. Englewood, Co.	OY-MCL
☐ N11AF	76	HS 125/600B	6057	NADA Airline Inc. Ocala, Fl.	N602CF
☐ N11AM	97	Learjet 60	60-118	International Associates of Machinists, Washington, DC.	N301BC
☐ N11AQ	68	Learjet 24	24-178	Sierra American Corp. Addison, Tx.	N723JW
☐ N11FH	78	Citation II	550-0012	Express Airlines I Inc/Northwest Airlink, Memphis, Tn.	C-GHOL
☐ N11HJ	72	Citation	500-0034	Robert Bolin, Wichita Falls, Tx.	(N111FS)
☐ N11LN	79	Westwind-1124	261	Newcastle Capital Group LLC. Dallas, Tx.	N39JN
☐ N11LX	74	Sabre-60	306-75	Lockheed Martin Tactical Defense Systems, Goodyear, Az	N509AB
☐ N11MN	76	Citation	500-0266	Jet Mavericks LLC. Indianapolis, In.	N40RF
☐ N11PM	04	390 Premier 1	RB-113	Raytheon Aircraft Co. Wichita, Ks.	
☐ N11SS	82	Citation II/SP	551-0436	D R Johnson Lumber Co/CO-GEN Co. Riddle, Or. (was 550-0437)	N437CF
☐ N11TM	78	Citation 1/SP	501-0060	Westwood Development Corp. Portland, Or.	N573L
☐ N11TS	86	Citation S/II	S550-0119	NTS Development Co. Louisville, Ky.	N11TR

Reg	Yr	Type	c/n	Owner/Operator	Prev Regn
❏ N11UB	98	Beechjet 400A	RK-212	MCFH Inc. Davis-Woodland, Ca.	N299AW
❏ N11UL	00	Hawker 800XP	8498	Universal Leaf Tobacco Co. Richmond, Va.	N809TA
❏ N11WF	99	Beechjet 400A	RK-236	Flower Foods Inc. Thomasville, Ga.	N2349V
❏ N11WM	99	Falcon 900EX	58	AzaAir Inc. Seattle, Wa.	N958EX
❏ N12AM	74	Citation	500-0235	WestJet LLC. Galesburg, Il.	N235CC
❏ N12BW	72	Sabre-40A	282-99	Barry Wehmiller Group Inc. St Louis, Mo.	N100FG
❏ N12CQ	93	Citation V	560-0231	Paloma Packing Inc. Santa Maria, Ca.	N501E
❏ N12CV	78	Citation 1/SP	501-0081	Paul Ruff, Springfield, Mo.	(N12CQ)
❏ N12EP	80	Falcon 10	175	Kenneth Bampfield, Vero Beach, Fl.	XA-LOK
❏ N12F	90	BAe 125/800B	8182	Wolfe Enterprises Inc. Columbus, Oh.	N128RS
❏ N12FN	75	Learjet 36	36-016	Flight Capital LLC. Madison, Ms.	N616DJ
❏ N12GP	69	Gulfstream 2	63	AZ3 Inc. Vernon, Ca.	(N20GP)
❏ N12GS	02	CitationJet CJ-2	525A-0127	Blue Sky Inc. Coatesville, Pa.	N5211A
❏ N12GY	99	CitationJet CJ-1	525-0374	C J L Enterprises Inc. Phoenix, Az.	N12GS
❏ N12L	98	Citation Excel	560-5002	TCF National Bank, Minneapolis, Mn.	N562XL
❏ N12MG	01	Beechjet 400A	RK-331	The Scotts Co. Columbus, Oh.	N5031D
❏ N12MW	00	Citation Encore	560-0542	Daggett Investment/Dakota Investment Corp. Wilmington, De.	(N120SB)
❏ N12NZ	99	Gulfstream 4SP	1376	Apollo Management LP. Ronkonkoma, NY.	N376GA
❏ N12PA	03	Hawker 800XP	8642	Poly Jet LLC/Poly-Flex Inc. Dallas-Love Field, Tx.	N642XP
❏ N12PB	68	Sabre-60	306-18	Commercial Aviation Enterprises Inc. Delray Beach, Fl.	N11AQ
❏ N12RN	95	Citation V Ultra	560-0316	Island Aircraft Associates Inc. Dallas, Tx.	(N5251Y)
❏ N12RP	79	Learjet 35A	35A-278	Stevens Aviation Inc. Greenville, SC.	N17GL
❏ N12ST	00	Learjet 60	60-205	SouthTrust Bank NA. Birmingham, Al.	N205ST
❏ N12TX	76	Falcon 10	90	Jetways Texas LLC. Dallas, Tx.	N14U
❏ N12U	89	Gulfstream 4	1112	United Technologies Corp. Hartford, Ct.	N12UT
❏ N12WF	99	Beechjet 400A	RK-228	Flowers Industries Inc. Thomasville, Ga.	N3228V
❏ N12WH	78	Citation 1/SP	501-0064	Willard Hanzlik/Nuevo Aviation Inc. Austin, Tx.	N96DS
❏ N13BK	76	Falcon 10	94	Steen Aviation Inc. Shreveport, La.	N54RS
❏ N13FE	66	DC 9-14	45706	Flight Services Group, Bridgeport, Ct.	N5NE
❏ N13FH	97	CitationJet	525-0185	Hertrich Aviation Inc. Seaford, De.	N83TR
❏ N13GB	91	Beechjet 400A	RK-13	TCC Air Services Inc. Greenwich, Ct.	N56BX
❏ N13GW	73	Westwind-1123	162	Jet Set Aircraft, Bogota, Colombia. (status ?).	XA-SDW
❏ N13J	02	Gulfstream 4SP	1482	Kaisen LLC. Raleigh, NC.	(N634S)
❏ N13M	02	CitationJet CJ-2	525A-0105	J L Mark Inc. Chandler, Az.	N.....
❏ N13NL	80	Westwind-Two	304	Westwind Services LLC. Little Rock, Ar.	N10NL
❏ N13ST	78	Citation 1/SP	501-0285	Varistar Corp. Fargo, ND. (was 500-0366).	N100BX
❏ N13SY	96	Beechjet 400A	RK-111	SY Air LLC. Tampa, Fl.	N412WP
❏ N14AZ	67	B 707-336C	19498	Grecoair Inc. El Paso, Tx.	9G-ACX
❏ N14CG	82	Falcon 50	100	Beta Aircraft Corp. Teterboro, NJ.	N102FJ
❏ N14CJ	84	Falcon 200	499	Jani King International Inc. Addison, Tx.	(N200CU)
❏ N14CK	81	Learjet 25G	25G-337	Pacific International Credit & Management, Dover, De.	LV-WBP
❏ N14CN	81	Westwind-Two	359	California Natural Products, Stockton, Ca.	C-GRGE
❏ N14DM	76	Learjet 24E	24E-341	Future Care Consultants Inc. Fort Lauderdale, Fl.	(N103JW)
❏ N14FE	98	Learjet 45	45-038	FEDEX, Memphis, Tn.	(N454RR)
❏ N14FN	73	Learjet 25C	25C-126	Flight Capital LLC. Madison, Ms.	(N162AC)
❏ N14GD	01	Challenger 604	5490	GG Aircraft LLC/Gordon Gund, Trenton, NJ.	N604GD
❏ N14HH	66	HS 125/731	25118	Dove Air Inc. Hendersonville, NC.	N227HF
❏ N14NA	92	Falcon 900B	124	Anschutz Corp. Denver, Co.	VP-BWS
❏ N14R	01	Global Express	9110	Rainin Air LLC/Rainin Instrument Co. Hillsboro, Or.	N700EL
❏ N14RM	80	Citation II/SP	551-0169	Guardian American Security, Southfield, Mi. (was 550-0126).	N700YM
❏ N14RZ	81	Citation II	550-0390	Mudd Air LC. Cedar Falls, Ia.	(N552AJ)
❏ N14T	01	Learjet 60	60-213	K B Graphics Inc. White Plains, NY.	N65T
❏ N14TU	93	Learjet 60	60-026	VGR Aviation LLC/Vector Group Ltd. Wilmington, De.	N14T
❏ N14VA	79	Citation 1/SP	501-0137	Randall Roth, Cornelius, NC.	N46SC
❏ N14VF	91	Citation V	560-0130	VF Jeanswear Inc. Greensboro-Highpoint, NC.	N130CV
❏ N15AS	94	Falcon 2000	3	Contran Corp. Dallas, Tx.	N2000A
❏ N15AW	73	Citation	500-0139	NST Corporate Aviation LC. Orlando, Fl.	N3771U
❏ N15AX	84	BAe 125/800B	8002	Air-X LLC. Opa Locka, Fl.	N882CW
❏ N15CV	97	Citation Bravo	550-0819	Cache Valley Electric Co. Logan, Ut.	N1259B
❏ N15CY	80	Citation 1/SP	501-0152	Theodor Huber, Wiesbaden, Germany.	VP-CCD
❏ N15EH	77	Learjet 35A	35A-126	Sinclair Oil Corp. Salt Lake City, Ut.	N744GL
❏ N15ER	79	Learjet 25D	25D-267	Richardson Investments Inc. San Antonio, Tx.	
❏ N15FE	98	Learjet 45	45-039	FEDEX, Memphis, Tn.	N456AS
❏ N15FJ	79	Citation 1/SP	501-0142	K3C Inc/Sierra Industries Inc. Uvalde, Tx.	(N123PL)
❏ N15H	77	Falcon 20F-5B	368	Wilson Aviation LLC. Glacier International, Mt.	N23A
❏ N15HF	70	Sabre-60	306-60	Williams International LLC. Waterford, Mi.	N15H
Reg	*Yr*	*Type*	*c/n*	*Owner/Operator*	*Prev Regn*

Reg	Yr	Type	c/n	Owner/Operator	Prev Regn
N15JA	78	Citation II	550-0035	Joyner Aviation LLC. Atlanta, Ga.	(N50GG)
N15LV	97	CitationJet	525-0191	Blue Heron Aviation Sales LLC. Melbourne, Fl.	C-FIMA
N15RH	83	Learjet 35A	35A-497	Camden Aviation Inc. St Charles, Il.	N21DA
N15RL	01	Citation X	750-0165	Levi, Ray & Shoup Inc. Springfield, Il.	N5257V
N15SK	96	Citation V Ultra	560-0395	Teterboro Aviation Inc. Teterboro, NJ.	(N19MU)
N15SL	71	Falcon 20F-5	256	JPLI LLC/Continental Aviation Services Inc. Naples, Fl.	N868DS
N15SN	88	Citation II	550-0566	Century Airconditioning Transportation LLC. Wilmington, De.	N15SP
N15TT	00	Citation X	750-0127	Cleo J Thompson, Ozona, Tx.	N52639
N15UC	99	Gulfstream V	589	The United Co. Bristol-Tri Cities, Tn.	N589GA
N15WH	76	Learjet 35A	35A-085	AirNet Systems Inc. Columbus, Oh. (orange).	
N15XM	81	Citation II	550-0308	John Lawson Rock & Oil Inc. Firebaugh, Ca.	N30SA
N16AZ	72	JetStar-8	5156	David Topokh, El Paso, Tx.	XB-DBT
N16DK	01	390 Premier 1	RB-19	DEKA Research & Development Corp. Manchester, NH.	N65TB
N16GS	02	Citation Excel	560-5278	Great Southern Wood Preserving, Abbeville, Al.	N.....
N16GX	99	Global Express	9016	Sky-Jet Aviation Inc. Wilmington, De.	N700AH
N16HC	66	Learjet 24	24-126	Hartford Holding Corp. Naples, Fl. (status ?).	(N345SF)
N16HL	78	Citation 1/SP	501-0059	Owners Jet Services Ltd. DuPage, Il.	ZS-EHL
N16KB	92	Citation VII	650-7008	F Kenneth Bailey Jr. Houston, Tx.	N909SB
N16KK	74	Learjet 25B	25B-174	Royal Air Freight Inc. Waterford, Mi.	N412SP
N16LG	74	Citation Eagle	500-0174	JH690 Inc. Lake St Louis, Mo.	N19AJ
N16LJ	86	Learjet 55	55-126	MBG LLC. Seattle, Wa.	N7260J
N16MF	89	Beechjet 400	RJ-65	Millenium Thoroughbreds Inc. Austin, Tx.	N1565B
N16MK	66	Jet Commander	84	Westar Aviation Inc. Miami, Fl.	N600ER
N16NK	99	Gulfstream V	585	Business Aircraft Corp. Coral Gables, Fl.	N18NK
N16NL	77	Citation 1/SP	501-0043	Orlando Jet Partners LLC. Altamonte Springs, Fl.	N10NL
N16PC	99	Learjet 45	45-050	Southern Company Services Inc. Atlanta, Ga.	
N16RP	85	Citation S/II	S550-0047	Rose Aviation LLC. Cresskill, NJ.	I-CEFI
N16RW	81	Challenger 600S	1013	Central Services LLC. St Louis, Mo.	N72SR
N16SU	84	Citation III	650-0025	Speciality Travel Services Inc. Oak Creek, Wi.	(N522GS)
N16TS	78	Citation II	550-0030	Cherokee Brick & Tile Co. Macon, Ga. (was 551-0077).	N4TS
N16VG	80	Citation 1/SP	501-0157	Gordon Rosenburg, San Ardo, Ca.	(N88BR)
N17A	80	Learjet 36A	36A-046	Avstar Inc. Seattle, Wa.	N146MJ
N17AH	80	Learjet 25D	25D-316	Spirit Wing Aviation Ltd. Guthrie, Ok. (Ff FJ44-2C 9 Jan 03)	(N782JR)
N17AN	99	Citation Excel	560-5030	Globe Leasing Inc. Chicago, Il.	N899BC
N17AZ	76	Learjet 35A	35A-080	Duty Free Aviation LLC. Glen Burnie, Md.	N10AZ
N17DD	89	BAe 125/800A	NA0437	LPSL Corporate Services Inc/Tucci Aviation LLC. Seattle, Wa.	C-FFTM
N17DM	82	Citation II	550-0417	VIP's Industries Inc. Salem, Or.	ZS-LHW
N17GX	99	Global Express	9045	Wing and a Prayer Inc/Glass Aviation Inc. San Jose, Ca.	C-GFKY
N17KD	76	Citation	500-0337	Sinclair-Kirkham-Conley LLC. Chesterfield, Mo.	(F-GNAB)
N17KJ	77	Gulfstream II SP	200	Not Yours LLC. Teterboro, NJ.	N281RB
N17KW	68	Gulfstream 2	28	K W Plastics Co. Troy, Al.	N68DM
N17LJ	76	Learjet 36	36-017	Premier Jets Inc. Hillsboro, Or.	(N361PJ)
N17MK	65	BAC 1-11/410AQ	054	Business Jet Services Ltd. Dallas, Tx.	N17VK
N17NC	80	Gulfstream 3	318	Saturn Productions Inc. Burbank, Ca.	N500WW
N17ND	82	Gulfstream 3	369	Jetaway Air Service LLC. Muskegon, Mi.	N740SS
N17TE	99	Challenger 604	5437	Turner Enterprises Inc/Flying T LLC. Atlanta, Ga.	N437FT
N17TJ	75	Falcon 10	43	Deerfleet LLC. Miami, Fl.	F-GIQP
N17UC	04	Challenger 300	20011	The United Co. Bristol-Tri Cities, Tn.	(N311DB)
N17VB	97	CitationJet	525-0206	Arizona Flight Procurement LLC. Lake Havasu City, Az.	
N17WC	83	Citation II	550-0478	Forest Hills Corp/Winegardner Companies, Memphis, Tn.	N214RW
N17WG	81	HS 125/700A	NA0290	Hawker Air LP/Jones & Granger, Houston, Tx.	N7WG
N18AC	98	Gulfstream 4SP	1344	Alberto-Culver USA Inc. Wheeling, Il.	N344GA
N18AN	93	Gulfstream 4SP	1228	AON Aviation Inc. Palwaukee, Il.	N464GA
N18AX	76	Learjet 35A	35A-087	Omni Air Express Inc. Tulsa, Ok.	(N862BD)
N18BA	82	HS 125/700A	NA0316	KATO Jet International LLC. Mankato, Mn.	(N501F)
N18BH	67	JetStar-731	5099	MIG Magic Inc. Portland, Or.	N62KK
N18BL	96	Learjet 31A	31A-126	Bobby LaBonte Enterprises Inc. Trinity, NC.	N22UF
N18CC	78	HS 125/700A	NA0222	Starlight Aviation Inc. Round Rock, Tx.	C-GNAZ
N18CG	98	Falcon 2000	57	Corning Inc. Hamilton, NY.	N2132
N18CV	75	Learjet 35	35-016	AeroFinance LLC/Alliance Air Inc. Opa Locka, Fl.	N1SC
N18FM	72	Citation	500-0014	N18FM LLC. Tulsa, Ok.	N800W
N18GA	97	CitationJet	525-0215	Griffin Industries Inc. Cold Springs, Ky.	
N18GB	94	Citation VII	650-7048	Green Bay Packaging Inc. Green Bay, Wi.	N51176
N18HC	81	Citation 1/SP	501-0223	J & S Wings LLC. Tuscaloosa, Al.	(N26HA)
N18HJ	88	Citation II	550-0587	Kinnarps AB. Falkoping, Sweden.	N1301S
N18HN	71	Falcon 20F-5	257	Navajo Refining Co. Dallas, Tx.	HB-VKO

| Reg | Yr | Type | c/n | Owner/Operator | Prev Regn |

Reg	Yr	Type	c/n	Owner/Operator	Prev Regn
N18MX	78	Falcon 10	117	High Speed Aviation Inc. Holland, Mi.	N923DS
N18NA	88	Citation II	550-0580	Go Flying High LLC. San Marcos, Tx.	N912BD
N18RF	00	Gulfstream V	628	Ivanhoe Capital Aviation LLC. Vancouver, BC. Canada.	N628GA
N18SH	81	HS 125/700A	NA0310	WFBNW NA. Salt Lake City, Ut.	N2640
N18SK	74	Falcon 10	34	Falconshare LLC. Ridgefield, Ct.	N220M
N18TM	02	Global Express	9090	SDA Enterprises Inc. West Palm Beach, Fl.	C-GIOD
N18WE	81	Learjet 35A	35A-377	Diamond Aviation LLC. Scottsdale, Az.	N10WF
N18WF	02	Global Express	9128	Westfield Aviation Inc. Sydney, NSW, Australia.	N700FY
N18WY	00	Global Express	9057	Citadel Investments Group LLC. Chicago, Il.	N18WF
N18WZ	00	Global Express	9059	Rank Services Ltd. Auckland, NZ.	N18WF
N19AJ	80	Citation II	550-0171	The Collins Group Inc. Jacksonville, Fl.	EI-BYN
N19CP	77	Citation II/SP	550-0003	Granite Development LLC. Atlanta, Ga. (was 551-0004)	YV-19CP
N19DD	83	Challenger 600S	1081	Challenger LLC. Arlington, Tx.	N456DK
N19ER	79	Citation II	550-0048	GWW LLC. Lompoc, Ca.	N10BF
N19HU	79	Citation II	550-0066	Batair LLC. Louisville, Ky.	(N410JP)
N19JM	78	Learjet 25D	25D-250	Viper Aviation Inc. Mooresville, NC.	N112JM
N19LT	90	Learjet 31	31-019	Wal-Mart Stores Inc. Rogers, Ar.	PT-OFL
N19MK	00	Citation Excel	560-5093	Moki Corp. Vero Beach, Fl.	N5203S
N19QC	94	Citation VI	650-0238	Stockton Equipment Leasing LLC. Danville, Ca.	N19UC
N19R	83	Diamond 1A	A043SA	Express Air LLC. Granite City, Il.	N322DM
N19RP	81	Learjet 35A	35A-363	Roaring Fork Partners LLC. Aspen, Co.	N183JC
N19SV	92	Citation VII	650-7002	SuperValu Inc. Minneapolis, Mn.	N95CC
N19UP	02	Learjet 31A	31a-237	Execujet Inc. Eighty-Four, Pa.	N23UP
N20AU	01	Citation Bravo	550-1012	Auburn University, Auburn, Al.	N.....
N20CC	77	Citation 1/SP	501-0262	Aircraft Owners LLC. Destin, Fl.	(N58T)
N20CF	77	Falcon 10	106	Contract Freighters Inc. Joplin, Mo.	N103MM
N20CL	84	Falcon 200	497	Bloomington Aircraft Rentals Inc. Bloomington, Mn.	N720HC
N20CR	83	Learjet 55	55-097	RVDH Development Corp/Shopko Stores Inc. Green Bay, Wi.	N40CR
N20DA	61	MS 760 Paris-2B	102	Semrau Aircraft Co. McKellar Airport, Tn.	N99HB
N20DK	78	Learjet 35A	35A-143	1 BMF LLC. Collierville, Tn.	OE-GER
N20EG	91	Gulfstream 4	1161	EGI Holdings LLC/Executive Fliteways Inc. Ronkonkoma, NY.	(N161TS)
N20FB	81	Citation II	550-0251	Sky High Aviation LLC. Stockton, Ca.	N550HF
N20FJ	67	Falcon 20C	119	Owners Jet Services Ltd. DuPage, Il.	F-GHFP
N20FL	99	Beechjet 400A	RK-247	Delhaize America Inc. Salisbury, NC.	N40252
N20FM	76	HS 125/F600A	6058	N20FM LLC. Tampa, Fl.	N658KA
N20G	93	Challenger 601-3R	5136	Goodyear Tire & Rubber Co. Akron, Oh.	N51GY
N20GP	02	CitationJet CJ-2	525A-0131	N83 Charlie Inc. Fort Wayne, In.	N51564
N20H	69	Gulfstream II SP	51	Hubbard Broadcasting Inc. St Paul, Mn.	N20HE
N20HF	68	Falcon 20D-5	191	31TJ LP-JT Aviation LLC & Lily Aviation LLC. Las Vegas, Nv.	OE-GCR
N20KH	78	Westwind-1124	223	Salisbury Holdings LLC. San Antonio, Tx.	N303PC
N20LW	75	Falcon 10	48	ConeJet LLC. Nashville, Tn.	LX-EPA
N20MY	68	Falcon 20C	136	Pilatus Business Aircraft Ltd. Jeffco Airport, Co.	LX-IAL
N20NL	04	390 Premier 1	RB-106	CNS Corp. Quincy, Il.	N61706
N20NW	72	Learjet 25B	25B-096	Airstar Aviation Inc. San Francisco, Ca.	N235JW
N20NY	66	Falcon 20C	61	Air Force Systems Command, Bedford, Ma.	N299NW
N20PA	85	Diamond 1A	A089SA	Lane Aviation Inc. Colorado Springs, Co.	N88CR
N20PL	02	Gulfstream G200	063	NP Air LLC/Taga Corp. Salt Lake City, Ut	N363GA
N20RM	77	Citation 1/SP	501-0025	Dowdle Butane Gas Co. Columbus, Ms.	N21BS
N20RZ	69	Learjet 25	25-024	Sky Link Jets Inc. Fort Lauderdale, Fl.	N20HJ
N20SM*	96	Citation V Ultra	560-0353	State of Mississippi, Jackson, Ms.	N353Z
N20T	78	Falcon 20F-5	381	Tuthill Corp. Chicago-Midway, Il.	N20TZ
N20TA	65	Learjet 23	23-062	Merit Capital LLC. Carson City, Nv.	N670MF
N20TX	73	Falcon 20F-5	296	Vanguard Health Management Inc. Nashville, Tn.	N19TX
N20UA	67	Falcon 20-5	91	Universal Avionics Systems Corp. Tucson, Az.	N777DC
N20VF	76	Falcon 20F-5	347	V F Corp. Greensboro-Highpoint, NC.	N347HS
N20VL	94	CitationJet	525-0069	Papa Golf Aviation LLC. Owasso, Ok.	N20FL
N20WE	00	Citation Excel	560-5115	Whelen Engineering Co. Chester, Ct.	N5157E
N20WN	77	Falcon 20F	370	Falcon Partners LLC. Salem, Or.	N269SR
N20XP	00	Learjet 31A	31A-197	Xpress Air Inc. Chattanooga, Tn.	
N20YL	95	Astra-1125SP	076	EAP Operating Inc. Fort Worth, Tx.	N699MQ
N21AC	95	Learjet 60	60-070	Alex Campbell Jr. Boca Raton, Fl.	N5035R
N21AM	84	Gulfstream 3	443	Hughes Electronics Corp. Van Nuys, Ca.	N5104
N21BD	02	Learjet 45	45-188	Columbus Transportation LLC. Columbus, Ga.	
N21CV	95	Citation V Ultra	560-0340	Eagle Aviation Inc. Columbia-Metropolitan, SC.	N5267T
N21DX	79	Westwind-1124	269	Deeluxe Transport Inc/Diamond Manufacturing Co. Wyoming, Pa	N50SL
N21EG	86	Citation S/II	S550-0087	Gander Mountain Co. Minneapolis, Mn.	N1274Z

Reg	Yr	Type	c/n	Owner/Operator	Prev Regn

Reg	Yr	Type	c/n	Owner/Operator	Prev Regn
☐ N21EL	99	Hawker 800XP	8396	Private Wings Ltd. Miami, Fl.	N23585
☐ N21EP	77	Citation 1/SP	501-0040	N21EP LLC/Infiniti Aviation LLC. Scottsdale, Az.	N501E
☐ N21FE	78	Falcon 20-5	399	McKinley Aircraft Holdings Inc. Akron-Canton, Oh.	N70U
☐ N21FN	70	Learjet 25	25-062	Hampton University, Newport News, Va.	N25ME
☐ N21HE	04	Falcon 2000EX EASY	46	Harrah's Operating Co. Las Vegas, Nv.	F-W...
☐ N21HQ	99	Citation X	750-0075	Harrah's Operating Co. Las Vegas, Nv.	N21HE
☐ N21HR	81	Westwind-Two	335	AIM Aircraft Leasing LLC. Franklin, Tn.	EC-GIB
☐ N21MA	00	Citation Excel	560-5089	M-A-M Leasing LLC. Cleveland-Cuyahoga, Oh.	N868JB
☐ N21NG	80	Learjet 35A	35A-343	Northrop Grumman Aviation Inc. Melbourne, Fl.	N21NA
☐ N21NR	84	Gulfstream 3	415	Nadir Industries Ltd. Tortola, BVI.	HZ-NR2
☐ N21PJ	80	Gulfstream 3	315	Pacific Jet/Flight Stream LLC. Burbank, Ca.	(N330PJ)
☐ N21RA	02	CitationJet CJ-2	525A-0092	Infinity Aviation Inc. St Augustine, Fl.	N.....
☐ N21SA	73	HS 125/F600A	6006	Scott Industrial Inc. Naperville, Il.	N606TS
☐ N21SF	77	Westwind-1124	214	John Beeson, Houston, Tx.	N46BK
☐ N21SL	99	Citation Bravo	550-0877	Schweitzer Engineering Laboratories, Pullman, Wa.	N5085J
☐ N21VC	95	CitationJet	525-0106	Mistral Aviation Ltd. Guernsey, C.I.	N5211A
☐ N22	95	Gulfstream V	501	Ford Motor Co. Detroit, Mi.	N501GV
☐ N22AF	91	Citation V	560-0129	C H C LLC. Memphis, Tn.	
☐ N22AX	91	Learjet 31A	31A-039	Axiom Capital Solutions LLC. Stoney Creek, NC.	N16ST
☐ N22EL	77	Citation 1/SP	501-0045	Santangelo Law Offices PC. Fort Collins, Co.	N833JL
☐ N22FM	83	Citation II	550-0461	Federal Mogul Corp. Southfield, Mi.	N12507
☐ N22FW	84	Falcon 20F-5	485	SRCG Holdings Inc/Richardson Aviation Inc. Fort Worth, Tx.	(N23SJ)
☐ N22G	93	Learjet 60	60-022	Goodyear Tire & Rubber Co. Akron, Oh.	N2602Z
☐ N22GA	78	Citation II	550-0031	Fitch Aviation Inc. Reno, Nv.	RP-C296
☐ N22GR	99	Citation Bravo	550-0892	Carlton Forge Works, Paramount, Ca.	(N84CF)
☐ N22HP	86	Citation S/II	S550-0103	Hamilton Ranches Inc. Itasca, Il.	N103QS
☐ N22HS	85	Falcon 200	507	Hal Sutton, Shreveport, La.	N50LG
☐ N22KW	99	Citation Excel	560-5062	Citation 22KW Inc. Columbus, Mt.	N5197A
☐ N22LC	03	Falcon 900EX EASY	136	Lowe's Companies Inc. North Wilkesboro, NC.	F-WWFN
☐ N22LQ	99	Citation V Ultra	560-0521	Lake Flyers LLC. Winston- Salem, NC.	N22LC
☐ N22LX	02	CitationJet CJ-2	525A-0109	Lexicon Inc. Little Rock, Ar.	N301EL
☐ N22LZ	78	Westwind-1124	236	Wagner Aeronautical/Aviation Corp. Central Point, Or.	(N236TS)
☐ N22MS	78	Learjet 35A	35A-209	Evergreen Equity Inc. McMinnville, Or.	N711DS
☐ N22NB	77	Sabre-75A	380-56	Sunwest Westwind Inc. Wilmington, De.	N14JD
☐ N22NG	02	Citation X	750-0204	Northrop Grumman Aviation Inc. Hawthorne, Ca.	N5197M
☐ N22NJ	73	Learjet 25C	25C-097	National Jets Inc/WER Aviation Corp. Tamarac, Fl.	I-SFER
☐ N22PC	88	Citation II	550-0583	DW Aviation LLC. Bloomfield, Mi.	(N228G)
☐ N22QF	01	Learjet 60	60-225	State Farm Insurance Companies, Bloomington, Il.	N22SF
☐ N22RD	77	Westwind-1124	203	N22RD Inc. Corpus Christi, Tx.	N880Z
☐ N22RG	97	Citation X	750-0031	Greenhill Aviation LLC. NYC.	N5061W
☐ N22SF	04	Challenger 604	5589	Bombardier Aerospace Corp. Windsor Locks, Ct.	N604SF
☐ N22T	92	Falcon 900B	119	Aplomado Inc. Portland, Or.	N477FJ
☐ N22UL	85	Citation S/II	S550-0039	Jeff Lion, Fresno, Ca.	
☐ N22WJ	67	Falcon 20-5B	113	World Jet Inc. Fort Lauderdale, Fl.	N400PG
☐ N23A	79	Learjet 35A	35A-233	Eagle Jet Aviation Inc. Las Vegas, Nv.	(N428TB)
☐ N23BJ	91	Falcon 900B	107	Air Laurel Inc. Laurel, Ms.	N823BJ
☐ N23BY	65	Learjet 23	23-009	Robert Younkin, Rogers, Ar.	N49CK
☐ N23CJ	67	HS 125/3A-RA	25152	Chestnut Hill Aviation Inc. Newton, Ma.	N50MJ
☐ N23FM	00	Falcon 50EX	296	Federal Mogul Corp. Southfield, Mi.	N50FJ
☐ N23M	99	Gulfstream V	579	3M Co. St Paul, Mn.	N579GA
☐ N23ND	66	Falcon 20C-5	48	Noble Drilling Services Inc. Houston, Tx.	N91CV
☐ N23NG	01	Citation Excel	560-5133	Northrop Grumman Aviation Inc. Hawthorn, Ca.	N.....
☐ N23NM	86	Citation S/II	S550-0121	MRRM PA. Charleston, SC.	(N20NM)
☐ N23RZ	74	Learjet 25B	25B-164	InterContinental Express LLC. Athens, Ga.	OB-1430
☐ N23SB	90	Challenger 601-3A	5074	United States Tobacco Co. White Plains, NY.	C-GLXH
☐ N23SR	01	Learjet 60	60-229	Sears Roebuck & Co. Chicago-Midway, Il.	
☐ N23TJ	76	Falcon 10	89	Mr Excitement Inc. Georgetown, De.	(N888WJ)
☐ N23VK	80	Citation 1/SP	501-0175	VK Aviation & Trading GmbH. Egelsbach, Germany.	VP-BVK
☐ N23VP	76	Falcon 10	91	RVP Leasing Co/Northern jet Management, Grand Rapids, Mi.	N790US
☐ N23YC	00	Citation Bravo	550-0923	W G Yates & Sons Construction Co. Philadelphia, Pa.	N676PB
☐ N23YZ	03	Citation Encore	560-0638	YZ Corp. Palm Beach, Fl.	N1269P
☐ N24AJ	74	Citation	500-0221	JMB Air Services Inc. Mobile, Al.	XC-GUH
☐ N24E	90	Citation II	550-0651	Million Air Richmond, Richmond, Va.	(N1311K)
☐ N24EP	01	Citation Excel	560-5213	Excel Ventures LLC. La Jolla, Ca.	N1130G
☐ N24ET	67	Learjet 24	24-148	AJJ LLC. Indianapolis, In.	N41MP
☐ N24FJ*	80	Westwind-1124	312	Jet Sales of Florida Inc. West Palm Beach, Fl.	N97HW

Reg	Yr	Type	c/n	Owner/Operator	Prev Regn
N24FW	76	Learjet 24E	24E-329	Hudson Flight Ltd. Pampa, Tx.	N329TJ
N24G	93	Learjet 60	60-018	Goodyear Tire & Rubber Co. Akron, Oh.	N4016G
N24GF	03	Citation Encore	560-0639	Grede Foundries Inc. Milwaukee, Wi.	N639CV
N24HX	92	Citation V	560-0165	Charles Anderson, Jacksonville, Tx.	C-GAPD
N24JD	91	Citation V	560-0140	Goodwyn Sales LLC. Memphis, Tn.	(N75GV)
N24JG*	87	BAe 125/800A	8084	Jeff Gordon Inc. Charlotte, NC.	N884CF
N24JK	92	Challenger 601-3A	5118	Star Bank NA/Central Investment Corp. Cincinnati-Lunken, Oh.	N824JK
N24KL	79	Westwind-1124	237	Orlando Financial Corp. Wilmington, De.	N28TJ
N24KT	95	Citation VII	650-7052	Jostens Inc. Minneapolis, Mn.	N24NB
N24LG	65	Learjet 24A	24A-011	Younkin Boreing Inc. Fort Worth, Tx.	N225LJ
N24NG	01	Citation Excel	560-5124	Northrop Grumman Aviation Inc. Hawthorn, Ca.	N5207A
N24NJ	65	Learjet 24	24-050	Planes 4 Sale LLC. Houston, Tx.	N24ET
N24PH	99	Citation Excel	560-5049	Pampelmousse Corp. Key Biscayne, Fl.	N5223Y
N24PR	88	Astra-1125	026	Progress Rail Services Corp. Albertville, Al.	N9VL
N24QT	01	Citation Bravo	550-0963	QuikTrip Corp. Tulsa, Ok.	N52114
N24S	74	Learjet 24D	24D-297	Metropolitan Air Inc. Baltimore, Md.	N8094U
N24SA	66	Learjet 24XR	24XR-117	Sundance Aviation Inc. Yukon, Ok.	N140EX
N24SR	01	Learjet 60	60-234	Sears Roebuck & Co. Chicago-Midway, Il.	N5013J
N24TH	01	Gulfstream 4SP	1475	Chelsea Aviation LLC. Dallas, Tx.	N475GA
N24TK	73	Learjet 24D	24D-268	Silverwood Inc. Athol, Id.	N98WJ
N24UD	00	Citation Excel	560-5147	C-Jay Aviation LLC. Cartersville, Ga.	N52059
N24VB	86	Citation III	650-0121	Word of Life Christian Center, Shreveport, La.	N121AG
N24XR	74	Learjet 24XR	24XR-283	Glass Investments Inc. Paris, Tx.	(N711SC)
N24YA	69	Learjet 24B	24B-206	Bobby Younkin Enterprises Inc. Springfield, Ar.	N116RM
N24YP	03	390 Premier 1	RB-95	Yates Petroleum Corp. Artesia, NM.	N6195S
N24YS	68	Gulfstream 2B	16	Fry's Electronics Inc. San Jose, Ca.	N38GL
N25AM	80	Learjet 25D	25D-321	CPN Television Inc. Clearwater, Fl.	
N25AN	79	Learjet 35A	35A-259	AirNet Systems Inc. Columbus, Oh. (black).	HK-3983X
N25BB	90	BAe 125/800A	NA0455	Baron & Budd PC. Dallas, Tx.	N195KC
N25CU	03	Hawker 400XP	RK-361	United Bottling Management LLC. Birmingham, Al.	N61661
N25CY	80	Learjet 25D	25D-302	Yelvington Transport Inc. Daytona Beach, Fl.	N702DA
N25EC	69	Learjet 25	25-026	Millennium Aircraft Holdings Ltd. Republic Airport, NY.	N281R
N25FM	70	Learjet 25	25-063	Royal Air Freight Inc. Waterford, Mi.	N24LT
N25FS	97	Citation Bravo	550-0823	Sarob/KFE Partnership Inc. San Diego, Ca.	(N823CB)
N25GG	02	Challenger 604	5536	BCMC Air LLC/Booth Creek Management Corp. Vail, Co.	N536MP
N25GV	02	Gulfstream V	674	East Coast Aviation II LLC. Ocala, Fl.	N674GA
N25GZ	84	Citation S/II	S550-0011	SP Express Inc. Wilmington, De.	N211QS
N25LJ	66	Learjet 24	24-123	Avstar Inc. Seattle, Wa.	N35EC
N25MB	96	Falcon 900B	163	Mellon Bank NA. Allegheny County, Pa.	VP-CGP
N25MC	02	390 Premier 1	RB-49	Mercury Travel Inc. Denver-Centennial, Co.	N5049U
N25MD	70	Learjet 25	25-054	Royal Air Freight Inc. Waterford, Mi.	N509G
N25MT	73	Learjet 25C	25C-129	American Aircraft Sales International Inc. Venice, Fl.	N25MR
N25MX	97	CitationJet	525-0220	Jan M Smith, Childress, Tx.	C-GHPP
N25NB	80	Learjet 25D	25D-326	Swing Wing Inc. Veedersburg, In.	N771CB
N25NG	02	Citation Excel	560-5250	Northrop Grumman Aviation Inc. Hawthorn, Ca.	N5095N
N25NY	80	Learjet 25D	25D-304	Savage Aviation Inc. Lebanon, Tn.	
N25PW	81	Learjet 25D	25D-342	Patterson & Wilder/P & W Aviation Inc. Pelham, Al.	(N325PJ)
N25QT	88	Citation II/SP	551-0584	QuikTrip Corp. Tulsa, Ok.	N550WV
N25RE	77	Learjet 25D	25D-227	Cav-Air Aircraft Inc. Hawarden, UK.	N227EW
N25SB	92	Challenger 601-3A	5115	United States Tobacco Co. White Plains, NY.	C-GLYC
N25TE	72	Learjet 25C	25C-087	F S Air Service Inc. Anchorage, Ak.	N99XZ
N25UJ	77	Learjet 25D	25D-215	Airojet Charters Inc. Fort Lauderdale, Fl.	N325JL
N25V	80	Challenger 600S	1015	4KS Aviation III Inc. Dallas, Tx.	144608
N25W	03	Hawker 800XP	8626	Watkins Associated Industries Inc. Lakeland, Fl.	N626XP
N25WJ	73	Learjet 25B	25B-105	Indiana Aircraft Charter LLC. Scherville, In.	LY-AJB
N25WX	98	Hawker 800XP	8359	Watkins Associated Industries Inc. Lakeland, Fl.	
N25XL	04	Citation Excel XLS	560-5536	Aircraft Guaranty Title & Trust LLC. Houston, Tx. (trustor ?	N.....
N26AT	73	Learjet 25B	25B-130	ATI Jet Sales LLC. El Paso, Tx.	N25PL
N26CB	01	Citation Bravo	550-1001	Brown Transport Inc. Holland, Mi.	N.....
N26CV	98	Citation Bravo	550-0861	SkyKing II LLC. Eugene, Or.	N26CB
N26DY	91	Citation V	560-0110	Pappas Telecasting Companies, Visalia, Ca.	N832QB
N26FN	75	Learjet 36	36-011	Flight Capital LLC. Madison, Ms.	N26MJ
N26GP	78	Learjet 35A	35A-157	Lithia Aircraft Inc. Medford, Or.	ZS-MWW
N26HG	89	Citation II/SP	551-0614	Harry Glauser, Houston, Tx.	D-ILAN
N26JP	93	Beechjet 400A	RK-74	Jefferson-Pilot Corp. Greensboro, NC.	N8146J
N26KL	84	Westwind-Two	409	Litehawk Aviation LLC/Litehouse Inc. Sandpoint, Id.	N217BM

| Reg | Yr | Type | c/n | Owner/Operator | Prev Regn |

Reg	Yr	Type	c/n	Owner/Operator	Prev Regn
N26LC	89	Learjet 31	31-006	Cappelli Development Corp. Valhalla, NY.	
N26ME	82	HS 125/700A	NA0315	F B L Jetco LLC. Issaquah, Wa.	N869KM
N26MJ	00	Citation X	750-0139	Independence Airlines Inc. Manchester, NH.	N5196U
N26PA	99	Beechjet 400A	RK-256	Professional Airways LLC. Cohasset, Ma.	N387AT
N26QB	95	CitationJet	525-0117	Master Craft Industrial Equipment Co. Tifton, Ga.	N26CB
N26QT	98	Citation V Ultra	560-0498	QuikTrip Corp. Tulsa, Ok.	(N24QT)
N26RL	97	CitationJet	525-0207	ZZ Enterprises, Kings Beach, Ca.	N31SG
N26SC	80	HS 125/700A	NA0283	Swiss Colony Inc/SC Aviation Inc. Monroe, Wi.	N93GR
N26T	86	Westwind-1124	418	B E & K Inc. Birmingham, Al.	N420MP
N26TZ	80	Westwind-1124	293	Westwind 293 LLC/Akins Ford Corp. Winder, Ga.	N26T
N26WJ	87	Falcon 50	181	MJBW Aviation LLC. Fort Worth, Tx.	N600CH
N26WP	01	Falcon 50EX	312	Weyerhaeuser Co. Tacoma, Wa.	F-WWHP
N27AJ	74	Falcon 10	31	International Union of Bricklayers & Allied Craftworkers, DC	(N29AA)
N27AX	76	Learjet 24D	24D-323	Omni Air Express Inc. Tulsa, Ok.	N453
N27BH	82	Challenger 600S	1051	Ben Hill Griffin Inc. Frostproof, Fl.	N91UC
N27BJ	71	Learjet 24B	24B-227	Key Lime Air. Englewood, Co.	N28AT
N27BL	78	Learjet 35A	35A-163	AirNet Systems Inc. Columbus, Oh. (red).	YV-173CP
N27CD	90	Gulfstream 4	1136	Schering Plough Corp. Morristown, NJ.	N401GA
N27CJ	02	CitationJet CJ-2	525A-0124	MGR Aviation LLC. Ann Arbor, Mi.	N.....
N27FL	99	Hawker 800XP	8426	Encanto Investments Inc. Tortola, BVI.	N426XP
N27L	72	Citation	500-0038	ConAero Inc. Houston, Tx.	(N207L)
N27MJ	77	Learjet 36A	36A-027	Flight Capital LLC. Madison, Ms.	N484HB
N27MX	04	Challenger 300	20014	Perpetual Aircraft Holdings LLC. Wilmington, De.	C-GZEJ
N27R	94	Falcon 2000	5	R J Reynolds Tobacco Co. Winston-Salem, NC.	F-WWMB
N27SF	73	Citation	500-0064	Seneca Foods Corp. Penn Yan, NY.	N564CC
N27SL	70	Gulfstream 2	84	Wiley Sanders Truck Lines Inc. Troy, Al.	N5101T
N27TB	85	Citation S/II	S550-0082	Bos Dairies LLC. Bakersfield, Ca.	N282QS
N27TS	83	Citation III	650-0006	Departures LLC. Dayton Beach, Fl.	N39RE
N27TT	77	Learjet 35A	35A-122	AirNet Systems Inc. Columbus, Oh. (blue).	OE-GMP
N27VP	97	Citation X	750-0027	Syracuse Jet Leasing LLC. Syracuse, NY.	N854WC
N27VQ	04	CitationJet CJ-2	525A-0221	Cessna Aircraft Co. Wichita, Ks.	N5153K
N27WW	77	Citation 1/SP	501-0264	Wildwood Industries Inc. Bloomington, Il. (was 500-0353).	N353WB
N27XL	98	Citation Excel	560-5010	N27XL Inc. Fort Lauderdale, Fl.	N52178
N28DM	04	CitationJet CJ-2	525A-0210	Machavia Inc. Long Beach, Ca.	N280DM
N28GA	97	CitationJet	525-0216	Griffin Industries Inc. Cold Springs, Ky.	
N28GP	00	Hawker 800XP	8489	Genuine Parts Co. Atlanta, Ga.	
N28MH	03	CitationJet CJ-2	525A-0161	Bear Air LLC. Duncansville, Pa.	N5100J
N28MJ	79	Learjet 35A	35A-224	M & J Leisure Ltd. Ogden, Ut.	N40RW
N28NP	99	Astra-1125SPX	118	Astra SPX LLC/Heitman Holdings Ltd. Waukegan, Il.	N529GA
N28PT	93	CitationJet	525-0017	Eagle Holding Corp. Las Vegas, Nv.	N525AE
N28R	95	Falcon 2000	7	R J Reynolds Tobacco Co. Winston-Salem, NC.	F-WWME
N28TS	73	HS 125/600A	6009	M F R Associates LLC. Wilmington, De.	(N183RM)
N28TX	92	Citation VII	650-7007	Bell Helicopter Textron Inc. Fort Worth, Tx.	N944L
N28YC	85	Gulfstream 3	455	Voyager YC Aviation LLC. Bozeman, Mt.	N147MR
N29AF	67	DC 9-15F	45826	U S Department of Energy, Albuquerque, NM.	CF-TON
N29B	00	Hawker 800XP	8518	Batelle Memeorial Institute, Columbus, Oh.	
N29CL	84	Westwind-Two	404	600 Flight Corp. Sugar Land, Tx.	N404W
N29GP	97	Hawker 800XP	8344	Genuine Parts Co. Atlanta, Ga.	
N29LJ	01	Learjet 60	60-240	Suzuki Del Caribe, San Juan, PR.	N5019V
N29MR	04	CitationJet CJ-2	525A-0206	Falco Aviation Inc. Douglas, IOM.	N.....
N29NW	82	Learjet 55	55-029	Jetstream Aviation, Allentown, Pa.	N100VA
N29QC	04	Citation Encore	560-0675	Questar Pipeline Co. Salt Lake City, Ut.	N.....
N29RE	02	Learjet 45	45-210	Allen Investments Inc. Southern Pines, NC.	N866RA
N29SM	02	Learjet 45	45-214	Sterling Motors Ltd. Santa Ana, Ca.	N214LF
N29SN	99	Learjet 31	31A-194	Carolina Packers Inc. Smithfield, NC.	N29SM
N29XA	86	Citation S/II	S550-0096	Interflight Inc. West Palm Beach, Fl. (rebuild ?).	N29X
N30AB	78	Westwind-1124	235	Albert Biedenharn Jr/Osborn Heirs Co. San Antonio, Tx.	N65A
N30AD	03	CitationJet CJ-2	525A-0165	Blue Yonder Holdings Inc. Fort Lauderdale, Fl.	N5243K
N30AF	84	Citation III	650-0049	Poppy Air LLC. Syosset, NY.	(N650AN)
N30AV	78	Citation II	550-0026	Hersey Mountain Air Inc/American Veladur Metal, Concord, NH.	(N2231B)
N30FT	98	Falcon 50EX	271	Intercon Inc. NYC.	N30FE
N30GF	83	Westwind-1124	401	Pelair Transport LLC. Houston, Tx.	N980S
N30GJ	00	Learjet 60	60-204	Publix Supermarkets Inc. Lakeland, Fl.	I-NATZ
N30GR	90	Citation II	550-0656	Eagle Investors LLC. Missoula, Mt.	
N30HD	02	CitationJet CJ-2	525A-0062	Roth Aircraft Inc. Sanford, Fl.	N5125J
N30HJ	79	Learjet 35A	35A-226	Hop-A-Jet Inc. Fort Lauderdale, Fl.	N1127M

Reg	Yr	Type	c/n	Owner/Operator	Prev Regn
N30JD	80	Citation II	550-0205	International Development Group Ltd. Kootenai, Id.	(N88727)
N30LB	96	Falcon 900EX	8	Great American Insurance Co. Cincinnati-Lunken, Oh.	F-WWFB
N30LJ	76	Learjet 25D	25D-209	Midsouth Services Inc. Clearwater, Fl.	N18NM
N30MP	66	B 727-21	18998	MP Aviation LLC. Costa Mesa, Ca.	N111JL
N30MR	78	Westwind-1124	225	Midwest Trophy Manufacturing Co. Del City, Ok.	N1124U
N30PA	79	Learjet 35A	35A-245	Big Sur Waterbeds Inc. Denver, Co.	N1526L
N30PC	03	Learjet 45	45-235	Southern Company Services Inc. Atlanta, Ga.	N50145
N30PR	68	Gulfstream II SP	35	Rutherford Oil Co. Houston, Tx.	N830TL
N30RL	90	Citation II	550-0653	Roseburg Lumber Co. Roseburg, Or.	N36854
N30SF	01	Learjet 45	45-175	Gulf States Toyota Inc. Houston, Tx.	N328RR
N30SJ	02	SJ 30-2	003	Sino Swearingen Aircraft Co. San Antonio, Tx.	
N30TH	98	Falcon 2000	66	Sony Aviation Inc. Teterboro, NJ.	F-WWMJ
N30WR	83	Gulfstream 3	380	Rollins Inc/LOR Inc. Atlanta, Ga.	N159B
N31AA	69	Learjet 25	25-041	Diamond Aviation Maintenance Inc. Deland, Fl. (status ?).	(N25RE)
N31CJ	01	CitationJet CJ-1	525-0474	Baird Air LLC. Springfield, Mo.	N.....
N31CR	79	Sabre-60	306-146	D D D Aero LLC. Concord, NH.	(N44DD)
N31D	01	Falcon 900C	191	Sentry Aviation Services LLC. Stevens Point, Wi.	F-WWVM
N31DP	76	Learjet 35	35-062	CJPJ Associates Inc. Little Falls, NJ.	N310BA
N31EP	68	HS 125/731	NA714	CME Constructors LLC. Santa Teresa, NM.	N811JA
N31EX	04	Falcon 2000EX EASY	31	Air Kaitar LLC/Kaitar Resources LLC. Tallahassee, Fl.	F-WWGJ
N31FF	92	Learjet 31A	31A-053	J H Siroonian Inc. Fresno, Ca.	(N44ZG)
N31FJ	74	Falcon 20E-5B	310	Dassault Falcon Jet Corp. Teterboro, NJ.	N831HG
N31GA	81	Citation II	550-0221	Green Aviation Corp. White Plains, NY.	N95AX
N31HD	97	CitationJet	525-0261	Hillsboro Air Services Inc. Hillsboro, Or.	(N61CV)
N31LJ	94	Learjet 31A	31A-097	Alpine Air Inc. Charleston, WV.	N50207
N31LT	66	Falcon 20C	69	Imperial Oil Co. Tampa, Fl.	N176BN
N31LW	73	Citation	500-0083	Mager Enterprises LLC. Fort Lauderdale, Fl.	VP-CHH
N31MC	79	Learjet 35A	35A-270	Jagee Travel LLC. Wilmington, De.	FAV-0013
N31MW	99	Learjet 31A	31A-171	Whiskey Tango LLC. Midland, Tx.	N129FX
N31NF	97	Learjet 31A	31A-151	Comtide Investments LLC. Columbus, Oh.	N583LJ
N31NS	95	Citation V Ultra	560-0286	Quinn Aire LLC. Rancho Santa Fe, Ca.	N57MB
N31PV	97	Learjet 31A	31A-130	Fabrica de Jabon Valdes, Guatemala City, Guatemala.	N5013N
N31SJ	01	Gulfstream G200	033	Ocean Air Charters, Carlsbad, Ca.	4X-CVK
N31TK	92	Learjet 31A	31A-059	Wal-Mart Stores Inc. Rogers, Ar.	(N67MP)
N31TR	79	B 727-212RE	21948	Triarc Companies Inc. Stewart, NY.	VR-COJ
N31UJ	95	Learjet 31A	31A-116	Averitt Air Charter Inc. Nashville, Tn.	N112HV
N31V	97	Learjet 45	45-015	Silver Lane Aviation LLC. NYC.	
N31WR	80	Learjet 35A	35A-313	AirNet Systems Inc. Columbus, Oh. (blue).	TR-LZI
N31WS	75	Learjet 35	35-027	Windstar Aviation Corp. Englewood, Co.	
N32AA	99	Beechjet 400A	RK-242	Advance Aircraft Co. Roanoke, Va.	N2322B
N32AJ	81	Learjet 36A	36A-048	Code Aviation LLC. La Jolla, Ca.	PT-WGM
N32B	88	Falcon 900	59	Black & Decker Corp. Baltimore, Md.	N442FJ
N32BC	96	Hawker 800XP	8321	Brunswick Corp. Waukegan, Il.	N691H
N32BD	98	Gulfstream V	548	Black & Decker Corp. Baltimore, Md.	N245TJ
N32BG	03	CitationJet CJ-1	525-0532	Lauralis Training LLC. Houston, Tx.	N.....
N32DD	76	Learjet 24E	24E-331	I Fly LLC. Springdale, Ar.	XA-REA
N32FM	81	Citation 1/SP	501-0210	Imperial Transport Inc. NYC.	N67848
N32GM	69	HS 125/731	NA728	Seminole Air LLC. Boca Raton, Fl.	N410PA
N32HJ	82	Learjet 35A	35A-463	Hop-A-Jet Inc. Fort Lauderdale, Fl.	N68LL
N32HM	78	Learjet 35A	35A-187	Original Honey Baked Ham Co. Atlanta, Ga.	N755GL
N32HP	83	Diamond 1A	A074SA	ST Air LLC/Stoughton Trailers, Stoughton, Wi.	N19GA
N32KB	72	HS 125/731	NA773	S S K Hawker Group LLC/O E M Controls Inc. Shelton, Ct.	C-FPPN
N32KJ	84	Learjet 55	55-093	Bellew Sky Inc. St Petersburg, Fl.	N725K
N32NG	97	Citation X	750-0039	Syracuse Jet Leasing LLC. Syracuse, NY.	N22NG
N32PA	77	Learjet 36A	36A-025	Phoenix Air Group Inc. Cartersville, Ga.	N800BL
N32PB	90	Citation V	560-0091	The South Beach Co. Palm Beach, Fl.	(N8GY)
N32PE	80	Learjet 35A	35A-327	Blue Canyon Inc. Smyrna, Tn.	N32PF
N32PJ	80	Learjet 35A	35A-320	Pacific Jet/Van Nuys Jet Partners LLC. Van Nuys, Ca.	N393JP
N32RZ	79	Learjet 35A	35A-238	White Industries Inc. Bates City, Mo. (status ?).	N500HZ
N32SG	02	390 Premier 1	RB-90	Sauvage Fuels Inc. Billings, Mt.	
N32TK	81	Citation II	550-0313	Centennial Management Inc. Aberdeen, SC. (was 551-0345).	N32TM
N32TX	84	Citation S/II	S550-0026	Therma-Tron-X Inc. Sturgeon Bay, Wi.	N24PF
N33BC	95	Hawker 800XP	8292	Brunswick Corp. Waukegan, Il.	N673H
N33BV	74	Falcon 10	33	Biovail Corporation International, Toronto, ON. Canada.	C-FBVF
N33D	00	Citation VII	650-7117	Dow Chemical Co. Midland, Mi.	N5263D
N33DT	94	CitationJet	525-0080	Delta Tango Inc. Des Moines, Ia.	N80CJ

Reg	Yr	Type	c/n	Owner/Operator	Prev Regn
N33EK	81	Citation II	550-0281	Reid Tool Supply Co. Muskegon, Mi.	N31RK
N33FW	97	CitationJet	525-0203	Duke Realty Services LP/Aire Corr LLC. Indianapolis, In.	N525GP
N33JW	74	Sabre-60	306-92	Government of Democratic Republic of Congo, Kinshasa.	N74AB
N33L	00	Citation VII	650-7118	Dow Chemical Co. Midland, Mi.	N5264U
N33LC	02	Falcon 50EX	326	Lowe's Companies Inc. North Wilkesboro, NC.	N37LC
N33M	99	Gulfstream V	594	3M Co. St Paul, Mn.	N594GA
N33NJ	80	Learjet 35A	35A-305	National Jets Inc. Fort Lauderdale, Fl.	N3VG
N33NL	03	Hawker 800XP	8643	Nick Corp. Lawrence, Ma.	(N843TS)
N33PA*	99	Challenger 604	5441	5441-604 Corp. Fort Lauderdale, Fl.	N441CL
N33PF	69	Learjet 25	25-028	RAB LLC. DuPage, Il.	N277LE
N33PJ	69	Gulfstream II SP	57	Pacific Jet/Bellevue Jet Partners LLC. Van Nuys, Ca.	(N333ST)
N33PT	78	Learjet 25D	25D-240	Bankair Inc. West Columbia, SC.	(N339BA)
N33RZ	76	Sabre-75A	380-47	Air N25BX Inc. Southfield, Mi.	N25BX
N33SJ	66	JetStar-731	5087	Craig Aviation Inc. Carlsbad-Palomar, Ca.	N75MG
N33TP	75	Learjet 24D	24D-321	Commonwealth Aviation Services Inc. Richmond, Va	C-FRNR
N33TR	80	Sabre-65	465-47	Trinity Industries Inc. Dallas, Tx.	N265A
N33TS	00	Citation Encore	560-0549	Devco Properties LLC. New Castle, De.	N11TS
N33VC	96	Hawker 800XP	8310	Silver Lake Aviation LLC/Million Air, Salt Lake City, Ut.	PT-WMG
N33WW	78	Citation 1/SP	501-0065	W R J Inc. Bloomfield Hills, Mi.	N2888A
N34AM	65	Sabre-40	282-31	Sabre Investments Ltd. St Louis, Mo.	N577VM
N34FS	84	Westwind-Two	417	Roundtree Aviation LLC. Shreveport, La.	(N99WF)
N34GB	84	Learjet 55	55-114	Reinalt-Thomas Corp. Scottsdale, Az.	N72608
N34GG	78	HS 125/700A	7034	Hawker 700 LLC. Lake Oswego, Or.	N402GJ
N34GN	02	390 Premier 1	RB-58	King Air LLC. Indianapolis, In.	N5158B
N34S	67	Gulfstream 2	5	Ozark Management Inc. Columbia, Mo.	N655TJ
N34TC	94	CitationJet	525-0083	Cosins Properties Inc. Atlanta, Ga.	(N421CP)
N34TJ	75	Falcon 10	41	Ace Air Inc/Ace Transportation Inc. New Orleans, La.	(N550BG)
N34TN	78	Learjet 25D	25D-249	Williams Development & Construction, Houston, Tx.	XA-FMU
N34U	00	Global Express	9070	United Technologies Corp. Hartford, Ct.	N700XR
N34WP	02	Citation Excel	560-5232	Weyerhaeuser Co/Paccar Inc. Tacoma, Wa.	N451W
N34WR	77	JetStar 2	5207	Nevada Sky Inc. Asheville, NC.	N176BN
N35AJ	75	Learjet 35	35-010	Romakowi LLC. Downers Grove, Il.	N888DE
N35AX	79	Learjet 35	35A-280	Superior Air Charter Inc. Medford, Or.	87-0026
N35AZ	79	Learjet 35A	35A-201	Hardsworth Aero LLC. Nashville, Tn.	XA-PIN
N35BG	81	Learjet 35A	35A-402	Tashi Corp. Medford, Or.	N7AB
N35BP	00	Galaxy-1126	016	BP Group Inc. Bradenton, Fl.	N40GX
N35CC	81	Sabre-65	465-59	Crown Controls Corp. New Bremen, Oh.	N8500
N35CD	99	Gulfstream V	603	Schering Plough Corp. Morristown, NJ.	N539GA
N35CR	74	Westwind-1123	176	Eumundi Trading Co. Wilmington, De.	N27AT
N35D	72	Westwind-1123	156	G W Taylor/Taylor Aircraft, Halfway, Mo.	N566MP
N35DL	80	Learjet 35A	35A-348	Melmik Aviation Inc. St Maarten, Netherlands Antilles.	N35TL
N35ED	79	Learjet 35A	35A-215	E H Darby & Co/Alpha Jet International, Muscle Shoals, Al.	N80GD
N35ET	99	Citation Bravo	550-0879	Bright World Inc. Minnetonka, Mn.	N4M
N35GC	79	Learjet 35A	35A-266	DLS Enterprises Inc. Arcola, Tx.	N922GL
N35GZ	85	Gulfstream 3	465	Trans Gulf Corp. Clearwater, Fl.	N33NT
N35HS	96	Citation VII	650-7072	Extreme Holdings Inc. Portland, Or.	N8494C
N35JN	82	Learjet 35A	35A-469	Taxi Jet Air Del Norte Inc. Houston, Tx.	N71MH
N35LH	85	Westwind-Two	413	Liberty Homes Inc. Goshen, In.	N413WW
N35NA	81	Learjet 35A	35A-381	Jetride Inc. Columbus, Oh.	N300CM
N35NK	82	Learjet 35A	35A-491	NAC-Nordic Aviation Contractors A/S. Skive, Denmark.	N394JP
N35RZ	94	Falcon 900B	137	RZ Aviation LLC/Ritz Camera Centers Inc. Leesburg, Va.	(N98DQ)
N35SA	00	Learjet 35A	35A-326	Precision Funding Inc. Little Rock, Ar.	N612DG
N35TJ	77	Learjet 35A	35A-137	C 22 LLC. Livingston, NJ.	N41FN
N35TN	82	Learjet 35A	35A-472	BCC Equipment Leasing Corp. Long Beach, Ca.	(N472AS)
N35UA	91	Learjet 35A	35A-665	UltraAir LLC. Omaha, Ne.	N291K
N35UJ	75	Learjet 35	35-007	Richmark Aircraft Leasing LLC. Boca Raton, Fl.	(N65FN)
N35UK	90	Learjet 35A	35A-662	Wal-Mart Stores Inc. Rogers, Ar.	G-BUSX
N35WB	80	Learjet 35A	35A-350	La Stella Corp. Pueblo, Co.	(N88NE)
N35WE	78	Learjet 35A	35A-156	American Air Network Alaska, Saratoga, Fl.	N190DA
N35WJ	73	Learjet 25B	25B-104	World Jet of Delaware Inc. Fort Lauderdale, Fl.	N128TJ
N35WP	74	HS 125/600B	6029	Schubach Aviation Inc. Carlsbad-Palomar, Ca.	N629TS
N35WR	79	Learjet 35A	35A-234	Wholesale Printing Products Inc. El Paso, Tx.	
N36DA	87	Falcon 200	510	Abbey Co/Montana Aviation LLC. Ontario, Ca..	N510LF
N36EP	01	Falcon 2000	172	JSM at Falcon LLC/Edgewood Properties Inc. Morristown, NJ.	N272EJ
N36FT	77	HS 125/700A	7013	Raytheon Aircraft Co. Wichita, Ks.	N96FT
N36H	96	Hawker 800XP	8332	L J Ventures LLC. Chicago, Il.	N332XP
Reg	*Yr*	*Type*	*c/n*	*Owner/Operator*	*Prev Regn*

Reg	Yr	Type	c/n	Owner/Operator	Prev Regn
N36HJ	81	Learjet 35A	35A-427	Hop-A-Jet Inc. Fort Lauderdale, Fl.	N358AC
N36MW	70	Gulfstream II SP	89	The Jet Place Inc. Tulsa, Ok.	N203A
N36PJ	81	Learjet 36A	36A-047	Pacific Jet/LR36 Partners LLC. Van Nuys, Ca.	OE-GMD
N36PN	68	Gulfstream 2B	42	B & G Leasing LLC. Southfield, Mi.	N1164A
N36PT	01	Citation Bravo	550-0966	Akio Hirato, Hillsboro, Or.	N51806
N36RG	95	CitationJet	525-0139	Lawrence Grey MD. Tampa, Fl.	N76AE
N36RR	67	Gulfstream 2B	4	RGR Technologies Inc. Lucas, Oh.	N8490P
N36RZ	67	Sabre-60	306-2	Ricardo Aramendia, Kenner, La.	(N27RZ)
N36SF	78	Westwind-1124	233	William J Ware, Houston, Tx.	N67DF
N36TH	04	Falcon 2000EX EASY	53	Sony Aviation, Teterboro, NJ.	F-WWMB
N36TJ	84	BAe 125/800A	8018	Black Creek Partners Inc. Plano, Tx.	(N525CF)
N36UP	02	Learjet 31A	31A-238	Thunderstone Aviation LLC. Boca Raton, Fl.	
N36WJ	79	Falcon 10	126	MJBW Aviation LLC. Fort Worth, Tx.	N26WJ
N36WL	81	Gulfstream 3	328	Martin Aviation Inc. Burbank, Ca.	N97AG
N37BE	83	Westwind-1124	396	Baldor Electric Co. Fort Smith, Ar.	8P-BAR
N37BG	02	CitationJet CJ-2	525A-0123	C M Gatton, Bristol-Tri Cities, Tn.	N5203S
N37BM	94	Learjet 31A	31A-096	Beach Air Travel Inc. Floyd Knobs, In.	N30TK
N37ER	81	Falcon 50	47	Falcon Leasing of South Florida LLC. Coconut Grove, Fl.	(N81CH)
N37FA	76	Learjet 35A	35A-091	J & S Properties LLC. Chicago, Il.	(N900JV)
N37HJ	79	Learjet 35A	35A-230	Hop-A-Jet Inc. Fort Lauderdale, Fl.	N356AC
N37HT	72	Learjet 24XR	24XR-243	Miracle Child Enterprises LLC. Palestine, Tx.	N57FL
N37MH	80	Citation II	550-0153	Charlie Brown Air Corp. State College, Pa.	N27MH
N37NY	88	B 737-4YO	23976	ITT Flight Operations Inc/New York Knicks, Allentown, Pa.	N773RA
N37RA	98	Learjet 31A	31A-153	Learjet Inc. Wichita, Ks.	RP-C6153
N37TA	75	Learjet 35	35-034	RLO Aviation Inc. Peoria, Il.	
N37TH	97	Falcon 2000	44	Chelsea Aviation LLC. Dallas, Tx.	N49MW
N37WH	94	Gulfstream 4SP	1243	Miami Dolphins/Huizenga Holdings Inc. Fort Lauderdale, Fl.	(N39WH)
N38AE	81	Westwind-Two	318	Time Compression Inc. New Castle, De.	N10FG
N38DD	82	Citation II	550-0340	Jet Set Aircraft Inc. Northridge, Ca.	ZP-TWN
N38LB	71	HS 125/731	NA770	Baron & Budd PC. Dallas, Tx.	N7170J
N38NS	97	Citation V Ultra	560-0411	Jackson National Life Insurance Co. Lansing, Mi.	PT-WNF
N38PS	78	Learjet 35A	35A-206	Sullivan Leasing Co. Durant, OK.	(N46KB)
N38SA	76	Citation	500-0297	Tropic Winds Hotel/Stanley L Allen, Myrtle Beach, SC.	N48DA
N38SW	99	Challenger 604	5423	SLW Aviation Inc. Houston, Tx.	N238SW
N38TJ	75	Falcon 20F-5B	339	FM Aircraft LLC. Aurora, Co.	SE-DSA
N38TT	81	Citation II	550-0268	Muntley Air LLC. Monterey, Ca. (was 551-0311)	N500FX
N38WP	99	Falcon 50EX	292	Weyerhaeuser Co/Paccar Inc. Tacoma, Wa.	N292EX
N39CB	76	Sabre-60	306-116	C U 2 LLC. Anoka, Mn.	N44WD
N39CD	84	Challenger 601	3030	Air Castle Worldwide Jet Charter Inc. Millville, NJ.	N34CD
N39CJ	93	CitationJet	525-0039	Bagwell Aviation LLC. Garner, NC.	N1958E
N39CK	68	Learjet 25	25-005	Kalitta Charters LLC. Detroit-Willow Run, Mi.	XA-SDQ
N39DK	82	Learjet 35A	35A-480	AirNet Systems Inc. Columbus, Oh. (green).	(N484)
N39EL	72	Learjet 24D	24D-251	By Jet Inc. Carson City, Nv.	N69XW
N39FN	74	Learjet 35	35-006	Flight Capital LLC. Madison, Ms.	N39DM
N39FS	62	Sabreliner CT-39A	276-33	BAe Systems Flight Systems Inc. Mojave, Ca.	N24480
N39H	91	Citation VI	650-0206	TVPX Inc. Concord, Ma.	PT-OKV
N39HF	93	Beechjet 400A	RK-65	Elk Air Partners LLC. Adrian, Mi.	(N81TT)
N39HH	79	Citation 1/SP	501-0132	HRH Aviation Inc. Dover, De.	N717JL
N39HJ	81	Learjet 35A	35A-337	Hop-A-Jet Inc. Fort Lauderdale, Fl.	N710AT
N39KM	69	Learjet 24B	24B-198	Aero-Jet Aviation Inc. Fort Lauderdale, Fl.	N21XB
N39LH	73	Citation	500-0089	Indiana Trading LLC. Elkhart, In.	EC-EBR
N39NP	98	Falcon 900EX	39	New Pembroke Ltd. Greensboro-Highpoint, NC.	VP-BID
N39PJ	77	Learjet 35A	35A-128	Pacific Jet Inc. Anchorage, Ak.	N257AL
N39RC	99	Citation Excel	560-5041	Warehouse Management Inc. Cincinnati-Lunken, Oh.	N1XL
N39RE	88	Challenger 601-3A	5020	AiRush Inc/Rush Enterprises Inc. San Antonio, Tx.	N604CF
N39RG	67	Sabre-40	282-82	Ronald Green, Quartz Hill, Ca.	XB-EQR
N39RP	84	Falcon 20F-5	478	Rich Aviation Inc. Buffalo, NY.	N300RT
N39TF	87	Citation S/II	S550-0139	Big Blue Express Inc. Omaha, Ne.	N706SB
N39TT	81	Falcon 20F	449	Nashville Air Associates Inc. Berry Field, Tn.	N457F
N39TW	91	Learjet 31A	31A-047	Liquid Magnetix Corp. Stony Brook, NY.	N31UK
N39WP	99	Falcon 50EX	294	Weyerhaeuser Co/Paccar Inc. Tacoma, Wa.	F-WWHV
N40	68	B 727-25QC	19854	FAA R&D Flight Program, Atlantic City, NJ.	N8171G
N40AJ	77	Citation 1/SP	501-0275	H B Aero LLC. Chesapeake, Va. (was 500-0362).	(N41AJ)
N40AN	79	Learjet 35A	35A-271	AirNet Systems Inc. Columbus, Oh. (green).	LV-OAS
N40BD	77	Learjet 35A	35A-140	Newcastle Corp. Wichita Falls, Tx.	N72TP
N40CJ	04	CitationJet CJ-1	525-0540	James Vannoy & Sons Construction Co. Jeffferson, NC.	N5127M
Reg	Yr	Type	c/n	Owner/Operator	Prev Regn

Reg	Yr	Type	c/n	Owner/Operator	Prev Regn
❏ N40CR	90	Learjet 55C	55C-144	NCR Corp. Dayton, Oh.	PT-OJH
❏ N40DK	84	Learjet 55	55-092	Corporate Jets Inc. Allegheny County, Pa.	N500FA
❏ N40FC	87	Citation III	650-0143	Frank's Casing Crew & Rental Tools, Lafayette, La.	N312CF
❏ N40GA	83	Diamond 1A	A040SA	Pennco Inc/Pennco Air LLC. Wilmington, De.	N188ST
❏ N40GG	78	Westwind-1124	229	Circus Air Inc. Zellwood, Fl.	N162E
❏ N40GT	73	Sabre-40A	282-126	American Sabre LLC. McPherson, Ks.	XA-SNI
❏ N40HB	00	Gulfstream 4SP	1407	Zeus LLC. Burbank, Ca.	N407QS
❏ N40KJ	03	Learjet 40	45-2002	Marine Charter Enterprises, Hillsboro, Or.	
❏ N40KW	98	Citation X	750-0040	Triad Hospitals Inc. Dallas, Tx.	N740VP
❏ N40LJ	04	Learjet 40	45-2009	Learjet Inc. Wichita, Ks.	
❏ N40LX	95	Learjet 40	45-001	Learjet Inc. Wichita, Ks. (Ff 31 Aug 02).	N45XL
❏ N40MA	88	Beechjet 400	RJ-42	Mahon Investments LLC. Columbia, Tn.	N442JC
❏ N40MF	00	Citation Bravo	550-0921	Dot Foods Inc. Mount Sterling, Il.	N5073G
❏ N40ML	04	Learjet 40	45-2024	Learjet Inc. Wichita, Ks.	N424LF
❏ N40NJ	73	Sabre-40A	282-134	ZMP Corp. Huntsville, Al.	N134JJ
❏ N40PC	04	Learjet 45	45-259	Learjet Inc. Wichita, Ks.	
❏ N40PK	79	Learjet 35A	35A-260	Med Air LLC. Lawrenceville, Ga.	
❏ N40PX	03	Learjet 40	45-2007	Air Max Aviation Inc. Carlsbad, Ca.	N50126
❏ N40SR	97	Gulfstream V	525	Essar Shipping Ltd. Mumbai, India.	N252JS
❏ N40TA	76	Westwind-1124	194	MRG Aviation Co. Englewood, Co.	N124FM
❏ N41AU	90	Astra-1125	041	NVLS 1 LLC. Tulatin, Or.	(N29UC)
❏ N41AV	69	Gulfstream II SP	61	PHRM Leasing LLC. Savannah, Ga.	N61LH
❏ N41C	83	Westwind-1124	398	Chevron USA Inc. New Orleans, La.	N59AP
❏ N41DP	03	Challenger 300	20010	Dean Phillips Inc. Essendon, VIC. Australia.	C-GZEB
❏ N41GT	79	Citation 1/SP	501-0297	Tobin Aviation Enterprises, Abilene, Tx. (was 500-0394).	N35LD
❏ N41HF	77	HS 125/700A	NA0208	Faith Aviation Ltd. Cincinnati, Oh.	N38PA
❏ N41HL	76	Citation	500-0338	I D I LLC. Springfield, Mo.	(N404JW)
❏ N41LF	02	CitationJet CJ-1	525-0501	Ludwig Law Firm Aviation Rental Inc. Little Rock, Ar.	N501CJ
❏ N41LV	80	Sabre-65	465-39	Royal Oak Enterprises Inc. Atlanta-DeKalb, Ga.	N203JK
❏ N41MH	65	Falcon 20C	14	Threhold Technology, Ontario, Ca.	N91JF
❏ N41NK	78	Learjet 25D	25D-238	Okun Air LLC. Indianapolis, In.	N300TL
❏ N41NW	75	Learjet 35	35-041	IDM Aviation Services LLC. Austin, Tx.	(N694PG)
❏ N41NY	59	MS 760 Paris	41	Your Aircraft Source LLC. Calhoun, Ga.	41
❏ N41PC	01	Learjet 45	45-190	Southern Company Services Inc. Atlanta, Ga.	
❏ N41PG	96	CitationJet	525-0175	Duke Realty Services LP/Aire Corr LLC. Indianapolis, In.	N175CP
❏ N41SM	81	Citation II	550-0231	Pacific Coast Enterprises LLC. Las Vegas, Nv.	N148DR
❏ N41VB	91	Gulfstream 4	1174	Viacom Inc/Paramount Pictures Corp. Van Nuys, Ca.	N6VB
❏ N41VP	02	Citation Encore	560-0626	Citation Technology Partners LLC. Hayward, Ca.	N.....
❏ N41WJ	81	Citation II	550-0237	Advanced Aviation LLC. Rancho Palos Verde, Ca.	ZS-NHO
❏ N42AJ	92	Beechjet 400A	RK-55	Alan Jay Logistics LLC. Sebring, Fl.	N404CC
❏ N42AS	68	HS 125/F3A	25150	Aero Toy Store LLC. Fort Lauderdale, Fl.	VP-BKY
❏ N42CM	76	Westwind-1124	189	AGG Aircraft Sales & Leasing Inc. Beverly, Ma.	N200DL
❏ N42EH	74	Falcon 10	28	DHB Consulting Group Inc. Burlington, Wi.	(N655DB)
❏ N42FB	00	Hawker 800XP	8467	First Tennessee Equipment Finance, Memphis, Tn.	N5732
❏ N42G	74	Falcon 10	20	Daily Transport LLC. Johnson-Bell Field, Missoula, Mt.	N113FJ
❏ N42HN	83	Learjet 35A	35A-507	C C Medflight Inc. Lawrenceville, Ga.	N42HP
❏ N42ND	96	Citation V Ultra	560-0400	University of Notre Dame, Notre Dame, In.	N916CG
❏ N42PH	81	Citation II	550-0304	BK Aviation Group LLC. Schaumburg, Il.	(N70PH)
❏ N42PJ	80	Learjet 35A	35A-285	Village Properties Inc. San Francisco, Ca.	N818WS
❏ N42PP	72	Gulfstream II SP	115	Bluegrass Gulfstream Investments LLC. Lexington, Ky.	N40AG
❏ N42SK	99	Falcon 50EX	290	660 AH Corp. Madison, NJ.	(N302WY)
❏ N42SR	83	Diamond 1	A038SA	Segrave Aviation Inc. Greenville, NC.	(N212PA)
❏ N42ST	96	Falcon 2000	39	Seagate Air LLC. San Jose, Ca.	N151AE
❏ N42TS	79	HS 125/700A	7067	Glieberman Aviation LLC. Novi, Mt.	N267TS
❏ N42US	80	Falcon 10	171	Aughrim Holding Co. Hillsboro, Or.	PT-OIC
❏ N42WJ	82	Falcon 20F	427	RPlane Inc. Houston, Tx.	I-ACTL
❏ N43DR	82	Learjet 25D	25D-353	Roever Evangelistic Associates Inc. Fort Worth, Tx.	N71AX
❏ N43EC	80	Falcon 10	168	Sequoia Properties Inc. Palwaukee, Il.	N175BL
❏ N43HF	04	Citation Excel XLS	560-5519	HF Express LP. San Luis Obispo, Ca.	N52655
❏ N43HJ	01	390 Premier 1	RB-41	Kinnarps AB. Falkoping, Sweden.	(N111HH)
❏ N43KW	98	Citation V Ultra	560-0487	Progress Energy Service Co. Raleigh, NC.	N46MW
❏ N43MF	80	Learjet 35A	35A-284	Med Flight Air Ambulance Inc. Albuquerque, NM.	OO-GBL
❏ N43ND	01	CitationJet CJ-2	525A-0041	Coulter Cadillac & Oldsmobile Inc. Phoenix, Az.	N.....
❏ N43NR	94	Learjet 60	60-043	Jupiter Aviation LLC. Darby, Pa.	C-GHKY
❏ N43NW	04	CitationJet CJ-1	525-0543	Nationwide Aviation LLC. Lake Havasu City, Az.	N5200U
❏ N43PJ	79	Learjet 28	28-004	Pacific Jet Inc. Teterboro, NJ.	N28AY
Reg	*Yr*	*Type*	*c/n*	*Owner/Operator*	*Prev Regn*

Reg	Yr	Type	c/n	Owner/Operator	Prev Regn
N43PR	87	Challenger 601-3A	5002	Town & Country Food Markets Inc. Wichita, Ks.	N585UC
N43QF	99	Learjet 60	60-159	State Farm Insurance Companies, Bloomington, Il.	N43SF
N43R	97	Challenger 604	5334	Rockwell Automation Inc. Milwaukee, Wi.	N604RC
N43RC	87	Citation S/II	S550-0149	Rohrer Corp. Wadsworth, Oh.	N810V
N43RJ	01	Gulfstream G100	136	Niznick Enterprises Inc. Las Vegas, Nv.	N68GX
N43RP	81	Westwind-Two	332	Petty Air LLC. Harrisburg, NC.	N332DF
N43SA	79	Citation II	550-0086	U S Customs Service, New Orleans NAS, La.	(XC-JCY)
N43SF	04	Challenger 604	5594	Bombardier Aerospace Corp. Windsor-Locks, Ct.	N594SF
N43SP	82	Citation 1/SP	501-0243	Spidela Inc. New Orleans, La.	N2624Z
N43TJ	77	Learjet 35A	35A-121	Golden Flight Enterprises LLC. Wadsworth, Oh.	(D-CFVG)
N43TS	69	HS 125/731	NA721	Aero Toy Store LLC. Fort Lauderdale, Fl.	N777GD
N43US	77	Falcon 10	110	Community Financial Services Inc. Atlanta, Ga.	N104DD
N43VS	85	Citation S/II	S550-0069	Kurt Manufacturing Co. Minneapolis, Mn.	(N12720)
N43W	82	Westwind-Two	374	H L Brown Operating LLC. Midland, Tx.	N33MK
N43WL	64	Sabre-40	282-15	Sabre Liner Aviation LLC. Midland, Tx.	N43W
N44AS	79	Citation II	550-0047	Julrich Aviation Inc. Broomfield, Co.	N66VM
N44CE	89	Gulfstream 4	1125	Caesar's Entertainment Inc. Las Vegas, Nv.	N49PP
N44CK	00	CitationJet CJ-1	525-0401	Koury Aviation Inc. Liberty, NC.	N142EA
N44CP	68	Learjet 25	25-006	Hartford Holding Corp. Naples, Fl.	N252SC
N44EG	87	Falcon 900	14	Bloomberg Services LLC. Morristown, NJ.	VP-BLP
N44EL	94	Learjet 60	60-036	U S Epperson Underwriting Co. Boca Raton, Fl.	N60LR
N44EV	76	Learjet 36A	36A-022	Maritime Sales & Leasing Inc. Newnan, Ga.	N36PD
N44FG	98	Citation V Ultra	560-0470	AFG Industries Inc. Blountville, Tn.	
N44FJ	93	CitationJet	525-0003	Cessna Finance Corp. Wichita, Ks.	N1326D
N44FM	79	Citation 1/SP	501-0156	Supreme Indiana Management LLC. Goshen, In.	N123FG
N44GT	93	Citation V	560-0252	Groendyke Transport Inc. Enid, Ok.	N252CV
N44HH	92	BAe 125/800A	NA0474	S-Prop LLC. Carmel, In.	N622AD
N44JC	01	Falcon 2000	164	John L Cox, Midland-Odessa, Tx.	F-WWVY
N44LC	98	Falcon 50EX	275	Lowe's Companies Inc. North Wilkesboro, NC.	(N44EQ)
N44LQ	98	Citation V Ultra	560-0482	Guardian Financial Management Inc. Burnsville, Mn.	N44LC
N44LV	96	Citation V Ultra	560-0397	Air Pronto LLC/Loves Country Stores Inc. Oklahoma City, Ok.	N560RC
N44LX	89	Gulfstream 4	1114	Trans Exec Air Service/Lexair Ltd. Van Nuys, Ca.	N314GA
N44M	94	Citation VII	650-7043	Seward Prosser Mellon, Ligonier, Pa.	N650DH
N44MM	84	Diamond 1A	A080SA	Mike Moser Inc. Rogers, Ar.	N275HS
N44PR	73	Westwind-1123	169	N44PR Inc. Corpus Christi, Tx.	N1100D
N44QF	01	Learjet 60	60-215	State Farm Insurance Companies, Bloomington, Il.	N44SF
N44QG	03	Learjet 45	45-237	Learjet Inc. Tucson, AZ.	N45QG
N44SF	04	Challenger 604	5601	State Farm Insurance Companies, Bloomington, Il.	C-G...
N44SH	01	Citation Encore	560-0613	44SH LLC/Bob Howard Pontiac GMC Inc. Oklahoma City.	(N448H)
N44SH*	04	Citation Sovereign	680-0023	44SH LLC/Bob Howard Pontiac GMC Inc. Oklahoma City.	N52235
N44SW	94	Citation II	550-0733	Steel Warehouse Co. South Bend, In.	N550TR
N44SZ	00	Learjet 31A	31A-193	Wyoming Associates Inc. Spartanburg, SC.	N44SF
N44TT	78	Learjet 35A	35A-211	InterContinental Express LLC. Athens, Ga.	N998JP
N45AC	87	Gulfstream 4	1036	Ashton Aviation LLC. Seattle, Wa.	N152A
N45AE	81	Learjet 35A	35A-422	GCA Aviation LLC. Tulsa, Ok.	N86BL
N45AF	78	Citation Eagle II	501-0284	Matthews Properties Inc. Fremont, Ca.	N729PX
N45AJ	00	Learjet 45	45-137	Suiza Foods Corp. Dallas, Tx.	(N45MU)
N45AX	03	Learjet 45	45-206	Omni Air Transport, Tulsa, Ok.	(PR-...)
N45BE	90	Citation II	550-0664	Chief Industries Inc. Grand Island, Ne.	N70PC
N45BK	69	Learjet 25	25-036	GoldStar International Inc. Port Arthur, Tx.	N15M
N45BR	98	Citation X	750-0045	Burlington Resources Oil & Gas Co. Houston, Tx.	N5109R
N45BS*	73	Learjet 25B	25B-111	PCH Aviation LLC. Palm Coast, Fl.	N825A
N45ED	66	Learjet 24	24-104	E H Darby & Co/Alpha Jet International, Muscle Shoals, Al.	N924ED
N45ET	00	Gulfstream 4SP	1405	Bright Flight Inc. Santa Fe, NM.	N310GA
N45FG	75	Learjet 36	36-010	Fremont Group/Bechtel Corp. Oakland, Ca.	N50SF
N45FS	79	Citation Eagle II	501-0102	Vanguard Investment & Consulting LLC. Atlanta, Ga.	N501CG
N45GA	90	Citation V	560-0064	Allied Properties of America Inc. Wilmington, De.	ZS-MVZ
N45GP	86	Citation S/II	S550-0110	Great Planes Industries LLC. Wheeling, Il.	N1291V
N45H	90	Astra-1125SP	050	45 Hotel Corp. Columbus, Oh.	N501JT
N45HC	01	Learjet 45	45-174	Harbert Aviation Inc. Birmingham, Al.	
N45HF	00	Learjet 45	45-121	HNT Properties LLC/Tenaska, Omaha, Ne.	(N666BG)
N45HG	97	Learjet 31A	31A-140	Asphalt Materials Inc. Indianapolis, In.	N314AC
N45JB	86	Falcon 200	505	Barron Aircraft LLC. Cannes, France.	N221FJ
N45KB	92	Citation V	560-0191	Advanced Drainage Systems Inc. Columbus, Oh.	N2JW
N45KG	82	HS 125/700A	7189	Kaman Corp. Hartford-Bradley, Ct.	N8KG
N45KJ	00	Learjet 45	45-301	Learjet Inc. Wichita, Ks.	

Reg	Yr	Type	c/n	Owner/Operator	Prev Regn

Reg	Yr	Type	c/n	Owner/Operator	Prev Regn
N45KK	97	Learjet 31A	31A-147	Blanco Oil Co. San Antonio, Tx.	N157EC
N45KX	03	Learjet 45	45-233	Carmax Auto Superstores Inc. Glan Allen, Va.	N5000E
N45LJ	04	Learjet 45	45-258	Learjet Inc. Wichita, Ks.	N5015U
N45LR	98	Learjet 45	45-013	Bullock Charter Inc. Princeton, Ma.	D-CFWR
N45ME	79	Citation II	550-0080	Suncrest Farms Inc. Phoenix, Az.	N22511
N45MH	00	CitationJet CJ-1	525-0386	PGM Air Inc. Caldwell, NJ.	N51993
N45ML	82	Citation II	550-0367	Commerce Aviation LLC/Airsuz LLC. Memphis, Tn.	N3MB
N45MM	78	Citation 1/SP	501-0070	GRL Investments LLC. Kalispell, Mt.	N628ZG
N45MR	01	Learjet 45	45-179	Speedbird Aviation LLC. Fort Wayne, In.	N541AL
N45NB*	03	390 Premier 1	RB-91	Air King Aviation LLC. Ootewah, Tn.	N24YD
N45NC	00	Falcon 50EX	302	National City Corp/NCC Services, Cleveland, Oh.	N302FJ
N45ND	01	390 Premier 1	RB-22	Raytheon Aircraft Co. Wichita, Ks.	N45NB
N45NF	01	Citation Bravo	550-0986	Samuel Roberts Noble Foundation Inc. Ardmore, Ok.	N986PA
N45NM	04	Learjet 45	45-253	HM International LLC. Tulsa, Ok.	N4008G
N45NP	02	Learjet 45	45-204	News Press & Gazette Co/NPG Aircraft Inc. St Joseph, Mo.	VH-ZZH
N45PH	83	Challenger 601	3004	Willis Leasing Finance Corp. Sausalito, Ca.	N501PC
N45PK	99	Learjet 31A	31A-186	Pike Electric Inc. Mount Airy, NC.	(N137FX)
N45RC	90	Citation V	560-0071A	CD Exploration Inc/CDX Gas Co. Addison, Tx.	N2728N
N45RK	92	Beechjet 400A	RK-43	Actuant Corp. Milwaukee, Wi.	N56400
N45SJ	96	Falcon 900EX	7	Sid Richardson Carbon & Gasoline Co. Fort Worth, Tx.	N907FJ
N45TK	01	Learjet 45	45-176	Speedbird Aviation LLC. Fort Wayne, In.	N5016S
N45TL	77	Citation 1/SP	501-0016	TLR Inc. Costa Mesa, Ca.	N17TJ
N45TP	96	Citation V Ultra	560-0405	RenAir Leasing Associates LLC. Jacksonville, Fl.	N137FA
N45UF	93	Learjet 31A	31A-072	Anderson Chemical Co. Macon, Ga.	(N14WT)
N45UG	01	Learjet 45	45-198	Universal Underwriters Service Corp. Kansas City, Mo.	N5048K
N45UJ	00	Learjet 45	45-080	DJT LLC/Carpenter Contractors of America Inc. Fl.	N42HP
N45UP	01	Learjet 45	45-170	Astra Holdings Inc/Hume & Johnson PA. Coral Springs, Fl.	N50154
N45VB	00	Learjet 45	45-043	Idaho Investments Inc. Idaho Falls, Id.	D-CRAN
N45VM	00	Citation Bravo	550-0918	Sierra Aviation Inc. Kansas City, Mo.	N5109R
N46E	04	Learjet 40	45-2010	Hunt Consolidated Inc. Dallas, Tx.	N50163
N46F	03	Challenger 604	5574	Hunt Consolidated Inc. Dallas, Tx.	N574F
N46GA	90	Citation V	560-0061	Frederick Air Charter LLC. Frederick, Md.	D-CNCI
N46HA	99	Falcon 2000	91	First Union Corp/Hawkaire, Charlotte, NC.	F-WWVK
N46JW	01	CitationJet CJ-2	525A-0046	J W Charter Inc. Houston, Tx.	N40RL
N46MK	83	Falcon 100	206	Merillat Industries Inc. Adrian, Mi.	N367F
N46PJ	78	Citation II/SP	551-0027	Citation Films International LLC. Seattle, Wa.	N522CC
N46SR	85	Challenger 601	3046	Arrowhead General Insurance Agency, San Diego, Ca.	LX-AEN
N46VE	00	Citation Excel	560-5077	V & E Aviation LLC. Indianapolis, In.	N221LC
N46WC	83	HS 125/700A	NA0334	Weldbend Corp. Chicago-Midway, Il.	N93GC
N47AN	84	Citation III	650-0054	JES Aircraft Services Inc. Columbia, Mo.	N17AN
N47CE	69	Jet Commander-B	137	Dove Air Inc. Hendersonville, NC.	XB-FKV
N47FH	93	CitationJet	525-0047	Pacific Sunset Inc. Malibu, Ca.	N47TH
N47HF	03	Citation Excel	560-5347	HF Express LP. Ventura, Ca.	N.....
N47HR	94	Gulfstream 4SP	1250	Laredo National Bank, Laredo, Tx.	VP-CBB
N47HV	73	HS 125/600A	6014	Aracel Inc. Tortola, BVI.	N47HW
N47HW	84	BAe 125/800A	8023	FHW Jr Inc. Havre, Mt.	N1910J
N47LP	81	Falcon 20F-5	457	High Valley Air Service Inc. Colorado Springs, Co.	N4362M
N47MR	72	Learjet 25B	25B-101	American Aircraft Sales International Inc. Fl. (status ?).	N821AW
N47PB	79	HS 125/700B	7055	MKJ Aviation Inc. Dallas, Tx.	(N755TS)
N47SE	80	Sabre-65	465-34	AIG Aviation Inc. Atlanta, Ga.	N65TS
N47SM	88	Citation II	550-0568	Pioneer Wings LLC. Scottsdale, Az.	N83KE
N47TH	95	CitationJet	525-0119	QEAT XX LLC. Naples, Fl.	N5264E
N47TL	81	Citation 1/SP	501-0200	National Marketing & Management Services LLC. Wilsall, Mt.	7Q-YTL
N47UF	80	Falcon 50	28	Premier Air Center Inc. East Alton, Il.	PH-LEM
N47VL	65	Sabre-40R	282-48	Jett Racing & Sales Inc. Laredo, Tx.	XA-RGC
N48AL	90	BAe 125/800A	8167	Lakha Air LLC. Seattle, Wa.	N825DA
N48AM	96	Learjet 31A	31A-123	American Medical Security Inc. Green Bay, Wi.	N323LJ
N48BV	85	Citation S/II	S550-0032	Regent Air Service Inc. Truckee, Ca.	N232WC
N48CC	98	Gulfstream 4SP	1363	Centex Corp. Dallas, Tx.	N463G
N48CG	96	Falcon 2000	41	Corning Inc. Hamilton, NY.	N2073
N48CT	73	Learjet 24XR	24XR-274	Aero Prodin S.A. Guatemala City, Guatemala.	(TG-...)
N48DD	66	HS 125/731	25115	Jet Services Enterprises Inc. Bethany, Ok.	N420JC
N48DK	78	Citation II/SP	551-0095	S & K Aviation Inc. Lake in the Hills, Il. (was 550-0049).	N402TJ
N48FB	81	HS 125/700A	NA0292	Grayford LLC. Dearborn, Mi.	N748FB
N48FN	71	Learjet 24D	24D-238	Hampton University, Newport News, Va.	N49DM
N48G	97	Falcon 50EX	258	Civic Center Corp/Anheuser Busch, Chesterfield, Mo.	VP-BST

Reg	Yr	Type	c/n	Owner/Operator	Prev Regn
N48GL	86	Falcon 50	168	Royal Jet Inc. La Jolla, Ca.	(N420JP)
N48GP	76	Learjet 35A	35A-069	The Aviation Co. Wilmington, NC.	N10AQ
N48GR	69	Learjet 25	25-048	G & R Machinery Sales LLC. Pharr, Tx.	XA-TCY
N48GX	00	Galaxy-1126	017	Southeast Frozen Foods Co. Miami, Fl.	4X-CVF
N48HC	81	Learjet 55	55-012	Manursing Associates LLC. Rye, NY.	N104BS
N48HF	03	Citation X	750-0220	HF Express LP. Ventura, Ca.	N52613
N48KH	81	Citation II	550-0295	Kir-Nie Aviation Corp. Quincy, Il.	N339MC
N48L	66	Learjet 24A	24A-107	Royal Air Freight Inc. Waterford, Mi.	
N48LB	79	HS 125/700B	7064	Baron & Budd PC. Dallas, Tx.	N395RD
N48MF	98	Beechjet 400A	RK-218	P T Management LLC. Portola Valley, Ca.	N3068M
N48NS	00	Citation Bravo	550-0939	Tower House Consultants Ltd. Jersey, Channel Islands.	VP-BNS
N48PL	97	Beechjet 400A	RK-138	Flyaway Acquisition Inc. Fort Worth, Tx.	N40PL
N48SD	83	Westwind-Two	399	Valy Aviation Corp. Wilmington, De.	N78WW
N48SE	92	Beechjet 400A	RK-48	Investment Capital Group LLC/ I C Jet, Sacramento, Ca.	N94HT
N48TC	01	390 Premier 1	RB-13	Tool Crib Aero Inc. Grand Forks, ND.	
N48TF	04	Learjet 45	45-248	Gulf States Toyota Inc. Houston, Tx.	N4004Y
N48WA	73	Learjet 25B	25B-136	Divine Aviation LLC. Burbank, Ca.	N753CA
N48WK	97	Falcon 2000	48	Las Brias LLC/Quail K LLC. Scottsdale, Az.	N701WG
N48WS	77	Sabre-60A	306-124	Whiteco Industries Inc. Merrillville, In.	N60RS
N48Y	84	BAe 125/800A	8009	Davison Transport Inc. Ruston, La.	N45Y
N49BE	78	Learjet 35A	35A-192	Mayo Aviation Inc. Englewood, Co.	N49PE
N49CT	81	Westwind-1124	314	Blue Sky Aviation LLC. Wichita, Ks.	N2HZ
N49FW	00	Citation Bravo	550-0948	Secretair LLC. Cincinnati, Oh.	N5264E
N49GS	76	Learjet 24F	24F-336	White Cloud Aviation LLC. Seattle, Wa.	N9LD
N49KW	02	Citation Bravo	550-1021	PPAL Inc. Kalamazoo, Mi.	N5174W
N49LD	92	Citation V	560-0175	McKee Foods Corp. Collegedale, Tn.	N1279Z
N49MJ	00	Citation Excel	560-5100	Melvin Joseph Construction Co. Georgetown, De.	N510XL
N49MN	88	Astra-1125	019	Astra 885 LLC/Actus Corp. Napa, Ca.	N49MW
N49NS	91	Citation V	560-0116	Seaman Corp. Lincoln, Ne.	N901RM
N49RF	94	Gulfstream 4SP	1246	NO&AA/U S Department of Commerce, MacDill AFB. Fl.	N407GA
N49SL	91	Gulfstream 4	1167	Sara Lee Corp. Chicago-Midway, Il.	N1SL
N49SM	87	Citation III	650-0132	Select Medical Corp. Harrisburg, Pa.	N24KT
N49U	79	Citation II	550-0082	Helicopters Inc. Calokia, Il.	N21DA
N49WA	73	Learjet 25B	25B-142	Fleet Unlimited Inc/Spirit Aviation, Van Nuys, Ca.	N70CE
N49WL	81	Learjet 35A	35A-457	O & S LLC. Waterford, Mi.	N113LB
N50AE	03	Hawker 800XP	8650	American Electric Power, Columbus, Oh.	N650XP
N50AM	72	Citation	500-0041	Phoenix Helicopters LLC. Dover, De.	N50AS
N50BH	82	Gulfstream 3	359	Crystal Jet Aviation Inc. Schenectady, NY.	(N25MT)
N50BN	88	BAe 125/800A	NA0430	Margent Air Services Inc. NYC.	N149VP
N50BV	77	Falcon 20F	365	J & R Aviation LLC. Warwick, RI.	N50BH
N50BZ	81	Falcon 50	80	ZG Aircraft Leasing LLC. Tampa, Fl.	N50SJ
N50CK	74	Learjet 25B	25B-157	Michigan Air Freight LLC. Ypsilanti, Mi.	N57CK
N50CR	69	Sabre-50	287-1	Rockwell Collins Inc. Cedar Rapids, Ia.	N287NA
N50CV*	95	Citation V Ultra	560-0293	River City Flying Service LLC. Portland, Or.	N131WC
N50DR	94	Citation V	560-0248	RWB Enterprises Inc. Norfolk, Va.	(N226U)
N50DS	02	Challenger 604	5544	First Southeast Aviation Corp. St Petersburg-Clearwater, Fl.	N604TS
N50EE	02	Gulfstream G400	1500	Idaho Associates LLC. Spartanburg, SC.	(N55GJ)
N50EF	84	Diamond 1A	A081SA	Eastern Foods Inc/Robert Brooks, Atlanta, Ga.	N750TJ
N50ET	01	CitationJet CJ-1	525-0476	Burlingame Industries Inc. Rialto, Ca.	N476CJ
N50FD	82	Westwind-1124	381	Sallie Mae Inc. Dulles, Va.	N381W
N50FF	91	Falcon 50	220	Maltese Journeys Inc. Portland, Or.	N528JR
N50FN	76	Learjet 35A	35A-070	Flight Capital LLC. Madison, Ms.	N543PA
N50GP	98	Citation V Ultra	560-0477	Gate Asphalt Co. Jacksonville, Fl.	N5085E
N50HC	90	Falcon 50	208	Group Holdings OR Inc. Fort Worth, Tx.	N50AE
N50HD	82	Falcon 50	83	Architectural Air LLC. Washington-Dulles, Va.	N881M
N50HM	85	Falcon 50	153	Health Management Associates Inc. Naples, Fl.	N16CP
N50J	83	Falcon 50	117	DHCI Partners LLC. Minneapolis, Mn.	N124HM
N50JP	80	Citation II	550-0143	First Insurance Agency Inc. Goodland, Ks.	N150RD
N50KC	01	Gulfstream V	659	Air Tiger 1 LLC. Oxford, Ct.	N589GA
N50KD	85	Falcon 50	145	Oakmont Corp. Reno, Nv.	(TC-...)
N50LQ	84	Falcon 50	148	KSL Recreation Corp. La Quinta, Ca.	N254NA
N50M	81	Westwind-1124	327	Jet Sets Inc. Sarasota, Fl.	4X-CRU
N50MJ	78	Learjet 35A	35A-164	K & K Jets LLC. Teterboro, NJ.	N248HM
N50MV	82	Falcon 50	124	Bloomberg Services LLC. Morristown, NJ.	VP-BFM
N50MW	85	Falcon 200	503	Transaction Systems Architects Inc. Omaha, Ne.	(N50MX)
N50NF	90	Citation II	550-0636	Global Energy Inc. Cincinnati, Oh.	N4EW

Reg	Yr	Type	c/n	Owner/Operator	Prev Regn

Reg	Yr	Type	c/n	Owner/Operator	Prev Regn
☐ N50NM	97	Falcon 50EX	266	MRRM PA.. Charleston, SC.	VP-BPA
☐ N50PA	79	Challenger 600S	1004	Prestige Air LLC. Las Vegas, Nv.	N640TS
☐ N50PM	03	390 Premier 1	RB-80	Mallen Industries Inc. Hilton Head, SC.	N50280
☐ N50PN	01	390 Premier 1	RB-11	Raytheon Aircraft Co. Wichita, Ks.	N50PM
☐ N50RL	86	Gulfstream 3	479	R & L Air LLC. Eugene, Or.	MM62025
☐ N50RW	74	Learjet 25B	25B-135	MBI LLC. Arlington, Va.	(N1RW)
☐ N50SF	88	Falcon 50	180	Fremont Group/Bechtel Corp. Oakland, Ca.	N2254S
☐ N50SJ	04	SJ 30-2	005	Sino Swearingen Aircraft Co. San Antonio, Tx.	
☐ N50SN	00	Falcon 50EX	310	First Quality Falcon LLC. Farmingdale, NY.	N50FQ
☐ N50TC	98	BBJ-72T	29024	Tracinda Corp. Van Nuys, Ca.	N1787B
☐ N50TG	99	Falcon 2000	96	Lake Capital LLC. Palwaukee, Il.	N88DD
☐ N50TQ	93	Astra-1125SP	065	Insurance Services Corp. Reading, Pa.	N50TG
☐ N50US	80	Citation II	550-0181	Bergeron Marine Service Inc. New Orleans, La.	N550GP
☐ N50XL	01	Citation Excel	560-5202	RJM Aviation Associates Inc. Berlin, Ct.	(N467SA)
☐ N51B	99	Beechjet 400A	RK-261	NACCO Industries Inc. Mayfield Heights, Oh.	N3261A
☐ N51C	90	Citation V	560-0084	Computer Service Professionals Inc. Jefferson City, Mo.	C-GHEC
☐ N51CD	96	CitationJet	525-0163	HD Aviation LLC. Little Canada, Mn.	N5138F
☐ N51EB	87	Beechjet 400	RJ-28	Sherr & Co. Hickory, NC.	N700LP
☐ N51FE	82	Falcon 50	121	McKinley Aircraft Holdings Inc. Akron-Canton, Oh.	N121FJ
☐ N51FL	00	Gulfstream V	646	Star Aircraft Leasing SA. Monaco.	N524GA
☐ N51GS	99	CitationJet	525-0317	General Shale Building Materials Inc. Bristol, Tn.	N317CJ
☐ N51HF	04	CitationJet CJ-3	525B-0011	Cessna Aircraft Co. Wichita, Ks.	(N110MG)
☐ N51HF	04	CitationJet CJ-3	525B-0008	HFL Express LLC. Ventura, Ca.	N.....
☐ N51JV	84	Citation III	650-0050	AMS Construction Co. Dallas, Tx.	(D-CVHA)
☐ N51LC	80	Learjet 35A	35A-302	AirNet Systems Inc. Columbus, Oh.	N631CW
☐ N51MF	86	Gulfstream 3	491	Ferrell Schultz Aviation LLC. Miami, Fl.	N101PT
☐ N51MJ	81	Falcon 50	54	Jensen Aviation LLC. Salt Lake City, Ut.	N100DV
☐ N51MN	95	Falcon 2000	14	MediaNews Services Inc. Denver, Co.	N70KS
☐ N51TV	83	Westwind-Two	402	Texas Television Inc. Corpus Christi, Tx.	N999LC
☐ N51V	88	Falcon 50	189	Starflight 50 LLC. Belle Chasse, La.	N51VT
☐ N51VC	00	Beechjet 400A	RK-288	International Veneer Co. South Hill, Va.	
☐ N51VL	85	Learjet 55	55-116	SP Aviation Inc. Hayward, Ca.	N51V
☐ N51WP	80	Citation 1/SP	501-0133	Weber Plywood & Lumber Co. Orange County, Ca.	(N955WP)
☐ N52AL	88	Beechjet 400	RJ-38	ALP Air LLC/Azalea Management & Leasing Inc. Asheville, NC.	N438DA
☐ N52AW	96	Beechjet 400A	RK-115	KA300 LLC. Reno, Nv.	(N369EA)
☐ N52CK	85	Citation S/II	S550-0076	Koury Aviation Inc. Liberty, NC.	N89TD
☐ N52CT	87	Learjet 55B	55B-131	Coyne International Enterprises Corp. Syracuse, NY.	N7260K
☐ N52DC	00	Falcon 2000	116	Dow Chemical Co. Ross Field, Mi.	N2216
☐ N52FT	85	Citation S/II	S550-0056	Texas Citation S/II Management LLC. San Antonio, Tx.	N550F
☐ N52GA	80	HS 125/700A	NA0270	Premier Aircraft Funding Inc. Miami, Fl.	PK-CTC
☐ N52JA	75	Falcon 10	59	Sportsmed Aviation LLC. Birmingham, Al.	N633WW
☐ N52LT	82	Citation II	550-0355	Berdan Holdings LLC/BLT Enterprises Inc. Oxnard, Ca.	N355DF
☐ N52MK	97	Gulfstream 4SP	1337	Michael Kittredge, Hobe Sound, Fl.	N637GA
☐ N52MW	00	Citation Excel	560-5144	Management West LLC. Aurora, Or.	N713DH
☐ N52N	85	Falcon 100	197	Long Island Airlines LLC. Farmingdale, NY.	N888G
☐ N52NW	69	Gulfstream 2	52	SFG Commercial Aircraft Leasing Inc. South Bend, In.	N211MT
☐ N52PK	93	CitationJet	525-0052	North Park Transportation Co. Billings, Mt.	N252CJ
☐ N52PM	74	Citation	500-0222	Alsate Aircraft Holdings LP. Farmington, NM.	N636SC
☐ N52RF	78	Citation II	550-0021	NO&AA/U S Department of Commerce, Stewart, NY.	N900LJ
☐ N52SM	92	BAe 1000A	NA1009	Sierra Pacific Industries Inc. Redding, Ca.	N125CJ
☐ N52TJ	73	Falcon 10	3	R V with Me Inc. Fresno, Ca.	(N149DG)
☐ N62TL	77	Citation I/SP	501-0053	Citizens Telephone Co. Brevard, NC.	N14EA
☐ N52WF	99	Citation V Ultra	560-0528	ThyssenKrupp-Waupaca, Waupaca, Wi.	
☐ N53BB	80	Citation 1/SP	501-0146	J R Tomkinson Inc. Newport Beach, Ca.	N194RC
☐ N53CG	97	CitationJet	525-0233	EHAD LLC. Powderly, Tx.	N233CJ
☐ N53DF	01	Challenger 604	5507	Sierra Land Group Inc. Burbank, Ca.	C-GLXB
☐ N53EZ	79	Citation 1/SP	501-0119	R & L West Group LLC. Bend, Or.	N77GJ
☐ N53FJ	81	Falcon 50	53	Dassault Falcon Jet Corp. Teterboro, NJ.	N22YP
☐ N53FL	68	Learjet 25	25-017	Airmark International, Corona, Ca.	N128JS
☐ N53FN	75	Learjet 35A	35A-021	LS Management Inc. Wichita, Ks.	N4415S
☐ N53FP	82	Citation II	550-0434	Heartland Aviation Inc. Eau Claire, Wi.	(D-CVAU)
☐ N53FT	81	Citation II	550-0276	Zesch Restaurants Inc. San Angelo, Tx.	C-GGFW
☐ N53GH	82	HS 125/700A	NA0314	G Howard Associates Inc. Ronkonkoma, NY.	(N106AE)
☐ N53GX	00	Global Express	9053	Mills Pride LP/White Rose Aviation Inc. W Palm Beach, Fl.	N700LJ
☐ N53HF	04	Citation X	750-0236	CHF Express LLC. Ventura, Ca.	N52462
☐ N53HJ	82	Learjet 55	55-037	JODA LLC/Worldwide Jet Charter Inc. Fort Lauderdale, Fl.	PT-OBR
Reg	*Yr*	*Type*	*c/n*	*Owner/Operator*	*Prev Regn*

48

Reg	Yr	Type	c/n	Owner/Operator	Prev Regn
☐ N53LM	80	Westwind-1124	311	John Lattimore Jr. McKinney, Tx.	N788MA
☐ N53MS	93	Beechjet 400A	RK-64	Image Air LLC. Warsaw, In.	N8164M
☐ N53PJ	60	MS 760 Paris-1R	53	R S Fox LP. Calhoun, Ga.	No 53
☐ N53RD	81	Citation	500-0415	Africano Aircraft Management LLC. Peoria, Il.	N50KR
☐ N53RG	81	Citation II	550-0257	RGCC LLC. Kansas City, Ks.	N187TA
☐ N53WA	75	Falcon 10	53	Double X LLC. Palo Alto, Ca.	I-LCJG
☐ N54	93	Learjet 60	60-009	FAA, Oklahoma City, Ok.	N26029
☐ N54AX	01	Gulfstream G200	054	Aspen Executive Air LLC. Aspen, Co.	N200GA
☐ N54BP	92	CitationJet	525-0002	Franklin Research Group Inc. Columbus, Oh.	N46JW
☐ N54CG	01	CitationJet CJ-1	525-0439	Craig Goess Inc/Greenville Toyota, Greenville, NC.	N395SD
☐ N54CJ	94	CitationJet	525-0054	American Aviation Inc. Henderson, NC.	N2638U
☐ N54DC	00	Falcon 2000	117	Dow Chemical Co. Ross Field, Mi.	N2217
☐ N54DD	90	Citation V	560-0089	International Jet Aviation Inc. Van Nuys, Ca.	ZS-MPT
☐ N54FN	72	Learjet 25C	25C-083	The Aviation Co. Wilmington, NC.	N200MH
☐ N54FT	79	Citation Eagle SP	501-0100	K3C Inc/Sierra Industries Inc. Uvalde, Tx.	C-GSUM
☐ N54HC	96	CitationJet	525-0157	Capital Partners Advisory Co/AM AV Inc. Baltimore, Md.	N57HC
☐ N54HD	92	Beechjet 400A	RK-49	Horne Properties Inc. Knoxville, Tn.	(N349HP)
☐ N54HF	85	Gulfstream 3	459	Midsouth Services Inc. St Petersburg-Clearwater, Fl.	N566C
☐ N54HP	97	Beechjet 400A	RK-160	AMPCO Inc. Riverhead, NY.	N2360F
☐ N54J	00	Falcon 2000	141	W W Grainger Inc. Palwaukee, Il.	N2000A
☐ N54JC	84	Challenger 601	3031	Tuck Aviation LLC/Alpha Mary Inc. Tucson, Az.	N303BX
☐ N54JV*	74	Citation	500-0163	Rimrock Properties LLC. Gallatin Gateway, Mt.	N8KH
☐ N54KB	00	Gulfstream V	627	Miranda International Aviation Inc. San Jose, Ca.	N627GA
☐ N54NW	82	Learjet 55	55-054	Surazel Aircraft LLC. Van Nuys, Ca.	HB-VHL
☐ N54PA	74	Learjet 36	36-004	Phoenix Air Group Inc. Cartersville, Ga.	N180GC
☐ N54PR	99	Gulfstream V	564	Prime Resources LLC/Prempal Rawat, Carson City, Nv.	N664GA
☐ N54RM	87	Citation II	550-0562	Chapparal Boats Inc. Nashville, Ga.	N813A
☐ N54SU	83	Challenger 600S	1053	Dunmore Realty LLC. Sacramento, Ca.	N54SK
☐ N54TG	98	Gulfstream V	523	Rochester Aviation Inc. Rochester, NY.	N790MC
☐ N54TK	85	Beechjet 400	RJ-5	Collins/Kelly Aviation Partners, Midland, Tx. (was A1005SA)	N77GA
☐ N54TN	92	Learjet 31A	31A-054	Tesalia Springs Co SA. Quito, Ecuador.	N82KL
☐ N54TS	75	Citation 1/SP	501-0643	J Edward Smith Jet LLC. Las Vegas, Nv. (was 500-0293).	N54CM
☐ N54WJ	77	HS 125/700A	7007	World Jet Inc. Fort Lauderdale, Fl.	N257WJ
☐ N54YR	85	Falcon 50	158	Phifer Wire Products Inc. Tuscaloosa, Al.	N142FJ
☐ N55	93	Learjet 60	60-013	FAA, Oklahoma City, Ok.	N26011
☐ N55AR	84	Learjet 55	55-105	Pacific Coast Group Inc. Las Vegas, Nv.	C-GQBR
☐ N55AS	90	Falcon 50	214	GKGF&S Acquisitions XXXI Inc. Indoianapolis, In.	N296FJ
☐ N55BH	84	Citation III	650-0041	International Industries Inc. Gilbert, WV.	
☐ N55CJ	99	CitationJet	525-0298	Pektron Aviation Inc. Gamston, UK.	G-RSCJ
☐ N55DG	83	Falcon 100	207	Griffin Ag Inc. Little Rock, Ar.	N456CM
☐ N55F	78	Learjet 35A	35A-147	AirNet Systems Inc. Columbus, Oh.	N717W
☐ N55FG	79	Westwind-1124	267	Vesuvius USA Corp. Champaign, Il.	N241CT
☐ N55FJ	76	Falcon 10	74	C J Aviation LLC. San Francisco, Ca.	N5JY
☐ N55FN	78	Learjet 35A	35A-202	Flight Capital LLC. Madison, Ms.	D-CGPD
☐ N55FT	72	Citation Longwing SP	500-0009	Guilford Transportation Industries, Portsmouth, NH.	N147WS
☐ N55G	68	HS 125/731	NA709	Dr Paul Madison, Michigan City, In.	(N2G)
☐ N55GR	74	Citation	500-0217	N55GR LLC. Woodinville, Wa.	N217S
☐ N55GV	97	Gulfstream V	515	WTC/Starjet Ltd.	V8-001
☐ N55HA	99	Citation Excel	560-5059	BellSouth Corp. Atlanta-Fulton County, Ga.	
☐ N55HF	95	Challenger 601-3R	5183	Hudson Foods Inc. Rogers, Ar.	N601HF
☐ N55HY	71	Gulfstream II SP	97	PacJet/Global Jet Shares Inc. Northbridge, Ca.	(N397L)
☐ N55KT	03	CitationJet CJ-2	525A-0177	Precision Dynamics International LLC. Chandler, Az.	N.....
☐ N55LC	01	Falcon 50EX	314	Lowe's Companies Inc. North Wilkesboro, NC.	N314EX
☐ N55LF	85	Learjet 55	55-112	55-112 LLC. Fort Lauderdale, Fl. (status ?).	EC-HAI
☐ N55LJ	82	Learjet 55	55-030	D & K Healthcare Resources, St Louis, Mo.	(N155CD)
☐ N55LS	79	Citation II/SP	551-0021	J & D Aircraft Sales LLC. Pasco, Wa.	N551CF
☐ N55NM	83	Learjet 55	55-085	HM International LLC. Tulsa, Ok.	N58FM
☐ N55NY	82	Learjet 55	55-020	Air New York LLC/Northeastern Aviation Corp. Melville, NY.	N35PF
☐ N55PX	98	CitationJet	525-0285	DW Enterprises LC. Wamego, Ks.	N55PZ
☐ N55RF	86	BAe 125/800A	8066	National Aircraft Leasing LLC. Anchorage, Ak.	N75CS
☐ N55RG	66	Gulfstream II SP	1	R W Galvin/Motorola Inc. Wheeling, Il.	N801GA
☐ N55RT	84	Learjet 55	55-095	Nuray Aircraft LLC. Charlotte, NC.	N8565Z
☐ N55RZ	71	HS 125/400A	NA764	ROC Air Service LLC. Thompson, Ga.	XB-CUX
☐ N55SC	95	Citation VII	650-7060	Fifty Five LLC. Midland, Tx.	N5218T
☐ N55SK	94	CitationJet	525-0063	Skyline Corp. Elkhart, In.	N2649J
☐ N55TD	90	Gulfstream 4	1131	Threshold Ventures Inc. Scottsdale, Az.	N679RW

Reg	Yr	Type	c/n	Owner/Operator	Prev Regn

Reg	Yr	Type	c/n	Owner/Operator	Prev Regn
☐ N55TP	81	Citation II	550-0256	TP Investments LLC. Northport, Al.	N75TP
☐ N55TY	97	Falcon 900EX	25	Tyco International Ltd. Portsmouth, NH.	N925EX
☐ N55UH	03	Gulfstream G550	5028	United Healthcare Services Inc. St Paul, Mn.	N928GA
☐ N55UJ	84	Learjet 55	55-090	Universal Jet Aviation Inc. Boca Raton, Fl.	N181EF
☐ N55VC	86	Learjet 55B	55B-130	R T Vanderbilt Co. White Plains, NY.	
☐ N55VR	95	Learjet 31	31-033C	Victoria Racing LLC. City of Industry, Ca.	N555VR
☐ N55WL	80	Citation II	550-0140	DT Aviation LLC. Sarasota, Fl.	N2646Z
☐ N56	94	Learjet 60	60-033	FAA, Oklahoma City, Ok.	N4031A
☐ N56AG	99	Galaxy-1126	011	Villair Ltd/Jet Aviation Business Jets, Geneva, Switzerland.	HB-IUU
☐ N56BE	01	Hawker 800XP	8527	B-200 Corp. Farmingdale, NY.	N813TA
☐ N56BP	79	Westwind-1124	268	Bradley Flight LLC. Denver, Co.	N41WH
☐ N56D	00	Gulfstream 4SP	1411	Snowbird Aviation LLC. Minneapolis, Mn.	N56MD
☐ N56EM	77	Learjet 35A	35A-144	AirNet Systems Inc. Columbus, Oh. (red).	N56HF
☐ N56GA	94	Citation V	560-0259	Dalton Aviation LLC. Eagle County, Co.	N37WP
☐ N56HA	99	Citation Excel	560-5063	First Union Corp/Hawkaire, Charlotte, NC.	N5200U
☐ N56JA	80	Learjet 35A	35A-342	AirNet Systems Inc. Columbus, Oh. (yellow).	YV-15CP
☐ N56L	93	Gulfstream 4SP	1213	Newsflight Inc. Los Angeles, Ca.	N416GA
☐ N56LF	92	Learjet 31A	31A-056	Wal-Mart Stores Inc. Rogers, Ar.	N303WB
☐ N56LT	80	Falcon 50	21	Level 3 Communications Inc. Broomfield, Co.	N770E
☐ N56LW	81	Citation 1/SP	501-0314	Larry Phillips, Fruitland Park, Fl.	N56MC
☐ N56MD	76	Learjet 25D	25D-214	H-F Aircraft LLC. Nederland, Tx.	N70TF
☐ N56MK	77	Citation 1/SP	501-0023	M L Kuhn Enterprises Inc. Whitesboro, Tx.	(N501FB)
☐ N56MM	76	Learjet 24F	24F-332	Northeastern Aviation Corp. Wilmington, De.	N13KL
☐ N56PA	77	Learjet 36A	36A-023	Phoenix Air Group Inc. Cartersville, Ga.	N6YY
☐ N56PB	81	Citation 1/SP	501-0219	Sound Container Inc. Renton, Wa.	N510GA
☐ N56PT	73	Learjet 24D	24D-276	JaGee Corp. Fort Worth, Tx.	N25CV
☐ N56RN	76	Sabre-60A	306-122	Reserve National Insurance Co. Oklahoma City, Ok.	N168H
☐ N56WE	78	Citation 1/SP	501-0056	Port City Castings Corp. Muskegon, Mi.	CC-CTE
☐ N57	94	Learjet 60	60-039	FAA, Oklahoma City, Ok.	N8071J
☐ N57BJ	85	Citation S/II	S550-0052	Plukair Delaware LLC. Wilmington, De.	N27GD
☐ N57CE	89	Citation III	650-0178	Dartswift Inc. Haverford, Pa.	N650BA
☐ N57CJ	85	Citation S/II	S550-0057	Raul Marquez, Edinburg, Tx.	N1UL
☐ N57EJ	01	CitationJet CJ-2	525A-0057	Exec-Jet Inc. Plainville-Robertson, Ct. (status ?).	N.....
☐ N57EL	02	Falcon 900EX	111	Enterprise Rent-A-Car Co. St Louis, Mo.	N101EX
☐ N57FC	81	Citation 1/SP	501-0229	Foxtrot Partners LLC. San Francisco, Ca.	N57MC
☐ N57FL	03	CitationJet CJ-2	525A-0198	Lill Air LLC/Frank Lill & Son Inc. Webster, NY.	N5162W
☐ N57HA	99	Citation Excel	560-5068	Wachovia Bank NA/Hawkaire, Charlotte, NC.	
☐ N57HC	02	CitationJet CJ-2	525A-0098	Bridgeport Associates Inc. Bedford, Ma.	N57HG
☐ N57HJ	76	Gulfstream 2	194	Flying Squirrel/GFS Manassas Air Services Inc. Arlington, Va	N194WA
☐ N57KW	02	Citation Excel	560-5214	Progress Energy Service Co. Raleigh, NC.	N.....
☐ N57LL	72	Citation	500-0025	Da Vinci Dental Studios Inc. West Hills, Ca.	N220W
☐ N57LN	90	BAe 125/800A	NA0464	Navellier Management Inc. Reno, Nv.	N341AP
☐ N57MC	03	Citation Bravo	550-1053	Massman Construction Co. Kansas City, Mo.	N.....
☐ N57MH	85	Learjet 55	55-113	Marriott International Inc. Washington, DC.	N236HR
☐ N57MK	89	Falcon 50	197	Klein Tools Inc. Palwaukee, Il.	N404JF
☐ N57MN	04	Falcon 2000EX EASY	50	McClatchy Newspapers Inc. Sacramento, Ca.	F-WWGO
☐ N57MQ	79	Sabre-65	465-11	Coastal Corp. Houston, Tx.	N5739
☐ N57NP	82	Gulfstream 3	340	Nicholas Price/BUMI Aviation LLC. Stuart, Fl.	N2LY
☐ N57NR	68	JetStar-731	5123	Aircraft Trading Center Inc. Tequesta, Fl.	N57NP
☐ N57PT	77	Westwind-1124	208	Thomas Aircraft Sales Inc. Mulvane, Ks.	N311DB
☐ N57RL	02	Citation Excel	560-5247	Florida Custom Coach Inc. Leesburg, Fl.	N7RL
☐ N57SF	82	Citation II	550-0402	F M Howell & Co. Elmira, NY. (was 551-0057).	N717PC
☐ N57TS	01	Learjet 31A	31A-236	Thunder Spring-Wareham LLC. Pocatello, Id.	N314DT
☐ N57TT	85	Gulfstream 3	471	Thompson Tractor Co. Birmingham, Al.	N583D
☐ N57WP	03	Citation Excel	560-5317	Weyerhaeuser Co. Tacoma, Wa.	N5269J
☐ N58	95	Learjet 60	60-057	FAA, Oklahoma City, Ok.	N50050
☐ N58AJ	85	Gulfstream 3	446	Air Sterling LLC/Richmor Aviation Inc. Columbia County, NY.	N446U
☐ N58BL	93	BAe 125/800A	8236	CDS Aviation LLC. Delray Beach, Fl.	(N39BL)
☐ N58CG	99	Falcon 900EX	47	Corning Inc. Hamilton, NY.	F-WWFO
☐ N58CW	77	Learjet 35A	35A-116	Worthington Ford of Alaska Inc. Anchorage, Ak.	N116AM
☐ N58EM	76	Learjet 35	35-046	N58EM LLC. West Columbia, SC.	VH-LJL
☐ N58FN	69	Learjet 24B	24B-184	Hampton University, Newport News, Va.	(N58FN)
☐ N58HA	00	Citation Excel	560-5099	Wachovia Bank NA/Hawkaire, Charlotte, NC.	N58XL
☐ N58HC	81	Learjet 25D	25D-341	Bankair Inc. West Columbia, SC.	XA-SAE
☐ N58HK	04	Citation Bravo	550-1086	David McClean Homes Ltd. Hawarden, UK.	N52446
☐ N58HT	81	Sabre-65	465-70	LTMC Inc. Macon, Ga.	N58CM

Reg	Yr	Type	c/n	Owner/Operator	Prev Regn

Reg	Yr	Type	c/n	Owner/Operator	Prev Regn
☐ N58JF	69	Gulfstream 2	65	Government of Democratic Republic of Congo, Kinshasa.	(N300FN)
☐ N58LC	00	Citation Excel	560-5109	Lusardi Construction Co. Carlsbad, Ca.	N561GR
☐ N58MM	79	Learjet 35A	35A-261	Aspen Base Operation Inc. Aspen, Co.	N63DH
☐ N58PM	92	BAe 125/800A	NA0472	Illinois Central Railroad Co. Chicago, Il.	N674BA
☐ N58SR	82	Learjet 55	55-058	Chrysler Aviation Inc. Van Nuys, Ca.	N129SP
☐ N58ST	99	Learjet 60	60-186	Servicios Aereos Sateca CA. Caracas, Venezuela.	N186ST
☐ N58TC	75	Citation	500-0261	LBR Aviation Leasing LLC/Riley Aviation Inc. Sturgis, Mi.	N711SF
☐ N58TS	66	JetStar-731	5079	Faith Landmark Ministries, Richmond, Va.	XA-MAZ
☐ N59	96	Learjet 60	60-080	FAA, Oklahoma City, Ok.	N8080W
☐ N59AJ	83	Gulfstream 3	413	ACG3 LLC. Helena, Mt.	N766WC
☐ N59AL	70	Learjet 24D	24D-236	Bastille Energy Corp. Oklahoma City, Ok.	N47TK
☐ N59AP	01	Gulfstream 4SP	1476	Computer Sciences Corp. El Segundo, Ca.	N476GA
☐ N59BR	02	Hawker 800XP	8599	BR Ventures Inc. Glen Burnie, Md.	N51169
☐ N59CC	73	Falcon 10	6	Vartec Properties Inc. Addison, Tx.	N32VC
☐ N59CF	90	Falcon 900B	98	Compass Foods Inc. Montvale, NJ.	(N903FJ)
☐ N59CJ	01	CitationJet CJ-2	525A-0059	DRDAN LLC/M & N Aviation Inc. San Juan, PR.	N.....
☐ N59DF	91	Citation V	560-0098	Sierra Land Group Inc. Burbank, Ca.	(N18SK)
☐ N59EC	01	Citation Excel	560-5123	JMZ LLC. Columbus, Oh.	N699BC
☐ N59FT	86	Citation III	650-0123	Citation 123 Corp. Coral Springs, Fl.	(N491SS)
☐ N59FY	81	Citation II/SP	551-0059	Fuqua Aviation LLC. Texarkana, Tx. (was 550-0397)	N59FA
☐ N59GB	82	Citation II/SP	551-0060	Tre Aviation Corp. Globe, Az.	(N60HW)
☐ N59HJ	82	Learjet 55	55-027	Hop-A-Jet Inc. Fort Lauderdale, Fl.	B-3980
☐ N59K	74	Sabre-60	306-82	Americana Aviation Inc. Albert Lea, Mn.	N60SL
☐ N59KC	96	Citation V Ultra	560-0363	KC LLC/AM AV Inc. Baltimore, Md.	N59KG
☐ N59KG	01	Citation Encore	560-0563	Krause Gentle Corp. Des Moines, Ia.	N51995
☐ N59MA	77	Citation 1/SP	501-0050	A & H Aircraft Sales Inc. Florence, Al.	N750LA
☐ N59NH	91	Citation V	560-0139	Pacific Coast Feather Co. Seattle, Wa.	(N75FV)
☐ N59TF	97	Citation V Ultra	560-0422	Teleflex Inc. Limerick, Pa.	N58RG
☐ N60AG	01	Citation Excel	560-5255	Arrowcrest Group P/L. Adelaide, SA. Australia.	N52081
☐ N60AN	97	Learjet 60	60-099	Jetride Inc. Columbus, Oh.	N212BX
☐ N60AV	79	Westwind-1124	254	Avjet Corp. Burbank, Ca.	N72HB
☐ N60BT	87	Westwind-1124	432	E E Treadaway, Houston, Tx.	N282SM
☐ N60CN	81	Falcon 50	79	Falcon Jet 50 Corp. San Juan, PR.	(N79FJ)
☐ N60EF	84	Diamond 1A	A070SA	Hooters of America Inc. Atlanta, Ga.	N84GA
☐ N60ES	94	CitationJet	525-0053	Cox & Perkins Exploration Inc. Houston, Tx.	(N603JC)
☐ N60EW	82	Citation 1/SP	501-0319	Jet Star Inc/IPM E F Weisert GmbH. Nuremberg, Germany.	N124KC
☐ N60FJ	78	Citation II/SP	551-0007	Flying J Inc, Brigham City, Ut.	YV-05CP
☐ N60GF	96	Learjet 60	60-077	EL Holdings LLC. Chicago, Il.	N227BX
☐ N60GG	93	Learjet 60	60-017	Booth Creek Management Corp. Vail, Co.	(N860AH)
☐ N60GT	58	MS 760 Paris-1A	8	David Bennett/Executive Aero,Colorado Springs, Co.	G-APRU
☐ N60GU	74	Gulfstream II SP	150	Bison Air Corp/Telford Aviation Inc. (stored Marana fm 4/03)	N319GP
☐ N60HD	97	Hawker 800XP	8334	Pelican Development LLC. Rolling Hills, Ca.	N80HD
☐ N60HM	82	Falcon 100	199	Dunbar Aviation LLC. Boston, Ma.	N96VR
☐ N60JC	70	Sabre-60	306-51	Airstream Aviation Inc. Delray Beach, Fl.	N141JA
☐ N60KF	95	Learjet 60	60-059	EL Holdings LLC. Chicago, Il.	N208BX
☐ N60KH	04	Learjet 60	60-272	Seven KH Aviation LLC. Beloit, Wi.	
☐ N60KJ	93	Learjet 60	60-005	Airtime LLC. Kenosha, Il.	(N205FX)
☐ N60LJ	04	Learjet 60	60-283	Learjet Inc. Wichita, Ks.	
☐ N60MG	94	Learjet 60	60-042	Chantilly Air Inc. Silver Spring, Md.	N90AQ
☐ N60MN	97	Learjet 60	60-100	Morris Newspaper Corp. Savannah, Ga.	N6100
☐ N60ND	75	Falcon 10	21	Shamrock Charter Inc. Fort Lauderdale, Fl.	N40WJ
☐ N60NF	00	Citation Encore	560-0562	OnFlight Inc. Cincinnati, Oh.	N5180K
☐ N60PC	00	Learjet 45	45-109	Southern Company Services Inc. Atlanta, Ga.	
☐ N60PT	99	Gulfstream 4SP	1379	Penske Jet Inc. Detroit, Mi.	N379GA
☐ N60QB	90	Citation V	560-0087	North American Jet LLC. Austin, Tx.	N600BW
☐ N60RD	93	Citation V	560-0244	Cirrus Connections Inc. Wilmington, De.	N244CV
☐ N60RL	04	Learjet 60	60-278	Learjet Inc. Wichita, Ks.	N5012K
☐ N60RU	98	Learjet 60	60-136	R & L Transfer Inc/R & L Carriers, Wilmington, Oh.	N60RL
☐ N60RY	97	Learjet 60	60-108	60-108 LLC. Fort Lauderdale, Fl.	(N220PX)
☐ N60S	81	Challenger 600S	1030	Platinum Jet Management, Fort Lauderdale, Fl.	(N196V)
☐ N60SB	04	Challenger 300	20019	Richards Group Inc. Dallas, Tx.	N319RG
☐ N60SL	78	Sabre-75A	380-60	Centurion Investments Inc. St Louis, Mo.	XA-RDY
☐ N60SR	93	Learjet 60	60-023	Bandag Inc. Muscatine, Ia.	N60SB
☐ N60TC	98	Falcon 2000	80	Tristram Colket Jr/Tekloc Enterprises, N Philadelphia, Pa.	N2CW
☐ N60TL*	89	Falcon 900	75	Capital Flight LLC. Bear, De.	N60RE
☐ N60TX	97	Learjet 60	60-097	COBAIR LLC. St Charles, Il.	N897R

Reg	Yr	Type	c/n	Owner/Operator	Prev Regn

Reg	Yr	Type	c/n	Owner/Operator	Prev Regn
☐ N60UJ	92	Learjet 60	60-007	Universal Jet Aviation Inc. Boca Raton, Fl.	(N204BX)
☐ N60VE	01	Learjet 60	60-222	Valero Energy, San Antonio, Tx.	N8088U
☐ N60WL	81	Learjet 35A	35A-382	Jet Sets Inc. Sarasota, Fl.	OE-GAF
☐ N60YC	03	Learjet 60	60-267	Quintette 1 LLC. West Palm Beach, Fl.	N50558
☐ N60ZD	99	Learjet 60	60-166	Airtime LLC. Kenosha, Wi.	N239FX
☐ N61CK	87	Citation III	650-0150	E & M Aviation LLC. Venice Municipal, Fl.	N150F
☐ N61CP*	04	Hawker 400XP	RK-402	Raytheon Aircraft Co. Wichita, Ks.	N485LX
☐ N61DF*	04	Citation Sovereign	680-0012	Cessna Aircraft Co. Wichita, Ks.	N970RC
☐ N61DN	98	Hawker 800XP	8386	Cintas Corp. Cincinnati, Oh.	N61DF
☐ N61DP	97	Learjet 60	60-122	RBS Lombard Inc. Chicago, Il.	N622LJ
☐ N61FB	74	Sabre-60	306-80	Fine Air Services Inc. Miami, Fl.	PT-KOT
☐ N61GB	02	Beechjet 400A	RK-341	N61GB LLC/Schneider National Inc. Green Bay, Wi.	N51241
☐ N61KB	97	Citation X	750-0021	W B Air One LLC. Houston, Tx.	N630M
☐ N61KW	00	Falcon 2000	137	Progress Energy Service Co. Raleigh, NC.	F-WWVM
☐ N61MA	80	Citation II	550-0176	Charter Services Inc. Mobile, Al.	(N24TR)
☐ N61SH	95	CitationJet	525-0095	Acme Research LLC. Dover, De.	(N5153K)
☐ N61SM	92	Beechjet 400A	RK-60	Superior Metal Products Inc. Lima, Oh.	N8260L
☐ N61TL	98	Citation V Ultra	560-0461	Empress Entertainment Inc. Chicago-Romeoville, Il.	N461VP
☐ N61TS	87	Falcon 900	13	Aspen Trading Corp. Miami, Fl.	(N297AP)
☐ N61VE	00	Learjet 60	60-224	Valero Energy, San Antonio, Tx.	
☐ N61WH	69	Gulfstream 2B	48	Hudson Capital Group Inc. Fort Lauderdale, Fl.	N711MC
☐ N61YP	98	CitationJet	525-0237	Air One Aviation Service LLG.	N237CJ
☐ N61ZZ	98	Learjet 60	60-128	Zulu Air Services, Greenwich, Ct.	(N660AN)
☐ N62BR	73	Citation	500-0093	Becknell Development LLC. Champaign, Il.	G-OCPI
☐ N62BX	95	Learjet 60	60-062	Bombardier Aerospace Corp. Windsor-Locks, Ct.	C-GLRS
☐ N62CH	84	Diamond 1A	A082SA	Realty Predevelopment Inc. Amarillo, Tx.	(N214PG)
☐ N62DM	72	Learjet 25B	25B-082	Butler National Inc. Newton, Ks.	N700FC
☐ N62GB	01	Citation Excel	560-5207	Graham Brothers Construction Co. Dublin, Ga.	N5076J
☐ N62GX	00	Gulfstream G200	031	RX Choice Inc/Rite Aid Corp. Harrisburg, Pa.	4X-CVH
☐ N62HM	95	Falcon 50	243	Hospital Management Associates Inc. Naples, Fl.	N724R
☐ N62MB	80	Learjet 35A	35A-282	West Bend Air Inc. West Bend, Wi.	N444CM
☐ N62ML	00	Gulfstream V	605	Gulfstream Aerospace Corp. Savannah, Ga.	N62MS
☐ N62MS	03	Gulfstream G550	5017	Melvin Simon & Assocs Inc. Indianapolis, In.	N917GA
☐ N62ND	81	Westwind-1124	379	Shaw Managed Services Inc. Baton Rouge, La.	N52FC
☐ N62NS	85	Citation S/II	S550-0072	Longhorn Aviation Inc. Jupiter, Fl.	TC-NMC
☐ N62PG	77	Learjet 36A	36A-031	Phoenix Air Group Inc. Cartersville, Ga.	N20UG
☐ N62SH*	03	CitationJet CJ-3	525B-0002	Cessna Aircraft Co. Wichita, Ks. (First flight 6 Nov 03).	N763CJ
☐ N62VE	96	Citation X	750-0004	Valero Energy, San Antonio, Tx.	N597U
☐ N62WA	96	Citation V Ultra	560-0360	Muscatine Corp. Muscatine, Ia.	N6780A
☐ N63AX	82	Learjet 55	55-063	Averitt Aviation Group Inc. Nashville, Tn.	(N63TN)
☐ N63CG	79	Citation 1/SP	501-0135	W L Paris Enterprises Inc. Louisville, Ky.	N49MP
☐ N63CR	85	Citation S/II	S550-0036	Rowe Aircraft Inc. Millington, Tn.	N63JU
☐ N63EM	73	HS 125/F400A	25272	Aviation Solutions LLC. Waterford, Mi.	N800JT
☐ N63GA	71	Learjet 24D	24D-241	Big Boys Toys Inc. Hialeah Gardens, Fl.	N363BC
☐ N63GC	89	Citation III	650-0179	ERG Aviation Inc/Ginn Development LLC. Bunnell, Fl.	N35FC
☐ N63HS	02	Gulfstream G550	5013	Air Simon Inc. Indianapolis, In.	N913GA
☐ N63JG	92	Citation V	560-0189	Jay Gee Holdings Inc. Hazleton, Pa.	N62HA
☐ N63JT	88	Citation S/II	S550-0156	Raley's, West Sacramento, Ca.	N901PV
☐ N63LB	00	Citation Bravo	550-0920	Lee Beverage Co. Oshkosh, Wi.	N5109W
☐ N63LF	96	CitationJet	525-0127	Appleton Orchard LLC. Hood River, Or.	N63LB
☐ N63LX	01	Citation Excel	560-5163	Lennox Industries Inc. Richardson, Tx.	N5166T
☐ N63MU	90	Gulfstream 4	1152	International Group Inc/SCM Assocs Inc. Penn Yan, NY.	N63M
☐ N63PP	83	Westwind-Two	394	Pogo Producing Co. Houston, Tx.	N21RA
☐ N63SE	00	Learjet 31A	31A-203	PWC Global Logistics Ltd & M H Alshaya Co.	
☐ N63TM	04	Citation Sovereign	680-0019	Cessna Aircraft Co. Wichita, Ks.	N5188N
☐ N63TS	75	Falcon 10	66	Grupo Vicini, Santo Domingo, Dominican Republic.	YV-70CP
☐ N63XG	77	Falcon 10	103	X-Gen Pharmaceuticals Inc. Islip, NY.	N26TJ
☐ N64AH	67	Jet Commander	94	Linea Aerea Puertorriquena Inc. Carlina, PR.	N94WA
☐ N64AL	87	Gulfstream 4	1013	Air Logic Sales Inc. Tampa, Fl.	N97FT
☐ N64BD	87	Falcon 900	16	Sky Aviation Corp. West Palm Beach, Fl.	VP-CBD
☐ N64BH	83	Citation 1/SP	501-0325	Pay & Save Inc. Littlefield, Tx.	N501LM
☐ N64CE	69	Learjet 24B	24B-205	Royal Air Freight Inc. Waterford, Mi.	(N721J)
☐ N64CF	82	Learjet 35A	35A-461	CF Industries Inc. Chicago, Il.	
☐ N64CP	79	Learjet 35A	35A-264	AirNet Systems Inc. Columbus, Oh. (green).	VR-CDI
☐ N64DH	66	Sabre-40R	282-52	Sunshine Aero Industries Inc. Crestview, Fl.	N282MC
☐ N64FE	87	Challenger 601-3A	5005	Omnicare Management Co. Covington, Ky.	N14GD

Reg	Yr	Type	c/n	Owner/Operator	Prev Regn
❏ N64HH	00	Learjet 45	45-087	American Industries Inc. Portland, Or.	N645HJ
❏ N64LE	95	Learjet 60	60-068	J-Air LLC. Van Nuys, Ca.	N823TR
❏ N64LX	01	Citation Excel	560-5164	Lennox Industries Inc. Richardson, Tx.	N5166U
❏ N64MA	65	Sabre-40	282-44	Chadco Aviation Inc. Dalton, Ga.	N600JS
❏ N64MP	82	Learjet 35A	35A-490	Atlantic Tele-Network Inc. St Thomas, USVI.	
❏ N64NB	92	Learjet 31A	31A-065	North Coast Aviation Inc. Pontiac, Mi.	N44SU
❏ N64PM	00	CitationJet CJ-1	525-0394	NowI LLC. Longboat Key, Fl.	N5132T.
❏ N64RT	81	Citation 1/SP	501-0191	Rubaiyat Trading Co. Birmingham, Al.	N98ME
❏ N64TF	79	Citation II	550-0064	HCE Leasing MO LLC. St Louis, Mo.	(N550TJ)
❏ N64VM	85	Beechjet 400	RJ-1	Verco Manufacturing/Nektor Industries Inc. Phoenix, Az.	
❏ N65A	73	Learjet 25B	25B-134	World Heir Inc. College Park, Ga.	N26FN
❏ N65AK	80	Sabre-65	465-35	Nelson Brothers Management Services, Birmingham, Al.	N2590E
❏ N65AR	88	Citation II	550-0585	Mountain Shadow Ventures LLC. Port Hadlock, Wa.	N89SE
❏ N65BP	91	Citation VI	650-0202	Alaska Communications Systems Group, Anchorage, Ak.	N202TJ
❏ N65BT	79	Sabre-65	465-3	Sabre 65 LLC. Kansas City, Mo.	N1CF
❏ N65CC	80	Sabre-65	465-46	Crown Controls Corp. New Bremen, Oh.	N65FF
❏ N65CE	83	Gulfstream 3	383	U S Army Corp of Engineers/Mississippi Valley Division.	83-0501
❏ N65CK	03	CitationJet CJ-2	525A-0185	Professional Flight Management LLC. Boca Raton, Fl.	N5257V
❏ N65DL	82	HS 125/700A	NA0321	Chestnut Ridge Air Ltd. NYC.	N165DL
❏ N65DV	89	Citation II	550-0624	Dole Fresh Vegetables Inc. Salinas, Ca.	N662AJ
❏ N65FA	86	BAe 125/800A	8065	Fraction Air Inc. Nashville, Tn.	N77CU
❏ N65FF	92	Challenger 601-3A	5122	Flying Fishawk LLC/FAF Manager Inc. Bedford, Ma.	N900CL
❏ N65HH	77	Sabre-65	465-1	H & H Color Lab Inc. Raytown, Mo.	(N117MN)
❏ N65JT	77	JetStar 2	5213	JWT Aircraft Holdings LLC. Phoenix, Az.	(N600JT)
❏ N65L	81	Sabre-65	465-76	Acopian Technical Co. Allentown, Pa.	
❏ N65MC	80	Sabre-65	465-36	WKC Corp. St Louis, Mo.	N424JM
❏ N65ML	81	Sabre-65	465-69	Midlifeair LLC. Benton Harbor, Mi.	N25KL
❏ N65PZ	01	CitationJet CJ-2	525A-0072	DAT-II LLC. Newark, De.	N5120U
❏ N65R	02	Gulfstream G200	072	Winn-Dixie Stores Inc. Jacksonville, Fl.	N272GA
❏ N65RA	85	Beechjet 400	RJ-9	Father & Son Aviation LLC. Georgetown, De.	N800FT
❏ N65RL	92	Citation V	560-0179	Levi, Ray & Shoup Inc. Springfield, Il.	N885M
❏ N65RZ	79	Learjet 35A	35A-236	Premier Aircraft Funding Inc. Miami, Fl.	EC-HLB
❏ N65SA	73	Citation	500-0114	Sundance Aviation Inc. Galesburg, Il.	I-AMCT
❏ N65SR	81	Sabre-65	465-54	Arrow Molded Plastics Inc. Circleville, Oh.	N1909R
❏ N65ST	02	Citation X	750-0211	REES Beehawk LLC/Beehawk Aviation Inc. Smyrna, Ga.	N954Q
❏ N65T	80	Sabre-65	465-43	Marotta Scientific Controls Inc. Montville, NJ.	N955PR
❏ N65TC	80	Sabre-65	465-30	AEC Properties LLC. Boston, Ma.	N89MM
❏ N65WH	72	Learjet 25B	25B-086	Dolphin Aviation Inc. Sarasota, Fl.	N23DB
❏ N65WS	73	Citation	500-0076	Promark Marketing & Sales Inc. Bentonville, Ar.	N500CV
❏ N65WW	81	Citation 1/SP	501-0194	Owners Jet Services Ltd. DuPage, Il.	N28JG
❏ N66AF	67	DC 9-15RC	47152	U S Department of Energy, Albuquerque, NM.	N65AF
❏ N66AM	96	CitationJet	525-0160	PCI LLC. Park Ridge, Il.	N5076J
❏ N66BE	97	CitationJet	525-0174	Apache Aviation LLC. Beaver Dam, Wi.	(N417Q)
❏ N66CF	75	Falcon 10	65	SAPI Air LLC. Hillsboro, Or.	(F-GJMA)
❏ N66DD	98	Gulfstream 4SP	1355	Duchossois Industries Inc. Palwaukee, Il.	N355GA
❏ N66EH	88	Citation S/II	S550-0158	SIT-JET Inc. Wilmington, De.	N158QS
❏ N66ES	97	CitationJet	525-0244	Starjet Air Inc/Royal Street Corp. Salt Lake City, Ut.	
❏ N66GE	80	Sabre-65	465-28	C & K Leasing Co. St Louis, Mo.	(N129BA)
❏ N66GZ	75	Sabre-60	306-99	Centurion Investments Inc. St Louis, Mo.	N66GE
❏ N66HD	87	Citation S/II	S550-0134	Harley-Davidson Sweden AB. Taeby, Sweden.	OY-GMJ
❏ N66KK	77	Learjet 35A	35A-095	Universal Pacific Investments Corp. Bend, Or.	N68UW
❏ N66LE	74	Citation Eagle	500-0170	DLJ Aviation LLC. Little Rock, Ar.	N818R
❏ N66LX	83	Westwind-Two	375	Providence Exploration & Production, Fort Smith, Ar.	N79AP
❏ N66MC	81	Citation II	550-0239	Cashman Holding LLC. Wayzata, Mn.	N4720T
❏ N66MS	81	Citation II	550-0399	Farmers Equipment Rental Inc. Fargo, ND. (was 551-0053)	(N6890C)
❏ N66MT	00	Citation Bravo	550-0913	Manatts Inc. Grinnell, Ia.	N232BC
❏ N66NJ	80	Learjet 35A	35A-296	National Jets Inc. Fort Lauderdale, Fl.	N51JA
❏ N66SG	00	Learjet 45	45-073	Woolsington Wunderbus Inc. Luton, IK.	N65U
❏ N66U	98	Citation V Ultra	560-0489	Spring Bay Aviation Inc. Ponte Vedra Beach, Fl.	
❏ N66W	02	Citation Excel	560-5320	Southern Bleacher Construction Co. Graham, Tx.	N5194J
❏ N67AS	05	390 Premier 1	RB-218	Raytheon Aircraft Co. Wichita, Ks.	
❏ N67BC	04	CitationJet CJ-2	525A-0225	Cessna Aircraft Co. Wichita, Ks.	N.....
❏ N67BK	01	Citation Bravo	550-0997	Beckley Flying Service Inc. Mount Hope, WV.	N5192E
❏ N67EL	95	Falcon 900B	153	Noble Drilling Services Inc. Houston, Tx.	N57EL
❏ N67GH	04	CitationJet CJ-2	525A-0217	Hughes & Hughes Investments Corp. Salt Lake City, Ut.	N5211F
❏ N67GW	03	Citation Encore	560-0641	Gary-Williams Energy Corp. Denver, Co.	N5270J

| Reg | Yr | Type | c/n | Owner/Operator | Prev Regn |

Reg	Yr	Type	c/n	Owner/Operator	Prev Regn
N67HB	75	Learjet 25B	25B-189	Water Soft Inc. Saxonburg, Pa.	N888DF
N67JR	66	B 727-30	18936	CityAir LLC. Van Nuys, Ca.	N18HH
N67LC	75	Falcon 10	49	AirSouth Inc. Jonesboro, Ar.	PT-LMO
N67PA	78	Learjet 35A	35A-208	67PA LLC. West Columbia, SC.	(N39DJ)
N67PC	01	Citation Bravo	550-1007	Avent LLC/Prent Corp. Janesville, Wi.	N717CB
N67PW	95	Falcon 50	248	67PW LLC. Teterboro, NJ.	N25UB
N67RX	00	Global Express	9067	Wander Inc. Morristown, NJ.	N700BK
N67TM	00	Gulfstream 4SP	1409	EMC Corp. Bedford, Ma.	N317GA
N67TW	00	Citation Excel	560-5122	TW Equipment Leasing Inc. Indianapolis, In.	N5211F
N67WB	97	Falcon 900EX	16	BDA/US Services Ltd & WRBC Transportation Inc. White Plains.	N916EX
N68AX	77	Learjet 25D	25D-216	Nader Sabouri, Lynchburg, Va.	N767SA
N68BC	93	Citation VII	650-7025	Quadion Corp. Minneapolis, Mn.	N442WJ
N68BP	68	Falcon 20C	155	Ozark Management Inc. Columbia, Mo.	N68BC
N68CB	99	Hawker 800XP	8453	Cracker Barrel Old Country Store Inc. Lebanon, Tn.	N802TA
N68CJ	96	CitationJet	525-0169	TXU Business Services Co. Dallas, Tx.	N5153K
N68CK	90	Citation V	560-0063	Koosharem Corp. Santa Barbara, Ca.	(N7FZ)
N68ED	94	Citation VI	650-0239	Betteroads Asphalt Corp. San Juan, PR.	N17QC
N68ES	01	Learjet 31A	31A-221	Premier Aviation Leasing LLC. Boise, Id.	
N68GA	75	HS 125/600A	6047	Sano Construction Corp. Whitestone, NY.	XA-RYK
N68GT	88	Falcon 100	217	Walnut Hill Cellular Telephone Co. David Wayne Airport, Tx.	F-GIFL
N68HC	00	Citation Excel	560-5103	HCA Squared LLC. Nashville, Tn.	N5218R
N68LP	01	Citation X	750-0169	Stardancer Leasing Co. Delray Beach, Fl.	N5248V
N68PC	98	Learjet 45	45-040	Southern Company Services Inc. Atlanta, Ga.	(N145MC)
N68PT	81	Westwind-1124	325	Thomas Aircraft Sales Inc. Mulvane, Ks.	N467MW
N68QB	76	Learjet 35A	35A-079	American Jet International Corp. Houston, Tx.	N500DS
N68TS	83	Citation II	550-0479	D & R Maintenance LLC. Brentwood, Tn.	N45NS
N69BH	79	Learjet 35A	35A-276	Midlantic Jet Charters Inc. Atlantic City, NJ.	N613RR
N69EC	85	Falcon 200	498	Ravenair LLC. Missoula, Mt.	N422L
N69FH	02	CitationJet CJ-2	525A-0068	AirMaryland LLC. Quincy, Ma.	N51444
N69GB*	74	Falcon 10	24	Greg Biffle Inc. Mooresville, NC.	N230RS
N69LD	85	Citation III	650-0080	McKee Foods Corp. Collegedale, Tn.	N1316E
N69LJ	94	Learjet 60	60-027	Federation International de l'Automobile,Geneva, Switzerland	N12FU
N69MT	67	JetStar-8	5107	OK Aircraft Parts Inc. Hollister, Ca. (status ?).	N7788
N69SB	03	Citation X	750-0212	Beneto Inc. Sacramento, Ca.	N4101Z
N69SW	76	Falcon 20F	356	CIT Group, Tempe, Az.	N11UF
N69VH	83	Learjet 55	55-062	Midlantic Jet Charters Inc. Atlantic City, NJ.	(N107MC)
N69WU	81	Sabre-65	465-51	JH Jet LLC. Helena, Mt.	N114LG
N69X	60	MS 760 Paris	90	AEI Fund Management Inc. St Paul, Mn.	(N5TA)
N69XW	74	Citation	500-0142	Blue Sky Jet Inc. San Diego-Montgomery, Ca.	N200GM
N70AE	99	Learjet 31A	31A-188	Allegheny Energy Service Corp. Hagerstown, Md.	
N70AG	97	Gulfstream V	522	Chargers Football LLC. San Diego, Ca.	N20HN
N70AX	78	Learjet 35A	35A-155	Averitt Air Charter Inc. Nashville, Tn.	N110AE
N70BG	77	Citation Eagle	501-0024	Centerville Aviation LLC. Kettering, Oh.	N724EA
N70BJ	92	Beechjet 400A	RK-39	Corporate Jet Partners LLC. Leesburg, Va.	N34VP
N70BR	98	Citation V Ultra	560-0478	Rosair Inc. Portland, Or.	N5095N
N70CA	75	Citation	500-0234	Scholten Roofing Co. Long Beach, Ca.	PH-CTG
N70CG	80	Citation 1/SP	501-0187	Stivers Midtown Lincoln-Mercury, Des Moines, Ia.	(N614DD)
N70CK	68	Falcon 20C	128	Michigan Air Freight LLC. Ypsilanti, Mi.	N228CK
N70EW	99	Global Express	9026	EWA Holdings LLC/East West Air Inc. Teterboro, NJ.	C-GEWV
N70HL	76	Sabre-60	306-102	LaValle Developers Inc. Youngstown, Oh.	N265TJ
N70HS	95	Falcon 900B	140	Linsang Logistics LLC. Manassas, Va.	VR-CES
N70JF	79	Learjet 25D	25D-278	White Industries Inc. Bates City, Mo. (status ?).	
N70KW	94	CitationJet	525-0050	Wilair Inc. Raleigh, NC.	N2634E
N70LF	96	Falcon 900EX	9	G C I Aviation/Gary Comer Inc. Chicago-O'Hare, Wi.	N909FJ
N70LJ*	78	Learjet 36A	36A-044	Jet ICU Leasing Inc. Ozona, Fl.	N286AB
N70MG	73	Citation	500-0063	Billionaire Business Jets LLC. Las Vegas, Nv.	OO-RST
N70NB	81	Citation 1/SP	501-0209	Synfuel Management LLC. Lexington, Ky.	N98RG
N70NE	87	BAe 125/800A	NA0407	Berkshire Leasing LLC. Pittsfield, Ma.	N552BA
N70PC	01	Learjet 45	45-172	Southern Company Services Inc. Atlanta, Ga.	
N70PL	80	Falcon 20F-5B	436	Pelican Leasing Inc. Little Rock, Ar.	N436RB
N70PS	98	Global Express	9012	American International Group, Teterboro, NJ.	C-GDGY
N70QB	81	HS 125/700A	NA0289	River Run Projects LLC. Nashua, NH.	N802RC
N70SK	70	Learjet 25	25-049	S K Logistics Inc. Jacksonville, Fl.	N70HJ
N70TH	92	Falcon 900B	117	Sony Aviation Inc. Teterboro, NJ.	N476FJ
N70TS	75	Citation	500-0281	Starbird Inc. Maitland, Fl.	N62TW
N70TT	01	Gulfstream G200	045	CJE Inc. Fort Worth, Tx.	N107GX
Reg	*Yr*	*Type*	*c/n*	*Owner/Operator*	*Prev Regn*

Reg	Yr	Type	c/n	Owner/Operator	Prev Regn
☐ N70VT	84	Diamond 1A	A085SA	Bec-Faye LLC. Greenville, NC.	(N911JJ)
☐ N70X	77	HS 125/700A	NA0207	Spectrum Air Services Inc. Atlanta, Ga.	N33RH
☐ N70XA	78	Citation II	550-0008	A D Aviation Ltd. Staverton, UK.	N70X
☐ N70XX	83	Diamond 1	A052SA	Apparelsoft Inc. Seeneca, SC.	I-FRAB
☐ N71BD	00	Gulfstream 4SP	1415	JJSA Aviation LLC. San Jose, Ca.	N415GA
☐ N71CC	73	Sabre-60A	306-71	Osprey Flight Management, Houston, Tx.	N1028Y
☐ N71CK	77	Learjet 36A	36A-035	Michigan Air Freight LLC. Ypsilanti, Mi.	VH-BIB
☐ N71FB	00	Learjet 31A	31A-205	Roxbury Technologies Inc. Zurich, Switzerland.	VP-CFB
☐ N71FS	94	Astra-1125SP	071	Pivotal Aviation 1 LLC. Phoenix, Az.	N60AJ
☐ N71GA	82	Citation II	550-0444	Green Aviation Corp. White Plains, NY.	N47SW
☐ N71GH	83	Diamond 1A	A071SA	Fox Air Inc. Jacksonville, Fl.	N70GA
☐ N71HR	01	CitationJet CJ-1	525-0494	Helderberg Aviation Inc. Schenectady, NY.	N.....
☐ N71KV	03	390 Premier 1	RB-71	KVOG LLC/KV Oil & Gas Inc. Lexington, Ky.	N4471P
☐ N71L	82	Citation 1/SP	501-0242	Lindair Inc. Sarasota, Fl.	N500BK
☐ N71LG	75	Learjet 35	35-019	Bombardier Capital Inc. Colchester, Vt.	N19NW
☐ N71LP	79	Citation 1/SP	501-0120	Star Aviators LLC. Princeton, WV.	OY-CPW
☐ N71LU*	83	Citation III	650-0019	Liberty University Inc. Lynchburg, Va.	N707MS
☐ N71M	76	Falcon 10	88	BAC Inc. Jackson, Wy.	F-GHER
☐ N71MT	92	BAe 125/800A	8230	Michelin North America Inc. Greenville, SC.	N678BA
☐ N71NK	98	Citation VII	650-7106	Flint Ink Corp. Detroit, Mi.	N716QS
☐ N71NP	01	Challenger 604	5504	Nationwide Mutual Insurance Co. Columbus, Oh.	C-GLYH
☐ N71PG	75	Learjet 36	36-013	Phoenix Air Group Inc. Cartersville, Ga.	D-CBRD
☐ N71RP	99	Citation X	750-0093	Time Warner Inc. Ronkonkoma, NY.	N993QS
☐ N71TJ	68	Falcon 20C-5	166	Bombardier Capital Inc. Colchester, Vt.	N33DY
☐ N71TS	76	Falcon 10	75	Ginju LLC. Alexandria, Va.	N97DX
☐ N71VR	96	Gulfstream 4SP	1290	Yona Venetian LLC/Las Vegas Sands Inc. Las Vegas, Nv.	N730BA
☐ N72AM	84	Citation S/II	S550-0004	Avondale Mills Inc. Monroe, Ga.	N554CA
☐ N72AV	78	Learjet 36A	36A-040	Cornua Legis Inc. Honolulu, Hi.	N500SV
☐ N72AX	81	Learjet 35A	35A-419	Omni Air International Inc. Tulsa, Ok.	N35SM
☐ N72BD	00	Gulfstream 4SP	1420	JJSA Aviation LLC. San Jose, Ca.	N420GA
☐ N72CK	78	Learjet 35A	35A-165	Kitty Hawk Charters Inc. Morristown, Tn.	N16BJ
☐ N72DA	77	Learjet 35A	35A-098	Duncan Aviation Inc. Lincoln, Ne.	(N998DJ)
☐ N72DJ	73	Citation	500-0072	General Aviation Services LLC. Lake Zurich, Il.	N114LA
☐ N72EL	86	Astra-1125	018	Liquid Aviation Inc. San Diego, Ca.	N72FL
☐ N72FC	95	Citation V Ultra	560-0347	Best Aviation Inc. Baldwin, Ga.	N5268V
☐ N72FD	99	Citation X	750-0072	D & F Partners LLC. Wilmington, De.	XA-VER
☐ N72GH	03	Hawker 400XP	RK-370	The Palmer Team Inc. Sacramento, Ca.	(N470CW)
☐ N72GW	76	JetStar 2	5205	Safari Air Inc. Easton, Md.	N454JB
☐ N72HG	86	Beechjet 400	RJ-11	Hantz Air LLC. Detroit-Willow Run, Mi. (was A1011SA).	N111BA
☐ N72JF	77	Learjet 35A	35A-088	AirNet Systems Inc. Columbus, Oh. (blue).	OE-GBR
☐ N72JW	00	CitationJet CJ-1	525-0406	James Walker Aircraft LLC. Lynchburg, Va.	N5124F
☐ N72LG	79	Learjet 35A	35A-228	Northwestern Arctic Air Inc. Anchorage, Ak.	N100NW
☐ N72LL	79	Learjet 35A	35A-275	Jet Management Inc. Sanford, Fl.	N235SC
☐ N72NP	98	Challenger 604	5385	Nationwide Mutual Insurance Co. Columbus, Oh.	C-GLXD
☐ N72PS	87	Falcon 900	18	American International Group, Teterboro, NJ.	N413FJ
☐ N72RK	94	Gulfstream 4SP	1248	Reebok International Ltd. Bedford, Ma.	N244DS
☐ N72SG	04	Citation Excel XLS	560-5508	SIG Aviation LLC/Strickland Insurance Group, Goldsboro, NC.	N.....
☐ N72TQ	64	Jet Commander	4	Liberty Scrap Metal, West Palm Beach, Fl. (status ?).	N72TQ
☐ N72VJ	80	Citation 1/SP	501-0149	JVB LLC. San Diego, Ca.	N96FP
☐ N72WC	85	Learjet 25G	25G-371	Wells Cargo Inc. Elkhart, In.	N4ZB
☐ N72WS	97	Falcon 900EX	14	American International Group, Teterboro, NJ.	F-WWFN
☐ N72WY	98	Challenger 604	5394	Fort Mitchell Construction LLC. Fort Mitchell, Ky.	N141DL
☐ N73B	76	Falcon 10	79	The Kroger Co. Cincinnati, Oh.	N160FJ
☐ N73CE	65	Learjet 23	23-068	Clark Enterprises Inc. Kula, Hi.	XB-GRR
☐ N73CK*	77	Learjet 35A	35A-092	Kalitta Charters LLC. Detroit-Willow Run, Mi.	N39WA
☐ N73CL	82	Westwind-Two	365	Polar Bear Express LLC. Las Vegas, Nv.	N2BG
☐ N73DJ	79	Learjet 25D	25D-273	Water Street Aviation LLC. Olympia, Wa.	N321AS
☐ N73DR	73	Sabre-40A	282-120	Dove Air Inc. Hendersonville, NC.	N73HP
☐ N73GH	97	Falcon 50EX	261	TCBY Ents/Hickinbotham Investments Inc. Little Rock, Ar.	(N97FJ)
☐ N73GP	86	Learjet 55B	55B-127	Novartis Services Inc. NYC.	HZ-AM2
☐ N73HM	88	Citation III	650-0169	Conway Air Corp. Chesterfield, Mo.	N749DC
☐ N73KH	93	Citation V	560-0220	Killam & Hurd, San Antonio, Tx.	N23UB
☐ N73M	98	Gulfstream V	547	3M Co. St Paul, Mn.	N647GA
☐ N73ME	01	Citation X	750-0155	Mountain Enterprises Inc. Lexington, Ky.	N551AM
☐ N73MP	74	Citation	500-0164	McLain Plumbing & Electric Service Inc. Philadelphia, Ms.	(N164GJ)
☐ N73PJ	03	390 Premier 1	RB-101	Phillips & Jordan Inc. Knoxville, Tn.	N101PN

Reg	Yr	Type	c/n	Owner/Operator	Prev Regn
N73RP	98	Gulfstream V	529	Time Warner Inc. Ronkonkoma, NY.	N529GA
N73ST	79	Citation II	550-0376	S & T Marketing Services LLC. Brooklyn, Mn. (was 551-0022).	N30EJ
N73TJ	79	Sabre-65	465-12	Tyringham Ridge Inc. Marlow, NH.	N529SC
N73UP	99	Hawker 800XP	8473	UnumProvident Corp. Chattanooga, Tn.	
N73WF	88	BAe 125/800A	NA0429	R-5 Holdings LLC. Bethlehem, Pa.	N106GC
N74A	68	Gulfstream 2B	36	MDA-Missile Defence Agency, Tulsa-R L Jones, Ok.	N901KB
N74FH	79	Citation Eagle	501-0138	Flybylight LLC. Carlsbad, Ca.	N501CE
N74FS	90	Falcon 900	85	Fayez Serofim & Co. Houston, Tx.	N461FJ
N74GR	82	Challenger 601	3001	GAR Aviation Ltd. San Antonio, Tx.	N789DR
N74HH	69	Gulfstream II SP	74	C & A Aircraft LLC. Scottsdale, Az.	N74TJ
N74HR	84	Citation 1/SP	501-0677	GAR Aircraft Holdings Inc. Houston, Tx.	N54CG
N74JA	82	Challenger 600S	1060	J A Interests Inc. Versailles, Ky.	N22AZ
N74JE	85	Citation S/II	S550-0074	John Eaves, Jackson, Ms.	N274PG
N74LL	74	Citation Eagle	500-0212	University Air LLC. Seekonk, Ma.	N92B
N74LM	85	Citation S/II	S550-0041	Blessey Travel Inc. Big Sky, Mt.	N74BJ
N74ND	86	BAe 125/800A	8063	Tulsair Beechcraft Inc. Tulsa, Ok.	N684C
N74NP	03	Hawker 800XP	8631	Nationwide Mutual Insurance Co. Columbus, Oh.	N631XP
N74PC	01	Hawker 800XP	8567	PNC Financial Services Group Inc. Allegheny County, Pa.	N50667
N74RD	78	Learjet 25D	25D-260	Private Jets LLC. Oklahoma City, Ok.	N43783
N74RP*	04	Gulfstream G550	5058	Gulfstream Aerospace Corp. Savannah, Ga.	N958GA
N74RQ	72	Gulfstream II SP	113	Cable Holdings Aviation Corp. White Plains, NY.	N74RT
N74RT	78	Gulfstream 2B	219	CHI Aviation Inc. Tompkins County, NY.	(N575E)
N74TS	82	Falcon 50	106	Aero Toy Store LLC. Fort Lauderdale, Fl.	N9300C
N74VC	80	Sabre-65	465-17	Aero-Auto Sales & Leasing Inc. Kent, Oh.	N32290
N74VF	88	Citation III	650-0156	Vernon Faulconer Inc. Lafayette, La.	N209A
N74ZC	04	Challenger 300	20018	Ziegler Inc. Minneapolis, Mn.	N84ZC
N75AX	79	Learjet 25D	25D-270	Aeroflight II Inc. Chicago, Il.	N123CG
N75B	91	Citation V	560-0156	Siegel-Robert Inc. St Louis, Mo.	N560L
N75BC	86	Westwind-1124	426	James Higgins MD Inc. Tulsa, Ok.	N426WW
N75BL	74	Learjet 25C	25C-156	Air Flight Inc/Spreng Enterprises Inc. Daytona Beach, Fl.	N613SZ
N75BS	74	Sabre-75A	380-12	Centurion Investments Inc. St Louis, Mo.	(N4WJ)
N75CC	92	Gulfstream 4	1182	Crown Controls Corp. New Bremen, Oh.	N202LS
N75CK	78	Learjet 25D	25D-256	Michigan Air Freight LLC. Ypsilanti, Mi.	N6LL
N75FC	01	CitationJet CJ-1	525-0455	Flying Crown Inc. Brooklyn, Oh.	N5183V
N75GM	74	Citation	500-0169	Aircraft Guaranty Title LLC. Houston, Tx.	(N676WE)
N75GP	86	Learjet 55B	55B-129	Gerber Products Co. Fremont, Mi.	
N75GW	75	Citation	500-0257	Heartland Aviation LLC. Scott, Ar.	N75FN
N75HS	97	Citation X	750-0037	Rex Realty Co. St Louis, Mo.	N51160
N75HU	00	Citation Excel	560-5119	Juno Industries Inc/Hughes Aviation, Orlando, Fl.	N357WC
N75MC	86	Citation S/II	S550-0109	Leche Inc. Key Biscayne, Fl.	(N50SL)
N75MT	92	BAe 125/800A	8231	Michelin North America Inc. Greenville, SC.	N685BA
N75PP	02	CitationJet CJ-2	525A-0132	Precision Punch Corp. Hartford-Brainard, Ct.	N5211F
N75RJ	91	Citation II	550-0692	K T & C Ltd. West Columbia, SC.	N692TT
N75RL	01	Beechjet 400A	RK-312	RLI Corp. Peoria, Il.	N5012U
N75RP	98	Gulfstream V	528	AOL Time Warner Inc. Ronkonkoma, NY.	N80RP
N75TE	99	Learjet 45	45-057	Temple Inland Forest Products Corp. Austin, Tx.	
N75TP	02	Citation Excel	560-5261	Crimson Excel LLC. Tuscaloosa, Al.	N5091J
N75VC	81	Sabre-65	465-71	NCI Operating Corp. Houston, Tx.	N75GL
N75WE	84	Falcon 50	152	Fisher Scientific International Inc. Portsmouth, NH.	N75W
N75WP	97	Citation V Ultra	560-0449	Salt River Project Ag/Power District, Phoenix, Az,	N555WK
N75Z	96	Citation V Ultra	560-0345	Dan's Classic Cars Inc. Grand Rapids, Mi.	(N560NS)
N75ZA	81	Citation II	550-0214	Laboratory Corp of America Holdings, Burlington, NC.	N75Z
N76AM	79	Falcon 10	157	JMK Aviation Trust, Fort Worth, Tx.	(N450CT)
N76AS	82	Citation II	550-0432	T & S Aircraft, Huntersville, NC.	I-ASAZ
N76AX	78	Learjet 25D	25D-254	Thomas Thornton, Austin, Tx.	I-AVJE
N76CK	68	Learjet 25	25-020	Kalitta Charters LLC. Detroit-Willow Run, Mi.	N500JS
N76CS	02	Hawker 800XP	8595	CSX Transportation Inc. Jacksonville, Fl.	N61495
N76ER	82	Westwind-Two	369	Air Ambulance Support Programmes Inc. Houston, Tx.	N85WC
N76FD	88	Falcon 900	41	Grindstone Aviation LLC. Lafayette Hill, Pa.	N404FF
N76HG	66	JetStar-731	5076	Pro Flights Inc. Henderson, Nv.	N69ME
N76MB	76	Falcon 10	83	Impact International Inc. Reno, Nv.	N67TJ
N76MC	93	Beechjet 400A	RK-58	Max Cap Corp. Hoffman Estates, Il.	PT-WHC
N76QF	99	Learjet 25D	60-156	State Farm Insurance Companies, Bloomington, Il.	N76SF
N76RP	00	Gulfstream 4SP	1440	AOL Time Warner Inc. Ronkonkoma, NY.	N997AG
N76TF	97	Citation V Ultra	560-0431	Teleflex Inc. Limerick, Pa.	N560JP
N76TJ*	76	HS 125/F600A	6070	Tennessee Jet Aircraft Sales Inc. Smyrna, Tn.	N365SB

Reg	Yr	Type	c/n	Owner/Operator	Prev Regn

Reg	Yr	Type	c/n	Owner/Operator	Prev Regn
N77BT	68	JetStar-731	5113	World Harvest Church Inc. Columbus, Oh.	N1962J
N77C	79	JetStar 2	5232	Trenton Foods/Parn Aviation Corp. Dover, De.	N90QP
N77CE	87	Falcon 900B	12	MidAmerican Energy Co. Des Moines, Ia.	N991AS
N77CP	98	Gulfstream V	565	Pfizer Inc. Mercer County Airport, NJ.	N460GA
N77CS	03	Hawker 800XP	8620	CSX Transportation Inc. Jacksonville, Fl.	N620XP
N77D*	95	Gulfstream 4SP	1266	FACE Aviation LLC. Allegheny County, Pa.	N77DY
N77DB	01	CitationJet CJ-1	525-0443	D'Arrigo Bros of California, Salinas, Ca.	N443CJ
N77DD	92	Citation II	550-0695	Davis Aviation, Belmar, NJ.	N7851M
N77FD	82	Citation 1/SP	501-0250	Ingles Markets Inc. Asheville, NC.	
N77FK	98	Gulfstream 4SP	1357	K Services Inc. Teterboro, NJ.	N357GA
N77HF	94	Citation VII	650-7036	Taft Sales & Leasing LLC. Dallas, Tx.	N95HF
N77HW	66	JetStar-6	5080	Delta Omni Corp. Corona, Ca.	N914P
N77LA	85	BAe 125/800A	8029	L2 Aviation Group/Aviation Charter Services, Indianapolis.	N600HS
N77LX	95	Citation VII	650-7051	Lexicon Inc. Little Rock, Ar.	N965JC
N77MR	77	Learjet 24E	24E-351	Goldenwings Inc. Bloomington, Il.	(N94BD)
N77ND	78	Citation II	550-0005	University of North Dakota, Grand Forks, ND.	OE-GKP
N77NJ	90	Learjet 35A	35A-658	National Jets Inc. Fort Lauderdale, Fl.	N162EM
N77NR	89	Citation V	560-0009	Nix, Patterson & Roach LLP. Longview-Gregg County, Tx.	N77HU
N77NT	81	Falcon 50	77	Nortel Networks Ltd. Nashville, Tn.	N992
N77PA	85	Citation S/II	S550-0051	Fleegs Air, Hamilton, Mt.	N132WC
N77PR	81	Citation II	550-0211	Triangle Consortium Corp. Kalispell, Mt.	N77PH
N77PY	94	Learjet 31A	31A-089	Wal-Mart Stores Inc. Rogers, Ar.	N77PH
N77SF	79	Falcon 10	141	Seneca Foods Corp. Penn Yan, NY.	N900D
N77TC	95	Hawker 800	8275	The Timken Co. Canton, Oh.	N905H
N77TE	82	Falcon 50	110	Temple Inland Forest Products Corp. Austin, Tx.	VR-BJA
N77UW	98	Citation Excel	560-5005	Meisenbach LLC. Seattle, Wa.	N166MB
N77VJ	65	Learjet 23	23-041	MTW Aerospace Inc. Montgomery, Al. (status ?)	C-GDDB
N77VR	99	CitationJet	525-0344	Ultimate Aviation Inc. Palwaukee, Il.	
N77WD	70	HS 125/731	NA748	Marlin Holdings Marketing LLC. Key West, Fl.	N62TW
N77WL	90	Gulfstream 4	1140	Presley CMR Inc. Santa Ana, Ca.	N827JM
N78AP	84	Citation III	650-0056	Apothecas Aviation LLC. Oyster Bay, NY.	N56JV
N78BR	97	Citation VII	650-7078	Newport Leasing Inc. Heathrow, Fl.	(N84NG)
N78CK	81	Citation II	550-0319	Marks Aviation LLC. Mobile, Al.	N76CK
N78GJ	80	Westwind-1124	310	Mid Oaks Investments LLC. Buffalo Grove, Il.	D-CBBD
N78LT	81	Falcon 50	75	Level 3 Communications Inc. Broomfield, Co.	N850CA
N78MC	77	Learjet 35A	35A-117	Midlantic Jet Charters Inc. Atlantic City, NJ.	N3155B
N78MD	01	Citation Bravo	550-0970	Montana Dakota Utilities Co. Bismarck, ND.	N367BP
N78PR	94	Learjet 31A	31A-090	Wal-Mart Stores Inc. Rogers, Ar.	N78PH
N78SD	00	Challenger 604	5469	Constructora Sambil CA. Caracas, Venezuela.	N469RC
N79AD	00	Global Express	9058	Arthur S DeMoss Foundation Inc. West Palm Beach, Fl.	N700AD
N79AN	93	Challenger 601-3R	5140	ElanAir Inc/Heritage Flight, Burlington, Vt.	N79AD
N79BK	79	Citation 1/SP	501-0111	Boyd Air Corp. Dallas, Tx.	N59WP
N79EL	98	Beechjet 400A	RK-214	G Kirkham/D F S Furniture Co. East Midlands, UK.	
N79FT	78	Citation 1/SP	501-0079	Foxtrot Tango LLC. Ramona, Ca.	N250GM
N79HM	93	Beechjet 400A	RK-70	TFC Investments LLC. Houston, Tx.	N73HM
N79KF	86	Citation III	650-0118	Klaussner Corporate Services Inc. Asheboro, NC.	N770MR
N79LB	04	CitationJet CJ-3	525B-0019	Cessna Aircraft Co. Wichita, Ks.	N.....
N79LC	79	Westwind-1124	257	Wilmington Aero Ventures Inc. Wilmington, De.	N124UF
N79NP	89	BAe 125/800A	NA0441	Raytheon Aircraft Co. Wichita, Ks.	N75NP
N79PF	00	Citation Excel	560-5151	Principal Life Insurance Co. Des Moines, Ia.	N5147B
N79PG	04	Citation Sovereign	680-0018	Cessna Aircraft Co. Wichita, Ks.	N.....
N79PM	98	Citation V Ultra	560-0459	Principal Life Insurance Co. Des Moines, Ia.	N5162W
N79RP	93	Gulfstream 4SP	1220	Time Warner Inc. Ronkonkoma, NY.	N449GA
N79RS	73	Citation	500-0107	Frank Harrison Haynes, Gainesville, Ga.	N40RW
N79SE	00	Learjet 31A	31A-206	Southeast Air Transportation Inc. Montgomery, Al.	N5000E
N79SF	78	Learjet 36A	36A-041	Phoenix Air Group Inc. Cartersville, Ga.	
N79TJ	79	Falcon 10	148	Pannar P/L. Rand, RSA.	N103PJ
N79TS	78	HS 125/700A	NA0233	Ocala Foxtrotter Ranch LLC. Aventura, Fl.	C-GABX
N80A	98	Gulfstream 4SP	1348	United States Steel Corp. Pittsburgh, Pa.	N348GA
N80AB	92	Citation V	560-0169	C5 LLC/IJAMMM Inc. Las Vegas, Nv.	N6888C
N80AJ	73	Citation	500-0100	PDQ Business Travel LLC. Countyline, Ok.	(N58BT)
N80AP	75	Learjet 24D	24D-312	Air Ambulance Professionals Inc. Fort Lauderdale, Fl.	N312NA
N80AR	81	Learjet 35A	35A-454	HME Enterprises Inc. Boca Raton, Fl.	(N80KR)
N80AT	00	Gulfstream 4SP	1410	Taubman Enterprises Inc. Waterford, Mi.	N318GA
N80AW	80	Citation II	550-0186	Arrow Industries Inc. Anaheim, Ca.	YV-187CP
N80BR	90	Gulfstream 4	1132	Scout Aviation LLC. NYC.	N604M

Reg	Yr	Type	c/n	Owner/Operator	Prev Regn
☐ N80C	02	CitationJet CJ-2	525A-0104	Eighty Charlie LLC. Eagle, Co.	N.....
☐ N80CJ	80	Citation 1/SP	501-0159	DJD Management Inc. Louisville, Ky.	N8189J
☐ N80CK	74	Learjet 24D	24D-309	Michigan Air Freight LLC. Ypsilanti, Mi.	N789AA
☐ N80DX	91	Beechjet 400A	RK-26	Data Exchange Corp. Camarillo, Ca.	N8097V
☐ N80E	04	Hawker 800XP	8680	United States Steel Corp. Pittsburgh, Pa.	N680XP
☐ N80EL	72	Learjet 25B	25B-092	Lanter Eye Care & Laser Surgery PC. Indianapolis, In.	N60DK
☐ N80F	00	Falcon 900EX	76	Anheuser Busch Companies Inc. St Louis, Mo.	F-WLJV
☐ N80FB	01	Hawker 800XP	8572	Action Transport Inc. Tupelo, Ms.	N5072L
☐ N80FD	79	Westwind-1124	260	Fisher Development Co. Lancaster, Pa.	(N503RH)
☐ N80GJ	88	BAe 125/800A	8136	Meurice Aviation Inc. Lawrenceville, Ga.	I-SDFG
☐ N80GM	80	Citation II	550-0147	Avcorp Inc. St Louis, Mo.	(N155JK)
☐ N80GR	02	Citation Encore	560-0616	Oil & Gas Rental Services Inc. Patterson, La.	N616CE
☐ N80HD	02	Hawker 800XP	8609	Harley-Davidson Motor Co.Milqwaukee, Wi.	N60159
☐ N80L	83	Gulfstream 3	406	United States Steel Corp. Pittsburgh, Pa,	N356GA
☐ N80LA	82	Citation II	550-0441	L Wood Aviation Inc. Austin, Tx.	G-RVHT
☐ N80LP	02	Citation Excel	560-5249	JEP Leasing LLC. Las Vegas, Nv.	N5096S
☐ N80PG	76	Learjet 35	35-063	Phoenix Air Group Inc. Cartersville, Ga.	N663CA
☐ N80PK	99	Hawker 800XP	8442	HEH Corp/HEH Nashville, Nashville, Tn.	N442XP
☐ N80R	02	Gulfstream G200	074	Winn-Dixie Stores Inc. Jacksonville, Fl.	N274GA
☐ N80RN	81	Sabre-65	465-53	Denison Jet Sales Corp. Landrum, SC.	N80R
☐ N80SF	81	Citation 1/SP	501-0189	501-0189 LLC. West Columbia, SC.	(N500SS)
☐ N80SL	79	Citation 1/SP	501-0294	Dr John Pate MD. El Paso, Tx. (was 500-0391).	N8EH
☐ N80TS	87	Beechjet 400	RJ-34	King Air 203 Leasing Inc. Caracas, Venezuela.	N7EY
☐ N80X	99	Citation Excel	560-5054	Capital City Press, Baton Rouge, La.	N1306V
☐ N81AX	79	Learjet 25D	25D-279	Med Air LLC. Lawrenceville, Ga.	N41ZP
☐ N81EB	77	Citation 1/SP	501-0003	T C Mueller Oil & Gas/TCM Air Inc. Fort Smith, Ar.	N781L
☐ N81ER	02	Citation Bravo	550-1015	R & J Aviation LLC. Farmington, Mi.	N5253S
☐ N81FR	76	Learjet 35A	35A-081	AirNet Systems Inc. Columbus, Oh.	N118DA
☐ N81KA	78	HS 125/700A	NA0227	Royster-Clark Inc. NYC.	N10CZ
☐ N81MR	86	Learjet 35A	35A-622	Wal-Mart Stores Inc. Rogers, Ar.	N610R
☐ N81MW	79	Learjet 25D	25D-277	Rocketown Tours Inc/I'll Lead You Home LLC. Nashville, Tn.	N321GL
☐ N81P	79	Falcon 10	153	Pilot Corp. McGhee-Tyson, Tn.	N344A
☐ N81PJ	61	MS 760 Paris-1R	81	EPS Aviation Stages Inc. Kelly, Wy.	No 81
☐ N81QH	83	Learjet 35A	35A-500	JAJALE Inc. Dallas, Tx.	N81CH
☐ N81RA	97	CitationJet	525-0194	Four Five Alpha LLC. Greenwich, Ct.	(N194VP)
☐ N81RR	79	Gulfstream 2TT	246	Geneva International Ltd. Arlington, Va.	N14LT
☐ N81SH	00	Citation Excel	560-5101	The Conair Group Inc. Pittsburgh, Pa.	N88845
☐ N81SN	98	Falcon 900EX	41	Amrash Aviation LLC. Greenville-Spartanburg, SC.	N5737
☐ N81TJ	90	Beechjet 400A	RK-14	Trimfoot Aviation/Crown Diversified Industries Inc. St Louis	(N414RK)
☐ N81TT	99	Galaxy-1126	006	Homelife Communities Group, Atlanta, Ga.	N7AU
☐ N81TX	76	Falcon 10	81	TXI Aviation Inc. Dallas, Tx.	N700BD
☐ N82A	89	Gulfstream 4	1068	Prudential Insurance Co. Newark, NJ.	N90AE
☐ N82AE	00	CitationJet CJ-1	525-0412	EDCO Products Inc. Hopkins, Mn.	N5161J
☐ N82AF	74	Sabre-80A	380-21	Aeropac Charters Inc. Manchester, NH.	N647JP
☐ N82AJ	78	Citation 1/SP	501-0282	European Air Service Inc.Vienna, Austria. (was 500-0376).	XA-SQX
☐ N82AX	80	Learjet 25D	25D-301	Tropical Jets of SRQ Inc. Sarasota, Fl.	N25CZ
☐ N82BE	99	Astra-1125SPX	113	BEF Aviation Co. Columbus, Oh.	(N297GA)
☐ N82BG	99	Citation X	750-0082	Double L T Aviation Inc. Rancho Santa Fe, Ca.	(N242LT)
☐ N82CA	69	HS 125/731	NA730	Lilly Beter Aviation PartnersInc. Boca Raton, Fl.	(N101HS)
☐ N82CG	80	Falcon 10	167	Joe Kirk Fulton, Lubbock, Tx.	(N111WW)
☐ N82CW	98	Challenger 604	5395	Costco Wholesale Inc. Seattle, Wa.	N606CC
☐ N82DT	78	Citation 1/SP	501-0289	W-II Investments Inc. Greenville, SC. (was 500-0375).	N501NZ
☐ N82EA	95	Hawker 800XP	8283	Aquila LLC. Bloomington, In.	N283BX
☐ N82GK	03	Hawker 800XP	8618	AGK82 LLC. Jersey, Channel Islands.	N618XP
☐ N82KK	97	Learjet 60	60-095	Krispy Kreme Doughnut Corp. Winston-Salem, NC. 'Donut 1'	(N82KD)
☐ N82MA	99	Citation Bravo	550-0891	R & J Aviation LLC. Farmington, Mi.	
☐ N82P	81	Citation 1/SP	501-0208	Pink Jeep Tours Inc. Sedona, Az.	(N25M)
☐ N82PJ	68	Falcon 20D	177	Peaks Aviation Services Inc. Denison, Tx.	N41BP
☐ N82RP	92	Falcon 900B	116	Rich Aviation Inc. Buffalo, NY.	N5VN
☐ N82ST	81	Falcon 50	85	Pioneer Private Aviation of Delaware, Minneapolis, Mn.	N254DV
☐ N82TN	78	Falcon 20F-5	384	Inland Paperboard & Packaging Inc. Austin, Tx. (status ?).	N120DE
☐ N82TS	74	Learjet 25B	25B-154	Lear 25 LLC. West Columbia, SC.	N47DK
☐ N82XP	89	BAe 125/800A	NA0447	SML LLC/Rouse Co. Baltimore, Md.	N95AE
☐ N83BG	82	Diamond 1	A018SA	THF Aviation LLC. St Louis, Mo.	(N831TJ)
☐ N83CG	83	Diamond 1A	A032SA	Advantage Jet Partners Inc. Albany, Ga.	(N996DR)
☐ N83CK	74	Learjet 25B	25B-183	Michigan Air Freight LLC. Ypsilanti, Mi.	N5LL

Reg	Yr	Type	c/n	Owner/Operator	Prev Regn
☐ N83CP	01	Gulfstream V	635	Pfizer Inc. Mercer County Airport, NJ.	N522GA
☐ N83CW	01	Gulfstream V	649	Costco Wholesale Inc. Seattle, Wa.	N649GA
☐ N83DC	00	CitationJet CJ-1	525-0380	Cor Group Inc. Strathmore, AB. Canada.	N525GB
☐ N83DM	81	Citation 1/SP	501-0227	DDM Holdings Inc. Wilmington, De.	N47CF
☐ N83EJ	99	Galaxy-1126	009	Gulfstream Aerospace LP. Dallas-Love, Tx.	N849GA
☐ N83FJ	81	Falcon 50	74	Civic Center Corp/Anheuser Busch, Chesterfield, Mo.	F-WZHA
☐ N83FN	75	Learjet 36	36-007	Flight Capital LLC. Madison, Ms.	N83DM
☐ N83GK	95	Citation VII	650-7050	Atlantic City LLC. Cincinnati-Lunken, Oh.	N33GK
☐ N83LJ	65	Learjet 23	23-076	AJM Airplane Co. Naples, Fl.	N50PJ
☐ N83M	98	Gulfstream V	557	3M Co. St Paul, Mn.	N657GA
☐ N83MD	80	HS 125/700A	NA0286	Mad Dog Aviation Inc. Seattle, Wa.	(N501MD)
☐ N83PP	85	Gulfstream 3	464	Park Place Entertainment Corp. Las Vegas, Nv.	N83AG
☐ N83RE	92	Citation V	560-0183	Van Ness Plastic Molding Co. Clifton, NJ.	N83RR
☐ N83SA	82	Diamond 1A	A030SA	Galaxy Air Services Inc. Sikeston, Mo.	(N800GC)
☐ N83SD	00	Citation Excel	560-5091	Wesdix Corp. Northbrook, Il.	N560CH
☐ N83SG	82	Westwind-Two	368	R & S Aircraft Investments LLC. Houston, Tx.	N368MD
☐ N83TE	75	Gulfstream 2B	156	Yellowstone Aviation LLC. Bozeman, Mt.	N525JT
☐ N83TF	02	Citation Encore	560-0636	Tomco II LLC. Nashville, Tn.	N.....
☐ N83TY	99	Falcon 50EX	288	Viper Aviation LLC. Englewood, Co.	N33TY
☐ N83WM	82	Learjet 55	55-043	Norwalk Aircraft Corp. Hackensack, NJ.	(N455EC)
☐ N84EA	83	Citation II	550-0484	Eagle Aviation Inc. Columbia-Metropolitan, SC.	N1253N
☐ N84EC	84	Citation S/II	S550-0014	American Aviation LLC. Eugene, Or.	N777AM
☐ N84FG	97	CitationJet	525-0192	Jet Motion LLC. Raleigh, NC.	N51444
☐ N84FM	02	390 Premier 1	RB-30	Fugate Aviation Inc. Wichita, Ks.	N84ML
☐ N84FN	74	Learjet 36	36-002	Flight Capital LLC. Madison, Ms.	N84DM
☐ N84GC	84	Citation II	550-0493	TVPX Inc. Concord, Ma.	N84AW
☐ N84GF*	82	Citation 1/SP	501-0254	Fisher Sand & Gravel Co. Glendive, Mt.	N66BK
☐ N84GV	99	Gulfstream V	584	EDS Information Services LLC. Dallas, Tx.	N584GA
☐ N84HP	81	Falcon 50	56	Hewlett-Packard Co. San Jose, Ca.	(N844J)
☐ N84NW	91	Falcon 50	216	Execujet Inc. Eighty-Four, Pa.	N56SN
☐ N84PH	84	Citation III	650-0062	Harron Aircraft LLC. Wilmington, De.	N475M
☐ N84PJ	98	Citation X	750-0048	Hampton Airways Inc. Sellersburg, In.	N5135A
☐ N84TJ	81	Falcon 10	188	Lakeview Transportation Corp. Los Angeles, Ca.	I-TFLY
☐ N84UP	99	Hawker 800XP	8484	UnumProvident Corp. Chattanooga, Tn.	
☐ N85	93	Challenger 601-3R	5138	FAA, Oklahoma City, Ok.	N138CC
☐ N85BN	85	Beechjet 400	RJ-7	Patterson Capital Corp. Los Angeles, Ca. (was A1007SA).	N25BN
☐ N85CC	96	Hawker 800XP	8307	New Bremen Investments Inc. Wapakoneta, Oh.	N307AD
☐ N85CL	01	Falcon 50EX	319	Cleveland Browns Transportation LLC. Berea, Oh.	(N319EX)
☐ N85D	00	Global Express	9078	Dole Foods Inc. Van Nuys, Ca.	N700AH
☐ N85EB	98	Citation V Ultra	560-0492	Elkhart Brass Manufacturing Co. Elkhart, In.	N41VR
☐ N85F	96	Falcon 50EX	253	JetCorp Aircraft Sales Inc. Chesterfield, Mo.	PT-WSC
☐ N85HH	80	HS 125/700A	7107	Highlandview Inc. Dallas, Tx.	(N38HH)
☐ N85HP	86	Falcon 50	163	Hewlett-Packard Co. San Jose, Ca.	(N854W)
☐ N85HS	69	Sabre-60	306-23	Anderson Aviation LLC. Kansas City, Mo.	N68MA
☐ N85JV	02	CitationJet CJ-2	525A-0085	AMI LLC/Amama LLC. Allegheny County, Pa.	N5185J
☐ N85JW	67	Jet Commander	95	Constellation Airways Inc. Sugarland, Tx.	CP-2259
☐ N85KH	85	BAe 125/800B	8028	SAN Services LLC. Cleveland, Oh.	G-TSAM
☐ N85M	01	Gulfstream V	648	MBNA Corp. Greater Wilmington, De.	N648GA
☐ N85MG*	85	BAe 125/800A	8035	Apogee Medical Management Inc. Eugene, Or.	N835CW
☐ N85MS	84	Citation III	650-0075	MS Advisors 1 LLC. Houston, Tx.	(N100MS)
☐ N85PL	01	390 Premier 1	RB-55	Lucky Dog Investments Inc. Newport Beach, Ca.	N390PL
☐ N85PT	80	Westwind-1124	285	Westwind Air LLC. Oklahoma City, Ok.	XA-LIJ
☐ N85SV	80	Learjet 35A	35A-347	Randall Aviation Inc. Fort Lauderdale, Fl.	OE-GNP
☐ N85TW	78	Learjet 25D	25D-251	Sierra American Corp. Addison, Tx.	TG-VOC
☐ N85V	99	Gulfstream V	595	Dart Container Corp. Sarasota, Fl.	(N595GV)
☐ N85VP	90	Citation V	560-0085	PHC-Aviation/Province Healthcare Co. Brentwood, Tn.	N891M
☐ N85WD	86	Gulfstream 4	1008	Week-Davies Aviation Inc. West Palm Beach, Fl.	N119R
☐ N86	94	Challenger 601-3R	5167	FAA, Oklahoma City, Ok.	N151CC
☐ N86BA	84	Citation S/II	S550-0001	Unlimited Aircraft Service Inc. San Juan, PR.	N151DD
☐ N86CE	94	Citation V Ultra	560-0265	Coca-Cola Enterprises Inc. Atlanta-Fulton County, Ga.	LV-WIJ
☐ N86CP	74	Sabre-60	306-76	Halford R Price, Phoenix, Az.	(N760SA)
☐ N86CW	95	Citation V Ultra	560-0342	Price Co/Costco Wholesale Inc. Seattle, Wa.	(N82CW)
☐ N86LA	93	CitationJet	525-0012	L O Aviation LLC. Little Rock, Ar.	N12PA
☐ N86PC	85	Citation S/II	S550-0017	C L Swanson Corp. Madison, Wi.	N88GD
☐ N86SG	82	Citation II	550-0350	Seymour Grubman, Beverly Hills, Ca.	
☐ N86SK	00	CitationJet CJ-1	525-0420	Aerotomas LLC. Billings, Mt.	N96SK

Reg	Yr	Type	c/n	Owner/Operator	Prev Regn
N86TW	97	Falcon 2000	43	Tallwood Management LLC. San Jose, Ca.	N43FJ
N86VP	85	Citation III	650-0089	Jet One LLC. Waterford, Mi.	(N229J)
N87	95	Challenger 601-3R	5190	FAA, Oklahoma City, Ok.	N190EK
N87BA	87	Citation S/II	S550-0131	Mechanical Tool & Engineering Co. Rockford, Il.	D-CHJH
N87GA	93	Citation V	560-0228	Gantt Aviation Inc. Georgetown, Tx.	XA-SLA
N87GJ	85	Westwind-Two	422	Purcell Co. Diamonhead, Ms.	N87GS
N87GS	79	Gulfstream 2	258	Shinn Enterprises Inc. New Orleans, La.	N437H
N87JK	91	Citation V	560-0115	Allied Home Mortgage Corp. Christensted, USVI.	N91YC
N87NY	61	MS 760 Paris	87	Your Aircraft Source LLC. Calhoun, Ga.	87
N87PT	80	Citation II	550-0174	Hargray Holdings Corp. Hilton Head, SC.	N666WW
N87SF	79	Citation II	550-0096	Seneca Foods Corp. Penn Yan, NY.	N30UC
N87SL	02	Citation X	750-0174	Schweitzer Engineering Laboratories, Pullman, Wa.	N174CX
N87TD	68	Gulfstream II SP	39	Pavair Inc. Van Nuys, Ca.	N87HB
N87TH	81	Falcon 10	178	David Donnini, Champaign, Il.	N79BP
N87TN	78	Falcon 20F-5B	385	Inland Paperboard & Packaging Inc. Austin, Tx.	N120WH
N88	04	Challenger 604	5588	FAA, Oklahoma City, Ok.	C-GLXU
N88AD	00	CitationJet CJ-1	525-0404	Lincoln Park Leasing LLC. Salem, Or.	(N746JB)
N88AF	02	Learjet 45	45-205	Lakeview (CPC) Air LLC. Kenosha, Wi.	N5052K
N88AJ	99	Citation Bravo	550-0885	A & J Management Services Inc. Menomonee Falls, Wi.	N820JM
N88BF	81	Sabre-65	465-60	Western Jet LLC. Milton, Wa.	(N688WS)
N88BG	76	Learjet 35A	35A-090	AirNet Systems Inc. Columbus, Oh. (yellow).	I-FIMI
N88BY	74	Learjet 25B	25B-168	Lear 25 LLC. West Columbia, SC.	N88BT
N88DD	02	Falcon 2000	204	Duchossois Industries Inc. Palwaukee, Il.	N2317
N88DJ	89	Citation III	650-0167	Dale Jarrett Inc. Conover, NC.	N832CC
N88DU	67	HS 125/731	25153	Hawker 25153 Inc. Fort Lauderdale, Fl.	N88DJ
N88EJ	99	Citation X	750-0088	Qualcomm Inc. San Diego, Ca.	N5130J
N88EL	03	390 Premier 1	RB-83	EL 88 Corp. Seattle, Wa.	N6183G
N88ER	01	390 Premier 1	RB-17	DP 64 LLC. Scottsdale, Az.	N88EL
N88EX	97	Citation V Ultra	560-0433	American Woodmark Corp. Winchester, Va.	N33LX
N88HD	03	Hawker 800XP	8616	Harley-Davidson Motor Co. Milwaukee, Wi.	N61216
N88HP*	99	Citation Excel	560-5050	Aero Advantage Inc. North Adams, Ma.	N184G
N88KC	03	CitationJet CJ-2	525A-0157	Victory Management Leasing Inc. Detroit, Mi.	N5270E
N88LC	03	Falcon 900EX EASY	137	Lowe's Companies Inc. North Wilkesboro, NC.	F-WWF0
N88LD	97	CitationJet	525-0181	M G A Inc. Dothan, Al.	N181CJ
N88LJ	74	Learjet 24D	24D-290	Aviation Pioneers LLC. Charleston, WV.	N24TK
N88MF	90	Astra-1125SP	048	Murfam Enterprises LLC. Rose Hill, NC.	N1125V
N88MM	02	390 Premier 1	RB-44	McMahans Furniture Co of Las Vegas, Carlsbad, Ca.	N5044X
N88MX	02	Falcon 2000	183	Maxim Aviation Co. Jeffco Airport, Co.	N2265
N88NJ	79	Learjet 25D	25D-294	National Jets Inc. Fort Lauderdale, Fl.	N161RA
N88NM	88	Citation II	550-0590	Star Aircraft LLC. Raleigh, NC.	N673CA
N88NW	76	Citation	500-0309	Peninsula Development Services Inc. Turnwater, Wa.	N791MA
N88TB	77	Citation 1/SP	501-0002	Gateway Aviation Inc. Carlsbad, Ca.	(N501WK)
N88UA	88	Beechjet 400	RJ-49	Razorback Foundation Inc. Fayetteville, Ar.	N1549J
N88V	99	Learjet 60	60-155	Jacura Delaware Inc. Highland Beach, Fl.	
N88WC	92	Citation V	560-0157	West Coast Charters LLC. Santa Ana, Ca.	N502TS
N88WR	98	BBJ-79U	29441	Seaflight Aviation Ltd. Athens, Greece.	N88WZ
N88WU	98	Citation Excel	560-5039	Barristair LC/Provost & Umphrey Law Firm, Beaumont, Tx.	N39JV
N88ZL	65	B 707-330B	18928	LOWA London-Washington Ltd. Boston, Ma.	N5381X
N89AC	84	Citation III	650-0029	Americredit Aviation LLC. Reno, Nv.	(N81TT)
N89AJ	75	Citation	500-0272	Asjet Aviation Inc. Wilmington, De.	N30JN
N89AM	83	Westwind-Two	389	Atherton & Murphy Investment Co. Tulsa-R L Jones, Ok.	N812G
N89BM	93	Falcon 50	237	Exchange Properties Corp. Bellevue, Wa.	N74BJ
N89D	79	Citation II	550-0056	Tidewater Jet Aviation LLC. Norfolk, Va.	N444FJ
N89ES	69	Learjet 24B	24B-197	EBJ Aviation LLC. Veradale, Wa.	N24FU
N89GA	80	Citation II	550-0122	Southern Aircraft Leasing Inc. Port Orange, Fl.	C-GCUL
N89GN	80	HS 125/700A	NA0272	Celtic Aviation Inc. Charleston, SC.	N77D
N89HB	89	Learjet 31	31-010	Hab-Air Inc/Venture Jets Inc. Lititz, Pa.	N311TS
N89HS	97	Astra-1125SPX	089	Axiom Intermediaries LLC. Stoney Creek, NC.	N918MK
N89LS	89	Citation II	550-0623	Les Schwab Warehouse Center Inc. Prineville, Or.	(N1255L)
N89MD	02	Citation Encore	560-0612	FutureSource Capital Corp. Bismarck, ND.	N5260U
N89MF	80	Citation 1/SP	501-0193	DM Farms of Rose Hill LLC. Rose Hill, NC.	N45MK
N89NC	04	Falcon 50EX	337	National City Corp. Cleveland, Oh.	N50FJ
N89RP	81	Learjet 35A	35A-410	Rich Aviation Inc. Buffalo, NY.	N820RP
N89TC	75	Learjet 35	35-026	West Knob Air LLC. Wilmington, De.	N54754
N89TJ	71	Gulfstream II SP	103	Bombardier Capital Corp. Colchester, Vt.	(N103WJ)
N90AH	75	Learjet 35	35-036	Cinnebar Solutions Inc. Winston-Salem, NC.	N76GP

Reg	Yr	Type	c/n	Owner/Operator	Prev Regn
☐ N90AJ	90	Astra-1125SP	052	Navajo Refining Co. Dallas, Tx.	
☐ N90AM	99	Gulfstream V	592	Really Quiet LLC. Mount Olive, NJ.	N592GA
☐ N90AR	93	Challenger 601-3R	5137	Elite Aviation LLC. Van Nuys, Ca.	N137CL
☐ N90BA	90	Learjet 31	31-018	Blackfriars Aviation LLC/Venture Jets Inc. Lititz, Pa.	(N20LL)
☐ N90BJ	92	Citation II	550-0710	Golden Shamrock Associates LLC. North Platte, Ne.	N510VP
☐ N90BL	91	Citation II	550-0682	Bourland & Leverich Aviation Inc. Pampa, Tx.	N682CJ
☐ N90CF	00	Citation Excel	560-5080	Columbia Forest Products Aviation Inc. Portland, Or.	N52141
☐ N90CJ	02	CitationJet CJ-2	525A-0149	Sunbelt Finance Inc. Jonesboro, Ar.	N.....
☐ N90EW	99	Global Express	9039	EWA Holdings LLC/East West Air Inc. San Jose, Ca.	N700GT
☐ N90FB	02	Hawker 800XP	8613	Action Transport Inc. Tupelo, Ms.	
☐ N90FF	80	HS 125/700A	NA0279	Dodson Aviation Inc. Wonderboom, RSA.	N1VQ
☐ N90FJ	65	Citation S/II	S550-0065	Flying J Inc. Brigham City, Ut.	N995DC
☐ N90JJ	88	Citation II	550-0571	Dan's Classic Cars Inc. Grand Rapids, Mi.	(N12990)
☐ N90KC	81	Westwind-Two	339	WFBNW NA. Salt Lake City, Ut.	N74AG
☐ N90LC	74	Falcon 10	23	GSO America Inc/L-Corp. Columbus, Oh.	N20WP
☐ N90MA	80	Citation II	550-0103	H C Paffenroth Inc. Palwaukee, II.	XA-JEZ
☐ N90MC	98	Learjet 60	60-130	Stoneridge Inc/Levitz Group Inc. Youngstown, Oh.	N630LJ
☐ N90NB	02	Citation Encore	560-0634	NBTY Inc. Bohemia, NY.	N5254Y
☐ N90NE	83	Learjet 55	55-075	FLC Co LP. Cleveland, Oh.	N55GH
☐ N90NF	01	Citation X	750-0170	OnFlight Inc. Cincinnati, Oh.	N5060K
☐ N90PT	83	Citation II	550-0465	Plummer Pontiac Cadillac GMC, Lodi, Ca.	N551WJ
☐ N90R	01	BBJ-7EL	32775	Swiflite Aircraft Corp. Van Nuys, Ca.	N376BJ
☐ N90TH	99	Falcon 900C	180	Sony Aviation Inc. Teterboro, NJ.	F-WWFX
☐ N90UG	00	Learjet 45	45-115	Universal Underwriters Service Corp. Kansas City, Mo.	
☐ N90WA	90	Learjet 31	31-028	Wal-Mart Stores Inc. Rogers, Ar.	
☐ N90WR	75	Learjet 35	35-022	AeroVision International LLC. Muskegon, Mi.	OY-BLG
☐ N90Z	82	Citation II	550-0336	Northern Jet, Iron Mountain, Mi.	N6830Z
☐ N91AG	02	Citation Encore	560-0606	Monsanto Co. St Louis, Mo.	N606CE
☐ N91AP	79	Citation 1/SP	501-0117	Smith Air Ltd. Hurst, Tx.	LV-MZG
☐ N91B	80	Citation II	550-0194	Beckett Enterprises/Scott Fetzer Co. Lakewood, Oh.	N88723
☐ N91BZ	80	Sabre-65	465-19	General Foam Plastics Corp. Mount Gilead, NC.	N65RC
☐ N91CH	85	BAe 125/800A	8030	CNC Aircraft Inc. Louisville, Ky.	N10WF
☐ N91CW	98	Gulfstream V	543	Costco Wholesale Inc. Seattle, Wa.	N643GA
☐ N91DP	93	Learjet 31A	31A-079	Pratt Industries (USA) Inc. Conyers, Ga.	N41DP
☐ N91HK	01	Hawker 800XP	8578	Mueller East Inc. Palm Beach International, Fl.	N50378
☐ N91KH	89	Challenger 601-3A	5038	Rhema Bible Church, Tulsa, Ok.	N78PP
☐ N91KL	03	Gulfstream G300	1507	L & L Manufacturing Co. Van Nuys, Ca.	N307GA
☐ N91KP	72	HS 125/600A	6003	Dr Paul Madison, Michigan City, In.	N91KH
☐ N91LA	03	Gulfstream G550	5027	Leucadia Aviation Inc. Salt Lake City, Ut.	N927GA
☐ N91LE	96	Learjet 60	60-091	Lone Star Steakhouse & Saloon Inc. Wichita, Ks.	N896R
☐ N91MK	81	Westwind-Two	324	Magnificent Frigate Aircraft LLC. Houston, Tx.	C-FCEJ
☐ N91ML	87	Citation S/II	S550-0132	Cherokee Aviation LLC. Louisville, Ky.	N91ME
☐ N91MS	81	Citation 1/SP	501-0173	TEC Equipment Inc. Portland, Or.	N25GT
☐ N91NA	77	Gulfstream 2B	198	Bopper Airways LLC/Indianapolis Colts Inc. Indianapolis, In.	N91LA
☐ N91PB	82	Falcon 100	198	Gulf Aire II Inc. Gulfport, Ms.	N1PB
☐ N91PN	72	Learjet 25B	25B-091	Aero Nash Inc. Tucson, Az.	VR-CCH
☐ N91SA	84	Westwind-Two	420	Geneva Woods Pharmacy Inc. Anchorage, Ak.	N420W
☐ N92AE	96	Gulfstream 4SP	1301	American Express Co. Stewart, NY.	N433GA
☐ N92B	83	Citation II	550-0471	Austin Air LLC. Cleveland, Oh.	(N623KC)
☐ N92BD	88	Citation II	550-0588	Southern Aviation Group Inc. Olive Branch, Ms.	N255CC
☐ N92BE	78	Citation 1/SP	501-0098	White Industries Inc. Bates City, Mo.	HB-VIC
☐ N92BL	77	Citation 1/SP	501-0026	B & B Aircraft LC. Jonesboro, Ar.	N92CC
☐ N92DE	96	Citation V Ultra	560-0391	Desert Eagle Distributing, El Paso, Tx.	N391CV
☐ N92FT	02	Hawker 800XP	8598	Rocky Mountain Aviation Inc. Santa Barbara, Ca.	(N800JA)
☐ N92JC	86	Citation S/II	S550-0115	The First W D Co. Rockford, II.	N92JT
☐ N92LA	02	Gulfstream G550	5002	Leucadia Aviation Inc/Baxter Investment LLC. NYC.	N550GA
☐ N92ME	85	Citation S/II	S550-0044	Old Dominion Freight Lines Inc. High Point, NC.	N92ME
☐ N92MG	82	Learjet 55	55-025	RDM Commerce Inc & Wilsonart International Inc. Temple, Tx.	N57FM
☐ N92ND	97	CitationJet	525-0186	Atlantic Aero Inc. Greensboro, NC.	N186CJ
☐ N92SM	73	Citation	500-0124	Standridge Color Corp. Social Circle, Ga.	N8FC
☐ N92SS	96	Citation V Ultra	560-0388	Southern States Co-operative Inc. Richmond, Va.	N5269A
☐ N92TS	75	Learjet 35	35-035	Lear 35-035 Holdings Inc. Fort Lauderdale, Fl.	N350TS
☐ N92UG	92	Learjet 31A	31A-050	Universal Underwriters Service Corp. Kansas City, Mo.	
☐ N92UP	97	Hawker 800XP	8309	Allyson Aviation LLC. Camarillo, Ca.	N5735
☐ N93AE	96	Gulfstream 4SP	1302	American Express Co. Stewart, NY.	(N98AE)
☐ N93AK	03	CitationJet CJ-2	525A-0181	Kennedy Rice Dryers Inc. Mer Rouge, La.	N5218T

| Reg | Yr | Type | c/n | Owner/Operator | Prev Regn |

Reg	Yr	Type	c/n	Owner/Operator	Prev Regn
N93AT	87	Gulfstream 4	1020	ASG/Tessler Aviation Leasing Corp. Jackson, Wy.	N9300
N93CL	85	Citation III	650-0074	Command Air LLC. Cahokia, Il.	(N194DQ)
N93CV	93	Citation V	560-0239	Rosebriar Transportation Inc. Dallas, Tx.	(N560RB)
N93DW	88	Challenger 601-3A	5025	Air Orange Inc. Orange County, Ca.	N11TK
N93EA	90	Citation V	560-0093	Eagle Aviation Inc. West Columbia, SC.	F-GKJL
N93GH	95	Falcon 2000	6	Allstate Insurance Co. Palwaukee, Il.	F-WQBL
N93GR	87	Falcon 900	24	Dumont Associates Inc. Morris Plains, NJ.	(N202WR)
N93KE	81	Westwind-1124	316	CU2 LLC/Copper Sales Inc. Anoka, Mn.	VH-ASR
N93LE	84	Learjet 35A	35A-592	La Stella Corp. Pueblo, Co.	N45KK
N93M	99	Gulfstream V	567	3M Co. St Paul, Mn.	N467GA
N93PE*	02	CitationJet CJ-2	525A-0093	Preco Electronics Inc. Boise, Id.	N96SK
N93S	01	Citation X	750-0189	U S Bank NA. St Paul, Mn.	N51984
N93SC	67	Jet Commander	90	Dodson International Parts Inc. Rantoul, Ks.	N1121E
N93SK	91	Learjet 31	31-031	SK Logistics Inc. Jacksonville, Fl.	N878MA
N93TS	71	HS 125/F400A	25264	Aero Toy Store LLC. Fort Lauderdale, Fl.	(N264TS)
N94AA	80	Learjet 35A	35A-295	AirNet Systems Inc. Columbus, Oh.	PT-LAA
N94AE	96	Gulfstream 4SP	1307	American Express Co. Stewart, NY.	N443GA
N94AF	77	Learjet 35A	35A-094	Ameriflight Inc. Burbank, Ca.	(N35PF)
N94AJ	72	Citation	500-0024	B & M Aviation LLC. Fairhope, Al.	VH-ICN
N94AL	01	CitationJet CJ-1	525-0432	Lima Mike Inc. Scottsdale, Az.	N51342
N94CK	99	Learjet 45	45-066	Kirkland Aviation Inc. Jackson, Tn.	
N94FL	84	Gulfstream 3	424	Texas Aviation Sales & Leasing LLC. Dallas, Tx.	N228G
N94GP	81	Learjet 35A	35A-411	Ridge Air LLC. Northbrook, Il.	PT-LBY
N94HE	94	Beechjet 400A	RK-89	Hughes-Ergon Co. Jackson, Ms.	N1560G
N94JT	86	BAe 125/800A	8071	LTJ LLC. Menlo Park, Ca.	N789LT
N94LD	83	Diamond 1A	A073SA	Chickasaw Nation, Ada, Ok.	N94LH
N94LH	96	Beechjet 400A	RK-112	Cameron Communications Corp. Sulphur, La.	N3272L
N94LT	96	Gulfstream 4SP	1313	Lucent Technologies Inc. Morristown, NJ.	N455GA
N94MZ	95	CitationJet	525-0094	Cessna Aircraft Co. Wichita, Ks.	(N51522)
N94RL	77	Learjet 35A	35A-096	LeTourneau Inc. Longview, Tx.	N96FA
N94SF*	79	Gulfstream 2TT	250	Share Force Two LLC. Orlando, Fl.	N309EL
N94TX	93	Citation V	560-0247	A & D Aircraft Corp. Manchester, NH.	
N94VP	90	Citation V	560-0094	Newco Leasing LLC. West Bend, Wi.	N1827S
N95AE	99	Gulfstream V	562	American Express Co. Stewart, NY.	N662GA
N95AG	96	Learjet 60	60-079	Delta Airelite Business Jets Inc. Cincinnati, Oh.	N319LJ
N95BD	77	JetStar 2	5208	Reinalt-Thomas Corp. Scottsdale, Az.	N38BG
N95BS	98	CitationJet	525-0283	Ferris Manufacturing Corp. Hinsdale, Il.	
N95CC	93	Citation VII	650-7030	Cessna Finance Corp. Wichita, Ks.	(N703VP)
N95CK	02	CitationJet CJ-1	525-0493	Southern Container Management Corp. Islip, NY.	N65CK
N95CM	81	HS 125/700A	NA0309	Crossmark Holdings Inc. Plano, Tx.	N309WM
N95EB	82	Challenger 600	1062	EBJ Aviation Holdings Inc. Norwell, Ma.	N68SD
N95FA	95	Beechjet 400A	RK-99	Regions Financial Corp. Birmingham, Al.	N3199Q
N95HC	94	Falcon 50	244	Harsco Corp. New Cumberland, Pa.	N50FJ
N95JK	80	Westwind-1124	283	McGriff, Seibels & Williams Inc. Birmingham, Al.	N17UC
N95NB	03	Citation Encore	560-0644	National Beef Packing LLC. Kansas City, Mo.	N8140S
N95RX	93	Citation VII	650-7035	Lyndy Aviation Inc. West Palm Beach, Fl.	PT-WLC
N95SJ	69	Gulfstream 2B	64	New World Aircraft LLC. Allentown, Pa.	N43RJ
N95TX	94	Citation VII	650-7037	Textron Inc. T F Green Airport, RI.	N737CC
N95UP	03	Hawker 800XP	8639	Colonial Companies Inc. Chattanooga, Tn.	N639XP
N95WK	84	Learjet 55	55-099	Cole/TDI Aviation LLC. White Plains, NY.	N17GL
N95XL	00	Citation Excel	560-5095	Sikeston Financial Corp. Panama City, Panama.	N5135A
N96	89	BAe 125/C-29A	8134	FAA, Oklahoma City, Ok.	88-0270
N96AX	85	Learjet 35A	35A-608	Conquest Air LLC. Sewickley, Pa.	N14T
N96CJ	02	CitationJet CJ-2	525A-0096	InnCal LLC. Stockton, Ca.	N5223D
N96CP	87	Citation III	650-0139	First American Corp. Santa Ana, Ca.	N4EG
N96DS	94	Challenger 601-3R	5146	SGI Air Holdings LLC/DLS Air LLC. Denver, Co.	N137MB
N96FB	73	Citation	500-0094	Delta Wings Inc. Carson City, Nv.	N80GB
N96FL	98	Astra-1125SPX	109	Doritos/Pepsico Inc. Addison, Tx.	
N96FN	78	Learjet 35A	35A-186	Flight Capital LLC. Madison, Ms.	N96DM
N96FT	01	Hawker 800XP	8568	Rocky Mountain Aviation Inc. Santa Barbara, Ca.	N4468K
N96G	01	CitationJet CJ-2	525A-0018	Reading Bakery Systems, Robesonia, Pa.	N5148N
N96GS	85	Learjet 35A	35A-606	Wings Service LP. Wilmington, De.	N3WP
N96JA	77	Gulfstream II SP	213	Jordan Industries-SLC/JI Aviation Inc. Deerfield, Il.	(N96BK)
N96LC	84	Citation 1/SP	501-0683	Attorney's Air Travel Inc. Atlanta, Ga.	(N49TA)
N96MR	81	Gulfstream 3	324	CityAir LLC. San Francisco, Ca.	N67JR
N96MT	96	Citation VII	650-7065	Windway Capital Corp. Sheboygan, Wi.	N650W

Reg	Yr	Type	c/n	Owner/Operator	Prev Regn

Reg	Yr	Type	c/n	Owner/Operator	Prev Regn
N96NB	04	Citation Encore	560-0673	John R Miller Enterprises LLC. Sula, Mt.	N5245U
N96NC	02	390 Premier 1	RB-86	Air Roxanne LLC. Rocky Mount, NC.	(N390TA)
N96RE	81	Sabre-65	465-52	Admiral Beverage Corp. Worland, Wy.	N500E
N96RX	98	Citation X	750-0044	Highland Leasing Corp. Woonsocket, RI.	N5103J
N96SG	65	HS 125/1A-522	25060	Gulf Air Group Corp. Houston, Tx.	XB-CXZ
N96TM	79	Westwind-1124	275	Wings of West Virginia LLC. Parkersburg, WV.	N6TM
N96TX	98	Citation X	750-0069	Textron Inc. T F Green Airport, RI.	N100FR
N96UT	89	Falcon 50	192	MidAmerican Energy Co. Des Moines, Ia.	N96LT
N97	89	BAe 125/C-29A	8154	FAA, Oklahoma City, Ok.	88-0272
N97AL	88	Citation III	650-0155	Cardinal Aviation LC. Charlottesville, Va.	N788NB
N97BG	82	Citation II	550-0428	Chancellor Services LLC. Grants Pass, Or.	N107WV
N97BH	95	Citation V Ultra	560-0290	Air Finance Corp. Van Nuys, Ca.	N5145P
N97CC	85	Citation S/II	S550-0045	Cite Investments LLC. Raleigh, NC.	T9-BIH
N97CE*	78	Learjet 35A	35A-203	CSE Aviation LLC/Electro Enterprises Inc. Oklahoma City, Ok.	N203RW
N97CJ	02	CitationJet CJ-2	525A-0097	Cessna Aircraft Co. Wichita, Ks.	N.....
N97DD	85	Citation III	650-0071	Bunker Aircraft Management Inc. Auburn, In.	N297DD
N97DK	98	Citation X	750-0035	Emerald Air Co. Oak Brook, Il.	N5071M
N97DQ	02	Global Express	9095	Egret Management LLC. NYC.	HB-IUJ
N97EM	83	Citation II	550-0481	Express Messenger Systems Inc. Phoenix, Az. (was 551-0481).	N481VP
N97FL	98	Astra-1125SPX	110	Pepsico Inc. Addison, Tx.	
N97FN	67	Learjet 25	25-003	Hampton University, Newport News, Va.	N97DM
N97FT	04	Gulfstream G450	4008	Fidelity National Financial, Jacksonville, Fl.	N608GA
N97LE	89	Learjet 35A	35A-648	La Stella Corp. Pueblo, Co.	N648J
N97PJ	62	MS 760 Paris-1R	97	Kenneth Holland, Santa Clarita, Ca.	No 97
N97SK	87	Citation S/II	S550-0127	73SK Corp. Wilmington, De.	N874JM
N97VF	96	CitationJet	525-0171	AMSCO Transportation inc. Ponca City, Ok.	N5153Z
N97VN	98	Citation Excel	560-5007	Veda Air LLC. London, Ky.	N83RR
N97WJ	67	Falcon 20C	101	J P Aviation Inc. Raleigh-Durham, NC.	N342F
N98	89	BAe 125/C-29A	8156	FAA, Oklahoma City, Ok.	88-0273
N98AC	02	Falcon 50EX	329	Allen Canning Co. Siloam Springs, Ar.	(N50FJ)
N98AG	99	Challenger 604	5402	J & S Service & Investment Ltd. Warsaw, Poland.	N14SP
N98AV	81	Citation 1/SP	501-0177	Luis Alvarez MD. PC. Lafayette, La.	N457CS
N98BL	95	Learjet 60	60-061	Devonwood LLC. Durham, NC.	(N63BL)
N98BM	76	Westwind-1124	193	Integrated Flight Resources Inc. Sugar Grove, Il.	N515LG
N98CG	74	Learjet 24D	24D-289	Memphis Aircraft Sales Inc. Memphis, Tn.	N289G
N98E	91	Citation V	560-0103	Cytex Plastics Inc. Houston, Tx.	(N67989)
N98FT	77	HS 125/700A	NA0216	Rocky Mountain Aviation Inc. Santa Barbara, Ca.	(N197FT)
N98JV	98	Learjet 60	60-135	Southern Plastics Inc/JVE Corp. Longview, Tx.	N135LJ
N98LC	76	Learjet 35A	35A-077	AirNet Systems Inc. Columbus, Oh.	ZS-NRZ
N98LT	95	Gulfstream 4SP	1278	Lucent Technologies Inc. Morristown, NJ.	VR-CTA
N98NX	93	Falcon 900B	128	Nextel Aviation Inc. Dulles, Va.	N11LK
N98Q	72	Citation	500-0040	Tri-State Care Flight LLC. Bullhead City, Az.	N600WM
N98RS	74	Learjet 25XR	25XR-148	Stern Holdings Inc. Dallas, Tx.	(N98JA)
N98XS	95	Citation VII	650-7058	XSEED Aviation LLC. Chicago-Du Page, Il.	N625CC
N99BB	96	Citation X	750-0005	Harris Air Inc. Logan, Ut.	N5263S
N99CJ	99	CitationJet	525-0333	Acme Air Inc. Columbia, SC.	
N99CK	80	Citation 1/SP	501-0153	Bingham Leasing LLC. Jackson, Tn.	(N484CS)
N99CN	81	Citation II	550-0396	Servicios Aeronauticos Sucre, Venezuela. (was 551-0065)	N99DE
N99FN	76	Learjet 35A	35A-071	RANAS, Nowra, NSW, Australia.	N199CJ
N99GA	92	Gulfstream 4	1198	Viad Corp. Phoenix, Az.	N425GA
N99GK	03	Learjet 40	45-2008	Gold Key Aviation Inc. Woody Creek, Co.	N2408
N99JB	99	CitationJet	525-0352	Jeff Burton Auto Sports Inc. Cornelius, NC.	N5185V
N99JD	82	Falcon 50	129	Central Financial Services Inc. Golden Valley, Mn.	N4903W
N99KW	03	Challenger 604	5564	Florida Wings Inc. Boca Raton, Fl.	N564BA
N99MC	74	Learjet 25B	25B-182	Air Ambulance Aircraft Inc. Sarasota, Fl.	N225JL
N99NJ	77	Learjet 25XR	25XR-220	National Jets Inc. Fort Lauderdale, Fl.	N220NJ
N99PD	80	Gulfstream 3	314	Hambrick Corp. Dallas, Tx.	(N99YD)
N99RS	78	Learjet 36A	36A-039	American Biomedical Group, Oklahoma City, Ok.	N25PK
N99SC	98	Gulfstream 4SP	1343	S S Platinum LLC/Skywalker Corporate Aviation, Lafayette, La	N343GA
N99TK	89	Citation II	550-0621	Pangel II LLC. Hailey, Id.	N102PA
N99UG	93	Challenger 601-3A	5126	UnitedGlobalCom Inc. Englewood, Co.	N21NY
N99WA	79	Falcon 10	150	Wheels of Africa, Rand Airport, South Africa.	N212NC
N99WJ	84	Gulfstream 3	431	Monarch Flight Inc. Charlotte, NC.	PK-CTP
N99ZC	99	Learjet 60	60-162	Plain Fish LLC. Wilmington, De.	
N100A	01	Global Express	9105	Mobil Corp. Dallas, Tx.	N700EC
N100AC	77	Falcon 20F-5	366	Amvest Mineral Services Inc. Charlottesville, Va.	N300CT

Reg	Yr	Type	c/n	Owner/Operator	Prev Regn
N100AG	93	BAe 125/800A	8238	R S Allen Aviation Inc. San Diego, Ca.	N70PM
N100AK	84	Gulfstream 3	437	Pacific Diversified Investments Inc. Anchorage, Ak.	N380TT
N100AR	02	Citation Excel	560-5241	Independence Airlines Inc. Manchester, NH.	N.....
N100AS	73	Falcon 20F-5B	274	City Aviation Services Inc. Detroit, Mi.	N260MB
N100AT	81	Learjet 35A	35A-436	Betaco Inc. Indianapolis, In.	N436BL
N100AW	97	Beechjet 400A	RK-150	Concesionario MB de Venezuela SA. Caracas.	N100AG
N100BC	87	Westwind-1124	438	Ball Corp. Broomfield, Co.	N438AM
N100BP	76	Sabre-75A	380-48	PSI Aviation Inc. Livonia, Mi.	N132DB
N100CH	94	CitationJet	525-0087	Coachmen Industries Inc. Elkhart, In.	N926CH
N100CJ	80	Citation II	550-0167	Midwest Airlines Transportation Corp. Wilmette, Il.	N88737
N100DS	90	Citation II	550-0639	DBS Transit Inc. Harrisburg, Pa.	N62RG
N100ED	01	Falcon 900C	195	National Industrial Development Corp. Tampa, Fl.	N195FJ
N100EG	82	Falcon 50	105	Condor Express Corp/Greenfield Aviation LLC. Bridgeport, Ct.	(N881L)
N100EJ	73	Sabre-75A	380-1	AVMATS/Centurion Investments Inc. St Louis, Mo.	N30GB
N100ES	01	Global Express	9108	Earth Star Inc. Burbank, Ca.	N700EK
N100FJ	77	Falcon 10	100	Smith Flooring Inc. St Louis, Mo.	(N217CP)
N100G	97	Astra-1125SPX	092	Hawk Flight Inc. Coatsville, Pa.	N8MN
N100GN	94	Gulfstream 4SP	1236	Gannett Co. Dulles, Va.	N478GA
N100GV	99	Gulfstream V	600	New World Jet Corp. Ronkonkoma, NY.	N650GA
N100HB	79	Citation II	550-0058	C E Leasing Inc. Tyrone, Ga.	N71CJ
N100HF	97	Gulfstream 4SP	1338	LHF Holdings Inc. Burlingame, Ca.	N401WT
N100HZ	84	Gulfstream 3	429	Harbour Group Industries Inc. St Louis, Mo.	N100HG
N100JF	81	HS 125/700A	NA0296	JHF LLC. Teterboro, NJ.	N700DA
N100JS	03	CitationJet CJ-2	525A-0176	JATO Aviation Inc. Northolt, UK.	N.....
N100KK	99	Learjet 45	45-065	Kohler Co. Kohler, Wi.	
N100KP	93	Falcon 50	232	King Pharmaceuticals Inc. Bristol, Tn.	N45NQ
N100KU	01	Citation Bravo	550-0813	University of Kansas, Lawrence, Ks.	N813CB
N100LR	82	Challenger 600S	1064	SynFuels Holdings Finance LLC. Birmingham, Al.	N75B
N100LX	81	Citation 1/SP	501-0220	Utah Jet Center LLC. Logan, Ut.	N100QH
N100NB	74	Learjet 25C	25C-181	AGA LLC. Spartanburg, SC.	N73TA
N100NG	01	Hawker 800XP	8537	Travel Guard Group Inc. Stevens Point, Wi.	
N100NR	03	Learjet 60	60-269	NRR Aviation LLC. Boca Raton, Fl.	N525MS
N100PF	00	CitationJet CJ-1	525-0390	PSF Associates LLC. Stratford, Ct.	N51396
N100QR	82	Challenger 600S	1043	Quick Flight Inc. Palm Beach, Fl.	N43NW
N100RR	81	Falcon 10	179	Rudd Performance Motorsports Inc. Greensboro, NC.	F-GERO
N100RS	82	Diamond 1A	A029SA	Word of Life Ministries Inc. Shreveport, La.	(N22CX)
N100SC	99	Citation Excel	560-5065	100 SC Partners/560 Inc. Chattanooga, Tn.	N5204D
N100SR	89	Astra-1125	037	Steven Rayman, Big Rock, Il.	N589TB
N100SY	90	Citation V	560-0054	Dumont Air LLC. Dallas, Tx.	(N748DC)
N100TM	02	Gulfstream V	692	Toyota Motor Sales USA Inc. Long Beach, Ca.	N692GA
N100U	91	BAe 1000A	NA1001	United Technologies Corp. Hartford, Ct.	G-BTTG
N100UP	88	Falcon 900B	44	Paget Holdings LLC. Westport, Ct.	HB-IBY
N100VR	01	Global Express	9098	DSC Enterprises Inc. Dulles, Va.	N149VB
N100WE	02	390 Premier 1	RB-45	Wiens Aviation LLC. Broomfield, Co.	N809RM
N100WN	79	Learjet 25D	25D-288	AirNet Systems Inc. Columbus, Oh.	(N40BC)
N100WP	90	Citation V	560-0073	Thunderbird Air LLC. Tempe, Az.	
N100WT	98	Citation Bravo	550-0858	Cheyenne Charters Inc. Dallas, Tx.	N1273Q
N100WY	01	Falcon 2000	178	WBY LLC. Carlsbad, Ca.	N884WY
N100Y	00	Citation Bravo	550-0919	Saratoga Inc. Lebanon, Or.	N52601
N100YP	88	Falcon 100	222	Villages Equipment Co. Leesburg, Fl.	N98VR
N101AJ	75	Learjet 36	36-008	Intermap Technologies Inc. Calgary, AB. Canada.	(N43A)
N101CC	00	Beechjet 400A	RK-277	Clark Distributing Co. Oakland, Ky.	(N566W)
N101CV	93	Gulfstream 4SP	1230	CSC Transport Inc. White Plains, NY.	9M-TRI
N101ET	82	Falcon 50	95	Morse Operations Inc. Fort Lauderdale, Fl.	N95FJ
N101FC	98	Hawker 800XP	8380	Field Container Aviation LLC. Elk Grove Village, Il.	N999JF
N101FG	98	Citation Bravo	550-0839	University Athletic Association Inc. Gainesville, Fl.	N839DW
N101HS	76	Falcon 10	82	Hirshfeld Steel Co. San Angelo, Tx.	N602NC
N101HW	94	Learjet 60	60-037	RMSC West Palm Beach Inc. Fort Lauderdale, Fl.	N637LJ
N101JL	01	Citation Bravo	550-1002	Link Snacks Inc. Rice Lake Regional, Wi.	N52397
N101KP	99	Citation V Ultra	560-0520	King Pharmaceuticals Inc. Bristol, Tn.	N620AT
N101L	00	Gulfstream G200	024	Landow 101 Inc. Bethesda, Md.	(N51GX)
N101MH	00	Gulfstream V	609	Standard & Poor's Securities Evaluations Inc. NYC.	N418SM
N101PC	66	BAC 1-11/401AK	073	Sky King Inc. Sacramento, Ca.	N401SK
N101PG	86	Citation III	650-0126	The Pape' Group Inc. Coburg, Or.	N311MA
N101PV	03	Falcon 2000EX	23	Vegso Aviation Inc. Boca Raton, Fl.	N223EX
N101RR	82	Citation 1/SP	501-0241	Parmley Aviation Services Inc. Council Bluffs, Ia.	C-GSTR
Reg	Yr	Type	c/n	Owner/Operator	Prev Regn

Reg	Yr	Type	c/n	Owner/Operator	Prev Regn
☐ N101U	01	CitationJet CJ-1	525-0454	Matrix Sales & Service Inc. Lewes, De.	N541CJ
☐ N101UD	04	Learjet 60	60-275	Unicorp Aviation Inc. Orlando, Fl.	
☐ N101UR	70	HS 125/F403A	25235	Unicorp Aviation Inc. Orlando, Fl.	N101UD
☐ N101VJ	81	Falcon 10	177	N434BC LLC. Wayne, Pa.	F-GFGB
☐ N101VS	70	Learjet 24B	24B-218	Advanced Technology Center, Buffalo, NY.	N682LJ
☐ N101WY	02	Citation Encore	560-0620	Department of Transportation, Cheyenne, Wy.	N.....
☐ N102AF	95	CitationJet	525-0122	Yankee Pacific LLC. Rye, NH.	N5264U
☐ N102AR	68	Learjet 25	25-012	White Industries Inc. Bates City, Mo.	N846YC
☐ N102BG	95	Gulfstream 4SP	1273	Berwind Corp. Philadelphia, Pa.	N372BG
☐ N102BQ	00	Falcon 50EX	305	AEC Properties LLC. Boston, Ma.	N102BG
☐ N102CE	95	Citation VII	650-7061	Centerpoint Energy Service Co. Houston, Tx.	N202CW
☐ N102CX	71	Gulfstream 2B	102	Clorox Co/KaiserAir Inc. Oakland, Ca.	N400CC
☐ N102FM	98	Gulfstream 4SP	1325	Inter-Americas Transport Inc. Westport, Ct.	(N24EE)
☐ N102FS	02	Citation Excel	560-5318	Three Eighteen Aviation Corp. New Haven, Ct.	N51743
☐ N102HB	82	Citation II	550-0409	Buzz-Air of Indiana Inc. East Chicago, In.	VR-CIT
☐ N102KP	99	Citation V Ultra	560-0527	King Pharmaceuticals Inc. Bristol, Tn.	N627AT
☐ N102LJ	97	Learjet 60	60-102	Williams International Air Inc. Rochester, NY.	LV-WXN
☐ N102PT	01	CitationJet CJ-1	525-0433	Symons Living Trust. San Francisco, Ca.	N5223D
☐ N102QS	04	Hawker 400XP	RK-380	NetJets, Columbus, Oh.	
☐ N102VP	74	Citation	500-0200	Airplane One LLC. Houston, Tx.	CS-DBM
☐ N102VS	74	Learjet 25B	25B-180	Arvin Calspan Corp/Veridian Flight Research, Roswell, NM.	N266BS
☐ N102WY	02	Citation Encore	560-0621	Department of Transportation, Cheyenne, Wy.	N.....
☐ N103CD	84	Gulfstream 3	418	World Heir Inc. College Park, Ga.	PT-ALK
☐ N103CJ	04	CitationJet CJ-3	525B-0003	Linweld Inc. Waverly, Ne.	N52059
☐ N103CS	01	CitationJet CJ-1	525-0438	CitationShares Sales Inc. White Plains, NY.	N51942
☐ N103F	66	HFB 320	1023	E O Ramonat, Murfresboro, Tn. (status ?).	N320AF
☐ N103HC	83	Diamond 1A	A068SA	SamCo Aviation LLC. Jacksonville, Fl.	(N68TK)
☐ N103HT	86	BAe 125/800A	8074	Hidalgo Trading LLC. Dallas-Love, Tx.	N850SM
☐ N103SV	03	Citation Sovereign	680-0003	Cessna Aircraft Co. Wichita, Ks.	N52114
☐ N103TA	69	Sabre-60	306-27	The Auction Inc. Danville, Ca.	(N105SS)
☐ N103VF	85	Citation S/II	S550-0046	Geo M Martin Co. Emeryville, Ca.	N760NB
☐ N104AE	77	HS 125/700A	NA0203	L & C Aircraft Sales & Leasing LLC. Portland, Me.	N620M
☐ N104AR	98	Gulfstream 4SP	1346	Greenaap Aviation Ltd.	N346GA
☐ N104CE	67	JetStar-8	5108	Wilson Air Service LLC. Andrews, NC.	XA-SWD
☐ N104CT	99	Citation X	750-0100	Townsend Engineering Co. Des Moines, Ia.	N5100J
☐ N104FL	03	Citation Bravo	550-1071	Department of Management Services, Tallahassee, Fl.	N5090A
☐ N104GA	04	Gulfstream G200	104	Rite Aid Corp. Harrisburg, Pa.	4X-C..
☐ N104HW	87	Citation II	550-0555	White Flood LLC. San Jose, Ca. (was 551-0555).	N93BA
☐ N104KW*	78	Falcon 10	122	Freedom Flotilla LLC. Austin, Tx.	N911UN
☐ N104PC	04	CitationJet CJ-2	525A-0212	Caymus Vineyards, Rutherford, Ca.	N5226B
☐ N104RS	79	Westwind-1124	273	C 23 Ltd. Lewes, De.	(N566PG)
☐ N104VV	69	Gulfstream II SP	53	Eagle Mountain International Church, Fort Worth, Tx.	N104CD
☐ N105BA	74	Learjet 25XR	25XR-152	Flites Inc. Batavia, Il.	XA-JSC
☐ N105BG	86	Citation S/II	S550-0105	Republic Aviation LLC. Chattanooga, Tn.	(N12907)
☐ N105BK	89	Falcon 900	70	Savin Investment Ltd. Tortola, BVI.	(VH-VIW)
☐ N105BN	91	Challenger 601-3A	5101	Barnes & Noble Inc. Teterboro, NJ.	(N108BN)
☐ N105CJ	04	CitationJet CJ-3	525B-0005	Berdan Holdings LLC. Oxnard, Ca.	N5270E
☐ N105FN	98	Astra-1125SPX	105	RAL Capital LLC. Scottsdale, Az.	HB-VMG
☐ N105GA	66	Learjet 24A	24A-116	Younkin Boreing Inc. Hot Springs, Ar. (status ?).	(N1420)
☐ N105HD	75	Sabre-75A	380-39	Sunrise Air Inc. Miami, Fl.	(N55HD)
☐ N105HS	65	HS 125/1A	25031	Select Aviation Inc. Waukesha, Wi.	N79AE
☐ N105JM	77	Citation 1/SP	501-0270	Apple Air LLC. Minot, ND.	N893CA
☐ N105LF	99	Falcon 2000	105	Oldbury Holdings Corp/Krystel Air Charter, Cranfield, UK..	N220EJ
☐ N105P	99	CitationJet	525-0336	Charles Putman, Glendive, Mt.	N51564
☐ N105PT	03	CitationJet CJ-2	525A-0155	Papa Tango LLC. Napa County, Ca.	N5180C
☐ N105SV	03	Citation Sovereign	680-0005	Magna Air Luftfahrt GmbH. Vienna, Austria.	N52229
☐ N105TB	68	Gulfstream 2	31	MIT Lincoln Labs/Air Force Material Command, Bedford, Ma.	N200CC
☐ N105TF	73	HFB 320	1055	Kalitta Flying Service Inc. Morristown, Tn.	N7865T
☐ N105UP	86	Challenger 601	3066	ARAMARK Services Inc. Philadelphia, Pa.	VP-CLE
☐ N105WC	81	Falcon 50	60	U S Leaseco Inc. Baltimore, Md.	CS-DFJ
☐ N105Y	83	Gulfstream 3	412	Occidental Petroleum Corp. Burbank, Ca.	N610CC
☐ N106BK	89	Falcon 900	76	Dunmore Homes LLC. Sacramento, Ca.	VH-WIZ
☐ N106CG	86	Beechjet 400	RJ-12	Twin Springs Aviation, St Louis, Mo.	N3112K
☐ N106CJ	93	CitationJet	525-0006	Citation 525 Inc/Northwest Stamping Inc. Eugene, Or.	N1326P
☐ N106CX	99	Citation X	750-0106	Mike's Airplane Rentals Inc. Tampa, Fl.	N52642
☐ N106DD	02	Beechjet 400A	RK-343	JCDE Air Inc. Portland, Me.	N806GG

Reg	Yr	Type	c/n	Owner/Operator	Prev Regn
N106EA	79	Citation 1/SP	501-0101	Mahaney Air LLC. Greenwich, Ct.	(N323JB)
N106KC	96	Beechjet 400A	RK-132	Cambata Aviation inc. Roanoke, Va.	N1087Z
N106QS	04	Hawker 400XP	RK-381	NetJets, Columbus, Oh.	
N106RW*	02	Falcon 900EX EASY	120	GTS-Global Transportation Systems Inc. Dulles, Va.	N900EX
N106SP	82	Citation II	550-0346	Stan Partee, Big Springs, Tx.	N550CF
N106ST	86	Citation III	650-0109	RNJ Holdings LLC. Lakeland, Fl.	N109ST
N106TW	76	Falcon 10	84	Titan International Inc. Quincy, Il.	N192MC
N107A	88	Gulfstream 4	1070	ARAMCO Associated Co. Dhahran, Saudi Arabia.	N407GA
N107CG	91	Citation VI	650-0207	Vesta Fire Insurance Corp. Birmingham, Al.	N334WC
N107EE	91	Citation II	550-0667	E & J Aircraft Sales & Leasing Inc. Longwood, Fl.	N167EA
N107EG	99	Citation Bravo	550-0894	Elmo Greer & Sons LLC. London-Corbin, Ky.	N550TE
N107GA	04	Gulfstream G200	107	Gulfstream Aerospace Corp. Dallas-Love, Tx.	4X-C..
N107HF	69	Learjet 25XR	25XR-029	Chipola Aviation Inc. Marianna, Fl.	N28LA
N107J	67	Falcon 20C	107	Flying Investment LLC/Jones Motorcars Inc. Fayetteville, Ar.	N213LS
N107LP	95	Learjet 31A	31A-107	LP Learjets LLC. New Castle, De.	N107TS
N107LT	81	HS 125/700A	NA0301	Lifetouch Inc/LT Flight Services Inc. Minneapolis, Mn.	N421SZ
N107RC	87	Citation S/II	S550-0150	Electrolux Home Products Inc. Augusta, Ga.	N150CJ
N107RM	83	Learjet 25D	25D-362	Fifty Four Sixty LLC. Mentor, Oh.	(N107MS)
N107RP	93	BAe 1000A	9038	Petersen Aviation, Van Nuys, Ca.	N125GM
N107TB	76	Falcon 10	77	Tennessee Jet Aircraft Sales Inc. Smyrna, Tn.	N53TS
N107WR	02	390 Premier 1	RB-73	Trigeant Air LLC/Seminole Aircraft Inc. Boca Raton, Fl.	(N107YR)
N108AR	85	Gulfstream 3	461	Flying Eagle Aviation LLC. Renton, Wa.	N104AR
N108BP	01	Hawker 800XP	8546	Avpro Inc. Baltimore, Md.	N50461
N108CG	98	Astra-1125SPX	108	Orne Equipment Leasing LLC. Portland, Me.	N302TS
N108CJ	95	CitationJet	525-0108	Vulcan Northwest Inc. Seattle-Tacoma, Wa.	N5211Q
N108DB	90	Gulfstream 4	1149	Blum Capital Partners LP. San Francisco, Ca.	N152KB
N108DD	04	Hawker 800XP	8700	JCDE Air Inc. Gorham, NC.	
N108EK	99	Citation Excel	560-5032	New Heights Aviation LLC. Minneapolis-Flying Cloud, Mn.	N165JB
N108FL	80	Learjet 25D	25D-300	Learjet 25D-300 LLC. Charleston, WV.	N659HX
N108JN	80	Learjet 35A	35A-358	Air Pegasus LLC. Tuscon, Az.	N358PG
N108KC	74	Falcon 10	8	Keller Companies Inc. Manchester, NH.	N88ME
N108LJ	95	Citation V Ultra	560-0337	Cessna Finance Corp. Wichita, Ks.	N5265N
N108MC	76	Citation	500-0322	W W Reynolds & R A Marks LLC. Mobile, Al.	N1AP
N108MS	02	BBJ-7BC	33102	Yona Aviation LLC. Needham, Ma.	N105QS
N108PJ	02	Beechjet 400A	RK-347	Pinjet Aviation LLC. McKinney, Tx.	N447CW
N108QS	04	Hawker 400XP	RK-382	NetJets, Columbus, Oh.	
N108R	67	Falcon 20DC	108	Kalitta Charters LLC. Detroit-Willow Run, Mi.	N101ZE
N108RB	77	Learjet 35A	35A-097	Lear CISA Inc. Wilmington, De.	N135J
N108RF	97	Citation Bravo	550-0805	David Gifford, Weston, Ma.	N5214K
N108WV	91	Citation VI	650-0204	Willamette Valley Co. Eugene, Or.	N811JT
N109CP	92	Beechjet 400A	RK-47	THV Seminars LLC/UCG Inc. Rockville, Md.	N408PC
N109GA	80	Citation II	550-0124	DMM Corp. Richmond, Il.	N124CR
N109GX	01	Gulfstream G100	142	Cook Aircraft Leasing Inc. Bloomington, In.	4X-CVK
N109HV	95	Learjet 31A	31A-105	American Air Charter Inc. Boca Raton, Fl.	N109FX
N109JC	79	Citation II	550-0099	Stroud Aviation Inc. Stroud, Ok.	N2664L
N109JR	01	Learjet 60	60-223	Ruan Inc. Des Moines, Ia.	N3006J
N109MC	76	Sabre-60	306-119	Westport Air Travel Inc. West Palm Beach, Fl.	N48MC
N109NT	03	Hawker 400XP	RK-374	Perkins Transportation Co. Atlanta, Ga.	N374XP
N109PW	83	Diamond 1A	A046SA	Fotex, Budapest, Hungary.	N900BT
N109SB	74	Sabre-75A	380-20	Sabre Direct, Raleigh, NC.	N773W
N109ST	90	Gulfstream 4	1151	S T Aviation LLC. Louis Center, Oh.	N80AT
N100WS	02	Citation Encore	560-0632	Southwestern Energy Co. Springdale, Ar.	N6521F
N110AB	75	Citation	500-0262	Air Amigos Inc. Tavares, Fl.	N110AF
N110AJ	78	Sabre-75A	380-70	VoyageAir Charter Inc. McKinney, Tx.	N1NR
N110BP	04	Challenger 604	5579	Popular Inc. San Juan, PR.	C-GLYC
N110BR	04	Citation Bravo	550-1100	Cessna Aircraft Co. Wichita, Ks.	N5203S
N110DS	80	Diamond 1A	A005SA	Diamond Jet 5 Inc. Upland, Ca.	N30HD
N110EJ	80	HS 125/700A	NA0273	Air Butler LLC. Northbrook, Il.	(N4477X)
N110ET	82	Learjet 55	55-023	Pontiac Aviation LLC. Southfield, Mi.	N7784
N110EX	00	Falcon 900EX	71	Sky River Consulting LLC. Las Vegas, Nv.	(N971EX)
N110FD	97	CitationJet	525-0241	Flournoy Aviation LLC. Columbus, Ga.	N209BS
N110FT	82	Learjet 35A	35A-471	Milam International Inc. Englewood, Co.	N95AP
N110GD	74	Gulfstream 2B	154	SA Holding LLC. NYC.	(N719SA)
N110HA	01	Gulfstream G200	035	Haworth Transportation Services LLC. Holland, Mi.	N59GX
N110J	79	Falcon 10	139	The Grigoriou Family LP. Statesville, NC.	(N610J)
N110JA	77	Citation 1/SP	501-0273	Meisner Aircraft Inc. Lake in the Hills, Il. (was 500-0363).	N302AJ
Reg	*Yr*	*Type*	*c/n*	*Owner/Operator*	*Prev Regn*

Reg	Yr	Type	c/n	Owner/Operator	Prev Regn
N110JB	81	Citation 1/SP	501-0172	IMI Holdings LLC/Sky King Inc. Asheville, NC.	HI-581SP
N110LA	75	Falcon 10	54	Lieblong Transport Delaware Inc. Conway, Ar.	N561D
N110LD	82	Citation II	550-0366	Warrington Development Corp. Gulf Shores, Al.	(N614GA)
N110LH	86	Citation S/II	S550-0118	Hallier Aviation LLC. Las Vegas, Nv.	N118AJ
N110MQ	01	CitationJet CJ-2	525A-0014	Teton Jet Inc. Newport, Ar.	N110MG
N110PP	84	Falcon 100	210	Flying G LLC. Atlanta-De Kalb, Ga.	N35WN
N110PR	01	390 Premier 1	RB-29	Raytheon Aircraft Co. Wichita, Ks.	N747BK
N110RA*	69	Learjet 25	25-025	Royal Air Freight Inc. Waterford, Mi.	(N111LM)
N110SC	99	Learjet 31A	31A-185	Steff's Co. Chattanooga, Tn.	N31LR
N110TP	78	Falcon 10	123	Liz Air LLC. Las Vegas, Nv.	N23WJ
N110WA	82	Citation II	550-0408	Musco Sports Lighting Inc. Oskaloosa, Ia.	N400TX
N111AC	66	Sabre-40	282-79	Airvac Inc. Rochester, In.	N35CC
N111AF	95	Learjet 31A	31A-111	Fernandez Aviation Inc. Birmingham, Mi.	N113AF
N111AM	95	CitationJet	525-0113	CJ Aero Group LLC. Wilmington, De.	N5214K
N111BB	75	Citation	500-0248	B & B Sales, Dallas, Tx.	(N70PB)
N111BF	96	CitationJet	525-0140	Big Sky Management Services Ltd. Missoula, Mt.	N725L
N111BP	67	Falcon 20C	111	Jones Motorcars Inc. Fayetteville, Ar.	N111AM
N111CX	98	Beechjet 400A	RK-210	Sabre Transportation Inc. Barboursville, WV.	
N111F	77	Sabre-60	306-126	Stuart Dingman, Manchester, NH.	HC-BUN
N111FA	80	Gulfstream 3	307	Falconcrest Aviation LLC. Carson City, Nv.	C-GGPM
N111FK	81	Challenger 600S	1027	FK Air LLC/Kelley & Farraro LLP. Fort Lauderdale, Fl.	N678CG
N111FW	95	Beechjet 400A	RK-102	Acme Management II Inc. Fort Worth, Tx.	N916GR
N111GD	75	Gulfstream 2	170	XTO Energy Corp. Fort Worth, Tx.	(N318GD)
N111GJ	02	CitationJet CJ-1	525-0500	Davison Transport Inc. Ruston, La.	N525CJ
N111GU	03	Citation Excel XLS	560-5504	Edinton Holdings USA Inc. Guatemala City, Guatemala.	N.....
N111GX	85	Gulfstream 3	454	Tesoro Petroleum Companies Inc. San Antonio, Tx.	N111G
N111HC	86	Gulfstream 3	482	Collins Brothers Corp. Las Vegas, Nv.	N268RJ
N111HZ	99	Falcon 2000	86	The Hertz Corp. Teterboro, NJ.	F-WWVF
N111JX	70	BAC 1-11/414EG	163	Select Aviation Inc. Waukesha, Wi.	N123H
N111KK	99	Learjet 45	45-061	Kohler Co. Kohler, Wi.	
N111LP	80	Westwind-1124	286	Junisa Inc. Georgetown, Tx.	N92FE
N111LX	00	Gulfstream V	608	Lexair Ltd/Trans-Exec Air Service Inc. Van Nuys, Ca.	N561GA
N111ME	74	Citation	500-0146	Ed Unicume, Scottsdale, Az.	N194AT
N111MP	73	Learjet 25XR	25XR-139	Amelia Airways Inc. Fort Lauderdale, Fl.	N605NE
N111QS	86	Citation S/II	S550-0111	Prestige Air LLC. Las Vegas, Nv.	(N777HN)
N111RZ	65	BAC 1-11/401AK	056	Rotec Industries Inc. Rockford, Il.	N491ST
N111UN	76	HS 125/600A	6055	Imeca Aviation LLC. Fort Lauderdale, Fl.	(N600GP)
N111VG	99	Hawker 800XP	8403	VG Aircraft LLC-Viking Global Investors LP. NYC.	N601RS
N111VV	90	Learjet 31	31-023	Inductotherm Industries Inc. Rancocas, NJ.	
N111VW	99	Falcon 2000	99	Volkswagen of America Inc. Pontiac, Mi.	N111VU
N111WB	74	Learjet 35	35-003	Aero-Jet Aviation Inc. Fort Lauderdale, Fl.	N703MA
N111Y	92	Citation VI	650-0223	Ingram Industries Inc. Nashville, Tn.	N1301D
N111ZN	96	Hawker 800XP	8327	Zenith National Insurance Corp. Van Nuys, Ca.	N327XP
N111ZS	79	HS 125/700A	7076	Hab-Air Inc. Allentown, Pa.	(N776TS)
N112CF	01	Challenger 604	5509	First Data Corp. Englewood, Co.	N604BG
N112CW	95	Citation V Ultra	560-0298	West Creek Aviation, Dallas, Tx.	N25CV
N112EB	79	Citation 1/SP	501-0112	Missouri Eagle LLC. Lebanon, Mo.	(N74PN)
N112FK	84	Learjet 55	55-102	FK Air LLC. Coral Gables, Fl.	PT-WSS
N112PR	87	Astra-1125	013	Tevis Technology Partners LLC. Menlo Park, Ca.	(N77JW)
N112SH	79	Citation II	550-0043	Canary Aircraft Sales Corp. Fort Smith, Ar.	N801JP
N113	66	B 727-30	18935	Grecoair Inc. El Paso, Tx.	N18G
N113AR	73	Gulfstream 2B	139	C A R LLC. Opa Locka, Fl.	N139CF
N113BG	02	CitationJet CJ-2	525A-0078	7G's Aviation LLC. Bakersfield, Ca.	N5162W
N113CS	88	Gulfstream 4	1049	113CS LLC. Oxford, Ct.	N372CM
N113SH	75	Citation	500-0285	SW Orthopaedic & Sports Medicine, Oklahoma City, Ok.	N86SS
N113VP	91	Citation V	560-0113	Kirkham Aviation Inc. Chesterfield, Mo.	N4
N114CJ	04	CitationJet CJ-3	525B-0014	Cessna Aircraft Co. Wichita, Ks.	N.....
N114FW	98	CitationJet	525-0307	Fred Gibbons Separate Property Trust, Los Altos Hills, Ca.	(N114FG)
N114LJ	99	Learjet 60	60-157	Animus Aviation Support LLC.	N236FX
N114M		BAe 146-100	E1068	Moncrief Oil, Fort Worth, Tx. 'Lucky Liz'	N861MC
N114PJ	97	Learjet 60	60-114	PRJ Holdings Inc. San Francisco, Ca.	N199SC
N114RA	75	Westwind-1123	179	Alberth Air Parts Inc. Cypress, Tx.	LV-WJU
N114SN	99	Astra-1125SPX	114	Sandals Resorts International Ltd. Nassau, Bahamas.	N114GA
N114WD	67	HS 125/3A	25114	Concourse Aerospace Corp. Fort Lauderdale, Fl.	XA-SGP
N115BB	98	CitationJet	525-0325	Hayden Air Inc. Portland, Or.	N764C
N115BX	96	Learjet 31A	31A-129	Averitt Aviation Group Inc. Nashville, Tn.	N115FX

Reg	Yr	Type	c/n	Owner/Operator	Prev Regn
N115CJ	02	CitationJet CJ-2	525A-0115	Conquest Services Inc. Petaluma, Ca.	N.....
N115CR	69	Sabre-60	306-43	A S Aviation Inc. Wilmington, De.	N10UM
N115FL	90	Gulfstream 4	1141	Tyco International Ltd. Portsmouth, NH.	N767EL
N115K	91	Citation V	560-0148	KaiserAir Inc. Oakland, Ca.	N560FB
N115QS	04	Hawker 400XP	RK-383	NetJets, Columbus, Oh.	
N115SK	02	Falcon 50EX	330	SAKS Inc. Memphis, Tn.	N330EX
N115TD	77	Falcon 10	96	TransDigm Inc. Cleveland, Oh.	N96TJ
N116AD	02	Beechjet 400A	RK-338	West Cherry Sales LLC. Memphis, Tn.	(N726PG)
N116AP	98	Beechjet 400A	RK-192	Raytheon Aircraft Co. Wichita, Ks.	N116AD
N116AS	99	Learjet 45	45-078	City Aviation Services Inc. Detroit, Mi.	N5016Z
N116CS	01	CitationJet CJ-1	525-0447	CitationShares Sales Inc. White Plains, NY.	N5120U
N116DD	72	JetStar-731	5155	Charles Joekel, Houston, Tx.	N84GA
N116HM	87	Gulfstream 4	1024	Wings Aviation International Inc. Franklin Lakes, NJ.	N96AE
N116JC	86	Astra-1125	014	CheckFree Services Corp. Norcross, Ga.	(N214TJ)
N116K	80	Citation II	550-0149	KaiserAir Inc. Oakland, Ca.	
N116LA	78	Citation II	550-0016	Lake Air Inc. Fort Lauderdale, Fl.	N204MC
N116LS*	87	Challenger 601-3A	5013	Starbucks Corp. Seattle, Wa.	N950FB
N116MA	77	Learjet 36A	36A-029	Dutch Navy, Valkenburg, Holland.	N16MA
N116PB	89	Astra-1125	032	Pelican Air LLC. Santa Ana, Ca.	N125MG
N116QS	04	Hawker 400XP	RK-385	NetJets, Columbus, Oh.	
N116RA	81	Challenger 600S	1011	RGA Holdings Inc. Teterboro, NJ.	N678ML
N116SC	62	Sabre-40R	282-1	Sabreliner Corp. St Louis, Mo. 'Sabre One'	(N351JM)
N116XP	04	Hawker 400XP	RK-416	Raytheon Aircraft Co. Wichita, Ks.	
N117AH	81	Westwind-Two	352	DPI Inc. Carson City, Nv.	N117JW
N117AJ	78	JetStar 2	5227	Real World Tours Inc. Nashville, Tn.	N171SG
N117DJ	79	Citation 1/SP	501-0127	DJ Aircraft Inc. Tolleson, Az.	N86SK
N117FJ	78	Gulfstream 2	229	J T Aviation Corp. Ronkonkoma, NY.	N702H
N117GL	78	Gulfstream 2	220	G & L Aviation Inc. Van Nuys, Ca.	N315TS
N117JJ	75	Gulfstream II SP	163	Gavilan Corp. Fort Lauderdale, Fl. 'El Condor'	N117JA
N117JW	81	Sabre-65	465-61	AmQuip Sales & Leasing Inc. Bethlehem, Pa.	N23BX
N117K	73	Learjet 24D	24D-272	Clay Lacy Aviation Inc. Van Nuys, Ca.	N51GL
N117MA	79	Citation 1/SP	501-0249	Maguire Products Inc. Aston, Pa.	(N82MP)
N117MS	81	Gulfstream 3	335	ITT Industries Inc. White Plains, NY.	HB-IMX
N117PK	84	Learjet C-21A	35A-513	Pert 35 Inc. Fenwick Island, De.	N35AQ
N117QS	04	Hawker 400XP	RK-391	Raytheon Aircraft Co. Wichita, Ks.	
N117SF	83	Falcon 50	137	Seneca Foods Corp. Penn Yan, NY.	N119FJ
N117TF	99	Global Express	9028	Tudor Investment Corp. Waterbury-Oxford, Ct.	C-GEZY
N117W	02	CitationJet CJ-2	525A-0079	Wallace Enterprises Inc. Atlanta-Fulton County, Ga.	N51872
N118AD	78	Falcon 10	118	Cooper/T Smith Stevedoring Co. Mobile, Al.	(N97RJ)
N118B	77	JetStar 2	5211	Four Star International Inc. Laredo, Tx.	N821MD
N118CS	01	CitationJet CJ-1	525-0457	CitationShares Sales Inc. White Plains, NY.	N.....
N118FN	77	Learjet 35A	35A-118	Aero-Jet Aviation Inc. Fort Lauderdale, Fl.	N88JA
N118HC	95	Learjet 60	60-067	Harbert Aviation Inc. Birmingham, Al.	N799SC
N118K	92	BAe 125/800A	NA0471	KaiserAir Inc. Oakland, Ca.	N57PM
N118KA	02	Gulfstream G200	065	Kandrew Air LLC. Burbank, Ca.	(N628RC)
N118LA	72	Citation	500-0039	White Industries Inc. Bates City, Mo.	PT-OOK
N118MB	73	Learjet 25B	25B-118	Kalitta Charters LLC. Detroit-Willow Run, Mi.	VP-CMB
N118MP	81	Westwind-Two	340	MVP Air LLC. Torrance, Ca.	N3RC
N118MT	90	Challenger 601-3A	5077	MTRM Realty LLC/Tennenbaum & Co. Van Nuys, Ca.	N64YP
N118RK	96	Citation V Ultra	560-0389	Telecommunications Financial Services, Baton Rouge, La.	N389JV
N118ST	02	Citation Excel	560-5287	SunTrust Banks Inc. Atlanta, Ga.	N.....
N119AG	00	Falcon 50EX	297	Allianz AG. Munich, Germany.	F-WWHY
N119BA	65	Learjet 23	23-084	Barr-Clay Auto Sales Inc. Coatesville, Pa.	N101JR
N119CS	01	CitationJet CJ-1	525-0466	ACH Hamburg Flug GmbH. Hamburg, Germany.	(D-ILLL)
N119GA	98	Challenger 604	5386	KTC Aviation LLC. Seattle, Wa.	N37DG
N119QS	04	Hawker 400XP	RK-394	Raytheon Aircraft Co. Wichita, Ks.	
N119RM	98	Citation X	750-0051	Red McCombs/APC Delaware Inc. San Antonio, Tx.	(N1419J)
N119U	91	Citation 1000A	9007	Randa LLC. Portland, Me.	N119PW
N120AP	88	BAe 125/800A	8120	APW North America Inc. Waukesha, Wi.	G-POSN
N120JC	79	HS 125/700A	NA0247	Southwestern Jet Charter Inc. Alton, Il.	N87AG
N120JP	83	Citation II	550-0468	Aero National Inc. Washington, Pa.	N123FH
N120NE	66	DC 9-15	45731	Genesis Aeronautics Inc. Van Nuys, Ca.	HB-IFA
N120Q	82	Citation II	550-0332	Therm-O-Disc Inc. Mansfield, Oh.	N12CQ
N120RA	67	Learjet 24	24-153	Royal Air Freight Inc. Waterford, Mi.	N153BR
N120RV	97	Learjet 31A	31A-137	Averitt Air Charter Inc. Nashville, Tn.	N120FX
N120SB	01	Citation Encore	560-0587	Palisades Aircraft Inc. Austin, Tx.	(N587K)
Reg	Yr	Type	c/n	Owner/Operator	Prev Regn

Reg	Yr	Type	c/n	Owner/Operator	Prev Regn
☐ N120YB	80	HS 125/700A	NA0282	Bemis Co Inc. Minneapolis, Mn.	N1982G
☐ N121AT	89	Falcon 100	226	Anthony Timberlands Inc. Phoenix, Az.	XA-RLX
☐ N121CG	86	Citation S/II	S550-0123	DJV Air Charters Inc. Tampa, Fl.	N1293A
☐ N121CK	65	Learjet 23	23-039	Aircraft Guaranty Title LLC. Houston, Tx.	XA-...
☐ N121CN	01	Citation Bravo	550-1000	Contrails LLC. Kerrville, Tx.	N5194B
☐ N121CP	00	CitationJet CJ-2	525A-0010	Skybank LLC/Pinnacle Bancorp Inc. Central City, Ne.	N5194J
☐ N121DF	01	Challenger 604	5480	Cintas Corp. Cincinnati-Lunken, Oh.	N480LB
☐ N121EB	00	CitationJet CJ-1	525-0405	Designer Programs Inc. Raleigh, NC.	N5125J
☐ N121ET	04	Challenger 604	5583	BWL Aviation LLC. Menlo Park, Ca.	C-GLXK
☐ N121EZ	96	Beechjet 400A	RK-109	Roger Snellenberger Development Corp. Indio, Ca.	N3269A
☐ N121GA	04	Gulfstream G450	4011	Gulfstream Aerospace Corp. Savannah, Ga.	
☐ N121GV	04	Gulfstream G200	094	Starship Enterprise Leasing LLC. Henderson, Nv.	N394GA
☐ N121GX	00	Gulfstream G200	014	Starship Enterprise Leasing LLC. Henderson, Nv.	N121GV
☐ N121JE	67	Sabre-60	306-4	JODA LLC. Chesterfield, Mo.	N1210
☐ N121JJ	88	Gulfstream 4	1075	Liamaj Aviation Inc. Houston, Tx.	N901K
☐ N121JM	99	Gulfstream 4SP	1399	Rim Air, Menlo Park, Ca.	N499GA
☐ N121L	99	Citation Bravo	550-0896	Hinton Aviation LLC. Byron Center, Mi.	
☐ N121LJ	96	Learjet 31A	31A-121	Renfro Corp. Mount Airy, NC.	
☐ N121PA	69	Jet Commander-A	129	Mach Aero International Corp. Tulsa, Ok.	N102CE
☐ N121PX	97	Learjet 31A	31A-141	Bombardier Aerospace Corp. Windsor Locks, Ct.	(N121HV)
☐ N121SG	91	Astra-1125SP	053	Cousins Properties Inc. Atlanta, Ga.	N853SP
☐ N121TL	00	Citation Excel	560-5073	Kirkwood Ventures LLC. Wilmington, De.	N79EA
☐ N122BN	01	Global Express	9103	Barnes & Noble Inc. Teterboro, NJ.	C-GIXO
☐ N122BX	97	Learjet 31A	31A-143	Priority Fulfillment Services Inc. Plano, Tx.	N122FX
☐ N122CS	01	CitationJet CJ-1	525-0469	CitationShares Sales Inc. White Plains, NY.	N52038
☐ N122DS	03	390 Premier 1	RB-100	D S Air Inc. Norfolk, Va.	
☐ N122DU	67	Gulfstream 2	6	Pincervale Ltd-UK/Jet Services Corp.(stored GVA since 7/02).	N122DJ
☐ N122EJ	86	Citation III	650-0122	Star XVI LLC. Jacksonville, Fl.	N65WL
☐ N122GV	01	Gulfstream G200	043	Starship Enterprise Leasing LLC. Henderson, Nv.	N103GX
☐ N122HM	80	Citation II	550-0129	Collins Investment Corp. Eden, Mn.	(N550RD)
☐ N122JW	79	Learjet 35A	35A-217	AirNet Systems Inc. Columbus, Oh. (yellow).	N111RF
☐ N122MP	83	Westwind-1124	390	Lemak International Aviation LLC. Birmingham, Al.	N59SM
☐ N122NC	98	Citation Bravo	550-0836	North Carolina Department of Commerce, Raleigh, NC.	N51872
☐ N122RS	01	Gulfstream 4SP	1417	Chiricahua Properties LLC. Tulsa, Ok.	(N417QS)
☐ N122SC	96	Falcon 2000	25	St Paul Aviation Inc. St Paul, Mn.	N96FG
☐ N122SM	02	CitationJet CJ-2	525A-0151	Granite Aviation Inc. Baltimore, Md.	N.....
☐ N122SP	82	Citation II/SP	551-0393	Phillips Energy Inc. Shreveport, La.	(N18CC)
☐ N122ST	67	Jet Commander-B	122	Plain Old Plane LLC. Birmingham, Al.	XA-SCV
☐ N122WS	86	Citation S/II	S550-0122	Advanced Drainage Systems Inc. Columbus, Oh.	I-TALG
☐ N123CD	64	Sabre-40	282-23	National Bank of Commerce, Germantown, Tn. (status ?).	(N55ME)
☐ N123DG	76	Learjet 24F	24F-342	Glynn Air Inc. Bartlesville, Ok.	N824GA
☐ N123EB	77	Citation 1/SP	501-0020	WCCP Aviation LLC. Van Nuys, Ca.	N32JJ
☐ N123GF	97	Citation Bravo	550-0817	Rock Jet Inc. Del Mar, Ca.	(YV-....)
☐ N123GM	81	Citation II	550-0333	Camelot Aviation Ventures Inc. Coral Gables, Fl.	N313CE
☐ N123JW	02	CitationJet CJ-2	525A-0152	Jacob Wood, Camarillo, Ca.	N.....
☐ N123KD	81	Citation 1/SP	501-0195	Kentucky Derby Hosiery Co. Hopkinsville, Ky.	N109DC
☐ N123KH	95	Challenger 604	5301	Nag's Head Capital Management LLC. New Haven, Ct.	N608CC
☐ N123LC	00	Gulfstream 4SP	1441	L & L Leasing LLC. White Plains, NY.	N1289M
☐ N123M	01	Gulfstream V	667	Open Road Airways Inc. Wheeling, Il.	N121BN
☐ N123MJ	65	Learjet 23	23-036	ATWRK Inc. Boulder, Co.	YV-278CP
☐ N123MR	02	Gulfstream 4SP	1492	Mandalay Resort Group, Las Vegas, Nv.	N392GA
☐ N123PL	82	Citation 1/SP	501-0234	MWBP Foundation LLC/Statsoft Inc. Tulsa, Ok.	N77PX
☐ N123RA	66	Falcon 20C	30	Royal Air Freight Inc. Waterford, Mi.	N514SA
☐ N123RC	81	Westwind-Two	349	Marck Aviation LLC. Grosse Pointe, Mi.	N728L
☐ N123RF	81	Citation II	550-0220	Whitney Education Group Inc. Cape Coral, Fl.	N4ZS
☐ N123S	03	CitationJet CJ-1	525-0525	RTS Consulting LLC. Far Hills, NJ.	N.....
☐ N123SL	01	Citation X	750-0168	Silverline Building Products, North Brunswick, NJ.	N1288B
☐ N123TL	85	Gulfstream 3	452	Oslo Express Inc. New Canaan, Ct.	VP-BNZ
☐ N123VP	79	Citation II	550-0111	World Acceptance Corp. Greenville, SC.	(N3184Z)
☐ N124CS	01	CitationJet CJ-1	525-0472	CitationShares Sales Inc. White Plains, NY.	N.....
☐ N124DC	74	Sabre-60	306-95	Drummond Company Inc. Birmingham, Al.	N999DC
☐ N124DT	83	Gulfstream 3	390	Air Troxel LLC. Holualoa, Hi.	N102AQ
☐ N124FX	98	Learjet 31A	31A-156	BBJS/FlexJets, Addison, Tx.	(N29RE)
☐ N124GR	81	Westwind-Two	315	Grupo Ruisanchez Corp. Fort Lauderdale, Fl.	(N89TJ)
☐ N124JL	66	Learjet 24	24-127	Dolphin Aviation Inc. Sarasota, Fl.	(N6462)
☐ N124NS*	77	Citation	500-0368	Centre of Neuro Skills/CFNS Inc. Dover, De.	N124NB

Reg	Yr	Type	c/n	Owner/Operator	Prev Regn
N124SD	79	Sabre-65	465-2	Fayette Aviation Inc. Venice, Fl.	N624DS
N124WW	76	Westwind-1124	201	B & D Holdings Inc. Pembroke Pines, Fl.	C-FOIL
N124ZT	77	Learjet 35A	35A-138	55JS LC. Salt Lake City, Ut.	N138NA
N125AS	82	HS 125/700A	NA0333	LHT Air Inc. Tupelo, Ms.	(N301AS)
N125CA	82	Falcon 100	196	Air Waukegan LLC. Waukegan, Il.	N573J
N125CF	70	HS 125/400A	NA759	Appletree Holding LLC. Nashua, NH.	(N400MR)
N125CK	71	HS 125/F400A	25266	Kitty Hawk Charters Inc. Morristown, Tn.	N135CK
N125CS	03	CitationJet CJ-1	525-0522	Acrylic Performance Inc. Pomona, Ca.	N138CS
N125DC	69	Gulfstream 2	55	Drummond Company Inc. Birmingham, Al.	N225SE
N125DG	01	CitationJet CJ-2	525A-0015	Fugal Aviation LLC. Pleasant Grove, Ut.	N.....
N125DH	71	HS 125/731	NA762	Hendon Air Charters LLC. Charlotte, NC.	N400GP
N125DJ	00	CitationJet CJ-1	525-0422	Crypton Air LLC. Flint, Mi.	N51881
N125DS	75	Citation	500-0258	Medic Air Corp. Reno, Nv.	N886CA
N125DT	74	TriStar 100	1079	Ultimate Air Corp/Donald Trump, NYC.	C-GIFE
N125EA	80	Citation 1/SP	501-0125	Eastern Alloys Inc. Maybrook, NY.	N69EP
N125F	67	HS 125/3A-RA	25151	Joseph Simons III, Aylett, Va.	G-AVTY
N125FS	97	Learjet 31A	31A-125	Frontier Spinning Mills Inc. Sanford, NC.	N527JG
N125FX	98	Learjet 31A	31A-157	AXA LLC/South Hill AXA Corp. Klamath Falls, Or.	
N125GK	67	HS 125/F3B	25127	Great Idea Corp. Fort Lauderdale, Fl.	G-KASS
N125GP	98	Learjet 31A	31A-162	Trans Air Inc. Dublin, Ireland.	N162LJ
N125GW	03	Learjet 45	45-236	GW Aviation LLP. Luton, UK.	N5018G
N125HF	85	Westwind-1124	408	Henig Aviation LLC. Montgomery, Al.	N408MJ
N125HH	85	BAe 125/800B	8034	Crusader Aviation Inc. Oxford, Ct.	N85DW
N125JJ	68	Gulfstream 2	15	J T Aviation Corp. Ronkonkoma, NY.	(N571BJ)
N125JR	65	HS 125/1A	25052	Aircraft R Us Inc. San Diego, Ca.	(N252MA)
N125JW	81	Learjet 25G	25G-352	A B Enterprises of Oregon, Redding, Ca.	N25FN
N125N	86	Citation III	650-0129	San Juan 55 Inc. Carolina, PR.	PT-LUO
N125NA	73	HS 125/F600A	6026	Yellowstone Aviation LLC. Bozeman, Mt.	(N125YD)
N125NX	71	Sabre-75	370-3	Select Aviation Inc. Waukesha, Wi.	N125N
N125PS	86	Challenger 601	3058	Omni Restaurant Consulting Co. Newport Beach, Ca.	C-GLXU
N125PT	78	Learjet 25D	25D-244	Jet East Transportation LLC. Manhasset Hills, NY.	N831LH
N125Q	86	Citation III	650-0128	Milliken & Co. Greenville, SC.	N628CC
N125QA	86	Citation S/II	S550-0125	Capital City Aviation Inc. Madison, Wi.	(N552SM)
N125RG	87	HS 125/700A	NA0263	Omnisure Consulting Group Inc. Love Field, Tx.	(N263TN)
N125SB	85	BAe 125/800A	8046	McClatchy Newspapers Inc. Sacramento, Ca.	N800BA
N125SJ	80	HS 125/700A	NA0275	Superstar Jet Corp. Sanford, Me.	(N550JP)
N125ST	89	Challenger 601-3A	5052	Cusick Consulting LLC. Boerne, Tx.	N652CW
N125TM	00	Hawker 800XP	8496	EMC Corp. Bedford, Ma.	
N125XX	80	HS 125/700A	NA0254	Surewings Inc/Ambrion Aviation, Luton, UK.	N124AR
N125ZZ	03	Hawker 800XP	8630	D & J Aviation Ltd. Luton, UK.	N630XP
N126CX	94	Learjet 60	60-049	Wingedfoot Services LLC. West Palm Beach, Fl.	N247N
N126KC	95	Hawker 800	8276	B2 Flight LLC. Portland, Or.	N667H
N126KD	03	Learjet 60	60-262	Kardan Inc. Northbrook, Il.	N5051A
N126KL	84	Learjet 55	55-096	Williams Air Service Inc. St Augustine, Fl.	N126KD
N126MT	84	Citation III	650-0044	Advent Aviation 1 LLC. Stewart, NY.	N129PJ
N126TF	97	Citation Bravo	550-0815	Fox Lumber Sales Inc. Hamilton, Mt.	N51038
N127BJ	73	Citation	500-0120	Corporate Aviation Analysis & Planning, Addison, Tx.	N999TC
N127BU	80	Citation II/SP	551-0179	Champagne Louis-Roederer, Reims-Prunay. (was 550-0134).	N203BE
N127GB	74	Learjet 25XR	25XR-175	GBONE Inc. Sherman Oaks, Ca.	N75SJ
N127GK	80	Gulfstream 3	311	Cove Partners LLC. Van Nuys, Ca.	N127BK
N127JJ	78	Citation II	550-0007	JJ's Jet LLC. Zanesville, Oh.	(N660TY)
N127KC	94	Hawker 800	8255	AVX Corp. Myrtle Beach, SC.	N946H
N127PM	78	Citation II	550-0027	Quest Aviation Inc. Carlsbad, Ca.	N222D
N127QS	99	BBJ-7BC	30327	NetJets, Columbus, Oh.	N1786B
N127RC	86	Citation S/II	S550-0088	C F R Investments Inc. Jacksonville, Fl.	N288QS
N127RP	93	BAe 1000A	9036	Petersen Aviation, Van Nuys, Ca.	(N108RP)
N127SF	97	Falcon 900EX	13	Seneca Flight Operations, Penn Yan, NY.	VP-BRO
N127SG	93	CitationJet	525-0046	JetEast LLC. Cincinnati, Oh.	N123JN
N127SR	97	Challenger 604	5358	SDRM LLC. Fort Lauderdale, Fl.	C-GJQN
N127VL	91	Learjet 31A	31A-036	Konem Aviation LLC. Maimi, Fl.	(N127V)
N127WL	74	Falcon 10	16	Westwood Lumber Co. Saginaw, Mi.	N416HC
N128AB	02	Gulfstream G400	1501	Prime Jet LLC. Van Nuys, Ca.	(N402QS)
N128CA	79	Learjet 35A	35A-248	Ameriflight Inc. Burbank, Ca.	C-GBFA
N128CS	99	CitationJet CJ-1	525-0361	CitationShares Sales Inc. White Plains, NY.	N361RB
N128FX	98	Learjet 31A	31A-163	BBJS/FlexJets, Addison, Tx.	
N128JL	02	390 Premier 1	RB-28	Premier 1 LLC. Wilmington, De.	N128RM

Reg	Yr	Type	c/n	Owner/Operator	Prev Regn
N128KG	69	Gulfstream 2	62	The Kipp Ginsburg Trust, Boca Raton, Fl.	N262PA
N128LR	78	Learjet 28	28-001	Elite Aviation LLC. Burbank, Ca.	N3AS
N128TS	95	Gulfstream 4SP	1263	DSA Aviation/Development Services of America, Seattle, Wa.	N263S
N128V	01	Learjet 60	60-226	3 Air LLC. Chicago, Il.	N3011F
N128YT	74	HS 125/600A	6035	White Industries Inc. Bates City, Mo.	(N635PA)
N129BT	87	Beechjet 400	RJ-29	Hoovestal Inc. Eagan, Mn.	XA-OAC
N129DV	82	Citation II	550-0365	Giddy Up N Go/Architectural Cost Control Systms, Dallas, Tx.	N100AY
N129JE	82	Falcon 50	127	Sackett Corp. NYC.	N1896F
N129KJ	00	Falcon 900C	184	Ohana Aircraft Ltd. Los Gatos, Ca.	F-WWFP
N129MC	96	Beechjet 400A	RK-129	Jet Equity Fleet LLC. Greenwich, Ct.	N1129X
N129ME	79	Learjet 24F	24F-357	Kingswood Aviation Inc. Los Gatos, Ca.	N288J
N129MH	03	Gulfstream G400	1517	Medco Health Solutions Inc. Franklin Lakes, NJ.	N517GA
N129PB	01	Citation Bravo	550-0973	Phoenix Bogo Inc. Wilmington, De.	N5245U
N129QS	99	BBJ-7BC	30329	NetJets, Columbus, Oh.	N1787B
N129SG	02	CitationJet CJ-2	525A-0129	Missoula Air LLC. Jackson, Wy.	N.....
N129TF	93	Challenger 601-3A	5129	TF Air LLC/TAG Aviation USA, White Plains, NY.	(N603AF)
N129TS	79	Learjet 35A	35A-253	Development Services of America Inc. Seattle, Wa.	N611SH
N129WA	67	Gulfstream 2B	9	John Wing Aviation Inc. Conroe, Tx.	N48EC
N130CE	73	Citation Eagle	500-0130	Tumac Industries Inc. Grand Junction, Co.	N800AB
N130CK	69	Learjet 25	25-038	Kalitta Charters LLC. Detroit-Willow Run, Mi.	N813JW
N130CS	02	CitationJet CJ-1	525-0490	CitationShares Sales Inc. White Plains, NY.	N52141
N130DW	74	Citation	500-0187	Far West Capital Inc. Salt Lake City, Ut.	N5FW
N130F	75	Learjet 35	35-044	AirNet Systems Inc. Columbus, Oh. (black).	(N44VW)
N130FX	98	Learjet 31A	31A-172	Downs Aircraft Inc. Bakersfield, Ca.	(N197PH)
N130GV	00	Gulfstream V	630	EDS Information Services LLC. Dallas, Tx.	N630GA
N130LC	92	BAe 125/800B	8228	Lakes Entertainment Inc. Minnetonka, Mn.	HB-VKV
N130LM	97	CitationJet	525-0214	Omni Leasing Corp. Lexington, Ky.	N130NM
N130RS	67	Learjet 24	24-138	Rocketplane Ltd Inc. Oklahoma City, Ok.	N94JJ
N130TM	01	Gulfstream V	660	Toyota Motor Sales USA Inc. Long Beach, Ca.	N533GA
N130TS	86	Citation III	650-0130	Hauck Casualty LLC. Cincinnati, Oh.	(N603HC)
N130WC	94	Citation V Ultra	560-0277	NetJets, Columbus, Oh.	N308QS
N130YB	80	HS 125/700A	NA0285	Curwood Inc. Oshkosh, Wi.	(N14WJ)
N131AP	86	Beechjet 400	RJ-10	Cor Aviation Inc. Orlando, Fl. (was A1010SA).	I-ALSE
N131BH	64	Sabre-40	282-18	Jett Racing & Sales Inc. Laredo, Tx.	N15TS
N131BR	93	Learjet 31A	31A-074	SMC Aviation LLC. Coeur d'Alene, Id.	N174TS
N131DA*	97	Learjet 31A	31A-136	Bombardier Aerospace Corp. Windsor Locks, Ct.	N119FX
N131EP	95	Falcon 2000	10	Westshore Aviation/Prince Transportation Inc. Holland, Mi.	N652PC
N131FX	99	Learjet 31A	31A-175	BBJS/FlexJets, Addison, Tx.	
N131GG	95	Learjet 31A	31A-113	Global Aviation LLC. Nicholasville, Ky.	(N642GG)
N131LA	70	HS 125/400A	NA750	N131LA LLC. Salem, Or.	XA-RWN
N131MV	66	Falcon 20C	31	Miami Valley Aviation Inc. Middletown, Oh.	N828AA
N131RG	96	CitationJet	525-0159	Administrative Concepts Inc. Long Beach, Ca.	N51872
N131TR	00	Learjet 60	60-216	WFBNW NA. Salt Lake City, Ut.	
N131TT	91	Learjet 31A	31A-049	Learshares 31 Inc. Fort Lauderdale, Fl.	N107GM
N132AH	96	CitationJet	525-0132	Air Prospect LLC. Louisville, Ky.	(N132RP)
N132CS	03	CitationJet CJ-1	525-0515	CitationShares Sales Inc. White Plains, NY.	N52141
N132EP	82	Falcon 20F-5B	463	Westshore Aviation/Prince Transportation Inc. Holland, Mi.	N134JA
N132FP	74	Gulfstream II SP	153	Crenshaw Christian Center Church, Van Nuys, Ca.	N110VW
N132FX	99	Learjet 31A	31A-177	BBJS/FlexJets, Addison, Tx.	
N132JC	01	Gulfstream G200	039	HM Aviation Inc. Wilmington, De.	(N302HM)
N132LA	69	Jet Commander-B	133	Alberto Herreros, Miami, Fl. (status ?).	XB-GBZ
N132MT	03	Citation Bravo	550-1080	Metal Technologies Inc. Auburn, In.	N.....
N132RL	67	HS 125/3A-RA	NA704	White Industries Inc. Bates City, Mo.	C-GSKV
N132TP*	84	Learjet 55	55-098	ARK Interests LLC. Wilmington, De.	N1324P
N133B	02	390 Premier 1	RB-68	BravoAir LLC. Leesburg, Va.	N50648
N133CS	02	CitationJet CJ-1	525-0502	CitationShares Sales Inc. White Plains, NY.	N51881
N133EJ	77	Learjet 35A	35A-133	Scott Smolen, N Tonawanda, NY.	N133GJ
N133EP	78	Falcon 10	131	Westshore Aviation/Prince Transportation Inc. Holland, Mi.	HB-VME
N133FX	99	Learjet 31A	31A-179	BBJS/FlexJets, Addison, Tx.	
N133JM	72	Citation	500-0028	Americana Aviation Inc. Albert Lea, Mn.	(N9LV)
N133VP	87	Citation S/II	S550-0133	Morrow Aviation Inc. Ormond Beach, Fl.	N431WM
N133WA	82	Citation II	550-0356	King Air E90 LLC. Apple Valley, Mn.	PT-OER
N134AR	99	BBJ-7AH	29749	BB Five Inc. DuPage, Il.	C6-TTB
N134AX	01	Gulfstream G200	034	JLT Aircraft Holding LLC. St Paul, Mn.	(N200GA)
N134BJ	97	Beechjet 400A	RK-134	Cabelas Inc. Sidney, Ne.	N1094D
N134BR	90	Gulfstream 4	1139	GSCP (NJ) Inc. Florham Park, NJ.	N331P

Reg	Yr	Type	c/n	Owner/Operator	Prev Regn

Reg	Yr	Type	c/n	Owner/Operator	Prev Regn
N134CM	97	Beechjet 400A	RK-144	Max Air LLC/Max Media LLC. Virginia Beach, Va.	
N134FA	92	Beechjet 400A	RK-34	HUSCO International Inc. Waukesha, Wi.	N721SS
N134FX	99	Learjet 31A	31A-195	BBJS/FlexJets, Addison, Tx.	
N134N	69	Jet Commander	134	UTCU LP. League City, Tx.	N7638S
N134RG	83	Diamond 1A	A037SA	TCA Leasing Inc. Duluth, Ga.	N109TW
N134RT*	81	HS 125/700A	NA0295	Thompson Management LLC. NYC.	N134NW
N134SW	04	390 Premier 1	RB-81	Sugar Woods Family Aviation LLC. Shreveport, La.	N390P
N134VS	81	Challenger 600	1034	Challenger Aircraft Holdings Inc. NYC.	LV-YLB
N134WE	77	Learjet 25XR	25XR-222	Air One Inc. Nashville, Tn.	N225TJ
N135AG	77	Learjet 35A	35A-132	N135AG LLC. West Columbia, SC.	N37TJ
N135BC	95	Challenger 800	7075	Burrell Colour, Crown Point, In.	N877SE
N135BJ	97	Beechjet 400A	RK-135	McNeil Transportation II LLC. Monroe, NC.	N1135A
N135CS	03	CitationJet CJ-1	525-0520	CitationShares Sales Inc. White Plains, NY.	N.....
N135DA	81	Learjet 35A	35A-405	Delta Airelite Business Jets Inc. Cincinnati, Oh.	N442DM
N135DE	91	Learjet 35A	35A-667	U S Department of Energy, Albuquerque, NM.	N91566
N135FA	76	Learjet 35A	35A-067	American Jet International Corp. Houston, Tx.	(N52FL)
N135GJ	77	Learjet 35A	35A-135	Maritime Sales & Leasing Inc. Newman, Ga.	I-ZOOM
N135HC	88	Citation III	650-0158	Southern Bag Corp Ltd & others, Madison, Ms.	N121AT
N135LR	82	Learjet 55	55-068	RL Aviation LLC. Van Nuys, Ca.	N38D
N135SG	03	EMB-135BJ Legacy	145706	United Aviation, Kuwait City, Kuwait.	PT-SAX
N135TP	82	Learjet 35A	35A-462	Aspen Furniture Designs Inc. Scottsdale, Az.	N7117
N135WC	94	Citation V Ultra	560-0261	BATT Partners LLC. Bossier City, La.	N305QS
N135WE	79	Learjet 35A	35A-240	M & W Inc. Smyrna, Tn.	N249B
N136DH	78	Learjet 36A	36A-036	Douglas Herbert Performance Parts, Concord, NC.	N36MJ
N136FX	99	Learjet 31A	31A-196	BBJS/FlexJets, Addison, Tx.	
N136JP	80	Learjet 35A	35A-359	J Spinner LLC. Denver, Co.	HB-VHB
N136MW	69	HFB 320	1036	Kalitta Flying Service Inc. Morristown, Tn.	(N92047)
N137FX	00	Learjet 31A	31A-201	BBJS/FlexJets, Addison, Tx.	N4003K
N137JC	91	Citation V	560-0137	Isle of Capri Casinos Inc. Biloxi, Ms.	N193G
N137RP	92	BAe 1000A	9021	Petersen Aviation, Van Nuys, Ca.	VP-CMZ
N137WC	76	Citation	500-0305	Air 1 Inc. St Cloud, Mn.	C-GMLC
N137WR	78	HS 125/700A	NA0225	Waddell & Reed Development Inc. Kansas City, Mo.	N995SA
N138AV	83	Falcon 50	138	Aerovertigo Inc/Aero Air LLC. Hillsboro, Or.	N380TJ
N138DM	81	Falcon 10	181	Jabil Circuit Inc. Fort Myers, Fl.	F-GJHG
N138F	98	Falcon 900B	174	First International Aviation Inc. Caracas, Venezuela.	N138FA
N138FJ	77	Falcon 20F	369	Ethox Chemicals Inc. Greensboro-High Point, NC.	N420J
N138J	80	Citation II	550-0118	Fairmont Partners One LLC. Los Angeles, Ca.	N118EA
N138M	98	Falcon 50EX	274	Motorola Inc. Schaumburg, Il.	F-WWHY
N138SA	73	Citation	500-0138	Miller Management Group Inc. Erie, Pa.	N3056R
N138SP	00	Citation X	750-0138	Mirage Enterprises Inc. Van Nuys, Ca.	N5241Z
N139LJ	05	Challenger 300	20039	Learjet Inc. Wichita, Ks.	C-G...
N139M	97	Hawker 8C^VP	8330	Brunswick Corp. Waukegan, Il.	N330XP
N139MY	85	Citation III	650-0072	MT Yack Aviation LLC. Wilmington, De.	N72ST
N139SK	83	Learjet 55	55-082	Airkraft LLC. Tallahassee, Fl.	N817AM
N139ST	89	Learjet 55C	55C-139	Building Exchange Co. Richmond, Va.	PT-GMN
N140AE	04	Global Express	9140	Bombardier Aerospace Corp. Windsor-Locks, Ct.	C-GAGQ
N140CA	73	Learjet 25B	25B-140	Cherry Air Inc. Addison, Tx.	N403AC
N140DA	02	CitationJet CJ-2	525A-0140	Dobber Aviation LLC. Tulsa-R L Jones, Ok.	N.....
N140DR	78	Westwind-1124	242	RAL Capital LLC. Scottsdale, Az.	N340DR
N140GB	02	Hawker 800XP	8594	OGB LLC. Pittsburgh-Atkinson, Ks.	N61904
N140GC	77	Learjet 25D	25D-225	B & C Flight Management Inc. Houston, Tx.	N808DS
N140JC	97	Learjet 60	60-106	Next Group LLC. Madison, Ms.	N106LJ
N140QS	04	Hawker 400XP	RK-406	NetJets, Columbus, Oh.	
N140RF	66	Sabre-40A	282-67	Centurion Investments Inc. St Louis, Mo.	N711T
N140SC	74	TriStar 500	1067	Orbital Sciences Corp. Bakersfield, Ca.	C-FTNJ
N140TS	87	Citation III	650-0141	Crest Jet LLC/Crest Industries LLC. Pineville, La.	N21WJ
N140VJ	87	Westwind-1124	435	Carlisle Air Corp. Portsmouth, NH.	N279JS
N141AB	02	Citation Bravo	550-1044	BAHACO LLC. Marina del Ray, Ca.	N52369
N141AL	81	HS 125/700A	NA0306	ADESA Inc & ALLETE Inc. Duluth, Mn.	N800MP
N141AQ	91	Citation V	560-0141	The Rothbury Corp. Midlothian, Va.	N6876S
N141DR	98	Beechjet 400A	RK-184	Quad C Management Inc. Charlottesville, Va.	N2314F
N141EX	04	Falcon 900EX EASY	141	Dassault Falcon Jet Corp. Teterboro, NJ.	F-WWFS
N141FM	82	Learjet 55	55-041	Integic Corp. Chantilly, Va.	HK-4016X
N141HL	97	Citation Bravo	550-0803	Hotel Lima LLC. New Orleans, La.	N550FB
N141JC	82	Citation II	550-0341	Silverhawk Aviation Inc. Lincoln, Ne.	(N367EA)
N141JF	71	Gulfstream 2	106	Aero Falcons LLC. Ontario, Ca.	(N473JF)

Reg	Yr	Type	c/n	Owner/Operator	Prev Regn
N141M	77	Citation 1/SP	501-0039	Reef Investments LLC. Pontiac, Mi.	N507DS
N141MH	83	Gulfstream 3	378	Cinema Aircraft Executive Transportation, Hillsboro, Or.	N920DC
N141RD	82	Challenger 600S	1041	AirButler LLC. Northbrook, Il.	N141TS
N141SL	78	Sabre-60	306-141	Revealing Truth Ministries, Tampa, Fl.	(N707GP)
N142AA	02	Citation Excel	560-5281	On Time Aviation Corp. Riyadh, Saudi Arabia.	(N68AA)
N142DA	77	Citation 1/SP	501-0004	EKA Aviation LLC. Dover, De.	N86JJ
N142EX	04	Falcon 900EX EASY	142	Dassault Falcon Jet Corp. Teterboro, NJ.	F-WWFU
N142HC	02	Gulfstream 4SP	1489	Delta Jet Ltd. Oxford, Ct.	N389GA
N142TJ	81	Citation II/SP	551-0359	The Langston Law Firm PA. Booneville, Ms.	(N551SE)
N143BP	03	Citation Bravo	550-1072	Cornerstone Aviation LLC. Aspen, Co.	N5148B
N143CK	73	Learjet 25B	25B-143	Cross & Kaufman Logging, Ashland, Or.	N113RF
N143CM	04	390 Premier 1	RB-114	Shoffner Aviation LLC. Raleigh, NC.	
N143DH	04	Citation Excel XLS	560-5514	Departures LLC. Daytona Beach, Fl.	N5086W
N143DZ	79	Sabre-60	306-142	CORE Projects Inc. Fresno, Ca.	(N700DA)
N143G	88	MD-87	49670	Otter Corp/422 Holdings Inc. Seattle, Wa.	N3H
N143GB	71	Learjet 24XR	24XR-233	Horizon Aircraft Maintenance LLC. Wichita, Ks.	(N56GH)
N143HM	98	Beechjet 400A	RK-205	Cast Masters Inc/Warmack & Co. Texarkana, Tx.	(N17CM)
N143KS	98	Gulfstream 4SP	1364	Spectacor Inc & Kalco Corp. Raleigh, NC.	N364GA
N143PL*	84	Citation III	650-0058	Fred J Lee LLC. Lawrenceville, Ga.	(N650JS)
N143V	68	Gulfstream II SP	17	Plains Exploration & Production Co. Houston, Tx.	N143G
N144BS	89	Challenger 601-3A	5033	Monte Carlo Associates LLC. Carvallis, Or.	N397Q
N144EM	02	CitationJet CJ-2	525A-0120	CJ2 LLC/Blue Sky Inc. Coatesville, Pa.	N5130J
N144EX	04	Falcon 900EX EASY	144	Dassault Falcon Jet Corp. Teterboro, NJ.	F-WWFW
N144GA	79	Citation II	550-0065	Trans-Equipment Services LLC/Spinx Co. Greenville, SC.	ZS-RCS
N144HM	99	Hawker 800XP	8431	M & M Air Inc. Dover, Fl.	
N144KK	01	Gulfstream V	669	Sheridan-Alii Aviation LLC. San Jose, Ca.	N569GA
N144MH	95	Citation VII	650-7059	Nashoba Inc. Dallas, Tx.	N76PR
N144PK	92	Gulfstream 4SP	1210	P K Aire Inc. Burbank, Ca.	N410QS
N144YD	02	CitationJet CJ-2	525A-0144	Pinstripe Inc. Stratford, Ct.	N.....
N144Z	00	Citation Bravo	550-0926	USDA Forest Service, Boise, Id.	N100Z
N145AM	76	Learjet 35A	35A-078	J C Jet Service Inc. Carrollton, Oh.	N45AW
N145AR	02	Learjet 45	45-203	ACR Enterprises LLC. Valley View, Tx.	
N145CG	01	Learjet 45	45-107	CTI of North Carolina Inc. Wilmington, NC.	
N145CX	00	Citation X	750-0145	Interstate Equipment Leasing Inc. Phoenix, Az.	(N745CW)
N145DF	84	Citation S/II	S550-0018	Star Diamond Co. Luton, UK.	N1AF
N145GM	99	Learjet 45	45-081	Tiara Air LLC. Naples, Fl.	N76TE
N145HC	02	Learjet 45	45-231	United States Aviation Co. Tulsa, Ok.	N30PF
N145K	99	Learjet 45	45-071	Koch Industries Inc. Wichita, Ks.	
N145SB	02	Learjet 45	45-142	KAG Services LLC. Eugene, Or.	(N450DS)
N145SH	73	Learjet 25B	25B-145	Valdosta Mall Inc. Duluth, Ga.	N2127E
N145SM	00	Citation Excel	560-5082	On Time Aviation Corp. Riyadh, Saudi Arabia.	
N145TA	74	Citation	500-0145	Sierra Foxtrot Charlie Inc. Kansas City, Mo.	(N415FC)
N145XL	01	Learjet 45	45-106	Xcel Energy Services Co. Minneapolis, Mn.	
N145XR	04	Learjet 45	45-251	LJ Leasing LLC. Bowling Green, Ky.	N40073
N146AS	02	Falcon 50EX	325	SeeCon Builders Inc. Concord, Ca.	N325EX
N146BA	96	Challenger 604	5327	TPS LLC. Bellevue, Wa.	D-AJAB
N146CT	01	Citation Bravo	550-0980	I D E Consultants Inc. Weston, Fl.	N312CS
N146EP	01	Citation Excel	560-5224	Complejo Educativo Parra Diaz, Caracas, Venezuela.	N5093L
N146EX	04	Falcon 900EX EASY	146	Dassault Falcon Jet Corp. Teterboro, NJ.	F-WWFZ
N146XL	01	Learjet 45	45-187	Southwestern Public Service Co. Amarillo, Tx.	N5030J
N147A	04	Westwind-1124	294	Salter Labs, Arvin, Ca.	HK-3884X
N147BJ	97	Beechjet 400A	RK-147	Aircraft Leasing International Inc. Teterboro, NJ.	
N147CA	77	Learjet 25D	25D-221	Palskids Inc. Poway, Ca.	YU-BKR
N147CK	67	Learjet 24	24-147	Kalitta Flying Service Inc. Morristown, Tn.	N147KH
N147CX	01	Citation X	750-0147	Interstate Equipment Leasing Inc. Phoenix, Az.	(N787CW)
N147G	87	Falcon 100	214	W W Grainger Inc. Palwaukee, Il.	N275FJ
N147RJ	91	Citation V	560-0147	Jackson Air Service LLC. Jackson, Wy.	N410J
N147SB*	96	Citation V Ultra	560-0380	Shields Real Estate LLC. Yakima, Wa.	N190KL
N147SC	73	Citation	500-0077	N147SC LLC/Humphrey Aviation LLC. Columbia, Md.	ZS-OAM
N147SW	02	Gulfstream G100	147	Contract Transportation Systems LP. Cleveland, Oh.	N147GA
N147TA	86	Citation III	650-0119	Tanimura & Antle Inc. Salinas, Ca.	N147PS
N147TW	68	Learjet 25	25-023	Sierra American Corp. Addison, Tx.	N767SC
N147X	81	Gulfstream 3	336	DX Service Co. Houston, Tx.	(N102PT)
N148ED	80	Citation 1/SP	501-0148	Tropic Aircraft Service Inc. Lakeland, Fl.	N148EA
N148FB	02	CitationJet CJ-2	525A-0148	Hawker Aviation Services LLC. Nashville, Tn.	N5132T
N148GB	98	Beechjet 400A	RK-185	Alpine Technologies Inc. Greenville, Tn.	(N450AT)
Reg	Yr	Type	c/n	Owner/Operator	Prev Regn

Reg	Yr	Type	c/n	Owner/Operator	Prev Regn
☐ N148H	77	Westwind-1124	206	Navajo Refining Co. Dallas, Tx.	N100ME
☐ N148J	83	Diamond 1A	A033SA	Air Charter & Sales LLC. Columbia, Mo.	N717DF
☐ N148M	97	Falcon 50EX	270	Motorola Inc. Schaumberg, Il.	N270EX
☐ N148MC	80	Falcon 20-5B	428	Mountaire Corp. Little Rock, Ar.	N98R
☐ N148TW	68	Falcon 20C	148	Sierra American Corp. Addison, Tx.	N148WC
☐ N148V	69	Gulfstream 2B	54	Bayoil (USA) Inc. Wilmington, De.	N955CC
☐ N149SB	03	Hawker 800XP	8654	Elk River Aviation Inc. Asheville, NC.	N654XP
☐ N149VB	97	Falcon 2000	53	JVB Aviation Falcon LLC. Broomfield, Co.	N149V
☐ N150BB	00	Challenger 604	5470	Janice B Brittingham, Dallas, Tx.	N604AC
☐ N150BC	98	Falcon 2000	67	Holiday Retirement Corp. Salem, Or.	F-WWMK
☐ N150BV	98	CitationJet	525-0320	Dynamic Aviation LLC/Steel Dynamics Inc. Fort Wayne, In.	
☐ N150CA	82	Diamond 1	A023SA	Charlie Air LLC. West Columbia, SC.	N22BN
☐ N150CT	03	Gulfstream G100	152	Gulfstream Aerospace LP. Fort Worth, Tx.	N352GA
☐ N150EX	79	Westwind-1124	262	Boomerang Air Inc. Wiley Post, Ok.	N79KP
☐ N150JP	92	Citation VII	650-7010	Ahold USA Holdings Inc. Chantilly, Va.	(N403BL)
☐ N150K	82	Falcon 50	108	Koch Industries Inc. Wichita, Ks.	N350X
☐ N150MH	84	Challenger 601	3021	McKesson Information Solutions Inc. Atlanta-De Kalb, Ga.	N966L
☐ N150MS	82	Learjet 55	55-049	Martin Sprocket & Gear Inc. Fort Worth, Tx.	D-CCHS
☐ N150NC	96	Hawker 800XP	8293	National City Corp. Cleveland, Oh.	N404CE
☐ N150RM	78	Citation 1/SP	501-0076	AMC II LLC. Greenville, NC.	N315MP
☐ N150RS	74	Learjet 25XR	25XR-162	Stern Holdings Inc. Dallas, Tx.	N97JJ
☐ N150SB	91	BAe 125/800B	8197	Pecos Aircraft Sales & Leasing LLC. Irving, Tx.	G-OMGE
☐ N150TF	99	Beechjet 400A	RK-240	T F Holding Corp. Harrisburg, Il.	N749SS
☐ N150TT	74	Citation	500-0176	Fostill West LLC. Chamblee, Ga.	G-TEFH
☐ N150TX	80	Falcon 50	13	DHM Aviation LLC. Dallas, Tx.	(N150NW)
☐ N151AG	66	Learjet 24	24-137	George Smith, Corona del Mar, Ca.	N72FP
☐ N151AS	74	Citation	500-0183	MTW Aerospace Inc. Montgomery, Al.	N112CP
☐ N151CS	04	CitationJet CJ-1	525-0529	CitationShares Sales Inc. White Plains, NY.	N50820
☐ N151DR	87	Citation III	650-0147	B & K Citation SII LLC. NYC.	N94BJ
☐ N151FD	04	Citation Bravo	550-1087	Bravo Enterprises LLC. McKinney, Tx.	N.....
☐ N151GR	01	Falcon 2000	151	Guthy-Renker Aviation, Palm Desert, Ca.	G-IBSF
☐ N151SD	94	Gulfstream 4SP	1249	NAJ/D S Advisors Inc. Palwaukee, Il.	N634S
☐ N151SG	65	HS 125/1A	25035	Canamera Holdings, Hillsborough, Or.	(N57TS)
☐ N151SP	77	Citation 1/SP	501-0021	Summa Peto LLC. Portola Valley, Ca.	ZS-MGL
☐ N151TM	03	Citation Bravo	550-1063	United American Insurance Co. McKinney, Tx.	N96TM
☐ N151WW	68	Learjet 24	24-170	Addison Aviation Services Inc. Addison, Tx.	N200DH
☐ N152CS	04	CitationJet CJ-1	525-0539	CitationShares Sales Inc. White Plains, NY.	N.....
☐ N152JH	02	Citation Encore	560-0615	Jack Henry & Associates Inc. Monett, Mo.	N5108G
☐ N152KV	96	CitationJet	525-0152	Plane House LLC. Indianapolis, In.	N152KC
☐ N153AG	65	Learjet 23	23-058	Great Oaks Institute of Technology, Cincinnati, Oh.	N7FJ
☐ N153CS	04	CitationJet CJ-1	525-0548	Cessna Aircraft Co. Wichita, Ks.	N5216A
☐ N153SG	04	Citation Bravo	550-1088	Henry Crown & Co. Palwaukee, Il.	N.....
☐ N154C	79	Gulfstream II SP	253	CONSOL Inc. Allegheny County, Pa.	N15TG
☐ N154FJ	80	HS 125/700A	NA0271	F-Jets LLC/F-Jets Charters LLC. Tampa, Fl.	N177JW
☐ N154G	88	Gulfstream 4	1044	Timberland Aviation Inc. Manchester, NH.	N1540
☐ N154JC	71	HS 125/731	25249	JHC Aviation LLC. Tucson, Az.	(N303BX)
☐ N154JH	01	Citation Encore	560-0555	Jack Henry & Associates Inc. Monett, Mo.	N5155G
☐ N154JS	00	Citation Encore	560-0540	J R Simplot Co. Boise, Id.	N540CV
☐ N154NS	94	Challenger 601-3R	5169	Norfolk Southern Railway Co. Norfolk, Va.	N773A
☐ N154PA	85	Falcon 50	154	Anschutz Corp. Denver, Co.	N404E
☐ N154RA	99	CitationJet	525-0304	RAB Aviation Holdings Inc. Wilmington, De.	EC-HBX
☐ N154RT	98	Learjet 31A	31A-154	Ruby Tuesday Inc. Knoxville, Tn.	N337RB
☐ N154SC	80	Citation 1/SP	501-0154	Alan Aviation LLC. Santa Monica, Ca.	CC-CWW
☐ N154VP	91	Citation V	560-0154	Moran Foods Inc/Save-A-Lot Ltd. St Louis, Mo.	N503T
☐ N155AC	88	Citation II	550-0573	AC Aviation Inc. Dover, De.	PT-OKM
☐ N155AM	77	Learjet 35A	35A-131	N155AM LLC. West Columbia, SC.	N26GD
☐ N155AN	03	Gulfstream G550	5029	Nissan North America Inc. Smyrna, Tn.	(N550RN)
☐ N155BC	85	Learjet 55	55-115	M M Coal Co & B & S Resources Inc. Columbus, Oh.	N633AC
☐ N155DB	90	Learjet 55C	55C-141	R & J Associates Inc. Santa Fe, NM.	
☐ N155FF*	80	Citation II	550-0155	Fox Flite Inc. Tulsa, Ok.	N215CW
☐ N155GM	82	Learjet 55	55-022	Fly 22 LLC. Livingston, NJ.	VP-BOL
☐ N155JC	82	Learjet 55	55-071	Stevens & Soldwisch Aircraft LLC. Denver, Co.	(N113YS)
☐ N155JH	01	Citation Encore	560-0568	Jack Henry & Associates Inc. Monett, Mo.	N52369
☐ N155LR	83	Learjet 55	55-074	RL Aviation LLC. Van Nuys, Ca.	N701DB
☐ N155ME	83	Westwind-1124	391	Shaw Managed Services Inc. Baton Rouge, La.	C-GMPF
☐ N155MK	74	Citation	500-0155	Joseph Tomkinson Inc. Newport Beach, Ca.	(N188DR)

Reg	Yr	Type	c/n	Owner/Operator	Prev Regn
N155MM	81	Gulfstream 3	325	N15MM LLC. Melville, NY.	N393U
N155NS	01	Hawker 800XP	8549	Norfolk Southern Railway Co. Norfolk, Va.	N51149
N155PT	94	Citation V	560-0257	Rig Corp/P J Taggares Co. Othello, Wa.	N1293L
N155RB	85	Learjet 55	55-117	Tulsair Beechcraft Inc. Tulsa, Ok.	N255MB
N155RM	01	390 Premier 1	RB-6	Jake's Fireworks Inc. Nevada, Mo.	N390R
N155SB	81	Learjet 55	55-013	Lencork LLC. Fort Lauderdale, Fl.	D-CUTE
N155SP	89	Learjet 55C	55C-137	SVW Air LLC. San Antonio, Tx.	N95SC
N155VP	91	Citation V	560-0155	Meyer Chatfield Aviation Services, N Philadelphia, Pa.	N40WP
N156BE	76	Falcon 10	87	Fuccillo Automotive Group Inc. Syracuse, NY.	N156BF
N156BF	03	Learjet 60	60-266	Fuccillo Automotive Group Inc. Syracuse, NY.	N266LJ
N156DB	81	Falcon 50	40	LKE LLC. Westport, Ct.	N150JT
N156DH	92	Beechjet 400A	RK-36	H & O Aviation LC. Wheeling, WV.	N57B
N156JH	01	Citation Encore	560-0575	Jack Henry & Associates Inc. Monett, Mo.	N5257C
N156JS	93	Learjet 31	31-033A	N156JS LLC. Coatesville, Pa.	N311LJ
N156ML	96	CitationJet	525-0156	Mark & Diana Levy, Paradise Valley, Az.	
N156NS	04	Hawker 800XP	8668	Norfolk Southern Railway Co. Norfolk, Va.	N668XP
N156PH	99	Learjet 45	45-027	Parker Hannifin International Corp. Cleveland, Oh.	
N156QS	00	BBJ-7BC	30756	NetJets, Columbus, Oh.	N1003W
N156WC	82	Falcon 50	89	NetJets, Columbus, Oh.	CS-DFI
N157AG	72	Learjet 24D	24D-252	Vail Jet Inc. Vail, Co.	(C6-BGF)
N157BM	88	Citation S/II	S550-0157	The Rivett Group LLC. Aberdeen, SD.	N157QS
N157DW	81	Citation II	550-0253	Woods & McCauley Aviation LLC. Counce, Tn. (was 551-0308).	N953FT
N157GA	86	Astra-1125	015	E & L Adventures LLC. Burbank, Ca.	N755PA
N157H	93	Gulfstream 4SP	1209	H J Heinz Co. Pittsburgh, Pa. 'Collegiality'	N445GA
N157JH	01	Citation Encore	560-0581	Jack Henry & Associates Inc. Monett, Mo.	N5269Z
N157JS	95	Learjet 31	31-033D	Equity Jets LLC. Coatesville, Pa.	N312LJ
N157PH	99	Learjet 45	45-030	Parker Hannifin International Corp. Cleveland, Oh.	N5012H
N157RP*	76	HS 125/600A	6067	Sub-Par Investments LLC. Wilmington, NC.	N822BD
N157SP	91	Astra-1125SP	057	Cementario Promociones y Ventas CA. Caracas, Venezuela.	YV-785CP
N157TW	68	Learjet 24	24-157	Sierra American Corp. Addison, Tx.	N659AT
N157WH	97	Beechjet 400A	RK-157	Hoovestol Inc. St Paul, Mn.	N897AT
N158CJ	03	CitationJet CJ-2	525A-0158	Zygmunt Solorz-Zak, Warsaw, Poland.	N.....
N158EC	01	Learjet 45	45-186	E C Aviation Services Inc. Holland-Tulip City, Mi.	
N158JA	97	Falcon 900EX	20	eBay Inc. San Jose, Ca.	N920EX
N158M	98	Falcon 50EX	273	Motorola Inc. Schaumburg, Il.	F-WWHX
N158PH	99	Learjet 45	45-047	Parker Hannifin International Corp. Cleveland, Oh.	
N158R	00	Learjet 31A	31A-189	Bombardier Aerospace Corp. Windsor Locks, Ct.	N316RS
N158TW	68	Falcon 20D	158	Sierra American Corp. Addison, Tx.	N450MA
N159AK	96	Beechjet 400A	RK-120	400A Air Charters LLC/Golden Eagle Air Inc. Farmingdale, NY.	N9146Z
N159EC	02	Learjet 45	45-229	E C Aviation Services Inc. Holland-Tulip City, Mi.	
N159JA*	04	Gulfstream G550	5062	Gulfstream Aerospace Corp. Savannah, Ga.	N962GA
N159KC	74	Citation	500-0159	M J Enterprises LLC. Springfield, Mo.	N97DD
N159LC	79	Citation 1/SP	501-0094	Midwest Aircraft Holdings LLC. Sugar Grove, Il.	N59CC
N159NB	74	Gulfstream 2B	140	Tikchik LLC. Anchorage, Ak.	N730TK
N160AG	68	HS 125/3A-RA	NA707	Aero Flight Service Inc. Fort Lauderdale, Fl.	SE-DHH
N160AN	98	Learjet 60	60-126	Jetride Inc. Dallas, Tx.	N224FX
N160CT	97	Hawker 800XP	8331	Coca-Cola Enterprises Inc. Atlanta-Fulton County, Ga.	N510BA
N160FJ	80	Falcon 10	160	Gemini Aircraft LLC. Carson City, Nv.	LX-JCG
N160GC	77	Learjet 36A	36A-030	Hudson Flight Ltd. Pampa, Tx.	(N36AX)
N160GH	98	Learjet 60	60-129	Hunt Corp/Lobo Aviation LLC. Scottsdale, Az.	N45US
N160H	84	Diamond 1A	A084SA	Avion Aircraft Sales LLC. Sanford, Fl.	N160S
N160LC	82	Challenger 600S	1068	Royal Pacific Aviation/Executive Flight, Pangborn Memorial.	N938WH
N160RM	98	Learjet 60	60-147	Rail Management Corp. Panama City Beach, Fl.	N133SR
N160TM	03	Gulfstream G400	1526	TAI Leasing Inc. Long Beach, Ca.	N526GA
N160W	72	Sabre-40A	282-101	Northrop Grumman Corp. Los Angeles, Ca.	N101RR
N160WC	86	Hawker 800 SP	8069	Washington Corps. Missoula, Mt. 'The Future is on the Wing'	N364WC
N160WS	96	Falcon 2000	28	American International Aviation Corp. Houston, Tx.	N596A
N161CC	74	Citation	500-0161	Universal Solutions Inc. Millville, NJ.	C-GHEC
N161CM	67	Sabre-60	306-5	White Industries Inc. Bates City, Mo.	(N477JM)
N161MM	02	Gulfstream G400	1511	Aircraft Properties LLC. West Palm Beach, Fl.	N201GA
N161NG	66	BAC 1-11/401AK	067	Northrop Grumman Corp. Baltimore, Md.	N765CF
N161TM	98	Citation Bravo	550-0867	Step 2 Co. Dover, Oh.	
N161WC	98	Global Express	9006	Washington Corps. Missoula, Mt.	N906GX
N161X	79	Westwind-1124	234	Westwind Aircraft LLC. Bend, Or.	N1124Z
N162EC	04	CitationJet CJ-3	525B-0026	Cessna Aircraft Co. Wichita, Ks.	N.....
N162JB	00	Hawker 800XP	8509	Lear Investment LLC/Lear Corp. Pontiac, Mi.	N983CE
Reg	Yr	Type	c/n	Owner/Operator	Prev Regn

Reg	Yr	Type	c/n	Owner/Operator	Prev Regn
N162JC	98	Gulfstream V	539	Jim Carrey/Pit Bull Productions Inc. Van Nuys, Ca.	N1GC
N162TJ	99	Citation Bravo	550-0888	Gulf Wide Aviation LLC. Baton Rouge, La.	N550BF
N162W	66	BAC 1-11/401AK	087	Northrop Grumman Corp. Los Angeles, Ca.	N173FE
N163AG	69	HS 125/3A-RA	25169	AVMATS/Centurion Investments Inc. St Louis, Mo.	N122AW
N163J	01	Falcon 2000	163	Elmet Air Inc. Fort Lauderdale, Fl.	F-WWVW
N163JM	88	Citation III	650-0163	Jetcraft Corp. Raleigh-Durham, NC.	N749CP
N163WC	77	Westwind-1124	217	Blue Water Aviation Inc. Chadds Ford, Pa.	N217WC
N163WG	86	Challenger 601	3057	Blue Water Aviation Inc. Chadds Ford, Pa.	N747TS
N163WW	81	Falcon 50	52	24th Century Air LLC. Williamsburg, Va.	N86AK
N164AS	01	Citation Excel	560-5192	Schwans Shared Services LLC. Marshall, Mn.	N192XL
N164CJ	02	CitationJet CJ-2	525A-0164	Barkley Transportation LLC. Dulles, Va.	N.....
N164GB	86	Falcon 50	164	Continental Aviation Services Inc. Naples, Fl.	N164MA
N164NW	68	Falcon 20C	164	Indigo Air, Chicago, Il.	N654E
N164RJ	99	BBJ-7BC	30328	Bausch & Lomb Inc. Rochester, NY.	N128QS
N164SB	98	Learjet 31A	31A-164	Leonda SA. Guatemala City, Guatemala.	N131GM
N164TC	92	Citation V	560-0174	Great Ozarks Aviation Co. Sprigfield, Mo.	N563C
N164W	66	BAC 1-11/401AK	090	Northrop Grumman Corp. Los Angeles, Ca.	G-AXCK
N164WC	86	BAe 125/800A	8072	Washington Corps. Missoula, Mt.	N747UP
N165CA	01	CitationJet CJ-1	525-0451	Captive Aire Systems Inc. Youngsville, NC.	N5135A
N165CM	77	Learjet 24E	24E-355	Kevin Simmons, Narrows, Va.	N500NH
N165G	83	Gulfstream 3	414	Harwinton Capital Corp. New Canaan, Ct.	N165ST
N165GA	03	Gulfstream G450	4005	Gulfstream Aerospace Corp. Savannah, Ga.	
N165HB	94	Beechjet 400A	RK-90	Covenant Transport Inc. Chattanooga, Tn.	N1570L
N165JF	94	Gulfstream 4SP	1251	Jet Flight Corp. Mount Kisco, NY.	N60PE
N165ST	88	Gulfstream 4	1053	JM Family Enterprises Inc. Fort Lauderdale, Fl.	N91AE
N165TW	66	Falcon 20C	65	Sierra American Corp. Addison, Tx.	C-GSKN
N165W	68	B 737-247	19605	Northrop Grumman Corp. Los Angeles, Ca.	N4508W
N166FA	80	Citation 1/SP	501-0166	Falcon Aviation LC. Durango, Co.	OY-INI
N166FB	97	Falcon 900EX	18	Bee Holdings LLC. Calgary, AB. Canada.	N18RF
N166GA	03	Gulfstream G450	4006	Professional Jet II LLC. Denver, Co.	
N166HL	94	Learjet 60	60-041	Schooner Inc/National Medical Care, Buffalo, NY.	N699SC
N166MC	83	Citation III	650-0003	Groupe Valois/Valavia SNC. Paris-Le Bourget, France.	OY-CGG
N166PC	74	Learjet 25B	25B-166	166PC LLC/Ocwen Inc. Dallas, Tx.	N918TD
N166RM	90	Astra-1125SP	047	B & J Astra LLC. Cincinnati, Oh.	N30AJ
N166WC	88	BAe 125/800A	NA0413	WC Leasing Corp/Washington Corps. Missoula, Mt.	N239R
N167BA	93	Learjet 31A	31A-087	Dulcich Jet LLC. Troutdale, Or.	OY-LJC
N167DD	86	BAe 125/800A	8068	JSDL Ltd/Jackson & Wade Services Inc. Overland Park, Ks.	N68HR
N168AS	76	Citation	500-0328	Ralph & Sandra Matteucci LLC. Las Vegas, Nv.	PT-LSF
N168BF	98	Hawker 800XP	8373	Pearson Assets Group Ltd. Singapore.	N3270X
N168BG	01	Citation Excel	560-5162	La Osa SA. Guatemala City, Guatemala.	N51511
N168CV	92	Citation V	560-0168	Lee Enterprises Inc. Davenport, Ia.	
N168DJ	69	Falcon 20-5B	168	Pacific Coast Group Inc. Las Vegas, Nv.	N514JJ
N168HH	99	Hawker 800XP	8398	Hwa Hsia (BVI) Corp. Wickhams City, BVI.	
N168LA	95	Challenger 601-3R	5179	Skykar Aviation Inc. Miami, Fl.	N168TS
N168NQ	02	Challenger 604	5531	Highfields Capital Management LP. Boston, Ma.	C-G...
N168VA	72	Gulfstream II SP	112	Vision Aviation Corp. Wilmington, De.	N87AG
N168W	65	Sabre-40	282-33	Northrop Grumman Corp. Los Angeles, Ca. (F-16 nose)	N903KB
N168WC	86	Gulfstream 4	1002	CNM Gulf Air LLC. Reno, Nv.	N440GA
N169CP	93	Citation V	560-0230	Del Valle Capital Corp. Modesto, Ca.	YV-169CP
N169EA	75	Gulfstream II SP	169	D Squared Aviation LLC. Burbank, Ca.	N169P
N169HM*	68	Gulfstream 2	13	LFP Inc/Flynt Aviation Inc. Van Nuys, Ca.	N269HM
N169KT	80	B 727-269	22359	WTC/Strong Aviation, Boston, Ma.	9K-AFA
N169LS	78	Falcon 10	115	SNF Inc. Fort Worth, Tx.	N636SC
N169PG*	98	Gulfstream V	563	Computer Associates International Inc. Islandia, NY.	N169CA
N169TA	85	Challenger 601	3041	Truman Arnold Companies, Texarkana, Tx.	N600MS
N169TT	89	Gulfstream 4	1113	TRT Leasing Inc. West Palm Beach, Fl.	N168TR
N169US	74	Learjet 24D	24D-298	AJM Airplane Co. Naples, Fl.	N470TR
N170CS	75	Falcon 10	58	CHANNIC Inc. Brookeville, Md.	(F-GHJL)
N170HL	86	Citation III	650-0125	Lichtin Corp. Raleigh, NC.	N650AF
N170LS	99	Learjet 45	45-029	N170LS Holdings LLC. Fort Lauderdale, Fl.	N290LJ
N170MD	73	Citation	500-0088	Denver Air LLC. Broomfield, Co.	PH-CTA
N170MK	80	Falcon 10	162	MK Aviation Inc. Statesville, NC.	(N713G)
N170MU	97	CitationJet	525-0170	Dealmaker LLC. Lexington, Ky.	N170BG
N170SW	99	Global Express	9042	Wal-Mart Stores Inc. Rogers, Ar.	N700WL
N170TM	02	CitationJet CJ-2	525A-0100	TitleMax Aviation Inc. Savannah, Ga.	N.....
N171JC	93	Gulfstream 4SP	1222	171JC LLC. Van Nuys, Ca.	N71RP

Reg	Yr	Type	c/n	Owner/Operator	Prev Regn
N171TG	95	Falcon 50EX	251	Tudor Investment Corp. Waterbury-Oxford, Ct.	N565
N171WH	78	Learjet 35A	35A-171	Hawk Communications.net LLC. Denver, Co.	N40DK
N171WJ	81	Citation 1/SP	501-0171	Owen Woodward, Breckenridge, Tx.	VH-BNK
N172CJ	01	CitationJet CJ-2	525A-0017	Space Exploration Technologies Corp. El Segundo, Ca.	N5162W
N172DH	04	CitationJet CJ-3	525B-0012	Delaney Aviation LLC. New Windsor, NY.	N5093D
N173A	80	Sabre-65	465-20	T-5 LLC/Tubular Steel Inc. St Louis, Mo.	N2544E
N173LC	98	Learjet 31A	31A-173	Seven KH Aviation LLC. Janesville, Wi.	
N173TR	85	BAe 125/800A	8039	Red Eye LLC. Florham Park, NJ.	N193TR
N173VP	89	Citation III	650-0173	Mercury Communications Inc. Coudersport, Pa.	N843G
N173WF	00	Citation X	750-0112	Westran Services Corp. Van Nuys, Ca.	N1107Z
N174AB	98	Beechjet 400A	RK-174	Black Ink Solutions Inc. Denver, Co.	N2204J
N174B	79	Falcon 10	142	Kroger Co. Cincinnati, Oh.	N5LP
N174BD	69	Falcon 20C	174	Phoenix Rising Aviation Inc. Greenland, Ar.	(D-CFAI)
N174DR	79	Citation II	550-0074	Robinson Industries Inc. Deland, Fl. (was 551-0109).	LX-THS
N174JS	01	Citation Encore	560-0572	J R Simplot Co. Boise, Id.	N.....
N174RD	75	Learjet 24XR	24XR-319	Hartford Holding Corp. Naples, Fl.	XC-SUP
N174VP*	92	Citation VII	650-7004	Moran Foods Inc/Save-A-Lot Ltd. St Louis, Mo.	N913SQ
N175BC	96	Falcon 2000	32	Barnard Aviation LLC. Bozeman, Mt.	N324CL
N175BG	83	Gulfstream 3	396	Bentley Aviation LLC. Van Nuys, Ca.	N800MK
N175BJ	97	Beechjet 400A	RK-175	WHW Transportation LLC. Jacksonville, Fl.	
N175CW	03	Citation Bravo	550-1065	Mississippi Aviation Services, Jackson, Ms.	N326CS
N175DP	00	Citation VII	650-7116	Milease LLC. Milwaukee, Wi.	N5268M
N175FJ	77	Falcon 10	97	Marmac Corp. Parkersburg, WV.	F-WPXF
N175J	89	Citation III	650-0168	BFB Aircraft LLC. Austin, Tx.	N1314H
N175SB	00	CitationJet CJ-1	525-0371	Salem Aviation, Jeddah, Saudi Arabia.	
N175SR	88	Citation III	650-0175	PDT Aviation LLC. Chicago-DuPage, Il.	N835KK
N175WS	03	Citation Excel	560-5327	American International Group, Teterboro, NJ.	N.....
N176AF	88	Citation III	650-0176	I M Group/Ilmor Engineering Inc. Coventry, UK.	N48TF
N176CF	96	Falcon 900B	160	CIGNA Corp. Bradley International, Ct.	F-WWFA
N176CL	02	Falcon 900EX	110	CIGNA Corp. Bradley International, Ct.	F-WWFI
N176MB	99	Learjet 60	60-176	M Bohlke Veneer Corp/MB Aviation Corp. Fairfield, Oh.	
N176WS	99	Learjet 31A	31A-176	Mid-America Aviation LLC. Lafayette, In.	
N177AM	90	Learjet 55C	55C-147	Florida Jet Service Inc. Fort Lauderdale, Fl.	N160NE
N177BB	88	Gulfstream 4	1073	Solar II Inc. Buffalo, NY.	N75PP
N177BC	74	Falcon 10	25	Perimeter Aviation Inc. Manchester, NH.	N719AL
N177EL	01	Citation X	750-0177	Rentair Inc/Ernst Langer, Hamburg, Germany.	N.....
N177JB	98	Learjet 31A	31A-161	Classic Auto Campus LLC. Mentor, Oh.	N3016X
N177JC	67	Jet Commander	77	Centennial Machine/Harrison Haynes, Gainesville, Ga.	N121JC
N177JF	96	CitationJet	525-0182	Rayco Industries Inc. Woooster, Oh.	N177JB
N177RE	93	CitationJet	525-0030	N177RE LLC. Portland, Or.	N1331X
N177RJ	87	Citation II	550-0550	RJ 1 LLC/Rinco of Delaware Inc. Canyon Lake, Tx.	N550FM
N178B	73	Gulfstream 2B	125	MDA-Missile Defence Agency, Tulsa-R L Jones, Ok.	N92NA
N178BR	03	Citation Excel	560-5354	HRL Ventures LLC. Chicago-Midway, Il.	(N71RL)
N178CP	74	Learjet 35	35-005	EPPS Air Service Inc. Atlanta-De Kalb, Ga.	N175J
N178HH	84	Gulfstream 3	448	WMA Aviation LLC. Lawrenceville, Ga.	N123AP
N179AE	02	Gulfstream G200	068	Capital Air Services Inc. Dallas-Love, Tx.	N368GA
N179DV	03	CitationJet CJ-2	525A-0172	RDV Corp. Grand Rapids, Mi.	N.....
N179T	70	Gulfstream 2B	86	NMP Enterprises LLC. Dallas-Love, Tx.	(N179DE)
N180AR	74	Gulfstream 2B	148	Azar Mineral Ltd. San Antonio, Tx.	N2815
N180CH	80	Challenger 600S	1005	N180CH Inc. Miami Beach, Fl.	N605TS
N180CP	96	Learjet 60	60-081	SFA of New Mexico Inc. Santa Fe, NM.	N60LJ
N180FW	82	Citation II	550-0364	Fralin Heywood, Roanoke, Va.	C-GLTG
N180NE	87	BAe 125/800A	NA0401	CIT Group, Tempe, Az.	N815CC
N181AP	87	Challenger 601-3A	5010	Tricom USA Inc. Jersey City, NJ.	N1812C
N181BR	01	Citation X	750-0181	Burlington Resources Oil & Gas Co. Houston, Tx.	N.....
N181CA	81	Learjet 35A	35A-420	Zulu Zulu LLC. Chicago-Du Page, Il.	N100KZ
N181CW	86	Gulfstream 4	1001	Flight Options LLC. Cleveland, Oh.	N981SW
N181EF	78	Learjet 35A	35A-190	Business Jets LLC/Executive Fliteways Inc. Ronkonkoma, NY.	(N208WR)
N181FH	87	BAe 125/800A	8098	Barr Laboratories Inc. Pomona, NY.	N300LS
N181G	84	Citation S/II	S550-0006	KS Aviation LLC. Bedford, NH.	N65DT
N181J	99	Challenger 604	5433	Alta Enterprises Inc. Bedford, Ma.	N433FS
N181JT	94	CitationJet	525-0081	CJ 181JT LLC. Rancho Cucamonga, Ca.	N5090V
N181MC	99	Falcon 50EX	279	MASCO Corp. Detroit-Metropolitan, Mi.	F-WWHE
N181RK	87	Falcon 200	515	Spiral Aviation LLC. Denver, Co.	XA-PFM
N181SG	92	Citation V	560-0181	Garaventa Co. Concord, Ca.	N1280R
N182K	80	Learjet 35A	35A-293	Robertson Asset Management Inc. Norfolk, Va.	

Reg	Yr	Type	c/n	Owner/Operator	Prev Regn
N183CM	01	Learjet 45	45-133	Stuart Jets LLC. Van Nuys, Ca.	N645KM
N183ML	99	Learjet 31A	31A-183	Bombardier Aerospace Corp. Windsor Locks, Ct.	N183DT
N183TX	03	CitationJet CJ-2	525A-0183	Orkney Air LLC. Wilmington, De.	N283CJ
N184GA	72	Falcon 20E	266	Grand Aire Express Inc. Toledo, Oh. (status ?).	N4115B
N184NA	74	Citation	500-0184	JDPCM&E LLC. Houston, Tx.	N67BF
N184PC	74	Sabre-80A	380-6	Sun Castle Aviation Inc. Las Vegas, Nv.	N711GD
N184TB	04	Hawker 800XP	8671	Thomas & Betts Corp. Memphis, Tn.	N671XP
N184TS*	74	Falcon 20-5B	313	Columbus Bank & Trust Co. Columbus, Ga.	N183TS
N185CX	01	Citation X	750-0185	THR Inc/Ritchie Capital Management LLC. DuPage, Il.	N45ST
N185G	04	Falcon 2000EX EASY	36	Boston Post Leasing LLC. Nashua, NH.	F-WWGR
N185GA	03	Gulfstream G450	4007	Gulfstream Aerospace Corp. Savannah, Ga.	
N186DS	90	Gulfstream 4	1154	Alcatel USA Resources Inc. Addison, Tx.	N151GX
N186SC	74	Citation	500-0186	W L Paris Enterprises Inc. Louisville, Ky.	(N510WL)
N186TW	00	CitationJet CJ-1	525-0416	Tallwood Management LLC. San Jose, Ca.	N8UC
N186XL	00	Citation Excel	560-5186	Russell Corp. Alexander City, Al.	N.....
N187AP	81	Challenger 600S	1035	Reeferway Ltd. Tortola, BVI.	N700CL
N187CA	75	Learjet 25B	25B-187	Aviation Dynamics Inc. Henderson, Nv.	YU-BJG
N187JN	82	Citation II	550-0335	Nemco Motor Sports Inc. Mooresville, NC.	N235TS
N187MG	03	CitationJet CJ-2	525A-0187	Whittier Hospital Management Inc. Haverhill, Ma.	N.....
N187PN	88	Falcon 50	187	Paradise Aviation (Jersey) Ltd. Athens, Greece.	VH-PPF
N187TJ	76	Westwind-1124	187	Jags of Sarasota Ltd. Sarasota, Fl.	N241RH
N188AK	99	Astra-1125SPX	121	Sallie Mae Inc. Dulles, Va.	N100AK
N188DC	76	Gulfstream 2	188	Avion LLC/Drummond Coal Inc. Birmingham, Al.	N555MU
N188DM	02	Falcon 50EX	327	Archer Daniels Midland Co. Decatur, Il.	N327EX
N188JR	03	CitationJet CJ-2	525A-0188	Tango Corp. Minden, Nv.	N5138J
N188JS	68	Gulfstream II SP	29	Bondstone Corp. Dallas-Love, Tx.	N941CW
N188KA	81	HS 125/700A	NA0294	Kookaburra Air LLC. Morristown, NJ.	N925DP
N188MR	78	Gulfstream 2	218	R S Aircraft, Englewood, Co.	N187PH
N188TG	96	Learjet 60	60-078	Drei T's LLC. O'Fallon, Mo.	N188TC
N188WS	01	Citation Excel	560-5179	Estopia Air LLC. Sunnyvale, Ca.	N86TW
N189CM	97	CitationJet	525-0189	Cottonaire LLC. Gastonia, NC.	
N189H	89	Citation V	560-0004	Honeywell International Inc. Morristown, NJ.	
N189JM	81	Falcon 10	189	Starflight LLC. New Orleans, La.	N812KC
N189K	90	Challenger 601-3A	5083	Swagelok/Crawford Fitting Co. Cleveland, Oh.	C-GLYA
N189WS	78	Gulfstream II SP	228	Willis, Stein Advisors LLC. Chicago, Il.	N157LH
N190AR	75	Learjet 25B	25B-190	World Jet of Delaware Inc. Fort Lauderdale, Fl.	XA-DAK
N190CS	76	Gulfstream II SP	190	Air Pip Inc. Chicago, Il.	N914CF
N190ES	90	Gulfstream 4	1135	Billionaire Inc. St Petersburg, Fl.	N100ES
N190H	77	Falcon 10	71	Owen Services LLC. Carter Lake, Ia.	(N202PV)
N190JK	95	Citation V Ultra	560-0303	PCH Aviation LLC. Palm Coast, Fl.	N190JH
N190K	81	Citation 1/SP	501-0192	Klabzuba Oil & Gas Inc. Fort Worth, Tx.	(N6781G)
N190MC	97	Falcon 2000	45	Masco Contractor Services, Daytona Beach, Fl.	N45SC
N190MQ	80	Falcon 50	26	WPE 50 LLC. Dallas, Tx.	N190MC
N190WP	01	Global Express	9104	McDonald's Corp. San Diego, Ca.	C-GJIU
N191KL	04	Citation Encore	560-0659	Kwik Lok Corp/KLC Transportation Ltd. Yakima, Wa.	N.....
N191LJ	01	Learjet 45	45-191	Dean Foods Co. Dallas, Tx.	(N432FX)
N191MC	98	Falcon 50EX	282	MASCO Corp. Detroit-Metropolitan, Mi.	F-WWHH
N191NQ	97	Beechjet 400A	RK-143	Cessna Finance Corp. Wichita, Ks.	N191NC
N191PP	02	CitationJet CJ-1	525-0487	Matrix Sales & Service Inc. Lewes, De.	CC-CMS
N191QS	00	BBJ-7BC	30791	NetJets, Columbus, Oh.	
N191VE	91	Citation V	560-0150	BigDaddy Aviation LLC. Abingdon, Va.	N191VF
N191VF	02	Citation Encore	560-0627	Primary Capital Management Inc. Las Vegas, Nv.	N191VB
N192CK	69	Falcon 20D	192	Kalitta Charters LLC. Detroit-Willow Run, Mi.	N192R
N192DW	80	Citation II	550-0192	David Wood, Coalinga, Ca.	YV-900CP
N192F*	98	Falcon 50EX	277	Freescale Semiconductor Inc. Austin, tx.	N198M
N192FG	76	Gulfstream II SP	192	Stockwood Inc. Morristown, NJ.	N273LP
N192NC	00	Hawker 800XP	8476	SCP Aviation LLC. Boca Raton, Fl.	N44676
N193DB	69	Learjet 24B	24B-193	Don Bessette Aviation Inc. Minot, ND.	N193JF
N193SB	93	Citation V	560-0229	B & C General Contractors Inc. Greensboro, NC.	N98GA
N193TR	82	Falcon 50	112	Wolf Springs Ranches Inc. Mankato, Co.	N144AD
N194JS	93	BAe 125/800A	8251	J R Simplot Co. Boise, Id.	N937H
N194K	89	Falcon 50	194	National Loss Control Services Corp. Long Grove, Il.	N95PH
N194SA	93	Citation V	560-0238	William Hobby, Houston, Tx.	N46WB
N194WM	97	Challenger 604	5340	Challenger Administration LLC/Mente Corp. Seattle, Wa.	N606CC
N195ME	95	CitationJet	525-0110	Methode Electronics Inc. Chicago, Il.	N5213S
N195SV	99	Falcon 50EX	293	Silver Ventures Inc. San Antonio, Tx.	N293EX

Reg	Yr	Type	c/n	Owner/Operator	Prev Regn
N195WS	87	Gulfstream 4	1050	ITT Flight Operations Inc. White Plains, NY.	N153RA
N196CF	69	Learjet 24B	24B-186	MTW Aerospace Inc. Montgomery, Al.	N73PS
N196HA	98	CitationJet	525-0256	Papercone Aviation LLC. Louisville, Ky.	
N196JS	80	Citation II	550-0196	Nesnah Aviation LLC. Holmen, Wi.	HB-VLS
N196KC	02	Falcon 2000	195	Kansas City Life Insurance Co. Kansas City, Ks.	N297QS
N196MG	87	BAe 125/800A	8081	Navellier Management Inc. Reno, Nv.	N196MC
N196PH	99	Learjet 45	45-056	E I DuPont de Nemours & Co. Des Moines, Ia.	
N196RG	00	Falcon 2000	135	RI-Relational Investors Aviation LLC. Carlsbad, Ca.	N222BN
N196RJ	81	Citation II	550-0207	D & B Drilling Inc. Wheatridge, Co.	N207BA
N196SB	04	Citation Excel XLS	560-5513	Ranger Corp. Everett, Wa.	N.....
N196SD	85	Citation III	650-0093	Southern Cross Ranch LLC. Monroe, NC.	N196SG
N196TB	69	Learjet 24B	24B-196	Brundage Management Co. San Antonio, Tx.	N196AF
N196TS	69	Falcon 20D	196	Aero Falcons LLC. Ontario, Ca.	(N142JF)
N197BE	92	Beechjet 400A	RK-33	Lubrizol Corp. Wickcliffe, Oh.	N197PF
N197CF	76	Learjet 25B	25B-197	SEC Management LLC. Hurst, Tx.	(N96DM)
N197CJ	03	CitationJet CJ-2	525A-0197	Kilo Alpha Services LLC. Texarkana, Tx.	N.....
N197HF	92	Citation II	550-0704	Hormel Foods Corp. Austin Municipal, Mn.	(N197GH)
N197LS	83	Learjet 25D	25D-363	La Stella Corp. Pueblo, Co.	XA-RSU
N197PH	99	Learjet 31A	31A-169	E I DuPont de Nemours & Co. Des Moines, Ia.	
N198DC	01	Challenger 604	5481	Dow Corning Corp. Midland, Mi.	N481KW
N198DF	03	Citation Excel	560-5337	Dairy Farmers of America Inc. Kansas City, Mo.	N51942
N198DL	66	JetStar-731	5083	Woods Aviation Inc. Palm Beach, Fl.	N817BD
N198GJ	78	Learjet 35A	35A-198	Lear 35-1 LLC. West Columbia, SC.	I-ALPT
N198GT	81	HS 125/700A	NA0288	LGT Aviation Inc. Santa Monica, Ca.	N700BW
N198HB	00	Learjet 60	60-198	United Furniture Equipment Rental Inc. Okolona, Ms.	
N198HF	91	Astra-1125SP	054	Hormel Foods Corp. Austin Municipal, Mn.	N70AJ
N198JA	75	Learjet 25B	25B-198	B & C Flight Management Inc. Houston, Tx.	N29TS
N198JH	97	CitationJet	525-0265	Jack Henry & Associates Inc. Monett, Mo.	
N198MR	84	Falcon 50	149	Jack Prewitt & Assocs Inc. Bedford, Tx.	N198M
N198ND	90	Citation II	550-0630	Dentressangle USA Inc. Lyon-Bron, France.	N198DF
N198SL	98	Citation Bravo	550-0835	Chesnuts Investments Inc. London-Corbin, Ky.	(N835VP)
N198TX	94	Citation VII	650-7047	Foundation Aircraft LLC. Roswell, Ga.	N1828S
N199BB	99	Citation Bravo	550-0895	George Schreyer Revocable Trust, Newport Coast, Ca.	
N199BT	80	Learjet 25D	25D-311	Commercial Bag Co. Normal, Il.	ZS-NJH
N199CK	74	Citation	500-0216	McKelvey Aviation One LLC. Marshfield, Ma.	N99CK
N199FG	92	Falcon 50	231	Fremont Group/Bechtel Corp. Oakland, Ca.	N10PP
N199HE	88	Astra-1125	027	Administaff Inc. Kingwood, Tx.	N199HF
N199HF	00	Gulfstream G200	028	Hormel Foods Corp. Austin Municipal, Mn.	N60GX
N199LX*	86	Gulfstream 4	1004	Paramount Aviation LLC. Cleveland, Oh.	N184CW
N199RM	03	390 Premier 1	RB-99	Robert Garriott, Austin, Tx.	N24YR
N199WW	76	Westwind-1124	199	Avwest International LLC. Boulder, Co.	D-CHDL
N200A	00	Global Express	9077	Mobil Corp. Fairfax, Va.	N100A
N200AB	69	Gulfstream 2	71	7-N Aircorp. Dallas, Tx.	N47A
N200AP	95	Citation X	750-0003	Air X Corp. Wilmington, De.	(N300VP)
N200AS	00	Citation Bravo	550-0934	Air Sierra Aviation Inc. Newport Beach, Fl.	N5260Y
N200AX	00	Gulfstream G200	022	Apex Babcock & Brown LLC. Concord, Ca.	N414KB
N200BA	02	Gulfstream G200	076	Bayou Helicopters Inc. Houston, Tx.	N376GA
N200CG	75	Citation	500-0230	Illinois Data Mart Inc. DuPage, Il.	N299TB
N200CH	02	Falcon 2000EX	4	Cardal Inc. Columbus-OSU, Oh.	F-WWGD
N200CP	72	Falcon 20E-5	275	CD Exploration Inc/CDX Gas Co. Addison, Tx.	(N999BG)
N200DE	98	Challenger 604	5390	Dunavant Enterprises Inc. Memphis, Tn.	N541DE
N200EE	66	BAC 1-11/212AR	083	Select Aviation Inc. Waukesha, Wi.	N490ST
N200FJ	84	Falcon 200	494	Windsong Air LLC. Westport, Ct.	EC-HEG
N200GA	03	Gulfstream G200	088	Moon, Sun & Stars Inc. Coral Gables, Fl.	(N721QS)
N200GF	87	Citation II/SP	551-0556	Golden Flake Snack Foods Inc. Birmingham, Al.	(N12979)
N200GN	98	Falcon 2000	68	Gannett Co. Dulles, Va.	F-WWMB
N200GP	97	Beechjet 400A	RK-172	General Parts Inc. Raleigh, NC.	N615HP
N200GT	68	Falcon 20C	137	Allied Signal Inc. Phoenix, Az.	N777PV
N200J	79	Falcon 20-5B	410	United Industries Corp. St Louis, Mo.	N200CP
N200JP	78	HS 125/700A	NA0238	Flights Unlimited LLC/Millco Inc. Canonsburg, Pa.	N120MH
N200JR	01	Citation Encore	560-0576	JRN Inc. Columbia, SC.	N.....
N200JX	64	BAC 1-11/203AE	015	Select Aviation Inc. Waukesha, Wi.	N583CQ
N200L	96	Falcon 900EX	2	Anheuser-Busch Companies Inc. St Louis, Mo.	F-WWFA
N200LB	04	390 Premier 1	RB-116	Briar Hill Leasing Inc. Lexington, Ky.	
N200LC	88	Gulfstream 4	1067	Aircraft Braking Services/K & F Industries Inc. NYC.	N145ST
N200LH	92	Citation VII	650-7005	Century Aviation of Colorado LLC. Telluride, Co.	N1259S

Reg	Yr	Type	c/n	Owner/Operator	Prev Regn

Reg	Yr	Type	c/n	Owner/Operator	Prev Regn
N200LJ	78	Learjet 35A	35A-200	World Jet Inc. Fort Lauderdale, Fl.	OO-LFY
N200LP	81	Diamond 1	A006SA	Central Flying Service Inc. Little Rock, Ar.	N750TJ
N200LS	00	Gulfstream 4SP	1449	Limited Inc. Columbus, Oh.	N449GA
N200LX	85	Citation S/II	S550-0061	Citation Aircraft LLC. Lebanon, NH.	N53JM
N200MT	98	Learjet 60	60-150	Aerospace Leasing LLC. Cincinnati, Oh.	N150BX
N200NC	80	Citation II	550-0184	Bavarian Aircraft LLC. Chanhassen, Mn.	(N20TV)
N200NE	95	Falcon 2000	22	Banc One Management Corp. Columbus, Oh.	F-WWMF
N200NK	99	Citation V Ultra	560-0511	EnKay Corp. Shreveport, La.	
N200NP	84	Falcon 200	488	Falcon West LLC. Sacramento, Ca.	N146CF
N200QC	72	Citation Longwing SP	500-0023	Mercy Med Flight, Fort Worth, Tx.	N50FT
N200RT	82	Falcon 50	126	Maguire Properties Inc. Los Angeles, Ca.	N52DQ
N200SC	95	Citation V Ultra	560-0326	560 Inc/100 SC Partners LP. Chattanooga, Tn.	(N711Z)
N200SG	93	Falcon 50	239	Hill Air Corp. Dallas, Tx.	N239FJ
N200SK	80	Gulfstream 3	319	SK Travel LLC. New Castle, De.	N319Z
N200SL	01	CitationJet CJ-1	525-0461	Sutherland Lumber & Home Centers Inc. Tulsa-R L Jones, Ok.	N5207A
N200ST	92	Astra-1125SP	061	Stewart Title Co. Sugarland, Tx.	N550M
N200TJ	96	Learjet 31A	31A-120	Oldwick Equipment Leasing Corp. Oldwick, NJ.	I-TYKE
N200TW	81	Learjet 35A	35A-397	Campbell Aircraft Holdings LLC. Coatsville, Pa.	D-CLAN
N200UP	81	Falcon 50	55	United Pan-Europe Communications NV. Amsterdam, Holland.	N96UH
N200VT	80	Citation II	550-0083	Gateway Aviation Inc. Van Nuys, Ca.	N54CC
N200WK	72	Falcon 20-5	261	TAG Aviation USA Inc. White Plains, NY.	N4368F
N200YB	02	Gulfstream G200	075	KFC US Properties Inc/Yum! Brands Inc. Louisville, Ky.	N875GA
N201CR	94	Falcon 2000	2	Romana Aircraft Inc. Santo Domingo, Dominican Republic.	F-GJHJ
N201GA	04	Gulfstream G200	101	Gulfstream Aerospace LP. Dallas-Love, Tx.	4X-C..
N201SU	01	Citation Encore	560-0586	IMP Inc. Paoli, Pa.	N52691
N201WR	02	Falcon 2000	201	Delaware Park LLC. Gaithersburg, Md.	F-WWFO
N202AR	84	Falcon 200	496	CIT Group, Tempe, Az.	N256JC
N202AV	99	Citation VII	650-7108	Avista Corp. Spokane, Wa.	
N202BG	94	CitationJet	525-0089	Brasfield & Gorrie LLC. Birmingham, Al.	N920MS
N202BT	82	Learjet 35A	35A-483	Books-A-Million Inc. Birmingham, Al.	(N483TJ)
N202CJ	04	CitationJet CJ-2	525A-0202	Cessna Aircraft Co. Wichita, Ks.	N.....
N202EX	02	Falcon 2000EX	2	Watsco Holdings Inc. Miami, Fl.	F-WWGA
N202JK	85	Citation III	650-0100	Kelgen Partnership LLP. Milwaukee, Wi.	N200LL
N202JS	73	Learjet 24D	24D-278	J R S Aviation Inc. St Petersburg, Fl.	N5695H
N202N	02	Learjet 60	60-258	LJ60 LLC. Wilmington, De.	
N202RL	00	Citation Excel	560-5117	RBL LLC/DB Aviation Inc. Waukegan, Il.	N5233J
N202SW	83	Citation II	550-0470	S T Wooten Corp. Wilson, NC.	N10RU
N202TH	00	Falcon 2000	130	Tyco International Ltd. Portsmouth, NH.	N99TY
N203	98	Challenger 604	5374	Jacura Delaware Inc. Highland Beach, Fl.	N97FJ
N203BA	85	Beechjet 400	RJ-3	P & I Inc. Leawood, Ks.	N508DM
N203BG	00	CitationJet CJ-1	525-0378	Brasfield & Gorrie LLC. Birmingham, Al.	N525CP
N203CW	87	Falcon 900	33	Cingular Wireless Aviation Holdings, Atlanta, Ga.	N931SB
N203GA	04	Gulfstream G200	103	Gulfstream Aerospace LP. Dallas-Love, Tx.	4X-C..
N203JE	91	Challenger 601-3A	5099	Inversiones Earon CA. Caracas, Venezuela.	N601DW
N203JL	69	Learjet 24B	24B-203	Bruce Leven, Mercer Island, Wa.	N203CK
N203NC	90	Falcon 50	203	Nova Chemicals Services Inc. Coraopolis, Pa.	C-GNCA
N203PM	88	Citation II	550-0578	N203PM LLC. Davenport, Ia.	PT-LQJ
N203QS	02	Falcon 2000	198	NetJets, Columbus, Oh.	F-WWVL
N203TA	96	Challenger 604	5316	Raytheon Travel Air Co. Wichita, Ks.	N200UL
N203TM	03	Hawker 800XP	8653	Cerner Corp. Kansas City, Mo.	N653XP
N204AB	01	Gulfstream G200	037	West Teton LLC. Newport Beach, Fl.	N337JD
N204AN	67	Falcon 20C	102	Nikki Air LLC. Las Vegas, Nv.	N403JW
N204BG	99	Citation V Ultra	560-0503	Brasfield & Gorrie LLC. Birmingham, Al.	VP-BDB
N204CA	78	Citation 1/SP	501-0283	James M Krueger, Newport Beach, Ca. (was 500-0377).	C-GPTC
N204CF	81	Citation II	550-0238	Corporate Flight Inc. Detroit, Mi.	N97S
N204DH	00	Beechjet 400A	RK-290	Drury Development Corp. St Louis, Mo.	N400QW
N204J	96	CitationJet	525-0164	John MacGuire, Santa Teresa, NM.	D-ICGT
N204JK	87	Challenger 601-3A	5015	Royal Oak Enterprises Inc. Atlanta-DeKalb, Ga.	N514RB
N204PM	81	Citation II	550-0320	Prewett Hosiery Sales, Fort Payne-Isbell, Al.	N57MB
N204QS	99	Falcon 2000	104	NetJets, Columbus, Oh.	F-WWVY
N204RT	00	Learjet 31A	31A-204	Ruby Tuesday Inc. Knoxville, Tn.	
N204TM	81	Westwind-1124	320	International Air Services CA Inc. Fort Lauderdale, Fl.	N60JP
N204TW	69	Falcon 20DC	204	Sierra American Corp. Addison, Tx.	EC-EGM
N205AJ	77	Westwind-1124	205	Eagle Leasing Inc. Alpharetta, Ga.	(N775JC)
N205BC	03	390 Premier 1	RB-69	Wheeler Trailer Inc. Chicago, Il.	
N205CM	94	Citation V	560-0250	Charlotte-Macklenberg Hospital Authority, Charlotte, NC.	N1291Y

Reg	Yr	Type	c/n	Owner/Operator	Prev Regn
N205EL	97	Challenger 604	5347	Invemed Aviation Services LLC. NYC.	N747TS
N205FH	99	CitationJet	525-0355	NorthJet Lease LLC. Edina, Mn.	N51396
N205JC	81	Falcon 20F-5B	440	Pere Marquette Group LLC. Grand Rapids, Mi.	N7000G
N205K	74	Falcon 20F-5B	319	Pacific Coast Group Inc. Las Vegas, Nv.	N77LA
N205WM	74	Falcon 20E-5	306	Wausau-Mosinee Paper Corp. Mosinee, Wi.	N76662
N205X	88	Gulfstream 4	1080	Occidental Petroleum Corp. Burbank, Ca.	N20XY
N205YY	04	CitationJet CJ-2	525A-0205	Big Skyy Aviation LLC. Portland, Or.	N5241Z
N206CX	01	Citation Excel	560-5206	NWW Excel Inc. Omaha, Ne.	N921DG
N206HY	94	Learjet 60	60-028	BBJS/FlexJets, Addison, Tx.	N206FX
N206LX	97	CitationJet	525-0205	Flight Options LLC. Cleveland, Oh.	N275CW
N207BS	01	CitationJet CJ-1	525-0445	Peco Air LLC. Baltimore, Md.	N445CJ
N207CA	68	Falcon 20D	153	Cherry Air Inc. Addison, Tx.	N70MD
N207EM	03	Falcon 2000	207	Robson Communities Inc. Scottsdale, Az.	F-WWVU
N207HF	77	Learjet 25D	25D-230	Chipola Aviation Inc. Marianna, Fl.	N7RL
N207JS	67	Falcon 20-5	117	Kenwood Financial LLC. Boca Raton, Fl.	F-GLMD
N207MJ	58	MS 760 Paris-2	2	Tej Jet of Del LLC. Dover, De.	N1EP
N207RG	76	Learjet 24E	24E-339	Tannelle Ltd. Silver Spring, Mo.	N52DD
N207TT	92	BAe 1000A	9008	LG Charter Inc. Boca Raton, Fl.	D-CADA
N207WW	77	Westwind-1124	207	Avwest International LLC. Boulder, Co.	D-CHAL
N208BH	00	Learjet 60	60-208	V3 LLC. Hailey, Id.	(N112MT)
N208R	91	BAe 1000A	NA1003	Raytheon Co. Lexington, Ma.	N14GD
N208VP	93	Citation V	560-0208	Dawg House Inc. Winston-Salem, NC.	N88G
N209CA	66	Falcon 20C	71	Source Investments LLC. Addison, Tx.	N195AS
N209CV	93	Citation V	560-0209	209 Aircraft Co LLC. Monticello, Mo.	
N209HR	00	Learjet 31A	31A-209	Laredo National Bank, Laredo, Tx.	N139FY
N209TM	03	Falcon 2000	209	Montalbano Enterprises LLC. DuPage, Il.	N209FS
N209TS	77	HS 125/700A	NA0209	HS700 LLC. Danbury, Ct.	N843CP
N210QS	03	Falcon 2000	211	NetJets, Columbus, Oh.	F-WWVY
N210RK	79	HS 125/700A	7073	Aspen Jet Inc. Blue Island, Il.	N701TA
N210WL	78	Learjet 35A	35A-210	Dickerson Associates Inc. West Columbia, SC.	XB-FNF
N211BR	74	Sabre-60	306-85	Flight Research Inc. Starksville, Ms.	N855CD
N211BX	96	Learjet 60	60-076	Bombardier Aerospace Corp. Windsor Locks, Ct.	N211FX
N211CC	91	Citation VI	650-0211	Crain Communications Inc. Detroit, Mi.	N333WC
N211DH	00	Gulfstream 4SP	1432	Hagadone Aviation LLC. Coeur d'Alene, Id.	N335GA
N211EC	80	Falcon 10	166	Easton Flying Partners LLC/Air Repair Inc. Easton, Md.	(N166SS)
N211GA	81	Diamond 1A	A011SA	Catawba Management Corp. Reston, Va.	(N77GA)
N211GM	97	CitationJet	525-0208	Spring House Inc. Alexandria, In.	N208JV
N211JC	80	Learjet 25D	25D-310	Associations Inc. Dallas, Tx.	(N211JE)
N211JL	81	Falcon 10	180	Planned Residential Communities Financial Co. Long Branch	N25MC
N211JS	79	Citation II	550-0098	Scolari's Warehouse Markets Inc. Sparks, Nv. (was 551-0140).	N212H
N211SJ	69	Gulfstream 2B	75	New World Aircraft LLC. Allentown, Pa.	N94TJ
N211ST	80	Westwind-Two	303	Western Airways Inc. Sugar Land, Tx.	N50QJ
N212AT	93	Gulfstream 4SP	1204	A T & T Corp. Morristown, NJ.	N435GA
N212AW	94	Gulfstream 4SP	1240	AT&T Wireless Inc. Seattle, Wa.	N333PV
N212BA	82	Gulfstream 3	353	Advance Flight Concepts Inc. Fort Lauderdale, Fl.	HZ-108
N212BH	02	Citation Bravo	550-1020	Avila Executive Aviation Inc. Santo Domingo, DR.	N5166T
N212BW	89	Citation V	560-0038	L & F Distributors Ltd. McAllen, Tx.	N2296S
N212FJ	79	Falcon 10	147	Aviation Charter Inc. Sioux City, Ia.	N125GA
N212K	93	Gulfstream 4	1192	A T & T Corp. Morristown, NJ.	N407GA
N212LD	87	Astra-1125	020	Seven Brothers Productions Inc. Burbank, Ca.	N279DP
N212M	77	Citation	501-0280	Makaira Aircraft Sales LLC. Collierville, Tn. (was 500-0373)	T9-BKA
N212R	69	Falcon 20DC	212	Kalitta Charters LLC. Detroit-Willow Run, Mi.	N31FE
N212RG	86	BAe 125/800B	8073	Onward & Upward LLC/Gilber Gagnon Howe LLC. Teterboro, NJ.	N2236
N212RR	97	Challenger 604	5336	RoRo 212 LLC. Cincinnati, Oh.	N310BX
N212T	97	Falcon 2000	52	A T & T Corp. Morristown, NJ.	F-WWMI
N212VZ	03	Gulfstream G400	1531	Verizon Communications, White Plains, NY.	N531GA
N213BA	85	Gulfstream 3	453	Avitrans Inc. Wilmington, De.	HZ-103
N213BK	98	Beechjet 400A	RK-216	B4A LLC/B A Karbank & Co. Kansas City, Mo.	N3050P
N213CA	78	Learjet 25D	25D-241	Delaware DI Properties LLC. Addison, Tx.	N713LJ
N213CC	81	Citation II	550-0213	RHA Air LLC. Little Rock, Ar.	N550HB
N213CF	79	Citation II	550-0112	C Fred Hudson, Ormond Beach, Fl.	N3FA
N213CJ	04	CitationJet CJ-2	525A-0213	Cessna Aircraft Co. Wichita, Ks.	N5244W
N213HP	87	Citation III	650-0133	Jet 213HP LLC/Addison Jet Center, Addison, Tx.	N250CM
N213JS	89	Citation II	550-0597	Idlewood Aviation Inc. Atlanta, Ga.	N400EX
N213LG	84	Diamond 1A	A079SA	Vanquish Aviation Inc. Tampa, Fl.	N574CF
N213PC	02	390 Premier 1	RB-75	Perryman Enterprises, Allegheny County, Pa.	
Reg	Yr	Type	c/n	Owner/Operator	Prev Regn

Reg	Yr	Type	c/n	Owner/Operator	Prev Regn
☐ N213QS	00	Falcon 2000	113	NetJets, Columbus, Oh.	F-WWVH
☐ N214AS	85	Falcon 200	501	Performance Investments Inc. Jacksonville, Fl.	N57TT
☐ N214DV	99	Falcon 50EX	289	Sequoia Millenium Falcon LLC. Menlo Park, Ca.	F-WWHQ
☐ N214JT	82	Citation II	550-0418	Moonlight Aviation LLC. Minneapolis, Mn.	N418CG
☐ N214MD	81	Citation II	550-0243	DMAC LLC. Dripping Springs, Tx.	XA-REN
☐ N214PN	85	Citation S/II	S550-0038	Philmar LLC. Oshkosh, Wi.	(N801CC)
☐ N214RW	02	Learjet 60	60-264	Midwest Onalaska Services LLC. La Crosse, Wi.	N40084
☐ N214TJ	99	Citation Bravo	550-0900	Branic Air LLC. Los Altos, Ca.	N327LN
☐ N214TS	89	Gulfstream 4	1121	Aero Toy Store LLC. Fort Lauderdale, Fl.	N811WW
☐ N214WM	98	Beechjet 400A	RK-197	Wilkes & McHugh PA. Tampa, Fl.	N3197A
☐ N214WY*	84	Gulfstream 3	441	Coastal Aviation Development LLC. NYC.	N80J
☐ N215BX	97	Learjet 60	60-101	Bombardier Capital Inc. Colchester, Vt.	N215FX
☐ N215EX	03	Falcon 2000EX	15	General Maritime Corp. Waterbury-Oxford, Ct.	(N97GM)
☐ N215KH	02	Falcon 2000	197	Concord Jet Service Inc. Concord, Ca.	N2290
☐ N215NA	81	Citation 1/SP	501-0215	Spence & Associates Inc. The Woodlands, Tx.	ZS-LXT
☐ N215QS	03	Falcon 2000	214	NetJets, Columbus, Oh.	N214FJ
☐ N215RE	03	Falcon 2000	215	RE/MAX International Inc. Greenwood Village, Co.	F-WWVC
☐ N215RS	78	HS 125/700A	NA0215	Aspen 1 LLC. Van Nuys, Ca.	N195XP
☐ N215RX	03	Citation X	750-0225	API Properties Nevada Inc. Granite Bay, Ca.	N5223D
☐ N215TP	89	Beechjet 400	RJ-64	S2 Yachts Inc. Holland, Mi.	N195JH
☐ N215TT	93	Learjet 31A	31A-076	BIK Rentals Inc. Concord, NC.	N518SA
☐ N216BX	97	Learjet 60	60-103	Bombardier Aerospace Corp. Windsor Locks, Ct.	N216FX
☐ N216CA	65	Falcon 20C	11	Delaware DI Properties LLC. Addison, Tx.	N983AJ
☐ N216CW	95	CitationJet	525-0116	Flight Options LLC. Cleveland, Oh.	(N202LX)
☐ N216RR	68	Gulfstream II SP	22	Skookum Air Inc. Irvine, Ca.	N217RR
☐ N216SA	65	Falcon 20DC	16	Smithair Inc. Lewis B Wilson Airport, Ga.	N216TW
☐ N217AJ	68	Falcon 20D	171	Owners Jet Services Ltd. DuPage, Il.	F-GICB
☐ N217AL	03	Citation X	750-0217	AML Leasing Inc. Burbank, Ca.	(N221AL)
☐ N217BX	97	Learjet 60	60-105	B C Aviation LLC. Reno, Nv.	N217FX
☐ N217CA	67	Falcon 20C	75	Source Investments LLC. Addison, Tx.	UR-EFB
☐ N217FS	81	Citation II	550-0273	Corporate Aviation Services Inc. Pepper Pike, Oh.	N68637
☐ N217JS	76	Learjet 24E	24E-345	J & S Aviation Leasing LLC. Nashville, Tn.	N435AS
☐ N217MB	98	Beechjet 400A	RK-217	Aristokraft Inc. Jasper, In.	
☐ N217MJ	02	Learjet 45	45-217	L217MJ LLC/My Jet LLC. Scottsdale, Az.	N401Q
☐ N217RJ	85	Citation III	650-0079	Skookum Air Inc. Irvine, Ca.	N69VC
☐ N217RR	88	Gulfstream 4	1042	Rutter Aviation LP/Skookum Air Inc. Irvine, Ca.	N68SL
☐ N217RT	81	Learjet 35A	35A-379	Dove Air Inc. Hendersonville, NC.	N18LH
☐ N217SA	81	Citation II	550-0217	MT Fluggesellschaft LLC. San Diego, Ca.	(D-IMME)
☐ N217TA	80	Learjet 35A	35A-289	Foxen Motorsports Inc. Santa Maria, Ca.	N36TJ
☐ N217WM	77	Learjet 25D	25D-217	M & V Airplane LLC. San Antonio, Tx.	N41H
☐ N218CA	69	Falcon 20DC	218	Delaware DI Properties LLC. Addison, Tx.	EC-EEU
☐ N218EC	00	Gulfstream V	656	Calpoint Funding LLC. Van Nuys, Ca.	(N218CP)
☐ N218JG	81	Citation 1/SP	501-0218	N218 Inc. Dover, De.	N218AM
☐ N218NB	98	Learjet 31A	31A-146	Well's Dairy Inc. Le Mars, Ia.	ZS-AGT
☐ N218PH	04	Falcon 2000	218	Pulte Homes Inc. Bloomfield, Mi.	F-WWVF
☐ N218QS	00	Falcon 2000	118	NetJets, Columbus, Oh.	F-WWVN
☐ N218TJ	65	HS 125/731	25018	On Time Aviation Corp. Jeddah, Saudi Arabia.	(P4-ZAW)
☐ N219CA	69	Falcon 20D	193	Delaware DI Properties LLC. Addison, Tx.	9Q-CTT
☐ N219CJ	97	CitationJet	525-0219	Dr F David Prentice, Houston, Tx.	N5197A
☐ N219FJ	04	Falcon 2000	219	Dassault Falcon Jet Corp. Teterboro, NJ.	F-W...
☐ N219FL	03	CitationJet CJ-2	525A-0111	TBAC LLC/Tickly Bender Realy Corp. Danbury, Ct.	N.....
☐ N219GA	00	Galaxy-1126	019	Gordon Management Inc. Chicago, Il.	N407LM
☐ N219JW	88	Falcon 100	219	Astec Industries Inc. Chattanooga, Tn.	PT-ORS
☐ N219MS	80	Citation II	550-0180	MDM Aviation LLC. Rochester, NY.	N3030T
☐ N219RB	78	Learjet 25D	25D-255	Pauli-Mar Investment Co. Centerline, Mi.	N717EP
☐ N219SJ	98	Beechjet 400A	RK-219	S J Aviation LLC. Novato, Ca.	N80BL
☐ N220AB	01	Falcon 2000	170	Pacific Connection Inc. Phoenix, Az.	F-W...
☐ N220AU	71	DC 10-10ER	46501	Project Orbis International Inc. NYC.	G-GCAL
☐ N220CA	69	Falcon 20DC	220	Addison Aviation Services Inc. Addison, Tx.	EC-EDL
☐ N220CM	88	Citation III	650-0160	Charter Manufacturing Co. Mequon, Wi.	N650PT
☐ N220DF	98	Falcon 2000	69	Siegel-Robert Inc. St Louis, Mo.	(N346SR)
☐ N220DH*	86	Westwind-Two	440	Nebrig & Assocs Inc. Denton, Tx.	N127SA
☐ N220GS	79	Learjet 35A	35A-220	Two Twenty LLC. Teterboro, NJ.	N373LP
☐ N220HM	81	Citation 1/SP	501-0182	HOM LLC/Hartsville Oil Mill, Darlington, SC.	VP-CAP
☐ N220JR	69	Gulfstream 2	50	Air Tiger Inc/Key Air Inc. Oxford, Ct.	N220FL
☐ N220LC	82	Challenger 600S	1071	Life Care Centers of America Inc. Cleveland, Tn.	N711DB

Reg	Yr	Type	c/n	Owner/Operator	Prev Regn

Reg	Yr	Type	c/n	Owner/Operator	Prev Regn
N220MT	78	Corvette	40	Meyer Tool Inc. Cincinnati-Lunken, Oh.	N200MT
N220TS	73	HS 125/600A	6021	MMI Inc. Lanseria, RSA.	N220TS
N221AM	73	Citation	500-0109	Aeromanagement Inc. Annapolis, Md.	I-AMCU
N221CM	81	Gulfstream 3	343	Trans-Exec Air Service Inc. Van Nuys, Ca.	N400AL
N221DG	03	Gulfstream G550	5020	David Geffen Co. Long Beach, Ca.	N920GA
N221HB	85	BAe 125/800A	8052	N221HB LLC. San Diego, Ca.	N233KC
N221LC	90	Challenger 601-3A	5066	Executive Flight Inc. Cleveland, Tn.	N566TS
N221PA	87	Astra-1125	016	Michigan Aircraft Sales LLC. Howell, Mi.	N221DT
N221PB	03	Hawker 800XP	8623	Fortune Brands Inc. Lincolnshire, Il.	(N823CW)
N221QS	04	Falcon 2000EX EASY	54	NetJets, Columbus, Oh.	F-WWMC.
N221SG	78	Learjet 35A	35A-182	Path Corp. Rehoboth Beach, De.	N3HA
N221TR	79	Learjet 35A	35A-221	Pak West Airlines Inc. Oakdale, Ca.	VH-FSY
N221TW	69	Falcon 20DC	221	Kitty Hawk Air Cargo Inc. Dallas, Tx.	EC-EIV
N221VP	01	Citation Encore	560-0585	Citation Technology Partners LLC. Hayward, Ca.	N5254Y
N222B	69	Learjet 25	25-047	Michigan Air Freight LLC. Ypsilanti, Mi.	(N68CK)
N222BE	82	Learjet 35A	35A-489	Mayo Aviation Inc. Englewood, Co.	
N222BG	81	Learjet 35A	35A-448	Goody's Family Clothing Inc. McGhee-Tyson, Tn.	N48MJ
N222GY	90	Gulfstream 4	1142	Gypsy Two LLC. Seattle, Wa.	N222
N222LH	82	Challenger 600S	1052	Lewis Hyman Inc. Van Nuys, Ca.	N152TS
N222LX	01	Gulfstream V	633	Lexair Ltd/Trans-Exec Air Service Inc. Van Nuys, Ca.	N633GA
N222MC	96	Challenger 604	5329	McCaw Communications Inc. Seattle, Wa.	(N222MZ)
N222MS	88	BAe 125/800A	NA0422	Stavola Aviation Inc. Anthony, Fl.	N125TR
N222MU	80	Falcon 10	164	C & H Travel LLC. Little Rock, Ar.	N228FJ
N222MW	00	Learjet 45	45-110	McWane Inc. Birmingham, Al.	N4002P
N222NB	79	Gulfstream 2B	245	222 Aviation LLC. Burbank, Ca.	N99WJ
N222NF	02	CitationJet CJ-2	525A-0074	Merak Aviation Inc. Opa Locka, Fl.	N5125J
N222NG	65	HS 125/1A	25016	World Jet of Delaware Inc. Fort Lauderdale, Fl.	N4997E
N222QS	00	Falcon 2000	122	NetJets, Columbus, Oh.	F-WWVR
N222TW	68	Learjet 24	24-161	Sierra American Corp. Addison, Tx.	N24KF
N222VV	80	Citation II/SP	551-0180	V O Aircraft Sales Inc. Melbourne, Fl. (was 550-0136).	(N729MJ)
N222WA	77	Citation 1/SP	501-0007	Unitco Air/Ralph Kiewit Jr. Van Nuys, Ca.	N5360J
N223AM	99	Citation Excel	560-5018	Automatic Aviation LLC. Orlando, Fl.	ZS-FCB
N223BG	71	Falcon 20F	250	Goody's Family Clothing Inc. McGhee-Tyson, Tn.	XA-HEW
N223DD	82	Falcon 50	128	Open Road Airways Inc. Wheeling, Il.	N733E
N223HD	99	Falcon 50EX	283	The Home Depot Inc. Atlanta-Fulton County, Ga.	N283FJ
N223J	82	Citation II	550-0412	Jet One LLC. Waterford, Mi.	N830VL
N223JV	91	Citation V	560-0131	Business Aviation Services/Daedalus Inc. Sioux Falls, SD.	PT-ORE
N223LB	80	Sabre-65	465-23	T-5 LLC/Tubular Steel Inc. St Louis, Mo.	(N904KB)
N223LC	78	Citation 1/SP	501-0055	Corus Hardware Corp. Catano, PR.	N145AJ
N223MD	01	Gulfstream V	665	Open Road Airways Inc. Wheeling, Il.	N845HS
N223TW	67	Falcon 20C	123	Sierra American Corp. Addison, Tx.	N45MR
N223WA	86	Westwind-1124	423	Texas International Gas & Oil Co. El Paso, Tx.	4X-CUC
N224CJ	97	CitationJet	525-0224	MKM Investment Co. Fernandina Beach, Fl.	
N224EA	80	HS 125/700B	7088	Atsinger Aviation LLC. Van Nuys, Ca.	N222HL
N224F	94	Challenger 601-3R	5163	Freeman Air Charter Inc. Stowe, Vt.	N980HC
N224GP	82	Westwind-1124	372	Ponder Investment Corp. Marshall, Tx.	N406CH
N224HD	04	Falcon 50EX	336	The Home Depot Inc. Atlanta-Fulton County, Ga.	F-WWHR
N224KC	86	Citation S/II	S550-0104	Tri-State Executive Air Inc. Boca Raton, Fl.	N12903
N224LJ	01	Learjet 31A	31A-224	Uptongrove Ltd. Dublin, Ireland.	(N800CH)
N224MC	97	Beechjet 400A	RK-165	Midmark Corp. Versailles, Oh.	N2225Y
N224N	92	Challenger 601-3A	5108	NLC Inc. Seattle, Wa.	N428CL
N224QS	00	Falcon 2000	124	NetJets, Columbus, Oh.	F-WWVU
N224WD	02	CitationJet CJ-2	525A-0122	Fall Line Equipment Co. Macon, Ga.	N5135A
N225AL	95	Astra-1125SP	075	AML Leasing LLC. Burbank, Ca.	(N175SP)
N225AR	01	Challenger 604	5500	Russell Aviation Leasing Inc. Sarasota, Fl.	C-GLXU
N225BJ	78	HS 125/700A	NA0231	World of Faith Christian Center Church, Southfield, Mi.	N125G
N225CC	89	Falcon 100	225	Subsonic Jet Prop Inc/ECFS Inc. Easton, Md.	(N814PJ)
N225CF	79	Learjet 35A	35A-225	CF Air LLC. Miami, Fl.	(N225DG)
N225CX	01	Gulfstream 4SP	1467	CXAir Holdings Inc. Princeton, NJ.	(N225BK)
N225DC	94	Gulfstream 4SP	1253	Avion LLC/Drummond Coal Inc. Birmingham, Al.	N676RW
N225HR	73	HS 125/600B	6017	Hollywood Air Inc. Tampa, Fl.	(N415BA)
N225J	81	Citation II	550-0283	Jet One LLC. Waterford, Mi.	N124GA
N225KA	68	Learjet 25	25-004	SAP LLP. Las Cruces, NM.	N251AF
N225KS	91	Falcon 900B	105	Russell Aviation LLC. Wolfeboro, NH.	N405EJ
N225LJ	98	Learjet 40	45-2025	Learjet Inc. Wichita, Ks.	
N225MS	67	Gulfstream II SP	8	Midsouth Services Inc. Clearwater, Fl.	N267PS
Reg	**Yr**	**Type**	**c/n**	**Owner/Operator**	**Prev Regn**

Reg	Yr	Type	c/n	Owner/Operator	Prev Regn
❑ N225N	91	Challenger 601-3A	5100	JBW Aircraft Leasing Co. Seattle, Wa.	N505M
❑ N225PB	01	Hawker 800XP	8558	Moen Inc. Lincolnshire, Il.	N51058
❑ N225TR	78	Gulfstream II SP	225	Frontier Oil Corp. Houston, Tx.	N289K
❑ N225WT	97	Citation Bravo	550-0821	DBM Aviation Inc. Las Vegas, Nv.	N77797
❑ N225WW*	02	CitationJet CJ-2	525A-0065	Waterway Plastics, Oxnard, Ca.	N225EL
❑ N226AL	88	Gulfstream 4	1057	Aircraft Holdings LLC. Southfield, Mi.	N222AD
❑ N226B	97	CitationJet	525-0200	Cottonaire LLC. Gastonia, NC.	N1276J
❑ N226CV	93	Citation V	560-0226	Penmor Aviation LLC. Boston, Ma.	N893CM
❑ N226CW	99	CitationJet	525-0326	Flight Options LLC. Cleveland, Oh.	(N211LX)
❑ N226CX	04	Citation X	750-0226	AML Leasing LLC. Burbank, Ca.	N.....
❑ N226HD	99	Global Express	9022	The Home Depot Inc. Atlanta-Fulton County, Ga.	N622AB
❑ N226QS	00	Falcon 2000	126	NetJets, Columbus, Oh.	F-WWVW
❑ N226R	70	Falcon 20DC	226	Kalitta Charters LLC. Detroit-Willow Run, Mi.	N21FE
❑ N226RM	74	Gulfstream II SP	145	Aviation Associates LLC. Houston, Tx.	N339H
❑ N226RS	01	Gulfstream 4SP	1479	Harbor Island Management LLC. Newport Beach, Ca.	N1479G
❑ N226WW	77	Westwind-1124	226	Avwest International LLC. Boulder, Co.	D-CHBL
❑ N227CK	70	Falcon 20DC	227	Kalitta Charters LLC. Detroit-Willow Run, Mi.	N227R
❑ N227CP	91	Challenger 601-3A	5097	Alesworth Inc. Panama City, Panama.	N120PA
❑ N227GM	75	Citation Eagle	500-0227	Golden Class Jet LLC. Fort Lauderdale, Fl.	(N776JS)
❑ N227KT	00	Learjet 31A	31A-208	1132 Investment Corp/U S Aviation Co. Tulsa, Ok.	N518JC
❑ N227LA	76	Gulfstream 2	193	American Aircraft Leasing Inc. Raleigh-Durham, NC.	N54JJ
❑ N227LT	70	HS 125/731	NA754	Avitrans Inc. Wilmington, De.	N711HL
❑ N227MK	73	Citation	500-0070	227MK Aviation Inc. NYC.	VP-CMO
❑ N227MM	79	HS 125/700A	NA0258	Betman Inc. Marlow Heights, MD.	N193RC
❑ N227QS	00	Falcon 2000	127	NetJets, Columbus, Oh.	F-WWVY
❑ N227RH	95	Challenger 601-3R	5177	Winnepeg LLC/Reyes Holdings LLC. Rosemont, Il.	N601UC
❑ N227SV	91	Gulfstream 4	1172	Assembly Pointe Aviation Inc. Schenectady, NY.	N85VM
❑ N227TS	68	Gulfstream II SP	27	Hollywood Entertainment Corp. Wilsonville, Or.	(N227TJ)
❑ N227WE	77	Falcon 20F-5	344	7700 Properties LLC. Oklahoma City, Ok.	(N731AE)
❑ N227WS	04	Citation Encore	560-0676	Wesley West Interests Inc. Houston, Tx.	N.....
❑ N228CC	80	Citation II	550-0133	Eastern Air Center Inc. Norwood, Ma.	C-GRIO
❑ N228DB	04	Citation X	750-0228	Dudmaston Ltd. Milan, Italy.	N228BD
❑ N228FJ	92	Falcon 50	228	Emmanuel Group. N Wilkesboro, NC.	C-GAZU
❑ N228FS	77	Citation 1/SP	501-0018	Tiforp Corp. Destin, Fl.	N228AJ
❑ N228FX	98	Learjet 60	60-132	BBJS/FlexJets, Addison, Tx.	
❑ N228H*	99	Global Express	9040	Flight Management LLC. Seattle, Wa.	N22BH
❑ N228MD	74	HS 125/600B	6037	Five Star Development Co/Blue Bonnett Air Resources, Dallas	N63810
❑ N228MH	80	Citation II/SP	551-0050	Jet II Aviation LLC. Wilmington, De. (was 550-0385).	N228AK
❑ N228N	94	Learjet 60	60-031	Salem Leasing Corp. Winston-Salem, NC.	N4031L
❑ N228RE	00	Gulfstream 4SP	1438	Cape Clear LLC. Westborough, Ma.	N388GA
❑ N228SW	77	Learjet 25D	25D-228	AirNet Systems Inc. Columbus, Oh.	
❑ N228TM	00	Hawker 800XP	8458	EMC Corp. Cork, Ireland.	N42685
❑ N229CE	04	Citation X	750-0229	Naples Citation LLC. Naples, Fl.	N5268A
❑ N229CJ	95	CitationJet	525-0129	B Four Flying Inc. Winfield, Ks.	N52642
❑ N229D	85	Westwind-Two	427	Diamond Management/24E-340 Inc. Tucson, Az.	N229N
❑ N229HD	91	Falcon 900B	108	The Home Depot Inc. Atlanta-Fulton County, Ga.	N511WM
❑ N229KD	97	Learjet 31A	31A-139	Kevin Harvick Inc. Kernersville, NC.	N131AR
❑ N229LJ	01	Learjet 31A	31A-229	Land-O-Sun Dairies LLC. Johnson City, Tn.	(N11TK)
❑ N229MC	81	Citation II	550-0229	Matsco Inc. Marietta, Ga.	C-FGAT
❑ N229QS	01	Falcon 2000	129	NetJets, Columbus, Oh.	F-WWVD
❑ N229R	70	Falcon 20DC	229	Kalitta Charters LLC. Detroit-Willow Run, Mi.	(N229CK)
❑ N229U	91	BAe 1000A	NA1002	United Technologies Corp. Hartford, Ct.	G-BTYN
❑ N229VP	93	Citation V	560-0219	Sierra Papa Inc. Bakersfield, Ca.	N318MN
❑ N229WJ	77	Learjet 25D	25D-229	World Jet of Delaware Inc. Fort Lauderdale, Fl.	CX-ECO
❑ N230AJ	89	Astra-1125	036	Brett Jett LLC/JED Air LLC. Rochester, NY.	N195FC
❑ N230BT	81	Falcon 50	62	Meteor Management LLC. Napa, Ca.	(CS-DFK)
❑ N230RA	70	Falcon 20DC	230	Kalitta Charters LLC. Detroit-Willow Run, Mi.	N26EV
❑ N230TS	68	HS 125/3A-RA	NA700	Core Investments Inc. Fort Lauderdale, Fl.	N946FS
❑ N231JH	81	Falcon 10	176	Knoxville Aircraft LLC. Knoxville, Tn.	N66HH
❑ N232CC	81	Learjet 35A	35A-367	CCI Corp. Tulsa, Ok.	N97RJ
❑ N232CF	84	Citation III	650-0067	Capital Funding Group Inc. Baltimore, Md.	N9AX
❑ N232CL	87	Falcon 900A	9	Werner Aire Inc. Omaha, Ne.	N193TR
❑ N232CW	78	Citation II	550-0032	High Sierra Inc. Wilmington, De.	N112JGS
❑ N232DM	79	Citation II	550-0079	Bruce Foods Corp. New Iberia, La.	N33RH
❑ N232FX	86	Learjet 35A	35A-620	Aviation Properties Inc/DB Aviation Inc. Waukegan, Il.	VR-BNI
❑ N232JR	98	Citation Bravo	550-0855	FJL Leasing Corp. Cincinnati, Oh.	N132LF

| Reg | Yr | Type | c/n | Owner/Operator | Prev Regn |

Reg	Yr	Type	c/n	Owner/Operator	Prev Regn
N232K	94	Gulfstream 4SP	1232	Barbara Fasken Oil & Ranch, Midland, Tx.	N471GA
N232LJ	01	Learjet 60	60-232	Bombardier Capital Inc. Colchester, Vt.	LV-ZYF
N232PR	87	Falcon 50	179	Diligence Transportation LLC. Boston, Ma.	N212Q
N232TN	78	HS 125/700A	NA0232	Coconut Grove Aviation LLC. Miami, Fl.	(N331CG)
N232TW	66	Falcon 20C	32	Sierra American Corp. Addison, Tx.	F-GIVT
N233BC	95	Falcon 50	241	Exchange Properties Corp. Bellevue, Wa.	F-OKSI
N233CA	73	Learjet 25B	25B-133	Addison Aviation Services Inc. Addison, Tx.	XA-RZY
N233CC	75	Learjet 35	35-031	CCI Corp. Tulsa, Ok.	N160AT
N233DB	74	Citation	500-0158	Southeast Automotive Inc. Nashville, Tn.	OY-TAM
N233JJ	74	Citation	500-0233	Blount Brothers Construction Inc. Shreveport, La.	N228S
N233KC	88	Falcon 900B	48	K Club Investments LLC/ACM Aviation Inc. San Jose, Ca.	N900MJ
N233MW	99	Beechjet 400A	RK-233	Whitefish Investment Partners LLC. Edina, Mn.	N2293V
N233TW	70	Learjet 24B	24B-221	Sierra American Corp. Addison, Tx.	N59JG
N233XL	01	Citation Excel	560-5233	Childish Creations International Inc. Norcross, Ga.	N.....
N234AQ	93	Citation V	560-0234	Midwest Air LLC. Homewood, Il.	
N234AT	74	Citation	500-0240	Mountain State University Inc. Beckley, WV.	N240CC
N234CA	65	Falcon 20C	17	Cherry Air Inc. Addison, Tx.	N55TH
N234DB	00	Gulfstream 4SP	1457	Skybird Aviation, Van Nuys, Ca.	N357GA
N234DC	75	Sabre-60	306-103	Jet Works Inc. Fort Myers, Fl.	N40TL
N234DK	98	Beechjet 400A	RK-182	Nantucket Express LLC. Oakbrook Terrace, Il.	N2322B
N234FJ	96	Falcon 2000	34	U S Bancorp Equipment Finance Inc. Portland, Or.	HB-IAY
N234G	65	Jet Commander	28	Aviation Business Corp. St Louis, Mo.	N77NR
N234GF	87	BAe 125/800A	8096	Law Flight LLC. Waterford, Mi.	N311JX
N234JW	77	Citation 1/SP	501-0037	A & G Coal Corp. Lonesome Pine, Va.	N19J
N234SV	77	Learjet 25D	25D-226	Valley Services, Van Nuys, Id.	N333SG
N235AC	92	Learjet 35A	35A-676	M-S Air Inc/Aviation Charter Services, Indianapolis, In.	(N620MJ)
N235CA	68	Falcon 20C	139	Cherry Air. Inc. Addison, Tx.	N900WB
N235CG	01	Learjet 60	60-230	Easy Flight LLC. Miami, Fl.	N826SR
N235DX	02	Gulfstream 4SP	1493	Dick's Sporting Goods Inc. Pittsburgh, Pa. (DA-CLASSIC).	N493GA
N235EA	76	Learjet 35	35-061	Dickerson Associates Inc. West Columbia, SC.	N238RC
N235HR	84	Learjet 55	55-094	Newport Federal Corp. Newport Beach, Fl.	(N236HR)
N235JS	78	Learjet 35A	35A-199	Management Co of South Carolina, Columbia, SC.	N444HC
N235KK	00	Gulfstream 4SP	1458	Kirschman Aviation, Altamonte Springs, Fl.	N358GA
N235LP	97	Gulfstream 4SP	1336	Crest Aviation LLC. Van Nuys, Ca.	N41CP
N235MC	80	Learjet 35A	35A-334	Smith's Food & Drug Centers Inc. Salt Lake City, Ut.	(N334AB)
N235SV	93	Citation VI	650-0235	BI-GO Markets Inc/Supervalu Inc. Minneapolis, Mn.	N235CM
N236CA	74	Learjet 25B	25B-161	Cherry Air Inc. Addison, Tx.	N61EW
N236LB	98	Citation Excel	560-5023	Jacob Stern & Sons Inc. Santa Barbara, Ca.	N236LD
N236LD	02	Citation Excel	560-5236	Casey Co. Long Beach, Ca.	N51072
N236QS	00	Falcon 2000	136	NetJets, Columbus, Oh.	F-WWVL
N236TW	70	Falcon 20F	236	Sierra American Corp. Addison, Tx.	N936NW
N237AF	79	Learjet 35A	35A-262	Ameriflight Inc. Burbank, Ca.	N237GA
N237BA	02	BBJ-7FD	33500	BCC Equipment Leasing Corp. Long Beach, Ca.	N237BA
N237FX	99	Learjet 60	60-158	Cessna Finance Corp. Wichita, Ks.	
N237GA	97	Challenger 604	5400	Sunbird Aviation LLC/Orange County, Costa Mesa, Ca.	(N237G)
N237TW	71	Learjet 24D	24D-237	Sierra American Corp. Addison, Tx.	N825DM
N237VP	93	Citation V	560-0237	Desert Sky LLC/United Leasing Inc. Evansville, In.	N893W
N237WR	79	HS 125/700A	NA0252	Waddell & Reed Development Inc. Kansas City, Mo.	N895CC
N238CA	69	Learjet 25	25-040	Source Investments LLC. Addison, Tx.	N23FN
N238FX	99	Learjet 60	60-163	BBJS/FlexJets, Addison, Tx.	
N238JA	77	Learjet 35A	35A-134	White Industries Inc. Bates City, Mo.	N235DH
N238PR	81	Learjet 35A	35A-394	Diligence Transportation LLC. Boston, Ma.	N232PR
N238SM	02	Citation Excel	560-5238	Continental Limited Inc. Detroit-Willow Run, Mi.	N5061P
N239AX	87	Falcon 900B	39	Aspen Executive Air LLC. Aspen, Co.	N573J
N239BD*	70	Falcon 20F	239	FM Aircraft LLC. Arlington, Tx.	N239CD
N239CA	74	Learjet 25B	25B-149	Cherry Air inc. Addison, Tx.	N149J
N239CW	99	CitationJet	525-0339	Flight Options LLC. Cleveland, Oh.	(N212LX)
N239RC	94	Learjet 60	60-046	Ray Charles Enterprises Inc. Van Nuys, Ca.	N214BX
N240AK	82	Challenger 600S	1067	Oak Air Ltd. Akron, Oh.	N205EL
N240B	99	Citation Excel	560-5057	ThyssenKrupp Budd Co. Pontiac, Mi.	N350RD
N240CF	74	Sabre-40A	282-132	Americana Aviation Inc. Albert Lea, Mn.	N70BC
N240CK	66	Falcon 20C-5	24	Kalitta Charters LLC. Detroit-Willow Run, Mi.	(N240FJ)
N240CM	90	Citation V	560-0048	JAS Investment Corp. Northbrook, Il.	N220CM
N240CX	99	Gulfstream 4SP	1370	Skyaire Inc. Arlington, Tx.	N370GA
N240FX	99	Learjet 60	60-167	BBJS/FlexJets, Addison, Tx.	
N240RS	83	Falcon 200	479	EHR Aviation Inc. Ponte Vedra Beach, Fl.	N349MG

Reg	Yr	Type	c/n	Owner/Operator	Prev Regn
N240TW	66	Falcon 20C	40	Sierra American Corp. Addison, Tx.	C-GSKQ
N240Z	01	Hawker 800XP	8565	Nissan North America Inc. Smyrna, Tn.	N4465M
N241BJ	88	Beechjet 400	RJ-41	Corporate Jet Partners LLC. Leesburg, Va.	(N270BJ)
N241CT	81	Westwind-Two	355	Chevron USA Inc. New Orleans, La.	N355JK
N241DS	85	Citation S/II	S550-0042	Westar Leasing Corp. San Diego, Ca.	N250AF
N241FB	92	Challenger 601-3A	5102	Skylands Aviation LLC. Dearborn, Mi.	N494LC
N241FT	81	Citation II	550-0241	Prana Inc. El Paso, Tx.	XA-TQL
N241FX	99	Learjet 60	60-172	BBJS/FlexJets, Addison, Tx.	
N241JA	66	Learjet 24	24-131	Milam International Inc. Englewood, Co.	N11FH
N241JC	71	Falcon 20E	241	Jetcraft Corp. Raleigh-Durham, NC.	I-FLYK
N241JS	03	Hawker 800XP	8652	SkyLand Leasing Corp. Seffner, Fl.	N652XP
N241LJ	03	Learjet 45	45-241	KPA LLC. Springfield, Mo.	
N241MH	81	Citation 1/SP	501-0214	Barbladon Aircraft Leasing LLC. Ponte Vedra Beach, Fl.	(N340AC)
N241RS	74	Falcon 10	18	SFG Commercial Aircraft Leasing Inc. South Bend, In.	N1TJ
N241RT	79	HS 125/700A	NA0242	Patron Aviation Corp. Atlanta, Ga.	N418BA
N241TR	88	Beechjet 400	RJ-45	Triton Boat LP/Bentz Companies, Ashland City, Tn.	N218RG
N242AC	02	Citation Encore	560-0609	AAA Cooper Transportation Inc. Dothan, Al.	N847HS
N242AL	83	HS 125/700A	NA0340	ADESA Inc & ALLETE Inc. Duluth, Mn.	N804WJ
N242DR	79	Learjet 35A	35A-242	Pacific Air Transport Inc. Houston-Hobby, Tx.	VH-FSZ
N242FX	99	Learjet 60	60-174	BBJS/FlexJets, Addison, Tx.	
N242GB	96	CitationJet	525-0151	NPC International Inc. Pittsburg, Ks.	N28DM
N242GS	78	Learjet 25D	25D-242	Outrageous Bluewater LP. McKinney, Tx.	(N242AF)
N242LJ	98	CitationJet	525-0242	DBS Corp. Chattanooga, Tn.	(N27FB)
N242ML	02	CitationJet CJ-1	525-0506	Branksome Aviation Inc. Banstead, UK.	N.....
N242MT	86	Learjet 35A	35A-621	Wal-Mart Stores Inc. Rogers, Ar.	PT-OTW
N242PF	79	Learjet 25D	25D-298	Hartford Holding Corp. Naples, Fl.	N298DR
N242RB	87	Learjet 55B	55B-132	Wyoming Associates Inc. Spartanburg, SC.	N122SU
N242SW	99	Citation Bravo	550-0908	Strongwell Corp. Bristol, Va.	N5264M
N242WT	82	Citation II/SP	551-0066	Knight Aviation LLC. Lafayette, La.	(N551GC)
N243CH	01	Citation Excel	560-5243	Caribbean Helicorp Inc. San Juan, PR.	N567CH
N243FJ	80	Falcon 20F-5	430	Dassault Falcon Jet Corp. Teterboro, NJ.	N660P
N243FX	99	Learjet 60	60-175	BBJS/FlexJets, Addison, Tx.	
N243SH	75	Citation	500-0243	Soaring Seagull LLC. Tulsa, Ok.	N53AJ
N244A	79	Falcon 10	145	Snap-Tite Inc. Erie. Pa.	N209FJ
N244DM	68	Gulfstream 2	21	Anthony Aiello, Chicago, Il.	N8PQ
N244DS	01	Gulfstream 4SP	1477	DS Aviation LLC. Indianapolis, In.	(N949AV)
N244FJ	81	Falcon 20F-5B	444	Dassault Falcon Jet Corp. Teterboro, NJ.	N665P
N244FX	99	Learjet 60	60-178	BBJS/FlexJets, Addison, Tx.	
N244JM	88	BAe 125/800A	NA0428	McAir Inc/Worthington Industries Inc. Worthington, Oh.	N582BA
N244LJ	79	Learjet 35A	35A-244	Cessna Finance Corp. Wichita, Ks.	(N116KV)
N244LS	01	Hawker 800XP	8569	L & G Management LLC. Palm City, Fl.	N4469X
N244RG	77	Learjet 35A	35A-154	Gillman/Universal-Ramsbar Inc. Houston, Tx.	N117RB
N245CC	81	Citation II	550-0212	Eastern Air Center Inc. Norwood, Ma.	(N6801V)
N245FX	99	Learjet 60	60-182	BBJS/FlexJets, Addison, Tx.	
N245J	02	Citation Excel	560-5245	Dana Flight Operations Inc. Swanton, Oh.	N50820
N245K	99	Learjet 45	45-076	Koch Industries Inc. Wichita, Ks.	
N245KC	01	Learjet 45	45-150	KeyCorp Aviation Co. Cleveland, Oh.	
N245MS	83	Learjet 55	55-077	GSS LLC. Atlanta, Ga.	N85NC
N245QS	01	Falcon 2000	145	NetJets, Columbus, Oh.	F-WWVZ
N245RS	74	HS 125/F600B	6027	Stern Holdings Inc. Addison, Tx.	N800NM
N245TT	02	Gulfstream G550	5003	WOTAN America Inc. Fort Lauderdale, Fl.	N703GA
N246AG	03	Falcon 900EX EASY	135	Cableair LLC. Monticello, NY.	F-WWFM
N246CB	98	Citation Bravo	550-0849	Swanson Charters Inc. Fort Myers, Fl.	N841JG
N246CM	81	Learjet 35A	35A-395	Massey Partners Ltd. Abilene, Tx.	N30GL
N246FX	99	Learjet 60	60-183	BBJS/FlexJets, Addison, Tx.	
N246GS	01	CitationJet CJ-1	525-0446	Advantage Flight Service Inc. Wilmington, De.	N5211A
N246JL	82	Challenger 600S	1046	Fugate Enterprises Inc/Executive Aircraft Corp. Wichita, Ks.	N46SR
N246NW	90	Citation V	560-0068	Northwestern Public Service Co. Huron, SD.	N712GF
N246V	99	Hawker 800XP	8417	National Gypsum Co. Charlotte, NC.	N747NG
N247CJ	92	Falcon 900B	122	RJP Services LLC. Waterbury-Oxford, Ct.	N612BH
N247CP	95	Learjet 60	60-052	Catterton Aviation LLC. Greenwich, Ct.	N120HV
N247CW	98	CitationJet	525-0247	Flight Options LLC. Cleveland, Oh.	(N208LX)
N247EM	88	Gulfstream 4	1045	Mariner Management LLC. Ronkonkoma, NY.	N227GH
N247FX	99	Learjet 60	60-187	BBJS/FlexJets, Addison, Tx.	
N247KB	99	Gulfstream 4SP	1375	KB Home Inc. Van Nuys, Ca.	N375GA
N247PL	70	Falcon 20F	247	North Star Aviation Inc. Mankato, Mn.	N70PL

Reg	Yr	Type	c/n	Owner/Operator	Prev Regn
☐ N247PS	93	Astra-1125SP	069	Gulfstream Aerospace Corp. Savannah, Ga.	N804JW
☐ N247RG	79	Gulfstream 3	252	247RG LLC. Addison, Tx.	XA-MEY
☐ N247VA	96	Vantage	001	VisionAire, Chesterfield, Mo. (Ff 16 Nov 96).	
☐ N247WE	98	Challenger 604	5369	World Wrestling Federation Entertainment Inc. White Plains.	N247WF
☐ N248AB	01	Gulfstream 4SP	1474	Prime Jet LLC. Van Nuys, Ca.	(N948AV)
☐ N248CJ	98	CitationJet	525-0248	Bill Putman, Glendive, Mt.	
☐ N248CK	78	Learjet 25D	25D-248	Kalitta Charters LLC. Detroit-Willow Run, Mi.	(N248LJ)
☐ N248CW	99	CitationJet	525-0348	Flight Options LLC. Cleveland, Oh.	(N213LX)
☐ N248FX	99	Learjet 60	60-188	BBJS/FlexJets, Addison, Tx.	
☐ N248HA	82	Citation II	550-0423	HoganAir LLC. Tampa, Fl.	C-FCCC
☐ N248JF	95	Falcon 2000	11	JF Aircraft Corp. Dearborn, Mi.	N721BS
☐ N248SL	00	Astra-1125SPX	125	Stim-Air Inc. Portland, Or.	N44GX
☐ N249FX	00	Learjet 60	60-193	BBJS/FlexJets, Addison, Tx.	
☐ N249HP	75	Learjet 24D	24D-301	RFS Aero Leasing Inc. Tucson, Az.	N31BG
☐ N249RM	00	Beechjet 400A	RK-285	Roma Aviation Corp. El Paso, Tx.	N249SB
☐ N250AJ	91	Beechjet 400A	RK-23	Anthony Costello, Rochester, NY.	(N960AJ)
☐ N250AL	02	Citation Encore	560-0605	Luhr Bros Inc. Columbia, Il.	N605CE
☐ N250DH	69	HS 125/731	NA718	Arnoni Aviation Inc. Houston, Tx.	XA-SSV
☐ N250DR	80	Citation II	550-0218	Delta Romeo Inc. Deland, Fl.	PT-LPP
☐ N250DV	02	Gulfstream V	691	RDV Corp. Grand Rapids, Mi.	N691GA
☐ N250FX	00	Learjet 60	60-194	BBJS/FlexJets, Addison, Tx.	
☐ N250GP	83	Diamond 1A	A069SA	Weston Aviation LLC.	(N501EZ)
☐ N250HP	99	Beechjet 400A	RK-250	Eagle Wings Inc. Lexington, Ky.	N2293V
☐ N250JE	92	BAe 125/800A	8237	Jet Equity Aviation LLC. White Plains, NY.	N237RA
☐ N250KD	89	Beechjet 400	RJ-60	U S Turbine Aircraft Sales Inc. Mason City, Ia.	XA-LEG
☐ N250LB	95	Gulfstream 4SP	1269	Lehman Brothers/Executive Fliteways Inc. Ronkonkoma, NY.	N677VU
☐ N250MS	69	Gulfstream II SP	45	Martin Sprocket & Gear Inc. Fort Worth, Tx.	N245GA
☐ N250SP	02	Hawker 800XP	8600	Sonoco Products Co. Darlington County, SC.	N61500
☐ N250SR	93	Citation V	560-0211	S E A LLC/Global Industries Inc. Grand Island, Ne.	N250SP
☐ N250VC	02	Gulfstream 4SP	1495	Dacion Corp. Teterboro, NJ.	N495GA
☐ N250VP	81	Citation II	550-0250	Tar Heel Air LLC. Fayetteville, NC.	N33GK
☐ N251AL	80	Learjet 25D	25D-313	Milam International Inc. Englewood, Co.	N727CS
☐ N251CP	01	Challenger 604	5524	251 Finance Inc. Caracas, Venezuela.	N251VG
☐ N251DS	77	Learjet 25D	25D-218	B & C Flight Management Inc. Houston, Tx.	N14NA
☐ N251DV	03	Gulfstream G400	1522	RDV Corp. Grand Rapids, Mi.	N522GA
☐ N251FX	00	Learjet 60	60-195	BBJS/FlexJets, Addison, Tx.	
☐ N251JA	74	Learjet 25B	25B-150	Milam International Inc. Englewood, Co.	N888RB
☐ N251JS	79	Gulfstream 2	251	Rubloff Development Group Inc. Rockford, Il.	N36GS
☐ N251KD	02	CitationJet CJ-2	525A-0133	251KD LLC. Wilson, Wy.	N.....
☐ N251MD	82	Learjet 25D	25D-356	DK Properties Inc. Newport Beach, Ca.	N25PT
☐ N251MG	75	Citation	500-0250	Michael Greer, Tupelo, Ms.	N251P
☐ N251QS	02	Falcon 2000	202	NetJets, Columbus, Oh.	F-WWVP
☐ N251TS	75	Learjet 25B	25B-201	VRBB Partners LLC. Miami Beach, Fl.	N59BL
☐ N252BK	73	Learjet 25B	25B-107	GoldStar International Inc. Port Arthur, Tx.	N25NB
☐ N252DH	93	BAe 125/800A	8244	Dafra Leasing LLC. Wilmington, De.	N530BA
☐ N252FX	00	Learjet 60	60-196	BBJS/FlexJets, Addison, Tx.	
☐ N252JK	96	CitationJet	525-0166	Kaney Citation LLC. Rockford, Il.	F-GRRM
☐ N252RP	01	Learjet 60	60-235	Kestral Technologies LLC. Chiacgo, Il.	N5013N
☐ N252RV	98	CitationJet	525-0252	Neighbourhood Restaurants, Hazard, Ky.	VP-CIS
☐ N252WJ	80	Learjet 35A	35A-349	World Jet Inc. Fort Lauderdale, Fl.	XA-TCI
☐ N253CM	00	Gulfstream V	610	Cargill Inc. Minneapolis, Mn.	(N610CM)
☐ N253CW	98	CitationJet	525-0253	Flight Options LLC. Cleveland, Oh.	(N209LX)
☐ N253DV	87	B 737-39A	23800	Magic Carpet Aviation Inc. Orlando, Fl.	N117DF
☐ N253FX	01	Learjet 60	60-241	BBJS/FlexJets, Addison, Tx.	N5026Q
☐ N253MT	72	HS 125/F400A	25253	Nevada Air Transport LLC. Carson City, Nv.	(N253CC)
☐ N253QS	01	Falcon 2000	153	NetJets, Columbus, Oh.	F-WWVK
☐ N253S	83	Learjet 55	55-053	I J Knight Inc. New Tripoli, Pa.	(N205EF)
☐ N253SJ	82	Falcon 50	107	ACI Pacific LLC. Agana, Guam.	F-WQBM
☐ N254AL	02	EMB-135BJ Legacy	145516	Swift Aviation Services Inc. Phoenix, Az.	PT-SAG
☐ N254CL	79	Learjet 25D	25D-275	Clay Lacy Aviation Inc. Van Nuys, Ca.	N211CD
☐ N254CR	76	Gulfstream 2	184	R & David Jacobs Group/Aviation Venture Inc. Cleveland, Oh.	N220GA
☐ N254CW	96	CitationJet	525-0154	Flight Options LLC. Cleveland, Oh.	(N204LX)
☐ N254FX	01	Learjet 60	60-247	BBJS/FlexJets, Addison, Tx.	
☐ N254GA	87	Gulfstream 4	1032	NetJets Middle East, Jeddah, Saudi Arabia.	N432QS
☐ N254RK	99	Beechjet 400A	RK-254	BJRK66 Inc. Dallas, Tx.	TC-BYD
☐ N254SC	72	Learjet 25B	25B-102	Dolphin Aviation Inc. Sarasota, Fl.	N64WH

Reg	Yr	Type	c/n	Owner/Operator	Prev Regn

Reg	Yr	Type	c/n	Owner/Operator	Prev Regn
N254SD	99	Gulfstream 4SP	1387	JMI Services Inc. San Diego, Ca.	N487GA
N254SJ	99	BBJ-7BC	30572	WFBNW NA. Salt Lake City, Ut. (trustor ?).	N171QS
N255AR	72	Learjet 24D	24D-255	World Jet of Delaware Inc. Fort Lauderdale, Fl.	XA-SMU
N255BD	01	Learjet 60	60-221	Georgia Services Group LLC. Columbus, Ga.	
N255CC	95	Challenger 604	5302	Apollo Aviation LLC. Englewood, Co.	(N150SE)
N255CM	97	Falcon 50EX	255	Cargill Inc. Minneapolis, Mn.	F-WWHC
N255DG	83	Diamond 1A	A056SA	Richmor Aviation Inc. Garfield County, Rifle, Co.	I-FRTT
N255DV	86	BAe 125/800A	8070	Amway Corp. Grand Rapids, Mi.	N528AC
N255DX	01	Hawker 800XP	8535	Quest Diagnostics Inc. Reading, Pa.	(N853QS)
N255FX	01	Learjet 60	60-220	BBJS/FlexJets, Addison, Tx.	N254FZ
N255GA	88	Gulfstream 4	1055	NetJets Middle East, Jeddah, Saudi Arabia.	XB-OEM
N255QS	01	Falcon 2000	155	NetJets, Columbus, Oh.	F-WWVM
N255RB	86	BAe 125/800A	8059	Regal-Beloit Corp. Janesville, Wi.	N355RB
N255RD	73	Citation	500-0069	Hernando Jet Center Inc. Brooksville, Fl.	\N969SE
N255RM	92	Citation V	560-0201	LOE Inc. Santa Fe, NM.	SU-EWA
N255TC	90	Citation II	550-0638	B & J of Destin Inc. Destin, Fl.	N1717L
N255TS	93	Gulfstream 4SP	1231	TransMeridian Aviation LLC. St Paul, Mn.	N250VZ
N255UJ	82	Learjet 55	55-032	EHR Aviation Inc. Ponte Vedra Beach, Fl.	N183SD
N255VP	87	Citation III	650-0152	Volare Partners LLC. Milwaukee, Wi.	N260VP
N256A	86	Falcon 50	172	Ameritas Life Insurance Co/Bridgemark Assocs. Lincoln, Ne.	N9000F
N256BC	94	Hawker 800	8256	Teterboro Aviation Inc. Teterboro, NJ.	(N256FS)
N256BM	82	Citation 1/SP	501-0256	Rick Mehrlich, Incline Village, Nv.	N256P
N256CC	01	Citation Bravo	550-0965	Carlisle Aviation LLC. Olive Branch, Ms.	N741PP
N256FX	02	Learjet 60	60-257	BBJS/FlexJets, Addison, Tx.	N50157
N256JB	98	CitationJet	525-0284	John Bowen, Satellite Beach, Fl.	
N256LK	97	Gulfstream V	514	Garthorpe Inc. Burbank, Ca.	N320K
N256V	79	Falcon 10	151	Thomas Harter Sr/Micro Dynamics Group, Chicago-O'Hare, Il.	N256W
N256W	03	Citation X	750-0221	Wendy's International Inc. Columbus, Oh.	N51042
N256WJ	73	HS 125/F600A	6008	Silverleaf Resorts Inc. Dallas, Tx.	XX508
N256WM	72	Learjet 24D	24D-256	M & V Airplane LLC. Roswell, NM.	N256MJ
N257CB	83	Diamond 1A	A050SA	Fikes Truck Line Inc. Hope, Ar.	N350DM
N257CW	80	Citation II	550-0157	Flight Options LLC. Cleveland, Oh.	N101BX
N257H	93	Gulfstream 4SP	1223	H J Heinz Co. Pittsburgh, Pa.	N935SH
N257SD	76	Learjet 35	35-064	Intercontinental Express LLC. Athens, Ga.	(N257DP)
N257V	78	Falcon 10	119	Jet Choice II LLC. St Paul, Mn.	N257W
N257W	99	Citation VII	650-7112	Wendy's International Inc. Columbus, Oh.	N5174W
N258A	81	Falcon 20F-5	438	HML Leasing LLC. Austin, Tx.	N256A
N258FX	02	Learjet 60	60-263	Learjet Inc. Wichita, Ks.	
N258G	81	Learjet 35A	35A-443	SWSTAR-M LLC. Solana Beach, Ca.	N135RJ
N258PE	68	Falcon 20D	163	Grand Aire Express Inc. Toledo, Oh.	N178GA
N258QS	01	Falcon 2000	158	NetJets, Columbus, Oh.	F-WWVP
N258SP	94	Hawker 800	8258	R-5 Holdings LLC. Bethlehem, Pa.	N910JN
N259DB	65	Learjet 23	23-064	Jet Investment Group Inc. Springfield, Il. (for rebuild ?).	ZS-MBR
N259DH	75	Citation	500-0259	West Star Construction Inc. Kingsburg, Ca.	RP-C1299
N259QS	01	Falcon 2000	159	NetJets, Columbus, Oh.	F-W...
N259RH	00	Hawker 800XP	8529	AutoStar LLC. Pittsburgh, Pa.	N814TA
N259SK	81	Gulfstream 3	327	Lasher Investment Management Service, Tampa, Fl.	N829MG
N259SP	01	Hawker 800XP	8531	Raytheon Aircraft Co. Wichita, Ks.	N4469F
N260AM	98	CitationJet	525-0260	Rancho Pacific Holdings LLC. Rancho Cucamongo, Ca.	D-IGZA
N260AN	98	Learjet 60	60-124	Jetride Inc. Dallas, Tx.	(N223BX)
N260BS	86	Citation S/II	S550-0080	BS-SII LLC. Coral Springs, Fl.	XA-TMI
N260CH	89	Gulfstream 4	1072	Crescent Heights of America Inc.	N500E
N260LF	90	Learjet 31	31-015	Landscapes Unlimited LLC. Lincoln, Ne.	N111TT
N260TB	93	Citation II	550-0720	The Bank, Birmingham, Al.	N848HS
N260UJ	93	Learjet 60	60-008	Richmark Aircraft Leasing LLC. Boca Raton, Fl.	N222HV
N260V	81	Challenger 600S	1022	DDH Aviation Inc. Fort Worth, Tx.	144610
N261JP	93	Beechjet 400A	RK-76	Jefferson-Pilot Corp. Greensboro, NC.	N8166A
N261PA	02	Hawker 800XP	8587	Executive Airways LLC. Plymouth, Ma.	N50657
N261PG	80	Learjet 35A	35A-329	Kladstrup-Wetzel Associates Ltd. Englewood, Co.	N261PC
N261SC	92	Learjet 31A	31A-061	Wal-Mart Stores Inc. Rogers, Ar.	N740F
N261WC	78	Learjet 25D	25D-261	Southeast Jet Leasing Inc. Deerfield Beach, Fl.	N24JK
N261WR	97	Citation V Ultra	560-0447	W R Meadows Inc. Hampshire, Il.	N51246
N262BK	98	CitationJet	525-0262	A & C Business Services Inc. Orlando, Fl.	N52547
N262PA	98	Beechjet 400A	RK-203	Lily Airways LLC. Plymouth, Ma.	N203RK
N262PC	98	Falcon 2000	78	Park Corp. Cleveland, Oh.	G-PYCO
N262QS	01	Falcon 2000	162	NetJets, Columbus, Oh.	F-W...

Reg	Yr	Type	c/n	Owner/Operator	Prev Regn
☐ N262Y	81	Citation II	550-0291	Colnan Inc. Tampa, Fl.	N40MA
☐ N263CT	98	CitationJet	525-0263	JKZ Properties Ltd. Arlington, Wa.	
☐ N264A	00	Global Express	9064	ALCOA, Allegheny County, Pa.	N700PL
☐ N264CL	78	Gulfstream II SP	227	Clay Lacy Aviation Inc. Van Nuys, Ca.	N200LS
☐ N264TW	77	Learjet 25D	25D-232	Chaparral Inc. Lubbock, Tx.	N500LW
☐ N265C	80	Sabre-65	465-33	M D Lung Inc/Patrick Industries Inc. Elkhart, In.	N465SR
☐ N265CP	80	Sabre-65	465-48	S & R Leasing LLC. Rome, Ga.	N265SP
☐ N265DC	65	Learjet 23	23-081	Intermountain Fixed Wing LC. Salt Lake City, Ut.	ZS-MDN
☐ N265DS	80	Sabre-65	465-45	GS Sabre 65 LLC. Pontiac, Mi.	N65DR
☐ N265GM	74	Sabre-60	306-84	Commercial Aviation Enterprises Inc. Delray Beach, Fl.	N55ZM
☐ N265H*	04	Falcon 900EX EASY	139	CNL Group Services Inc. Orlando, Fl.	N139EX
☐ N265KC	76	Sabre-80A	380-49	Grayson Air Service LLC. Detroit, Mi.	(N480CF)
☐ N265M	80	Sabre-65	465-31	Aero Charter Inc. St Louis, Mo.	N65FC
☐ N265MK	74	Sabre-60	306-90	N265 LLC. St Louis, Mo.	N123FG
☐ N265MP	72	Falcon 20F	265	JNM Air Delaware LLC. St Louis, Mo.	N606RP
☐ N265QS	01	Falcon 2000	165	NetJets, Columbus, Oh.	F-WWVE
☐ N265SC	73	Sabre-40A	282-117	Sunshine Aero Industries Inc. Crestview, Fl.	(N298AS)
☐ N265SJ	98	Gulfstream 4SP	1351	Mokulele LLC. Dulles, Va.	N451QS
☐ N265ST	91	Gulfstream 4	1179	JM Family Enterprises Inc. Fort Lauderdale, Fl.	N41QR
☐ N265TS	00	Citation Bravo	550-0942	Arcadia Aviation LLC. Wilmington, De.	N72SG
☐ N265TW	78	Learjet 25D	25D-265	Chaparrel Inc. Lubbock, Tx.	N69GF
☐ N265U	77	Sabre-60	306-132	Pre-Fab Transit Co. Champaign, Il.	N60AG
☐ N265WS	81	Sabre-65	465-62	Signco Transportation LLC. Merrillville, In.	(N65BT)
☐ N266CJ	98	CitationJet	525-0266	Baltimore Clipper Inc. Van Nuys, Ca.	
☐ N266TW	73	Learjet 24D	24D-266	Sierra American Corp. Addison, Tx.	N266BS
☐ N267BB	79	Citation II	550-0067	Bohlke International Airways Inc. St Croix, USVI.	N267CW
☐ N267BW	98	Challenger 604	5391	United Healthcare Services Inc. St Paul, Mn.	N788SC
☐ N267JE	80	HS 125/700A	NA0267	Jackson Financial Services Inc. Decatur, Ga.	N36GS
☐ N267WG	94	Citation V Ultra	560-0267	West Gaines Seed & Delinting Inc. Seminole, Tx.	N267VP
☐ N268FJ	97	Falcon 50EX	268	Dassault Falcon Jet Corp. Teterboro, NJ.	F-WQBL
☐ N268PA	01	Beechjet 400A	RK-323	M M & S Airways LLC. New Bedford, Ma.	N5003G
☐ N268QS	01	Falcon 2000	168	NetJets, Columbus, Oh.	(N2260)
☐ N268WC	79	Learjet 25D	25D-268	DMK Ventures LLC. Huntsville, Al.	(N829AA)
☐ N268WS	03	Learjet 60	60-268	Wingedfoot Services LLC. West Palm Beach, Fl.	N5011L
☐ N269JR	99	Citation X	750-0073	ROI Development Corp/Newmar, Santa Ana, Ca.	N999CX
☐ N269QS	01	Falcon 2000	169	NetJets, Columbus, Oh.	F-WWVJ
☐ N269RC	73	Citation	500-0078	Magnetic Land Inc. Las Vegas, Nv.	N110CK
☐ N269SW	78	Falcon 10	125	Lynch Air LLC. Rancho Santa Fe, Ca.	XA-SAR
☐ N269TA	89	Citation V	560-0006	Truman Arnold Companies, Texarkana, Tx.	N570MH
☐ N270CW	88	Citation II	550-0570	Flight Options LLC. Cleveland, Oh.	N570WD
☐ N270HC	84	BAe 125/800A	8020	Hawker 800 LLC. Irvine, Ca.	(N251TJ)
☐ N270KA	81	HS 125/700A	NA0307	Crusader Aviation Inc. Oxford, Ct.	N270MC
☐ N270LC	79	Westwind-1124	245	Moser, Patterson & Sheridan LLP. Houston, Tx.	N404CB
☐ N270MC	83	Gulfstream 3	374	Key Air Inc/Parke Aviation Corp. Scarborough Manor, NY.	N24GA
☐ N270NF	80	Citation 1/SP	501-0144	Air Justice LLC/Lundy & Davis LLP. Lake Charles, La.	N270SF
☐ N270PM	74	Citation	500-0196	Metroline Equipment Leasing LLC. Troy, Mi.	(N711FW)
☐ N270SC	93	Gulfstream 4SP	1229	Trans-Exec Air Service Inc. Van Nuys, Ca.	N830EC
☐ N270V	81	Challenger 600S	1017	4KS Aviation III Inc. Dallas, Tx.	114609
☐ N270WS	89	Learjet 55C	55C-138	Weather Shield Inc. Medford, Wi.	N338FP
☐ N271AC	74	Citation	500-0218	Dominion Air Charter Inc. Louisa County, Va.	N4AC
☐ N271CA	90	Citation V	560-0071	Chandler USA Inc. Chandler, Ok.	
☐ N271DV	00	Falcon 900EX	68	Poplar Glen LLC. Seattle, Wa.	N390DE
☐ N271L	04	Learjet 60	60-271	Learjet Inc. Wichita, Ks.	
☐ N271MB	80	Sabre-65	465-24	Wm F & Michael D Murphy Partnership, East Moline, Il.	N777SK
☐ N271SC	93	Learjet 31A	31A-071	Wal-Mart Stores Inc. Rogers, Ar.	N742F
☐ N272BC	04	Learjet 45	45-252	Bissell Inc. Grand Rapids, Mi.	N40076
☐ N272DN	78	Falcon 10	135	American Equity Investment Properties, Des Moines, Ia.	N707CX
☐ N272MH	04	Citation Sovereign	680-0015	Cessna Aircraft Co. Wichita, Ks.	N......
☐ N272MW	02	Gulfstream G200	058	Thermo Properties II LLC. Denver, Co.	(N702QS)
☐ N273CA	69	Learjet 25	25-039	Source Investments LLC. Addison, Tx.	(N25VJ)
☐ N273JC	98	Falcon 2000	73	Via Feliz LLC/Woodland Aviation Inc. San Jose, Ca.	(N97LT)
☐ N273LJ	79	Learjet 35A	35A-273	Jetride Inc. Columbus, Oh.	N103CL
☐ N273LP	01	Learjet 45	45-185	Louisiana-Pacific Corp. Hillsboro, Or.	
☐ N273LR	70	Learjet 25	25-058	ATI Jet Sales LLC. El Paso, Tx.	N273LP
☐ N273MC	00	Learjet 60	60-181	Meredith Corp. Des Moines, Ia.	
☐ N273MG	85	Learjet 55	55-119	Hermann Aviation Inc. St Louis, Mo.	N273MC

Reg	Yr	Type	c/n	Owner/Operator	Prev Regn
N273RA	97	Astra-1125SPX	097	Rite Aid Corp. Harrisburg, Pa.	
N273S	98	Challenger 604	5396	Shamrock Aviation Inc. Teterboro, NJ.	N604SH
N274CA	68	Sabre-60	306-31	Conrad Aviation Technologies Inc. Centerville, Oh.	N307D
N274HM	81	Westwind-Two	342	CBA Flight Services Inc. Paramus, NJ.	N204AB
N274JS	79	Learjet 35A	35A-274	First Star Inc. Hollister, Ca.	N274FD
N274K	79	Westwind-1124	274	C L Frates & Co. Oklahoma City, Ok.	N701W
N274MA	66	Jet Commander	74	Constellation Airways Inc. Sugarland, Tx.	(N149SF)
N275BB	04	Citation Bravo	550-1075	Citation Oil & Gas Corp. Houston, Tx.	N5162W
N275E	71	Learjet 24D	24D-245	Rocket Air LLC. Olympia, Wa.	(N44KB)
N275GK	75	Citation	500-0275	North American Air LLC. Hudson, Fl.	(N275BH)
N275HH	90	Falcon 50	207	RLG Test Flight Services LLC. Austin, Tx.	N369EG
N275QS	98	Falcon 2000	75	NetJets, Columbus, Oh.	F-WWMK
N275RA	97	Astra-1125SPX	098	Rite Aid Corp. Harrisburg, Pa.	
N276A	02	Citation Excel	560-5276	Alfa Aircraft Holdings LLC. Montgomery, Al.	N.....
N276GC	99	Challenger 604	5431	The Graham Companies, York, Pa.	C-GLWR
N277AL	84	Learjet 55	55-104	ATI Jet Sales LLC. El Paso, Tx.	N18CQ
N277AT*	86	Falcon 200	509	Arrow Trading Inc. Fort Lauderdale, Fl.	N200WY
N277GA	02	Gulfstream G200	077	Executive Services Inc. Scottsdale, Az.	4X-CVH
N277JM	81	Citation II/SP	551-0035	Air Cruise/John Myers, Long Beach, Ca.	N277HM
N277MG	67	Jet Commander-A	127	Kendall Aircraft Sales Inc. Sarasota, Fl.	N550K
N277QS	02	Falcon 2000	177	NetJets, Columbus, Oh.	F-WWMD
N277RC	93	Citation V	560-0210	Richard & Mary Cree, Jackson, Wy.	N420DM
N277RP	87	Gulfstream 4	1026	Harbour Group Industries Inc. St Louis, Mo.	(N277AG)
N277TW	73	Learjet 24D	24D-277	Sierra American Corp. Addison, Tx.	N57BC
N277WW	80	Westwind-1124	277	Avwest International LLC. Boulder, Co.	D-CHCL
N278GA	02	Gulfstream G200	078	TASair Aviation SA. Nyon, Switzerland.	(HB-IUS)
N278GS	02	Falcon 2000	193	Gilead Sciences Inc. Foster City, Ca.	N239QS
N278QS	98	Falcon 2000	77	NetJets, Columbus, Oh.	F-WWMM
N279DM	79	Learjet 35A	35A-214	AirNet Systems Inc. Columbus, Oh. (black).	
N279LE	73	Learjet 25B	25B-112	Tee Time Air LLC. Brookfield, Wi.	(YV-....)
N280AJ	98	Beechjet 400A	RK-164	U S Airports Air Charters Inc. Rochester, NY.	(N69LS)
N280BC	03	Falcon 50EX	332	Liberty Mutual Insurance Co. Bedford, Ma.	N332EX
N280BG	82	Falcon 50	109	Soloflex Inc. Hillsboro, Or.	N280BC
N280BQ	89	Falcon 900B	71	Liberty Mutual Insurance Co. Bedford, Ma.	N280BC
N280C	79	Learjet 25D	25D-280	Steve Sandlin, Las Vegas, Nv.	(N510L)
N280K	98	Challenger 604	5365	Eastman Kodak Co. Rochester, NY.	N618DC
N280PM	80	Citation II	550-0188	Planemasters Ltd. DuPage, Il.	N38NA
N280QS	02	Falcon 2000	181	NetJets, Columbus, Oh.	F-WWMM
N280R	69	Learjet 24B	24B-188	Spirit Wing Aviation Ltd. Guthrie, Ok.	N230R
N280TA	80	Citation II	550-0206	Sesame Street Productions Inc. Boca Raton, Fl.	XA-SQW
N281BT	80	HS 125/700A	NA0281	THR LLC. Dallas-Love, Tx.	N403DP
N281CW	96	CitationJet	525-0131	Flight Options LLC. Cleveland, Oh.	(N203LX)
N281FP	73	Learjet 24D	24D-281	Valhi Inc. Dallas, Tx.	N23MJ
N281QS	98	Falcon 2000	81	NetJets, Columbus, Oh.	F-WWVA
N281VP	94	Citation V Ultra	560-0281	P & M Leasing Inc. Green Bay, Wi.	N511ST
N282AC	67	Learjet 24	24-145	USA Jet Airlines Inc. Detroit-Willow Run, Mi.	(XA-LNA)
N282CJ	02	CitationJet CJ-2	525A-0082	C I Automobiles Ltd. Guernsey, C.I.	N5183V
N282QT	01	Gulfstream V	673	G F Management LLC. Durham, NC.	N873GA
N282T	75	Falcon 10	42	CDECRE Inc. Chicago, Il.	N100UB
N282WW	77	Sabre-60	306-134	IVEFA CA-Venezuela/Gadsden Holdings Inc. Miami, Fl.	N323EC
N283CW	92	Citation II	550-0713	Business Transportation Services Ltd. Columbus, Oh.	N95HE
N283DF	03	Citation II	550-0456	Iradewinds 12/21 Inc. Sherman, Tx.	C-GMPQ
N283S	00	Global Express	9080	Shamrock Aviation Inc. Teterboro, NY.	C-GHFH
N283SA	67	Falcon 20C	83	Smithair Inc. Lewis B Wilson Airport, Ga.	(N82SR)
N284CP	96	Citation V Ultra	560-0358	Cook Sales Inc. Carbondale, Il.	N30TV
N284DB	69	HS 125/731	NA715	284DB Inc. Newtown Square, Pa.	N824TJ
N284QS	02	Falcon 2000	185	NetJets, Columbus, Oh.	F-WWML
N284RJ	77	Citation 1/SP	501-0005	Rockbridge Consulting Inc. Santa Barbara, Ca.	N143EP
N284TJ	79	Learjet 25D	25D-284	InterContinental Express LLC. Athens, Ga.	XC-CFM
N285AL	87	BAe 125/800A	8085	Air Logic Sales Inc. Tampa, Fl.	G-WBPR
N285CC	95	Citation V Ultra	560-0285	TXU Business Services Co. Dallas, Tx.	N147VC
N285CP	81	Falcon 50	44	CITGO Petroleum Corp. Tulsa, Ok.	N44MK
N285DH	82	Learjet 55	55-026	Insurance Investors Inc. Austin, Tx.	N1324B
N285MC	86	Citation S/II	S550-0102	Aromaco Aircraft Sales & Rental Inc. Heber Springs, Ar.	N287MC
N285TW	73	Falcon 20E	285	Sierra American Corp. Addison, Tx.	N285AP
N285XP	95	Hawker 800XP	8285	Fremont Administrative Services Corp. Van Nuys, Ca.	N808H

Reg	Yr	Type	c/n	Owner/Operator	Prev Regn
☐ N286CW	93	CitationJet	525-0026	Flight Options LLC. Cincinnati, Oh.	(N214LX)
☐ N286MC	97	Citation VII	650-7076	Maytag Corp. Newton, Ia.	
☐ N286PC	80	Citation 1/SP	501-0164	C L Swanson Corp. Madison, Wi.	N170JS
☐ N286WL	80	Learjet 35A	35A-286	Orion Aviation International LLC. Huntsville, Al.	PT-LSW
☐ N286ZT	99	Falcon 50EX	286	Horizon Americas Inc. Wilmington, De.	VP-BMI
☐ N287DL	74	HS 125/600A	6040	Jet Global Inc. Jacksonville, Fl.	(N301JJ)
☐ N287KB	89	MD-87	49768	KEB Aircraft Sales Inc. Danville, Ca.	D-ALLJ
☐ N287MC	99	Citation VII	650-7096	Maytag Corp. Newton, Ia.	N5162W
☐ N287SA	76	Falcon 20F	349	J B Aviation Inc. Jacksonville, Fl.	N767AG
☐ N288AG	98	CitationJet	525-0288	Professional Equipment Management, Red Lodge, Mt.	
☐ N288CW	97	CitationJet	525-0218	Flight Options LLC. Cleveland, Oh.	(N207LX)
☐ N288DF	74	Learjet 24D	24D-288	Blue Sky Partners LLC. Pampa, Tx.	
☐ N288FF	95	Learjet 31A	31A-108	Bogey Free LLC. St Petersburg, Fl.	(N288BF)
☐ N288G	01	CitationJet CJ-2	525A-0035	Airdine LLC. Novato, Ca.	N51564
☐ N288HL	02	Citation Encore	560-0599	Tigerpaw Investments LLC. Lakeland, Fl.	N52690
☐ N288JP	79	Learjet 35A	35A-288	Prior Aviation Service Inc. Buffalo, NY.	N288JE
☐ N288KA	83	Gulfstream 3	391	Kookaburra Air LLC. Morristown, NJ.	N14SY
☐ N288MM	85	Citation 1/SP	501-0689	Coldwater Veneer Inc. Coldwater, Mi.	N88MM
☐ N288SP	75	Citation	500-0241	American Aviation LLC. Las Vegas, Nv.	XB-EPN
☐ N288Z	99	Global Express	9024	Chamarac Inc. White Plains, NY.	N700BH
☐ N289K	93	Challenger 601-3A	5132	Swagelok/Crawford Fitting Co. Cleveland, Oh.	N610DB
☐ N290CA	78	Westwind-1124	216	Club Air Inc. Greenwood, Tx.	(N65BK)
☐ N290CP	77	Westwind-1124	219	Westwind Partners Inc/CP Investment Ltd. Caracas, Venezuela.	YV-190CP
☐ N290EC	89	BAe 125/800A	NA0444	Ethyl Corp. Richmond, Va.	N596BA
☐ N290QS	03	Falcon 2000	190	NetJets, Columbus, Oh.	F-WWVA
☐ N290VP	79	Citation II	550-0090	Heritage Food Service Equipment, Fort Wayne, In.	N410NA
☐ N291BC	89	Falcon 50	199	Boise Cascade Corp. Boise, Id.	N287FJ
☐ N291CW	98	CitationJet	525-0301	Flight Options LLC. Cleveland, Oh.	N270J
☐ N291DV	00	Citation Excel	560-5146	Fall River Aviation LLC. Corvallis, Or.	N.....
☐ N292ME	80	Learjet 35A	35A-292	Aircraft Specialists Inc. Sellersburg, In.	N634H
☐ N292PC	82	Falcon 50	99	Powers Construction Co/Rogers Aviation LLC. Florence, SC.	N816M
☐ N292QS	99	Falcon 2000	93	NetJets, Columbus, Oh.	F-WWVM
☐ N292SG	01	CitationJet CJ-1	525-0423	Gregory Poole Equipment Co. Raleigh-Durham, NC.	N62SH
☐ N293BC	83	Falcon 50	135	Boise Cascade Corp. Boise, Id.	N125FJ
☐ N293MC	74	Learjet 24D	24D-293	Jack Air LLC. Morrison, Co.	N917BF
☐ N293P	90	Astra-1125SP	049	293P LLC & 1125SP LLC. Belleair, Fl.	(N1TM)
☐ N293RT*	85	Citation S/II	S550-0023	ROCK-TENN Co. Atlanta, Ga.	N94RT
☐ N294AT	98	CitationJet	525-0294	Piney Branch Motors Inc/Allied Trailers, Savage, Md.	
☐ N294CW	95	CitationJet	525-0114	Flight Options LLC. Cleveland, Oh.	(N215LX)
☐ N294NW	69	Learjet 25	25-031	Miami Valley Aviation Inc. Middletown, Oh.	(N294M)
☐ N294RT	94	Citation V Ultra	560-0264	ROCK-TENN Co. Atlanta, Ga.	N264U
☐ N294S	97	Astra-1125SPX	094	Contract Transportation Systems LP. Cleveland, Oh.	
☐ N295BM	95	Citation V Ultra	560-0295	Milloaks LLC/Okland Construction Co. Salt Lake City, Ut.	N80EP
☐ N295DS	95	CitationJet	525-0091	DSW Development Corp. Cape Girardeau, Mo.	N5138F
☐ N295FA	93	Beechjet 400A	RK-68	Gilleland Aviation Inc. Georgetown, Tx.	(N419LX)
☐ N295JR	89	BAe 125/800A	NA0440	James River Financial Corp. Manakin-Sabot, Va.	N74NP
☐ N295NW	74	Learjet 24XR	24XR-295	Universal Pacific Investments Corp. Bend, Or.	N590CH
☐ N295PS	01	Learjet 31A	31A-230	Teknon LLC. Hillsboro, Or.	N5004Z
☐ N295TW	65	Falcon 20C	5	Sierra American Corp. Addison, Tx.	F-GJPR
☐ N296CW	81	Citation II	550-0306	Flight Options LLC. Cleveland, Oh. (was 551-0341).	N341CW
☐ N296DC	98	CitationJet	525-0296	Dement Construction Co. Jackson, Tn.	
☐ N296QS	02	Falcon 2000	196	NetJets, Columbus, Oh.	F-WWVI
☐ N296RG	81	HS 125/700A	NA0293	RI-Relational Investors Aviation LLC. Carlsbad, Ca.	N996RP
☐ N296TS	94	Learjet 60	60-029	Aero Toy Store LLC. Fort Lauderdale, Fl.	C-GFAX
☐ N297GB	93	Gulfstream 4SP	1208	Great Buy Inc. Van Nuys, Ca.	VP-BNY
☐ N297MC	99	Gulfstream 4SP	1393	Frontliner Inc. San Diego, Ca.	N393GA
☐ N297PF	75	Falcon 10	56	MCJM LLC/Pinnacle Data Services Inc. Houston, Tx.	N56WJ
☐ N297S	74	Citation	500-0197	Aircare International Inc. Austin, Tx.	XA-SRB
☐ N298AG	84	BAe 125/800A	8014	Hawker II LLC. Portland, Me.	N94WN
☐ N298BP	81	HS 125/700A	NA0298	Brooks Pride Corp. Salem, NH.	N298TS
☐ N298DC	01	Challenger 604	5503	Dow Corning Corp. Midland, Mi.	C-GLYA
☐ N298HM	78	Westwind-1124	240	JFB Aircraft Westwind Inc. Sarasota, Fl.	N72787
☐ N298NW	80	Learjet 35A	35A-298	America Air Network Alaska, Sarasota, Fl.	I-FLYC
☐ N298QS	99	Falcon 2000	98	NetJets, Columbus, Oh.	F-WWVR
☐ N298W	88	Falcon 900	45	Fisher Scientific International Inc. Portsmouth, NH.	N64BE
☐ N299CW	97	CitationJet	525-0199	Flight Options LLC. Cleveland, Oh.	(N205LX)

Reg	Yr	Type	c/n	Owner/Operator	Prev Regn
N299DB	75	Falcon 10	50	Northern Aircraft Leasing LLC. Bozeman, Mt.	N411SC
N299DH	03	Citation Encore	560-0645	Las Vegas Aviation III LLC. Bozeman, Mt.	N5269A
N299GS	74	HS 125/F600A	6046	MV Flight Service LLC. Weslaco, Tx.	(N299DG)
N299HS	03	Citation Bravo	550-1049	Cessna Aircraft Co. Wichita, Ks.	N249CB
N299JC	73	Falcon 20F	299	Jones Motorcars Inc. Fayetteville, Ar.	(N669AC)
N299MW	79	Learjet 25D	25D-299	J C Jet Service Inc. Carrollton, Oh.	(N5B)
N299QS	86	Citation S/II	S550-0099	Professional Leasing Services LLC. Fremont, Oh.	(N777FD)
N299SC	97	Learjet 60	60-112	Coyote Air LLC. Houston, Tx.	
N299SG	94	Learjet 60	60-025	Integrated Payment Systems Inc. Englewood, Co.	N299SC
N299TW	74	Learjet 24D	24D-299	Chaparrel Inc. Lubbock, Tx.	XB-GJS
N299WB	80	HS 125/700A	NA0265	Weisnell LLC/JDP EHP ET, Houston, Tx.	N91CM
N300A	81	Falcon 50	64	Domino's Pizza LLC. Ann Arbor, Mi.	N418S
N300AA	02	Learjet 45	45-211	Ewing Irrigation Products Inc. Albuquerque, NM.	N50490
N300AK	01	Citation Encore	560-0593	Arizona-Kentucky LLC. Ashland, Ky.	N121LS
N300AR	83	Diamond 1A	A041SA	Superstition Springs Enterprises Inc. Phoenix, Az.	N300AA
N300BA	68	Falcon 20-5	142	Bon Aero Inc. St Charles, Il.	XA-RNB
N300BC	03	Challenger 604	5563	Ball Corp. Broomfield, Co.	N563BA
N300BL	89	BAe 125/800A	8155	Pinnacle Entertainment Inc. Las Vegas, Nv.	N238AJ
N300BV	00	CitationJet CJ-1	525-0418	Hammill CJ-1 LLC. Toledo, Oh.	N51444
N300CQ	01	Hawker 800XP	8555	CEQUEL III Aviation LLC. St Louis, Mo.	N820TA
N300CR	91	Challenger 601-3A	5092	Crane Aerospace, White Plains, NY.	HB-IKV
N300CS	97	Citation Bravo	550-0818	CitationShares Sales Inc. White Plains, NY.	N818AJ
N300CV	74	Falcon 20F	322	Falcon Air LLC. Tampa, Fl.	N464M
N300DA	02	Citation Excel	560-5270	Crete Carrier Corp. Lincoln, Ne.	N356WC
N300DL	96	CitationJet	525-0148	Blue Heron Aviation Sales LLC. Melbourne, Fl.	XB-ATH
N300GB	99	Beechjet 400A	RK-262	FAC Logistics LLC. Rocky Mount, NC.	
N300GC	81	Citation II	550-0311	Guinn Construction Co. Bakersfield, Ca.	N211SP
N300GF	02	Citation Bravo	550-1046	Gordon Food Service Inc. Grand Rapids, Mi.	N.....
N300GP	98	Citation Bravo	550-0856	Wilbur & Orville Inc. Grand Rapids, Mi.	N300GF
N300JC	02	Learjet 45	45-209	CeCo Enterprises LLC. Las Vegas, Nv.	(N435FA)
N300JD	02	Citation X	750-0202	Deere & Co. Moline, Il.	N.....
N300JE	99	Learjet 45	45-094	Eckerd Fleet Inc. Clearwater, Fl.	
N300JZ	81	Gulfstream 3	875	UJZ LLC/Zimmerman & Partners Advertising, Boca Raton, Fl.	(N845FW)
N300K	99	Gulfstream V	587	Ford Motor Co. Detroit, Mi.	N587GA
N300L	96	Gulfstream V	507	Leonore Annenberg, Philadelphia, Pa.	N507GV
N300PY	97	Citation Bravo	550-0806	Alfa Air LLC. Simsbury, Ct.	N52141
N300QS	95	Citation V Ultra	560-0322	NetJets, Columbus, Oh.	N850BA
N300RB	84	BAe 125/800B	8013	Ligon Air LLC. Birmingham, Al.	(N500RH)
N300RD	67	Gulfstream 2	3	Rubloff Aviation LLC. Rockford, Il.	(N417RD)
N300SC	76	Learjet 25D	25D-208	N300SC Inc. Fort Lauderdale, Fl.	N500MP
N300SF	76	Falcon 20F	258	Safe Flight Instrument Corp. White Plains, NY.	N20AE
N300SJ	00	Citation Excel	560-5107	SJ Travel LLC. Bristol, Tn.	I-NYNY
N300SL	03	390 Premier 1	RB-110	Roll International Corp. Van Nuys, Ca.	N701KB
N300TC	78	Westwind-1124	241	American Aviation Inc. Brooksville, Fl.	N789TE
N300TE	79	Learjet 35A	35A-237	Great Dane Airlines Inc. Albuquerque, NM.	N300TW
N300TK	82	HS 125/700A	NA0337	Wilson Holdings Inc. Montgomery, Al.	N300TW
N300TS	80	Diamond 1	A003SA	Infinity Aviation LLC. Norman, Ok.	N300DM
N300TW	83	Challenger 600S	1080	Wilson Holdings Inc. Montgomery, Al.	N3JL
N300UJ	80	Gulfstream 3	316	Universal Jet Aviation Inc. Boca Raton, Fl.	(N69EH)
N300WY	84	Gulfstream 3	427	C & S Aviation LLC. Dallas, Tx.	N87AC
N300XL	80	Westwind-1124	276	TSTI LC. Houston, Tx.	N800XL
N301K	99	Gulfstream V	591	Ford Motor Co. Detroit, MI.	N591GA
N301KF	80	Westwind-Two	301	KGF Aviation LLC. Seattle, Wa.	N230JS
N301PC	82	Westwind-Two	377	Dude Inc. Fort Smith, Ar.	4X-CUJ
N301PE	92	BAe 1000A	9031	Peabody Holding Co. St Louis, Mo.	N301PH
N301QS	04	Citation Sovereign	680-0010	NetJets, Columbus, Oh.	N5135A
N301R	65	Falcon 20C	3	Kalitta Charters LLC. Detroit-Willow Run, Mi.	N92MH
N301RJ	95	Learjet 60	60-054	F1 Air LLC. Wilmington, De.	VP-BMM
N301TT	68	Falcon 20C	160	AVMATS/Centurion Investments Inc. St Louis, Mo.	N100UF
N302CS	97	Citation Bravo	550-0820	CitationShares Sales Inc. White Plains, NY.	N820CB
N302EJ	95	Citation V Ultra	560-0302	Interstate Equipment Leasing Inc. Phoenix, Az.	(N602SA)
N302GC	02	EMB-135LR Legacy	145600	Embraer, Nashville, Tn.	PT-...
N302PC	82	Challenger 600S	1072	Lower Cross Corp. Stamford, Ct.	(N190SC)
N302PE*	04	Hawker 800XP	8693	Peabody Energy Corp. St Louis, Mo.	N693XP
N302QS	97	Citation V Ultra	560-0402	NetJets, Columbus, Oh.	N5200U
N302ST	80	Gulfstream 3	302	S T Aviation LLC. Louis Center, Oh.	N109ST

Reg	Yr	Type	c/n	Owner/Operator	Prev Regn
N302TB	04	Hawker 400XP	RK-384	Moser Engine Service Inc. Gillette, Wy.	N84XP
N303A*	79	Citation 1/SP	501-0092	Aardvark Aircraft Sales Corp. Wilmington, De.	N501X
N303BC	96	Hawker 800XP	8324	NBC Air LLC. Las Vegas, Nv.	N324XP
N303CB	92	Citation V	560-0190	Taft Sales & Leasing LLC. Dallas, Tx.	(N214LS)
N303CJ	04	CitationJet CJ-3	525B-0031	Cessna Aircraft Co. Wichita, Ks.	N.....
N303CP	00	Citation Encore	560-0539	Folsom Lake Aviation LLC. Folsom, Ca.	N539CE
N303CS	97	Citation Bravo	550-0814	CitationShares Sales Inc. White Plains, NY.	PT-WNH
N303EJ	75	Learjet 24D	24D-303	White Industries Inc. Bates City, Mo.	PT-LOJ
N303FZ	89	Falcon 100	218	Bogey Bird Inc. Indianapolis, In.	N130DS
N303GC	03	EMB-135LR Legacy	145608	Embraer, Nashville, Tn.	PT-...
N303PC	86	Citation III	650-0110	J C Pace Holding Co & Kimball Inc. Fort Worth, Tx.	N76D
N303QS	95	Citation V Ultra	560-0343	NetJets, Columbus, Oh.	N60AE
N303RH	80	Citation 1/SP	501-0303	River Holdings Aviation LLC. Daytona Beach. (was 500-0397)	N370TP
N304CS	98	Citation Bravo	550-0847	CitationShares Sales Inc. White Plains, NY.	N133AV
N304JR*	93	Beechjet 400A	RK-63	Rookis Inc. Santa Rosa Beach, Fl.	N163RK
N304QS	97	Citation V Ultra	560-0408	NetJets, Columbus, Oh.	N560NS
N304SE	00	Beechjet 400A	RK-304	Sklar Transport LLC. Shreveport, La.	N5004Y
N304TS	80	Gulfstream 3	304	Nomad Transportation LLC. Van Nuys, Ca.	VR-BSL
N304TT	81	Challenger 600S	1033	Carballo Aviation LLC. Tulsa. Ok.	N357RT
N305AR	80	Learjet 25D	25D-314	Moyal Aircraft Sales LLC. NYC.	N95BP
N305BB	78	Westwind-1124	228	Professional Air Leasing LLC. Miami, Fl.	4X-CLZ
N305CC	99	Global Express	9027	Carnival Corp. Fort Lauderdale, Fl.	C-GEZX
N305CJ	95	CitationJet	525-0105	Aqua Sun Investments LLC. Ormond Beach, Fl.	(D-IAFD)
N305CS	97	Citation Bravo	550-0825	CitationShares Sales Inc. White Plains, NY.	(N45HV)
N305GA	04	Gulfstream G200	105	Gulfstream Aerospace LP. Dallas-Love, Tx.	4X-C..
N305JA	03	Hawker 800XP	8625	OAC Air LLC. Little Rock, Ar.	N625XP
N305LM	00	Gulfstream 4SP	1443	HGA LLC. Dallas, Tx.	N443GA
N305PA	66	DC 9-15	45740	PharmAir Corp. Miami, Fl.	N911KM
N305S	76	Citation	500-0301	Odegaard Aviation Inc. Kindred, ND.	OE-FNG
N305SC*	03	Hawker 800XP	8662	Studio City Aviation 04 LLC. Studio City, Ca.	N662XP
N305TC	89	Gulfstream 4	1116	National City Leasing Corp. Louisville, Ky.	N971L
N306CJ	01	CitationJet CJ-2	525A-0016	Aqua Sun Investments LLC. Middleburg Heights, Oh.	(N547AC)
N306CS	99	Citation Bravo	550-0881	CitationShares Sales Inc. White Plains, NY.	(N312RD)
N306JA	76	Learjet 24D	24D-306	Trovarsi LLC. Mesquite, Tx.	(N243RK)
N306PA	84	Citation III	650-0053	Jetcorp LLC/Edco Disposal Corp. Lemon Grove, Pa.	N367G
N306QS	94	Citation V Ultra	560-0266	NetJets, Columbus, Oh.	N288JR
N306R*	96	Learjet 60	60-084	JRM Air LLC. Cleveland, NC.	N100R
N306SA	69	Sabre-60	306-40	Addison Aircraft Sales Inc. Holly Lake Ranch, Tx.	XA-SBX
N306TR	95	Citation V Ultra	560-0306	Dover Motorsports Inc. Dover, De.	N49MJ
N306TT	90	Gulfstream 4	1148	T Bird Aviation Inc. Du Page, Il.	HB-IEJ
N307CS	01	Citation Bravo	550-0974	CitationShares Sales Inc. White Plains, NY.	N.....
N307HF	71	Learjet 25B	25B-075	Chipola Aviation Inc. Marianna, Fl.	N82025
N307QS	95	Citation V Ultra	560-0307	NetJets, Columbus, Oh.	N5233J
N308A	92	Citation II	550-0703	ARAMCO Associated Co. Dhahran, Saudi Arabia.	
N308AB	02	Gulfstream 4SP	1496	Prime Jet LLC. Van Nuys, Ca.	N496GA
N308BW	81	Learjet 35A	35A-438	William Walker Properties Inc. Tulsa, Ok.	N308R
N308CS	01	Citation Bravo	550-0976	CitationShares Sales Inc. White Plains, NY.	N5168Y
N308DD	79	HS 125/700A	NA0250	Hollywood Aviation Inc. Van Nuys, Ca.	(N900JG)
N308DM	02	Falcon 50EX	328	Archer Daniels Midland Co. Decatur, Il.	N328EX
N308DT	04	Citation Bravo	550-1094	Tippman Aviation LLC. Fort Wayne, In.	N.....
N308EE	69	Gulfstream 2	68	Executive Charter LLC. Chicago, Il.	N308EL
N308GT	00	CitationJet CJ-2	525A-0004	Mark Solomon, Fort Lauderdale, Fl.	(N699JM)
N308HG	80	Gulfstream 3	308	The Glimcher Co. Columbus, Oh.	N308GA
N308TW	79	Citation II	550-0044	Dove Air Inc Hendersonville, NC. (was 551-0092)	(N452AJ)
N308U	04	Falcon 2000EX EASY	37	United Technologies Corp. Windsor Locks, Ct.	F-WWGS
N309AK	02	Beechjet 400A	RK-348	400A Air Charters LLC/Golden Eagle Air Inc. Farmingdale, NY.	N448CW
N309CS	01	Citation Bravo	550-0977	CitationShares Sales Inc. White Plains, NY.	N5172M
N309QS	99	Citation V Ultra	560-0509	NetJets, Columbus, Oh.	
N310AS	99	Hawker 800XP	8443	Ali-Air Inc. Gainesville, Fl.	
N310EL	87	Gulfstream 4	1021	Eli Lilly & Co. Indianapolis, In.	EC-HGH
N310LJ	99	Learjet 45	45-031	Yamhill Finance Ltd. Ecuador.	9V-ATH
N310ME	80	Learjet 35A	35A-310	Aircraft Specialists Inc. Sellersburg, In.	N8280
N310PE	81	Challenger 600S	1012	Priester Aviation LLC. Wheeling, Il.	N167SC
N310ZM	02	Learjet 45	45-218	AllTech Inc. Nicholasville, Ky.	N50163
N311AG	71	B 727-17	20512	Vallejo Co. San Francisco, Ca.	N767RV
N311BD	79	Gulfstream 2TT	236	Newcastle Corp. Wichita Falls, Tx.	N311DH

| Reg | Yr | Type | c/n | Owner/Operator | Prev Regn |

Reg	Yr	Type	c/n	Owner/Operator	Prev Regn
N311BX	97	Challenger 604	5342	Bombardier Aerospace Corp. Windsor Locks, Ct.	N311FX
N311CS	01	Citation Bravo	550-0979	KTSC LLC. Madisonville, Tx.	N52475
N311CW	83	Citation III	650-0011	Flight Options LLC. Cleveland, Oh.	N17TN
N311DG	92	Citation V	560-0167	Zoe Aviation & Charter Service Inc. Euless, Tx.	N211DG
N311EL	89	Gulfstream 4	1095	Eli Lilly & Co. Indianapolis, In.	N469GA
N311GL	01	Beechjet 400A	RK-311	The Country Shop Inc. Hickory, NC.	N711GL
N311HS	00	Beechjet 400A	RK-296	Pizzagali Properties LLC/PPL Aviation, Burlington, Vt.	
N311JA	88	Falcon 900	63	CMS Energy Corp/Act Two Inc. Pontiac, Mi.	N75W
N311LJ	75	Learjet 24D	24D-311	Lake Scene Inc. Houston, Tx.	(N76PW)
N311ME	79	Citation 1/SP	501-0118	Ed Unicume, Scottsdale, Az.	N61572
N311QS	95	Citation V Ultra	560-0311	NetJets, Columbus, Oh.	(N5244F)
N311TP	81	Citation 1/SP	501-0196	Robert Rapaport, Palm Beach, Fl.	(N311TT)
N311VP	81	Citation 1/SP	501-0311	Aurora Aircraft Co. Asuncion, Paraguay. (was 500-0405).	(N501PY)
N312AL	83	Learjet 55	55-089	LevAir Ltd. Palm Beach International, Fl.	N628PT
N312AM	96	Challenger 604	5312	Marin Conveyancing Corp. Lake Success, NY.	(N905SB)
N312CJ	01	CitationJet CJ-2	525A-0031	Sterna Aviation Ltd. Ronaldsway, IOM.	N5204D
N312EL	89	Gulfstream 4	1105	Eli Lilly & Co. Indianapolis, In.	N408GA
N312K	75	Falcon 20F-5	324	Falcon Acquisitions LLC. Carson City, Nv.	N324TC
N312NC	81	Citation II	550-0290	Progress Aviation Corp. Dallas, Tx.	N217LG
N312P	00	Falcon 900EX	67	Marmon Group Inc. Chicago-Midway, Il.	N967EX
N312QS	95	Citation V Ultra	560-0312	NetJets, Columbus, Oh.	(N52457)
N313BW	00	Learjet 45	45-108	AND Inc. Stamford, Ct.	N50154
N313CC	03	Falcon 2000EX	12	Comcast Cable Communication Holdings, N Philadelphia, Pa.	F-WWGK
N313CQ	85	BAe 125/800A	8043	Purcell Tire Co. Potosi, Mo.	N313CC
N313CR	04	CitationJet CJ-2	525A-0234	Cessna Aircraft Co. Wichita, Ks.	N.....
N313CS	01	Citation Bravo	550-0981	Advocare International LLC. Carrollton, Tx.	N5093L
N313CV	95	Citation V Ultra	560-0313	Jet Serv Corp. Winamac, In.	N5246Z
N313GH	00	Falcon 2000	125	Allstate Insurance Co. Palwaukee, Il.	F-WWVV
N313HC	01	Citation Encore	560-0603	Hibernia Aviation Corp. Mobile, Al.	N603CV
N313JS	66	JetStar-731	5086	Seagull Aircraft Corp. Fort Lauderdale, Fl.	(N65JW)
N313K	79	Falcon 20F	404	Falcon Acquisitions LLC. Carson City, Nv.	N28C
N313P	02	BBJ-7BC	33010	Keller & Tate Management LLC. Reno, Nv.	(N104QS)
N313QS	95	Citation V Ultra	560-0325	NetJets, Columbus, Oh.	N96AT
N313RG	96	Gulfstream V	504	Renco Group Inc. NYC.	N504GV
N313TW	76	Westwind-1124	190	21st Century Air Inc/Mikal Watts, Corpus Christi, Tx.	N190WW
N314CS	01	Citation Bravo	550-1004	CitationShares Sales Inc. White Plains, NY.	N.....
N314ER	68	HS 125/3A-RA	NA710	Flite Services Inc. Lakeland, Fl.	(N767LC)
N314GA	04	Gulfstream G450	4014	Gulfstream Aerospace Corp. Savannah, Ga.	
N314MK	91	Learjet 31A	31A-040	Bodor Corp. Warsaw, In.	N340LJ
N314QS	97	Citation V Ultra	560-0441	NetJets, Columbus, Oh.	
N314RW	90	Citation V	560-0051	Red Wing Shoe Co. Red Wing, Mn.	N599SG
N314SG	97	Learjet 31A	31A-133	Bend Properties Inc. Irvine, Ca.	N331ZX
N314SL	00	Citation VII	650-7115	Jefferson Smurfit Corp. St Louis, Mo.	N5267K
N314TC*	98	Hawker 800XP	8400	TNC Corp. Chicago, Il.	N404JC
N314TW	74	Falcon 20E	314	Sierra American Corp. Addison, Tx.	F-GDLU
N314XS	91	Learjet 31A	31A-048	Global Select Capital Inc. Van Nuys, Ca.	N43SE
N315AJ	66	Learjet 24	24-108	Charter Airlines Inc. Las Vegas, Nv.	N900JA
N315BX	98	Challenger 604	5377	Bombardier Aerospace Corp. Windsor Locks, Ct.	N315FX
N315CS	96	Citation V Ultra	560-0371	Pheasant Kay-Bee Toy Inc. Nashua, NH.	N371CV
N315EJ	93	Citation V	560-0215	Intrepid Aviation LLC. Denver, Co.	N23NS
N315ES	83	Citation II	550-0459	7-11 Air Corp. Teterboro, NJ.	N15TV
N315MK	82	Challenger 600S	1047	Athenian Air Link, Athens, Greece.	(N500EX)
N315MR	97	CitationJet	525-0198	M G A Inc. Dothan, Al.	N51522
N315QS	95	Citation V Ultra	560-0315	NetJets, Columbus, Oh.	(N5250K)
N315R	90	Beechjet 400A	RK-9	Citation LLC. Evansville, In.	(N150TF)
N315TS	00	BBJ-7CU	30772	Tutor-Saliba Corp. Van Nuys, Ca.	N1784B
N316CS	02	Citation Bravo	550-1010	CitationShares Sales Inc. White Plains, NY.	N5228J
N316CW	83	Citation III	650-0016	Flight Options LLC. Cleveland, Oh.	N32MG
N316EC	87	BAe 125/800A	NA0403	Park-Ohio Industries Inc. Cleveland, Oh.	N89NC
N316EQ	75	Sabre-75A	380-38	Jose Manuel Figueroa, McAllen, Tx.	N316EC
N316GS	00	Global Express	9075	Citiflight Inc. White Plains, NY.	C-GHEI
N316LP	81	Diamond 1A	A012SA	L P M Air Inc. Pensacola, Fl.	N112GA
N316MH	86	Citation S/II	S550-0108	Shilo Management Corp. Portland, Or.	N108QS
N316QS	99	Citation V Ultra	560-0516	NetJets, Columbus, Oh.	
N316SR	00	Learjet 45	45-119	Stull Ranches LLC. Anaheim, Ca.	N5016V
N317BX*	99	Challenger 604	5407	BBJS/FlexJets, Addison, Tx.	N317FX

Reg	Yr	Type	c/n	Owner/Operator	Prev Regn
☐ N317CC	01	Hawker 800XP	8532	Cozzens & Cudahy Air Inc. Milwaukee, Wi.	
☐ N317CS	02	Citation Bravo	550-1019	CitationShares Sales Inc. White Plains, NY.	N5231S
☐ N317HC	80	Citation II	550-0185	Tassa HN Inc. Wilmington, De.	N511DL
☐ N317JQ	82	Citation 1/SP	501-0317	OTW Farms LLC. Hollister, Ca.	5N-AVL
☐ N317JS	83	Westwind-Two	385	Westpark Air Inc. Sugar Land, Tx.	N962MV
☐ N317M	02	Falcon 2000	188	MBNA Corp. Greater Wilmington, De.	N317MZ
☐ N317MJ	89	Gulfstream 4	1122	Lyon Aviation Inc/Majjec Jhett LLC. Pittsfield, Ma.	N317M
☐ N317ML	00	Gulfstream 4SP	1446	MBNA Corp. Greater Wilmington, De.	N317M
☐ N317MN	01	Falcon 2000	146	MBNA Corp. Greater Wilmington, De.	N866AV
☐ N317MQ	01	Falcon 2000	152	MBNA Corp. Greater Wilmington, De.	N70XC
☐ N317MR	01	Falcon 2000	144	MBNA Corp. Greater Wilmington, De.	N317ML
☐ N317PC	02	Hawker 400XP	RK-357	Airpak Financial Corp. Guatemala City, Guatemala.	N5057Z
☐ N317QS	95	Citation V Ultra	560-0317	NetJets, Columbus, Oh.	(N52526)
☐ N317TC	72	HS 125/600A	6007	Landa Property Management Inc. Austin, Tx.	N3007
☐ N317TT	80	Learjet 35A	35A-317	Inter Island Yachts Inc. Zephyr Cove, Nv.	N98TE
☐ N317VS	80	Learjet 25D	25D-317	Capital Auto Sales Inc. Denver, Co.	N317TS
☐ N318CS	02	Citation Bravo	550-1029	CitationShares Sales Inc. White Plains, NY.	N5270J
☐ N318CT	90	Citation V	560-0081	Century Tel Service Group LLC. Monroe, La.	N560HP
☐ N318FX	99	Challenger 604	5415	BBJS/FlexJets, Addison, Tx.	C-GLWT
☐ N318GA	92	Falcon 50	233	Garden Air LLC. Morristown, NJ.	N48HB
☐ N318MM	01	Citation Excel	560-5220	Schwans Shared Services LLC. Marshall, Mn.	N5112K
☐ N318NW	80	Learjet 35A	35A-318	Hollywood Entertainment Corp. Wilsonville, Or.	N103CF
☐ N318QS	97	Citation V Ultra	560-0418	NetJets, Columbus, Oh.	N5112K
☐ N318SP	75	Gulfstream II SP	168	Euro Airways Inc. San Francisco. (stored GVA since 9/02).	N317AF
☐ N319CS	02	Citation Bravo	550-1036	CitationShares Sales Inc. White Plains, NY.	N.....
☐ N319FX	99	Challenger 604	5418	Bombardier Aerospace Corp. Windsor Locks, Ct.	C-GLXS
☐ N319QS	99	Citation V Ultra	560-0519	NetJets, Columbus, Oh.	
☐ N319SC	97	Learjet 31A	31A-131	Apple Hospitality Air LLC. Richmond, Va.	N31LR
☐ N320AF	76	HFB 320	1061	Kalitta Flying Service Inc. Morristown, Tn.	(D-CEDL)
☐ N320FX	99	Challenger 604	5425	Boca Air LLC. Richardson, Tx.	C-GLXH
☐ N320GX	02	Global Express	9116	Texas Instruments Inc. McKinney, Tx.	N700EW
☐ N320MD	82	Westwind-1124	366	M-D Building Products Inc. Oklahoma City, Ok.	N65TD
☐ N320QS	95	Citation V Ultra	560-0321	NetJets, Columbus, Oh.	N5262W
☐ N320RG	74	Citation	500-0236	Aerocor LLC. Chicago-Gary, Il.	N742K
☐ N321AN	79	Learjet 35A	35A-272	Anderson News Corp .Knoxville, Tn.	N500EF
☐ N321AR	87	Citation III	650-0151	Exodus Aviation LLC. Pineview, NY.	N660AF
☐ N321BN	96	Gulfstream 4SP	1300	BNB LLC. Franklin Park, Il.	(N500BL)
☐ N321FX	99	Challenger 604	5427	BBJS/FlexJets, Addison, Tx.	C-GLWV
☐ N321GG	98	Citation V Ultra	560-0474	Ultra Investments Inc. Coral Springs, Fl.	N474VP
☐ N321GL	93	Learjet 31A	31A-085	Starwood Industries Inc. Richmond, Va.	N531AT
☐ N321MS	00	Hawker 800XP	8515	Morteza Ejabat Trust, Portland, Or.	N321EJ
☐ N321SF	00	Galaxy-1126	021	Smithfield Foods Inc. Newport News, Va.	N41GX
☐ N321TS	80	Citation 1/SP	501-0155	VTS Clima Gulf FZCO, Dubai, UAE.	N299D
☐ N322AU	76	Learjet 24D	24D-326	MedJets LLC. Cedar Knolls, NJ.	N326KE
☐ N322BC	82	HS 125/700A	NA0322	TCA Air LLC/Bratton Capital Inc. Wilmington, De.	C-FCHT
☐ N322BJ	03	390 Premier 1	RB-93	RB93 LLC/Cole Inc. Three Lakes, Wi.	
☐ N322CP	93	Falcon 900B	134	Gallagher Enterprises LLC. Pueblo, Co.	N88YF
☐ N322CS	03	Citation Bravo	550-1052	CitationShares Sales Inc. White Plains, NY.	N.....
☐ N322FX	99	Challenger 604	5434	BBJS/FlexJets, Addison, Tx.	C-GLXY
☐ N322GC	81	Learjet 55	55-008	Caulkins Investment Co. Denver, Co.	N551SC
☐ N322GT	02	Citation Bravo	550-1030	Throgmartin Leasing LLC. Murrells Inlet, SC.	N52397
☐ N322K	94	Fokker 70	11521	Ford Motor Co. Detroit, MI.	PH-MKS
☐ N322MA	82	Citation II/SP	551-0378	Mary-Ali 322 LLC. Wilmington, De.	(F-OGVA)
☐ N322QS	97	Citation V Ultra	560-0421	NetJets, Columbus, Oh.	
☐ N322RR	87	Falcon 200	514	Rogers Enterprises of Idaho LLC. Tyler, Tx.	N87AG
☐ N322RS	76	Learjet 24D	24D-322	R & S Aircraft LLC. Melbourne, Fl.	(N322TJ)
☐ N322TS	88	Learjet 31	31-002	Daniela 2001 Inc. Wilmington, De.	N350DS
☐ N323FX	00	Challenger 604	5447	BBJS/FlexJets, Addison, Tx.	C-GLYC
☐ N323JH	84	Gulfstream 3	434	World Healing Center Church Inc. Irving, Tx.	(N73ET)
☐ N323L	91	BAe 125/800B	8212	Jetcraft Corp. Raleigh-Durham, NC.	RP-C8008
☐ N323LM	01	CitationJet CJ-2	525A-0020	Thunder Aviation Acquisitions Inc. Spirit of St Louis, Mo.	N904AM
☐ N323P	97	Astra-1125SPX	096	Allease Inc. Tuscaloosa, Al.	N96AL
☐ N323QS	95	Citation V Ultra	560-0323	NetJets, Columbus, Oh.	N5097H
☐ N323SK	02	CitationJet CJ-2	525A-0134	Haas Racing Team LLC. Camarillo, Ca.	N.....
☐ N324AM	01	390 Premier 1	RB-42	Raytheon Aircraft Co. Wichita, Ks.	N390CK
☐ N324B	90	Challenger 601-3A	5069	Ripplewood Aviation LLC. NYC.	N655CN

Reg	Yr	Type	c/n	Owner/Operator	Prev Regn

Reg	Yr	Type	c/n	Owner/Operator	Prev Regn
☐ N324CS	03	Citation Bravo	550-1059	CitationShares Sales Inc. White Plains, NY.	N.....
☐ N324FX	00	Challenger 604	5454	BBJS/FlexJets, Addison, Tx.	C-GLXQ
☐ N324JC	76	Citation	500-0324	Foxdale Aviation Inc. Ronaldsway, IOM.	(N721HW)
☐ N324K	95	Fokker 70	11545	Ford Motor Co. Detroit, Mi.	PH-EZH
☐ N324L	81	Citation 1/SP	501-0197	Lee Lewis Construction Co. Lubbock, Tx.	N100SN
☐ N324QS	97	Citation V Ultra	560-0423	NetJets, Columbus, Oh.	N5073G
☐ N324SA	85	BAe 125/800A	8047	J L Leasing LLC. Farmingdale, NY.	N84FA
☐ N324SM	99	Global Express	9023	Raptor Air LP.	C-GEZD
☐ N324TW	76	Learjet 24D	24D-324	Chaparrel Inc. Lubbock, Tx.	XA-SCY
☐ N325CS	03	Citation Bravo	550-1061	CitationShares Sales Inc. White Plains, NY.	N5267K
☐ N325FX	00	Challenger 604	5457	BBJS/FlexJets, Addison, Tx.	C-GLXW
☐ N325JF	01	EMB-135ER	145499	Intel Corp/Executive Jet Management Inc. Cincinnati, Oh.	PT-...
☐ N325LW	81	Westwind-Two	334	RER Aviation LLC. Sugar Land, Tx.	N40MP
☐ N325NW	80	Learjet 35A	35A-325	AeroMedic LLC. Greenwich, Ct.	I-FFLY
☐ N325QS	97	Citation V Ultra	560-0425	NetJets, Columbus, Oh.	
☐ N326B	98	CitationJet	525-0302	The Buckle Inc. Kearney, Ne.	N302CJ
☐ N326CB	69	JetStar-8	5143	Centurion Investments Inc. St Louis, Mo. (status ?).	N620JB
☐ N326DD	78	Learjet 35A	35A-173	326DD LLC. West Columbia, SC.	YU-BPY
☐ N326EW	98	Falcon 2000	58	Leco Corp. South Bend, In.	N2133
☐ N326FX	00	Challenger 604	5464	BBJS/FlexJets, Addison, Tx.	C-GLWR
☐ N326HG	83	Learjet 35A	35A-501	Chantilly Air Inc. Silver Spring, Md.	N35HW
☐ N326JD	01	Gulfstream 4SP	1460	57 Aviation Services LLC. White Plains, NY.	(N326LM)
☐ N326MA	01	Citation Excel	560-5159	Michael Anderson, Victoria, Tx.	N336MA
☐ N326QS	99	Citation V Ultra	560-0526	NetJets, Columbus, Oh.	
☐ N326RG*	04	Challenger 300	20026	Bombardier Aerospace Corp. Windsor Locks, Ct.	C-FDHV
☐ N326VW	66	Falcon 20C-5	27	Grand Aire Express Inc. Toledo, Oh.	N174GA
☐ N327FX	00	Challenger 604	5466	BBJS/FlexJets, Addison, Tx.	C-GLWV
☐ N327JJ	81	Gulfstream 3	329	CFW LLC. White Plains, NY.	(N329N)
☐ N327LJ	00	Hawker 800XP	8490	Cavallino Air LLC. Los Gatos, Ca.	N50490
☐ N327QS	95	Citation V Ultra	560-0327	NetJets, Columbus, Oh.	(N51038)
☐ N327SA	85	Westwind-Two	428	Sonic Financial Corp. Charlotte, NC.	(N92BE)
☐ N327TL	98	Gulfstream 4SP	1339	Thomas H Lee Co. Boston, Ma.	N339GA
☐ N328AC	00	Dornier Do328JET	3132	ACA Private Shuttle, Dulles, Va.	D-C...
☐ N328BX	96	Challenger 604	5328	GE Capital Mietfinanz GmbH. Koeln, Germany.	(A6-EJB)
☐ N328CJ	99	CitationJet	525-0328	BK Aviation LLC. Shellyville, Ky.	
☐ N328CS	03	Citation Bravo	550-1074	Frontera Produce Ltd. McAllen, Tx.	N.....
☐ N328FX	00	Challenger 604	5474	BBJS/FlexJets, Addison, Tx.	C-GLXM
☐ N328GT	01	Dornier Do328JET	3183	Ultimate Jetcharters, Canton, Oh.	D-C...
☐ N328JK	69	Learjet 24B	24B-212	JFleet Inc. Fort Worth, Tx.	N328TL
☐ N328NA	80	Citation 1/SP	501-0168	Citation Partners LLC. Signal Mountain, Tn.	N601WT
☐ N328PC	81	Westwind-Two	328	Pella Corp. Pella, Ia.	C-GPFC
☐ N328PM	01	Dornier Do328JET	3184	Altria Corporate Services Inc. White Plains, NY.	D-B...
☐ N328PT	01	Dornier Do328JET	3199	Pacelli Beteiligungs GmbH. Munich.	D-....
☐ N328QS	97	Citation V Ultra	560-0428	NetJets, Columbus, Oh.	
☐ N328RC*	04	Challenger 300	20028	Rouse Transportation LLC. Baltimore, Md.	C-FDIA
☐ N328SA	84	Westwind-Two	425	Sonic Financial Corp. Charlotte, NC.	(N365QX)
☐ N329CS	03	Citation Bravo	550-1077	CitationShares Sales Inc. White Plains, NY.	N.....
☐ N329FX	02	Challenger 604	5541	BBJS/FlexJets, Addison, Tx.	C-GLXO
☐ N329JC	85	Citation S/II	S550-0059	Laredo National Bank, Laredo, Tx.	N829JC
☐ N329JS	77	JetStar 2	5206	White Industries Inc. Bates City, Mo.	XA-JML
☐ N329K	02	Falcon 2000	182	Ford Motor Co. Detroit, Mi.	N2000A
☐ N330DE	86	BAe 125/800A	8060	Duke Energy Corp. Houston, Tx.	N330X
☐ N330FX	01	Challenger 604	5487	BBJS/FlexJets, Addison, Tx.	C-GLWT
☐ N330G	66	HS 125/731	25087	Calibur Aviation LLC. Colleyville, Tx.	N66AM
☐ N330K	02	Falcon 2000	189	Ford Motor Co. Detroit, Mi.	N2000A
☐ N330L	81	Learjet 25D	25D-330	Butler National Inc. Newton, Ks.	N330LJ
☐ N330MC	97	Falcon 900EX	21	MCI Communications Corp. Dulles, Va.	(N331MC)
☐ N330QS	95	Citation V Ultra	560-0329	NetJets, Columbus, Oh.	N5105F
☐ N330TP	94	Challenger 601-3R	5142	Washington Times Aviation Inc. Washington-Dulles, Va.	VR-CJJ
☐ N330TS	01	Beechjet 400A	RK-330	VIG Leasing Corp. Wilmington, De.	N33NL
☐ N330TW	76	Learjet 24E	24E-330	Sierra American Corp. Addison, Tx.	N511AT
☐ N330VP	95	Citation V Ultra	560-0330	J & N Leasing LLC. Spokane, Wa.	N851WC
☐ N330WR	81	Gulfstream 3	337	Orkin Inc. Atlanta-DeKalb, Ga.	N456SW
☐ N331BN	04	Gulfstream G200	095	Burlington Northern/Santa Fe Railway, Fort Worth, Tx.	N595GA
☐ N331CC	89	Citation V	560-0044	Del Papa Distribution Co LP. Houston, Tx.	N111VP
☐ N331DC	91	Challenger 601-3A	5093	Interstate Distributor Co. Tacoma, Wa.	N375H

Reg	Yr	Type	c/n	Owner/Operator	Prev Regn

Reg	Yr	Type	c/n	Owner/Operator	Prev Regn
N331EX	03	Falcon 50EX	331	SE Leasing LLC/Rooms To Go Inc. Seffner, Fl.	F-WWHM
N331FX	01	Challenger 604	5491	BBJS/FlexJets, Addison, Tx.	C-G...
N331MC	97	Falcon 900EX	22	WISC Ltd. Greater Wilmington, De.	(N21HJ)
N331MS	99	CitationJet	525-0330	JMS Partners LLC. Jackson, Mi.	N330CJ
N331N	90	Learjet 31	31-022	Harbor Jet LLC. Alpena, Mi.	
N331PR	97	Citation Bravo	550-0831	Poly-Resyn Inc. DuPage, Il.	N5145P
N331QS	95	Citation V Ultra	560-0331	NetJets, Columbus, Oh.	N51072
N331SK	92	Astra-1125SP	063	Winnebago Industries Inc. Forest City, Ia.	(N60RV)
N331TH	96	Challenger 604	5325	KAD Aviation LLC. San Jose, Ca.	N60CT
N331TP	97	Challenger 604	5350	Washington Times Aviation Inc. Washington-Dulles, Va.	C-GLXU
N332CS	04	Citation Bravo	550-1081	CitationShares Sales Inc. White Plains, NY.	N.....
N332FX	02	Challenger 604	5543	BBJS/FlexJets, Addison, Tx.	(N605BA)
N332K	01	Learjet 45	45-169	Kiewit Engineering Co. Omaha, Ne.	N77HN
N332LC	96	Citation V Ultra	560-0332	Cessna Finance Corp. Wichita, Ks.	(N5108G)
N332QS	99	Citation V Ultra	560-0523	NetJets, Columbus, Oh.	
N332SE	76	Citation	500-0332	World of God Fellowship Inc/Daystar TV Network, Bedford, Tx.	LV-LZR
N333BD	00	Citation Bravo	550-0958	Lake Aircraft Rental LLC. Longview, Tx.	N5168Y
N333DP	72	HS 125/731	NA775	Doane Products Co. Joplin, Mo.	N17HV
N333EB	99	Citation Bravo	550-0893	EBAA Iron Inc. Eastland, Tx.	N5073G
N333EC	91	Falcon 900B	106	Flying Falcon Inc. Miami, Fl.	N332EC
N333FJ	73	Falcon 10	1	World Jet Inc. Fort Lauderdale, Fl.	F-BJLH
N333GJ	85	Challenger 601	3042	Advance America Cash Advance Centers, Spartanburg, SC.	N900CC
N333GZ	65	HS 125/1A-522	25070	White Industries Inc. Bates City, Mo.	N470TS
N333J	04	CitationJet CJ-1	525-0531	Ruan Inc. Des Moines, Ia.	N5211A
N333JH	76	Citation Eagle	500-0292	Harvey Foods Inc. Nashville, Ga.	N501HK
N333KC	75	Learjet 35	35-037	Lockwood Systems Ltd. Carson City, Nv.	N45TK
N333KE	74	Falcon 10	14	Falconmitch Inc. Tyler, Tx.	N31TJ
N333KK	83	Challenger 600S	1082	Kohler Inc. Kohler, Wi.	N777KZ
N333MG	88	Challenger 601-3A	5035	Griffco Aviation Inc. Santa Monica, Ca.	N606CC
N333MS	80	HS 125/700A	7115	King Air International LLC.	N125YY
N333NM	65	Sabre-40	282-45	Commercial Aviation Enterprises Inc. Delray Beach, Fl.	N333GM
N333PC	95	Hawker 800XP	8277	Polco Inc. Washington, DC.	N97SH
N333PY	97	Gulfstream 4SP	1317	Perry Capital LLC. Teterboro, NJ.	N929WT
N333QS	95	Citation V Ultra	560-0333	NetJets, Columbus, Oh.	(N5109R)
N333RL	92	BAe 1000B	9027	Becker Aviation LLC. Troy, Mi.	N333RU
N333RY	69	Learjet 24B	24B-202	J 2 Partnership, San Antonio, Tx. (status ?)	N814JR
N333TW	68	Learjet 24	24-168	Sierra American Corp. Addison, Tx.	N155BT
N333VS	93	CitationJet	525-0034	Nowak Aviation Inc. Warwick, RI.	N9GU
N333WM	96	Citation V Ultra	560-0385	Morris Communications Corp. Augusta, Ga.	N5109R
N334AF	01	Learjet 45	45-143	Ashley Furniture Industries Inc. Arcadia, Wi.	N145GS
N334BD	02	CitationJet CJ-1	525-0486	Cherokee Aircraft Rental LLC. Longview, Tx.	N5211A
N334CS	04	Citation Bravo	550-1089	CitationShares Sales Inc. White Plains, NY.	N.....
N334ED	81	Citation II	550-0228	Wings LLC. Pelham, Al.	VH-EXM
N334FX	04	Challenger 604	5586	New York Life Insurance Co. NYC.	C-GLXQ
N334JC	90	Gulfstream 4	1134	Gulfstream International Corp. Savannah, Ga.	VP-BJD
N334KC	83	Diamond 1A	A034SA	G W S Enterprises LLC. Coleman, Ok.	N303P
N334MC	96	Gulfstream 4SP	1289	MCI Communications Corp. Dulles, Va.	N800WC
N334PS	74	HS 125/600A	6032	Canrose Air 1 LLC. Orem, Ut.	N801BC
N334QS	97	Citation V Ultra	560-0434	NetJets, Columbus, Oh.	
N334RC	73	Citation	500-0062	Eagle Air Services Inc. Wilmington, De.	N4KH
N335AS	78	Learjet 35A	35A-170	Jet 1 Inc. Naples, Fl.	N335NA
N335AT	74	Learjet 35	35-009	Trossi Holding SA/Elian Holdings Inc. Wilmington, De.	PT-LGR
N335CS	04	Citation Bravo	550-1091	CitationShares Sales Inc. White Plains, NY.	N.....
N335CT	99	CitationJet	525-0335	Mag Air LLC. Concord, NC.	N335CJ
N335H	79	Gulfstream 2TT	238	Halliburton Energy Services Inc. Dallas, Tx.	N831GA
N335J	01	CitationJet CJ-1	525-0425	Baron Real Estate Group LLC. Newton, Ma.	N5188A
N335JB	01	390 Premier 1	RB-15	1st Trading USA Inc. Coral Gables, Fl.	(N153SW)
N335JJ	03	CitationJet CJ-2	525A-0162	J Alesi, Annemasse, France.	N.....
N335MG	87	Learjet 35A	35A-626	Eagle Jet Aviation Inc/Milt's Eagle LLC. Las Vegas, Nv.	(N385MG)
N335PR	89	Learjet 35A	35A-647	PIA LLC. Atlanta, Ga.	ZS-DJB
N335QS	95	Citation V Ultra	560-0335	NetJets, Columbus, Oh.	
N335RD	78	Learjet 35A	35A-216	RDC Marine Inc. Houston, Tx.	N142LG
N335TW	75	Falcon 20F	335	Chaparral Leasing Inc. Newton, Ks.	(N301FC)
N335UJ	82	Learjet 35A	35A-492	Richmark Aircraft Leasing LLC. Boca Raton, Fl.	N37SV
N335VB	80	Westwind-1124	297	Pauls Operations Inc. Aurora, Co.	N801SM
N336CS	04	Citation Bravo	550-1095	CitationShares Sales Inc. White Plains, NY.	N.....

Reg	Yr	Type	c/n	Owner/Operator	Prev Regn
N336MA	78	Citation II	550-0036	Mac Aircraft Inc. Las Vegas, Nv.	N789BR
N336QS	95	Citation V Ultra	560-0336	NetJets, Columbus, Oh.	N5265B
N336RJ	79	Sabre-65	465-10	Six Star Inc. Winter Park, Fl.	N77TC
N336UB	99	Learjet 45	45-046	Aero Holding LLC. Fort Lauderdale, Fl.	N136MA
N336XL	03	Citation Excel	560-5336	Jim & Mike Leasing LLC. Columbus-Bolton, Oh.	(N336BC)
N337CS	04	Citation Bravo	550-1097	CitationShares Sales Inc. White Plains, NY.	N51488
N337FP	90	Learjet 31	31-020	Mid-America Aviation LLC. Lafayette, In.	N31LJ
N337QS	97	Citation V Ultra	560-0437	NetJets, Columbus, Oh.	
N337RE	84	BAe 125/800A	8024	Bar-Ned Aviation LLC. Tompkins County, NY.	N802D
N337WR	94	Hawker 800	8273	Waddell & Reed Development Inc. Kansas City, Mo.	N258RA
N338CL	77	Gulfstream 2B	199	C & L Aviation LLC. Nashville, Tn.	N900TJ
N338CS	04	Citation Bravo	550-1084	CitationShares Sales Inc. White Plains, NY.	N52141
N338FJ	04	Falcon 50EX	338	The Glebe Group Inc. Oklahoma City, Ok.	F-WWHT
N338MM	88	Gulfstream 4	1076	Franklin Templeton Travel Inc. San Mateo, Ca.	HZ-MNC
N338QS	04	Citation Sovereign	680-0011	NetJets, Columbus, Oh.	N5135K
N338R	95	Citation V Ultra	560-0338	R P Air Inc. St Paul, Mn.	N592M
N338TP	00	Global Express	9073	Washington Times Aviation Inc. Washington-Dulles, Va.	N700XN
N339BC	82	Learjet 55	55-039	Chilton Aviation Inc. Wilmington, De.	VR-BQF
N339CA	77	HS 125/700A	NA0213	Cambata Aviation Inc. Roanoke, Va.	N370RR
N339CS	04	Citation Bravo	550-1085	CitationShares Sales Inc. White Plains, NY.	N5068R
N339PM	65	Sabre-40	282-38	PM Transportation LLC. Chicago, Il.	N921JG
N339QS	95	Citation V Ultra	560-0339	NetJets, Columbus, Oh.	
N340AK	99	Challenger 604	5405	Oak Air Ltd. Akron, Oh.	N811BP
N340EX	04	Falcon 50EX	340	Dassault Falcon Jet Corp. Teterboro, NJ.	F-WWHV
N340QS	99	Citation V Ultra	560-0514	NetJets, Columbus, Oh.	
N341AP	03	Falcon 2000EX	24	Air Products & Chemicals Inc. Allentown, Pa.	N224EX
N341AR	99	CitationJet	525-0341	Ahern Rentals Inc. Las Vegas, Nv.	
N341CS	04	Citation Bravo	550-1106	CitationShares Sales Inc. White Plains, NY.	N.....
N341K	01	Learjet 45	45-157	Kiewit Engineering Co. Omaha, Ne.	N545RA
N341KA	73	Falcon 20F	281	Falcon Acquisitions LLC. Carson City, Nv.	N341K
N341QS	96	Citation V Ultra	560-0341	NetJets, Columbus, Oh.	
N342CC	82	Citation II	550-0414	Charter Services Inc. Mobile, Al.	(N414VP)
N342CS	04	Citation Bravo	550-1101	Cessna Aircraft Co. Wichita, Ks.	N5264U
N342K	01	Learjet 45	45-171	Kiewit Engineering Co. Omaha, Ne.	N171DP
N342QS	95	Citation V Ultra	560-0324	NetJets, Columbus, Oh.	N55LQ
N342TC	94	Challenger 601-3R	5155	Sun Microsystems Inc. Portland, Or.	C-GLWV
N343CA	76	Learjet 25B	25B-202	Jim Donaldson/Cherry Air Inc. Dallas, Tx.	YU-BRA
N343CC	96	Citation V Ultra	560-0368	Westvaco Corp. NYC.	N5194J
N343CM	81	Citation II	550-0195	Blue Lake Air LLC. Alica, Ar.	N61CK
N343DF	94	Gulfstream 4SP	1241	Parkview Acquisition Inc. NYC.	N169CA
N343DP	86	Gulfstream 3	483	Meridian Equipment Co. Albany, NY.	N343DF
N343K	00	Challenger 604	5476	Eastman Kodak Co. Rochester, NY.	(N329FX)
N343MG	90	Falcon 900	95	M G Transportation Inc. West Palm Beach, Fl.	N478A
N343PR	01	390 Premier 1	RB-7	Town & Country Food Markets Inc. Wichita, Ks.	
N343QS	97	Citation V Ultra	560-0444	NetJets, Columbus, Oh.	
N343RK	73	Learjet 25B	25B-110	Maxfly Aviation Inc. Fort Lauderdale, Fl.	N52SD
N344AA	93	Gulfstream 4SP	1207	7-11 Air Corp. Teterboro, NJ.	(N77VU)
N344CA	76	Learjet 25B	25B-203	Jim Donaldson/Cherry Air Inc. Dallas, Tx.	YU-BRB
N344CM	00	Falcon 50EX	300	Cargill Inc. Minneapolis, Mn.	F-WWHB
N344GW	81	Gulfstream 3	344	U S Department of Energy, Albuquerque, NM.	N344DD
N344QS	95	Citation V Ultra	560-0344	NetJets, Columbus, Oh.	N5268M
N344RJ	76	Citation	500-0340	Roy Johnson, Addison, Tx.	N26NS
N345AA	92	Gulfstream 4	1186	7-11 Air Corp. Teterboro, NJ.	8P-MAK
N345AP	97	Falcon 50EX	254	Air Products & Chemicals Inc. Allentown, Pa.	N50AE
N345AW	01	Learjet 45	45-182	Saturn of Kansas City Inc. Kansas City, Mo.	N50248
N345BS	75	Westwind-1124	181	Linrose Aviation Inc. Longview, Tx.	N325LJ
N345CC	86	Citation S/II	S550-0095	Air Charters LLC. Salt Lake City, Ut.	N200NV
N345CJ	02	CitationJet CJ-2	525A-0136	Brantigan Research, Santa Fe, NM.	N5141F
N345FH	68	Falcon 20C	146	Grand Aire Express Inc. Toledo, Oh. (still N182GA 9/04).	N182GA
N345GC	88	Astra-1125	023	Flying Wings LLC. Clearwater, Fl.	N23TJ
N345GL	70	HS 125/400A	NA753	Hawkeye Aviation Transportation Inc. Des Moines, Ia.	N840H
N345K	01	Learjet 45	45-151	Koch Industries Inc. Wichita, Ks.	
N345LC	00	Gulfstream 4SP	1442	L & L Leasing LLC. White Plains, NY.	N481FB
N345MA	99	Learjet 45	45-054	Richards Aviation Inc. Memphis, Tn.	
N345MC	69	Learjet 25	25-046	MCOCO Inc/Air America Jet Charter, Houston, Tx.	N33PT
N345MG	99	CitationJet CJ-1	525-0372	Anderson Aviation Inc. Lake Forest, Il.	N372CP

Reg	Yr	Type	c/n	Owner/Operator	Prev Regn
N345N	81	Citation 1/SP	501-0204	Butler Properties Aviation LLC. Atlanta, Ga.	(N345HB)
N345QS	97	Citation V Ultra	560-0445	NetJets, Columbus, Oh.	N5000R
N345RJ	83	Learjet 55	55-078	R J Corman Aviation Services LLC. Lexington, Ky.	N55VK
N345RL	01	Learjet 45	45-180	Knollwood LLC. Houston, Tx.	N880LJ
N345SV	01	Learjet 45	45-140	Blue Sky 45 LLC. Van Nuys, Ca.	XA-AED
N345TR	81	Westwind-Two	345	R & S Airways Inc. Ocala, Ks.	N534R
N345WB	99	Learjet 45	45-036	Ameriair Leasing LLC/Corum Homes LLC. Miami, Fl.	
N346BA	97	Challenger 604	5361	Boeing Executive Flight Operations, Seattle, Wa.	C-GLXD
N346CM	00	Citation Bravo	550-0915	Massey Partners Ltd. Abilene, Tx.	N915BB
N346QS	04	Citation Sovereign	680-0013	NetJets, Columbus, Oh.	N5136J
N346XL	03	Citation Excel	560-5346	Florida Power & Light Co. Opa Locka, Fl.	N517CS
N347GA	81	Westwind-Two	347	Executive Time Management Inc. Atlanta, Ga.	N178HH
N347JV	81	Learjet 25D	25D-347	West Jet LLC. Salt Lake City, Ut.	N347AC
N347QS	96	Citation V Ultra	560-0357	NetJets, Columbus, Oh.	N81SH
N348DH	83	Westwind-1124	386	Remuda Resources Inc/Dan J Harrison III, Catarina, Tx.	N68WW
N348K	90	Falcon 50	205	Kiewit Engineering Co. Omaha, Ne.	N52JJ
N348MC	95	Hawker 800XP	8290	Monsanto Co. St Louis, Mo.	N670H
N348QS	95	Citation V Ultra	560-0348	NetJets, Columbus, Oh.	N52682
N348W	76	Sabre-60	306-94	Platina Investment Corp. Wiley Post, Ok.	N217RN
N349BA	00	BBJ-73Q	30789	Boeing Executive Flight Operations, Seattle, Wa.	
N349JC	76	Falcon 10	70	Northern Jet Management Inc. Grand Rapids, Mi.	VP-BCH
N349JR	93	Challenger 601-3A	5130	L T Exchange Corp. Oklahoma City, Ok.	N601SR
N349K	87	Falcon 900	10	Elk Mountain Ventures Inc. Omaha, Ne.	N5MC
N349MC	77	Westwind-1124	224	Harter Aviation LLC. Houston, Tx.	N2756T
N349SF	94	CitationJet	525-0049	Smithfield Foods Inc. Newport News, Va.	N49CJ
N350BV	03	CitationJet CJ-2	525A-0186	Banjo Corp/Canine Aviation LLC. Crawfordsville, In.	N5247U
N350C	00	Gulfstream V	612	Rikio Co. Tokyo, Japan.	N569GA
N350DA	81	Learjet 35A	35A-366	Dalton Aviation LLC. Amherst, NY.	N119CP
N350EF	81	Learjet 35A	35A-385	Executive Flight Inc. Pangborn Memorial, Wa.	N535MC
N350JH	75	Learjet 25B	25B-200	Mar-El Aviation Inc. Nashville, Tn.	N680BC
N350JS	80	Falcon 50	15	Jet Source Inc. Carlsbad, Ca.	(N595CW)
N350M	91	Citation VI	650-0203	Murphy Oil Corp. El Dorado, Ar.	N4612Z
N350PL	82	HS 125/700A	NA0338	Pelco Sales Inc. Clovis, Ca.	N797FA
N350WB	82	Falcon 50	102	Wagner & Brown Inc. Midland, Tx.	(N50WB)
N350WC	01	Citation Excel	560-5226	Williams Aviation Inc. Tulsa, Ok.	N5196U
N350ZE	02	Challenger 604	5547	Nissan North America Inc. Barrigada, Guam.	C-GLYA
N351AC	92	Learjet 31A	31A-051	Alpha Charlie Inc. Mountville, Pa.	N1905H
N351AM	81	Learjet 35A	35A-409	Aspen Base Operation Inc. Aspen, Co.	N35FE
N351AS	78	Learjet 35A	35A-146	L35 LLC. Meridian, Id.	N55AS
N351C	79	Westwind-1124	264	Dundon Management LLC. Dallas, Tx.	N88PV
N351CW	02	390 Premier 1	RB-53	Chandler Real Estate Inc. Helena, Mt.	N351CB
N351EF	77	Learjet 35A	35A-125	Executive Flight Inc. Pangborn Memorial, Wa.	N125GA
N351GL	73	Learjet 35	35-001	Learjet Inc. Wichita, Ks. (experimental).	N731GA
N351N	65	Learjet 23	23-054	LandAir Mapping Inc. Atlanta, Ga.	N351NR
N351PJ	76	Learjet 35A	35A-074	Premier Jets Inc. Hillsboro, Or.	N198T
N351QS	98	Citation V Ultra	560-0451	NetJets, Columbus, Oh.	N5124F
N351SP	95	Hawker 800XP	8280	Sonoco Products Co. Darlington County, SC.	G-BWDC
N351TC	04	Hawker 800XP	8675	Taylor Companies, Hagerstown, Md.	N675XP
N351TX	77	Learjet 35A	35A-127	CIT Group, Tempe, Az.	N727GL
N351WC	01	Citation Excel	560-5225	Cardinal Glass Industries Inc. Minnetonka, Mn.	(N351CG)
N352AF	98	Falcon 900B	172	Fayair Inc. Dover, De.	N177FJ
N352EF	91	Learjet 31A	31A-046	Executive Flight Inc. Pangborn Memorial, Wa.	N131PT
N352HS	85	Learjet 35A	35A-596	Evergreen Aircraft Sales & Leasing, McMinnville, Or.	N826CO
N352MD	77	Learjet 24F	24F-352	CPA Aviation Inc. Tulsa, Ok.	(N449JS)
N352QS	96	Citation V Ultra	560-0352	NetJets, Columbus, Oh.	N5153X
N352WB	81	Falcon 50	71	Wagner & Brown Inc. Midland, Tx.	J2-KBA
N353CA	69	Sabre-60	306-28	Charter America Inc. Miami, Fl.	N741RL
N353EF	81	Learjet 35A	35A-364	Harborview Medical Center, Seattle, Wa.	N490BC
N353FT*	82	Citation II	550-0353	First Team Air LLC. Maitland, Fl. (was 551-0398).	N477KM
N353GA	04	Gulfstream G100	153	Jet 1 Holdings Inc. Wilmington, De. (trustor ?).	4X-CVJ
N353PJ	73	Citation	500-0104	All Altitude Aviation Inc. Edgewater, Fl.	(N3330)
N353QS	99	Citation V Ultra	560-0530	NetJets, Columbus, Oh.	
N353VA	83	Gulfstream 3	371	Venusair LLC. Burbank, Ca.	N681FM
N353WC	01	Citation X	750-0180	Williams Companies Inc. Tulsa, Ok.	N51511
N354CL	83	Learjet 35A	35A-493	Clay Lacy Aviation Inc. Van Nuys, Ca.	N493CH
N354EF	81	Learjet 35A	35A-378	Executive Flight Inc. Pangborn Memorial, Wa.	N354ME

Reg	Yr	Type	c/n	Owner/Operator	Prev Regn

Reg	Yr	Type	c/n	Owner/Operator	Prev Regn
N354GA	04	Gulfstream G100	154	Gulfstream Aerospace LP. Fort Worth, Tx.	4X-...
N354LQ	76	Learjet 35	35-055	Addison Express LLC. Addison, Tx.	C-GCJD
N354PM	75	Learjet 35	35-015	Addison Express LLC. Addison, Tx.	(N335SS)
N354QS	96	Citation V Ultra	560-0356	NetJets, Columbus, Oh.	N5153Z
N354RB	02	390 Premier 1	RB-54	Raytheon Aircraft Co. Wichita, Ks.	ZS-MGK
N354TC	96	Challenger 601-3R	5192	Hilton Hotels Corp. Van Nuys, Ca.	C-GLYC
N354WC	02	Citation X	750-0191	Williams Companies Inc. Tulsa, Ok.	N5267G
N355AC	70	HS 125/F403B	25227	Midsouth Services Inc. Clearwater, Fl.	N227MS
N355CC	98	Challenger 604	5393	CP Management LLC. Baltimore, Md.	C-GLYA
N355CD	81	Sabre-65	465-57	Sound Trak Inc. Omaha, Ne.	N903K
N355EJ	94	Citation V	560-0255	American Air Travelers Inc. Stuart, Fl.	N255WA
N355MC	76	Falcon 20F-5B	355	MCI Communications Corp. Dulles, Va.	N803WC
N355UJ	82	Learjet 55	55-033	Richmark Aircraft Leasing LLC. Boca Raton, Fl.	N398AC
N356BR	82	Gulfstream 3	356	Stephens Institute/Academy of Art College, San Francisco, Ca	N356TJ
N356JW	90	Learjet 35A	35A-656	Air Bear Inc. Amarillo, Tx.	N335SB
N356MS	04	Global 5000	9149	Bombardier Aerospace Corp. Windsor Locks, Ct.	C-FAIY
N356SA	94	Citation V	560-0256	Swift Aviation Services Inc. Phoenix, Az.	N356EJ
N356SR	82	HS 125/700A	NA0318	Schumacher Aircraft LLC. Mount Prospect, Il.	N114BA
N356WA	97	Learjet 60	60-123	Wilsonart International Inc. Temple, Tx.	
N357BE	04	Citation Encore	560-0663	Basin Electric Power Co-Operative, Bismark, ND.	N5266F
N357EC	04	Citation Excel XLS	560-5510	Entergy Services Inc. New Orleans, La.	N41118
N357EF	80	Learjet 35A	35A-323	Executive Flight Inc. Pangborn Memorial, Wa.	N735A
N357J	03	CitationJet CJ-2	525A-0184	Changes in Altitude Aviation Inc. Tampa, Fl.	N.....
N357JV	99	CitationJet	525-0357	Lewco Air LLC. Baton Rouge, la.	
N357KM	85	Gulfstream 3	435	Komar Aviation LLC. Long Beach, Ca.	N32KA
N357LJ	80	Learjet 35A	35A-357	Jetride Inc. Columbus, Oh.	N104SB
N357PR	82	Gulfstream 3	348	From the Heart Minisitries Inc. Temple Hills, Md.	N756S
N357PS	76	Falcon 20F-5	357	Falcon Acquisitions LLC. Carson City, Nv.	N342KF
N358BJ	02	BBJ-7ES	33542	Boeing Business Jets, Seattle, Wa.	
N358QS	97	Citation V Ultra	560-0455	NetJets, Columbus, Oh.	N51396
N358WC	00	Citation X	750-0121	Williams Communications Aircraft LLC. Tulsa, Ok.	(XB-...)
N359CW	88	Citation III	650-0159	Flight Options LLC. Cleveland, Oh.	N267TG
N359EC	00	Citation Encore	560-0559	UCC Washington Park Inc. Trenton, NJ.	(N659SA)
N359EJ	78	Learjet 35A	35A-193	Harborview Medical Center, Seattle, Wa.	N9EE
N359GW	04	Citation Bravo	550-1076	G W Air Charter LLC. Appleton, Wi.	N51872
N359V	98	Astra-1125SPX	102	Valmont Industries Inc. Valley, Ne.	N525M
N359WC	00	Citation Excel	560-5129	Williams Communications Aircraft LLC. Tulsa, Ok.	N5214J
N359WJ	67	Sabre-60	306-1	Commercial Aviation Enterprises Inc. Delray Beach, Fl.	XA-REC
N360AN	98	Learjet 60	60-137	Jetride Inc. Dallas, Tx.	N229FX
N360CA*	81	Diamond 1A	A009SA	Charlie Air LLC. West Columbia, SC.	N318RS
N360HS	99	Citation Bravo	550-0889	Auctionair LLC. Cottonwood, Az.	N619JM
N360JG	83	Learjet 25D	25D-360	Pegasus Aviation LLC. Nashville, Tn.	N618P
N360LA	00	Global Express	9087	Luft Aviation Charter P/L. Melbourne.	N700BQ
N360LJ	80	Learjet 35A	35A-360	Big Sky LLC. Farmington, Mo.	(N987DK)
N360M	84	Citation S/II	S550-0022	Murphy & Pruet Family Investments, El Dorado, Ar.	N258P
N360MB	80	Gulfstream 3	306	FKA Distributing Co/Homedics Inc. Pontiac, Mi.	N104BK
N360MC	77	Citation 1/SP	501-0036	House of Raeford Farms Inc. Raeford, NC.	HI-493
N360QS	98	Citation V Ultra	560-0460	NetJets, Columbus, Oh.	N5157E
N361AS	00	Beechjet 400A	RK-287	Munn River LLC. Barnes Municipal, Westfield, Ma.	N4467E
N361DB	99	Citation Bravo	550-0884	Radio Flyer 884 LLC. St Louis, Mo.	N1318Y
N361DE	85	Citation 1/SP	501-0687	Details Services LLC. Mooresville, NC.	N361DB
N361EC*	03	Citation Excel	560-5515	Entergy Services Inc. New Orleans, La.	N4118K
N361EE	96	Citation VII	650-7057	TSI Telecommunication Services Inc. Wiley Post, Ok.	N653EJ
N361PJ	74	Learjet 36	36-003	Premier Jets Inc. Hillsboro, Or.	N55CJ
N361QS	95	Citation V Ultra	560-0361	NetJets, Columbus, Oh.	N5156B
N362CP	82	Citation II	550-0403	Colonial Pipeline Co. Atlanta, Ga. (was 551-0058).	N637EH
N362FL	99	CitationJet CJ-1	525-0362	National Energy Resorces Inc. Knoxville, Tn.	N362PE
N362FW	80	Learjet 35A	35A-362	Eric Stirling, Fairbanks, Ak.	N633DS
N363QS	99	Citation V Ultra	560-0536	NetJets, Columbus, Oh.	
N363TD	78	Citation 1/SP	501-0068	North West Air Travel LLC. Albany, Or.	N68EA
N364CL	81	Learjet 35A	35A-383	Clay Lacy Aviation Inc. Van Nuys, Ca.	N66FE
N364CW	88	Citation III	650-0164	Flight Options LLC. Cleveland, Oh.	N164AF
N364G	89	Gulfstream 4	1091	General Electric Co. Stewart, NY.	N467GA
N365AT	99	Hawker 800XP	8449	Draupner Services LLC. Sanford, Fl.	N41431
N365EA	91	Citation V	560-0107	Quest II LLC. Moline, Il.	N560RJ
N365G	89	Gulfstream 4	1101	General Electric Co. Stewart, NY.	N404GA

Reg	Yr	Type	c/n	Owner/Operator	Prev Regn
☐ N365GA*	94	Astra-1125SP	072	Gulfstream Aerospace Corp. Savannah, Ga.	N32TM
☐ N365GL	96	Learjet 31A	31A-128	Gurley-Leep Oldsmobile Cadillac Inc. Mishawaka, In.	(N469)
☐ N365N	80	Learjet 35A	35A-300	Newell Rubbermaid Inc. Rockford, Il.	
☐ N365TC	68	Gulfstream II SP	41	Trans Continental Jet Shares LLC. Rockledge, Fl.	N416K
☐ N366F	88	Gulfstream 4	1041	Connell Industries Inc. Boston, Ma.	N433GA
☐ N366G	98	BBJ-75V	28581	General Electric Co. Stewart, NY.	N1787B
☐ N366JA*	82	Gulfstream 3	366	Air Castle Worldwide Jet Charter Inc. Millville, NJ.	N333LX
☐ N366LJ	83	Learjet 25D	25D-366	Toscana Construction Inc. McAllen, Tx.	ZS-CAT
☐ N366QS	98	Citation V Ultra	560-0466	NetJets, Columbus, Oh.	
☐ N366TS	98	Learjet 31A	31A-166	South Skys LLC. Miami, Fl.	N811PS
☐ N366TT	79	Learjet 35A	35A-227	My Jet LLC. Hayward, Ca.	N902JC
☐ N367DA*	85	Learjet 35A	35A-599	Global Holding Corp. Portland, Or.	N58GL
☐ N367G	98	BBJ-75V	28579	General Electric Co. Stewart, NY.	
☐ N367JC	90	Citation V	560-0069	Walter Air Corp. Houston, Tx.	N857WC
☐ N367QS	96	Citation V Ultra	560-0367	NetJets, Columbus, Oh.	N5161J
☐ N367WW	82	Westwind-1124	367	Fred Hallmark, Warrior, Al.	N455S
☐ N368AG	89	Gulfstream 4	1087	Blue Sky Group Inc. Van Nuys, Ca.	N110TM
☐ N368BE	00	Citation Encore	560-0546	Basin Electric Power, Bismarck, ND.	N5151D
☐ N368CE	95	B 737-33A	27456	Club Excellence Inc/Finova Capital Corp. Paramus, NJ.	9M-CHG
☐ N368D	84	Learjet 25D	25D-368	U S Marshals Service, Oklahoma City, Ok.	N8567J
☐ N368DS	73	Gulfstream 2B	123	The Scruggs Law Firm PA. Oxford, Ms.	N344AB
☐ N369B	97	Citation X	750-0030	The Buckle Inc. Kearney, Ne.	(N855WC)
☐ N369BA	80	Learjet 35A	35A-312	369BA LLC. West Columbia, SC.	LV-OFV
☐ N369BG	87	Falcon 900B	40	B/G Enterprises LLC. Indianapolis, In.	N145W
☐ N369EA	85	Beechjet 400	RJ-2	Elliott Aviation Aircraft Sales Inc. Des Moines, Ia.	N402FB
☐ N370AS	59	MS 760 Paris	30	Your Aircraft Source LLC. Calhoun, Ga.	30
☐ N370BA	04	Citation Excel XLS	560-5525	Credomatic of Florida Inc. Miami, Fl.	N5264A
☐ N370BC	86	B 737-205	23468	Basic Capital Management Inc. Addison, Tx.	HZ-TBA
☐ N370DE	99	Hawker 800XP	8441	Duke Energy Corp. Houston, Tx.	N800PB
☐ N370FC	03	Hawker 400XP	RK-378	Franklin Corp. Starkville, Ms.	
☐ N370JL	83	Gulfstream 3	401	JGL Aviation LLC. Broomfield, Co.	N97AG
☐ N370KP	82	Falcon 50	103	Southern Cross Ranch LLC. Monroe, NC.	N83MP
☐ N370SC	93	Learjet 31A	31A-070	Wal-Mart Stores Inc. Rogers, Ar.	(N270SC)
☐ N370TP	84	Citation III	650-0059	TP Aviation LLC. DeLand, Fl.	N660AA
☐ N370V	80	Challenger 600S	1014	448 Alliance Corp. Fort Worth, Tx.	144607
☐ N371AS	59	MS 760 Paris	34	Your Aircraft Source LLC. Calhoun, Ga.	34
☐ N371BC	01	BBJ2-8EF	32971	Boeing Business Jets, Seattle, Wa.	
☐ N371CF	02	Beechjet 400A	RK-351	International Coffee & Fertilizer Trading Co. Guatemala City	N6051C
☐ N371P	03	Citation Excel	560-5371	Dana Flight Operations Inc. Swanton, Oh.	N.....
☐ N371QS	98	Citation V Ultra	560-0471	NetJets, Columbus, Oh.	N5188A
☐ N372BG	03	Gulfstream G550	5038	Berwind Corp/Contrail Aviation LLC. Philadelphia, Pa.	N938GA
☐ N372CM	00	Gulfstream 4SP	1451	Cordelia S May, Ligonier, Pa.	N351GA
☐ N372G	97	Challenger 604	5351	General Electric Co. Stewart, NY.	N374G
☐ N372Q	67	Jet Commander	112	Plain Old Plane LLC. Birmingham, Al.	N773WB
☐ N372QS	96	Citation V Ultra	560-0372	NetJets, Columbus, Oh.	N76CK
☐ N373AS	59	MS 760 Paris	36	Airborne Turbine LP. San Luis Obispo, Ca.	36
☐ N373DJ	84	Citation III	650-0038	Westjet Leasing LLC. Fort Collins, Co.	N366GE
☐ N373G	03	Challenger 604	5556	GE Air Transport Services Inc. White Plains, NY.	C-GLWZ
☐ N373QS	96	Citation V Ultra	560-0373	NetJets, Columbus, Oh.	
☐ N373RR	83	Gulfstream 3	373	Roberts Aviation LLC. St Louis, Mo.	N373GS
☐ N373RS	97	Falcon 50EX	259	Kalamazoo Group LLC. Mattawan, Mi.	VP-CHG
☐ N374AS	59	MS 760 Paris	38	Airborne Turbine LP. San Luis Obispo, Ca.	38
☐ N374FD	85	Airbus A300C4-620	374	Flight Director Inc. Austin, Tx. (status ?).	A6-PFD
☐ N374G	98	Challenger 604	5368	General Electric Co. Stewart, NY.	N368G
☐ N374QS	98	Citation V Ultra	560-0475	NetJets, Columbus, Oh.	
☐ N375AS	59	MS 760 Paris	44	Airborne Turbine LP. San Luis Obispo, Ca.	44
☐ N375DT	03	Hawker 400XP	RK-372	CarDan Air Inc/Towbin Management Inc. Las Vegas, Nv.	N6172V
☐ N375NW	83	Gulfstream 3	375	Pacific Jet/EHR Aviation Inc. Van Nuys, Ca.	(N75GJ)
☐ N375QS	96	Citation V Ultra	560-0375	NetJets, Columbus, Oh.	
☐ N376BE	83	Westwind-Two	376	N376BE Inc. Scottsdale, Az.	N376WA
☐ N376D	75	Sabre-60A	306-101	Salyer Farms Airport, Corcoran, Ca.	N60FS
☐ N376MB	01	Learjet 31A	31A-234	MB Aviation Corp. Fairfield, Oh.	N5028E
☐ N376PJ	83	Gulfstream 3	376	Hansen Prero Aviation LLC. Bellevue, Wa.	N376EJ
☐ N376QS	94	Citation V Ultra	560-0276	NetJets, Columbus, Oh.	N183AJ
☐ N377GS	01	CitationJet CJ-2	525A-0077	Grand Sport Leasing LLC. Cincinnati-Lunken, Oh. (status ?).	N5148N
☐ N377HS	75	Sabre-75A	380-36	Centurion Investments Inc. St Louis, Mo.	XB-MCB

Reg		Yr	Type		c/n		Owner/Operator		Prev Regn

Reg	Yr	Type	c/n	Owner/Operator	Prev Regn
N377HW	85	Falcon 50	156	Pro Flights Inc. Fort Lauderdale, Fl.	N4MR
N377JE	83	Citation III	650-0013	Air LLC/Dubois County Flight Services, Huntingburg, In.	N313QS
N377QS	96	Citation V Ultra	560-0377	NetJets, Columbus, Oh.	N450RA
N377RX	83	Gulfstream 3	377	Sea-Ya Enterprises LLC. Sarasota, Fl.	N760AC
N377SC	00	Falcon 900EX	66	Steelcase Inc. Grand Rapids, Mi.	F-WWFA
N377SF	98	Citation X	750-0068	Mandan LLC. Chicago, Il.	N5100J
N378AS	59	MS 760 Paris	45	Airborne Turbine LP. San Luis Obispo, Ca.	45
N378C	76	Falcon 10	73	Falcon Flight Group LLC. Dover, De.	VR-BNT
N379QS	98	Citation V Ultra	560-0479	NetJets, Columbus, Oh.	N5125J
N379XX	83	Gulfstream 3	394	Nexxus Products Inc. Santa Barbara, Ca. 'Jheri Reading'	N311GA
N380AK	97	Citation Bravo	550-0809	Marbo Enterprises LLC. Houma, La.	N300AK
N380BC	74	Sabre-80A	380-17	Bryce Corp/F C Leasing Inc. Memphis, Tn.	N1115
N380CF	77	Sabre-75A	380-51	Habari Inc. Rancho Cucamonga, Ca.	N382LS
N380CW	84	Citation III	650-0030	Flight Options LLC. Cleveland, Oh.	N650SC
N380DE	94	Hawker 800	8269	Duke Energy Corp. Houston, Tx.	N380X
N380FP	77	Sabre-75A	380-54	Fowler Marketing Express LLC. Fresno, Ca.	N910BH
N380GG	02	Hawker 800XP	8591	Titan Aviation LLC. Dallas, Tx.	N61791
N380GK	76	Sabre-75A	380-44	Cayenne Aviation LP. Houston, Tx.	N2440G
N380RD	89	Citation V	560-0026	WWB LLC. Eden Prairie, Mn.	N350RD
N381BJ	78	Citation	501-0286	Jetstream Holdings Inc. Wilmington, De. (was 500-0381).	(N789AA)
N381CW	86	Citation III	650-0111	Flight Options LLC. Cleveland, Oh.	N500CM
N381VP	80	Citation II	550-0381	Teton Leasing LLC. Pocatello, Id. (was 551-0049).	N391KC
N382AA	66	Jet Commander	56	Mach Aero International Corp. Tulsa, Ok.	(N53AA)
N382EM	02	CitationJet CJ-1	525-0496	Rotorwing LLC. Coldwater, Mi.	N5223P
N382G	02	Gulfstream G200	079	General Dynamics Corp. Pontiac, Mi.	N379GA
N382QS	96	Citation V Ultra	560-0382	NetJets, Columbus, Oh.	
N382TC	75	Learjet 35	35-039	The Nordam Group Inc. Tulsa, Ok.	N1HP
N383DT	98	Challenger 604	5383	Novell Inc. Salt Lake City, Ut.	C-GLYK
N383MB	03	Challenger 604	5568	Zulu Equipment LLC. Seattle, Wa.	N604JC
N383QS	98	Citation V Ultra	560-0483	NetJets, Columbus, Oh.	
N383SF	96	Astra-1125SPX	083	Smithfield Foods Inc. Newport News, Va.	
N384AT	74	Westwind-1123	175	Dodson International Parts Inc. Rantoul, Ks. (status ?).	(N571MC)
N384CF	81	Learjet 35A	35A-384	CF Palwaukee LLC. Pal-Waukee, Il.	N811DD
N384CW	87	Citation III	650-0144	Flight Options LLC. Cleveland, Oh.	N2605
N384JW	80	Learjet 35A	35A-316	N384JW LLC/Winner Aviation Corp. Youngstown, Oh.	N89GK
N384K	78	Falcon 20F-5B	387	Quality Shipyards Inc. New Orleans, La.	N676DW
N385AC	68	Falcon 20C	144	Falcon Leasing Inc. Elko, Nv.	N911RG
N385CT	04	Challenger 604	5592	Caterpillar Inc. Peoria, Il.	C-GLYH
N385CW	87	Citation III	650-0145	Flight Options LLC. Cleveland, Oh.	N29AU
N385MG	05	Citation Excel XLS	560-5556	Cessna Aircraft Co. Wichita, Ks.	N.....
N386AM	80	Citation II/SP	551-0191	S F Aircraft Inc. St Thomas, USVI.	N127KR
N386CH	01	EMB-135LR	145467	Intel Corp/Executive Jet Management Inc. Cincinnati, Oh.	PT-...
N386CM	80	Learjet 35A	35A-283	Giddy Up N Go/Architectural Cost Control Systems, Dallas, Tx	N205FL
N386CW	90	Citation III	650-0186	Flight Options LLC. Cleveland, Oh.	N186VP
N386K*	95	Challenger 601-3R	5174	Lear 45-086 Holding Corp. Fort Lauderdale, Fl.	N28KA
N386QS	98	Citation V Ultra	560-0486	NetJets, Columbus, Oh.	
N387CL	98	Challenger 604	5387	Allied Caribbean Inc. Coral Gables, Fl.	N316FX
N387FJ*	83	Falcon 200	487	Dassault Falcon Jet Corp. Teterboro, NJ.	N137TA
N387HA	79	Learjet 35A	35A-251	Highland Associates Inc. Birmingham, Al.	N251CT
N387PA	01	Gulfstream G100	145	General Cigar Holdings Transportation Inc. Teterboro, NJ.	N264GA
N387RE	88	Citation II	550-0575	McNeill & Assocs Ltd. Germantown, Tn.	N337RE
N387SC	80	Citation II	550-0142	Cavalear LLC. Boca Raton, Fl.	PT-LCR
N388BS	99	Hawker 800XP	8423	Tanara Inc. Dallas-Love Field, Tx.	N925JF
N388CW	86	Gulfstream 3	489	Deniston Enterprises Inc. Baltimore, Md.	N888CW
N388GM	76	Citation	500-0323	Thomas Pacific Construction Inc. San Rafael, Ca.	(N268GM)
N388GS	99	Falcon 900EX	55	Citiflight Inc. White Plains, NY.	(N399CG)
N388MM	86	Gulfstream 3	490	Franklin Templeton Travel Inc. San Mateo, Ca.	N28R
N388PD	87	Learjet 35A	35A-630	Dooney & Bourke PR Inc. Yabucoa, PR.	N742P
N388PS	02	CitationJet CJ-1	525-0492	P & S Aerowest Inc. Forney, Tx.	N492CJ
N388SB	81	Citation II	550-0245	Sierra Bravo Aviation LLC. Wichita, Ks.	N505GP
N388WW	83	Westwind-1124	388	Expan Leasing II LLC. Pontiac, Mi.	N900H
N389AT	79	Learjet 25D	25D-297	Spirit Wing Aviation Ltd. Guthrie, Ok.	N24KW
N389KA	81	Learjet 35A	35A-389	L F S T LLC. Las Cruces, NM.	N79AX
N390AG	77	Falcon 20F	360	A G Aviation LLC. Palwaukee, Il.	N865VP
N390AJ	81	Citation II	550-0326	J & M Leasing LLC. Dublin, Oh.	(N390JP)
N390BW	01	390 Premier 1	RB-12	Raytheon Aircraft Co. Wichita, Ks.	XA-TSN

Reg	Yr	Type	c/n	Owner/Operator	Prev Regn
N390DP	02	390 Premier 1	RB-34	Davison Transport Inc. Ruston, La.	
N390GS	95	Falcon 2000	21	Citigroup/The Travelers Inc. White Plains, NY.	F-WWMA
N390JK	01	390 Premier 1	RB-39	Kelley Aviation Associates Inc. Amarillo, Tx.	N39KT
N390JW	01	390 Premier 1	RB-78	A & G Coal Co. Lonesome Pine, Va.	
N390QS	98	Citation V Ultra	560-0490	NetJets, Columbus, Oh.	
N390RA	98	390 Premier 1	RB-1	Raytheon Aircraft Co. Wichita, Ks. (Ff 23 Dec 98).	
N390RC	02	390 Premier 1	RB-56	Hawker Pacific P/L. Yagoona, NSW.	
N390TC	99	390 Premier 1	RB-3	Raytheon Aircraft Co. Wichita, Ks. (Ff 17 Sep 99).	
N391AN	79	Citation II	550-0084	International Aviation Network, Santa Monica.(was 551-0129).	(N467MW)
N391BC	99	Citation Bravo	550-0909	Best Chairs Inc. Ferdinand, In.	N44KW
N391QS	98	Citation V Ultra	560-0493	NetJets, Columbus, Oh.	
N391SH	83	Gulfstream 3	392	Aircraft Network LLC. Dallas-Love, Tx.	N801WC
N392FV	84	Challenger 601	3032	Sugar Pine Aviation LLC. Merlin, Or.	N111GX
N392QS	97	Citation V Ultra	560-0429	NetJcts, Columbus, Oh.	
N392RG	99	CitationJet	525-0340	Race Glaze LLC. Lannon, Wi.	
N392SM	00	CitationJet CJ-1	525-0392	Pacific Flight Services LLC. Santa Barbara, Ca.	N5165T
N393BB	88	Beechjet 400	RJ-39	Brown & Brown Inc. Daytona Beach, Fl.	N48SR
N393BD	93	Gulfstream 4SP	1205	USA Video Distribution LLC. NYC.	N8203K
N393CW	86	Citation III	650-0113	Flight Options LLC. Cincinnati, Oh.	N652JM
N393E	85	Citation S/II	S550-0053	AEGON USA Inc. Cedar Rapids, la.	N1223N
N393QS	96	Citation V Ultra	560-0393	NetJets, Columbus, Oh.	N5156V
N393S	83	Falcon 20F	473	Sunoco Inc. Philadelphia, Pa.	N473SH
N393TA	98	Learjet 60	60-143	TA393 LLC. Miami, Fl.	N6666A
N394AK	01	Gulfstream 4SP	1470	Talon Air/Roxann Management Corp. Farmingdale, NY.	N34UH
N394BB	03	Hawker 400XP	RK-364	Brown & Brown Inc. Daytona Beach, Fl.	
N394QS	96	Citation V Ultra	560-0394	NetJets, Columbus, Oh.	N5093Y
N394TR	94	Gulfstream 4SP	1252	Triarc Companies Inc. Stewart, NY.	N252C
N394WJ	00	Citation Excel	560-5086	Copart Inc. Benicia, Ca.	N269JR
N395EJ	76	HS 125/600B	6060	T-Bird Aviation Inc Tampa, Fl.	N422TR
N395GA	81	Sabre-65	465-65	Christopher's Jet World LLC. Golden, Co.	(N600WE)
N395HB	99	Beechjet 400A	RK-253	Florida Rock Industries Inc. Jacksonville, Fl.	N4053T
N395HE	90	Citation II	550-0641	Sewanee Investments LLC. Houston, Tx.	PT-WON
N395LJ	94	Learjet 31A	31A-095	Wal-Mart Stores Inc. Rogers, Ar.	OK-AJD
N395QS	98	Citation V Ultra	560-0496	NetJets, Columbus, Oh.	
N395R	92	Citation V	560-0188	Ryan's Family Steak Houses Inc. Greer, SC.	N64PM
N395TJ	83	Westwind-Two	395	Alaska Flight Services LLC. Tuscaloosa, Al.	N395SR
N395WB	83	Diamond 1A	A045SA	Watts Brothers Cable Construction, Owensboro, Ky.	N545TP
N395WJ	03	Citation Excel	560-5330	Agile Aviation LLC. San Jose, Ca.	(N638Q)
N396CF	70	Gulfstream II SP	96	Hollywood Aviation Inc. Burbank, Ca.	XA-EYA
N396M	82	Citation II	550-0362	Peter Sturdivant LLC. Hailey, Id.	(N440PJ)
N396QS	96	Citation V Ultra	560-0396	NetJets, Columbus, Oh.	N50938
N396U	98	Gulfstream 4SP	1350	Unisys Corp. Trenton, NJ.	N330GA
N396V	80	Challenger 600S	1009	4KS Aviation III Inc. Dallas, Tx.	144606
N397AT	00	Learjet 45	45-105	ITC Service Co. Valley, Al.	N105LJ
N397CA	97	Beechjet 400A	RK-136	Cambata Aviation Inc. Roanoke, Va.	N780TP
N397CW	86	Citation III	650-0107	Flight Options LLC. Cleveland, Oh.	N650JG
N397JJ	98	Gulfstream 4SP	1354	ACE INA/Recovery Services International Inc. Philadelphia..	N397J
N397SC	72	Citation Eagle	500-0019	B&B Leasing LLC/Independent Stave Co. Lebanon, Mo.	OB-1280
N398AC	93	Falcon 50	240	Iowa Land & Building Co. Cedar Rapids, la.	(N200BN)
N398CJ	00	CitationJet CJ-1	525-0398	DK Airways Corp/M & N Aviation Inc. San Juan, PR.	N5183V
N398CW	85	Citation III	650-0098	Flight Options LLC. Cleveland, Oh.	N54HC
N398LS	98	Citation Bravo	550-0853	Les Schwab Warehouse Center Inc. Prineville, Or.	N5086W
N398QS	99	Citation V Ultra	560-0522	NetJets, Columbus, Oh.	
N398RS	98	Citation Excel	560-5009	Roaring Springs Ranch Inc. Portland, Or.	N52113
N399AZ	81	Learjet 35A	35A-399		PT-OVC
N399BA	81	Learjet 35A	35A-371	Bankair Inc. West Columbia, SC.	LV-ALF
N399CB	95	Gulfstream 4SP	1261	P Dussmann Inc. Los Angeles, Ca.	N469GA
N399DM	81	Diamond 1A	A008SA	Paul Sadler, Henderson, Tx.	(N56SK)
N399FG	77	Falcon 20F-5	373	Flex Air Ltd/Flight Star Corp. Chicago-Midway, Il.	N620CC
N399FL	83	Challenger 600S	1083	Challenger 600 LLC/The Air Group, Chesterfield, Mo.	N471SB
N399G	96	CitationJet	525-0183	Dineair Corp. Holmdel, NJ.	N97CJ
N399GS	00	Global Express	9074	Citiflight Inc. White Plains, NY.	C-GHEA
N399HS	04	Citation Encore	560-0678	Cessna Aircraft Co. Wichita, Ks.	N5203J
N399MM	82	Diamond 1A	A017SA	H2 Enterprises LLC. Sarasota, Fl.	(N33MM)
N399QS	99	Citation V Ultra	560-0510	NetJets, Columbus, Oh.	
N399RA	98	Beechjet 400A	RK-200	MaLeCo, Salem, Or.	VP-CKK

Reg	Yr	Type	c/n	Owner/Operator	Prev Regn

Reg	Yr	Type	c/n	Owner/Operator	Prev Regn
☐ N399RP	82	Diamond 1A	A020SA	C C Medflight Inc. Lawrenceville, Ga.	(N911JJ)
☐ N399RV	84	Gulfstream 3	423	Vinson Media Group LLC. St Louis, Mo.	N225SF
☐ N399W	01	Citation X	750-0171	Williams International LLC. Waterford, Mi.	N51160
☐ N400	03	Challenger 604	5572	Indianapolis Motor Speedway LLC. Indianapolis, In.	N572MS
☐ N400AJ	97	Beechjet 400A	RK-137	Schuele German Technologies GmbH. Bad Radolfszell, Germany	N1117Z
☐ N400CC	88	Gulfstream 4	1046	KaiserAir Inc. Oakland, Ca.	N119K
☐ N400CP	00	Gulfstream G100	131	Gulf 100 Inc. Coral Springs, Fl.	N57GX
☐ N400CT	98	Beechjet 400A	RK-179	CTS Corp/NIBCO Inc. Elkhart, In.	N75GK
☐ N400D	70	Gulfstream II SP	100	KFLP Air LLC. Boulder, Co.	XB-FVL
☐ N400DB	71	Sabre-75	370-4	Banner Associates Inc. Lake Forest, Il.	N370BH
☐ N400DW	88	Beechjet 400	RJ-40	Forsythe West Investments Inc. Chesterfield, Mo.	N3240M
☐ N400EP	70	Learjet 24XR	24XR-215	Abofamalom Inc. Palm Harbor, Fl.	(N57JR)
☐ N400FF	83	Learjet 35A	35A-498	Charter Rent LLC. Elmira, NY.	N498JR
☐ N400FJ	02	Gulfstream 4SP	1494	Fletcher Jones Management Group Inc. Las Vegas, Nv.	N494GA
☐ N400FR	70	HS 125/400A	NA751	Romair Inc. Fort Lauderdale, Fl.	HC-BTT
☐ N400FT	95	Beechjet 400A	RK-101	Featherlite Aviation Co. Cresco, Ia.	ZS-JRO
☐ N400GA	04	Gulfstream G400	1516	CMA Services LLC. Fort Lauderdale, Fl.	N516GA
☐ N400GJ	87	Beechjet 400	RJ-23	C C Medflight Inc. Lawrenceville, Ga.	N3123T
☐ N400GK	82	Diamond 1	A019SA	Soaring Seagull LLC. Tulsa, Ok.	N319DM
☐ N400GR	01	Beechjet 400A	RK-335	Texas State Bank, McAllen, Tx.	N5015B
☐ N400GX	99	Global Express	9037	MicroStrategy Inc. Dulles, Va.	N777VU
☐ N400HD	98	Beechjet 400A	RK-191	Two Rivers Aviation LLC. Sioux City, SD.	N367EA
☐ N400HF	00	Gulfstream 4SP	1444	AEC Properties LLC. Boston, Ma.	(N444GV)
☐ N400HH	82	Diamond 1	A025SA	400HH Inc. Lebanon, NJ.	N1843A
☐ N400HS	01	Beechjet 400A	RK-314	H S Aero Services LLC/Condor Express Corp. Danbury, Ct.	N5014G
☐ N400HT	04	CitationJet CJ-2	525A-0208	Hudson Thompson Development LLC. Georgetown, De.	N.....
☐ N400J	97	Gulfstream 4SP	1330	Johnson & Johnson, Mercer County Airport, NJ.	N324GA
☐ N400JD	04	Citation X	750-0235	Deere & Co. Moline, Il.	N.....
☐ N400JE	77	Learjet 35A	35A-120	AirNet Systems Inc. Columbus, Oh. (blue).	(N400RV)
☐ N400JH	93	Citation VI	650-0226	Hans Management Corp. Savannah, Ga.	N1302A
☐ N400KG	98	Beechjet 400A	RK-221	DRG Star Management LLC. San Francisco, Ca.	N18BR
☐ N400KP	01	Beechjet 400A	RK-308	Kingston Aviation LLC. Idaho Falls, Id.	N51008
☐ N400KS	89	Citation V	560-0041	4KS Aviation III Inc. Dallas, Tx.	VH-NTH
☐ N400LC	70	HS 125/400A	NA743	DeJarnette Enterprises Inc. Lee's Summit, Mo.	HK-3653
☐ N400LV	76	Learjet 35A	35A-083	Aeronautical Resources Corp. Aventura, Fl.	YV-100CP
☐ N400LX	97	Citation V Ultra	560-0453	L J Associates Inc. Latrobe, Pa.	N453CV
☐ N400M	73	Gulfstream II SP	132	Lorien Aviation Inc. Van Nuys, Ca.	N873GA
☐ N400MC	97	Citation V Ultra	560-0440	Clayton Aviation/RCM Industries Inc. Il. (was 560-0424).	PT-WSN
☐ N400ML	83	Diamond 1A	A064SA	American Medical Equipment & Security, Miami, Fl.	N2225J
☐ N400MP	99	Gulfstream 4SP	1369	Tisma Holdings Inc. Dulles, Va.	N469G
☐ N400MR	78	JetStar 2	5228	Jack Prewitt/Landstar Properties LLC. Bedford, Tx.	N400MP
☐ N400MS	72	Learjet 24D	24D-246	Air Services Inc. Carrollton, Ga.	N500MS
☐ N400MV	00	Beechjet 400A	RK-286	Michigan Veneer Ltd. Pewamo, Mi.	
☐ N400NF	84	Diamond 1A	A091SA	Heartland Management Co. Topeka, Ks.	N400HG
☐ N400NR	76	Sabre-75A	380-41	JHM Leasing Corp. Pittsfield, Ma.	N400N
☐ N400NS	91	Beechjet 400A	RK-28	Hendricks & Partners Aviation LLC. Phoenix, Az.	(N902PC)
☐ N400PC	84	Citation III	650-0057	Tyler Jet LLC. Tyler, Tx.	N31TJ
☐ N400PJ	76	Gulfstream II SP	183	G II Jet Partners LLC. Van Nuys, Ca.	N806WC
☐ N400PR	69	HS 125/400A	NA732	Aircraft Aloft II LLC. Spring, Tx.	N732TS
☐ N400PU	97	Beechjet 400A	RK-156	Purdue Research Foundation, West Lafayette, In.	N2056E
☐ N400RB	99	Citation X	750-0076	JRB Capital LC. Louisville, Ky.	N5197M
☐ N400RE	86	Citation S/II	S550-0093	Evernham Motorsports LLC. Statesville, NC.	N93QS
☐ N400RG	67	B 727-22	19149	MBI Aviation Inc. Wilmington, De. 'Al Bashaer'	N7085U
☐ N400RM	75	Citation Longwing SP	500-0290	RMDD LLC. Oxford, Ms.	N896MB
☐ N400RS	74	Sabre-75A	380-25	R2D2 LLC. Stuart, Fl.	N13NH
☐ N400RY	01	Beechjet 400A	RK-355	Robert Yates Racing Inc. Concord, NC.	N767SB
☐ N400SH	95	Beechjet 400A	RK-100	Oneok Inc. Tulsa, Ok.	N1570B
☐ N400TB	92	Challenger 601-3A	5120	Taco Bell Corp. Santa Ana, Ca.	(N500TB)
☐ N400TE	98	Beechjet 400A	RK-187	Tharaldson Equipment Inc. Fargo, ND.	N2298S
☐ N400TL	01	Beechjet 400A	RK-339	LGI Training LLC. Conroe, Tx.	N439CW
☐ N400UF	82	Diamond 1A	A022SA	Cardi-Air Ambulance Service LLC. San Angelo, Tx.	(N397SL)
☐ N400VC	78	Learjet 25XR	25XR-235	N W Aircraft LLC. San Antonio, Tx.	N400JS
☐ N400VK	90	Beechjet 400A	RK-3	Northport Air Inc. Tuscaloosa, Al.	N400VG
☐ N400VP	96	Beechjet 400A	RK-110	Childress Aviation, Atlanta, Ga.	(N400A)
☐ N400WD	00	CitationJet CJ-2	525A-0002	WD Forty Something LLC. Hillsboro, Or.	N765CT
☐ N400WK	93	Citation VI	650-0231	Truck Body Aviation Inc. Lynchburg, Va.	N67SF

Reg	Yr	Type	c/n	Owner/Operator	Prev Regn
N400WY	85	Gulfstream 3	467	C & S Aviation LLC. Dallas, Tx.	N551AC
N400XP	04	Hawker 400XP	RK-400	Raytheon Aircraft Co. Wichita, Ks.	
N401AJ	74	Learjet 25B	25B-171	Travel Lear Charter Service Inc. Oklahoma City, Ok.	N888LR
N401DP	81	Learjet 25D	25D-329	Palm Air, Memphis, Tn.	N83TE
N401EG	04	Learjet 40	45-2021	Learjet Inc. Wichita, Ks.	
N401FT	03	Gulfstream G400	1523	EJS-Executive Jet Shares Inc. Brazil.	N423GA
N401G	83	Citation 1/SP	501-0320	Young Family Trust, Portola Valley, Ca.	N70467
N401GJ	87	Beechjet 400	RJ-26	C C Medflight Inc. Lawrenceville, Ga.	N91MT
N401HF	03	Gulfstream G550	5039	Central Management Services Inc. Camarillo, Ca.	N939GA
N401JW	75	Falcon 10	46	Hudson Flight Ltd. Pampa, Tx.	N908RF
N401KC	01	Citation Bravo	550-0969	The 401(K) Companies Inc. Austin, Tx.	N5228J
N401KH	95	Citation V Ultra	560-0304	Kindred Healthcare Inc. Louisville, Ky.	N47VC
N401LG	01	CitationJet CJ-2	525A-0037	FB Air LLC/Fletcher Bright Co. Chattanooga, Tn..	N5221Y
N401LJ	02	Learjet 40	45-2001	Wall Design Inc. Irvine, Ca. (Ff 5 Sep 02).	N40LJ
N401MC	89	Citation V	560-0034	Moyer Aviation Inc. Ulysses, Ks.	N895LD
N401NK	99	Challenger 604	5409	PACPAL LLC. Seattle, Wa.	C-GETU
N401QS	00	Gulfstream 4SP	1408	NetJets, Columbus, Oh.	(N448QS)
N401SR	03	Gulfstream G450	4001	Gulfstream Aerospace Corp. Savannah, Ga (Ff 30 Apr 03)	
N401WJ	99	Gulfstream V	599	Avalon Capital Group Inc. La Jolla, Ca.	N496GA
N401WT	93	Astra-1125SP	068	MESH LLC. Hillsboro, Or.	N1125Z
N402AC	66	HS 125/1A-522	25103	Lomax International Inc. Miami, Fl.	N60HU
N402CW	90	Beechjet 400A	RK-2	Flight Options LLC. Cleveland, Oh.	N272BQ
N402DP	81	Learjet 35A	35A-439	Palm Air, Memphis, Tn.	N35LW
N402FB	99	Beechjet 400A	RK-255	Farm Bureau Life Insurance Co. Des Moines, Ia.	N960JJ
N402FG	90	Falcon 900B	87	Flex Air Ltd. Urbana, Il.	N33GG
N402FT	03	Gulfstream G400	1527	EJS-Executive Jet Shares Inc. Brazil.	N327GA
N402GS	93	Beechjet 400A	RK-71	Commonwealth Aviation Services Inc. Richmond, Va.	N73BL
N402JP	95	Gulfstream 4SP	1283	Colleen Corp. Philadelphia, Pa.	N401JL
N402LM	03	Gulfstream G200	082	Lockheed Martin Corp. Baltimore, Md.	N282GA
N403CB	85	Citation III	650-0099	403CB LLC. Glenview, Il.	N26SD
N403CW	95	Beechjet 400A	RK-103	Flight Options LLC. Cleveland, Oh.	(N422LX)
N403DP	81	Learjet 35A	35A-446	Palm Air, Memphis, Tn.	N794GC
N403ET	99	Citation V Ultra	560-0535	Yardelle Investment Management LLC. Fort Worth, Tx.	(N57ML)
N403FW	81	Learjet 35A	35A-403	All American Jet Inc. Hudson, Fl.	N100HW
N403LM	03	Gulfstream G200	083	Lockheed Martin Corp. Baltimore, Md.	N283GA
N403QS	99	Gulfstream 4SP	1403	NetJets, Columbus, Oh.	N403GA
N403SR	03	Gulfstream G450	4003	Gulfstream Aerospace Corp. Savannah, Ga. (Ff 22 Jul 03).	
N403TB	03	Gulfstream 4	1191	TB Aviation LLC. Westminster, Md.	N317MB
N403W	84	Westwind-1124	403	NIBCO Inc. Elkhart, In.	4X-CUH
N403WY	82	Challenger 600S	1059	K-N Partners LLC. Houston, Tx.	N103HB
N404A	99	Falcon 900EX	56	BellSouth Corp. Atlanta-Fulton County, Ga.	N956EX
N404AC	99	Gulfstream 4SP	1384	Apache Corp. Houston, Tx.	(HZ-KS3)
N404BL	03	Hawker 400XP	RK-367	Bausch & Lomb Inc. Rochester, NY.	
N404BT	99	Citation Excel	560-5038	BellSouth Corp. Atlanta-Fulton County, Ga.	N5214K
N404F	99	Falcon 900EX	49	WCF-William C Ford Aircraft Corp. Detroit, Mi.	N949EX
N404G	90	Citation V	560-0095	Cushing Stone Co. Amsterdam, NY.	N707CV
N404HS	99	Gulfstream 4SP	1404	H & S Ventures LLC. Newport Beach, Ca.	N404HA
N404JW	74	Falcon 10	29	Hudson Flight Ltd. Pampa, Tx.	N999F
N404KS	81	Citation II	550-0334	Bentley Aviation LLC. Columbia, SC.	(N755BP)
N404M	00	Gulfstream V	654	Bristol-Myers Squibb Co. White Plains, NY.	VP-BLA
N404MK	03	Learjet 40	45-2003	Keller Uchida Realty Resources LLC. Portland, Or.	
N404MM	00	Citation Excel	560-5161	Martin Marietta Materials Inc. Raleigh, NC.	N.....
N404MS	00	Beechjet 400A	RK-283	Mississippi State University Foundation, Starkville, Ms.	N600SB
N404QS	96	Gulfstream 4SP	1304	NetJets, Columbus, Oh.	N436GA
N404R	00	Falcon 900EX	81	BellSouth Corp. Atlanta-Fulton County, Ga.	N404N
N404RP	78	Citation II	550-0024	Blue Horizon LLC. Kalamazoo, Mi.	N413CK
N404SB	00	Citation Excel	560-5069	BellSouth Corp. Atlanta-Fulton County, Ga.	N5201M
N404SJ	03	SJ 30-2	004	Sino Swearingen Aircraft Co. San Antonio, Tx.	N709JB
N404SS	97	Dornier Do328JET	3090	BellSouth Corp. Atlanta-Fulton County, Ga.	D-CDYY
N404ST	03	Falcon 900C	200	The Travelers Indemnity Co. Windsor Locks, Ct.	N207FJ
N404VL	00	Global Express	9085	The Von Liebig Office Inc. Naples, Fl.	N700GQ
N404WC	68	Jet Commander-A	128	Aquarius Air LLC. Roanoke, Va.	(N386JM)
N404XT	99	Gulfstream 4SP	1366	XTO Energy Corp. Fort Worth, Tx.	N404M
N405CC	96	Challenger 800	7099	Carnival Cruise Lines/Fun Air Corp. Fort Lauderdale, Fl.	N305CC
N405CW	00	Beechjet 400A	RK-305	Flight Options LLC. Cleveland, Oh.	(N466LX)
N405DC	81	Falcon 50	42	Tower Operating LLC. Oklahoma City, Ok.	N185BA

Reg	Yr	Type	c/n	Owner/Operator	Prev Regn
❑ N405DW	81	HS 125/700A	7130	Leaseco Aviation Inc. Orangevale, Ca.	N405TP
❑ N405FX	99	Learjet 45	45-026	BBJS/FlexJets, Addison, Tx.	
❑ N405GJ	80	Learjet 35A	35A-354	Pinnacle Towers Inc. Sarasota, Fl.	N212GA
❑ N405HG	01	Gulfstream V	661	Kimberly-Clark Corp. Dallas, Tx.	N561GA
❑ N405JW	66	Falcon 20-5	54	Black Creek Partners Inc. Plano, Tx.	N380RA
❑ N405LM	98	Gulfstream V	541	Lockheed Martin Corp. Baltimore, Md.	N641GA
❑ N405PC	89	Learjet 35A	35A-651	Ventures Acquisition LLC. McMinnville, Or.	HB-VJK
❑ N406CW	90	Beechjet 400A	RK-6	Flight Options LLC. Cleveland, Oh.	N401EE
❑ N406FX	00	Learjet 45	45-089	BBJS/FlexJets, Addison, Tx.	
❑ N406PW	74	Sabre-75A	380-2	P & W Aviation Inc. Wilmington, NC.	N642TS
❑ N406TS	85	Beechjet 400	RJ-6	Teton Aviation Inc. Teton Village, Wy. (was A1006SA).	YV-838CP
❑ N406VJ	90	Citation V	560-0056	Montana Jet LLC. Bozeman, Mt.	N560AE
❑ N407CW	00	Beechjet 400A	RK-307	Flight Options LLC. Cleveland, Oh.	(N467LX)
❑ N407GC	94	Gulfstream 4SP	1242	Brokerage & Management Corp. NYC.	N982HC
❑ N407RA	95	Learjet 31A	31A-103	Renar Charter Services LLC. Jensen Beach, Fl.	N766AJ
❑ N407W	84	Westwind-Two	407	Cross Creek Aviation Inc. Dallas, Tx.	4X-CUK
❑ N408CW	96	Beechjet 400A	RK-108	Flight Options LLC. Cleveland, Oh.	(N424LX)
❑ N408JD	84	Citation III	650-0035	Eagle Jets LLC. Jonesboro, Ga.	N400JD
❑ N408LN	01	Gulfstream G200	036	Gulfstream Aerospace LP. Dallas-Love, Tx.	N408LM
❑ N408MG	80	Learjet 35A	35A-328	Millenium Air Xpress, Van Nuys, Ca.	N392JP
❑ N408PC*	01	Beechjet 400A	RK-325	Pridgeon & Clay Inc. Grand Rapids, Mi.	N275BC
❑ N408QS	96	Gulfstream 4SP	1308	NetJets, Columbus, Oh.	N446GA
❑ N409AV	98	Hawker 800XP	8347	Avjet Corp. Burbank, Ca.	N40PL
❑ N409FX	99	Learjet 45	45-095	BBJS/FlexJets, Addison, Tx.	
❑ N409GB	03	Citation Sovereign	680-0006	Green Bay Packaging Inc. Green Bay, Wi.	N5264U
❑ N409GL	73	Sabre-40A	282-122	SabreJet LLC. Jacksonville-Craig, Fl.	N188PS
❑ N409KC	90	Challenger 601-3A	5075	VoltronAir LLC. St Louis, Mo.	N601Z
❑ N409LM	02	Gulfstream G200	059	Lockheed Martin Corp. Baltimore, Md.	(OY-RAK)
❑ N409S	75	Citation Eagle	500-0238	NMJ Group LLC. Albuquerque, NM.	VP-CON
❑ N409ST	87	Citation II	550-0559	Jesscom International LLC. Fort Lauderdale. (was 551-0559)	OO-MMP
❑ N409WT	63	Jet Commander	3	GeoCom Enterprises Inc. Fort Lauderdale, Fl.	N400WT
❑ N410BD	84	Learjet 35A	35A-594	Oxford LLC. Easton, Md.	OY-LJA
❑ N410CW	01	Beechjet 400A	RK-310	Flight Options LLC. Cleveland, Oh.	(N468LX)
❑ N410DM	92	Citation V	560-0184	Dibrell Brothers Tobacco Co. Danville, Va.	N873DB
❑ N410DW	89	Citation V	560-0021	GordonAir Inc. Johnson City, Tn.	N669AJ
❑ N410FX	00	Learjet 45	45-101	BBJS/FlexJets, Addison, Tx.	
❑ N410LM	99	Gulfstream V	578	Lockheed Martin Corp. Baltimore, Md.	N21GN
❑ N410M	99	Gulfstream V	575	Bristol-Myers Squibb Co. White Plains, NY.	N475GA
❑ N410NA	97	Citation V Ultra	560-0435	Noble Energy Inc. Houston, Tx.	N52352
❑ N410WW	99	Global Express	9047	William Wrigley/Zeno Air Inc. Chicago, Il.	C-GFLU
❑ N411AJ	04	Learjet 40	45-2011	My Jet LLC. Scottsdale, Az.	N51001
❑ N411BA	82	Learjet 35	35-024	Divine Aviation LLC. Van Nuys, Ca.	N241RT
❑ N411FB	66	HS 125/1A-522	25074	Florida Football Enterprises Inc. Fort Lauderdale, Fl.	N300GB
❑ N411FX	00	Learjet 45	45-102	BBJS/FlexJets, Addison, Tx.	
❑ N411GA	73	HS 125/600A	6024	Arnoni Aviation Ltd. Houston, Tx. (status ?).	N669SC
❑ N411HB	85	Westwind-Two	419	Alcole Enterprises LLC. Woodland Hills, Ca.	N51MN
❑ N411MY	03	CitationJet CJ-1	525-0512	Sweatmore Air LLC. Scottsdale, Az.	N.....
❑ N411PA	77	HS 125/700A	NA0211	Boca Airplane Leasing Corp/PAS Inc. Boca Raton, Fl.	(N602JJ)
❑ N411QS	96	Gulfstream 4SP	1311	NetJets, Columbus, Oh.	N449GA
❑ N411RE	82	Diamond 1A	A016SA	A La Jet LLC. Oklahoma City, Ok.	N706JH
❑ N411SK	00	Learjet 60	60-201	Bombardier Aerospace Corp. Windsor Locks, Ct.	N411ST
❑ N411SP	83	Diamond 1A	A049SA	Olympia Investments Inc. Pleasanton, Ca.	XA-SOD
❑ N411ST	04	Challenger 300	20031	Benson Football Inc. Metairie, La.	N131LJ
❑ N411TJ	83	Challenger 601	3010	Idaho Rivers LLC. Mountain View, Ca.	N601BD
❑ N411WW	92	Gulfstream 4SP	1203	William Wrigley/Zeno Air Inc. Chicago, Il.	N410WW
❑ N412AB	84	Falcon 200	492	Arkansas Best Corp. Fort Smith, Ar.	N803F
❑ N412DP	82	HS 125/700A	NA0312	Commercial Defeasance LLC. Charlotte, NC.	N500GS
❑ N412ET	02	Citation Bravo	550-1041	E T MacKenzie LLC. Grand Ledge, Mi.	N5206T
❑ N412FX	00	Learjet 45	45-103	BBJS/FlexJets, Addison, Tx.	
❑ N412JT*	71	Gulfstream II SP	101	Diamond Air Inc. Richmond Heights, Oh.	N512JT
❑ N412PE	84	Citation II	550-0483	Summit Express Inc. San Jose, Ca.	N483SC
❑ N412SE	81	Citation 1/SP	501-0225	Richard Carroll, Newport Beach, Ca.	TG-KIT
❑ N413CK	92	Citation V	560-0194	American Proteins Inc. Cumming, Ga.	N852WC
❑ N413LC	90	Learjet 35A	35A-659	CP Transportation Inc. Gillespie Field, San Diego, Ca.	(N878LP)
❑ N413QS	03	Gulfstream G400	1521	NetJets, Columbus, Oh.	N221GA
❑ N414CC	02	Falcon 2000	206	Med Equip Inc/Forest Health Industries, Grand Rapids, Mi.	N2319

Reg	Yr	Type	c/n	Owner/Operator	Prev Regn
N414DH	03	Gulfstream G200	081	AirBill Inc. Portsmouth, NH.	N881GA
N414DK	00	Gulfstream G200	023	Sterling Advisors LP. Northbrook, Il.	N414DH
N414FW	02	CitationJet CJ-2	525A-0081	Direct Air Charters LLC. Lumberton, NJ.	N51342
N414FX	00	Learjet 45	45-111	BBJS/FlexJets, Addison, Tx.	
N414KD	03	Gulfstream G200	084	Oakmont Corp. Los Angeles, Ca.	N284GA
N414KL	84	Learjet 35A	35A-595	Krueger International Inc. Green Bay, Wi.	N85PM
N414PE	87	BAe 125/800A	8090	Palikea Eheu LLC. Laguna Beach, Ca.	N901RP
N414RF	79	HS 125/700A	NA0244	Hollywood Aviation Inc. Burbank, Ca.	N230DP
N414TE	01	390 Premier 1	RB-4	TyRose Investments Inc. Wilmington, De.	N842PM
N415AJ	89	Citation II	550-0600	Tulip Aviation Inc. Granville, Il.	PT-LSR
N415BJ	94	Hawker 800	8257	Planemasters Ltd. DuPage, Il.	N802DC
N415CS	99	CitationJet CJ-1	525-0373	Wilson Construction Co. Canby, Or.	
N415FW	99	Citation X	750-0095	Mile High Aircraft LLC. Chicago, Il.	
N415FX	00	Learjet 45	45-112	BBJS/FlexJets, Addison, Tx.	
N415LJ	66	Learjet 23	23-092	Skycare Inc. Smyrna, Tn.	N344WC
N415NP	93	Learjet 60	60-024	Nie Planes LLC. Boise, Id.	LV-WFM
N415PG	94	Gulfstream 4SP	1238	Parkside Aviation Corp. San Francisco, Ca.	(N92LU)
N415TH	84	Westwind-Two	415	Leetwood North LLC/R W Leet Electric Inc. Kalamazoo, Mi.	N415EL
N415WW	93	Gulfstream 4SP	1226	1226 Enterprises LLC. Burbank, Ca.	N50MG
N416BA	96	Citation V Ultra	560-0359	Business Air LLC. Cleveland, Oh.	ZS-SMB
N416BD	02	Challenger 604	5548	Glenoak LLC. Boston, Ma.	N548LP
N416CC	82	Citation II	550-0416	Berry Leasing Co LP. Madera, Ca.	N12167
N416CG	76	Gulfstream 2	180	Kingsway Aviation Inc. Wilmington, De.	N702JA
N416FX	00	Learjet 45	45-113	BBJS/FlexJets, Addison, Tx.	
N416HF	90	Citation V	560-0037	Norcross Helicopters Inc. Rochester, NY.	N17LK
N416KC	01	Falcon 50EX	318	Spenaero Inc. Salt Lake City, Ut.	F-WWHX
N416KD	78	Gulfstream 2	231	KDF Corp. Dallas-Love, Tx.	N47EC
N416QS	97	Gulfstream 4SP	1316	NetJets, Columbus, Oh.	N427GA
N416SJ	72	JetStar-731	5153	World Jet Inc. Fort Lauderdale, Fl.	N416KD
N416WM	86	Gulfstream 3	487	ADI/Hi Flite Inc. Rochester Hills, Mi.	N618KM
N417AM	85	Learjet 55	55-123	Florida Jet Service Inc. Fort Lauderdale, Fl.	N150NE
N417BA	79	Learjet 35A	35A-257	MCA-Midwest Corporate Aviation Lear 24 LP. Wichita, Ks.	N275DJ
N417CL	92	Challenger 601-3A	5107	EDS Information Services LLC. Dallas, Tx.	C-GLWZ
N417CW	91	Beechjet 400A	RK-17	Flight Options LLC. Cleveland, Oh.	(N401LX)
N417EK	72	Gulfstream II SP	110	East Harris County Othopaedic Association, Houston, Tx.	N92AG
N417FX	00	Learjet 45	45-114	BBJS/FlexJets, Addison, Tx.	
N417JD	01	Citation Excel	560-5231	TVPX Inc. Concord, Ma.	N231XL
N417KT	84	Diamond 1A	A083SA	Jet Linx Aviation Corp. Omaha, Ne.	N83TK
N417KW	00	Citation Bravo	550-0933	AeroSolutions Group Inc. Bethesda, Md.	N5262X
N417Q*	00	CitationJet CJ-1	525-0385	Wing and a Prayer Inc/Glass Aviation Inc. San Jose, Ca.	N417C
N417RC	85	Citation S/II	S550-0055	Crossland Aviation LLC. Basalt, Co.	N87FL
N417WW	68	Learjet 24	24-171	Artemis Aviation Group LLC. Wilmington, De.	N737FN
N418CA	75	Learjet 36A	36A-018		PT-ACC
N418CW	91	Beechjet 400A	RK-18	Flight Options LLC. Cleveland, Oh.	(N402LX)
N418FX	00	Learjet 45	45-120	BBJS/FlexJets, Addison, Tx.	
N418KC	96	CitationJet	525-0130	First Interstate Bancsystem Inc. Billings, Mt.	N416KC
N418MG	88	Beechjet 400	RJ-54	Florida Air LLC. Jacksonville, Fl.	XB-FDH
N418MN	01	Learjet 45	45-130	Aerometro LLC. Houston, Tx.	N4001G
N418QA	87	Gulfstream 4	1018	Quest Softair Inc. Santa Ana, Ca.	N43KS
N418RD	77	HS 125/700A	NA0210	Rubloff Aviation LLC. Rockford, Il.	OY-JPJ
N418SG	03	Gulfstream G550	5040	Indigo Management Co. Van Nuys, Ca.	N940GA
N419CW	91	Beechjet 400A	RK-19	Flight Options LLC. Cleveland, Oh.	(N405LX)
N419FX	00	Learjet 45	45-125	BBJS/FlexJets, Addison, Tx.	
N419MB	94	Beechjet 400A	RK-85	All Services Inc. Overland Park, Ks.	N419MS
N419MS	70	Gulfstream II SP	81	Rubin Consulting Group Inc. Arlington Heights, Il.	N151SD
N419TK	00	Astra-1125SPX	122	419 Flight LLC. Chicago, Il.	(N297GA)
N419WC	74	Falcon 10	11	Willow Creek Association, Barrington, Il.	(N11WC)
N420CC	91	Gulfstream 4	1164	KaiserAir Inc. Oakland, Ca.	N300GX
N420CE	01	Gulfstream G100	139	Ceridian Corp. Minneapolis, Mn.	N100GA
N420CH	01	CitationJet CJ-2	525A-0027	Four Twenty Charlie LLC/CRH Investments, Fife, Wa.	N5194J
N420CL	79	Falcon 50	10	Channelock Inc. Franklin-Venango Regional, Pa.	N65B
N420DH	01	Beechjet 400A	RK-326	Duc Housing Partners Inc. Los Gatos, Ca.	N749RH
N420DM	97	Citation V Ultra	560-0464	Platt Electric Supply Inc. Beaverton, Or.	
N420FX	00	Learjet 45	45-126	BBJS/FlexJets, Addison, Tx.	
N420GL	78	Falcon 20F	391	Channelock Inc. Meadville, Pa.	N420CL
N420HA	03	HA-420 HondaJet	P001	Honda R & D Americas Inc. Union, Oh. (Ff 3 Dec 2003)	

Reg	Yr	Type	c/n	Owner/Operator	Prev Regn
N420JC	81	Gulfstream 3	326	James McMahan, Van Nuys, Ca.	(N326DD)
N420JM	81	Westwind-1124	363	River East Transportation Inc. Chicago, Il.	(N723JM)
N420KK	00	Falcon 900EX	84	Krispy Kreme Doughnut Corp. Winston-Salem, NC.	(N82KK)
N420PC	81	Citation 1/SP	501-0237	Jon Veechie, Green Bay, Wi.	(N712VE)
N420QS	97	Gulfstream 4SP	1320	NetJets, Columbus, Oh.	N437GA
N420RC	82	Gulfstream 3	354	MTF Corp. Coral Gables, Fl.	N16NK
N420ST	88	Challenger 601-3A	5027	Card Aeronautics LLC. Kansas City, Mo.	N420SZ
N421AL	00	Global Express	9051	Ann Lurie Revocable Trust, Chicago, Il.	N700DZ
N421FX	01	Learjet 45	45-145	BBJS/FlexJets, Addison, Tx.	N50145
N421SZ	00	Global Express	9056	Equity Group Investments LLC. Chicago-Midway, Il.	N700DU
N422AB	02	Citation Excel	560-5285	ABF Aviation LLC/Arkansas Best Corp. Fort Smith, Ar.	N285XL
N422BC	84	Citation III	650-0024	Bradley Fixtures Corp. Menomonee Falls, Wi.	N650SL
N422CP	99	Learjet 60	60-171	Pohlad Companies Inc. Minneapolis, Mn.	
N422CW	91	Beechjet 400A	RK-22	Flight Options LLC. Cleveland, Oh.	(N404LX)
N422DA	77	Citation 1/SP	501-0051	Dominion Citation Group LC. Richmond, Va.	N303CB
N422FX	01	Learjet 45	45-135	BBJS/FlexJets, Addison, Tx.	N4004Y
N422ML	99	Gulfstream 4SP	1367	Premiere Radio Networks, Sherman Oaks, Ca.	(HZ-KS2)
N422QS	97	Gulfstream 4SP	1322	NetJets, Columbus, Oh.	N445GA
N422TK	83	Gulfstream 3	395	T-Bird Aviation Inc. Tampa, Fl.	N395EJ
N422X	79	HS 125/700A	NA0253	Carl Reichardt/KaiserAir Inc. Oakland, Ca.	(N831CJ)
N423FX	01	Learjet 45	45-134	BBJS/FlexJets, Addison, Tx.	N4004Q
N423SJ	88	BAe 125/800A	NA0423	American Seafoods Group LLC. Seattle, Wa.	N204SM
N424BT	89	Beechjet 400	RJ-62	B J Tidwell Industries Inc. San Antonio, Tx.	N333RS
N424CJ	04	CitationJet CJ-2	525A-0224	Cessna Aircraft Co. Wichita, Ks.	N5264N
N424CS	79	Westwind-1124	255	Sam Susser, Corpus Christi, Tx.	N202MW
N424DA	72	Citation	500-0029	Bodmer Financing Co. Zurich, Switzerland.	C-GDWN
N424FX	01	Learjet 45	45-146	BBJS/FlexJets, Addison, Tx.	
N424HH	04	Citation Excel XLS	560-5534	Cessna Aircraft Co. Wichita, Ks.	N5165P
N424JR	84	Westwind-Two	405	Allan Kanner & Assocs LLC. New Orleans, La.	N420CE
N424KW	99	Learjet 60	60-153	Kennard Warfield Jr. Dulles, Va.	(N235BX)
N424LB	85	Citation III	650-0076	Jet Flight Services Inc. Wilmington, De.	XA-SEP
N424MP	00	Astra-1125SPX	129	El Portal SA.	N52GX
N424QS	98	Gulfstream 4SP	1324	NetJets, Columbus, Oh.	N457GA
N424R	74	Sabre-75A	380-15	Roblene Enterprises Inc. Ormond Beach, Fl.	N22JW
N424RJ	77	HS 125/700A	7010	Rickell Aircraft Enterprises inc. Austin, Tx.	N425RJ
N424RS	72	Learjet 24D	24D-258	Aloha Jet Inc. Bear, De.	(N24DZ)
N424TG	81	Citation II	550-0258	TD Air LLC. Allegheny County, Pa.	N550PR
N424TV	96	CitationJet	525-0145	Darrold Cannan Jr. Wichita Falls, Tx.	N145CJ
N424XT	74	Falcon 20-5B	316	XTO Energy Corp. Fort Worth, Tx.	N242CT
N425AS	80	Learjet 35A	35A-281	Jetlease LLC. Fargo, ND.	N425M
N425CW	01	Beechjet 400A	RK-345	Flight Options LLC. Cleveland, Oh.	(N474LX)
N425FX	01	Learjet 45	45-147	BBJS/FlexJets, Addison, Tx.	
N425JF	66	Falcon 20C	64	Kendall Aircraft Sales Inc. Sarasota, Fl.	N513AG
N425JL	73	Learjet 25B	25B-127	Dolphin Aviation Inc. Sarasota, Fl.	N222AK
N425M	92	Learjet 31A	31A-055	GEICO Corp. Washington, DC.	N666RE
N425RA	81	Learjet 25D	25D-351	Ryan Leasing Inc. Wichita, Ks.	N425RH
N425RJ	83	Falcon 200	484	Fant Aircraft Enterprises LLC. Houston, Tx.	N24JG
N425SA	81	Learjet 35A	35A-425	Symbolic Aviation Inc. Holly Lake Ranch, Tx.	N111KZ
N425SD	77	HS 125/700A	NA0212	448 Alliance Corp. Fort Worth, Tx.	(N125MJ)
N425WN	86	Challenger 601	3052	Navellier Management Ltd. Reno, Nv.	VP-CRX
N426CF	97	Challenger 604	5338	Montgomery Capital of Delaware LLC. Fort Washington, Pa.	N70RP
N426CM	00	Citation X	750-0117	VMD Aviation LLC/Flannery Properties, Portland, Or.	N50612
N426ED	00	CitationJet CJ-1	525-0426	Sunseeker Air Inc. Bend, Or.	N5197A
N426FX	01	Learjet 45	45-142	BBJS/FlexJets, Addison, Tx.	
N426JN	98	Learjet 60	60-142	J P Air Charter Inc. Ontario, Ca.	N642LJ
N426PF	89	Challenger 601-3A	5046	Sagitta LLC. Waukegan, Il.	N818TY
N426QS	00	Gulfstream 4SP	1426	NetJets, Columbus, Oh.	N426GA
N426RJ	77	Westwind-1124	218	TL Marketing LLC. Pleasant View, Tn.	N425RJ
N426TA	69	Learjet 24B	24B-181	Windwalker Aero Corp. Naperville, Il.	N254JT
N427CD	02	Citation Encore	560-0633	CD Exploration Inc/CDX Gas Co. Addison, Tx.	(N860Q)
N427CJ	75	Falcon 10	67	Superior Transportation Inc. Sioux City, Ia.	D-COME
N427CW	90	Beechjet 400A	RK-27	Flight Options LLC. Cleveland, Oh.	(N405LX)
N427SS	84	Citation 1/SP	501-0681	Sierra Sierra Enterprises Inc. Minden, Nv.	N82LS
N427TL*	81	Learjet 55	55-006	Marantha Transportation LLC. Rancho Mirage, Ca.	N228PK
N428AS	02	Gulfstream 4SP	1487	Market Air LLC. Virginia Beach, Va.	N487GA
N428CC	91	Falcon 50	225	Colony Capital LLC. Oklahoma City, Ok.	N32TC
Reg	Yr	Type	c/n	Owner/Operator	Prev Regn

Reg	Yr	Type	c/n	Owner/Operator	Prev Regn
N428DA	64	JetStar-6	5048	814K LLC. Pleasant View, Tn.	(N130LW)
N428FX	01	Learjet 45	45-164	BBJS/FlexJets, Addison, Tx.	
N428JD	86	Beechjet 400	RJ-13	Dewberry Air LLC. Dover, De.	(N400TN)
N428M	99	Gulfstream 4SP	1382	Swiflite Aircraft Corp. Burbank, Ca.	N1GC
N428QS	97	Gulfstream 4SP	1328	NetJets, Columbus, Oh.	N328GA
N428RJ	73	Citation	500-0082	Marathon Aircraft Inc. Little Rock, Ar.	N482RJ
N428WE	93	Beechjet 400A	RK-72	BMSB Inc/Burger Management South Bend Inc. South Bend, In.	N910SH
N429DA	66	HS 125/1B-S522	25090	American Aircraft Sales International Inc. Fl. (status ?).	N102TW
N429FX	01	Learjet 45	45-165	BBJS/FlexJets, Addison, Tx.	
N429SA	96	Gulfstream 4SP	1314	USAA, San Antonio, Tx.	N461GA
N430CW	91	Beechjet 400A	RK-30	Flight Options LLC. Cleveland, Oh.	(N406LX)
N430FX	01	Learjet 45	45-166	BBJS/FlexJets, Addison, Tx.	
N430GR	01	CitationJet CJ-1	525-0430	American Land Development Corp. Hoover, Al.	N52081
N430JH	04	CitationJet CJ-1	525-0530	Harvey Aircraft LLC. Flora, Ms.	N5244F
N430JW	74	Learjet 24XR	24XR-285	Magnolia River Development LLC. Summerdale, Al.	N995DR
N430LR	92	BAe 1000A	9030	Raytheon Aircraft Co. Wichita, Ks.	N530QS
N430MP	73	Sabre-40A	282-113	Nautical Science Foundation, Fort Lauderdale, Fl.	N430MB
N430PT	85	Westwind-1124	430	P T Air LLC. Seattle, Wa.	N430BJ
N430SA	94	Citation VII	650-7041	USAA, San Antonio, Tx.	(N449SA)
N431AS	81	Learjet 35A	35A-431	Gill Aviation LLC/Restoration St Louis Inc. St Louis, Mo.	N431CW
N431BC	89	Learjet 31	31-005	Bovis Construction Corp. Charlotte, NC.	(N963Y)
N431CB	94	Challenger 601-3R	5164	C R Bard Inc. Morristown, NJ.	N164CC
N431CW	91	Beechjet 400A	RK-31	Flight Options LLC. Cleveland, Oh.	(N407LX)
N431FX	01	Learjet 45	45-177	BBJS/FlexJets, Addison, Tx.	
N431JT	84	Gulfstream 3	417	Hunters Glen Inc/TTG Enterprises Ltd. Dallas, Tx.	N300M
N431YD	01	CitationJet CJ-1	525-0431	Farrish Air LLC. Richmond, Va.	N51993
N432AC	04	Citation X	750-0231	Apache Aviation Inc. Houston, Tx.	N5190R
N432AQ	89	BAe 125/800A	NA0434	Apache Corp. Houston, Tx.	N432AC
N432CC	79	Sabre-65	465-6	Tonkawa Inc/Carlson Companies Inc. St Paul, Mn.	N2CC
N432CJ	01	CitationJet CJ-2	525A-0043	PT Air LLC. Murrels Inlet, SC.	N52002
N432CW	91	Beechjet 400A	RK-32	Flight Options LLC. Cleveland, Oh.	(N408LX)
N432FX	01	Learjet 45	45-197	BBJS/FlexJets, Addison, Tx.	
N432JW	78	Learjet 36A	36A-043	Medivac Partners LLC. Bellevue, Wa.	(N143JW)
N432MC	02	Challenger 604	5532	United of Omaha Life Insurance Co. Omaha, Ne.	N532DM
N432RJ	01	Citation Bravo	550-0967	Directors Air Corp. Abilene, Tx.	N967CB
N433DD	78	Learjet 35A	35A-161	Business Jet Leasing Inc. Salt Lake City, Ut.	YV-65CP
N433FX	01	Learjet 45	45-192	BBJS/FlexJets, Addison, Tx.	
N433GM	85	Westwind-Two	433	Meir Inc. Hartford, Ct.	N433WR
N433LF	84	Citation III	650-0027	LCG Transportation LLC/TCL Realty Inc. Naples, Fl.	N650NY
N434FX	02	Learjet 45	45-212	BBJS/FlexJets, Addison, Tx.	N50111
N434SB	82	Citation II	550-0426	Air Century Inc. Tampa, Fl.	(N426VP)
N434UM	74	Citation	500-0190	Marlin Air Inc. Detroit, Mi.	N602BC
N435CW	92	Beechjet 400A	RK-35	Icon Corporate Air LLC. Las Vegas, Nv.	(N409LX)
N435GA	03	Gulfstream G400	1535	Gulfstream Aerospace Corp. Savannah, Ga.	
N435GM	73	Gulfstream II SP	137	RMQ Ltd-Reaud, Morgan & Quinn Inc. Beaumont, Tx.	N485GM
N435JF	97	Falcon 2000	47	JF Aircraft Corp. Dearborn, Mi.	N800BL
N435JL	75	Learjet 35	35-018	White Industries Inc. Bates City, Mo. (status ?).	(N435EC)
N435MS	76	Learjet 35	35-054	Monte Sol Jet Inc. Santa Fe, NM.	N109MC
N435T	00	Falcon 900EX	63	Tribune Co. Chicago-Midway, Il.	N900EX
N435UJ	75	Learjet 35	35-025	E H R Aviation Inc. Ponte Vedra Beach, Fl.	(N188JA)
N436QS	00	Gulfstream 4SP	1436	NetJets, Columbus, Oh.	N436GA
N437CW	99	Beechjet 400A	RK-237	Flight Options LLC. Cleveland, Oh.	(N443LX)
N437GA	00	Gulfstream 4SP	1437	National Air Services, Jeddah, Saudi Arabia.	
N437MC	02	Challenger 604	5537	United of Omaha Life Insurance Co. Omaha, Ne.	N537DR
N437SJ	86	Westwind-Two	437	Davison Transport Inc. Ruston, La.	N437WW
N438LX	98	Beechjet 400A	RK-202	Flight Options LLC. Cleveland, Oh.	N742TA
N438MC	97	Citation V Ultra	560-0438	Contract Transport Inc. Indianapolis, In.	(PT-WQE)
N438PM	99	Hawker 800XP	8425	Carpau Corp. Tarpon Springs, Fl.	N89BR
N438SP	99	Citation Bravo	550-0882	Southern Pipe & Supply Co. Meridian, Ms.	N12MA
N439WW	86	Westwind-Two	439	Cimarex Energy Co. Denver, Co.	4X-CUG
N440AS	99	Falcon 2000	102	American Standard Co/Amstan Air Inc. Teterboro, NJ.	N515TK
N440BC	70	HS 125/400A	NA744	Boles Parts Supply Inc/BPS Aviation LLC. Atlanta, Ga.	N711BP
N440CE	00	Citation Bravo	550-0937	Elizabeth Prothro, Wichita Falls, Tx.	N51666
N440CW	92	Beechjet 400A	RK-40	Flight Options LLC. Cleveland, Oh.	(N410LX)
N440DM	81	Learjet 55	55-005	MBK Aviation Services LLC. Fort Lauderdale, Fl.	(N94TJ)
N440DS	90	Beechjet 400A	RK-8	Carolina's of Charleston LLC. Charleston, SC.	

Reg	Yr	Type	c/n	Owner/Operator	Prev Regn

Reg	Yr	Type	c/n	Owner/Operator	Prev Regn
☐ N440KT	72	Learjet 24D	24D-249	Spirit Wing Aviation Ltd. Guthrie, Ok.	N249RA
☐ N440MC	83	Learjet 35A	35A-495	McClane Company Inc. Temple, Tx.	
☐ N440RC	00	Beechjet 400A	RK-269	Rineco Chemical Industries Inc. Little Rock, Ar.	N400MR
☐ N440RD	72	HS 125/F403B	25270	Rubloff Aviation LLC. Rockford, Il.	N400GP
☐ N440TC	89	Gulfstream 4	1115	Meridian Services Inc. Teterboro, NY.	N410MY
☐ N441BC	89	Astra-1125	033	JB Holdings LLC. Anchorage, Ak.	N52KS
☐ N441PC	92	Learjet 35A	35A-668	Allmetal Inc. Wheeling, Il.	N9168Q
☐ N441QS	98	Gulfstream 4SP	1341	NetJets, Columbus, Oh.	N341GA
☐ N441TC	74	Citation	500-0140	Lee Petrutsas, Brackettville, Tx.	N4ZK
☐ N442CW	92	Beechjet 400A	RK-42	Flight Options LLC. Cleveland, Oh.	(N411LX)
☐ N442JB	73	Citation	500-0117	Tom Dean, Long Beach, Ca.	N161WC
☐ N442KM	85	Citation S/II	S550-0060	N/S One LLC/Aero Film, Santa Monica, Ca.	N260QS
☐ N442LW	01	Citation Bravo	550-1028	Wachob Leasing Co/U S Aviation Co. Tulsa, Ok.	N.....
☐ N442NR	04	Citation Bravo	550-1078	Refuse Equipment Manufacturing, Riyadh, Saudi Arabia.	N.....
☐ N442QG	73	Gulfstream 2	133	Wing Aviation Inc. Conroe, Tx.	N444QG
☐ N442RM	74	Sabre-60	306-73	Private Manufacturing Inc. Austin, Tx.	XA-TNW
☐ N442SR	03	Gulfstream G450	4002	Gulfstream Aerospace Corp. Savannah, Ga. (Ff 12 Jun 03).	
☐ N442WJ	99	Citation X	750-0099	Cessna Aircraft Co. Wichita, Ks.	N442WT
☐ N442WT	04	Citation X	750-0233	Wilson Trailer Co. Sioux City, Ia.	N51612
☐ N443M	00	Hawker 800XP	8519	O'Gara Aviation LLC. Atlanta, Ga.	
☐ N443RK	75	Learjet 35	35-023	Florida Jet Center, Fort Lauderdale, Fl.	N886CS
☐ N444CR	75	Falcon 10	45	Chelsea Enterprises LLC/Air Repair Inc. Easton, Md.	C-FTEN
☐ N444CW	84	Citation III	650-0064	Lithia Aircraft Inc. Medford, Or.	N650TC
☐ N444CX	00	Citation X	750-0125	Bitz Aviation Inc. Allegheny County, Pa.	N5061W
☐ N444EA	04	Citation Bravo	550-1079	Edgar Aviation LLC. Kansas City, Ks.	N1271B
☐ N444EP	85	Westwind-Two	436	Brothers Equipment Leasing LLC. Charlotte, NC.	N100AK
☐ N444EX	95	Citation VII	650-7056	M D C Holdings Inc. Denver, Co.	N60PL
☐ N444G	81	Citation II	550-0209	Thomas F Mitts MD Inc/Wadwelle Inc. Visalia, Ca.	(N877GB)
☐ N444GA	80	Gulfstream 3	301	MW Sky LLC/Men's Wearhouse LLC. Houston, Tx.	N110BR
☐ N444GG	94	Citation V Ultra	560-0262	Elias-Savion-Fox LLC. Allegheny County, Pa.	N262CV
☐ N444HC	93	Learjet 31A	31A-064	John Sessa, Fort Lauderdale, Fl.	N142GT
☐ N444MK	78	Learjet 25D	25D-252	Vail Jet Inc. Vail, Co.	N44FH
☐ N444MW	01	Learjet 45	45-131	McWane Inc. Birmingham, Al.	
☐ N444PE	84	Falcon 50	143	P & E Properties Inc. Teterboro, NJ.	N77CP
☐ N444QG	00	Gulfstream 4SP	1453	Quad/Graphics Inc. Waukesha, Wi.	N453GA
☐ N444RH	02	CitationJet CJ-2	525A-0099	Jacket Express LLC. Reno, Nv.	N5223P
☐ N444SS	01	390 Premier 1	RB-16	Savant Aircraft Corp. Houston, Tx.	N151KD
☐ N444TG	81	Learjet 25D	25D-327	Gaines Motor Lines Inc. Hickory, NC.	(N327BC)
☐ N444TW	77	Learjet 24F	24F-348	Sierra American Corp. Addison, Tx.	N8BG
☐ N444WB	77	Learjet 35A	35A-105	Aero-Jet Aviation Inc. Fort Lauderdale, Fl.	(D-CHRC)
☐ N444WJ	75	Falcon 10	64	Worldwide Charter LLC. Marathon, Fl.	N718CA
☐ N444WW	79	Learjet 25D	25D-283	JFleet Inc. Fort Worth, Tx.	N312GK
☐ N445A	81	Westwind-1124	362	AK Steel Corp. West Mifflin, Pa.	4X-CUP
☐ N445BL	82	Westwind-1124	382	Jet Services Enterprises Inc. Bethany, Ok.	N999BL
☐ N445CW	93	Beechjet 400A	RK-45	Flight Options LLC. Cleveland, Oh.	(N412LX)
☐ N445N	02	Learjet 45	45-202	NIBCO Inc. Elkhart, In.	N5048Q
☐ N446CW	02	Beechjet 400A	RK-346	Flight Options LLC. Cleveland, Oh.	(N475LX)
☐ N446D	81	Falcon 20F-5B	446	QWest Communications Corp. Denver-Centennial, Co.	N270RA
☐ N446M	98	Beechjet 400A	RK-199	Motion Industries Inc. Atlanta, Ga.	N739TA
☐ N448AS	04	Challenger 300	20027	American Seafoods Group LLC. Seattle, Wa.	C-GZEH
☐ N448CC	92	BAe 1000A	NA1007	Continental Carrier Inc. Columbus, Oh.	N600LS
☐ N448CW	03	Hawker 400XP	RK-368	Flight Options LLC. Cleveland, Oh.	
☐ N448GR	93	Astra-1125SP	070	GR Aviation Corp. Fort Lauderdale, Fl.	(N100GQ)
☐ N448W	78	Sabre-75A	380-63	Platina Investment Corp. Wiley Post, Ok.	N75RS
☐ N449DT	77	Citation Eagle II	501-0012	Four Futures Corp. Az. (Ff FJ44 Eagle II 30 Sep 00).	N15FJ
☐ N449ML	00	Global Express	9055	WFC Air Inc. Teterboro, NJ.	C-GFWZ
☐ N450AJ	82	Challenger 600	1075	Jones Airways LLC. Cleveland, Tn.	N751DB
☐ N450AR	97	Gulfstream V	520	Aspen 1 LLC. Orange, Ca.	N17GV
☐ N450BC	99	Learjet 45	45-075	Cunningham Charter Corp. Anna, Il.	
☐ N450BF	87	Gulfstream 4	1015	Bowen Family Homes Inc. Buford, Ga.	VP-BRF
☐ N450CL	81	Falcon 50	76	Werner Aire Inc. Omaha, Ne.	N411WW
☐ N450CP	73	Falcon 20F-5	289	Carolina Blue Air Corp. Greensboro, NC.	N75TJ
☐ N450CW	92	Beechjet 400A	RK-50	Flight Options LLC. Cleveland, Oh.	(N413LX)
☐ N450DR	82	Falcon 50	113	DoctAir Inc. Vienna, Va.	N75RZ
☐ N450GA	03	Gulfstream G450	4004	Gulfstream Aerospace Corp. Savannah, Ga. (Ff 18 Sep 03)	N404SR
☐ N450K	88	Falcon 50	186	Kimball International Transit Inc. Huntingburg, In.	N278FJ
Reg	Yr	Type	c/n	Owner/Operator	Prev Regn

Reg	Yr	Type	c/n	Owner/Operator	Prev Regn
☐ N450LX*	99	Beechjet 400A	RK-260	Flight Options LLC. Cleveland, Oh.	N787TA
☐ N450MC	81	Learjet 35A	35A-368	McLane Co. Temple, Tx.	N99KW
☐ N450RS	84	Citation III	650-0061	Refreshment Services Inc. Springfield, Il.	N650TC
☐ N450T	98	Citation X	750-0054	Beehawk Aviation Inc. Smyrna, Ga.	N45ST
☐ N450TJ	98	Learjet 45	45-012	JACO Oil Co. Bakersfield, Ca.	D-CMLP
☐ N451AJ	02	CitationJet CJ-2	525A-0110	Velox Aircraft LLC. Port Hueneme, Ca.	N.....
☐ N451CL	01	Learjet 45	45-149	Werner Aire Inc. Omaha, Ne.	
☐ N451CS	99	Gulfstream V	570	Saban Entertainment/5161 Corp. Burbank, Ca.	N470GA
☐ N451DP	71	Falcon 20F	249	Dad's Products Inc. Meadville, Pa.	N777JF
☐ N451GA	93	Gulfstream 4SP	1221	Amgen Inc. Thousand Oaks, Ca.	
☐ N451N	03	Learjet 45	45-230	Newell Rubbermaid Inc. Rockford, Il.	N4008G
☐ N451ST	01	Learjet 45	45-200	JM Family Enterprises Inc. Fort Lauderdale, Fl.	
☐ N451WM	99	Learjet 45	45-091	Wal-Mart Stores Inc. Rogers, Ar.	(N408BX)
☐ N452AJ	98	Citation V Ultra	560-0494	Jones Airways LLC. Cleveland, Tn.	N86GR
☐ N452CJ	99	Learjet 45	45-090	Wal-Mart Stores Inc. Rogers, Ar.	N407FX
☐ N452DA	81	Learjet 35A	35A-452	Duncan Aviation Inc. Lincoln, Ne.	N279SP
☐ N452LJ	96	Learjet 45	45-002	Learjet Inc. Wichita, Ks. (Ff 6 Apr 96).	N45LJ
☐ N452QS	98	Gulfstream 4SP	1352	NetJets, Columbus, Oh.	N352GA
☐ N452ST	02	Learjet 45	45-201	JM Family Enterprises Inc. Fort Lauderdale, Fl.	N473LP
☐ N453AM	82	Learjet 35A	35A-453	Anderson News Corp. Knoxville, Tn.	(N802EC)
☐ N453CW	92	Beechjet 400A	RK-53	Flight Options LLC. Cleveland, Oh.	(N414LX)
☐ N453DP	74	HS 125/600A	6044	Arnoni Aviation Inc. Houston, Tx. (status ?).	N454DP
☐ N453GS	83	Challenger 601	3011	The Bistate Oil Co. NYC.	N202PH
☐ N453JS	94	Falcon 900B	144	Joseph Scott, Boise, Id.	N144FJ
☐ N453LJ	96	Learjet 45	45-003	Learjet Inc. Wichita, Ks. (Ff 24 Apr 96).	
☐ N453MA	79	Learjet 25D	25D-291	3M Aviation LLC. Alpharetta, Ga.	(N477MM)
☐ N453S	82	Citation II	550-0445	Selman Hangar, Monroe, La. (was 551-0445).	N1248K
☐ N453SB	74	Falcon 20F	308	Sierra Bravo Graco Inc. Baltimore, Md.	N81AJ
☐ N453TM	90	BAe 125/800A	8203	EMC Corp. Bedford, Ma.	N228G
☐ N454AC	77	Citation 1/SP	501-0015	McClain Enterprises Inc. Mountain Home, Ar.	N4446P
☐ N454BE*	85	Gulfstream 3	472	Bellew Sky Inc. St Petersburg, Fl.	N780RA
☐ N454CG	00	Learjet 45	45-085	George's Enterprises LLC. Springdale, Ar.	
☐ N454DP	81	Falcon 10	130	WJE Aircraft LLC. Denver, Co.	N432EZ
☐ N454JB	82	Gulfstream 3	345	Shaw Managed Services Inc. Baton Rouge, La.	N76TJ
☐ N454LC	01	Learjet 45	45-123	Lamar Air LLC. Baton Rouge, La.	
☐ N454QS	00	Gulfstream 4SP	1454	NetJets, Columbus, Oh.	N454GA
☐ N454RT	98	Citation V Ultra	560-0454	Malphrus Construction Co. Ridgeland, SC.	TC-ROT
☐ N455BE	82	Challenger 600S	1069	Bellew Sky Inc. St Petersburg, Fl.	(N818E)
☐ N455BK	79	HS 125/700A	NA0256	Oral Roberts Evangelistic Association, Tulsa, Ok.	(N830LR)
☐ N455CW	03	Hawker 400XP	RK-365	Flight Options LLC. Cleveland, Oh.	
☐ N455DW	87	Beechjet 400	RJ-20	Dudley Walker, Martinsville, Va.	N901P
☐ N455RH	85	Learjet 55	55-110	Hunt Aviation Inc. Indianapolis, In.	N55GY
☐ N455SH	87	Astra-1125	017	DDMR LLC. Tampa, Fl.	(N800JS)
☐ N456AB	80	Citation II	550-0249	Bell Helicopter Textron Inc. Fort Worth, Tx. (was 551-0236).	N39GA
☐ N456CG	81	Learjet 25D	25D-343	LDL Aircraft Leasing LLC. Pittsfield, Ma.	N3797L
☐ N456CL	81	Learjet 35A	35A-456	Jet Charter Inc. Van Nuys, Ca.	N711CD
☐ N456CW	92	Beechjet 400A	RK-56	Flight Options LLC. Cleveland, Oh.	(N415LX)
☐ N456JG	96	Beechjet 400A	RK-119	Rymeg LLC/Tricam Industries, Eden Prairie, Mn.	(N456NS)
☐ N456JW	99	Citation Excel	560-5033	456JW Inc. Reno, Nv.	N5211Q
☐ N456PR	99	Astra-1125SPX	116	Portland Holding Inc. Wilmington, De.	N527GA
☐ N456R	79	Citation 1/SP	501-0292	Peddler LLC. Cedar Rapids, Ia. (was 500-0383)	YV-2295P
☐ N456SL*	04	Citation Excel XLS	560-5528	Cessna Aircraft Co. Wichita, Ks.	N579BJ
☐ N457CW	92	Beechjet 400A	RK-57	Flight Options LLC. Cleveland, Oh.	(N416LX)
☐ N457DS	88	Gulfstream 4	1077	Dankjold Reed Aviation LLC. Palm Beach, Fl.	N477TS
☐ N457HL	82	Challenger 600S	1063	Henry IV LLC/Dankjold Reed Aviation LLC. Palm Beach, Fl.	N409CC
☐ N457JC	85	Gulfstream 3	457	GTE Southwest Inc. San Angelo, Tx.	N972G
☐ N458BE	84	Gulfstream 3	440	Billionaire Inc. St Petersburg, Fl.	N71RP
☐ N458CK	92	Citation V	560-0160	Adler Group Inc. Opa Locka, Fl.	ZS-NDT
☐ N458HC	89	Beechjet 400	RJ-58	K & P Aviation LLC. Tampa, Fl.	N258BJ
☐ N458MT	98	CitationJet	525-0316	J M Thomas Forest Products Co. Ogden, Ut.	N316EJ
☐ N458N	79	Citation II	550-0061	Dr William Reed Jr. Overland Park, Ks.	N456N
☐ N458SM	04	CitationJet CJ-1	525-0541	Woodland Leasing LLC. Woodland, Ca.	N.....
☐ N459BN	02	Gulfstream G200	071	Burlington Northern/Santa Fe Railway, Fort Worth, Tx.	(N706QS)
☐ N459CS	02	Challenger 604	5546	Computer Sciences Corp. El Segundo, Ca.	N604BA
☐ N459NA	01	CitationJet CJ-1	525-0459	Nephrology Associates PC. Cape Girardeau, Mo.	N.....
☐ N460AN	98	Learjet 60	60-127	Jetride Inc. Dallas, Tx.	(N225BX)

| *Reg* | *Yr* | *Type* | *c/n* | *Owner/Operator* | *Prev Regn* |

Reg	Yr	Type	c/n	Owner/Operator	Prev Regn
N460AS	01	390 Premier 1	RB-8	Flight Options LLC. Cleveland, Oh.	
N460BG	96	Learjet 60	60-090	Bellew Sky Inc. St Petersburg, Fl.	PT-WMO
N460CP	83	Citation III	650-0021	Health Systems Management Inc. Tifton, Ga.	N650SS
N460F	89	Challenger 601-3A	5055	Hunt Oil Co. Dallas, Tx.	N46F
N460L	02	390 Premier 1	RB-46	Jetflight Aviation Inc. Salzburg, Austria.	
N460PG	85	Gulfstream 3	460	Magic Johnson Entertainment Inc. Beverly Hills, Ca.	(N32MJ)
N460QS	98	Gulfstream 4SP	1360	NetJets, Columbus, Oh.	N360GA
N461CW	93	Beechjet 400A	RK-61	Data Recognition Corp. Maple Grove, Mn.	(N417LX)
N461EA	89	Beechjet 400	RJ-61	B D Aire LLC. Wilmington, De.	N701LP
N461GT	83	Gulfstream 3	411	Airmont Ltd-Deeside Trading Co. Reno, Nv.	N966H
N462B	89	Citation V	560-0016	James Koehler, Aberdeen, SD.	N68HQ
N462CS	01	Gulfstream 4SP	1462	Credit Suisse First Boston Inc. White Plains, NY.	N462GA
N462CW	92	Beechjet 400A	RK-62	Flight Options LLC. Cleveland, Oh.	(N418LX)
N462QS	95	Gulfstream 4SP	1262	NetJets, Columbus, Oh.	N496GA
N463HK	68	Gulfstream 2	11	Don King Productions, Deerfield Beach, Fl. 'Only in America'	N611TJ
N463LM	82	Gulfstream 3	370	Kaizen Aviation Inc. Jacksonville, Fl.	N697BJ
N464AM	83	Diamond 1A	A090SA	Jet N464AM LLC/Jet Solutions LLC. Birmingham, Al.	C-GLIG
N464C	03	CitationJet CJ-2	525A-0118	Loren Cook Co. Springfield-Branson, Mo.	N5163C
N464CL	66	Learjet 24A	24A-096	Clay Lacy Aviation Inc. Van Nuys, Ca.	N1972L
N464QS	95	Gulfstream 4SP	1264	NetJets, Columbus, Oh.	N499GA
N464TF	99	Learjet 60	60-185	First Data Technologies Inc. Englewood, Co.	
N465NW	82	Learjet 35A	35A-465	465NW LLC. West Columbia, SC.	
N465QS	01	Gulfstream 4SP	1463	NetJets, Columbus, Oh.	N463GA
N465SP	81	Sabre-65	465-72	William Bolthouse Farms Inc. Bakersfield, Ca.	OO-RSE
N465TS	80	Sabre-65	465-15	T-5 LLC/Tubular Steel Inc. St Louis, Mo.	XA-ZUM
N466AE	91	BAe 125/800A	NA0466	Central & South West Services Inc. Dallas, Tx.	N466CS
N466CW	03	Hawker 400XP	RK-366	Flight Options LLC. Cleveland, Oh.	
N466SS	89	Citation II	550-0626	Capital Buyers of Delaware Inc. Conway, Ar.	LV-WOZ
N466TS	88	Gulfstream 4	1066	Aero Toy Store LLC. Fort Lauderdale, Fl.	N118R
N467MW	93	Astra-1125SP	067	Sunstate Aviation LLC. Phoenix, Az.	N267SP
N467QS*	04	Gulfstream G400	1533	NetJets, Columbus, Oh.	N533GA
N468GA	00	Gulfstream 4SP	1468	M&P Co/Ceramica Cleopatra Co. Cairo, Egypt.	
N468KL	89	Challenger 601-3A	5036	LK Air Inc. Menlo Park, Ca.	N225N
N468RB	77	Sabre-60	306-133	Taylor's Aviation Services LLC. Marion, Oh.	N400JH
N468RW	01	CitationJet CJ-1	525-0468	Warren Inc. Collins, Ms.	N.....
N469BB	81	Learjet 35A	35A-434	Joseph Bourget, Phoenix, Az.	N4401
N469DE	99	Citation Bravo	550-0883	Credomatic of Florida Inc. Miami, Fl.	
N469DN	98	Citation V Ultra	560-0469	Ultra Capital LLC. Jackson, Ms.	N7010R
N469WC*	76	Westwind-1124	202	Business Limo LLC. Denton, Tx.	N59PT
N470BC	03	Hawker 800XP	8651	Architectural Air LLC. Washington-Dulles, Va.	N651XP
N470DP	95	Citation V Ultra	560-0291	McCreary Investment LLC. Denver, Co.	N744R
N470SK	03	Citation Excel	560-5348	Sugar Creek Inc. Olathe, Ks.	N.....
N471CJ	01	CitationJet CJ-1	525-0471	Empire Properties LLC. Marietta, Ga.	N768R
N471CR	01	Gulfstream 4SP	1471	Education Finance Resources Corp. Dulles, Va.	N471GA
N471CW	97	Beechjet 400A	RK-161	Flight Options LLC. Cleveland, Oh.	(N428LX)
N471WR	01	Citation Bravo	550-0987	Alpine Aviation LLC. Yakima, Wa.	N987GR
N472QS	99	Gulfstream 4SP	1372	NetJets, Columbus, Oh.	N372GA
N473CW	92	Gulfstream 4	1194	Compuware Corp. Farmington Hills, Mi.	N77QR
N473JE	96	Beechjet 400A	RK-121	Jet Ex LLC. Wayzata, Mn.	N419MS
N473KT	84	Gulfstream 3	438	Karthe Corp/Chrysler Pentastar Aviation, Waterford, Mi.	N911KT
N473LP	01	Learjet 45	45-196	Louisiana-Pacific Corp. Hillsboro, Or.	N50353
N473TC	69	Learjet 25	25-043	Tulsair Beechcraft Inc. Tulsa, Ok.	N234ND
N474D	00	Gulfstream 4SP	1445	Millard Drexler Inc. San Francisco, Ca.	N445QS
N474PC	02	CitationJet CJ-2	525A-0087	Pio-Trans Inc. Cleveland, Tn.	N.....
N475AT	79	Westwind-1124	270	Air Ambulance by Air Trek Inc. Punta Gorda, Fl.	N501DT
N475DH	02	CitationJet CJ-2	525A-0090	Design Homes Inc. Prairie du Chien, Wi.	N.....
N475DJ	82	Gulfstream 3	358	Baymark Development Corp. Norfolk Va.	(N1149E)
N475EZ	83	Falcon 20F	475	Garrett Aviation Services Inc. Springfield, Il.	T 11-5/45-0
N475HM	99	Hawker 800XP	8451	General American Enterprises Inc. Little Rock, Ar.	N41534
N475LC	01	Gulfstream 4SP	1472	Starflite International Corp. New Braunfels, Tx.	N4DA
N475QS	95	Gulfstream 4SP	1275	NetJets, Columbus, Oh.	N459GA
N475WA	83	Citation II	550-0475	Potomac Street Partners LLP. Englewood, Co.	N870MH
N476BJ	97	Beechjet 400A	RK-176	MG Aviation LLC. Richmond, Va.	
N476LC	86	Citation S/II	S550-0091	Braxton Management Services LLC. Great Falls, Mt.	N241LA
N476LX	04	Hawker 400XP	RK-376	Flight Options LLC. Cleveland, Oh.	N476CW
N476MK	00	Falcon 50EX	301	Merck & Co. Mercer County, NJ.	N301EX

Reg	Yr	Type	c/n	Owner/Operator	Prev Regn
☐ N477A	79	Citation II/SP	550-0374	M & B Holdings of Delaware LLC. Gulf Shores. (was 551-0020).	(N999LL)
☐ N477DM	98	Challenger 604	5398	Delta Airelite Business Jets Inc. Cincinnati, Oh.	N597DM
☐ N477GG	74	Gulfstream 2B	155	477 Aviation LLC/Fashion Resources Inc. Van Nuys, Ca.	XA-GAC
☐ N477JB	93	Gulfstream 4SP	1214	Jerry Bruckheimer Inc. Van Nuys, Ca.	N2615B
☐ N477JE	89	Citation II	550-0620	One Aviation LLC. Huntingburg, In.	(N508AJ)
☐ N477LC	87	Citation S/II	S550-0153	Braxton Management Services LLC. Great Falls, Mt.	N242LA
☐ N477LX	04	Hawker 400XP	RK-377	Flight Options LLC. Cleveland, Oh.	N477CW
☐ N477QS	99	Gulfstream 4SP	1377	NetJets, Columbus, Oh.	N377GA
☐ N477RP	94	Gulfstream 4SP	1247	Petersen Aviation, Van Nuys, Ca.	N14UH
☐ N477SA	03	Gulfstream G400	1529	USAA, San Antonio, Tx.	N529GA
☐ N477SJ	85	Gulfstream 3	477	Meregrass Inc. Dallas, Tx.	01 USCG
☐ N477X	74	Sabre-60	306-78	Thoroughbred Leasing Inc. Morgantown, WV.	N140JA
☐ N478GS	01	Gulfstream 4SP	1478	Braxton Management Services LLC. Great Falls, Mt.	N378GA
☐ N478LX	04	Hawker 400XP	RK-387	Flight Options LLC. Cleveland, Oh.	
☐ N478PM	97	Citation X	750-0014	Reese International Ltd. Austin, Tx.	(N14VP)
☐ N479LX	04	Hawker 400XP	RK-388	SSC Aviation 04 LLC. Englewood, Co.	
☐ N480CC	87	Citation S/II	S550-0129	Crounse Corp. Paducah, Ky.	N87TH
☐ N480DG	89	Citation V	560-0015	Genter Airways LLC. Van Nuys, Ca.	N580MR
☐ N480JJ	00	Learjet 31A	31A-212	Fontana Aviation Inc. Concord, NC.	N31KJ
☐ N480LX	04	Hawker 400XP	RK-398	Flight Options LLC. Cleveland, Oh.	
☐ N480QS	99	Gulfstream 4SP	1380	NetJets, Columbus, Oh.	N380GA
☐ N480RL	91	Citation V	560-0109	Rand Consulting Inc. San Francisco, Ca.	N109VP
☐ N481CW	89	Beechjet 400A	RK-1	Flight Options LLC. Cleveland, Oh. (was RJ-51).	(N401CW)
☐ N481FM	79	Learjet 35A	35A-218	RSB Investments Inc/Skyward Aviation, Washington, Pa.	(N83TE)
☐ N481MC	75	Westwind-1123	184	Deer Horn Aviation LC. Midland, Tx.	CC-CRK
☐ N481NS	82	Westwind-1124	378	AirCorp Inc. Tuscaloosa, Al.	C-GXKF
☐ N481QS	96	Gulfstream 4SP	1281	NetJets, Columbus, Oh.	N470GA
☐ N482CP	81	Learjet 25D	25D-331	Carmike Cinemas Inc. Columbus, Ga.	N462B
☐ N482CW	99	Beechjet 400A	RK-222	Flight Options LLC. Cleveland, Oh.	(N440LX)
☐ N482DM	84	Diamond 1A	A088SA	Avis Aviation LLC. St Louis, Mo.	
☐ N483BA	01	Challenger 604	5483	Boeing Executive Flight Operations, Seattle, Wa.	C-GLYK
☐ N483DM	74	Learjet 24D	24D-291	InterContinental Express LLC. Athens, Ga.	N488DM
☐ N483FG	80	HS 125/700A	7094	Plane 1 LLC. Oakbrook Terrace, Il.	N415RD
☐ N484CJ	02	CitationJet CJ-1	525-0484	Fegotila Inc. Staverton, UK.	N5211F
☐ N484CW	01	Beechjet 400A	RK-334	Flight Options LLC. Cleveland, Oh.	(N473LX)
☐ N484JC	03	Hawker 800XP	8644	Johnson Controls Inc. Milwaukee, Wi.	N644XP
☐ N484MM	98	Citation V Ultra	560-0491	Phantom Sales Inc. Plantation, Fl.	N404MM
☐ N484T	02	Citation X	750-0199	Target Corp. Minneapolis, Mn.	N5245L
☐ N484TL	70	Gulfstream II SP	93	Boxing Cat Productions Inc. Burbank, Ca.	N62K
☐ N485AC	82	Learjet 35A	35A-485	Sunward Corp. Billings, Mt.	N710WL
☐ N485AK	81	Citation II	550-0193	AKSM Equipment LLC. Columbus, Oh.	N260J
☐ N485GM	83	Gulfstream 3	387	RMQ Ltd-Reaud, Morgan & Quinn Inc. Beaumont, Tx.	N620JA
☐ N485LT	00	Hawker 800XP	8485	Surewing Inc/Ambrion Aviation, Luton, UK.	N44515
☐ N486BG	93	Challenger 601-3A	5133	Berkley Aviation Inc. Fort Lauderdale, Fl.	N121FF
☐ N486CW	82	Diamond 1	A026SA	FractionAir Inc. Nashville, Tn.	(N26FA)
☐ N486QS	99	Gulfstream 4SP	1386	NetJets, Columbus, Oh.	N486GA
☐ N486TM	00	EMB-135ER	145364	Intel Corp/Executive Jet Management Inc. Cincinnati, Oh.	PT-...
☐ N487DT	03	390 Premier 1	RB-85	D/T Carson Enterprises Inc. Murrieta, Ca.	N4485B
☐ N487FW	82	Learjet 35A	35A-487	Delta Leasing Inc. Stuart, Fl.	N391JR
☐ N487GS	68	B 737-247	19600	Charlotte Hornets/Shinn Enterprises Inc. Charlotte, NC.	N307VA
☐ N487QS	95	Gulfstream 4SP	1287	NetJets, Columbus, Oh.	N484GA
☐ N488CH	04	Global Express	9150	Bombardier Aerospace Corp. Windsor Locks, Ct.	C-FAIV
☐ N488CP	99	Citation Excel	560-5055	Space Shuttle Aircraft Leasing Co. Salem, Or.	(N560KN)
☐ N488DM	80	Sabre-65	465-26	Marshall Air LLC. Scottsdale, Az.	N31SJ
☐ N488GR	64	JetStar-6	5051	Sound Corp. Carson City, Nv.	N488JS
☐ N488HP	00	Hawker 800XP	8488	Aero Timber Partners LLC. Atlanta, Ga.	N50788
☐ N488PC	02	390 Premier 1	RB-57	New Age Electronics Inc. Van Nuys, Ca.	N457K
☐ N488RC	01	390 Premier 1	RB-23	Raytheon Aircraft Co. Wichita, Ks.	N488PC
☐ N488SR	02	CitationJet CJ-1	525-0488	Chaparral Aviation Inc. San Jose, Ca.	N525WH
☐ N489BB*	83	Falcon 200	489	489BB LLC. Lake Park, Fl.	N489TK
☐ N489CB	01	CitationJet CJ-1	525-0489	Cimarron Aviation Inc. Bend, Or.	N489ED
☐ N489QS	99	Gulfstream 4SP	1389	NetJets, Columbus, Oh.	N389GA
☐ N489SA*	83	BAe 125/800A	8053	Summit Aviation Corp. Farmingdale, NY.	N484RA
☐ N489SS	84	Citation II	550-0489	Sierra Sierra Enterprises Inc. Minden, Nv.	(N801TA)
☐ N490CC	84	Citation II	550-0490	Norcross Aviation LLC. Rochester, NY. (was 551-0490)	(N490CD)
☐ N490JC	03	Hawker 400XP	RK-373	Freight Handlers Inc. Fuquay Varina, NC.	N373XP

| Reg | Yr | Type | c/n | Owner/Operator | Prev Regn |

Reg	Yr	Type	c/n	Owner/Operator	Prev Regn
❑ N490QS	02	Gulfstream 4SP	1488	NetJets, Columbus, Oh.	N488GA
❑ N491AN	83	Westwind-1124	393	International Aviation Network, Santa Monica, Ca.	N53WW
❑ N491BT	83	Diamond 1A	A054SA	IBT Inc. Merriam, Ks.	N141H
❑ N491CW	94	Beechjet 400A	RK-91	Flight Options LLC. Cleveland, Oh.	(N420LX)
❑ N491EC	02	Gulfstream 4SP	1491	Eastman Chemical Co. Bristol-Tri Cities Regional, Tn.	N491GA
❑ N491JB	89	Citation III	650-0182	MAG Air LLC. Concord, NC.	N682CC
❑ N491PT	73	Citation	500-0102	Sunflower Air LLC. Wilmington, De.	N491BT
❑ N492A	84	Gulfstream 3	425	Sonic Financial Corp. Charlotte, NC.	N425SP
❑ N492JT	70	Gulfstream II SP	82	John Travolta/Atlo Inc. Jumbolair Aviation Community, Ocala.	N728T
❑ N492MA	83	Citation II	550-0472	Petro Wings LC. Pampa, Tx. (status ?).	N12511
❑ N492QS	99	Gulfstream 4SP	1392	NetJets, Columbus, Oh.	N392GA
❑ N493CW	94	Beechjet 400A	RK-93	Flight Options LLC. Cleveland, Oh.	(N421LX)
❑ N493QS	96	Gulfstream 4SP	1293	NetJets, Columbus, Oh.	N415GA
❑ N493S	00	Falcon 2000	134	Dassault Falcon Jet Corp. Teterboro, NJ.	SX-DCF
❑ N494AT	87	BAe 125/800A	NA0404	Vodafone UK, Farnborough, UK.	N916PT
❑ N494CW	90	Beechjet 400A	RK-4	Flight Options LLC. Cleveland, Oh.	N771EL
❑ N494PA	83	Learjet 35A	35A-505	CJ Systems Aviation Group Inc. Allegheny County, Pa.	N505EE
❑ N494RG	98	Hawker 800XP	8378	Regions Financial Corp. Birmingham, Al.	
❑ N495BA	01	Challenger 604	5495	Boeing Executive Flight Operations, Seattle, Wa.	C-GLXK
❑ N495CM	80	Citation II	550-0151	BBS 1 LLC/Barrett Business Services Inc. Portland, Or.	N35HC
❑ N495CW	90	Beechjet 400A	RK-5	Flight Options LLC. Cleveland, Oh.	(N405CW)
❑ N495QS	96	Gulfstream 4SP	1295	NetJets, Columbus, Oh.	N417GA
❑ N496AS	96	Beechjet 400A	RK-117	Executive AirShare Corp. Wichita, Ks.	N12MQ
❑ N497CW	00	Beechjet 400A	RK-297	Flight Options LLC. Cleveland, Oh.	N699TA
❑ N497DM	97	Challenger 604	5359	Delta Airelite Business Jets Inc. Cincinnati, Oh.	C-GLWR
❑ N497PT	80	HS 125/700A	NA0266	JMAC266 LLC. Washington, DC.	N86MD
❑ N498AB	00	Citation Excel	560-5116	Romeo Delta Enterprises LLC. Bedford, Ma.	N5246Z
❑ N498CS	90	Citation III	650-0180	Pheasant Kay-Bee Toy Inc. Nashua, NH.	N768NB
❑ N498QS	99	Gulfstream 4SP	1398	NetJets, Columbus, Oh.	N398GA
❑ N498RS	70	HS 125/731	NA749	SkyBus Inc. Fort Lauderdale, Fl.	N498R
❑ N498YY	02	CitationJet CJ-1	525-0498	John Mills Aviation Services LLP. Luton, UK.	N5201J
❑ N499EH	78	Learjet 25D	25D-239	Eddie & Ercie Hill, Wichita Falls, Tx.	N45H
❑ N499NH	81	Sabre-65	465-56	Newman Racing, Lincolnshire, Il.	N65TL
❑ N499P	87	Beechjet 400	RJ-31	Citation Jet Premier Inc. Brookfield, Wi.	N114AP
❑ N499PB	65	JetStar-6	5063	Friendship Aviation Inc. Clearwater, Fl.	N499PB
❑ N499QS	96	Gulfstream 4SP	1299	NetJets, Columbus, Oh.	N423GA
❑ N499RC	86	Citation S/II	S550-0090	Racing Champions Corp/T-Bird Aviation Inc. Chicago-DuPage.	N113VP
❑ N499SA	98	Citation VII	650-7088	USAA, San Antonio, Tx.	
❑ N499WM	98	Citation Bravo	550-0869	Weis Markets Inc. Sunbury, Pa.	N98RX
❑ N500	99	Challenger 604	5419	Indianapolis Motor Speedway LLC. Indianapolis, In.	C-GLYK
❑ N500AD	73	Citation	500-0091	Investment Leasing LLC. St Charles, Mo.	(N1899)
❑ N500AF	86	Falcon 50	170	AFLAC Inc. Columbus, Ga.	N293K
❑ N500AT	91	Citation V	560-0146	Circuit City Stores Inc. Richmond, Va.	N2000M
❑ N500BN	02	Hawker 800XP	8608	Argent Marketing Services LLC. White Plains, NY.	N61708
❑ N500CD	97	Gulfstream 4SP	1321	Cendant Corp. Ronkonkoma, NY.	(N600CC)
❑ N500CG	98	Learjet 45	45-009	Tessa Two Inc/Chip Ganassi Racing, Indianapolis, In.	N459LJ
❑ N500CW	04	CitationJet CJ-1	525-0542	Cessna Aircraft Co. Wichita, ks.	N5125J
❑ N500DB	77	JetStar 2	5219	Banner Associates Inc. Lake Forest, Il.	(LY-EWC)
❑ N500DG	88	Beechjet 400	RJ-43	Multi Media Games Inc. Austin, Tx.	N401CG
❑ N500E	94	Gulfstream 4SP	1235	Exxon Mobil Corp. Houston, Tx.	N100A
❑ N500ED	79	Learjet 35A	35A-241	500ED LLC. West Columbia, SC.	N500EX
⤶ N500EF	83	Gulfstream 3	400	Jet Wings Inc. Fort Lauderdale, Fl.	(N990ML)
❑ N500EL	74	Citation	500-0173	White Industries Inc. Bates City, Mo.	N59CL
❑ N500ES	66	JetStar-731	5075	Rubloff Development Group Inc. Rockford, Il.	N1DB
❑ N500ET	74	Citation	500-0180	Sunshine Air Inc. Double Springs, Al.	N772C
❑ N500FA*	86	Astra-1125	011	Transeastern Properties Inc. Coral Springs, Fl.	N991RV
❑ N500FK	90	Citation V	560-0047	Circuit City Stores Inc. Richmond, Va.	N2666A
❑ N500FM	80	HS 125/700A	NA0280	First Magnus Financial Corp. Tucson, Az.	N280VC
❑ N500FR	91	Citation VI	650-0208	Circuit City Stores Inc. Richmond, Va.	I-TALW
❑ N500FZ	90	Citation V	560-0018	Waverly Investors LLC. Highland Park, Il.	N114CP
❑ N500GF	86	Gulfstream 3	488	Waffle House Inc. Norcross, Ga.	(N45PG)
❑ N500GR	73	Citation	500-0098	G J R Leasing Inc/Reebaire Aircraft Inc. Hot Springs, Ar.	PH-CTC
❑ N500GV	96	Gulfstream V	506	Datel Holdings Ltd. Farnborough, UK.	(N110LE)
❑ N500HF	93	BAe 125/800A	8249	AEH Aviation Inc. Wilmington, De.	(N826SU)
❑ N500HY	97	Beechjet 400A	RK-153	NACCO Materials Handling Group Inc. Greenville, SC.	N153BJ
❑ N500J	91	BAe 125/800A	NA0469	Johnson & Johnson, Mercer County Airport, NJ.	N671BA
Reg	Yr	Type	c/n	Owner/Operator	Prev Regn

Reg	Yr	Type	c/n	Owner/Operator	Prev Regn
N500JD	78	Falcon 20-5	378	JHD Aircraft Sales Co. Memphis, Tn.	N305AR
N500JE	94	Learjet 31A	31A-088	RP Sales & Leasing Inc. Sandford, Fl.	N508J
N500JS	78	Learjet 35A	35A-169	Ultra Wheel Co. Buena Park, Ca.	N48CN
N500JW	78	Gulfstream 2TT	234	Jet-A-Way Charters LLC. Willimantic, Ct.	(N956MJ)
N500KE	81	Westwind-1124	360	The Ride Inc. Anchorage, Ak.	N816S
N500LG	79	Learjet 28	28-005	Jet Manager Inc. Hanford, Ca.	N8LL
N500LJ	02	Beechjet 400A	RK-340	Civilcad Constructors SA. Santo Domingo, Dominican Republic.	N51540
N500LR	87	Challenger 601-3A	5012	Circuit City Stores Inc. Richmond, Va.	N1868M
N500LS	98	BBJ-73T	29054	Limited Inc. Columbus, Oh.	N6067E
N500M	97	Astra-1125SPX	091	Cook Aircraft Leasing Inc. Bloomington, In.	N500MZ
N500MA	72	Gulfstream 2B	119	MA 500 Inc. Nazareth, Pa.	N305SJ
N500MG	02	Citation Encore	560-0624	Pacific Monarch Resorts Inc. Santa Ana, Ca.	N1242K
N500ML	73	Citation	500-0074	M & L Aviation LLC. Cashmere, Wa.	PT-OOF
N500MP	99	Learjet 31A	31A-198	N500MP LLC. Grand Rapids, Mi.	
N500N	02	Falcon 50EX	323	NASCAR Inc. Daytona Beach, Fl.	N323EX
N500ND	80	Learjet 35A	35A-351	World Jet Inc. Fort Lauderdale, Fl.	N500DD
N500NH	82	Falcon 20F-5B	470	Haas Enterprises LLC. Lincolnshire, Il.	N470G
N500NJ	73	Citation	500-0113	Northern Air Inc. Grand Rapids, Mi.	N684H
N500PC	90	Challenger 601-3A	5071	PepsiCo Inc. White Plains, NY.	C-GLWT
N500PE	99	Challenger 604	5440	Applera Corp. White Plains, NY.	C-GLXU
N500PG	85	Challenger 601	3039	Air Kelso LLC. Teterboro, NJ.	N639CL
N500PP	83	Diamond 1A	A061SA	Diamond Aviation of Jackson LLC. Jackson, Mi.	N18T
N500PR	02	Challenger 800	7846	Penske Jet Inc. Detroit, Mi.	N846PR
N500PX	98	Citation Excel	560-5017	Phoenix Construction Services Inc. Panama City, Fl.	N600BJ
N500R	03	Falcon 2000EX	13	NASCAR Inc. Daytona Beach, Fl.	F-WWGL
N500RH	85	Gulfstream 3	451	Hendrick Motorsports Inc. Harrisburg, NC.	N351FJ
N500RL	73	Gulfstream 2	122	R Lacy Inc Oil & Gas Production, Longview, Tx.	N84A
N500RP	00	Learjet 60	60-206	Penske Jet Inc. Detroit, Mi.	(N254FX)
N500RR	83	Falcon 200	491	Sonic Financial Corp. Charlotte, NC.	N843MG
N500SK	73	Citation	500-0129	M H Aviation LLC. Cleveland, Tn.	N8114G
N500SV	03	CitationJet CJ-2	525A-0153	Peoples Management of South Texas Inc. Laredo, Tx.	N5223P
N500SW	76	Learjet 24D	24D-325	Performance Aircraft Leasing Inc. Aspen, Co.	(N117CC)
N500TH	99	Beechjet 400A	RK-246	Lin R Rogers Electrical Contractors, Winston Salem, NC.	
N500TM	73	Citation Eagle	500-0112	Heizer Aviation Inc. St Louis, Mo.	N515DC
N500TS	99	Citation Bravo	550-0886	True Speed Enterprises II Inc. Indianapolis, In.	N550KH
N500UB	90	Citation V	560-0052	Pomeroy Transport Inc. Stamford, Ct.	N500LE
N500UJ	90	Citation V	560-0062	Harris Air Inc. Logan, Ut.	(N405RH)
N500VC	91	Citation V	560-0144	Vancreb LLC. Corvallis, Or.	N2000X
N500WN	69	F 28-1000	11016	Wayne Newton/Desert Eagle LLC. Las Vegas, Nv.	N43AE
N500WR	91	Learjet 31A	31A-038	Diamond Aviation II Inc. Concord, NC.	N131NA
N500XY	66	HS 125/731	25119	Chestnut Hill Aviation Inc. Newton, Ma.	N213H
N500ZA	77	Learjet 24F	24F-350	Onager Co. Odessa, Tx.	N741GL
N501AF	78	Citation 1/SP	501-0139	Newport Aeronaut LLC. Bellevue, Wa.	N888BH
N501AT	77	Citation 1/SP	501-0017	TAS Enterprises LLC. Bellevue, Wa.	N100WJ
N501BB	79	Citation 1/SP	501-0087	HBC Aviation LLC. Fargo, ND.	N501SJ
N501BE	77	Citation 1/SP	501-0263	Freeman Holdings Aircraft LLC. Topeka, Ks. (was 500-0352)	(N501BF)
N501BP	81	Citation 1/SP	501-0231	Central Virginia Aircraft Sales Inc. Lynchburg, Va.	N29HE
N501CB	78	Citation 1/SP	501-0281	501CB LLC. Reno, Nv. (was 500-0372).	N501SJ
N501CD	78	Citation 1/SP	501-0066	David MacHugh, Pasco, Wa.	VP-CTB
N501CF	79	Citation 1/SP	501-0128	WL Aircraft Inc. Richmond, Va.	N900MM
N501CP	77	Citation 1/SP	501-0034	Consolidated Pipe & Supply Co. Birmingham, Al.	N444MV
N501CT	00	Hawker 800XP	8512	Century Tel Service Group LLC. Monroe, La.	
N501CV	01	Gulfstream V	639	CSC Transport Inc. White Plains, NY.	N639GA
N501CW	90	Citation V	560-0050	Flight Options LLC. Cleveland, Oh.	N208BC
N501D	79	Citation 1/SP	501-0298	S Aviation LLC. Las Vegas, Nv.	VR-CMS
N501DA*	81	Citation 1/SP	501-0205	Dove Air Inc. Hendersonville, NC.	N6784T
N501DB	02	Falcon 900C	196	Konfara Co. Scottsdale, Az.	N196FJ
N501DD	77	Citation 1/SP	501-0035	Dukes Deux Leasing Co. Scottsdale, Az.	N35JF
N501DG	74	Citation	500-0194	Southeastern Aviation Group LLC. Clinton, Tn.	N194TS
N501DP	80	Citation 1/SP	501-0162	Dunn Equipment Leasing LLC. Daytona Beach, Fl.	N446V
N501DR	79	Citation 1/SP	501-0141	Eagle Aviation LLC. Wilmington, De.	N501GG
N501DY	82	Citation 1/SP	501-0240	GBC Technologies Inc. Carrollton, Ga.	N77UB
N501E	73	Citation	500-0364	Personal Airliner Ltd. Guernsey, C.I.	G-ORJB
N501EA	77	Citation 1/SP	501-0054	Sierra Tel Business Systems/S T Air Services, Oakhurst, Ca.	N2BT
N501EJ	73	Citation	500-0119	Lynch Flying Service Inc. Billings, Mt.	N95Q
N501EK	78	Citation 1/SP	501-0078	WCI Communities Inc. Fort Myers, Fl.	N13BT

Reg	Yr	Type	c/n	Owner/Operator	Prev Regn

Reg	Yr	Type	c/n	Owner/Operator	Prev Regn
☐ N501EM	79	Citation 1/SP	501-0134	Solitaire Inc. Portland, Or.	N501LW
☐ N501F	95	Hawker 800XP	8286	U S Filter Corp. Palm Springs, Ca.	N807H
☐ N501FJ	80	Citation 1/SP	501-0167	Quest Energy LLC. Portland, Or.	N723JM
☐ N501FP	80	Citation 1/SP	501-0161	Flying Service NV. Antwerp, Belgium.	XB-FXO
☐ N501G	81	Citation 1/SP	501-0202	DWT Inc. Oklahoma City, Ok.	N477KM
☐ N501GB	74	Citation	500-0231	Guiffre Organization Ltd. Watertown, Wi.	N500SJ
☐ N501GF	83	HS 125/700B	7208	Waffle House Inc. Norcross, Ga.	G-BLSM
☐ N501HG	82	Citation 1/SP	501-0221	Georgia Aviation & Technical College, Eastman, Ga.	(N643VP)
☐ N501HH*	84	Citation 1/SP	501-0679	J K Aviation LLC. Pueblo West, Co.	N73SK
☐ N501HS	79	Citation 1/SP	501-0096	Garry Lewis, Baton Rouge, La.	N660KC
☐ N501JC	75	Citation	500-0252	Biplane Adventures Inc. Quakertown, Pa.	N244WJ
☐ N501JD	79	Citation 1/SP	501-0129	J & D Aircraft Sales LLC. Pasco, Wa.	PT-LQQ
☐ N501JE	83	Citation 1/SP	501-0253	NetFirst Financial Inc/NF Investments Inc. Atlanta, Ga.	N2650Y
☐ N501JF	76	Citation	500-0343	WB Aviation LLC. Atlanta, Ga.	C-FOSM
☐ N501JG	77	Citation 1/SP	501-0038	Challenger Aircraft Charters LLC. Newport, RI.	N315S
☐ N501JJ	77	Citation 1/SP	501-0269	Josef Eoff, Salem, Or. (was 500-0357).	XB-GVY
☐ N501JM	81	Citation 1/SP	501-0226	R & R Aviation LLC. Wilmington, De.	N226VP
☐ N501JP	94	Citation II	550-0730	The Pyle Group LLC. Madison, Wi.	(N650JP)
☐ N501JS	90	Citation V	560-0066	Fun Times Boat Inc. Slidell, La.	N60S
☐ N501KC	79	Falcon 200	401	Symbolic Aviation Inc. La Jolla, Ca.	N699GA
☐ N501KG	75	Citation	500-0279	Faith Christian Family Church, Panama City Beach, Fl.	N120S
☐ N501KK	81	Citation 1/SP	501-0181	Barnhill & Associates LLC. Amarillo, Tx.	N250SR
☐ N501KR	93	CitationJet	525-0033	King Ranch Inc. Houston, Tx.	N116AP
☐ N501LB	74	Citation	500-0165	Executive Business Jet Inc. Wilmington, De.	(N501FF)
☐ N501LC	80	Citation II	550-0146	ILC Interests Ltd. San Antonio, Tx.	(N611RR)
☐ N501LH	76	Citation	500-0342	Americraft Carton Inc. Kansas City, Mo.	N501DR
☐ N501MB	79	Citation 1/SP	501-0122	Wistar Management Corp. West Palm Beach, Fl.	(N501MD)
☐ N501MD	73	Falcon 20E	284	Mad Dog Aviation Inc. Seattle, Wa.	(N801MD)
☐ N501MT	83	Citation 1/SP	501-0675	Imaginary Images Inc. Richmond-Chesterfield, Va.	N8900M
☐ N501PC	97	Falcon 50EX	265	PepsiCo Inc. White Plains, NY.	N9550A
☐ N501PV	77	Citation 1/SP	501-0028	Jet Lease Partners Inc. Missoula, Mt.	N1234X
☐ N501RC	80	Citation 1/SP	501-0165	New Hampshire Jet Holdings Inc. Nashua, NH.	N165NA
☐ N501RM	78	Citation 1/SP	501-0093	Ban Air Ltd. Wilton, Ct.	N623LB
☐ N501RS	79	Citation 1/SP	501-0097	C C Services of Nevada Inc. Clearwater, Fl.	N479JS
☐ N501SP	77	Citation 1/SP	501-0019	Fleming Aircraft Sales, St Paul, Mn.	(N301MC)
☐ N501SS	78	Citation	500-0374	Jeff Jobe, Bend, Or.	(N505BB)
☐ N501T	82	Citation 1/SP	501-0244	H & D Aviation LLC. Charlotte, NC.	N176FB
☐ N501TJ	77	Citation 1/SP	501-0013	VoiceNet Air Inc. Ivyland, Pa.	VR-BJK
☐ N501TL	74	Citation	500-0207	True Love Foundation LLC. Morton Grove, Il.	(N107SE)
☐ N501TP	84	Citation 1/SP	501-0684	Stage Aviation Inc. Carmel, Ca.	N3683G
☐ N501VC	81	Citation 1/SP	501-0184	Virgo Commodities Corp. Brownsville, Tx.	N433MM
☐ N501VP	77	Citation 1/SP	501-0261	Aberrone LLC. Wilmington, De. (was 500-0351).	N7NE
☐ N501WB	80	Citation 1/SP	501-0158	Bannen Enterprises/Davric Corp. Medford, Or.	N1MX
☐ N501WD	83	Citation 1/SP	501-0251	TOH Aircraft Partners LLC. Birmingham, Al.	N501RG
☐ N501XP	04	Hawker 800XP	8701	Raytheon Aircraft Co. Wichita, Ks.	
☐ N502BC	00	Citation Excel	560-5098	Wellmark Inc/Blue Cross & Blue Shield, Des Moines, Ia.	N200PF
☐ N502BE	74	Citation	500-0195	Makena Hawaii Inc. Kailua, Hi.	N500LJ
☐ N502BG	78	Falcon 20F-5	388	Cobalt Resources LLC. Jackson, Wy.	N756
☐ N502CC	79	Citation 1/SP	501-0113	L Robert Kimball & Assocs Inc. Edensburg, Pa.	N200ES
☐ N502CL	78	Citation II/SP	551-0002	The Stephenson Aviation Trust, Lake in the Hills, Il.	N39ML
☐ N502E	93	Citation V	560-0234	Emerson Electric Co. St Louis, Mo.	
☐ N502EA	05	Eclipse 500	EX500-...	Eclipse Aviation Corp. Albuquerque, NM.	
☐ N502GF	83	HS 125/700B	7210	Waffle House Inc. Norcross, Ga.	G-BLTP
☐ N502HE	92	Challenger 601-3A	5111	Heckmann Enterprises Inc. Palm Springs, Ca.	N502F
☐ N502JB	82	Falcon 50	115	Sails In Concert Inc. Tallahassee, Fl.	N569CC
☐ N502JL	00	Global Express	9050	Hanover Aviation Inc. Orlando, Fl.	VP-COP
☐ N502JM	04	Learjet 40	45-2017	MALCO Aircraft Sales & Leasing LLC. Las Vegas, Nv.	N5009T
☐ N502KA	96	Gulfstream V	502	Kataiba Al Ghanim, Kuwait.	N502GV
☐ N502PC	92	Challenger 601-3A	5121	PepsiCo Inc. White Plains, NY.	C-GLYK
☐ N502PG	79	Falcon 10	144	Coppergate LLC. Carmel, In.	N502BG
☐ N502QS	00	Gulfstream V	601	NetJets, Columbus, Oh.	N536GA
☐ N502RD	72	Citation	500-0043	Citation 500-043 Leasing Inc. Caracas, Venezuela.	(N96EJ)
☐ N502RP	00	Learjet 60	60-199	Penske Jet Inc. Detroit, Mi.	N253FX
☐ N502TN	02	CitationJet CJ-1	525-0505	Midwest Transplant Network, Westwood, Ks.	N.....
☐ N502XL	04	Citation Excel XLS	560-5502	Distribution Air LLC. Springfield, Mo.	N52144
☐ N503BC	01	Learjet 60	60-239	The Brinks Co. Richmond, Va.	(ZS-SCT)

Reg	Yr	Type	c/n	Owner/Operator	Prev Regn

Reg	Yr	Type	c/n	Owner/Operator	Prev Regn
N503CC	72	Citation	500-0003	JetPlus LLC. Little Rock, Ar.	
N503CG	97	Dornier Do328JET	3086	Chip Ganassi/SABCO Racing Inc. Mooresville, NC.	5N-SPD
N503CS	01	Citation Excel	560-5205	CitationShares Sales Inc. White Plains, NY.	N5100J
N503EA	04	Eclipse 500	EX500-108	Eclipse Aviation Corp. Albuquerque, NM.	
N503EZ	82	Falcon 50	84	Garrett Aviation Services Inc. Springfield, Il.	N2711B
N503MG	66	B 727-191	19392	Roush Racing Inc. Livonia, Mi.	N503RA
N503PC	97	Falcon 50EX	263	PepsiCo Inc. White Plains, NY.	N8550A
N503QS	90	BAe 1000A	9003	NetJets, Columbus, Oh.	G-ELRA
N503RP	01	Learjet 60	60-227	Omicron Transportation Inc. Reading, Pa.	N253FX
N503XS	04	Citation Excel XLS	560-5503	Cessna Aircraft Co. Wichita, Ks.	N.....
N504BW	91	Citation V	560-0128	BorgWarner Inc. Chicago, Il.	N85KC
N504CC	99	Citation V Ultra	560-0504	Casto Plane LLC. Columbus, Oh.	
N504CS	02	Citation Excel	560-5229	CitationShares Sales Inc. White Plains, NY.	N5105F
N504D	79	Citation Eagle	500-0387	Vortex Services Inc. New Orleans, La.	N484KA
N504EA	05	Eclipse 500	EX500-...	Eclipse Aviation Corp. Albuquerque, NM.	
N504F	80	Learjet 35A	35A-340	National Waterworks Inc. Waco, Tx.	N11YM
N504PK	04	Citation Excel	560-5369	Pike Electric Inc. Mount Airy, NC.	N678QS
N504QS	00	Gulfstream V	613	Anchor Marketing, Bar Harbor Island, Fl.	N570GA
N504T	94	Citation VII	650-7040	Fall Creek Partners LLC. Chicago-Du Page, Il.	N1265B
N504TS	87	Challenger 601-3A	5004	Aero Toy Store LLC. Fort Lauderdale, Fl.	N618DC
N505AG	99	Citation Bravo	550-0905	Mike Rutherford, Houston, Tx.	N5101J
N505AJ	67	Falcon 20C	89	Amermex Inc. Laredo, Tx.	N71CP
N505BB	83	Citation 1/SP	501-0323	T & T Ball Corp. Wilmington, De.	(N142AL)
N505BG	80	Citation 1/SP	501-0185	Gunn Oil Co. Wichita Falls, Tx.	N501LL
N505CF	79	Citation 1/SP	501-0130	Coburn's Inc. St Cloud, Mn.	N102HS
N505CS	02	Citation Excel	560-5252	CitationShares Sales Inc. White Plains, NY.	N5145V
N505DH	83	Learjet 35A	35A-504	505 LLC/Norbridge Inc. Fort Lauderdale, Fl.	G-RAFF
N505EA	05	Eclipse 500	EX500-...	Eclipse Aviation Corp. Albuquerque, NM.	
N505EH	83	Learjet 55	55-067	TVPX Inc. Concord, Ma.	N127GT
N505FX	03	Challenger 300	20006	BBJS/FlexJets, Addison, Tx.	N5014F
N505GA	98	Galaxy-1126	005	CC Center LLC. San Rafael, Ca.	4X-IGB
N505HG	75	Learjet 36	36-009	General Transervice Inc. New Castle, De.	N505RA
N505JH	79	Citation 1/SP	501-0126	Jackson Hole Air Charter Inc. Jackson, Wy.	N505SP
N505K	72	Citation	500-0004	HCEA PA. Houston, Tx.	N5005
N505MA	98	Citation X	750-0057	Syracuse Jet Leasing LLC. Syracuse, NY.	
N505QS	91	BAe 1000A	9005	NetJets, Columbus, Oh. (was NA1000).	N410US
N505RJ	77	Citation 1/SP	501-0009	Richard J Rico Revocable Trust, Vacaville, Ca.	N505BC
N505RP	83	Citation II	550-0450	Boston Air Charter Co. Norfolk, Ma.	N15EA
N505RR	97	Falcon 2000	46	Sonic Aviation Inc. Charlotte, NC.	CS-DCM
N505RX	01	Gulfstream V	675	Aventis Pharmaceuticals Inc. Allentown, Pa.	N675GA
N505TC	81	Falcon 50	57	Thornton Corp. Van Nuys, Ca.	N138E
N506BA	83	Falcon 50	230	Air Bahnik LLC/Executive Fliteways Inc. Ronkonkoma, NY.	F-OMON
N506CS	02	Citation Excel	560-5267	CitationShares Sales Inc. White Plains, NY.	N5246Z
N506E	93	Citation V	560-0236	Emerson Electric Co. St Louis, Mo.	
N506EA	05	Eclipse 500	EX500-...	Eclipse Aviation Corp. Albuquerque, NM.	
N506FX	03	Challenger 300	20007	BBJS/FlexJets, Addison, Tx.	C-G...
N506QS	00	Gulfstream V	623	NetJets, Columbus, Oh.	N623GA
N506TF	77	Citation 1/SP	501-0001	Ozark Management LLC. Columbia, Mo.	N51CJ
N506TS	87	Challenger 601-3A	5006	Aero Toy Store LLC. Fort Lauderdale, Fl.	C-GENA
N507AS	00	Falcon 50EX	311	Albertsons Inc. Boise, Id.	F-WWHO
N507CS	02	Citation Excel	560-5282	CitationShares Sales Inc. White Plains, NY.	N5094D
N507CW	81	Diamond 1A	A007SA	Flight Options LLC. Cleveland, Oh.	(N485CW)
N507F	82	HS 125/700A	NA0324	K2 Inc. Carlsbad, Ca.	(N880CR)
N507FX	03	Challenger 300	20008	BBJS/FlexJets, Addison, Tx.	C-GZDV
N507HF	70	Learjet 25	25-057	Chipola Aviation Inc. Marianna, Fl.	(N225EA)
N507QS	01	Gulfstream V	625	NetJets, Columbus, Oh.	N625GA
N507R	82	Challenger 600S	1077	94 Trading LLC. Wilmington, De.	(N940DH)
N507SA	00	Gulfstream 4SP	1456	AMB Group LLC. Atlanta, Ga.	N396GA
N508BP	99	Hawker 800XP	8419	Pilgrim's Pride Corp. Pittsburgh, Tx.	N419XP
N508CJ	02	CitationJet CJ-1	525-0508	Richardson Arrow LLC. Wilmington, De.	N5225K
N508CS	02	Citation Excel	560-5294	CitationShares Sales Inc. White Plains, NY.	N5068R
N508FX	03	Challenger 300	20009	BBJS/FlexJets, Addison, Tx.	C-GZDY
N508GA	04	Gulfstream G200	108	Gulfstream Aerospace LP. Dallas-Love, Tx.	4X-C..
N508GP	81	Learjet 35A	35A-424	Flight Capital LLC. Madison, Ms.	N2844
N508KD	93	Citation V	560-0245	Da-Ro Investments LLC. Scottsdale, Az.	(N508DW)
N508P	02	Gulfstream V	693	Hewlett Packard Co. San Jose, Ca.	N693GA

Reg	Yr	Type	c/n	Owner/Operator	Prev Regn

Reg	Yr	Type	c/n	Owner/Operator	Prev Regn
☐ N508QS	01	Gulfstream V	631	NetJets, Columbus, Oh.	N631GA
☐ N508SR	77	Learjet 24E	24E-347	Roger Claypool, Paia, Hi.	N500SR
☐ N508TL	98	CitationJet	525-0281	LaBonte Racing Inc. Winston Salem, NC.	N500TL
☐ N508VM	75	HS 125/F600B	6045	JJM Leasing LLC. Mundelein, Il.	G-BGYR
☐ N509CS	02	Citation Excel	560-5310	CitationShares Sales Inc. White Plains, NY.	N.....
☐ N509FX	03	Challenger 300	20012	BBJS/FlexJets, Addison, Tx.	C-GZEH
☐ N509QC	80	HS 125/700A	NA0277	WRS Air LLC. Plano, Tx.	(N799FL)
☐ N509QS	00	Gulfstream V	637	NetJets, Columbus, Oh.	N637GA
☐ N510AJ	77	Citation 1/SP	501-0031	Santa Ynez Valley Construction Co. Solvang, Ca.	XA-SDI
☐ N510BC	83	Diamond 1A	A057SA	BC Aviation/Bruno Capital Management Corp. Birmingham, Al.	N334WM
☐ N510BM	69	Falcon 20D	215	Grand Aire Express Inc. Toledo, Oh.	N619GA
☐ N510CL	73	Falcon 10	9	The Stephenson Aviation Trust, Lake in the Hills, Il.	N149TJ
☐ N510FX	04	Challenger 300	20017	BBJS/FlexJets, Addison, Tx.	C-GZEP
☐ N510GP	82	Citation II	550-0421	Uniform Code Council Inc. Van Nuys, Ca.	(N801TA)
☐ N510JC	80	Citation II	550-0197	Five Ten Group LLC. Incline Village, Nv.	HB-VIT
☐ N510MG	98	Gulfstream 4SP	1349	OM Group Inc. Cleveland, Oh.	N616DG
☐ N510MS	69	Learjet 24B	24B-204	DK Turbines LLC. Hollister, Ca.	N510ND
☐ N510MT	91	Citation V	560-0122	Biomet Inc/Air Warsaw Inc. Warsaw, In.	(N710MT)
☐ N510NJ	81	Citation 1/SP	501-0180	Northern Air Inc. Grand Rapids, Mi.	N650MW
☐ N510RH	70	Gulfstream II SP	80	Rick Hendrick Motorsports Inc. Harrisburg, NC.	N500RH
☐ N510SD	88	Citation III	650-0161	Marlin Air Inc. Detroit, Mi.	N500AE
☐ N510SR	69	Gulfstream 2B	70	Related Companies LP. Teterboro, NJ.	N908CE
☐ N510US	78	Gulfstream II SP	223	Adams Investment Enterprises LLC. Ventura, Ca.	N257H
☐ N510WS	73	Falcon 20-5B	292	World Savings & Loan Association, Oakland, Ca.	N733S
☐ N511AB	81	Citation II	550-0299	Elizabeth Cardide Die Co. Allegheny County. (was 551-0339).	HB-VIR
☐ N511AC	95	CitationJet	525-0098	Avis Industrial Corp. Upland, In.	N5156D
☐ N511AJ	70	Learjet 25	25-055	SunTrust Bank, Miami, Fl.	N65RC
☐ N511AT	74	Citation	500-0166	Air Ambulance by Air Trek Inc. Punta Gorda, Fl.	N8DE
☐ N511BA	69	Gulfstream 2	49	Okun Air LLC. Indianapolis, In.	(N49JS)
☐ N511BP	99	CitationJet	525-0332	Alabama Farmers Cooperative, Decatur, Al.	(N332VP)
☐ N511CS	03	Citation Excel	560-5324	CitationShares Sales Inc. White Plains, NY.	N.....
☐ N511DR	94	Citation V Ultra	560-0274	Loretto Aviation LLC. San Jose, Ca.	(N511DP)
☐ N511FL*	67	Falcon 20C-5	122	T-Bird Aviation Inc. Chicago-DuPage, Il.	N302TT
☐ N511FX	04	Challenger 300	20021	BBJS/FlexJets, Addison, Tx.	C-G...
☐ N511JP	00	Citation Bravo	550-0959	Northshore Air LLC. Mandeville, La.	N418KW
☐ N511KA	78	HS 125/700A	NA0237	Crusader Aviation Inc. Oxford, Ct.	N511GP
☐ N511PA	89	Gulfstream 4	1111	Apex Oil Co. Clayton, Mo.	N111ZT
☐ N511QS	01	Gulfstream V	647	NetJets, Columbus, Oh.	N647GA
☐ N511TC	94	CitationJet	525-0074	Semitool Inc. Cambridge, UK.	N26581
☐ N511TD	69	JetStar-8	5145	Centurion Investments Inc. St Louis, Mo.	XA-JFE
☐ N511TH	01	Citation Encore	560-0561	Triad Hospitals Inc. Dallas, Tx.	N120SB
☐ N511TS	67	JetStar-731	5101	Anthony Holdings International Inc. West Mifflin, Pa.	N800AF
☐ N511WP	01	Learjet 45	45-183	West Point Stevens Inc. La Grange-Callaway, Ga.	N5025K
☐ N511WV	91	Citation V	560-0138	Cin-Jet Inc. Cincinnati, Oh.	OY-FFV
☐ N512C	00	Gulfstream 4SP	1428	A T & T Wireless Inc. Seattle, Wa.	N330GA
☐ N512CC	72	Citation	500-0012	K3C Inc/Sierra Industries Inc. Uvalde, Tx.	XC-FIU
☐ N512CS	03	Citation Excel	560-5326	CitationShares Sales Inc. White Plains, NY.	N.....
☐ N512FX	04	Challenger 300	20022	BBJS/FlexJets, Addison, Tx.	C-GZDS
☐ N512SD	73	Gulfstream II SP	130	The Provident Bank, Cincinnati, Oh.	N518GS
☐ N513AC	70	Falcon 20D	242	Westway Air Inc. Sugar Land, Tx.	(N242MA)
☐ N513EF	97	Citation V Ultra	560-0412	Eagle Aviation Inc. West Columbia, SC.	N412CW
☐ N513LR	91	BAe 1000A	NA1004	Raytheon Aircraft Co. Wichita, Ks.	(N513RA)
☐ N513ML	03	Hawker 800XP	8641	M P Air Inc/Mylan Pharmaceuticals Inc. Morgantown, WV.	N641XP
☐ N513MW	97	Gulfstream V	510	BMW GmbH. Munich, Germany.	N598GA
☐ N513RV	03	CitationJet CJ-1	525-0513	La Mesa RV Center Inc. Eugene, Or.	N52591
☐ N514AJ	74	HS 125/600B	6033	A J Foyt Enterprises Inc. Waller, Tx.	N600HS
☐ N514BC	00	Citation Bravo	550-0947	J Oliver Cunningham, Phoenix, Az.	N947CB
☐ N514CS	03	Citation Excel	560-5328	CitationShares Sales Inc. White Plains, NY.	N.....
☐ N514DS	97	CitationJet	525-0255	D S Aviation Inc. Irving, Tx.	
☐ N514FX	04	Challenger 300	20023	BBJS/FlexJets, Addison, Tx.	N513FX
☐ N514QS	91	BAe 1000A	NA1005	NetJets, Columbus, Oh.	N125CJ
☐ N515BP	80	Challenger 600S	1006	Affiliated Computer Services Inc. Dallas-Love, Tx.	N296V
☐ N515CS	03	Citation Excel	560-5335	CitationShares Sales Inc. White Plains, NY.	N.....
☐ N515EV	03	CitationJet CJ-2	525A-0211	Everair LLC. Niagara Falls, NY.	N.....
☐ N515GM	00	BBJ-7BC	30782	Kevinair LLC. Van Nuys, Ca.	N1006F
☐ N515KK	84	Diamond 1A	A086SA	Kent Kelly/Diamond Aircraft Leasing Corp. Montgomery, Al.	N486DM

Reg	Yr	Type	c/n	Owner/Operator	Prev Regn
N515MW	92	Beechjet 400A	RK-38	Moore Wallace North America Inc. Stamford, Ct.	N522EF
N515PL	89	Gulfstream 4	1092	NBL LLC. Bozeman, Mt.	N18RF
N515PV	02	Falcon 2000	192	Sentry Aviation Services LLC. Stevens Point, Wi.	N2000A
N515QS	91	BAe 1000A	NA1006	NetJets, Columbus, Oh.	N1000E
N515TC	81	Learjet 25D	25D-354	Eagle Wings Aviation Inc. St Joseph, Mo.	N3795U
N515TJ	99	Beechjet 400A	RK-229	Drake Aviation Inc. Bloomfield Hills, Mi.	N3129X
N515WA	98	Beechjet 400A	RK-215	Aalfs Manufacturing Inc. Sioux City, SD.	N3038W
N515WE	74	Citation	500-0208	Southern Air Services Inc. Tuscaloosa, Al.	(N508CC)
N516CC	00	Galaxy-1126	020	Morgan Flight LLC. Naples, Fl.	N46GX
N516FX	04	Challenger 300	20036	BBJS/FlexJets, Addison, Tx.	C-F...
N516GH	98	Gulfstream V	553	MDL Consulting Associates LLC. Nashua, NH.	N653GA
N516QS	01	Gulfstream V	658	NetJets, Columbus, Oh.	N532GA
N516SM	91	Challenger 601-3A	5089	U S Cable Corp. West Palm Beach, Fl.	N968L
N517AF	98	Citation Bravo	550-0846	Flying U LLC. Elkhorn, Ne.	N5101J
N517AM	84	Learjet 55	55-108	aaiPharma Inc. Wilmington, NC.	(N551AM)
N517CC*	96	Learjet 31A	31A-117	Carmike Cinemas Inc. Columbus, Ga.	N317LJ
N517CW	80	Falcon 50	17	Flight Options LLC. Cleveland, Oh.	(N550LX)
N517FX	04	Challenger 300	20038	BBJS/FlexJets, Addison, Tx.	C-G...
N517GP	98	Learjet 31A	31A-152	Smail Aviation Inc. Latrobe, Pa.	
N517LR	92	BAe 1000A	9017	Raytheon Aircraft Co. Wichita, Ks.	N517QS
N517PJ	99	Falcon 2000	94	Tait Aviation LLC. San Jose, Ca.	N48HA
N518CL	95	Challenger 601-3R	5180	Applera Corp. White Plains, NY.	C-GLYO
N518EJ	80	Falcon 50	18	AmQuip Sales & Leasing Inc. Bensalem, Pa.	(N10UG)
N518GS	02	Learjet 45	45-225	George Strait Productions Inc. San Antonio, Tx.	N436FX
N518JG	00	Learjet 31A	31A-219	Joe Gibbs Racing Inc. Concord, NC.	N214PW
N518M	05	Hawker 800XP	8737	Raytheon Aircraft Co. Wichita, Ks.	
N518MV	81	Citation II/SP	551-0046	JFM Development LLC. Byron, Ca.	N81GD
N518N	87	Citation II	550-0563	Neuhoff Aviation Inc. Dallas, Tx.	G-THCL
N518SB	79	Learjet 55C	55C-139A	La Stella Corp. Pueblo, Co. (was 55-002)	N518SA
N519AA	79	Citation II	550-0053	Extreme Auto & Marine Inc. Warren, Oh.	N550EC
N519AF	83	Gulfstream 3	393	A & F Aircraft Leasing LLC. Van Nuys, Ca.	N33GZ
N519CW	80	Falcon 50	19	Flight Options LLC. Cleveland, Oh.	(N551LX)
N519M	05	Hawker 800XP	8747	Raytheon Aircraft Co. Wichita, Ks.	
N519MZ	01	Challenger 604	5519	Bombardier Aerospace Corp. Windsor Locks, Ct.	P4-AVJ
N520AF	94	Falcon 50	247	AFLAC Inc. Columbus, Ga.	N740R
N520AW	81	Falcon 20F-5B	453	AWI (Nevada) Inc. Las Vegas, Nv.	N189MM
N520CH	97	Beechjet 400A	RK-162	Concord Hospitality Enterprises Inc. Raleigh, NC.	OY-SIS
N520CM	99	Citation X	750-0107	Caremark RX Inc. Birmingham, Al.	N107CX
N520DB	63	MS 760 Paris-2	101	Eaglehead Aviation Inc. Tifton, Ga.	N444ET
N520E	90	Gulfstream 4	1138	Exxon Mobil Corp. Houston, Tx.	(N501E)
N520G	00	Citation Excel	560-5083	Oldenburg Aviation Inc. Milwaukee, Wi.	N52144
N520JF	97	Hawker 800XP	8317	Scott Reichelm/TAG Aviation Inc. White Plains, NY.	N520BA
N520JM	02	CitationJet CJ-2	525A-0086	Blue Ribbon Jet LLC. Hyrum, Ut.	N5132T
N520MP	85	Westwind-1124	421	Interselect Inc. Dallas, Tx.	N317MQ
N520QS	92	BAe 1000A	NA1008	NetJets, Columbus, Oh.	N676BA
N520SC	01	Learjet 60	60-233	Stryker Corp. Kalamazoo, Mi.	N33DC
N520SP	04	Hawker 800XP	8669	Star North Aviation Inc. Latrobe, Pa.	N669XP
N520SR	79	Learjet 25D	25D-272	Reagan Buick Oldsmobile Inc. Omaha, Ne.	N717AN
N520WS	88	Beechjet 400	RJ-53	World Savings & Loan Association, Oakland, Ca.	N53EB
N521CD	03	Falcon 2000EX	21	Cendant Corp. Ronkonkoma, NY.	N221EX
N521CS	04	Citation Excel	560-5362	CitationShares Sales Inc. White Plains, NY.	N.....
N521FL	66	Falcon 20-5	68	IFL Group Inc. Waterford, Mi.	N458SW
N521FP	97	Citation X	750-0016	Universal Forest Products Inc. Grand Rapids, Mi.	N206PC
N521JK	94	Hawker 800	8262	Spankie LLC. Van Nuys, Ca.	N959H
N521LF	91	Citation V	560-0132	Interlease Aviation Corp. Van Nuys, Ca.	N226JV
N521PF	93	CitationJet	525-0005	P F Flyers Inc. Lakeland, Fl.	N58KJ
N521RA	99	Citation Excel	560-5076	Shea Aviation Inc. Newton, NC.	
N521TM	92	Citation II	550-0705	Idaho Power Co. Boise, Id.	
N521WH*	01	Learjet 31A	31A-220	WDH Aviation LLC/Richards Aviation Inc. Memphis, Tn.	N521CH
N522AC	03	Gulfstream G400	1524	RDV Corp. Grand Rapids, Mi.	N524GA
N522CS	04	Citation Excel	560-5364	CitationShares Sales Inc. White Plains, NY.	N.....
N522EE	03	Hawker 800XP	8621	Energy Education of Montana Inc. Wichita Falls, Tx.	(N621XP)
N522EL	02	Beechjet 400A	RK-342	TT Transport LLC. Memphis, Tn.	N522EE
N522JA	95	Citation V Ultra	560-0288	Seminole Aviation LLC. Seminole, Ok.	N5141F
N522RA	00	Citation Excel	560-5136	Peach Aviation LLC. Thomasville, GA.	N560JP
N522WK	83	Learjet 55	55-088	Jet Corp. Chesterfield, Mo.	N901JC

Reg	Yr	Type	c/n	Owner/Operator	Prev Regn

Reg	Yr	Type	c/n	Owner/Operator	Prev Regn
❏ N523AC*	03	Gulfstream G400	1528	Amway Corp. Grand Rapids, Mi.	N528GA
❏ N523BT	98	CitationJet	525-0311	Beall Lessors Inc. Portland, Or.	
❏ N523CS	04	Citation Excel XLS	560-5507	CitationShares Sales Inc. White Plains, NY.	N.....
❏ N523CW	80	Falcon 50	23	Flight Options LLC. Cleveland, Oh.	(N553LX)
❏ N523JM	92	Challenger 601-3A	5106	Worthington Industries/McAir Inc. Worthington, Oh.	(N601PR)
❏ N523KW	98	Citation Excel	560-5015	Capital Excel Inc. Wichita, Ks.	N5223D
❏ N523NA	81	Guardian HU-25B	439	NASA, Langley Research Centre, Hampton, Va.	2125
❏ N523QS	92	BAe 1000A	NA1010	NetJets, Columbus, Oh.	N679BA
❏ N523WC	03	Falcon 2000	212	N523WC LLC/Marion Plaza Inc. Youngstown, Oh.	N523W
❏ N523WG	87	BAe 125/800A	8086	Jen-Air LLC. DuPage, Il.	(N523W)
❏ N524AC	02	Gulfstream V	686	Alticor Inc. Grand Rapids, Mi.	N686GA
❏ N524AN	89	Gulfstream 4	1119	Harrinford Ltd. Tortola, BVI.	N768J
❏ N524CJ	03	CitationJet CJ-1	525-0524	Commander Properties Inc. Kenner, La.	N5202D
❏ N524DW	71	Learjet 25B	25B-081	Charter Airlines Inc. Las Vegas, Nv.	N66TJ
❏ N524HC	95	Learjet 31A	31A-114	Harbert Corp. Birmingham, Al.	
❏ N524LP	04	Hawker 400XP	RK-386	PIN Aviation LLC. Irving, Tx.	
❏ N524LR	92	BAe 1000A	9024	Raytheon Aircraft Co. Wichita, Ks.	N524QS
❏ N524MA	78	Citation II	550-0029	Penn Warranty Corp. Taylor, Pa.	N550TJ
❏ N524PA	75	Learjet 35	35-033	Phoenix Air Group Inc. Cartersville, Ga.	N31FN
❏ N524SF	98	CitationJet	525-0240	CPL Aviation/C P Lockyer Inc. Coventry, UK.	N525GM
❏ N525AD	04	CitationJet CJ-1+	525-0600	Cessna Aircraft Co. Wichita, Ks. (was 525-0536)	N52369
❏ N525AL	93	CitationJet	525-0011	JetCo Holdings Inc. Guernsey, Channel Islands.	(N1327N)
❏ N525AM	04	CitationJet CJ-1	525-0538	Rancho Pacific Holdings LLC. Rancho Cucamonga, Ca.	N51564
❏ N525AR	00	CitationJet CJ-1	525-0395	A R Wings Inc. Pittsburgh, Pa.	N5183U
❏ N525AS	00	CitationJet CJ-1	525-0363	All-State Industries Inc. Des Moines, Ia.	
❏ N525BP	01	CitationJet CJ-1	525-0479	BPI Aviation LLC. Sioux City, Ia.	N5200R
❏ N525BR	01	CitationJet CJ-1	525-0444	WS Aviation LLC. Birmingham, Al.	(N525WS)
❏ N525BT	96	CitationJet	525-0161	Vichon Nevelle (Nevada) Inc. Las Vegas, Nv.	N5076K
❏ N525CC	00	CitationJet CJ-2	525A-0007	Cessna Aircraft Co. Wichita, Ks.	(N8CQ)
❏ N525CD	99	CitationJet CJ-1	525-0360	C & D Aerospace, Garden Grove, Ca.	N31CJ
❏ N525CG	02	CitationJet CJ-2	525A-0125	Cessna Aircraft Co. Riyadh, Saudi Arabia.	N525CC
❏ N525CH	94	CitationJet	525-0078	Cooper Hosiery Mills Inc. Fort Payne, Al.	N5085E
❏ N525CK	02	CitationJet CJ-2	525A-0128	Dr Charles Key MD. Dallas, Tx.	N5204D
❏ N525CM	95	CitationJet	525-0093	International Auto Brokers Inc. Paradise Valley, Az.	I-IDAG
❏ N525CU	98	CitationJet	525-0292	Flying Enterprises LLC. Albuquerque, NM.	N171W
❏ N525CW	93	Citation V	560-0225	Flight Options LLC. Cleveland, Oh.	N1823S
❏ N525DC	97	CitationJet	525-0195	Pacific Cataract & Laser Institute, Chehalis-Centralia, Wa.	(N525ST)
❏ N525DG	01	CitationJet CJ-2	525A-0084	Direct Jet Charter LLC. Greensboro, NC.	N.....
❏ N525DL	02	CitationJet CJ-2	525A-0050	North Central Management Inc. Madison, Wi.	N.....
❏ N525DM*	99	CitationJet	525-0314	Marco Opthalmic Inc. Jacksonville, Fl.	N428PC
❏ N525DP	99	CitationJet	525-0318	Means to Go LLC. Altoona, Pa.	
❏ N525DR	98	CitationJet	525-0308	Aqua Blue Aviation Inc. San Diego, Ca.	N72SG
❏ N525DT	00	CitationJet CJ-2	525A-0003	Leonard Green & Partners LP. Van Nuys, Ca.	N132CJ
❏ N525DV	02	CitationJet CJ-2	525A-0119	Pacific Cataract & Laser Institute, Chehalis-Centralia, Wa.	N.....
❏ N525DY	98	CitationJet	525-0306	Torrance Hangar Development LLC. Rolling Hills, Ca.	N4RH
❏ N525EC	98	CitationJet	525-0246	Entertainment Co. Sevierville, Tn.	
❏ N525EZ	02	CitationJet CJ-2	525A-0080	Eli's Bread Inc. NYC.	N5135K
❏ N525F	94	CitationJet	525-0058	Semitool Europe, Salzburg, Austria.	N526CK
❏ N525FT	99	CitationJet CJ-1	525-0367	G & G Aviation LLC.	N51872
❏ N525GM	02	CitationJet CJ-2	525A-0150	IntegriAir LLC. New Haven, Ct.	N.....
❏ N525GP	98	Learjet 31A	31A-155	Georgia Pacific Corp. Atlanta, Ga.	
❏ N525GV	91	CitationJet	525-0001	Guardian Enterprises Inc. Portland, Or.	N525VP
❏ N525HB	01	CitationJet CJ-2	525A-0040	Harold Bagwell, Garner, NC.	N.....
❏ N525HC	98	CitationJet	525-0270	Springfield Flying Service Inc. Springfield, Mo.	N5194J
❏ N525HS	93	CitationJet	525-0035	Cloud Eleven Inc. Zurich, Switzerland.	N1779E
❏ N525HV	97	CitationJet	525-0201	Hy-Vee Inc. West Des Moines, Ia.	N5156D
❏ N525J	97	CitationJet	525-0184	National Pacific Fund Inc. Beckeley, Ca.	N5185V
❏ N525JD	02	CitationJet CJ-2	525A-0130	JD Air Inc. Wyckoff, NJ.	N51396
❏ N525JJ	02	CitationJet CJ-1	525-0497	Stanley Bank, Kansas City, Ks.	N132CS)
❏ N525JL	00	CitationJet CJ-1	525-0407	Lewis Investment Co. Birmingham, Al.	N51872
❏ N525JM	96	CitationJet	525-0134	Keen Transport Inc. Carlisle, Pa.	(N525KT)
❏ N525JV	93	CitationJet	525-0010	Flying B's LLC. Rogers, Ar.	ZS-MVX
❏ N525KA	96	CitationJet	525-0162	Carolex Air LLC. Chattanooga, Tn.	(N39GA)
❏ N525KA	92	CitationJet	525-0019	Physical Systems Inc. Carson City, Nv.	(N525SP)
❏ N525KN	93	CitationJet	525-0007	R & B Air LLC. Cary, NC.	(N1327E)
❏ N525KR	03	CitationJet CJ-2	525A-0160	Rombauer Vineyards Inc. St Helena, Ca.	N.....

| Reg | Yr | Type | c/n | Owner/Operator | Prev Regn |

Reg	Yr	Type	c/n	Owner/Operator	Prev Regn
☐ N525LB	00	CitationJet CJ-1	525-0388	JetEast LLC. Cincinnati, Oh.	N525MH
☐ N525LC	82	Citation II	550-0349	United Builders Service Inc. Jeffco Airport, Co.	N600SZ
☐ N525LF	00	CitationJet CJ-1	525-0382	Mallard Air LLC. El Cerrito, Ca.	N5124F
☐ N525LM	00	CitationJet CJ-1	525-0427	MML Investments LLC. Medford, Or.	N128GW
☐ N525LP	97	CitationJet	525-0196	LP Adventures Inc. Wilmington, De.	N250GM
☐ N525LW	94	CitationJet	525-0082	Orion Aviation International LLC. Hintsville, Al.	D-IHHS
☐ N525M	99	CitationJet	525-0334	West Land Holdings LLC. Memphis, Tn.	(N44FE)
☐ N525MB	93	CitationJet	525-0036	Falcon Aviation Inc. Columbus, Oh.	N1782E
☐ N525MC	93	CitationJet	525-0018	McCoy Corp. San Marcos, Tx.	(N1328X)
☐ N525MF	98	CitationJet	525-0313	SMJ Delaware Inc. Wilmington, De.	N525MR
☐ N525ML	00	CitationJet CJ-1	525-0402	N525ML LLC. Las Vegas, Nv.	N.....
☐ N525MP	01	CitationJet CJ-2	525A-0012	PAWS LLC. Las Vegas, Nv.	
☐ N525MR	03	CitationJet CJ-2	525A-0173	Philips Holding LLC. Minneapolis-Flying Cloud, Mn.	N.....
☐ N525MW	00	CitationJet CJ-1	525-0370	P D Gaus, Duesseldorf, Germany.	N5145P
☐ N525NA	94	CitationJet	525-0048	Jackson Food Stores Inc. Meridian, Id.	N500HC
☐ N525NP	01	CitationJet CJ-1	525-0458	Deanna Enterprises LLC. Baton Rouge, La.	LX-MSP
☐ N525P	96	CitationJet	525-0165	Augusta Aviation LLC. Augusta, Ga.	D-IHCW
☐ N525PB	97	CitationJet	525-0232	JCL Corp. Bentonville, Ar.	N525PF
☐ N525PE	02	Citation Bravo	550-1031	Plastic Engineering Co. Sheboygan, Wi.	N.....
☐ N525PF	01	CitationJet CJ-2	525A-0023	Fenske Media Corp. Rapid City, SD.	N5135K
☐ N525PL	93	CitationJet	525-0043	Chandelle Investment Corp. Portland, Or.	N2616L
☐ N525PM	02	CitationJet CJ-2	525A-0067	Continental Management Co. Douglas, IOM.	N5141F
☐ N525PS	94	CitationJet	525-0061	Omyaviation Inc. Proctor, Vt.	N61CJ
☐ N525PT	95	CitationJet	525-0125	Herman Briones, Santiago, Chile.	N525PE
☐ N525PV	80	Citation 1/SP	501-0188	Rio Grande Chemical (GP) LLC. McAllen, Tx.	N251CT
☐ N525QS	92	BAe 1000A	9025	NetJets, Columbus, Oh.	N292H
☐ N525RA	96	CitationJet	525-0167	A-One Flight LLC/Fly Away Inc. Alpharetta, Ga.	N1EF
☐ N525RC	97	CitationJet	525-0178	Rydell Co. Sioux Falls, SD.	
☐ N525RD	91	Citation V	560-0106	Phillips Plastics Corp. Phillips, Wi.	N60SH
☐ N525RF	00	CitationJet CJ-1	525-0411	525RF LLC. Hampton, Va.	N51575
☐ N525RK	00	CitationJet CJ-1	525-0413	Graham National Bank, Bethany, Ok.	N5185J
☐ N525RM	97	CitationJet	525-0225	Molded Fiber Glass Companies, Ashtabula, Oh.	
☐ N525RP	93	CitationJet	525-0023	Acme Rocket Sleds Inc. Van Nuys, Ca.	N525RF
☐ N525RW	02	CitationJet CJ-2	525A-0060	Warren Manufacturing Inc. Birmingham, Al.	N57HC
☐ N525SD	89	Challenger 601-3A	5056	Skye Gryphon LLC. Hooksatt, NH.	N153NS
☐ N525SM	03	CitationJet CJ-2	525A-0175	SMI Air LLC/Systems & Methods Inc. Carrollton, Ga.	N.....
☐ N525TF	94	CitationJet	525-0067	TFP Corp. Medina, Oh.	N594JB
☐ N525TG	01	CitationJet CJ-2	525A-0021	Means to Go LLC. Altoona, Pa.	
☐ N525TJ	01	CitationJet CJ-2	525A-0024	Champlain Air Inc. Plattsburgh, NY.	N5216A
☐ N525TW	68	Learjet 25	25-011	Sierra American Corp. Addison, Tx.	N108GA
☐ N525VG	98	CitationJet	525-0239	Av Solutions Inc. Flint, Mi.	PT-XJS
☐ N525VV	02	CitationJet CJ-2	525A-0113	CJ2-113 LLC. Wilmington, De.	N.....
☐ N525WB	94	CitationJet	525-0079	Barnet Vistas LLC. Spartanburg, SC.	N179CJ
☐ N525WC	95	CitationJet	525-0107	Option Air LLC. Boston, Ma.	N5211F
☐ N525WD	02	CitationJet CJ-2	525A-0107	WD Aviation Inc. Louisville, Ky.	N.....
☐ N525WM	97	CitationJet	525-0213	Carolex Air LLC. Chattanooga, Tn.	
☐ N525WW	94	CitationJet	525-0060	Walters & Wolff, Fremont, Ca.	XA-TRI
☐ N525XX	81	Westwind-1124	336	Trans Alliance Inc. Plainfield, Il.	N255RB
☐ N525ZZ	01	CitationJet CJ-2	525A-0055	The Des Moines Co. Des Moines, Ia.	N207BS
☐ N526AC	89	BAe 125/800A	8169	Alticor Inc. Grand Rapids, Mi.	N47CG
☐ N526CP	95	CitationJet	525-0099	HawgWild Air LLC. Springdale, Ar.	N525CP
☐ N526EE	00	Gulfstream 4SP	1406	Grass Green LLC.	N404GA
☐ N526EZ	00	CitationJet CJ-1	525-0400	Federated Rural Electric Management, Lenexa, Ks.	(N88798)
☐ N526GP	99	Learjet 31A	31A-181	Georgia Pacific Corp. Atlanta, Ga.	N134FX
☐ N526HV	03	CitationJet CJ-2	525A-0139	Hy-Vee Inc. Des Moines, Ia.	N5228Z
☐ N527AC	87	BAe 125/800A	NA0405	Alticor Inc. Grand Rapids, Mi.	N542BA
☐ N527CJ	03	CitationJet CJ-1	525-0527	Labat-Anderson Inc. McLean, Va.	N5211Q
☐ N527DS	81	Citation II	550-0287	JFS Leasing Corp. Atlanta, Ga.	(N221JS)
☐ N527EW	83	Citation 1/SP	501-0322	Rockville Investments (Jersey) Ltd. Jersey, C.I. (AVB 5EW).	(N769EW)
☐ N527GP	99	Learjet 31A	31A-182	Georgia Pacific Corp. Atlanta, Ga.	N136FX
☐ N527JA	90	Challenger 601-3A	5058	Endeavour Partners LLC. Matthews, NC.	N101SK
☐ N527JG	03	Gulfstream G400	1519	Gibbs International Inc. Spartanburg, SC.	N519GA
☐ N527M	86	BAe 125/800A	8054	Marathon Oil Co. Findlay, Oh.	G-5-15
☐ N527PA	76	Learjet 36A	36A-019	Phoenix Air Group Inc. Cartersville, Ga.	N540PA
☐ N527SC	02	Citation Excel	560-5260	Spartech Corp. Spirit of St Louis, Mo.	N.....
☐ N528AP	83	Gulfstream 3	399	Arrow Plane LLC. Salt Lake City, Ut.	N188TJ
Reg	*Yr*	*Type*	*c/n*	*Owner/Operator*	*Prev Regn*

Reg	Yr	Type	c/n	Owner/Operator	Prev Regn
N528BP	03	Hawker 800XP	8646	Pilgrims Pride Corp. Pittsburgh, Tx.	N646XP
N528CJ	04	CitationJet CJ-1	525-0528	Hi Fli Aviation Too LLC. Charleston, SC.	N.....
N528GP	99	Challenger 604	5401	Georgia Pacific Corp. Atlanta, Ga.	N98FJ
N528JR	88	Falcon 900	51	Hartvig Aviation LLC. Mclean, Va.	N9RG
N528KW	92	Citation V	560-0224	Five in Five LLC. Dallas, Tx.	N523KW
N528M	86	BAe 125/800A	8055	Marathon Oil Co. Findlay, Oh.	G-5-504
N528QS	04	Gulfstream G550	5042	NetJets, Columbus, Oh.	N942GA
N528RR	90	Astra-1125SP	042	RFP Aeronautical Corp. Irving, Tx.	N588R
N529AL	90	Gulfstream 4	1123	WFBNW NA. Salt Lake City, Ut. (trustor ?).	I-LUBI
N529D	84	Challenger 601	3025	Trust Aviation Inc. Manchester, NH.	N529DM
N529DB	97	Challenger 800	7152	Hardwicke Properties LLC. Wilmington, De.	N655CC
N529DM	03	Challenger 604	5575	Trust Aviation Inc. Manchester, NH.	C-GLWT
N529GP	99	Challenger 604	5412	Georgia Pacific Corp. Atlanta, Ga.	N99FJ
N529KF	95	Learjet 60	60-064	EL Holdings LLC. Chicago, Il.	N210HV
N529M	99	Hawker 800XP	8446	Marathon Oil Co. Houston, Tx.	
N529MM	80	Falcon 50	29	Meisner Aircraft Inc. Lake in the Hills, Il.	N529CW
N529PC	99	CitationJet CJ-2	525A-0001	PJC Ventures LLC. Dover, De.	N525AZ
N529TS	77	JetStar 2	5209	GLE Aircraft LLC. Sunny Isles Beach, Fl.	N297US
N530AG	00	CitationJet CJ-1	525-0409	Chatham Air LLC. Chatham, Ma.	(N334DB)
N530AR	87	Falcon 50	175	Miami Valley CTC Inc. Dayton, Oh.	(VP-B..)
N530DG	94	Falcon 50	245	Gallagher Enterprises LLC. Pueblo, Co.	N720ME
N530DL	80	Westwind-1124	287	Leprino Foods, Broomfield, Co.	N146BF
N530GA	79	Gulfstream II SP	247	EG Air LLC. Detroit, Mi/MG-75 Inc. Waterford, Mi.	N75MG
N530KF	66	B 727-61	19176	Grecoair Inc. El Paso, Tx.	N2777
N530P	81	Citation II	550-0310	Business Aircraft Group Inc. Cleveland, Oh.	N7798D
N530SM*	04	Hawker 800XP	8697	Raytheon Aircraft Co. Wichita, Ks.	N697XP
N531AB	75	Sabre-60	306-98	Hubert Jet LLC. Pontiac, Mi.	N169AC
N531AF	98	Gulfstream V	531	Vulcan Northwest Inc. Seattle-Tacoma, Wa.	(N8CA)
N531AJ	75	Learjet 35	35-011	Western Aviation Services Inc. Englewood, Co.	N408RB
N531CM	85	Citation S/II	S550-0033	Myers Group V Inc. Omaha, Ne.	N550ST
N531CW	77	Learjet 25D	25D-231	DZT Inc. Lawrenceville, Ga.	N225HW
N531MD	95	Gulfstream 4SP	1280	Yona Venetian LLC. Las Vegas, Nv.	N468GA
N531RA	00	Learjet 31A	31A-192	R A Aviation LLC. Chattanooga, Tn.	N50088
N531RC	01	Citation Excel	560-5184	Great Dane Financial LLC. Chicago, Il.	N184XL
N531SK	92	Learjet 31A	31A-043	SK Logistics Inc. Jacksonville, Fl.	N43LJ
N532CC	00	Citation Excel	560-5111	Charlotte Pipe & Foundry Co. Charlotte, NC.	N5141F
N532MA	89	Citation V	560-0036	Edens & Avant Realty Inc. Columbia, SC.	(N560EJ)
N532PJ	99	Hawker 800XP	8448	Master Four LLC/Town Fair Tire Centers Inc. Oxford, Ct.	N41280
N532SP	00	Gulfstream V-SP	632	Gulfstream Aerospace Corp. Savannah, Ga. (Ff 31 Aug 01).	N5SP
N533CC	01	Citation Excel	560-5201	Ruddick Corp. Charlotte, NC.	N5096S
N533MA	79	Citation II	550-0078	Four Twenty One Inc. Oklahoma City, Ok.	(N277A)
N533QS	92	BAe 1000A	9033	NetJets, Columbus, Oh.	N850BL
N534CC	99	Citation Excel	560-5025	Ruddick Corp. Charlotte, NC.	
N534H	90	Citation III	650-0196	Hillenbrand Industries Inc. Batesville, In.	N896EC
N534TX	95	CitationJet	525-0092	Golondrina Air Inc. Sandia, Tx.	N523AS
N535AF	78	Learjet 35A	35A-191	Ameriflight Inc. Burbank, Ca.	N35SE
N535BC	03	Hawker 800XP	8655	WAC Charter Inc. Aurora, Co.	N655XP
N535BP	03	Citation Encore	560-0646	Beef Products Inc. Sioux City, Ia.	N846QS
N535CD	03	390 Premier 1	RB-96	C & D Aerospace, Santa Ana, Ca.	
N535CE	02	Citation Encore	560-0635	Latium Jet Services Inc. Staverton, UK.	N5257C
N535CJ	04	CitationJet CJ-1	525-0535	JAC USA Inc. NYC.	N5090A
N535LR	95	CitationJet	525-0128	L R Green Co/Poster Display Co. Indianapolis, In.	N5092D
N535QS	93	BAe 1000A	9035	NetJets, Columbus, Oh.	N160BA
N535TA	75	Learjet 35	35-013	B & C Flight Management Inc. Houston, Tx.	N35BN
N535V	98	Gulfstream V	535	GVX Inc/Dart Container Corp. Sarasota, Fl.	N775US
N536KN	76	Learjet 35A	35A-073	Grand Aire Express Inc. Toledo, Oh.	N610GA
N538XL	04	Citation Excel XLS	560-5538	Cessna Aircraft Co. Wichita, Ks.	N5163C
N539LB	93	Learjet 31A	31A-078	Bettcher Industries Inc. Birmingham, Al.	N112CM
N539PG	74	Sabre-60	306-79	Sharecraft LLC. North Canton, Oh.	N43JG
N539QS	93	BAe 1000A	9039	NetJets, Columbus, Oh.	N169BA
N539WA	00	Citation Encore	560-0556	Westchester Air Inc. Jonesville, Tx.	N5165P
N540B	79	HS 125/700A	NA0255	Virginia Binger/Jucamcyn Theaters Corp. Minneapolis, Mn.	N125AJ
N540CH	96	Gulfstream 4SP	1306	Chase Manhattan Bank, White Plains, NY.	N441GA
N540CS	04	Citation Excel XLS	560-5516	CitationShares Sales Inc. White Plains, NY.	N.....
N540EA	75	Gulfstream II SP	174	Jetmark Aviation LLC/Richmor Aviation Inc. Waterbury-Oxford.	N900ES
N540LR*	93	BAe 1000A	9040	Raytheon Aircraft Co. Wichita, Ks.	N540QS

Reg	Yr	Type	c/n	Owner/Operator	Prev Regn

Reg	Yr	Type	c/n	Owner/Operator	Prev Regn
N540M	00	Gulfstream V	597	Marathon Oil Co. Findlay, Oh.	N302K
N540W	95	Gulfstream 4SP	1265	Harpo Productions-Oprah Winfrey/Leap of Faith Inc. Chicago.	N465GA
N541CS	04	Citation Excel XLS	560-5521	CitationShares Sales Inc. White Plains, NY.	N.....
N541CV	00	Citation Encore	560-0541	CUNA Mutual Life Insurance Co. Waverly, Ia.	(N486BG)
N541CW	80	Diamond 1	A004SA	Turbine Aircraft Marketing Inc. San Angelo, Tx.	(N541TM)
N541LR*	93	BAe 1000A	9041	Raytheon Aircraft Co. Wichita, Ks.	N541QS
N541PA	76	Learjet 35	35-053	Phoenix Air Group Inc. Cartersville, Ga.	N53FN
N541RL	89	Astra-1125	034	Northsky Flights LLC. Eagle Point, Or.	N511WA
N541S	86	Citation III	650-0115	CGW Inc/Starter Jet II LLC. Atlanta, Ga.	N1419J
N542CS	04	Citation Excel XLS	560-5523	CitationShares Sales Inc. White Plains, NY.	N.....
N542QS	93	BAe 1000A	9042	NetJets, Columbus, Oh.	N941H
N542SA	83	Learjet 35A	35A-503	Jetstream Inc. Portland, Or.	N77NR
N543CM	99	Learjet 45	45-062	Caremark RX Inc. Birmingham, Al.	N512RB
N543H	02	Gulfstream V	688	Hewlett-Packard Co. San Jose, Ca.	(N254W)
N543LE	00	Citation Encore	560-0543	Land's End Inc. Dodgeville, Wi.	N51995
N543SC	87	Citation S/II	S550-0144	Rogue Valley Aircraft Leasing LLC. Ashland, Or.	N6516V
N544CM	86	Falcon 50	173	Carpau Corp. Tarpon Springs, Fl.	PT-LJI
N544PA	79	Learjet 35A	35A-247	Phoenix Air Group Inc. Cartersville, Ga.	N523PA
N544QS	94	Hawker 1000	9044	NetJets, Columbus, Oh.	N956H
N544RA	84	Falcon 50	144	Four Directions Air Inc. Verona, NY.	(LX-FTJ)
N544XL	99	Citation Excel	560-5044	437 North Main Partners LP. Butler, Pa.	N5218T
N545CS	98	Gulfstream 4SP	1361	Campbell Soup Co. Camden, NJ.	N361GA
N545EC	01	Learjet 45	45-199	EFCO Corp/JKS LLC. Monett, Mo.	
N545GA	78	Citation II	550-0040	State of Georgia DoT, Atlanta, Ga. (was 551-0085).	(N551GA)
N545GM	78	HS 125/700A	NA0228	GR Corp. Albuquerque, NM.	N555CR
N545K	04	Learjet 45	45-244	Koch Industries Inc. Wichita, Ks.	N5009V
N545PA	77	Learjet 36A	36A-028	Phoenix Air Group Inc. Cartersville, Ga.	N75TD
N545QS	94	Hawker 1000	9045	NetJets, Columbus, Oh.	G-5-801
N545RW	96	CitationJet	525-0141	BHR Air Service LLC. Pleasant Hill, Ca.	N725CF
N545TC	98	Beechjet 400A	RK-213	TECP Aviation Inc. Chicago, Il.	N175PS
N545TG	04	CitationJet CJ-1	525-0545	Interstate Warehousing Inc. Fort Wayne, In.	N.....
N546BZ	92	Beechjet 400A	RK-41	Brazeway Inc. Adrian, Mi.	N920SA
N546CS	04	Citation Excel XLS	560-5524	CitationShares Sales Inc. White Plains, NY.	N5267G
N546QS	94	Hawker 1000	9046	NetJets, Columbus, Oh.	N962H
N547CS	04	Citation Excel XLS	560-5542	CitationShares Sales Inc. White Plains, NY.	N5267K
N547FP	89	Challenger 601-3A	5047	Fox Paine & Co. Sacramento, Ca.	N140CH
N547JG	78	Learjet 25D	25D-264	Goodman Aviation Inc. Las Vegas, Nv.	N502JC
N547K	81	Falcon 50	46	Z-Line Designs Inc. Livermore, Ca.	N347K
N547PA	75	Learjet 36	36-012	Phoenix Air Group Inc. Cartersville, Ga.	N712JE
N547QS	94	Hawker 1000	9047	NetJets, Columbus, Oh.	N296H
N547ST	05	CitationJet CJ-1	525-0547	Southern Tire Aviation LLC. Columbia, Ms.	N.....
N548QS	95	Hawker 1000	9048	NetJets, Columbus, Oh.	N802H
N549CS	04	Citation Excel XLS	560-5546	CitationShares Sales Inc. White Plains, NY.	N51881
N549PA	77	Learjet 35A	35A-119	Phoenix Air Group Inc. Cartersville, Ga.	(N64DH)
N549QS	96	Hawker 1000	9049	NetJets, Columbus, Oh.	G-5-837
N550A	84	Citation S/II	S550-0009	Coyote Air LLC. Houston, Tx.	N1256Z
N550AB	90	Citation II	550-0633	Embry-Riddle Aeronautical University, Daytona Beach, Fl.	N7AB
N550AJ	87	Citation S/II	S550-0141	Red Hawk Aviation LLC. Phoenix, Az.	N26JJ
N550AK	82	Learjet 55	55-045	Jet Shares LLC. Lexington, Ky.	(N123LC)
N550AL	83	Citation II	550-0462	Family Video Movie Club Inc. Springfield, Il.	N501DK
N550AS	85	Citation S/II	S550-0020	Norsan Financial & Leasing Inc. Pittsburg, Ca.	(N1259R)
N550BB	95	Citation Bravo	550-0734	Cessna Aircraft Co. Wichita, Ks. (Ff 19 Apr 95).	(N1214J)
N550BC	97	Citation Bravo	550-0804	Brindlee Air Travel LLC. Huntsville, Al.	N804CB
N550BJ	81	Citation II	550-0277	Network Power Systems Inc. Raleigh-Durham, NC.	N550WJ
N550BP	81	Citation II/SP	550-0246	Toy Air Inc. Detroit-Willow Run, Mi. (was 551-0296).	N551TK
N550BT	86	Citation S/II	S550-0085	Browning Brothers LLC. Ogden, Ut.	N143BP
N550CA	80	Citation II	550-0152	DJL LLC. Anchorage, Ak.	N88840
N550CG	79	Citation II	550-0095	Jet Blue LLC. Fort Lauderdale, Fl.	N100UF
N550CL	79	Falcon 50	8	International Aviation LLC. Palwaukee, Il.	N508EJ
N550CS	04	Citation Excel XLS	560-5551	Cessna Aircraft Co. Wichita, Ks.	N.....
N550CU	80	Citation II	550-0175	CAAIR Corp. Wilmington, De.	C-GHWW
N550CW	83	Challenger 600S	1084	Jayhawk Inc. Dallas, Tx.	N175ST
N550CZ	87	Citation S/II	S550-0128	Farmington Aviation Inc. Farmington, Ct.	N370M
N550DA	80	Citation II	550-0170	Jet U S Inc. New Castle, De.	N508CV
N550DL*	88	Citation S/II	S550-0155	Leis Air LLC. Honolulu, Hi.	N155GB
N550DR	79	Citation II	550-0052	Spirit of Freedom Foundation Inc. Cleveland, Oh.	PH-CTZ

Reg	Yr	Type	c/n	Owner/Operator	Prev Regn
☐ N550DS	88	Citation S/II	S550-0154	Mount Ida LLC. Meredith, NH.	N660AJ
☐ N550DW	84	Citation II	550-0487	The Charles Machine Works Inc. Perry, Ok.	N444BL
☐ N550F	84	Citation S/II	S550-0010	Fagen Inc. Granite Falls, Mn.	N422MJ
☐ N550FP	02	Citation Bravo	550-1024	Flying Service NV. Antwerp, Belgium.	N5254Y
☐ N550GA	04	Gulfstream G550	5043	Blixseth Group Inc. Rancho Mirage, Ca.	N943GA
☐ N550GB	80	Citation II/SP	551-0201	DeVries International Inc. Irvine, Ca. (was 550-0131).	N550JB
☐ N550GH	99	Citation Bravo	550-0898	B R M Management LLC. Rancho Santa Fe, Ca.	
☐ N550GM	82	Citation II	550-0344	Sureflight LLC. Albuquerque, NM.	PT-LKR
☐ N550GV	03	Gulfstream G550	5022	Fly Away Ltd. Manaus, Brazil.	N922GA
☐ N550GW	02	Gulfstream G550	5006	Grand Warehouse Inc. Tokyo, Japan.	N906GA
☐ N550H	98	Hawker 800XP	8356	Happy Hawker LLC. Seattle, Wa.	
☐ N550HB	84	Westwind-Two	414	The KBH Corp. Clarksdale, Ms.	N524RH
☐ N550HC	86	Citation S/II	S550-0116	First Financial Resources Inc. Denton, Tx.	N125CG
☐ N550HG	83	Learjet 55	55-083	Harbour Group Industries Inc. St Louis, Mo.	N551AS
☐ N550HH	96	Citation Bravo	550-0802	Continental Resources Inc. Enid, Ok.	N802CB
☐ N550HT	86	Citation S/II	S550-0107	Lawrence Finch, Concord, Ca.	N713DH
☐ N550J	98	Citation Bravo	550-0848	John Mayes, Palo Alto, Ca.	N997HT
☐ N550JC	78	Citation II	550-0038	Ryan Aerospace Corp. Belmar, NJ.	(N842CC)
☐ N550KA	80	Citation II	550-0279	CVG Logistics LLC/Commercial Vehicle Group Inc. New Albany.	N566CC
☐ N550KG	00	Citation Bravo	550-0949	Klein Gilhousen, Bozeman, Mt.	
☐ N550KJ	98	Citation Bravo	550-0854	K Jet Inc. Chicago, Il.	N550KH
☐ N550KL	98	Citation Bravo	550-0844	FCAL Aviation LLC/Jennmar Corp. Pittsburgh, Pa.	
☐ N550KM	85	Citation S/II	S550-0081	TEB Charter Services Inc. Seneca, NM.	N168HC
☐ N550KR	93	Citation II	550-0727	Two Gs Aviation LLC/Rice Enterprises LLC. Cordova, Tn.	N550DG
☐ N550KW	82	Citation II	550-0411	EDCO Disposal Corp. Lemon Grove, Ca.	C-FMPP
☐ N550LA	78	Citation II	550-0006	Ronson Aviation Inc. Trenton, NJ.	N725RH
☐ N550LH	79	Citation II	550-0105	Heartland Aviation Inc, Eau Claire, Wi.	N105BA
☐ N550MJ	81	Citation II	550-0215	Midwest Jet LLC. Marshall, Mn.	N40MT
☐ N550MT	03	Gulfstream G550	5026	Cleopatra Group/Abou El Enein LLC. Cairo, Egypt.	N926GA
☐ N550PA	80	Citation II	550-0191	Golden Investments Kansas Inc. Independence, Ks.	C-GWCJ
☐ N550PD	01	Citation Bravo	550-0995	Patterson-UTI Aviation LLC. Snyder, Tx.	N.....
☐ N550PF	00	Citation Bravo	550-0925	University of Alabama, Tuscaloosa, Al.	5N-DUK
☐ N550PG	81	Citation II	550-0216	FSA Aviation LLC. Oklahoma City, Ok.	(N911NJ)
☐ N550PL	87	Citation S/II	S550-0130	Cessna Aircraft Co. Wichita, Ks.	N302PC
☐ N550PM	78	Citation II	550-0219	Planemasters Ltd. DuPage, Il. (was 551-0008).	N550RP
☐ N550PW	80	Citation II	550-0159	Plato Woodwork/Wood I Fly LLC. St Louis, Mn.	N444GB
☐ N550QS	96	Hawker 1000	9050	NetJets, Columbus, Oh.	G-5-846
☐ N550RB	80	Citation II	550-0117	Dixie Capital Corp. Richmond, Va.	N150HE
☐ N550RM	92	Citation II	550-0698	Orbital Enterprises Inc. Eugene, Or.	YV-911CP
☐ N550RS	74	Citation Longwing SP	500-0202	Santiago Communities Inc. Orange, Ca.	(N108WT)
☐ N550RV	84	Citation S/II	S550-0012	Guaranty Air Inc. Junction City, Or.	N550TB
☐ N550SA	81	Citation II	550-0248	Security Aviation Inc. Anchorage, Ak.	N6804C
☐ N550SF	79	Citation II	550-0110	Sanford Farms Inc. Hartford-Brainard, Ct.	N122G
☐ N550SJ	86	Citation S/II	S550-0100	Bed Rock Inc/Tri State Motor Transit Co. Joplin, Mo.	N300QW
☐ N550SP	87	Citation S/II	S550-0151	Rocking N Air Inc. Camarillo, Ca.	N151Q
☐ N550T	01	CitationJet CJ-2	525A-0025	Sand Castle Enterprises/Taft Broadcasting Co. Charlotte, SC.	N51396
☐ N550TA	81	Citation II/SP	551-0039	Sunday Unlimited, Coeur d'Alene, Id.	N71LP
☐ N550TC	82	Learjet 55	55-034	Continental Jet LLC/Blackhawk Construction Co. Wilmington.	N123LC
☐ N550TF	93	CitationJet	525-0013	Setzer Wood LLC. Lexington, Ky.	N550T
☐ N550TL	92	Citation II	550-0716	SB Jets LLC. Redmond, Or.	VP-CTF
☐ N550TM	00	Citation Bravo	550-0936	Pilot International Inc. Wichita, Ks.	N5101J
☐ N550TT	81	Citation II	550-0266	N550TT LLC. Lynchburg, Va.	N825JV
☐ N550TW	89	Citation II	550-0603	Conquest Air Corp. Shreveport, La.	N560AB
☐ N550U	77	Citation Eagle	501-0047	Valcom Services LLC. Roanoke, Va.	N550T
☐ N550VC	00	Citation Bravo	550-0924	SJK Leasing Corp. Las Vegas, Nv.	XT-COK
☐ N550VW	81	Citation II	550-0307	S & T Leasing LLP. Norwood, Ma.	N37BM
☐ N550WB	81	Citation II	550-0230	Southeast Equipment Co. Cambridge, Oh.	N550EK
☐ N550WG	01	Citation Bravo	550-0953	Woodland Eagle LLC. Wilmington, De.	C-GZEK
☐ N550WL	81	Citation II	550-0223	W L Paris Enterprises Inc. Louisville, Ky.	N239CD
☐ N550WM	92	Falcon 50	229	Jabil Circuit Inc. Fort Myers, Fl.	C-GMID
☐ N550WS	98	Citation Bravo	550-0845	Spence Enterprises 1 Inc. Crystal Lake, Il.	N51817
☐ N550WW	92	Citation V	560-0180	Wasser & Winters Co. West Linn, Or.	N1280K
☐ N551BB	81	Citation II/SP	551-0038	Bromma Air Maintenance AB. Stockholm-Bromma, Sweden.	N103M
☐ N551BC	79	Citation II	550-0242	Boulder Capital Inc. Mill Valley, Ca. (was 551-0012).	N1955E
☐ N551BP	82	Citation II	550-0424	Kinnaird Properties, Lafayette, Ca.	N271CG
☐ N551CL	80	Citation II/SP	551-0215	W M Cramer Lumber Co. Hickory, NC.	N500PX

Reg   Yr Type   c/n   Owner/Operator   Prev Regn

Reg	Yr	Type	c/n	Owner/Operator	Prev Regn
N551CW	81	Falcon 50	51	Flight Options LLC. Cleveland, Oh.	(N554LX)
N551CZ	78	Citation II	550-0028	Central Connecticut Aircraft LLC. Plainville, Ct.	N310AV
N551EA	81	Citation II/SP	551-0360	Ernesto Ancira Jr. Wilmington, De. (was 550-0328).	N24CJ
N551G	01	Citation Bravo	550-0968	Auto Glass Center of Kansas Inc. Cedar Rapids, Ia.	N51612
N551GA	00	Gulfstream V	606	Amgen Inc. Thousand Oaks, Ca.	N53HS
N551HH	78	Citation II/SP	551-0071	Hanford Hotels Inc. Newport Beach, Ca.	N551DS
N551MF	81	Learjet 55	55-015	Importadora Fenix SA. Santo Domingo, Dominican Republic.	N27DD
N551MS	80	Citation Eagle	501-0147	Michael Simpson, Bridgeport, Tx.	N27TS
N551QS	96	Hawker 1000	9051	NetJets. Columbus, Oh.	G-5-859
N551RF	86	Citation S/II	S550-0097	Rio Fox LLC. McAllen, Tx.	N551BE
N551SS	02	Falcon 2000	186	Siebel Systems Inc. San Jose, Ca.	N2270
N551V	98	Citation Bravo	550-0850	Iowa Aviators LC. Mason City, Ia.	N551G
N551VB	02	Hawker 800XP	8617	Auto Central Services Inc. Sarasota, Fl.	N617XP
N551WL	81	Citation II	550-0261	W L Paris Enterprises Inc. Louisville, Ky.	N50AZ
N552AJ	78	Citation 1/SP	501-0074	CWCWA LLC. Las Vegas, Nv.	N28GC
N552BE	87	Citation S/II	S550-0138	Beverly Enterprises Inc. Fort Smith, Ar.	(N501BE)
N552CB	02	Citation Bravo	550-1026	Shenandoah Services LC. Harrisonburg, Va.	N5180K
N552HV	00	Citation Encore	560-0552	CCM Leasing LLC. Helena, Mt.	N55HV
N552JT	73	Gulfstream II SP	135	J T Aviation Corp. Ronkonkoma, NY.	N515JT
N552QS	97	Hawker 1000	9052	NetJets, Columbus, Oh.	G-5-863
N552SK	00	Learjet 60	60-219	Red River Resources Inc. Belgrade, Mt.	N660KS
N552SM	00	Citation Bravo	550-0929	Focal Point Lighting LLC. Chicago, Il.	N5086W
N552TC	04	Citation Encore	560-0674	Timothy Hoiles, Colorado Springs, Co.	N52601
N553CW	94	Citation V	560-0253	Flight Options LLC. Cleveland, Oh.	N20LT
N553JT	80	Gulfstream 3	305	J T Aviation Corp. Ronkonkoma, NY.	N552JT
N553M	89	Falcon 50	201	Marmon Group Inc. Chicago-Midway, Il.	N54DA
N553MJ	87	Citation II	550-0553	Rat Pack LLC/WB Aviation Inc. Panama City Beach, Fl.	N5XR
N553V	78	Learjet 35A	35A-141	Mayo Shaw LLC. Englewood, Co.	N553M
N554CL	82	Learjet 55	55-040	Clay Lacy Aviation Inc. Van Nuys, Ca.	N55HK
N554EJ	95	Citation V Ultra	560-0328	Ultra Partnership LLC. Cleveland, Oh.	(N554UJ)
N554T	86	Citation S/II	S550-0124	T & T Enterprises LLC. Santa Clara, Ca.	N52CK
N555BK	00	Citation Bravo	550-0916	Koop Aviation BV. Groningen-Eelde, Holland.	N5265N
N555DH	85	Citation III	650-0090	Den-Star Aviation Inc. Minneapolis, Mn.	N1DH
N555DS	81	Citation II	550-0275	Delmar Systems Inc. West Linn, Or.	N550CP
N555DZ	81	Falcon 10	186	Aviation Enterprises Inc. Bedford, Tx.	N555DH
N555GL*	83	Gulfstream 3	403	George Levin, Fort Lauderdale, Fl.	N403WJ
N555HD	84	Gulfstream 3	444	Colonial Acquisitions Ltd. Hanover, Ma.	N110MT
N555HM	00	Citation Bravo	550-0950	S & D Coffee Inc. Concord, NC.	
N555KK	94	Beechjet 400A	RK-92	QSA LLC. Fort Smith, Ar.	N3240J
N555KT	82	Citation II	550-0420	APS Air Inc. Cedar Rapids, Ia. (was 551-0419)	I-AGSM
N555KW	78	Citation 1/SP	501-0063	M H E Inc. Bryan, Oh. (was 500-0476).	N501BA
N555LG	93	Challenger 601-3A	5127	Leonard Green & Partners LP. Van Nuys, Ca.	N718R
N555LJ	69	Learjet 24B	24B-195	Butler National Inc. Newton, Ks.	(N46LM)
N555PG	99	Citation V	560-0102	BTM Enterprises Inc. Frisco, Tx.	N560BA
N555RE	83	Gulfstream 3	409	Raleigh Holdings LLC. Santa Monica, Ca.	N828MG
N555RT	81	Citation II/SP	551-0323	Ret Butler Communications Corp. Steamboat Springs, Co.	N819Y
N555SD	81	Learjet 25D	25D-333	Diamond Shamrock/Joe Brand Inc. Laredo, Tx.	N34MJ
N555SR	83	Falcon 20F-5	455	Ray Industries Inc/Sea Ray Boats Inc. McGhee-Tyson, Tn.	F-GKAL
N555VR	04	Learjet 45	45-257	Victoria Racing LLC. City of Industry, Ca.	N5012H
N555WD	97	Challenger 604	5355	WDW Aviation Inc/Executive Flight Service, Jacksonville, Fl.	C-GLWV
N555WF	99	Citation Excel	560-5064	The South Financial Group Inc. Greenville, SC.	N2JW
N555WH	78	Learjet 36A	36A-037	Rikuo Corp. Van Nuys, Ca.	RP-C5128
N555WL	98	Citation V Ultra	560-0488	Golf Air Ltd. Bloomfield Hills, Mi.	N555WF
N556AR	98	Gulfstream V	556	MWM AG. Zug, Switzerland.	N656GA
N556BG	98	Citation V Ultra	560-0499	Bull Aviation Inc. Guatemala City, Guatemala.	
N556HJ	82	Learjet 55	55-028	Hop-A-Jet Inc. Fort Lauderdale, Fl.	N556GA
N557CS	85	Citation S/II	S550-0016	Rabbit Hill Industries Inc. White Plains, NY.	N85MP
N557PG	01	Citation Encore	560-0557	National Aircraft Leasing Corp. Greenville, De.	N221CE
N558CG	01	Citation Encore	560-0558	Jeffrey Ludwig PA. Jacksonville, Fl.	N558V
N558HJ	82	Learjet 55	55-048	JODA LLC/Worldwide Jet Charter Inc. Fort Lauderdale, Fl.	N558AC
N558R	99	Citation Excel	560-5075	Rogers Group Inc. Nashville, Tn.	
N559AM	99	Citation VII	650-7107	TXU Business Services Co. Dallas, Tx.	
N559GV	98	Gulfstream V	559	Gulfstream Aerospace Corp. Savannah, Ga.	N659GA
N559LC	74	Gulfstream 2	152	Little Caesar Enterprises Inc. Pontiac, Mi.	N62WB
N560A	96	Citation V Ultra	560-0364	Alcoa Fujikura Ltd. Brentwood, Tn.	N991PC
N560AF	90	Citation V	560-0100	Falcon CCV LLC. Dallas, Tx.	N560WE

Reg	Yr	Type	c/n	Owner/Operator	Prev Regn

Reg	Yr	Type	c/n	Owner/Operator	Prev Regn
☐ N560AG	95	Citation V Ultra	560-0301	Flying Service NV. Antwerp, Belgium.	VR-BQB
☐ N560AN	98	Learjet 60	60-138	Jetride Inc. Dallas, Tx.	(N230BX)
☐ N560BC	89	Citation V	560-0032	Broin & Associates Inc. Sioux Falls, SD.	N96MY
☐ N560BJ	97	Citation V Ultra	560-0436	Bon Travay LLC/B&J Smith Investments Inc. Scottsdale, Az.	N96FC
☐ N560BP	92	Citation V	560-0172	Apple Restaurants Management Co. Duluth, Ga.	N172CV
☐ N560BT	99	Citation Excel	560-5031	Dorand Aviation LLC. Portland, Or.	N531BJ
☐ N560CE	98	Citation Excel	560-5012	Hesco Parts Corp. Louisville, Ky.	I-JETS
☐ N560CF	89	Citation V	560-0040	Max Air Group LLC/Corporate Flight Inc. Detroit, Mi.	N91NL
☐ N560CG	00	Citation Excel	560-5121	Cardinal Glass Industries Inc. Minnetonka, Mn.	N5223Y
☐ N560CH	01	Citation Encore	560-0611	CMH Homes Inc. Knoxville, Tn.	N98AQ
☐ N560CJ	90	Citation V	560-0086	Spyglass Entertainment Group LLC. Van Nuys, Ca.	N560CX
☐ N560CK	93	Citation V	560-0207	Koury Aviation Inc. Liberty, NC.	N780BF
☐ N560CM	02	Citation Excel	560-5277	Hensley & Co. Phoenix, Az.	N5076K
☐ N560CR	04	Citation Encore	560-0662	Cumberland Resources Corp. Charlottesville, Va.	N5212M
☐ N560CX	01	Citation Encore	560-0582	Schoonover Enterprises LLC. Shreveport, La.	N843HS
☐ N560DE	02	Citation Excel	560-5284	NV Sea-Invest International Services, Antwerp, Belgium.	N5109W
☐ N560DP	01	Citation Excel	560-5212	Union Underwear Co. Bowling Green, Ky.	N5090Y
☐ N560EL	90	Citation V	560-0049	Eastway Aviation Inc. Ronkonkoma, NY.	(N2672X)
☐ N560EM	94	Citation V Ultra	560-0278	OIA Air Corp. Nashua, NH.	VH-FHJ
☐ N560EP	91	Citation V	560-0101	Eastway Aviation Inc. Ronkonkoma, NY.	N560DM
☐ N560ER	89	Citation V	560-0003	560 Company Inc. Anchorage, Ak.	N560BA
☐ N560FN	89	Citation V	560-0024	The Compass Group Inc. Hilton Head, SC.	N4CS
☐ N560G	91	Citation V	560-0112	Corporate Flight South Inc. St Petersburg, Fl.	N145MK
☐ N560GB	99	Citation Excel	560-5027	Accent Stripe Inc. Orchard Park, NY.	N5202D
☐ N560GL	90	Citation V	560-0079	Aviation Charter/Great Lakes Chemical Corp. W Lafayettte, In	(N2746C)
☐ N560GS	94	Citation V Ultra	560-0263	Cochran, Cherry, Givens & Smith PC. Albany, Ga.	N979C
☐ N560GT	91	Citation V	560-0142	Georges Tranchant/Techni Airplane LLC. Paris-Le Bourget.	N560FA
☐ N560H	89	Citation V	560-0017	Emerald Holding Co. Pittsburgh, Pa.	N89BM
☐ N560HC	89	Citation V	560-0020	Collins Brothers Corp. Las Vegas, Nv.	N520CV
☐ N560JC	04	Citation Excel XLS	560-5541	Cessna Aircraft Co. Wichita, Ks.	N5201J
☐ N560JG	04	Citation Excel XLS	560-5531	Cessna Aircraft Co. Wichita, Ks.	N52229
☐ N560JM	89	Citation V	560-0010	Apex Aviation Corp. Napa, Ca.	N643RT
☐ N560JP	02	Citation Excel	560-5311	JDP Aircraft II Inc. Raleigh, NC.	N712KC
☐ N560JR	89	Citation V	560-0027	North American Jet LLC. Austin, Tx.	(N12289)
☐ N560JW	01	Citation Encore	560-0560	Scion LLC. Allen, Ky.	N5180C
☐ N560KL	02	Citation Encore	560-0622	C Kevin Landry. Bedford-Hanscom, Ma.	N5197A
☐ N560KT	02	Citation Excel	560-5127	Knight Flight Services LLC. Charlotte, NC.	N.....
☐ N560L	98	Citation Excel	560-5011	Lozier Corp. Omaha, Ne.	N52141
☐ N560LC	95	Citation V Ultra	560-0296	Landmark Communications Inc. Norfolk, Va.	(N5163C)
☐ N560LT	94	Citation V Ultra	560-0275	Life Time Fitness Inc. Eden Prairie, Mn.	(N560LW)
☐ N560ME	89	Citation V	560-0012	Caribbean Helicorp Inc. San Juan, PR.	(ZP-...)
☐ N560MH	91	Citation V	560-0105	Bell Aviation Inc. West Columbia, SC.	N147VG
☐ N560MR	01	Citation Encore	560-0594	Citation Associates Inc. Roanoke, Va.	N52446
☐ N560NY	01	Citation Excel	560-5198	Trans-Marine Management Corp. Tampa, Fl.	N552MA
☐ N560PA	91	Citation V	560-0136	Performance Air LLC. Gaithersburg, Md.	N999AD
☐ N560PK	91	Citation V	560-0133	Solaire LLC. Corvallis, Or.	N93DW
☐ N560PS	91	Citation V	560-0120	Phil Smith Management Inc. Pompano Beach, Fl.	N1824S
☐ N560RA	66	Falcon 20C	56	Kalitta Charters LLC. Detroit-Willow Run, Mi.	N388AJ
☐ N560RG	00	Citation Encore	560-0551	Galland Aviation LLC. Portland, Or.	N52670
☐ N560RK	96	Citation V Ultra	560-0407	LigonAir LLC. Allegheny County, Pa.	F-OHRU
☐ N560RL	91	Citation V	560-0135	M J Enterprises LLC. Springfield, Mo.	N560BB
☐ N560RM	04	Citation Encore	560-0658	Moore Air LLC.MIV Assocs LLC. Oklahoma City, Ok.	N52234
☐ N560RN	95	Citation V Ultra	560-0309	Rocking N Air Inc. Camarillo, Ca.	N212BD
☐ N560RP	91	Citation V	560-0158	RDD Leasing Inc. Lake in the Hills, Il.	N801AB
☐ N560RS	03	Citation Excel	560-5323	Eastway Aviation LLC & Group Outcome LLC. Islip, NY.	N606Q
☐ N560RV*	97	Citation V Ultra	560-0417	TVPX Inc. Concord, Ma.	N525BA
☐ N560RW	92	Citation V	560-0196	RBW Enterprises Inc. West Conshohocken, Pa.	N357AZ
☐ N560S	01	Citation Excel	560-5190	SISMA Aviation Inc. Jersey, Channel Islands. (AVB 4S).	N51038
☐ N560SB	80	HS 125/700A	NA0274	N560SB LLC. Fort Myers, Fl.	(OY-VIA)
☐ N560SE	96	Citation V Ultra	560-0390	PDX VFR LLC. Portland, Or.	N390VP
☐ N560SH	83	Gulfstream 3	404	Safari Aero/Safari Charters Ltd. Fort Pierce, Fl.	(N24TJ)
☐ N560TA	97	Citation V Ultra	560-0430	Citcon Inc. Portsmouth, NH.	C-GLIM
☐ N560TE	01	Citation Encore	560-0595	Thumb Energy Inc. Bad Axe-Huron, Mi.	N.....
☐ N560TG	04	Citation Encore	560-0668	November 50TG Investments LLC. Wilmington, De.	N5214L
☐ N560TH	01	Citation Excel	560-5215	TJH Air Inc/Westair Flying Services Ltd. Blackpool, UK.	VP-CPC
☐ N560TS*	03	Challenger 604	5560	Bombardier Aerospace Corp. Windsor Locks, Ct.	N604CC

Reg	Yr	Type	c/n	Owner/Operator	Prev Regn

Reg	Yr	Type	c/n	Owner/Operator	Prev Regn
N560VR	98	Citation V Ultra	560-0480	Viking Aircraft LLC/Viking Range Corp. Greenwood, Ms.	N71JJ
N560VU	97	Citation Encore	707	Cessna Aircraft Co. Wichita, Ks. (was 560-0424).	N5079V
N560WD	97	Citation V Ultra	560-0399	WD2 Associates, Houston, Tx.	N97NB
N560WH	89	Citation V	560-0013	Exchange Air Partners LLC. Oakhurst, NJ.	(N1217P)
N560XL	96	Citation Excel	706	Cessna Aircraft Co. Wichita, Ks. (Ff 29 Feb 96).	
N561AC	93	Citation V	560-0218	JW & JA Inc/Aire Corr LLC. Indianapolis, In.	N5GE
N561AS	80	Citation II	550-0383	Premier Communications Inc. Oklahoma City, Ok.	N551AB
N561B	89	Citation V	560-0008	J G Boswell Co. Burbank, Ca.	
N561BC	98	CitationJet	525-0257	International Bank of Commerce, Laredo, Tx.	N26DK
N561BP	00	Citation Excel	560-5134	BT Aviation LP/Greater Ozarks Aviation Co. Springfield, Mo.	N52352
N561CC	97	Citation V Ultra	560-0416	Air Land Leasing LLC. Madera, Ca.	N416VP
N561EJ	89	Citation V	560-0035	WE Enterprises LLC. Franklin Lakes, NJ.	N36H
N561JS	96	Citation V Ultra	560-0413	Enhancement of Illinois Inc. Springfield, Il.	N8041R
N561PS	84	Citation S/II	S550-0013	Paul Broadhead Interests Inc. Meridian, Ms.	N389L
N561TS	90	Citation V	560-0057	Southern Aircraft & Transportation, Laredo, Tx.	N561BC
N561VP	87	Citation V	560-0001	Tradition Aviation LLC. Bermuda Dunes, Ca.(was S550-0136).	N1217V
N561XL	96	Citation Excel	560-5001	Cessna Aircraft Co. Wichita, Ks.	
N562DB	04	Citation Excel XLS	560-5532	Bell Leasing Inc. Phoenix, Az.	N5270E
N562DD	00	Citation Excel	560-5108	Bell Leasing Inc. Albuquerque, NM.	N562DB
N562ME	03	Challenger 604	5562	Mercury Engineering Executive Travel Ltd. Dublin, Ireland.	N562BA
N562MS	70	Sabre-60	306-44	Jet Air LLC. Cincinnati, Oh.	HC-BQU
N562R	69	Sabre-60	306-37	Southeast Turbine Aircraft Sales Inc. Palm beach, Fl.	N4SE
N562TS	02	Citation Excel	560-5178	Turquoise Delaware Inc. San Antonio, Tx.	
N563CH	01	Citation Excel	560-5182	CHR Aviation LLC. Minneapolis-Flying Cloud, Mn.	N98RX
N563TS	90	Challenger 601-3A	5063	Aero Toy Store LLC. Fort Lauderdale, Fl.	N50DS
N564BR	81	HS 125/700A	NA0287	Kaleidoscope Aviation Corp. Kansas City, Mo.	(N731GA)
N564CL	70	Learjet 25	25-060	Clay Lacy Aviation Inc. Van Nuys, Ca.	N695LJ
N564TJ	97	Citation V Ultra	560-0432	Branch Aircraft Leasing Inc. Ocala, Fl.	N856WC
N565A	04	Citation Sovereign	680-0024	Cessna Aircraft Co. Wichita, Ks.	N5241R
N565AB	99	Citation Excel	560-5072	CCA Industries Inc. Richmond, Va.	N52178
N565CC	73	Citation	500-0065	Trendway Corp. Holland, Mi.	(N565TW)
N565EJ	90	Citation V	560-0099	A Clifford Edwards, Billings, Mt.	N560GM
N565JP	93	CitationJet	525-0041	James Pugh Jr. Winter Park, Fl.	F-HADA
N565JW	91	Citation V	560-0149	S C Johnson & Son Inc/Johnson's Wax, Racine, Wi.	(N68786)
N565NC	87	Citation II	550-0565	Idaho Potato Packers Inc. Blackfoot, Id.	N565JS
N565RV	97	Gulfstream 4SP	1323	Xamex Investments Inc. Champlain, NY.	N503PC
N565SS	72	Citation	500-0017	Dallas Citation LLC. Dallas, Tx.	N49EA
N565ST	02	Gulfstream G550	5015	JM Family Enterprises Inc. Fort Lauderdale, Fl.	N915GA
N565V	77	Citation 1/SP	501-0267	Shanair Inc. Memphis, Tn. (was 500-0355).	N565VV
N565VV	80	Citation II/SP	551-0181	565VV Ltd. Union Hill, Il.	N29B
N566YT	67	Falcon 20C	94	Grand Aire Express Inc. Toledo, Oh.	N614GA
N567CA	79	Citation II	550-0092	Accessories Inc. Allison Park, Pa.	F-GNLF
N567EA	73	Citation	500-0067	Eastern Fishing & Rental Tools Inc. Laurel, Ms.	(N949SA)
N567F	92	Citation V	560-0171	Federated Corporate Services Inc. Cincinnati-Lunken, Oh.	N573F
N567JP	00	CitationJet CJ-2	525A-0011	Aircraft Brokers Inc. Estero, Fl.	N51881
N567MC	03	Citation Excel	560-5357	Maurice McAlister, Bullhead, Az.	N5161J
N567RA	76	Falcon 10	80	Air Bob Inc. Houston, Tx.	(N803RA)
N567T	01	390 Premier 1	RB-37	Traylor Brothers Inc. Henderson, Ky.	N452A
N567WB	79	Citation 1/SP	501-0109	PSM Associates LLC. Rose Hill, NC.	N30RE
N568DM	02	Citation Excel	560-5325	ADM Milling Co/Archer Daniels Midland Co. Decatur, Il.	N52397
N568PA	78	Learjet 35A	35A-205	CFF Air Inc/Phoenix Air, Cartersville, Ga.	N59FN
N568RL	97	Citation V Ultra	560-0443	23CG LLC. Dallas, Tx.	N24UD
N568TN	69	Gulfstream II SP	67	VOZ LLC. San Jose, Ca.	N67PR
N568WC	90	Citation V	560-0083	WCAO Aviation/World Class Automotive Operations, Humble, Tx.	N22LP
N569BW	81	Falcon 50	45	Quality Jet LLC. Chattanooga, Tn.	N9BX
N569CW	90	Gulfstream 4	1145	Countrywide Home Loans Inc. Van Nuys, Ca.	N797CD
N569D	72	Falcon 20F	259	Mass Development LLC. Oklahoma City, Ok.	N569DW
N569DM	02	CitationJet CJ-2	525A-0088	Exec-Jet Inc. Bristol, Ct.	N.....
N569DW	88	Falcon 100	220	Quality Jet LLC. Chattanooga, Tn.	N702NC
N570AM	03	Learjet 45	45-238	National Dairy Holdings LP. Dallas, Tx.	
N570BJ	89	Citation V	560-0030	The O'Leary Group Inc. Charlotte, NC.	XB-MTS
N570D	82	Citation 1/SP	501-0257	Old Dominion Freight Lines Inc. High Point, NC.	N12NM
N570EJ	92	Citation V	560-0164	Lynch Flying Service Inc. Billings, Mt.	N392BS
N570R	81	Sabre-65	465-75	Frontenac Properties Inc/Aero Charter Inc. Chesterfield, Mo.	N2581E
N571BA	03	Challenger 604	5571	Boeing Co. Chicago, Il.	N604BA
N571BC	88	Citation II	550-0599	International Bank of Commerce, Laredo, Tx.	VR-BYE

Reg	Yr	Type	c/n	Owner/Operator	Prev Regn
❏ N571CH	79	HS 125/700A	NA0251	Roto-Rooter Inc. Cincinnati, Oh.	M810CR
❏ N573AB	97	Citation V Ultra	560-0427	ABC Netherlands Inc. Carolina, PR.	N11LQ
❏ N573AC	90	Challenger 601-3A	5060	Ashton Aviation LLC. Seattle, Wa.	N506BA
❏ N573BA	03	Challenger 604	5573	The Boeing Co. Chicago, Il.	C-GLXB
❏ N573BB	91	Citation V	560-0108	BBI-Blue Beacon International Inc. Salina, Ks.	N73MN
❏ N573CW	82	Falcon 50	73	Flight Options LLC. Cleveland, Oh.	(N556LX)
❏ N573LR	78	Learjet 35A	35A-153	Casey Tool & Machine Co. Casey, Il.	N573LP
❏ N573M	03	Citation Bravo	550-1066	Menard Inc. Eau Claire, Wi.	N.....
❏ N573TR	91	Falcon 50	217	Trident Seafoods Corp. Sand Point, Ak.	N573AC
❏ N574BB	89	Citation V	560-0022	BBI-Blue Beacon International Inc. Salina, Ks.	N211MA
❏ N574DA	95	Learjet 60	60-055	Fielding Aviation LLC. St Louis, Mo.	N660CB
❏ N574M	99	Citation Bravo	550-0910	Menard Inc. Eau Claire, Wi.	N5207V
❏ N575BW	80	Citation II	550-0116	Texarkana Holdings Inc. Mesquite, Tx.	N669MA
❏ N575CT	95	Gulfstream 4SP	1284	Chevron Corp. Oakland, Ca.	N90AM
❏ N575E	86	Gulfstream 4	1007	E I Aviation LLC. Miami, Fl.	N59JR
❏ N575EW	87	Citation S/II	S550-0140	Gainesville Aircraft Sales Inc. Gainesville, Fl.	C-GLCR
❏ N575GH	82	Learjet 55	55-042	American Jet International Corp. Houston, Tx.	D-CMTM
❏ N575M	99	Citation Bravo	550-0911	Menard Inc. Eau Claire, Wi.	N52655
❏ N575RD	73	Citation	500-0075	White Industries Inc. Bates City, Mo. (status ?)	(N600TT)
❏ N575SG	85	Citation S/II	S550-0064	Mary Rose Aviation Inc. Houston, Tx.	N200CV
❏ N575WW	76	Learjet 35	35-043	Executive Jet Services Inc. Carlsbad, Ca.	C-GVCA
❏ N577JC	00	Citation X	750-0122	Dragon Leasing Corp. DuPage, Il.	N800W
❏ N577JT	78	Citation 1/SP	501-0057	Citation Aviation LLC. Birmingham, Al.	N577VM
❏ N577T	89	BAe 125/800B	8149	612 Corp. Miami, Fl.	N155T
❏ N577VM	98	Citation Bravo	550-0863	Walls Aircraft LLC/Cleveland Newspapers Inc. Birmingham, Al.	N709JW
❏ N577VN	89	Citation II	550-0615	T S Air LLC. Granite City, Il.	N577VM
❏ N578BB	85	Citation S/II	S550-0037	Bermuda Air Medivac Services Ltd. Hamilton, Bermuda.	N573BB
❏ N578FP	90	Challenger 601-3A	5078	Fox Paine & Co. Sacramento, Ca.	N553DF
❏ N578M	89	Citation II	550-0612	Premier Air Center Inc. East Alton, Il.	(N534M)
❏ N579CE	01	Citation Encore	560-0579	Next Century Aviation Inc. Sausalito, Ca.	N5259Y
❏ N579L	88	Citation II	550-0579	Roby Inc. Marysville, Oh.	(N13001)
❏ N579TG	84	Gulfstream 3	433	TIG Productions/Time Warner Entertainment Co. Burbank, Ca.	N399CB
❏ N580R	73	Citation	500-0127	Mid Continent Corp. Sunset Hills, Mo.	N500R
❏ N580RC	01	Citation Excel	560-5166	Rosewood Resources Inc. Dallas, Tx.	N5068R
❏ N580RJ	02	Beechjet 400A	RK-329	Hincojet LLC/The Hinman Co. Kalamazoo, Mi.	N5129U
❏ N580SH	01	Citation Bravo	550-0994	Carolina Mat Flight Director LLC. Plymouth, NC.	N.....
❏ N581AS	80	Learjet 35A	35A-311	JT Leasing Inc. Naples, Fl.	N121JT
❏ N581MB	72	Gulfstream II SP	109	Marquez Brothers Aviation LLC. Las Vegas, Nv.	N73AW
❏ N581RA	95	Learjet 31A	31A-106	Lear N89TC LLC/N A Degerstrom Inc. Spokane, Wa.	N531RA
❏ N581SF	02	390 Premier 1	RB-47	FKM Enterprises LLC. Minneapolis, Mn.	(N145SD)
❏ N581TS	01	Challenger 604	5482	The Bendini Group Inc. Tupelo, Ms.	N322LA
❏ N582EJ	81	Falcon 50	82	JBNB Falcon LLC. Newport Beach, Ca.	N150BP
❏ N583AJ	92	Gulfstream 4	1184	Jerome Moss, Van Nuys, Ca.	(N805JM)
❏ N583BS	79	Learjet 35A	35A-258	SRC Enterprises Inc. Chicago, Il.	(N218CR)
❏ N583CC	75	B 737-291	21069	Gund Business Enterprises Inc. Cleveland, Oh.	N15255
❏ N583CE	01	Citation Encore	560-0583	Lakeside Industries Inc. Issaquah, Wa.	N52591
❏ N583CW	91	Citation V	560-0123	Flight Options LLC. Cleveland, Oh.	(N321VP)
❏ N583PS	00	Learjet 45	45-136	PSS World Medical Inc. Jacksonville, Fl.	(N136LJ)
❏ N583VC	84	BAe 125/800A	8003	Vitesse Corp. Greenfield, In.	N803BA
❏ N585AC	69	Falcon 20D	205	Falcon Air Charter LLC. Addison, Tx.	N915SA
❏ N585D	94	Gulfstream 4SP	1258	E I DuPont de Nemours & Co. New Castle, De.	N400UP
❏ N585DG	94	CitationJet	525-0057	Direct Jet Charter LLC. Greensboro, NC.	N525DG
❏ N585DM	79	Citation II	550-0371	Mixed Wing LLC. Wilmington, De.	C-GJCN
❏ N585G	94	Beechjet 400A	RK-94	Greg Garrison Productions, Van Nuys, Ca.	HB-VLN
❏ N585JC	00	Gulfstream V	618	Johnson Controls Inc. Milwaukee, Wi.	N585GA
❏ N585KS	00	Citation Bravo	550-0945	Horizon Aviation Leasing LLC. Naples, Fl.	N5109R
❏ N585M	99	Citation X	750-0096	Menard Inc. Eau Claire, Wi.	
❏ N585PC	04	Citation Excel	560-5366	Fowler Foods of Delaware LLC. Jonesboro, Ar.	N5216A
❏ N585PK	01	CitationJet CJ-1	525-0452	Pegasus StarFlight LLC. Watsonville, Ca.	(N107PK)
❏ N585T	01	Citation X	750-0197	Target Corp. Minneapolis, Mn.	N.....
❏ N585TC	83	Diamond 1A	A060SA	FractionAir Inc. Nashville, Tn.	(N300SJ)
❏ N585TH	02	Citation Bravo	550-1035	Jaguar Aviation Inc. Mount Vernon, Tx.	N.....
❏ N585VC	02	Hawker 800XP	8585	Vitesse Corp. Greenfield, In.	(N885VC)
❏ N586CC	92	Citation V	560-0186	Runway Air LLC. Newport, Ky.	N583N
❏ N586CS	97	Falcon 50EX	260	Valkyrie Aviation Corp. Seattle, Wa.	F-WWHK
❏ N586D	00	Gulfstream 4SP	1439	E I DuPont de Nemours & Co. New Castle, De.	N439GA

Reg	Yr	Type	c/n	Owner/Operator	Prev Regn
☐ N586RE	80	Citation II	550-0199	U S Customs Service, Oklahoma City, Ok.	N67983
☐ N586SF	97	Beechjet 400A	RK-151	The South Financial Group Inc. Greenville, SC.	N115CD
☐ N587VV	78	HS 125/700A	7046	Full Court Aviation Inc. Dover, De.	N828AN
☐ N588AC	00	Citation Bravo	550-0912	Northstar Aviation Inc/ACEMCO Inc. Grand Haven, Mi.	N5117U
☐ N588CG	75	Learjet 24D	24D-304	Michigan Air Freight LLC. Ypsilanti, Mi.	N500CG
☐ N588GS	01	Falcon 900EX	104	Citiflight Inc. White Plains, NY.	F-WWFA
☐ N589DC	66	Falcon 20C	45	Grand Aire Express Inc. Toledo, Oh.	N175GA
☐ N589HM	98	Gulfstream V	554	Cirrus Gas 5 LLC. Dallas, Tx.	N654GA
☐ N589MT	01	Challenger 604	5502	Andaman Aviation Inc. Northolt, UK.	HB-JRY
☐ N590A	89	Citation V	560-0029	Alascom Inc. Anchorage, Ak.	(N1229C)
☐ N590CH	68	Gulfstream II SP	19	Bombardier Capital Inc. Colchester, Vt.	(N213DC)
☐ N590CW	80	Falcon 50	20	Flight Options LLC. Cleveland, Oh.	(N552LX)
☐ N590DA	84	Gulfstream 3	445	Oslo Express Inc. New Canaan, Ct.	N599DA
☐ N590HM	90	Gulfstream 4	1153	Cirrus Gas 4 LLC. Luton, UK.	N589HM
☐ N591CF	04	Citation Encore	560-0661	CC Services Inc. Bloomington, Il.	N5162W
☐ N591DK	02	Citation Encore	560-0591	David Kashtan, La Selva Beach, Ca.	N.....
☐ N591M	99	Citation V Ultra	560-0533	Modine Manufacturing Co. Racine, Wi.	
☐ N591SC	83	Learjet 55	55-091	Texas Aviation Sales & Leasing LLC. Dallas, Tx.	(N567SC)
☐ N592DR	01	CitationJet CJ-2	525A-0028	Delta Romeo LLC. Portola Valley, Ca.	D-IBBB
☐ N592HC	02	390 Premier 1	RB-92	Bozeman 592 LLC. Bozeman, Mt.	N62LW
☐ N592VP	90	Citation V	560-0092A	Rocketman Rocketeers LC. Austin, Tx.	(N713HH)
☐ N592WP	75	Citation	500-0253	Miyasaka & Soilfume Inc. Watsonville, Ca.	N8TG
☐ N593CW	93	Citation V	560-0223	Flight Options LLC. Cleveland, Oh.	N223VP
☐ N593HR	87	BAe 125/800A	8089	593HR Inc. Nashville, Tn.	N862CE
☐ N593M	99	Citation V Ultra	560-0525	Modine Manufacturing Co. Racine, Wi.	N5093Y
☐ N594G	83	Citation II	550-0482	Growmark Inc. Bloomington, Il.	N62WG
☐ N594M*	94	Citation V Ultra	560-0279	Ultra Air LLC. Jackson, Ms.	N361EC
☐ N594RJ	88	Challenger 601-3A	5029	R J Corman Aviation Services LLC. Lexington, Ky.	N83LC
☐ N594WP	91	Citation II	550-0693	S & M Brands Inc. Keysville, Va.	VP-BTR
☐ N595DC*	75	Citation	500-0265	Davis Companies Air LLC. Newberry, Fl.	N501SC
☐ N595MA	04	Citation Encore	560-0680	Cessna Aircraft Co. Wichita, Ks.	N5245L
☐ N595PA	97	Learjet 31A	31A-150	PA Lear 31A-150 LLC. Springdale, Ar.	N316AS
☐ N595PC	97	Citation Bravo	550-0826	Rite Flite Aviation Ltd. Cleveland, Oh.	N51072
☐ N595PE	98	Gulfstream 4SP	1373	Platinum Equity LLC. Van Nuys, Ca.	N106KA
☐ N596GA	99	Gulfstream V	596	Aero Graphics Inc. Manassas, Va.	N596GA
☐ N597CS	97	Citation 1/SP	501-0293	James Parker, Lynchburg, Va. (was 500-0389).	N850MA
☐ N597JA	04	Challenger 604	5597	Jetcraft Corp. Raleigh-Durham, NC.	C-GLWT
☐ N598C	86	Citation III	650-0112	Aurora Ventures LLC. Minneapolis, Mn.	N93DK
☐ N598CA	80	Citation II	550-0187	Staff Air System Inc. Wilmington, De.	C-GHOM
☐ N598CW	92	Citation V	560-0198	Flight Options LLC. Cleveland, Oh.	(N198VP)
☐ N598GS	70	Gulfstream II SP	85	Centralise Leasing Corp. Irvine, Ca.	N524MM
☐ N598JC	77	Falcon 10	112	Merrill Pacific Holdings LLC/Aero Air LLC. Portland, Or.	N12MB
☐ N598JL	87	Beechjet 400	RJ-19	Jet Linx Aviation Corp. Omaha, Ne.	N101CC
☐ N598JM	78	Westwind-1124	222	Morgan & Weisbrod LLP. Dallas, Tx.	N3RC
☐ N598KW	86	Citation S/II	S550-0098	K Air Leasing Inc. Fort Wayne, In.	N598WC
☐ N599BR	82	Citation 1/SP	501-0258	Jack Wall Aircraft Sales Inc. Memphis, Tn.	N16KW
☐ N599CN	88	Gulfstream 4	1065	Illinois Central Railroad Co. Chicago, Il.	N511C
☐ N599CT	00	Learjet 31A	31A-200	Lestralaur LLC. Friday Harbor, Wa.	N797WB
☐ N599DA	01	Challenger 604	5498	Delphi Automotive Systems LLC. Troy, Mi.	N598DA
☐ N599JL	86	Beechjet 400	RJ-14	Jet Linx Aviation Corp. Omaha, Ne.	(N770TB)
☐ N600AE	76	HS 125/F600A	6068	Air Eagle LLC. Detroit, Mi.	N501R
☐ N600AK	99	Global Express	9033	Colwend LLC/Dallah Al Baraka, Jeddah, Saudi Arabia.	C-GFAN
☐ N600AL	00	CitationJet CJ-1	525-0383	Willowbrook Ford Inc. Willowbrook, Il.	N5231S
☐ N600AM	97	Challenger 604	5345	Secure Aviation LLC. Fort Lauderdale, Fl.	N345BA
☐ N600AS	94	Learjet 60	60-040	Chickasaw Nation, Ada, Ok.	N660AS
☐ N600AT	87	Citation II	550-0551	B & B Aviation LLC. Grove City, Oh. (was 551-0551).	N487LD
☐ N600AW	03	Learjet 31	31A-242	Tucker Investments LLC. Bentonville, Ar.	(PR-BOI)
☐ N600BD	81	Challenger 600S	1020	Sherwood Stars LLC. Santa Ana, Ca.	N808TM
☐ N600BG	95	Gulfstream 4SP	1268	Sleep Air LLC. Teterboro, NJ.	(N888MF)
☐ N600BW	04	Citation Encore	560-0671	BorgWarner Inc. Chicago, Il.	N52457
☐ N600C	82	Learjet 55	55-047	Fayez Sarofim & Co. Houston, Tx.	
☐ N600CD	78	Falcon 20F-5	377	Rapid Leasing Inc. Cedar Rapids, Ia.	N377RP
☐ N600CG	83	Diamond 1A	A055SA	Concorde Group Aviation Inc. Oak Harbor, Wa.	N600MS
☐ N600CK	91	Gulfstream 4	1169	CRK Studio LLC. Waterbury, Ct.	N600DW
☐ N600DR	98	Gulfstream 4SP	1356	Dominion Resources Inc. Richmond, Va.	(JY-TWO)
☐ N600DT	75	Learjet 35	35-017	MartinAir Inc. Richmond, Va.	N456MS

Reg	Yr	Type	c/n	Owner/Operator	Prev Regn

Reg	Yr	Type	c/n	Owner/Operator	Prev Regn
N600EA	85	Citation S/II	S550-0015	Estancia Aviation LLC. Gresham, Or.	C-GMTV
N600EF	96	Citation V Ultra	560-0376	Kennedy Aviation LLC. Los Altos, Ca.	N600LF
N600EG	66	HS 125/731	25075	Yemille Valencia de Garza, San Antonio, Tx.	(N95TJ)
N600ES	99	Challenger 604	5439	Earth Star Inc. Burbank, Ca.	C-GLXQ
N600G	76	HS 125/F600A	6066	Giant Industries Inc. Scottsdale, Az.	N800JP
N600GA	93	Learjet 60	60-021	GAF Holdings Inc. Visalia, Ca.	N600LG
N600GG	97	Learjet 60	60-115	North American Jet Charter Inc. Banning, Ca.	N500ZH
N600GL	68	Sabre-60A	306-24	OTW Farms LLC. Hollister, Ca.	(N600GE)
N600GM	79	Learjet 25D	25D-290	Milam International Inc. Englewood, Co.	N321RB
N600GW	83	Diamond 1A	A044SA	Glacier Properties LLC. Mobile, Al.	N606JM
N600HL	74	Falcon 10	19	Falcon Flyers Inc. Wilmington, De.	LX-TRG
N600HR	93	CitationJet	525-0038	C J Sales LLC. Santa Rosa Beach, Fl.	N135MM
N600J	92	BAe 125/800A	NA0470	Johnson & Johnson, Mercer County Airport, NJ.	N672BA
N600JD	94	Citation VI	650-0236	Deere & Co. Moline, Il.	N1303M
N600JM	96	Falcon 900EX	5	Otari LLC. Boeing Field, Seattle, Wa.	N500VM
N600KM	84	Citation S/II	S550-0008	Kreuter Engineering Inc. New Paris, In.	(N40KM)
N600L	02	Learjet 60	60-259	Lincoln National Life Insurance Co. Fort Wayne, In.	N40075
N600LC	03	Learjet 60	60-265	Lincoln National Life Insurance Co. Fort Wayne, In.	N40086
N600LF	01	Citation Encore	560-0569	G C I Aviation/Gary Comer Inc. Waukesha, Wi.	N1315C
N600LN	96	Learjet 60	60-082	Lincoln National Life Insurance Co. Fort Wayne, In.	N682LJ
N600MK	72	HS 125/600A	6004	Boyington Capital Group LLC. Plano, Tx.	N5AH
N600ML	01	Learjet 60	60-217	Deerfield Aviation LLC. Fort Lauderdale, Fl.	N60LJ
N600N	97	Falcon 50EX	256	Anheuser-Busch Companies Inc. St Louis, Mo.	VP-CBT
N600NY	78	Westwind-1124	231	Taughannock Aviation Corp. Tomkins County, NY.	N331GW
N600PJ	92	Learjet 60	60-004	Pacific Jet/L60 Jet Partners LLC. Van Nuys, Ca.	N194AL
N600RA	77	Corvette	36	Intermountain Timber Products LLC. Cottage Grove, Or.	N601RC
N600RM	78	Citation 1/SP	501-0044	Capital City Aviation Inc. Madison, Wi.	N50US
N600SJ	68	Sabre-60	306-15	Addison Aircraft Sales Inc. Holly Lake Ranch, Tx. (status ?)	N604MK
N600ST	03	Citation Bravo	550-1054	Sandair LLC. Redmond, Or.	N254CB
N600SV	68	HS 125/731	25159	Pan-Jet LLC/Pan Holdings Inc. Andover, Ma.	N67TJ
N600TC	80	Westwind-Two	299	Employee Benefit Management Services Inc. Billings, Mt.	(N67TJ)
N600VC	93	Gulfstream 4SP	1227	VC Aviation Services LLC. Pontiac, Mi.	N626TC
N600WD	74	Falcon 20E-5	300	WRRCO Inc. Beaumont, Tx.	N300FJ
N600WG	82	Falcon 50	98	Greenleaf Corp. Saegertown, Pa.	N50MM
N600WJ	80	Challenger 600S	1007	HRS Solutions LLC. Davisburg, Mi.	144604
N600YB	04	Gulfstream G200	096	Yum Restaurant Services Group, Louisville, Ky.	N196GA
N601AA	86	Challenger 601	3061	Solar II Inc. Buffalo, NY.	N597FJ
N601AB	01	Gulfstream G200	047	AmSouth Bank, Birmingham, Al.	N110GX
N601AE	85	Challenger 601	3050	Kendall-Jackson Wine Estates Ltd. Santa Rosa, Ca.	N95SR
N601AF	89	Challenger 601-3A	5045	Airgas Inc. New Castle, De.	N500GS
N601BC	79	Citation II	550-0091	Hickory Springs Manufacturing Co. Hickory, NC.	N527AG
N601BE	92	Challenger 601-3A	5103	BE Aerospace Inc. Wellington, Fl.	N76CS
N601BW	94	Challenger 601-3R	5150	Bindley Western Industries Inc. Indianapolis, In.	N602CC
N601CM	83	Challenger 600	1079	Waste Connections Transportation Co. Portland, Or.	N601SA
N601CT	82	Challenger 600S	1049	International Consolidated Technologies LLC. Las Vegas, Nv.	N600CF
N601CV	94	Challenger 601-3R	5144	Summit Seafood Supply Inc. Houston, Tx.	N347BA
N601DR	96	Hawker 800XP	8299	Dominion Resources Inc. Richmond, Va.	(N32BC)
N601DT	88	Challenger 601-3A	5024	Verde Capital Corp/Drivetime, Phoenix, Az.	N601NB
N601EC	90	Challenger 601-3A	5064	Virginia Air Corp. Richmond, Va.	N564TS
N601FJ	84	Challenger 601	3023	Sierra Mike Aviation II LLC. Concord, NC.	N601KE
N601FR	87	Challenger 601-3A	5003	Furniture Row Leasing LLC. Lakewood, Co.	HB-IKT
N601FS	93	Challenger 601-3A	5119	JDC Support Services LLC. Mobile, Al.	N519DB
N601GB	85	Challenger 601	3044	Challenger Leasing LLC. Bellevue, Wa.	N955DB
N601GG	00	Learjet 60	60-192	North American Jet Charter Inc. Banning, Ca.	
N601GL	70	Sabre-60A	306-50	Sabre Fifty Inc. Buenos Aires, Argentina.	XB-FSZ
N601GT	85	Challenger 601	3062	International Game Technology, Reno, Nv.	N601HP
N601HW	94	Challenger 601-3R	5154	Wal-Mart Stores Inc. Rogers, Ar.	C-FJLA
N601JA	75	HS 125/600A	6051	Hawker Aviation Services LLC. Nashville, Tn.	N95TS
N601JE	91	Challenger 601-3A	5086	Private Jet Charters LLC. Teterboro, NJ.	N343KA
N601JG	83	Challenger 601	3006	Glidewell Laboratories, Newport Beach, Ca.	N256SD
N601JM	85	Challenger 601	3048	Airborne Charter Inc. Santa Monica, Ca.	(N628WC)
N601KF	95	Challenger 601-3R	5175	Kentucky Fried Chicken Corp/Yum! Brands Inc. Louisville, Ky.	N306BX
N601KJ	95	Challenger 601-3R	5187	Veinte-Siete LLC. NYC.	C-GLXK
N601KK	82	Challenger 600S	1061	Kamilla Aircraft Holdings Inc. Fort Lauderdale, Fl.	(N661TS)
N601LG	87	Challenger 601-3A	5008	Caribbean Marine/South Seas Helicopter Co Inc. Carlsbad, Ca.	N601EG
N601LJ	92	Learjet 60	60-001	Learjet Inc. Wichita, Ks.	
Reg	Yr	Type	c/n	Owner/Operator	Prev Regn

Reg	Yr	Type	c/n	Owner/Operator	Prev Regn
☐ N601LS	93	Challenger 800	7008	Limited Inc. Columbus, Oh.	N501LS
☐ N601MD	98	Gulfstream V	538	Open Road Airways Inc. Wheeling, Il.	N538GA
☐ N601PR	85	Challenger 601	3045	Paige Charters Inc. Boca Raton, Fl.	N998JR
☐ N601QS	02	Citation Excel	560-5301	NetJets, Columbus, Oh.	N.....
☐ N601RC	86	Challenger 601	3055	Rockwell Collins Inc. Cedar Rapids, Ia.	N608RP
☐ N601RL	88	Challenger 601-3A	5028	A T Massey Coal Co. Richmond, Va.	(N601EA)
☐ N601S	86	Challenger 601	3060	The Bistate Oil Co. NYC.	C-GLXY
☐ N601ST	90	Challenger 601-3A	5081	John & June Rogers/Sky Trek Aviation, Modesto, Ca.	HL7202
☐ N601TP	94	Challenger 601-3R	5156	The Pyle Group LLC. Madison, Wi.	N255CC
☐ N601TX	83	Challenger 601	3005	Pegasus IV Inc/TXI Aviation Inc. Dallas, Tx.	C-FAAL
☐ N601UP	92	Challenger 601-3A	5123	Union Pacific Railroad Co. Omaha, Ne.	C-GLWR
☐ N601VH	89	Challenger 601-3A	5043	Vector Research Ltd. Durham, NC.	N601BH
☐ N601WJ	82	Challenger 600S	1065	K Aviation LLC. Sarasota, Fl.	144602
☐ N601WM	88	Challenger 601-3A	5026	Tower LLC. Chicago, Il.	C-GLWT
☐ N601WW	82	Challenger 600S	1076	White Cloud Co. White Plains, NY.	I-BLSM
☐ N602AB	01	Gulfstream G200	048	AmSouth Bank, Birmingham, Al.	N112GX
☐ N602AT	89	Citation II	550-0606	Economic Development Partnership, Birmingham, Al.	N770BB
☐ N602CW	83	Challenger 601	3002	Flight Options LLC. Cleveland, Oh.	N750GT
☐ N602DV*	02	390 Premier 1	RB-121	Raytheon Aircraft Co. Wichita, Ks.	(N72DV)
☐ N602JR	70	HS 125/731	NA752	Vernon Sorenson MD. Santa Barbara, Ca.	N700FA
☐ N602PM	99	Gulfstream 4SP	1402	Altria Corporate Services Inc. White Plains, NY.	(N602AG)
☐ N602QS	04	Citation Excel XLS	560-5518	NetJets, Columbus, Oh.	N52699
☐ N602VC	01	Gulfstream G200	038	VC Aviation Services LLC. Pontiac, Mi.	N168EC
☐ N603CS	95	Gulfstream 4SP	1257	Phelps Dodge Corp. Phoenix, Az.	(N99PD)
☐ N603MA	80	Sabre-65	465-16	Denison Jet Sales Corp. Landrum, SC.	N920CC
☐ N603PM	00	Gulfstream 4SP	1452	Altria Corporate Services Inc. White Plains, NY.	(N603AG)
☐ N603QS	01	Citation Excel	560-5203	NetJets, Columbus, Oh.	N.....
☐ N603SC	97	Learjet 60	60-096	Flextronics Photonics PPT Inc. Hillsboro, Or.	N8086L
☐ N603TS	75	HS 125/600A	6041	Corp Industrial Delta SA. Toluca, Mexico.	N808RP
☐ N604AB	96	Challenger 604	5306	California Choice Benefit Administration, Orange, Ca.	N309BX
☐ N604AS	79	Learjet 25D	25D-292	B & C Flight Management Inc. Houston, Tx.	N711VK
☐ N604B	97	Challenger 604	5335	Stream Enterprises LLC. Punta Gorda, Fl.	N801P
☐ N604BB	04	Challenger 604	5582	MA Aviation LLC/MidAmerica Charters Ltd. Fargo, ND.	C-GLXH
☐ N604BM	97	Challenger 604	5354	ARAMARK Services Inc. Philadelphia, Pa.	(N604AG)
☐ N604CB	01	Challenger 604	5526	Colonial Bank, Montgomery, Al.	N804CB
☐ N604CD	04	Challenger 604	5591	Aero Toy Store LLC. Fort Lauderdale, Fl.	C-GLYA
☐ N604CE	00	Challenger 604	5446	Coca-Cola Enterprises Inc. Atlanta-Fulton County, Ga.	C-GLWZ
☐ N604CL	03	Challenger 604	5570	Hershey Foods Corp. Hershey, Pa.	C-GLYH
☐ N604CP	96	Challenger 604	5321	C Cary Patterson, Addison, Tx.	C-FZPG
☐ N604CS	04	Citation Sovereign	680-0007	CitationShares Sales Inc. White Plains, NY.	N52081
☐ N604CT	96	Challenger 604	5314	RCM Management Services GP Inc. Houston, Tx.	C-GLWZ
☐ N604DH	97	Challenger 604	5344	Advance PCS, Irving, Tx.	N344BA
☐ N604FJ	86	Challenger 601-3A	5001	Carco Leasing/Carco Training Inc. Plano, Tx.	(N59FJ)
☐ N604GM	98	Challenger 604	5399	Western Aviation Inc. Guatemala City, Guatemala.	C-GLXB
☐ N604GR	00	Challenger 604	5478	Goodrich Corp. Richfield, Oh.	N478BA
☐ N604GS	85	Learjet 35A	35A-604	Six Hundred Four Corp. Teterboro, NJ.	N73LP
☐ N604GW	99	Challenger 604	5424	Cook Aircraft Leasing Inc. Bloomington, In.	G-DAAC
☐ N604HC	02	Challenger 604	5555	Harbert Aviation Inc. Birmingham, Al.	N555VV
☐ N604HJ	98	Challenger 604	5382	Brunner & Lay Inc. Franklin Park, Il.	C-GLXS
☐ N604JR	00	Challenger 604	5449	Knight Ridder Leasing Co. Opa Locka, Fl.	N604GT
☐ N604JS	96	Challenger 604	5311	Great Point Advisors LLC. Boston, Ma.	(N989DH)
☐ N604KJ	02	Challenger 604	5554	Marine Charter Enterprises, Hillsboro, Or.	C-GLWV
☐ N604LA	99	Challenger 604	5436	Trey Aviation LLC. St Paul, Mn.	C-GLXF
☐ N604LC	98	Challenger 604	5373	L & L Leasing LLC. White Plains, NY.	HB-ILL
☐ N604LJ	03	CitationJet CJ-2	525A-0180	Lan Jet LLC. Gadsden, Al.	N.....
☐ N604MC	04	Challenger 604	5581	Dean Foods Co. Dallas, Tx.	C-GLXF
☐ N604ME	92	Challenger 601-3A	5112	Executive Air Solutions Inc. Van Nuys, Ca.	N404AB
☐ N604MU	99	Challenger 604	5406	Suiza Foods Corp. Dallas, Tx.	C-GLXS
☐ N604PA	03	Challenger 604	5566	Prime Aire Inc. Springfield, Mo.	C-GLXU
☐ N604QS	01	Citation Excel	560-5204	NetJets, Columbus, Oh.	N.....
☐ N604RP	00	Challenger 604	5473	Nestle Purina PetCare Co. St Louis, Mo.	C-GLXK
☐ N604RS	02	Challenger 604	5551	M/I Schottenstein Homes Inc. Columbus, Oh.	N551BT
☐ N604RT	01	Challenger 604	5497	Sonic Aviation LLC. Jackson, Wy.	C-GLXO
☐ N604S	85	Learjet 35A	35A-597	Sandler Management Group, Norfolk, Va.	N355CA
☐ N604SA	97	Challenger 604	5341	Sandler Management Group LLC. Norfolk, Va.	C-GJBA
☐ N604SB	03	Challenger 604	5569	Polear Inc. Camarillo, Ca.	C-GZVZ

Reg	Yr	Type	c/n	Owner/Operator	Prev Regn

Reg	Yr	Type	c/n	Owner/Operator	Prev Regn
☐ N604SC	04	Challenger 604	5593	Bombardier Aerospace Corp. Windsor Locks, Ct.	C-GLYK
☐ N604SH	80	Challenger 600S	1008	Mountain Aviation LC. Cheyenne, Wy.	(D-C...)
☐ N604SR	03	Challenger 604	5558	North Allegheny Corp. Helena, Mt.	C-G...
☐ N604ST	00	Challenger 604	5479	SMC Aviation-Seatankers Management Co. Oslo, Norway.	ZS-CMB
☐ N604SX	01	Challenger 604	5492	Conklin Corp/Aircraft N604SX, Pleasant Valley, NY.	N711SX
☐ N604TS	99	Challenger 604	5420	Aero Toy Store LLC. Fort Lauderdale, Fl.	VP-BCO
☐ N604UP	01	Challenger 604	5496	Astra Holdings Inc/Hume & Johnson PA. Coral Springs, Fl.	N496DB
☐ N604VF	00	Challenger 604	5444	Dwight Management LLC. Minneapolis, Mn.	C-GLWV
☐ N604VK	01	Challenger 604	5493	Valda Kohar/VDK LLC. Lexington, Ma.	C-G...
☐ N604VM	96	Challenger 604	5304	Global Aviation Delaware LLC. NYC.	C-GITG
☐ N604W	99	Challenger 604	5421	Commander Airways Inc. Tampa, Fl.	N604JP
☐ N604WF	03	Challenger 604	5561	Westfield Corp. Los Angeles, Ca.	N561CC
☐ N604WS	00	Challenger 604	5471	Wingedfoot Services LLC. West Palm Beach, Fl.	N471MK
☐ N604ZH	98	Challenger 604	5376	Zimmer Inc. Warsaw, In.	N604CD
☐ N605CH	00	Gulfstream V	621	Chase Manhattan Bank, White Plains, NY.	(N605M)
☐ N605FX	03	Learjet 40	45-2004	BBJS/FlexJets, Addison, Tx.	N40082
☐ N605QS	03	Citation Excel	560-5321	NetJets, Columbus, Oh.	N.....
☐ N605T	96	Challenger 601-3R	5191	Avion LLC/Airmax LLC. Englewood, Co.	N191BE
☐ N605TC	02	390 Premier 1	RB-52	Tomcat Air LLP. Redington Beach, Fl.	N60152
☐ N605VF	04	Global 5000	9152	Bombardier Aerospace Corp. Windsor Locks, Ct.	C-FBPK
☐ N606AM	83	Falcon 100	205	Flight Management Corp/Dart Container Corp. Sarasota, Fl.	N700DW
☐ N606AT	93	Citation VI	650-0225	Longborough Aviation Inc/GDTC Ltd. 3taverton, UK.	N1301Z
☐ N606BR	92	Learjet 60	60-006	SMC Aviation LLC. Coeur d'Alene, Id.	N606TS
☐ N606FX	03	Learjet 40	45-2005	BBJS/FlexJets, Addison, Tx.	N40083
☐ N606GA	04	Gulfstream G200	106	Gulfstream Aerospace LP. Dallas-Love, Tx.	4X-C..
☐ N606GB	78	Learjet 25D	25D-245	New World Racing Inc. Charlotte, NC.	(N25PW)
☐ N606JR	97	CitationJet	525-0231	Roush Racing Inc. Livonia, Mi.	N5223D
☐ N606KK	76	Citation	500-0306	Karl Klement, West Hartford, Ct.	N36SJ
☐ N606L	93	Learjet 60	60-020	HAALO Ltd. Las Vegas, Nv.	N600L
☐ N606MA	76	Westwind-1124	196	McCrory Air LLC. Birmingham, Al.	N863AB
☐ N606PM	02	Gulfstream G300	1512	Altria Corporate Services Inc. Richmond, Va.	N512GA
☐ N606QS	03	Citation Excel	560-5338	NetJets, Columbus, Oh.	N5094D
☐ N606RP	04	Challenger 604	5578	Nestle Purina PetCare Co. St Louis, Mo.	C-GLWZ
☐ N606SM	74	Learjet 25B	25B-185	TMS Aviation LLC. Wilmington, NC.	N988AC
☐ N607BF	83	Learjet 55	55-056	607BF Inc/Flynn Enterprises Inc. Chicago, Il.	N156JC
☐ N607CF	76	Sabre-60	306-118	W R Fry/CC2B Trust, San Jose, Ca.	N607SR
☐ N607DB	98	CitationJet	525-0269	Charolais Corp. Madisonville, Ky.	N5219T
☐ N607FX	04	Learjet 40	45-2012	BBJS/FlexJets, Addison, Tx.	
☐ N607PM	03	Gulfstream G300	1509	Altria Corporate Services Inc. Milwaukee, Wi.	N509GA
☐ N607QS	03	Citation Excel	560-5340	NetJets, Columbus, Oh.	N50820
☐ N607RP	95	Challenger 601-3R	5184	Nestle Purina PetCare Co. St Louis, Mo.	N605RP
☐ N608BG	84	Gulfstream 3	430	BSI Holdings Inc. Paradise Valley, Az.	N600BG
☐ N608CE	01	Citation Encore	560-0608	York International Corp. Harrisburg-Capital City, Pa.	N52059
☐ N608CL	92	Gulfstream 4	1193	Cassandra Lee Flight Operations LLC. Carmel, Ca.	N620KA
☐ N608CT	90	Citation V	560-0065	Century Tel Service Group LLC. Monroe, La.	N560JV
☐ N608DB	97	CitationJet	525-0179	R R Dawson Bridge Co. Lexington, Ky.	N877GS
☐ N608FX	04	Learjet 40	45-2014	BBJS/FlexJets, Addison, Tx.	
☐ N608GF	82	Learjet 35A	35A-477	Avatar Air Inc. Highland Beach, Fl.	N155RD
☐ N608MD	77	Gulfstream 2	197	Senterra Consulting LLC. Houston, Tx.	(N217AH)
☐ N608MM	95	CitationJet	525-0104	Allegis Corp. Minneapolis, Mn.	N606MM
☐ N608PM	02	Gulfstream 4SP	1486	Altria Corporate Services Inc. White Plains, NY.	(N608AG)
☐ N608QS	02	Citation Excel	560-5308	NetJets, Columbus, Oh.	N.....
☐ N609CC	99	Challenger 604	5438	OD Aviation Inc. Delray Beach, Fl.	C-GLXM
☐ N609FX	04	Learjet 40	45-2022	BBJS/FlexJets, Addison, Tx.	N5013U
☐ N609PM	02	Gulfstream G300	1510	Altria Corporate Services Inc. Milwaukee, Wi.	N510GA
☐ N609QS	04	Citation Excel XLS	560-5522	NetJets, Columbus, Oh.	N51872
☐ N610AB	83	Gulfstream 3	398	Air Lake Lines Inc. Brooklyn Center, Mn.	N777RZ
☐ N610AS	95	Falcon 2000	8	Broad River Aviation Inc. Fort Lauderdale, Fl.	F-WWMF
☐ N610CB	02	Citation Bravo	550-1014	Ocotillo Partners LLC. Scottsdale, Az.	N52475
☐ N610GD	85	Citation S/II	S550-0034	Continental Motorcars Inc. Melbourne, Fl.	N59EC
☐ N610GR	01	Citation X	750-0163	B F Goodrich Co. Akron, Oh.	N5253S
☐ N610HC	86	Astra-1125	012	Diamond Shamrock Refining & Marketing Co. San Antonio, Tx.	N27BH
☐ N610JB	89	Citation II	550-0610	Bays Hotel Corp. Chicago-Romeoville, Il.	N610BL
☐ N610JR	86	Learjet 55	55-125	Tele/Com Air Inc. Sugar Grove, Il.	
☐ N610LJ	86	Learjet 35A	35A-610	EPC Transport Inc. Denver, Co.	(N354GE)
☐ N610MC	99	Gulfstream 4SP	1368	May Department Stores Co. St. Louis, Mo.	N1967M

Reg	Yr	Type	c/n	Owner/Operator	Prev Regn

Reg	Yr	Type	c/n	Owner/Operator	Prev Regn
☐ N610QS	01	Citation Excel	560-5210	NetJets, Columbus, Oh.	N.....
☐ N610RA	70	Sabre-60	306-54	Golden Aviation de Mexico SA. Naulcalpan.	N97SC
☐ N610SE	81	Westwind-Two	346	Hudson Flight Ltd. Pampa, Tx.	N610HC
☐ N610SM	98	Astra-1125SPX	101	Sallie Mae Inc. Dulles, Va.	(N291WK)
☐ N610TS	93	Learjet 60	60-010	Eastern Aviation LLC. Wilmington, De.	N561TC
☐ N610TT	80	Citation 1/SP	501-0170	Tradewind LLC. Dover, De.	N170EA
☐ N611AT	79	Citation 1/SP	501-0103	Vermeer Manufacturing Co. Pella, Ia.	N49WC
☐ N611DB	75	Learjet 24D	24D-318	Air Center Helicopters Inc. St Thomas, USVI.	N114JT
☐ N611GA	65	Falcon 20C	9	Grand Aire Express Inc. Toledo, Oh.	LV-WMF
☐ N611JM	92	Gulfstream 4	1178	JFM Inc. Chicago-Du Page, Il.	N909LS
☐ N611JW	96	Falcon 900B	162	Tristram Inc/Florida Marlins, Boca Raton, Fl.	N162FJ
☐ N611MC	79	HS 125/700A	NA0257	May Department Stores Co. St. Louis, Mo.	N125HS
☐ N611PA	94	Beechjet 400A	RK-78	Suncoast Aviation Inc. Durham, NC.	N8278Z
☐ N611QS	05	Citation Excel XLS	560-5548	NetJets, Columbus, Oh.	N5168Y
☐ N611TG	87	Beechjet 400	RJ-27	Swing Plance Aviation LLC.	(N427CW)
☐ N611WM	99	Beechjet 400A	RK-249	Wilkes & McHugh PA. Tampa, Fl.	N4249K
☐ N611XP	04	Hawker 400XP	RK-411	Raytheon Aircraft Co. Wichita, Ks.	
☐ N612AC	88	Gulfstream 4	1059	Levitical Equipment & Leasing LP. Houston-Hobby, Tx.	N199WW
☐ N612EQ	81	Learjet 55	55-003	B & E Aircraft Sales LLC. Coral Gables, Fl.	(N553GJ)
☐ N612GA	65	Falcon 20C	8	Grand Aire Express Inc. Toledo, Oh.	N190BD
☐ N612MC	82	HS 125/700A	NA0317	May Department Stores Co. St. Louis, Mo.	N700SS
☐ N612QS	02	Citation Excel	560-5312	NetJets, Columbus, Oh.	N.....
☐ N612VR	79	Citation II/SP	551-0026	JWR Enterprises Inc. Dover, De. (was 550-0377).	N32PB
☐ N613GY	02	Citation Excel	560-5300	Native American Air Services Inc. Mesa, Az.	N5085E
☐ N613MC	81	HS 125/700A	7151	May Department Stores Co. St. Louis, Mo.	N161G
☐ N614AF	95	Challenger 601-3R	5171	Beacon Capital Partners LLC. Nashua, NH.	N213MC
☐ N614AP	86	BAe 125/800A	8057	GW Enterprises/Wingate Healthcare Holdings Inc. Needham, Ma	N614AF
☐ N614B	04	CitationJet CJ-3	525B-0017	Cessna Aircraft Co. Wichita, Ks.	N.....
☐ N614BG	04	Hawker 800XP	8704	Raytheon Aircraft Co. Wichita, Ks.	
☐ N614CM	00	Gulfstream V	614	CYMI Investments Sub Inc. Dayton, Oh.	N571GA
☐ N614RD	86	Gulfstream 4	1006	Cor Aviation LLC. Carlsbad, Ca.	N3338
☐ N615HB	81	Learjet 35A	35A-444	G A Robinson III, Memphis, Tn.	N615HP
☐ N615HP	99	Beechjet 400A	RK-231	General Parts Inc. Raleigh, NC.	N781TP
☐ N615MS*	87	Falcon 900B	25	MSS Falcon 900 LLC. Van Nuys, Ca.	N660BD
☐ N615QS	04	Citation Excel	560-5360	NetJets, Columbus, Oh.	N5079V
☐ N615RG	98	Citation Excel	560-5016	Aircraft Leasing & Sales Inc. Wichita, Ks.	
☐ N615SR	00	Falcon 50EX	298	Cooper Industries Inc. Houston, Tx.	F-WWHZ
☐ N616CC	00	Gulfstream 4SP	1455	AMFM Air Services Inc. San Antonio, Tx.	N455GA
☐ N616CS	04	Citation Sovereign	680-0016	Cessna Aircraft Co. Wichita, Ks.	N.....
☐ N616DC	99	Global Express	9025	DJW Aviation II LLC/ACM Aviation Inc. Monterey, Ca.	N700AQ
☐ N616DF	82	Challenger 600S	1038	Western States Property Development, Carson City, Nv.	N65HJ
☐ N616KG	03	Gulfstream G400	1534	Kraft Group LLC. Foxboro, Ma.	(N650PW)
☐ N616NA	69	Learjet 25	25-035	National Aeronautics, Cleveland, Oh.	N33TR
☐ N616QS	03	Citation Excel	560-5345	NetJets, Columbus, Oh.	N.....
☐ N617BG	83	Diamond 1A	A067SA	Turbine Aircraft Marketing Inc. San Angelo, Tx.	N63DR
☐ N617PD	02	Citation Excel	560-5273	Cobalt Aviation II LLC. N Philadelphia, Pa.	N1268D
☐ N617QS	04	Citation Excel XLS	560-5509	NetJets, Columbus, Oh.	N.....
☐ N617TM	99	Hawker 800XP	8411	JetSet LLC. Las Vegas, Nv.	
☐ N618AJ	81	Challenger 600S	1018	GECC, Danbury, Ct.	N771WW
☐ N618BR	65	Learjet 23	23-082A	Robert West Jr. Orinda, Ca.	(N118LS)
☐ N618GH	87	Falcon 200	513	Corporate Flight Services LLC. Newtown Square, Pa.	N5UQ
☐ N618QS	04	Citation Excel XLS	560-5506	NetJets, Columbus, Oh.	N.....
☐ N618R	94	Learjet 60	60-044	Contessa Food Products Inc. Van Nuys, Ca.	(N1618R)
☐ N619KK	88	Gulfstream 4	1062	Virtucon LLC/First Commercial Corp. San Diego, Ca.	N104JG
☐ N619MC	76	Gulfstream 2	196	May Department Stores Co. St. Louis, Mo.	N610MC
☐ N619MJ	82	Learjet 55	55-021	Robert E Sutton, Englewood, Co.	I-LOOK
☐ N620A	79	Falcon 20F-5	412	AWI (Nevada) Inc. Las Vegas, Nv.	N12FU
☐ N620BB	01	CitationJet CJ-1	525-0467	Brian Shore, Oyster Bay, NY.	N5157E
☐ N620DS	88	Gulfstream 4	1040	GR1040 Inc. Los Angeles, Ca.	N74RP
☐ N620HF*	88	Challenger 601-3A	5021	Gotham Enterprises & Affiliates LLC. NYC.	N621CF
☐ N620JH	95	Gulfstream 4SP	1272	AirStar Corp. Salt Lake City, Ut	N621JA
☐ N620JM	78	Learjet 35A	35A-207	Aspen Base Operation Inc. Aspen, Co.	N3PW
☐ N620K	00	Global Express	9052	Eastman Kodak Co. Rochester, NY.	N752DS
☐ N620KE	01	Gulfstream G100	137	PPD Aeronautics LLC. Wilmington, NC.	N75GX
☐ N620M	01	Gulfstream 4SP	1473	TADIC Inc. Kansas City, Mo.	XA-EOF
☐ N620S	81	Challenger 600S	1031	Beech Street Corp. Macon, Ga.	C-GLXS

Reg	Yr	Type	c/n	Owner/Operator	Prev Regn
N620TC	93	CitationJet	525-0014	Golden Eagle Aviation Inc. Southfield, Mi.	N70TR
N621CH	96	Hawker 800XP	8303	CSG Systems International Inc. Englewood, Co.	N876H
N621JH	00	Gulfstream 4SP	1423	Huntsman Chemical Corp/Airstar Corp. Salt Lake City, Ut.	N423GA
N621KB	01	Gulfstream G200	044	Sheridan-Alii Aviation LLC. San Jose, Ca.	N621KD
N621KD	02	Gulfstream G550	5001	ALII Aviation LLC/Exponent Inc. San Jose, Ca.(Ff 18 Jul 02).	N5SP
N621QS	02	Citation Excel	560-5280	NetJets, Columbus, Oh.	N.....
N621S	83	Gulfstream 3	381	Westgate Aviation LLC. Orlando, Fl.	N1871R
N621SC	01	Gulfstream 4SP	1481	SCS Services LLC. San Jose, Ca.	N281GA
N621SV*	04	Citation Sovereign	680-0021	Titlemax Aviation Inc. Savannah, Ga.	N1276L
N622EX	91	Citation II	550-0679	Mobile Crane Services Inc. Ottumwa, Ia.	N250GM
N622PC	99	Citation Excel	560-5024	PNB Aero Services Inc. Love Field, Tx.	N654EL
N622PG	78	Citation II	550-0037	PGC Services Inc. Amarillo, Tx.	(N37GA)
N622QS	02	Citation Excel	560-5286	NetJets, Columbus, Oh.	N.....
N622RR	68	Gulfstream II SP	12	R-Squared LLC. Dallas-Love, Tx.	N794SB
N622SV	00	Galaxy-1126	015	Simon Ventures Inc/NIC Air Inc. Naples, Fl.	N38GX
N622VH	90	Citation II	550-0635	Dubois County Flight Services Inc. Huntingburg, In.	(N214CP)
N622WM	90	Challenger 601-3A	5084	AirBill Inc. NYC.	N399CF
N623BM	77	Gulfstream 2	205	Bill Mullis Enterprises Inc. Sarasota, Fl.	N205BL
N623CW	88	Challenger 601-3A	5023	Flight Options LLC. Cleveland, Oh.	N175ST
N623DS	90	Citation II	550-0662	United Rotary Brush Corp. Olathe, Ks.	N911QB
N623KC*	90	Citation V	560-0076	Austin Air LLC. Cleveland, Oh.	N94NB
N623MS	82	Gulfstream 3	351	Yuna Aviation LLC. Needham, Ma	N18TM
N623PM	92	Citation VII	650-7018	CB Transport Inc/Compass Bank, Birmingham, Al.	N119RM
N623QS	02	Citation Excel	560-5299	NetJets, Columbus, Oh.	N.....
N623TS	96	Challenger 604	5323	Aero Toy Store LLC. Fort Lauderdale, Fl.	N604DS
N624AT	01	Citation Excel	560-5174	ALLTEL Corp. Little Rock, Ar.	N5223X
N624B	03	Hawker 400XP	RK-369	Bunn-O-Matic Corp. Springfield, Il.	N369XP
N624BP	89	Gulfstream 4	1093	Triangle Air Services Inc. Teterboro, NJ.	N399PA
N624GJ	95	Gulfstream 4SP	1267	Peregrine Aviation LLC. Seattle, Wa.	N301K
N624KM	78	Westwind-1124	227	K & M Equipment Co. Van Nuys, Ca.	N64FG
N624N	02	Gulfstream V	681	ITT Industries Inc. White Plains, NY.	(N519QS)
N624PD	70	HS 125/731	NA756	Bristol Capital Advisors LLC. Van Nuys, Ca.	N400JK
N624PP	81	Gulfstream 3	320	Blue Skies Aircraft Holdings LLC. NYC.	N624BP
N624QS	02	Citation Excel	560-5302	NetJets, Columbus, Oh.	(N118ST)
N624VA	70	B 727-17	20327	Enterprise Aviation LLC. Grand Rapids, Mi.	N529AC
N625AT	01	Citation Excel	560-5175	ALLTEL Corp. Little Rock, Ar.	N52114
N625AU	81	Learjet 25D	25D-340	Yelvington Transport Inc. Daytona Beach, Fl.	N980A
N625BL	87	Learjet C-21A	35A-625	Air Shares LLC. Sanford, Fl.	86-0375
N625PG	98	CitationJet	525-0282	Montpelier Partners LLC. Bridgeport, Ct.	
N625QS	03	Citation Excel	560-5319	NetJets, Columbus, Oh.	N.....
N625W	95	Beechjet 400A	RK-106	Stuart Family Land & Cattle Inc. Lincoln, Ne.	N1HS
N626AT	01	Citation Excel	560-5239	ALLTEL Corp. Little Rock, Ar.	N239XL
N626BM	88	Learjet 35ZR	35A-634	Jet Air Holdings Inc. Wilmington, De.	I-EAMM
N626CG	85	BAe 125/800A	8041	Keystone Aviation LLC/Million Air, Salt Lake City, Ut.	N71NP
N626EK	96	Falcon 900B	157	EK LLC. Fairfield, Ia.	N1868S
N626GA	00	Gulfstream V	626	Fightertown Inc. Miami, Fl.	(N5JR)
N626JS	97	Gulfstream 4SP	1334	J W Childs Associates Inc. Bedford, Ma.	N434QS
N626KM	93	Learjet 60	60-012	Lear 60 LLC. Van Nuys, Ca.	N147CC
N626LJ	97	Learjet 60	60-119	J W Childs Associates Inc. Bedford, Ma.	N119LJ
N626QS	01	Citation Excel	560-5126	NetJets, Columbus, Oh.	
N626RB	93	Citation V	560-0221	Robert Millard, Stratford, Ct.	N701DK
N626TC*	61	MS 760 Paris	88	Airborne Turbine Inc. San Luis Obispo, Ca.	N88NY
N627BC	98	Citation Bravo	550-0868	A T Massey Coal Co. Richmond, Va.	N5117U
N627CW	84	Challenger 601	3027	Paramount Aviation LLC. Cleveland, Oh.	(N603LX)
N627E	79	Citation 1/SP	501-0123	Orion Aviation LLC. El Paso, Tx.	N627L
N627JG	72	Falcon 20E	267	JBH Aviation LLC. Spartanburg, SC.	N731G
N627KR	90	Challenger 601-3A	5059	147RK LLC. Roseland, NJ.	C-GZNC
N627L	98	Citation Bravo	550-0843	EETEM Inc. Indianapolis, In.	N5079V
N627QS	02	Citation Excel	560-5227	NetJets, Columbus, Oh.	N5197M
N627R	00	Citation X	750-0132	Camden News Publishing Co. Little Rock, Ar.	N51055
N627XL	01	Citation Excel	560-5149	Lord Leasing Inc. Cary, NC.	N.....
N628BS	72	Citation	500-0045	Chippewa Aerospace Inc. Myrtle Beach, SC.	(N628FS)
N628CB	01	Citation Bravo	550-0991	Cimarron Aviation Inc. Bend, Or.	N4190A
N628CC	99	Falcon 2000	95	Comcast Cable Communication Holdings, N Philadelphia, Pa.	F-WWVO
N628DB	79	Learjet 35A	35A-246	Ameriplan USA Corp. Dallas, Tx.	N1DC
N628GZ	87	Learjet 35A	35A-628	debis Financial Services Inc. Norwalk, Ct.	CX-VRH

Reg	Yr	Type	c/n	Owner/Operator	Prev Regn
☐ N628HC	73	Gulfstream 2	134	EICO II Corp. NYC.	N555KH
☐ N628QS	02	Citation Excel	560-5305	NetJets, Columbus, Oh.	N.....
☐ N628SA	00	Falcon 2000	128	Swift Aviation Services Inc. Phoenix, Az.	N228EJ
☐ N629DM	99	CitationJet CJ-1	525-0369	Altrua America Jet Services LLC. Tallahassee, Fl.	N5200U
☐ N629QS	02	Citation Excel	560-5306	NetJets, Columbus, Oh.	N.....
☐ N629RM	85	Citation III	650-0096	RDM Enterprises LLC. Denver, Co.	N702SW
☐ N629TD	70	Gulfstream II SP	92	Triple Diamond Gulfstream LLC. Wheeling, Il.	(N584DM)
☐ N629WH	80	Westwind-Two	305	Willard Hammonds II, Corpus Christi, Tx.	N717EA
☐ N630CC	80	Citation II	550-0130	Chestnut's Investments Inc. Wilmington, De.	N778C
☐ N630QS	00	Citation Excel	560-5130	NetJets, Columbus, Oh.	N52113
☐ N630S	90	Astra-1125SP	046	Fountainhead Sales & Leasing Corp. Braselton, Ga.	N140DR
☐ N630SJ	80	Learjet 35A	35A-344	New World Aircraft LLC. Allentown, Pa.	N344MC
☐ N630TF	01	CitationJet CJ-2	525A-0022	Horizon Aviation LLC. Smyrna, Ga.	(N117W)
☐ N631AT	99	Learjet 31A	31A-191	Bombardier Aerospace Corp. Windsor Locks, Ct.	
☐ N631CC	95	Learjet 31A	31A-104	Cleveland Construction Inc. Cleveland, Oh.	N104BX
☐ N631EA	90	Citation II	550-0631	WWB LLC. Eden Prairie, Mn.	XA-ICP
☐ N631M	96	Citation V Ultra	560-0383	Ferdinand Stent, Stone Mountain, Ga.	N63TM
☐ N631PP	97	Beechjet 400A	RK-155	Wilder Aviation Sales & Leasing Inc. Clearwater, Fl.	N631RP
☐ N631QS	01	Citation Excel	560-5131	NetJets, Columbus, Oh.	N52136
☐ N631RP	02	Citation Excel	560-5254	Ring Power Corp. Jacksonville, Fl.	N51743
☐ N631SF	93	Learjet 31A	31A-075	Sanderson Farms Inc. Laurel, Ms.	(N418RT)
☐ N632BL	01	Citation Excel	560-5171	Pacific Simon LLC. Wilmington, De.	SU-EWB
☐ N632FW	96	Hawker 800XP	8294	Marine R Corp. Naples, Fl.	N404BS
☐ N632PB	91	Learjet 31	31-033	Modern Transportation Co. Owensboro, Ky.	(N131WS)
☐ N632PE	68	HS 125/1A	25058	located Freetown, Sierra Leone. (status ?).	(EC-...)
☐ N632QS	01	Citation Excel	560-5132	NetJets, Columbus, Oh.	N5225K
☐ N633AT	73	Citation	500-0087	Air Ambulance by Air Trek Inc. Punta Gorda, Fl.	(N911CJ)
☐ N633CW	83	Challenger 601	3013	Flight Options LLC. Cleveland, Oh.	(N602LX)
☐ N633EE	85	Citation S/II	S550-0058	A K Guthrie, Big Spring, Tx.	N1271E
☐ N633QS	04	Citation Excel XLS	560-5526	NetJets, Columbus, Oh.	N5194B
☐ N633RP	02	Citation Excel XLS	560-5501	Cessna Aircraft Co. Wichita, Ks. (was 560-5313)	N562XL
☐ N633SA	93	Citation V	560-0235	Sumlin Aviation LLC. Hickory, NC.	N92BF
☐ N633SF	02	Learjet 31A	31A-241	Sanderson Farms Inc. Laurel, Ms.	N335AF
☐ N633SL	69	Sabre-60	306-33	Sabreliner 633SL Inc. Independence, Ks.	CC-CGT
☐ N633W	87	Falcon 50	184	Pet Supermarket Inc/West Air LLC. Sunrise, Fl.	N25ME
☐ N634H	87	Falcon 50	178	Hillenbrand Industries Inc. Batesville, In.	N59PM
☐ N635AV	92	Gulfstream 4SP	1185	Avery Dennison Corp/Air Group Inc. Van Nuys, Ca.	N485GA
☐ N635E	99	Falcon 2000	106	PLA Aircraft Corp. Dearborn, Mi.	F-W...
☐ N635QS	03	Citation Excel	560-5358	NetJets, Columbus, Oh.	N5235G
☐ N636BC	89	Astra-1125	039	British Creek Air LLC. Denver, Co.	XA-JRM
☐ N636GD	87	Gulfstream 4	1012	GDR Aviation LLC. NYC.	(N713VL)
☐ N636MF	97	Gulfstream V	512	Ropa Two Corp. Teterboro, NJ.	N512GA
☐ N636N	78	Citation 1/SP	501-0069	Carbontec Energy Corp. McMinnville, Or.	N501EF
☐ N636QS	02	Citation Excel	560-5304	NetJets, Columbus, Oh.	N.....
☐ N637GA	03	Gulfstream G550	5037	Gulfstream Aerospace Corp. Savannah, Ga.	
☐ N637QS	01	Citation Excel	560-5137	NetJets, Columbus, Oh.	
☐ N638QS	04	Citation Excel	560-5363	NetJets, Columbus, Oh.	N.....
☐ N638XP	03	Hawker 800XP	8638	Raytheon Aircraft Co. Wichita, Ks.	
☐ N639AT*	80	Westwind-Two	308	Air Ambulance by Air Trek Inc. Punta Gorda, Fl.	N628KM
☐ N639QS	01	Citation Excel	560-5139	NetJets, Columbus, Oh.	
☐ N640BA	90	Learjet 35A	35A-664	Beta Aire Ltd. Toledo, Oh.	C-GRMJ
☐ N640CH	99	Challenger 604	5428	Chase Manhattan Bank, White Plains, NY.	C-GLYO
☐ N640QS	02	Citation Excel	560-5240	NetJets, Columbus, Oh.	N51055
☐ N641QS	02	Citation Excel	560-5295	NetJets, Columbus, Oh.	N50820
☐ N642AC	99	Beechjet 400A	RK-224	AC Expeditions LLC. St Augustine, Fl.	N51NP
☐ N642AG	02	EMB-135BJ Legacy	145642	Apollo Group, Scottsdale, Az.	PT-SAQ
☐ N642BJ	77	Citation Eagle	501-0032	YNR Aviation Ltd. Rochester, Mn.	N85WP
☐ N642LF	03	Citation Encore	560-0642	Lufkin Industries Inc. Lufkin, Tx.	N.....
☐ N642RP	69	Sabre-60	306-46	AVMATS/Centurion Investments Inc. St Louis, Mo.	N100FN
☐ N643CR	82	Challenger 600	1055	Monfort Aviation LLC. Eaton, Co.	N217MB
☐ N643RT	89	Citation V	560-0019	Thomas Wathen Trust, Santa Barbara, Ca.	N61TW
☐ N643TD	82	Citation II	550-0438	Lynn Durham, Midland, Tx.	N437CC
☐ N645AM	88	Learjet 35A	35A-645	Samanta SpA. Naples, Italy.	N43TR
☐ N645G	76	Learjet 35	35-056	Parmley Aviation Services Inc. Council Bluffs, Ia.	N106GL
☐ N645QS	00	Citation Excel	560-5145	NetJets, Columbus, Oh.	N52645
☐ N646QS	01	Citation Excel	560-5246	NetJets, Columbus, Oh.	N.....
Reg	Yr	Type	c/n	Owner/Operator	Prev Regn

Reg	Yr	Type	c/n	Owner/Operator	Prev Regn
N647JP	67	Falcon 20-5	120	Luiginos Inc. Duluth, Mn.	N20AF
N647QS	05	Citation Excel XLS	560-5547	NetJets, Columbus, Oh.	N5156D
N647TS	94	Learjet 60	60-047	HCE Leasing LLC. Cleveland, Oh.	(N225LC)
N649TT	90	Falcon 900	82	Larry Townes, Lewisville, Ar.	(N561CM)
N650AS	83	Citation III	650-0002	650-0002 Inc. Naples, Fl.	(N650BG)
N650AT	94	Citation VII	650-7053	Apogent Technologies Inc. Portsmouth, NH.	N128SL
N650BA*	89	Citation III	650-0170	Home Air Inc/Home Place Inc. Gainesville, Ga.	N32JJ
N650BW	84	Citation III	650-0028	Jet Management Inc. Sanford, Fl.	N38ED
N650CB	85	Citation III	650-0084	Southwest Cartage Inc. Annapolis, Md.	(N431CQ)
N650CC	90	Citation III	650-0193	Murphy Oil Corp. El Dorado, Ar.	N55HD
N650CD	84	Citation III	650-0066	O'Gara Aviation LLC. Las Vegas, Nv.	N138V
N650CE	86	Citation III	650-0106	Clark Transportation Co. Bethesda, Md.	N106CC
N650CG	84	Citation III	650-0023	C G Bretting Manufacturing Co. Ashland, Wi.	N38DD
N650CH	88	Citation III	650-0154	Daryl Verdoorn, Eden Prairie, Mn.	N696HC
N650CJ	94	Citation VII	650-7044	Tailwind East LLC. Turkey, NC.	N7005
N650CM	92	Citation V	560-0177	CM Aviation LLC. Santa Barbara, Ca.	N242AC
N650CP	92	Citation VII	650-7016	CFP Leasing LLC. Wheeling, Il.	N650RP
N650DA	86	Citation III	650-0114	Duncan Aviation Inc. Lincoln, Ne.	N651AF
N650DR	89	Citation III	650-0181	DeJet Aviation Inc. Knoxville, Tn.	N743CC
N650FC	87	Citation III	650-0146	Frank's Casing Crew & Rental Tools, Lafayette, La.	XA-PIP
N650FP	90	Citation III	650-0188	Flying Service NV. Antwerp, Belgium.	N587S
N650GC	92	Citation VI	650-0216	WJM Aviation LLC. Romeoville, Il.	N650KC
N650GE	93	Astra-1125SP	064	Gaylord Broadcasting Corp. Nashville, Tn.	4X-CUG
N650GH	84	Citation III	650-0034	Chattern Inc. Chattanooga, Tn.	(N45US)
N650HC	86	Citation III	650-0124	Findlay Management Group, Henderson, Nv.	N7HV
N650J	83	Citation III	650-0022	Highlands Aviation Corp. Houston, Tx.	
N650JB	00	Citation VII	650-7113	Realty Investment Co. Silver Spring, Md.	PP-JRA
N650JL*	98	Citation VII	650-7101	Littlefield 2000 Trust, El Sobrante, Ca.	N612AB
N650K	93	Citation VII	650-7034	Convergent Consulting Corp. Dallas, Tx.	VP-CDW
N650KB	85	Citation III	650-0078	M Robert Miller Inc. Ashville, NY.	N650WL
N650LA	83	Citation III	650-0004	William Lynch Associates, Boston, Ma.	N650GT
N650LR	89	Learjet 35A	35A-650	Wal-Mart Stores Inc. Rogers, Ar.	N135MW
N650LW	83	Citation III	650-0010	DeBordieu/Dallas II Inc. Dallas, Tx.	OK-NKN
N650MM	84	Citation III	650-0048	Preco Electronics Inc. Boise, Id.	N986M
N650PW	03	Gulfstream G400	1530	Bohemian Breweries Inc. Fort Collins, Co.	N330GA
N650QS	01	Citation Excel	560-5150	NetJets, Columbus, Oh.	N5100J
N650RL	94	Citation VII	650-7029	Central PA Cellular Telephone Co. Pensacola, Fl.	XA-SOK
N650RP	88	Citation III	650-0157	Trillium Staffing Inc. Kalamazoo, Mi.	N10JP
N650SB	83	Citation III	650-0018	Trishan Air Inc. Santa Barbara, Ca.	N275WN
N650SG	90	Citation III	650-0191	South Street Aviation LC/AM AV Inc. Baltimore, Md.	N650TJ
N650TA	85	Citation III	650-0088	Thunder Aviation Acquisitions Inc. Spirit of St Louis, Mo.	(N590AQ)
N650TS	92	Citation VI	650-0219	White Rose Ltd. UK.	(N211MA)
N650TT	84	Citation III	650-0046	Mobile Fractional Leasing LLC. Mobile, Al.	N57TT
N650VW	90	Citation III	650-0184	MI Home Products Inc. Middletown, Pa.	N11288
N650W	94	Citation VI	650-0237	Orion Aviation International LLC. Huntsville, Al.	(N656LE)
N650WB	83	Citation III	650-0020	Woodland Aircraft Leasing Inc. St Paul, Mn.	N10PN
N650WC	90	Citation II	550-0627	Towne Management Co. Youngstown, Oh.	N17FL
N650WE	84	Citation III	650-0040	533MA LLC. Vancouver, Wa.	HB-VIY
N650X	81	Falcon 50	69	Radnor Management Inc. Radnor, Pa.	N80FJ
N650Z	86	Citation III	650-0108	Bohemian Breweries Inc. Fort Collins, Co.	(N1302U)
N651AT	84	Citation III	650-0063	MBO Aviation LLC. Earlsboro, Ok.	N650AT
N651BP	83	Citation III	650-0017	Kinnaird Air Oregon, Portland, Or.	(N650BP)
N651CC	00	Citation VII	650-7119	United Foods Inc. Bells, Tn.	N5152X
N651CG	82	Citation III	650-0001	Point Aerospace Corp. Dover, De.	N651CC
N651CJ	99	CitationJet CJ-1	525-0365	Vinci Aviation Inc. Rancho Santa Fe, Ca.	N5130J
N651CV	84	Citation III	650-0036	Summit Seafood Supply Inc. Houston, Tx.	N650BS
N651CW	86	Challenger 601	3051	Flight Options LLC. Cleveland, Oh.	(N604LX)
N651EJ	95	Citation V	650-0241	Three Angels Broadcasting Co. Frankford, Il.	N651JM
N651LJ	66	Learjet 24A	24A-125	Steven Lysdale, Bellevue, Wa.	
N651MK	81	Sabre-65	465-73	Stempre Listo LLC/Energy Services Inc. Dover, De.	N64MQ
N651QS	02	Citation Excel	560-5251	NetJets, Columbus, Oh.	N.....
N652CV	84	Citation III	650-0055	Seafood Holding Supply Inc. Houston, Tx.	N16AS
N652ND	75	Citation	500-0277	Carothers Construction Inc. Water Valley, Ms.	N67MA
N652NR	03	Citation Encore	560-0652	Cross Jet Inc. Wellesbourne Mountford, UK.	N.....
N652QS	01	Citation Excel	560-5152	NetJets, Columbus, Oh.	
N653AC	94	Challenger 601-3R	5153	Adelaide LLC. Greensboro, NC.	OY-APM

Reg	Yr	Type	c/n	Owner/Operator	Prev Regn
N653CW	89	Challenger 601-3A	5053	Flight Options LLC. Cleveland, Oh.	(N611LX)
N654AT	94	Beechjet 400A	RK-88	RBJ Industries Inc. Minneapolis-St Cloud, Mn.	N1549W
N654CE	04	Citation Encore	560-0654	Wells Fargo Bank NA. Salt Lake City, Ut. (trustor ?).	N52653
N655CM*	86	Beechjet 400	RJ-17	CH Aircraft LLC. St Louis, Mo.	N455FD
N655TH	98	Learjet 60	60-141	Great Bay Aviation LLC. Portsmouth, NH.	N163BA
N656PS	78	Citation II	550-0009	California Oregon Broadcasting, Medford, Or.	N744DC
N656Z	04	Citation Encore	560-0656	Rainier Fruit Co. Yakima, Wa.	N.....
N657T	94	Citation VII	650-7042	Hershey Foods Corp. Middletown, Pa.	N1265K
N658CF*	82	Challenger 600S	1058	Freeman Jet LLC. Topeka, Ks.	N60HJ
N659FM	95	Falcon 2000	17	Thayer Services LLC. Manassas, Va.	N89TY
N659QS	04	Citation Excel	560-5359	NetJets, Columbus, Oh.	N.....
N660AS	00	Learjet 60	60-191	ASCO Inc/ASCO Transport Inc. St Louis, Mo.	N30154
N660BC	95	Learjet 60	60-063	BC Air LLC/Prestige Builders Group Corp. Miami, Fl.	N8270
N660CC	01	Beechjet 400A	RK-319	Burt Aviation Corp. Rochester Hills, Mi.	N689TA
N660EG	95	Falcon 900B	152	Georgica Enterprises LLC. Ronkonkoma, NY.	N337MC
N660HC	99	Learjet 45	45-058	Holder Construction/DEC-District Equipment Co. Atlanta, Ga.	RP-C1944
N660PA*	93	Citation VI	650-0230	Mutual Assurance Agency Inc. Birmingham, Al.	N616AT
N660Q	88	Citation III	650-0162	Excellent Aviation Rentals Inc. Houston, Tx.	N275GC
N660RM	82	Challenger 600S	1054	Romeo Mike Aviation Inc. Fort Lauderdale, Fl.	N602AS
N660XP	04	Hawker 800XP	8660	Rockwell Collins Inc. Cedar Rapids, Ia.	
N661AC	74	Citation	500-0121	N661AC Inc. Wilmington, De.	N3QE
N661AJ	92	Citation V	560-0176	Shepherd's Chapel Inc. Gravette, Ar.	PT-WOM
N661GA	98	Gulfstream V	561	Lear Investment LLC/Lear Corp. Pontiac, Mi.	
N661JN	91	BAe 125/800A	NA0468	Jackson National Life Insurance Co. Lansing, Mi.	N410BT
N662CB	03	Citation Bravo	550-1062	Information Technology Inc. Lincoln, Ne.	N.....
N662P	01	Falcon 50EX	320	CONOCO-Phillips, Houston, Tx.	F-WWHZ
N662QS	02	Citation Excel	560-5262	NetJets, Columbus, Oh.	N.....
N663MK	01	Falcon 900EX	94	Merck & Co. Mercer County, NJ.	N994EX
N663P	00	Gulfstream 4SP	1434	CONOCO-Phillips, Houston, Tx.	N434GA
N663PD	87	Gulfstream 4	1022	Paul Davril Inc. Los Angeles, Ca.	N23MU
N663QS	02	Citation Excel	560-5263	NetJets, Columbus, Oh.	N.....
N664AC	01	Hawker 800XP	8566	A C Corp. Washington-Dulles, DC.	N4466Z
N664AJ	89	Citation II	550-0613	Airplane One LLC. Northport, Al.	PT-OAC
N664CE	04	Citation Encore	560-0664	Active Organics, Lewisville, Tx.	N5151D
N664CL	68	Learjet 24	24-167	Clay Lacy Aviation Inc. Van Nuys, Ca.	N888B
N664CW	86	Challenger 601	3064	Flight Options LLC. Cleveland, Oh.	(N606LX)
N664QS	02	Citation Excel	560-5264	NetJets, Columbus, Oh.	N5066U
N664SS	83	Citation II	550-0458	Hoeweler Group Inc. Cincinnati, Oh.	N25MK
N665CH	02	CitationJet CJ-1	525-0504	Volante Aviation Inc. Cranfield, UK.	N52081
N665DP	93	CitationJet	525-0028	Catbird Aviation LLC. Raleigh, NC.	G-GRGG
N665QS	01	Citation Excel	560-5165	NetJets, Columbus, Oh.	N5109W
N666BE	04	Falcon 2000EX EASY	32	Formula One Management Ltd. Biggin Hill, UK.	F-WWGK
N666CT	87	Challenger 601-3A	5007	Polygon Air Corp. White Plains, NY.	N17TZ
N666K	90	Astra-1125	040	Aerojet Inc. Gaithersburg, Md.	N279DS
N666KL	81	Westwind-1124	321	Aero Jet Charter Inc. Washington, DC.	N666K
N666LN	84	Citation S/II	S550-0005	Sky Eagle Corp. Reno, Nv.	(N1256G)
N666MW	75	Learjet 24D	24D-305	Triple Six Lear LLC. Wilmington, De.	N510PA
N666MX	02	Citation Excel	560-5292	ComJet BV. Rotterdam, Holland.	N5101J
N666TK	82	Learjet 55	55-038	Polygon Air Corp. White Plains, NY.	N50AF
N666TR	96	Challenger 604	5309	Janus Transair Corp. Belchertown, Ma.	C-GHRK
N667CX	68	Gulfstream II SP	10	Oslo Express Inc. New Canaan, Ct.	N51TJ
N667LC	96	Challenger 604	5324	Loews Corp/Clinton Court Corp. Teterboro, NJ.	N601CC
N667MB	83	Learjet 55	55-073	Jedami Jet LLC. Hollywood, Fl.	N155V
N667P	00	Gulfstream 4SP	1447	CONOCO-Phillips, Houston, Tx.	N447GA
N667QS	04	Citation Excel	560-5365	NetJets, Columbus, Oh.	N.....
N668AJ	82	Citation II	550-0442	DAC Aviation LLC. Douglas, Ga.	N442ME
N668CB	03	Citation Bravo	550-1068	Information Technology Inc. Lincoln, Ne.	N.....
N668JT	75	Gulfstream 2	162	Plan 15 Aviation LLC. Elmira-Corning, NY.	N666JT
N668P	01	Falcon 50EX	315	CONOCO-Phillips, Houston, Tx.	F-WWHU
N668QS	02	Citation Excel	560-5268	NetJets, Columbus, Oh.	N.....
N668S	76	Citation	500-0314	Nolan's RV Center Inc. Denver, Co.	N66ES
N668VB	97	CitationJet	525-0228	Winfield Consumer Products Inc. Winfield, Ks.	N668VP
N668VP	01	Learjet 31A	31A-232	Vic Air LLC. Winston-Salem, NC.	N5008S
N669B	03	Citation Bravo	550-1060	Hines Jetcorp LLC. Spring Lake, Mi.	N.....
N669BJ	99	Gulfstream 4SP	1397	S & H Automotive Products Inc. Fort Lauderdale, Fl.	N397GA
N669W	96	Citation VII	650-7066	Elmet Air Inc. NYC.	N766CG

Reg	Yr	Type	c/n	Owner/Operator	Prev Regn

Reg	Yr	Type	c/n	Owner/Operator	Prev Regn
N670C	72	Sabre-75A	370-7	Jett Aire Florida One Inc. Palm Beach, Fl.	N670C
N670CE	04	Citation Encore	560-0670	Acrylic Encore Inc. Pomona, Ca.	N5243K
N670H	81	Sabre-65	465-58	Honeywell International Inc. Phoenix, Az.	N670AS
N670JD	84	Citation S/II	S550-0019	Amber Services Inc. Chicago, Il.	N550TB
N670MW	04	Citation Excel XLS	560-5511	Marvin Lumber & Cedar Co. Warroad, Mn.	N52609
N670QS	01	Citation Excel	560-5170	NetJets, Columbus, Oh.	
N670XP	04	Hawker 800XP	8670	Raytheon Aircraft Co. Wichita, Ks.	
N671LE	01	Gulfstream V	671	BG Aviation LLC. NYC.	N571GA
N671LW	70	Gulfstream 2	90	Scott Aviation Inc. DuPage, Il.	N20GP
N671QS	00	Citation Excel	560-5071	NetJets, Columbus, Oh.	N51881
N671TS	92	Learjet 35A	35A-671	Aero Toy Store LLC. Fort Lauderdale, Fl.	N671BX
N671WM	02	Falcon 2000	194	Waste Management Inc. Andrau Airpark-Houston, Tx.	F-WWVF
N672PS*	99	Galaxy-1126	010	GC International LLC. Lawrenceville, Ga.	N121LS
N672SA	94	Citation V Ultra	560-0272	Interstate Equipment Leasing Inc. Phoenix, Az.	N372EJ
N673BA	01	Falcon 2000	173	Bank of America NA. Charlotte, NC.	F-WWVR
N673LR	80	Citation II	550-0179	Tyburn Management Ltd. Allegheny County, Pa.	N673LP
N673TS	92	Challenger 600S	1073	VKC Consulting LLC. Bar Harbor, Fl.	(N600EC)
N674AC	82	Diamond 1A	A024SA	Pre-Paid Legal Services Inc. Ada, Ok.	N450PC
N674BP	95	Learjet 60	60-074	Tafel Motors Inc/Peterson Air LLC. Louisville, Ky.	N620JF
N674G	82	Citation II	550-0435	Findlay Industries Inc. Findlay, Oh. (was 551-0434).	N390DA
N674JM	01	CitationJet CJ-1	525-0485	Evan Morgan Massey, Richmond-Chesterfield County, Va.	N52136
N674LJ	93	Learjet 35A	35A-G74	Novada N674LJ LLC. San Antonio, Tx.	N900JE
N674RW	97	Gulfstream V	524	Coca-Cola Co. Atlanta, Ga.	N400JD
N674SF	99	Beechjet 400A	RK-232	Dakota-Jet LLP. Grand Forks, ND.	N2355N
N675QS	02	Citation Excel	560-5275	NetJets, Columbus, Oh.	N.....
N675RW	98	Gulfstream V	526	Coca-Cola Co. Atlanta, Ga.	N526GA
N675SS	88	Citation II	550-0576	Structural Steel Services Inc. Meridian-Key Field, Ms.	N438SP
N676BA	01	Falcon 2000	176	Bank of America NA. Charlotte, NC.	F-WWMC
N676BB	03	Citation Excel	560-5349	Becker Trading Co. Vero Beach, Fl.	N.....
N676CC	84	Citation 1/SP	501-0676	Lud Corrao Revocable Family Trust, Reno, Nv.	N76JY
N676DG	75	Citation	500-0256	G & G Group LLC. Parsons, Tn.	N131SB
N676GA	02	Gulfstream V	676	Gulfstream Aerospace Corp. Savannah, Ga.	
N676GH	04	Hawker 800XP	8676	Jack Prewitt & Assocs Inc. Bedford, Tx.	N676XP
N676JB	03	Hawker 800XP	8619	LRB LLC. Burbank, Ca.	N61719
N676QS	01	Citation Excel	560-5176	NetJets, Columbus, Oh.	
N676TC	00	Astra-1125SPX	128	Alpine Cascade Corp. Santa Barbara, Ca.	N179DC
N677AS	02	390 Premier 1	RB-33	American Specialty Insurance Services, Fort Wayne, In.	N50843
N677CT	80	Learjet 35A	35A-307	K & M Equipment Co. Van Nuys, Ca.	(N119HB)
N677GA	02	Gulfstream V	677	Gulfstream Aerospace Corp. Savannah, Ga.	(N677F)
N677GS	91	Citation II	550-0669	Golden Shamrock Associates LLC. North Platte, Ne.	N846HS
N677JM	78	Citation 1/SP	501-0052	Flying M LLC. Page, Az.	N900MC
N677QS	04	Citation Excel	560-5367	NetJets, Columbus, Oh.	N.....
N677RP	89	Gulfstream 4	1085	Petersen Aviation, Van Nuys, Ca.	N864CE
N677RW	92	Gulfstream 4	1177	Coca-Cola Co. Atlanta, Ga.	(I-LADB)
N678MA	82	Falcon 50	116	Ovation Air Group Inc. Carlsbad, Ca.	XB-SOL
N678SB	92	BAe 1000B	9016	Gray & Co. New Orleans, La.	N291H
N679GA	02	Gulfstream V	679	Gulfstream Aerospace Corp. Savannah, Ga.	
N679QS	02	Citation Excel	560-5279	NetJets, Columbus, Oh.	N.....
N680AF	93	Learjet 31A	31A-068	Alaska Flight Services LLC. Tuscaloosa, Al.	C-GWXK
N680AR	04	Citation Sovereign	680-0025	Cessna Aircraft Co. Wichita, Ks.	N5247S
N680CJ	69	Learjet 24B	24B-211	Diplomat Aviation Inc. Tulsa, Ok.	N413WF
N680CS	02	Citation Sovereign	709	Cessna Aircraft Co. Wichita, Ks. (First Flight 27 Feb 02).	
N680DF	01	Falcon 2000	180	International Paper Co. White Plains, NY.	(N203DD)
N680GA	01	Gulfstream V	680	BMA Charter s r o, Prague, Czech Republic.	
N680GW	96	Citation V Ultra	560-0369	Grady-White Boats Inc. Greenville, NC.	N5200
N680JB	03	CitationJet CJ-2	525A-0190	Cedar Hill Investment LLC. Silver Spring, Md.	N5141F
N680PH	04	Citation Sovereign	680-0030	Cessna Aircraft Co. Wichita, Ks.	N.....
N681CE	04	Citation Encore	560-0681	Sierra Pacific Industries, Anderson, Ca.	N5265B
N681CS	02	Citation Sovereign	680-0001	Cessna Aircraft Co. Wichita, Ks. (First Flight 27 Jun 02).	
N681QS	01	Citation Excel	560-5181	NetJets, Columbus, Oh.	
N681XP	04	Hawker 800XP	8681	United States Steel Corp. Pittsburgh, Pa.	
N682B	89	BAe 125/800A	NA0431	E I DuPont de Nemours & Co. New Castle, De.	N585BA
N682DB	03	Citation Sovereign	680-0009	Cessna Aircraft Co. Wichita, Ks.	N.....
N682HC	84	Citation 1/SP	501-0682	Herman Carruth, Duluth, Ga.	N682DC
N683E	87	BAe 125/800A	NA0410	E I DuPont de Nemours & Co. New Castle, De.	N555BA
N683EC	75	Gulfstream 2	157	Westshore Aviation/Prince Transportation Inc. Holland, Mi.	N658PC

Reg	Yr	Type	c/n	Owner/Operator	Prev Regn

Reg	Yr	Type	c/n	Owner/Operator	Prev Regn
N683EL	86	Learjet 35A	35A-614	35A-614 LLC. Coeur d'Alene, Id.	N335EA
N683PF	86	Citation S/II	S550-0083	BKMS BigSky LLC. San Jose, Ca.	N883PF
N684AT	81	Gulfstream 3	339	Mill Creek Systems LLC. Vail, Co.	N339A
N684DK	04	Hawker 800XP	8684	Monsanto Co. St Louis, Mo.	
N684GA	02	Gulfstream V	684	Gulfstream Aerospace Corp. Savannah, Ga.	
N684HA	77	Learjet 35A	35A-113	AirNet Systems Inc. Columbus, Oh. (blue).	(N113AN)
N684JW	81	Learjet 25D	25D-350	AirCorp Inc. Tuscaloosa, Al.	(N428CH)
N684KF	03	Falcon 2000	213	JCG Aviation LLC/Koch Meat Co. Park Ridge, Il.	N212QS
N684QS	00	Citation Excel	560-5084	NetJets, Columbus, Oh.	N5211A
N685FF	84	HS 125/731	25121	Spirit of Faith Christian Center, Temple Hills, Md.	N125LK
N685RC	98	Learjet 31A	31A-149	TRC Realty Co. Burlington, Vt.	N1904S
N685SF*	70	Gulfstream II SP	94	Spirit of Faith Christian Center, Temple Hills, Md.	N18AQ
N685TA	02	Gulfstream V	685	G IV Corp/American Home Products, Morristown, NJ.	N585GA
N686AB	02	Learjet 31A	31A-239	AirBrock LLC. Waccaboc, NY.	
N686SC	98	Beechjet 400A	RK-211	KA Corp/Webb Road Development Inc. Whitefish, Mt.	N3028U
N686TA	01	Beechjet 400A	RK-328	Flight Options LLC. Cleveland, Oh.	(N472LX)
N686TR	96	Beechjet 400A	RK-127	U-Haul Comapny of Oregon, Portland, Or.	N696TR
N687QS	01	Citation Excel	560-5187	NetJets, Columbus, Oh.	
N688CF	74	Citation	500-0147	Big Chief Aviation Inc. Goshen, In.	N494G
N688DB	03	CitationJet CJ-2	525A-0192	Paradise Companies LLC. Natchez, Ms.	N.....
N688G	04	Hawker 800XP	8688	Giant Industries Inc. Scottsdale, Az.	
N688GS	73	Learjet 25B	25B-123	Royal Air Freight Inc. Waterford, Mi.	N906SU
N688JD	99	Citation Bravo	550-0902	Conex International Corp. Jasper, Tx.	N770UM
N688QS	02	Citation Excel	560-5188	NetJets, Columbus, Oh.	N.....
N689AM	03	Hawker 800XP	8665	Alpha Mike Aviation Inc. Winnetka, Il.	N665XP
N689TA	01	Beechjet 400A	RK-327	Flight Options LLC. Cleveland, Oh.	(N471LX)
N689VP	91	Citation II	550-0689	HNB Investments LLC. San Diego, Ca.	XA-JYO
N689W	84	Citation III	650-0045	Liz Air LLC. Las Vegas, Nv.	N669W
N690DM	81	Citation 1/SP	501-0222	Space City Aviation, Austin, Tx.	N25HS
N690EW	79	Citation II	550-0108	Krew Supershuttle LLC. Dallas, Tx.	N36NA
N690JC	80	Learjet 25D	25D-320	Skytech Aviation Inc. Addison, Tx.	OO-LFR
N690QS	00	Citation Excel	560-5090	NetJets, Columbus, Oh.	N51246
N691AN	03	EMB-135BJ Legacy	145699	Wind Spirit LLC. Santa Monica, Ca.	PT-...
N691QS	02	Citation Excel	560-5290	NetJets, Columbus, Oh.	N.....
N691RC	89	Gulfstream 4	1079	Wham Leasing Corp. Teterboro, NJ.	N479TS
N691TA	01	Beechjet 400A	RK-317	Flight Options LLC. Cleveland, Oh.	(N469LX)
N692BE	85	Citation III	650-0092	Hollywood Air Inc. Pinellas Park, Fl.	N692CC
N692EB	69	Gulfstream 2B	775	Motor Air LLC. San Bernardino, Ca.	N4PC
N692FG	70	Learjet 25	25-052	Lear 25-052 Inc. Chula Vista, Ca.	N692FC
N692QS	00	Citation Excel	560-5092	NetJets, Columbus, Oh.	N5125J
N693SH	88	Falcon 900B	43	Dittmer Trading LLC. Chicago, Il.	N388Z
N694JC	81	Challenger 600S	1026	IDM Aviation Services LLC. Austin, Tx.	(N507WY)
N694JP	99	Falcon 900EX	59	Liberty Mutual Insurance Co. Bedford, Ma.	N959EX
N694LM	77	Citation	500-0354	IDM Aviation Services LLC. Austin, Tx.	N354RC
N694QS	01	Citation Excel	560-5194	NetJets, Columbus, Oh.	N.....
N695BK	99	Beechjet 400A	RK-235	Big Country Air LLC. Fargo, ND.	
N695QS	02	Citation Excel	560-5293	NetJets, Columbus, Oh.	N.....
N695XP	04	Hawker 800XP	8695	Bob Air LLC/Thompson & Co of Tampa Inc. Tampa, Fl.	
N696CM	01	Citation Bravo	550-0978	Alabama National Bancorp. Birmingham, Al.	N52475
N696HC	01	Falcon 50EX	316	Henry Crown & Co. Palwaukee, Il.	N316EX
N696MJ	75	Gulfstream 2B	165	A P Enterprises LLC. Vero Beach, Fl.	N183V
N696PA	92	Learjet 31A	31A-060	PA Lear 31A-060 LLC. Springdale, Ar.	N156EC
N696QS	02	Citation Excel	560-5296	NetJets, Columbus, Oh.	N.....
N696RB*	97	Learjet 31A	31A-145	BAC Transportation Inc. Stockton, Ca.	N89RF
N696RV	67	Jet Commander	118	JTS Aviation Inc. Amarillo, Tx.	N381DA
N696ST	97	CitationJet	525-0187	Dr Robert Knollenberg, Boulder, Co.	N5130J
N696TA	00	Beechjet 400A	RK-301	Flight Options LLC. Cleveland, Oh.	(N465LX)
N696US	80	Sabre-65	465-18	United Space Alliance LLC. Houston, Tx.	N4M
N696VP	92	Citation II	550-0696	RLH Enterprises LLC. Chicago, Il.	N67NC
N697A	01	Gulfstream V	662	ALCOA Inc. Allegheny County, Pa.	N662GA
N697MB	74	Citation	500-0224	Dove Air Inc. Hendersonville, NC.	N145CM
N697MC	85	Citation III	650-0097	RTW Aviation Inc. Greensboro, NC.	N725WH
N697QS	01	Citation Excel	560-5197	NetJets, Columbus, Oh.	N.....
N697TA	00	Beechjet 400A	RK-299	Flight Options LLC. Cleveland, Oh.	
N697US*	80	Sabre-65	465-49	United Space Alliance LLC. Houston, Tx.	N82CR
N698CW	83	Challenger 601	3008	Flight Options LLC. Cleveland, Oh.	(N600LX)

Reg	Yr	Type	c/n	Owner/Operator	Prev Regn

Reg	Yr	Type	c/n	Owner/Operator	Prev Regn
☐ N698MM	97	Learjet 31A	31A-142	Marime Max Inc/Delaware Av Lease LLC. Clearwater, Fl.	ZS-EAG
☐ N698PW	96	Beechjet 400A	RK-114	Deep South Aviation Inc. Fort Worth, Tx.	N363K
☐ N698RS	83	Challenger 601	3014	Ariana LLC/Republic Industries Inc Fort Lauderdale, Fl.	N292GA
☐ N698TA	00	Beechjet 400A	RK-298	Flight Options LLC. Cleveland, Oh.	
☐ N699CW	87	Challenger 601-3A	5009	Flight Options LLC. Cleveland, Oh.	(N610LX)
☐ N699DA	01	Learjet 60	60-237	Delphi Automotove Systems LLC. Troy, Mi.	
☐ N699MC	03	Falcon 2000EX	25	Mazama Capital Management Inc. Hillsboro, Or.	N225EX
☐ N699QS	01	Citation Excel	560-5199	NetJets, Columbus, Oh.	N.....
☐ N699RD	70	Sabre-60	306-53	Sabreliner Corp. St Louis, Mo.	(N999LG)
☐ N699ST	81	Learjet 35A	35A-441	Sterling Aviation LLC. Miami, Fl.	RP-C1404
☐ N699TS	72	HS 125/F600A	6001	Aviation Solutions LLC. Farmington Hills, Mi.	N773JC
☐ N699TW	66	Falcon 20DC	50	Kitty Hawk Air Cargo Inc. Dallas, Tx.	EC-EDO
☐ N699XP	04	Hawker 800XP	8699	Raytheon Aircraft Co. Wichita, Ks.	
☐ N700AJ	03	Adams A700	0001	Adams Aircraft Industries, Englewood, Co. (Ff 27 Jul 03).	N700JJ
☐ N700AL	75	Falcon 10	55	SBM Aviation Inc. Jackson-Thompson, Ms.	(N700PD)
☐ N700BX	00	Global Express	9068	Wilmington Trust Co. Wilmington, De.	(N889JC)
☐ N700CE	84	HS 125/700A	7213	Codale Electric Supply Inc. Salt Lake City, Ut.	(N703MJ)
☐ N700CH	95	Learjet 60	60-056	Cardal Inc. Columbus-OSU, Oh.	N117RJ
☐ N700CJ	93	CitationJet	525-0027	Bruun Aircraft LLC. Hillsboro, Or.	N816RD
☐ N700CN	90	Gulfstream 4	1133	Copley Press Inc. Carlsbad, Ca.	N443GA
☐ N700EW	04	Global Express	9142	Bombardier Aerospace Corp. Windsor Locks, Ct.	C-GAGT
☐ N700FA	04	Hawker 400XP	RK 300	Raytheon Aircraft Co. Wichita, Ks.	
☐ N700FH	79	Falcon 10	158	Flex Air Ltd/Flight Star Corp. Chicago-Midway, Il.	N790FH
☐ N700FS	99	Gulfstream 4SP	1400	Agro-Industrial Management, West Palm Beach, Fl.	N215TM
☐ N700FW	77	HS 125/700A	NA0205	Jackson Financial Services Inc. Decatur, Ga.	N807TC
☐ N700GB	02	Global Express	9124	Bombardier Aerospace Corp. Windsor Locks, Ct.	C-FZVN
☐ N700GD	89	Gulfstream 4	1104	Stanford Aircraft LLC. Miami, Fl.	N600ML
☐ N700GG	78	Learjet 36A	36A-038	North American Jet Charter Inc. Banning, Ca.	N548PA
☐ N700GW	98	CitationJet	525-0275	Joe Morten & Son Inc. South Sioux City, Ne.	
☐ N700HH	78	HS 125/700A	NA0240	Hotel Hotel Aircraft Inc. St Louis, Mo.	N130BA
☐ N700HX	97	Global Express	9005	Oakley Inc. Foothill Ranch, Ca.	VP-CPC
☐ N700JA	77	Citation 1/SP	501-0272	Solley Air LLC. Wilmington, De.	N700JR
☐ N700JC	81	Sabre-65	465-74	Oxley Petroleum Co. Tulsa, Ok.	
☐ N700JR	04	Citation Encore	560-0666	Johnny Ribeiro Builder Air LLC. Las Vegas, Nv.	N51160
☐ N700KS	01	Global Express	9109	Amblin Entertainment Inc/Dreamworks LLC. Burbank, Ca.	N700DU
☐ N700LH	01	Citation X	750-0148	Limerick Holdings LLC/The Broe Companies Inc. Denver, Co.	N.....
☐ N700LP	81	HS 125/700A	NA0311	Orcas Air Inc. Santa Monica, Wa.	N425WN
☐ N700LS	00	Gulfstream 4SP	1412	Limited Inc. Columbus, Oh.	N412GA
☐ N700LW	77	Citation Eagle 400SP	501-0033	James Hammond, Plymouth, Mn.	N411ME
☐ N700MD	77	Westwind-1124	212	Kal Kustom NW Inc. Salem, Or.	N900CS
☐ N700MG	01	Hawker 800XP	8540	Abbott Laboratories Inc. Waukeagn, Il.	(XA-...)
☐ N700MH	86	Citation III	650-0127	James Hammond, Minneapolis, Mn.	(N95UJ)
☐ N700ML	99	Global Express	9043	Regent Entertainment, Santa Monica, Ca.	N700BU
☐ N700MP	81	Falcon 50	70	HOP Air One GP Inc. Frisco, Tx.	N306ES
☐ N700NH	81	HS 125/700A	NA0304	Nighthawk Management LLC. Allegheny County, Pa.	N96PR
☐ N700NW	79	HS 125/700A	NA0246	Howe Electric Inc. Fresno, Ca.	N79HC
☐ N700NY	81	HS 125/700A	NA0299	Alwyn LLC. Mankato, Mn.	N703JP
☐ N700QS	01	Gulfstream G200	052	NetJets, Columbus, Oh.	N294GA
☐ N700R	04	Hawker 800XP	8692	NASCAR Inc. Daytona Beach, Fl.	N37092
☐ N700RR	78	HS 125/700A	NA0217	Roberts Aircraft LLC. St Louis, Mo.	(N6960)
☐ N700RY	83	Citation III	650-0005	Radioactive LLC. Cincinnati, Oh.	N693BA
☐ N700SA	81	HS 125/700A	NA0339	JI. Leasing LLC. Valhalla, NY.	PT-ORJ
☐ N700SB	81	Gulfstream 3	334	Heir to Air Inc. Van Nuys, Ca.	N41PG
☐ N700SJ	76	Learjet 35A	35A-082	AirNet Systems Inc. Columbus, Oh. (was orange now red).	N700GB
☐ N700SW	00	Citation X	750-0142	Safeway Insurance Co. Westmont, Il.	N5172M
☐ N700TR	70	HS 125/731	NA745	Career Aviation Academy Inc. Las Vegas, Nv.	N400XJ
☐ N700VC	72	Citation Eagle	500-0011	Faith Life Church Inc. Branson, Mo.	C-GJEM
☐ N700VT	81	HS 125/700A	7158	V T Inc. Kansas City, Mo.	XB-DZN
☐ N700WC	78	HS 125/700A	7022	Airplane One LLC. Houston, Tx.	N109AF
☐ N701AS	76	Learjet 35A	35A-047	AirNet Systems Inc. Columbus, Oh. (blue).	N13MJ
☐ N701BG	87	Citation S/II	S550-0142	Black Gold Potato Sales Inc. Grand Forks, ND.	C-GCRG
☐ N701CP	00	Beechjet 400A	RK-272	Central Plains Steel Co/Richard Owen LLC. Kansas City, Ks.	N3237H
☐ N701CR	00	Citation Excel	560-5141	Globe Leasing Inc. Chicago, Il.	N17AN
☐ N701CW	76	HS 125/700A	7001	Continental Carrier Inc. Columbus, Oh.	(N807CW)
☐ N701DA	78	Learjet 35A	35A-180	DavisAir Inc. Allegheny County, Pa.	N44HG
☐ N701DF	02	390 Premier 1	RB-59	JIK Mission Lakes Manager Inc. Fort Lauderdale, Fl.	

| Reg | Yr | Type | c/n | Owner/Operator | Prev Regn |

Reg	Yr	Type	c/n	Owner/Operator	Prev Regn
N701FW	80	Sabre-65	465-21	Freeman Jet LLC. Topeka, Ks.	(N265CA)
N701HA	92	Citation VII	650-7001	Blue Pacific Aviation Inc. Wilmington, De.	N404JF
N701JH	78	JetStar 2	5230	MidAmerica Jet Inc. Owensboro, Ky.	N901EH
N701KB	03	390 Premier 1	RB-103	Southeast Kansas Leasing LLC. Pittsburg, Ks.	N61930
N701LX*	00	Citation X	750-0114	Flight Options LLC. Cleveland, Oh.	N114CX
N701MS	76	HS 125/F600A	6061	MCS Leasing Inc. Carlsbad-Paolmar, Ca.	N331DC
N701S	69	Gulfstream II SP	69	Gulfway Air Inc. Sugar Land, Tx.	N440DR
N701SC	71	Learjet 24XR	24XR-235	MCA-Taylor Lear 24 LLC. Wichita, Ks.	N51VL
N701SF	02	CitationJet CJ-2	525A-0071	Air Frantz Inc. White Plains, NY.	N34RL
N701TF	02	CitationJet CJ-2	525A-0112	TVPX Inc. Tampa, Fl.	N525U
N701TP	97	CitationJet	525-0190	Geostar Leasing Corp. Mount Pleasant, Pa.	N708TF
N701TS	77	HS 125/700A	NA0201	Tecno Transport International, Fort Lauderdale, Fl.	G-IECL
N701VV	02	Citation Bravo	550-1033	Miller Container Aviation Inc. Moline-Quad City, Il.	N933BB
N701WC	03	Falcon 50EX	333	Liberty Mutual Insurance Co. Bedford, Ma.	N334EX
N701WH	98	Global Express	9010	N2T Inc/Oakley Inc. Bellingham, Wa.	C-GDGQ
N702CA	80	Falcon 20-5B	429	Busey Corp. Urbana, Il.	N149MC
N702DM	84	Gulfstream 3	428	D Q Automobiles/Papa Grande Management Co. Irving, Tx.	N760G
N702GA	04	Gulfstream G200	102	Gulfstream Aerospace LP. Dallas-Love, Tx.	4X-C..
N702GH	02	Gulfstream 4SP	1497	GEH Air Transportation LLC. White Plains, NY.	(N497QS)
N702HC	73	HS 125/600A	6023	Donali Eugene Radle, Sarasota, Fl.	N523MA
N702JH	83	Diamond 1A	A035SA	MidAmerica Jet Inc. Owensboro, Ky.	N135GA
N702LP	94	Beechjet 400A	RK-87	Leggett & Platt Inc. Joplin, Mo.	N1567L
N702QS	02	Gulfstream G200	070	NetJets, Columbus, Oh.	N268GA
N702R	97	Learjet 60	60-113	Raytheon Aircraft Co. Wichita, Ks.	N700R
N703JH	81	Diamond 1A	A010SA	MidAmerica Jet Inc. Owensboro, Ky.	N300DH
N703LP	91	Beechjet 400A	RK-20	Celero Energy LP. Midland, Tx.	N870P
N703QS	02	Gulfstream G200	060	NetJets, Columbus, Oh.	N270GA
N703TM	91	Falcon 50	218	Carlisle Holdings LLC. Bedford, Ma.	N750FJ
N703TS	78	HS 125/700A	7031	Hawker 700 Holding Management Inc. Miami, Fl.	(N703JN)
N703VZ	87	BAe 125/800A	NA0408	GTE Southwest Inc. White Plains, NY.	N309G
N704DA	81	Citation II	550-0202	D + A Investments LLC. Albuquerque, NM.	N550NE
N704JA	84	Gulfstream 3	432	Chancellor Media Air Services Corp. Austin, Tx.	(N997CM)
N704JM	98	Hawker 800XP	8367	United Aircraft Holdings LLC. Concord, NC.	OY-GIP
N704MF	00	Global Express	9065	MC Group, Hillsboro, Or.	N711SW
N704T	99	390 Premier 1	RB-2	Raytheon Aircraft Co. Wichita, Ks.	
N705AC	77	Westwind-1124	209	SMA LLC. Clearwater, Fl.	N222LH
N705JA	82	Gulfstream 3	360	Jet Aviation Private Fleet LLC. Burbank, Ca.	N90LC
N705LP	99	Beechjet 400A	RK-251	Leggett & Platt Inc. Joplin, Mo.	N3106Y
N705QS	02	Gulfstream G200	061	NetJets, Columbus, Oh.	N271GA
N705SG	00	Citation Excel	560-5142	Union of Operating Engineers, Van Nuys, Ca.	N5093D
N705SP	85	Citation S/II	S550-0048	Sportsmans Market Inc. Batavia, Oh.	N999TJ
N706CJ*	00	Learjet 60	60-207	King Aircraft Ltd. White Plains, NY.	N777VQ
N706CR	99	Learjet 60	60-168	Bombardier Aerospace Corp. Windsor Locks, Ct.	N706CJ
N706JA	81	Gulfstream 3	322	Tropical Development LLC. Provo, Ut.	N606ES
N706LP	01	Beechjet 400A	RK-336	Leggett & Platt Inc. Joplin, Mo.	(N706PL)
N706NA	92	Citation II	550-0706	JLF Aircraft Inc. Los Gatos, Ca.	7Q-YLF
N706SA	90	Learjet 31	31-026	RGM LLC. Charleston, WV.	(N184RM)
N706VP	96	Citation X	750-0006	Syracuse Jet Leasing LLC. Syracuse, NY.	N484H
N706XP	04	Hawker 800XP	8706	Raytheon Aircraft Co. Wichita, Ks.	
N707AM	80	Falcon 10	159	Air Vandia LLC. Conway, Ar.	N707DC
N707BC	87	Astra-1125SPX	093	Westwind Acquisition LLC. Dulles, Va.	N149TD
N707CA	63	B 707-351C	18586	Omega Air Inc. Washington, DC.	P4-FDH
N707CG	80	Falcon 10	165	Gresham & Assocs Inc. Stockbridge, Ga.	N56LP
N707GW	01	Gulfstream V	629	Goodwill, Tokyo, Japan.	N711RQ
N707HP	04	Citation Bravo	550-1096	WFBNW NA. Salt Lake City, Ut. (trustor ?).	(N877B)
N707JA	85	Gulfstream 3	447	Jet Aviation Private Fleet LLC. Burbank, Ca.	N144PK
N707JT	64	B 707-138B	18740	John Travolta/Atlo Inc. Jumbolair Aviation Community, Ocala.	N707XX
N707JU	79	B 707-3W6C	21956	Omega Air Inc. Washington, DC.	CN-CCC
N707LG	75	B 707-3M1C	21092	Omega Air Inc. San Antonio, Tx.	A-7002
N707MM	00	Falcon 2000	131	Massachusetts Mutual Life Insurance Co. Bedford, Ma.	F-WWVG
N707MQ	77	B 707-368C	21368	Almeda Corp, San Antonio, Tx.	HZ-HM3
N707NV	92	Learjet 31A	31A-063	NV707 LLC. Oakville, Ca.	N995AW
N707PE	89	BAe 125/800A	NA0442	Louisiana Aviation LLC. Whitefish, Mt.	N4444J
N707PF	82	Citation II	550-0452	Eagle Creek Aviation Inc. Longview, Tx.	N707PE
N707QS	02	Gulfstream G200	066	NetJets, Columbus, Oh.	N276GA
N707SC	65	Learjet 24	24-065	Dolphin Aviation Inc. Sarasota, Fl.	N957SC

| Reg | Yr | Type | c/n | Owner/Operator | Prev Regn |

Reg	Yr	Type	c/n	Owner/Operator	Prev Regn
☐ N707SG	03	Gulfstream G200	087	Grossman Company Properties Inc. Santa Monica, Ca.	(N747SG)
☐ N707SK	59	B 707-138B	17702	Mideast Jet, Jeddah, Saudi Arabia.	N707KS
☐ N707TA	96	Hawker 800XP	8296	Ryan Hawker 707 LLC. Rockford, Il.	(N812LX)
☐ N707TF	71	Westwind-1123	155	Ferrante Aviation Inc. Vandergrift, Pa.	N707TE
☐ N707W	79	Citation 1/SP	501-0085	Wellons Inc. Sherwood, Or.	N25DD
☐ N707WB	93	Falcon 900B	132	The Home Depot Inc. Atlanta-Fulton County, Ga.	N132FJ
☐ N707XP	04	Hawker 800XP	8707	Raytheon Aircraft Co. Wichita, Ks.	
☐ N708GP	03	CitationJet CJ-2	525A-0154	RSF Management Services Inc. Rancho Santa Fe, Ca.	N5091J
☐ N708QS	02	Gulfstream G200	069	NetJets, Columbus, Oh.	N279GA
☐ N708SP	97	Learjet 45	45-014	Tappetto Magico Inc. Wilmington, De.	
☐ N708TA	98	Beechjet 400A	RK-178	Flight Options LLC. Cleveland, Oh.	(N430LX)
☐ N709EL	92	Beechjet 400A	RK-52	Gal Air Inc. Atlanta, Ga.	(N709EW)
☐ N709RS	92	Citation II	550-0709	R S & I Oregon Inc. Portland, Or.	N709VP
☐ N709TA	98	Beechjet 400A	RK-180	Flight Options LLC. Cleveland, Oh.	(N480CW)
☐ N709TB	74	Citation	500-0214	Roby Inc. Marysville, Oh.	N214CA
☐ N710A	88	BAe 125/800B	8110	ARAMCO Associated Co. Dhahran, Saudi Arabia.	D-CMIR
☐ N710AW	97	Citation X	750-0033	Allied Waste Industries Inc. Scottsdale, Az.	N5093D
☐ N710EC	02	Gulfstream G400	1502	Chouest Air Inc. Houma, La.	N202GA
☐ N710GS	75	Learjet 35	35-032	Flight Capital LLC. Madison, Ms.	N711MA
☐ N710HL	82	Challenger 600S	1050	Caesh Air LLC. St Charles, Il.	N82CN
☐ N710JC	78	Falcon 10	120	Minnesota Choice Aviation LLC. St Paul, Mn.	N402JW
☐ N710LC	90	Citation V	560-0058	Rockies West LLC/Lanz Cabinet Shop Inc. Eugene, Or.	N62GA
☐ N710LM	89	Challenger 601-3A	5037	Liberty Media Group. Denver, Co.	N212LM
☐ N710MT	94	Citation V	560-0254	Biomet Inc/Air Warsaw Inc. Warsaw, In.	N586GB
☐ N710QS	99	Citation VII	650-7100	NetJets, Columbus, Oh.	
☐ N710SA	80	Westwind-1124	296	Sun Air Inc. Laredo, Tx.	N89TJ
☐ N710TA	98	Beechjet 400A	RK-183	Flight Options LLC. Cleveland, Oh.	(N432LX)
☐ N710TV	68	Learjet 24	24-159	Royal Air Freight Inc. Waterford, Mi.	(N269AL)
☐ N710VF	89	Challenger 601-3A	5050	VILLCo Aviation LLC. Pontiac, Mi.	(N25GG)
☐ N710VL*	76	Citation	500-0302	Jefferson County Racing Association, Montgomery, Al.	(N777QE)
☐ N711AJ	01	390 Premier 1	RB-18	Hoffler Air LLC. Chesapeake, Va.	N88MM
☐ N711BE	02	CitationJet CJ-2	525A-0116	Guaranty Development Co. Bozeman, Mt.	N5233J
☐ N711BX	98	CitationJet	525-0299	Donald Baker, Tucson, Az.	N711BE
☐ N711CW	65	Learjet 24	24-055	Premier Jets Inc. Hillsboro, Or.	N511WH
☐ N711EC	97	Beechjet 400A	RK-167	Romero Leasing Inc. Stuttgart, Ar.	N2267B
☐ N711EG	82	Gulfstream 3	349	Entrepreneurial Asset Management LLC. Newport Beach, Ca.	N6458
☐ N711FG	94	Learjet 31A	31A-092	Frontier Shoppes Inc. Las Vegas, Nv.	N50302
☐ N711FJ	79	Falcon 10	149	Embee Inc. Santa Ana, Ca.	(N830SR)
☐ N711GA	81	Challenger 600S	1025	Green Aviation Corp. White Plains, NY.	(OY-CKO)
☐ N711GD	03	Hawker 800XP	8612	Sunflower Aircraft Inc. Joplin, Mo.	N50522
☐ N711GF	96	Citation VII	650-7075	IPD-Indeck Power Overseas LLC. Wheeling, Il.	N52613
☐ N711GL	90	Gulfstream 4	1130	G & L Aviation Inc. Van Nuys, Ca.	N404LM
☐ N711HA	02	Citation Bravo	550-1039	Hoyt Air Inc. Albuquerque, NM.	N320CS
☐ N711HE	04	Falcon 2000EX EASY	47	Harrah's Operating Co. Reno, Nv.	F-W...
☐ N711HF	87	Falcon 100	213	Hartford Holding Corp. Naples, Fl.	F-WKAE
☐ N711HQ	99	Citation X	750-0078	Harrah's Operating Co. Las Vegas, Nv.	N711HE
☐ N711JC	75	Falcon 10	69	Object Development Corp. Santa Ana, Ca.	N7TJ
☐ N711KE	80	Westwind-1124	288	Kauffman Engineering/Hawk Holdings Inc. Zionsville, In.	N48AH
☐ N711LS	04	Global 5000	9155	The Whitewind Co. Windsor Locks, Ct.	C-FBPT
☐ N711LV	93	Citation VI	650-0232	Union Financial Services Inc. Lincoln, Ne.	(N512MT)
☐ N711MC	02	Global Express	9121	N & M D Investment Corp. Fort Lauderdale, Fl.	N700FN
☐ N711MD	85	Citation S/II	S550-0066	Cabot Air LLC. Boston, Ma.	N1272P
☐ N711MN	97	Global Express	9002	Qualcomm Inc. San Diego, Ca.	N711MC
☐ N711MQ	76	Gulfstream 2B	189	ABCO Aviation Inc. Houston, Tx.	N404AC
☐ N711MT	76	Citation	500-0316	January Transport Inc. Oklahoma City, Ok.	(N127CJ)
☐ N711NB	92	Citation VII	650-7009	First National Bank, McCallen, Tx.	N709VP
☐ N711NK	04	Citation Excel XLS	560-5533	Spartan Air Flight LLC. Wilmington, De.	N.....
☐ N711NV	87	Citation II/SP	551-0557	Nevada Department of Transport, Carson City. (was 550-0557).	N1298C
☐ N711PC	76	Learjet 24D	24D-327	World of Faith Christian Center Church, Southfield, Mi.	N327GJ
☐ N711R	99	Learjet 45	45-049	Cockrell Resources Inc. Houston, Tx.	
☐ N711RL	03	Gulfstream G550	5010	Ralph & Ricky Lauren/RL Wings LLC. NYC.	N910GA
☐ N711RZ	68	Gulfstream 2	25	Heritage Jets Inc. Bear, De.	N711RL
☐ N711SW	88	Gulfstream 4	1033	Wynn Resorts Ltd/Las Vegas Jet, Las Vegas, Nv.	N6458
☐ N711SX	02	Global Express	9125	Acme Operating Co. Cleveland, Oh.	N700FR
☐ N711T	87	Falcon 50	176	Grey Falcon LLC. N Philadelphia, Pa.	N568VA
☐ N711TF	75	Falcon 10	52	Contemporary Industries Leasing Corp. Omaha, Ne.	N860E

Reg	Yr	Type	c/n	Owner/Operator	Prev Regn
N711UF	84	Gulfstream 3	421	Frank Fertitta Enterprises Inc. Las Vegas, Nv.	N921FF
N711VF	82	Citation 1/SP	501-0236	Gem Air Inc & Ameristar Casinos Inc. Las Vegas, Nv.	N26227
N711VH	84	Citation III	650-0047	Trio Holdings LLC. Hackensack, NJ.	N33BQ
N711VL	72	Gulfstream II SP	120	Macon Co Greyhound Park Inc. Montgomery, Al.	C-GTEW
N711VT	99	Citation X	750-0101	Aerohead Aviation Inc. Scottsdale, Az.	N881G
N711WD	79	Learjet 25D	25D-282	Orion Construction Group LLC. Appleton, Wi.	
N711WG	00	CitationJet CJ-1	525-0424	Midwest Transport LLC. St Joseph, Mo.	N28SW
N711WM	96	Challenger 800	7140	Coast Hotels & Casinos Inc. Las Vegas, Nv.	N140WC
N711WV	78	Falcon 20F-5	396	SBR Inc. Parkersburg, WV.	N711GL
N712CC	87	Gulfstream 4	1028	SAH Enterprises Inc. Santa Monica, Ca. 'Camille'.	N712CW
N712DP	80	Learjet 25D	25D-319	Don Prudhomme Leasing Inc. Carlsbad, Ca.	N680JC
N712EJ	01	Learjet 31A	31A-231	R H Bluestein & Co. Birmigham, Mi.	XA-VTR
N712JC	98	Citation X	750-0052	Air Franci Inc. Houston, Tx.	N5000R
N712KM	77	Citation	500-0348	Klotz Aviation LLC. Garden City, Ks.	C-GCLQ
N712MQ	71	Gulfstream 2	104	ABCO Aviation Inc. Houston, Tx.	C-FHPM
N712PD	79	Citation II	550-0069	August Doppes, Glenshaw, Pa.	C-FFCL
N712QS	02	Gulfstream G200	073	NetJets, Columbus, Oh.	N673GA
N712R	67	Learjet 24	24-156	Royal Cake Co. Winston Salem, NC.	N111RP
N712TA	98	Beechjet 400A	RK-186	Flight Options LLC. Cleveland, Oh.	(N433LX)
N713DH	04	Citation Excel XLS	560-5527	HMC Aviation Inc. New Smyrna Beach, Fl.	N5254Y
N713HC	96	Challenger 604	5308	5308 Acquistion LLC/HCC Insurance Holdings Inc. Belgrade, Mt	N982J
N713JD	78	Citation 1/SP	501-0075	Jordan Foster Aviation Inc. Jacksonville, Fl.	N51ET
N713MC	79	Falcon 20F-5B	392	Stephen Haight Construction, Sioux Falls, SD..	(N392FJ)
N713QS	99	Citation VII	650-7103	NetJets, Columbus, Oh.	
N713SA	73	Citation	500-0132	Highlands Management Group Inc. Scottsdale, Az.	(N992HG)
N713SN	87	Falcon 50	182	Alaska Eastern Inc. Eureka, Ca.	N250AS
N713SS	68	HS 125/400A	NA712	Bill Austin Aircraft & Yacht Sales, Sparta, Tn.	N712VS
N713XP	04	Hawker 800XP	8713	Raytheon Aircraft Co. Wichita, Ks.	
N714RM	03	Citation Bravo	550-1057	Raj Consulting LLC. Santa Ana, Ca.	N5245U
N715CG	02	Learjet 45	45-208	CG Cars LLC/Carl Gregory Cars Inc. Fort Payne, Al.	N5050G
N715JS	72	Citation	500-0001	Jerry Savelle Ministries International, Crowley, Tx.	N501KG
N715PS	90	Citation V	560-0055	Eagle Aviation Inc. Aiken, SC.	N209CP
N715QS	97	Citation VII	650-7105	NetJets, Columbus, Oh.	
N715TA	98	Beechjet 400A	RK-189	Flight Options LLC. Cleveland, Oh.	(N434LX)
N715WS	74	Falcon 20F-5B	305	Venture Jet Partners LLC. San Diego, Ca.	N34EW
N716CB	72	Citation	500-0055	Town & Country Supermarkets Inc. West Allis, Wi.	N999SF
N716DB	85	BAe 125/800A	8048	Western Leasing Co. Green Bay, Wi.	C-GCIB
N716DD	86	Citation S/II	S550-0120	J Bar B Aviation LLC. Waelder, Tx.	N716DB
N716TE	72	Gulfstream 2	116	Trans-Exec Air Service Inc. Van Nuys, Ca.	(N410LR)
N717AJ	78	Learjet 35A	35A-183	Sky Chief Air Inc. Brentwood, Tn.	N183FD
N717AM	84	Learjet 55	55-100	Florida Jet Service Inc. Fort Lauderdale, Fl.	(N500NB)
N717CF	98	Beechjet 400A	RK-177	711EE LLC. Carthage, NC.	N2277G
N717DD	98	Beechjet 400A	RK-207	Carlton-Bates Co. Little Rock, Ar.	N3015F
N717DM	82	Citation II	550-0436	GRM Aviation Inc. St Helena, Ca.	N711Z
N717EA	02	Beechjet 400A	RK-354	Earnhardt Aviation LLC. Scottsdale, Az.	N5084U
N717EP*	82	Learjet 55	55-016	Flaum Management Co. Rochester, NY.	N646G
N717GK	01	Citation Bravo	550-0971	Gould Investment Management LLC. Bellevue, Wa.	N717KQ
N717HB	83	Learjet 55	55-066	HBE Corp. Chesterfield, Mo.	N50DD
N717JB	96	Learjet 60	60-093	Arbor Aviation Enterprises LLC. Ronkonkoma, NY.	N129JR
N717JM	86	Citation III	650-0138	Miami Jet Professionals LLC. Miami, Fl.	N35PN
N717LA	80	Falcon 50	32	Papalote Aviation LLP/Miller of Dallas, Dallas, Tx.	N80TR
N717MB	00	Citation Excel	560-5114	MPW Industrial Services Group, Newark-Heath, Oh.	N20SB
N717MT	89	BAe 125/800A	NA0443	TTG Enterprises LLC. White Plains, NY.	N360DE
N717NA	01	CitationJet CJ-1	525-0437	Andrews Flight of Alabama Inc. Birmingham, Al.	N5185V
N717TG	01	Beechjet 400A	RK-320	The Answer Group Inc. Fort Lauderdale, Fl.	N4469E
N717VB	02	CitationJet CJ-2	525A-0137	Starlight Air LLC. Tacoma Narrows, Wa.	N.....
N717VL	04	Citation Bravo	550-1108	Cessna Aircraft Co. Wichita, Ks.	N.....
N718AN	95	Learjet 60	60-065	Anderson Management Services, Knoxville, Tn.	N30W
N718CK	82	Citation II	550-0368	Ryacon Airways Inc/Brendon Group Inc. Wilmington, De.	N94MF
N718DW	81	Falcon 50	81	SmithKline-Beckman/Colleen Corp. Philadelphia, Pa.	N89FJ
N718HC	85	BAe 125/800B	8040	Noblestar Consulting Inc. Dallas, Tx.	N713HC
N718JS	69	Gulfstream 2	66	SEI-Sykes Enterprises Inc. Tampa, Fl.	N165U
N718KS	04	Falcon 2000	216	KSI Services Inc. Dulles, Va.	F-WWVD
N718MC	98	Gulfstream V	549	Radical Ventures LLC/Mark Cuban, Dallas, Tx.	N317JD
N718SA	81	Citation 1/SP	501-0179	Harris Air Inc. Logan, Ut.	(N406RH)
N718TA	98	Beechjet 400A	RK-195	Flight Options LLC. Cleveland, Oh.	(N435LX)

Reg	Yr	Type	c/n	Owner/Operator	Prev Regn
N719CC	80	Westwind-1124	290	Bears Aviation LLC. Wilmington, De.	N800JJ
N719D	94	CitationJet	525-0075	Ross Aviation Inc. Cortland, Oh.	N719L
N719EH	88	Citation II	550-0572	Valhalla Air LLC. Palm Beach International, Fl.	N193SS
N719HG	83	Citation III	650-0007	Hantz Air LLC. Ypsilanti, Mi.	N52SY
N719L	01	390 Premier 1	RB-25	North American Air Charter Corp. Marlborough, Ma.	N808W
N719RM	90	Citation V	560-0092	Friedman, Fleischer & Lowe LLC. San Francisco, Ca.	XB-RTT
N720CC	00	Learjet 45	45-072	SouthTrust Bank NA. Atlanta, Ga.	I-ERJC
N720CH	89	Gulfstream 4	1118	N720CH Inc. Miami, Fl.	N418TT
N720DC	66	B 727-77	19253	Santa Barbara Aerospace Inc. Santa Barbara, Ca.	N448DR
N720DF	74	Falcon 10	26	Saturn Aviation Inc. Fort Wayne, In.	N707AM
N720DR	77	Gulfstream II SP	209	E R Aviation LLC. Salt Lake City, Ut.	N277T
N720JC	72	Falcon 20F-5	273	Jet Choice II LLC. St Paul, Mn.	N596DA
N720JR	62	B 720-047B	18451	J Raphael/J A R Aircraft Services Inc. Richardson, Tx.	N720JR
N720JW	76	Gulfstream II SP	178	Deerport Aviation Corp. Taipei, Taiwan.	N42LC
N720LH	78	Gulfstream 2TT	233	LCH LLC. Westport, Ct.	N233RS
N720LM	92	Challenger 601-3A	5104	Liberty Media Group. Denver, Co.	N212CT
N720MC	81	Westwind-Two	358	MKC Consolidated LLC. Love Field, Tx.	N787RP
N720ML	02	Falcon 900EX	115	Northwestern Mutual Life Insurance Co. Milwaukee, Wi.	F-WWFN
N720PT	78	HS 125/700A	NA0223	Pinnacle Trading LLC. Fresno, Ca.	N154JD
N720PW	60	B 720-023B	18021	Pratt & Whitney Canada Inc. Montreal, PQ. Canada.	C-FWXI
N720QS	03	Gulfstream G200	085	NetJets, Columbus, Oh.	N285GA
N720TA	97	Hawker 800XP	8320	Flight Options LLC. Cleveland, Oh.	(N813I X)
N720WW	79	Learjet 35A	35A-254	WPW Aircraft LLC. Scottsdale, Az.	N254US
N721AS	77	Learjet 35A	35A-101	Jet 1 Inc. Naples, Fl.	N109JU
N721BS	02	Learjet 45	45-227	Volante LLC. Las Vegas, Nv.	N437FX
N721CC	93	Citation II	550-0721	Munoco LC. El Dorado, Ar.	N1207B
N721CP	97	Learjet 45	45-006	Lear 006 Holding Ltd. Fort Lauderdale, Fl.	N456LM
N721DR	80	Citation II	550-0164	Citation Partners Inc. Fort Lauderdale, Fl.	N916RC
N721EC*	80	Learjet 35A	35A-355	East Coast Jets Inc. Allentown, Pa.	N351WB
N721FF	01	Gulfstream 4SP	1484	Frank Fertitta Enterprises Inc. Las Vegas, Nv.	N484GA
N721G	92	Challenger 601-3A	5109	Abbey Challenger LLC. Boston, Ma.	N721S
N721HM	96	Falcon 900B	158	Quantitative Financial Strategies, Stamford, Ct.	N404VC
N721J	04	Challenger 604	5590	Starbucks Corp. Seattle, Wa.	C-GLXY
N721LH	73	HS 125/600A	6025	NAT Aviation USA Inc. Miami, Fl.	C-GTPC
N721MC	88	Challenger 601-3A	5031	Marnell Corrao Associates, Las Vegas, Nv.	N908CL
N721MF	81	B 727-2X8	22687	Wedge Group Europe, Paris, France.	N4523N
N721MJ	94	Learjet 31A	31A-098	Maui Jim Inc. Peoria, Il.	N148C
N721MM	89	MD-87	49767	MGM Mirage Inc. Las Vegas, Nv.	N721EW
N721PA	65	JetStar-731	5054	Pan American Enterprises Ltd. Tampa, Fl.	N354CA
N721QS	04	Gulfstream G200	092	NetJets, Columbus, Oh.	N492GA
N721RL	99	Gulfstream 4SP	1394	High Tech Aircraft Corp. Portsmouth, NH.	N394GA
N721RM	75	HS 125/600B	6053	CIT Group, Tempe, Az.	N5NR
N721S	01	Citation V	668	Starbucks Flight Operations, Seattle, Wa.	N568GA
N721T	01	Citation Bravo	550-0993	Sadler/Chauncey LLC. Scottsdale, Az.	N5244W
N721VT	01	Citation X	750-0167	V T Inc. Kansas City, Mo.	N4165Y
N722A	90	BAe 125/800A	NA0461	ARAMCO Associated Co. Dhahran, Saudi Arabia.	N461W
N722AZ	00	Gulfstream G100	132	Sentinel Air LLC. Rutherford, Ca.	N775DF
N722CC	84	BAe 125/800A	8008	Rosemore Inc. Baltimore, Md.	G-5-11
N722DJ	81	Challenger 600S	1029	Djurin Aviation Inc. Waukegan, Il.	N600TN
N722EM	85	Learjet 25D	25D-372	The Myler Co. Crawfordsville, In.	N5NC
N722HP	86	Challenger 601	3054	HSPT LLC. Carlsbad, Ca.	N50TG
N722JB	95	Falcon 2000	13	Clos de Berry Management Ltd. Dayton, Oh.	N2004
N722JS	95	Learjet 31A	31A-109	BLT Aviation/Building&Land Technology Corp. Bridgeport, Ct.	(N9VL)
N722MM	88	Gulfstream 4	1052	MGM Mirage Inc. Las Vegas, Nv.	N152TS
N722Q	58	MS 760 Paris	9	David Bennett/Executive Aero, Colorado Springs, Co.	N334RK
N722QS	04	Gulfstream G200	093	NetJets, Columbus, Oh.	N393GA
N722SG	94	CitationJet	525-0088	Southwest Gas Corp. Las Vegas, Nv.	N188CJ
N722TA	97	Hawker 800XP	8322	Flight Options LLC. Cleveland, Oh.	(N814LX)
N722TS	02	CitationJet CJ-2	525A-0138	Harden Aviation LLC. Haleyville-Posey Field, Al.	N.....
N723CC	82	Learjet 55	55-036	Air Clayco Inc. St Louis, Mo.	N155HM
N723HH	94	Challenger 601-3R	5165	Hawker 723 Holdings Inc. Fort Lauderdale, Fl.	N723HA
N723JR	81	Citation 1/SP	501-0190	Allsup's Convenience Stores Inc. Clovis, NM.	N40AW
N723JW	67	Learjet 24	24-142	Charter Airlines Inc. Las Vegas, Nv.	N777MR
N723MM	82	Gulfstream 3	357	MGM Mirage Inc. Las Vegas, Nv.	N891MG
N723QS	04	Gulfstream G200	099	NetJets, Columbus, Oh.	N499GA
N723RE	00	Citation Bravo	550-0944	Edinton Holdings USA Inc. Guatemala City, Guatemala.	N5267J

Reg	Yr	Type	c/n	Owner/Operator	Prev Regn
N724AF	99	Global Express	9031	Vulcan Northwest Inc. Seattle-Tacoma, Wa.	N700FN
N724B	77	HS 125/700A	NA0204	BOY-CEN Air LLC. Traverse City, Mi.	G-BERX
N724CC	98	Citation X	750-0062	Clear Channel Communications Inc. San Antonio, Tx.	
N724CL	66	B 727-51	19121	Clay Lacy Aviation Inc. Van Nuys, Ca.	N299LA
N724DB	82	Gulfstream 3	372	Keystone Foods Corp. Philadelphia, Pa.	N500EX
N724DS	69	Falcon 20D-5B	198	Amjet Aviation Co. Atlanta, Ga.	N339TG
N724EA	80	HS 125/700A	NA0264	Ace Boca Aviation LLC. Wilmington, De.	N161WC
N724HB	89	Beechjet 400	RJ-55	AirLouie LLC. Tampa, Fl.	N780GT
N724KW	99	Beechjet 400A	RK-263	MidAmerican Holding Co. Kansas City, Mo.	N724MH
N724QS*	04	Gulfstream G200	100	NetJets, Columbus, Oh.	N500GA
N724TS	69	HS 125/731	NA724	New Light Church World Outreach Centre, Houston, Tx.	C-FSDH
N725CC	93	Citation II	550-0725	Air Fred LLC. Fresno, Ca.	N222FA
N725DM	81	Falcon 10	184	Roppe Corp. Columbus, Oh.	N4AC
N725DS	97	Citation Bravo	550-0822	Data Sales Financial Co. Burnsville, Mn.	N2029E
N725FL	82	Citation II	550-0369	Aircraft Managing Holdings Inc. Wilmington, De.	N725BF
N725JG	79	Falcon 20F-5B	416	25 Hitman JG LLC. Henderson, Nv.	N416F
N725LB	02	Global Express	9129	Moore Capital Management LLC. New York, NY.	N700FZ
N725PA	93	Falcon 50	236	Kiewit Engineering Co. Omaha, Ne.	XA-HHF
N725SC*	96	Learjet 60	60-083	SunCal Management LLC. Irvine, Ca.	N255RK
N725WH	65	HS 125/731	25042	White Industries Inc. Bates City, Mo.	(N42FD)
N726AG	05	CitationJet CJ-3	525B-0029	Cessna Aircraft Co. Wichita, Ks.	N.....
N726AM	93	Citation II	550-0726	AM Aircraft LLC. Las Vegas, Nv.	N726BM
N726MR	74	Falcon 10	35	Air 4 Aviation LLC/Tri-C Aviation Inc. Houston, Tx.	N83TJ
N726PG	02	Beechjet 400A	RK-337	Wheless Industries Inc. New Orleans, La.	N5037L
N726RP	02	CitationJet CJ-2	525A-0114	Larmont Investments Inc. Panama City, Panama.	N.....
N726RW	88	Gulfstream 4	1039	Pacific Jet Inc. Van Nuys, Ca.	N1901M
N726SC	94	CitationJet	525-0051	Southaire Inc. Memphis, Tn.	N808HS
N726TA	98	Hawker 800XP	8363	Flight Options LLC. Cleveland, Oh.	(N816LX)
N726TM	00	CitationJet CJ-1	525-0414	Alpha Echo Aviation LLC. Charlevoix, Mi.	N5223P
N726WR	68	Learjet 25	25-007	Aviation Equipment Resources Inc. Van Nuys, Ca.	(N58JA)
N727AT	80	Westwind-1124	284	RHF Ventures, Stockton, Ca.	N217BL
N727BT	93	Learjet 31A	31A-082	Wal-Mart Stores Inc. Rogers, Ar.	PT-MVI
N727C	84	Citation II	550-0485	McKelvey Aviation One LLC. Marshfield, Ma.	PT-WBV
N727CF	65	B 727-22	18323	PDC 1999 LLC. Fort Worth, Tx.	VR-BMC
N727CP	89	Learjet 31	31-009	O'Gara Aviation LLC. Atlanta, Ga.	N173PS
N727EC	64	B 727-30	18365	Atlantic Aircraft Inc. Kingshill, USVI.	N700TE
N727EF	85	Citation S/II	S550-0043	Sierra Industries Ltd. Uvalde, Tx.	N727NA
N727GG	66	B 727-95	19252	Trans Gulf Corp. Clearwater, Fl.	HZ-WBT2
N727GP	67	B 727-21	19260	Malibu Consulting Corp. Los Angeles, Ca.	N727LA
N727HC	67	B 727-35	19835	Clay Lacy Aviation Inc. Burbank, Ca.	N900CH
N727LM	80	Learjet 25D	25D-308	L & M Forwarding Inc. Laredo, Tx.	N102RR
N727PX	67	B 727-21	19261	Paxson Communications Management Co. West Palm Beach, Fl.	N260GS
N727RE	81	B 727-282	22430	Palace Air Inc. Las Vegas, Nv.	N6167D
N727S	90	Challenger 601-3A	5062	Rainier Aviation Inc. Seattle, Wa.	N142B
N727TA	77	HS 125/700A	NA0202	Provident Bank, Cincinnati, Oh.	N333ME
N727TK	74	Citation Eagle SP	500-0141	GE Engine Services, Tempe, Az.	XB-EWQ
N727TS	76	Falcon 10	76	Ajax Aviation Ltd/East Coast Flight Services, Easton, Md.	F-BYCC
N727VJ	67	B 727-44	19318	UBICS/UB Group, Bangalore, India.	N44MD
N727WF	68	B 727-23	20045	Peninsular Aviation LLC.	N2913
N727YB	03	Citation Excel	560-5332	Yellowbird Aviation LLC. New Haven, Ct.	N.....
N728A	69	DC 8-72	46081	ARAMCO Associated Co. Houston, Tx.	N8971U
N728AZ	81	Westwind-Two	351	Air Francis LLC. San Francisco, Ca.	N722AZ
N728LB	96	Gulfstream 4SP	1296	Jetstream Ventures LLC. Wilmington, De.	N725LB
N728LW	78	Falcon 50	3	Laurence Carr, Anchorage, Ak.	N8805
N728MC	79	Citation 1/SP	501-0115	Polymer Compounds Inc. Coral Gables, Fl.	N95RE
N728MG*	81	Learjet 55	55-004	Jet Partners LLC. Teterboro, NJ.	N155PJ
N728PX	68	JetStar-731	5112	Paxson Communications Management Co. West Palm Beach, Fl.	N499PC
N728TA	98	Hawker 800XP	8364	Flight Options LLC. Cleveland, Oh.	(N817LX)
N729AT	99	Hawker 800XP	8402	Moonfire Marine LLC. Wilmington, De.	N23550
N729KF	01	Challenger 604	5513	KW Flight LLC. Bozeman, Mt.	N604NG
N729SB	04	Learjet 45	45-254	Sky Blue Aviation LLC. Irvine, Ca.	
N729TA	98	Hawker 800XP	8374	Flight Options LLC. Cleveland, Oh.	(N818LX)
N730BH	03	EMB-135BJ	145730	Briad Restaurant Group, Florham Park, NJ.	PT-SHG
N730CA	80	Westwind-Two	295	Seven Bar Flying Service Inc. Dallas, Tx.	N555CW
N730LM	01	Falcon 900EX	101	Liberty Media Group. Denver, Co.	(N875F)
N730M	94	Learjet 60	60-048	Snap-On Aviation LLC. Waukegan, Wi.	N648LJ
Reg	Yr	Type	c/n	Owner/Operator	Prev Regn

Reg	Yr	Type	c/n	Owner/Operator	Prev Regn
☐ N730TA	98	Hawker 800XP	8383	Flight Options LLC. Cleveland, Oh.	(N819LX)
☐ N731DL	78	HS 125/700A	NA0234	Aim Leasing LLC. Newark, De.	N205BS
☐ N731JR	90	BAe 125/800A	NA0451	Veda Air LLC. London, Ky.	N883EJ
☐ N731TA	00	Beechjet 400A	RK-273	Flight Options LLC. Cleveland, Oh.	(N455LX)
☐ N731UG	02	390 Premier 1	RB-70	Corporacion 731CP Inc. Caracas, Venezuela.	N5070W
☐ N731WL	65	JetStar-731	5070	Central Business Jets Inc. Burnsville, Mn.	N712TE
☐ N733A	04	Hawker 800XP	8687	Humana Inc. Louisville, Ky.	N61987
☐ N733CF	90	Challenger 601-3A	5057	C R Bard Inc. Morristown, NJ.	N830CD
☐ N733E	82	Learjet 55	55-057	Fisher Aviation LLC. Wilmington, De.	N733EY
☐ N733EY	92	Challenger 601-3A	5113	CB Applications LLC. White Plains, NY.	N163MR
☐ N733H	02	Hawker 800XP	8590	Humana Inc. Louisville, Ky.	(N590VC)
☐ N733K	03	Hawker 800XP	8645	Humana Inc. Louisville, Ky.	N645XP
☐ N733M	93	Falcon 50	242	JAPC Inc. Louisville, Ky.	N9000F
☐ N733PA	86	B 737-205	23466	CONOCO-Phillips Alaska, Anchorage, Ak.	N733AR
☐ N733TA	97	Hawker 800XP	8337	Flight Options LLC. Cleveland, Oh.	(N815LX)
☐ N735TA	00	Beechjet 400A	RK-274	Flight Options LLC. Cleveland, Oh.	(N456LX)
☐ N736BP	86	B 737-205	23465	CONOCO-Phillips Alaska, Anchorage, Ak.	LN-SUU
☐ N736LB	04	CitationJet CJ-2	525A-0203	Cessna Aircraft Co. Wichita, Ks.	N.....
☐ N736LE	69	HS 125/731	NA736	Lady Edith Hawker Flight LLC/Wittsend Aviation, Wittman, Md.	N800AF
☐ N737A	00	B 737-7AX	30181	ARAMCO Associated Co. Dhahran, Saudi Arabia.	
☐ N737AG	99	BBJ-7BF	30496	Fun Air Corp. Miami, Fl.	N180AD
☐ N737BZ	98	BBJ-73Q	29102	Boeing Business Jets, Seattle, Wa. Ff 4 Sep 98.	
☐ N737CC	99	BBJ-74Q	29135	Mideast Jet, Jeddah, Saudi Arabia.	N60436
☐ N737DX	90	B 737-408	24804	Sports Jet LLC/BancBoston Transport Leasing Inc. Boston, Ma.	TF-FIC
☐ N737ER	00	BBJ-7CJ	30754	BBJ One Inc. Jeddah, Saudi Arabia.	N61MJ
☐ N737GG	99	BBJ-74Q	29136	Mideast Jet, Jeddah, Saudi Arabia.	N1779B
☐ N737M	03	BBJ2-8EQ	33361	EIE Eagle Inc Estab.	N737SP
☐ N737MM	88	Beechjet 400	RJ-35	Milgard Leasing LP. Tacoma, Wa.	N71GA
☐ N737RJ	82	Citation 1/SP	501-0238	SetJets LLC. Bellevue, Wa.	N995PA
☐ N737WH	98	BBJ-75T	29142	Huizenga Holdings Inc. Fort Lauderdale, Fl.	N700WH
☐ N738A	00	B 737-7AX	30182	ARAMCO Associated Co. Dhahran, Saudi Arabia.	N1785B
☐ N738K	93	Citation VI	650-0222	Air GTI Inc/Gordon Trucking Inc. Tacoma, Wa.	N733K
☐ N739A	00	B 737-7AX	30183	ARAMCO Associated Co. Dhahran, Saudi Arabia.	N1786B
☐ N739TA	99	Beechjet 400A	RK-257	Flight Options LLC. Cleveland, Oh.	(N449LX)
☐ N740BA	97	Gulfstream V	516	BankAmerica/KaiserAir Inc. Oakland, Ca.	N555CS
☐ N740E	98	Learjet 45	45-023	Eaton Corp. Cleveland, Oh.	
☐ N740EJ	70	Learjet 24B	24B-222	MTW Aerospace Inc. Montgomery, Al.	N740F
☐ N740JA	88	Gulfstream 4	1074	RL Transportation LLC. Newport Beach, Ca.	VP-BKT
☐ N740K	89	Gulfstream 4	1094	MVOC LLC. San Diego, Ca.	(N628NP)
☐ N740SS	98	Gulfstream V	532	Shorenstein Management Inc. San Francisco, Ca.	N282QA
☐ N740TA	96	Beechjet 400A	RK-123	Flight Options LLC. Cleveland, Oh.	N110TG
☐ N740TF	00	Learjet 45	45-074	Clarcor Inc. Rockford, Il.	N815A
☐ N741AM	79	JetStar 2	5236	Aircraft Management Co. Sarasota, Fl.	N34TR
☐ N741C	80	Westwind-1124	292	ECP Westwind LLC. Fort Wayne, In.	N292JC
☐ N741CC	97	CitationJet	525-0227	Wings 0227 LLC. Wilmington, De.	
☐ N741E	97	Learjet 45	45-011	Eaton Corp. Cleveland, Oh.	
☐ N741JC	81	Citation II	550-0316	Columbus Christian Center Inc. Columbus, Oh.	N129TS
☐ N741MR*	74	Falcon 20F	312	Mitchell Aviation LLC. Phoenix, Az.	N132AP
☐ N741PC	02	CitationJet CJ-2	525A-0066	Corporacion Mariposa SA. Guatemala City, Guatemala.	N51396
☐ N741T	82	Citation II	550-0363	Tennyson Enterprises Inc. Ottumwa, Ia.	N363SP
☐ N741TA	98	Beechjet 400A	RK-201	Flight Options LLC. Cleveland, Oh.	(N437LX)
☐ N742E	98	Learjet 45	45-025	Eaton Corp. Cleveland, Oh.	
☐ N742PB	99	BBJ-73U	29200	Chartwell Partners LLC. Burbank, Ca.	
☐ N743A	01	B 737-7AXC	30184	ARAMCO Associated Co. Dhahran, Saudi Arabia.	
☐ N743E	97	Learjet 45	45-016	Eaton Corp. Cleveland, Oh.	
☐ N743JG	02	CitationJet CJ-2	525A-0056	Latitude 45 Inc. Chicago-DuPage, Il.	N5202D
☐ N743TA	00	Beechjet 400A	RK-271	Flight Options LLC. Cleveland, Oh.	(N454LX)
☐ N744AT	78	Citation II	550-0017	Air Ambulance by Air Trek Inc. Punta Gorda, Fl.	N771ST
☐ N744DB	95	Learjet 60	60-053	RSJ Industries LLC. Wilmington, De.	N360UJ
☐ N744N	93	Learjet 31A	31A-069	Prior Aviation Service Inc. Buffalo, NY.	(N169SC)
☐ N744TA	99	Beechjet 400A	RK-245	Flight Options LLC. Cleveland, Oh.	(N446LX)
☐ N744X	81	Falcon 50	58	Kroger Dedicated Logistics Co. Cincinnati-Lunken, Oh.	N72FJ
☐ N745A	01	B 737-7AXC	30185	ARAMCO Associated Co. Dhahran, Saudi Arabia.	
☐ N745CC	03	Citation Bravo	550-1051	Fred Beans Ford Inc. Doylestown, Pa.	N251CB
☐ N745E	97	Learjet 45	45-008	Eaton Corp. Cleveland, Oh.	
☐ N745K	04	Learjet 45	45-245	Koch Industries Inc. Wichita, Ks.	N5010U

Reg	Yr	Type	c/n	Owner/Operator	Prev Regn

Reg	Yr	Type	c/n	Owner/Operator	Prev Regn
N745RS	88	Gulfstream 4	1063	M Ventures LLC/Wenner Media LLC. Islip, NY.	N720LH
N745TA	97	Beechjet 400A	RK-145	Flight Options LLC. Cleveland, Oh.	(N425LX)
N745TC	04	Learjet 45	45-260	Thompson Machinery Commerce Corp. La Vergne, Tn.	
N745UP	97	Hawker 800XP	8336	Avpro Inc. Baltimore, Md.	N2286U
N746TA	97	Beechjet 400A	RK-146	Flight Options LLC. Cleveland, Oh.	(N426LX)
N746UP	00	Hawker 800XP	8522	Union Pacific Railroad Co. Omaha, Ne.	N812TA
N747AC	97	CitationJet	525-0202	Rio Bravo Helicopters Corp. Laredo, Tx.	N202CJ
N747AN	86	Learjet 55	55-121	Worrell Investment Co. Charlottesville, Va.	N155SC
N747CP	83	Learjet 35A	35A-502	Kress Enterprises Inc. Brimfield, Il.	N8565X
N747CX	81	Falcon 20F-5B	442	MorAir Inc/ACXIOM Inc. Little Rock, Ar.	I-SREG
N747DP	02	Learjet 60	60-251	Bretford Manufacturing Inc. Waukegan, Il.	N50458
N747GM	80	Learjet 35A	35A-308	Chariot Air LLC/Addison Jet Center, Addison, Tx.	(N7LA)
N747JB	89	Citation II/SP	551-0617	N747JB Inc/John Bleakley Ford Inc. Douglasville, Ga.	N450GM
N747NB	68	Gulfstream 2	20	Eddie Long, Lithonia, Ga.	N331P
N747RL	04	Citation Sovereign	680-0002	Lewis Aeronautical LLC. San Antonio, Tx.	(N682CS)
N747RR	94	Beechjet 400A	RK-95	Mannesmann Dematic Rapistan Corp. Grand Rapids, Mi.	HS-UCM
N747SC	66	Learjet 24	24-019	Dolphin Aviation Inc. Sarasota, Fl.	N100EA
N747SG	97	Learjet 60	60-109	Grossman Company Properties Inc. Santa Monica, Ca.	N707SG
N747TX	94	Citation VII	650-7046	Textron Inc. T F Green Airport, RI.	N746BR
N747Y	96	Challenger 604	5305	Dana Flight Operations Inc. Swanton, Oh.	N747
N748MN	78	Gulfstream II SP	215	Merle Norman Cosmetics Inc. Van Nuys, Ca.	N816GA
N748RE	04	CitationJet CJ-2	525A-0215	Hawk Air LLC. Waukegan, Il.	N.....
N749CP	89	Falcon 50	200	SLMF LLC. Minneapolis-Anoka, Mn.	N595JS
N749DC	96	Citation V Ultra	560-0370	Dobson Communications Corp. Oklahoma City, Ok.	N607RJ
N749DX	02	Citation X	750-0173	Dobson Communications Corp. Oklahoma City, Ok.	N173CX
N749GA	03	Gulfstream G100	149	Aircraft Guaranty Title LLC. Houston, Tx.	4X-C..
N749P	98	Citation X	750-0046	Foster Poultry Farms, Eugene, Or.	N749DX
N749RL	00	Citation Encore	560-0554	Encore Aircraft Ventures LLC. Burlington, Vt.	N747RL
N749SS	02	Learjet 60	60-252	Smith Aircraft Leasing LLC. Talladega, Al.	N5051X
N749TA	97	Beechjet 400A	RK-149	Flight Options LLC. Cleveland, Oh.	(N427LX)
N750BA	98	Gulfstream V	558	BankAmerica/KaiserAir Inc. Oakland, Ca.	N658GA
N750BL	02	Citation X	750-0178	Badger Liquor Co. Fond du Lac, Wi.	N275NM
N750BP	99	Citation X	750-0111	BLR Leasing LLC/Beeler Properties Inc. Sugar Land, Tx.	N5264A
N750CC	80	Sabre-65	465-37	Marathon Aviation Inc. Georgetown, De.	N750CS
N750CW	96	Citation X	750-0008	Sierra Stellar Inc. Encinatas, Ca.	N708VP
N750CX	93	Citation X	703	Model 750 Citation X first flight 21 December 1993.	
N750DF	84	Falcon 50	140	DFE Partners, Springfield, Ma.	N303JW
N750DM	01	Citation X	750-0146	Morgan's Mach One Machine LLC. Aspen, Co.	N5152X
N750EC	96	Citation X	750-0007	SCB Enterprises Inc. Reno, Nv.	N52655
N750FB	95	Citation VII	650-7049	Richmor Aviation Inc. Columbia County, NY.	N900FL
N750FL	94	Citation V Ultra	560-0268	KM & Z Aviation LLC, Charlotte, NC.	N269CM
N750GM	98	Citation X	750-0066	General Mills Inc. Minneapolis, Mn.	
N750H	86	Falcon 50-40	171	White Lodging Services, Gypsum, Co.	(N650AS)
N750HS	99	Citation X	750-0103	HealthSouth Aviation Inc. Birmingham, Al.	N96TX
N750JB	98	Citation X	750-0063	Sweatmore Air LLC. Scottsdale, Az.	N51038
N750JC	86	Falcon 50	162	Minnesota Choice Aviation LLC. St Paul, Mn.	N244AD
N750JJ	98	Citation X	750-0065	J J Gumberg Co. Pittsburgh, Pa.	(N965QS)
N750MC	90	Falcon 50	202	McLeod USA Integrated Business Systems, Cedar Rapids, Ia.	N202CP
N750NS	01	Citation X	750-0172	Aviation Beauport Ltd. Jersey, C.I. (AVB 6NS).	N5066U
N750PP	84	Citation 1/SP	501-0686	Peter Pfendler, Petaluma, Ca.	N6763M
N750PT	99	Citation X	750-0109	PCMT Aviation LLC. Mountain View, Ca.	N900EJ
N750RA	72	Gulfstream II SP	117	Reliance Aviation Management LLC. Fort Lauderdale, Fl.	N7500
N750RL	97	Citation X	750-0025	Rosebud Air LLC/Westcor Aviation, (2500th Citation built).	N50612
N750RV	90	BAe 125/800A	NA0453	Rayovac Corp. Madison, Wi.	(N750PB)
N750SL	87	Citation II	550-0554	Kern Global Service LLC. Bakersfield, Ca.	(N705JT)
N750SP	76	Westwind-1124	198	WGL Capital Corp. Aspen, Co.	N71PT
N750SW	81	Gulfstream 3	338	Safeway Inc. Oakland, Ca.	(N338RJ)
N750TA	99	Beechjet 400A	RK-226	Flight Options LLC. Cleveland, Oh.	N59BP
N750TX	01	Citation X	750-0150	Textron Inc. T F Green Airport, RI.	N750MD
N750VP	96	Citation X	750-0022	Arlie Air LLC. Eugene, Or.	(N750AG)
N750WM	04	Citation X	750-0230	WM Aviation LLC/Southland Aviation Corp. Maitland, Fl.	N.....
N750XX	99	Citation X	750-0094	Stephenson Air Services Inc. Atherton, Ca.	N51038
N751BC	01	Gulfstream G200	049	International Bank of Commerce, Laredo, Tx.	N290GA
N751BH	98	Citation X	750-0059	Bob Herd/Ty-Tex Exploration Inc. Tyler, Tx.	(N570BH)
N751CA	73	Learjet 25B	25B-122	Critical Air Medicine Inc. San Diego, Ca.	N122WC
N751GM	02	Citation X	750-0207	AESR LLC. Minneapolis, Mn.	N5152X

Reg	Yr	Type	c/n	Owner/Operator	Prev Regn

Reg	Yr	Type	c/n	Owner/Operator	Prev Regn
N751PJ	60	MS 760 Paris-1R	51	Alexandair Inc. de Kooy/Den Helder, Holland.	No 51
N751PL	02	Citation Excel	560-5237	Preformed Line Products Co. Cleveland, Oh.	N5061W
N751TA	99	Beechjet 400A	RK-225	Flight Options LLC. Cleveland, Oh.	
N752BA	01	Gulfstream V	640	Bank of America NA. Charlotte, NC.	N580GA
N752BP	00	Learjet 60	60-184	BLR Leasing LLC/Beeler Properties Inc. Sugar Land, Tx.	N184LJ
N752CC	79	Citation II	550-0018	U S Customs Service, Oklahoma City, Ok.	(N3225M)
N752CM	80	HS 125/700A	7082	BRBF Inc/Taughannock Aviation Corp. Ithaca, NY.	N70HF
N752EA	73	Learjet 25B	25B-137	Mike Naughton Ford Inc. Aurora, Co.	N752CA
N752S	99	Falcon 2000	82	Shell Aviation Corp. Houston, Tx.	F-WWVB
N752TA	99	Hawker 800XP	8397	Flight Options LLC. Cleveland, Oh.	(N820LX)
N753BP	01	Learjet 60	60-238	BLR Leasing LLC/Beeler Properties Inc. Sugar Land, Tx.	N5018U
N753CC	80	Citation II	550-0109	U S Customs Service, Oklahoma City, Ok.	N2665N
N753CJ	03	CitationJet CJ-3	525B-0001	Cessna Aircraft Co. Wichita, Ks. (FF 8 Aug 03).	N753CJ
N753JC*	80	Falcon 50	25	Minnesota Choice Aviation LLC. St Paul, Mn.	N502EZ
N753S	99	Falcon 2000	88	Shell Aviation Corp. Houston, Tx.	F-WWVH
N753TA	99	Beechjet 400A	RK-230	Flight Options LLC. Cleveland, Oh.	(N441LX)
N754BA	02	Gulfstream G550	5007	Bank of America NA. Charlotte, NC.	N907GA
N754GL	78	Learjet 35A	35A-197	Ameriflight Inc. Burbank, Ca.	
N754JB	71	Gulfstream II SP	105	Newport/Signal Air Inc. Costa Mesa, Ca.	N711TE
N754SE	94	Citation X	750-0001	Loyd's Business Jets Ltd. Warsaw, Poland.	TC-ATV
N754TA	99	Hawker 800XP	8406	Flight Options LLC. Cleveland, Oh.	(N821LX)
N755A	98	Astra-1125SPX	103	Galoncevinticinoo Ino. Pompano Beach, Fl.	
N755PA	01	Gulfstream G200	042	SanMar Corp/MJL Air Partners LLC. Issaquah, Wa.	N701HB
N755RV	98	Challenger 604	5370	Rayovac Corp. Madison, Wi.	N320CL
N755TA	01	Beechjet 400A	RK-324	Flight Options LLC. Cleveland, Oh.	(N470LX)
N755VT	89	Learjet 55C	55C-142	Aerohead Aviation Inc. Scottsdale, Az.	N555MX
N755WJ	70	HS 125/400A	NA755	Unizan Bank NA. Columbus, Oh.	(N871MA)
N756AF	91	B 757-23A	24923	Vulcan Northwest Inc. Seattle-Tacoma, Wa.	N680FM
N757AF	91	B 757-2J4	25155	Vulcan Northwest Inc. Seattle-Tacoma, Wa.	N115FS
N757AL	77	Learjet 35A	35A-130	P & D Aviation LLC. Mesa, Ca.	(N116PR)
N757BJ	83	B 757-236	22176	Luxury Air LLC. Charlotte, NC.	N267PW
N757CE	94	Beechjet 400A	RK-86	Grand Casinos Inc. Gulfport, Ms.	(N72PP)
N757CK	89	Citation V	560-0028	Koury Aviation Inc. Liberty, NC.	N6FZ
N757CP	02	CitationJet CJ-2	525A-0069	Falcon LLC. Indianapolis, In.	N51564
N757CX	79	Falcon 20F-5	408	ACXIOM Corp. Little Rock, Ar.	N408PA
N757EG	03	Citation Sovereign	680-0017	Erickson Group,	N5248V
N757M	87	BAe 125/800A	NA0402	Dan Air LLC. Klamath Falls, Or.	N1125
N757MA	97	B 757-24Q	28463	Mideast Jet, Jeddah, Saudi Arabia.	
N757WS	98	Beechjet 400A	RK-169	Williams Marketing Services Inc. Joplin, Mo.	N2329N
N758CC	97	Challenger 604	5353	Challenger Management LLC. Beckley, WV.	VH-LAM
N758CX	98	Citation X	750-0058	U S Bancorp Equipment Finance Inc. Portland, Or.	(N87N)
N758S	82	Citation II	550-0407	Straubel Investments LLC. Davenport, Ia.	(N950FC)
N759WR	04	Gulfstream G550	5063	Gulfstream Aerospace Corp. Savannah, Ga.	N963GA
N760	96	Falcon 900EX	3	Anheuser Busch Companies Inc. St Louis, Mo.	JA50TH
N760A*	70	Learjet 25	25-051	UCL Aircraft Sales LLC. San Antonio, Tx.	N76UM
N760AR	61	MS 760 Paris-2B	108	Thomas Winship, Carefree, Az.	PH-MSX
N760FM	62	MS 760 Paris-2	111	FM Aero Inc. Calhoun, Ga.	C6-BEV
N760FR	61	MS 760 Paris-1A	72	National Test Pilots School, Mojave, Ca.	F-BJLV
N760PJ	59	MS 760 Paris	27	Airborne Turbine LP. San Luis Obispo, Ca.	27
N760R	61	MS 760 Paris-2B	104	Upper Limits Sales & Leasing Inc.	N760P
N760S	59	MS 760 Paris	43	B Air Inc. Alexandria, Va.	N760C
N760X	59	MS 760 Paris	28	Paul Gernhardt, Ashburn, Va.	I-SNAI
N763D	89	Citation V	560-0007	Aspect Aviation/Aspect Energy LLC. Denver, Co.	N717MB
N764KF	78	Learjet 25D	25D-234	LMF Jet LLC. Clearwater, Fl.	N18BL
N764LA	69	Falcon 20D	211	Grand Aire Express Inc. Toledo, Oh.	N618GA
N764RH	76	Learjet 25D	25D-210	Rusco Co. Memphis, Tn.	N75TJ
N765A	88	Gulfstream 4	1069	ARAMCO Associated Co. Dhahran, Saudi Arabia.	N459GA
N765TS	71	HS 125/731	NA765	Songbird Aviation II LLC. Nashville, Tn.	N68CB
N765WT	89	Challenger 601-3A	5039	W W Tichenor & Co/Stargazer Aviation, San Antonio, Tx.	N811BR
N766AE	81	Citation II	550-0203	Citation Holdings Corp. Wilmington, De.	(N857BT)
N766JS	67	B 727-27	19535	Aircraft Guaranty LLC. Las Vegas, Nv.	N60FM
N766MH	83	Citation III	650-0015	Marketing Management Inc. Fort Worth, Tx.	N15QS
N767A	03	B 767-2AXER	33685	ARAMCO Associated Co. Houston, Tx.	
N767BS	01	Citation Excel	560-5191	Briggs & Stratton Corp. Milwaukee, Wi.	N5090A
N767CB	83	Gulfstream 3	397	Aviation 1 LLC. Morristown, NJ.	N692TV
N767FL	96	Gulfstream V	503	FL Aviation Inc. Morristown, NJ.	N503GV

Reg	Yr	Type	c/n	Owner/Operator	Prev Regn
N767JH	72	Sabre-40A	282-98	Americana Aviation Inc. Albert Lea, Mn.	N516LW
N767KS	98	B-767-29N	28270	Mideast Jet, Jeddah, Saudi Arabia.	
N767W	02	CitationJet CJ-2	525A-0168	Kendall/Hunt Publishing Co. Dubuque, Ia.	N.....
N768TA	98	Beechjet 400A	RK-168	Flight Options LLC. Cleveland, Oh.	(N429LX)
N769BH	75	Falcon 10	60	Ben Hicks Aviation Ltd. Grand Prairie, Tx.	N69WJ
N769H	80	Citation II	550-0158	Honeywell International Inc. Olathe, Ks.	N258CW
N769JW	98	Falcon 2000	72	Devon Energy Corp. Wiley Post, Ok.	N96LT
N769SC	74	Falcon 10	7	Southern Cross Aircraft LLC. Fort Lauderdale, Fl.	HB-VKE
N770BB	91	B 757-2J4	25220	Yucaipa Management Co. Burbank, Ca.	VP-CAU
N770BC	00	Learjet 60	60-203	Franke & Co. Scottsdale, Az.	
N770BM	89	Learjet 35A	35A-654	Heights Aviation, Tucson, Az.	N8189
N770CC	80	HS 125/700A	NA0278	Newco Aviation LLC. Vestal, NY.	N130AP
N770CH	01	Learjet 31A	31A-222	Cardal Inc. Columbus-OSU, Oh.	N200CH
N770FG	67	Falcon 20-5B	116	Timothy Flynn, Las Vegas, Nv.	F-GLMM
N770HS	82	HS 125/700A	NA0336	Hip Air LLC. Portland, Or.	VT-SRR
N770JM	04	Citation Excel	560-5370	McDonough Capital LLC. Deerfield, Il.	N5270P
N770JR	62	JetStar-731	5037	Winterbok Inc. Southport, Ct.	N552JH
N770MC	75	Citation 20F	330	Jetcraft Corp. Raleigh-Durham, NC.	(N227LA)
N770MP	85	Falcon 50	161	Air Travel Inc. NYC.	N301JJ
N770RR	72	Falcon 20F	272	Midwest Freightways Aircraft Leasing, Aurora, Il.	N20FE
N770SC	88	Gulfstream 4	1056	Station Casinos Inc/STN Aviation Inc. Las Vegas, Nv.	N33MX
N771B	79	Westwind-1124	258	Living World International Inc. Saginaw-Tri City, Mi.	N58FB
N771HR	74	Citation	500-0206	I H R Administrative Services Inc. Wichita Falls, Tx.	VH-LGL
N771SB	81	Learjet 35A	35A-401	Seven Bar Flying Service Inc. Dallas, Tx.	(N177SB)
N771SV	98	Hawker 800XP	8391	N717CF LLC. Naples, Fl.	N391XP
N772AW	71	Westwind-1124	154	Talktelcom Inc. Carson City, Nv.	D-CBBE
N772SB	84	Citation II	550-0498	Bridgeway Enterprises Inc. Spicewood, Tx.	N78FK
N772WH	69	B 737-112	19772	Savannah Aviation LLC. San Antonio, Tx.	XC-UJL
N773AA	68	HS 125/731	NA713	MV Flight Service LLC. Westlaco, Tx.	N272B
N773CA	98	Citation Bravo	550-0840	DeJarnette Enterprises Inc. Lee's Summit, Mo.	(N442SW)
N773DL	78	Learjet 35A	35A-174	ICI Realty Inc. Dallas-Love, Tx.	N38AM
N773JC	84	Challenger 601	3029	IngenierosConsultores CentroComercial PuenteCristal, Caracas	N629TS
N773MJ	93	Gulfstream 4SP	1225	Silver Stream Aviation LLC. NYC.	N816GS
N773TA	00	Beechjet 400A	RK-279	Flight Options LLC. Cleveland, Oh.	(N458LX)
N774TS	71	HS 125/731	NA774	Simba Air LLC. Dover, De.	G-5-821
N775M	92	Citation VII	650-7017	M & I Marshall & Ilsley Bank, Milwaukee, Wi.	
N775TA	00	Beechjet 400A	RK-276	Flight Options LLC. Cleveland, Oh.	(N457LX)
N776DF	95	CitationJet	525-0111	Songbird Aviation Inc. Bloomfield Hills, Mi.	N52136
N776JS	82	Learjet 35A	35A-476	Airspeed Holdings LLC. Boca Raton, Fl.	N777LB
N776LB	03	CitationJet CJ-2	525A-0191	Continental Lending Group LLC. Denver, Co.	N.....
N776MA	75	Gulfstream 2B	166	Deniston Enterprises Inc/Prime Airborne, Sikorsky, Ct.	XA-SWP
N777AM*	89	Astra-1125	038	American Aviation LLC/Medical Concepts Inc. Eugene, Or.	N930UC
N777AS	98	B 777-24Q	29271	Mideast Jet, Jeddah, Saudi Arabia.	
N777AY	76	JetStar 2	5201	Space Master Buidling Systems LLC. Atlanta, Ga.	N745DM
N777CJ	03	CitationJet CJ-2	525A-0182	Bramac LLC. Jeffco Airport, Co.	N.....
N777DB	01	Hawker 800XP	8551	Cosmos Air LLC/Bigelow Companies, Las Vegas, Nv.	N190NC
N777DC	84	Westwind-Two	410	Skyliner Inc. Omaha, Ne.	N26VB
N777DM	80	Learjet 35A	35A-297	Business Jet Leasing Inc. Salt Lake City, Ut.	N38US
N777DY	03	CitationJet CJ-2	525A-0189	Oregon Flight Services LLC. Portland, Or.	N5124F
N777EH	78	HS 125/700B	7020	Charter Equipment Leasing LLC. Bellevue, Wa.	N311JD
N777FC	86	Falcon 200	508	Ferro Corp/BP America Inc. Cleveland, Oh.	XA-RKE
N777FE	87	Beechjet 400	RJ-30	Aspen Executive Air LLC. Aspen, Co.	N468MJ
N777FH	01	Citation Excel	560-5148	Sho-Deen Inc. Aurora, Il.	N52234
N777FL	00	Astra-1125SPX	124	James Warren, Portland, Or.	N42GX
N777GD	81	Challenger 600S	1023	EHR Aviation Inc. Ponte Vedra Beach, Fl.	(N333TS)
N777GG	79	Citation 1/SP	501-0108	M G Aviation Inc. Ashland, Ky.	N777AJ
N777HD	83	Westwind-1124	397	Jesse Duplantis Ministries, New Orleans, La.	N11CS
N777JF	04	390 Premier 1	RB-105	Kensington Transcom Inc. Gaithersburg, Md.	N5105
N777JJ	72	Citation Eagle	500-0056	Air USA Inc. Quincy, Il.	N52ET
N777JV	03	Citation Excel	560-5342	Threshold Leasing LLC. Fort Worth, Tx.	N7337F
N777KK	00	Gulfstream 4SP	1429	Kohler Co. Kohler, Wi.	N429GA
N777KY	75	B 727-2B6	21068	Team Aviation LLC. Charlotte, NC.	N119GA
N777LB	82	Learjet 35A	35A-473	Speedbird Inc. Cincinnati, Oh.	N35TH
N777LD	84	Learjet 35A	35A-314	Lowell Dunn Co. Hialeah, Fl.	(N118GM)
N777MC	00	Learjet 60	60-180	Meredith Corp. Des Moines, Ia.	
N777MN*	01	Falcon 2000	147	M D C Holdings Inc. Denver, Co.	N999BE

Reg	Yr	Type	c/n	Owner/Operator	Prev Regn
N777MQ	01	390 Premier 1	RB-20	Raytheon Aircraft Co. Wichita, Ks.	(N390BP)
N777MW	86	Gulfstream 3	485	McWane Inc. Birmingham, Al.	N721CW
N777MX	84	Citation III	650-0051	Duke Woody Aviation LLC. Denver, Co.	N651BH
N777NG	01	Citation Bravo	550-0992	Tazio Aviation Inc/Peter Neumark, Hawarden-Chester, UK.	N52086
N777NJ	04	CitationJet CJ-3	525B-0009	Cessna Aircraft Co. Wichita, Ks.	N51806
N777PZ	68	JetStar-731	5128	Accrued Investments Inc. Houston-Hobby, Tx.	N128BP
N777RN	65	HS 125/1A	25027	Triton Ranch & Cattle Co. Henderson, Nv.	N125BH
N777SA	88	Gulfstream 4	1081	Management Investment Enterprises LLC. Ventura, Ca.	(N955HC)
N777SL	76	Citation	500-0307	NKC Inc. & WCS Inc. Troy, Al.	N2613
N777TX	72	Learjet 25C	25C-084	Z Line Designs Inc. Livermore, Ca.	F-BYAL
N777VC	04	Challenger 300	20016	CMK Air LLC/Vencom Group Inc. Lake Forest, Il.	N316LJ
N777WY	81	Citation II	550-0264	U S Energy Corp & Crested Corp. Riverton, Wy.	N550KC
N777XS	83	Citation III	650-0008	Coushatta Tribe of Louisiana, Oakdale, La.	N926CR
N777YC	85	Learjet 55	55-120	Yellow Cab Service Corp of Florida, West Palm Beach, Fl.	N120LJ
N777ZC	88	Citation III	650-0153	C-Flair LLC/ExcelAire Service Inc. Ronkonkoma, NY.	N47CM
N778BC	04	Citation Encore	560-0657	Justice Aviation LLC. Beckley, WV.	N5214L
N778GM	72	Learjet 25B	25B-078	G M Miller & Co. Suwanee, Ga.	N778JC
N778JA	72	HS 125/1A	NA778	Pegasus & Crew Inc. Dania Beach, Fl.	N88AF
N778JC	81	Citation II/SP	551-0369	John Jr LLC. Columbus, Oh.	N68BK
N778JM	79	Citation II	550-0072	Premier Aviation LLC/Colman Funding, San Francisco, Ca.	N770JM
N778MA	04	CitationJet CJ-2	525A-0222	Cessna Aircraft Co. Wichita, Ks.	N.....
N779AZ	95	Challenger 601-3R	5176	Pittco Inc. Memphis, Tn.	N600DH
N779DC	84	Diamond 1A	A072SA	CMRS-Catholic Mutual Relief Society of America, Omaha, Ne.	N777DC
N779LC	70	Gulfstream 2B	88	Letica Corp. Pontiac, Mi.	N80WD
N779QS	97	Citation VII	650-7079	NetJets, Columbus, Oh.	
N779SG	88	Falcon 900B	46	U S Foodservice Inc. Columbia, Md.	(N946TS)
N780CF	78	Citation II	550-0014	CarFaye Inc. Eugene, Or.	N780GT
N780CS	01	Citation Excel	560-5168	Pegasus Air LLC. Scottsdale, Az.	N565DR
N780E	91	Gulfstream 4	1165	IBM Corp. Dutchess County Airport, NY.	N460GA
N780F	97	Gulfstream V	530	IBM Corp. Dutchess County Airport, NY.	N530GA
N780RH	02	Gulfstream 4SP	1498	Huffco Group LLC. Houston, Tx.	N398GA
N780SP	91	Falcon 900B	93	Riverside Aviation LLC. Bridgeport, Ct.	N900Q
N780TA	99	Hawker 800XP	8437	Flight Options LLC. Cleveland, Oh.	(N825LX)
N781JR	72	HS 125/731	NA779	Veda Air LLC. London, Ky.	N731JR
N781TA	95	Hawker 800XP	8281	Flight Options LLC. Cleveland, Oh.	N281XP
N782QS	98	Citation VII	650-7082	NetJets, Columbus, Oh.	
N782TA	95	Hawker 800XP	8282	Flight Options LLC. Cleveland, Oh.	(N811LX)
N782TP	99	Beechjet 400A	RK-243	York Aviation Inc. York, Pa.	
N783FS	95	Falcon 2000	9	Farspo LLC/Thornton Aircraft, Van Nuys, Ca.	N209FJ
N783H	91	Citation VI	650-0210	Towanda Leasing Inc. Houston, Tx.	(N650RA)
N783TA	99	Beechjet 400A	RK-234	Flight Options LLC. Cleveland, Oh.	(N442LX)
N784BX	98	Falcon 2000	56	Cockrell Resources Inc. Houston, Tx.	TC-CYL
N785QS	98	Citation VII	650-7085	NetJets, Columbus, Oh.	N5112K
N785TA	99	Beechjet 400A	RK-239	Flight Options LLC. Cleveland, Oh.	(N444LX)
N786TA	99	Beechjet 400A	RK-248	Flight Options LLC. Cleveland, Oh.	(N447LX)
N786YA	00	Learjet 31A	31A-215	Samsher Flight Management Inc. Las Vegas, Nv.	N30051
N787JD	88	Citation II	550-0589	Jet Duluth LLC. Duluth, Mn.	N679BC
N787LP	96	Learjet 60	60-087	Southeastern Asset Management Inc. Memphis, Tn.	N410ST
N787QS	98	Citation VII	650-7087	NetJets, Columbus, Oh.	N5163C
N787WH	81	B 737-2V6	22431	Huizenga Holdings Inc. Fort Lauderdale, Fl.	N737WH
N788CG	00	Falcon 900EX	79	Corning Inc. Hamilton, NY.	F-WWFS
N788FS	81	Westwind-Two	319	Gateway Aviation Inc. Van Nuys, Ca.	N783FS
N789CA	94	Astra-1125SP	074	Citation Jet Premier Inc. Brookfield, Wi.	N500AJ
N789CF	66	BAC 1-11/422EQ	119	Kori Air Inc. Reno, Nv.	(N114MX)
N789CN	00	Citation Excel	560-5070	CN Aviation LLC. Santa Ana, Ca. (status ?).	N507VP
N789DD	80	Citation	500-0404	Jim Clark & Associates Inc. Oklahoma City, Ok.	G-ZAPI
N789DJ	82	Diamond 1A	A015SA	Romero Leasing Inc. Stuttgart, Ar.	N789DD
N789LB	93	BAe 125/800A	8248	Air Group/Superior Industries International Inc. Burbank.	N388H
N789MB	04	Challenger 300	20020	Mathis Brothers Furniture Co. Oklahoma City, Ok.	C-GZET
N789ME	98	Falcon 50EX	276	Mid American Energy Holdings Co. Omaha, Ne.	N128M
N789PR	01	Gulfstream G200	050	Gulfstream Aerospace LP. Dallas-Love, Tx.	N789RR
N789QS	98	Citation VII	650-7089	NetJets, Columbus, Oh.	
N789RR	04	Gulfstream G550	5045	Black Diamond Aviation Inc. Tampa, Fl.	N945GA
N789SG	76	Sabre-60	306-121	Model Transportation LLC. Burbank, Ca.	XA-SYS
N789SR	93	Learjet 31A	31A-083	North Slope Borough Search & Rescue, Barrow, Ak.	N40363
N789TA	00	Beechjet 400A	RK-268	Flight Options LLC. Cleveland, Oh.	(N453LX)

Reg	Yr	Type	c/n	Owner/Operator	Prev Regn
N789TR	83	Gulfstream 3	405	448 Alliance Corp. Fort Worth, Tx.	N789TP
N789TT	82	Citation II	550-0343	Tahoe-Teton Associates Inc. Menlo Park, Ca.	G-ORCE
N790AL	85	Citation S/II	S550-0024	Lauren Alexa Leasing LLC. Laguna Niguel, Ca.	N34NS
N790FH	91	Astra-1125SP	056	Pioneer Aviation LLC. Eugene, Or.	N3175T
N790JC	87	Falcon 900	17	Minnesota Choice Aviation LLC. St Paul, Mn.	N944AD
N790JR	84	Westwind-Two	424	Journal Register Co. Trenton, NJ.	N424W
N790L	95	Falcon 2000	15	IBM Corp. White Plains, NY.	F-WWMO
N790M	95	Falcon 2000	19	IBM Corp. White Plains, NY.	F-WWMC
N790QS	98	Citation VII	650-7090	NetJets, Columbus, Oh.	
N790SS	03	Hawker 400XP	RK-363	E F Edwards LLC. Santa Ana, Ca.	(N363XP)
N790TA	99	Beechjet 400A	RK-252	Flight Options LLC. Cleveland, Oh.	
N790Z	96	Falcon 2000	31	IBM Corp. White Plains, NY.	N2032
N791QS	98	Citation VII	650-7091	NetJets, Columbus, Oh.	
N791TA	95	Hawker 800XP	8291	Flight Options LLC. Cleveland, Oh.	N291SJ
N792MA	81	Citation II	550-0302	Grafair Inc. Vero Beach, Fl. (status ?)	N133BC
N792QS	98	Citation VII	650-7092	NetJets, Columbus, Oh.	
N792TA	99	Beechjet 400A	RK-264	Flight Options LLC. Cleveland, Oh.	(N451LX)
N793AA	79	Citation 1/SP	501-0106	Airline Transport Professionals Corp. Wilmington, De.	D-IANE
N793BG	83	Westwind-Two	392	SynFuels Holdings Finance LLC. Birmingham, Al.	N95WC
N793CJ	93	CitationJet	525-0021	NorthJet Lease LLC. Edina, Mn.	(N1329G)
N793CT	94	Challenger 601-3R	5148	Caterpillar Inc. Peoria, Il.	C-GLXD
N793RC	01	Hawker 800XP	8550	Raymond Transportation Corp. Binghampton, NY.	
N793TA	99	Beechjet 400A	RK-244	Flight Options LLC. Cleveland, Oh.	(N445LX)
N794QS	98	Citation VII	650-7094	NetJets, Columbus, Oh.	
N794SB	76	Gulfstream II SP	176	Capital Aircraft Group LLC. Dallas, Tx.	N15UG
N794TA	00	Beechjet 400A	RK-282	Flight Options LLC. Cleveland, Oh.	(N459LX)
N794TK	82	Westwind-Two	373	Lifestyle Aviation Inc. Coburg, Or.	N555DH
N795A	81	HS 125/700B	7127	W W Aircraft LLC. Garrettsville, Oh.	HB-VLC
N795BA	04	Gulfstream G550	5031	Bank of America NA. Charlotte, NC.	N931GA
N795BM	01	CitationJet CJ-1	525-0481	Bill Miller Equipment Sales Inc. Eckhart Mines, Md.	N4DF
N795HG	98	Citation X	750-0053	Greens Comet LLC/Fast Greens LLC. Tucson, Az.	(N795HC)
N795QS	99	Citation VII	650-7095	NetJets, Columbus, Oh.	
N795TA	00	Beechjet 400A	RK-284	Flight Options LLC. Cleveland, Oh.	(N460LX)
N796CH	85	BAe 125/800A	8049	Palmetto Aviation LLC. Hickory, NC.	N93CT
N796HR	96	Astra-1125SPX	085	CPX Charter Inc. Covington, Ky.	N796HP
N796TA	00	Beechjet 400A	RK-289	Flight Options LLC. Cleveland, Oh.	
N797CB	96	Learjet 60	60-086	H E Butt Grocery Co. San Antonio, Tx.	N686LJ
N797CM	88	Gulfstream 4	1064	HM LLC. Manassas, Va.	N7RP
N797CS	82	Learjet 55	55-018	CommScope Inc of NC. Catawba, NC.	N599EC
N797CW	81	Citation II	550-0232	U S Customs Service, Oklahoma City, Ok.	N929DS
N797EP*	88	BAe 125/800A	NA0426	Equity Office Properties Management Corp. Chicago-Midway.	N726EP
N797PA	97	Learjet 60	60-098	PA Lear 60-098 LLC. Carrollton, Tx.	N218BX
N797QS	98	Citation VII	650-7097	NetJets, Columbus, Oh.	
N797SE	80	Citation 1/SP	501-0151	CMC Aviation LLC. Denver, Co.	N797SF
N797SF	80	Citation II	550-0200	Hilltex Properties Inc/Charter Jet Aviation LLC. Addison.	(N810MG)
N797TA	99	Beechjet 400A	RK-265	Flight Options LLC. Cleveland, Oh.	(N452LX)
N797TE	01	Citation Bravo	550-0962	Tampa Electric/Peoples Gas System Inc. Tampa, Fl.	N5212M
N797WC	00	Falcon 2000	140	Land Sea Air Leasing Corp. Van Nuys, Ca.	N797SM
N797WQ	77	JetStar 2	5216	Pacific Exchange Corp. Van Nuys, Ca.	N797WC
N798TA	98	Beechjet 400A	RK-198	Flight Options LLC. Cleveland, Oh.	(N436LX)
N799JC	01	Hawker 800XP	8544	Johnson Controls Inc. Milwaukee, Wi.	
N799RM	04	Hawker 800XP	8708	Raytheon Aircraft Co. Wichita, Ks.	
N799S	02	Hawker 800XP	8588	CYMI Investments Sub Inc. Dayton, Oh.	N44888
N799SM	98	Beechjet 400A	RK-220	Dental Health Resources LLC. Effingham, Il.	N220BJ
N799TA	98	Beechjet 400A	RK-209	Flight Options LLC. Cleveland, Oh.	(N439LX)
N799WW	01	Global Express	9092	Wideworld Services Ltd.	N15FX
N800AB	99	Citation Bravo	550-0875	Check Clearing House Aviation LLC. Glenwood Springs, Co.	TG-BAC
N800AF	89	BAe 125/800A	8158	Air 4 Aviation LLC/Tri-C Resources Inc. Houston, Tx.	N158TN
N800AH	04	Hawker 800XP	8679	Armor Holdings Aircraft LLC. Jacksonville, Fl.	N679XP
N800AL	97	Gulfstream 4SP	1340	Abbott Laboratories Inc. Waukegan, Il.	N1TF
N800AR	82	Gulfstream 3	362	Perpetual Corp & Lazy Lane Farms, Washington, DC.	N408M
N800AW	78	Learjet 35A	35A-149	AirNet Systems Inc. Columbus, Oh. (blue). (status ?).	(N40AN)
N800BD	91	Falcon 50	224	Becton-Dickinson & Co. Teterboro, NJ.	XA-BEG
N800BF	78	Citation 1/SP	501-0080	Bravo-Fox LLC.	N37LA
N800BN	04	Challenger 604	5600	Jetcraft Corp. Raleigh-Durham, NC.	C-G...
N800BQ	88	Gulfstream 4	1034	JSH Properties Inc. Bellevue, Wa.	N800BG

Reg	Yr	Type	c/n	Owner/Operator	Prev Regn

Reg	Yr	Type	c/n	Owner/Operator	Prev Regn
N800BT	82	Challenger 600S	1044	Direct Jet Services LLC. Kansas City, Mo.	N55AR
N800BV	87	BAe 125/800B	8097	Daybreak Properties Inc. Lebanon, Mo.	N170BA
N800BW	02	Citation Encore	560-0640	Borg Warner Air/Fluid System, Pontiac, Mi.	N640CE
N800CC	94	Hawker 800XP	8266	Charter Communications Inc. St Louis, Mo.	N414XP
N800CD	74	Sabre-75A	380-23	Kastlemar Inc. Wilmington, De.	N102RD
N800CH	01	Learjet 31A	31A-223	Cardal Inc. Columbus-OSU, Oh.	N8064K
N800CJ*	76	Citation	500-0330	SK Jets Inc. Fort Lauderdale, Fl.	N141SG
N800CQ	03	Hawker 800XP	8636	General Parts Inc. Raleigh, NC.	(N203GP)
N800CS	02	390 Premier 1	RB-62	CAT Scale Co/CS Flight Services Inc. Moline, Il.	N6162Z
N800DA	66	HS 125/1A-522	25047	Dabia Corp. Wilmington, De.	(N717GF)
N800DN	90	BAe 125/800A	NA0462	Kangaroo Aviation LLC. Menlo Park, Ca.	N800DR
N800DR	00	Hawker 800XP	8478	Dominion Resources Inc. Richmond, Va.	N806TA
N800DT	81	Citation 1/SP	501-0198	Liberty Press Group, Ardmore, New Zealand.	N198VP
N800DW	68	Falcon 20-5	135	Marigot LLC. Waukegan, Il.	N194MC
N800EC	87	BAe 125/800A	NA0411	Energy Corp of America, Denver, Co.	N600LS
N800EG	83	Falcon 200	495	Greenfield Aviation LLC. Bridgeport, Ct.	C-GSCR
N800EH	01	Beechjet 400A	RK-322	Agri Beef Co. Boise, Id.	N800EL
N800EL	03	Hawker 800XP	8622	American Bizjet Corp. Panama City, Panama.	N622XP
N800EM	03	Hawker 800XP	8649	Killer Creek LLC. St Thomas, USVI.	N649XP
N800FD	98	Hawker 800XP	8390	Federated Investors Inc. Pittsburgh, Pa.	(N800SG)
N800FF	79	Falcon 20F	406	Devcon Construction Inc. Tualatin, Or.	G-BGOP
N800FH	84	BAe 125/800A	800G	Q Iloward & Assocs Inc. Ronkonkoma, NY.	(N886CW)
N800FL	84	BAe 125/800A	8005	Bir Aviation Corp. Indianapolis, In.	N601UU
N800GA	79	Learjet 28	28-003	Gorilla Aviation LLC. Denver, Co.	N28GW
N800GD	67	JetStar-731	5100	Call Plane Solutions Inc. Waukesha, Wi.	N510TS
N800GE	69	HS 125/400A	NA735	Gan Eden Air Inc. Santa Fe, NM.	N165AG
N800GF	94	Beechjet 400A	RK-96	Aero Gat Inc. St Louis, Mo.	N824JM
N800GG	68	Learjet 25	25-008	Company Air, Thousand Oaks, Ca.	N88NJ
N800GH	99	Falcon 2000	89	Leading Edge LLC/CSM Corp. St Paul, Mn.	N2000A
N800GJ	80	Learjet 35	35A-352	S P Aviation Inc/Silverado Partners, Hayward, Ca.	N35CZ
N800GM	85	Citation III	650-0077	Triple S Aerospace LLC. Pleasant Beach, NJ.	N701AG
N800GN	98	Hawker 800XP	8372	Global Securitized Investments Ltd. San Jose, Ca.	LV-ZHY
N800GP	78	Learjet 35A	35A-158	AGA Aviation LLC. Wheeling, Il.	N158NE
N800GW	98	CitationJet	525-0276	Joe Morten & Son Inc. South Sioux City, Ne.	
N800HH	82	Challenger 600S	1074	Aircraft No 1074 LLC. St Paul, Mn.	HZ-RFM
N800HT	02	Hawker 400XP	RK-356	Bella Aves LLC. Charleston, SC.	N800GR
N800J	97	Gulfstream 4SP	1333	Johnson & Johnson, Mercer County Airport, NJ.	N333GA
N800JH	98	Falcon 2000	63	J & J Aviation LLC. Eagle, Co.	N804JH
N800LF	00	Hawker 800XP	8492	NADA Airline Inc. Ocala, Fl.	N800FJ
N800LJ	81	Learjet 55	55-009	N800LJ Inc. Coconut Grove, Fl.	N559BC
N800LL	86	BAe 125/800B	8079	Q Air LLC/Executive Fliteways Inc. Ronkonkoma, NY.	9M-DDW
N800M	80	Sabre-65	465-41	Fitness Management Corp. West Bloomfield, Mi.	N2556E
N800MA	01	Learjet 45	45-189	Old Mountain Air Inc. Waukegan, Il.	N5030N
N800MC	90	Citation III	650-0195	McLeod USA Integrated Business Systems, Cedar Rapids, Ia.	C-GAPT
N800MJ	92	BAe 125/800A	8226	Gulf Hawk LLC/Panattoni Development Co. Dallas-Love, Tx.	N709EA
N800MK	98	Astra-1125SPX	106	SPX Leasing LLC. Cincinnati, Oh.	N876GA
N800MT	90	Citation II	550-0647	Executive Air Taxi Corp. Bismarck, ND.	N140MD
N800NB	97	CitationJet	525-0212	National By-Products LLC. Des Moines, Ia.	N67VW
N800NJ	96	Hawker 800XP	8314	N90BJ Inc. Warsaw, In.	OM-SKY
N800NP	70	HS 125/731	NA758	Charter Jet LLC. Alexandria, Va.	N731MS
N800NS	03	Hawker 800XP	8633	Novamerican Tube Holdings Inc. Montreal, Canada.	N633XP
N800PA	89	BAe 125/800A	NA0438	Metz Family Enterprises LLC. Sharon, Ct.	N753G
N800PC	98	Hawker 800XP	8369	PNC Financial Services Group Inc. Allegheny County, Pa.	
N800PE	00	Hawker 800XP	8508	PandaAir Corp. Dallas, Tx.	N5008S
N800PJ	00	Gulfstream G200	026	Asset Management Co. Palo Alto, Ca.	N56GX
N800PL*	04	Hawker 800XP	8696	Raytheon Aircraft Co. Wichita, Ks.	N36896
N800PM	78	Gulfstream 2TT	224	PAM Aviation LLC/Phil Mickelson, Scottsdale, Az.	N90CP
N800PP	66	Falcon 20C	44	Company Air, Thousand Oaks, Ca.	(N773HS)
N800PW	96	Astra-1125SPX	079	Au Revoir Ltd. Santa Fe, NM.	C-FCFP
N800QC	89	BAe 125/800A	NA0445	Quikrete International Inc. Atlanta-DeKalb, Ga.	N174NW
N800QS	02	Citation Encore	560-0598	NetJets, Columbus, Oh.	N5250P
N800R	04	Hawker 800XP	8694	NASCAR Inc. Daytona Beach, Fl.	N36894
N800RF	79	Learjet 25D	25D-281	Spring Creek LLC. Ripon, Ca.	N555PG
N800RK	96	CitationJet	525-0158	Rice Lake Weighing Systems Inc. Rice Lake, Wi.	N800RL
N800RL	04	CitationJet CJ-2	525A-0220	Rice Lake Weighing Systems Inc. Rice Lake, Wi.	N.....
N800RM	83	BAe 125/800B	8001	Romeo Mike Aviation Inc. Fort Lauderdale, Fl.	N801CR

Reg	Yr	Type	c/n	Owner/Operator	Prev Regn
N800RR	79	Citation II	550-0089	Raven Air LLC. Wiley Post, Ok.	N81CC
N800RT	69	Gulfstream II SP	47	Robert E Torray & Co. Bethesda, Md.	N800FL
N800S	87	BAe 125/800A	8082	Gilricho Inc. Van Nuys, Ca.	(N601BX)
N800SB	77	Falcon 10	104	Sunbelt Sportswear, San Antonio, Tx.	N913VL
N800SD	00	Beechjet 400A	RK-270	Burkland Distributors Inc/Bur-Con LLC. Peoria, Il.	N3231H
N800SE	88	BAe 125/800A	NA0425	Shasta Enterprises, Red Bluff, Ca.	N110MH
N800TG	72	HS 125/731	NA780	TGINN Jets LLC. Bingham, Mi.	N265DL
N800TL	99	Hawker 800XP	8394	Air Excellence LLC. Akron, Oh.	N800ER
N800TV	80	Citation II	550-0172	Tropical Village Aircraft Corp. Orlando, Fl.	N412P
N800TW	79	Citation 1/SP	501-0136	T W Inc. Ashland, Ky.	N66AG
N800UK	01	Hawker 800XP	8577	Liberty Aviation Co, Leeds-Bradford, UK.	N51027
N800VA	00	Citation Bravo	550-0956	University of Virginia Foundation, Charlotteville, Va.	N572PB
N800VC	88	BAe 125/800A	NA0415	A & R Jet Leasing LLC. Coral Gables, Fl.	N560BA
N800VT	02	CitationJet CJ-2	525A-0103	Clausen Investments Inc/V-T Industries Inc. Storm Lake, Ia.	N5218R
N800WA	88	BAe 125/800A	NA0414	W W Aircraft LLC. Garrettsville, Oh.	N4361Q
N800WC	00	CitationJet CJ-2	525A-0006	Air Wolff LLC. Portland, Or.	N411GC
N800WG	89	BAe 125/800A	8152	David Oyedepo Ministries, Lagos, Nigeria.	(N42US)
N800WH	86	BAe 125/800A	8080	Hawker Holdings LLC. Ronkonkoma, NY.	N800BP
N800WP	00	Hawker 800XP	8459	Raytheon Aircraft Co. Wichita, Ks.	N800WW
N800WV	87	Beechjet 400	RJ-24	Giles Automotive Inc. Lafayette, La.	N800WW
N800WW*	03	Hawker 800XP	8661	KTW & PNW Transport LLC. Tucson, Az.	N661XP
N800WY	01	Hawker 800XP	8556	M & N Aviation, Casper, Wy.	N51556
N800XL	68	Gulfstream 2	24	Cedar Enterprises LLC. Richardson, Tx.	(N800XC)
N800XM	99	Hawker 800XP	8414	AEA Services LLC. Saddle River, NJ.	EI-RNJ
N800XP	01	Hawker 800XP	8541	M & N Aviation, Casper, Wy.	N50441
N800ZZ	89	Astra-1125	028	Palm Coast Leasing Inc. Fort Lauderdale, Fl.	N816HB
N801BB	96	Citation Bravo	550-0801	Bandyco LLC. Stanford, Ky.	N5135K
N801CE	94	BAe 125/800A	8253	Cummins Inc. Columbus, In.	N942H
N801CF	90	BAe 125/800A	NA0452	Shuert Industries LLC/Corporate Flight Inc. Detroit, Mi.	XA-SIV
N801CT	90	Learjet 31	31-017	Inter-Tel Technologies Inc. Reno, Nv.	N600AW
N801CW	84	BAe 125/800A	8012	Flight Options LLC. Cleveland, Oh.	(N801LX)
N801DL	90	Falcon 50	206	Indefensible Corp. Miami, Fl.	VP-BMF
N801DM	93	B 757-256	26240	Dallas Mavericks/MLW Aviation LLC. Dallas, Tx.	N286CD
N801G	96	Astra-1125SPX	081	General Dynamics C45, Taunton, Ma.	N800AJ
N801MB	99	Hawker 800XP	8440	Brass Aviation Inc. Fairfield, NJ.	N40488
N801MJ	85	Gulfstream 3	450	Bay Hawk LLC/Panattoni Development Co. Portland, Or.	N888VS
N801P*	90	BAe 125/800A	NA0456	Piedmont Hawthorne Aviation Inc. Winston Salem, NC.	N152NS
N801PN	00	Global Express	9062	Sabrina Aviation Corp. Punta Gorda, Fl.	N700CJ
N801QS	01	Citation Encore	560-0601	NetJets, Columbus, Oh.	N5239J
N801RA	80	HS 125/700A	7100	Rusco Co. Memphis, Tn.	N858JR
N801RS	96	Astra-1125SPX	084	Richard Schaden PC. Birmingham, Mi.	N795HB
N801SC	69	Falcon 20D	206	CIT Group, Tempe, Az.	N632PB
N801SS	80	Sabre-65	465-40	Stephen Susman PC. Houston, Tx.	N465PM
N801WB	95	Hawker 800XP	8287	Novell Inc. Salt Lake City, Ut.	(N287XP)
N801WM	00	Hawker 800XP	8503	Waste Management Inc. Andrau Airpark-Houston, Tx.	N802WM
N802AB	93	Citation V	560-0217	Matsco Inc. Marietta, Ga.	N602AB
N802CC	76	Gulfstream 2	187	Rubloff Aviation LLC. Rockford, Il.	N202GA
N802CE	94	Hawker 800	8270	Cummins Inc. Columbus, In.	N297H
N802DC	02	Hawker 800XP	8562	Naples Jet Charter Inc. Naples, Fl.	(N877S)
N802DR	04	Hawker 800XP	8667	Dominion Resources Inc. Richmond, Va.	N667XP
N802HH	02	Hawker 4000 Horizon	RC-2	Raytheon Aircraft Co. Wichita, Ks. (Ff 10 May 02).	
N802TA	99	Hawker 800XP	8454	Flight Options LLC. Cleveland, Oh.	(N826LX)
N802X	88	BAe 125/800A	NA0418	Exxon Mobil Corp. Houston, Tx.	N563BA
N803BF	82	HS 125/700A	7178	Tapatio Inc. Corpus Christi, Tx.	N178WB
N803CE	94	Hawker 800	8271	Cummins Inc. Columbus, In.	N298H
N803E	86	Beechjet 400	RJ-16	SMC Corp. Bend, Or.	(N440MP)
N803HH	02	Hawker 4000 Horizon	RC-3	Raytheon Aircraft Co. Wichita, Ks.	
N803JL	89	BAe 125/800A	NA0436	Jet Linx Aviation Corp. Omaha, Ne.	N160NW
N803RR	90	Challenger 601-3A	5073	Alsco Inc. Salt Lake City, Ut.	N5073
N803TA	00	Hawker 800XP	8455	Flight Options LLC. Cleveland, Oh.	(N827LX)
N803X	88	BAe 125/800A	NA0420	Exxon Mobil Corp. Houston, Tx.	N565BA
N804AC	98	Hawker 800XP	8368	Albemarle Corp. Richmond, Va.	
N804BH	02	Hawker 800XP	8596	Mahaska Bottling Co. Oskaloosa, Ia.	N596XP
N804HH	04	Hawker 4000 Horizon	RC-4	Raytheon Aircraft Co. Wichita, Ks. (Ff 29 Apr 04).	
N804JJ	77	Falcon 10	105	Biokine Inc. Lawrenceville, Ga.	N16WJ
N804PA	79	Sabre-65	465-4	Studer Group Travel LLC. Gulf Breeze, Fl.	N800TW
Reg	Yr	Type	c/n	Owner/Operator	Prev Regn

Reg	Yr	Type	c/n	Owner/Operator	Prev Regn
N804QS	02	Citation Encore	560-0610	NetJets, Columbus, Oh.	N52699
N804TF	81	Learjet 35A	35A-404	Lion Aviation LLC. Richmond, Va.	N404DP
N804X	88	BAe 125/800A	NA0421	Exxon Mobil Corp. Houston, Tx.	N566BA
N805CD	83	HS 125/700A	7209	GER Consulting Inc. Stuart, Fl.	N127SR
N805HH	04	Hawker 4000 Horizon	RC-5	Wichita Air Services Inc. Wichita, Ks.	
N805QS	00	Hawker 800XP	8505	NetJets, Columbus, Oh.	N50005
N805SM	69	Jet Commander-B	145	RAA Enterprises Inc. Wilmington, De.	N145AJ
N805VC	94	CitationJet	525-0076	Numenor Ventures LLC. Montecito, Ca.	N4TF
N805VZ	99	Challenger 604	5410	Verizon Aviation Corp. Teterboro, NJ.	N199BA
N805X	91	BAe 125/800A	NA0465	Exxon Mobil Corp. Houston, Tx.	N637BA
N806AC	00	Gulfstream V	622	Casden Aircraft LLC. Burbank, Ca.	N304K
N806CB	65	HS 125/731	25038	Dove Air Inc. Hendersonville, NC.	N42CK
N806LJ	65	Learjet 23	23-073	A Liner 8 Aviation, Livonia, Mi.	
N806MN	03	CitationJet CJ-2	525A-0194	Sanguis LLC/Mobren Transport Inc. Sioux City, la.	N.....
N806QS	02	Citation Encore	560-0614	NetJets, Columbus, Oh.	N5296X
N806XM	99	Hawker 800XP	8418	Mobil Corp. Fairfax, Va.	N31046
N807CC	77	Gulfstream 2TT	212	Lear 35 LLC. Van Nuys, Ca.	N551MD
N807JW	98	Astra-1125SPX	100	Jeld-Wen Inc. Klamath Falls, Or.	
N807MB	92	Citation II	550-0694	Burford's Tree Surgeons Inc. Birmingham, Al.	N550KE
N807QS	02	Citation Encore	560-0617	NetJets, Columbus, Oh.	N5207A
N807TA	00	Hawker 800XP	8483	Flight Options LLC. Cleveland, Oh.	(N030LX)
N807Z	89	Challenger 601-3A	5040	Native Air Services Inc. Mesa, Az.	N652CN
N808BL	03	Hawker 800XP	8634	Bausch & Lomb Inc. Rochester, NY.	
N808G	91	Challenger 601-3A	5098	The GAP Inc/TAG Aviation USA, San Francisco, Ca.	N812GS
N808HG	94	Challenger 601-3R	5157	Kimberly-Clark Integrated Services Inc. Roswell, Ga.	N800KC
N808L	82	Falcon 100	200	Brunner & Lay Inc. Franklin Park, Il.	N80BL
N808QS	02	Citation Encore	560-0619	NetJets, Columbus, Oh.	N52135
N808RP	77	JetStar 2	5215	Rico-Perez Products Inc. Miami, Fl.	N80TS
N808T	98	Gulfstream 4SP	1342	Odin Aviation Inc. Burbank, Ca.	N555KC
N808TA	01	Hawker 800XP	8548	Flight Options LLC. Cleveland, Oh.	(N835LX)
N808TH	96	Citation V Ultra	560-0378	Royal Travel SA. Panama City, Panama.	(N378VP)
N808V	01	390 Premier 1	RB-5	Frank Fletcher Premier One Inc. Little Rock, Ar.	N155GD
N808W	98	Learjet 31A	31A-165	Danny Souders, Denver-Jeffco, Co.	N885TW
N808WA	98	CitationJet	525-0290	Mill Creek Aviation Inc. Antioch, Il.	
N809BA	98	Hawker 800XP	8388	OD Aviation Inc. Delray Beach, Fl.	(N809TP)
N809C	00	Gulfstream 4SP	1450	CONOCO-Phillips, Houston, Tx.	N370GA
N809F	81	Falcon 10	182	Florida Falcon Holdings Inc. Wilmington, De.	N111MU
N809JC	80	Westwind-1124	298	NFA Corp. Waukegan, Il.	N298CM
N809JW	00	Gulfstream G100	135	Jeld-Wen Inc. Klamath Falls, Or.	N58GX
N809R	98	Learjet 60	60-146	Mitchell Enterprise Group LLC. Coconut Grove, Fl.	N800R
N809SG	04	EMB-135BJ Legacy	14500809	Meadow Lane Air Partners LLC. Southampton, NY.	PT-SII
N810CW	84	BAe 125/800A	8010	Options Financing LLC. Cleveland, Oh.	(N800LX)
N810D	97	Challenger 604	5331	Jet Express Transit Corp. Morristown, NJ.	C-GLYH
N810GS	79	HS 125/700A	7061	Nebrig & Assocs Inc. Denton, Tx.	N700SF
N810HS	72	HS 125/400A	25271	Centurion Investments Inc. St Louis, Mo.	N70AP
N810JW	01	Gulfstream G100	138	Jeld-Wen Inc. Klamath Falls, Or.	N80GX
N810KB*	80	HS 125/700B	7118	KBA/Bridges & Shields LLC. East Point, Ga.	N619TD
N810LX	89	BAe 125/800A	NA0432	Flight Options LLC. Cleveland, Oh.	N805CW
N810MT	84	Challenger 601	3026	Biomet Inc/Air Warsaw Inc. Warsaw, In.	N716HP
N810QS	02	Citation Encore	560-0625	NetJets, Columbus, Oh.	N
N810RA	67	Falcon 20C	81	Kalitta Charters LLC. Detroit-Willow Run, Mi.	N93RS
N810SS	96	CitationJet	525-0137	Viaticus LLC. Park City, Ut.	(N525SE)
N810TM	02	Gulfstream 4SP	1483	Toyota Motor Sales USA Inc. Long Beach, Ca.	N483GA
N810V	93	BAe 125/800B	8224	Vee-Jay Equipment LLC. Pontiac, Mi.	N478PM
N811AA	68	Falcon 20D	187	USA Jet Airlines Inc. Detroit-Willow Run, Mi.	N750R
N811AG	98	Falcon 2000	71	Tyco International Ltd. Portsmouth, NH.	N811TY
N811AV	00	Falcon 900EX	74	Avaya Inc. Morristown, NJ.	N315KP
N811CW	84	BAe 125/800A	8011	Flight Options LLC. Cleveland, Oh.	N186G
N811DF	79	Gulfstream II SP	244	Flynn Financial Corp. San Francisco, Ca.	N509TT
N811JW	01	Gulfstream G100	140	Jeld-Wen Inc. Klamath Falls, Or.	4X-CVK
N811MT	81	Challenger 600S	1024	CPH Aircraft LLC/Capital Pacific Holdings Inc. Newport Beach	N810MT
N811QS	03	Hawker 800XP	8614	NetJets, Columbus, Oh.	
N811RC	02	CitationJet CJ-2	525A-0058	Rico Marketing Corp. Flint-Bishop, Mi.	N52035
N811ST	01	Citation Excel	560-5193	SunTrust Banks Inc. Atlanta, Ga.	N.....
N811VC	81	Westwind-1124	331	C & E Holdings Inc. Madison, Md.	N228L
N811VG	79	Citation II/SP	551-0017	Pacific Coast Aviation Inc. Sacrament, Ca.	N811VC

Reg	Yr	Type	c/n	Owner/Operator	Prev Regn
☐ N812AA	66	Falcon 20C	57	USA Jet Airlines Inc. Detroit-Willow Run, Mi.	N711KG
☐ N812G	97	Challenger 604	5330	The GAP Inc/TAG Aviation USA, San Francisco, Ca.	C-GLYO
☐ N812GA	04	Gulfstream G450	4012	Gulfstream Aerospace Corp. Savannah, Ga.	
☐ N812QS	02	Citation Encore	560-0628	NetJets, Columbus, Oh.	N.....
☐ N812WN	80	Sabre-65	465-25	First State Trucking Inc. Selbyville, De.	N324ZR
☐ N812XL*	81	Challenger 600S	1016	XL Capital Partners Inc. Colorado Springs, Co.	N920RV
☐ N813AS	78	Learjet 35A	35A-167	AirNet Systems Inc. Columbus, Oh. (was orange now black).	N725P
☐ N813BR	67	Sabre-60	306-8	Chadco Aviation Inc. Dalton, Ga.	N613BR
☐ N813CW	99	Hawker 800XP	8413	Flight Options LLC. Cleveland, Oh.	(N822LX)
☐ N813JD	98	Citation Bravo	550-0838	K-Tek Corp. Prairieville, La.	N49KW
☐ N813LS	69	Falcon 20-5B	185	SGI-Sheakley Group Inc/Irish Air LLC. Cincinnati, Oh.	N147X
☐ N813P	77	JetStar 2	5222	Takoje Corp. Reno, Nv.	A6-CPC
☐ N813TL	66	DC 9-15	45732	U S Department of Justice, Pineville, La.	N29
☐ N813VZ	94	Challenger 601-3R	5160	Verizon Aviation Corp. Teterboro, NJ.	N94BA
☐ N814CM	92	Citation V	560-0170	HNI Corp. Muscatine, Ia.	(N417H)
☐ N814D	71	HS 125/400A	NA761	813BR LLC. Pleasant View, Tn.	XA-RIL
☐ N814ER	75	Citation	500-0280	Flite Services Inc. Lakeland, Fl.	N102AD
☐ N814GF	96	Learjet 60	60-085	Papy LLC. Coral Gables, Fl.	N89KW
☐ N814K	76	JetStar 2	5204	618BR LLC. Pleasant View, Tx.	N202ES
☐ N814PS	94	Challenger 601-3R	5159	Med 4 Home Inc. Tampa, Fl.	C-GICI
☐ N814RW	67	DC 9-15F	47011	U S Marshals Service, Oklahoma City, Ok.	N179DE
☐ N814T	67	Jet Commander	106	Maxfly Aviation Inc. Fort Lauderdale, Fl.	N814K
☐ N815CE	81	Citation II	550-0204	Seaport Aviation Inc. Wilmington, De.	(N300PR)
☐ N815CM	91	Citation V	560-0104	HON Industries Inc. Muscatine, Ia.	(N416H)
☐ N815DD	81	Learjet 35A	35A-414	TCL Air Inc. Ridgewood, NJ.	N196SP
☐ N815E	96	Learjet 31A	31A-118	Wal-Mart Stores Inc. Rogers, Ar.	N815A
☐ N815H	87	Citation S/II	S550-0146	Universal Connections Ltd. Caracas, Venezuela.	N81SH
☐ N815JW	01	Gulfstream G200	053	Jeld-Wen Inc. Klamath Falls, Or.	(N601AV)
☐ N815L	77	Learjet 35A	35A-142	EPPS Air Service Inc. Atlanta-De Kalb, Ga.	N815A
☐ N815MA	82	Citation II	550-0406	Citation Air Travel Inc. Dover, De.	HH-JPD
☐ N815MC	96	CitationJet	525-0142	Kestrel Inc/Madison Chemical Co. Madison, In.	N5068R
☐ N815PA	01	Challenger 604	5511	PepsiAmericas Inc. Minneapolis, Mn.	C-GLWX
☐ N815QS	04	Hawker 800XP	8705	NetJets, Columbus, Oh.	
☐ N815RK	85	Westwind-1124	416	Rance King Properties Inc. Long Beach, Ca.	N303TS
☐ N815TA	01	Hawker 800XP	8534	Flight Options LLC. Cleveland, Oh.	(N833LX)
☐ N816AA	73	Falcon 20E	290	USA Jet Airlines Inc. Detroit-Willow Run, Mi.	I-TIAL
☐ N816CC	00	Challenger 604	5451	Wind & Lion Aviation LLC. Menlo Park, Ca.	(N120MT)
☐ N816CW	84	BAe 125/800A	8016	Flight Options LLC. Cleveland, Oh.	N906SB
☐ N816DK	00	Beechjet 400A	RK-291	Connor Air Services Inc. Fulton County, Ga.	N3191L
☐ N816FC	94	CitationJet	525-0059	Fortney Companies Inc. La Crosse, Wi.	N71GW
☐ N816GA	04	Gulfstream G450	4016	Gulfstream Aerospace Corp. Savannah, Ga.	
☐ N816JW	98	Gulfstream G200	097	Jeld-Wen Inc. Klamath Falls, Or.	N397GA
☐ N816MC	82	Learjet 55	55-035	Macon USA Corp. Wilmington, De.	VP-CUC
☐ N816QS	99	Hawker 800XP	8416	NetJets, Columbus, Oh.	
☐ N816SP	88	Challenger 601-3A	5030	Glacier Bay Capital LLC. Portsmouth, NH.	N816SQ
☐ N816SQ	01	Global Express	9106	Sprint/United Management Co. Kansas City, Mo.	N916SQ
☐ N817AA	70	Falcon 20DC	233	USA Jet Airlines Inc. Detroit-Willow Run, Mi.	I-TIAG
☐ N817AM	83	Learjet 55	55-069	Florida Jet Service Inc. Fort Lauderdale, Fl.	N102ST
☐ N817GR	83	Diamond 1A	A062SA	Betony Enterprises LLC & AN Ryder LLC. Tiburon, Ca.	N616MM
☐ N817MB	92	Citation VII	650-7012	Koury Aviation Inc. Liberty, NC.	N317MB
☐ N817MF	85	Gulfstream 3	466	Monroe Business Ventures LLC. Farmingdale, NY.	N102AK
☐ N817MQ	92	Citation VII	650-7015	Teena Koury, Liberty, NC.	N317MQ
☐ N817PD	90	Citation V	560-0075	Cobalt Aviation II LLC. N Philadelphia, Pa.	(N619PD)
☐ N817QS	01	Hawker 800XP	8517	NetJets, Columbus, Oh.	
☐ N818AA	66	Falcon 20C	36	USA Jet Airlines Inc. Detroit-Willow Run, Mi.	OE-GUS
☐ N818BA	87	Gulfstream 4	1017	NJL Enterprises LLC. Greenwich, Ct.	N402KC
☐ N818DA	77	Gulfstream II SP	208	Aspen 1 LLC. Van Nuys, Ca.	C-FNCG
☐ N818JH	81	Westwind-Two	341	JUD LLC. Anglewood, NJ.	N52KS
☐ N818KC	75	HS 125/700A	NA0206	Ogden Flight Services Group Inc. Bridgeport, Ct.	N701NW
☐ N818LD	77	Sabre-75A	380-30	L D Holdings LLC. Sussex, NJ.	N818DW
☐ N818LS	99	Global Express	9035	The Whitewind Co. Windsor Locks, Ct.	N711LS
☐ N818ME	00	Gulfstream 4SP	1431	Cape Clear LLC. Westborough, Ma.	(N818RM)
☐ N818MV	90	BAe 125/800A	8186	MVA Aircraft Leasing Inc. Greenwich, Ct.	N818G
☐ N818RF	03	Gulfstream G550	5018	Aircraft Overseas (Cayman) Ltd.	N518GA
☐ N818TH	96	Challenger 604	5315	Tommy Hilfeger USA Inc. NYC.	N818LS
☐ N818TJ	83	Gulfstream 3	384	GKW Unified Holdings LLC. Los Angeles, Ca.	N112GS

Reg	Yr	Type	c/n	Owner/Operator	Prev Regn

Reg	Yr	Type	c/n	Owner/Operator	Prev Regn
N819AA	66	Falcon 20C	26	USA Jet Airlines Inc. Detroit-Willow Run, Mi.	N11827
N819AP	01	Hawker 800XP	8559	Matadoro Management Investment LLC. Menlo Park, Ca.	N50459
N819DM	81	HS 125/700A	NA0326	TBC LLC/Jayco Associates Inc. Tampa, Fl.	N194WC
N819GY	78	Sabre-75A	380-66	Centurion Investments Inc. St Louis, Mo.	N943CC
N819RC	76	Westwind-1124	192	HRS Solutions LLC. Davisburg, Mi.	N319BG
N820AA	67	Falcon 20C	118	USA Jet Airlines Inc. Detroit-Willow Run, Mi.	F-GGKE
N820CE	99	CitationJet CJ-1	525-0368	Commercial Envelope Manufacturing Co. Deer Park, NY.	N5185J
N820CT	78	HS 125/700A	NA0229	Nebrig & Assocs Inc. Denton, Tx.	N825CT
N820FJ	90	Citation III	650-0183	Kerr-McGee Corp. Will Rogers, Ok.	(N820F)
N820L	65	Learjet 23	23-020	Butler National Inc. Newton, Ks.	N388R
N820MC	79	Citation II	550-0106	W D Larson Companies Ltd. Bloomington, Mn.	(N820MQ)
N820MG	69	HS 125/731	NA739	Mediacom Communications Corp. Middletown, NY.	N820MC
N820MS	90	Gulfstream 4	1147	Koloa Aviation Inc. Honolulu, Hi.	N200PM
N820QS	03	Citation Encore	560-0650	NetJets, Columbus, Oh.	N5260Y
N820TM	02	Gulfstream G300	1508	Toyota Motors Sales USA Inc. Long Beach, Ca.	N508GA
N821AA	69	Falcon 20D	203	USA Jet Airlines Inc. Detroit-Willow Run, Mi.	N36P
N821DG	02	Citation Excel	560-5297	David Goldner/Altare LLC. Boca Raton, Fl.	(N721DG)
N821QS	89	Hawker 800XP	8709	NetJets, Columbus, Oh.	
N822AA	69	Falcon 20D	195	USA Jet Airlines Inc. Detroit-Willow Run, Mi.	N195MP
N822BL	85	BAe 125/800B	8022	Branch Law Firm Aviation Ltd. Albuquerque, NM.	N4257R
N822CA	02	Learjet 45	45-215	ConAgra Foods Inc. Omaha, Ne.	N5018G
N822HA*	03	Citation II	550-0464	Hill Aircraft & Leasing Corp. Atlanta-Fulton County, Ga.	N117TA
N822TP	95	Falcon 2000	20	The Travelers Indemnity Co. Windsor Locks, Ct.	N389GS
N823AA	70	Falcon 20D	228	USA Jet Airlines Inc. Detroit-Willow Run, Mi.	OE-GRU
N823CA	02	Learjet 45	45-221	ConAgra Inc. Omaha, Ne.	N40078
N823CT	90	Citation II	550-0650	Denver Air LLC. Broomfield, Co.	N824CT
N823DF	00	Global Express	9066	DDF Y2K Family Trust, Hillsboro, Or.	N708SC
N823ET	03	Hawker 400XP	RK-360	Cheyenne American Corp. Anaheim, Ca.	N6200D
N823GA	86	Gulfstream 4	1005	Guardian Services Inc. Ontario, Ca.	VR-BJZ
N823NA	81	Citation II	550-0236	Proctor & Gamble Pharmaceuticals Inc. Norwich, NY.	LN-AAD
N823PM	03	Citation Bravo	550-1064	TBN Group. Reno, Nv.	N.....
N823TT	00	Beechjet 400A	RK-278	Raytheon Aircraft Co. Wichita, Ks.	N4378P
N824CA	96	Gulfstream 4SP	1309	ConAgra inc. Omaha, Ne.	N309GA
N824CB	97	Citation Bravo	550-0824	LJ Associates Inc/LJ Aviation, Latrobe, Pa.	N5121N
N824CC	82	Learjet 55	55-024	Charles Collins Aviation Inc. Carlsbad-Palomar, Ca.	N900FA
N824CW	88	BAe 125/800A	NA0417	Flight Options LLC. Cleveland, Oh.	(N809LX)
N824DS	76	Falcon 10	92	Limousin Air LLC. Nashville, Tn.	N724DS
N824DW	84	Diamond 1A	A075SA	Jet Linx Aviation Corp. Omaha, Ne.	N11WF
N824ES	94	CitationJet	525-0066	Scope Leasing Inc. Columbus, Oh.	(N823ES)
N824GB	03	Hawker 400XP	RK-371	G D Barnes Consulting LLC. Orange County, Ca.	N401CW
N824MG	84	Learjet 55	55-106	Lear II LLC. Bellevue, Wa.	N318JH
N824QS	00	Hawker 800XP	8523	NetJets, Columbus, Oh.	N5023J
N824SS	87	Beechjet 400	RJ-18	WillTim LLC. Fort Worth, Tx.	N595PT
N825AC	92	Learjet 31A	31A-058	Purwin LLC. Van Nuys, Ca.	N298CH
N825AM	76	Learjet 24E	24E-340	Mercurius Aviation Inc. Waco, Tx.	N457GM
N825CA	02	Learjet 45	45-220	ConAgra Foods Inc. Omaha, Ne.	N40077
N825CT	00	Hawker 800XP	8497	Cooper Tire & Rubber Co. Findlay, Oh.	N51197
N825GA	00	Citation X	750-0143	Galt Aviation LLC. San Jose, Ca.	N51744
N825JW	85	Citation III	650-0082	LNW Consulting/Wolff Urban Management Inc. Van Nuys, Ca.	N4VY
N825LJ	83	Learjet 35A	35A-496	Skyways Inc. Pottsville, Pa.	N496SW
N825LM	01	Gulfstream V	655	Penobscot Properties LLC. New Castle, De.	N629GA
N825MG	82	Learjet 55	55-055	Lear 1 LLC. Bellevue, Wa.	N970F
N825PS	81	Citation 1/SP	501-0224	Dawson Oil Co. LaCrosse, Wi.	N456CE
N825QS	04	Citation Encore	560-0655	NetJets, Columbus, Oh.	N.....
N825SB	68	Sabre-40	282-92	San Bernardino County Sheriff, Rialto, Ca.	158382
N825SG	04	EMB-135BJ Legacy	14500825	Swift Aviation Services Inc. Phoenix, Az.	PT-SIK
N826AA	67	Falcon 20C	67	USA Jet Airlines Inc. Detroit-Willow Run, Mi.	N821AA
N826AC	93	Citation V	560-0242	Aerial Services Group LLC. Naples, Fl.	N605AT
N826CA	02	Learjet 45	45-222	ConAgra Foods Inc. Santa Ana, Ca.	N673LB
N826CT	88	BAe 125/800A	NA0412	Cooper Tire & Rubber Co. Findlay, Oh.	N825PS
N826CW	85	BAe 125/800A	8026	Flight Options LLC. Cleveland, Oh.	N6TU
N826GA	94	Hawker 800	8263	PPG Industries Inc. Allegheny County, Pa.	N961H
N826GW	77	Gulfstream II SP	210	PF Air LLC/W Polisseni Inc. Fairport, NY.	N30FW
N826HS	98	CitationJet	525-0305	Overall Management 1 LLC. Solvang, Ca.	N.....
N826JS	04	Challenger 604	5587	Bombardier Aerospace Corp. Windsor Locks, Ct.	C-GLXS
N826K	98	Falcon 900EX	36	Alten Consulting LLC. St Louis, Mo.	N326K

Reg	Yr	Type	c/n	Owner/Operator	Prev Regn

Reg	Yr	Type	c/n	Owner/Operator	Prev Regn
☐ N826RT	81	Citation II/SP	551-0056	Ron Adkison, Henderson, Tx.	N36WJ
☐ N826SS	93	Learjet 60	60-015	Jet Operations LLC. Bellevue, Wa.	(N960HL)
☐ N827AA	74	Falcon 20E	298	USA Jet Airlines Inc. Detroit-Willow Run, Mi.	OE-GNN
☐ N827CR	80	Learjet 35A	35A-332	Inter Continental Express LLC. Hosford, Fl.	N543WW
☐ N827DP	90	Citation II	550-0660	Drug Plastics & Glass Co. Boyertown, Pa.	N160SP
☐ N827GA	99	Gulfstream 4SP	1391	PPG Industries Inc. Allegheny County, Pa.	N391GA
☐ N827K	92	Gulfstream 4	1180	BC Enterprises LC. Rifton, NY.	N709LS
☐ N827SA	99	Hawker 800XP	8438	WEKEL SA. Bogota, Colombia.	VP-BHZ
☐ N827SL	77	Sabre-75A	380-53	Palmair LLC. Milwaukie, Or.	N380SR
☐ N827SS*	93	Learjet 60	60-014	Lear 60 Leasing LLC. Fort Lauderdale, Fl.	N7US
☐ N828AF	85	Citation S/II	S550-0067	Summit Group Inc/ARTC, Columbia, SC.	N900DM
☐ N828CA	02	Learjet 45	45-159	ConAgra Foods Inc. Omaha, Ne.	N5001J
☐ N828CW	99	Hawker 800XP	8428	Flight Options LLC. Cleveland, Oh.	(N823LX)
☐ N828NS	00	Hawker 800XP	8464	National Air Services, Jeddah, Saudi Arabia.	HZ-KRSA
☐ N828QS	01	Hawker 800XP	8528	NetJets, Columbus, Oh.	
☐ N828SK	88	Challenger 601-3A	5018	JCI Transportation LLC. Chattanooga, Tn.	N893AC
☐ N828SS	80	Citation II/SP	551-0205	Sierra Stone Co. Dallas, Tx. (was 550-0161)	HB-VIO
☐ N829AA	72	Learjet 25B	25B-100	USA Jet Airlines Inc. Detroit-Willow Run, Mi.	N25TK
☐ N829CA	82	Learjet 35A	35A-459	Antilles Aircraft Leasing Inc. Dover, De. (status ?).	N969MT
☐ N829CB	98	Citation Bravo	550-0829	Westair Flying Services Ltd. Blackpool, UK.	N5096S
☐ N829JC	02	Citation Excel	560-5291	Henry Crown & Co. Palwaukee, Il.	N5086W
☐ N829NL	73	Gulfstream 2	128	New Light Church World Outreach Centre, Houston, Tx.	N128TS
☐ N829NS	00	Hawker 800XP	8475	National Air Services, Jeddah, Saudi Arabia.	HZ-KRSB
☐ N829RN	00	EMB-135ER	145361	Intel Corp/Executive Jet Management Inc. Cincinnati, Oh.	PT-...
☐ N830	84	Westwind-1124	406	Triumph Aviation Inc. Wayne, Pa.	N100CH
☐ N830AA	66	Falcon 20C	55	USA Jet Airlines Inc. Detroit-Willow Run, Mi.	N520FD
☐ N830C	87	Westwind-Two	442	Air Travel Services Inc. Nashville, Tn.	N71WF
☐ N830EF	87	Gulfstream 4	1023	EFB Aviation LLC. Arlington, Va.	(N830FB)
☐ N830KE	98	Citation Bravo	550-0830	LP 207 LLC. Greenville, NC.	N5076J
☐ N830RA	66	Falcon 20C	66	Allegra Unlimited Inc. Oak Brook, Il.	N766NW
☐ N831DC	88	BAe 125/800B	8112	La Paloma Verde Inc. Lawrenceville, Ga.	N331DC
☐ N831DF	70	HS 125/731	25231	Gore Creek Aviation LLC. Eagle, Co.	N831NW
☐ N831GA	90	Citation III	650-0194	TP Air LLC/Timber Products Co. Eugene, Or.	N2606
☐ N831S	93	CitationJet	525-0031	Emerald Coast Aviation LLC. Wilmington, De.	N31CJ
☐ N831V	04	CitationJet CJ-3	525B-0013	Cessna Aircraft Co. Wichita, Ks.	N5228Z
☐ N832CB	92	Citation VII	650-7020	Mount Hood Transport Inc. Klamath Falls, Or.	N700RR
☐ N832CW	99	Hawker 800XP	8432	Flight Options LLC. Cleveland, Oh.	(N824LX)
☐ N832QS*	04	Hawker 800XP	8683	Raytheon Aircraft Co. Wichita, Ks.	N61343
☐ N832SC	00	Challenger 604	5461	Delta Airelite Business Jets Inc. Cincinnati, Oh.	C-GLYK
☐ N832UJ	98	Citation Bravo	550-0832	Great River Energy, Elk River, Mn.	PT-WSO
☐ N833AV	99	Falcon 900C	181	Avaya Inc. Morristown, NJ.	HB-IUY
☐ N833CW	85	BAe 125/800A	8033	Flight Options LLC. Cleveland, Oh.	(N802LX)
☐ N833JP	85	BAe 125/800A	8044	Hawker 800 LLC. Salt Lake City, Ut.	N72NP
☐ N833QS	99	Hawker 800XP	8433	NetJets, Columbus, Oh.	
☐ N834AF	01	Learjet 31A	31A-225	Wal-Mart Stores Inc. Rogers, Ar.	N334AF
☐ N834DC	85	Citation S/II	S550-0035	Young Family Trust, Portola Valley, Ca.	XA-THO
☐ N834H	89	Citation III	650-0177	Hillenbrand Industries Inc. Batesville, In.	N707HJ
☐ N834QS	04	Citation Encore	560-0669	NetJets, Columbus, Oh.	N5216A
☐ N836LX	01	Hawker 800XP	8552	Flight Options LLC. Cleveland, Oh.	N817TA
☐ N836QS	99	Hawker 800XP	8348	NetJets, Columbus, Oh.	
☐ N837AC	04	CitationJet CJ-1	525-0537	Aho Construction 1 Inc. Vancouver, Wa.	N.....
☐ N837MA	73	Citation	500-0096	C & M Aero Inc. Wilmington, De.	(N187AP)
☐ N838QS	97	Hawker 800XP	8338	NetJets, Columbus, Oh.	
☐ N838RC	04	Learjet 60	60-276	RC Airways Inc. Luton, UK.	N5000E
☐ N839LX	03	Hawker 800XP	8657	Flight Options LLC. Cleveland, Oh.	(N857CW)
☐ N840CC	99	Citation Excel	560-5040	Blue Cross & Blue Shield Inc. Jacksonville, Fl.	N54HA
☐ N840FJ	91	Falcon 50	223	Kerr-McGee Corp. Will Rogers, Ok.	N633L
☐ N840GL*	77	Falcon 10	109	GLCC/SMC Aircraft Services LLC. Port Meadville, Pa.	N89EC
☐ N840LX	04	Hawker 800XP	8666	Flight Options LLC. Cleveland, Oh.	(N866LX)
☐ N840MQ	82	Citation II	550-0427	Armstrong Aircraft LLC. Madison, Wi.	N840MC
☐ N840QS	97	Hawker 800XP	8340	NetJets, Columbus, Oh.	
☐ N840R	90	Citation III	650-0197	NASCAR Inc. Daytona Beach, Fl.	N800R
☐ N840RG	79	Gulfstream 2TT	235	R & G Aviation LLC. Huntsville, Al.	N430RG
☐ N840SW	93	Learjet 31A	31A-084	Woodgrain Millwork Transportation, Ontario, Ca.	N196HA
☐ N841DW	01	Citation Excel	560-5177	William Victor Aviation Ltd. Jacksonville, Fl.	N5061P
☐ N841GA	03	Gulfstream G550	5041	Gulfstream Aerospace Corp. Savannah, Ga.	
Reg	Yr	Type	c/n	Owner/Operator	Prev Regn

Reg	Yr	Type	c/n	Owner/Operator	Prev Regn
N841LX	04	Hawker 800XP	8702	Raytheon Aircraft Co. Wichita, Ks.	
N841TF	81	Learjet 35A	35A-416	Dreamstream Aviation LLC. Prescott, Az.	N841TT
N841W	98	Citation Bravo	550-0841	Big Sky LLC. Oklahoma City, Ok.	N841WS
N841WS	04	Hawker 800XP	8674	Walter Scott International Ltd. Edinburgh, Scotland.	N674XP
N842CB	98	Citation Bravo	550-0842	Louisiana Aircraft LLC. Oklahoma City, Ok.	N86AJ
N842QS	01	Hawker 800XP	8542	NetJets, Columbus, Oh.	
N843B	70	HS 125/731	NA742	Phaeton LLC. East Haven, Ct.	N74RT
N843CP	93	Learjet 60	60-011	N74B LLC. Salem, Or.	N611TS
N843CW	01	Hawker 800XP	8543	Flight Options LLC. Cleveland, Oh.	(N834LX)
N843LX*	96	Hawker 800XP	8297	Flight Options LLC. Cleveland, Oh.	N725TA
N844DR	98	Citation Bravo	550-0860	Donald Air LLC. Monroee, NC.	(N860J)
N844F	82	Falcon 100	201	Semitool Inc. Cambridge, UK.	N100NW
N844GA	90	Astra-1125SP	044	Gertel & Suchoski Aviation LLC. Fort Pierce, Fl.	N676TC
N844GF	89	Gulfstream 4	1107	Ford Aviation LLC. San Francisco, Ca.	N844GS
N844HS	01	Citation Encore	560-0596	HealthSouth Aviation Inc. Birmingham, Al.	N52235
N844L	75	Learjet 35	35-014	Nevada Jet Aviation Inc. Las Vegas, Nv.	N190GC
N844NX	85	Falcon 50	147	Western Stone & Metal Corp. Englewood, Co.	N526CC
N844QS	02	Citation Encore	560-0629	NetJets, Columbus, Oh.	N.....
N844SL	67	Falcon 20C	77	Grand Aire Express Inc. Toledo, Oh. (still N613GA 9/04).	N613GA
N844TM	04	Citation Encore	560-0660	Munoz Bermudez Inc. Santurce, PR.	N5264M
N844UP	01	Falcon 2000	156	Union Pacific Railroad Co. Omaha, Ne.	F-WWVN
N845CW	85	BAo 125/000A	8045	Flight Options LLC. Cleveland, Oh.	(N803LX)
N845GA	99	Galaxy-1126	012	Lions Air AG. Zurich, Switzerland.	(HB-IGK)
N845QS	01	Hawker 800XP	8545	NetJets, Columbus, Oh.	N50445
N845RL	99	Learjet 45	45-022	Four S's LLC. Greenville, NC.	(XA-RUR)
N846L*	83	Citation II	550-0477	Legendary Air Inc. Destin, Fl.	N344KK
N847C	84	Citation S/II	S550-0003	Transit Air Services Inc. Morristown, NJ.	N847G
N847CW	03	Hawker 800XP	8647	Flight Options LLC. Cleveland, Oh.	(N837LX)
N848C	89	Beechjet 400	RJ-63	F&S LLC/Triple S Hauling Inc. Columbia, Mo.	
N848CC	98	Challenger 604	5367	MHS Consulting Corp. St Louis, Mo.	N145DL
N848CW	03	Hawker 800XP	8648	Flight Options LLC. Cleveland, Oh.	
N848D	78	Citation II	550-0039	Carter County Bank/Summers-Taylor Inc. Tn. (was 551-0084).	ZP-TYO
N848DM	02	Citation Excel	560-5329	Archer Daniels Midland Co. Decatur, Il.	N.....
N848G	97	Citation V Ultra	560-0465	Sibsair LLC. Grand Rapids, Mi.	N465CV
N848N	97	Hawker 800XP	8371	ITT Flight Operations Inc. Allentown, Pa.	
N848RJ	86	Gulfstream 3	492	N848RJ Inc. Burbank, Ca.	N188TC
N849HS	81	Westwind-Two	344	U S Technology Corp. Canton, Oh.	N311BR
N850CC	80	Sabre-65	465-38	LMI LLC. Alpharetta, Ga.	N850CS
N850CT	04	Hawker 800XP	8677	Copeland Corp. Dayton, Oh.	N677XP
N850DG	98	CitationJet	525-0268	Delta Health Group Inc. Pensacola, Fl.	
N850EP	81	Falcon 50	39	Fisher Controls International LLC. St Louis, Mo.	N326FB
N850FB	94	Challenger 601-3R	5162	FleetBoston Financial Corp. Boston, Ma.	N850FL
N850J	97	Hawker 800XP	8311	DePuy Orthopaedics Inc. Warsaw, In.	N800RD
N850K	03	Falcon 2000	210	Koch Industries Inc. Wichita, Ks.	N2325
N850PM	81	Citation II	550-0210	D & R Ventures LLC. Sherman Oaks, Ca.	XA-KMX
N850PT*	03	Citation X	750-0222	PCMT Aviation LLC. Mountain View, Ca.	N222CX
N850TC	92	BAe 1000A	9032	Taubman Centers Inc. Waterford, Mi.	N300LS
N851CW	86	BAe 125/800A	8051	Flight Options LLC. Cleveland, Oh.	(N804LX)
N851EL	03	Gulfstream G300	1515	Pleasant Travel Service, Van Nuys, Ca.	N415GA
N851GA	04	Gulfstream G550	5051	Gulfstream Aerospace Corp. Savannah, Ga.	
N852A	87	BAe 125/800A	8083	Rycho Aviation LLC. Bethosda, Md.	(N805AF)
N852GA	75	HS 125/600A	6048	Rivers Corp. Wilmington, De.	TC-COS
N852QS	99	Hawker 800XP	8452	NetJets, Columbus, Oh.	
N852SP	80	Citation II	550-0382	Stephens Pipe&Steel Transportation Inc. Russell Springs, Ky.	N551TT
N854SM	71	HS 125/731	NA766	Conrad Kulatz, West Palm Beach, Fl.	N150SA
N855DG	80	Falcon 20-5	432	Dollar General Corp. Nashville-Berry Field, Tn.	N237PT
N855FC	97	Beechjet 400A	RK-141	Flow Companies Inc. Winston-Salem, NC.	N874JD
N855GA	92	BAe 125/800A	8211	Guardian Aviation Services LLC. Teterboro, NJ.	N151TC
N855JB	04	390 Premier 1	RB-104	George Inc. Wilmington, De.	N5104G
N855PT	82	Learjet 55	55-046	Jet 55 LLC. Manhasset Hills, NY.	N55HL
N855QS	98	Hawker 800XP	8355	NetJets, Columbus, Oh.	
N855RB	97	Gulfstream V	509	EMAX LLC. Charlottesville, Va.	N509GV
N855SA	82	Gulfstream 3	363	Atsinger Aviation LLC. Van Nuys, Ca.	N77EK
N855TJ	03	Falcon 2000EX	19	Lark Aviation LLC. Manchester, NH.	N528BD
N856AF	88	BAe 125/800A	NA0427	Alfa Fox LLC/Chief Executive Air, NYC.	N45Y
N856BB	00	CitationJet CJ-1	525-0381	Dempsey Boyd, Clayton, Al.	N5185J

Reg	Yr	Type	c/n	Owner/Operator	Prev Regn
☐ N856F	01	Falcon 2000	138	M & K Premier Air LLC. St Louis, Mo.	N799BC
☐ N856JB	65	Learjet 23	23-052	John Kowal/Skyway Enterprises Inc. Kissimmee, Fl.	N360EJ
☐ N857AA	99	Citation Bravo	550-0901	JV Jet Services LLC. Norfolk, Va.	N5058J
☐ N857ST	98	Gulfstream 4SP	1345	Seminole Tribe of Florida, Hollywood, Fl.	N457ST
☐ N858MK	00	Learjet 45	45-141	KMI Management LLC. Indianapolis, In.	N142HQ
☐ N858PJ	81	Challenger 600S	1028	SJC Consulting Inc. Rancho Santa Fe, Ca.	YV-1111CP
☐ N858QS	04	Hawker 800XP	8691	NetJets, Columbus, Oh.	
☐ N860DB*	01	CitationJet CJ-1	525-0434	Shelburne Limestone Corp. Colchester, Vt.	N860DD
☐ N860FJ	97	Falcon 900EX	30	Kerr-McGee Corp. Will Rogers, Ok.	N662P
☐ N860JB	88	Gulfstream 4	1054	JBNB Falcon LLC. Dover, De.	(N1DC)
☐ N860MX	73	Learjet 25B	25B-109	B & C Flight Management Inc. Houston, Tx.	C-GSAS
☐ N860PD	95	Learjet 60	60-073	Parker Drilling Co. Tulsa, Ok.	N256M
☐ N860QS	04	Hawker 800XP	8698	NetJets, Columbus, Oh.	
☐ N860S	76	Learjet 35A	35A-086	Houck Leasing Inc. Fort Pierce, Fl.	N86CS
☐ N860W	97	Citation VII	650-7086	DW Enterprises LC. Wamego, Ks.	N5134Z
☐ N861CE	94	Citation V Ultra	560-0273	Coca-Cola Enterprises Inc. Atlanta-Fulton County, Ga.	N61JB
☐ N861CW	86	BAe 125/800A	8061	Flight Options LLC. Cleveland, Oh.	(N805LX)
☐ N861QS	98	Hawker 800XP	8361	NetJets, Columbus, Oh.	
☐ N862CW	86	BAe 125/800A	8062	Dan Air LLC. Klamath Falls, Or.	(N806LX)
☐ N862KM	99	Beechjet 400A	RK-227	Bravo Romeo II LLC/Red Star Investments Inc. Las Vegas, Nv.	N362KM
☐ N862QS	98	Hawker 800XP	8362	NetJets, Columbus, Oh	
☐ N863CA	01	Learjet 45	45-160	ConAgra Foods Inc. Omaha, Ne.	N455DE
☐ N863CE	95	Hawker 800XP	8289	Coca-Cola Enterprises Inc. Atlanta-Fulton County, Ga.	N515GP
☐ N863QS	99	Hawker 800XP	8463	NetJets, Columbus, Oh.	
☐ N863RD	95	Citation V Ultra	560-0287	Premier Electric Aviation LLC. Naples, Fl.	N117MR
☐ N863TM	04	Falcon 2000	217	TME Aviation LLC. Orlando, Fl.	F-WWVE
☐ N864QS	01	Hawker 800XP	8564	NetJets, Columbus, Oh.	
☐ N865AM	03	Hawker 400XP	RK-358	AMFI LLC/Accurate Metal Fabricators Inc. Orange County, Ca.	N5158D
☐ N865CA	01	Learjet 45	45-193	ConAgra Inc. Omaha, Ne.	N434FX
☐ N865EC*	92	Citation VII	650-7014	Entergy Services Inc. New Orleans, La.	N864EC
☐ N865M	00	Citation Encore	560-0550	Cessna Aircraft Co. Wichita, Ks.	N51072
☐ N865SM	98	Hawker 800XP	8365	SummitJets Inc. Newport Beach, Ca.	
☐ N866CA	01	Learjet 45	45-184	ConAgra Inc. Omaha, Ne.	N45VP
☐ N866CW	99	Hawker 800XP	8466	Flight Options LLC. Cleveland, Oh.	(N829LX)
☐ N866G	00	Gulfstream G200	025	General Dynamics Network Systems, Needham, Ma.	N302MC
☐ N866RB	99	Hawker 800XP	8405	Raytheon Aircraft Co. Wichita, Ks.	N866RR
☐ N866RR	03	Hawker 800XP	8624	Reynolds & Reynolds Co. Dayton, Oh.	N624XP
☐ N867CW	86	BAe 125/800B	8067	Flight Options LLC. Cleveland, Oh.	(N807LX)
☐ N867JC	80	Citation II	550-0166	Bart Palmisano Sr. Metairie, La.	N367JC
☐ N867QS	02	Hawker 800XP	8576	NetJets, Columbus, Oh.	
☐ N868AG	75	Gulfstream II SP	167	Blue Sky Group Inc. Van Nuys, Ca.	N368AG
☐ N868BT	82	Falcon 50	93	Sirius Inc. Corvallis, Or.	N844X
☐ N868JB	01	Citation Excel	560-5180	HealthTrust Inc/HCA Squared LLC. Nashville, Tn.	N.....
☐ N868JT	95	Citation V Ultra	560-0310	Florida Power & Light Co. Opa Locka, Fl.	N410CV
☐ N868SM	79	Gulfstream 2B	254	Tricycle Aviation LLC. Van Nuys, Ca.	N706TS
☐ N868WC	90	BAe 125/800A	NA0449	World Class Automotive Operations, Dallas, Tx.	N800WT
☐ N869GR	01	CitationJet CJ-1	525-0478	Fun Bike Center Inc. San Diego, Ca.	N5233J
☐ N870CM	01	Challenger 604	5488	Caremark RX Inc. Birmingham, Al.	N604CC
☐ N870GA	04	Gulfstream G550	5070	Gulfstream Aerospace Corp. Savannah, Ga.	
☐ N871MM	01	Falcon 900EX	89	MMC Executive Services Inc. Teterboro, NJ.	N990EX
☐ N872AT	95	Hawker 800XP	8278	Raytheon Aircraft Co. Wichita, Ks.	G-BVZK
☐ N872EC	01	Falcon 2000	143	Entergy Services Inc. New Orleans, La.	N2230
☐ N872QS	00	Hawker 800XP	8472	NetJets, Columbus, Oh.	N44722
☐ N872RD	81	Citation II	550-0226	RDO Aviation Co. Park Rapids, Mn.	N872RT
☐ N873G	83	Challenger 601	3009	Air Castle Corp. Santa Monica, Ca.	(N651AC)
☐ N873JC	00	Dornier Do328JET	3118	Johnson Controls Inc. Milwaukee, Wi.	D-B...
☐ N873QS	02	Hawker 800XP	8573	NetJets, Columbus, Oh.	
☐ N874A	96	Gulfstream 4SP	1285	Anadarko Petroleum Corp. Houston, Tx.	N477GA
☐ N874C	93	Gulfstream 4SP	1219	Hewlett-Packard Co. San Jose, Ca.	N87HP
☐ N874QS	99	Hawker 800XP	8474	NetJets, Columbus, Oh.	
☐ N874RA	82	Gulfstream 3	361	Thundervolt LLC. Sandy, Ut.	(N874RR)
☐ N874WD	92	Astra-1125SP	062	Williamson-Dickie Manufacturing Co. Fort Worth, Tx.	N866Q
☐ N875CA	80	Sabre-65	465-42	MA Inc. oshkosh, Wi.	N45NP
☐ N875G	84	Challenger 601	3019	Home Air Inc/Home Place Inc. Gainesville, Ga.	N375G
☐ N875HS	82	Westwind-1124	370	Monroe LLC. Washington, DC.	N471TM
☐ N875LP	96	Hawker 800XP	8308	Thomas H Lee Co. Boston, Ma.	N345BR

Reg	Yr	Type	c/n	Owner/Operator	Prev Regn
N875QS	98	Hawker 800XP	8375	NetJets, Columbus, Oh.	
N876C	86	Learjet 35A	35A-616	Dycom Industries Inc. Palm Beach, Fl.	N876CS
N876G	95	Citation VII	650-7062	Bath Iron Works, Bath, Me.	N5262Z
N876H	02	Challenger 604	5542	Household International Inc. Palwaukee, Il.	C-GLXQ
N876MA	75	Falcon 10	63	Deniston Enterprises Inc/Prime Airborne, Sikorsky, Ct.	N70TS
N876MC	70	Learjet 24B	24B-217	Royal Air Freight Inc. Waterford, Mi.	C-FZHT
N876QS	02	Hawker 800XP	8586	NetJets, Columbus, Oh.	
N876SC*	96	Falcon 2000	24	Steelcase Inc. Grand Rapids, Mi.	N376SC
N876WB	77	Citation	500-0347	Schaefer Ambulance Service Inc. Van Nuys, Ca.	N500XY
N877A	01	Gulfstream 4SP	1461	Anadarko Petroleum Corp. Houston, Tx.	(N874RA)
N877B	04	Citation Bravo	550-1110	Cessna Aircraft Co. Wichita, Ks.	N.....
N877DM	95	Hawker 800XP	8279	Saturn Jets LLC. Waco, Tx.	N817H
N877FL	99	Beechjet 400A	RK-223	LandAmerica Financial Group Inc. Richmond, Va.	N777FL
N877G	95	Citation VII	650-7063	General Dynamics Land Systems, Sterling Heights, Mi.	N95CC
N877H	00	Challenger 604	5445	Household International Inc. Palwaukee, Il.	N604HD
N877J	93	Beechjet 400A	RK-69	Knier & Associates Inc. Cary, NC.	N877S
N877JG	75	Falcon 20F	325	GHS Liner LLC. Belleville, Mi.	(N325MC)
N877RB	95	Citation V Ultra	560-0318	SSS Ultra LLC. Miami Beach, Fl.	N877RF
N877RF	01	Citation Excel	560-5219	Reinhart FoodService Inc. La Crosse, Wi.	N5079H
N877S	01	Hawker 800XP	8560	Sparks Companies Inc. Fort Morgan, Co.	N50740
N877SL	96	Hawker 800XP	8323	Cresair Inc. Northvale, NJ.	N877S
N877W	04	390 Premier 1	RB-107	Georgia Crown Distributing Co. Columbus, Ga.	N61717
N878AG*	00	Citation Bravo	550-0941	Funair Corp. Miami, Fl.	N900SS
N878G	97	Gulfstream 4SP	1331	General Dynamics Corp. Dulles, DC.	N331GA
N878RM	83	Challenger 601	3012	Aviation Associates LLC. Houston, Tx.	N23BN
N878SM	97	Gulfstream 4SP	1319	Symax Aviation Inc. West Palm Beach, Fl.	N429GA
N879QS	98	Hawker 800XP	8379	NetJets, Columbus, Oh.	
N880CH	90	Astra-1125SP	045	Cloud Nine Aviation LLC. Los Angeles, Ca.	VH-FIS
N880CM	02	Citation Bravo	550-1032	W & M Air Inc. Somerset, Pa.	N.....
N880CR	97	Challenger 604	5356	Omnicare Management Co. Covington, Ky.	(N605AG)
N880DP	74	DC 9-32	47635	Detroit Pistons/Round Ball One Corp. Detroit, Mi.	N880RB
N880ET	01	Challenger 604	5514	Delek Group, Tel Aviv, Israel.	C-GJOE
N880G	95	Gulfstream 4SP	1286	General Dynamics Corp. Dulles, DC.	N464SP
N880GC	87	Gulfstream 4	1016	Guardian Industries Corp. Detroit, Mi.	N29GY
N880M	80	BAe 125/800A	8027	Intertape Polymer Mangement Corp. Bradenton, Fl.	N80CC
N880QS	02	Hawker 800XP	8570	NetJets, Columbus, Oh.	(N873QS)
N880RJ	75	Gulfstream II SP	159	Bentley Autojet LLC. New Castle, De.	(N397JT)
N880SP	96	Hawker 800XP	8298	D Squared Aviation LLC. Gary, In.	N298XP
N880WD	91	Gulfstream 4	1170	J Porter Enterprises Inc. Romulus, Mi.	N997BC
N880WE	78	Gulfstream 2	217	HBJ Leasing LLC. Waterford, Mi.	N880WD
N880Z	84	Learjet 35A	35A-591	Paper Moon Aviation Corp. Wheeling, Il.	N9ZB
N881CA	83	Learjet 35A	35A-508	United Agri Products Inc. Greeley, Co.	N7777B
N881CW	99	Hawker 800XP	8461	Flight Options LLC. Cleveland, Oh.	(N828LX)
N881DM	74	Sabre-40A	282-137	Michael Dorn Inc. Burbank, Ca.	(N666VC)
N881KS	98	CitationJet	525-0300	Kansas State University, Salina, Ks.	N300CQ
N881Q	00	Falcon 900EX	80	International Paper Co. White Plains, NY.	F-WWFV
N881TW	97	Challenger 604	5348	Terayan Communication Corp. Santa Clara, Ca.	C-GLWR
N882C	90	Challenger 601-3A	5065	Transit Air Services Inc. Morristown, NJ.	N601BF
N882CA	01	Learjet 45	45-155	ConAgra Foods Inc. Omaha, Ne.	N145MC
N882GA	96	Astra-1125SPX	082	DCT Services LLC. Denver, Co.	N121GV
N882KB	03	Citation X	750-0216	F Korbel & Brothers Inc. Guerneville, Ca.	N1268F
N882QS	00	Hawker 800XP	8482	NetJets, Columbus, Oh.	N43182
N882RB	85	Citation S/II	S550-0075	David Hutton, Killen, Al.	N882KB
N882SC	84	Learjet 35A	35A-590	ATI Jet Sales LLC. El Paso, Tx.	(N822SF)
N883KB	85	Citation III	650-0095	Beneto Inc. Sacramento, Ca.	N882KB
N883PF	00	Citation Excel	560-5085	Prestage Farms Inc. Clinton, NC.	N85XL
N883RT	94	Citation V	560-0260	W Heywood Fralin, Roanoke, Va.	N888RT
N883XL	74	Citation	500-0177	DiamondAire LLC. Waco, Tx.	(N431LC)
N884B	00	Citation Excel	560-5140	ElanAir Inc/Heritage Flight, Burlington, Vt.	N52655
N884BB	99	Citation Excel	560-5036	Olympus Aviation Inc. Minneapolis, Mn.	N36XL
N884L	93	Gulfstream 4SP	1212	Hewlett-Packard Co. San Jose, Ca.	N88HP
N884TW	01	Learjet 60	60-244	Trans West Air Service Inc. Salt Lake City, Ut.	N5031R
N884VC	02	Hawker 800XP	8584	Vitesse Corp. Greenfield, In.	N51384
N885	86	Falcon 900	6	Anheuser-Busch Companies Inc. St Louis, Mo.	N80F
N885BB	00	Citation Excel	560-5135	Olympus Aviation Inc. Minneapolis, Mn.	LV-ZXW
N885G	97	Gulfstream V	518	General Dynamics Corp. Dulles, DC.	(N55GV)

Reg	Yr	Type	c/n	Owner/Operator	Prev Regn

Reg	Yr	Type	c/n	Owner/Operator	Prev Regn
☐ N885KT	01	Gulfstream V	699	Troutt LLC. Tulsa, Ok. (was s/n 666).	N699GA
☐ N885M	99	Hawker 800XP	8410	Jimbob Aviation Inc. Westfield, Ma.	N315BK
☐ N885RR*	01	Gulfstream G200	055	Rabbit Run LLC. Dulles, Va.	N885AR
☐ N885TA	86	Gulfstream 4	1003	Yellowstone Aviation & Marine LLC. Bozeman, Mt.	N685TA
☐ N885TW	04	Challenger 300	20037	Learjet Inc. Wichita, Ks.	C-GZDS
☐ N886CA	01	Learjet 45	45-154	ConAgra Foods Inc. Omaha, Ne.	N3008P
☐ N886DC	98	Falcon 900B	177	FJ 900 Inc/Danaher Corp. Washington, DC.	F-WWFY
☐ N886DT	85	Gulfstream 3	463	Southlake Aviation LLC. Fort Worth, Tx.	N463GE
☐ N886G	02	Gulfstream G200	057	Electric Boat Corp. Groton, Ct.	N299GA
☐ N886QS	00	Hawker 800XP	8486	NetJets, Columbus, Oh.	
☐ N886R	79	Learjet 35A	35A-269	Colorado Structures Inc. Colorado Springs, Co.	N211WH
☐ N886S	78	HS 125/700A	7025	James Crystal Aviation LLC. West Palm Beach, Fl.	N7782
☐ N887DT	78	JetStar 2	5223	Deep South Aviation Inc. Fort Worth, Tx.	N886DT
☐ N887PA	88	Astra-1125	025	S Hawk Holdings Inc. Indianapolis-Terry, In.	N387PA
☐ N887QS	99	Hawker 800XP	8387	NetJets, Columbus, Oh.	
☐ N887WM	99	Global Express	9041	Challenger Administration LLC/Mente Corp. Seattle, Wa.	N195WM
☐ N887WS	02	Global Express	9120	Williams-Sonoma Inc. San Francisco, Ca.	N700FG
☐ N888AZ	84	Challenger 601	3024	C & C Enterprises Inc. Tompkins County, NY.	N93CR
☐ N888CJ	66	HS 125/1A	25084	Hawker Holdings Inc. Fort Lauderdale, Fl.	N890RC
☐ N888CP	88	Learjet 31	31-003	Ten Air Aircraft Corp. Minneapolis, Mn.	N331CC
☐ N888CW	98	Gulfstream V	545	Countrywide Home Loans Inc. Van Nuys, Ca.	N5GV
☐ N888CX	99	Learjet 45	45-044	Compar Foundation, Belgrade, Serbia.	D-CLUB
☐ N888DH	87	Challenger 601-3A	5014	R D Hubbard Enterprises Inc. Palm Springs, Ca.	N311GX
☐ N888DV	85	Learjet 25G	25G-370	Moana Management LLC. Sacramento, Ca.	N972H
☐ N888ES	90	Gulfstream 4	1120	C&S Aviation LLC/Executive Software International , Burbank.	N20H
☐ N888FA	72	Learjet 24D	24D-257	Intermountain Fixed Wing LC. Salt Lake City, Ut.	C-GHDP
☐ N888FJ	73	Falcon 10	4	Stone Aviation LLC. Denton, Tx.	EC-FTV
☐ N888FL	77	Citation 1/SP	501-0014	L & L Aviation Inc. Vicksburg, Ms.	N22TP
☐ N888GL	03	CitationJet CJ-2	525A-0201	Garmin International Inc. Olathe, Ks.	N.....
☐ N888JL	75	Citation	500-0242	Triple Eight LLC/Dialysis Laboratories Inc. Deland, Fl.	(N884DR)
☐ N888KU	94	CitationJet	525-0068	Sencon International Inc. Miami, Fl.	N303LC
☐ N888LK	02	Gulfstream G550	5012	Deerport Aviation Corp. Taipei, Taiwan.	N812GA
☐ N888LV*	82	Gulfstream 3	347	GC Asset Management LLC/Midtown Equities, NYC.	N545JT
☐ N888MC	66	Learjet 24	24-106	Kempt Ville Plane Parts Ltd. Wilmington, De.	N103RB
☐ N888ME	81	Falcon 50	41	Texas Aero Aircraft Sales Group, Waco, Tx.	N888MF
☐ N888MJ	73	Citation 1/SP	501-0446	First Choice Equipment Co. Glen Allen, (was s/n 500-0097).	N63CF
☐ N888ML	04	EMB-135BJ Legacy	14500818	New Macau Landmark Management Ltd.	PT-SIM
☐ N888MX	89	Gulfstream 4	1110	Maxim Aviation Co. Jeffco Airport, Co.	N526EE
☐ N888PM	92	Gulfstream 4	1195	Red, White & Blue Pictures Inc. Van Nuys, Ca.	N867CE
☐ N888RA	96	CitationJet	525-0135	Richard Auhll, Santa Barbara, Ca.	N5207A
☐ N888RK	98	CitationJet	525-0331	Kom Activity BV. Rotterdam, Holland.	
☐ N888RL	81	Citation II	550-0254	Heard, Robbins, Cloud et al, Houston, Tx.	N888RT
☐ N888RT	99	Citation Excel	560-5047	R T Oliver Investments Inc. Norman-University, Ok.	N838RT
☐ N888SF	02	CitationJet CJ-1	525-0480	Steiner Film Aviation Inc. Munich, Germany.	N5223Y
☐ N888SQ	96	Gulfstream 4SP	1305	Sprint/United Management Co. Kansas City, Mo.	N439GA
☐ N888SV	97	Citation V Ultra	560-0442	778 LLC. Huron, SD.	(N156JH)
☐ N888TJ	71	HS 125/731	25250	Crusader Aero Inc. Bata, Equatorial Guinea.	N7SJ
☐ N888TW	74	Learjet 24D	24D-292	Sierra American Corp. Addison, Tx.	N800PC
☐ N888TX	92	Citation VII	650-7003	Image Aviation LLC. Alpharetta, Ga.	(N650RJ)
☐ N888WS	94	Challenger 601-3R	5170	Williams-Sonoma Inc. San Francisco, Ca.	N166A
☐ N888XL	89	Citation II	550-0598	Citation II LLC. Richardson, Tx.	N7WY
☐ N888YF	02	BBJ-7BC	33036	Evergreen International SA. Panama City, Panama.	N110QS
☐ N888ZZ	84	BAe 125/800A	8017	Current Aviation Group Inc.	N217RM
☐ N889B	02	Citation Bravo	550-1047	MedEquip Inc. Grand Raoids, Mi.	N5231S
☐ N889CA	00	Learjet 45	45-132	ConAgra Inc. Omaha, Ne.	N132LJ
☐ N889DW	97	Learjet 60	60-117	New Vistas LLC. Seattle, Wa.	
☐ N889FA	80	Citation II/SP	551-0036	First American Title Insurance Co. Santa Ana, Ca.	N3170B
☐ N889G	01	Gulfstream G200	046	General Dynamics Network Systems, Needham, Ma.	PR-MEN
☐ N889JC	75	Gulfstream II SP	158	Amador LLC. Dallas, Tx.	N2S
☐ N889NC	99	BBJ-7AV	30070	Newsflight Inc. Los Angeles, Ca.	N18NC
☐ N889RA*	80	Sabre-65	465-22	The Glebe Group Inc. Oklahoma City, Ok.	N883RA
☐ N890A	99	Gulfstream 4SP	1396	Aluminum Co of America, West Mifflin, Pa.	N396GA
☐ N890CW	01	Hawker 800XP	8510	Flight Options LLC. Cleveland, Oh.	(N831LX)
☐ N890FH	01	Falcon 900EX	99	Med Equip Inc/Forest Health Industries, Grand Rapids, Mi.	N996EX
☐ N890MC	90	Citation III	650-0199	McLeod USA Integrated Business Systems, Cedar Rapids, Ia.	N65KB
☐ N890SP	01	Hawker 800XP	8530	NiSource Corporate Services Co. Gary, In.	

Reg	Yr	Type	c/n	Owner/Operator	Prev Regn

Reg	Yr	Type	c/n	Owner/Operator	Prev Regn
N890TJ	68	Gulfstream 2	23	Bizjet International Sales & Support Inc. Tulsa, Ok.	N7TJ
N891CA	74	Citation	500-0168	Gulf Atlantic Airways/University Air Center, Gainesville, Fl	(N46JA)
N892PB	79	Citation II	550-0070	Tansoar Inc. Rogers, Ar.	N550KA
N892QS	03	Hawker 800XP	8592	RenaissanceRe Holdings Ltd. Hamilton, Bermuda.	
N892SB	78	Falcon 20F-5B	379	Security Benefit Group Inc. Topeka, Ks.	N62570
N892TM	72	Gulfstream II SP	121	Trayton Aviation LLC. Burbank, Ca.	N721PL
N893CW	02	Hawker 800XP	8603	Flight Options LLC. Cleveland, Oh.	(N803CW)
N893QS	99	Hawker 800XP	8393	NetJets, Columbus, Oh.	
N894C	01	CitationJet CJ-2	525A-0013	GHIZ Enterprises Inc. Thousand Oaks, Ca.	N8940
N894CA	98	Hawker 800XP	8366	Collins & Aikman Corp. Charlotte, NC.	(CS-MAI)
N894TW	81	Westwind-1124	354	Bulard Air Services LLC. NYC.	N124LS
N895CC	82	Challenger 600S	1039	Blue Bear Air Inc. Bozeman, Mt.	N722HP
N895J	70	Learjet 24B	24B-213	E M Aviation Inc. Laredo, Tx.	N95AB
N895QS	03	Hawker 800XP	8606	NetJets, Columbus, Oh.	N60506
N896CG	03	Citation Bravo	550-1055	Gallo Air Inc. Guatemala City, Guatemala.	N.....
N896CW	00	Hawker 800XP	8516	Flight Options LLC. Cleveland, Oh.	(N832LX)
N896QS	03	Hawker 800XP	8640	NetJets, Columbus, Oh.	N640XP
N897CW	86	BAe 125/800A	8077	Flight Options LLC. Cleveland, Oh.	(N808LX)
N897MC	99	Citation Bravo	550-0914	Manitowoc Co. Manitowoc, Wi.	N5105F
N898CB	91	Citation V	560-0097	Jetco V LLC. Danbury, Ct.	(N6790L)
N898CT	98	Falcon 2000	60	Nortom Corp. Concord, Ca.	N524SA
N898EW	93	Challenger 601-3A	5134	WFBNW NA. Salt Lake City, Ut.	N511WN
N898MC	02	Citation Excel	560-5244	Manitowoc Co. Manitowoc, Wi.	N244XL
N898PA	97	Learjet 60	60-111	PA Lear 60-111 LLC. Carrollton, Tx.	N221FX
N898QS	02	Hawker 800XP	8593	NetJets, Columbus, Oh.	
N898R	99	Challenger 604	5408	Resources Aviation Inc. Fort Lauderdale, Fl.	C-GLXW
N898TA	00	Beechjet 400A	RK-295	Flight Options LLC. Cleveland, Oh.	(N463LX)
N899AB	78	HS 125/700A	NA0230	Ogden Flight Services Group Inc. Bridgeport, Ct.	N881S
N899B	03	Citation Bravo	550-1073	Northern Air Inc. Grand Rapids, Mi.	N.....
N899CS	92	Learjet 31A	31A-052	CommScope Inc of NC. Catawba, NC.	N75MC
N899DC	99	Citation Bravo	550-0899	Dixie Chopper Bravo LLC. Coatesville, In.	N5076K
N899DM	78	HS 125/700A	7028	ASG Inc/Markin Aviation LLC. New Windsor, NY.	N7728
N899GA	69	Gulfstream 2	43	Helicopter Systems Inc. Mesa, Az.	(N247LG)
N899MA	80	Citation II	550-0121	Mississippi Aviation Services, Jackson, Ms.	N896MA
N899SC	02	Hawker 800XP	8602	SCI Texas Funeral Services Inc. Houston, Tx.	N61702
N899TA	00	Beechjet 400A	RK-292	Flight Options LLC. Cleveland, Oh.	(N462LX)
N899U	02	Falcon 2000	199	International Paper Co. White Plains, NY.	N2295
N900AD	71	HS 125/400A	NA769	MBNA Corp. Greater Wilmington, De.	N369JH
N900AJ	69	Learjet 25	25-027	Smartparts Inc. Fort Lauderdale, Fl.	N500DL
N900AK	71	Gulfstream II SP	108	Private Jet Inc. New Canaan, Ct.	N200GH
N900AL	89	Gulfstream 4	1097	Abbott Laboratories Inc. Waukegan, Il.	N402GA
N900BF	77	Gulfstream II SP	206	J I Aviation LLC/Apex Oil Co. St Louis, Mo.	N2PK
N900BJ	77	Learjet 35A	35A-123	N900BJ LLC. West Columbia, SC.	N900JE
N900BT	00	CitationJet CJ-1	525-0377	Techni Airplane LLC. Armonk, NY.	N15C
N900BZ	98	Falcon 900EX	37	ZG Aircraft Leasing LLC/Boulder Aviation LLC. Tampa, Fl.	N327K
N900CH	97	Falcon 50EX	264	Cardinal Healthcare/Cardal Inc. Columbus, Oh.	C-6BHD
N900CM	01	Falcon 50EX	321	Excel Corp. Wichita, Ks.	N321EX
N900CP	79	HS 125/700A	NA0248	Allied Services Inc. Norfolk, Va.	N900CQ
N900CS	91	Falcon 900B	104	Charles Schwab & Co. San Francisco, Ca.	N881G
N900CX	97	Falcon 900EX	19	ACXIOM Corp. Little Rock, Ar.	N96DS
N900DB	78	JetStar 2	5225	Banner Associates Inc. Lake Forest, Il.	TC-IHS
N900DH	72	Gulfstream 2	111	Business Jet Services Ltd. Dallas-Love, Tx.	N900BR
N900DL	89	Astra-1125	030	Duro-Last Inc/Duro-Last Roofing Inc. Sigourney, Ia.	N902G
N900DP	81	Challenger 600S	1036	BusAv/Del Inc. Aiken, SC.	N66MF
N900DS	93	CitationJet	525-0032	Great Southern Bank, Springfield, Mo.	N32VP
N900DV	94	Falcon 900B	148	Vecellio Management Services Inc. West Palm Beach, Fl.	N522AC
N900DW	99	Falcon 900B	179	Whiteco Industries Inc. Merrillville, In.	N900FJ
N900E	93	Citation V	560-0206	N900E LLC. Stuart, Fl.	N560TX
N900EB	04	Citation Sovereign	680-0008	Subaru of New England Inc. Norwood, Ma.	N.....
N900ES	98	Challenger 604	5381	Earth Star Inc. Burbank, Ca.	C-GLYH
N900FH	96	Falcon 900EX	6	Airwork Jet Ltd. Auckland, NZ.	N143DL
N900FS	76	Westwind-1124	191	Franks Petroleum Inc. Shreveport, La.	(N900RR)
N900G	75	Citation	500-0268	Zesch Restaurants Inc. San Angelo, Tx.	A6-RKH
N900GB	87	Gulfstream 4	1025	B-Jet LLC/TISMA Inc. Dulles, Va.	N928ST
N900GC	76	Citation	500-0298	Granite Construction Co. Watsonville, Ca.	N5298J
N900GG	70	Learjet 24B	24B-216	Mach Aviation LLC. Houston, Tx.	N777LB

Reg	Yr	Type	c/n	Owner/Operator	Prev Regn
☐ N900GW	99	CitationJet	525-0323	Joe Morten & Son Inc. South Sioux City, Ne.	
☐ N900H	90	Challenger 601-3A	5080	Hoak Travel Inc. Dallas, Tx.	N903TA
☐ N900HA	01	CitationJet CJ-2	525A-0039	Auberach Aeronautic Asociates Inc. East Hampton, NY.	(N525L)
☐ N900HC	03	Falcon 900EX EASY	127	Group Falcon EX Holdings LLC. Portland, Or.	F-WWFD
☐ N900HD	01	Falcon 900EX	103	NII Aviation Inc. Dulles, Va.	N103FJ
☐ N900HE	89	Falcon 900	68	Group Holdings EG Inc. Fort Worth, Tx.	N900HC
☐ N900HG	95	Falcon 900EX	1	Jetflight Aviation Inc. Lugano-Agno, Switzerland.	PH-ERP
☐ N900JC	78	Learjet 35A	35A-178	AirNet Systems Inc. Columbus, Oh.	(N104AA)
☐ N900JT	81	HS 125/700A	NA0303	J T Inc. Southfield, Mi.	N678W
☐ N900KD	93	Falcon 900B	131	Oakmont Corp. Los Angeles, Ca.	N900VT
☐ N900KJ	02	Falcon 900C	199	Kendall-Jackson Wine Estates Ltd. Santa Rosa, Ca.	N199FJ
☐ N900KX	01	Falcon 900EX	98	Juniper Networks/Adventair LLC-VC Jets LLC. San Jose, Ca.	N998EX
☐ N900LA	83	Gulfstream 3	379	Sonoran Charters LLC. Scottsdale, Az.	N28QQ
☐ N900LC	00	Falcon 900C	186	DB Aviation Inc. Waukegan, Il.	F-WWFJ
☐ N900LM	87	Citation S/II	S550-0145	CB Capital Aviation LLC. Centerville, Oh.	4X-CPT
☐ N900LS	99	Gulfstream 4SP	1401	Limited Inc. Columbus, Oh.	N401GA
☐ N900MF	79	Citation II	550-0338	KAF Flying LLC. Menlo Park, Ca.. (was 551-0016).	N900SE
☐ N900MG	88	Falcon 900B	67	The Scotts Co. Columbus, Oh.	N900MA
☐ N900MJ	99	Falcon 900EX	57	ACM Aviation Inc. San Jose, Ca.	N900MT
☐ N900MK	98	Falcon 900EX	29	McKesson Information Solutions Inc. Atlanta-De Kalb, Ga.	N25UD
☐ N900MN	93	Citation VII	650-7027	MNI Equipment Inc. Scottsdale, Az.	N657ER
☐ N900MV	03	Falcon 900EX EASY	131	Bloomberg Services LLC. Monmouth County, NJ.	VP-BFM
☐ N900NA	66	Learjet 24A	24A-111	RBS Aviation Group Inc. Hampton, Ga.	N44WD
☐ N900NB	01	Falcon 900C	190	New World Jet Corp. Ronkonkoma, NY.	F-WWFI
☐ N900NE	89	Falcon 900	83	Banc One Management Corp. Columbus, Oh.	N900WG
☐ N900P	01	Learjet 45	45-173	Riverside Financial LLC. Wisconsin Dells, Wi.	
☐ N900PJ	82	Learjet 55	55-064	L55 Jet Partners LLC. Anchorage, Ak.	N121LT
☐ N900PS	91	Citation V	560-0118	Papa Sierra LLC. San Luis Obsipo, Ca.	N626SL
☐ N900Q	96	Falcon 900EX	10	TP Aviation LLC/Tarrant Partners LP. Fort Worth, Tx.	N22CS
☐ N900QS	00	Citation X	750-0123	NetJets, Columbus, Oh.	(N51038)
☐ N900R	94	Learjet 31A	31A-101	NASCAR Inc. Daytona Beach, Fl.	N293SA
☐ N900RA*	67	Falcon 20C	59	Royal Air Freight Inc. Waterford, Mi.	N159MV
☐ N900RL	90	Gulfstream 4	1150	RL Aviation LLC. Van Nuys, Ca.	N386AG
☐ N900RX*	99	Falcon 900C	183	Roux Investment Management LLC. Campbell, Ca.	(N900WP)
☐ N900SA	66	DC 9-15	45775	HW Aviation LLC. Chicago, Il.	N40SH
☐ N900SB	97	Falcon 900EX	26	SBC Management Services Inc. San Antonio, Tx.	F-WWFX
☐ N900SJ	87	Falcon 900	19	Sid R Bass Inc. Fort Worth, Tx.	N414FJ
☐ N900SM	89	Citation V	560-0014	Servicemaster Holding Corp. Downers Grove, Il.	(N650ST)
☐ N900SN	02	Falcon 900EX	117	First Quality/SN 117 Inc. Farmingdale, NY.	(N900EX)
☐ N900SX	94	Falcon 900B	139	Elon Musk, El Segundo, Ca.	(N523AG)
☐ N900TA	74	Citation	500-0182	Mapleleaf Acquisitions Inc. Wilmington, De.	N23W
☐ N900TG	95	Falcon 900B	155	CSIM Air LLC. Portland, Oh.	N155FJ
☐ N900TN	83	Westwind-Two	400	AirCorp Inc. Tuscaloosa, Al.	N900PA
☐ N900TR	97	Falcon 900B	170	TRT Juniper Holdings LLC. Corpus Christi, Tx.	N900DA
☐ N900UD*	91	Citation VI	650-0213	Cessna Aircraft Co. Wichita, Ks.	N900JD
☐ N900VL	88	Falcon 900B	60	Outfitter Aviation LLC. Medford, Or.	N91TH
☐ N900VP	80	Westwind-1124	289	Venture Air LLC. Newark, De.	VR-CIL
☐ N900WK	88	Falcon 900B	57	Kellogg Co. Battle Creek, Mi.	N441FJ
☐ N900WR	00	Gulfstream 4SP	1416	Wayne Reaud, Beaumont, Tx.	N416GA
☐ N900WY	04	Challenger 300	20035	M & N Aviation, Casper, Wy.	C-GZET
☐ N900YP	02	Falcon 900EX	114	Villages Equipment Co. Leesburg, Fl.	(N114EX)
☐ N901C	77	JetStar 2	5218	BCJ Aviation LLC. Van Nuys, Ca.	N816RD
☐ N901CJ	98	CitationJet	525-0278	Inca Aviation LLC. Scottsdale, Az.	N100SM
☐ N901DK	04	Citation Excel XLS	560-5505	Keffer Management Co. Charlotte, NC.	N.....
☐ N901EB	00	CitationJet CJ-2	525A-0008	CMH Homes Inc. Knoxville, Tn.	N900EB
☐ N901FH	81	Gulfstream 3	333	Coca-Cola Bottling Co Consolidated, Charlotte, NC.	N50PM
☐ N901GW	01	CitationJet CJ-1	525-0470	Joe Morten & Son Inc. South Sioux City, Ne.	N.....
☐ N901K	97	Hawker 800XP	8329	Ada Rossin/Rosetree Inc. Allegheny County, Pa.	N329XP
☐ N901MD	98	Falcon 900EX	38	MacDermid Inc. Arapahoe, Co.	N68CG
☐ N901MK	85	Falcon 50	157	McKesson Information Solutions Inc. Atlanta-De Kalb, Ga.	N911HB
☐ N901NB	82	Citation 1/SP	501-0255	Robert Morgan Enterprises, Tracy, Ca.	N400LX
☐ N901P	00	Learjet 31A	31A-199	Nielsen-Wurster Group Inc. Princeton, NJ.	N900P
☐ N901QS	99	Citation X	750-0102	Sun Microsystems Inc. Portland, Or.	N51995
☐ N901SB	02	Falcon 900EX EASY	122	SBC Management Services Inc. San Antonio, Tx.	F-WWFX
☐ N901SS	00	Falcon 900C	187	EOS Aviation LLC. San Jose, Ca.	N181FJ
☐ N901TA	93	Challenger 601-3R	5141	Flight Options LLC. Cleveland, Oh.	(N613LX)

Reg	Yr	Type	c/n	Owner/Operator	Prev Regn
N901TF	99	Falcon 50EX	285	Tyson Foods Inc. Bentonville, Ar.	F-WWHM
N901WG	73	Gulfstream 2	126	Gary, Williams et al, Stuart, Fl. 'Wings of Justice'	N416K
N902	96	Gulfstream 4SP	1310	Owens-Illinois General Inc. Swanton, Oh.	(N2425)
N902AG	02	Challenger 604	5512	AGCO Corp. DeKalb-Peachtree, Ga.	N512SH
N902DD	73	Citation	500-0126	Del Mar Citation LLC. Las Vegas, Nv.	N404MA
N902DK	94	Citation II	550-0732	Keffer Management Co. Charlotte, NC.	N101AF
N902F	93	Citation VII	650-7022	TF Aircraft LLC/TGF Investments LP. Palatine, Il.	N902RM
N902L	02	Gulfstream G400	1504	Pinehurst Timber LLC. Portland, Or.	(N402QS)
N902MP	03	Challenger 604	5559	MP Air Inc. Morgantown, WV.	N559JA
N902NC	90	Falcon 900	97	Newell Co. Rockford, Il.	(N900UU)
N902P	86	Beechjet 400	RJ-15	Flightworks Inc. Hickory, NC.	N73BE
N902QS	95	Citation X	750-0002	NetJets, Columbus, Oh.	N752CX
N902RD	03	390 Premier 1	RB-74	Hensel Phelps Construction Co. Leesburg, Va.	N61474
N902RL	83	Learjet 55	55-087	RL Aviation LLC. Van Nuys, Ca.	N554PF
N902SB	00	Falcon 50EX	308	SBC Management Services Inc. San Antonio, Tx.	F-WWHL
N902TA	93	Challenger 601-3R	5139	Flight Options LLC. Cleveland, Oh.	(N612LX)
N902TF	00	Falcon 50EX	303	Tyson Foods Inc. Bentonville, Ar.	F-WWHE
N902VP	91	Citation VI	650-0209	Gonsalves & Santucci Inc. Concord, Ca.	N198D
N902WC	68	B 737-247	19613	Nordam Group Inc. Tulsa, Ok.	N308VA
N902WG	81	B 737-2H6	22620	Gary Aircraft, Stuart, Fl.	N22620
N903AG	94	Learjet 60	60-045	AGCO Corp. DeKalb-Peachtree, Ga.	N711VJ
N903AI	76	Learjet 35A	35A-084	ALCO Holdings LLC/Agnew Co. Portland, Or.	(N696JH)
N903AM	97	Learjet 60	60-104	Med 4 Home Inc. Tampa, Fl.	N83WM
N903CG	01	Beechjet 400A	RK-333	Sims Enterprises Inc. Norfolk, Va.	(N72FL)
N903FH	01	Citation Excel	560-5160	Coca-Cola Bottling Co Consolidated, Charlotte, NC.	N595A
N903G	84	Gulfstream 3	422	Owens-Illinois General Inc. Swanton, Oh.	N407CA
N903HC	96	Learjet 45	45-010	Hytrol Conveyor Co. Jonesboro, Ar.	N41DP
N903JC	83	Learjet 55	55-081	Pacific Coast Group Inc. Las Vegas, Nv.	N777MQ
N903QS	01	Citation X	750-0162	NetJets, Columbus, Oh.	
N903SB	00	Falcon 50EX	309	SBC Management Services Inc. San Antonio, Tx.	F-WWHM
N903SC	77	HS 125/700A	NA0218	Caribbean Skies Aviation LLC. St Thomas, USVI.	N804FF
N903TF	02	Global Express	9097	Tyson Foods Inc. Bentonville, Ar.	C-GIPD
N903VP	99	Citation Bravo	550-0903	David Albin, Santa Fe, NM.	N14HB
N904BB	99	Citation Bravo	550-0904	Nunes Co. Salinas, Ca.	N5093Y
N904BW*	85	BAe 125/800A	8042	Robert Mondavi Corp. Oakland, Ca.	N804RM
N904DP	02	CitationJet CJ-1	525-0503	BusAv/Del Inc. Aiken, SC.	N.....
N904DS	02	Global Express	9118	DSWA LLC/Snyder Communications LP. Dulles, Va.	N700EZ
N904GP	89	BAe 125/800A	NA0448	Godwin Pumps of America Inc. Bridgeport, NJ.	N60TG
N904LX*	04	EMB-135BJ Legacy	145780	Flight Options LLC. Cleveland, Oh.	N780SG
N904QS	03	Citation X	750-0210	NetJets, Columbus, Oh.	N51666
N904SB	99	Falcon 50EX	284	SBC Management Services Inc. San Antonio, Tx.	F-WWHL
N904SJ	89	Citation II	550-0604	SJ Aire Aviation Co. Laredo, Tx.	N887SA
N905B*	00	Falcon 2000	132	JRB Air LLC. Bellevue, Wa.	N97NX
N905FJ	86	Falcon 900	5	Maughold Ltd. Roadtown, Tortola, BVI.	(D-ACDC)
N905LC	88	Citation II	550-0581	Special Services Corp. Greenville, SC.	(N13007)
N905QS	01	Citation X	750-0105	NetJets, Columbus, Oh.	
N906AS	00	Citation Encore	560-0547	A T Shaw Co. Concord, Ca.	N68MA
N906QS	03	Citation X	750-0206	NetJets, Columbus, Oh.	
N906TF	98	Challenger 604	5366	Tyson Foods Inc. Fayetteville, Ar.	C-GJFC
N906WK	91	Falcon 900	102	Kellogg Co. Battle Creek, Mi.	N467FJ
N907DF	86	Citation III	650-0120	Duraflame Inc. Stockton, Ca.	N30NM
N907JE	95	Beechjet 400A	RK-107	Bleka Aviation LLC. Romeoville, Il.	N733MK
N907QS	02	Citation X	750-0201	NetJets, Columbus, Oh.	
N907R	82	Learjet 35A	35A-488	Thomas Thornton, Austin, Tx.	N900R
N907RT	75	Citation	500-0255	JODA LLC. Chesterfield, Mo.	(N255RG)
N907TF	77	Falcon 10	107	Tyson Foods Inc. Bentonville, Ar.	N91BP
N907WS	89	Challenger 601-3A	5048	Shidler Investment Corp. Honolulu, Hi.	N716RD
N908CA	95	Falcon 900B	151	CMI Aviation Inc. Urbana, Il.	EC-HHK
N908CH	78	Falcon 20F-5	383	Lear 55 LLC/Bestjets of Million Air St Louis LLC. Mo.	N900CH
N908JB	91	Falcon 900B	112	Strange Bird Inc. Los Angeles, Ca.	N248AG
N908JE	69	B 727-31	20115	JEGE Inc. Wilmington, De.	N505LS
N908QS	03	Citation X	750-0108	NetJets, Columbus, Oh.	N51744
N908R	92	Beechjet 400A	RK-44	Wolverine Tube Inc. Huntsville-Decatur, Al.	N404VP
N908TF	77	Falcon 10	102	Tyson Foods Inc. Bentonville, Ar.	N61BP
N908VZ	97	Hawker 800XP	8313	Verizon Communications, White Plains, NY.	N84BA
N909AS	93	Falcon 900B	127	Albertsons Inc. Boise, Id.	N390F

Reg	Yr	Type	c/n	Owner/Operator	Prev Regn

Reg	Yr	Type	c/n	Owner/Operator	Prev Regn
☐ N909GA	04	Gulfstream G450	4009	Rabbit Run LLC. Washington, DC.	
☐ N909JE	74	Gulfstream 2B	151	Hyperion Air Inc. Wilmington, De.	(N988JE)
☐ N909M	98	CitationJet	525-0249	Marseille-Kliniken AG/VDSE GmbH. Hamburg, Germany.	N5214L
☐ N909MK	79	Gulfstream II SP	241	M K Aviation LLC. Southfield, Mi.	(N902MK)
☐ N909MM	01	Falcon 900EX	88	Massachusetts Mutual Life Insurance Co. Bedford, Ma.	F-W...
☐ N909PM	98	Falcon 900B	176	Danaher Corp. Washington, DC.	(N900SM)
☐ N909PS	77	Citation 1/SP	501-0008	Silversteel America Inc/Aviation Beauport Ltd. Jersey, C.I.	N900PS
☐ N909QS	96	Citation X	750-0009	NetJets, Columbus, Oh.	N96TX
☐ N909RR	81	Gulfstream 3	332	Ramsey Asset Management LLC. McLean, Va.	N921AS
☐ N909RX	94	Gulfstream 4SP	1239	Hoechst Marion Roussel Inc. Kansas City, Mo.	N1JN
☐ N909SK	95	Learjet 60	60-060	SK Logistics Inc. St Augustine, Fl.	N175BA
☐ N909ST	98	Beechjet 400A	RK-194	Star Transport Inc. Morton, Il.	N194BJ
☐ N909TF	75	Falcon 10	51	Tyson Foods Inc. Bentonville, Ar.	N51BP
☐ N910CN	81	Falcon 50	59	Skyfarm LLC. Hillsborough, Ca.	N900JB
☐ N910CS	92	Falcon 900B	126	Charles Schwab & Co. San Francisco, Ca.	N733HL
☐ N910DC	98	Gulfstream V	544	Chrysler Pentastar Aviation, Waterford, Mi.	N644GA
☐ N910DP	85	Citation III	650-0081	Westair Corp. Duluth, Ga.	(N881BA)
☐ N910G	78	Citation 1/SP	501-0083	AeroJet LLC. Gardner, Il.	N101LD
☐ N910GA	04	Gulfstream G450	4010	Gulfstream Aerospace Corp. Savannah, Ga.	
☐ N910HM	91	Citation II	550-0674	Marklite LLC. Manassas, Va.	N65TP
☐ N910JD	99	Hawker 800XP	8420	DMG Air LLC/Dawson Management Group Inc. Big Fork, Mt.	N31340
☐ N910JW	87	Falcon 900	31	S C Johnson & Son Inc/Johnson's Wax, Racine, Wi.	N900FJ
☐ N910KB	83	Challenger 601	3007	David Booth & co-owners, Van Nuys, Ca.	N711SZ
☐ N910MT	79	Citation II	550-0075	S L Air International LLC. Hinsdale, Il.	N710MT
☐ N910MW	01	Falcon 900EX	85	Wilson Aviation LLC. Glacier International, Mt.	(N410MW)
☐ N910Q	95	Falcon 900B	156	Tarrant Partners LP. Fort Worth, Tx.	HL7301
☐ N910QS	00	Citation X	750-0110	NetJets, Columbus, Oh.	
☐ N910RB	81	Citation II	550-0267	New York Central Mutual Fire Insurance Co. Edmeston, NY.	XA-AOC
☐ N910S	90	Gulfstream 4	1155	200 PS Aircraft Holdings Inc. Chicago, Il.	N1761B
☐ N910V	01	Gulfstream V	636	200 PS Aircraft Holdings Inc. Chicago, Il.	N556GA
☐ N911AE	77	Learjet 35A	35A-109	Keystone Aviation LLC/Million Air, Salt Lake City, Ut.	N506GP
☐ N911AJ	74	Learjet 25B	25B-163	AASP-Air Ambulance Support Programmes Inc. Houston, Tx.	(N65RC)
☐ N911CB	01	Citation Encore	560-0604	Commerce Bank NA. Kansas City, Mo.	N.....
☐ N911CR	71	JetStar-731	5150	Juan Rodriguez, Sarasota/Advanced Airways Inc. Lantana, Fl.	N721CR
☐ N911CU	78	Westwind-1124	246	Medic Air Corp. Reno, NV.	N101SV
☐ N911DG	69	Falcon 20C	162	Aero Taxi Rockford Inc. Rockford, Il.	(N389AC)
☐ N911DT	82	Falcon 20F-5B	471	Alpha Charlie Aviation LLC. Addison, Tx.	N44JQ
☐ N911DX	83	Learjet 35A	35A-499	Sales Operating Control Services, Littleton, Co.	N1TS
☐ N911GM	72	Citation	500-0048	JetSet International, Wilmington, De.	N67JR
☐ N911LM	71	Learjet 25C	25C-070	Covenant Sales & Leasing Inc. New Orleans, La.	C-FHZU
☐ N911ML	79	Learjet 35A	35A-256	Buck Air LLC. Monterey, Ca.	(N66PJ)
☐ N911MM	77	Citation Eagle	501-0030	MercMed LLC/Mercury Air Group Inc. Burbank, Ca.	(N911MU)
☐ N911NP	98	CitationJet	525-0273	Kingfisher Aviation LC. Waterloo, Ia.	(N525HC)
☐ N911RF	73	Learjet 25B	25B-138	Covenant Sales & Leasing Inc. New Orleans, La.	N73LJ
☐ N911SP	78	Westwind-1124	244	FlightStar Inc. Van Nuys, Ca.	N124PA
☐ N912CW	01	EMB-135BJ Legacy	145412	Flight Options LLC. Cleveland, Oh.	(N135JM)
☐ N912DA	69	Jet Commander-B	147	Agro Air Associates Inc. Miami, Fl.	(N888MP)
☐ N912QS	96	Citation X	750-0012	NetJets, Columbus, Oh.	N966H
☐ N912SH	96	Beechjet 400A	RK-128	The Harrell Corp. Tampa, Fl.	N1108Y
☐ N912TB	90	Learjet 31	31-024	Bradshaw Aviation LLC. Addison, Tx.	N92EC
☐ N913BJ	89	Citation V	560-0011	Walco Air LLC/Walters Management LLC. Greenville, SC.	N700TF
☐ N913GA	04	Gulfstream G450	4013	Gulfstream Aerospace Corp. Savannah, Ga.	
☐ N913MC	87	Beechjet 400	RJ-22	Napa Valley Jet Partners LLC. Napa, Ca.	N913SF
☐ N913MK	84	Gulfstream 3	407	Mary Kay Inc. Dallas, Tx.	N407GA
☐ N913QS	99	Citation X	750-0113	NetJets, Columbus, Oh.	
☐ N913RC	73	Citation	500-0059	East Alabama Feed Supplements Co. Fulton County, Ga.	N40PD
☐ N913V	83	HS 125/700A	NA0345	Heritage Aviation LLC. Jacksonville, Fl.	(N313VR)
☐ N914BD	02	Gulfstream V	690	J B Ivey & Co. Salisbury, NC.	N690GA
☐ N914CD	74	Citation	500-0150	James Lee Sr. Portland, Or.	N9V
☐ N914DD	89	Falcon 900	80	Dillard Department Stores Inc. Little Rock, Ar.	N914BD
☐ N914DM	81	Westwind-1124	357	MCL Transportation Inc. Chicago, Il.	N357BC
☐ N914J	00	Gulfstream V	615	Metromedia Aircraft Co. Teterboro, NJ.	N572GA
☐ N914KA	78	Gulfstream II SP	214	Krystal Air LLC. Hillsboro, Or.	N214NW
☐ N914MH	70	Gulfstream II SP	91	Cinema Aircraft Executive Transportation, Hillsboro, Or.	N81FC
☐ N914MM	79	Westwind-1124	250	The Wisdom Center Inc. Denton, Tx.	(N250KD)
☐ N914SH	98	Beechjet 400A	RK-193	HSI Air Travel LLC. Boulder, Co.	N13US

Reg	Yr	Type	c/n	Owner/Operator	Prev Regn
N914SP	04	Citation Sovereign	680-0020	Olympia Investments Inc. Pleasanton, Ca.	N5245U
N914X	95	Challenger 601-3R	5185	Xerox Corp. White Plains, NY.	N611CC
N915AM	01	Hawker 800XP	8574	WFBNW NA. Salt Lake City, Ut.	N51274
N915BD	91	Challenger 601-3A	5091	Dillard Department Stores Inc. Little Rock, Ar.	C-GLXM
N915GA	04	Gulfstream G450	4015	Gulfstream Aerospace Corp. Savannah, Ga.	
N915QS	97	Citation X	750-0015	NetJets, Columbus, Oh.	N326SU
N915RB	98	Citation X	750-0042	FHC Flight Services Inc. Norfolk, Va.	N95CM
N915RP	75	Citation	500-0270	Romeo Papa Holdings Inc. El Paso, Tx.	N501DR
N915US	76	Learjet 24B	24B-189	MTW Aerospace Inc. Montgomery, Al. (status ?).	N711DX
N916BD	94	Learjet 31A	31A-093	Dillard Department Stores Inc. Little Rock, Ar.	N4031K
N916CS	00	Citation Excel	560-5153	Avlease LLC. Ann Arbor, Mi.	N5105F
N916GR	02	Gulfstream G200	067	Gene Reed Enterprises Inc. Charleston, SC.	N367GA
N916QS	00	Citation X	750-0116	NetJets, Columbus, Oh.	
N916RC	73	Citation	500-0061	Swanson Charters Inc. Punta Gorda, Fl.	N52AJ
N917BD	94	Learjet 31A	31A-094	Dillard Department Stores Inc. Little Rock, Ar.	N31AX
N917BE	80	Westwind-1124	291	Basler Electric Co. Highland, Il.	N124WK
N917EE	01	Citation Excel	560-5158	Capital Air Services Inc. Dallas-Love, Tx.	N5151D
N917GA	04	Gulfstream G450	4017	Gulfstream Aerospace Corp. Savannah, Ga.	
N917GL	02	Global Express	9117	Texas Instruments Inc. McKinney, Tx.	N700EY
N917JC	94	Falcon 50	250	Tiercel Ltd Quito, Ecuador.	N277JW
N917JG	83	Falcon 200	490	Tiercel Ltd. St Thomas, USVI.	N917JC
N917R	98	Global Express	9008	Navair LLC. Ronkonkoma, NY.	(N90005)
N917RG	04	CitationJet CJ-3	525B-0010	Cessna Aircraft Co. Wichita, Ks.	N5097H
N917SB	80	Falcon 50	14	Air Zenith LLC. White Plains, NY.	N955E
N917SC	81	Learjet 35A	35A-440	N917SC Ltd. Fort Lauderdale, Fl.	(N354EM)
N917VZ	96	Gulfstream 4SP	1292	Verizon Communications, White Plains, NY.	N1GT
N917W	91	Gulfstream 4	1158	Evergreen International Aviation Inc. McMinnville, Or.	N17582
N918BD	92	Citation V	560-0173	Aerocentro de Servicios CA. Caracas, Venezuela.	N68881
N918BG	80	Gulfstream 3	300	BHG Flights LLC/ECFS Inc. Easton, Md.	N71TJ
N918CC	97	Gulfstream 4SP	1335	Astor Street Asset Management Inc. Chicago, Il.	N720BA
N918JM	00	Falcon 50EX	304	999 Aviation LLC. DuPage, Il.	F-WWHF
N918MJ	94	Astra-1125SPX	073	MJB Tri-Motor LLC. DuPage, Il.	N173W
N918QS	03	Citation X	750-0223	NetJets, Columbus, Oh.	N.....
N918SS	79	Westwind-1124	263	Jetstream Enterprises LLC. Chicago, Il.	N29PC
N919BT	85	Westwind-Two	434	Navsink Corp. Newark, De.	N187EC
N919CT	88	Gulfstream 4	1051	Cell Therapeutics Inc. Seattle, Wa.	N399CC
N919DS	00	Astra-1125SPX	127	General Dynamics Decision Systems Inc. Scottsdale, Az.	N247PS
N919QS	03	Citation X	750-0224	NetJets, Columbus, Oh.	N.....
N919RT	02	Hawker 800XP	8607	CJC Equipment LLC. Teterboro, NJ.	N60507
N919SA	03	Falcon 900EX EASY	124	Synthes (USA)/IMP Inc. Chester County, Pa.	F-WWFZ
N919SF	03	Hawker 800XP	8635	Swift & Co International Sales Corp. Greeley, Co.	N635XP
N920DB	87	Falcon 900B	20	Conanicut Aviation LLC. Danbury, Ct.	N256DV
N920DC	98	Gulfstream V	534	Chrysler Pentastar Aviation, Waterford, Mi.	(N158JJ)
N920DS	02	Global Express	9113	Delaware Global Operations Inc. Wilmington, De.	C-GKCG
N920DY	81	Sabre-65	465-50	Anahbig Aviation Inc. Laredo, Tx.	(N920DG)
N920G	76	Falcon 20F-5	352	PAWS LLC. Muncie, In.	N4466F
N920QS	00	Citation X	750-0120	NetJets, Columbus, Oh.	
N920TB	94	Gulfstream 4SP	1254	JS Aviation LLC. Aventura, Fl.	N920DS
N921CC	81	Sabre-65	465-67	U S Europe Africa Trade Inc. Wilmington, De.	N65AR
N921EC	01	Falcon 50EX	313	Pamina LLC. Toms River, NJ.	F-WQBM
N921MB	78	Sabre-60	306-135	Eagle Investments International Inc. Miami, Fl.	N60AM
N921ML	67	Falcon 20C	99	AMI/Marion Merrell Dow-Marion Laboratories Inc. Kansas City.	N982F
N922AC	92	Citation V	560-0187	Autocam Corp. Kentwood, Mi.	N80GE
N922GK	04	HS 125/400A	NA726	Ken-Gil Aviation Inc. Palm Beach, Fl.	N922RR
N922H	99	Falcon 2000	97	Honeywell International Inc. Morristown, NJ.	N620AS
N922JW	87	Falcon 900	36	S C Johnson & Son Inc/Johnson's Wax, Racine, Wi.	N91MK
N922MS*	67	JetStar-731	5097	Edgewood Capital LLC. Belton, Mo. (status ?).	N1BL
N922SL	78	Citation II	550-0034	Summerland LLC. Summerland, Fl.	N60CC
N923AR	94	CitationJet	525-0055	Aero Connections LLC. Banner Elk, NC.	N2639Y
N923HB	77	Falcon 10	99	Helms Briscoe Performance Group Inc. Scottsdale, Az.	N63BA
N923JH	92	Citation II	550-0708	Charter Service LLC/Comair Jet Express, Cincinnati, Oh.	N720WC
N923PC	01	Citation Excel	560-5169	Union Planters Corp. Olive Branch, Ms.	N.....
N923QS	97	Citation X	750-0023	NetJets, Columbus, Oh.	N5000R
N923S	86	Citation S/II	S550-0092	Arkansas Wholesale Lumber Co. Searcy, Ar.	N92QS
N923SK	95	Learjet 60	60-050	EL Holdings LLC. Chicago, Il.	N207BX
N924AM	78	Learjet 35A	35A-188	SGIII LLC/Sachs Group Inc. Wheeling, Il.	N999JF

Reg	Yr	Type	c/n	Owner/Operator	Prev Regn
☐ N924BW	74	Learjet 25B	25B-158	AirNet Systems Inc. Columbus, Oh.	N71RB
☐ N924JE	00	Citation Excel	560-5138	AEE Holdings Inc. Atlanta, Ga.	N704JW
☐ N924JM	96	Hawker 800XP	8312	JMC Highflyer LLC. Scottsdale, Az.	N251X
☐ N924QS	00	Citation X	750-0124	NetJets, Columbus, Oh.	
☐ N924WJ	83	Falcon 50	141	LCG Enterprises LLC. Waterbury-Oxford, Ct.	N96NX
☐ N925AJ	94	Falcon 2000	4	Seneca Livestock Co. Eugene, Or.	F-WWMA
☐ N925BC	97	Falcon 50EX	257	BASF Corp. Morristown, NJ..	F-OKSY
☐ N925BE	67	Falcon 20C	80	Laino LLC. Orland Park, Il.	N24TW
☐ N925CA	85	Learjet 35A	35A-605	Spud Walks II Inc. Denver, Co.	N825CA
☐ N925DM	82	Learjet 35A	35A-486	Milam International Inc. Englewood, Co.	N810CC
☐ N925DW	76	Learjet 25D	25D-213	Leaseco Aviation Inc. Orangevale, Ca.	N803PF
☐ N925GS	82	Falcon 50	90	AIW Inc/American Ironworks Inc. Baltimore, Md.	N4351M
☐ N925MJ	83	Diamond 1	A065SA	Power Design Inc. St Petersburg, Fl.	N16MF
☐ N926CB*	00	Citation VII	650-7114	CB Transport Inc/Compass Bank, Birmingham, Al.	N68BR
☐ N926CC	01	CitationJet CJ-1	525-0491	Classic Century Training LLC. Arlington, Tx.	N491LT
☐ N926EC	01	Citation Bravo	550-1016	Grouper LLC. Bozeman, Mt.	N926ED
☐ N926HC	85	Citation III	650-0094	Maund Automotive Group LP. Austin, Tx.	N650SP
☐ N926MC	78	HS 125/700A	NA0214	MC Aviation Corp. Van Nuys, Ca.	N926TC
☐ N926NY	68	Gulfstream II SP	33	FTO Co. Tompkins County, NY.	N327TC
☐ N926QS	97	Citation X	750-0026	NetJets, Columbus, Oh.	N5066U
☐ N926RM	87	Citation II	550-0567	CB of Gainesville LLC. Gainesville, Fl.. (was 551-0567).	N41BH
☐ N926TF	03	CitationJet CJ-1	525-0519	TFF LLC. Nashville, Tn.	N.....
☐ N927DJ	00	Learjet 31A	31A-210	Schwab Industries Inc. Dover, Oh.	
☐ N927SK	99	Learjet 45	45-051	Kesler Enterprises LLC/Bodor Corp. Warsaw, In.	N145KC
☐ N928CD	97	Learjet 60	60-110	A L Inc. Omaha, Ne.	N60LJ
☐ N928CW	02	EMB-135BJ Legacy	145528	Flight Options LLC. Cleveland, Oh.	VP-CVD
☐ N928DA	00	Citation Bravo	550-0928	Dove Air Inc. Hendersonville, NC.	PH-DYN
☐ N928RD	74	Citation	500-0204	103BL LLC. Quakertown, Pa.	N204Y
☐ N929AK	03	Hawker 800XP	8627	800XP Holdings LLC. Farmingdale, NY.	N627XP
☐ N929CG	77	Sabre-75A	380-52	N929CG LLC. St Thomas, USVI.	(N929GC)
☐ N929EJ	97	Citation X	750-0029	Executive Jet Sales Inc. Columbus, Oh.	(N992QS)
☐ N929GW	99	Learjet 60	60-165	Publix Supermarkets Inc. Lakeland, Fl.	
☐ N929HG	98	Falcon 2000	79	M C Aviation LLC. Tulsa, Ok.	(N772MC)
☐ N929JH	97	Learjet 31A	31A-132	Bunch of Birdies LLC. St Petersburg, Fl.	N116BX
☐ N929ML	82	Falcon 50	92	Flightstar Inc/Executive Fliteways Inc. Ronkonkoma, NY.	(N881J)
☐ N929QS	00	Citation X	750-0129	NetJets, Columbus, Oh.	
☐ N929SR	80	Learjet 35A	35A-287	T & M Air LLC. Eagle County, Co.	N71HS
☐ N929T	80	Falcon 50	24	Eagle II LLC/Semitool Inc. Kalispell, Mt.	N280RT
☐ N929VC	01	CitationJet CJ-1	525-0453	DECIT Inc. Pottsville, Pa.	N902RD
☐ N929WG	01	Gulfstream G200	056	Fort Calumet Corp. Chicago-Midway, Il.	N298GA
☐ N929WQ	90	BAe 125/800A	NA0459	Fort Calumet Corp. Chicago-Midway, Il.	N929WG
☐ N930MG	88	Beechjet 400	RJ-52	California Jet Shares, Concord, Ca.	N196JH
☐ N930QS	00	Citation X	750-0130	NetJets, Columbus, Oh.	
☐ N930SD	99	Falcon 2000	90	DABS LLC. Miami, Fl.	F-WQBM
☐ N931FD	96	Learjet 31A	31A-124	Family Dollar Inc. Charlotte, NC.	
☐ N931QS	98	Citation X	750-0064	NetJets, Columbus, Oh.	N964EJ
☐ N931RS	99	Learjet 31A	31A-184	Russell Stover Candies Inc. Kansas City, Mo.	
☐ N932FD	99	Learjet 31A	31A-187	Family Dollar Inc. Charlotte, NC.	
☐ N932QS	97	Citation X	750-0032	NetJets, Columbus, Oh.	
☐ N933JC	79	Sabre-75A	380-72	Flight 180 LLC/Bingham Financial, Detroit-Willow Run, Mi.	N555JR
☐ N933JJ	98	Gulfstream 4SP	1347	Coanda Inc. Mendham, NJ.	N988H
☐ N933NA	66	Learjet 23	23-049	Earth Resources Laboratory, Stennis, Ms.	(N933N)
☐ N933PA	82	Gulfstream 3	367	Aircraft Leasing Group LLC. Opa Locka, Fl.	N300FS
☐ N933PB	02	Citation Encore	560-0618	Cessna Finance Corp. Wichita, Ks.	N51995
☐ N933QS	00	Citation X	750-0133	NetJets, Columbus, Oh.	
☐ N933SH	83	Citation III	650-0009	HCT Air LLC. Seekonk, Ma.	N933DB
☐ N934AM	97	CitationJet	525-0230	Quarry Lane LLC. Van Nuys, Ca.	(N904AM)
☐ N934BD	01	Citation X	750-0152	Nighthawk Ventures LLC. San Jose, Ca.	OH-PPJ
☐ N934GA	03	Gulfstream G550	5034	Gulfstream Aerospace Corp. Savannah, Ga.	
☐ N934H	89	Citation III	650-0172	Hillenbrand Industries Inc. Batesville, In.	N672CC
☐ N934QS	98	Citation X	750-0034	NetJets, Columbus, Oh.	
☐ N935H	92	BAe 125/800A	NA0475	Rent-A-Center Addison LLC. Plano, Tx.	N800CJ
☐ N935QS	99	Citation X	750-0135	NetJets, Columbus, Oh.	
☐ N936QS	98	Citation X	750-0036	NetJets, Columbus, Oh.	N5085E
☐ N937QS	00	Citation X	750-0137	NetJets, Columbus, Oh.	
☐ N938CC	98	Citation X	750-0038	Flight Options LLC. Cleveland, Oh.	(N700LX)

| Reg | Yr | Type | c/n | Owner/Operator | Prev Regn |

Reg	Yr	Type	c/n	Owner/Operator	Prev Regn
N938D	82	Citation II	550-0454	BH & D Aviation Inc. Palm Coast, Fl.	N93BD
N938QS	02	Citation X	750-0183	NetJets, Columbus, Oh.	
N938W	82	Citation II	550-0448	A E S Industries, Tallahassee, Al.	(N39HD)
N939CK	74	Falcon 20E	317	Hasta Manana Inc/Ceka Aviation Inc. San Jose, Ca.	HB-VEV
N939GP	96	Beechjet 400A	RK-125	The Polisseni Family LP/PF Air LLC. Rochester, NY.	N400KL
N939QS	02	Citation X	750-0193	NetJets, Columbus, Oh.	N.....
N939TW	92	Citation V	560-0185	Rodney Robertson, Albuquerque, NM.	N989TW
N940CC	65	Sabre-40	282-34	Coastal Corp/ANR Coal Co. Roanoke, Va.	N400CS
N940EX	04	Falcon 900EX EASY	140	Dassault Falcon Jet Corp. Teterboro, NJ.	F-WWFR
N940P	95	Learjet 60	60-071	J P Air Charter Inc. Ontario, Ca.	N60LJ
N940SW	94	CitationJet	525-0071	Golden Rule Financial Corp. Indianapolis, In.	N26509
N941AM	02	Gulfstream 4SP	1499	GC Air LLC. Anaheim, Ca.	N499GA
N941CE	80	HS 125/700A	NA0259	Corporate Eagle Capital LLC. Pontiac, Mi.	N128CS
N941HC	90	BAe 125/800A	NA0458	Robinson Leasing Inc. Driggs, Id.	N940HC
N941JC	76	Citation	500-0310	Elite Transportation Services Inc. Clearwater, Fl.	N222VV
N941QS	01	Citation X	750-0141	NetJets, Columbus, Oh.	N5068R
N941RM	98	Citation V Ultra	560-0476	CAVU Inc. Saratoga, Ca.	N150S
N942CC	78	Sabre-75A	380-64	Air 3 Travel Services Inc. Akron, Oh.	N75Y
N942CJ	02	CitationJet CJ-2	525A-0094	Will-Flite Aviation Ltd. Shreveport, La.	N.....
N942DS	65	HS 125/731	25032	Dove Air Inc. Hendersonville, NC.	N98TJ
N942QS	97	Citation X	750-0024	NetJets, Columbus, Oh.	N504SU
N942WC	82	Westwind-1124	383	James Aviation LLC. Bristol, Tn.	N84VV
N943CE	81	HS 125/700A	NA0300	Corporate Eagle Capital LLC. Pontiac, Mi.	N700SA
N943JB	03	Falcon 2000EX	18	TS Servicing Co. Baltimore, Md.	F-GUHB
N943QS	97	Citation X	750-0043	NetJets, Columbus, Oh.	N5090Y
N943RC	81	Citation 1/SP	501-0206	Princess Aviation LLC/Horne Ford Inc. Pinetop, Az.	N943LL
N944AH	98	Citation Excel	560-5008	DDAC LLC/Pacific Assembly Inc. Palwaukee, Il.	SE-RBC
N944BB	03	Hawker 800XP	8611	Zargeo Inc. Santa Teresa, NM.	(N944PP)
N944D	96	Citation X	750-0011	Honeywell Inc. Minneapolis, Mn.	N944H
N944H	03	Gulfstream G550	5016	Honeywell International Inc. Morristown, NJ.	N916GA
N944KM	76	Learjet 24E	24E-334	Global Charters LLC. Louisville, Ky.	N66MJ
N944M	82	Westwind-Two	364	Richland LLC. Columbia, SC.	RP-C2480
N944NA	74	Gulfstream 2	144	NASA Johnson Space Center, Houston, Tx.	HB-ITR
N944QS	01	Citation X	750-0144	NetJets, Columbus, Oh.	
N945CC	79	Sabre-65	465-13	Air Medical Partners II Inc. San Diego, Ca.	(N950CS)
N945CE	81	HS 125/700A	NA0297	Corporate Eagle Capital LLC. Pontiac, Mi.	N589UC
N945ER	85	Citation S/II	S550-0021	Upson Aviation II LLC. Fort Lauderdale, Fl.	N320DG
N945FD	01	Learjet 45	45-122	Family Dollar Inc. Charlotte, NC.	
N945MA	88	MD-87	49725	Miami Air International, Miami, Fl.	VP-BPO
N945NA	72	Gulfstream 2	118	NASA Johnson Space Center, Houston, Tx. (NASA 650).	(N651NA)
N945W	80	Learjet 35A	35A-301	Walthall Asset Management Corp. Dallas, Tx.	N98AC
N946GA	04	Gulfstream G550	5046	Gulfstream Aerospace Corp. Savannah, Ga.	
N946GM	77	Westwind-1124	215	Gary Markel Enterprises Inc. St Petersburg, Fl.	N500WH
N946NA	74	Gulfstream 2	146	NASA Johnson Space Center, Houston, Tx.	N897GA
N946QS	02	Citation X	750-0195	NetJets, Columbus, Oh.	N5241R
N946TC	03	Citation Excel	560-5331	CFA Aviation LLC/Chick-Fil-A Inc. Atlanta, Ga.	N6430S
N947CE	81	HS 125/700A	NA0291	Corporate Eagle Capital LLC. Pontiac, Mi.	N45AF
N947GA	04	Gulfstream G550	5047	White Lotus LLC/Aviation Legal Group PA. Fort Lauderdale, Fl	
N947GS	79	Learjet 35A	35A-250	Saldana Air LLC. Chicago, Il.	N63LF
N947LF	99	Falcon 900EX	44	Menajian Inc/Leopoldo Fernandez, Dulles, Va.	N900PL
N947ML	71	DC 9-32	47514	Homfeld II LLC. Eastpointe, Mi.	PH-MAX
N947NA	74	Gulfstream 2	147	NASA Johnson Space Center, Houston, Tx.	N898GA
N947QS	98	Citation X	750-0047	NetJets, Columbus, Oh.	N5091J
N947TC	78	Learjet 25D	25D-233	InterContinental Express LLC. Athens, Ga.	N75LM
N948DC	80	Citation II	550-0123	Nashville Air Inc. Wilmington, De.	N748DC
N948GA	04	Gulfstream G550	5048	Gulfstream Aerospace Corp. Savannah, Ga.	
N948MA	89	MD-87	49778	U S Marshals Service, Oklahoma City, Ok.	VP-BOO
N948NA	74	Gulfstream 2	222	NASA Johnson Space Center, Houston, Tx.	N5253A
N948QS	01	Citation X	750-0149	NetJets, Columbus, Oh.	N52601
N949CC	80	Westwind-1124	280	Unitex Properties Inc. Marshall, Tx.	N508R
N949CE	83	HS 125/700A	NA0343	Corporate Eagle Capital LLC. Pontiac, Mi.	N524M
N949GA	04	Gulfstream G550	5049	Gulfstream Aerospace Corp. Savannah, Ga.	
N949GP	99	Global Express	9049	GPR Aviation LLC. Hillsboro, Or.	N471DG
N949L	66	DC 9-14	45844	International Airline Support Group, Miami, Fl.	N8963
N949NA	78	Gulfstream II SP	221	NASA Johnson Space Center, Houston, Tx.	N827K
N949QS	98	Citation X	750-0049	NetJets, Columbus, Oh.	N5153K

Reg   Yr   Type   c/n   Owner/Operator   Prev Regn

Reg	Yr	Type	c/n	Owner/Operator	Prev Regn
☐ N949SA*	81	Citation II	550-0329	P & L Aviation II Inc. Ridgeland, Ms.	N491N
☐ N950CM	96	Gulfstream 4SP	1315	Oaktree Capital Management, Van Nuys, Ca.	N315GA
☐ N950DM	86	Gulfstream 4	1010	Fairmont Aviation Inc. Greenwich, Ct.	N824CA
☐ N950F	88	Falcon 50	191	Russell Stover Candies Inc. Kansas City, Mo.	N282FJ
☐ N950G	77	Learjet 36A	36A-032	Asjet Aviation Inc. Wilmington, De.	(N16AJ)
☐ N950GA	04	Gulfstream G550	5050	Gulfstream Aerospace Corp. Savannah, Ga.	
☐ N950H	00	Falcon 50EX	307	Highlands Aviation Corp. Farnborough, UK.	F-WWHK
☐ N950HB	00	Gulfstream 4SP	1464	First Marblehead Corp. Boston, Ma.	N950AV
☐ N950NA	76	Gulfstream II SP	185	NASA Johnson Space Center, Houston, Tx.	N297GB
☐ N950P	97	CitationJet	525-0234	Intrepid Aviation Acquisition Service, Germantown, Tn.	(N91GH)
☐ N950PC	96	Hawker 800XP	8300	Hawker Aviation LLC/The Claremont Co. Bedford, Ma.	N800VF
☐ N950QS	98	Citation X	750-0050	NetJets, Columbus, Oh.	N5156D
☐ N950SF	88	Falcon 900B	50	Bechtel Equipment Operations, Louisville, Ky.	(N711WK)
☐ N950SP	81	Learjet 35A	35A-450	Jet Air Inc. Cincinnati, Oh.	N450KK
☐ N950SW	88	Challenger 601-3A	5032	Safeway Inc. Oakland, Ca.	N601ER
☐ N950TC	96	Citation V Ultra	560-0384	TCAir LLC. Los Altos, Ca.	(N86DD)
☐ N951DB	76	Westwind-1124	195	JODA LLC. Chesterfield, Mo.	N195ML
☐ N951QS	01	Citation X	750-0151	NetJets, Columbus, Oh.	
☐ N951RK	76	Gulfstream II SP	191	Kenair Inc. West Palm Beach, Fl.	N675RW
☐ N952CH	00	Citation Bravo	550-0952	Big Dog Aviation Inc. Elmhurst, Il.	N5268V
☐ N952GA	04	Gulfstream G550	5052	Gulfstream Aerospace Corp. Savannah, Ga.	
☐ N952QS	02	Citation X	750-0200	NetJets, Columbus, Oh.	N.....
☐ N952VS	98	Learjet 31A	31A-168	Inversiones Occilear Inc. Fort Lauderdale, Fl.	YV-952CP
☐ N953C	92	Citation V	560-0163	KM Aircraft Corp. Houston, Tx.	N529X
☐ N953F	89	Citation V	560-0005	Affordable Equity Partners Inc. Columbia, Mo.	
☐ N953FA	89	Challenger 601-3A	5041	Mondoil Enterprises LLC. Mora, NM.	(N541TS)
☐ N953JF	84	Citation III	650-0043	John Fabick Tractor Co. Fenton, Mo.	N643CC
☐ N953QS	01	Citation X	750-0153	NetJets, Columbus, Oh.	
☐ N954H	94	Hawker 800	8259	Pomeroy Computer Resources, Hebron, Ky.	(N966L)
☐ N955EA	73	Learjet 24D	24D-279	Exec Air Montana Inc. Helena, Mt.	N101AR
☐ N955GA	04	Gulfstream G550	5055	Gulfstream Aerospace Corp. Savannah, Ga.	
☐ N955H	99	Gulfstream 4SP	1383	Honeywell Inc. Minneapolis, Mn.	N383GA
☐ N955JS	01	Learjet 31A	31A-228	Jesus Silva, Houston, Tx.	N3018P
☐ N955QS	98	Citation X	750-0055	NetJets, Columbus, Oh.	N5068R
☐ N956GA	04	Gulfstream G550	5056	Beehawk Aviation Inc. Smyrna, Ga.	
☐ N956PP	89	Astra-1125	029	PrintPack Inc. Atlanta, Ga.	N131DA
☐ N956QS	01	Citation X	750-0156	NetJets, Columbus, Oh.	
☐ N957F	98	Astra-1125SPX	104	Navesink Corp. Wilmington, De.	(N104GA)
☐ N957GA	04	Gulfstream G550	5057	Gulfstream Aerospace Corp. Savannah, Ga.	
☐ N957H	94	Hawker 800	8260	KORK Inc. Peoria, Il.	G-5-800
☐ N957MB	73	HS 125/F600A	6015	Marquez Brothers Aviation LLC. Las Vegas, Nv.	N700XJ
☐ N957P	02	Gulfstream G200	062	Navigator Investments LLC. Chiacgo, Il.	N362GA
☐ N958DM	02	Falcon 900EX	119	Archer Danield Midland Co. Decatur, Il.	N119EX
☐ N958PP	83	Diamond 1A	A031SA	ROM Corp. Belton, Mo.	N956PP
☐ N958QS	01	Citation X	750-0158	NetJets, Columbus, Oh.	
☐ N959GA	04	Gulfstream G550	5059	Gulfstream Aerospace Corp. Savannah, Ga.	
☐ N959SA	76	Learjet 35A	35A-076	AirNet Systems Inc. Columbus, Oh. (blue).	
☐ N960CD	91	Citation V	560-0121	Coos & Deschutes LLC. Redmond, Or.	N821VP
☐ N960CR	98	Citation V Ultra	560-0500	Progressive Casualty Insurance Co. Cleveland-Cuyahoga, Oh.	N35TF
☐ N960FA	81	Westwind-Two	348	Anne H Bass, Fort Worth, Tx.	N348SJ
☐ N960GA	04	Gulfstream G550	5060	Gulfstream Aerospace Corp. Savannah, Ga.	
☐ N960JH	03	Citation Encore	560-0643	Medallion Exploration, Salt Lake City, Ut.	N5264N
☐ N960QS	01	Citation X	750-0160	NetJets, Columbus, Oh.	
☐ N960S	82	Falcon 50	86	Outback Steakhouse/Boomerang Air Inc. Tampa, Fl.	N86JC
☐ N960TX	79	Falcon 20F-5B	403	Interstate Equipment Inc. Bozeman, Mt.	(N175BC)
☐ N961EX	99	Falcon 900EX	61	LAPA SA. Buenos Aires, Argentina. 'Southern Star'	F-WWFL
☐ N961MR	92	Learjet 60	60-003	AM & JB Inc. Cleveland, Oh.	N60LJ
☐ N961QS	98	Citation X	750-0061	NetJets, Columbus, Oh.	N5109R
☐ N961SV	99	Gulfstream 4SP	1395	Harmony Management Inc. Burbank, Ca.	N395GA
☐ N961V	96	Gulfstream 4SP	1298	Swiflite Aircraft Corp. Burbank, Ca.	N501PC
☐ N962CW	01	EMB-135BJ Legacy	145462	Flight Options LLC. Cleveland, Oh.	(N254JM)
☐ N962J	82	Citation II	550-0453	D & D Aviation, Grandview, Mo.	N962JC
☐ N962QS	00	Citation X	750-0126	NetJets, Columbus, Oh.	N5076K
☐ N964C	81	Sabre-65	465-66	Saint Gobain Containers, Muncie, In.	
☐ N964GA	04	Gulfstream G550	5064	Gulfstream Aerospace Corp. Savannah, Ga.	
☐ N964H	98	Challenger 604	5363	Harris Corp. Melbourne, Fl.	C-GLXF

Reg	Yr	Type	c/n	Owner/Operator	Prev Regn
N964QS	01	Citation X	750-0164	NetJets, Columbus, Oh.	
N965GA	04	Gulfstream G550	5065	Gulfstream Aerospace Corp. Savannah, Ga.	
N965LC	01	CitationJet CJ-1	525-0462	Lane Construction Corp. Meriden, Ct.	N5197A
N965M	00	Falcon 900EX	65	Motorola Inc. Palwaukee, Il.	N965EX
N966GA	04	Gulfstream G550	5066	Gulfstream Aerospace Corp. Savannah, Ga.	
N966H	03	Falcon 900EX EASY	126	Honeywell International Inc. Morristown, NJ.	F-WWFC
N966JM	93	Citation V	560-0240	Johnson Machinery Co. Riverside, Ca.	N91ME
N966QS	01	Citation X	750-0166	NetJets, Columbus, Oh.	
N966SW	94	Citation V Ultra	560-0284	Old Dominion Freight Lines Inc. High Point, NC.	(N369TC)
N967GA	04	Gulfstream G550	5067	Gulfstream Aerospace Corp. Savannah, Ga.	
N967QS	98	Citation X	750-0067	NetJets, Columbus, Oh.	
N968GA	04	Gulfstream G550	5068	Gulfstream Aerospace Corp. Savannah, Ga.	
N969	93	Learjet 31A	31A-086	Synfuel Management LLC. Lexington, Ky.	N166BA
N969GA	04	Gulfstream G550	5069	Gulfstream Aerospace Corp. Savannah, Ga.	
N969JD*	99	Learjet 60	60-154	Northern Flights LLC/Trakair, Winooski, Vt.	N233FX
N969RE	01	390 Premier 1	RB-14	390 LLC. North Las Vegas, Nv.	
N969SG	92	Gulfstream 4	1197	Moon Doggie Aircraft Services Corp. Addison, Tx.	XA-CAG
N970QS	98	Citation X	750-0070	NetJets, Columbus, Oh.	
N970S	93	Falcon 50	238	Outback Steakhouse/Boomerang Air Inc. Tampa, Fl.	3E-DVL
N970SJ	90	Gulfstream 4	1146	New World Aircraft LLC. Allentown, Pa.	N776US
N970SK	02	Citation X	760-0186	Oshkosh Truck Corp. Appleton, Wi.	N5188N
N970SU	96	CitationJet	525-0173	Dobber Aviation LLC. Tulsa-R L Jones, Ok.	N51564
N970WJ	80	Learjet 25D	25D-324	SalJet LLC. Columbus, Ga.	XA-POP
N971DM	03	CitationJet CJ-1	525-0510	Senate Inc/Xclusive Jet Charter, Bornemouth-Hurn, UK.	N1DM
N971EC	85	Gulfstream 4	1000	Emmis Communications Corp. Indianapolis, In.	N404DB
N971EQ	68	Gulfstream 2B	32	Emmis Communications Corp. Indianapolis, In.	N971EC
N971K	81	Learjet 35A	35A-373	I J Knight Inc. New Tripoli, Pa.	N97AN
N971QS	99	Citation X	750-0071	NetJets, Columbus, Oh.	
N972NR*	78	Sabre-75A	380-65	Compass Acquisition & Development, Dallas, Tx.	N69JN
N972PF	01	390 Premier 1	RB-38	Plastic Ingenuity Inc. Cross Plains, Wi.	
N972TF	69	Jet Commander-B	138	Oduyemi Gabriel, Lagos, Nigeria. (status ?)	N5BA
N972VZ	91	Citation VI	650-0212	Verizon Communications, White Plains, NY.	N805GT
N973HR	02	Learjet 60	60-260	Hoffman-LaRoche Inc. Nutley, NJ.	N257FX
N973M	00	Falcon 900EX	73	Motorola Inc. Palwaukee, Il.	F-WWFI
N974JD	02	Hawker 800XP	8589	Raytheon Aircraft Co. Wichita, Ks.	N51289
N975CM	97	Beechjet 400A	RK-166	New England Aviation Management LLC. Canton, Ma.	N2299T
N975DM	02	CitationJet CJ-2	525A-0083	Dynamic International of Wisconsin Inc. Waukesha, Wi.	N.....
N975GR	84	Diamond 1A	A077SA	Cutter Aviation Inc. Phoenix, Az.	N66PL
N975HM	01	Citation Bravo	550-0975	L IG Air Inc. Islip, NY.	N.....
N975QS	02	Citation X	750-0175	NetJets, Columbus, Oh.	
N975RD	04	Hawker 400XP	RK-390	R R Donnelley & Sons Co. Chicago, Il.	N480LX
N975RR	02	Beechjet 400A	RK-349	Moeller Transport Leasing Inc. Lima-Allen County, Oh.	N449CW
N976BS	68	Learjet 25	25-016	ATI Jet Sales LLC. El Paso, Tx.	(N35WE)
N976GA	80	Citation II	550-0165	GAS Aircraft Capital LLC. Wheeling, Il.	ZS-LHU
N976SR	80	Sabre-65	465-29	Copper Station Holdings LLC. Columbia, SC.	N6NR
N977AR	97	Learjet 31A	31A-134	Meita LLC. Chandler, Az.	N118BX
N977CP	03	Falcon 2000EX	17	CITGO Petroleum Corp. Tulsa, Ok.	N217EX
N977DM	99	CitationJet	525-0338	Bluegrass Aero LLC. Cincinnati, Oh.	N525RL
N977LP	00	Falcon 900EX	77	Lima Papa LLC. Farmingdale, NY.	F-WWFQ
N977MR	02	Citation Encore	560-0623	Plane Truth LLC/Mandalay Resort Group. Las Vegas, Nv.	N51993
N977QS	99	Citation X	750 0077	NetJets, Columbus, Oh.	
N977TW	65	Falcon 20C	13	Sierra American Corp. Addison, Tx.	F-BTCY
N978E	77	Learjet 36A	36A-024	Chrysler Aviation Inc. Van Nuys, Ca.	N38D
N978QS	02	Citation X	750-0187	NetJets, Columbus, Oh.	N.....
N978W	81	Falcon 50	49	TAS LLC/Aero Taxi Inc. Greater Wilmington, De.	N43BE
N979CB	93	Gulfstream 4SP	1217	Design Professionals LLC. NYC.	(N711PE)
N979QS	99	Citation X	750-0079	NetJets, Columbus, Oh.	
N979RF	81	Learjet 35A	35A-376	Jedami Jet LLC. Hollywood, Fl.	XA-SBF
N980DM	77	Citation 1/SP	501-0062	PAS Flight Systems LLC. Scottsdale, Az.	N900DM
N980S	94	Falcon 50	249	Outback Steakhouse/Boomerang Air Inc. Tampa, Fl.	N247CJ
N981CE	01	Hawker 800XP	8563	Corporate Eagle Capital LLC. Pontiac, Mi.	N4469M
N981LB	04	CitationJet CJ-1	525-0546	Cessna Aircraft Co. Wichita, Ks.	N5188N
N982AR	98	Beechjet 400A	RK-206	Arvinmeritor Inc. Troy, Mi.	N30046
N982B	71	Gulfstream 2B	98	PrivateSky Aviation/Ninety-Eight Aviation LLC. Butte, Mt.	N883ES
N982MC	77	Falcon 10	114	Music City Charter Inc. McGhee-Tyson, Tn.	N108TG
N982NA	82	Citation II	550-0345	304 MC Ltd. Liverpool, NY.	N267TC

Reg	Yr	Type	c/n	Owner/Operator	Prev Regn
N982QS	02	Citation X	750-0182	NetJets, Columbus, Oh.	
N982RK	80	Gulfstream 3	310	Water Over Mountain Holdings LLC. Burlington, NC.	(N373LP)
N983CC	80	Falcon 10	163	RMH Teleservices Inc. Addison, Tx.	(N73TJ)
N983J	00	Global Express	9072	Jacobs Family Trust, Central Point, Or.	N700LN
N983MC	77	Falcon 10	111	Music City Charter Inc. McGhee-Tyson, Tn.	N10HE
N983QS	99	Citation X	750-0083	NetJets, Columbus, Oh.	
N984BK	98	Citation Bravo	550-0857	Farm Leasing Inc. Atlanta, Ga.	VP-CCP
N984GC	98	Hawker 800XP	8377	Gainey Aircraft Corp.Grand Rapids.(Millenium Hawker 1000th).	N1251K
N984QS	99	Citation X	750-0084	NetJets, Columbus, Oh.	
N984SA	83	Diamond 1A	A063SA	Media Aviation Associates LLC. Montgomery, Al.	N51BE
N984TS	00	Global Express	9084	McDonald's Corp. San Diego, Ca.	N908BX
N986DS	83	Citation 1/SP	501-0321	Oncourse Charter LLC. Rogers, Ar.	N510SJ
N986MA	93	Learjet 31A	31A-080	Mescalero Apache Tribe, Mescalero, NM.	N80LJ
N986QS	99	Citation X	750-0086	NetJets, Columbus, Oh.	N888CN
N987CJ	88	Citation S/II	S550-0152	Bibler Aviation Inc. Russellville, Ar.	N843G
N987G	89	Astra-1125	031	Peekey Lumbus LC. Del Mar, Ca.	N987GK
N987GK	90	Falcon 900B	88	Shadowfax LLC. Carlsbad, Ca.	N987QK
N987LP	91	Learjet 35A	35A-670	Johnson Aviation LLC. Columbus, In.	N787LP
N987QS	99	Citation X	750-0087	NetJets, Columbus, Oh.	
N987RC*	80	Falcon 50	31	Rockford Falcon Jet LLC & ROR Jet LLC. Grand Rapids, Mi.	N292FH
N987SA	75	Gulfstream II SP	172	S/A Holdings LLC. Columbia County, NY.	N903AG
N988AA	81	Learjet 25D	25D-348	aaiPharma Inc. Wilmington, NC.	N522JS
N988AS	78	Learjet 25D	25D-257	B & C Flight Management Inc. Houston, Tx.	N377Q
N988H	03	Falcon 900EX EASY	125	Honeywell International Inc. Phoenix, Az.	F-WWFB
N988QC	81	Learjet 35A	35A-455	Moyle Petroleum Co. Rapid City, SD.	N455NE
N988T	88	Falcon 900B	65	Semitool Inc. Kalispell, Mt.	(N990MQ)
N989AL	78	Learjet 35A	35A-212	Air Ambulance Professionals Inc. Fort Lauderdale, Fl.	N291A
N989QS	99	Citation X	750-0089	NetJets, Columbus, Oh.	
N989SC	74	Citation	500-0148	Genesis Air LLC. Columbus, Ms.	LV-WXJ
N989TL	68	Learjet 24	24-160	Booth Ranches/F Otis Booth Jr. Van Nuys, Ca.	N4791C
N989TV	81	Citation II	550-0285	Citation Ventures LLC. South Burlington, Vt.	N989TW
N989TW	98	Citation Excel	560-5014	Wamburg Financial Corp. Barrington, Il.	(N16SN)
N990AK	97	Challenger 604	5337	Oak Management Corp. Westport, Ct.	N270RA
N990AL	72	Citation	500-0033	W-K Inc. Leawood, Ks.	(N130AL)
N990BB	88	Falcon 900B	42	Bresnan Aviation LLC. Greenwich, Ct.	N901BB
N990DK	98	Citation Excel	560-5019	Cottonaire LLC. Gastonia, NC.	N980DK
N990H	97	Falcon 900EX	17	Honeywell International Inc. Morristown, NJ.	N600AS
N990HC	99	Hawker 800XP	8412	Harsco Corp. New Cumberland, Pa.	N30682
N990JM	01	Citation Bravo	550-0990	Ironwood Services Inc. Flint, Mi.	N5154J
N990M	89	Citation II	550-0608	Menzil Enterprises Inc. Allegheny County, Pa.	N608AM
N990MC	03	Falcon 900EX EASY	123	MASCO Corp. Detroit-Metropolitan, Mi.	N990ML
N990MF	99	Citation Excel	560-5052	Caledonia Leasing LLC. Mundelein, Il.	N5228Z
N990PT	75	Sabre-65	306-114	Taylor Energy Co. New Orleans, La.	N65RN
N990QS	02	Citation X	750-0190	NetJets, Columbus, Oh.	N.....
N990S	81	Westwind-Two	322	Outback Steakhouse/Boomerang Air Inc. Tampa, Fl.	N2AV
N990WM	98	Falcon 900EX	40	Indigo Airship Leasing Ltd. Page Field-Fort Myers, Fl.	N606DR
N991BM	79	Citation II	550-0114	Sunfresh Inc. Royal City, Wa.	(N900BM)
N991CX	99	Citation X	750-0091	Flight Options LLC. Cleveland, Oh.	(N791CW)
N991DB	99	Learjet 60	60-177	Riverhorse Investments Inc. Van Nuys, Ca.	N60LR
N991LF	99	Gulfstream V	576	International Lease Finance Corp. Van Nuys, Ca.	N476GA
N991RF	86	Falcon 900B	3	Prisa Leasing LLC. Santa Barbara, Ca.	N327F
N991TD	66	Learjet 24	24-124	Ruhe Sales Inc. Leipsic, Oh.	XA-RTV
N991TW	97	Challenger 604	5333	Ross Investments Inc. Oakland, Ca.	N600MS
N992HE	01	Citation Bravo	550-1006	Whayne Supply Co. Louisville, Ky.	N106BB
N992TD	65	Learjet 23	23-035	Ruhe Sales Inc. Lepsic, Oh.	(N10QX)
N993	80	Falcon 50	38	SDR LLC. Maitland, Fl.	N58FJ
N993DS	81	Westwind-Two	356	Fedrick Aviation LLC. Napa, Ca.	N38TJ
N993EX	01	Falcon 900EX	93	KAD Aviation LLC. San Jose, Ca.	F-WWFL
N993GL	02	CitationJet CJ-1	525-0509	Cresair Inc. Northvale, NJ.	(N904DP)
N993H	99	Beechjet 400A	RK-241	Horton Transportation Inc. Minneapolis, Mn.	N3241Q
N993TD	68	Learjet 24	24-166	Air Cargo Express Inc. Fort Wayne, In.	N124HF
N994CT	94	Challenger 601-3R	5161	Caterpillar Inc. Peoria, Il.	C-GLWZ
N994GC	00	Gulfstream 4SP	1435	Guidant Corp. Indianapolis, In.	N435GA
N994GG	69	Gulfstream 2	77	J & M Plane LLC. Chiacgo, Il.	N994GC
N994TD	68	Learjet 24	24-179	Air Cargo Express Inc. Fort Wayne, In.	XA-RQP
N995CK	67	Falcon 20C	95	Kalitta Charters LLC. Detroit-Willow Run, Mi.	N950RA

Reg	Yr	Type	c/n	Owner/Operator	Prev Regn
N995CR	80	Learjet 35A	35A-304	Champion Racing Aviation LLC. Boca Raton, Fl.	(N97QA)
N995CW	01	EMB-135BJ Legacy	145495	Flight Options LLC. Cleveland, Oh.	PR-LEG
N995DP	85	Learjet 35A	35A-600	A Duie Pyle Inc. Coatesville, Pa.	N823CP
N995MA	97	Challenger 604	5362	MAG Aviation Co.	N607PM
N995RD	74	Sabre-80A	380-9	Jet Harbor Inc. Fort Lauderdale, Fl.	N383CF
N995SK	97	Falcon 900B	166	Tiburon Transportation Ltd. Santa Rosa, Ca.	F-GLHI
N995TD	67	Learjet 24	24-149	Air Cargo Express Inc. Fort Wayne, In.	N64HB
N996AG	98	Falcon 2000	64	American General Corp. Houston, Tx.	F-WWMH
N996CR	83	Learjet 55	55-060	Champion Racing Aviation LLC. Boca Raton, Fl.	N255TS
N996JS	96	Learjet 31A	31A-119	MRK LLC. Dallas-Love, Tx.	N114HY
N996QS	02	Citation X	750-0196	NetJets, Columbus, Oh.	
N996TD	75	Learjet 24D	24D-320	Ruhe Sales Inc. Leipsic, Oh.	S5-BAB
N997CB	00	Citation Excel	560-5102	H E Butt Grocery Co. San Antonio, Tx.	N5135K
N997EA	92	Citation V	560-0178	Ernie Elliott Aviation Inc. Dawsonville, Ga.	N500PX
N997MX	83	Diamond 1	A036SA	Metal Exchange Corp. Matthews, NC.	N18BA
N997QS	03	Citation X	750-0208	NetJets, Columbus, Oh.	
N998AL	02	Learjet 31A	31A-240	Alex Lyon & Son, Syracuse, NY.	
N998AM	98	Global Express	9009	Pan Asia Industries Ltd. Torrance, Ca.	N813SQ
N998BC	90	Citation II	550-0665	Professional Office Services Inc. Waterloo, Ia.	N665MC
N998CK	67	Falcon 20C	98	Kalitta Charters LLC. Detroit-Willow Run, Mi.	N980R
N998CX	99	Citation X	750-0098	Swift Aviation Services Inc. Phoenix, Az.	(N798CW)
N998EA	79	Citation 1/SP	501-0104	Ernie Elliott Aviation Inc. Dawsonville, Ga.	N33HC
N998QS	02	Citation X	750-0198	NetJets, Columbus, Oh.	
N998SA	98	Citation V Ultra	560-0485	Cessna Aircraft Co. Wichita, Ks.	
N999AM	74	Citation	500-0232	JMK Aviation Trust, Fort Worth, Tx.	N126R
N999AZ	81	Westwind-Two	343	Water Taxi LLC. St Thomas, USVI.	N343RD
N999BL	86	Astra-1125	024	Brunswick Corp. Waukegan, Il.	N300JJ
N999BW	67	BAC 1-11/419EP	120	Business Jet Services Ltd. Dallas-Love, Tx.	N87BL
N999CB	85	Citation S/II	S550-0054	Charles Brewer Ltd. Phoenix, Az.	N57MB
N999CY	80	HS 125/700A	NA0261	Consumer Marketing Services Inc. Liverpool, NY.	N983GT
N999EA	85	Citation S/II	S550-0077	Ernie Elliott Aviation Inc. Dawsonville, Ga.	N202WC
N999EH	87	Falcon 900	15	999EH LLC/East Hampton Air, East Hampton, NY.	(N115FJ)
N999FA	81	Learjet 35A	35A-386	White Industries Inc. Bates City, Mo.	N13VG
N999GG	00	Learjet 31A	31A-216	Chimney Creek Ranch, Goldsboro, NC.	N40077
N999GP	00	Gulfstream 4SP	1422	Gary Primm/Primadonna Resorts Inc. Las Vegas, Nv.	N422GA
N999GR	79	Citation II	550-0097	RAC Corp. Pompano Beach, Fl.	N202CE
N999HC	85	Citation S/II	S550-0030	H S Industries LLC. Groton, Ct.	(N999GL)
N999JF	95	Beechjet 400A	RK-98	J F Air Inc. Houston, Tx.	N866BB
N999LL	80	Falcon 10	152	Gryphon Ventures Inc. Houston, Tx.	N152WJ
N999LX	89	Gulfstream 4	1099	CKE Associates LLC. Van Nuys, Ca.	N199QS
N999MC	84	Westwind-Two	412	Billabong Air LLC. Tampa, Fl.	N50HS
N999MF	69	Learjet 25	25-050	Rainbow Chaser West Inc. Evergreen, Co.	N55FN
N999MK	81	Citation II/SP	551-0304	Kaftan Ventures LLC. Pontiac, Mi.	N304KT
N999MS	81	Citation 1/SP	501-0230	C & G Air LLC/Buffalo Coal Co. Oakland, Md.	9A-DVR
N999ND	77	Learjet 35A	35A-112	Mercurius Aviation Inc. Waco, Tx.	N299LR
N999PJ	61	MS 760 Paris-2	89	Tej Jet of Del LLC. Dover, De.	F-BJLY
N999PM	00	Falcon 900EX	70	Pacific Marine Leasing Inc. Phoenix, Az.	N970EX
N999PW	80	Citation 1/SP	501-0160	2141 Corp. Atlanta, Ga.	C-GAAA
N999QS	02	Citation X	750-0203	NetJets, Columbus, Oh.	
N999TF	82	Challenger 600S	1042	MDC Aviation LLC/MDC Homes, Alpharetta, Ga.	(N939CG)
N999TH	87	Falcon 200	512	Journal Publishing Co. Albuquerque, NM.	N45WH
N999VK	01	Challenger 604	5499	VKRM Aviation LLC. Los Altos Hills, Ca.	N499KR
N999WA	71	Learjet 24D	24D-242	JetSet Airlines LLC. Costa Mesa, Ca.	N1972G
N999WE	02	CitationJet CJ-2	525A-0126	CJ2 Aviation LLC/Bill Elliott Racing Team, Statesville, NC.	N534CJ
N999WS	81	Citation 1/SP	501-0186	Airflite Inc. Shawnee, Ok.	N37HW
N1000E	94	CitationJet	525-0077	W E Hess Co/WRHC LLC. Chickasha, Ok.	N50820
N1000W	92	Citation V	560-0204	Ashland Inc. Ashland-Boyd, Ky.	N1283Y
N1023C	01	EMB-135LR	145550	CONOCO-Phillips, Houston, Tx.	PT-...
N1040	00	Gulfstream V	650	Cox Enterprises Inc. Atlanta, Ga.	N520GA
N1082A	88	Gulfstream 4	1082	Burlington Resources Oil & Gas Co. Houston, Tx.	
N1083Z	96	Beechjet 400A	RK-131	Universal Health Management LLC. Detroit, Mi.	
N1086	88	Gulfstream 4	1086	Stockwood Inc. Morristown, NJ.	N23SY
N1090X	04	Challenger 604	5576	Xerox Corp. White Plains, NY.	C-GLWV
N1094L	00	Citation Excel	560-5094	Mission City Management Inc. San Antonio, Tx.	
N1116R	96	Beechjet 400A	RK-116	CTB Inc. Milford, In.	
N1121R	69	Jet Commander-A	125	Albert Lea Airport Inc. Albert Lea, Mn.	N30LS

Reg	Yr	Type	c/n	Owner/Operator	Prev Regn

Reg	Yr	Type	c/n	Owner/Operator	Prev Regn
❑ N1123G	75	Gulfstream II SP	160	Leonard Green & Partners LP. Van Nuys, Ca.	N919TG
❑ N1125	88	Astra-1125	021	Gulfstream Aerospace Corp. Savannah, Ga.	N1125S
❑ N1125A	90	Astra-1125SP	051	Parsons & Whittemore Inc. Rye Brook, NY.	
❑ N1125J	96	Astra-1125SP	078	Kroger Co. Cincinnati, Oh.	
❑ N1125K	89	Astra-1125	035	State Street Corp. Stratford, Ct.	
❑ N1125M	82	Learjet 55	55-065	Bayer Corp. Pittsburgh, Pa.	(N565B)
❑ N1125S	00	Gulfstream G100	134	PGA Tour Golf Course Prop. Ponte Vedre, Fl.	N64GX
❑ N1127K	98	CitationJet	525-0293	Charles Hutter, Carson City, Nv.	
❑ N1128B	99	Falcon 2000	83	Florida Power & Light Co. Opa Locka, Fl.	F-WWVC
❑ N1129E	00	Citation Excel	560-5112	Decant Air LLC. Santa Barbara, Ca.	N52547
❑ N1129L	99	Citation V Ultra	560-0507	Siebel Systems Inc. San Jose, Ca.	N5059N
❑ N1129M	84	Learjet 55	55-101	Bayer Corp. Pittsburgh, Pa.	C-FNRG
❑ N1140A	76	Learjet 35	35-045	AirNet Systems Inc. Columbus, Oh. (red).	(N40AN)
❑ N1200N	92	Citation II	550-0681	U S Customs Service, Oklahoma City, Ok. (XC-LHA as required)	(N6776Y)
❑ N1218C	71	Gulfstream II SP	99	FBX Aviation LLC. Atlanta, Ga.	N900MP
❑ N1220W	02	CitationJet CJ-2	525A-0146	Overland West Investments Inc. Ogden, Ut.	N.....
❑ N1221J	00	Learjet 60	60-209	Turner Holdings LLC. Dallas, Tx.	N40085
❑ N1249P	82	Citation II	550-0451	Camperdown Co. Greenville, SC.	
❑ N1250V	82	Citation II	550-0439	Aquila Air LLC/PN Air LP. Cincinnati, Oh.	N511WS
❑ N1252D	83	Citation II	550-0476	Esto Logistics LLC. Jeffersonville, In.	
❑ N1254C	99	Citation VII	650-7098	CB Transport Inc/Compass Bank, Birmingham, Al.	N621AB
❑ N1254X	84	Citation II	550-0494	U S Customs Service, Phoenix, Az.	XC-JBR
❑ N1255J	03	CitationJet CJ-2	525A-0101	F3 Aviation Corp. Steamboat Springs, Co.	(N533JF)
❑ N1255K	84	Citation II	550-0505	U S Customs Service, Oklahoma City, Ok.	XC-JAY
❑ N1257B	84	Citation II	550-0497	U S Customs Service, Oklahoma City, Ok.	(XC-JBQ)
❑ N1258B	02	Citation Bravo	550-1037	Northern Air Inc. Grand Rapids, Mi.	N5180C
❑ N1277E	02	CitationJet CJ-2	525A-0076	Heaven Express LLC. Watsonville, CA.	N5156D
❑ N1286C	93	Citation V	560-0222	FMR Group LLC. Norwalk, Ct.	
❑ N1308L	04	CitationJet CJ-3	525B-0004	Solitaire Air LLC/C3SP LLC. Fort Worth, Tx.	N5207A
❑ N1326A	02	Citation Excel	560-5272	Airplane International Holdings Inc. Wilmington, De.	N5079V
❑ N1327J	93	CitationJet	525-0009	ZellAir LLC. Akron, Oh.	
❑ N1329G	96	CitationJet	525-0146	Radomir Zivanic/Novabank SA. Attica, Greece.	(OE-FGG)
❑ N1400M	87	Citation III	650-0140	Mustang Fuel Corp. Oklahoma City, Ok.	N4FC
❑ N1419J	90	Citation VI	650-0201	Kenneth Anderson, Memphis, Tn.	N347BG
❑ N1454	82	Gulfstream 3	350	JP Air Charter Inc. Ontario, Ca.	N1454H
❑ N1454H	00	Gulfstream V	619	Amerada Hess Corp. Trenton, NJ.	N608GA
❑ N1500	83	Challenger 600S	1078	Wegmans Food Markets Inc. Rochester, NY.	N53SR
❑ N1540	99	Gulfstream V	580	Cox Enterprises Inc. Atlanta, Ga.	N580GA
❑ N1547B	88	Beechjet 400	RJ-47	Aviation Team Inc. Fort Lauderdale, Fl.	
❑ N1620	92	Gulfstream 4SP	1206	Cox Enterprises Inc. Atlanta, Ga.	N1040
❑ N1624	97	Gulfstream 4SP	1318	Chevron USA Inc. New Orleans, La.	N418GA
❑ N1625	98	Gulfstream 4SP	1358	Chevron USA Inc. New Orleans, La.	N358GA
❑ N1630	01	Hawker 800XP	8557	Cox Enterprises Inc. Atlanta, Ga.	N51457
❑ N1640	98	Hawker 800XP	8376	Cox Enterprises Inc. Atlanta, Ga.	
❑ N1776E	78	HS 125/700A	NA0226	Voyager Aviation LLC. Belgrade, Mt.	N7WC
❑ N1776H	87	BAe 125/800A	8091	320 LLC. Helena, Mt.	N165BA
❑ N1818C	99	Gulfstream 4SP	1385	Ab Initio Software Corp. Bedford, Ma.	N577VU
❑ N1818S	93	Falcon 900B	136	Stephens Group Inc. Little Rock, Ar.	N137FJ
❑ N1823D	69	Gulfstream II SP	59	The Air Group Inc. Van Nuys, Ca.	N879GA
❑ N1829S	98	Falcon 50EX	280	Stephens Group Inc. Little Rock, Ar.	N50FJ
❑ N1836S	00	Citation Excel	560-5143	Stephens Group Inc. Little Rock, Ar.	N5096S
❑ N1837S	98	Citation Excel	560-5155	Stephens Group Inc. Little Rock, Ar.	N5095N
❑ N1838S	02	Citation Excel	560-5322	Stephens Group Inc. Little Rock, Ar.	N5196U
❑ N1839S	01	Falcon 50EX	317	Stephens Group Inc. Little Rock, Ar.	F-WWHW
❑ N1848T	99	CitationJet	525-0350	Knapheide Manufacturing Co. Quincy, Il.	N1348T
❑ N1865M	85	Citation S/II	S550-0071	Milliken & Co. Greenville, SC.	N571CC
❑ N1867M	02	Citation Excel	560-5303	Mericos Aviation Ltd. Van Nuys, Ca.	N.....
❑ N1868M	00	Global Express	9069	Metropolitan Life Insurance Co. NYC.	N700LD
❑ N1871R	01	Citation Encore	560-0580	CFG-Citizens Financial Group Service Corp. Providence, RI.	N580CE
❑ N1873	01	Citation X	750-0128	George Koch Sons Inc. Evansville, In.	N67CX
❑ N1881Q	79	Falcon 20F-5B	414	Emerson Power Transmissions Inc. Tomkins County, NY.	N412F
❑ N1884	81	Challenger 600S	1032	Jamboree Elite LLC/Newport Federal Corp. Newport Beach, Ca.	(N31DC)
❑ N1886G	93	Citation II	550-0722	Airlease LLC. Meridian, Id.	XA-SMT
❑ N1896V	97	Falcon 50EX	262	New York Times Co. Bradley, Ct.	N262EX
❑ N1897A	97	Hawker 800XP	8326	1897 Corp. Chicago, Il.	N326XP
❑ N1897S	77	Falcon 20-5	376	J M Smucker Co. Akron-Canton, Oh.	N1892S

| *Reg* | *Yr* | *Type* | *c/n* | *Owner/Operator* | *Prev Regn* |

Reg	Yr	Type	c/n	Owner/Operator	Prev Regn
N1900W	90	Gulfstream 4	1124	Whirlpool Corp. Benton Harbor, Mi.	N420GA
N1902P	93	Challenger 601-3R	5135	J C Penney Corp. Dallas, Tx.	N1902J
N1903G	96	Challenger 604	5326	Tri C Inc/Gaylord Broadcasting, Oklahoma City, Ok.	N908G
N1904P	92	Challenger 601-3A	5116	J C Penney Corp. Dallas, Tx.	N841PC
N1904S	99	Learjet 45	45-053	1904 LLC/Spitzer Management Inc. Elyria, Oh.	N3211Q
N1904W	94	Gulfstream 4SP	1237	Whirlpool Corp. Benton Harbor, Mi.	N480GA
N1910A	90	BAe 125/800A	NA0454	Hallmark Cards Inc. Kansas City, Mo.	N616BA
N1910H	96	Hawker 800XP	8318	Hallmark Cards Inc. Kansas City, Mo.	N318XP
N1920	91	Beechjet 400A	RK-21	Perdue Farms Inc. Salisbury, Md.	N717VA
N1925M	96	Gulfstream 4SP	1282	Mannco LLC. Sylmar, Ca.	N9KN
N1926S	99	Learjet 31A	31A-180	Ararat Rock Products Co. Mount Airy, NC.	
N1927G	96	Falcon 2000	35	W W Grainger Inc. Palwaukee, Il.	N27WP
N1929Y	99	Falcon 2000	84	Oak Spring Farms LLC. Dulles, Va.	F-WWVD
N1932K	94	Learjet 31A	31A-099	Advance America Cash Advance Centers, Spartanburg, SC.	N1932P
N1932P	02	Gulfstream G400	1514	Mozart Investments Inc. Roanoke, Va.	N314GA
N1940	92	Learjet 60	60-002	McMullen Consultants/Executive Fliteways Inc. Ronkonkoma.	N190AS
N1944P	02	Jet Commander-C	142	Pittsburgh Institute of Aeronautics, Pittsburgh, Pa.	N51038
N1956M	85	Gulfstream 3	469	Hill Air Corp. Dallas, Tx.	JY-HZH
N1958N	85	Citation S/II	S550-0073	Milliken & Co. Greenville, SC.	(N1273E)
N1961S	99	Citation Bravo	550-0890	Union Air I I C. Camp Douglas, Wi.	
N1962J	98	Citation Bravo	550-0862	Eagle Mountain International Church, Fort Worth, Tx.	N442SW
N1066L	65	Learjet 24A	24A-012	Clay Lacy Aviation Inc. Van Nuys, Ca.	N1969L
N1983Y	83	Learjet 55	55-079	Anderson & Anderson LLC. Florence, Al.	(N2855)
N1987	02	Challenger 604	5550	Petsmart Leasing Inc. Scottsdale, Az.	N250CC
N1989D	02	Hawker 800XP	8580	Hensel Phelps Construction Co. Leesburg, Va.	(N880QS)
N1990C	95	Gulfstream 4SP	1276	Citadel Investment Group LLC. Chicago, Il.	N1955M
N1993	82	Falcon 100	195	Mingawair Inc. Wilmington, De.	TS-IAM
N2000	69	Gulfstream II SP	56	Model Transportation LLC. Van Nuys, Ca.	N690PC
N2000L	99	Falcon 2000	92	Millard Refrigerated Services Inc/MPS Inc. Omaha, Ne.	N2191
N2000X	94	Citation V	560-0249	Ashland Inc. Ashand-Boyd, Ky.	N733M
N2002P	95	Gulfstream 4SP	1279	J C Penney Corp. Dallas, Tx.	N466GA
N2006	74	Sabre-40A	282-135	Air Camis Inc. Canton, Oh.	(N67BK)
N2015M	94	BAe 125/800A	8254	Raytheon Aircraft Co. Wichita, Ks.	N943H
N2032	89	BAe 125/800A	8175	U S Marshals Service, Oklahoma City, Ok.	N175U
N2033	87	BAe 125/800A	8093	U S Marshals Service, Oklahoma City, Ok.	N317CQ
N2093A	69	Learjet 24B	24B-194	Butler National Inc. Newton, Ks.	(N62FN)
N2094L	72	Learjet 25B	25B-095	Royal Air Freight Inc. Waterford, Mi.	G-GRCO
N2107Z	93	Gulfstream 4SP	1211	Vista Capital Management LLC. Van Nuys, Ca.	N447GA
N2112L	00	Falcon 2000	112	Siebel Systems Inc. San Jose, Ca.	N2000A
N2143H	59	B 707-123B	17644	Ess Jay Air Inc. Beaumont, Tx.	HZ-DAT
N2150H	77	Westwind-1124	210	Jet Flight LLC. Shreveport, La.	N428JF
N2158U	79	Citation 1/SP	501-0091	RBK Aviation Inc. Wilson, NY.	N2158U
N2235V	98	Beechjet 400A	RK-181	Suncoast Aviation Inc. Durham, NC.	
N2243	81	Citation 1/SP	501-0212	Smiley Investment Co. Little Rock, Ar.	N70AA
N2250G	01	CitationJet CJ-2	525A-0047	Hickory Aviation LLC. Adel, Ia.	N5148N
N2273Z	97	Beechjet 400A	RK-173	TCC Air Services Inc. Greenwich, Ct.	
N2351K	89	Citation II	550-0594	U S Customs Service, Oklahoma City, Ok.	N1302X
N2411A	85	Citation III	650-0103	Kempthorn Inc. Canton, Oh.	N407LM
N2500B	96	Citation OT-47B	560-0386	U S Dept of State, Oklahoma City, Ok.	N615L
N2617U	82	Citation 1/SP	501-0235	Corporate Consulting & Financial Inc/ACM, San Jose, Ca.	(N31CF)
N2648X	79	Citation 1/SP	501-0105	NCI Operating Corp. Houston, Tx.	(N231LC)
N2663Y	89	Citation II	550-0602	U S Customs Service, Oklahoma City, Ok.	XC-JAZ
N2700	79	Sabre-65	465-7	R-Plane Inc. Houston, Tx.	N2000
N2734K	89	Citation II	550-0595	U S Customs Service, New Orleans NAS, La.	XC-JCV
N2929*	04	Gulfstream G550	5053	Gulfstream Aerospace Corp. Savannah, Ga.	N953GA
N3007	00	Hawker 800XP	8487	Empire Airlines Inc. Lebanon, Mo.	N51387
N3008	87	BAe 125/800A	8092	WFBNW NA. Salt Lake City, Ut.	N3007
N3034B	68	Learjet 24	24-176	MTW Aerospace Inc. Montgomery, Al.	PT-CXJ
N3121B	87	Beechjet 400	RJ-21	FractionAir Inc. Nashville, Tn.	
N3170B*	86	Citation III	650-0136	Spring Mountain Enterprises Inc. Costa Mesa, Az.	N650DF
N3197Q	95	Beechjet 400A	RK-97	Dani Howard, Mooresville, NC.	
N3215K	84	Learjet 35A	35A-589		PT-GAP
N3235U	95	Beechjet 400A	RK-105	B W Aviation LLC. Allegheny County, Pa.	(N423LX)
N3262M	91	Citation II	550-0652	U S Customs Service, Oklahoma City, Ok. (XC-HJF as required)	(N1311P)
N3280G	66	Sabre-40	282-70	United CCM Corp. San Antonio, Tx. (status ?).	N34LP
N3337J	97	Beechjet 400A	RK-159	Woodbridge Logistics LLC. Brattleboro, Vt.	N2159P

Reg	Yr	Type	c/n	Owner/Operator	Prev Regn
N3444B	92	Citation V	560-0192	Figg Transportation Inc. Tallahassee, Fl.	N238JC
N3490L	74	Citation	500-0128	USP Investments LLC. Yachats, Or.	N501AR
N3616	01	Citation Encore	560-0571	Caterpillar Inc. Peoria, Il.	N5244W
N3722Z	04	390 Premier 1	RB-122	Raytheon Aircraft Co. Wichita, Ks.	
N3723A	04	390 Premier 1	RB-123	Raytheon Aircraft Co. Wichita, Ks.	
N3725F	04	390 Premier 1	RB-125	Raytheon Aircraft Co. Wichita, Ks.	
N3726G	04	390 Premier 1	RB-126	Raytheon Aircraft Co. Wichita, Ks.	
N3901A*	03	390 Premier 1	RB-102	Raytheon Aircraft Co. Wichita, Ks.	N6182F
N4000K	00	Citation Excel	560-5081	Kimball International Transit Inc. Huntingburg, In.	
N4000R	01	Hawker 4000 Horizon	RC-1	Raytheon Aircraft Co. Wichita, Ks. (Ff 11 Aug 01).	
N4107W	04	Citation Excel XLS	560-5530	Germanium Corp of America Inc. Clinton, NY.	N5270J
N4108E	00	CitationJet CJ-1	525-0410	Commercial Aviation Inc. Kerrville, Tx.	(N292SG)
N4200	99	Falcon 2000	87	Key Corp Aviation Co. Cleveland, Oh.	N287QS
N4200K	96	Citation V Ultra	560-0354	Kimball International Transit Inc. Huntingburg, In.	N5157E
N4275K	00	Beechjet 400A	RK-275	Harbor Air LC/Sun Aviation Inc. Vero Beach, Fl.	
N4350M	84	Falcon 50	142	MeadWestvaco Corp. Dayton, Oh.	N132FJ
N4358N	76	Learjet 35	35-065	AirNet Systems Inc. Columbus, Oh. (green).	N425DN
N4395D	02	390 Premier 1	RB-65	Lider Taxi Aereo SA. Belo Horizonte, MG.Brazil.	
N4402	90	BAe 125/800A	NA0460	GMRI Leasing Inc. Orlando, Fl.	N632BA
N4403	00	Hawker 800XP	8480	GMRI Leasing Inc. Orlando, Fl.	
N4405	01	Citation Bravo	550-1023	GMRI Leasing Inc. Orlando, Fl.	N.....
N4415M	76	Learjet 35A	35A-072	L S Management Inc. Wichita, Ks.	N2015M
N4415S	79	Learjet 35A	35A-232	L S Management Inc. Wichita, Ks.	N8281
N4415W	79	Learjet 35A	35A-229	L S Management Inc. Wichita, Ks.	N415LS
N4425*	98	Falcon 900EX	32	Owens Corning Fiberglas Corp. Swanton, Oh.	N2425
N4426	94	Hawker 800	8272	Owens Corning Fiberglas Corp. Swanton, Oh.	N2426
N4428*	95	Hawker 800	8274	Owens Corning Fiberglas Corp. Swanton, Oh.	N2428
N4447P	81	Learjet 25D	25D-338	Houck Leasing Inc. Fort Pierce, Fl.	XA-LOF
N4467X	00	Beechjet 400A	RK-267	Galena Air Services Co. Denver, Co.	
N4480W	00	Beechjet 400A	RK-280	Kentucky Apparel LP. Tompkinsville, Ky.	
N4483W	01	Beechjet 400A	RK-313	Tulip Air BV. Rotterdam, Holland.	(PH-BBC)
N4488W	83	Learjet 25D	25D-367	Whitesell of Carolina Inc. High Point, NC.	VT-SWP
N4500X	84	Gulfstream 3	416	Platinum Dunes Productions, Van Nuys, Ca.	(N500XB)
N4545	98	Learjet 45	45-045	Rancho del Sol LLC. Byron, Ca.	
N4614N	90	Citation II	550-0659	U S Customs Service, Oklahoma City, Ok.	XC-HGZ
N4895Q	92	Citation V	560-0199	Amistad Aviation Inc. Amistad, NM.	N78950
N5000X	00	Gulfstream V	611	Teratorn LLC. Seattle, Wa.	N568GA
N5001J	01	Learjet 45	45-169	Learjet inc. Wichita, Ks.	
N5010X	01	390 Premier 1	RB-10	Raytheon Aircraft Co. Wichita, Ks. (status ?).	
N5011L	04	Learjet 45	45-256	Learjet Inc. Wichita, Ks.	
N5026	03	CitationJet CJ-2	525A-0159	Overseas Transcom Corp. Jacksonville, Fl.	N.....
N5101	98	Gulfstream V	550	General Motors Corp. Detroit, Mi.	N650GA
N5102	98	Gulfstream V	551	General Motors Corp. Detroit, Mi.	N651GA
N5112	96	Citation X	750-0010	General Motors Corp. Detroit, Mi.	N5225K
N5113	97	Citation X	750-0013	General Motors Corp. Detroit, Mi.	N5241Z
N5114	97	Citation X	750-0017	General Motors Corp. Detroit, Mi.	N51072
N5115	96	Citation X	750-0018	General Motors Corp. Detroit, Mi.	N95CC
N5116	97	Citation X	750-0019	General Motors Corp. Detroit, Mi.	N5109W
N5117	95	Citation VII	650-7064	General Motors Corp. Detroit, Mi.	HB-VLP
N5119	90	BAe 125/800A	8177	NSI Leasing LLC/National System Inc. Maryland Heights, Mo.	N217AL
N5161R	71	JetStar-731	5161	5161 Romeo LLC. Chicago, Il.	LY-AMB
N5165T	04	Citation Excel XLS	560-5543	Cessna Aircraft Co. Wichita, Ks.	
N5173F	00	Citation Excel	560-5173	Dana Flight Operations Inc. Swanton, Oh.	N51743
N5175U	73	B 737/T-43A	20689	EG&G/Department of the Air Force, McCarran, Nv.	72-0282
N5176Y	74	B 737/T-43A	20692	EG&G/Department of the Air Force, McCarran, Nv.	72-0285
N5177C	74	B 737/T-43A	20693	EG&G/Department of the Air Force, McCarran, Nv.	72-0286
N5183U	04	Citation X	750-0238	Cessna Aircraft Co. Wichita, Ks.	
N5225G	68	Falcon 20D	181	LVA Management & Consulting Inc. Lawrenceville, Ga.	N817JS
N5227G	04	CitationJet CJ-3	525B-0006	Cessna Aircraft Co. Wichita, Ks.	
N5228J	04	Citation X	750-0237	Cessna Aircraft Co. Wichita, Ks.	
N5260Y	04	Citation Sovereign	680-0026	Cessna Aircraft Co. Wichita, Ks.	
N5268V	04	Citation X	750-0239	Cessna Aircraft Co. Wichita, Ks.	
N5269S	04	Citation Excel XLS	560-5545	Cessna Aircraft Co. Wichita, Ks.	
N5270K	04	Citation Sovereign	680-0014	Cessna Aircraft Co. Wichita, Ks.	
N5294E	74	B 737/T-43A	20691	EG&G/Department of the Air Force, McCarran, Nv.	72-0284
N5294M	74	B 737/T-43A	20694	EG&G/Department of the Air Force, McCarran, Nv.	72-0287
Reg	Yr	Type	c/n	Owner/Operator	Prev Regn

Reg	Yr	Type	c/n	Owner/Operator	Prev Regn
☐ N5314J	91	Citation II	550-0663	U S Customs Service, New Orleans NAS, La.	(XC-JCX)
☐ N5319*	96	Challenger 604	5319	Stanford Aviation 5555 LLC. Miami, Fl.	N2SA
☐ N5322	02	Falcon 50EX	322	Vulcan Aggregates LLC. Birmingham, Al.	F-WWHB
☐ N5349	97	Challenger 604	5349	Apex Babcock & Brown LLC. Concord, Ca.	N312BX
☐ N5373D	96	Citation OT-47B	560-0381	U S Dept of State, Oklahoma City, Ok.	N214L
☐ N5408G	91	Citation II	550-0666	U S Customs Service, Oklahoma City, Ok. (XC-JBS as required)	XC-JBS
☐ N5572	83	Learjet 55	55-072	Milam International Inc. Englewood, Co.	SX-BNS
☐ N5616	00	Gulfstream V	616	Halliburton Energy Services Inc. Houston, Tx.	N141HC
☐ N5731	86	Falcon 900	8	Guild Investments LLC. Northbrook, Il.	N406FJ
☐ N5734	97	Hawker 800XP	8304	Air Time Aviation LLC. Bethesda, Md.	N802JT
☐ N5736	00	Hawker 800XP	8471	Ogden & Sons plc. Leeds-Bradford, UK.	N43642
☐ N5879	61	MS 760 Paris-2B	107	CJT Holdings LLC. Dallas, Tx.	PH-MSW
☐ N5956B	00	Gulfstream 4SP	1469	Oakmont Holdings LLC. Van Nuys, Ca.	N269GA
☐ N6001L	80	Citation II	550-0169	U S Customs Service, New Orleans NAS, La.	(XC-JDA)
☐ N6015Y	04	390 Premier 1	RB-115	Raytheon Aircraft Co. Wichita, Ks.	
☐ N6110	93	Citation VII	650-7023	AESR LLC. Minneapolis, Mn.	N1262G
☐ N6111F	04	390 Premier 1	RB-111	Charlie Aviation LLC/Azzar Store Equipment Inc. Grand Rapids	
☐ N6117G	04	390 Premier 1	RB-117	Raytheon Aircraft Co. Wichita, Ks.	
☐ N6118C	04	390 Premier 1	RB-118	Raytheon Aircraft Co. Wichita, Ks.	
☐ N6119C	04	390 Premier 1	RB-119	Roberts Properties Inc. Atlanta, Ga.	
☐ N6120U	04	390 Premier 1	RB-120	Raytheon Aircraft Co. Wichita, Ks.	
☐ N6124W	04	390 Premier 1	RB-124	Raytheon Aircraft Co. Wichita, Ks.	
☐ N6144S	02	Beechjet 400A	RK-344	Hall Auto World Inc. Norfolk, Va.	
☐ N6177Y	67	Learjet 24	24-151	Adventure Capital Group Expedition, Fort Lauderdale, Fl.	N53GH
☐ N6453	03	Falcon 2000EX	26	Nike Inc/Aero Air LLC. Hillsboro, Or.	N226EX
☐ N6555L	67	Falcon 20C	85	Threshold Ventures Inc. Scottsdale, Az.	VH-JSY
☐ N6637G	91	Citation II	550-0670	U S Customs Service, New Orleans NAS. (XC-JEG as required).	(XC-JCZ)
☐ N6666R	01	Falcon 900EX	102	Burnett Aviation Co. Fort Worth, Tx.	N6666P
☐ N6757M	02	Challenger 604	5545	McCormick & Co. Baltimore-Martin County, Md.	N334FX
☐ N6763L	91	Citation II	550-0673	U S Customs Service, Oklahoma City, Ok. (XC-HHA as required)	XC-HHA
☐ N6775C	91	Citation II	550-0677	U S Customs Service, Oklahoma City, Ok. (XC-HJC as required)	
☐ N6776T	92	Citation II	550-0680	U S Customs Service, Oklahoma City, Ok. (XC-HJE as required)	
☐ N6846T	90	Citation II	550-0625	White Oak Flight Service Inc. Beckley, WV.	N625EA
☐ N7050V	83	Diamond 1A	A058SA	Marvin Lumber & Cedar Co. Warroad, Mn.	VR-BKA
☐ N7070A	85	Citation S/II	S550-0068	Omega Air Inc. Dublin, Ireland.	N4049
☐ N7074X	70	Learjet 24B	24B-223	Interlease Aviation Corp. Northfield, Il. (status ?).	D-CFVG
☐ N7092C	78	Learjet 35A	35A-184	Cefaratti International Inc. Coronado, Ca.	HB-VFO
☐ N7148J	75	Sabre-75A	380-33	AVMATS, Chesterfield, Mo.	N129MS
☐ N7200K	66	Learjet 23	23-099	RBS Aviation Group Inc. Hampton, Ga.	
☐ N7270B	73	B 727-232	20641	Clay Lacy Aviation Inc. Van Nuys, Ca.	N18786
☐ N7374	01	Hawker 800XP	8524	Sportsmen's Aviation Group LLC. Florence, Or.	N4224H
☐ N7381	65	B 720-060B	18977	Raytheon Co. Lexington, Ma. (status ?).	N440DS
☐ N7418F	99	Citation X	750-0074	Wings Associates Inc. White Plains, NY.	N2418F
☐ N7490A	82	HS 125/700A	NA0320	Oehmig Aviation LLC. Houston, Tx.	N700HW
☐ N7600	04	Hawker 400XP	RK-395	SAS Institute Inc. Cary, NC.	
☐ N7600G	01	Citation X	750-0159	State Jet Services LLC/SAS Institute Inc. Cary, NC.	N1128V
☐ N7600K	02	BBJ-7BC	32628	SAS Institute Inc. Cary, NC.	N102QS
☐ N7601	94	Gulfstream 4SP	1245	Unocal Corp. Van Nuys, Ca.	(N7602)
☐ N7601R	60	MS 760 Paris-1R	60	William Spriggs, Santa Paula, Ca.	No 60
☐ N7700T	82	Citation 1/SP	501-0248	Distribution Air LLC. Springfield, Mo.	(N711EG)
☐ N7715X	03	CitationJet CJ-2	525A-0178	BH Aviation Inc. Santa Ana, Ca.	N52655
☐ N7715Y	00	CitationJet CJ-1	525-0387	John Needham, Austin, Tx.	N7715X
☐ N7734T	98	Learjet 60	60-139	Tejas Aviation Management, Fort Worth, Tx.	N370AT
☐ N7777B	91	Citation VI	650-0214	Bergstrom Pioneer Auto & Truck Leasing, Neenah, Wi.	N771JB
☐ N7810W	73	Learjet 25B	25B-117	Crow Executive Air Inc. Toledo-Metcalf, Oh.	N731CW
☐ N7895Q	01	Citation Encore	560-0564	Corporate Aviation, Raleigh, NC.	N5241R
☐ N7996	84	BAe 125/800A	8019	Amweld Building Products Inc/W W Aircraft LLC. Garrettsville	(N800NW)
☐ N8005	98	Citation Excel	560-5006	RAW Inc. Raleigh, NC.	N5141F
☐ N8005Y	73	Learjet 25B	25B-121	Source Investments LLC. Addison, Tx.	XA-SAL
☐ N8030F	89	BAe 125/C-29A	8131	Bombardier Aerospace Corp. Windsor Locks, Ct.	N95
☐ N8040A	76	Learjet 35	35-048	AirNet Systems Inc. Columbus, Oh. (black).	F-GHMP
☐ N8064A	80	Learjet 35A	35A-324	Airlift Trading Ltd. Auckland, NZ.	G-JETG
☐ N8073R	91	Beechjet 400A	RK-24	Raytheon Aircraft Co. Wichita, Ks.	
☐ N8085T	92	Beechjet 400A	RK-51	L & K Consulting Inc. Grand Junction, Co.	
☐ N8100E	96	Falcon 900EX	4	Emerson Electric Co. St Louis, Mo.	N204FJ
☐ N8130S	02	Citation Encore	560-0631	Peri Ventures LLC. Reno, Nv.	N813QS

Reg	Yr	Type	c/n	Owner/Operator	Prev Regn

Reg	Yr	Type	c/n	Owner/Operator	Prev Regn
N8167Y	93	Beechjet 400A	RK-67	Annett Holdings Inc. Des Moines, Ia.	
N8186	02	Hawker 800XP	8604	CYMI Investments Sub Inc. Dayton, Oh.	N60664
N8200E	87	Falcon 900B	34	Emerson Electric Co. St Louis, Mo.	N8100E
N8239E	92	Beechjet 400A	RK-46	Nulife Aviation LLC. Sarasota, Fl.	
N8271	95	Learjet 60	60-066	F E R M Inc. Miami Lakes, Fl.	N5006K
N8279G	93	Beechjet 400A	RK-79	Frances Dittmer Projects Inc. Garfield County, Rifle, Co.	OH-RIF
N8283C	94	Beechjet 400A	RK-83	Advanced Flightworks LLC. Dover, De.	XA-MII
N8288R	95	CitationJet	525-0090	Interwings Charter of N America, Capetown, RSA.	N5136J
N8300E	80	Falcon 50	33	Emerson Electric Co. St Louis, Mo.	N8100E
N8341C	96	CitationJet	525-0150	Air Commander LLC. St Paul, Mn.	ZS-NUW
N8344M	88	Citation II	550-0577	JWM Acquisition Associates LLC. Cary, NC.	N827JB
N8400E	84	Falcon 50	150	Emerson Electric Co. St Louis, Mo.	N8200E
N8500	72	Sabre-40A	282-108	Haws Aviation LLC. Huntsville, Al.	N85CC
N8860	66	DC 9-15	45797	Richard Mellon Scaife, Latrobe, Pa.	(EC-BAX)
N8940	02	CitationJet CJ-2	525A-0091	Mac-Tech Inc. Wellington, Ks.	N.....
N9035Y	61	MS 760 Paris-1A	86	North Pacific Aircraft Development Co. Helena, Mt.	F-BJLX
N9072U	86	Citation S/II	S550-0106	Harper Cattle Aviation LLC. Arlington, Tx.	N666TR
N9108Z	75	Learjet 36	36-005	B & C Flight Management Inc. Houston, Tx.	LV-LOG
N9180K	99	CitationJet	525-0342	Cessna Aircraft Co. Wichita, Ks.	N342AC
N9253V	91	Gulfstream 4	1176	Media Consulting Services LLC. Greenwich, Ct.	VP-CRY
N9292X	97	Hawker 800XP	8315	Warner Road Aviation Inc. Steamboat Springs, Co.	N2169X
N9395Y	79	HS 125/700A-2	NA0243	Air 4 Aviation LLC/Tri-C Aviation Inc. Houston, Tx.	N104JG
N9700T	92	Citation V	560-0203	Hutchens Industries inc/Tandem Air LLC. Springfield, Mo.	N7700L
N9700X	95	Challenger 601-3R	5186	Cameron-Henkind Corp. White Plains, NY.	N612CC
N9867	04	Hawker 800XP	8678	CYMI Investments Sub Inc. Dayton, Oh.	N678XP
N9871R	04	Falcon 2000EX EASY	43	CFG Service Corp. Providence, RI.	F-WWGY
N9999M	89	Gulfstream 4	1090	Star Plane Inc. NYC.	VP-CYM
N9999V	81	HS 125/700A	NA0308	Vinson Group LLC. St Louis, Mo.	N10CN
N10123	71	Gulfstream 2TT	107	Geosar LLC. Van Nuys, Ca.	N5113H
N10857	91	BAe 125/800B	8213	Raytheon Aircraft Co. Little Rock, Ar.	G-BURV
N11887	73	Sabre-75A	380-4	Jose Manuel Figueroa, McAllen, Tx.	XA-RLP
N12068	93	Citation II	550-0719	La Oso SA. Guatemala City, Guatemala.	(N550BG)
N12549	84	Citation II	550-0501	U S Customs Service, Oklahoma City, Ok.	
N12659	74	Sabre-75A	380-16	AVMATS, Chesterfield, Mo.	N126MS
N14456	00	Gulfstream 4SP	1430	Bandwidth LLC/Avjet Corp. Burbank, Ca.	N530JD
N24237	85	Citation III	650-0102	Beasley Broadcasting Group, Naples, Fl.	N406LM
N26494	89	Citation II	550-0605	U S Customs Service, Oklahoma City, Ok.	(N1304B)
N26496	89	Citation II	550-0607	U S Customs Service, New Orleans NAS. La.	(XC-JCW)
N26621	89	Citation II	550-0593	U S Customs Service, Oklahoma City, Ok.	(XC-JBT)
N30156	73	Westwind-1123	165	RAA Enterprises Inc. Wilmington, De.	N22RD
N31496	04	Hawker 400XP	RK-396	Aerolineas Ejecutivas SA. Toluca, Mexico.	
N36607	04	Hawker 400XP	RK-407	Raytheon Aircraft Co. Wichita, Ks.	
N36701	04	Hawker 400XP	RK-401	Raytheon Aircraft Co. Wichita, Ks.	
N36803	04	Hawker 400XP	RK-403	Raytheon Aircraft Co. Wichita, Ks.	
N36907	04	Hawker 400XP	RK-417	Raytheon Aircraft Co. Wichita, Ks.	
N36997	04	Hawker 400XP	RK-397	Flight Options LLC. Cleveland, Oh.	
N37010	04	Hawker 800XP	8710	Raytheon Aircraft Co. Wichita, Ks.	
N37108	04	Hawker 400XP	RK-408	Raytheon Aircraft Co. Wichita, Ks.	
N37115	04	Hawker 400XP	RK-415	Raytheon Aircraft Co. Wichita, Ks.	
N37201	91	Citation II	550-0655	U S Customs Service, New Orleans NAS, La.	
N37204	04	Hawker 400XP	RK-404	Raytheon Aircraft Co. Wichita, Ks.	
N37211	04	Hawker 800XP	8711	Raytheon Aircraft Co. Wichita, Ks.	
N37310	04	Hawker 400XP	RK-410	Raytheon Aircraft Co. Wichita, Ks.	
N37312	04	Hawker 400XP	RK-412	Raytheon Aircraft Co. Wichita, Ks.	
N37971	82	Learjet 25D	25D-358	Caulkins Investment Co. Denver, Co.	
N40593	65	Jet Commander	41	Mach Aero International Corp. Tulsa, Ok.	(N499TR)
N44982	99	Gulfstream V	581	Bayard Foreign Marketing LLC. Portland, Or.	N8068V
N45678	03	Citation Bravo	550-1056	Department of Justice, Fort Worth, Tx.	N52601
N46190	66	HS 125/731	25108	White Industries Inc. Bates City, Mo. (status ?).	C-GTTS
N46253	78	Citation	500-0369	White Industries Inc. Bates City, Mo. (status ?).	C-GVER
N50078	04	390 Premier 1	RB-109	Bechcraft Vertrieb & Service GmbH. Augsburg, Germany.	
N50111	04	Learjet 40	45-2019	Learjet Inc. Wichita, Ks.	
N50153	04	Learjet 40	45-2020	Learjet Inc. Wichita, ks.	
N50446	66	Falcon 20C	21	Sierra American Corp. Addison, Tx.	C-FTUT
N50553	04	Hawker 800XP	8703	Raytheon Aircraft Co. Wichita, Ks.	
N50727	04	Hawker 400XP	RK-389	Pluck Air LLC/Tony Downs Food Co. St James, Mn.	

Reg	Yr	Type	c/n	Owner/Operator	Prev Regn
N51099	74	Citation	500-0203	International Turbine Service Inc. Grapevine, Tx.	CC-PZM
N52526	04	Citation X	750-0234	Cessna Aircraft Co. Wichita, Ks.	
N52639	04	Citation Excel XLS	560-5517	Cessna Aircraft Co. Wichita, Ks.	
N60322	04	390 Premier 1	RB-112	Raytheon Aircraft Co. Wichita, Ks.	
N61908	04	390 Premier 1	RB-108	Beechcraft Vertrieb & Service GmbH. Augsburg, Germany.	
N61998	03	390 Premier 1	RB-98	Raytheon Aircraft Co. Wichita, Ks.	
N63357	67	Jet Commander	99	N22RD Inc. Corpus Christi, Tx.	N22RD
N77058	88	Challenger 601-3A	5017	Kimberly-Clark Corp. Dallas, Tx.	N202HG
N77215	96	CitationJet	525-0149	Moonchild Aviation LLC. Los Angeles, Ca.	(N67GU)
N77702	02	Learjet 45	45-224	Miller's Professional Imaging, Pittsburgh, Pa.	N822GA
N77794	94	CitationJet	525-0073	Executive Wings Inc. Wexford, Pa.	N2656G
N79711	00	BBJ-7BQ	30547	Dallah Al Baraka, Jeddah, Saudi Arabia.	(HZ-DG5)
N80364	76	Citation Eagle	500-0299	Farnley Investments Ltd. Dublin, Ireland.	OY-TKI
N82400	93	Beechjet 400A	RK-75	RDK Charter Services LLC. Elkhart, In.	
N87319	93	CitationJet	525-0037	Aircraft Marketing Inc. Albuquerque, NM.	EC-IAB
N89319	74	Citation	500-0223	Aircraft Marketing Inc. Albuquerque, NM.	I-CLAD
N99114	73	Sabre-40A	282-128	Jett Aire Florida One Inc. Palm Beach, Fl.	XA-LIX
Military					
00-1051	01	Citation UC-35C	560-0565	U S Army, B-2/228th AVN,	(00-0002)
00-1052	01	Citation UC-35C	560-0574	U S Army, PATD,	N52526
00-1053	01	Citation UC 35C	560-0577	U S Army, PATD,	N5207V
U1	00	Gulfstream C-37A	653	USCG, Washington, DC.	N527GA
01-0005	02	BBJ-7DM (C-40B)	33080	USAF, 1st AS/89th AW, Andrews AFB. Md.	N374BC
01-0015	01	BBJ-7DM (C-40B)	32916	USAF, 65th AS, 15ABW, Hickam AFB. Hi.	N378BJ
01-0028	00	Gulfstream C-37A	620	USAF, 310 Airlift Squadron, MacDill AFB. Fl.	N535GA
01-0029	00	Gulfstream C-37A	624	USAF, 310 Airlift Squadron, MacDill AFB. Fl.	N624GA
01-0030	01	Gulfstream C-37A	663	USAF, 310 Airlift Squadron, MacDill AFB. Fl.	N663GA
01-0040	00	BBJ-7DM (C-40B)	29971	USAF, 1st AS/89th AW, Andrews AFB. Md.	N371BJ
01-0065	00	Gulfstream C-37A	652	USAF, Hickam AFB. Hi.	N582GA
01-0076	01	Gulfstream V	645	USAF,	N645GA
01-0301	01	Citation UC-35C	560-0589	U S Army, PATD,	N5151D
02-0201	00	BBJ-7CPS (C-40C)	30755	D C ANG, 201st Airlift Squadron, Andrews AFB. Md.	N752BC
02-0202	99	BBJ-7CPS (C-40C)	30753	D C ANG, 201st Airlift Squadron, Andrews AFB. Md.	N754BC
02-0203	02	BBJ-7BC (C-40C)	33434	USAF,	N236BA
02-1863	01	Gulfstream C-37A	670	U S Army. 'Gettysburg'	N670GA
03-0016	03	Citation UC-35D	560-0649	U S Army,	N5267T
03-0726	04	Citation UC-35C	560-0667	U S Army,	N52462
150972	60	Sabreliner T-39D	285-4	U. S. Navy, Pensacola NAS, Fl.	
150977	60	Sabreliner T-39D	285-9	U. S. Navy, Pensacola NAS, Fl.	
150992	61	Sabreliner T-39D	285-24	U. S. Navy, Naval Weapons Center, China Lake, Ca.	
151337	61	Sabreliner T-39D	285-26	U. S. Navy, Pensacola NAS, Fl.	
158380	68	Sabreliner CT-39E	282-95	U. S. Navy, Pensacola NAS, Fl.	N425NA
158381	68	Sabreliner CT-39E	282-93	U. S. Navy, VRC-50, Cubi Point, Phillipines. (status ?).	N4701N
158843	71	Sabreliner CT-39G	306-52	23. U S Navy, NAS Pensacola, Fl.	N955R
158844	71	Sabreliner CT-39G	306-55	U. S. Navy,	N5419
159361	73	Sabreliner CT-39G	306-65	U. S. Navy, Code 30, VR-24, NAF Sigonella, Italy.	N8364N
159364	74	Sabreliner CT-39G	306-69	25. U S Navy, NAS Pensacola, Fl.	
159365	74	Sabreliner CT-39G	306-70	U. S. Marine Corps, El Toro MCAS, Ca.	
160053	75	Sabreliner CT-39G	306-104	U S Navy,	N65795
160054	75	Sabreliner CT-39G	306-105	22. U S Navy, NAS Pensacola, Fl.	N65796
160055	75	Sabreliner CT-39G	306-106	Station Operations & Engineering Sqn. Cherry Point MCAS, NC.	N65797
160056	75	Sabreliner CT-39G	306-107	Station Operations & Engineering Sqn. Cherry Point MCAS, NC.	N65798
163691	86	Gulfstream C-20D	480	U S Navy, VR-1, CFLSW, Andrews AFB. Md.	N302GA
163692	86	Gulfstream C-20D	481	USMC/USN, VR-1, CFLSW, Andrews AFB. Md.	N304GA
165093	92	Gulfstream C-20G	1187	USN, VR-48, Andrews AFB. Md. 'City of Anapolis'	N481GA
165094	92	Gulfstream C-20G	1189	USN, VR-48, Andrews AFB. Md. 'City of Baltimore'	N402GA
165151	92	Gulfstream C-20G	1199	U S Navy, VR-51, Code RG, Kaneohe, Hi.	N428GA
165152	92	Gulfstream C-20G	1201	U S Navy, VR-51, Code RG, Kaneohe, Hi.	N431GA
165153	92	Gulfstream C-20G	1200	USMC, MASD, NAF Washington, Andrews AFB. Md.	N430GA
165509	64	Sabre T-39N	282-9	01. U S Navy, Pensacola NAS, Fl.	N301NT
165510	66	Sabre T-39N	282-81	02. U S Navy, Pensacola NAS, Fl.	N302NT
165511	65	Sabre T-39N	282-29	03. U S Navy, Pensacola NAS, Fl.	N303NT
165512	63	Sabre T-39N	282-2	04. U S Navy, Pensacola NAS, Fl.	N304NT
165513	66	Sabre T-39N	282-66	05. U S Navy, Pensacola NAS, Fl.	N305NT
165514	65	Sabre T-39N	282-30	06. U S Navy, Pensacola NAS, Fl.	N306NT
165515	66	Sabre T-39N	282-72	07. U S Navy, Pensacola NAS, Fl.	N307NT
Reg	*Yr*	*Type*	*c/n*	*Owner/Operator*	*Prev Regn*

Reg	Yr	Type	c/n	Owner/Operator	Prev Regn
165516	67	Sabre T-39N	282-90	08. U S Navy, Pensacola NAS, Fl.	N308NT
165517	66	Sabre T-39N	282-61	09. U S Navy, Pensacola NAS, Fl.	N309NT
165518	66	Sabre T-39N	282-77	10. U S Navy, Pensacola NAS, Fl.	N310NT
165519	64	Sabre T-39N	282-19	11. U S Navy, Pensacola NAS, Fl.	N311NT
165520	65	Sabre T-39N	282-32	12. U S Navy, Pensacola NAS, Fl.	N312NT
165521	68	Sabre T-39N	282-94	13. U S Navy, Pensacola NAS, Fl.	N313NT
165523	64	Sabre T-39N	282-20	14. U S Navy, Pensacola NAS, Fl.	N315NT
165524	66	Sabre T-39N	282-60	15. U S Navy, Pensacola NAS, Fl.	N316NT
165740	99	Citation UC-35C	560-0524	USMC, MWHS-4/EZ, New Orleans NAS, La.	N5091J
165741	99	Citation UC-35C	560-0529	USMC, MWHS-4/EZ, New Orleans NAS, La.	N5097H
165829	00	B 737-7AF (C-40A)	29979	U S Navy, VR-59/RY, NAS Fort Worth JRB, Tx.	N1003N
165830	00	B 737-7AF (C-40A)	29980	U S Navy, VR-59/RY, NAS Fort Worth JRB, Tx.	N1003M
165831	00	B 737-7AF (C-40A)	30200	U S Navy, VR-59/RY, NAS Fort Worth JRB, Tx.	N1786B
165832	01	B 737-7AF (C-40A)	30781	U S Marine Corp, VR-58/JV, 'City of St Augustine'	
165833	01	B 737-7AF (C-40A)	32597	U S Navy, VR-58/JV, 'City of Dallas'	
165834	02	B 737-7AF (C-40A)	32598	U S Navy, VR-58/JV,	
165835	04	B 737-7AF (C-40A)	33826	U S Navy,	N6065Y
165939	01	Citation UC-35D	560-0570	U S Marine Corp. MWHS-1,	N5262W
166374	02	Citation UC-35D	560-0592	U S Marine Corp, VM/HQUSMC,	N5180C
166375	00	Gulfstream V	657	U S Navy, 'Spirit of Midway Island'	N587GA
166474	02	Citation UC-35D	560-0630	USMC, MWHS-1,	N5180K
166500	04	Citation UC-35D	560-0651	USMC, MCAS Miramar,	N5156D
166712	04	Citation UC-35	560-0672	United States Navy,	N5253G
166713	04	Citation UC-35	560-0677	United States Navy,	N5079V
2101	77	Guardian HU-25B	374	USCG, Cape Cod, Ma.	N1045F
2102	78	Guardian HU-25B	386	USCG, Miami, Fl.	N149F
2103	78	Guardian HU-25B	394	FAA, Sandia National Laboratory, Albuquerque, NM.	N178F
2104	78	Guardian HU-25C	390	USCG, Miami, Fl.	N173F
2105	78	Guardian HU-25D	398	USCG, Corpus Christi, Tx.	N183F
2109	79	Guardian HU-25A	407	USCG, Cape Cod, Ma.	N406F
2110	79	Guardian HU-25A	411	USCG, AR & SC, Elizabeth City, NC.	N408F
2111	79	Guardian HU-25B	413	USCG, AR & SC, Elizabeth City, NC. (status ?).	N410F
2112	79	Guardian HU-25C	415	USCG, Corpus Christi, Tx.	N413F
2113	79	Guardian HU-25A	417	USCG, Miami, Fl.	N416FJ
2114	79	Guardian HU-25A	418	USCG, Miami, Fl.	N417F
2117	80	Guardian HU-25A	421	USCG, Miami, Fl.	N422F
2118	80	Guardian HU-25B	423	USCG, ATC, Mobile, Al.	N423F
2120	80	Guardian HU-25A	425	USCG, ATC, Mobile, Al.	N425F
2121	80	Guardian HU-25A	431	USCG, ATC, Mobile, Al.	N429F
2128	81	Guardian HU-25A	445	USCG, Miami, Fl.	N449F
2129	81	Guardian HU-25C	447	USCG, Miami, Fl.	N455F
2131	81	Guardian HU-25C	452	USCG, Cape Cod, Ma.	N459F
2133	81	Guardian HU-25C	456	USCG, Cape Cod, Ma.	N462F
2134	81	Guardian HU-25A	458	USCG, Miami, Fl.	N465F
2135	81	Guardian HU-25C	459	USCG, Miami, Fl.	N466F
2136	81	Guardian HU-25A	460	USCG, Corpus Christi, Tx.	N467F
2139	82	Guardian HU-25C	466	USCG, Miami, Fl.	N473F
2140	82	Guardian HU-25C	467	USCG, Cape Cod, Ma.	N474F
2141	77	Guardian HU-25C	371	USCG, Cape Cod, Ma.	N1039F
59-2873	59	Sabreliner CT-39B	270-1	USAF/4950th Test Wing-ASD, Edwards AFB. Ca.	
60-3474	60	Sabreliner CT-39B	270-3	USAF/4950th Test Wing-ASD, Edwards AFB. Ca.	
61-0670	61	Sabreliner T-39A	265-73	USAF,	
62-4125	62	C-135B	18465	USAF, 58th MAS, Ramstein AB. Germany.	
62-4126	62	C-135B	18466	USAF, 89th MAW, Andrews AFB. Md.	
62-4127	62	C-135B	18467	USAF, 89th MAW, Andrews AFB. Md.	
62-4129	62	C-135B	18469	USAF, 89th MAW, Andrews AFB. Md.	
62-4130	62	C-135B	18470	USAF, 89th MAW, Andrews AFB. Md.	
62-4488	62	Sabreliner CT-39A	276-41	USAF, ANG, Andrews AFB. Md.	
721	95	Citation OT-47B	560-0365	FAP,	N2500D
73-1681	75	C-9C	47668	USAF, SAM, 1st MAS/89th MAW, Andrews AFB. Md.	
73-1682	75	C-9C	47670	USAF, SAM, 1st MAS/89th MAW, Andrews AFB. Md.	
73-1683	75	C-9C	47671	USAF, SAM, 99th AS, Andrews AFB. Md.	
82-8000	87	B 747-2G4B	23824	VC-25A, Presidential aircraft, 89th MAW, Andrews AFB. Md.	
830500	83	Gulfstream C-20A	382	U S Navy, C-in-C USNE, Sigonella, Italy.	83-0500
83-0502	83	Gulfstream 3	389	C-20A, NASA, Edwards AFB. Ca.	N310GA
84-0064	84	Learjet C-21A	35A-510	USAF, 375th AW/458th AS/84th ALF,	N7263D
Reg	**Yr**	**Type**	**c/n**	**Owner/Operator**	**Prev Regn**

Reg	Yr	Type	c/n	Owner/Operator	Prev Regn
☐ 84-0065	84	Learjet C-21A	35A-511	USAF, 375th AW/458th AS/332nd ALF,	N7263E
☐ 84-0066	84	Learjet C-21A	35A-512	USAF, 375th AW/457th AS/AFFSA,	N7263F
☐ 84-0068	84	Learjet C-21A	35A-514	USAF, 76th AW/86th AW (USAFE), Ramstein AB. Germany.	N7263K
☐ 84-0069	84	Learjet C-21A	35A-515	USAF, KS/314th AW/45th AS, Keesler AFB. Ms.	N7263L
☐ 84-0070	84	Learjet C-21A	35A-516	USAF, KS/314th AW/45th AS, Keesler AFB. Ms.	N7263N
☐ 84-0071	84	Learjet C-21A	35A-517	USAF, KS/314th AW/45th AS, Keesler AFB. Ms.	N7263R
☐ 84-0072	84	Learjet C-21A	35A-518	USAF, KS/314th AW/45th AS, Keesler AFB. Ms.	N7263X
☐ 84-0073	84	Learjet C-21A	35A-519	USAF, 375th AW/457th AS, Andrews AFB. Md.	N400AD
☐ 84-0074	84	Learjet C-21A	35A-520	USAF, 375th AW/457th AS, Andrews AFB. Md.	N400AK
☐ 84-0075	84	Learjet C-21A	35A-521	USAF, 375th AW/457th AS, Andrews AFB. Md.	N400AN
☐ 84-0076	84	Learjet C-21A	35A-522	USAF, 375th AW/457th AS, Andrews AFB. Md.	N400AP
☐ 84-0077	84	Learjet C-21A	35A-523	USAF, 375th AW/457th AS, Andrews AFB. Md.	N400AQ
☐ 84-0078	84	Learjet C-21A	35A-524	USAF, 375th AW/457th AS, Andrews AFB. Md.	N400AS
☐ 84-0079	84	Learjet C-21A	35A-525	USAF, 375th AW/457th AS, Andrews AFB. Md.	N400AT
☐ 84-0080	84	Learjet C-21A	35A-526	USAF, 375th AW457th AS, Andrews AFB. Md.	N400AU
☐ 84-0081	84	Learjet C-21A	35A-527	USAF, 76th AS/86th AW (USAFE), Stuttgart AB. Germany.	N400AX
☐ 84-0082	84	Learjet C-21A	35A-528	USAF, 76th AS/86th AW (USAFE), Stuttgart AB. Germany.	N400AY
☐ 84-0083	84	Learjet C-21A	35A-529	USAF, 76th AS/86th AW (USAFE), Stuttgart AB. Germany.	N400AZ
☐ 84-0084	84	Learjet C-21A	35A-530	USAF, 76th AS/86th AW (USAFE), Ramstein AB. Germany.	N400BA
☐ 84-0085	84	Learjet C-21A	35A-531	USAF, 76th AS/86th AW (USAFF), Ramstein AD. Germany.	N400FY
☐ 84-0086	84	Learjet C-21A	35A-532	USAF, 76th AS/86th AW (USAFE), Ramstein AB. Germany.	N400BN
☐ 84-0087	84	Learjet C-21A	35A-533	USAF, 76th AS/86th AW (USAFE), Ramstein AB. Germany.	N400BQ
☐ 84-0088	84	Learjet C-21A	35A-534	USAF, 375th AW/458th AS/311th ALF,	N400BU
☐ 84-0089	84	Learjet C-21A	35A-535	USAF, 375th AW/458th AS/311th ALF,	(N61905)
☐ 84-0090	84	Learjet C-21A	35A-536	USAF, 375th AW/456th AS/311th ALF,	N400BZ
☐ 84-0091	84	Learjet C-21A	35A-537	USAF, 375th AW/458th AS/311th ALF,	N400CD
☐ 84-0092	85	Learjet C-21A	35A-538	USAF, 375th AW/458th AS/311th ALF,	N400CG
☐ 84-0093	85	Learjet C-21A	35A-539	USAF, 375th AW/458th AS/311th ALF,	N400CJ
☐ 84-0094	85	Learjet C-21A	35A-540	USAF, 375th AW/457th AS/47th ALF,	N400CK
☐ 84-0095	85	Learjet C-21A	35A-541	USAF, 375th AW/457th AS/47th ALF,	N400CQ
☐ 84-0096	85	Learjet C-21A	35A-542	USAF, 375th AW/457th AS/47th ALF,	N400CR
☐ 84-0098	85	Learjet C-21A	35A-544	USAF, 475th AW/457th AS/47th ALF,	N400CV
☐ 84-0099	85	Learjet C-21A	35A-545	USAF, 475th AW/457th AS/47th ALF,	N400CX
☐ 84-0100	85	Learjet C-21A	35A-546	USAF, 475th AW/457th AS/47th ALF,	N400CY
☐ 84-0101	85	Learjet C-21A	35A-547	USAF, 374th AW/459th AS, (PACAF), Yokota AB. Japan.	N400CZ
☐ 84-0102	85	Learjet C-21A	35A-548	USAF, 374th AW/459th AS, (PACAF), Yokota AB. Japan.	N400DD
☐ 84-0103	85	Learjet C-21A	35A-549	USAF, 375th AW/458th AS/84th ALF,	N400DJ
☐ 84-0104	85	Learjet C-21A	35A-550	USAF, 375th AW/458th AS/84th ALF,	N400DL
☐ 84-0105	85	Learjet C-21A	35A-551	USAF, 375th AW/458th AS/84th ALF,	N400DN
☐ 84-0106	85	Learjet C-21A	35A-552	USAF, 314th AW/45th AS,	N400DQ
☐ 84-0107	85	Learjet C-21A	35A-553	USAF, 375th AW/458th AS/84th ALF,	N400DR
☐ 84-0108	85	Learjet C-21A	35A-554	USAF, 76th AS/86th AW, (USAFE), Ramstein AB. Germany.	N400DU
☐ 84-0109	85	Learjet C-21A	35A-555	USAF, 76th AS/86th AW, (USAFE), Ramstein AB. Germany.	N400DV
☐ 84-0110	85	Learjet C-21A	35A-556	USAF, 76th AS/86th AW, (USAFE), Ramstein AB. Germany.	N400DX
☐ 84-0111	85	Learjet C-21A	35A-557	USAF, 76th AS/86th AW, (USAFE), Ramstein AB. Germany.	N400DY
☐ 84-0112	85	Learjet C-21A	35A-558	USAF, 76th AS/86th AW, (USAFE), Ramstein AB. Germany.	N400DZ
☐ 84-0113	85	Learjet C-21A	35A-559	USAF, 375th AW/457th AS/12th ALF,	N400EC
☐ 84-0114	85	Learjet C-21A	35A-560	USAF, 375th AW/457th AS/12th ALF,	N400EE
☐ 84-0115	85	Learjet C-21A	35A-561	USAF, 375th AW/457th AS/12th ALF,	N400EF
☐ 84-0116	85	Learjet C-21A	35A-562	USAF, 375th AW/457th AS/12th ALF,	N400EG
☐ 84-0117	85	Learjet C-21A	35A-563	USAF, 375th AW/457th AS/12th ALF,	N400EJ
☐ 84-0118	85	Learjet C-21A	35A-564	USAF, 375th AW/458th AS, Scott AFB. Il.	N400EK
☐ 84-0119	85	Learjet C-21A	35A-565	USAF, 375th AW/458th AS, Scott AFB. Il.	N400EL
☐ 84-0120	85	Learjet C-21A	35A-566	USAF, 375th AW/458th AS, Scott AFB. Il.	N400EM
☐ 84-0122	85	Learjet C-21A	35A-568	USAF, 375th/AW457th AS, Andrews AFB. Md.	N400EQ
☐ 84-0123	85	Learjet C-21A	35A-569	USAF, 375th AW/457th AS,	N400ER
☐ 84-0124	85	Learjet C-21A	35A-570	USAF, 375th AW/457th AS,	N400ES
☐ 84-0125	85	Learjet C-21A	35A-571	USAF, 375th AW/457th AS,	N400ET
☐ 84-0126	85	Learjet C-21A	35A-572	USAF, 375th AW/458th AS/332nd ALF	N400EU
☐ 84-0127	85	Learjet C-21A	35A-573	USAF, 375th AW/458th AS,	N400EV
☐ 84-0128	85	Learjet C-21A	35A-575	USAF, 375th AW/458th AS,	N400EY
☐ 84-0129	85	Learjet C-21A	35A-576	USAF, 375th AW/458th AS,	N400EZ
☐ 84-0130	85	Learjet C-21A	35A-577	USAF, 374th AW/459th AS,	N400FE
☐ 84-0131	85	Learjet C-21A	35A-578	USAF, 374th AW/459th AS,	N400FG
☐ 84-0132	85	Learjet C-21A	35A-579	USAF, 375th AW/457th AS/84th ALF,	N400FH
☐ 84-0133	85	Learjet C-21A	35A-580	USAF, 375th AW/458th AS/332nd ALF,	N400FK

Reg	Yr	Type	c/n	Owner/Operator	Prev Regn
84-0134	85	Learjet C-21A	35A-581	USAF, RA/12th FTW (ABTC), Randolph AFB. Tx.	N400FM
84-0135	85	Learjet C-21A	35A-582	USAF, RA/12th FTW (ABTC), Randolph AFB. Tx.	N400FN
84-0137	85	Learjet C-21A	35A-585	USAF, 375th AW/458th AS/332nd ALF,	N400FR
84-0139	85	Learjet C-21A	35A-587	USAF, 375th AW/457th AS/12th ALF,	N400FU
84-0140	85	Learjet C-21A	35A-588	USAF, 375th AW/458th AS,	N400FV
84-0141	85	Learjet C-21A	35A-584	USAF, FF/1st FW (ACC), Langley AFB. Va.	N400FQ
84-0142	85	Learjet C-21A	35A-586	USAF, 375th AW/458th AS,	N400FT
85-0049	85	Gulfstream 3	456	C-20C, U. S. Army, 99th AS/89th AW, Andrews AFB. Md.	N336GA
85-0050	85	Gulfstream 3	458	C-20C, U. S. Army, 99th AS/89th AW, Andrews AFB. Md.	N338GA
86-0201	85	Gulfstream 3	470	USAF, C-20B, 99th AS/89th AW, Andrews AFB. Md.	N344GA
86-0202	85	Gulfstream 3	468	USAF, C-20B, 99th AS/89th AW, Andrews AFB. Md.	N342GA
86-0203	85	Gulfstream 3	475	USAF, C-20B, 99th AS/89th AW, Andrews AFB. Md.	N312GA
86-0204	85	Gulfstream 3	476	USAF, C-20B, 99th AS/89th AW, Andrews AFB. Md.	N314GA
86-0206	85	Gulfstream 3	478	USAF, C-20B, 99th AS/89th AW, Andrews AFB. Md.	N318GA
86-0374	87	Learjet C-21A	35A-624	USAF, Peterson AFB. Co.	
86-0377	87	Learjet C-21A	35A-629	USAF, Peterson AFB. Co.	
86-0403	85	Gulfstream 3	473	USAF, C-20D, 99th AS/89th AW, Andrews AFB. Md.	N326GA
87-0139	86	Gulfstream C-20E	497	U S Army, PATFD, Hickam AFB. Hi.	N7096G
87-0140	86	Gulfstream C-20E	498	U S Army, OSACOM PAT Flight Det. Andrews AFB. Md.	N7096E
89-0284	92	Jayhawk T-1A	TT-5	USAF, VN/71 FTW 26 FTS, Vance AFB. Ok.	N2876B
90-0300	92	Gulfstream 4	1181	USAF, C-20G, 99th AS, Andrews AFB. Md.	N473GA
90-0400	91	Jayhawk T-1A	TT-3	USAF, XL/47 FTW 86 FTS, Laughlin AFB. Tx.	N2892B
90-0401	92	Jayhawk T-1A	TT-7	USAF, XL/47 FTW 86 FTS, Laughlin AFB. Tx.	N2869B
90-0402	92	Jayhawk T-1A	TT-8	USAF, XL/47 FTW 86 FTS, Laughlin AFB. Tx.	N2868B
90-0403	92	Jayhawk T-1A	TT-9	USAF, VN/71 FTW 26 FTS, Vance AFB. Ok.	
90-0404	92	Jayhawk T-1A	TT-6	USAF, RA/12 FTW 99 FTS, Randolph AFB. Tx.	N2872B
90-0405	92	Jayhawk T-1A	TT-4	USAF, RA/12 FTW 99 FTS, Randolph AFB. Tx.	
90-0406	92	Jayhawk T-1A	TT-11	USAF, XL/47 FTW 86 FTS, Laughlin AFB. Tx.	
90-0407	92	Jayhawk T-1A	TT-10	USAF, CB/14 FTW, Columbus AFB. Ms.	
90-0408	92	Jayhawk T-1A	TT-12	USAF, CB/14 FTW, Columbus AFB. Ms.	
90-0409	92	Jayhawk T-1A	TT-13	USAF, CB/14 FTW, Columbus AFB. Ms.	
90-0410	92	Jayhawk T-1A	TT-14	USAF, VN/71 FTW 26 FTS, Vance AFB. Ok.	
90-0411	92	Jayhawk T-1A	TT-15	USAF, VN/71 FTW 26 FTS, Vance AFB. Ok.	
90-0412	91	Jayhawk T-1A	TT-2	USAF, CB/14 FTW, Columbus AFB. Ms. (was RK-15).	N2887B
90-0413	92	Jayhawk T-1A	TT-16	USAF, CB/14 FTW, Columbus AFB. Ms.	
91-0075	92	Jayhawk T-1A	TT-18	USAF, XL/47 FTW 86 FTS, Laughlin AFB. Tx.	
91-0076	92	Jayhawk T-1A	TT-17	USAF, XL/47 FTW 86 FTS, Laughlin AFB. Tx.	
91-0077	91	Jayhawk T-1A	TT-1	USAF, VN/71 FTW 26 FTS, Vance AFB. Ok. (was RK-12).	N2886B
91-0078	92	Jayhawk T-1A	TT-19	USAF, XL/47 FTW 86 FTS, Laughlin AFB. Tx.	
91-0079	92	Jayhawk T-1A	TT-20	USAF, XL/47 FTW 86 FTS, Laughlin AFB. Tx.	
91-0080	92	Jayhawk T-1A	TT-21	USAF, VN/71 FTW 26 FTS, Vance AFB. Ok.	
91-0081	92	Jayhawk T-1A	TT-22	USAF, XL/47 FTW 86 FTS, Laughlin AFB. Tx.	
91-0082	92	Jayhawk T-1A	TT-23	USAF, XL/47 FTW 86 FTS, Laughlin AFB. Tx.	
91-0083	92	Jayhawk T-1A	TT-24	USAF, XL/47 FTW 86 FTS, Laughlin AFB. Tx.	
91-0084	92	Jayhawk T-1A	TT-25	USAF, VN/71 FTW 26 FTS, Vance AFB. Ok.	
91-0085	92	Jayhawk T-1A	TT-26	USAF, XL/47 FTW 86 FTS, Laughlin AFB. Tx.	
91-0086	92	Jayhawk T-1A	TT-27	USAF, XL/47 FTW 86 FTS, Laughlin AFB. Tx.	
91-0087	92	Jayhawk T-1A	TT-28	USAF, XL/47 FTW 86 FTS, Laughlin AFB. Tx.	
91-0088	92	Jayhawk T-1A	TT-29	USAF, VN/71 FTW 26 FTS, Vance AFB. Ok.	
91-0089	92	Jayhawk T-1A	TT-30	USAF, XL/47 FTW 86 FTS, Laughlin AFB. Tx.	
91-0090	93	Jayhawk T-1A	TT-31	USAF, XL/47 FTW 86 FTS, Laughlin AFB. Tx.	
91-0091	93	Jayhawk T-1A	TT-32	USAF, XL/47 FTW 86 FTS, Laughlin AFB. Tx.	
91-0092	93	Jayhawk T-1A	TT-33	USAF, XL/47 FTW 86 FTS, Laughlin AFB. Tx.	
91-0093	93	Jayhawk T-1A	TT-34	USAF, XL/47 FTW 86 FTS, Laughlin AFB. Tx. (status ?).	
91-0094	93	Jayhawk T-1A	TT-35	USAF, XL/47 FTW 86 FTS, Laughlin AFB. Tx.	
91-0095	93	Jayhawk T-1A	TT-36	USAF, VN/71 FTW 26 FTS, Vance AFB. Ok.	
91-0096	93	Jayhawk T-1A	TT-37	USAF, RA/12 FTW 99 FTS, Randolph AFB. Tx.	
91-0097	93	Jayhawk T-1A	TT-38	USAF, XL/47 FTW 86 FTS, Laughlin AFB. Tx.	
91-0098	93	Jayhawk T-1A	TT-39	USAF, VN/71 FTW 26 FTS, Vance AFB. Ok.	
91-0099	93	Jayhawk T-1A	TT-40	USAF, RA/12 FTW 99 FTS, Randolph AFB. Tx.	
91-0100	93	Jayhawk T-1A	TT-41	USAF, CB/14 FTW, Columbus AFB. Ms.	
91-0101	93	Jayhawk T-1A	TT-42	USAF, RA/12 FTW 99 FTS, Randolph AFB. Tx.	
91-0102	93	Jayhawk T-1A	TT-43	USAF, RA/12 FTW 99 FTS, Randolph AFB. Tx.	
91-0108	91	Gulfstream C-20F	1162	U S Army, OSACOM PAT Flight Det. Andrews AFB. Md.	N7096B
92-0330	93	Jayhawk T-1A	TT-44	USAF, RA/12 FTW 99 FTS, Randolph AFB. Tx.	
92-0331	93	Jayhawk T-1A	TT-45	USAF, RA/12 FTW 99 FTS, Randolph AFB. Tx.	
Reg	Yr	Type	c/n	Owner/Operator	Prev Regn

Reg	Yr	Type	c/n	Owner/Operator	Prev Regn
☐ 92-0332	93	Jayhawk T-1A	TT-46	USAF, RA/12 FTW 99 FTS, Randolph AFB. Tx.	
☐ 92-0333	93	Jayhawk T-1A	TT-47	USAF, RA/12 FTW 99 FTS, Randolph AFB. Tx.	
☐ 92-0334	93	Jayhawk T-1A	TT-48	USAF, RA/12 FTW 99 FTS, Randolph AFB. Tx.	
☐ 92-0335	93	Jayhawk T-1A	TT-49	USAF, RA/12 FTW 99 FTS, Randolph AFB. Tx.	
☐ 92-0336	93	Jayhawk T-1A	TT-50	USAF, RA/12 FTW 99 FTS, Randolph AFB. Tx.	
☐ 92-0337	93	Jayhawk T-1A	TT-51	USAF, RA/12 FTW 99 FTS, Randolph AFB. Tx.	
☐ 92-0338	93	Jayhawk T-1A	TT-52	USAF, RA/12 FTW 99 FTS, Randolph AFB. Tx.	
☐ 92-0339	93	Jayhawk T-1A	TT-53	USAF, RA/12 FTW 99 FTS, Randolph AFB. Tx.	
☐ 92-0340	93	Jayhawk T-1A	TT-54	USAF, RA/12 FTW 99 FTS, Randolph AFB. Tx.	
☐ 92-0341	93	Jayhawk T-1A	TT-55	USAF, VN/71 FTW 26 FTS, Vance AFB. Ok.	
☐ 92-0342	93	Jayhawk T-1A	TT-56	USAF, XL/47 FTW 86 FTS, Laughlin AFB. Tx.	
☐ 92-0343	93	Jayhawk T-1A	TT-57	USAF, VN/71 FTW 26 FTS, Vance AFB. Ok.	
☐ 92-0344	93	Jayhawk T-1A	TT-58	USAF, XL/47 FTW 86 FTS, Laughlin AFB. Tx.	
☐ 92-0345	93	Jayhawk T-1A	TT-59	USAF, XL/47 FTW 86 FTS, Laughlin AFB. Tx.	
☐ 92-0346	93	Jayhawk T-1A	TT-60	USAF, XL/47 FTW 86 FTS, Laughlin AFB. Tx.	
☐ 92-0347	93	Jayhawk T-1A	TT-61	USAF, XL/47 FTW 86 FTS, Laughlin AFB. Tx.	
☐ 92-0348	93	Jayhawk T-1A	TT-62	USAF, XL/47 FTW 86 FTS, Laughlin AFB. Tx.	
☐ 92-0349	93	Jayhawk T-1A	TT-63	USAF, XL/47 FTW 86 FTS, Laughlin AFB. Tx.	
☐ 92-0350	93	Jayhawk T-1A	TT-64	USAF, XL/47 FTW 86 FTS, Laughlin AFB. Tx.	
☐ 92-0351	93	Jayhawk T-1A	TT-65	USAF, VN/71 FTW 26 FTS, Vonce AFB. Ok.	
☐ 92-0352	93	Jayhawk T-1A	TT-66	USAF, XL/47 FTW 86 FTS, Laughlin AFB. Tx.	
☐ 92-0353	93	Jayhawk T-1A	TT-67	USAF, RA/12 FTW 99 FTS, Randolph AFB. Tx.	
☐ 92-0354	93	Jayhawk T-1A	TT-68	USAF, XL/47 FTW 86 FTS, Laughlin AFB. Tx.	
☐ 92-0355	93	Jayhawk T-1A	TT-69	USAF, XL/47 FTW 86 FTS, Laughlin AFB. Tx.	
☐ 92-0356	94	Jayhawk T-1A	TT-70	USAF, XL/47 FTW 86 FTS, Laughlin AFB. Tx.	
☐ 92-0357	94	Jayhawk T-1A	TT-71	USAF, XL/47 FTW 86 FTS, Laughlin AFB. Tx.	
☐ 92-0358	94	Jayhawk T-1A	TT-72	USAF, XL/47 FTW 86 FTS, Laughlin AFB. Tx.	
☐ 92-0359	94	Jayhawk T-1A	TT-73	USAF, RA/12 FTW 99 FTS, Randolph AFB. Tx.	
☐ 92-0360	94	Jayhawk T-1A	TT-74	USAF, XL/47 FTW 86 FTS, Laughlin AFB. Tx.	
☐ 92-0361	94	Jayhawk T-1A	TT-75	USAF, XL/47 FTW 86 FTS, Laughlin AFB. Tx.	
☐ 92-0362	94	Jayhawk T-1A	TT-76	USAF, XL/47 FTW 86 FTS, Laughlin AFB. Tx.	
☐ 92-0363	94	Jayhawk T-1A	TT-77	USAF, CB/14 FTW, Columbus AFB. Ms.	
☐ 92-0375	94	Gulfstream 4SP	1256	C-20H, USAF, 76th AS,	N438GA
☐ 92-9000	87	B 747-2G4B	23825	VC-25A, Presidential aircraft, 89th MAW, Andrews AFB. Md.	
☐ 93-0621	94	Jayhawk T-1A	TT-78	USAF, XL/47 FTW 86 FTS, Laughlin AFB. Tx.	
☐ 93-0622	94	Jayhawk T-1A	TT-79	USAF, XL/47 FTW 86 FTS, Laughlin AFB. Tx.	
☐ 93-0623	94	Jayhawk T-1A	TT-80	USAF, XL/47 FTW 86 FTS, Laughlin AFB. Tx.	
☐ 93-0624	94	Jayhawk T-1A	TT-81	USAF, XL/47 FTW 86 FTS, Laughlin AFB. Tx.	
☐ 93-0625	94	Jayhawk T-1A	TT-82	USAF, XL/47 FTW 86 FTS, Laughlin AFB. Tx.	
☐ 93-0626	94	Jayhawk T-1A	TT-83	USAF, XL/47 FTW 86 FTS, Laughlin AFB. Tx.	
☐ 93-0627	94	Jayhawk T-1A	TT-84	USAF, XL/47 FTW 86 FTS, Laughlin AFB. Tx.	
☐ 93-0628	94	Jayhawk T-1A	TT-85	USAF, XL/47 FTW 86 FTS, Laughlin AFB. Tx.	
☐ 93-0629	94	Jayhawk T-1A	TT-86	USAF, XL/47 FTW 86 FTS, Laughlin AFB. Tx.	
☐ 93-0630	94	Jayhawk T-1A	TT-87	USAF, RA/12 FTW 99 FTS, Randolph AFB. Tx.	
☐ 93-0631	94	Jayhawk T-1A	TT-88	USAF, RA/12 FTW 99 FTS, Randolph AFB. Tx.	
☐ 93-0632	94	Jayhawk T-1A	TT-89	USAF, XL/47 FTW 86 FTS, Laughlin AFB. Tx.	
☐ 93-0633	94	Jayhawk T-1A	TT-90	USAF, XL/47 FTW 86 FTS, Laughlin AFB. Tx.	
☐ 93-0634	94	Jayhawk T-1A	TT-91	USAF, XL/47 FTW 86 FTS, Laughlin AFB. Tx.	
☐ 93-0635	94	Jayhawk T-1A	TT-92	USAF, XL/47 FTW 86 FTS, Laughlin AFB. Tx.	
☐ 93-0636	94	Jayhawk T-1A	TT-93	USAF, XL/47 FTW 86 FTS, Laughlin AFB. Tx.	
☐ 93-0637	94	Jayhawk T-1A	TT-94	USAF, XL/47 FTW 86 FTS, Laughlin AFB. Tx.	
☐ 93-0638	94	Jayhawk T-1A	TT-95	USAF, VN/71 FTW 26 FTS, Vance AFB. Ok.	
☐ 93-0639	94	Jayhawk T-1A	TT-96	USAF, VN/71 FTW 26 FTS, Vance AFB. Ok.	
☐ 93-0640	94	Jayhawk T-1A	TT-97	USAF, XL/47 FTW 86 FTS, Laughlin AFB. Tx.	
☐ 93-0641	94	Jayhawk T-1A	TT-98	USAF, VN/71 FTW 26 FTS, Vance AFB. Ok.	
☐ 93-0642	94	Jayhawk T-1A	TT-99	USAF, VN/71 FTW 26 FTS, Vance AFB. Ok.	
☐ 93-0643	94	Jayhawk T-1A	TT-100	USAF, VN/71 FTW 26 FTS, Vance AFB. Ok.	
☐ 93-0644	95	Jayhawk T-1A	TT-101	USAF, VN/71 FTW 26 FTS, Vance AFB. Ok.	
☐ 93-0645	95	Jayhawk T-1A	TT-102	USAF, VN/71 FTW 26 FTS, Vance AFB. Ok.	
☐ 93-0646	95	Jayhawk T-1A	TT-103	USAF, VN/71 FTW 26 FTS, Vance AFB. Ok.	
☐ 93-0647	95	Jayhawk T-1A	TT-104	USAF, VN/71 FTW 26 FTS, Vance AFB. Ok.	
☐ 93-0648	95	Jayhawk T-1A	TT-105	USAF, VN/71 FTW 26 FTS, Vance AFB. Ok.	
☐ 93-0649	95	Jayhawk T-1A	TT-106	USAF, VN/71 FTW 26 FTS, Vance AFB. Ok.	
☐ 93-0650	95	Jayhawk T-1A	TT-107	USAF, VN/71 FTW 26 FTS, Vance AFB. Ok.	
☐ 93-0651	95	Jayhawk T-1A	TT-108	USAF, XL/47 FTW 86 FTS, Laughlin AFB. Tx.	
☐ 93-0652	95	Jayhawk T-1A	TT-109	USAF, XL/47 FTW 86 FTS, Laughlin AFB. Tx.	

Reg	Yr	Type	c/n	Owner/Operator	Prev Regn

Reg	Yr	Type	c/n	Owner/Operator	Prev Regn
❏ 93-0653	95	Jayhawk T-1A	TT-110	USAF, VN/71 FTW 26 FTS, Vance AFB. Ok.	
❏ 93-0654	95	Jayhawk T-1A	TT-111	USAF, VN/71 FTW 26 FTS, Vance AFB. Ok.	
❏ 93-0655	95	Jayhawk T-1A	TT-112	USAF, VN/71 FTW 26 FTS, Vance AFB. Ok.	
❏ 93-0656	95	Jayhawk T-1A	TT-113	USAF, VN/71 FTW 26 FTS, Vance AFB. Ok.	
❏ 94-0114	95	Jayhawk T-1A	TT-114	USAF, CB/14 FTW, Columbus AFB. Ms.	
❏ 94-0115	95	Jayhawk T-1A	TT-115	USAF, VN/71 FTW 26 FTS, Vance AFB. Ok.	
❏ 94-0116	95	Jayhawk T-1A	TT-116	USAF, VN/71 FTW 26 FTS, Vance AFB. Ok.	
❏ 94-0117	95	Jayhawk T-1A	TT-117	USAF, VN/71 FTW 26 FTS, Vance AFB. Ok.	
❏ 94-0118	95	Jayhawk T-1A	TT-118	USAF, VN/71 FTW 26 FTS, Vance AFB. Ok.	
❏ 94-0119	95	Jayhawk T-1A	TT-119	USAF, VN/71 FTW 26 FTS, Vance AFB. Ok.	
❏ 94-0120	95	Jayhawk T-1A	TT-120	USAF, VN/71 FTW 26 FTS, Vance AFB. Ok.	
❏ 94-0121	95	Jayhawk T-1A	TT-121	USAF, VN/71 FTW 26 FTS, Vance AFB. Ok.	
❏ 94-0122	95	Jayhawk T-1A	TT-122	USAF, VN/71 FTW 26 FTS, Vance AFB. Ok.	
❏ 94-0123	95	Jayhawk T-1A	TT-123	USAF, VN/71 FTW 26 FTS, Vance AFB. Ok.	
❏ 94-0124	95	Jayhawk T-1A	TT-124	USAF, VN/71 FTW 26 FTS, Vance AFB. Ok.	
❏ 94-0125	95	Jayhawk T-1A	TT-125	USAF, VN/71 FTW 26 FTS, Vance AFB. Ok.	
❏ 94-0126	95	Jayhawk T-1A	TT-126	USAF, VN/71 FTW 26 FTS, Vance AFB. Ok.	
❏ 94-0127	95	Jayhawk T-1A	TT-127	USAF, VN/71 FTW 26 FTS, Vance AFB. Ok.	
❏ 94-0128	95	Jayhawk T-1A	TT-128	USAF, VN/71 FTW 26 FTS, Vance AFB. Ok.	
❏ 94-0129	95	Jayhawk T-1A	TT-129	USAF, VN/71 FTW 26 FTS, Vance AFB. Ok.	
❏ 94-0130	95	Jayhawk T-1A	TT-130	USAF, VN/71 FTW 26 FTS, Vance AFB. Ok.	
❏ 94-0131	96	Jayhawk T-1A	TT-131	USAF, CB/14 FTW, Columbus AFB. Ms.	
❏ 94-0132	96	Jayhawk T-1A	TT-132	USAF, CB/14 FTW, Columbus AFB. Ms.	
❏ 94-0133	96	Jayhawk T-1A	TT-133	USAF, VN/71 FTW 26 FTS, Vance AFB. Ok.	
❏ 94-0134	96	Jayhawk T-1A	TT-134	USAF, CB/14 FTW, Columbus AFB. Ms.	
❏ 94-0135	96	Jayhawk T-1A	TT-135	USAF, CB/14 FTW, Columbus AFB. Ms.	
❏ 94-0136	96	Jayhawk T-1A	TT-136	USAF, CB/14 FTW, Columbus AFB. Ms.	
❏ 94-0137	96	Jayhawk T-1A	TT-137	USAF, CB/14 FTW, Columbus AFB. Ms.	
❏ 94-0138	96	Jayhawk T-1A	TT-138	USAF, CB/14 FTW, Columbus AFB. Ms.	
❏ 94-0139	96	Jayhawk T-1A	TT-139	USAF, CB/14 FTW, Columbus AFB. Ms.	
❏ 94-0140	96	Jayhawk T-1A	TT-140	USAF, CB/14 FTW, Columbus AFB. Ms.	
❏ 94-0141	96	Jayhawk T-1A	TT-141	USAF, CB/14 FTW, Columbus AFB. Ms.	
❏ 94-0142	96	Jayhawk T-1A	TT-142	USAF, CB/14 FTW, Columbus AFB. Ms.	
❏ 94-0143	96	Jayhawk T-1A	TT-143	USAF, CB/14 FTW, Columbus AFB. Ms.	
❏ 94-0144	96	Jayhawk T-1A	TT-144	USAF, CB/14 FTW, Columbus AFB. Ms.	
❏ 94-0145	96	Jayhawk T-1A	TT-145	USAF, CB/14 FTW, Columbus AFB. Ms.	
❏ 94-0146	96	Jayhawk T-1A	TT-146	USAF, CB/14 FTW, Columbus AFB. Ms.	
❏ 94-0147	96	Jayhawk T-1A	TT-147	USAF, CB/14 FTW, Columbus AFB. Ms.	
❏ 94-0148	96	Jayhawk T-1A	TT-148	USAF, CB/14 FTW, Columbus AFB. Ms.	
❏ 94-1569	97	Astra C-38A	088	USAF, 201st Airlift Wing, Maryland ANG, Andrews AFB. Md.	N398AG
❏ 94-1570	97	Astra C-38A	090	USAF, 201st Airlift Wing, Maryland ANG. Andrews AFB. Md.	N399AG
❏ 95-0040	96	Jayhawk T-1A	TT-149	USAF, CB/14 FTW, Columbus AFB. Ms.	
❏ 95-0041	96	Jayhawk T-1A	TT-150	USAF, CB/14 FTW, Columbus AFB. Ms.	
❏ 95-0042	96	Jayhawk T-1A	TT-151	USAF, CB/14 FTW, Columbus AFB. Ms.	
❏ 95-0043	96	Jayhawk T-1A	TT-152	USAF, CB/14 FTW, Columbus AFB. Ms.	
❏ 95-0044	96	Jayhawk T-1A	TT-153	USAF, CB/14 FTW, Columbus AFB. Ms.	
❏ 95-0045	96	Jayhawk T-1A	TT-154	USAF, CB/14 FTW, Columbus AFB. Ms.	
❏ 95-0046	96	Jayhawk T-1A	TT-155	USAF, CB/14 FTW, Columbus AFB. Ms.	
❏ 95-0047	96	Jayhawk T-1A	TT-156	USAF, XL/47 FTW 86 FTS, Laughlin AFB. Tx.	
❏ 95-0048	96	Jayhawk T-1A	TT-157	USAF, CB/14 FTW, Columbus AFB. Ms.	
❏ 95-0049	96	Jayhawk T-1A	TT-158	USAF, CB/14 FTW, Columbus AFB. Ms.	
❏ 95-0050	96	Jayhawk T-1A	TT-159	USAF, CB/14 FTW, Columbus AFB. Ms.	
❏ 95-0051	96	Jayhawk T-1A	TT-160	USAF, CB/14 FTW, Columbus AFB. Ms.	
❏ 95-0052	96	Jayhawk T-1A	TT-161	USAF, CB/14 FTW, Columbus AFB. Ms.	
❏ 95-0053	96	Jayhawk T-1A	TT-162	USAF, CB/14 FTW, Columbus AFB. Ms.	
❏ 95-0054	96	Jayhawk T-1A	TT-163	USAF, CB/14 FTW, Columbus AFB. Ms.	
❏ 95-0055	96	Jayhawk T-1A	TT-164	USAF, CB/14 FTW, Columbus AFB. Ms.	
❏ 95-0056	96	Jayhawk T-1A	TT-165	USAF, CB/14 FTW, Columbus AFB. Ms.	
❏ 95-0057	96	Jayhawk T-1A	TT-166	USAF, CB/14 FTW, Columbus AFB. Ms.	
❏ 95-0058	96	Jayhawk T-1A	TT-167	USAF, CB/14 FTW, Columbus AFB. Ms.	
❏ 95-0059	97	Jayhawk T-1A	TT-168	USAF, CB/14 FTW, Columbus AFB. Ms.	
❏ 95-0060	97	Jayhawk T-1A	TT-169	USAF, CB/14 FTW, Columbus AFB. Ms.	
❏ 95-0061	97	Jayhawk T-1A	TT-170	USAF, CB/14 FTW, Columbus AFB. Ms.	
❏ 95-0062	97	Jayhawk T-1A	TT-171	USAF, CB/14 FTW, Columbus AFB. Ms.	
❏ 95-0063	97	Jayhawk T-1A	TT-172	USAF, RA/12 FTW 99FTS, Randolph AFB. Tx.	
❏ 95-0064	97	Jayhawk T-1A	TT-173	USAF, CB/14 FTW, Columbus AFB. Ms.	

Reg   *Yr*   *Type*   *c/n*   *Owner/Operator*   *Prev Regn*

Reg	Yr	Type	c/n	Owner/Operator	Prev Regn
☐ 95-0065	97	Jayhawk T-1A	TT-174	USAF, CB/14 FTW, Columbus AFB. Ms.	
☐ 95-0066	97	Jayhawk T-1A	TT-175	USAF, XL/47 FTW 86 FTS, Laughlin AFB. Tx.	
☐ 95-0067	97	Jayhawk T-1A	TT-176	USAF, XL/47 FTW 86 FTS, Laughlin AFB. Tx.	
☐ 95-0068	97	Jayhawk T-1A	TT-177	USAF, CB/14 FTW, Columbus AFB. Ms.	
☐ 95-0069	97	Jayhawk T-1A	TT-178	USAF, VN/71 FTW 26 FTS, Vance AFB. Ok.	
☐ 95-0070	97	Jayhawk T-1A	TT-179	USAF, VN/71 FTW 26 FTS, Vance AFB. Ok.	
☐ 95-0071	97	Jayhawk T-1A	TT-180	USAF, VN/71 FTW 26 FTS, Vance AFB. Ok.	
☐ 95-0123	96	Citation UC-35A	560-0387	U S Army, B-1/214th AVN, Wiesbaden, Germany.	N5108G
☐ 95-0124	96	Citation UC-35A	560-0392	U S Army, B-1/214th AVN, Wiesbaden, Germany.	N5124F
☐ 96-0107	97	Citation UC-35A	560-0404	U S Army, C/2-228th AVN,.	N5201M
☐ 96-0108	97	Citation UC-35A	560-0410	U S Army, Puerto Rico RFC,	N5211A
☐ 96-0109	97	Citation UC-35A	560-0415	U S Army, A/6 52nd Aviation, Kastner AAF, NAF Atsugi, Japan.	N52457
☐ 96-0110	97	Citation UC-35A	560-0420	U S Army, A/6 52nd Aviation, Kastner AAF, NAS Atsugi, Japan.	N51942
☐ 96-0111	98	Citation UC-35A	560-0426	U S Army, C/6-52nd AVN,	N5101J
☐ 97-0049	98	Gulfstream C-37A	566	U S Army, Andrews AFB. Md.	N466GA
☐ 97-0101	98	Citation UC-35A	560-0452	U S Army, B-1/214th AVN, Wiesbaden, Germany.	N5130J
☐ 97-0102	98	Citation UC-35A	560-0456	U S Army, B-1/214th AVN, Wiesbaden, Germany.	N51444
☐ 97-0103	98	Citation UC-35A	560-0462	U S Army, B6/52nd Aviation, Dobbins ARB. Ga.	N5183U
☐ 97-0104	98	Citation UC-35A	560-0468	U S Army, Puerto Rico RFC,	N51042
☐ 97-0105	98	Citation UC-35A	560-0472	U S Army, B-1/214th AVN, Wiesbaden, Germany.	N5079II
☐ 97-0400	98	Gulfstream C-37A	521	UGAF, 99th AS, Andrews AFB. Md.	
☐ 97-0401	98	Gulfstream C-37A	542	USAF, 99th AS, Andrews AFB. Md.	N642GA
☐ 98-0001	98	B 757-2G4 (VC-32A)	29025	USAF, 99th AS, Andrews AFB. Md.	N3519L
☐ 98-0002	98	B 757-2G4 (VC-32A)	29026	USAF, 99th AS, Andrews AFB. Md.	N3519M
☐ 98-0006	99	Citation UC-35A	560-0495	U S Army, A Det.1/6-52nd AVN.	
☐ 98-0007	99	Citation UC-35A	560-0501	U S Army, Alska RFC,	N51896
☐ 98-0008	99	Citation UC-35A	560-0505	U S Army, Alaska RFC,	N52229
☐ 98-0009	99	Citation UC-35A	560-0508	U S Army, Puerto Rico RFC,	N5085E
☐ 98-0010	99	Citation UC-35A	560-0513	U S Army, B-6/52nd AVN,	N5061W
☐ 99-0003	98	B 757-2G4 (VC-32A)	29027	USAF, 89th MAW, Andrews AFB. Md.	
☐ 99-0004	98	B 757-2G4 (VC-32A)	29028	USAF, 89th MAW, Andrews AFB. Md.	
☐ 99-0100	99	Citation UC-35A	560-0532	U S Army, B-6/52nd AVN,	N5268V
☐ 99-0101	99	Citation UC-35A	560-0534	U S Army, B-6/52nd AVN,	N5112K
☐ 99-0102	00	Citation UC-35A	560-0538	U S Army, B-1/214th AVN, Wiesbaden, Germany.	N51143
☐ 99-0103	00	Citation UC-35B	560-0545	U S Army, B-2/228th AVN,	N5091J
☐ 99-0104	00	Citation UC-35B	560-0548	U S Army, Puerto Rico RFC,	N5097H
☐ 99-0402	99	Gulfstream C-37A	571	USAF, SHAPE, Chievres, Belgium.	N671GA
☐ 99-0404	99	Gulfstream C-37A	590	USAF, 99th AS, Andrews AFB. Md.	N590GA

OB = PERU   Total 12

Civil

Reg	Yr	Type	c/n	Owner/Operator	Prev Regn
☐ OB-1396	75	F 28-1000	11100	Government of Peru, Lima.	FAP-390
☐ OB-1626	91	Citation V	560-0124	Southern Peru Copper Corp. Lima.	N124VP
☐ OB-1703	85	Astra-1125	004	ATSA-Aero Transporte SA. Lima.	N425TS
☐ OB-1792T	86	Citation S/II	S550-0086	Aero Transporte SA. Lima.	4X-COO

Military

Reg	Yr	Type	c/n	Owner/Operator	Prev Regn
☐ 700		Falcon 20	...	FAP, Grupo Aereo 8, Las-Palmas-Lima. (s/n 434 ?).	
☐ FAP 300	80	Falcon 20F	434	FAP, Grupo Aereo 8, Las Palmas-Lima.	OB-1433
☐ FAP 352	83	B 737-282	23042	FAP, Grupo Aereo 8, Las Palmas-Lima.	VT-PDC
☐ FAP 356	95	B 737-528	27426	FAP, Grupo Aereo 8, Las Palmas-Lima.	PRP-001
☐ FAP 370	69	DC 8-62CF	46078	FAP, Grupo Aereo 8, Las Palmas-Lima.	HB-IDK
☐ FAP 371		DC 0-62CF	45984	FAP, Grupo Aereo 8, Las Palmas-Lima.	HB-IDH
☐ FAP 524	83	Learjet 36A	36A-051	Peruvian Air Force, Lima-Las Palmas.	OB-1431
☐ FAP 525	83	Learjet 36A	36A-052	Peruvian Air Force, Lima-Las Palmas.	OB-1432

OD = LEBANON   Total 1

Civil

Reg	Yr	Type	c/n	Owner/Operator	Prev Regn
☐ OD-FNF	81	HS 125/700B	7124	Fahed Fadel, Jeddah, Saudi Arabia.	HZ-DA4

OE = AUSTRIA   Total 96

Civil

Reg	Yr	Type	c/n	Owner/Operator	Prev Regn
☐ OE-...	04	Citation X	750-0232	ULL 3 Beteiligungs u Management GmbH. Vienna.	N232CX
☐ OE-FBS	87	Citation II/SP	551-0574	Airlink Luftverkehrs GmbH. Salzburg.	N60GF
☐ OE-FCM	76	Citation	500-0294	Cable TV Airlines SRL. Loreto. Italy.	OY-VIP
☐ OE-FCY	04	CitationJet CJ-2	525A-0204	Jetalliance Flugbetriebs AG. Vienna.	N.....
☐ OE-FDM	79	Citation 1/SP	501-0140	Goldeck-Flug GmbH. Klagenfurt.	N96CF
☐ OE-FGD	93	CitationJet	525-0020	Glock GmbH. Klagenfurt.	(OO-LFU)
☐ OE-FGI	98	CitationJet	525-0254	Ing. Robert Baumann Luftfahrt GmbH. Klagenfurt.	N5193V
Reg	Yr	Type	c/n	Owner/Operator	Prev Regn

Reg	Yr	Type	c/n	Owner/Operator	Prev Regn
☐ OE-FGN	75	Citation	500-0291	Airlink Luftverkehrs GmbH. Salzburg.	N291DS
☐ OE-FHH	82	Citation 1/SP	501-0246	Rath Aviation GmbH. Salzburg.	N26LC
☐ OE-FHW	79	Citation 1/SP	501-0121	DAEDALOS Flugbetriebs GmbH. Graz.	D-IANO
☐ OE-FJU	98	CitationJet	525-0295	Jetalliance Flugbetriebs AG. Vienna.	N5209E
☐ OE-FLG	95	CitationJet	525-0103	Alpla Air Charter GmbH. Hard.	D-IVHA
☐ OE-FMA	97	CitationJet	525-0188	AVAG Air GmbH. Salzburg.	D-IVIN
☐ OE-FMS	79	Citation 1/SP	501-0239	Oldenburg Kunstoff-Technik GmbH. Kassel, Germany.	N164CB
☐ OE-FMU	93	CitationJet	525-0040	Ulrich Schroeder, Vienna.	N525AJ
☐ OE-FPA	87	Citation II/SP	551-0552	Airlink Luftverkehrs GmbH. Salzburg.	
☐ OE-FPS	03	CitationJet CJ-2	525A-0142	Rath Aviation GmbH. Salzburg.	N5207A
☐ OE-FRR	95	CitationJet	525-0124	RUKA GmbH. Salzburg.	(ZS-BSS)
☐ OE-FSS	97	CitationJet	525-0226	Aero-Charter Krifka GmbH. Wels.	TC-LIM
☐ OE-FUJ	01	CitationJet CJ-1	525-0544	Jetalliance Flugbetriebs AG. Vienna.	N.....
☐ OE-GAA	91	Citation V	560-0111	Tyrol Air Ambulance GmbH. Innsbruck.	(N6802T)
☐ OE-GBA	79	Citation II	550-0085	Bannert Air GmbH. Vienna.	N57AJ
☐ OE-GBC	93	Citation II	550-0717	Bannert Air GmbH. Vienna.	SE-RBM
☐ OE-GBD	00	Gulfstream G100	133	Bannert Air GmbH. Vienna.	D-CGMA
☐ OE-GCB	99	Citation V Ultra	560-0517	Goldeck-Flug GmbH. Klagenfurt.	N424HH
☐ OE-GCC	91	Citation V	560-0125	Goldeck-Flug GmbH. Klagenfurt.	N6809V
☐ OE-GCD	99	Citation V Ultra	560-0497	Goldeck-Flug GmbH. Klagenfurt.	N497EA
☐ OE-GCF	88	Learjet 55C	55C-136	Schaffer GmbH. Vienna.	N155PS
☐ OE-GCH	92	Citation VII	650-7006	COMTEL Air Luftverkehrs GmbH. Vienna.	TC-KOC
☐ OE-GCI	78	Citation II	550-0041	WWW Bedarfsluftfahrt mbH. Vienna.	N177HH
☐ OE-GCN	83	Citation III	650-0014	COMTEL Air Luftverkehrs GmbH. Vienna.	(N855DH)
☐ OE-GCO	83	Citation III	650-0012	COMTEL Air Luftverkehrs GmbH. Vienna.	N15VF
☐ OE-GCP	93	Citation V	560-0214	Krono Air GmbH. Salzburg.	N1285D
☐ OE-GDA	92	Citation V	560-0200	Austro Control GmbH/Jetalliance Flugbetriebs AG. Vienna.	
☐ OE-GDI	99	Learjet 45	45-037	MAP Executive Flight Service GmbH. Vienna.	N50145
☐ OE-GDM	92	Citation II	550-0707	Red Bull GmbH. Salzburg.	(SE-DYY)
☐ OE-GEG	04	Citation Excel XLS	560-5529	Jetalliance Flugbetriebs AG. Vienna.	N5262X
☐ OE-GEJ	04	Citation Encore	560-0665	Jetalliance Flugbetriebs AG. Vienna.	N5200R
☐ OE-GEO	00	Hawker 800XP	8477	Schaffer GmbH. Vienna.	N44767
☐ OE-GGB	04	Learjet 40	45-2018	Cirrus Airlines Luftfahrt GmbH. Saarbruecken, Germany.	N5018G
☐ OE-GHM	97	Beechjet 400A	RK-148	Jetalliance Flugbetriebs AG. Vienna.	N663AJ
☐ OE-GHP	01	Citation Bravo	550-0998	Air Executive GmbH. Salzburg.	N5165P
☐ OE-GHU	97	Hawker 800XP	8335	Goldeck-Flug GmbH. Klagenfurt.	OY-RAC
☐ OE-GII	99	Learjet 60	60-169	Amira Air GmbH. Vienna.	N5014F
☐ OE-GIL	79	Citation II	550-0060	Air-Styria Luftfahrtunternehmen GmbH. Graz.	N315CK
☐ OE-GKK	99	Citation Bravo	550-0872	Jetfly Airline GmbH. Linz.	N5093L
☐ OE-GLL	03	Citation Bravo	550-1069	Jetfly Airline GmbH. Linz.	N5093Y
☐ OE-GLS	00	Citation VII	650-7110	Tyrolean Jet Service GmbH. Innsbruck.	N657JW
☐ OE-GME	00	Citation Excel	560-5113	Jetalliance Flugbetriebs AG. Vienna.	N52178
☐ OE-GMI	96	Citation V Ultra	560-0362	Jetalliance Flugbetriebs AG. Vienna.	N5183U
☐ OE-GMR	01	Learjet 60	60-248	TUPACK Verpackungen GmbH. Vienna.	N5038N
☐ OE-GNI	01	Learjet 60	60-236	Niki Luftfahrt GmbH. Vienna.	I-INL
☐ OE-GNL	94	Learjet 60	60-032	Amira Air GmbH. Vienna.	N5013D
☐ OE-GNW	03	Citation Excel	560-5339	Jetalliance Flugbetriebs AG & Zenith Airways GmbH. Vienna.	N51143
☐ OE-GPA	02	Citation Excel	560-5265	AVAG Air GmbH. Salzburg.	N5100J
☐ OE-GPG	91	Astra-1125SPX	115	ABC Bedarfsflug GmbH/Fly Tyrol, Innsbruck.	C-GRGE
☐ OE-GPH	01	Citation Encore	560-0590	Porsche Konstruktionen KG. Salzburg.	N5166T
☐ OE-GPS	98	Citation Bravo	550-0837	Tyrol Air Ambulance GmbH. Innsbruck.	N5185J
☐ OE-GPZ	99	Citation Excel	560-5067	International Jet Management GmbH. Vienna.	HB-VMZ
☐ OE-GRR	82	Learjet 55	55-059	Goldeck-Flug GmbH. Klagenfurt.	N59LJ
☐ OE-GTF	04	Learjet 60	60-281	Air Executive GmbH. Salzburg.	
☐ OE-GTI	99	Citation Excel	560-5037	Air Executive GmbH. Salzburg.	D-CIII
☐ OE-GTZ	98	Citation Bravo	550-0864	Taxiflug GmbH Dornbirn, Dornbirn.	N864CB
☐ OE-GUK	96	Beechjet 400A	RK-124	Jetalliance Flugbetriebs AG. Vienna.	N124BG
☐ OE-HAA	04	Do 328-310 ENVOY	3200	Club 328 Ltd. Southampton, UK.	D-BDXN
☐ OE-HAB	04	Do 328-310 ENVOY	3210	Club 328 Ltd. Southampton, UK.	D-BDXQ
☐ OE-HET	83	Challenger 600S	1085	Jetalliance Flugbetriebs AG. Vienna.	N600ST
☐ OE-HGG	03	Citation X	750-0214	Glock GmbH. Klagenfurt.	N5154J
☐ OE-HIT	91	Falcon 50	222	Friedrich Karl Flick, Vienna.	D-BELL
☐ OE-HLE	85	Challenger 601	3047	Goldeck-Flug GmbH. Klagenfurt.	N601TJ
☐ OE-HMS	99	Dornier Do328JET	3121	Tyrolean Jet Service GmbH. Innsbruck.	D-BDXI
☐ OE-HPS	03	Falcon 50EX	334	Rath Aviation GmbH. Salzburg.	N335EX
☐ OE-HRR	04	Challenger 300	20033	TUPACK Verpackungen GmbH. Vienna.	C-FCMG

Reg   Yr   Type   c/n   Owner/Operator   Prev Regn

Reg	Yr	Type	c/n	Owner/Operator	Prev Regn
☐ OE-HTG	01	Dornier Do328JET	3162	Grossmann Air Service GmbH. Vienna.	D-B...
☐ OE-HTI	03	Gulfstream G200	089	Ion Tiriac Air SA/Jetalliance Flugbetriebs AG. Vienna.	N289GA
☐ OE-HTJ	99	Dornier Do328JET	3114	Tyrolean Jet Service GmbH. Innsbruck.	D-BDXA
☐ OE-IAS	04	EMB-135BJ Legacy	14500832	Jetalliance Flugbetriebs AG. Vienna.	(N832SG)
☐ OE-ICF	87	Falcon 900B	22	COMTEL Air Luftverkehrs GmbH. Vienna.	N54DC
☐ OE-IDM	99	Falcon 900EX	51	Red Bull GmbH. Salzburg.	F-GVDP
☐ OE-IEL	01	Global Express	9099	Tyrolean Jet Service GmbH. Innsbruck.	C-GZKL
☐ OE-IFA	92	MD-83	49809	Al Ghanim Corp/Jetalliance Flugbetriebs AG. Vienna.	3B-AGC
☐ OE-IGS	99	Global Express	9044	COMTEL Air Luftverkehrs GmbH Vienna.	I-MOVE
☐ OE-IIA	01	Gulfstream V	641	International Jet Management GmbH. Vienna.	HB-IIZ
☐ OE-IJA	91	Gulfstream 4	1157	Jetalliance Flugbetriebs AG. Vienna.	N457GA
☐ OE-IKP	04	Challenger 604	5599	Amira Air GmbH. Vienna.	C-G...
☐ OE-IMB	04	Challenger 604	5585	Jetalliance Flugbetriebs AG. Vienna.	(D-ARTN)
☐ OE-INF	96	Challenger 604	5303	Air Executive GmbH. Salzburg.	OY-TNF
☐ OE-INI	04	Challenger 604	5595	Air Executive GmbH. Salzburg.	C-FCOE
☐ OE-ISA	03	EMB-135BJ Legacy	145711	Jetalliance Flugbetriebs AG. Vienna.	N135SL
☐ OE-ISN	04	EMB-135BJ Legacy	14500851	Jetalliance Flugbetriebs AG. Vienna.	PT-SIO
☐ OE-ITA	95	B 737-3L9	27924	Ion Tiriac Air SA/Jetalliance Flugbetriebs AG. Vienna.	N730PA
☐ OE-IVK	04	Falcon 900EX EASY	138	MAP Executive Flight Service GmbH. Vienna.	F-WWFP
☐ OE-IVV	04	Gulfstream G550	5054	Jetalliance Flugbetriebs AG. Vienna.	N954GA
☐ OE-IVY	02	Gulfstream V	687	Jetalliance Flugbetriebs AG. Vienna.	N687GA
☐ OE-IWP	04	EMB-135BJ Legacy	14500841	Jetalliance Flugbetriebs AG. Vienna.	PT-SIN
☐ OE-IYA	99	Challenger 604	5435	Transair GmbH. Vienna.	N604PN

OH = FINLAND Total 15

Civil

Reg	Yr	Type	c/n	Owner/Operator	Prev Regn
☐ OH-FEX	03	Falcon 2000EX	27	Merropoint OY/Airfix Aviation OY. Helsinki.	F-WWGZ
☐ OH-FIX	02	Falcon 2000	179	AI Air Ltd/Airfix Aviation OY. Helsinki-Vantaa.	F-WWMF
☐ OH-FPC	76	Falcon 20F	345	Lillbacka Jetair OY. Kauhava.	N133AP
☐ OH-IPJ	00	Learjet 45	45-104	Baltika Brewery, St Petersburg, Russia.	N40012
☐ OH-KNE	81	Diamond 1	A014SA	Jetflite OY. Helsinki.	N339DM
☐ OH-ONE	00	Citation Excel	560-5157	Planmeca OY/Jetflite OY. Helsinki.	N40577
☐ OH-PPI	00	Citation X	750-0115	IPP OY/Airfix Aviation, Helsinki-Vantaa.	N5085E
☐ OH-PPR	02	Falcon 900EX	118	Airfix Aviation OY, Helsinki-Vantaa.	F-WWFS
☐ OH-WIC	00	Challenger 604	5452	Jetflite OY. Helsinki.	N452WU
☐ OH-WIF	81	Falcon 20F	461	Jetflite OY. Helsinki.	N353CP
☐ OH-WIN	84	Falcon 20F-5B	481	Jetflite OY. Helsinki.	N250RA
☐ OH-WIP	77	Falcon 20F-5B	359	Jetflite OY. Helsinki.	N369CE

Military

Reg	Yr	Type	c/n	Owner/Operator	Prev Regn
☐ LJ-1	81	Learjet 35A	35A-430	Finnish Air Force, Air Support Squadron, Jyvaskyla.	N10870
☐ LJ-2	82	Learjet 35A	35A-451	Finnish Air Force, Air Support Squadron, Jyvaskyla.	N1462B
☐ LJ-3	82	Learjet 35A	35A-470	Finnish Air Force, Air Support Squadron, Jyvaskyla.	N3810G

OK = CZECH REPUBLIC / CZECHIA Total 6

Civil

Reg	Yr	Type	c/n	Owner/Operator	Prev Regn
☐ OK-SLA	99	CitationJet	525-0310	Silesia Air, Ostrava.	D-IIJS
☐ OK-SLN	04	EMB-135BJ Legacy	145796	ABA-Air a.s. Prague.	PT-SIF
☐ OK-SLS	90	Citation V	560-0088	Silesia Air, Ostrava.	D-CMCM
☐ OK-UZI	89	Beechjet 400	RJ-56	Czech Government-Civil Aviation Inspectorate, Prague.	G-BSZP
☐ OK-VSZ	02	Citation Bravo	550-1040	ABA-Air a.s. Prague.	N12378

Military

Reg	Yr	Type	c/n	Owner/Operator	Prev Regn
☐ 5105	92	Challenger 601-3A	5105	Czech Government, Prague.	OK-BYA

OO = BELGIUM Total 27

Civil

Reg	Yr	Type	c/n	Owner/Operator	Prev Regn
☐ OO-ACT	02	Falcon 900C	194	Flying Service NV. Antwerp.	F-WWFZ
☐ OO-FLN	03	CitationJet CJ-2	525A-0179	ZBG Services NV/Airventure BV. Antwerp.	N179FZ
☐ OO-FPA	02	Citation Excel	560-5248	Flying Service NV. Cannes-Mandelieu, France.	HB-VNR
☐ OO-FYG	02	Citation Bravo	550-1027	Flying Service NV. Antwerp.	N52691
☐ OO-GFD	99	Falcon 2000	101	Abelag Aviation, Brussels.	N399FA
☐ OO-IAR	03	Falcon 2000EX	8	Flying Group NV. Antwerp.	F-GUTD
☐ OO-KRC*	04	Challenger 604	5577	ComJet BV. Rotterdam, Holland.	N577CJ
☐ OO-LCM	72	Citation	500-0036	Abelag Aviation, Brussels.	N18HJ
☐ OO-LFN	04	Learjet 45	45-250	Abelag Aviation, Brussels.	N40050
☐ OO-LFS	98	Learjet 45	45-018	Abelag Aviation, Brussels.	N418LJ
☐ OO-LFV	82	Learjet 35A	35A-481	Abelag Aviation, Brussels.	N27NR
☐ OO-MDN	72	Falcon 20F-5B	262	Abelag Aviation, Brussels.	D2-ESV
☐ OO-MLG	99	Citation Excel	560-5028	Abelag Aviation, Brussels.	CS-DDB

Reg	Yr	Type	c/n	Owner/Operator	Prev Regn

Reg	Yr	Type	c/n	Owner/Operator	Prev Regn
☐ OO-PHI	95	CitationJet	525-0115	Flying Service NV. Antwerp.	N52141
☐ OO-SKP	84	Citation S/II	S550-0007	Sky-Service BV. Wevelgem.	CS-DCE
☐ OO-SKV	91	Citation V	560-0153	Sky-Service BV. Wevelgem.	SE-DYZ
☐ OO-TME	02	Learjet 60	60-255	Toyota Motor Marketing Europe, Brussels.	N5013U
☐ OO-VMB	98	Falcon 2000	74	Flying Service NV. Antwerp.	F-GJSC

Military

☐ CA-01	85	Airbus A310-222	372	Belgian Defence, 21 Sqn. 15TW, Melsbroek.	9V-STN
☐ CA-02	85	Airbus A310-222	367	Belgian Defence, 21 Sqn. 15TW, Melsbroek.	9V-STM
☐ CD-01	91	Falcon 900B	109	Belgian Defence, 21 Sqn. 15TW, Melsbroek.	G-BTIB
☐ CE-01	01	EMB-135LR	145449	Belgian Defence, 21 Sqn. 15TW, Melsbroek.	PT-SUU
☐ CE-02	01	EMB-135LR	145486	Belgian Defence, 21 Sqn. 15TW, Melsbroek.	
☐ CE-03	01	EMB-145LR	145526	Belgian Defence, 21 Sqn. 15TW, Melsbroek.	PT-STR
☐ CE-04	01	EMB-145LR	145548	Belgian Defence, 21 Sqn. 15TW, Melsbroek.	PT-...
☐ CM-01	73	Falcon 20E	276	BAF 31, Belgian Defence, 21 Sqn. Melsbroek.	F-WNGL
☐ CM-02	73	Falcon 20E-5	278	BAF 32, Belgian Defence, 21 Sqn. Melsbroek.	F-WQBN

OY = DENMARK   Total   45

Civil

☐ OY-BZT	81	Citation II	550-0259	Benair A/S. Stauning.	N810JT
☐ OY-CCJ	82	Learjet 35A	35A-468	North Flying A/S. Aalborg.	N486LM
☐ OY-CEV	75	Citation	500-0329	North Flying A/S. Aalborg.	N4999H
☐ OY-CKE	95	Citation VII	650-7070	Danfoss Aviation/Air Alsie A/S. Sonderborg.	N654EJ
☐ OY-CKI	01	Falcon 2000	154	Air Alsie A/S. Sonderborg.	F-WWVL
☐ OY-CLD	90	Challenger 601-3A	5070	Eurojet Italia SRL. Milan, Italy.	(D-AAFX)
☐ OY-CLN	04	Falcon 2000EX EASY	35	Danfoss Aviation/Air Alsie A/S. Sonderborg.	F-WWGQ
☐ OY-CVS	04	Global Express	9139	Blue Aviation,	C-FYZP
☐ OY-CYV	82	Citation II	550-0440	North Flying A/S. Aalborg.	N120TC
☐ OY-EKC	01	Citation Excel	560-5217	Lego Systems A/S. Billund.	(OY-LEG)
☐ OY-ELY	80	Citation II	550-0139	Jet Plane Corp ApS. Bolzano, Italy.	(PT-WQG)
☐ OY-FFB	81	Citation	500-0406	Karlog Air A/S. Sonderborg.	SE-DET
☐ OY-GGG	94	Citation VII	650-7039	Grundfos A/S. Bjerringbro/Air Alsie A/S. Sonderborg.	D-CACM
☐ OY-GGR	04	CitationJet CJ-2	525A-0216	Amicrop/Flyjet, Roskilde.	N51246
☐ OY-GKC	01	Citation Excel	560-5189	Lego Systems A/S. Billund.	N5073G
☐ OY-GMC	78	Citation II	550-0025	UN/Aviation Assistance A/S. Roskilde.	9H-ACR
☐ OY-GMK	79	Citation II	550-0071	Aviation Assistance A/S. Roskilde.	(OY-GMB)
☐ OY-JAI	74	Citation	500-0193	Karlog Air A/S. Sonderborg.	N293S
☐ OY-JET	02	CitationJet CJ-2	525A-0089	Weibel Scientific A/S. Roskilde.	N.....
☐ OY-JEV	81	Citation II	550-0284	Weibel Scientific A/S. Roskilde.	I-ARIB
☐ OY-JMC	98	CitationJet	525-0277	Himmark Air A/S. Nordberg.	N277CJ
☐ OY-JPJ	84	Citation III	650-0060	Dantax A/S-North Flying A/S. Aalborg.	N220TV
☐ OY-LGI	01	Learjet 60	60-243	Execujet Scandinavia A/S-Graff Aviation Ltd. UK.	N50287
☐ OY-LJF	00	Learjet 60	60-173	Execujet Scandianvia A/S. Roskilde.	
☐ OY-LJJ	00	Learjet 45	45-116	Execujet Scandinavia A/S. Roskilde.	N50111
☐ OY-MMM	99	Challenger 604	5430	Maersk Air A/S. Copenhagen.	C-GFOE
☐ OY-MSI	99	Global Express	9032	Execujet Scandinavia A/S. Stansted, UK.	G-CBNP
☐ OY-NLA	84	Citation III	650-0070	Norwegian Air Ambulance Ltd. Oslo, Norway.	LN-NLD
☐ OY-OKK	03	Falcon 900EX EASY	128	Lego Systems A/S. Billund.	F-WWFE
☐ OY-PCW	75	Citation	500-0278	Executive Jet Services ApS. Billund.	(VP-BBE)
☐ OY-PDN	82	Citation II/SP	551-0412	Nassau Doors A/S. Ringe.	N413VP
☐ OY-PHN	84	Falcon 100	209	Pharma Nord ApS. Billund.	HB-VKR
☐ OY-RAA	92	BAe 125/800B	8235	Maersk Air A/S. Copenhagen.	(PH-WOL)
☐ OY-RGG	02	CitationJet CJ-1	525-0495	FlyJet A/S. Copenhagen.	N5246Z
☐ OY-SBR	75	Corvette	23	North Flying A/S. Aalborg.	F-BVPF
☐ OY-SBT	76	Corvette	33	North Flying A/S. Aalborg. (status ?).	F-BTTT
☐ OY-SML	98	CitationJet	525-0258	Skan Service ApS. Billund.	N108CR
☐ OY-TMA	83	Citation II	550-0457	Nilan A/S. Hedensted.	N63TM
☐ OY-UCA	04	CitationJet CJ-2	525A-0209	Air Alsie A/S. Sonderborg.	N5085E
☐ OY-VIS	91	Citation II	550-0672	DRT/Dansk Radio Teknik A/S. Billund.	(N394MA)

Military

☐ C-080	98	Challenger 604	5380	RDAF, ESK.721, Aalborg.	C-GEGM
☐ C-168	00	Challenger 604	5468	RDAF, ESK.721, Aalborg.	C-GHRJ
☐ C-172	00	Challenger 604	5472	RDAF, ESK.721, Aalborg.	C-GHRZ
☐ F-249	79	Gulfstream 3	249	RDAF, ESK.721, Vaerlose-Copenhagen.	N901GA
☐ F-313	80	Gulfstream 3	313	RDAF, ESK.721, Vaerlose-Copenhagen.	

Reg	Yr	Type	c/n	Owner/Operator	Prev Regn

PH	=	NETHERLANDS			*Total*	**20**

Civil

Reg	Yr	Type	c/n	Owner/Operator	Prev Regn
☐ PH-BPS	74	Falcon 20F-5B	321	Jet Management Europe BV. Amsterdam.	N104SB
☐ PH-CJI	00	Citation Excel	560-5128	Cartier Europe BV. Amsterdam.	N5228Z
☐ PH-CTX	81	Citation II	550-0398	Dynamic Air BV. Eindhoven.	N398S
☐ PH-DYE	00	Citation Bravo	550-0927	Jet Management Europe BV. Amsterdam.	N5061P
☐ PH-ECI	99	CitationJet	525-0321	Exact Nederland BV. Rotterdam.	D-IAAS
☐ PH-ECL	01	CitationJet CJ-2	525A-0054	Exact Nederland BV. Rotterdam.	D-IAAS
☐ PH-EDM	01	Falcon 900C	188	EDM Air BV/Jet Management Europe BV. Amsterdam.	F-WWFZ
☐ PH-EZF	96	Fokker 70	11576	PT Caltex Pacific Indonesia/Pelita, Jakarta. 'Rokan'	
☐ PH-FIS	03	CitationJet CJ-1	525-0514	KNSF Vastgoed Management BV. Amsterdam.	N514RV
☐ PH-HMA	01	Citation Bravo	550-0972	Heerema Engineering, Rotterdam.	N52462
☐ PH-ILC	96	Falcon 900B	161	AZ Exclusive Travel BV. Eindhoven.	G-GSEB
☐ PH-KBX	94	Fokker 70	11547	Dutch Royal Flight, Amsterdam.	PH-...
☐ PH-LAB	92	Citation II	550-0712	NLR-National Aerospace Laboratory, Amsterdam.	N12030
☐ PH-MEX	92	Citation VI	650-0217	Excellent Air GmbH. Stadtlohn, Germany.	N217CM
☐ PH-MGT	93	CitationJet	525-0042	Jet Netherlands BV. Amsterdam.	N96GD
☐ PH-OLI	88	Falcon 900	35	Jet Netherlands BV. Amsterdam.	F-GNDK
☐ PH-RSA	00	Citation Excel	560-5110	Cartier Europe BV. Amsterdam.	N5200Z
☐ PH-SOL	01	CitationJet CJ-1	525-0417	Jet Management Europe BV. Amsterdam.	(PH-SLD)
☐ PH-VBG	02	Falcon 2000EX	5	Jet Netherlands BV. Amsterdam.	F-GUDN

Military

☐ V-11	86	Gulfstream 4	1009	RNAF, 334 Squadron, Eindhoven.	VR-BOY

PK	=	INDONESIA			*Total*	**21**

Civil

☐ PK-...	03	Hawker 400XP	RK-362		N362XP
☐ PK-CAH	92	Learjet 31A	31A-066	Directorate of Civil Aviation, Jakarta.	N26006
☐ PK-CAJ	93	Learjet 31A	31A-077	Directorate of Civil Aviation, Jakarta.	N26002
☐ PK-OCF	68	B 737-247	19601	Airfast Indonesia PT/Freeport-McMoRan Inc. New Orleans, La.	N466AC
☐ PK-OCG	70	B 737-293	20335	Airfast Indonesia PT/Freeport-McMoRan Inc. New Orleans, La.	N469AC
☐ PK-OCI	70	B 737-230C	20255	Airfast Indonesia PT/Freeport-McMoRan Inc. New Orleans, La.	N800WA
☐ PK-OSP	89	BAe 146/CC2	E1124	Government of Indonesia, Jakarta.	G-CBXY
☐ PK-PJF	66	BAC 1-11/401AK	065	Citra Aviation PT. Jakarta.	N117MR
☐ PK-PJJ	93	BAe 146/RJ-85	E2239	Pelita Air Service/Government of Indonesia, Jakarta.'Wamema'	G-5-239
☐ PK-PJK	83	F 28-4000	11192	Caltex/Pelita Air Service, Jakarta.	PH-EXW
☐ PK-PJL	76	F 28-4000	11111	Pelita Air Service, Jakarta.	PH-EXA
☐ PK-PJM	81	F 28-4000	11178	Pelita Air Service, Jakarta. 'Matak'	PH-EXW
☐ PK-PJN	90	Fokker 100	11288	Pelita Air Service, Jakarta. 'Lengguru'	PH-LMU
☐ PK-PJY	79	F 28-4000	11146	Pelita Air Service, Jakarta. 'Arun'	PH-EXN
☐ PK-RJW	71	F 28-1000	11045	Post Ekspres Prima, Jakarta. 'Anugerah'	PH-PBX
☐ PK-TRI	68	Falcon 20F	173	Indonesian Air Transport, Jakarta.	N729S
☐ PK-TRU	80	BAC 1-11/492GM	262	Indonesian Air Transport, Jakarta.	G-BLDH
☐ PK-TST	68	BAC 1-11/423ET	118	Indonesian Air Transport, Jakarta.	G-BEJM
☐ PK-TVO	01	Hawker 800XP	8579	Travira Air, Jakarta.	N50309
☐ PK-VBA	66	B 727-25	18970	PENAS/Bakrie Aviation, Jakarta.	N680AM

Military

☐ A-2801	71	F 28-1000	11042	TNI-AU, SkU 17, Jakarta.	PK-PJT

PP	=	BRAZIL			*Total*	**289**

Civil

☐ PP-AAF	03	Falcon 2000EX	16	Metro Taxi Aereo Ltda. Sao Paulo, SP.	F-WWGO
☐ PP-AIO	85	Citation III	650-0087	State Government of the Amazonas, Manaus, AM.	N37VP
☐ PP-ANA	03	Hawker 800XP	8637	CEUMA, Sao Luis, MA.	N637XP
☐ PP-BIA	02	Challenger 604	5539	Braco SA. Sao Paulo, SP.	N539AB
☐ PP-BMG	03	Citation Bravo	550-1045	Banco BMG SA. Belo Horizonte, MG.	N52690
☐ PP-CFF	00	Falcon 2000	110	Iguatemi Shopping Centers SA. Sao Paulo, SP.	N2194
☐ PP-CRS	99	CitationJet	525-0346	Varbra SA. Sao Paulo, SP.	N5136J
☐ PP-EIF	84	Citation 1/SP	501-0680	State Government of Parana, Curitiba, PR.	PT-LFR
☐ PP-ERR	75	Learjet 35	35-008	State Government of Roraima, Boa Vista, RR.	PT-LFS
☐ PP-ESC	89	Citation II	550-0618	Sec. Est. Casa Civil S Catarina, Florianopolis, SC.	PT-LXG
☐ PP-ISJ	94	Citation V	560-0258	Aero Express Taxi Aereo Ltda.	N60NS
☐ PP-JAA	84	Learjet 36A	36A-055	Lider Taxi Aereo SA. Sao Paulo, SP.	N365AS
☐ PP-JBS	00	CitationJet CJ-1	525-0408	Agropecuaria Fribol Ltda.	N408GR
☐ PP-JET	00	CitationJet CJ-1	525-0384	GOF Air Ltda.	N5148B
☐ PP-JFM	99	Citation Excel	560-5045	Martins Com Serv de Distrib SA.	N5221Y
☐ PP-JGV	00	Citation Excel	560-5105	TAM Jatos Executivos Marilia SA. Sao Paulo, SP.	PR-RAA

Reg	Yr	Type	c/n	Owner/Operator	Prev Regn

Reg	Yr	Type	c/n	Owner/Operator	Prev Regn
❏ PP-JQM	98	Citation X	750-0056	Caiua Servicos de Electricidade SA. Sao Paulo, SP.	N5105F
❏ PP-LEM	74	Citation	500-0171	ATA-Aerotaxi Abaeta Ltda. Salvador, BA.	PT-LIX
❏ PP-OAA	00	Citation Bravo	550-0954	Usina Alto Alegre SA. Presidente Prudente, SP.	N5079V
❏ PP-ORM	00	Citation Bravo	550-0930	Delta Publicidade SA.	N5086U
❏ PP-PMV	00	Falcon 50EX	299	Morro Vermelho Taxi Aerea Ltda. Sao Paulo, SP.	N299EX
❏ PP-RAA	99	Citation Excel	560-5034	TAM Jatos Executivos Marilia SA. Sao Paulo, SP.	N52113
❏ PP-UQF	04	Hawker 400XP	RK-379		N979XP
❏ PP-WRV	00	Beechjet 400A	RK-258	WRV Empreend e Particip Ltda.	(PP-LUA)
❏ PP-XJO	00	EMB-135BJ Legacy	145363	Embraer SA. Sao Paulo, SP.	
❏ PP-YOF	99	CitationJet	525-0356	Box 3 Video Publicidade e Producao Ltda. Embu Guacu, SP.	N5213S
❏ PR-...	04	Citation Excel XLS	560-5535		N5141F
❏ PR-AAA	00	Citation Excel	560-5120	Cia Tecidos Norte de Minas Cotemias,	N5211Q
❏ PR-ABV	01	CitationJet CJ-1	525-0428	Cia Cervejaria Brahma, Sao Paulo, SP.	N5203J
❏ PR-ACC	02	Citation Excel	560-5274	Morro Vermelho Taxi Aereo Ltda. Sao Paulo, SP.	N5060K
❏ PR-AJG	99	Citation VII	650-7111		N226W
❏ PR-AMA	01	390 Premier 1	RB-21	JAT Aerotaxi Ltda. Brasilia, DF.	N390MB
❏ PR-ARA	01	CitationJet CJ-1	525-0441	Alphaville Urbanismo SA. Alphaville, SP.	N5200R
❏ PR-BBS	02	BBJ-7BC	32575	Banco Safra SA. Sao Paulo, SP.	N182QS
❏ PR-BER	01	390 Premier 1	RB-40	Frigorifico Bertin Ltda. Sao Paulo, SP.	N51140
❏ PR-CIM	01	390 Premier 1	RB-32		N5132D
❏ PR-DBB	95	Hawker 800XP	8284	Unimed N N F C Trabajos Med Ltda.	(N919H)
❏ PR-EMS	02	Citation Excel	560-5223	EMS Industria Farmaceutica Ltda. S B de Campo, SP.	N5086R
❏ PR-EOB	01	CitationJet CJ-1	525-0483	Aerofar Taxi Aereo Ltda. Campo de Marte, SP.	N5250E
❏ PR-EXP	01	CitationJet CJ-1	525-0482		N5211Q
❏ PR-FEP	98	Citation Bravo	550-0833		N833PA
❏ PR-FNP	97	Citation X	750-0028	N Piquet/TAM Jatos Executivos Marilia SA. Sao Paulo, SP.	N100FF
❏ PR-GAM	02	Citation Excel	560-5256	Amaggi Export Import Ltda.	N4107V
❏ PR-GPA	00	Falcon 900EX	82	Grupo Pao de Acucar SA. Sao Paulo, SP.	N982EX
❏ PR-JAQ	98	Citation X	750-0060	Monte Cristalina SA.	N98CX
❏ PR-JET	01	CitationJet CJ-2	525A-0042	Global Taxi Aereo Ltda. Sao Paulo, SP.	N52342
❏ PR-JRR	03	390 Premier 1	RB-84		N61784
❏ PR-JST	02	CitationJet CJ-2	525A-0044	Transportadora Julio Simoes Ltda.	N5241Z
❏ PR-JTS	83	Diamond 1A	A066SA	Jet Sul Taxi Aereo Ltda. Curitiba, PR.	N88ME
❏ PR-LAM	01	Citation Encore	560-0600	Lojas Americanas SA. Rio de Janeiro, RJ.	N52369
❏ PR-LJM	01	CitationJet CJ-1	525-0456	Soc Acucereira Monteriso de Barros SA.	N5185J
❏ PR-LRJ	98	Learjet 31A	31A-158		N126BX
❏ PR-LTA	84	BAe 125/800B	8025	Lider Aviacao SA. Belo Horizonte, MG.	C-GGYT
❏ PR-LUG	01	Hawker 800XP	8553	LUG Taxi Aereo Ltda. Maceio, AL.	N51453
❏ PR-MVB	02	Beechjet 400A	RK-350	Dogen Holdings Ltd. Belo Horizonte, MG.	N61850
❏ PR-NBR	02	Citation Excel	560-5289	CBMM-Cia Brasileiro de Metal e Mineracao, Sao Paulo, SP.	N5105F
❏ PR-OFT	00	Gulfstream G200	027	Andrade Gutierrez SA. Belo Horizonte, MG.	N878CS
❏ PR-OPP	01	Hawker 800XP	8547	Grupo Odebrecht SA. Rio de Janeiro, RJ.	N4469N
❏ PR-ORE	03	EMB-135BJ Legacy	145625	Companhia Vale Do Rio Doce, Rio de Janeiro, RJ.	PT-SDN
❏ PR-OTA	04	Learjet 45	45-242	OceanAir,	N45SY
❏ PR-PPN	04	Falcon 2000EX EASY	40	Distribuidor Farmaceutica Panarello Ltda.	N240EX
❏ PR-PTL	94	Citation VII	650-7038		N398W
❏ PR-RIO	03	EMB-135BJ Legacy	145717	Consorcio Unibanco BW. Rio de Janeiro.	PT-SAZ
❏ PR-SCB	94	Learjet 31A	31A-100		N31LK
❏ PR-SCR	04	Citation Encore	560-0653		N5265N
❏ PR-SOL	88	BAe 125/800B	8133	Nacional Taxi Aereo Ltda. Goiania, GO.	N800FK
❏ PR-SUL	67	Falcon 20C	129	Jet Sul Taxi Aereo Ltda. Curitiba, PR.	N119LA
❏ PR-TOP	01	CitationJet CJ-2	525A-0061	Box 3 Video Publicidade e Producao Ltda. Embu Guacu, SP.	N5214J
❏ PR-VGD	95	CitationJet	525-0120	Intertel Comerco e Construcao Ltda. Sao Paulo, SP.	N525CZ
❏ PR-VRD	01	Citation Excel	560-5211	Seguranca Taxi Aereo Ltda. Sao Jose do Rio, SP.	N5076K
❏ PR-WQT	03	Falcon 2000EX	22	Varbra SA. Sao Paulo, SP.	N218EX
❏ PR-WYW	93	Falcon 50	234	Walduck Wanderley/Wanair Taxi Aereo Ltda. Belo Horizonte.	PT-AAF
❏ PR-XDY	00	Citation X	750-0118	Conforto Empreendimentoes Particapacoes, Campinas, SP.	N753BD
❏ PR-XJS	00	Learjet 60	60-189	Transporte Julio Simoes SA/Taxi Aereo Weston Ltda. Recife.	N189LJ
❏ PT-FJA	99	CitationJet	525-0337	Laboratorios Neo Quimica SA.	
❏ PT-FNP	99	CitationJet	525-0319	AUTOCRAC. Brasilia, DF.	
❏ PT-FPP	98	Citation Excel	560-5003	Distribuidora Farmaceutica Panarello, Goiania, GO.	(PT-WZO)
❏ PT-FTB	90	Citation V	560-0060	Taxi Aereo Marilia SA. Sao Paulo, SP.	N60MF
❏ PT-FTC	01	CitationJet CJ-2	525A-0048	Igreja Universal do Reino de Deus,	N5183U
❏ PT-FTE	02	CitationJet CJ-2	525A-0053	Taxi Aerea Marilia SA. Sao Paulo, SP.	N5194J
❏ PT-FTG	02	CitationJet CJ-2	525A-0117	Taxi Aerea Marilia SA. Sao Paulo, SP.	N5214K
❏ PT-FTR	03	CitationJet CJ-2	525A-0141	Taxi Aerea Marilia SA. Sao Paulo, SP.	N51872

Reg	Yr	Type	c/n	Owner/Operator	Prev Regn

Reg	Yr	Type	c/n	Owner/Operator	Prev Regn
☐ PT-FZA	01	Learjet 31A	31A-214	Dalari Financial Inc. Maceio, AL.	N124DF
☐ PT-GAF	94	Hawker 800	8261	Banjet Taxi Aereo Ltda. Belo Horizonte, MG.	N958H
☐ PT-IIQ	72	Learjet 25C	25C-089	Delmar Taxi Aereo Ltda. Tatui, SP.	(N890K)
☐ PT-ISO	73	Learjet 25C	25C-115	Golden Key Participacoes Ltda. Camboriu, SC.	
☐ PT-JAA	90	BAe 125/800B	8190	Lider Taxi Aereo SA. Belo Horizonte, MG.	PT-OHB
☐ PT-JKQ	74	Learjet 24D	24D-284	Proserc Proc. Dados SDVA Ltda. Curitiba, PR.	
☐ PT-JMJ	73	Citation	500-0134	TAMIG-Mendes Junior Engenharia SA. Belo Horizonte, MG.	N134CC
☐ PT-KBR	74	Citation	500-0156	DS Air Taxi Aereo Ltda. Rio de Janeiro, RJ.	
☐ PT-KIR	73	Citation	500-0103	Hedge Asses e Cons Empr Ltda. Brasilia, DF.	N103CC
☐ PT-KPA	74	Citation	500-0181	Taxi Aereo Weston Ltda. Recife, PE.	N181CC
☐ PT-KPB	74	Citation	500-0188	Aeronet Informatica Ltda. Imperatriz, MA.	N5223J
☐ PT-KZR	79	Learjet 35A	35A-252	Lider Taxi Aereo SA. Belo Horizonte, MG.	N28CR
☐ PT-LBN	73	Citation	500-0079	Mario Celso Lopes, Andradina, SP.	N40JF
☐ PT-LBW	70	Learjet 25XR	25XR-056	Eucatur Emp Uniao Casc Tur Ltda. Cascavel, PR.	N780A
☐ PT-LCC	81	Citation Eagle	500-0413	Banco Rural SA. Belo Horizonte, MG.	(PT-LBZ)
☐ PT-LCD	77	Learjet 35A	35A-103	Premier Taxi Aereo Ltda. Sao Paulo, SP.	N50MJ
☐ PT-LDH	72	Citation	500-0049	Bradesco Leasing SA. Arrend. Mercantil, Osasco, SP.	PT-FXB
☐ PT-LDI	77	Citation	500-0335	Safra Leasing SA. Arrend Mercantil, S C do Sul, SP.	N2937L
☐ PT-LDM	82	Learjet 35A	35A-494	ELO Particip e Administracao Ltda.	
☐ PT-LDR	88	Learjet 55B	55B-134	BRATA-Brasilia Taxi Aereo Ltda. Brasilia, DF.	N7261D
☐ PT LDY	79	Woctwind-1124	251	TAMIG-Mendes Junior Engenharia SA. Belo Horizonte, MG	CX-CMJ
☐ PT-LEA	74	Learjet 25B	25B-155	Christos Argyrios Mitropoulos,	N24TA
☐ PT-LEB	82	Learjet 35A	35A-474	Soc. de Taxi Aereo Weston Ltda. Recife, PE.	N37975
☐ PT-LEN	72	Learjet 25B	25B-093	Pires do Rio CITEP C I F Aco Ltda. S Caet do Sul, SP.	N33NM
☐ PT-LET	83	Learjet 55	55-080	LUG Taxi Aereo Ltda. Maceio, AL.	N85632
☐ PT-LGW	85	Learjet 35A	35A-598	State Government of Minas Gerais, Belo Horizonte, MG.	N8567T
☐ PT-LHB	85	BAe 125/800B	8031	CTEEP-Cia Transm Energ Elet Paulista,	PT-ZAA
☐ PT-LHC	85	Citation III	650-0086	Interavia Taxi Aereo Ltda. Sao Paulo, SP.	(N1317X)
☐ PT-LHK	69	HS 125/400B	25197	Jet Sul Taxi Aereo Ltda. Curitiba, PR.	PP-EEM
☐ PT-LHR	82	Learjet 55	55-044	SOTAN-Soc. de Taxi Aereo Nordeste Ltda. Maceio, AL.	N3797C
☐ PT-LHT	82	Learjet 35A	35A-479	Constructora Queiroz Galvao SA. Rio de Janeiro, RJ.	N30SA
☐ PT-LIV	84	Citation II	550-0499	Reali Taxi Aereo Ltda. Sao Paulo, SP.	N550PT
☐ PT-LJF	81	Citation II/SP	551-0289	Hyram G Delado Garcete, Dourados, MS. (was 550-0244).	N551BW
☐ PT-LJJ	81	Citation II	550-0247	Renda Partiipacoes,	(N85NA)
☐ PT-LJK	81	Learjet 35A	35A-372	Lider Taxi Aereo SA. Belo Horizonte, MG.	N372AS
☐ PT-LJL	86	Citation S/II	S550-0084	Banco Rural SA. Belo Horizonte, MG.	N1274N
☐ PT-LJQ	86	Citation S/II	S550-0113	Taxi Aereo Sinuelo Ltda. Vespasiano, MG.	N553CC
☐ PT-LKD	78	Learjet 24F	24F-356	LMS/Intersul Aviacao Executiva Ltda. Sao Paulo, SP.	N113JS
☐ PT-LKS	86	Citation S/II	S550-0114	Aeromil Taxi Aereo Ltda. Sao Paulo, SP.	N1292A
☐ PT-LLN	74	Learjet 25C	25C-176	BCN Leasing SA. Barueri, SP.	N28KV
☐ PT-LLS	80	Learjet 35A	35A-303	Viacao Araguarina Ltda. Goiania, GO.	N771A
☐ PT-LLT	81	Citation II	550-0327	Banorte Leasing SA. Barueri, SP.	N74JN
☐ PT-LLU	80	Citation II	550-0132	Taxi Aereo Piracicaba Ltda. Sao Paulo, SP.	(N330MG)
☐ PT-LMM	80	Learjet 25D	25D-323	NTA-Nacional Taxi Aereo Ltda. Goiania, GO.	N6YY
☐ PT-LMS	74	Learjet 24D	24D-296	Sul America Taxi Aereo Ltda. Sao Paulo, SP.	N500DJ
☐ PT-LMY	87	Learjet 35A	35A-627	Objetiva Taxi Aereo Ltda. Belo Horizonte, MG.	N7260T
☐ PT-LNC	81	Citation II	550-0222	Defensa Agrochemeical Corp AVV.	N17RG
☐ PT-LNE	66	Learjet 24	24-114	Adhemar Goncalves Moreira Neto, Belo Horizonte, MG.	N99DM
☐ PT-LNN	83	Diamond 1A	A048SA	Jet Sul Taxi Aereo Ltda. Curitiba, PR. (status ?)	N335DM
☐ PT-LOE	81	Learjet 35A	35A-393	Jet Sul Taxi Aereo Ltda. Curitiba, PR.	N700WJ
☐ PT-LOG	75	Citation	500-0284	Adriano Cocelli SA. Riberao Preto, SP.	N37DW
☐ PT-LOS	74	Citation	500-0329	Oeste Redes Aereas-ORA Taxi Aereo SA. Cuiaba, MT.	N6034F
☐ PT-LOT	77	Learjet 35A	35A-093	Antena um Radiodifusao Ltda. Rio de Janeiro, RJ.	N44PT
☐ PT-LPH	73	Learjet 24D	24D-275	Nova Prospera Mineracao SA. Belo Horizonte, MG.	N216HB
☐ PT-LPK	78	Citation II	550-0010	ATA-Aerotaxi Abaete Ltda. Salvador, BA.	N806C
☐ PT-LPN	81	Citation II	550-0294	Constructora Barbosa Mello SA. Belo Horizonte, MG.	N323CJ
☐ PT-LQK	76	Learjet 24E	24E-333	Rubens de Carvalho,	N75GR
☐ PT-LQP	88	BAe 125/800B	8116	Tirreno Taxi Aereo Ltda. Sao Paulo, SP.	G-5-592
☐ PT-LQR	75	Citation	500-0246	Reali Taxi Aereo Ltda. Sao Paulo, SP.	N227VG
☐ PT-LSJ	78	Learjet 35A	35A-181	Lider Taxi Aereo SA. Belo Horizonte, MG.	N5114G
☐ PT-LTB	89	Citation III	650-0166	PONTAX-Ponta Grossa Taxi Aereo Ltda. Sao Paulo, SP.	N1313J
☐ PT-LTI	75	Citation	500-0226	Cervejaria Belco SA. Sao Manuel, SP.	N100AD
☐ PT-LTJ	81	Citation II	550-0225	Produtos Electricos Corona Ltda. Sao Paulo, SP.	N258CC
☐ PT-LUA	77	Citation	500-0346	Silvio Name Jr, Curitiba, PR.	N56DV
☐ PT-LUE	85	Citation III	650-0091	TAM Jatos Executivos Marilia SA. Sao Paulo, SP.	N58HC
☐ PT-LUG	80	Learjet 35A	35A-356	JK Taxi Aereo Ltda. Brasilia, DF.	N800WJ

Reg	*Yr*	*Type*	*c/n*	*Owner/Operator*	*Prev Regn*

Reg	Yr	Type	c/n	Owner/Operator	Prev Regn
PT-LUK	83	Learjet 55	55-086	Soc. de Taxi Aereo Weston Ltda. Recife, PE.	N8227P
PT-LUZ	81	Learjet 25D	25D-335	Transportadora Rio Itaipu Ltda. Rio de Janeiro, RJ.	N27KG
PT-LVD	88	Falcon 100	223	Brasil Warrant Administracao Ltda. Sao Paulo, SP.	N126FJ
PT-LVF	89	Citation III	650-0171	Confianca Factoring F Merc Ltda. Cuiaba, MT.	N1354G
PT-LXH	73	Citation	500-0133	Nacional Expresso Ltda. Uberlandia, MG.	N1270K
PT-LXO	88	Learjet 55C	55C-135	Manaca Taxi Aereo Ltda. Sao Paulo, SP.	N1055C
PT-LXX	89	Learjet 31	31-007	Cia Brasileira de Cartuchos, Sao Paulo, SP.	N3819G
PT-LZP	80	Learjet 35A	35A-339	Construtora Andrade Gutierrez SA. Belo Horizonte, MG.	N1500
PT-LZQ	89	Citation V	560-0045	Bunge Alimentos SA.	N2665Y
PT-MBZ	88	Astra-1125	022	Serv Jet Serv Pecas P/Avioes Ltda. Brasilia, DF.	4X-CUT
PT-MGS	92	Citation VII	650-7021	State Government of Minas Gerais, Belo Horizonte, MG.	N1262B
PT-MIL	95	CitationJet	525-0086	Viacao Barao de Maua Ltda. Sao Paulo, SP.	N5093L
PT-MJC	94	CitationJet	525-0085	Radio Record SA. Sao Paulo.	VR-CDN
PT-MMO	83	Citation II	550-0455	Nor-Jet Particip. e Serv. Ltda. Bauru, SP.	N90SF
PT-MMV	97	Citation Bravo	550-0811	Morro Vermelho Taxi Aereo Ltda. Sao Paulo, SP.	N5221Y
PT-MPE	93	CitationJet	525-0015	TAM Jatos Executivos Marilia SA. Sao Paulo, SP.	N115CJ
PT-MPL	97	Beechjet 400A	RK-158	MPE Montagens, Rio de Janeiro, RJ.	N2358X
PT-MSK	00	Citation Excel	560-5087	Casa Bahia Comercial Ltda. Curitiba, PR.	N5165T
PT-MSP	98	CitationJet	525-0259	Flexiveix Diadema Ltda.	N5235G
PT-OAG	82	Citation II	550-0357	ZLC Intermed. de Negocios SC Ltda. Goiania, GO.	N29FA
PT-OBD	71	Learjet 24B	24B-228	DIMASA/Oliveira Silva Taxi Aereo Ltda. Manaus, AM.	N150AB
PT-OCZ	80	Learjet 35A	35A-361	BRATA-Brasilia Taxi Aereo Ltda. Brasilia, DF.	PT-FAT
PT-ODC	84	Citation 1/SP	501-0678	MRV Servicos de Engenharia Ltda.	(N26AA)
PT-ODL	90	Citation II	550-0640	Primo Schincariol Ind. Cerv. Ref. SA. Itu. SP.	N1308V
PT-ODZ	90	Citation II	550-0645	Antonio Wagner Da C Henriques, Belo Horizonte, MG.	N1310C
PT-OEX	90	Falcon 900	92	Banco Safra SA. Sao Paulo, SP.	N463FJ
PT-OHD	79	Learjet 25D	25D-296	Superjet Aerotaxi Ltda. Florianapolis, SC.	N55MJ
PT-OIG	72	Citation	500-0005	Luiz Carlos Sella e Outro, Curitiba, PR.	N815HC
PT-OJF	73	Citation	500-0131	Noronha Taxi Aereo Ltda. Teresina, PI.	N457CA
PT-OJG	91	Citation II	550-0676	EMS Industria Farmaceutica Ltda. S B de Campo, SP.	N67741
PT-OKP	83	Citation II	550-0460	Parana Jet Taxi Aereo Ltda. Curitiba, PR. (was 551-0460).	N6523A
PT-OMS	75	Citation	500-0251	ATA-Aerotaxi Abaete Ltda. Salvador, BA.	N790EA
PT-OMT	74	Citation	500-0179	ATA-Aerotaxi Abaete Ltda. Salvador, BA.	N179EA
PT-OMU	91	Citation VI	650-0205	TAM Jatos Executivos Marilia SA. Sao Paulo, SP.	N2630N
PT-OOI	91	BAe 125/800B	8214	Grupo OK Benefica Cia Nacional de Pneus Ltda. Brasilia, DF.	VR-CCX
PT-OOL	73	Citation	500-0060	Nort Jet Taxi Aereo Ltda. Belem, PA.	N712G
PT-OPJ	81	Learjet 35A	35A-396	ABC Taxi Aereo Ltda. Uberlandia, MG.	N74JL
PT-OQD	75	Citation	500-0244	Superjet Taxi Aereo Ltda. Florianopolis, SC.	N516AB
PT-ORA	90	Learjet 55C	55C-146	Soc. de Taxi Aereo Weston Ltda. Recife, PE.	N9125M
PT-ORC	92	Citation V	560-0195	TAM-Jatos Executivos Marilia SA. Rio de Janeiro, RJ.	N1282N
PT-OSD	75	Citation	500-0325	Anicuns SA. Alcool e Derivados,	N60MP
PT-OSM	88	Citation S/II	S550-0160	EBTA-Empresa Baiana de Taxi Aereo Ltda. Salvador, BA.	N550GT
PT-OSW	90	BAe 125/800B	8184	Construtora Cowan Ltda. Belo Horizonte, MG.	G-5-678
PT-OTC	90	BAe 125/800B	8194	Centaurus Taxi Aereo Ltda. Rio de Janeiro, RJ.	G-5-692
PT-OTQ	72	Citation	500-0046	Diogenes Setti Sobreira, Rio de Janeiro, RJ.	N929RW
PT-OTS	93	Citation V	560-0213	Guaxupe Taxi Aereo Ltda. Guaxupe, MG.	N12845
PT-OVK	72	Citation	500-0027	Douglas Aldred, Sao Paulo, SP.	N777AN
PT-OVU	93	Citation VII	650-7033	Banco Bradesco SA. Rio de Janeiro, RJ.	N1264B
PT-OVV	89	Citation II	550-0616	Delta National Bank Trust Co. NYC. USA.	(D-IAFA)
PT-OVZ	91	Learjet 31A	31A-037	Aztur Taxi Aereo e Turismo Ltda. Porte Alegre, RS.	N31TF
PT-OXT	83	Diamond 1A	A039SA	Himaco Hidraulicos e Maquinas Ltda. Porto Alegre, RS.	N399MJ
PT-POK	86	Learjet 35A	35A-619	Partpar Administ e Particip Ltda. Rio de Janeiro, RJ.	N8568V
PT-PRR	00	CitationJet CJ-1	525-0403	Remar Admin e Comercio SA.	N51817
PT-SAS	03	EMB-135BJ Legacy	145678	Embraer SA. Sao Paulo, SP.	
PT-SIB	04	EMB-135BJ Legacy	145770	Embraer SA. Sao Paulo, SP.	
PT-SIC	04	EMB-135BJ Legacy	145775	Embraer SA. Sao Paulo, SP.	
PT-SIP	04	EMB-135BJ Legacy	14500854	Embraer SA. Sao Paulo, SP.	
PT-SIQ	04	EMB-135BJ Legacy	14500863	Embraer SA. Sao Paulo, SP.	
PT-WAL	90	BAe 125/800B	8198	Construtora Cowan Ltda. Belo Horizonte, MG.	G-5-694
PT-WBC	96	Astra-1125SPX	086	Companhia Cervejaria Brahma, Rio de Janeiro, RJ.	N793A
PT-WBY	72	Citation	500-0008	Clipper Agencia de Viagens Ltda. Aracaju, SE.	ZP-TYP
PT-WEW	68	Learjet 24	24-158	Pedro Muffato e Cia Ltda. Cascavel, PR.	N220PM
PT-WFD	95	Citation V Ultra	560-0308	Serveng Civilsan SA Emp Assoc Eng. Brasilia, DF.	N5235G
PT-WFT	74	Citation	500-0154	TASUL-Taxi Aereo Sul Ltda. Porto Alegre, RS.	N54MC
PT-WGF	80	Learjet 35A	35A-322	Vector Taxi Aereo Ltda. Belo Horizonte, MG.	N305SC
PT-WHB	93	Beechjet 400A	RK-73	Lider Taxi Aereo SA. Belo Horizonte, MG.	N8070Q

| Reg | Yr | Type | c/n | Owner/Operator | Prev Regn |

Reg	Yr	Type	c/n	Owner/Operator	Prev Regn
☐ PT-WHD	93	Beechjet 400A	RK-77	Lider Taxi Aereo SA. Belo Horizonte, MG.	N8277Y
☐ PT-WHE	93	Beechjet 400A	RK-81	Lider Taxi Aereo SA. Belo Horizonte, MG.	N8167G
☐ PT-WHF	93	Beechjet 400A	RK-82	Lider Taxi Aereo SA. Belo Horizonte, MG.	N8282E
☐ PT-WHG	92	Beechjet 400A	RK-54	Lider Taxi Aereo SA. Belo Horizonte, MG.	N80938
☐ PT-WIB	87	Citation S/II	S550-0137	Bertol Aerotaxi Ltda. Porte Alegre, RS.	N100TB
☐ PT-WIV	95	Learjet 31A	31A-110	Du Valle Transporta Com. e Agro. Ltda. Sao Paulo, SP.	N40130
☐ PT-WJS	96	Beechjet 400A	RK-122	Frigorifico Bertin Ltda. Sao Paulo. SP.	N1102B
☐ PT-WJZ	81	Citation II	550-0318	TAM Jetos Exexutivos Marilia SA. Rio de Janeiro, RJ.	PT-LJT
☐ PT-WKL	74	Learjet 24D	24D-294	Isaias Santos de Carvalho, Curitiba, PR. (status ?).	PP-EIW
☐ PT-WKQ	91	Citation II	550-0675	BLD Leasing LLC. Miami, Foteleza, CE.	N275BD
☐ PT-WLO	97	Learjet 31A	31A-122	Usiminas Admin Partipacoes S. Med, Belo Horizonte, MG.	N122LJ
☐ PT-WLX	97	CitationJet	525-0176	JCA Holding Participacoes Ltda. Rio de Janeiro, RJ.	N5161J
☐ PT-WLY	96	Citation VII	650-7074	Companhia Muller de Bebidas,	N5183V
☐ PT-WMA	96	Hawker 800XP	8301	Lider Taxi Aereo SA. Belo Horizonte, MG.	N1105Z
☐ PT-WMZ	97	Citation V Ultra	560-0406	Taxi Aereo Marilia SA. Sao Paulo, SP.	N5203S
☐ PT-WQH	98	Citation VII	650-7083	Banco Bradesco SA. Rio de Janeiro, RJ.	
☐ PT-WQI	98	CitationJet	525-0238	Saturno Taxi Aereo Ltda.	N5203S
☐ PT-WQS	99	Citation 900EX	53	Braco SA. Sao Paulo, SP.	N953EX
☐ PT-WSB	97	Learjet 31A	31A-135	VIP Jet Aero Taxi Ltda. Curitiba, PR.	N80645
☐ PT-WSF	80	Falcon 10	169	Flysul Aerotaxi Ltda. Porte Alegre, RS.	(N107AF)
☐ PT-WUM	99	Citation X	750-0092	Consorcia Voa Ltda. Rio de Janeiro, RJ.	N5066U
☐ PT-WVG	99	Hawker 800XP	8395	Interavia Taxi Aereo Ltda. Sao Paulo, SP.	N23577
☐ PT-WVH	97	Citation V Ultra	560-0409	Seguranca Taxi Aereo Ltda. Sao Jose do Rio, SP.	(N409VP)
☐ PT-WYC	98	Falcon 2000	59	Grendene SA. Sao Paulo, SP.	N2146
☐ PT-WYU	99	Citation Excel	560-5060	Citrosuco Paulista SA. Matao, SP.	N5201J
☐ PT-XAC	98	CitationJet	525-0280	Andriano Coselli SA. Ribeirao Preto, SP.	N5151D
☐ PT-XCF	97	Citation V Ultra	560-0450	Equip Taxi Aereo Ltda. Sao Jose dos Pinhais, PR.	N51246
☐ PT-XCL	99	Citation Excel	560-5020	Ventura Holding, Sao Paulo, SP.	PT-XCL
☐ PT-XDB	98	CitationJet	525-0274	Empresa Brasileira de Distribuidora Ltda. Belem, Pa.	
☐ PT-XFG	99	Citation VII	650-7099	Cell Star do Brasil,	N5141F
☐ PT-XFS	97	Learjet 60	60-121	Soc. de Taxi Aereo Weston Ltda. Recife, PE.	N621LJ
☐ PT-XGS	99	Learjet 60	60-164		N60LJ
☐ PT-XIB	99	Citation Excel	560-5043	Brasil Duty Free Shop Ltda. Rio de Janeiro, RJ.	N5218R
☐ PT-XLI	80	Learjet 35A	35A-299	Lider Taxi Aereo SA. Belo Horizonte, MG.	(PT-PMV)
☐ PT-XLR	99	Learjet 45	45-048	Lojas Riachuelo SA. Sao Paulo, SP.	
☐ PT-XMM	98	CitationJet	525-0267	Taxi Aereo Jet News Ltda. Belem, PA.	N5201J
☐ PT-XPP	97	Learjet 31A	31A-148	Radio e Televisao Iguacu SA. Curitiba, PR.	(PT-XIT)
☐ PT-XSC	99	Falcon 900EX	60	Sucocitrico Cutrale Ltda. Sao Paulo, SP.	N960EX
☐ PT-XSX	99	Citation Bravo	550-0873	Frigorifico Quatro Marcos Ltda.	N5109R
☐ PT-XTA	89	Learjet 31	31-013	Target Aviacao Executiva SA. Sao Paulo, SP.	N213PA

Military

Reg	Yr	Type	c/n	Owner/Operator	Prev Regn
☐ 2101	04	Airbus A319-133X	2263	FAB/Republica Federativa do Brasil,	D-AVWJ
☐ 2113	67	HS 125/3A-RA	NA701	FAB, GTE=Grupo do Transporte Especiale, Brasilia.	N125HS
☐ 2401	68	B 707-345C	19840	FAB=Forca Aerea Brasileira.	PP-VJY
☐ 2710	87	Learjet 35A	35A-631	Brazilian Air Force,	N3818G
☐ 2711	87	Learjet 35A	35A-632	Brazilian Air Force,	N1461B
☐ 2712	87	Learjet 35A	35A-633	Brazilian Air Force,	N39416
☐ 2713	88	Learjet 35A	35A-636	Brazilian Air Force,	
☐ 2714	88	Learjet 35A	35A-638	Brazilian Air Force,	
☐ 2715	88	Learjet 35A	35A-639	Brazilian Air Force,	
☐ 2716	88	Learjet 35A	35A-640	Brazilian Air Force.	N8568Y
☐ 2717	88	Learjet 35A	35A-641	Brazilian Air Force,	N7261H
☐ 2718	88	Learjet 35A	35A-642	Brazilian Air Force,	N7262X
☐ 6700	01	EMB-145RS	145257	Brazilian Air Force,	PP-XRU
☐ EC93-2125	68	HS 125/3B-RC	25164	FAB=Forca Aerea Brasileira. Flight inspection.	
☐ EU93-2119	73	HS 125/403B	25274	FAB, G.E.I.V., Rio-Santos Dumont. (flight calibration).	G-5-20
☐ EU93-2121	68	HS 125/3B-RC	25165	FAB, G.E.I.V., Rio-Santos Dumont. (flight calibration).	VC93-2121
☐ EU93-6050	99	BAe U-125A	8401	FAB, G.E.I.V., Rio-Santos Dumont. (flight calibration).	N23592
☐ EU93-6051	99	BAe U-125A	8421	FAB, G.E.I.V., Rio-Santos Dumont. (flight calibration).	N31820
☐ EU93-6052	99	BAe U-125A	8434	FAB, G.E.I.V., Rio-Santon Dumont. (flight calibration).	N40027
☐ EU93-6053	99	BAe U-125A	8447	FAB, G.E.I.V., Rio-Santos Dumont. (flight calibration).	N40310
☐ FAB6000	86	Learjet 35A	35A-613	FAB=Forca Aerea Brasileira.	N4289X
☐ FAB6001	86	Learjet 35A	35A-615	FAB=Forca Aerea Brasileira.	N7260E
☐ FAB6002	86	Learjet 35A	35A-617	FAB=Forca Aerea Brasileira.	N4289Z
☐ FAB6100	89	Learjet 55C	55C-140	FAB=Forca Aerea Brasileira.	PT-OCA
☐ VC93-2120	68	HS 125/3B-RC	25162	FAB, GTE=Grupo do Transporte Especiale, Brasilia.	

Reg	Yr	Type	c/n	Owner/Operator	Prev Regn

Reg	Yr	Type	c/n	Owner/Operator	Prev Regn
VC93-2123	68	HS 125/3B-RC	25167	FAB, GTE=Grupo do Transporte Especiale, Brasilia.	
VC93-2124	68	HS 125/3B-RC	25168	FAB, GTE=Grupo do Transporte Especiale, Brasilia.	
VC96-2115	76	B 737-2N3	21165	FAB, GTE=Grupo do Transporte Especiale, Brasilia.	
VC96-2116	76	B 737-2N5	21166	FAB, GTE=Grupo do Transporte Especiale, Brasilia.	
VU93-2114	70	HS 125/400A	NA740	FAB, GTE=Grupo do Transporte Especiale, Brasilia.	N702P
VU93-2117	69	HS 125/400A	NA738	FAB, GTE=Grupo do Transporte Especiale, Brasilia	N702D
VU93-2118	69	HS 125/400A	NA729	FAB, GTE=Grupo do Transporte Especiale, Brasilia.	N702SS
VU93-2126	73	HS 125/403B	25277	FAB, GTE=Grupo do Transporte Especiale, Brasilia.	
VU93-2127	73	HS 125/403B	25288	FAB, GTE=Grupo do Transporte Especiale, Brasilia.	
VU93-2128	73	HS 125/403B	25289	FAB, GTE=Grupo do Transporte Especiale, Brasilia.	G-5-16

P2   =   PAPUA NEW GUINEA   Total   2

Civil

Reg	Yr	Type	c/n	Owner/Operator	Prev Regn
P2-MBD	79	Citation II	550-0076	Airlines of PNG Ltd. Port Moresby.	VH-XDD
P2-TAA	80	Citation II	550-0145	Trans Air P/L. Port Moresby.	P2-MBN

P4   =   ARUBA   Total   38

Civil

Reg	Yr	Type	c/n	Owner/Operator	Prev Regn
P4-ALM	01	Citation Excel	560-5218	Fayco International AVV/Al Misehal Commercial Group, Riyadh.	N218AM
P4-AMF	91	BAe 125/800B	8201	Petrovair/Wasserstein Investments AVV.	G-BWSY
P4-AOB	70	HS 125/731	NA747	AVCOM/Evolga AVV. Moscow-Vnukovo, Russia.	N125NW
P4-AOC	66	HS 125/731	25079	AVCOM/Evolga AVV. Moscow-Vnukovo, Russia.	N942WN
P4-AOD	81	HS 125/700A	NA0313	AVCOM/Evolga AVV. Moscow-Vnukovo, Russia.	N419RD
P4-AOE	81	HS 125/700A	7136	AVCOM/Evolga AVV. Moscow-Vnukovo, Russia.	N318CD
P4-AVM	00	Learjet 60	60-197	AVMAX Group Inc. Calgary, AB. Canada.	N23PZ
P4-AVN	79	Falcon 10	128	AVCOM/Evolga AVV. Moscow-Vnukovo, Russia.	N228SJ
P4-CBH	66	BAC 1-11/401AK	088	Jetline Inc. Sharjah, UAE.	HZ-MAJ
P4-CRJ	98	Challenger 800	7176	HCX Aviation AVV/Global Jet Luxembourg, Luxembourg.	LX-GJC
P4-DCE	69	DC 8-62H	46071	Jetline Inc. Sharjah, UAE.	P4-CBA
P4-EPI	93	Challenger 601-3A	5125	V-S Aviation AVV/Bollening Trading Ltd. Limassol, Cyprus.	(N14DP)
P4-FAY	01	Challenger 604	5508	Fayco International AVV/Al Misehal Commercial Group, Riyadh.	N528DK
P4-FSH	80	B 747SP-31	21963	Crestwind Aviation, Cincinnati, Oh. USA.	A6-SMM
P4-GJC	99	BBJ-7CG	30751	Tanzanite Investments AVV/Silver Arrows, Geneva, Switzerland	N888GW
P4-IKR	98	Falcon 2000	70	Ikaros Aviation AVV. Kiev, Ukraine.	N207QS
P4-IVM	03	EMB-135BJ	145686	Pacific Information Technology Inc. Moscow, Russia.	N686SG
P4-JLB	80	BAC 1-11/492GM	260	ARABASCO/Mercury Aviation, Jeddah, Saudi Arabia.	VP-CHM
P4-JLD	67	B 727-193	19620	Joylud Dist International/Government of Tatarstan.	VP-CWC
P4-JLI	80	B 727-2K5	21853	Jetline Inc. Mitiga, Libya.	HZ-HR4
P4-LJG	04	Citation X	750-0227	Ven Air Ltd. Dublin, Ireland.	N5267J
P4-MED	74	TriStar 100	1064	Eagle Jet Aviation Inc. Tucson, Az. USA.	N787M
P4-MES	02	B 767-33AER	33425	Crocus Corp AVV/Global Jet Luxembourg SA. Luxembourg.	N595HA
P4-MMG	65	B 727-30	18368	Amel Aruba Ltd & MME Aviation (Cayman Islands).	VP-CMM
P4-NJR	62	B 720-047B	18453	JR Executive Aruba AVV. Beirut, Lebanon.	HZ-KA4
P4-NSN	86	B 757-2M6	23454	Government of Kazakhstan, Almaty, Kazakhstan.	VR-CRK
P4-OBE	81	HS 125/700B	7142	United Slinx Corp AVV /Aero Rent, Moscow, Russia.	G-BJDJ
P4-ONE	67	B 727-22	19148	Joss AVV. Aruba. (stored San Antonio).	N341TC
P4-PHS	90	B 737-53A	24970	BGL Corp AVV.	P4-FZT
P4-SIS	03	EMB-135BJ Legacy	145586	Evolga AVV/AVCOM, Moscow, Russia.	PT-...
P4-SKI	78	B 727-212	21460	Precision International Services Ltd. Bouremouth-Hurn, UK.	VP-CBQ
P4-SNT	01	Hawker 800XP	8538	Daedelos AVV. Oranjestad.	N538LD
P4-TAK	00	Gulfstream 4SP	1425	Uni Oil AG/Mint Juleps Investment AVV. Almaty, Kazakhstan	XA-ABA
P4-TAT	03	Challenger 604	5567	Royal Turbo Jet AVV. Kazan, Russia.	C-FAOL
P4-TBN	99	BBJ-7BH	29791	TBN Aviation AVV. Riyadh, Saudi Arabia.	N348BA
P4-VJR	75	HS 125/600B	6049	JR Executive Aruba AVV.	HZ-KA5
P4-VVP	02	EMB-135BJ Legacy	145549	Evolga AVV. Moscow, Russia.	PT-SAJ
P4-YJR	64	B 727-30	18366	JR Executive Aruba AVV. Beirut, Lebanon.	N727JR

RA   =   RUSSIA / RUSSIAN FEDERATION   Total   10

Civil

Reg	Yr	Type	c/n	Owner/Operator	Prev Regn
RA-02801	80	HS 125/700B	7097	Meridian Air/Magnitogorsk & Tjazhprom, Moscow.	G-5-810
RA-02803	81	HS 125/700B	7139	Jet 2000 Business Jets, Moscow-Vnukovo.	G-5-875
RA-02807	86	BAe 125/800B	8076	Aero Rent/Master Group, Moscow.	G-5-535
RA-02850	80	HS 125/700B	7112	SIAT-Sibaviatrans, Krasnoyamsk.	G-SVLB
RA-09000	92	Falcon 900B	118	Gazprom/Gazkomplektimpex, Ostafyevo.	F-GNFI
RA-09001	94	Falcon 900B	123	Gazprom/Gazkomplektimpex, Ostafyevo.	F-WWFL
RA-09003	68	Falcon 20D	183	AVCOM, Moscow-Vnukovo.	EC-EFR
RA-09004	99	Falcon 20C	170	Jet 2000 Business Jets, Moscow-Vnukovo. (stored GVA).	F-GHPA
RA-10201	00	Gulfstream 4SP	1465	UTair Aviation/Surguneftegaz, Khanty-Mansisk.	N465GA

Reg	Yr	Type	c/n	Owner/Operator	Prev Regn
☐ RA-3077K	67	Sabre-60	306-13	Aeroclub KVS, Moscow.	N306CF

RP = PHILIPPINES   *Total*   17

Civil

Reg	Yr	Type	c/n	Owner/Operator	Prev Regn
☐ RP-1250	79	F 28-3000	11153	Government of Philippines, Manila.	PH-ZBV
☐ RP-C....	69	Learjet 24B	24B-182	Wilma's Flight Service Inc. Tamuning, Guam.	N155J
☐ RP-C1180	90	Citation II	550-0658	Rio Tuba Nickel Mining Corp.	N550MZ
☐ RP-C125	65	HS 125/1A-522	25033	Makar Properties Development Inc. Cebu.	N125LL
☐ RP-C1426	81	Learjet 35A	35A-426	Columbian Motors/Subic International Air Charter, Manila.	N1128J
☐ RP-C1747	73	Learjet 24XR	24XR-264	Subic International Air Charter Inc. Subic Bay.	PI-C1747
☐ RP-C1911	80	Falcon 10	174	Associated Brokerage Systems Inc. Manila.	N402ES
☐ RP-C1958	00	Learjet 45	45-100	Subic International Air Charter Inc. Subic Bay.	N45LJ
☐ RP-C2424	70	Learjet 24B	24B-226	Marlin Bay Helicopters, Port Vila, Vanuatu.	N335RY
☐ RP-C4007	92	B 737-332	25996	Government of Philippines, Manila.	RP-C2000
☐ RP-C6003	02	Learjet 60	60-254	Subic International Air Charter Inc. Subic Bay.	N5054J
☐ RP-C610	80	Learjet 35A	35A-338	United Coconut Planters Bank, Manila.	N610GE
☐ RP-C6178	99	Learjet 31A	31A-178	Subic International Air Charter Inc. Subic Bay.	N50145
☐ RP-C7808	94	Falcon 900B	125	Jet Eagle International Ltd. Subic Bay.	VP-BSK
☐ RP-C848	65	Learjet 23	23-072	Air Ads Inc. Manila.	N2SN
☐ RP-C8576	02	Hawker 800XP	8571	Challenger Aero Corp. Subic Bay.	N4471N
☐ RP-C8822	94	Learjet 31A	31A-041	Asia Pacific Helicopters, Manila.	N319CH

SE = SWEDEN   *Total*   35

Civil

Reg	Yr	Type	c/n	Owner/Operator	Prev Regn
☐ SE-DDY	80	Citation II	550-0115	Flyco NV/Inter Air AB. Malmo-Sturup. (INR 303).	OY-CCU
☐ SE-DEG	75	Citation	500-0276	HYPO Bautrager GmbH.	N29EB
☐ SE-DEY	77	Citation	500-0370	Holland Alcomix BV. Amsterdam, Holland.	N36897
☐ SE-DEZ	77	Citation 1/SP	501-0279	Stella Aviation Charter BV. Teuge, Holland. (was 500-0371)	N66HD
☐ SE-DHO	78	Learjet 35A	35A-195	SAAB Nyge-Aero AB. Skavsta. (Target 01).	N555JE
☐ SE-DHP	76	Learjet 35A	35A-075	SAAB Nyge-Aero AB. Skavsta. (Target 02)	N30FN
☐ SE-DLB	81	Falcon 100	183	Andersson Business Jet AB. Stockholm-Bromma.	N183SR
☐ SE-DLZ	82	Citation	500-0411	Jiv Air AB. Goeteborg-Saeve.	G-NCMT
☐ SE-DRS	91	Beechjet 400A	RK-37	Stralfors AB/PA-Flyg AB. Ljungbby-Feringe.	N8014Q
☐ SE-DRZ	76	Citation	500-0315	ETM/West Air Sweden AB. Lidkoeping-Hovby.	(OY-TCP)
☐ SE-DUZ	74	Citation	500-0143	Polvere di Stelle SRL. Ancona, Italy.	N767BA
☐ SE-DVD	97	Hawker 800XP	8339	Birgma Sweden AB. Joenkoping.	N23395
☐ SE-DVE	97	Falcon 900EX	23	Volvo AB/Blue Chip Jet AB. Goeteborg-Saeve.	F-WWFS
☐ SE-DVP	89	Falcon 100	224	Andersson Business Jet AB. Stockholm-Bromma.	F-WWZN
☐ SE-DVT	90	Citation II	550-0634	Volvo Aero AB/Volvo Aero Corp. Trollhaettan.	N550SB
☐ SE-DVY	92	Citation VII	650-7011	EFS-European Flight Service AB. Goeteborg-Saeve.	N700VP
☐ SE-DYB	87	Falcon 100	216	Andersson Business Jet AB. Stockholm-Bromma.	(N71M)
☐ SE-DYE	98	Hawker 800XP	8382	Volvo AB/Blue Chip Jet AB. Goeteborg-Saeve.	N23451
☐ SE-DYR	79	Citation II/SP	551-0132	Dafgards AB. Lidkoeping-Hovby. (was 550-0087).	C-GTBR
☐ SE-DYV	98	Hawker 800XP	8385	Volvo AB/Blue Chip Jet AB. Goeteborg-Saeve.	G-05-02
☐ SE-DYX	99	Citation Excel	560-5029	EFS-European Flight Service AB. Goeteborg-Saeve.	N5203S
☐ SE-DZZ	81	Learjet 35A	35A-415	Flyair Ltd/East Air KB. Stockholm-Bromma.	D-COSY
☐ SE-RBK	81	Citation II	550-0315	Waltair Europe AB. Noerrkoping.	N59GU
☐ SE-RBO	00	Beechjet 400A	RK-303	Stralfors AB/PA-Flyg AB. Ljungbby-Feringe.	N400HD
☐ SE-RBX	99	Citation Excel	560-5056	Open Air AB/NEX Time Jet AB-Nextjet, Stockholm.	N688AG
☐ SE-RBY	02	Citation Bravo	550-1038	Stall Palema AB/AB Benders Takpanneindustri, Lidkoping-Hovby	(N551VP)
☐ SE-RBZ	78	Citation 1/SP	501-0061	Hastens Sangar AB. Vasteras.	N202CF
☐ SE-RCA	78	Learjet 35A	35A-175	SAAB Nyge-Aero AB. Skavsta. (Target 03).	D-CDWN
☐ SE-RDX	03	Gulfstream G550	5019	EFS-European Flight Service AB. Goeteborg-Saeve.	N919GA

Military

Reg	Yr	Type	c/n	Owner/Operator	Prev Regn
☐ 102001	87	Gulfstream 4/Tp 102	1014	Swedish Air Force, Bromma. (Code 021 of F16).	N779SW
☐ 102002	93	Gulfstream 4/Tp 102B	1215	Swedish Air Force, Linkoeping-Malmen. (Code 022 of F16).	N426GA
☐ 102003	93	Gulfstream 4/Tp 102B	1216	Swedish Air Force, Linkoeping-Malmen. (Code 023 of F16).	N440GA
☐ 102004	95	Gulfstream 4/Tp 102C	1274	Swedish Air Force, Uppsala. (Code 024 of F16).	LV-WOM
☐ 86001	65	Sabre-40/Tp 86	282-49	Defense Material Administration, Linkoeping.	N905KB
☐ 86002	67	Sabre-40/Tp 86	282-91	Defence Material Administration, Linkoeping.	N40NR

SP = POLAND   *Total*   1

Civil

Reg	Yr	Type	c/n	Owner/Operator	Prev Regn
☐ SP-KCL	04	CitationJet CJ-1	525-0526		N526LC

ST = SUDAN   *Total*   4

Civil

Reg	Yr	Type	c/n	Owner/Operator	Prev Regn
☐ ST-PRE	65	JetStar-6	5071	Government of Sudan, Khartoum.	SU-DAH

Reg	Yr	Type	c/n	Owner/Operator	Prev Regn

Reg	Yr	Type	c/n	Owner/Operator	Prev Regn
□ ST-PRS	77	Falcon 20F	372	Government of Sudan, Khartoum.	F-WRQV
□ ST-PSA	90	Falcon 900	84	Government of Sudan, Khartoum.	F-WQBM
□ ST-PSR	82	Falcon 50	114	Government of Sudan, Khartoum.	F-WPXM

SU = EGYPT   Total   18

Civil

Reg	Yr	Type	c/n	Owner/Operator	Prev Regn
□ SU-AXJ	74	B 707-366C	20919	Government of Egypt, Cairo. (r/c Egyptian 01)	
□ SU-AXN	73	Falcon 20-5B	294	Government of Egypt, Cairo.	F-BVPM
□ SU-AYD	77	Falcon 20-5B	361	Government of Egypt, Cairo.	F-WMKF
□ SU-AZJ	76	Falcon 20-5B	358	Government of Egypt, Cairo.	F-WRQY
□ SU-BNC	97	Gulfstream 4SP	1329	Government of Egypt, Cairo.	N329GA
□ SU-BND	97	Gulfstream 4SP	1332	Government of Egypt, Cairo.	N332GA
□ SU-BNO	01	Gulfstream 4SP	1424	Government of Egypt, Cairo.	N328GA
□ SU-BNP	00	Gulfstream 4SP	1427	Government of Egypt, Cairo.	N427GA
□ SU-BPE	03	Gulfstream G400	1506	Government of Egypt, Cairo.	N306GA
□ SU-BPF	03	Gulfstream G400	1518	Government of Egypt, Cairo.	N218GA
□ SU-EWC	99	Citation Excel	560-5042	Executive Wings Aviation, Cairo.	N42XL
□ SU-GGG	94	Airbus A340-211	061	Government of Egypt, Cairo.	F-W...
□ SU-MSG	00	Learjet 45	45-069	Artoc Group Investment & Development, Cairo.	N50157
□ SU-OAE	68	Falcon 20D-5B	175	Pyramid Airlines, Cairo.	HB-VJW
□ SU-PIX	82	HS 125/700B	7184	National Aviation Co. Cairo.	G-36-2

Military

Reg	Yr	Type	c/n	Owner/Operator	Prev Regn
□ SU-BGM	88	Gulfstream 4	1048	Egyptian Air Force/Arab Republic of Egypt, Cairo.	N448GA
□ SU-BGU	85	Gulfstream 3	439	Egyptian Air Force/Arab Republic of Egypt, Cairo.	N17586
□ SU-BGV	85	Gulfstream 3	442	Egyptian Air Force/Arab Republic of Egypt, Cairo.	N17587

SX = GREECE   Total   10

Civil

Reg	Yr	Type	c/n	Owner/Operator	Prev Regn
□ SX-BMK	99	Citation Bravo	550-0907	Hellados Hotels/Mitsis Co. Athens.	HB-VMM
□ SX-BTV	86	Learjet 55	55-124	Aegean Aviation Ltd. Athens.	N58CQ
□ SX-DCA	04	Falcon 2000EX	29	Interjet SA. Athens.	F-WWGD
□ SX-DCE	02	Citation Excel	560-5288	Interjet SA. Athens.	N5117U
□ SX-DCI	96	Citation V Ultra	560-0366	Interjet Hellenic Aviation SA. Athens.	N52352
□ SX-DCM	99	Citation Excel	560-5051	Interjet SA. Athens.	N1324B

Military

Reg	Yr	Type	c/n	Owner/Operator	Prev Regn
□ 209	99	EMB-135LR	145209	Greek Air Force/Government, Athens.	PT-SFX
□ 374	01	EMB-135EW	145374	Greek Air Force/Government, Athens.	PP-XHL
□ 484	02	EMB-135BJ Legacy	145484	Greek Air Force/Government, Athens.	PT-...
□ 678	02	Gulfstream V	678	MoD/Government of Greece, Elefis.	N678GA

S5 = SLOVENIA   Total   4

Civil

Reg	Yr	Type	c/n	Owner/Operator	Prev Regn
□ S5-BAA	86	Learjet 35A	35A-618	Government of Slovenia, Ljubljana.	SL-BAA
□ S5-BAX	85	Citation S/II	S550-0028	Smelt Air/GIO Business Aviation, Ljubljana.	HB-VHH
□ S5-BAY	99	CitationJet	525-0315	Gan Air, Ljubljana.	D-IAME
□ S5-BBB	01	CitationJet CJ-2	525A-0019	Air Sierra Slovenia, Ljubljana.	N67GH

S9 = SAO TOME & PRINCIPE   Total   1

Civil

Reg	Yr	Type	c/n	Owner/Operator	Prev Regn
□ S9-NAD	65	JetStar-6	5065	Transafrik, Sao Tome. (status ?).	N1966G

TC = TURKEY   Total   34

Civil

Reg	Yr	Type	c/n	Owner/Operator	Prev Regn
□ TC-AHS	00	Hawker 800XP	8504	Ahsel Air Transportation Co. Ankara.	N5004B
□ TC-AKK	97	Falcon 900B	171	Mach Air, Istanbul.	F-WWFW
□ TC-ANC	91	BAe 125/800B	8208	Tekfen Air Transport, Istanbul.	G-5-700
□ TC-ANT	93	Citation VI	650-0229	Emair-Emelki Ticaret Havacilik Ithalat-Ihraca, Ankara.	N1302X
□ TC-ARC	97	Learjet 60	60-094	Arkasair Havacilik ve Ticaret AS. Izmir.	N93BA
□ TC-DGC	01	Falcon 2000	166	Dogan Havacilik, Istanbul.	(N2259)
□ TC-ELL	94	Learjet 60	60-030	Cukurova Holding AS. Istanbul.	N164PA
□ TC-GGG	75	Falcon 20E	326	Form Air, Istanbul.	TC-CEN
□ TC-KON	98	Citation VII	650-7084	Super Air, Gaziantep.	N1127G
□ TC-LAA	93	Citation V	560-0212	DHMI Hava Taksi, Ankara.	N1284X
□ TC-LAB	93	Citation V	560-0216	DHMI Hava Taksi, Ankara.	N1285N
□ TC-LEY	69	HFB 320	1043	Genel Air AS. Istanbul.	16+03
□ TC-LMA	02	Citation Excel	560-5242	Limak Ins AS. Ankara.	N51042
□ TC-MDG	92	Challenger 601-3A	5110	MNG Airlines, Istanbul.	N308BX
□ TC-MEK	93	Learjet 60	60-016	Cukurova Holding AS. Istanbul.	N50163
□ TC-MHS	03	390 Premier 1	RB-77		N6177A

Reg	Yr	Type	c/n	Owner/Operator	Prev Regn

Reg	Yr	Type	c/n	Owner/Operator	Prev Regn
☐ TC-MKA	01	Citation Bravo	550-0960	Bon Air AS. Istanbul.	N960CB
☐ TC-MSB	97	Beechjet 400A	RK-170	Sky Line Ulasim Ticaret AS. Ankara.	TC-MCX
☐ TC-NEO	97	Beechjet 400A	RK-130	Nurol Aviation, Ankara.	N1130B
☐ TC-NOA	77	JetStar 2	5220	Genel Air AS. Istanbul.	A6-KAH
☐ TC-PLM	01	Falcon 2000	160	Palavia One Co. Malta.	VP-CGM
☐ TC-PRK	02	Falcon 2000	191	Park Havalicik/Park Group,	F-GUYM
☐ TC-RMK	01	Falcon 2000	157	KOC Holding AS/Set Air, Istanbul.	F-WWVQ
☐ TC-SSS	78	JetStar 2	5226	Genel Air AS. Istanbul.	N308SG
☐ TC-STR	99	Hawker 800XP	8415	Rumeli Air, Istanbul.	TC-BHD
☐ TC-TAN	00	Challenger 604	5459	DOGUS Air, Istanbul.	N459MT
☐ TC-TEK	92	BAe 125/800B	8229	Tekfen Air Transport, Istanbul.	N229RY

Military

Reg	Yr	Type	c/n	Owner/Operator	Prev Regn
☐ 001	87	Gulfstream 4	1027	TC-GAP. Government of Turkey, Istanbul.	TC-GAP
☐ 002	88	Gulfstream 4	1043	Government of Turkey, Istanbul.	TC-ATA
☐ 003	91	Gulfstream 4	1163	Turkish Air Force, 224 Filo, Etimesgut-Ankara.	N458GA
☐ 84-007	84	Citation II	550-0502	Turkish Air Force, 224 Filo, Etimesgut. (flight calibration)	12-001
☐ 84-008	84	Citation II	550-0503	Turkish Air Force, 224 Filo, Etimesgut. (flight calibration)	12-002
☐ 93-004	93	Citation VII	650-7024	Turkish Air Force, 224 Filo, Etimesgut-Ankara.	93-7024
☐ 93-005	93	Citation VII	650-7026	Turkish Air Force, 224 Filo, Etimesgut-Ankara.	93-7026

TG = GUATEMALA   Total   4

Civil

Reg	Yr	Type	c/n	Owner/Operator	Prev Regn
☐ TG-AIR	93	Learjet 31A	31A-067	Aceros de Guatemala SA. Guatemala City.	N9173M
☐ TG-RIE	81	Citation 1/SP	501-0216	Trans RIF SA. Guatemala City.	TG-RIF
☐ TG-RIF	94	CitationJet	525-0072	Trans RIF SA. Guatemala City.	N2651R
☐ TG-TJF	66	BAC 1-11/401AK	089	Tikal Jets, Guatemala City. 'Quirigua'	N97JF

TJ = CAMEROON   Total   2

Civil

Reg	Yr	Type	c/n	Owner/Operator	Prev Regn
☐ TJ-AAM	78	B 727-2R1	21636	Government of Cameroun, Yaounde.	
☐ TJ-AAW	86	Gulfstream 3	486	Government of Cameroun, Yaounde.	N316GA

TL = CENTRAL AFRICAN REPUBLIC   Total   1

Civil

Reg	Yr	Type	c/n	Owner/Operator	Prev Regn
☐ TL-FCA	60	Caravelle 3	42	Government of Central African Republic. (wfu ?).	TL-KAB

TN = CONGO BRAZZAVILLE   Total   1

Civil

Reg	Yr	Type	c/n	Owner/Operator	Prev Regn
☐ TN-ADI	75	Corvette	9	Government of Congo Republic, Brazzaville. (status ?).	F-OCRN

TR = GABON   Total   5

Civil

Reg	Yr	Type	c/n	Owner/Operator	Prev Regn
☐ TR-KSP	97	Gulfstream 4SP	1327	Government of Gabon, Libreville.	(TR-KHD)
☐ TR-LDB	90	BAe 125/800B	8192	Ste. Crossair, Zurich/Air Affaires Gabon, Libreville.	G-5-691
☐ TR-LEX	97	Falcon 900EX	24	Government of Gabon/El Hadj Omar Bongo, Libreville.	F-WWFU
☐ TR-LFB	67	HS 125/3B	25130	Avirex SA. Libreville.	F-BSIM
☐ TR-LTZ	69	DC 8-73CF	46053	Government of Gabon, Libreville.	N8638

TS = TUNISIA   Total   3

Civil

Reg	Yr	Type	c/n	Owner/Operator	Prev Regn
☐ TS-IAY	84	Airbus A300B4-620	354	Government of Libya, Tripoli, Libya.	A6-SHZ
☐ TS-IOO	99	BBJ-7H3	29149	Government of Tunisia, Tunis.	N5573L
☐ TS-JAM	82	Falcon 50	125	Tunisavia, Tunis.	HB-IBQ

TT = CHAD   Total   1

Civil

Reg	Yr	Type	c/n	Owner/Operator	Prev Regn
☐ TT-AAI	79	Gulfstream 2	240	Government of Tchad, N'Djamena.	5A-DDR

TU = IVORY COAST   Total   5

Civil

Reg	Yr	Type	c/n	Owner/Operator	Prev Regn
☐ TU-TIZ	76	F 28-1000C	11099	Air Ivoire, Abidjan.	PH-VAB

Military

Reg	Yr	Type	c/n	Owner/Operator	Prev Regn
☐ TU-VAA	87	Fokker 100	11245	Government of Ivory Coast, Abidjan.	PH-CDI
☐ TU-VAD	87	Gulfstream 4	1019	Government of Ivory Coast, Abidjan.	N17584
☐ TU-VAF	85	Gulfstream 3	462	Government of Ivory Coast, Abidjan.	N303GA
☐ TU-VAJ		F 28-4000VIP	11124	Government of Ivory Coast, Abidjan.	TU-VAZ

T9 = BOSNIA-HERZEGOVINA   Total   1

Civil

Reg	Yr	Type	c/n	Owner/Operator	Prev Regn
☐ T9-SBA	80	Citation	500-0399	Air Service R.S/Republic of Srpska,	YU-BML

Reg	Yr	Type	c/n	Owner/Operator	Prev Regn

UK	**=**	**UZBEKISTAN**		*Total*	**1**

Civil

Reg	Yr	Type	c/n	Owner/Operator	Prev Regn
☐ UK-80001	97	BAe 146/RJ-85	E2312	Government of Uzbekistan, Tashkent.	G-6-312

UN	**=**	**KAZAKHSTAN**		*Total*	**2**

Civil

Reg	Yr	Type	c/n	Owner/Operator	Prev Regn
☐ UN-B1111	66	BAC 1-11/401AK	078	Orient Eagle Airways, Almaty.	P4-CCL
☐ UN-B6701		B 767-2DXER	32954	Government of Kazakhstan, Almaty.	

UR	**=**	**UKRAINE**		*Total*	**4**

Civil

Reg	Yr	Type	c/n	Owner/Operator	Prev Regn
☐ UR-CCB	68	Falcon 20-5	141	CABI Airlines Ltd/KABI Avia, Donetzk.	(UR-BCA)
☐ UR-CCC	93	Falcon 50	235	CABI Airlines Ltd/KABI Avia, Donetzk.	(UR-ACA)
☐ UR-CCF	90	Falcon 50	212	CABI Airlines Ltd/KABI Avia, Donetzk.	LX-APG
☐ UR-NIK	67	Falcon 20C	112	Sirius Air Co. Donetzk.	UR-CCD

VH	**=**	**AUSTRALIA**		*Total*	**82**

Civil

Reg	Yr	Type	c/n	Owner/Operator	Prev Regn
☐ VH-...	04	Learjet 45	45-262		
☐ VH-ACE	87	Falcon 900	37	Remorex P/L. Perth, WA.	VH-FCP
☐ VH-AJG	80	Westwind-1124	281	Pel-Air Aviation P/L. Sydney, NSW.	(N200XJ)
☐ VH-AJJ	79	Westwind-1124	248	Pel-Air Aviation P/L. Sydney, NSW.	N25RE
☐ VH-AJK	79	Westwind-1124	256	Pel-Air Aviation P/L. Sydney, NSW.	4X-CNB
☐ VH-AJP	78	Westwind-1124	238	Pel-Air Aviation P/L. Sydney, NSW.	4X-CMJ
☐ VH-AJV	80	Westwind-1124	282	Pel-Air Aviation P/L. Sydney, NSW.	N186G
☐ VH-ANE	03	CitationJet CJ-1	525-0521	Malmet (QLD) P/L. Parafield, SA.	N521CJ
☐ VH-BZL	97	Beechjet 400A	RK-139	Buzz Aviation P/L. Sydney, NSW.	VH-MZL
☐ VH-CCC	89	Gulfstream 4	1083	Crown Ltd/Jet City P/L. Melbourne, VIC.	HB-ITZ
☐ VH-CCJ	79	Citation 1/SP	501-0089	CCJ P/L. Ascot, QLD.	VH-LJG
☐ VH-CPE	85	Falcon 200	504	Consolidated Press Holdings P/L. Sydney, NSW.	N702SB
☐ VH-CXJ	01	Learjet 45	45-152	BAe Systems Flight Training (Australia) P/L. Parafield, SA.	N5014E
☐ VH-EJK	96	Learjet 45	45-007	Execujet Australia P/L. Sydney, NSW.	ZS-OPD
☐ VH-EJY	80	Citation II	550-0141	Executive Jet Charter P/L. Aitkenvale, QLD.	VH-INX
☐ VH-EMM	72	Citation	500-0051	Doug Kefford, Footscray, VIC.	VH-ICX
☐ VH-EMO	85	Citation S/II	S550-0063	ESSO Australia Resources P/L. Melbourne, VIC.	(N12717)
☐ VH-ESM	86	Learjet 35A	35A-611	RANAS, Nowra, NSW.	N611TW
☐ VH-EXB	97	Beechjet 400A	RK-154	Executive Airlines P/L. Essendon, VIC.	VH-BJC
☐ VH-FGK	98	Citation Bravo	550-0852	Melbourne Air Holdings P/L. Essendon, VIC.	N5076J
☐ VH-HKX	72	Citation Eagle	500-0050	Metropolis City Promotions P/L. Essendon, VIC.	N333PP
☐ VH-HVH	77	Citation Eagle	500-0349	Sterling Aviation P/L. Bankstown, NSW.	VH-HVM
☐ VH-HVM	01	Citation Bravo	550-0984	Carrington Investments P/L. Southland Centre, VIC.	(N984VP)
☐ VH-ING	99	Citation VII	650-7104	Inghams Enterprises P/L. Bankstown, NSW.	N5148B
☐ VH-JCR	79	Learjet 35A	35A-231	Jet City P/L. Melbourne, VIC.	N62DK
☐ VH-JCX	86	Learjet 36A	36A-057	Jet City P/L. Melbourne, VIC.	HB-VIF
☐ VH-KEF	96	Hawker 800XP	8295	Prime Aviation P/L. Essendon, VIC.	VH-LAT
☐ VH-KNS	81	Westwind-1124	323	Pel-Air Aviation P/L. Sydney, NSW.	N816H
☐ VH-KNU	81	Westwind-1124	317	Pel-Air Aviation P/L. Sydney, NSW.	VH-UUZ
☐ VH-KXL	95	CitationJet	525-0100	Edwards Coaches P/L. Armdale, NSW.	VH-CIT
☐ VH-LAW	01	Falcon 900C	192	Walker Corp P/L. Sydney, NSW.	N192LW
☐ VH-LMP	92	BAe 1000B	9022	Boston LHF P/L-Santos Ltd. Adelaide, SA.	G-5-734
☐ VH-MCX	78	Falcon 10	134	McCafferty's Air Charter P/L. Toowoomba, QLD.	N509TC
☐ VH-MOJ	96	CitationJet	525-0138	Dramatic Investments P/L. Blaxland, NSW.	N5211F
☐ VH-MOR	02	CitationJet CJ-2	525A-0063	Morgan & Co P/L. Perth, Wa.	N5208F
☐ VH-MZL	03	Learjet 60	60-270	Sydney Jet Charter P/L. Sydney, NSW.	N5012K
☐ VH-NCP	89	Gulfstream 4	1108	News Ltd. Sydney, NSW.	N522AC
☐ VH-NGA	83	Westwind-Two	387	Pel-Air Aviation P/L. Sydney, NSW.	N97AL
☐ VH-OCV	04	Learjet 60	60-273	Execujet Australia P/L. Sydney, NSW.	N4002P
☐ VH-OVB	81	Learjet 35A	35A-400	Shortstop Charter P/L. Melbourne, VIC.	VH-RHQ
☐ VH-OYC	79	Citation II	550-0102	Pearl Aviation Australia P/L. Perth, WA.	VH-JPG
☐ VH-PFA	90	Learjet 35A	35A-661	ST Aerospace Engineering P/L. Seletar, Singapore.	N1268G
☐ VH-PFS	01	Learjet 45	45-168	ST Aerospace Engineering P/L. Seletar, Singapore.	N50088
☐ VH-PPD	00	Falcon 900C	185	Paspaley Pearling Co P/L. Darwin, NT.	HB-IGT
☐ VH-PPF	84	Learjet 35A	35A-593	Paspaley Pearling Co P/L. Perth, WA.	N593PN
☐ VH-PSM	79	Citation II	550-0054	Shortstop Jet Charter P/L. Essendon, VIC.	VH-OYW
☐ VH-PSU	99	Citation V Ultra	560-0515	Queensland Police Service, Brisbane, QLD.	N51042
☐ VH-SCC	03	Citation Bravo	550-1058	MacArthur Jet Charter, Camden, NSW.	N52691
☐ VH-SCD	82	Citation II	550-0339	DHM Aircraft Sales P/L-Dream Aviation, Moorebank, NSW.	VH-KTK

Reg	Yr	Type	c/n	Owner/Operator	Prev Regn
☐ VH-SGY	97	Hawker 800XP	8328	Queensland Government Air Wing, Brisbane, QLD.	N328XP
☐ VH-SLD	78	Learjet 35A	35A-145	Pel Air Aviation P/L-RANAS, Nowra, NSW.	(N166AG)
☐ VH-SLE	81	Learjet 35A	35A-428	Pel Air Aviation P/L-RANAS, Nowra, NSW.	N17LH
☐ VH-SLF	81	Learjet 36A	36A-049	Pel Air Aviation P/L-RANAS, Nowra, NSW.	N136ST
☐ VH-SLJ	75	Learjet 36	36-014	Pel Air Aviation P/L-RANAS, Nowra, NSW.	N200Y
☐ VH-SMF	95	Citation V Ultra	560-0320	Maroomba Airlines, Perth, WA.	N320VP
☐ VH-SOU	76	Citation	500-0333	D K Thornton/Sydney Jet Charter, Sydney-Bankstown, NSW.	N275AL
☐ VH-SQD	99	Learjet 45	45-033	Singapore Airlines Flying College P/L. Maroochydore, QLD.	9V-ATI
☐ VH-SQM	99	Learjet 45	45-035	Singapore Airlines Flying College P/L. Maroochydore, QLD.	9V-ATJ
☐ VH-SQR	01	Learjet 45	45-195	Singapore Airlines Flying College P/L. Maroochydore, QLD.	N5040Y
☐ VH-SQV	02	Learjet 45	45-207	Singapore Airlines Flying College P/L. Maroochydore, QLD.	N5000E
☐ VH-TEN	03	Citation X	750-0215	Balmoral Air P/L. Artarmon, NSW.	N215CX
☐ VH-VGX	00	Global Express	9079	Pratt Holdings P/L. Melbourne, VIC.	(N217JC)
☐ VH-VLJ	81	Learjet 35A	35A-432	JV Aviation Management Services P/L. Melbourne, VIC.	G-HUGG
☐ VH-VLZ	91	Citation II	550-0690	Orkdale P/L. Main Beach, QLD.	OE-GLZ
☐ VH-WNZ	79	Citation II	550-0057	Tasman Australia Airlines P/L. Paradise Point, QLD.	(N2661N)
☐ VH-WSM	00	Astra-1125SPX	123	Pearl Aviation Australia P/L. Brisbane, QLD.	(C-GWST)
☐ VH-XCJ	97	Citation Bravo	550-0810	Mount Craigie Holdings P/L. Rosebud West, VIC.	VH-MGC
☐ VH-XGG	91	Gulfstream 4	1156	The Gandel Group P/L. Melbourne, VIC.	VH-TGG
☐ VH-ZLE	82	Citation II	550-0347	China Southern WA Flying College P/L. Jandakot, WA.	ZS-LEE
☐ VH-ZLT	99	Citation Bravo	550-0878	China Southern WA Flying College P/L. Jandakot, WA.	N5135K
☐ VH-ZMD	75	Citation	500-0263	Australasian Jet P/L. Essendon, VIC.	VH-AQS
☐ VH-ZZH	00	Challenger 604	5456	Avwest P/L. Perth, WA.	VH-MXK
Military					
☐ A20-261	76	B 707-368C	21261	RAAF, 33 Squadron, Richmond, NSW.	N7486B
☐ A20-623	68	B 707-338C	19623	RAAF, 33 Squadron, Richmond, NSW. 'City of Sydney'	C-GRYN
☐ A20-624	68	B 707-338C	19624	RAAF, 33 Squadron, Richmond, NSW. 'Richmond Town'	VH-EAD
☐ A20-627	68	B 707-338C	19627	RAAF, 33 Squadron, Richmond, NSW. (status ?).	VH-EAG
☐ A20-629	68	B 707-338C	19629	RAAF, 33 Squadron, Richmond, NSW.	C-GGAB
☐ A36-001	00	BBJ-7DF	30790	RAAF, 34 Squadron, Fairbairn, Canberra, ACT.	N10040
☐ A36-002	00	BBJ-7DT	30829	RAAF, 34 Squadron, Fairbairn, Canberra, ACT.	N372BJ
☐ A37-001	02	Challenger 604	5521	RAAF, 34 Squadron, Fairbairn, Canberra, ACT.	N521RF
☐ A37-002	02	Challenger 604	5534	RAAF, 34 Squadron, Fairbairn, Canberra, ACT.	N534RF
☐ A37-003	01	Challenger 604	5538	RAAF, 34 Squadron, Fairbairn, Canberra, ACT.	N538RF

VP-B = BERMUDA   *Total*   105

Reg	Yr	Type	c/n	Owner/Operator	Prev Regn
Civil					
☐ VP-B..	94	Challenger 601-3R	5149		N63ST
☐ VP-BAA	66	B 727-51	19123	Marbyia Investments Ltd/KAK Aviation Ltd. Malaga, Spain.	N727AK
☐ VP-BAB	66	B 727-76	19254	Marbyia Investments Ltd/KAK Aviation Ltd. Malaga, Spain.	N682G
☐ VP-BAC	99	Gulfstream V	588	TAG Aviation SA. Geneva, Switzerland.	N588GA
☐ VP-BAE	03	390 Premier 1	RB-66	Kesko Bermuda Ltd.	N50586
☐ VP-BAT	79	B 747SP-21	21648	Worldwide Aircraft Holding Co. Bournemouth-Hurn, UK.	VR-BAT
☐ VP-BBA	67	BAC 1-11/422EQ	126	Jetline Inc. Sharjah, UAE.	PK-TSR
☐ VP-BBD	92	Falcon 50	226	Blue Heron Aviation Ltd/Chagoury Brothers, Lagos, Nigeria.	F-WQBN
☐ VP-BBJ	98	BBJ-72U	29273	JABJ/Picton II Ltd. Geneva, Switzerland.	(N1GN)
☐ VP-BBT	98	B 737-705	29089	Ford Motor Co. Stansted, UK.	LN-TUB
☐ VP-BBU	98	B 737-705	29090	Ford Motor Co. Stansted, UK.	LN-TUC
☐ VP-BBV	74	Falcon 10	22	Valiant Aviation Ltd.	F-GJLL
☐ VP-BBW	98	BBJ-78J	30076	Altitude 41 Ltd/GAMA Aviation Ltd. Farnborough, UK.	P4-CZT
☐ VP-BCC	02	Regional Jet	7717	Consolidated Contractors Co. Athens, Greece.	C-GZSQ
☐ VP-BCI	00	Challenger 000	7351	Consolidated Contractors Co. Athens, Greece.	N351BA
☐ VP-BCM	99	Hawker 800XP	8404	Magic Condor Ltd. Cannes, France.	N30289
☐ VP-BCV	02	Falcon 2000	187	Vitesse Corp. Greenfield, In. USA.	N87FJ
☐ VP-BCX	01	Falcon 900C	193	S K M Ltd. Moscow, Russia.	F-WQBL
☐ VP-BDD	99	Global Express	9017	Aero Toy Store LLC. Fort Lauderdale, Fl. USA.	C-GEIR
☐ VP-BDJ	68	B 727-23	20046	Donald Trump/D J Aerospace (Bermuda) Ltd. NYC.	VR-BDJ
☐ VP-BDL	00	Falcon 2000	111	Sioux Co. Luton, UK.	F-WWVF
☐ VP-BDS	97	CitationJet	525-0180	Ekron Ltd/AVCON AG. Zurich, Switzerland.	(N133AV)
☐ VP-BEC	97	Falcon 900B	165	Longtail Aviation Ltd.	G-EVES
☐ VP-BEE	02	Falcon 900EX	109	Sonair, Luanda, Angola.	F-WWFG
☐ VP-BEF	04	Falcon 900EX EASY	130	Sonair, Luanda, Angola.	F-WWFH
☐ VP-BEH	00	Falcon 900EX	75	Go Ahead Vacations Ltd. Stockholm, Sweden.	(F-GYDP)
☐ VP-BEJ	90	Challenger 601-3A	5061	Eurojet Holdings Ltd. Stansted, UK.	(N575MA)
☐ VP-BEL	99	BBJ-74T	29139	Execujet Air Charter AG. Zurich.	N21KR
☐ VP-BEN	99	Global Express	9020	Symphony Master Ltd. Kuala Lumpur, Malaysia.	N700GK
☐ VP-BER	03	Falcon 2000EX	10	Birgma Sweden AB. Stockholm, Sweden.	(SE-RBV)
Reg	*Yr*	*Type*	*c/n*	*Owner/Operator*	*Prev Regn*

Reg	Yr	Type	c/n	Owner/Operator	Prev Regn
VP-BEZ	98	Learjet 60	60-149	Palm Tree Aviation Ltd. Cairo, Egypt. 'El Ahmaf'	SU-EZI
VP-BFA	01	BBJ-7BC	30884	Royal Squadron, Amman, Jordan.	N184QS
VP-BFF	76	Gulfstream II SP	186	Shukra Nigeria Ltd.	VP-BJV
VP-BFH	98	Falcon 900B	173	Al Hokair Aviation Ltd. Riyadh, Saudi Arabia.	PH-LBA
VP-BGC	97	Falcon 900C	169	Parc Aviation Ltd. Paris-Le Bourget, France.	F-GRDP
VP-BGD	78	Falcon 10	113	Speed Aero, Dorval, PQ. Canada.	LX-DPA
VP-BGE	75	Citation	500-0287	Ross Aviation Ltd. Bristol-Filton, UK.	(VP-CAW)
VP-BGG	99	Global Express	9018	Global Air Ltd/Mideast Jet, Jeddah, Saudi Arabia.	C-GEVO
VP-BGN	02	Gulfstream G550	5011	Rockfield Holdings Ltd/Jetclub AG. Farnborough, UK.	(N522QS)
VP-BGO	99	Challenger 604	5404	Sun International Management Ltd. Nassau, Bahamas.	C-GLYO
VP-BHB	92	BAe 125/800A	NA0473	GAMA Aviation Ltd. Farnborough, UK.	N25WN
VP-BHH	00	Challenger 604	5448	Mouawad SA. Jeddah, Saudi Arabia.	TC-DHH
VP-BHM	69	DC 8-62	46111	Brisair Ltd/Sheikh El Khereiji, Saudi Arabia.	VR-BHM
VP-BHN	01	BBJ2-8AN	32438	Rafic Hariri/Saudi Oger Ltd. Riyadh.	N1786B
VP-BHO	81	Citation 1/SP	501-0207	Cardinal Aviation Ltd.	OE-FYC
VP-BHS	01	Challenger 604	5505	Consolidated Contractors International, Farnborough, UK.	N505JD
VP-BIE	01	Challenger 601	3016	Inflite Executive Charter Ltd. Stansted, UK.	N601CL
VP-BIF	71	B 727-1H2	20533	Next Century Aviation Inc. Sausalito, Ca.	VP-BIL
VP-BIH	96	Challenger 601-3R	5193	Netwind Express Ltd.	(N601HJ)
VP-BJB	99	BBJ-7BC	30330	Sigair Ltd/Sheikh El Khereiji, Saudi Arabia.	N130QS
VP-BJD	02	Gulfstream V	672	Transworld Oil America Inc. Newark, NJ.	N672GA
VP-BJH	98	Challenger 604	5397	Red Sea Aviation Ltd/JABJ AG. Zurich, Switzerland.	HB-IIV
VP-BJR	03	CitationJet CJ-2	525A-0147	Joest Racing GmbH. Mannheim, Germany.	N5188W
VP-BJS	82	Learjet 35A	35A-464	Dole Fresh Fruit International, Costa Rica.	N464WL
VP-BKB	01	Hawker 800XP	8539	AVCON AG. Zurich/AAK Co. Beirut, Lebanon.	N51239
VP-BKH	87	Gulfstream 4	1029	Specialised Transportation (Bermuda) Ltd. Isle of Man.	VP-BKI
VP-BKK	70	HS 125/731	25238	Air 125 Ltd. Hurn, UK.	G-36-1
VP-BKS	93	B 767-3P6ER	27254	Kalair USA Corp/Mideast Jet, Jeddah, Saudi Arabia.	A40-GW
VP-BKZ	99	Gulfstream V	602	Dennis Vanguard International Ltd. Birmingham, UK.	N602GV
VP-BLA	03	Gulfstream G550	5024	ISPAT Group Ltd. Luton, UK.	N924GA
VP-BLB	89	Falcon 900B	49	Maritime Investment & Shipping/Stavros Niarchos, Athens.	VR-BLB
VP-BLD	68	JetStar-731	5117	Magnair Ltd. Palma, Spain.	(N858SH)
VP-BLH	00	Gulfstream G200	029	Global Aviation Ltd. Frankfurt, Germany.	N61GX
VP-BLM	90	Falcon 900B	72	Globus Travel/Aileron/Sen Montegazza, Lugano, Switzerland.	VR-BLM
VP-BLT	81	Westwind-Two	337	Island Aviation Ltd/Longtail Aviation, Hamilton.	N2518M
VP-BLV	76	Citation	500-0344	Santom Ltd	VR-BLV
VP-BMD	83	HS 125/700B	7200	Air VIP Ltd. Athens, Greece.	VR-BMD
VP-BMG	00	Challenger 604	5460	Westbury Jet Ltd. Fort Myers, Fl. USA.	N460WJ
VP-BMJ	01	Falcon 2000EX	1	Ormond Ltd. Saudi Arabia. (Ff 25 Oct 01).	F-WMEX
VP-BMS	99	Falcon 900EX	42	Flying Lion/Stork Ltd. Boca Raton, Fl. USA.	N942EX
VP-BMT	01	Gulfstream G100	144	Execujet Charter AG. Zurich, Switzerland.	N262GA
VP-BMW	02	Gulfstream G100	146	Execujet Charter AG. Zurich, Switzerland.	N646GA
VP-BNA	67	B 727-21	19262	Skyways International Inc. Houston, Tx. USA.	VR-BNA
VP-BNF	97	Challenger 604	5332	Quantex Financial/Sural CA. Caracas, Venezuela.	C-FZRR
VP-BNL	00	Gulfstream V	607	Nebula Ltd/GAMA Aviation Ltd. Farnborough, UK.	N303K
VP-BNN	94	Gulfstream 4SP	1255	Nebula Ltd/GAMA Aviation Ltd. Farborough, UK.	N600PM
VP-BNR	03	Gulfstream G550	5033	Eiger Jet Ltd/Rashid Engineering, Riyadh, Saudi Arabia.	N933GA
VP-BNS	98	Challenger 604	5384	JABJ AG/Mobinil Mobil Services, Cairo, Egypt.	HB-IVV
VP-BNT	00	Falcon 2000	121	Mikati Communications Corp. Beirut, Lebanon.	(F-GVDA)
VP-BOA	92	Challenger 601-3A	5114	SAMCO Aviation, Riyadh, Saudi Arabia.	VR-BOA
VP-BOK	02	Global Express	9101	Falconair/Rembrandt Tobacco Group, Capetown, RSA.	C-GIXJ
VP-BON	92	Astra-1125SP	060	Aerocentro de Servicios CA. Caracas, Venezuela.	VR-BON
VP-BOR	86	Gulfstream 3	484	Rida Aviation Ltd. Houston, Tx. USA.	N506T
VP-BOY	80	HS 125/700B	7109	B-Jet Ltd. Beirut, Lebanon.	VP-BTZ
VP-BPC	94	Falcon 900B	142	Middle East Jet Services, Beirut, Lebanon.	N103DT
VP-BPW	94	Falcon 900B	135	J N Somers/Tower House Consultants Ltd. Jersey, C.I.	VR-BPW
VP-BRH	99	B 777-2ANER	29953	R B Hariri/Saudi Oger Ltd. Riyadh, Saudi Arabia.	
VP-BRM		BBJ-75U	28976	Dobro Ltd. Stansted, UK.	(VP-BOC)
VP-BRT	02	BBJ-7BC	32970	JABJ AG. Zurich, Switzerland.	N707BZ
VP-BSA	89	Falcon 50	196	Shell Aircraft Ltd. Rotterdam, Holland.	D-BNTH
VP-BSD	00	Citation Excel	560-5088	Murtagh Aviation, St Mawgan, UK.	N52081
VP-BSF	89	Gulfstream 4	1098	Wings Venture Ltd. Greenwich, Ct. USA.	N7800
VP-BSH	01	Gulfstream 4SP	1466	Shell Aircraft Ltd. Rotterdam, Holland.	N266GA
VP-BSK	99	Hawker 800XP	8409	Flycraft Ltd/Aurela Co Ltd. Vilnius, Lithuania.	N929AL
VP-BSL	90	Falcon 50	209	Shell Aircraft Ltd. Rotterdam, Holland.	N96DS
VP-BSM	98	Gulfstream V	555	Rashid Engineering, Riyadh, Saudi Arabia.	N655GA

Reg	Yr	Type	c/n	Owner/Operator	Prev Regn

Reg	Yr	Type	c/n	Owner/Operator	Prev Regn
☐ VP-BUS	90	Gulfstream 4	1127	JABJ AG/Urs Schwarzenbach, Farnborough, UK.	VR-BUS
☐ VP-BVP	04	Falcon 2000EX EASY	45	Blue Air Ltd. Brazil.	F-W...
☐ VP-BVT	00	Gulfstream 4SP	1419	International Jet Club Ltd. Farnborough, UK.	EI-CVT
☐ VP-BWR	99	BBJ-79T	29317	USAL Ltd. Geneva, Switzerland.	N1787B
☐ VP-BXP	00	Hawker 800XP	8494	Vulcan Aviation Ltd.	N808TA
☐ VP-BYA	01	BBJ-7AN	29972	Saudi Oger Ltd. Riyadh, Saudi Arabia.	N1786B
☐ VP-BYS	99	Gulfstream 4SP	1381	Eiger Jet/Saudi Oger Ltd. Riyadh, Saudi Arabia.	VP-BIV
☐ VP-BYY	99	Global Express	9030	Executive Jets Ltd/Mideast Jet, Jeddah, Saudi Arabia.	C-GFAD
☐ VP-BZL	01	BBJ2-8DV	32915	LOWA London-Washington Ltd. Boston, Ma. USA.	D-ABZL

VP-C = CAYMAN ISLANDS   Total   75

Civil

Reg	Yr	Type	c/n	Owner/Operator	Prev Regn
☐ VP-CAB	91	Falcon 900B	101	ASW Airservice Werkflugdienst GmbH. Hamburg, Germany.	D-ALME
☐ VP-CAD	98	CitationJet	525-0297	Reynard Motor Sport, Bremen, Germany.	N316MJ
☐ VP-CAI	99	Citation Excel	560-5048	Chester Holding Ltd. Georgetown.	N548XL
☐ VP-CAR	86	Citation III	650-0135	Wheels Aviation Industries,	N135AF
☐ VP-CAT	81	Citation 1/SP	501-0232	Melman Investments Ltd. Guernsey, Channel Islands.	VR-CAT
☐ VP-CBB	01	BBJ2-8AW	32806	Bosco Aviation Ltd. Riyadh, Saudi Arabia.	N757BC
☐ VP-CBM	94	Citation II	550-0729	Bernard Matthews plc. Norwich, UK.	VR-CBM
☐ VP-CBS	89	Challenger 601-3A	5044	Aprilia Holdings Inc. Tel Aviv, Israel.	VP-CMC
☐ VP-CBW	89	Gulfstream 4	1096	Rolls Royce plc. Farnborough, UK.	VR-CBW
☐ VP CBX	97	Gulfstream V	511	Tak Aviation, Farnborough, UK.	N511GA
☐ VP-CCG	66	BAC 1-11/401AK	081	ARAVCO Ltd. Bournemouth-Hurn, UK.	VR-CCG
☐ VP-CCL	84	Falcon 200	482	SHK Jeans Co. Braunschweig, Germany.	(N94TJ)
☐ VP-CCO	81	Citation II	550-0321	Comptec Components SA/Flight Consultancy Services,	N321GA
☐ VP-CCR	90	Challenger 601-3A	5079	Shoreditch Investments Ltd. Jeddah, Saudi Arabia.	VR-CCR
☐ VP-CDE	92	BAe 125/800B	8234	Arven Ltd. Opa Locka, Fl. USA.	VR-CDE
☐ VP-CDF	01	Global Express	9093	Eaglewind Ltd/Willenborg Flug GmbH. Mannheim, Germany.	C-GZVZ
☐ VP-CEA	00	Hawker 800XP	8520	Complex Aircraft Ltd. Jersey, C.I.	OE-GEA
☐ VP-CEB	01	Global Express	9083	Silver Arrows SA. Luton, UK.	C-GKLF
☐ VP-CEC	99	BBJ-7AW	30031	JABJ AG/Bugshan Construction Co. Jeddah, Saudi Arabia.	N73715
☐ VP-CED	99	Citation Bravo	550-0870	Iceland Frozen Foods plc. Luton, UK.	N50612
☐ VP-CEZ	03	Falcon 900EX EASY	134	Executive Jet Charter Ltd. Bristol-Filton, UK.	F-WWFL
☐ VP-CFA	02	EMB-135BJ Legacy	145637	Alfal/Sheikh Fahad Al Athel, Riyadh, Saudi Arabia.	PT-SAP
☐ VP-CFG	81	Citation 1/SP	501-0176	GDTC Ltd. Staverton, UK.	VR-CFG
☐ VP-CFL	96	Falcon 900B	164	Proair Charter Transport GmbH. Frankfurt, Germany.	G-MLTI
☐ VP-CFT	90	Challenger 601-3A	5067	Meral Holdings Ltd/Jetclub AG. Zurich, Switzerland.	HB-IUF
☐ VP-CGA	99	Falcon 2000	100	Volkswagenwerke AG. Braunschweig, Germany.	F-WWVT
☐ VP-CGB	94	Falcon 900B	145	Volkswagenwerke AG. Braunschweig, Germany.	VR-CGB
☐ VP-CGC	99	Falcon 2000	107	Volkswagenwerke AG. Braunschweig, Germany.	F-WWVB
☐ VP-CGE	97	Citation VII	650-7077	Duke of Westminster/Grosvenor Estates, Chester-Hawarden.	(N582JF)
☐ VP-CGG	04	Citation Excel	560-5361	Grampian Food Group Ltd. Leeds-Bradford, UK.	N361XL
☐ VP-CGS	01	Global Express	9102	Jet Aviation Business Jets AG. Zurich, Switzerland.	HB-IGS
☐ VP-CHK	79	B 737-2S9	21957	Executive Air Transport AG. Zurich, Switzerland.	PK-HHS
☐ VP-CHW	98	Gulfstream G200	004	Weber Management GmbH. Stuttgart, Germany.	(N711JQ)
☐ VP-CIC	87	Challenger 601-3A	5011	TAG Aviation Inc. Stansted, UK.	VR-CIC
☐ VP-CID	94	Falcon 900B	130	Haider Ltd. Riyadh, Saudi Arabia.	VR-CID
☐ VP-CIE	01	Airbus A319-133X	1589	Bugshan Construction Co. Riyadh, Saudi Arabia.	D-AVYF
☐ VP-CIP	99	Gulfstream 4SP	1371	TAG Aviation SA. Geneva, Switzerland.	N371GA
☐ VP-CJA	96	Falcon 2000	18	Gerhard Berger GmbH. Cannes-Mandelieu, France.	EI-LJR
☐ VP-CJF	87	Falcon 900B	26	Jet Wings Ltd/Jetline Sharjah, UAE.	N900RN
☐ VP CJL	66	BAC 1 11/401AK	086	Jetlinc Inc. Sharjah, UAE.	N325V
☐ VP-CJN	70	B 727-76	20371	Starling Aviation (Cayman) Ltd.	5X-AMM
☐ VP-CJP	88	Challenger 601-3A	5022	ARAVCO Ltd. Farnborough, UK.	N449MC
☐ VP-CJR	82	Citation II	550-0354	Broome & Wellington (Aviation) Ltd.. Manchester, UK.	VR-CJR
☐ VP-CKA	71	B 727-82	20489	SAMCO Aviation, Riyadh, Saudi Arabia.	VR-CKA
☐ VP-CKN	02	Hawker 800XP	8615	Westdeutsche Gipswerke Baldwin & Nikolaus Knauf, Nuremberg	N61515
☐ VP-CLB	98	Falcon 900EX	34	Volkswagenwerke AG. Braunschweig, Germany.	F-WWF.
☐ VP-CLD	82	Citation II	550-0323	Pan Maritime/Dovey Aviation, Cardiff, Wales.	(N323AM)
☐ VP-CLM	66	BAC 1-11/401AK	072	Aeroleasing SA. Grand Cayman.	N119DA
☐ VP-CLO	01	Falcon 900EX	90	LUK-Avia Inc. Moscow, Russia.	F-WWFG
☐ VP-CLU	79	HS 125/700A	NA0245	LUK-Avia Inc. Moscow, Russia.	N81QV
☐ VP-CLX	80	HS 125/700B	7091	LUK-Avia Inc. Moscow, Russia.	G-OCAA
☐ VP-CME		B 767-231	22567	Sheikh Mustafa Idrees, Saudi Arabia.	(N515DL)
☐ VP-CMG	97	Gulfstream V	519	JABJ AG/SAP AG Systems, Walldorf. Germany.	N597GA
☐ VP-CMI	69	BAC 1-11/212AR	183	Ashmawi Aviation, Malaga, Spain. 'Sabah' (status ?).	VR-CMI
☐ VP-CMN	67	B 727-46	19282	IDG (Cayman) Ltd.	VR-CMN

THE REGISTRY ARUBA A.V.V.
THE FLAG OF CHOICE WITH CONVENIENCE...

Ministry of Transport & Communications
DEPARTMENT OF CIVIL AVIATION
SABANA BERDE 73-B
ORANJESTAD, ARUBA

ARE YOU CONSIDERING REGISTERING YOUR AIRCRAFT IN A CREDIBLE CATEGORY 1 ASSESSED COUNTRY, FOR POLITICAL FISCAL, ECONOMIC, COMMERCIAL OR ANY OTHER REASON?

Worldwide Commercial Jet and Regional Commuter Airlines, Financial Groups, Aircraft owners and Operators value our services for efficiency, cost containment, financial benefits, premier tax haven, high safety standards, reliability, maintenance conformity, regulations compliance to JAA & FAA requirements, quickness and much more. . . Call us today.

For information and a Brochure, contact:

International Air Safety Office
8750 NW 36th Street, Suite 210
Miami, Florida 33178 USA
Tel: (305) 471-9889
Fax: (305) 471-8122 or 8561

ONE STEP FOR SAFETY, QUALITY AND DEPENDABILITY

Aruba Registry is open to all Aircraft Owners and Operators

INTERNATIONAL AIR SAFETY OFFICE
Administrators of the Intl. Aviation Program of Aruba

P4-EPI   Challenger 601-3A   JetPhotosNet (Supplied by Registry of Aruba)

P4-GJC   BBJ   Jose Rodriguez (Supplied by Registry of Aruba)

P4-VVP   EMB-135BJ Legacy   Stefan Hengermier (Supplied by Reg. of Aruba)

Reg	Yr	Type	c/n	Owner/Operator	Prev Regn
☐ VP-CMP	84	HS 125/700B	7214	Costair Ltd/Viamax, Athens, Greece.	P4-CMP
☐ VP-CNF	96	CitationJet	525-0153	Foster Aviation Ltd. Biggin Hill, UK.	(N525EF)
☐ VP-CNP	86	Gulfstream 3	496	Fitzwilton plc. Dublin, Ireland.	N843HS
☐ VP-COM	76	Citation	500-0318	Rapid 3864 Ltd/Colin McGill, Biggin Hill, UK.	VR-COM
☐ VP-CPA	77	Gulfstream II SP	204	Global Aviation/Chief Harry Akande, Ibadan, Nigeria.	VR-CPA
☐ VP-CPH	98	Beechjet 400A	RK-188		N2298W
☐ VP-CPT	91	BAe 1000B	9004	Remo Investments, Biggin Hill, UK.	VR-CPT
☐ VP-CRB	97	Learjet 60	60-125	Lisanne Ltd. Guernsey, Channel Islands. 'La Petite Souris'	N60LR
☐ VP-CRS	99	Galaxy-1126	008	Rostrum Aircraft Ltd. Salzburg, Austria.	(N288GA)
☐ VP-CSA	81	B 737-2W8	22628	SAMCO Aviation, Riyadh, Saudi Arabia.	A6-ESJ
☐ VP-CSF	99	Gulfstream 4SP	1390	Mohammed Fakhry/MSF Aviation, Luton, UK.	N1874M
☐ VP-CSM	66	JetStar-731	5092	Ashmawi Aviation, Malaga, Spain.	VR-CSM
☐ VP-CSN	97	Citation V Ultra	560-0401	Scottish & Newcastle Breweries plc. Edinburgh, Scotland.	N401CV
☐ VP-CTJ	79	Citation II	550-0073	Flight Consultancy Services, Biggin Hill, UK.	F-GBTL
☐ VP-CUB	77	Gulfstream 2B	207	U B Ltd. Bangalore, India. "Sidharta"	(VT-UBG)
☐ VP-CVL	00	Learjet 45	45-059	Interdean, London/Interdean AG. Munich, Germany.	N50153
☐ VP-CVP	00	Beechjet 400A	RK-300	Sky Jet Flugservice GmbH. Baden-Baden, Germany.	N4001M
☐ VP-CVX	00	Airbus A319CJ-133X	1212	Volkswagenwerke AG. Braunschweig, Germany.	(D-AIKA)
☐ VP-CZY	79	B 727-2P1	21595	Dunview Ltd-Zarki Yamani/JABJ AG. Zurich, Switzerland.	N727MJ
☐ VR-CKO	68	DC 9-15	47151	K A K Aviation Ltd. Malaga, Spain. (status ?).	VR-CKE

VT = INDIA — Total 33

Civil

Reg	Yr	Type	c/n	Owner/Operator	Prev Regn
☐ VT-...	02	Gulfstream G100	148		4X-CVI
☐ VT-AAA	82	HS 125/700A	NA0323	Reliance Transport & Travel Ltd. Mumbai.	N2830
☐ VT-AMA	88	Gulfstream 4	1060	Reliance Transport & Travel Ltd. Mumbai.	N1SF
☐ VT-BAV	01	Gulfstream G100	143	Aditya Birla Technologies, Mumbai.	N261GA
☐ VT-COT	96	Falcon 2000	36	Tata Iron & Steel Co. Mumbai.	F-GNBL
☐ VT-CSP	04	Citation Excel	560-5368	Poonawalla Group, Pune.	N12686
☐ VT-DHA	01	Global Express	9111	Reliance Industries Ltd. Mumbai.	C-GJTK
☐ VT-EHS	82	Learjet 29	29-003	Aviation Research Centre/Government of India Agency, Delhi.	N289CA
☐ VT-EIH	84	Learjet 29	29-004	Aviation Research Centre/Government of India Agency, Delhi.	N294CA
☐ VT-EQZ	67	HS 125/3B	25133	India International Airways P/L. Delhi.	G-ILLS
☐ VT-ETG	86	Citation S/II	S550-0089	Rusi H Modi/Tata Engineering Services Ltd. Calcutta.	VT-RHM
☐ VT-EUN	82	Citation II	550-0352	Asia Aviation Ltd. Delhi.	N352AM
☐ VT-EUX	95	Citation V Ultra	560-0299	State Government of Tamil Nadu, Madras.	N5168F
☐ VT-JSP	04	CitationJet CJ-2	525A-0207	Jindal Group, New Delhi.	N1267B
☐ VT-KMB	87	Citation S/II	S550-0135	Grasim India Ltd. Bombay.	N2235
☐ VT-OBE	84	HS 125/700B	7215	Oberoi Group/East India Hotels Ltd., New Delhi.	VH-HSP
☐ VT-OPJ	95	CitationJet	525-0112	Jindal Iron & Steel Co Ltd. Mumbai.	N1006F
☐ VT-RAY	89	BAe 125/800B	8165	Raymond Woollen Mills Ltd. Mumbai.	ZS-BPG
☐ VT-RPG	98	Beechjet 400A	RK-190	Spencer Travel Services Ltd. Chennai.	N325JG
☐ VT-TAT	98	Falcon 2000	65	Taj Air Ltd. Mumbai.	(F-OIBA)
☐ VT-TBT	97	Falcon 2000	49	Taj Air Ltd. Mumbai.	F-WQBK
☐ VT-TEL	88	Beechjet 400	RJ-46	Spencer Travel Services Ltd. Bangalore.	N146JB
☐ VT-UBG	71	HS 125/F400B	25254	United Breweries Group/UB Ltd. Bangalore. 'Leana'	G-5-624

Military

Reg	Yr	Type	c/n	Owner/Operator	Prev Regn
☐ 0126	00	Astra-1125SPX	126		4X-CVJ
☐ K2412	83	B 737-2A8	23036	Indian Air Force, Delhi.	VT-EHW
☐ K2413	83	B 737-2A8	23037	Indian Air Force, Delhi.	VT-EHX
☐ K2899	68	B 707-337C	19988	Indian Air Force, Delhi.	VT-DXT
☐ K2900	67	B 707-337C	19248	Indian Air Force, Delhi.	VT-DVB
☐ K2980	84	Gulfstream SRA-1	420	Indian Air Force, New Delhi. (used VT-ENR 1987-2003).	N47449
☐ K2981	86	Gulfstream SRA-1	494	Indian Air Force, New Delhi.	N370GA
☐ K2982	86	Gulfstream SRA-1	495	Indian Air Force, New Delhi.	N371GA
☐ K3186	71	B 737-2A8	20484	Indian Air Force, Delhi.	VT-EAK
☐ K3187	70	B 737-2A8	20483	Indian Air Force, Delhi.	VT-EAJ

V5 = NAMIBIA — Total 5

Civil

Reg	Yr	Type	c/n	Owner/Operator	Prev Regn
☐ V5-CDM	91	Citation V	560-0151	Consolidated Diamond Mines,	ZS-NDU
☐ V5-NAG	94	Learjet 31A	31A-091	Government of Namibia, Windhoek.	N5019Y
☐ V5-NAM	91	Falcon 900B	103	Government of Namibia, Windhoek.	F-WWFJ
☐ V5-NPC	97	Learjet 31A	31A-138	NamPower, Windhoek.	N138LJ
☐ V5-OGL	73	Citation	500-0080	T M Domenig, Omaruru.	ZS-NGR

V8	**=**	**BRUNEI**		*Total*	**3**

Civil

Reg	Yr	Type	c/n	Owner/Operator	Prev Regn
❑ V8-ALI	91	B 747-430	26426	Government of Brunei, Bandar Seri Begawan.	(D-ABVM)
❑ V8-BKH	94	Airbus A340-212	046	Government of Brunei, Bandar Seri Begawan.	V8-PJB
❑ V8-MHB	93	B 767-27G (ER)	25537	Government of Brunei, Bandar Seri Begawan.	V8-MJB

XA	**=**	**MEXICO**		*Total*	**522**

Civil

Reg	Yr	Type	c/n	Owner/Operator	Prev Regn
❑ XA-...	91	Citation V	560-0127		N127VP
❑ XA-...	78	HS 125/700A	NA0224		N200GY
❑ XA-...	83	Learjet 25D	25D-361		N804RH
❑ XA-...	76	HS 125/600A	6071	Monterrey Jet Center, Monterrey, NL.	N171TS
❑ XA-...	83	HS 125/700A	NA0344		N11YR
❑ XA-...	62	Sabreliner CT-39A	276-25	Jett Paqueteria SA. San Luis Potosi.	N39RG
❑ XA-...	65	HS 125/1A	25053		N25JT
❑ XA-...	89	BAe 125/C-29A	8129	Servicios Privados de Aviacion SA. Toluca, Mexico.	N8029Z
❑ XA-...	65	HS 125/731	25066		N373DH
❑ XA-...	80	Learjet 25D	25D-295		N25HF
❑ XA-...	69	HS 125/400A	NA722		(N280CH)
❑ XA-...	73	Sabre-40A	282-112		N40ZA
❑ XA-...	80	HS 125/700A	NA0260		N184TB
❑ XA-...	84	Citation 1/SP	501-0685		N501EG
❑ XA-...	73	Sabre-40A	282-124		N70ES
❑ XA-...	71	JetStar-8	5148	TAESA-Transportes Aereos Ejecutivos SA. Toluca.	XA-OLI
❑ XA-...	80	Gulfstream 3	312	Aircraft Guaranty Title LLC. Houston, Tx.	N312NW
❑ XA-...	74	Citation	500-0199		C-FGAT
❑ XA-...	60	Sabreliner CT-39A	265-15	Jett Paqueteria SA. San Luis Potosi.	N510TD
❑ XA-...	89	Citation II	550-0619		N550BD
❑ XA-...	91	Beechjet 400A	RK-16		N416CW
❑ XA-...	76	Learjet 24D	24D-308	Jose Fernandez,	N89AA
❑ XA-...	65	Sabre-40	282-41		N240AC
❑ XA-...	81	Citation II	550-0227		N227DR
❑ XA-...	94	Citation VI	650-0234	GEC CEF Mexico SA. Mexico City.	(N735A)
❑ XA-...	78	Sabre-60	306-140	Golden Aviation de Mexico SA. Naulcalpan.	N26SQ
❑ XA-...	90	Citation III	650-0198		N650BC
❑ XA-...	77	HS 125/600A	6064		N125HF
❑ XA-...	92	Citation II	550-0711		N58LC
❑ XA-...	69	HS 125/731	NA719		N545S
❑ XA-...	81	Citation 1/SP	501-0201		N953SL
❑ XA-...	84	Gulfstream 3	426		N703JA
❑ XA-...	01	Learjet 31A	31A-235		N317K
❑ XA-...	84	Learjet 25D	25D-369		N369D
❑ XA-...	02	Beechjet 400A	RK-352	Transportes Castores de Baja California, Leon, GTO.	N6052U
❑ XA-...	80	Learjet 25D	25D-315		N315FW
❑ XA-...	77	Sabre-60	306-131		(N131SE)
❑ XA-...	98	Beechjet 400A	RK-171		N287CD
❑ XA-...	66	HS 125/1A-522	25107	Aeromedica SA. Toluca.	XA-HFM
❑ XA-...	79	HS 125/700A	NA0241	Aero Sami SA. Garza Garcia, NL.	(N388BS)
❑ XA-...	67	HS 125/3A-R	25148	Intervuelos Nacionales SA.	(N819P)
❑ XA-AAA	69	Learjet 24B	24B-208	Aerofreight SA.	N14PT
❑ XA-AAF*		Sabreliner T-39D	277-7	noted Davis-Monthan as 150548 4/04.	N956M
❑ XA-AAG*		Sabreliner T-39D	277-2	noted at Davis-Monthan as 150543 4/04.	N960M
❑ XA-AAH*	61	Sabreliner T-39D	285-25	noted Davis Monthan as 151336 4/04.	N961M
❑ XA-AAI*		Sabreliner T-39D	277-6	noted at Davis Monthan as 150547 4/04.	N959M
❑ XA-AAJ*	60	Sabreliner T-39D	285-1	noted Davis-Monthan as 150969 4/04.	N957M
❑ XA-AAK	84	Citation II	550-0486	Fiesta Inn/Sky Aeronautical Services SA. Puebla La Noria.	(N35PN)
❑ XA-AAL	79	JetStar 2	5231	Aircraft Transportadora SA.	XA-TPJ
❑ XA-AAS	80	Learjet 25D	25D-305	Aeroni Air Taxi SA. Toluca.	N188R
❑ XA-AAW*	67	Sabreliner CT-39E	282-85	Jett Paquetaria SA. San Luis Potosi. (status ?).	N958M
❑ XA-AAY	75	Falcon 10	27	Servicios Ejecutivos Tampico SA. Tampico.	N38DA
❑ XA-ABE	99	Citation Bravo	550-0887	Aero Roca SA. Celaya.	N887BB
❑ XA-ACA	68	Falcon 20D	179	Sirvair Corp. Toluca.	(N669JL)
❑ XA-ACD	76	Sabre-80A	380-50	Aero Jets Corporativos SA. Torreon.	XA-TDQ
❑ XA-ACH	92	Citation VI	650-0218	Servicios Aeronaticos del Oriente SA.	XA-MTZ
❑ XA-ACN	74	HS 125/600A	6038	Aero Central SA. Jurica, Quintana Roo.	N199SG
❑ XA-ACX	85	Learjet 25D	25D-373	AITSA-Aerotransportes Internacionales de Torreon SA.	EC-EGY

Reg	Yr	Type	c/n	Owner/Operator	Prev Regn

Reg	Yr	Type	c/n	Owner/Operator	Prev Regn
☐ XA-ADJ	65	Learjet 24	24-060	Aeronaves TSM SA. Saltillo.	N90J
☐ XA-ADR	68	HS 125/3A-RA	NA706		N777GA
☐ XA-AEE	68	HS 125/3A-RA	NA703		N140JS
☐ XA-AEI	74	Citation	500-0213	Almaver SA.	(N213CE)
☐ XA-AET	00	Hawker 800XP	8502	Aereo Taxi Mexicano SA. Toluca.	N4469B
☐ XA-AEX	02	BBJ-7EJ	32774	Grupo Omnilife SA/Omniflys SA. Guadalajara, JAL.	N1784B
☐ XA-AFA	01	Beechjet 400A	RK-316	Aerolineas Ejecutivas SA. Toluca.	N3216X
☐ XA-AFG	77	Sabre-60	306-130	Aerolineas Sol SA. Toluca.	XB-JMM
☐ XA-AFH	81	Learjet 25D	25D-332	PRI, Toluca.	XB-DZQ
☐ XA-AFP	73	Gulfstream II SP	136	Aeromundo Ejecutivo SA. Toluca.	XA-ABA
☐ XA-AFS	99	Beechjet 400A	RK-259	Aerolineas Ejecutivas SA. Toluca.	N3259Z
☐ XA-AFU	90	Citation II	550-0661	Aero Ejecutivo Nieto SA. Celaya.	N3444P
☐ XA-AFW	66	Sabre-40	282-63	Aviones de Sonora SA. Hermosillo.	N325K
☐ XA-AFX	98	Learjet 31A	31A-159	S A E, Toluca.	N127BX
☐ XA-AGA	79	Citation 1/SP	501-0095	Puerto Vallarta Taxi Aereo SA. Puerto Vallarta.	N612DS
☐ XA-AGL	70	HS 125/731	NA757	Aeroservicios Sipse SA. Merida, Yucatan.	N900WG
☐ XA-AGN	79	Citation II	550-0077	Antair SA. Toluca.	XA-PIJ
☐ XA-AGT	70	Sabre-60	306-58	Golden Aviation de Mexico SA. Naulcalpan.	N529CF
☐ XA-AHM	75	Gulfstream 2	161	Antair SA/Grupo Acerero del Norte SA. Toluca.	XA-RUS
☐ XA-AIM	00	Learjet 45	45-077	Transportes Aereos de Xalapa SA. Toluca.	N770DS
☐ XA-AJL	73	Learjet 25B	25B-120	Aero J L SA. Toluca.	N120SL
☐ XA-ALA	88	Falcon 50	188	Servicios Integrales de Aviacion SA. Toluca.	N160AF
☐ XA-ALF	00	Learjet 45	45-127	El Caminante Taxi Aereo SA. Guadalajara, JAL.	N421FY
☐ XA-ALV	73	Learjet 25B	25B-124	Airlink US-MX SA. Guadalajara.	N33TW
☐ XA-AMI	80	HS 125/700A	NA0269	Servicios Privados de Aviacion SA. Toluca.	(N61GF)
☐ XA-AMT		Hawker 800XP	...	noted Houston 9/04.	
☐ XA-AMX		Hawker 800	...	noted Fort Lauderdale 4/04.	
☐ XA-APE	99	Falcon 900B	178	Aero Personal SA. Toluca.	N179FJ
☐ XA-ARA	70	Gulfstream II SP	79	Aereo Transportes Comercial SA. Toluca. (status ?).	XA-STO
☐ XA-ASR		Citation	...	noted Las Vegas 11/04.	
☐ XA-AST	97	Challenger 604	5357	Vitro SA/Aeroempresarial SA. Monterrey, NL.	N604FS
☐ XA-ATE	77	Sabre-60	306-123	Aero Transportes Empresariales SA. Toluca.	N97SC
☐ XA-AVE	01	Falcon 2000	175	Aerolineas Ejecutivas SA. Toluca.	N2258
☐ XA-AVV	71	Learjet 25XR	25XR-079		XA-SVG
☐ XA-BAL	98	Gulfstream V	546	Aerovics SA. Toluca.	N646GA
☐ XA-BCE	65	JetStar-731	5053	Banco Nacional de Comercio Exterior SNC. Toluca.	XC-JCC
☐ XA-BEB	69	JetStar-731	5132	TAESA. Toluca. 'Ishtar - Goddess of Luck'	XA-PSD
☐ XA-BEG	98	Falcon 900EX	33	Servicios Ejecutivos Continental SA. Tampico.	XA-TMH
☐ XA-BET	75	Citation	500-0296	Aerodinamica de Monterrey SA. Monterrey, NL.	N269BF
☐ XA-BNG	87	Beechjet 400	RJ-33	Servicios Aereos Gana SA. San Luis Potosi.	XA-JJA
☐ XA-BNO	80	Learjet 35A	35A-336	TAESA-Transportes Aereos Ejecutivos SA. Toulca.	(N336EA)
☐ XA-BRE	95	Learjet 60	60-058	TAESA-Transportes Aereos Ejecutivos SA. Toluca.	N92BL
☐ XA-BRG	91	Learjet 31	31-032	Aerolineas Commerciales SA. Morelia.	XA-AAP
☐ XA-BUX	78	Learjet 35A	35A-176	Transportes Aereos Tecnico Ejecutivo SA. Monterrey, NL.	(N67GA)
☐ XA-CAH	97	CitationJet	525-0210	Chilchota Taxi Aereo SA. Durango.	N999EB
☐ XA-CAP	03	Citation Bravo	550-1070	Chilchota Taxi Aereo SA. Durango.	N327CS
☐ XA-CCC	77	Learjet 25XR	25XR-219	Aerotaxis Dos Mil SA. Saltillo.	N55SL
☐ XA-CEG	79	Falcon 10	146	Aeroservicios Regiomontanos SA.	N461AS
☐ XA-CEN	68	Sabre-60	306-26	Aerologic SA. Toluca.	(N377EM)
☐ XA-CHA	93	BAe 125/800A	8241	Transportes Aereos Sierra Madre SA. Monterrey, NL.	N540BA
☐ XA-CHP	68	Sabre-60	306-22	Aerotrans Privados SA/Seguros Chapultepec SA. Toluca.	(N450CE)
☐ XA-CMG	66	BAC 1-11/401AK	079	Grupo Adelac,	N880P
☐ XA-CPQ	98	Gulfstream V	533	Commander Mexicana SA. Toluca.	N533GA
☐ XA-CUR	77	Sabre-60	306-127	Peninter Aerea SA. Merida.	N60DD
☐ XA-CVD	81	Learjet 35A	35A-370	Novedades Editores SA. Toluca.	XA-OFA
☐ XA-CVE	77	JetStar 2	5214		N50KP
☐ XA-CZG	78	Learjet 35A	35A-162	Aerojobeni SA. Toluca.	N222SL
☐ XA-DAN	68	HS 125/3A-RA	25158	Aero Dan SA. Saltillo.	(N702GA)
☐ XA-DCS	66	HS 125/3A	25078	Aero Dan SA. Saltillo.	(N16PJ)
☐ XA-DET	76	Learjet 24F	24F-337	AEMSA/Gutsa Construcciones SA.	XA-GEO
☐ XA-DGP	99	CitationJet	525-0329	Aeroservicios de Nuevo Leon SA. Guadalupe, NL.	
☐ XA-DIJ	73	Learjet 24D	24D-269	Jet Rent SA. Toluca.	
☐ XA-DRM	03	Citation Excel	560-5307	Export Air del Peru SA.	N.....
☐ XA-DSC	71	Sabre-60	306-56	TAESA-Transportes Aereos Ejecutivos SA. Toluca.	XA-RXP
☐ XA-DUC	72	Falcon 20F	269	Aerolineas Ejecutivas SA. Toluca.	XA-NAY
☐ XA-DUQ	84	Falcon 50	146	Duque Jet SA.	N7228K
Reg	Yr	Type	c/n	Owner/Operator	Prev Regn

Reg	Yr	Type	c/n	Owner/Operator	Prev Regn
☐ XA-EAJ	99	Gulfstream V	604	Desarollo Milaz SA/Aero Personal SA. Toluca.	N551GA
☐ XA-EHR	68	Gulfstream 2B	30	Sirvair Corp. Toluca.	N30438
☐ XA-EKT	79	JetStar 2	5234	Aerotaxis Metropolitanos SA. Toluca.	(N234TS)
☐ XA-EMO	69	JetStar-8	5140	TAESA-Transportes Aereos Ejecutivos SA. Toluca.	XA-JCG
☐ XA-EOF	02	Gulfstream G550	5008	Jet Ejecutivos SA. Toluca.	N908GA
☐ XA-ERH	81	Gulfstream 3	323	Sirvair Corp. Toluca.	N323G
☐ XA-ESC	75	Gulfstream II SP	164	Viajes Ejecutivos Mexicanos SA. Toluca.	N80AG
☐ XA-EYA	99	Gulfstream 4SP	1388	Ronso SA. Toluca.	N4SP
☐ XA-FEX	99	Falcon 900EX	46	Execujet Mexico SA. Monterrey, NL.	N946EX
☐ XA-FFF	75	Learjet 35	35-042		N270CS
☐ XA-FIR	93	Citation II	550-0718	Aero Taxi Autlan SA. Toluca.	N12060
☐ XA-FLM	77	Falcon 20F	364	Transpais Aereo SA. Monterrey, NL.	N285U
☐ XA-FLY	02	Learjet 60	60-250	Fly-Mex SA.	N50433
☐ XA-FMR	79	Learjet 25D	25D-274	Aero Copter SA. Toluca.	XA-RZE
☐ XA-FMT	92	Learjet 35A	35A-672		N45KK
☐ XA-FMX	00	Citation X	750-0119	Aerocer SA. Monterrey, NL.	N5223X
☐ XA-FNY	77	Gulfstream II SP	211	Naviera Mexicana SA. Toluca.	N7079N
☐ XA-FTN	66	Sabre-40	282-80	Taxi Aereo Turistico SA. Acapulco.	N40WH
☐ XA-FVK	80	Falcon 50	35	Aerolineas Ejecutivas SA. Toluca.	N350AF
☐ XA-GAO	02	Beechjet 400A	RK-353	Aerolineas Ejecutivas SA. Toluca.	N353AE
☐ XA-GAP	79	Sabre-65	465-R	Commander Mexicana SA/El Heraldo de Mexico SA. Toluca.	N10581
☐ XA CDM		Citation	...	noted Los Angeles 10/04.	
☐ XA-GCC		BAe 125/	...	noted Scottsdale, Az. 1/04.	
☐ XA-GCH	81	Falcon 50	50	Comercial Aerea SA. Chihuahua.	N247BV
☐ XA-GDO	81	Learjet 35A	35A-449	Guja SA. Mexico City.	N449QS
☐ XA-GDW	61	Sabreliner CT-39A	265-86	Jett Paqueteria SA. Quetzalcoatl.	XB-GDW
☐ XA-GGG	73	Learjet 25B	25B-147	Aero Rentas de Coahuila SA. Saltillo.	N147BP
☐ XA-GHR	78	Sabre-75A	380-58	Taxirey SA. Monterrey.	XA-SEB
☐ XA-GIC	04	Hawker 800XP	...	noted Las Vegas 8/04.	
☐ XA-GIH	74	Sabre-60	306-72	Transportes Aereos de Xalapa SA. Jalapa.	N97SC
☐ XA-GLG	02	Hawker 800XP	8583		N50983
☐ XA-GMD	99	Falcon 50EX	291	Grupo Modelo SA/Diblo Corporativo SA.	N294EX
☐ XA-GME	93	Challenger 601-3A	5128	Mexico Transportes Aereos SA. Toluca.	C-FPOX
☐ XA-GMO	03	Citation Sovereign	680-0004		N5233J
☐ XA-GNI	03	Falcon 2000EX	20	Transportes Aereos Mexiquenses SA. Toluca.	N219EX
☐ XA-GRB	98	Challenger 604	5375	Aerolineas de Tuhuacan SA. Tehuacan, Puebla.	N604HP
☐ XA-GRR	02	Learjet 40	45-2013		N5018G
☐ XA-GTC	69	HS 125/731	NA734	Aeronaves del Nordeste SA.	(N38TS)
☐ XA-GTE	01	Hawker 800XP	8554	Aerolineas Ejecutivas SA. Toluca.	(5B-CKG)
☐ XA-GUA	90	Challenger 601-3A	5076		N5TM
☐ XA-GUR		Sabre-60	...	State Government of Quintana Roo,	
☐ XA-GYR	64	Sabre-40	282-6	Servicios Aereos Ilsa SA. Torreon.	XA-SBS
☐ XA-HFM	04	Learjet 45	45-246	Aeromedica SA. Toluca.	N5012G
☐ XA-HHF	99	Falcon 2000	85	Aerotaxi Grupo Tampico SA. Tampico.	N344GC
☐ XA-HNY	73	JetStar-8	5162	Naviera Mexicana SA. Toluca.	N10JJ
☐ XA-HVP	84	Citation III	650-0032	Aerotron, Puerto Vallarta, Guadalajara.	N332FW
☐ XA-ICF	02	Hawker 800XP	8581	Aerolineas Ejecutivas SA. Toluca.	N50661
☐ XA-ICG	68	Falcon 20C	159	Aerotaxis Dos Mil SA. Toluca.	N96RT
☐ XA-ICK	74	Sabre-60	306-86	Servicios Aereos del Centro SA. Toluca.	N60TG
☐ XA-ICO	01	Citation Excel	560-5196	Ingenerios Civiles Associados SA. Toluca,	N51038
☐ XA-IGE	04	Challenger 604	5580		C-FADG
☐ XA III	72	Falcon 20F	264	Aerotaxis Dos Mil SA. Toluca.	N264TN
☐ XA-ILV	76	Gulfstream 2	195	Transpais Aereo SA. Monterrey, NL.	N71TP
☐ XA-IMY	95	Challenger 601-3R	5189	Corporativo Grupo IMSA SA. Garcia Garcia, NL.	N203G
☐ XA-ISR	94	Falcon 900B	147	Aeroxtra SA. Toluca.	N147FJ
☐ XA-JAI	82	HS 125/700A	NA0319		N319NW
☐ XA-JCE	74	Sabre-60	306-93	Transporte Ejecutivo Aereo SA. Toluca.	N507U
☐ XA-JET	03	Hawker 800XP	8628	Aerolineas Ejecutivas SA. Toluca.	N628XP
☐ XA-JEX	79	Citation	500-0395	Aerotaxi Villa Rica SA. Veracruz.	N2651S
☐ XA-JFE	01	Challenger 604	5525	Transporte Ejecutivo Aereo SA. Toluca.	N525E
☐ XA-JHE	03	Gulfstream G200	086	Servicios Ejecutivos Gose SA.	N286GA
☐ XA-JIQ	75	Learjet 24D	24D-317	Servicios de Alquiler Aereo SA. Toluca.	N45AJ
☐ XA-JJJ	82	Learjet 35A	35A-460	Servicios Aereos del Centro SA. Toluca.	XA-MPS
☐ XA-JJS	98	Learjet 60	60-131	Aero Lider SA/Arrendadora Banamex SA. Toluca.	N131LJ
☐ XA-JMF	01	Learjet 45	45-178	Aerobono SA. Toluca.	N50207
☐ XA-JML	77	Sabre-60	306-125		XA-AEV

Reg	*Yr*	*Type*	*c/n*	*Owner/Operator*	*Prev Regn*

Reg	Yr	Type	c/n	Owner/Operator	Prev Regn
XA-JMS	02	Hawker 800XP	8582	Servicios Aereos Denim SA. Durango.	(N170SK)
XA-JOC	80	Learjet 25D	25D-303	Jet Rent SA. Toluca.	
XA-JPX		Hawker 800XP	...	noted Orlando 11/04.	
XA-JRF	75	Sabre-80A	380-32	Aerotaxis de Aguascalientes SA. Aguascalientes.	N198GB
XA-JRH	85	Learjet 35A	35A-609	Aero Ermes SA. Monterrey, NL.	N788QC
XA-JRV	74	Citation	500-0136	Sisteme Aeronautica, Naucalpan.	N136SA
XA-JSC	74	Learjet 25XR	25XR-173	Aeroejecutivos de Baja California SA. Tijuana, BC.	N104BW
XA-JYC	90	Learjet 31	31-030	Jomar Taxi Aereo SA.	N255DY
XA-JZL	94	Challenger 601-3R	5158	Servicios Aeronauticas Zeta SA. Juarez, Chihuahua.	XA-MKI
XA-KCM	81	Learjet 35A	35A-418	Taxi Aereo de Mexico SA/Kimberly Clark SA. Toluca.	
XA-KIM	83	Challenger 601	3015	Taxi Aereo de Mexico SA/Kimberly Clark SA. Toluca.	N374G
XA-KKK	74	Learjet 25B	25B-169	Aerotaxis Dos Mil SA. Toluca.	N59FL
XA-KMX	84	Citation III	650-0039	PACCAR Mexico Logistics Inc. Mexicali, BC.	N171L
XA-KOF	65	HS 125/1A	25065	Aerovias del Golfo SA. Veracruz.	N1YE
XA-LEY	85	Citation III	650-0073	Aereo Transportes del Humaya SA.	N85DA
XA-LIO	75	Falcon 10	40	Transpais Aereo SA. Monterrey, NL.	N15SJ
XA-LLL	68	Learjet 25	25-015	Rajet Aeroservicios SA. Ramos Arizpe, Coah.	N125U
XA-LML	73	Sabre-40A	282-115	Aerotron, Puerto Vallarta, Guadalajara.	XA-GCH
XA-LNK	68	Learjet 24	24-174	Airlink US-MX SA. Guadalajara.	N77GJ
XA-LOF	01	Citation Bravo	550-0989	AeroVirel SA.	N5270E
XA-LRJ	82	Learjet 25D	25D-359	Servicios Aereos del Centro SA. Toluca.	N116JR
XA-LRX	00	Learjet 45	45-067	Aviacion Comercial de America SA. Monterrey, NL.	N5087B
XA-MAM	85	Falcon 200	506	International Charter Services SA. Tampico.	N147TA
XA-MAV	01	Falcon 2000	149	Aviacion Ejecutiva Mexicana SA. Toluca.	N2235
XA-MBM	66	HS 125/731	25101	Grupo Salinas y Rochas SA.	N78AG
XA-MDK	02	Gulfstream G200	080	Aerolineas Marcos SA. Toluca.	N380GA
XA-MDM	97	Learjet 60	60-089	Aeroservicios Dinamicos SA. Toluca.	N8089Y
XA-MEV		Falcon 20	...	noted Teterboro 9/04.	
XA-MEX	98	Beechjet 400A	RK-196	Aerolineas Ejecutivas SA. Toluca.	N2283T
XA-MIK	65	JetStar-731	5066	TAESA-Transportes Aereos Ejecutivos SA. Toluca. (status ?).	XA-SAE
XA-MJE	66	Sabre-40	282-65	Aerojet Corporativo SA.	XA-GGR
XA-MJI		HS 125/	...	noted Orlando 11/04.	
XA-MKI	01	Gulfstream V	664	Servicios Aeronauticas Zeta SA. Juarez, Chihuahua.	(N564QS)
XA-MMM	75	Falcon 10	36	Antair SA. Toluca.	N76AF
XA-MSA	74	Falcon 20F	327	Aereo Saba SA. Monterrey, NL.	N327BC
XA-NGS	98	Global Express	9014	Vitro SA/Aeroempresarial SA. Monterrey, NL.	C-FRGX
XA-NLA	69	Learjet 24	24-180	Aerolineas Amanecer SA. Toluca. (status ?).	XA-SBR
XA-NLK	66	Learjet 24	24-109	Aerolineas Amanacer SA.	N900DL
XA-NTE		Hawker 800XP	...	noted Los Angeles 2/04.	
XA-OAC	88	Beechjet 400	RJ-36		N52GA
XA-OEM	98	Gulfstream V	540	Aerolineas Sol SA. Toluca.	N640GA
XA-OLE	91	Learjet 31A	31A-044	Operadora de Lineas Ejecutivas SA.	XA-MJG
XA-ORA	01	Learjet 60	60-245	Avemex SA. Toluca.	N50330
XA-ORO	80	Learjet 35A	35A-290		XA-RAV
XA-OVR	02	Global Express	9119	Corporacion Aero Angeles SA. Toluca.	C-GZOW
XA-PAZ	80	Learjet 25D	25D-309	Transportes La PAZ SA. Matehuala.	XB-DKS
XA-PES	69	JetStar-8	5130	SACSA, Toluca.	XA-TZV
XA-PIH	72	Sabre-40A	282-102	Verataxis SA. Vera Cruz.	(N157AT)
XA-PIU	80	Learjet 25D	25D-293	Servicios Aereos Estrella SA. Toluca.	N97JP
XA-POG	72	Learjet 25B	25B-080	TAESA-Transportes Aereos Ejecutivos SA. Toluca.	N30AP
XA-PVR		Learjet 35A	...	noted Fort Worth 10/04.	
XA-PYR	74	Westwind-1124	174	Aerotron, Puerto Vallarta, Guadalajara.	N760C
XA-RAP	74	Sabre-60	306-88	Servicios Privados de Aviacion SA. Toluca.	N22CG
XA-RAR	87	Beechjet 400	RJ-32	Servicios Aereos Interestatales SA. Monterrey, NL.	N31432
XA-RBP	68	Gulfstream II SP	14	TAESA-Transportes Aereos Ejecutivos SA. Toluca.	XA-RBS
XA-RBS	89	Gulfstream 4	1102	Aerotaxis Metropolitanos SA. Toluca.	N910B
XA-RCM		Gulfstream G4	...	noted Las Vegas 11/04.	
XA-RDD	65	HS 125/1A	25030	Aerotaxis Metropolitanos SA. Toluca.	XA-MBM
XA-RED	65	Sabre-40	282-26	Aereo Centro SA. Quintana Roo.	N300CH
XA-RES		sabre-	...	noted Toluca 3/04.	
XA-RET	02	Falcon 2000	184	Casa Cuervo SA./Aeroservicios Ejecutivos SA. Toluca.	N2261
XA-RFB	74	Sabre-60	306-87	Aero Quimmco SA. Monterrey.	N200CE
XA-RGB	03	Falcon 900EX EASY	129	GRUMA-Grupo Maseca SA/TATESA, Toluca.	N129EX
XA-RGG	93	BAe 1000A	9037	Aero Services Vanguardia SA.	XA-TGK
XA-RGH	81	Learjet 35A	35A-412	Sistemas Aeronauticos 2000 SA. Toluca.	N314C
XA-RGS	90	Citation III	650-0189	SARSA, Monterrey, NL.	N26174

Reg	Yr	Type	c/n	Owner/Operator	Prev Regn
☐ XA-RIN	78	Learjet 35A	35A-152	Lineas Aereas Ejecutivas de Durango SA. Durango.	N964CL
☐ XA-RIR	69	Sabre-60	306-36	Servicios Aereos del Centro SA. Toluca.	N436CC
☐ XA-RIZ	72	Westwind-1123	160	Servicios Aereos del Mar SA. Acapulco.	XA-MUI
☐ XA-RLH	73	Sabre-40A	282-129	Aerotaxis Latino Americanos SA. Culiacan.	(N99FF)
☐ XA-RLL	74	Sabre-60	306-83	Servindustria Aeronautica SA. Celaya.	N99FF
☐ XA-RLS	70	Sabre-60	306-57	Organizacion de Servicios Ejecutivos Aereos SA. (status ?).	N465JH
☐ XA-RMA	66	Falcon 20C	39	Aeroextra SA. Toluca.	XB-EDU
☐ XA-RNK	90	Learjet 31	31-021	Taxi Aereo del Noroeste SA. Cuidada Obregon, Sonora.	N3802G
☐ XA-ROY		JetStar	...	noted Teterboro 4/04.	
☐ XA-RPS	56	Sabre-40	282-56	Servicios Aereos de Los Angeles SA. Puebla.	N85DA
☐ XA-RPT	68	HS 125/3A-RA	NA708	Aerodan SA. Saltillo.	N75GN
☐ XA-RSP	66	HS 125/1A	25091	Aerotaxi Monse SA. Morelos. (stored at FXE since 1993).	N65FC
☐ XA-RSR	65	HS 125/1A-522	25017	Aerotaxi Monse SA. Morelos. (stored at FXE since 1993).	N333M
☐ XA-RTM	65	Sabre-40R	282-39	Transportes Ejecutivos SA. Mexico City.	XA-RKQ
☐ XA-RUY	96	Hawker 800XP	8302	Aerolineas Ejecutivas SA. Toluca.	N302XP
☐ XA-RVT	78	Sabre-60	306-138	Aero Danta SA. Mexico City.	N702JR
☐ XA-RVV	90	Falcon 50	213	Aerolineas Ejecutivas SA. Toluca.	N295FJ
☐ XA-RYB	94	Hawker 1000	9043	Aero Servicio Corporativo SA. Monterey, NL.	(N881JT)
☐ XA-RYE	73	Citation	500-0068	Cia Mexicana de Aeroplanos SA. Toluca.	XB-FDN
☐ XA-RYH	81	Learjet 25D	25D-334		N23W
☐ XA-RYJ	71	Sabre-75	370-5	Servicios Aereos Corporativos SA. Puerto Vallarta.	N250BC
☐ XA-RYM	86	RAe 125/000A	8075		N3GU
☐ XA-RZD	91	Challenger 601-3A	5087	Aerotrans Privados SA/Consorcio Industrial Escorpion,Toluca.	N601CC
☐ XA-SAH	78	Sabre-60	306-137	Aviones Ejecutivos JFA SA. Tuxtla Gutierrez Militar.	N18X
☐ XA-SAI	74	HS 125/600A	6016	Omnirent Aviones SA. Toluca.	N99SC
☐ XA-SAU	78	HS 125/700A	NA0220	Aero Gisa SA/Grupo Industrial Saltillo SA. Saltillo.	N725CC
☐ XA-SBV	75	Sabre-60A	306-109	Aero Rey SA. Del Norte, NL.	N602KB
☐ XA-SCE	73	Learjet 24D	24D-271	Aerovias Castillo SA. Guadalajara.	N4305U
☐ XA-SDI	01	Citation Bravo	550-0983	Hoteles Dinamicos SA. Guadalajara.	N51055
☐ XA-SDT	92	Citation V	560-0162	Stars de Mexico SA. Toluca.	N68864
☐ XA-SDU	84	Citation III	650-0052	Servicios Aeronauticos Zeta SA. Juarez, Chihuahua.	N20MW
☐ XA-SEY	81	Citation 1/SP	501-0228	Verataxis SA. Vera Cruz.	N228EA
☐ XA-SFE	73	Citation	500-0125	Arrendadora Bance SA. San Luis Potosi.	C-FCFP
☐ XA-SFQ	72	HS 125/400A	NA768	Aero Cheyenne SA. Monterrey.	N2155P
☐ XA-SIM	92	Falcon 900B	114	Aerolineas Mexicanos JS SA. Toluca.	N474FJ
☐ XA-SJC	92	Citation V	560-0197	Taxi Aereos del Noroeste SA. Obregon.	(EI-DUN)
☐ XA-SJM	77	Sabre-60	306-128	Servicios Aereos Denim SA. Durango.	(N24TK)
☐ XA-SJN	83	Learjet 25D	25D-365	DGO-JET SA. Durango.	N365CM
☐ XA-SJS	71	Learjet 25B	25B-076	SACSA, Toluca.	N77KW
☐ XA-SLB	93	Citation VI	650-0228	Gof-Air SA. Toluca.	N228CM
☐ XA-SLP	72	HS 125/600A	6002	Aero Magar SA. Guadalajara.	N602MM
☐ XA-SLR	66	HS 125/3A	25112	Maria del Pilar Oliver Gaya Vd. Toluca.	XB-FFV
☐ XA-SMF	67	Sabre-60A	306-6	Aerotaxi Monse SA. Morelos.	XA-ADC
☐ XA-SMR	66	Sabre-40	282-71	Aerolineas Ejecutivas Tarascas SA. Morelia, Michoacan.	N957CC
☐ XA-SOL	01	Challenger 604	5501	Aerolineas Ejecutivas SA. Toluca.	N501AJ
☐ XA-SON	79	HS 125/700A	NA0268	Aero Sami SA. Monterrey, NL.	N501MM
☐ XA-SOR	94	Challenger 601-3R	5147	Aeropycsa SA. Toluca.	C-FRJX
☐ XA-SOY	69	JetStar-8	5142	Compania Ejecutiva SA. Toluca.	N23FE
☐ XA-SPM	80	Sabre-65	465-14	Aero Toluca International SA. Toluca.	N25SR
☐ XA-SPQ	93	Citation VII	650-7028	Aero Personal SA. Toluca.	N728CM
☐ XA-SQA	73	Sabre-40A	282-125	Jett Paqueteria SA. Quetzalcoatl.	XB-NIB
☐ XA-SQV	80	Citation II	550-0198	Servicios Aereos Especializados Mexicanos SA. Del Norte.	XC-DOK
☐ XA-SSS	82	Falcon 50	119	Associados Latinamericanos de Transporte Aereo SA.	N57DC
☐ XA-SSU	70	Learjet 24D	24D-230	Aero-Jet Express SA/Arrendadora Union SA. Guadalajara.	N32287
☐ XA-SSV		Sabre-	...	noted Miami 11/04.	
☐ XA-STE		Hawker 800XP	...	noted Miami 10/04,	
☐ XA-STI	74	Sabre-60	306-89	Multiservicios Aereos Queretanos SA. Queretaro.	N86RM
☐ XA-SVG	75	Sabre-60	306-97	Golden Aviation de Mexico SA. Naulcalpan.	N15DJ
☐ XA-SVX	75	Learjet 35	35-012	Aerotransportes de Toluca SA.	N97TJ
☐ XA-TAB	85	Falcon 100	204	Aerovics SA. Toluca.	F-WGTG
☐ XA-TCA	70	Learjet 24B	24B-224	Servicios Aereos SAAR SA. Veracruz.	(N51GJ)
☐ XA-TCN	78	JetStar 2	5229		N222MF
☐ XA-TDD	95	Falcon 50EX	252	Transportacion Aerea del Norte SA. Monterrey, NL.	N50FJ
☐ XA-TDK	72	Gulfstream 2	114	Omni Flys SA. Guadalajara.	N25BF
☐ XA-TDQ	00	Beechjet 400A	RK-281	Aero Jets Corporativos SA. Torreon.	N4081L
☐ XA-TDU	96	Falcon 2000	29	CEMEX SA/Aviacion Comercial de America SA. Monterrey.	N2028

	Reg	Yr	Type	c/n	Owner/Operator	Prev Regn
❏	XA-TDX	62	Sabreliner CT-39A	276-27	Jett Paqueteria SA. Quetzalcoatl.	XB-GDV
❏	XA-TEL	97	Falcon 900B	168	TELMEX/Aero Frisco SA. Mexico City.	N167FJ
❏	XA-TFD	60	Sabreliner CT-39A	265-10	Jett Paqueteria SA. San Luis Potosi. (status ?).	N510TA
❏	XA-TFL	61	Sabreliner CT-39A	265-48	Jett Paqueteria SA. Quetzalcoatl.	N6CF
❏	XA-TGO	62	Sabreliner T-39A	276-6	Jett Paqueteria SA. San Luis Potosi.	N6552R
❏	XA-THD	79	Learjet 35A	35A-243	Servicios de Taxi Aereo SA. Toluca.	N152TJ
❏	XA-THF	67	Jet Commander	109	Millenium Air Servicios Aereos Integrados SA. Guadalajara.	TG-VWA
❏	XA-TIE	83	Learjet 25D	25D-364	Aero Silza SA. Chihuahua.	N25TZ
❏	XA-TIW	62	Sabreliner CT-39A	276-44	Jett Paqueteria SA. San Luis Potosi.	N63811
❏	XA-TIX	62	Sabreliner CT-39A	276-21	Jett Paqueteria SA. San Luis Potosi.	N63611
❏	XA-TIY	60	Sabreliner CT-39A	265-14	Jett Paqueteria SA. Quetzalcoatl.	60-3486
❏	XA-TJU	62	Sabreliner CT-39A	276-8	Jett Paqueteria SA. San Luis Potosi.	N4314B
❏	XA-TJY	62	Sabreliner CT-39A	276-39	Jett Paqueteria SA. San Luis Potosi.	N265WB
❏	XA-TJZ	61	Sabreliner CT-39A	265-76	Jett Paqueteria SA. San Luis Potosi.	N4313V
❏	XA-TKQ	87	BAe 125/800A	NA0409	Crelan SA.	N875SC
❏	XA-TKW	64	Sabre-40	282-13	Jett Paqueteria SA. San Luis Potosi.	N502RR
❏	XA-TKY	77	Citation 1/SP	501-0029	Aerotaxi Paba SA.	(N45AQ)
❏	XA-TKZ	01	Citation Excel	560-5208	AVEMEX SA. Toluca.	N5109W
❏	XA-TMF	75	Sabre-60	306-100	Hunter's del Valle SA. Monterrey, NL.	XB-LAW
❏	XA-TMX	96	Citation VII	650-7069	Aero Frisco SA. Toluca.	N5117U
❏	XA-TMZ	85	Citation III	650-0068	Servicios Aeronauticos del Oriente SA.	N650AJ
❏	XA-TNP	61	Sabreliner CT-39A	265-62	Jett Paqueteria SA. San Luis Potosi.	(N6581K)
❏	XA-TNY	69	HS 125/731	NA727	Aeroservicio Azteca SA.	N100RH
❏	XA-TOF	76	Citation	500-0345	Aeronaves del Nordeste SA.	(N747KL)
❏	XA-TOM	81	Sabre-65	465-55	Industrial Perforadora de Campeche SA. Toluca.	XB-RYO
❏	XA-TOY		JetStar	...	noted Teterboro 4/04.	
❏	XA-TPB	89	BAe 125/800A	8176	Aero Sami SA. Monterrey, NL.	N176WA
❏	XA-TPD	69	JetStar-731	5134	SACSA, Toluca. (status ?).	XA-JMN
❏	XA-TPU	79	Sabre-60	306-143	Horizontes Aereos SA.	XA-SUN
❏	XA-TQA	84	Citation II	550-0504	Aerotaxi del Potosi SA. San Luis Potosi.	N72SL
❏	XA-TQR	62	Sabreliner CT-39A	276-4	Jett Paqueteria SA. San Luis Potosi.	N31403
❏	XA-TRE	92	Citation VII	650-7019	AVEMEX SA. Toluca.	XA-TCZ
❏	XA-TRQ	66	Learjet 24	24-112	Aeronaves TSM SA. Saltillo.	N104GA
❏	XA-TSS	70	Sabre-60	306-63	TAESA-Transportes Aereos Ejecutivos SA. Toluca.	XB-ZNP
❏	XA-TSZ	79	Sabre-75A	380-71	Aero Util SA. Toluca.	N80HK
❏	XA-TTE	65	JetStar-731	5058		N200DW
❏	XA-TTG	01	CitationJet CJ-1	525-0475	Aero Barloz SA. Monterrey, NL.	N475CJ
❏	XA-TTH		BAe 125/	...	noted Toluca 2/03,	
❏	XA-TTS	00	Beechjet 400A	RK-302	Aerolineas Ejecutivas SA. Toluca.	N5002G
❏	XA-TTT	69	Learjet 24B	24B-199	Aerotaxis Dos Mil SA. Saltillo.	N70TJ
❏	XA-TUD	74	Sabre-75A	380-5	First Sabre SA.	N71460
❏	XA-TUL	89	Learjet 31	31-012	Verataxis SA. Vera Cruz.	XA-RUU
❏	XA-TVG	01	Challenger 604	5520	Operadora Turistica Aurora SA.	N520JR
❏	XA-TVH	91	Citation II	550-0668		(N866VP)
❏	XA-TVI	84	BAe 125/800A	8004	Aeroservicios Ejecutivos Corporativos SA. Toluca.	XA-RET
❏	XA-TVK	67	JetStar-731	5098		(N963Y)
❏	XA-TVQ	82	Falcon 50	94	Aerolineas Sol SA. Toluca.	(XA-AFG)
❏	XA-TVZ	76	Sabre-60	306-113		N113T
❏	XA-TWH	80	Learjet 25D	25D-289	Hoteles Dinamicos SA. Guadalajara.	N321GE
❏	XA-TWW	01	Beechjet 400A	RK-332	Aerolineas Ejecutivas SA. Toluca.	N5032H
❏	XA-TXB	90	Falcon 50	210	Taxi Aereo de Veracruz SA. Jalapa.	F-GICN
❏	XA-TYD	01	Beechjet 400A	RK-321		N379DR
❏	XA-TYH	00	Hawker 800XP	8491	Crelan SA.	N51191
❏	XA-TYK	02	Hawker 800XP	8597	Aerolineas Ejecutivas SA. Toluca.	N597XP
❏	XA-TYZ		Sabre-	...	noted Houston-Hobby 3/04.	
❏	XA-TZF	01	Challenger 604	5527	Aero Silza SA. Chihuahua.	N554SC
❏	XA-TZI	96	Learjet 60	60-088	Aero Silza SA. Chihuahua.	XA-TZF
❏	XA-UAF	03	Citation Excel	560-5356		N519CS
❏	XA-UAG	01	Learjet 45	45-139	Universidad Autonoma de Guadalajara AC. Jalisco.	N45VL
❏	XA-UAM	96	Citation VII	650-7073		N1887M
❏	XA-UAW	03	Hawker 400XP	RK-359	Aerolineas Ejecutivas SA. Toluca.	N61959
❏	XA-UBH		Sabre-75	...	noted Las Vegas 10/04.	
❏	XA-UCN	88	Falcon 50	177		N14NE
❏	XA-UCV	03	Hawker 400XP	RK-375	Aerolineas Ejecutivas SA. Toluca.	N375XP
❏	XA-UUU	79	Learjet 25D	25D-276		N188TA
❏	XA-UVA	01	Citation Bravo	550-0999	Taxi Aereo del Norte SA. Monterrey, NL.	N5270E

Reg	Yr	Type	c/n	Owner/Operator	Prev Regn
XA-VEL	69	Sabre-60	306-42	Arrendadora Financiera Dina SA. Merida.	N128JC
XA-VIG	97	Learjet 60	60-116	Servicios Aereos Interestatales SA. Monterrey, NL.	N166LJ
XA-VMC	73	Learjet 25B	25B-114	Aeroejecutivos de Baja California SA. Tijuana, BC.	N114HC
XA-VRO	99	Beechjet 400A	RK-238	Aerolineas Ejecutivas SA. Toluca.	XA-DOS
XA-VTO	93	Falcon 900B	129	Aeroempresarial SA/Vitro Corporativo SA. Monterrey, NL.	N483FJ
XA-VYA	81	Learjet 25D	25D-336	El Caminante Taxi Aereo SA. Guadalajara, JAL.	N6345N
XA-VYC	99	Learjet 45	45-034	El Caminante Taxi Aereo SA. Guadalajara, JAL.	N454LP
XA-WWW	75	Learjet 25B	25B-193	Rajet Aeroservicios SA. Ramos Arizpe, Coah.	N125TN
XA-XGX		Citation	...	noted Houston 10/04.	
XA-XIS	93	Citation VII	650-7032	AVEMEX SA. Toluca.	N12637
XA-YYY	79	Learjet 25D	25D-263	Rajet Aeroservicios SA. Ramos Arizpe, Coah.	N825D
XA-ZAP	77	Learjet 35A	35A-129	Aerolineas Ejecutivas SA. Toluca.	N229X
XA-ZTA	98	Learjet 60	60-134	Servicios Aeronauticas Zeta SA. Juarez, Chihuahua.	N134LJ
XA-ZTH	89	Learjet 31	31-004	Servicios Especiales del Pacifico Jalisco, Silao	
XA-ZUL	01	390 Premier 1	RB-9	Aerolineas Ejecutivas SA. Toluca.	XA-IAS
XA-ZYZ	93	Learjet 31A	31A-073	Transportes Aereos Pegaso SA. Toluca.	N46UF
XA-ZZZ	81	Learjet 25D	25D-346	Aero Rentas de Coahuila SA. Saltillo.	N71AX
XB-...	77	Sabre-60	306-129	Moldes y Plasticos de Monterrey SA. Monterrey, NL.	N60ML
XB-...	75	Sabre-75A	380-40		N14TN
XB-...	69	HS 125/400A	NA737	Salvador Gaxiola Espinoza, Gudalajara, JAL.	N400KD
XB-ADR	66	Learjet 24	24-103	Aeronaves TSM SA. Saltillo.	N105EC
XB-ADZ	73	HS 125/600A	6018	Aero Continental SA.	XA-TNX
XB-AGV	82	Citation II	550-0430	Arrendadora y Commercial Industrial del Golfo SA.	N56FT
XB-AMO	74	Citation	500-0152	Fabricas Orion SA. Monterrey, NL.	N2782D
XB-BON	90	Citation II	550-0654	Benjamin Trapero Bustamente, Los Mochis-Topolbampo.	XA-RZB
XB-DBS	73	JetStar-8	5159	Sindicato Petrolero Mexicano SA. Mexico City.	N520M
XB-DGA		CitationJet	...	noted San Antonio 2/04.	
XB-DVF	81	Citation	500-0408	Alonso Ayala Rodriguez, Del Monte, NL.	XA-LUD
XB-DZD	77	Learjet 24F	24F-349	Impulsora Azucarera del Noroes, Culiacan.	XA-CAP
XB-DZR	73	Learjet 24D	24D-273	Sindicato Nacional de Trabaja Education, Toluca.	XC-DOP
XB-EEP	85	Citation S/II	S550-0070	Marca-Tel International SA. Monterrey, NL.	N570RC
XB-ESS	73	Sabre-40A	282-123	Cafe Descafeinado de Chis. Cordoba.	XA-APD
XB-ESX	70	Sabre-60A	306-47	Grupo Corporativo Cever SA. Toluca.	XA-ZOM
XB-ETV	75	Sabre-60	306-96	Aceros San Luis SA. San Luis Potosi.	N315JM
XB-FKT	90	Learjet 31	31-029	Zeferino Romero Bringas, Tehuacan.	N9173L
XB-FMK	79	HS 125/700A	NA0249	Juan R Brittingham SA. Monterrey, NL..	N799SC
XB-FNW	79	Learjet 35A	35A-255	Adame Barocio Alfonso, Toluca.	XB-LHS
XB-FRP	69	HS 125/400A	NA720	Productos Rolmex SA. Monterrey, NL.	XA-RMN
XB-GBF	75	Citation	500-0273	Jaime M Benavides Pompa, Monterrey, NL.	XA-RUR
XB-GCC	93	BAe 125/800A	8252	Federico Terrazas Torres,	N938H
XB-GDJ	81	Citation	500-0412	Constructora y Pavimentadora SA. Leon, Guanjuato.	XA-LUV
XB-GHO	67	Learjet 24	24-141	Jesus Arturo Armenta Castro, Apodaca, NL.	XB-FJW
XB-GLZ	81	Citation II	550-0303	Lineas de Producciones SA y Perforadora Central SA. Toluca.	N450CC
XB-GNF	72	HS 125/403A	NA776	Desarollo Inmobiliario SA. Monterrey, NL.	XA-SGM
XB-GRN	84	Citation III	650-0069	Exploradora del Sal SA.	N910M
XB-GSP	77	Sabre-75A	380-55	Treviso Ballesteros Lillia, Del Norte, NL.	XB-RDB
XB-HDL	67	Sabre-60	306-7	Aerovias Ejecutivas SA. Toluca.	XA-SND
XB-HGE	81	Learjet 25D	25D-325	Materiales y Construcciones SA.	N325JB
XB-HJS	76	Sabre-60	306-110	Alfonso Celis Romero, Tehuacan, Puebla.	N75GM
XB-HRA	67	Falcon 20C	127	Transpais Aereo SA. Monterrey, Nl	XB-GCR
XB-HZF	83	Citation II	550-0473	My Jet SA. Munterrey, NL.	N484MA
XB-IJW	74	Citation	500-0198		N997CA
XB-IKY	90	Citation II	550-0642	Aero Citro SA. Vera Cruz.	XA-SEX
XB-INI	96	Beechjet 400A	RK-126	Servicios Aereos de Chihuahua SA.	N197SD
XB-IPX		Hawker 800XP	...	noted Orlando 1/04.	
XB-IXT	73	Citation	500-0110		N172MA
XB-JDG		Citation	...	noted San Antonio 10/04.	
XB-JGI		Sabre-	...	noted San Antonio 10/04.	
XB-JHD		Citation	...	noted Las Vegas 10/04.	
XB-JHE	89	Beechjet 400	RJ-48	Industrial Patrona SA. Veracruz, Guadalajara.	N1548D
XB-JLJ	81	Citation II	550-0274	Operado Intergrupo SA.	N75GA
XB-JLU	81	Learjet 25D	25D-328	Arrendadora y Comercial Immobiliaria de Sol SA.	N518JG
XB-JMR	68	Sabre-60	306-35	Cia J M Romo SA. Aguascalientes.	N3456B
XB-JTN	82	HS 125/700A	NA0331	Jamil Textil SA. Toluca.	N900BL
XB-MAR	69	HS 125/400A	NA731	Taxi Aereo Nacional SA. Sotelo.	XA-MAR
XB-MGM	77	Learjet 25D	25D-224	Transporte Aereo MGM SA. Guadalajara, JAL.	N80X

Reg	Yr	Type		c/n	Owner/Operator		Prev Regn

Reg	Yr	Type	c/n	Owner/Operator	Prev Regn
☐ XB-MSV		Hawker 800XP	...	noted Opa Locka 2/04.	
☐ XB-MYE	65	Learjet 23	23-066	Maclovio Hernandez, Vera Cruz.	N211TS
☐ XB-PBT	72	Citation	500-0054		(N54FT)
☐ XB-RGO	73	Sabre-40A	282-114	Regio Empresas y Copropietarios, Del Norte, NL.	XB-RGS
☐ XB-TRY	74	Citation Eagle SP	500-0210	Grupo Tor Rey SA.	N501TK
☐ XC-...	80	Westwind-1124	279	State Government of Colima, Colima.	N400TF
☐ XC-AA70	68	Gulfstream 2	18	Procurad General de la Republica, Mexico City.	XA-LZZ
☐ XC-AA89	76	Sabre-75A	380-46	Procurad General de la Republica, Mexico City.	XC-HFY
☐ XC-AAC	68	Sabre-60	306-21	Procurad General de la Republica, Mexico City.	XB-QND
☐ XC-AAJ	68	Sabre-60	306-20		XA-TLL
☐ XC-COL	69	Jet Commander-B	135	State Government of Colima, Colima.	N1121N
☐ XC-CUZ	79	Learjet 35A	35A-213	Fonseca Alvarez Guillermo, San Luis Potosi.	(N935NA)
☐ XC-DDA	75	Sabre-75A	380-34	DGAC, Mexico City.	N97SC
☐ XC-DGA	72	Citation	500-0010	SCT/DGAC Verificaciones, Mexico City.	XC-FIT
☐ XC-DIP	73	Falcon 20E	282	Transporte Aereo Federal, Mexico City.	N282C
☐ XC-FEZ	81	Citation	500-0409	SCT/DGAC Verificaciones, Mexico City.	N67815
☐ XC-FIV	72	Citation	500-0013	SCT/DGAC Verificaciones, Mexico City.	N513CC
☐ XC-GAW	81	Citation	500-0410	State Government of Tamaulipas, Victoria.	N6780Z
☐ XC-GTO	80	Citation	500-0396	State Government of Guanajuato, Guanajuato.	(XA-JEW)
☐ XC-GUB	80	Learjet 25D	25D-306	SARH/Ministry of Agriculture, Mexico City.	XA-DUB
☐ XC-HGY	69	Sabre-60	306-38	Aerotaxis del Golfo SA. Acapulco, Guerrero.	XA-DCO
☐ XC-HHJ	81	Learjet 35A	35A-435	State Government of Chiapas, Tuxtla Gutierrez.	N435N
☐ XC-HIE	79	Learjet 29	29-002	PF-201, Policia Federal Preventiva, Mexico City.	XC-DFS
☐ XC-HIS	80	Learjet 25D	25D-312	State Government of Chiapas, Tuxtla Gutierrez.	N94MJ
☐ XC-HIX	71	Falcon 20E	248	Governor of the State of Sinaloa, Bachigualato.	XB-VRM
☐ XC-IST	79	Learjet 29	29-001	ISSSTE/Institute of Security Social Services, Mexico City.	N929GL
☐ XC-JDC	79	Sabre-60	306-145	Governor of the State of Campeche.	XA-LOQ
☐ XC-JDX	65	Learjet 23	23-070	Procurad General de la Republica, Mexico City.	XC-AA104
☐ XC-LGD	65	Learjet 23	23-037	Comision Nacional del Agua, Mexico City.	XC-AA28
☐ XC-LHB		Citation	...	Procurad General/Mexican Customs Service.	
☐ XC-MMM	72	Citation	500-0035	State Government of Michoacan,	XA-JOV
☐ XC-NSP	75	Learjet 25B	25B-194	CONASUPO, Toluca.	XB-GPJ
☐ XC-PFJ	73	Falcon 20E	287	Secretaria de Gobernacion, Mexico City.	XA-SAG
☐ XC-PFN	75	Sabre-60	306-111	PF-213, Policia Federal Preventiva, Mexico City.	XA-SKB
☐ XC-PFP	72	Learjet 24D	24D-260	PF-..., Policia Federal Preventiva, Mexico City.	XA-GBA
☐ XC-PFT	75	Gulfstream II SP	175	PF-210, Policia Federal Preventiva, Mexico City.	XA-FNY
☐ XC-PGM	90	Citation II	550-0644	PGR/PJF-Policia Judicial Federal, Mexico City.	(N1310B)
☐ XC-PGN	89	Citation III	650-0165	Procurad General de la Republica, Mexico City.	(N650GJ)
☐ XC-PGP	91	Citation II	550-0648	Procurad General de la Republica, Mexico City.	N1260G
☐ XC-RPP	78	Learjet 25D	25D-236	Secretaria de Hacienda y Credito Publico, Aguascalientes.	N1466B
☐ XC-SCT	80	Citation II	550-0138	SCT, Mexico City. 'Mexico es Primero'.	N2646X
☐ XC-SEY	68	Falcon 20C	169	ASA, Mexico City.	N4370F
☐ XC-SKI	68	JetStar-8	5124	Secretaria de la Reforma Agraria, Toluca.	XA-SKI
☐ XC-SON	78	Falcon 20F-5	393	State Government of Sonora, Bachigualato.	XC-FVH
☐ XC-SST	94	Citation II	550-0731	DGAC, Mexico City.	N550BP
☐ XC-VMC	00	Learjet 45	45-028		HB-VMC
☐ XC-VSA	79	Learjet 28	28-002	State Government of Tabasco, Villahermosa. 'El Chontal'	N511DB
Military					
☐ 3501	65	B 727-64	18912	EA302, Santa Lucia.	(XB-DLM)
☐ 3503	65	B 727-14	18908	EA302, Santa Lucia.	10503/XC-F
☐ 3504	65	B 727-14	18909	EA302, Santa Lucia.	10504/XC-F
☐ 3505		B 727-264	22661	EA302, Santa Lucia.	XA-MXA
☐ 3506		B 727-264	22662	EA302, Santa Lucia.	XA-MXB
☐ 3908	69	JetStar-8	5144	Ministry of Defence, Mexico City.	10201
☐ 3909	80	Learjet 35A	35A-321	Ministry of Defence, Mexico City.	TP-106
☐ 3929	73	Citation	500-0090	EA501, Santa Lucia.	ETE-1329
☐ AMT-203	69	Sabre-60	306-34	Marina Transporte, Mexico City.	MTX-04
☐ MTX-01	98	Learjet 60	60-152	Secretaria de Marina, Mexico City.	N50126
☐ MTX-02	99	Learjet 31A	31A-174	Secretaria de Marina, Mexico City.	N9VL
☐ MTX-03	81	Learjet 25D	25D-339	Secretaria de Marina, Mexico City.	N21HR
☐ TP-104	75	Learjet 35	35-028	CGATP, Mexico City.	XC-IPP
☐ TP-105	81	Learjet 36A	36A-050	CGATP, Mexico City.	XC-AA24
☐ XC-UJB	89	B 737-33A	24095	TP-02, Estado Mayor Presidencial, Mexico City.	N731XL
☐ XC-UJF	78	Sabre-60	306-144	Aeropuertos y Servicios Auxiliares, Mexico City.	XC-AA51
☐ XC-UJM	87	B 757-225	22690	TP-02, C-GTAP, Mexico City.	XC-UJM/TP
☐ XC-UJN	82	Gulfstream 3	352	TP-06, Presidencia de la Republica, Chiapas.	HB-ITM
Reg	*Yr*	*Type*	*c/n*	*Owner/Operator*	*Prev Regn*

Reg	Yr	Type	c/n	Owner/Operator	Prev Regn
☐ XC-UJO	83	Gulfstream 3	386	TP-07, Government of Mexico, Mexico City.	N902KB
☐ XC-UJS	78	Sabre-60	306-139	Procurad General de la Republica, Mexico City.	XC-UJE
☐ XC-UJU	78	Sabre-75A	380-68	Procurad General de la Republica, Mexico City.	XC-UJD

XT = BURKINA FASO   *Total*   1

Civil

☐ XT-BBE	66	B 727-14	18990	Government of Burkina Faso, Ouagadougou.	N21UC

XU = CAMBODIA   *Total*   2

Civil

☐ XU-008	75	Falcon 20E	323	Government of Cambodia, Phnom Penh.	OE-GLF
☐ XU-888	69	F 28-1000	11012	President Airlines, Phnom Penh.	XU-001

XY = MYANMAR   *Total*   1

Military

☐ 4400	82	Citation II	550-0358	MoD/Myanmar Air Force, Mingaladon.	N6801Q

YA = AFGHANISTAN   *Total*   1

Civil

☐ YA-GAB		HS 125/	...	noted Termez, Uzbekistan 3/04.	

YI = IRAQ   *Total*   7

Civil

☐ YI-AHH	76	Falcon 20F	307	Ministry of Defence, Muthana. (photo-recce).	F-WRQR
☐ YI-AHJ	78	Falcon 20F	343	Ministry of Defence, Muthana. (photo-recce).	F-WRQR
☐ YI-AKB	79	JetStar 2	5235	Government/Iraqi Airways, Baghdad. (status ?).	N4055M
☐ YI-AKC	79	JetStar 2	5237	Government/Iraqi Airways, Baghdad. (status ?).	N4058M
☐ YI-AKD	79	JetStar 2	5238	Government/Iraqi Airways, Baghdad. (status ?).	N4062M
☐ YI-AKE	79	JetStar 2	5239	Government/Iraqi Airways, Baghdad. (status ?).	N4063M
☐ YI-AKF	79	JetStar 2	5240	Government/Iraqi Airways, Baghdad. (status ?).	N4065M

YK = SYRIA   *Total*   3

Military

☐ YK-ASA	75	Falcon 20F	328	Government of Syria, Damascus.	(N4459F)
☐ YK-ASB	75	Falcon 20F	331	Government of Syria, Damascus.	F-WRQS
☐ YK-ASC	91	Falcon 900	100	Government of Syria, Damascus.	F-WWFB

YL = LATVIA   *Total*   4

Civil

☐ YL-MAR	99	Hawker 800XP	8389	PAREX/VIP Avia Ltd. Riga.	YR-VPA
☐ YL-NST	99	Hawker 800XP	8424	PAREX/VIP Avia Ltd. Riga.	N1899K
☐ YL-VIP	87	BAe 125/800B	8078	PAREX/VIP Avia Ltd. Riga.	G-88-01
☐ YL-WBD	99	Challenger 604	5442	PAREX/VIP Avia Ltd. Riga.	G-POAJ

YR = ROMANIA   *Total*   1

Civil

☐ YR-BRE	86	BAC 1-11/561RC	405	Romavia/Government of Romania, Bucharest.	

YU = YUGOSLAVIA   *Total*   4

Civil

☐ YU-BNA	81	Falcon 50	43	Government of Yugoslavia, Belgrade.	72102
☐ YU-BRZ	91	Learjet 31A	31A-045	Avio Service, Belgrade.	N67SB
☐ YU-BSM	97	Citation Bravo	550-0808	Prince Aviation, Belgrade.	SE-DVZ
☐ YU-BVV	81	Citation II	550-0272	Prince Aviation, Belgrade.	SE-DVV

YV = VENEZUELA   *Total*   62

Civil

☐ YV-...	78	Citation 1/SP	501-0071		N509P
☐ YV-....	74	Citation Longwing SP	500-0167	Seven Clouds CA. Caracas.	N801KT
☐ YV-....	71	HS 125/400A	NA760	Gregory Hurtado, Caracas.	N456WH
☐ YV-....	72	Citation	500-0047	Jorge Lopez, Caracas.	N7281Z
☐ YV-....	69	HS 125/731	NA723	Inversiones Alfamaq CA. Caracas.	N444HH
☐ YV-03CP	67	JetStar-731	5106	Servicios Aerofacility SA. Caracas.	YV-03CP
☐ YV-1049CP	78	Learjet 25D	25D-253		N321AU
☐ YV-1055CP	81	Citation II	550-0312		(VH-ARZ)
☐ YV-1122CP	71	HS 125/F400B	25248		N189RR
☐ YV-1133CP	76	Citation	500-0317		N317VP
☐ YV-1144CP	72	Sabre-40A	282-106		N854RB
☐ YV-122CP		Hawker 800XP	...	noted Fort Lauderdale 9/04.	
☐ YV-12CP	82	Learjet 55	55-031	Coca-Cola OCAAT C.A. Caracas.	
☐ YV-162CP	81	Citation II	550-0300	Aero Servicios ALAS C.A. Caracas.	N68881

Reg	Yr	Type	c/n	Owner/Operator	Prev Regn

Reg	Yr	Type	c/n	Owner/Operator	Prev Regn
☐ YV-203CP	70	Learjet 25C	25C-061	Tranarg C.A. Caracas.	N9CN
☐ YV-21CP	73	Citation	500-0115	Transportes Inland, Caracas.	YV-TAFA
☐ YV-2426P	81	Citation II/SP	551-0313	(was 550-0270).	N270CF
☐ YV-2454P	67	Jet Commander	96		(N2ES)
☐ YV-2482P	74	Westwind-1123	172	West Wind Air C.A. Caracas.	YV-58CP
☐ YV-2567P	80	Citation II/SP	551-0223	Inversiones Marafuera CA. Caracas.	(N28GZ)
☐ YV-2605P	79	Citation 1/SP	501-0131	Autotek CA. Caracas.	N301PP
☐ YV-2671P	79	Citation II/SP	551-0015	Inversiones Lunfa CA. Caracas.	YV-213CP
☐ YV-2711P	00	Citation Bravo	550-0943	Inversiones SCL 12 SA. Caracas.	N706CP
☐ YV-332CP	81	Westwind-Two	330	Transporte 330 SA/Cia Tamesis SA. Caracas.	N723K
☐ YV-376CP	90	Citation II	550-0637	Miralta CA. Caracas.	N1258U
☐ YV-388CP	71	HFB 320	1057	Inversiones Guraica CA. Caracas.	VR-CYR
☐ YV-432CP	81	Learjet 35A	35A-437	Constructora Pedeca CA. La Carlota.	N3803G
☐ YV-450CP	91	Falcon 50	219	PDVSA-Petroleos de Venezuela SA. Caracas.	N129FJ
☐ YV-455CP	83	Falcon 50	136	PDVSA-Petroleos de Venezuela SA. Caracas.	N50HC
☐ YV-462CP	79	Falcon 50	4	Petroleos de Venezuela SA. Caracas.	YV-O-SATA
☐ YV-52CP	77	Citation	500-0367	Construcciones CADE.	N36906
☐ YV-55CP	74	Citation	500-0215	SABENPE, Caracas.	YV-T-OOO
☐ YV-572CP	75	Corvette	17	Aerocolon S.A. Caracas. (status ?).	F-ODTM
☐ YV-701CP	91	Citation II	550-0683	Luis Mendoza, Caracas.	(N6777X)
☐ YV-713CP	83	Citation II/SP	551-0463	Promociones Orizaba CA.. Caracas.	YV-05C
☐ YV-754CP	97	Beechjet 400A	RK-152		N97FB
☐ YV-771CP	95	Astra-1125SP	077	Transporte Polar CA. Caracas.	N771CP
☐ YV-772CP	01	Gulfstream G200	041	Transporte Polar CA. Caracas.	N101GX
☐ YV-778CP	82	Citation II	550-0405	Consolid-Air S.A.	YV-604P
☐ YV-810CP	83	Citation II	550-0467	Distribuidora Sal Bahia SA.	N64CM
☐ YV-811CP	91	Citation V	560-0134	Banco del Caribe S.A. Caracas.	N6812D
☐ YV-815CP	66	HS 125/731	25098	Inversiones Desirio CA.	N29CR
☐ YV-824CP	68	Learjet 24	24-173	Editorial Roderick, Puerto Ordaz.	N623RC
☐ YV-881CP	72	Citation	500-0052	Transportes Lehmacorp CA.	YV-2628P
☐ YV-888CP	81	Citation II	550-0135	Inversiones Brancom SA. Caracas.	N550BP
☐ YV-901CP	72	Citation	500-0058	Corporacion 385 CA. Caracas.	N6145Q
☐ YV-939CP	72	Citation	500-0031	Executive Air C.A. Caracas.	YV-646CP
☐ YV-968CP	01	Beechjet 400A	RK-306	Wyngs Aviation CA. Caracas.	N4056V
☐ YV-O-CVG-2	78	Citation II/SP	551-0006	EDELCA-Electrificaciones de Caroni,	YV-06CP
Military					
☐ 0001	01	Airbus A319CJ-133X	1468	Government of Venezuela, Caracas.	D-AVYQ
☐ 0002	78	Citation II	550-0011	FAV, MoD, Caracas.	(N98876)
☐ 0006	72	Learjet 24D	24D-250	FAV, MoD, Caracas. (status ?).	N85CD
☐ 0018	80	Falcon 50	22	FAV, MoD, Caracas.	N50FL
☐ 0207	76	B 737-2N1	21167	Republica Bolivariana de Venezuela, Caracas.	0001
☐ 0222	73	Citation	500-0092	FAV, MoD, Caracas.	N592CC
☐ 0442	70	Falcon 20D	235	FAV, Palo Negro AB. Maracau.	(N442)
☐ 1650	83	Falcon 20F	476	FAV, MoD, Caracas.	F-ZJTD
☐ 1967		Citation	...	FAV, MoD, Caracas.	
☐ 2222	81	Citation II	550-0224	FAV, MoD, Caracas.	YV-O-MTC-
☐ 5761	66	Falcon 20C	23	FAV, Palo Negro AB. Maracau.	(N582G)
☐ 5840	69	Falcon 20D	216	FAV, Palo Negro AB. Maracau.	N9FE
☐ YV-2338P	82	Citation II	550-0449	FAV, MoD, Caracas.	(FAV1107)

Z = ZIMBABWE — Total 1

Civil

Reg	Yr	Type	c/n	Owner/Operator	Prev Regn
☐ Z-WPD	87	BAe 146 Statesman	E2065	Air Zimbabwe/Government of Zimbabwe,	G-5-065

ZK = NEW ZEALAND — Total 5

Civil

Reg	Yr	Type	c/n	Owner/Operator	Prev Regn
☐ ZK-KFB	98	Gulfstream 4SP	1362	Air National Corporate Ltd. Auckland.	(N888LF)
☐ ZK-TBM	03	CitationJet CJ-1	525-0511	Christchurch Helicopters Ltd. Christchurch.	N5212M
☐ ZK-XVL	89	Learjet 35A	35A-649	Auckland Air Charter Ltd. Auckland.	N35QB
Military					
☐ NZ7571		B 757-2K2	26633	RNZAF, Ohakea.	PH-TKA
☐ NZ7572		B 757-2K2	26634	RNZAF, Ohakea.	PH-TKB

ZP = PARAGUAY — Total 3

Civil

Reg	Yr	Type	c/n	Owner/Operator	Prev Regn
☐ ZP-AGD	71	Westwind-1123	151	Humberto Dominguez Dibb, Asuncion.	N88WP
☐ ZP-TDF	68	HS 125/400A	NA711	Government of Paraguay, Asuncion.	N601JJ
☐ ZP-TZH	74	Citation	500-0185	L C Santi, Asuncion.	N500AZ
Reg	Yr	Type	c/n	Owner/Operator	Prev Regn

Civil

Reg	Yr	Type	c/n	Owner/Operator	Prev Regn
ZS-...	99	Hawker 800XP	8429	NAC P/L. Rand.	N68HD
ZS-...	03	Hawker 800XP	8659	NAC P/L. Rand.	N659XP
ZS-...	03	Hawker 800XP	8658	NAC P/L. Rand.	N658XP
ZS-ACE	82	Citation 1/SP	501-0245	ZS-KMO P/L. Lanseria.	A2-AGM
ZS-ALT	02	Challenger 604	5552	Chartertech Partnership, Lanseria.	N552CC
ZS-AOL	01	Gulfstream V	634	Anglo Operations Ltd. Johannesburg.	N534GA
ZS-ARG	80	Citation II/SP	551-0163	Mineag Air Partnership P/L. Lanseria.	D-IGRC
ZS-AVM	02	390 Premier 1	RB-31	Cape Air Charter Partnership P/L. Capetown.	N3231K
ZS-BAR	02	Learjet 45	45-219	Barloworld Ltd. Lanseria.	N4003K
ZS-BXR	73	Learjet 25XR	25XR-141	King Air Services Partnership, Lanseria.	N25HA
ZS-CAG	82	HS 125/700B	7172	King Air Services Partnership, Lanseria.	N355WJ
ZS-CAL	69	HS 125/F3B-RA	25172	King Air Services Partnership, Lanseria.	(G-5-506)
ZS-CAR	86	Citation S/II	S550-0078	Civil Aviation Authority, Johannesburg.	N1273X
ZS-CDS	97	Citation V Ultra	560-0414	Metcash Aviation P/L. Lanseria.	N5235G
ZS-CEW	80	Learjet 35A	35A-341	Chartwell Aviation P/L. Lanseria.	N259WJ
ZS-CJT	03	CitationJet CJ-2	525A-0163	ZSCJT Partnership,	N5151D
ZS-CWD	78	Citation 1/SP	501-0049	Containerworld P/L. Durban.	OY-SVI
ZS-DAV	95	Falcon 900B	149	Hawker Air Services P/L. Lanseria.	VP-BPI
ZS-DCA	00	Learjet 45	45-117	Daimler Chrysler/DC Aviation P/L. Pretoria.	N40081
ZS-DCI	99	Learjet 45	45-052	Searay 45 Charters Partnership, Capetown.	(ZS-SCT)
ZS-DDA	03	Hawker 800XP	8601	Beechjet Charter Partnership P/L. Pinegowrie.	N61101
ZS-DDM	02	390 Premier 1	RB-63	Fourie's Poultry Farm P/L. Potchefstrom.	N6163T
ZS-DDT	00	Hawker 800XP	8465	Pinnacle Point Resorts P/L. Capetown.	N43265
ZS-DSA	72	Citation	500-0044	D S Avnit, Lanseria.	N501VH
ZS-EDA	87	Citation S/II	S550-0126	Extra Dimensions Aviation P/L. Lanseria.	(N127RC)
ZS-ESA	00	Global Express	9061	Government of Rwanda, Kigali.	ZS-ESA
ZS-FOX	76	Falcon 10	72	Awesome Aviation P/L-Medicair, Grand Central.	N50TY
ZS-FUL*	04	Learjet 45	45-270		
ZS-FUN	77	Learjet 24F	24F-354	Awesome Aviation P/L-Medicair, Grand Central.	PT-LYE
ZS-GJB	02	Global Express	9122	Kangra Group P/L. Lanseria.	N700FW
ZS-IDC	03	Citation Excel	560-5352	Kindoc Airways P/L. Lanseria.	N5245D
ZS-IPE	83	HS 125/700A	NA0342	S D Davidson/Sam Air Ltd. Port Elizabeth.	(ZS-IPI)
ZS-KJY	68	Learjet 24	24-165	MCC Aviation P/L. Lanseria.	V5-KJY
ZS-LDV	82	Citation	500-0418	Parbair Trust, Lanseria.	N2628B
ZS-LME	70	HS 125/403B	25242	Lanseria Aviation P/L. Lanseria.	3D-ABZ
ZS-LOW	02	Learjet 45	45-228	Barloworld Capital P/L. Lanseria.	N5012Z
ZS-LPE	69	HS 125/400B	25184	TCT Leisure P/L. Lanseria.	SAAF04
ZS-LWU	69	Learjet 24B	24B-209	King Air Services Partnership, Lanseria.	N14BC
ZS-LXH	76	Learjet 25D	25D-206	Nelair Aviation Services P/L. Nelspruit.	N206EQ
ZS-MAN	66	HS 125/1B	25067	Sabre Pharmaceuticals P/L. Lanseria.	Z-TBX
ZS-MCU	73	Citation	500-0137	Moraine Freight P/L. Lanseria.	N12ME
ZS-MDA	91	Astra-1125SP	055	Global Equities Aviation P/L. Benmore.	N120GA
ZS-MGD*	05	Falcon 2000EX EASY	51		F-W...
ZS-MGJ	69	Learjet 24XR	24XR-207	Nelair Aviation Services P/L. Nelspruit.	N457JA
ZS-MGK	03	390 Premier 1	RB-67	Mawenzi Resources & Finance Co. Lanseria.	N6167D
ZS-MHN	89	Beechjet 400	RJ-59	South African Police Services, Wonderboom.	N1559U
ZS-MTD	74	Learjet 25B	25B-160	Brachloty Trading Rental Trust, Tzaneen.	3D-AEZ
ZS-NDX	91	Citation V	560-0152	De Beers Consolidated Mines Ltd. Johannesburg.	N6882R
ZS-NGG	73	Learjet 24XR	24XR-280	Nelair Aviation Services P/L. Nelspruit. (repaired).	N79RS
ZS-NGL	92	Citation V	560-0202	Sappi Manufacturing P/L. Lanseria.	N1283V
ZS-NGS	93	Citation V	560-0241	De Beers Consolidated Mines Ltd. Johannesburg.	N241CV
ZS-NII	80	Citation II	550-0168	Rossair Executive Air Charter P/L. Lanseria.	N68GA
ZS-NNM	67	BAC 1-11/409AY	108	Nationwide Air Charter P/L. Lanseria.	G-BGTU
ZS-NUZ	96	Citation V Ultra	560-0398	Falconair/Rembrandt Tobacco Group, Capetown.	N5061W
ZS-NYG	73	Learjet 25C	25C-098	The Core Computer Business P/L. Morningside.	N502MH
ZS-NYV	95	Learjet 31A	31A-115	Government of Kwazulu-Natal, Ulundi.	N31NR
ZS-OEA	73	Learjet 24XR	24XR-267	Trans African Aviation P/L.. Fourways.	N267MP
ZS-OFM	98	Citation V Ultra	560-0467	Kindoc Airways P/L. Lanseria.	N5096S
ZS-OGS	75	Citation	500-0260	Kiara Air P/L. Ballito.	N260RD
ZS-OHZ	00	Citation Excel	560-5079	Anglo Operations Ltd. Johannesburg.	N5218T
ZS-OIE	83	Citation II	550-0480	Sukramark P/L. Malelane.	N380MS
ZS-OIF	70	HS 125/731	NA746	W von Wedel Aviation P/L. Lanseria.	N103RR
ZS-OML	94	Learjet 31A	31A-170	Execujet Air Charter P/L. Lanseria.	(OY-LJN)
ZS-ONE	71	Citation Eagle	500-0002	J & D Aviation CC. Lanseria.	C-FCPW
Reg	Yr	Type	c/n	Owner/Operator	Prev Regn

Reg	Yr	Type	c/n	Owner/Operator	Prev Regn
☐ ZS-ONG	99	Falcon 50EX	287	Falconair/Rembrandt Tobacco Group, Capetown.	F-WWHO
☐ ZS-ORW	88	Beechjet 400	RJ-37	Skyinvest Administration P/L-Skyfalcon, Tokai.	N31437
☐ ZS-OSG	01	Challenger 604	5486	Government of Zambia, Lusaka, Zambia.	N486EJ
☐ ZS-OUU	87	Beechjet 400	RJ-25	Cape Air Charter Partnership P/L. Capetown.	N425BJ
☐ ZS-OXY	87	BAe 125/800A	8095	NAC P/L. Rand.	N40255
☐ ZS-PBA*	79	Learjet 35A	35A-263	Dodson International Parts Inc. Lanseria. (status ?).	N2422J
☐ ZS-PDG	00	Learjet 45	45-092	Friedshelf 366 P/L. Capetown.	(ZS-PPR)
☐ ZS-PFE	03	390 Premier 1	RB-94	Waste Product Utilisation P/L. Lanseria.	N6194N
☐ ZS-PFG	73	Citation Eagle	500-0122	Pro-Med Construction CC. Lanseria.	N122AP
☐ ZS-PJE	65	HS 125/731	25023	Marsess Mining Investments P/L. Pretoria.	(N89FF)
☐ ZS-PKD	04	Gulfstream G200	098	Baobab Aviation P/L. Lanseria.	N398GA
☐ ZS-PKR	00	Falcon 2000	114	Pepkor Group P/L-Flicape P/L. Capetown.	F-WWVI
☐ ZS-PLC	69	HS 125/731	NA733	Landonia Trust Co. Houghton.	N243JB
☐ ZS-PMA	73	Citation Eagle	500-0123	Spring Lights 1 P/L. Johannesburg.	VH-ECD
☐ ZS-PNP	00	Learjet 31A	31A-202	Pick N'Pay P/L. Capetown.	N4003L
☐ ZS-PRM	01	390 Premier 1	RB-24	NAC P/L. Rand.	(ZS-PRF)
☐ ZS-PTL	01	Learjet 45	45-181	Rodo Investments P/L. Lanseria.	N5024E
☐ ZS-PZA	03	Hawker 800XP	8632	Pezula Private Estate P/L-Crucial Trade 101 P/L. Knysa.	N632XP
☐ ZS-RCC	73	Citation	500-0106	Jet Air Charter P/L. Lanseria	N606CC
☐ ZS-RKV	79	Citation II	550-0051	Mouritzen Family Trust, Randburg.	N678CA
☐ ZS-RSA	01	BBJ-7ED	32627	Government of South Africa. Waterkloof AFB. 'Inkwazi'	N373BJ
☐ ZS-SAB	99	Citation X	750-0080	South African Breweries Ltd. Lanseria.	N5165T
☐ ZS-SEA	79	Falcon 10	156	ESCOM/Sapphire Executive Air, Grand Central.	SE-DEK
☐ ZS-SEB	80	Falcon 10	127	ESCOM/Sapphire Executive Air, Grand Central.	(N7RZ)
☐ ZS-SES	78	Learjet 35A	35A-185	Aircraft Africa Contracts Co P/L. Lanseria.	OE-GAV
☐ ZS-SGS	03	390 Premier 1	RB-72	Skyros Properties P/L. Capetown.	N535BR
☐ ZS-SMT	67	HS 125/3B	25128	Skymaster Trust, Johannesburg.	F-GECR
☐ ZS-SOS	84	Falcon 200	493	International SOS Assistance P/L. Lanseria.	VH-ECG
☐ ZS-SSM	68	Learjet 25XR	25XR-022	ZS-SSM Partnership, Lanseria.	N111WB
☐ ZS-TEX	82	Gulfstream 3	355	African Air Solutions, Lanseria.	N355TS
☐ ZS-TJS	00	Learjet 45	45-083	Tokyo Sexwale, Lanseria.	OY-LJG
☐ ZS-TMG	74	Citation	500-0149	COMAV, Menlo Park.	N149PJ
☐ ZS-TOW	82	Learjet 35A	35A-475	NAC P/L. Rand.	(N42AJ)
☐ ZS-TOY	70	Learjet 24B	24B-219	Landonia Trust CC. Upington.	N977GA
☐ ZS-UCH	02	Citation Encore	560-0607	Newshelf 681 P/L. Lanseria.	N5270K
☐ ZS-YES	01	Learjet 45	45-194	Yes Air P/L. Capetown.	N5014E
☐ ZS-ZZZ*	78	Learjet 35A	35A-172	Naturelink Airlines P/L. Wonderboom, RSA.	N50AK
Military					
☐ ZS-CAQ	83	Falcon 50	133	South African Air Force, Pretoria.	HB-IEA
☐ ZS-CAS	82	Falcon 50	91	South African Air Force, Pretoria.	ZS-BMB
☐ ZS-LIG	83	Citation II	550-0474	South African Air Force, Pretoria.	N12514
☐ ZS-MLN	81	Citation II/SP	551-0285	South African Air Force, Waterkloof AFB.	VDF-030
☐ ZS-NAN	91	Falcon 900B	99	South African Air Force, Waterkloof AFB.	F-WWFE

Z3 = MACEDONIA
Total 1

Civil

☐ Z3-BAA	76	Learjet 25B	25B-205	Government of Macedonia, Skopje.	YU-BKJ

3A = MONACO
Total 2

Civil

☐ 3A-MGR	01	Falcon 2000	167	Prince Rainier, Nice, France.	F-WWVG
☐ 3A-MRB	82	Citation II/SP	551-0421	Boutsen Aviation, Monaco. (was 550-0422).	D-IAWA

3B = MAURITIUS
Total 2

Civil

☐ 3B-GFI	81	Challenger 600S	1019	Generale Aviation et Finance Internationale Ltd. Lumbumbashi	ZS-NER
☐ 3B-XLA	87	Falcon 900B	7	XL Aviation, Geneva, Switzerland.	TR-LCJ

3C = EQUATORIAL GUINEA
Total 5

Civil

☐ 3C-EGE	02	BBJ-7FB/W	33367	Government of Equatorial Guinea, Malabo.	N377JC
☐ 3C-ONM	97	Falcon 900B	167	Government of Equatorial Guinea, Malabo.	F-GUEQ
☐ 3C-QQU	66	JetStar-731	5082	Jetline Inc. Sharjah, UAE.	(P4-CBJ)
☐ 3C-QRF	66	BAC 1-11/401AK	061	Jetline Inc. Sharjah, UAE.	P4-CBI
☐ 3C-QRK	76	JetStar 2	5202	Jetline Inc. Sharjah, UAE.	P4-CBG

3D = SWAZILAND
Total 3

Civil

☐ 3D-BOE	65	B 727-30	18933	Government of Democratic Republic of Congo, Kinshasa.	N7271P
Reg	Yr	Type	c/n	Owner/Operator	Prev Regn

Reg	Yr	Type	c/n	Owner/Operator	Prev Regn
☐ 3D-JNM	66	B 727-89	19139	Global Airways,	N511DB
☐ 3D-KMJ	68	B 727-22C	19892		NZ7271

4X = ISRAEL   Total   23

Civil

Reg	Yr	Type	c/n	Owner/Operator	Prev Regn
☐ 4X-CLK	77	Westwind-1124	213	Noy Aviation Ltd. Tel Aviv.	N30YM
☐ 4X-CLL	01	Gulfstream G200	040	Memorand Management (1998) Ltd. Tel Aviv.	N90GX
☐ 4X-CMF	01	Challenger 604	5522	Fishman Properties Ltd/Noy Aviation Ltd. Tel Aviv.	C-GKCB
☐ 4X-CMG	80	Citation 1/SP	501-0143	MGK Holding Ltd. Tel Aviv.	N501MG
☐ 4X-CMR	90	Citation III	650-0185	MGK Holding Ltd. Tel Aviv.	(N650MG)
☐ 4X-CMY	98	Challenger 604	5388	Merhav MNF Ltd/Noy Aviation Ltd. Tel Aviv.	C-GDVM
☐ 4X-CMZ	00	Challenger 604	5450	Jet Link, Tel Aviv.	N450DK
☐ 4X-COE	97	Challenger 604	5352	Chim-Nir Aviation Services Ltd. Herzlia.	C-GBKE
☐ 4X-COG	00	Gulfstream G200	018	Chim-Nir Aviation, Tel Aviv.	N18GZ
☐ 4X-CPU	00	Citation Excel	560-5074	Arkia Israeli Airlines Ltd. Tel Aviv.	N466LM
☐ 4X-CRU	04	Hawker 800XP	8682	Ray Aviation Ltd. Tel Aviv.	N682XP
☐ 4X-CZD	79	Citation II/SP	551-0117	Gesher-Aviri Co. Tel Aviv. (was 550-0063).	N551AD
☐ 4X-WIA	84	Astra-1125	002	Israel Aircraft Industries Ltd. Tel Aviv. (status ?).	

Military

Reg	Yr	Type	c/n	Owner/Operator	Prev Regn
☐ 4X-...	02	Gulfstream G550	5014	ISDAF, Tel Aviv.	N014CA
☐ 4X-...	04	Gulfstream G550	5044	ISDAF, Tel Aviv.	N944GA
☐ 4X-JY.	77	B 707-3P1C	21334	275, ISDAF, Tel Aviv.	A7-AAA
☐ 4X-JYB	72	B 707-3H7C	20629	255, ISDAF, Tel Aviv.	4X-BYR
☐ 4X-JYH	65	B 707-3J6B	20721	264, ISDAF, Tel Aviv.	B-2416
☐ 4X-JYJ	76	Westwind-1124N	185	927, ISDAF/195 Squadron, Tel Aviv.	N1123U
☐ 4X-JYO	76	Westwind-1124N	186	931, ISDAF/195 Squadron, Tel Aviv.	N1123R
☐ 4X-JYQ	69	B 707-344C	20110	242, ISDAF, Tel Aviv.	4X-BYQ
☐ 4X-JYR	71	Westwind-1124N	152	929, ISDAF/195 Squadron, Tel Aviv.	4X-CJC
☐ 4X-JYV	75	B 707-3L6C	21096	272, ISDAF, Tel Aviv.	P4-MDJ

5A = LIBYA   Total   8

Civil

Reg	Yr	Type	c/n	Owner/Operator	Prev Regn
☐ 5A-DAG	68	Falcon 20C	143	Air Jamahiriya, Tripoli.	F-WMKH
☐ 5A-DAJ	69	JetStar-8	5136	Libyan Air Ambulance/Ministry of Health, Tripoli.	LAAF001
☐ 5A-DAK	76	B 707-3L5C	21228	Government of Libya, Tripoli.	
☐ 5A-DCK	78	Corvette	38	Libyan Air Ambulance/Ministry of Health, Tripoli.	F-ODIF
☐ 5A-DCM	81	Falcon 50	68	Government of Libya, Tripoli.	F-WZHQ
☐ 5A-DCO	70	Falcon 20C	190	Air Jamahiriya, Tripoli.	LAAF002
☐ 5A-DDQ	70	BAC 1-11/414EG	158	Libyan Arab Airlines, Tripoli.	C5-LKI
☐ 5A-DDS	79	Gulfstream 2	242	Libyan Arab Airlines, Tripoli.	

5B = CYPRUS   Total   7

Civil

Reg	Yr	Type	c/n	Owner/Operator	Prev Regn
☐ 5B-...	66	HS 125/1A	25088	J A T Overseas Ltd. Nicosia.	N1230B
☐ 5B-CHE	68	JetStar-731	5114	Medavia Ltd. Nicosia. (status ?).	N26GL
☐ 5B-CJG	98	Astra-1125SPX	099	Columbia Ship Management Ltd. Larnaca.	N987A
☐ 5B-CKK	91	Challenger 601-3A	5094	Palmyra Aviation Ltd. Athens, Greece.	VP-BZT
☐ 5B-CKL	00	Hawker 800XP	8495	Lexata Aviation Ltd. Athens, Greece.	C-GGCH
☐ 5B-CKN	04	Falcon 50EX	339	CSM Aviation Co. Larnarca.	F-WWHU
☐ 5B-DBE	65	B 727-30	18371	Skylink Services Ltd. Larnarca.	9M-SAS

5H = TANZANIA   Total   2

Civil

Reg	Yr	Type	c/n	Owner/Operator	Prev Regn
☐ 5H-CCM	78	F 28-3000	11137	Government of Tanzania, Dar es Salaam. 'Uhuru na Umoja'	PH-ZBS
☐ 5H-ONE	03	Gulfstream G550	5030	Government of Tanzania, Dar es Salaam.	N830GA

5N = NIGERIA   Total   39

Civil

Reg	Yr	Type	c/n	Owner/Operator	Prev Regn
☐ 5N-AGV	76	Gulfstream 2	177	Federal Government of Nigeria, Lagos.	N17587
☐ 5N-AGZ	89	BAe 125/800B	8143	Aero Contractors Ltd/Central Bank, Lagos.	5N-NPF
☐ 5N-ALH	66	HS 125/1B	25089	Aero Contractors Ltd. Lagos.	OO-SKJ
☐ 5N-AOC	81	Learjet 25D	25D-322	AIC Co Ltd. Ibadan. (stored Dusseldorf since 11/00).	
☐ 5N-APN	75	Citation	500-0286	Nigerian Police Force, Lagos.	N286CC
☐ 5N-AVK	82	HS 125/700B	7160	Federal Civil Aviation Authority, Lagos.	G-5-19
☐ 5N-AVM	82	Citation 1/SP	501-0233	Federal Civil Aviation Authority, Lagos.	N26264
☐ 5N-AVV	67	HS 125/3B	25138	Intercontinental Airlines Ltd. Lagos.	I-BOGI
☐ 5N-AYA	90	Citation II	550-0632	Federal Government of Nigeria, Lagos.	N12570
☐ 5N-BBF	69	B 727-231	20049	Aviation Development Co/ADC Airlines, Lagos.	N44316
☐ 5N-BBG	69	B 727-231	20050	Aviation Development Co/ADC Airlines, Lagos.	N74317
Reg	Yr	Type	c/n	Owner/Operator	Prev Regn

Reg	Yr	Type	c/n	Owner/Operator	Prev Regn
☐ 5N-BCI	73	Citation	500-0085	AshakaCem plc. Lagos.	(N64AJ)
☐ 5N-BEL	85	Citation S/II	S550-0079	Air Logistics/Airlog,	N97LB
☐ 5N-BEX	83	HS 125/700A	7197	Executive Jet Services Ltd. Lagos.	(N2QL)
☐ 5N-BGR	01	Learjet 45	45-163	Capital Aviation Services BV. Kaduna.	N427BX
☐ 5N-BPC	81	HS 125/700A	NA0305	Associated Aviation Ltd. Lagos.	N305TH
☐ 5N-CCC	66	BAC 1-11/401AK	069	Kabo Air, Kano.	VR-CCS
☐ 5N-DAO	82	HS 125/700A	NA0329	Associated Aviation Ltd. Lagos.	N190WC
☐ 5N-EAS	70	HS 125/403B	25217	Executive Airline Services Ltd. Lagos.	G-ULFR
☐ 5N-EMA	76	HS 125/600A	6069	Southern Airlines Ltd. Lagos.	N369TS
☐ 5N-FGE	90	Falcon 900	96	Federal Government of Nigeria, Lagos.	5N-OIL
☐ 5N-FGN	82	B 727-2N5	22825	Federal Government of Nigeria, Lagos.	5N-AGY
☐ 5N-FGO	88	Falcon 900	52	Federal Government of Nigeria, Lagos.	F-WWFC
☐ 5N-FGP	90	Gulfstream 4	1126	Federal Government of Nigeria, Lagos.	N426GA
☐ 5N-FGR	92	BAe 1000B	9018	Federal Government of Nigeria, Lagos.	G-5-741
☐ 5N-FGS	01	Gulfstream V	643	Federal Government of Nigeria, Lagos.	N523GA
☐ 5N-GGG	68	BAC 1-11/423ET	154	Kabo Air, Kano.	G-BEJW
☐ 5N-MAO	82	HS 125/700A	NA0332	King Airlines & Travel Ltd. Lagos.	N332WE
☐ 5N-MAY	76	HS 125/600B	6062	King Airlines & Travel Ltd. Lagos.	G-TMAS
☐ 5N-MAZ	82	HS 125/700B	7169	King Airlines & Travel Ltd. Lagos.	B-HSS
☐ 5N-MBM	66	BAC 1-11/401AK	068	Albarka Air Services, Abuja. (status ?).	N263PC
☐ 5N-NPC	88	BAe 125/800B	8109	Aero Contractors Ltd/Nigerian National Petroleum Co. Lagos.	G-5-104
☐ 5N-NPF	80	Citation II	550-0125	Nigerian Police Force, Lagos.	N125RR
☐ 5N-SPE	01	Dornier Do328JET	3151	Shell Petroleum Ltd. Lagos.	D-BDXT
☐ 5N-SPM	01	Dornier Do328JET	3141	Shell Petroleum Ltd. Lagos.	D-BDXR
☐ 5N-SPN	99	Dornier Do328JET	3120	Shell Petroleum Ltd. Lagos.	D-BABA
☐ 5N-VVV	66	BAC 1-11/401AK	080	Kabo Air, Kano. (status ?).	HZ-BL1
☐ 5N-WMA	68	HS 125/400B	25178	World Mission Agency, Lagos. (status ?).	G-OOSP
☐ 5N-YET	73	HS 125/600A	6013	Associated Aviation Ltd. Lagos.	VR-CDG

5R = MADAGASCAR
Total 4

Civil

☐ 5R-MBR	75	Corvette	16	Aeromarine, Antananarivo-Ivato.	5R-MVN
☐ 5R-MHF	80	Citation II/SP	551-0171	Ste Henri Fraise Fils et Cie, Tananarive-Ivato.	ZS-PMC
☐ 5R-MHK	76	Corvette	34	Trimeta SA. Ivato.	CN-TCS

Military

☐ 5R-MRM		B 737-3Z9	24081	Government of Madagascar, Ivato.	OE-ILG

5T = MAURITANIA
Total 1

Civil

☐ 5T-CJP	79	B 727-294	22044	Government of Mauritania, Nouakchott.	ZS-OBM

5U = NIGER
Total 1

Military

☐ 5U-BAG	78	B 737-2N9C	21499	Government of Niger Republic, Niamey. 'Monts Baghezan'	(5U-MAF)

5V = TOGO
Total 2

Civil

☐ 5V-TAI	74	F 28-1000	11079	Government of Togo, Lome.	5V-MAB
☐ 5V-TGE	74	B 707-3L6B	21049	Government of Togo, Lome.	P4-TBN

5X = UGANDA
Total 1

Civil

☐ 5X-UEF	00	Gulfstream 4SP	1413	Government of Uganda, Kampala.	N413GA

5Y = KENYA
Total 3

Civil

☐ 5Y-MNG	99	Citation Bravo	550-0876	Phoenix Aviation Ltd. Nairobi.	N876CB
☐ 5Y-TWE	88	Citation II	550-0569	Transworld Safaris (K) Ltd. Nairobi.	G-OSNB

Military

☐ KAF308	95	Fokker 70	11557	Government of Kenya, Nairobi.	PH-MXM

6V = SENEGAL
Total 1

Civil

☐ 6V-AEF	75	B 727-2M1	21091	Government of Senegal, Dakar. 'Pointe de Sangomar'	N40104

7O = YEMEN
Total 2

Civil

☐ 7O-ADC	85	BAe 125/800B	8037	Sunrise Trading, Sana'a. 'Anisa IV'.	4W-ACN
☐ 7O-YMN	79	B 747SP-27	21786	Government of Yemen, Sana'a.	A7-AHM

Reg	Yr	Type		c/n	Owner/Operator	Prev Regn

7P = LESOTHO — Total 2

Civil

Reg	Yr	Type	c/n	Owner/Operator	Prev Regn
☐ 7P-DPT	65	B 727-30	18370	Aero Africa, Maseru.	3D-DPT
☐ 7P-TCB	69	Gulfstream 2B	73	David Topokh, Pietersburg, RSA.	3D-TCB

7Q = MALAWI — Total 1

Military

Reg	Yr	Type	c/n	Owner/Operator	Prev Regn
☐ MAAW-J1	86	BAe 125/800B	8064	Government of Malawi, Zomba.	G-5-514

7T = ALGERIA — Total 8

Civil

Reg	Yr	Type	c/n	Owner/Operator	Prev Regn
☐ 7T-VCW	82	HS 125/700B	7163	E.N. pour l'Exploitation Meteorlogique et Aeronautique.	G-5-12
☐ 7T-VHP	79	JetStar 2	5233	Government of Palestine, Gaza.	YI-AKA
☐ 7T-VVL	68	HS 125/3B	25131	Sahara Airlines, Algiers.	3A-MDE

Military

Reg	Yr	Type	c/n	Owner/Operator	Prev Regn
☐ 7T-VPC	00	Gulfstream 4SP	1418	Government of Algeria, Algiers.	N418GA
☐ 7T-VPG	00	Gulfstream V	617	Government of Algeria, Algiers.	N5G
☐ 7T-VPM	00	Gulfstream 4SP	1421	Government of Algeria, Algiers.	N421GA
☐ 7T-VPR	96	Gulfstream 4SP	1288	Government of Algeria, Algiers.	N403GA
☐ 7T-VPS	96	Gulfstream 4SP	1291	Government of Algeria, Algiers.	N412GA

8P = BARBADOS — Total 1

Civil

Reg	Yr	Type	c/n	Owner/Operator	Prev Regn
☐ 8P-MAK	98	Gulfstream V	537	Augusto Lopez/Helicol SA. Bogota, Colombia.	N537GA

9A = CROATIA — Total 1

Civil

Reg	Yr	Type	c/n	Owner/Operator	Prev Regn
☐ 9A-CRO	96	Challenger 604	5322	Government of Croatia/Republika Hrvatska, Zagreb.	N604CL

9G = GHANA — Total 2

Military

Reg	Yr	Type	c/n	Owner/Operator	Prev Regn
☐ G-530	77	F 28-3000	11125	Government/Ghana Air Force, Accra.	PH-ZBP
☐ G-540	86	Gulfstream 3	493	Government/Ghana Air Force, Accra.	N40QJ

9H = MALTA — Total 1

Civil

Reg	Yr	Type	c/n	Owner/Operator	Prev Regn
☐ 9H-AEE	99	Learjet 60	60-170	Government of Malta/Eurojet Ltd. Luqa.	D-COWS

9K = KUWAIT — Total 6

Civil

Reg	Yr	Type	c/n	Owner/Operator	Prev Regn
☐ 9K-AHI	84	Airbus A300C-620	344	Government of Kuwait, Kuwait City.	PK-MAY
☐ 9K-AJD	98	Gulfstream V	560	Kuwait Airways Corp. Kuwait City.	N660GA
☐ 9K-AJE	99	Gulfstream V	569	Kuwait Airways Corp. Kuwait City.	N469GA
☐ 9K-AJF	99	Gulfstream V	573	Kuwait Airways Corp. Kuwait City.	N673GA
☐ 9K-AKD	03	Airbus A320-212	2046	Government of Kuwait, Kuwait City. 'Al-Mobarakiya'	F-WWBG
☐ 9K-ALD	93	Airbus A310-308	648	Government of Kuwait, Kuwait City. 'Al-Salmiya'	F-WWCR

9M = MALAYSIA — Total 11

Civil

Reg	Yr	Type	c/n	Owner/Operator	Prev Regn
☐ 9M-ABC	96	Gulfstream 4SP	1312	Flightplan Jet Club Ltd/T Ananda Krishnan, Kuala Lumpur.	N453GA
☐ 9M-AZZ	92	BAe 125/800B	8219	Government of Sarawak/Hornbill Skyways, Kuching.	G-5-740
☐ 9M-BCR	66	Falcon 20C	35	F R Aviation Ltd. Hurn, UK.	N809P
☐ 9M-BDK	75	Falcon 20EW	304	F R Aviation Ltd. Hurn, UK.	G-FRAD
☐ 9M-CAL	94	Learjet 60	60-034	Civil Aviation Directorate, Kuala Lumpur.	N5034Z
☐ 9M-FCL	95	Learjet 60	60-072	Department of Civil Aviation, Kuala Lumpur.	N5072L
☐ 9M-ISJ	89	Gulfstream 4	1106	Government of Johore, Johore Bahru.	N17608

Military

Reg	Yr	Type	c/n	Owner/Operator	Prev Regn
☐ M28-01	75	F 28-1000	11088	9M-EBE, TUDM, 2 Sku, Subang.	FM2101
☐ M37-01	88	Falcon 900	64	9M-..., TUDM, 2 Sku, Subang.	N446FJ
☐ M48-02	02	Global Express	9096	TUDM, 2 Sku, Subang.	M52-01
☐ M53-01	99	BBJ-7H6	29274	TUDM, 2 Sku, Subang.	9M-BBJ

9Q = CONGO KINSHASA — Total 4

Civil

Reg	Yr	Type	c/n	Owner/Operator	Prev Regn
☐ 9Q-CBC	71	HS 125/F600B	25258	SCIBE Airlift, Kinshasa.	TL-ADK
☐ 9Q-CDC	66	B 727-30	18934	Democratic Republic of Congo, Kinshasa. 'Hewa Bora'	9Q-RDZ
☐ 9Q-CGF	74	HS 125/600B	6031	Forrest Industries, Lumbumbashi.	9Q-CFW
☐ 9Q-CPR	71	HS 125/403B	25247	Shabair SPRL. Lumbumbashi.	9Q-CSN

Reg	Yr	Type	c/n	Owner/Operator		Prev Regn
9U = **BURUNDI**					**Total** 1	
Civil						
☐ 9U-BTB	81	Falcon 50	66	Government of Burundi, Bujumbura.		N4413N
9XR = **RWANDA**					**Total** 1	
Civil						
☐ 9XR-CH		Caravelle 3	209	Government of Rwanda, Kigali.		F-RIJFM

*** Denotes reserved registration**

Total Bizjets	13883

Business Jets - Written Off /Withdrawn From Use

A4O = OMAN
Civil

Reg	Yr	Type	c/n	Owner/Operator	Prev Regn
☐ A4O-AB		VC 10-1103	820	Wfu. Displayed at Brooklands Museum, Weybridge, UK.	G-ASIX

A6 = UNITED ARAB EMIRATES
Civil

Reg	Yr	Type	c/n	Owner/Operator	Prev Regn
☐ A6-SHK	1987	BAe 146 Statesman	E1091	Wfu. Located Bournemouth-Hurn UK.	G-BOMA

B = CHINA
Civil

Reg	Yr	Type	c/n	Owner/Operator	Prev Regn
☐ B-7023	1992	Citation VI	650-0221	W/o Xichang, China. 2 Sep 02.	B-4107

B = CHINA - TAIWAN
Civil

Reg	Yr	Type	c/n	Owner/Operator	Prev Regn
☐ B-98181	1993	Learjet 35A	35A-675	W/o target towing Eastern Taiwan. 17 Sep 94.	N2602M

Military

Reg	Yr	Type	c/n	Owner/Operator	Prev Regn
☐ 18351	1961	B 720-051B	18351	Wfu. Preserved at Kangshan AB Museum, Taiwan.	N721US
☐ 2721	1967	B 727-109	19399	Wfu.	B-1818
☐ 2722	1967	B 727-109	19520	Wfu. Located Taiching, Taiwan.	B-1820
☐ 2723	1969	B 727-109C	20111	Wfu. Located Nankang, Taiwan.	B-1822
☐ 2724	1967	B 727 121C	19818	Wfu.	B-188

C = CANADA
Civil

Reg	Yr	Type	c/n	Owner/Operator	Prev Regn
☐ C-FBCL	1972	Citation	500-0042	Wfu. Cx C- 6/97.	N542CC
☐ CF-BRL	1972	Sabre-40A	282-107	W/o Frobisher Bay, NT. Canada. 27 Feb 74.	N40NR
☐ C-FCFL	1970	HS 125/400A	NA741	W/o Labrador, NF. Canada. 9 Dec 77.	G-AXTT
☐ CF-CFL	1969	HS 125/400A	NA725	W/o Labrador, NF, Canada. 11 Nov 69.	
☐ C-FDTF	1966	JetStar-6	5088	Wfu. Located Atlantic Canada Museum Halifax, NS.	N9244R
☐ C-FDTX	1961	JetStar-6	5018	Wfu. Located Rockcliffe Museum, Ottawa, ON. Canada.	N9287R
☐ C-FEYG	1966	Jet Commander	81	W/o Winnipeg, MT. Canada. 26 May 78.	CF-KBI
☐ C-FHLL	1965	HS 125/1A	25034	Wfu. Accident 4/83. Wing fitted to s/n 25027. YHU 10/95.	
☐ C-FMTC	1966	HS 125/1A-522	25104	Wfu. Parts at Lakeland, Fl. USA.	N140AK
☐ C-FMWW	1982	Westwind-Two	380	W/o Meadowlake, SK. Canada. 27 Jan 94.	N380DA
☐ C-FRBC	1973	JetStar-8	5160	Wfu. Parted out 1988.	(N60EE)
☐ C-FSKC	1972	Citation	500-0018	W/o Rawlins, Wy. USA. 25 Jul 98.	N70841
☐ C-FTBZ	1994	Challenger 604	5991	W/o Wichita, Ks. USA. 10 Oct 00. (prototype Ff 18 Sep 94).	C-GLYA
☐ C-GBRW	1973	Learjet 36	36-001	Wfu. Cx C- 4/97. College of Aeronautics, Montreal St Hubert.	N26GL
☐ C-GBWA	1973	Learjet 24D	24D-261	Wfu. Located Detroit-Willow Run, Mi. USA.	D-COOL
☐ C-GCGR-X	1978	Challenger 600	1001	W/o Mojave, Ca. USA. 3 Apr 80.	
☐ C-GESZ	1972	Citation	500-0022	Wfu.	N800JD
☐ C-GKHA	1965	Falcon 20C	19	Wfu. Last located Ottawa-Rockcliffe, Canada. Cx C- 4/04.	(N41PD)
☐ C-GMEA	1968	HS 125/3A-RA	NA702	Wfu. Located Arnoni Aviation Inc. Houston, Tx. USA.	N813PR
☐ C-GNVT	1979	Falcon 10	138	W/o Kuujjuaq, PQ. Canada. 14 Aug 01.	N236DJ
☐ C-GPUN	1976	Learjet 35	35-058	W/o Queen Charlotte Island, BC. Canada. 11 Jan 95.	
☐ C-GWPB	1967	Falcon 20C	92	Wfu. Located B C Institute of Technology, Vancouver, Canada.	117503
☐ C-GXFZ	1972	Citation	500-0032	W/o Orillia, ON. Canada. 26 Sep 84.	(N5364U)
☐ C-GYCJ	1987	Citation II	550-0561	W/o Sandspit, BC. Canada. 12 Nov 02.	N234RA

Military

Reg	Yr	Type	c/n	Owner/Operator	Prev Regn
☐ 144612	1979	Challenger 600S	1002	Wfu. Located at Heritage Park, Winnipeg, Mt. Canada.	C-GCGS-X
☐ 144613	1984	Challenger 601	3035	W/o Shearwater, NS. Canada. 24 Apr 95.	C-GCUN

CC = CHILE
Military

Reg	Yr	Type	c/n	Owner/Operator	Prev Regn
☐ E-302	1984	Citation III	650-0033	W/o Concepcion, Chile. 9 Jul 92.	CC-ECE

D = GERMANY
Civil

Reg	Yr	Type	c/n	Owner/Operator	Prev Regn
☐ D-ASDB	1977	VFW 614	G19	Wfu. Located RAF St Athan, UK.	OY-RRW
☐ D-AXDB	1977	VFW 614	G18	Wfu. Located Nordholtz, Germany.	(OY-RGT)
☐ D-CARA	1966	HFB 320	1021	Wfu. Cx D- 3 Jul 84. Displayed at Finkenwerder, Germany.	
☐ D-CARE	1966	HFB 320	1022	Wfu. Located at Finow Museum, Germany.	
☐ D-CARY	1967	HFB 320	1026	Wfu. Located Laatzen Museum, Hanover, Germany.	TC-FNS
☐ D-CASH	1987	Citation II	550-0564	W/o Salzburg, Austria. 19 Feb 96.	N674CA
☐ D-CASY	1968	HFB 320	1029	W/o Blackpool, UK. 29 Jun 72.	
☐ D-CATY	1977	Learjet 35A	35A-114	W/o Moscow, Russia. 15 Dec 94.	(N851L)
☐ D-CBNA	1967	Falcon 20C	63	W/o Narsarsuaq, Greenland. 4 Aug 01.	PH-LPS
☐ D-CBUR	1977	Falcon 10	98	W/o Friesenheim, Germany. 8 Aug 96.	F-WPXG

Reg	Yr	Type	c/n	Owner/Operator	Prev Regn

Reg	Yr	Type	c/n	Owner/Operator	Prev Regn
☐ D-CDFA	1975	Learjet 36	36-006	W/o Libya. 26 Mar 80.	D-CAFO
☐ D-CDPD	1974	Learjet 25B	25B-177	W/o North Atlantic. 18 May 83.	N74SW
☐ D-CHFB	1964	HFB 320	V1	W/o Torrejon, Spain. 12 May 65.	
☐ D-CHVB	1989	Citation II	550-0629	W/o Allendorf, Germany 25 Jan 95.	N1256T
☐ D-CIRO	1969	HFB 320	1044	W/o Texel Island, Netherlands. 18 Dec 70.	
☐ D-CLOU	1964	HFB 320	V2	Wfu. Located at Deutsches Museum, Munich, Germany.	
☐ D-COCO	1982	Learjet 35A	35A-466	W/o Cologne-Bonn, Germany. 7 Jun 93. (parts at Dodsons, Ks)	N600WJ
☐ D-COSA	1971	HFB 320	1056	Wfu. Located Niederaltaich, Germany.	
☐ D-IAEC	1981	Citation 1/SP	501-0203	W/o Blankensee Airport, Lubeck, Germany. 31 May 87.	N67830
☐ D-IEVX	2001	CitationJet CJ-2	525A-0036	W/o Milan, Italy. 8 Oct 01.	N5246Z
☐ D-IHAQ	1965	Learjet 23	23-007	W/o Zurich, Switzerland. 12 Dec 65.	N826L
☐ D-IHLZ	1970	Learjet 24B	24B-225	W/o Mariensiel, Germany. 18 Jun 73.	N618R
☐ D-IJHM	1980	Citation II/SP	551-0033	W/o Kassel, Germany. 19 May 82.	N88692
☐ D-IMMM	2001	CitationJet CJ-1	525-0460	W/o Florence, Italy. 12 Mar 04.	N5185V
Military					
☐ 10+01	1968	B 707-307C	19997	Wfu. to NATO as LX-N19997.	(68-11071)
☐ 10+02	1968	B 707-307C	19998	Wfu. to USAF for E-8C J-STARS.	(68-11072)
☐ 10+04	1968	B 707-307C	20000	Wfu. to NATO as LX-N20000.	(68-11074)
☐ 16+06	1969	HFB 320	1048	Wfu. Located Luftwaffe Museum Gatow-Berlin, Germany.	D-CISI
☐ 16+08	1966	HFB 320	1025	Wfu. Located Manching, Germany.	D-9537
☐ 16+22	1976	HFB 320	1059	W/o Schwabmuenchen, Germany. 27 Nov 76.	98+25
☐ 16+26	1979	HFB 320ECM	1063	Wfu. Located Luftwaffe Museum Gatow-Berlin, Germany.	D-CANU
☐ CA+102	1962	JetStar-6	5035	W/o Bremen, Germany. 16 Jan 68.	(62-12167)

EC = SPAIN

Civil

Reg	Yr	Type	c/n	Owner/Operator	Prev Regn
☐ EC-CGG	1973	Citation	500-0108	W/o Barcelona, Spain. 22 Nov 74.	N108CC
☐ EC-CKR	1975	Learjet 25B	25B-184	W/o Northolt, UK. 13 Aug 96.	
☐ EC-DFA	1978	Learjet 35A	35A-196	W/o Palma, Spain. 13 Aug 80.	HB-VFU
☐ EC-DQC	1976	Corvette	24	Wfu. Sold as spares 2/91.	F-BVPI
☐ EC-DQE	1976	Corvette	26	Wfu. Cx EC- 8/97, Fuselage at Dieupentale, France.	F-GDAY
☐ EC-DQG	1976	Corvette	27	W/o Cordoba, Spain. 25 Nov 00.	F-BVPH
☐ EC-ECB	1969	Falcon 20DC	210	W/o Las Palmas, Canary Islands. 30 Sep 87.	N66VG
☐ EC-EFI	1968	Falcon 20D	189	W/o Nr Keflavik, Iceland. 11 Oct 87.	N444BF
☐ EC-EGS	1974	HS 125/600A	6034	Wfu. Parts at Spirit of St Louis, Mo. USA.	EC-115
☐ EC-EGT	1966	HS 125/1A-522	25080	Wfu. Parts at Dodsons, Rantoul, Ks. USA.	N23KL
☐ EC-EHF	1973	HS 125/600A	6011	Wfu. Parts at Dodsons, Rantoul, Ks. USA .	N81D
☐ EC-EKK	1967	Falcon 20C	106	Wfu. Located Madrid-Barajas, Spain.	N31V
☐ EC-FGX	1965	JetStar-731	5062	Wfu. Cx USA 5/97.	EC-697

EI = EIRE

Military

Reg	Yr	Type	c/n	Owner/Operator	Prev Regn
☐ 236	1971	HS 125/F600B	25256	W/o Casement-Dublin, Ireland. 27 Nov 79.	G-AYBH

EL = LIBERIA

Civil

Reg	Yr	Type	c/n	Owner/Operator	Prev Regn
☐ EL-VDY	1971	Falcon 20E	245	Wfu. Parts at Dodsons, Rantoul, Ks. USA.	HB-VDY

EP = IRAN

Civil

Reg	Yr	Type	c/n	Owner/Operator	Prev Regn
☐ EP-AGX	1973	Falcon 20E	283	W/o Kermanshah, Iran. 21 Nov 74.	F-WRQS
Military					
☐ 5-3020	1976	Falcon 20E	348	W/o Ardebil, Iran. 3 March 97.	5-4039
☐ 5-9001	1976	Falcon 20F	351	W/o Iran. 15 Feb 91.	F-WMKJ
☐ 5-9002	1976	Falcon 20F	353	W/o Iran. 31 Jan 91.	F-WRQP

F = FRANCE

Civil

Reg	Yr	Type	c/n	Owner/Operator	Prev Regn
☐ F-BJET	1959	MS 760 Paris-1A	39	Wfu. Located Reims-Prunay, France.	F-WJAA
☐ F-BKMF	1964	HS 125/1	25007	W/o Nice, France. 5 Jun 66.	HB-VAH
☐ F-BLKL	1964	MS 760 Paris-3	01	Wfu. Located Reims-Prunay, France.	F-WLKL
☐ F-BMSS	1965	Falcon 20F	2	Wfu.	F-WMSS
☐ F-BRNL	1969	Learjet 24B	24B-183	W/o Toulouse, France. 18 Dec 85.	OY-AGZ
☐ F-BSQN	1972	Falcon 10	03	Wfu. CoA expiry 4/81.	F-WSQN
☐ F-BSRL	1969	Learjet 24B	24B-210	W/o Provins Nr Paris, France. 10 Jun 85.	ZS-LLG
☐ F-BSTM	1965	AC 680V-TU	1540-6	Wfu. Cx F- 18 Nov 91. Museum exhibit Pelegry-Perpignan.	F-WSTM
☐ F-BTTU	1977	Corvette	37	W/o St Yan, France. 31 Jul 90.	
☐ F-BUQN	1973	Corvette	3	W/o Toulouse, France. 16 Oct 00.	F-WUQN
☐ F-BUQP	1974	Corvette	4	Wfu. Located Toulouse-Blagnac, France.	F-WUQP

Reg	Yr	Type	c/n	Owner/Operator	Prev Regn

Reg	Yr	Type	c/n	Owner/Operator	Prev Regn
☐ F-BVPB	1974	Corvette	6	Wfu. Cx F- 26 Nov 99. Located Paris-Le Bourget, France.	F-OGJL
☐ F-BXPT	1965	Learjet 23	23-014	Wfu. CoA expiry 11 Mar 93. Cx F- 10/00.	(HB-VEL)
☐ F-BXQL	1961	MS 760 Paris-2B	105	Wfu. Located at Reims-Prunay, France.	N760Q
☐ F-GAMA	1965	Learjet 23	23-023	Wfu. Located Perigeux Technical school, France.	HB-VEL
☐ F-GAPY	1965	Learjet 23	23-027	Wfu. at White Industries, Bates City, Mo. USA.	(N108TW)
☐ F-GBTC	1978	Falcon 10	124	W/o Chalons-Vatry Nr Paris, France. 15 Jan 86.	F-WPUY
☐ F-GDAE	1966	Falcon 24	24-105	Wfu. Last located Allibaudiere, Troyes, France.	TR-LYB
☐ F-GDAV	1965	Learjet 23	23-017	W/o Lisbon, Portugal. 30 Jan 89.	F-GBTA
☐ F-GDHR	1982	Learjet 55	55-070	W/o Nr Jakiri, Cameroun. 5 Feb 87.	
☐ F-GHLN	1972	Falcon 20E	255	W/o Paris-Le Bourget, France. 20 Jan 95.	VH-MIQ
☐ F-GJCC	1967	Falcon 20C	72	Wfu. Last located Middletown, Oh, USA.	(N172MV)
☐ F-GJGB	1975	Falcon 10	47	W/o Besancon, France. 30 Sep 93.	N79PB
☐ F-GJHK	1977	Falcon 10	108	W/o Brest, France. 26 Mar 92.	(F-GFJK)
☐ F-GJMA	1978	Falcon 10	116	W/o Madrid, Spain. 27 Sep 96.	N525RC
☐ F-GKPP	1961	MS 760 Paris-2	98	W/o Calvi, Corsica. Oct 91.	3A-MPP
☐ F-WAMD		Falcon 30	01	Wfu. Located Vitrolles Engineering University, Marseille.	
☐ F-WDFJ	1977	Falcon 20G	362	Wfu. Located Istres, France. (20G prototype).	F-WATF
☐ F-WFAL	1970	Falcon 10	01	W/o Romorantin-Loire Valley, France. 31 Oct 72.	
☐ F-WLKB	1963	Falcon 20C	01	Wfu. Located Musee de l'Air, Paris-Le Bourget	F-BLKB
☐ F-WMSH	1965	Falcon 20C	1	Wfu. Donated to Rene Lemaire for Bordeaux-Merignac museum.	F-ZACV
☐ F-WNDB	1976	Falcon 50	1	Wfu. Displayed Conservatoire de l'Air et l'Espace, Bordeaux.	F-BNDB
☐ F-WRSN	1970	Corvette	01	W/o Marseilles, France. 23 Mar 71.	(F-WSSE)
☐ F-WZIH	1966	HFB 320	1024	Wfu. at Musee de l'Air, Paris-Le Bourget, France.	16+07

Military

Reg	Yr	Type	c/n	Owner/Operator	Prev Regn
☐ 141	1963	Caravelle 3	141	Wfu. Located at Musee de l'Air, Paris-Le Bourget, France.	F-BJTK
☐ 154	1968	Falcon 20C	154	W/o Rambouillet, France. 22 Jan 76.	F-WLCV
☐ 39	1975	Falcon 10MER	39	W/o Toul-Rosieres, France. 30 Jan 80.	F-WPUX
☐ F-RHFA	1966	Falcon 20C	49	Wfu. Located at Villacoublay, Paris, France.	F-TEOA
☐ F-UGWP	1975	Falcon 20E	309	W/o Nr Villacoublay-Paris, France. 2 Dec 91.	F-RAFU
☐ F-ZACB	1971	Falcon 10	02	Wfu. Located ENSAE at Lespinet near Toulouse, France.	F-ZJTA

G   = GREAT BRITAIN

Civil

Reg	Yr	Type	c/n	Owner/Operator	Prev Regn
☐ G-ARVF		VC 10-1101	808	Wfu. Located Hermeskiel collection Nr Trier, Germany	
☐ G-ARYA	1962	HS 125/1	25001	Wfu. Located London Colney museum, Herts, UK.	
☐ G-ARYB	1962	HS 125/1	25002	Wfu. Located Midlands Air Museum, Coventry, UK.	
☐ G-ARYC	1963	HS 125/1	25003	Wfu. Located Mosquito Aircraft Museum, Hatfield, UK.	
☐ G-ASNU	1964	HS 125/1	25005	Wfu. Cx G- 18 Nov 91. Last located Lagos, Nigeria .	D-COMA
☐ G-ASSM	1965	HS 125/1-522	25010	Wfu. Located Kensington Science Museum, London, UK.	G-ASSM
☐ G-ATPD	1966	HS 125/1B-522	25085	Wfu. Located Bournemouth-Hurn, UK.	5N-AGU
☐ G-ATPE	1966	HS 125/1B-522	25092	Wfu. Cx G- 14 Mar 90.	
☐ G-AVGW	1967	HS 125/3B	25120	W/o Luton, UK. 23 Dec 67.	
☐ G-AXDM	1969	HS 125/403B	25194	Wfu. Located Farnborough, UK. Cx G- 11/03.	
☐ G-AXPS	1967	HS 125/3B	25135	W/o Edinburgh, Scotland. 20 Jul 70.	HB-VAY
☐ G-AZCH	1969	HS 125/3B-RA	25154	Wfu. Central fuselage in use as a mobile display, Luton, UK.	EP-AHK
☐ G-BBRT	1974	HS 125/600B	6036	Wfu. Fuselage used in paint spraying trials, Chester, UK.	
☐ G-BCUX	1974	HS 125/600B	6043	W/o Dunsfold, UK. 20 Nov 75.	
☐ G-BKBH	1975	HS 125/600B	6052	Wfu. Cx G- 15 Jul 99. Located Southampton, UK.	5N-DNL
☐ G-BKRL	1988	Leopard	001	Wfu. Cx G- 1/99.	
☐ G-BOCB	1966	HS 125/1B-522	25106	Wfu. Cx G- 22 Feb 95.	G-OMCA
☐ G-BPCP	1980	Citation	500-0403	W/o Jersey, Channel Islands. 1 Oct 80.	N1710E
☐ G-DBAL	1966	HS 125/3B	25117	Wfu. Cx G- 4/93.	G-BSAA
☐ C-EXLR	1990	BAe 1000B	8151	Wfu. Instructional airframe at Raytheon, Wichita, Ks. USA.	
☐ G-FIVE	1963	HS 125/1	25004	Wfu. Wings used in rebuild of s/n 25008, but not finalised.	G-ASEC
☐ G-GMAC	1988	Gulfstream 4	1058	W/o Teterboro, NJ. USA. 1 Dec 04.	VP-BME
☐ G-JETB	1981	Citation II	550-0288	W/o Southampton, UK. 26 May 1993.	G-MAMA
☐ G-JSAX	1969	HS 125/3B-RA	25157	Wfu. Broken up 4/86 at Southampton, UK.	G-GGAE
☐ G-LORI	1971	HS 125/403B	25246	Wfu. at Lagos, Nigeria.	G-AYOJ
☐ G-MURI	1988	Learjet 35A	35A-646	W/o Lyon-Satolas, France. 2 May 00.	N712JB
☐ G-OBOB	1966	HS 125/3B	25069	W/o Columbia, Mo. USA. 30 Jan 89. (parts at White Inds.).	G-BAXL
☐ G-OHEA	1967	HS 125/3B-RA	25144	Wfu. Cx G- 6/94. Last located Cranfield, UK.	G-AVRG
☐ G-OMGB	1974	HS 125/600B	6039	Wfu. at Luton, UK. TT 6944. Parts at Hooks Airport, Tx. USA.	EC-EAO
☐ G-OMGC	1975	HS 125/600B	6056	Wfu. at Luton, UK. TT 6404. Parts at Hooks Airport, Tx. USA.	G-BKCD
☐ G-TACE	1970	HS 125/403B	25223	Wfu. Cx G-1 /90. Last located Dunsfold, UK.	G-AYIZ
☐ G-UESS	1976	Citation	500-0326	W/o Stornaway, Scotland. 8 Dec 83.	N45LC
☐ G-YUGO	1966	HS 125/1B-522	25094	Wfu. Cx G- 3/93. Last located Biggin Hill, UK.	G-ATWH

Reg	Yr	Type	c/n	Owner/Operator	Prev Regn

Military

Reg	Yr	Type	c/n	Owner/Operator	Prev Regn
❏ XS710/O	1965	Dominie T1	25012	Wfu. Instructional airframe as 9259M, RAF Cosford, UK.	XS710
❏ XS714/P	1966	Dominie T1	25054	Wfu. Fire school RAF Manston, UK.	
❏ XS726/T	1965	Dominie T1	25044	Wfu. Instructional airframe as 9273M, RAF Cosford, UK.	
❏ XS729/G	1965	Dominie T1	25049	Wfu. Instructional airframe as 9275M, RAF Cosford, UK.	
❏ XS732/B	1966	Dominie T1	25056	Wfu.	
❏ XS733/Q	1966	Dominie T1	25059	Wfu. Instructional airframe as 9276M, RAF Cosford, UK.	
❏ XS734/N	1966	Dominie T1	25061	Wfu. Instructional airframe as 9260M, RAF Cosford, UK.	
❏ XS735/R	1966	Dominie T2	25071	Wfu. Instructional airframe at RAF St Athan, UK.	
❏ XS738/U	1966	Dominie T1	25077	Wfu. Instructional airframe as 9274M, RAF Cosford, UK.	
❏ XW930	1966	HS 125/1	25009	Wfu. Located Jordan's scrapyard Portsmouth, UK.	G-ATPC
❏ ZF130	1976	HS 125/600B	6059	Wfu.	(9M-DMF)

HB = SWITZERLAND

Civil

Reg	Yr	Type	c/n	Owner/Operator	Prev Regn
❏ HB-PAA	1960	MS 760 Paris	69	Wfu. Cx HB- 25 Jun 84. Located Montelimar-Ancone.	J-4117
❏ HB-VAM	1965	Learjet 23	23-044	W/o Innsbruck, Austria. 28 Aug 72.	N22B
❏ HB-VAP	1966	Falcon 20C	37	W/o Goose Bay, NF, Canada. 1 Oct 67.	(N11WA)
❏ HB-VCG	1970	Falcon 20D	231	W/o St Moritz, Switzerland. 20 Feb 72.	F-WPXE
❏ HB-VFS	1978	Learjet 36A	36A-042	W/o Zarzaitine, Algeria. 23 Sep 95.	N39391
❏ HB-VLV	1990	Citation V	560-0077	W/o Zurich, Switzerland. 20 Dec 01.	N42NA

HC = ECUADOR

Military

Reg	Yr	Type	c/n	Owner/Operator	Prev Regn
❏ AEE-402	1976	Sabre-75A	380-45	W/o Quito, Ecuador. 10 Dec 92.	FAE-045
❏ FAE-068	1966	Sabre-40R	282-68	W/o Quito, Ecuador. 3 Jun 88.	N4469N

HK = COLOMBIA

Civil

Reg	Yr	Type	c/n	Owner/Operator	Prev Regn
❏ HK-3885	1973	Citation	500-0135	W/o Pereira, Colombia. 7 Mar 97.	YV-717CP

HP = PANAMA

Military

Reg	Yr	Type	c/n	Owner/Operator	Prev Regn
❏ HP-500A	1965	B 727-44C	18894	Wfu. (to N61944 and bu). Located Opa Locka, Fl. USA.	FAP 400

HS = THAILAND

Military

Reg	Yr	Type	c/n	Owner/Operator	Prev Regn
❏ 33-333	1990	B 737-3Z6	24480	W/o Nr Khon Kaen, Thailand. 30 Mar 93.	

HZ = SAUDI ARABIA

Civil

Reg	Yr	Type	c/n	Owner/Operator	Prev Regn
❏ HZ-AA1	1973	HS 125/600B	6019	Wfu. Cx G- 3/93. Last located Dunfold, UK.	(G-FANN)
❏ HZ-ABM2	1966	BAC 1-11/401AK	060	Wfu. Last located Jeddah, Saudi Arabia.	HZ-MAA
❏ HZ-FMA	1966	HS 125/1B	25105	Wfu. Located Jeddah, Saudi Arabia.	G-AYRY
❏ HZ-FNA	1965	JetStar-8	5056	Wfu. Last located Spirit of St Louis, Mo. USA.	HZ-FK1
❏ HZ-GP5	1975	Learjet 25XR	25XR-199	W/o Narssarssuaq, Greenland. 11 Jan 82.	HZ-RI1
❏ HZ-HM2	1975	B 707-368C	21081	Wfu. Cx HZ- 8/03.	HZ-HM1
❏ HZ-TAS	1962	B 707-321B	18338	Wfu. Last located Manston, UK.	N98WS
❏ HZ-TNA	1968	JetStar-731	5120	Wfu. Last located at Geneva, Switzerland.	N40DC
❏ SA-R-7		DH Comet 4C	6461	W/o Cuneo, Italy. 20 Mar 63.	

I = ITALY

Civil

Reg	Yr	Type	c/n	Owner/Operator	Prev Regn
❏ I-AIFA	1976	Learjet 36A	36A-021	W/o Forli, Italy. 10 Dec 79.	N3524F
❏ I-ALSU	1990	Beechjet 400A	RK-11	W/o Parma, Italy. 27 Nov 91. (parts at Dodsons, Ks. USA).	N5680Z
❏ I-AMME	1975	Learjet 24D	24D-310	W/o Bari, Italy. 6 Feb 76.	HB-VDU
❏ I-AVJG	1978	Learjet 35A	35A-189	W/o Portofino, Italy. 24 Oct 99.	N727JP
❏ I-CIST	1985	Citation III	650-0085	W/o Roma-Ciampino, Italy. 4 Nov 00.	N650DA
❏ I-COTO	1979	Learjet 25D	25D-285	Wfu. Broken up 10/86 at Paris-Le Bourget, France.	N422G
❏ I-DRIB	1969	Falcon 20D	201	Wfu. CoA expiry 13 Apr 93.	D-CELL
❏ I-ERJC	2000	Learjet 45	45-093	W/o Milan, Italy. 1 Jun 03.	(PT-XLF)
❏ I-KILO	1981	Learjet 55	55-007	W/o Seville, Spain 4 Apr 94. (parts at Griffin, Ga. USA).	N41ES
❏ I-MCSA	1977	Learjet 35A	35A-099	W/o Palermo, Sicily. 22 Feb 78.	HB-VFC
❏ I-MOCO	1981	Learjet 35A	35A-445	W/o Nuremberg, Germany. 7 Feb 01.	HB-VHG
❏ I-NICK	1968	Sabre-40	282-25	Wfu. Parts at White Industries, Bates City, Mo. USA.	N40SJ
❏ I-NLAE	1968	Falcon 20C	134	W/o Kiel-Holtenau, Germany. 25 Sep 91.	N897D
❏ I-PIAI	1968	PD 808	503	W/o San Sebastian, Spain. 18 Jun 68.	
❏ I-RACE	1964	HS 125/1	25006	Wfu.	HB-VAG
❏ I-SNAF	1968	HS 125/3B	25145	Wfu.	G-AVXL
❏ I-SNAP	1961	MS 760 Paris	99	W/o Milan, Italy. 27 Oct 62.	
❏ I-VIGI	1981	Diamond 1	A013SA	W/o Parma, Italy. 15 Oct 99.	N81HH

Reg	Yr	Type	c/n	Owner/Operator	Prev Regn

Military

Reg	Yr	Type	c/n	Owner/Operator	Prev Regn
☐ MM577	1968	PD 808-TA	501	Wfu. RS-48. Located Pratica di Mare, Italy.	
☐ MM61948	1969	PD 808-VIP	506	Wfu. at Pratica di Mare, Italy.	
☐ MM61949	1969	PD 808-VIP	507	Wfu. at Pratica di Mare, Italy.	
☐ MM61951	1969	PD 808-VIP	509	Wfu. Located Pratica di Mare, Italy.	
☐ MM61952	1969	PD 808-GE2	510	Wfu. Located Pratica di Mare, Italy.	
☐ MM61953	1969	PD 808-TP	511	W/o Venice, Italy. 15 Sep 93.	
☐ MM61956	1969	PD 808-TP	514	Wfu. Located Pratica di Mare, Italy.	
☐ MM61957	1970	PD 808-TP	515	Wfu. Located Pratica di Mare, Italy.	
☐ MM61958	1970	PD 808-GE1	505	Wfu. Located Practica di Mare, Italy.	
☐ MM61959	1970	PD 808-GE1	516	Wfu. Located Pratica di Mare, Italy.	
☐ MM61960	1970	PD 808-GE1	517	Wfu. Located Pratica di Mare, Italy.	
☐ MM61961	1970	PD 808-GE1	518	Wfu. Last flight 17 May 03.	
☐ MM61962	1970	PD 808-GE1	519	Wfu. Located Pratica di Mare, Italy.	
☐ MM61963	1970	PD 808-GE1	520	Wfu. Located Ditallandia, Castel Volturno, Italy.	
☐ MM62013	1974	DC 9-32	47600	W/o ground collision Moscow-Vnukovo, Russia. 8 Feb 99.	
☐ MM62014	1970	PD 808-RM	521	Wfu. Located Pratica di Mare, Italy.	
☐ MM62015	1970	PD 808-RM	522	Wfu. Located Pratica di Mare, Italy.	I-PIAY
☐ MM62016	1970	PD 808-RM	523	Wfu. Located Pratica di Mare, Italy.	
☐ MM62017	1970	PD 808-RM	524	Wfu. Located Pratica di Maro, Italy.	

JA = JAPAN

Civil

Reg	Yr	Type	c/n	Owner/Operator	Prev Regn
☐ JA8246	1984	Diamond 1A	A092SA	W/o Sado Island, Japan. 23 Jul 86.	
☐ JA8438	1976	Citation	500-0321	Wfu. Cx JA 17 Sep 96. Located Yokohama, Japan.	N5321J

Military

Reg	Yr	Type	c/n	Owner/Operator	Prev Regn
☐ 9202	1986	Learjet U36A	36A-056	W/o Iwakuni AB. Japan. 21 May 03.	N3802G
☐ 9203	1990	Learjet U36A	36A-058	W/o Shikoku Island, Japan. 28 Feb 91.	N4290J

JY = JORDAN

Civil

Reg	Yr	Type	c/n	Owner/Operator	Prev Regn
☐ JY-AEW	1976	Learjet 35	35-052	W/o Riyadh, Saudi Arabia. 28 Apr 77.	
☐ JY-AFC	1976	Learjet 36A	36A-020	W/o Amman, Jordan. 21 Sep 77.	

LN = NORWAY

Civil

Reg	Yr	Type	c/n	Owner/Operator	Prev Regn
☐ LN-AAA	1967	Falcon 20CC	73	Wfu. Parted out at Memphis, Tn. USA.	LX-AAA
☐ LN-AAB	1965	Falcon 20C	12	Wfu. Parted out at Memphis, Tn. USA.	N51SF
☐ LN-AAE	1980	Citation II/SP	551-0245	W/o Bardufoss, Norway. 15 Nov 89.	N224CC
☐ LN-FOE	1967	Falcon 20C	62	W/o Norwich, England. 12 Dec 73.	(N17401)

LV = ARGENTINA

Civil

Reg	Yr	Type	c/n	Owner/Operator	Prev Regn
☐ LV-ALW	1981	HS 125/700B	7133	W/o Salta, Argentina. 11 Apr 85.	LV-PMM
☐ LV-JXA	1971	Learjet 24D	24D-240	Wfu. Located at Olathe Johnson/Century Airport, Ks. USA.	LV-PRB
☐ LV-MMV	1978	Learjet 25D	25D-259	W/o Posadas, Argentina. 23 Sep 89.	LV-PAW
☐ LV-RDB	1965	Jet Commander	12	W/o Moron, Argentina. 1991.	N344DA
☐ LV-TDF	1982	Learjet 35A	35A-478	W/o Ushula, Argentina. 15 May 84.	N3815G
☐ LV-WEN	1969	Jet Commander-B	126	W/o Cordoba, Argentina. 29 Sep 94.	N87DL
☐ LV-WHZ	1967	Jet Commander	108	Wfu. Located Aeroparque Buenos Aires, Argentina.	N77ST
☐ LV-WLH	1966	Falcon 20C	34	W/o Nr Salta, Argentina 7 Feb 97.	LV-PHV
☐ LV-WMR	1966	Learjet 24	24-135	W/o Pasadas. Argentina. 28 Aug 95.	N77LB
☐ LV-WND	1973	Sabre-40A	282-131	Wfu. Located San Fernando, Argentina.	N82R
☐ LV-WOF	1968	Sabre-60	306-25	Wfu. Located San Fernando, Argentina.	(OB-1550)
☐ LV-WPO	1967	Sabre-60	306-3	W/o Cordoba, Argentina. 16 Jul 98.	N160CF

Military

Reg	Yr	Type	c/n	Owner/Operator	Prev Regn
☐ 5-T-10-074		F 28-3000M	11147	Wfu. Located Ezeiza, Argentina.	PH-EXW
☐ T-24	1980	Learjet 35A	35A-333	W/o Pebble Island, Falklands, South Atlantic. 7 Jun 82.	

N = USA

Civil

Reg	Yr	Type	c/n	Owner/Operator	Prev Regn
☐ N.....	1991	Learjet 35A	35A-666	Wfu. Aircraft not built.	
☐ N1AH	1981	Learjet 35A	35A-398	W/o Great Falls, Mt. USA. 16 May 97.	N3797A
☐ N1DC	1994	Learjet 60	60-035	W/o Troy, Al. USA. 14 Jan 01.	N116AS
☐ N1DK	1974	Citation	500-0175	W/o Allegheny County, Pa. USA. 6 Jan 98.	N175CC
☐ N1EC	1966	Jet Commander	51	Wfu. Cx USA 8/94. Parts at Dodsons, Rantoul, Ks. USA.	N18JL
☐ N1EM	1966	JetStar-6	5077	W/o Chicago, Il. USA. 25 Mar 76.	N1924V
☐ N1JR	1975	Learjet 25B	25B-188	W/o Waterville, Me. USA. 28 Jul 84. (parts at White Inds.).	A40-AJ
☐ N1JS	1979	Westwind-1124	249	Wfu.	4X-CMU

Reg	Yr	Type	c/n	Owner/Operator	Prev Regn

Reg	Yr	Type	c/n	Owner/Operator	Prev Regn
☐ N1JU	1965	Jet Commander	13	Wfu. Parts at White Industries, Bates City, Mo. USA.	N1JU
☐ N1PT	1967	Jet Commander	93	Wfu. Cx USA 11/94.	(N999RA)
☐ N1R	1960	B 720-023B	18022	Wfu. To USAF 4/83 for KC-135E spares.	N7536A
☐ N1SJ	1962	Sabreliner CT-39A	276-45	Wfu. Located San Jose University, San Jose, Ca. USA.	62-4492
☐ N2CA	1979	Citation II/SP	551-0024	W/o Mountain View, Mo. USA. 18 Dec 82.	N26628
☐ N2TE	1958	MS 760 Paris	5	W/o Nr John Wayne Airport, Ca. USA. 30 Nov 96.	(N760LB)
☐ N2WU	1966	Jet Commander	72	Wfu. Located at Don Torcuato, Argentina.	VR-CAU
☐ N3MF	1966	HS 125/1A-522	25093	Wfu. Used in repair of s/n 25271.	N306L
☐ N3QL	1965	JetStar-731	5064	Wfu. Parts at Dodsons, Rantoul, Ks. USA.	N3QS
☐ N3VL	1975	Westwind-1123	180	Wfu. Cx USA 4/01.	N192LH
☐ N3ZA	1965	Learjet 23	23-024	Wfu. Cx USA 5/91. Parts at White Industries, Mo. USA.	N3ZA
☐ N4LG	1967	Sabre-60	306-9	Wfu. Located Greenville Tech Foundation Inc. SC. USA.	N5071L
☐ N4SX	1966	JetStar-8	5081	Wfu. Cx USA 11/87.	N4SP
☐ N5JR	1966	Jet Commander	49	Wfu. Parts at White Industries, Bates City, Mo. USA.	N430C
☐ N5NG	1973	HS 125/600A	6020	Wfu. Last located at Monterrey-Mexico as XA-NTE.	XA-NTE
☐ N5UJ	1972	Learjet 25B	25B-088	W/o Pittsburgh, Pa. USA. 23 Nov 01.	N125JL
☐ N6CD	1974	Citation	500-0151	Wfu. Cx USA 11/91. Parts at White Industries, Mo. USA.	N151CC
☐ N6ES	1961	JetStar-6	5023	Wfu. Parts at White Industries, Bates City, Mo. USA. (3/88).	N2ES
☐ N6NE	1961	JetStar-731	5006	Wfu. Last located fire dump Southampton, UK. (wef 2/97).	(VR-CCC)
☐ N6NF	1968	Learjet 25	25-021	Wfu. Displayed at Ozark Municipal Airport, Dothan, Al. USA.	N40SN
☐ N7ES	1969	HFB 320	1045	Wfu. Located Opa Locka, Fl. USA.	N4ZA
☐ N7GP	1965	Learjet 23	23-082	Wfu. Located at Tara Field, Ga. USA.	(N216SA)
☐ N7RC	1978	Citation II	550-0019	W/o Walker's Cay, Bahamas. 26 Apr 95. (parts at Dodsons).	N900AF
☐ N8FE	1969	Falcon 20DC	199	Wfu. Located Steven F Udvar-Hazy Center , Dulles, Va. USA.	N4388F
☐ N8GE	1966	Jet Commander	63	Wfu. Parts at White Industries, Bates City, Mo. USA.	N8GA
☐ N8MQ	1972	Learjet 25B	25B-085	Wfu. Cx USA 3/98. Located Nr Lake City Airport, Fl. USA.	N8MA
☐ N8RA	1967	Jet Commander	104	Wfu.	N87B
☐ N9FE	1967	Falcon 20DC	84	Wfu. Exhibited at FEDEX Corporate HQ. Memphis, Tn. USA.	(N150FE)
☐ N10BD	1983	Learjet 35A	35A-506	Wfu. Cx USA 3/03. Located Denver International, Co. USA.	N317BG
☐ N10EA	1965	Jet Commander	39	Wfu. Located at Copenhagen, Denmark.	N16FP
☐ N10GE	1977	Citation 1/SP	501-0022	W/o Nr Harrison Airport, Ar. USA. 21 May 85.	(N800WC)
☐ N10LN	1968	HS 125/3A-RA	25156	Wfu. Last located Lakeland, Fl. USA.	N522M
☐ N10MB	1972	Westwind-1123	157	Wfu. Parts at OK Aircraft, Gilroy, Ca. USA.	(N820RT)
☐ N10SL	1964	Sabre-40	282-11	Wfu. Located at Fort Lauderdale Executive, Fl. USA.	XA-...
☐ N10UJ	1977	Westwind-1124	204	Wfu. Cx USA 5/03.	(N100XJ)
☐ N10YJ	1975	Falcon 10	57	W/o White Plains, NY. USA 30 Jun 97.	(N50YJ)
☐ N11QM	1966	Learjet 23	23-091	Wfu. Cx USA 12/89.	N110M
☐ N11UE	1962	JetStar-6	5038	Wfu. Last located at El Mirage, Ca. USA.	(N44KF)
☐ N12AR	1969	Falcon 20D	200	Wfu. Cx USA 5/03.	YV-876P
☐ N12MK	1969	Learjet 24B	24B-192	W/o Palm Springs, Ca. USA. 6 Jan 77.	N1919W
☐ N13MJ	1975	Learjet 24D	24D-314	W/o Elizabeth City, NC. USA. 6 Nov 82.	N501MH
☐ N14TX	1977	Learjet 36A	36A-033	W/o Stephenville, NF. Canada. 6 Dec 96.	N762L
☐ N15EC	1962	Sabreliner CT-39A	276-22	Wfu. East Coast Technical School, Hanscom, Ma. USA.	62-4469
☐ N15NY	1979	Citation 1/SP	501-0110	W/o Akron, Oh. USA. 2 Aug 79.	(N26481)
☐ N15TW	1977	Learjet 35A	35A-106	W/o Minneapolis, Mn. USA. 8 Dec 85. (parts at Taylorville).	N101BG
☐ N15TX	1974	Falcon 10	13	Wfu. Cx USA 2/93.	N777SN
☐ N16SK	1967	Jet Commander	101	Wfu. Cx USA 5/88. Located Bodo Aviation Museum, Norway.	N16MA
☐ N17FN	1970	Learjet 24B	24B-220	Wfu. Parts at Dodsons, Rantoul, Ks. USA.	N248J
☐ N17SL	1966	HS 125/1A-522	25082	Wfu. Parts at White Industries, Bates City, Mo. USA.	N1MY
☐ N18CA	1965	Jet Commander	5	Wfu. Cx USA 10/86. Parts at Dodsons, Rantoul, Ks. USA.	C-GKFT
☐ N19BG	1973	Sabre-40A	282-118	Wfu. Cx USA 8/95. Parts at AVMATS Paynesville, Mo. USA.	PT-JNJ
☐ N19LH	1979	Learjet 35A	35A-279	W/o Avon Park, Fl. USA. 15 Jul 97.	
☐ N20EP	1965	Learjet 23	23-008	Wfu. Displayed at White Industries, Bates City, Mo. USA.	N20BD
☐ N20K	1969	Jet Commander-C	144	Wfu. Parts at White Industries, Bates City, Mo. USA.	(N920KP)
☐ N20M	1966	Learjet 23	23-094	W/o Detroit, Mi. USA. 15 Dec 72.	N417LJ
☐ N21AK	1966	Jet Commander	59	Wfu.	N59JC
☐ N21CC	1973	Citation	500-0099	Wfu. Last located Addison, Tx. USA.	N599CC
☐ N22FM	1974	Citation	500-0229	W/o Wichita, Ks. USA. 26 Apr 83.	
☐ N22RB	1967	JetStar-8	5093	Wfu. Cx USA 10/90.	N76EB
☐ N23AC	1988	Gulfstream 4	1047	W/o Pal-Waukee Chicago, Il. USA. 30 Oct 96.	N461GA
☐ N23AJ	1965	Learjet 23	23-053	Wfu. Cx USA 9/92.	F-BTQK
☐ N23ST	1959	MS 760 Paris	50	W/o New Mexico, USA. 11 Sep 90.	N42BL
☐ N23TJ	1965	Learjet 23	23-033	Wfu. See www.airzoo.org	N60DH
☐ N24RZ	1974	Learjet 25B	25B-159	W/o Fort Lauderdale, Fl. USA. 22 Feb 04.	OB-1429
☐ N24SA	1965	Learjet 23	23-025	Wfu. Cx USA 6/89.	N508M
☐ N24VM	1965	Learjet 24	24-051	Wfu. Cx USA 8/88. Parts at White Industries, Mo. USA.	N70JC
Reg	Yr	Type	c/n	Owner/Operator	Prev Regn

Reg	Yr	Type	c/n	Owner/Operator	Prev Regn
N24WX	1966	Learjet 24	24-101	Wfu. Located San Carlos, Az. USA.	XA-SGU
N24YE	1965	Learjet 24	24-087	Wfu. Cx USA 1/03.	N24YA
N25BR	1989	Beechjet 400	RJ-57	W/o Rome, Ga. USA. 11 Dec 91.	
N25TA	1975	Learjet 25B	25B-196	W/o New Mexico. USA. 11 Apr 80.	N711WD
N26BA	1967	Learjet 24	24-134	Wfu. Parts at Dodsons, Rantoul, Ks. USA.	N911TR
N26TL	1965	HS 125/1A	25037	Wfu. Cx USA 8/92.	(N389DA)
N27BD	1966	Jet Commander	53	Wfu. Cx USA 1/95. Parts at White Industries, Mo. USA.	N925HB
N27MD	1967	Jet Commander	102	Wfu. Parts at White Industries, Bates City, Mo. USA.	
N27R	1974	Falcon 20E	303	W/o Naples, Fl. USA. 12 Nov 76.	N4445F
N28CK	1969	Learjet 25	25-045	Wfu. Located Montgomery, Al. USA.	N24FN
N28ST	1965	Learjet 23	23-013	W/o Nr Guatemala City, Guatemala. 31 Jul 87.	N37BL
N29FN	1968	Learjet 25	25-018	Wfu. Parts at Brandis Aviation, Taylorville, Il. USA.	(N23FN)
N29LB	1966	Jet Commander	61	W/o Many Airport, La. USA. 19 Dec 80.	N29LP
N30AD	1969	Jet Commander-C	143	Wfu. Cx USA 4/99. Located Boeing Field, Wa. USA.	N41
N30AN	1974	Westwind-1123	173	Wfu. Parts at El Mirage, Ca. USA.	N30JM
N30BE	1964	Sabre-40	282-14	Wfu. Parts at AVMATS Paynesville, Mo. USA.	(N30PN)
N30CC	1974	Sabre-60A	306-81	Wfu. Cx USA 12/95. Parts at AVMATS Paynesville, Mo. USA.	N6ND
N30DK	1980	Learjet 35A	35A-345	W/o San Diego, Ca. USA. 24 Oct 04.	N345LJ
N30EM	1976	Learjet 24E	24E-338	Wfu. Cx USA 12/89. Parts at Taylorville, Il. USA.	N30LM
N30SJ	1991	SJ 30-2	001	Wfu. Cx USA 10/99.	
N30W	1964	Sabre-40	282-5	W/o Perryville, Mo. USA. 21 Dec 67.	
N31BP	1968	JetStar-731	5125	Wfu. Last located Fort Lauderdale Executive, Fl. USA.	N48UC
N31CK	1965	Learjet 23	23-079	Wfu. Last located El Mirage, Ca. USA.	N240AQ
N31SK	1966	Learjet 24	24-118	W/o Vail, Co. USA. 27 Mar 87.	N1919W
N32CA	1966	Learjet 24	24-132	Wfu. Cx USA 9/01.	N238R
N32WE	1973	Westwind-1123	164	Wfu. Parts at White Industries, Bates City, Mo. USA.	N9114S
N33UT	1962	Sabreliner CT-39A	276-34	Wfu. Located University of Tennessee, Tullahoma, Tn. USA.	62-4481
N34NW	1967	Jet Commander	117	Wfu. Parts at White Industries, Bates City, Mo. USA.	N54WC
N34SW	1967	Jet Commander	97	Wfu. Parts at Hollister, Ca. USA.	N3082B
N34W	1965	Sabre-40	282-47	W/o Midland, Tx. USA. 4 Jan 74.	N740R
N36MK	1966	HS 125/1A	25073	W/o Boise, Id. USA. 28 Dec 70.	N372GM
N36PT	1966	Jet Commander	79	Wfu. Cx USA 1/97.	N100LL
N37BL	1965	Learjet 23	23-069	W/o Oakdale, Ca. USA. 4 Mar 98.	(N34TR)
N37CP	1965	Learjet 23	23-028	Wfu. Parts at White Industries, Bates City, Mo. USA.	N5QY
N37SJ	1965	Jet Commander	38	Wfu. Parts at White Industries, Bates City, Mo. USA.	N106CJ
N38B	1971	King Air 200	BB-1	Wfu. Project shelved 1978.	
N38DJ	1975	Learjet 25B	25B-191	W/o Sheboygan, Wi. USA. 12 Jun 92. (parts at Hampton, Ga.).	N78BT
N39DM	1975	Learjet 35	35-040	W/o San Clemente Island, Ca. USA. 5 Mar 86.	C-GGYV
N39Q	1968	JetStar-8	5126	Wfu. Parted out 1983.	N39E
N40BC	1973	Learjet 25B	25B-128	W/o Pueblo, Co. USA. 6 Jul 79. (parts at White Industries).	N1MX
N40BP	1965	Sabre-40	282-40	Wfu. Parts at Clarksville, Mo. USA.	N40BP
N40LB	1968	Learjet 25	25-009	W/o Omaha, Ne. USA. 25 Sep 73.	9Q-CHC
N40LB	1965	Sabre-40	282-36	Wfu. Located Fort Lauderdale Executive, Fl. USA.	N200MP
N40PC	1973	HS 125/600A	6010	W/o McLean, Va. USA. 28 Apr 77.	N23BH
N40UA	1966	Jet Commander	40	Wfu. Parts at White Industries, Bates City, Mo. USA.	N40AJ
N41GS	1964	Sabre-40	282-16	Wfu. Last located 10/88 Miami International, Fl. USA.	N40GP
N42		Convair 880	55	Wfu.	N112
N42QB	1965	Jet Commander	6	Wfu. Parts at White Industries, Bates City, Mo. USA.	N420P
N43AR	1972	JetStar-8	5154	Wfu. Located Fort Lauderdale Executive, Fl. USA.	XC-SRH
N43CF	1966	Sabre-40	282-59	Wfu. Cx USA 8/95.	N40SE
N44	1969	Jet Commander-A	130	W/o Latrobe, Pa. USA. 2 Nov 88.	N84
N44CJ	1967	Learjet 24	24-146	W/o Felt, Ok. USA. 1 Oct 81.	N235Z
N44GA	1966	Learjet 24	24-129	W/o Santa Catalina, Ca. USA. 30 Jan 84.	C-GSAX
N44PA	1973	Learjet 25B	25B-144	W/o Carlsbad, Ca. USA. 23 Dec 91.	N10NT
N45BP	1978	HS 125/700A	NA0219	W/o Beaumont, Tx. USA. 20 Sep 03.	N219TS
N45CP	1972	Learjet 25XR	25XR-073	W/o Lexington, Ky. USA. 30 Aug 02.	N888DB
N46	1964	B 727-30	18360	Wfu. Cx USA 8/94.	N97
N46TE	1979	Gulfstream 2	243	W/o Little Rock, Ar. USA. 19 Jan 90.	N119RC
N47BA	1976	Learjet 35	35-060	W/o Aberdeen, SD. USA. 25 Oct 99.	(N590CH)
N48AJ	1968	Learjet 24	24-172	Wfu. at White Industries, Bates City, Mo. USA.	N234WR
N48BA	1967	Learjet 24	24-152	Wfu. Parts at Dodsons, Rantoul, Ks. USA.	N9LM
N48CG	1966	Sabre-40	282-75	Wfu. Cx USA 12/83. Parts at Clarksville, Mo. USA.	(N48CE)
N48CQ	1976	Gulfstream 2	181	Wfu. Last located Tulsa, Ok. USA.	N48CC
N49RJ	1966	Sabre-40	282-69	Wfu. Last loacted at Fort Lauderdale Executive, Fl. USA.	N777VZ
N49UC	1967	JetStar-731	5110	Wfu. Parted out 1991.	N788S
N50AS	1966	HS 125/1A-522	25083	Wfu. Cx USA 9/92.	N538
Reg	Yr	Type	c/n	Owner/Operator	Prev Regn

Reg	Yr	Type	c/n	Owner/Operator	Prev Regn
N50BA	1965	Learjet 24	24-043	Wfu. Cx USA 8/89 as N43AC.	(N43AC)
N50BK	1985	Citation S/II	S550-0031	W/o Big Bear, Ca. USA. 13 Aug 02.	N54WJ
N50CD	1965	Sabre-40	282-42	Wfu. Cx USA 10/91. Parts at Paynesville, Mo. USA.	N500RK
N50DG	1968	Sabre-60	306-19	Wfu. Cx USA 10/98.	N8000U
N50HH	1965	HS 125/1A-522	25022	W/o Bedford, In. USA. 2 Aug 86. (parts at O K Aircraft, Ca.)	N100GB
N50JP	1966	Jet Commander	69	Wfu. Cx USA 10/97. Parts at Dodsons, Rantoul, Ks. USA.	N10SN
N50MM	1973	Citation	500-0118	Wfu. Display fuselage for Aviation Fabrications Inc. Mo. USA	N972GW
N50PL	1981	Westwind-Two	338	W/o Pocono Mountains, Nr Scranton, Pa. USA. 12 Dec 99.	N114WL
N50SK	1980	Westwind-Two	309	W/o Bowie County, Tx. USA. 4 Apr 86.	N240S
N50TE	1976	Falcon 10	86	Wfu. Parts at White Industries, Bates City, Mo. USA.	N411WW
N50UD	1961	JetStar-6	5019	Wfu. Parts noted 1990 at N Perry & Fort Lauderdale, Fl. USA.	N50UD
N51CA	1969	Learjet 25	25-030	W/o Newark, NJ. USA. 30 Mar 83.	N45DM
N51DB	1978	Learjet 25XR	25XR-246	W/o Nr Medina, Saudi Arabia. 24 Oct 86.	N40162
N51FN	1976	Learjet 35	35-059	W/o Carlsbad, Ca. USA. 2 Apr 90. (parts at White Industries)	N221Z
N52	1974	Sabre-75A	380-10	Wfu. Cx USA 9/95. Located Burlington, Vt. USA.	
N52AN	1972	Citation	500-0030	Wfu.	N530CC
N53CC	1981	Citation II	550-0400	W/o Roxboro, NC. USA. 1 Oct 89.	N888EB
N55NC	1965	JetStar-6	5060	Wfu. Last located Fort Lauderdale, Fl. USA. Cx USA 7/88.	N31F
N55NJ	1968	Learjet 24	24-162	Wfu. Parts at Dodsons, Rantoul, Ks. USA.	N835AG
N55RF	1965	HS 125/731	25020	Wfu. Cx USA 8/03.	N125TJ
N56B	1965	BAC 1-11/401AK	055	Wfu. Cx USA 8/91.	N1JR
N57TA	1981	Learjet 55	55-010	W/o Waterkloof AFB. Pretoria, South Africa. 13 Nov 81.	
N59RD	1963	B 707-441	17905	Wfu. Cx USA 7/89.	PP-VJA
N60	1975	Sabre-75A	380-28	Wfu. Cx USA 6/96.	
N60BC	1968	JetStar-8	5116	Wfu. Parts at Spirit of St Louis, Mo. USA.	N3HB
N60CD	1965	Jet Commander	44	Wfu. Parts at Dodsons, Rantoul, Ks. USA.	N69GT
N60JN	1967	Sabre-60	306-14	Wfu. Parts at Perryville, Mo. USA.	N43GB
N60MB	1974	Falcon 10	15	W/o Stapleton-Denver, Co. USA. 3 Apr 77.	N109FJ
N60XL	1987	Learjet 60	55C-001	Wfu. Cx USA 9/96.	N551DF
N61RH	1965	Sabre-40	282-27	Wfu. Located College of Technology, Tulsa, Ok. USA.	N111EA
N61RS	1983	Westwind-Two	384	W/o Taos, NM. USA. 8 Nov 02.	(N50MF)
N61TJ	1979	Gulfstream 2	256	Wfu. Parts at Dodsons, Rantoul, Ks. USA.	(N135WJ)
N61TS	1965	Learjet 23	23-029	Wfu. Parted out 10/85.	N66AS
N63CK	1967	Learjet 24	24-119	Wfu. Parts at Dodsons, Rantoul, Ks. USA.	N61CK
N63HJ	1981	Challenger 600S	1021	Wfu. Cx USA 10/04.	N914XA
N64	1975	Sabre-75A	380-35	W/o Liberal, Ks. USA. 29 Sep 86.	
N65TS	1965	HS 125/1A-522	25043	Wfu. Parts at Dodsons, Rantoul, Ks. USA	N522ME
N66HA	1967	HS 125/3A	25126	W/o Houston, Tx. USA. 13 Aug 89.	N510X
N66JE	1981	Westwind-1124	326	W/o ground fire Denver, Co. USA. 21 Feb 95.	(N88JE)
N66MP	1961	JetStar-6	5015	Wfu. Last located at S Seattle Community College, Wa. USA.	N9064F
N67KM	1974	Sabre-75A	380-7	W/o Watertown, SD. USA. 14 Jun 75.	
N67TS	1966	HS 125/1A-522	25097	Wfu. Cx USA 11/01.	N89HB
N68LU	1968	Learjet 24	24-163	Wfu. Located Lewis University, Romeoville, Il. USA.	N65WM
N69KB	1965	Learjet 23	23-042	Wfu. Cx USA 12/91. Parts at White Industries, Mo. USA.	N701RZ
N70FJ	1978	Citation 1/SP	501-0073	W/o Nr Hailey, Id. USA. 15 Mar 03.	(N840MC)
N70HC	1972	Sabre-75	370-8	Wfu. Cx USA 4/96. Parts at AVMATS Paynesville, Mo. USA.	N3TE
N71JC	1989	Learjet 31	31-008	W/o Amory, Ms. USA. 2 Sep 97. (parts at Griffin, Ga.).	
N74AG	1966	JetStar-731	5072	Wfu. Cx USA 11/99.	N74AG
N74BS	1973	Sabre-60	306-64	Wfu. Located AVMATS Spirit of St Louis, Mo. USA.	N96CP
N75CN	1975	Sabre-75A	380-31	Wfu. Parts at Dodsons, Rantoul, Ks. USA.	N62
N77AP	1965	Sabre-40	282-37	W/o New Orleans, La. USA. 7 Nov 77.	N265W
N77BT	1967	HS 125/3A-RA	25155	Wfu. Last located Montgomery, Al. USA.	(N158AG)
N77FV	1965	Jet Commander	26	Wfu. Cx USA 10/88.	N10MC
N77JL	1974	Learjet 24XR	24XR-286	W/o Belleville, Il. USA. 12 Nov 03.	N57DB
N77NJ	1969	Learjet 25	25-033	Wfu. Cx USA 7/03.	YV-88CP
N77NT	1965	Jet Commander	7	Wfu. Cx USA 11/91.	N77NT
N77RS	1973	Learjet 25C	25C-094	W/o Anchorage, Ak. USA. 4 Dec 78. (parts at White Inds.).	N97J
N77VK	1965	HS 125/731	25051	Wfu. Cx USA 1/87.	C6-BEY
N78JR	1966	Falcon 20C	70	Wfu. Parted out 3/89. Last located El Mirage, Ca. USA.	(N400NL)
N79DD	1975	Citation	500-0254	W/o San Luis Obispo, Ca. USA. 24 Sep 90.	N29991
N80DH	1969	Learjet 24B	24B-191	Wfu. Cx USA 3/89. Parts at Dodsons, Rantoul, Ks. USA.	(N44TL)
N80TN	1974	Sabre-75A	380-19	Wfu. Cx USA 6/02.	N80HG
N81MC	1977	Learjet 24F	24F-344	W/o St Thomas, USVI. 10 Nov 84.	
N82ML	1967	Sabre-40	282-83	Wfu. Cx USA 3/95. Parts at AVMATS Paynesville, Mo. USA.	N160TC
N83CE	1965	Learjet 23	23-074	Wfu. Located Gilbert Community College, Chandler, Az.	XB-GRQ
N84GP	1983	Peregrine	551	Wfu. Located Oklahoma Air & Space Museum Exhibit, USA.	N9881S
Reg	**Yr**	**Type**	**c/n**	**Owner/Operator**	**Prev Regn**

Reg	Yr	Type	c/n	Owner/Operator	Prev Regn
N85	1968	Sabre-40	282-97	W/o Nr Recife, Brazil. 14 Jan 76.	N4706N
N85DW	1975	Sabre-75A	380-27	W/o Ironwood, Mi. USA. 14 Aug 00.	N90GW
N85JM	1976	Falcon 10	85	W/o Aurillac, France. 17 Feb 93. (parts at White Industries)	(N95DW)
N85VT	1985	Gulfstream 3	449	W/o Houston, Tx. USA. 22 Nov 04.	N85V
N86	1967	Sabre-40	282-86	Wfu. Cx USA 9/92.	N2255C
N86BE	1978	Learjet 35A	35A-194	W/o Marianna, Fl. USA. 5 Apr 00.	N86BL
N86CC	1966	Learjet 24	24-115	Wfu. Parts at Brandis Aviation, Taylorville, Il. USA.	N591DL
N87CM	1964	Sabre-40	282-21	Wfu. Parts at AVMATS Paynesville, Mo. USA.	N168D
N87DG	1965	Jet Commander	14	Wfu. Cx USA 7/94. Parts at White Industries, Mo. USA.	N87DC
N88	1967	Sabre-40	282-88	Wfu. Located Hampton University, Newport News, Va. USA.	N2237C
N88B	1965	Learjet 24	24-015	Wfu. Located Pima County Museum, Tucson, Az. USA.	
N88CH	1961	Convair 880	58	Wfu. Located Bonza Bay, East London, RSA.	VR-HGF
N88HA	1990	Challenger 601-3A	5072	W/o Nr Bassett-Rock County Airport, Ne. USA. 20 Mar 94.	N609K
N88JF	1966	Learjet 24A	24A-110	W/o Detroit, Mi. USA. Oct 86. (parts at Taylorville, Il.).	N35JF
N88JM	1961	JetStar-731	5011	Wfu. Fuselage noted 1988 at Lincoln, Ne. USA.	N159B
N88MR	1966	HS 125/1A	25013	Wfu. Cx USA 6/86. Parts at White Industries, Mo. USA.	N4646S
N88NB	1963	BAC 1-11/201AC	005	Wfu. Cx USA 8/89.	N97KR
N89	1967	Sabre-40	282-89	Wfu. Parted out 10/91.	N2276C
N89MR	1965	Jet Commander	9	Wfu. Parts at OK Aircraft, Gilroy, Ca. USA.	(N90KK)
N90AG	1999	Challenger 604	5414	W/o Birmingham, UK. 4 Jan 02.	N604AG
N90HM	1973	Westwind-1123	170	Wfu. Cx USA 5/94.	N150HR
N90ME	1965	JetStar-6	5057	Wfu. Last located 5/88 at Memphis, Tn. USA.	N90ME
N91MJ	1979	Citation II	550-0101	W/o Marco Island, Fl. USA. 31 Dec 95.	(N42BM)
N92GS	1962	B 720-047B	18452	Wfu. Last located Miami, Fl. USA.	N93146
N93BE	1965	Jet Commander	27	Wfu. Parts at White Industries, Bates City, Mo. USA.	N93B
N93BP	1968	Learjet 24	24-169	Wfu. Parts at Dodsons, Rantoul, Ks. USA.	N927AA
N93BR	1970	Learjet 24D	24D-231	Wfu. Parts at Brandis Aviation, Taylorville, Il, USA.	N37DH
N95B	1965	Jet Commander	19	Wfu. Instructional airframe Norway 5/88.	
N95GS	1961	JetStar-6	5014	Wfu. Parted out in 1989 at Miami, Fl. USA.	N54BW
N95TC	1975	Learjet 35	35-020	W/o Waco, Tx. USA. 20 Dec 84. (parts at White Industries).	XA-BUK
N96AA	1967	Learjet 24	24-139	Wfu. Parts at Dodsons, Rantoul, Ks. USA.	N481EZ
N96BB	1964	JetStar-6	5049	Wfu. Located at S Seattle Community College, Wa. USA.	N96B
N96CK	1965	Learjet 23	23-016	Wfu. Last located El Mirage, Ca. USA.	N7GF
N96GS	1965	JetStar-731	5068	W/o Miami, Fl. USA. 6 Jan 90.	N9231R
N96TS	1973	Westwind-1123	159	Wfu. Parts were at Hollister, Ca. USA.	N344CK
N97DM	1972	Learjet 24D	24D-253	W/o San Clemente Island, Ca. USA. 5 Mar 86.	N417JD
N98KT	1961	Caravelle 6R	102	Wfu. Located at Van Nuys, Ca. USA.	N2296N
N98SC	1965	Jet Commander	32	Wfu. Located Washington County, Pa. USA.	N101BU
N99FT	1965	JetStar-731	5055	Wfu. Last located scrapyard Long Beach, Ca. USA.	N707EZ
N99GS	1965	Jet Commander	31	Wfu.	N399D
N99S	1981	Sabre-65	465-64	W/o Toronto, Canada. 11 Jan 83.	
N99TC	1966	Learjet 23	23-098	Wfu. Parts at Brandis Aviation, Taylorville, Il. USA.	N711AE
N99W	1965	Jet Commander	46	Wfu. Cx USA 2/99.	N202ST
N100DL	1969	Learjet 24B	24B-201	Wfu. Parts at White Industries, Bates City, Mo. USA.	C-GTFA
N100EP	1978	Learjet 35A	35A-150	W/o Allegheny County Airport, Pa. USA. 11 May 87.	
N100MK	1968	Learjet 25	25-019	W/o Sandusky, Oh. USA. 21 Oct 78.	N88FP
N100RC	1966	Jet Commander	60	W/o Lexington, Ky. USA. 14 Nov 70.	N6545V
N100SQ	1966	Learjet 24	24-113	Wfu. Cx USA 10/81.	N204Y
N100TA	1965	Learjet 23	23-045	W/o Savannah, Ga. USA. 6 May 82.	N711MR
N100TR	1966	Jet Commander	76	Wfu. Parts at Hollister, Ca. USA.	N100DR
N100VQ	1967	Learjet 24	24-140	Wfu. Located St Petersburg-Clearwater, Fl. USA.	N100VC
N100WM	1966	Jet Commander	73	Wfu. Located at Sarasota, Fl. USA.	N100W
N101AD	1972	HS 125/731	NA777	Wfu. Parted out 10/91. (fuselage at Tulsa, Ok. USA.).	(N425JF)
N101LB	1965	Jet Commander	8	Wfu. Parts at Tucson, Az. USA.	(N1MM)
N101PP	1966	Learjet 23	23-085	W/o Windsor Locks, Ct. USA. 4 Jun 84.	N385J
N102CJ	1966	Jet Commander	78	Wfu. Located at Opa Locka, Fl. USA.	N866DH
N104SL	1972	Sabre-40A	282-104	Wfu. Cx USA 1/01.	XA-SEU
N104SS	1968	Sabre-60	306-30	Wfu. Parts at White Industries, Bates City, Mo. USA.	N1116A
N106TF	1969	HFB 320	1042	Wfu. Located Louisville, Ky. USA.	(N603GA)
N107CJ	1964	Sabre-40	282-12	Wfu. Cx USA 1/97.	N368DA
N108PA	1975	Learjet 25B	25B-195	Wfu.	OB-M-1004
N110FS	1966	Sabre-40	282-58	Wfu. Parts at Spirit of St Louis, Mo. USA.	N1101G
N111DC	1968	HFB 320	1030	Wfu. Located at Monroe, Mi. USA.	(N247GW)
N111LR	1997	CitationJet	525-0222	W/o Atlanta, Ga. USA. 4 Apr 98.	
N111M	1965	Falcon 20C	10	Wfu. Cx USA 8/87. Parts at AVMATS Paynesville, Mo. USA.	N810F
N111NF	1973	Westwind-1123	168	Wfu. Loacted at Dallas-Love Field, Tx. USA.	N66SM
Reg	Yr	Type	c/n	Owner/Operator	Prev Regn

Reg	Yr	Type	c/n	Owner/Operator	Prev Regn
N111TD	1965	Jet Commander	11	Wfu. Last located St Simons Island, Ga. USA.	(N55CM)
N111YL	1965	Jet Commander	42	Wfu. Cx USA 7/94.	N111Y
N112TJ	1961	JetStar-731	5029	Wfu. Last located El Mirage, Ca. USA.	(N1406)
N114GB	1966	Learjet 23	23-022	Wfu. Parts at White Industries, Bates City, Mo. USA.	N456SC
N115DX	1968	JetStar-8	5111	Wfu. Parted out 8/91.	N115MR
N116KX	1966	Jet Commander	87	Wfu. Parts were at Hollister, Ca. USA.	N430DC
N118AF	1974	Westwind-1123	177	Wfu. Cx USA 10/91.	(N114ED)
N118BA	1966	JetStar-6	5091	Wfu. Cx USA 5/93. Parts at White Industries, Mo. USA.	N118B
N119MA	1969	Learjet 24B	24B-200	Wfu. Parts at White Industries, Bates City, Mo. USA.	N246CM
N120AR	1966	JetStar-8	5089	Wfu.	(N85DL)
N120ES	1977	Citation 1/SP	501-0041	W/o San Salvador, El Salvador 24 Apr 95. (parts at Dodsons).	N173SK
N120TA		BAC 1-11/520FN	236	Wfu.	PP-SDS
N121AJ	1966	Jet Commander	57	Wfu. Cx USA 4/82.	N770WL
N121DJ	1967	Falcon 20C	121	Wfu. Last located at Dodsons, Rantoul, Ks. USA.	N500BG
N121EL	1968	Learjet 25	25-010	Wfu. Located Kingston University, UK.	(N82UH)
N121FJ	1981	Falcon 100	192	W/o Rancho Murieta Airport, Ca. USA. 15 Oct 87.	N100FJ
N121GW	1965	Falcon 20C	4	W/o Memphis, Tn. USA. 18 May 78.	N116JD
N121HM	1965	Jet Commander	18	Wfu. Instructional airframe at Copenhagen, Denmark.	N1166Z
N122M	1965	Learjet 23	23-065A	Wfu. Last located El Mirage, Ca. USA.	(N156AG)
N123AC	1966	HS 125/3A	25122	Wfu. Parts at OK Aircraft, Gilroy, Ca. USA.	N255CB
N123CB	1970	Learjet 24D	24D-232	W/o Butte, Mt. USA. 17 Apr 71.	
N123CV	1974	Westwind-1123	178	Wfu. Cx USA 8/04.	N999U
N123DR	1973	Westwind-1123	158	Wfu. Located Aeroparque Buenos Aires, Argentina.	N1123G
N123RE	1967	Learjet 24	24-154	W/o Lancaster, Ca. USA. 17 Oct 78.	N11AK
N124RM	1966	JetStar-731	5078	Wfu. Cx USA 3/04.	N515AJ
N124TV	1973	Gulfstream 2	124	Wfu. Last located Mojave, Ca. USA.	(N98DEF)
N124VS	1966	Jet Commander	64	Wfu. Located Manila, Philippines.	N124JB
N125AW	1966	HS 125/1A	25057	Wfu. American Flight&Technology Center, Pontiac, Mi. USA.	N188K
N125CA	1970	Falcon 20DC	208	W/o Catersville, Al. USA. 29 Jun 89.	N300JJ
N125CM	1971	HS 125/400A	NA767	Wfu. Cx USA 6/95. Parts at AVMATS Paynesville, Mo. USA.	N28GE
N125E	1966	HS 125/1A-522	25110	W/o Hobby-Houston, Tx. USA. 29 Jun 83.	N3125B
N125FD	1966	HS 125/3A	25123	Wfu. Parts at Dodsons, Rantoul, Ks. USA.	N44PW
N125NE	1979	Learjet 25D	25D-271	W/o Gulf of Mexico. 21 May 80.	(N183AP)
N126R	1968	Falcon 20C	126	W/o El Paso, Tx. USA. 28 Aug 98.	N102ZE
N127MS	1974	Sabre-75A	380-18	Wfu. Cx USA 6/95. Parts at Perryville, Mo. USA.	N55
N127MW	1959	HFB 320	1027	W/o Aberdeen, SD. USA. 5 Oct 84.	N905MW
N128GA	1966	BAC 1-11/401AK	058	Wfu.	N128TA
N128SD	1969	HFB 320	1035	Wfu. Located Monroe, Mi. USA.	PH-HFC
N129DM	1969	Learjet 24B	24B-187	Wfu.	N5WJ
N129K	1966	Jet Commander	70	Wfu. Parts at White Industries, Bates City, Mo. USA.	N1194Z
N130MR	1995	CitationJet	525-0097	W/o Buda, Tx. USA. 26 Mar 00.	N234WS
N130MW	1968	HFB 320	1033	Wfu. Located Monterey, Ca. USA.	N132MW
N131MS	1975	Sabre-75A	380-22	Wfu. Cx USA 6/95. Parts at Perryville, Mo. USA.	N132MS
N132MW	1968	HFB 320	1032	Wfu. Located Monterey, Ca. USA.	N130MW
N133BL	1966	Learjet 24	24-133	Wfu. Cx USA 3/04.	N133DF
N133ME	1966	Jet Commander	50	Wfu.	N612JC
N133W	1965	Learjet 23	23-021	W/o Burbank, Ca. USA. 1 Apr 78.	N427NJ
N135PT	1984	Learjet C-21A	35A-509	W/o Groton, Ct. USA. 4 Aug 03.	N826RD
N136DH	1965	HS 125/1A	25036	Wfu. Cx USA 7/95.	C-FPQG
N137GL	1978	Learjet 25D	25D-237	W/o Detroit, Mi. USA. 19 Jan 79.	(N28BP)
N138BF	2000	SJ 30-2	002	W/o N of Del Rio, Tx. USA. 26 Apr 03.	
N138SR	1959	B 707-138B	17697	W/o Hangar fire Port Harcourt, Nigeria. 28 Aug 98.	(N138MJ)
N140MM	1964	Sabre-40	282-8	Wfu. Cx USA 9/96.	N369N
N140RC	1965	Learjet 23	23-048	Wfu. Last located Montgomery, Al. USA.	N48MW
N144CP	1969	Learjet 24B	24B-185	Wfu. Parts at Dodsons, Rantoul, Ks. USA.	N44CP
N148E	1966	Jet Commander	22	W/o Burbank, Ca. USA. 13 Sep 68.	N200M
N148PE	1960	JetStar-6	5002	Wfu. Parted out at Minneapolis, Mn. USA. (during 1987).	N81JJ
N149HP	1979	Falcon 10	154	Wfu. Parts at White Industries, Bates City, Mo. USA.	N777FJ
N149SF	1969	Jet Commander-B	149	Wfu. Cx USA 11/03.	(N803AU)
N151TB	1974	Sabre-80A	380-11	Wfu. Cx USA 11/04.	N265SR
N153TW	1969	Learjet 25	25-053	W/o Lansing, NY. USA. 24 Aug 01.	N37GB
N154AG	1965	Learjet 23	23-034	Wfu. Located Museum of Flight, Seattle, Wa. USA.	N24FF
N155AG	1969	Learjet 25	25-037	Wfu. Fuselage used for display by Best Aeronet Ltd.	N28AA
N155TJ	1967	JetStar-731	5104	Wfu. Last Located Fort Lauderdale Excecutive, Fl. USA.	N155AV
N158DP	1961	JetStar-8	5013	Wfu. Parts at White Industries, Bates City, Mo. USA. (3/88).	(N5AX)
N159DP	1966	Jet Commander	52	Wfu. Located Aviation Museum, Darwin, Australia.	N159MP

Reg	Yr	Type	c/n	Owner/Operator	Prev Regn
☐ N162JB	1970	Sabre-60	306-62	Wfu. Cx USA 8/01.	N62CF
☐ N163DC	1967	Jet Commander	89	Wfu. Located New Orleans Lakefront, La. USA.	N10BK
☐ N163DL	1973	Westwind-1123	163	Wfu. Cx USA 10/97. Parts at Dodsons, Rantoul, Ks. USA.	N47DC
☐ N163WS	1969	Jet Commander-B	141	Wfu. Cx USA 12/03.	5N-EZE
☐ N165WC	1968	Falcon 20C-PW300	140	Wfu. Located Detroit Willow Run, Mi. USA.	N314AE
☐ N167G	1977	JetStar 2	5212	Wfu. Cx USA 7/03.	(N95SR)
☐ N169RF	1969	Sabre-60	306-45	W/o Phoenix, Az. USA. 7 Nov 92.	N742K
☐ N171CC	1968	JetStar-8	5127	Wfu. Located El Mirage, Ca. USA. (as N171SG).	N636
☐ N171GA	1969	HFB 320	1039	Wfu. Last located Toledo, Oh. USA.	N208MM
☐ N171JL	1966	JetStar-731	5074	Wfu. Cx USA 10/01.	N171JL
☐ N171MC	1974	Falcon 10	30	Wfu. Parts at White Industries, Bates City, Mo. USA.	N191MC
☐ N172AC	1963	Jet Commander	1	Wfu.	N112AC
☐ N173EL	1975	Gulfstream 2TT	173	Wfu. Last located Van Nuys, Ca. USA.	(N444ML)
☐ N173GA	1971	HFB 320	1052	Wfu. Located Jefferson Technical College, Louisville, Ky.	PT-IDW
☐ N175FS	1965	Learjet 24A	24A-031	Wfu. Last located Griffin, Ga. USA.	N202BA
☐ N176GA	1971	HFB 320	1053	Wfu. Last located Toledo, Oh. USA.	PT-IOB
☐ N179GA	1967	Falcon 20C	100	W/o St Louis, Mo. USA. 8 Apr 03.	I-VEPA
☐ N181MA	1979	Diamond-Two	A001SA	Wfu. Located Wichita-Beech Field, USA.	JQ8001
☐ N183GA	1968	Falcon 20C	147	W/o Swanton, Oh. USA. 8 Apr 03.	N41154
☐ N196KC	1966	Jet Commander	68	W/o Fayetteville, Ar. USA. I Jul 68.	N619JC
☐ N197JS	1965	JetStar-731	5069	Wfu. Cx USA 2/99.	XA-PGO
☐ N200CK	1962	JetStar-6	5039	Wfu. Last located 7/90 at Spirit of St Louis, Mo. USA.	N200CK
☐ N200JE	1968	Falcon 20C	133	Wfu. Parts at Dodsons, Rantoul, Ks. USA.	N133FJ
☐ N200LF	1966	Jet Commander	47	Wfu. Parts at White Industries, Bates City, Mo. USA.	N222HM
☐ N200PR	2003	390 Premier 1	RB-79	W/o Blackbushe, UK. 7 Apr 04.	
☐ N200RC	1969	Jet Commander-B	140	W/o Tampa, Fl. USA. 25 Sep 73.	4X-CPG
☐ N202DN	1983	Falcon 100	202	W/o Lawrence, Ks. USA. 9 Dec 01.	N80WJ
☐ N203M	1967	Jet Commander	120	Wfu. Cx USA 1/85.	N200M
☐ N204C	1974	Gulfstream 2	143	W/o Kota Kinabalu, Borneo. 4 Sep 91.	N334
☐ N204RC	1968	Gulfstream 2	34	W/o Caracas, Venezuela. 17 Jun 91.	N500JR
☐ N207JC	1976	Learjet 25D	25D-207	Wfu. Parts at White Industries, Bates City, Mo. USA.	I-LEAR
☐ N210RS	1973	Falcon 20C	18	Wfu. Cx USA 8/96.	N9DM
☐ N211MB	1970	Learjet 25	25-059	W/o Port au Prince, Haiti. 3 Aug 80.	N425JX
☐ N212AP	1972	JetStar-8	5147	Wfu. Located Greenwood, Ms. USA.	N718R
☐ N212CW	1966	Jet Commander	75	Wfu. Parts at White Industries, Bates City, Mo. USA.	N1121R
☐ N212NE	1976	Learjet 25D	25D-212	Wfu. Parted out 1989.	N911MG
☐ N213AP	1968	JetStar-8	5122	Wfu. Cx USA 3/89.	N1107M
☐ N217A	1974	HS 125/600B	6030	Wfu.	G-TOMI
☐ N219TT	1975	Sabre-75A	380-24	Wfu. Cx USA 2/95. Located Tulsa Technology Center, Ok. USA.	N58
☐ N220JC	1983	Learjet 55	55-050	W/o Boca Raton, Fl. USA. 23 Jun 00.	(N55UJ)
☐ N220RB	1960	DC 8-21	45280	Wfu. Located Datang Shan Museum, Beijing, China.	N8003U
☐ N221PH	1966	Sabre-40	282-55	Wfu. Cx USA 8/86, Parts at AVMATS, Mo. USA.	(N221PX)
☐ N222FJ	1997	Williams V-Jet II	001	Wfu. Located EAA Museum Oshkosh, Wi. USA.	
☐ N222KN	1968	JetStar-8	5118	Wfu. Parted out 1988.	N333KN
☐ N222WL	1981	Citation II	550-0208	Wfu. Cx USA 3/91.	N54RC
☐ N224SC	1966	Learjet 24A	24A-100	W/o Gainesville, Ga. USA. 26 Sep 99. (parts at Griffin, Ga).	N427LJ
☐ N225LS	1965	Sabre-40	282-51	Wfu. Parts at Paynesville, Mo. USA.	(N51MN)
☐ N227GA	1969	Gulfstream II SP	76	Wfu. Cx USA 4/04. Last located Van Nys, Ca. USA.	N227G
☐ N232RA	1970	Falcon 20DC	232	W/o Binghampton, NY. USA. 15 Feb 89.	N27EV
☐ N234CM	1970	Learjet 24B	24B-214	W/o Nr Monclova, Mexico. 16 Dec 88.	N42NF
☐ N234F	1965	Learjet 23	23-063	W/o Palm Springs, Ca. USA. 14 Nov 65.	
☐ N234MR	1966	Learjet 24	24-130	Wfu. Cx USA 10/87.	N330J
☐ N234UM	1973	Citation	500-0105	Wfu. Cx USA 12/04.	N32W
☐ N235KC	1966	HS 125/1A	25096	W/o Grand Bahama, Bahamas. 21 Nov 66.	G-ATNR
☐ N235R	1965	Learjet 23	23-032	W/o Clarendon, Tx. USA. 23 Apr 66.	
☐ N236BN	1979	HS 125/700A	NA0236	W/o Jackson, Wy. USA. 20 Dec 00.	N64HA
☐ N236JP	1967	Jet Commander	116	W/o Marion, Va. USA. 31 Oct 69.	N4743E
☐ N240AA	1966	Jet Commander	82	Wfu. Cx USA 9/03.	N103BW
☐ N241H	1979	Sabre-65	465-5	W/o Molokai-Hoolehua, Hi. USA. 11 May 00.	(N60CR)
☐ N244RD	1966	Learjet 24	24-120	Wfu. Parts at Dodsons, Rantoul, Ks. USA.	PT-LMF
☐ N250EC	1972	Sabre-40A	282-110	Wfu. Cx USA 4/04.	N477A
☐ N250UA	1967	Jet Commander-A	121	W/o Flatwood, La. USA. 27 Apr 78.	N1121R
☐ N253K	1974	Falcon 10	10	W/o Meigs-Chicago, Il. USA. 30 Jan 80. (parts at White Inds)	N105FJ
☐ N257TM	1966	Sabre-40	282-76	Wfu. Cx USA 6/02.	N256CM
☐ N267L	1965	JetStar-6	5067	W/o Luton, UK. 29 Mar 81.	(N267AD)
☐ N280AT	1978	Westwind-1124	247	W/o Panama City, Panama. 2 Jul 04.	N280AZ
Reg	Yr	Type	c/n	Owner/Operator	Prev Regn

Reg	Yr	Type	c/n	Owner/Operator	Prev Regn
❏ N287W	1969	Falcon 20D	194	Wfu. Parts at AVMATS Paynesville, Mo. USA.	N297W
❏ N300HW	1965	HS 125/1A	25021	Wfu. Parts at White Industries, Bates City, Mo. USA.	N711WJ
❏ N300JA	1974	Learjet 24D	24D-282	W/o Dutch Harbour, Ak. USA. 2 Dec 79.	D-INKA
❏ N300PL	1978	Learjet 25D	25D-247	Wfu. Parted out following accident 12/83.	
❏ N301AJ	1966	Jet Commander	48	W/o Cozumel, Mexico. 13 Aug 90.	N502U
❏ N302EJ	1975	Learjet 24D	24D-302	W/o Puerta Vallarta, Mexico. 14 Apr 83.	N39DM
❏ N303AF	1967	Learjet 24	24-144	Wfu. Parts at White Industries, Bates City, Mo. USA.	N700C
❏ N303GA	1980	Gulfstream 3	303	W/o Aspen, Co. USA. 29 Mar 01.	N1761W
❏ N305AJ	1967	Jet Commander	100	Wfu. Parts at OK Aircraft, Gilroy, Ca. USA.	N11WP
❏ N308WC	1961	JetStar-6	5020	Wfu. Cx USA 8/88.	(N777NN)
❏ N309CK	1981	Westwind-Two	350	W/o Irvine, Ca. USA. 15 Dec 93.	N777LU
❏ N309LJ	1969	Learjet 25	25-034	Wfu. Located Gloucester-Staverton, UK.	N309AJ
❏ N316M	1965	Learjet 23	23-061	W/o Lake Michigan, USA. 19 Mar 66.	
❏ N320MC	1968	HFB 320	1034	W/o Phoenix, Az. USA. 9 Mar 73.	N320J
❏ N320MJ	1969	B 707-321B	20028	W/o Marana, Az. USA. 20 Sep 90.	VR-CBN
❏ N320W	1965	Jet Commander	15	Wfu. Parts at White Industries, Bates City, Mo. USA.	N125K
❏ N321AF	1976	HFB 320	1060	Wfu. at Hollister, Ca. USA.	(D-CCCH)
❏ N322AF	1975	HFB 320	1058	Wfu. at Hollister, Ca. USA.	16+21
❏ N323AF	1979	HFB 320	1062	Wfu. at Hollister, Ca. USA.	N323AF
❏ N324AF	1980	HFB 320	1064	Wfu. at Hollister, Ca. USA.	16+27
❏ N325AF	1980	HFB 320	1065	Wfu. at Hollister, Ca. USA.	16+28
❏ N329J	1957	JetStar	1001	Wfu. pending move to Museum of Flight, Seattle, Wa. USA..	
❏ N331DP	1965	Learjet 23	23-067	W/o Dayton, Oh. USA. 18 Jan 90.	N720UA
❏ N331DP	1965	Learjet 23	23-059	Wfu. Located at Detroit, Mi. (N331DP transferred to 23-067).	N31DP
❏ N332PC	1965	Learjet 23	23-056	W/o Flint, Mi. USA. 6 Jan 77. (parts at White Inds.).	N362EJ
❏ N333AV	1966	Falcon 20C	28	Wfu. College of Aeronautics, Montreal St Hubert, Canada.	C-GEAQ
❏ N333BG	1967	Jet Commander	98	Wfu. Cx USA 6/97.	N301L
❏ N333CG	1978	Learjet 25D	25D-262	W/o Salina, Ks. USA. 12 Jun 01.	N440F
❏ N333GB	1966	BAC 1-11/401AK	076	Wfu. Last located San Antonio, Tx. USA.	VR-BHS
❏ N333SV	1968	Jet Commander	114	Wfu. Cx USA 1/98. Parts at Hollister, Ca. USA.	N85MR
❏ N334JC	1976	Citation	500-0334	Wfu. Cx USA 3/98.	ZS-MPI
❏ N338EC	1965	Sabreliner-731	5061	Wfu.	N333EC
❏ N349M	1965	Jet Commander	23	Wfu. Parts at White Industries, Bates City, Mo. USA.	N2100X
❏ N350JF	1979	Learjet 35A	35A-219	W/o over Adwa, Ethiopia. 29 Aug 99.	N502G
❏ N360HK	1973	Westwind-1123	166	Wfu.	C-GDOC
❏ N366AA	1974	Learjet 25B	25B-151	W/o Briggsdale, Co. USA. 31 Aug 74.	
❏ N380AA	1969	JetStar-8	5131	Wfu. Cx USA 3/92.	N212JW
❏ N386G	1965	Jet Commander	43	Wfu. Parted out 1989.	N121CS
❏ N388LS	1981	Learjet 35A	35A-388	W/o Lebanon, NH. USA. 24 Dec 96.	N388PD
❏ N390RB	2001	390 Premier 1	RB-26	W/o Herrera Santo Domingo, Dominican Republic. 7 Jan 03.	(N390HR)
❏ N395BB	1979	Falcon 20F	395	Wfu. As OD-PAL. Parts at White Industries Inc. Mo. USA.	OD-PAL
❏ N397F	1969	Gulfstream 2	72	W/o Burlington, Vt. USA. 22 Feb 76.	
❏ N397QS	1999	Citation V Ultra	560-0531	W/o Leakey, Tx. USA. 2 May 02.	
❏ N397RD	1968	Gulfstream 2	37	Wfu. Cx USA 11/02. Last located El Mirage, Ca. USA.	N994JD
❏ N399P	1967	Sabre-40	282-87	Wfu. Donated Pittsburgh Institute of Aeronautics, Pa. USA.	N36P
❏ N400CP	1965	Jet Commander	30	W/o Burlington, Vt. USA. 21 Jan 71.	N401V
❏ N400M	1961	JetStar-6	5008	W/o Saranac Lake, NY. USA. 27 Dec 72.	N500Z
❏ N400PH	1968	HS 125/400A	NA716	W/o Lexington, Ky. USA. 5 Dec 87.	N888CR
❏ N400VG	1996	Beechjet 400A	RK-113	W/o Beckley, WV. USA. 17 Apr 99.	N3263N
❏ N401DE	1967	Jet Commander	92	Wfu. Cx USA 3/89.	N33PS
❏ N401MS	1968	Sabre-60	306-17	Wfu. Cx USA 8/01.	N13SL
❏ N401RD	1975	Citation	500-0267	Wfu. Parts at Dodsons, Rantoul, Ks. USA.	(N4090P)
❏ N403M	1969	Jet Commander	132	W/o Salt Lake City, Ut. USA. 16 Dec 69.	N200M
❏ N405PC	1980	Citation 1/SP	501-0150	W/o Depere, Wi. USA. 3 Apr 01.	N73FW
❏ N408TR	1964	Sabre-40	282-4	Wfu. Located Toledo Public Schools, Swanton, Oh. USA.	N111MS
❏ N409MA	1970	Gulfstream 2	83	W/o Quito, Ecuador. 4 May 95.	(N48MS)
❏ N411BW	1985	Diamond-Two	A1008SA	Wfu. Parts at Dodsons, Rantoul, Ks. USA.	
❏ N418MA	1980	Citation II	550-0144	W/o Mineral Wells, Tx. USA. 18 Nov 03.	RP-C689
❏ N422BC	1980	Westwind-Two	302	W/o Milwaukee, Wi. USA. 26 Dec 99.	N100AK
❏ N425JA	1966	Falcon 20C	51	Wfu. Cx USA 10/94.	N425JF
❏ N428JX	1973	Learjet 25B	25B-103	W/o Richmond, In. USA. 3 Jul 75.	
❏ N431NA	1960	Sabreliner T-39D	285-2	Wfu. Cx USA 12/91.	USN 150970
❏ N431NA	1960	Sabreliner CT-39A	265-16	Wfu. Located Des Moines Educational Resources, Ia. USA.	USAF 60-348
❏ N432EJ	1965	Learjet 23	23-028A	W/o Muskegon, Mi. USA. 25 Oct 67.	N803LJ
❏ N434AN	1964	JetStar-731	5050	Wfu. Last located at Griffin, Ga. USA.	HZ-THZ
❏ N434EJ	1965	Learjet 23	23-046	W/o Pellston, Mi. USA. 9 May 70.	(N822LJ)
Reg	Yr	Type	c/n	Owner/Operator	Prev Regn

Reg	Yr	Type	c/n	Owner/Operator	Prev Regn
N440HM	1980	Learjet 35A	35A-294	W/o Greenville, SC. USA. 27 Feb 97	N35VP
N440RM	1961	JetStar-6	5016	Wfu. Last located Roswell, NM. USA.	N712GW
N442NE	1981	Learjet 35A	35A-442	W/o Morristown, NJ. USA. 26 Jul 88. (parts at White Inds.).	N35BK
N444TJ	1969	Jet Commander-B	146	Wfu. Parts at Griffin, Ga. USA.	N926JM
N445	1965	Jet Commander	37	Wfu. Last located scrapyard near Wiley Post, Ok. USA.	N723JB
N448GG	1965	Learjet 23	23-057	Wfu. Parts at Dodsons, Rantoul, Ks. USA.	N448GC
N454LJ	1996	Learjet 45	45-004	W/o Wallops Island, Va. USA. 27 Oct 98.	
N454RN	1966	Learjet 24	24-121	W/o Atlanta, Ga. USA. 26 Feb 73.	N454GL
N455JA	1974	Learjet 24XR	24XR-300	W/o Gulkana, Ak. USA. 20 Aug 85.	N300EJ
N456JA	1973	Learjet 24XR	24XR-265	W/o Nr Juneau, Ak. USA. 24 Oct 85.	N32WL
N458J	1973	Learjet 25XR	25XR-106	W/o Columbus, Oh. USA. 1 Jul 91.	N458JA
N460MC	1967	Falcon 20C	105	Wfu. Parts at Spirit of St Louis, Mo. USA.	N97FJ
N463LJ		Learjet 25	25-001	Wfu. Used in construction of s/n 25-002.	
N467H	1963	Sabre-40	282-3	Wfu. Located Van Nuys, Ca. USA.	(N57QR)
N480LR	1972	HFB 320	1054	Wfu. Cx USA 1/87. GTCC Aviation Center, Greensboro, NC.	N896HJ
N481DH	1969	Jet Commander-B	139	Wfu. Parts at White Industries, Bates City, Mo. USA.	N188G
N500AD	1972	Citation	500-0006	Wfu. Cx USA 5/91.	(N500AH)
N500BF	1965	Learjet 23	23-010	Wfu. Located Detroit-Willow Run, Mi. USA.	N400BF
N500CC	1969	Citation	669	Wfu. Cx USA 1/78.	
N500EA	2002	Eclipse 500	EX500-100	Wfu. Retired after 55 flights with TT 54 hours on 22 Oct 03.	
N500FM	1966	Learjet 23	23-088	W/o Columbia, Tn. USA. 2 Jul 91. (parts at Detroit).	(N500LH)
N500HH	1974	Citation	500-0189	Wfu. Cx USA 5/01. Located Addison, Tx. USA.	N189CC
N500J	1969	Gulfstream 2	60	W/o Hot Springs, Va. USA. 26 Sep 76.	N892GA
N500JJ	1959	B 707-138B	17699	Wfu.	G-AVZZ
N500JR	1966	Jet Commander	65	W/o North Platte, SD. USA. 26 Sep 66.	
N500JW	1964	Learjet 23	23-005	Wfu. Cx USA 8/87. Parts at Willow Run Detroit, Mi. USA.	N15BE
N500MA	1962	JetStar-731	5033	Wfu. Cx USA 9/02. Last located Conroe, Tx. USA.	N50EC
N500MF	1965	Jet Commander	34	Wfu. Parts at White Industries, Bates City, Mo. USA.	TG-OMF
N500NL	1974	Sabre-75A	380-8	W/o 23 Feb 75.	N5107
N500RW	1978	Learjet 35A	35A-148	W/o Teterboro, NJ. USA. 24 May 88.	N333RP
N500WN	1969	JetStar-8	5135	Wfu. Located AVMATS Spirit of St Louis, Mo. USA.	(N500FG)
N501AL	1961	JetStar-6	5012	Wfu. Derelict by 3/94 at Opa Locka, Fl. USA.	N500SJ
N501CC	1970	Citation	701	Wfu. Smithsonian 'Business Wings' exhibit, DC (was s/n 670).	
N501EZ	1978	Citation 1/SP	501-0058	W/o Grannis, Ar. USA. 2 Dec 98.	N211X
N501GP	1972	Citation	500-0026	W/o Bluefield, WV. USA. 21 Jan 81.	N526CC
N501PS	1974	Learjet 25B	25B-153	W/o Detroit, Mi. USA. 26 May 77.	
N503U	1966	Jet Commander	83	W/o nr Guatamala City, Guatamala. 19 Dec 95.	C-GHPR
N505PF	1965	Learjet 23	23-006	Wfu. Exhibit Kansas Aviation Museum, Mo. USA.	N111JD
N515VW	1968	Learjet 25	25-013	W/o Delemont, Switzerland. 17 Apr 69.	
N520S	1966	JetStar-731	5084	W/o Westchester, NY. USA. 11 Feb 81.	N901E
N521M	1967	HS 125/3A	25129	W/o Findlay, Oh. USA. 12 Dec 72.	G-AVDM
N521PA	1979	Learjet 35A	35A-239	W/o Fresno, Ca. USA. 14 Dec 94. Cx USA 5/95.	N239GJ
N525CJ	1991	CitationJet	702	Wfu. Modified to CJ-2 prototype with s/n 708.	
N525KL	1996	CitationJet	525-0136	W/o Point Lookout, Mo. USA. 10 Dec 99.	N52081
N530G	1967	JetStar-731	5096	Wfu. Cx USA 3/04.	N9252R
N535PC	1980	Learjet 35A	35A-291	W/o Aspen, Co. USA. 13 Feb 91.	N7US
N540CL	1965	Learjet 23	23-026	Wfu. Parts at Hollister, Ca. USA.	N404DB
N545BF	1970	JetStar-8	5146	Wfu. Cx USA 8/92.	N499AS
N546PA	1980	Learjet 36A	36A-045	W/o Astoria, Or. USA. 3 Dec 02.	N13FN
N547JL	1979	Sabre-75A	380-69	W/o Marion, Ks. USA. 20 Jul 98.	N111VX
N550CC	1977	Citation	686	Wfu.	
N555AJ	1971	Citation	500-0007	W/o Denver, Co. USA. 19 Nov 79.	N500LF
N555DM	1965	Jet Commander	25	Wfu. Parts at Dodsons, Rantoul, Ks. USA.	
N555LB	1968	Learjet 24	24-177	Wfu. Last located El Mirage, Ca. USA.	(N524DW)
N555PB	1964	JetStar-6	5047	Wfu. Last located Rockland, Me. USA. Cx USA 10/90.	N409MA
N555PT	1966	Sabre-40	282-53	Wfu. Cx USA 2/91. Parts at AVMATS, Mo. USA.	N600BP
N555SG	1966	JetStar-8	5090	Wfu. Last located Fort Lauderdale, Fl. USA.	N55CJ
N556AT	1972	Citation	500-0020	Wfu. Cx USA 2/93.	C-FBAX
N560CC	1977	Citation V	550-0001	Wfu. Located Wichita Area Technical College, Ks. USA.	N5050J
N560MC	1965	Jet Commander	24	Wfu.	(N7GW)
N560VP	1989	Citation V	560-0002	W/o La Carlota, Caracas, Venezuela. 15 Nov 04.	N101HB
N564MG	1961	JetStar-6	5021	Wfu. Fuselage only 5/88 at Memphis, Tn. USA.	C-FETN
N565KC	1969	Gulfstream 2TT	46	Wfu. Last located Islip, NY. USA.	N505JT
N566NA	1972	Learjet 25	25-064	Wfu. Located John C Stennis Space Center, Ms. USA.	N266GL
N567DW	1965	Sabre-40	282-35	Wfu. Parts at AVMATS Paynesville, Mo. USA.	N341AR
N580NJ	1966	Jet Commander	58	Wfu. Cx USA 12/00.	CP-2263

Reg	Yr	Type	c/n	Owner/Operator	Prev Regn
N580WE	1968	Jet Commander-A	123	Wfu. Cx USA 7/02. Parts at Dodsons, Rantoul, Ks. USA.	N1121A
N600K	1969	Jet Commander-B	148	Wfu. Cx USA 6/99. Parts at Hollister, Ca. USA.	(N22LL)
N600XJ	1969	Learjet 24B	24B-190	W/o Helendale, Ca. USA. 23 Dec 03.	N190BP
N601JJ	1967	JetStar-8	5102	Wfu. Cx USA 2/00.	N601JJ
N602GA	1969	HFB 320	1041	Wfu. Last located Toledo, Oh. USA.	N92045
N604AN	1975	Corvette	18	Wfu. Cx USA 12/90. To Spain for spares.	F-BTTO
N604GA	1969	HFB 320	1037	W/o Howell Island, Chesterfield, Mo. USA. 30 Nov 04.	YV-999P
N605GA	1969	HFB 320	1038	Wfu. Located Jefferson Technical College, Louisville, Ky.	N301AT
N611JC	1963	Jet Commander	2	Wfu. Test airframe for static fatigue.	
N614GB	1977	VFW 614	G14	Wfu. Located Oldenburg, Germany.	(OY-RGB)
N617CC	1981	Citation 1/SP	501-0211	Wfu. Cx USA 6/96.	N6785C
N617GA	1967	Falcon 20C	88	Wfu. Last located at Bates City, Mo. USA.	N41CD
N621ST	1964	HS 125/1A	25014	Wfu. Broken up for spares 3/85. Cx USA 6/02.	XA-JUZ
N626CC	1984	Citation III	650-0026	Wfu. Damaged on production line 1984, now test airframe.	
N627WS	1974	Learjet 25B	25B-170	W/o Houston, Tx. USA. 13 Jan 98.	N98796
N630N	1966	Sabre-40	282-73	Wfu. Cx USA 6/85. Parts at Spirit of St Louis, Mo. USA.	N630M
N650	1980	Citation VII	697	Wfu. Located Wichita-Mid Continent, Ks. USA.	
N650CC	1979	Citation	696	Wfu. Cx USA 11/89.	
N650DH	1966	BAC 1-11/2400	059	Wfu. Cx USA 12/92.	N700JA
N658TC	1969	Learjet 25	25-044	W/o Victoria, Tx. USA. 18 Jan 72.	N962GA
N660A	1968	Learjet 24	24-155	Wfu. Parts at El Mirage, Ca. USA. (as N464CL).	N210FP
N661LJ		Learjet 25	25-002	Wfu. AiResearch engine tests.	
N666BT	1965	Falcon 20C	7	Wfu. Last located at Oklahoma City, Ok. USA.	XA-ACI
N666TW	1973	Learjet 25B	25B-116	W/o Del Rio, Tx. USA. 19 Sep 03.	(N818GY)
N678BC	1967	JetStar-731	5109	Wfu. Cx USA 11/92.	N968BN
N690LJ	1965	Learjet 23	23-078	W/o Orlando, Fl. USA. 30 Nov 67.	
N700CW	1974	Citation	500-0205	W/o Eagle Pass, Tx. USA. 1 Apr 83.	(N541NC)
N700DK	1981	Falcon 10	191	W/o Pal-Waukee, Il. USA. 23 Sep 85.	N256FJ
N701JA	1967	Gulfstream II SP	7	Wfu. Cx USA 11/03. Last located 12/04 at Van Nuys, Ca. USA.	N118NP
N705EA	1968	HS 125/731	NA705	Wfu. Last located at Bates City, Mo. USA.	N25MJ
N706A	1964	Sabre-40	282-7	Wfu. Last located Opa Locka, Fl. USA.	XA-STU
N707FH	1966	Sabre-40	282-74	Wfu. Cx USA 10/02.	N707TG
N707RZ	1962	B 707-328	18375	Wfu. Broken up at Fort Lauderdale, Fl. USA.	F-BHSU
N710JW	1965	Jet Commander	35	Wfu. Cx USA 11/92.	N7HL
N710K	1962	MS 760 Paris	112	Wfu. Located Mojave, Ca. USA.	N7277X
N710MB	1984	Diamond 1A	A078SA	W/o Nr Goodland, Ks. USA. 15 Dec 93.	N378DM
N711AF	1975	Learjet 35	35-029	W/o 100km South of Katab, Egypt. 11 Aug 79.	
N711EV	1973	Gulfstream II SP	129	Wfu. Cx USA 10/03.	N626TC
N711JT	1967	Jet Commander	91	W/o Tullahoma, Tn. USA. 13 Mar 75.	N73535
N711WM	1982	Citation II/SP	551-0388	W/o 6 Nov 86.	
N711Z	1960	JetStar	1002	Wfu. Displayed as USAF 89001 at Andrews AFB, Md. USA.	N329K
N715MH	1973	Learjet 25B	25B-132	W/o Ciudad Victoria, Mexico. 26 Oct 01.	N715JF
N717JM	1961	JetStar-6	5009	Wfu. Cx USA 8/84.	(HB-VET)
N720Q	1969	Gulfstream 2	58	W/o Kline, SC. USA. 24 Jun 74.	N878GA
N722KS	1968	Falcon 20C	130	Wfu. Last located Ontario, Ca,. USA. Cx USA 3/04.	(N130TJ)
N723GL	1977	Learjet 35A	35A-107	W/o College Station-Easterwood, Tx. USA. 12 Dec 85.	
N724LG	1967	Learjet 24	24-143	Wfu. Last located El Mirage, Ca. USA.	(N24WF)
N727RL	1964	B 727-25	18253	Wfu.	EL-GOL
N727US	1978	Sabre-75A	380-61	Wfu. Cx USA 10/99. Parts at AVMATS St Louis, Mo. USA.	9L-LAW
N730CP	1972	Sabre-40A	282-103	Wfu. Located Toledo, Oh. USA.	N730CA
N731L	1966	JetStar-731	5095	Wfu. Cx USA 11/03.	N780RH
N739R	1966	Sabre-40	282-78	W/o Ventura, Ca. USA. 16 May 67.	
N743R	1968	Sabre-60	306-11	W/o Montrose, Ca. USA. 13 Apr 73.	N723R
N745F	1965	Learjet 23	23-077	W/o Perris, Ca. USA. 30 Jul 88.	(N611CA)
N747E	1964	Sabre-40	282-22	W/o Buenos Aires, Argentina. 22 Dec 94.	N747
N747GB	1969	JetStar-8	5141	Wfu. Located Lagos, Nigeria.	N3982A
N747LB	1966	Jet Commander-B	55	Wfu. Cx USA 11/03.	N11MC
N750SB	1968	HFB 320	1031	Wfu. Located Opa Locka, Fl. USA.	N300SB
N751CR	1966	Jet Commander	88	Wfu. Located at OK Aircraft, Gilroy, Ca. USA.	N70CS
N754DB	1968	Learjet 25	25-014	Wfu. Cx USA 5/04.	N14LJ
N760J	1958	MS 760 Paris	6	Wfu.	N84J
N760M	1959	MS 760 Paris	49	W/o Evadale, Tx. USA. 3 May 69.	
N760T	1961	MS 760 Paris-2B	103	Wfu. Located Mojave, Ca. USA.	N760N
N769K	1974	Citation	500-0228	Wfu. Parts at White Industries, Bates City, Mo. USA.	N6365C
N771WB	1969	Sabre-60	306-29	Wfu. Destroyed by fire as N771WW. (parts at White Inds).	N771WW
N774W	1975	Sabre-75A	380-37	Wfu. Cx USA 9/03.	N65
Reg	**Yr**	**Type**	**c/n**	**Owner/Operator**	**Prev Regn**

Reg	Yr	Type	c/n	Owner/Operator	Prev Regn
N777EP	1960	JetStar-6	5004	Wfu. Located at Gracelands, Memphis, Tn. USA.	N69HM
N777PQ	1970	HFB 320	1050	Wfu.	N777PZ
N777PY	1997	Gulfstream V	508	Wfu. Last located Savannah, Ga. USA.	N777TY
N779XX	1983	Challenger 601	3018	W/o Milan, Italy. 7 Feb 85.	C-GBXW
N780PV	1965	Jet Commander	36	Wfu. Cx USA 5/88. Was instructional airframe Norway.	N730PV
N784B	1982	Falcon 50	118	W/o Teterboro, NJ. USA. 10 Nov 85.	(N183B)
N787R	1974	Sabre-60	306-77	Wfu. Parts at AVMATS Spirit of St Louis, Mo. USA.	N180AR
N787WB	1977	JetStar 2	5210	W/o Austin, Tx. USA 27 Nov 98.	N707WB
N793NA	1959	B 707-138B	17700	Wfu. Located, Tucson, Az.	VP-BDE
N797SC	1969	Learjet 25	25-042	Wfu. Located Deland, Fl. USA.	(N125WD)
N800CS	1966	Sabre-40	282-64	Wfu. Cx USA 2/90.	N9000S
N801	1969	JetStar-8	5138	Wfu. Located Greenville Technical College, SC. USA.	N31DK
N801L	1963	Learjet 23	23-001	W/o Wichita, Ks. USA. 4 Jun 64.	
N802L	1964	Learjet 23	23-002	Wfu. Located Steven F Udar-Hazy Center, Dulles, Va.	
N804LJ	1965	Learjet 23	23-015A	W/o Jackson, Mi. USA. 21 Oct 65.	
N804LJ	1964	Learjet 23	23-004	Wfu. Re-certificated s/n 23-015A. Subsequently W/o 21 Oct 65	
N805C	1981	Challenger 600	1037	W/o Sun Valley, Id. USA. 3 Jan 83.	C-GLYE
N805F	1966	Falcon 20C	60	W/o Boca Raton, Fl. USA. 5 Jul 71.	N885F
N805NA	1966	Learjet 24A	24A-102	W/o Victorville, Ca. USA. 7 Jun 01.	N706NA
N808JA	1965	Learjet 23	23-050A	W/o in ground firo 23 May 82.	N808LJ
N811HI	1970	Citation 1/SP	501-0114	Wfu. Parts at White Industries Inc. Bates City, Mo. USA.	(N725RH)
N813AA	1966	Falcon 20C	25	Wfu. Last located Detroit-Willow Run, Mi. USA.	TG-GGA
N813M	1978	Learjet 35A	35A-151	Wfu. Stolen ex Wichita 13 Apr 84. Cx USA 6/86.	N711L
N814NA	1960	JetStar-6	5003	Wfu. Located Plant 42 Heritage Park, Palmdale, Ca. USA.	NASA14
N821LG	1980	Falcon 10	170	W/o Nr West Chester, Pa. USA. 2 Feb 86.	N236FJ
N822LJ	1965	Learjet 23	23-080	W/o Detroit, Mi. USA. 9 Dec 67.	
N824LJ	1966	Learjet 23	23-083	Wfu. Located Kalamazoo Air Zoo, Kalamazoo, Mi. USA.	
N830G	1968	Gulfstream 2	44	Wfu. Cx USA 1/02.	N585A
N831LC	1966	HS 125/1A-522	25095	W/o Nr San Diego, Ca. USA. 16 Mar 91.	N25AW
N831RA	1968	Learjet 24	24-164	Wfu. Last located Dodsons, Rantoul, Ks.	(XA-TKC)
N833NA	1961	B 720-061	18066	W/o Edwards AFB. Ca. USA. 1 Dec 84.	N2697V
N848C	1966	Jet Commander	54	Wfu. Cx USA 8/88.	N6534V
N856MA	1969	Sabre-60	306-41	W/o Democratic Republic of Congo in 2003.	(N62DW)
N864CL	1970	Learjet 24B	24B-229	W/o San Francisco, Ca. USA. 9 Oct 84.	N551AS
N866JS	1965	Learjet 23	23-018	W/o Richmond, Va. USA. 6 May 80. (parts at White Inds.).	N866DB
N873LP	1977	Learjet 35A	35A-104	W/o Auburn, Al. USA. 22 Sep 85.	N87W
N880A	1968	Gulfstream 2	38	Wfu. Cx USA 4/95. Located Detroit Willow Run, Mi. USA.	N80A
N880EP	1960	Convair 880	38	Wfu. Located at Elvis Presley's Graceland Estate, Memphis.	N8809E
N881FC	1968	Learjet 24	24-175	Wfu. Last located FXE, USA. Cx USA 3/93.	N28BK
N888AR	1966	Falcon 20C	33	W/o Acapulco, Mexico. 7 Aug 76.	N369EJ
N888DL	1971	HFB 320	1051	Wfu. Cx USA 8/90.	N6ZA
N888RW	1962	JetStar-6	5040	Wfu. Cx USA 6/88.	(N88892)
N897WA	1962	B 707-321B	18339	Wfu.	OE-IEB
N900CD	1966	HS 125/3A	25111	Wfu. Cx USA 7/99. Parts at White Industries, Mo. USA.	N177GP
N900CR	1962	JetStar-731	5036	Wfu. Last located 10/99 at Griffin, Ga. USA.	N90KR
N900WJ	1982	Diamond 1A	A028SA	W/o Dallas, Tx. USA. 27 Jan 00.	N331DC
N902GT	1967	Gulfstream II SP	2	Wfu. Cx USA 7/03.	N434JW
N910MH	1965	Jet Commander	45	Wfu. Located College of Aeronautics, La Guardia, NY. USA.	N121PG
N911AS	1965	HS 125/1A	25039	Wfu. Last located Montgomery, Al. USA.	N125TB
N912AS	1967	HS 125/3A	25124	Wfu. Located Montgomery, Al. USA.	N552N
N920G	1974	Sabre-60	306-74	W/o Lancaster, Pa. USA. 27 Dec 74.	
N921FP	1984	Learjet 55	55-103	W/o Rutland, Vt. USA. 6 Aug 86.	
N925R	1966	Jet Commander	80	Wfu.	N173AR
N930GL	1980	Learjet 35A	35A-330	Wfu. Cx USA 7/91.	
N945MC	1975	Falcon 10	37	Wfu. Cx USA 1/04. Last located at Griffin, Ga. USA.	N72GW
N946JR	1968	Sabre-60	306-10	Wfu. Parts at AVMATS Paynesville, Mo. USA.	N125MC
N957TH	1966	Falcon 20C	38	Wfu. Parts at Elsberry, Mo. USA.	N1107M
N959SC	1965	Learjet 23	23-045A	W/o Detroit City, Mi. USA. 23 Jul 91.	F-BSUX
N960CC	1959	B 707-123B	17634	Wfu. Last located Amarillo, Tx. USA.	N707AR
N970GA	1971	Falcon 20F	246	Wfu. Last located at Bates City, Mo. USA.	(F-GLMT)
N971AS	1961	JetStar-731	5007	Wfu. Last located Atlanta-Peachtree, USA..	N72CT
N984HF	1969	HS 125/731	NA717	W/o Sparta, Tn. USA. 7 Nov 85.	N100HF
N984JD	1987	Learjet 31	31-001	Wfu. Cx USA 4/99. Parts at Dodsons, Rantoul, Ks. USA.	N311DF
N988MT	1962	Sabreliner CT-39A	276-32	Wfu. Located Metro Aviation Tech Career Center, OKC. USA.	62-4479
N990L	1966	Falcon 20C	43	W/o Dallas NAS, Tx. USA. 8 Mar 75.	N872F
N991PC	1989	Citation V	560-0043	W/o Eagle River, Wi. USA. 30 Dec 95.	(N2665F)
Reg	Yr	Type	c/n	Owner/Operator	Prev Regn

Reg	Yr	Type	c/n	Owner/Operator	Prev Regn
N996JR	1996	CitationJet	525-0147	W/o Coupeville, Wa. USA. 22 Jul 03.	N52178
N997TD	1972	Learjet 24D	24D-247	W/o Sierra Blanca, Tx. USA. 10 Dec 01.	N247DB
N998RD	1967	Jet Commander	103	Wfu. at Dodsons, Rantoul, Ks. USA.	N77HH
N999BH	1980	Learjet 25D	25D-318	W/o nr Santa Fe, NM. USA. 5 Sep 93.	N522TA
N999CV	1974	Citation	500-0211	Wfu. Parts at White Industries, Bates City, Mo. USA.	N999CB
N999HG	1974	Learjet 25B	25B-178	W/o Sanford, NC. USA. 8 Sep 77.	N999MV
N1001U		Caravelle 6R	86	Wfu. Located Pima Air Museum, Tucson, Az. USA.	PT-DUW
N1021B	1966	Learjet 23	23-086	W/o Racine, Wi. USA. 6 Nov 69.	
N1121E	1965	Jet Commander	20	Wfu. Parts at Hollister, Ca. USA.	N334LP
N1121F	1969	Jet Commander-B	150	W/o La Carbonera, Zacatecas, Mexico. 21 May 97.	N121FM
N1121G	1966	Jet Commander	67	Wfu. Parts at Dodsons, Rantoul, Ks. USA.	N650M
N1121M	1967	Jet Commander	111	Wfu. Parts at Long Beach, Ca. USA.	C-GDJW
N1121N	1967	Jet Commander	110	Wfu. Parts were at Hollister, Ca. USA.	N16GH
N1123E	1967	HS 125/3A-R	25149	Wfu. Malaysian Institute of Aviation Technology,Kuala Lumpur	N99KR
N1123H	1973	Westwind-1123	167	Wfu. Parts at White Industries, Bates City, Mo. USA.	N873EJ
N1135K	1965	HS 125/1A	25019	W/o Des Moines, Ia. USA. 24 Feb 66.	N1125G
N1151K	1968	JetStar-731	5115	Wfu. Cx USA 9/96.	N8300E
N1181G	1981	Falcon 50	72	W/o Lake Geneva, Wi. USA. 12 May 85. (parts at Paynesville).	N82FJ
N1218S	1982	Citation II/SP	551-0428	W/o Cordele, Ga. USA. 22 Dec 99.	(N147RP)
N1501	1965	Falcon 20C	15	Wfu. Last located Detroit-Willow Run, Mi. USA.	N151CG
N1777T	1966	Jet Commander	62	Wfu. Last located at Tucson, Az. USA.	C-GKFS
N1846	1966	Falcon 20C	47	W/o Parkersburg, WV. USA. 13 Mar 68.	N875F
N1863T	1966	Sabre-40	282-62	Wfu. Cx USA 8/87.	
N1909D	1966	Sabre-40	282-57	Wfu. Cx USA 4/97. Parts at AVMATS St Louis, Mo. USA.	N1909R
N1929P	1962	Sabreliner CT-39A	276-48	Wfu. Pittsburgh Institute of Aeronautics. USA. (or Taiwan ?)	N6612S
N1963A	1966	Learjet 23	23-097	Wfu. Parts at Tara Field, Hampton, Ga. USA. .	N1968A
N1965W	1962	Sabreliner CT-39A	276-9	Wfu. Located Westwood College of Aviation Technology, Ca.	62-4456
N1966J	1966	Jet Commander	66	Wfu. Parts at White Industries, Bates City, Mo. USA.	
N1968W	1966	Learjet 23	23-089	Wfu. Cx USA 4/01. Parts at Dodson's, Ottawa, Ks. USA.	N969B
N2114E	1973	HS 125/600A	6022	Wfu. Located Hooks Airport, Tx. USA.	XA-XET
N2120Q	1967	Westwind-1123	107	Wfu.	CA-01
N2200A	1975	Sabre-75A	380-26	Wfu. Last located Spirit of St Louis, Mo. USA.	N128MS
N2265Z	1976	Sabre-75A	380-43	Wfu. Parts at Clarksville, Mo. USA.	N6NR
N2286D	1982	Learjet 35A	35A-482	W/o Straits of Malacca, Malaysia. 14 Feb 93.	N482U
N2503L	1965	Learjet 23	23-047	Wfu. Parts at Dodsons, Rantoul, Ks. USA.	N444WC
N2579E	1965	Jet Commander	21	Wfu. Parts at White Industries, Bates City, Mo. USA.	CF-WOA
N2627U	1982	Citation 1/SP	501-0247	W/o Wichita, Ks. USA. 12 Nov 82.	(N24CH)
N2954T	1966	Falcon 20C	58	Wfu. Parted out 1987.	HB-VDG
N3080	1966	JetStar-6	5094	Wfu.	N3030
N3118M	1969	HS 125/400A	25199	Wfu. Parts at Dodson's, Rantoul, Ks. USA.	(N905Y)
N3274Q	1966	HS 125/1A	25102	Wfu. Cx USA 12/95.	XB-AKW
N3278	1969	Sabre-60	306-32	Wfu. Parts at AVMATS Spirit of St Louis, Mo. USA.	N4743N
N3504	1960	Sabreliner CT-39A	265-32	Wfu. Located Parks College Aviation School, St Louis. USA.	60-3504
N3507W	1960	Sabreliner CT-39A	265-35	Wfu. Located West Los Angeles College, Ca. USA.	60-3507
N3833L	1967	B 720-047B	19523	Wfu. To USAF for KC-135E spares 9/83.	5V-TAD
N4060K		Sabre-UTX	246-1	Wfu. Mock up until 1967, and subsequently broken up.	
N4253A	1973	HS 125/600B	6005	Wfu. Cx USA 6/95. Parts at White Industries, Mo. USA.	EC-EAC
N4400E	1965	HS 125/1A	25026	Wfu. Parts at Spirit of St Louis, Mo. USA.	(XA-...)
N4550T	1968	BAC 1-11/204AF	135	Wfu. Cx USA 12/93.	HZ-MO1
N5027Q	2001	Learjet 60	60-242	W/o Santa Cruz do Sul, Brazil. 7 Oct 02.	(PR-LDF)
N5038	1959	B 707-123B	17652	Wfu.	N7525A
N5075L	1968	Sabre-60A	306-16	Wfu. Cx USA 5/95. Parts at AVMATS Paynesville, Mo. USA.	N38UT
N5094B	1968	Jet Commander	105	Wfu. Parts at White Industries, Bates City, Mo. USA.	C-GWPV
N5269A	1998	Citation VII	650-7109	W/o ground accident Wichita, Ks. USA. Dec 99.	(N709QS)
N5565	1973	Sabre-40A	282-119	W/o Oklahoma City, Ok. USA. 15 Jan 74.	N8341N
N5863		Convair 880	48	Wfu. Cx USA 10/86.	N58RD
N5878	1961	MS 760 Paris-2B	106	Wfu.	PH-MSV
N6555C	1967	Falcon 20C	78	Wfu. Located Greenville/Donaldson Center, SC. USA.	VH-JSX
N6581E	1961	Sabreliner CT-39A	265-82	Wfu. Located Spokane Community College, Wa. USA.	61-0679
N6887Y	1981	Citation II	550-0293	W/o Billings, Mt. USA. 19 Dec 92.	
N7028F	1969	Jet Commander-A	131	Wfu. Located Fairmont State College, Fairmont, WV. USA.	N43
N7143N	1961	Sabreliner CT-39A	265-70	Wfu. Last located Fujairah, UAE.	61-0667
N7145V	1960	JetStar-731	5001	Wfu. Parts at White Industries, Bates City, Mo. USA. (4/98).	N11
N7158Q	1969	HFB 320	1040	Wfu. Cx USA 3/99. Last located El Mirage, Ca. (as I-ITAL).	I-ITAL
N7201U	1959	B 720-022	17907	Wfu. Scrapped at Luton, UK. 13 Jul 82.	
N7224U	1962	B 720-022	18077	Wfu. Cx USA 2/87.	
Reg	**Yr**	**Type**	**c/n**	**Owner/Operator**	**Prev Regn**

Reg	Yr	Type	c/n	Owner/Operator	Prev Regn
☐ N7572N	1971	Sabre-75	370-1	Wfu. Used as parts in other test aircraft.	
☐ N7775	1966	JetStar-6	5073	Wfu. Cx USA 12/86.	
☐ N7842M	1966	Falcon 20C	42	W/o Fort Worth, Tx. USA. 16 Jan 74.	N1503
☐ N8000Z	1973	HS 125/600A	6012	Wfu. Cx USA 12/95. Parts at Hooks Airport, Tx. USA.	EC-EOQ
☐ N8070U	1967	Jet Commander-B	124	Wfu. Parts at O K Aviation Inc. Monterey, Ca. USA.	XA-RQT
☐ N8221M	1984	Diamond 1A	A076SA	W/o Jasper Hinton, Alberta, Canada as C-GLIG. 1 Mar 95.	C-GLIG
☐ N8534	1968	Jet Commander	113	Wfu. Last located Deland, Fl. USA.	4X-CPB
☐ N8733	1969	B 707-331B	20062	Wfu. To USAF for KC-135E spares 5/86.	
☐ N9023W	1965	Jet Commander	10	Wfu. Instructional airframe Norwegian Mechanics School.	N5BP
☐ N9166Y	1961	Sabreliner CT-39A	265-80	Wfu. Located Helena VoTec Center, Helena, Mt. USA.	61-0677
☐ N9258U	1978	Falcon 10	132	Wfu. Parts at White Industries, Bates City, Mo. USA.	TC-ATI
☐ N9503Z	1964	Sabre-40	282-10	W/o Blaine, Mn. USA. 7 Mar 73.	N525N
☐ N9739B	1964	JetStar-6	5052	Wfu. Last located Bi-States Park, St Louis, Mo. USA.	C-FDTM
☐ N10855	1990	BAe 1000B	8159	Wfu. Cx USA 7/03.	G-OPFC
☐ N12058	1984	Citation T-47A	552-0004	W/o hangar fire Forbes Field, Topeka, Ks. USA. 20 Jul 93.	(162758)
☐ N12065	1985	Citation T-47A	552-0011	W/o hangar fire Forbes Field, Topeka, Ks. USA. 20 Jul 93.	(162765)
☐ N12269	1985	Citation T-47A	552-0015	W/o hangar fire Forbes Field, Topeka, Ks. USA. 20 Jul 93.	(162769)
☐ N12557	1984	Citation T-47A	552-0003	W/o hangar fire Forbes Field, Topeka, Ks. USA. 20 Jul 93.	(162757)
☐ N12564	1985	Citation T-47A	552-0010	W/o hangar fire Forbes Field, Topeka, Ks. USA. 20 Jul 93.	(162764)
☐ N12566	1985	Citation T-47A	552-0012	Wfu. Located Technical School, Columbus-Bolton, Oh.	(162766)
☐ N12568	1985	Citation T-47A	552-0014	Wfu. Located at Cessna Experimental, Wichita, Ks. USA.	(162768)
☐ N12600	1985	Citation T-47A	552-0006	W/o hangar fire Forbes Field, Topeka, Ks. USA. 20 Jul 93.	(162760)
☐ N12756	1984	Citation T-47A	552-0002	W/o hangar fire Forbes Field, Topeka, Ks. USA. 20 Jul 93.	(162756)
☐ N12761	1984	Citation T-47A	552-0007	W/o hangar fire Forbes Field, Topeka, Ks. USA. 20 Jul 93.	(162761)
☐ N12762	1985	Citation T-47A	552-0008	W/o hangar fire Forbes Field, Topeka, Ks. USA. 20 Jul 93.	(162762)
☐ N12763	1985	Citation T-47A	552-0009	W/o hangar fire Forbes Field, Topeka, Ks. USA. 20 Jul 93.	(162763)
☐ N12855	1984	Citation T-47A	552-0001	W/o hangar fire Forbes Field, Topeka, Ks. USA. 20 Jul 93.	(167255)
☐ N12859	1984	Citation T-47A	552-0005	W/o hangar fire Forbes Field, Topeka, Ks. USA. 20 Jul 93.	(162759)
☐ N12967	1985	Citation T-47A	552-0013	W/o hangar fire Forbes Field, Topeka, Ks. USA. 20 Jul 93.	(162767)
☐ N21092	1961	Sabreliner CT-39A	265-42	Wfu. Blackhawk Technical College, Janesville, Wi. USA.	61-0639
☐ N29019	1970	Sabre-75	370-6	Wfu. Cx USA 10/91. Parts at AVMATS Paynesville, Mo. USA.	(N30EV)
☐ N29977	1966	HS 125/1A	25028	Wfu. Cx USA 4/91. Parts at White Industries, Mo. USA.	XA-ESQ
☐ N32010	1961	Sabreliner CT-39A	265-83	Wfu. Central Missouri State University, Warrensburg, Mo.USA.	61-0680
☐ N32508	1961	Sabreliner T-39D	285-17	Wfu. National Museum of Naval Aviation, Pensacola, Fl. USA.	150985
☐ N35403	1980	Citation II/SP	551-0029	W/o Ainsworth, Ne. USA. 1 Jan 05. (was 550-0379).	N450GM
☐ N40180	1976	Falcon 10	93	Wfu. Parts at White Industries, Bates City, Mo. USA.	F-BYCV
☐ N41953	1971	HS 125/F400A	25268	Wfu. Located Arnoni Aviation Inc. Houston, Tx. USA.	(N268TS)
☐ N65618	1962	Sabreliner CT-39A	276-42	Wfu. Northwestern Community College, Rangely, Co. USA.	62-4489
☐ N71543	1975	Sabre-75A	380-29	Wfu. Last located University of Illinois.	N132MS
☐ N72028	1974	Sabre-75A	380-14	Wfu. Parts at Dodsons, Rantoul, Ks. USA.	N53
☐ N91669	1965	Jet Commander	17	Wfu. Parts at OK Aircraft, Gilroy, Ca. USA.	C-FSUA
☐ N98386	1965	Learjet 23	23-040	Wfu. Cx USA 8/82.	(N12HJ)
Military					
☐ 150542		Sabreliner T-39D	277-1	Wfu. Stored China Lake, Ca. USA.	
☐ 150544		Sabreliner T-39D	277-3	Wfu. at AMARC 3/85 as 7T-006. Tt 5872.	
☐ 150545		Sabreliner T-39D	277-4	Wfu.	
☐ 150546		Sabreliner T-39D	277-5	Wfu. at AMARC 7/85 as 7T-014. Tt 9124.	
☐ 150549		Sabreliner T-39D	277-8	Wfu. at AMARC 3/85 as 7T-011. Tt 7886.	
☐ 150550		Sabreliner T-39D	277-9	Wfu. at AMARC.	
☐ 150551		Sabreliner T-39D	277-10	Wfu. at AMARC 10/81 as 7T-002.	
☐ 150971	1960	Sabreliner T-39D	285-3	Wfu. at AMARC as 7T-001.	
☐ 150973	1960	Sabreliner T-39D	285-5	Wfu. at AMARC 4/85 as 7T-013. Tt 7155.	
☐ 150974	1960	Sabreliner T-39D	285-6	Wfu. at AMARC 7/85 as 7T-015. Tt 8737.	
☐ 150975	1960	Sabreliner T-39D	285-7	Wfu. at AMARC 3/85 as 7T-007. Tt 9524.	
☐ 150976	1960	Sabreliner T-39D	285-8	Wfu. at AMARC 7/85 as 7T-016. Tt 7943.	
☐ 150978	1961	Sabreliner T-39D	285-10	Wfu. at AMARC 3/85 as 7T-009. Tt 7576.	
☐ 150979	1961	Sabreliner T-39D	285-11	Wfu. at AMARC 7/85 as 7T-017. Tt 8631.	
☐ 150980	1961	Sabreliner T-39D	285-12	Wfu. at AMARC 3/85 as 7T-004.	
☐ 150981	1961	Sabreliner T-39D	285-13	Wfu. at AMARC 3/85 as 7T-012. Tt 8184.	
☐ 150982	1961	Sabreliner T-39D	285-14	Wfu. at AMARC 2/86 as 7T-022. Tt 8188.	
☐ 150983	1961	Sabreliner T-39D	285-15	Wfu. at AMARC 2/86 as 7T-023. Tt 9833.	
☐ 150984	1961	Sabreliner T-39D	285-16	Wfu. at AMARC 3/85 as 7T-010. Tt 8552.	
☐ 150986	1961	Sabreliner T-39D	285-18	Wfu. Preserved Robins AFB. Ga. USA.	
☐ 150987	1961	Sabreliner T-39D	285-19	Wfu. Preserved at NAS Patuxent River, Md. USA.	
☐ 150988	1961	Sabreliner T-39D	285-20	Wfu. at AMARC 3/85 as 7T-005. Tt 9208.	
☐ 150989	1961	Sabreliner T-39D	285-21	Wfu. Stored China Lake, Ca. USA.	
Reg	*Yr*	*Type*	*c/n*	*Owner/Operator*	*Prev Regn*

Reg	Yr	Type	c/n	Owner/Operator	Prev Regn
❑ 150990	1961	Sabreliner T-39D	285-22	Wfu. at AMARC 2/86 as 7T-024. Tt 9804.	
❑ 150991	1961	Sabreliner T-39D	285-23	Wfu. at AMARC 7/84 as 7T-003. Tt 8677.	
❑ 151338	1961	Sabreliner T-39D	285-27	Wfu. Southern Museum of Flight, Birmingham, Al. USA.	
❑ 151339	1961	Sabreliner T-39D	285-28	Wfu. Preserved NAS Pensacola, Fl. USA.	
❑ 151340	1961	Sabreliner T-39D	285-29	Wfu. at AMARC 1/86 as 7T-018. Tt 8563.	
❑ 151341	1961	Sabreliner T-39D	285-30	Wfu. at AMARC 1/86 as 7T-019. Tt 10118.	
❑ 151342	1961	Sabreliner T-39D	285-31	Wfu. Located Milwaukee Area Techical College, Wi. USA.	
❑ 151343	1961	Sabreliner T-39D	285-32	Wfu. NAS Pensacola, Fl. USA.	
❑ 157352	1965	Sabreliner CT-39E	282-46	W/o Alameda AFB. Ca. USA. 21 Dec 75.	test
❑ 157353	1967	Sabreliner CT-39E	282-84	Wfu. At AMARC 5/00.	N2254B
❑ 158383	1968	Sabreliner CT-39E	282-96	Wfu. Parts at Dodsons, Rantoul, Ks. USA.	N4705N
❑ 159362	1973	Sabreliner CT-39G	306-66	Wfu. at Mojave, Ca. USA.	N8365N
❑ 159363	1973	Sabreliner CT-39G	306-67	Wfu. Located Edwards AFB. Ca. USA.	
❑ 160057	1975	Sabreliner CT-39G	306-108	W/o Glenview NAS, USA. 3 Mar 91.	N65799
❑ 165522	1965	Sabre T-39N	282-28	W/o Nr Pensacola NAS, Fl. USA. 8 May 02.	N314NT
❑ 165525	1972	Sabre T-39N	282-100	W/o Nr Pensacola, Fl. USA. 8 May 02.	N317NT
❑ 165938	2001	Citation UC-35D	560-0567	W/o Miramar, Ca. USA. 10 Mar 04.	N5268A
❑ 2106	1978	Guardian HU-25A	402	Wfu. at AMARC as 410007 10/95.	N187F
❑ 2107	1979	Guardian HU-25D	409	Wfu. at AMARC as 410018 9/01.	N407F
❑ 2108	1979	Guardian HU-25A	405	Wfu. at AMARC as 410016 8/01.	N405F
❑ 2115	1979	Guardian HU-25A	419	Wfu. at AMARC as 410017 9/01.	N419F
❑ 2116	1980	Guardian HU-25A	420	Wfu. at AMARC as 410005 /95.	N420F
❑ 2119	1980	Guardian HU-25A	424	Wfu. at AMARC as 410002 /94. (not noted 11/03).	N424F
❑ 2122	1980	Guardian HU-25B	433	Wfu. at AMARC as 410020 9/01.	N432F
❑ 2123	1980	Guardian HU-25A	435	Wfu. Last located Alton-St Louis, Mo. USA.	N433F
❑ 2124	1980	Guardian HU-25A	437	Wfu. at AMARC 2/02.	N435F
❑ 2126	1981	Guardian HU-25B	441	Wfu. at AMARC 2/02.	N445F
❑ 2127	1981	Guardian HU-25A	443	Wfu. at AMARC as 410001 /94.	N447F
❑ 2130	1981	Guardian HU-25C	450	Wfu. at AMARC 11/03.	N458F
❑ 2132	1981	Guardian HU-25B	454	Wfu. at AMARC as 410019 9/01.	N461F
❑ 2137	1981	Guardian HU-25A	462	Wfu. at AMARC 3/02.	N470F
❑ 2138	1982	Guardian HU-25A	464	Wfu. at AMARC as 41009 10/95.	N472F
❑ 58-6970	1959	C-137B	17925	Wfu. Located Boeing Museum of Flight, Seattle, Wa. USA.	
❑ 58-6971	1959	C-137B	17926	Wfu. Located Pima County Museum, Tuscon, Az. USA.	
❑ 58-6972	1959	C-137B	17927	Wfu.	
❑ 59-2868	1959	Sabreliner CT-39A	265-1	Wfu. Located Albuquerque, NM. USA.	(N2259V)
❑ 59-2869	1959	Sabreliner CT-39A	265-2	Wfu. Dept of General Services, Memphis, Tn. USA.	(N4999G)
❑ 59-2870	1959	Sabreliner T-39A	265-3	Wfu. at AMARC.	
❑ 59-2871	1959	Sabreliner T-39A	265-4	W/o Eglin AFB. Fl. USA. 13 Nov 69.	
❑ 59-2872	1959	Sabreliner CT-39A	265-5	Wfu. at AMARC 6/84 as TG015. Tt 12728.	(N2296C)
❑ 59-2874	1959	Sabreliner NT-39B	270-2	Wfu. at AMARC as TG0103.	
❑ 59-5958	1961	JetStar-6	5010	Wfu. Displayed Travis AFB Museum, Ca. USA.	59-5958
❑ 59-5959	1962	JetStar-6	5026	Wfu. C-140A, USAF located at Scott AFB. Il. USA.	
❑ 59-5960	1962	JetStar-6	5028	Wfu. Last located Greenville, Tx. USA.	
❑ 59-5961	1962	JetStar-6	5030	W/o Robins AFB. Ga. USA. 7 Nov 62.	
❑ 59-5962	1962	JetStar-6	5032	Wfu. Last located at Edwards AFB. Ca. USA.	
❑ 60-3475	1960	Sabreliner CT-39B	270-4	Wfu. at AMARC as TG098.	
❑ 60-3476	1960	Sabreliner NT-39B	270-5	Wfu. at AMARC as TG0102.	
❑ 60-3477	1960	Sabreliner CT-39B	270-6	Wfu. at AMARC as TG0101.	
❑ 60-3478	1959	Sabreliner CT-39B	265-6	Wfu. at AMARC.	
❑ 60-3479	1959	Sabreliner CT-39A	265-7	Wfu. at AMARC 8/85 as TG082. Tt 22494.	
❑ 60-3480	1960	Sabreliner CT-39A	265-8	Wfu. at AMARC 6/84 as TG013.	
❑ 60-3481	1960	Sabreliner CT-39A	265-9	Wfu. Lane Community College, Eugene, Or. USA.	
❑ 60-3483	1960	Sabreliner CT-39A	265-11	Wfu. Preserved at Travis AFB. Ca. USA.	
❑ 60-3485	1960	Sabreliner CT-39A	265-13	Wfu. Western International Aviation, Tucson, Az. USA.	
❑ 60-3489	1960	Sabreliner CT-39A	265-17	Wfu. Houston Community College, Houston, Tx. USA.	
❑ 60-3491	1960	Sabreliner CT-39A	265-19	Wfu. at AMARC 5/84 as TG009. Tt 20372.	
❑ 60-3492	1960	Sabreliner CT-39A	265-20	Wfu. Thief River Falls Technical Institute, Mn. USA.	
❑ 60-3493	1960	Sabreliner CT-39A	265-21	Wfu. Instructional airframe at Moses Lake, Wa. USA.	
❑ 60-3494	1960	Sabreliner CT-39A	265-22	Wfu. at AMARC 12/85 as TG094. Tt 18375.	
❑ 60-3495	1960	Sabreliner CT-39A	265-23	Wfu. Preserved at Scott AFB. Il. USA.	
❑ 60-3496	1960	Sabreliner CT-39A	265-24	Wfu. Cochise Community College, Douglas, Az. USA.	
❑ 60-3497	1960	Sabreliner CT-39A	265-25	Wfu. R J Daley College, Chicago, Il. USA.	
❑ 60-3498	1960	Sabreliner CT-39A	265-26	Wfu. Williams Gateway, Chandler Municipal, Az. USA.	
❑ 60-3499	1960	Sabreliner CT-39A	265-27	Wfu. at AMARC 10/84 as TG037. Tt 20506.	
❑ 60-3500	1960	Sabreliner CT-39A	265-28	Wfu. Le Tourneau College, Longview, Tx. USA.	
Reg	Yr	Type	c/n	Owner/Operator	Prev Regn

Reg	Yr	Type	c/n	Owner/Operator	Prev Regn
☐ 60-3501	1960	Sabreliner CT-39A	265-29	Wfu. at AMARC 12/85 as TG093. Tt 15817.	
☐ 60-3502	1960	Sabreliner CT-39A	265-30	Wfu. Dr R Smirnow, NYC. USA.	
☐ 60-3503	1960	Sabreliner GCT-39A	265-31	Wfu. Located museum at Aurora Municipal, Il. USA.	
☐ 60-3505	1960	Sabreliner CT-39A	265-33	Wfu. preserved at Edwards Flight Test Museum, Ca. USA.	
☐ 60-3506	1960	Sabreliner T-39A	265-34	W/o Colorado Springs, Co. USA. 9 Feb 74.	
☐ 60-3508	1960	Sabreliner CT-39A	265-36	Wfu. Lake Area Vocational Technical College, Waterstown, SD.	
☐ 61-0634	1961	Sabreliner CT-39A	265-37	Wfu. Preserved at Dyess AFB. Tx. USA.	
☐ 61-0635	1961	Sabreliner CT-39A	265-38	Wfu. Regional Vocational Technical Institute, Lafayette, La.	
☐ 61-0636	1961	Sabreliner CT-39A	265-39	Wfu. at AMARC 9/85 as TG089. Tt 19841.	
☐ 61-0637	1961	Sabreliner CT-39A	265-40	Wfu. at AMARC 10/84 as TG035. Tt 21729.	
☐ 61-0638	1961	Sabreliner CT-39A	265-41	Wfu. Keesler AFB. Ms. USA.	
☐ 61-0640	1961	Sabreliner T-39A	265-43	W/o Halifax County Airport, NC. USA. 16 Apr 70.	
☐ 61-0641	1961	Sabreliner CT-39A	265-44	Wfu. Rock Valley College, Rockford, Il. USA.	
☐ 61-0642	1961	Sabreliner CT-39A	265-45	Wfu. at AMARC 12/84 as TG045. Tt 17270.	
☐ 61-0643	1961	Sabreliner CT-39A	265-46	Wfu. at AMARC 9/84 as TG022. Tt 20288.	
☐ 61-0644	1961	Sabreliner T-39A	265-47	W/o Andrews AFB. Md. USA. 7 May 63.	
☐ 61-0646	1961	Sabreliner T-39A	265-49	W/o. Richmond, Va. USA. 14 May 75.	
☐ 61-0647	1961	Sabreliner CT-39A	265-50	Wfu. Community College, Costa Mesa, Ca. USA.	
☐ 61-0648	1961	Sabreliner CT-39A	265-51	Wfu. DMI Aviation, Tucson, Az. USA.	
☐ 61-0649	1961	Sabreliner T-39A	265-52	Wfu. Portland Airport Museum, Portland, Or. USA.	(N1064)
☐ 61-0650	1961	Sabreliner CT-39A	265-53	Wfu. Everett Community College, Seattle, Wa. USA.	
☐ 61-0651	1961	Sabreliner CT-39A	265-54	Wfu. Florence Technical College, Florence, SC. USA.	
☐ 61-0652	1961	Sabreliner CT-39A	265-55	Wfu. at AMARC 9/85 as TG087. Tt 16815.	(N4999H)
☐ 61-0653	1961	Sabreliner CT-39A	265-56	Wfu. Community College, San Francisco, Ca. USA.	
☐ 61-0654	1961	Sabreliner CT-39A	265-57	Wfu. Embry-Riddle Aeronautical University, Daytona Beach.	
☐ 61-0655	1961	Sabreliner CT-39A	265-58	Wfu. P Regina, Granada Hills, Ca. USA.	
☐ 61-0656	1961	Sabreliner CT-39A	265-59	Wfu. at AMARC 5/84 as TG010. Tt 21617.	
☐ 61-0657	1961	Sabreliner CT-39A	265-60	Wfu. Located Westwood College of Aeronautics yard, Houston.	
☐ 61-0658	1961	Sabreliner CT-39A	265-61	Wfu.	
☐ 61-0660	1961	Sabreliner CT-39A	265-63	Wfu. Preserved at McClellan AFB. Ca. USA.	
☐ 61-0661	1961	Sabreliner T-39A	265-64	W/o Paine Field, Wa. USA. 29 Jul 62.	
☐ 61-0662	1961	Sabreliner CT-39A	265-65	Wfu. Parts at AVMATS Paynesville, Mo. USA.	
☐ 61-0663	1961	Sabreliner CT-39A	265-66	Wfu.	
☐ 61-0664	1961	Sabreliner CT-39A	265-67	Wfu. Duel Vocational Institute, Tracy, Ca. USA.	
☐ 61-0665	1961	Sabreliner CT-39A	265-68	Wfu. at AMARC 10/84 as TG028. Tt 19423.	
☐ 61-0666	1961	Sabreliner CT-39A	265-69	Wfu. at AMARC 6/84 as TG014. Tt 20336.	
☐ 61-0668	1961	Sabreliner CT-39A	265-71	Wfu. Thief River Falls Technical Institute, Mn. USA.	
☐ 61-0669	1961	Sabreliner CT-39A	265-72	Wfu. Metro Aviation Center, Oklahoma City, Ok. USA.	
☐ 61-0671	1961	Sabreliner CT-39A	265-74	Wfu. Keesler AFB. Ms. USA.	
☐ 61-0672	1961	Sabreliner T-39A	265-75	W/o Kunsong, Korea. 13 Mar 79.	
☐ 61-0674	1961	Sabreliner T-39A	265-77	Wfu. Preserved Norton AFB. Ca. USA.	
☐ 61-0675	1961	Sabreliner T-39A	265-78	Wfu.	
☐ 61-0676	1961	Sabreliner CT-39A	265-79	Wfu. at AMARC 12/84 as TG049. Tt 21692.	
☐ 61-0678	1961	Sabreliner CT-39A	265-81	Wfu. at AMARC 5/84 as TG012. Tt 14666.	
☐ 61-0681	1961	Sabreliner CT-39A	265-84	Wfu. Willow Run Museum, Detroit, Mi. USA.	
☐ 61-0682	1961	Sabreliner CT-39A	265-85	Wfu. Dross Metals, Tucson, Az. USA.	
☐ 61-0684	1961	Sabreliner CT-39A	265-87	Wfu.	
☐ 61-0685	1961	Sabreliner CT-39A	265-88	Wfu. at U S Army Aviation Museum, Fort Rucker, Al. USA.	61-0685
☐ 61-2488	1961	JetStar-6	5017	Wfu. VC-140B, USAF/preserved Warner Robins AFB. Ga. USA.	N9286R
☐ 61-2489	1961	JetStar-6	5022	Wfu. Located Pima County Museum, Tucson, Az. USA..	
☐ 61-2490	1961	JetStar-6	5024	Wfu. at AMAHC as CL-004 4/87.	
☐ 61-2491	1962	JetStar-6	5027	Wfu. Located Rhein-Main, Frankfurt, Germany.	
☐ 61-2492	1962	JetStar-6	5031	Wfu. Located Wright-Patterson Museum, Oh. USA.	
☐ 61-2493	1962	JetStar-6	5034	Wfu. at AMARC as CL003 2/84.	
☐ 62-4197	1962	JetStar-6	5041	Wfu. at AMARC as CL007 7/87.	
☐ 62-4198	1962	JetStar-6	5042	Wfu. Broken up at Mildenhall, UK. 1/92.	
☐ 62-4199	1962	JetStar-6	5043	Wfu. at AMARC as CL002 2/84.	
☐ 62-4200	1963	JetStar-6	5044	Wfu. at AMARC as CL005 6/87.	
☐ 62-4201	1963	JetStar-6	5045	Wfu. Located at Hill AFB. Ut. USA.	
☐ 62-4448	1962	Sabreliner T-39A	276-1	W/o Erfurt, East Germany. 28 Jan 64.	
☐ 62-4449	1962	Sabreliner CT-39A	276-2	Wfu. Located Pima County Museum, Tucson, Az. USA.	
☐ 62-4450	1962	Sabreliner CT-39A	276-3	Wfu. Western International Aviation, Tucson, Az. USA.	
☐ 62-4452	1962	Sabreliner CT-39A	276-5	Wfu. at Travis AFB. Ca. USA.	
☐ 62-4454	1962	Sabreliner CT-39A	276-7	Wfu. at AMARC 8/84 as TG018. Tt 20878.	
☐ 62-4457	1962	Sabreliner CT-39A	276-10	Wfu. at AMARC 11/83 as TG002. Tt 19944.	
☐ 62-4458	1962	Sabreliner T-39A	276-11	W/o Clark AFB. Philippines. 25 Mar 65.	
Reg	Yr	Type	c/n	Owner/Operator	Prev Regn

Reg	Yr	Type	c/n	Owner/Operator	Prev Regn
☐ 62-4459	1962	Sabreliner CT-39A	276-12	Wfu. Located Clover Park VoTec College, Tacoma, Wa.	
☐ 62-4460	1962	Sabreliner T-39A	276-13	W/o Torrejon AB. Spain. 28 Feb 70.	
☐ 62-4461	1962	Sabreliner CT-39A	276-14	Wfu. at Robins AFB. Ga. USA.	
☐ 62-4462	1962	Sabreliner CT-39A	276-15	Wfu. Trident Technical College, Charleston, SC.	
☐ 62-4463	1962	Sabreliner CT-39A	276-16	Wfu. at AMARC as TG100.	
☐ 62-4464	1962	Sabreliner CT-39A	276-17	Wfu. Utah State University, Salt Lake City, Ut.	
☐ 62-4465	1962	Sabreliner T-39A	276-18	Wfu. at March AFB. Ca.	
☐ 62-4466	1962	Sabreliner CT-39A	276-19	Wfu. Davis Aerospace High School, Detroit, Mi.	
☐ 62-4467	1962	Sabreliner CT-39A	276-20	Wfu. Guilford TCC Aviation Center, Greensboro, NC. USA.	
☐ 62-4470	1962	Sabreliner T-39A	276-23	Wfu. at Maxwell AFB. Al. USA.	
☐ 62-4471	1962	Sabreliner CT-39A	276-24	Wfu. at Ramstein AB. Germany.	
☐ 62-4473	1962	Sabreliner CT-39A	276-26	Wfu. to Dr R Smirnow, NYC. USA.	62-4473
☐ 62-4475	1962	Sabreliner CT-39A	276-28	Wfu. Milwaukee Technical College, Wi. USA.	
☐ 62-4476	1962	Sabreliner T-39A	276-29	Wfu. at AMARC as TG099.	
☐ 62-4477	1962	Sabreliner CT-39A	276-30	Wfu. Milwaukee Technical College, Milwaukee, Wi. USA.	
☐ 62-4478	1962	Sabreliner T-39A	276-31	Wfu. Located Wright-Patterson Museum, Oh. USA.	
☐ 62-4482	1962	Sabreliner T-39A	276-35	Wfu. at Kelly AFB. Tx. USA.	
☐ 62-4483	1962	Sabreliner CT-39A	276-36	Wfu. Indian Hills Community College, Ottumwa, Ia. USA.	
☐ 62-4484	1962	Sabreliner CT-39A	276-37	Wfu. at Kadena AB. Okinawa, Japan.	
☐ 62-4485	1962	Sabreliner T-39A	276-38	Wfu. fire dump Yokota AB. Japan.	
☐ 62-4487	1962	Sabreliner T-39A	276-40	Wfu. Displayed at SAC Museum, Ne. USA.	
☐ 62-4490	1962	Sabreliner CT-39A	276-43	Wfu. Located at Lawrenceville/Gwinnett County, Ga. USA.	
☐ 62-4493	1962	Sabreliner CT-39A	276-46	Wfu. College of Technology, Williamsport, Pa. USA.	
☐ 62-4494	1962	Sabreliner CT-39A	276-47	Wfu. at Chanute AFB. Il. USA.	
☐ 62-4496	1962	Sabreliner T-39A	276-49	W/o Scranton, Pa. USA. 20 Apr 85.	
☐ 62-4497	1962	Sabreliner CT-39A	276-50	Wfu. East Coast Technical College, Bedford-Hanscom, Ma. USA.	
☐ 62-4498	1962	Sabreliner CT-39A	276-51	Wfu. Salt Lake City Community College, Ut. USA.	
☐ 62-4499	1962	Sabreliner T-39A	276-52	W/o 24 Jun 69.	
☐ 62-4500	1962	Sabreliner CT-39A	276-53	Wfu. Milwaukee Area Technical College, Wi. USA.	
☐ 62-4501	1962	Sabreliner CT-39A	276-54	Wfu. O'Fallon Technical College, St Louis, Mo. USA.	
☐ 62-4502	1962	Sabreliner T-39A	276-55	W/o Langley AFB. Va. USA 31 Dec 68.	
☐ 62-6000	1962	C-137C	18461	Wfu. Located USAF Museum, nr Wright-Patterson AFB.	
☐ 72-0283	1972	B 737-253 (CT-43A)	20690	Wfu. TH0003 at AMARC 1/03.	
☐ 72-7000	1972	C-137C	20630	Wfu. Located Presidential Library, Simi Valley, Santa Monica	N8459
☐ 84-0097	1985	Learjet C-21A	35A-543	W/o Ellsworth AFB. SD. USA. 2 Feb 02.	N400CU
☐ 84-0121	1985	Learjet C-21A	35A-567	W/o Alabama, USA. 15 Jan 87.	N400EN
☐ 84-0136	1985	Learjet C-21A	35A-583	W/o Thomas Russell Field, Alexander City, Al. USA. 17 Apr 95	N400FP
☐ 84-0138	1985	Learjet C-21A	35A-574	Wfu. at AMARC.	N400EX
☐ 84-0193	1974	B 727-30	18362	Wfu. Located Davis Monthan AFB. USA.	N78
☐ N8052V	1960	Sabreliner CT-39A	265-18	Wfu. Located S Seattle Community College, Wa. USA.	60-3490

OB = PERU
Civil

☐ OB-1319	1973	Sabre-40A	282-127	W/o Buenos Aires, Argentina. 3 Sep 93.	OB-T-1919

OE = AUSTRIA
Civil

☐ OE-FAN	1976	Citation	500-0289	W/o Mount Creisa, Sardinia. 24 Feb 04.	N939KS
☐ OE-FAP	1975	Citation	500-0300	W/o as OE-FAP Greece 6 Oct 84. (parts at Dodsons, Ks.).	(N500CX)
☐ OE-FFK	1979	Citation 1/SP	501-0124	W/o Nr Salzburg, Austria. 26 Oct 88.	N95RE

OH = FINLAND
Civil

☐ OH-CAR	1974	Citation	500-0144	W/o Nr Helsinki, Finland. 19 Nov 87.	N332H
☐ OH-FFW	1970	Falcon 20F	243	W/o Montreal, Canada. 1 Mar 72.	F-WMKH
☐ OH-GLB	1973	Learjet 24D	24D-262	Wfu. Located Rovaniemi, Finland.	N110PS

OY = DENMARK
Civil

☐ OY-SBS	1975	Corvette	21	W/o Nice, France. 3 Sep 79.	F-BVPE

Military

☐ F-330	1981	Gulfstream 3	330	W/o Vagar, Faroe Islands. 3 Aug 96.	

PK = INDONESIA
Civil

☐ PK-CIR	1967	Falcon 20C	90	Wfu. Located at Jakarta International, Indonesia.	VH-CIR
☐ PK-DJW	1968	HS 125/3B-RA	25147	Wfu. Located near Halim-Jakarta airport, Indonesia.	PK-PJR

Military

☐ A-1645	1965	JetStar-6	5059	Wfu. Museum exhibit at Yogjakarta-Adisutjipto, Indonesia.	T-1645

Reg	Yr	Type	c/n	Owner/Operator	Prev Regn

☐ A-9446	1964	JetStar-6	5046	Wfu. Last located Halim-Jakarta, Indonesia.	T-9446

PP = BRAZIL

Civil

Reg	Yr	Type	c/n	Owner/Operator	Prev Regn
☐ PP-FMX	1966	Learjet 23	23-090	W/o Rio de Janeiro, Brazil. 30 Aug 69.	
☐ PP-SED	1973	Sabre-40A	282-121	Wfu. Cx USA 8/97.	N8349N
☐ PT-ASJ	1976	Falcon 10	95	W/o Rio de Janeiro, Brazil. 17 Feb 89.	N173FJ
☐ PT-CMY	1974	Learjet 25C	25C-108	W/o Juiz de Fora, Brazil. 6 Apr 90.	
☐ PT-CXK	1966	Learjet 24	24-122	W/o Rio-Galeon, Brazil. 4 May 73.	N461LJ
☐ PT-DVL	1971	Learjet 25B	25B-077	W/o Sao Paulo, Brazil. 12 Nov 76.	
☐ PT-DZU	1971	Learjet 24D	24D-244	W/o Sao Paulo, Brazil. 23 Aug 79.	
☐ PT-IBR	1972	Learjet 25C	25C-072	W/o Sao Paulo, Brazil. 26 Sep 76.	N256GL
☐ PT-ILJ	1973	Citation	500-0057	W/o Rio, Brazil. 3 Jul 97. (parts at Dodsons, Ks. USA).	N557CC
☐ PT-ISN	1973	Learjet 25C	25C-113	W/o Belo Horizonte, Brazil. 4 Nov 89. Cx PT- 1/90.	
☐ PT-JBQ	1973	Learjet 25B	25B-119	W/o Rio Branco, Brazil. 4 Sep 82.	N3810G
☐ PT-JDX	1973	Learjet 25C	25C-131	W/o Congonhas, Brazil. 26 Dec 78.	N3803G
☐ PT-JXS	1974	Citation	500-0162	W/o Belem, Brazil. 16 Mar 75.	
☐ PT-KBC	1974	Learjet 25C	25C-165	W/o Riberao Preto, Brazil. 4 Jun 96.	
☐ PT-KIU	1974	Citation	500-0172	W/o Aracatuba, Brazil. 12 Nov 76.	N172CC
☐ PT-KKV	1974	Learjet 25C	25C-172	W/o Macre, Brazil. 20 Feb 88, rebuilt, w/o again 11 Jan 91.	
☐ PT-KPE	1975	Learjet 24D	24D-315	Wfu. Located at San Paulo Congonhas, Brazil.	
☐ PT-KYR	1979	Learjet 25D	25D-266	W/o 23 Aug 86.	
☐ PT-KZY	1976	Learjet 25B	25B-204	W/o Uberaba, Brazil. 16 May 82.	N472J
☐ PT-LAU	1971	Learjet 24D	24D-239	W/o Brasilia, Brazil. 10 Sep 94.	N83MJ
☐ PT-LCN	1974	Learjet 24D	24D-287	W/o Florianapolis, Brazil. 4 Apr 84.	N92565
☐ PT-LCV	1972	Learjet 24D	24D-254	Wfu.	N13606
☐ PT-LEM	1973	Learjet 24D	24D-270	W/o Riberao Preto, Brazil. 7 Apr 99.	N3979P
☐ PT-LGJ	1985	Citation S/II	S550-0025	W/o Rio de Janeiro, Brazil. 6 Sep 88.	(N12596)
☐ PT-LHU	1973	Learjet 25C	25C-099	W/o Icuape, Brazil. 28 Jul 92. Cx PT- 10/94.	PT-FAF
☐ PT-LIG	1985	Learjet 55	55-111	W/o Guanabara Bay, Brazil. 9 Nov 94. (parts at Dodsons).	N7260G
☐ PT-LIH	1981	Learjet 35A	35A-433	W/o Uberlandia, Brazil. 15 Mar 91.	(N93RC)
☐ PT-LIY	1975	Citation	500-0219	W/o Marilia, Brazil. 1 Dec 02.	N408CA
☐ PT-LKQ	1965	Learjet 23	23-038	Wfu. Bu at Michigan Institute of Aeronautics,Detroit, USA.	N175BA
☐ PT-LKT	1986	Citation S/II	S550-0117	W/o Sao Paulo-Congonhas, Brazil. 1 Dec 92. Cx PT- 10/94.	N1292N
☐ PT-LLL	1978	Learjet 25D	25D-258	W/o Nr Brasilia, Brazil. 18 Mar 91.	N258MD
☐ PT-LMA	1977	Learjet 24F	24F-353	W/o Macre, Brazil. 24 Feb 88.	N63BW
☐ PT-LME	1980	Citation II/SP	551-0023	W/o Soracaba, Brazil. 23 Jul 03.	N34DL
☐ PT-LML	1978	Citation II	550-0013	W/o Criciuma, Santa Catarina, Brazil. 15 Aug 97.	N21SV
☐ PT-LPZ	1972	Citation	500-0015	Wfu. Located Sao Paulo, Brazil.	N14JL
☐ PT-LQG	1975	Citation	500-0271	W/o Canelo, Rio Sul, Brazil. 31 Oct 97.	N53FB
☐ PT-LSD	1978	Learjet 25D	25D-243	W/o Sierra de Cantareira, Sao Paulo, Brazil. 2 Mar 96.	N711JT
☐ PT-OEF	1977	Learjet 35A	35A-102	W/o Morelia, Mexico. 2 May 92.	N232R
☐ PT-OMV	1990	Citation VI	650-0200	W/o Nr Bogota, Colombia. 23 Mar 94.	N650CM

Military

☐ VC93-2122	1968	HS 125/3B-RC	25166	W/o Brasilia, Brazil. 18 Jun 79.	
☐ VU93-2129	1973	HS 125/403B	25290	W/o Carajas, Brazil. 9 Sep 87.	

P4 = ARUBA

Civil

☐ P4-AFE	1980	B 747SP-31	21962	Wfu.	TF-ABN
☐ P4-AMB	1972	HS 125/400B	25252	Wfu.	N48US
☐ P4-DRS	1975	B 707-368C	21104	Wfu. Located San Antonio, Tx. USA.	ST-DRS

RP = PHILIPPINES

Civil

☐ RP-C1500	1975	Citation	500-0225	W/o between Cagayan & Butuan, Philippines. 1 Feb 97.	VH-OIL
☐ RP-C1980	1979	Falcon 20F	400	W/o Davao City, Philippines. 24 Apr 96.	F-WRQR
☐ RP-C911	1960	B 707-321	17606	Wfu. Located at Manila as 'Club 707' restaurant.	N728PA

SE = SWEDEN

Civil

☐ SE-DCY	1969	Jet Commander	136	W/o Stockholm, Sweden. 4 Dec 69.	N5044E
☐ SE-DLK	1976	Westwind-1124	197	W/o Umeaa, Sweden. 21 Sep 92.	N29CL

SU = EGYPT

Civil

☐ SU-DAF	1962	JetStar-6	5025	Wfu.	(ST-JRM)
☐ SU-DAG	1968	JetStar-8	5121	Wfu. Located Cairo, Egypt.	(ST-PRM)

SX = GREECE
Civil

Reg	Yr	Type	c/n	Owner/Operator	Prev Regn
☐ SX-ASO	1971	Learjet 25B	25B-074	W/o Antibes, France. 18 Feb 72.	N251GL
☐ SX-BSS	1966	HS 125/3A	25116	Wfu. Located Thessaloniki, Greece.	N726CC

TC = TURKEY
Civil

☐ TC-NSU	1969	HFB 320	1046	Wfu.	16+04
☐ TC-OMR	1969	HFB 320	1047	Wfu.	16+05
☐ TC-YIB	1983	Diamond 1A	A051SA	Wfu. Parts at Dodsons, Rantoul, Ks. USA.	D-CFGV

TL = CENTRAL AFRICAN REPUBLIC
Civil

| ☐ TL-AAI | | Caravelle 3 | 10 | Wfu. Broken up at Paris-Orly 2/83. | F-BNGE |

TN = CONGO BRAZZAVILLE
Civil

| ☐ TN-ADB | 1975 | Corvette | 22 | W/o Nkayi, Congo Republic. 30 Mar 79. | F-ODFE |

TR = GABON
Civil

| ☐ TR-KHB | 1973 | Gulfstream 2 | 127 | W/o Ngaoundere, Cameroun. 6 Feb 80. | N17581 |
| ☐ TR-LZT | 1975 | Corvette | 20 | Wfu. Located Toulouse-Blagnac, France. | (F-GKJB) |

TT = CHAD
Civil

| ☐ TT-AAM | | Caravelle 6R | 100 | Wfu. Cx TT- 5/80. Last located N'Djamena, Chad. | (TT-AAD) |

TY = BENIN
Civil

☐ TY-BBK	1976	Corvette	29	W/o Lagos, Nigeria. 16 Nov 81.	F-OBZP
☐ TY-BBR	1971	B 707-336B	20457	W/o Sebha, Libya. 13 Jun 85.	9G-ADB
☐ TY-BBW	1962	B 707-321	18084	Wfu.	TY-AAM

VH = AUSTRALIA
Civil

☐ VH-AJS	1977	Westwind-1124	221	W/o Alice Springs, Australia. 27 Apr 95.	(N969EG)
☐ VH-ANQ	1975	Citation Eagle	500-0283	W/o Cairns, Australia. 11 May 90.	N18AF
☐ VH-CAO	1965	HS 125/3B	25015	Wfu. Located Schofields, Richmond, NSW. Australia.	(N750D)
☐ VH-ECE	1966	HS 125/3B	25062	Wfu. Located The Oaks, Nr Camden, NSW. Australia.	
☐ VH-FSA	1974	Citation	500-0237	W/o Prosperine, Queensland, Australia. 20 Feb 84.	N14TT
☐ VH-FWO	1967	Falcon 20C	110	Wfu. Parts at Springfield, Il. USA.	C-FWRA
☐ VH-IWJ	1982	Westwind-1124	371	W/o Botany Bay, Australia. 10 Oct 85.	4X-CUH
☐ VH-LCL	1980	Citation 1/SP	501-0145	W/o Lord Howe Island. 22 Apr 90. (parts at Dodsons, Ks.).	(N2652Z)
☐ VH-LLW	1979	Westwind Sea Scan	253	Wfu. Last located Jandakot, WA. Australia.	N253MD
☐ VH-LLX	1979	Westwind Sea Scan	259	Wfu.	N315JM
☐ VH-LLY	1979	Westwind Sea Scan	272	Wfu. Last located Jandakot, WA. Australia.	N723R
Military					
☐ A20-103	1975	B 707-368C	21103	W/o Nr RAAF E Sale, VIC. Australia. 29 Oct 91.	HZ-ACG

VP-B = BERMUDA
Civil

☐ VP-BIA	1963	DC 8-52	45658	Wfu. Last located Lasham, UK.	VR-BIA
☐ VP-BLN	1983	Gulfstream 3	402	W/o Lac du Bourget, Chambery, France. 6 Feb 98.	VR-BLN
☐ VR-BJB	1970	Falcon 20F	244	W/o Lugano, Switzerland. 15 Jan 88. (parts at Dodsons, Ks.)	(OE-GCS)
☐ VR-BJI	1971	JetStar-731	5149	Wfu. Parted out 7/91.	N110MZ
☐ VR-BLJ	1968	Gulfstream 2	40	W/o Jos, Nigeria. 20 Jun 96.	N1039
☐ VR-BMB	1970	HS 125/400B	25240	Wfu. Last located Stansted, UK.	VR-BKN
☐ VR-BZA	1970	B 707-336C	20375	Wfu. Located Lake Charles, La. USA.	VR-BZA

VP-C = CAYMAN ISLANDS
Civil

| ☐ VR-CAN | 1961 | B 707-138B | 18067 | Wfu. | 9Y-TDC |
| ☐ VR-CCY | 1966 | JetStar-6 | 5085 | Wfu. Located Abu Dhabi Higher College of Technology, UAE. | S9-NAE |

VT = INDIA
Civil

| ☐ VT-ERO | 1965 | Jet Commander | 33 | Wfu. Parts at Hollister, Ca. USA. | N104CJ |

XA = MEXICO
Civil

☐ XA-ADC	1966	BAC 1-11/211AH	084	Wfu. Last located San Antonio, Tx. USA.	S9-TAE
☐ XA-BBA	1977	Learjet 25D	25D-223	W/o Washington-Dulles, USA. 18 Jun 94.	XA-RWH
☐ XA-COL	1966	HS 125/1A	25086	W/o Acalpulco, Mexico. 12 Oct 73.	N3699T

| Reg | Yr | Type | c/n | Owner/Operator | Prev Regn |

Reg	Yr	Type	c/n	Owner/Operator	Prev Regn
XA-CUZ	1972	HS 125/400A	NA772	W/o Cancun, Mexico. 26 Dec 80.	N69BH
XA-EEU	1966	Sabre-40	282-54	W/o ground accident Mexico 1980.	N256CT
XA-GBP	1963	B 727-25	18252	Wfu.	XB-GBP
XA-HOK	1964	Sabre-40	282-17	Wfu. Parts at AVMATS Paynesville, Mo. USA.	N900CS
XA-ISH	1985	BAe 125/800A	8036	W/o Nr Tampico, Mexico. 27 Oct 03.	N621MT
XA-JLV	1967	Learjet 24	24-136	Wfu.	N24LW
XA-KEW	1980	HS 125/700A	NA0276	W/o Norte-Monterrey, Mexico. 2 May 81.	G-5-14
XA-KUT	1974	HS 125/600A	6028	W/o Houston, Tx. USA. 18 Jan 88. (parts at Dodsons, Ks).	C-GDHW
XA-LAN	1979	Learjet 35A	35A-267	W/o Hermosillo, Mexico. 8 Jan 93.	N39418
XA-NOG	1981	Learjet 25D	25D-349	W/o Tijuana, Mexico. 2 Sep 93.	N20GT
XA-POJ	1972	Westwind-1123	161	Wfu. Parts at Dodsons, Rantoul, Ks. USA.	N33WD
XA-PUF	1972	Westwind-1123	153	Wfu. Parts were at Hollister, Ca. USA.	N223WW
XA-PUL	1972	JetStar-8	5151	Wfu.	N45K
XA-RNR	1970	Sabre-60	306-49	Wfu.	XA-POR
XA-ROK	1969	JetStar-8	5133	Wfu.	HZ-WT1
XA-RQB	1967	Learjet 24XR	24XR-150	Wfu. Last located at Dodsons, Rantoul, Ks. USA.	N24XR
XA-RQI	1969	Learjet 25	25-032	Wfu. Exhibit main terminal Mexico City 1994.	XA-ZYZ
XA-RRC	1972	Learjet 24D	24D-259	Wfu. Parts at White Industries, Bates City, Mo. USA.	N22MH
XA-RRK	1976	Learjet 24D	24D-307	W/o Tampico, Mexico. 2 Jan 98.	N307BJ
XA-RVG	1969	JetStar-731	5139	Wfu. Parts at Griffin, Ga. USA. Cx USA 2/97	(N1189A)
XA-RZC	1965	Learjet 23	23-071	Wfu. Parts at Dodsons, Rantoul, Ks. USA.	(N6262T)
XA-SBC	1966	II3 125/1A-522	25068	Wfu. Parts at Dodsons, Rantoul, Ks. USA.	(N5274U)
XA-SHA	1966	Jet Commander	86	Wfu. Parts at Dodsons, Rantoul, Ks. USA.	XA-RIW
XA-SLH	1969	Sabre-60	306-39	Wfu. Cx USA 4/00. Parts at AVMATS SUS, Mo. USA.	(N82197)
XA-SLQ	1973	Citation	500-0111	W/o Ensenada, Mexico. 6 Feb 96.	XA-SHO
XA-SMH	1973	Citation	500-0084	W/o Aleman, Veracruz, Mexico. 25 March 94.	XB-FPK
XA-SMQ	1965	Sabre-40	282-50	Wfu. Parts at AVMATS Spririt of St Louis, Mo. USA.	(N282CA)
XA-SOC	1972	JetStar-8	5152	Wfu. Located Toluca, Mexico.	N113KH
XA-SWF	1981	Learjet 35A	35A-391	W/o Nr Tepic Airport, Mexico. 23 Jun 95.	N888PT
XA-TAL	1966	HS 125/1A-522	25064	W/o Toluca, Mexico. 9 Jul 99.	XB-GGK
XA-TAV	1967	JetStar-8	5103	Wfu. Located Aruba, Netherlands Antilles.	XA-TAZ
XA-TDG	1973	JetStar-8	5158	Wfu. Located Mexico City, Mexico.	XA-FHR
XA-TDP	1966	Learjet 24	24-128	Wfu. Parts at Dodsons, Rantoul, Ks. USA.	(N128WD)
XA-TFC	1960	Sabreliner CT-39A	265-12	W/o Monterrey, Mexico. 16 May 97. USA.	XB-GDU
XA-TZW	1969	JetStar-8	5129	Wfu. Located Toluca, Mexico.	XA-TJW
XA-ZZZ	1979	Learjet 25D	25D-287	Wfu. Parts at White Industries, Bates City, Mo. USA.	N20AD
XB-BBL	1973	Sabre-40A	282-116	Wfu. Located Toluca, Mexico.	N4PH
XB-DLV	1961	JetStar-8	5005	Wfu. Cx USA as N22265 6/02.	(N22265)
XB-DUH	1972	JetStar-8	5157	Wfu. Displayed as N001DI at Dodsons,Rantoul, Ks. USA.	N29WP
XB-FJI	1967	Jet Commander	115	Wfu. Located Monterrey, Mexico.	N500VF
XB-GJO	1973	Sabre-75	370-9	Wfu. Parts at Spirit of St Louis, Mo. USA.	(N370SL)
XB-JOY	1973	Learjet 24D	24D-263	W/o Mexico City, Mexico. 29 Jun 76.	N3812G
XC-AA26	1968	Sabre-60A	306-12	Wfu.	XC-HHL
XC-AA73	1972	Sabre-40A	282-105	Wfu. Located Mexico City, Mexico.	XA-SCN
XC-HAD	1966	Jet Commander	85	Wfu.	N201S
XC-PGE	1974	Sabre-40A	282-130	Wfu. Located Mexico City, Mexico.	XC-PGE
XC-TIJ	1970	HFB 320	1049	W/o San Diego, Ca. USA. 6 Jun 84.	XC-DGA

Military

Reg	Yr	Type	c/n	Owner/Operator	Prev Regn
MTX-02	1975	Learjet 24D	24D-313	W/o Mexico City, Mexico. 20 Nov 98. (at White Industries).	MTX-01
XC-UJC	1978	Sabre-75A	380-67	W/o Saltillo, Mexico. 26 Oct 89. (parts at AVMATS, Mo.).	TP-103
XC-UJI	1969	B 737-247	20127	W/o Lomar, Bonita, Mexico. 14 May 99.	B-12001

YI = IRAQ

Civil

Reg	Yr	Type	c/n	Owner/Operator	Prev Regn
YI-AKH	1982	HS 125/700B	7187	W/o as destroyed during Gulf War 2/91,	YI-AKH
YI-AKI	1983	Gulfstream 3	408	W/o as destroyed during Gulf War 2/91.	9K-AEG
YI-AKJ	1984	Gulfstream 3	419	W/o as destroyed during Gulf War 2/91.	9K-AEH

YU = YUGOSLAVIA

Civil

Reg	Yr	Type	c/n	Owner/Operator	Prev Regn
YU-BJH	1975	Learjet 25B	25B-186	W/o Sarajevo, Yugoslavia. 18 Jan 77.	

YV = VENEZUELA

Civil

Reg	Yr	Type	c/n	Owner/Operator	Prev Regn
YV-123CP	1965	Jet Commander	16	Wfu.	N177A
YV-160CP	1977	Westwind-1124	211	W/o La Aurora, Guatemala City, Guatemala. 19 Feb 97.	4X-CLI
YV-O-MAC-	1976	Citation	500-0336	W/o Caracas, Venezuela. Jun 79.	N336CC

Reg	Yr	Type	c/n	Owner/Operator	Prev Regn

ZK = NEW ZEALAND
Military

Reg	Yr	Type	c/n	Owner/Operator	Prev Regn
☐ NZ7272	1968	B 727-22C	19895	Wfu. Located RNZAF Ground Training Wing Woodbourne..	N7438U
☐ NZ7273	1968	B 727-22C	19893	Wfu. Last located Blenheim, New Zealand.	N7436U

ZS = SOUTH AFRICA
Civil

Reg	Yr	Type	c/n	Owner/Operator	Prev Regn
☐ N89XL	1974	Westwind-1123	171	Wfu. Located Lanseria, RSA.	(ZS-ODP)
☐ ZS-JBA	1971	HS 125/400B	25259	Wfu. Cx ZS- 3/03. Last located Lanseria, RSA.	SAAF05
☐ ZS-JWC	1965	Learjet 23	23-030	Wfu. Parts for ZS-MDN 23-081. Located Provo, Ut. USA..	N431CA

Military

Reg	Yr	Type	c/n	Owner/Operator	Prev Regn
☐ SAAF01	1969	HS 125/400B	25177	W/o Devil's Peak, South Africa. 26 May 71.	G-AWXN
☐ SAAF02	1969	HS 125/400B	25181	W/o Devil's Peak, South Africa. 26 May 71.	G-AXLU
☐ SAAF03	1969	HS 125/400B	25182	W/o Devil's Peak, South Africa. 26 May 71.	G-AXLV

3D = SWAZILAND
Civil

Reg	Yr	Type	c/n	Owner/Operator	Prev Regn
☐ 3D-ART	1975	Falcon 10	61	W/o Magoebaskloof, Transvaal, RSA. 3 Oct 86.	F-BFDG

4X = ISRAEL
Civil

Reg	Yr	Type	c/n	Owner/Operator	Prev Regn
☐ 4X-...	1985	Astra-1125	003	Wfu. static and fatigue test airframe.	
☐ 4X-AIP	1978	Westwind-1124	243	W/o Rosh-Pina, Israel. 23 Jul 96.	N215SC
☐ 4X-COA	1966	Jet Commander	71	Wfu. Located at Hatzerim Air Force Museum, Israel.	N721GB
☐ 4X-COJ	1965	Jet Commodore	29	W/o Tel Aviv, Israel. 21 Jan 70.	N615JC
☐ 4X-IGA	1997	Galaxy-1126	003	Wfu. Located Tel Aviv, Israel.	
☐ 4X-WIN	1984	Astra-1125	001	Wfu. Broken up by 31 Aug 86.	

5A = LIBYA
Civil

Reg	Yr	Type	c/n	Owner/Operator	Prev Regn
☐ 5A-DAD	1965	Learjet 23	23-075	W/o Damascus, Syria. 5 Jun 67.	
☐ 5A-DAR	1977	JetStar 2	5221	W/o en route Tripoli-Algeria, North Africa. 16 Jan 83.	N5547L

5N = NIGERIA
Civil

Reg	Yr	Type	c/n	Owner/Operator	Prev Regn
☐ 5N-AAN	1967	HS 125/3B	25125	Wfu. Located Kingston University, Newcastle, UK.	F-GFMP
☐ 5N-AER	1968	HS 125/1B-522	25099	Wfu. Located Zaria, Nigeria.	(N2246)
☐ 5N-AMF	1967	HFB 320	1028	W/o Abidjan, Ivory Coast. 25 Jul 77.	D-CASU
☐ 5N-AMR	1978	Citation II	550-0045	W/o Bauchi, Nigeria. 21 May 91.	N4CR
☐ 5N-AOG	1967	HS 125/3B-RA	25143	Wfu.	G-AVXK
☐ 5N-AOL	1975	HS 125/600B	6050	Wfu. Located Lagos, Nigeria.	G-BLOI
☐ 5N-ASQ	1981	Learjet 25D	25D-344	W/o Lagos, Nigeria. 22 Jul 83.	N37943
☐ 5N-ASZ	1966	HS 125/1B	25063	Wfu. Broken up at Southampton-UK 11/86.	G-ONPN
☐ 5N-AVZ	1967	HS 125/3B-RA	25113	Wfu. Located Lagos, Nigeria.	G-AVDX
☐ 5N-AWB	1966	HS 125/1B	25025	Wfu.	(F-OCGK)
☐ 5N-AWD	1964	HS 125/1	25008	Wfu.	G-ASSI
☐ 5N-AWS	1975	HS 125/600B	6042	W/o Casablanca, Morocco. 31 Dec 86.	(G-5-505)
☐ 5N-AXO	1983	HS 125/700B	7196	W/o Kano, Nigeria. 17 Jan 96.	G-5-766
☐ 5N-AXP	1983	HS 125/700B	7203	W/o Kaduna, Nigeria. 31 Dec 85.	G-5-14
☐ 5N-BDC	1967	BAC 1-11/412EB	111	W/o Libreville, Gabon. 28 Aug 01.	EL-LIB
☐ 5N-HHH	1966	BAC 1-11/401AK	064	Wfu. Located Southend, UK.	HZ-NB2
☐ 5N-RNO	1975	HS 125/600B	6054	W/o Lagos, Nigeria. May 01.	5N-YFS

5T = MAURITANIA
Civil

Reg	Yr	Type	c/n	Owner/Operator	Prev Regn
☐ 5T-RIM	1961	Caravelle 6R	91	Wfu.	5T-MAL

5V = TOGO
Civil

Reg	Yr	Type	c/n	Owner/Operator	Prev Regn
☐ 5V-TAA	1974	Gulfstream 2	149	W/o Lome, Togo. 26 Dec 74.	N17586
☐ 5V-TAG	1968	B 707-312B	19739	W/o Niamey, Niger. 21 Sep 00.	N600CS

6V = SENEGAL
Civil

Reg	Yr	Type	c/n	Owner/Operator	Prev Regn
☐ 6V-AAR	1959	Caravelle 3	5	Wfu. Located Dakar, Senegal.	6V-ACP

7T = ALGERIA
Civil

Reg	Yr	Type	c/n	Owner/Operator	Prev Regn
☐ 7T-VHB	1978	Gulfstream 2	230	W/o Nr Qotur, NW Iranian Border. 3 May 82.	N17586
☐ 7T-VRE	1969	Falcon 20C	156	W/o 30 May 81.	F-WMKI

9K = KUWAIT
Military

Reg	Yr	Type	c/n	Owner/Operator	Prev Regn
☐ KAF 320		DC 9-32	47691	W/o during Gulf War 2/91.	160749

9M = MALAYSIA
Civil

| ☐ 9M-HLG | 1972 | HS 125/400B | 25257 | Wfu. | G-BATA |

Military

| ☐ M24-01 | 1969 | HS 125/400B | 25189 | Wfu. Stored RMAF Subang, Malaysia. | FM1801 |
| ☐ M24-02 | 1969 | HS 125/400B | 25209 | Wfu. Stored RMAF Subang, Malaysia. | FM1802 |

9Q = CONGO KINSHASA
Civil

| ☐ 9Q-CBC | 1972 | Learjet 24D | 24D-248 | W/o Kinshasa, Zaire. 18 Jan 94. | OO-LFA |

Military

| ☐ 9T-MSS | 1968 | B 707-382B | 19969 | Wfu. Located Lisbon, Portugal. | CS-TBD |

9V = SINGAPORE
Civil

| ☐ 9V-ATD | 1993 | Learjet 31 | 31-033B | W/o between Phuket & Ranong, Thailand. 21 Jul 97. | N2600S |

9XR = RWANDA
Civil

| ☐ 9XR-NN | 1979 | Falcon 50 | 6 | W/o Kigali, Rwanda. 6 Apr 94. | N815CA |
| ☐ 9XR-RA | 1964 | BAC 1-11/201AC | 011 | Wfu. Last located Lanseria, RSA. | EL-ALD |

BizJets- totals by type   *Total Jets*   13883

390 Premier 1	125	Citation Bravo	306	Falcon 100	34
AC 690A-TU	1	Citation Eagle	30	Falcon 10MER	6
Adams A700	1	Citation Eagle 400SP	1	Falcon 20	2
Airbus A300	3	Citation Eagle II	3	Falcon 200	33
Airbus A310	19	Citation Eagle SP	3	Falcon 2000	219
Airbus A319	22	Citation Encore	129	Falcon 2000EX	29
Airbus A320	2	Citation Excel	373	Falcon 2000EX EASY	24
Airbus A330	1	Citation Excel XLS	49	Falcon 20-5	15
Airbus A340	8	Citation II	591	Falcon 20-5B	16
Astra C-38A	2	Citation II/SP	78	Falcon 20C	92
Astra-1125	33	Citation III	196	Falcon 20C-5	6
Astra-1125SP	36	Citation Longwing SP	5	Falcon 20C-5B	1
Astra-1125SPX	51	Citation OT-47B	5	Falcon 20D	28
B 707	40	Citation S/II	156	Falcon 20D-5	2
B 720	5	Citation Sovereign	27	Falcon 20D-5B	2
B 727	73	Citation UC-35	2	Falcon 20DC	14
B 737	70	Citation UC-35A	20	Falcon 20E	40
B 747	23	Citation UC-35B	2	Falcon 20E-5	8
B 757	18	Citation UC-35C	7	Falcon 20E-5B	5
B 767	8	Citation UC-35D	5	Falcon 20ECM	2
B 777	2	Citation V	260	Falcon 20EW	20
BAC 1-11	34	Citation V Ultra	249	Falcon 20F	52
BAe 1000A	31	Citation VI	40	Falcon 20F-5	29
BAe 1000B	9	Citation VII	118	Falcon 20F-5B	31
BAe 125/	2	Citation X	240	Falcon 20GF	1
BAe 125/800A	176	CitationJet	356	Falcon 20SNA	3
BAe 125/800B	63	CitationJet CJ-1	187	Falcon 20SP	1
BAe 125/C-29A	5	CitationJet CJ-1+	1	Falcon 50	241
BAe 125/CC3	6	CitationJet CJ-2	227	Falcon 50 SURMAR	4
BAe 146 Statesman	1	CitationJet CJ-3	21	Falcon 50-40	1
BAe 146/CC2	3	Corvette	28	Falcon 50EX	90
BAe 146/RJ-85	4	DC 10	2	Falcon 7X	1
BAe 146-100	4	DC 8	13	Falcon 900	60
BAe 146-200	1	DC 9	14	Falcon 900A	1
BAe U-125A	31	Diamond 1	18	Falcon 900B	117
BBJ	73	Diamond 1A	67	Falcon 900C	25
BBJ2	10	Do 328-310 ENVOY	2	Falcon 900EX	118
Beechjet 400	62	Dominie T1	3	Falcon 900EX EASY	29
Beechjet 400A	351	Dominie T2	8	Fokker 100	2
Beechjet 400T	13	Dornier Do328JET	14	Fokker 70	5
C-135B	5	Eclipse 500	5	Galaxy-1126	15
C-9C	3	EMB-135BJ	2	Gardian	5
Caravelle 3	2	EMB-135BJ Legacy	32	Global 5000	12
Challenger 300	40	EMB-135ER	3	Global Express	146
Challenger 600	5	EMB-135EW	1	Guardian HU-25A	11
Challenger 600S	75	EMB-135LR	5	Guardian HU-25B	5
Challenger 601	65	EMB-135LR Legacy	2	Guardian HU-25C	9
Challenger 601-3A	133	EMB-145LR	2	Guardian HU-25D	1
Challenger 601-3R	59	EMB-145RS	1	Gulfstream 2	74
Challenger 604	301	F 28-1000	11	Gulfstream 2B	42
Challenger 800	14	F 28-3000	5	Gulfstream 2TT	16
Citation	313	F 28-4000	6	Gulfstream 3	188
Citation 1/SP	288	Falcon 10	162	Gulfstream 4	192

Aircraft	Count	Aircraft	Count	Aircraft	Count
Gulfstream 4/Tp 102	1	Jayhawk T-1A	180	Sabre-40A	28
Gulfstream 4/Tp 102B	2	Jet Commander	19	Sabre-40R	5
Gulfstream 4/Tp 102C	1	Jet Commander-A	4	Sabre-50	1
Gulfstream 4SP	291	Jet Commander-B	7	Sabre-60	102
Gulfstream C-20A	1	Jet Commander-C	1	Sabre-60A	9
Gulfstream C-20D	2	JetStar	2	Sabre-65	75
Gulfstream C-20E	2	JetStar 2	37	Sabre-75	5
Gulfstream C-20F	1	JetStar-6	6	Sabre-75A	45
Gulfstream C-20G	5	JetStar-731	33	Sabre-80A	7
Gulfstream C-37A	11	JetStar-8	16	Sabreliner CT-39A	16
Gulfstream G100	24	Learjet 23	27	Sabreliner CT-39B	2
Gulfstream G200	90	Learjet 24	45	Sabreliner CT-39E	3
Gulfstream G300	8	Learjet 24A	7	Sabreliner CT-39G	9
Gulfstream G300MPA	2	Learjet 24B	34	Sabreliner T-39A	2
Gulfstream G4	1	Learjet 24D	63	Sabreliner T-39D	9
Gulfstream G400	26	Learjet 24E	15	Sentinel R1	5
Gulfstream G450	17	Learjet 24F	11	SJ 30-2	3
Gulfstream G550	69	Learjet 24XR	14	TriStar 100	2
Gulfstream II SP	101	Learjet 25	40	TriStar 500	4
Gulfstream SRA-1	3	Learjet 25B	79	Vantage	1
Gulfstream U-4	5	Learjet 25C	16	VFW 614	1
Gulfstream V	180	Learjet 25D	143	Westwind-1123	14
Gulfstream V-SP	1	Learjet 25G	4	Westwind-1124	157
HA-420 HondaJet	1	Learjet 25XR	15	Westwind-1124N	3
Hawker 1000	10	Learjet 28	5	Westwind-Two	84
Hawker 4000 Horizon	5	Learjet 29	4		
Hawker 400XP	58	Learjet 31	37		
Hawker 800	21	Learjet 31A	206		
Hawker 800 SP	1	Learjet 35	59		
Hawker 800XP	423	Learjet 35A	492		
HFB 320	6	Learjet 35ZR	1		
HS 125/	2	Learjet 36	15		
HS 125/1A	12	Learjet 36A	35		
HS 125/1A-522	12	Learjet 40	25		
HS 125/1B	2	Learjet 45	262		
HS 125/1B-S522	1	Learjet 55	118		
HS 125/3A	3	Learjet 55B	8		
HS 125/3A-R	1	Learjet 55C	14		
HS 125/3A-RA	12	Learjet 60	278		
HS 125/3B	6	Learjet C-21A	78		
HS 125/3B-RA	1	Learjet U36A	4		
HS 125/3B-RC	5	Leopard	1		
HS 125/400A	25	McDonnell 220	1		
HS 125/400B	6	MD-11	2		
HS 125/403A	1	MD-83	1		
HS 125/403B	8	MD-87	5		
HS 125/600A	29	MS 760 Paris	14		
HS 125/600B	10	MS 760 Paris-1A	3		
HS 125/700A	170	MS 760 Paris-1R	5		
HS 125/700A-2	1	MS 760 Paris-2	4		
HS 125/700B	31	MS 760 Paris-2B	4		
HS 125/731	60	PD 808	1		
HS 125/F3A	1	PD 808-GE2	1		
HS 125/F3B	1	PD 808-TA	1		
HS 125/F3B-RA	2	PD 808-TP	1		
HS 125/F400A	8	PD 808-VIP	1		
HS 125/F400B	2	Regional Jet	2		
HS 125/F403A	1	Sabre-	4		
HS 125/F403B	2	Sabre T-39N	15		
HS 125/F600A	11	Sabre-40	23		
HS 125/F600B	3	Sabre-40/Tp 86	2		

Business Jets
Cross-Reference by Construction Number

Aerospatiale

Corvette

c/n	reg
01	wo
1	F-ZVMV
2	F-ZVMW
3	wo
4	wfu
5	CN-TDE
6	wfu
7	F-BVPK
8	F-GJAS
9	TN-ADI
10	F-ZVMX
11	F-GKGA
12	F-GMOF
13	F-GFDH
14	F-GIRH*
15	EC-HHZ
16	5R-MBR
17	YV-572CP
18	wfu
19	EC-HIA
20	wfu
21	wo
22	wo
23	OY-SBR
24	wfu
25	F-BVPG
26	wfu
27	wo
28	F-GPLA
29	wo
30	F-GLEC
31	F-GJAP
32	F-GILM
33	OY-SBT
34	5R-MHK
35	F-ODSR
36	N600RA
37	wo
38	5A-DCK
39	F-GJLB
40	N220MT

Airbus

Airbus

c/n	reg
004	D-ACME
009	JY-ABH
026	A7-HHK
046	V8-BKH
061	SU-GGG
151	HZ-WBT4
204	D-ASFB
344	9K-AHI
354	TS-IAY
367	CA-02
372	CA-01
374	N374FD
418	F-RADC
421	F-RADA
422	F-RADB
425	15003
431	HZ-NSA
444	15004
446	15001
473	A7-AAF
482	15002
487	A7-HJJ
495	A7-HHH
498	10+21
499	10+22
503	10+23
523	10+27
550	T 22-1
551	T 22-2
591	44-444
648	9K-ALD
910	A6-ESH
913	G-OMAK
927	A7-AAG
1002	MM62173
1053	D-ADNA
1157	MM62174
1212	VP-CVX
1256	F-GSVU
1335	A7-HHJ
1468	0001
1485	F-RBFA
1556	F-RBFB
1589	VP-CIE
1656	A7-CJA
1727	D-APAC
1795	MM62209
1880	D-APAD
1908	60221
1947	D-APAA
1955	D-APAB
1999	F-GYAS
2046	9K-AKD
2263	2101
2341	A7-CJB

Boeing

707

c/n	reg
17606	wfu
17634	wfu
17644	N2143H
17652	wfu
17696	HZ-123
17697	wo
17699	wfu
17700	wfu
17702	N707SK
17905	wfu
18067	wfu
18084	wfu
18334	CNA-NS
18338	wfu
18339	wfu
18375	wfu
18586	N707CA
18740	N707JT
18757	T 17-2
18926	903
18928	N88ZL
19000	904
19164	TM 17-4
19248	K2900
19443	902
19498	N14AZ
19623	A20-623
19624	A20-624
19627	A20-627
19629	A20-629
19635	68-19635
19716	FAC-1201
19739	wo
19840	2401
19866	68-19866
19969	wfu
19988	K2899
19997	wfu
19998	wfu
20000	wfu
20025	D2-MAN
20028	wo
20060	T 17-1
20062	wfu
20110	4X-JYQ
20375	wfu
20457	wo
20629	4X-JYB
20715	D2-TPR
20721	4X-JYH
20919	SU-AXJ
21049	5V-TGE
21081	wfu
21092	N707LG
21096	4X-JYV
21103	wo
21104	wfu
21228	5A-DAK
21261	A20-261
21334	4X-JY.
21367	T 17-3
21368	N707MQ
21396	1001
21956	N707JU

720

c/n	reg
17907	wfu
18021	N720PW
18022	wfu
18024	C-FETB
18066	wo
18077	wfu
18351	wfu
18451	N720JR
18452	wfu
18453	P4-NJR
18977	N7381
19523	wfu

727

c/n	reg
18252	wfu
18253	wfu
18323	N727CF
18360	wfu
18362	wfu
18363	EP-PLN
18365	N727EC
18366	P4-YJR
18368	P4-MMG
18370	7P-DPT
18371	5B-DBE
18894	wfu
18908	3503
18909	3504
18912	3501
18933	3D-BOE
18934	9Q-CDC
18935	N113
18936	N67JR
18970	PK-VBA
18990	XT-BBE
18998	N30MP
19006	HZ-OCV
19121	N724CL
19123	VP-BAA
19124	HZ-DG1
19139	3D-JNM
19148	P4-ONE
19149	N400RG
19176	N530KF
19252	N727GG
19253	N720DC
19254	VP-BAB
19260	N727GP
19261	N727PX
19262	VP-BNA
19282	VP-CMN
19318	N727VJ
19392	N503MG
19394	J2-KBA
19399	wo
19402	D2-EVG
19403	D2-EVD
19520	wfu
19535	N766JS
19620	P4-JLD
19818	wfu
19835	N727HC
19854	N40
19859	C-FPXD
19892	3D-KMJ
19893	wfu
19895	wfu
20045	N727WF
20046	VP-BDJ
20049	5N-BBF
20050	5N-BBG
20111	wfu
20115	N908JE
20228	JY-HS1
20327	N624VA
20371	VP-CJN
20489	VP-CKA
20512	N311AG
20523	LV-JTD
20533	VP-BIF
20641	N7270B
21010	JY-HS2
21068	N777KY
21091	6V-AEF
21460	P4-SKI
21595	VP-CZY
21636	TJ-AAM
21824	A9C-BA
21853	P4-JLI
21948	N31TR
22044	5T-CJP
22359	N169KT
22362	HZ-AB3
22430	N727RE
22661	3505
22662	3506
22687	N721MF
22825	5N-FGN
22968	HZ-HR3

737

c/n	reg
19600	N487GS
19601	PK-OCF
19605	N165W
19613	N902WC
19772	N772WH
20127	wo
20255	PK-OCI
20335	PK-OCG
20483	K3187
20484	K3186
20689	N5175U
20690	wfu
20691	N5294E
20692	N5176Y
20693	N5177C
20694	N5294M
21069	N583CC
21165	VC96-2115
21166	VC96-2116
21167	0207
21317	EP-AGA
21499	5U-BAG
21957	VP-CHK
22050	N5WM
22431	N787WH
22600	HZ-MIS
22620	N902WG
22628	VP-CSA
23036	K2412
23037	K2413
23042	FAP 352
23059	22-222
23152	85101
23465	N736BP
23466	N733PA
23468	N370BC
23800	N253DV
23976	N37NY
24081	5R-MRM
24095	XC-UJB
24480	wo
24804	N737DX
24866	HS-HRH
24970	P4-PHS
25502	B-4018
25503	B-4019
25504	AP-BEH
25996	RP-C4007
26855	EZ-A001
27426	FAP 356
27456	N368CE
27906	55-555
27924	OE-ITA
28081	B-4020
28082	B-4021
28492	B-10001
28866	921
29089	VP-BBT
29090	VP-BBU
29979	165829
29980	165830
30139	3701
30181	N737A
30182	N738A
30183	N739A
30184	N743A
30185	N745A
30200	165831
30781	165832
32597	165833
32598	165834
33826	165835

747

c/n	reg
21648	VP-BAT
21649	A9C-HMH
21652	HZ-HM1B
21785	A40-SO
21786	70-YMN
21961	A6-SMR
21962	wfu
21963	P4-FSH
21992	A40-SP
22750	HZ-AIJ
23070	HZ-HM1A
23610	A6-ZSN
23824	82-8000
23825	92-9000
24730	20-1101
24731	20-1102
25880	HZ-WBT3
26426	V8-ALI
26903	A6-HRM
26906	A6-MMM
28551	A6-UAE
28961	A6-YAS
32445	A4O-OMN
33684	A9C-HMK

757

c/n	reg
22176	N757BJ
22690	XC-UJM
23454	P4-NSN
24527	HB-IEE
24923	N756AF
25155	N757AF
25220	N770BB
25345	EZ-A010
25487	TP-01
25495	HZ-HMED

26240	N801DM		
26633	NZ7571		
26634	NZ7572		
28463	N757MA		
29025	98-0001		
29026	98-0002		
29027	99-0003		
29028	99-0004		

767

22567	VP-CME
25537	V8-MHB
27254	VP-BKS
27255	HZ-WBT6
28270	N767KS
32954	UN-B6701
33425	P4-MES
33685	N767A

777

29271	N777AS
29953	VP-BRH

BBJ

28579	N367G
28581	N366G
28076	VP-BRM
29024	N50TC
29054	N500LS
29102	N737BZ
29135	N737CC
29136	N737GG
29139	VP-BEL
29142	N737WH
29149	TS-IOO
29188	HZ-TAA
29200	N742PB
29233	N4AS
29251	A6-HRS
29268	A6-AIN
29269	A6-RJZ
29272	FAC-001
29273	VP-BBJ
29274	M53-01
29317	VP-BWR
29441	N88WR
29749	N134AR
29791	P4-TBN
29857	A6-RJY
29858	A6-DAS
29865	HB-IIO
29866	HB-IIP
29971	01-0040
29972	VP-BYA
30031	VP-CEC
30070	N889NC
30076	VP-BBW
30327	N1270S
30328	N164RJ
30329	N129QS
30330	VP-BJB
30496	N737AG
30547	N79711
30572	N254SJ
30751	P4-GJC
30752	HB-IIQ
30753	02-0202
30754	N737ER
30755	02-0201
30756	N1560QS
30772	N315TS
30782	N515GM
30789	N349BA
30790	A36-001
30791	N1910S
30829	A36-002
30884	VP-BFA
32438	VP-BHN
32450	A6-MRM
32451	HZ-102
32575	PR-BBS
32627	ZS-RSA
32628	N7600K

32774	XA-AEX
32775	N90R
32777	G-OBBJ
32805	HZ-101
32806	VP-CBB
32807	HL7770
32825	A6-HEH
32915	VP-BZL
32916	01-0015
32970	VP-BRT
32971	N371BC
33010	N313YP
33036	N888YF
33079	EW-001PA
33080	01-0005
33102	N108MS
33361	N737M
33367	3C-EGE
33405	HZ-MF1
33434	02-0203
33473	A6-AUH
33499	HZ-MF2
33500	N237BA
33542	N358BJ

DC-0

45280	wfu
45570	F-RAFE
45658	wo
45819	F-RAFC
45984	FAP 371
46013	F-RAFG
46043	F-ZVMT
46053	TR-LTZ
46067	HB-IGH
46071	P4-DCE
46078	FAP 370
46081	N728A
46084	HZ-HM11
46111	VP-BHM
46130	F-RAFF

DC-9/MD80 Series

45706	N13FE
45731	N120NE
45732	N813TL
45740	N305PA
45775	N900SA
45797	N8860
45826	N29AF
45844	N949L
47011	N814RW
47151	VR-CKO
47152	N66AF
47514	N947ML
47595	MM62012
47600	wo
47635	N880DP
47691	wo
49670	N143G
49725	N945MA
49767	N721MM
49768	N287KB
49778	N948MA
49809	OE-IFA

DC-10

46501	N220AU
47907	N10MB

MD-11

48532	HZ-HM7
48533	HZ-AFA1

Bombardier

Learjet 23

23-001	wo
23-002	wfu
23-003	N3BL
23-004	wfu
23-005	wfu
23-006	wfu
23-007	wo
23-008	wfu

23-009	N23BY
23-010	wfu
23-013	wo
23-014	wfu
23-015A	wfu
23-016	wfu
23-017	wo
23-018	wfu
23-020	N820L
23-021	wo
23-022	wfu
23-023	wfu
23-024	wfu
23-025	wfu
23-026	wfu
23-027	wfu
23-028	wfu
23-028A	wfu
23-029	wfu
23-030	wfu
23-032	wo
23-033	wfu
23-034	wfu
23-035	N992TD
23 036	N123MJ
23-037	XC-LGD
23-038	wfu
23-039	N121CK
23-040	wfu
23-041	N77VJ
23-044	wo
23-045	wo
23-045A	wo
23-046	wo
23-047	wfu
23-048	wfu
23-049	N933NA
23-050A	wo
23-052	N856JB
23-053	wfu
23-054	N351N
23-056	wo
23-057	wfu
23-058	N153AG
23-059	wfu
23-061	wo
23-062	N20TA
23-063	wo
23-064	N259DB
23-065A	wfu
23-066	XB-MYE
23-067	wo
23-068	N73CE
23-069	wo
23-070	XC-JDX
23-071	wfu
23-072	RP-C848
23-073	N806LJ
23-074	wfu
23-075	wo
23-076	N83LJ
23-077	wo
23-078	wo
23-079	wfu
23-080	wo
23-081	N265DC
23-082	wfu
23-082A	N618BR
23-083	wfu
23-084	N119BA
23-085	wo
23-086	wo
23-088	wo
23-089	wfu
23-090	wo
23-091	wo
23-092	N415LJ
23-093	N7GF
23-094	wo
23-095	N9RA

23-097	wfu
23-098	wfu
23-099	N7200K

Learjet 24

24A-011	N24LG
24A-012	N1965L
24-015	wfu
24-019	N747SC
24-031	wfu
24-043	wfu
24-050	N24NJ
24-051	wfu
24-055	N711CW
24-060	XA-ADJ
24-065	N707SC
24-087	wfu
24A-096	N464CL
24A-100	wo
24-101	wfu
24A-102	wo
24-103	XB-ADR
24-104	N45ED
24-105	wfu
24-106	N888MC
24A-107	N40L
24-108	N315AJ
24-109	XA-NLK
24-110	wo
24A-111	N900NA
24-112	XA-TRQ
24-113	wfu
24-114	PT-LNE
24-115	wo
24A-116	N105GA
24XR-117	N24SA
24-118	wo
24-119	wfu
24-120	wfu
24-121	wo
24-122	wo
24-123	N25LJ
24-124	N991TD
24A-125	N651LJ
24-126	N16HC
24-127	N124JL
24-128	wfu
24-129	wo
24-130	wo
24-131	N241JA
24-132	wfu
24-133	wo
24-134	wfu
24-135	wo
24-136	wfu
24-137	N151AG
24-138	N130RS
24-139	wfu
24-140	wfu
24-141	XB-GHO
24-142	N723JW
24-143	wfu
24-144	wfu
24-145	N282AC
24-146	wo
24-147	N147CK
24-148	N24ET
24-149	N995TD
24XR-150	wfu
24-151	N6177Y
24-152	wfu
24-153	N120RA
24-154	wo
24-155	wfu
24-156	N712R
24-157	N157TW
24-158	PT-WEW
24-159	N710TV
24-160	N989TL
24-161	N222TW
24-162	wfu

24-163	wfu
24-164	wo
24-165	ZS-KJY
24-166	N993TD
24-167	N664CL
24-168	N333TW
24-169	wfu
24-170	N151WW
24-171	N417WW
24-172	wfu
24-173	YV-824CP
24-174	XA-LNK
24-175	wo
24-176	N3034B
24-177	wfu
24-178	N11AQ
24-179	N994TD
24-180	XA-NLA
24B-181	N426TA
24B-182	RP-C....
24B-183	wo
24B-184	N58FN
24B-185	wfu
24B-186	N196CF
24B-187	wfu
24B-188	N280R
24B-189	N915US
24B-190	wfu
24B-191	wfu
24B-192	wo
24B-193	N193DB
24B-194	N2093A
24B-195	N555LJ
24B-196	N196TB
24B-197	N89ES
24B-198	N39KM
24B-199	XA-TTT
24B-200	wfu
24B-201	wfu
24B-202	N333RY
24B-203	N203JL
24B-204	N510MS
24B-205	N64CE
24B-206	N24YA
24XR-207	ZS-MGJ
24B-208	XA-AAA
24B-209	ZS-LWU
24B-210	wo
24B-211	N680CJ
24B-212	N328JK
24B-213	N895J
24B-214	wo
24XR-215	N400EP
24B-216	N900GG
24B-217	N876MC
24B-218	N101VS
24B-219	ZS-TOY
24B-220	wfu
24B-221	N233TW
24B-222	N740EJ
24B-223	N7074X
24B-224	XA-TCA
24B-225	wo
24B-226	RP-C2424
24B-227	N27BJ
24B-228	PT-OBD
24B-229	wo
24D-230	XA-SSU
24D-231	wfu
24D-232	wo
24XR-233	N143GB
24D-234	LV-JTZ
24XR-235	N701SC
24D-236	N59AL
24D-237	N237TW
24D-238	N48FN
24D-239	wo
24D-240	wfu
24D-241	N63GA
24D-242	N999WA
24XR-243	N37HT

24D-244	wo	24D-325	N500SW	25-047	N222B	25B-133	N233CA	25D-214	N56MD
24D-245	N275E	24D-326	N322AU	25-048	N48GR	25B-134	N65A	25D-215	N25UJ
24D-246	N400MS	24D-327	N711PC	25-049	N70SK	25B-135	N50RW	25D-216	N68AX
24D-247	wo	24D-328	D-CMMM	25-050	N999MF	25B-136	N48WA	25D-217	N217WM
24D-248	wo	24E-329	N24FW	25-051	N760A*	25B-137	N752EA	25D-218	N251DS
24D-249	N440KT	24E-330	N330TW	25-052	N692FG	25B-138	N911RF	25XR-219	XA-CCC
24D-250	0006	24E-331	N32DD	25-053	wo	25XR-139	N111MP	25XR-220	N99NJ
24D-251	N39EL	24F-332	N56MM	25-054	N25MD	25B-140	N140CA	25D-221	N147CA
24D-252	N157AG	24F-333	PT-LQK	25-055	N511AJ	25XR-141	ZS-BXR	25XR-222	N134WE
24D-253	wo	24E-334	N944KM	25XR-056	PT-LBW	25B-142	N49WA	25D-223	wo
24D-254	wfu	24E-335	N2DD	25-057	N507HF	25B-143	N143CK	25D-224	XB-MGM
24D-255	N255AR	24F-336	N49GS	25-058	N273LR	25B-144	wo	25D-225	N140GC
24D-256	N256WM	24F-337	XA-DET	25-059	wo	25B-145	N145SH	25D-226	N234SV
24D-257	N888FA	24E-338	wfu	25-060	N564CL	25C-146	I-BMFE	25D-227	N25RE
24D-258	N424RS	24E-339	N207RG	25C-061	YV-203CP	25B-147	XA-GGG	25D-228	N228SW
24D-259	wfu	24E-340	N825AM	25-062	N21FN	25XR-148	N98RS	25D-229	N229WJ
24D-260	XC-PFP	24E-341	N14DM	25-063	N25FM	25B-149	N239CA	25D-230	N207HF
24D-261	wfu	24E-342	N123DG	25-064	wfu	25B-150	N251JA	25D-231	N531CW
24D-262	wfu	24E-343	N7EJ	25C-070	N911LM	25B-151	wo	25D-232	N264TW
24D-263	wo	24F-344	wo	25C-071	LV-ZTH	25XR-152	N105BA	25D-233	N947TC
24XR-264	RP-C1747	24F-345	N217JS	25C-072	wo	25B-153	wo	25D-234	N764KF
24XR-265	wo	24E-346	HP-....	25XR-073	wo	25B-154	N82TS	25XR-235	N400VC
24D-266	N266TW	24F-347	N508SR	25B-074	wo	25B-155	PT-LEA	25D-236	XC-RPP
24XR-267	ZS-OEA	24F-348	N444TW	25B-075	N307HF	25C-156	N75BL	25D-237	wo
24D-268	N24TK	24F-349	XB-DZD	25B-076	XA-SJS	25B-157	N50CK	25D-238	N41NK
24D-269	XA-DIJ	24E-350	N500ZA	25B-077	wo	25B-158	N924BW	25D-239	N499EH
24D-270	wo	24E-351	N77MR	25B-078	N778GM	25B-159	wo	25D-240	N33PT
24D-271	XA-SCE	24F-352	N352MD	25XR-079	XA-AVV	25B-160	ZS-MTD	25D-241	N213CA
24D-272	N117K	24F-353	wo	25B-080	XA-POG	25B-161	N236CA	25D-242	N242GS
24D-273	XB-DZR	24F-354	ZS-FUN	25B-081	N524DW	25XR-162	N150RS	25D-243	wo
24XR-274	N48CT	24E-355	N165CM	25B-082	N62DM	25B-163	N911AJ	25D-244	N125PT
24D-275	PT-LPH	24F-356	PT-LKD	25C-083	N54FN	25B-164	N23RZ	25D-245	N606GB
24D-276	N56PT	24F-357	N129ME	25C-084	N777TX	25C-165	wo	25XR-246	wo
24D-277	N277TW	Learjet 25		25B-085	wfu	25B-166	N166PC	25D-247	wfu
24D-278	N202JS	25-001	wfu	25B-086	N65WH	25B-167	C-GBFP	25D-248	N248CK
24D-279	N955EA	25-002	wfu	25C-087	N25TE	25B-168	N88BY	25D-249	N34TN
24XR-280	ZS-NGG	25-003	N97FN	25C-088	wo	25B-169	XA-KKK	25D-250	N19JM
24D-281	N281FP	25-004	N225KA	25C-089	PT-IIQ	25B-170	wo	25D-251	N85TW
24D-282	wo	25-005	N39CK	25B-090	C-FPUB	25B-171	N401AJ	25D-252	N444MK
24XR-283	N24XR	25-006	N44CP	25B-091	N91PN	25C-172	wo	25D-253	YV-1049CP
24D-284	PT-JKQ	25-007	N726WR	25B-092	N80EL	25XR-173	XA-JSC	25D-254	N76AX
24XR-285	N430JW	25-008	N800GG	25B-093	PT-LEN	25B-174	N16KK	25D-255	N219RB
24XR-286	wo	25-009	wo	25C-094	wo	25XR-175	N127GB	25D-256	N75CK
24D-287	wo	25-010	wo	25B-095	N2094L	25C-176	PT-LLN	25D-257	N988AS
24D-288	N288DF	25-011	N525TW	25B-096	N20NW	25B-177	wo	25D-258	wo
24D-289	N98CG	25-012	N102AR	25C-097	N22NJ	25B-178	wo	25D-259	wo
24D-290	N88LJ	25-013	wo	25C-098	ZS-NYG	25C-179	C-GSKL	25D-260	N74RD
24D-291	N483DM	25-014	wfu	25C-099	wo	25B-180	N102VS	25D-261	N261WC
24D-292	N888TW	25-015	XA-LLL	25B-100	N829AA	25C-181	N100NB	25D-262	wo
24D-293	N293MC	25-016	N976BS	25B-101	N47MR	25B-182	N99MC	25D-263	XA-YYY
24D-294	PT-WKL	25-017	N53FL	25B-102	N254SC	25B-183	N83CK	25D-264	N547JG
24XR-295	N295NW	25-018	wfu	25B-103	wo	25B-184	wo	25D-265	N265TW
24D-296	PT-LMS	25-019	wo	25B-104	N35WJ	25B-185	N606SM	25D-266	wo
24D-297	N24S	25-020	N76CK	25B-105	N25WJ	25B-186	wo	25D-267	N15ER
24D-298	N169US	25-021	wfu	25XR-106	wo	25B-187	N187CA	25D-268	N268WC
24D-299	N299TW	25XR-022	ZS-SSM	25B-107	N252BK	25B-188	wo	25D-269	LV-WOC
24XR-300	wo	25-023	N147TW	25C-108	wo	25B-189	N67HB	25D-270	N75AX
24D-301	N249HP	25-024	N20RZ	25C-109	N860MX	25B-190	N190AR	25D-271	wo
24D-302	wo	25-025	N110RA*	25C-110	N343RK	25B-191	wo	25D-272	N520SR
24D-303	N303EJ	25-026	N25EC	25B-111	N45BS*	25B-192	FAB 008	25D-273	N73DJ
24D-304	N588CG	25-027	N900AJ	25B-112	N279LE	25B-193	XA-WWW	25D-274	XA-FMR
24D-305	N666MW	25-028	N33PF	25C-113	wo	25B-194	XC-NSP	25D-275	N254CL
24D-306	N306JA	25XR-029	N107HF	25B-114	XA-VMC	25B-195	wfu	25D-276	XA-UUU
24D-307	wo	25-030	wo	25C-115	PT-ISO	25B-196	wo	25D-277	N81MW
24D-308	XA-...	25-031	N294NW	25C-116	wo	25B-197	N197CF	25D-278	N70JF
24D-309	N80CK	25-032	wfu	25B-117	N7810W	25B-198	N198JA	25D-279	N81AX
24D-310	wo	25-033	wfu	25B-118	N118MB	25XR-199	wo	25D-280	N280C
24D-311	N311LJ	25-034	wfu	25B-119	wo	25B-200	N350JH	25D-281	N800RF
24D-312	N80AP	25-035	N616NA	25B-120	XA-AJL	25B-201	N251TS	25D-282	N711WD
24D-313	wo	25-036	N45BK	25B-121	N8005Y	25B-202	N343CA	25D-283	N444WW
24D-314	wo	25-037	wfu	25B-122	N751CA	25B-203	N344CA	25D-284	N284TJ
24D-315	wfu	25-038	N130CK	25B-123	N688GS	25B-204	wo	25D-285	wfu
24D-316	LV-LRC	25-039	N273CA	25B-124	XA-ALV	25B-205	Z3-BAA	25D-286	N9QM
24D-317	XA-JIQ	25-040	N238CA	25B-125	N10VG	25D-206	ZS-LXH	25D-287	wo
24D-318	N611DB	25-041	N31AA	25C-126	N14FN	25D-207	wfu	25D-288	N100WN
24XR-319	N174RD	25-042	wfu	25B-127	N425JL	25D-208	N300SC	25D-289	XA-TWH
24D-320	N996TD	25-043	N473TC	25B-128	wo	25D-209	N30LJ	25D-290	N600GM
24D-321	N33TP	25-044	wo	25C-129	N25MT	25D-210	N764RH	25D-291	N453MA
24D-322	N322RS	25-045	wfu	25B-130	N26AT	25D-211	FAB 010	25D-292	N604AS
24D-323	N27AX	25-046	N345MC	25C-131	wo	25D-212	wfu	25D-293	XA-PIU
24D-324	N324TW			25B-132	wo	25D-213	N925DW	25D-294	N88NJ

Reg	Code
25D-295	XA-...
25D-296	PT-OHD
25D-297	N389AT
25D-298	N242PF
25D-299	N299MW
25D-300	N108FL
25D-301	N82AX
25D-302	N25CY
25D-303	XA-JOC
25D-304	N25NY
25D-305	XA-AAS
25D-306	XC-GUB
25D-307	LV-OEL
25D-308	N727LM
25D-309	XA-PAZ
25D-310	N211JC
25D-311	N199BT
25D-312	XC-HIS
25D-313	N251AL
25D-314	N305AR
25D-315	XA-...
25D-316	N17AH
25D-317	N317VS
25D-318	wo
25D-319	N712DP
25D-320	N690JC
25D-321	N25AM
25D-322	5N-AOC
25D-323	PT-LMM
25D-324	N970WJ
25D-325	XB-HGE
25D-326	N25NB
25D-327	N444TG
25D-328	XB-JLU
25D-329	N401DP
25D-330	N330L
25D-331	N482CP
25D-332	XA-AFH
25D-333	N555SD
25D-334	XA-RYH
25D-335	PT-LUZ
25D-336	XA-VYA
25G-337	N14CK
25D-338	N4447P
25D-339	MTX-03
25D-340	N625AU
25D-341	N58HC
25D-342	N25PW
25D-343	N456CG
25D-344	wo
25D-345	LV-WLG
25D-346	XA-ZZZ
25D-347	N347JV
25D-348	N988AA
25D-349	wo
25D-350	N684JW
25D-351	N425RA
25G-352	N125JW
25D-353	N43DR
25D-354	N515TC
25D-355	LV-WRE
25D-356	N251MD
25D-357	LV-WXY
25D-358	N37971
25D-359	XA-LRJ
25D-360	N360JG
25D-361	XA-...
25D-362	N107RM
25D-363	N197LS
25D-364	XA-TIE
25D-365	XA-SJN
25D-366	N366LJ
25D-367	N4488W
25D-368	N368D
25D-369	XA-...
25G-370	N888DV
25G-371	N72WC
25D-372	N722EM
25D-373	XA-ACX

Learjet 28

Reg	Code
28-001	N128LR
28-002	XC-VSA
28-003	N800GA
28-004	N43PJ
28-005	N500LG

Learjet 29

Reg	Code
29-001	XC-IST
29-002	XC-HIE
29-003	VT-EHS
29-004	VT-EIH

Learjet 31

Reg	Code
31-001	wfu
31-002	N322TS
31-003	N888CP
31-004	XA-ZTH
31-005	N431BC
31-006	N26LC
31-007	PT-LXX
31-008	wo
31-009	N727CP
31-010	N89HB
31-011	HB-VJI
31-012	XA-TUL
31-013	PT-XTA
31-014	N5VG
31-015	N260LF
31-016	N1DE
31-017	N801CT
31-018	N90BA
31-019	N19LT
31-020	N337FP
31-021	XA-RNK
31-022	N331N
31-023	N111VV
31-024	N912TB
31-025	I-AIRW
31-026	N706SA
31-027	N2FU
31-028	N90WA
31-029	XB-FKT
31-030	XA-JYC
31-031	N93SK
31-032	XA-BRG
31-033	N632PB
31-033A	N156JS
31-033C	wo
31-033C	N55VR
31-033D	N157JS
31-034	CS-DDZ
31A-035	N3VJ
31A-036	N127VL
31A-037	PT-OVZ
31A-038	N500WR
31A-039	N22AX
31A-040	N314MK
31A-041	RP-C8822
31A-042	D-CURT
31A-043	N531SK
31A-044	XA-OLE
31A-045	YU-BRZ
31A-046	N352EF
31A-047	N39TW
31A-048	N314XS
31A-049	N131TT
31A-050	N92UG
31A-051	N351AC
31A-052	N899CS
31A-053	N31FF
31A-054	N54TN
31A-055	N425M
31A-056	N56LF
31A-057	D-CSAP
31A-058	N825AC
31A-059	N31TK
31A-060	N696PA
31A-061	N261SC
31A-062	AP-BEK
31A-063	N707NV
31A-064	N444HC
31A-065	N64NB
31A-066	PK-CAH
31A-067	TG-AIR
31A-068	N680AF
31A-069	N744N
31A-070	N370SC
31A-071	N271SC
31A-072	N45UF
31A-073	XA-ZYZ
31A-074	N131BR
31A-075	N631SF
31A-076	N215TT
31A-077	PK-CAJ
31A-078	N539LB
31A-079	N91DP
31A-080	N986MA
31A-081	LV-YMB
31A-082	N727BT
31A-083	N789SR
31A-084	N840SW
31A-085	N321GL
31A-086	N969
31A-087	N167BA
31A-088	N500JE
31A-089	N77PY
31A-090	N78PR
31A-091	V5-NAG
31A-092	N711FG
31A-093	N916BD
31A-094	N917BD
31A-095	N395LJ
31A-096	N37BM
31A-097	N31LJ
31A-098	N721MJ
31A-099	N1932K
31A-100	PR-SCB
31A-101	N900R
31A-102	C-GWXP
31A-103	N407RA
31A-104	N631CC
31A-105	N109HV
31A-106	N581RA
31A-107	N107LP
31A-108	N288FF
31A-109	N722JS
31A-110	PT-WIV
31A-111	N111AF
31A-112	LX-PCT
31A-113	N131GG
31A-114	N524HC
31A-115	ZS-NYV
31A-116	N31UJ
31A-117	N517CC*
31A-118	N815E
31A-119	N996JS
31A-120	N200TJ
31A-121	N121LJ
31A-122	PT-WLO
31A-123	N48AM
31A-124	N931FD
31A-125	N125FS
31A-126	N18BL
31A-127	HB-VLR
31A-128	N365GL
31A-129	N115BX
31A-130	N31PV
31A-131	N319SC
31A-132	N929JH
31A-133	N314SG
31A-134	N977AR
31A-135	PT-WSB
31A-136	N131DA*
31A-137	N120RV
31A-138	V5-NMC
31A-139	N229KD
31A-140	N45HG
31A-141	N121PX
31A-142	N698MM
31A-143	N122BX
31A-144	JA01CP
31A-145	N696RB*
31A-146	N218NB
31A-147	N45KK
31A-148	PT-XPP
31A-149	N685RC
31A-150	N595PA
31A-151	N31NF
31A-152	N517GP
31A-153	N37RA
31A-154	N154RT
31A-155	N525GP
31A-156	N124FX
31A-157	N125FX
31A-158	PR-LRJ
31A-159	XA-AFX
31A-160	LX-EAR
31A-161	N177JB
31A-162	N125GP
31A-163	N128FX
31A-164	N164SB
31A-165	N808W
31A-166	N366TS
31A-167	LX-OMC
31A-168	N952VS
31A-169	N197PH
31A-170	ZS-OML
31A-171	N31MW
31A-172	N130FX
31A-173	N173LC
31A-174	MTX-02
31A-175	N131FX
31A-176	N176WS
31A-177	N132FX
31A-178	RP-C6178
31A-179	N133FX
31A-180	N1926S
31A-181	N526GP
31A-182	N527GP
31A-183	N183ML
31A-184	N931RS
31A-185	N110SC
31A-186	N45PK
31A-187	N932FD
31A-188	N70AE
31A-189	N158R
31A-190	N8TG
31A-191	N631AT
31A-192	N531RA
31A-193	N44SZ
31A-194	N29SN
31A-195	N134FX
31A-196	N136FX
31A-197	N20XP
31A-198	N500MP
31A-199	N901P
31A-200	N599CT
31A-201	N137FX
31A-202	ZS-PNP
31A-203	N63SE
31A-204	N204RT
31A-205	N71FB
31A-206	N79SE
31A-207	D-CSIE
31A-208	N227NT
31A-209	N209HR
31A-210	N927DJ
31A-211	N5NC
31A-212	N480JJ
31A-213	D-CMRM
31A-214	PT-FZA
31A-215	N786YA
31A-216	N999GH
31A-217	N10SE
31A-218	N1ED
31A-219	N518JG
31A-220	N521WH*
31A-221	N68ES
31A-222	N770CH
31A-223	N800CH
31A-224	N224LJ
31A-225	N834AF
31A-226	N7SN
31A-227	D-CGGG
31A-228	N955JS
31A-229	N229LJ
31A-230	N295PS
31A-231	N712EJ
31A-232	N668VP
31A-233	EI-MAX
31A-234	N376MB
31A-235	XA-...
31A-236	N57TS
31a-237	N19UP
31A-238	N36UP
31A-239	N686AB
31A-240	N998AL
31A-241	N633SF
31A-242	N600AW

Learjet 35

Reg	Code
35-001	N351GL
35-002	C-GVVA
35-003	N111WB
35-004	C-GIRE
35-005	N178CP
35-006	N39FN
35-007	N35UJ
35-008	PP-ERR
35-009	N335AT
35-010	N35AJ
35-011	N531AJ
35-012	XA-SVX
35-013	N535TA
35-014	N844L
35-015	N354PM
35-016	N18CV
35-017	N600DT
35-018	N435JL
35-019	N71LG
35-020	wo
35A-021	N53FN
35-022	N90WR
35-023	N443RK
35-024	N411BA
35-025	N435UJ
35-026	N89TC
35-027	N31WS
35-028	TP-104
35-029	wo
35-030	C-GKPE
35-031	N233CC
35-032	N710GS
35-033	N524PA
35-034	N37TA
35-035	N92TS
35-036	N90AH
35-037	N333KC
35-038	C-FBFP
35-039	N382TC
35-040	wo
35-041	N41NW
35-042	XA-FFF
35-043	N575WW
35-044	N130Г
35-045	N1140A
35-046	N58EM
35A-047	N701AS
35-048	N8040A
35-049	LV-ZZF
35-050	351
35-051	N2BA
35-052	wo
35-053	N541PA
35-054	N435MS
35-055	N354LQ
35-056	N645G
35-057	C-GTDE
35-058	wo
35-059	wo
35-060	wo
35-061	N235EA
35-062	N31DP
35-063	N80PG

35-064	N257SD	35A-145	VH-SLD	35A-226	N30HJ	35A-307	N677CT	35A-388	wo
35-065	N4358N	35A-146	N351AS	35A-227	N366TT	35A-308	N747GM	35A-389	N389KA
35-066	352	35A-147	N55F	35A-228	N72LG	35A-309	C-GUAC	35A-390	C-FPRP
35A-067	N135FA	35A-148	wo	35A-229	N4415W	35A-310	N310ME	35A-391	wo
35A-068	T-781	35A-149	N800AW	35A-230	N37HJ	35A-311	N581AS	35A-392	N1XL
35A-069	N48GP	35A-150	wo	35A-231	VH-JCR	35A-312	N369BA	35A-393	PT-LOE
35A-070	N50FN	35A-151	wfu	35A-232	N4415S	35A-313	N31WR	35A-394	N238PR
35A-071	N99FN	35A-152	XA-RIN	35A-233	N23A	35A-314	N777LD	35A-395	N246CM
35A-072	N4415M	35A-153	N573LR	35A-234	N35WR	35A-315	D-CCAA	35A-396	PT-OPJ
35A-073	N536KN	35A-154	N244RG	35A-235	LV-ZSZ	35A-316	N384JW	35A-397	N200TW
35A-074	N351PJ	35A-155	N70AX	35A-236	N65RZ	35A-317	N317TT	35A-398	wo
35A-075	SE-DHP	35A-156	N35WE	35A-237	N300TE	35A-318	N318NW	35A-399	N399AZ
35A-076	N959SA	35A-157	N26GP	35A-238	N32RZ	35A-319	T-23	35A-400	VH-OVB
35A-077	N98LC	35A-158	N800GP	35A-239	wo	35A-320	N32PJ	35A-401	N771SB
35A-078	N145AM	35A-159	D-CAPO	35A-240	N135WE	35A-321	3909	35A-402	N35BG
35A-079	N68QB	35A-160	D-CCCA	35A-241	N500ED	35A-322	PT-WGF	35A-403	N403FW
35A-080	N17AZ	35A-161	N433DD	35A-242	N242DR	35A-323	N357EF	35A-404	N804TF
35A-081	N81FR	35A-162	XA-CZG	35A-243	XA-THD	35A-324	N8064A	35A-405	N135DA
35A-082	N700SJ	35A-163	N27BL	35A-244	N244LJ	35A-325	N325NW	35A-406	ER-LGA
35A-083	N400LV	35A-164	N50MJ	35A-245	N30PA	35A-326	N35SA	35A-407	C-GIWO
35A-084	N903AL	35A-165	N72CK	35A-246	N628DB	35A-327	N32PF	35A-408	LV-AIT
35A-085	N15WH	35A-166	N10UF	35A-247	N544PA	35A-328	N408MG	35A-409	N351AM
35A-086	N860S	35A-167	N813AS	35A-248	N128CA	35A-329	N261PG	35A-410	N89RP
35A-087	N18AX	35A-168	C-FZQP	35A-249	C-FICU	35A-330	wfu	35A-411	N94GP
35A-088	N72JF	35A-169	N500JS	35A-250	N947GS	35A-331	D-CGFC	35A-412	XA-RGH
35A-089	D-CCHB	35A-170	N335AS	35A-251	N387HA	35A-332	N827CR	35A-413	D-CFCF
35A-090	N88BG	35A-171	N171WH	35A-252	PT-KZR	35A-333	wo	35A-414	N815DD
35A-091	N37FA	35A-172	ZS-ZZZ*	35A-253	N129TS	35A-334	N235MC	35A-415	SE-DZZ
35A-092	N73CK*	35A-173	N326DD	35A-254	N720WW	35A-335	N3MB	35A-416	N841TF
35A-093	PT-LOT	35A-174	N773DL	35A-255	XB-FNW	35A-336	XA-BNO	35A-417	LX-ONE
35A-094	N94AF	35A-175	SE-RCA	35A-256	N911ML	35A-337	N39HJ	35A-418	XA-KCM
35A-095	N66KK	35A-176	XA-BUX	35A-257	N417BA	35A-338	RP-C610	35A-419	N72AX
35A-096	N94RL	35A-177	D-CITY	35A-258	N583BS	35A-339	PT-LZP	35A-420	N181CA
35A-097	N108RB	35A-178	N900JC	35A-259	N25AN	35A-340	N504F	35A-421	D-CDSF
35A-098	N72DA	35A-179	D-CGFA	35A-260	N40PK	35A-341	ZS-CEW	35A-422	N45AE
35A-099	wo	35A-180	N701DA	35A-261	N58MM	35A-342	N56JA	35A-423	D-CAVE
35-100	C-GRFO	35A-181	PT-LSJ	35A-262	N237AF	35A-343	N21NG	35A-424	N508GP
35-101	N721AS	35A-182	N221SG	35A-263	ZS-PBA*	35A-344	N630SJ	35A-425	N425SA
35-102	wo	35A-183	N717AJ	35A-264	N64CP	35A-345	wo	35A-426	RP-C1426
35-103	PT-LCD	35A-184	N7092C	35A-265	8..	35A-346	EC-IIC	35A-427	N36HJ
35-104	wo	35A-185	ZS-SES	35A-266	N35GC	35A-347	N85SV	35A-428	VH-SLE
35-105	N444WB	35A-186	N96FN	35A-267	wo	35A-348	N35DL	35A-429	800
35-106	wo	35A-187	N32HM	35A-268	D-CGFB	35A-349	N252WJ	35A-430	LJ-1
35-107	wo	35A-188	N924AM	35A-269	N886R	35A-350	N35WB	35A-431	N431AS
35A-108	D-CJPG	35A-189	wo	35A-270	N31MC	35A-351	N500ND	35A-432	VH-VLJ
35A-109	N911AE	35A-190	N181EF	35A-271	N40AN	35A-352	N800GJ	35A-433	wo
35A-110	N4J	35A-191	N535AF	35A-272	N321AN	35A-353	C-GDJH	35A-434	N469BB
35A-111	I-LIAD	35A-192	N49BE	35A-273	N273LJ	35A-354	N405GJ	35A-435	XC-HHJ
35A-112	N999ND	35A-193	N359EF	35A-274	N274JS	35A-355	N721EC*	35A-436	N100AT
35A-113	N684HA	35A-194	wo	35A-275	N72LL	35A-356	PT-LUG	35A-437	YV-432CP
35A-114	wo	35A-195	SE-DHO	35A-276	N69BH	35A-357	N357LJ	35A-438	N308BW
35A-115	T-21	35A-196	wo	35A-277	N2WQ	35A-358	N108JN	35A-439	N402DP
35A-116	N58CW	35A-197	N754GL	35A-278	N12RP	35A-359	N136JP	35A-440	N917SC
35A-117	N78MC	35A-198	N198GJ	35A-279	wo	35A-360	N360LJ	35A-441	N699ST
35A-118	N118FN	35A-199	N235JS	35A-280	N35AX	35A-361	PT-OCZ	35A-442	wo
35A-119	N549PA	35A-200	N200LJ	35A-281	N425AS	35A-362	N362FW	35A-443	N258G
35A-120	N400JE	35A-201	N35AZ	35A-282	N62MB	35A-363	N19RP	35A-444	N615HB
35A-121	N43TJ	35A-202	N55FN	35A-283	N386CM	35A-364	N353EF	35A-445	wo
35A-122	N27TT	35A-203	N97CE*	35A-284	N43MF	35A-365	D-CFAI	35A-446	N403DP
35A-123	N900BJ	35A-204	D-CFTG	35A-285	N42PJ	35A-366	N350DA	35A-447	D-COKE
35A-124	C-GTJL	35A-205	N568PA	35A-286	N286WL	35A-367	N232CC	35A-448	N222BG
35A-125	N351EF	35A-206	N38PS	35A-287	N929SR	35A-368	N450MC	35A-449	XA-GDO
35A-126	N15EH	35A-207	N620JM	35A-288	N288JP	35A-369	T-24	35A-450	N950SP
35A-127	N351TX	35A-208	N67PA	35A-289	N217TA	35A-370	XA-CVD	35A-451	LJ-2
35A-128	N39PJ	35A-209	N22MS	35A-290	XA-ORO	35A-371	N399BA	35A-452	N452DA
35A-129	XA-ZAP	35A-210	N210WL	35A-291	wo	35A-372	PT-LJK	35A-453	N453AM
35A-130	N757AL	35A-211	N44TT	35A-292	N292ME	35A-373	N971K	35A-454	N80AR
35A-131	N155AM	35A-212	N989AL	35A-293	N182K	35A-374	HZ-106	35A-455	N9880C
35A-132	N135AG	35A-213	XC-CUZ	35A-294	wo	35A-375	HZ-107	35A-456	N456CL
35A-133	N133EJ	35A-214	N279DM	35A-295	N94AA	35A-376	N979RF	35A-457	N49WL
35A-134	N238JA	35A-215	N35ED	35A-296	N66NJ	35A-377	N18WE	35A-458	N4EA
35A-135	N135GJ	35A-216	N335RD	35A-297	N777DM	35A-378	N354EF	35A-459	N829CA
35A-136	T-22	35A-217	N122JW	35A-298	N298NW	35A-379	N217RT	35A-460	XA-JJJ
35A-137	N35TJ	35A-218	N481FM	35A-299	PT-XLI	35A-380	C-GAJS	35A-461	N64CF
35A-138	N124ZT	35A-219	wo	35A-300	N365N	35A-381	N35NA	35A-462	N135TP
35A-139	D-CGFD	35A-220	N220GS	35A-301	N945W	35A-382	N60WL	35A-463	N32PJ
35A-140	N40BD	35A-221	N221TR	35A-302	N51LC	35A-383	N364CL	35A-464	VP-BJS
35A-141	N553V	35A-222	D-CGFG	35A-303	PT-LLS	35A-384	N384CF	35A-465	N465NW
35A-142	N815L	35A-223	D-CGRC	35A-304	N995CR	35A-385	N350EF	35A-466	wo
35A-143	N20DK	35A-224	N28MJ	35A-305	N33NJ	35A-386	N999FA	35A-467	HZ-MS1
35A-144	N56EM	35A-225	N225CF	35A-306	N9ZD	35A-387	D-CARL	35A-468	OY-CCJ

35A-469	N35JN	35A-550	84-0104	35A-631	2710	36A-035	N71CK	45-052	ZS-DCT
35A-470	LJ-3	35A-551	84-0105	35A-632	2711	36A-036	N136DH	45-053	N1904S
35A-471	N110FT	35A-552	84-0106	35A-633	2712	36A-037	N555WH	45-054	N345MA
35A-472	N35TN	35A-553	84-0107	35A-634	N626BM	36A-038	N700GG	45-055	G-OLDF
35A-473	N777LB	35A-554	84-0108	35A-635	40208	36A-039	N99RS	45-056	N196PH
35A-474	PT-LEB	35A-555	84-0109	35A-636	2713	36A-040	N72AV	45-057	N75TE
35A-475	ZS-TOW	35A-556	84-0110	35A-638	2714	36A-041	N79SF	45-058	N660HC
35A-476	N776JS	35A-557	84-0111	35A-639	2715	36A-042	wo	45-059	VP-CVL
35A-477	N608GF	35A-558	84-0112	35A-640	2716	36A-043	N432JW	45-060	N1MG
35A-478	wo	35A-559	84-0113	35A-641	2717	36A-044	N70LJ*	45-061	N111KK
35A-479	PT-LHT	35A-560	84-0114	35A-642	2718	36A-045	wo	45-062	N543CM
35A-480	N39DK	35A-561	84-0115	35A-643	D-CGFJ	36A-046	N17A	45-063	N10J
35A-481	OO-LFV	35A-562	84-0116	35A-644	C-GMMY	36A-047	N36PJ	45-064	EC-ILK
35A-482	wo	35A-563	84-0117	35A-645	N645AM	36A-048	N32AJ	45-065	N100KK
35A-483	N202BT	35A-564	84-0118	35A-646	wo	36A-049	VH-SLF	45-066	N94CK
35A-484	T-25	35A-565	84-0119	35A-647	N335PR	36A-050	TP-105	45-067	XA-LRX
35A-485	N485AC	35A-566	84-0120	35A-648	N97LE	36A-051	FAP 524	45-068	I-ERJD
35A-486	N925DM	35A-567	wo	35A-649	ZK-XVL	36A-052	FAP 525	45-069	SU-MSG
35A-487	N487FW	35A-568	84-0122	35A-650	N650LR	36A-053	HY-984	45-070	LX-IMS
35A-488	N907R	35A-569	84-0123	35A-651	N405PC	36A-054	9201	45-071	N145K
35A-489	N222BE	35A-570	84-0124	35A-652	N2KZ	36A-055	PP-JAA	45-072	N720CC
35A-490	N64MP	35A-571	84-0125	35A-653	LX-LAR	36A-056	wo	45-073	N66SG
35A-491	N35NK	35A-572	84-0126	35A-654	N770BM	36A-057	VH-JCX	45-074	N740TF
35A-492	N335UJ	35A-573	84-0127	35A-655	C-GMMA	36A-058	wn	45-075	N450BC
35A-493	N354CL	35A-574	wfu	35A-656	N356JW	36A-059	9204	45-076	N245K
35A-494	PT-LDM	35A-575	84-0128	35A-657	N10AH	36A-060	9205	45-077	XA-AIM
35A-495	N440MC	35A-576	84-0129	35A-658	N77NJ	36A-061	9206	45-078	N116AS
35A-496	N825LJ	35A-577	84-0130	35A-659	N413LC	36A-062	D-CGFE	45-079	N5FE
35A-497	N15RH	35A-578	84-0131	35A-660	C-GLJQ	36A-063	D-CGFF	45-080	N45UJ
35A-498	N400FF	35A-579	84-0132	35A-661	VH-PFA	*Learjet 45*		45-081	N145GM
35A-499	N911DX	35A-580	84-0133	35A-662	N35UK	45-002	N452LJ	45-082	N1HP
35A-500	N81QM	35A-581	84-0134	35A-663	D-CCCB	45-003	N453LJ	45-083	ZS-TJS
35A-501	N326HG	35A-582	84-0135	35A-664	N640BA	45-004	wo	45-084	HB-VML
35A-502	N747CP	35A-583	wo	35A-665	N35UA	45-005	G-ZXZX	45-085	N454CG
35A-503	N542SA	35A-584	84-0141	35A-666	wfu	45-006	N721CP	45-086	C-GMRO
35A-504	N505DH	35A-585	84-0137	35A-667	N135DE	45-007	VH-EJK	45-087	N64HH
35A-505	N494PA	35A-586	84-0142	35A-668	N441PC	45-008	N745E	45-088	C-FMGL
35A-506	wfu	35A-587	84-0139	35A-669	C-GWFG	45-009	N500CG	45-089	N406FX
35A-507	N42HN	35A-588	84-0140	35A-670	N987LP	45-010	N903HC	45-090	N452CJ
35A-508	N881CA	35A-589	N3215K	35A-671	N671TS	45-011	N741E	45-091	N451WM
35A-509	wo	35A-590	N882SC	35A-672	XA-FMT	45-012	N450TJ	45-092	ZS-PDG
35A-510	84-0064	35A-591	N880Z	35A-673	C-GPDO	45-013	N45LR	45-093	wo
35A-511	84-0065	35A-592	N93LE	35A-674	N674LJ	45-014	N708SP	45-094	N300JE
35A-512	84-0066	35A-593	VH-PPF	35A-675	wo	45-015	N31V	45-095	N409FX
35A-513	N117PK	35A-594	N410BD	35A-676	N235AC	45-016	N743E	45-096	C-GDMI
35A-514	84-0068	35A-595	N414KL	*Learjet 36*		45-017	D-CESH	45-097	D-CMSC
35A-515	84-0069	35A-596	N352HS	36-001	wfu	45-018	OO-LFS	45-098	N6FE
35A-516	84-0070	35A-597	N604S	36-002	N84FN	45-019	C-GLRJ	45-099	N7FE
35A-517	84-0071	35A-598	PT-LGW	36-003	N361PJ	45-020	C-GVVZ	45-100	RP-C1958
35A-518	84-0072	35A-599	N367DA*	36-004	N54PA	45-021	HB-VMB	45-101	N410FX
35A-519	84-0073	35A-600	N995DP	36-005	N9108Z	45-022	N845RL	45-102	N411FX
35A-520	84-0074	35A-601	HY-986	36-006	wo	45-023	N740E	45-103	N412FX
35A-521	84-0075	35A-602	HY-987	36-007	N83FN	45-024	C-FBCL	45-104	OH-FFX
35A-522	84-0076	35A-603	HY-988	36-008	N101AJ	45-025	N742E	45-105	N397AT
35A-523	84-0077	35A-604	N604GS	36-009	N505HG	45-026	N405FX	45-106	N145XL
35A-524	84-0078	35A-605	N925CA	36-010	N45FG	45-027	N156PH	45-107	N145CG
35A-525	84-0079	35A-606	N96GS	36-011	N26FN	45-028	XC-VMC	45-108	N313BW
35A-526	84-0080	35A-607	D-CGFH	36-012	N547PA	45-029	N170LS	45-109	N60PC
35A-527	84-0081	35A-608	N96AX	36-013	N71PG	45-030	N157PH	45-110	N222MW
35A-528	84-0082	35A-609	XA-JRH	36-014	VH-SLJ	45-031	N310LJ	45-111	N414FX
35A-529	04-0083	35A-610	N610LJ	36-015	N10FN	45-032	N4FE	45-112	N415FX
35A-530	84-0084	35A-611	VH-ESM	36-016	N12FN	45-033	VH-SQD	45-113	N416FX
35A-531	84-0085	35A-612	D-CGFI	36-017	N17LJ	45-034	XA-VYC	45-114	N417FX
35A-532	84-0086	35A-613	FAB6000	36A-018	N418CA	45-035	VH-SQM	45-115	N90UG
35A-533	84-0087	35A-614	N683EL	36A-019	N527PA	45-036	N345WB	45-116	OY-LJJ
35A-534	84-0088	35A-615	FAB6001	36A-020	wo	45-037	OE-GDI	45-117	ZS-DCA
35A-535	84-0089	35A-616	N876C	36A-021	wo	45-038	N14FE	45-118	N5XP
35A-536	84-0090	35A-617	FAB6002	36A-022	N44EV	45-039	N15FE	45-119	N316SR
35A-537	84-0091	35A-618	S5-BAA	36A-023	N56PA	45-040	N68PC	45-120	N418FX
35A-538	84-0092	35A-619	PT-POK	36A-024	N978E	45-041	C-GPDQ	45-121	N45HF
35A-539	84-0093	35A-620	N232FX	36A-025	N32PA	45-042	N10R	45-122	N945FD
35A-540	84-0094	35A-621	N242MT	36A-026	N8UA	45-043	N45VB	45-123	N454LC
35A-541	84-0095	35A-622	N81MR	36A-027	N27MJ	45-044	N888CX	45-124	G-OLDL
35A-542	84-0096	35A-623	40207	36A-028	N545PA	45-045	N4545	45-125	N419FX
35A-543	wo	35A-624	86-0374	36A-029	N116MA	45-046	N336UB	45-126	N420FX
35A-544	84-0098	35A-625	N625BL	36A-030	N160GC	45-047	N158PH	45-127	XA-ALF
35A-545	84-0099	35A-626	N335MG	36A-031	N62PG	45-048	PT-XLR	45-128	N10NL
35A-546	84-0100	35A-627	PT-LMY	36A-032	N950G	45-049	N711R	45-129	N9CH
35A-547	84-0101	35A-628	N628GZ	36A-033	wo	45-050	N16PC	45-130	N418MN
35A-548	84-0102	35A-629	86-0377	36A-034	B-4599	45-051	N927SK	45-131	N444MW
35A-549	84-0103	35A-630	N388PD					45-132	N889CA

c/n	Reg
45-133	N183CM
45-134	N423FX
45-135	N422FX
45-136	N583PS
45-137	N45AJ
45-138	G-OLDJ
45-139	XA-UAG
45-140	N345SV
45-141	N858MK
45-142	N145SB
45-143	N334AF
45-144	D-CEMM
45-145	N421FX
45-146	N424FX
45-147	N425FX
45-148	D-CDEN
45-149	N451CL
45-150	N245KC
45-151	N345K
45-152	VH-CXJ
45-153	C-GCMP
45-154	N886CA
45-155	N882CA
45-156	G-OLDC
45-157	N341K
45-158	LX-DSL
45-159	N828CA
45-160	N863CA
45-161	G-OLDR
45-162	N426FX
45-163	5N-BGR
45-164	N428FX
45-165	N429FX
45-166	N430FX
45-167	G-GMAA
45-168	VH-PFS
45-169	N5001J
45-169	N332K
45-170	N45UP
45-171	N342K
45-172	N70PC
45-173	N900P
45-174	N45HC
45-175	N30SF
45-176	N45TK
45-177	N431FX
45-178	XA-JMF
45-179	N45MM
45-180	N345RL
45-181	ZS-PTL
45-182	N345AW
45-183	N511WP
45-184	N866CA
45-185	N273LP
45-186	N158EC
45-187	N146XL
45-188	N21BD
45-189	N800MA
45-190	N41PC
45-191	N191LJ
45-192	N433FX
45-193	N865CA
45-194	ZS-YES
45-195	VH-SQR
45-196	N473LP
45-197	N432FX
45-198	N45UG
45-199	N545EC
45-200	N451ST
45-201	N452ST
45-202	N445N
45-203	N145AR
45-204	N45NP
45-205	N88AF
45-206	N45AX
45-207	VH-SQV
45-208	N715CG
45-209	N300JC
45-210	N29RE
45-211	N300AA
45-212	N434FX

c/n	Reg
45-213	D-CEWR
45-214	N29SM
45-215	N822CA
45-216	C-GHCY
45-217	N217MJ
45-218	N310ZM
45-219	ZS-BAR
45-220	N825CA
45-221	N823CA
45-222	N826CA
45-223	C-FNRG
45-224	N77702
45-225	N518GS
45-226	I-ERJE
45-227	N721BS
45-228	ZS-LOW
45-229	N159EC
45-230	N451N
45-231	N145HC
45-232	LV-ARD
45-233	N45KX
45-234	258
45-235	N30PC
45-236	N125GW
45-237	N44QG
45-238	N570AM
45-239	C-GJCY
45-240	N9FE
45-241	N241LJ
45-242	PR-OTA
45-243	G-IOOX
45-244	N545K
45-245	N745K
45-246	XA-HFM
45-247	N3AS
45-248	N48TF
45-249	C-GLRS
45-250	OO-LFN
45-251	N145XR
45-252	N272BC
45-253	N45NM
45-254	N729SB
45-255	C-FSDL
45-256	N5011L
45-257	N555VR
45-258	N45LJ
45-259	N40PC
45-260	N745TC
45-261	LX-IMS*
45-262	VH-...
45-270	ZS-FUL*
45-301	N45KJ

Learjet 55

c/n	Reg
55-003	N612EQ
55-004	N728MG*
55-005	N440DM
55-006	N427TL*
55-007	wo
55-008	N322GC
55-009	N800LJ
55-010	wo
55-011	LY-LRJ
55-012	N48HC
55-013	N155SB
55-014	N1CG
55-015	N551MF
55-016	N717EP*
55-017	D-CCGN
55-018	N797CS
55-019	C-GSWP
55-020	N55NY
55-021	N619MJ
55-022	N155GM
55-023	N110ET
55-024	N824CC
55-025	N92MG
55-026	N285DH
55-027	N59HJ
55-028	N556HJ
55-029	N29NW

c/n	Reg
55-030	N55LJ
55-031	YV-12CP
55-032	N255UJ
55-033	N355UJ
55-034	N550TC
55-035	N816MC
55-036	N723CC
55-037	N53HJ
55-038	N666TK
55-039	N339BC
55-040	N554CL
55-041	N141FM
55-042	N575GH
55-043	N83WM
55-044	PT-LHR
55-045	N550AK
55-046	N855PT
55-047	N600C
55-048	N558HJ
55-049	N150MS
55-050	wo
55-051	D-CATL
55-052	D-COOL
55-053	N253S
55-054	N54NW
55-055	N825MG
55-056	N607BF
55-057	N733E
55-058	N58SR
55-059	OE-GRR
55-060	N996CR
55-061	D-CFUX
55-062	N69VH
55-063	N63AX
55-064	N900PJ
55-065	N1125M
55-066	N717HB
55-067	N505EH
55-068	N135LR
55-069	N817AM
55-070	wo
55-071	N155JC
55-072	N5572
55-073	N667MB
55-074	N155LR
55-075	N90NE
55-076	C-GKTM
55-077	N245MS
55-078	N345RJ
55-079	N1983Y
55-080	PT-LET
55-081	N903JC
55-082	N139SK
55-083	N550HG
55-084	D-CWDL
55-085	N55NM
55-086	PT-LUK
55-087	N902RL
55-088	N522WK
55-089	N312AL
55-090	N55UJ
55-091	N591SC
55-092	N40DK
55-093	N32KJ
55-094	N235HR
55-095	N55RT
55-096	N126KL
55-097	N20CR
55-098	N132TP*
55-099	N95WK
55-100	N717AM
55-101	N1129M
55-102	N112FK
55-103	wo
55-104	N277AL
55-105	N55AR
55-106	N824MG
55-107	D-CWAY
55-108	N517AM
55-109	D-CVIP
55-110	N455RH

c/n	Reg
55-111	wo
55-112	N55LF
55-113	N57MH
55-114	N34GB
55-115	N155BC
55-116	N51VL
55-117	N155RB
55-118	C-FCLJ
55-119	N273MG
55-120	N777YC
55-121	N747AN
55-122	D-CGBR
55-123	N417AM
55-124	SX-BTV
55-125	N610JR
55-126	N16LJ
55B-127	N73GP
55B-128	N8MF
55B-129	N75GP
55B-130	N55VC
55B-131	N52CT
55B-132	N242RB
55B-133	EC-INS
55B-134	PT-LDR
55C-135	PT-LXO
55C-136	OE-GCF
55C-137	N155SP
55C-138	N270WS
55C-139	N139ST
55C-139A	N518SB
55C-140	FAB6100
55C-141	N155DB
55C-142	N755VT
55C-143	D-CMAD
55C-144	N40CR
55C-145	N10CR
55C-146	PT-ORA
55C-147	N177AM

Learjet 60

c/n	Reg
55C-001	wfu
60-001	N601LJ
60-002	N1940
60-003	N961MR
60-004	N600PJ
60-005	N60KJ
60-006	N606BR
60-007	N60UJ
60-008	N260UJ
60-009	N54
60-010	N610TS
60-011	N843CP
60-012	N626KM
60-013	N55
60-014	N827SS*
60-015	N826SS
60-016	TC-MEK
60-017	N60GG
60-018	N24G
60-019	D-CRAN*
60-020	N606L
60-021	N600GA
60-022	N22G
60-023	N60SR
60-024	N415NP
60-025	N299SG
60-026	N14TU
60-027	N69LJ
60-028	N206HY
60-029	N296TS
60-030	TC-ELL
60-031	N228N
60-032	OE-GNL
60-033	N56
60-034	9M-CAL
60-035	wo
60-036	N44EL
60-037	N101HW
60-038	C-FJGG
60-039	N57
60-040	N600AS

c/n	Reg
60-041	N166HL
60-042	N60MG
60-043	N43NR
60-044	N618R
60-045	N903AG
60-046	N239RC
60-047	N647TS
60-048	N730M
60-049	N126CX
60-050	N923SK
60-051	D-CHER
60-052	N247CP
60-053	N744DB
60-054	N301RJ
60-055	N574DA
60-056	N700CH
60-057	N58
60-058	XA-BRE
60-059	N60KF
60-060	N909SK
60-061	N98BL
60-062	N62BX
60-063	N660BC
60-064	N529KF
60-065	N718AN
60-066	N8271
60-067	N118HC
60-068	N64LE
60-069	D-CITA
60-070	N21AC
60-071	N940P
60-072	9M-FCL
60-073	N860PD
60-074	N674BP
60-075	N9CU
60-076	N211BX
60-077	N60GF
60-078	N188TG
60-079	N95AG
60-080	N59
60-081	N180CP
60-082	N600LN
60-083	N725SC*
60-084	N306R*
60-085	N814GF
60-086	N797CB
60-087	N787LP
60-088	XA-TZI
60-089	XA-MDM
60-090	N460BG
60-091	N91LE
60-092	C-FBLJ
60-093	TC-ARC
60-094	N82KK
60-095	N603SC
60-096	N60TX
60-097	N797PA
60-098	N60AN
60-099	N60MN
60-100	N60MN
60-101	N215BX
60-102	N102LJ
60-103	N216BX
60-104	N903AM
60-105	N217BX
60-106	D-CFFB
60-107	N60RY
60-108	N747SG
60-109	N928CD
60-110	N898PA
60-111	N299SC
60-112	N702R
60-113	N114PJ
60-114	N600GG
60-115	XA-VIG
60-116	N889DW
60-117	N11AM
60-118	N626LJ
60-119	D-CSIX
60-120	PT-XFS
60-121	

c/n	Reg	c/n	Reg
60-122	N61DP	60-203	N770BC
60-123	N356WA	60-204	N30GJ
60-124	N260AN	60-205	N12ST
60-125	VP-CRB	60-206	N500RP
60-126	N160AN	60-207	N706CJ*
60-127	N460AN	60-208	N208BH
60-128	N61ZZ	60-209	N1221J
60-129	N160GH	60-210	C-FGJC
60-130	N90MC	60-211	D-CHLE
60-131	XA-JJS	60-212	LX-RPL
60-132	N228FX	60-213	N14T
60-133	C-FBCD	60-214	D-CIMM
60-134	XA-ZTA	60-215	N44QF
60-135	N98JV	60-216	N131TR
60-136	N60RU	60-217	N600ML
60-137	N360AN	60-218	EI-IAW
60-138	N560AN	60-219	N552SK
60-139	N7734T	60-220	N255FX
60-140	T-10	60-221	N255BD
60-141	N655TH	60-222	N60VE
60-142	N426JN	60-223	N109JR
60-143	N393TA	60-224	N61VE
60-144	D-CKKK	60-225	N22QF
60-145	LX-PRA	60-226	N128V
60-146	N809R	60-227	N503RP
60-147	N160RM	60-228	N10ST
60-148	D-CETV	60-229	N23SR
60-149	VP-BEZ	60-230	N235CG
60-150	N200MT	60-231	D-CDNX
60-151	N9ZM	60-232	N232LJ
60-152	MTX-01	60-233	N520SC
60-153	N424KW	60-234	N24SR
60-154	N969JD*	60-235	N252RP
60-155	N88V	60-236	OE-GNI
60-156	N76QF	60-237	N699DA
60-157	N114LJ	60-238	N753BP
60-158	N237FX	60-239	N503BC
60-159	N43QF	60-240	N29LJ
60-160	D-CDNY	60-241	N253FX
60-161	N99ZC	60-242	wo
60-162	N238FX	60-243	OY-LGI
60-163	PT-XGS	60-244	N884TW
60-164	N929GW	60-245	XA-ORA
60-165	N60ZD	60-246	D-CWHS
60-166	N240FX	60-247	N254FX
60-167	N706CR	60-248	OE-GMR
60-168	OE-GII	60-249	D-CLUB
60-169	9H-AEE	60-250	XA-FLY
60-170	N422CP	60-251	N747DP
60-171	N241FX	60-252	N749SS
60-172	OY-LJF	60-253	C-FBLU
60-173	N242FX	60-254	RP-C6003
60-174	N243FX	60-255	OO-TME
60-175	N176MB	60-256	D-CCGG
60-176	N991DB	60-257	N256FX
60-177	N244FX	60-258	N202N
60-178	C-FCNR	60-259	N600L
60-179	N777MC	60-260	N973HR
60-180	N273MC	60-261	D-CROB
60-181	N245FX	60-262	N126KD
60-182	N246FX	60 263	N250FX
60-183	N752BP	60-264	N214RW
60-184	N464TF	60-265	N600LC
60-185	N58ST	60-266	N156BF
60-186	N247FX	60-267	N60YC
60-187	N248FX	60-268	N268WS
60-188	PR-XJS	60-269	N100NR
60-189	ES-PVS	60-270	VH-MZL
60-190	N660AS	60-271	N271L
60-191	N601GG	60-272	N60KH
60-192	N249FX	60-273	VH-OCV
60-193	N250FX	60-274	D-CSIM
60-194	N251FX	60-275	N101UD
60-195	N252FX	60-276	N838RC
60-196	P4-AVM	60-277	LX-LOU
60-197	N198HB	60-278	N60RL
60-198	N502RP	60-281	OE-GTF
60-199	A6-EJA	60-283	N60LJ
60-200	N411SK	**Learjet 40**	
60-201	N1RB	45-001	N40LX

c/n	Reg	c/n	Reg
45-2001	N401LJ	1057	N6MW
45-2002	N40KJ	1058	N658CF*
45-2003	N404MK	1059	N403WY
45-2004	N605FX	1060	N74JA
45-2005	N606FX	1061	N601KK
45-2006	D-CNIK	1062	N95EB
45-2007	N40PX	1063	N457HL
45-2008	N99GK	1064	N100LR
45-2009	N40LJ	1065	N601WJ
45-2010	N46E	1066	D-BSNA
45-2011	N411AJ	1067	N240AK
45-2012	N607FX	1068	N160LC
45-2013	XA-GRR	1069	N455BE
45-2014	N608FX	1070	D-BUSY
45-2015	I-ERJG	1071	N220LC
45-2016	I-ELYS	1072	N302PC
45-2017	N502JM	1073	N673TS
45-2018	OE-GNN	1074	N800HH
45-2019	N50111	1075	N450AJ
45-2020	N50153	1076	N601WW
45-2021	N401EG	1077	N507R
45-2022	N609FX	1078	N1500
45-2024	N40ML	1079	N601CM
45-2025	N225LJ	1080	N300TW
Challenger 600		1081	N19DD
1001	wo	1082	N333KK
1002	wfu	1083	N399FL
1004	N50PA	1084	N550CW
1005	N180CH	1085	OE-HET
1006	N515BP	**Challenger 601**	
1007	N600WJ	1003	C-GCGT
1008	N604SH	3001	N74GR
1009	N396V	3002	N602CW
1010	N7JM	3003	C-GESR
1011	N116RA	3004	N45PH
1012	N310PE	3005	N601TX
1013	N16RW	3006	N601JG
1014	N370V	3007	N910KB
1015	N25V	3008	N698CW
1016	N812XL*	3009	N873G
1017	N270V	3010	N411TJ
1018	N618AJ	3011	N453GS
1019	3B-GFI	3012	N878RM
1020	N600BD	3013	N633CW
1021	wfu	3014	N698RS
1022	N260V	3015	XA-KIM
1023	N777GD	3016	VP-BIE
1024	N811MT	3017	C-FBYJ
1025	N711GA	3018	wo
1026	N694JC	3019	N875G
1027	N111FK	3020	C-GCFI
1028	N858PJ	3021	N150MH
1029	N722DJ	3022	C-GCFG
1030	N60S	3023	N601FJ
1031	N620S	3024	N888AZ
1032	N1884	3025	N529D
1033	N304TT	3026	N810MT
1034	N134VS	3027	N627CW
1035	N187AP	3028	C-FBEL
1036	N900DP	3029	N773JC
1037	wo	3030	N39CD
1038	N616DF	3031	N54JC
1039	N895CC	3032	N392FV
1040	144601	3033	HB-ILK
1041	N141RD	3034	C-GSAP
1042	N999TF	3035	wo
1043	N100QR	3036	144614
1044	N800BT	3037	144615
1045	C-GBKB	3038	144616
1046	N246JL	3039	N500PG
1047	N315MK	3040	12+02
1048	C-GDDR	3041	N169TA
1049	N601CT	3042	N333GJ
1050	N710HL	3043	12+03
1051	N27BH	3044	N601GB
1052	N222LH	3045	N601PR
1053	N54SU	3046	N46SR
1054	N660RM	3047	OE-HLE
1055	N643CR	3048	N601JM
1056	N1HZ	3049	12+04

c/n	Reg
3050	N601AE
3051	N651CW
3052	N425WN
3053	12+05
3054	N722HP
3055	N601RC
3056	12+06
3057	N163WG
3058	N125PS
3059	12+07
3060	N601S
3061	N601AA
3062	N601GT
3063	C-FURG
3064	N664CW
3065	LX-GDC
3066	N105UP
Challenger 601-3A	
5001	N604FJ
5002	N43PR
5003	N601FR
5004	N504TS
5005	N64FE
5006	N500T3
5007	N666CT
5008	N601LG
5009	N699CW
5010	N181AP
5011	VP-CIC
5012	N500LR
5013	N116LS*
5014	N888DH
5015	N204JK
5016	C-GQWI
5017	N77058
5018	N828SK
5019	C-GHGC
5020	N39RE
5021	N620HF*
5022	VP-CJP
5023	N623CW
5024	N601DT
5025	N93DW
5026	N601WM
5027	N420ST
5028	N601RL
5029	N594RJ
5030	N816SP
5031	N721CW
5032	N950SW
5033	N144BS
5034	C-GIOH
5035	N333MG
5036	N468KL
5037	N710LM
5038	N91KH
5039	N765WT
5040	N807Z
5041	N953FA
5042	HR-IKS
5043	N601VH
5044	VP-CBS
5045	N601AF
5046	N426PF
5047	N547FP
5048	N907WS
5049	B-MAI
5050	N710VF
5051	C-GQBQ
5052	N125ST
5053	N653CW
5054	N3FE
5055	N460F
5056	N525SD
5057	N733CF
5058	N527JA
5059	N627KR
5060	N573AC
5061	VP-BEJ
5062	N727S

C/N	Reg	C/N	Reg	C/N	Reg	C/N	Reg	C/N	Reg
5063	N563TS	5145	C-GDPF	5330	N812G	5411	N3PC	5492	N604SX
5064	N601EC	5146	N96DS	5331	N810D	5412	N529GP	5493	N604VK
5065	N882C	5147	XA-SOR	5332	VP-BNF	5413	C-FSJR	5494	D-ANKE
5066	N221LC	5148	N793CT	5333	N991TW	5414	wo	5495	N495BA
5067	VP-CFT	5149	VP-B..	5334	N43R	5415	N318FX	5496	N604UP
5068	C-FNNS	5150	N601BW	5335	N604B	5416	G-FTSL	5497	N604RT
5069	N324B	5151	C-GMMI	5336	N212RR	5417	D-AETV	5498	N599DA
5070	OY-CLD	5152	G-FBFI	5337	N990AK	5418	N319FX	5499	N999VK
5071	N500PC	5153	N653AC	5338	N426CF	5419	N500	5500	N225AR
5072	wo	5154	N601HW	5339	C-GNCR	5420	N604TS	5501	XA-SOL
5073	N803RR	5155	N342TC	5340	N194WM	5421	N604W	5502	N589MT
5074	N23SB	5156	N601TP	5341	N604SA	5422	D-ADNE	5503	N298DC
5075	N409KC	5157	N808HG	5342	N311BX	5423	N38SW	5504	N71NP
5076	XA-GUA	5158	XA-JZL	5343	C-GHKY	5424	N604GW	5505	VP-BHS
5077	N118MT	5159	N814PS	5344	N604DH	5425	N320FX	5506	C-FHYL
5078	N578FP	5160	N813VZ	5345	N600AM	5426	JY-ONE	5507	N53DF
5079	VP-CCR	5161	N994CT	5346	HZ-SJP3	5427	N321FX	5508	P4-FAY
5080	N900H	5162	N850FB	5347	N205EL	5428	N640CH	5509	N112CF
5081	N601ST	5163	N224F	5348	N881TW	5429	701	5510	B-7696
5082	N6BB	5164	N431CB	5349	N5349	5430	OY-MMM	5511	N815PA
5083	N189K	5165	N723HH	5350	N331TP	5431	N276GC	5512	N902AG
5084	N622WM	5166	HB-IVS	5351	N372G	5432	C-GPGD	5513	N729KF
5085	I-DAGS	5167	N86	5352	4X-COE	5433	N181J	5514	N880ET
5086	N601JE	5168	C-GRPF	5353	N758CC	5434	N322FX	5515	EI-IRE
5087	XA-RZD	5169	N154NS	5354	N604BM	5435	OE-IYA	5516	N1DG
5088	C-GPOT	5170	N888WS	5355	N555WD	5436	N604LA	5517	LN-SUN
5089	N516SM	5171	N614AF	5356	N880CR	5437	N17TE	5518	N8SP
5090	HB-ITK	5172	C-FUND	5357	XA-AST	5438	N609CC	5519	N519MZ
5091	N915BD	5173	D-AKUE	5358	N127SR	5439	N600ES	5520	XA-TVG
5092	N300CR	5174	N386K*	5359	N497DM	5440	N500PE	5521	A37-001
5093	N331DC	5175	N601KF	5360	C-GZEK	5441	N33PA*	5522	4X-CMF
5094	5B-CKK	5176	N779AZ	5361	N346BA	5442	YL-WBD	5523	B-7697
5095	N2FE	5177	N227RH	5362	N995MA	5443	JY-TWO	5524	N251CP
5096	C-FJJC	5178	B-MAC	5363	N964H	5444	N604VF	5525	XA-JFE
5097	N227CP	5179	N168LA	5364	C-FBNS	5445	N877H	5526	N604CB
5098	N808G	5180	N518CL	5365	N280K	5446	N604CE	5527	XA-TZF
5099	N203JE	5181	C-FCIB	5366	N906TF	5447	N323FX	5528	D-AJAG
5100	N225N	5182	HL7577	5367	N848CC	5448	VP-BHH	5529	HB-JRA
5101	N105BN	5183	N55HF	5368	N374G	5449	N604JR	5530	HB-JRB
5102	N241FB	5184	N607RP	5369	N247WE	5450	4X-CMZ	5531	N168NQ
5103	N601BE	5185	N914X	5370	N755RV	5451	N816CC	5532	N432MC
5104	N720LM	5186	N9700X	5371	C-GGWH	5452	OH-WIC	5533	144617
5105	5105	5187	N601KJ	5372	G-LVLV	5453	C-FHGC	5534	A37-002
5106	N523JM	5188	N10FE	5373	N604LC	5454	N324FX	5535	144618
5107	N417CL	5189	XA-IMY	5374	N203	5455	C-GCDF	5536	N25GG
5108	N224N	5190	N87	5375	XA-GRB	5456	VH-ZZH	5537	N437MC
5109	N721G	5191	N605T	5376	N604ZH	5457	N325FX	5538	A37-003
5110	TC-MDG	5192	N354TC	5377	N315BX	5458	C-GZPX	5539	PP-BIA
5111	N502HE	5193	VP-BIH	5378	D-ASTS	5459	TC-TAN	5540	HB-JRC
5112	N604ME	5194	A9C-BXD	5379	C-GQPA	5460	VP-BMG	5541	N329FX
5113	N733EY	**Challenger 604**		5380	C-080	5461	N832SC	5542	N876H
5114	VP-BOA	5301	N123KH	5381	N900ES	5462	D-AHLE	5543	N332FX
5115	N25SB	5302	N255CC	5382	N604HJ	5463	D-AHEI	5544	N50DS
5116	N1904P	5303	OE-INF	5383	N383DT	5464	N326FX	5545	N6757M
5117	C-FBCR	5304	N604VM	5384	VP-BNS	5465	C-GLBB	5546	N459CS
5118	N24JK	5305	N747Y	5385	N72NP	5466	N327FX	5547	N350ZE
5119	N601FS	5306	N604AB	5386	N119GA	5467	G-REYS	5548	N416BD
5120	N400TB	5307	LX-FAZ	5387	N387CL	5468	C-168	5549	N2JW
5121	N502PC	5308	N713HC	5388	4X-CMY	5469	N78SD	5550	N1987
5122	N65FF	5309	N666TR	5389	D-AUKE	5470	N150BB	5551	N604RS
5123	N601UP	5310	C-GPFC	5390	N200DE	5471	N604WS	5552	ZS-ALT
5124	C-FBOM	5311	N604JS	5391	N267BW	5472	C-172	5553	HB-JRZ
5125	P4-EPI	5312	N312AM	5392	C-FCDE	5473	N604RP	5554	N604KJ
5126	N99UG	5313	N3HB	5393	N355CC	5474	N328FX	5555	N604HC
5127	N555LG	5314	N604CT	5394	N72WY	5475	D-ASIE	5556	N373G
5128	XA-GME	5315	N818TH	5395	N82CW	5476	N343K	5557	C-GAWH
5129	N129TF	5316	N203TA	5396	N273S	5477	A9C-BXB	5558	N604SR
5130	N349JR	5317	C-FNNT	5397	VP-BJH	5478	N604GR	5559	N902MP
5131	N6JB	5318	HB-IVR	5398	N477DM	5479	N604ST	5560	N560TS*
5132	N289K	5319	N5319*	5399	N604GM	5480	N121DF	5561	N604WF
5133	N486BG	5320	HZ-AFA2	5400	N237GA	5481	N198DC	5562	N562ME
5134	N898EW	5321	N604CP	5401	N528GP	5482	N581TS	5563	N300BC
5135	N1902P	5322	9A-CRO	5402	N98AG	5483	N483BA	5564	N99KW
5136	N20G	5323	N623TS	5403	D-ADND	5484	C-GWLL	5565	D-ABCD
5137	N90AR	5324	N667LC	5404	VP-BGO	5485	LX-FBY	5566	N604PA
5138	N85	5325	N331TH	5405	N340AK	5486	ZS-OSG	5567	P4-TAT
5139	N902TA	5326	N1903G	5406	N604MU	5487	N330FX	5568	N383MB
5140	N79AN	5327	N146BA	5407	N317BX*	5488	N870CM	5569	N604SB
5141	N901TA	5328	N328BX	5408	N898R	5489	C-GGBL	5570	N604CL
5142	N330TP	5329	N222MC	5409	N401NK	5490	N14GD	5571	N571BA
5144	N601CV			5410	N805VZ	5491	N331FX	5572	N400

c/n	reg.		c/n	reg.
5573	N573BA		7152	N529DB
5574	N46F		7176	P4-CRJ
5575	N529DM		7180	B-4007
5576	N1090X		7189	B-4010
5577	OO-KRC*		7193	B-4011
5578	N606RP		7351	VP-BCI
5579	N110BP		**7846**	**N500PR**
5580	XA-IGE		**Regional Jet**	
5581	N604MC		7508	G-ELNX
5582	N604BB		**7717**	**VP-BCC**
5583	N121ET		**Global Ex/5000/ASTOR**	
5584	C-FAWU		9001	C-FBGX
5585	OE-IMB		9002	N711MN
5586	N334FX		9003	C-FBDR
5587	N826JS		9004	N1TK
5588	N88		9005	N700HX
5589	N22SF		9006	N161WC
5590	N721J		9007	EC-IUQ
5591	N604CD		9008	N917R
5592	N385CT		9009	N998AM
5593	N604SC		9010	N701WH
5594	N43SF		9011	HB-IHQ
5595	OE-INI		9012	N70PS
5596	C-FCSD		9013	LX-GEX
5597	N59/JA		9014	XA-NGS
5598	C-FDJN		9015	HB-JEN
5599	OE-IKP		9016	N16GX
5600	N800BN		9017	VP-BDD
5601	N44SF		9018	VP-BGG
5602	C-FDBJ		9019	HL7576
5991	**wo**		9020	VP-BEN
Challenger 300			9021	N8VB
20001	C-GJCJ		9022	N226HD
20002	C-GJCF		9023	N324SM
20003	C-GIPX		9024	N288Z
20004	C-GJCV		9025	N616DC
20005	C-GIPZ		9026	N70EW
20006	N505FX		9027	N305CC
20007	N506FX		9028	N117TF
20008	N507FX		9029	HZ-AFA
20009	N508FX		9030	VP-BYY
20010	N41DP		9031	N724AF
20011	N17UC		9032	OY-MSI
20012	N509FX		9033	N600AK
20013	I-SDFC		9034	JA005G
20014	N27MX		9035	N818LS
20015	A6-SMS		9036	HB-ITG
20016	N777VC		9037	N400GX
20017	N510FX		9038	G-LOBL
20018	N74ZC		9039	N90EW
20019	N60SB		9040	N228H*
20020	N789MB		9041	N887WM
20021	N511FX		9042	N170SW
20022	N512FX		9043	N700ML
20023	N514FX		9044	OE-IGS
20024	C-FAUZ		9045	N17GX
20025	EC-JEG		9046	N1TS
20026	N326RG*		9047	N410WW
20027	N448AS		9048	N4GX
20028	N328RC*		9049	N949GP
20029	HB-JEC*		9050	N502JL
20030	C-FDIH		9051	N421AL
20031	N411ST		9052	N620K
20032	C-FDIJ		9053	N53GX
20033	OE-HRR		9054	HB-IKZ
20034	C-FCXJ		9055	N449ML
20035	N900WY		9056	N421SZ
20036	N516FX		9057	N18WY
20037	N885TW		9058	N79AD
20038	N517FX		9059	N18WZ
20039	N139LJ		9060	EC-IBD
20042	**A7-AAN***		9061	ZS-ESA
Challenger 800			9062	N801PN
7008	N601LS		9063	B-HMA
7075	N135BC		9064	N264A
7099	N405CC		9065	N704MF
7136	HB-IDJ		9066	N823DF
7138	B-4005		9067	N67RX
7140	N711WM		9068	N700BX
7149	B-4006		9069	N1868M

c/n	reg.		c/n	reg.		c/n	reg.
9070	N34U		9151	C-FBOC		686	wfu
9071	D-ADNB		9152	N605VF		696	wfu
9072	N983J		9153	C-FBPJ		701	wfu
9073	N338TP		9154	C-FBPL		500-0001	N715JS
9074	N399GS		9155	N711LS		500-0002	ZS-ONE
9075	N316GS		9156	C-FBPZ		500-0003	N503CC
9076	LX-VIP		9157	C-FBQD		500-0004	N505K
9077	N200A		9158	C-FCOG		500-0005	PT-OIG
9078	N85D		9159	C-FCOI		500-0006	wfu
9079	VH-VGX		9160	C-FCOJ		500-0007	wo
9080	N283S		9161	C-FCOK		500-0008	PT-WBY
9081	F-GVML		9162	C-FCOZ		500-0009	N55FT
9082	JA006G		**9163**	**C-FCPH**		500-0010	XC-DGA
9083	VP-CEB		**British Aerospace**			500-0011	N700VC
9084	N984TS		**BAC 1-11**			500-0012	N512CC
9085	N404VL		005	wfu		500-0013	XC-FIV
9086	HB-INJ		011	wfu		500-0014	N18FM
9087	N360LA		015	N200JX		500-0015	wo
9088	C-GNCB		054	N17MK		500-0016	C-GPLN
9089	EC-IFS		055	wfu		500-0017	N565SS
9090	N18TM		056	N111RZ		500-0018	wo
9091	N1FE		058	wfu		500-0019	N397SC
9092	N799WW		059	wfu		500-0020	wfu
9093	VP-CDF		060	wfu		500-0021	N7GJ
9094	A6-EJB		061	3C-QRF		500-0022	wfu
9095	N97DQ		064	wfu		500-0023	N200QC
9096	M48-02		065	PK-PJF		500-0024	N94AJ
9097	N903TF		067	N161NG		500-0025	N57LL
9098	N100VR		068	5N-MBM		500-0026	wo
9099	OE-IEL		069	5N-CCC		500-0027	PT-OVK
9100	N1SA		072	VP-CLM		500-0028	N133JM
9101	VP-BOK		073	N101PC		500-0029	N424DA
9102	VP-CGS		076	wfu		500-0030	wfu
9103	N122BN		078	UN-B1111		500-0031	YV-939CP
9104	N190WP		079	XA-CMG		500-0032	wo
9105	N100A		080	5N-VVV		500-0033	N990AL
9106	N816SQ		081	VP-CCG		500-0034	N11HJ
9107	ZJ690		083	N200EE		500-0035	XC-MMM
9108	N100ES		084	wfu		500-0036	OO-LCM
9109	N700KS		086	VP-CJL		500-0037	EC-GTS
9110	N14R		087	N162W		500-0038	N27L
9111	VT-DHA		088	P4-CBH		500-0039	N118LA
9112	C-GBLX		089	TG-TJF		500-0040	N98Q
9113	N920DS		090	N164W		500-0041	N50AM
9114	N1SL		108	ZS-NNM		500-0042	wfu
9115	LX-PAK		111	wo		500-0043	N502RD
9116	N320GX		118	PK-TST		500-0044	ZS-DSA
9117	N917GL		119	N789CF		500-0045	N628BS
9118	N904DS		120	N999BW		500-0046	PT-OTQ
9119	XA-OVR		126	VP-BBA		500-0047	YV-....
9120	N887WS		135	wfu		500-0048	N911GM
9121	N711MC		154	5N-GGG		500-0049	PT-LDH
9122	ZS-GJB		158	5A-DDQ		500-0050	VH-HKX
9123	ZJ691		163	N111JX		500-0051	VH-EMM
9124	N700GB		183	VP-CMI		500-0052	YV-881CP
9125	N711SX		236	wfu		500-0053	I-AEAL
9126	A7-AAM		259	G-MAAH		500-0054	XB-PBT
9127	C-GERS		260	P4-JLB		500-0055	N716CB
9128	N18WF		262	PK-TRU		500-0056	N777JJ
9129	N725LB		263	ZH763		500-0057	wo
9130	C-GLRM		**405**	**YR-BRE**		500-0058	YV-901CP
9131	ZJ692		**BAe 146**			500-0059	N913RC
9132	ZJ693		E1006	G-OFOA		500-0060	PT-OOL
9133	G-XPRS		E1017	G-BLRA		500-0061	N916RC
9134	A7-GEX		E1021	ZE700		500-0062	N334RC
9135	ZJ694		E1029	ZE701		500-0063	N70MG
9136	C-GZPV		E1068	N114M		500-0064	N27SF
9137	C-GZPW		E1091			500-0065	N565CC
9138	C-GZRA		E1124	PK-OSP		500-0066	C-GQCC
9139	OY-CVS		E1144	G-OFOM		500-0067	N567EA
9140	N140AE		E2018	G-TBAE		500-0068	XA-RYE
9141	C-GAGS		E2065	Z-WPD		500-0069	N255RD
9142	N700EW		E2239	PK-PJJ		500-0070	N227MK
9143	C-FAGU		E2306	A9C-HWR		500-0071	D2-EDC
9144	C-FAGV		E2312	UK-80001		500-0072	N72DJ
9145	C-FAHN		**E2390**	**A9C-BDF**		500-0073	C-FKMC
9146	C-FAHQ		**Cessna**			500-0074	N500ML
9147	C-FAHX		**500 Citation I**			500-0075	N575RD
9148	C-FAIO		669	wfu		500-0076	N65WS
9149	N356MS					500-0077	N147SC
9150	N488CH					500-0078	N269RC

Reg		Reg		Reg		Reg		Reg	
500-0079	PT-LBN	500-0161	N161CC	500-0242	N888JL	500-0324	N324JC	501-0022	wo
500-0080	V5-OGL	500-0162	wo	500-0243	N243SH	500-0325	PT-OSD	501-0023	N56MK
500-0081	I-PEGA	500-0163	N54JV*	500-0244	PT-OQD	500-0326	wo	501-0024	N70BG
500-0082	N428RJ	500-0164	N73MP	500-0245	D-IAJJ	500-0327	5327	501-0025	N20RM
500-0083	N31LW	500-0165	N501LB	500-0246	PT-LQR	500-0328	N168AS	501-0026	N92BL
500-0084	wo	500-0166	N511AT	500-0247	C-GMAJ	500-0329	OY-CEV	501-0027	JA8380
500-0085	5N-BCI	500-0167	YV-....	500-0248	N111BB	500-0330	N800CJ*	501-0028	N501PV
500-0086	D-ICIA	500-0168	N891CA	500-0249	N1GG	500-0331	G-LOFT	501-0029	XA-TKY
500-0087	N633AT	500-0169	N75GM	500-0250	N251MG	500-0332	N332SE	501-0030	N911MM
500-0088	N170MD	500-0170	N66LE	500-0251	PT-OMS	500-0333	VH-SOU	501-0031	N510AJ
500-0089	N39LH	500-0171	PP-LEM	500-0252	N501JC	500-0334	wfu	501-0032	N642BJ
500-0090	3929	500-0172	wo	500-0253	N592WP	500-0335	PT-LDI	501-0033	N700LW
500-0091	N500AD	500-0173	N500EL	500-0254	wo	500-0336	wo	501-0034	N501CP
500-0092	0222	500-0174	N16LG	500-0255	N907RT	500-0337	N17KD	501-0035	N501DD
500-0093	N62BR	500-0175	wo	500-0256	N676DG	500-0338	N41HL	501-0036	N360MC
500-0094	N96FB	500-0176	N150TT	500-0257	N75GW	500-0339	G-DJAE	501-0037	N234JW
500-0095	I-....	500-0177	N883XL	500-0258	N125DS	500-0340	N344RJ	501-0038	N501JG
500-0096	N837MA	500-0178	EC-IBA	500-0259	N259DH	500-0341	C-FDMB	501-0039	N141M
500-0097	N500GR	500-0179	PT-OMT	500-0260	ZS-OGS	500-0342	N501LH	501-0040	N21EP
500-0098	wfu	500-0180	N500ET	500-0261	N58TC	500-0343	N501JF	501-0041	wo
500-0099	wfu	500-0181	PT-KPA	500-0262	N110AB	500-0344	VP-BLV	501-0042	I-AROM
500-0100	N80AJ	500-0182	N900TA	500-0263	VH-ZMD	500-0345	XA-TOF	501-0043	N16NL
500-0101	C-GKCZ	500-0183	N151AS	500-0264	G-JTNC	500-0346	PT-LUA	501-0044	N600RM
500-0102	N491PT	500-0184	N184NA	500-0265	N595DC*	500-0347	N876WB	501-0045	N22EL
500-0103	PT-KIR	500-0185	ZP-TZH	500-0266	N11MN	500-0348	N712KM	501-0046	N5VP
500-0104	N353PJ	500-0186	N186SC	500-0267	wfu	500-0349	VH-HVH	501-0047	N500U
500-0105	wfu	500-0187	N130DW	500-0268	N900G	500-0354	N694LM	501-0048	I-OTEL
500-0106	ZS-RCC	500-0188	PT-KPB	500-0269	D-ICCC	500-0356	AE-185	501-0049	ZS-CWD
500-0107	N79RS	500-0189	wfu	500-0270	N915RP	500-0358	I-UUNY	501-0050	N59MA
500-0108	wo	500-0190	N434UM	500-0271	wo	500-0361	F-GKIR	501-0051	N422DA
500-0109	N221AM	500-0191	LV-YRB	500-0272	N89AJ	500-0364	N501E	501-0052	N677JM
500-0110	XB-IXT	500-0192	I-AMCY	500-0273	XB-GBF	500-0367	YV-52CP	501-0053	N52TL
500-0111	wo	500-0193	OY-JAI	500-0274	N5LK	500-0368	N124NS*	501-0054	N501EA
500-0112	N500TM	500-0194	N501DG	500-0275	N275GK	500-0369	N46253	501-0055	N223LC
500-0113	N500NJ	500-0195	N502BE	500-0276	SE-DEG	500-0370	SE-DEY	501-0056	N56WE
500-0114	N65SA	500-0196	N270PM	500-0277	N652ND	500-0374	N501SS	501-0057	N577JT
500-0115	YV-21CP	500-0197	N297S	500-0278	OY-PCW	500-0378	C-GBNE	501-0058	wo
500-0116	EC-HRH	500-0198	XB-IJW	500-0279	N501KG	500-0386	LQ-MRM	501-0059	N16HL
500-0117	N442JB	500-0199	XA-...	500-0280	N814ER	500-0387	N504D	501-0060	N11TM
500-0118	wfu	500-0200	N102VP	500-0281	N70TS	500-0392	D-ISSS	501-0061	SE-RBZ
500-0119	N501EJ	500-0201	F-GRCH	500-0282	HB-VNU	500-0395	XA-JEX	501-0062	N980DM
500-0120	N127BJ	500-0202	N550RS	500-0283	wo	500-0396	XC-GTO	501-0063	N555KW
500-0121	N661AC	500-0203	N51099	500-0284	PT-LOG	500-0399	T9-SBA	501-0064	N12WH
500-0122	ZS-PFG	500-0204	N928RD	500-0285	N113SH	500-0401	I-FARN	501-0065	N33WW
500-0123	ZS-PMA	500-0205	wo	500-0286	5N-APN	500-0403	wo	501-0066	N501CD
500-0124	N92SM	500-0206	N771HR	500-0287	VP-BGE	500-0404	N789DD	501-0067	HB-VJB
500-0125	XA-SFE	500-0207	N501TL	500-0288	N1DA	500-0406	OY-FFB	501-0068	N363TD
500-0126	N902DD	500-0208	N515WE	500-0289	wo	500-0408	XB-DVF	501-0069	N636N
500-0127	N580R	500-0209	EC-HFA	500-0290	N400RM	500-0409	XC-FEZ	501-0070	N45MM
500-0128	N3490L	500-0210	XB-TRY	500-0291	OE-FGN	500-0410	XC-GAW	501-0071	YV-...
500-0129	N500SK	500-0211	wfu	500-0292	N333JH	500-0411	SE-DLZ	501-0072	N1HA
500-0130	N130CE	500-0212	N74LL	500-0293	wo	500-0412	XB-GDJ	501-0073	wo
500-0131	PT-OJF	500-0213	XA-AEI	500-0294	OE-FCM	500-0413	PT-LCC	501-0074	N552AJ
500-0132	N713SA	500-0214	N709TB	500-0295	N10FG	500-0415	N53RD	501-0075	N713JD
500-0133	PT-LXH	500-0215	YV-55GP	500-0296	XA-BET	500-0418	ZS-LDV	501-0076	N150RM
500-0134	PT-JMJ	500-0216	N199CK	500-0297	N38SA	501-0280	N212M	501-0077	I-....
500-0135	wo	500-0217	N55GR	500-0298	N900GC	501-0286	N381BJ	501-0078	N501EK
500-0136	XA-JRV	500-0218	N271AC	500-0299	N80364	500-5585	D-CTLX*	501-0079	N79FT
500-0137	ZS-MCU	500-0219	wo	500-0300	wo	**500 Citation I/SP**		501-0080	N800BF
500-0138	N138SA	500-0220	G-ORHE	500-0301	N305S	501-0001	N506TF	501-0081	N12CV
500-0139	N15AW	500-0221	N24AJ	500-0302	N710VL*	501-0002	N88TB	501-0082	N5WF
500-0140	N441TC	500-0222	N52PM	500-0303	N8DX	501-0003	N81EB	501-0083	N910G
500-0141	N727TK	500-0223	N89319	500-0304	N10UH	501-0004	N142DA	501-0084	EC-ISP
500-0142	N69XW	500-0224	N697MB	500-0305	N137WC	501-0005	N284RJ	501-0085	N707W
500-0143	SE-DUZ	500-0225	wo	500-0306	N606KK	501-0006	I-ERJA	501-0086	EC-INJ
500-0144	wo	500-0226	PT-LTI	500-0307	N777SL	501-0007	N222WA	501-0087	N501BB
500-0145	N145TA	500-0227	N227GM	500-0308	F-GSMC	501-0008	N909PS	501-0088	N3WT
500-0146	N111ME	500-0228	wfu	500-0309	N88NW	501-0009	N505RJ	501-0089	VH-CCJ
500-0147	N688CF	500-0229	wo	500-0310	N941JC	501-0010	EC-EDN	501-0090	N3GN
500-0148	N989SC	500-0230	N200CG	500-0311	I-RAGW	501-0011	N1UM	501-0091	N2158U
500-0149	ZS-TMG	500-0231	N501GB	500-0312	F-GJDG	501-0012	N449DT	501-0092	N303A*
500-0150	N914CD	500-0232	N999AM	500-0313	HB-VLE	501-0013	N501TJ	501-0093	N501RM
500-0151	wfu	500-0233	N233JJ	500-0314	N668S	501-0014	N888FL	501-0094	N159LC
500-0152	XB-AMO	500-0234	N70CA	500-0315	SE-DRZ	501-0015	N454AC	501-0095	XA-AGA
500-0153	N2RM	500-0235	N12AM	500-0316	N711MT	501-0016	N45TL	501-0096	N501HS
500-0154	PT-WFT	500-0236	N320RG	500-0317	YV-1133CP	501-0017	N501AT	501-0097	N501RS
500-0155	N155MK	500-0237	wo	500-0318	VP-COM	501-0018	N228FS	501-0098	N92BE
500-0156	PT-KBR	500-0238	N409S	500-0319	F-GKID	501-0019	N501SP	501-0099	I-FLYA
500-0157	EC-HPQ	500-0239	PT-LOS	500-0320	I-CARY	501-0020	N123EB	501-0100	N54FT
500-0158	N233DB	500-0240	N234AT	500-0321	wfu	501-0021	N151SP	501-0101	N106EA
500-0159	N159KC	500-0241	N288SP	500-0322	N108MC			501-0102	N45FS
500-0160	C-GNSA			500-0323	N388GM				

Serial	Reg	Serial	Reg	Serial	Reg	Serial	Reg	Serial	Reg
501-0103	N611AT	501-0184	N501VC	501-0267	N565V	525-0032	N900DS	525-0113	N111AM
501-0104	N998EA	501-0185	N505BG	501-0269	N501JJ	525-0033	N501KR	525-0114	N294CW
501-0105	N2648X	501-0186	N999WS	501-0270	N105JM	525-0034	N333VS	525-0115	OO-PHI
501-0106	N793AA	501-0187	N70CG	501-0272	N700JA	525-0035	N525HS	525-0116	N216CW
501-0107	EC-GJF	501-0188	N525PV	501-0273	N110JA	525-0036	N525MB	525-0117	N26QB
501-0108	N777GG	501-0189	N80SF	501-0275	N40AJ	525-0037	N87319	525-0118	D-IRWR
501-0109	N567WB	501-0190	N723JR	501-0279	SE-DEZ	525-0038	N600HR	525-0119	N47TH
501-0110	wo	501-0191	N64RT	501-0281	N501CB	525-0039	N39CJ	525-0120	PR-VGD
501-0111	N79BK	501-0192	N190K	501-0282	N82AJ	525-0040	OE-FMU	525-0121	D-ICSS
501-0112	N112EB	501-0193	N89MF	501-0283	N204CA	525-0041	N565JP	525-0122	N102AF
501-0113	N502CC	501-0194	N65WW	501-0284	N45AF	525-0042	PH-MGT	525-0123	D-IRKE
501-0114	wfu	501-0195	N123KD	501-0285	N13ST	525-0043	N525PL	525-0124	OE-FRR
501-0115	N728MC	501-0196	N311TP	501-0289	N82DT	525-0044	D-IDBW	525-0125	N525PT
501-0116	N7TK	501-0197	N324L	501-0292	N456R	525-0045	LV-AMB	525-0126	D-IMPC
501-0117	N91AP	501-0198	N800DT	501-0293	N597CS	525-0046	N127SG	525-0127	N63LF
501-0118	N311ME	501-0199	N7SV	501-0294	N80SL	525-0047	N47FH	525-0128	N535LR
501-0119	N53EZ	501-0200	N47TL	501-0297	N41GT	525-0048	N525NA	525-0129	N229CJ
501-0120	N71LP	501-0201	XA-...	501-0298	N501D	525-0049	N349SF	525-0130	N418KC
501-0121	OE-FHW	501-0202	N501G	501-0302	N7EN	525-0050	N70KW	525-0131	N281CW
501-0122	N501MB	501-0203	wo	501-0303	N303RH	525-0051	N726SC	525-0132	N132AH
501-0123	N627E	501-0204	N345N	501-0311	N311VP	525-0052	N52PK	525-0133	EC-GIE
501-0124	wo	501-0205	N501DA*	501-0314	N56LW	525-0053	N60ES	525-0134	N525JM
501-0125	N125EA	501-0206	N943RC	501-0317	N317JQ	525-0054	N54CJ	525-0135	N888RA
501-0126	N505JH	501-0207	VP-BHO	501-0319	N60EW	525-0055	N923AR	525-0136	wo
501-0127	N117DJ	501-0208	N82P	501-0320	N401G	525-0056	JA8420	525-0137	N810SS
501-0128	N501CF	501-0209	N70NB	501-0321	N986DS	525-0057	N585DG	525-0138	VH-MOJ
501-0129	N501JD	501-0210	N32FM	501-0322	N527EW	525-0058	N525F	525-0139	N36RG
501-0130	N505CF	501-0211	wfu	501-0323	N505BB	525-0059	N816FC	525-0140	N111BF
501-0131	YV-2605P	501-0212	N2243	501-0324	JA8493	525-0060	N525WW	525-0141	N545RW
501-0132	N39HH	501-0213	I-AUNY	501-0325	N64BH	525-0061	N525PS	525-0142	N815MC
501-0133	N51WP	501-0214	N241MH	501-0446	N888MJ	525-0062	C-GINT	525-0143	D-IALL
501-0134	N501EM	501-0215	N215NA	501-0643	N54TS	525-0063	N55SK	525-0144	D-IDAG
501-0135	N63CG	501-0216	TG-RIE	501-0675	N501MT	525-0064	D-IHEB	525-0145	N424TV
501-0136	N800TW	501-0217	N7MZ	501-0676	N676CC	525-0065	EC-FZP	525-0146	N1329G
501-0137	N14VA	501-0218	N218JG	501-0677	N74HR	525-0066	N824ES	525-0147	wo
501-0138	N74FH	501-0219	N56PB	501-0678	PT-ODC	525-0067	N525TF	525-0148	N300DL
501-0139	N501AF	501-0220	N100LX	501-0679	N501HH*	525-0068	N888KU	525-0149	N77215
501-0140	OE-FDM	501-0221	N501HG	501-0680	PP-EIF	525-0069	N20VL	525-0150	N8341C
501-0141	N501DR	501-0222	N690DM	501-0681	N427SS	525-0070	D-ISGW	525-0151	N242GB
501-0142	N15FJ	501-0223	N18HC	501-0682	N682HC	525-0071	N940SW	525-0152	N152KV
501-0143	4X-CMG	501-0224	N825PS	501-0683	N96LC	525-0072	TG-RIF	525-0153	VP-CNF
501-0144	N270NF	501-0225	N412SE	501-0684	N501TP	525-0073	N77794	525-0154	N254CW
501-0145	wo	501-0226	N501JM	501-0685	XA-...	525-0074	N511TC	525-0155	I-EDEM
501-0146	N53BB	501-0227	N83DM	501-0686	N750PP	525-0075	N719D	525-0156	N156ML
501-0147	N551MS	501-0228	XA-SEY	501-0687	N361DE	525-0076	N805VC	525-0157	N54HC
501-0148	N148ED	501-0229	N57FC	501-0688	D-IMRX	525-0077	N1000E	525-0158	N800RK
501-0149	N72VJ	501-0230	N999MS	501-0689	N288MM	525-0078	N525CH	525-0159	N131RG
501-0150	wo	501-0231	N501BP	*525 CitationJet*		525-0079	N525WB	525-0160	N66AM
501-0151	N797SE	501-0232	VP-CAT	702	wfu	525-0080	N33DT	525-0161	N525BT
501-0152	N15CY	501-0233	5N-AVM	525-0001	N525GV	525-0081	N181JT	525-0162	N525JW
501-0153	N99CK	501-0234	N123PL	525-0002	N54BP	525-0082	N525LW	525-0163	N51CD
501-0154	N154SC	501-0235	N2617U	525-0003	N44FJ	525-0083	N34TC	525-0164	N204J
501-0155	N321TS	501-0236	N711VF	525-0004	N7CQ	525-0084	D-ITSV	525-0165	N525P
501-0156	N44FM	501-0237	N420PC	525-0005	N521PF	525-0085	PT-MJC	525-0166	N252JK
501-0157	N16VG	501-0238	N737RJ	525-0006	N106CJ	525-0086	PT-MIL	525-0167	N525RA
501-0158	N501WB	501-0239	OE-FMS	525-0007	N525KN	525-0087	N100CH	525-0168	D-IRON
501-0159	N80CJ	501-0240	N501DY	525-0008	C-GDKI	525-0088	N722SG	525-0169	N68CJ
501-0160	N999PW	501-0241	N101RR	525-0009	N1327J	525-0089	N202BG	525-0170	N170MU
501-0161	N501FP	501-0242	N71L	525-0010	N525JV	525-0090	N8288R	525-0171	N97VF
501-0162	N501DP	501-0243	N43SP	525-0011	N525AL	525-0091	N295DS	525-0172	D-IFUP
501-0163	I-CIGR	501-0244	N501T	525-0012	N86LA	525-0092	N5341X	525-0173	N970SU
501-0164	N286PC	501-0245	ZS-ACE	525-0013	N550TF	525-0093	N525CM	525-0174	N66BE
501-0165	N501RC	501-0246	OE-FHH	525-0014	N620TC	525-0094	N94MZ	525-0175	N41PG
501-0166	N166FA	501-0247	wo	525-0015	PT-MPE	525-0095	N61SH	525-0176	PT-WLX
501-0167	N501FJ	501-0248	N7700T	525-0016	D-IKOP	525-0096	D-ICEE	525-0177	F-HASC
501-0168	N328NA	501-0249	N117MA	525-0017	N28PT	525-0097	wo	525-0178	N525RC
501-0169	C-GFEE	501-0250	N77FD	525-0018	N525MC	525-0098	N511AC	525-0179	N608DB
501-0170	N610TT	501-0251	N501WD	525-0019	N525KA	525-0099	N526CP	525-0180	VP-BDS
501-0171	N171WJ	501-0252	I-TOIO	525-0020	OE-FGD	525-0100	VH-KXL	525-0181	N88LD
501-0172	N110JB	501-0253	N501JE	525-0021	N793CJ	525-0101	F-GPFC	525-0182	N177JF
501-0173	N91MS	501-0254	N84GF*	525-0022	G-BVCM	525-0102	LX-LOV	525-0183	N399G
501-0174	N1AG	501-0255	N901NB	525-0023	N525RP	525-0103	OE-FLG	525-0184	N525J
501-0175	N23VK	501-0256	N256BM	525-0024	F-HAOA	525-0104	N608MM	525-0185	N13FH
501-0176	VP-CFG	501-0257	N570D	525-0025	D-IBBA	525-0105	N305CJ	525-0186	N92ND
501-0177	N98AV	501-0258	N599BR	525-0026	N286CW	525-0106	N21VC	525-0187	N696ST
501-0178	G-FLVU	501-0259	D-IEIR	525-0027	N700CJ	525-0107	N525WC	525-0188	OE-FMA
501-0179	N718SA	501-0260	N7UF	525-0028	N665DP	525-0108	N108CJ	525-0189	N189CM
501-0180	N510NJ	501-0261	N501VP	525-0029	D-IWHL	525-0109	C-GDWS	525-0190	N701TP
501-0181	N501KK	501-0262	N20CC	525-0030	N177RE	525-0110	N195ME	525-0191	N15LV
501-0182	N220HM	501-0263	N501BE	525-0031	N831S	525-0111	N776DF	525-0192	N84FG
501-0183	CS-AYY	501-0264	N27WW			525-0112	VT-OPJ	525-0193	D-ILCB

Serial	Reg	Serial	Reg	Serial	Reg	Serial	Reg	Serial	Reg
525-0194	N81RA	525-0275	N700GW	525-0356	PP-YOF	525-0435	G-CJAD	525-0516	EC-IRB
525-0195	N525DC	525-0276	N800GW	525-0357	N357JV	525-0436	EC-HVQ	525-0517	D-IFDH
525-0196	N525LP	525-0277	OY-JMC	525-0358	G-HMMV	525-0437	N717NA	525-0518	D-ILLL
525-0197	EC-HIN	525-0278	N901CJ	525-0359	F-GTRY	525-0438	N103CS	525-0519	N926TF
525-0198	N315MR	525-0279	D-IGME	**525 CitationJet CJ-1**		525-0439	N54CG	525-0520	N135CS
525-0199	N299CW	525-0280	PT-XAC	525-0360	N525CD	525-0440	C-GPWM	525-0521	VH-ANE
525-0200	N226B	525-0281	N508TL	525-0361	N128CS	525-0441	PR-ARA	525-0522	N125CS
525-0201	N525HV	525-0282	N625PG	525-0362	N362FL	525-0442	D-IFIS	525-0523	F-HAJD
525-0202	N747AC	525-0283	N95BS	525-0363	N525AS	525-0443	N77DB	525-0524	N524CJ
525-0203	N33FW	525-0284	N256JB	525-0364	C-FTKX	525-0444	N525BR	525-0525	N123S
525-0204	B-4108	525-0285	N55PX	525-0365	N651CJ	525-0445	N207BS	525-0526	SP-KCL
525-0205	N206LX	525-0286	D-ICEY	525-0366	D-IRMA	525-0446	N246GS	525-0527	N527CJ
525-0206	N17VB	525-0287	C-GBPM	525-0367	N525FT	525-0447	N116CS	525-0528	N528CJ
525-0207	N26RL	525-0288	N288AG	525-0368	N820CE	525-0448	EC-J..	525-0529	N151CS
525-0208	N211GM	525-0289	D-ISHW	525-0369	N629DM	525-0449	JA525A	525-0530	N430JH
525-0209	D-ILAT	525-0290	N808WA	525-0370	N525MW	525-0450	I-BOAT	525-0531	N333J
525-0210	XA-CAH	525-0291	F-GPLF	525-0371	N175SB	525-0451	N165CA	525-0532	N32BG
525-0211	D-IMMD	525-0292	N525CU	525-0372	N345MG	525-0452	N585PK	525-0533	D-IPMI
525-0212	N800NB	525-0293	N1127K	525-0373	N415CS	525-0453	N929VC	525-0534	JA100C
525-0213	N525WM	525-0294	N294AT	525-0374	N12GY	525-0454	N101U	525-0535	N535CJ
525-0214	N130LM	525-0295	OE-FJU	525-0375	HB-VNL	525-0455	N75FC	525-0537	N837AC
525-0215	N18GA	525-0296	N296DC	525-0376	C-GTRG	525-0456	PR-LJM	525-0538	N525AM
525-0216	N28GA	525-0297	VP-CAD	525-0377	N900BT	525-0457	N118CS	525-0539	N152CS
525-0217	D-IEWS	525-0298	N55CJ	525-0378	N203BG	525-0458	N525NP	525-0540	N40CJ
525-0218	N288CW	525-0299	N711BX	525-0379	I-IMMI	525-0459	N459NA	525-0541	N458SM
525-0219	N219CJ	525-0300	N881KS	525-0380	N83DC	525-0460	wo	525-0542	N500CW
525-0220	N25MX	525-0301	N291CW	525-0381	N856BB	525-0461	N200SL	525-0543	N43NW
525-0221	D-IWIL	525-0302	N326B	525-0382	N525LF	525-0462	N965LC	525-0544	OE-FUJ
525-0222	wo	525-0303	D-IMMI	525-0383	N600AL	525-0463	361	525-0545	N545TG
525-0223	D-IGAS	525-0304	N154RA	525-0384	PP-JET	525-0464	362	525-0546	N981LB
525-0224	N224CJ	525-0305	N826HS	525-0385	N417Q*	525-0465	363	525-0547	N547ST
525-0225	N525RM	525-0306	N525DY	525-0386	N45MH	525-0466	N119CS	525-0548	N153CS
525-0226	OE-FSS	525-0307	N114FW	525-0387	N7715Y	525-0467	N620BB	525-0600	N525AD
525-0227	N741CC	525-0308	N525DR	525-0388	N525LB	525-0468	N468RW	**525A CitationJet CJ-2**	
525-0228	N668VB	525-0309	D-IBMS	525-0389	D-IDAS	525-0469	N122CS	708	N2CJ
525-0229	LX-FOX	525-0310	OK-SLA	525-0390	N100PF	525-0470	N901GW	525A-0001	N529PC
525-0230	N934AM	525-0311	N523BT	525-0391	LX-IIH	525-0471	N471CJ	525A-0002	N400WD
525-0231	N606JR	525-0312	F-GTMD	525-0392	N392SM	525-0472	N124CS	525A-0003	N525DT
525-0232	N525PB	525-0313	N525MF	525-0393	D-IBIT	525-0473	LX-MRC	525A-0004	N308GT
525-0233	N53CG	525-0314	N525DM*	525-0394	N64PM	525-0474	N31CJ	525A-0005	I-LALL
525-0234	N950P	525-0315	S5-BAY	525-0395	N525AR	525-0475	XA-TTG	525A-0006	N800WC
525-0235	LX-GCA	525-0316	N458MT	525-0396	D-IMAC	525-0476	N50ET	525A-0007	N525CC
525-0236	D-ISWA	525-0317	N51GS	525-0397	I-RVRP	525-0477	D-INOC	525A-0008	N901EB
525-0237	N61YP	525-0318	N525DP	525-0398	N398CJ	525-0478	N869GR	525A-0009	F-HAPP
525-0238	PT-WQI	525-0319	PT-FNP	525-0399	D-ITAN	525-0479	N525BP	525A-0010	N121CP
525-0239	N525VG	525-0320	N150BV	525-0400	N526EZ	525-0480	N888SF	525A-0011	N567JP
525-0240	N524SF	525-0321	PH-ECI	525-0401	N44CK	525-0481	N795BM	525A-0012	N525MP
525-0241	N110FD	525-0322	LX-YSL	525-0402	N525ML	525-0482	PR-EXP	525A-0013	N894C
525-0242	N242LJ	525-0323	N900GW	525-0403	PT-PRR	525-0483	PR-EOB	525A-0014	N110MQ
525-0243	CC-PVJ	525-0324	G-IUAN	525-0404	N88AD	525-0484	N484CJ	525A-0015	N125DG
525-0244	N66ES	525-0325	N115BB	525-0405	N121EB	525-0485	N674JM	525A-0016	N306CJ
525-0245	G-SFCJ	525-0326	N226CW	525-0406	N72JW	525-0486	N334BD	525A-0017	N172CJ
525-0246	N525EC	525-0327	LV-AXN	525-0407	N525JL	525-0487	N191PP	525A-0018	N96G
525-0247	N247CW	525-0328	N328CJ	525-0408	PP-JBS	525-0488	N488SR	525A-0019	S5-BBB
525-0248	N248CJ	525-0329	XA-DGP	525-0409	N530AG	525-0489	N489CB	525A-0020	N323LM
525-0249	N909M	525-0330	N331MS	525-0410	N4108E	525-0490	N130CS	525A-0021	N525TG
525-0250	HB-VMT	525-0331	N888RK	525-0411	N525RF	525-0491	N926CC	525A-0022	N630TF
525-0251	N1JB	525-0332	N511BP	525-0412	N82AE	525-0492	N388PS	525A-0023	N525PF
525-0252	N252RV	525-0333	N99CJ	525-0413	N525RK	525-0493	N95CK	525A-0024	N525TJ
525-0253	N253CW	525-0334	N525M	525-0414	N726TM	525-0494	N71HR	525A-0025	N550T
525-0254	OE-FGI	525-0335	N335CT	525-0415	EC-ISS	525-0495	OY-RGG	525A-0026	D-IHAP
525-0255	N514DS	525-0336	N105P	525-0416	N186TW	525-0496	N382EM	525A-0027	N420CH
525-0256	N196HA	525-0337	PT-FJA	525-0417	PH-SOL	525-0497	N525JJ	525A-0028	N592DR
525-0257	N561BC	525-0338	N977DM	525-0418	N300BV	525-0498	N498YY	525A-0029	D-IKJS
525-0258	OY-SML	525-0339	N239CW	525-0419	N7XE*	525-0499	HB-VNP	525A-0030	D-ISJP
525-0259	PT-MSP	525-0340	N392RG	525-0420	N86SK	525-0500	N111GJ	525A-0031	N312CJ
525-0260	N260AM	525-0341	N341AR	525-0421	D-ILME	525-0501	N41LF	525A-0032	D-IOBO
525-0261	N31HD	525-0342	N9180K	525-0422	N125DJ	525-0502	N133CS	525A-0033	HB-VNO
525-0262	N262BK	525-0343	D-IURS	525-0423	N292SG	525-0503	N904DP	525A-0034	D-IJOA
525-0263	N263CT	525-0344	N77VR	525-0424	N711WG	525-0504	N665CH	525A-0035	N288G
525-0264	D-IPCS	525-0345	G-ZIZI	525-0425	N335J	525-0505	N502TN	525A-0036	wo
525-0265	N198JH	525-0346	PP-CRS	525-0426	N426ED	525-0506	N242ML	525A-0037	N401LG
525-0266	N266CJ	525-0347	I-DAGF	525-0427	N525LM	525-0507	364	525A-0038	I-IMMG
525-0267	PT-XMM	525-0348	N248CW	525-0428	PR-ABV	525-0508	N508CJ	525A-0039	N900HA
525-0268	N850DG	525-0349	D-ICWB	525-0429	EC-IVJ	525-0509	N993GL	525A-0040	N525HB
525-0269	N607DB	525-0350	N1848T	525-0430	N430GR	525-0510	N971DM	525A-0041	N43ND
525-0270	N525HC	525-0351	LX-SUP	525-0431	N431YD	525-0511	ZK-TBM	525A-0042	PR-JET
525-0271	HB-VNK	525-0352	N99JB	525-0432	N94AL	525-0512	N411MY	525A-0043	N432CJ
525-0272	N4GA	525-0353	D-ICOL	525-0433	N102PT	525-0513	N513RV	525A-0044	PR-JST
525-0273	N911NP	525-0354	D-IMMP*	525-0434	N860DB*	525-0514	PH-FIS	525A-0045	N3ST
525-0274	PT-XDB	525-0355	N205FH			525-0515	N132CS		

Serial	Reg.
525A-0046	N46JW
525A-0047	N2250G
525A-0048	PT-FTC
525A-0049	D-IEFD
525A-0050	N525DL
525A-0051	N6M
525A-0052	D-ISCH
525A-0053	PT-FTE
525A-0054	PH-ECL
525A-0055	N525ZZ
525A-0056	N743JG
525A-0057	N57EJ
525A-0058	N811RC
525A-0059	N59CJ
525A-0060	N525RW
525A-0061	PR-TOP
525A-0062	N30HD
525A-0063	VH-MOR
525A-0064	EC-IEB
525A-0065	N225WW*
525A-0066	N741PC
525A-0067	N525PM
525A-0068	N69FH
525A-0069	N757CP
525A-0070	D-ILAM
525A-0071	N701SF
525A-0072	N65PZ
525A-0073	I-LVNB
525A-0074	N222PF
525A-0075	HP-1461
525A-0076	N1277E
525A-0077	N377GS
525A-0078	N113BG
525A-0079	N117W
525A-0080	N525EZ
525A-0081	N414FW
525A-0082	N282CJ
525A-0083	N975DM
525A-0084	N525DG
525A-0085	N85JV
525A-0086	N520JM
525A-0087	N474PC
525A-0088	N569DM
525A-0089	OY-JET
525A-0090	N475DH
525A-0091	N8940
525A-0092	N21RA
525A-0093	N93PE*
525A-0094	N942CJ
525A-0095	I-DEUM
525A-0096	N96CJ
525A-0097	N97CJ
525A-0098	N57HC
525A-0099	N444RH
525A-0100	N170TM
525A-0101	N1255J
525A-0102	D-IWIR
525A-0103	N800VT
525A-0104	N80C
525A-0105	N13M
525A-0106	D-IUAC
525A-0107	N525WD
525A-0108	D-ICMS
525A-0109	N22LX
525A-0110	N451AJ
525A-0111	N219FL
525A-0112	N701TF
525A-0113	N525VV
525A-0114	N726RP
525A-0115	N115CJ
525A-0116	N711BE
525A-0117	PT-FTG
525A-0118	N464C
525A-0119	N525DV
525A-0120	N144EM
525A-0121	N5YD
525A-0122	N224WD
525A-0123	N37BG
525A-0124	N27CJ
525A-0125	N525CG
525A-0126	N999WE

Serial	Reg.
525A-0127	N12GS
525A-0128	N525CK
525A-0129	N129SG
525A-0130	N525JD
525A-0131	N20GP
525A-0132	N75PP
525A-0133	N251KD
525A-0134	N323SK
525A-0135	N4RP
525A-0136	N345CJ
525A-0137	N717VB
525A-0138	N722TS
525A-0139	N526HV
525A-0140	N140DA
525A-0141	PT-FTR
525A-0142	OE-FPS
525A-0143	D-ISUN
525A-0144	N144YD
525A-0145	N7GZ
525A-0146	N1220W
525A-0147	VP-BJR
525A-0148	N148FB
525A-0149	N90CJ
525A-0150	N525GM
525A-0151	N122SM
525A-0152	N123JW
525A-0153	N500SV
525A-0154	N708GP
525A-0155	N105PT
525A-0156	JA525B
525A-0157	N88KC
525A-0158	N158CJ
525A-0159	N5026
525A-0160	N525KR
525A-0161	N28MH
525A-0162	N335JJ
525A-0163	ZS-CJT
525A-0164	N164CJ
525A-0165	N30AD
525A-0166	D-IAMO
525A-0167	D-ILDL
525A-0168	N767W
525A-0169	F-GPUJ
525A-0170	C6-...
525A-0171	CC-CHE
525A-0172	N179DV
525A-0173	N525MR
525A-0174	D-IDMH
525A-0175	N525SM
525A-0176	N100JS
525A-0177	N55KT
525A-0178	N7715X
525A-0179	OO-FHN
525A-0180	N604LJ
525A-0181	N93AK
525A-0182	N777CJ
525A-0183	N183TX
525A-0184	N357J
525A-0185	N65CK
525A-0186	N350BV
525A-0187	N18/MG
525A-0188	N188JR
525A-0189	N777DY
525A-0190	N680JB
525A-0191	N776LB
525A-0192	N668DB
525A-0193	D-IKAL
525A-0194	N806MN
525A-0195	D-IMAX
525A-0196	D-INOB
525A-0197	N197CJ
525A-0198	N57FL
525A-0199	I-GOSF
525A-0200	F-GZUJ
525A-0201	N888GL
525A-0202	N202CJ
525A-0203	N736LB
525A-0204	OE-FCY
525A-0205	N205YY
525A-0206	N29MR
525A-0207	VT-JSP

Serial	Reg.
525A-0208	N400HT
525A-0209	OY-UCA
525A-0210	N28DM
525A-0211	N515EV
525A-0212	N104PC
525A-0213	N213CJ
525A-0214	N1DM
525A-0215	N748RE
525A-0216	OY-GGR
525A-0217	N67GH
525A-0218	D-IPVD
525A-0219	F-HEOL
525A-0220	N800RL
525A-0221	N27VQ
525A-0222	N778MA
525A-0223	D-IWAN*
525A-0224	N424CJ
525A-0225	N67BC
525A-0230	D-IGRO*
525A-0234	N313CR

525B CitationJet CJ-3

Serial	Reg.
711	N3CJ
525B-0001	N753CJ
626b 0002	NG29II*
525B-0002	N103CJ
525B-0003	N1308L
525B-0005	N105CJ
525B-0006	N5227G
525B-0007	N7CC
525B-0008	N51HF
525B-0009	N777NJ
525B-0010	N917RG
525B-0011	N51HF
525B-0012	N172DH
525B-0013	N831V
525B-0014	N114CJ
525B-0017	N614B
525B-0019	N79LB
525B-0025	N7NE*
525B-0026	N162EC
525B-0029	N726AG
525B-0031	N303CJ

550 Citation II

Serial	Reg.
550-0004	F-GNCP
550-0005	N77ND
550-0006	N550LA
550-0007	N127JJ
550-0008	N70XA
550-0009	N656PS
550-0010	PT-LPK
550-0011	0002
550-0012	N11FH
550-0013	wo
550-0014	N780CF
550-0016	N116LA
550-0017	N744AT
550-0018	N752CC
550-0019	wo
550-0021	N52RF
550-0024	N404RP
550-0025	OY-GMC
550-0026	N30AV
550-0027	N127PM
550-0028	N551CZ
550-0029	N524MA
550-0030	N16TS
550-0031	N22GA
550-0032	N232CW
550-0033	LX-GDL
550-0034	N922SL
550-0035	N15JA
550-0036	N336MA
550-0037	N622PG
550-0038	N550JC
550-0039	N848D
550-0040	N545GA
550-0041	OE-GCI
550-0042	C-FPEL
550-0043	N112SH
550-0044	N308TW

Serial	Reg.
550-0045	wo
550-0046	C-GRHC
550-0047	N44AS
550-0048	N19ER
550-0050	F-GMCI
550-0051	ZS-RKV
550-0052	N550DR
550-0053	N519AA
550-0054	VH-PSM
550-0055	N10EG
550-0056	N89D
550-0057	VH-WNZ
550-0058	N100HB
550-0060	OE-GIL
550-0061	N458N
550-0062	C-GDLR
550-0064	N64TF
550-0065	N144GA
550-0066	N19HU
550-0067	N267BB
550-0068	N1WB
550-0069	N712PD
550-0070	N892PB
550-0071	OY CMK
550-0072	N778JM
550-0073	VP-CTJ
550-0074	N174DR
550-0075	N910MT
550-0076	P2-MBD
550-0077	XA-AGN
550-0078	N533MA
550-0079	N232DM
550-0080	N45ME
550-0081	I-AROO
550-0082	N49U
550-0083	N200VT
550-0084	N391AN
550-0085	OE-GBA
550-0086	N43SA
550-0089	N800RR
550-0090	N290VP
550-0091	N601BC
550-0092	N567CA
550-0094	G-RDBS
550-0095	N550CG
550-0096	N87SF
550-0097	N999GR
550-0098	N211JS
550-0099	N109JC
550-0100	C-GLMK
550-0101	wo
550-0102	VH-OYC
550-0103	N90MA
550-0104	301
550-0105	N550LH
550-0106	N820MC
550-0108	N690EW
550-0109	N753CC
550-0110	N550SF
550-0111	N123VP
550-0112	N213CF
550-0113	C-FIMP
550-0114	N991BM
550-0115	SE-DDY
550-0116	N575BW
550-0117	N550RB
550-0118	N138J
550-0121	N899MA
550-0122	N89GA
550-0123	N948DC
550-0124	N109GA
550-0125	5N-NPF
550-0127	G-ESTA
550-0129	N122HM
550-0130	N630CC
550-0132	PT-LLU
550-0133	N228CC
550-0135	YV-888CP
550-0138	XC-SCT
550-0139	OY-ELY
550-0140	N55WL

Serial	Reg.
550-0141	VH-EJY
550-0142	N387SC
550-0143	N50JP
550-0144	wo
550-0145	P2-TAA
550-0146	N501LC
550-0147	N80GM
550-0148	N116K
550-0150	N1SV
550-0151	N495CM
550-0152	N550CA
550-0153	N37MH
550-0154	G-JETJ
550-0155	N155FF*
550-0156	EC-IAX*
550-0157	N257CW
550-0158	N769H
550-0159	N550PW
550-0162	N1UA
550-0164	N721DR
550-0165	N976GA
550-0166	N867JC
550-0167	N100CJ
550-0168	Z8-NII
550-0169	N6001L
550-0170	N550DA
550-0171	N19AJ
550-0172	N800TV
550-0174	N87PT
550-0175	N550CU
550-0176	N61MA
550-0179	N673LR
550-0180	N219MS
550-0181	N50US
550-0182	F-HACA
550-0183	G-JMDW
550-0184	N200NC
550-0185	N317HC
550-0186	N80AW
550-0187	N598CA
550-0188	N280PM
550-0189	D-CCCF
550-0190	F-GZLC
550-0191	N550PA
550-0192	N192DW
550-0193	N485AK
550-0194	N91B
550-0195	N343CM
550-0196	N196JS
550-0197	N510JC
550-0198	XA-SQV
550-0199	N586RE
550-0200	N797SF
550-0201	N1GH
550-0202	N704DA
550-0203	N766AE
550-0204	N815CE
550-0205	N30JD
550-0206	N280TA
550-0207	N196RJ
550-0208	wfu
550-0209	N444G
550-0210	N850PM
550-0211	N77PR
550-0212	N245CC
550-0213	N213CC
550-0214	N75ZA
550-0215	N550MJ
550-0216	N550PG
550-0217	N217SA
550-0218	N250DR
550-0219	N550PM
550-0220	N123RF
550-0221	N31GA
550-0222	PT-LNC
550-0223	N550WL
550-0224	2222
550-0225	PT-LTJ
550-0226	N872RD
550-0227	XA-...
550-0228	N334ED

Serial	Reg.	Serial	Reg.	Serial	Reg.	Serial	Reg.	Serial	Reg.
550-0229	N229MC	550-0321	VP-CCO	550-0435	N674G	550-0568	N47SM	550-0654	XB-BON
550-0230	N550WB	550-0322	N5TR	550-0436	N717DM	550-0569	5Y-TWE	550-0655	N37201
550-0231	N41SM	550-0323	VP-CLD	550-0438	N643TD	550-0570	N270CW	550-0656	N30GR
550-0232	N797CW	550-0324	HB-VLQ	550-0439	N1250V	550-0571	N90JJ	550-0657	CC-DGA
550-0234	C-FLPD	550-0326	N390AJ	550-0440	OY-CYV	550-0572	N719EH	550-0658	RP-C1180
550-0235	I-PNCA	550-0327	PT-LLT	550-0441	N80LA	550-0573	N155AC	550-0659	N4614N
550-0236	N823NA	550-0329	N949SA*	550-0442	N668AJ	550-0575	N387RE	550-0660	N827DP
550-0237	N41WJ	550-0332	N120Q	550-0443	EC-IMF	550-0576	N675SS	550-0661	XA-AFU
550-0238	N204CF	550-0333	N123GM	550-0444	N71GA	550-0577	N8344M	550-0662	N623DS
550-0239	N66MC	550-0334	N404KS	550-0445	N453S	550-0578	N203PM	550-0663	N5314J
550-0241	N241FT	550-0335	N187JN	550-0446	U 20-2	550-0579	N579L	550-0664	N45BE
550-0242	N551BC	550-0336	N90Z	550-0447	HB-VIS	550-0580	N18NA	550-0665	N998BC
550-0243	N214MD	550-0337	N3FW	550-0448	N938W	550-0581	N905LC	550-0666	N5408G
550-0245	N388SB	550-0338	N900MF	550-0449	YV-2338P	550-0582	FAC-1211	550-0667	N107EE
550-0247	PT-LJJ	550-0339	VH-SCD	550-0450	N505RP	550-0583	N22PC	550-0668	XA-TVH
550-0248	N550SA	550-0340	N38DD	550-0451	N1249P	550-0585	N65AR	550-0669	N677GS
550-0249	N456AB	550-0341	N141JC	550-0452	N707PF	550-0586	F-GGGA	550-0670	N6637G
550-0250	N250VP	550-0343	N789TT	550-0453	N962J	550-0587	N18HJ	550-0671	G-VUEA
550-0251	N20FB	550-0344	N550GM	550-0454	N938D	550-0588	N92BD	550-0672	OY-VIS
550-0252	N6JU	550-0345	N982NA	550-0455	PT-MMO	550-0589	N787JD	550-0673	N6763L
550-0253	N157DW	550-0346	N106SP	550-0456	N283DF	550-0590	N88NM	550-0674	N910HM
550-0254	N888RL	550-0347	VH-ZLE	550-0457	OY-TMA	550-0592	U 20-3	550-0675	PT-WKQ
550-0255	I-JESO	550-0348	C-GSCX	550-0458	N664SS	550-0593	N26621	550-0676	PT-OJG
550-0256	N55TP	550-0349	N525LC	550-0459	N315ES	550-0594	N2351K	550-0677	N6775C
550-0257	N53RG	550-0350	N86SG	550-0460	PT-OKP	550-0595	N2734K	550-0678	EC-FES
550-0258	N424TG	550-0351	I-ALKA	550-0461	N22FM	550-0596	EC-HGI	550-0679	N622EX
550-0259	OY-BZT	550-0352	VT-EUN	550-0462	N550AL	550-0597	N213JS	550-0680	N6776T
550-0260	N6HF	550-0353	N353FT*	550-0463	N822HA*	550-0598	N888XL	550-0681	N1200N
550-0261	N551WL	550-0354	VP-CJR	550-0465	N90PT	550-0599	N571BC	550-0682	N90BL
550-0263	I-....	550-0355	N52LT	550-0466	N10LY	550-0600	N415AJ	550-0683	YV-701CP
550-0264	N777WY	550-0356	N133WA	550-0467	YV-810CP	550-0601	G-CBTU	550-0684	C-FJXN
550-0265	CN-TKK	550-0357	PT-OAG	550-0468	N120JP	550-0602	N2663Y	550-0685	C-FJWZ
550-0266	N550TT	550-0358	4400	550-0469	I-....	550-0603	N550TW	550-0686	C-FKCE
550-0267	N910RB	550-0362	N396M	550-0470	N202SW	550-0604	N904SJ	550-0687	C-FKDX
550-0268	N38TT	550-0363	N741T	550-0471	N92B	550-0605	N26494	550-0688	C-FKEB
550-0269	N1MM	550-0364	N180FW	550-0472	N492MA	550-0606	N602AT	550-0689	N689VP
550-0271	N1NL	550-0365	N129DV	550-0473	XB-HZF	550-0607	N26496	550-0690	VH-VLZ
550-0272	YU-BVV	550-0366	N110LD	550-0474	ZS-LIG	550-0608	N990M	550-0691	C-GAPV
550-0273	N217FS	550-0367	N45ML	550-0475	N475WA	550-0609	F-GLTK	550-0692	N75RJ
550-0274	XB-JLJ	550-0368	N718CK	550-0476	N1252D	550-0610	N610JB	550-0693	N594WP
550-0275	N555DS	550-0369	N725FL	550-0477	N846L*	550-0611	F-GGGT	550-0694	N807MB
550-0276	N53FT	550-0371	N585DM	550-0478	N17WC	550-0612	N578M	550-0695	N77DD
550-0277	N550BJ	550-0376	N73ST	550-0479	N68TS	550-0613	N664AJ	550-0696	N696VP
550-0279	N550KA	550-0378	D-CIFA	550-0480	ZS-OIE	550-0615	N577VN	550-0697	D-CHEP
550-0280	C-GKAU	550-0381	N381UP	550-0481	N97EM	550-0616	PT-OVV	550-0698	N550RM
550-0281	N33EK	550-0382	N852SP	550-0482	N594G	550-0618	PP-ESC	550-0699	C-FKLB
550-0282	G-JETC	550-0383	N561AS	550-0483	N412PE	550-0619	XA-...	550-0700	C-FJCZ
550-0283	N225J	550-0390	N14RZ	550-0484	N84EA	550-0620	N477JE	550-0701	C-FLZA
550-0284	OY-JEV	550-0393	I-FLYD	550-0485	N727C	550-0621	N99TK	550-0702	C-FMFM
550-0285	N989TV	550-0396	N99CN	550-0486	XA-AAK	550-0622	LX-VAZ	550-0703	N308A
550-0286	N2GG	550-0398	PH-CTX	550-0487	N550DW	550-0623	N89LS	550-0704	N197HF
550-0287	N527DS	550-0399	N66MS	550-0488	C-FCSS	550-0624	N65DV	550-0705	N521TM
550-0288	wo	550-0400	wo	550-0489	N489SS	550-0625	N6846T	550-0706	N706NA
550-0289	C-FTMS	550-0402	N57SF	550-0490	N490CC	550-0626	N466SS	550-0707	OE-GDM
550-0290	N312NC	550-0403	N362CP	550-0491	I-AVRM	550-0627	N650WC	550-0708	N923JH
550-0291	N262Y	550-0405	YV-778CP	550-0492	I-AVGM	550-0628	IGM-628	550-0709	N709RS
550-0292	C-FTOM	550-0406	N815MA	550-0493	N84GC	550-0629	wo	550-0710	N90BJ
550-0293	wo	550-0407	N758S	550-0494	N1254X	550-0630	N198ND	550-0711	XA-...
550-0294	PT-LPN	550-0408	N110WA	550-0495	N10TC	550-0631	N631EA	550-0712	PH-LAB
550-0295	N48KH	550-0409	N102HB	550-0497	N1257B	550-0632	5N-AYA	550-0713	N283CW
550-0296	G-BJIR	550-0410	C-GNWM	550-0498	N772SB	550-0633	N550AB	550-0714	G-SPUR
550-0297	B-4104	550-0411	N550KW	550-0499	PT-LIV	550-0634	SE-DVT	550-0715	LV-YHC
550-0299	N511AB	550-0412	N223J	550-0501	N12549	550-0635	N622VW	550-0716	N550TL
550-0300	YV-162CP	550-0414	N342CC	550-0502	84-007	550-0636	N50NF	550-0717	OE-GBC
550-0301	B-4103	550-0415	F-GJYD	550-0503	84-008	550-0637	YV-376CP	550-0718	XA-FIR
550-0302	N792MA	550-0416	N416CC	550-0504	XA-TQA	550-0638	N255TC	550-0719	N12068
550-0303	XB-GLZ	550-0417	N17DM	550-0505	N1255K	550-0639	N100DS	550-0720	N260TB
550-0304	N42PH	550-0418	N214JT	550-0550	N177RJ	550-0640	PT-ODL	550-0721	N721CC
550-0305	B-4105	550-0419	G-FJET	550-0551	N600AT	550-0641	N395HE	550-0722	N1886G
550-0306	N296CW	550-0420	N555KT	550-0553	N553MJ	550-0642	XB-IKY	550-0723	N5NE
550-0307	N550VW	550-0421	N510GP	550-0554	N750SL	550-0643	G-EJEL	550-0724	LV-WEJ
550-0308	N15XM	550-0423	N248HA	550-0555	N104HW	550-0644	XC-PGM	550-0725	N725CC
550-0309	N530P	550-0424	N551BP	550-0558	LV-WJN	550-0645	PT-ODZ	550-0726	N726AM
550-0310	N300GC	550-0425	U 20-1	550-0559	N409ST	550-0646	N9VF	550-0727	N550KR
550-0311	YV-1055CP	550-0426	N434SB	550-0561	wo	550-0647	N800MT	550-0728	LV-WJO
550-0312	N32TK	550-0427	N840MQ	550-0562	N54RM	550-0648	XC-PGP	550-0729	VP-CBM
550-0313	SE-RBK	550-0428	N97BG	550-0563	N518N	550-0649	HB-VMH	550-0730	N501JP
550-0315	N741JC	550-0430	XB-AGV	550-0564	wo	550-0650	N823CT	550-0731	XC-SST
550-0316	PT-WJZ	550-0432	N76AS	550-0565	N565NC	550-0651	N24E	550-0732	N902DK
550-0318	N78CK	550-0433	N7ZU	550-0566	N15SN	550-0652	N3262M	550-0733	N44SW
550-0320	N204PM	550-0434	N53FP	550-0567	N926RM	550-0653	N30RL		

Citation Bravo

Serial	Reg	Serial	Reg	Serial	Reg	Serial	Reg
550-0734	N550BB	550-0879	N35ET	550-0960	TC-MKA	550-1041	N412ET
550-0801	N801BB	550-0880	N7YA	550-0961	HK-4250	550-1042	G-ORDB
550-0802	N550HH	550-0881	N306CS	550-0962	N797TE	550-1043	CS-DHH
550-0803	N141HL	550-0882	N438SP	550-0963	N24QT	550-1044	N141AB
550-0804	N550BC	550-0883	N469DE	550-0964	HB-VMY	550-1045	PP-BMG
550-0805	N108RF	550-0884	N361DB	550-0965	N256CC	550-1046	N300GF
550-0806	N300PY	550-0885	N88AJ	550-0966	N36PT	550-1047	N889B
550-0807	C-GPGA	550-0886	N500TS	550-0967	N432RJ	550-1048	CS-DHI
550-0808	YU-BSM	550-0887	XA-ABE	550-0968	N551G	550-1049	N299HS
550-0809	N380AK	550-0888	N162TJ	550-0969	N401KC	550-1050	A9C-BXC
550-0810	VH-XCJ	550-0889	N360HS	550-0970	N78MD	550-1051	N745CC
550-0811	PT-MMV	550-0890	N1961S	550-0971	N717GK	550-1052	N322CS
550-0812	C-FJBO	550-0891	N82MA	550-0972	PH-HMA	550-1053	N57MC
550-0813	N100KU	550-0892	N22GR	550-0973	N129PB	550-1054	N600ST
550-0814	N303CS	550-0893	N333EB	550-0974	N307CS	550-1055	N896CG
550-0815	N126TF	550-0894	N107EG	550-0975	N975HM	550-1056	N45678
550-0816	C-FMCI	550-0895	N199BB	550-0976	N308CS	550-1057	N714RM
550-0817	N123GF	550-0896	N121L	550-0977	N309CS	550-1058	VH-SCC
550-0818	N300CS	550-0897	G-GHPG	550-0978	N696CM	550-1059	N324CS
550-0819	N15CV	550-0898	N550GH	550-0979	N311CS	550-1060	N669B
550-0820	N302CS	550-0899	N899DC	550-0980	N146CT	550-1061	N325CS
550-0821	N225WT	550-0900	N214TJ	550-0981	N313CS	550-1062	N662CB
550-0822	N726DS	550-0901	N857AA	550-0982	C-GVIJ	550-1063	N151TM
550-0823	N25FS	550-0902	N688JD	550-0983	XA-GDI	550-1064	N823PM
550-0824	N824CB	550-0903	N903VP	550-0984	VH-HVM	550-1065	N175CW
550-0825	N305CS	550-0904	N904BB	550-0985	G-FCDB	550-1066	N573M
550-0826	N595PC	550-0905	N505AG	550-0986	N45NF	550-1067	N6TM
550-0827	D-CCAB	550-0906	HB-VNZ	550-0987	N471WR	550-1068	N668CB
550-0828	N6FR	550-0907	SX-BMK	550-0988	I-FJTC	550-1069	OE-GLL
550-0829	N829CB	550-0908	N242SW	550-0989	XA-LOF	550-1070	XA-CAP
550-0830	N830KE	550-0909	N391BC	550-0990	N990JM	550-1071	N104FL
550-0831	N331PR	550-0910	N574M	550-0991	N628CB	550-1072	N143BP
550-0832	N832UJ	550-0911	N575M	550-0992	N777NG	550-1073	N899B
550-0833	PR-FEP	550-0912	N588AC	550-0993	N721T	550-1074	N328CS
550-0834	D-CALL	550-0913	N66MT	550-0994	N580SH	550-1075	N275BB
550-0835	N198SL	550-0914	N897MC	550-0995	N550PD	550-1076	N359GW
550-0836	N122NC	550-0915	N346CM	550-0996	CC-LLM	550-1077	N329CS
550-0837	OE-GPS	550-0916	N555BK	550-0997	N67BK	550-1078	N442NR
550-0838	N813JD	550-0917	G-IDAB	550-0998	OE-GHP	550-1079	N444EA
550-0839	N101FG	550-0918	N45VM	550-0999	XA-UVA	550-1080	N132MT
550-0840	N773CA	550-0919	N100Y	550-1000	N121CN	550-1081	N332CS
550-0841	N841W	550-0920	N63LB	550-1001	N26CB	550-1082	CS-DHJ
550-0842	N842CB	550-0921	N40MF	550-1002	N101JL	550-1083	I-PABL
550-0843	N627L	550-0922	I-FJTB	550-1003	1003	550-1084	N338CS
550-0844	N550KL	550-0923	N23YC	550-1004	N314CS	550-1085	N339CS
550-0845	N550WS	550-0924	N550VC	550-1005	CS-DHA	550-1086	N58HK
550-0846	N517AF	550-0925	N550PF	550-1006	N992HE	550-1087	N151FD
550-0847	N304CS	550-0926	N144Z	550-1007	N67PC	550-1088	N153SG
550-0848	N550J	550-0927	PH-DYE	550-1008	D2-ECE	550-1089	N334CS
550-0849	N246CB	550-0928	N928DA	550-1009	CS-DHB	550-1090	CS-DHK
550-0850	N551V	550-0929	N552SM	550-1010	N316CS	550-1091	N335CS
550-0851	N7NN	550-0930	PP-ORM	550-1011	C-FRST	550-1092	CS-DHL
550-0852	VH-FGK	550-0931	C-FAMJ	550-1012	N20AU	550-1093	CS-DHM
550-0853	N398LS	550-0932	I-MTVB	550-1013	CS-DHC	550-1094	N308DT
550-0854	N550KJ	550-0933	N417KW	550-1014	N610CB	550-1095	N336CS
550-0855	N232JR	550-0934	N200AS	550-1015	N81ER	550-1096	N707HP
550-0856	N300GP	550-0935	G-IPAL	550-1016	N926EC	550-1097	N337CS
550-0857	N984BK	550-0936	N550TM	550-1017	CS-DHD	550-1098	CS-DHN
550-0858	N100WT	550-0937	N440CE	550-1018	D-CEFM*	550-1099	CS-DHO*
550-0859	I-BENN	550-0938	EC-HRO	550-1019	N317CS	550-1100	N110BR
550-0860	N844DR	550-0939	N48NS	550-1020	N212BH	550-1101	N342CS
550-0861	N26CV	550-0940	G-FIRM	550-1021	N49KW	550-1103	LZ-AVB
550-0862	N1962J	550-0941	N878AG*	550-1022	CS-DHE	550-1106	N341CS
550-0863	N577VM	550-0942	N265TS	550-1023	N4405	550-1108	N717VL
550-0864	OE-GTZ	550-0943	YV-2711P	550-1024	N550FP	550-1110	N877B
550-0865	D-CPPP	550-0944	N723RE	550-1025	CS-DHF		
550-0866	D-CHZF	550-0945	N585KS	550-1026	N552CB		
550-0867	N161TM	550-0946	HB-VMX	550-1027	OO-FYG		
550-0868	N627BC	550-0947	N514BC	550-1028	N442LW		
550-0869	N499WM	550-0948	N49FW	550-1029	N318CS		
550-0870	VP-CED	550-0949	N550KG	550-1030	N322GT		
550-0871	I-GIWW	550-0950	N555HM	550-1031	N525PE		
550-0872	OE-GKK	550-0951	LN-SUV	550-1032	N880CM		
550-0873	PT-XSX	550-0952	N952CH	550-1033	N701VV		
550-0874	D-CHAN	550-0953	N550WG	550-1034	CS-DHG		
550-0875	N800AB	550-0954	PP-OAA	550-1035	N585TH		
550-0876	5Y-MNG	550-0955	HB-VMW	550-1036	N319CS		
550-0877	N21SL	550-0956	N800VA	550-1037	N1258B		
550-0878	VH-ZLT	550-0957	G-IKOS	550-1038	SE-RBY		
		550-0958	N333BD	550-1039	N711HA		
		550-0959	N511JP	550-1040	OK-VSZ		

S550 Citation II

Serial	Reg	Serial	Reg
S550-0001	N86BA	S550-0049	B-4101
S550-0002	CC-CWW	S550-0050	B-4102
S550-0003	N847C	S550-0051	N77PA
S550-0004	N72AM	S550-0052	N57BJ
S550-0005	N666LN	S550-0053	N393E
S550-0006	N181G	S550-0054	N999CB
S550-0007	OO-SKP	S550-0055	N417RC
S550-0008	N600KM	S550-0056	N52FT
S550-0009	N550A	S550-0057	N57CJ
S550-0010	N550F	S550-0058	N633EE
S550-0011	N25GZ	S550-0059	N329JC
S550-0012	N550RV	S550-0060	N442KM
S550-0013	N561PS	S550-0061	N200LX
S550-0014	N84EC	S550-0062	I-AVVM
S550-0015	N600EA	S550-0063	VH-EMO
S550-0016	N557CS	S550-0064	N575SG
S550-0017	N86PC	S550-0065	N90FJ
S550-0018	N145DF	S550-0066	N711MD
S550-0019	N670JD	S550-0067	N828AF
S550-0020	N550AS	S550-0068	N7070A
S550-0021	N945ER	S550-0069	N43VS
S550-0022	N360M	S550-0070	XB-EEP
S550-0023	N293RT*	S550-0071	N1865M
S550-0024	N790AL	S550-0072	N62NS
S550-0025	wo	S550-0073	N1958N
S550-0026	N32TX	S550-0074	N74JE
S550-0027	N5WC	S550-0075	N882RB
S550-0028	S5-BAX	S550-0076	N52CK
S550-0029	HB-VMJ	S550-0077	N999EA
S550-0030	N999HC	S550-0078	ZS-CAR
S550-0031	wo	S550-0079	5N-BEL
S550-0032	N48BV	S550-0080	N260BS
S550-0033	N531CM	S550-0081	N550KM
S550-0034	N610GD	S550-0082	N27TB
S550-0035	N834DC	S550-0083	N683PF
S550-0036	N63CR	S550-0084	PT-LJL
S550-0037	N578BB	S550-0085	N550BT
S550-0038	N214PN	S550-0086	OB-1792T
S550-0039	N22UL	S550-0087	N21EG
S550-0040	C-FEMA	S550-0088	N127RC
S550-0041	N74LM	S550-0089	VT-ETG
S550-0042	N241DS	S550-0090	N499RC
S550-0043	N727EF	S550-0091	N476LC
S550-0044	N92ME	S550-0092	N923S
S550-0045	N97CC	S550-0093	N400RE
S550-0046	N103VF	S550-0094	N1H
S550-0047	N16RP	S550-0095	N345CS
S550-0048	N705SP		

c/n	Reg
S550-0096	N29XA
S550-0097	N551RF
S550-0098	N598KW
S550-0099	N299QS
S550-0100	N550SJ
S550-0101	C-FABF
S550-0102	N285MC
S550-0103	N22HP
S550-0104	N224KC
S550-0105	N105BG
S550-0106	N9072U
S550-0107	N550HT
S550-0108	N316MH
S550-0109	N75MC
S550-0110	N45GP
S550-0111	N111QS
S550-0112	A2-MCB
S550-0113	PT-LJQ
S550-0114	PT-LKS
S550-0115	N92JC
S550-0116	N550HC
S550-0117	wo
S550-0118	N110LH
S550-0119	N11TS
S550-0120	N716DD
S550-0121	N23NM
S550-0122	N122WS
S550-0123	N121CG
S550-0124	N554T
S550-0125	N125QA
S550-0126	ZS-EDA
S550-0127	N97SK
S550-0128	N550CZ
S550-0129	N480CC
S550-0130	N550PL
S550-0131	N87BA
S550-0132	N91ML
S550-0133	N133VP
S550-0134	N66HD
S550-0135	VT-KMB
S550-0137	PT-WIB
S550-0138	N552BE
S550-0139	N39TF
S550-0140	N575EW
S550-0141	N550AJ
S550-0142	N701BG
S550-0143	N1VA
S550-0144	N543SC
S550-0145	N900LM
S550-0146	N815H
S550-0147	CS-DDV
S550-0148	D-CSFD
S550-0149	N43RC
S550-0150	N107RC
S550-0151	N550SP
S550-0152	N987CJ
S550-0153	N477LC
S550-0154	N550DS
S550-0155	N550DL*
S550-0156	N63JT
S550-0157	N157BM
S550-0158	N66EH
S550-0159	N9GY
S550-0160	PT-OSM

551 Citation II/SP

c/n	Reg
550-0003	N19CP
550-0246	N550BP
550-0374	N477A
551-0002	N502CL
551-0003	I-MESK
551-0006	YV-O-CVG-:
551-0007	N60FJ
551-0010	D-ICAC
551-0015	YV-2671P
551-0017	N811VG
551-0018	D-IEAR
551-0021	N55LS
551-0023	wo
551-0024	wo
551-0026	N612VR

c/n	Reg
551-0027	N46PJ
551-0029	wo
551-0031	N5TQ
551-0033	wo
551-0035	N277JM
551-0036	N889FA
551-0038	N551BB
551-0039	N550TA
551-0046	N518MV
551-0050	N228MH
551-0051	D-ICTA
551-0056	N826RT
551-0059	N59FY
551-0060	N59GB
551-0066	N242WT
551-0071	N551HH
551-0095	N48DK
551-0117	4X-CZD
551-0122	N10LR
551-0132	SE-DYR
551-0133	HB-VDO
551-0141	CC-CWZ
551-0149	N5WT
551-0163	ZS-ARG
551-0169	N14RM
551-0171	5R-MHF
551-0174	EI-CIR
551-0179	N127BU
551-0180	N222VV
551-0181	N565VV
551-0191	N386AM
551-0201	N550GB
551-0205	N828SS
551-0214	N9SS
551-0215	N551CL
551-0223	YV-2567P
551-0245	wo
551-0285	ZS-MLN
551-0289	PT-LJF
551-0304	N999MK
551-0313	YV-2426P
551-0323	N555RT
551-0335	D-ILCC
551-0355	I-ALPG
551-0359	N142TJ
551-0360	N551EA
551-0361	LV-APL
551-0369	N778JC
551-0378	N322MA
551-0388	wo
551-0393	N122SP
551-0396	LV-WXD
551-0401	D-IMME
551-0412	OY-PDN
551-0421	3A-MRB
551-0428	wo
551-0431	N4NM
551-0457	N11SS
551-0463	YV-713CP
551-0496	LX-PRS
551-0500	N9CR
551-0552	OE-FPA
551-0556	N200GF
551-0557	N711NV
551-0560	D-IMMF
551-0574	OE-FBS
551-0584	N25QT
551-0591	N1AT
551-0614	N26HG
551-0617	N747JB

560 Citation V/Ultra

c/n	Reg
550-0001	wfu
560-0001	N561VP
560-0002	wo
560-0003	N560ER
560-0004	N189H
560-0005	N953F
560-0006	N269TA
560-0007	N763D
560-0008	N561B

c/n	Reg
560-0009	N77NR
560-0010	N560JM
560-0011	N913BJ
560-0012	N560ME
560-0013	N560WH
560-0014	N900SM
560-0015	N480DG
560-0016	N462B
560-0017	N560H
560-0018	N500FZ
560-0019	N643RT
560-0020	N560HC
560-0021	N410DW
560-0022	N574BB
560-0023	N3FA
560-0024	N560FN
560-0025	CNA-NV
560-0026	N380RD
560-0027	N560JR
560-0028	N757CK
560-0029	N590A
560-0030	N570BJ
560-0031	D-CHDE
560-0032	N560BC
560-0033	C-GAPC
560-0034	N401MC
560-0035	N561EJ
560-0036	N532MA
560-0037	N416HF
560-0038	N212BW
560-0039	CNA-NW
560-0040	N560CF
560-0041	N400KS
560-0042	D-CAWU
560-0043	wo
560-0044	N331CC
560-0045	PT-LZQ
560-0046	G-CJAE
560-0047	N500FK
560-0048	N240CM
560-0049	N560EL
560-0050	N501CW
560-0051	N314RW
560-0052	N500UB
560-0053	C-FACO
560-0054	N100SY
560-0055	N715PS
560-0056	N406VJ
560-0057	N561TS
560-0058	N710LC
560-0059	F-GKHL
560-0060	PT-FTB
560-0061	N46GA
560-0062	N500UJ
560-0063	N68CK
560-0064	N45GA
560-0065	N608CT
560-0066	N501JS
560-0067	JA119N
560-0068	N246NW
560-0069	N367JC
560-0070	F-GJXX
560-0071	N271CA
560-0071A	N45RC
560-0072	JA120N
560-0073	N100WP
560-0074	C-GBNX
560-0075	N817PD
560-0076	N623KC*
560-0077	wo
560-0078	D-CSUN
560-0079	N560GL
560-0080	JA8576
560-0081	N318CT
560-0082	C-FETJ
560-0083	N568WC
560-0084	N51C
560-0085	N85VP
560-0086	N560CJ
560-0087	N60QB
560-0088	OK-SLS

c/n	Reg
560-0089	N54DD
560-0090	LV-AHX
560-0091	N32PB
560-0092	N719RM
560-0092A	N592VP
560-0093	N93EA
560-0094	N94VP
560-0095	N404G
560-0096	N10TD
560-0097	N898CB
560-0098	N59DF
560-0099	N565EJ
560-0100	N560AF
560-0101	N560EP
560-0102	N555PG
560-0103	N98E
560-0104	N815CM
560-0105	N560MH
560-0106	N525RD
560-0107	N365EA
560-0108	N573BB
560-0109	N480RL
560-0109A	N4MM
560-0110	N26DY
560-0111	OE-GAA
560-0112	N560G
560-0113	N113VP
560-0114	D-CZAR
560-0115	N87JK
560-0116	N49NS
560-0117	D-CMEI
560-0118	N900PS
560-0119	F-GLIM
560-0120	N560PS
560-0121	N960CD
560-0122	N510MT
560-0123	N583CW
560-0124	OB-1626
560-0125	OE-GCC
560-0126	LV-RED
560-0127	XA-...
560-0128	N504BW
560-0129	N22AF
560-0130	N14VF
560-0131	N223JV
560-0132	N521LF
560-0133	N560PK
560-0134	YV-811CP
560-0135	N560RL
560-0136	N560PA
560-0137	N137JC
560-0138	N511WV
560-0139	N59NH
560-0140	N24JD
560-0141	N141AQ
560-0142	N560GT
560-0143	N10TB
560-0144	N500VC
560-0145	D-CFLY
560-0146	N500AT
560-0147	N147RJ
560-0148	N115K
560-0149	N565JW
560-0150	N191VE
560-0151	V5-CDM
560-0152	ZS-NDX
560-0153	OO-SKV
560-0154	N154VP
560-0155	N155VP
560-0156	N75B
560-0157	N88WC
560-0158	N560RP
560-0159	D-CLEO
560-0160	N458CK
560-0161	TR 20-01
560-0162	XA-SDT
560-0163	N953C
560-0164	N570EJ
560-0165	N24HX
560-0166	HB-VMV
560-0167	N311DG

c/n	Reg
560-0168	N168CV
560-0169	N80AB
560-0170	N814CM
560-0171	N567F
560-0172	N560BP
560-0173	N918BD
560-0174	N164TC
560-0175	N49LD
560-0176	N661AJ
560-0177	N650CM
560-0178	N997EA
560-0179	N65RL
560-0180	N550WW
560-0181	N181GA
560-0182	C-FCRH
560-0183	N83RE
560-0184	N410DM
560-0185	N939TW
560-0186	N586CC
560-0187	N922AC
560-0188	N395R
560-0189	N63JG
560-0190	N303CB
560-0191	N45KB
560-0192	N3444B
560-0193	TR 20-02
560-0194	N413CK
560-0195	PT-ORC
560-0196	N560RW
560-0197	XA-SJC
560-0198	N598CW
560-0199	N4895Q
560-0200	OE-GDA
560-0201	N255RM
560-0202	ZS-NGL
560-0203	N9700T
560-0204	N1000W
560-0205	F-GLYC
560-0206	N900E
560-0207	N560CK
560-0208	N208VP
560-0209	N209CV
560-0210	N277RC
560-0211	N250SR
560-0212	TC-LAA
560-0213	PT-OTS
560-0214	OE-GCP
560-0215	N315EJ
560-0216	TC-LAB
560-0217	N802AB
560-0218	N561AC
560-0219	N229VP
560-0220	N73KH
560-0221	N626RB
560-0222	N1286C
560-0223	N593CW
560-0224	N528KW
560-0225	N525CW
560-0226	N226CV
560-0227	LV-WDR
560-0228	N87GA
560-0229	N193SB
560-0230	N169CP
560-0231	N1CQ
560-0232	N502E
560-0233	0233
560-0234	N234AQ
560-0235	N633SA
560-0236	N506E
560-0237	N237VP
560-0238	N194SA
560-0239	N93CV
560-0240	N966JM
560-0241	ZS-NGS
560-0242	N826AC
560-0243	D-CAMS
560-0244	N60RD
560-0245	N508KD
560-0246	LV-WGY
560-0247	N94TX
560-0248	N50DR

560-0249	N2000X	560-0330	N330VP	560-0416	N561CC	560-0498	N26QT	560-0563	N59KG
560-0250	N205CM	560-0331	N331QS	560-0417	N560RV*	560-0499	N556BG	560-0564	N7895Q
560-0251	LV-WGO	560-0332	N332LC	560-0418	N318QS	560-0500	N960CR	560-0566	C-FAMI
560-0252	N44GT	560-0333	N333QS	560-0419	EC-GOV	560-0501	98-0007	560-0568	N155JH
560-0253	N553CW	560-0334	N4TL	560-0420	96-0110	560-0502	D2-EBA	560-0569	N600LF
560-0254	N710MT	560-0335	N335QS	560-0421	N322QS	560-0503	N204BG	560-0571	N3616
560-0255	N355EJ	560-0336	N336QS	560-0422	N59TF	560-0504	N504CC	560-0572	N174JS
560-0256	N356SA	560-0337	N108LJ	560-0423	N324QS	560-0505	98-0008	560-0573	C-FALI
560-0257	N155PT	560-0338	N338R	560-0424	N325QS	560-0506	G-OGRG	560-0575	N156JH
560-0258	PP-ISJ	560-0339	N339QS	560-0425	96-0111	560-0507	N1129L	560-0576	N200JR
560-0259	N56GA	560-0340	N21CV	560-0426	N573AB	560-0508	98-0009	560-0578	D-CAUW
560-0260	N883RT	560-0341	N341QS	560-0427	N328QS	560-0509	N309QS	560-0579	N579CE
560-0261	N135WC	560-0342	N86CW	560-0428	N392QS	560-0510	N399QS	560-0580	N1871R
560-0262	N444GG	560-0343	N303QS	560-0429	N560TA	560-0511	N200NK	560-0581	N157JH
560-0263	N560GS	560-0344	N344QS	560-0430	N76TF	560-0512	N10AU	560-0582	N560CX
560-0264	N294RT	560-0345	N75Z	560-0431	N564TJ	560-0513	98-0010	560-0583	N583CE
560-0265	N86CE	560-0346	C-GFCL	560-0432	N88EX	560-0514	N340QS	560-0584	N7HB
560-0266	N306QS	560-0347	N72FC	560-0433	N334QS	560-0515	VH-PSU	560-0585	N221VP
560-0267	N267WG	560-0348	N348QS	560-0434	N410NA	560-0516	N316QS	560-0586	N201SU
560-0268	N750FL	560-0349	JA001A	560-0435	N560BJ	560-0517	OE-GCB	560-0587	N120SB
560-0269	C-GRCC	560-0351	C-GAWR	560-0436	N337QS	560-0518	JA02AA	560-0588	C-GJEI
560-0270	N4FC	560-0352	N352QS	560-0437	N438MC	560-0519	N319QS	560-0590	OE-GPH
560-0271	HB-VNB	560-0353	N20SM*	560-0438	N6NY	560-0520	N101KP	560-0591	N591DK
560-0272	N672SA	560-0354	N4200K	560-0439	N400MC	560-0521	N22LQ	660 0603	N300AK
560-0273	N861CE	560-0355	HK-4304	560-0440	N314QS	560-0522	N398QS	560-0594	N560MR
560-0274	N511DR	560-0356	N354QS	560-0441	N888SV	560-0523	N332QS	560-0595	N560TE
560-0275	N560LT	560-0357	N347QS	560-0442	N568RL	560-0524	165740	560-0596	N844HS
560-0276	N376QS	560-0358	N284CP	560-0443	N343QS	560-0525	N593M	560-0597	JA002A
560-0277	N130WC	560-0359	N416BA	560-0444	N345QS	560-0526	N326QS	560-0598	N800QS
560-0278	N560EM	560-0360	N62WA	560-0445	HB-VLZ	560-0527	N102KP	560-0599	N288HL
560-0279	N594M*	560-0361	N361QS	560-0446	N261WR	560-0528	N52WF	560-0600	PR-LAM
560-0280	HB-VNA	560-0362	OE-GMI	560-0447	C-GSUN	560-0529	165741	560-0601	N801QS
560-0281	N281VP	560-0363	N59KC	560-0448	N75WP	560-0530	N353QS	560-0602	N9CN
560-0282	D-CBEN	560-0364	N560A	560-0449	PT-XCF	560-0531	wo	560-0603	N313HC
560-0283	N1CH	560-0366	SX-DCI	560-0450	N351QS	560-0532	99-0100	560-0604	N911CB
560-0284	N966SW	560-0367	N367QS	560-0451	97-0101	560-0533	N591M	560-0605	N250AL
560-0285	N285CC	560-0368	N343CC	560-0452	N400LX	560-0534	99-0101	560-0606	N91AG
560-0286	N31NS	560-0369	N680GW	560-0453	N454RT	560-0535	N403ET	560-0607	ZS-UCH
560-0287	N863RD	560-0370	N749DC	560-0454	N358QS	560-0536	N363QS	560-0608	N608CE
560-0288	N522JA	560-0371	N315CS	560-0455	97-0102	560-0537	G-TTFN	560-0609	N242AC
560-0289	LV-WLS	560-0372	N372QS	560-0456	G-GRGS	560-0538	99-0102	560-0610	N804QS
560-0290	N97BH	560-0373	N373QS	560-0457	LV-YMA	560-0545	99-0103	560-0611	N560CH
560-0291	N470DP	560-0375	N375QS	560-0458	N79PM	560-0548	99-0104	560-0612	N89MD
560-0292	HL7501	560-0376	N600EF	560-0459	N360QS	560-0565	00-1051	560-0613	N44SH
560-0293	N50CV*	560-0377	N377QS	560-0460	N61TL	560-0567	wo	560-0614	N806QS
560-0294	HL7502	560-0378	N808TH	560-0461	97-0103	560-0570	165939	560-0615	N152JH
560-0295	N295BM	560-0379	C-GWCR	560-0462	D-CEMG	560-0574	00-1052	560-0616	N80GR
560-0296	N560LC	560-0380	N147SB*	560-0463	N420DM	560-0577	00-1053	560-0617	N807QS
560-0297	HL7503	560-0382	N382QS	560-0464	N848G	560-0589	01-0301	560-0618	N933PB
560-0298	N112CW	560-0383	N631M	560-0465	N366QS	560-0592	166374	560-0619	N808QS
560-0299	VT-EUX	560-0384	N950TC	560-0466	ZS-OFM	560-0630	166474	560-0620	N101WY
560-0300	HL7504	560-0385	N333WM	560-0467	97-0104	560-0649	03-0016	560-0621	N102WY
560-0301	N560AG	560-0387	95-0123	560-0468	N469DN	560-0651	166500	560-0622	N560KL
560-0302	N302EJ	560-0388	N92SS	560-0469	N44FG	560-0667	03-0726	560-0623	N977MR
560-0303	N190JK	560-0389	N118RK	560-0470	N371QS	560-0672	166712	560-0624	N500MG
560-0304	N401KH	560-0390	N560SE	560-0471	97-0105	560-0677	166713	560-0625	N810QS
560-0305	LV-WMT	560-0391	N92DE	560-0472	N1CF	*Citation Encore*		560-0626	N41VP
560-0306	N306TR	560-0392	95-0124	560-0473	N321GG	707	N560VU	560-0627	N191VF
560-0307	N307QS	560-0393	N393QS	560-0474	N340QS	560-0539	N303CP	560-0628	N812QS
560-0308	PT-WFD	560-0394	N394QS	560-0475	N941RM	560-0540	N154JS	560-0629	N844QS
560-0309	N560RN	560-0395	N15SK	560-0476	N50GP	560-0541	N541CV	560-0631	N8130S
560-0310	N868JT	560-0396	N396QS	560-0477	N70BR	560-0542	N12MW	560-0632	N109WS
560-0311	N311QS	560-0397	N44LV	560-0478	N379QS	560-0543	N543LE	560-0633	N427CD
560-0312	N312QS	560-0398	ZS-NUZ	560-0479	N560VR	560-0544	D-CASA	560-0634	N90NB
560-0313	N313CV	560-0399	N560WD	560-0480	C-GXCG	560-0546	N368BE	560-0635	N535CE
560-0314	C-FYMM	560-0400	N42ND	560-0481	N44LQ	560-0547	N906AS	560-0636	N83TF
560-0315	N315QS	560-0401	VP-CSN	560-0482	N383QS	560-0549	N33TS	560-0637	CS-DIG
560-0316	N12RN	560-0402	N302QS	560-0483	C-GYMM	560-0550	N865M	560-0638	N23YZ
560-0317	N317QS	560-0403	JA01TM	560-0484	N998SA	560-0551	N560RG	560-0639	N24GF
560-0318	N877RB	560-0404	96-0107	560-0485	N386QS	560-0552	N552HV	560-0640	N800BW
560-0319	N2RC	560-0405	N45TP	560-0486	N43KW	560-0553	G-KDMA	560-0641	N67GW
560-0320	VH-SMF	560-0406	PT-WMZ	560-0487	N555WL	560-0554	N749RL	560-0642	N642LF
560-0321	N320QS	560-0407	N560RK	560-0488	N66U	560-0555	N154JH	560-0643	N960JH
560-0322	N300QS	560-0408	N304QS	560-0489	N390QS	560-0556	N539WA	560-0644	N95NB
560-0323	N323QS	560-0409	PT-WVH	560-0490	N484MM	560-0557	N557PG	560-0645	N299DH
560-0324	N342QS	560-0410	96-0108	560-0491	N85EB	560-0558	N558CG	560-0646	N535BP
560-0325	N313QS	560-0411	N38NS	560-0492	N391QS	560-0559	N359EC	560-0647	C-GDSH
560-0326	N200SC	560-0412	N513EF	560-0493	N452AJ	560-0560	N560JW	560-0648	C-GTOG
560-0327	N327QS	560-0413	N561JS	560-0494	98-0006	560-0561	N511TH	560-0650	N820QS
560-0328	N554EJ	560-0414	ZS-CDS	560-0495	N395QS	560-0562	N60NF	560-0652	N652NR
560-0329	N330QS	560-0415	96-0109	560-0496	OE-GCD			560-0653	PR-SCR

Serial	Reg	Serial	Reg	Serial	Reg	Serial	Reg	Serial	Reg
560-0654	N654CE	560-5054	N80X	560-5135	N885BB	560-5216	CS-DNY	560-5297	N821DG
560-0655	N825QS	560-5055	N488CP	560-5136	N522RA	560-5217	OY-EKC	560-5298	C-GSEC
560-0656	N656Z	560-5056	SE-RBX	560-5137	N637QS	560-5218	P4-ALM	560-5299	N623QS
560-0657	N778BC	560-5057	N240B	560-5138	N924JE	560-5219	N877RF	560-5300	N613GY
560-0658	N560RM	560-5058	HB-VNC	560-5139	N639QS	560-5220	N318MM	560-5301	N601QS
560-0659	N191KL	560-5059	N55HA	560-5140	N884B	560-5221	CS-DNW	560-5302	N624QS
560-0660	N844TM	560-5060	PT-WYU	560-5141	N701CR	560-5222	N2HB	560-5303	N1867M
560-0661	N591CF	560-5061	HB-VMO	560-5142	N705SG	560-5223	PR-EMS	560-5304	N636QS
560-0662	N560CR	560-5062	N22KW	560-5143	N1836S	560-5224	N146EP	560-5305	N628QS
560-0663	N357BE	560-5063	N56HA	560-5144	N52MW	560-5225	N351WC	560-5306	N629QS
560-0664	N664CE	560-5064	N555WF	560-5145	N645QS	560-5226	N350WC	560-5307	XA-DRM
560-0665	OE-GEJ	560-5065	N100SC	560-5146	N291DV	560-5227	N627QS	560-5308	N608QS
560-0666	N700JR	560-5066	HB-VMU	560-5147	N24UD	560-5228	G-IPAX	560-5309	C-GMKZ
560-0668	N560TG	560-5067	OE-GPZ	560-5148	N777FH	560-5229	N504CS	560-5310	N509CS
560-0669	N834QS	560-5068	N57HA	560-5149	N627XL	560-5230	G-NETA	560-5311	N560JP
560-0670	N670CE	560-5069	N404SB	560-5150	N650QS	560-5231	N417JD	560-5312	N612QS
560-0671	N600BW	560-5070	N789CN	560-5151	N79PF	560-5232	N34WP	560-5314	CS-DFO
560-0673	N96NB	560-5071	N671QS	560-5152	N652QS	560-5233	N233XL	560-5315	CS-DFP
560-0674	N552TC	560-5072	N565AB	560-5153	N916CS	560-5234	C-FCXL	560-5316	D-CWWW
560-0675	N29QC	560-5073	N121TL	560-5154	HB-VNI	560-5235	CS-DNZ	560-5317	N57WP
560-0676	N227WS	560-5074	4X-CPU	560-5155	N1837S	560-5236	N236LD	560-5318	N102FS
560-0678	N399HS	560-5075	N558R	560-5156	N2ZC	560-5237	N751PL	560-5319	N625QS
560-0680	N595MA	560-5076	N521RA	560-5157	OH-ONE	560-5238	N238SM	560-5320	N66W
560-0681	N681CE	560-5077	N46VE	560-5158	N917EE	560-5239	N626AT	560-5321	N605QS
560-0683	F-HILM*	560-5078	C-FPWC	560-5159	N326MA	560-5240	N640QS	560-5322	N1838S
Citation Excel/XLS		560-5079	ZS-OHZ	560-5160	N903FH	560-5241	N100AR	560-5323	N560RS
706	N560XL	560-5080	N90CF	560-5161	N404MM	560-5242	TC-LMA	560-5324	N511CS
560-5001	N561XL	560-5081	N4000K	560-5162	N168BG	560-5243	N243CH	560-5325	N568DM
560-5002	N12L	560-5082	N145SM	560-5163	N63LX	560-5244	N898MC	560-5326	N512CS
560-5003	PT-FPP	560-5083	N520G	560-5164	N64LX	560-5245	N245J	560-5327	N175WS
560-5004	AP-...	560-5084	N684QS	560-5165	N665QS	560-5246	N646QS	560-5328	N514CS
560-5005	N77UW	560-5085	N883PF	560-5166	N580RC	560-5247	N57RL	560-5329	N848DM
560-5006	N8005	560-5086	N394WJ	560-5167	G-REDS	560-5248	OO-FPA	560-5330	N395WJ
560-5007	N97VN	560-5087	PT-MSK	560-5168	N780CS	560-5249	N80LP	560-5331	N946TC
560-5008	N944AH	560-5088	VP-BSD	560-5169	N923PC	560-5250	N25NG	560-5332	N727YB
560-5009	N398RS	560-5089	N21MA	560-5170	N670QS	560-5251	N651QS	560-5333	N2
560-5010	N27XL	560-5090	N690QS	560-5171	N632BL	560-5252	N505CS	560-5334	CS-DFQ
560-5011	N560L	560-5091	N83SD	560-5172	HB-VNH	560-5253	C-FTIL	560-5335	N515CS
560-5012	N560CE	560-5092	N692QS	560-5173	N5173F	560-5254	N631RP	560-5336	N336XL
560-5013	N1PB	560-5093	N19MK	560-5174	N624AT	560-5255	N60AG	560-5337	N198DF
560-5014	N989TW	560-5094	N1094L	560-5175	N625AT	560-5256	PR-GAM	560-5338	N606QS
560-5015	N523KW	560-5095	N95XL	560-5176	N676QS	560-5257	CS-DFM	560-5339	OE-GNW
560-5016	N615RG	560-5096	C-GCXL	560-5177	N841DW	560-5258	C-GWII	560-5340	N607QS
560-5017	N500PX	560-5097	C-GLMI	560-5178	N562TS	560-5259	G-XLMB	560-5341	N3
560-5018	N223AM	560-5098	N502BC	560-5179	N188WS	560-5260	N527SC	560-5342	N777JV
560-5019	N990DK	560-5099	N58HA	560-5180	N868JB	560-5261	N75TP	560-5343	G-WINA
560-5020	PT-XCL	560-5100	N49MJ	560-5181	N681QS	560-5262	N662QS	560-5344	I-CMAL
560-5021	D-CMIC	560-5101	N81SH	560-5182	N563CH	560-5263	N663QS	560-5345	N616QS
560-5022	HZ-FYZ	560-5102	N997CB	560-5183	G-IAMS	560-5264	N664QS	560-5346	N346XL
560-5023	N236LB	560-5103	N68HC	560-5184	N531RC	560-5265	OE-GPA	560-5347	N47HF
560-5024	N622PC	560-5104	LX-JCD	560-5185	G-SIRS	560-5266	G-CBRG	560-5348	N470SK
560-5025	N534CC	560-5105	PP-JGV	560-5186	N186XL	560-5267	N506CS	560-5349	N676BB
560-5026	C-GJRB	560-5106	HB-VND	560-5187	N687QS	560-5268	N668QS	560-5350	LV-AIW
560-5027	N560GB	560-5107	N300SJ	560-5188	N688QS	560-5269	HB-VAA	560-5351	N1HS
560-5028	OO-MLG	560-5108	N562DD	560-5189	OY-GKC	560-5270	N300DA	560-5352	ZS-IDC
560-5029	SE-DYX	560-5109	N58LC	560-5190	N560S	560-5271	LN-SUX	560-5353	EC-ISQ
560-5030	N17AN	560-5110	PH-RSA	560-5191	N767BS	560-5272	N1326A	560-5354	N178BR
560-5031	N560BT	560-5111	N532CC	560-5192	N164AS	560-5273	N617PD	560-5355	CS-DFR
560-5032	N108EK	560-5112	N1129E	560-5193	N811ST	560-5274	PR-ACC	560-5356	XA-UAF
560-5033	N456JW	560-5113	OE-GME	560-5194	N694QS	560-5275	N675QS	560-5357	N567MC
560-5034	PP-RAA	560-5114	N717MB	560-5195	D-CVHI	560-5276	N276A	560-5358	N635QS
560-5035	N4JS	560-5115	N20WE	560-5196	XA-ICO	560-5277	N560CM	560-5359	N659QS
560-5036	N884BB	560-5116	N498AB	560-5197	N697QS	560-5278	N16GS	560-5360	N615QS
560-5037	OE-GTI	560-5117	N202RL	560-5198	N560NY	560-5279	N679QS	560-5361	VP-CGG
560-5038	N404BT	560-5118	B-7019	560-5199	N699QS	560-5280	N621QS	560-5362	N521CS
560-5039	N88WU	560-5119	N75HU	560-5200	C-GXCO	560-5281	N142AA	560-5363	N638QS
560-5040	N840CC	560-5120	PR-AAA	560-5201	N533CC	560-5282	N507CS	560-5364	N522CS
560-5041	N39RC	560-5121	N560CG	560-5202	N50XL	560-5283	CS-DFN	560-5365	N667QS
560-5042	SU-EWC	560-5122	N67TW	560-5203	N603QS	560-5284	N560DE	560-5366	N585PC
560-5043	PT-XIB	560-5123	N59EC	560-5204	N604QS	560-5285	N422AB	560-5367	N677QS
560-5044	N544XL	560-5124	N24NG	560-5205	N503CS	560-5286	N622QS	560-5368	VT-CSP
560-5045	PP-JFM	560-5125	N4JB	560-5206	N206CX	560-5287	N118ST	560-5369	N504PK
560-5046	A9C-BXA	560-5126	N626QS	560-5207	N62GB	560-5288	SX-DCE	560-5370	N770JM
560-5047	N888RT	560-5127	N560KT	560-5208	XA-TKZ	560-5289	PR-NBR	560-5371	N371P
560-5048	VP-CAI	560-5128	PH-CJI	560-5209	HB-VNS	560-5290	N691QS	560-5372	CS-DFS
560-5049	N24PH	560-5129	N359WC	560-5210	N610QS	560-5291	N829JC	560-5501	N633RP
560-5050	N88HP*	560-5130	N630QS	560-5211	PR-VRD	560-5292	N666MX	560-5502	N502XL
560-5051	SX-DCM	560-5131	N631QS	560-5212	N560DP	560-5293	N695QS	560-5503	N503XS
560-5052	N990MF	560-5132	N632QS	560-5213	N24EP	560-5294	N508CS	560-5504	N111GU
560-5053	I-BENT	560-5133	N23NG	560-5214	N57KW	560-5295	N641QS	560-5505	N901DK
		560-5134	N561BP	560-5215	N560TH	560-5296	N696QS	560-5506	N618QS

560-5507	N523CS	650-0036	N651CV	650-0117	F-GGAL	650-0198	XA-...	650-7034	N650K
560-5508	N72SG	650-0037	I-GASD	650-0118	N79KF	650-0199	N890MC	650-7035	N95RX
560-5509	N617QS	650-0038	N373DJ	650-0119	N147TA	**650 Citation VI**		650-7036	N77HF
560-5510	N357EC	650-0039	XA-KMX	650-0120	N907DF	650-0200	wo	650-7037	N95TX
560-5511	N670MW	650-0040	N650WE	650-0121	N24VB	650-0201	N1419J	650-7038	PR-PTL
560-5512	CS-DFT	650-0041	N55BH	650-0122	N122EJ	650-0202	N65BP	650-7039	OY-GGG
560-5513	N196SB	650-0042	C-GPOP	650-0123	N59FT	650-0203	N350M	650-7040	N504T
560-5514	N143DH	650-0043	N953JF	650-0124	N650HC	650-0204	N108WV	650-7041	N430SA
560-5515	N361EC*	650-0044	N126MT	650-0125	N170HL	650-0205	PT-OMU	650-7042	N657T
560-5516	N540CS	650-0045	N689W	650-0126	N101PG	650-0206	N39H	650-7043	N44M
560-5517	N52639	650-0046	N650TT	650-0127	N700MH	650-0207	N107CG	650-7044	N650CJ
560-5518	N602QS	650-0047	N711VH	650-0128	N125Q	650-0208	N500FR	650-7045	CC-CPS
560-5519	N43HF	650-0048	N650MM	650-0129	N125N	650-0209	N902VP	650-7046	N747TX
560-5520	CS-DFU	650-0049	N30AF	650-0130	N130TS	650-0210	N783H	650-7047	N198TX
560-5521	N541CS	650-0050	N51JV	650-0131	303	650-0211	N211CC	650-7048	N18GB
560-5522	N609QS	650-0051	N777MX	650-0132	N49SM	650-0212	N972VZ	650-7049	N750FB
560-5523	N542CS	650-0052	XA-SDU	650-0133	N213HP	650-0213	N900UD*	650-7050	N83GK
560-5524	N546CS	650-0053	N306PA	650-0134	D-CARE	650-0214	N7777B	650-7051	N77LX
560-5525	N370BA	650-0054	N47AN	650-0135	VP-CAR	650-0215	N650GC	650-7052	N24KT
560-5526	N633QS	650-0055	N652CV	650-0136	N3170B*	650-0216	I-BLUB	650-7053	N650AT
560-5527	N713DH	650-0056	N78AP	650-0137	N4Y	650-0217	PH-MEX	650-7054	LV-WTN
560-5528	N456SL*	650-0057	N400PC	650-0138	N717JM	650-0218	XA-ACH	650-7055	D-CMPI
560-5529	OE-GEG	650-0058	N143PL*	650-0139	N96CP	650-0219	N650TS	650-7056	N444EX
560-5530	N4107W	650-0059	N370TP	650-0140	N1400M	650-0220	B-7022	650-7057	N361EE
560-5531	N560JG	650-0060	OY-JPJ	650-0141	N140TS	650-0221	wo	650-7058	N98XS
560-5532	N562DB	650-0061	N450RS	650-0142	D-CRHR	650-0222	N738K	650-7059	N144MH
560-5533	N711NK	650-0062	N84PH	650-0143	N40FC	650-0223	N111Y	650-7060	N55SC
560-5534	N424HH	650-0063	N651AT	650-0144	N384CW	650-0224	N1UP	650-7061	N102CE
560-5535	PR-...	650-0064	N444CW	650-0145	N385CW	650-0225	N606AT	650-7062	N876G
560-5536	N25XL	650-0065	C-FIMO	650-0146	N650FC	650-0226	N400JH	650-7063	N877G
560-5537	I-TAKA	650-0066	N650CD	650-0147	N151DR	650-0227	N2UP	650-7064	N5117
560-5538	N538XL	650-0067	N232CF	650-0148	N7HF	650-0228	XA-SLB	650-7065	N96MT
560-5539	B-3642	650-0068	XA-TMZ	650-0149	D-CBPL	650-0229	TC-ANT	650-7066	N669W
560-5540	B-3643	650-0069	XB-GRN	650-0150	N61CK	650-0230	N660PA*	650-7067	C-FTOR
560-5541	N560JC	650-0070	OY-NLA	650-0151	N321AR	650-0231	N400WK	650-7068	N7AB
560-5542	N547CS	650-0071	N97DD	650-0152	N255VP	650-0232	N711LV	650-7069	XA-TMX
560-5543	N5165T	650-0072	N139MY	650-0153	N777ZC	650-0233	CC-DAC	650-7070	OY-CKE
560-5545	N5269S	650-0073	XA-LEY	650-0154	N650CH	650-0234	XA-...	650-7071	HS-DCG
560-5546	N549CS	650-0074	N93CL	650-0155	N97AL	650-0235	N235SV	650-7072	N35HS
560-5547	N647QS	650-0075	N85MS	650-0156	N74VF	650-0236	N600JD	650-7073	XA-UAM
560-5548	N611QS	650-0076	N424LB	650-0157	N650RP	650-0237	N650W	650-7074	PT-WLY
560-5551	N550CS	650-0077	N800GM	650-0158	N135HC	650-0238	N19QC	650-7075	N711GF
560-5556	N385MG	650-0078	N650KB	650-0159	N359CW	650-0239	N68ED	650-7076	N286MC
560-5570	N10VQ	650-0079	N217RJ	650-0160	N220CM	650-0240	D-CAKE	650-7077	VP-CGE
650 Citation III		650-0080	N69LD	650-0161	N510SD	650-0241	N651EJ	650-7078	N788R
650-0001	N651CG	650-0081	N910DP	650-0162	N660Q	**650 Citation VII**		650-7079	N779QS
650-0002	N650AS	650-0082	N825JW	650-0163	N163JM	697	wfu	650-7080	CS-DNF
650-0003	N166MC	650-0083	N5NR	650-0164	N364CW	650-7001	N701HA	650-7081	CS-DNG
650-0004	N650LA	650-0084	N650CB	650-0165	XC-PGN	650-7002	N19SV	650-7082	N782QS
650-0005	N700RY	650-0085	wo	650-0166	PT-LTB	650-7003	N888TX	650-7083	PT-WQH
650-0006	N27TS	650-0086	PT-LHC	650-0167	N88DJ	650-7004	N174VP*	650-7084	TC-KON
650-0007	N719HG	650-0087	PP-AIO	650-0168	N175J	650-7005	N200LH	650-7085	N785QS
650-0008	N777XS	650-0088	N650TA	650-0169	N73HM	650-7006	OE-GCH	650-7086	N860W
650-0009	N933SH	650-0089	N86VP	650-0170	N650BA*	650-7007	N28TX	650-7087	N787QS
650-0010	N650LW	650-0090	N555DH	650-0171	PT-LVF	650-7008	N16KB	650-7088	N499SA
650-0011	N311CW	650-0091	PT-LUE	650-0172	N934H	650-7009	N711NB	650-7089	N789QS
650-0012	OE-GCO	650-0092	N692BE	650-0173	N173VP	650-7010	N150JP	650-7090	N790QS
650-0013	N377JE	650-0093	N196SD	650-0174	D-CLUE	650-7011	SE-DVY	650-7091	N791QS
650-0014	OE-GCN	650-0094	N926HC	650-0175	N175SR	650-7012	N817MB	650-7092	N792QS
650-0015	N766MH	650-0095	N883KB	650-0176	N176AF	650-7013	N2NT	650-7093	C3-DNE
650-0016	N316CW	650-0096	N629RM	650-0177	N834H	650-7014	N865EC*	650-7094	N794QS
650-0017	N651BP	650-0097	N697MC	650-0178	N57CE	650-7015	N817MQ	650-7095	N795QS
650-0018	N650SB	650-0098	N398CW	650-0179	N63GC	650-7016	N650CP	650-7096	N287MC
650-0019	N71LU*	650-0099	N403CB	650-0180	N498CS	650-7017	N775M	650-7097	N797QS
650-0020	N650WB	650-0100	N202JK	650-0181	N650DR	650-7018	N623PM	650-7098	N1254C
650-0021	N460CP	650-0101	N9NL	650-0182	N49JB	650-7019	XA-TRE	650-7099	PT-XFG
650-0022	N650J	650-0102	N24237	650-0183	N820FJ	650-7020	N832CB	650-7100	N710QS
650-0023	N650CG	650-0103	N2411A	650-0184	N650VW	650-7021	PT-MGS	650-7101	N650JL*
650-0024	N422BC	650-0104	C-GOXB	650-0185	4X-CMR	650-7022	N902F	650-7102	D-CNCJ
650-0025	N16SU	650-0105	I-FEEV	650-0186	N386CW	650-7023	N6110	650-7103	N713QS
650-0026	wfu	650-0106	N650CE	650-0187	D-CRRR	650-7024	93-004	650-7104	VH-ING
650-0027	N433LF	650-0107	N397CW	650-0188	N650FP	650-7025	N68BC	650-7105	N715QS
650-0028	N650BW	650-0108	N650Z	650-0189	XA-RGS	650-7026	93-005	650-7106	N71NK
650-0029	N89AC	650-0109	N106ST	650-0190	D-C...	650-7027	N900MN	650-7107	N559AM
650-0030	N380CW	650-0110	N303PC	650-0191	N650SG	650-7028	XA-SPQ	650-7108	N202AV
650-0031	N1ZC	650-0111	N381CW	650-0192	LN-AAU	650-7029	N650RL	650-7109	wo
650-0032	XA-HVP	650-0112	N598C	650-0193	N650CC	650-7030	N95CC	650-7110	OE-GLS
650-0033	wo	650-0113	N393CW	650-0194	N831GA	650-7031	N4QN	650-7111	PR-AJG
650-0034	N650GH	650-0114	N650DA	650-0195	N800MC	650-7032	XA-XIS	650-7112	N257W
650-0035	N408JD	650-0115	N541S	650-0196	N534H	650-7033	PT-OVU	650-7113	N650JB
		650-0116	C-FJJG	650-0197	N840FH			650-7114	N926CB*

650-7115	N314SL	750-0046	N749P	750-0127	N15TT	750-0208	N997QS	22	VP-BBV
650-7116	N175DP	750-0047	N947QS	750-0128	N1873	750-0209	N7SB	23	N90LC
650-7117	N33D	750-0048	N84PJ	750-0129	N929QS	750-0210	N904QS	24	N69GB*
650-7118	N33L	750-0049	N949QS	750-0130	N930QS	750-0211	N65ST	25	N177BC
650-7119	N651CC	750-0050	N950QS	750-0131	C-GAPT	750-0212	N69SB	26	N720DF
680 Sovereign		750-0051	N119RM	750-0132	N627R	750-0213	N9NG	27	XA-AAY
709	N680CS	750-0052	N712JC	750-0133	N933QS	750-0214	OE-HGG	28	N42EH
680-0001	N681CS	750-0053	N795HG	750-0134	CS-DCT	750-0215	VH-TEN	29	N404JW
680-0002	N747RL	750-0054	N450T	750-0135	N935QS	750-0216	N882KB	30	wfu
680-0003	N103SV	750-0055	N955QS	750-0136	N1DH	750-0217	N217AL	31	N27AJ
680-0004	XA-GMO	750-0056	PP-JQM	750-0137	N937QS	750-0218	D-BLDI	32	32
680-0005	N105SV	750-0057	N505MA	750-0138	N138SP	750-0219	D-BKLI	33	N33BV
680-0006	N409GB	750-0058	N758CX	750-0139	N26MJ	750-0220	N48HF	34	N18SK
680-0007	N604CS	750-0059	N751BH	750-0140	D-BLUE	750-0221	N256W	35	N726MR
680-0008	N900EB	750-0060	PR-JAQ	750-0141	N941QS	750-0222	N850PT*	36	XA-MMM
680-0009	N682DB	750-0061	N961QS	750-0142	N700SW	750-0223	N918QS	37	wfu
680-0010	N301QS	750-0062	N724CC	750-0143	N825GA	750-0224	N919QS	38	F-GBRF
680-0011	N338QS	750-0063	N750JB	750-0144	N944QS	750-0225	N215RX	39	wo
680-0012	N61DF*	750-0064	N931QS	750-0145	N145CX	750-0226	N226CX	40	XA-LIO
680-0013	N346QS	750-0065	N750JJ	750-0146	N750DM	750-0227	P4-LJG	41	N34TJ
680-0014	N5270K	750-0066	N750GM	750-0147	N147CX	750-0228	N228DB	42	N282T
680-0015	N272MH	750-0067	N967QS	750-0148	N700LH	750-0229	N229CE	43	N17TJ
680-0016	N616CS	750-0068	N377SF	750-0149	N948QS	750-0230	N750WM	44	C-FZOP
680-0017	N757EG	750-0069	N96TX	750-0150	N750TX	750-0231	N432AC	45	N444CR
680-0018	N79PG	750-0070	N970QS	750-0151	N951QS	750-0232	OE-...	46	N401JW
680-0019	N63TM	750-0071	N971QS	750-0152	N934BD	750-0233	N442WT	47	wo
680-0020	N914SP	750-0072	N72FD	750-0153	N953QS	750-0234	N52526	48	N20LW
680-0021	N621SV*	750-0073	N269JR	750-0154	N8JC	750-0235	N400JD	49	N67LC
680-0023	N44SH*	750-0074	N7418F	750-0155	N73ME	750-0236	N53HF	50	N299DB
680-0024	N565A	750-0075	N21HQ	750-0156	N956QS	750-0237	N5228J	51	N909TF
680-0025	N680AR	750-0076	N400RB	750-0157	B-7021	750-0238	N5183U	52	N711TF
680-0026	N5260Y	750-0077	N977QS	750-0158	N958QS	750-0239	N5268V	53	N53WA
680-0030	N680PH	750-0078	N711HQ	750-0159	N7600G	**Citation T-47A**		54	N110LA
750 Citation X		750-0079	N979QS	750-0160	N960QS	552-0001	wo	55	N700AL
703	N750CX	750-0080	ZS-SAB	750-0161	I-KETO	552-0002	wo	56	N297PF
750-0001	N754SE	750-0081	N1BS	750-0162	N903QS	552-0003	wo	57	wo
750-0002	N902QS	750-0082	N82BG	750-0163	N610GR	552-0004	wo	58	N170CS
750-0003	N200AP	750-0083	N983QS	750-0164	N640QS	552-0005	wo	59	N52JA
750-0004	N62VE	750-0084	N984QS	750-0165	N15RL	552-0006	wo	60	N769BH
750-0005	N99BB	750-0085	D-BTEN	750-0166	N966QS	552-0007	wo	61	wo
750-0006	N706VP	750-0086	N986QS	750-0167	N721VT	552-0008	wo	62	N6VG
750-0007	N750EC	750-0087	N987QS	750-0168	N123SL	552-0009	wo	63	N876MA
750-0008	N750CW	750-0088	N88EJ	750-0169	N68LP	552-0010	wo	64	N444WJ
750-0009	N909QS	750-0089	N989QS	750-0170	N90NF	552-0011	wo	65	N66CF
750-0010	N5112	750-0090	C-GCUL	750-0171	N399W	552-0012	wfu	66	N63TS
750-0011	N944D	750-0091	N991CX	750-0172	N750NS	552-0013	wo	67	N427CJ
750-0012	N912QS	750-0092	PT-WUM	750-0173	N749DX	552-0014	wfu	68	F-GFPF
750-0013	N5113	750-0093	N71RP	750-0174	N87SL	552-0015	wo	69	N711JC
750-0014	N478PM	750-0094	N750XX	750-0175	N975QS	**Citation OT-47B**		70	N349JC
750-0015	N915QS	750-0095	N415FW	750-0176	N1AP	560-0350	FAC-5760	71	N190H
750-0016	N521FP	750-0096	N585M	750-0177	N177EL	560-0365	721	72	ZS-FOX
750-0017	N5114	750-0097	C-GIGT	750-0178	N750BL	560-0374	FAC-5761	73	N378C
750-0018	N5115	750-0098	N998CX	750-0179	HB-JEZ	560-0381	N5373D	74	N55FJ
750-0019	N5116	750-0099	N442WJ	750-0180	N353WC	560-0386	N2500B	75	N71TS
750-0020	N8JQ	750-0100	N104CT	750-0181	N181BR	**Dassault**		76	N727TS
750-0021	N61KB	750-0101	N711VT	750-0182	N982QS	*Falcon 10/100*		77	N107TB
750-0022	N750VP	750-0102	N901QS	750-0183	N938QS	01	wo	78	C-FEXD
750-0023	N923QS	750-0103	N750HS	750-0184	I-JETX	1	N333FJ	79	N73B
750-0024	N942QS	750-0104	N5T	750-0185	N185CX	02	wfu	80	N567RA
750-0025	N750RL	750-0105	N905QS	750-0186	N970SK	2	C-GRIS	81	N81TX
750-0026	N926QS	750-0106	N106CX	750-0187	N978QS	03	wfu	82	N101HS
750-0027	N27VP	750-0107	N520CM	750-0188	C-FTEN	3	N52TJ	83	N76MB
750-0028	PR-FNP	750-0108	N908QS	750-0189	N93S	4	N888FJ	84	N106TW
750-0029	N929EJ	750-0109	N750PT	750-0190	N990QS	5	F-BVPR	85	wo
750-0030	N369B	750-0110	N910QS	750-0191	N354WC	6	N59CC	86	wfu
750-0031	N22RG	750-0111	N750BP	750-0192	N5FF	7	N769SC	87	N156BE
750-0032	N932QS	750-0112	N173WF	750-0193	N939QS	8	N108KC	88	N71M
750-0033	N710AW	750-0113	N913QS	750-0194	G-CDCX	9	N510CL	89	N23TJ
750-0034	N934QS	750-0114	N701LX*	750-0195	N946QS	10	wo	90	N12TX
750-0035	N97DK	750-0115	OH-PPI	750-0196	N996QS	11	N419WC	91	N23VP
750-0036	N936QS	750-0116	N916QS	750-0197	N585T	12	N10F	92	N824DS
750-0037	N75HS	750-0117	N426CM	750-0198	N998QS	13	wfu	93	wfu
750-0038	N938CC	750-0118	PR-XDY	750-0199	N484T	14	N333KE	94	N13BK
750-0039	N32NG	750-0119	XA-FMX	750-0200	N952QS	15	wo	95	wo
750-0040	N40KW	750-0120	N920QS	750-0201	N907QS	16	N127WL	96	N115TD
750-0041	C-GIWZ	750-0121	N358WC	750-0202	N300JD	17	F-GNDZ	97	N175FJ
750-0042	N915RB	750-0122	N577JC	750-0203	N999QS	18	N241RS	98	wo
750-0043	N943QS	750-0123	N900QS	750-0204	N22NG	19	N600HL	99	N923HB
750-0044	N96RX	750-0124	N924QS	750-0205	C-GSUX	20	N42G	100	N100FJ
750-0045	N45BR	750-0125	N444CX	750-0206	N906QS	21	N60ND	101	101
		750-0126	N962QS	750-0207	N751GM			102	N908TF

No	Reg	No	Reg	No	Reg	No	Reg	No	Reg
103	N63XG	184	N725DM	36	N818AA	117	N207JS	198	N724DS
104	N800SB	185	185	37	wo	118	N820AA	199	wfu
105	N804JJ	186	N555DZ	38	wfu	119	N20FJ	200	wfu
106	N20CF	187	N5CA	39	XA-RMA	120	N647JP	201	wfu
107	N907TF	188	N84TJ	40	N240TW	121	wfu	202	N9TE
108	wo	189	N189JM	41	041	122	N511FL*	203	N821AA
109	N840GL*	190	C-FBNW	42	wo	123	N223TW	204	N204TW
110	N43US	191	wo	43	wo	124	F-ZACC	205	N585AC
111	N983MC	192	wo	44	N800PP	125	0125	206	N801SC
112	N598JC	193	EC-HVV	45	N589DC	126	wo	207	G-FRAP
113	VP-BGD	194	F-GIPH	46	EC-EHC	127	XB-HRA	208	wo
114	N982MC	195	N1993	47	wo	128	N70CK	209	G-FRAR
115	N169LS	196	N125CA	48	N23ND	129	PR-SUL	210	wo
116	wo	197	N52N	49	wfu	130	wfu	211	N764LA
117	N18MX	198	N91PB	50	N699TW	131	F-ZACD	212	N212R
118	N118AD	199	N60HM	51	wfu	132	G-FFRA	213	G-FRAK
119	N257V	200	N808L	52	D-CLBR	133	wfu	214	G-FRAO
120	N710JC	201	N844F	53	053	134	wo	215	N510BM
121	F-GDLR	202	wo	54	N405JW	135	N800DW	216	5840
122	N104KW*	203	I-FJDC	55	N830AA	136	N20MY	217	17103
123	N110TP	204	XA-TAB	56	N560RA	137	N200GT	218	N218CA
124	wo	205	N606AM	57	N812AA	138	F-ZACR	219	TM 11-3
125	N269SW	206	N46MK	58	wfu	139	N235CA	220	N220CA
126	N36WJ	207	N55DG	60	N900NA*	140	wfu	221	N2211W
127	ZS-SEB	208	F-GSLZ	60	wo	141	UR-CCB	222	TM 11-2
128	P4-AVN	209	OY-PHN	61	N20NY	142	N300BA	223	G-FRAH
129	129	210	N110PP	62	wo	143	5A-DAG	224	G-FRAM
130	N454DP	211	F-GELT	63	wo	144	N385AC	225	C-FONX
131	N133EP	212	CNA-NZ	64	N425JF	145	F-ZACU	226	N226R
132	wfu	213	N711HF	65	N165TW	146	N345FH	227	N227CK
133	133	214	N147G	66	N830RA	147	wfu	228	N823AA
134	VH-MCX	215	F-GHPB	67	N826AA	148	N148TW	229	N229R
135	N272DN	216	SE-DYB	68	N521FL	149	EC-EQP	230	N230CA
136	F-GFMD	217	N68GT	69	N31LT	150	HC-BSS	231	wo
137	C-GTVO	218	N303FZ	70	wfu	151	G-FRAL	232	wo
138	wo	219	N219JW	71	N209CA	152	CNA-NN	233	N817AA
139	N110J	220	N569DW	72	wfu	153	N207CA	234	I-LIAC
140	F-GHDX	221	F-GPFD	73	wfu	154	wo	235	0442
141	N77SF	222	N100YP	74	N8TP	155	N68BP	236	N236TW
142	N174B	223	PT-LVD	75	N217CA	156	wo	237	EC-JDV
143	143	224	SE-DVP	76	F-GJDB	157	C-GRSD	238	F-RAEE
144	N502PG	225	N225CC	77	N844SL	158	N158TW	239	N239BD*
145	N244A	226	N121AT	78	wfu	159	XA-ICG	240	HB-VMN
146	XA-CEG		*Falcon 20/200 Guardian*	79	F-ZACT	160	N301TT	241	N241JC
147	N212FJ	01	wfu	80	N925BE	161	N10RZ	242	N513AC
148	N79TJ	1	wfu	81	N810RA	162	N911DG	243	wo
149	N711FJ	2	wfu	82	G-FRAS	163	N258PE	244	wo
150	N99WA	3	N301R	83	N283SA	164	N164NW	245	wfu
151	N256V	4	wo	84	wfu	165	CNA-NM	246	wfu
152	N999LL	5	N295TW	85	N6555L	166	N71TJ	247	N247PL
153	N81P	6	EC-EDC	86	F-ZACG	167	F-RAEB	248	XC-HIX
154	wfu	7	wfu	87	G-FRAT	168	N168DJ	249	N451DP
155	F-GTOD	8	N612GA	88	wfu	169	XC-SEY	250	N223BG
156	ZS-SEA	9	N611GA	89	N505AJ	170	RA-09004	251	EP-IPA
157	N76AM	10	wfu	90	wfu	171	N217AJ	252	F-ZACA
158	N700FH	11	N216CA	91	N20UA	172	I-LIAB	253	TM 11-1
159	N707AM	12	wfu	92	wfu	173	PK-TRI	254	F-GPAB
160	N160FJ	13	N977TW	93	F-RAED	174	N174BD	255	wo
161	I-CREM	14	N41MH	94	N566YT	175	SU-OAE	256	N15SL
162	N170MK	15	wfu	95	N995CK	176	F-GHDT	257	N18HN
163	N983CC	16	N216SA	96	F-ZACB	177	N82PJ	258	N300SF
164	N222MU	17	N234CA	97	G-FRAU	178	G-FRBA	259	N569D
165	N707CG	18	wfu	98	N998CK	179	XA-ACA	260	F-RAEA
166	N211EC	19	wfu	99	N921ML	180	I-GOBJ	261	N200WK
167	N82CG	20	G-FRAJ	100	wo	181	N5225G	262	OO-MDN
168	N43EC	21	N50446	101	N97WJ	182	F-UKJA	263	F-ZACY
169	PT-WSF	22	F-ZACS	102	N204AN	183	RA-09003	264	XA-III
170	wo	23	5761	103	F-GPAA	184	EC-HCX	265	N265MP
171	N42US	24	N240CK	104	F-ZACW	185	N813LS	266	N184GA
172	N10NC	25	wfu	105	wfu	186	F-UKJE/463	267	N627JG
173	N8LT	26	N819AA	106	wfu	187	N811AA	268	F-RAEF
174	RP-C1911	27	N326VW	107	N107J	188	F-ZACX	269	XA-DUC
175	N12EP	28	wfu	108	N108R	189	wo	270	G-FRAI
176	N231JH	29	LV-WMM	109	C-FIGD	190	5A-DCO	271	F-GKDB
177	N101VJ	30	N123RA	110	wfu	191	N20HF	272	N770RR
178	N87TH	31	N131MV	111	N111BP	192	N192CK	273	N720JC
179	N100RR	32	N232TW	112	UR-NIK	193	N219CA	274	N100AS
180	N211JL	33	wo	113	N22WJ	194	wfu	275	N200CP
181	N138DM	34	wo	114	G-FRAW	195	N822AA	276	CM-01
182	N809F	35	9M-BCR	115	F-UKJG	196	N196TS	277	J 753
183	SE-DLB			116	N770FG	197	C-GTAK	278	CM-02

279	D-CLBE	360	N390AG	441	wfu	5	F-RAFI	86	N960S
280	F-GPAD	361	SU-AYD	442	N747CX	6	wo	87	C-GLRP
281	N341KA	362	wfu	443	wfu	7	7	88	F-GYOL
282	XC-DIP	363	N3VF	444	N244FJ	8	N550CL	89	N156WC
283	wo	364	XA-FLM	445	2128	9	F-GGCP	90	N925GS
284	N501MD	365	N50BV	446	N446D	10	N420CL	91	ZS-CAS
285	N285TW	366	N100AC	447	2129	11	F-GGVB	92	N929ML
286	EP-AGY	367	EP-SEA	448	48	12	CNA-NO	93	N868BT
287	XC-PFJ	368	N15H	449	N39TT	13	N150TX	94	XA-TVQ
288	F-ZACV	369	N138FJ	450	wfu	14	N917SB	95	N101ET
289	N450CP	370	N20WN	451	F-UKJC	15	N350JS	96	C-FMFL
290	N816AA	371	2141	452	2131	16	F-HBBM	97	C-FPDO
291	F-RAEG	372	ST-PRS	453	N520AW	17	N517CW	98	N600WG
292	N510WS	373	N399FG	454	wfu	18	N518EJ	99	N292PC
293	I-GOBZ	374	2101	455	N555SR	19	N519CW	100	N14CG
294	SU-AXN	375	F-ZACZ	456	2133	20	N590CW	101	EP-TFA
295	G-FRAF	376	N1897S	457	N47LP	21	N56LT	102	N350KP
296	N20TX	377	N600CD	458	2134	22	0018	103	N370KP
297	CS-DCK	378	N500JD	459	2135	23	N523CW	104	HB-IGR
298	N827AA	379	N892SB	460	2136	24	N929T	105	N100EG
299	N299JC	380	I-ULJA	461	OH-WIF	25	N753JC*	106	N74TS
300	N600WD	381	N20T	462	wfu	26	N190MQ	107	N253SJ
301	EP-AKC	382	N10AZ	463	N132EP	27	27/F-RAFK	108	N150K
302	F-GOPM	383	N908CH	464	wfu	28	N47UF	109	N280BG
303	wo	384	N82TN	465	65	29	N529MM	110	N77TE
304	9M-BDK	385	N87TN	466	2139	30	30/F-ZVMB	111	F-GMOT
305	N715WS	386	2102	467	2140	31	N987RC*	112	N193TR
306	N205WM	387	N384K	468	J 468	32	N717LA	113	N450DR
307	F-GYPB	388	N502BG	469	J 469	33	N8300E	114	ST-PSR
308	N453SB	389	I-CMUT	470	N500NH	34	F-RAFL	115	N502JB
309	wo	390	2104	471	N911DT	35	XA-FVK	116	N678MA
310	N31FJ	391	N420GL	472	72	36	36	117	N50J
311	F-BVPN	392	N713MC	473	N393S	37	F-HAIR	118	wo
312	N741MR*	393	XC-SON	474	N1HF	38	N993	119	XA-SSS
313	N184TS*	394	2103	475	N475EZ	39	N850EP	120	EP-TFI
314	N314TW	395	wfu	476	1650	40	N156DB	121	N51FE
315	D-CLBB	396	N711WV	477	77	41	N888ME	122	5-9013
316	N424XT	397	F-GBTM	478	N39RP	42	N405DC	123	F-GPSA
317	N939CK	398	2105	479	N240RS	43	YU-BNA	124	N50MV
318	15-2233	399	N21FE	480	80	44	N285CP	125	TS-JAM
319	N205K	400	wo	481	OH-WIN	45	N569BW	126	N200RT
320	EP-FIF	401	N501KC	482	VP-CCL	46	N547K	127	N129JE
321	PH-BPS	402	wfu	483	F-UKJI	47	N37ER	128	N223DD
322	N300CV	403	N960TX	484	N425RJ	48	C-FBVF	129	N99JD
323	XU-008	404	N313K	485	N22FW	49	N978W	130	C-GSRS
324	N312K	405	wfu	486	N6VF	50	XA-GCH	131	F-GOAL
325	N877JG	406	N800FF	487	N387FJ*	51	N551CW	132	132
326	TC-GGG	407	2109	488	N200NP	52	N163WW	133	ZS-CAQ
327	XA-MSA	408	N757CX	489	N489BB*	53	N53FJ	134	F-HALM
328	YK-ASA	409	wfu	490	N917JG	54	N51MJ	135	N293BC
329	D-CMET	410	N200J	491	N500RR	55	N200UP	136	YV-455CP
330	N770MC	411	2110	492	N412AB	56	N84HP	137	N117SF
331	YK-ASB	412	N620A	493	ZS-SOS	57	N505TC	138	N138AV
332	TM 11-4	413	2111	494	N200FJ	58	N744X	139	N7GX
333	15-2235	414	N1881Q	495	N800EG	59	N910CN	140	N750DF
334	EP-FIC	415	2112	496	N202AR	60	N105WC	141	N924WJ
335	N335TW	416	N725JG	497	N20CL	61	HB-IES	142	N4350M
336	5-2802	417	2113	498	N69EC	62	N230BT	143	N444PE
337	YI-AHH	418	2114	499	N14CJ	63	C-FKCI	144	N544RA
338	EP-FID	419	wfu	500	C-GRPM	64	N300A	145	N50KD
339	N38TJ	420	wfu	501	N214AS	65	F-GPPF	146	XA-DUQ
340	5-2803	421	2117	502	HB-VNG	66	9U-BTB	147	N844NX
341	F-GYSL	422	F-RAEH	503	N50MW	67	T-783	148	N50LQ
342	F-RAEC	423	2118	504	VH-CPE	68	5A-DCM	149	N198MR
343	YI-AHJ	424	wfu	505	N45JB	69	N650X	150	N8400E
344	N227WE	425	2120	506	XA-MAM	70	N700MP	151	MM62020
345	OH-FPC	426	HB-VNM	507	N22HS	71	N352WB	152	N75WE
346	5-2804	427	N42WJ	508	N777FC	72	wo	153	N50HM
347	N20VF	428	N148MC	509	N277AT*	73	N573CW	154	N154PA
348	wo	429	N702CA	510	N36DA	74	N83FJ	155	MM62021
349	N287SA	430	N243FJ	511	EC-JBH	75	N78LT	156	N377HW
350	5-3021	431	2121	512	N999TH	76	N450CL	157	N901MK
351	wo	432	N855DG	513	N618GH	77	N77NT	158	N54YR
352	N920G	433	wfu	514	N322RR	78	F-RAFJ	159	HB-ISD
353	wo	434	FAP 300	515	N181RK	79	N60CN	160	N4VF
354	5-9003	435	wfu	*Falcon 50/50EX*		80	N50BZ	161	N770MP
355	N355MC	436	N70PL	1	wfu	81	N718DW	162	N750JC
356	N69SW	437	wfu	2	F-GSER	82	N582EJ	163	N85HP
357	N357PS	438	N258A	3	N728LW	83	N50HD	164	N164GB
358	SU-AZJ	439	N523NA	4	YV-462CP	84	N503EZ	165	LX-FMR
359	OH-WIP	440	N205JC			85	N82ST	166	N5VF

No.	Reg	No.	Reg	No.	Reg	No.	Reg	No.	Reg
167	N2FQ	248	N67PW	329	N98AC	68	N900HE	149	ZS-DAV
168	N48GL	249	N980S	330	N115SK	69	I-SNAX	150	HB-IUW
169	F-GUAJ	250	N917JC	331	N331EX	70	N105BK	151	N908CA
170	N500AF	251	N171TG	332	N280BC	71	N280BQ	152	N660EG
171	N750H	252	XA-TDD	333	N701WC	72	VP-BLM	153	N67EL
172	N256A	253	N85F	334	OE-HPS	73	T 18-5	154	LX-LFA
173	N544CM	254	N345AP	335	C-GMII	74	T 18-4	155	N900TG
174	N8KG	255	N255CM	336	N224HD	75	N60TL*	156	N910Q
175	N530AR	256	N600N	337	N89NC	76	N106BK	157	N626EK
176	N711T	257	N925BC	338	N338FJ	77	T 18-3	158	N721HM
177	XA-UCN	258	N48G	339	5B-CKN	78	LX-GES	159	LX-COS
178	N634H	259	N373RS	340	N340EX	79	N6BX	160	N176CF
179	N232PR	260	N586CS	*Falcon 900 A/B/C*		80	N914DD	161	PH-ILC
180	N50SF	261	N73GH	1	G-HMEI	81	I-TLCM	162	N611JW
181	N26WJ	262	N1896T	2	F-RAFP	82	N649TT	163	N25MB
182	N713SN	263	N503PC	3	N991RF	83	N900NE	164	VP-CFL
183	I-CAFD	264	N900CH	4	F-RAFQ	84	ST-PSA	165	VP-BEC
184	N633W	265	N501PC	5	N905FJ	85	N74FS	166	N995SK
185	F-GKBZ	266	N50NM	6	N885	86	F-GVAE	167	3C-ONM
186	N450K	267	F-OHFO	7	3B-XLA	87	N402FG	168	XA-TEL
187	N187PN	268	N268FJ	8	N5731	88	N987GK	169	VP-BGC
188	XA-ALA	269	F-GJBZ	9	N232CL	89	I-NUMI	170	N900TR
189	N51V	270	N148M	10	N349K	90	T 18-2	171	TC-AKK
190	CS-TMJ	271	N30FT	11	F-GKHJ	91	C3-DFH	172	N352AF
191	N950F	272	C-GKCI	12	N77CE	92	PT-OEX	173	VP-BFH
192	N96UT	273	N158M	13	N61TS	93	N780SP	174	N138F
193	MM62026	274	N138M	14	N44EG	94	CS-DFB	175	CS-TMQ
194	N194K	275	N44LC	15	N999EH	95	N343MG	176	N909PM
195	17401	276	N789ME	16	N64BD	96	5N-FGE	177	N886DC
196	VP-BSA	277	N192F*	17	N790JC	97	N902NC	178	XA-APE
197	N57MK	278	C-G...	18	N72PS	98	N59CF	179	N900DW
198	17402	279	N181MC	19	N900SJ	99	ZS-NAS	180	N90TH
199	N291BC	280	N1829S	20	N920DB	100	YK-ASC	181	N833AV
200	N749CP	281	C-GNET	21	HZ-AFT	101	VP-CAB	182	EC-JBB
201	N553M	282	N191MC	22	OE-ICF	102	N906WK	183	N900RX*
202	N750MC	283	N223HD	23	I-BEAU	103	V5-NAM	184	N129KJ
203	N203NC	284	N904SB	24	N93GR	104	N900CS	185	VH-PPD
204	EC-HHS	285	N901TF	25	N615MS*	105	N225KS	186	N900LC
205	N348K	286	N286ZT	26	VP-CJF	106	N333EC	187	N901SS
206	N801DL	287	ZS-ONG	27	N5VJ	107	N23BJ	188	PH-EDM
207	N275HH	288	N83TY	28	N1S	108	N229HD	189	C-GMND
208	N50HC	289	N214DV	29	C-GTCP	109	CD-01	190	N900NB
209	VP-BSL	290	N42SK	30	I-DIES	110	C-GJPG	191	N31D
210	XA-TXB	291	XA-GMD	31	N910JW	111	N8BX	192	VH-LAW
211	MM62029	292	N38WP	32	N10MZ	112	N908JB	193	VP-BCX
212	UR-CCF	293	N195SV	33	N203CW	113	HZ-SAB2	194	OO-ACT
213	XA-RVV	294	N39WP	34	N8200E	114	XA-SIM	195	N100ED
214	N55AS	295	I-FJDN	35	PH-OLI	115	LX-MEL	196	N501DB
215	D-BOOK	296	N23FM	36	N922JW	116	N82RP	197	LX-GJL
216	N84NW	297	N119AG	37	VH-ACE	117	N70TH	198	C-GAZU
217	N573TR	298	N615SR	38	T 18-1	118	RA-09000	199	N900KJ
218	N703TM	299	PP-PMV	39	N239AX	119	N22T	200	N404ST
219	YV-450CP	300	N344CM	40	N369BG	120	F-GRAX	201	LX-FTA
220	N50FF	301	N476MK	41	N76FD	121	HB-IFQ	202	F-WWFF
221	17403	302	N45NC	42	N990BB	122	N247CJ	203	F-WWFY
222	OE-HIT	303	N902TF	43	N693SH	123	RA-09001	*Falcon 900EX*	
223	N840FJ	304	N918JM	44	N100UP	124	N14NA	1	N900HG
224	N800BD	305	N102BQ	45	N298W	125	RP-C7808	2	N200L
225	N428CC	306	LX-AKI	46	N779SG	126	N910CS	3	N760
226	VP-BBD	307	N950H	47	F-GNMF	127	N909AS	4	N8100E
227	C-GGFP	308	N902SB	48	N233KC	128	N98NX	5	N600JM
228	N228FJ	309	N903SB	49	VP-BLB	129	XA-VTO	6	N900FH
229	N550WM	310	N50SN	50	N950SF	130	VP-CID	7	N45SJ
230	N506BA	311	N507AS	51	N528JR	131	N900KD	8	N30LB
231	N199FG	312	N26WP	52	5N-FGO	132	N707WB	9	N70LF
232	N100KP	313	N921EC	53	JA8570	133	N5UU	10	N900Q
233	N318GA	314	N55LC	54	I-FICV	134	N322CP	11	F-GOYA
234	PR-WYW	315	N668P	55	C-GSMR	135	VP-BPW	12	F-HAXA
235	UR-CCC	316	N696HC	56	JA8571	136	N1818S	13	N127SF
236	N725PA	317	N1839S	57	N900WK	137	N35RZ	14	N72WS
237	N89BM	318	N416KC	58	HB-IGL	138	C-FGFI	15	C-G0AG
238	N970S	319	N85CL	59	N32B	139	N900SX	16	N67WB
239	N200SG	320	N662P	60	N900VL	140	N70HS	17	N990H
240	N398AC	321	N900CM	61	HZ-AFZ	141	C-GHML	18	N166FB
241	N233BC	322	N5322	62	LX-LFB	142	VP-BPC	19	N900CX
242	N733M	323	N500N	63	N311JA	143	CS-DDI	20	N158JA
243	N62HM	324	LX-IRE	64	M37-01	144	N453JS	21	N330MC
244	N95HC	325	N146AS	65	N988T	145	VP-CGB	22	N331MC
245	N530DG	326	N33LC	66	CS-TMK	146	N4MB	23	SE-DVE
246	F-GTJF	327	N188DM	67	N900MG	147	XA-ISR	24	TR-LEX
247	N520AF	328	N308DM			148	N900DV		

No.	Reg.
25	N55TY
26	N900SB
27	I-FLYW
28	HB-IAH
29	N900MK
30	N860FJ
31	HZ-OFC4
32	N4425*
33	XA-BEG
34	VP-CLB
35	HB-IAQ
36	N826K
37	N900BZ
38	N901MD
39	N39NP
40	N990WM
41	N81SN
42	VP-BMS
43	EC-HOB
44	N947LF
45	MM62171
46	XA-FEX
47	N58CG
48	G-CBHT
49	N404F
50	F-GPNJ
51	OE-IDM
52	MM62172
53	PT-WQS
54	HB-IUX
55	N388GS
56	N404A
57	N900MJ
58	N11WM
59	N694JP
60	PT-XSC
61	N961EX
62	EC-HNU
63	N435T
64	D-AJAD
65	N965M
66	N377SC
67	N312P
68	N271DV
69	C-FJOI
70	N999PM
71	N110EX
72	N2BD
73	N973M
74	N811AV
75	VP-BEH
76	N80F
77	N977LP
78	G-DAEX
79	N788CG
80	N881Q
81	N404R
82	PR-GPA
83	HB-IGI
84	N420KK
85	N910MW
86	HB-IGX
87	C-GGMI
88	N909MM
89	N871MM
90	VP-CLO
91	I-CAEX
92	HB-IFJ
93	N993EX
94	N663MK
95	HB-IGY
96	HB-JSY
98	N900KX
99	N890FH
100	JA55TH
101	N730LM
102	N6666R
103	N900HD
104	N588GS
105	G-LCYA
106	LX-ZAK

No.	Reg.
107	F-HBOL
108	N9WV
109	VP-BEE
110	N176CL
111	N57EL
112	G-JJMX
113	F-HRBS*
114	N900YP
115	N720ML
116	MM62210
117	N900SN
118	OH-PPR
119	N958DM

Falcon 900EX EASY

No.	Reg.
97	F-WNCO
120	N106RW*
121	F-GSEF
122	N901SB
123	N990MC
124	N919SA
125	N988H
126	N966H
127	N900HC
128	OY-OKK
129	XA-RGB
130	VP-BEF
131	N900MV
132	G-JPSX
133	D-AZEM
134	VP-CEZ
135	N246AG
136	N22LC
137	N88LC
138	OE-IVK
139	N265H*
140	N940EX
141	N141EX
142	N142EX
143	F-WWFV
144	N144EX
145	F-WWFX
146	N146EX
148	F-WWFG

Falcon 2000

No.	Reg.
1	F-GMOE
1	VP-BMJ
2	N201CR
2	N202EX
3	N15AS
3	HB-IAJ
4	N925AJ
4	N200CH
5	N27R
5	PH-VBG
6	N93GH
6	F-WXEY
7	N28R
7	D-BIRD
8	N610AS
8	OO-IAR
9	N783FS
9	HB-IGQ
10	N131EP
10	VP-BER
11	N248JF
11	I-NATS
12	I-SNAW
12	N313CC
13	N722JB
13	N500R
14	N51MN
14	HB-IAU
15	N790L
15	N215EX
16	HB-IAW
16	PP-AAF
17	N659FM
17	N977CP
18	VP-CJA
18	N943JB

No.	Reg.
19	N790M
19	N855TJ
20	N822TP
20	XA-GNI
21	N390GS
21	N521CD
22	N200NE
22	PR-WQT
23	N10JP*
23	N101PV
24	N876SC*
24	N341AP
25	N122SC
25	N699MC
26	HB-ISF
26	N6453
27	F-GJSK
27	OH-FEX
28	N160WS
28	N2CC
29	XA-TDU
29	SX-DCA
30	HB-IAZ
31	N790Z
32	N175BC
33	HB-IAX
34	N234FJ
35	N1927G
36	VT-COT
37	EC-GNK
38	N8QM
39	N42ST
40	N1C
41	N48CG
42	HB-IBH
43	N86TW
44	N37TH
45	N190MC
46	N505RR
47	N435JF
48	N48WK
49	VT-TBT
50	D-BEST
51	N2AT
52	N212T
53	N149VB
54	I-JAMY
55	HB-IVM
56	N784BX
57	N18CG
58	N326EW
59	PT-WYC
60	N898CT
61	HB-IVN
62	HB-IVO
63	N800JH
64	N996HG
65	VT-TAT
66	N30TH
67	N150BC
68	N200GN
69	N220DF
70	P4-IKR
71	N811AG
72	N769JW
73	N273JC
74	OO-VMB
75	N275QS
76	F-WQBN
77	N278QS
78	N262PC
79	N929HG
80	N60TC
81	N281QS
82	N752S
83	N1128B
84	N1929Y
85	XA-HHF
86	N111HZ
87	N4200
88	N753S

No.	Reg.
89	N800GH
90	N930SD
91	N46HA
92	N2000L
93	N292QS
94	N517PJ
95	N628CC
96	N50TG
97	N922H
98	N298QS
99	N111VW
100	VP-CGA
101	OO-GFD
102	N440AS
103	I-FLYP
104	N2040S
105	N105LF
106	N635E
107	VP-CGC
108	I-FLYV
109	CS-DNP
110	PP-CFF
111	VP-BDL
112	N2112L
113	N2130S
114	ZS-PKR
115	CS-DNQ
116	N52DC
117	N54DC
118	N2180S
119	D-BDNL
120	CS-DNR
121	VP-BNT
122	N2220S
123	LZ-OOI
124	N2240S
125	N313GH
126	N2260S
127	N2270S
128	N628SA
129	N2290S
130	N202TH
131	N707MM
132	N905B*
133	F-WQBK
134	N493S
135	N196RG
136	N2360S
137	N61KW
138	N856F
139	CS-DNS
140	N797WC
141	N54J
142	HZ-KSDC
143	N872EC
144	N317MR
145	N2450S
146	N317MN
147	N777MN*
148	CS-DFC
149	XA-MAV
150	EC-HYI
151	N151GR
152	N317MQ
153	N2530S
154	OY-CKI
155	N2550S
156	N844UP
157	TC-RMK
158	N2580S
159	N2590S
160	TC-PLM
161	I-DDVF
162	N2620S
163	N163J
164	N44JC
165	N2650S
166	TC-DGC
167	3A-MGR
168	N2680S
169	N2690S

No.	Reg.
170	N220AB
171	F-ORAV
172	N36EP
173	N673BA
174	CS-DFD
175	XA-AVE
176	N676BA
177	N2770S
178	N100WY
179	OH-FIX
180	N680DF
181	N2800S
182	N329K
183	N88MX
184	XA-RET
185	N2840S
186	N551SS
187	VP-BCV
188	N317M
189	N330K
190	N2900S
191	TC-PRK
192	N515PV
193	N2780S
194	N671WM
195	N196KC
196	N2960S
197	N215KH
198	N2030S
199	N899U
200	I-SEAE
201	N201WR
202	N251QS
203	I-ARIF
204	N88DD
205	CS-DFE
206	N414CC
207	N207EM
208	G-GEDY
209	N209TM
210	N850K
211	N2100S
212	N523WC
213	N684KF
214	N215QS
215	N215RE
216	N718KS
217	N863TM
218	N218PH
219	N219FJ

Falcon 2000 EASY

No.	Reg.
30	D-BERT
31	N31EX
32	N666BE
33	D-BILL
34	HB-JEG
35	OY-CLN
36	N185G
37	N308U
38	N3BM
39	CS-TLP
40	PR-PPN
41	CS-DFF
42	F-GUTC
43	N9871R
44	CS-DFG
45	VP-BVP
46	N21HE
47	N711HE
49	F-WWGN
50	N57MN
51	ZS-MGD*
52	F-WWMA
53	N36TH
54	N2210S

Dornier

328JET

No.	Reg.
3086	N503CG
3090	N404SS
3114	OE-HTJ

c/n	Reg
3118	N873JC
3120	5N-SPN
3121	OE-HMS
3132	N328AC
3141	5N-SPM
3151	5N-SPE
3162	OE-HTG
3183	N328GT
3184	N328PM
3199	N328PT
3216	D-BADC

Dornier 328 ENVOY

c/n	Reg
3200	OE-HAA
3210	OE-HAB

Embraer

EMB-135/145

c/n	Reg
145209	209
145257	6700
145361	N829RN
145363	PP-XJO
145364	N486TM
145374	374
145412	N912CW
145449	CE-01
145462	N962CW
145467	N386CH
145484	484
145486	CE-02
145495	N995CW
145499	N325JF
145516	N254AL
145526	CE-03
145528	N928CW
145540	EC-IIR
145548	CE-04
145549	P4-VVP
145550	N1023C
145555	HB-JEA
145586	P4-SIS
145600	N302GC
145608	N303GC
145625	PR-ORE
145637	VP-CFA
145642	N642AG
145644	HB-JED
145678	PT-SAS
145686	P4-IVM
145699	N691AN
145706	N135SG
145711	OE-ISA
145717	PR-RIO
145730	N730BH
145770	PT-SIB
145775	PT-SIC
145780	N904LX*
145796	OK-SLN
14500809	N809SG
14500818	N888ML
14500825	N825SG
14500832	OE-IAS
14500841	OE-IWP
14500851	OE-ISN
14500858	PT-SIP
14500863	PT-SIQ

Fokker

F 28

c/n	Reg
11012	XU-888
11016	N500WN
11028	T-03
11042	A-2801
11045	PK-RJW
11079	5V-TAI
11088	M28-01
11099	TU-TIZ
11100	OB-1396
11104	EP-PAZ
11111	PK-PJL
11124	TU-VAJ
11125	G-530
11137	5H-CCM
11145	5-P-20-074
11146	PK-PJY
11147	wfu
11150	5-T-21-074
11153	RP-1250
11178	PK-PJM
11192	PK-PJK
11203	T-50
11992	FAC-0001

Fokker 100

c/n	Reg
11245	TU-VAA
11288	PK-PJN

Fokker 70

c/n	Reg
11521	N322K
11545	N324K
11547	PH-KBX
11557	KAF308
11576	PH-EZF

Gulfstream

Gulfstream 2

c/n	Reg
1	N55RG
2	wfu
3	N300RD
4	N36RR
5	N34S
6	N122DU
7	wfu
8	N225MS
9	N129WA
10	N667CX
11	N463HK
12	N622RR
13	N169HM*
14	XA-RBP
15	N125JJ
16	N24YS
17	N143V
18	XC-AA70
19	N590CH
20	N747NB
21	N244DM
22	N216RR
23	N890TJ
24	N800XL
25	N711RZ
26	N4RT
27	N227TS
28	N17KW
29	N188JS
30	XA-EHR
31	N105TB
32	N971EQ
33	N926NY
34	wo
35	N30PR
36	N74A
37	wfu
38	wfu
39	N87TD
40	wo
41	N365TC
42	N36PN
43	N899GA
44	wfu
45	N250MS
46	wfu
47	N800RT
48	N61WH
49	N511BA
50	N220JR
51	N20H
52	N52NW
53	N104VV
54	N148V
55	N125DC
56	N2000
57	N33PJ
58	wo
59	N1823D
60	wo
61	N41AV
62	N128KG
63	N12GP
64	N95SJ
65	N58JF
66	N718JS
67	N568TN
68	N308EE
69	N701S
70	N510SR
71	N200AB
72	wo
73	7P-TCB
74	N74HH
75	N211SJ
76	wfu
77	N994GG
78	HP-1A
79	XA-ARA
80	N510RH
81	N419MS
82	N492JT
83	wo
84	N27SL
85	N598GS
86	N179T
87	N779LC
88	N36MW
89	N671LW
90	N914MH
91	N629TD
92	N484TL
93	N685SF*
94	N2DF
95	N396CF
96	N55HV
97	N982B
98	N1218C
99	N400D
100	N412JT*
101	N102CX
102	N89TJ
103	N712MQ
104	N754JB
105	N141JF
106	N10123
107	N900AK
108	N581MB
109	N417EK
110	N900DH
111	N168VA
112	N74RQ
113	XA-TDK
114	N42PP
115	N716TE
116	N750RA
117	N945NA
118	N500MA
119	N711VL
120	N892TM
121	N500RL
122	N368DS
123	wfu
124	N178B
125	N901WG
126	wo
127	N829NL
128	wfu
129	N512SD
130	N2JR
131	N400M
132	N442QG
133	N628HC
134	N552JT
135	XA-AFP
136	N435GM
137	N6JW
138	N113AR
139	N159NB
140	JA8431
141	N948NA
142	N5RD
143	wo
144	N944NA
145	N226RM
146	N946NA
147	N947NA
148	N180AR
149	wo
150	N60GU
151	N909JE
152	N559LC
153	N132FP
154	N110GD
155	N477GG
156	N83TE
157	N683EC
158	N889JC
159	N880RJ
160	N1123G
161	XA-AHM
162	N668JT
163	N117JJ
164	XA-ESC
165	N696MJ
166	N776MA
167	N868AG
168	N318SP
169	N169EA
170	N111GD
171	HZ-AFH
172	N987SA
173	wfu
174	N540EA
175	XC-PFT
176	N794SB
177	5N-AGV
178	N720JW
179	HZ-PCA
180	N416CG
181	wfu
182	CNA-NL
183	N400PJ
184	N254CR
185	N950NA
186	VP-BFF
187	N802CC
188	N188DC
189	N711MQ
190	N190CS
191	N951RK
192	N192FG
193	N227LA
194	N57HJ
195	XA-ILV
196	N619MC
197	N608MD
198	N91NA
199	N338CL
200	N17KJ
201	HZ-AFI
202	A9C-BG
203	HZ-AFJ
204	VP-CPA
205	N623BM
206	N900BF
207	VP-CUB
208	N818DA
209	N720DR
210	N826GW
211	XA-FNY
212	N807CC
213	N96JA
214	N914KA
215	N748MN
216	HZ-HA1
217	N880WE
218	N188MR
219	N74RT
220	N117GL
221	N949NA
222	N948NA
223	N510US
224	N800PM
225	N225TR
226	N5DL
227	N264CL
228	N189WS
229	N117FJ
230	wo
231	N416KD
232	N10RQ
233	N720LH
234	N500JW
235	N840RG
236	N311BD
237	EC-FRV
238	N335H
239	HZ-AFK
240	TT-AAI
241	N909MK
242	5A-DDS
243	wo
244	N811DF
245	N222NB
246	N81RR
247	N530GA
248	N7WG
250	N94SF*
251	N251JS
253	N154C
254	N868SM
255	N4NR
256	wfu
257	N1CC
258	N87GS
775	N692EB

Gulfstream 3

c/n	Reg
249	F-249
252	N247RG
300	N918BG
301	N444GA
302	N302ST
303	wo
304	N304TS
305	N553JT
306	N360MB
307	N111FA
308	N308HG
309	N1NA
310	N982RK
311	N127GK
312	XA-...
313	F-313
314	N99PD
315	N21PJ
316	N300UJ
317	HZ-DG2
318	N17NC
319	N200SK
320	N624PP
321	N9KI
322	N706JA
323	XA-ERH
324	N96MR
325	N155MM
326	N420JC
327	N259SK
328	N36WL
329	N327JJ
330	wo
331	HZ-RC3
332	N909RR
333	N901FH
334	N700SB
335	N117MS
336	N147X
337	N330WR
338	N750SW
339	N684AT
340	N57NP
341	N1PR

342	N1JK	423	N399RV	1002	N168WC	1083	VH-CCC	1164	N420CC
343	N221CM	424	N94FL	1003	N885TA	1084	HB-IMY	1165	N780E
344	N344GW	425	N492A	1004	N199LX*	1085	N677RP	1166	HZ-AFY
345	N454JB	426	XA-...	1005	N823GA	1086	N1086	1167	N49SL
346	HZ-HR2	427	N300WY	1006	N614RD	1087	N368AG	1168	A40-AB
347	N888LV*	428	N702DM	1007	N575E	1088	N1JN	1169	N600CK
348	N357PR	429	N100HZ	1008	N85WD	1089	911	1170	N880WD
349	N711EG	430	N608BG	1009	V-11	1090	N9999M	1171	N3SA
350	N1454	431	N704JA	1010	N950DM	1091	N364G	1172	N227SV
351	N623MS	432	N579TG	1011	A6-HHH	1092	N515PL	1173	OK1
352	XC-UJN	433	N323JH	1012	N636GD	1093	N624BP	1174	N41VB
353	N212BA	434	N357KM	1013	N64AL	1094	N740K	1175	G-EVLN
354	N420RC	435	N10EH	1014	102001	1095	N311EL	1176	N9253V
355	ZS-TEX	436	N100AK	1015	N450BF	1096	VP-CBW	1177	N677RW
356	N356BR	437	N473KT	1016	N880GC	1097	N900AL	1178	N611JM
357	N723MM	438	SU-BGU	1017	N818BA	1098	VP-BSF	1179	N265ST
358	N475DJ	439	N458BE	1018	N4180A	1099	N999LX	1180	N827K
359	N50BH	440	N590DA	1019	TU-VAD	1100	B-8080	1181	90-0300
360	N705JA	441	N214WY*	1020	N93AT	1101	N365G	1182	N75CC
361	N874RA	442	SU-BGV	1021	N310EL	1102	XA-RBS	1183	HB-IBX
362	N800AR	443	N21AM	1022	N663PD	1103	C-FHPM	1184	N583AJ
363	N855SA	444	N555HD	1023	N830EF	1104	N700GD	1185	N635AV
364	HZ-AFN	445	N590DA	1024	N116HM	1105	N312EL	1186	N345AA
365	CNA-NU	446	N58AJ	1025	N900GB	1106	9M-ISJ	1187	165093
366	N366JA*	447	N707JA	1026	N277RP	1107	N844GF	1188	HL7222
367	N933PA	448	N178HH	1027	001	1108	VH-NCP	1189	165094
368	C-GBBB	449	wo	1028	N712CC	1109	EC-IKP	1190	JA001G
369	N17ND	450	N801MJ	1029	VP-BKH	1110	N888MX	1191	N403TB
370	N463LM	451	N500RH	1030	N1WP	1111	N511PA	1192	N212K
371	N353VA	452	N123TL	1031	HZ-AFU	1112	N12U	1193	N608CL
372	N724DB	453	N213BA	1032	N254GA	1113	N169TT	1194	N473CW
373	N373RR	454	N111GX	1033	N711SW	1114	N44LX	1195	N888PM
374	N270MC	455	N28YC	1034	N800BQ	1115	N440TC	1196	A40-AC
375	N375NW	456	85-0049	1035	HZ-AFV	1116	N305TC	1197	N969SG
376	N376PJ	457	N457JC	1036	N45AC	1117	G-HARF	1198	N99GA
377	N377RX	458	85-0050	1037	HZ-103	1118	N720CH	1199	165151
378	N141MH	459	N54HF	1038	HZ-AFW	1119	N524AN	1200	165153
379	N900LA	460	N460PG	1039	N726RW	1120	N888ES	1201	165152
380	N30WR	461	N108AR	1040	N620DS	1121	N214TS	1202	HB-ITF
381	N621S	462	TU-VAF	1041	N366F	1122	N317MJ	1203	N411WW
382	830500	463	N886DT	1042	N217RR	1123	N529AL	1204	N212AT
383	N65CE	464	N83PP	1043	002	1124	N1900W	1205	N393BD
384	N818TJ	465	N35GZ	1044	N154G	1125	N44CE	1206	N1620
385	HZ-MS3	466	N817MF	1045	N247EM	1126	5N-FGP	1207	N344AA
386	XC-UJO	467	N400WY	1046	N400CC	1127	VP-BUS	1208	N297GB
387	N485GM	468	86-0202	1047	wo	1128	HZ-MFL	1209	N157H
388	N8JL	469	N1956M	1048	SU-BGM	1129	N8MC	1210	N144PK
389	83-0502	470	86-0201	1049	N113CS	1130	N711GL	1211	N2107Z
390	N124DT	471	N57TT	1050	N195WS	1131	N55TD	1212	N884L
391	N288KA	472	N454BE*	1051	N919CT	1132	N80BR	1213	N56L
392	N391SH	473	86-0403	1052	N722MM	1133	N700CN	1214	N477JB
393	N519AF	474	D2-ECB	1053	N165ST	1134	N334JC	1215	102002
394	N379XX	475	86-0203	1054	N860JB	1135	N190ES	1216	102003
395	N422TK	476	86-0204	1055	N255GA	1136	N27CD	1217	N979CB
396	N175BG	477	N477SJ	1056	N770SC	1137	N7RX	1218	N5MC
397	N767CB	478	86-0206	1057	N226AL	1138	N520E	1219	N874C
398	N610AB	479	N50RL	1058	wo	1139	N134BR	1220	N79RP
399	N528AP	480	163691	1059	N612AC	1140	N77WL	1221	N451GA
400	N500EF	481	163692	1060	VT-AMA	1141	N115FL	1222	N171JC
401	N370JL	482	N111HC	1061	HB-IWZ	1142	N222GY	1223	N257H
402	wo	483	N343DP	1062	N619RK	1143	HZ-AFX	1224	C-GEIV
403	N555GL*	484	VP-BOR	1063	N745RS	1144	B-3999	1225	N773MJ
404	N560SH	485	N777MW	1064	N797CM	1145	N569CW	1226	N415WW
405	N789TR	486	TJ-AAW	1065	N599CN	1146	N970SJ	1227	N600VC
406	N80L	487	N416WM	1066	N466TS	1147	N820MS	1228	N18AN
407	N913MK	488	N500GF	1067	N200LC	1148	N306TT	1229	N270SC
408	wo	489	N388CW	1068	N82A	1149	N108DB	1230	N101CV
409	N555RE	490	N388MM	1069	N765A	1150	N900RL	1231	N255TS
410	HZ-AFR	491	N51MF	1070	N107A	1151	N109ST	1232	N232K
411	N461GT	492	N848RJ	1071	N1	1152	N63MU	1233	A6-OME
412	N105Y	493	G-540	1072	N260CH	1153	N590HM	1234	I-LXGR
413	N59AJ	494	K2981	1073	N177BB	1154	N186DS	1235	N500E
414	N165G	495	K2982	1074	N740JA	1155	N910S	1236	N100GN
415	N21NR	496	VP-CNP	1075	N121JJ	1156	VH-XGG	1237	N1904W
416	N4500X	497	87-0139	1076	N338MM	1157	OE-IJA	1238	N415PG
417	N431JT	498	87-0140	1077	N457DS	1158	N917W	1239	N909RX
418	N103CD	875	N300JZ	1078	G-DNVT	1159	HB-IKR	1240	N212AW
419	wo		*Gulfstream 4/G300/400*	1079	N691RC	1160	251	1241	N343DF
420	K2980	1000	N971EC	1080	N205X	1161	N20EG	1242	N407GC
421	N711UF	1001	N181CW	1081	N777SA	1162	91-0108	1243	N37WH
422	N903G			1082	N1082A	1163	003	1244	JA002G

1245	N7601	1326	95-3254	1407	N40HB	1488	N490QS	514	N256LK
1246	N49RF	1327	TR-KSP	1408	N401QS	1489	N142HC	515	N55GV
1247	N477RP	1328	N428QS	1409	N67TM	1490	N1TM	516	N740BA
1248	N72RK	1329	SU-BNC	1410	N80AT	1491	N491EC	517	HB-IMJ
1249	N151SD	1330	N400J	1411	N56D	1492	N123MR	518	N885G
1250	N47HR	1331	N878G	1412	N700LS	1493	N235DX	519	VP-CMG
1251	N165JF	1332	SU-BND	1413	5X-UEF	1494	N400FJ	520	N450AR
1252	N394TR	1333	N800J	1414	N5VS	1495	N250VC	521	97-0400
1253	N225DC	1334	N626JS	1415	N71BD	1496	N308AB	522	N70AG
1254	N920TB	1335	N918CC	1416	N900WR	1497	N702GH	523	N54TG
1255	VP-BNN	1336	N235LP	1417	N122RS	1498	N780RH	524	N674RW
1256	92-0375	1337	N52MK	1418	7T-VPC	1499	N941AM	525	N40SR
1257	N603CS	1338	N100HF	1419	VP-BVT	1500	N50EE	526	N675RW
1258	N585D	1339	N327TL	1420	N72BD	1501	N128AB	527	N5SA
1259	N4PG	1340	N800AL	1421	7T-VPM	1502	N710EC	528	N75RP
1260	N3PG	1341	N441QS	1422	N999GP	1503	A6-RJA	529	N73RP
1261	N399CB	1342	N808T	1423	N621JH	1504	N902L	530	N780F
1262	N462QS	1343	N99SC	1424	SU-BNO	1505	A6-RJB	531	N531AF
1263	N128TS	1344	N18AC	1425	P4-TAK	1506	SU-BPE	532	N740SS
1264	N464QS	1345	N857ST	1426	N426QS	1507	N91KL	533	XA-CPQ
1265	N540W	1346	N104AR	1427	SU-BNP	1508	N820TM	534	N920DC
1266	N77D*	1347	N933JJ	1428	N512C	1509	N607PM	535	N535V
1267	N624GJ	1348	N80A	1429	N777KK	1510	N609PM	536	N5UH
1268	N600BG	1349	N510MG	1430	N14456	1511	N161MM	537	8P-MAK
1269	N250LB	1350	N396U	1431	N818ME	1512	N606PM	538	N601MD
1270	75-3251	1351	N265SJ	1432	N211DH	1513	N4UC	539	N162JC
1271	75-3252	1352	N452QS	1433	N1SN	1514	N1932P	540	XA-OEM
1272	N620JH	1353	A9C-BAH	1434	N663P	1515	N851EL	541	N405LM
1273	N102BG	1354	N397JJ	1435	N994GC	1516	N400GA	542	97-0401
1274	102004	1355	N66DD	1436	N436QS	1517	N129MH	543	N91CW
1275	N475QS	1356	N600DR	1437	N437GA	1518	SU-BPF	544	N910DC
1276	N1990C	1357	N77FK	1438	N228RE	1519	N527JG	545	N888CW
1277	N5GF	1358	N1625	1439	N586D	1520	HZ-MF3	546	XA-BAL
1278	N98LT	1359	05-3255	1440	N76RP	1521	N413QS	547	N73M
1279	N2002P	1360	N460QS	1441	N123LC	1522	N251DV	548	N32BD
1280	N531MD	1361	N545CS	1442	N345LC	1523	N401FT	549	N718MC
1281	N481QS	1362	ZK-KFB	1443	N305LM	1524	N522AC	550	N5101
1282	N1925M	1363	N48CC	1444	N400HF	1525	HZ-MF4	551	N5102
1283	N402JP	1364	N143KS	1445	N474D	1526	N160TM	552	N9SC
1284	N575CT	1365	HZ-MS4	1446	N317ML	1527	N402FT	553	N516GH
1285	N874A	1366	N404XT	1447	N667P	1528	N523AC*	554	N589HM
1286	N880G	1367	N422ML	1448	N1LB	1529	N477SA	555	VP-BSM
1287	N487QS	1368	N610MC	1449	N200LS	1530	N650PW	556	N556AR
1288	7T-VPR	1369	N400MP	1450	N809C	1531	N212VZ	557	N83M
1289	N334MC	1370	N240CX	1451	N372CM	1532	HZ-MF5	558	N750BA
1290	N71VR	1371	VP-CIP	1452	N603PM	1533	N467QS*	559	N559GV
1291	7T-VPS	1372	N472QS	1453	N444QG	1534	N616KG	560	9K-AJD
1292	N917VZ	1373	N595PE	1454	N454QS	1535	N435GA	561	N661GA
1293	N493QS	1374	N1PG	1455	N616CC	Gulfstream G450		562	N95AE
1294	HZ-KAA	1375	N247KB	1456	N507SA	4001	N401SR	563	N169PG*
1295	N495QS	1376	N12NZ	1457	N234DB	4002	N442SR	564	N54PR
1296	N728LB	1377	N477QS	1458	N235KK	4003	N403SR	565	N77CP
1297	LV-WSS	1378	N2PG	1459	D-AJGK	4004	N450GA	566	97-0049
1298	N961V	1379	N60PT	1460	N326JD	4005	N165GA	567	N93M
1299	N499QS	1380	N480QS	1461	N877A	4006	N166GA	568	N5HN
1300	N321BN	1381	VP-BYS	1462	N462CS	4007	N185GA	569	9K-AJE
1301	N92AE	1382	N428M	1463	N465QS	4008	N97FT	570	N451GA
1302	N93AE	1383	N955H	1464	N950HB	4009	N909GA	571	99-0402
1303	85-3253	1384	N404AC	1465	RA-10201	4010	N910GA	572	HB-IIS
1304	N404QS	1385	N1818C	1466	VP-BSH	4011	N121GA	573	9K-AJF
1305	N888SQ	1386	N486QS	1467	N225CX	4012	N812GA	574	N1KE
1306	N540CH	1387	N254SD	1468	N468GA	4013	N913GA	575	N410M
1307	N94AE	1388	XA-EYA	1469	N5956B	4014	N314GA	576	N991LF
1308	N408QS	1389	N489QS	1470	N394AK	4015	N915GA	577	HB-IVZ
1309	N824CA	1390	VP-CSF	1471	N471CR	4016	N816GA	578	N410LM
1310	N902	1391	N827GA	1472	N475LC	4017	N917GA	579	N23M
1311	N411QS	1392	N492QS	1473	N620M	Gulfstream V/G500/550		580	N1540
1312	9M-ABC	1393	N297MC	1474	N248AB	501	N22	581	N44982
1313	N94LT	1394	N721RL	1475	N24TH	502	N502KA	582	EC-IRZ
1314	N429SA	1395	N961SV	1476	N59AP	503	N767FL	583	HZ-MS5
1315	N950CM	1396	N890A	1477	N244DS	504	N313RG	584	N84GV
1316	N416QS	1397	N669BJ	1478	N478QS	505	EI-WGV	585	N16NK
1317	N333PY	1398	N498QS	1479	N226RS	506	N500GV	586	N2N
1318	N1624	1399	N121JM	1480	CS-DKA	507	N300L	587	N300K
1319	N878SM	1400	N700FS	1481	N621SC	508	wfu	588	VP-BAC
1320	N420QS	1401	N900LS	1482	N13J	509	N855RB	589	N15UC
1321	N500CD	1402	N602PM	1483	N810TM	510	N513MW	590	99-0404
1322	N422QS	1403	N403QS	1484	N721FF	511	VP-CBX	591	N301K
1323	N565RV	1404	N404HS	1485	N5NG	512	N636MF	592	N90AM
1324	N424QS	1405	N45ET	1486	N608PM	513	HB-IVL	593	I-DEAS
1325	N102FM	1406	N526EE	1487	N428AS			594	N33M

(Serial / Registration listing)

No.	Reg.	No.	Reg.
595	N85V	677	N677GA
596	N596GA	678	678
597	N540M	679	N679GA
598	N1SF	680	N680GA
599	N401WJ	681	N624N
600	N100GV	682	G-JCBV
601	N502QS	683	JA500A
602	VP-BKZ	684	N684GA
603	N35CD	685	N685TA
604	XA-EAJ	686	N524AC
605	N62ML	687	OE-IVY
606	N551GA	688	N543H
607	VP-BNL	689	JA501A
608	N111LX	690	N914BD
609	N101MH	691	N250DV
610	N253CM	692	N100TM
611	N5000X	693	N508P
612	N350C	699	N885KT
613	N504QS	5001	N621KD
614	N614CM	5002	N92LA
615	N914J	5003	N245TT
616	N5616	5004	HB-IGM
617	7T-VPG	5005	N4CP
618	N585JC	5006	N550GW
619	N1454H	5007	N754BA
620	01-0028	5008	XA-EOF
621	N605CH	5009	N1HC
622	N806AC	5010	N711RL
623	N5060S	5011	VP-BGN
624	01-0029	5012	N888LK
625	N507QS	5013	N63HS
626	N626GA	5014	4X-...
627	N54KB	5015	N565ST
628	N18RF	5016	N944H
629	N707GW	5017	N62MS
630	N130GV	5018	N818RF
631	N508QS	5019	SE-RDX
632	N532SP	5020	N221DG
633	N222LX	5021	N5DA
634	ZS-AOL	5022	N550GV
635	N83CP	5023	N1GN
636	N910V	5024	VP-BLA
637	N509QS	5025	HB-JEE
638	HB-IIY	5026	N550MT
639	N501CV	5027	N91LA
640	N752BA	5028	N55UH
641	OE-IIA	5029	N155AN
642	CS-DKB	5030	5H-ONE
643	5N-FGS	5031	N795BA
644	HZ-MS5A	5032	G-HRDS
645	01-0076	5033	VP-BNR
646	N51FL	5034	N934GA
647	N5110S	5035	N1TF
648	N85M	5036	N1BN
649	N83CW	5037	N637GA
650	N1040	5038	N372BG
651	N1DC	5039	N401HF
652	01-0065	5040	N418SG
653	01	5041	N841GA
654	N404M	5042	N528QS
655	N825LM	5043	N550GA
656	N218EC	5044	4X-...
657	166375	5045	N789RR
658	N516QS	5046	N946GA
659	N50KC	5047	N947GA
660	N130TM	5048	N948GA
661	N405HG	5049	N949GA
662	N697A	5050	N950GA
663	01-0030	5051	N851GA
664	XA-MKI	5052	N952GA
665	N223MD	5053	N2929*
666	N123M	5054	OE-IVV
667	N721S	5055	N955GA
668	N144KK	5056	N956GA
669	02-1863	5057	N957GA
670	N671LE	5058	N74RP*
671	VP-BJD	5059	N959GA
672	N282QT	5060	N960GA
673	N25GV	5062	N159JA*
674	N505RX	5063	N759WR
675	N676GA	5064	N964GA
676	N676GA		
5065	N965GA		
5066	N966GA		
5067	N967GA		
5068	N968GA		
5069	N969GA		
5070	N870GA		

HFB
HFB 320

No.	Reg.
V1	wo
V2	wfu
1021	wfu
1022	wfu
1023	N103F
1024	wfu
1025	wfu
1026	wfu
1027	wo
1028	wo
1029	wo
1030	wfu
1031	wfu
1032	wfu
1033	wfu
1034	wo
1035	wfu
1036	N136MW
1037	wo
1038	wfu
1039	wfu
1040	wfu
1041	wfu
1042	wfu
1043	TC-LEY
1044	wo
1045	wfu
1046	wfu
1047	wfu
1048	wfu
1049	wo
1050	wfu
1051	wfu
1052	wfu
1053	wfu
1054	wfu
1055	N105TF
1056	wfu
1057	YV-388CP
1058	wfu
1059	wo
1060	wfu
1061	N320AF
1062	wfu
1063	wfu
1064	wfu
1065	wfu

Israeli Aircraft Indu
Astra-1125 SPX

No.	Reg.
001	wfu
002	4X-WIA
003	wfu
004	OB-1703
011	N500FA*
012	N610HC
013	N112PR
014	N116JC
015	N157GA
016	N221PA
017	N455SH
018	N72EL
019	N49MN
020	N212LD
021	N1125
022	PT-MBZ
023	N345GC
024	N999BL
025	N887PA
026	N24PR
027	N199HE
028	N800ZZ
029	N956PP
030	N900DL
031	N987G
032	N116PB
033	N441BC
034	N541RL
035	N1125K
036	N230AJ
037	N100SR
038	N777AM*
039	N636BC
040	N666K
041	N41AU
042	N528RR
043	N1M
044	N844GA
045	N880CH
046	N630S
047	N166RM
048	N88MF
049	N293P
050	N45H
051	N1125A
052	N90AJ
053	N121SG
054	N198HF
055	ZS-MDA
056	N790FH
057	N157SP
058	C-FDAX
059	LX-GOL
060	VP-BON
061	N200ST
062	N874WD
063	N331SK
064	N650GE
065	N50TQ
066	C-FMHL
067	N467MW
068	N401WT
069	N247PS
070	N448GR
071	N71FS
072	N365GA*
073	N918MJ
074	N789CA
075	N225AL
076	N20YL
077	YV-771CP
078	N1125J
079	N800PW
080	C-GSSS
081	N801G
082	N882GA
083	N383SF
084	N801RS
085	N796HR
086	PT-WBC
087	C-FRJZ
088	94-1569
089	N89HS
090	94-1570
091	N500M
092	N100G
093	N707BC
094	N294S
095	C6-JET
096	N323P
097	N273RA
098	N275RA
099	5B-CJG
100	N807JW
101	N610SM
102	N359V
103	N755A
104	N957F
105	N105FN
106	N800MK
107	D-CRIS
108	N108CG
109	N96FL
110	N97FL
111	HB-VOA
112	N1MC
113	N82BE
114	N114SN
115	OE-GPG
116	N456PR
117	C-FTDB
118	N28NP
119	B-20001
120	C-GPDA
121	N188AK
122	N419TK
123	VH-WSM
124	N777FL
125	N248SL
126	0126
127	N919DS
128	N676TC
129	N424MP
130	C-GBSW

G100

No.	Reg.
131	N400CP
132	N722AZ
133	OE-GBD
134	N1125S
135	N809JW
136	N43RJ
137	N620KE
138	N810JW
139	N420CE
140	N811JW
141	CC-CWK
142	N109GX
143	VT-BAV
144	VP-BMT
145	N387PA
146	VP-BMW
147	N147SW
148	VT-...
149	N749GA
150	C-FHRL
151	C-GTDO
152	N150CT
153	N353GA
154	N354GA

Galaxy

No.	Reg.
003	wfu
005	N505GA
006	N81TT
007	HB-IUT
008	VP-CRS
009	N83EJ
010	N672PS*
011	N56AG
012	N845GA
013	HB-IGP
015	N622SV
016	N35BP
017	N48GX
019	N219GA
020	N516CC
021	N321SF

G200

No.	Reg.
004	VP-CHW
014	N121GX
018	4X-COG
022	N200AX
023	N414DK
024	N101L
025	N866G
026	N800PJ
027	PR-OFT
028	N199HF
029	VP-BLH
030	B-HWB
031	N62GX
032	HB-JEB
033	N31SJ
034	N134AX

#	Reg	#	Reg	#	Reg	#	Reg	#	Reg
035	N110HA	6	wfu	87	wfu	168	wfu	249	wfu
036	N408LN	7	wfu	88	wfu	169	N44PR	250	N914MM
037	N204AB	8	wfu	89	wfu	170	wfu	251	PT-LDY
038	N602VC	9	wfu	90	N93SC	171	wfu	252	N1WS
039	N132JC	10	wfu	91	wo	172	YV-2482P	253	wfu
040	4X-CLL	11	wfu	92	wfu	173	wfu	254	N60AV
041	YV-772CP	12	wo	93	wfu	174	XA-PYR	255	N424CS
042	N755PA	13	wfu	94	N64AH	175	N384AT	256	VH-AJK
043	N122GV	14	wfu	95	N85JW	176	N35CR	257	N79LC
044	N621KB	15	wfu	96	YV-2454P	177	wfu	258	N771B
045	N70TT	16	wfu	97	wfu	178	wfu	259	wfu
046	N889G	17	wfu	98	wfu	179	N114RA	260	N80FD
047	N601AB	18	wfu	99	N63357	180	wfu	261	N11LN
048	N602AB	19	wfu	100	wfu	181	N345BS	262	N150EX
049	N751BC	20	wfu	101	wfu	182	LV-WYL	263	N918SS
050	N789PR	21	wfu	102	wfu	183	LV-WLR	264	N351C
051	LN-SUS	22	wo	103	wfu	184	N481MC	265	N7DJ
052	N700QS	23	wfu	104	wfu	185	4X-JYJ	266	N5HQ
053	N815JW	24	wfu	105	wfu	186	4X-JYO	267	N55FG
054	N54AX	25	wfu	106	N814T	187	N187TJ	268	N56BP
055	N885RR*	26	wfu	107	wfu	188	C-GRDP	269	N21DX
056	N929WG	27	wfu	108	wfu	189	N42CM	270	N475AT
057	N886G	28	N234G	109	XA-THF	190	N313TW	271	C-FJOJ
058	N272MW	29	wo	110	wfu	191	N900FS	272	wfu
059	N409LM	30	wo	111	wfu	192	N819RC	273	N104RS
060	N703QS	31	wfu	112	N372Q	193	N98BM	274	N274K
061	N705QS	32	wfu	113	wfu	194	N40TA	275	N96TM
062	N957P	33	wfu	114	wfu	195	N951DB	276	N300XL
063	N20PL	34	wfu	115	wfu	196	N606MA	277	N277WW
064	N2BG	35	wfu	116	wo	197	wo	278	C-GHYD
065	N118KA	36	wfu	117	wfu	198	N750SP	279	XC-...
066	N707QS	37	wfu	118	N696RV	199	N199WW	280	N949CC
067	N916GR	38	wfu	119	LV-WES	200	N4WG	281	VH-AJG
068	N179AE	39	wfu	120	wfu	201	N124WW	282	VH-AJV
069	N708QS	40	wfu	121	wo	202	N469WC*	283	N95JK
070	N702QS	41	N40593	122	N122ST	203	N22RD	284	N727AT
071	N459BN	42	wfu	123	wfu	204	wfu	285	N85PT
072	N65R	43	wfu	124	wfu	205	N205AJ	286	N111LP
073	N712QS	44	wfu	125	N1121R	206	N148H	287	N530DL
074	N80R	45	wfu	126	wo	207	N207WW	288	N711KE
075	N200YB	46	wfu	127	N277MG	208	N57PT	289	N900VP
076	N200BA	47	wfu	128	N404WC	209	N705AC	290	N719CC
077	N277GA	48	wo	129	N121PA	210	N2150H	291	N917BE
078	N278GA	49	wfu	130	wo	211	wo	292	N741C
079	N382G	50	wfu	131	wfu	212	N700MD	293	N26TZ
080	XA-MDK	51	wfu	132	wo	213	4X-CLK	294	N147A
081	N414DH	52	wfu	133	N132LA	214	N21SF	295	N730CA
082	N402LM	53	wfu	134	N134N	215	N946GM	296	N710SA
083	N403LM	54	wfu	135	XC-COL	216	N290CA	297	N335VB
084	N414KD	55	wfu	136	wo	217	N163WC	298	N809JC
085	N720QS	56	N382AA	137	N47CE	218	N426RJ	299	N600TC
086	XA-JHE	57	wfu	138	N972TF	219	N290CP	300	N10MV
087	N707SG	58	wfu	139	wfu	220	N9RD	301	N301KF
088	N200GA	59	wfu	140	wo	221	wo	302	wo
089	OE-HTI	60	wo	141	wfu	222	N598JM	303	N211ST
090	B-KMJ	61	wo	142	N1944P	223	N20KH	304	N13NL
091	N2HL	62	wfu	143	wfu	224	N349MC	305	N629WH
092	N721QS	63	wfu	144	wfu	225	N30MR	306	HK-4204X
093	N722QS	64	wfu	145	N805SM	226	N226WW	307	N4SQ
094	N121GV	65	wo	146	wfu	227	N624KM	308	N639AT*
095	N331BN	66	wfu	147	N912DA	228	N305BB	309	wo
096	N600YB	67	wfu	148	wfu	229	N40GG	310	N78GJ
097	N816JW	68	wo	149	wfu	230	N1KT	311	N53LM
098	ZS-PKD	69	wfu	150	wo	231	N600NY	312	N24FJ*
099	N723QS	70	wfu	151	ZP-AGD	232	N4MH	313	C-GDSR
100	N724QS*	71	wfu	152	4X-JYR	233	N36SF	314	N49CT
101	N201GA	72	wfu	153	wfu	234	N161X	315	N124GR
102	N702GA	73	wfu	154	N772AW	235	N30AB	316	N93KE
103	N203GA	74	N274MA	155	N707TF	236	N22LZ	317	VH-KNU
104	N104GA	75	wfu	156	N35D	237	N24KL	318	N38AE
105	N305GA	76	wfu	157	wfu	238	VH-AJP	319	N788FS
106	N606GA	77	N177JC	158	wfu	239	HK-2485W	320	N204TM
107	N107GA	78	wfu	159	wfu	240	N298HM	321	N666KL
108	N508GA	79	wfu	160	XA-RIZ	241	N300TC	322	N990S
Commander/Westwind		80	wfu	161	wfu	242	N140DR	323	VH-KNS
1	wfu	81	wo	162	N13GW	243	wo	324	N91MK
2	wfu	82	wfu	163	wfu	244	N911SP	325	N68PT
3	N409WT	83	wo	164	wfu	245	N270LC	326	wo
4	N72TQ	84	N16MK	165	N30156	246	N911CU	327	N50M
5	wfu	85	wfu	166	wfu	247	wo	328	N328PC
		86	wfu	167	wfu	248	VH-AJJ	329	N7HM

330	YV-332CP	411	HC-BVX	5045	wfu	5126	wfu	1079	N125DT
331	N811VC	412	N999MC	5046	wfu	5127	wfu	1247	HZ-ABI
332	N43RP	413	N35LH	5047	wfu	5128	N777PZ	1249	HZ-HM6
333	HR-PHO	414	N550HB	5048	N428DA	5129	wfu	1250	HZ-HM5
334	N325LW	415	N415TH	5049	wfu	5130	XA-PES	**Morane Saulnier**	
335	N21HR	416	N815RK	5050	wfu	5131	wfu	*MS760 Paris*	
336	N525XX	417	N34FS	5051	N488GR	5132	XA-BEB	01	wfu
337	VP-BLT	418	N26T	5052	wfu	5133	wfu	2	N207MJ
338	wo	419	N411HB	5053	XA-BCE	5134	XA-TPD	5	wo
339	N90KC	420	N91SA	5054	N721PA	5135	wfu	6	wfu
340	N118MP	421	N520MP	5055	wfu	5136	5A-DAJ	8	N60GT
341	N818JH	422	N87GJ	5056	wfu	5137	1004	9	N722Q
342	N274HM	423	N223WA	5057	wfu	5138	wfu	27	N760PJ
343	N999AZ	424	N790JR	5058	XA-TTE	5139	wfu	28	N760X
344	N849HS	425	N328SA	5059	wfu	5140	XA-EMO	30	N370AS
345	N345TR	426	N75BC	5060	wfu	5141	wfu	34	N371AS
346	N610SE	427	N229D	5061	wfu	5142	XA-SOY	36	N373AS
347	N347GA	428	N327SA	5062	wfu	5143	N326CB	38	N374AS
348	N960FA	429	C-FROY	5063	N499PB	5144	3908	39	wfu
349	N123RC	430	N430PT	5064	wfu	5145	N511TD	41	N41NY
350	wo	431	C-FGGH	5065	S9-NAD	5146	wfu	43	N760S
351	N728AZ	432	N60BT	5066	XA-MIK	5147	wfu	44	N375AS
352	N117AH	433	N433GM	5067	wo	5148	XA-...	45	N378AS
353	EC-GSL	434	N919BT	5068	wo	5149	wfu	49	wo
354	N894TW	435	N140VJ	5069	wfu	5150	N911CR	50	wo
355	N241CT	436	N444EP	5070	N731WL	5151	wfu	51	N751PJ
356	N993DS	437	N437SJ	5071	ST-PRE	5152	wfu	53	N53PJ
357	N914DM	438	N100BC	5072	wfu	5153	N416SJ	60	N7601R
358	N720MC	439	N439WW	5073	wfu	5154	wfu	69	wfu
359	N14CN	440	N220DH*	5074	wfu	5155	N116DD	72	N760FR
360	N500KE	441	C-FZEI	5075	N500ES	5156	N16AZ	81	N81PJ
361	N3AV	442	N830C	5076	N76HG	5157	wfu	86	N9035Y
362	N445A	**Lockheed**		5077	wo	5158	wfu	87	N87NY
363	N420JM	*JetStar*		5078	wfu	5159	XB-DBS	88	N626TC*
364	N944M	1001	wfu	5079	N58TS	5160	wfu	89	N999PJ
365	N73CL	1002	wfu	5080	N77HW	5161	N5161R	90	N69X
366	N320MD	5001	wfu	5081	wfu	5162	XA-HNY	97	N97PJ
367	N367WW	5002	wfu	5082	3C-QQU	5201	N777AY	98	wo
368	N83SG	5003	wfu	5083	N198DL	5202	3C-QRK	99	wo
369	N76ER	5004	wfu	5084	wo	5203	1003	101	N520DB
370	N875HS	5005	wfu	5085	wfu	5204	N814K	102	N20DA
371	wo	5006	wfu	5086	N313JS	5205	N72GW	103	wfu
372	N224GP	5007	wfu	5087	N33SJ	5206	N329JS	104	N760R
373	N794TK	5008	wo	5088	wfu	5207	N34WR	105	wfu
374	N43W	5009	wfu	5089	wfu	5208	N95BD	106	wfu
375	N66LX	5010	wfu	5090	wfu	5209	N529TS	107	N5879
376	N376BE	5011	wfu	5091	wfu	5210	wo	108	N760AR
377	N301PC	5012	wfu	5092	VP-CSM	5211	N118B	111	N760FM
378	N481NS	5013	wfu	5093	wfu	5212	wfu	112	wfu
379	N62ND	5014	wfu	5094	wfu	5213	N65JT	**Piaggio**	
380	wo	5015	wfu	5095	wfu	5214	XA-CVE	*PD808*	
381	N50FD	5016	wfu	5096	wfu	5215	N808RP	501	wfu
382	N445BL	5017	wfu	5097	N922MS*	5216	N797WQ	502	MM578
383	N942WC	5018	wfu	5098	XA-TVK	5217	N1MJ	503	wo
384	wo	5019	wfu	5099	N18BH	5218	N901C	504	I-PIAL
385	N317JS	5020	wfu	5100	N800GD	5219	N500DB	505	wfu
386	N348DH	5021	wfu	5101	N511TS	5220	TC-NOA	506	wfu
387	VH-NGA	5022	wfu	5102	wfu	5221	wo	507	wfu
388	N388WW	5023	wfu	5103	wfu	5222	N813P	508	MM61950
389	N89AM	5024	wfu	5104	wfu	5223	N887DT	509	wfu
390	N122MP	5025	wfu	5105	HZ-MA1	5224	N6QZ	510	wfu
391	N155ME	5026	wfu	5106	YV-03CP	5225	N900DB	511	wo
392	N793BG	5027	wfu	5107	N69MT	5226	TC-SSS	512	MM61954
393	N491AN	5028	wfu	5108	N104CE	5227	N117AJ	513	MM61955
394	N63PP	5029	wfu	5109	wfu	5228	N400MR	514	wfu
395	N395TJ	5030	wo	5110	wfu	5229	XA-TCN	515	wfu
396	N37BE	5031	wfu	5111	wfu	5230	N701JH	516	wfu
397	N777HD	5032	wfu	5112	N728PX	5231	XA-AAL	517	wfu
398	N41C	5033	wfu	5113	N77BT	5232	N77C	518	wfu
399	N48SD	5034	wfu	5114	5B-CHE	5233	7T-VHP	519	wfu
400	N900TN	5035	wo	5115	wfu	5234	XA-EKT	520	wfu
401	N30GF	5036	wfu	5116	wfu	5235	YI-AKB	521	wfu
402	N51TV	5037	N770JR	5117	VP-BLD	5236	N741AM	522	wfu
403	N403W	5038	wfu	5118	wfu	5237	YI-AKC	523	wfu
404	N29CL	5039	wfu	5119	N1DB	5238	YI-AKD	524	wfu
405	N424JR	5040	wfu	5120	wfu	5239	YI-AKE	**Raytheon**	
406	N830	5041	wfu	5121	wfu	5240	YI-AKF	*Diamond*	
407	N407W	5042	wfu	5122	wfu	**Tristar**		A001SA	wfu
408	N125HF	5043	wfu	5123	N57NR	1064	P4-MED		
409	N26KL	5044	wfu	5124	XC-SKI	1067	N140SC		
410	N777DC			5125	wfu				

Cessna Citation / Beechjet / Hawker production list

c/n	Reg		c/n	Reg
A002SA	JA8248		A083SA	N417KT
A003SA	N300TS		A084SA	N160H
A004SA	N541CW		A085SA	N70VT
A005SA	N110DS		A086SA	N515KK
A006SA	N200LP		A087SA	I-AVEB
A007SA	N507CW		A088SA	N482DM
A008SA	N399DM		A089SA	N20PA
A009SA	N360CA*		A090SA	N464AM
A010SA	N703JH		A091SA	N400NF
A011SA	N211GA		A092SA	wo
A012SA	N316LP		A1008SA	wfu

Beechjet 400

c/n	Reg
RJ-1	N64VM
RJ-2	N369EA
RJ-3	N203BA
RJ-4	N8YM
RJ-5	N54TK
RJ-6	N406TS
RJ-7	N85BN
RJ-9	N65RA
RJ-10	N131AP
RJ-11	N72HG
RJ-12	N106CG
RJ-13	N428JD
RJ-14	N599JL
RJ-15	N902P
RJ-16	N803E
RJ-17	N655CM*
RJ-18	N824SS
RJ-19	N598JL
RJ-20	N455DW
RJ-21	N3121B
RJ-22	N913MC
RJ-23	N400GJ
RJ-24	N800WV
RJ-25	ZS-OUU
RJ-26	N401GJ
RJ-27	N611TG
RJ-28	N51EB
RJ-29	N129BT
RJ-30	N777FE
RJ-31	N499P
RJ-32	XA-RAR
RJ-33	XA-BNG
RJ-34	N80TS
RJ-35	N737MM
RJ-36	XA-OAC
RJ-37	ZS-ORW
RJ-38	N52AL
RJ-39	N393BB
RJ-40	N400DW
RJ-41	N241BJ
RJ-42	N40MA
RJ-43	N500DG
RJ-44	I-TOPJ
RJ-45	N241TR
RJ-46	VT-TEL
RJ-47	N1547B
RJ-48	XB-JHE
RJ-49	N88UA
RJ-50	N8HQ
RJ-51	N930MG
RJ-52	N520WS
RJ-53	N418MG
RJ-54	N724HB
RJ-55	OK-UZI
RJ-56	wo
RJ-57	N458HC
RJ-58	ZS-MHN
RJ-59	N250KD
RJ-60	N461EA
RJ-61	N424BT
RJ-62	N848C
RJ-63	N215TP
RJ-65	N16EM

Citation (A-series continued)

c/n	Reg		c/n	Reg
A013SA	wo		A048SA	PT-LNN
A014SA	OH-KNE		A049SA	N411SP
A015SA	N789DJ		A050SA	N257CB
A016SA	N411RE		A051SA	wfu
A017SA	N399MM		A052SA	N70XX
A018SA	N83BG		A053SA	JA30DA
A019SA	N400GK		A054SA	N491BT
A020SA	N399RP		A055SA	N600CG
A021SA	N4LK		A056SA	N255DG
A022SA	N400UF		A057SA	N510BC
A023SA	N150CA		A058SA	N7050V
A024SA	N674AC		A059SA	N1JC
A025SA	N400HH		A060SA	N585TC
A026SA	N486CW		A061SA	N500PP
A027SA	N7PW		A062SA	N817GR
A028SA	wo		A063SA	N984SA
A029SA	N100RS		A064SA	N400ML
A030SA	N83SA		A065SA	N925MJ
A031SA	N958PP		A066SA	PR-JTS
A032SA	N83CG		A067SA	N617BG
A033SA	N148J		A068SA	N103HC
A034SA	N334KC		A069SA	N250GP
A035SA	N702JH		A070SA	N60EF
A036SA	N997MX		A071SA	N71GH
A037SA	N134RG		A072SA	N779DC
A038SA	N42SR		A073SA	N94LD
A039SA	PT-OXT		A074SA	N32HP
A040SA	N40GA		A075SA	N824DW
A041SA	N300AR		A076SA	wo
A042SA	N8LE		A077SA	N975GR
A043SA	N19R		A078SA	wo
A044SA	N600GW		A079SA	N213LG
A045SA	N395WB		A080SA	N44MM
A046SA	N109PW		A081SA	N50EF
A047SA	N2WC		A082SA	N62CH

400A/Hawker 400XP

c/n	Reg		c/n	Reg
RK-1	N481CW		RK-2	N402CW
RK-3	N400VK		RK-4	N494CW
RK-5	N495CW		RK-88	N654AT
RK-6	N406CW		RK-89	N94HE
RK-7	N9PW		RK-90	N165HB
RK-8	N440DS		RK-91	N491CW
RK-9	N315R		RK-92	N555KK
RK-10	D-CEIS		RK-93	N493CW
RK-11	wo		RK-94	N585G
RK-13	N13GB		RK-95	N747RR
RK-14	N81TJ		RK-96	N800GF
RK-16	XA-...		RK-97	N3197Q
RK-17	N417CW		RK-98	N999JF
RK-18	N418CW		RK-99	N95FA
RK-19	N419CW		RK-100	N400SH
RK-20	N703LP		RK-101	N400FT
RK-21	N1920		RK-102	N111FW
RK-22	N422CW		RK-103	N403CW
RK-23	N250AJ		RK-104	LV-WPE
RK-24	N8073R		RK-105	N3235U
RK-25	D-CLBA		RK-106	N625W
RK-26	N80DX		RK-107	N907JE
RK-27	N427CW		RK-108	N408CW
RK-28	N400NS		RK-109	N121EZ
RK-29	I-IPIZ		RK-110	N400VP
RK-30	N430CW		RK-111	N13SY
RK-31	N431CW		RK-112	N94LH
RK-32	N432CW		RK-113	wo
RK-33	N197BE		RK-114	N698PW
RK-34	N134FA		RK-115	N52AW
RK-35	N435CW		RK-116	N1116R
RK-36	N156DH		RK-117	N496AS
RK-37	SE-DRS		RK-118	LV-WTP
RK-38	N515MW		RK-119	N456JG
RK-39	N70BJ		RK-120	N159AK
RK-40	N440CW		RK-121	N473JE
RK-41	N546BZ		RK-122	PT-WJS
RK-42	N442CW		RK-123	N740TA
RK-43	N45RK		RK-124	OE-GUH
RK-44	N908R		RK-125	N939GP
RK-45	N445CW		RK-126	XB-INI
RK-46	N8239E		RK-127	N686TR
RK-47	N109CP		RK-128	N912SH
RK-48	N48SE		RK-129	N129MC
RK-49	N54HD		RK-130	TC-NEO
RK-50	N450CW		RK-131	N1083Z
RK-51	N8085T		RK-132	N106KC
RK-52	N709EL		RK-133	I-TOPB
RK-53	N453CW		RK-134	N134BJ
RK-54	PT-WHG		RK-135	N135BJ
RK-55	N42AJ		RK-136	N397CA
RK-56	N456CW		RK-137	N400AJ
RK-57	N457CW		RK-138	N48PL
RK-58	N76MC		RK-139	VH-BZL
RK-59	N5PF		RK-140	A6-FLJ
RK-60	N61SM		RK-141	N855FC
RK-61	N461CW		RK-142	N9WW
RK-62	N462CW		RK-143	N191NQ
RK-63	N304JR*		RK-144	N134CM
RK-64	N53MS		RK-145	N745TA
RK-65	N39HF		RK-146	N746TA
RK-66	I-AVSS		RK-147	N147BJ
RK-67	N8167Y		RK-148	OE-GHM
RK-68	N295FA		RK-149	N749TA
RK-69	N877J		RK-150	N100AW
RK-70	N79HM		RK-151	N586SF
RK-71	N402GS		RK-152	YV-754CP
RK-72	N428WE		RK-153	N500HY
RK-73	PT-WHB		RK-154	VH-EXB
RK-74	N26JP		RK-155	N631PP
RK-75	N82400		RK-156	N400PU
RK-76	N261JP		RK-157	N157WH
RK-77	PT-WHD		RK-158	PT-MPL
RK-78	N611PA		RK-159	N3337J
RK-79	N8279G		RK-160	N54HP
RK-80	AP-BEX		RK-161	N471CW
RK-81	PT-WHE		RK-162	N520CH
RK-82	PT-WHF		RK-163	I-TOPD
RK-83	N8283C		RK-164	N280AJ
RK-84	D-CHSW		RK-165	N224MC
RK-85	N419MB		RK-166	N975CM
RK-86	N757CE		RK-167	N711EC
RK-87	N702LP		RK-168	N768TA
RK-169	N757WS		RK-210	N111CX
RK-170	TC-MSB		RK-211	N686SC
RK-171	XA-...		RK-212	N11UB
RK-172	N200GP		RK-213	N545TC
RK-173	N2273Z		RK-214	N79EL
RK-174	N174AB		RK-215	N515WA
RK-175	N175BJ		RK-216	N213BK
RK-176	N476BJ		RK-217	N217MB
RK-177	N717CF		RK-218	N48MF
RK-178	N708TA		RK-219	N219SJ
RK-179	N400CT		RK-220	N799SM
RK-180	N709TA		RK-221	N400KG
RK-181	N2235V		RK-222	N482CW
RK-182	N234DK		RK-223	N877FL
RK-183	N710TA		RK-224	N642AC
RK-184	N141DR		RK-225	N751TA
RK-185	N148GB		RK-226	N750TA
RK-186	N712TA		RK-227	N862KM
RK-187	N400TE		RK-228	N12WF
RK-188	VP-CPH		RK-229	N515TJ
RK-189	N715TA		RK-230	N753TA
RK-190	VT-RPG		RK-231	N615HP
RK-191	N400HD		RK-232	N674SF
RK-192	N116AP		RK-233	N233MW
RK-193	N914SH		RK-234	N783TA
RK-194	N909ST		RK-235	N695BK
RK-195	N718TA		RK-236	N11WF
RK-196	XA-MEX		RK-237	N437CW
RK-197	N214WM		RK-238	XA-VRO
RK-198	N798TA		RK-239	N785TA
RK-199	N446M		RK-240	N150TF
RK-200	N399RA		RK-241	N993H
RK-201	N741TA		RK-242	N32AA
RK-202	N438LX		RK-243	N782TP
RK-203	N262PA		RK-244	N793TA
RK-204	I-ASER		RK-245	N744TA
RK-205	N143HM		RK-246	N500TH
RK-206	N982AR		RK-247	N20FL
RK-207	N717DD		RK-248	N786TA
RK-208	HI-766SP		RK-249	N611WM
RK-209	N799TA			

RK-250	N250HP	RK-331	N12MG
RK-251	N705LP	RK-332	XA-TWW
RK-252	N790TA	RK-333	N903CG
RK-253	N395HB	RK-334	N484CW
RK-254	N254RK	RK-335	N400GR
RK-255	N402FB	RK-336	N706LP
RK-256	N26PA	RK-337	N726PG
RK-257	N739TA	RK-338	N116AD
RK-258	PP-WRV	RK-339	N400TL
RK-259	XA-AFS	RK-340	N500LJ
RK-260	N450LX*	RK-341	N61GB
RK-261	N51B	RK-342	N522EL
RK-262	N300GB	RK-343	N106DD
RK-263	N724KW	RK-344	N6144S
RK-264	N792TA	RK-345	N425CW
RK-265	N797TA	RK-346	N446CW
RK-266	N10FL	RK-347	N108PJ
RK-267	N4467X	RK-348	N309AK
RK-268	N789TA	RK-349	N975RR
RK-269	N440RC	RK-350	PR-MVB
RK-270	N800SD	RK-351	N371CF
RK-271	N743TA	RK-352	XA-...
RK-272	N701CP	RK-353	XA-GAO
RK-273	N731TA	RK-354	N717EA
RK-274	N735TA	RK-355	N400RY
RK-275	N4275K	RK-356	N800HT
RK-276	N775TA	RK-357	N317PC
RK-277	N101CC	RK-358	N865AM
RK-278	N823TT	RK-359	XA-UAW
RK-279	N773TA	RK-360	N823ET
RK-280	N4480W	RK-361	N25CU
RK-281	XA-TDQ	RK-362	PK-...
RK-282	N794TA	RK-363	N790SS
RK-283	N404MS	RK-364	N394BB
RK-284	N795TA	RK-365	N455CW
RK-285	N249RM	RK-366	N466CW
RK-286	N400MV	RK-367	N404BL
RK-287	N361AS	RK-368	N448CW
RK-288	N51VC	RK-369	N624B
RK-289	N796TA	RK-370	N72GH
RK-290	N204DH	RK-371	N824GB
RK-291	N816DK	RK-372	N375DT
RK-292	N899TA	RK-373	N490JC
RK-293	EC-HTR	RK-374	N109NT
RK-294	HS-TPD	RK-375	XA-UCV
RK-295	N898TA	RK-376	N476LX
RK-296	N311HS	RK-377	N477LX
RK-297	N497CW	RK-378	N370FC
RK-298	N698TA	RK-379	PP-UQF
RK-299	N697TA	RK-380	N102QS
RK-300	VP-CVP	RK-381	N106QS
RK-301	N696TA	RK-382	N108QS
RK-302	XA-TTS	RK-383	N115QS
RK-303	SE-RBO	RK-384	N302TB
RK-304	N304SE	RK-385	N116QS
RK-305	N405CW	RK-386	N524LP
RK-306	YV-968CP	RK-387	N478LX
RK-307	N407CW	RK-388	N479LX
RK-308	N400KP	RK-389	N50727
RK-309	I-VITH	RK-390	N975RD
RK-310	N410CW	RK-391	N117QS
RK-311	N311GL	RK-392	AP-BNO
RK-312	N75RL	RK-393	CS-DMA
RK-313	N4483W	RK-394	N119QS
RK-314	N400HS	RK-395	N7600
RK-315	N6MF	RK-396	N31496
RK-316	XA-AFA	RK-397	N36997
RK-317	N691TA	RK-398	N480LX
RK-318	HB-VNE	RK-399	N700FA
RK-319	N660CC	RK-400	N400XP
RK-320	N717TG	RK-401	N36701
RK-321	XA-TYD	RK-402	N61CP*
RK-322	N800EH	RK-403	N36803
RK-323	N268PA	RK-404	N37204
RK-324	N755TA	RK-406	N140QS
RK-325	N408PC*	RK-407	N36607
RK-326	N420DH	RK-408	N37108
RK-327	N689TA	RK-410	N37310
RK-328	N686TA	RK-411	N611XP
RK-329	N580RJ	RK-412	N37312
RK-330	N330TS	RK-415	N37115
		RK-416	N116XP
		RK-417	N36907

Beechjet 400T

TX-1	41-5051
TX-2	41-5052
TX-3	41-5053
TX-4	41-5054
TX-5	41-5055
TX-6	51-5056
TX-7	51-5057
TX-8	51-5058
TX-9	71-5059
TX-10	01-5060
TX-11	21-5011
TX-12	21-5012
TX-13	41-5063

Jayhawk

TT-1	91-0077	TT-64	92-0350	TT-145	94-0145
TT-2	90-0412	TT-65	92-0351	TT-146	94-0146
TT-3	90-0400	TT-66	92-0352	TT-147	94-0147
TT-4	90-0405	TT-67	92-0353	TT-148	94-0148
TT-5	89-0284	TT-68	92-0354	TT-149	95-0040
TT-6	90-0404	TT-69	92-0355	TT-150	95-0041
TT-7	90-0401	TT-70	92-0356	TT-151	95-0042
TT-8	90-0402	TT-71	92-0357	TT-152	95-0043
TT-9	90-0403	TT-72	92-0358	TT-153	95-0044
TT-10	90-0407	TT-73	92-0359	TT-154	95-0045
TT-11	90-0406	TT-74	92-0360	TT-155	95-0046
TT-12	90-0408	TT-75	92-0361	TT-156	95-0047
TT-13	90-0409	TT-76	92-0362	TT-157	95-0048
TT-14	90-0410	TT-77	92-0363	TT-158	95-0049
TT-15	90-0411	TT-78	93-0621	TT-159	95-0050
TT-16	90-0413	TT-79	93-0622	TT-160	95-0051
TT-17	91-0076	TT-80	93-0623	TT-161	95-0052
TT-18	91-0075	TT-81	93-0624	TT-162	95-0053
TT-19	91-0078	TT-82	93-0625	TT-163	95-0054
TT-20	91-0079	TT-83	93-0626	TT-164	95-0055
TT-21	91-0080	TT-84	93-0627	TT-165	95-0056
TT-22	91-0081	TT-85	93-0628	TT-166	95-0057
TT-23	91-0082	TT-86	93-0629	TT-167	95-0058
TT-24	91-0083	TT-87	93-0630	TT-168	95-0059
TT-25	91-0084	TT-88	93-0631	TT-169	95-0060
TT-26	91-0085	TT-89	93-0632	TT-170	95-0061
TT-27	91-0086	TT-90	93-0633	TT-171	95-0062
TT-28	91-0087	TT-91	93-0634	TT-172	95-0063
TT-29	91-0088	TT-92	93-0635	TT-173	95-0064
TT-30	91-0089	TT-93	93-0636	TT-174	95-0065
TT-31	91-0090	TT-94	93-0637	TT-175	95-0066
TT-32	91-0091	TT-95	93-0638	TT-176	95-0067
TT-33	91-0092	TT-96	93-0639	TT-177	95-0068
TT-34	91-0093	TT-97	93-0640	TT-178	95-0069
TT-35	91-0094	TT-98	93-0641	TT-179	95-0070
TT-36	91-0095	TT-99	93-0642	TT-180	95-0071
TT-37	91-0096	TT-100	93-0643		
TT-38	91-0097	TT-101	93-0644		
TT-39	91-0098	TT-102	93-0645		
TT-40	91-0099	TT-103	93-0646		
TT-41	91-0100	TT-104	93-0647		
TT-42	91-0101	TT-105	93-0648		
TT-43	91-0102	TT-106	93-0649		
TT-44	92-0330	TT-107	93-0650		
TT-45	92-0331	TT-108	93-0651		
TT-46	92-0332	TT-109	93-0652		
TT-47	92-0333	TT-110	93-0653		
TT-48	92-0334	TT-111	93-0654		
TT-49	92-0335	TT-112	93-0655		
TT-50	92-0336	TT-113	93-0656		
TT-51	92-0337	TT-114	94-0114		
TT-52	92-0338	TT-115	94-0115		
TT-53	92-0339	TT-116	94-0116		
TT-54	92-0340	TT-117	94-0117		
TT-55	92-0341	TT-118	94-0118		
TT-56	92-0342	TT-119	94-0119		
TT-57	92-0343	TT-120	94-0120		
TT-58	92-0344	TT-121	94-0121		
TT-59	92-0345	TT-122	94-0122		
TT-60	92-0346	TT-123	94-0123		
TT-61	92-0347	TT-124	94-0124		
TT-62	92-0348	TT-125	94-0125		
TT-63	92-0349	TT-126	94-0126		
		TT-127	94-0127		
		TT-128	94-0128		
		TT-129	94-0129		
		TT-130	94-0130		
		TT-131	94-0131		
		TT-132	94-0132		
		TT-133	94-0133		
		TT-134	94-0134		
		TT-135	94-0135		
		TT-136	94-0136		
		TT-137	94-0137		
		TT-138	94-0138		
		TT-139	94-0139		
		TT-140	94-0140		
		TT-141	94-0141		
		TT-142	94-0142		
		TT-143	94-0143		
		TT-144	94-0144		

HS/BAe125/Dominie

NA700	N230TS
NA701	2113
NA702	wfu
NA703	XA-AEE
NA704	N132RL
NA705	wfu
NA706	XA-ADR
NA707	N160AG
NA708	XA-RPT
NA709	N55G
NA710	N314ER
NA711	ZP-TDF
NA712	N713SS
NA713	N773AA
NA714	N31EP
NA715	N284DB
NA716	wo
NA717	wo
NA718	N250DH
NA719	XA-...
NA720	XB-FRP
NA721	N43TS
NA722	XA-...
NA723	YV-....
NA724	N724TS
NA725	wo
NA726	N922GK
NA727	XA-TNY
NA728	N32GM
NA729	VU93-2118
NA730	N82CA
NA731	XB-MAR
NA732	N400PR
NA733	ZS-PLC
NA734	XA-GTC
NA735	N800GE
NA736	N736LE
NA737	XB-...
NA738	VU93-2117
NA739	N820MG
NA740	VU93-2114
NA741	wo
NA742	N843B

NA743	N400LC	25044	wfu	25125	wfu	25289	VU93-2128	NA0204	N724B
NA744	N440BC	25045	XS727/D	25126	wo	25290	wo	NA0205	N700FW
NA745	N700TR	25046	LV-YGC	25127	N125GK	*125-600*		NA0206	N818KC
NA746	ZS-OIF	25047	N800DA	25128	ZS-SMT	6001	N699TS	NA0207	N70X
NA747	P4-AOB	25048	XS728/E	25129	wo	6002	XA-SLP	NA0208	N41HF
NA748	N77WD	25049	wfu	25130	TR-LFB	6003	N91KP	NA0209	N209TS
NA749	N498RS	25050	XS730/H	25131	7T-VVL	6004	N600MK	NA0210	N418RD
NA750	N131LA	25051	wfu	25132	G-OCBA	6005	wfu	NA0211	N411PA
NA751	N400FR	25052	N125JR	25133	VT-EQZ	6006	N21SA	NA0212	N425SD
NA752	N602JR	25053	XA-...	25135	wo	6007	N317TC	NA0213	N339CA
NA753	N345GL	25054	wfu	25138	5N-AVV	6008	N256WJ	NA0214	N926MC
NA754	N227LT	25055	XS731/J	25140	C6-MED	6009	N28TS	NA0215	N215RS
NA755	N755WJ	25056	wfu	25143	wfu	6010	wo	NA0216	N98FT
NA756	N624PD	25057	wfu	25144	wfu	6011	wfu	NA0217	N700RR
NA757	XA-AGL	25058	N632PE	25145	wfu	6012	wfu	NA0218	N903SC
NA758	N800NP	25059	wfu	25147	wfu	6013	5N-YET	NA0219	wo
NA759	N125CF	25060	N96SG	25148	XA-...	6014	N47HV	NA0220	XA-SAU
NA760	YV-....	25061	wfu	25149	wfu	6015	N957MB	NA0221	C-GTOR
NA761	N814D	25062	wfu	25150	N42AS	6016	XA-SAI	NA0222	N18CC
NA762	N125DH	25063	wfu	25151	N125F	6017	N225HR	NA0223	N720PT
NA763	N1QH	25064	wo	25152	N23CJ	6018	XB-ADZ	NA0224	XA-...
NA764	N55RZ	25065	XA-KOF	25153	N88DU	6019	wfu	NA0225	N137WR
NA765	N765TS	25066	XA-...	25154	wfu	6020	wfu	NA0226	N1776E
NA766	N854SM	25067	7S-MAN	25155	wfu	6021	N220TS	NA0227	N81KA
NA767	wfu	25068	wfu	25156	wfu	6022	wfu	NA0228	N545GM
NA768	XA-SFQ	25069	wo	25157	wfu	6023	N702HC	NA0229	N820CT
NA769	N900AD	25070	N333GZ	25158	XA-DAN	6024	N411GA	NA0230	N899AB
NA770	N38LB	25071	wfu	25159	N600SV	6025	N721LH	NA0231	N225BJ
NA771	N4WC	25072	XS736/S	25162	VC93-2120	6026	N125NA	NA0232	N232TN
NA772	wo	25073	wo	25164	EC93-2125	6027	N245RS	NA0233	N79TS
NA773	N32KB	25074	N411FB	25165	EU93-2121	6028	wo	NA0234	N731DL
NA774	N774TS	25075	N600EG	25166	wo	6029	N35WP	NA0235	N10C
NA775	N333DP	25076	XS737/K	25167	VC93-2123	6030	wfu	NA0236	wo
NA776	XB-GNF	25077	wfu	25168	VC93-2124	6031	9Q-CGF	NA0237	N511KA
NA777	wfu	25078	XA-DCS	25169	N163AG	6032	N334PS	NA0238	N200JP
NA778	N778JA	25079	P4-AOC	25171	D2-FEZ	6033	N514AJ	NA0239	C-GKPM
NA779	N781JR	25080	wfu	25172	ZS-CAL	6034	wfu	NA0240	N700HH
NA780	N800TG	25081	XS739/F	25177	wo	6035	N128YT	NA0241	XA-...
25001	wfu	25082	wfu	25178	5N-WMA	6036	wfu	NA0242	N241RT
25002	wfu	25083	wfu	25181	wo	6037	N228MD	NA0243	N9395Y
25003	wfu	25084	N888CJ	25182	wo	6038	XA-ACN	NA0244	N414RF
25004	wfu	25085	wfu	25184	ZS-LPE	6039	wfu	NA0245	VP-CLU
25005	wfu	25086	wo	25189	wfu	6040	N287DL	NA0246	N700NW
25006	wfu	25087	N330G	25194	wfu	6041	N603TS	NA0247	N120JC
25007	wo	25088	5B-...	25197	PT-LHK	6042	wo	NA0248	N900CP
25008	wfu	25089	5N-ALH	25199	wfu	6043	wo	NA0249	XB-FMK
25009	wfu	25090	N429DA	25209	wfu	6044	N453DP	NA0250	N308DD
25010	wfu	25091	XA-RSP	25215	D2-EXR	6045	N508VM	NA0251	N571CH
25011	XS709/M	25092	wfu	25217	5N-EAS	6046	N299GS	NA0252	N237WR
25012	wfu	25093	wfu	25219	D2-FFH	6047	N68GA	NA0253	N422X
25013	wfu	25094	wfu	25223	wfu	6048	N852GA	NA0254	N125XX
25014	wfu	25095	wo	25227	N355AC	6049	P4-VJR	NA0255	N540B
25015	wfu	25096	wo	25231	N831DF	6050	wfu	NA0256	N455BK
25016	N222NG	25097	wfu	25235	N101UR	6051	N601JA	NA0257	N611MC
25017	XA-RSR	25098	YV-815CP	25238	VP-BKK	6052	wfu	NA0258	N227MM
25018	N218TJ	25099	wfu	25240	wfu	6053	N721RM	NA0259	N941CE
25019	wo	25100	N6SS	25242	ZS-LME	6054	wo	NA0260	XA-...
25020	wfu	25101	XA-MBM	25243	N4ES	6055	N111UN	NA0261	N999CY
25021	wfu	25102	wfu	25246	wfu	6056	wfu	NA0262	N3RC
25022	wo	25103	N402AC	25247	9Q-CPR	6057	N11AF	NA0263	N126RG
25023	ZS-PJE	25104	wfu	25248	YV-1122CP	6058	N20FM	NA0264	N724EA
25024	XS711/L	25105	wfu	25249	N154JC	6059	wfu	NA0265	N299WB
25025	wfu	25106	wfu	25250	N888TJ	6060	N395EJ	NA0266	N497PT
25026	wfu	25107	XA-...	25251	LV-AXZ	6061	N701MS	NA0267	N267JE
25027	N777RN	25108	N46190	25252	wfu	6062	5N-MAY	NA0268	XA-SON
25028	wfu	25109	N4CR	25253	N253MT	6063	N9AZ	NA0269	XA-AMI
25029	N10D	25110	wo	25254	VT-UBG	6064	XA-...	NA0270	N52GA
25030	XA-RDD	25111	wfu	25255	N4QB	6065	N4SA	NA0271	N154FJ
25031	N105HS	25112	XA-SLR	25257	wfu	6066	N600G	NA0272	N89GN
25032	N942DS	25113	wfu	25259	wfu	6067	N157RP*	NA0273	N110EJ
25033	RP-C125	25114	N114WD	25260	D2-EFM	6068	N600AE	NA0274	N560SB
25034	wfu	25115	N48DD	25264	N93TS	6069	5N-EMA	NA0275	N125SJ
25035	N151SG	25116	wfu	25266	N125CK	6070	N76TJ*	NA0276	wo
25036	wfu	25117	wfu	25268	wfu	6071	XA-...	NA0277	N509QC
25037	wfu	25118	N14HH	25269	AP-BGI	25256	wo	NA0278	N770CC
25038	N806CB	25119	N500XY	25270	N440RD	25258	9Q-CBC	NA0279	N90FF
25039	wfu	25120	wo	25271	N810HS	*125-700*		NA0280	N500FM
25040	XS712/A	25121	N685FF	25272	N63EM	NA0201	N701TS	NA0281	N281BT
25041	XS713/C	25122	wfu	25274	EU93-2119	NA0202	N727TA	NA0282	N120YB
25042	N725WH	25123	wfu	25277	VU93-2126	NA0203	N104AE	NA0283	N26SC
25043	wfu	25124	wfu	25288	VU93-2127			NA0284	N10UC

Reg#	Reg	Reg#	Reg	Reg#	Reg	Reg#	Reg	Reg#	Reg
NA0285	N130YB	7076	N111ZS	NA0431	N682B	8039	N173TR	8154	N97
NA0286	N83MD	7082	N752CM	NA0432	N810LX	8040	N718HC	8155	N300BL
NA0287	N564BR	7085	N10TN	NA0433	N9UP	8041	N626CG	8156	N98
NA0288	N198GT	7088	N224EA	NA0434	N432AQ	8042	N904BW*	8158	N800AF
NA0289	N70QB	7091	VP-CLX	NA0435	C-GMTR	8043	N313CQ	8164	HZ-130
NA0290	N17WG	7094	N483FG	NA0436	N803JL	8044	N833JP	8165	VT-RAY
NA0291	N947CE	7097	RA-02801	NA0437	N17DD	8045	N845CW	8167	N48AL
NA0292	N48FB	7100	N801RA	NA0438	N800PA	8046	N125SB	8169	N526AC
NA0293	N296RG	7103	G-GIRA	NA0439	C-GKPP	8047	N324SA	8175	N2032
NA0294	N188KA	7107	N85HH	NA0440	N295JR	8048	N716DB	8176	XA-TPB
NA0295	N134RT*	7109	VP-BOY	NA0441	N79NP	8049	N796CH	8177	N5119
NA0296	N100JF	7112	RA-02850	NA0442	N707PE	8050	G-OURA	8180	G-BZNR
NA0297	N945CE	7115	N333MS	NA0443	N717MT	8051	N851CW	8182	N12F
NA0298	N298BP	7118	N810KB*	NA0444	N290EC	8052	N221HB	8184	PT-OSW
NA0299	N700NY	7124	OD-FNF	NA0445	N800QC	8053	N489SA*	8186	N818MV
NA0300	N943CE	7127	N795A	NA0446	N82XP	8054	N527M	8190	PT-JAA
NA0301	N107LT	7130	N405DW	NA0447	N904GP	8055	N528M	8192	TR-LDB
NA0302	C-GLIG	7133	wo	NA0448	N868WC	8056	G-JETI	8194	PT-OTC
NA0303	N900JT	7136	P4-AOE	NA0449	C-GAGU	8057	N614AP	8197	N150SB
NA0304	N700NH	7139	RA-02803	NA0450	N731JR	8058	G-JJSI	8198	PT-WAL
NA0305	5N-BPC	7142	P4-OBE	NA0451	N801CF	8059	N255RB	8201	P4-AMF
NA0306	N141AL	7151	N613MC	NA0452	N750RV	8060	N330DE	8203	N453TM
NA0307	N270KA	7158	N700VT	NA0453	N1910A	8061	N861CW	8208	TC-ANC
NA0308	N9999V	7160	5N-AVK	NA0454	N25BB	8062	N862CW	8210	HB-VMI
NA0309	N95CM	7163	7T-VCW	NA0455	N801P*	8063	N74ND	8211	N855GA
NA0310	N18SH	7166	EC-HRQ	NA0456	C-GKGD	8064	MAAW-J1	8212	N323L
NA0311	N700LP	7169	5N-MAZ	NA0457	N941HC	8065	N65FA	8213	N10857
NA0312	N412DP	7172	ZS-CAG	NA0458	N929WQ	8066	N55RF	8214	PT-OOI
NA0313	P4-AOD	7175	G-MKSS	NA0459	N4402	8067	N867CW	8215	29-3041
NA0314	N53GH	7178	N803BF	NA0460	N722A	8068	N167DD	8219	9M-AZZ
NA0315	N26ME	7181	ZD620	NA0461	N800DN	8069	N160WC	8222	G-VIPI
NA0316	N18BA	7183	ZD703	NA0462	N57LN	8070	N255DV	8224	N810V
NA0317	N612MC	7184	SU-PIX	NA0463	N805X	8071	N94JT	8226	N800MJ
NA0318	N356SR	7187	wo	NA0464	N466AE	8072	N164WC	8227	39-3042
NA0319	XA-JAI	7189	N45KG	NA0465	N2QG	8073	N212RG	8228	N130LC
NA0320	N7490A	7190	ZD621	NA0466	N661JN	8074	N103HT	8229	TC-TEK
NA0321	N65DL	7194	ZD704	NA0467	N500J	8075	XA-RYM	8230	N71MT
NA0322	N322BC	7196	wo	NA0468	N600J	8076	RA-02807	8231	N75MT
NA0323	VT-AAA	7197	5N-BEX	NA0469	N118K	8077	N897CW	8232	C-FBUR
NA0324	N507F	7200	VP-BMD	NA0470	N58PM	8078	YL-VIP	8233	G-BYHM
NA0325	C-GOGM	7203	wo	NA0471	VP-BHB	8079	N800LL	8234	VP-CDE
NA0326	N819DM	7205	ZE395	NA0472	N44HH	8080	N800WH	8235	OY-RAA
NA0327	C-GAAA	7208	N501GF	NA0473	N935H	8081	N196MG	8236	N58BL
NA0328	N2HP	7209	N805CD	8001	N800RM	8082	N800S	8237	N250JE
NA0329	5N-DAO	7210	N502GF	8002	N15AX	8083	N852A	8238	N100AG
NA0330	XB-JTN	7211	ZE396	8003	N583VC	8084	N24JG*	8239	C-GMLR
NA0331	5N-MAO	7212	LY-BSK	8004	XA-TVI	8085	N285AL	8240	G-CJAA
NA0332	N125AS	7213	N700CE	8005	N800FL	8086	N523WG	8241	XA-CHA
NA0333	N46WC	7214	VP-CMP	8006	N800FH	8087	C-FIGO	8242	49-3043
NA0334	C-GJBJ	7215	VT-OBE	8007	C-GWLE	8088	G-BTAB	8243	C-GSCL
NA0335	N770HS	*125-800/Hawker 800XP*		8008	N722CC	8089	N593HR	8244	N252DH
NA0336	N300TK	NA0401	N180NE	8009	N48Y	8090	N414PE	8245	52-3001
NA0337	N350PL	NA0402	N757M	8010	N810CW	8091	N1776H	8246	HB-VKW
NA0338	N700SA	NA0403	N316EC	8011	N811CW	8092	N3008	8247	52-3002
NA0339	N242AL	NA0404	N494AT	8012	N801CW	8093	N2033	8248	N789LB
NA0340	I-CIGH	NA0405	N527AC	8013	N300RB	8094	D-CFAN	8249	N500HF
NA0341	ZS-IPE	NA0406	C-FSCI	8014	N298AG	8095	ZS-OXY	8250	52-3003
NA0342	N949CE	NA0407	N70NE	8015	C-GWFM	8096	N234GF	8251	N194JS
NA0343	XA-...	NA0408	N703VZ	8016	N816CW	8097	N800BV	8252	XB-GCC
NA0344	N913V	NA0409	XA-TKQ	8017	N888ZZ	8098	N181FH	8253	N801CE
7001	N701CW	NA0410	N683E	8018	N36TJ	8099	N10YJ	8254	N2015M
7007	N54WJ	NA0411	N800EC	8019	N7996	8106	G-OLDD	8255	N127KC
7010	N424RJ	NA0412	N826CT	8020	N270HC	8109	5N-NPC	8256	N256BC
7013	N36FT	NA0413	N166WC	8021	G-RCEJ	8110	N710A	8257	N415BJ
7020	N777EH	NA0414	N800WA	8022	N822BL	8112	N831DC	8258	N258SP
7022	N700WC	NA0415	N800VC	8023	N47HW	8115	G-TCAP	8259	N954H
7025	N886S	NA0416	C-GCGS	8024	N337RE	8116	PT-LQP	8260	N957H
7028	N899DM	NA0417	N824CW	8025	PR-LTA	8118	HZ-105	8261	PT-GAF
7031	N703TS	NA0418	N802X	8026	N826CW	8120	N120AP	8262	N521JK
7034	N34GG	NA0419	HZ-BL2	8027	N880M	8129	XA-...	8263	N826GA
7037	G-IFTE	NA0420	N803X	8028	N85KH	8130	G-OSPG	8264	HB-VLF
7040	G-OWDB	NA0421	N804X	8029	N77LA	8131	N8030F	8265	HB-VLG
7046	N587VV	NA0422	N222MS	8030	N91CH	8133	PR-SOL	8266	N800CC
7054	G-OURB	NA0423	N423SJ	8031	PT-LHB	8134	N96	8267	I-SIRF
7055	N47PB	NA0424	N800SE	8032	HZ-WBT5	8136	N80GJ	8268	62-3004
7061	N810GS	NA0425	N797EP*	8033	N833CW	8143	5N-AGZ	8269	N380DE
7062	EI-WJN	NA0426	N856AF	8034	N125HH	8146	HZ-109	8270	N802CE
7064	N48LB	NA0427	N244JM	8035	N85MG*	8148	HZ-110	8271	N803CE
7067	N42TS	NA0428	N73WF	8036	wo	8149	N577T	8272	N4426
7070	G-DEZC	NA0429	N50BN	8037	70-ADC	8152	N800WG	8273	N337WR
7073	N210RK			8038	C-FDDD	8153	HB-VHV	8274	N4428*

8275	N77TC	8356	N550H	8437	N780TA	8518	N29B	8599	N59BR
8276	N126KC	8357	258-357	8438	N827SA	8519	N443M	8600	N250SP
8277	N333PC	8358	D-CJET	8439	CS-DNL	8520	VP-CEA	8601	ZS-DDA
8278	N872AT	8359	N25WX	8440	N801MB	8521	HB-VNJ	8602	N899SC
8279	N877DM	8360	92-3012	8441	N370DE	8522	N746UP	8603	N893CW
8280	N351SP	8361	N861QS	8442	N80PK	8523	N824QS	8604	N8186
8281	N781TA	8362	N862QS	8443	N310AS	8524	N7374	8605	C-GJKI
8282	N782TA	8363	N726TA	8444	LX-ARC	8525	B-3993	8606	N895QS
8283	N82EA	8364	N728TA	8445	12-3017	8526	B-3995	8607	N919RT
8284	PR-DBB	8365	N865SM	8446	N529M	8527	N56BE	8608	N500BN
8285	N285XP	8366	N894CA	8447	EU93-6053	8528	N828QS	8609	N80HD
8286	N501F	8367	N704JM	8448	N532PJ	8529	N259RH	8610	42-3022
8287	N801WB	8368	N804AC	8449	N365AT	8530	N890SP	8611	N944BB
8288	72-3005	8369	N800PC	8450	I-DLOH	8531	N259SP	8612	N711GD
8289	N863CE	8370	02-3013	8451	N475HM	8532	N317CC	8613	N90FB
8290	N348MC	8371	N848N	8452	N852QS	8533	32-3021	8614	N811QS
8291	N791TA	8372	N800GN	8453	N68CB	8534	N815TA	8615	VP-CKN
8292	N33BC	8373	N168BF	8454	N802TA	8535	N255DX	8616	N88HD
8293	N150NC	8374	N729TA	8455	N803TA	8536	B-3996	8617	N551VB
8294	N632FW	8375	N875QS	8456	G-JMAX	8537	N100NG	8618	N82GK
8295	VH-KEF	8376	N1640	8457	CS-DNO	8538	P4-SNT	8619	N676JB
8296	N707TA	8377	N984GC	8458	N228TM	8539	VP-BKB	8620	N77CS
8297	N843LX*	8378	N494RG	8459	N800WP	8540	N700MG	8621	N522EE
8298	N880SP	8379	N870QS	8460	C FIIND	8541	N000XP	8622	N800EL
8299	N601DR	8380	N101FC	8461	N881CW	8542	N842QS	8623	N221PB
8300	N950PC	8381	02-3014	8462	LV-ZTR	8543	N843CW	8624	N866RR
8301	PT-WMA	8382	SE-DYE	8463	N863QS	8544	N799JC	8625	N305JA
8302	XA-RUY	8383	N730TA	8464	N828NS	8545	N845QS	8626	N25W
8303	N621CH	8384	G-LAOR	8465	ZS-DDT	8546	N108BP	8627	N929AK
8304	N5734	8385	SE-DYV	8466	N866CW	8547	PR-OPP	8628	XA-JET
8305	72-3006	8386	N61DN	8467	N42FB	8548	N808TA	8629	N61729
8306	82-3007	8387	N887QS	8468	CS-DNT	8549	N155NS	8630	N125ZZ
8307	N85CC	8388	N809BA	8469	22-3019	8550	N793RC	8631	N74NP
8308	N875LP	8389	YL-MAR	8470	B-3991	8551	N777DB	8632	ZS-PZA
8309	N92UP	8390	N800FD	8471	N5736	8552	N836LX	8633	N800NS
8310	N33VC	8391	N771SV	8472	N872QS	8553	PR-LUG	8634	N808BL
8311	N850J	8392	LX-GBY	8473	N73UP	8554	XA-GTE	8635	N919SF
8312	N924JM	8393	N893QS	8474	N874QS	8555	N300CQ	8636	N800CQ
8313	N908VZ	8394	N800TL	8475	N829NS	8556	N800WY	8637	PP-ANA
8314	N800NJ	8395	PT-WVG	8476	N192NC	8557	N1630	8638	N638XP
8315	N9292X	8396	N21EL	8477	OE-GEO	8558	N225PB	8639	N95UP
8316	C-GDII	8397	N752TA	8478	N800DR	8559	N819AP	8640	N896QS
8317	N520JF	8398	N168HH	8479	CS-DNU	8560	N877S	8641	N513ML
8318	N1910H	8399	CS-DNJ	8480	N4403	8561	I-ALHO	8642	N12PA
8319	C-FIPE	8400	N314TC*	8481	HZ-KSRC	8562	N802DC	8643	N33NL
8320	N720TA	8401	EU93-6050	8482	N882QS	8563	N981CE	8644	N484JC
8321	N32BC	8402	N729AT	8483	N807TA	8564	N864QS	8645	N733K
8322	N722TA	8403	N111VG	8484	N84UP	8565	N240Z	8646	N528BP
8323	N877SL	8404	VP-BCM	8485	N485LT	8566	N664AC	8647	N847CW
8324	N303BC	8405	N866RB	8486	N886QS	8567	N74PC	8648	N848CW
8325	82-3008	8406	N754TA	8487	N3007	8568	N96FT	8649	N800EM
8326	N1897A	8407	12-3015	8488	N488HP	8569	N244LS	8650	N50AE
8327	N111ZN	8408	B-3990	8489	N28GP	8570	N880QS	8651	N470BC
8328	VH-SGY	8409	VP-BSK	8490	N327LJ	8571	RP-C8576	8652	N241JS
8329	N901K	8410	N885M	8491	XA-TYH	8572	N80FB	8653	N203TM
8330	N139M	8411	N617TM	8492	N800LF	8573	N873QS	8654	N149SB
8331	N160CT	8412	N990HC	8493	12-3018	8574	N915AM	8655	N535BC
8332	N36H	8413	N813CW	8494	VP-BXP	8575	B-3997	8656	CS-DFX
8333	92-3009	8414	N800XM	8495	5B-CKL	8576	N867QS	8657	N839LX
8334	N60HD	8415	TC-STR	8496	N125TM	8577	N800IJK	8658	ZS-...
8335	OE-GHU	8416	N816QS	8497	N825CT	8578	N91HK	8659	ZS-...
8336	N745UP	8417	N246V	8498	N11UL	8579	PK-TVO	8660	N660XP
8337	N733TA	8418	N806XM	8499	CS-DNV	8580	N1989D	8661	N800WW*
8338	N838QS	8419	N508BP	8500	C-FPCE	8581	XA-ICF	8662	N305SC*
8339	SE-DVD	8420	N910JD	8501	B-3992	8582	XA-JMS	8663	CS-DFY
8340	N840QS	8421	EU93-6051	8502	XA-AET	8583	XA-GLG	8664	CS-DFW
8341	92-3010	8422	CS-DNM	8503	N801WM	8584	N884VC	8665	N689AM
8342	258-342	8423	N388BS	8504	TC-AHS	8585	N585VC	8666	N840LX
8343	258-343	8424	YL-NST	8505	N805QS	8586	N876QS	8667	N802DR
8344	N29GP	8425	N438PM	8506	I-RONY	8587	N261PA	8668	N156NS
8345	D-CBMW	8426	N27FL	8507	C-GIBU	8588	N799S	8669	N520SP
8346	258-346	8427	12-3016	8508	N800PE	8589	N974JD	8670	N670XP
8347	N409AV	8428	N828CW	8509	N162JB	8590	N733H	8671	N184TB
8348	92-3011	8429	ZS-...	8510	N890CW	8591	N380GG	8672	N1CA*
8349	C-FEPC	8430	CS-DNK	8511	CS-DNX	8592	N892QS	8673	CS-DFZ
8350	258-350	8431	N144HM	8512	N501CT	8593	N898QS	8674	N841WS
8351	258-351	8432	N832CW	8513	22-3020	8594	N140GB	8675	N351TC
8352	258-352	8433	N833QS	8514	D-CHEF	8595	N76CS	8676	N676GH
8353	258-353	8434	EU93-6052	8515	N321MS	8596	N804BH	8677	N850CT
8354	N2G	8435	CS-DNN	8516	N896CW	8597	XA-TYK	8678	N9867
8355	N855QS	8436	N836QS	8517	N817QS	8598	N92FT	8679	N800AH

8680	N80E	9045	N545QS	RB-72	ZS-SGS	282-23	N123CD	282-110	wfu
8681	N681XP	9046	N546QS	RB-73	N107WR	282-24	N8AF	282-111	N7KG
8682	4X-CRU	9047	N547QS	RB-74	N902RD	282-25	wfu	282-112	XA-...
8683	N832QS*	9048	N548QS	RB-75	N213PC	282-26	XA-RED	282-113	N430MP
8684	N684DK	9049	N549QS	RB-76	N1XH	282-27	wfu	282-114	XB-RGO
8685	N36685	9050	N550QS	RB-77	TC-MHS	282-28	wo	282-115	XA-LML
8686	CS-DRA	9051	N551QS	RB-78	N390JW	282-29	165511	282-116	wfu
8687	N733A	9052	N552QS	RB-79	wo	282-30	165514	282-117	N265SC
8688	N688G	**Premier 1**		RB-80	N50PM	282-31	N34AM	282-118	wfu
8689	F-HBFP	RB-1	N390RA	RB-81	N134SW	282-32	165520	282-119	wo
8690	CS-DRB	RB-2	N704T	RB-82	D-IBBB	282-33	N168W	282-120	N73DR
8691	N858QS	RB-3	N390TC	RB-83	N88EL	282-34	N940CC	282-121	wfu
8692	N700R	RB-4	N414TE	RB-84	PR-JRR	282-35	wfu	282-122	N409GL
8693	N302PE*	RB-5	N808V	RB-85	N487DT	282-36	wfu	282-123	XB-ESS
8694	N800R	RB-6	N155RM	RB-86	N96NC	282-37	wo	282-124	XA-...
8695	N695XP	RB-7	N343PR	RB-87	B-8006	282-38	N339PM	282-125	XA-SQA
8696	N800PL*	RB-8	N460AS	RB-88	G-OMJC	282-39	XA-RTM	282-126	N40GT
8697	N530SM*	RB-9	XA-ZUL	RB-89	D-IWWW	282-40	wfu	282-127	wo
8698	N860QS	RB-10	N5010X	RB-90	N32SG	282-41	XA-...	282-128	N99114
8699	N699XP	RB-11	N50PN	RB-91	N45NB*	282-42	wfu	282-129	XA-RLH
8700	N108DD	RB-12	N390BW	RB-92	N592HC	282-43	FAE-043	282-130	wfu
8701	N501XP	RB-13	N48TC	RB-93	N322BJ	282-44	N64MA	282-131	wfu
8702	N841LX	RB-14	N969RE	RB-94	ZS-PFE	282-45	N333NM	282-132	N240CF
8703	N50553	RB-15	N335JB	RB-95	N24YP	282-47	wo	282-133	I-RELT
8704	N614BG	RB-16	N444SS	RB-96	N535CD	282-48	N47VL	282-134	N40NJ
8705	N815QS	RB-17	N88ER	RB-97	G-FRYL	282-49	86001	282-135	N2006
8706	N706XP	RB-18	N711AJ	RB-98	N61998	282-50	wfu	282-136	CP-2317
8707	N707XP	RB-19	N16DK	RB-99	N199RM	282-51	wfu	282-137	N881DM
8708	N799RM	RB-20	N777MQ	RB-100	N122DS	282-52	N64DH	**Sabre 50**	
8709	N821QS	RB-21	PR-AMA	RB-101	N73PJ	282-53	wfu	287-1	N50CR
8710	N37010	RB-22	N45ND	RB-102	N3901A*	282-54	wo	**Sabre 60**	
8711	N37211	RB-23	N488RC	RB-103	N701KB	282-55	wfu	306-1	N359WJ
8712	N370R	RB-24	ZS-PRM	RB-104	N855JB	282-56	XA-RPS	306-2	N36RZ
8713	N713XP	RB-25	N719L	RB-105	N777JF	282-57	wfu	306-3	wo
8737	N518M	RB-26	wo	RB-106	N20NL	282-58	wfu	306-4	N121JE
8747	N519M	RB-27	D-IFMC	RB-107	N877W	282-59	wfu	306-5	N161CM
125-1000		RB-28	N128JL	RB-108	N61908	282-60	165524	306-6	XA-SMF
NA1001	N100U	RB-29	N110PR	RB-109	N50078	282-61	165517	306-7	XB-HDL
NA1002	N229U	RB-30	N84FM	RB-110	N300SL	282-62	wfu	306-8	N813BR
NA1003	N208R	RB-31	ZS-AVM	RB-111	N6111F	282-63	XA-AFW	306-9	wfu
NA1004	N513LR	RB-32	PR-CIM	RB-112	N60322	282-64	wfu	306-10	wfu
NA1005	N514QS	RB-33	N677AS	RB-113	N11PM	282-65	XA-MJE	306-11	wo
NA1006	N515QS	RB-34	N390DP	RB-114	N143CM	282-66	165513	306-12	wfu
NA1007	N448CC	RB-35	D-IAGG	RB-115	N6015Y	282-67	N140RF	306-13	RA-3077K
NA1008	N520QS	RB-36	N1XT	RB-116	N200LB	282-68	wo	306-14	wfu
NA1009	N52SM	RB-37	N567T	RB-117	N6117G	282-69	wfu	306-15	N600SJ
NA1010	N523QS	RB-38	N972PF	RB-118	N6118C	282-70	N3280G	306-16	wfu
8151	wfu	RB-39	N390JK	RB-119	N6119C	282-71	XA-SMR	306-17	wfu
8159	wfu	RB-40	PR-BER	RB-120	N6120U	282-72	165515	306-18	N12PB
9003	N503QS	RB-41	N43HJ	RB-121	N602DV*	282-73	wfu	306-19	wfu
9004	VP-CPT	RB-42	N324AM	RB-122	N3722Z	282-74	wfu	306-20	XC-AAJ
9005	N505QS	RB-43	N1EG	RB-123	N3723A	282-75	wfu	306-21	XC-AAC
9007	N119U	RB-44	N88MM	RB-124	N6124W	282-76	wfu	306-22	XA-CHP
9008	N207TT	RB-45	N100WE	RB-125	N3725F	282-77	165518	306-23	N85HS
9012	I-....	RB-46	N460L	RB-126	N3726G	282-78	wo	306-24	N600GL
9016	N678SB	RB-47	N581SF	RB-218	N67AS	282-79	N111AC	306-25	wfu
9017	N517LR	RB-48	D-IATT	**Sabre**		282-80	XA-FTN	306-26	XA-CEN
9018	5N-FGR	RB-49	N25MC	**Sabre 40**		282-81	165510	306-27	N103TA
9021	N137RP	RB-50	D-ISXT	282-1	N116SC	282-82	N39RG	306-28	N353CA
9022	VH-LMP	RB-51	LX-LCG	282-2	165512	282-83	wfu	306-29	wfu
9023	N524LR	RB-52	N605TC	282-3	wfu	282-86	wfu	306-30	wfu
9024	N525QS	RB-53	N351CW	282-4	wfu	282-87	wfu	306-31	N274CA
9025	N525QS	RB-54	N354RB	282-5	wo	282-88	wfu	306-32	wfu
9026	G-GDEZ	RB-55	N85PL	282-6	XA-GYR	282-89	wfu	306-33	N633SL
9027	N333RL	RB-56	N390RC	282-7	wfu	282-90	165516	306-34	AMT-203
9028	D-CBWW	RB-57	N488PC	282-8	wfu	282-91	86002	306-35	XB-JMR
9029	EZ-B021	RB-58	N34GN	282-9	165509	282-92	N825SB	306-36	XA-RIR
9030	N430LR	RB-59	N701DF	282-10	wo	282-94	165521	306-37	N562R
9031	N301PE	RB-60	LX-PRE	282-11	wfu	282-97	wo	306-38	XC-HGY
9032	N850TC	RB-61	EC-IOZ	282-12	wfu	282-98	N767JH	306-39	wfu
9033	N533QS	RB-62	N800CS	282-13	XA-TKW	282-99	N12BW	306-40	N306SA
9034	G-GMAB	RB-63	ZS-DDM	282-14	wfu	282-100	wfu	306-41	wo
9035	N535QS	RB-64	LX-PMR	282-15	N43WL	282-101	N160W	306-42	XA-VEL
9036	N127RP	RB-65	N4395D	282-16	wfu	282-102	XA-PIH	306-43	N115CR
9037	XA-RGG	RB-66	VP-BAE	282-17	wfu	282-103	wfu	306-44	N562MS
9038	N107RP	RB-67	ZS-MGK	282-18	N131BH	282-104	wfu	306-45	wo
9039	N539QS	RB-68	N133B	282-19	165519	282-105	wfu	306-46	N642RP
9040	N540LR*	RB-69	N205BC	282-20	165523	282-106	YV-1144CP	306-47	XB-ESX
9041	N541LR*	RB-70	N731UG	282-21	wfu	282-107	wo	306-48	N4NT
9042	N542QS	RB-71	N71KV	282-22	wo	282-108	N8500	306-49	wfu
9043	XA-RYB					282-109	FAE-047		
9044	N544QS								

Reg	ID
306-50	N601GL
306-51	N60JC
306-52	158843
306-53	N699RD
306-54	N610RA
306-55	158844
306-56	XA-DSC
306-57	XA-RLS
306-58	XA-AGT
306-59	N10LX
306-60	N15HF
306-61	N1JX
306-62	wfu
306-63	XA-TSS
306-64	wfu
306-65	159361
306-66	wfu
306-67	wfu
306-68	FAE-049
306-69	159364
306-70	159365
306-71	N71CC
306-72	XA-GIH
306-73	N442RM
306-74	wo
306-75	N11LX
306-76	N86CP
306-77	wfu
306-78	N477X
306-79	N539PG
306-80	N61FB
306-81	wfu
306-82	N59K
306-83	XA-RLL
306-84	N265GM
306-85	N211BR
306-86	XA-ICK
306-87	XA-RFB
306-88	XA-RAP
306-89	XA-STI
306-90	N265MK
306-91	LV-WXX
306-92	N33JW
306-93	XA-JCE
306-94	N348W
306-95	N124DC
306-96	XB-ETV
306-97	XA-SVG
306-98	N531AB
306-99	N66GZ
306-100	XA-TMF
306-101	N376D
306-102	N70HL
306-103	N234DC
306-104	160053
306-105	160054
306-106	160055
306-107	160056
306-108	wo
306-109	XA-SBV
306-110	XB-HJS
306-111	XC-PFN
306-112	CC-CTC
306-113	XA-TVZ
306-115	FAB 001
306-116	N39CB
306-117	FAE-001A
306-118	N607CF
306-119	N109MC
306-120	N1GM
306-121	N789SG
306-122	N56RN
306-123	XA-ATE
306-124	N48WS
306-125	XA-JML
306-126	N111F
306-127	XA-CUR
306-128	XA-SJM
306-129	XB-...
306-130	XA-AFG
306-131	XA-...
306-132	N265U
306-133	N468RB
306-134	N282WW
306-135	N921MB
306-137	XA-SAH
306-138	XA-RVT
306-139	XC-UJS
306-140	XA-...
306-141	N141SL
306-142	N143DZ
306-143	XA-TPU
306-144	XC-UJF
306-145	XC-JDC
306-146	N31CR

Sabre 65

Reg	ID
465-1	N65HH
465-2	N124SD
465-3	N65BT
465-4	N804PA
465-5	wo
465-6	N432CC
467-7	N2700
465-8	XA-GAP
465-9	N0QV
465-10	N336RJ
465-11	N57MQ
465-12	N73TJ
465-13	N945CC
465-14	XA-SPM
465-15	N465TS
465-16	N603MA
465-17	N74VC
465-18	N696US
465-19	N91BZ
465-20	N173A
465-21	N701FW
465-22	N889RA*
465-23	N223LB
465-24	N271MB
465-25	N812WN
465-26	N488DM
465-27	N4CS
465-28	N66GE
465-29	N976SR
465-30	N65TC
465-31	N265M
465-32	HB-VCN
465-33	N265C
465-34	N47SE
465-35	N65AK
465-36	N65MC
465-37	N750CC
465-38	N850CC
465-39	N41LV
465-40	N801SS
465-41	N800M
465-42	N875CA
465-43	N65T
465-44	N7NR
465-45	N265DS
465-46	N65CC
465-47	N33TR
465-48	N265CP
465-49	N697US*
465-50	N920DY
465-51	N69WU
465-52	N96RE
465-53	N80RN
465-54	N65SR
465-55	XA-TOM
465-56	N499NH
465-57	N355CD
465-58	N670H
465-59	N35CC
465-60	N88BF
465-61	N117JW
465-62	N265WS
465-63	N2NL
465-64	wo
465-65	N395GA
465-66	N964C
465-67	N921CC
465-68	N6NR
465-69	N65ML
465-70	N58HT
465-71	N75VC
465-72	N465SP
465-73	N651MK
465-74	N700JC
465-75	N570R
465-76	N65L
306-114	N990PT

Sabre 75

Reg	ID
370-1	wfu
370-2	N10M
370-3	N125NX
370-4	N400DB
370-5	XA-RYJ
370-6	wfu
370-8	wfu
370-9	wfu

Sabre 75A

Reg	ID
370-7	N670C
380-1	N100EJ
380-2	N406PW
380-3	T-11
380-4	N11887
380-5	XA-TUD
380-7	wo
380-8	wo
380-10	wfu
380-12	N75BS
380-13	AE-175
380-14	wfu
380-15	N424R
380-16	N12659
380-18	wfu
380-19	wfu
380-20	N109SB
380-22	wfu
380-23	N800CD
380-24	wfu
380-25	N400RS
380-26	wfu
380-27	wo
380-28	wfu
380-29	wfu
380-30	N818LD
380-31	wfu
380-33	N7148J
380-34	XC-DDA
380-35	wo
380-36	N377HS
380-37	wfu
380-38	N316EQ
380-39	N105HD
380-40	XB-...
380-41	N400NR
380-42	N3RP
380-43	wfu
380-44	N380GK
380-45	wo
380-46	XC-AA89
380-47	N33RZ
380-48	N100BP
380-51	N380CF
380-52	N929CG
380-53	N827SL
380-54	N380FP
380-55	XB-GSP
380-56	N22NB
380-57	JY-AFH
380-58	XA-GHR
380-59	N1LT
380-60	N60SL
380-61	wfu
380-62	JY-AFP
380-63	N448W
380-64	N942CC
380-65	N972NR*
380-66	N819GY
380-67	wo
380-68	XC-UJU
380-69	wo
380-70	N110AJ
380-71	XA-TSZ
380-72	N933JC

Sabre 80

Reg	ID
380-6	N184PC
380-9	N995RD
380-11	wfu
380-17	N380BC
380-21	N82AF
380-30	XA-JRF
380-49	N265KC
380-50	XA-ACD

Sabreliner T-39A(265)

Reg	ID
265-1	wfu
265-2	wfu
265-3	wfu
265-4	wo
265-5	wfu
265-7	wfu
265-8	wfu
265-9	wfu
265-10	XA-TFD
265-11	wfu
265-12	wo
265-13	wfu
265-14	XA-TIY
265-15	XA-...
265-16	wfu
265-17	wfu
265-18	wfu
265-19	wfu
265-20	wfu
265-21	wfu
265-22	wfu
265-23	wfu
265-24	wfu
265-25	wfu
265-26	wfu
265-27	wfu
265-28	wfu
265-29	wfu
265-30	wfu
265-31	wfu
265-32	wfu
265-33	wfu
265-34	wo
265-35	wfu
265-36	wfu
265-37	wfu
265-38	wfu
265-39	wfu
265-40	wfu
265-41	wfu
265-42	wfu
265-43	wo
265-44	wfu
265-45	wfu
265-46	wfu
265-47	wo
265-48	XA-TFL
265-49	wo
265-50	wfu
265-51	wfu
265-52	wfu
265-53	wfu
265-54	wfu
265-55	wfu
265-56	wfu
265-57	wfu
265-58	wfu
265-59	wfu
265-60	wfu
265-61	wfu
265-62	XA-TNP
265-63	wfu
265-64	wo
265-65	wfu
265-66	wfu
265-67	wfu
265-68	wfu
265-69	wfu
265-70	wfu
265-71	wfu
265-72	wfu
265-73	61-0670
265-74	wfu
265-75	wo
265-76	XA-TJZ
265-77	wfu
265-78	wfu
265-79	wfu
265-80	wfu
265-81	wfu
265-82	wfu
265-83	wfu
265-84	wfu
265-85	wfu
265-86	XA-GDW
265-87	wfu
265-00	wfu

Sabreliner T-39A(276)

Reg	ID
276-1	wo
276-2	wfu
276-3	wfu
276-4	XA-TQR
276-5	wfu
276-6	XA-TGO
276-7	wfu
276-8	XA-TJU
276-9	wfu
276-10	wfu
276-11	wo
276-12	wfu
276-13	wo
276-14	wfu
276-15	wfu
276-16	wfu
276-17	wfu
276-18	wfu
276-19	wfu
276-20	wfu
276-21	XA-TIX
276-22	wfu
276-23	wfu
276-24	wfu
276-25	XA-...
276-26	wfu
276-27	XA-TDX
276-28	wfu
276-29	wfu
276-30	wfu
276-31	wfu
276-32	wfu
276-33	N39FS
276-34	wfu
276-35	wfu
276-36	wfu
276-37	wfu
276-38	wfu
276-39	XA-TJY
276-40	wfu
276-41	62-4488
276-42	wfu
276-43	wfu
276-44	XA-TIW
276-45	wfu
276-46	wfu
276-47	wfu
276-48	wfu
276-49	wo
276-50	wfu
276-51	wfu
276-52	wo
276-53	wfu
276-54	wfu
276-55	wo

Sabreliner T-39B

265-6	wfu
270-1	59-2873
270-2	wfu
270-3	60-3474
270-4	wfu
270-5	wfu
270-6	wfu

Sabreliner T-39D

277-1	wfu
277-2	XA-AAG*
277-3	wfu
277-4	wfu
277-5	wfu
277-6	XA-AAI*
277-7	XA-AAF*
277-8	wfu
277-9	wfu
285-1	XA-AAJ*
285-2	wfu
285-3	wfu
285-4	150972
285-5	wfu
285-6	wfu
285-7	wfu
285-8	wfu
285-9	150977
277-10	wfu
285-10	wfu
285-11	wfu
285-12	wfu
285-13	wfu
285-14	wfu
285-15	wfu
285-16	wfu
285-17	wfu
285-18	wfu
285-19	wfu
285-20	wfu
285-21	wfu
285-22	wfu
285-23	wfu
285-24	150992
285-25	XA-AAH*
285-26	151337
285-27	wfu
285-28	wfu
285-29	wfu
285-30	wfu
285-31	wfu
285-32	wfu

Sabreliner T-39E

282-46	wo
282-84	wfu
282-85	XA-AAW*
282-93	158381
282-95	158380
282-96	wfu

Swearingen

SJ 30

001	wfu
002	wo
003	N30SJ
004	N404SJ
005	N50SJ

VFW

VFW614

G14	wfu
G17	D-ADAM
G18	wfu
G19	wfu

Biz-Jet Database

If you need more information then call us for a quote.

We can supply a database updated monthly or a simple report.

Data Includes:

Registration
Registration Country
Construction Number
Aircraft Type
Engine Manufacturer
Engine Model
Year of manufacturer
Base of Operation
Operator/Owners Name
Operator/Owners Address
Contact
Telephone Number
Fax Number
Purchase date
History of Aircraft

BUCHair UK Ltd, 78 High Street,
Reigate, Surrey, RH2 9AP
Tele: +44 (0)1737 224747   Fax: +44 (0)1737 226777
Email buchair_uk@compuserve.com

BIZ TURBOPROPS 2004

BizProps - Country Index

Country	Prefix	Page
ALGERIA	7T	445
ANGOLA	D2	300
ARGENTINA	LV	316
ARUBA	P4	424
AUSTRALIA	VH	427
AUSTRIA	OE	417
BAHAMAS	C6	298
BANGLADESH	S2	425
BELGIUM	OO	417
BELIZE	V3	431
BERMUDA	VP-B	430
BOLIVIA	CP	297
BOTSWANA	A2	289
BRAZIL	PP	419
BULGARIA	LZ	317
BURKINA FASO	XT	435
CAMEROON	T.I	427
CANADA	C	290
CAYMAN ISLANDS	VP-C	430
CHILE	CC	296
CHINA	B	289
CHINA - HONG KONG	B-H	289
CHINA - TAIWAN	B	290
COLOMBIA	HK	308
CONGO BRAZZAVILLE	TN	427
CONGO KINSHASA	9Q	446
COSTA RICA	TI	427
CROATIA	9A	446
CYPRUS	5B	444
CZECH REPUBLIC / CZECHIA	OK	417
DENMARK	OY	418
DOMINICAN REPUBLIC	HI	307
ECUADOR	HC	307
EGYPT	SU	425
EIRE	EI	301
EL SALVADOR	YS	435
FINLAND	OH	417
FRANCE	F	302
GABON	TR	427
GERMANY	D	298
GHANA	9G	446
GREAT BRITAIN	G	305
GREECE	SX	425
GUATEMALA	TG	426
HONDURAS	HR	311
ICELAND	TF	426
INDIA	VT	430
INDONESIA	PK	419
IRAN	EP	302
ISRAEL	4X	443
ITALY	I	312
IVORY COAST	TU	427
JAMAICA	6Y	445
JAPAN	JA	313
KAZAKHSTAN	UN	427
KENYA	5Y	445
KOREA	HL	311
LIBYA	5A	444
LUXEMBOURG	LX	317
MADAGASCAR	5R	444
MALAWI	7Q	445
MALAYSIA	9M	446
MALI	TZ	427
MALTA	9H	446
MAURITANIA	5T	444
MAURITIUS	3B	443
MEXICO	XA	432
MONACO	3A	443
MOROCCO	CN	297
MOZAMBIQUE	C9	298
NAMIBIA	V5	431
NETHERLANDS	PH	418
NETHERLANDS ANTILLES	PJ	418
NEW ZEALAND	ZK	439
NIGER	5U	444
NIGERIA	5N	444
NORWAY	LN	315
OMAN	A4O	289
PAKISTAN	AP	289
PANAMA	HP	311
PAPUA NEW GUINEA	P2	424
PARAGUAY	ZP	440
PERU	OB	416
PHILIPPINES	RP	424
POLAND	SP	425
PORTUGAL	CS	297
QATAR	A7	289
ROMANIA	YR	435
SAO TOME & PRINCIPE	S9	426
SAUDI ARABIA	HZ	312
SENEGAL	6V	445
SEYCHELLES	S7	426
SIERRA LEONE	9L	446
SLOVAKIA	OM	417
SLOVENIA	S5	426
SOMALIA	6O	445
SOUTH AFRICA	ZS	440
SPAIN	EC	301
SRI LANKA	4R	443
SUDAN	ST	425
SWAZILAND	3D	443
SWEDEN	SE	424
SWITZERLAND	HB	306
TANZANIA	5H	444
THAILAND	HS	312
TOGO	5V	444
TURKEY	TC	426
TURKS & CAICOS ISLANDS	VQ-T	
UGANDA	5X	445
UNITED ARAB EMIRATES	A6	289
URUGUAY	CX	298
USA	N	317
VENEZUELA	YV	435
VIETNAM	VN	430
YUGOSLAVIA	YU	435
ZAMBIA	9J	446
ZIMBABWE	Z	439

Business TurboProps - By Country within Continent includes Civil And Military

Total Props	9903

Africa

7T	=	ALGERIA	14
D2	=	ANGOLA	26
A2	=	BOTSWANA	12
XT	=	BURKINA FASO	2
TJ	=	CAMEROON	3
TN	=	CONGO BRAZZAVILLE	1
9Q	=	CONGO KINSHASA	11
SU	=	EGYPT	6
TR	=	GABON	3
9G	=	GHANA	1
TU	=	IVORY COAST	3
5Y	=	KENYA	32
5A	=	LIBYA	4
5R	=	MADAGASCAR	1
7Q	=	MALAWI	1
TZ	=	MALI	1
5T	=	MAURITANIA	2
3B	=	MAURITIUS	2
CN	=	MOROCCO	17
C9	=	MOZAMBIQUE	5
V5	=	NAMIBIA	10
5U	=	NIGER	2
5N	=	NIGERIA	15
S9	=	SAO TOME & PRINCIPE	4
6V	=	SENEGAL	2
9L	=	SIERRA LEONE	1
6O	=	SOMALIA	1
ZS	=	SOUTH AFRICA	186
ST	=	SUDAN	3
3D	=	SWAZILAND	1
5H	=	TANZANIA	5
5V	=	TOGO	3
5X	=	UGANDA	1
9J	=	ZAMBIA	10
Z	=	ZIMBABWE	11
Total for Continent			**402**

Australasia

VH	=	AUSTRALIA	169
ZK	=	NEW ZEALAND	10
P2	=	PAPUA NEW GUINEA	8
Total for Continent			**187**

Central America

P4	=	ARUBA	2
C6	=	BAHAMAS	3
V3	=	BELIZE	1
VP-	=	CAYMAN ISLANDS	2
TI	=	COSTA RICA	11
HI	=	DOMINICAN REPUBLIC	3
YS	=	EL SALVADOR	1
TG	=	GUATEMALA	18
HR	=	HONDURAS	7
6Y	=	JAMAICA	1
PJ	=	NETHERLANDS ANTILLES	3
HP	=	PANAMA	40
VQ	=	TURKS & CAICOS ISLANDS	2
Total for Continent			**94**

Europe

OE	=	AUSTRIA	18
OO	=	BELGIUM	11
LZ	=	BULGARIA	2
9A	=	CROATIA	1
5B	=	CYPRUS	2
OK	=	CZECH REPUBLIC / CZECHIA	7
OY	=	DENMARK	26
EI	=	EIRE	3
OH	=	FINLAND	13
F	=	FRANCE	211
D	=	GERMANY	163
G	=	GREAT BRITAIN	59
SX	=	GREECE	15
TF	=	ICELAND	4
I	=	ITALY	45
LX	=	LUXEMBOURG	22
9H	=	MALTA	1
3A	=	MONACO	4
PH	=	NETHERLANDS	24
LN	=	NORWAY	22
SP	=	POLAND	4
CS	=	PORTUGAL	4
YR	=	ROMANIA	3
OM	=	SLOVAKIA	2
S5	=	SLOVENIA	3
EC	=	SPAIN	38
SE	=	SWEDEN	28
HB	=	SWITZERLAND	54

TC	=	TURKEY	18	
YU	=	YUGOSLAVIA	4	

Total for Continent   811

Far East

S2	=	BANGLADESH	2
B	=	CHINA	12
B-	=	CHINA - HONG KONG	2
B	=	CHINA - TAIWAN	3
VT	=	INDIA	59
PK	=	INDONESIA	21
JA	=	JAPAN	107
UN	=	KAZAKHSTAN	1
HL	=	KOREA	6
9M	=	MALAYSIA	10
AP	=	PAKISTAN	9
RP	=	PHILIPPINES	28
S7	=	SEYCHELLES	3
4R	=	SRI LANKA	2
HS	=	THAILAND	26
VN	=	VIETNAM	1

Total for Continent   292

Middle East

EP	=	IRAN	24
4X	=	ISRAEL	29
A4	=	OMAN	1
A7	=	QATAR	1
HZ	=	SAUDI ARABIA	4
A6	=	UNITED ARAB EMIRATES	4

Total for Continent   63

North America

VP-	=	BERMUDA	9
C	=	CANADA	435
XA	=	MEXICO	227
N	=	USA	6432

Total for Continent   7103

South America

LV	=	ARGENTINA	98
CP	=	BOLIVIA	16
PP	=	BRAZIL	306
CC	=	CHILE	27
HK	=	COLOMBIA	192
HC	=	ECUADOR	20
ZP	=	PARAGUAY	14
OB	=	PERU	31
CX	=	URUGUAY	2
YV	=	VENEZUELA	245

Business TurboProps - By Country

| AP | = | PAKISTAN | | | Total | 9 |

Civil

Reg	Yr Type	c/n	Owner/Operator	Prev Regn
☐ AP-BBR	90 DHC 6-300	782	Oil & Gas Development Corp.	C-GEVP
☐ AP-BCQ	85 Conquest II	441-0352	Government of Punjab, Lahore.	N1213N
☐ AP-BCY	85 Conquest II	441-0350	Government of Sind, Karachi.	N12127
☐ AP-BFK	91 Reims/Cessna F406	F406-0059	M Nawaz, Karachi.	N3122E
☐ AP-CAA	77 King Air 200	BB-278	Directorate of Civil Aviation, Karachi.	AP-CAD

Military

☐ 11667	81 Gulfstream 840	11667	Pakistan Army,	N5919K
☐ 11733	84 Gulfstream 840	11733	Pakistan Army,	N56GA
☐ 927	82 King Air B200	BB-927	Pakistan Air Force, Rawalpindi.	N18262
☐ J 752	65 Fokker F 27-200	10281	Pakistan Air Force, 12 Squadron Chakala, Islamabad.	AP-ATW

| A2 | = | BOTSWANA | | | Total | 12 |

Civil

☐ A2-AEZ	79 King Air 200	BB-421	Kalahari Air Services & Charter, Gaborone.	N4488L
☐ A2-AGO	90 King Air B200	BB-1353	De Beers Botswana Mining Co P/L. Orapa.	N15599
☐ A2-AHT	80 Conquest 1	425-0011	B L C Aviation Ltd.	N6161P
☐ A2-AHV	83 King Air F90-1	LA-212	Sladden International P/L. Gaborone.	N6726P
☐ A2-AHZ	76 King Air 200	BB-95	Air Charter Botswana P/L. Gaborone.	ZS-JPD
☐ A2-AJK	80 King Air 200	BB-704	Botswana Ash,	ZS-KLO
☐ A2-BHM	81 King Air B200	BB-903	Broadhurst Motors, Gaborone.	ZS-LBE
☐ A2-DBH	81 King Air C90	LJ-988	Air Charter Botswana P/L. Gaborone.	ZS-LUU
☐ A2-KAS	80 King Air 200	BB-614	Air Charter Botswana P/L. Gaborone.	ZS-LKA
☐ A2-MXI	79 King Air 200T	BT-5	Maxi Save, (was BB-469).	N205EC
☐ A2-OLM	01 Beech 1900D	UE-423	Debswana Diamond Co P/L. Gaborone.	

Military

☐ OB-2	90 King Air B200	BB-1352	Government/Botswana Defence Force, Gaborone.	N5568V

| A40 | = | OMAN | | | Total | 1 |

Civil

☐ A40-CQ	84 Dornier 228-100	7028	Royal Oman Police, Seeb.	D-IBLN

| A6 | = | UNITED ARAB EMIRATES | | | Total | 4 |

Civil

☐ A6-...	68 King Air B90	LJ-397		ZS-OYS
☐ A6-GAK	02 Pilatus PC-12/45	479		HB-FPE

Military

☐ 801	96 King Air 350	FL-131	United Arab Emirates Air Force.	A6-MHH
☐ 802	96 King Air 350	FL-132	United Arab Emirates Air Force.	A6-KHZ

| A7 | = | QATAR | | | Total | 1 |

Civil

☐ A7-AHK	90 King Air B200	BB-1350	Sheikh Ahmad bin Hamad bin Khalid Al Thani, Doha.	(N147VC)

| B | = | CHINA | | | Total | 12 |

Civil

☐ B-3551	85 King Air B200	BB-1204	CAAC Special Services Division, Beijing.	N6927C
☐ B-3552	85 King Air B200	BB-1205	CAAC Special Services Division, Beijing.	N6927D
☐ B-3553	85 King Air B200	BB-1206	CAAC Special Services Division, Beijing.	N6927G
☐ B-3581	94 King Air 350	FL-111	CAAC Special Services Division, Beijing.	N8139K
☐ B-3582	94 King Air 350	FL-113	CAAC Special Services Division, Beijing.	N8291Y
☐ B-3583	00 King Air 350	FL-318	CAAC Special Services Division, Beijing.	N3218Z
☐ B-3621	90 PA-42 Cheyenne IIIA	5501051	CAAC Flying College, Guanghan.	(D-IOSG)
☐ B-3622	90 PA-42 Cheyenne IIIA	5501052	CAAC Flying College, Guanghan.	(D-IOSG)
☐ B-3623	90 PA-42 Cheyenne IIIA	5501054	CAAC Flying College, Guanghan.	N92409
☐ B-3624	90 PA-42 Cheyenne IIIA	5501056	CAAC Flying College, Guanghan.	N9241D
☐ B-3625	92 PA-42 Cheyenne IIIA	5501059	CAAC Flying College, Guanghan.	(OE-FAB)
☐ B-3626	94 PA-42 Cheyenne IIIA	5501060	CAAC Flying College, Guanghan.	N9115X

| B-H | = | CHINA - HONG KONG | | | Total | 2 |

Civil

☐ B-HRS	98 BAe Jetstream 41	41102	Government Flying Service, Chek Lap Kok.	G-4-102
☐ B-HRT	98 BAe Jetstream 41	41104	Government Flying Service, Chek Lap Kok.	G-BXWN

| Reg | Yr Type | c/n | Owner/Operator | Prev Regn |

B = CHINA - TAIWAN *Total* 3

Civil

Reg	Yr	Type	c/n	Owner/Operator	Prev Regn
☐ B-00135	91	King Air 350	FL-52	Civil Aeronautical Administration, Taipei.	B-135
☐ B-13152	79	King Air 200	BB-449	Government of Taiwan, Taipei.	N2068L
☐ B-13153	93	King Air 350	FL-108	Department of Forests/Council of Agriculture, Taipei.	(VH-...)

C = CANADA *Total* 435

Civil

Reg	Yr	Type	c/n	Owner/Operator	Prev Regn
☐ C-FABR	93	King Air 350	FL-100	Execaire Inc/IMP Group Ltd. Dorval, PQ.	N350AM
☐ C-FAFD	70	King Air 100	B-42	Kenn Borek Air Ltd. Calgary, AB.	LN-VIP
☐ C-FAFE	79	King Air B100	BE-72	Alta Flights (Charters) Inc. Edmonton, AB.	ZS-MZS
☐ C-FAFS	77	King Air B100	BE-31	Alta Flights (Charters) Inc. Edmonton, AB.	N80DB
☐ C-FAFT	75	King Air/Catpass 250	BB-57	Alta Flights (Charters) Inc. Edmonton, AB.	N121DA
☐ C-FAFZ	81	King Air B100	BE-121	Alta Flights (Charters) Inc. Edmonton, AB.	VT-AVB
☐ C-FAIP	74	King Air A100	B-193	Air Inuit Ltd. Kuujjuaq, PQ.	F-GXAB
☐ C-FAJV	98	Pilatus PC-12/45	234	Bearskin Lake Air Service Ltd. Thunder Bay, ON.	HB-FRE
☐ C-FAKN	77	King Air 200	BB-216	Alkan Air Ltd. Whitehorse, Yukon. NT.	LN-VIU
☐ C-FAKP	72	Rockwell 690	11040	Air Spray (1967) Ltd. Edmonton, AB.	N690DC
☐ C-FAMB	87	King Air B200	BB-1281	Air Mikicow Ltd. Fort McMurray, AB.	N856TC
☐ C-FAMF	76	SA-226T Merlin 3A	T-274	Perimeter Aviation Ltd. Winnipeg, MT.	I-SWAA
☐ C-FAMO	69	BAe HS 748-2A	1669	Aerial Recon Surveys Ltd. Whitecourt, AB.	
☐ C-FAMU	73	King Air A100	B-166	Voyageur Airways Ltd. North Bay, ON.	N221SS
☐ C-FANF	69	SA-26T Merlin 2A	T26-32	Keewatin Air Ltd. Rankin Inlet, NT.	N742G
☐ C-FAPP	73	King Air A100	B-169	Voyageur Airways Ltd. North Bay, ON.	N305TZ
☐ C-FASB	73	King Air A100	B-163	Thunder Airlines Ltd. Thunder Bay, ON.	SE-ING
☐ C-FASF	01	Pilatus PC-12/45	416	RJM Aviation Ltd/Airsprint, Ottawa, ON.	N416PC
☐ C-FASN	77	King Air B100	BE-17	Arctic Sunwest Charters, Yellowknife, NT.	(N1981B)
☐ C-FASP	00	Pilatus PC-12/45	331	Airsprint Inc. Calgary, AB.	HB-FRP
☐ C-FASR	00	Pilatus PC-12/45	353	RJM Aviation Ltd/Airsprint, Edmonton, AB.	N353PC
☐ C-FATA	77	King Air 200	BB-283	Air Tindi Ltd. Yellowknife, NT.	N283JP
☐ C-FATR	70	681 Turbo Commander	6020	Ministic Air Ltd. Winnipeg, MT.	N114MR
☐ C-FAWE	68	Gulfstream 1	188	Propair Inc. Rouyn-Noranda, PQ.	HB-LDT
☐ C-FAXN	66	680V Turbo Commander	1546-9	Aero Aviation Centre (1981) Ltd. Edmonton, AB.	N2549E
☐ C-FBCN	74	King Air 200	BB-7	Kenn Borek Air Ltd. Calgary, AB.	
☐ C-FBGS	74	King Air A100	B-204	Voyageur Airways Ltd. North Bay, ON.	N108JL
☐ C-FBPT	65	King Air 90	LJ-13	Toranda Leasing Inc. Calgary, AB.	N99W
☐ C-FCAW	70	SA-26AT Merlin 2B	T26-172E	Carson Air Ltd. Williams Lake, BC.	N135SR
☐ C-FCDF	80	King Air F90	LA-81	Concord Drilling Fluids Ltd. Calgary, AB.	N444MF
☐ C-FCEC	81	Cheyenne II-XL	8166030	Craig Evan Corp/CEC Flightexec, London, ON.	N76TW
☐ C-FCEF	79	PA-31T Cheyenne II	7920069	Craig Evan Corp/CEC Flightexec, London, ON.	N250KA
☐ C-FCGB	75	King Air/Catpass 250	BB-24	Bar XH Air Inc. Medicine Hat, AB.	N183MC
☐ C-FCGC	77	King Air/Catpass 250	BB-236	North Cariboo Flying Service Ltd. Fort St John, BC.	N46KA
☐ C-FCGE	66	King Air A90	LJ-118	Buffalo Airways Ltd. Hay River, NT.	
☐ C-FCGH	67	King Air A90	LJ-203	Buffalo Airways Ltd. Hay River, NT.	
☐ C-FCGI	67	King Air A90	LJ-220	Northwestern Air, Fort Smith, Ar.	
☐ C-FCGL	77	King Air/Catpass 250	BB-190	Northern Thunderbird Air Inc. Smithers, BC.	N190MD
☐ C-FCGM	77	King Air 200	BB-217	North Cariboo Flying Service Ltd. Fort St John, BC.	N200CD
☐ C-FCGN	68	King Air A90	LJ-313	AeroPro, Ste Foy, PQ.	
☐ C-FCGT	76	King Air/Catpass 250	BB-159	Koowatin Air Ltd. Winnipeg, MT.	N47FH
☐ C-FCGU	78	King Air/Catpass 250	BB-301	Air Tindi Ltd. Yellowknife, NT.	N611SW
☐ C-FCGW	77	King Air/Catpass 250	BB-207	Air Nunavut Ltd. Iqaluit, NT.	N111WH
☐ C-FCJV	98	Pilatus PC-12/45	240	Bearskin Lake Air Service Ltd. Thunder Bay, ON.	N240PD
☐ C-FCLH	83	King Air F90	LA-184	Falcon Air Services, Saskatoon, SK.	OY-CCC
☐ C-FCMJ	71	681B Turbo Commander	6054	Perimeter Aviation Ltd. Winnipeg, MT.	N21HC
☐ C-FCZZ	73	Rockwell 690A	11106	Conair Group Inc. Abbotsford, BC.	N57106
☐ C-FDAM	69	King Air/Catpass 250	B-8	North Cariboo Flying Service Ltd. Fort St John, BC.	N59T
☐ C-FDGP	82	King Air B200	BB-1022	Fast Air Ltd. Winnipeg, MT.	N220RJ
☐ C-FDJQ	71	King Air 100	B-84	Flying Colours Corp. Peterborough, ON.	TI-AYN
☐ C-FDOR	72	King Air A100	B-103	Maritime Air Charter Ltd. Halifax, NS.	
☐ C-FDOS	72	King Air A100	B-106	Air Satellite Inc. Baie Comeau, PQ.	
☐ C-FDOU	72	King Air A100	B-112	Propair Inc. Rouyn-Noranda, PQ.	
☐ C-FDOV	72	King Air A100	B-117	5H Management Co/National Aviation Centre, Prince Albert, SK	
☐ C-FDOY	72	King Air A100	B-120	C E P Atmosphair Inc. St-Jean Chrysostome, PQ.	
☐ C-FDTC	99	King Air 350	FL-234	Avionair Inc. Dorval, PQ.	N3234K
☐ C-FEQB	79	PA-31 Cheyenne II	7920071	491549 Alberta Ltd. Calgary, AB.	SX-ABU
Reg	Yr	Type	c/n	Owner/Operator	Prev Regn

Reg	Yr	Type	c/n	Owner/Operator	Prev Regn
☐ C-FEVC	82	King Air B200	BB-973	Le Fevre & Co Property Agents Ltd. Victoria, BC.	N53TM
☐ C-FFFG	75	Mitsubishi MU-2L	662	Thunder Airlines Ltd. Thunder Bay, ON.	N5191B
☐ C-FFNV	77	PA-31T Cheyenne II	7720058	Integra Air Inc. Lethbridge, AB.	N167DA
☐ C-FFSS	80	MU-2 Marquise	783SA	IMP Group Ltd/Execaire Inc. Ottawa, ON.	N81604
☐ C-FFST	03	P-180 Avanti	1063	Avia Aviation Ltd. Calgary, AB.	N137PA
☐ C-FGEM	80	MU-2 Solitaire	434SA	886875 Ontario Inc. St Catherines, ON.	N24MW
☐ C-FGFL	00	Pilatus PC-12/45	339	Airsprint Inc. Calgary, AB.	HB-FRU
☐ C-FGFZ	78	King Air 200	BB-403	Provincial Airlines Ltd. St Johns, NF.	N147K
☐ C-FGIN	73	King Air A100	B-164	AeroPro, Ste Foy, PQ.	N164RA
☐ C-FGNL	74	King Air A100	B-184	Province of Newfoundland, St Johns, NF.	
☐ C-FGRE	98	Pilatus PC-12/45	241	Chartright Air Inc. Toronto, ON.	HB-FRL
☐ C-FGSX	83	Cheyenne II-XL	8166048	Aviation Commercial Aviation, Hearst, ON.	N600XL
☐ C-FGWA	79	PA-31T Cheyenne II	7920045	Craig Evan Corp/CEC Flightexec, London, ON.	N52LS
☐ C-FGWD	97	King Air B200	BB-1599	GWD Management Inc, Burlington, ON.	N200V
☐ C-FGWT	85	Gulfstream 900	15042	Grenfell Regional Health Services Board, St Anthony, NF.	N71GA
☐ C-FGXE	88	King Air C90A	LJ-1179	Dept of Transport, Ottawa, ON.	N179RC
☐ C-FGXG	86	King Air C90A	LJ-1139	Dept of Transport, Ottawa, ON.	N121RL
☐ C-FGXH	88	King Air C90A	LJ-1162	Dept of Transport, Ottawa, ON.	N477JA
☐ C-FGXJ	88	King Air C90A	LJ-1178	Dept of Transport, Ottawa, ON.	N357CY
☐ C-FGXL	88	King Air C90A	LJ-1189	Dept of Transport, Ottawa, ON.	(N203SL)
☐ C-FGXO	89	King Air C90A	LJ-1200	Dept of Transport, Ottawa, ON.	N68TW
☐ C-FGXQ	89	King Air C90A	LJ-1192	Dept of Transport, Hamilton, ON.	N616SC
☐ C-FGXS	89	King Air C90A	LJ-1207	Dept of Transport, Ottawa, ON.	N207RC
☐ C-FGXT	90	King Air C90A	LJ-1230	Dept of Transport, Ottawa, ON.	N1564P
☐ C-FGXU	86	King Air C90A	LJ-1140	Dept of Transport, Winnipeg, MT.	N8841
☐ C-FGXX	87	King Air C90A	LJ-1151	Dept of Transport, Winnipeg, MT.	N126RL
☐ C-FGXZ	88	King Air C90A	LJ-1177	Dept of Transport, Edmonton, AB.	(N357CA)
☐ C-FHBO	63	Gulfstream 1	104	Petro Canada Inc. Calgary, AB.	N719G
☐ C-FHGG	75	King Air A100	B-207	Integra Air Inc. Lethbridge, AB.	N727LE
☐ C-FHLP	76	King Air C90	LJ-685	H L Powell Trucking Ltd. Grand Prairie, AB.	C-FATW
☐ C-FHSP	82	Conquest II	441-0265	Juan Air (1979) Ltd. Sidney, BC.	N441E
☐ C-FHVM	01	PA-46-500TP Meridian	4697091	Voortman Cookies Ltd. Burlington, ON.	
☐ C-FHWI	67	King Air A90	LJ-309	Grondair/Grondin Transport Inc. St Frederic, PQ.	N329H
☐ C-FIDN	69	King Air 100	B-3	North Cariboo Flying Service Ltd. Fort St John, BC.	N128RC
☐ C-FIFE	76	Mitsubishi MU-2L	683	Nav Air Charter Inc. Victoria, BC.	OY-CEF
☐ C-FIFO	79	King Air 200	BB-527	Provincial Airlines Ltd. St Johns, NF.	N662L
☐ C-FIJV	98	Pilatus PC-12/45	222	Bearskin Lake Air Service Ltd. Thunder Bay, ON.	C-FKEN
☐ C-FIPO	01	PA-46-500TP Meridian	4697060	Image Air Charter Inc. Mississauga, ON.	
☐ C-FJAK	81	Cheyenne II-XL	8166028	Centerline (Windsor) Ltd. Windsor, ON.	N355SS
☐ C-FJEL	78	Mitsubishi MU-2N	706SA	Thunder Airlines Ltd. Thunder Bay, ON.	N866MA
☐ C-FJHP	68	King Air B90	LJ-325	Air Roberval Ltd. Roberval, PQ.	N900LD
☐ C-FJOL	98	King Air 350	FL-208	Skyservice Aviation Inc. Dorval, PQ.	N23086
☐ C-FJVB	81	PA-31T Cheyenne II	8120012	Lochhead-Haggerty Engineering & Manufacturing, Vancouver.	C-FZIH
☐ C-FKBU	77	King Air 200	BB-285	Kenn Borek Air Ltd. Calgary, AB.	C-GQXF
☐ C-FKIO	78	Mitsubishi MU-2N	725SA	Transwest Air Ltd. Prince Albert, SK.	N888RH
☐ C-FKJI	76	King Air 200	BB-105	Walsten Air Service (1986) Ltd. Kenora, ON.	N71TZ
☐ C-FKPA	99	Pilatus PC-12/45	275	Air Bravo Corp. Bracebridge, ON.	N275PC
☐ C-FKPI	99	Pilatus PC-12/45	250	Peace Air Ltd. Peace River, AB.	N250PB
☐ C-FKPX	02	Pilatus PC-12/45	451	Pascan Aviation Inc. Ste Foy, PQ.	HB-FSJ
☐ C-FKRB	98	Pilatus PC-12/45	233	Wasaya Airways LP. Thunder Bay, ON.	HB-FRD
☐ C-FKSL	00	Pilatus PC-12/45	324	North American Charters Ltd. Thunder Bay, ON.	N324PC
☐ C-FKTL	80	Conquest 1	425-0008	Kal Air Ltd. Vernon, BC.	N811NA
☐ C-FKTN	83	Conquest 1	425-0190	Kal Aviation Group Inc. Vernon, BC.	N444RU
☐ C-FKUL	98	Pilatus PC-12/45	204	Peace Air Ltd. Peace River, AB.	ZS-PAY
☐ C-FKVL	00	Pilatus PC-12/45	307	Peace Air Ltd. Peace River, AB.	N307PB
☐ C-FLRB	72	King Air A100	B-131	Little Red Air Service Ltd. Fort Vermilion, AB.	N102FG
☐ C-FLRD	79	King Air A100	B-243	Little Red Air Service Ltd. Fort Vermilion, AB.	N63SJ
☐ C-FLRM	83	King Air B200	BB-1115	C-K Air Service Ltd. Toronto-Pearson, ON.	N764NB
☐ C-FLTC	74	King Air C90	LJ-631	Little Red Air Service Ltd. Fort Vermilion, AB.	N103FG
☐ C-FLTS	73	King Air A100	B-149	Skyward Aviation Ltd. Winnipeg, MT.	N883CA
☐ C-FMDF	01	Pilatus PC-12/45	365	David Fountain, Halifax, NS.	N365PC
☐ C-FMHB	76	PA-31T Cheyenne II	7620023	491549 Alberta Ltd. Calgary, AB.	SX-ABT
☐ C-FMHD	92	King Air 350	FL-87	Aviation CMP Inc. St Georges, PQ.	C-GSCL
☐ C-FMKD	68	King Air B90	LJ-376	North Cariboo Flying Service Ltd. Fort St John, BC.	N300RV
☐ C-FMPA	96	Pilatus PC-12	164	RCMP-GRC Air Services, Winnipeg, MT.	HB-FRZ

Reg	Yr	Type	c/n	Owner/Operator	Prev Regn
☐ C-FMPB	99	Pilatus PC-12/45	283	RCMP-GRC Air Services, Ottawa, ON.	N1983R
☐ C-FMPE	00	Pilatus PC-12/45	314	RCMP-GRC Air Services, Edmonton, AB.	HB-FQZ
☐ C-FMPN	99	Pilatus PC-12/45	296	RCMP-GRC Air Services, Ottawa, ON.	HB-FQK
☐ C-FMPO	98	Pilatus PC-12/45	229	RCMP-GRC Air Aervices, Edmonton, AB.	HB-FRA
☐ C-FMPW	00	Pilatus PC-12/45	315	RCMP-GRC Air Services, Prince Albert, SK.	HB-FRA
☐ C-FMWM	70	King Air 100	B-59	Northern Thunderbird Air Inc. Smithers, BC.	N702JL
☐ C-FMXY	70	King Air 100	B-40	North Cariboo Flying Service Ltd. Fort St John, BC.	N923K
☐ C-FNCB	78	King Air E90	LW-287	Pentastar Transportation Ltd. Spruce Grove, AB.	N23660
☐ C-FNCN	69	King Air B90	LJ-468	Grondair/Grondin Transport inc. St Frederic, PQ.	N1FC
☐ C-FNED	76	King Air C90	LJ-680	Alberta Central Airways Ltd. Lac La Biche, AB.	N928RD
☐ C-FNGA	90	P-180 Avanti	1007	Cascades Inc. St Hubert, PQ.	I-RAII
☐ C-FNIL	02	King Air 350	FL-354	North Cariboo Flying Service Ltd. Fort St John, BC.	N354H
☐ C-FNRM	81	Gulfstream 840	11692	Morgan Air Services Co. Calgary, AB.	N152X
☐ C-FNWC	81	Conquest II	441-0216	Fast Air Ltd. Winnipeg, MT.	N441DM
☐ C-FNYM	76	PA-31T Cheyenne II	7620033	Northern Youth Programs Foundation, Dryden, BC.	N44TC
☐ C-FOGP	83	King Air B100	BE-134	Max Aviation Inc. St Hubert, PQ.	N363EA
☐ C-FOGY	76	King Air 200	BB-168	Propair Inc. Rouyn-Noranda, PQ.	N10VW
☐ C-FOPD	97	Pilatus PC-12/45	182	Province of Ontario Provincial Police, Sault Ste Marie, ON.	C-FKAC
☐ C-FOUR	73	Mitsubishi MU-2J	606	Shootor Airoouricr Corp. Saskatoon, 3K.	N338MA
☐ C-FPAJ	73	King Air A100	B-151	Propair Inc. Rouyn-Noranda, PQ.	N324B
☐ C-FPBC	78	King Air B100	BE-44	Celtic Tech Jet Ltd. Gloucester, ON.	N300MP
☐ C-FPCI	01	Pilatus PC-12/45	399	Wasaya Airways LP. Thunder Bay, ON.	N399PB
☐ C-FPCP	00	King Air 350	FL-317	Sunwest Home Aviation Ltd. Calgary, AB.	(XA-...)
☐ C-FPCZ	01	Pilatus PC-12/45	433	RJM Aviation Ltd/Airsprint, Calgary, AB.	HB-FRU
☐ C-FPLG	75	King Air A100	B-224	Aeropro, Ste Foy, PQ.	N16SM
☐ C-FPQQ	88	King Air B200	BB-1304	Little Red Air Service Ltd. Fort Vermilion, AB.	(VT-...)
☐ C-FPWR	91	King Air 350	FL-62	Churchill Falls (Labrador) Corp. Churchill Falls, NF.	N82882
☐ C-FQOV	70	King Air 100	B-38	Little Red Air Service Ltd. Fort Vermilion, AB.	N931M
☐ C-FRJE	78	PA-31T Cheyenne II	7820002	Westair Aviation Inc. Kamloops, BC.	C-GCUL
☐ C-FROM	73	Mitsubishi MU-2J	601	Nav Air Charter Inc. Victoria, BC.	N308MA
☐ C-FROW	74	Mitsubishi MU-2J	628	Nav Air Charter Inc. Victoria, BC.	N4202M
☐ C-FRWK	81	MU-2 Marquise	1521SA	Thunder Airlines Ltd. Thunder Bay, ON.	N437MA
☐ C-FSAO	98	King Air B200	BB-1610	Slave Air (1988) Ltd. Slave Lake, AB.	N713TA
☐ C-FSAT	96	King Air B200	BB-1526	Slave Air (1988) Ltd. Slave Lake, AB.	N417MC
☐ C-FSEA	84	Conquest 1	425-0192	Sunlite Electric (St Paul) Ltd. St Paul, AB.	N1221T
☐ C-FSFI	83	Conquest II	441-0316	Airco Aircraft Charters Ltd. Edmonton, AB.	N800SR
☐ C-FSIK	78	King Air B100	BE-39	Max Aviation Inc. St Hubert, PQ.	N129CP
☐ C-FSKA	78	King Air A100	B-239	Sunrise Electric Ltd/Skyward Aviation Ltd. Thompson, MT.	N154TC
☐ C-FSKC	80	Conquest II	441-0139	Skyward Aviation Ltd. Thompson, MT.	N441LL
☐ C-FSKG	80	Conquest II	441-0120	Skyward Aviation Ltd. Thompson, MT.	N544AL
☐ C-FSKQ	76	King Air 200	BB-99	Sontair Ltd. Chatham, ON.	5Y-SEL
☐ C-FSRK	97	Pilatus PC-12/45	202	Wasaya Airways LP. Thunder Bay, ON.	ZS-SRK
☐ C-FSTP	02	P-180 Avanti	1055	Avia Aviation Ltd. Calgary, AB.	N925GS
☐ C-FSVC	68	SA-26T Merlin 2A	T26-19	Keewatin Air Ltd. Rankin Inlet, NT.	N2JE
☐ C-FTIX	78	SA-226AT Merlin 4A	AT-066	GE Canada Asset Financing Inc. Vancouver, BC.	N5455M
☐ C-FTLB	87	King Air 300	FA-137	Bar XH Air Inc. Medicine Hat, AB.	C-GMBA
☐ C-FTMA	73	King Air A100	B-174	Montair Aviation Inc. Delta, BC.	N151A
☐ C-FTML	70	Mitsubishi MU-2G	525	Kitts Aviation, Lloydminster, AB.	N360JK
☐ C-FTOO	72	Mitsubishi MU-2J	549	Nav Air Charter Inc. Victoria, BC.	N65198
☐ C-FTPE	93	King Air C90B	LJ-1342	Tatham Process Engineering Inc. Toronto, ON.	
☐ C-FTWO	75	Mitsubishi MU-2L	672	Nav Air Charter Inc. Victoria, BC.	N709US
☐ C-FUFW	66	King Air 90	LJ-84	College d'Enseignement General et Professionel, Longueil, PQ	N619GS
☐ C-FVAX	83	Conquest 1	425-0178	North Cariboo Flying Service Ltd. Calgary, AB.	(N90GM)
☐ C-FVPC	00	Pilatus PC-12/45	358	V Kelner Pilatus Center Inc. Thunder Bay, ON.	HB-FSK
☐ C-FVPK	98	Pilatus PC-12/45	211	RJM Aviation Ltd/Airsprint, Ottawa, ON.	ZS-OEW
☐ C-FWAV	99	Pilatus PC-12/45	280	Wasaya Airways Ltd. Thunder Bay, ON.	HB-FSY
☐ C-FWPG	71	King Air 100	B-67	Airco Aircraft Charters Ltd. Edmonton, AB.	N26KW
☐ C-FWPN	70	King Air 100	B-51	Alberta Central Airways Ltd. Lac La Biche, AB.	N16SW
☐ C-FWPT	83	Cheyenne II-XL	8166066	Sawridge Energy Ltd. Slave Lake, AB.	N9170C
☐ C-FWRL	78	Conquest II	441-0079	9519 Investments Ltd. Prince George, BC.	N441KR
☐ C-FWRM	72	King Air A100	B-125	Propair Inc. Rouyn-Noranda, PQ.	N89JM
☐ C-FWUT	76	PA-31T Cheyenne II	7620039	Ashe Aircraft Enterprises Ltd. Calgary, AB..	N82031
☐ C-FWWK	89	King Air 300	FA-182	Carrier Lumber Ltd. Prince George, BC.	N8840A
☐ C-FWWQ	80	King Air 200	BB-667	West Wind Aviation Inc. Saskatoon, SK.	N667NA
☐ C-FWXB	82	King Air B200	BB-1058	Northern Thunderbird Air Inc. Prince George, BC.	N220DK
Reg	**Yr**	**Type**	**c/n**	**Owner/Operator**	**Prev Regn**

Reg	Yr	Type	c/n	Owner/Operator	Prev Regn
☐ C-FWXI	85	King Air B200	BB-1224	Beaver Air Services LP. The Pas, MT.	C-GTLA
☐ C-FWYF	71	King Air 100	B-89	Airco Aircraft Charters Ltd. Edmonton, AB.	N169RA
☐ C-FWYN	70	King Air 100	B-47	Airco Aircraft Charters Ltd. Edmonton, AB.	C-GNAX
☐ C-FWYO	70	King Air 100	B-28	Airco Aircraft Charters Ltd. Edmonton, AB.	N27JJ
☐ C-FXAJ	72	King Air A100	B-122	Air Mikisew Ltd. Fort McMurray, AB.	N8181Z
☐ C-FXRJ	81	King Air B100	BE-115	4229291 Canada Inc. Ville St Laurent, PQ.	N104LS
☐ C-FYBV	75	PA-31T Cheyenne II	7520015	Ashe Aircraft Enterprises Ltd. Calgary, AB.	N11232
☐ C-FYUT	99	Pilatus PC-12/45	254	Pascan Aviation Inc. Ste Foy, PQ.	N254PC
☐ C-FYZS	98	Pilatus PC-12/45	227	Keewatin Air Ltd. Winnipeg, MT.	HB-FQY
☐ C-FZNQ	77	King Air/Catpass 250	BB-264	Air Nunavut Ltd. Iqaluit, NT.	N456CJ
☐ C-FZPW	81	King Air B200	BB-940	Keewatin Air Ltd. Winnipeg, MT.	N519SA
☐ C-FZRQ	72	Rockwell 690	11025	Air Spray (1967) Ltd. Red Deer, AB.	N100LS
☐ C-FZVW	81	King Air 200	BB-787	Voyageur Airways Ltd. North Bay, ON.	N26G
☐ C-FZVX	77	King Air 200	BB-231	Voyageur Airways Ltd. North Bay, ON.	N200FH
☐ C-G...	73	King Air A100	B-165		C-GTLA
☐ C-G...	05	PA-46-500TP Meridian	4697200		
☐ C-GAAL	73	Rockwell 690A	11104	Conair Group Inc. Abbotsford, BC.	N690AZ
☐ C-GACA	88	King Air 1300	BB-1309	Alberta Central Airways Ltd. Lac La Biche, AB.	N4277C
☐ C-GACN	90	King Air 1300	BB-1384	Alberta Central Airways Ltd. Lac La Biche, AB.	N575T
☐ C-GADI	81	King Air B200	BB-853	West Wiind Aviation LP. Saskatoon, SK.	N44SR
☐ C-GAIK	72	King Air A100	B-104	Air Inuit Ltd. Kuujjuaq, PQ.	C-GCFD
☐ C-GAMC	80	MU-2 Marquise	785SA	Thunder Airlines Ltd. Thunder Bay, ON.	N273MA
☐ C-GAPK	74	King Air A100	B-198	Transwest Air Ltd. Prince Albert, SK.	N712AS
☐ C-GARO	72	King Air 200	BB-2	Pratt & Whitney Canada Inc. Longueil, PQ.	N200KP
☐ C-GASI	72	King Air A100	B-126	Thunder Airlines Ltd. Thunder Bay, ON.	N23BW
☐ C-GASW	72	King Air A100	B-108	Thunder Airlines Ltd. Thunder Bay, ON.	N110JJ
☐ C-GAVI	74	King Air A100	B-201	Kenn Borek Air Ltd. Calgary, AB.	G-BBVM
☐ C-GAWP	97	Pilatus PC-12/45	187	102662 Canada Inc/ExpressAir, Ottawa, ON.	HB-FSV
☐ C-GBBG	95	King Air B200	BB-1507	Newfoundland Labrador Air Transport Ltd. Deer Lake, NF.	N232JS
☐ C-GBBS	81	King Air 200	BB-757	Air Express Ontario Inc. Oshawa, ON.	N948MB
☐ C-GBCI	02	P-180 Avanti	1057	Craig Evan Corp/CEC Flightexec, London, ON.	N333BH
☐ C-GBFO	81	Cheyenne II-XL	8166069	Aviation Commercial Aviation, Hearst, ON.	N511SC
☐ C-GBJV	98	Pilatus PC-12/45	237	Wasaya Airways LP. Thunder Bay, ON.	HB-FRH
☐ C-GBOT	81	PA-42 Cheyenne III	8001063	Craig Evan Corp/CEC Flightexec, London, ON.	C-FCEH
☐ C-GBTL	96	Pilatus PC-12/45	159	Pascan Aviation Inc. Ste Foy, PQ.	N159PB
☐ C-GBTS	91	TBM 700	19	Brucelandair International, Kitchener, ON.	N635DS
☐ C-GBVX	80	King Air B100	BE-99	North Cariboo Flying Service Ltd. Fort St John, BC.	N524BA
☐ C-GBXW	97	Pilatus PC-12	170	Wasaya Airways LP. Thunder Bay, ON.	N170PD
☐ C-GBYN	85	King Air B200	BB-1232	Adlair Aviation (1983) Ltd. Yellowknife, NT.	N209CM
☐ C-GBZM	69	SA-26AT Merlin 2B	T26-122	Air Dorval Ltee. Dorval, PQ.	N63SC
☐ C-GCFB	81	King Air C90	LJ-929	NAV Canada, Vancouver, BC.	N81DD
☐ C-GCFF	79	King Air 200	BB-474	NAV Canada, Macdonald-Cartier, ON.	
☐ C-GCFL	70	King Air B90	LJ-500	NAV Canada, Ottawa, ON.	N20WC
☐ C-GCFM	80	King Air C90	LJ-886	North Cariboo Flying Service Ltd. Calgary, AB.	N15SL
☐ C-GCFZ	79	King Air C90	LJ-849	NAV Canada, Vancouver, BC.	N6647P
☐ C-GCIL	83	Conquest II	441-0314	North Cariboo Flying Service Ltd. Calagry, AB.	XB-CSB
☐ C-GCYB	83	Conquest II	441-0298	Image Air Charter Inc. Toronto-Buttonville, ON.	N245DL
☐ C-GDCL	74	Rockwell 690A	11192	Conair Group Inc. Abbotsford, BC.	N57192
☐ C-GDEF	78	SA-226AT Merlin 4A	AT-069	Propair Inc. Rouyn-Noranda, PQ.	(N558AC)
☐ C-GDFJ	76	King Air B100	BE-15	Dynamic Flight Services Inc. Calgary, AB.	N300DG
☐ C-GDFZ	70	King Air B100	BE-16	Dynamic Flight Services Inc. Calgary, AB.	N331GB
☐ C-GDGD	97	Pilatus PC-12/45	193	North American Charters Ltd. Thunder Bay, ON.	N193PC
☐ C-GDLG	81	Conquest 1	425-0063	Kildair Service Ltd. St Paul de Joliette, PQ.	N425TY
☐ C-GDPB	82	King Air B200C	BL-44	Air Tindi Ltd. Yellowknife, NT.	N18379
☐ C-GDPI	73	King Air A100	B-156	Voyageur Airways Ltd. North Bay, ON.	N21RX
☐ C-GEAS	90	King Air 350	FL-17	Province of Saskatchewan, Regina, SK.	N56872
☐ C-GEBA	76	PA-31T Cheyenne II	7620029	Beaver Air Services LP. The Pas, MT.	N177JE
☐ C-GEHS	80	MU-2 Marquise	763SA	Thunder Airlines Ltd. Thunder Bay, ON.	N26AP
☐ C-GEJE	03	King Air 350	FL-385	Grant Executive Jets Inc. Earlton, ON.	N5085T
☐ C-GEOS	76	Rockwell 690A	11279	Geographic Air Survey Ltd. Edmonton, AB.	N57180
☐ C-GEOW	98	Pilatus PC-12/45	244	Nakina Outpost Camps & Air Service Ltd. Nakina, ON.	HB-FRO
☐ C-GFAB	66	680V Turbo Commander	1601-43	Province of New Brunswick, Fredericton, NB.	N577RH
☐ C-GFAM	79	PA-31T Cheyenne II	7920042	Georgian Express Ltd. Toronto, ON.	(N777LE)
☐ C-GFIL	99	Pilatus PC-12/45	268	North American Charters Ltd. Thunder Bay, ON.	N268PC
☐ C-GFKS	79	King Air A100	B-247	Thunder Airlines Ltd. Thunder Bay, ON.	N153TC

Reg	Yr	Type	c/n	Owner/Operator	Prev Regn
☐ C-GFLA	99	Pilatus PC-12/45	293	RCMP-GRC Air Services, Ottawa, ON.	N293PC
☐ C-GFOL	75	King Air 200	BB-27	La Loge Mecatina Inc. La Romaine, PQ.	N120DP
☐ C-GFOX	03	P-180 Avanti	1065	RCMP-GRC Air Services, Ottawa, ON.	N126PA
☐ C-GFPP	72	Rockwell 690	11032	Air Spray (1967) Ltd. Red Deer, AB.	N349AC
☐ C-GFSA	97	King Air 350	FL-174	Province of Alberta, Edmonton, AB.	
☐ C-GFSB	75	King Air 200	BB-84	Fast Air Ltd. Winnipeg, MT.	
☐ C-GFSG	75	King Air 200	BB-671	Province of Alberta, Edmonton, AB.	
☐ C-GFSH	81	King Air B200	BB-912	Province of Alberta, Edmonton, AB.	
☐ C-GGDC	80	MU-2 Marquise	796SA	IMP Group Ltd/Execaire Inc. Toronto-Pearson, ON.	N700MA
☐ C-GGGQ	83	King Air B200	BB-1128	Aliant Telecom Inc. St John, NB.	
☐ C-GGKJ	78	King Air B100	BE-49	Alta Flights (Charters) Inc. Edmonton, Ab.	N400RK
☐ C-GGOO	73	Rockwell 690	11068	Air Spray (1967) Ltd. Edmonton, AB.	N9168N
☐ C-GGPS	78	PA-31T Cheyenne II	7820023	Craig Evan Corp/CEC Flightexec. London, ON.	
☐ C-GHDP	81	King Air B200	BB-891	Keewatin Air Ltd. Winnipeg, MT.	N888HG
☐ C-GHOC	74	King Air A100	B-194	Kenn Borek Air Ltd. Calgary, AB.	N57237
☐ C-GHOP	76	King Air 200	BB-120	Sunwest Home Aviation Ltd. Calgary, AB.	N6773S
☐ C-GHQG	85	King Air 300	FA-39	Government of Canada, Ottawa, ON.	N339WD
☐ C-GHVR	68	King Air B90	LJ-337	Northern Lights College, Dawson Creek, BC.	
☐ C-GHWF	73	Rockwell 690A	11134	Conair Group Inc. Abbotsford, BC.	N45VT
☐ C-GHYT	72	King Air U-21J	B-98	L & A Aviation Ltd/Landa Aviation, Hay River, NT.	N998RC
☐ C-GILM	72	King Air A100	B-124	Voyageur Airways Ltd. North Bay, ON. (status ?).	N100SJ
☐ C-GIND	81	King Air B200C	BL-42	Voyageur Airways Ltd. North Bay, ON.	N819CD
☐ C-GISH	73	King Air A100	B-152	Voyageur Airways Ltd. North Bay, ON.	(N67LG)
☐ C-GITC	01	TBM 700B	223	1087485 Alberta Ltd. Calgary, AB.	N700BY
☐ C-GIZX	73	King Air A100	B-172	Air Creebec Inc. Val D'Or, PQ.	N735DB
☐ C-GJBQ	74	King Air A100	B-191	Aeropro, Ste Foy, PQ.	N214CK
☐ C-GJBV	72	King Air A100	B-100	Voyageur Airways Ltd. North Bay, ON.	N100S
☐ C-GJFO	72	Rockwell 690	11035	Air Spray (1967) Ltd. Edmonton, AB.	N15VZ
☐ C-GJFY	81	King Air 200	BB-812	Sunwest Home Aviation Ltd. Calgary, AB.	C-GYUI
☐ C-GJHF	81	Conquest 1	425-0080	Abell Aviation Inc. Toronto-Pearson, ON.	N880EA
☐ C-GJHW	73	King Air A100	B-175	Transwest Air Ltd. Prince Albert, SK.	N92DL
☐ C-GJJF	72	King Air A100	B-123	Voyageur Airways Ltd. North Bay, ON.	N741EB
☐ C-GJJT	81	King Air 200	BB-828	Voyageur Airways Ltd. North Bay, ON.	N62GA
☐ C-GJKS	70	King Air 100	B-14	North American Charters Ltd. Thunder Bay, ON.	N402G
☐ C-GJLI	78	King Air 200	BB-347	Western Air Service (1986) Ltd. Kenora, ON.	N424CR
☐ C-GJLJ	77	King Air A100	B-235	Propair Inc. Rouyn-Noranda, PQ.	N23517
☐ C-GJLK	90	King Air 350	FL-13	Carson Air Ltd. Vancouver, BC.	N301JW
☐ C-GJLP	73	King Air A100	B-148	Propair Inc. Rouyn-Noranda, PQ.	N67V
☐ C-GJMM	01	P-180 Avanti	1037	Marivent Corp. St Bruno, PQ.	(N180UJ)
☐ C-GJPT	75	PA-31T Cheyenne II	7520039	Province of Saskatchewan, Regina, SK.	
☐ C-GJSU	71	King Air 100	B-88	Kenn Borek Air Ltd. Calgary, AB.	N100ZM
☐ C-GKAJ	77	King Air A100	B-232	Bearskin Lake Air Service Ltd. Thunder Bay, ON.	N400WH
☐ C-GKAY	97	Pilatus PC-12	178	1401277 Ontario Ltd. Thunder Bay, ON.	N178PC
☐ C-GKBB	73	King Air C90	LJ-607	Kenn Borek Air Ltd. Calgary, AB.	N48DA
☐ C-GKBN	75	King Air 200	BB-29	Kenn Borek Air Ltd. Calgary, AB.	LN-ASG
☐ C-GKBP	79	King Air 200	BB-505	Kenn Borek Air Ltd. Calgary, AB.	C-GKBP
☐ C-GKBQ	70	King Air 100	B-62	Kenn Borek Air Ltd. Calgary, AB.	LN-NLB
☐ C-GKBZ	71	King Air 100	B-85	Kenn Borek Air Ltd. Calgary, AB.	LN-PAJ
☐ C-GKNP	80	King Air B100	BE-89	Airsprint Inc. Calgary, AB.	N737MG
☐ C-GKNR	00	Pilatus PC-12/45	308	Kivalliq Air Ltd. Winnipeg, MT.	HB-FQV
☐ C-GKPC	75	PA-31T Cheyenne II	7520021	Kelly Panteluk Construction Ltd. Salmon Arm, SK.	C-GZQD
☐ C-GKPL	98	Pilatus PC-12/45	245	Wasaya Airways Ltd. Thunder Bay, ON.	ZS-DET
☐ C-GKSC	81	King Air F90	LA-113	Sanjel Corp. Calgary, AB.	N890CA
☐ C-GLAG	79	PA-31T Cheyenne II	7920027	Cascades Inc. St Hubert, PQ.	N71QS
☐ C-GLBL	82	Conquest II	441-0250	Airspec Corp Ltd. Toronto, ON.	N441MC
☐ C-GLCE	02	Pilatus PC-12/45	475	Road Trailer Rentals Inc. Buttonville, ON.	N475PC
☐ C-GLEM	91	P-180 Avanti	1009	Cascades Inc. St Hubert, PQ.	D-IHMO
☐ C-GLER	04	PA-46-500TP Meridian	4697185	DFM Aviation LP. Ste Julie, PQ.	
☐ C-GLGE	79	Conquest II	441-0086	Alta Flights (Charters) Inc. Edmonton, AB.	C-GAGE
☐ C-GLKA	68	SA-26T Merlin 2A	T26-20	Keewatin Air Ltd. Rankin Inlet, NT.	N77WF
☐ C-GLLS	98	King Air B200	BB-1601	Province of Saskatchewan, Regina, SK.	N2303F
☐ C-GLPG	73	King Air A100	B-159	AeroPro, Ste Foy, PQ.	N110KF
☐ C-GLRR	66	King Air A90	LJ-134	Little Red Air Service Ltd. Fort Vermilion, AB.	N38LA
☐ C-GMAG	76	King Air A100	B-229	Northern Hawk Aviation Ltd. Richmond, BC.	N100HC
☐ C-GMBC	92	King Air C90B	LJ-1300	Bombardier/Canadian Aviation Training Centre, Southport, MT.	

Reg	Yr Type	c/n	Owner/Operator	Prev Regn
☐ C-GMBD	92 King Air C90B	LJ-1301	Bombardier/Canadian Aviation Training Centre, Southport, MT.	
☐ C-GMBG	92 King Air C90B	LJ-1304	Bombardier/Canadian Aviation Training Centre, Southport, MT.	
☐ C-GMBH	92 King Air C90B	LJ-1309	Bombardier/Canadian Aviation Training Centre, Southport, MT.	
☐ C-GMBW	92 King Air C90B	LJ-1310	Bombardier/Canadian Aviation Training Centre, Southport, MT.	
☐ C-GMBX	92 King Air C90B	LJ-1313	Bombardier/Canadian Aviation Training Centre, Southport, MT.	
☐ C-GMBY	92 King Air C90B	LJ-1317	Bombardier/Canadian Aviation Training Centre, Southport, MT.	
☐ C-GMBZ	92 King Air C90B	LJ-1319	Bombardier/Canadian Aviation Training Centre, Southport, MT.	
☐ C-GMDF	76 PA-31T Cheyenne II	7620019	Bar XH Air Inc. Medicine Hat, AB.	
☐ C-GMEH	02 King Air 350	FL-353	Clearwater Fine Foods Inc. Upper Tantallon, NS.	N6153V
☐ C-GMOC	79 King Air/Catpass 250	BB-513	Alkan Air Ltd. Whitehorse, Yukon, NT.	N513SA
☐ C-GMPE	98 Pilatus PC-12/45	184	RCMP-GRC Air Services, Prince George, BC.	HB-FSS
☐ C-GMPI	99 Pilatus PC-12/45	239	RCMP-GRC Air Services, Ottawa, ON.	HB-FRJ
☐ C-GMPP	01 Pilatus PC-12/45	374	RCMP-GRC Air Services, Winnipeg, MT.	N374PC
☐ C-GMPW	99 Pilatus PC-12/45	274	RCMP-GRC Air Services, Ottawa, ON.	N274PC
☐ C-GMPY	00 Pilatus PC-12/45	311	RCMP-GRC Air Services, Edmonton, AB.	N311PB
☐ C-GMPZ	99 Pilatus PC-12/45	272	RCMP-GRC Air Services, Montreal, PQ.	HB-FSQ
☐ C-GMWR	75 King Air 200	BB-68	Provincial Airlines Ltd. St Johns, NF.	N844N
☐ C-GMYM	01 PA-46-500TP Meridian	4697114	Mackenzie Capital Corp. Bracebridge,	
☐ C-GNAA	70 King Air 100	B-24	La Loche Airways Ltd. Edmonton, AB.	N382WC
☐ C-GNAJ	72 King Air A100	B-107	Northern Air Charter (PR) Inc. Peace River, AB.	LN-AAH
☐ C-GNAM	89 King Air 1300	BB-1339	Northern Air Charter (PR) Inc. Peace River, AB.	(N131AZ)
☐ C-GNAR	74 King Air A100	B-190	Peace Air Ltd. Peace River, AB.	LN-AAG
☐ C-GNAX	92 King Air B200	BB-1419	Northern Air Charter (PR) Inc. Peace River, AB.	N146SB
☐ C-GNBB	79 King Air 200	BB-479	Pentastar Transportation Ltd. Spruce Grove, AB.	N200UQ
☐ C-GNDI	76 PA-31T Cheyenne II	7620036	Fast Air Ltd. Winnipeg, MT.	N73TB
☐ C-GNEP	84 Conquest 1	425-0221	Pacific Western Helicopters Ltd. Prince George, BC.	N904RM
☐ C-GNEX	75 King Air A100	B-211	Thunder Airlines Ltd. Thunder Bay, ON.	
☐ C-GNKP	75 PA-31T Cheyenne II	7520008	Province of Saskatchewan, Regina, SK.	
☐ C-GNLA	90 King Air 350	FL-26	Government of Newfoundland & Labrador, St Johns, NF.	N59TF
☐ C-GOGS	99 King Air 350	FL-269	Province of Ontario, Sault Ste Marie, ON.	N3169N
☐ C-GOGT	79 King Air 200	BB-535	Beaver Air Services LP. The Pas, MT.	
☐ C-GOIC	99 King Air 350	FL-272	Province of Ontario, Sault Ste Marie, ON.	N3172N
☐ C-GPAI	03 Pilatus PC-12/45	491	Pascan Aviation Inc. Ste Foy, PQ.	HB-FQY
☐ C-GPBA	75 King Air A100	B-215	Exact Air Inc. St Honore, PQ.	N552GA
☐ C-GPCB	70 King Air 100	B-45	North Cariboo Flying Service Inc. Fort St John, BC.	N704S
☐ C-GPCD	75 King Air 200	BB-76	Provincial Airlines Ltd. St Johns, NF.	N500DR
☐ C-GPCL	74 SA-226AT Merlin 4	AT-017	Perimeter Aviation Ltd. Winnipeg, MT.	N5RT
☐ C-GPCO	04 Pilatus PC-12/45	603	V Kelner Pilatus Center Inc. Thunder Bay, ON.	
☐ C-GPCP	76 King Air 200	BB-140	Pacific Coastal Airlines Ltd. Richmond, BC.	
☐ C-GPEA	76 King Air/Catpass 250	BB-170	Prince Edward Air Ltd. Moncton, NB.	N869MA
☐ C-GPIA	04 P-180 Avanti	1072	Avia Aviation Ltd. Calgary, AB.	N157PA
☐ C-GPIM	80 PA-31T Cheyenne II	8020065	Westair Aviation Inc. Kamloops, BC.	C-GNAM
☐ C-GPJL	81 King Air B100	BE-107	Max Aviation Inc. St Hubert, PQ.	N3699B
☐ C-GPNB	92 King Air C90B	LJ-1305	Province of New Brunswick, Fredericton, NB.	N488JR
☐ C-GPPC	95 King Air 350	FL-127	Sunwest Home Aviation Ltd. Calgary, AB.	
☐ C-GPRO	73 SA-226T Merlin 3	T-239	Southern Aviation Ltd. Regina, SK.	N833S
☐ C-GPRU	77 King Air B100	BE-26	Max Aviation Inc. St Hubert, PQ.	N36WH
☐ C-GPSB	81 PA-42 Cheyenne III	8001030	Swanberg Air Inc. Grand Prairie, AB.	N855GA
☐ C-GPSP	78 Conquest II	441-0058	Hauts-Monts Inc. Ste Foy, PQ.	OY-BHM
☐ C-GPSQ	78 Conquest II	441-0076	Hauts-Monts Inc. Beauport, PQ.	N441RC
☐ C-GPTA	65 Gulfstream 1	162	Ptarmigan Airways Ltd. Yellowknife, NT.	N300GP
☐ C-GQJG	77 King Air 200	BB-249	Aviation Starlink Inc. Dorval, PQ.	
☐ C-GQNJ	77 King Air 200	BB-275	Walsten Air Service (1986) Ltd. Kenora, ON..	
☐ C-GRBA	98 Pilatus PC-12/45	238	843420 Alberta Ltd/Pilatus 238 Ltd. Edmonton, AB.	N238PC
☐ C-GRBF	70 SA-26AT Merlin 2B	T26-171E	Peace Air/Roberts Brothers Farming Ltd. Falher, AB.	N50AK
☐ C-GRDC	98 Pilatus PC-12/45	214	Pascan Aviation Inc. Ste Foy, PQ.	PT-XTG
☐ C-GRHD	83 Conquest 1	425-0167	Gary L Redhead Holdings Ltd. Regina, SK.	N6872L
☐ C-GRJP	98 Pilatus PC-12/45	196	RJM Aviation Ltd/Airsprint, Calgary, AB.	N196PC
☐ C-GRJZ	00 King Air 350	FL-285	Jetport Inc. Hamilton, ON.	N3185J
☐ C-GRMS	97 Pilatus PC-12/45	200	Road Trailer Rentals Inc. Buttonville, ON.	N200PD
☐ C-GRSL	74 King Air C90	LJ-609	AeroPro, Ste Foy, PQ.	N38BA
☐ C-GSAA	91 PA-42 Cheyenne IIIA	5501057	Province of Saskatchewan, Saskatoon, SK.	N120GA
☐ C-GSAE	00 King Air B200	BB-1748	Province of Saskatchewan, Saskatoon, SK.	N50848
☐ C-GSAV	01 King Air B200	BB-1790	Province of Saskatchewan, Saskatoon, SK.	N4470T
☐ C-GSFI	83 Conquest 1	425-0177	Sunwest Home Aviation Ltd. Calgary, AB.	C-GRJM
Reg	**Yr Type**	**c/n**	**Owner/Operator**	**Prev Regn**

Reg	Yr	Type	c/n	Owner/Operator	Prev Regn
☐ C-GSFM	68 King Air B90		LJ-422	Kenn Borek Air Ltd. Calgary, AB.	N513SC
☐ C-GSKH	82 Conquest II		441-0264	Skyward Aviation Ltd. Thompson, MT.	N254WS
☐ C-GSSK	86 Conquest II		441-0362	Alta Flights (Charters) Inc. Edmonton, AB.	D-IAGA
☐ C-GSVQ	66 680V Turbo Commander		1544-8	Northern Lights College, Dawson Creek, BC.	N146E
☐ C-GSWF	82 King Air B100		BE-129	Sunwest Home Aviation Ltd. Calgary, AB.	C-GSWF
☐ C-GSWG	82 King Air B100		BE-131	Sunwest Home Aviation Ltd. Calgary, AB.	N6354H
☐ C-GSWX	93 Beech 1900D		UE-63	Sunwest Home Aviation Ltd. Calgary, AB.	
☐ C-GSYN	70 King Air 100		B-61	Adlair Aviation (1983) Ltd. Yellowknife, NT.	N418LA
☐ C-GTEM	99 King Air 350		FL-236	Skyservice Aviation Inc. Dorval, PQ.	N2346S
☐ C-GTFP	76 PA-31T Cheyenne II		7620016	491549 Alberta Ltd. Calgary, AB.	N57524
☐ C-GTLF	70 King Air 100		B-72	Skyward Aviation Ltd. Winnipeg, MT.	N5476R
☐ C-GTLS	70 King Air 100		B-35	North Cariboo Flying Service Ltd. Fort St John, BC.	N178WM
☐ C-GTMA	68 King Air B90		LJ-348	Province of Alberta, Edmonton, AB.	N805K
☐ C-GTMM	79 PA-31T Cheyenne 1		7904008	Marivent Corp.	N528DS
☐ C-GTMW	70 SA-226AT Merlin 4		AT-002	Provincial Airlines Ltd. St Johns, NF.	N39RD
☐ C-GTOL	80 PA-31T Cheyenne 1		8004028	Tech-Aero Inc. Calgary, AB.	N2325V
☐ C-GTUC	77 King Air 200		BB-268	Air Tindi Ltd. Yellowknife, NT.	N565RA
☐ C-GTWW	75 King Air C90		LJ-657	Walsten Air Service (1986) Ltd. Kenora, ON.	N9030R
☐ C-GUPP	73 King Air A100		B 157	Thunder Airlines Ltd. Thunder Bay, ON.	N123CS
☐ C-GVIK	76 King Air B100		BE-7	Max Aviation Inc. St Hubert, PQ.	N57HT
☐ C-GVKA	78 PA-31T Cheyenne II		7920008	Westair Aviation Inc. Kamloops, BC.	
☐ C-GVKC	98 Pilatus PC-12/45		207	Kivalliq Air Ltd. Winnipeg, MT.	ZS-OEV
☐ C-GVKK	78 PA-31T Cheyenne II		7820038	The Craig Evan Corp/Flight Exec, London, ON.	N679MM
☐ C-GWEW	73 Rockwell 690		11057	Conair Group Inc. Abbotsford, BC.	N376TC
☐ C-GWRK	02 P-180 Avanti		1061	Avia Aviation Ltd. Calgary, AB.	N129PA
☐ C-GWSL	75 SA-226AT Merlin 4A		AT-028	Max Aviation Inc. St Hubert, PQ.	N5341M
☐ C-GWUY	75 King Air 200		BB-77	North-Wright Airways Ltd. Norman Wells, NT.	N300CP
☐ C-GWWA	70 King Air 100		B-27	Kenn Borek Air Ltd. Calgary, AB.	G-BOFN
☐ C-GWWN	74 King Air 200		BB-14	West Wind Aviation Inc. Saskatoon, SK.	N418CS
☐ C-GWWQ	71 King Air 100		B-76	Alta Flights (Charters) Inc. Edmonton, AB.	N300DA
☐ C-GWXH	83 King Air B200		BB-1126	Citicapital Ltd. Toronto, ON.	C-GTLG
☐ C-GWXM	88 King Air B200C		BL-130	Western Express Air Lines Inc. Vancouver, BC.	N362TD
☐ C-GXBF	76 PA-31T Cheyenne II		7620010	Canlynx Airways Inc. Mississauga, ON.	N54988
☐ C-GXCD	76 PA-31T Cheyenne II		7620026	Ashe Aircraft Enterprises Ltd. Calgary, AB.	
☐ C-GXHD	89 King Air 1300		BB-1338	Bar XH Air Inc. Medicine Hat, AB.	(OY-...)
☐ C-GXHF	89 King Air 1300		BB-1343	Bar XH Air Inc. Medicine Hat, AB.	5Y-ECO
☐ C-GXHG	90 King Air 1300		BB-1383	Bar XH Air Inc. Medicine Hat, AB.	N913YW
☐ C-GXHN	80 King Air 200		BB-693	Bar XH Air Inc. Medicine Hat, AB.	N245JS
☐ C-GXHP	70 King Air A100		B-132	Bar XH Air Inc. Medicine Hat, AB.	XB-SLG
☐ C-GXHR	88 King Air 1300		BB-1305	Bar XH Air Inc. Medicine Hat, AB.	5Y-EOB
☐ C-GXHS	88 King Air 1300		BB-1302	Bar XH Air Inc. Medicine Hat, AB.	PT-WYY
☐ C-GXHW	80 King Air 200		BB-710	Bar XH Air Inc. Medicine Hat, AB.	N850C
☐ C-GXRX	70 King Air 100		B-36	Shuswap Flight Centre Ltd. Salmon Arm, BC.	N600CB
☐ C-GXTC	77 PA-31T Cheyenne II		7720052	Venture Aviation Services Ltd. Vancouver, BC.	(N82165)
☐ C-GYQK	73 King Air A100		B-153	Pascan Aviation Inc. Ste Foy, PQ.	N120AS
☐ C-GYSC	97 King Air B200		BB-1579	Sanjel Corp. Calgary, AB.	(N886AT)
☐ C-GZGZ	00 Pilatus PC-12/45		357	Soltron Realty Inc. Dorval, PQ.	N7725X
☐ C-GZNS	82 MU-2 Marquise		1550SA	Thunder Airlines Ltd. Thunder Bay, ON.	N64WB
☐ C-GZON	72 Rockwell 690		11020	Air Spray (1967) Ltd. Edmonton, AB.	N14CV
☐ C-GZRP	84 PA-42 Cheyenne IIIA		5501011	Helicopter Transport Services, Carp, ON.	N100CS
☐ C-GZRX	80 King Air 200		BB-574	North Cariboo Flying Service Ltd. Fort St John, BC.	N75WL
☐ C-GZUZ	73 King Air A100		B-143	491549 Alberta Ltd. Calgary, AB.	N151U
☐ C-GZYO	78 King Air 200		BB-383	Air Nunavut Ltd. Iqaluit, NT.	N384DB

CC = CHILE
Total 27

Civil

Reg	Yr	Type	c/n	Owner/Operator	Prev Regn
☐ CC-...	78 PA-31T Cheyenne II		7820035	Bull & Bear Inc. Tobalaba.	N5MQ
☐ CC-...	79 PA-31T Cheyenne II		7920082		N109TT
☐ CC-...	90 King Air B200		BB-1368		N558FM
☐ CC-CBD	83 PA-31T Cheyenne 1		8104070	Aerobenic SA. Santiago.	(D-IIHW)
☐ CC-CLY	71 King Air 100		B-79	Maquinarias Pivcevic E Hijos Ltda/Aerovias DAP. Punta Arenas	CC-PIE
☐ CC-COT	67 King Air A90		LJ-227	Maquinarias Pivcevic E Hijos Ltda/Aerovias DAP. Punta Arenas	CC-PIR
☐ CC-CPB	01 King Air B200		BB-1796	Transportes y Servicios Aereos SA. Santiago.	N4126T
☐ CC-CVT	99 King Air C90B		LJ-1556	Bonir Ltda. Santiago.	N3156F
☐ CC-CVZ	69 King Air B90		LJ-441	Turismo Aereo Chile Ltda. Santiago.	CC-PBZ

Reg	Yr Type	c/n	Owner/Operator	Prev Regn

Reg	Yr	Type	c/n	Owner/Operator	Prev Regn
☐ CC-CWD	81 PA-31T Cheyenne 1		8104071	Aero Cardal Ltda. Tobalaba.	CC-CRU
☐ CC-CZC	79 PA-31T Cheyenne II		7920072	Servicios Aereos El Loa SA. Chuquicamata.	N620P
☐ CC-CZX	80 PA-31T Cheyenne II		8020069	Elalba SA & Westfield Business, Los Cerillos.	CC-CNH
☐ CC-DIV	81 King Air B200CT		BN-1	D.G.A.C. Santiago. (was BL-24).	CC-EAA
☐ CC-DSN	75 King Air E90		LW-153	D.G.A.C. Santiago.	CC-EAB
☐ CC-PBT	81 PA-31T Cheyenne 1		8104063	Metalurgica Ducasse Ltda. Santiago.	N2568Y
☐ CC-PCY	81 PA-31T Cheyenne II		8120028	Inversiones Antilco Ltda. Santiago.	N59KC
☐ CC-PHM	79 PA-31T Cheyenne 1		7904054	Industria Metalurgica del Norte, Santiago.	CC-CPV
☐ CC-PJH	81 PA-31T Cheyenne II		8120049	Inversiones Cerro Negrao Ltda. Quillota.	CC-CNT
☐ CC-PML	84 Cheyenne II-XL		1166002	Banco O Higgins/Rimac SA. Santiago. (was 8166074).	N2580Z
☐ CC-PNS	81 PA-31T Cheyenne 1		8104002	Constructora Raul del Rio SA. Santiago.	N780CA
☐ CC-PTA	81 Cheyenne II-XL		8166070	Banco O Higgins y Forest Quinen, Santiago.	N333X
☐ CC-PVE	81 Cheyenne II-XL		8166038	Soc de Servicios Latinoamericana Ltda. Santiago.	N161TC
☐ CC-PWH	81 PA-31T Cheyenne 1		8104023	Transportes Modern Air SA. Tobalaba.	CC-CWK
☐ CC-PZB	78 PA-31T Cheyenne II		7820020	San Andreas Ltda. Santiago.	CC-CZB
Military					
☐ 331	75 King Air A100		B-219	Fuerza Aerea de Chile, Gr 10, Santiago.	CC-ESA
☐ 336	96 King Air B200		BB-1530	Fuerza Aerea de Chile, Gr 10, Santiago.	
☐ C-51	80 PA-31T Cheyenne II		8020090	Carabineros de Chile, Tobalaba.	CC-PMZ

CN = **MOROCCO**   *Total*   17

Civil

Reg	Yr	Type	c/n	Owner/Operator	Prev Regn
☐ CN-...	03 King Air 350	FL-374			N6174N
☐ CN-...	67 King Air A90	LJ-217			F-GJRD
☐ CN-CDF	80 King Air 200	BB-577		Royal Air Maroc, Casablanca.	
☐ CN-CDN	80 King Air 200	BB-713		Royal Air Maroc, Casablanca.	N36741
☐ CN-RLE	97 King Air 350	FL-170		Regional Air Lines, Casablanca.	N2015G
☐ CN-TAX	80 King Air C90	LJ-922		Omnium Nord Africain, Casablanca.	F-GCPN
☐ CN-TPH	82 King Air B200	BB-1006		Ste de Production Agricole, Anfa.	N680CB
Military					
☐ CNA-NB	74 King Air A100	B-181		Government of Morocco, Rabat.	
☐ CNA-NC	74 King Air A100	B-182		Government of Morooco, Rabat.	
☐ CNA-ND	74 King Air A100	B-183		Government of Morocco, Rabat.	
☐ CNA-NE	74 King Air A100	B-186		Government of Morocco, Rabat.	
☐ CNA-NF	74 King Air A100	B-187		Government of Morocco, Rabat.	
☐ CNA-NG	82 King Air B200	BB-1072		Government of Morocco, Rabat.	
☐ CNA-NH	82 King Air B200	BB-1073		Government of Morocco, Rabat.	
☐ CNA-NI	82 King Air B200C	BL-57		Government of Morocco, Rabat.	
☐ CNA-NX	89 King Air 300	FA-207		Government of Morocco, Rabat.	
☐ CNA-NY	89 King Air 300	FA-208		Government of Morocco, Rabat.	

CP = **BOLIVIA**   *Total*   16

Civil

Reg	Yr	Type	c/n	Owner/Operator	Prev Regn
☐ CP-...	73 Rockwell 690A	11107			N813PR
☐ CP-....	73 King Air E90	LW-28		Aero Centro SA. La Paz.	N2XZ
☐ CP-1678	81 PA-31T Cheyenne II	8120017		Luis A Gomez,	EB-004
☐ CP-1934	69 680W Turbo Commander	1835-40			N81LC
☐ CP-2042	70 681 Turbo Commander	6025			N10HG
☐ CP-2078	80 Gulfstream 980	95004		Juan Carlos Vaca Artega, Santa Cruz.	N100TB
☐ CP-2182	73 Rockwell 690	11055			N100MB
☐ CP-2224	79 Rockwell 690B	11564		Aero Inca Ltda. La Paz.	N401SP
☐ CP-2266	77 Rockwell 690B	11395		Aeroeste Ltda/Dr. Jorge Velasco Monasterio, Santa Cruz.	N816PC
Military					
☐ EB-50	CASA 212-300	369		Ejercito de Bolivia, La Paz.	
☐ FAB 0..	74 King Air 200	BB-11		Fuerza Aerea Boliviana, La Paz.	FAB 001
☐ FAB 018	81 King Air 200C	BL-28		Fuerza Aerea Boliviana, Esc 810, La Paz.	
☐ FAB 026	King Air 90	...		Fuerza Aerea Boliviana, La Paz.	
☐ FAB 028	73 Rockwell 690	11067		Fuerza Aerea Boliviana, La Paz.	CP-1076
☐ FAB 030	Rockwell 690	...		Fuerza Aerea Boliviana, La Paz.	
☐ FAB-042	King Air E90	...		Fuerza Aerea Boliviana, La Paz.	

CS = **PORTUGAL**   *Total*   4

Civil

Reg	Yr	Type	c/n	Owner/Operator	Prev Regn
☐ CS-ASG	77 Rockwell 690B	11452		OMNI Aviacao & Tecnologia Ltda. Cascais-Tires.	N115SB
☐ CS-DCP	66 King Air A90	LM-22		K & K Aircraft, Funchal.	N7034K
☐ CS-DDF	83 King Air/Catpass 250	BB-1129		OMNI Aviacao & Tecnologia Ltda. Cascais-Tires.	N66404

Reg	Yr	Type	c/n	Owner/Operator	Prev Regn

Reg	Yr	Type	c/n	Owner/Operator	Prev Regn
☐ CS-DDU	80	King Air 200	BB-640	OMNI Aviacao & Tecnologia Ltda. Cascais-Tires.	N47CF

CX = URUGUAY   Total   2

Civil

Reg	Yr	Type	c/n	Owner/Operator	Prev Regn
☐ CX-...	85	Gulfstream 1000	96093		C-FALI

Military

Reg	Yr	Type	c/n	Owner/Operator	Prev Regn
☐ AU-871	78	King Air 200T	BT-4	Uruguayan Navy. (was BB-408).	N2067D

C6 = BAHAMAS   Total   3

Civil

Reg	Yr	Type	c/n	Owner/Operator	Prev Regn
☐ C6-...	68	Mitsubishi MU-2F	122	Bahamas Customs Service, Nassau.	N98MA
☐ C6-...	93	King Air 350	FL-95		N8145E
☐ C6-...	04	King Air B200	BB-1851		N6151C

C9 = MOZAMBIQUE   Total   5

Civil

Reg	Yr	Type	c/n	Owner/Operator	Prev Regn
☐ C9-ASK	81	King Air C90	LJ-954	Airplus SARL, Maputo.	F-GDCC
☐ C9-ASV	81	King Air 200C	BL-21	LAM-Linhas Aereas de Mocambique, Maputo.	N3831T
☐ C9-ENH	80	King Air 200	BB-626	ENH-Nacional Hidrocarbonetos de Mocambique, Maputo.	C9-ASS
☐ C9-JTP	76	PA-31T Cheyenne II	7620012	Reliable Fork Lift & Truck Services, Alrode.	ZS-JTP
☐ C9-PMZ	82	King Air B200	BB-1076	Pedro Mendez/Airplus, Maputo.	ZS-MTW

D = GERMANY   Total   163

Civil

Reg	Yr	Type	c/n	Owner/Operator	Prev Regn
☐ D-C...	89	King Air 300	FA-192	Beechcraft Vertrieb & Service GmbH. Augsburg.	N900RB
☐ D-C...	04	King Air 350	FL-410		
☐ D-CACB	83	King Air B200T	BT-27	German Flight Inspection, Braunschweig. (was BB-1105).	N7244R
☐ D-CADN	93	King Air 350	FL-101	R+R Flugzeughandels u Vermietungs GmbH. Kamenz.	N82311
☐ D-CAMM	91	King Air 350	FL-64	AERO Flugcharter/Business Air Charter GmbH. Gera.	
☐ D-CBIN	82	SA-227AT Merlin 4C	AT-440B	Binair GmbH. Munich.	I-FSAD
☐ D-CCBW	91	King Air 350	FL-46	Aero-Flugcharter/Business Air Charter GmbH. Gera.	N81623
☐ D-CCCC	82	SA-227AT Merlin 4C	AT-511	Northern Air Freight GmbH. Flensburg. 'City of Flensburg'	N600N
☐ D-CFMA	92	King Air 350	FL-76	FCS-Flight Calibration Services GmbH. Braunschweig.	N8274U
☐ D-CFMB	93	King Air 350	FL-97	FCS-Flight Calibration Services GmbH. Braunschweig.	N8297L
☐ D-CKWM	94	King Air 350	FL-124	WEKA Firmengruppe GmbH. Augsburg.	N3198N
☐ D-CLOG	00	King Air 350	FL-276	Kronotrans Speditions GmbH.	N3176T
☐ D-CNAY	81	SA-227AT Merlin 4C	AT-493	Hahn Airlines GmbH. Hahn.	PH-RAX
☐ D-COEB	99	King Air 350	FL-255	Dr August Oekter/Teuto Air Lufttaxi GmbH. Bielefeld.	N3205M
☐ D-COLA	92	King Air 350	FL-75	Private Wings Flugcharter GmbH. Berlin-Schoenefeld.	HB-GJB
☐ D-CSAG	99	Beech 1900D	UE-353	Strathmann AG/FLM Aviation KG. Hamburg. 'SAG 2'	N23527
☐ D-CSKY	96	King Air 350	FL-130	Intro Verwaltungs GmbH/Aero-Dienst GmbH. Templehof.	N5651Q
☐ D-CUNO	00	King Air 350	FL-311	Beechcraft Vertrieb & Service GmbH. Augsburg.	N5011K
☐ D-EICO	01	PA-46-500TP Meridian	4697125		N5361C
☐ D-EPKD	00	PA-46-500TP Meridian	4697019		OY-GPT
☐ D-ESSS	01	PA-46-500TP Meridian	4697070		D-FOXI
☐ D-FALF	99	TBM 700B	157		F-WWRN
☐ D-FAPC*	04	Pilatus PC-12/45	579		
☐ D-FBFS	92	TBM 700A	74	Brose Fahrzeugteile GmbH/BFS Flugservice GmbH. Coburg.	F-OHBK
☐ D-FBFT	04	TBM 700C	302	Brose Fahrzeugteile GmbH/BFS Flugservice GmbH. Coburg.	
☐ D-FBOY	00	TBM 700B	171		F-WWRP
☐ D-FCRF	01	PA-46-500TP Meridian	4697063		N253MM
☐ D-FCJA	97	Pilatus PC-12	177	Christian F Ahrenkiel GmbH. Hamburg.	HB-FSM
☐ D-FGYY	00	TBM 700B	162		
☐ D-FIRE	99	TBM 700B	137	Ulrich Brunner Ofen und Heiztechnik GmbH. Eggenfelden.	
☐ D-FIVE	01	TBM 700B	186		
☐ D-FKAI	04	TBM 700C	288		
☐ D-FNRE	99	TBM 700A	142	Richard Engstler Elastometall GmbH. Ottersweier.	
☐ D-FSJP	98	TBM 700	130		N38KJ
☐ D-FTAN	92	TBM 700	24	Diamond Aircraft GmbH. Siegerland.	PH-AJS
☐ D-I...	04	King Air C90B	LJ-1716	Beechcraft Vertrieb & Service GmbH. Augsburg.	N61716
☐ D-IAAC	78	Conquest II	441-0073	Ruediger Kueckelhaus/CCF Manager Airline GmbH. Cologne.	N88834
☐ D-IAAH	90	King Air C90A	LJ-1247	Dipl. Kfm. Steuerberater Dietmar Volkmann, Nuremberg.	N5651J
☐ D-IABC	67	680V Turbo Commander	1684-65	Air Tempelhof Flug GmbH. Tempelhof-Berlin.	EC-HDE
☐ D-IAHT	77	Mitsubishi MU-2P	352SA	H Teegen, Straubing.	N41AD
☐ D-IAJK	97	King Air B200	BB-1565	Avanti Air GmbH. Siegerland.	D-IMGI
☐ D-IAKK	87	King Air B200	BB-1265	Vibro Air Flugservice GmbH. Moenchengladbach.	N550TF

Reg	Yr	Type	c/n	Owner/Operator	Prev Regn

Reg	Yr	Type	c/n	Owner/Operator	Prev Regn
☐ D-IANA	95	King Air B200	BB-1517	KLW Mietflug/Dix Aviation, Paderborn-Lippstadt.	N3217V
☐ D-IAPA	81	PA-31T Cheyenne 1	8104032	VBG-Verwaltungs u Beteiligungs GmbH. Goerlitz.	N5SL
☐ D-IATM	97	King Air B200	BB-1595		N713FP
☐ D-IBAB	92	King Air 300LW	FA-225	Hans Grohe GmbH. Schiltach.	N82396
☐ D-IBAD	85	King Air B200	BB-1229	PTL-Pilot Training GmbH. Landshut.	
☐ D-IBAG	74	Rockwell 690A	11211	Vorgebirgs-Residenz Bonn-Edenich GmbH. Saarbruecken.	
☐ D-IBAR	87	King Air B200	BB-1280	Lindner Hotels AG. Dusseldorf/ACH Hamburg Flug, Hamburg.	
☐ D-IBDH	92	King Air C90B	LJ-1307	Peene-Werft GmbH. Peenemuende.	N8053U
☐ D-IBER	89	King Air 300LW	FA-184	DSF Flugdienst AG. Siegerland.	
☐ D-IBFE	00	King Air B200	BB-1716	Beechcraft Berlin Aviation GmbH. Tempelhof.	N3216G
☐ D-IBFS	89	King Air B200	BB-1349	Heberger Bau GmbH/Silver Clound Air GmbH. Speyer.	D-IBFS
☐ D-IBFT	96	King Air B200	BB-1535	Brose Fahrzeugteile GmbH/BFS Flugservice GmbH. Coburg.	N1135Z
☐ D-IBHL	84	SA-227TT Merlin 3C	TT-512A	Reederei und Schiffmakler Egon Oldendorf oHG. Luebeck.	N123GM
☐ D-IBIW	80	PA-31T Cheyenne 1	8004011	BIW-Beratung fuer Industrie u Wirtschaft GmbH. Weinstadt.	N76TG
☐ D-IBMC	81	King Air C90	LJ-931	Garant Import und Export GmbH. Hamm.	HB-GIE
☐ D-IBMP	87	King Air B200	BB-1284	B200 Flug Charter Leer GmbH/ACH Hamburg Flug GmbH. Hamburg.	N6321V
☐ D-IBNK	89	King Air 300LW	FA-204	Marxer Anglangen u Maschinenbau GmbH. Friedberg.	N5662T
☐ D-IBSA	81	PA-31T Cheyenne II	8120033	Frau Amalie-Barbara Fuchs/Fuchs Mineraloelwerke, Mannheim.	N42TW
☐ D-ICGA	81	Cheyenne II-XL	8166056	Skyline Flights GmbH. Hanover.	N550TL
☐ D-ICGB	84	PA-42 Cheyenne IIIA	5501007	Cirrus Aviation Luftfahrt GmbH. Saarbruecken.	N834CM
☐ D-ICHG	91	King Air B200	BB-1400	Avanti Air GmbH. Siegerland.	N8085D
☐ D-ICHS	85	Conquest 1	425-0233	Karl-Heinz SengewaldA W Aerowest GmbH. Hannover.	N80938
☐ D-ICIR	83	King Air B200	BB-1051	Cirrus Aviation Luftfahrt GmbH. Saarbruecken.	(G-BJWG)
☐ D-ICKM	82	King Air B200	BB-1005	WM Aero Charter GmbH. Stuttgart.	OE-FKW
☐ D-ICMF	81	Conquest 1	425-0102	IMCON Immobilenentwicklungs und Betriebs GmbH. Herne.	N151GA
☐ D-ICWM	82	King Air B200C	BL-49	WM Aero Charter GmbH. Stuttgart.	N51CV
☐ D-IDAK	75	King Air C90	LJ-647	Transavia GmbH. Speyer.	LX-DAK
☐ D-IDAX	84	Conquest 1	425-0209		D-IMPC
☐ D-IDBU	84	PA-42 Cheyenne IIIA	5501029	DSF Flugdienst AG. Siegerland.	N700CC
☐ D-IDCV	00	King Air C90B	LJ-1622	Beechcraft Vertrieb & Service GmbH. Augsburg.	N4172Q
☐ D-IDEA	80	SA-226T Merlin 3B	T-322	Gerhard Schmid, Flensburg.	(N330JP)
☐ D-IDIA	90	PA-42 Cheyenne IIIA	5501055	ACH Hamburg Flug GmbH. Hamburg.	N955TA
☐ D-IDIX	99	King Air C90B	LJ-1571	Dix Aviation, Paderborn.	N90KA
☐ D-IDSF	81	PA-42 Cheyenne III	8001009	Diamond Aircraft Service GmbH. Siegerland.	N849AM
☐ D-IEAH	89	King Air C90A	LJ-1216	Fischerwerke Artur Fischer GmbH. Donaueschingen.	N1562Z
☐ D-IEBE	91	King Air C90A	LJ-1267	Ebenhoeh Kies-u-Sandwerke GmbH/Isarflug GmbH. Munich.	A6-FAE
☐ D-IEBM	91	King Air 300	FA-217	EBM Motoren Ventilatoren, Mulfingen.	N911RB
☐ D-IEDI	98	King Air B200	BB-1633	Flyer SA AG. Weiterstadt.	N2345M
☐ D-IEFB	81	King Air B200	BB-897	Flugbereitschaft GmbH. Karlsruhe.	N200TM
☐ D-IFFB	93	King Air 300LW	FA-224	Strathmann AG/FLM Aviation KG. Hamburg.	N56449
☐ D-IFHI	81	King Air C90	LJ-977	Ailana Vermoegens und Grundstuecksverwaltungs GmbH. Munich.	N1813P
☐ D-IFHZ	84	PA-31T Cheyenne 1A	1104016	Zollern Flugdienste GmbH. Mengen.	N91201
☐ D-IFMI	85	King Air C90A	LJ-1101	Fritz Mueller, Ingelfingen.	N17EL
☐ D-IFSH	84	PA-42 Cheyenne IIIA	5501014	FSH Schul u Charter GmbH. Leipzig.	N45SL
☐ D-IFUN	80	King Air 200	BB-575	Grenzland Air Service, Stadtlohn.	D-ISJP
☐ D-IGKN	84	King Air C90A	LJ-1077	Lufttaxi Flug GmbH. Dortmund.	N4111U
☐ D-IGOB	92	P-180 Avanti	1016	Cirrus Aviation Luftfahrt GmbH. Saarbruecken.	I-PJAT
☐ D-IHAH	94	King Air C90B	LJ-1370	Beechcraft Vertrieb & Service GmbH. Augsburg.	N1570C
☐ D-IHBP	95	King Air C90B	LJ-1424	Berger Bau GmbH/Comair Reise u Charter GmbH. Vilshofen.	N3252J
☐ D-IHDE	77	King Air C90	LJ-725	ATF-Air Transport Flug GmbH. Bindlach.	
☐ D-IHHE	93	King Air C90B	LJ-1327	FVG-Flugzeugvermietungs GmbH. Saarbruecken.	N8227P
☐ D-IHJK	81	PA-31T Cheyenne 1	8104057	H J Kuepper/Avanti Air GmbH. Siegerland.	N62BW
☐ D-IHJL	84	PA-31T Cheyenne 1A	1104015	LLT Immobilienentwicklungs GmbH.	S5-CEJ
☐ D-IHKM	87	King Air C90A	LJ-1158	Porta Flug GmbH. Porta Westfalica.	N38H
☐ D-IHLA	83	PA-42 Cheyenne IIIA	8301001	Cirrus Aviation Luftfahrt GmbH. Saarbruecken.	C-GNRD
☐ D-IHMV	93	King Air C90B	LJ-1325	Aircharter Flugservice GmbH. Donaueschingen.	N8135M
☐ D-IHSI	80	Gulfstream 980	95039	Air Evertz,	N9790S
☐ D-IHSW	92	King Air C90B	LJ-1315	Kapp Werkzeugmaschinenfabrik GmbH. Coburg.	N8103E
☐ D-IHUC	81	Gulfstream 980	95069	Team Air Flugservice GmbH. Munich.	N695EC
☐ D-IHVA	84	PA-42 Cheyenne IIIA	5501025	Fahrzeugelektrik Pirna GmbH. Pirna.	
☐ D-IIAH	00	King Air B200	BB-1741	A Haring, Donaueschingen.	N2341K
☐ D-IICE	77	King Air 200	BB-269	Excellent Air GmbH. Amsterdam, Holland.	N269D
☐ D-IIHA	72	King Air C90	LJ-562	Dr Joachim von Meister, Bad Homburg.	(N333FJ)
☐ D-IIKM	85	King Air C90A	LJ-1120	Kurt Jaeger, Berlin.	N7237K
☐ D-IIWB	93	King Air C90B	LJ-1340	ACH Hamburg Flug GmbH. Hamburg.	N10799

Reg	Yr	Type	c/n	Owner/Operator	Prev Regn
☐ D-IIXX	82	PA-31T Cheyenne 1	8104066		D-IHMM
☐ D-IJET	02	P-180 Avanti	1056	Vibrogruppe Air Flugservice GmbH. Moenchengladbach.	
☐ D-IJLF	86	Conquest II	441-0358	Wilhelm Gronbach GmbH. Muehldorf-am-Inn.	N85DJ
☐ D-IKES	81	King Air C90	LJ-942	Dehner Garten-Center GmbH. Augsburg.	
☐ D-IKET	80	PA-31T Cheyenne II	8020017	Karosserie Entwicklung Thurner, Landshut.	N154CA
☐ D-IKEW	78	PA-31T Cheyenne II	7820066	Kress Elektrik GmbH. Bisingen.	N6108A
☐ D-IKIM	93	King Air C90B	LJ-1324	Rudolf Kimmerle Gewerbebau, Augsburg.	N82430
☐ D-IKIW	74	King Air C90	LJ-641	Air Evex Westfalia Flug GmbH. Paderborn.	N7128H
☐ D-IKKY	80	MU-2 Solitaire	420SA	Golden Europe Jet de Luxe Club E V. Stuttgart.	I-SOLT
☐ D-IKLN	90	King Air B200	BB-1369		(N567DM)
☐ D-IKMS	96	King Air C90B	LJ-1441		F-GSDM
☐ D-IKOB	81	King Air B200	BB-921	MediAir GmbH. Munich.	N244JB
☐ D-ILCE	80	PA-31T Cheyenne 1	8004053	DSF Flugdienst AG. Siegerland.	
☐ D-ILGA	84	PA-31T Cheyenne 1A	1104014	ElektroMstr. Willy Stuecker, Brokdorf.	N9382T
☐ D-ILGI	85	King Air C90A	LJ-1090	Georg Wissler, Aschaffenburg-Grossostheim.	N7210H
☐ D-ILIN	79	King Air 200	BB-545	EAS-Executive Air Service Flug GmbH. Mannheim.	OY-CBY
☐ D-ILLF	97	King Air B200	BB-1568	Fischer Flug GmbH. Lahr.	N1067V
☐ D-ILPC	83	Conquest 1	425-0131	Ueber den Wolken GmbH. Hamburg.	OE-FAM
☐ D-ILYS	85	Conquest II	441-0355	Lufttaxi Flug GmbH. Dortmund	N355VB
☐ D-IMIM	81	PA-42 Cheyenne III	8001048	MediAir GmbH. Munich.	N830CM
☐ D-IMON	77	King Air 200	BB-276	Bonair Business Charter GmbH. Cologne.	TF-ELT
☐ D-IMWK	84	SA-227TT Merlin 300	TT-529	LTO-Lufttransport Muenster-Osnabrueck GmbH. Munster.	N3109S
☐ D-INAS		King Air	...	noted Prestwick 10/04.	
☐ D-INGA	80	Conquest 1	425-0003	Westavia GmbH. Moenchengladbach.	N98751
☐ D-INNN	81	PA-31T Cheyenne II	8120102	Raiffeisenbank Vilshofener Land eG. Vilshofen.(was 8120067).	N822SW
☐ D-INUS	90	Reims/Cessna F406	F406-0043	Flugdienst Fehlhaber GmbH. Cologne.	
☐ D-INWK	75	SA-226T Merlin 3A	T-255	Rudas Studios KG/Air Traffic GmbH. Duesseldorf.	N5349M
☐ D-IOHL	85	Conquest II	441-0357	Ohlair Charterflug KG. Kiel.	PH-BMP
☐ D-IONE	80	PA-42 Cheyenne III	8001002	DSF Flugdienst AG. Siegerland.	N61QR
☐ D-IOSA	87	PA-42 Cheyenne IIIA	5501040	Lufthansa Flight Training GmbH. Bremen.	N9578N
☐ D-IOSB	87	PA-42 Cheyenne IIIA	5501042	Lufthansa Flight Training GmbH. Bremen.	
☐ D-IOSC	87	PA-42 Cheyenne IIIA	5501043	Lufthansa Flight Training GmbH. Bremen.	D-IOKP
☐ D-IOSD	87	PA-42 Cheyenne IIIA	5501044	Lufthansa Flight Training GmbH. Bremen.	
☐ D-IOTT	79	PA-31T Cheyenne II	7920010	Dr Bernd Koenes, Erkelenz.	N6196A
☐ D-IPOS	82	Conquest 1	425-0120	Dr Peters GmbH/MSR-Flug Charter GmbH. M-Osnabrueck.	N425R
☐ D-IPSY	97	King Air B200	BB-1591	Winter & Kamp GmbH/ACM Air Charter Minninger, Baden-Baden.	N1819H
☐ D-IQAS	84	PA-42 Cheyenne 400LS	5527022	Quick Air Service GmbH. Cologne.	N322KW
☐ D-IRIS	85	King Air F90-1	LA-229	Frau Uta Ackermans-Meynen, Kerken.	N7209Z
☐ D-ISAZ	82	King Air B200	BB-983	Bizair Flug GmbH. Berlin-Tempelhof.	(N983AJ)
☐ D-ISHY	88	Reims/Cessna F406	F406-0027	Flugdienst Fehlhaber GmbH. Cologne.	PH-FWH
☐ D-ISIG	81	PA-31T Cheyenne 1	8104055	Schindler Ingenieur GmbH. Aschaffenburg.	N123AT
☐ D-ISIX	94	King Air C90B	LJ-1355	Brinkmann Maschinenfabrik GmbH. Schloss Holte.	N995PA
☐ D-ISTB	85	King Air F90-1	LA-227	A & G Bumueller Grossbaeckerei u Konditorei, Stuttgart.	N330VP
☐ D-ISTC	81	MU-2 Solitaire	436SA		(N928VF)
☐ D-ITCH	86	King Air C90A	LJ-1138	Roland & Meckbach GmbH. Kassel-Calden.	N17KA
☐ D-ITLL	82	King Air F90	LA-192	Tamsen Ferrari, RR & Bentley Import & Export GmbH. Stuhr.	N17TS
☐ D-ITOP	00	King Air C90B	LJ-1606	VHM Schul und Charterflug GmbH. Essen.	N4206U
☐ D-IUDE	93	King Air C90B	LJ-1323	Wolfgang Preinfalk Werkzeug & Machinenbau GmbH. Sulzbach.	N90KA
☐ D-IUTA	80	Gulfstream 840	11639	Wilhelm Huelpert, Dortmund.	HB-LOL
☐ D-IVIP	99	King Air B200	BB-1672	VHM Schul und Charterflug GmbH. Essen.	
☐ D-IWID	96	King Air C90B	LJ-1450	Widerker Aircraft GmbH. Stuttgart.	N3265K
☐ D-IWKB	98	King Air B200	...	Wittgensteiner Rehakliniken GmbH/Avanti Air GmbH. Frankfurt.	
☐ D-IWSH	93	King Air B200	BB-1462	Diamond Air Service GmbH. Stuttgart.	N82425
☐ D-IXXX	84	Cheyenne II-XL	1166003	FSH Schul u Charter GmbH. Leipzig.	D-ICDU
☐ D-IZAC	77	King Air B100	BE-29	Zell Air GmbH. Muehlheim.	D-IERI
☐ D-IZZY	99	P-180 Avanti	1034	Air Go Flugservice GmbH. Hahn.	N680JP

D2 = ANGOLA
Total 26

Civil

Reg	Yr	Type	c/n	Owner/Operator	Prev Regn
☐ D2-...	79	King Air 200T	BT-8	(was BB-530).	ZS-OPR
☐ D2-ALS	66	King Air 90	LJ-80		ZS-NED
☐ D2-EAA	73	Rockwell 690A	11132	Directorate of Civil Aviation, Luanda.	CR-LAA
☐ D2-EBF	81	King Air 200	BB-836	Gira Globo Ltda Aeronautica. Luanda.	S9-NAQ
☐ D2-EBG	78	King Air 200	BB-334	Manewa Taxi Aereo Ltda. Luanda.	ZS-NRT
☐ D2-ECN	85	Reims/Cessna F406	F406-0002	SAL-Sociedade de Aviacao Ligeira SA. Luanda.	PH-MNS

☐ D2-ECO	86 Reims/Cessna F406	F406-0011	SAL-Sociedade de Aviacao Ligeira SA. Luanda.	D-IDAA
☐ D2-ECP	87 Reims/Cessna F406	F406-0016	SAL-Sociedade de Aviacao Ligeira SA. Luanda.	PH-LAS
☐ D2-ECQ	87 Reims/Cessna F406	F406-0019	SAL-Sociedade de Aviacao Ligeira SA. Luanda.	G-CVAN
☐ D2-ECX	90 King Air B200	BB-1362	SAL-Sociedade de Aviacao Ligeira SA. Luanda.	N1565F
☐ D2-ECY	89 King Air B200C	BL-135	SAL-Sociedade de Aviacao Ligeira SA. Luanda.	S9-NAP
☐ D2-EDD	95 King Air B200	BB-1512	Harlow Resources Ltd. Roadtown, Tortola, BVI.	N700FT
☐ D2-EMX	79 King Air 200	BB-480	Intertransit, Luanda. 'Rita Yara'	ZS-MJH
☐ D2-EOJ	90 King Air B200	BB-1371	Equator Leasing 14 Ltd. Luanda.	N56616
☐ D2-EQC	68 King Air B90	LJ-324	SONANGOL Aeronautica - Helipetrol, Luanda.	N892DF
☐ D2-ERK	81 King Air B200	BB-937	U N WFP-World Food Programme - Skylink Canada,	C9-ATW
☐ D2-ESP	90 King Air B200	BB-1391	SONANGOL Aeronautica - Helipetrol, Luanda.	N8048W
☐ D2-EXB	65 Gulfstream 1	166	Intertransit/GMX-Grupo Mello Xavier, Luanda.	4X-ARG
☐ D2-EXC	61 Gulfstream 1	80	Intertransit, Luanda.	F-GGGY
☐ D2-EXD	64 Gulfstream 1	124	Intertransit, Luanda.	ZS-NKT
☐ D2-EXW	76 King Air 200	BB-101	Government of Angola, Luanda.	ZS-MGR
☐ D2-FEG	82 King Air B200	BB-1060	Tropicana, Luanda.	ZS-TON
☐ D2-FEI	80 King Air 200	BB-620	Transteco, Luanda.	ZS-OGV
☐ D2-FFK	82 King Air B200	BB-1026	Tropicana, Luanda.	N153D
☐ D2-FFL	76 King Air 200	BB-126	Gira Globo Ltda Aeronautica, Luanda. 'Capembe'	ZS-PBB
☐ D2-FMD	80 King Air/Catpass 250	BT-18	Capricorn Systems Ltd. Lanseria, RSA. (was BB-695).	N123PW

EC = **SPAIN** Total 38

Civil

☐ EC-CHE	74 King Air A100	B-195	FAASA Aviacion, Palma del Rio.	E23-2
☐ EC-DHF	79 PA-31T Cheyenne II	7920073	Dominguez Toledo SA/Mayoral, Malaga.	N23699
☐ EC-DSA	66 680T Turbo Commander	1564-20	Ambulancias Insulares SA. Palma de Mallorca. (status ?).	I-ARBO
☐ EC-DXA	76 Rockwell 690A	11328	Tur Air SA. Madrid. 'Don Mendo'	D-IHVB
☐ EC-EAG	68 680W Turbo Commander	1776-14	Ambulancias Insulares SA. Palma de Mallorca. (status ?).	N680W
☐ EC-EIH	74 Rockwell 690A	11212	Ambulancias Insulares SA. Palma de Mallorca. (status ?).	N690BT
☐ EC-EIL	72 Rockwell 690	11007	Ambulancias Insulares SA. Palma de Mallorca. (status ?).	N171TT
☐ EC-EVJ	60 Gulfstream 1	39	Stellair, Madrid.	EC-376
☐ EC-EXB	65 Gulfstream 1	153	Stellair, Madrid.	EC-433
☐ EC-EZO	60 Gulfstream 1	41	Stellair, Madrid. (status ?).	EC-494
☐ EC-FIO	60 Gulfstream 1	40	Stellair, Madrid.	EC-493
☐ EC-FPF	91 TBM 700	12	Arturo Beltran SA. Zaragoza.	F-OHBD
☐ EC-GBB	76 King Air 200	BB-182	PMS SA/Flightline SL. Barcelona-El Prat.	EC-727
☐ EC-GBI	75 SA-226AT Merlin 4A	AT-041	Aeroway SL. Madrid.	EC-867
☐ EC-GFK	77 SA-226AT Merlin 4A	AT-062	Flightline SL/Ibertrans Aerea SL. Barcelona-El Prat.	EC-125
☐ EC-GHZ	79 King Air 200	BB-555	Urgemer Canarias SL. Las Palmas.	D-IFOR
☐ EC-GIJ	68 King Air B90	LJ-382	Aqua Air, Barcelona.	F-WQCC
☐ EC-GJZ	69 SA-26AT Merlin 2B	T26-149	Air Business SL. Madrid.	EC-202
☐ EC-GOK	74 Mitsubishi MU-2J	635	Airnor - Aeronaves del Noroeste SL. Ponteareas.	OY-ARV
☐ EC-GOY	71 King Air C90	LJ-527	Rivaflecha SL/BKS Air, Bilbao.	N55SG
☐ EC-GSQ	95 King Air 350	FL-128	TAS-Transportes Aereos del Sur SA. Seville.	N128FL
☐ EC-HBF	80 SA-226AT Merlin 4A	AT-074	Flightline SL/MRW Worldwide Courier, Barcelona-El Prat.	EC-GDR
☐ EC-HHO	77 King Air 200	BB-262	Sky Services Aviation SL. Madrid-Torrejon.	N92V
☐ EC-HMA	73 King Air C90	LJ-577	Rivafleca SL/BKS Air, Bilbao.	N57KA
☐ EC-HNH	73 Rockwell 690	11058	Trabajos Aereos SA. Cuatro Vientos.	N690PJ
☐ EC-IBK	01 King Air 350	FL-328	Gestair Executive Jet SA. Madrid-Torrejon.	N4328W
☐ EC-IIP	84 PA-42 Cheyenne 400LS	5527018	Aerodynamics Malaga SL. Malaga.	D-IIAQ
☐ EC-ILE	01 King Air B200	BB-1792	Helisureste SA. Palma. 'Mutxamel'	N5092K
☐ EC-ISH	03 Pilatus PC-12/45	498	Norestair SL. Barcelona-El Prat.	HB-FPG
☐ EC-IUV	78 King Air 200	BB-366		D-IBHK
☐ EC-IUX	03 King Air B200	BB-1840	Transportes Aereos del Sur SA. Seville.	N816LD
☐ EC-IVZ	03 PA-46-500TP Meridian	4697170	Gavina, Sabadell.	N3046P
☐ EC-J..	94 King Air B200	BB-1478	Inversiones Aeronauticas Baleares, Palma.	D-IHAN

Military

☐ 42-..	74 King Air C90	LJ-624	Grupo 42, Getafe.	EC-CHC
☐ 42-..	73 King Air C90	LJ-603	Grupo 42, Getafe.	EC-CDI
☐ 42-..	73 King Air C90	LJ-608	Grupo 42, Getafe.	EC-CDK
☐ 42-...	73 King Air C90	LJ-605	Grupo 42, Getafe.	EC-CDJ
☐ E 22-01	75 King Air C90	LJ-666	42-30, Grupo 42, Getafe.	EC-COL

EI = **EIRE** Total 3

Civil

☐ EI-DMG	80 Conquest II	441-0165	Dawn Meats Group Ltd. Waterford.	N140MP
Reg	Yr Type	c/n	Owner/Operator	Prev Regn

Reg	Yr Type	c/n	Owner/Operator	Prev Regn
☐ EI-TBM	02 TBM 700B	232	Folens Management Services Ltd. Weston.	F-OIKH

Military

☐ 240	80 King Air 200	BB-672	Irish Air Corps. Casement-Dublin.	

EP = IRAN
Total 24

Civil

☐ EP-AGU	70 681 Turbo Commander	6012	Government of Iran, Tehran.	N9061N
☐ EP-AGV	72 Rockwell 690	11045	Government of Iran, Tehran.	
☐ EP-AGW	72 Rockwell 690	11047	Government of Iran, Tehran.	
☐ EP-AHL	74 Rockwell 690A	11143	Sazemane Sanoye Nazami, Tehran.	N57142
☐ EP-AHM	74 Rockwell 690A	11182	State Television Company of Iran, Tehran.	
☐ EP-AKI	73 Rockwell 690	11075	Department of Forest Protection, Tehran.	
☐ EP-FIA	69 680W Turbo Commander	1849-45	Directorate of Civil Aviation, Tehran.	
☐ EP-FIB	69 680W Turbo Commander	1850-46	Directorate of Civil Aviation, Tehran.	
☐ EP-FSS	69 680W Turbo Commander	1848-44	Directorate of Civil Aviation, Tehran.	
☐ EP-KCD	75 Rockwell 690A	11256	Iran Asseman Airlines, Tehran.	

Military

☐ 4-901	73 Rockwell 690	11077	Iranian Army, Mehrabad.	
☐ 4-902	73 Rockwell 690	11078	Iranian Army, Mehrabad.	
☐ 4 003	73 Rockwell 690	11079	Iranian Army, Mehrabad.	
☐ 501	73 Rockwell 690	11076	Iranian Navy, Mehrabad.	
☐ 5-2505	74 Rockwell 690A	11183	Iranian Navy, Mehrabad.	
☐ 5-280	71 681B Turbo Commander	6062	Iranian Air Force, Tehran.	
☐ 5-281	72 681B Turbo Commander	6068	Iranian Air Force, Tehran.	
☐ 5-282	72 681B Turbo Commander	6072	Iranian Air Force, Tehran.	
☐ 5-4035	76 Rockwell 690A	11294	Iranian Navy, Mehrabad.	N9187N
☐ 5-4036	76 Rockwell 690A	11295	Iranian Navy, Mehrabad.	N81427
☐ 5-4037	76 Rockwell 690A	11333	Iranian Navy, Mehrabad.	N57196
☐ 5-4038	76 Rockwell 690A	11334	Iranian Navy, Mehrabad.	N81467
☐ 6-3201	74 Rockwell 690A	11181	Iranian Police Wing, Tehran.	N57196
☐ 6-3202	76 Rockwell 690A	11293	Iranian Police Wing, Tehran.	N81467

F = FRANCE
Total 211

Civil

☐ F-....	93 Reims/Cessna F406	F406-0072		
☐ F-....	00 King Air B200	BB-1698		
☐ F-ASFA	73 King Air E90	LW-47	SEFA, Muret. (status ?)	
☐ F-BOSY	66 King Air A90	LJ-128	Altagna, Bastia-Poretta, Corsica.	D-IMTW
☐ F-BRNO	69 King Air B90	LJ-482	Oceanis Promotion SAS. Montpellier.	HB-GEE
☐ F-BTQP	65 King Air 90	LJ-40	Air Bor SARL. Dijon-Longvic.	I-GNIS
☐ F-BVTB	73 King Air C90	LJ-579	Ste FFM, Marseille.	D-INAF
☐ F-BXAP	71 King Air C90	LJ-522	Air Normandie, Le Havre-Octeville.	D-IHVB
☐ F-BXAS	75 Rockwell 690AT	11240	Ste Turbomeca, Pau.	F-WXAS
☐ F-BXON	75 King Air E90	LW-161	Champagne Airlines, Reims.	
☐ F-BXPY	76 King Air C90	LJ-684	Atlantic-Ste Francaise de Developpement Thermique, La Roche	
☐ F-BXSI	76 King Air 200	BB-128	DARTA Aero Charter, Paris-Le Bourget.	
☐ F-BXSK	76 PA-31T Cheyenne II	7620020	Air Bor SARL. Dijon-Longvic.	
☐ F-BXSL	75 King Air C90	LJ-648	Herve Coral, Le Landin.	
☐ F-GALD	76 PA-31T Cheyenne II	7620032	Ste SITRAM Inox, St Benoit du Sault.	
☐ F-GALN	76 King Air 200T	BT-1	IGN France, Creil. (was BB-186).	
☐ F-GALP	77 King Air 200T	BT-2	IGN France, Creil. (was BB-203).	
☐ F-GALZ	76 King Air E90	LW-199	Ste Transport Air Centre, Roanne-Renaison.	
☐ F-GBLU	79 King Air C90	LJ-822	Icare Franche Comte, Montbeliard.	(F-GNCY)
☐ F-GBPB	66 King Air 90	LJ-98	Air Bor SARL. Dijon-Longvic.	OY-ANP
☐ F-GBPZ	79 King Air C90	LJ-860	AVDEF-Aviation Defence Service, Nimes-Garons.	
☐ F-GCGA	80 King Air C90	LJ-894	Airailes, Colmar-Houssen.	
☐ F-GCLD	74 King Air C90	LJ-637	Altagna, Bastia-Poretta, Corsica.	N95DD
☐ F-GCLH	80 PA-31T Cheyenne II	8020044	SARL Clovis, Troyes.	N2330V
☐ F-GCTR	81 King Air F90	LA-115	Starcraft, Toussus Le Noble.	
☐ F-GDAK	81 King Air F90	LA-141	Air Service Vosges, Epinal-Mirecourt.	
☐ F-GDJS	83 King Air B200	BB-1116	Aero Entreprise, Toussus le Noble.	(D-ILOC)
☐ F-GEFZ	81 Conquest 1	425-0059	Les Ailes Roussillonnaises, Montpellier.	LN-AFB
☐ F-GEJV	72 King Air A100	B-129	Phenix Aviation, Le Havre.	N235B
☐ F-GEOU	81 King Air C90	LJ-941	Air Service Vosges, Epinal-Mirecourt.	N3804C
☐ F-GEQM	80 MU-2 Marquise	790SA	Ste Financiere Delot et Compagnie, Orleans.	N279MA
☐ F-GERP	73 SA-226AT Merlin 4	AT-012	CEGEBAIL, Marcq en Baroeul.	N111MV
Reg	Yr Type	c/n	Owner/Operator	Prev Regn

Reg	Yr	Type	c/n	Owner/Operator	Prev Regn
F-GERS	80	King Air 200	BB-753	Air Taxi SAT, Blois Le Breuil.	N3705B
F-GESJ	74	King Air E90	LW-97	Transport Air Centre-Lyon/Ste Aerostock, Paris-Le Bourget.	F-WZIG
F-GETI	80	King Air F90	LA-19	LST, Toussus Le Noble.	N90NS
F-GETJ	78	King Air E90	LW-296	Air 5P.F, Castres-Mazamet.	(F-GZZB)
F-GEXK	68	King Air B90	LJ-331	Air Provence International, Marseille.	N886BD
F-GEXL	76	King Air 200	BB-202	Aviasud Aerotaxi, Nice-Cote d'Azur.	N2425X
F-GEXV	74	King Air A100	B-199	Phenix Aviation, Le Havre.	N110TD
F-GFDJ	74	King Air E90	LW-86	Taxi Air Fret SA. Toussus-le-Noble.	(N505N)
F-GFEA	76	PA-31T Cheyenne II	7620011	France Europe Aviajet, Paris-Le Bourget.	N76PT
F-GFEF	63	Gulfstream 1	122	DIWAN, Rennes-St Jacques.	N707MP
F-GFHC	77	King Air C90	LJ-717	Locavia France, Nantes-Atlantique.	N200BX
F-GFHQ	68	King Air B90	LJ-347	Y P Aviation, Pointoise-Cormeilles.	N777SB
F-GFIR	68	King Air B90	LJ-434	Ocean Airlines, Montpellier.	C-GRCN
F-GFJR	81	Conquest 1	425-0032	Ste Vitreenne d'Abattage, Rennes.	N6773B
F-GFLE	75	PA-31T Cheyenne II	7520002	Ste Prestavia SA. Coulommiers.	N90589
F-GFUV	77	PA-31T Cheyenne II	7720063	SWAP, Paris-Le Bourget.	N3948A
F-GFVN	82	King Air F90	LA-166	Electronique Mecanique et Conseil SARL. Toussus Le Noble.	HB-GHM
F-GGCH	81	PA-31T Cheyenne II	8120056	Airways SA. Agen-La Garenne.	N51TW
F-GGLA	80	King Air 200	BB-744	Chalair, Caen-Carpiquet.	F-GGPJ
F-GGLN	79	King Air 200	BB-439	Air Net GIE. Montpellier.	N500JA
F-GGLV	73	King Air A100	B-150	Air Bretagne, Noyal-Pontivy.	N51BL
F-GGMS	75	King Air 200	BB-80	ASE/Ste Aeronautique Auboise, Troyes.	N444TW
F-GGMV	80	King Air 200	BB-616	Trans Helicoptere Service, Lyon-Bron.	SE-IUN
F-GGPR	80	King Air 200	BB-681	Aero Services France, Paris-Le Bourget.	LN-AXA
F-GGRV	77	PA-31T Cheyenne II	7720036	Airlec Air Espace SA. Bordeaux-Merignac.	N41RC
F-GGVG	78	SA-226T Merlin 3B	T-293	Airlec Air Espace SA. Bordeaux-Merignac.	D-IBBB
F-GHBB	71	King Air C90	LJ-510	SAL SA. Luxembourg/Air Entreprise International, Paris.	D-ILHB
F-GHBD	72	King Air C90	LJ-545	Travelair Enterprises, Pointoise-Cormeiles.	D-ILHD
F-GHDO	67	King Air A90	LJ-206	Ste Aero Stock, Toussus-le-Noble. (status ?)	F-BTAK
F-GHEM	78	King Air C90	LJ-760	OMI-Optique Medicale Industrielle, Point a Pitre, Guadaloupe	N700JP
F-GHFE	72	King Air C90	LJ-544	Lux Aero SA. Pointoise.	(F-GHFC)
F-GHHV	72	King Air A100	B-91	Air Bretagne, Noyal-Pontivy.	N9050V
F-GHIV	80	King Air F90	LA-22	Air Poitiers/Iso Air, Vouille.	(N444EM)
F-GHJV	77	PA-31T Cheyenne II	7720067	G F R, Annemasse.	N900SF
F-GHLB	78	King Air 200	BB-349	Seine Aviation/Chalair, Caen-Carpiquet.	(N349JW)
F-GHOC	78	King Air 200	BB-406	DARTA Aero Charter, Paris-Le Bourget.	G-OEMS
F-GHSV	80	King Air 200	BB-622	Lima Papa SARL/Air Normandie, Le Havre-Octeville.	N212BF
F-GHTA	78	PA-31T Cheyenne II	7820015	Yankee Delta, Montpellier.	N107BK
F-GHUV	78	King Air E90	LW-278	Avialim, Limoges.	N700MA
F-GHVF	82	SA-227AT Merlin 4C	AT-423	Compagnie Aeronautique Europeenne, Marseille-Marignane.	N10NB
F-GHVV	80	King Air 200	BB-676	Seine Aviation/Chalair, Caen-Carpiquet.	N970AA
F-GICA	88	King Air 300	FA-146	Soframa Holding & Sacha Boileau, Noumea, New Caledonia.	N2650C
F-GICE	68	King Air B90	LJ-363	Michel Bidoux/Air Transport Pyrenees SA. Pau.	N303WJ
F-GIFC	69	King Air B90	LJ-456	EAL-Europe Air Lines, Montpellier.	D-ILTY
F-GIFK	80	King Air F90	LA-62	Loc Air SA. Perpignan.	(F-HAAG)
F-GIII	80	PA-31T Cheyenne II	8020037	SAS Weishardt International, Agen-La Garenne.	N805SW
F-GIJB	74	King Air 200	BB-13	Seine Aviation/Chalair, Caen-Carpiquet.	N83MA
F-GIZB	81	King Air C90	LJ-955	Atlantique Air Assistance, Nantes-Atlantique.	N768SB
F-GJAD	72	King Air E90	LW-3	Ste Grenobloise d'Electronique et d'Automatisme, Grenoble.	N888BH
F-GJBS	83	King Air B200	BB-1181	Aerophoto Europe Investigation, Moulins-Montbeuguy.	N6725Y
F-GJCR	78	King Air E90	LW-251	Dassault Aviation, Istres.	N7ZU
F-GJFA	87	King Air B200	BB-1270	SEFA, Muret.	N30391
F-GJFC	89	King Air B200	BB-1347	SEFA, Muret.	
F-GJFE	91	King Air B200	BB-1399	SEFA, Muret.	
F-GJJJ	74	King Air A100	B-196	Regourd Aviation, Paris-Le Bourget.	N773SK
F-GJMJ	82	King Air B200	BB-1032	Alsair SA. Colmar-Houssen.	I-CUVI
F-GJPD	80	King Air E90	LW-328	Trans Helicoptere Service, Lyon-Bron.	N551M
F-GJPE	77	PA-31T Cheyenne II	7720042	Ste Air Mont Blanc, Sallanches.	YU-BKT
F-GJRK	77	King Air C90	LJ-710	Icare Enterprises, Funchal, Madeira.	3A-MON
F-GKCV	77	King Air 200	BB-251	Aero Services France, Paris-Le Bourget.	I-BMPE
F-GKEL	76	King Air A100	B-228	Locavia France, Nantes-Atlantique.	ZS-LVL
F-GKII	79	King Air 200	BB-515	Sogelease France SA/Chalair SA. Caen-Carpiquet.	(F-HADA)
F-GKRR	81	PA-31T Cheyenne II	8120015	La Paparre et Fils, Agen-La Garenne.	N107TT
F-GKSP	95	King Air C90B	LJ-1409	Transport'Air, Avignon.	(F-GKDG)
F-GKYY	02	King Air 350	FL-357	SOFIM, Orleans St Denis de l'Hotel.	N61907
Reg	Yr	Type	c/n	Owner/Operator	Prev Regn

Reg	Yr	Type	c/n	Owner/Operator	Prev Regn
☐ F-GLBZ	91	TBM 700	32	SOCATA/TBM SA. Tarbes.	N356M
☐ F-GLIF	77	King Air 200	BB-192	Trans Helicoptere Service, Lyon-Bron.	F-OGPQ
☐ F-GLLA	85	King Air C90A	LJ-1093	Lorraine Aviation SARL. Nancy-Essey.	HB-GHN
☐ F-GLLH	83	King Air B200	BB-1109	COMATA SNC. Lorient.	N900ED
☐ F-GLPT	79	SA-226T Merlin 3B	T-298	Airlec Air Espace SA. Bordeaux-Merignac.	VH-AWU
☐ F-GLRP	81	PA-31T Cheyenne II	8120064	Helijet/Air Star, Chambery.	F-ZBFZ
☐ F-GLRZ	91	King Air C90A	LJ-1296	Groupe Entremont SNC. Annecy.	(F-GJDK)
☐ F-GMGB	90	King Air B200	BB-1390	IGN France, Creil.	(F-GLOP)
☐ F-GMLT	92	King Air B200T	BT-34	IGN France, Creil. (was BB-1426).	N56361
☐ F-GMLV	01	TBM 700B	219	Salvagnini Nederland BV. Vicenza, Italy.	
☐ F-GMPM	92	King Air C90B	LJ-1303	Ste O C I M Location et Cie, Toussus-le-Noble.	(F-GIAO)
☐ F-GMRN	78	King Air E90	LW-304	EAL-Europe Air Lines, Montpellier.	N113SB
☐ F-GMTO	74	SA-226AT Merlin 4A	AT-031	Etat Francais Meteo France, Bretigny.	N22KW
☐ F-GNEE	93	King Air C90B	LJ-1328	G I E Avion Ecco, Lyon-Bron.	N90HB
☐ F-GNEG	90	King Air B200	BB-1377	Airailes, Colmar-Houssen.	HB-GIR
☐ F-GNMA	92	King Air C90A	LJ-1299	Franciscair SAS. Lyon-Bron.	N8253D
☐ F-GNMP	79	King Air C90	LJ-828	Boust Air SAS, St Etienne Boutheon.	(F-GPJC)
☐ F-GNOE	97	King Air 350	FL-183	SNC Beech 200, Pointoise.	HB-GJL
☐ F-GNPD	77	King Air 200	BB-199	AVDEF-Aviation Defence Service, Nimes-Garons.	I N-PAD
☐ F-GOAE	92	King Air B300C	FM-1	Ste Eolia/Aerope 3S Aviation, Pointoise. (status ?).	V5-RTZ
☐ F-GOBK		ATR 42-320	264	France Telecom, Lannion-Servel.	F-SEBK
☐ F-GOCF	78	King Air 200	BB-397	TGB SARL. La Rochelle.	LX-GDB
☐ F-GOOO	89	King Air 300	FA-175	Air Vendee Investissements, Nantes.	N175NJ
☐ F-GOSB	00	King Air 350	FL-301	S. A. ACCOR, Toussus Le Noble.	N4211V
☐ F-GPAC	81	King Air B200	BB-920	AVDEF-Aviation Defense Service, Nimes-Garons.	SE-LMM
☐ F-GPAS	77	King Air 200	BB-209	SARL West Aero/Ocean Airlines, La Rochelle.	D-IACS
☐ F-GPBF	79	PA-31T Cheyenne II	7920094	Bretagne Angleterre Irlande SA. Rennes.	OH-PYE
☐ F-GPDV	75	King Air 200	BB-37	Au Gre du Vent, St Die.	ZS-NXH
☐ F-GPGH	94	King Air 350	FL-120	PGA Motors Holding et Joseph Landreau, Poitiers-Biard.	D-CBBB
☐ F-GPLK	95	King Air C90B	LJ-1391	SNC Airco, Brive.	3A-MRL
☐ F-GPRH	93	King Air 300LW	FA-226	SNC Partnair, Paris-Le Bourget.	F-OHRT
☐ F-GQJD	75	King Air C90	LJ-667	Avialim, Limoges.	N888GN
☐ F-GRAI	91	Reims/Cessna F406	F406-0061	Reims Aviation Industries SA. Reims-Prunay.	N406CT
☐ F-GRAJ	01	Pilatus PC-12/45	406	Nicodis/SA Lavel Distribution, Lavel-Entrammes.	
☐ F-GRPS	78	PA-31T Cheyenne II	7820010	Pastej SARL. Annemasse.	(LX-GPP)
☐ F-GRSO	80	King Air 200C	BL-11	Manag'Air, Amiens-Gilsy.	(F-GYMD)
☐ F-GSEB	83	King Air B200	BB-1110	J M Communication, Paris-Le Bourget.	TR-LDU
☐ F-GSIN	77	King Air 200	BB-239	Chalair, Caen-Carpiquet.	N517JM
☐ F-GTCR	01	King Air C90B	LJ-1660	Toucanair SA. Paris-le Bourget.	N4470M
☐ F-GTEF	79	King Air 200	BB-560	PG Air, Paris-Le Bourget.	LN-MAA
☐ F-GTEM	93	King Air 350	FL-80	Oyonnair SARL. Lyon-Bron.	PH-BRN
☐ F-GTJM	99	TBM 700B	145	Ouest Participations, Paris-Le Bourget.	
☐ F-GULJ	79	King Air 200	BB-561	Air Taxi SAT, Blois Le Breuil.	(F-GZAT)
☐ F-GULM	89	King Air C90A	LJ-1226	Rapido SA. Laval.	N369B
☐ F-GVJB	00	Pilatus PC-12/45	359	Transaltis, Charlerois, Belgium.	HB-FSN
☐ F-GVRM	66	King Air A90	LJ-121	Mitjavila SNC. Perpignan.	N948RM
☐ F-GXES	81	PA-42 Cheyenne III	8001043	Air Bor SARL. Dijon-Longvic.	D-IYES
☐ F-GYGL	92	King Air C90B	LJ-1321	Romadol SARL. Funchal, Madeira.	D-IOMG
☐ F-GZJM	76	SA-226T Merlin 3A	T-264	Georges Kern, Haguenan.	LX-LAP
☐ F-GZPE	03	P-180 Avanti	1064	Bio Merieux & Pan Europeenne Air Service, Chambery.	
☐ F-GZRB	00	TBM 700B	166	SOCATA, Paris-Le Bourget.	F-OHBZ
☐ F-HAAA	76	King Air E90	LW-175	Regourd Aviation, Paris-Le Bourget.	F-BXSN
☐ F-HAAG	80	King Air 200	BB-722	Paris Sud Affaires, Toussus-Le-Noble.	3A-MBD
☐ F-HADR	99	King Air C90B	LJ-1583	Delta Romeo SAS. Marseille-Marignane.	N902PU
☐ F-HHAM	94	King Air C90B	LJ-1361	DARTA Aero Charter, Paris-Le Bourget.	N5521T
☐ F-HJCM	85	King Air C90A	LJ-1098	Sogefima SA. Toulouse-Blagnac.	N294TT
☐ F-ODGS	77	PA-31T Cheyenne II	7720041	Franck Jean Gallo, Noumea, New Caledonia.	TS-LAZ
☐ F-ODMM	80	PA-31T Cheyenne II	8020084	Ste Pacific Perles, Papeete, Tahiti.	F-WFLQ
☐ F-OGOG	88	Reims/Cessna F406	F406-0026	Air Guyane, Cayenne-Rochambeau.	
☐ F-OHCP	81	King Air 200	BB-831	High Commissioner of French Polynesia, Papeete, Tahiti.	F-ODUA
☐ F-OHJK	96	King Air B200	BB-1544	Air Archipels, Faaa-Tahiti.	N1094S
☐ F-OINC	86	King Air B200	BB-1244	Haut Commissariat de Nouvelle Caledonie, Noumea.	F-GSFA
☐ F-OSPJ	03	Reims/Cessna F406	F406-0091	Air St Pierre SA. St Pierre et Miquelon Islands.	
☐ F-WKDL	91	TBM 700	03	SOCATA/TBM SA. Tarbes.	
☐ F-WKPG	91	TBM 700	02	SOCATA/TBM SA. Tarbes.	

	Reg	Yr Type	c/n	Owner/Operator	Prev Regn
☐	F-WQFA	94 Reims/Cessna F406	F406-0073	Reims Aviation Industries SA. Reims-Prunay.	G-BVJT
☐	F-WTBM	83 TBM 700	01	SOCATA/TBM SA. Tarbes.	

Military

	Reg	Yr Type	c/n	Owner/Operator	Prev Regn
☐	F-MABM	87 Reims/Cessna F406	F406-0008	008/ABM, EAAT, Rennes-St Jacques.	
☐	F-MABN	86 Reims/Cessna F406	F406-0010	010/ABN, EAAT, Rennes-St Jacques.	
☐	F-MABO	94 TBM 700	99	99/ABO, EAAT, Rennes-St Jacques.	
☐	F-MABP	94 TBM 700	100	100/ABP, EAAT, Rennes-St Jacques.	
☐	F-MABQ	96 TBM 700	115	115/ABQ, EAAT, Rennes-St Jacques.	
☐	F-MABR	98 TBM 700	136	136/ABR, EAAT, Rennes-St Jacques.	
☐	F-MABS	99 TBM 700	139	139/ABS, EAAT, Rennes-St Jacques.	
☐	F-MABT	99 TBM 700B	156	156/ABT, EAAT, Rennes-St Jacques.	
☐	F-MABU	99 TBM 700B	159	159/ABU, EAAT, Rennes-St Jacques.	
☐	F-MABV	99 TBM 700B	160	160/ABV, EAAT, Rennes-St Jacques.	
☐	F-RAXA	92 TBM 700	33	33/43-XA, ETE.043, Bordeaux-Merignac.	F-..ID
☐	F-RAXB	92 TBM 700	35	35/43-XB, ETE.043, Bordeaux-Merignac.	
☐	F-RAXC	93 TBM 700	70	70/43-XC, ETE.043, Bordeaux-Merignac.	
☐	F-RAXD	93 TBM 700	77	77/65-XD, COTAM, ETEC.065, Villacoublay.	
☐	F-RAXE	93 TBM 700	78	78/44-XE, ETE.044 Aix-Les-Milles.	
☐	F-RAXF	93 TBM 700	80	80/41-XF, ETE.041, Metz-Frescarty.	
☐	F-RAXG	92 TBM 700	94	94/44-XG,	
☐	F-RAXH	92 TBM 700	95	95/65-XH, COTAM, ETEC.065 Villacoublay.	
☐	F-RAXI	94 TBM 700	103	103/41-XI, ETE.041 Metz-Frescarty.	
☐	F-RAXJ	94 TBM 700	104	104/41-XJ, ETE.041 Metz-Frescarty.	
☐	F-RAXK	94 TBM 700	105	105/65-XK, COTAM, ETEC.065 Villacoublay.	
☐	F-RAXL	92 TBM 700	93	93/43-XL,	
☐	F-RAXM	95 TBM 700	111	111/65-XM, COTAM, ETEC.065 Villacoublay.	
☐	F-RAXN	96 TBM 700	117	117/44-XN, ETE.044, Aix-Les-Milles.	
☐	F-RAXO	97 TBM 700	125	125/65-XO, COTAM, ETEC.065 Villacoublay.	
☐	F-RAXP	95 TBM 700	110	110/41-XP, ETE.041 Metz-Frescarty.	
☐	F-RAXQ	98 TBM 700	131	131/65-XQ, COTAM,	
☐	F-RAXR	99 TBM 700B	146	146/65-XR, COTAM, ETEC.065 Villacoublay.	
☐	F-RAXS	99 TBM 700B	147	147/65-XS, COTAM,	
☐	F-ZBAB	88 Reims/Cessna F406	F406-0025	French Customs, Paris-Dugny.	
☐	F-ZBBB	89 Reims/Cessna F406	F406-0039	French Customs, Paris-Dugny.	F-WZDS
☐	F-ZBBF	71 King Air C90	LJ-518	Securite Civile, Paris.	F-BTCA
☐	F-ZBCE	89 Reims/Cessna F406	F406-0042	French Customs, Paris-Dugny.	F-WKRA
☐	F-ZBCF	95 Reims/Cessna F406	F406-0077	French Customs, Paris-Dugny.	F-WZDZ
☐	F-ZBCG	93 Reims/Cessna F406	F406-0066	French Customs, Paris-Dugny.	F-WZDT
☐	F-ZBCH	94 Reims/Cessna F406	F406-0075	French Customs, Paris-Dugny.	
☐	F-ZBCI	93 Reims/Cessna F406	F406-0070	French Customs, Paris-Dugny.	
☐	F-ZBCJ	94 Reims/Cessna F406	F406-0074	French Customs, Paris-Dugny.	
☐	F-ZBEP	85 Reims/Cessna F406	F406-0006	French Customs, Paris-Dugny.	
☐	F-ZBES	85 Reims/Cessna F406	F406-0017	French Customs, Paris-Dugny.	
☐	F-ZBFA	83 Reims/Cessna F406	F406-01	French Customs, Paris-Dugny.	F-GGRA
☐	F-ZBFJ/98	83 King Air B200	BB-1102	GMA/Ministry of the Interior, Marseille-Marignane.	(F-GKDO)
☐	F-ZBFK/96	81 King Air B200	BB-876	GMA/Ministry of the Interior, Marseille-Marignane.	F-GHSC
☐	F-ZBGA	99 Reims/Cessna F406	F406-0086	French Customs, Paris-Dugny.	F-WWSR
☐	F-ZBGB	02 Reims/Cessna F406	F406-0090	French Customs, Paris-Dugny.	
☐	F-ZBMB/97	90 King Air B200	BB-1379	GMA/Ministry of the Interior, Marseille-Marignane.	F-GJFD
☐	F-ZVMN	94 TBM 700	106	106/MN, CEV-Centre d'Essais en Vol, Bretigny.	

G = GREAT BRITAIN   Total   59

Civil

	Reg	Yr Type	c/n	Owner/Operator	Prev Regn
☐	G-BGRE	79 King Air 200	BB-568	Martin Baker (Engineering) Ltd. Chalgrove.	
☐	G-BKFY	82 King Air C90A	LJ-1028	Blackbrook Aviation LP. Luton.	N213CT
☐	G-BLKP	84 BAe Jetstream 31	634	Global Aviation Ltd. Humberside.	G-31-634
☐	G-BMKD	84 King Air C90A	LJ-1069	Alan Bristow, Cranleigh.	N223CG
☐	G-BNDY	85 Conquest 1	425-0236	Standard Aviation Ltd. Newcastle.	N1262T
☐	G-BPPM	82 King Air B200	BB-1044	GAMA Aviation Ltd. Fairoaks.	N7061T
☐	G-BRGN	84 BAe Jetstream 31	637	Cranfield University, Cranfield.	G-BHLC
☐	G-BVMA	81 King Air 200	BB-797	Dragonfly Aviation Services LP. Cardiff.	G-VPLC
☐	G-BYCP	82 King Air B200	BB-966	London Executive Aviation, London City.	F-GDCS
☐	G-BZNE	00 King Air 350	FL-286	Gavyn Davies, London.	N4486V
☐	G-CCPU	04 Pilatus PC-12/45	549	Technical Flight Services Ltd. Bournemouth-Hurn.	HB-FQE
☐	G-CCWY	04 Pilatus PC-12/45	568	Meridian Aviation Group Ltd. Bournemouth-Hurn.	HB-F..

Reg	Yr Type	c/n	Owner/Operator	Prev Regn

Reg	Yr	Type	c/n	Owner/Operator	Prev Regn
☐ G-CEGP	80 King Air 200		BB-726	CEGA Aviation Ltd. Goodwood.	N50AJ
☐ G-CEGR	78 King Air 200		BB-351	Henfield Lodge Aviation Ltd/CEGA Aviation Ltd. Goodwood.	N68CP
☐ G-CLOW	81 King Air 200		BB-821	Clowes Estates Ltd/Eastern Air Executive, Sturgate.	N821RC
☐ G-DERI	01 PA-46-500TP Meridian		4697078	Intesa Leasing SpA. Milan, Italy.	N51151
☐ G-DERK	02 PA-46-500TP Meridian		4697152	Derek Priestley, Jersey, Cl.	N165MA
☐ G-ERAD	99 King Air C90B		LJ-1565	GKL Management Services, Cranleigh.	N213NC
☐ G-FCED	81 Cheyenne II-XL		8166013	Air Medical Fleet Ltd. Oxford.	C-FCED
☐ G-FIND	89 Reims/Cessna F406		F406-0045	Atlantic Express Ltd. Coventry.	OY-PEU
☐ G-FPLA	82 King Air B200		BB-944	Flight Precision Ltd. Durham Tees Valley.	N31WL
☐ G-FPLB	82 King Air B200		BB-1048	Flight Precision Ltd. Durham Tees Valley.	N739MG
☐ G-FPLC	81 Conquest II		441-0207	Flight Precision Ltd. Durham Tees Valley.	G-FRAX
☐ G-FPLD	92 King Air B200		BB-1433	Flight Precision Ltd. Durham Tees Valley.	N43CE
☐ G-FRYI	76 King Air 200		BB-210	London Executive Aviation, London City.	G-OAVX
☐ G-HAMA	75 King Air 200		BB-30	GAMA Aviation Ltd. Fairoaks.	N244JB
☐ G-IJYS	86 BAe Jetstream 31		715	Air Kilroe Ltd /Eastern Airways Ltd. Humberside.	G-BTZT
☐ G-IMGL	97 King Air B200		BB-1564	IM Aviation Ltd/Rangemile, Coventry.	VP-CMA
☐ G-KVIP	79 King Air 200		BB-487	Capital Trading Aviation Ltd. Filton.	G-CBFS
☐ G-LEAF	87 Reims/Cessna F406		F406-0018	Atlantic Express Ltd. Coventry.	EI-CKY
☐ G-MAFA	89 Reims/Cessna F406		F406-0036	Directflight Ltd. Prestwick.	G-DFLT
☐ G-MAFB	96 Reims/Cessna F406		F406-0080	Directflight Ltd. Prestwick.	F-WWSR
☐ G-MAMD	97 King Air B200		BB-1549	Forest Aviation Ltd. Doncaster.	N1069S
☐ G-MOUN	00 King Air B200		BB-1734	Geoffrey Mountain, Leeds-Bradford.	N123NA
☐ G-OMNH	76 King Air 200		BB-108	Newborne Ltd/Sterling Aviation Ltd. Norwich.	N108BM
☐ G-ORJA	97 King Air B200		BB-1570	Air West Ltd/Centerline Air Charter Ltd. Bristol-Lulsgate.	N1120Z
☐ G-ORTH	75 King Air E90		LW-136	Kilo Aviation Ltd. Liverpool.	G-DEXY
☐ G-OWAX	78 King Air 200		BB-302	Context GB Ltd/Pool Aviation (NW) Ltd. Blackpool.	N86Y
☐ G-PFFN	79 King Air 200		BB-456	The Puffin Club Ltd. Leicester.	N456CD
☐ G-RACI	79 King Air C90		LJ-819	Foxdale Consulting Ltd. Douglas, IOM.	G-SHAM
☐ G-RKJT	01 PA-46-500TP Meridian		4697111	Harpin Ltd. York.	N338DB
☐ G-ROWN	80 King Air 200		BB-684	Valentia Air Ltd. Oxford.	G-BHLC
☐ G-SFPA	91 Reims/Cessna F406		F406-0064	Fisheries Protection Agency, Edinburgh.	
☐ G-SFPB	91 Reims/Cessna F406		F406-0065	Fisheries Protection Agency, Edinburgh.	
☐ G-SFSG	77 King Air E90		LW-239	Geminair Ltd. Thruxton.	N24SM
☐ G-SGEC	00 King Air B200		BB-1747	Bridgtown Plant Ltd. Staverton.	N214FW
☐ G-SPOR	97 King Air B200		BB-1557	Select Plant Hire Co/Platinum Air Charter Ltd. Southend.	N57TL
☐ G-TURF	87 Reims/Cessna F406		F406-0020	Atlantic Express Ltd. Coventry.	EI-CND
☐ G-VSBC	88 King Air B200		BB-1290	BAe Systems Marine Ltd. Walney Aerodrome.	N3185C
☐ G-WELL	76 King Air E90		LW-198	CEGA Aviation Ltd. Goodwood.	(N7PB)
☐ G-WVIP	80 King Air 200		BB-625	Capital Trading Aviation Ltd. Filton.	N869AM
☐ G-ZAPT	01 King Air B200C		BL-141	Titan Airways Ltd. Stansted.	N200KA
Military					
☐ G-RAFJ	03 King Air B200S		BB-1829	RAF, 45(R) Squadron, Cranwell.	N6129N
☐ G-RAFK	03 King Air B200		BB-1830	RAF, 45(R) Squadron, Cranwell.	N50130
☐ G-RAFL	03 King Air B200S		BB-1832	RAF, 45(R) Squadron, Cranwell.	N5032K
☐ G-RAFM	03 King Air B200S		BB-1833	RAF, 45(R) Squadron, Cranwell.	N51283
☐ G-RAFN	03 King Air B200S		BB-1835	RAF, 45(R) Squadron, Cranwell.	N60275
☐ G-RAFO	03 King Air B200S		BB-1836	RAF, 45(R) Squadron, Cranwell.	N60476
☐ G-RAFP	03 King Air B200S		BB-1837	RAF, 45(R) Squadron, Cranwell.	N61037

HB = SWITZERLAND

Total 54

Civil					
☐ HB-FOB	93 Pilatus PC-12M Eagle		P-02	Pilatus Flugzeugwerke AG. Stans.	
☐ HB-FOG	96 Pilatus PC-12/45		134	Gruppe Ruestung, Berne.	
☐ HB-FOI	96 Pilatus PC-12		157	FOI Plane AG. St Moritz.	
☐ HB-FOL	97 Pilatus PC-12		166	Pilatus Flugzeugwerke AG. Stans.	HB-FSB
☐ HB-FOO	97 Pilatus PC-12/45		290	Dislocato Universal SA/Lions Air AG. Zurich.	
☐ HB-FOP	99 Pilatus PC-12/45		291	Translem SA. Sion.	
☐ HB-FOQ	00 Pilatus PC-12/45		349	Aero Gear AG/Lions Air AG. Zurich.	(ZS-SRO)
☐ HB-FOR	99 Pilatus PC-12/45		257	Cemex Investments AG. Schaan, Liechtenstein.	N653CA
☐ HB-FOS	00 Pilatus PC-12/45		366	Sasset AG/Lions Air AG. Zurich.	
☐ HB-FOT	95 Pilatus PC-12/45		121	Pilatus Flugzeugwerke AG. Stans.	ZS-PVT
☐ HB-FOU	00 Pilatus PC-12/45		368	Bahlsen Management AG/Execujet Switzerland AG. Zurich.	
☐ HB-FOV	97 Pilatus PC-12/45		190	Pilatus Flugzeugwerke AG. Stans.	ZS-OFN
☐ HB-FOW	01 Pilatus PC-12/45		411	Future Finance Corp AG. Cham.	
☐ HB-FOX	00 Pilatus PC-12/45		334	Lions Air AG. Zurich.	

Reg	Yr	Type	c/n	Owner/Operator	Prev Regn

Reg	Yr Type	c/n	Owner/Operator	Prev Regn
☐ HB-FOY	01 Pilatus PC-12/45	386	Central Aviation AG/Lions Air AG. Zurich.	
☐ HB-FOZ	00 Pilatus PC-12/45	352	Nicolas Schilling SA. Neuchatel.	(ZS-TLA)
☐ HB-FPB	02 Pilatus PC-12/45	381	Camdoe AG/Avcon Ltd. Zurich.	HB-FSO
☐ HB-FPC	01 Pilatus PC-12/45	422	Moliair AG. Altenrhein.	HB-FRK
☐ HB-FPJ	03 Pilatus PC-12/45	490	Gonagall Trading Corp/Lions-Air AG. Zurich.	
☐ HB-FPK	03 Pilatus PC-12/45	513	Swiss Business Air,	
☐ HB-FPL	99 Pilatus PC-12/45	247	Lions Air AG. Zurich.	(PH-CVA)
☐ HB-FPR	04 Pilatus PC-12/45	544	Pilatus Flugzeugwerke AG. Stans.	
☐ HB-FPX	04 Pilatus PC-12/45	566	Pilatus Flugzeugwerke AG. Stans.	
☐ HB-FQP	04 Pilatus PC-12/45	606	Pilatus Flugzeugwerke AG. Stans.	
☐ HB-FQQ	04 Pilatus PC-12/45	605	Pilatus Flugzeugwerke AG. Stans.	
☐ HB-FRL	04 Pilatus PC-12/45	611	Pilatus Flugzeugwerke AG. Stans.	
☐ HB-GHD	80 King Air F90	LA-50	Air Evasion SA. Lausanne.	F-GCLS
☐ HB-GHK	81 Gulfstream 1000	96023	Gofir SA Aerotaxi, Lugano.	ZS-KZV
☐ HB-GHV	88 King Air 300	FA-170	ATG Swiss First GmbH. Zug.	
☐ HB-GIL	77 King Air 200	BB-194	Air Glaciers SA. Sion.	HB-GIL
☐ HB-GJD	80 King Air 200C	BL-7	Zimex Business Aviation AG. Zurich.	F-GJBJ
☐ HB-GJF	95 King Air C90B	LJ-1407	Air-N AG. Lausanne.	
☐ HB-GJH	81 King Air C90	LJ-972	Flying Devil SA. Lausanne.	N18080
☐ HB-GJI	79 King Air 200	BB-451	Air Glaciers SA. Sion.	D-IBOW
☐ HB-GJM	77 King Air 200	BB-255	Air Glaciers SA. Sion.	N32KD
☐ HB-GJR	02 King Air 350	FL-340	BergAir SA. Lausanne.	N5070M
☐ HB-GJS	04 King Air 350	FL-404	Breitling SA. Grenchen.	N6204G
☐ HB-GPG	78 King Air 200	BB-307	Pocair SA. La Chaux de Fonds.	N703HT
☐ HB-GPH	97 King Air B200	BB-1569	Pinkerton AG. Baar.	EI-WHE
☐ HB-GPI	91 King Air 300LW	FA-220	Technomag AG. Berne.	N41GA
☐ HB-KEI	91 TBM 700	3	Contaco Establishment, Cascais, Portugal.	F-GJTS
☐ HB-KFR	01 TBM 700B	195	Olivier Rochat, Lausanne.	(N700EN)
☐ HB-KOL	01 TBM 700B	218	Aerolift AG. Zurich.	N700NE
☐ HB-LLK	79 PA-31T Cheyenne 1	7904014	Kogno Anstalt, Vaduz. Liechstenstein.	N401PT
☐ HB-LNL	80 PA-31T Cheyenne II	8020083	Daniel Knutti, Magglingen-Macolin.	N54JB
☐ HB-LNX	81 Cheyenne II-XL	8166050	Transwing AG. Grenchen.	N700XL
☐ HB-LOE	81 Conquest 1	425-0016	Mecaplex AG. Grenchen.	ZS-KST
☐ HB-LQP	80 PA-31T Cheyenne 1	8004044	Ursella Holding AG. Berne.	OO-JMR
☐ HB-LRV	78 PA-31T Cheyenne II	7820017	Thomke AG. Stans.	N82222
☐ HB-LTE	01 P-180 Avanti	1042	Ovala AG. Lugano.	
☐ HB-LTI	80 PA-31T Cheyenne II	8020091	Symbios Orthopedie SA. Yverdon.	F-GIPL
☐ HB-LTM	85 PA-42 Cheyenne 400LS	5527028	Thomke Management AG. Grenchen.	N4119X
☐ HB-LTN	03 P-180 Avanti	1066	Hara International AG. Altenrhein.	
Military				
☐ T-721	93 King Air 350C	FN-1	Swiss Air Force, Berne.	HB-GII

HI = **DOMINICAN REPUBLIC** *Total* 3

Civil

Reg	Yr Type	c/n	Owner/Operator	Prev Regn
☐ HI-678CT	69 Gulfstream 1	323	Caribe SA. Santo Domingo.	HI-678CA
☐ HI-701SP	82 King Air B200	BB-984	Corp Aeroportuaria del Este,	N9RU
☐ HI-776SP	88 King Air C90A	LJ-1163		N777J

HC = **ECUADOR** *Total* 20

Civil

Reg	Yr Type	c/n	Owner/Operator	Prev Regn
☐ HC-...	80 King Air 200	BB-703		N703KH
☐ HC-...	80 Gulfstream 980	95026		N903L
☐ HC-...	83 Gulfstream 900	15023		N88RC
☐ HC-...	81 King Air C90-1	LJ-986	San Sierra Aero Servicios, Quito.	N18300
☐ HC-...	92 King Air 350	FL-85		N8080C
☐ HC-BHU	80 Gulfstream 840	11634	TAESA. Quito. (status ?).	N5886K
☐ HC-BIF	81 PA-31T Cheyenne II	8120019	Ecuavia SA. Guayaquil.	N2425X
☐ HC-BPY	71 681B Turbo Commander	6049	Aviopacifico SA. Guayaquil.	N587KA
☐ HC-BUD	81 Gulfstream 840	11669	SAEREO SA. Quito.	N844MA
☐ HC-BXH	82 Conquest II	441-0268	Union de Bananeros Ecuatorianos, Quito.	VP-BPH
☐ HC-BXT	80 Gulfstream 840	11615	San Eduardo Distribuidora SA. Quito.	N811EC
☐ HC-BYO	98 Beech 1900D	UE-317	ICARO-Instituto Civil Aeronautico SA. Quito.	N2290B
☐ HC-DAC	76 King Air E90	LW-178	Directorate of Civil Aviation, Quito.	
Military				
☐ AEE-101	81 King Air 200	BB-811	Ministry of National Defence, Quito.	AEE-001
☐ ANE-231	81 King Air 200	BB-771	Aviacion Naval Ecuatoriana, Guayaquil.	N3831Q
Reg	**Yr Type**	**c/n**	**Owner/Operator**	**Prev Regn**

Reg	Yr	Type	c/n	Owner/Operator	Prev Regn
☐ ANE-232	85	King Air 300	FA-75	Aviacion Naval Ecuatoriana, Guayaquil.	N7247A
☐ ANE-233	80	King Air 200	BB-580	Aviacion Naval Ecuatoriana, Guayaquil.	N48450
☐ ANE-234	79	King Air 200	BB-458	Aviacion Naval Ecuatoriana, Guayaquil.	N169DB
☐ FAE-001	70	BAe HS 748-2A	1684	Government of Ecuador, Quito.	HC-AUK
☐ IGM-240	78	King Air A100	B-242	Instituto Geografico Militar, Ejercito-army photo survey.	

HK = COLOMBIA

Civil

Total   192

Reg	Yr	Type	c/n	Owner/Operator	Prev Regn
☐ HK-...	80	Gulfstream 980	95001	Gustavo Durango, Cali.	N980AA
☐ HK-...	84	King Air 300	FA-22		N72069
☐ HK-....	79	PA-31T Cheyenne II	7920088		N171DA
☐ HK-....	74	King Air E90	LW-90		N114AT
☐ HK-....	79	Conquest II	441-0110		N84CH
☐ HK-....	85	Gulfstream 1000	96080		N960AC
☐ HK-....	80	Gulfstream 840	11604	Carlos Alberto Cortez, Bogota.	N5855K
☐ HK-....	75	SA-226T Merlin 3A	T-253		N959M
☐ HK-....	70	681 Turbo Commander	6014	David Quinones, Medellin.	N681SM
☐ HK-....	80	Gulfstream 840	11602	ALICOL-Aerolineas Intercolombianos Ltda. Bogota.	N2647C
☐ HK-....	83	King Air F90	LA-198	Central Charter de Colombia SA. Bogota.	N198FM
☐ IIK-....	93	King Air D200	BB-1452		N15HV
☐ HK-....	81	Gulfstream 980	95080		N999ST
☐ HK-....	77	Rockwell 690B	11386		N568H
☐ HK-....	81	King Air F90	LA-84		N122GA
☐ HK-....	86	King Air 300	FA-99	Amazonian Investment Inc. Bogota.	N6293V
☐ HK-....	95	DHC 8-202	391	BPX Colombia SA. Bogota.	C-GFBW
☐ HK-....	81	PA-31T Cheyenne 1	8104007		N914CR
☐ HK-....	82	Gulfstream 900	15010	Turbine Group Inc. Melbourne, Fl. USA. (status ?).	N900BE
☐ HK-....	67	King Air A90	LJ-210	David Quinones, Medellin.	N43TT
☐ HK-....	67	King Air A90	LJ-248	Elias Valera Morales, Bogota.	N562P
☐ HK-1770G	74	Rockwell 690A	11216	Instituto Geografico Agustin Codazzi, Bogota.	N57216
☐ HK-1977	70	681 Turbo Commander	6035	SEARCA-Servicio Aereo de Capurgana Ltda.	HK-1977W
☐ HK-1982	72	Rockwell 690	11014	TAS-Transporte Aereo de Santander,	HK-1982W
☐ HK-2055	72	Rockwell 690	11005	ARPA-Aerolineas Regionales de Paz de Ariporo Ltda.	HK-2055W
☐ HK-2060W	72	Mitsubishi MU-2K	243	Agropecuaria Las Garzas y Cia Ltda.	HK-2060X
☐ HK-2120P	74	Mitsubishi MU-2J	621	Carlos Alberto Aragon Orozco,	HK-2120
☐ HK-2218W	78	Rockwell 690B	11453	Fabrica de Dulces Colombina Ltda.	N81736
☐ HK-2281	72	Rockwell 690	11033	AVIEL-Aviones Ejecutivos Ltda. Bogota.	HK-2281P
☐ HK-2282P	73	Rockwell 690A	11128	Gabriel Antonio Valencia Rendon,	HK-2282W
☐ HK-2285P	67	680T Turbo Commander	1632-57	Jimenez Alfonso Mejia,	HK-2285
☐ HK-2291X	77	Rockwell 690B	11364	Mineros de Antioquia SA.	HK-2291
☐ HK-2347	79	PA-31T Cheyenne II	7920076	HELICONDOR-Helicopteros El Condor Ltda/Helicafe Ltda.	HK-2347P
☐ HK-2376P	71	681 Turbo Commander	6043	Martha Lucy Hernandez de Dominguez,	HK-2376
☐ HK-2390W	77	Conquest II	441-0016	Norman Gonzalez y Asociados Ltda.	N36938
☐ HK-2403	76	Mitsubishi MU-2L	678	Jorge Alfonso Diaz Clavijo,	HK-2403W
☐ HK-2414P	76	Rockwell 690A	11296	Nestor Manuel Gutierrez Sanchez,	HK-2414
☐ HK-2455	80	PA-31T Cheyenne II	8020047	LIRA-Lineas Aereas de Uraba Ltda.	HK-2455
☐ HK-2479W	80	SA-226T Merlin 3B	T-320	AGROCASA Ltda/Inversiones Agropecuarias Casanare,	HK-2479
☐ HK-2491	76	King Air E90	LW-183	Interamericana de Aviacion SA. Bogota.	YV-940P
☐ HK-2495P	80	Gulfstream 840	11633	Dario Maja Velasquez,	N5885K
☐ HK-2538P	80	Conquest II	441-0114	Pozo Hernando Buitrago,	HK-2538X
☐ HK-2551P	78	Rockwell 690B	11489	Francisco Antonio Molina Laverde,	N7701L
☐ HK-2585P	80	PA-31T Cheyenne II	8020077	Giraldo Eliecer Giraldo,	(N2519V)
☐ HK-2596	81	King Air C90	LJ-957	AEROTACA SA-Aerotransportes Casanare/Aerotaxi Casanare	HK-2596G
☐ HK-2601	80	Gulfstream 840	11651	Lopez Montoya Cia S C S.	N840JP
☐ HK-2631G	81	PA-31T Cheyenne II	8120032	Ministerio de Obras Publicas y Transporte, Bogota.	HK-2631X
☐ HK-2642P	81	PA-31T Cheyenne II	8120037	Hector Gomez Alvarez,	
☐ HK-2684X	81	PA-42 Cheyenne III	8001068		N4099Y
☐ HK-2749P	81	Cheyenne II-XL	8166019	Adriana Gomez Larroche,	HK-2749X
☐ HK-2772X	81	PA-42 Cheyenne III	8001059	Fernando Rafael Llanos Avila,	HK-2772X
☐ HK-2909P	82	Gulfstream 1000	96045	Jorge Arturo Buelvas Marchena,	HK-2909
☐ HK-2926P	82	Cheyenne T-1040	8275015	Felipe Sandoval Rincon,	HK-2926
☐ HK-2951	82	Gulfstream 1000	96049	Aerotayrona Ltda.	HK-2951P
☐ HK-2963	81	Cheyenne II-XL	8166053	Supertiendas y Droguerias Olimpicas SA/Char Hermanos Ltda.	N174CC
☐ HK-3000G	81	PA-42 Cheyenne III	8001062	Unidad Administrativa Especial/Aeronautica Civil de Colombia	HK-3000X
☐ HK-3009	83	Conquest II	441-0273	Helicopteros El Condor-Helicondor Ltda/Helicafe Ltda.	HK-3009P

Reg	Yr	Type	c/n	Owner/Operator	Prev Regn
☐ HK-3036P	82	Conquest 1	425-0118	Pedro Antonio Pineda Duque,	N6881Q
☐ HK-3043P	81	PA-31T Cheyenne II	8120051	Juan Climaco Prieto Cabrera,	(N2525Y)
☐ HK-3060	82	Gulfstream 1000	96039	ATTA-Asociacion Tolimense de Transporte Aereo Ltda.	HK-3060W
☐ HK-3074P	81	Cheyenne II-XL	8166035	Giraldo Arteaga Salvador Dario,	HK-3074
☐ HK-3117W	81	Cheyenne II-XL	8166073	Carvajal SA.	HK-3117X
☐ HK-3147X	73	Rockwell 690A	11122		N9229Y
☐ HK-3192W	85	Gulfstream 1000	96077	Aero Charter Ltda.	HK-3192X
☐ HK-3193	85	Gulfstream 1000	96086	AEROES-Aerolineas Especiales/Taxi Aereo Aereos Ltda.	HK-3193X
☐ HK-3214	81	King Air B200	BB-854	Servialas de Colombia Ltda	HK-3214X
☐ HK-3218	83	Gulfstream 1000	96061	AVIEL-Aviones Ejecutivos Ltda. Bogota.	N184BB
☐ HK-3239W	82	Gulfstream 1000	96010	Aero Antigua Ltda.	HK-3239X
☐ HK-3253P	85	Gulfstream 1000	96074	Mario Montoya Gomez,	HK-3253X
☐ HK-3275	85	Gulfstream 1000	96076	Hector Fabio Gonzalez Martinez,	HK-3275X
☐ HK-3277P	80	King Air C90	LJ-892	Lazaro Estrada Ospina,	HK-3277W
☐ HK-3279	84	Gulfstream 1000	96072	Aerocarbones del Cesar Ltda/Aerocarbon,	HK-3279W
☐ HK-3283W	85	Gulfstream 1000	96099	Compania Exploradora del Pacifico Ltda.	HK-3293
☐ HK-3290P	81	Gulfstream 840	11653	Irene Leonor Clamote Lagnoo,	HK-3290
☐ HK-3291P	85	Gulfstream 1000	96088	Diamar Ltda.	HK-3291W
☐ HK-3314W	75	Rockwell 690A	11255	SIRVE-Sociedad Importadora de Repuestos y Vehiculos Ltda.	HK-3314
☐ HK-3324P	85	Gulfstream 1000	96100	Adriana Lopez Cardona,	N111VP
☐ HK-3366X	82	Gulfstream 1000	96033	LAPAZ Colombia, Paz de Ariporo.	G-I000
☐ HK-3367	82	Gulfstream 1000	96018	SERPA-Servicios Aereos del Pacifico,	YV-416CP
☐ HK-3379W	79	Rockwell 690B	11525	Velez y Valencia Compania S en C.	HK-3379
☐ HK-3381G	87	PA-42 Cheyenne IIIA	5501039	IDEMA-Instituto de Mercadeo Agropecuaria, Bogota.	HK-3381X
☐ HK-3385P	82	Gulfstream 840	11728	Hector Eduardo Tautna Cinturia,	HK-3385X
☐ HK-3389P	82	Gulfstream 1000	96037	Oscar Alberto Morales Salazar,	HK-3389
☐ HK-3390	82	Gulfstream 1000	96047	Air Caribe Ltda. Cartagena.	HK-3390X
☐ HK-3391W	82	Gulfstream 1000	96059	Aerominas de Colombia Ltda.	HK-3391
☐ HK-3397W	88	PA-42 Cheyenne 400LS	5527037	AGRONASUR-Agropecurias y Ganaderias del Sur Ltda.	N9561N
☐ HK-3401	78	Conquest II	441-0059	VIANA-Vias Aereas Nacionales Ltda. Arauca.	N441MS
☐ HK-3406	81	Gulfstream 980	95062	JET-Jet Express Ltda/Cia Sinuana de Transp. Aer Costa Ltda.	N92MT
☐ HK-3407	81	Gulfstream 980	95075	LIRA-Lineas Aereas de Uraba Ltda.	HK-3407X
☐ HK-3408	81	Gulfstream 980	95050	Servicios Aereos de la Capital Ltda. Bogota.	HK-3408X
☐ HK-3418	84	Conquest II	441-0333	SADA-Sociedad Aeronautica de Armenia Ltda.	HK-3418P
☐ HK-3424	80	Gulfstream 840	11611	APEL Express SA/Aerolineos Petroleros del Llano,	N35DR
☐ HK-3429W	79	King Air C90	LJ-831	NADAL Ltda/Asesores de Seguros y Servicios Generales,	HK-3429X
☐ HK-3432	85	King Air B200	BB-1227	SAVA-Servicios Aereos del Valle/Aviaco Ltda. Bogota.	N7237A
☐ HK-3433X	88	King Air 300	FA-159	Caja de Credito Agraria Industrial y Minero, Bogota.	N3083B
☐ HK-3439	82	Gulfstream 1000	96021	Aeroejecutivos Colombia SA. Bogota.	N132PR
☐ HK-3444	81	Gulfstream 980	95057	Servicios Aereos de la Capital Ltda. Bogota.	HK-3444X
☐ HK-3447P	82	Gulfstream 840	11722	Alvaro Jose Salgado Calle,	HK-3447
☐ HK-3450	81	Gulfstream 980	95083	RAA-Rutas Aereas Araucanas Ltda. Arauca.	HK-3450W
☐ HK-3451	86	PA-42 Cheyenne 400LS	5527033	SATURNO-Servicio Aereo Turistico del Nororiente Ltda.	N827PC
☐ HK-3455	81	Gulfstream 980	95065	RAA-Rutas Aereas Aruacanas Ltda. Arauca.	HK-3455X
☐ HK-3456W	83	Conquest II	441-0271	Aero Antigua Ltda.	HK-3456
☐ HK-3461	81	Gulfstream 980	95043	ALICOL-Aerolineas Intercolombianos Ltda. Bogota.	HK-3461X
☐ HK-3465P	73	Rockwell 690	11059	Sergio Jose Cardona Jimenez,	HK-3465X
☐ HK-3466	74	Rockwell 690A	11165	Helitaxi Ltda. Bogota.	N690LP
☐ HK-3472X	80	PA-31T Cheyenne II	8020043	F de Jesus Ocampo de Sepulveda. (status ?).	
☐ HK-3474	80	Gulfstream 980	95016	RAA-Rutas Aereas Aruacanas Ltda. Arauca.	N7050S
☐ HK-3481	81	Gulfstream 980	95079	Alfuturo Aereo Ltda/Aerocali Luego Alfuturo Air Ltda.	N9831S
☐ HK-3484	80	Gulfstream 980	95022	LAR-Lineas Aereas de Rionegro Ltda.	N20HG
☐ HK-3497	84	Conquest II	441-0335	LAR-Lineas Aereas de Rionegro Ltda.	HK-3497X
☐ HK-3505	84	King Air F90-1	LA-221	Aeropei Ltda.	HK-3505W
☐ HK-3507	82	King Air B200	BB-974	Lineas Aereas de Los Libertadores/Lineas Aereas Petroleras,	N1861B
☐ HK-3512	82	Conquest II	441-0261	AEROLLANO Ltda/Aerovias del Llano, Villavicencio (Meta).	N261DW
☐ HK-3514	74	Rockwell 690A	11221	Julio Cesar Gerena Diaz,	N132RD
☐ HK-3529	85	Conquest II	441-0348	VIANA-Vias Aereas Nacionales Ltda. Arauca.	HK-3529X
☐ HK-3532	85	Conquest II	441-0356	Aeroexpresso de la Sabana Ltda.	N441CS
☐ HK-3534	86	King Air 300	FA-96	SAETA-Servicios Aereos del Metay Territorios Nacionales Ltda	N2586E
☐ HK-3540E	83	Conquest II	441-0287	ARO-Aerovias Regionales del Oriente,	HK-3540
☐ HK-3547	85	King Air 300	FA-86	AEROATLANTICO-Aerovias del Atlantico Ltda.	N955AA
☐ HK-3550	83	Conquest II	441-0320	SARPA-Servicios Aereos Panamericanos Ltda. Puerto Asis.	N189WS
☐ HK-3554	82	King Air B200	BB-1068	TAG-Trans Aereo de Girardot/Taxi Aereo Girardot Ltda.	N2157L
☐ HK-3556P	85	King Air 300	FA-47	Martha Lucia Obando Pena,	N961AA

Reg	Yr	Type	c/n	Owner/Operator	Prev Regn
❏ HK-3561	77	Rockwell 690B	11365	Helitaxi Ltda. Bogota.	LV-LZS
❏ HK-3562	82	Conquest II	441-0232	CALAMAR Ltda. Calamar (Vaupes).	N443WS
❏ HK-3568	83	Conquest II	441-0309	LARCO-Lineas Aereas de Corozal Ltda.	N441MT
❏ HK-3573	82	Conquest II	441-0251	SARPA-Servicios Aereos Panamericanos Ltda. Puerto Asis.	N711GF
❏ HK-3580W	64	Gulfstream 1	145	Compania Rural de Occidente Ltda.	HK-3329X
❏ HK-3596	82	Conquest II	441-0276	Aerotaxi de Valledupar Ltda. Bogota.	HK-3596X
❏ HK-3597	73	Rockwell 690A	11110	Aerotaxi de Valledupar Ltda. Bogota.	HK-3597X
❏ HK-3611	84	Conquest II	441-0324	Taxi Aereo de Caldas Ltda.	N1209P
❏ HK-3613	81	Conquest II	441-0206	Aero Antigua Ltda.	N7049Y
❏ HK-3615	82	Conquest II	441-0239	Cx HK- 7/95 to ?	N45TF
❏ HK-3620X	80	Conquest II	441-0152	Aerotaxi de Valledupar Ltda. Bogota.	N2628X
❏ HK-3648	86	King Air 300	FA-100	Aerolimosina Ltda. (status ?).	N2614C
❏ HK-3654	86	King Air 300LW	FA-101	Aerotaxi del Quindio Ltda.	G-BSTF
❏ HK-3656	76	Rockwell 690A	11314	SERCU-Servicios Aereos de Cucuta Ltda. (status ?).	N14AD
❏ HK-3659	85	King Air 300	FA-60	APEL Express SA/Aerolineas Petroleras del Llano,	N285KA
❏ HK-3680	80	Gulfstream 840	11620	Air Tropical Ltda. Bahia Solano.	G-BXYZ
❏ HK-3681	61	Gulfstream 1	78	Aerotaxi de Valledupar Ltda. Bogota.	N33CP
❏ HK-3693X	82	PA-42 Cheyenne III	8001075	HELIVALLE/Helicopteros del Valle Ltda.	N4998M
❏ HK-3700	82	Gulfstream 840	11721	APEL Express SA/Aerolineas Petroleras del Llano.	XA-...
❏ HK-3704X	90	King Air/Catpass 250	BB-1392	BP Exploration Co Colombia Ltda. Bogota.	N8026J
❏ HK-3705	75	King Air 200	BB-63	Aerotaxi del Quindio Ltda.	HK-3705X
❏ HK-3819	81	Gulfstream 980	95059	SAHO-Servicios Aereos Horizonte Ltda.	N9811S
❏ HK-3822	77	King Air 200	BB-248	AERUBA-Aerotaxi de Uraba Ltda. (status ?).	N123PM
❏ HK-3828	84	King Air 300	FA-10	Aerotaxi del Quindio Ltda.	N13PD
❏ HK-3860	88	King Air 300	FA-169	SADA-Sociedad Aeronautica de Armenia Ltda.	XA-PUD
❏ HK-3907	73	King Air E90	LW-39	AERVAL-Aereos y Valores Ltda. Bogota.	OB-1466
❏ HK-3912	81	Gulfstream 840	11668	Taxi Aereo del Uraba Ltda.	YV-2413P
❏ HK-3922P	78	King Air 200	BB-352	Oscar Alberto Monsalve Arbelaez,	YV-...
❏ HK-3923X	79	King Air 200	BB-450	JET-Jet Express Ltda/Cia Sinuana de Transp. Aer Costa Ltda.	C-GJCM
❏ HK-3935W	81	King Air F90	LA-151	Air Charter Ltda.	YV-445CP
❏ HK-3936	75	King Air 200	BB-75	TAXOR-Taxi Aereo de la Orinoquia Ltda.	N70LA
❏ HK-3941W	78	King Air 200	BB-333	Air Charter Ltd. (status ?).	TC-AUY
❏ HK-3961X	84	Gulfstream 1000	96069	Danilo Botero Bustos, Bogota.	N6151T
❏ HK-3965X		King Air E90	...		
❏ HK-3990X	90	King Air 1300	BB-1376	APSA-Aeroexpresso Bogota SA. Bogota.	N914YW
❏ HK-3995X	77	King Air 200	BB-196		LN-FKF
❏ HK-4065W	81	Gulfstream 840	11673	Servicios Aereos y Terrestres Ltda.	YV-779CP
❏ HK-4095X		King Air 200	...	noted 9/97.	
❏ HK-4108X	75	King Air 200	BB-60	S A de Capurgana Ltda.	N530JA
❏ HK-4179X	81	PA-31T Cheyenne II	8120062	Jardines de Paz SA.	HK-3025
❏ HK-4236	76	King Air 200	BB-135	Helicargo SA. Medellin.	N402RG
❏ HK-4256	82	King Air B200	BB-1049	Helicargo SA. Medellin. (now HK-4282X ?).	N6144H
❏ HK-853W	69	King Air B90	LJ-458	Jorge Hernando Carvajal Administradores Ltda y Cia S En C.	HK-353P
❏ HP-1457	87	King Air 300	FA-123	Airleasing International Corp.	HK-3670
Military					
❏ ARC-101		King Air 200	...		
❏ ARC-301		PA-31T Cheyenne	...	noted 9/97.	
❏ ARC-601		Rockwell 690	...	noted 9/97.	
❏ ARC-701		Gulfstream 1	...	noted 9/00.	
❏ EJC-103		Gulfstream 1000	...	Colombian Army, Bogota.	
❏ EJC-108		King Air 200	...	Colombian Army, Bogota.	
❏ EJC-114	85	Gulfstream 1000	96083	Colombian Army, Bogota.	HK-3376
❏ EJC-115	81	Gulfstream 980	95066	Colombian Army, Bogota.	HK-2682P
❏ EJC-116		King Air 90	...	Colombian Army, Bogota. (noted 9/00).	
❏ EJC-117	80	King Air 200	BB-694	Colombian Army, Bogota.	PT-OTO
❏ EJC-118	98	King Air/Catpass 250	BB-1615	Colombian Army, Bogota.	N170L
❏ FAC-225		King Air 200	...	Fuerza Aerea Colombiana, Bogota-El Dorado. (noted 9/00).	
❏ FAC-5198	82	Gulfstream 1000	96030	Fuerza Aerea Colombiana, Bogota-El Dorado.	HK-....
❏ FAC-542	66	680V Turbo Commander	1563-19	Fuerza Aerea Colombiana, Bogota-El Dorado.	HK-2539G
❏ FAC-5553	81	Gulfstream 980	95055	Fuerza Aerea Colombiana, Bogota-El Dorado.	FAC-553
❏ FAC-5570	78	King Air C90	LJ-752	Fuerza Aerea Colombiana, Bogota-El Dorado.	FAC-570
❏ FAC-5739	75	PA-31T Cheyenne II	7520014	Fuerza Aerea Colombiana, Bogota-El Dorado.	N8TK
❏ FAC-5750		King Air 200	...	Fuerza Aerea Colombiana, Bogota-El Dorado.	
❏ PNC-0225	99	King Air B200	BB-1644	Policia Nacional de Colombia, Bogota.	N3055K
❏ PNC-203		King Air 200	...	Policia Nacional de Colombia, Bogota.	
Reg	**Yr**	**Type**	**c/n**	**Owner/Operator**	**Prev Regn**

Reg	Yr	Type	c/n	Owner/Operator	Prev Regn
☐ PNC-204	77	Conquest II	441-0031	Policia Nacional de Colombia, Bogota.	N918FE
☐ PNC-205		Gulfstream 1000	...	Policia Nacional de Colombia, Bogota.	
☐ PNC-208		King Air 300	...	Policia Nacional de Colombia, Bogota.	
☐ PNC-209	77	King Air 200	BB-212	Policia Nacional de Colombia, Bogota.	N910L
☐ PNC-210	77	King Air 200	...	Policia Nacional de Colombia, Bogota.	
☐ PNC-225		King Air B200	...	Policia Nacional de Colombia, Bogota.	

HL = KOREA   Total   6

Military

Reg	Yr	Type	c/n	Owner/Operator	Prev Regn
☐ 98-1001	98	Reims/Cessna F406	F406-0081	Republic of Korea Navy, Seoul.	F-WWSR
☐ 98-1002	98	Reims/Cessna F406	F406-0082	Republic of Korea Navy, Seoul.	F-WWSS
☐ 98-1003	98	Reims/Cessna F406	F406-0083	Republic of Korea Navy, Seoul.	F-W...
☐ 98-1004	99	Reims/Cessna F406	F406-00..	Republic of Korea Navy, Seoul.	F-W...
☐ 98-1005	99	Reims/Cessna F406	F406-0084	Republic of Korea Navy, Seoul.	F-WSSU
☐ 98-1006	99	Reims/Cessna F406	F406-0085	Republic of Korea Navy, Seoul.	F-W...

HP = PANAMA   Total   40

Civil

Reg	Yr	Type	c/n	Owner/Operator	Prev Regn
☐ HP-...	85	Gulfstream 1000	96081		N600BM
☐ HP-...	82	Conquest II	441-0277	Revise SA.	N441HT
☐ HP-...	82	Gulfstream 900	15003		N900RH
☐ HP-...	85	Gulfstream 1000	96082		N89GA
☐ HP-...	82	Gulfstream 900	15004		N5838N
☐ HP-...	82	Gulfstream 1000	96003		N17CG
☐ HP-...	79	Rockwell 690B	11565	TRANSPASA, Panama-Paitilla.	N81HK
☐ HP-...	76	King Air 200	BB-164	Air Anstro Services SA. Panama City.	N70PQ
☐ HP-...	04	King Air 350	FL-395		N61185
☐ HP-...	84	Conquest II	441-0328	City Investments Ltd. Panama City.	N12093
☐ HP-....	65	King Air 90	LJ-55	Air Anstro Services SA. Panama City.	N711BP
☐ HP-....	77	King Air 200	BB-237	Blue Water Reef International Research, Panama City.	N114JF
☐ HP-....	76	King Air 200	BB-330		N127TT
☐ HP-....	71	King Air C90	LJ-520		N1869
☐ HP-....	73	Rockwell 690	11073	Heliatlantic SA. El Dorado.	N680AD
☐ HP-....	65	King Air 90	LJ-5		N357JR
☐ HP-....	75	King Air 200	BB-33	Transportes Aereos de Maracay, Panama City.	N90806
☐ HP-....	77	King Air 200	BB-300	Transportes Aereos de Maracay, Panama City.	F-GHLV
☐ HP-....	78	King Air 200	BB-362	Baru Air SA. Panama City.	N506AB
☐ HP-....	78	King Air C-12C	BC-63	Eduardo Finol de Leon, Caracas, Venezuela.	N712GA
☐ HP-....	73	Rockwell 690A	11102		N697JM
☐ HP-....	67	King Air A90	LJ-296		N30EH
☐ HP-1069	77	SA-226T Merlin 3A	T-288	Inversiones Humbolt SA. Panama City.	HP-1069P
☐ HP-1136AP	68	SA-26AT Merlin 2B	T26-113	Raul Arias/Apair SA. Paitilla.	N878SC
☐ HP-1149P	82	Gulfstream 1000	96031	World Interstate Corp.	C-FDGD
☐ HP-1180	83	King Air B200	BB-1131	Bocas Fruit Co. Panama City.	N6642Z
☐ HP-1182	90	King Air 300	FA-209	Motta Internacional SA. Panama City.	N148M
☐ HP-1189	84	Conquest II	441-0332	Marucci Holdings SA.	N888FL
☐ HP-1316	88	King Air B200T	BT-33	Bocas Fruit Co. Panama City. (was BB-1301).	N600RD
☐ HP-1336APP	73	King Air A100	B-173	Aeroperlas SA/Apair SA. El Dorado.	C-GAST
☐ HP-1415	77	Rockwell 690B	11354	Beltline Corp. Panama City.	HK-2490W
☐ HP-1433	68	680W Turbo Commander	1820-34	Cx HP- to ?	HK-3975X
☐ HP-1500	01	King Air C90B	LJ-1648	Aeronaves del Atlantico SA. El Dorado.	N3178H
☐ HP-1512	77	King Air 200	BB-311	Transportes Aereos del Toro SA.	N370TC
☐ HP-1515	98	King Air B200	BB-1611	May's Zona Libre SA. Panama City.	N2287J
☐ HP-2888	91	King Air B300C	FM-2	Blue Cascade Inc.	N749RH
☐ HP-5000H	77	King Air E90	LW-240	Helix-Craft Trading/Caribe Express SA.	N500EA
☐ HP-77PE	77	Rockwell 690B	11368	Aviacion Panamena SA. Panama City.	N77PE
☐ HP-809	80	PA-31T Cheyenne II	8020015	Colony Trading SA.	N2353W
☐ HP-960P	80	King Air 200	BB-617	Stowage SA. (status ?).	HP-960

HR = HONDURAS   Total   7

Civil

Reg	Yr	Type	c/n	Owner/Operator	Prev Regn
☐ HR-...	76	Rockwell 690A	11302	San Pedro Aviation Inc. Tegucigalpa.	N302BA
☐ HR-...	67	Mitsubishi MU-2B	021		N22JZ
☐ HR-ANL	79	King Air 200	BB-481	Comercial y Invesriones Galatia SA. (status ?)	N144K
☐ HR-ASY	82	King Air B200	BB-1063		N4359T
☐ HR-IAH	66	King Air A90	LJ-122	Islena Airlines, La Ceiba.	N860K

Reg	Yr	Type	c/n	Owner/Operator	Prev Regn

Reg	Yr Type	c/n	Owner/Operator	Prev Regn
☐ HR-JFA	81 PA-42 Cheyenne III	8001056	AVE SA.	
Military				
☐ FAH-006	83 Gulfstream 1000	96060	Fuerza Aerea Honduras, Tegucigalpa.	HK-3194X

HS = THAILAND — Total 26

Civil

Reg	Yr Type	c/n	Owner/Operator	Prev Regn
☐ HS-ADS	99 King Air B200	BB-1678	Aeronautical Radio of Thailand, Bangkok.	N2287L
☐ HS-DCB	76 King Air 200	BB-132	Aeronautical Radio of Thailand, Bangkok.	HS-FFI
☐ HS-DCF	88 King Air B200	BB-1315	Aeronautical Radio of Thailand, Bangkok.	HS-AFI
☐ HS-ITD	96 King Air 350	FL-151	Italian/Thai Development Co. Bangkok.	N10817
☐ HS-SLA	91 King Air 350	FL-53	Siam Land Flying Co. Bangkok.	HS-TFI
☐ HS-SLB	90 King Air C90A	LJ-1243	Siam Land Flying Co. Bangkok.	HS-TFH
☐ HS-TFG	78 Rockwell 690B	11482	Thai Flying Service Co. Bangkok.	N745T

Military

Reg	Yr Type	c/n	Owner/Operator	Prev Regn
☐ 00923	73 King Air E90	LW-26	Royal Thai Army, Don Muang.	01769
☐ 0169	Beech 1900C-1	UC-169	Royal Thai Army, Don Muang.	N.....
☐ 0170	Beech 1900C-1	UC-170	Royal Thai Army, Don Muang.	N.....
☐ 0342	78 King Air 200	BB-342	Royal Thai Army, Don Muang.	794
☐ 1112	95 Dornier 228-212	8226	Royal Thai Navy,	D-CBDF
☐ 1113	95 Dornier 228-212	8227	Royal Thai Navy,	D-CCCP
☐ 1114	96 Dornier 228-212	8228	Royal Thai Navy,	D-C...
☐ 1165	83 King Air B200	BB-1165	Royal Thai Army, Don Muang.	N6922P
☐ 2011	96 King Air 350	FL-146	KASET, Bangkok.	N3268Z
☐ 2012	96 King Air 350	FL-147	KASET, Bangkok.	N3269W
☐ 41060	95 BAe Jetstream 41	41060	Royal Thai Army, Don Muang.	G-BWGW
☐ 41094	96 BAe Jetstream 41	41094	Royal Thai Army, Don Muang.	G-BWTZ
☐ 60501	79 SA-226AT Merlin 4A	AT-071	Royal Thai Air Force, Bangkok.	60301
☐ 60502	79 SA-226AT Merlin 4A	AT-072	Royal Thai Air Force, Bangkok.	60302
☐ 60503	79 SA-226AT Merlin 4A	AT-073	Royal Thai Air Force, Bangkok.	60303
☐ 81491	76 Rockwell 690A	11340	Royal Thai Survey Dept. Bangkok.	11340
☐ 93303	92 King Air B200	BB-1436	Royal Thai Survey Dept. Bangkok.	N1564M
☐ 93304	92 King Air B200	BB-1441	Royal Thai Survey Dept. Bangkok.	56385
☐ 93305	92 King Air B200	BB-1443	Royal Thai Survey Dept. Bangkok.	56379

HZ = SAUDI ARABIA — Total 4

Civil

Reg	Yr Type	c/n	Owner/Operator	Prev Regn
☐ HZ-PC2	87 Beech 1900C-1	UC-4	Directorate of Civil Aviation,	N3078C
☐ HZ-SN6	72 SA-226AT Merlin 4	AT-007	DHL/SNAS WorldWide Express, Bahrain.	N2610
☐ HZ-SN8	82 SA-227AT Merlin 4C	AT-434	DHL/SNAS WorldWide Express, Bahrain.	N3110F
☐ HZ-SS1	72 Rockwell 690	11006	Saudi Arabian Photo Co. Riyadh.	N690SP

I = ITALY — Total 45

Civil

Reg	Yr Type	c/n	Owner/Operator	Prev Regn
☐ I-AESW	02 TBM 700B	225	Tango Bravo Mike SARL. Milan.	F-OIKG
☐ I-ASMI	83 King Air B200	BB-1124	Assicuratrice Milanese, Parma.	LX-DUC
☐ I-BCOM	00 P-180 Avanti	1040	Air Walser SRL. Milan.	
☐ I-BPAE	04 P-180 Avanti	1081	Blue Panorama Airlines, Rome.	
☐ I-BPAF	04 P-180 Avanti	1086	Blue Panorama Airlines, Rome.	HB-FQU
☐ I-CGAT	75 PA-31T Cheyenne II	7520033	Compagnia Generale Aeronautica, Genoa.	N54964
☐ I-CGTT	78 PA-31T Cheyenne II	7820045	Soc. New Bristol SRL. Milan.	N82288
☐ I-DPCR	95 P-180 Avanti	1032	Protezione Civile, Genoa.	(D-IMLP)
☐ I-DPCS	99 P-180 Avanti	1033	Protezione Civile, Genoa.	
☐ I-FXRB	00 P-180 Avanti	1035	Fox Air SRL. Bologna.	
☐ I-FXRC	00 P-180 Avanti	1045	Fox Air SRL. Bologna.	
☐ I-FXRE	02 P-180 Avanti	1049	Loop SpA/Fox Air SRL. Bologna.	
☐ I-FXRF	02 P-180 Avanti	1060	EuroSkyLink, Coventry, UK.	
☐ I-HYDR	75 PA-31T Cheyenne II	7520034	Compagnia Generale Aeronautica, Genoa.	N54966
☐ I-LIAT	80 PA-31T Cheyenne 1	8004052	Soc. R F Celada SpA. Milan.	N2316X
☐ I-LIPO	74 King Air C90	LJ-616	Soc. Coronet SpA. Milan.	SE-GXD
☐ I-MAGJ	75 Rockwell 690A	11265	Aviomar SRL. Roma-Urbe.	N81540
☐ I-MTOP	03 King Air B200	BB-1825	Toscana Jet, Florence.	N4485Z
☐ I-NARB	74 SA-226AT Merlin 4	AT-020	BESIT SNC. Servizi Aerei, Olbia. 'Cises'	N747BD
☐ I-NARC	75 SA-226AT Merlin 4A	AT-035	BESIT SNC. Servizi Aerei, Olbia.	N90090
☐ I-NARW	77 SA-226AT Merlin 4A	AT-058	BESIT SNC. Servizi Aerei, Olbia.	D-ICFB
☐ I-PALS	75 PA-31T Cheyenne II	7620005	Soc. PAL SRL. Pollone (BI).	N54979
☐ I-PIAH	81 King Air 200	BB-777	Interfly SRL. Breschia.	

Reg	Yr Type	c/n	Owner/Operator	Prev Regn

Reg	Yr	Type	c/n	Owner/Operator	Prev Regn
☐ I-POMO	79	PA-31T Cheyenne 1	7904030	Soc. Adria Fly Shipping SAS. Udine.	N601PT
☐ I-SASA	80	PA-31T Cheyenne 1	8004024	Soc. Alibrixia Nord SRL. Brescia.	N2321V
☐ I-TREP	87	PA-42 Cheyenne IIIA	5501045	Soc. Alitalia Flying School, Rome.	
☐ I-TREQ	87	PA-42 Cheyenne IIIA	5501046	Soc. Alitalia Flying School, Rome.	
☐ I-TRER	87	PA-42 Cheyenne IIIA	5501047	Soc. Alitalia Flying School, Rome.	

Military

Reg	Yr	Type	c/n	Owner/Operator	Prev Regn
☐ MM62159	94	P-180 Avanti	1023	AMI, 36 Stormo, Giola del Colle.	
☐ MM62160	94	P-180 Avanti	1024	AMI, 14 Stormo, Pratica di Mare.	
☐ MM62161	94	P-180 Avanti	1025	AMI, Sq Coll e Soccorso, Milan.	
☐ MM62162	94	P-180 Avanti	1028	AMI, 14 Stormo, Pratica di Mare.	
☐ MM62163	94	P-180 Avanti	1029	AMI, 14 Stormo, Pratica di Mare.	
☐ MM62164	94	P-180 Avanti	1030	AMI, Centro Sperimentale, Pratica di Mare.	
☐ MM62165	96	ATR 42-400MP	500	GF-13. AMI/Guardia di Finanza,	F-WWEW
☐ MM62166	96	ATR 42-400MP	502	GF-14. AMI/Guardia di Finanza,	F-WWEM
☐ MM62167	94	P-180 Avanti	1026	Cavelleria dell'Aria, ACTL 28 Gr Sqd 'Tucano', Roma-Ciampino	(D-IMED)
☐ MM62168	92	P-180 Avanti	1027	Cavelleria dell'Aria, ACTL 28 Gr Sqd 'Tucano', Roma-Ciampino	F-GMRM
☐ MM62169	9	P-180 Avanti	1031	Cavellaria dell'Aria, ACTL 28 Gr Sqd 'Tucano', Roma-Ciampino	
☐ MM62199	01	P-180 Avanti	1041	AMI, 14 Stormo, Pratica di Mare.	
☐ MM62200	01	P-180 Avanti	1047	AMI, 14 Stormo, Pratica di Mare.	
☐ MM62201	01	P-180 Avanti	1053	AMI, 14 Stormo, Pratica di Mare.	
☐ MM62202	02	P-180 Avanti	1058	AMI, 14 Stormo, Pratica di Mare.	
☐ MM62203	02	P-180 Avanti	1071	AMI, 14 Stormo, Practica di Mare.	I-RAII
☐ MM62204	03	P-180 Avanti	...	AMI, 14 Stormo, Practica di Mare.	

JA = JAPAN   *Total*   107

Civil

Reg	Yr	Type	c/n	Owner/Operator	Prev Regn
☐ JA....	02	King Air C90B	LJ-1690		N61669
☐ JA....	03	King Air 350	FL-382		N61942
☐ JA003G	98	SAAB 2000	051	JCAB, Tokyo.	SE-051
☐ JA004G	98	SAAB 2000	054	JCAB, Tokyo.	SE-O54
☐ JA007C	93	King Air C90B	LJ-1350	C Itoh Aviation Co. Shikabe.	N492JW
☐ JA01EP	98	King Air B200	BB-1604	Seiko Epson Corp. Kagoshima-Makarazaki.	N1017V
☐ JA01KA	99	King Air C90B	LJ-1567	Kawasaki Heavy Industries, Gifu.	N31279
☐ JA21EG	99	King Air C90B	LJ-1591	Gios Kodomo, Okayama-Konan.	N400TG
☐ JA353N	02	King Air 350	FL-345	Noevir Co. Makurazaki.	N5045L
☐ JA376N	03	King Air 350	FL-376	Noevir Co. Kagoshima.	N6176C
☐ JA8599	95	Pilatus PC-12	128	Ando Shokai/Auto Panther, Kagoshima.	HB-FQT
☐ JA8600	81	Gulfstream 980	95070	Asia Air Survey Co. Tokyo-Chofu.	N35SA
☐ JA868A	00	King Air 350	FL-292	JCG-Japanese Coast Guard, Shin-Chitose.	N3192N
☐ JA869A	00	King Air 350	FL-295	JCG-Japanese Coast Guard, Sendai.	N3195T
☐ JA8705	92	King Air B200	BB-1431	Naka Nihon Air Service Co. Nagoya.	N82696
☐ JA870A	00	King Air 350	FL-297	JCG-Japanese Coast Guard, Hiroshima.	N3197N
☐ JA8817	80	King Air 200T	BT-13	JCG-Japanese Coast Guard, Yao. (was BB-609).	N60587
☐ JA8818	80	King Air 200T	BT-14	JCG-Japanese Coast Guard, Niigata. (was BB-627).	(9Q-CTZ)
☐ JA8819	80	King Air 200T	BT-15	JCG-Japanese Coast Guard, Chitose. (was BB-647).	N6059D
☐ JA881C	97	King Air C90B	LJ-1470	Japcon Inc. Konan.	N1099Z
☐ JA8820	80	King Air 200T	BT-16	JCG-Japanese Coast Guard, Sendai. (was BB-665).	N60603
☐ JA8824	81	King Air 200T	BT-17	JCG-Japanese Coast Guard, Ishigaki. (was BB-798).	N3718Q
☐ JA8826	81	Gulfstream 980	95078	Naka Nihon Air Service Co. Nagoya.	N9830S
☐ JA8828	74	SA-226AT Merlin 4	AT-016	Showa Aviation Co. Osaka-Yao.	N76MX
☐ JA8829	82	King Air 200T	BT-22	JCG-Japanese Coast Guard, Naha. (was BB-991).	N1841K
☐ JA8833	83	King Air B200T	BT-28	JCG-Japanese Coast Guard, Kagoshima. (was BB-1117).	N1846M
☐ JA8844	86	King Air C90A	LJ-1141	Nishi Nihon Iryo Service, Oita.	N2736D
☐ JA8845	87	King Air C90A	LJ-1142	Flying Training, Sendai.	N2860A
☐ JA8846	87	King Air C90A	LJ-1143	Taian Kensetsu, Nagoya.	N7239S
☐ JA8847	87	King Air C90A	LJ-1144	Flying Training, Sendai.	N7239U
☐ JA8848	87	King Air C90A	LJ-1145	Flying Training, Sendai.	N7239Y
☐ JA8850	87	King Air C90A	LJ-1149	Flying Training, Sendai.	N7240E
☐ JA8851	87	King Air C90A	LJ-1150	Flying Training, Sendai.	N7240K
☐ JA8853	85	PA-42 Cheyenne 400LS	5527026	Bell Hand Club Co. Chofu.	(N429BX)
☐ JA8854	87	King Air B200T	BT-31	JCG-Japanese Coast Guard, Yao. (was BB-1264).	N72392
☐ JA8855	85	Conquest 1	425-0235	Konan Co. Tokunoshima.	N1262P
☐ JA8860	88	King Air B200T	BT-32	JCG-Japanese Coast Guard, Fukuoka. (was BB-1289).	N3184A
☐ JA8867	87	PA-42 Cheyenne 400LS	5527035	Mainichi Shimbun, Tokyo.	N9295A
☐ JA8881	91	King Air 300	FA-219	Japan Digital Laboratories, Honda.	N6080W

Reg	Yr	Type	c/n	Owner/Operator	Prev Regn

Reg	Yr	Type	c/n	Owner/Operator	Prev Regn
☐ JA8882	91	King Air C90A	LJ-1290	JAL Capital,	N81763
☐ JA8883	91	King Air C90A	LJ-1291	JAL Capital,	N8178W
☐ JA8884	91	King Air C90A	LJ-1292	JAL Capital,	N81826
☐ JA8894	92	TBM 700	38	Geos, Okayama.	F-OHBG
☐ JA8951	96	SAAB 340B-SAR	385	JCG-Japanese Coast Guard, Tokyo-Haneda.	SE-C85
☐ JA8952	97	SAAB 340B-SAR	405	JCG-Japanese Coast Guard, Tokyo-Haneda.	SE-C...
Military					
☐ 22003	72	Mitsubishi LR-1	803	JG-2003, JGSDF, Tachikawa. (was s/n 230).	
☐ 22007	76	Mitsubishi LR-1	807	JG-2007, JGSDF, Osaka-Yao. (was s/n 334).	
☐ 22008	77	Mitsubishi LR-1	808	JG-2008, JGSDF, Kasuminome. (was s/n 359).	
☐ 22009	78	Mitsubishi LR-1	809	JG-2009, JGSDF, Osaka-Yao. (was s/n 376).	
☐ 22010	78	Mitsubishi LR-1	810	JG-2010, JGSDF, Sapporo-Okadama. (was s/n 394).	
☐ 22013	81	Mitsubishi LR-1	813	JG-2013, JGSDF, Sapporo-Okadama. (was s/n 442).	
☐ 22014	81	Mitsubishi LR-1	814	JG-2014, JGSDF, Takayubaru. (was s/n 443).	
☐ 22015	81	Mitsubishi LR-1	815	JG-2015, JGSDF, Osaka-Yao. (was s/n 444).	
☐ 22016	83	Mitsubishi LR-1	816	JG-8016, JGSDF, Utsonimiya. (was s/n 456).	
☐ 22017	83	Mitsubishi LR-1	817	JG-8017, JGSDF, Sapporo-Okadama. (was s/n 457).	
☐ 22018	85	Mitsubishi LR-1	818	JG-2018, JGSDF, Kisarazu. (was s/n 465).	
☐ 22019	85	Mitsubishi LR-1	819	JG 2019, JGSDF, Naha. (was s/n 463).	
☐ 22020	85	Mitsubishi LR-1	820	JG-2020, JGSDF, Kasuminome. (was s/n 466).	
☐ 23051	98	King Air 350 (LR-2)	FL-176	JG-3051, JGSDF, Utsunomiya.	N11309
☐ 23052	98	King Air 350 (LR-2)	FL-186	JG-3052, JGSDF, Kisarazu.	N11310
☐ 23053	00	King Air 350 (LR-2)	FL-266	JG-3053, JGSDF, Naha.	N31379
☐ 23054	00	King Air 350 (LR-2)	FL-307	JG-3054, JGSDF, Takayubaru.	N5007H
☐ 23055	01	King Air 350 (LR-2)	FL-331	JG-3055, JGSDF,	N350KD
☐ 23-3226	81	Mitsubishi MU-2E	926	JASDF. (was s/n 455).	
☐ 23-3227	85	Mitsubishi MU-2E	927	JASDF. (was s/n 464).	
☐ 6808	80	King Air TC90	LJ-916	JMSDF, 202nd Air Training Squadron, Tokushima AB.	N67233
☐ 6809	80	King Air TC90	LJ-917	JMSDF, 202nd Air Training Squadron, Tokushima AB.	N6724D
☐ 6810	81	King Air TC90	LJ-976	JMSDF, 202nd Air Training Squadron, Tokushima AB.	N3832G
☐ 6811	81	King Air TC90	LJ-980	JMSDF, 202nd Air Training Squadron, Tokushima AB.	N3832K
☐ 6812	82	King Air TC90	LJ-1042	JMSDF, 202nd Air Training Squadron, Tokushima AB.	N18460
☐ 6813	82	King Air TC90	LJ-1043	JMSDF, 202nd Air Training Squadron, Tokushima AB.	N1846B
☐ 6814	82	King Air TC90	LJ-1044	JMSDF, 202nd Air Training Squadron, Tokushima AB.	N1846D
☐ 6815	82	King Air TC90	LJ-1047	JMSDF, 202nd Air Training Squadron, Tokushima AB.	N1846F
☐ 6816	83	King Air TC90	LJ-1060	JMSDF, 202nd Air Training Squadron, Tokushima AB.	N1875Z
☐ 6817	83	King Air TC90	LJ-1061	JMSDF, 202nd Air Training Squadron, Tokushima AB.	N1876Z
☐ 6818	83	King Air TC90	LJ-1062	JMSDF, 202nd Air Training Squadron, Tokushima AB.	N6886S
☐ 6819	84	King Air TC90	LJ-1083	JMSDF, 202nd Air Training Squadron, Tokushima AB.	N6923Z
☐ 6820	84	King Air TC90	LJ-1084	JMSDF, 202nd Air Training Squadron, Tokushima AB.	N69237
☐ 6821	85	King Air TC90	LJ-1110	JMSDF, 202nd Air Training Squadron, Tokushima AB.	N7238J
☐ 6822	87	King Air TC90	LJ-1146	JMSDF, 202nd Air Training Squadron, Tokushima AB.	N72400
☐ 6823	93	King Air TC90	LJ-1335	JMSDF, 202nd Air Training Squadron, Tokushima AB.	N82323
☐ 6824	93	King Air TC90	LJ-1336	JMSDF, 202nd Air Training Squadron, Tokushima AB.	N82326
☐ 6825	93	King Air TC90	LJ-1337	JMSDF, 202nd Air Training Squadron, Tokushima AB.	N82349
☐ 6826	93	King Air TC90	LJ-1338	JMSDF, 202nd Air Training Squadron, Tokushima AB.	N82366
☐ 6827	93	King Air TC90	LJ-1339	JMSDF, 202nd Air Training Squadron, Tokushima AB.	N82376
☐ 6828	00	King Air TC90	LJ-1584	JMSDF, 202nd Air Training Squadron, Tokushima AB.	N3184F
☐ 6829	00	King Air TC90	LJ-1592	JMSDF, 202nd Air Training Squadron, Tokushima AB.	N40490
☐ 6830	00	King Air TC90	LJ-1596	JMSDF, 202nd Air Training Squadron, Tokushima AB.	N43046
☐ 6831	00	King Air TC90	LJ-1634	JMSDF, 202nd Air Training Squadron, Tokushima AB.	N50344
☐ 6832	00	King Air TC90	LJ-1636	JMSDF, 202nd Air Training Squadron, Tokushima AB.	N50785
☐ 6833	00	King Air TC90	LJ-1638	JMSDF, 202nd Air Training Squadron, Tokushima AB.	N50778
☐ 83-3223	78	Mitsubishi MU-2E	923	JASDF. (was s/n 377).	
☐ 83-3224	78	Mitsubishi MU-2E	924	JASDF. (was s/n 378).	
☐ 9102	82	King Air UC-90	LJ-1038	JMSDF-Japanese Maritime Self Defence Force.	N1839D
☐ 9301	88	King Air LC-90	LJ-1182	JMSDF-Japanese Maritime Self Defence Force.	
☐ 9302	90	King Air LC-90	LJ-1248	JMSDF-Japanese Maritime Self Defence Force.	N56633
☐ 9303	90	King Air LC-90	LJ-1249	JMSDF-Japanese Maritime Self Defence Force, Atsugi.	N56638
☐ 9304	91	King Air LC-90	LJ-1281	JMSDF-Japanese Maritime Self Defence Force, Atsugi.	N81538
☐ 9305	91	King Air LC-90	LJ-1282	JMSDF-Japanese Maritime Self Defence Force.	N8154G
☐ 93-3225	81	Mitsubishi MU-2E	925	JASDF. (was s/n 445).	
☐ JA861A	97	King Air 350	FL-180	JCG-Japanese Coast Guard, Kagoshima.	N18327
☐ JA862A	97	King Air 350	FL-188	JCG-Japanese Coast Guard, Naha.	N18297
☐ JA863A	98	King Air 350	FL-191	JCG-Japanese Coast Guard, Yonago.	N11191
Reg	*Yr*	*Type*	*c/n*	*Owner/Operator*	*Prev Regn*

Reg	Yr Type	c/n	Owner/Operator	Prev Regn
☐ JA864A	98 King Air 350	FL-193	JCG-Japanese Coast Guard, Yonago.	N11250
☐ JA865A	98 King Air 350	FL-195	JCG-Japanese Coast Guard, Ishigaki.	N11278
☐ JA866A	98 King Air 350	FL-218	JCG-Japanese Coast Guard, Fukuoka.	N2352N
☐ JA867A	98 King Air 350	FL-222	JCG-Japanese Coast Guard, Niigata.	N23272

LN = NORWAY   Total 22

Civil

Reg	Yr Type	c/n	Owner/Operator	Prev Regn
☐ LN-ABU	80 Conquest II	441-0162	Bergen Air Transport A/S. Bergen.	N800AB
☐ LN-ACE	73 Rockwell 690	11121	Helitrans A/S. Trondheim.	S5-CAI
☐ LN-FAH	77 Rockwell 690B	11367	Helitrans A/S. Trondheim.	OY-BEJ
☐ LN-FWA	81 Gulfstream 840	11681	Helitrans A/S. Trondheim.	SE-IUV
☐ LN-FWB	80 Gulfstream 840	11613	Helitrans A/S. Trondheim.	SE-GSS
☐ LN-MOB	80 King Air 200	BB-584	Lufttransport A/S. Tromso.	N400WP
☐ LN-MOC	93 King Air B200	BB-1449	Lufttransport A/S. Tromso.	N200KA
☐ LN-MOD	93 King Air B200	BB-1459	Lufttransport A/S. Tromso.	N8163R
☐ LN-MOE	93 King Air B200	BB-1460	Lufttransport A/S. Tromso.	N8164G
☐ LN-MOF	93 King Air B200	BB-1461	Lufttransport A/S. Tromso.	N8261E
☐ LN-MOG	93 King Air B200	BB-1465	Lufttransport A/S. Tromso.	N8214T
☐ LN-MOH	93 King Air B200	BB-1466	Lufttransport A/S. Tromso.	N8216Z
☐ LN-MOI	93 King Air B200	BB-1470	Lufttransport A/S. Tromso.	N8225Z
☐ LN-MOJ	89 King Air B200	BB-1334	Lufttransport A/S. Tromso.	TC-SKO
☐ LN-MON	96 King Air B200	BB-1537	Lufttransport A/S. Tromso.	ZS-ARL
☐ LN-MOO	99 King Air B200	BB-1692	Lufttransport A/S. Tromso.	N29AH
☐ LN-MOT	97 King Air B200	BB-1590	Lufttransport A/S. Tromso.	D-IHUT
☐ LN-NOA	81 King Air B200	BB-829	Sundt Air A/S. Oslo-Gardemoen.	N829AJ
☐ LN-SFT	80 SA-226T Merlin 3B	T-342	Helitrans A/S. Trondheim.	N342NX
☐ LN-SUZ	96 King Air B200	BB-1547	Sundt Air A/S. Oslo-Gardemoen.	N780CA
☐ LN-TWL	83 King Air B200	BB-1144	Trans Wing A/S. Oslo.	N120AJ
☐ LN-VIZ	83 King Air B200	BB-1136	SAAB Norsk Flyjeneste A/S. Sandefjord-Torp.	D-IDOK

LV = ARGENTINA   Total 98

Civil

Reg	Yr Type	c/n	Owner/Operator	Prev Regn
☐ LQ-BLU	PA-42 Cheyenne 400LS	...	Corte Suprema de Justica Nacional, Buenos Aires.	
☐ LQ-PIE	King Air C90B	...		
☐ LQ-ZRB	99 King Air C90B	LJ-1552	Gobierno Santiago del Estero, Santiago del Estero.	N3132D
☐ LV-...	97 King Air C90B	LJ-1466		N466SC
☐ LV-...	75 King Air E90	LW-135		N74VR
☐ LV-...	04 King Air B200	BB-1877		N61767
☐ LV-...	04 King Air 350	FL-420		
☐ LV-...	00 King Air C90B	LJ-1617		N363K
☐ LV-...	03 King Air B200	BB-1817		N5117M
☐ LV-APF	81 PA-42 Cheyenne III	8001026	Government Province of Catamarca, Catamarca.	LQ-APF
☐ LV-BNA	77 Rockwell 690B	11419	Government Province of Cordoba.	LV-PYH
☐ LV-JJW	69 King Air B90	LJ-449	Jose Luis Colombero, Cordoba.	LV-PIZ
☐ LV-LEY	72 Rockwell 690	11019	CATA Linea Aerea S A C I F I., Buenos Aires.	LQ-LEY
☐ LV-LRH	75 Rockwell 690A	11236	Odol SA. (status ?).	LV-PTT
☐ LV-LTB	75 Rockwell 690A	11238	Government Province of Jujuy, San Salvador.	LV-PUA
☐ LV-LTC	75 Rockwell 690A	11241	SAPSE-Servicios Aereos Patagonicas, Viedma, Rio Negro.	LV-PUB
☐ LV-LTU	75 Rockwell 690A	11261	SASA-Sudamericana de Aviacion SA. Buenos Aires.	LV-PUI
☐ LV-LTV	75 PA-31T Cheyenne II	7520022	Government Province of Corrientes.	LV-PTS
☐ LV-LTX	75 Rockwell 690A	11258	SASA-Sudamericana de Aviacion SA. Buenos Aires.	LV-PUH
☐ LV-LTY	74 Rockwell 690A	11230	Government Province of Tucuman.	LV-PTY
☐ LV-LZL	75 Rockwell 690A	11246	Emepa SA. Buenos Aires.	LV-PUW
☐ LV-LZM	75 Rockwell 690A	11268	Banco Mercantil Argentino SA. Buenos Aires.	LV-PUX
☐ LV-LZO	75 PA-31T Cheyenne II	7620003	Esco SA. Buenos Aires.	LV-LZO
☐ LV-MAW	77 Rockwell 690B	11398	TAN-Transportes Aereos Neuquen, Neuquen. `Collon Cora'	LV-PVN
☐ LV-MBY	77 Rockwell 690B	11412	Government Province of Chaco, Resistencia.	LV-PXN
☐ LV-MCV	77 Mitsubishi MU-2P	361SA	Industrias Metalurgica Pescarmona, Buenos Aires.	LV-PYI
☐ LV-MDG	77 PA-31T Cheyenne II	7720065	Ver Part. Vinelli,	LV-PYD
☐ LV-MDN	78 Rockwell 690B	11442	Government Province of Cordoba.	LV-PYT
☐ LV-MGC	77 Mitsubishi MU-2N	704SA	T A F T SRL. Buenos Aires.	LV-PZT
☐ LV-MMY	78 Conquest II	441-0075	Government Province of Buenos Aires.	LV-PBA
☐ LV-MNR	79 PA-31T Cheyenne II	7920017	Government Province of Rioja.	LV-P..
☐ LV-MNU	79 PA-31T Cheyenne II	7920003	Government Province of Formosa.	LV-DMO
☐ LV-MOD	79 PA-31T Cheyenne II	7920033	Government Province of Santa Cruz.	LV-P..
☐ LV-MOE	79 PA-31T Cheyenne II	7920050	Government Province of Catamarca, Catamarca.	LV-P..

Reg	Yr	Type	c/n	Owner/Operator	Prev Regn
☐ LV-MRT	78	Conquest II	441-0082	Government Province of Buenos Aires.	LV-PAZ
☐ LV-MRU	78	Conquest II	441-0077	Government Province of Buenos Aires.	LV-PBB
☐ LV-MTU	79	PA-31T Cheyenne II	7920080	Inst. Argentina de Sanidad y Calidad, Buenos Aires.	LV-P..
☐ LV-MYA	79	Rockwell 690B	11558	Government Province of Santa Fe.	LV-PDH
☐ LV-MYX	79	PA-31T Cheyenne 1	7904045	Chincul S A C A I., Buenos Aires.	LV-P..
☐ LV-OAP	79	PA-31T Cheyenne II	7920065	Inst. Argentina de Sanidad y Calidad, Buenos Aires.	LV-PCJ
☐ LV-OBB	80	King Air E90	LW-330	Aerorutas S A T A, Buenos Aires.	LV-PFJ
☐ LV-OEI	80	Gulfstream 840	11612	Government Province of La Pampa, Santa Rosa.	LV-PGD
☐ LV-OFT	80	King Air 200	BB-699	Don Roberto S A A C I., Buenos Aires.	LV-PIF
☐ LV-OFX	67	680V Turbo Commander	1682-63	Empesur SA. Rio Gallegos, Santa Cruz.	AE-129
☐ LV-OGF	80	PA-31T Cheyenne II	8020013	Emp. Dist. de Energia Norte SA. Buenos Aires.	LV-P..
☐ LV-ROC	88	King Air C90A	LJ-1180	Petrel Aereos Servicios SRL. Buenos Aires.	LV-PAJ
☐ LV-RZB	69	SA-26AT Merlin 2B	T26-143	Coronaire SA. Quimes.	LV-PFR
☐ LV-VHO	68	King Air B90	LJ-428	Orion Aviacion SA. Buenos Aires.	N74GR
☐ LV-VHR	68	King Air B90	LJ-323	Aviajet SA. San Fernando.	N90SM
☐ LV-WDO	71	King Air 100	B-82	Navy Jet SA.	AE-100
☐ LV-WEW	81	King Air 200	BB-870	Tenil SA. Buenos Aires.	N200EL
☐ LV-WFP	75	King Air E90	LW-129	Servicio Aerocomercial Essair, Venado Tuerto, Santa Fe.	N423JD
☐ LV-WGP	79	King Air 200	BB-558	Minera del Altoplano SA. Don Torcuato.	N58JR
☐ LV-WHV	78	King Air E90	LW-259	Starman SA. Buenos Aires.	N269JB
☐ LV-WIO	80	King Air 200	BB-606	Cheyenne SA. Buenos Aires.	N29AJ
☐ LV-WIP	93	King Air 300LW	FA-229	G & M S A, Buenos Aires.	LV-PHI
☐ LV-WIR	73	SA-226T Merlin 3	T-232	Hawk Air SA. Don Torcuato.	N56TA
☐ LV-WJE	94	King Air C90B	LJ-1354	Granbril SACIFIA, Lanus, Buenos Aires.	N8294Z
☐ LV-WJY	74	Mitsubishi MU-2J	644	Parala SRL. Buenos Aires.	N494WC
☐ LV-WLT	92	King Air 300	FA-221	TIA SA. Don Torcuato.	N70FL
☐ LV-WMA	93	King Air 300	FA-222	Banco Mercantil Argentino SA. Buenos Aires.	N8273L
☐ LV-WMG	95	King Air C90B	LJ-1395	Aero Federal SA. Don Torcuato.	LV-PHZ
☐ LV-WNC	75	SA-226AT Merlin 4A	AT-036	Hawk Air SA. Don Torcuato.	N642TS
☐ LV-WOR	96	King Air B200	BB-1521	Heli-Air SA. Don Torcuato.	N3241N
☐ LV-WOS	80	King Air 200	BB-639	Promas SA. La Rioja.	N550E
☐ LV-WPB	95	King Air C90B	LJ-1416	Government Province of Chubut, Rawson, Chubut.	N3254E
☐ LV-WPM	80	King Air/Catpass 250	BB-729	Government Province of La Pampa, Santa Rosa.	N743R
☐ LV-WRM	68	King Air B90	LJ-333	Alas del Sur SA. Neuquen.	OB-1495
☐ LV-WXG	81	PA-42 Cheyenne III	8001044	Sancor SA. Sunchales Oeste, Santa Fe.	ZP-TYZ
☐ LV-WYC	97	King Air B200	BB-1566	Government Province of Salta.	N1106J
☐ LV-WZR	73	King Air E90	LW-70	VIP Air SA. Buenos Aires.	N5911P
☐ LV-YBP	97	King Air C90B	LJ-1489	Olmedo Agropecuaria Rosario de la Frontera,	N1069F
☐ LV-YCS	97	King Air B200	BB-1588	Per Trans SA. Buenos Aires.	N3247Q
☐ LV-YLC	98	King Air 350	FL-190	Aero Baires SACI. Buenos Aires.	N2290V
☐ LV-YTB	98	King Air B200	BB-1616	Petrel Aereos Servicios SRL. Buenos Aires.	N2294B
☐ LV-ZPY	81	King Air F90	LA-89	Bravo Foxtrot SRL. Buenos Aires.	N77PA
☐ LV-ZRG	99	King Air B200	BB-1652	Gobierno Provincia del Chaco, Chaco.	N3152K
☐ LV-ZSX	95	Pilatus PC-12	133	Horizon Americas Inc. San Fernando.	N133CZ
☐ LV-ZTE		King Air B200	...	noted 5/01.	
☐ LV-ZTO	67	King Air A90	LJ-292	Flight Express, Buenos Aires.	N100JF
☐ LV-ZTV	99	King Air B200	BB-1703		N3203Z
☐ LV-ZXX	00	King Air 350	FL-310	Gobierno Provincia de Santa Cruz, Santa Cruz.	N5010H
☐ LV-ZXZ	70	King Air B90	LJ-489	La Delicia Felipe Fort, Buenos Aires.	N90RZ
☐ LV-ZYB	99	King Air B200	BB-1690		N600DF

Military

Reg	Yr	Type	c/n	Owner/Operator	Prev Regn
☐ 4-F-43/0743	79	King Air 200	BB-460	FA1-EAN4/EAR4, Argentine Naval Base, Punta Indio.	4-G-43/07
☐ 4-G-41/0697	75	King Air 200	BB-54	FA1/EAN4/EA4R, Argentine Naval Base, Punta Indio.	5-T-31/06
☐ 4-G-42/0698	75	King Air 200	BB-71	FA1/EAN4-EA4R, Argentine Naval Base, Punta Indio.	5-T-32/06
☐ 4-G-45/0745	79	King Air 200	BB-488	FA1-EAN4/EAR4, Argentine Naval Base, Punta Indio.	
☐ 4-G-47/0747	79	King Air 200	BB-546	FA1-EAN4/EAR4, Argentine Naval Base, Punta Indio.	
☐ 4-G-48/0748	79	King Air 200	BB-549	FA1-EAN4/EAR4, Argentine Naval Base, Punta Indio.	
☐ AE-176	77	SA-226T Merlin 3A	T-275	Argentine Army,	N5393M
☐ AE-178	77	SA-226T Merlin 3A	T-280	Argentine Army,	N5397M
☐ AE-179	77	SA-226T Merlin 3A	T-281	Argentine Army,	N5399M
☐ AE-180	79	SA-226AT Merlin 4A	AT-071E	Argentine Army. (was TC-286).	N5656M
☐ AE-181	77	SA-226AT Merlin 4A	AT-063	Argentine Army,	TS-01
☐ AE-182	78	SA-226AT Merlin 4A	AT-064	Argentine Army,	TS-02
☐ GN-810	00	Pilatus PC-12/45	294	Gendarmerie Nacional, Campo de Mayo.	HB-FQI
☐ LV-RTC	79	King Air 200	BB-471	Argentine Navy, Buenos Aires.	4-G-44/0

Reg	*Yr*	*Type*	*c/n*	*Owner/Operator*	*Prev Regn*

LX = LUXEMBOURG

Civil

Reg	Yr Type	c/n	Owner/Operator	Prev Regn
☐ LX-ACR	81 PA-31T Cheyenne 1	8104067	Leander Reichle Stassenbau GmbH. Gerolstein, Germany.	D-IACR
☐ LX-ALX	82 King Air B200	BB-951	JDP LUX SA/Wings Luxembourg, Paris-Le Bourget, France.	N37HR
☐ LX-APB	79 King Air C90	LJ-867	Hawker Pacific Asia Pte Ltd. Seletar.	3A-MKB
☐ LX-FUN	01 PA-46-500TP Meridian	4697050	N Rollinger/Helios Service SARL. Saumur.	N123SX
☐ LX-JDP	77 King Air/Catpass 250	BB-303	JDP Lux SA/JDP & Financiere de Rosario, Paris, France.	F-GHCS
☐ LX-JFA	92 TBM 700	63	Jetfly Aviation SA. Luxembourg.	F-GLJS
☐ LX-JFD	01 TBM 700B	199	Jetfly Aviation SA. Luxembourg.	F-OIKC
☐ LX-JFE	01 TBM 700B	208	Jetfly Aviation SA. Luxembourg.	F-OIKE
☐ LX-JFF	01 TBM 700B	212	Jetfly Aviation SA. Luxembourg.	F-OIKF
☐ LX-JFH	03 Pilatus PC-12/45	522	Jetfly Aviation SA. Luxembourg.	HB-...
☐ LX-JFI	04 Pilatus PC-12/45	574	Jetfly Aviation SA. Luxembourg.	HB-...
☐ LX-LAB	03 Pilatus PC-12/45	531	Dublet et Cie.	(LX-DOG)
☐ LX-LLM	91 King Air C90A	LJ-1261	Adaya SA. Brussels, Belgium.	F-GJSD
☐ LX-LTX	78 King Air E90	LW-297	Sky-Service BV. Wevelgem, Belgium.	SE-IKD
☐ LX-NOP	76 SA-226T Merlin 3A	T-259	CAE Aviation,	CF-01
☐ LX-NRJ	76 SA-226T Merlin 3A	T-265	CAE Aviation,	CF-05
☐ LX-PBL	98 King Air C90B	LJ-1539	Locadis SA. Orleans, France.	D-IGAH
☐ LX-PIX	76 SA-226T Merlin 3A	T-267	Aerodata International Surveys BV. Antwerp, Belgium.	CF-06
☐ LX-RAD	70 King Air A90	LM-126	Cicade SA. Gosselies, Belgium.	N7171A
☐ LX-RSO	76 SA-226T Merlin 3A	T-260	CAE Aviation,	CF-02
☐ LX-RST	78 PA-31T Cheyenne II	7820027	Luxembourg Air Rescue as. Luxembourg.	F-GGPJ
☐ LX-SEA	86 King Air 300	FA-94	Aeroservice Amtec Corp/Fly Air SA. Annemasse, France.	F-GVPE

LZ = BULGARIA

Civil

Reg	Yr Type	c/n	Owner/Operator	Prev Regn
☐ LZ-YUK	75 King Air 200	BB-82	Naftex Bulgarian Aviation Co. Varna.	LZ-FEO

Military

Reg	Yr Type	c/n	Owner/Operator	Prev Regn
☐ 020	03 Pilatus PC-12M	518	Bulgarian Air Force, 16 Transport AB, Sofia-Vrazhdebna.	HB-FPH

N = USA

Civil

Reg	Yr Type	c/n	Owner/Operator	Prev Regn
☐ N1BK	85 King Air 300	FA-76	Paul Covey, San Antonio, Tx.	N404SD
☐ N1BM	81 Conquest 1	425-0042	Acme Aviation Inc. Idabell, Ok.	N67735
☐ N1DK	76 King Air C90	LJ-676	Blac Bear Reserve Equipment Co. Cary, NC.	N605DK
☐ N1GF	82 King Air C90-1	LJ-1031	Sawtooth Inc. Dothan, Al.	N397CA
☐ N1HX	78 King Air 200	BB-361	Danni's Aviation LLC. Memphis, Tn.	N334RR
☐ N1JG	78 Rockwell 690B	11510	Gay Company Inc. Austin, Tx.	N1NG
☐ N1JW	95 Pilatus PC-12	116	Pilatus Partners LLC. Tuscaloosa, Al.	N491PC
☐ N1KA	81 King Air B200	BB-899	CMH Homes Inc/Clayton Homes, Maryville, Tn.	N18544
☐ N1KG	75 Rockwell 690A	11235	Keith Graham Jr. Austin, Tx.	N46BA
☐ N1LF	01 King Air B200	BB-1778	Sizewise Rentals Inc. Ellis, Ks.	N4368X
☐ N1MA	79 King Air F90	LA-3	Alan & Diane Gaudenti, Rancho Palos Verde, Ca.	(N87AG)
☐ N1MN	84 SA-227TT Merlin 3C	TT-486A	Devcon Construction Inc/Ceka Aviation, San Jose, Ca.	N86SH
☐ N1MT	79 King Air C90	LJ-824	Delta State University, Cleveland, Ms.	N724TD
☐ N1MW	88 King Air 300	FA-151	Michael Waltrip Inc. Sherrill's Ford, NC.	C-FMHD
☐ N1NP	91 King Air C90A	LJ-1289	Nebraska Public Power District, Columbus, Ne.	N563AC
☐ N1PD	94 King Air 350	FL-121	JLJ Equipment Leasing Corp. Pottersville, NJ.	N351EB
☐ N1PN	94 King Air B100	BE-32	Clark Airways LLC/John W Clark Oil Co. Dover, De.	N712MA
☐ N1RQ	01 PA-46-500TP Meridian	4697112	Quast Aviation LLC. Maple Plain, Mn.	N53415
☐ N1SC*	90 King Air 350	FL-9	South Carolina Department of Commerce, Columbia, SC.	N2SC
☐ N1SP	77 King Air C-12C	BC-42	Delaware State Police, Dover, De.	N6SP
☐ N1TC	95 Pilatus PC-12	130	Marcare Air LLC. San Luis Obispo, Ca.	HB-FQU
☐ N1TR	78 King Air A100	B-238	Trinity River Authority, Arlington, Tx.	N9100S
☐ N1TX	81 King Air 200	BB-800	State of Texas, Austin, Tx.	N200GA
☐ N1UC	75 King Air E90	LW-140	Flight Operations LLC. Naples, Fl.	N8069S
☐ N1UV	71 King Air C90	LJ-511	Aviation Advisors International Inc. Sarasota, Fl.	N45BA
☐ N1VQ	77 Rockwell 690B	11369	First Star Inc. Hollister, Ca.	N369GM
☐ N1WJ	65 King Air 90	LJ-60	RidgeAire Inc. Jacksonville, Tx.	N763K
☐ N1WV	98 King Air 350	FL-223	West Virginia Office of Travel Management, Charleston, WV.	N3033U
☐ N1YC	69 SA-26AT Merlin 2B	T26-131	Van Lewis Inc. Henderson, Tx.	N4251R
☐ N1YS	79 King Air 200	BB-430	Raytheon Aviation LLC. Wilmington, De.	N1BS
☐ N1Z	00 King Air B200	BB-1759	Niznick Enterprises Inc. Las Vegas, Nv.	N541AS
☐ N2DB	72 Rockwell 690	11028	Keith Brown, Denver, Co.	N9228N

Reg	Yr Type	c/n	Owner/Operator	Prev Regn

Reg	Yr	Type	c/n	Owner/Operator	Prev Regn
☐ N2DS	78	PA-31T Cheyenne II	7820081	Alpine Aviation Inc. White Lake, Mi.	N34CA
☐ N2FJ	76	PA-31T Cheyenne II	7620050	JP2 LLC. Willoughby, Oh.	(N39RP)
☐ N2GL	82	SA-227TT Merlin 3C	TT-426A	Finair LLC. Ponte Vedra Beach, Fl.	N4491E
☐ N2GZ	67	Mitsubishi MU-2B	025	Tarrant County Junior College, Fort Worth, Tx.	N2GT
☐ N2JB	00	Pilatus PC-12/45	342	Breco International,	(ZS-SRJ)
☐ N2MP	76	King Air C-12C	BC-32	State Highway Patrol, Jefferson City, Mo.	76-22556
☐ N2NA	62	Gulfstream 1	96	NASA, OSF Johnson Space Centre, Houston, Tx.	N1NA
☐ N2NC	83	Conquest II	441-0307	North Carolina Dept of Transportation, Raleigh, NC.	N8617K
☐ N2PX	86	King Air B200	BB-1260	Publix Super Markets Inc. Lakeland, Fl.	
☐ N2PY	77	King Air 200	BB-200	Ameris Health Systems LLC. Nashville, Tn.	N2PX
☐ N2RA	77	Mitsubishi MU-2P	366SA	Julia Cummings, Lafayette, Ca.	N66UP
☐ N2SM	97	King Air 350	FL-185	Oso Rio LLC. Houston, Tx.	N18269
☐ N2TS	85	Beech 1900C	UB-39	SABCO Racing Inc. Mooresville, NC.	N404SS
☐ N2TX	81	King Air B100	BE-103	Robert Schumacher/Texland Aviation Co. Abilene, Tx.	N3699T
☐ N2U	77	King Air 200	BB-263	Helicopters Inc. Cahokia, Il.	N48Q
☐ N2UV	69	King Air B90	LJ-480	Charles Greene, Fort Lauderdale, Fl.	N92BA
☐ N2UW	77	King Air 200T	BT-3	University of Wyoming, Laramie, Wy. (was BB-270).	
☐ N2UZ*	86	PA-42 Cheyenne 400LS	5527034	Tango Lima Aviation LLC. Terryville, Ct.	JA8878
☐ N2VA	83	Gulfstream 1000	96062	Department of Aviation, Richmond, Va.	N120GA
☐ N2WF	02	TBM 700B	220	Leasing Systems LLC. Sewalls Point, Fl.	VH-TBO
☐ N2YF	96	Pilatus PC-12	140	Tactair Fluid Controls Inc. Liverpool, NY.	N129DH
☐ N3AH	87	King Air 300	FA-130	American Aviation Charters LLC. Lafayette, La.	N9UP
☐ N3AT	81	King Air C90	LJ-933	Appalachian Tire Products Inc. Charleston, WV.	N3709S
☐ N3AW	77	Conquest II	441-0036	Arrowhead Co. Round Mountain, Tx.	N36968
☐ N3CG	67	680V Turbo Commander	1680-62	KingAir Aircraft Services LLC. Mooresville, NC.	N3CC
☐ N3CR	81	King Air 200	BB-850	Richard Childress Racing Enterprises Inc. Welcome, NC.	N2UH
☐ N3DE	78	King Air 200	BB-332	Champion Air LLC. Mooresville, NC.	N23807
☐ N3DF	65	King Air 90	LJ-36	Donald Bush, Warner Robins, Ga.	(N312DS)
☐ N3GC	73	King Air C90	LJ-576	AlliedSignal Avionics Inc. Everett, Wa.	
☐ N3GT	73	Mitsubishi MU-2K	277	Donald & Gail Taylor Trust, Albuquerque, NM.	N390K
☐ N3KF	71	King Air C90	LJ-530	Ohio Medical Transportation Inc. Columbus, Oh.	N404VW
☐ N3LS	67	King Air E90	LW-245	DZM Inc. Houston, Tx.	N18DV
☐ N3NC	82	Conquest II	441-0238	North Carolina Dept of Transportation, Raleigh, NC.	N95TD
☐ N3PX	84	King Air B200	BB-1173	Comair Leasing LLC. Easley, SC.	N2842B
☐ N3RK	81	Cheyenne II-XL	8166022	Superior Distributing Co. Fostoria, Oh.	N81502
☐ N3TJ	78	Rockwell 690B	11471	Blood Vessel Inc. Dover, De.	(N622HC)
☐ N3TK	80	Conquest II	441-0158	Centaur Corp. Irvine, Ca.	N36EF
☐ N3UN	78	Mitsubishi MU-2N	720SA	Turbine Aircraft Marketing Inc. San Angelo, Tx.	VH-MIT
☐ N3WM	78	Conquest II	441-0068	MVY Air II Inc. Morristown, NJ.	N88827
☐ N3WU	76	Rockwell 690A	11336	Aero Air LLC. Hillsboro, Or.	N16GL
☐ N3ZC	85	King Air B200	BB-1207	Zachary Construction Corp. San Antonio, Tx.	(N321SF)
☐ N4AT	77	King Air 200	BB-281	Speedy LLC. Monterey, Ca.	N315JW
☐ N4FB	67	680V Turbo Commander	1688-68	Fernando Rodrigo, Miami, Fl.	N4F
☐ N4KU	89	King Air B200	BB-1323	N4KU LLC/First Management Inc. New Country, Ks.	(N769WT)
☐ N4MD	99	TBM 700B	153	Airborne Inc. Wilmington, De.	(N40DN)
☐ N4MR	76	King Air E90	LW-184	Roberts Aviation LLC. Bossier City, La.	N899GP
☐ N4NF	88	King Air 300LW	FA-165	Nash Finch Co. Rapid City, SD.	N886CA
☐ N4NU	01	King Air B200	BB-1782	University of Nebraska Foundation, Lincoln, Ne.	N4482Z
☐ N4PT	81	King Air B200	BB-879	Pope & Talbot Inc. Portland, Or.	
☐ N4PZ	75	Rockwell 690A	11269	Phillip Zeeck Inc. Odessa, Tx.	N690DM
☐ N4QL	81	King Air B200	BB-942	Quarry Lane LLC. Moorpark, Ca.	N707NV
☐ N4RX	79	PA-31T Cheyenne 1	7904012	IMFESA/Ernesto S Botello, Santo Domingo, Dominican Republic.	(N204MB)
☐ N4RY	65	King Air 90	LJ-8	Additive Services Inc. Hudson, NH.	(N16CG)
☐ N4TJ	75	King Air 200	BB-40	Jaco Oil Co. Bakersfield, SC.	N35TT
☐ N4TS	03	Pilatus PC-12/45	509	First Virtual Air LLC. Wolf Creek, Mt.	N509PB
☐ N4WE	87	PA-42 Cheyenne 400LS	5527041	All Planes Inc. Wilmington, De.	N9518N
☐ N4YF	01	King Air C90B	LJ-1658	Jomeg Aviation LLC. New Castle, Pa.	
☐ N4YS	92	King Air 350	FL-82	W R Fry/CC2B Trust, Palo Alto, Ca.	N8182C
☐ N5AH*	80	King Air F90	LA-53	Empire Air LLC. Torrance, Ca.	N514LM
☐ N5BR	93	TBM 700	89	Lloyd Rasner, Corona del Mar, Ca.	D-FEIN
☐ N5CE	83	Conquest 1	425-0135	Avion Capital Corp. Anchorage, Ak.	N6884D
☐ N5D	78	PA-31T Cheyenne II	7820080	William Packer, Orchard, Mi.	N6097A
☐ N5DM	00	Pilatus PC-12/45	355	News Flight Inc. NYC.	HB-FSG
☐ N5HG	82	Conquest II	441-0247	HRL Ventures LLC. Chicago Ridge, Il.	N6857T
☐ N5HT	91	TBM 700	9	Quik-Cook Inc. Rochester, NY.	N969RF
Reg	*Yr*	*Type*	*c/n*	*Owner/Operator*	*Prev Regn*

Reg	Yr	Type	c/n	Owner/Operator	Prev Regn
N5LC	80	MU-2 Solitaire	433SA	Manitoba Leasing Corp. Lancaster, NY.	N209MA
N5LE	77	King Air 200	BB-195	B-Air LLC. Nashville, Tn.	YV-92CP
N5LJ	75	Mitsubishi MU-2P	321SA	Lane's Valley Forge Aviation Inc. Collegeville, Pa.	N513DQ
N5MK	79	King Air 200	BB-537	LHI Air Corp. West Palm Beach, Fl.	N700BX
N5NW	82	King Air F90	LA-199	Northwest Composites, Marysville, Wa.	N211NA
N5PA	81	PA-42 Cheyenne III	8001051	Saperston Asset Management, Buffalo, NY.	N810L
N5PP	02	PA-46-500TP Meridian	4697145	Air Alliant LLC. Palo Alto, Ca.	
N5PU	84	Conquest 1	425-0198	Bruce Lampert PC. Broomfield, Co.	N5PP
N5PX	79	King Air 200	BB-554	N5 Papa Xray LLC. Wilmington, De.	N204BR
N5RB	81	PA-31T Cheyenne 1	8104042	Equity Management Inc. Columbus, Oh.	N12WZ
N5RE	68	680W Turbo Commander	1818-32	Pennsylvania College of Technology, Williamsport, Pa.	N3RA
N5ST	77	King Air 200	BB-289	Mayo Aviation Inc. Englewood, Co.	N7MB
N5SY	81	PA-42 Cheyenne III	8001069	Dialysis Clinic Inc. Nashville, Tn.	N5SS
N5TA	77	King Air C90	LJ-724	MacDonald Enterprises Inc. Spencerville, Oh.	N5TW
N5TW	93	King Air B200	BB-1471	Backe Aviation Inc. Bonita Springs, Fl.	
N5UN	80	King Air 200	BB-697	Western Skies Aviation LLC. Arnold, Ca.	N5ON
N5WG	67	King Air A90	LJ-289	G M B Aviation Inc. Fort Worth, Tx.	N35P
N5WN*	94	Pilatus PC-12	104	Universal Helair Inc. Orlando, Fl.	N813PC
N5XM	94	King Air 350	FL-115	C & C Aviation LLC. Worcester, Ma.	N35DT
N5Y	67	King Air A90	LJ-272	Carrier Enterprises Corp. Wilmington, De.	
N6BZ	82	Gulfstream 900	15008	Red Sea Nevada Inc. Dallas, Tx.	ZS-KZT
N6DM	03	PA-46-500TP Meridian	4697154	Strategic Organizational Management Ltd. Denver, Co.	N3055C
N6E	70	681 Turbo Commander	6002	Cardozo Technologies Inc. Manor, Tx.	N9052N
N6HU	78	King Air 200	BB-319	Harding University Inc. Searcy, Ar.	N300WJ
N6KE	80	MU-2 Marquise	766SA	William Denniston Jr. Lake Forest, Il.	(N6KU)
N6KF	75	Mitsubishi MU-2L	659	Flight Line Inc. Denver, Co.	N5JE
N6KZ	67	King Air A90	LJ-238	Gregg Aviation Inc. Wilmington, De.	N190RF
N6PX	77	King Air 200	BB-205	Royal Air Charters Inc. Shreveport, La.	N6PW
N6UD	82	King Air B200	BB-1055	Braun Racing LLC. Winamac, In.	N6LD
N6VJ	81	King Air F90	LA-88	Hansen Group A/S. Staverton, UK.	F-GVJV
N6VP	77	Conquest II	441-0019	Verama Inc. Wilmington, De.	(N55CC)
N6WU	99	King Air B200	BB-1668	L J Associates Inc. Latrobe, Pa.	N3168F
N7BF	68	King Air B90	LJ-350	Rainbow International Airlines Inc. St Thomas, USVI.	(N579B)
N7DD	74	Mitsubishi MU-2K	297	Business Air Inc. Bennington, Vt.	N106GB
N7FL	78	PA-31T Cheyenne II	7820082	Liberty Charter Inc. Wilmington, De.	N6100A
N7HN	84	MU-2 Marquise	1563SA	Soft Computer Consultants Inc. Palm Harbor, Fl.	(D-IOMX)
N7KS	79	Rockwell 690B	11521	California Architectural Lighting, Portland, Or.	N81746
N7NA	82	King Air/Catpass 250	BB-997	NASA HQ/OSSA, Washington, DC.	
N7NW	80	Conquest II	441-0186	Aztlan Corp. Ashland, Or.	N2724S
N7PA	92	King Air B200	BB-1444	Warren Spieker Jr. Soledad, Ca.	N663CS
N7RC	85	King Air 300	FA-58	Ring Container Technologies, Olive Branch, Ms.	N555WF
N7SL	59	Gulfstream 1	11	Sanders Lead Co. Troy, Al.	N100EL
N7TD	78	King Air E90	LW-276	Twin Disc Inc. Racine, Wi.	N125L
N7TW	69	King Air B90	LJ-478	Rush Aviation Inc. Oxford, Al.	N40WS
N7VA	80	King Air 200	BB-670	Department of Aviation, Richmond, Va.	N1VA
N7VR	78	PA-31T Cheyenne 1	7804010	Woftam Inc. Lock Haven, Pa.	N93TW
N7WF	82	Conquest 1	425-0119	Foxtrot Inc. Wichita Falls, Tx.	N17RC
N7WU	75	King Air E90	LW-142	State of Washington, Olympia, Wa.	N7WS
N7YR	03	Pilatus PC-12/45	532	Shikari Capital LLC. Portland, Or.	N532WA
N7ZT	01	Pilatus PC-12/45	385	Zia Air LLC. San Luis Obispo, Ca.	HB-FQD
N8AM	77	King Air 200	BB-274	Consolidated Aviation LLC. Wilmington, De.	N1MM
N8BG	77	King Air 200	BB-267	Colonel Science LLC. Santa Ynez, Ca.	N267TT
N8CF	80	PA-31T Cheyenne II	8020062	Copto Inc. Jacksonville, Fl.	N5452J
N8E	62	Gulfstream 1	94	N8E LLC. Newton, Ga.	N794G
N8EF	80	King Air 200	BB-721	Reigan Pegasus LLC. Green Mountain Falls, Co.	N610HG
N8EG	92	TBM 700	34	Doug Carlson, Aspen, Co.	
N8FR	81	Conquest 1	425-0095	Frank Rhodes Jr. Newport Beach, Ca.	N68481
N8GT	85	King Air C90A	LJ-1103	Business Aircraft Leasing Inc. Nashville, Tn.	N55LC
N8KT	69	SA-26AT Merlin 2B	T26-158E	Davidson Air Inc. Little Rock, Ar.	N256WC
N8MG	78	King Air C90	LJ-747	W W Reynolds & R A Marks LLC. Mobile, Al.	N529JH
N8NA	82	King Air B200	BB-950	NASA/OSSA, Wallops Island, Va.	
N8NX	81	King Air 200	BB-774	AFAB LLC. Naples, Fl.	N3738B
N8PC	71	Mitsubishi MU-2F	193	A Lamas, Buenos Aires, Argentina.	N1210W
N8RW	82	MU-2 Marquise	1548SA	Titan Aviation LC. West Palm Beach, Fl.	N47RW
N8RY	81	PA-42 Cheyenne III	8001036	Y T Timber Inc. Boise, Id.	N3JQ
Reg	Yr	Type	c/n	Owner/Operator	Prev Regn

Reg	Yr	Type	c/n	Owner/Operator	Prev Regn
⌁ N8SV	79	King Air 200	BB-506	King Air IV Inc. Bellevue, Wa.	N945BV
⌁ N8UM	01	PA-46-500TP Meridian	4697067	Sabe Aviation Inc. Naples, Fl.	N44SK
⌁ N8VL	83	Gulfstream 840	11732	Brays Air LLC. Sheldon, SC.	N29DS
⌁ N9DA	82	King Air C90	LJ-944	Tampa Aircraft Holding Inc. Tampa, Fl.	N944TT
⌁ N9DC	01	King Air C90B	LJ-1668	Silver Wings LLC. Central Point, Or.	N4468F
⌁ N9EE	03	TBM 700C	286	Air Alliant LLC. Palo Alto, Ca.	N386MA
⌁ N9HW	69	King Air B90	LJ-459	Michael Mullins, Germantown, Tn.	N2JR
⌁ N9KG	77	Rockwell 690B	11426	STV Ltd. Hillsboro, Or.	(N690DM)
⌁ N9LE	01	TBM 700B	224	Lou Air Associates Inc. St Petersburg, Fl.	N700XL
⌁ N9NB	78	Mitsubishi MU-2N	728SA	SDS Project LLC. Austin, Tx.	N9NC
⌁ N9VC	78	King Air C90	LJ-763	Dakota King Air LLC/Executive Air Taxi Corp. Bismark, ND.	N78JD
⌁ N9WR	81	King Air B200	BB-913	Automotive Advantage Inc. Frederick, Md.	(N501E)
⌁ N10AG	80	King Air B100	BE-100	Auto Glass Specialist Inc. Madison, Wi.	N3688F
⌁ N10AY	65	King Air 90	LJ-88	A C McPhie, Bend, Or. (status ?).	(N90233)
⌁ N10BQ	74	PA-31T Cheyenne II	7400005	West Tenessee Aviation Inc. Union City, Tn.	(N80BC)
⌁ N10BY	80	King Air 200	BB-642	Hill Top Aircraft Inc. Tyler, Tx.	N30MK
⌁ N10CS	80	PA-31T Cheyenne 1	8004007	Trimair Inc. Dothan, Al.	N118BW
⌁ N10CW	03	King Air B200	BB-1846	South Holland Trust & Savings Bank, South Holland, Il.	
⌁ N10EC	85	King Air B200	BB-1211	State of Tennessee, Nashville, Tn.	N7220C
⌁ N10FB	82	Conquest 1	425-0117	Western Farm Bureau Service Co. Laramie, Wy.	N123SC
⌁ N10HT	80	MU-2 Marquise	778SA	EPPS Air Service Inc. Atlanta, Ga.	N264MA
⌁ N10JE	65	King Air 90	LJ-10	APA Enterprises Inc. Poughskeepsie, NY.	N10J
⌁ N10K	90	King Air 350	FL-4	Department of Central Services, Oklahoma City, Ok.	N97DL
⌁ N10MD	78	King Air C90	LJ-750	N10MD LLC. Huntsville, Al.	N214D
⌁ N10MR	77	Mitsubishi MU-2P	351SA	Agri-Systems, Hardin, Mt.	N10FR
⌁ N10PF	97	Pilatus PC-12	165	Powell Solidaire Inc. Sacramento, Ca.	N65KW
⌁ N10RM	81	Conquest 1	425-0074	Golden Eagle Aviation LLC. Orlando, Fl.	N146GA
⌁ N10TM	69	King Air B90	LJ-476	Air Amteck LLC. Lexington, Ky.	N41AA
⌁ N10TQ	90	2000 Starship	NC-8	Raytheon Aircraft Co. Wichita, Ks.	N10TX
⌁ N10TX	89	King Air 350	FL-1	Bryan Hardeman, Albuquerque, NM.	N552TR
⌁ N10UN	97	King Air 350	FL-158	Universal Avionics Systems Corp. Tucson, Az.	N1095Q
⌁ N10UT	76	Mitsubishi MU-2M	346	NFM Inc. Henderson, Nv.	(N45PD)
⌁ N10VU	81	MU-2 Solitaire	438SA	Chester Upham Jr. Mineral Wells, Tx.	N99LC
⌁ N10WG	79	King Air E90	LW-310	Wings to Go Leasing Co. Doylestown, Pa.	LV-MRN
⌁ N10XJ	74	King Air E90	LW-117	Reynolds Texas Properties LC. Dallas, Tx.	N76PW
⌁ N10YP	67	King Air A90	LJ-265	Gary Yost, Sherman, Tx.	(N126AT)
⌁ N11	73	King Air C-12C	BD-1	FAA, Oklahoma City, Ok.	73-1205
⌁ N11AB	78	King Air 200	BB-305	KS Air Charter/Ken Small Construction Inc. Bakersfield, Ca.	N30XY
⌁ N11CT	68	680W Turbo Commander	1773-11	Bob Jones University Inc. Greenville, SC.	N4852E
⌁ N11DT	72	King Air E90	LW-11	Marjet Inc. Honolulu, Hi.	N241B
⌁ N11FL	67	King Air A90	LJ-301	Core Investments Inc. Fort Lauderdale, Fl. (status ?).	N800Q
⌁ N11FT	81	King Air C90	LJ-958	SKS Management Inc. Cocoa, Fl.	N505MT
⌁ N11GS	88	King Air 300	FA-147	GCS Enterprises Inc. Sulphur Springs, Tx.	N860CC
⌁ N11HM	66	680V Turbo Commander	1620-51	R W Hawkins, Columbia, Il.	N680MH
⌁ N11HY	77	Rockwell 690B	11403	Harvey & Linda Peel, Tijeras, NM.	N29973
⌁ N11JJ	69	King Air 100	B-2	Vintage Props & Jets Inc. New Smyrna Beach, Fl.	N3RC
⌁ N11SJ	74	Mitsubishi MU-2K	285	R & J AG Manufacturing Inc. Ashland, Oh.	N111JE
⌁ N11SN	82	King Air C90-1	LJ-1036	Paradise View Motors Inc. Santa Barbara, Ca.	(N59WP)
⌁ N11TE	98	King Air 350	FL-211	Tractor & Equipment Co. Birmingham, Al.	N715CG
⌁ N11TN	68	King Air B90	LJ-419	M & C Aviation Inc. Bronx, NY.	N11TE
⌁ N11UN	63	Gulfstream 1	102	Sky Bus Inc. Fort Lauderdale, Fl.	C6-UNO
⌁ N12	73	King Air C-12C	BD-8	FAA, Oklahoma City, Ok.	73-1212
⌁ N12AX	78	King Air E90	LW-293	Corporate Aircraft Leasing LLC. Winston-Salem, NC.	N12AU
⌁ N12CF	79	King Air 200	BB-534	N12CF LLC/Bremer Family Trust, Corona, Ca.	
⌁ N12DE	78	Rockwell 690B	11501	Dealers Electrical Supply Co. Waco, Tx.	N25CL
⌁ N12DT	78	Conquest II	441-0040	Write Stuff Aviation Inc. Fort Lauderdale, Fl.	(N441RA)
⌁ N12DZ	01	Pilatus PC-12/45	390	Zipp Express Inc. Fort Myers, Fl.	N46CE
⌁ N12GJ	72	King Air E90	LW-12	Building Ideas Inc. Palo Alto, Ca.	RP-C289
⌁ N12GR	79	PA-31T Cheyenne II	7920058	RG International Aircraft Corp. Medley, Fl.	N179SW
⌁ N12JD	98	Pilatus PC-12/45	228	Mariposa Group LLC. Salina, Ks.	HB-FQZ
⌁ N12LA	73	King Air E90	LW-49	Jay Bird Air LLC. Dublin, Oh.	N777AJ
⌁ N12MA	04	TBM 700C	318	SOCATA Aircraft, Pembroke Pines, Fl.	
⌁ N12MF	81	SA-226T Merlin 3B	T-417	5-T Aviation LLC. Eunice, La.	N89RP
⌁ N12MU	71	681B Turbo Commander	6051	Miami Univesrity, Oxford, Oh.	N200M
⌁ N12NG	80	King Air 200	BB-581	Northrop Grumman Aviation Inc. Melbourne, Fl.	N14NA

| Reg | Yr | Type | c/n | Owner/Operator | Prev Regn |

Reg	Yr Type	c/n	Owner/Operator	Prev Regn
N12NL	81 Conquest 1	425-0069	Dapcon Consulting Inc. Chicago, Il.	N634M
N12RA	69 Mitsubishi MU-2F	177	BH Jr Motorsports Inc. White House, Tn.	N177SA
N12RW	61 Gulfstream 1	82	Air Cess/CCET Aviation Enterprise, Ras Al Khaimah, UAE.	SE-LFV
N12SJ	76 Mitsubishi MU-2M	333	Air 1st Aviation Companies Inc. Aiken, SC.	N521MA
N12TW	77 PA-31T Cheyenne II	7720017	196 East LLC. Exeter, NH.	N19AC
N12WC	69 SA-26AT Merlin 2B	T26-118	RKC Properties LLC. Tampa, Fl.	N1224S
N13GZ	99 King Air C90B	LJ-1590	Eagle Air Med Corp. Blanding, Ut.	PT-WXH
N13LY	00 King Air B200	BB-1718	A Better Road Aviation LLC. Jacksonville, Fl.	N3018C
N13NW	79 Conquest II	441-0090	North West Group Inc. Denver, Co.	N4061K
N13YS	77 Mitsubishi MU-2L	694	TRE Aviation Corp. Globe, Az.	N800PC
N14BM	81 Conquest 1	425-0076	Albert Sickinger, Bloomfield Hills, Mi.	N67735
N14C	73 King Air E90	LW-62	Dynamic Aviation Group Inc. Bridgewater, Va.	N16NM
N14CF	75 King Air A100	B-209	Beech Transportation Inc. Eden Prairie, Mn.	N100AN
N14CP	73 King Air C90	LJ-585	Dynamic Aviation Group Inc. Bridgewater, Va.	
N14EA	78 PA-31T Cheyenne II	7820006	Fitch Aviation Inc. Reno, Nv.	F-GFPV
N14FJ	79 Conquest II	441-0118	Land Safely LLC. Monmouth Beach, NJ.	5N-DOV
N14GV	01 PA-46-500TP Meridian	4697092	Number One for Great Veneers LLC. Wilmington, De.	
N14HG	82 King Air B200	BB-1071	Steady Compass LLC. Minden, Nv.	N82BS
N14NG	87 King Air B200	BB-1276	Northrop Grumman Aviation Inc. Montgomery-San Diego, Ca.	N40TD
N14NM	73 King Air E90	LW-35	Corporate Aircraft Partners Inc. Cleveland, Oh.	N811JB
N14NW	80 Conquest II	441-0171	North West Group Inc. Denver, Co.	C-GKMA
N14PX	81 PA-31T Cheyenne 1	8104060	Family Extended Care of Winter Haven, Miami, Fl.	N74ML
N14RD	01 Pilatus PC-12/45	384	RDC Marine Inc. Houston, Tx.	HB-FQC
N14SB	77 King Air E90	LW-214	Clayton Motors Inc. Knoxville, Tn.	N17603
N14TF	81 King Air 200	BB-810	Jetstream Air LLC. Colfax, NC.	N711AE
N14TP	72 SA-226T Merlin 3	T-220	Interair Lease LLC. Fort Smith, Ar.	N905RK
N14V	68 King Air B90	LJ-411	Donald Warren, Clinton, Ar.	N807K
N14VL	81 MU-2 Marquise	1514SA	JPW Aviation LLC. Clarksdale, Ms.	YV-108CP
N14YS	74 Mitsubishi MU-2K	290	Barry Simpson Aircraft Sales Inc. Colorado Springs, Co.	N4186Y
N15	81 King Air F90	LA-138	FAA, Oklahoma City, Ok.	
N15CC	67 Mitsubishi MU-2B	023	AV Solutions Inc. Flint, Mi.	N555VK
N15CD	74 Rockwell 690A	11177	Philip Sellers Co. Montgomery, Al.	N16TB
N15CN	80 SA-226T Merlin 3B	T-339	St John & Deal Inc. Ponte Vedra Beach, Fl.	N15CC
N15CT	67 King Air A90	LJ-192	Charles Thomas, Loves Park, Il.	N792K
N15DB	82 Conquest II	441-0278	Sierra Pacific Industries Inc. Redding, Ca.	N98718
N15EK	95 Pilatus PC-12	120	Quest Diagnostics Inc. Reading, Pa.	N112AF
N15EW	03 King Air 350	FL-388	EWC Aviation Corp. McKinney, Tx.	N4488H
N15KA	79 King Air 200	BB-457	American Aviation Inc. Brooksville, Fl.	(N825AA)
N15KW	81 Cheyenne II-XL	8166014	Alfons Ribitsch, Torrance, Ca.	(N31KP)
N15PX	85 King Air 300	FA-82	D & S Industries of Louisiana LLC. New Orleans, La.	(N317BC)
N15SB	02 TBM 700	247	N15SB LLC. Chatham, NJ.	F-WWRN
N15SF	79 Rockwell 690B	11528	EMS Air Services of NY Inc. Canandaigua, NY.	N690SH
N15ST	83 Conquest 1	425-0140	Nicholas Street/The United Co. Blountville, Tn.	N5829J
N15TR	81 MU-2 Solitaire	446SA	Northwest Aviation LLC. Fargo, ND.	N81MW
N15WD	91 King Air 350	FL-57	Byram Properties/By-Car Inc. Austin, Tx.	(N114JB)
N15WN	73 King Air E90	LW-78	G L Wilson Building Co. Statesville, NC.	N4378W
N15WS	90 King Air 350	FL-33	Peconic Aviation LLC. Wst Palm Beach, Fl.	N882CA
N15YS	73 Mitsubishi MU-2J	598	Brown Air LLC. Cedar Falls, Ia.	C-FMBL
N16	80 King Air C90	LJ-893	FAA, Oklahoma City, Ok.	
N16GF	96 King Air B200	BB-1531	G F Air LLC. Charleston, SC.	N1081F
N16KM	81 King Air C90	LJ-961	Cox-Flanders Aircraft LLC. Evansville, In.	XA-ISL
N16KW	96 King Air C90B	LJ-1435	F C Stone Group Inc. Des Moines, Ia.	N1095M
N16LH	77 King Air E90	LW-217	Antlers Natural Gas Enterprises, Colorado Springs, Co.	
N16NG	78 DHC 6-300	596	Northrop Grumman Aviation Inc. Hawthorne, Ca.	N16NA
N16WG	85 King Air F90-1	LA-226	Rialto Riverside Corp. Corona, Ca.	N6690L
N17	80 King Air C90	LJ-896	FAA, Oklahoma City, Ok.	
N17CK	85 Reims/Cessna F406	F406-0001	Clint Aero Inc. St Thomas, USVI.	PH-ALO
N17HF	73 Rockwell 690A	11127	Meyer Co. Garfield Heights, Oh.	N199WP
N17HG	81 MU-2 Marquise	1510SA	Castlehill Aviation LLC. Ashburn, Va.	N417MA
N17HM	76 King Air 200	BB-94	King Aviation Inc. Hillsborough, Ca.	N28AH
N17JG	68 680W Turbo Commander	1802-24	Tulsa County Area VoTec School, Tulsa, Ok.	N102US
N17KK	93 King Air C90B	LJ-1318	Av Advantage LLC. Bloomfield Hills, Mi.	N131SA
N17LH	01 PA-46-500TP Meridian	4697007	Paul Sciarra, Montclair, NJ.	
N17NM	77 King Air E90	LW-237	Seven Bar Flying Service Inc. Albuquerque, NM.	N5NM
N17PA	92 P-180 Avanti	1017	Aurora Aviation Inc. Batavia, Il.	D-IJCL

Reg	Yr	Type	c/n	Owner/Operator	Prev Regn
N17SA	66	King Air A90	LJ-164	Flanagan Enterprises (Nevada) Inc. Carson City, Nv.	N8GF
N17SE	76	King Air E90	LW-169	Air Serv International Inc. Warrenton, Va.	N600KC
N17TU	75	PA-31T Cheyenne II	7520035	Midwest Flying Service Inc. Sheldon, Ia.	N66LD
N17VV	84	SA-227TT Merlin 300	TT-536	ABM Air LLC. Wilmington, De.	N72WC
N17WT	66	King Air 90	LJ-86	Jeffair LLC. Fayetteville, Ga.	N60RJ
N17ZD	82	Gulfstream 1000	96017	International Air Service Inc. Opa Locka, Fl. (status ?).	(N17QC)
N18	81	King Air F90	LA-145	FAA, Oklahoma City, Ok.	
N18AF	95	King Air B200	BB-1497	N220PB LLC. Mesa, Az.	N508BM
N18AH	72	King Air A100	B-118	Joe Dan Manis, Laurinburg, NC.	N100MX
N18BF	69	Mitsubishi MU-2F	173	AMCAP Leasing LLC. Houston, Tx.	N887Q
N18CJ	77	King Air 200	BB-260	Memphis Aircraft Sales Inc. Memphis, Tn.	N1SC
N18CM	84	King Air F90-1	LA-219	Trace Transportation/Trace Die Cast Inc. Bowling Green, Ky.	N8YK
N18KA	78	King Air 200	BB-360	Century Aviation of Colorado LLC. Telluride, Co.	N210PH
N18KK	71	681B Turbo Commander	6055	Karl Koster, Fremont, Ca.	N9127N
N18KW	81	PA-31T Cheyenne II	8120059	Shave-Aire LLC/Barrier Island Realty Inc. Kitty Hawk, NC.	N20WE
N18RN*	00	King Air 350	FL-300	Roberts Properties Inc. Atlanta, Ga.	N1CR
N18SR	00	TBM 700B	161	Modern Aero Inc. Eden Prairie, Mn.	I-AESR
N18XJ	97	King Air C90B	LJ-1500	Mick J Dubea, Beaumont, Tx.	(N200JG)
N18ZX	78	PA-31T Cheyenne II	7820014	Paoo Aviation Corp. Norfolk, Va.	C-GSBC
N19	80	King Air C90	LJ-909	FAA, Oklahoma City, Ok.	
N19CX	01	PA-46-500TP Meridian	4697077	Ken Pritchett, Bend, Or.	N797BG
N19DA	80	King Air B100	BE-87	Dominion Air Leasing Inc. Richmond, Va.	N980KA
N19GA	81	Mitsubishi MU-2P	454SA	Quest for Life Church, Banner Elk, NC.	I-FRTL
N19GD	93	King Air 350	FL-96	Gorman-Rupp Co. Mansfield, Oh.	N19GR
N19GR	04	King Air 350	FL-414	Gorman-Rupp Co. Mansfield, Oh.	N36814
N19GU	73	Mitsubishi MU-2J	574	Bush Field Aircraft Co. Augusta, Ga.	N243MA
N19LW	81	King Air C90	LJ-991	FAKA Air LLC. Washington, DC.	N504AB
N19NC	89	King Air 300	FA-183	Haydn Cutler, Wake Forest, NC.	N1549D
N19NG	87	Beech 1900C-1	UC-2	Northrop Grumman Aviation Inc. Hawthorne, Ca.	N19NA
N19RK	80	King Air F90	LA-12	Ring Container Technologies, Olive Branch, Ms.	N200E
N19SG	00	TBM 700B	194	Aircraft Guaranty Title LLC. Houston, Tx.	
N19UM	71	King Air C90	LJ-524	SKET Maschinen u Anlagenbau GmbH. Memmingen, Germany.	N19CM
N20	80	King Air C90	LJ-912	FAA, Oklahoma City, Ok.	
N20AE	81	King Air 200	BB-843	American Jet San Antonio, San Antonio, Tx.	D-IFES
N20BL	66	King Air A90	LJ-163	Business Aircraft Sales Corp. Chattanooga, Tn.	N2RR
N20BM	67	680V Turbo Commander	1698-75	Swanson Air LLC. Fort Wayne, In.	N420J
N20BP	76	Rockwell 690A	11341	Brass & Stainless Designs Inc. Dallas, Tx.	N81493
N20DH	87	King Air B200	BB-1263	Hughes-Sasser Ltd. Beeville, Tx.	N263SW
N20DL	80	PA-31T Cheyenne 1	8004045	Central Iowa Energy Co-operative, Cedar Rapids, Ia.	N26DV
N20EB	76	Rockwell 690A	11282	Texas Aerospace Services Inc. Abilene, Tx.	N429K
N20EF	69	SA-26AT Merlin 2B	T26-157	Air Cargo Carriers Inc. Milwaukee, Wi.	N20ER
N20EW	88	King Air 300	FA-152	Western Heritage Investments Corp. Missoula, Mt.	D-CIMB
N20FD	98	King Air C90B	LJ-1528	LegendAir LLC. Nashville, Tn.	N2273A
N20KV	69	SA-26AT Merlin 2B	T26-154	Kayser Ventures Ltd. Geneva, Il.	N71SF
N20KW	85	King Air 300	FA-44	K & W Restaurants Inc. Winston Salem, NC.	N48EB
N20LB	96	King Air B200	BB-1541	Silver Dollar City Inc. Branson, Mo.	N1003W
N20LH	74	King Air E90	LW-80	Southern Mechanical Plumbing Inc. Sunnyvale, Ca.	N3ZC
N20MA	78	Rockwell 690B	11514	Miniter Resource Partners Inc. Norwell, Ma.	N14BU
N20ME	78	Rockwell 690B	11440	Wrangler Aviation Corp. Norman, Ok.	N47CF
N20NK	85	King Air 300	FA-51	Big Bale Aviation Inc. Wilmington, De.	N20NL
N20RA	85	Beech 1900C	UB-42	EG&G, Las Vegas, Nv.	(N272HK)
N20RE	81	King Air 200	BB-758	Rodney Mitchell, Granite Bay, Ca.	
N20S	78	King Air E90	LW-267	Robert Schiffenhaus, Espoo, Finland.	N23726
N20TN	79	PA-31T Cheyenne II	7920019	Donald Cornforth MD Inc. Bakersfield, Ca.	N20TV
N20WL	77	PA-31T Cheyenne II	7720011	Hamblen Aero Inc. Morristown, Tn.	N51BJ
N20WP	77	King Air C90	LJ-738	WP Flight LLC. Apopka, Fl.	N239C
N20WS	73	King Air E90	LW-30	Southeast Airmotive Corp. Charlotte, NC.	(N24TF)
N21	80	King Air C90	LJ-902	FAA, Oklahoma City, Ok.	N5
N21CJ	80	MU-2 Marquise	789SA	Bankair Inc. West Columbia, SC.	N278MA
N21DE	76	King Air 200	BB-117	Silverton Air LLC. Bardstown, Ky.	N1DE
N21FG	81	King Air 200	BB-839	Department of Fish & Game, Sacramento, Ca.	N3849B
N21HP	77	Mitsubishi MU-2P	357SA	Richland Aviation, Sidney, Mt.	N2HP
N21JA	74	Mitsubishi MU-2J	614	Bankair Inc. West Columbia, SC.	N998CA
N21LE	02	King Air C90B	LJ-1682	UL-ECO Inc. Tampa, Fl.	N6082A
N21NM	80	King Air E90	LW-336	Seven Bar Flying Service Inc. Albuquerque, NM.	N675J

Reg	Yr Type	c/n	Owner/Operator	Prev Regn
N21SP	74 King Air C90	LJ-630	Southern Produce Distributors Inc. Fiason, NC.	N22BM
N22BB	67 King Air A90	LJ-241	Robert Spillman, Elyria, Oh.	N27UU
N22BD	85 King Air 300	FA-84	Bill Davis Racing Inc. Thomasville, NC.	N121RH
N22BJ	72 King Air A100	B-133	Silverhawk Aviation Inc. Lincoln, Ne.	N1200Z
N22CG	80 Conquest II	441-0119	Jubilee Airways Inc. Glasgow, Scotland.	N26231
N22CK	79 Rockwell 690B	11524	Acme Aviation LLC. Swanson, Il.	N81773
N22DT	80 PA-31T Cheyenne II	8020057	Conyan Aviation Inc. Boise, Id.	N806CM
N22DW	80 SA-226T Merlin 3B	T-317	MACI Leasing Corp. Edison, NJ.	N10143
N22EQ	72 SA-226T Merlin 3	T-221	Los Encinos Inc. Dover, De.	N264B
N22ER	72 King Air E90	LW-18	Mary Rogers, San Antonio, Tx.	N22EH
N22ET	68 680W Turbo Commander	1793-23	R Con Aviation Inc. Billings, Mt.	N22RT
N22F	82 King Air B200	BB-1025	Wesley West Interests Inc. Houston, Tx.	(N2227F)
N22FS	96 King Air C90B	LJ-1452	Frank & Rona Singer Living Trust, Huntington Beach, Ca.	N548JG
N22GW	70 SA-26AT Merlin 2B	T26-169	Peterson Corporate Travel LLC. Nashville, Tn.	N227CH
N22HD	04 King Air C90B	LJ-1720	MJF Aero Inc. Hockessin, De.	
N22LP	01 Pilatus PC-12/45	402	DTI/Oldham Associates LLC. Springville, Ut.	N9DC
N22MZ	69 Mitsubishi MU-2F	158	Africano Aircraft Management LLC. Peoria, Il.	PT-BPY
N22NR	70 SA-26AT Merlin 2B	T26-173	Sunwest S E Kansas LP. Independence, Ks.	N99RK
N22RT	70 681 Turbo Commander	6001	J & J Service, Tulsa, Ok.	N66CP
N22ST	PA-46 Turbo Malibu	4636122	Sijben, Maastricht, Holland.	
N22TL	80 King Air E90	LW-334	Peake Motor Co. Kenner, La.	
N22TP	82 King Air B200	BB-979	Telavia Aircraft Sales/Tango Papa Aviation, Telluride, Co.	N6120C
N22UC	78 PA-31T Cheyenne 1	7804007	Blue Sky Aviation Inc. Hermiston, Or.	N244GC
N22VF	81 Cheyenne II-XL	8166018	Cape Smythe Air Service Inc. Barrow, Ak.	N5UB
N22WF	79 PA-31T Cheyenne II	7920007	On-Air LLC. Sweickley, Pa.	(N53TR)
N22WZ	00 TBM 700B	173	Jerry Fussel, Wilson, Wy.	
N22XY	73 Mitsubishi MU-2J	599	Air Flight Enterprises Inc. Port Orange, Fl.	N121BA
N22YC	81 Cheyenne II-XL	8166020	W G Yates & Sons Construction Co. Philadelphia, Ms.	N11YC
N23AE	73 SA-226T Merlin 3	T-241	Explosive Professionals Inc. Worthington, Ky.	N73542
N23EA	80 Conquest II	441-0183	Jackson Air Inc. Jackson, Oh.	N120EA
N23EH	01 King Air B200	BB-1776	Holm Improvement Inc. Maitland, Fl.	N4476M
N23MV	77 PA-31T Cheyenne II	7720044	Texair LLC. Logan, NM.	N4015Y
N23RF	04 P-180 Avanti	1080	Trek Ventures LLC. Annapolis, Md.	G-OESL
N23ST	78 King Air 200	BB-375	Moody Holdings Inc. Portland, Or.	N89FC
N23TC	79 King Air 200	BB-453	DIHE Inc. Van Nuys, Ca.	N1284
N23WJ	88 King Air B200	BB-1297	Peter, Scott & Palmer LLC. Cashiers, NC.	N55FJ
N23WP	80 PA-31T Cheyenne II	8020004	PFC Inc/Stingray Boat Co. Hartsville, SC.	N51RL
N23WS	83 King Air B200	BB-1143	Dovey Air Inc. Birmingham, Mi.	(N330BH)
N24BL	88 King Air 300	FA-153	Bennett Lumber Products Inc. Princeton, Id.	N21CY
N24CC	74 Rockwell 690A	11201	JWS Inc. Bozeman, Mt.	N50ST
N24DD	79 PA-31T Cheyenne II	7920074	Summit Helicopters Inc. Cloverdale, Va.	N204EF
N24DS	00 King Air C90B	LJ-1616	Truck Driver Institute of Alabama, Oxford, Al.	N342P
N24GJ	78 King Air C90	LJ-769	C C Medflight Inc. Lawrenceville, Ga.	N911UM
N24GN	82 King Air B200	BB-953	Flat Creek Development Co. Jackson, Wy.	N953L
N24GT	75 Rockwell 690A	11254	Rogers Helicopters Inc. Clovis, Ca.	XA-RMZ
N24PT	77 Conquest II	441-0015	Donald Aircraft LLC. Wilmington, De.	N441TJ
N24QF	84 Conquest 1	425-0181	John McDermott, Ankeny, Ia.	(N24QL)
N24SP	74 King Air C-12L	BB-3	Kentucky State Police, Frankfort, Ky.	71-21058
N24WC	78 Mitsubishi MU-2N	705SA	Mobile Instrument Service & Repair Inc. Bellefontaine, Oh.	N865MA
N24YC	97 King Air C90B	LJ-1484	W G Yates & Sons Construction Co. Philadelphia, Ms.	N1134D
N25BD	72 Rockwell 690	11009	Haas Chemical Co. Melrose, Fl.	N9209N
N25BE	70 681 Turbo Commander	6041	Midwestern Jet Sales & Service Inc. Oklahoma City, Ok.	N9101N
N25CE	77 Rockwell 690B	11400	Denmark Investments Inc. Murrieta, Ca.	(N3TJ)
N25CS	82 King Air B200	BB-948	Three Guys LLC. Austin, Tx.	N150RH
N25DL	77 King Air C90	LJ-716	Sunmor Aviation Ltd. Dayton, Tx.	N25KW
N25GK	90 King Air B200	BB-1373	KASA Marine Ltd/Alto LLC. Traverse City, Mi.	N25GE
N25GM	79 MU-2 Solitaire	412SA	Rod Aero Aircraft Brokerage, Fort Lauderdale, Fl.	N814HH
N25HB	96 King Air C90B	LJ-1453	Hempt Brothers Inc. Camp Hill, Pa.	N1092G
N25KA	81 King Air 200	BB-783	Eric Stirling, Fairbanks, Ak.	N3714P
N25MG	79 PA-31T Cheyenne II	7920059	Beyond Aviation LLC. Fort Wayne, In.	N63SC
N25MR	80 King Air 200	BB-611	D & R Maintenance LLC. Brentwood, Tn.	N1JP
N25ND	80 PA-31T Cheyenne II	8020005	The UND Aerospace Foundation, Grand Forks, ND.	N25AS
N25RZ	79 Rockwell 690B	11518	EAL Inc/Executive Aviation Logistics, Chino, Ca.	(N91AV)
N25TG	77 King Air E90	LW-238	Custom Air Services Inc. Chattanooga, Tn.	N707DC
N25WC	98 King Air B200	BB-1640	Georgia Air South Inc. Valdosta, Ga.	N351SC

Reg	Yr Type	c/n	Owner/Operator	Prev Regn

Reg	Yr Type	c/n	Owner/Operator	Prev Regn
☐ N26BE	78 King Air 200	BB-388	Manchester Plastics Ltd. Troy, Mi.	N388MC
☐ N26DV	83 PA-31T Cheyenne 1A	8304003	Vogel Paint & Wax Co. Orange City, Ia.	VH-SJJ
☐ N26JB	81 PA-31T Cheyenne 1	8104020	Airlock Ltd. St Paris, Oh.	N31WM
☐ N26KC	01 PA-46-500TP Meridian	4697113	Kelly Cornell, Atlantis, Fl.	N6DM
☐ N26KH	04 Pilatus PC-12/45	592	Concord Jet Service Inc. Portland, Or.	HB-FRD
☐ N26PK	80 Conquest II	441-0143	Hauts-Monts Inc. Beauport, PQ. Canada.	(N66TR)
☐ N26SL	79 PA-31T Cheyenne II	7920091	Sierra Lima LLC. Bozeman, Mt.	N19GA
☐ N26UT	81 King Air B200	BB-901	Watson Engineering Inc. Taylor, Mi.	
☐ N26VW	02 Pilatus PC-12/45	478	Canvasback Enterprises LP. Kerrville, Tx.	N478PC
☐ N27BF	81 PA-31T Cheyenne 1	8104038	Dr Barry Jeffries, Atlanta, Ga.	N130CC
☐ N27BM	91 King Air C90B	LJ-1288	Tri-State Aero Inc. Evansville, In.	N90KB
☐ N27CS	79 King Air B100	BE-63	Profile Aviation Services Inc. Hickory, NC.	N924RM
☐ N27CV	83 King Air B200	BB-1161	Valley International Properties, Stuart, Fl.	N77CV
☐ N27DK	04 PA-46-500TP Meridian	4697196	TJD Corp. Wilmington, De.	
☐ N27GE	92 King Air 350	FL-86	Rebel Express LLC. Salinas, Ca.	(N60CC)
☐ N27KM	77 PA-31T Cheyenne II	7720051	U S Naval Research Laboratory, Washington, DC.	85-1609
☐ N27RC	83 King Air B200	BB-1134	Camacho Express LLC/Caribe Imported Cigars Inc. Miami, Fl.	N98LP
☐ N27SE	82 King Air F90	LA-194	SL Aviation LC. Charleston, WV.	N6685P
☐ N27TJ	81 MU-2 Marquise	1511SA	Pavair Corp. Greenwich, Ct.	N418MA
☐ N27VE	85 Gulfstream 1000B	96202	Edelbrock Corp. Torrance, Ca.	N695P
☐ N27WH	80 King Air F90	LA-23	DRJ Group Inc. Ocala, Fl.	N14TT
☐ N28BG	77 PA-31T Cheyenne II	7720005	GRL Investments LLC. Kalispell, Mt.	N444ET
☐ N28C	75 King Air A100	B-216	Dynamic Aviation Group Inc. Bridgewater, Va.	JDFT-3
☐ N28CG	94 Dornier 328-100	3024	Corning Inc. Corning, NY.	N95CG
☐ N28DA	82 PA-42 Cheyenne III	8001078	John J Gee Wax & Co. West Grove, Pa.	N22HD
☐ N28DC	68 Mitsubishi MU-2D	106	Eastern New Mexico University, Roswell, NM.	N518TQ
☐ N28GC	89 King Air 300	FA-172	Grupe Commercial Co. Stockton, Ca.	N34BS
☐ N28J	78 King Air 200	BB-348	Sierra Pacific Industries Inc. Redding, Ca.	
☐ N28KC	78 King Air 200	BB-356	W A A M Inc. Goulds, Fl.	N9KA
☐ N28KP	79 King Air C90	LJ-845	State of Montana, Helena, Mt.	N28KC
☐ N28M	75 King Air E90	LW-147	K & K Aircraft Inc. Bridgewater, Va.	N553MA
☐ N28MS	74 King Air E90	LW-100	Rocky Mountain Holdings LLC. Provo, Ut.	N31FN
☐ N28NK	04 PA-46-500TP Meridian	4697191	New Piper Aircraft Inc. Vero Beach, Fl.	
☐ N28TC	78 Rockwell 690B	11449	Lewisburg Transportation LLC. Wilmington, De.	D-ICSM
☐ N28TM	82 King Air C90-1	LJ-1029	Five Star Aero LLC. Strafford, Mo.	N6567C
☐ N28VM	01 King Air B200	BB-1772	Van Metre Air LLC. Burke, Va.	N4472C
☐ N28VU	80 King Air 200	BB-743	Shiver Security Systems Inc. Cincinnati, Oh.	N111LP
☐ N28WN	81 Cheyenne II-XL	8166026	Malco Leasing Corp. Danbury, Ct.	N77UH
☐ N29DE	67 680V Turbo Commander	1699-76	World Wide Wings, Duncan, Ok.	N7029P
☐ N29EC	85 King Air 300	FA-66	E C Aviation Services Inc. Zeeland, Mi.	N17ME
☐ N29GA	83 Gulfstream 900	15025	Powell Group, Baton Rouge, La.	
☐ N29HF	80 King Air 200	BB-685	Sherwood McGuigan, Midland, Tx.	N29CH
☐ N29JS	01 P-180 Avanti	1046	Pelham Air LLC. Wilmington, De.	N124PA
☐ N29KG	79 Rockwell 690B	11548	Rocky Mountain Aviation Inc. Chino, Ca.	N81625
☐ N29LA	80 PA-31T Cheyenne II	8020076	Exeat Aviation Inc. Marco Island, Fl.	F-GNAC
☐ N29LH	04 PA-46-500TP Meridian	4697179	H & M Bay Inc. Federalsburg, Md.	
☐ N29M	74 King Air E90	LW-88	Dynamic Aviation Group Inc. Bridgewater, Va.	F-GELL
☐ N29PR	70 681 Turbo Commander	6018	Alfred Balitzer, Claremont, Ca.	PT-DQX
☐ N29TB	79 King Air C90	LJ-846	AHG Hotels LLC. Greenville, SC.	OY-MBA
☐ N29TF	84 PA-42 Cheyenne IIIA	5501003	Hawker Partners LLC. Darien, Ct.	(N340BH)
☐ N30BG	71 681B Turbo Commander	6059	Vvoortech Inc. Council Bluffs, Ia.	N333RK
☐ N30CN	95 King Air C90B	LJ-1415	Streamline Air LLC. Santa Barbara, Ca.	
☐ N30DU	77 PA-31T Cheyenne II	7720054	Scheufler Inc. Valley City, Oh.	(N98AS)
☐ N30FE	88 King Air 300	FA-148	Fresh Express Inc. Salinas, Ca.	N3086D
☐ N30GC	73 King Air A100	B-177	Federated Department Stores Inc. Miami, Fl.	(N100BX)
☐ N30GK	80 King Air C90	LJ-923	Procoil Aviation LLC. Marshall, Tx.	XA-REH
☐ N30GT	80 King Air F90	LA-37	Hodge Law Firm, Spartanburg, SC.	
☐ N30HF	71 King Air C90	LJ-506	Franklin Academy Inc. Cleveland, Tn.	N63TH
☐ N30HS	69 SA-26AT Merlin 2B	T26-156	Bowers Aire Ltd. Palacios, Tx.	N112A
☐ N30KC	77 King Air E90	LW-241	Kingsford Manufacturing Co. Oakland, Ca.	N17844
☐ N30MA	78 Mitsubishi MU-2P	371SA	Wilson Construction Delaware Corp. Wilmington, De.	ZK-ECR
☐ N30MC	89 King Air 300	FA-199	Madden Contracting Co. Minden, La.	N42GA
☐ N30NH	80 King Air F90	LA-48	SQH Air Corp. Menlo Park, Ca.	C-FOMH
☐ N30PH	80 King Air 200	BB-635	Longvue Properties LLC. Greensburg, La.	N30PM
☐ N30RR	73 Mitsubishi MU-2K	263	Tony Equipment Leasing Corp. Lewes, De.	N10VU
Reg	Yr Type	c/n	Owner/Operator	Prev Regn

Reg	Yr	Type	c/n	Owner/Operator	Prev Regn
☐ N30SE	78	King Air 200	BB-313	A & M Holdings LLC. Stuttgart, Ar. (status ?).	N23313
☐ N30TF	69	SA-26AT Merlin 2B	T26-162	Merlin Aviation LLC. St Louis, Mo.	C-FTEL
☐ N30VP	97	King Air B200	BB-1560	Valley Proteins Inc. Winchester, Va.	N1103B
☐ N30W	78	King Air C-12C	BC-72	Dynamic Aviation Group Inc. Bridgewater, Va.	N200EJ
☐ N31A	78	King Air E90	LW-281	DavisAir Inc. Allegheny County, Pa.	N502SC
☐ N31AD	81	Conquest 1	425-0049	Allaire Dupont, Chesapeake, Md.	N67741
☐ N31AT	77	SA-226AT Merlin 4A	AT-057	White Industries Inc. Bates City, Mo. (status ?).	N31264
☐ N31BR	85	CASA 212-200	294	FS Air Service Inc. Anchorage, Ak.	
☐ N31DV	74	Rockwell 690A	11154	Dunn Vineyards LLC. Angwin, Ca.	N102JK
☐ N31DX	00	Pilatus PC-12/45	343	Riley Aviation Leasing LLC. Salt Lake City, Ut.	HB-FRM
☐ N31FM	81	King Air 200	BB-869	Colemill Enterprises Inc. Nashville, Tn.	N2135J
☐ N31HL	81	PA-31T Cheyenne II	8120060	Lawrence F Grey MD. Tampa, Fl.	N816JA
☐ N31JV	82	SA-227TT Merlin 3C	TT-453	JV Air LLC. La Porte, Tx.	N944KR
☐ N31JZ	81	Cheyenne II-XL	8166062	DHZ Inc. Cincinnati, Oh.	N310JD
☐ N31MB	80	PA-31T Cheyenne 1	8004013	J R Cummins LLC. Lexington, Ky.	
☐ N31SN	68	King Air B90	LJ-362	SafeFlight Inc. Poughkeepsie, NY.	N31SV
☐ N31SV	95	King Air B200	BB-1514	Sioux Valley Hospital Association, Sioux Falls, SD.	N214SE
☐ N31TL	81	King Air F90	LA-133	Sothern Lady Inc. Lakeland, Fl.	N1803P
☐ N31WC	79	King Air 200	BB-465	VDC Aircraft inc. Miamisburg, Oh.	N24SA
☐ N31WP	74	King Air E90	LW-99	N31WP King Air E90 LP. Houston, Tx.	N31JJ
☐ N32BA	69	King Air B90	LJ-475	Sky's The Limit Inc. Hutchinson, Mn.	N500RK
☐ N32BW	79	Rockwell 690B	11545	Northern Precision Instruments LLC. Wentworth, NH.	N25LS
☐ N32CK	01	PA-46-500TP Meridian	4697123	Alpine Falcon LLC. Dover, De.	N633P
☐ N32CM	80	King Air C90	LJ-881	Red Spot Paint & Varnish Co. Evansville, In.	N32SJ
☐ N32EC	77	Mitsubishi MU-2N	699SA	Security Air Service LLC. Murrels Inlet, SC.	N859MA
☐ N32FH	65	King Air 90	LJ-74	Special Ops Aviation Inc. Norfolk, Va.	XA-RMH
☐ N32GA	74	Rockwell 690A	11215	Petroleum Helicopters Inc. Lafayette, La.	N215BA
☐ N32JP	88	King Air C90A	LJ-1172	Price Services Inc. Monticello, Ar.	N904TD
☐ N32KC	95	King Air 350	FL-125	Wilson & Assocs of Delaware LC. Little Rock, Ar.	N32KQ
☐ N32KE	01	PA-46-500TP Meridian	4697048	Group Growth Services Inc. Richmond, In.	
☐ N32KW	78	PA-31T Cheyenne II	7820090	Exec Air Montana Inc. Helena, Mt.	D-IJPG
☐ N32LJ	82	King Air B200	BB-993	Larry Collins, Portland, Tn.	N32TJ
☐ N32MA	82	King Air C90	LJ-1023	McRight-Smith Capital LP. McInney, Tx.	N731RJ
☐ N32MT	87	King Air C90A	LJ-1155	Management Specialities LLC/Dunham Price Inc. Westlake, La.	N3077Y
☐ N32P	66	King Air A90	LM-31	Dynamic AvLease Inc. Bridgewater, Va.	N7040J
☐ N32PH	81	Gulfstream 840	11691	Petroleum Helicopters Inc. Lafayette, La.	N800BM
☐ N32PR	76	Rockwell 690A	11332	Core Corp. Boulder, Co.	(N216PL)
☐ N32SV	81	King Air 200	BB-865	Sioux Valley Hospital Association, Sioux Falls, SD.	N531BB
☐ N32WC	87	King Air B200	BB-1285	West Coast Charters LLC. Santa Ana, Ca.	N280JR
☐ N32WS	76	Rockwell 690A	11339	R & S Aviation LLC. Neenah, Wi.	ZS-JRL
☐ N33AR	97	King Air B200	BB-1577	Itochu Aviation Inc. El Segundo, Ca.	C-FLXM
☐ N33BK	91	King Air B200	BB-1403	BK Associates Inc. Atlanta, Ga.	N8094Q
☐ N33DE	83	Conquest II	441-0308	State of North Carolina, Raleigh, NC.	N87494
☐ N33EW	81	MU-2 Marquise	1519SA	Florida Express Corp. Wilmington, De.	N331W
☐ N33JA	99	Pilatus PC-12/45	261	Jet Capital Inc. Edwards, Co.	N654CA
☐ N33LA	01	King Air B200	BB-1777	NPP Inc. Valdosta, Ga.	N4347X
☐ N33MC	81	PA-31T Cheyenne II	8120050	James Costello, Bend, Or.	N194MA
☐ N33MS	81	PA-31T Cheyenne II	8120036	Maurice Shacket, West Bloomfield, Mi.	N25WA
☐ N33SB	67	King Air A90	LJ-252	David Harden, Washington, Pa.	N728K
☐ N33WG	72	Rockwell 690	11038	Big Eye Helicopters, Agana, Guam.	(N38PR)
☐ N34AL	80	MU-2 Marquise	792SA	Flight Line Inc. Salt Lake City, Ut.	N66LA
☐ N34CE	81	King Air C90	LJ-932	Trans Oceano LLC. San Jose, Costa Rica.	(N90CE)
☐ N34ER	88	PA-42 Cheyenne 400LS	5527036	Starwood Air LLC. Missoula, Mt.	D-IONE
☐ N34GA	82	Gulfstream 1000	96057	Franklin Realty Group Inc. Blue Bell, Pa.	(N9977S)
☐ N34HA	67	King Air A90	LJ-315	Hawk Aviation Inc. Hanahan, SC.	XB-FJM
☐ N34HM	77	PA-31T Cheyenne II	7720003	Pace Aviation Ltd. Reno, Nv.	N28FM
☐ N34LT	92	King Air B200	BB-1437	Corporate Airways Inc. Thomasville, Ga.	N8059Y
☐ N34MF	76	King Air E90	LW-163	Denison Jet Sales Corp. Landrum, SC.	(N112CM)
☐ N34RT	76	Rockwell 690A	11315	Aircraft Resource Center Inc. St Paul, Mn.	N34SC
☐ N34SM	77	SA-226T Merlin 3A	T-279	Flight Solutions Inc. Hendersonville, Tn.	N5396M
☐ N34UA	69	SA-26AT Merlin 2B	T26-145	James Heth, Lindale, Tx.	
☐ N34UP	73	King Air C-12C	BC-6	Eagles Quest LLC. Wayne, Mi.	N530SP
☐ N35	78	King Air 200	BB-88	FAA, Oklahoma City, Ok.	N4
☐ N35CM	73	King Air E90	LW-51	Southern Air Services Inc. Tuscaloosa, Al.	N7LR
☐ N35GR	85	King Air B200	BB-1167	JNG Services Inc. Lexington, Ky.	N18CM

Reg	Yr	Type	c/n	Owner/Operator	Prev Regn
N35HC	94	King Air C90B	LJ-1375	Bruce Barclay, Mechanicsburg, Pa.	XA-TDW
N35KD	75	King Air 200	BB-35	KD Air LLC. Big Fork, Mt.	N200YY
N35LW	85	King Air 300LW	FA-63	L Wood Aviation Inc. Austin, Tx.	D-IILG
N35RR	81	MU-2 Marquise	1525SA	Flight Line Inc. Denver, Co.	N442MA
N35RT	78	PA-31T Cheyenne II	7820018	Townsend Engineering Co. Des Moines, Ia.	N353T
N35TK	81	Conquest 1	425-0088	Allied Resources Inc. Warwick, RI.	N425BW
N35TV	73	King Air C90	LJ-572	Hartford Holding Corp. Naples, Fl.	N46RF
N36AG	83	Gulfstream 1000	96058	L C Leasing Co. Annapolis, Md.	HP-11GT
N36AT	80	MU-2 Solitaire	426SA	JS Holdings LLC. Indianapolis, In.	N181RS
N36CP	76	King Air 200	BB-178	Chartair Inc. Waterford, Mi.	N355AF
N36DD	69	King Air B90	LJ-464	Mapleleaf Acquisitions Inc. Wilmington, De.	N813K
N36G	67	Mitsubishi MU-2B	035	Buckeye Holding Ltd. Newark, De.	N601CT
N36GS	88	King Air B200	BB-1298	Andrew Heller, Austin, Tx.	N734A
N36JF	78	Rockwell 690B	11478	MMDEX LLC. Carlisle, Pa.	N81797
N36JT	80	Gulfstream 980	95024	Aerographics Inc. Manassas, Va.	N66FP
N36LC	81	SA-226T Merlin 3B	T-387	Simmonds King Air Inc. Marietta, Ga.	N777JE
N36PE	69	SA-26AT Merlin 2B	T26-164	BGT Minerals LLC. Aledo, Tx.	N50MA
N36SW	78	Rockwell 690B	11505	Eagle Leasing Inc. Midland City, Al.	N28WR
N36TW	80	PA-31T Cheyenne II	8020075	Esposita Aviation Inc. Wilmington, De.	
N37AL	79	MU-2 Marquise	752SA	White Industries Inc. Bates City, Mo.	N11WQ
N37BW	73	Rockwell 690A	11129	Damin Sir Paul Inc. Boca Raton, Fl.	(N500AL)
N37CB	79	King Air 200	BB-532	Diversified Capital Investments LLC. Central City, Ky.	(N731RC)
N37CN	78	King Air C90	LJ-745	Business & Pleasure Air Charter LC. Schulenberg, Tx.	N384H
N37DA	97	Pilatus PC-12	195	Duncan Aviation Inc. Lincoln, Ne.	C-FKAE
N37GA	87	King Air B200	BB-1272	Legacy Air LLC. Missoula, Mt.	VT-EQD
N37GP	65	King Air 90	LJ-15	APA Enterprises Inc. Poughkeepsie, NY.	N733KL
N37H	66	King Air A90	LM-48	Dynamic AvLease Inc. Bridgewater, Va.	N7059H
N37HB	77	PA-31T Cheyenne II	7720020	R L RiemenschneiderEnterprises Co. Redmond, Or.	N37RT
N37HC	74	King Air E90	LW-108	Cochran Rental Co. Cochran, Ga.	N37X
N37KK	73	Mitsubishi MU-2J	588	Bar Aircraft Leasing Co. Clarkston, Mi.	N32CK
N37KW	89	PA-42 Cheyenne 400LS	5527039	Phoenix Air LLC. Augusta, Ga.	C-FPQA
N37NC	81	King Air 200	BB-781	National Commerce Bancorporation, Memphis, Tn.	N469JW
N37PC	79	King Air B100	BE-66	J & M Leasing LLC. Dublin, Oh.	N6032E
N37PJ	79	PA-31T Cheyenne 1	7904003	Rock Leasing, Las Vegas, Nv.	N800CM
N37PS	81	Conquest 1	425-0050	Sterry Family Trust, Sumers, Mt.	N425FB
N37RR	79	Rockwell 690B	11552	Rose Isle Aviation LLC. Orlando, Fl.	N888SL
N37SB	82	Gulfstream 840	11724	Stephen R Butter, Longview, Tx.	N5962K
N37TW	81	PA-31T Cheyenne 1	8104006	Virga Corp/Virga Enviromental Corp. Loveland, Co.	(N816CM)
N37XX	85	King Air C90A	LJ-1112	N37XX LLC. Aromas, Ca.	N66LM
N38AA	80	Conquest II	441-0163	Capital City Aviation Inc. Madison, Wi.	(N38BR)
N38AF	85	PA-42 Cheyenne 400LS	5527029	RASair LLC. Manchester, NH.	N689CA
N38BE	71	Mitsubishi MU-2F	210	Avmanco 1 Ltd/Steven Bernstein, Dickens, Tx.	N34DD
N38CG	95	Dornier 328-100	3034	Corning Inc. Corning, NY.	D-CDXA
N38H	92	King Air 350	FL-71	Axiom Capital II LLC. Destin, Fl.	N56456
N38JV	92	King Air B200	BB-1439	J & J Maintenance Inc. Austin, Tx.	N423PC
N38LM	77	Rockwell 690B	11424	Jet Works Inc. Fort Myers, Fl.	CP-2299
N38RE	81	PA-31T Cheyenne 1	8104028	Javelin Air Inc. Blakely, Ga.	N241AC
N38RP	77	King Air C90	LJ-722	The Card Plane LLC. Birmingham, Al.	N35HP
N38RY	87	King Air 300	FA-134	Robert Yates Racing Inc. Charlotte, NC.	N28RY
N30TA	81	SA-226T Merlin 3B	T-397	Armstrong International Inc. Stuart, Fl.	
N38TR	80	King Air C90	LJ-908	TRC Aviation LLC. Signal Mountain, Tn.	N1078
N38TW	81	PA-31T Cheyenne 1	8104008	Tango Whiskey inc. Wilmington, De.	
N38V	66	King Air A90	LM-105	Dynamic AvLease Inc. Bridgewater, Va.	N7148A
N38VT	80	PA-31T Cheyenne II	8020022	Cavalier Motor Co. Mechanicsville, Va.	N38V
N38VV	91	King Air B200	BB-1412	Ward Air LLC. Rockville, Md.	N38V
N38WA	74	Rockwell 690A	11169	Airborne Support Inc. Houma, La.	XB-FLF
N38WV	96	King Air B200	BB-1554	Colcaribe Investments SA. Barranquilla, Colombia.	N88WV
N38XJ	98	King Air C90B	LJ-1512	United Interstate Financial Services, Van Nuys, Ca.	
N39A	83	Conquest 1	425-0138	Barcar LC. Vero Beach, Fl.	N6884Q
N39AS	68	680W Turbo Commander	1721-1	Southern Turbines Inc. Vero Beach, Fl. (was 1721-92).	N954HE
N39EH	79	PA-31T Cheyenne II	7920020	Country Foods Inc. Polson, Mt.	N224EC
N39FB	88	King Air C90A	LJ-1165	ICI Seeds/Farm Bureau Life Insurance Co. Des Moines, Ia.	(N325A)
N39GK	00	P-180 Avanti	1039	Meyer Tool Inc. Cincinnati, Oh.	N120PA
N39K	80	PA-31T Cheyenne II	8020053	Go Fast Inc. Wilmington, De.	N440PA
N39MS	75	SA-226T Merlin 3A	T-257	Khan Aviation Inc. Elkhart, In.	N45BB
Reg	Yr	Type	c/n	Owner/Operator	Prev Regn

Reg	Yr	Type	c/n	Owner/Operator	Prev Regn
N39PH	79	King Air 200C	BL-3	TriState CareFlight LLC. Bullhead City, Az.	N141GS
N39Q	66	King Air A90	LM-106	Dynamic AvLease Inc. Bridgewater, Va.	N7154W
N39TL	81	PA-31T Cheyenne 1	8104012	Panhandle Telecommunications & Systems, Guymon, Ok.	N39TW
N40AM	80	MU-2 Solitaire	427SA	Scope Leasing Inc. Columbus, Oh.	N166MA
N40BA	69	King Air B90	LJ-444	Munoz Bermudez Inc. San Juan, PR.	(HI-...)
N40BC	84	King Air B200	BB-1169	MOCI Leasing Inc. Dover, De.	N90LP
N40FK	84	PA-42 Cheyenne 400LS	5527003	212 Aviation Corp. Des Moines, Ia.	(N42AJ)
N40GZ*	04	King Air 350	FL-400	Jorge C Zamora-Quezada, Mission, Tx.	N40TH
N40HE	79	King Air 200	BB-569	Baru Air SA. Panama City, Panama.	(N977BA)
N40JJ	78	Mitsubishi MU-2P	383SA	PLSR LLC. Plano, Tx.	N10JJ
N40KC	75	Mitsubishi MU-2M	322	Keller Companies Inc. Manchester, NH.	N20KC
N40MH	90	King Air C90A	LJ-1258	Brunner Drilling & Manufacturing Inc. Elroy, Wi.	N80CK
N40PD*	81	PA-31T Cheyenne II	8120044	Powell Development Co. Kirkland, Wa.	N666JK
N40PJ	99	King Air B200	BB-1660	Phillips & Jordan Inc. Robbinsville, NC.	
N40PT	88	King Air B200	BB-1291	Laurel Aviation Inc. Decatur, Il.	D-CIRA
N40R	73	King Air C-12C	BC-7	Dynamic Aviation Group Inc. Bridgewater, Va.	N380SA
N40RA	76	King Air 200	BB-104	John Simmons/Captex Land Corp. Austin, Tx.	
N40SM	79	Rockwell 690B	11559	First Windsor Inc. Mendota Heights, De.	
N40TT	75	PA-31T Cheyenne II	7520023	Ocean Aircraft Ltd. Chesapeake, Va.	N314GA
N40WG	78	Rockwell 690B	11459	Malibu Boats West Inc. Merced, Ca.	N333KD
N40XJ	00	King Air C90B	LJ-1640	Rydell Chevrolet Inc. Waterloo, Ia.	
N41AK	82	King Air F90	LA-188	I & S Graham Aviation, Glasgow, Scotland.	(N46BA)
N41HH	75	King Air E90	LW-146	Sundancer Enterprises LLC. Norman, Ok.	N141DA
N41J	66	King Air A90	LM-89	Dynamic Aviation, Bridgewater, Va.	N7113Z
N41LH	65	Gulfstream 1	156	Executive Jet Support Ltd. UK. (status ?).	(N159KK)
N41T	70	Rockwell 690	11001	Altair Aircraft LLC. Gainesvile, Fl. (was s/n 6031).	N700CB
N41WC	68	King Air B90	LJ-430	Beech Transportation Inc. Eden Prairie, Mn.	N551SS
N41WE	78	King Air E90	LW-280	Mountain Flight Service Inc. Steamboat Springs, Co.	N4820M
N41WL	80	King Air F90	LA-60	Hudson Ford Nissan, Madisonville, Ky.	(N100WL)
N42AF	81	MU-2 Marquise	1539SA	EPPS Air Service Inc. Atlanta, Ga.	ZS-MRJ
N42CQ	67	King Air A90	LJ-245	Oklahoma State Department Vo-Tech, Stillwater, Ok.	(N221ML)
N42CV	80	PA-31T Cheyenne II	8020067	Eagle Air LLC. Lafayette, La.	N793S
N42DT	82	Conquest II	441-0234	Richard Devirian, Torrance, Ca.	N41CR
N42EL	00	King Air 350	FL-302	Raytheon Aircraft Co. Wichita, Ks.	N4302J
N42LJ	79	King Air 200	BB-564	Smith Newspapers Inc. Fort Payne, Al.	ZS-KHK
N42LW	99	King Air B200	BB-1688	RPJ Aircraft Investors LLC. Camarillo, Ca.	
N42PC	74	King Air E90	LW-85	KL Aviation HC LLC. Indianapolis, In.	N20RF
N42QB	84	PA-42 Cheyenne 400LS	5527015	Kladstrup-Wetzel Associates Ltd. Engelwood, Co.	ZK-RUR
N42SC	96	King Air B200	BB-1550	CLC Leasing Inc. Dallas, Tx.	(N42SQ)
N42SL	82	Gulfstream 900	15013	OPEC Air LLC. Shreveport, La.	N900AB
N43AJ	77	King Air 200	BB-243	Marvin Blount Jr. Greenville, NC.	N300US
N43BG	94	King Air 350	FL-117	Boyd Central Region Inc. Memphis, Tn.	N1553V
N43BH	83	Conquest 1	425-0130	B H Aviation Inc/Hughes Supply Inc. Orlando, Fl.	N68823
N43CB	74	SA-226T Merlin 3	T-246	Bahamas Red Bird Inc. North Miami, Fl.	N43FG
N43JT	67	King Air A90	LJ-286	Alexander Consutling Services Inc. Griffin, Ga.	(N67PT)
N43MB	69	King Air B90	LJ-463	Abrotec GmbH. Magdeburg, Germany.	(N300A)
N43PC	78	King Air E90	LW-253	Prototype Equipment Corp. Lake Forest, Il.	N709DB
N43TA	92	King Air B200	BB-1432	Louisiana Aircraft LLC. Oklahoma City, Ok.	N8037J
N43TL	97	King Air B200	BB-1582	T-L Irrigation Co. Hastings, Ne.	N1130R
N43VM	00	PA-46-500TP Meridian	4697005	Borealis Investments, Washington, DC.	
N43WA	70	King Air B90	LJ-501	Willis Enterprises Inc. Montesano, Wa.	N865MA
N43WH	81	PA-31T Cheyenne II	8120068	Big Timber Ltd. Clovis, NM.	D-IJOE
N43WS	72	King Air E90	LW-16	Colemill Enterprises Inc. Nashville, Tn.	N80NC
N44AX	80	MU-2 Solitaire	416SA	Downs Aircraft Inc. Wilmington, De.	(N613CF)
N44DT	78	PA-31T Cheyenne II	7820043	Enchantment Aviation Inc. Elephant Butte, NM.	(N82267)
N44GK	78	King Air E90	LW-298	Seven Bar Flying Service Inc. Albuquerque, NM.	(N118SB)
N44GL	75	SA-226AT Merlin 4A	AT-032	SouthBank, Huntsville, Al.	N44PB
N44HP	77	King Air C90	LJ-702	Belk Farms, Bermuda Dunes, Ca.	
N44HT	79	PA-31T Cheyenne II	7920061	Cheyenne Airways LLC. Kansas City, Mo.	N117FN
N44KA*	00	King Air B200	BB-1711	JF Aviation Associates Inc. Jupiter, Fl.	
N44KS	86	SAAB 340A	050	Goodyear Tire & Rubber Co. Akron, Oh.	N340SA
N44KT	76	King Air 200	BB-154	Orval Yarger, Normal, Il.	N44KA
N44KU	74	Mitsubishi MU-2J	647	Bankair Inc. West Columbia, SC.	(N110SS)
N44MR	81	King Air 200C	BL-27	Delta Life Insurance Co. Thomasville, Ga.	N3827Z
N44MV	74	King Air E90	LW-107	Brad Gray, North Bend, Or.	N96TB
Reg	Yr	Type	c/n	Owner/Operator	Prev Regn

Reg	Yr Type	c/n	Owner/Operator	Prev Regn
☐ N44MX	81 MU-2 Marquise	1526SA	Swallow Aviation & Investment Inc. Green Cove Springs, Fl.	N44MM
☐ N44NC	77 Rockwell 690B	11387	Abaco LLC. Nashville, Tn.	(N790CB)
☐ N44NL	94 King Air B200	BB-1492	Pronto Enterprises Trust, Pittsburgh, Pa.	
☐ N44PA	81 King Air F90	LA-149	Sassafras Aviation LLC. Knoxville, Tn.	(N10DR)
☐ N44RG	68 King Air B90	LJ-417	Southern Stars Aviation LLC. Montgomery, Al.	N29TC
☐ N44UF	75 King Air 200	BB-36	Maxair Inc. Appleton, Wi.	N816RB
☐ N44US	75 King Air 200	BB-56	D K & L LLC. Indianapolis, In.	N55BN
☐ N44VR	80 MU-2 Solitaire	432SA	SamaritanAir Inc. Anchorage, Ak.	N15WF
☐ N45A	77 King Air C-12C	BC-48	Dynamic Aviation Group Inc. Bridgewater, Va.	77-22937
☐ N45AR	92 Beech 1900D	UE-12	Range Systems Engineering Co. West Palm Beach, Fl.	N138MA
☐ N45AZ	77 Rockwell 690B	11383	State of Arizona, Phoenix, Az.	YV-149CP
☐ N45CE	74 Mitsubishi MU-2J	653	M & M Aircraft Inc. Cape Coral, Fl.	N350HE
☐ N45CF	80 King Air 200	BB-736	Angel Flight Business Inc. Suwanee, Ga.	N577L
☐ N45FL	94 2000A Starship	NC-45	L-3 Communications AeroTech LLC. Madison, Ms.	N8215Q
☐ N45LG	82 Gulfstream 1000	96050	MGS Training Corp. Laredo, Tx.	N900EC
☐ N45LU	76 King Air B100	BE-8	Parks College of St Louis University, St Louis, Mo.	N688DS
☐ N45MF	74 King Air A100	B-202	Metro Aviation Inc. Shreveport, La.	N72TA
☐ N45MW	82 SA-227AT Merlin 4C	AT-452	Wilder Aviation Sales & Leasing, Clearwater, Fl.	N3010Q
☐ N45PF*	04 King Air C90B	LJ-1703	Raytheon Aircraft Co. Wichita, Ks.	(N713US)
☐ N45PJ	01 PA-46-500TP Meridian	4697031	Vaughan Air LLC. Wilmington, De.	
☐ N45PM	00 Pilatus PC-12/45	367	Time Tool Inc. Hillsboro, Or.	HB-FSR
☐ N45PR	66 King Air A90	LJ-145	Al's Aerial Spraying, Ovid, Mi.	N89991
☐ N45RF*	85 Gulfstream 1000	96089	U S Dept of Commerce/NOAA, MacDill AFB. Fl.	N7812
☐ N45RL	72 King Air C90	LJ-565	Aviapana SA. Panama City, Panama.	N711MP
☐ N45RR*	04 King Air B200	BB-1853	RWR Brokers Inc. Van Nuys, Ca.	N6193R
☐ N45SA	80 King Air C90	LJ-903	SAF Ltd/Safari Aviation, Lihue, Hi.	N1UM
☐ N45SQ	00 King Air B200	BB-1719	Sky Quest LLC. Hunting Valley, Oh.	N45RR
☐ N45TT	67 King Air A90	LJ-312	Eclipse Enterprises inc. Pensacola, Fl. (status ?)	N675SB
☐ N46AE	99 King Air C90B	LJ-1582	Meymar Drive Inc. White Fish, Mt.	
☐ N46AK	79 MU-2 Marquise	754SA	EPPS Air Service Inc. Atlanta, Ga.	XB-FBY
☐ N46AR	92 Beech 1900D	UE-27	Range Systems Engineering Co. West Palm Beach, Fl.	
☐ N46AX	67 King Air A90	LJ-317	Golden Valley Aviation, Clinton, Mo.	N46A
☐ N46BE	75 King Air A100	B-214	BCD Holding Inc. Fort Lauderdale, Fl.	HZ-AFC
☐ N46BM	99 King Air B200	BB-1663	Myers Aviation LLC. Worcester, Pa.	(N512BC)
☐ N46BR	81 King Air 200	BB-852	South Coast Lumber Co. Brookings, Or.	
☐ N46DT	65 King Air 90	LJ-7	White Industries Inc. Bates City, Mo.	C-GJBK
☐ N46FD	85 PA-42 Cheyenne 400LS	5527027	Essex Air LLC. Essex, Ct.	HP-1341
☐ N46FL	95 King Air 350	FL-129	Texas Estrellas Inc. Tyler, Tx.	
☐ N46HA	77 Rockwell 690B	11381	William Greene, Elizabethton, Tn.	N81593
☐ N46HL	84 PA-42 Cheyenne 400LS	5527017	52HL LLC/Metro Corp. Philadelphia, Pa.	N410TW
☐ N46JK	73 King Air A100	B-154	White Skies Aviation LLC. Montgomery, Al.	N919WM
☐ N46JX	82 King Air F90	LA-171	Alyair LLC. Terrell, Tx.	N46JW
☐ N46KC	80 SA-226T Merlin 3B	T-332	John L Cox, Midland, Tx.	(N46KM)
☐ N46NA	70 SA-226T Merlin 3	T-206	Avtrend Inc. Miami, Fl.	N11RM
☐ N46PL	01 PA-46-500TP Meridian	4697054	Avco Leasing Inc. Wilmington, De.	D-FKAI
☐ N46PV	01 PA-46-500TP Meridian	4697046	Flying Machines LLC. Seattle, Wa.	
☐ N46RP	76 King Air E90	LW-193	Chrysalis Leasing LLC. Madison, Wi.	(N6410X)
☐ N46SA	73 SA-226T Merlin 3	T-231	Priority Air Inc. Terrytown, La.	N20QN
☐ N46TF	01 King Air B200	BB-1780	Trajen Inc. Bryan, Tx.	N4480Y
☐ N46WE	02 PA-46-500TP Meridian	4697134	Whelen Engineering Co. Chester, Ct.	
☐ N47AW	75 King Air E90	LW-104	LVNCS LLC. Madison, Wi.	N75KC
☐ N47BH	78 King Air E90	LW-275	James Hall & James Branton, San Antonio, Tx.	N4725M
☐ N47CA	79 PA-31T Cheyenne II	7920043	Westlog Inc/CAL-ORE Life Flight, Brookings, Or.	
☐ N47CK	71 681B Turbo Commander	6058	White Industries Inc. Bates City, Mo.	N4ME
☐ N47DG	82 King Air B200	BB-1040	Norsan Consulting & Management Inc. Tucker, Ga.	N27LJ
☐ N47EP	79 Rockwell 690B	11520	DBL Inc. Jupiter, Fl.	(N471HP)
☐ N47HM	67 680V Turbo Commander	1691-70	Cochise Community College, Douglas, Az.	N4585E
☐ N47JF	80 PA-31T Cheyenne II	8020031	Minnetrista Corp. Muncie, In.	N102AR
☐ N47JR	80 Conquest II	441-0160	Rusk Cattle Co. Austin, Tx.	D-IAAV
☐ N47LC	73 King Air E90	LW-64	Mercer Ranches, Prosser, Wa.	N213DS
☐ N47RM	03 King Air B200	BB-1820	V A Resources LLC. Casper, Wy.	N6020Z
☐ N47SW	83 King Air C90-1	LJ-1057	Interstate Mechanical Corp. Phoenix, Az.	N424TV
☐ N47TT	80 Gulfstream 840	11600	Leslie Farming, Miles City, Mt.	N840FC
☐ N48A	73 King Air C-12C	BC-12	K & K Aircraft Inc. Bridgewater, Va.	(N9TW)
☐ N48BA	81 Gulfstream 840	11665	Speciality Rentals Inc. Hammond, La. (status ?).	D-IWKW
Reg	Yr Type	c/n	Owner/Operator	Prev Regn

Reg	Yr	Type	c/n	Owner/Operator	Prev Regn
☐ N48BS	80 Conquest II		441-0125	The Brothers Signal Co. Leesburg, Va.	N375K
☐ N48CR	80 King Air 200		BB-599	West Texas Gas Inc. Midland, Tx.	
☐ N48CS	86 King Air B200		BB-1247	General Equipment & Manufacturing Co. Louisville, Ky.	N392DF
☐ N48GS	81 PA-42 Cheyenne III		8001028	The Grease Spot Inc. Kankakee, Il.	N52WA
☐ N48HH	79 SA-226T Merlin 3B		T-304	MAJA Co. Topeka, Ks.	F-GBOP
☐ N48NP	81 MU-2 Solitaire		447SA	Niles Chemical Paint Co. Niles, Mi.	(N348CP)
☐ N48PA	59 Gulfstream 1		18	Anthony Aiello, DuPage, Il.	N3UP
☐ N48PG	97 Pilatus PC-12/45		191	Devnick LLC. Oklahoma City, Ok.	(N242PM)
☐ N48RA	78 PA-42 Cheyenne III		7801004	David Whitt, Texarkana, Tx.	XA-RLW
☐ N48TA	78 King Air E90		LW-283	Tidewater Aero LLC & Stanton Aviation LLC. Norfolk, Va.	N845MC
☐ N48TE	77 King Air E90		LW-230	Group III Aviation Inc. Saginaw, Mi.	N48T
☐ N48W	78 King Air E90		LW-254	Platina Investment Corp. Wiley Post, Ok.	N22654
☐ N48XP	66 King Air 90		LJ-109	K & K Aircraft Inc. Bridgewater, Va.	N48N
☐ N49AC	80 PA-31T Cheyenne 1		8004021	James Cook III, Panama City, Fl.	N2317V
☐ N49B	81 PA-31T Cheyenne II		8120055	Grimans Air LLC. Wilmington, De.	N19BG
☐ N49CH	79 King Air F90		LA-2	Alternative Energy Inc. Bangor, Me.	N58AB
☐ N49CL	99 King Air 350		FL-268	The Jones Co. Waycross, Ga.	
☐ N49E	78 King Air B100		BE-47	American Bridge Co. Pittsburgh, Pa.	N4996M
☐ N49GM	83 Conquest 1		425-0165	Hans Kuen GmbH. Hard, Austria.	D-IRGW
☐ N49GN	68 King Air B90		LJ-381	Gemair Inc. Wilmington, De.	N48A
☐ N49H	80 SA-226T Merlin 3B		T-310	Howell Instruments Inc. Fort Worth, Tx.	N400FF
☐ N49JG	81 King Air B200		BB-884	Air VP Carter LLC/Mooney LLC. Louisville, Ky.	C-FLOR
☐ N49K	76 King Air C-12C		BD-26	Dynamic Aviation Group Inc. Bridgewater, Va.	76-0169
☐ N49KC	78 King Air 200		BB-318	Beech Transportation Inc. Eden Prairie, Mn.	
☐ N49LL	92 King Air C90B		LJ-1316	Davis Capital LLC. Edwards, Co.	N8114P
☐ N49LM	96 Pilatus PC-12		163	M L Morse LLC/Mikalix Aviation Group, Great Falls, Va.	HB-FRY
☐ N49NM	93 PA-31T Cheyenne II		7520006	IVO Inc. Ontario, Or.	N19NM
☐ N49PH	80 King Air F90		LA-33	King Aero LLC. Santa Rosa, Ca.	N90FL
☐ N49R	73 King Air C-12C		BD-2	Dynamic Aviation Group Inc. Bridgewater, Va.	N390SA
☐ N49SK	82 King Air B200		BB-1090	J & B Wood Enterprises LLC. Wilmington, De.	N54SK
☐ N49SS	78 King Air B100		BE-37	Cooper Container Corp. Maynardville, Tn.	N111XP
☐ N50AJ	79 King Air 200		BB-434	Lakeway Leasing Inc. Morristown, Tn.	N68AA
☐ N50AW	81 King Air F90		LA-142	Thoroughbred Aviation Ltd. Newark, De.	N1815T
☐ N50DX	74 Rockwell 690A		11227	Christopher Zupsic, Clovis, Or.	N131JN
☐ N50DY	82 King Air B200		BB-1061	Apex Aviation Corp. Napa, Ca.	N50DR
☐ N50EB	75 King Air E90		LW-128	FNB Investments LLC. Mesa, Az.	N1CB
☐ N50K	74 Mitsubishi MU-2K		305	M & P Enterprises Inc. White Plains, Md.	N465MA
☐ N50KG	82 King Air B200		BB-1066	Kenco Group, Chattanooga, Tn.	N356WG
☐ N50KV	68 SA-26AT Merlin 2B		T26-115	Southland Leasing Co. Inman, SC.	N1223S
☐ N50LG	80 SA-226T Merlin 3B		T-315	Air-1 Leasing LLC. Fort Scott, Ks.	N315DB
☐ N50MF	82 Conquest II		441-0262	CS Systems Inc. Irvine, Ca.	N489WC
☐ N50MT	79 SA-226T Merlin 3B		T-308	Worldwide Aircraft Services Inc. Springfield, Mo.	N900TX
☐ N50RV	80 King Air E90		LW-338	D W Davies Co. Racine, Wi.	(N199DW)
☐ N50ST	91 TBM 700		20	David Blakeslee, Marina del Rey, Ca.	N95BM
☐ N50VP	88 King Air C90A		LJ-1185	Comm-Craft Inc. Winfield, La.	N44GP
☐ N50WF	81 Gulfstream 840		11701	Northern Air Transport Inc. Mora, Mn.	N5953K
☐ N50WG	01 P-180 Avanti		1050	Crossbow 50 LLC. Carlsbad, Ca.	N134PA
☐ N51CU	83 Conquest 1		425-0171	Mercy Healthcare North, Redding, Ca.	D-IBBP
☐ N51DM	82 Gulfstream 1000		96014	Donald & E L Mashburn, Oklahoma City, Ok.	N9934S
☐ N51DN	72 King Air E90		LW-7	D-W Corp. Des Moines, Ia.	N51SG
☐ N51EE	80 King Air 200		BB-634	Bates & Associates Inc. Bainbridge, Ga.	N851MK
☐ N51FT	79 PA-31T Cheyenne 1		7904028	Forum Flyers LLC. Uvalde, Tx.	N5WC
☐ N51JK	81 PA-31T Cheyenne II		8120025	Triple J Aviation Ltd. Fort Collins, Co.	D-ICPA
☐ N51KC	80 PA-42 Cheyenne III		8001001	S A Comunale Co. Barbertown, Oh.	C-FWCC
☐ N51RD	78 PA-31T Cheyenne II		7820056	Nailen Investments Inc. Dothan, Al.	N4NH
☐ N51WF	81 Gulfstream 840		11684	ThyssenKrupp-Waupaca, Waupaca, Wi.	N5936K
☐ N52C	85 King Air 300		FA-40	Aristokraft Inc. Jasper, In.	N1MC
☐ N52CD	69 Mitsubishi MU-2F		174	Mike Chappell & Co LLC. Durham, NC.	C-FCCD
☐ N52EL	67 King Air A90		LJ-204	Allied Signal Corp. Fort Lauderdale, Fl.	N165U
☐ N52GP	81 King Air 200		BB-766	Global Industries Ltd. Sulphur, La.	N510H
☐ N52GT	78 King Air 200		BB-377	The Messenger Inc. Union City, Tn.	N41GT
☐ N52HL	80 PA-31T Cheyenne 1		8004023	4QC LLC/Metro Corp. Philadelphia, Pa.	N4QG
☐ N52KA	73 King Air E90		LW-42	Kenneth Rogers, Oklahoma City, Ok.	
☐ N52PF	79 PA-31T Cheyenne 1		7904023	Papa Fox LLC. Yuma, Az.	N52PC
☐ N52PY	74 Rockwell 690A		11196	Tumbleweed Corp. Lathrop, Ca.	N52PB
Reg	Yr	Type	c/n	Owner/Operator	Prev Regn

Reg	Yr	Type	c/n	Owner/Operator	Prev Regn
❏ N52SF	75 King Air 200		BB-106	SAK Aviation Inc. Pittsburgh, Pa.	N383AS
❏ N52SZ	99 King Air B200		BB-1686	Sheetz Aviation Inc. Altoona, Pa.	
❏ N52TT	79 PA-31T Cheyenne II		7920057	Minuteman Aviation Inc. Missoula, Mt.	N102E
❏ N53AM	79 PA-31T Cheyenne II		7920037	Collen Clark, Dallas, Tx.	N610MW
❏ N53CE	76 King Air E90		LW-160	Engineering & Manufacturing Services Inc. Huntsville, Al.	N251SR
❏ N53CK	78 King Air 200		BB-329	Causey Aviation Service Inc. Liberty, NC.	N311GA
❏ N53DA	82 SA-227TT Merlin 3C		TT-438	Nimbus Corp. Shaw Island, Wa.	(N312ST)
❏ N53EC	72 King Air C90		LJ-552	Leo Naeger, Fair Oaks Ranch, Tx.	VH-WNT
❏ N53GA	85 King Air B200		BB-1201	Selge Leasing Inc. Niles, Mi.	D-IMMM
❏ N53KA	81 King Air B200		BB-880	KAB 200 LLC. Atherton, Ca.	YV-1006CP
❏ N53MD	71 King Air 100		B-86	Lynch Flying Service Inc. Billings, Mt.	N500Y
❏ N53PB	02 King Air C90B		LJ-1678	Sun Realty of Nags Head Inc. Kill Devil Hills, NC.	N786P
❏ N53PE	87 King Air 300		FA-133	Platt Electric Supply Inc. Beaverton, Or.	N900GB
❏ N53PK	01 PA-46-500TP Meridian		4697093	Robert D Rash & Assocs Inc. Rowlett, Tx.	N249C
❏ N53RF	74 Rockwell 690A		11153	NO&AA/U S Department of Commerce, Minneapolis, Mn.	N57074
❏ N53RT	81 King Air 200		BB-808	Robert Tobin & Associates Inc. St Joseph, Mo.	N808EB
❏ N53TA	78 PA-31T Cheyenne II		7820083	Indiana Paging Network Inc. Michigan City, In.	N53TM
❏ N53TD	78 King Air B100		BE-53	Corporate Flight Inc. Detroit, Mi.	N2037C
❏ N53TJ	89 King Air C90A		LJ-1209	K K S Aviation Inc/Sky Trek Aviation, Modesto, Ca.	N3030C
❏ N53TM	97 King Air 350		FL-165	Katherine Meredith, Des Moines, Ia.	(N393CF)
❏ N54AM	97 King Air C90B		LJ-1506	Alice Manufacturing Co. Greenville, SC.	N988P
❏ N54CF	68 King Air B90		LJ-374	Greenair Corp. Memphis, Tn.	N32SV
❏ N54CK	68 Mitsubishi MU-2F		135	Kalitta Leasing LLC. Ypsilanti, Mi.	N66CL
❏ N54DA	84 PA-42 Cheyenne 400LS		5527006	EMI Flight Services Inc. Denver, Co.	N7MZ
❏ N54EC	71 King Air C90		LJ-526	Aircraft Sales Corp. Crystal Lake, Il.	ZS-MLO
❏ N54EZ	79 PA-31T Cheyenne 1		7904031	Air Success LLC. Fremont, Oh.	(N673BB)
❏ N54FB	85 King Air B200		BB-1212	Farm Bureau Life Insurance Co. Des Moines, Ia.	N7221Y
❏ N54GA	83 Gulfstream 1000		96066	Flight Asset Management Inc. Dallas, Tx.	
❏ N54GP	75 SA-226AT Merlin 4A		AT-034	Double EE Ranch Inc. Wilmington, De.	N717CC
❏ N54JW	70 King Air 100		B-60	Dodson Aviation Inc. Ottawa, Ks.	N2FA
❏ N54PC	75 Mitsubishi MU-2M		319	Saxton Leasing Inc. Plymouth, Mi.	N475CA
❏ N54PT	80 King Air E90		LW-331	PT Pope Ranch Inc. Portland, Or.	RP-C319
❏ N54UM	80 Gulfstream 980		95025	Trust Aviation Inc. Miami, Fl.	N9779S
❏ N54WW	67 King Air A90		LJ-209	Concrete Structures of the Midwest, Chicago, Il.	N90BE
❏ N54YC	90 King Air 300		FA-212	AirColor LLC. Wilmington, De.	N5070W
❏ N55AC	81 Conquest 1		425-0020	Rice Industries Inc. Wichita, Ks.	N200MT
❏ N55BK	96 Pilatus PC-12/45		160	JK Moving & Storage Inc. Sterling, Va.	N160PC
❏ N55CE	71 SA-226AT Merlin 4		AT-004	U S Army Corps of Engineers, Omaha, Ne.	
❏ N55EP	98 King Air C90B		LJ-1520	Generation 2000 LLC. Pahrump, Nv.	
❏ N55FY	67 King Air A90		LJ-194	APA Enterprises Inc. Poughkeepsie, NY.	N55FW
❏ N55GD	78 PA-31T Cheyenne II		7820003	Pro Air LLC. Manhattan, Ks.	N547TA
❏ N55HC	75 King Air E90		LW-134	MSK Aircraft LLC. Pearland, Tx.	N663LS
❏ N55HL	90 King Air B200		BB-1367	Air Fred LLC/Manufacturers Acceptance Corp. Fresno, Ca.	N67JB
❏ N55JS	74 Rockwell 690A		11195	The ServiCenter Inc. Bethany, Ok.	N690DD
❏ N55KW	81 PA-31T Cheyenne II		8120007	WTM Transport Management BV. Amstelveen, Holland.	N2369X
❏ N55MG	68 King Air B90		LJ-391	T & T Delaware Aviation LLC. Wilmington, De.	N22JJ
❏ N55MN	85 King Air C90		LJ-974	State of Minnesota DoT, St Paul, Mn.	N555RA
❏ N55MP	99 King Air B200		BB-1679	Maxon Corp. Muncie, In.	
❏ N55PC	84 King Air B200		BR-1170	CTEH Leasing LLC. Little Rock, Ar.	N6930P
❏ N55R	76 PA-31T Cheyenne II		7620055	Larry Risley, Farmington, NM.	N85KA
❏ N55WF	85 King Air C90A		LJ-1114	Perry Park Investments Inc. Larkspur, Co.	N808W
❏ N55WJ	77 Rockwell 690B		11427	Dogwood Aviation LLC. Alpharetta, Ga.	N46802
❏ N55ZG	01 PA-46-500TP Meridian		4697082	Highlands Aviation LLC. Aspen, Co.	N262TL
❏ N56AP	81 King Air B200		BB-882	Dove Leasing LLC. Wilmington, De.	N56AY
❏ N56AY	95 King Air B200		BB-1511	A Y McDonald Industries Inc. Dubuque, Ia.	N507EF
❏ N56CC	77 King Air 200		BB-189	AGEV Air Inc. Lafayette, La.	N392K
❏ N56CD*	75 King Air 200		BB-64	Commander Inc. Lyon, Ms.	N608DK
❏ N56DA	79 King Air 200		BB-486	Robert C Hayes, Concord, NC.	N56RA
❏ N56DL	77 King Air C90		LJ-732	Southwind Air Inc. Memphis, Tn.	N473LP
❏ N56EZ	03 Pilatus PC-12/45		488	Devco-Air SP.z.o.o. Warsaw, Poland.	(SP-KEZ)
❏ N56HT	77 King Air E90		LW-215	Pritchard Transportation LLC. Pascagoula, Ms.	I-MCCC
❏ N56KA	81 King Air 200		BB-763	Vigil Aviation LLC. Concord, NC.	N50PM
❏ N56RT	81 King Air 200		BB-817	Rust Family LLC. Albuquerque, NM.	
❏ N56WF	91 TBM 700		8	Zero Five Kilo Corp. Nashua, NH.	JA8892
❏ N57AG	68 King Air B90		LJ-343	Patricia Williams, Fitzgerald, Ga.	N880X
Reg	*Yr*	*Type*	*c/n*	*Owner/Operator*	*Prev Regn*

Reg	Yr Type	c/n	Owner/Operator	Prev Regn
❏ N57EC	74 Rockwell 690A	11178	Joe Walravenl, Eastland, Tx.	N124SB
❏ N57EM	67 King Air A90	LJ-295	Richard Harvey, Tyler, Tx.	N57FM
❏ N57GA	79 King Air 200	BB-477	G & A Aviation LLC. Greenwood, SC.	F-GILB
❏ N57HQ	92 TBM 700	90	B H Sports Marketing & Aviation Inc. Bear, De.	N57HC
❏ N57KE	91 King Air 350	FL-61	Eberl's Management LLC. Lakewood, Co.	N350CS
❏ N57LT	02 Pilatus PC-12/45	474	Lexington Turbo LLC. Lexington, Ma.	HB-FQE
❏ N57MA	68 King Air B90	LJ-414	Thomas Howell Kiewit (USA) Inc. Miami, Fl. (stolen 6/92).	C-GVCC
❏ N57MR	76 PA-31T Cheyenne II	7620022	Republic Investment Group LLC. Windham, NH.	N57MK
❏ N57RS	74 Rockwell 690A	11149	International Steel & Tube SA. Santo Domingo, D R.	N5KW
❏ N57SC	90 King Air 350	FL-34	HRB Systems Inc. State College, Pa.	N987HT
❏ N57SL	92 TBM 700	57	U S Financial Services Inc. Wilmington, De.	
❏ N57TJ	80 King Air B100	BE-102	Sky High LLC. Missoula, Mt.	(N91L)
❏ N57TM	80 King Air F90	LA-34	A T T Aviation Inc. Lafayette, La.	N43WS
❏ N57TX	98 King Air 350	FL-225	Spence Enterprises, Eldorado Hills, Ca.	N57TS
❏ N57VA	96 King Air 350	FL-154	Venture Services of Kentucky Inc. Chattanooga, Tn.	N160AR
❏ N58AC	65 King Air 90	LJ-77	Sunny South Inc. Gainesville, Fl.	N56SQ
❏ N58AM	84 PA-31T Cheyenne 1A	1104005	Air Medical Ltd. New Braunfels, Tx.	N2427W
❏ N58AS	82 King Air B200C	BL-50	Aviation Specialities Inc. Washington, DC.	N54HF
❏ N58CA	69 Mitsubishi MU-2F	170	F J Grieser Co. Miami, Fl.	N239MA
❏ N58ES	84 King Air 300	FA-17	Penn Leasing Ltd. Muskegon, Mi.	N71FA
❏ N58EZ	81 King Air F90	LA-97	Avico Partners/Wilshire Capital Holdings LLC. Columbia, SC.	N371CP
❏ N58GA	82 King Air B200	BB-1003	Legal Eagle Associates Inc. Hattiesburg, Ms.	I-MEPE
❏ N58HP	00 TBM 700B	170	Hartzell Propeller Inc. Piqua, Oh.	
❏ N58KA	65 King Air 90	LJ-58	Leonard Sallustro, Throgg Station, NY.	C-GXHD
❏ N58PL	81 Cheyenne II-XL	8166024	Exec Air Montana Inc. Helena, Mt.	N2586Y
❏ N58VS	00 Pilatus PC-12/45	341	DMH Inc. Forest Grove, Or.	HB-FRW
❏ N59EK	80 King Air F90	LA-58	Air Cosbar LLC. Aspen, Co.	N67TM
❏ N59EZ	81 SA-226T Merlin 3B	T-394	Financial Southern Corp. Wilmington, De.	N1QL
❏ N59KA	73 King Air C90	LJ-589	American Furniture Inc. Albuquerque, NM.	
❏ N59KS	75 Mitsubishi MU-2L	664	O'Connell Meares Investments Ltd. Tampa, Fl.	N555BC
❏ N59MS	95 King Air C90B	LJ-1405	Snijder Air Service Inc. Antwerp, Belgium.	
❏ N59RT	79 Conquest II	441-0111	WFBNW NA. Salt Lake City, Ut.	N462AC
❏ N59RW	73 Mitsubishi MU-2K	267	D O Aviation Inc. Indianapolis, In.	N313MA
❏ N59WF	01 PA-46-500TP Meridian	4697042	Pyxis LLC. Wilmington, De.	
❏ N60AA	83 King Air B200	BB-1099	Crown Aircraft Investments Inc. Boca Raton, Fl.	(N160TT)
❏ N60AR	00 King Air B200	BB-1743	Arrow Med Tech LLC. Reading, Pa.	N4443V
❏ N60AZ	75 Mitsubishi MU-2M	329	Air 1st Aviation Companies Inc. Aiken, SC.	N35VS
❏ N60B	74 Rockwell 690A	11172	Interlease Aviation Corp. Northfield, Il.	(D-IIGI)
❏ N60BA	74 King Air E90	LW-79	Bemidji Aviation Services Inc. Bemidji, Mn.	N12AK
❏ N60CM	96 King Air 350	FL-139	Mewbourne Oil Co. Tyler, Tx.	
❏ N60DB	77 Rockwell 690B	11420	H T Haralambos, Rolling Hills, Ca.	N813AW
❏ N60FL	81 MU-2 Marquise	1512SA	Flight Line Inc. Denver, Co.	HB-LQB
❏ N60JW	80 PA-31T Cheyenne 1	8004031	Southern Tank Leasing Inc. Demopalis, Al.	N2349V
❏ N60KA	73 King Air C90	LJ-586	Caribe Air LLC. Wilmington, De.	
❏ N60KC	80 MU-2 Marquise	781SA	Keller Companies Inc. Manchester, NH.	N7045X
❏ N60KW	78 King Air C90	LJ-800	Robert James, Fallbrook, Ca.	N2032N
❏ N60MH	78 King Air E90	LW-290	Commercial Aviation Services Inc. Miami, Fl.	N79NS
❏ N60NB	81 MU-2 Marquise	1528SA	Dogfox Airways Inc. Wilmington, De.	5Y-BIZ
❏ N60PD	75 King Air 200	BB-58	CWW Inc. Englewood, Co.	N60PC
❏ N60TJ	77 King Air B100	BE-21	ARK Leasing Inc. Newport Beach, Ca.	N17821
❏ N60TR	81 Conquest II	441-0203	Frank Ford Smith Jr. Austin, Tx.	N441Z
❏ N60VP	97 King Air C90B	LJ-1516	Sonic Angel Air Inc. Daphene, Al.	
❏ N60WA	81 PA-31T Cheyenne II	8120013	Arturo Ortega, William Island, Fl. USA.	YV-1995B
❏ N60YP	00 King Air 350	FL-304	Yates Petroleum Corp. Artesia, NM.	N44866
❏ N61AP	84 King Air B200	BB-1192	James McMahan, Van Nuys, Ca.	N6743D
❏ N61BA	78 Mitsubishi MU-2N	729SA	B & H Air LLC. Victoria, Tx.	C-FHXZ
❏ N61GJ	79 MU-2 Solitaire	398SA	Craig Sjoberg & Assocs Inc. Pleasanton, Ca.	N61DP
❏ N61GN	95 King Air C90B	LJ-1421	N61GN LLC. Chattanogga, Tn.	N3252B
❏ N61GT	01 P-180 Avanti	1051	IGT-International Game Technology, Reno, Nv.	N129PA
❏ N61HA	95 Beech 1900D	UE-175	Wachovia Bank of Georgia NA. Atlanta, Ga.	N995WS
❏ N61HT	68 King Air B90	LJ-358	King Aire Inc. Charleston, WV.	N934LD
❏ N61JB	80 MU-2 Solitaire	417SA	Pro Flight LLC. Greenville, SC.	N29JS
❏ N61KA	89 King Air 300LW	FA-200	SDT Leasing LLC. Grants Pass, Or.	OY-CCZ
❏ N61Q	66 King Air A90	LM-92	Dynamic Aviation, Bridgewater, Va.	N7123C
❏ N61SB	63 Gulfstream 1	115	Apex Aviation Group Inc. Southlake, Tx.	C-FASC
Reg	**Yr Type**	**c/n**	**Owner/Operator**	**Prev Regn**

Reg	Yr	Type	c/n	Owner/Operator	Prev Regn
N62BL	78	King Air E90	LW-272	Robert Landry, Jonesboro, Ar.	(N301HC)
N62DL	77	King Air 200	BB-208	ZMM Services LLC. Tampa, Fl.	N188WG
N62E	80	PA-31T Cheyenne II	8020074	Star Air LLC/AGT Enterprises Inc. Prairie du Chien, Wi.	(N47DR)
N62FB	94	King Air B200	BB-1482	Texas Farm Bureau Building Corp. Waco, Tx.	N77CX
N62LM	92	TBM 700	67	Primus Leasing Corp. Wilmington, De.	
N62LT	01	PA-46-500TP Meridian	4697027	Dana Hunter, Lake Havasu City, Az.	
N62SK	78	King Air C90	LJ-784	VIM Inc. Fayetteville, WV.	YV-254CP
N62WC	89	King Air B200	BB-1326	West Coast Charters LLC. Santa Ana, Ca.	N38LA
N62WM	04	PA-46-500TP Meridian	4697177	H & M Bay Inc. Federalsburg, Md.	
N63BV	78	King Air E90	LW-256	Mayo Aviation Inc. Englewood, Co.	N63BW
N63CA	78	PA-31T Cheyenne II	7820033	Speciality Industries, Red Lion, Pa.	OO-DGS
N63CM	80	PA-31T Cheyenne II	8020039	YT Timber Inc. Boise, Id.	N2584W
N63DL	80	Gulfstream 840	11601	Larry Lehmkuhl, Placida, Fl.	N840CM
N63LP	84	King Air 300	FA-18	JMC Aviation LLC. Scottsdale, Az.	N63LB
N63SK	80	King Air 200	BB-747	IED-Innovative Electronic Designs, Louisville, Ky.	N117CM
N63TP	97	TBM 700	128	Hot Air LLC. Cambridge, Ma.	N128PC
N64C*	66	King Air A90	LM-32	Dynamic Aviation Group Inc. Bridgewater, Va.	
N64DC	79	King Air 200	BB-492	Pontiac Flight Service Inc. Waterford, Mi.	N200PD
N64GA	81	King Air 200	BB-790	Den Beste Transportation Inc. Windsor, Ca.	D-IAMB
N64GG	99	King Air 350	FL-274	Specsavers Aviation Ltd. Guernsey, C.I.	(N350GL)
N64KA	73	King Air C90	LJ-606	ABC Aviation LLC. Magnolia, Ms.	
N64LG	72	Mitsubishi MU-2K	240	H D Murphy & Assocs Inc. Wellman, Ia.	N222HL
N64MD	82	MU-2 Marquise	1561SA	Marquise Investments LLC. Memphis, Tn.	N486MA
N64PS	81	Gulfstream 840	11702	Peter Schiff, Cookeville, Tn.	N5954K
N64WF	99	Pilatus PC-12/45	298	PC-12 LLC. Frankfort, Ky.	HB-FQM
N65AF	04	Pilatus PC-12/45	565	Angel Fire Express LLC. Angel Fire, NM.	HB-FSM
N65CL	92	King Air C90B	LJ-1306	Coastal Lumber Co. Weldon, NC.	N422RJ
N65EB	78	King Air 200	BB-325	Clement Aviation Inc. Fort Dodge, Ia.	F-GGAK
N65EZ	84	PA-31T Cheyenne 1A	1104013	Hotel Charlie LLC. Wilmington, De.	N20MR
N65GP	92	King Air C90B	LJ-1320	Triangle Air Corp. San Juan, PR.	N8119N
N65JA	66	King Air A90	LM-34	JAARS Inc. Waxhaw, NC.	N7042R
N65JG	81	MU-2 Marquise	1523SA	Copper Beach Development Inc. Wilmington, De.	N439MA
N65KA	74	King Air C90	LJ-611	Vernon Johnson, Bailey, NC.	
N65KG	84	PA-31T Cheyenne 1A	1104017	Kevin Glasheen, Wolfforth, Tx.	EC-HCQ
N65MT	80	King Air F90	LA-34	Hendricks Aviation Inc. Troy, Al.	D-IAGB
N65RT	76	King Air 200	BB-97	Professional Travel Inc. La Porte, In.	N7EG
N65TA	72	King Air C90	LJ-538	Grove Aviation LLC. Gulfport, Ms.	VH-LLS
N65TB	99	Pilatus PC-12/45	263	Dalks Leasing Inc. Wilmington, De.	N329PA
N65TW	81	King Air B200	BB-902	Seven Bar Flying Service Inc. Albuquerque, NM.	N5TW
N65U*	67	King Air A90	LM-87	Dynamic Aviation Group Inc. Bridgewater, Va.	
N65V*	66	King Air A90	LM-113	Dynamic Aviation Group Inc. Bridgewater, Va.	
N66	87	King Air 300	FF-1	FAA, Oklahoma City, Ok. (was FA-126).	
N66AD	68	King Air B90	LJ-380	Freefall Express Inc. Keene, NH.	C-GHLA
N66BS	80	King Air F90	LA-40	Simmons Inc of Virginia, Bristol, Va.	N6748P
N66BZ	83	Conquest II	441-0306	Wiley Equipment Leasing LLC. Wilmington, De.	(N441DM)
N66CK	98	King Air C90B	LJ-1529	Carson & Co. Bon Secour, Al.	
N66CY	72	Mitsubishi MU-2J	562	AJM Airplane Co. Naples, Fl.	N29CY
N66FF	80	MU-2 Solitaire	430SA	Econo-Air Inc. Middletown, NY.	N856JC
N66FV	67	680V Turbo Commander	1676-59	Valley International Airport, Harlingen, Tx.	N580M
N66GS	67	King Air A90	LJ-237	Mile-Hi Skydivers Inc. Longmont, Co.	N232A
N66GW	74	Rockwell 690A	11174	Resource 21 LLC. Englewood, Co.	N6B
N66JC	81	Cheyenne II-XL	8166029	G & T Partners LLC. Gainesville, Ga.	N346JC
N66KA	73	King Air C90	LJ-582	National Flight Services Inc. Swanton, Oh.	
N66LM	83	King Air B200	BB-1158	LMC Leasing Inc/Latt Maxcy Corp. Frostproof, Fl.	N419TW
N66LP	80	King Air F90	LA-21	Peterson Farms Inc. Decatur, Il.	
N66MD	69	SA-26AT Merlin 2B	T26-159	Donald Paolucci/Mohican Air Service Inc. Fairview Park, Oh.	N14JK
N66MF	84	PA-42 Cheyenne IIIA	5501009	MTW Aerospace Inc. Montgomery, Al.	N66MT
N66RE	67	King Air A90	LJ-307	Bear Air Inc. Campbell, Ca.	N966CY
N66TJ	75	King Air 200	BB-42	Tyler Jet LLC. Tyler, Tx.	N3GY
N66TL	84	King Air C90	LJ-636	Skycorp Executive Charters Inc. Everett, Wa.	N222BJ
N66TW	80	PA-31T Cheyenne 1	8004030	Marine Transportation Services Inc. Houston, Tx.	N2347V
N67	87	King Air 300	FF-2	FAA, Oklahoma City, Ok. (was FA-129).	
N67BA	81	Conquest 1	425-0007	IMIC Aviation Inc. Columbia, SC.	C-GJEB
N67BS	81	King Air B100	BE-104	Team Health Inc. Knoxville, Tn.	N67KA
N67BW	01	PA-46-500TP Meridian	4697011	New Piper Aircraft Inc. Vero Beach, Fl.	
Reg	Yr	Type	c/n	Owner/Operator	Prev Regn

Reg	Yr	Type	c/n	Owner/Operator	Prev Regn
N67CC	00	King Air C90	LJ-1619	David Auth, Hobe Sound, Fl.	N90VF
N67CG	79	Rockwell 690B	11540	ESI Inc of Tennessee, Kennesaw, Ga.	N81697
N67CL	87	King Air C90A	LJ-1154	Coastal Lumber Co. Weldon, NC.	N3076U
N67FE	82	Gulfstream 840	11729	Furnas Electric Co. Sugar Grove, Il.	N5967K
N67GA	76	King Air 200	BB-176	Aviation Advisors International Inc. Sarasota, Fl.	F-GFMJ
N67JE	81	Conquest 1	425-0058	John & Colleen Gerken, Sandpoint, Id.	N67CA
N67JG	81	PA-31T Cheyenne II	8120052	Hans-Juergen Guido, Regensburg, Germany.	D-IFGN
N67K	66	King Air A90	LM-24	Dynamic Aviation Group Inc. Bridgewater, Va.	N7035B
N67PD	81	Cheyenne II-XL	8166033	High Country Investments Inc. Bend, Or.	N42NE
N67PL	72	King Air C90	LJ-566	Driscoll Aviation Inc. Fort Lauderdale, Fl.	N67PC
N67PS	74	King Air E90	LW-112	Timberland Aviation Inc. Eufaula, Al.	N3034W
N67SD	89	King Air B200	BB-1327	Pratt Street Aviation LLC/AM AV Inc. Baltimore, Md.	(N204BF)
N67SM	70	Mitsubishi MU-2F	183	Turbine Aircraft Parts Inc. San Angelo, Tx.	N221KP
N67TC	74	Rockwell 690A	11233	MBH Services Ltd. Southend, UK.	HR-AAJ
N67V	79	King Air E90	LW-309	Quality Plus Inc. Omaha, Ne.	N90SR
N67X	66	King Air A90	LM-14	Dynamic AvLease Inc. Bridgewater, Va.	N70224
N68	87	King Air 300	FF-3	FAA, Oklahoma City, Ok.	
N68AJ	84	King Air C90A	LJ-1071	W Hampton Pitts, Nashville, Tn.	ZS-LOK
N68AM	82	King Air F90	LA-172	Avondale Mills Inc. Monroe, Ga.	(N808DS)
N68BJ	79	PA-31T Cheyenne II	7920029	Arrow Leasing Ltd. Norwood, Ma.	TG-VDG
N68CD	68	King Air B90	LJ-366	Pacific Coast Enterprises LLC. Las Vegas, Nv.	N66CD
N68CL	81	MU-2 Solitaire	448SA	Robert & Cynthia Peterson Living Trust, Harrodsburg, Ky.	N231LC
N68DA	76	King Air B100	BE-14	Dominion Air Leasing Inc. Richmond, Va.	N86FD
N68DK	80	King Air F90	LA-56	Rogue Aviation LLC. Grants Pass, Or.	N777AQ
N68FA	82	King Air B200	BB-1088	Hoar Construction LLC. Birmingham, Al.	N868HC
N68FB	00	King Air B200	BB-1710	FBL Leasing Services Inc. Des Moines, Ia.	C6-MIP
N68HS	84	Conquest II	441-0331	Hastings Books, Music & Video, Amarillo, Tx.	N1210D
N68MN	00	King Air B200	BB-1704	Green King Inc. Wilmington, De.	N3204W
N68MT	81	Cheyenne II-XL	8166060	Stokes & O'Steen LLC. Jacksonville, Fl.	N66MT
N68MY	83	King Air B200	BB-1142	Myco Industries Inc. Artesia, NM.	N23YP
N68PK	99	Pilatus PC-12/45	265	Knight Flight LLC. Wilmington, De.	HB-FSJ
N68PM	76	King Air E90	LW-188	Benchmark Aviation LLC. Baton Rouge, La.	N16TE
N68TD	73	Rockwell 690	11066	Wells & West Inc. Murphy, NC.	N36WR
N68TN	75	Mitsubishi MU-2L	675	Air 1st Aviation Companies Inc. Aiken, SC.	N835MA
N68VH	70	681 Turbo Commander	6007	Forte Management Corp. Cincinnati, Oh.	LV-JOJ
N69	88	King Air 300	FF-4	FAA, Oklahoma City, Ok.	
N69AD	81	King Air F90	LA-143	Zulu Golf Aviation LLC. Aspen, Co.	N624LF
N69CD	76	King Air 200	BB-156	Glady's Enterprises Inc. El Paso, Tx.	N69LD
N69FG	98	Pilatus PC-12/45	225	R J Aviation Equipment Inc. Wilmington, De.	HB-FQW
N69GA	84	Gulfstream 1000	96071	Kudu Aviation Inc. Fort Lauderdale, Fl.	
N69LS	03	King Air B200	BB-1841	Universal Aviation LLC. Fort Lauderdale, Fl.	N6191N
N69PC	81	PA-42 Cheyenne III	8001023	Cheyenne III Inc. Gainesville, Ga.	N5PF
N69ST	74	SA-226AT Merlin 4A	AT-030	OM Enterprise Inc. Michigan City, In.	N5440F
N70	88	King Air 300	FF-5	FAA, Oklahoma City, Ok.	
N70AB	77	King Air C90	LJ-712	Turbo Air Inc. Boise, Id.	C-GUNG
N70AJ	77	King Air 200	BB-206	Aspen Medical Consultants/Marketing, Phoenix, Az.	(N30AJ)
N70CM	01	King Air C90B	LJ-1670	TPW Aviation LLC. Cedartown, Ga.	N4470K
N70CU	81	King Air B200	BB-888	Corair of Delaware LLC. Louisville, Ky.	N700U
N70FC	73	SA-226T Merlin 3	T-226	William D Fisher Enterprises LLC. Richmond, In.	N41BA
N70GM	82	Conquest 1	425-0108	Alpha Delta Aviation Inc. Van Buren, Ar.	D-IAAX
N70GW	81	PA-31T Cheyenne 1	8104004	Minion Morgans Inc. Oxford, Mi.	N4WP
N70JL	71	King Air 100	B-87	Aeroflite Inc. Marion, Il.	N125DB
N70KC	80	MU-2 Marquise	775SA	Keller Companies Inc. Manchester, NH.	N93GN
N70LG	83	King Air B200C	BL-67	Bombardier Capital Inc. Colchester, Vt.	TR-LBP
N70LT	99	TBM 700B	151	Woodstock Aviation Inc. Santa Rosa, Ca.	(N950WA)
N70MD	74	Rockwell 690A	11210	Briteway Carstar Collision Center, Bend, Or.	N1SS
N70MN	93	King Air B200	BB-1447	State of Minnesota DoT, St Paul, Mn.	N8138V
N70MV	73	King Air E90	LW-48	Zamaga inc. Bethesda, Md.	OK-DKH
N70RB	79	King Air 200	BB-603	Bell Construction Co. Brentwood, Tn.	N91TR
N70RD	79	King Air 200	BB-426	Jennings Osborne, Little Rock, Ar.	N220CB
N70RF	70	681 Turbo Commander	6013	E M Travels & Sales Inc. Opa Locka, Fl.	N60BC
N70SW	74	King Air E90	LW-101	Yankee Flying Ltd. Salinas, Ca.	N111PC
N70TJ	79	PA-31T Cheyenne 1	7904019	J H Leasing Inc. Wilmington, De.	N506TQ
N70TW	79	PA-31T Cheyenne 1	7904043	Bob Ewing, Jasper, Tx.	
N70U	66	King Air A90	LM-51	Dynamic AvLease Inc. Bridgewater, Va.	N7063W
Reg	**Yr**	**Type**	**c/n**	**Owner/Operator**	**Prev Regn**

Reg	Yr	Type	c/n	Owner/Operator	Prev Regn
N70VM	67 King Air A90	LJ-300	Texas Biz Jet, Fort Worth, Tx.	N222MB
N70VR	01 King Air C90B	LJ-1651	TSI Leasing Inc-Valley Research, South Bend, In.	
N71	88 King Air 300	FF-6	FAA, Oklahoma City, Ok.	
N71BX	74 King Air E90	LW-74	J-Law Aviation LLC. Fayetteville, NC.	N713X
N71DP	81 MU-2 Marquise	1502SA	Jaax Flying Service/Marquise Investments LLC. Calexico, Ca.	VH-MVU
N71EE	01 TBM 700B	192	Lincoln Aviation Inc. Rodelillo, Chile.	F-WWRJ
N71EN	74 King Air C90	LJ-632	Premier West Bancorp. Medford, Or.	N71FN
N71HE	81 Conquest 1	425-0085	Codding Investments Inc. Santa Rosa, Ca.	N5HE
N71KA	73 King Air C90	LJ-578	David & Catherine Paine, Templeton, Ca.	N84JH
N71MR	83 Gulfstream 1000	96054	Boomerang Financial Corp. Wilmington, De.	N8LB
N71RD	69 Gulfstream 1	322	Saican Air (SA) Inc. Wonderboom, RSA.	N9QM
N71TP	00 Pilatus PC-12/45	371	Ted Lamb Co. Prescott, Az.	HBFSU
N71VE	72 Rockwell 690	11043	Cooper Aerial Surveys Ltd. Sandtoft, UK.	N71VT
N71VG	91 King Air C90A	LJ-1279	Flightcraft Inc. Portland, Or.	(N904MK)
N71VT	80 King Air 200	BB-709	Virginia Polytechnic Institute & State University.	(N202VT)
N71WB	75 King Air E90	LW-127	Air Charter Express Inc. High Ridge, Mo.	N711RQ
N72	88 King Air 300	FF-7	FAA, Oklahoma City, Ok.	
N72CF	69 SA-26AT Merlin 2B	T26-132	Tinnon Real Estate Holdings LLC. henton, Ar.	N425MC
N72DK	85 King Air 300	FA-42	First National Bank Group, McAllen, Tx.	N791X
N72EE	04 P-180 Avanti	1074	Lincoln Aviation Inc, Rodelillo, Chile.	
N72GA	85 King Air 300	FA-72	Line Power Manufacturing Co. Bristol, Va.	(N82LP)
N72MM	79 King Air 200	BB-497	Northeastern Aviation Corp. Wilmington, De.	N73CA
N72PK	96 King Air C90B	LJ-1449	Keith Thompson Aviation LLC. Atlanta, Ga.	
N72RE	02 King Air 350	FL-344	816 Charter LLC. Houston, Tx.	N5044B
N72RL	79 King Air 200	BB-509	Waypoint LLC. Danbury, Ct.	N72DD
N72SE	80 King Air 200	BB-596	Southern Energy Homes Inc. Addison, Al.	N918JN
N72TB	80 Gulfstream 840	11619	WFBNW NA. Salt Lake City, Ut. (trustor ?).	N16TG
N72TG	90 King Air C90A	LJ-1252	Tom Growney Equipment Inc. Albuquerque, NM.	N92CD
N73	88 King Air 300	FF-8	FAA, Oklahoma City, Ok.	
N73BG	80 PA-31T Cheyenne 1	8004027	R W Air Services Inc. Hatfield, Pa.	(N701GP)
N73DW	81 Conquest 1	425-0089	Bell Aviation Inc. West Columbia, SC.	N74JW
N73EF	80 Gulfstream 840	11617	Executive Flight Inc. Pangborn Memorial, Wa.	N840LC
N73HC	69 SA-26AT Merlin 2B	T26-138	H-1 Syatems Inc/Midwest Air Charter, Washington, In.	N52L
N73MA	79 MU-2 Solitaire	414SA	Anaconda Aviation Corp. Boca Raton, Fl.	N72TJ
N73MC	73 King Air C90	LJ-600	Hamer-Senter Aircraft LLC. Fort Worth, Tx.	N3PR
N73MW	75 King Air 200	BB-22	Royal Palm Airlease Inc. Deerfield Beach, Fl.	N7300R
N73PG	00 King Air C90B	LJ-1607	BR Aircraft LLC. Sacramento, Ca.	N782P
N73YP	01 PA-46-500TP Meridian	4697080	Mid-America Freightways Inc. Evergreen, Co.	
N74	88 King Air 300	FF-9	FAA, Oklahoma City, Ok.	
N74AW	85 King Air B200	BB-1233	Southern Securities Ltd. Greensboro, NC.	N887T
N74AX	96 Pilatus PC-12	149	Concepts Aviation Inc. Wilmington, De.	N15TP
N74B	02 King Air C90B	LJ-1680	Centennial Air Transport LLC. Newport News, Va.	N790W
N74BY	77 Conquest II	441-0039	Calvert Aviation Corp. Cockeysville, Md.	N36972
N74EF	80 Gulfstream 840	11614	Harborview Medical Center, Seattle, Wa.	N74RF
N74GB	74 Rockwell 690A	11206	Color Fast Industries Inc. Colton, Ca.	N75RR
N74GS	83 King Air B200	BB-1135	Krohn Air Services Ltd. Springfield, Oh.	N399LA
N74JV	71 King Air 100	B-74	Vernon Sorenson MD. Bakersfield, Ca.	N3500E
N74LV	82 King Air B200	BB-1074	Cx USA 2/94 to ?	C-GTDX
N74ML	83 King Air B200	BB-1123	Miller Livestock Co. Bakersfield, Ca.	(N282TA)
N74RG	99 King Air B200	BB-1651	Kansas City Royals Baseball Corp. Kansas City, Mo.	N32434
N74RR	81 King Air B100	BE-122	Mansfield Oil Co & Onyx Petroleum Inc. Gainesville, Ga.	XB-ESH
N74TF	03 King Air 350	FL-370	Tripifoods Inc. Buffalo, NY.	N6170D
N74TW	79 PA-31T Cheyenne II	7920067	I R Investments OCFI, Sebastian, Fl.	(N4301L)
N75	88 King Air 300	FF-10	FAA, Oklahoma City, Ok.	
N75AH	80 King Air 200	BB-741	Air Holdings Inc. Helena, Mt.	N80GS
N75AP	79 King Air B100	BE-57	HP Aviation LLC. Canton, Oh.	N57AK
N75AW	81 PA-42 Cheyenne III	8001046	Andrew & Williamson Sales Co. San Diego, Ca.	N148CA
N75FL	83 PA-42 Cheyenne IIIA	8301002	Mustang Enterprises Co. Santa Fe, NM.	(N830AM)
N75GR	75 King Air A100	B-210	Silverhawk Aviation Inc. Lincoln, Ne.	N75ZZ
N75HW	85 Conquest 1	425-0232	G & W Air Inc. Middletown, Oh.	N50JN
N75JP	76 King Air E90	LW-158	Prior Aviation Service Inc. Buffalo, NY.	N940SR
N75LA	71 King Air 100	B-75	Luis Arturo Alvardo, Miami, Fl.	C-FCSD
N75LS	84 PA-42 Cheyenne IIIA	5501017	Freeman Decorating Co. Dallas, Tx.	N4118H
N75LV	82 King Air B200	BB-1075	Cook-Fort Worth Children's Medical Center, Fort Worth, Tx.	C-GTDY
N75LW	74 King Air E90	LW-75	Loronix Information Systems Inc. Durango, Co.	XB-AEU

Reg	Yr	Type	c/n	Owner/Operator	Prev Regn
N75ME	85	King Air 300	FA-57	Golden Rule Financial Corp. Indianapolis, In.	N75MC
N75MS	83	King Air F90-1	LA-204	Dodson International Parts Inc. Ottawa, Ks.	XA-PEM
N75MX	71	SA-226T Merlin 3	T-218	Flight Research, Hattiesburg, Ms.	N990M
N75PG	95	King Air C90B	LJ-1390	Dasch Air LLC. Walnut Creek, Ca.	N3237K
N75RM	78	SA-226T Merlin 3A	T-290	Riverside Manufacturing Co. Moultrie, Ga.	N5450M
N75RS	71	King Air C90	LJ-533	C C Services of Nevada Inc. Clearwater, Fl.	N739K
N75TF	78	PA-31T Cheyenne II	7820075	High Air Inc. Plano, Tx.	N781CW
N75TW	80	PA-31T Cheyenne 1	8004016	NCMC Inc. Greeley, Co.	
N75U	74	Rockwell 690A	11218	Alan Huggins, Gilroy, Ca.	N690TP
N75V	66	King Air A90	LM-103	Dynamic Aviation Group Inc. Bridgewater, Va.	N7143Y
N75WA	81	PA-31T Cheyenne 1	8104101	Robinette Aviation LLC. Bristol, Tn.	D-IASW
N75WD	91	King Air 350	FL-51	MSI Aviation LLC. Maitland, Fl.	N8055J
N75X	82	SA-227TT Merlin 3C	TT-421	D & S Inc. Irving, Tx.	N1014B
N75ZT	82	King Air B200	BB-967	Behlen Manufacturing Co. Columbus, Ne.	N75Z
N76	88	King Air 300	FF-11	FAA, Oklahoma City, Ok.	
N76EC	74	Rockwell 690A	11208	North American Financial Inc. Hayward, Ca.	N74RR
N76HH	81	Gulfstream 980	95076	Eagle Air Inc. Memphis, Tn.	N9828S
N76HM	81	King Air 200C	BL-17	H & M Rentals, Iowa City, Ia.	5Y-JMR
N76MG	01	PA-46-500TP Meridian	4697056	Monroe Motors Inc. Colorado Springs, Co.	
N76PM	98	King Air 350	FL-200	Pine Street Associates LLC. Monroe, La.	N2122M
N76Q	66	King Air A90	LM-15	Dynamic AvLease Inc. Bridgewater, Va.	N7026H
N76SK	74	King Air E90	LW-115	Malouf Aero LLC. Greenwood, Ms.	N37MC
N76WA	76	Rockwell 690A	11342	Avilon Inc. Colorado Springs, Co.	XA-RPD
N77	88	King Air 300	FF-12	FAA, Oklahoma City, Ok.	
N77CA	80	King Air 200	BB-717	Frances Christmann, Pinedale, NY.	
N77CV	98	King Air B200	BB-1625	Pennsylvania State University, University Park, Pa.	
N77DA	66	King Air A90	LJ-146	Nebo Chevrolet, Dardanelle, Ar.	N49EL
N77DK	81	MU-2 Solitaire	449SA	Daniel Knopper, West Bloomfield, Mi.	N22TG
N77HD	91	King Air B200	BB-1397	Arkansas State Highway & Transportation Dept. Little Rock.	N8062J
N77HE	81	King Air C90	LJ-969	Midwest Corporate Aviation Inc. Wichita, Ks.	9Q-CHE
N77HS	85	Gulfstream 900	15041	Harrison Steel Castings Co. Attica, In.	N82BA
N77JX	73	King Air E90	LW-54	Barry Richardson, Marston, Mo.	N771HM
N77ML	81	Conquest II	441-0202	Martin & Evelyn Lutin Family Trust, Van Nys, Ca.	N449DR
N77NB	79	King Air C90	LJ-818	Nicola Banking System Inc. Chickasha, Ok.	N97SF
N77NL	77	PA-31T Cheyenne II	7720038	New South Inc. Charleston, SC.	N82136
N77PF	70	King Air 100	B-70	Air Charter Service Inc. Washington, Pa.	N25JL
N77PV	80	King Air F90	LA-68	Summit Air Inc. Jacksonville, Fl.	N99LM
N77QX	80	King Air 200	BB-659	Dallas Air Corp. Wilmington, De.	N77CX
N77R	83	Conquest II	441-0288	Barker Homes Inc. Sparks, Nv.	N352RT
N77SA	83	Conquest II	441-0329	Security Aviation Inc. Anchorage, Ak.	N12099
N77SS	67	King Air A90	LJ-230	K & K Aircraft Inc. Bridgewater, Va.	N93BA
N77WF	72	King Air E90	LW-4	Thomas Stanton, McAllen, Tx.	N44EC
N77WM	86	King Air C90A	LJ-1133	Air Flite III Inc. Saginaw, Mi.	N300HH
N77YP	82	Conquest 1	425-0111	Taylor Aviation LLC. Columbia, SC.	N50FS
N77ZA	00	Pilatus PC-12/45	300	PMC Distribution Inc. Orange, Va.	C-FNAS
N78	88	King Air 300	FF-13	FAA, Oklahoma City, Ok.	
N78BA	74	Rockwell 690A	11166	SSG Equipment Leasing LLC. Winston-Salem, NC.	N77HS
N78CA	79	PA-31T Cheyenne II	7920062	TMC210 LLC. Hampton, Va.	F-GIYV
N78CC	03	PA-46-500TP Meridian	4697163	Carl Conti, Melbourne, Fl.	
N78CH	70	681 Turbo Commander	6038	Wrangler Aviation Corp. Norman, Ok.	N46JC
N78CP	74	SA-226T Merlin 4A	AT-029	White Industries Inc. Bates City, Mo.	N294A
N78CS	73	SA-226T Merlin 3A	T-229	Stratus Air LLC. Ventura, Ca.	N105BB
N78CT	81	King Air 200	BB-761	Springfield Aviation LLC. Santa Cruz, Ca.	N107TM
N78DA	76	King Air B100	BE-11	Dominion Air Leasing Inc. Richmond, Va.	N1911L
N78FS	79	MU-2 Solitaire	409SA	Smith & Gray Aero Inc. Mount Sterling, Ky.	N990MA
N78NA	77	Rockwell 690B	11401	George Davis, Rancho Cucamonga, Ca.	N28SE
N78PG	00	Pilatus PC-12/45	370	STC Acquisitions Inc. Wilmington, De.	N373KM
N78PK	81	MU-2 Marquise	1522SA	Zwana LLC. Fairhaven, Ma.	C-GFFH
N78TT	78	Rockwell 690B	11509	Pace Electronics/Electroair Inc. Sodus, NY.	(N269PK)
N78WD	78	Mitsubishi MU-2P	368SA	Pleasure Craft Marine Engines, Canal Winchester, Oh.	N16TQ
N79	88	King Air 300	FF-14	FAA, Oklahoma City, Ok.	
N79BE	77	Rockwell 690B	11408	Elcor Corp. St Louis, Mo.	(N690SA)
N79CF	79	King Air/Catpass 250	BB-441	Bering Air Inc. Nome, Ak.	
N79CT	79	King Air E90	LW-303	RR Enterprises Inc/Randall Stores Inc. Mitchell, SD.	N20351
N79EC	80	King Air F90	LA-74	Engineered Component Sales Inc. Southfield, Mi.	N81PS

Reg	Yr	Type	c/n	Owner/Operator	Prev Regn
N79FB	79	PA-31T Cheyenne II	7920016	Paddington Associates Inc. Newark, De.	N6180A
N79GA	79	King Air 200	BB-556	Elliott Aviation Aircraft Sales Inc. Des Moines, Ia.	I-ARBX
N79HS	61	Gulfstream 1	79	Emery Worldwide, Palo Alto, Ca.	N190DM
N79JS	90	King Air B200	BB-1370	JDS Aviation Inc/Scully Co. Jenkintown, Pa.	N200BM
N79PE	04	King Air C90B	LJ-1724	Raytheon Aircraft Co. Wichita, Ks.	
N79PH	82	Gulfstream 1000	96029	Anodyne Corp. Nashua, NH.	N282AC
N79SZ	83	Gulfstream 900	15024	Eagle Air Inc. Memphis, Tn.	N5911N
N79TE	85	King Air 300	FA-67	SPP Travel LLC. Wilmington, De.	N55SC
N80	88	King Air 300	FF-15	FAA, Oklahoma City, Ok.	
N80BC	97	King Air B200	BB-1571	Carter's Shooting Center Inc. Spring, Tx.	
N80BT	92	King Air B200	BB-1429	JW & JA Inc/Aire Corr Inc. Indianapolis, In.	RP-C1995
N80BZ	87	King Air 300	FA-117	Tucker Inc. Ellicott City, Md.	N80X
N80CP	79	PA-31T Cheyenne II	7920040	Cheyenne Shares LLC. Willoughby, Oh.	
N80DG	66	King Air A90	LJ-131	John Judice, Shreveport, La.	N700S
N80HH	79	MU-2 Marquise	732SA	Mitts Corp. Gainesville, Fl.	(N30MA)
N80JN	74	Mitsubishi MU-2J	626	Westair Aviation Ltd. Shannon, Ireland.	EC-GLU
N80M	81	King Air F90	LA-150	Axmer Aviation Inc. Franksville, Wi.	N700RL
N80MA	77	PA-31T Cheyenne II	7720043	Sims Enterprises, Kaysville, Ut.	(F-GJDK)
N80PA	77	King Air 200	BB-234	Bradley Herricks, Midland, Tx.	N200JC
N80RT	78	King Air 200	BB-370	HLW LLC. Sioux City, Ia.	N117WD
N80TB	76	Rockwell 690A	11300	Platt Valley Aero LLC. Nogal, NM.	N471SC
N80VP	01	King Air B200	BB-1769	Goff Air LLC. Traverse City, Mi.	N520GM
N80WM	81	King Air 200	BB-863	South Florida Water Management Division, West Palm Beach.	N44919
N80Y	67	King Air A90	LM-79	Dynamic Aviation Group Inc. Bridgewater, Va.	N65U
N81	88	King Air 300	FF-16	FAA, Oklahoma City, Ok.	
N81AT	70	King Air B90	LJ-490	Dallas Offset Inc. Dallas, Tx.	N881LT
N81BL	03	PA-46-500TP Meridian	4697160	Badger Land Equipment Leasing Inc. Franklin, Wi.	
N81GC	80	King Air F90	LA-73	6646K Inc. Tulsa, Ok.	N369BR
N81JN	81	Gulfstream 840	11660	National Childrens Leukemia Foundation, NYC.	(N140WJ)
N81LT	81	King Air B200	BB-892	Vermdeco Aviation LPC. Wilmington, De.	(SE-IIS)
N81MF	78	Mitsubishi MU-2P	375SA	Mesquite Air Services Inc. Lake Havasu City, Az.	N17JQ
N81MP	73	King Air C90	LW-72	Pegasus Aviation Inc. Cleveland, Oh.	N102MC
N81NA	81	King Air C90	LJ-993	M & H International Spedition u Logistik GmbH. Neuensalz.	RP-C...
N81PA	99	King Air 350	FL-250	Pennsylvania DoT Bureau of Aviation, New Cumberland, Pa.	N3092K
N81PF	76	King Air 200	BB-158	North Bay Charter LLC. Reno, Nv.	N81PA
N81PN	77	Conquest II	441-0037	Conquest Aviation Inc. Redding, Ca.	N441TH
N81RZ	80	King Air 200	BB-739	Vacuum Industrial Pollution International Inc. Baton Rouge.	VT-ESR
N81SD	81	King Air F90	LA-130	Bi-Lo Inc. Maudlin, SC.	
N81TF	81	King Air 200	BB-750	BB-750 Leasing LLC. Fort Lauderdale, Fl.	(N750TT)
N81WE	79	PA-31T Cheyenne II	7920060	MEK Inc .Leburn, Ky.	N31WE
N81WS	84	SA-227TT Merlin 3C	TT-480	Tuf-N-Lite Aircraft Inc. Springboro, Oh.	N500DB
N81WU	80	King Air 200	BB-576	Aero King Inc/Provost & Umphrey Law Firm, Beaumont, Tx.	N505SC
N82HR	94	Pilatus PC-12	106	Harris Farms Inc. Coalinga, Ca.	N106WA
N82PC	80	PA-31T Cheyenne II	8020082	Automatic Business Products, New Smyrna Beach, Fl.	N2580V
N82PG	82	PA-42 Cheyenne III	8001070	Mitch Probasco, Floydata, Tx.	N721CA
N82PK	97	King Air B200	BB-1596	HEH Corp. Brentwood, Tn.	
N82TW	80	PA-31T Cheyenne 1	8004034	Dugan Funeral Services Inc. Fremont, Ne.	(N81TW)
N82WC	78	Mitsubishi MU-2P	393SA	Scott Dann, Libertyville, Il.	N9SR
N82WU	98	King Air 350	FI -197	Flying High Inc/Provost & Umphrey Law Firm, Beaumont, Tx.	
N82XL	81	Cheyenne II-XL	8166034	9009-9177 Canada USA Inc. Wilmington, De.	HK-3603X
N83	88	King Air 300	FF-18	FAA, Oklahoma City, Ok.	
N83A	78	Conquest II	441-0050	Peacock Aviation Inc. Omaha, Ne.	N55FC
N83AJ	03	Pilatus PC-12/45	495	Beach Aviation Inc. Palisades Verdes Est, Ca.	N495PC
N83CA	80	PA-31T Cheyenne II	8020072	Inductotherm Industries Inc. Rancocas, NJ.	C-FEVC
N83CH	81	Conquest 1	425-0025	Kenneth Karas, Tehachapl, Ca.	N53MS
N83FE	77	King Air E90	LW-219	Aviation Holdings Ltd. Houston, Tx.	N77AG
N83FM	68	King Air B90	LJ-341	Kenneth McLeod, Chandler, Az.	N91NC
N83G	73	Rockwell 690	11064	Don McCormack, Oklahoma City, Ok.	N830
N83GA	79	King Air 200	BB-518	Guardian Eagle Co. Eden Prairie, Mn.	VH-MKR
N83GF	83	Conquest 1	425-0132	Fisher Sand & Gravel Co. Dickinson, ND.	N6883R
N83KA	83	King Air B200	BB-1111	McCoy Leasing LLC. Chattanooga, Tn.	ZS-LVK
N83LS	96	King Air C90B	LJ-1461	Luck Stone, Richmond, Va.	N1076K
N83MG	81	PA-31T Cheyenne 1	8104047	J & B Watkins 1997 Family Trust, San Marcos, Ca.	N2420Y
N83P	82	King Air C90-1	LJ-1027	Kyanite Mining Corp. Dillwyn, Va.	
N83PH	82	King Air B200	BB-976	Arnold & Arnold Real Estate Inc. Naples, Fl.	N83RH
Reg	Yr	Type	c/n	Owner/Operator	Prev Regn

Reg	Yr	Type	c/n	Owner/Operator	Prev Regn
N83RH	90	King Air 300	FA-213	Moga Management LLC. Fairfax, Va.	N5647Q
N83RZ	82	King Air B200	BB-1024	Rozzo Jets Inc. Fort Lauderdale, Fl.	SU-PAA
N83TC	70	King Air B90	LJ-483	Gordon Aviation Inc. Wilmington, De.	N210K
N83WA	83	Gulfstream 1000	96063	United Auto Equipment Leasing LLC. Portland, Or.	N61508
N83WE	78	King Air E90	LW-289	Miner's Inc. Hermantown, Mn.	N222MC
N83XL	81	Cheyenne II-XL	8166075	North Shore Properties, Erie, Pa.	N2325W
N84	88	King Air 300	FF-19	FAA, Oklahoma City, Ok.	
N84CA	76	King Air 200	BB-166	Buffalo Air LLC. Waterford, Mi.	N89MP
N84CQ	80	King Air 200	BB-691	Navacorp III LLC. NYC.	N84CC
N84GA	80	SA-226T Merlin 3B	T-312	REG Management LLC/Giles Automotive Inc. Lafayette, La.	N90NB
N84GU	79	Rockwell 690B	11522	Aircraft Investments Inc. Batesville, Ar.	N691TP
N84HS	92	TBM 700	50	Skypath Inc. Daytona Beach, Fl.	(N67LF)
N84JL	80	King Air F90	LA-18	J-L Chieftain Inc. Longview, Tx.	N65SF
N84LJ	79	Conquest II	441-0084	Lovejoy Industries/L J Aircraft Inc. Oak Brook, Il.	N441GN
N84P	83	King Air C90	LJ-1045	Divine Aviation LLC. El Dorado Hills, Ca.	
N84PA	81	King Air 200	BB-835	Pennsylvania DoT Bureau of Aviation, New Cumberland, Pa.	N81CT
N84PC	81	King Air B200	BB-860	Triss Corp. Melvindale, Mi.	N488AD
N84SH	01	PA-46-500TP Meridian	4697059	Muncie Aviation Co. Muncie, In.	
N84TP	80	King Air C90	LJ-911	Andercraft Products Inc. Rancho Cucamonga, Ca.	N107K
N85AB	74	Rockwell 690A	11167	Eagle Creek Aviation Services Inc. Indianapolis, In.	N36BA
N85DR	78	King Air C90	LJ-767	Sunshine Sales & Leasing Inc. Clearwater, Fl.	(N85PR)
N85EM	81	Cheyenne II-XL	8166055	Cheyenne Sales & Leasing LLC/Tiffin Aire Inc. Tiffin, Oh.	(CP-1699)
N85FC	81	King Air 200	BB-785	Woodway Aero Holdings Co. Houston, Tx.	RP-C582
N85GA	85	King Air B200	BB-1228	Crown Aviation LLC. Mesa, Az.	D-IMGL
N85GC	81	PA-31T Cheyenne II	8120009	Gerard Comboul Aviation Inc. Nice, France.	D-IHMS
N85HB	81	PA-31T Cheyenne II	8120021	Michael Spear, Columbia, Md.	N80WA
N85PJ	82	King Air F90	LA-163	W & P Air LLC. Dawsonville, Ga.	N154AJ
N85SL	84	PA-42 Cheyenne 400LS	5527005	Sierra Aviation Inc. Bishop, Ca.	HP-2001
N85TB	79	King Air C90	LJ-833	Corporate Air Travel, Reno, Nv.	(N45AW)
N85TK	02	PA-46-500TP Meridian	4697128	Meridian Air LLC. Dover, De.	
N86BM	75	King Air A100	B-206	Silverhawk Aviation Inc. Lincoln, Ne.	N86PA
N86EA	81	Conquest 1	425-0082	Stone Power Sales & Service Inc. Casper, Wy.	N6846T
N86JG	84	King Air C90A	LJ-1076	Allen County Aviation/John Galvin, Lima, Oh.	N69275
N86LD	00	King Air C90B	LJ-1631	Dion Aircraft Sales Inc. Key West, Fl.	N4031K
N86MG	67	King Air A90	LJ-264	Aviation Parts Exchange Inc. Southlake, Tx.	N86JR
N86TR	77	King Air B100	BE-22	Edward Baloian, Fresno, Ca.	N50SS
N87BT	67	680V Turbo Commander	1705-81	City of New York, Long Island City, NY.	N87D
N87CA	78	King Air A100	B-240	Midwest Regional Airlines Inc. Eldon, Mo.	(N112CM)
N87CF	83	King Air B200	BB-1122	Feltus Aviation LLC. Little Rock, Ar.	N6606R
N87CH	72	King Air E90	LW-20	Dionisio Arriola, Moses Lake, Wa.	N84LS
N87E	66	King Air A90	LM-5	Dynamic AvLease Inc. Bridgewater, Va.	N7007Q
N87HB	90	King Air C90A	LJ-1251	Mountain Air Cargo Inc. Denver, NC.	N5607X
N87JE	77	King Air B100	BE-27	ARCH Air Medical Service Inc. Englewood, Co.	(N297SL)
N87LP	78	King Air 200	BB-331	Soin International LLC. Dayton, Oh.	N111WA
N87MM	68	King Air B90	LJ-415	Engines Inc. Weiner, Ar.	N210X
N87NW	78	King Air B100	BE-42	Mountain Flight Service Inc. Steamboat Springs, Co.	N700SB
N87SA	82	King Air B200	BB-1089	James F Humphreys & Assocs LLC. Charleston, WV.	(N69JH)
N87V	70	King Air A90	LM-130	Dynamic Aviation, Bridgewater, Va.	N71764
N87WS	77	Conquest II	441-0009	Fairway Ltd. Nantwich, UK.	N777ED
N87WZ	78	Rockwell 690B	11511	Royce International Investment Co. Santa Barbara, Ca.	N81795
N87XX	81	King Air B100	BE-105	Aeropac Charters Inc. Manchester, NH.	N28PH
N87YC	99	King Air 350	FL-246	Yankee Charlie LLC/Barbara Deanne, Houston, Tx.	N3106P
N87YP	81	PA-31T Cheyenne II	8120053	Ridge Finance Corp. Cranford, NJ.	N53TW
N87YQ	87	King Air 300	FA-131	Alpine Industries/EcoQuest International, Greeneville, Tn.	N87YC
N88B	81	Cheyenne II-XL	8166023	F McLeskey, Virginia Beach, Va.	N2577Y
N88BC	79	PA-31T Cheyenne II	7920032	WPC Ltd. Bluefield, WV.	N23139
N88BJ	80	Gulfstream 840	11627	MAX 1 LLC. Aspen, Co.	N24A
N88FA	79	King Air B100	BE-74	Crow Executive Air Inc. Toledo-Metcalf, Oh.	N56FL
N88GL	81	King Air C90	LJ-945	Austin Lopez, St John, USVI.	N979C
N88GW	81	Conquest II	441-0187	Hamburg Aero Leasing LP. Hamburg, NY.	N405JB
N88HL	82	MU-2 Marquise	1542SA	Rough Ryder Aircraft Corp. Wilmington, De.	N468MA
N88HM	71	King Air C90	LJ-502	Western Flyers Air Service, McAllen, Tx.	N881K
N88JH	89	King Air B200	BB-1331	Teton Aviation LLC. Jackson, Wy.	N5530H
N88MT	81	King Air 200	BB-830	Standard Commercial Tobacco Co. Wilson, NC.	N88P
N88NT	99	Pilatus PC-12/45	285	The Newtron Group Inc. Baton Rouge, La.	N285PS

Reg	Yr	Type	c/n	Owner/Operator	Prev Regn
N88PD	90	King Air C90A	LJ-1242	Pipe Distributors Inc. Houston, Tx.	N15696
N88QM	81	PA-31T Cheyenne 1	8104025	RB LLC. Tequesta, Fl.	N2476X
N88QT	82	Conquest II	441-0228	Start Renting Inc/SRI Sky LLC. Madison, Wi.	(N363PD)
N88RP	70	King Air B90	LJ-491	OMNI Energy Services Corp. Lafayette, La.	N88RB
N88RY	87	King Air 300	FA-122	Robert Yates Racing Inc. Charlotte, NC.	N112HF
N88SD	75	King Air C90	LJ-661	BHA Leasing Inc. Standish, Me.	N26CS
N88SP	66	King Air A90	LJ-116A	Air Reldan Inc. New Orleans, La.	N885K
N88TL	81	King Air B100	BE-113	BWOC Air Services Inc. Columbus, Ga.	N1888M
N88TR	73	King Air E90	LW-57	Cushing Stone Co. Amsterdam, NY.	N86TR
N88U	98	TBM 700	135	SOCATA Aircraft, Pembroke Pines, Fl.	
N88WF	95	TBM 700	102	Kansas Aircraft Corp. New Century, Ks.	(N102WF)
N88WV	99	King Air 350	FL-253	WIV Air LLC. Van Nuys, Ca.	N525BA
N88XJ	98	King Air C90B	LJ-1525	James Frost, Avon, Co.	
N89DR	78	Mitsubishi MU-2N	713SA	R & M Foods Inc. Hattiesburg, Ms.	N874MA
N89F	66	King Air A90	LM-124	Dynamic Aviation, Bridgewater, Va.	N72014
N89KA	89	King Air C90A	LJ-1227	Executive King Air LLC. Portland, Or.	N200SY
N89SC	81	MU-2 Marquise	1516SA	Nashville Air Flights Inc. Nashville, Tn.	N4SY
N89ST	01	PA-46-500TP Meridian	4697008	First South Development & Investment Co. Greensboro, NC.	N62WM
N89TM	73	King Air C90	IJ-610	Gormin AT Inc. Salem, Or.	(N169WD)
N89UA	89	King Air B200	BB-1336	University of Arkansas, Fayetteville, Ar.	N131BP
N89WA	96	King Air B200	BB-1540	DeBruce Grain Inc. Kansas City, Mo.	
N90AT	76	Rockwell 690A	11272	Angelina Air Inc. Pompano Beach, Fl.	N888PB
N90AW	76	King Air C90	LJ-697	Krider Construction Inc. Pineville, Or.	C-GSAX
N90BD	81	King Air F90	LA-134	Robert DeLong, San Clemente, Ca.	N993M
N90BF	75	King Air E90	LW-124	First Air Leasing Inc. Greenville, SC.	N90GK
N90BP	77	King Air C90	LJ-718	Air Medical Leasing Inc. Lawrenceville, Ga.	
N90CB	69	King Air B90	LJ-473	Aeronca Inc. Middletown, Oh.	N9390C
N90CH	96	King Air C90B	LJ-1445	Chartco LLC. Salisbury, NC.	N209P
N90CN	95	King Air C90B	LJ-1410	Nogle & Black Aviation Inc. Tuscola, Il.	N771SG
N90CP*	03	TBM 700	285	Century Enterprises Group LLC. Fort Lauderdale, Fl.	N706CA
N90CT	75	King Air C90	LJ-645	Robert Schroeder, Kaukauna, Wi.	(N999MJ)
N90DN	68	King Air B90	LJ-437	Business Aircraft Leasing Inc. Nashville, Tn.	N12JG
N90EJ	78	King Air C90	LJ-749	Edwards Jet Center, Billings, Mt.	N552R
N90EL	73	King Air C90	LJ-592	Blue Sky Jet Inc. Spring Valley, Ca.	N383DA
N90ET	80	King Air F90	LA-20	ETS Laboratories, Helena, Ca.	(N85JG)
N90FA	66	King Air A90	LJ-133	Gateway Technical College, Kenosha, Wi.	N90SA
N90FS	80	PA-31T Cheyenne II	8020011	James Beasley, Philadelphia, Pa.	N73CA
N90GA	90	King Air B200	BB-1359	Stark Truss Co. Canton, Oh.	RP-C4188
N90GB	69	King Air B90	LJ-469	David F Q Younges, Medellin, Colombia.	XA-COG
N90GN	66	King Air A90	LJ-157	C & F Ranch LC. Oklahoma City, Ok.	N288HH
N90GT	84	SA-227TT Merlin 3C	TT-534	E C Menzies Electrical Inc. Essendon, VIC. Australia.	N139F
N90KS	98	King Air C90B	LJ-1517	Kimco Staffing & Services Inc. Irvine, Ca.	N90KA
N90LB	73	King Air C90	LJ-573	Front Page Corp. Douglas, Ga.	N707RW
N90LF	79	King Air C90	LJ-852	CJ Systems Aviation Group Inc. Allegheny County, Pa.	YV-250CP
N90LG	68	King Air B90	LJ-351	Dodson International Parts Inc. Ottawa, Ks.	N62BW
N90MT	89	King Air C90A	LJ-1223	Elvira Minotti, Taverne, Switzerland.	OY-JAB
N90MU	76	King Air C90	LJ-679	J & D Aircraft Sales LLC. Pasco, Wa.	N90ML
N90MV	77	King Air C90	LJ-701	Lagniappe Air LLC. Edmond, Ok.	N90LJ
N90NA	81	King Air F90	LA-104	Conquest Charter Inc. Carson City, Nv.	D-IEEE
N90NM	68	King Air B90	LJ-404	John Antunis, Hilton Head, SC.	N90MT
N90PB	76	King Air 200	BB-125	Grant Aviation Inc. Anchorage, Ak.	TG-UGA
N90PH	73	King Air E90	LW-60	HLC Hotels Inc. Savannah, Ga.	N999TB
N90PR	96	King Air C90B	LJ-1437	East Pike Auto Inc. Zanesville, Oh.	N1067L
N90PW	76	King Air C90	LJ-681	Longin Consultants Inc. Burlington, Wi.	N1581L
N90RK	99	King Air C90B	LJ-1554	True North Aviation LLC. New Smyrna Beach, Fl.	(N90ND)
N90RT	81	King Air F90	LA-146	Save Mart Supermarkets/Sky Trek Aviation, Modesto, Ca.	N90TX
N90SB	81	King Air F90	LA-154	Red River Cellular Telephone Co. Texarkana, Tx.	(C-GFFY)
N90TD	82	King Air F90	LA-183	Fairfield Manley LLC.	N82WC
N90TP	80	King Air F90	LA-66	Triton Air Inc. Wilmington, De.	(YV-373CP
N90TW	84	PA-42 Cheyenne IIIA	5501013	La Stella Corp. Pueblo, Co.	N40833
N90VM	81	PA-31T Cheyenne 1	8104031	Monaghan Management Corp. Commerce City, Co.	(N90FJ)
N90VP	67	King Air A90	LJ-276	APA Enterprises Inc. Deland, Fl.	N574M
N90WE	88	King Air 300LW	FA-164	Warren Equipment Co. Midland, Tx.	N42AJ
N90WG	79	PA-31T Cheyenne II	7920044	C W Aviation Inc. Bryan, Tx.	PT-OTF
N90WJ	71	King Air C90	LJ-525	Blackhawk Technical College, Janesville, Wi.	N70MT

Reg	Yr	Type	c/n	Owner/Operator	Prev Regn
N90WL	69	King Air B90	LJ-461	W L Paris Enterprises Inc. Louisville, Ky.	N453SR
N90WP	94	King Air C90B	LJ-1383	Alpha Aircraft Charter Ltd. Girard, Oh.	
N90WT	73	King Air E90	LW-31	Aviacion Lider SA. Lima, Peru.	N17GD
N90WW	84	PA-31T Cheyenne 1A	1104004	Voyager Aviation LLC. Racine, Wi.	N15AT
N90XS*	81	King Air E90	LW-342	Flying King LLC. Chanhassen, Mn.	N3741M
N90YA	81	Conquest 1	425-0090	Quinn Aire LLC. Rancho Santa Fe, Ca.	N90GA
N90ZH	73	King Air C90	LJ-594	Lancaster Airport LLC. Lancaster, Tx.	N3094W
N91CT	78	Rockwell 690B	11428	Clemson University, Clemson, SC.	N91CS
N91HT	85	King Air B200	BB-1183	Hawkeye Aviation LLC. Pikeville, Ky.	N44MH
N91KA	90	King Air C90A	LJ-1232	Pacific Flight Services Inc. Reno, Nv.	XA-RGL
N91LW	82	King Air C90	LJ-1001	HCA Wesley Medical Center, Wichita, Ks.	N88EL
N91MM	71	Mitsubishi MU-2F	198	Anderson Aerial Spraying Service, Canby, Mn.	N71MF
N91RK	76	King Air A100	B-226	Crystal Aviation LLC. Atlantic Beach, NC.	N9126S
N91S	70	King Air A90	LU-15	Dynamic Aviation, Bridgewater, Va.	N71998
N91TJ	78	King Air C90	LJ-744	Cannon Air LLC. Scottsdale, Az.	N771PS
N91TS	80	PA-31T Cheyenne II	8020050	McCranie Motor & Tractor Inc. Macon, Ga.	C-FSRW
N92DN	88	King Air 300	FA-149	Straitix Leasing LLC. Norcross, Ga.	N92DE
N92DV	78	King Air E90	LW-292	Air Methods Corp/KMRC Guardian Air Inc. Flagstaff, Az.	N7MA
N92FC	90	King Air C90A	LJ-1235	Longleaf AIF LLC. Hilton Head, SC.	D-IABB
N92JQ	81	Conquest II	441-0223	Conquest LLC. Woodruff, Wi.	N92JC
N92JR	81	King Air 200	BB-751	Tennair LLC. Clarksville, Tn.	N751EB
N92S	70	King Air A90	LU-5	Dynamic Aviation, Bridgewater, Va.	N7199B
N92TC	71	Mitsubishi MU-2F	209	Rosewood Aviation Inc. Nashville, Tn.	N212CC
N92TW	90	King Air 350	FL-3	Noel Aviation Interests Ltd. Odessa, Tx.	(N350PC)
N92WC	89	King Air B200	BB-1330	Doug Jackson, Newport Coast, Ca.	N681PC
N92WG	66	King Air A90	LJ-182	Southern Pioneer Life Insurance Co. Trumann, Ar.	N92W
N93A	73	King Air E90	LW-63	Alpha Horizon LLC/Fairway Ford Isuzu Inc. Greenville, SC.	N808GA
N93AH	73	Mitsubishi MU-2J	581	Trans Check Inc. Carlsbad, Ca.	N161WC
N93AJ	77	King Air B100	BE-18	Air Jet Inc. Cary, NC.	N818PA
N93BJ	81	King Air F90	LA-136	News Wholesalers of Michigan Inc. Westland, Mi.	(N215DM)
N93CN	80	PA-31T Cheyenne 1	8004029	Jerry & Corrine Nothman, Portland, Or.	N49GG
N93D	77	King Air B100	BE-23	A & Q LLC. Ada, Mi.	N13KA
N93GA	86	King Air 300	FA-93	CC Aviation LLC/Dulany Aviation Inc. Wilmington, De.	(N92CC)
N93HC	77	Conquest II	441-0011	Horizons Inc. Rapid City, SD.	N900JT
N93KA	80	King Air F90	LA-24	John Braly, Boerne, Tx.	
N93LL	01	PA-46-500TP Meridian	4697045	2802 E Old Tower Rd. Phoenix, AZ 85034.	
N93LP	80	King Air C90	LJ-901	Mid America Drilling Equipment Inc. Ocala, Fl.	N23LF
N93MA	82	Gulfstream 1000	96035	Eagle Air Inc. Memphis, Tn. (now XC-HFZ ?).	D-IBER
N93ME	77	Rockwell 690B	11414	2141 Corp. Atlanta, Ga.	VH-PCD
N93NM	82	Gulfstream 1000	96020	National Childrens Leukemia Foundation, NYC.	(N139WJ)
N93NP	84	King Air B200	BB-1184	N Philadelphia Aviation Corp/Summit Aviation, Middletown, De	N27SE
N93QR	03	King Air C90B	LJ-1696	King Air 90B LLC. Wadsworth, Il.	N61906
N93RA	68	680W Turbo Commander	1722-2	American Aviation Ground Services, Miami, Fl. (was 1722-93).	N93D
N93RY	66	King Air A90	LJ-174	Air Capital Insurance LLC. Wichita, Ks.	(N193SF)
N93SF	76	King Air B100	BE-13	Sugar Fox LLC. Greenville, NC.	N4213S
N93SH	79	PA-31T Cheyenne 1	7904029	Dan Cox, Warden, Wa.	N29CA
N93WT	80	King Air B100	BE-80	Wes-Tex Drilling Co. Abilene, Tx.	N13DR
N93ZC	80	King Air 200	BB-654	LuxAire LLC. Apple Valley, Mn.	XB-BXU
N94AC	78	Rockwell 690B	11486	Apollo Aviation Inc. Glastonbury, Ct.	N34EF
N94CD	81	King Air C90	LJ-939	Brown Aviation LLC. Charlotte, NC.	N26803
N94EA	85	Gulfstream 1000	96094	Midtex Investments Inc. Austin, Tx.	N131GA
N94EG	81	PA-31T Cheyenne 1	8104033	Boston Air Charter LLC. Norfolk, Ma.	N881SW
N94EW	81	PA-42 Cheyenne III	8001054	Derby Air LLC. Willoughby, Oh.	N29HS
N94FG	79	King Air 200	BB-433	Flex-Air Ltd. Urbana, Il.	N133GA
N94HB	80	King Air C90	LJ-904	Central Flying Service Inc. Little Rock, Ar.	N90HB
N94JD	81	King Air F90	LA-139	Gap Air Inc. Johnstown, Pa.	N333EB
N94KC	76	King Air 200	BB-172	Alliant Hospitals Inc. Louisville, Ky.	N68RR
N94MG	90	King Air C90A	LJ-1229	MGA Services Inc. Hoover, Al.	D-IAFF
N94PA	82	Gulfstream 1000	96005	Quasar Aviation, Dover, De.	N815S
N94SA	65	Gulfstream 1	157	World Sales & Turbine Co. El Dorado, Panama.	N741G
N94TK	94	King Air C90B	LJ-1358	Tem-Kil Co. Macogdoches, Tx.	N80927
N95AB	81	Gulfstream 1000	96012	Talon Erectors Inc. Hagerstown, Md.	N695BA
N95AC	81	SA-226T Merlin 3B	T-381	F S Air Service Inc. Anchorage, Ak.	N80MJ
N95AN	95	King Air B200	BB-1506	Bear Lake Aviation LLC. Destin, Fl.	N202TS
N95CT	85	King Air B200	BB-1235	Jajale Inc. Dallas, Tx.	N43CE
Reg	Yr	Type	c/n	Owner/Operator	Prev Regn

Reg	Yr	Type	c/n	Owner/Operator	Prev Regn
☐ N95GA	93	King Air B200	BB-1467	Pride Mobility Products Corp. Exeter, Pa.	(N929AK)
☐ N95JM	76	Rockwell 690A	11289	Valley Oil/Pond LLC. Salem, Or.	(N27JT)
☐ N95LB	73	King Air E90	LW-24	James Tate, Christiansted, USVI.	N95RB
☐ N95PC	85	King Air C90A	LJ-1109	Jim Hankins Air Service Inc. Jackson, Ms.	
☐ N95TT	81	King Air B200	BB-917	M B Aviation LLC. Pawleys Island, SC.	(N115SB)
☐ N95VR	81	PA-42 Cheyenne III	8001049	Golden Eagle Aviation Inc/Henry Luken, Bradenton, Fl.	C-FIZG
☐ N96AG	67	King Air A90	LJ-260	Aviation Group LLC. Concord, NC.	N303NH
☐ N96AH	75	King Air C90	LJ-643	Jemco of Pensacola Inc. Pensacola, Fl.	N909HC
☐ N96AM	00	King Air B200	BB-1713	Texas A & M University, College Station, Tx.	N3053Q
☐ N96CE	96	King Air B200	BB-1536	CAIAIR Inc. Beaumont, Tx.	N10436
☐ N96DQ	79	King Air C90	LJ-814	Cavalier Aire Inc. Wilmington, De.	N96DC
☐ N96FA	85	King Air C90A	LJ-1111	Flad & Assocs Inc. Madison, Wi.	N240EA
☐ N96GP	89	King Air B200	BB-1322	BosAir Ltd/North Star Realty Services LLC. Chicago, Il.	N391L
☐ N96KA	90	King Air 350	FL-36	Louis Beecherl LLC. Wanut Springs, Tx.	(N825G)
☐ N96MA	78	PA-31T Cheyenne 1	7804005	Headstrong Inc. Lyon, Ms.	N6095A
☐ N96RL	68	SA-26AT Merlin 2B	T26-116	JB Aviation Tucson LLC. Tucson, Az.	N100AW
☐ N96TT	80	King Air F90	LA-26	Katemo Corp. Princeton, NJ.	N6668C
☐ N96VC	79	SA-226T Merlin 3B	T-303	National Childrens Leukemia Foundation, NYC.	N5654M
☐ N97AB	70	SA-226T Merlin 3	T-203	Reese Airoroft Inc. Indianapolls, In.	N5273M
☐ N97CV	97	King Air C90B	LJ-1492	Bergen Associates, Georgetown, De.	N2029Z
☐ N97DR	96	King Air 350	FL-133	Danchar Inc/Sun Aviation Inc. Vero Beach, Fl.	
☐ N97EB	86	King Air 300	FA-97	MAACO Enterprises Inc. King of Prussia, Pa.	N50NL
☐ N97KA	97	King Air C90B	LJ-1469	Crutchfield Corp. Charlottesville, Va.	
☐ N97LL	01	PA-46-500TP Meridian	4697058	Air Northeast LLC. Lynn, Ma.	
☐ N97PC	80	PA-31T Cheyenne II	8020034	DR Holdings LLC. Franklin, NC.	N4241Y
☐ N97SZ	83	King Air B200	BB-1166	Zimmerman Development Inc. Los Angeles, Ca.	D-ITAB
☐ N97TW	79	PA-31T Cheyenne II	7920051	Roger Mellon, Lakeland, Fl.	
☐ N97WC	90	King Air B200	BB-1382	West Coast Charters LLC. Santa Ana, Ca.	N678RM
☐ N97WD	80	King Air B100	BE-97	KA South Inc. Hilton Head Island, SC.	N43RJ
☐ N97WE	97	King Air B200	BB-1586	Wagner Equipment Co. Englewood, Co.	N3181Q
☐ N98AJ	78	Rockwell 690B	11458	Cascadian Aviation LLC. Bellevue, Wa.	ZS-KEF
☐ N98AR*	79	King Air C90	LJ-829	ALARO Inc. Giddings, Tx.	(N11FX)
☐ N98AT	76	PA-31T Cheyenne II	7620014	Custom Fabric & Repair Inc. Marshfield, Wi.	(N460LC)
☐ N98B	66	King Air 90	LJ-87	Aerosports Inc. Applegate, Or.	
☐ N98BK	98	King Air C90B	LJ-1522	Mid-State Bank & Trust, Arroyo Grande, Ca.	N58XJ
☐ N98DA	97	King Air B200	BB-1555	Adam Aviation/First American Bank Texas SSB. Bryan, Tx.	
☐ N98EP	85	Conquest 1	425-0230	Ernest Pestana Inc. Incline Village, Nv.	N1227V
☐ N98GF	80	PA-31T Cheyenne 1	8004009	Cattle Baron Restaurants Inc. Roswell, NM.	N2412W
☐ N98HB	67	King Air A90	LJ-285	Hermann Bodmer & Co. Zurich, Switzerland.	PH-IND
☐ N98HF	74	King Air E90	LW-89	T & R Aircraft LLC. Memphis, Tn.	N77PA
☐ N98KS	97	King Air C90B	LJ-1502	N98KS LLC. Fresno, Ca.	N5UL
☐ N98NF	98	TBM 700	133	Baker Air LLC. San Francisco, Ca.	F-WWRP
☐ N98PJ	76	Rockwell 690A	11320	Sports VIP Inc. Davidson, NC.	N220HC
☐ N98PM	75	King Air E90	LW-131	McGriff, Seibels & Williams Inc. Birmingham, Al.	N98PC
☐ N98TB	78	PA-31T Cheyenne II	7820040	Plane Stupid Inc. Littleton, Co.	N68MB
☐ N98TG	79	PA-31T Cheyenne 1	7904027	NCMC Inc. Greeley, Co.	N98TW
☐ N98UC	81	SA-226T Merlin 3B	T-378	Southwest First Street Corp. Highlands, NC.	N1011P
☐ N98WP	97	King Air C90B	LJ-1493	T & A Aviation LLC. Texarkana, Ar.	(N98WS)
☐ N99AC	75	King Air E90	LW-120	BYB Southeast LLC. Jonesboro, Ar.	(N870BB)
☐ N99BT	73	Mitsubishi MU-2J	591	S & W Aircraft Sales Inc. Wilmington, De.	N295MA
☐ N99EL	59	Gulfstream 1	7	MissionAir Inc. Kissimmee, Fl.	N5VX
☐ N99JW	82	SA-227TT Merlin 3C	TT-450	GDE Aviation LLC. Destin, Fl.	N53PC
☐ N99KF	79	PA-31T Cheyenne II	7920093	SST Corp. Klamath Falls, Or.	N2416R
☐ N99LL	82	King Air B200	BB-994	Alabama River Pulp Co. Purdue Hill, Al.	N25CN
☐ N99ML	03	King Air B200	BB-1844	Black River Construction Services, Black River Falls, Wi.	N18ST
☐ N99MN	96	King Air C90B	LJ-1460	Business Aircraft Leasing Inc. Nashville, Tn.	N99ML
☐ N99SR	74	Mitsubishi MU-2K	315	Jetset Ltd. Lanseria, RSA.	N505MA
☐ N99U*	90	King Air 350	FL-20	Helicopters Inc. Cahokia, Il.	N350NJ
☐ N99VA	77	PA-31T Cheyenne II	7720007	Avro Ltd. Las Vegas, Nv.	N721RP
☐ N99WC	76	Rockwell 690A	11308	Special Investments Inc. Encino, Ca.	N81419
☐ N100AQ	89	King Air 300	FA-190	1st Source Leasing Inc. South Bend, In.	N17TW
☐ N100BY	84	MU-2 Marquise	1565SA	Spark Technologies & Innovations NV. Curacao.	N530DP
☐ N100BZ	85	King Air 300	FA-32	M & S Aviation LLC/Echo Aviation LC. Tempe, Az.	N100BE
☐ N100CC	83	Conquest 1	425-0170	Honey B LLC/Honey Buckets, Puyallup, Wa.	N68721
☐ N100CE	80	SA-226T Merlin 3B	T-325	Crescent Equipment LLC. Wilmington, De.	HC-BUA

Reg	Yr Type	c/n	Owner/Operator	Prev Regn
N100CF	72 Mitsubishi MU-2F	229	Errol Forman, Champaign, Il.	N217MA
N100CM	80 PA-31T Cheyenne II	8020073	Langdale Industries, Valdosta, Ga.	N2474V
N100EC	75 King Air E90	LW-150	Metsource Inc. Knoxville, Tn.	N23AE
N100FL	85 King Air 300	FA-34	Dept of Management Services, Tallahassee, Fl.	N865M
N100GL	70 681 Turbo Commander	6028	Ecological Services International, Los Fresnos, Tx.	N9028N
N100JD	97 King Air C90B	LJ-1472	Estrella Aviation LLC. Phoenix, Az.	N1099L
N100KA	70 King Air 100	B-11	On-Air LLC. Sewickley, Pa.	
N100KB	79 King Air C90	LJ-820	CarinaStar Assets LLC. Hilton Head, SC.	
N100KE	74 Mitsubishi MU-2P	313SA	Internet Jet Sales Ltd. White Mills, Pa.	N100KP
N100LA*	85 King Air B200	BB-1200	Voyager Aviation LLC. Racine, Wi.	N6816A
N100NP	80 MU-2 Solitaire	423SA	Fountainbleu Management Services, New Orleans, La.	N156MA
N100PY	81 King Air B200	BB-890	Coastal Aircraft Leasing LLC. Panama City, Fl.	N100PX
N100RU	96 King Air C90B	LJ-1433	Rental Uniform Service of Florence, Charleston, SC.	N3254A
N100SM	99 King Air C90	LJ-1561	State of Missouri, Jefferson City, Mo.	N3171A
N100SN	69 SA-26AT Merlin 2B	T26-129	Blair Aviation Ltd. Dallas, Tx.	N784AF
N100TW	78 King Air B100	BE-51	ZMax LLC. Athens, Ga.	N1DA
N100UE	66 King Air A90	LJ-138	CASC Inc. Cedartown, Ga.	N100UF
N100V	78 King Air C90	LJ-796	Reliance Air LLC. Conway, Ar.	
N100VK	94 PA-46 Turbo Malibu	1	Toys 4 Boys Inc. Beaumont, Tx.	
N100WB	66 King Air A90	LJ-139	Brown Boy Aviation, Royal City, Wa.	N1515T
N100WG	95 Pilatus PC-12	131	Walter Grubmueller,	N88EL
N100WQ	78 PA-31T Cheyenne II	7820084	JS Aircraft LLC. Eden, NC.	N450DA
N100YC	99 Pilatus PC-12/45	281	Passport Leasing Corp. Fort Lauderdale, Fl.	HB-FSZ
N101BS	68 King Air B90	LJ-375	Bruce Scheffer/Valparaiso International, Valparaiso, In.	N110BS
N101BU	85 King Air C90A	LJ-1107	CHL II LLC. Coral Springs, Fl.	N72260
N101CA	82 Conquest 1	425-0142	State of Texas, Austin, Tx.	OH-CIK
N101CS	76 King Air C-12C	BC-41	Profile Aviation Services Inc. Hickory, NC.	N257AG
N101GQ	79 King Air 200	BB-427	American Capital Corp. Chesterfield, Mo.	N101CC
N101MC	73 SA-226T Merlin 3A	T-234	Cappaert Air Planes LLC. Vicksburg, Ms.	N531LP
N101SG	01 King Air B200	BB-1785	Andair Inc. McAllen, Tx.	N4455U
N101SN	81 King Air B100	BE-118	Trace Air Inc. Fort Worth, Tx.	N4700K
N102AE	90 PA-42 Cheyenne IIIA	5501053	Cobalt Aviation III LLC. Philadelphia, Pa.	PT-WQA
N102AJ	75 King Air C90	LJ-649	NST Corporate Aviation LC. Orlando, Fl.	OO-MCL
N102BX	79 MU-2 Marquise	748SA	Bankair Inc. West Columbia, SC.	N102BG
N102FK*	81 King Air C90	LJ-982	State of Florida, Tallahassee, Fl.	N1820P
N102LF	70 King Air 100	B-65	Lynch Flying Service Inc. Billings, Mt.	N102RS
N102PG	84 King Air 300	FA-19	The Pape' Group Inc. Coburg, Or.	N101PC
N102RR	00 Pilatus PC-12/45	316	South Texas Airfreight Inc. San Antonio, Tx.	(ZS-SRO)
N102SL	02 P-180 Avanti	1052	Skyline Aviation Services Inc. Stewart, NY.	N139PA
N102WK	80 King Air F90	LA-36	Willis Knighton Medical Center, Shreveport, La.	N6736C
N103AL	85 King Air 300	FA-62	Kiawah Aviation LLC. Kiawah Island, SC.	N215P
N103AP	75 King Air E90	LW-126	Pamplemousse Corp. Key Biscayne, Fl.	RP-C201
N103BE*	03 King Air 350	FL-369	Raytheon Aircraft Co. Wichita, Ks.	N100BE
N103BL	75 King Air C90	LJ-650	Aircraft N103BL Holding LLC. Radnor, Pa.	N103FL
N103BN	77 King Air C-12C	BC-47	Harrison County Sheriffs Department, Gulfport, Ms.	77-22936
N103CB	81 King Air F90	LA-98	L & L Aviation LLC. Bossier City, La.	N77JT
N103CW	85 King Air 300	FA-64	Flying Pigs LLC. Greensboro, NC.	(N64HF)
N103PA	70 SA-226T Merlin 3	T-202	Aircraft Guaranty Corp. Germany.	C-FDAC
N103PM	78 King Air 200	BB-304	National Investments Leasing Inc. Wilmington, De.	N451DB
N103RC	75 Mitsubishi MU-2L	673	River City Aviation Inc. West Memphis, Ar.	N4565E
N103RN	98 King Air 350	FL-231	Noel Corp. Yakima, Wa.	N231PK
N103SL	02 P-180 Avanti	1059	AvantAir Inc. Stewart, NY.	N128PA
N104AJ	88 King Air C90A	LJ-1164	Luwe Flug Inc. Lux & Weigl, Bayreuth, Germany.	ZS-MIL
N104BH	01 PA-46-500TP Meridian	4697104	French Onion LLC. Langhorne, Pa.	
N104CX	82 King Air B200	BB-1004	Crux Subsurface Inc. Spokane, Wa.	N104AK
N104JB	80 MU-2 Solitaire	435SA	John Broome Ranches, Oxnard, Ca.	N213MA
N104LC	78 King Air C90	LJ-757	Ivy Aircraft LLC. Hot Springs, Ar.	N23675
N104TA	77 SA-226T Merlin 3A	T-289	Berry Aviation Inc. San Marcos, Tx	(F-GBBD)
N105FC	81 Conquest 1	425-0094	105 LLC. San Francisco, Ca.	N104HW
N105K	66 King Air 90	LJ-113	Airlift California Inc. Hollister, Ca.	N16CS
N105LV	84 PA-42 Cheyenne 400LS	5527010	Bank of Las Vegas, Las Vegas, Nv.	N24KW
N105MA	81 PA-31T Cheyenne 1	8104015	T-G Air Power Inc. Buffalo, NY.	N381SW
N105MW	98 Pilatus PC-12/45	235	Management West LLC. Aurora, Or.	N235AH
N105RG	69 King Air B90	LJ-454	W L Barefoot LLC. Four Oaks, NC.	N105RJ
N105SL	03 P-180 Avanti	1068	AvantAir Inc. Stewart, NY.	
Reg	Yr Type	c/n	Owner/Operator	Prev Regn

Reg	Yr	Type	c/n	Owner/Operator	Prev Regn
☐ N105TC	84	King Air C90A	LJ-1086	Blossman Gas of N Carolia Inc. Asheville, NC.	N18182
☐ N105VY	81	King Air B100	BE-109	Atlantic KingAir Inc. New Gretna, NJ.	N3811F
☐ N105WM	78	Mitsubishi MU-2N	709SA	Richland LLC. Columbia, SC.	N105NM
☐ N106PA	79	King Air 200	BB-428	JWG Inc. Winston-Salem, NC.	G-BFWI
☐ N106SL	03	P-180 Avanti	1070	AvantAir Inc. Stewart, NY.	
☐ N106TT	80	Gulfstream 840	11630	Skytel Inc. Fort Lauderdale, Fl.	D-INRO
☐ N107AJ	82	King Air F90	LA-189	Westerman Ltd. Addison, Tx.	ZS-LFP
☐ N107FL	76	King Air 200	BB-150	Advocate Air LLC. Houston, Tx.	N203SF
☐ N107GL	79	Rockwell 690B	11554	Western Eagle Express LLC. Brawley, Ca.	N84WA
☐ N107JJ	74	Rockwell 690A	11209	John Jacobs, Chicago, Il.	N500TS
☐ N107MG	82	King Air B200	BB-924	BK Associates Inc. Atlanta, Ga.	N52YR
☐ N107PC	83	Cheyenne II-XL	8166046	Maca Inc. Wilmington, DE.	(N18KW)
☐ N107SB	72	Mitsubishi MU-2F	226	Hilgy's LP Gas Inc. Tomahawk, Wi.	N187SB
☐ N107SC	78	King Air C90	LJ-788	Golden Eagle Partnership LC. San Antonio, Tx.	N2030W
☐ N107SL	03	P-180 Avanti	1073	AvantAir Inc. Stewart, NY.	
☐ N108AL	80	King Air 200	BB-730	Gene Reed Enterprises Inc. N Charleston, SC.	N103AL
☐ N108EB	81	King Air B100	BE-108	Andrie Inc. Muskegon, Mi.	N38005
☐ N108JC*	98	Pilatus PC-12/45	209	J W Connolly of Sewickley, Pa.	N209PB
☐ N108KU	73	King Air C90	LJ-568	Magic Express Airlines Inc. Wilmington, De.	N100KU
☐ N108NL*	79	PA-31 Cheyenne II	7920092	McDonald Properties LC. Fairfield, Ia.	N73TW
☐ N108NT	97	King Air 350	FL-168	Bear Creek Aviation LLC. Cincinnati, Oh.	N109NT
☐ N108SA	77	Rockwell 690B	11416	Lund Assocs Inc. Rapid City, SD.	N81658
☐ N108TJ	79	Conquest II	441-0108	Martin's Super Markets Inc. South Bend, In.	N104RD
☐ N108UC	80	PA-31T Cheyenne II	8020018	Inductotherm Industries Inc. Rancocas, NJ.	N802HC
☐ N109DT	85	King Air C90A	LJ-1102	Schoeneman Beauty Supply, Pottsville, Pa.	N682TA
☐ N109GE	94	King Air B200	BB-1476	Weavair Inc. NYC.	ZS-ODU
☐ N109MD	85	King Air B200	BB-1213	Mike Duncan/MBD Inc. Dover, De.	N74AL
☐ N109MS	90	P-180 Avanti	1008	Draceana Corp. Stamford, Ct.	N1LY
☐ N109TM	76	King Air 200	BB-124	Breezey II LLC. Duck, NC.	N124AJ
☐ N110BM	76	King Air 200	BB-110	D & B Air Corp. Austin, Tx.	OE-FIM
☐ N110CE	81	King Air B100	BE-120	Clark Transportation Co. Bethesda, Md.	N2QE
☐ N110EL	65	King Air 90	LJ-71	Tradewinds Air LLC. Stockbridge, Ga.	N1100X
☐ N110G	81	King Air 200	BB-792	Gared Graphics Inc. Van Nuys, Ca.	
☐ N110GC	77	Mitsubishi MU-2P	363SA	Engineered Products Co. San Juan, PR.	(N178GV)
☐ N110MA	74	Mitsubishi MU-2J	616	AIC Aviation Inc. Sullivan, In.	SE-IUB
☐ N110PM	97	King Air C90B	LJ-1481	Mueller Transportation inc. Springfield, Mo.	N1101U
☐ N110RB	64	Gulfstream 1	126	Intermediaries International Inc. Del Mar, Ca.	N63AU
☐ N110VU*	73	King Air A100	B-176	Colemill Enterprises Inc. Nashville, Tn.	N3076W
☐ N111AA	79	King Air F90	LA-6	Blue Water Aviation LLC. Oakman, Al.	C-GSSA
☐ N111AB	81	SA-226T Merlin 3B	T-407	Catterton Aviation LLC. Greenwich, Ct.	
☐ N111CT	76	PA-31 Cheyenne II	7620047	Stanley Thomas, Fort Worth, Tx.	N82039
☐ N111CZ	79	SA-226T Merlin 3B	T-297	Nassau Aircraft Holdings LLC. Garden City, Ga.	N92427
☐ N111FV	74	King Air E90	LW-105	Excel Dealer Services Inc. Surf City, NC.	N111FW
☐ N111HF	71	Mitsubishi MU-2F	208	DBH Attachments Inc. Adamsville, Tn.	N288MA
☐ N111JA	74	King Air E90	LW-84	Executive Air Charter of New Orleans, New Orleans, La.	TF-DCA
☐ N111JW*	01	King Air B200	BB-1767	Jakat LLC. Sapello, NM.	N806G
☐ N111KA	83	King Air C90-1	LJ-1051	PP & J LLC/Cyclone Drilling Inc. Gillette, Wy.	HP-976P
☐ N111KU	86	Conquest 1	425-0226	Herbert Baskin, Berkley, Ca.	(N264HB)
☐ N111KV	79	PA-31T Cheyenne II	7920035	American Medflight Inc. Reno, Nv.	N110MP
☐ N111M	98	King Air 350	FL-210	Ingram Industries Inc. Nashville, Tn.	N350WH
☐ N111MD	99	King Air B200	BB-1665	Argosy Aircraft Inc. Reno, Nv.	
☐ N111MU	94	King Air C90SE	LJ-1362	Neurodiagnostic Testing Services Inc. Huntersville, NC.	N111MD
☐ N111NS	81	King Air 200C	BL-36	Columbia Helicopters Inc. Aurora, Or.	
☐ N111PV	81	King Air 200	BB-772	Tarbert Aviation/MacAllister Machinery Co. Indianapolis, In.	(N917GP)
☐ N111RF	75	PA-31T Cheyenne II	7520037	Dosmatic USA Inc. Carollton, Tx.	(N111BF)
☐ N111SF	91	King Air 350	FL-45	Furrow Services LLC. Knoxville, Tn.	(N350FT)
☐ N111SK	67	680V Turbo Commander	1710-85	Bergman Photographic Services Inc. Portland, Or.	N111ST
☐ N111SS	84	King Air 300	FA-4	KA Rentals LLC. Edina, Mn.	(N788SC)
☐ N111SU	84	Conquest 1	425-0205	Pilgrims Holdings Ltd. Hickory Corners, Mi.	N105TC
☐ N111TC	79	King Air E90	LW-305	T C Aviation Inc. Brentwood, Ca.	N942RM
☐ N111UT	78	King Air 200	BB-374	University of Tennessee, Alcoa, Tn.	N7QR
☐ N111VR	91	P-180 Avanti	1006	DLZ Aircraft Inc. Columbus, Oh.	N34S
☐ N111YF	77	King Air B100	BE-30	DeJarnette Enterprises Inc. Lee's Summit, Mo.	N110EC
☐ N112AB	85	King Air 300	FA-85	Cloudscape Inc. Ruidoso, NM.	N92GC
☐ N112AF	99	Pilatus PC-12/45	266	Alpha Flying Inc. Nashua, NH.	HB-FSK

Reg	Yr Type	c/n	Owner/Operator	Prev Regn
N112BB	81 PA-31T Cheyenne 1	8104021	Neil Whitesell, Muscle Shoals, Al.	N633AB
N112BC	81 PA-42 Cheyenne III	8001027	Williams Group International Inc. Stone Mountain, Ga.	
N112BL	77 PA-31T Cheyenne II	7720037	North Dakota Department of Transport, Bismarck, ND.	
N112CE	85 Gulfstream 1000	96097	Clark Transportation Co. Bethesda, Md.	N134GA
N112CS	84 SA-227TT Merlin 3C	TT-541	Cal-Ark Inc. Little Rock, Ar.	N348KN
N112ED	80 PA-31T Cheyenne II	8020060	E H Derby & Co/Alpha Jet Interrnational, Muscle Shoals, Al.	N703CJ
N112EF	73 Rockwell 690A	11123	E F W Aircraft Sales Corp. Dover, De.	N122PG
N112EM	76 Rockwell 690A	11330	E Micah Aviation Inc. Cincinnati, Oh.	N567H
N112MA	77 Mitsubishi MU-2N	689SA	Somerset Spring & Alighment Inc. Raritan, NJ.	C-FTAD
N113CT	70 681 Turbo Commander	6006	Jack Wellborne/Highlander Trust, Idabel, Ok.	N2725B
N113GS	80 SA-226T Merlin 3B	T-330	GRD Contractors Inc. Costa Mesa, Ca.	YV-788CP
N113RC	75 PA-31T Cheyenne II	7520009	Tripp Ag Inc/Searcy Farm Supply LLC. Searcy, Ar.	(N117BL)
N113SD	73 Mitsubishi MU-2J	600	Air Flight Enterprises Inc. Port Orange, Fl.	N707TT
N113SL	92 P-180 Avanti	1020	AvantAir Inc. Stewart, NY.	D-ITCN
N113US	87 King Air B200	BB-1283	Pampelmousse LLC/United Supermarkets Inc. Lubbock, Tx.	N200KA
N113WC	80 PA-42 Cheyenne III	8001005	C & D Investments Inc. Fort Smith, Ar.	N13TT
N114CW	66 King Air A90	LJ-114	Colorado Well Service Inc. Rangely, Co.	N114KA
N114DB	85 King Air C90A	LJ-1097	Qualim V LLC. Providence, RI.	OY-JAJ
N114HB	96 King Air B200	BB-1533	Mattic/Navajo Inc. Onalaska, Wi.	N14HB
N114JR	80 PA-31T Cheyenne 1	8004037	Oman Sales Inc/The Sleep Shop, Lubbock, Tx.	N900PC
N114SB	76 King Air 200	BB-161	Seven Bar Flying Service Inc. Albuquerque, NM.	N131PA
N115AB	74 Rockwell 690A	11231	Daedalus Enterprises LLC. Great Falls, Mt.	N115BH
N115AP	68 Mitsubishi MU-2F	136	Lagonia Holdings LLC/MAL Aircraft Sales, Cordova, Tn.	N75RJ
N115CT	99 King Air B200	BB-1669	Kavak Enterprises Ltd. Roadtown , Tortola, BVI.	
N115DT	75 King Air A100	B-212	Air Serv International Inc. Redlands, Ca.	N115D
N115GA	85 Gulfstream 1000B	96201	Horizon Aircraft Sales Inc. Miami, Fl.	
N115GB	99 King Air 350	FL-237	Graham Brothers Construction Co. Dublin, Ga.	N310TK
N115KC	02 TBM 700B	239	Pegasus 115 LLC. Miami, Fl.	
N115KU	82 King Air C90-1	LJ-1040	University of Kansas, Kansas City, Ks.	N115MX
N115PA	66 King Air A90	LJ-117	APA Enterprises Inc. Poughskeepsie, NY.	N10430
N115PC	78 PA-31T Cheyenne II	7820001	Eagles WingsAviation LLC. Monroeville, Al.	(N300PR)
N116AF	96 Pilatus PC-12	137	Fargo Transportation Inc. Chestnut Hill, Ma.	(N316WF)
N116DG	81 King Air B100	BE-116	BDG LLC. Hutchinson, Ks.	N116AC
N116JP	81 PA-42 Cheyenne III	8001050	Turbines Inc. Terre Haute, In.	N4098K
N116RJ	72 King Air U-21J	B-96	Air Norman LLC. Denver, NC.	N96GJ
N117CP	67 King Air A90	LM-68	K K Aircraft Inc. Bridgewater, Va.	(N73Q)
N117FH	76 King Air E90	LW-194	Collins Aviation LLC. Midland, Tx.	N194KA
N117H	79 MU-2 Marquise	751SA	GoBuyAir LLC. Flint, Mi.	N948MA
N117MF	78 King Air C90	LJ-779	Mercy Flights Inc. Medford, Or.	(N107RE)
N117PW	01 PA-46-500TP Meridian	4697030	Johnson Potato Co. Walhalla, ND.	
N117TJ	80 King Air F90	LA-17	RaCon Inc. Tuscaloosa, Al.	N19EG
N117WF	95 Pilatus PC-12	117	Fisher Auto Parts Inc. Staunton, Va.	(N12FA)
N118AF	97 Pilatus PC-12	175	CED Management Services Inc. Northbrook, Il.	HB-FSK
N118CR	76 Rockwell 690A	11276	Hokie Airco Inc. Roanoke, Va.	N57172
N118GW	87 King Air 300	FA-119	Majestic Aviation Inc. Bakersfield, Ca.	N688RL
N118NL	81 King Air B100	BE-111	Architectural Cost Control Systems, Dallas, Tx.	N400TJ
N118P	74 Mitsubishi MU-2J	646	Newair LLC. Newport, Ar.	N113P
N118WC	80 PA-31T Cheyenne II	8020020	Halair Inc. Wilmington, De.	N113WC
N119AF	98 Pilatus PC-12/45	215	Alpha Flying Inc. Nashua, NH.	HB-FQS
N119AR	04 King Air B200	BB-1867	AR Equipment/Armstrong Transfer & Storage Co. Morrisville.	N6167R
N119EB	77 PA-31T Cheyenne II	7720012	Michael Harper, Duncanville, Tx.	N79ML
N119RL	79 PA-31T Cheyenne 1	7904002	Versa Air II LLC. Racine, Wi.	D-IEIS
N119SA	89 King Air C90A	LJ-1196	Sara Air LLC. Greensboro, NC.	N484JA
N120FA	82 SA-227AT Merlin 4C	AT-461	Transair America Inc. Buffalo Grove, Il.	F-GGLF
N120FS	79 King Air 200	BB-562	BK LLC/Dubois County Flight Services, Huntingburg, In.	(N777JE)
N120JM	84 SA-227AT Merlin 4C	AT-577	Path Corp. Rehoboth Beach, De.	N31136
N120MG	79 King Air B100	BE-70	King Air LLC. Hilton Head Island, SC.	N926HS
N120NA	83 King Air B200	BB-1120	Washington State Patrol, Olympia, Wa.	N6609K
N120P	81 King Air 200	BB-786	Duckwall-ALCO Stores Inc. Abilene, Ks.	
N120PR	83 King Air B200T	BT-29	Commonwealth of Puerto Rico, San Juan, PR.(was BB-1097).	N150BA
N120RC	81 King Air F90	LA-117	R R Cassidy Inc. Baton Rouge, La.	N7775
N120RL	79 King Air 200T	BT-9	Global Aircraft Leasing Inc. Griffin, Ga. (was BB-551).	JA8814
N120SC	78 SA-226AT Merlin 4A	AT-067	River City Aviation Inc. West Memphis, Ar.	C-FJTL
N120SL	01 PA-46-500TP Meridian	4697057	AvantAir Inc. Stewart, NY.	C-FGDM
N120TM	81 SA-226T Merlin 3B	T-405	OG LLC. Birmingham, Al.	N189CC
Reg	Yr Type	c/n	Owner/Operator	Prev Regn

Reg	Yr	Type	c/n	Owner/Operator	Prev Regn
N120TT	84	King Air C90A	LJ-1073	Banyan Aircraft Sales LLC. Fort Lauderdale, Fl.	HP-1152
N120WW	01	PA-46-500TP Meridian	4697047	Aircraft Guaranty Title LLC. Houston, Tx.	LX-ILE
N121B	72	King Air E90	LW-21	Goodland Regional Medical Center, Goodland, Ks.	
N121CA	73	King Air C-12C	BD-9	California Department of Justice, Sacramento, Ca.	73-1213
N121CH	73	Mitsubishi MU-2K	265	Air 1st Aviation Companies Inc. Aiken, SC.	SE-IOY
N121CS	81	PA-42 Cheyenne III	8001032	Flying Moose LLC/Bennett Law Office PA. Mizzoula, Mt.	N432R
N121EG	73	King Air E90	LW-71	Falcon Executive Inc. Mesa, Az.	
N121EH	81	Cheyenne II-XL	8166039	Pensacola Aircraft LLC. Pensacola, Fl.	N121LH
N121JW	76	Rockwell 690A	11299	Aero Charter Services Inc. Bloomsburg, Pa.	(N121DK)
N121KB	68	SA-26T Merlin 2A	T26-33	Eastern Aviation & Marine Underwriters, Towson, Md.	N1215S
N121LB	79	King Air 200	BB-475	Berry Air LLC. Tahlequah, Ok.	
N121LH	90	PA-42 Cheyenne IIIA	5501049	O G Packing Co. Anchorage, Ak.	N949TA
N121P	81	King Air C90	LJ-970	Lane Aviation Corp. Columbus, Oh.	
N121RF	95	Pilatus PC-12	114	Richard A Foreman Associates Inc. Wilmington, De.	N114SV
N121TD	78	King Air C-12C	BC-74	Idaho Department of Law Enforcement, Boise, Id.	78-23138
N121WH	92	P-180 Avanti	1019	Calzada LLC. Los Angeles, Ca.	D-IHRA
N122CK	78	Mitsubishi MU-2P	374SA	Lycoming Aviation Inc. Williamsport, Pa.	N9HA
N122K	77	King Air C90	LJ-707	Dycom Aviation LLC. Greensboro, NC.	(N32HF)
N122MA	71	Mitsubishi MU-2F	207	ZMP Corp. Huntsville, Al.	
N122PA	00	P-180 Avanti	1038	Piaggio Avanti 1038 LLC. Great Meadow, NJ.	I-FXRD
N122RF	76	King Air 200	BB-122	Smart Air Service Inc. Wilmington, De.	(N719HT)
N122TP	88	King Air B200	BB-1293	Tango Papa Aviation LLC. Telluride, Co.	N3127K
N122U	70	King Air 100	B-32	Coastal Wings Inc. Nantucket, Ma.	C-GSAM
N122ZZ	69	King Air 100	B-6	Marco Jet LLC. Sarasota, Fl.	N169MM
N123AF	85	King Air 300	FA-46	Tecnicard Inc. Miami, Fl.	N7222V
N123AG	81	PA-42 Cheyenne III	8001031	Aqua Glass Corp. Adamsville, Tn.	N123CN
N123AT	89	King Air C90A	LJ-1224	Bluestem Asset Management LLC. Charlottesville, Va.	PT-OBF
N123BL	80	King Air B100	BE-83	Skyway K West LLC. Clarksville, Tn.	N412FC
N123CH	80	King Air F90	LA-32	Automobile Transport Co. Jacksonville, Fl.	N969MC
N123EA	79	PA-31T Cheyenne II	7920028	Eastern Air Center Inc. Norwood, Ma.	N10MC
N123LH	82	SA-227TT Merlin 3C	TT-433	North Park Aviation LLC. San Marcos, Tx.	C-GFCE
N123LL	80	King Air C90	LJ-885	Page Air Inc. Midlothian, Va.	N1WB
N123ME	86	Conquest II	441-0359	Active Research Technologies LLC. Lewisville, Tx.	N40FJ
N123MH	74	King Air E90	LW-104	Mark Osborn, Birmingham, Al.	N133PL
N123ML	97	King Air B200	BB-1587	George Beitzel, Chappaqua, NY.	N32700
N123SK	72	King Air C90	LJ-540	Metair LLC. Tulsa, Ok.	(N690CA)
N123V	67	King Air A90	LJ-258	Milwaukee Area Technical College, Milwaukee, Wi.	N915BD
N123WH	82	King Air B100	BE-126	JLEE Industries LLC. Beaver, WV.	(N512DS)
N123ZC	02	TBM 700B	229	Jasper Industries Ltd. Wilmington, De.	F-HELO
N124BK	80	King Air F90	LA-15	KLM Oil Properties LLC. Nara Visa, NM.	N237JS
N124CM	84	King Air 300	FA-24	Carter Machinery Co Inc. Salem, Va.	N300KA
N124DA	98	King Air 350	FL-228	Allen Aviation LLC. Richmond, Va.	N272SW
N124EB	94	King Air 350	FL-126	Natural Selection Foods, San Juan Baitista, Ca.	N102CS
N124GA	82	King Air B200	BB-1039	Pinnacle Resources Inc. Pine Bluff, Ar.	HB-GHS
N124LL	03	King Air C90B	LJ-1695	Longleaf Aviation LLC. Newton, Ga.	
N124PC	98	Pilatus PC-12/45	217	Aviation Consultants of Aspen Inc. Hollis, NH.	HB-FQJ
N124PS	03	Pilatus PC-12/45	502	Duck Pond Aviation II LLC. San Jose, Ca.	HB-FRH
N124SA	67	King Air A90	LJ-306	Smyrna Air Center Inc. Smyrna, Tn.	YV-2683P
N124UV	95	Pilatus PC-12	124	Unionville Aviation Inc. Wilmington, De.	N124PB
N125A	68	King Air B90	LJ-360	David Swetland, Cleveland, Oh.	N1250B
N125D	81	King Air B100	BE-114	James Naples/New Boston General Hospital Inc. New Boston, Tx	
N125KW	81	King Air B200	BB-939	Kankakee B200 Leasing LLC. Kankakee, Il.	N164TC
N125MM	80	Gulfstream 840	11605	Malibu Aviation Co. Concord, NH.	HB-GPB
N125NC	82	King Air B200	BB-1023	N Carolina Department of Commerce, Raleigh, NC.	N62546
N125PG	82	Conquest 1	425-0125	Douglas Barkdull, Scottsdale, Az.	N125VE
N125RG	82	SA-227TT Merlin 3C	TT-441	Sunlight Corp. Greenwich, Ct.	YV-277CP
N125SC	83	Conquest 1	425-0136	James E Simon Co. Cheyenne, Wy.	N6884G
N125TS	92	King Air B200	BB-1422	Tri-State Generation & Transmission Inc. Broomfield, Co.	N422BW
N125VH	77	King Air B100	BE-25	Valley Hope Association, Norton, Ks.	N125U
N125WG*	75	SA-226T Merlin 3A	T-250	Gamble Aviation LLC. Shreveport, La.	N311RV
N125WZ	01	PA-46-500TP Meridian	4697032	125WZ Ltd. Dallas, Tx.	
N126DS	90	King Air 350	FL-31	ISC Aviation LLC. Fort Mill, SC.	(N331JH)
N126M	80	Gulfstream 980	95033	Barbee's Freeway Ford Inc. Denver, Co.	N8774P
N126MM	01	King Air C90B	LJ-1669	Technical Film Systems Inc. Van Nuys, Ca.	N4469Z
N126SP	85	King Air B200	BB-1209	Aero Care Services LLC. Mendham, NJ.	(N53GA)
Reg	Yr	Type	c/n	Owner/Operator	Prev Regn

Reg	Yr	Type	c/n	Owner/Operator	Prev Regn
N127BB	80	Conquest 1	425-0012	Sound Security Inc. Portland, Or.	N127DC
N127DC	82	King Air F90	LA-177	King Air F90 Charter LLC. Zanesville, Oh.	N418DY
N127EC	78	King Air E90	LW-299	ATSTM LLC. Milwaukee, Wi.	N127BB
N127GA	77	King Air 200	BB-312	Beech Transportation Inc. Eden Prairie, Mn.	F-GEBC
N127HT	67	King Air A90	LJ-215	Southwest Aviation Specialist LLC. Tulsa, Ok.	HB-GEV
N127MC	85	Conquest 1	425-0231	McCoy Corp. San Marcos, Tx.	N12270
N127MJ	83	King Air B200	BB-1132	King Air Charter LLC. Zanesville, Oh.	N152C
N127TA	80	King Air 200	BB-636	Pacific International Marketing, Salinas, Ca.	N806TC
N127Z	74	King Air A100	B-179	USDA Forest Service, Boise, Id.	N20EG
N128CM	01	Pilatus PC-12/45	403	Eagle Cap Leasing Inc. Enterprises, Or.	HB-FQT
N128EZ	80	Conquest II	441-0128	Air Zieba LP.	N441TM
N128JP	80	King Air F90	LA-25	F90 Partners LLC. Thunderbolt, Ga.	N616CP
N128MG	97	King Air 350	FL-182	Martin Gas Transport Inc. Kilgore, Tx.	N381MG
N128PA	91	P-180 Avanti	1013	Piaggio America Inc. Greenville, SC.	I-FXRA
N128SB	97	King Air C90B	LJ-1503	Digger Pine Enterprises LLC. Saratoga, Ca.	N9MU
N128VT	92	King Air B200	BB-1442	Missouri Dept of Conservation, Jefferson City, Mo.	N128V
N129AF	64	Gulfstream 1	129	Aerial Films Inc. Morristown, NJ.	N113GA
N129C	73	King Air E90	LW-61	CPC International Apple Co. Yakima, Wa.	N120GR
N129EJ	01	PA-46-500TP Meridian	4697065	Patrick McCall, Orange, Ca.	
N129LA	66	King Air A90	LJ-129	Aviones Inc. Wilmington, De.	N7202L
N129LC	79	PA-31T Cheyenne 1	7904042	129LC LLC/High Air Inc. Plano, Tx.	N247R
N129RP*	84	King Air C90A	LJ-1075	Philcrest Properties Inc. Tulsa, Ok.	N68474
N129RW*	68	King Air B90	LJ-369	Royis Ward, Corpus Christi, Tx.	N70CU
N129TB	81	Gulfstream 840	11676	Semitool Inc. Kalispell, Mt.	N5928K
N129TT	82	King Air B200	BB-1078	Eric Travel Inc. Stewart, Mn.	(N781HM)
N130AT	80	King Air B100	BE-88	Roche Biomedcal Lab Inc. Burlington, NC.	
N130CT	79	King Air 200	BB-578	Southeast Airmotive Corp. Charlotte, NC.	N303DK
N130DM	68	King Air B90	LJ-385	FMCO Promotions, Little Rock, Ar.	N33AS
N130MS	79	MU-2 Marquise	750SA	Prima Group Marketing LLC. Helena, Mt.	N947MA
N130TT	78	Rockwell 690B	11495	T & T Air Charter LLC. Kingmont, WV.	N76EC
N131DF	79	PA-31T Cheyenne 1	7904015	Great Bear Aviation Co. Chicago, Il.	N23235
N131JN	02	Pilatus PC-12/45	446	DLN Aviation Inc. Lafayette, La.	N446PC
N131PC	78	PA-31T Cheyenne II	7820009	W Brent Davis, Springfield, Mo.	
N131SJ	76	King Air 200	BB-131	BM Devco Inc. Larkspur, Ca.	TC-TAB
N131SP	83	King Air F90-1	LA-206	Kaufmann Land & Development LLC. Denver, Co.	(N4UC)
N131TC	77	King Air 200	BB-271	Trical Inc. Hollister, Ca.	N69BK
N132AS	81	King Air C90	LJ-928	ASI Holdings Inc. Albany, Ga.	N5095K
N132BK	81	MU-2 Marquise	1529SA	Flight Line Inc. Salt Lake City, Ut.	N818R
N132CC	84	King Air 300	FA-11	Club Car Inc. Augusta, Ga.	N732P
N132CW	77	SA-226T Merlin 3B	T-276	Continental Wingate Co. Needham, Ma.	N188SC
N132DD	79	King Air E90	LW-308	N2DD Inc. Newark, De.	N2DD
N132HS	72	King Air E90	LW-8	Medway Air Ambualnce Inc. Lawrenceville, Ga.	N132B
N132JH	73	Rockwell 690A	11126	C & F Aviation, Norman, Ok.	(N345SP)
N132K	81	King Air B200	BB-938	Dan & Bruce Harrison, Houston, Tx.	
N132MC	92	King Air B200	BB-1395	Louisiana Aircraft LLC. Oklahoma City, Ok.	N8049H
N132N	82	King Air B200	BB-1053	David & Diane Miller, Bandon, Or.	(N212DM)
N133DL	80	Gulfstream 840	11616	Safeguards International Inc. Charlotte, NC.	D-IGEL
N133FM	81	PA-42 Cheyenne III	8001010	Plane 1 Leasing Co. Naples, Fl.	YV-O-ICA-1
N133GA	89	King Air B200	BB-1321	Mid-America Apartments LP. Memphis, Tn.	F-GILI
N133K	94	King Air B200	BB-1487	Super King Partners LLC. Fayetteville, NC.	(D-IAJK)
N133LA	67	King Air C90	LJ-537	Owners Jet Services Ltd. St Charles, Il.	N537EC
N133NL	01	King Air 350	FL-332	B & W Consulting LLC. Reserve, La.	N4332U
N133PA	02	P-180 Avanti	1062	RGH Aviation LLC. Edwards, Co.	
N134G	01	PA-46-500TP Meridian	4697041	SEH Aviation Corp. Wilmington, De.	
N134M	03	PA-46-500TP Meridian	4697169	Cos Aircraft LLC. Colorado Springs, Co.	
N134MA	70	Mitsubishi MU-2G	507	Nashville Jets Inc. Murfreesboro, Tn.	
N134W	65	King Air 90	LJ-52	Lucaya Air Enterprise Inc. Opa Locka, Fl.	N90BL
N134WJ	89	King Air B200C	BL-134	Evergreen Equity Inc. McMinnville, Or.	SE-LMP
N135CL	77	PA-31T Cheyenne II	7720019	Smokey's Smokehouse Inc. Spanish Fork, Ut.	N75465
N135FL	02	PA-46-500TP Meridian	4697105	Aviation Advantage LLC. Wilmington, De.	
N135JM	01	PA-46-500TP Meridian	4697072	P & M Land Ventures LLC. Oceanside, Ca.	C-GNSS
N135MA	80	PA-31T Cheyenne II	8020025	The Title Company Inc. La Crosse, Wi.	N2407W
N135MK	84	King Air 300	FA-3	Osprey Flight Management Inc. Houston, Tx.	N67683
N136AJ	90	King Air B200C	BL-136	Balmoral Central Contracts Inc.	ZS-SON
N136JH	70	King Air 100	B-25	Sky Med Inc. Haleiwa, Hi.	N352NR

345

Reg	Yr Type	c/n	Owner/Operator	Prev Regn
☐ N136MB	78 King Air B100	BE-50	CanDo Air LLC. Charleston, SC.	N955FC
☐ N136PA	04 P-180 Avanti	1092	Piaggio America Inc. Greenville, SC.	
☐ N136SP	80 Cheyenne II-XL	8166001	Pense Brothers Drilling Co. Frederickstown, Md.	VH-RSW
☐ N137BW	78 Rockwell 690B	11446	Ken Thompson Inc. Cypress, Ca.	N117SA
☐ N137CP	69 SA-26AT Merlin 2B	T26-136	Air Jordan LLC. Newport News, Va.	N51LF
☐ N137CW	79 PA-31T Cheyenne 1	7904052	Airvest LLC. Bristol, Va.	N72TW
☐ N137D	82 King Air B100	BE-128	Barnes Global Network, Charleston, SC.	(N56TJ)
☐ N137JT	80 PA-31T Cheyenne II	8020014	J & T Implements LLC. Belton, Mo.	N801ST
☐ N138JM	91 TBM 700	7	Muncie Aviation Co. Muncie, In.	D-FGYY
☐ N139B	72 King Air C90	LJ-563	Rocky Mountain Air PMG LLC. Hamilton, Mt.	
☐ N139CS	81 PA-31T Cheyenne II	8120004	Chandler Aviation Corp. Ashland, Oh.	C-GSSC
☐ N139SC	79 King Air C90	LJ-868	Aerostar Executive Aviation Inc. San Antonio, Tx.	F-GERL
☐ N140CM	70 Mitsubishi MU-2F	190	Marlin Crane Inc. Greenwood, In.	N111MA
☐ N140CP	77 Mitsubishi MU-2P	362SA	Kozarksy Aviation Inc. Atlanta, Ga.	N801L
☐ N140GA	80 King Air 200	BB-715	Pezold Air Charters LLC. Columbus, Ga.	ZS-NOC
☐ N140PA	67 King Air A90	LJ-297	Wright Brothers Aircraft Title Inc. Oklahoma City, Ok.	N839K
☐ N141CE	03 King Air 350	FL-387	Raytheon Aircraft Co. Wichita, Ks.	N5117S
☐ N141CT	80 King Air 200	BB-651	Cenac Towing Co. Houma, La.	N132GA
☐ N141DA	93 King Air 350	FL-92	L & K Inc. Omaha, Ne.	(N141DB)
☐ N141GA	80 PA-31T Cheyenne 1	8004022	Stratford Aviation Co. Lincoln, Ne.	G-BHTP
☐ N141K	97 King Air 350	FL-161	Victor One Four One LLC. Lincoln, Ma.	OY-LEL
☐ N141RR	65 King Air 90	LJ-38	APA Enterprises Inc. Poughkeepsie, NY.	C-GGGL
☐ N141SM	84 King Air 300	FA-23	Spencer Air inc. Mooresville, NC.	N313MP
☐ N141TC	84 PA-42 Cheyenne IIIA	5501021	Joseph Meyer, Edwardsville, Il.	N200JH
☐ N141VY	99 Pilatus PC-12/45	256	Mitek Corp/Elijah Reed Corp. Wilmington, De.	HB-FSA
☐ N142BK	79 MU-2 Marquise	733SA	Air 1st Aviation Companies Inc. Aiken, SC.	N533MA
☐ N142CE	04 King Air 350	FL-391	Raytheon Aircraft Co. Wichita, Ks.	N5091G
☐ N142EB	82 King Air B200	BB-1042	MITC Aviation LLC. Prairie Village, Ks.	N447AC
☐ N142JC	80 King Air B100	BE-93	Valley Plating Inc. Green Bay, Wi.	XC-IMC
☐ N142LT	00 Pilatus PC-12/45	312	Lyle Turner, Rancho Santa Fe, Ca.	HB-FQY
☐ N142WJ	80 Conquest II	441-0142	Robinson Air Crane Inc. Opa Locka, Fl.	XC-AA11
☐ N143DE	80 King Air 200	BB-585	Affiliated Leasing Inc. Greenwood, SC.	N43PE
☐ N143JA	75 Mitsubishi MU-2M	324	BAR Realty Corp. San Juan, PR.	N512MA
☐ N143Z	DHC 6-300	437	USDA Forest Service, Boise, Id.	
☐ N144JB	85 Gulfstream 900	15039	Skytel Inc. Fort Lauderdale, Fl.	N61GA
☐ N144JT	98 TBM 700B	144	Menter Aviation LLC. Slinger, Wi.	
☐ N144PL	84 PA-42 Cheyenne 400LS	5527014	PL Flight LLC. Kirkland, Wa.	N400SN
☐ N145AF*	04 King Air C90B	LJ-1721	Raytheon Aircraft Co. Wichita, Ks.	N6196S
☐ N145AJ	95 King Air B200	BB-1501	Atlanta Jet Inc. Lawrenceville, Ga.	PR-DPS
☐ N145FS	81 MU-2 Solitaire	437SA	Professional Aviation Sales & Service, Millington, Tn.	N666AM
☐ N145JP	81 King Air 200	BB-818	Jepco Air Inc. Chattanooga, Tn.	N80QB
☐ N145MJ	76 King Air C-12C	BC-24	My Jet Inc. Cary, NC.	N716GA
☐ N145MR	81 King Air F90	LA-125	Aviation M R LLC. Wilmington, De.	N65MM
☐ N146FL	80 King Air F90	LA-59	Keep Holdings Inc. Wilmington, De.	G-FLTI
☐ N146GW	83 Conquest 1	425-0146	C & E Cattle Co. Yuma, Az.	N146FW
☐ N146MD	81 King Air B200	BB-886	Don Oppliger Trucking Inc/Jamie & Mary LLC. Clovis, NM.	N111JW
☐ N146MH	81 King Air B200	BB-885	MHG Leasing Inc. Greenville, SC.	N146BC
☐ N146PC	96 PC-12 Spectre	146	Pilatus Business Aircraft Ltd. Jeffco Airport, Co.	N777JF
☐ N147NA	82 King Air B200	BB-1047	C C Medflight Inc. Lawrenceville, Ga.	ZS-LIL
☐ N148Z	69 King Air B90	LJ-472	USDA Forest Service, Washington, DC.	(N204FW)
☐ N149CC*	88 King Air 300	FA-145	Cianbro Corp. Baltimore, Md.	N145NA
☐ N149CM	88 King Air C90A	LJ-1184	KBC Air LLC/Cogswell Motors Inc. Russellville, Ar.	N483JA
☐ N149Z	82 King Air B200C	BL-124	USDA Forest Service, Washington, DC.	N107Z
☐ N150GW	98 King Air C90B	LJ-1531	Southwest Tape & Label Inc. Anthony, NM.	N2309J
☐ N150MX	04 Pilatus PC-12/45	580	Queen Street PC-12 LLC. Phoenix, Az.	HB-FQR
☐ N150PB	96 Pilatus PC-12	150	Foghorn Flite LLC. Pendleton, In.	HB-FRL
☐ N150TJ	76 King Air B100	BE-3	Pennington Seed Inc. Madison, Ga.	N9103S
☐ N150TK	84 Cheyenne II-XL	1166008	Tiffin Aire Inc. Tiffin, Oh.	N150RC
☐ N150TW	73 King Air E90	LW-50	Chaparral Inc/Ameristar Jet Charter Inc. Dallas, Tx.	N88GC
☐ N150VE	76 King Air C90	LJ-678	Allied Aviation LLC. Cookville, Tn.	N9091S
☐ N150YA	82 King Air B100	BE-124	Hospital Investors Management Corp. Englewood Cliffs, NJ.	(N150YR)
☐ N150YR	82 King Air B100	BE-132	Central Control Inc. Alexandria, La.	
☐ N151CF	96 King Air B200	BB-1551	Goldwind Inc.	N969TS
☐ N151E	00 King Air 350	FL-298	Waterloo Industries Inc. Waterloo, Ia.	N4298H
☐ N151EL	78 King Air 200	BB-371	Americana Aviation Inc. Albert Lea, Mn.	N151E
Reg	*Yr Type*	*c/n*	*Owner/Operator*	*Prev Regn*

Reg	Yr	Type	c/n	Owner/Operator	Prev Regn
N151GS	80	PA-31T Cheyenne II	8020024	Strausser Enterprises Inc. Easton, Pa.	N103SP
N151MP	81	Cheyenne II-XL	8166063	Minnkota Power Co-Operative, Grand Forks, ND.	N776AK
N151WT	83	King Air B200	BB-1151	KO Aviation LLC. Cleves, Oh.	XA-MCB
N152AL	04	PA-46-500TP Meridian	4697182	Aeromed Equipment Leasing LLC. Minnetonka, Mn.	
N152D	75	King Air E90	LW-119	Frances Nordstrom, Lemoore, Ca.	N102CU
N152PC	04	Pilatus PC-12/45	552	Shurley Air LLC. Wilmington, De.	HB-FSU
N152RP	86	King Air B200	BB-1255	Partidas Air LLC/JRW Aviation Inc. Dallas, Tx.	(N86KA)
N152TW	76	King Air 200	BB-152	Chapparal Inc/Ameristar Jet Charter Inc. Dallas, Tx.	N1223C
N152WE	81	King Air F90	LA-152	S & H Air Service LLC. Lafayette, La.	HP-1215
N152WW	75	King Air C90	LJ-654	Excell Aviation LLC/Jetflite Inc. Gulf Stream, Fl.	N917K
N153JA	70	King Air 100	B-53	EN Aviation Inc. Cordova, Tn.	N153JW
N153JM	83	Conquest 1	425-0153	Mark Jacobson & Associates Inc. Bingham Farms, Mi.	C-GAGE
N153ML	75	King Air 200	BB-23	John Powell, Colorado Springs, Co.	N814KA
N153PB	96	Pilatus PC-12/45	153	E L Thompson & Son Inc. St Croix, USVI.	HB-FRO
N153PM	80	King Air C90	LJ-876	Carver Aero Inc. Davenport, la.	N876NA
N154CA	80	PA-31T Cheyenne II	8020085	Fedair Inc. Wilmington, De.	D-IIPA
N154DF	98	King Air B200	BB-1649	Moss Supply Co. Charlotte, NC.	N154DE
N154DR	01	PA-46-500TP Meridian	4697034	Jessee Kent, Big Sky, Mt.	N4189N
N154L	77	SA-226T Merlin 3A	T-284	Sun Development & Management Corp. Indianapolis, In.	(N28TA)
N154WC	70	Mitsubishi MU-2G	509	Schuybroeck Aviation Inc. Dover, De.	C-GBOX
N155A	91	King Air C90A	LJ-1257	GutterGuard LLC. Chamblee, Ga.	N8255A
N155AS	73	Mitsubishi MU-2J	589	Turbine Aircraft Marketing Inc. San Angelo, Tx.	N293MA
N155AV	85	King Air B200	BB-1216	Teton Leasing LLC. Pocatello, Id.	(N210AC)
N155CA	78	PA-31T Cheyenne II	7820024	Reno Flying Service Inc. Reno, Nv.	YV-...
N155LS	78	King Air E90	LW-286	Mac-Air LLC. Middleboro, Ma.	N18754
N155MA	67	Mitsubishi MU-2B	014	Roy Lieske, Milwaukee, Wi.	N4WD
N155MC	78	PA-31T Cheyenne II	7820069	CartretteLLC. Greenville, NC.	N168DA
N155QS	75	King Air 200	BB-79	C & H Aviation LLC. La Crosse, Wi.	N155RJ
N155RG	89	King Air C90A	LJ-1219	The Rasmussen Group, Des Moines, la.	N771AW
N156GA	83	Conquest 1	425-0134	M-W Air LC. Lubbock, Tx.	HB-LNT
N156SB	96	Pilatus PC-12	156	Yoyo LLC. Bremerton, Wa.	HB-FRR
N156SW	03	Pilatus PC-12/45	514	Classic Flight Corp. Forney, Tx.	HB-FRQ
N157A	82	King Air B200C	BL-53	Aviation Specialities Inc. Washington, DC.	N320JS
N157CA	82	MU-2 Marquise	1558SA	Flight Line Inc. Denver, Co.	N5PQ
N157CB	78	King Air C90	LJ-758	L & R Investments LLC. Crossett, Ar.	N900SC
N157JB	91	TBM 700	6	Milton Holcombe, Dallas, Tx.	N700ZL
N157LL	81	PA-42 Cheyenne III	8001058	Lima/Lima Aviation Services LLC. Lakeland, Fl.	N4098T
N157MA	80	MU-2 Solitaire	424SA	Dr Marius Maxwell/Sabre Investments Inc. Paducah, Ky.	
N158CA	68	SA-26AT Merlin 2B	T26-107	S & J Enterprises Inc. Fort Lauderdale, Fl.	C-GMOU
N158TJ	81	PA-42 Cheyenne III	8001057	Frank L Woodworth Inc. Pittsfield, Me.	(N821TB)
N159DG	79	PA-31T Cheyenne II	7920024	Garbo Lobster Co. Groton, Ct.	N111HT
N159GS	69	Gulfstream 1	200	Gyrocam G-1 Inc. Sarasota, Fl.	N255TK
N160AB	91	King Air 300	FA-216	Aaron Rents Inc. Atlanta, Ga.	N160AC
N160AC	03	King Air 350	FL-367	Elkhorn Aviation LLC. Hayward, Ca.	N6167K
N160EA	69	SA-26AT Merlin 2B	T26-165	JBI Holdings Inc. Wilmington, De.	C-GMZG
N160MW	04	King Air 350	FL-407	Midwest Jet Inc. Mattoon, Il.	
N160NA	77	PA-31T Cheyenne II	7720060	S & H Sales LP. Kalispell, Mt.	XB-JIC
N160SF	75	King Air 200	BB-32	La Quinta Air Corp. Palm Springs, Ca.	N100SF
N160SM	98	King Air 350	FL-215	Stowers Machinery Corp. Knoxville, Tn.	N160AC
N160SP	81	MU-2 Marquise	1506SA	Jerry Woolf DDS Inc. Bakersfield, Ca.	N15MV
N160TR	79	PA-31T Cheyenne II	7920036	BHS Direct Inc. UK.	N81918
N160TT	79	King Air E90	LW-309	Pacific International Gulf Systems, Chicago, Il.	N630AM
N161AJ	96	Pilatus PC-12	161	Garrett Gruener, Berkeley, Ca.	VH-FAM
N161RC	90	King Air B200	BB-1356	Rieke Corp. Auburn, In.	N5598N
N162PA	77	King Air 200	BB-232	Aero Lima/John Air Services Inc. Miami, Fl. (status ?).	YV-112CP
N162Q	83	King Air B200	BB-1104	EZ Flight LLC. Chatsworth, Ga.	N1628
N163SA	79	PA-31T Cheyenne II	7920025	White Industries Inc. Bates City, Mo.	N6195A
N164DB	04	PA-46-500TP Meridian	4697176	Flightline Group Inc. Tallahassee, Fl.	
N164PA	60	Gulfstream 1	54	Phoenix Air Group Inc. Cartersville, Ga.	N26AJ
N164PG	00	TBM 700B	164	SOCATA Aircraft, Pembroke Pines, Fl.	F-WWRR
N164ST	01	PA-46-500TP Meridian	4697064	Sarabe Inc. Salisbury, Md.	
N165BC	80	Gulfstream 840	11646	Ian Herzog A Professional Corp. Santa Monica, Ca.	N65Y
N165KC	79	PA-31T Cheyenne 1	7904022	Casey's Services Co. Ankeny, la.	N46CR
N165PA	63	Gulfstream 1	119	Phoenix Air Group Inc, Cartersville, Ga.	YV-28CP
N165SW	79	PA-31T Cheyenne 1	7904051	Mihada Inc. Auburn, Al.	N49RM

Reg	Yr	Type	c/n	Owner/Operator	Prev Regn
☐ N166PM	03	PA-46-500TP Meridian	4697166	Aero Toys Inc. Orlando, Fl.	N772SE
☐ N166SA	88	King Air 300	FA-166	Palm Leasing LLC. Youngstown, Oh.	9J-AFI
☐ N166SB	00	Pilatus PC-12/45	310	Edge Wireless LLC. Mukilteo, Wa.	HB-FQW
☐ N166WT	80	PA-31T Cheyenne 1	8004020	H & M Properties Inc. Jacksonville, NC.	N700BS
☐ N167AR	99	Pilatus PC-12/45	279	J Smith Marketing Inc. Clearwater, Fl.	HB-FSX
☐ N167BB	83	King Air C90-1	LJ-1054	BuzzEd LLC. Elgin, Il.	N10AV
☐ N167PA	63	Gulfstream 1	117	Phoenix Air Group Inc. Cartersville, Ga.	YV-08CP
☐ N167R	78	Rockwell 690B	11437	Central Bank & Trust Co. Lexington, Ky.	HL5261
☐ N168MA	83	Conquest 1	425-0155	Binova Produce Inc. Nogales, Az.	YV-266CP
☐ N168PA	60	Gulfstream 1	56	Phoenix Air Group Inc. Cartersville, Ga.	YV-46CP
☐ N169DC	80	PA-31T Cheyenne 1	8004048	Dakota Aircraft Inc. Pierre, SD.	(N55JP)
☐ N169DR	89	King Air C90A	LJ-1205	New South Communications Inc. Meridian, Ms.	N1552F
☐ N169P	01	King Air C90B	LJ-1647	RACC, Wichita, Ks.	N169P
☐ N170AS	72	King Air A100	B-127	Samoa Aviation Inc. Pago Pago, American Samoa.	C-GJVK
☐ N170S*	04	King Air C90B	LJ-1708	Shanair LLC. Visalia, Ca.	N974C
☐ N170SE	00	King Air B200	BB-1740	Mango Air Inc. Visalia, Ca.	N170S
☐ N171AF	79	PA-31T Cheyenne II	7920089	Aero Oro LLC. Colorado Springs, Co.	N101AF
☐ N171AT	66	680V Turbo Commander	1616-49	Harold Wright, Anchorage, Ak.	N311PD
☐ N171CP	99	King Air 350	FL-244	InterCity Investments Properties Inc. Dallas, Tx.	N2344N
☐ N171DR	81	Gulfstream 840	11683	Antonio Enriquez, Seattle, Wa.	N60VS
☐ N171JP	77	PA-31T Cheyenne II	7720028	Frost Flying Inc. Marianna, Ar.	N29JM
☐ N171MA	80	MU-2 Solitaire	431SA	Drug & Laboratory Disposal Inc. Plainwell, Mi.	
☐ N171PA	68	Gulfstream 1	192	Phoenix Air Group Inc. Cartersville, Ga.	YV-76CP
☐ N171PC	68	SA-26AT Merlin 2B	T26-103	White Industries Inc. Bates City, Mo.	N136SP
☐ N172JS	97	Pilatus PC-12	171	J B Scott, Boise, Id.	N171PD
☐ N172PB	97	Pilatus PC-12	172	Locker Inc. Texico, NM.	HB-FSH
☐ N173DB	78	Rockwell 690B	11485	DMB Packing Corp. Newman, Ca.	N46NH
☐ N173KS	97	Pilatus PC-12	173	Grafe Auction Co. Spring Valley, Mn.	HB-FSI
☐ N173PA	66	Gulfstream 1	175	Phoenix Air Group Inc. Cartersville, Ga.	YV-453CP
☐ N173PL	81	King Air F90	LA-106	Gavin Air LLC. Yalesville, Ct.	C-GQGA
☐ N173RC	76	King Air 200	BB-173	LPTP Inc. Rayne, La.	N55FG
☐ N173S	92	King Air B300C	FM-4	Stevens Express Leasing Inc. Memphis, Tn.	N8275P
☐ N174MA	79	MU-2 Marquise	753SA	Bankair Inc. West Columbia, SC.	N100BY
☐ N174WB	81	King Air 200	BB-804	BACE International Inc. Charlotte, NC.	N3824P
☐ N175AA	81	PA-42 Cheyenne III	8001017	Trial Support Services Inc. Mesquite, Tx.	XA-SEK
☐ N175AZ	82	King Air C90	LJ-1006	Kirkland's Inc. Jackson, Tn.	N123NA
☐ N175CA	79	MU-2 Marquise	736SA	Air 1st Aviation Companies Inc. Aiken, SC.	N711PD
☐ N175DB	63	680V Turbo Commander	1519-95	Richard Rohrman, Shawnee Mission, Ks. (status ?).	N1161Z
☐ N175GM	79	King Air 200	BB-501	Eye Fly Inc. Wilmington, De.	N175BM
☐ N175SA	76	King Air 200	BB-183	General Atomics Inc. San Diego, Ca.	N418GA
☐ N175WB	04	PA-46-500TP Meridian	4697181	Caysal LLC. Dover, De.	
☐ N176BJ	69	Mitsubishi MU-2F	144	Turbine Aircraft Marketing Inc. San Angelo, Tx.	N11KR
☐ N176CS	80	PA-31T Cheyenne 1	8004054	Intercept Inc. Norcross, Ga.	N176FE
☐ N176FB	81	PA-42 Cheyenne III	8001041	P R Transportation LLC. Washington, NC.	G-BWTX
☐ N176M	82	King Air B200	BB-1029	APACO Inc. Ooltewah, Tn.	N95BD
☐ N176TW	74	King Air E90	LW-76	Ameristar Jet Charter Inc. Dallas, Tx.	ZS-LJF
☐ N177CN	84	King Air B200	BB-1191	Pine Telephone Co. Broken Bow, Ok.	(YV-....)
☐ N177LA	85	King Air B200	BB-1203	DXP Holdings Inc. Houston, Tx.	N177JE
☐ N177MK	75	King Air E90	LW-149	Trans-Equipment Services Inc. Greenville, SC.	N177KA
☐ N178CD	81	PA-31T Cheyenne II	8120046	Mathew Emmens, Durham, NC.	N101DH
☐ N178JM	96	King Air C90B	LJ-1430	Boutsen Aviation, Monte Carlo, Monaco.	OK-BKS
☐ N178LA	82	King Air F90	LA-178	S C Anderson Inc. Bakersfield, Ca.	N53G
☐ N179D	85	King Air C90A	LJ-1091	Gem City Properties LLC. Laramie, Wy.	
☐ N180AV	92	P-180 Avanti	1018	Din Aero Inc. Troy, Mi.	N220TW
☐ N180BP	90	P-180 Avanti	1004	Jo-Lee LLC. Portland, Or.	I-RAIH
☐ N180HM	01	P-180 Avanti	1043	Snowwis Aviation LLC. Siloam Springs, Ar.	N122PA
☐ N181BG	93	P-180 Avanti	1015	GeeBee LLC/MNP Corp. Utica, Mi.	N180SH
☐ N181CG	77	King Air E90	LW-225	Another Road Aviation LLC. Jacksonville, Fl.	(N419HM)
☐ N181DC	75	PA-31T Cheyenne II	7520026	Western Agro Inc. Mayaguez, PR.	N180JS
☐ N181MD	83	Conquest II	441-0295	Birchwood Lumber & Veneer Co. Birchwood, Wi.	N6837R
☐ N181NK	66	King Air A90	LJ-142	Jack Wall Aircraft Sales Inc. Memphis, Tn.	N101NK
☐ N181PC	03	TBM 700C	261	Longslow Food Group Inc. Colwyn Bay, Wales.	
☐ N181SW	81	PA-31T Cheyenne 1	8104001	MacFarlane Co USA LLC. El Dorado, Ar.	
☐ N181Z	73	King Air E90	LW-52	USDA/Forest Service Fire & Aviation, Boise, Id.	N74171
☐ N182CA	81	King Air F90	LA-121	Price Construction Inc. Big Spring, Tx.	N82DD
Reg	**Yr**	**Type**	**c/n**	**Owner/Operator**	**Prev Regn**

Reg	Yr	Type	c/n	Owner/Operator	Prev Regn
N182ME	78	PA-31T Cheyenne II	7820021	Universal Turbine Parts Inc. Prattville, Al.	N102FL
N183K	61	Gulfstream 1	84	Transcontinental Aviation Inc. Greensboro, NC.	N184K
N183MA	72	Mitsubishi MU-2F	217	Turbine Aircraft Marketing Inc. San Angelo, Tx.	
N183PA	69	Gulfstream 1	199	Phoenix Air Group Inc. Cartersville, Ga.	YV-83CP
N183PC	97	Pilatus PC-12	183	Hughes Unlimited Inc. Port Bolivar, Tx.	HB-FSR
N183SA	73	King Air C90	LJ-571	Signature Air Inc. Canonsburg, Pa.	D-ILKB
N184AE	01	PA-46-500TP Meridian	4697026	Airmann LLC. Shelbyville, Tn.	N184AL
N184D	87	King Air 300	FA-132	Cross County Carriers Ltd. Cincinnati, Oh.	N1845
N184K	85	SAAB 340A	029	Indiana University Foundation, Bloomington, In.	N98AL
N184PA	62	Gulfstream 1	97	Phoenix Air Group Inc. Cartersville, Ga.	YV-85CP
N184RB	01	PA-46-500TP Meridian	4697087	Marine Transportation Services Inc. Houston, Tx.	
N184VB	80	Conquest II	441-0184	Diplomat Freight Services Inc. Annapolis, Md.	(N184DF)
N185DH	81	King Air B200	BB-905	Insurance Investors Inc. Austin, Tx.	N79GS
N185MA	72	Mitsubishi MU-2F	219	James Paige Jr. Daytona Beach, Fl.	
N185MV	82	King Air B200	BB-1034	Midwest Aviation, Marshall, Mn.	N185MC
N185PA	59	Gulfstream 1	26	Phoenix Air Group Inc. Cartersville, Ga.	YV-82CP
N185PB	97	Pilatus PC-12	185	Roger & Gayle Block, Gardnerville, Nv.	HB-FST
N185XP	82	King Air B200	BB-952	U S Department of Energy, Las Vegas, Nv.	N1852B
N186DD	81	King Air F90	LA-83	Just Comare LLC. Newton, NJ.	N771JB
N186E	79	Rockwell 690B	11566	DPA Transco LLC. Newport Beach, Ca.	N186EC
N186EB	84	King Air B200	BB-1186	Executive Business Aviation Inc. Nashville, Tn.	ZS-NBA
N186GA	78	PA-31T Cheyenne II	7820086	W & V LLC. Macon, Ga.	N44CS
N186PA	59	Gulfstream 1	23	Phoenix Air Group Inc. Cartersville, Ga.	N193PA
N186WF	97	Pilatus PC-12	186	186WF Inc. San Francisco, Ca.	N186WF
N187CP	79	PA-31T Cheyenne II	7920054	Electromatic International Inc. Hollywood, Fl.	(N690CA)
N187JD	03	PA-46-500TP Meridian	4697180	Jeff Dinklage Agri-Business Inc. Wisner, Ne.	
N187SB	77	Mitsubishi MU-2N	698SA	Keystone Advertising Inc. East Freedom, Pa.	N263ND
N187SC	79	PA-31T Cheyenne 1	7904020	Aviation Parts Exchange Inc. Bedford, Tx.	N800MP
N187Z	68	SA-26T Merlin 2A	T26-29	U S Department of Agriculture, Washington, DC.	N22CE
N188BF	81	King Air F90	LA-105	Flagship Aviation LLC. Hamel, Mn.	D-IAWK
N188CA	79	PA-31T Cheyenne 1	7904004	Knarf Equipment Inc. Fort Washington, Pa.	(N188EC)
N188DF	84	Conquest 1	425-0188	J P Air Charter Inc. Ontario, Ca.	N188CP
N188JB	81	King Air F90	LA-107	Burkhart Enterprises Inc. Tulsa, Ok.	N700BK
N188MC	93	King Air 350	FL-93	MASCO Corp. Taylor, Mi.	N82678
N188PC	97	Pilatus PC-12	188	Fly One Eight Eight Inc. Wilmington, De.	HB-FSW
N188RM	74	Mitsubishi MU-2K	298	Kelly Green Seeds Inc. Farwell, Tx.	PT-OFV
N189GH	79	PA-31T Cheyenne II	7920084	Patriot Leasing Corp. Kenner, La.	N666JL
N189JR	80	King Air F90	LA-61	DMD Inc. Springfield, Il.	N444RS
N189MC	96	King Air 350	FL-136	MASCO Corp. Taylor, Mi.	N35017
N190BT	65	King Air 90	LJ-59	Tiger Pass Properties Inc. Gretna, La.	N1909R
N190FD	80	King Air F90	LA-42	Alfred Tria Jr. Princeton, NJ.	(D-ILIM)
N190JL	65	King Air 90	LJ-69	APA Enterprises Inc. Poughskepsie, NY.	N120DP
N190PA	68	Gulfstream 1	195	Phoenix Air Group Inc. Cartersville, Ga.	N1900W
N190RM	72	King Air F90	LW-1	Alden Aviation Inc. Georgetown, De.	N64RJ
N190SS	92	King Air C90A	LJ-1298	J & H Kramer Inc. Redwood City, Ca.	N170AJ
N191A	78	King Air C90	LJ-765	Punta Gorda Transport LLC. Punta Gorda, Fl.	5N-WNL
N191MA	81	PA-31T Cheyenne 1	8104019	B & E Leasing LLC. Dubuque, Ia.	N817QT
N191SP	99	Pilatus PC-12/45	284	PBCB LLC. Bellevue, Wa.	N284LK
N191WB	91	King Air C90B	LJ-1295	Wild Blue Yonder of Oklahoma LLC. Goldsby, Ok.	N91LY
N192PA	65	Gulfstream 1	149	Phoenix Air Group Inc. Cartersville, Ga.	N684FM
N192PC	97	Pilatus PC-12	192	Finnoff International LLC. Boulder, Co.	HB-FQA
N192SA	76	King Air 200	BB-92	Sky Way Aircraft Inc. St Petersburg, Fl.	C-FJRT
N192TB	81	Cheyenne II-XL	8166015	Cheyenne Leasing LLC. West Palm Beach, Fl.	N131XL
N193A	71	King Air C90	LJ-503	International Airline Training Academy Inc. Tucson, Az.	
N193AA	79	MU-2 Marquise	741SA	AEF LC VII, Pensacola, Fl.	(N98CF)
N193FS	91	King Air 300	FA-218	Flexsteel Industries Inc. Dubuque, Ia.	N770GX
N193PA	64	Gulfstream 1	125	Phoenix Air Group Inc. Cartersville, Ga.	N5NA
N194TR	83	King Air B200	BB-1146	Tony Green & Assocs Inc. Boone, NC.	N60FC
N195AA	79	PA-31T Cheyenne 1	7904001	Bondy's Air Inc. Dover, De.	D-ILOR
N195AE	89	King Air 300	FA-195	Air Eagle LLC. Detroit, Mi.	N1554U
N195AL	86	King Air 300	FA-102	Red Stripe Air LLC. Odessa, Tx.	(N886DT)
N195DP	66	King Air 90	LJ-89	Skydive Alabama Inc. Decatur, Il.	N195DR
N195FW	81	Conquest II	441-0195	Beach Manufacturing Co. Donnelsville, Oh.	(N2626B)
N195MA	70	King Air 100	B-20	W L Paris Enterprises Inc. Louisville, Ky.	(N28WL)
N195PA	62	Gulfstream 1C	88	Phoenix Air Group Inc. Cartersville, Ga.	C-GPTN
Reg	Yr	Type	c/n	Owner/Operator	Prev Regn

Reg	Yr Type	c/n	Owner/Operator	Prev Regn
☐ N196MA	80 MU-2 Marquise	764SA	Cebolla Inc. Pharr, Tx.	
☐ N196PA	64 Gulfstream 1	139	Phoenix Air Group Inc. Cartersville, Ga.	C-FRTU
☐ N196PP	80 King Air 200	BB-668	Mike Vaughn Custom Sports Inc. Oxford, Mi.	N1MW
☐ N197AS	81 King Air F90	LA-116	Asset Sales Inc. Indian Trail, NC.	N3825E
☐ N197CC	78 King Air C90	LJ-783	Carl Carr, Destin, Fl.	N197SC
☐ N197PA	62 Gulfstream 1	93	Phoenix Air Group Inc. Cartersville, Ga.	N137C
☐ N198DM	85 King Air B200	BB-1198	Air Logic Sales Inc. Lakeland, Fl.	VT-JKC
☐ N198KA	66 King Air A90	LJ-162	Assure Aviation LLC. Memphis, Tn.	N198T
☐ N198MA	72 Mitsubishi MU-2J	563	Turbine Aircraft Marketing Inc. San Angelo, Tx.	
☐ N198PA	59 Gulfstream 1C	27	Phoenix Air Group Inc. Cartersville, Ga.	N415CA
☐ N198PP	92 King Air C90B	LJ-1314	Peterson Toyota Inc. Lumberton, NC.	N8022Q
☐ N198X	98 TBM 700	138	Wrenn Aircraft Inc. Asheville, NC.	N242CA
☐ N199BC	80 King Air F90	LA-30	Eagle Air LLC. Metairie, La.	(N483JM)
☐ N199CG	01 King Air C90B	LJ-1661	CG Aviation LLC. Asheboro, NC.	N5061X
☐ N199CM	99 Pilatus PC-12/45	262	K & A Aero LLC. Eureka, Ca.	HB-FSG
☐ N199CP	01 PA-46-500TP Meridian	4697099	Rent Lease Aviation LLC. Virginia Beach, Wa.	C-GPDP
☐ N199MA	81 PA-31T Cheyenne 1	8104005	We-Lease LC. Johnston, Ia.	N944JG
☐ N199MH	81 King Air/Catpass 250	BB-855	Russian Hill Partners Inc. San Francisco, Ca.	N223HC
☐ N199ND	76 PA-31T Cheyenne II	7620035	RLG Aircraft Leasing LLC. Wilmington, De.	N197TA
☐ N199TT	76 King Air E90	LW-157	Magic Aviation LLC. Ankeny, Ia.	N81AS
☐ N199WF	98 Pilatus PC-12/45	199	Catch 31 Inc. Wilmington, De.	HB-FQH
☐ N199Y	91 King Air 350	FL-66	Task Aviation LLC. Richmond, Va.	VP-CRI
☐ N200AE	66 Gulfstream 1	169	Termnet Merchant Services Inc. Atlanta, Ga.	N400WF
☐ N200AF	75 King Air 200	BB-102	Quebec Enterprises Inc. Burbank, Ca.	N997MA
☐ N200AJ	73 King Air A100	B-146	Royal Air Freight Inc. Waterford, Mi.	N410SB
☐ N200AU	79 King Air 200	BB-432	Al Ochoa Farms Inc. Lind, Wa.	N33KM
☐ N200BC	75 King Air 200	BB-55	SR Forwarding Inc. Laredo, Tx.	G-OAKM
☐ N200BH	80 King Air 200	BB-587	Giradi, Keese & Crane, Van Nuys, Ca.	
☐ N200BT	77 King Air 200	BB-293	Crystal Aviation LLC. Atlantic Beach, NC.	(N202QS)
☐ N200CJ	76 King Air 200	BB-143	Four Kings Air LLC. Montello, Wi.	N1PC
☐ N200DA	83 King Air B200	BB-1095	Nion LLC. New Century, Ks.	N170L
☐ N200DK	82 Gulfstream 1000	96019	Coast Aircraft Brokerage Inc. Tarzana, Ca.	(N9939S)
☐ N200DT	68 680W Turbo Commander	1763-9	Commander Services Inc. Hayward, Ca.	N97011
☐ N200EC	76 King Air 200	BB-134	Chouest Air Inc. Houma, La.	D-IAAK
☐ N200ET	78 King Air C-12C	BC-73	Air Serv International Inc. Redlands, Ca.	78-23137
☐ N200EW	83 King Air B200	BB-1163	Have A Heart Leasing LLC. Chillicothe, Oh.	N200DB
☐ N200EZ	74 King Air 200	BB-9	Fabio Ortega, Medellin, Colombia.	N5PC
☐ N200FB	79 PA-31T Cheyenne 1	7904037	E-Z Mart Stores Inc. Texarkana, Ar.	N2332R
☐ N200FM	75 King Air 200	BB-81	Professional Aviation Sales & Service, Millington, Tn.	N18DN
☐ N200FV	77 King Air 200	BB-299	ZZ Leasing Inc. Memphis, Tn.	N6111
☐ N200GS	85 King Air B200	BB-1214	Navajo Nation, Window Rock, Az.	N7225D
☐ N200HD	82 King Air B200	BB-987	Oahu Properties LLC. Tuscaloosa, Al.	N358ST
☐ N200HF	04 King Air B200	BB-1858	Hunt Aviation LLC. Ruston, La.	N6158Q
☐ N200HK	99 King Air B200	BB-1677	Advanced Flightworks II LLC. Austin, Tx.	N200HF
☐ N200HV	97 King Air C90B	LJ-1478	Hy-Vee Food Stores Inc. West Des Moines, Ia.	N1108M
☐ N200HW	97 King Air B200	BB-1561	HW3 Operating LLC. Fort Worth, Tx.	N224RT
☐ N200HX	86 King Air B200	BB-1243	Helicopter Express Inc. Lawrenceville, Ga.	N84CC
☐ N200JC	98 Jetcruzer 500	002	AASI Aircraft, Long Beach, Ca.	
☐ N200JL	76 King Air 200	RR-127	John Lyddon, Las Vegas, Nv.	N2127L
☐ N200JQ	74 Rockwell 690A	11224	Corona Aircraft Inc. Corona, Ca.	N200JN
☐ N200KP	85 King Air B200	BB-1215	Boundary Layer Research Inc. Everett, Wa.	PH-ACZ
☐ N200MH	69 SA-26AT Merlin 2B	T26-148	Lionel Nerwich, Farmersville, Tx.	N540MC
☐ N200MJ	82 King Air B200	BB-1012	Prior Aviation Service Inc. Buffalo, NY.	N14BW
☐ N200MP	84 King Air B200	BB-1174	Wildcat Leasing Inc. Plano, Tx.	(N696AC)
☐ N200NA	82 King Air B200	BB-1079	Trueb Emulsions Chemie AG. Switzerland.	HB-GDL
☐ N200NB	77 PA-31T Cheyenne II	7720035	Medical Imaging Consultants PC. Lavista, Ne.	
☐ N200ND	98 King Air B200	BB-1612	North Dakota Department of Transport, Bismarck, ND.	
☐ N200NR	91 King Air B200	BB-1380	Fox Flite Inc. Tulsa, Ok.	N77HN
☐ N200NW	99 King Air B200	BB-1691	Viking Transport/Northland Aluminum Products, St Louis Park.	
☐ N200NY	76 King Air C-12C	BC-25	New York State Police, Latham, NY.	N1172J
☐ N200PG	79 PA-31T Cheyenne II	7920015	Road Builders Inc. Lincoln, Ne.	N200GH
☐ N200PL	78 King Air 200	BB-410	Polaris Industries Inc. Minneapolis, Mn.	N275Z
☐ N200PU	94 King Air B200	BB-1477	Purdue University, Lafayette, In.	N8301D
☐ N200QQ	79 King Air 200	BB-521	Quincy Newspapers Inc. Quincy, Il.	N355TW
☐ N200QS	83 King Air B200	BB-1130	NetJets International Inc. Oklahoma City, Ok.	N16KK
Reg	*Yr Type*	*c/n*	*Owner/Operator*	*Prev Regn*

Reg	Yr	Type	c/n	Owner/Operator	Prev Regn
☐ N200RE	76	King Air E90	LW-164	Growth Ventures Leasing Inc. East Jordan, Mi.	
☐ N200RM	73	King Air E90	LW-45	Phoenix Partners Leasing LLC. University Place, Wa.	N777SS
☐ N200RR	87	King Air B200	BB-1282	Texas Dept of Criminal Justice, Huntsville, Tx.	N3082C
☐ N200RS	94	King Air B200	BB-1481	Patterson Aviation LLC. Omaha, Ne.	N1559W
☐ N200RW	77	King Air 200	BB-242	Dodson International Parts Inc. Ottawa, Ks. (status ?)	N24201
☐ N200RX	72	Mitsubishi MU-2J	548	National Seating & Mobility Inc. Franklin, Tn.	N68DA
☐ N200SE	85	King Air B200	BB-1208	King Flyers Partners LP. Magnolia, Tx.	N7213K
☐ N200SN	80	SA-226T Merlin 3B	T-354	N200SN LLC. Charlotte, NC.	N656PS
☐ N200SV	84	King Air B200	BB-1187	Waterside Aircraft Sales LLC. Old Saybrook, Ct.	N610SW
☐ N200TB	67	680V Turbo Commander	1708-83	East Coast Aero Technical School, Holden, Ma.	N500HY
☐ N200TG	73	King Air C90	LJ-583	Gemi Trucking Inc. Eatonton, Ga.	N21WB
☐ N200TK	85	King Air B200	BB-1240	Deblu Air LLC. Wilmington, De.	N90BL
☐ N200TP	77	King Air 200	BB-191	3 Lone Stars LLC. Arlington, Tx.	N1PC
☐ N200TR	84	King Air C90A	LJ-1067	Taylor Ramsey Enterprises Inc. Lynchburg, Va.	N224P
☐ N200TS	78	PA-31T Cheyenne 1	7804002	Hayes LLC. Wilmington, De.	N94TB
☐ N200TT	81	Gulfstream 980	95073	Aero Executive International Inc. Scottsdale, Az. (status ?)	N9825S
☐ N200U	95	King Air C90B	LJ-1389	Ohio University, Athens, Oh.	CC-CTW
☐ N200UW	83	King Air B200	BB-1155	University of Wyoming, Laramie, Wy.	N155NA
☐ N200VA	77	King Air 200	BB-246	Continental Air Care Inc. Yerington, Nv.	(N138CC)
☐ N200VC	00	King Air 350	FL-316	Vectren Aero Inc. Evansville, In.	N3216L
☐ N200WB	84	King Air 300	FA-5	Spud Air LLC/Alford Farms Inc. Pasco, Wa.	N224BB
☐ N200WZ	76	King Air 200	BB-89	Holmes Aviation LLC. Des Moines, Ia.	N16BF
☐ N200XL	81	Cheyenne II-XL	8166010	J Jeffrey Brausch & Co. Medina, Oh.	
☐ N200ZC	75	King Air 200	BB-41	Honeywell International Inc. Morristown, NJ.	
☐ N200ZK	96	King Air B200	BB-1553	Rani Aviation Inc. Mala-Mala, RSA.	ZS-NZK
☐ N200ZT	90	King Air B200	BB-1393	MJP Aviation LLC. Winthrop Harbor, Il.	N73LC
☐ N201CH	76	King Air 200	BB-103	Marcraft LLC. Mesquite, Nv.	
☐ N201KA	79	King Air 200	BB-417	R & B Aircraft leasing LLC. Galesburg, Il.	HB-GHF
☐ N201SM	67	SA-26T Merlin 2A	T26-5	J Sills, Lakeland, Fl.	N400P
☐ N201UV	76	Mitsubishi MU-2L	680	Royal Air Freight Inc. Waterford, Mi.	N201U
☐ N202AJ	79	King Air 200	BB-511	Yaris Air Transport Inc. Panama City, Panama.	N200LW
☐ N202HC	78	PA-31T Cheyenne II	7820036	TufAir LLC. Frankfort, Ky.	N82251
☐ N202MC	78	Mitsubishi MU-2P	369SA	Southern Aircraft Consultancy Inc. St Just, UK.	N755MA
☐ N202WS	75	SA-226AT Merlin 4A	AT-037	Dash 10 Charters Inc. Austin, Tx.	N216GA
☐ N203BS	79	King Air 200	BB-476	Bill Smith, Oklahoma City, Ok.	N6040T
☐ N203HC	98	King Air B200	BB-1602	Hytrol Conveyor Co. Jonesboro, Ar.	N2302S
☐ N203LG	81	King Air B200	BB-926	CWW Inc. Englewood, Co.	N68GK
☐ N203PC	78	King Air E90	LW-258	Flying Swan Inc. Wilmington, De.	N20316
☐ N203RC	03	King Air B200	BB-1822	Warren Manufacturing Inc. Birmingham, Al.	N6022Q
☐ N203RD	77	King Air E90	LW-203	PBSA Aviation Corp. Fort Lauderdale, Fl.	YV-O-SAS-
☐ N203RR	84	King Air 300	FA-27	Jetman LC. Fort Worth, Tx.	N300PE
☐ N203TS	99	King Air B200	BB-1689	Execuflight LLC. Monroeville, Al.	
☐ N203TW	92	King Air B200	BB-1417	Bedford Partners LLC/Tradewind Aviation LLC. White Plains.	N511HA
☐ N204JS	81	King Air 200	BB-842	Eric Stirling, Fairbanks, Ak.	N38473
☐ N204W	98	King Air 350	FL-204	State of Wisconsin, Madison, Wi.	N2301Q
☐ N204WB	84	King Air B200	BB-1179	Helicopters of Northwest Florida Inc. Navarre, Fl.	N444WB
☐ N205BN	77	Rockwell 690B	11404	Boone Newspapers Inc. Tuscaloosa, Al.	N100MF
☐ N205MS	81	King Air C90	LJ-948	McGriff, Siebels & Williams Inc. Birmingham, Al.	N4495U
☐ N205PA	04	P-180 Avanti	1088	Piaggio America Inc. Greenville, SC.	
☐ N205SM	83	King Air F90-1	LA-205	Lewis Air Fleet LLC. Ponte Vedra Beech, Fl.	N6690R
☐ N205SP	03	King Air B200	BB-1826	Colorado State Patrol, Denver, Co.	N200KA
☐ N205ST	81	King Air C90	LJ-965	SDI Leasing LLC. Houston, Tx.	N205SP
☐ N206BN	78	Rockwell 690B	11455	Boone Newspapers Inc. Tuscaloosa, Al.	N13PF
☐ N206K	85	King Air 300	FA-36	Diamond 1A Inc. Divide, Co.	
☐ N206P	79	King Air 200	BB-466	WBJ Aviation LLC. Elm City, NC.	N200TW
☐ N207BA	75	Mitsubishi MU-2L	666	Bill Austin Aircraft & Yacht Sales, Sparta, Tn.	SE-IVA
☐ N207CM	86	King Air B200	BB-1246	Carolinas Medical Center, Charlotte, NC.	(N210CM)
☐ N207DB	81	King Air 200	BB-862	Hermes Aviation LLC/Sky Trek Aviation, Modesto, Ca.	N260F
☐ N207HB	95	King Air B200	BB-1516	Hill Brothers Leasing Co. Falkner, Ms.	N1CQ
☐ N207P	95	King Air C90B	LJ-1406	S & B Equipment Leasing Inc. Broadview Heights, Oh.	
☐ N207RS	83	Conquest 1	425-0195	Flying Machines LLC. Myrtle Beach, SC.	(N316LR)
☐ N207SB	71	King Air 100	B-69	Ken Schrader Racing Inc. Concord, NC.	(N501KS)
☐ N207SS	80	Conquest II	441-0136	Tampa Bay Aircraft Sales Inc. Clearwater, Fl.	N441HC
☐ N208CL	76	Rockwell 690A	11297	Beecher Securities Inc. Houston, Tx.	N514GP
☐ N208CW	00	King Air B200	BB-1720	Flight Options LLC. Cleveland, Oh.	N608TA
Reg	**Yr**	**Type**	**c/n**	**Owner/Operator**	**Prev Regn**

Reg	Yr Type	c/n	Owner/Operator	Prev Regn
☐ N208F	81 King Air 200	BB-851	Air Transportation LLC. Ridgeland, Ms.	N200E
☐ N208RC	80 King Air F90	LA-46	King Air Corp. Miami, Fl.	ZP-TZF
☐ N208SR	75 King Air A100	B-208	Inter-Island Air inc. San Juan, PR.	9Y-TJA
☐ N208SW	80 King Air 200	BB-720	MDM Craft LLC. Caledonia, NY.	N202SW
☐ N208TS	95 King Air B200	BB-1510	J J & P LLC. Petaluma, Ca.	N991WS
☐ N209CM	98 King Air B200	BB-1613	Chatlotte Mecklenburg Hospital Authority, Charlotte, NC.	N299RJ
☐ N209KC	01 PA-46-500TP Meridian	4697009	Air Dover Corp. Wilmington, De.	
☐ N209ST	04 PA-46-500TP Meridian	4697209	New Piper Aircraft Inc. Vero Beach, Fl.	
☐ N210AJ	81 King Air F90	LA-131	Tailplane Corp. Wilmington, De.	N42SY
☐ N210CL	04 TBM 700C	303	Orgeron Investments LLC. Golden Meadow, La.	
☐ N210CM	80 King Air 200	BB-621	Charlotte Macklenburg Hospital, Charlotte, NC.	N207CM
☐ N210EC	84 King Air C90A	LJ-1070	State of Tennessee, Nashville, Tn.	N67554
☐ N210PT	98 Pilatus PC-12/45	210	Robert Pitre, Albuquerque, NM.	HB-FQR
☐ N211AD	85 Gulfstream 1000	96092	Allison Development Corp. Charlotte, NC.	N127GA
☐ N211AE	77 PA-31T Cheyenne II	7720064	Hap's Aerial Enterprises Inc. Sellersburg, In.	N60DR
☐ N211BE	74 Mitsubishi MU-2J	641	Chisos Corp. Houston, Tx.	N114MA
☐ N211CP	81 King Air 200	BB-843	Davis Lee Enterprises LLC. Guntersville, Al.	N3850K
☐ N211EZ	01 PA-46-500TP Meridian	4697117	Brand New Entertainment LLC. Sausalito, Ca	N53353
☐ N211HV	02 King Air B200	BB-1799	University Athletic Association Inc. Gainesville, Fl.	N5099H
☐ N211PC	80 King Air C90	LJ-910	Rancho Vaquero Ltd. Laredo, Tx.	TC-FRT
☐ N211RV	70 Mitsubishi MU-2G	502	Mits 502 LLC. Lansing, Il. (was s/n 153).	C-FAXP
☐ N212D	67 King Air A90	LJ-234	Central Missouri State University, Warrenburg, Mo.	N800BP
☐ N212GA	91 King Air B200	BB-1406	General Aviation Services LLC. Lake Zurich, Il.	5B-CJM
☐ N212HH	79 PA-31T Cheyenne 1	7904010	Thomas G Smith, Alexandria, La.	N25BF
☐ N212JB	85 King Air B200	BB-1238	Beech 212JB LP. El Paso, Tx.	(N86GA)
☐ N212LT	04 Pilatus PC-12/45	595	Plane Holdings Inc. Maastricht, Holland.	HB-FRG
☐ N212LW	92 King Air B200	BB-1420	Power Flame Inc. Parsons, Ks.	N210SA
☐ N212PB	98 Pilatus PC-12/45	212	Arbor Financial Corp. Glenbrook, Nv.	HB-FQT
☐ N212WP	65 King Air 90	LJ-62	Volunteer Machinery Sales Co. Portland, Tn.	N512WP
☐ N213DB	93 King Air B200	BB-1450	Marshall Air Systems Inc. Charlotte, NC.	N8059Q
☐ N213PA	84 SA-227TT Merlin 3C	TT-518	Delaris Inc. St Thomas, USVI.	N861CG
☐ N213RW	76 King Air E90	LW-167	Polaris Industries Inc. Minneapolis, Mn.	(N199PL)
☐ N213SC	69 SA-26AT Merlin 2B	T26-135	Baskidball Equipment Leasing LLC. Dallas, Tx.	N124PS
☐ N213UV	76 King Air C-12C	BC-28	N1089V Inc. Wilmington, De.	(ZS-LES)
☐ N214EC	85 King Air 300	FA-50	Shamrock Aviation Inc. Warren, Mi.	N85GA
☐ N214KF	99 King Air C90	LJ-1570	Chemtool Inc. Crystal Lake, Il.	N3252W
☐ N214LA	85 Conquest 1	425-0214	Lanier LLC. New Orleans, La.	D-ISAR
☐ N214P	91 King Air C90A	LJ-1293	Navajo Nation, Window Rock, Az.	
☐ N214SC	74 King Air E90	LW-94	Aviacion Lider SA. Lima, Peru.	N35KA
☐ N214TP	03 King Air B200	BB-1855	Platinum Aviation LLC/TAG Manufacturing, Monte Sereno, Ca.	N6155T
☐ N215AA	81 King Air 200C	BL-15	Petro Wings LC. Pampa, Tx.	N159AG
☐ N215HC	03 King Air B200	BB-1848	Plane Lease Co. Minneapolis, Mn.	N5148Q
☐ N215MH	82 MU-2 Marquise	1544SA	W & O Leasing LLC. Wilmington, De.	N202DT
☐ N215SD	01 PA-46-500TP Meridian	4697049	Integrity Aero LLC. San Antonio, Tx.	
☐ N216BJ	84 Conquest 1	425-0216	R W Refrigeration Distribution Co. Springfield, Mo.	VH-EGT
☐ N216CD	75 Mitsubishi MU-2K	323	Camile Landry, Baton Rouge, La.	N511MA
☐ N216KC	98 Pilatus PC-12/45	216	Airmans Aviation Co. Fort Smith, Ar.	N4PC
☐ N216LJ	67 King Air A90	LJ-190	CNS Ventures LLC. Houston, Tx.	N216AJ
☐ N216RP	82 King Air B200	BB-1015	Primorc Inc. Adrian, Mi.	N901EB
☐ N216TM	02 Pilotus PC-12/45	441	JAF Aviation LLC. Denver, Co.	HB-FSA
☐ N217CS	82 Cheyenne T-1040	8275014	Cape Smythe Air Service Inc. Barrow, Ak.	C-FYPL
☐ N217DH	02 TBM 700B	243	TVPX Inc. Concord, Ma.	F-WWRI
☐ N217EB	96 Pilatus PC-12	154	Allair Air Services Corp. Wall, NJ.	N144PC
☐ N218MS	81 Gulfstream 980	95041	Say-Air LLC. Nashua, NH.	N3U
☐ N218WA	98 Pilatus PC-12/45	218	Innovative Health Systems Inc. Folsom, Ca.	HB-FQK
☐ N219CS	82 Cheyenne T-1040	8275005	Universal Turbine Parts Inc. Prattville, Al. (status ?).	C-GPBC
☐ N219MA	81 MU-2 Solitaire	440SA	Southwind Ventures Inc. Wilmington, De.	
☐ N219PC	98 Pilatus PC-12/45	219	Blossom Air Inc. Kenai, Ak.	HB-FQL
☐ N219SC	80 PA-31T Cheyenne 1	8004040	Wyman Consulting Associates Inc. Hanover, NH.	N744WP
☐ N220AA	76 King Air B100	BE-5	Abilene Aero Charter/Lubbock Aero Charter, Abilene, Tx.	N577RW
☐ N220AJ	96 King Air B200	BB-1539	US Airports Air Charters Inc. Rochester, NY.	N1089S
☐ N220CG	04 King Air 350	FL-397	Offshore Energy Services Inc. Lafayette, La.	
☐ N220CL	00 Pilatus PC-12/45	364	Jonathan Aviation Ltd. Whitestone, NY.	HB-FSP
☐ N220FS*	76 PA-31T Cheyenne II	7620052	Honker Air LLC/Styline Industries Inc. Huntingburg, In.	N577JE
☐ N220JB	80 King Air 200	BB-638	Memphis Aereo Co SA. Memphis, Tn.	N8DX
Reg	**Yr Type**	**c/n**	**Owner/Operator**	**Prev Regn**

Reg	Yr	Type	c/n	Owner/Operator	Prev Regn
N220JM	04	PA-46-500TP Meridian	4697183	BD & GD LLC. Tucson, Az.	
N220KW	73	King Air A100	B-185	N220KW LLC. Wenatchee, Wa.	N818AS
N220MA	02	TBM 700C	248	Angel Peralta, El Paso, Tx.	N220MA
N220N	81	MU-2 Solitaire	450SA	Air 1st Aviation Companies Inc. Aiken, SC.	N220W
N220PB	76	King Air E90	LW-168	King Air LLC. Mesa, Az.	(N616DD)
N220TB	82	King Air B200	BB-1057	Rocky Mountain Holdings LLC. Provo, Ut.	F-GILY
N220TT	79	King Air 200	BB-462	Shann Air Inc/Shannahan Crane & Hoist Inc. St Louis, Mo.	G-MOAT
N221BG	78	King Air 200	BB-354	Goody's Family Clothing Inc. Alcoa, Tn.	N550JC
N221G	98	King Air 350	FL-198	Gage Marketing Group LLC. Minneapolis, Mn.	(N64GG)
N221K	81	Gulfstream 980	95077	Nayko Inc. Portland, Or.	N9829S
N221MA	80	MU-2 Marquise	771SA	Turbine Aircraft Marketing Inc. San Angelo, Tx.	N248NW
N221MM	88	King Air 300	FA-161	Franklin/Templeton Travel Inc. San Mateo, Ca.	N3113A
N221PC	98	Pilatus PC-12/45	221	Stephen Scherer, St Louis, Mo.	HB-FQM
N221RC	81	PA-31T Cheyenne 1	8104046	Four-O Management LLC. Lubbock, Tx.	N478PC
N221SP	84	King Air B90	BB-1180	AEI Holding LLC. Ashland, Ky.	VR-BNN
N221TC	83	King Air B100	BE-136	Texas Christian University, Fort Worth, Tx.	N18348
N222AG	82	King Air F90	LA-159	Gaits LLC. Fishers, In.	N76HC
N222CM	95	Pilatus PC-12	111	Briar Lakes Productions Inc. Athens, Tx.	HB-FQE
N222DM	73	King Air C-12C	BC-15	Los Angeles Police Department, Van Nuys, Ca.	N382PD
N222FA	78	Mitsubishi MU-2N	714SA	Helitech Inc. Hampton, Va.	N994PE
N222GW	79	PA-31T Cheyenne 1	7904050	Dodson International Parts Inc. Ottawa, Ks.	N2512R
N222HH	85	MU-2 Marquise	1569SA	Hoover Inc. Nashville, Tn.	N502MA
N222KA	75	King Air 200	BB-84	Washington State Patrol, Olympia, Wa.	
N222LA	78	King Air 200	BB-409	Abilene Aero Charter/Lubbock Aero Charter, Abilene, Tx.	N220TA
N222LP	80	King Air B100	BE-85	Line Power Manufacturing Co. Bristol, Va.	N6723T
N222ME	76	Rockwell 690A	11338	Stormy Petrel LLC. Atlanta, Ga.	N46906
N222MV	71	SA-226T Merlin 3	T-212	Aeromax Inc. Columbus, Oh.	VR-BHQ
N222PV	97	King Air 350	FL-167	Peavey Electronics Corp. Meridian, Ms.	OY-GIG
N222SL	79	PA-31T Cheyenne 1	7904046	Dr James Langley MD. Golden, Co.	N23658
N222WJ	85	King Air C90A	LJ-1106	Lock Haven Aircraft Sales Inc. Lock Haven, Pa.	N6690C
N223CH	68	King Air B90	LJ-321	Emerald Air Services Ltd. Fayetteville, Ar.	N269RR
N223CS	82	Cheyenne T-1040	8275008	Cape Smythe Air Service Inc. Barrow, Ak.	N315SC
N223JB	78	Mitsubishi MU-2N	724SA	Burton Air Corp. Fairfax, Va.	N300GM
N223JR	85	King Air 300	FA-45	Delta Coals Inc. Nashville, Tn.	N7220L
N223LH	76	King Air A100	B-223	LELAH Holdings LP. Reno, Nv.	N233AL
N223P	94	King Air 350	FL-106	BB&T Corp. Winston-Salem, NC.	N793EM
N224CC	89	King Air C90A	LJ-1218	James Harris, Houston, Tx.	N15628
N224CR	91	King Air 350	FL-60	Dartswift Inc. Rosemont, Pa.	(N65GR)
N224EZ*	85	Gulfstream 1000B	96206	Marjo Ventures Inc. Lake Geneva, Wi.	N97315
N224HR	71	SA-226T Merlin 3	T-217	Presgar Transportation Corp. Lutz, Fl.	(N217PG)
N224LB	73	King Air A100	B-162	Allison Aviation LLC. Wilmington, De.	N96AL
N224P	85	King Air B200	BB-1230	Branch Banking & Trust Co. Elm City, NC.	
N225CA	81	PA-31T Cheyenne 1	8104024	Windward Aviation Corp. Katonah, NY.	SE-IUG
N225CM	03	King Air 350	FL-378	San Diego Diversified Builder Services, El Cajon, Ca.	N4478H
N225DF	85	Conquest 1	425-0225	D Mark Group/Phoenix Aerospace Investments, Eau Claire, Wi.	N902DP
N225LH	76	King Air C-12C	BC-33	Department of Public Safety, Montgomery, Al.	76-22557
N225MA	01	PA-46-500TP Meridian	4697106	Coppergate LLC. Carmel, In.	N2HD
N225MM	78	Rockwell 690B	11442	SABAW Trading LLC. Seabroo, Tx.	N81764
N225PT	82	Cheyenne II-XL	8166032	Perair Corp. New Hyde Park, NY.	(N107MQ)
N225WC	04	King Air B200	BB-1862	WCAO Aviation/World Class Automotive Operations, Humble, Tx.	N6162X
N225WL	85	King Air B200	BB-1226	Floyd's Equipment Inc. Sikeston, Mo.	(N346EA)
N226DD	77	SA-226T Merlin 3A	T-286	T & G Leasing Inc. Lighthouse Point, Fl.	XB-ZAO
N226DL	01	PA-46-500TP Meridian	4697039	Fly Grado LLC. St Louis, Mo.	N139KC
N226FC	79	SA-226T Merlin 3B	T-306	Rosebriar Transportation Inc. Dallas, Tx.	N5661M
N226JW	68	King Air B90	LJ-406	Tahoe Aviation Inc. Carson City, Nv.	N438
N226K	98	King Air 350	FL-226	RSE Aviation Sales & Leasing LLC. Lawrenceville, Ga.	
N226N	01	Pilatus PC-12/45	414	JD Plane LLC. Bellevue, Wa.	N905B
N226PB	02	TBM 700B	226	Top Ten Aviation Inc/Thai Flying School, Don Muang, Thailand	N226GS
N226SR	76	SA-226T Merlin 3A	T-270	Falcon Flight, Telluride, Co.	N953AE
N227BC	76	King Air A100	B-227	C B Aviation Inc. Gainesville, Fl.	N77715
N227KM	92	King Air 350	FL-91	Stuart Investment Co. Wilmington, De.	N350KA
N227TM	74	PA-31T Cheyenne II	7400008	Mehl, Grifin & Bartek Ltd. Arlington, Va.	N66837
N227TT	82	SA-227TT Merlin 3C	TT-444	Tarrant Aviation LLC. Dover, De.	VH-UZA
N228CX	93	TBM 700	84	Bernard Holmes, Southend, UK.	
N228RA	76	King Air E90	LW-197	Air Methods Corp/Flagstaff Medical Center Inc. Flagstaff, Az	N222JD
Reg	Yr	Type	c/n	Owner/Operator	Prev Regn

Reg	Yr Type	c/n	Owner/Operator	Prev Regn
N228WP	72 Mitsubishi MU-2F	228	Wayne Perry Construction Inc. Buena Park, Ca.	N963MA
N229EM	77 King Air C-12C	BC-59	MTW Aerospace Inc. Montgomery, Al.	77-22948
N229J*	00 King Air C90B	LJ-1629	James R Vannoy & Sons Construction, Jefferson, NC.	N224JV
N230DC	86 King Air B200	BB-1256	Metro Enterprises LLC. Dover, De.	N1847S
N230PG	98 Pilatus PC-12/45	230	U-Haul Co of Oregon, Portland, Or.	OY-TUS
N231CM	02 PA-46-500TP Meridian	4697146	PB One Aviation LLC. Austin, Tx.	
N231PT	74 PA-31T Cheyenne II	7400003	Premark Realty LC. Ashburn, Va.	(N177PT)
N231SW	79 PA-31T Cheyenne 1	7904007	Hummer 1 LLC. Camden, SC.	
N232AL	75 King Air A100	B-222	Para Drop, Elroy, Az.	(N304TC)
N232DH	79 PA-31T Cheyenne 1	7904021	DDK Enterprises LLC. Fayetteville, NC.	N23263
N232GM	84 Conquest 1	425-0219	Mook Enterprises LLC. Scottsdale, Az.	N242GB
N232JS	79 King Air 200	BB-446	Biddulph Oldsmobile Inc. Peoria, Az.	N885HT
N232PS	76 PA-31T Cheyenne II	7620018	Weather Modification Inc. Fargo, ND.	SX-BFR
N233PS	78 PA-31T Cheyenne II	7820039	Aerolease LLC. Fargo, ND.	SX-BFQ
N233RC	81 Conquest II	441-0263	Rico Marketing Inc. Flint, Mi.	N815MC
N234CC	79 Conquest II	441-0100	Lindow Aircraft Corp. Steamboat Springs, Co.	N388DR
N234CW	85 King Air F90	LA-236	Jaqua Aviation LLC. Laguna Beach, Ca.	(N230RM
N234K	84 PA-31T Cheyenne II	7520001	Weather Modification Inc. Fargo, ND.	N668DH
N234KW	82 King Air B90	RR-1065	General Atomics Inc. San Diego, Ca.	D-ICOA
N234RG	03 Pilatus PC-12/45	520	WFBNW NA. Salt Lake City, Ut.	HB-FRV
N234TK	77 King Air B100	BE-24	Main Street Equipment & Leasing Inc. Lexington, Ky.	N187J
N234Z	04 PA-46-500TP Meridian	4697194	Granite Securities LLC. Medford, Or.	
N235GA	85 Gulfstream 1000B	96209	GAC/U S Government,	
N235KT	58 Fairchild F-27F	16	Jeppesen Development Inc. Howey on the Hills, Fl.	N101FG
N235TW	03 PA-46-500TP Meridian	4697157	John Buchanan, Big Fork, Mt.	
N236CP	76 King Air B100	BE-9	Medic Air Corp. Reno, Nv.	(N360BA)
N236JS	81 King Air F90	LA-90	ITC Development Inc. Huntington, WV.	N290DK
N238GA	85 Gulfstream 1000B	96210	GAC/U S Government,	
N240AJ	98 King Air B200	BB-1619	US Airports Air Charters Inc. Rochester, NY.	N719TA
N240DH	85 SA-227AT Merlin 4C	AT-602B	Ameriflight Inc/DHL Airways Inc. Cincinnati, Oh.	N3117P
N240K	68 King Air B90	LJ-340	Merlin Associates Inc. Princeton, NJ.	N925B
N240NM	73 SA-226T Merlin 3	T-240	Hollycorp Aviation LLC. Dallas, Tx.	N76U
N240RE	73 King Air C90	LJ-570	Drewcy Inc. Denton, Tx.	N240RL
N240S	73 King Air 300	FA-116	Data Supplies Inc. Duluth, Ga.	N2998X
N241CW	78 King Air B100	BE-54	GECC. Danbury, Ct.	N2025S
N241DH	85 SA-227AT Merlin 4C	AT-607B	Ameriflight Inc/DHL Airways Inc. Cincinnati, Oh.	N3118A
N241PM	03 PA-46-500TP Meridian	4697150	Rearden Aviation LLC. Helena, Mt.	C-GMCM
N241TL	99 TBM 700B	150	Conquest Air LLC. Sewickley, Pa.	(N700EV)
N242DH	85 SA-227AT Merlin 4C	AT-608B	Ameriflight Inc/DHL Airways Inc. Cincinnati, Oh.	N3118G
N242JH	98 Pilatus PC-12/45	232	Center Charter LLC. San Francisco, Ca.	HB-FRC
N242LF	81 King Air F90	LA-86	Metro Aviation Inc. Shreveport, La.	N249RC
N242NA	85 King Air B200	BB-1242	Brooks Aviation/American Education Centers, Pittsburgh, Pa.	LV-ZFC
N242NS	91 King Air C90A	LJ-1271	Magnolia Aviation Sales LLC. Corinth, Ms.	
N242RA	80 PA-42 Cheyenne III	8001003	Ross Aviation Inc. Cortland, Oh.	N8EA
N243DH	85 SA-227AT Merlin 4C	AT-609B	Ameriflight Inc/DHL Airways Inc. Cincinnati, Oh.	N3118H
N244AB	80 PA-31T Cheyenne 1	8004015	The Parton Companies, Rutherfordton, NC.	N2442W
N244CH	81 King Air 200	BB-801	CEH Inc. Drummond Island, Mi.	N123WN
N244DH	85 SA-227AT Merlin 4C	AT-618B	Ameriflight Inc/DHL Airways Inc. Cincinnati, Oh.	
N244JP	76 King Air 200	BB-109	Destin Airways LLC. Atlanta-DeKalb, Ga.	N908R
N244JS	81 King Air 200	BB-754	Business Aviation Services, Sioux Falls, SD	N242DM
N244MP	79 Rockwell 690B	11531	GOR Commercial Enterprises Inc. Miami, Fl.	N101RF
N244SA	74 SA-226T Merlin 3	T-244	Central Oregon Builders Inc. Bend, Or.	RP-C203
N245CF	76 Rockwell 690A	11313	MWJ Industries LLC. Fort Smith, Ar.	N245CT
N245DH	85 SA-227AT Merlin 4C	AT-624B	Ameriflight Inc/DHL Airways Inc. Cincinnati, Oh.	
N246CA	80 King Air F90	LA-27	Conover Aviation LLC. Bend, Or.	N40BR
N246DH	85 SA-227AT Merlin 4C	AT-625B	Ameriflight Inc/DHL Airways Inc. Cincinnati, Oh.	
N246MC	78 Rockwell 690B	11448	Olen Spurgeon, Washington, Il.	XC-COL
N246SD	04 King Air 350	FL-394	Spring Valley Ranch LLC. Dublin, Ca.	N6194U
N246W	82 MU-2 Marquise	1552SA	Pamida Inc. Omaha, Ne.	N478MA
N247B	73 King Air A100	B-139	Aviation Charter Services, Indianapolis, In.	
N247DH	85 SA-227AT Merlin 4C	AT-626B	Ameriflight Inc/DHL Airways Inc. Cincinnati, Oh.	
N247JM	82 King Air B200	BB-996	JM Associates Inc. Little Rock, Ar.	N707CG
N247LM	81 PA-31T Cheyenne 1	8104043	Mystair Inc. Dover, De.	N527JC
N248DA	03 PA-46-500TP Meridian	4697156	Andair LLC. Lakeland, Fl.	N156SE
N248DH	85 SA-227AT Merlin 4C	AT-630B	Ameriflight Inc/DHL Airways Inc. Cincinnati, Oh.	
Reg	Yr Type	c/n	Owner/Operator	Prev Regn

Reg	Yr	Type	c/n	Owner/Operator	Prev Regn
N248DJ	84	PA-42 Cheyenne 400LS	5527021	Sunni Sailing Inc. Orlando, Fl.	N4RP
N248J	81	Cheyenne II-XL	8166009	Jomax Construction Co. Great Bend, Ks.	N2488Y
N249CP	79	King Air C90	LJ-841	Guardian Aircraft Leasing LLC. Albuquerque, NM.	YV-249CP
N249DH	85	SA-227AT Merlin 4C	AT-631B	Ameriflight Inc/DHL Airways Inc. Cincinnati, Oh.	
N249PA	65	King Air 90	LJ-21	Loan Guarantee Insurance Agency Inc. Irvine, Ca.	N5Y
N249WM	75	King Air E90	LW-139	Richards Aviation Inc. Memphis, Tn.	N345KA
N250CT	78	PA-31T Cheyenne II	7820011	CT Aviation LLC. Albuquerque, NM.	N884CA
N250SA	00	PA-46-500TP Meridian	4697004	Smith Air LLC. Walnut Creek, Ca.	(N711HQ)
N250TM	81	King Air 200	BB-822	Trafficmaster plc. Cranfield, UK.	F-GIND
N250TT	78	PA-31T Cheyenne II	7820050	J S Holding Inc. Fort Scott, Ks.	F-GGPV
N250U	67	King Air A90	LJ-213	Dr G William Woods, New Ulm, Tx.	N417CS
N251ES	75	Rockwell 690A	11251	Schwertner Farms Inc. Schwertner, Tx.	N690RC
N251LL	84	King Air 300	FA-2	Radeco Inc. Baytown, Tx.	C-GFES
N252CP	01	King Air B200	BB-1791	ATM Air LLC. Birmingham, Al.	N4471C
N252RC	87	King Air C90A	LJ-1152	Big Spring Aircraft Sales LLC. Huntsville, AL.	C-FGXA
N253AS	97	King Air 350	FL-155	Executive AirShare Corp. Wichita, Ks.	N253MS
N253JM	79	Rockwell 690B	11551	Montgomery Aviation LLC. St Louis, Mo.	N358HF
N253PC	99	Pilatus PC-12/45	253	Mission Holdings LLC. Polson, Mt.	HB-FRM
N255DW	01	PA-46-500TP Meridian	4697020	Bonair Inc. Boulder, Co.	
N256DD	82	Conquest II	441-0256	Berry Leasing LLC. Madera, Ca.	N256DP
N256TA	67	King Air A90	LJ-256	Flanagan Enterprises (Nevada) Inc. Carson City, Nv.	C-FOLR
N257CQ	95	King Air C90B	LJ-1419	Absher Air Inc. Somerset, Ky.	N257CG
N257NA	77	King Air 200	BB-257	KA Aircraft Charter Inc. Juno Beach, Fl.	(N257BH)
N257YA	98	King Air B200	BB-1622	Pruitt Tran Inc/Pruitt Corp. Toccoa, Ga.	N30365
N258AG	77	King Air C-12C	BC-44	Eagle Aviation LLC. Hickory, NC.	77-22933
N258JC	76	King Air E90	LW-191	Blackjack Air LLC. Waco, Tx.	N63EC
N258VB	82	Conquest II	441-0258	High Plains Pizza Inc. Great Falls, Mt.	(N6859Y)
N258WC	99	Pilatus PC-12/45	258	Charles Weinreis LLC. Minatare, Ne.	HB-FSC
N259SC	72	King Air E90	LW-17	Aircraft Guaranty Title LLC. Houston, Tx.	(N906BB)
N259WA	99	Pilatus PC-12/45	259	Pegasus Air Inc. Naples, Fl.	HB-FSD
N260CB	73	Mitsubishi MU-2J	573	Clyde Barton, Lake Jackson, Tx.	N203GA
N260G	96	King Air B200	BB-1525	260G Corp/GPI Aviation Inc. University Park, Pa.	N1015X
N260HS	99	Pilatus PC-12/45	260	Jen-Linz Ltd. Oklahoma City, Ok.	(N472SW)
N260WE	79	Rockwell 690B	11536	EMS Air Services of NY Inc. Canandaiga, NY.	N81707
N261AC	78	King Air 200	BB-321	BaronAir LLC. Fort Worth, Tx.	N38JL
N261BC	00	King Air B200	BB-1757	Cherokee Ford Inc. Woodstock, Ga.	N4357Y
N261GB	85	King Air C90A	LJ-1119	Magic Leasing LLC. Orland Park, Il.	N386CP
N261KW	73	Mitsubishi MU-2K	264	Sea Empty Equipment Inc. Merrimack, NH.	N264KW
N261MA	80	MU-2 Marquise	758SA	Robert & Cynthia Peterson Living Trust, Harrodsburg, Ky.	N777FL
N261WB	75	Mitsubishi MU-2M	330	Roy Kinsey Jr. Pensacola, Fl.	N261WR
N262J	03	TBM 700C	292	Sales Force Management Inc. Wilmington, De.	
N262MM	01	PA-46-500TP Meridian	4697040	LK Aero Corp. Brigantine, NJ.	
N262SA	78	SA-226T Merlin 3B	T-292	Merlin III B Associates Inc. Stuart, Fl.	(N1AQ)
N263AL	95	Pilatus PC-12	112	Lost Tree Aviation Inc. Indianapolis, In.	HB-FQG
N263CM	72	SA-226T Merlin 3	T-223	Damax Inc. Las Vegas, Nv.	N2630M
N263CW	03	TBM 700C	263	Cuprum Aviation LLC. Angola, In.	N700BU
N263SP	00	King Air B200	BB-1737	Marvin Lumber & Cedar Co. Warroad, Mn.	N4437S
N264B	01	PA-46-500TP Meridian	4697028	Comfly Corp. Middleburn, Ct.	
N264KW	79	MU-2 Solitaire	403SA	Dr Kenneth Wolf MD. Lewiston, Me.	N12LE
N264PA	80	King Air B100	BE-86	Air East Inc. Johnstown, Pa.	N85KA
N264SP	00	King Air B200	BB-1756	Indiana State Police, Indianapolis, In.	N5056U
N264WF	99	Pilatus PC-12/45	264	Ali-Gator Air LLC. Fairborn, Oh.	HB-FSI
N265EJ	81	King Air B200	BB-911	A Clifford Edwards, Billings, Mt.	N411CC
N265EX	80	Gulfstream 980	95032	Benchmark Ventures Ltd. Wilmington, De.	N9785S
N266EB	77	King Air 200	BB-266	Weekend Air Charter Services Inc. Trenton, NJ.	ZS-NNS
N266M	82	SA-227TT Merlin 3C	TT-424	Air Charter Ltd. Wausau, Wi.	N900AK
N266RD	01	King Air B200	LJ-1633	Windy City Express LLC/Condor Express Corp. Danbury, Ct.	N4473M
N266RH	81	King Air 200	BB-778	Big Laurel LLC. NYC.	N36CP
N267CB*	04	King Air B200	BB-1873	DeltaCore Charter Services LLC. Redmond, Wa.	N6113P
N267R	78	Rockwell 690B	11456	DLZ Aircraft Inc. Columbus, Oh.	D-IGLB
N267WF	99	Pilatus PC-12/45	267	Emerging Growth Advisors Inc. Baltimore, Md.	HB-FSL
N268CB	87	King Air 300	FA-121	Cass Ford Inc. El Paso, Tx.	N42AJ
N269AB	99	Pilatus PC-12/45	297	Bear Creek Aviation LLC. Baltimore, Md.	N269AF
N269AF*	03	Pilatus PC-12/45	526	M & N Equipment LLC. Casper, Wy.	N526PB
N269BW	80	King Air 200	BB-618	Big Country Charters LLC. Fayetteville, Ar.	HB-GID

Reg	Yr	Type	c/n	Owner/Operator	Prev Regn
☐ N269DE	71 SA-226T Merlin 3		T-208	A Z Aviation, Berryville, Ar. (status ?).	N429LC
☐ N269JG	81 King Air C90		LJ-949	J & G Aviation LLC. Mountain View, Ar.	N100HS
☐ N269JP	94 Pilatus PC-12		105	May Trucking Co. Salem, Or.	(N91MT)
☐ N269LS	81 King Air 200		BB-799	Chetcam LLC. Northridge, Ca.	N250DL
☐ N269PB	99 Pilatus PC-12/45		269	Rocky Mountain Group Technologies LLC. Evergreen, Co.	HB-FSN
☐ N269PM	68 SA-26T Merlin 2A		T26-26	Richard Viola, Canyon Lake, Ca.	C-GWKA
☐ N269SC	76 King Air C90		LJ-683	Community Health Associates Inc. Nashville, Tn.	(F-GVEP)
☐ N270DP	79 Rockwell 690B		11541	Commander Aviation LLC. Raleigh, NC.	N690BD
☐ N270M	67 King Air A90		LJ-288	Clark Brothers Felt, Waco, Tx.	
☐ N271BC	85 King Air 300		FA-48	Robert & Colleen Haas, San Francisco, Ca.	N7221N
☐ N271SS	00 Pilatus PC-12/45		306	I S & S Aviation LLC. Wilmington, De.	HB-FQT
☐ N271TW	79 MU-2 Marquise		734SA	MooToo 1 Inc. Newark, De.	(N331J)
☐ N271WN	67 King Air A90		LJ-226	Carole Broderick, Pinellas Park, Fl.	N14TG
☐ N272EA	02 King Air C90B		LJ-1686	Pinnacle Country Club Inc. Milan, Il.	
☐ N272MA	03 TBM 700C		272	Flight Level LLC. Madison, Wi.	
☐ N272MC	73 Mitsubishi MU-2K		272	RLSPP LLC. Plano, Tx.	N10BK
☐ N273AF	99 Pilatus PC-12/45		273	Alpha Flying Inc. Nashua, NH.	HB-FSR
☐ N273AZ	79 Conquest II		441-0104	Two Guys & A Plane Ltd. Toledo, Oh.	N8194Z
☐ N273NA	78 King Air E90		I W-273	Dale Danks Jr. Jackson, Ms.	N10SA
☐ N273TA	92 King Air 350		FL-69	Tanimura & Antle Inc. Salinas, Ca.	N8230Q
☐ N274GC	85 Conquest II		441-0349	Pro Aviation II LLC. Ogden, Ut.	N12125
☐ N274KA	78 King Air E90		LW-274	Martin Aviation Corp. NYC.	C-GTIO
☐ N274SB	78 PA-31T Cheyenne II		7820074	Lyddon Aero Center Inc. Liberal, Ks.	N787SW
☐ N275BT	00 King Air 350		FL-275	Executive AirShare Corp. Wichita, Ks.	(N350RC)
☐ N275CA	01 TBM 700B		200	Sierra Hotel Aviation LLC. Greenwich, Ct.	
☐ N275FA	95 King Air C90B		LJ-1403	Casco Transport Inc. Catano, PR.	N903SE
☐ N275LA	91 King Air C90A		LJ-1275	Davis Petroleum Products LLC. Glasgow, UK.	TC-AEM
☐ N275LE	68 King Air B90		LJ-373	Take-Off LLC. Santa Rosa Beach, Fl.	N99KA
☐ N275X	79 King Air 200		BB-502	K A 200 Inc/Western Airways Inc. Sugar Land, Tx.	N77PA
☐ N276CN	99 Pilatus PC-12/45		276	P & M Land Ventures LLC. Oceanside, Ca.	C-GMAE
☐ N276JB	98 King Air 350		FL-219	Allen Concrete & Masonry Inc. Raleigh, NC.	
☐ N276VM	66 King Air 90		LJ-81	Emersum Air Corp. Carroll, Oh.	N950K
☐ N277DG	81 PA-31T Cheyenne 1		8104058	Ideal Aviation LLC. Meridian, Ms.	(N130A)
☐ N277GE	90 King Air B200		BB-1389	Glass Equipment Development Inc. Twinsburg, Oh.	N389SA
☐ N277JB	76 King Air 200		BB-116	Flying Angels Inc. Apopka, Fl.	N92TA
☐ N277JJ	82 King Air B200		BB-1043	Full Gospel Baptist Church, New Orlaeans, La.	(N666JJ)
☐ N277PC	99 Pilatus PC-12/45		277	C & R Aviation LLC. Incline Village, Nv.	HB-FSV
☐ N277RS	79 King Air 200		BB-461	Soin International LLC. Dayton, Oh.	N33TG
☐ N277SP	80 King Air F90		LA-77	All Systems Satellite Distributors, Newark, NJ.	N827DP
☐ N277SW	81 King Air C90		LJ-968	NE Aviation LLC. Lewisville, Tx.	VH-FOP
☐ N277WC	03 King Air B200		BB-1824	Legal Aire Services Inc. Jacksonville, Fl.	N6124A
☐ N278AB	82 King Air C90-1		LJ-1012	Alton Blakely Aviation Inc. Stanford, Ky.	N617LM
☐ N278SW	82 King Air C90-1		LJ-1011	Citation Ventures Inc. Long Beach, Ca.	VH-FDW
☐ N278WC	99 Pilatus PC-12/45		278	Airwolff II LLC. Portland, Or.	HB-FSW
☐ N279DD	77 Rockwell 690B		11373	Robert Perkins, Carmel, Ca.	N911AC
☐ N280RA	75 King Air 200		BB-53	P & S Transport LLC. Shreveport, La.	N6ES
☐ N280SC	80 King Air 200		BB-664	Silverhawk Aviation Inc. Lincoln, Ne.	(N364EA)
☐ N280TT	77 King Air 200		BB-280	Sunquest Executive Air Charter Inc. Van Nuys, Ca.	F-GJPD
☐ N280YR	82 King Air B200		BB-943	B & H Aviation LLC. Butler, Pa.	N250YR
☐ N281JH	79 King Air 200		BB-516	B100 Aviation LLC. Smyrna, Tn.	N231JH
☐ N281MA	73 Mitsubishi MU-2K		261	William Powell, Lake Havasu City, Az.	
☐ N281WB	03 Pilatus PC-12/45		483	Right Rudder Inc. Fort Lauderdale, Fl.	N483PC
☐ N282CT	82 King Air B200		BB-1002	Indianapolis Aviation Inc. Fishers, In.	N6169S
☐ N282DB	77 King Air E90		LW-209	E-90 LLC. Parker, Co.	N32NS
☐ N282JD	01 King Air B200		BB-1779	Millennium Aviation New York LLC. Rochester, NY.	N624TA
☐ N282MS	71 Mitsubishi MU-2F		194	Agroaplica Corp. Santo Domingo, Dominican Republic.	N440EZ
☐ N282PC	81 Cheyenne II-XL		8166006	Mini Max Warehouses Inc. Florence, SC.	N38WA
☐ N282SJ	81 King Air 200		BB-925	Big Air LLC. Stockton, Ca.	N115D
☐ N282SW	01 PA-46-500TP Meridian		4697073	Williams Enterprises Inc. Carmi, Il.	
☐ N282TC	85 King Air E90		LW-311	TLC King Air One LLC. Burlington, NC.	N505RP
☐ N283B	76 King Air C-12C		BC-35	A H Charters Inc. Belle Chasse, La.	N7067B
☐ N283BS	91 TBM 700		16	Seymour Transport Inc. Grammer, In.	N700CT
☐ N283CB*	96 King Air 350		FL-135	W C Bradley Co & Columbus Bank & Trust Co. Columbus, Ga.	N3263M
☐ N283KA	75 King Air 200		BB-83	Med Air LLC. Lawrenceville, Ga.	RP-C711
☐ N284K	80 King Air 200		BB-608	Indiana University Foundation, Bloomington, In.	N16AS
Reg	*Yr Type*		*c/n*	*Owner/Operator*	*Prev Regn*

Reg	Yr	Type	c/n	Owner/Operator	Prev Regn
☐ N284PM	77 King Air C90	LJ-734	Dawkins, Thompson & Thompson LLC. Hartsville, SC.	(N700BN)
☐ N285KW	84 Cheyenne II-XL	1166007	La Oso SA. Guatemala City, Guatemala. (was 1122001)	D-IAQA
☐ N286AF	76 Rockwell 690A	11286	Mojoe LLC. Wilmington, De.	ZS-NXK
☐ N287CB	82 Cheyenne II-XL	8166051	Cottingham & Butler Insurance Service Inc. Dubuque, Ia.	N30VB
☐ N287PC	99 Pilatus PC-12/45	287	DGM Leasing, Oceanside, Ca.	HB-FQD
☐ N288CR	78 King Air E90	LW-269	Home Aviation LLC/Horne Ford Inc. Pinetop, Az.	N288CB
☐ N288KM	95 King Air B200	BB-1508	E J Aviation LLC. Scottsdale, Az.	N3208T
☐ N288RA	69 King Air 100	B-5	Cool Tours Inc. Guaynabo, PR.	N280CA
☐ N289PB	99 Pilatus PC-12/45	289	Philip Rosenbaum, Austin, Tx.	N289PB
☐ N290AJ	80 King Air C90	LJ-871	King Leasing Inc. Durham, NC.	N29EB
☐ N290CC	66 King Air A90	LJ-132	Jett Aire Florida One Inc. Fort Lauderdale, Fl.	ZP-TYF
☐ N290DP	71 King Air C90	LJ-529	Dodson International/Nion LLC, Rantoul, Ks.	LV-WJP
☐ N290GC	74 Mitsubishi MU-2K	310	R & J Enterprises of North Carolina, Murphy, NC.	VH-MUK
☐ N290K	80 King Air E90	LW-337	June & John Rogers/Sky Trek Aviation, Modesto, Ca.	
☐ N290KA	73 King Air E90	LW-59	Vamco International Inc. Pittsburgh, Pa.	N992MA
☐ N290MC	77 King Air E90	LW-206	Maconix Ltd. Minster, Oh.	N6406S
☐ N290PA	71 King Air C90	LJ-519	Simply Living Ltd. Galesburg, Il.	N82307
☐ N290PF	76 Rockwell 690A	11290	Aero Air LLC. Hillsboro, Or.	N100JJ
☐ N290RD	66 King Air A90	LJ-167	Ceonco Inc. Fayetteville, Ar.	N789TW
☐ N290RS	79 PA-31T Cheyenne 1	7904033	JSA Aviation LLC. Pineville, La.	N627NB
☐ N290SJ	77 King Air 200	BB-290	Citation Ventures Inc. Las Vegas, Nv.	YV-161CP
☐ N290TA	73 SA-226T Merlin 3	T-228	Transport Aviation Partners Inc. Las Vegas, Nv.	N610ED
☐ N291CC	77 King Air C90	LJ-728	D L Morgan Aviation Inc. Charleston, SC.	N275L
☐ N291DF	98 King Air C90B	LJ-1534	Davis & Floyd Inc. Greenwood, SC.	N268P
☐ N291MB	74 Mitsubishi MU-2K	291	Interncontinental Jet Inc. Tulsa, Ok.	CP-1147
☐ N291MM	73 King Air E90	LW-32	H McMurrey, Houston, Tx.	N123PP
☐ N291PA	77 King Air 200	BB-291	Business Aircraft Solutions Inc. East Alton, Il.	N769
☐ N291RB	74 Rockwell 690A	11161	Ron Blackwell Ford Inc. Bentonville, Ar.	XA-RZS
☐ N292A	66 King Air 90	LJ-99	Placebo Air LLC. Ridgecrest, Ca.	N73679
☐ N292SN	92 King Air B200	BB-1425	Sierra Nevada Helicopters Inc. Lebanon, NH.	N212SN
☐ N292Z	66 680T Turbo Commander	1566-22	Pegasus Force, Homestead, Fl.	OB-T-924
☐ N294DR	04 PA-46-500TP Meridian	4697184	Front Range Radiation Oncology PC. Littleton, Co.	
☐ N295CP	88 King Air B200	BB-1295	Rocky Top Building Products Inc. Rocky Mount, Va.	N95MW
☐ N295PC	99 Pilatus PC-12/45	295	Seminole Tribe of Florida, Hollywood, Fl.	HB-FQJ
☐ N296AS	77 King Air C90	LJ-704	JSW Investments Inc/Aero-Smith Inc. Martinsburg, WV.	N1565L
☐ N298D	00 King Air C90B	LJ-1603	Laursen Aviation Inc. Auburn, Ca.	N445D
☐ N299AK	03 King Air B200	BB-1850	B200 Air Charters LLC. Great Neck, NJ.	N6150Q
☐ N299AL	03 King Air B200	BB-1823	Aviation Specialities Inc. Washington, DC.	N299AK
☐ N299AM	98 Pilatus PC-12/45	236	University of Utah Hospitals & Clinic, Salt Lake City, Ut.	HB-FRG
☐ N299D	67 King Air A90	LJ-257	Sun Charter LLC. St Petersburg, Fl.	C-FXNB
☐ N299EC	81 SA-226T Merlin 3B	T-410	Smith & Sons Aircraft LLC. Stuart, Fl.	(D-IFLY)
☐ N299K	79 King Air C90	LJ-839	Hartford Holding Corp. Naples, Fl.	9G-SAM
☐ N299KP	84 King Air F90-1	LA-218	King Air 200 Partners LLC. Palo Alto, Ca.	N218BA
☐ N299MK	90 King Air B200	BB-1357	Boman & Kemp Manufacturing Inc. Ogden, Ut.	D-IBSY
☐ N299MS	69 King Air B90	LJ-457	Tuff Country Inc. West Jordan, Ut.	N405BC
☐ N299RP	98 King Air C90B	LJ-1537	Utility Air Inc. Moberly, Mo.	N99ML
☐ N299VM	85 King Air C90A	LJ-1125	Skyline Crest Enterprises LLC. Antioch, Ca.	N299KA
☐ N300AE	94 TBM 700	97	Yankee Bravo Inc. Ponte Verde, Fl.	
☐ N300AJ	82 King Air B200	BB-965	Trey Aviation LLC. Allen, Tx.	N184MQ
☐ N300AL	80 SA-226T Merlin 3B	T-326	M & C Leasing Inc. Hammond, In.	N19J
☐ N300AZ	04 TBM 700C	300	SOCATA Aircraft, Pembroke Pines, Fl.	
☐ N300CH	75 King Air E90	LW-148	U S Helicopters Inc & Diamond Aviation Inc. Marshville, NC.	N300KD
☐ N300CW	87 King Air 300	FA-115	TumiAir Inc. Woodside, Ca.	XC-AA20
☐ N300DM	82 King Air F90	LA-165	Las Montanas Aviation LLC. Tucson, Az.	N686LD
☐ N300ET	90 King Air B200	BB-1381	SET AIR LLC/Air-Care Inc. Rocky Mount, NC.	N215P
☐ N300FL	98 King Air B200	BB-1629	Fleet Financial Group Inc. Providence, RI.	N2221Z
☐ N300FN	84 King Air C90A	LJ-1066	J & E Piledriving Inc. Syracuse, NY.	N300FL
☐ N300HB	79 King Air 200	BB-566	Whiting Wings/Whiting Systems Inc. Alexander, Ar.	N200ER
☐ N300HH	85 King Air 300	FA-80	Barrett, Burke, Wilson et al, Addison, Tx.	(N257BB)
☐ N300HV	85 King Air 300	FA-29	Central Cooling Co. Fremont, Ca.	N72146
☐ N300KA	90 King Air 350	FL-28	Malone Aero Sales LLC. Atlanta, Ga.	N220CL
☐ N300MC	86 King Air 300	FA-91	Ridgeway Enterprises Inc/Rose Packing Co. Barrington, Il.	N990PT
☐ N300MT	75 King Air E90	LW-143	Executive Air Taxi Corp. Bismarck, ND.	N300BA
☐ N300NK	83 Conquest II	441-0318	Enkay Corp. Shreveport, La.	N1208M
☐ N300PH	89 King Air 300	FA-201	Big Sky Caravan LLC. Ennis, Mt.	
Reg	Yr Type	c/n	Owner/Operator	Prev Regn

Reg	Yr Type	c/n	Owner/Operator	Prev Regn
☐ N300PP	88 King Air 300LW	FA-171	B V Handel en Exploitatienmaatschappij Ruygrok,	D-COIL
☐ N300PR	84 King Air 300	FA-13	Echo Maintenance Ltd. Port Arthur, Tx.	(N500GC)
☐ N300PT	73 SA-226T Merlin 3	T-233	Clinical Evalutations inc. Houston, Tx.	N84LC
☐ N300PU	99 King Air B200	BB-1657	Purdue University, Lafayette, La.	
☐ N300PV	81 PA-31T Cheyenne II	8120038	Lucian McElroy, Metamora, Mi.	N806CA
☐ N300R	02 King Air 350	FL-362	NASCAR Inc. Daytona Beach, Fl.	N6162K
☐ N300RC	89 King Air 300	FA-177	JPT Associates LLC. Minneapolis, Mn.	(N350CD
☐ N300RX	73 Mitsubishi MU-2J	572	Turbine Aircraft Marketing Inc. San Angelo, Tx.	N986MA
☐ N300SE	85 King Air 300	FA-68	Georgia Theatre Co. St Simons Island, Ga.	N10QY
☐ N300SR	81 PA-31T Cheyenne 1	8104022	Seastar Inc. Carmel, In.	N77NH
☐ N300SV	87 King Air 300	FA-112	Furry Bird LLC. Durango, Co.	F-GJHH
☐ N300TA	80 King Air F90	LA-9	Michael Williams, LaPorte, In.	N200FA
☐ N300TM	91 King Air 350	FL-50	Taylor & Martin/T & M Enterprises Inc. Fremont, Ne.	N202PV
☐ N300TN	88 King Air 300	FA-168	Wahoo Air LLC/Agency Solutions, Tampa, Fl.	N300TM
☐ N300TP	87 King Air B200	BB-1279	Otter Tail Power Co. Fergus Falls, Mn.	N58AB
☐ N300TR	74 King Air 200	BB-6	Mutual Assurance Agency Inc. Birmingham, Al.	N301TT
☐ N300VA	80 King Air C90	LJ-877	Virginia Student Aid Founndation, Charlottesvillo, Va.	N66877
☐ N300WP	79 PA-31T Cheyenne 1	7904006	D K & L LLC. Indianapolis, In.	N6182
☐ N301CG	85 King Air 300	FA 87	John Lister, Hondo, Tx. (status ?).	N899EA
☐ N301D	01 PA-46-500TP Meridian	4697043	312D Leasing Inc. Jupiter, Fl.	N5077Y
☐ N301GM	77 Mitsubishi MU-2L	696	Currituck Inc. Elizabeth City, NC.	N856MA
☐ N301HC	85 King Air B200	BB-1219	Intermountain Health Care Services, Salt Lake City, Ut.	N200YB
☐ N301PS	80 King Air 200	BB-657	Corporate Air Inc. Fort Wayne, In.	
☐ N301SL	91 P-180 Avanti	1011	AvantAir Inc. Stewart, NY.	N130AV
☐ N301TA	79 PA-31T Cheyenne 1	7904041	Ralph Norton MD. Houston, Tx.	N65CK
☐ N301TS	79 King Air B100	BE-76	Energy Aviation LLC. Atlanta, Ga.	N812WJ
☐ N302MB	77 King Air 200	BB-272	Clayton Aviation Inc. Franklin Park, Il.	N202KA
☐ N302NC	84 King Air 300	FA-9	BCDL Air LLC. Wilmington, De.	N930G
☐ N302PB	00 Pilatus PC-12/45	302	Neptune Colorado LLC. Reno, Nv.	HB-FQO
☐ N302TA	80 PA-31T Cheyenne II	8020046	David York, Menlo Park, Ca.	N1879D
☐ N302WC	77 Rockwell 690B	11399	Wick Communications Co/Shanks Mare LLC. Sierra Vista, Az.	N1ER
☐ N303AG	72 Mitsubishi MU-2K	239	Falconmitch Inc. Tyler, Tx.	N222LR
☐ N303CA	86 King Air C90A	LJ-1134	Dunlap & Kyle Co. Batesville, Ms.	D-IEVO
☐ N303G	77 Rockwell 690B	11355	Clemson University, Clemson, SC.	N303G
☐ N303GM	82 Gulfstream 1000	96042	South Pacific Air Transport, Houston, Tx.	N9962S
☐ N303JD	00 Pilatus PC-12/45	303	Lisgar II LLC. Lincoln, Ca.	N912RP
☐ N303JW*	02 PA-46-500TP Meridian	4697149	James Warren, Ashland, Or.	
☐ N303MA	77 SA-226T Merlin 3A	T-278	Calark, Mabelvale, Ar.	N475MG
☐ N304JS	88 King Air 300	FA-142	JFOX3 LLC. Wilmington, De.	N27TB
☐ N304LG	77 King Air E90	LW-231	Seven Bar Flying Service Inc. Albuquerque, NM.	N4954S
☐ N304PR*	00 Pilatus PC-12/45	304	Pacific Real Estate Consulting LLC. Larkspur, Ca.	N304PT
☐ N304SC	92 Cheyenne T-1040	8275017	SouthCentral Air Inc. Kenai, Ak.	N9096C
☐ N304SL	04 P-180 Avanti	1077	AvantAir Inc. Stewart, NY.	N205PA
☐ N305CW	75 Mitsubishi MU-2L	667	Murray Aviation Inc. Ypsilanti, Mi.	N300CW
☐ N305DS	75 Mitsubishi MU-2M	328	Florida Fast Flight Corp. Miami Lakes, Fl.	N5PC
☐ N305JS	79 King Air 200	BB-472	Mountain View Aviation LLC. Mountain View, Ar.	G-WRCF
☐ N305PC	97 Beech 1900D	UE-299	BCC Equipment Leasing Corp. Long Beach, Ca.	
☐ N305SA	86 King Air 300	FA-111	SteakAir Inc. Little Rock, Ar.	N391MT
☐ N305SL	04 P-180 Avanti	1083	AvantAir Inc. Stewart, NY.	
☐ N305TT	81 King Air C90	LJ-992	O'Mar Inc. Wilmer, Al.	HB-GJA
☐ N306M	86 King Air 300	FA-98	Jackson Air Charter Inc. Jackson, Ms.	N30SM
☐ N306SL	04 P-180 Avanti	1084	AvantAir Inc. Stewart, NY.	N306SL
☐ N307PA	79 SA-226T Merlin 3B	T-307	James Mason, DeKalb, Il.	N606PS
☐ N307SL	04 P-180 Avanti	1091	AvantAir Inc. Stewart, NY.	
☐ N308SL	04 P-180 Avanti	1093	AvantAir Inc. Stewart, NY.	
☐ N310JM	01 PA-46-500TP Meridian	4697069	Doverdel LLC. Wilmington, De.	
☐ N310MA	69 Mitsubishi MU-2F	167	Jackson Tennessee Leasing Co. Jackson, Tn.	N549LK
☐ N311AC	81 PA-31T Cheyenne II	8120016	Dr Peter Sones, Atlanta, Ga.	N241PS
☐ N311AV	78 King Air 200	BB-336	Colemill Enterprises Inc. Nashville, Tn.	N50TW
☐ N311CM	80 King Air B100	BE-101	L J Associates Inc. Latrobe, Pa.	N3695A
☐ N311DS	80 King Air F90	LA-41	RidgAire Inc. Jacksonville, Tx.	N37JT
☐ N311G	01 King Air B200	BB-1760	Jet Sharing Aviation LLC. Boca Raton, Fl.	N4360N
☐ N311GC	80 King Air F90	LA-55	RTE Enterprises Inc. Van Nuys, Ca.	N300GC
☐ N311GM	96 King Air 350	FL-138	Garan Manufacturing Corp. Starkville, Ms.	N350P
☐ N311KB	73 King Air C-12C	BD-3	Orange County Sheriffs Office, Orlando, Fl.	N140MT
Reg	**Yr Type**	**c/n**	**Owner/Operator**	**Prev Regn**

Reg	Yr	Type	c/n	Owner/Operator	Prev Regn
☐ N311LM	77	PA-31T Cheyenne II	7720016	Freefall Express inc. Keene, NH.	C-FACM
☐ N311MP	83	King Air B200	BB-1112	Med-Pro Leasing, Oklahoma City, Ok.	(N7090U)
☐ N311RF	85	King Air 300	FA-33	Samaritan's Purse Inc. Boone, NC.	N250PD
☐ N311RN*	74	Mitsubishi MU-2K	311	Northern Jet Sales LLC. Murfreesboro, Tn.	N311JB
☐ N311SC	82	Cheyenne T-1040	8275006	SouthCentral Air Inc. Kenai, Ak.	N9176Y
☐ N311SR	66	King Air 90	LJ-107	Barber Aviation Inc. Brookville, Pa.	N7BQ
☐ N312BC	94	Pilatus PC-12	101	CPG Leasing LLC. Wayzata, Mn. (was s/n P-03).	HB-FOC
☐ N312DB	85	King Air 300	FA-35	Drone Aviation LLC. Snellville, Ga.	N26JP
☐ N312DE	85	King Air 300	FA-49	Atlantic Coast Carriers Inc. Fayetteville, NC.	N984SW
☐ N312JC	88	King Air B200	BB-1312	Mobile Bay Air LLC. Theodore, Al.	N506EB
☐ N312MA	73	Mitsubishi MU-2K	266	Raymond Kinney & Finley Ledbetter, Gainesville, Tx.	
☐ N312ME	82	King Air B200C	BL-46	Aviation Specialities Inc. Washington, DC.	N3125J
☐ N312PC	96	Pilatus PC-12	144	James Aviation Inc. Erie, Pa.	HB-FRF
☐ N312RL	97	King Air 350	FL-164	Belk Simpson Co. Greenville, SC.	C-FOIL
☐ N312SB	88	King Air B200	BB-1313	Robins Aviation LLC. Warner Robins, Ga.	N138JH
☐ N312VF	67	King Air A90	LJ-299	L & S Supply LLC. Dalton, Ga.	(N312MH)
☐ N313BA	89	King Air 300	FA-178	Beta Aire Ltd/Heidtman Steel Products Inc. Toledo, Oh.	ZS-MNG
☐ N313BB	84	PA-42 Cheyenne IIIA	5501016	Browning Brothers LLC. Ogden, Ut.	N94CS
☐ N313D	82	SA-227AT Merlin 4C	AT-464	Mana-Igreja Crista Inc. Tulsa, Ok.	N30364
☐ N313DW	96	King Air C90B	LJ-1434	Durair Inc. Sedona, Az.	
☐ N313EE	80	King Air 200	BB-708	Mirax Aviation Inc. Carmel, In.	N313EL
☐ N313ES	88	King Air B200	BB-1300	Hull Properties Inc. Augusta, Ga.	(N43GJ)
☐ N313KY	86	King Air 300	FA-110	Yellow Iron LLC/Reese Air LLP. Las Vegas, Nv.	ZS-NPL
☐ N313PC	91	PA-42 Cheyenne 400LS	5527044	Precision Concrete Construction Co. White Marsh, Md.	N495CA
☐ N314DD	80	PA-31T Cheyenne 1	8004025	North Wind Aviation Corp. Fort Wayne, In.	N2323V
☐ N314GK	80	PA-31T Cheyenne 1	8004026	N731PC LLC. Toledo, Oh.	N76CP
☐ N314P	82	King Air F90	LA-170	Sunrise Aviation LLC. Ridgefield, Ct.	N605CC
☐ N314SC	82	Cheyenne T-1040	8275007	Universal Turbine Parts Inc. Prattville, Al.	N9180Y
☐ N314TD	80	PA-31T Cheyenne II	8020056	PL Flight LLC. Kirkland, Wa.	N144RL
☐ N315MS	78	King Air 200	BB-404	INHS Leasing LLC. Spokane, Wa.	N777PR
☐ N315N	01	King Air B200	BB-1766	Norma One LLC. Johns Island, SC.	(N4GP)
☐ N316CA*	83	Conquest II	441-0315	Crusader Air LLC. Cleveland, Tn.	N441HF
☐ N316EN	77	Mitsubishi MU-2M	349SA	Land Design Inc. Southern Pines, NC.	N734MA
☐ N316JP	81	King Air B200	BB-923	Tonic Air Inc. Sharpsburg, Ga.	N200MG
☐ N316MS	78	King Air 200	BB-412	INHS Leasing LLC. Spokane, Wa.	N2030P
☐ N316PR	80	MU-2 Marquise	761SA	Flyin Cloud LLC. Myrtle Beach, SC.	N678RH
☐ N316WB	80	PA-31T Cheyenne 1	8004057	Breathwit Marine Contractors Inc. Dickenson, Tx.	N316JP
☐ N317NA	98	Pilatus PC-12/45	223	Native Air Services Inc. Mesa, Az.	N223PD
☐ N317P	92	King Air 350	FL-74	Lakeside Industries Inc. Issaquah, Wa.	
☐ N317RT	99	King Air B200	BB-1694	O'Reilly II Aviation, Springfield, Mo.	(ZS-...)
☐ N318AK	78	Conquest II	441-0070	Precision Leasing Inc. Delray Beach, Fl.	N621SC
☐ N318F	73	King Air C90	LJ-574	Pacific Coast Enterprises LLC. Las Vegas, Nv.	(N1097S)
☐ N318MT	00	Pilatus PC-12/45	318	Micron Technology Inc. Boise, Id.	HB-FRB
☐ N318TK	73	Rockwell 690A	11136	AED Aviation Inc. Wilmington, De.	N333CA
☐ N318W	78	King Air 200	BB-402	USDA Forest Service, Boise, Id.	N400QK
☐ N318WA	77	Rockwell 690B	11444	Websta's Aviation Services Inc. St Croix, USVI.	N690TG
☐ N319BF	81	Gulfstream 840	11675	Jose Manuel Gardilla,	N39SA
☐ N319EE	04	King Air 350	FL-401	Energy East Corp. New Gloucester, Me.	
☐ N319TB	04	TBM 700C	319	SOCATA Aircraft, Pembroke Pines, Fl.	
☐ N320CA	03	P-180 Avanti	1069	Eastlake Avanti LLC. Eastlake, Co.	N143PA
☐ N320SS	83	Conquest 1	425-0139	QEAT XXI LLC. Indianapolis, In.	N383SS
☐ N321CW	99	TBM 700B	155	Carson Wealth Management Group Inc. Omaha, Ne.	N345HB
☐ N321DM	77	King Air E90	LW-250	Aerostar Executive Aviation Inc. San Antonio, Tx.	N600EF
☐ N321DZ	68	King Air B90	LJ-367	B T P Inc. Missoula, Mt.	N9711B
☐ N321F	78	King Air C-12C	BC-70	Dynamic Aviation Group Inc. Bridgewater, Va.	78-23134
☐ N321LB	81	Cheyenne II-XL	8166012	Strategic Technology Resources LLC. Roswell, NM.	N888PT
☐ N321LH	84	PA-42 Cheyenne 400LS	5527012	JANA Aviation Inc. Wilmington, De.	C-GRGE
☐ N321P	78	King Air RC-12D	GR-10	Dynamic Aviation Group Inc. Bridgewater, Va. (was BP-6).	78-23145
☐ N321PH	69	SA-26AT Merlin 2B	T26-140	Princess Aviation Group Inc. Stuart, Fl.	N718GL
☐ N321PL	00	Pilatus PC-12/45	321	Jim Air Inc. Anchorage, Ak.	HB-FRD
☐ N321TP	80	MU-2 Marquise	780SA	Ted Price Sr. Ventura, Ca.	N16HA
☐ N322GB	80	MU-2 Solitaire	419SA	Flying Services Inc. Corpus Christi, Tx.	N153MA
☐ N322GK	80	King Air F90	LA-64	Milford Bostik, Waco, Tx.	N3698H
☐ N322MR	00	King Air C90B	LJ-1611	LSR LLC. Hattiesburg, Ms.	N530AC
☐ N322P	83	Conquest II	441-0274	Herbert & Marigrace Boyer, Novato, Ca.	N98468

Reg	Yr	Type	c/n	Owner/Operator	Prev Regn
N322R	78	King Air C90	LJ-746	Morningstar Capital Investments LLC. Scottsdale, Az.	(N122RG)
N322TA	80	MU-2 Marquise	760SA	Indiana State Medical Association, Indianapolis, In.	N321RC
N322TC	92	King Air C90B	LJ-1302	KJV Aviation Inc. Petersburg, WV.	N5670D
N323HA	79	King Air E90	LW-323	Dale Aviation Inc. Rapid City, SD.	N323KA
N323RR	78	King Air 200	BB-380	R & R Aviation of the Carolinas, Charlotte, NC.	N59GS
N324EC	72	King Air U-21J	B-99	Eagle Creek Aviation, Longview, Tx.	N100GJ
N324JS	02	TBM 700B	230	Flamingo 700 Inc. Wilmington, De.	N242CA
N325JM	99	King Air 350	FL-235	FHC Flight Services Inc. Norfolk, Va.	
N325MA	75	Mitsubishi MU-2M	325	Hahn Transportation Ltd. Decatur, Il.	N440RB
N325MW	00	Pilatus PC-12/45	325	325MW Inc. Los Altos Hills, Ca.	(ZS-SRI)
N325WP	89	King Air 300	FA-173	Blue Ridge King Inc. Martinsville, Va.	N89GA
N325WR	80	King Air F90	LA-10	Apple Sauce Inc. Crestview Hills, Il.	N325WP
N326AJ	78	King Air 200	BB-396	Century Aviation of Colorado LLC. Telluride, Co.	(N98HH)
N326KW	90	King Air/Catpass 250	BB-1360	Bering Air Inc. Nome, Ak.	HK-3703X
N326MS	80	SA-226T Merlin 3B	T-313	Royal Estates Inc. Forney, Tx.	RP-C323
N326PA	00	Pilatus PC-12/45	362	Pappa Alpha LLC. Los Altos Hills, Ca.	HB-FSM
N326PT	99	King Air C90B	LJ-1581	Eve Flying Inc. North Caldwell, NJ.	N32211
N326RS	83	Conquest II	441-0326	IAS Air LLC. Shelley, Id.	N171SP
N326RT	79	King Air 200	BB 653	Tarp-It Inc. Ellensburg, Wa.	N83JN
N327R	99	King Air 350	FL-259	Stockton Equipment Leasing LLC. Stockton, Ca.	C-GDKI
N327RB	78	King Air 200	BB-335	Deffenbaugh Industries Inc. Shawnee, Ks.	N327RK
N327YR	02	Pilatus PC-12/45	457	Yellow Rose Aviation LLC. Golden, Co.	N457PC
N328AJ	99	King Air 350	FL-245	Aries Aviation LLC. Columbus, Oh.	N350G
N328DC	94	Dornier 328-100	3019	Pacific Gas & Electric Co. San Francisco, Ca.	
N328KK	81	Cheyenne II-XL	8166068	Kent Kelly/Bristol Aircraft Leasing LLC. Montgomery, Al.	N612BB
N328PA	00	Pilatus PC-12/45	328	Atoll Holdings Ltd.	HB-FRM
N329HS	80	SA-226T Merlin 3B	T-323	Cypress Aviation Inc. Marks, Ms.	(N329HP)
N329KK	81	PA-31T Cheyenne 1	8104011	Kent Kelly/Bristol Aircraft Leasing LLC. Montgomery, Al.	(N839CH)
N329NG	00	Pilatus PC-12/45	329	Beta Equipment Services of NH Inc. Hampton, NH.	(ZS-SRJ)
N330CS	89	King Air B200	BB-1337	Concord Service Corp/Cable Services, Williamsport, Pa.	N1550U
N330DM	92	P-180 Avanti	1014	Glenbrook Aviation Inc. Fort Wayne, In.	N705PA
N330ES	78	Rockwell 690B	11476	Earth Search Sciences Inc. McCall, Id.	N690SC
N330V	79	King Air C90	LJ-811	Cross Atlantic Express LLC. Wilmington, De.	
N331AM	66	King Air A90	LJ-144	White Industries Inc. Bates City, Mo.	(N3DG)
N331GM	80	SA-226T Merlin 3B	T-331	Kings Bay Airmotive Inc. Tampa, Fl.	N331TB
N331H	61	Gulfstream 1	70	Dodson International Parts Inc. Ottawa, Ks.	N770G
N331KB	78	PA-31T Cheyenne 1	7804009	Kelbrach Aviation LLC. Overland Park, Ks.	N6125A
N331MA	80	MU-2 Marquise	768SA	Turbine Aircraft Marketing Inc. San Angelo, Tx.	N36MF
N331MP	83	Conquest II	441-0312	Martin's Famous Pastry Shoppe Inc. Chambersburg, Pa.	N514MC
N331RC	73	Rockwell 690A	11137	Ace Air Inc. Lafayette, La.	N876MC
N332DE	76	King Air C90	LJ-674	Delta Echo LLC. Sioux Falls, SD.	N9074S
N332DM	80	Conquest II	441-0167	Fury Management of Delaware Inc. Wilmington, De.	N312KJ
N332SA	85	PA-42 Cheyenne 400LS	5527025	Golden Air Inc. Dothan, Al.	N325KW
N332SM	81	PA-42 Cheyenne III	8001020	Coosa Air Inc. Rome, Ga.	N332SA
N333AP	83	King Air B200	BB-1137	Andy Petree Racing Inc. East Flat Rock, NC.	N133LJ
N333BM	97	King Air C90B	LJ-1504	CTW Trading LLC. Tulsa, Ok.	
N333DV	88	King Air 300	FA-144	Vincent Aviation Inc. Van Nuys, Ca.	N950JM
N333F	68	SA-26AT Merlin 2B	T26-100	Marvin Perry, Morrilton, Ar.	(N500SN
N333G	66	King Air 90	LJ-101	Bramco Aircraft Leasing, Miami, Fl.	N42B
N333HC	74	Rockwell 690A	11150	Robert Holt, Midland, Tx.	N47150
N333LE	77	King Air E90	LW-223	Standridge Color Corp. Social Circle, Ga.	N7UM
N333M	99	King Air 350	FL-243	Advanced Aquacultural Technologies & others, Warsaw, In.	N3043S
N333MM	00	PA-46-500TP Meridian	4697010	Robert Lunday Jr. Covington, Wa.	
N333P	80	PA-31T Cheyenne II	8020002	Victorian Aviation Ltd. Mendon, Ma.	(N4LH)
N333RD	81	King Air B200	BB-915	Kato Jet International LLC. Mankato, Mn.	ZS-LFT
N333RK	78	Mitsubishi MU-2P	380SA	Orison B Curpier Co. Cooperstown, NY.	ZS-NIY
N333TL	82	King Air C90	LJ-999	Scope Leasing Inc. Columbus, Oh.	N333TP
N333TN	80	PA-31T Cheyenne II	8020089	Betnr Engineering & Construction Corp. Pittsfield, Ma.	D-IGEM
N333TP	88	King Air B200	BB-1292	Textile Printing Co. Chattanooga, Tn.	N3109Y
N333TX	76	Mitsubishi MU-2M	332	PWB Air Inc. Brady, Tx.	(N4DM)
N333UJ	83	Conquest 1	425-0179	Ugly John's Aircraft LLC. Afton, Ok.	N918CK
N333UP	82	Gulfstream 1000	96015	Anderson Fought, Portland, Or.	N325MM
N333WC	85	King Air 300	FA-55	DDMR LLC/Walkabout Air Inc.Tampa, Fl.	N321EC
N333WF	78	Mitsubishi MU-2P	387SA	Jaax Flying Service/Solitaire Investments LLC. Calexico, Ca.	N8TB
N333WT	81	King Air F90	LA-91	SumTranz LLC/Sumter Petroleum Co. Sumter, SC.	N641PE

Reg	Yr	Type	c/n	Owner/Operator	Prev Regn
☐ N333XX	79	PA-31T Cheyenne II	7920038	Robert Arnot, South Newbury, NH.	N333CE
☐ N334CA	79	PA-31T Cheyenne 1	7904034	Quik Flight LLC. Scotia, NY.	C9-ENT
☐ N334EB	73	Mitsubishi MU-2J	568	Bankair inc. West Columbia, SC.	N99SL
☐ N335KW	89	King Air B200	BB-1335	McKnight LLC. Virginia Beach, Va.	(N10SA)
☐ N335MA	02	TBM 700B	235	Lewis Martin, Bloomington, Il.	
☐ N335S	77	King Air 200	BB-227	Skyways Ltd. Huron, SD.	N90BR
☐ N335TA	79	King Air 200	BB-514	Bell Aviation Inc. West Columbia, SC.	(N435TA)
☐ N335WH	00	Pilatus PC-12/45	335	Presco Inc. Lafayette, La.	N335PB
☐ N336JM	81	King Air E90	LW-345	ASI Holdings Inc. Albany, Ga.	N173AS
☐ N337C	80	Conquest II	441-0126	Chapman Corp. Washington, Pa.	N98630
☐ N337DR	82	Gulfstream 900	15007	Douglas Reichardt/Southern Nevada Jet, Henderson, Nv.	N695LD
☐ N337KC	84	Conquest II	441-0337	Kinsley Construction, York, Pa.	XA-PEH
☐ N337TF	01	PA-46-500TP Meridian	4697094	Aero Equipment Leasing Inc. Indianapolis, In.	N221FP
☐ N337TP	00	Pilatus PC-12/45	326	Washington Times Aviation Inc. Washington, DC.	PT-TPU
☐ N338CM	77	Mitsubishi MU-2N	703SA	W W & D Ltd. Hinsdale, Il.	N333GM
☐ N338DB	03	PA-46-500TP Meridian	4697155	Oakfield Aviation Inc. Wilmington, De.	N53677
☐ N338PC	00	Pilatus PC-12/45	338	Sierra Star Leasing LLC. Dover, De.	HB-FRT
☐ N339JG	82	King Air B100	BE-130	Country Air Services LLC. Mascoutah, Il.	C-GTCL
☐ N339KA	80	King Air E90	LW-339	Blaha Air Services Inc. Rocky River, Oh.	LV-VFC
☐ N340SS	85	SAAB 340A	022	Meregrass Inc. Dallas, Tx.	N804CE
☐ N341DB	89	King Air 300	FA-185	B-Air LC. Sikeston, Mo.	N1191K
☐ N341MH	80	King Air E90	LW-341	H & D Aviation LC. Palmetto, Fl.	RP-C1990
☐ N341MM*	03	PA-46-500TP Meridian	4697168	Schoenleben Aero Inc. Celina, Oh.	N2HD
☐ N343CW	00	Pilatus PC-12/45	340	Winn LLC. Wilmington, De.	HB-FRV
☐ N343RR*	04	PA-46-500TP Meridian	4697197	Access Yacht Sales Inc. Key Largo, Fl.	
☐ N344DP	95	King Air C90B	LJ-1414	210 Destinations Co. Bethesda, Md.	N523P
☐ N344KL	73	Mitsubishi MU-2K	257	Flight Service Co. Munhall, Pa.	N344K
☐ N344L	94	King Air 350	FL-107	Synergy International LLC. Grand Haven, Mi.	N4S
☐ N345BH	01	King Air C90B	LJ-1645	Aurora Aviation Inc. McGregor, Tx.	XA-TXE
☐ N345CM	77	Mitsubishi MU-2J	11402	Smith Aircraft Management LLC. Shreveport, La.	N81638
☐ N345DF	78	PA-31T Cheyenne II	7820088	State of Nevada, Carson City, Nv.	N4491C
☐ N345DG	98	King Air B200	BB-1653	GAF Holdings Inc. Visalia, Ca.	N653ME
☐ N345RF*	00	Pilatus PC-12/45	345	Claire Air LLC. Addison, Il.	N1983R
☐ N345SA	72	Mitsubishi MU-2J	557	European Aircraft Leasing Inc. Dover, De.	OH-MIC
☐ N345T	68	SA-26AT Merlin 2B	T26-105	Tschetter Enterprises Inc. Naples, Fl.	
☐ N345TP	80	Conquest 1	425-0005	AVCO Express LLC. Summerville, SC.	N6SK
☐ N345TT	68	680W Turbo Commander	1791-21	Thunder Commander Ltd. Van Nuys, Ca.	N77JL
☐ N345V	72	King Air E90	LW-23	Rich Jones Aviation, Alexandria, NM.	
☐ N345WK	97	King Air B200	BB-1580	Olde Dominion Aviation LLC. Winter Park, Fl.	N200KA
☐ N346VL	72	Mitsubishi MU-2F	231	Diamond, Lakee & Pearson Resources, Austin, Tx.	N666MA
☐ N347D	85	King Air B200	BB-1197	Bill Putnam, Mills, Wy.	
☐ N347KC	00	Pilatus PC-12/45	347	Task Force Tips Inc. Valparaiso, In.	HB-FSA
☐ N348AC	67	King Air A90	LJ-196	St Louis Public Schools Gateway Institute of Technology, Mo.	N300DD
☐ N348PC	00	Pilatus PC-12/45	348	J Luis Franco, McAllen, Tx.	HB-FSB
☐ N350AB	98	King Air 350	FL-212	Rolling Plains Well Service Inc. Midland, Tx.	N2341F
☐ N350AJ	90	King Air 350	FL-22	Three Stars Aviation LLC/Caprock Energy Inc. Wilmington, De.	ZS-NGI
☐ N350AT	73	King Air E90	LW-58	Executive Wings Inc. Wexford, Pa.	N250HP
☐ N350BD	94	King Air 350	FL-123	Deep South Aviation Inc. Southlake, Tx.	N30YR
☐ N350BF	89	King Air 300	FA-187	Bassett Furniture Industries Inc. Bassett, Va.	N89GC
☐ N350BG	98	King Air 350	FL-217	Ruby-Forrest Ltd. Suwanee, Ga.	N350FC
☐ N350BS	90	King Air 350	FL-6	Raytan LLC. Joliet, Il.	N100BG
☐ N350BW	00	King Air 350	FL-278	Cibolo LLC. St Helens, Or.	
☐ N350CS	98	King Air 350	FL-214	Srair LLC. Riviera Beach, Fl.	N350WG
☐ N350D	01	King Air 350	FL-334	Southlake Aviation Management Inc. Southlake, Tx.	N5034F
☐ N350DR	91	King Air 350	FL-63	DeRoyal Industries Inc. Powell, Tn.	(N10DR)
☐ N350DW	88	King Air 300	FA-157	W I Aviation LLC. Wilmington, De.	YV-1077CP
☐ N350EB	91	King Air 350	FL-49	Pinefield Consulting Inc. Portsmouth, NH.	N27BH
☐ N350FH	90	King Air 350	FL-10	Piedmont Hawthorne Aviation Inc. Winston-Salem, NC.	N305RL
☐ N350FW	04	King Air 350	FL-421	Air Excursions LLC. Chicago, Il.	
☐ N350GA	90	King Air 350	FL-16	Gasser Air Co. Youngstown, Oh.	N48HP
☐ N350HA	04	King Air 350	FL-393	Hawks Transportation LLC. Omaha, Ne.	N6193S
☐ N350J	00	King Air 350	FL-314	DePuy Orthopaedics Inc. Warsaw, In.	N4314X
☐ N350JB	98	King Air 350	FL-213	Land Rover Denver East Inc. Aurora, Co.	
☐ N350JR	00	King Air 350	FL-312	Integral Resources LLC/J C Williams Co. Modesto, Ca.	HB-GJN
☐ N350KG	97	King Air 350	FL-156	N350KG LLC. Seattle, Wa.	N470MN

Reg	Yr	Type	c/n	Owner/Operator	Prev Regn
N350KS	00	King Air 350	FL-323	State of Kansas, Topeka, Ks.	N4323W
N350LL	97	King Air 350	FL-157	TFM Enterprises LLC. Atlanta, Ga.	N1093Q
N350MC	81	SA-226T Merlin 3B	T-400	Sanair Corp. Boston, Ma.	N10126
N350MR	90	King Air 350	FL-14	Marni Resources Inc. Corpus Christi, Tx.	N996AM
N350MS	01	King Air 350	FL-326	C W Avery Leasing Corp. Plainfield, Il.	(N326PK)
N350NY	00	King Air 350	FL-283	State of New York Power Authority, White Plains, NY.	N4083L
N350P	91	King Air 350	FL-47	SSM Aviation Corp/ABQ Aviation LLC. Albuquerque, NM.	N326MX
N350RG	80	MU-2 Marquise	773SA	International Amusement Ltd. Durand, Mi.	N259MA
N350RR	03	King Air 350	FL-365	Gulf & Ohio Airways Inc. Knoxville, Tn.	N6165J
N350S	97	King Air 350	FL-179	The Shoe Show Inc. Concord, NC.	N744W
N350TC	79	King Air B100	BE-62	True Blue Air LLC. Cedar Falls, Ia.	N991DM
N350TF	98	King Air 350	FL-202	Apple Aviation LLC. Stockbridge, Ga.	N2217C
N350TJ	82	King Air B100	BE-125	Home Health Holdings Inc. Silsbee, Tx.	N314EB
N350TL	02	King Air 350	FL-347	Raytheon Aircraft Corp. Wichita, Ks.	N350TT
N350TR	91	King Air 350	FL-67	Thompson Realty Co. Shoal Creek, Al.	(N850TR)
N350TV	00	King Air 350	FL-319	Tennessee Valley Authority, Muscle Shoals, Al.	N4319T
N350VM	91	King Air 350	FL-41	Hawk Aviation LLC. Farmington Hills, Mi.	N25CU
N350WA	78	King Air C90	LJ-762	BW & KW LLC. Wilmington, De.	N178RC
N350WD	99	King Air 350	FL-256	Dallas Capital Management Inc. Van Nuys, Ca.	
N350WP	00	King Air 350	FL-282	Alpha Aircraft Charter Ltd. Girard, Oh.	
N351CB	04	King Air 350	FL-396	Coin Builders Aviation Inc. Mosinee-Central, Wi.	N6196H
N351DD*	99	King Air 350	FL-257	Dyson, Dyson & Dunn Inc. Winnetka, Il.	N257MM
N351GC	91	King Air 350	FL-56	University of South Carolina, Columbia, SC.	N350DK
N351GR	79	King Air E90	LW-324	Outlook Marketing LLC. Narrows, Va.	N2043C
N351MA	78	King Air 200	BB-359	Old Glory Inc. Tulsa, Ok.	N359K
N351MP	00	King Air 350	FL-305	MAC Papers Inc. Jacksonville, Fl.	N3132M
N351PC	00	Pilatus PC-12/45	351	Spur Leasing LLC. Evansville, In.	HB-FSD
N351SA	92	King Air B200	BB-1423	RT Leasing LLC. Atlanta, Ga.	P2-MBH
N352GR	74	King Air E90	LW-93	Lance Alm, Chicago, Il.	N655F
N353KM	03	Pilatus PC-12/45	534	N353KM LLC. Carefree, Az.	HB-FSH
N354AF	00	Pilatus PC-12/45	354	Alpha Flying Inc. Nashua, NH.	HB-FSF
N355DM	00	King Air 350	FL-320	Texas KA350 Partners LLC. McAllen, Tx.	N380MS
N355ES	83	Conquest 1	425-0158	Leavenworth Excavating & Equipment, Leavenworth, Ks.	N25QL
N355JS	78	King Air E90	LW-257	JPS Aviation LLC. Syracuse, NY.	N711BX
N355PM	01	PA-46-500TP Meridian	4697071	PEM Aviation LLC. Plymouth, Mi.	
N356AJ	78	Mitsubishi MU-2P	381SA	AJ Inc. Dover, De.	N103RB
N356CC	03	King Air B200	BB-1843	Buena Suerte LLC/Ten Thirteen Inc. Los Angeles, Ca.	N6043T
N356F	01	TBM 700B	207	Stephen Robertson, Jackson, Wy.	
N356GA	79	King Air 200	BB-447	Best Storage Construction LLC. Reno, Nv.	N300CT
N357BB	90	King Air 350	FL-27	BDF Airgroup LLC. Addison, Tx.	(N73GB)
N357CC	82	King Air F90	LA-180	Conklin Instrument Corp. Pleasant Valley, NY.	N999KK
N357HP	82	King Air C90-1	LJ-1030	Department of Public Safety, Jackson, Ms.	N6504H
N357RL	03	King Air 350	FL-373	R & L Carriers Inc. Wilmington, Oh.	N6173K
N357ST	81	Gulfstream 980	95074	Memphis Eagle Ltd. Dover, De.	(N123MZ)
N359CV	01	Pilatus PC-12/45	382	Passmore Aviation LLC. Pryor, Ok.	HB-FQB
N359GP	84	Cheyenne II-XL	1166001	Great Plains Communications Inc. Blair, NE.	N835MW
N359MB	02	King Air 350	FL-359	MasterBrand Cabinets Inc. Jasper, In.	
N360C	70	King Air 100	B-21	Black Hawk Aviation Inc. Paris, Tn.	N11AG
N360CB	01	King Air 350	FL-336	Raytheon Aircraft Co. Wichita, Ks.	N4336P
N360DA	99	Pilatus PC-12/45	270	On The Rise Aviation LLC. Dover, De.	(N880TR)
N360EA	85	King Air B200	BB-1231	TransMontaigne Transport Inc. Englewood, Co.	OE-FJB
N360MP	84	King Air C90A	LJ-1085	Aracel Inc. Tortola, BVI.	N720CT
N360RA	79	MU-2 Marquise	740SA	Hirschfield Steel Co. San Angelo, Tx.	XA-EFU
N360X	01	King Air B200	BB-1783	Oxford Mining Co. Coshocton, Oh.	N625TA
N361EA	83	King Air B200	BB-1103	Pride Air Inc. Lake Village, Ar.	N57SC
N361GB	95	Pilatus PC-12	132	Radio Flyer II Inc. Lincoln, Il.	N361DB
N361JA	76	Mitsubishi MU-2L	681	Flight Line Inc. Salt Lake City, Ut.	C-GJWM
N361JC	77	PA-31T Cheyenne II	7720062	Sandy Land Underground Water Distribution, Plains, Tx.	N68LM
N361MA	80	MU-2 Solitaire	429SA	Motors Management Group Inc. Richmond, Va.	N77DB
N361TD	87	King Air B200C	BL-128	Desa Air Inc. Dover, De.	N128TJ
N362D	78	King Air E90	LW-265	Jet Arizona Inc. Tucson, Az.	
N362SH	76	Rockwell 690A	11316	Flight Plan One LLC/Bay Cast Inc. Bay Cast, Mi.	(N690PB)
N363CA	86	King Air B200	BB-1250	Van Ness Management LLC. Lubbock, Tx.	N2519Y
N363D	95	King Air B200	BB-1503	Wolfcreek Management LLC. Portland, Or.	N363K
N363EA	96	King Air B200	BB-1538	JA Investments Inc/Consolidated Biscuit Co. McComb, Oh.	PH-VMP
Reg	Yr	Type	c/n	Owner/Operator	Prev Regn

Reg	Yr	Type	c/n	Owner/Operator	Prev Regn
☐ N364BC	78	King Air B100	BE-35	Frederick Kaiser, Kerrville, Tx.	N564BC
☐ N364EA	80	King Air 200	BB-689	Omni Dynamic Aviation LLC. Fort Wayne, In.	N187MQ
☐ N364WA	77	Rockwell 690B	11439	Trojan Leasing Inc. Troy, Oh.	D-IADH
☐ N366EA	81	King Air 200	BB-841	Cashiers Planning Group Inc. Atlanta, Ga.	N841K
☐ N366GW	79	King Air E90	LW-320	Joe Morten & Son Inc. South Sioux City, Ne.	N366JM
☐ N366SB	63	Fairchild F-27F	97	Beartooth Communications Inc. Helena, Mt.	N20W
☐ N366SL	03	King Air 350	FL-366	Aero Federal SA. Don Torcuato, Argentina.	
☐ N367LF*	78	King Air 200	BB-405	Life Logistics LLC. St Louis, Mo.	N350AC
☐ N367RA	78	King Air 200	BB-367	October Investments LLC. Whitefish, Mt.	ZS-NPO
☐ N368DC	00	Beech 1900D	UE-368	Dow Chemical Co. Midland, Mi.	
☐ N369CD	76	King Air E90	LW-162	Enchantment Aviation Inc. Elephant Butte, NM.	N36GS
☐ N369GA	81	King Air C90	LJ-934	Eastway Aviation LLC. Ronkonkoma, NY.	F-GCTA
☐ N369SA	76	King Air C-12C	BC-23	Air Lannan LLC. Santa Fe, NM.	N200LW
☐ N369TA	81	King Air 200	BB-820	Pinnacle Air Services Inc. Bloomington, In.	N935SJ
☐ N370AE	87	SA-227AT Merlin 4C	AT-506	GAS/Wilson Inc. Lake Zurich, Il.	N87FM
☐ N370K	66	680V Turbo Commander	1570-25	Riley Air Charters Inc. Santa Ana, Ca.	N222JK
☐ N370MA	78	Mitsubishi MU-2P	370SA	Robert Nass Inc. Asheville Regional, Pa.	N370AC
☐ N370X	69	SA-26AT Merlin 2B	T26-106	Twins Charter Aircraft Inc. Miami Beach, Fl.	
☐ N372GT	01	Pilatus PC-12/45	372	Pacific Detroit Realty LLC. Portland, Or.	HB-FSV
☐ N372JB	80	King Air 200	BB-719	Ernie Ball Inc. San Luis Obispo, Ca.	N3722Y
☐ N373CA	93	PA-42 Cheyenne III	8001037	CCH Aviation LLC. Great Falls, Va.	HK-3618W
☐ N373KM	00	Pilatus PC-12/45	373	Pilatus Montana LLC. Cameron, Mt.	(N373GE)
☐ N373LP	81	Conquest 1	425-0141	JAD Aviation Inc. Bloomington, Il.	D-IIGA
☐ N373Q	81	PA-42 Cheyenne III	8001014	Dynamic Engineering Inc. Fort Smith, Ar.	C-GAKA
☐ N375AA	74	Rockwell 690A	11179	Miroslav Liska, Bend, Or.	N57179
☐ N375AC	75	Mitsubishi MU-2M	327	Celco Constantine Engineering Laboratories, Wilmington, De.	N515MA
☐ N375CA	74	Mitsubishi MU-2J	643	Cars & Planes Inc. Jacksonville, Fl.	N881DT
☐ N375RD	00	PA-46-500TP Meridian	4697003	Richard Dumais, Richardson, Tx.	
☐ N376KC	01	Pilatus PC-12/45	376	Kaiser Midwest Inc. Marble Hill, Mo.	HB-FSZ
☐ N376RC	78	King Air 200	BB-376	BTD Inc/Business Air, Denton, Tx.	N409GA
☐ N376WS	80	PA-31T Cheyenne II	8020064	Polar Star Co. Hodges, SC.	(N32WS)
☐ N377AC*	96	Pilatus PC-12/45	162	A & C Aviation, Fort Myers, Fl.	(N871GM)
☐ N377CA	83	Conquest II	441-0289	Arturo Saldana, Coppell, Tx.	N88638
☐ N377L	00	Pilatus PC-12/45	346	Alexander Lidow, El Segundo, Ca.	HB-FRZ
☐ N377NJ	68	Mitsubishi MU-2D	104	Northern Jet Sales LLC. Murfreesboro, Tn.	N151JB
☐ N377P	84	King Air C90A	LJ-1087	Mid South Aviation LLC. Nashville, Tn.	N7252S
☐ N378HH	01	Pilatus PC-12/45	378	Harrison Airplane Leasing LLC. Phoenix, Az.	PH-WMC
☐ N378SF	78	King Air 200	BB-378	Jerri Trigg, Houston, Tx.	N200BP
☐ N379JG	81	SA-226T Merlin 3B	T-414	Gettel Investments Inc. Sarasota, Fl.	N271DC
☐ N379VM	73	King Air E90	LW-27	379VM LLC. Jeffco Airport, Co.	N999ES
☐ N380SC	79	King Air C90	LJ-862	M & M Aircraft Inc. Cape Coral, Fl.	F-GMJP
☐ N381CR	87	Beech 1900C	UB-69	RCR Air Inc. Welcome, NC.	N331CR
☐ N381PD	73	King Air C-12C	BC-14	Los Angeles Police Department, Van Nuys, Ca.	N381PD
☐ N381R	78	King Air 200	BB-385	Jack Air LLC. Morrison, Co.	N81RD
☐ N381SC	94	King Air C90B	LJ-1381	Southern Cross Aircraft LLC. Fort Lauderdale, Fl.	LV-P..
☐ N382MB	81	PA-31T Cheyenne II	8120057	Roppe Corp. Postoria, Oh.	N9087Y
☐ N382ME	79	King Air 200	BB-436	City Furniture Inc. Tamarac, Fl.	N83KA
☐ N383AA	72	King Air E90	LW-13	383AA LLC. Ontario, Or.	N21DJ
☐ N383JP	80	King Air 200	BB-615	Moreland Aircraft LLC. Bakersfield, Ca.	RP-C704
☐ N383SS	80	Conquest II	441-0161	Joseph Skilken & Co. Columbus, Oh.	N2721D
☐ N385GH	81	Conquest II	441-0066	Superior Aviation Inc. Ford Airport, Mi.	N185GA
☐ N385MC	82	King Air B200	BB-1017	McAninch Corp. Des Moines, Ia.	N200PH
☐ N386GA	78	King Air C90	LJ-775	Advatage Air Inc. Terry, Ms.	HB-GIW
☐ N387AS	95	King Air C90B	LJ-1417	Executive AirShare Corp. Wichita, Ks.	N3217X
☐ N387CC	80	SA-226T Merlin 3B	T-360	Hiers Properties LLC. Hockessin, De.	N118BR
☐ N387GA	77	King Air C90	LJ-726	Midwest Maule Inc. Crystal Lake, Il.	(N469PC)
☐ N387GC	01	King Air C90B	LJ-1655	Gary Crossley Ford Inc. Liberty, Mo.	N5154E
☐ N387W	01	Pilatus PC-12/45	387	State of Wisconsin, Madison, Wi.	HB-FQJ
☐ N388NC	01	MU-2 Solitaire	452SA	Village Builders Inc. Newfield, NJ.	(D-IBBB)
☐ N388PC	01	Pilatus PC-12/45	388	SDD Holdings Inc. Atlanta, Ga.	HB-FQE
☐ N388TW	01	PA-46-500TP Meridian	4697018	James Gero, Rockwall, Tx.	
☐ N389AS	96	King Air C90B	LJ-1438	Terry Aviation Inc. Fort Worth, Tx.	N3268M
☐ N389W	01	Pilatus PC-12/45	389	State of Wisconsin, Madison, Wi.	HB-FQN
☐ N390L	81	King Air C90	LJ-987	Richard Rehn, Ritzville, Wa.	ZS-LZP
☐ N390MD	01	King Air 350	FL-333	Maryland State Police, Baltimore, Md.	N4483Y
Reg	Yr	Type	c/n	Owner/Operator	Prev Regn

Reg	Yr Type	c/n	Owner/Operator	Prev Regn
☐ N390PS	78 King Air E90	LW-279	Pro Air Inc. Columbus, Ne.	N390MT
☐ N391BT	81 King Air C90	LJ-983	Vector Aviation LLC. Jackson, Mi.	N491BT
☐ N391EC	01 Pilatus PC-12/45	391	PC-12 Holding Inc. Santo Domingo, Dominican Republic.	HB-FQG
☐ N391GM	80 SA-226T Merlin 3B	T-391	Continental Air Care Inc. Yerington, Nv.	F-GCTC
☐ N391RR	90 King Air 350	FL-23	Kojaian Aviation LLC. Bloomfield Hills, Mi.	(F-GKIZ)
☐ N392KC	78 King Air 200	BB-392	Fresh Air DeKalb LLC. Naperville, Il.	N392CF
☐ N392P	78 MU-2 Solitaire	392SA	Berg Steel Pipe Corp. Panama City, Fl.	D-IFMU
☐ N392TW	68 King Air B90	LJ-392	Victor Manuel Moncada, Medellin, Colombia.	N121HC
☐ N392WC	01 Pilatus PC-12/45	392	Justice LLC. Columbus, Ga.	HB-FQH
☐ N393AF	01 Pilatus PC-12/45	393	Alpha Flying Inc. Nashua, NH.	HB-FQI
☐ N393CE	85 King Air F90	LA-230	Langston Air LLC. Pelzer, SC.	N393CF
☐ N393JW	77 King Air 200	BB-292	Flyboys LLC. Ephrata, Wa.	(N393JM)
☐ N394AL	68 King Air B90	LJ-394	Skydive Virginia Inc. McGaheysville, Va.	C-GASR
☐ N394B	99 King Air C90B	LJ-1553	Piedmont Hawthorne Aviation Inc. Winston-Salem, NC.	
☐ N394S	96 King Air 350	FL-144	Raytheon Aircraft Credit Corp. Wichita, Ks.	N1084W
☐ N395AM	83 King Air B200	BB-1101	Amcast Industrial Corp. Dayton, Oh.	N48CE
☐ N395CA	84 Cheyenne II-XL	1166005	Cheyenne Air LLC. Ellensburg, Va.	HB-LRM
☐ N395DR	81 PA-42 Cheyenne III	8001065	Lauren Manufacturing Co. New Philadelphia, Oh.	N742RB
☐ N395KT	00 P-180 Avanti	1044	AvantAir Inc. Stewart, NY.	N128PA
☐ N395MB	91 King Air 350	FL-39	Mammoth Beach LLC. El Segundo, Ca.	N390TT
☐ N395PC	01 Pilatus PC-12/45	395	Lindsey Aviation Services, Haslet, Tx.	HB-FQP
☐ N395SM	02 PA-46-500TP Meridian	4697129	Samuel Maness, Apollo Beach, Fl.	N302MM
☐ N395W	01 Pilatus PC-12/45	394	State of Wisconsin, Madison, Wi.	HB-FQO
☐ N396CA	82 King Air C90-1	LJ-1035	Claxton Poultry Farms, Claxton, Ga.	F-GLJD
☐ N396FW	80 PA-42 Cheyenne III	8001021	David Olson, Houston, Tx.	C-FWAB
☐ N396PS	69 SA-26AT Merlin 2B	T26-151	U R One Investments Inc. Bear, De.	C-GSWJ
☐ N397SA	74 King Air C-12L	BB-4	Commonwealth Aviation LLC. Hickory, NC.	N200LN
☐ N397WM	88 King Air C 300	FA-156	West Michigan Aviation Services, Holland, Mi.	N642BL
☐ N398J	01 Pilatus PC-12/45	398	Oklahoma Cardiovascular Associates, Oklahoma City, Ok.	HB-FQL
☐ N398SP	81 PA-31T Cheyenne 1	8104027	Astro Aviation LLC. Waterford, Mi.	N681SW
☐ N399AE	03 King Air B200	BB-1834	Cloverleaf Cold Storage Co. Sioux City, Ia.	N6034P
☐ N399AM	99 Pilatus PC-12/45	249	University of Utah Hospitals & Clinic, Salt Lake City, Ut.	(F-GTTT)
☐ N399AS	83 King Air B200C	BL-65	Capital Aerolease, Bethesda, Md.	N870CA
☐ N399BM	78 King Air 200	BB-399	Baylor University, Waco, Tx.	F-GIRM
☐ N399CW	98 King Air B200	BB-1646	Warren Manufacturing Inc. Birmingham, Al.	
☐ N399GM	72 Rockwell 690	11030	The Turbine Group Inc. Vero Beach, Fl.	VH-WLO
☐ N399SA	74 King Air C-12L	BB-5	Stanford & Assocs Inc. Fredricksburg, Va.	N200KE
☐ N399TW*	83 King Air F90-1	LA-203	Trans West Aero LLC. La Jolla, Ca.	OY-CVC
☐ N399WS	99 King Air C90B	LJ-1547	Nance Air Inc. Melbourne, Fl.	
☐ N400AC	76 King Air B100	BE-12	Midlantic Jet Charters Inc. Atlantic City, NJ.	
☐ N400AL	89 King Air 350	FL-2	Abbott Laboratories Inc. Waukegan, Il.	N350KR
☐ N400BW	98 Pilatus PC-12/45	224	RAW Inc. Raleigh, NC.	N224PB
☐ N400BX	76 King Air C90	LJ-686	Mark Ray, Cameron, Il.	N100BT
☐ N400CM	76 PA-31T Cheyenne II	7620040	Robert Brocker, Youngstown, Oh.	
☐ N400DC	69 SA-26AT Merlin 2B	T26-167	Parts & Turbines Inc. St Simons Island, Ga.	N5353M
☐ N400DG	68 SA-26T Merlin 2A	T26-9	Hodges Packing Co. Palestine, Tx.	N22EK
☐ N400DS	78 Rockwell 690B	11512	Commander LLC. Newport Beach, Ca.	N81872
☐ N400ES	78 Mitsubishi MU-2P	389SA	Triple J Flying Inc. Olds, Ia.	(N543JF)
☐ N400GW	97 King Air B200	BB-1583	Gary Whitman, Charleston, SC.	N424RA
☐ N400KW	78 King Air 200	BB-337	K & D S Trust, Irondale, Al.	N600AM
☐ N400LJ	80 PA-31T Cheyenne 1	8004012	Federal Airways Corp. Wilmington, De.	N41PN
☐ N400LP	67 680V Turbo Commander	1697-74	Country Club Investment & Development, Fairmont, WV.	N400LR
☐ N400PS	79 MU-2 Solitaire	411SA	West Texas Executive Leasing Inc. San Angelo, Tx.	N8LC
☐ N400PT	98 PA-46-400TP Meridian	4697E1	New Piper Aircraft Inc. Vero Beach, Fl.	
☐ N400RV	79 King Air C90	LJ-853	BreeMac Capital Corp. Wilmington, De.	N6LD
☐ N400RX	73 Mitsubishi MU-2J	593	BSA Design Inc. Indianapolis, In.	C-GJAV
☐ N400SG	74 Mitsubishi MU-2J	634	Pan American Importing Corp. Wilmington, De.	C-GODE
☐ N400VB	84 PA-42 Cheyenne 400LS	5527002	Kelleher Corp. San Rafael, Ca. (was 8427002).	N400PS
☐ N400WS	81 Cheyenne II-XL	8166044	Aspen Air Inc. Albuquerque, NM.	N31KW
☐ N401BL	87 King Air 300	FA-125	Bi-Lo Inc. Mauldin, SC.	N488GA
☐ N401CG	99 King Air B200	BB-1666	Cardinal Glass Industries Inc. Minnetonka, Mn.	N444MT
☐ N401EM	81 King Air C90	LJ-950	Eagle Med/Ballard Aviation Inc. Wichita, Ks.	N108TT
☐ N401HC	88 King Air B200	BB-1294	Intermountain Health Care Services, Salt Lake City, Ut.	N294WT
☐ N401JC	75 Mitsubishi MU-2M	326	ATI Performance Products Inc. Baltimore, Md.	N700LW
☐ N401MM	99 PA-46-400TP Meridian	4697001	New Piper Aircraft Inc. Vero Beach, Fl.	
Reg	Yr Type	c/n	Owner/Operator	Prev Regn

Reg	Yr	Type	c/n	Owner/Operator	Prev Regn
☐ N401NS	85 King Air 300	FA-28		Naylor Inc. Atlanta, Ga.	N481NS
☐ N401PD	01 Pilatus PC-12/45	401		Arend Corp. Oakland, Ca.	HB-FQS
☐ N401SK	03 King Air B200	BB-1828		Steven Kennedy/SLK Family LLC. Blanco, Tx.	N61808
☐ N401SM	99 Pilatus PC-12/45	255		Air Penn Inc. Chamblee, Ga.	HB-FRV
☐ N401VA	82 Cheyenne T-1040	8275001		ASE Aircraft Inc. Las Vegas, Nv.	N2489Y
☐ N402EM	80 King Air C90	LJ-914		Ballard Aviation Inc. Wichita, Ks.	N914TT
☐ N402GW	02 PA-46-500TP Meridian	4697120		Gary Whitman, Charleston, SC.	N551S
☐ N402JL	04 King Air 350	FL-402		Health Systems Inc. Sikeston, Mo.	N6182Z
☐ N402KA	77 King Air 200	BB-296		Aviation Charter Services, Indianapolis, In.	N402CJ
☐ N402MM	99 PA-46-400TP Meridian	4697002		New Piper Aircraft Inc. Vero Beach, Fl.	
☐ N403EM	82 King Air C90	LJ-1000		Ballard Aviation Inc. Wichita, Ks.	N982FA
☐ N403J	99 King Air B200	BB-1700		JimsAir Aviation Services Inc. San Diego, Ca.	N70VP
☐ N403MM	99 PA-46-400TP Meridian	4697E3		New Piper Aircraft Inc. Vero Beach, Fl.	
☐ N404EW	89 King Air 300	FA-186		Seidner-Miller Inc. Glendora, Ca.	(N700FT)
☐ N404FA	82 King Air B200	BB-981		Joe Falk Motorsports/Falk Air Corp. Norfolk, Va.	N481BC
☐ N404J	02 King Air B200	BB-1793		JimsAir Aviation Services Inc. San Diego, Ca.	N5093X
☐ N404JP	82 King Air C90-1	LJ-1039		Parish Planes LLC. Tullahoma, Tn.	N6746S
☐ N404PT	99 King Air B200	BB-1674		Kendall LLC. Palo Alto, Ca.	(HC-...)
☐ N404SC	79 King Air C90	LJ-843		Jay Hall Jr. Cheshire, Oh.	N843CP
☐ N405J	94 King Air 350	FL-112		Jimsair Aviation Services Inc. San Diego, Ca.	N850SJ
☐ N405SA	80 SA-226T Merlin 3B	T-329		Sequoia Air, Inglewood, Ca.	N626PS
☐ N406CP	81 Gulfstream 840	11655		Palumbo Aircraft Sales Inc. Uniontown, Oh.	YV-406CP
☐ N406GV	90 Reims/Cessna F406	F406-0049		Gussic Ventures LLC. Anchorage, Ak.	9M-PNS
☐ N406P	90 Reims/Cessna F406	F406-0050		Priority Air Charter LLC. Kidron, Oh.	VH-RCA
☐ N406RL	99 King Air C90B	LJ-1574		Baron Charter Service LLC. Oklahoma City, Ok.	(N286WA)
☐ N406RS	79 PA-31T Cheyenne II	7920048		Travel Services LLC. Rantool, Il.	N404AF
☐ N406SD	91 Reims/Cessna F406	F406-0063		Bering Strait School District, Unalakleet, Ak.	PH-GUI
☐ N407GW	89 King Air C90A	LJ-1221		Augusta Aviation Inc. Augusta, Ga.	N400GW
☐ N407MA	81 MU-2 Marquise	1503SA		H & F Executive Aviation Inc. Wilmington, De.	
☐ N408C	88 King Air 300	FA-155		Cutter Aviation Inc. Phoenix, Az.	N155BM
☐ N408LB	01 Pilatus PC-12/45	408		Felicity Air LLC. San Francisco, Ca.	HB-FQY
☐ N408SH	81 PA-31T Cheyenne 1	8104052		DGA Inc. Nebraska City, Ne.	N422HV
☐ N408WG	84 PA-42 Cheyenne 400LS	5527008		HLW LLC. Lexington, SC.	(N31WE)
☐ N409DR	01 Pilatus PC-12/45	377		Collett Transportation/Collett Land Co. Charlotte, NC.	N377PC
☐ N409LV*	04 King Air 350	FL-409		Andrmar Air LLC. Las Vegas, Nv.	N6109U
☐ N409RA	79 King Air 200	BB-429		Anthony Aviation Center Inc. Pompano Beach, Fl.	N574GS
☐ N410CA	81 Cheyenne II-XL	8166005		Waldinger Corp. Des Moines, Ia.	N127GP
☐ N410MC	78 King Air C90	LJ-761		MK Leasing Inc. Melbourne, Fl.	N25HB
☐ N410MF	79 Conquest II	441-0093		Ocean Mist Farms, Castroville, Ca.	N441K
☐ N410SP	70 King Air A90	LM-136		Samaritan's Purse Inc. Boone, NC.	N7181Z
☐ N410TH	68 680W Turbo Commander	1790-20		Charles Bella, El Paso, Tx.	N5061E
☐ N410VE	81 Conquest 1	425-0097		Miami Air Corp. Wilmington, De.	N6849D
☐ N411BG	84 PA-42 Cheyenne 400LS	5527004		DP Air LLC. Portland, Or.	N4119B
☐ N411BL	79 King Air 200	BB-448		Beacon Light Missionary Baptist Church, New Orleans, La.	N700HM
☐ N411CC	95 King Air B200	BB-1520		Sunshine Aviation LLC. Roseburg, Or.	(N265EJ)
☐ N411DL	77 PA-31T Cheyenne II	7720057		Burt Aviation & Transportation LLC. Saginaw, Mi.	C-GGVB
☐ N411FT	69 King Air B90	LJ-443		Arin Travel LLC. Wilmington, De.	N796K
☐ N411LM	77 PA-31T Cheyenne II	7720069		Mansfield Industrial Coatings Inc. Pensacola, Fl.	N45TX
☐ N411MV	00 Pilatus PC-12/45	344		Cowtown Investments LLC. Portola Valley, Ca.	HB-FRX
☐ N411RA	80 King Air 200	BB-712		Moe Air LLC. Newton, NC.	N200BM
☐ N411RJ	81 King Air F90	LA-124		EZ Acceptance Inc. San Diego, Ca.	N627AC
☐ N411RS	66 King Air 90	LJ-106		Sundance Aviation Inc. Yukon, Ok.	N271MB
☐ N412KC	96 Pilatus PC-12	129		MRV Air LC. Reno, Nv.	N426DW
☐ N412MA	67 King Air A90	LJ-214		K & K Aircraft Inc. Bridgewater, Va.	N985AA
☐ N412MD	01 Pilatus PC-12/45	412		Senate Inc. Wilmington, De.	N10778
☐ N412SH	87 King Air B200	BB-1269		THD Properties LLC. Chicago, Il.	N21NV
☐ N412SR	72 King Air E90	LW-2		Hogue Ranches Inc. Prosser, Wa.	N710TK
☐ N413DM	81 King Air 200	BB-768		McDowell Aviation LP. Dripping Springs, Tx.	N37392
☐ N414GN	75 King Air E90	LW-156		Newberg Flying Enterprises Inc. Chicago, Il.	(N5PC)
☐ N415HS	83 King Air F90-1	LA-210		Sogibo Inc. Wilmington, De.	N415RB
☐ N415PB	01 Pilatus PC-12/45	415		Mercury Travel Inc. Lakewood, Co.	HB-FRI
☐ N415RB	95 King Air B200	BB-1513		Barnhill Contracting Co. Tarboro, NC.	N3217N
☐ N415TM	01 King Air B200	BB-1752		McLinch Aviation Corp. Fairfield, Ct.	N4362F
☐ N416BK	79 King Air C90	LJ-816		King Taylor Inc. Nashville, Tn.	N40PS
☐ N416CS	84 King Air B200	BB-1182		Short Field LLC. Bellevue, Wa.	N67262
Reg	Yr Type	c/n		Owner/Operator	Prev Regn

Reg	Yr Type	c/n	Owner/Operator	Prev Regn
N416DY	89 King Air 300	FA-197	Yancey Brothers Co. Austell, Ga.	N59AH
N416LF	92 P-180 Avanti	1012	LDF Support Group Inc. Wichita, Ks.	N500GC
N416MR	67 King Air A90	LJ-267	Flyboys LLC. Ephrata, Wa.	N416LF
N416P	80 King Air F90	LA-67	Metro Aviation Inc. Shreveport, La.	N614ME
N417KC	01 Pilatus PC-12/45	417	Bedrock Aviation LLC. Holly, Mi.	HB-FRF
N417VN	89 King Air C90A	LJ-1202	Henna Revocable Trust, Pacifica, Ca.	HB-GIZ
N418J	00 King Air B200	BB-1705	Winds Aloft LLC. Houston, Tx.	
N419R	78 PA-31T Cheyenne II	7820034	Reno Flying Service Inc. Reno, Nv.	N82249
N419SC	80 Conquest II	441-0149	419 Aviation Inc. Inverness, Il.	N600VT
N419WA	01 Pilatus PC-12/45	419	Charter US LLC. Liberty, SC.	HB-FRH
N420AF	01 Pilatus PC-12/45	420	Alpha Flying Inc. Nashua, NH.	HB-FRJ
N420DB	80 Conquest II	441-0129	Mid-South Agricultural Products Inc. Lafayette, La.	(N441BD)
N420DW	01 Pilatus PC-12/45	404	Richard Wikert, Fremont, Ne.	HB-FQU
N420MA	82 Conquest 1	425-0116	RGS Investments Inc. Milwaukee, Wi.	(N425TS)
N420PA	78 PA-42 Cheyenne III	7800001	New Piper Aircraft Inc. Vero Beach, Fl.	
N420TA	79 King Air 200	BB-420	Kohner Aviation Inc. Dover, De.	N210SU
N421HV	91 King Air B200	LJ-1266	DLC Aero LLC. Willmar, Mn.	
N422AS*	04 King Air C90B	LJ-1714	ALL Star Advertising Agency Inc. Baton Rouge, La.	NG172Y
N422MU	00 Pilatus PC-12/45	336	Chinook Inc. Colorado Springs, Co.	N336PC
N422PM	95 King Air C90B	LJ-1412	Kleber Aviation, Pars-Le Bourget, France.	N14GG
N422Z	81 King Air F90	LA-135	Paul Walton, Indianapolis, In.	
N423JB	82 Cheyenne II-XL	8166052	G L Wilson & Sioux City Truck Sales Inc. Sioux City, Ia.	D-IOKA
N423KC	82 PA-42 Cheyenne III	8001074	Central Arkansas Nursing Centers Inc. Fort Smith, Ar.	CX-ROU
N423TG	81 Conquest II	441-0200	Commercial Developers Inc. Wichita, Ks.	N313GA
N423WA	01 Pilatus PC-12/45	423	Western Aircraft Inc. Boise, Id.	HB-FRM
N424BS	76 King Air 200	BB-179	Command Aircraft Parts & Recovery, Bunnell, Fl. (status ?).	N630DB
N424CM	80 PA-31T Cheyenne 1	8004002	Martin Medical Consulting Inc. Springfield, Il.	(N2499R)
N424CP	82 King Air F90	LA-182	W C McQuaide Inc. Johnstown, Pa.	(N107MC)
N424EM	93 King Air C90B	LJ-1351	Ballard Aviation Inc. Wichita, Ks.	N493JX
N424PB	01 Pilatus PC-12/45	424	Skytech Inc. Baltimore, Md.	HB-FRL
N424PP	69 680W Turbo Commander	1821-35	Corona Aircraft Inc. Corona, Ca.	TG-DAM
N424RA	02 King Air B200	BB-1797	Edward Rorer, Villanova, Pa.	N5097G
N424SW	71 King Air 100	B-80	Windham Aviation Inc. Williamantic, Ct.	N99KA
N425AD	84 Conquest 1	425-0220	Avgroup Financial Corp. Las Vegas, Nv.	N188RB
N425AL	81 Conquest 1	425-0100	Abbott-Long Inc. Montrose, Co.	N70HB
N425AP	80 King Air 200	BB-682	Tradewind Air LLC. Yorklyn, De.	N208JS
N425AR	81 Conquest 1	425-0065	SB Aircraft LLC. Polson, Mt.	N6844S
N425AT	80 Conquest 1	425-0004	Med-Trade Inc. Northbrook, Il.	N425TF
N425BA	81 Conquest 1	425-0046	Quad Fund Inc. Mount Pleasant, Tx.	(N911MM)
N425BS	84 Conquest 1	425-0210	Johnson Ford, Lancaster, Ca.	N721VB
N425CL	84 Conquest 1	425-0206	ICM Inc. Colwich, Ks.	N12238
N425D	82 Conquest 1	425-0121	Smoore Inc/Titanium Luxury Club LLC. Scottsdale, Az.	N944JV
N425DC	83 Conquest 1	425-0185	Kent Audio Visual/Kent Business Systems Inc. Wichita, Ks.	N6874L
N425DD	81 Conquest 1	425-0083	NorCal Beverage Co. West Sacramento, Ca.	N6846X
N425DH	81 Conquest 1	425-0066	Quinn Aire LLC. Rancho Sante Fe, Ca.	N6844T
N425DM	81 Conquest 1	425-0098	J Thomas Solano, Ponte Vedra Beach, Fl.	(N425TS)
N425DR	84 Conquest 1	425-0199	Inter-City Air Ltd. Channel Islands.	VP-BDR
N425DT	79 Rockwell 690B	11519	G & A Services Inc. Wilmington, De.	CP-2225
N425E	81 Conquest 1	425-0096	Western Pneumatics/WP Air LLC. Eugene, Or.	N425EA
N425EC	80 MU-2 Marquise	793SA	WEC Ltd. Paradise Valley, Az.	HZ-AMA
N425EM	83 Conquest 1	425-0164	Kudzu International Inc. Hagerstown, Md.	D-IJOY
N425ET	81 Conquest 1	425-0072	DJT Inc. Lawton, Ok.	(N425TB)
N425EZ	83 Conquest 1	425-0099	Conquest 99 LLC. Greenwich, Ct.	N404EW
N425FG	83 Conquest 1	425-0186	Glover Feed Mills Inc. Mount Pleasant, Tx.	N444AK
N425GM	81 Conquest 1	425-0033	Dodeca Resources Inc. Henderson, Nv.	D-IAJA
N425HB	81 Conquest 1	425-0073	Conquest Aviation/Howard Baker, Huntsville, Tn.	N550SC
N425HD	82 Conquest 1	425-0113	Hiland Dairy Foods Co. Springfield, Mo.	N6851L
N425HJ	83 Conquest 1	425-0169	Robert Lloyd Electric Co. Wichita Falls, Tx.	ZS-AMC
N425HS	81 Conquest 1	425-0044	Flying Partners NV. Antwerp, Belgium.	N555BE
N425JB	81 Conquest 1	425-0043	John MacGuire, Santa Teresa, NM.	N550SC
N425JH	82 Conquest 1	425-0124	MGP Ingredients Inc. Atchison, Ks.	N425DS
N425JP	81 Conquest 1	425-0038	Al Hogan, Rockport, Tx.	N3FC
N425KC	83 Conquest 1	425-0174	The Plumbers Warehouse, Carson, Ca.	N384MA
N425KD	85 Conquest 1	425-0203	Executive Aircraft Leasing Inc. Columbia City, In.	N45TP
N425LA	81 Conquest 1	425-0092	GEM Aircraft Leasing Inc. Rochester, Mn.	N40RD

Reg	Yr	Type	c/n	Owner/Operator	Prev Regn
N425LC	81	Conquest 1	425-0054	Gwil & Gale Evans LLC. Bend, Or.	N425SM
N425LD	83	Conquest 1	425-0149	State of Texas, Austin, Tx.	N425EJ
N425LG	82	Conquest 1	425-0107	Team G Motorsports LC/Viron International Corp. Owosso, Mi.	N1NL
N425MM	81	Gulfstream 840	11699	Aardex Corp. Lakewood, Co.	XB-DYZ
N425N	84	Conquest 1	425-0218	Tailwind LLC. Silver City, NM.	N425GV
N425NC	84	Conquest 1	425-0207	Kindle Ford Mercury Lincoln Inc. Cape May, NJ.	(N13EB)
N425NP	86	Conquest 1	425-0224	JH Aircraft Management Inc. Jackson, Wy.	N850GM
N425NW	81	Conquest 1	425-0070	Air Giant LLC. Watsonville, Ca.	N6854P
N425PC	84	Conquest 1	425-0193	Hughes-Sasser Ltd. Beeville, Tx.	N214KC
N425PG	85	Conquest 1	425-0200	425PG LLC. Dover, De.	N17HM
N425PJ	83	Conquest 1	425-0157	Skyline Aviation LLC. Orem, Ut.	(N68860)
N425PL	81	Conquest 1	425-0010	Starline Aviation Inc. Mount Vernon, Wa.	N813JL
N425PV	82	Conquest 1	425-0104	Westmoreland Mechanical Testing & Research, Latrobe, Pa.	N425MB
N425RM	83	Conquest 1	425-0180	Mar Aviation Corp. Youngstown, Oh.	N68731
N425RR	75	Rockwell 690A	11259	Rami Aviation Ltd/Ford Farm Racing, Fairoaks, UK.	VP-BRR
N425SF	81	Conquest 1	425-0037	Presbyterian Medical Services, Santa Fe, NM.	N6773L
N425SG	83	Conquest 1	425-0166	Sgavit Aviation LLC/Accutronics Inc. Denver, Co.	(N802JH)
N425SP	83	Conquest 1	425-0184	Scope Leasing Inc. Columbus, Oh.	VH-JER
N425SR	83	Conquest 1	425-0133	Coleman Oil & Gas Inc. Farmington, Ma.	(N83WF)
N425SW	81	Conquest 1	425-0061	Gryphon Aviation LLC. Camp Hill, Pa.	D-IAGT
N425SX	82	Conquest 1	425-0106	John Adler, Boca Raton, Fl.	N425GA
N425TB	84	Conquest 1	425-0068	Donnell Properties LLC. Wichita Falls, Tx.	(N425PF)
N425TC	80	Conquest 1	425-0014	Stearman Farm Inc. Farmington, Ar.	(N6770W)
N425TM	84	Conquest 1	425-0217	Six L's Packing Co. Clinton, NC.	(N526LS)
N425TV	83	Conquest 1	425-0176	Conquest Aircraft Leasing LLC. Miami, Fl.	ZS-LDR
N425TW	83	Conquest 1	425-0161	Teton West Construction, Rexburg, Id.	N707NY
N425TX	81	Conquest 1	425-0039	C Hadlai Hull, Chicago, Il.	D-INWG
N425WB	81	Conquest 1	425-0028	Peter Skeat, Flamwood, South Africa.	N67224
N425WL	84	Conquest 1	425-0197	Lantis Enterprises Inc. Spearfish, SD.	N501
N425WT	83	Conquest 1	425-0175	Irwin International Inc. Corona, Ca.	(D-ILPC)
N425XP	81	Conquest 1	425-0064	Wingding Aviation LLC. Wilmington, De.	ZS-MIG
N426EM	93	King Air C90B	LJ-1352	Ballard Aviation Inc. Wichita, Ks.	N494JY
N427DD	78	PA-31T Cheyenne II	7820029	Dunagan Property Management Inc. Huntsville, Al.	N78UA
N427DM	79	King Air C90	LJ-804	First Washington Management Group Inc. Dover, De.	N429DM
N427RB	89	King Air C90A	LJ-1208	N427RB Inc. McLean, Va.	N621WP
N427SP	73	SA-226AT Merlin 4	AT-018	Blaine Air LLC. Columbus, Oh.	N600TA
N427TA	77	PA-31T Cheyenne II	7720027	TAB LLC/Blacklidge Emulsions Inc. Gulfport, Ms.	XB-HGY
N427WA	01	Pilatus PC-12/45	427	Western Aircraft Inc. Boise, Id.	HB-FRP
N428DC	01	PA-46-500TP Meridian	4697124	Heritage Aircraft LLC. Indianapolis, In.	
N428P	80	King Air 200	BB-745	Air Croghan LLC. Boulder, Co.	N3698S
N428SJ	72	Rockwell 690	11016	Arlie & Co. Eugene, Or.	(C-....)
N429AP	78	PA-31T Cheyenne II	7820076	Alan Pesch, Stonington, Ct.	N29CA
N429DM	77	King Air E90	LW-221	RKA Inc. Wilmington, De.	N400SF
N429MM	01	PA-46-500TP Meridian	4697105	Stallion Enterprises LLC. Osprey, Fl.	
N429PC	01	Pilatus PC-12/45	429	National Limousine Service Inc. Leawood, Ks.	HB-FRR
N429PL	97	King Air B200	BB-1574	Learner Financial Corp. Walnut Creek, Ca.	(N429LF)
N429WM	81	MU-2 Marquise	1520SA	S & S Aviation Inc. Baltimore, Md.	N777MJ
N430DA	73	Mitsubishi MU-2K	253	Bush Field Aircraft Co. Augusta, Ga.	
N430JT	92	King Air B300C	FM-3	Lindsey Aviation Services, Haslet, Tx.	N8230Q
N430MC	81	King Air B200	BB-904	John DeNault/KJB Air, Fullerton, Ca.	(N202KC)
N431AC	75	PA-31T Cheyenne II	7520024	Inter-Tel Inc. Chandler, Az.	N431LS
N431CF	81	Cheyenne II-XL	8166002	Reliant Air Charter Inc. Danbury, Ct.	C-FKEY
N431GW	80	PA-31T Cheyenne II	8020088	M C Aviation Inc. Barrington, Il.	N58GG
N431MC	85	PA-42 Cheyenne 400LS	5527031	AngelBear LLC. Gaylord, Mi.	N41199
N431R	71	King Air 100	B-71	Vintage Props & Jets Inc. New Smyrna Beach, Fl.	N7771R
N431S	82	SA-227TT Merlin 3C	TT-431	Arens Industries inc. Northfield, Il.	N431SA
N431WC	01	Pilatus PC-12/45	431	Pelican Pacific Air LLC. Pleasanton, Ca.	HB-FRT
N432CV	95	Pilatus PC-12	119	Ray Dolby, San Francisco, Ca.	HB-FQM
N432FA	80	King Air 200	BB-592	BBP Aviation LLC. Green Bay, Wi.	N26SJ
N432LM*	04	King Air B200	BB-1871	Panhandle Consulting LLC/Thompson Grading Inc. Dallas, Ga.	N6171R
N432MH	01	Pilatus PC-12/45	432	Magnum Hunter Production Inc.	N432PC
N432NA	59	Fairchild F-27F	35	Southeastern Oklahoma State University, Durant, Ok.	N768RL
N433HC	02	King Air B200	BB-1807	Hill Construction Corp. San Juan, PR.	N5007L
N434BW	94	King Air 350	FL-109	B W Aviation LLC. Hendersonville, NC.	N510WP
N434CA	82	CASA 212-200	286	Fayard Enterprises Inc. Louisburg, NC.	

Reg	Yr Type	c/n	Owner/Operator	Prev Regn
N434CC	79 Rockwell 690B	11537	RORAN Investments Inc. San Francisco, Ca.	N611MT
N435A	67 King Air A90	LJ-229	APA Enterprises Inc. Deland, Fl.	
N435DM	99 TBM 700B	154	Miller Welding & Iron Works Inc. Washington, Il.	
N435PC	01 Pilatus PC-12/45	435	Bounty Air Leasing LLC. Coral Gables, Fl.	HB-FRV
N437CF	66 King Air A90	LJ-140	TN-TX LLC. Smyrna, Tn.	N50GH
N437JB	03 King Air C90B	LJ-1687	Bill & Jodean Bradford Investments Inc. Dallas, Tx.	N6187L
N437WF	82 King Air B200	BB-962	LJ Air Inc. Wood Dale, Il.	N719HC
N438CA	98 King Air C90B	LJ-1541	Columbus Airways Inc. Columbus, In.	
N438GP	87 PA-42 Cheyenne 400LS	5527038	UMI Investments Inc. Coral Gables, Fl.	HK-3459P
N438HT	79 King Air 200	BB-438	3 Lone Stars LLC. Arlington, Tx.	N438BM
N439BA	81 MU-2 Solitaire	439SA	Tahoe Helicopters Inc. Bakersfield, Ca.	D-IBBB
N439PW	99 King Air C90B	LJ-1589	Paul Wood, Lake Forest, Il.	
N439WA	77 King Air E90	LW-216	Auro King Air/JHM Florida Hotels Management Inc. Greenville.	N190DB
N439WC	02 Pilatus PC-12/45	439	Peninsular Capital Advisors LLC. Charlottesville, Va.	HB-FSD
N440CA	85 PA-42 Cheyenne IIIA	5501027	SunStarr Aviation LLC. Fond du Lac, Wi.	D-IHGO
N440CC	74 Rockwell 690A	11191	C F P & P Inc. Fort Vernon, In.	N616SD
N440HC	82 Conquest 1	425-0145	G & A Investments LLC. Akron, Oh.	N801FD
N440KF	80 King Air C90	LJ-878	MJLG LLC. Nantucket, Ma.	N440KC
N440S	81 Cheyenne II-XL	8166016	Seneca Properties Inc. Sandusky, Oh.	N400XL
N440SM	70 King Air 100	B-44	Diamond Aviation Corp. Deland, Fl.	(N101PF)
N44UST	75 King Air 200	BB-65	Shelby Tigers Aviation LLC. Memphis, Tn.	(N901BR)
N440TP	65 King Air 90	LJ-17	Apex Aviation Group Inc. Southlake, Tx.	(N110AS)
N440WA	80 King Air 200	BB-700	Wilson & Associates of Delaware LLC. Little Rock, Ar.	N200PY
N441A	79 Conquest II	441-0094	Aviation Technologies Inc. Tulsa, Ok.	N555GD
N441AB	83 Conquest II	441-0284	WDG Management Services LC. Vernon, Tx.	N6888C
N441AD	81 Conquest II	441-0226	Conquest Aviation Inc. Wilmington, De.	N6281R
N441AE	82 Conquest II	441-0280	Aldridge Electric Inc. Libertyville, Il.	N986MC
N441AG	84 Conquest II	441-0327	Harvard Aviation Investment Corp. Las Vegas, Nv.	(N1209X)
N441AR	80 Conquest II	441-0148	Chrysalis 1 Inc. Fayetteville, Ar.	N170MA
N441BB	81 Conquest II	441-0217	Head Inc. Columbus, Oh.	N441WM
N441BH	80 Conquest II	441-0145	Quest Air Charters Inc. San Marcos, Ca.	N31CR
N441BL	83 Conquest II	441-0322	Bravo Lima LLC. Newport Beach, Ca.	N536MA
N441BW	77 Conquest II	441-0034	Wisconsin Aviation Inc. Watertown, Wi.	(N248DJ)
N441CA	78 Conquest II	441-0046	G G Trucking Inc. Franklin, Wi.	(N36989)
N441CC	78 Conquest II	441-0008	Oregon Atlantic Aviation LLC. Eugene, Or.	N441CP
N441CD	82 Conquest II	441-0259	Seminis Vegetable Seeds Inc. Saticoy, Ca.	N87HT
N441CG	95 King Air C90B	LJ-1398	Servicios Aereos del Caribe, Barranquilla, Colombia.	N996TT
N441CJ	80 Conquest II	441-0117	PFD Supply Corp. Carlinville, Il.	(N2623Z)
N441CT	78 Conquest II	441-0048	Aberdeen Flying Service, Aberdeen, SD.	N60FJ
N441CX	83 Conquest II	441-0305	Western Slope Auto Co. Grand Junction, Co.	N441FB
N441DB	83 Conquest II	441-0300	Alpha Victor Ltd. Dayton, Oh.	N68439
N441DD	84 Conquest II	441-0341	High Times Inc. Bentonville, Ar.	N441PM
N441DK	80 Conquest II	441-0176	Felts Field Aviation Inc. Spokane, Wa.	N139ML
N441DN	84 Conquest II	441-0325	Shippers Air Corp. Quincey, Il.	N325CM
N441DR	77 Conquest II	441-0035	Dove Air Inc. Hendersonville, NC.	G-FRAZ
N441DS	77 Conquest II	441-0028	Delmar Systems Inc. West Linn, Or.	N36955
N441DZ	79 Conquest II	441-0089	Dura Supreme Inc. Howard Lake, Mn.	N90GC
N441EB	78 Conquest II	441-0049	Plane Space Inc. West Palm Beach, Fl.	N441FW
N441EC	80 Conquest II	441-0179	BEE Aviation Inc. Sturgis, Ky.	N415PA
N441EE	79 Conquest II	441-0083	Flight Research Inc. Starkville, Ms.	N26BJ
N441EP	83 Conquest II	441-0283	Exxel LLC. Bellingham, Wa.	C-GMSL
N441EW	81 Conquest II	441-0214	Kenneth & Carol Lindstrom, Morton, Il.	N837RE
N441G	81 Conquest II	441-0230	Robinson Manufacturing Co. Dayton, Tn.	N14PN
N441HH	77 Conquest II	441-0007	Norcal Products Inc. Yreka, Ca.	ZS-PES
N441HK	84 Conquest II	441-0336	Gem Air LLC. Bakersfield, Ca.	N441JD
N441HS	84 Conquest II	441-0330	Phoenix Aircraft Sales & Rental Inc .Jacksonville, Fl.	(N747VB)
N441HT	79 Conquest II	441-0085	HANAH Travel & Leasing LLC. Alvin, Tx.	N347AP
N441JA	80 Conquest II	441-0137	Cheyenne Aviation Inc. Wilmington, De.	N301KB
N441JC	80 Conquest II	441-0156	Farmers Investment Co. Sahuarita, Az.	N829JQ
N441JK	81 Conquest II	441-0197	A L Stuart & Co. Stamford, Ct.	N8108Z
N441JR	83 Conquest II	441-0303	SR Aviation Inc. Wilmington, De.	N6860A
N441KM	78 Conquest II	441-0044	Kreuter Engineering Inc. New Paris, In.	N549GS
N441KP	78 Conquest II	441-0062	Alpha Victor Ltd. Dayton, Oh.	N76DA
N441KW*	78 Conquest II	441-0078	Freedom Flotilla LLC. Austin, Tx.	N441FC
N441LA	81 Conquest II	441-0210	Lee Aero LLC. Wichita, Ks.	N525MA

Reg	Yr Type	c/n	Owner/Operator	Prev Regn
☐ N441LB	78 Conquest II	441-0080	PlaneCo LLC. Lincoln, Ne.	N441BL
☐ N441LS	85 Conquest II	441-0342	Liberty Steel Products Inc/Meander Air LLC. Jackson, Oh.	N30832
☐ N441M	80 Conquest II	441-0122	Davandy LLC. St Louis, Mo.	(N441P)
☐ N441MD	79 Conquest II	441-0103	Keystone Aerial Surveys Inc. Philadelphia, Pa.	N441CE
☐ N441ME	83 Conquest II	441-0266	Scientific Flight Service. Washington, DC.	N800YM
☐ N441MJ	77 Conquest II	441-0024	Big Bear Charter Corp. Park City, Ut.	YS-111N
☐ N441MT	83 Conquest II	441-0297	Marine Terminals Air Inc. Mount Pleasant, SC.	N6838T
☐ N441MW	83 Conquest II	441-0286	First Port Air Inc. Omaha, Ne.	C-FUDY
☐ N441ND	80 Conquest II	441-0123	SR Real Estate LLC. Chaicgo, Il.	(N441JH)
☐ N441P	77 Conquest II	441-0032	Sisi Corp. St Louis, Mo.	N441M
☐ N441PG	82 Conquest II	441-0245	DPA LLC. Harlem, Mt.	C-GMSL
☐ N441PJ	84 Conquest II	441-0321	K Transit LLC. Branson, Md.	C-FNNC
☐ N441PP	93 Conquest II	441-0292	Air Construction Inc. McKinney, Tx.	N666HC
☐ N441PS	78 Conquest II	441-0045	S O Altfillisch Inc. Glendora, Ca.	N441JA
☐ N441PW	82 Conquest II	441-0240	Four Star Greenhouse Sales Inc. Carleton, Mi.	N413PC
☐ N441PZ	85 Conquest II	441-0351	Steven Silver, Hinsdale, Il.	N369PC
☐ N441RB	77 Conquest II	441-0029	John DeJoria. (status ?).	(N36956)
☐ N441RJ	80 Conquest II	441-0151	Hilltop Aviation LLC. Summit, NJ.	N2628M
☐ N441RK	78 Conquest II	441-0074	Chancellor Enterprises Ltd. Midland, Tx.	N1962J
☐ N441RS	81 Conquest II	441-0221	Ralph Steiger, Covina, Ca.	N881CD
☐ N441S	83 Conquest II	441-0323	Conquest Leasing LLC. Sheridan, Wy.	N323JG
☐ N441SA	80 Conquest II	441-0172	Security Aviation Inc. Anchorage, Ak.	N441VP
☐ N441SB	83 Conquest II	441-0301	Hondo LLC. Phoenix, Az.	N328VP
☐ N441SC	77 Conquest II	441-0012	Exports Inc. Sweet Grass, Mt.	N36932
☐ N441SM	80 Conquest II	441-0134	D & H Airways LLC. Fort Collins, Co.	N441DE
☐ N441ST	77 Conquest II	441-0014	RAL Enterprises Inc.	N441AA
☐ N441SX	82 Conquest II	441-0248	Pratt & Tobin PC. East Alton, Il.	N441JV
☐ N441TA	81 Conquest II	441-0204	Thomas Appleton, Hidden Hills, Ca.	N2727L
☐ N441TF	79 Conquest II	441-0072	Burlington Aviation LLC. Burlington, Wa.	C-FMSP
☐ N441UC	85 Conquest II	441-0344	Unit Corp. Tulsa, Ok.	N441ML
☐ N441VB	80 Conquest II	441-0115	Avian Corp. Edina, Mn.	RP-C549
☐ N441VC	80 Conquest II	441-0192	DG Financial Consulting & Leasing, Longview, Tx.	N441DW
☐ N441VH	81 Conquest II	441-0225	Satellite Aero Inc. Jackson, Wy.	N6854D
☐ N441WD	79 Conquest II	441-0107	JJA Holdings LLC. Birmingham, Al.	C-FGPK
☐ N441WJ	81 Conquest II	441-0194	WMJ Aviation LLC. Canton, Ga.	N26RF
☐ N441WL	78 Conquest II	441-0041	Lantis Enterprises Inc. Spearfish, SD.	N458HR
☐ N441WP	79 Conquest II	441-0098	Aero Transporte Nationale, Brownsville, Tx.	(N35DD)
☐ N441WT	82 Conquest II	441-0242	MCM Transport Inc. Aberdeen, NC.	N3127R
☐ N441X	82 Conquest II	441-0254	M/V Forger Inc. Portland, Or.	N410MA
☐ N441YA	81 Conquest II	441-0231	Paxton Media Group Inc. Paducah, Ky.	HK-3647X
☐ N442JA	77 Conquest II	441-0013	Pegasus & Crew Inc. Fort Lauderdale, Fl.	N441BG
☐ N442KA	79 King Air 200	BB-442	Nielsons Inc. Cortez, Co.	
☐ N443CL	79 King Air E90	LW-318	Ventana Aviation LLC. Salinas, Ca.	N943CL
☐ N443DW	83 Conquest II	441-0313	DWE Aviation Inc. Wilmington, NC.	N313DS
☐ N443H	80 Conquest 1	425-0002	Robert Hogue MD. Brownwood, Tx.	N74HR
☐ N443PE	89 BAe Jetstream 31	777	Petty Enterprises, Las Vegas, Nv.	N425AE
☐ N443TC	77 King Air B100	BE-20	Hanley Co. Knoxville, Tn.	N525WE
☐ N444AD	80 King Air 200	BB-733	Dept of Public Safety, Anchorage, Ak.	
☐ N444AK	84 Conquest II	441-0334	Black Hills Aviation Inc. Alamogordo, NM.	N334FW
☐ N444BK	89 King Air B200	BB-1332	Koop Aviation BV. Groningen-Eelde, Holland.	D-ICSM
☐ N444BN	78 PA-31T Cheyenne II	7820028	Wildflower of Delaware LLC. Dover, De.	N82232
☐ N444CM	96 Pilatus PC-12	152	Airco Associates LLC. Minneapolis, Mn.	HB-FRN
☐ N444EB	79 King Air 200	BB-444	Herb Tobman, Las Vegas, Nv.	ZS-LZU
☐ N444EG	84 King Air 200	BB-624	Creola Inc/Brazos Machinery & Equipment Inc. Clute, Tx.	N202BB
☐ N444FF	73 Mitsubishi MU-2K	260	Intercontinental Jet Inc. Tulsa, Ok.	N790CA
☐ N444FT	00 Pilatus PC-12/45	322	Flying Turtle LLC. Nantucket, Ma.	N124MK
☐ N444KA	83 King Air B200	BB-1160	ERG Aviation Inc. Palm Coast, Fl.	N388CP
☐ N444KF	83 Conquest 1	425-0191	Texia Energy Management Inc. Houston, Tx.	N1221N
☐ N444KK	83 King Air F90	LA-209	Darryl Unruh, Asheville, NC.	N6727U
☐ N444LB	82 SA-227TT Merlin 3C	TT-428A	Corporate Aviation LLC. Lafayette, La.	
☐ N444LN	81 PA-42 Cheyenne III	8001045	Plaza Enterprises LLC. Missoula, Mt.	N169TC
☐ N444LP	02 King Air B200	BB-1816	BCS Produce Co. San Diego, Ca.	N5016K
☐ N444NR	79 Rockwell B600	11549	Cosgrove Aircraft Service Inc. Hauppauge, NY.	N444NC
☐ N444PC	79 PA-31T Cheyenne II	7920066	Business Aircraft Center Inc. Danbury, Ct.	N111AM
☐ N444PS	74 King Air C90	LJ-615	Northwest Boring Co. Woodinville, Wa.	(N38DG)

Reg	Yr	Type	c/n	Owner/Operator	Prev Regn
N444RC	75	PA-31T Cheyenne II	7520030	Four R C Corp. Baton Rouge, La.	N54959
N444RK	83	King Air B100	BE-137	McWorth Management Co. Paris, Tn.	N65187
N444RR	83	Conquest 1	425-0128	Sasnak Management Corp. Wichita, Ks.	N444RH
N444SC	81	PA-42 Cheyenne III	8001034	PA42 LLC. Exeter, NH.	N74FB
N444WC	82	Cheyenne II-XL	8166054	E S Wagner Co. Oregon, Oh.	N176RS
N444WD	82	Gulfstream 1000	96006	Dawson Farms LLC. Delhi, La.	(N496MA)
N444WE	82	MU-2 Marquise	1551SA	Marquise Enterprises LLC.	N444WF
N444WG	69	King Air B90	LJ-455	Hayward Aviation Inc. Hayward, Wi.	PT-OYD
N445AE	78	Conquest II	441-0043	Physicians Aviation Inc. Wichita, Ks.	N445WS
N445CR	79	King Air C90	LJ-838	Claire Rice, Palm Desert, Ca.	N445DR
N446AS	96	King Air C90B	LJ-1446	Executive AirShare Corp. Wichita, Ks.	N222NF
N447PC	02	Pilatus PC-12/45	447	Skytech Inc. Baltimore, Md.	HB-FSG
N447TF	03	King Air 350	FL-364	Continental Datalabel Inc. Elgin, Il.	N5084V
N447WS	81	Conquest II	441-0198	K & W Aviation Inc/Wings Aloft Inc. Seattle, Wa.	C-FCWZ
N448CP	77	King Air E90	LW-232	CPL Aviation Inc. Bald Knob, Ar.	N112SB
N449BY	02	Pilatus PC-12/45	449	Blue Yonder Airways LLC. Houston, Tx.	HD-FSH
N449LC	74	Rockwell 690A	11187	Blue Water Aviation Inc. Jupiter, Fl.	HC-BPX
N450DW	01	King Air 350	FL-325	White Mountain Insurance Group. White River Junction, Vt.	N5025L
N450FS	76	Mitsubishi MU-2M	338	Professional Aviation Sales & Service, Millington, Tn.	N456PS
N450HC	81	Cheyenne II-XL	8166021	Simplifly Aviation LLC. Wilmington, De.	N300XL
N450LM	90	King Air 350	FL-5	Shelter Enterprises Inc. Columbia, Mo.	N5634E
N450MA	73	Mitsubishi MU-2J	587	Intercontinental Jet Inc. Tulsa, Ok.	N212BA
N450MW	84	PA-42 Cheyenne 400LS	5527013	Northeast Air Charter Inc. Greenwich, Ct.	N32KK
N450PC	02	Pilatus PC-12/45	450	Departures Leasing LLC. Colorado Springs, Co.	HB-FSF
N450WH	87	King Air B200	BB-1275	A T Williams Oil Co. Winston-Salem, NC.	N98RY
N451A	93	King Air C90B	LJ-1348	Gilardi Aviation Ltd. Sidney, Oh.	
N451DM	00	Pilatus PC-12/45	350	Air Fox Hollow LLC. Menlo Park, Ca.	HB-FSC
N451WS	79	Conquest II	441-0096	RJF Avionics LLC. Wilmington, De.	N8977N
N452MA	81	MU-2 Marquise	1533SA	Far West Ventures Inc. Palm Beach, Fl.	
N452MD	02	Pilatus PC-12/45	452	MDR Aviation Inc. Columbia, Ms.	HB-FSK
N452TT	69	King Air B90	LJ-452	Ameri-Air Leasing Corp. Miami, Fl.	D-ILKA
N453PC	02	Pilatus PC-12/45	453	J & J Aviation LLC. Las Vegas, Nv.	HB-FSL
N454CA	81	PA-31T Cheyenne 1	8104053	SunStarr Aviation LLC. Fond du lac, Wi.	G-JVAJ
N454DC	82	King Air B200	BB-995	D C & Associates of S Carolina Inc. Columbia, SC.	XA-RVJ
N454EA	78	Conquest II	441-0054	Topo Bird LLC. Yarmouth, Me.	C-GRSL
N454LF	98	King Air 350	FL-209	JAMM Aviation Inc. Columbus, Oh.	N2303B
N454MA	81	MU-2 Marquise	1535SA	Flight Line Inc. Denver, Co.	
N454P	94	King Air C90B	LJ-1372	McDowell Pharmaceutical LLC. Kansas City, Mo.	(N121EB)
N454PS	02	Pilatus PC-12/45	454	Shelaero LLC. De Kalb, Ga.	HB-FSM
N455DK	97	Pilatus PC-12/45	194	Doug Bradley Trucking Inc. Salina, Ks.	N216
N455JW	81	PA-42 Cheyenne III	8001040	Gas'N Shop Inc. Lincoln, Ne.	N456JW
N455LG	04	PA-46-500TP Meridian	4697203	New Piper Aircraft Inc. Vero Beach, Fl.	
N455MM	80	PA-31T Cheyenne II	8020087	Mike Miklus III Inc. Newark, De.	N26PJ
N455SC	03	King Air 350	FL-384	Spartan Chemical Co. Swanton, Oh.	N5084Y
N455SE	02	King Air 350	FL-356	BR Aircraft LLC. Sacramento, Ca.	N455SC
N455SG	01	PA-46-500TP Meridian	4697096	Graftaire LLC. Shreveport, La.	
N455WM	02	Pilatus PC-12/45	455	McClone Enterprises LLC. Shingle Spring, Ca.	HB-FSN
N456AC	83	PA-31T Cheyenne 1	8104068	John Godfrey, Horseshoe Bay, tx.	XA-RLB
N456CS	76	King Air 200	BB-177	Plains Exploration & Production Co. Houston, Tx.	
N456ES	83	King Air B200	BB-1107	Instant Air Inc. Linden, NJ.	N564BC
N456FC	83	Conquest 1	425-0127	Lamar Leasing Co. Lamar, In.	N6882V
N456GT	82	Conquest II	441-0294	G T Aviation Inc. Wilmington, De.	N294VB
N456PC	02	Pilatus PC-12/45	456	Cummins Aviation LLC. Wilmington, De.	HB-FSQ
N456PF	78	King Air 200	BB-413	Cowan Watts Flying Service LLC. Pasco, Wa.	N2061B
N456PP	03	King Air C90B	LJ-1699	Bookcircus.com.LLC. Tulsa, Ok.	N90KP
N456Q	89	King Air 300	FA-181	Quinn Co. Fresno, Ca.	(N458Q)
N456V	98	Pilatus PC-12/45	201	Riverbend Enterprises Inc. Idaho Falls, Id.	HB-FOM
N457CP	67	King Air A90	LJ-275	Texas State Technical College, Waco, Tx.	N457SR
N457G	69	SA-26AT Merlin 2B	T26-150	Sun Charter LLC. St Petersburg, Fl.	N4257X
N457TG	80	PA-31T Cheyenne II	8020059	VT Air LLC. Corvalllis, Or.	N457TC
N458BB	85	MU-2 Solitaire	458SA	Beeline Flight Inc. Wilmington, De.	XB-FQM
N458DL	02	Pilatus PC-12/45	458	HLS Air Inc. San Diego, Ca.	N458PC
N459CA	02	TBM 700B	238	Rand Insurance Inc. Riverside, Ct.	(N700EF)
N459DF	01	King Air B200	BB-1761	California Dept of Forestry & Fire, Sacramento, Ca.	N4461C
N459MA	02	TBM 700C	259	Tri-M Communications Inc. Santa Barbara, Ca.	
Reg	Yr	Type	c/n	Owner/Operator	Prev Regn

Reg	Yr Type	c/n	Owner/Operator	Prev Regn
N459PC	02 Pilatus PC-12/45	459	Alan Ross, Tulsa, Ok.	HB-FST
N459SA	85 MU-2 Solitaire	459SA	Solitaire Leasing LLC. Wilmington, De.	OY-CGW
N460FS	73 Mitsubishi MU-2K	280	Professional Aviation Sales & Service, Millington, Tn.	N10BK
N460K	77 Rockwell 690B	11392	Aero Horizons Inc. Deland, Fl.	LV-MAG
N460PB	02 Pilatus PC-12/45	460	Carolina Express LLC. Fairmont, Mn.	HB-FSU
N461BB	01 PA-46-500TP Meridian	4697016	Meridian Leasing LLC. Rockport, Me.	
N461LM	96 TBM 700	122	Smarter Charter Inc. Tampa, Fl.	F-GLBJ
N461MA	74 Mitsubishi MU-2K	301	Good Aviation LLC. Grand Rapids, Mi.	N10T
N462MA	74 Mitsubishi MU-2K	302	Copper Station Holdings LLC. Columbia, SC.	
N462PC	02 Pilatus PC-12/45	462	NW Aircraft Sales & Leasing LLC. Scappoose, Or.	HB-FSW
N463DC	76 SA-226T Merlin 3A	T-273	Jaime Hernandez, Brownsville, Tx.	N5390M
N463DP	79 King Air 200	BB-463	Gula Charter Service LLC. Camp Hill, Pa.	VH-ITH
N463JT	02 Pilatus PC-12/45	463	Mountain Air Charter LLC. Jordan Valley, Or.	HB-FRD
N464AB	67 King Air A90	LJ-224	CLS Investments Inc. Edinburg, Tx.	N464AL
N464G	67 King Air A90	LJ-202	Diamond Air Inc. Waco, Tx.	(N474DP)
N465PC	02 Pilatus PC-12/45	465	Fischer Industries Air LLC. Sebastian, Fl.	HB-FSY
N465SK	01 PA-46-500TP Meridian	4697013	Malibu Financial Corp. Dover, De.	
N466MW	87 King Air B200	BB-1273	Chandelle Development LLC. Denver, Co.	N30486
N466SA	01 Pilatus PC-12/45	443	Skyair AG. Zurich, Switzerland.	HB-...
N467BC	99 King Air B200	BB-1647	Bright Coop Inc. Nacogdoches, Tx.	N50PU
N467BW	72 King Air A100	B-130	Trevor & Associates Inc. Marrion, Oh.	N83TM
N467MA	85 MU-2 Marquise	1567SA	Earthmark Travel LLC. Fort Myers, Fl.	PT-LPB
N468SP	84 MU-2 Marquise	1566SA	Samaritan's Purse Inc. Boone, NC.	5Y-SPR
N469AF	02 Pilatus PC-12/45	469	Alpha Flying Inc. Nashua, NH.	HB-FQB
N469B	78 King Air C90	LJ-803	J B F Inc. South Point, Oh.	N75GA
N469BL	69 SA-26AT Merlin 2B	T26-139	AER Aviation Inc. Dallas, Tx.	C-FCAR
N469MA	82 MU-2 Marquise	1543SA	Via Air Inc. Charlotte, NC.	TF-FHM
N469TA	82 King Air B200	BB-959	Oryx LLC. Naples, Fl.	N28CN
N470AH	02 Pilatus PC-12/45	470	Pilatus Aviation LLC. San Jose, Ca.	N470WA
N470MM	00 Beech 1900D	UE-394	Schwans Shared Services LLC. Marshall, Mn.	N41255
N470SC	90 King Air 350	FL-35	Poly-Foam International Inc. Fremont, Oh.	N550TP
N470TC	79 King Air 200	BB-424	MacAviation LLC. Jonesboro, Ar.	F-GMCR
N471CD	83 SA-227AT Merlin 4C	AT-549	Ashley Aire Inc. Upper Marlboro, Md.	89-1471
N471JS	83 Gulfstream 900	15031	Etheridge Enterprises Inc. Jackson, Ms.	(N901TE)
N473GG	78 PA-31T Cheyenne II	7820026	Dietrich Transport Inc. Norristown, Pa.	N570AB
N473PC	02 Pilatus PC-12/45	473	N473PC LLC. Spokane, Wa.	HB-FQD
N475JA	87 King Air C90A	LJ-1147	Progress Instruments Inc. Lee Summit, Mo.	
N476D	02 Pilatus PC-12/45	476	HPM Investments Inc. Bornemouth-Hurn, UK.	HB-FQG
N477B	78 Conquest II	441-0055	Joplin Regional Stockyards Inc. Carthage, Mo.	HB-LFF
N477HC	03 PA-46-500TP Meridian	4697171	Copperman Enterprises LLC. Naples, Fl.	
N477JM	79 King Air 200	BB-538	Two Aviation, Greensboro, NC.	5N-AVH
N478CR	97 King Air C90B	LJ-1474	ALG Aircraft LLC. Delano, Ca.	N205P
N479MA	82 MU-2 Marquise	1553SA	Gulf Transportation & Equipment Inc. Panama City, Fl.	
N479SW	79 PA-31T Cheyenne 1	7904047	Chesnut's Investments Inc. London, Ky.	
N479VK	73 SA-226AT Merlin 4	AT-009	Metroliner LLC. Swanton, Oh.	N615GA
N480BC	68 SA-26AT Merlin 2B	T26-108	Air Sales Inc. Hollister, Ca.	N122NK
N480BR	90 King Air B200	BB-1355	Russcor Financial Inc. Scottsdale, Az.	OH-WIB
N480EA	81 Conquest 1	425-0035	Metroplains Development LLC. St Paul, Mn.	N402NG
N480K	79 Rockwell 690B	11543	SB Aircraft Sales, Boulder, Co.	(N117FA)
N480MA	82 MU-2 Marquise	1554SA	I M LLC. San Diego, Ca.	
N480TC	97 King Air B200	BB-1600	Cardinal AG Co. Eden Prairie, Mn.	
N480WH	02 Pilatus PC-12/45	480	Frank Howard No 1 LLC. Colorado Springs, Co.	HB-FQK
N481SW	81 PA-31T Cheyenne 1	8104016	Charles White Construction Co. Clarksdale, Ms.	
N481TL	02 Pilatus PC-12/45	481	481TL LLC. Hartford, Ct.	HB-FQL
N482TC	83 PA-31T Cheyenne 1	8104072	Craig Massey, Richmond, Va.	
N482WA	03 Pilatus PC-12/45	482	Lilly Leasing LLC. Wilmington, NC.	HB-FQP
N484AS	80 PA-31T Cheyenne 1	8004055	AirSure Limited Properties Inc. Golden, Co.	N619RB
N484SC	78 PA-31T Cheyenne II	7820022	Strategic Technology Resources LLC. Roswell, NM.	N9DK
N485AT	89 King Air C90A	LJ-1203	Advanced Technology Services Inc. Peoria, Il.	N115MZ
N485K	79 King Air 200	BB-485	Steven Aviation LLC. Wichita, Ks.	N120K
N485PC	03 Pilatus PC-12/45	485	Pilatus Leasing LLC. Beachwood, Oh.	HB-FQS
N485R	80 King Air 200	BB-605	Crown Air LLC. Arlington, Wa.	N605EA
N486PB	03 Pilatus PC-12/45	486	Distinctive Sky LLC. Mokena, Il.	HB-FQT
N487JH	78 King Air B100	BE-43	Col Management LLC. Lake Charles, La.	N544FD
N487LM	03 Pilatus PC-12/45	517	BTI Aviation LLC. Colorado Springs, Co.	HB-FRT
Reg	Yr Type	c/n	Owner/Operator	Prev Regn

Reg	Yr	Type	c/n	Owner/Operator	Prev Regn
☐ N487PC	03	Pilatus PC-12/45	487	Abbey Leasing Co. Bonita Springs, Fl.	HB-FQU
☐ N488FT	81	King Air F90	LA-137	Team Financial Inc. Birmingham, Al.	N200MW
☐ N488XJ	98	King Air C90B	LJ-1527	Wilkes & McHugh PA. Tampa, Fl.	
☐ N489GA	79	Rockwell 690B	11530	R & D Tire Mold Co. Mount Pleasant, Tn.	N81734
☐ N489JG	03	Pilatus PC-12/45	489	GCM Aviation LLC. Hillsborough, NJ.	HB-FQW
☐ N489SC	80	Gulfstream 840	11635	Blue & Gold Mountain Air LLC. Parkersburg, WV.	N331SC
☐ N490J	92	King Air C90B	LJ-1312	Southern Aviation Group Inc. Wilmington, De.	N490JT
☐ N490MA	74	Mitsubishi MU-2J	640	Earthmark Travel LLC. Fort Myers, Fl.	
☐ N490TN	92	King Air 350	FL-89	TennOhio Transportation Co. Columbus, Oh.	N8112F
☐ N490W	01	King Air C90B	LJ-1649	OSI Software Inc. San Leandro, Ca.	N4479W
☐ N491JV	93	King Air C90B	LJ-1349	Omnione LLC. Albany, Or.	
☐ N491MB	81	Cheyenne II-XL	8166007	Travel Services LLC. Rantoul, Il.	N187GA
☐ N492PA	70	King Air B90	LJ-492	Istvan Bessenyei, Budapest, Hungary.	(N946WA)
☐ N492WA	03	Pilatus PC-12/45	492	Cascade WA LLC. Seattle, Wa.	HB-FQZ
☐ N494MA	86	King Air 300	FA-108	Sterling Air Finance LLC. St Clair Shores, Mi.	OY-LKT
☐ N494PC	03	Pilatus PC-12/45	494	Kendall Jackson Wine Estates, Medford, Or.	(N621J)
☐ N495MA	74	Mitsubishi MU-2K	306	Bedrock Resources Inc. Ocala, Fl.	
☐ N495NM	78	King Air C90	LJ-781	State of New Mexico, Santa Fe, NM.	N4953M
☐ N495TM	97	King Air C90B	LJ-1495	Turbine Aircraft Marketing Inc. San Angelo, Tx.	D-IDIX
☐ N495Y	04	King Air C90B	LJ-1707	Arkwest Aviation LLC. Danville, Ar.	
☐ N496DT	03	Pilatus PC-12/45	496	Normac Aviation Ltd. Wilmington, De.	HB-FRD
☐ N497P	85	King Air C90A	LJ-1126	Piedmont Hawthorne Aviation Inc. Winston-Salem, NC.	N300CK
☐ N497PC	03	Pilatus PC-12/45	497	Bureau of Immigration & Customs Enforcement, Washington, DC.	HB-F..
☐ N498AC	77	King Air 200	BB-287	PS Air Inc. Cedar Rapids, la.	N429E
☐ N499TT	79	King Air 200	BB-499	Pacific Bonding Corp. Carlsbad, Ca.	N6051C
☐ N499WC	78	Rockwell 690B	11499	AeroMitchell Inc. City of Industry, Ca.	N81832
☐ N500CP*	94	2000A Starship	NC-50	Starship Transport LLC. Newport Beach, Ca.	N8285Q
☐ N500CR	80	King Air 200	BB-714	Horizon Air Inc. Georgetown, Ky.	N7CC
☐ N500CS	81	King Air 200	BB-773	Wells Fargo Bank NW NA. Weston, Ireland.	N83JE
☐ N500DW	79	King Air 200	BB-523	DarWal Inc. Harrisburg, NC.	N196MP
☐ N500EQ	94	King Air C90B	LJ-1387	Red Drive IV LLC. Houston, Tx.	N500ED
☐ N500FC	87	King Air 300	FA-124	Fibres Aviation LLC. Augusta, Ga.	N1845C
☐ N500FF	98	TBM 700	141	SOCATA Aircraft, Pembroke Pines, Fl.	
☐ N500GN	75	King Air 200	BB-62	Gannett Co. Dulles, Va.	N300GN
☐ N500KA	81	King Air 200	BB-819	Palmer Aviation Leasing LLC. Germantown, Tn.	N425P
☐ N500KD	80	King Air B100	BE-79	Winner Aviation Corp. Vienna, Oh.	N500JE
☐ N500KR	77	King Air C90	LJ-708	NC Stste Bureau of Investigation, Raleigh, NC.	N500KS
☐ N500KS	75	King Air 200	BB-59	Ken Schrader Racing Inc. Concord, NC.	N504WR
☐ N500LM	84	PA-42 Cheyenne 400LS	5527016	James Smith, Kalispell, Mt.	
☐ N500LP	83	King Air B200	BB-1141	Neal Hawthorn, Longview, Tx.	N66549
☐ N500MS	75	King Air E90	LW-123	Mike Skinner Enterprises Inc. Greensboro, NC.	N121GW
☐ N500MY	78	PA-31T Cheyenne 1	7804004	Tri Rotor Spray & Chemical, Ulysses, Ks.	N500MT
☐ N500NK	03	Pilatus PC-12/45	500	Peoples Choice Consulting LLC. Irvine, Ca. (400th PC-12).	N500ZP
☐ N500PB	81	Cheyenne II-XL	8166027	Broyhill Industries Inc. Lenoir, NC.	N2602Y
☐ N500PJ	75	Mitsubishi MU-2L	668	Premier Jets Inc. Portland, Or.	N500RM
☐ N500PS	72	Mitsubishi MU-2F	224	Turbine Aircraft Marketing Inc. San Angelo, Tx.	N190MA
☐ N500PV	79	King Air 200	BB-452	B-Fast Corp. Newton, Pa.	N500PR
☐ N500RJ	83	Conquest II	441-0302	Edward Jankowski, Mancos, Co.	N68599
☐ N500RN	62	Gulfstream 1	95	USAF, 89th Operations Group, Andrews AFB. Md.	(N700MA)
☐ N500SE	01	PA-46-500TP Meridian	4697118	Air FMS Inc. Galesburg, Il.	
☐ N500SX	80	SA-226T Merlin 3B	T-366	Merlin Aviation Inc. Indianapolis, In.	N911JZ
☐ N500VA	98	King Air C90B	LJ-1519	WeatherBell Aviation LLC. Martinsville, Va.	N800JF
☐ N500VL	03	King Air 350	FL-383	WB Air Time LLC. Virginia Beach, Va.	N6183S
☐ N500W	80	King Air 200	BB-600	B & R Motorsports LLC. Greenwich, Ct.	N15KA
☐ N500WD	83	Conquest 1	425-0147	Wil-Flite Aviation LLC. Longview, Tx.	N500MC
☐ N500WF	81	King Air B200	BB-947	William Flowers, Dothan, Al.	G-FOOD
☐ N500XX	73	Mitsubishi MU-2K	250	Econo-Air Inc. Middletown, NY.	N740FN
☐ N501AR	03	PA-46-500TP Meridian	4697162	Hide-Away Ironing Boards Inc. Tulsa, Ok.	N563MA
☐ N501EB	79	King Air 200	BB-422	Precision Holdings LLC. Kimberly, Id.	N551E
☐ N501HC	88	King Air B200	BB-1306	Intermountain Health Care Services, Salt Lake City, Ut.	N1553E
☐ N501MS	74	King Air C90	LJ-626	J&R Air LLC/Chicago Adhesive Products Co. Romeoville, Il.	N500MS
☐ N501P	04	King Air C90B	LJ-1732	Raytheon Aircraft Co. Wichita, Ks.	
☐ N501PB	03	Pilatus PC-12/45	501	Capital Holdings 121 LLC. Vero Beach, Fl.	HB-FRG
☐ N501PM	92	P-180 Avanti	1022	PM Aircraft Leasing LLC. Conroe, Tx.	F-GMCP
☐ N501PT	79	PA-31T Cheyenne 1	7904048	Sky Trek LLC. San Diego, Ca.	

Reg	Yr Type	c/n	Owner/Operator	Prev Regn
N501TD	81 King Air F90	LA-82	Burkhalter Transport Inc. Columbus, Ms.	N531DS
N501WN	65 Gulfstream 1	165	Erin Miel Inc. Las Vegas, Nv.	N500WN
N502BR	80 Conquest II	441-0135	U S Leasing & Financial Inc. Wilmington, De.	N93RK
N502DT	77 Rockwell 690B	11413	DT Industries Inc. Lebanon, Mo.	N690DT
N502MS	82 King Air C90-1	LJ-996	Kiowa Aviation LLC. Galesburg, Il.	HB-GDA
N502NC	81 Conquest 1	425-0056	D & D Aviation Inc. Grandview, Mo.	N56DA
N502SE	77 King Air C90	LJ-740	Aerolease LLC. Fargo, ND.	(N390YH)
N502SP	79 King Air F90	LA-4	EDT Towage Inc. Larnaca, Cyprus.	N1HE
N502WC	76 SA-226T Merlin 3A	T-268	Westra Construction Inc. Waupun, Wi.	N4273X
N503AA	74 Mitsubishi MU-2J	633	Turbine Aircraft Marketing Inc. San Angelo, Tx.	(N56JS)
N503AB	70 King Air 100	B-18	Aero Transit Inc. Apple Valley, Ca.	(N901AT)
N503CB	82 King Air C90	LJ-997	CTB Inc. Goshen, In.	N1853T
N503F	76 King Air 200	BB-185	RLD Leasing Inc. Downers Grove, Il.	N265EB
N503M	66 King Air A90	LJ-158	Robert Spillman, Elyria, Oh.	(N900WM)
N503P	79 King Air 200	BB-437	Griffin Brothers Aviation Inc. Cornelius, NC.	N500MT
N503RH	89 Beech 1900C-1	UC-78	Hendrick Motorsports Inc. Charlotte, NC.	N1568D
N503RM*	80 King Air 200	BB-673	KingDon LLC. Morresville, NC.	N502RH
N503WJ	79 King Air 200	BB-503	Variety Wholesalers Inc. Raleigh, NC.	RP-C304
N503WR	79 PA-31T Cheyenne 1	7904016	M M Air Inc. Flowood, Ms.	N93CV
N503WS	03 Pilatus PC-12/45	503	Priority Aircraft Inc. Blairsville, Pa.	N503PB
N504CB	75 King Air E90	LW-125	Executive Aircraft Services Inc. Elizabethtown, NC.	N543MB
N504GF	83 King Air B200	BB-1156	Waffle House Inc. Norcross, Ga.	N66825
N504RH	88 Beech 1900C	UB-72	Rick Hendrick Motorsports Inc. Harrisburg, NC.	OY-JRS
N504SR	03 PA-46-500TP Meridian	4697165	Synergy Aviation LLC. Salt Lake City, Ut.	
N504TF	04 King Air 350	FL-399	Teixeira Farms Inc. Santa Maria, Ca.	
N505AM	81 King Air B200	BB-919	Flight Management Co/Dart Container Corp. Sarasota, Fl.	N160AD
N505FK	73 King Air C-12C	BC-18	Monroe County Sheriffs Department, Key West, Fl.	N465MC
N505FS	85 SA-227AT Merlin 4C	AT-591	F S Air Service Inc. Anchorage, Ak.	N176SW
N505HC	82 Conquest II	441-0257	Span Construction & Engineering Inc. Madera, Ca.	N100YA
N505MW	75 King Air E90	LW-155	Golden Eagle Associates Ltd. Dallas, Tx.	N505GA
N505P	03 Pilatus PC-12/45	505	POMCO Equipment Inc. Syracuse, NY.	HB-FRK
N505RH	86 Beech 1900C	UB-56	Rick Hendrick Motorsports Inc. Harrisburg, NC.	OY-JRP
N505RT	68 680W Turbo Commander	1752-5	Twin City Leasing Corp. Kansas City, Mo.	N5051E
N505WR	84 King Air 300	FA-15	J M Air Inc. Pinedale, Wy.	
N506F	86 King Air C90A	LJ-1129	BuzzEd LLC. Elgin, Il.	N817F
N506GT	80 King Air 200	BB-612	Foster Poultry Farms Inc. Livingston, Ca.	
N506MV	99 King Air 350	FL-261	Foster Poultry Farms Inc. Livingston, Ca.	N350GT
N507AM	01 Pilatus PC-12/45	418	Alatex LLC. Wilmington, De.	N418PB
N507BE	80 King Air 200	BB-735	Aviation Enterprises LLC/Basin Electric Power, Bismark, ND.	N508JA
N507EB	82 King Air 350	FL-81	JRW Aviation Inc. Dallas, Tx.	N8053R
N507K	79 King Air 200	BB-507	OK Consultants Inc. Monterey, Ca.	F-GEJY
N507RC	03 Pilatus PC-12/45	507	Ritzcraft Aviation LLC. Mifflinburg, Pa.	N507PB
N507SC	00 King Air B200	BB-1738	Co-Mar of Dayton Inc. Bowling Green, Ky.	
N507W	67 King Air A90	LJ-269	BTP Inc. Missoula, Mt.	N788K
N508CB	04 King Air C90B	LJ-1715	Bankers Capital Corp. Brandon, Ms.	
N508MV	81 King Air B200	BB-877	Triangle Air Services Inc. Woodcliff Lakes, NJ.	N711BU
N509FP	04 King Air B200	BB-1886	Raytheon Aircraft Co. Wichita, Ks.	
N509RH	95 SAAB 2000	030	Hendrick Motorsports Inc. Charlotte, NC.	N5125
N510GS	99 King Air B200	BB-1746	Flyaway Inc. Fort Worth, Tx.	N518GS
N510LC	77 PA-31T Cheyenne II	7720068	Packless Industries/Packless Metal Hose, Waco, Tx.	(N69XX)
N510ME	79 King Air E90	LW-312	Carroll Laing, Wichita Falls, Tx.	N505BG
N510UF	04 King Air B200	BB-1872	United Fire & Casualty Co. Cedar Rapids, Ia.	N6172W
N511AS	87 King Air B200	BB-1286	Textile Rubber & Chemical Co. Dalton, Ga.	N800GF
N511D	97 King Air 350	FL-172	Bunn-O-Matic Corp. Springfield, Il.	
N511KV	96 King Air C90B	LJ-1422	GQuest Technology LLC. Greensboro, NC.	N2123Y
N511PB	03 Pilatus PC-12/45	511	AVP Holdings of Delaware LLC. Overland Park, Ks.	HB-FRO
N511RH	95 SAAB 2000	020	Hendrick Motorsports Inc. Charlotte, NC.	N5123
N511RZ	93 King Air B200	BB-1458	Air Med Services Inc. Lafayette, La.	N457TQ
N511SD	99 King Air B200	BB-1683	DashDale Aviation LLC. Fort Dodge, Ia.	
N512DC	02 King Air 350	FL-342	Crider Transportation LLC. Stillmore, Ga.	N4472S
N512FS	79 SA-226T Merlin 3B	T-299	F S Air Service Inc. Anchorage, Ak.	N55ZP
N512G	65 King Air 90	LJ-64	American Aircraft Inc. Newton, Ks.	N512Q
N512JD	66 680T Turbo Commander	1584-36	Seaquest Expeditions Inc. Eugene, Or.	N512JC
N512KA	79 King Air/Catpass 250	BB-512	Warocon Inc. Nassau, Bahamas.	N333TS
N512RR	79 King Air C90	LJ-832	Ruhl Develpment LLC. Davenport, Ia.	N10QW
Reg	Yr Type	c/n	Owner/Operator	Prev Regn

Reg	Yr Type	c/n	Owner/Operator	Prev Regn
N513DM	82 MU-2 Marquise	1560SA	Incoe Corp. Troy, Mi.	N486MA
N513KL	81 King Air F90	LA-123	Mager Enterprises LLC. Dover, De.	N211EC
N514GP	94 BAe Jetstream 41	41038	Georgia Pacific Corp. Atlanta, Ga.	N438JX
N514MA	82 King Air B200	BB-1007	M Aviation Services of Florida LLC. Tallahassee, Fl.	G-SBAS
N514NA	68 680W Turbo Commander	1772-10	NASA Langley Research Center, Hampton, Va.	83-24126
N514RD	79 King Air 200C	BL-5	Evergreen Helicopters Inc. McMinnville, Or.	N14RD
N514RS	94 2000A Starship	NC-51	Robert Scherer III, Charlotte, NC.	N6204U
N514TB	90 King Air B200	BB-1351	Tejas Enterprises LLC. Houston, Tx.	N777JV
N515AF	03 Pilatus PC-12/45	515	Alpha Flying Inc. Nashua, NH.	HB-FRR
N515AM	80 Gulfstream 980	95008	Allen Myland Inc. Broomall, Pa.	N9761S
N515AS	72 King Air A100	B-90	Elias R V Morales, Valencia Caracobo, Venezuela.	(YV-2423P
N515BC	75 King Air E90	LW-121	R S D Technologies LLC. Fenton, Mi.	N500TR
N515CK	00 King Air B200	BB-1726	Lone Wolf Aviation LLC. Brighton, Mi.	N515CL
N515CR	84 King Air B200	BB-1175	Travel King Inc. Atlanta, Ga.	SE-IXA
N515GA	82 PA-31T Cheyenne 1	8104050	Ingram Aviation LLC. San Braunfels, Tx.	N49WA
N515M	82 PA-42 Cheyenne III	8001079	AeroSolutions Group Inc. Bethesda, Md.	N515DW
N515RC	84 PA-42 Cheyenne IIIA	5501018	WMJ Corp. Colorado Springs, Co.	N516GA
N515RP	00 Pilatus PC-12/45	330	Sunrise Community Inc. Miami, Fl.	HB-FRO
N516BA	99 King Air 350	FL-247	3DL Management LLC. Santa Ana, Ca.	N350TG
N516S	83 Cheyenne II XL	8166076	KC Leasing LLC. Salt Lake City, Ut.	N51GS
N516WB	65 King Air 90	LJ-70	University of Alaska, Fairbanks, Ak.	N516W
N517AB	82 King Air F90	LA-174	Broin & Associates Inc. Sioux Falls, SD.	N766RB
N517HP	79 Rockwell 690B	11517	B-H Sales Inc. Richmond, In.	N101RW
N518NA	67 King Air A90	LM-80	Lake Technical Institute, Watertown, SD.	66-18080
N518TS	86 King Air C90A	LJ-1130	Allied Aircraft LLC/Tower Industries Inc. Anaheim, Ca.	(N581TS)
N519CC	83 Gulfstream 1000	96068	Eagle Air Inc. Memphis, Tn.	N62GA
N519HB	80 Gulfstream 980	95013	L C Leasing Co. Annapolis, Md.	N500TH
N519PC	03 Pilatus PC-12/45	519	Spring Creek Research LLC. Santa Barbara, Ca.	HB-FRU
N520CS	71 681B Turbo Commander	6061	Medic Air Corp. Reno, Nv.	(N22FF)
N520DD	80 King Air 200	BB-738	Quail Creek Petroleum Management, Oklahoma City, Ok.	N66TS
N520DG	00 King Air B200	BB-1753	David R Webb Co. Edinburgh, In.	
N520HP	01 PA-46-500TP Meridian	4697012	Dana Brent, Greenleaf, Or.	
N520JG	68 Gulfstream 1	197	Joe Gibbs Racing Inc. Charlotte, NC.	N197RM
N520MC	75 King Air 200	BB-43	Mayo Aviation Inc. Englewood, Co.	N500UR
N520RM	83 Conquest 1	425-0129	Joseph Thibodeau PC. Denver, Co.	(N425JT)
N521DG	00 King Air B200	BB-1723	Interforest Corp. Darlington, Pa.	N3223R
N521LB	77 King Air E90	LW-249	Baron & Budd PC. Dallas, Tx.	N68CC
N521M	87 Beech 1900C	UB-68	Raytheon Aircraft Co. Wichita, Ks.	N30CY
N521PC	03 Pilatus PC-12/45	521	Clover Mechanical LLC. Ottawa, Il.	HB-FRW
N521PM	77 PA-31T Cheyenne II	7720048	Hadden Enterprises Inc. Pembroke, Ky.	N82163
N522AS	75 PA-31T Cheyenne II	7520007	Aerial Services Inc. Cedar Falls, Ia.	OH-PNT
N522DJ	04 Pilatus PC-12/45	539	DRJ Group Inc. Ocala, Fl.	N539PS
N522TG	80 King Air 200	BB-727	N522TG LLC/JP Air Charter Inc. Ontario, Ca.	N1955E
N522WD	80 Conquest 1	425-0015	Maliboo LLC. Wando, SC.	N40RD
N523CJ	73 King Air E90	LW-40	Medical Advocacy Services for Healthcare, Fort Worth, Tx.	N155CG
N523GM	98 King Air B200	BB-1598	Saddle Creek Corp. Lakeland, Fl.	N706TA
N523JL	03 Pilatus PC-12/45	523	Tradewind Aviation LLC. White Plains, NY.	HB-FRY
N523PD	79 PA-31T Cheyenne 1	7904044	Small Newspaper Services LLC. Kankakee, Il.	N23569
N524AM	79 PA-31T Cheyenne II	7920039	Associazione Romana Aersportiva,	F-GLLG
N524CM	01 Pilatus PC-12/45	410	Carlmax Aviation LLC. New Orleans, La.	N10VQ
N524FS	80 King Air 200	BB-590	WFBNA NA/Littleton Overseas Inc. BVI.	F-GIDV
N524GM	01 King Air B200C	BL-142	N840GR Inc. Wilmington, De.	(N840GR)
N524GT	03 Pilatus PC-12/45	524	Airport Equipment Rentals Inc. Fairbanks, Ak.	HB-FRZ
N524MR	79 King Air 200	BB-524	Charles Perme, Harrison, Ar.	D-ILPC
N524PM	01 PA-46-500TP Meridian	4697024	Champ Systems Inc. Sacramento, Ca.	
N524SC	70 King Air 100	B-37	Star Care V, Lincoln, Ne.	N627L
N524TS	88 King Air C90A	LJ-1187	Flying Partners LLC. Baton Rouge, La.	(N15PT)
N525BC	99 King Air 350	FL-252	TVPX Inc. Concord, Ma.	N3252B
N525DF	00 King Air 350	FL-366	Ventex Operating Corp. Nocona, Tx.	
N525JA	81 King Air 200	BB-873	Jetz Air Inc. Topeka, Ks.	N117CA
N525JK	67 King Air A90	LJ-305	Dynamic Aviation Group Inc. Bridgewater, Va.	N732NM
N525SK	83 King Air B200	BB-1148	ORRA Enterprises Inc. Wilmington, De.	N345MB
N525ZS	71 King Air 100	B-66	Baru Air SA. Panama City, Panama.	HP-1411
N526RR	67 King Air A90	LJ-263	HDH Aviation Corp. Poughkeepsie, NY.	N526BT
N527AF	70 Mitsubishi MU-2G	527	Air 1st Aviation Companies Inc. Aiken, SC.	VH-MNU

Reg	Yr Type	c/n	Owner/Operator	Prev Regn
N527MA	01 PA-46-500TP Meridian	4697127	David Smith, Wadsworth, Oh.	
N527PB	03 Pilatus PC-12/45	527	Special Exploration Co. Stillwater, Ok.	HB-FSC
N527TS	00 TBM 700B	184	GTS Enterprises Inc. Canton, Ga.	
N528AF	70 Mitsubishi MU-2G	528	Air 1st Aviation Companies Inc. Aiken, SC.	VH-UZB
N528AM	85 King Air 300	FA-59	Sause Brothers Ocean Towing Co. Coos Bay, Or.	N7233U
N528DS	81 PA-42 Cheyenne III	8001012	Danny Ray Smith, Tuscaloosa, Al.	N25LA
N528EJ	03 Pilatus PC-12/45	528	EJ Leasing LLC. Fargo, ND.	HB-FSD
N528WG	76 King Air 200	BB-151	Tigress Air III LLC/ECFS Inc. Easton, Md.	N98CM
N529NA	83 King Air B200	BB-1091	NASA Langley Research Center, Hampton, Va.	N9NA
N529PM	01 PA-46-500TP Meridian	4697029	BGM Inc. Ranchos De Ta. NM.	
N529PS	03 Pilatus PC-12/45	529	Century Aircraft LLC. Wilmington, De.	N529PB
N530CH	92 King Air C90B	LJ-1322	UNC Medical Air Inc. Chapel Hill, NC.	N500QT
N530HP	01 PA-46-500TP Meridian	4697101	Mugsy Aviation Inc. Dover, De.	
N530WC	03 Pilatus PC-12/45	530	Hawkins Aviation LLC. Boise, Id.	HB-FSK
N531CB	83 King Air B100	BE-133	Big River Aviation LLC/Wood & Associates, Bonne Terre, Mo.	N531CM
N531CS	72 King Air C90	LJ-549	Staffmed Aviation LLC. Greensboro, NC.	N600DJ
N531GK	77 Rockwell 690B	11394	Astur Air Corp. Sarasota, Fl.	LV-MAU
N531MB	85 King Air 300	FA-69	Morgan Executive Services Inc. Garden City, Ga.	N300TB
N531MC	84 PA-42 Cheyenne 400LS	5527007	MS Management Services Inc. Hartford, Ct.	N400SL
N533DM	74 Mitsubishi MU-2N	652SA	Turbine Aircraft Marketing Inc. San Angelo, Tx.	N533MA
N533M	81 Conquest II	441-0222	Terra Diamond Industrial Inc. Salt Lake City, Ut.	N500GM
N533P	87 King Air B200	BB-1278	C W Parker Aviation LLC. Pinehurst, NC.	D-IAIR
N533PC	03 Pilatus PC-12/45	533	MG Aviation Inc. Dover, De.	HB-FSG
N534M	98 Beech 1900D	UE-333	Menard Inc. Eau Claire, Wi.	N23235
N535BB	04 Pilatus PC-12/45	596	Pilatus Business Aircraft Ltd. Jeffco Airport, Co.	
N535M	98 Beech 1900D	UE-332	Menard Inc. Eau Claire, Wi.	
N535MJ	04 Pilatus PC-12/45	535	Oxford Hill LLC. Westminster, Md.	HB-FSI
N535WM	75 Mitsubishi MU-2L	655	Bankair Inc. West Columbia, SC.	N535MA
N536BW	04 King Air 350	FL-432	Raytheon Aircraft Co. Wichita, Ks.	
N536M	98 Beech 1900D	UE-334	Menard Inc. Eau Claire, Wi.	
N537PC	04 Pilatus PC-12/45	537	Royce Leasing LLC. Indian Wells, Ca.	HB-F..
N538AM	86 King Air/Catpass 250	FA-107	Changer Inc. Greeneville, SC.	N538AS
N539DP	65 King Air 90	LJ-53	P & H Inc. Statesville, NC.	N818MS
N540CB	87 King Air 300	FA-135	Pepco Inc. Rocky Mount, NC.	HB-GHY
N540GA	98 King Air C90B	LJ-1557	State of Georgia DoT, Atlanta, Ga.	N557SA
N540GC	81 Conquest 1	425-0026	JoJo Aircraft LLC. Raleigh, NC.	N540GA
N540SP	73 King Air C-12C	BC-5	Baja Air Inc. California City, Ca.	73-22254
N540WJ	80 King Air F90	LA-54	HPG Management Inc. Santa Monica, Ca.	HK-2484
N541AA	82 King Air C90-1	LJ-1041	Platinum 23 Leasing Co. Fort Lauderdale, Fl.	PT-OVN
N541MM	80 King Air F90	LA-71	U I S Inc. Fairfield, Il.	N45WL
N541PB	04 Pilatus PC-12/45	541	Bureau of Immigration & Customs Enforcement, Washington, DC.	HB-FSO
N541SC	87 King Air 300	FA-138	King Air N541SC LLC. Los Banos, Ca.	N30757
N542KA	79 King Air 200	BB-542	WCAO Aviation/World Class Automotive Operations, Humble, Tx.	N978GA
N543GA	99 King Air C90B	LJ-1558	State of Georgia DoT, Atlanta, Ga.	
N543GC	81 Conquest 1	425-0101	Astec Industries Inc. Chattanooga, Tn.	N543GA
N543HC	00 King Air C90B	LJ-1620	Burk Royalty Co. Wichita Falls, Tx.	N3220E
N543PB	04 Pilatus PC-12/45	543	PC-12 LLC. Knoxville, Tn.	HB-FSQ
N543S	66 680T Turbo Commander	1556-14	Mark Lundell, Paradise Valley, Az.	
N544AF	71 Mitsubishi MU-2G	544	Air 1st Aviation Companies Inc. Aiken, SC.	VH-KOF
N544CB	81 MU-2 Marquise	1536SA	D & B Truck & Trailer Repair Services, Nashville, Tn.	N157GA
N544GA	82 Gulfstream 900	15015	State of Georgia DoT, Atlanta, Ga.	N27MW
N544PS	86 King Air 300	FA-90	PWS Air LLC. Portland, Or.	N1115
N544UP	83 SA-227AT Merlin 4C	AT-544	Ameriflight Inc. Burbank, Ca.	N68TA
N545C	01 King Air C90B	LJ-1654	TS Aviation Inc. Naples, Fl.	
N545LC	80 King Air 200	BB-339	Charlie Romeo LLC. Little Rock, Ar.	N339AJ
N546C	04 King Air C90B	LJ-1723	Raytheon Aircraft Co. Wichita, Ks.	
N546PB	04 Pilatus PC-12/45	546	Mountain State Equipment Leasing, Wodland Park, Co.	HB-FSL
N547AF	04 Pilatus PC-12/45	547	Alpha Flying Inc. Nashua, NH.	HB-FSS
N547GA	99 King Air C90B	LJ-1559	State of Georgia DoT, Atlanta, Ga.	
N547GC	81 Conquest 1	425-0084	Norton Packaging Inc. Hayward, Ca.	N547GA
N547TA	77 Mitsubishi MU-2P	364SA	Turbine Aircraft Holdings LLC. Dallas, Tx.	N749MA
N548GQ	70 681 Turbo Commander	6027	Stanley Perkins, San Diego, Ca.	N681AS
N548UP	83 SA-227AT Merlin 4C	AT-548	Ameriflight Inc. Burbank, Ca.	N548SA
N549BR	79 King Air C90	LJ-809	Kendzicky Aviation LLC. Whitmore Lake, Mi.	N922DT
N549GA	00 King Air C90B	LJ-1613	State of Georgia DoT, Atlanta, Ga.	N5013J

Reg	Yr Type	c/n	Owner/Operator	Prev Regn
☐ N550BE	73 SA-226T Merlin 3	T-224	Cowboy Aviation LLC. Longmont, Co.	N5307M
☐ N550MM	81 Cheyenne II-XL	8166017	Lima Alpha Corp. Allentown, Pa.	N2536Y
☐ N550SW	04 King Air C90B	LJ-1700	Chieftain LLC. Islamorada, Fl.	N923P
☐ N551JL	81 King Air 200	BB-788	Raymond Shefland, Bemidji, Mn.	
☐ N551TP	00 King Air 350	FL-303	Tecumseh Products Co. Tecumseh, Mi.	(N75WP)
☐ N552E	01 King Air C90B	LJ-1662	Amalgamated Stuff Inc. Needham, Ma.	(XA-...)
☐ N552TP	00 King Air 350	FL-281	Tecumseh Products Co. Tecumseh, Mi.	
☐ N552TT	83 King Air B200	BB-1159	Sunshine Airways of N O LLC. Metairie, La.	(D-IRUS)
☐ N553AM	81 Conquest II	441-0219	Anderson Merchandisers Inc. Amarillo, Tx.	N555WA
☐ N553CA	03 Pilatus PC-12/45	553	Pinnacle Jets LLC. Debary, Fl.	HB-FSV
☐ N554CF	73 King Air E90	LW-66	Viking Aviation LLC. Jonesboro, Ar.	(N106TB)
☐ N555AL	90 King Air C90A	LJ-1268	Tri Aviation Inc. Belle Vernon, Pa.	N525P
☐ N555AM	73 SA-226T Merlin 3	T-227	Edgewater Ventures LLC. Santa Monica, Ca.	N142NR
☐ N555AT	81 PA-31T Cheyenne 1	8104054	MARKAY Enterprises Ltd. Wilmington, De.	N818SW
☐ N555C	68 Mitsubishi MU-2F	129	ISD, Rivervalls, Mn.	N555S
☐ N555CK	76 King Air C90	LJ-677	CJS LLC. Gulfport, Ms.	N555WF
☐ N555DX	85 King Air 300	FA-65	Quest Diagnostics Inc. Reading, Pa.	N332CP
☐ N555EW	99 Pilatus PC-12/45	271	Safe Landings LLC. Billings, Mt.	HB-FSW
☐ N555FT	80 Conquest II	441-0124	S & J Operating Co. Wichita Falls, Tx.	N2G24N
☐ N555FW	77 King Air E90	LW-248	Justin Brands Inc. Fort Worth, Tx.	N9FC
☐ N555HJ*	94 King Air C90B	LJ-1378	HJS Transport LLC. Newark, De.	N3083K
☐ N555HP	95 TBM 700	108	STS Inc. Dover, De.	
☐ N555JJ	77 Conquest II	441-0004	R A Swick & Assocs Inc. Toledo, Oh.	N555JK
☐ N555MS	80 King Air C90	LJ-872	Mott Oil Inc. Bessemer, Al.	N6668U
☐ N555MT	77 Rockwell 690B	11418	Taylor Aircraft Holdings Inc. Short Hills, NJ.	N773CA
☐ N555PE	04 Pilatus PC-12/45	555	Lindbergh Jets Inc. Portland, Or.	HB-FSW
☐ N555PM	76 PA-31T Cheyenne II	7620028	Reflection Two LLC. Burlington, NC.	N531PT
☐ N555TP	82 Conquest 1	425-0110	Ian Air LLC. Troy, Mi.	N6851A
☐ N555TT	76 King Air E90	LW-170	Southeast Air Charters LLC. Alexandria, La.	N500TL
☐ N555VW	93 King Air C90B	LJ-1330	Victor Whiskey LLC. San Francisco, Ca.	N266F
☐ N555WQ	00 King Air 350	FL-287	Iron Eagle Inc. Fayetteville, Ar.	N555WF
☐ N555ZA	91 King Air 350	FL-48	Sunstream Air LLC. Portland, Or.	N309M
☐ N556BA	97 King Air B200	BB-1556	Home Air Inc/Home Place Inc. Gainesville, Ga.	YV-1031CP
☐ N556BR	89 PA-42 Cheyenne IIIA	5501040	Trec LLC & Castlebay LLC. Shrewsbury, Ma.	N925RM
☐ N556HL	04 Pilatus PC-12/45	556	HL Ventures LLC. Los Altos, Ca.	HB-FSX
☐ N556UP	83 SA-227AT Merlin 4C	AT-556	Ameriflight Inc. Burbank, Ca.	N3113B
☐ N557CA	04 TBM 700C	306	TBMCO Development LLC. Southern Shores, NC.	
☐ N557DF*	04 Pilatus PC-12/45	557	Gulf States Toyota Inc. Houston, Tx.	HB-FSR
☐ N557P	02 King Air C90B	LJ-1689	Atlantic Transportation Wilmington, Wilmington, NC.	
☐ N558AC	68 SA-26AT Merlin 2B	T26-144	Haynie Enterprises Inc. Reno, Nv.	N913DM
☐ N558AF	04 Pilatus PC-12/45	558	Alpha Flying Inc. Nashua, NH.	HB-FSY
☐ N559CA	01 TBM 700B	213	Fred Parsons, Alexandria, Va.	
☐ N559PB	04 Pilatus PC-12/45	559	Aviation Sales Inc. Englewood, Co.	HB-FSZ
☐ N560UP	83 SA-227AT Merlin 4C	AT-560	Ameriflight Inc. Burbank, Ca.	N3113A
☐ N561SS	79 King Air 200	BB-464	Harrisburg Jet Center Inc. New Cumberland, Pa.	N79SE
☐ N561ST	04 Pilatus PC-12/45	561	Cosmic Air Inc. Lakewood, Oh.	HB-FQA
☐ N561UP	83 SA-227AT Merlin 4C	AT-561	Ameriflight Inc. Burbank, Ca.	N3113F
☐ N562HP	03 PA-46-500TP Meridian	4697139	SC Aviation LLC. Wilmington, De.	
☐ N562NA	97 Pilatus PC-12	174	Native Air Services Inc. Mesa, Az.	N174PC
☐ N562PB	04 Pilatus PC-12/45	562	West Branch Air Services LLC. Alger, Mi.	HB-FQB
☐ N563MC	68 King Air B90	LJ-384	Cirrus Aircraft Shares Inc/Hamer Trading Inc. Williamsburg.	N736K
☐ N563TM	04 Pilatus PC-12/45	563	Trebro Manufacturing LLC. Billings, Mt.	HB-FQC
☐ N564AC	80 Conquest II	441-0147	Erickson Air Crane Inc. Central Point, Or.	N999BE
☐ N564CA	79 King Air B100	BE-58	Carver Aero Inc. Davenport, Ia.	N100P
☐ N565C	03 PA-46-500TP Meridian	4697173	Rio 42 Equipment LLC. Lubbock, Tx.	
☐ N565M	85 Beech 1900C	UB-43	Raytheon Aircraft Co. Wichita, Ks.	N34GT
☐ N566CA	67 King Air A90	LJ-184	RAA Enterprise Inc. Wilmington, De.	N858K
☐ N566TC	83 King Air B200	BB-1145	Pelican Aircraft Inc. Nassau, Bahamas.	C6-TTC
☐ N566UP	83 SA-227AT Merlin 4C	AT-566	Ameriflight Inc. Burbank, Ca.	N3113N
☐ N567FH	04 Pilatus PC-12/45	567	Island Air Inc. Kalispell, Mt.	HB-FQF
☐ N567GJ	74 King Air E90	LW-95	Clement Aviation Inc. Fort Dodge, Ia.	OY-CFO
☐ N567JD	82 King Air B200	BB-949	Appalachian Services Inc. Pikeville, Ky.	N61415
☐ N567R	73 Rockwell 690	11051	Irvin Marx Jr. Dallas, Tx.	N500R
☐ N567US	98 King Air B200	BB-1634	United Supermarkets of Oklahoma Inc. Altus, Ok.	N567PK
☐ N568K	81 King Air B100	BE-106	SRI General Partner LLC. Houston, Tx.	(N59SS)
Reg	Yr Type	c/n	Owner/Operator	Prev Regn

Reg	Yr	Type	c/n	Owner/Operator	Prev Regn
N568SA	99	King Air C90B	LJ-1568	RPJ Aircraft Investors LLC. Santa Monica, Ca.	
N569AF	04	Pilatus PC-12/45	569	Alpha Flying, Nashua, NH.	HB-FQG
N569GR	96	King Air C90B	LJ-1447	Osage Air LLC. Baton Rouge, La.	(N9690B)
N569SC	82	King Air B200	BB-1084	Swiss Colony Inc/SC Aviation Inc. Monroe, Wi.	N284KW
N569UP	83	SA-227AT Merlin 4C	AT-569	Ameriflight Inc. Burbank, Ca.	N31134
N571PC	04	Pilatus PC-12/45	571	SKA Consulting LLC. Westlake Village, Ca.	HB-FQI
N572P	94	King Air B200	BB-1483	Blue Sky Aviation, Waukesha, Wi.	XA-TFE
N572PC	04	Pilatus PC-12/45	572	Ridge Air LLC. Lincoln, Ne.	HB-FQJ
N573G	82	SA-227AT Merlin 4C	AT-446	Ameriflight Inc. Burbank, Ca.	N3008L
N573MA	69	Mitsubishi MU-2F	162	Bohlke International Airways Inc. St Croix, USVI.	N875Q
N573P*	95	King Air C90B	LJ-1413	Piedmont Hawthorne Aviation Inc. Winston-Salem, NC.	(N90KA)
N574P	99	King Air C90B	LJ-1548	Piedmont Hawthorne Aviation Inc. Winston-Salem, NC.	LV-ZPS
N575C	71	King Air C90	LJ-532	David Lilly, Alentown, Pa.	N57SC
N575CA	80	MU-2 Solitaire	425SA	Sea & Air Sales LLC. Orlando, Fl.	N111GP
N575PC	04	Pilatus PC-12/45	575	Groendyke Transport Inc. Enid, Ok.	HB-FQL
N576RG	04	Pilatus PC-12/45	576	Bob Air Acquisitions LLC. Concord, Ma.	HB-FQM
N577BF	04	Pilatus PC-12/45	577	Geoduck Aviation LLC. Seattle, Wa.	HB-FQN
N577D	70	King Air 100	B-22	Vintage Props & Jets Inc. New Smyrna Beach, Fl.	N577L
N577DC	67	King Air A90	LJ-308	Cosco Aviation Services, Crestview, Fl.	N970GA
N577PW	84	Conquest 1	425-0194	LA Aviation LLC. Cary, NC.	N12214
N578BM	79	King Air 200	BB-588	Faraway Enterprises Inc. Addison, Tx.	N132GA
N578DC	04	Pilatus PC-12/45	570	Nicholas Elliott & Jordan LLC. Tampa, Fl.	N570DC
N579MC	98	King Air 350	FL-230	Deer Horn Aviation LC. Midland, Tx.	N3059F
N579PS	70	King Air B90	LJ-496	Wheaton Evangelistic Association Inc.. Hamilton, Al.	N878K
N580AC	95	King Air C90B	LJ-1388	Anderson Columbia Co. Lake City, Fl.	N83KK
N580AF	73	Mitsubishi MU-2J	580	Intercontinental Jet Inc. Tulsa, Ok.	CP-2390
N580BK	82	King Air B200	BB-1000	John Newcombe Enterprises Inc. Blacksburg, Va.	N74RN
N580PA	82	King Air F90	LA-158	F-90 LLC. Durham, NC.	N122SC
N580RA	73	King Air C90	LJ-580	Kelley Aviation Inc. Deer Park, Il.	(F-GFYI)
N580S	79	King Air B100	BE-77	Bott Radio Network Inc. Gravois Mills, Mo.	N55US
N581B	84	King Air C90A	LJ-1170	J G Boswell Co. Burbank, Ca.	N4131S
N581PC	04	Pilatus PC-12/45	581	Fair Equipment LLC. Denver, Co.	HB-FQY
N581RJ	80	King Air F90	LA-14	BMW's Prosthetica & Orthotics LLC. Jackson, Ms.	N205BC
N582C	03	TBM 700C	274	J F Air Traffic Inc. Temple, Tx.	
N582DT	04	Pilatus PC-12/45	582	Bizplane LLC. Carolina Beach, NC.	HB-FQS
N582JF	74	SA-226AT Merlin 4A	AT-027	Foods USA/JGF Farms, Koeltzton, Mo.	N824MD
N582SE	04	PA-46-500TP Meridian	4697188	Will Snead, Dalhart, Tx.	
N583AT	99	King Air 350	FL-258	SCANA Services Inc. Columbia, SC.	N3258R
N584JV	04	Pilatus PC-12/45	584	Juniper Valley LLC. Salem, Or.	HB-FQS
N584PS	75	PA-31T Cheyenne II	7620008	Caribbean Eagle Inc. Miami, Fl.	C-FYTK
N585CE	85	King Air B200	BB-1194	Air Progress LLC. Overland Park, Ks.	HK-4297X
N585PA	81	Conquest 1	425-0047	Park Avenue Group Inc. Stuart, Fl.	5Y-KXU
N585PB	04	Pilatus PC-12/45	585	Pilatus Business Aircraft Ltd. Jeffco Airport, Mo.	HB-FQV
N585R	88	King Air C90A	LJ-1169	Baron Leasing Corp. Cresco, Pa.	N30844
N586BC	85	King Air B200	BB-1223	Blue Cross & Blue Shield, Chattanooga, Tn.	N7231M
N586DV	79	Rockwell 690B	11553	Commander LLC. Albuquerque, NM.	N27VG
N586PB	04	Pilatus PC-12/45	586	Pilatus Business Aircraft Ltd. Jeffco Airport, Mo.	HB-FQW
N586TC	75	King Air C90	LJ-653	Focus Enterprises Inc. Valparaiso, In.	N585TC
N586UC	83	King Air B200	BB-1118	PTS Aircraft Sales LLC. Canton, Oh.	N913PG
N587M	68	King Air B90	LJ-361	Jacquin Aviation Inc. Morris, Il.	N530M
N587PB	95	King Air C90B	LJ-1408	Air Montgomery Ltd. Leeds-Bradford, UK.	N749RN
N588KC	04	Pilatus PC-12/45	588	Pilatus Business Aircraft Ltd. Jeffco Airport, Mo.	HB-FRA
N588SA	99	King Air C90B	LJ-1588	Eagle Air Med Corp. Blanding, Ut.	
N588SD	01	King Air C90B	LJ-1663	Richard Zic/Sierra Delta LLC. Chicago, Il.	N5133W
N588XJ	98	King Air C90B	LJ-1530	Harmon Foods Inc. Jacksonville, Fl.	
N589AC	04	Pilatus PC-12/45	589	Pilatus Business Aircraft Ltd. Jeffco Airport, Co.	
N589H	91	P-180 Avanti	1010	Western Airways Inc. Sugar Land, Tx.	(N1JW)
N590GM	99	King Air C90B	LJ-1594	Scenic Aviation Inc. Blanding, Ut.	
N590SA	68	King Air B90	LJ-401	X-Press Charter Services Inc. Longview, Tx.	N500NA
N591AF	04	Pilatus PC-12/45	591	Alpha Flying Inc. Nashua, NH.	HB-F..
N592Q	85	Conquest II	441-0361	Kelley Air Inc. Burlington, Ma.	N592G
N593BJ	77	King Air 200	BB-297	H & O Aviation LLC. Wheeling, WV.	P2-IAH
N593DJ	77	King Air 200	BB-277	H & O Aviation LLC. Wheeling, WV.	N200AP
N593MA	92	King Air 350	FL-68	McCardell Properties Inc. Auburn Hills, Mi.	N877V
N593PC	04	Pilatus PC-12/45	593	Pilatus Business Aircraft Ltd. Jeffco Airport, Co.	HB-FRE
Reg	Yr	Type	c/n	Owner/Operator	Prev Regn

Reg	Yr Type	c/n	Owner/Operator	Prev Regn
N594WA	04 Pilatus PC-12/45	594	Pilatus Business Aircraft Ltd. Jeffco Airport, Co.	
N595RC	81 King Air C90	LJ-964	Granberry Supply Corp. Phoenix, Az.	(N501GS)
N595TM	90 King Air C90A	LJ-1255	Binder Corp. Wilmington, De.	N55495
N596CU	77 King Air C90	LJ-721	Image Air LLC. Elmira, NY.	N111AA
N597CH	04 Pilatus PC-12/45	597	Pilatus Business Aircraft Ltd. Jeffco Airport, Co.	
N597P	00 King Air C90B	LJ-1597	Flyby Aviation LLC. Wilmington, De.	LV-ZTP
N598AC	92 King Air 350	FL-78	Iowa Land & Buidling Co. Cedar Rapids, Ia.	N551ES
N598HC	04 Pilatus PC-12/45	598	Pilatus Business Aircraft Ltd. Jeffco Airport, Co.	
N599PB	04 Pilatus PC-12/45	599	Pilatus Business Aircraft Ltd. Jeffco Airport, Co.	
N599TR	65 Gulfstream 1	160	Aerial Films Inc. Sarasota, Fl.	(N965CJ)
N600AC	76 King Air E90	LW-185	N600AC LLC. Tucson, Az.	
N600BF	67 King Air A90	LJ-193	James Vecchio, Grand Prairie, Tx.	N600BW
N600BM	84 Gulfstream 840	11734	Butler Machinery Co. Fargo, ND.	N1931S
N600BS	81 Cheyenne II-XL	8166045	Aero Transport Propfessionals Inc. Hot Springs, Ar.	N9138Y
N600CB	91 King Air 350	FL-38	Basha's - Chapman Group, Chandler, Az.	N350SR
N600CM	83 Gulfstream 900	15020	City Aviation Services Inc. Detroit, Mi.	N102VF
N600CX	73 King Air E90	LW-43	Michael Miller & Associates Inc. Alexandria, Va.	D-INAC
N600DL	75 SA-226T Merlin 3A	T-252	A H A of Delaware Inc. Gulf Breeze, Fl	(D-IBIN)
N600DM	78 King Air 200	BB-414	Jack Adams Co. Olive Branch, Ms.	N5VG
N600FE	81 King Air C90	LJ-935	Richmor Aviation Inc. Hudson, NY.	N600FL
N600FL	99 King Air C90B	LJ-1540	TVPX Inc. Concord, Ma.	N2187J
N600KA	88 King Air 300	FA-143	Global Aviation LP. Cheyenne, Wy.	N300KA
N600MM	80 Gulfstream 980	95029	Bush Field Aircraft Co. Augusta, Ga.	(N700MM)
N600P	68 SA-26T Merlin 2A	T26-6	Bell Leasing Inc. Mesquite, Tx.	
N600PE	04 Pilatus PC-12/45	600	Pilatus Business Aircraft Ltd. Jeffco Airport. (500th PC-12)	
N600RL	01 King Air B200	BB-1800	RML Aircraft Services LLC. Wichita, Ks.	N314FW
N600WM	80 King Air F90	LA-75	Cam-Trans Inc. Wilmington, De.	N3686B
N600WS	78 Rockwell 690B	11435	Sunbelt Communications Co. Las Vegas, Nv.	N200M
N601BM	97 Pilatus PC-12	181	Butler Machinery Co. Fargo, ND.	HB-FSB
N601CF	75 King Air 200	BB-25	EPPS Air Service Inc. Atlanta, Ga.	N1555N
N601DM	79 King Air C90	LJ-825	R & L Air LLC. Eugene, Or.	N11LS
N601HT	00 Pilatus PC-12/45	337	CIGI Direct Insurance Services Inc. Salida, Co.	HB-FSJ
N601JT	80 SA-226T Merlin 3B	T-319	Day Star Aviation LLC. Aberdeen, SD.	N808LB
N601LM	72 King Air A100	B-116	Lloyd's Aviation LLC. Syracuse, NY.	N100GV
N601PC	76 King Air A100	B-225	Leavitt Group Wings LLC. Cedar City, Ut.	N723W
N601SD*	74 Mitsubishi MU-2J	610	Jefferson County Sheriff's Office, Beaumont, Tx.	N92ST
N601TA	66 King Air A90	LJ-120	Turbine Power Inc. Oklahoma City, Ok.	N601T
N601WT	82 Gulfstream 900	15016	Stuart Aviation Inc. Wilmington, De.	N950TJ
N602EB	79 King Air F90	LA-5	X95 LLC. NYC.	N90FD
N602MJ	02 King Air B200	BB-1801	Blue Bird Holdings Corp. Wilmington, De.	N5001Q
N603PA	68 King Air B90	LJ-403	Blue Water Aircraft Inc. Wilmington, De.	(N603RE)
N603TA	98 King Air B200	BB-1623	US Airports Air Charters Inc. Van Nuys, Ca.	(N250AJ)
N603WM	89 King Air 300	FA-198	White Mountain Holdings Insurance Group Ltd. Hanover, NH.	N16TB
N604DK	82 King Air F90	LA-193	Fresno Flight LLC. Fresno, Ca.	N193GM
N604RR	80 Conquest II	441-0140	Inversiones Leasing Plane 2004, Caracas, Venezuela.	C-GCTA
N604TA	99 King Air B200	BB-1680	Flight Options LLC. Cleveland, Oh.	
N604WP	04 Pilatus PC-12/45	604	Pilatus Business Aircraft Ltd. Jeffco Airport, Co.	
N605TA	00 King Air B200	BB-1708	Flight Options LLC. Cleveland, Oh,	
N605TQ	00 Pilatus PC-12/45	320	Tomcat Air LLP. Redington Beach, Fl.	N605TC
N606AJ	86 King Air B200	BB-1257	Aircraft Technical Service Inc. Van Nuys, Ca.	G-IJJB
N607DK	81 King Air F90	LA-140	Trinity Lighting Inc. Jonesboro, Ar.	N190GM
N607KW	82 King Air B200	BB-977	Nie Planes LLC. Boise, Id.	N733NM
N607MA	01 PA-46-500TP Meridian	4697107	D V Trading Inc. Boca Raton, Fl.	
N607TA	00 King Air B200	BB-1715	Flight Options LLC. Cleveland, Oh.	
N608JR	84 King Air B200	BB-1197	Rosfam Airplane Co. Birmingham, Mi.	N200LU
N609SA	00 King Air C90B	LJ-1609	Seven Rivers Inc. Carlsbad, NM.	
N609TA	00 King Air B200	BB-1725	Flight Options LLC. Cleveland, Oh.	
N610CA	80 MU-2 Marquise	788SA	Bankair Inc. West Columbia, SC.	N277MA
N610GH	94 Pilatus PC-12	103	Quality Leasing Inc. Fort Walton Beach, Fl.	HB-FOD
N610P	75 PA-31T Cheyenne II	7620002	Forrest Wood, Flippin, Ar.	N54977
N610TA	98 King Air B200	BB-1609	US Airports Air Charters Inc. Rochester, NY.	(N260AJ)
N611	82 Gulfstream 900	15018	Department of the Interior, Boise, Id.	N5886N
N611AY	73 King Air C90	LJ-601	Frami Corp. Wilmington, De.	N99CD
N611CF	89 King Air C90A	LJ-1198	James Kirvida, Osceola, Wi.	N486JD
N611DD	79 King Air C90	LJ-806	DashDale Aviation LLC. Fort Dodge, Ia.	N105CG

Reg	Yr Type	c/n	Owner/Operator	Prev Regn

Reg	Yr	Type	c/n	Owner/Operator	Prev Regn
N611ND	94	King Air A90	LM-11	K & K Aircraft Inc. Bridgewater, Va.	(N49K)
N611R	77	King Air E90	LW-244	Zim Air LLC. Okoboji, Ia.	OY-ASU
N611RR	80	PA-31T Cheyenne 1	8004006	Versa Air III LLC. Racine, Wi.	(N611RP)
N611TA	00	King Air B200	BB-1730	Flight Options LLC. Cleveland, Oh.	
N612DT	60	Gulfstream 1	52	Mission Air Services LLC. San Antonio, Tx.	(N18TZ)
N612SA	76	King Air C-12C	BC-29	Stanford & Associates Inc. Fredricksburg, Va.	(N42J)
N612TA	00	King Air B200	BB-1735	Flight Options LLC. Cleveland, Oh.	
N613BR	65	King Air 90	LJ-9	Skydive Monroe, Monroe, Ga.	N649MC
N613CS	80	King Air 200	BB-613	AvFuel Corp. Ann Arbor, Mi.	N2TX
N613HC	77	PA-31T Cheyenne II	7720053	Cross Island Cruising Inc. Dover, De.	(N779SW)
N613NA	98	Pilatus PC-12/45	197	Native Air Services Inc. Mesa, Az.	N197PC
N613RF	84	King Air C90A	LJ-1068	RHF Interests Inc. Shreveport, La.	N666PC
N613TA	97	King Air B200	BB-1581	Townley Manufacturing Co. Candler, Fl.	N12MY
N614ML	92	King Air 350	FL-84	Oliver Aviation Inc/Love Box Co. Wichita, Ks.	N8084J
N614SA	00	King Air C90B	LJ-1614	Global Air Support LLC. Penrose, Co.	
N615AA	67	King Air A90	LJ-298	McGee Industries LLC. Ridgecrest, Ca.	N788W
N615C	59	Gulfstream 1	16	Erin Miel Inc .Las Vegas, Nv.	N202HA
N615DP	76	Rockwell 690A	11317	HSFCA Ltd. Quincy, Il.	N615
N615SB	78	Rockwell 690B	11457	Sair LLC. Indianapolis, In.	N691CP
N615TA	01	King Air B200	BB-1745	Flight Options LLC. Cleveland, Oh.	
N616CG	81	Conquest 1	425-0087	MidAir Pacific LLC. Eugene, Or.	N616MG
N616GB	81	King Air 200	BB-752	Business Aviation Services, Sioux Falls, SD	N300QW
N616PS	80	SA-226T Merlin 3B	T-316	Custom Destination Charters Inc. St Petersburg, Fl.	N51DA
N616TA	01	King Air B200	BB-1749	Flight Options LLC. Cleveland, Oh.	
N617BB	70	Mitsubishi MU-2G	522	HDL Research Lab Inc. Brenham, Tx.	N147MA
N617DW	80	PA-31T Cheyenne 1	8004042	Abraham Melawer, Houston, Tx.	(N612AM)
N617KM	85	King Air C90A	LJ-1095	Refrigeration Supplies Distributor, Monterey Park, Ca.	N850CE
N617MM	99	King Air C90B	LJ-1587	Centerville Aviation LLC. Kettering, Oh.	
N617TA	01	King Air B200	BB-1751	Flight Options LLC. Cleveland, Oh.	
N618	90	King Air B200	BB-1378	U S Department of the Interior, Boise, Id.	N5637Y
N618RD	78	King Air E90	LW-301	R D Baron Inc. Port Washington, NY.	N550P
N618SW	81	Cheyenne II-XL	8166036	Cheyenne LLC. Allegheny County, Pa.	
N618TA	01	King Air B200	BB-1754	Flight Options LLC. Cleveland, Oh.	
N619JB	81	PA-42 Cheyenne III	8001011	Win Win Aviation LLC. Newark, De.	N795KW
N619TA	01	King Air B200	BB-1758	Flight Options LLC. Cleveland, Oh.	
N620DB	79	PA-31T Cheyenne II	7920055	ALCO Plane LLC. Dover, De.	N23407
N620WE	78	King Air C90	LJ-743	W H Ebert Corp. San Jose, Ca.	N161AC
N621CG*	74	Mitsubishi MU-2J	631	Heartland Aviation LLC. Mount Juliet, Tn.	N629TM
N621TA	73	Mitsubishi MU-2J	605	Metro Enviromental Associates Inc. Washington, Ga.	XB-ARE
N621TB	68	King Air B90	LJ-334	Atlanta Northside Aviation Inc. Kennesaw, Ga.	N722TS
N621TD	85	King Air C90A	LJ-1123	JHF Aircraft Holdings LLC. Memphis, Tx.	N917BH
N622AJ	83	Cheyenne II-XL	8166071	World Wide Aviation Inc . Wilmington, De.	N8EE
N622BB	84	PA-31T Cheyenne 1A	1104012	Wells Dairy Inc. Le Mars, Ia.	N284BB
N622KM	79	King Air 200	BB-491	K & M Equipment Co. Van Nuys, Ca.	N622DC
N622MM	83	Conquest 1	425-0187	Santa Fe Investments Inc. Wilmington, De.	(N425KA)
N623AW	67	King Air A90	LJ-282	HDH Aviation Corp. Poughkeepsie, NY.	N853K
N623BB	67	King Air A90	LJ-277	His Ministries International Inc. Panama City, Fl.	N228CF
N623R	66	King Air A90	LJ-173	JGM Air LLC. Destin, Fl.	XB-SFS
N623VP	81	King Air 200	BB-769	HKR&W LLC. Hilton Head Island, SC.	N769AJ
N624CB	80	Conquest II	441-0166	Industrials International Inc. St Thomas, USVI.	I-GEFI
N625GA	04	King Air B200	BB-1884	Raytheon Aircraft Co. Wichita, Ks.	
N625N	91	King Air B200	BB-1394	Sterling Jet Charters LLC. Fort Myers, Fl.	N625W
N626SA	71	King Air 100	B-78	Fly Conversions LLC. Marion, Wi.	RP-C282
N626TA	02	King Air B200	BB-1786	Don Fanetti Trucking, Franklin, Wi.	(N716GS)
N627FB	81	King Air B200	BB-928	Fletcher Bright Co/FB Aire Inc. Chattanooga, Tn.	N553HC
N627PC	84	PA-42 Cheyenne IIIA	5501010	Reinbeck Motors Co. Reinbeck, Ia.	N627KW
N628DS	82	King Air B200	BB-1013	Friehe Farms, Moses Lake, Wa.	N623DS
N629DF	04	Pilatus PC-12/45	590	Delta Fox II LLC. Holland, Mi.	
N629GT	01	P-180 Avanti	1048	First National Bank of Florida, Naples, Fl.	N74BJ
N629JG	03	King Air C90B	LJ-1688	Basche Properties II LLC. Cleveland, Oh.	
N629MC	03	Pilatus PC-12/45	516	T & M Enterprises LP. Portland, Or.	HB-FRS
N629MU	74	Mitsubishi MU-2J	629	Global Aircraft Industries of AZ LLC. Virginia, RSA.	ZS-NDM
N629SC	72	King Air A100	B-137	Big Blue Inc. Fort Lauderdale, Fl.	PT-OVQ
N629SK	01	Pilatus PC-12/45	413	Karol Atmosfera LLC. Boston, Ma.	N413AF
N629TG	82	SA-227AT Merlin 4C	AT-427	Thomas Ganley, Brecksville, Oh.	N66GA
Reg	Yr	Type	c/n	Owner/Operator	Prev Regn

Reg	Yr Type	c/n	Owner/Operator	Prev Regn
❏ N630DB	76 King Air 200	BB-187	Medpeak LLC. Palm Coast, Fl.	
❏ N630HA	74 Mitsubishi MU-2J	630	Turbine Aircraft Marketing Inc. San Angelo, Tx.	OY-BIS
❏ N630MW	81 Cheyenne II-XL	8166011	Atwell Investments LC. Adel, Ia.	N218SW
❏ N631BA*	67 Mitsubishi MU-2B	031	Bill Austin Aircraft & Yacht Sales, Sparta, Tn.	N222GS
❏ N631ME	04 King Air 350	FL-430	Raytheon Aircraft Co. Wichita, Ks.	
❏ N631PC	81 PA-42 Cheyenne III	8001060	National Group Protection Inc. Charlottesville, Va.	(N623KW)
❏ N632DS	88 King Air 300	FA-141	Rockwell-Ditzler Assocs Inc. Houston, Tx.	N3080F
❏ N632RR	81 King Air F90	LA-111	Dunmore Homes LLC. Roseville, Ca.	HB-GHO
❏ N633RB	01 PA-46-500TP Meridian	4697061	Gardner Aircraft Sales Inc. Daytona Beach, Fl.	
❏ N633ST	73 SA-226T Merlin 3	T-237	Bluebird Properties Inc. Sullivan, Mo.	C-FCPH
❏ N633WC	81 PA-31T Cheyenne 1	8104036	Werner Construction Co. Hastings, NE.	N75BR
❏ N634B	73 King Air C-12C	BC-19	Turbo Air Inc. Boise, Id.	73-22268
❏ N634TT	86 King Air B200	BB-1252	Ted Taylor, Birmingham, Al.	N125GA
❏ N635AF	77 King Air C90	LJ-736	Airhole LLC. Beaumont, Tx.	N19HT
❏ N635B	77 King Air C-12C	BC-49	Jet Sales & Services Inc. Sarasota, Fl.	77-22938
❏ N635SF	03 King Air B200	BB-1847	Sanderson Farms Inc. Laurel, Ms.	N61847
❏ N636B	77 King Air C-12C	BC-61	Robert Kline, Reading, Pa.	77-22950
❏ N636CR	81 PA-31T Cheyenne II	8120014	Camilo H Rodriguez P. Panama City, Panama.	(N322JD)
❏ N636GW	80 King Air E90	LW-332	Iowa Rotocast Plastics Inc. Decorah, Ia.	N636JM
❏ N636SP	77 SA-226T Merlin 3A	T-285	BLN Engineering LLC. Wilmington, De.	N6SP
❏ N637B	78 King Air C-12C	BC-62	Jet Sales & Services Inc. Sarasota, Fl.	78-23126
❏ N637WG	74 Mitsubishi MU-2J	637	Bankair Inc. West Columbia, SC.	N951MS
❏ N637WM	01 King Air B200	BB-1768	Wyoming Machinery Co. Casper, Wy.	N4268V
❏ N638D	68 King Air B90	LJ-424	Turbine Power Inc. Bridgewater, Va.	
❏ N639B	78 King Air C-12C	BC-67	McIntosh Enterprises LLC. Boise, Id.	78-23131
❏ N640MA	73 Mitsubishi MU-2J	590	Intercontinental Jet Inc. Tulsa, Ok.	N54US
❏ N640MW	Beech 1900C-1	UC-1	Marvin Lumber & Cedar Co. Warroad, Mn.	N3114B
❏ N641TS	80 King Air 200	BB-641	D K & L LLC. Indianapolis, In.	N641TC
❏ N642DH	68 King Air B90	LJ-420	Diamond Airways Inc. Columbus, Oh.	N759KX
❏ N642JL	85 King Air 300	FA-30	OMCO Equipment LLC/Ohio Molding Corp. Wickliffe, Oh.	N70CR
❏ N642TD	78 King Air C90	LJ-766	Southwest Financial Inc. Garden City, Ks.	N44VC
❏ N642TF	78 King Air 200	BB-363	Chardan Aero Corp. Stuart, Fl.	N96GA
❏ N643EA	01 King Air C90B	LJ-1643	BPPM Inc. Dover, De.	
❏ N643JW	78 Rockwell 690B	11492	KCK Services LLC/Key City Leasing Co. Sioux City, Ia.	C-FACC
❏ N644EM	81 MU-2 Marquise	1534SA	Earle Martin, Houston, Tx.	N667AM
❏ N644SP	76 King Air C90	LJ-696	Monroe Air Center LLC. Monroe, La.	(N525PC)
❏ N646DR	80 King Air 200	BB-646	TEAM Industries Inc/Anoka Air Charter, Minneapolis.	N646BM
❏ N647JM	83 King Air B200	BB-1147	Sherrohil LLC. Dover, De.	N6627V
❏ N648JG	04 King Air C90	LJ-1706	JEG Diversified Healthcare Inc. Van Nuys, Ca.	N5066N
❏ N649JC	80 King Air 200	BB-649	IT & Associates Inc. Oklahoma City, Ok.	N777JE
❏ N650DM*	92 TBM 700	85	DVDMLS Inc. Moline, Il.	PH-TBD
❏ N650JT	79 King Air B100	BE-60	Varsity Carpet Service/Professsional Aviation Inc.Dalton, Ga	(N650UT)
❏ N650RS	80 PA-31T Cheyenne II	8020071	Altitude Inc. Lakewood, Oh.	(N658RS)
❏ N652L	80 King Air E90	LW-329	Legacy Homes LLC. Montgomery, Al.	F-GJBG
❏ N653PC	94 Dornier 328-100	3027	Prince Transportation Inc. Holland, Mi.	D-CDHM
❏ N653TB	80 King Air 200	BB-586	TAB Aircraft Leasing LLC. Atlanta, Ga.	ZS-MGG
❏ N654BA	82 King Air B200C	BL-54	Department of the Air Force, McCarran, Nv.	N6563C
❏ N654C	65 King Air 90	LJ-12	Turbine Power Inc. Bridgewater, Va.	N90MR
❏ N654JC	01 Pilatus PC-12/45	437	Jeticopter LLC. Mountain View, Ca.	HB-FRZ
❏ N655BA	80 King Air 200	BB-655	Western Airways Inc. Sugar Land, Tx.	G-OGAT
❏ N655JG	92 King Air B200	BB-1440	Illinois Valley Paving Co. Winchester, Il.	N8046N
❏ N655PC	80 Gulfstream 980	95015	Arvest Bank Group Inc. Bentonville, Ar.	N9768S
❏ N655SC	99 King Air 350	FL-239	Standridge Color Corp. Social Circle, Ga.	N455SF
❏ N656BA	01 King Air C90B	LJ-1656	Hogan Aircraft LLC. Ruston, La.	
❏ N657PP	03 King Air 350	FL-375	Peterson Tractor Co/Peterson Cat Inc. San Leandro, Ca.	N6175F
❏ N659PC	69 Gulfstream 1	196	Conquest Air LLC. Sewickley, Pa.	N134PA
❏ N660GW	75 King Air C90	LJ-673	Clement Aviation Inc. Fort Dodge, Ia.	N660JM
❏ N660M	74 King Air 200	BB-10	Quality Concepts LLC. Bourbonnais, Il.	(N980DB)
❏ N660MW	93 King Air/Catpass 250	BB-1428	Marvin Lumber & Cedar Co. Warroad, Mn.	N8265V
❏ N660PB	90 King Air B200	BB-1364	Pter Stent & William Wilson III, Menlo Park, Ca.	N5510Y
❏ N661BA	83 King Air B200C	BL-61	Department of the Air Force, McCarran, Nv.	N6564C
❏ N661DP	80 MU-2 Marquise	798SA	Great River Finance Co. La Grange, Mo.	VH-MIU
❏ N661DW	92 TBM 700	61	Danwell Corp. Springfield, Il.	
❏ N661TC	81 PA-31T Cheyenne II	8120022	Blue Goose Aviation LLC. Roseburg, Or.	N127AT
❏ N661WP	04 Pilatus PC-12/45	578	Electro-Methods Holdings LLC. Windsor, Ct.	HB-FQO
Reg	Yr Type	c/n	Owner/Operator	Prev Regn

Reg	Yr Type	c/n	Owner/Operator	Prev Regn
☐ N662BA	83 King Air B200C	BL-62	Department of the Air Force, McCarran, Nv.	N6566C
☐ N662JS	76 King Air E90	LW-176	Hughes Flying Service Inc. Miami, Fl.	N70EA
☐ N665JK	75 King Air C90	LJ-665	Primecare Medical Inc. Penbrook, Pa.	EC-COK
☐ N665TM	81 Conquest II	441-0215	M Curve Aviation, Effingham, Il.	ZS-KPB
☐ N666DC	73 King Air E90	LW-44	Blue Ash Industrial Supply Co. Cincinnati, Oh.	N166A
☐ N666GT	04 Pilatus PC-12/45	573	3976 Bellinger Lane, Medford, OR 97501.	HB-FQK
☐ N666MN	66 680T Turbo Commander	1568-24	Regional Missouri Bank, Marceline, Mo.	N2637M
☐ N666SP	74 Mitsubishi MU-2K	286	MX Aviation LLC/Marine Oil Services of New York LLC. Va.	(N66AW)
☐ N666ZT	79 King Air E90	LW-315	MAG Management Corp. Akron, Oh.	HB-GGU
☐ N667CC	03 King Air B200	BB-1827	WNC Aviation Rentals LLC. Asheville, NC.	N50807
☐ N667RB	03 Pilatus PC-12/45	484	Rye Aviation Services Inc. Rye Beach, NH.	N484AF
☐ N668K	01 King Air 350	FL-329	Aviaserv LLC/FLRT Inc. Van Nuys, Ca.	N350KA
☐ N668WJ	75 King Air C90	LJ-668	World Jet of Delaware Inc. Fort Lauderdale, Fl.	F-OGOX
☐ N669HS	69 SA-26AT Merlin 2B	T26-161	Canamera Holdings LLC. Las Vegas, Nv.	N59TP
☐ N669SP	68 SA-26AT Merlin 2B	T26-101	Edgewater Ventures LLC. Santa Monica, Ca.	N11PM
☐ N669WB	80 PA-31T Cheyenne 1	8004018	Poquito Valley Partnership, Prescott Valley, Az.	N32JP
☐ N670AT	69 King Air B90	LJ-481	RS Air LLC. West Palm Beach, Fl.	G-BVRS
☐ N670TA	98 King Air B200	BB-1631	Flight Options LLC. Cleveland, Oh.	N670DF
☐ N671LL	66 King Air A90	LJ-148	Sky King Charters LLC. Cincinnati, Oh.	N671L
☐ N675BC	97 King Air 350	FL-178	Prewitt Leasing Inc. Bedford, Tx.	N675PC
☐ N675PC	02 King Air 350	FL-352	Pacific Coast Jet Charter Inc. Rancho Cordova, Ca.	N5152H
☐ N676DM	71 681B Turbo Commander	6048	Frank Harrison Haynes, Gainesville, Ga.	N911JM
☐ N676J	76 King Air E90	LW-179	Seven Bar Flying Service Inc. Albuquerque, NM.	N211MH
☐ N677J	78 King Air E90	LW-294	RJA Corp-Richard J Andrews, Houston, Tx.	N9DF
☐ N677JE	00 King Air B200	BB-1702	Air Plane LLC. Huntingburg, In.	N581FM
☐ N677KA	67 680V Turbo Commander	1677-60	H F Payne Construction Co. Monrovia, Md.	N2UL
☐ N677WA	75 Rockwell 690A	11243	Mediplane Inc. Santa Rosa, Ca.	(N911RX)
☐ N678SS	82 King Air B200	BB-1021	Southern Systems Inc. Memphis, Tn.	N195KA
☐ N679BK	76 Mitsubishi MU-2L	679	Intercontinental Jet Inc. Tulsa, Ok.	C-FYBN
☐ N680AS	95 BAe Jetstream 41	41030	AlliedSignal Inc. Morristown, NJ.	N410JA
☐ N680CA	74 Mitsubishi MU-2J	642	Air 1st Aviation Companies Inc. Aiken, SC.	N492MA
☐ N680FS	67 680V Turbo Commander	1687-67	Commander Aviation LLC/Witwer Construction, Fort Wayne, In.	N42TF
☐ N680JD	68 680W Turbo Commander	1792-22	Michael Knudsen, Anaheim, Ca.	N43WL
☐ N680KM	68 680W Turbo Commander	1812-29	Great American Financial Services, Portland, Or.	N500NR
☐ N681DC	70 681 Turbo Commander	6036	Darrell Clendenen, Corona, Ca.	RP-C1977
☐ N681EV	90 King Air C90A	LJ-1228	Timber Air LLC. Rocky Mount, Va.	N190JS
☐ N682C	02 PA-46-500TP Meridian	4697130	South Shore Aviation Partners LLC. Wilmington, De.	
☐ N682DR	76 King Air 200	BB-130	Air Services Inc. Traverse City, Mi.	N323MB
☐ N682KA	76 King Air C90	LJ-682	Pezold Air Charters LLC. Columbus, Ga.	N3980D
☐ N683GW	02 King Air C90B	LJ-1683	Pajaros LLC/Gowan Co. Yuma, Az.	N6183A
☐ N685BC	02 King Air 350	FL-355	Columbus Bank & Trust Co/WCB Air LLC. Columbus, Ga.	N6055H
☐ N686AC	82 King Air B100	BE-127	The G W Van Keppel Co. Kansas City, Ks.	N666AC
☐ N686GW	84 King Air C90A	LJ-1082	ABC AirGroup LLC/Concorde Companies, Tampa, Fl.	N666GW
☐ N687AE	79 Conquest II	441-0087	AirEvac Services Inc. Lafayette, La.	N441DW
☐ N687HB	76 Mitsubishi MU-2L	687	Golden Eagle Aviation Inc. Portsmouth, Va.	XB-ARF
☐ N687L	66 680V Turbo Commander	1560-17	RAF Air Cargo Inc. Wilmington, De.	N419S
☐ N688JB	90 King Air 350	FL-18	Barnett Investments Inc. LaVerne, Ca.	HK-3988X
☐ N688LL	98 King Air B200	BB-1617	Pulaski Services Inc. Little Rock, Ar.	
☐ N688RA	76 Mitsubishi MU-2L	688	Royal Air Freight Inc. Waterford, Mi.	N688MA
☐ N689AE	83 Conquest II	441-0281	AirEvac Services Inc. Lafayette, La.	N6832C
☐ N689JV	78 King Air 200	BB-338	Richmor Aviation Inc. Hudson, NY.	VR-BGN
☐ N689EB	76 King Air C90	LJ-689	Elliott Aviation Flight Services Inc. Des Moines, la.	(N45FE)
☐ N690AC	79 Rockwell 690B	11527	Gisler Management Inc. Bend, Or.	N81765
☐ N690AH	73 Rockwell 690A	11119	Handmade Homes Inc. Enid, Ok.	XA-RTQ
☐ N690AR	74 Rockwell 690A	11155	Reno Group Leasing LLC. Indianapolis, In.	N155TA
☐ N690AS	76 Rockwell 690A	11277	Pickett LLC. Huntsville, Al.	(N690TA)
☐ N690AT	74 Rockwell 690A	11202	Central Air Southwest, Kansas City, Mo.	N600PB
☐ N690AX	77 Rockwell 690B	11384	Eagle Creek Aviation Services Inc. Indianapolis, In.	N690KC
☐ N690BA	78 Rockwell 690B	11513	RAB Aviation Inc. Mantua, Oh.	(N690KG)
☐ N690BH	77 Rockwell 690B	11361	Bradley Howard, Van Nuys, Ca.	N100AM
☐ N690BK	78 Rockwell 690B	11508	Symen Van der Linden LLC. Chandler, Az.	N307CL
☐ N690BM	76 Rockwell 690A	11311	William Latham, Haymarket, Va.	N57118
☐ N690CB	78 Rockwell 690B	11477	Byerly Aviation Inc. Peoria, Il.	C-FHNL
☐ N690CC	77 Rockwell 690B	11379	Edgar Cruft, Tijeras, NM.	
☐ N690CE	73 Rockwell 690A	11103	Dynamic Engineering Inc. Fort Smith, Ar.	N690MF
Reg	Yr Type	c/n	Owner/Operator	Prev Regn

Reg	Yr Type	c/n	Owner/Operator	Prev Regn
☐ N690CF	74 Rockwell 690A	11168	Contract Freighters Inc. Joplin, Mo.	N690AZ
☐ N690CH	79 Rockwell 690B	11542	Blue Skies Air LLC. Portland, Or.	N76DT
☐ N690CP	78 Rockwell 690B	11451	Three Sisters Corp. Monroeville, Pa.	N71MA
☐ N690DB	74 Rockwell 690A	11226	Martin Container Inc/Swift Transportation Co. Phoenix, Az.	N717AP
☐ N690DS	75 Rockwell 690A	11262	Title Financial Group, Blackfoot, Id.	N57104
☐ N690E	84 PA-42 Cheyenne IIIA	5501020	Teufel Nursery Inc. Hillsboro, Or.	(N700LT)
☐ N690EH	76 Rockwell 690A	11309	Surdex Corp. Chesterfield, Mo.	N2NQ
☐ N690EM	73 Rockwell 690A	11125	Saybrook III LLC. Toledo, Oh.	N690AE
☐ N690ES	77 Rockwell 690B	11388	William Rabb, Boulder, Co.	N532
☐ N690FD	77 Rockwell 690B	11393	Tennessee Jet Corp. Wilmington, De.	N699GN
☐ N690G	73 King Air E90	LW-34	Pepper Air LLC. Metairie, La.	(N387SC)
☐ N690GF	76 Rockwell 690B	11357	GJF Enterprises Inc. Daytona Beach, Fl.	N690GH
☐ N690GG	77 Rockwell 690B	11411	2141 Corp. Atlanta, Ga.	N95GR
☐ N690GK	72 Rockwell 690	11031	La Mansion de Sarita Inc/N690 LLP. Fort Worth, Tx.	N84DT
☐ N690GS	77 Rockwell 690A	11363	Semrau Aircraft Co. Jackson, Tn.	N690JB
☐ N690GZ	76 Rockwell 690A	11319	George Zimmermann, West Palm Beach, Fl.	N690AJ
☐ N690HB	74 Rockwell 690A	11205	J Brooks LLC. Louisville, Ky.	N9007
☐ N690HF	76 Rockwell 690A	11298	Mid-South Aircraft Sales, Clarksville, Ar.	(N80LE)
☐ N690HM	74 Rockwell 690A	11159	U S Aircraft Leasing Inc. Dover, De.	N2ES
☐ N690HS	78 Rockwell 090B	11431	M Morgan Holdings Inc. Wilmington, De.	N72RF
☐ N690HT	78 Rockwell 690B	11467	Extraordinaire Inc. Washington, DC.	N690PG
☐ N690JH	79 Rockwell 690B	11529	Extreme Auto & Marine Inc. Vienna, Oh.	N226BP
☐ N690JJ	74 Rockwell 690A	11171	Pacific Commerce Co. R Santa Margarita, Ca.	N690EM
☐ N690JK	78 Rockwell 690B	11480	IESI TX GP Corp. Fort Worth, Tx.	N81799
☐ N690JT	77 Rockwell 690B	11353	N31WD LLC. Seattle, Wa.	C-GHQG
☐ N690L	97 King Air B200	BB-1573	Air Logistics LLC. Lafayette, La.	N702TA
☐ N690LL	79 Rockwell 690B	11544	Flying Raven LLC. Wilsall, Mt.	N690BE
☐ N690LS	78 Rockwell 690B	11475	Office Management Systems Inc. Columbus, Ms.	N690CA
☐ N690MG	77 Rockwell 690B	11423	TM1 LLC. Fort Wayne, In.	N81674
☐ N690NA	77 Rockwell 690B	11359	Dove Air Inc. Hendersonville, NC.	XB-OCI
☐ N690PT	75 Rockwell 690A	11252	Bandana Trading Inc. San Luis Obispo, Ca.	(N690AR)
☐ N690RA	72 Rockwell 690	11010	R W Armstrong PC. Brownsville, Tx.	XA-RYF
☐ N690RC	76 Rockwell 690A	11310	Nightengale Aviation LLC. Beltsville, Md.	N331JA
☐ N690RD	78 Rockwell 690B	11350	DeJarnette Enterprises Inc. Lee's Summit, Mo.	HK-2051W
☐ N690RE	76 Rockwell 690A	11271	Byerly Aviation Inc. Peoria, Il.	N690RC
☐ N690RK	73 Rockwell 690A	11138	Surry Chemicals Aviation LLC. Mount Airy, NC.	N690EC
☐ N690RP	78 Rockwell 690B	11493	Andrew Foss, San Jose, Ca.	N1HR
☐ N690SC	83 King Air B200	BB-1139	Dan Craine, Port Arkansas, Tx.	N256BD
☐ N690SD	76 Rockwell 690A	11287	Sedgwick County, Wichita, Ks.	N777HE
☐ N690SG	74 Rockwell 690A	11146	Amber Aviation Inc. Beaver Creek, Oh.	F-OHJE
☐ N690SM	76 Rockwell 690A	11337	First Wing Inc. Carmel, In.	N1547A
☐ N690SS	79 Rockwell 690B	11550	Arkie Flies Inc. Orlando, Fl.	N9LV
☐ N690TC	77 Rockwell 690B	11385	TM1 LLC. Fort Wayne, In.	VH-EXT
☐ N690TD	76 Rockwell 690A	11307	Genesis Aircraft Marketing LLC. Bethany, Ok. (status ?).	(N46AZ)
☐ N690TH*	78 Rockwell 690B	11487	Atlanta Channel Inc. Panama City, Fl.	N690LH
☐ N690TP	82 Gulfstream 900	15001	Seybert Arcraft LLC. Indianapolis, In.	N711DW
☐ N690TR	72 Rockwell 690	11034	Career Aviation Sales Inc. Oakdale, Ca.	EC-EFS
☐ N690TW	85 PA-42 Cheyenne IIIA	5501026	Trans-West Inc. Denver, Co.	N31KF
☐ N690WC	72 Rockwell 690	11017	West Coast Airlines/Wadell Engineering Corp. Burlingame, Ca.	N101RQ
☐ N690WD	74 Rockwell 690A	11176	JHH Aircraft Inc. Lancaster, Ca.	LV-LMU
☐ N690WP	79 Rockwell 690B	11561	Bob Mitchell, Sallisaw, Ok.	N9196Q
☐ N690WS	74 Rockwell 690A	11194	Burelbach Industries Corp. Rickreall, Or.	N953HF
☐ N690XY	78 Rockwell 690B	11433	Just Plane Corp. Sioux City, Ia.	(N690BW)
☐ N691AS	90 King Air C90A	LJ-1240	HTBE LLC. Lake Oswego, Or.	N1565X
☐ N691PA	79 King Air C90A	11526	QT Aviation LLC. Duncan, Ok.	N64EZ
☐ N692M	77 King Air E90	LW-228	Morrow Aviation Inc. Ormond Beach, Fl.	N53BB
☐ N692T	79 Rockwell 690B	11555	Delta Oil Inc. Wilmington, De.	N150SP
☐ N692W	02 King Air C90B	LJ-1692	RyandAm Aviation LLC. Fairfield, Ca.	
☐ N693MA	03 TBM 700C	293	Muncie Aviation Co. Muncie, In.	
☐ N693VM	75 Rockwell 690A	11234	Bryan Medlock Jr. Dallas, Tx.	N698CE
☐ N694CT	03 King Air C90B	LJ-1694	Air 1 Aviation Services LLC. Baltimore, Md.	N90KA
☐ N695AB	81 Gulfstream 1000	96055	ASA Aircraft LLC. Framingham, Ma.	CP-2050
☐ N695AM	82 Gulfstream 1000	96007	Red Fox Leasing Inc. Louisville, Ky.	(N63361U)
☐ N695CT	85 Gulfstream 1000	96096	Challenge Tool & Manufacturing Inc. New Haven, In.	N695CT
☐ N695GG	82 Gulfstream 1000	96036	Golden Giant Inc. Kenton, Oh.	N20GT
Reg	*Yr Type*	*c/n*	*Owner/Operator*	*Prev Regn*

Reg	Yr	Type	c/n	Owner/Operator	Prev Regn
N695GH	85	Gulfstream 1000	96078	Green Aircraft Leasing Inc. Peoria, Il.	N85NM
N695GJ	82	Gulfstream 1000	96011	La Mansion Aviation Inc. Fort Worth, Tx.	N5422P
N695HT	82	Gulfstream 1000	96038	Farsight Technologies Inc. Las Vegas, Nv.	N707TS
N695JJ	76	King Air C90	LJ-695	Butler Aviation Inc. Houma, La.	N93BB
N695MG	85	Gulfstream 1000B	96204	Goelst Aviation LLC. Winston-Salem, NC.	N30059
N695NC	82	Gulfstream 1000	96032	251 Finance Inc. Coral Springs, Fl.	VH-GAB
N695PC	00	Pilatus PC-12/45	305	ESPD LLC. Cornelius, NC.	HB-FQS
N695RC	85	Gulfstream 1000	96087	Rialto Concrete Products Inc. Conroe, Tx.	N722SG
N696JB	70	King Air 100	B-26	Dolph Briscoe Jr. Uvalde, Tx.	N610KR
N696RA	81	King Air F90	LA-87	421 Corp. Denham Springs, La.	N200SC
N697MP	72	King Air C90	LJ-554	Dove Air Inc. Hendersonville, NC.	N697MB
N697P	85	King Air B200	BB-1217	Petro Star Inc. Anchorage, Ak.	(N204GR)
N698GN	66	680V Turbo Commander	1589-40	Michael Franzblau, Los Angeles, Ca.	N699GN
N698P	98	King Air B200	BB-1621	Schuett Enterprises Inc. Fort Lauderdale, Fl.	
N699KM	75	SA-226T Merlin 3A	T-256	American Aviation Inc. Brooksville, Fl.	N311GM
N699MW	85	King Air 300	FA-73	M A Inc. Oshkosh, Wi.	N408G
N699RK*	79	SA-226T Merlin 3B	T-300	K'Berger Inc. Del Rio, Tx.	N193CS
N699SB	76	Rockwell 690A	11280	Bryant Racing Inc. Anaheim, Ca.	(N53AR)
N700AD	02	TBM 700C	250	TBM 700-234 Aircraft Partners LLC. Hinsdale, NH.	
N700AN	98	TBM 700	132	Gerald Mercer, Columbus, Oh.	F-WWRO
N700AQ	02	TBM 700C	252	Hunter Corp. Santa Barbara, Ca.	
N700AT	73	King Air A100	B-136	Tonka Bay Transport LLC. Tonka Bay, Mn.	(N45PL)
N700AU	01	TBM 700B	185	SOCATA Aircraft, Pemboke Pines, Fl.	N700AJ
N700AZ	02	TBM 700C	254	Frank Air Leasing LLC. Springfield, Pa.	
N700BA	80	King Air B100	BE-84	Byerly Aviation Inc. Peoria, Il.	N300TN
N700BD	04	TBM 700C	320	SOCATA Aircraft, Pembroke Pines, Fl.	
N700BE	79	King Air 200	BB-528	Scope Leasing Inc. Columbus, Oh.	N203BC
N700BF	92	TBM 700	53	Den Enterprises LLC. Carefree, Az.	
N700BK	02	TBM 700C	262	M H Ventures LLC. Wilmington, De.	
N700BN	01	TBM 700B	203	William Dixon Jr. Kentfield, Ca.	
N700BQ	04	TBM 700C	298	Cuatro Aviation LLC. Los Angeles, Ca.	
N700BS	91	TBM 700	11	B & D Thermal Protection Consulting Inc. Daytona Beach, Fl.	N877PC
N700CB	00	TBM 700B	176	Fifth Third Leasing Co. Cincinnati, Oh.	F-WWRO
N700CC	96	TBM 700	113	Ronald Canada, Knoxville, Tn.	F-OHBU
N700CF	96	TBM 700	123	James Findeiss, Fort Lauderdale, Fl.	N700TB
N700CL	03	TBM 700C	266	Jupiter Training Inc. Garland, Tx.	
N700CP	76	King Air C90	LJ-700	CKL Enterprises LLC. Pelham, Al.	N700FC
N700CS	95	TBM 700	109	Michael Rosenberg, Chapel Hill, NC.	
N700CT	02	TBM 700B	236	Vladigor Investments Inc. San Francisco, Ca.	
N700CV	01	TBM 700B	221	Agnondas LLC. Palo Alto, Ca.	F-WWRJ
N700CZ	04	TBM 700C	301	OKAY Inc. Wilmington, De. (trustor ?).	
N700DD	78	King Air E90	LW-288	Sammann Corp. Michigan City, In.	N717US
N700DE	91	TBM 700	4	Commercial Bag Co. Normal, Il.	N701MR
N700DH	74	King Air E90	LW-114	Avolare Enterprises LLC. Tucson, Az.	N89L
N700DQ	03	TBM 700C	271	Tahoe Investments Inc. Los Altos Hills, Ca.	
N700DT	98	TBM 700	134	Delta Tango Corp. Whitefish, Mt.	F-WWRR
N700DZ	03	TBM 700C	295	Timothy Diestel, Bend, Or.	
N700EG	03	TBM 700C	284	Lemoine Investments Inc. Hoboken, NJ.	
N700EJ	03	TBM 700C	291	Comstock Crosser & Assocs Development LLC. Ca.	
N700EK	04	TBM 700C	304	Boardroom Aviation LLC. Reno, Nv.	
N700EL	01	TBM 700B	209	Air Twinlite Inc. Dolls Grove, Ireland.	N701AR
N700ER	01	TBM 700B	198	Exchange Enterprise Group LLC. Indianapolis, In.	
N700EV	03	TBM 700C	287	MG Air Transport LLC. Newport, NC.	
N700EZ	04	TBM 700C	307	DBW Aviation LLC. Anaheim, Ca.	
N700FT	03	TBM 700	267	William Foster, Sherborn, Ma.	
N700GE	02	TBM 700C	255	David Wolfe, Tempe, Az.	
N700GJ	02	TBM 700B	241	RBL Aviation LLC. Carlsbad, Ca.	(N702RM)
N700GM	91	King Air C90A	LJ-1283	MICO Inc. North Mankata, Mn.	D-IHMW
N700GN	02	TBM 700C	246	Winged Horse LLC. Anchorage, Ak.	F-WWRJ
N700GQ	03	TBM 700C	289	ALS Aviation LLC. Culver City, Ca.	
N700GT	03	TBM 700C	276	Enstrom Candies Inc. Grand Junction, Co.	
N700GV	03	TBM 700C	290	SOCATA Aircraft, Pembroke Pines, Fl.	
N700HD	04	TBM 700C	313	Cutter SW Aircraft Sales LLC. Phoenix, Az.	
N700HK	93	TBM 700	60	Daniel Lee, Wilson, Wy.	(N95DW)
N700HL	03	TBM 700C	281	Conrad Aviation LLC. Simpsonville, SC.	

Reg	Yr Type	c/n	Owner/Operator	Prev Regn
☐ N700HM	03 TBM 700C	297	SOCATA Aircraft, Pembroke Pines, Fl.	
☐ N700HN	01 TBM 700B	204	Doyle Hartman, Aspen, Co.	
☐ N700HY	03 TBM 700C	278	Cutter Southwest Aircraft Sales LLC. Phoenix, Az.	
☐ N700JD	03 TBM 700C	264	Juliette Delta LLC. Frankfort, In.	N700MZ
☐ N700KB	00 King Air C90B	LJ-1615	Aspenwood Directories Inc. Colorado Springs, Co.	N3151P
☐ N700KD*	04 TBM 700C	305	Centennial Homes Inc. Novato, Ca.	N700DN
☐ N700KH	01 TBM 700B	210	N700KH LLC. Dublin, Oh.	N708AV
☐ N700KL	92 TBM 700	88	C Kevin Landry, Lincoln, Ma.	
☐ N700KM	99 TBM 700B	158	Frederick Croatti, Londonderry, NH.	
☐ N700KP	02 TBM 700B	228	Blu Vu LLC. Reno, Nv.	
☐ N700KV	04 TBM 700C	296	SOCATA Aircraft, Pembroke Pines, Fl.	
☐ N700KW	76 King Air 200	BB-115	Eastern Tennessee Subway Development, Kmoxville, Tn.	N335TM
☐ N700L	82 Gulfstream 1000	96034	MAX 1 LLC. Aspen, Co.	(N24A)
☐ N700LF	02 TBM 700	270	Sunbeam Aviation LLC. Wilmington, De.	(N700HS)
☐ N700LL	93 TBM 700	86	Evergreen III LLC. Seattle, Wa.	
☐ N700MB	67 King Air A90	LJ-233	Micro-Asian Air Inc. Barrigada, Guam.	N100HT
☐ N700MK	02 TBM 700C	251	Spring Brook Marina Inc. Seneca, Il.	F-WWNP
☐ N700MV	91 TBM 700	13	Agrest Enterprises LLC. Wilmington, De.	(LX-JFB)
☐ N700MX	91 TBM 700	14	Medox LLC. Middleton, Wi.	N292RG
☐ N700NA	94 King Air B200	BB-1491	Penn State University, University Park, Pa.	JA8614
☐ N700NC	72 King Air A100	B-138	Ascension Aviation LLC. Gaylord, Mi.	N600DK
☐ N700ND	01 TBM 700B	217	S & S Aviation LLC. Boise, Id.	F-HIGH
☐ N700PC	80 Gulfstream 980	95023	James Lindsey Jr Family Trust, Van Nuys, Ca.	N888SF
☐ N700PG	98 King Air 350	FL-233	Blue Cross & Blue Shield, Chattanooga, Tn.	N700PE
☐ N700PK	92 TBM 700	52	UIS Aviation Services Inc. Pleasant Grove, Ut.	F-OHEV
☐ N700PQ	77 Rockwell 690B	11389	Rogers Helicopters Inc. Clovis, Ca.	N700PC
☐ N700PT	03 TBM 700C	268	Links Aero LLC. Shalimar, Fl.	
☐ N700PU	91 TBM 700	15	John Montgomery, Orinda, Ca.	
☐ N700PV	01 TBM 700B	215	SOCATA Aircraft, Pembroke Pines, Fl.	
☐ N700PW	01 TBM 700B	211	David Lau, Watertown, Wi.	
☐ N700PX	02 TBM 700C	249	Unimax Aviation Inc. Portland, Or.	F-WWRK
☐ N700QD	01 TBM 700B	174	Quest Diagnostics Inc. Teterboro, NJ.	F-GLBC
☐ N700RF	91 King Air C90A	LJ-1262	Pelico Inc/Anoka Air Charter Inc. Minneapolis, Mn.	N200HV
☐ N700RG	78 PA-31T Cheyenne II	7820042	OFEK Holding Corp. Wilmington, De.	N400RT
☐ N700RK	02 TBM 700C	253	Kritser Equipment Leasing LLC. Colorado Springs, Co.	N700BH
☐ N700RX	72 Mitsubishi MU-2K	241	Internet Jet Sales Ltd. White Mills, Pa.	C-GJAV
☐ N700S	01 TBM 700B	193	Speedbird Aviation Inc/Sanjay Singh, Fairoaks, UK.	
☐ N700SF	91 TBM 700	26	Air Frantz Inc. Greenwich, Ct.	
☐ N700SL	02 TBM 700C	257	Mitchell Aviation Innovations LLC. Wayland, Ma.	
☐ N700SP	94 TBM 700	98	Hokanson Equipment Leasing LLC. Indianapolis, In.	
☐ N700SY	03 TBM 700C	283	Skytran LLC. Charlotte, NC.	
☐ N700TB	03 TBM 700C	256	SOCATA Aircraft, Pembroke Pines, Fl.	
☐ N700TG	78 King Air C-12C	BC-75	The Telford Group Inc. Bangor, Me.	N900RF
☐ N700TJ	91 TBM 700	27	Flying Bees Aviation LLC. Columbus, Oh.	N700WD
☐ N700TK	04 TBM 700C	311	Columbia Aircraft Sales Inc. Groton, Ct.	
☐ N700TL	01 TBM 700B	227	XFM Systems Inc. Encinitas, Ca.	
☐ N700U	03 King Air 350	FL-363	Ohio University, Athens, Oh.	N6043M
☐ N700VA	02 TBM 700B	233	SOCATA Aircraft, Pembroke Pines, Fl. (status ?).	F-OIKI
☐ N700VB	02 TBM 700B	237	ATM Leasing Inc. Wilmington, De.	F-OIKJ
☐ N700VD	01 TBM 700B	190	International Aircraft Marketing & Management, New Castle.	N705AV
☐ N700VF	81 PA-42 Cheyenne III	8001053	WBY Enterprises LLC. Jackson, Tn.	N543FM
☐ N700VJ	00 TBM 700B	163	N700VJ LLC. Wilmington, De.	N700DN
☐ N700VM	92 TBM 700	72	VMO Corp. Coral Gables, Fl.	
☐ N700VP	00 TBM 700B	180	SAAIR LLC. Dover, Ma.	(D-FWIR)
☐ N700VX	96 TBM 700	118	KP Equipment LLC. Billings, Mt.	F-GLBI
☐ N700WA	79 MU-2 Solitaire	400SA	Wemco Aviation Inc. Wilmington, De.	N40MZ
☐ N700WD	77 King Air E90	LW-218	Whiskey Delta LLC. Stuart, Fl.	HP-1246
☐ N700WE	01 TBM 700B	214	Greystone Aviation Inc. Newport Beach, Ca.	N703AV
☐ N700WJ	81 Conquest 1	425-0036	Bighorn Airways Inc. Sheridan, Wy.	(N32TJ)
☐ N700WK	00 TBM 700B	175	Riverton Air LLC. Wilmington, De.	D-FFBU
☐ N700WS	00 TBM 700B	172	MK Leasing LLC. Scottsdale, Az.	F-GLBT
☐ N700WT	93 TBM 700	91	Jerry's Enterprises Inc. Edina, Mn.	
☐ N700XS	02 TBM 700C	260	Sooner Turbine Aviation LLC. Miami, Fl.	N738C
☐ N700YN	01 TBM 700B	222	TBM Aviation LLC. Simsbury, Ct.	F-WWRK
☐ N700Z	79 King Air 200	BB-443	Bramco Inc. Louisville, Ky.	
Reg	Yr Type	c/n	Owner/Operator	Prev Regn

Reg	Yr	Type	c/n	Owner/Operator	Prev Regn
N700ZA	04 TBM 700C		317	SOCATA Aircraft, Pembroke Pines, Fl.	
N700ZB	04 TBM 700C		321	SOCATA Aircraft, Pembroke Pines, Fl.	
N700ZP	04 TBM 700C		322	SOCATA Aircraft, Pembroke Pines, Fl.	
N700ZR	93 TBM 700		87	Nova Aviation LLC. Fort Lauderdale, Fl.	N874RJ
N700ZZ	96 TBM 700		116	Tycor Leasing LLC. Tuscon, Az.	N116VL
N701AT	68 King Air B90		LJ-390	Elias R V Morales, Valencia Carabobo, Venezuela.	N701AT
N701AV	00 TBM 700B		179	D James Bidzos, Mill Valley, Ca.	(N69FR)
N701BN	61 Gulfstream 1		74	Battelle Pacific Northwest Laboratories, Pasco, Wa.	N5619D
N701CR	83 Conquest 1		425-0148	Tech II Inc. Springfield, Oh.	N425EK
N701ES	92 TBM 700		46	Nantucket Leasing LLC. Mineola, NY.	N844S
N701FC	00 King Air 350		FL-291	Forum Communications Co. Fargo, ND.	
N701GT	02 P-180 Avanti		1054	AvantAir Inc. Stewart, NY.	N137PA
N701LT	95 TBM 700		107	Baker Aviation LLC. Versailles, Ky.	F-GLLL
N701MK	97 TBM 700		124	MAK Equipment Leasing LLC. Northampton, Pa.	N701PP
N701NC	78 King Air 200		BB-324	Merrog Inc. Wilmington, De.	N111SF
N701PT	80 PA-31 Cheyenne 1		8004008	Natoli Engineering Co. Chesterfield, Mo.	(N701DH)
N701QD	97 TBM 700B		126	Quest Diagnostics Inc. Teterboro, NJ.	N811SW
N701RJ	70 King Air 100		B-23	Planes 4 Sale LLC. Houston, Tx.	N711AU
N701X	76 King Air E90		LW-165	Gold Aviation Services Inc. Fort Lauderdale, Fl.	N700DH
N701XP	79 King Air C90		LJ-826	Matthew Shieman, Morag, Ca.	(N20GT)
N702AA	01 TBM 700B		216	Lantech Leasing LLC. Louisville, Ky.	
N702AR	03 TBM 700C		275	ISNET Aviation Inc. UK.	
N702AV	00 TBM 700B		182	Panther Aviation LLC. Los Altos Hills, Ca.	
N702BM	91 TBM 700		2	Fabry Air Corp. Wilmington, De.	N100PB
N702DK	90 King Air C90A		LJ-1259	Cheyenne Ventures LLC. Richmond, Va.	N712JC
N702GS	00 TBM 700B		177	Monroe Group II Inc. Northbrook, Il.	F-WWRP
N702H	96 TBM 700		112	Anchor Equipment Leasing LLC. Cincinnati, Oh.	N12WY
N702JL	81 King Air B100		BE-110	Health Systems Inc. Sikeston, Mo.	N702R
N702MA	82 King Air B200		BB-1010	Michigan Aeronautics Commission, Lansing, Mi.	N62FC
N702MB	04 TBM 700C		314	TBM 700 Inc. Wilmington, De.	
N702QD	00 TBM 700B		165	Quest Diagnostics Inc. Teterboro, NJ.	N700DY
N702XP	78 King Air E90		LW-266	Air 4M LLC. Southlake, Tx.	N215HC
N703CA	03 TBM 700C		273	Well Air Inc. Brewster, NY.	
N703DM	69 Mitsubishi MU-2F		138	Eumundi Trading Co. Wilmington, De.	N252DC
N703HT	77 King Air 200		BB-228	Hidalgo Trading LLC. Ponte Vedra Beach, Fl.	N79KF
N703JR	76 King Air C-12C		BC-22	Jacksonville Sheriff's Department, Jacksonville, Fl.	N200NG
N703JT	80 King Air F90		LA-39	University of South Carolina Athletics Dept. Columbia, SC.	YV-342CP
N703QD	99 TBM 700B		129	Quest Diagnostics Inc. Teterboro, NJ.	LX-JFC
N703RM	00 King Air B200		BB-1699	Rushmark Properties LLC. Fairfax, Va.	N3199B
N703X	80 King Air 200		BB-737	SouperKruser Inc/Gold Aviation Services Inc. Fort Lauderdale	N38GM
N704QD	01 TBM 700B		188	Quest Diagnostics Inc. Teterboro, NJ.	
N706AV	01 TBM 700B		191	Thionville Laboratories Inc. New Orleans, La.	
N706DG	79 King Air 200		BB-548	Davis-Garvin Agency Inc/D-G Air LLC. Columbia, SC.	N78SC
N706DM	67 Mitsubishi MU-2B		038	Bush Field Aircraft Co. Augusta, Ga.	N8BL
N706KC	76 Rockwell 690A		11343	BRS Services Inc. Reno, Nv.	N706US
N706TA	99 King Air B200		BB-1656	Southwest Aircraft Charter LC. Mesa, Az.	
N707AF	78 Mitsubishi MU-2N		707SA	Gustl Spreng Enterprises Inc. Daytona Beach, Fl.	VH-NMU
N707AV	01 TBM 700B		197	Eleigh Aviation LLC. Carson City, Nv.	F-WWRK
N707CB	81 Conquest 1		425-0023	Flying High Ventures Inc. Sun River, Or.	N23AW
N707CV	81 PA-31T Cheyenne 1		8104013	Romana Air Corp. San Juan, PR.	N212GM
N707FA	01 King Air 350		FL-337	F & W Corp. San Juan, PR.	N5037A
N707MA	83 Conquest II		441-0285	Caribbean Air & Marine Service, Memphis, Tn.	D-IIAA
N707ML	75 PA-31T Cheyenne II		7520017	Flight Capital LLC. Madison, Ms.	(N5RZ)
N707SS	71 King Air 100		B-81	OTW Farms LLC. Hollister, Ca.	N858B
N707TL	76 King Air E90		LW-173	Transworld Leasing Corp. San Antonio, Tx.	N1573L
N707WD	81 PA-31T Cheyenne II		8120103	Airex LLC. Hilton Head, SC. (was 8120065).	N182TC
N708DG	71 King Air C90		LJ-508	Hinds Community College, Raymond, Ms.	N706DG
N708DM	73 Mitsubishi MU-2K		271	Bush Field Aircraft Co. Augusta, Ga.	N23HR
N708EF	91 TBM 700		21	Mulligan Aviation, Annapolis, Md.	(N554CA)
N708PW	91 TBM 700		29	Third Moment Aviation LLC. NYC.	N700PW
N709FN	74 Mitsubishi MU-2K		308	Bush Field Aircraft Co. Augusta, Ga.	N709DM
N709MC	00 TBM 700B		168	JMC Leasing Inc. St Petersburg, Fl.	
N710G	78 Mitsubishi MU-2N		710SA	Turbine Aircraft Marketing Inc. San Angelo, Tx.	I-MLST
N710JB	01 King Air B200		BB-1784	Sunset Leasing Inc. Sarasota, Fl.	N4484W
N710NC	78 King Air 200		BB-322	Ascension Aviation LLC. Gaylord, Mi.	N715MA

385

Reg	Yr Type	c/n	Owner/Operator	Prev Regn
N711AW	81 King Air 200	BB-755	One Alpha Whiskey LLC. Odessa, Tx.	N71TB
N711BN	73 King Air C90	LJ-588	Liberte Air Corp. St Croix, USVI.	N711BL
N711CR	74 King Air 200	BB-16	RidgeAire Inc. Jacksonville, Tx.	N700CP
N711DB	67 King Air A90	LJ-311	Billings Flying Service Inc. Billings, Mt.	F-GNBA
N711ER	81 PA-31T Cheyenne 1	8104056	Aviation Inc. Fulton, Ms.	(D-IAHM)
N711FN	81 Cheyenne II-XL	8166043	Alabama Electric Co-operative Inc. Andalusia, Al.	N820SW
N711GE	81 Conquest II	441-0209	Haggen Inc. Bellingham, Wa.	N2728G
N711GM	70 King Air 100	B-31	T & W Leasing, Mesquite, Tx.	N38HB
N711HV	77 King Air E90	LW-246	Kaden Airmotive Inc. Dallas, Tx.	N711NV
N711KB	80 King Air 200	BB-593	Charter Aviation/Venture Aviation Group LLC Greenville, SC.	(N209JS)
N711KP	76 King Air C90	LJ-692	Peter Messina & Assocs Ltd. Itasca, Il.	(N692RC
N711L	84 King Air F90-1	LA-222	U S Investments Ltd. Crystal Bay, Nv.	N69283
N711LD	81 PA-31T Cheyenne 1	8104040	JAS Enterprises LLC. Pittsford, NY.	N981SR
N711MB	80 Conquest II	441-0116	Baldini's Inc. Sparks, Nv.	N441GE
N711MZ	81 King Air 200	BB-849	Champion Air LLC. Mooresville, NC.	N74F
N711PB	77 Rockwell 690B	11356	Ohio Kentucky Oil Corp. Lexington, Ky.	N653PC
N711PM	02 TBM 700B	234	Lewis & Lewis Attorneys, Clarksdale, Ms.	N811SV
N711RD	79 PA-31T Cheyenne II	7920068	J E L Farms Ltd. Hale Center, Tx.	N40JC
N711RE	77 King Air A100	B-233	Tulip City Air Service Inc. Holland, Mi.	N99HE
N711RJ	94 King Air 350	FL-116	Butler Automotive Group Inc. Macon, Ga.	D-CAAA
N711SB	01 PA-46-500TP Meridian	4697075	Cash South LLC. Georgetown, De.	
N711TN	80 King Air 200	BB-628	Francille Corp. Germantown, Tn.	N6739P
N711TZ	77 King Air E90	LW-226	W/o Kremmling, Co. USA. 19 Mar 03.	N976
N711VK	69 Mitsubishi MU-2F	157	The Granite Guy LLC. Indianapolis, In.	N157AF
N711VM	79 King Air 200	BB-544	Crabtree Aviation LLC. Knoxville, Tn.	N711VH
N711VN	90 King Air 350	FL-7	Lifeline Aviation LLC. Porterville, Ca.	N7350C
N711VV	90 King Air B200	BB-1365	Maynard Aviation LLC. Hackensack, NJ.	N963GM
N712BC	02 Pilatus PC-12/45	448	SAH East Coast LLC. Teterboro, NJ.	HB-FSP
N712GJ	81 King Air B200	BB-840	Mortgage Solutions of Colorado, Colorado Springs, Co.	N840RC
N712GK	82 King Air 200	BB-1035	KS Air 3-7-12 LLC. Charlotte, NC.	N96ZZ
N712RH	03 King Air B200	BB-1839	AMR Aviation LLC. Baton Rouge, La.	N5039X
N713EA	04 King Air C90B	LJ-1713	Elliott Aviation Aircraft Sales Inc. Des Moines, Ia.	N546C
N713RH	87 King Air B200	BB-1274	Falcon Air LLC. Olive Branch, Ms.	(N47AJ)
N713US	04 King Air C90B	LJ-1727	Raytheon Aircraft Co. Wichita, Ks.	
N715CA	81 PA-31T Cheyenne II	8120063	Giumarra Brothers Fruit Co. Los Angeles, Ca.	
N715CQ	92 King Air 200	BB-1421	International Muffler Co. Schulenberg, Tx.	(N538KB
N715HL	99 Pilatus PC-12/45	292	Iliamna Air Taxi Inc. Iliamna, Ak.	N292PB
N715MC	91 TBM 700	30	Beartooth Aviation LLC. Eden Prairie, Mn.	
N715RD	80 King Air 200	BB-707	Central Virginia Aircraft Sales Inc. Lynchburg, Va.	N627BC
N715TL	04 Pilatus PC-12/45	548	TNH Leasing LLC. Iliamna, Ak.	HB-FST
N715WA	73 King Air A100	B-168	Colemill Enterprises Inc. Nashville, Tn.	F-GFVM
N716AV	04 King Air B200	BB-1876	Snowy Range Aviation LLC. Cheyenne, Wy.	
N716CC	81 Conquest II	441-0213	Home Air Inc/Home Place Inc. Gainesville, Ga.	N6851Y
N716MA	04 TBM 700C	310	Muncie Aviation Co. Muncie, In.	
N716TA	95 King Air B200	BB-1509	Flight Options LLC. Cleveland, Oh.	N109NT
N716WA	80 PA-31T Cheyenne II	8020042	Westlog Inc/CAL-ORE Life Flight, Smith River, Ca.	(N414CW
N717D	80 King Air B100	BE-91	DeCol Aviation Inc. Altoona, Pa.	N6740D
N717DC	87 King Air B200	BB-1261	Danella Companies Inc. Plymouth Meeting, Pa.	N2997N
N717ES	80 PA-42 Cheyenne III	8001004	Thompson Travel LLC. West Columbia, SC.	N42WZ
N717HT	76 King Air 200	BB-133	Sun Quest Executive Charter Inc. Van Nuys, Ca.	N113RL
N717JG	75 King Air C90	LJ-672	RPJ Aircraft Investors LLC. Santa Monica, Ca.	(N11AB)
N717LW	98 King Air B200	BB-1642	Greater Media Services Inc. Braintree, Ma.	N3051S
N717PD	70 SA-26AT Merlin 2B	T26-178	Ziegler Family Trust, Portland, Or.	N61775
N717PS	76 Mitsubishi MU-2L	686	Royal Air Freight Inc. Waterford, Mi.	N23RA
N717RA	65 Gulfstream 1	167	Riverside International Airlines Inc. Riverside, Ca.	C-GDWN
N717RD	89 King Air C90A	LJ-1199	J & S Yacht Services Inc. Wilmington, De.	N487JD
N717RS	60 Gulfstream 1	38	Riverside International Airlines Inc. Riverside, Ca.	N333AH
N717VL	98 King Air 350	FL-207	Mustang Interests LLC. Llano, Tx.	N2308R
N717X	73 King Air C90	LJ-581	Bert Nelson, Dallas, Tx.	N717XP
N717Y	91 TBM 700	17	J H Van Zant II, Albany, Tx.	
N718JP	96 Pilatus PC-12	155	Pezold Air Charters LLC. Columbus, Ga.	N361FB
N718K	68 King Air B90	LJ-371	B90 King Group LLC. Austin, Tx.	
N718MB	91 King Air C90A	LJ-1287	MPW Industrial Services Group Inc. Hebron, Oh.	N881JT
N718RJ	97 King Air B200	BB-1597	AAA Cooper Transportation Corp. Dothan, Al.	
N719RA	60 Gulfstream 1	28	Dodson International Parts Inc. Ottawa, Ks.	N118X

Reg	Yr	Type	c/n	Owner/Operator	Prev Regn
☐ N720AF	04	King Air C90	LJ-1718	Stevens Aviation Inc. Greenville, SC.	
☐ N720AM	87	King Air C90B	LJ-1490	Myers Aviation LLC. Worcester, Pa.	(N520AM)
☐ N720C	73	King Air A100	B-171	Oscar Charlie LLC. Hollywood, Md.	C-FJFH
☐ N720JK	69	Mitsubishi MU-2F	154	Wolfhunter Aviation LLC. Kokomo, In.	(N81LJ)
☐ N720MP	82	King Air B200	BB-1080	Idlewood Aviation Inc. Atlanta-DeKalb, Ga.	N72GG
☐ N720RD	77	King Air C90	LJ-720	Greenway Medical Technologies, Carrollton, Ga.	VT-EFP
☐ N721FC	68	Mitsubishi MU-2D	111	East Mississippi Community Co. Mayhew, Ms.	N858Q
☐ N721ML	82	Gulfstream 900	15002	SLFH Air LLC/Stephen LaFrance Holdings Inc. Pine Bluff, Ar.	N721MR
☐ N721NB	00	King Air 350	FL-288	First National Bank, Edinburg, Tx.	N168ET
☐ N721RD	80	King Air 200	BB-677	Drinkard Development Inc. Cullman, Al.	N200KK
☐ N721SR	00	TBM 700B	181	122 Ventures Inc. Atlanta, Ga.	
☐ N721SW	79	King Air 200	BB-519	S & W Ready Mix Concrete Co. Clinton, NC.	(N747P)
☐ N721TB	77	Rockwell 690B	11352	David C Poole Co. Greenville, SC.	N46JC
☐ N722EJ	74	Rockwell 690A	11175	Sun West Aviation Inc. Tucson, Az.	XA-SPW
☐ N722ER	85	PA-42 Cheyenne 400LS	5527023	Relinquished Aviation II LLC. Boston, Ma.	C-GMFI
☐ N722GA	80	Conquest II	441-0153	Classen Airways LLC. Oklahoma City, Ok.	C-FMSK
☐ N722JB	01	King Air C90B	LJ-1652	JSB Aviation LLC. Wichita Falls, Tx.	N722JM
☐ N722KR	84	King Air C90A	LJ-1065	Sunbird Aviation Inc. Belgrade, Mt.	N900LE
☐ N722LJ	66	680V Turbo Commander	1538-5	Performance Plus LLC. Seattle, Wa.	N100BP
☐ N722PT	85	King Air F90-1	LA-235	Penkhus Motor Co. Colorado Springs, Co.	N901GS
☐ N722SR	92	TBM 700	49	Go-Mav Inc. Simi Valley, Ca.	N567T
☐ N723AC	76	Rockwell 690A	11249	Keystone Senior Capital Corp. Indianapolis, In.	N161JB
☐ N723JP	79	PA-31T Cheyenne II	7920009	Missouri Forge Inc. Doniphan, Mo.	N723JR
☐ N723KR	01	PA-46-500TP Meridian	4697033	Greater South Agency Inc. Columbia, SC.	
☐ N724A	96	DHC 8-202	440	ARAMCO Associated Co. Houston, Tx.	C-GFBW
☐ N724DM	98	TBM 700	143	Air Men Inc. Concord, Ma.	N709DM
☐ N724DR	00	King Air C90B	LJ-1612	Lands End Aviation LLC. Los Altos Hills, Ca.	N3212Y
☐ N724HS	04	Pilatus PC-12/45	564	HS Holdings Group LLC. Oakland Park, Fl.	N564PB
☐ N724KH	96	King Air C90B	LJ-1426	Cloud Nine Corp. Batesville, In.	N724KW
☐ N724RN	01	TBM 700B	202	Ronald Nelson, Pasadena, Ca.	N709AV
☐ N725A	96	DHC 8-202	441	ARAMCO Associated Co. Houston, Tx.	C-GFCF
☐ N725AR	80	King Air C90	LJ-879	Baker Street Holding LLC. Phoenix, Az.	N6656D
☐ N725FN	73	Mitsubishi MU-2K	248	Bush Field Aircraft Co. Augusta, Ga.	N725DM
☐ N725JT	81	MU-2 Solitaire	451SA	Corsair Enterprises Inc. Bamberg County, SC.	N1728S
☐ N725MC	76	King Air 200	BB-169	N725MC Inc. Lafayette, Ca.	N200KA
☐ N725RA	80	King Air 200	BB-725	Barnett Investments Inc. LaVerne, Ca.	TP-209
☐ N725SV	78	Conquest II	441-0051	Sunview Air Inc. Delano, Ca.	N986SG
☐ N726CB	00	King Air B200	BB-1750	Henry Broadcasting Nevada Inc. San Francisco, Ca.	N4150T
☐ N726FN	74	Mitsubishi MU-2K	284	Aviation Systems & Manufacturing, Tuskegee, Al.	N726DM
☐ N726T	96	King Air 350	FL-149	B E & K Inc. Birmingham, Al.	N42ED
☐ N727BW	81	King Air 200	BB-861	AUG Inc. Augusta, Ga.	N727DD
☐ N727CC	82	Gulfstream 1000	96027	United States Aviation Underwriters, NYC.	N9947S
☐ N727DP	75	SA-226AT Merlin 4A	AT-039	Paragon Scientific Corp/Mark Kyle, Austin, Tx.	N439BW
☐ N727MT	78	King Air E90	LW-271	S V Leasing LLC. Park City, Ut.	N123LN
☐ N727PC	81	PA-42 Cheyenne III	8001025	Cheyenne Air LLC. Lafayette, La.	(D-IBTV)
☐ N727RS	81	King Air B100	BE-112	Montana Sky Fly LLC. Hamilton, Mt.	N990SV
☐ N727SM	78	PA-31T Cheyenne II	7820019	CSC Inc. Manhattan, Il.	N9113Y
☐ N727TP	81	MU-2 Marquise	1517SA	Ted Price Sr. Ventura, Ca.	(N321TP)
☐ N728DS	78	King Air C90	LJ-773	Central Bank, Lebanon, Mo.	N8TZ
☐ N728F	67	Mitsubishi MU-2B	019	Internet Jet Sales Ltd. White Milla, Pa.	N3551X
☐ N728FN	74	Mitsubishi MU-2K	303	DGH P/L. Brunswick, VIC. Australia.	N728DM
☐ N729CC	79	Rockwell 690B	11539	Structural Steel Services Inc. Meridian, Ms.	N81699
☐ N729MS	76	King Air B100	BE-2	King B100 LLC/Rensselaer Iron & Steel Inc. Rensselaer, NY.	N43KA
☐ N730EJ	75	King Air A100	B-217	Eric Jacobs, Radnor, Pa.	(F-GNAK)
☐ N730PT	77	PA-31T Cheyenne II	7720008	Twin Otter International Ltd. Las Vegas, Nv.	XA-HAY
☐ N730SS	77	Rockwell 690B	11415	DLZ Aircraft Inc. Columbus, Oh.	N700SS
☐ N731BH	86	Conquest II	441-0360	Hubbard Air LLC. Berwyn, Pa.	N441RW
☐ N731CJ	79	MU-2 Marquise	731SA	Rok-Mor Inc. Murrells Inlet, SC.	N81FR
☐ N731KA	77	King Air C90	LJ-731	White Industries Inc. Bates City, Mo.	N37PT
☐ N731TM	91	TBM 700	5	Melvin Rushton, Dallas, Tx.	N800GS
☐ N732WJ	79	King Air C90	LJ-869	Southold Aviation LLC. Palm Beach, Fl.	)
☐ N733NM	93	King Air 350	FL-104	Niagara Mohawk Power Corp. Syracuse, NY.	N8207D
☐ N733P	01	PA-46-500TP Meridian	4697052	Angus Mercer, Charlotte, NC.	
☐ N736P	85	King Air 300	FA-53	CSL 340 Corp. Truro, Ma.	
☐ N737E	74	Rockwell 690A	11189	Green Fairways Inc. Chicago, Il.	(N300CG)

Reg	Yr	Type	c/n	Owner/Operator	Prev Regn
❏ N738R	71	King Air C90	LJ-517	Pine Tree Aviation LLC. Boulder, Co.	N738RH
❏ N740GL	80	King Air 200	BB-650	UNHCR, Lanseria, South Africa.	N33TJ
❏ N740P	85	King Air B200	BB-1218	Navajo Nation, Window Rock, Az.	
❏ N740PB	75	Mitsubishi MU-2L	657	Maple Point Aviation of Ohio Inc. Columbus, Oh.	N740PC
❏ N740PC	85	King Air 300	FA-78	Oglethorpe Power Corp. Tucker, Ga.	N72479
❏ N741FN	75	Mitsubishi MU-2L	658	Air 1st Aviation Company of Oklahoma, Tulsa, Ok.	N740DM
❏ N741MA	77	Mitsubishi MU-2P	355SA	Bio Vim Inc. Naples, Fl.	N54EC
❏ N742GR	70	SA-26AT Merlin 2B	T26-172	Toys 4 Boys Inc. Beaumont, Tx.	N120FS
❏ N743JA	73	King Air E90	LW-73	William Arrington, Pampa, Tx.	(N743EC)
❏ N744CH	78	Rockwell 690B	11470	CH Aviation Inc. Wilmington, De.	N86MP
❏ N744JD	73	Rockwell 690A	11135	Tomato Express Inc Lexington, Ky.	N160G
❏ N744P	04	King Air C90B	LJ-1709	Blue Gander LLC. Newark, De.	
❏ N746KF	79	King Air 200	BB-473	Sierra 24 Leasing LLC. Fremont, Oh.	N510CB
❏ N747AW	01	PA-46-500TP Meridian	4697017	Sydney Aircraft Leasing Inc. Wilmington, De.	N123AD
❏ N747HN	80	King Air 200	BB-658	Pacific Coast Enterprises LLC. Las Vegas, Nv.	N127AP
❏ N747RE	77	PA-31T Cheyenne II	7720032	Weather Modification Inc. Fargo, ND.	(N748NL)
❏ N747SF	82	King Air C90	LJ-1003	James Leasing, Union City, Tn.	N90DL
❏ N747SY	82	MU-2 Marquise	1556SA	Yukon Air Inc, Wilmington, De.	N277JR
❏ N748SB	01	King Air 350	FL-321	Nectar of the Gods Air Inc. San Juan, PR.	N541GA
❏ N750AA	73	SA-226AT Merlin 4	AT-011	Damax Inc. Las Vegas, Nv.	PT-WGH
❏ N750CA	79	MU-2 Solitaire	407SA	Templeton Aircraft LLC. Washington, DC.	N979MA
❏ N750FC	70	King Air 100	B-58	PHP Aviation LLC. Houston, Tx.	C-FJLJ
❏ N750HG	80	King Air 200	BB-644	Isis Air SA. Panama City, Panama.	YV-O-CVI
❏ N750KC	77	King Air 200	BB-224	Magnum Tool Co. Colorado Springs, Co.	N215PA
❏ N750MD*	04	King Air B200	BB-1878	Davis Development Inc. Stockbridge, Ga.	
❏ N750RC	74	King Air C90	LJ-640	The Ruth Co. Lexington, Ky.	N942M
❏ N750TT	77	King Air 200	BB-215	Carolina Turbine Sales Inc. Tyler, Tx.	ZS-NGC
❏ N751BR	78	Rockwell 690B	11436	B & R Aviation LLC. Van Nuys, Ca.	N690FR
❏ N751J*	91	TBM 700	25	Sweatmore Air Inc. Scottsdale, Az.	N751JB
❏ N751JT	81	Conquest 1	425-0122	Phoenix Digital Data LLC. Columbia, SC.	N6882D
❏ N751KC	80	King Air C90	LJ-887	J A Peterson Enterprises Inc. Shawnee Mission, Ks.	N887CF
❏ N751PC	66	King Air A90	LJ-143	White Industries Inc. Bates City, Mo.	(N280KA
❏ N752MM	04	PA-46-500TP Meridian	4697192	SDCC Management Inc. Aubrey, Tx.	
❏ N754TW	78	King Air C90	LJ-754	Air Leisure LLC/Broadband International, Medley, Fl.	N303QC
❏ N755DM	94	TBM 700	101	ISDM Inc. Prairie Village, Ks.	
❏ N755MA	72	Mitsubishi MU-2J	553	Air 1st Aviation Company of Oklahoma, Tulsa, Ok.	N7034K
❏ N755PG	90	TBM 700	1	Gardner Aircraft Sales Inc. Daytona Beach, Fl.	D-FTBM
❏ N755Q	68	Mitsubishi MU-2F	131	PA Charter Inc. Gibsonia, Pa.	C6-BFA
❏ N756Q	68	Mitsubishi MU-2F	132	Dean Phillips Inc. Essendon, VIC.	
❏ N757H	81	Conquest 1	425-0006	City Link Airlines, Silver City, NM.	C-GMSV
❏ N758K	67	King Air A90	LJ-316	Hill County Claims Management Inc. Center Point, Tx.	XB-BZQ
❏ N759A	96	DHC 8-202	435	ARAMCO Associated Co. Houston, Tx.	C-G...
❏ N759AF	80	MU-2 Marquise	759SA	Golden Eagle Aviation II LLC. Portsmouth, Va.	LV-ODZ
❏ N760MM	82	PA-42 Cheyenne III	8001102	Mawson & Mawson Inc. Langhorne, Pa.	N4114A
❏ N760NP	75	King Air 200	BB-46	MEBE Inc. Oklahoma City, Ok.	N760NB
❏ N761K	68	King Air B90	LJ-426	Jordan Foster Aviation Inc. Deland, Fl.	(N713JF
❏ N762JC	80	MU-2 Marquise	762SA	T Bradley Harris LLC. Morgantown, WV.	OY-SUH
❏ N762KA	81	King Air 200	BB-762	Aircraft Guaranty Trust LLC. Houston, Tx.	RP-C465
❏ N762NB	81	King Air B200	BB-893	Sky High Air LLC. Orangeburg, SC.	
❏ N762VM	87	SA-227AT Merlin 4C	AT-695B	F Major LLC. Houston, Tx.	N2709Z
❏ N764CA	91	King Air B200	BB-1408	King Air 200 LLC/Carver Aero Inc. Muscatine, Ia.	N74RF
❏ N764K	74	King Air A100	B-178	United Air Services Co. Cobham, Va.	N3078W
❏ N765TC	80	King Air 200	BB-716	LNC Corp. Nashville, Tn.	F-ODYR
❏ N765WA	81	King Air 200	BB-765	N765WA Aviation LLC. Heber City, Ut.	N242LC
❏ N766LF*	04	King Air B200	BB-1864	Luihn Food Systems Inc. Raleigh, NC.	N6084C
❏ N766MA	78	Mitsubishi MU-2P	373SA	Frank Sanderson, Hampton, Va.	
❏ N766RB	82	King Air F90	LA-196	Norman Black, Atlanta, Ga.	CC-CTE
❏ N767CW	94	TBM 700	96	High Sierra Inc. Los Angeles, Ca.	
❏ N767DM	81	Cheyenne II-XL	8166042	Snowbow Inc. Fairbanks, Ak.	N500XL
❏ N767HP	99	TBM 700B	152	SOCATA Aircraft, Pembroke Pines, Fl.	
❏ N767JT	00	Pilatus PC-12/45	327	Teerling Aviation Inc. Lockport, Il.	HB-FRL
❏ N767LD	68	King Air B90	LJ-425	Lloyd Douglas Enterprises LLC. Aledo, Tx.	N93WB
❏ N767MC	73	King Air C90	LJ-595	New Life Aviation Group Inc. Laurelton, NY.	(N595A
❏ N767TP	01	PA-46-500TP Meridian	4697036	Cross Development of Missouri, Wentzville, Mo.	
❏ N767WF	78	King Air 200	BB-314	Alpha Leasing Inc. Schaumberg, Il.	N101BP
Reg	Yr	Type	c/n	Owner/Operator	Prev Regn

Reg	Yr Type	c/n	Owner/Operator	Prev Regn
N768MB	80 PA-31T Cheyenne 1	8004041	Hitch Enterprises Inc. Guymon, Ok.	N769MB
N768WT	90 King Air 350	FL-25	Beech Transportation Inc. Eden Prairie, Mn.	N769WT
N769CM	02 Pilatus PC-12/45	464	Jackson Ridge Montana LLC. Billings, Mt.	N464WC
N769D	80 King Air F90	LA-52	Dailey Equipment Co. Jackson, Ms.	
N769GR	98 King Air C90B	LJ-1509	Rite Flite Aviation Ltd. Cleveland, Oh.	
N769JS	01 TBM 700B	187	West Coast Trens Inc. Huntington Beach, Ca.	
N769MB	79 King Air 200	BB-571	American Health Centers Inc. Parsons, Tn.	N702AS
N770AJ	91 King Air C90A	LJ-1272	Double S Ranch Inc. Beaumont, Tx.	(N41AJ)
N770D	80 King Air B100	BE-90	Brodock Executive Air Inc. Utica, NY.	N67460
N770DC	00 TBM 700B	183	Broadway Two LLC. Dover, De.	
N770G	99 Pilatus PC-12/45	299	J2W Aviation LLC. Providence, RI.	HB-FPF
N770HM	81 King Air B200	BB-916	Blue Lake Air LLC/David Smith Farms Inc. Jonesboro, Ar.	(N770SF)
N770JH	90 King Air 350	FL-8	Skynight LLC/Skyview Cooling Co. Yuma, Az.	N124BB
N770MA	74 Mitsubishi MU-2J	625	Turbine Aircraft Marketing Inc. San Angelo, Tx.	N22522
N770MG	75 PA-31T Cheyenne II	7520029	Fly Me LLC. Tupelo, Ms.	N43SQ
N770RL	70 King Air 100	B-46	Ra-Lin & Associates, Carrollton, Ga.	(N770RU)
N770RW	74 Mitsubishi MU-2J	627	The F4 Phantom II Corp. Santa Fe, NM.	5Y-BJX
N770SD	80 King Air F90	LA-72	Holiday Management Co. Evansville, In.	N90SK
N770U	96 King Air B200	BB-1546	Air Rehab & Sales Inc. Jacksonville, Fl.	N770M
N770VF	01 King Air C90B	LJ-1641	V F Management Co. Roanoke, Va.	N654P
N771AK	77 King Air C-12C	BC-56	Alaska Dept of Public Safety, Anchorage, Ak.	77-22945
N771BA	78 Rockwell 690B	11429	Eagle Creek Aviation Services Inc. Indianapolis, In.	(D-ILAT)
N771CW	78 King Air B100	BE-52	Grand Prix Aviation LLC. Cordova, Tn.	N771S
N771FF	82 Gulfstream 900	15014	S E C Inc. Athens, Ga.	N5869N
N771HC	76 King Air 200	BB-147	Advance Food Co. Enid, Ok.	N777FL
N771HM	99 King Air 350	FL-262	HMHC Inc. Plymouth Meeting, Pa.	N725BA
N771JB	02 King Air C90B	LJ-1676	Laurel Aviation Enterprises, St James, NY.	N5076G
N771KT	01 Pilatus PC-12/45	361	East Coast Transportation Inc. Randolph, NY.	HB-FSX
N771MG	98 King Air B200	BB-1636	RPJ Aircraft Investors LLC. Santa Monica, Ca.	(N771SQ)
N771PA	83 King Air C90-1	LJ-1055	EJI Sales Inc. Montvale, NJ.	N303D
N771PD	01 King Air C90B	LJ-1635	MarBry Holdings LLC. Statesville, NC.	N5035M
N771SC	99 King Air B200	BB-1693	Wal-Mart Leasing Inc. Bentonville, Ar.	N773TP
N771SW	77 PA-31T Cheyenne II	7720002	Western Kansas Ground Water Management, Scott City, Ks.	N505GP
N772AF	82 King Air B200	BB-1001	AMF Aviation LLC. Tallahassee, Fl.	N94QD
N772DA	80 MU-2 Marquise	772SA	EPPS Air Service Inc. Atlanta, Ga.	I-MPLT
N772MA	78 Mitsubishi MU-2P	382SA	Jetprop Inc. Waterloo, Ia.	
N772SL	78 SA-226T Merlin 3A	T-258	Jet Operators LLC. Frisco, Tx.	N828CM
N773	83 King Air F90-1	LA-214	Blossom Agency, Indianapolis, In.	N77P
N773PW	79 King Air C90	LJ-864	Key Share Transportation LLC. Wilmington, De.	N199TD
N773S	67 King Air A90	LJ-283	Union Air LLC. Searcy, Ar.	
N773TP	00 King Air B200	BB-1722	Utah Aeronautical Operations, Salt Lake City, Ut.	
N774DK	96 Pilatus PC-12	167	Franklin M Orr Jr Trust, Stanford, Ca.	HB-FSC
N774KV	81 Cheyenne II-XL	8166057	State of Nebraska, Lincoln, Ne.	N9168Y
N774MA	78 Mitsubishi MU-2P	384SA	Robbins Management Group Inc. Panama City, Fl.	(N127RM)
N775CA	83 PA-42 Cheyenne IIIA	5501004	Northern Aircraft Sales, Bismarck, ND.	D-IEEF
N775D	99 King Air C90B	LJ-1579	Business Aircraft Leasing Inc. Nashville, Tn.	
N775DM	78 King Air C90	LJ-764	Antioch Air Corp. Jacksonville, Fl.	N201KA
N776CC	72 Mitsubishi MU-2J	560	Artis James Jr/Sparc Co. Diamondhead, Ms.	N195MA
N776DC	77 King Air E90	LW-235	Bush Sneed, Nashville, Tn.	C-FBCS
N776L	70 King Air 100	B-54	Dodson International Parts Inc. Rantoul, Ks.	N1776L
N776RM	86 King Air B200	BB-1245	Dave, Bruce & S LLC. Clara City, Mn.	N76RJ
N777AG	98 King Air B200	BB-1638	General Council of the Assemblies of God, Springfield, Mo.	N770TP
N777AJ	94 King Air B200	BB-1498	General Council of the Assemblies of God, Springfield, Mo.	N777AG
N777AQ	80 King Air 200	BB-583	DeWaynes Quality Metal Coatings Inc. Lesington, Tn.	N777AG
N777AT	66 King Air A90	LJ-166	White Industries Inc. Bates City, Mo.	N28J
N777AW	79 King Air 200	BB-536	Three C's LLC/Advanced Wireless Comms, Lakeville, Mn.	N33FM
N777DQ	79 King Air B100	BE-59	L J Associates Inc. Latrobe, Pa.	(N47KS)
N777EB	79 King Air C90	LJ-863	Sunshine Aviation LLC. Red Bay, Al.	N200SC
N777EL	79 Rockwell 690B	11538	Westak of Oregon Inc. Forest Grove, Or.	N81701
N777FX	04 PA-46-500TP Meridian	4697211	Cx USA 1/05 to ?	
N777G	81 PA-31T Cheyenne 1	8104065	Northwestern Aviation Inc. Des Moines, Ia.	N2580Y
N777GF	72 King Air C90	LJ-564	Aeronca Inc. Middletown, Oh.	N246DA
N777GS	79 King Air A100	B-241	CJ Systems Aviation Group Inc. Allegheny County, Pa.	N777GF
N777HF	99 King Air B200	BB-1645	777MOC 1 LLC. Capitola, Ca.	N615WH
N777HZ	74 SA-226T Merlin 3A	T-249	James A Tammaro MD PC. Lake Havasu City, Az.	N249RL

Reg	Yr	Type	c/n	Owner/Operator	Prev Regn
N777JX	99	Pilatus PC-12/45	288	MY Aviation LLC. Media, Pa.	N777JF
N777KA	78	King Air E90	LW-285	Liberty Transportation LLC. Woodbridge, Ct.	
N777LE	81	PA-31T Cheyenne II	8120104	Leading Edge Aviation Services Inc. Santa Ana. (was 8120069)	C-FZIC
N777LP	78	Mitsubishi MU-2N	719SA	Lincoln Leasing Co. Lincoln, Ne.	N911JE
N777MG	01	PA-46-500TP Meridian	4697066	Scotts Co. Marysville, Oh.	N5327Y
N777NP	65	King Air 90	LJ-67	APA Enterprises Inc. Poughkeepsie, NY.	(N21AM
N777NV	81	Gulfstream 840	11680	Nevada Department of Transportation, Carson City, Nv.	N680WA
N777SS	80	King Air 200	BB-661	King Air Shares LLC. Bakersfield, Ca.	N111JW
N777SW	01	King Air B200	BB-1773	Oasis Sales Corp. Joplin, Mo.	N623TA
N777TE	74	Rockwell 690A	11162	Tex Edwards Co. Pensacola, Fl.	N124HQ
N777VG	90	King Air B200	BB-1366	Alan Vester Management Corp. Littleton, NC.	N777AG
N777VK	69	Mitsubishi MU-2F	179	Transparent Technology Services Corp. Palm Beach, Fl.	N4WQ
N777WM	79	MU-2 Solitaire	397SA	Monee DR LLC. Missoula, Mt.	N666SP
N777XW	78	Conquest II	441-0065	Werco Manufacturing Inc. Broken Arrow, Ok.	N1228W
N777YN	01	King Air C90B	LJ-1657	Jeffrey Morgan, Scottsdale, Az.	N777MN
N778HA	81	PA-31T Cheyenne II	8120008	Missionair Inc. Danbury, Ct.	D-ICBH
N779DD	92	King Air C90A	LJ-1297	Basha's - Chapman Group, Chandler, Az.	N8239Q
N779JM	88	King Air C90A	LJ-1183	J & M Aviation Inc. Howell, Mi.	N482JA
N779M	80	SA-226T Merlin 3B	T-363	Tru-Truss Inc. Lacey, Wa.	(N155AF
N779MJ	89	King Air C90A	LJ-1197	AM Management Inc. Iowa City, Ia.	N485JD
N779VF	90	King Air C90A	LJ-1254	Fulling Mill LLC. Bronxville, NY.	N770VF
N780BP	73	Rockwell 690	11052	Long Star Air Service Inc. Miami, Fl.	N1230D
N780RC	81	King Air 200	BB-780	D W Machine Products Inc. Highland, Il.	F-GIHK
N782MA	78	MU-2 Solitaire	390SA	Tri-Air LLC. Springfield, Mo.	
N783MA	78	Mitsubishi MU-2P	391SA	Mitchell Slayman, Bakersfield, Ca.	
N783MC	73	King Air C-12C	BC-2	U S Customs Service, Oklahoma City, Ok.	N7064B
N783ST	80	Conquest II	441-0170	Silver Eagle Air Enterprises Inc. Roaring Springs, Pa.	N720JM
N784LB	90	King Air B200	BB-1374	Lima Bravo LLC. Sparta, Mi.	N899HC
N785JH	00	P-180 Avanti	1036	Promotional Researchers Inc. Charlottesville, Va.	N126PA
N785JP	04	King Air C90B	LJ-1710	MCA-Plane LLC/Motor Consultants of America Inc. Flint, Mi.	
N785MA	03	TBM 700C	280	Astro Aviation LLC. Waterford, Mi.	
N785P	04	King Air C90B	LJ-1712	Piedmont Hawthorne Aviation Inc. Winston-Salem, NC.	
N786AH	78	PA-31T Cheyenne II	7820053	SonFlight LLC. Andover, Ma.	C-GJJE
N786CB	76	King Air B100	BE-4	Aeronaut Ltd. Nassau, Bahamas.	N9104S
N786DD	84	King Air B200	BB-1171	Lawrence Contracting Co. Gilberton, Pa.	N86DD
N786RM	99	King Air C90B	LJ-1545	ESEC Investments LLC. Tampa, Fl.	N3145F
N786SR	82	King Air B200	BB-1016	North Slope Borough Search & Rescue, Barrow, Ak.	(N38AJ)
N787K	66	King Air 90	LJ-102	Ameron-Enmar Finishes Division, Little Rock, Ar.	
N787LB	85	PA-42 Cheyenne IIIA	5501030	Lawrence Aviation Inc. Austin, Tx.	N637KC
N787TT	78	King Air C90	LJ-787	Care Free Air LLC. San Jose, Ca.	TC-NAZ
N788BB	76	PA-31T Cheyenne II	7620051	Slick Corp. Fort Worth, Tx.	N631W
N788JL	84	Conquest 1	425-0202	Executive Turbine Sales Inc. Sarasota, Fl.	VH-EGO
N788RB	00	TBM 700B	167	Blissco Inc. Tulsa, Ok.	
N788SF	04	King Air B200	BB-1857	Suncrest Farms Inc. Van Nuys, Ca.	N5157G
N788SW	79	King Air E90	LW-327	Sugar Whiskey LLC. Nashville, Tn.	G-JGAL
N788TA	99	King Air B200	BB-1648	Flight Options LLC. Cleveland, Oh.	
N789CH	79	PA-31T Cheyenne II	7920079	American Medflight Inc. Reno, Nv.	N555HC
N789G	62	Gulfstream 1	89	Yellow Tail G-1 LLC. San Antonio, Tx.	
N789KP	01	King Air C90B	LJ-1664	Northeast Executive Jet LLC. Reading, Ma.	N5064L
N789LL	03	King Air 350	FL-386	Leavitt Leasing Co. Los Angeles, Ca.	N5086P
N789SB	97	King Air 350	FL-143	Superior Industries International Inc. Fayetteville, Ar.	N2392S
N790A	82	King Air C90-1	LJ-1016	Ninety LLC/Butler Aviation Inc. Houma, La.	N790A
N790P	03	King Air 350	FL-379	Olson Phillips Aviation LLC. Destin, Fl.	N61679
N790RB	78	King Air E90	LW-262	Leestown Aviation KA Inc. Dover, De.	N7ZW
N790RM	79	King Air 200	BB-445	Radnor Management Inc. Radnor, Pa.	N364SE
N790SD	79	PA-31T Cheyenne II	7920004	Silverwings Air Ambulance Ltd.. Silver City, NM.	N790SV
N790TB	99	TBM 700B	148	SOCATA Aircraft, Pembroke Pines, Fl.	(N700E
N791DC	91	King Air B200	BB-1402	Air Methods Corp/Deaconess Medical Center Inc. Billings, Mt.	N91CD
N791EB	81	King Air 200	BB-791	TCAS Enterprises LLC. Colleyville, Tx.	TC-ACN
N792JM	88	King Air 300	FA-140	Jamestown Metal Marine Sales Inc. Boca Raton, Fl.	N117DH
N792SG	01	Pilatus PC-12/45	380	S&SG LLC. La Jolla, Ca.	N380PF
N793DC	91	King Air B200	BB-1404	Air Methods Corp/Deaconess Medical Center Inc. Billings, Mt.	N93CD
N793WB	01	King Air 350	FL-324	Falcon Air Services LLC. Mesa, Az.	(N797W
N794A	84	PA-42 Cheyenne IIIA	5501015	DADCO Inc/Flugdienst Carlos de Pilar, Graefelfing, Germany.	D-ILSW
N794B	81	Conquest 1	425-0017	Ganz Air LLC. Belmont, Ma.	N58CH
Reg	**Yr**	**Type**	**c/n**	**Owner/Operator**	**Prev Regn**

Reg	Yr	Type	c/n	Owner/Operator	Prev Regn
☐ N794CE	79	King Air B100	BE-69	LMJ Inc. Wake Forest, NC.	N794WB
☐ N794MA	80	MU-2 Marquise	794SA	West Texas Executive Leasing Inc. San Angelo, Tx.	N54CE
☐ N794P	04	King Air C90B	LJ-1704	Pee Dee Electricom Inc. Darlington, SC.	
☐ N794PF	81	Conquest 1	425-0018	Prestage Farms of South Carolina LLC. Camden, SC.	N425CF
☐ N795CA	79	King Air 200	BB-559	Plane South Leasing Inc. Dunwoody, Ga.	N559BM
☐ N795PA	78	King Air 200	BB-328	Aircraft Acquisition LLC. Duluth, Ga.	(D-IDOL)
☐ N795TB	84	SA-227TT Merlin 300	TT-483A	WFBNW NA. Salt Lake City, Ut.	N328AJ
☐ N797CF	78	King Air C90	LJ-797	Daedalus Inc/Business Aviation Services, Sioux Falls, SD.	N61GA
☐ N797RW	80	Conquest II	441-0185	Tech II Inc. Springfield, Oh.	N999DF
☐ N798K	66	King Air A90	LJ-178A	Jacquin Aviation Inc. Morris, Il.	
☐ N799DD	72	King Air A100	B-102	Finkbeiner Aviation, Little Rock, Ar.	N777SD
☐ N799GK	78	King Air C90	LJ-799	Southwest Jet Inc. Belton, Mo.	ZP-TXE
☐ N800BJ	97	King Air 350	FL-184	Southern Cross Ranch LLC. Monroe, NC.	(N100PX)
☐ N800BK	81	King Air F90	LA-119	BK Aviation Inc. Grand Prairie, Tx.	(N800C)
☐ N800BS	98	King Air B200	BB-1620	BancorpSouth Bank, Tupelo, Ms.	
☐ N800BY	72	Mitsubishi MU-2F	221	Louis Provenza, Slidell, La.	N800BR
☐ N800CA	00	Beech 1900D	UE-383	Ruand Inc. Osage Beech, Mo.	N31686
☐ N800CG	81	King Air 200	BB-826	American Mine Research Inc. Rocky Gap, Va.	N1CB
☐ N800EB	79	PA-31T Cheyenne II	7920046	Southern Sky Inc. Miami, Fl.	N700LT
☐ N800ED	76	Mitsubishi MU-2M	339	Rydal Services Inc. Rydal, Pa.	N60NJ
☐ N800GS	99	TBM 700B	149	Sutliff Chevrolet Co. Harrisburg, Pa.	
☐ N800HA	77	King Air 200	BB-220	Hill Aircraft & Leasing Corp. Atlanta-Fulton County, Ga.	N75VF
☐ N800KT	89	King Air B200	BB-1346	Nevown Inc. Spartanburg, SC.	
☐ N800LD	78	SA-226T Merlin 3A	T-291	Schutts Aviation LLC. Fort Worth, Tx.	N19SD
☐ N800MG	86	King Air B200	BB-1259	MGI Aviation Ltd. Kidlington-Oxford, UK.	D-IDSM
☐ N800MM	81	SA-226T Merlin 3B	T-375	KLT Enterprises Inc/Public Safety Center, Eugene, Or.	(N98FT)
☐ N800NR	87	King Air B200	BB-1262	A N Rusche Land & Investment LLC. Houston, Tx.	N90TM
☐ N800PG	91	King Air C90A	LJ-1286	C-Air Ltd. Columbus, Oh.	N301ER
☐ N800PK	82	King Air B200	BB-982	King Air 982 LLC. Carlsbad-Palomar, Ca.	N800JR
☐ N800RE	84	King Air 300	FA-7	EEI Holding Corp. Springfield, Il.	N800EB
☐ N800RP	74	King Air C90	LJ-628	Marion Plywood Corp/MPC of Marion LLC. Marion, Wi.	(N800KD)
☐ N800TT	82	King Air B200	BB-957	JENCO Inc. Greensboro, NC.	N200HW
☐ N801AR	89	King Air 300	FA-191	Albritton News Bureau Inc. Washington, DC.	(N881AR)
☐ N801BS	00	King Air C90B	LJ-1601	Stephen Parker, Odessa, Tx.	N903TS
☐ N801CA	81	PA-31T Cheyenne 1	8104018	La Stella Corp. Pueblo, Co.	
☐ N801EB	73	Rockwell 690A	11111	RWT Transport LLC. Chapel Hill, NC.	XA-...
☐ N801HL	80	PA-31T Cheyenne II	8020016	Eastern Mountain Air LLC. Dover, De.	N2355W
☐ N801JW	82	PA-42 Cheyenne III	8001072	Hortmont Aviation Services Inc. New Hope, Pa.	N63WA
☐ N801KM	67	King Air A90	LJ-218	Covenant Sales & Leasing Inc. New Orleans, La.	N380M
☐ N801NA	83	King Air B200	BB-1164	NASA, Edwards AFB. Ca.	N701NA
☐ N801WA	01	PA-46-500TP Meridian	4697062	Shamrock Services Inc. San Angelo, Tx.	C-GEMO
☐ N802BS	01	King Air 350	FL-338	BancorpSouth Bank, Tupelo, Ms.	N3238S
☐ N802DG	79	King Air C90	LJ-807	Hillsborough County Mosquito Control, Tampa, Fl.	N877WL
☐ N802DJ	69	SA-26AT Merlin 2B	T26-117	Spartan Fleet Management Inc. Tryon, NC.	C-GYLP
☐ N802HS	95	Pilatus PC-12	118	Keystone Builders Resource Group Inc. Richmond, Va.	HB-FQL
☐ N802MM	03	PA-46-500TP Meridian	4697148	Renlim LLC. Atlanta, Fl.	
☐ N802MW	82	PA-42 Cheyenne III	8001081	MIC-PLANE Inc. Baltimore, Md.	N881AM
☐ N802RD	80	King Air B100	BE-96	Wisconsin Aviation Inc. Watertown, Wi.	N55TJ
☐ N803HC	81	King Air F90	LA-99	Hudson Company of Tennessee Inc. Henagar, Al.	N711KW
☐ N804	80	King Air 200	BB-724	Transcom Services LLC. Pottsville, Pa.	(N200WB)
☐ N804C	84	Cheyenne II-XL	1166006	Relco Locomotives Inc. Minooka, Il. (was s/n 1122001).	(N42RL)
☐ N804JH	01	PA-46-500TP Meridian	4697044	Avex Inc. Camarillo, Ca.	
☐ N806JW	96	King Air 350	FL-140	Jeld-Wen Inc. Klamath Falls, Or. (5000th King Air).	N1070D
☐ N806W	61	Gulfstream 1	67	U S Immigration & Naturalization Service, Pineville, La.	N5241Z
☐ N807M	82	SA-227AT Merlin 4C	AT-454	Ameriflight Inc. Burbank, Ca.	N3013T
☐ N807RS	00	King Air C90B	LJ-1602	Romeo Sierra LLC. Montecito, Ca.	(N700KB)
☐ N808DS	98	King Air B200	BB-1628	MT King Air LLC. Virginia Beach, Va.	
☐ N808GU	66	680V Turbo Commander	1579-32	Kenneth Erickson, San Diego, Ca.	N6536V
☐ N808NC	85	Gulfstream 1000	96085	Intermap Technologies Inc. Calgary, AB. Canada.	N205AB
☐ N808NT	81	Gulfstream 980	95081	Eagle Air Inc. Memphis, Tn.	N888NT
☐ N808PK	78	Mitsubishi MU-2P	385SA	High Country Aviation Inc. Tulsa, Ok.	LV-MLT
☐ N808SW	78	King Air C90	LJ-801	SLWNC Inc. Raleigh, NC.	TC-CSA
☐ N808TC	83	King Air F90-1	LA-211	Valhalla Aviation Inc. Los Angeles, Ca.	(N808TC)
☐ N808WD	99	King Air B200	BB-1685	State of Texas, Austin, Tx.	
☐ N809E	84	PA-42 Cheyenne IIIA	5501006	Cheyenne Aircraft LLC. Searcy, Ar.	N942PC

Reg	Yr Type	c/n	Owner/Operator	Prev Regn
N810EC	81 Gulfstream 980	95071	Fini SA. (status ?).	N9823S
N810HM	83 PA-31T Cheyenne 1A	8304002	Basham, Boutwell, Miller, Gher & Assocs. Eastview, Ky.	N910HM
N810JB	76 King Air 200	BB-139	BS LLC. Vernon, In.	N170SP
N810K	82 King Air B200	BB-1045	ASI Holdings Inc. Albany, Ga.	N810V
N811DA	81 PA-42 Cheyenne III	8001029	B & C Flight Management Inc. Houston, Tx.	N40PT
N811FA	80 King Air 200	BB-678	Fallstreak Aviation LLC. Roswell, Ga.	N811VG
N811GA	79 King Air C90	LJ-810	GA Associates LLC. Chesteron, In.	ZS-MZG
N811LC	89 King Air 300	FA-194	CRO Realty Inc. Deerfield Beach, Fl.	(N811DC
N811R	86 King Air C90A	LJ-1131	Precision Funding of Arkansas Inc. Little Rock, Ar.	N72508
N811SW	02 TBM 700C	240	Samir Wahby, Fort Dodge, Ia.	F-WWRO
N811VT	78 King Air 200	BB-323	Berryman Investments Inc. Boerne, Tx.	N4430V
N812AC	66 King Air A90	LJ-123	Britannia Aircraft Ltd. Dover, De.	N815K
N812BJ	84 PA-42 Cheyenne 400LS	5527020	Skyview Unlimited LC. Hillsborough, Or.	N402TW
N812CP	81 King Air F90	LA-127	Forest Hill Management Co. Forest Hill, Md.	YV-02CP
N812DP	75 King Air 200	BB-69	Coquille Air Inc. Eugene, Or.	N204JS
N812KB	75 King Air E90	LW-144	Cajun Flight LLC. Rochester, NY.	YV-66CP
N812LP	00 King Air C90B	LJ-1600	Larry Plummer, Camarillo, Ca.	
N812P	65 King Air 90	LJ-2	Cascade Air Services Inc. Issaquah, Wa.	N812Q
N813AR	78 PA-31T Cheyenne II	7820013	Dawson Construction Co. Gadsen, Al.	(N813AM
N813BL	79 King Air B100	BE-55	M-C Industries Inc. Topeka, Ks.	N546BZ
N813JB	80 King Air C90	LJ-899	JWC Investments LLC. Denver, Co.	N6732V
N813ZM	83 Conquest 1	425-0159	Fred Hibberd Jr. The Dalles, Or.	N425BB
N814CP	85 King Air C90A	LJ-1127	RMJ Aviation Inc. Forest Hill, Md.	(N779JM
N814G	66 King Air 90	LJ-104	John Crossno, Decatur, Il.	(N819C)
N814SS	80 SA-226T Merlin 3B	T-314	Dallas Fort Worth Sarcoma Group, Dallas, Tx.	N963DC
N814W	78 PA-31T Cheyenne II	7820073	Allen Lund Co. La Canada, Ca.	N7703L
N815BC	83 Gulfstream 840	11731	RBR Aircraft inc. Albuquerque, NM.	N840DA
N815D	89 King Air 300	FA-188	Family Video Movie Club Inc. Glenview, Il.	N423MK
N816BC	04 PA-46-500TP Meridian	4697195	New Piper Aircraft Inc. Vero Beach, Fl.	
N816CM	81 PA-31T Cheyenne 1	8104009	Silverhawk Aviation Inc. Lincoln, Ne.	
N816DE	99 King Air 350	FL-232	Pennington Aviation Inc. Baton Rouge, La.	N816DK
N816RL	76 King Air E90	LW-187	Peter Earp, Staverton, UK.	N66BP
N817CJ	79 PA-31T Cheyenne II	7920005	Riders in the Sky Inc. Amarillo, Tx.	N6166A
N817DP	87 King Air C90A	LJ-1156	ASMI Air LLC/Alan Silvestri Music Inc. Carmel Highlands, Ca.	N18264
N818AG	01 King Air B200	BB-1771	Servicios Aereos Occidentales, Lima, Peru.	N4271V
N818L	66 680V Turbo Commander	1558-16	Turcotte Enterprises Inc. Houston, Tx.	N818EC
N818PF	82 King Air B200	BB-1059	Patrick Farrah, Glenbrook, Nv.	N382AG
N818PL	82 Conquest 1	425-0109	Telsmith Inc. Mequon, Wi.	N66LL
N818RA	97 Pilatus PC-12	179	H I S LLC. Los Altos Hills, Ca.	N179SS
N818WV	03 King Air 350	FL-381	Water Valley Land LLC. Longmont, Co.	N350PL
N819EE	97 King Air 350	FL-187	R & F Wings LLC/Raymours Furniture Co. Liverpool, NY.	N319EE
N819MH	77 King Air C90	LJ-735	Windward Charter Ltd. Indianapolis, In.	N190TT
N819MK	77 PA-31T Cheyenne II	7720018	Esrair LLC/GSR Development LLC. Holmes Beach, Fl.	3A-MBA
N819SW	81 PA-31T Cheyenne 1	8104059	J Enterprises Inc. Wichita, Ks.	
N820BC	83 PA-42 Cheyenne III	8001105	B C Air LC. Moundridge, Ks.	N620MV
N820RD	74 King Air E90	LW-82	Par Five Aviation LLC. Brookfield, Wi.	YV-0-MA
N820SM	04 TBM 700C	316	SOCATA Aircraft, Pembroke Pines, fl.	
N821CS	02 King Air C90B	LJ-1674	N821CS LLC. Miami, Fl.	N4484T
N821J	03 PA-46-500TP Meridian	4697172	Cornerstone Managcment Group LLC. Paris, Tn.	
N821MA	75 Mitsubishi MU-2N	661SA	Legg Hudson Kovach LLC. Milton, De.	
N821TB	84 King Air 300	FA-6	Rumrunner of Naples LLC. Naples, Fl.	N64SS
N821U	65 King Air 90	LJ-19	Special Ops Aviation Inc. Norfolk, Va.	
N822BA	82 King Air F90	LA-191	E & J Aviation LLC. Wyoming, De.	(F-GRLN
N822VK	90 King Air 300	FA-211	Villa Katharine LLC. Commerce, Ga.	N701JP
N823DB	81 Conquest 1	425-0086	Centurion Equity Inc. Orlando, Fl.	N40RN
N823EB	98 King Air 350	FL-227	Denison Aviation LLC. Indianapolis, In.	
N823MA	75 Mitsubishi MU-2L	663	Turbine Aircraft Marketing Inc. San Angelo, Tx.	YV-409F
N823SB	76 Rockwell 690A	11304	San Bernadino County Sheriff's Department, Rialto, Ca.	(N29AA)
N823SD	04 King Air 350	FL-390	Stafford Development Co. Tifton, Ga.	N777YC
N823SE	99 King Air 350	FL-263	Raytheon Aircraft Co. Wichita, Ks.	N823SD
N824AC	78 King Air E90	LW-291	Chappell Smith & Assocs Inc. Franklin, Tn.	5U-ABV
N824JH	82 Cheyenne II-XL	8166040	Cloud Management Services LLC. Sarasota, Fl.	(N4DF)
N824S	82 King Air B200	BB-1064	BEP LLC/Bum Bros Materials Inc. Tuscaloosa, Al.	N129D
N824VA	81 PA-31T Cheyenne 1	8104039	Elaine Matheson, Kennewick, Wa.	(N54EM
N825B	82 Conquest 1	425-0123	Certified Leasing Co. Bakersfield, Ca.	N6882L
Reg	Yr Type	c/n	Owner/Operator	Prev Regn

Reg	Yr	Type	c/n	Owner/Operator	Prev Regn
N825JG	89	King Air 300	FA-196	Strand Aviation Inc. Wilmington, De.	N325JG
N825K	66	King Air 90	LJ-91	Spirit Fighters Inc. Wilmington, De.	N2085W
N825KA	81	King Air 200	BB-825	Brock Enterprises Inc. Beaumont, Tx.	XC-FUS
N825RT	81	King Air 200	BB-795	Raintree Express Inc. Tannersville, Pa.	N828JB
N825SP	80	Conquest II	441-0127	Steel Holdings Inc. Manhattan, Ks.	N322AN
N825ST	89	King Air B200	BB-1320	June & John Rogers/Sky Trek Aviation, Modesto, Ca.	N300LX
N825SW	82	Cheyenne II-XL	8166058	Hilton Enterprises Inc. Panama City, Fl.	
N825TS	00	King Air 350	FL-308	Aspen Air Inc. Little Rock, Ar.	
N826CM	82	PA-31T Cheyenne 1	8104048	Comcorps Inc. Mount Pleasant, SC.	
N826MA	84	King Air 300	FA-8	Anderson Hay & Grain Co. Ellensburg, Wa.	N300PK
N826RM	80	PA-31T Cheyenne 1	8004033	Eighty-Eight Inc/Action Airlines Inc. Groton, Ct.	N855RM
N827CC	85	King Air 300	FA-43	Calcot Ltd. Bakersfield, Ca.	N85TH
N827DL	86	King Air 300	FA-103	Equipos del Puerto SA. Guatemala City, Guatemala.	HP-1298
N827RM	82	King Air B100	BE-123	Farroll Equipment Co. Arroyo Grande, Ca.	N55FR
N827T	66	King Air 90	LJ-83	Quest Aviation Inc. Fort White, Fl.	(YV-980P)
N827VG	02	TBM 700B	242	Victor Charlie Partners LLC. Naples, Fl.	
N828AJ	04	King Air 350	FL-406	Air Jordan LLC. Newport News, Va.	
N828FC	96	King Air C90B	LJ-1436	Blackbird Caye Enterprises Inc. Belize.	N823FC
N828FM	82	King Air B200	BB-1069	South Aviation Inc. Fort Lauderdale, Fl.	LV-ZSE
N829BC	91	TBM 700	31	Berry Companies Inc. Wichita, Ks.	N701PF
N830EM	70	King Air 100	B-29	White Industries Inc. Bates City, Mo.	N8300E
N831CH	80	PA-31T Cheyenne 1	8004047	The RAFTT Corp. Houston, Tx.	(N911DW)
N831E	01	King Air C90B	LJ-1650	John Crump Automotive Inc. Jasper, Al.	N5150K
N831TM	98	King Air B200	BB-1635	JetSet LLC. Las Vegas, Nv.	N567A
N832AD	83	Conquest II	441-0311	Donald & Alice Fehrenbach, Chandler, Az.	XA-OAC
N833RL	81	King Air 200	BB-833	PTC Aviation Corp. Fort Lauderdale, Fl.	HP-1469
N835CC	83	Gulfstream 840	11730	State of New Mexico, Santa Fe, NM.	N28GA
N835MA	85	Conquest 1	441-0343	Cook Aircraft Leasing Inc. Bloomington, In.	N12114
N836MA	78	SA-226AT Merlin 4A	AT-068	Javelin Conversions Inc. Houston, Tx.	(N26LE)
N838RA	92	TBM 700	71	Chester Prior, Echo, Or.	N888RA
N840BC	81	Gulfstream 840	11663	Golden Eagle & Equipment & Leasing LLC. Buellton, Ca.	N840NB
N840CF	80	Gulfstream 840	11624	Francis Partners Ltd. Crowley, La.	N840XL
N840CP	99	King Air B200	BB-1658	CPSM Air, Burlingame, Ca.	N207CW
N840JC	80	Gulfstream 840	11643	Semitool Inc. Kalispell, Mt.	(N5895K)
N840JK	81	Gulfstream 840	11697	JJK Aviation LLC. Bristol, Tn.	N840AA
N840JW	81	Gulfstream 840	11658	Westerman Ltd. Addison, Tx.	N840FK
N840KB	80	Gulfstream 840	11640	Basswood Inc. Portland, Or.	N840VB
N840LC	80	Gulfstream 840	11647	Indiana Aircraft Sales Inc. Indianapolis, In.	HK-3460P
N840LE	81	Gulfstream 840	11709	O Henriksen/Crystal Ltd. Guernsey, Channel Islands.	N690BA
N840MA	74	Mitsubishi MU-2J	612	Air 1st Aviation Companies Inc. Aiken, Sc.	N799MA
N840MD	81	Gulfstream 840	11693	Hangen Equipment Leasing LLC. Wellsville, Ks.	N79SA
N840MG	80	Gulfstream 840	11638	Grupo Texpasa SA. Guatemala City, Guatemala.	N3XY
N840SB	83	King Air F90-1	LA-202	Intri-Plex Technologies Inc. Goleta, Ca.	N777AS
N840SE	80	Gulfstream 840	11610	Maya Air LLC. Telluride, Co.	N840AA
N840SM	81	Gulfstream 840	11700	G & V Aviation Corp. Fort Lauderdale, Fl.	(N83SA)
N840TW	81	Gulfstream 840	11689	PDMA Aviation Inc. Indianapolis, In.	N265JH
N840V	82	Gulfstream 840	11727	Mid Kansas Agri Co. Pawnee Rock, Ks.	N5965K
N840VM	80	Gulfstream 840	11607	Commercial Aviation Services Inc. Miami, Fl.	N840EA
N842DS	79	King Air A100	B-244	Brewer Aviation LLC. Duncan, Ok.	N942DS
N843BC	82	King Air B200	BB-1011	C Vincent Phillips MD. Bakersfield, Ca.	N20SM
N843BH	01	TBM 700B	196	H & H Air Inc. Washington, In.	F-WWRI
N843FC	82	King Air B200	BB-1030	Food City Aviation LLC & W-L Aviation LLC. Abingdon, Va.	N360SC
N844C	79	King Air C90	LJ-866	Better Minerals & Aggregates Co. Berkeley Springs, WV.	N6664P
N844MP	84	King Air B200	BB-1168	BB1168 LLC. Newark, De.	N179MC
N846BB	69	SA-26AT Merlin 2B	T26-149E	Merlin Wings LLC. Sandy, Ut.	N200BC
N846BE	84	King Air 300	FA-16	MD Airways Inc. Derby, Ks.	
N846CM	75	King Air 200	BB-18	Frontier Refining & Marketing, Englewood, Co.	N346CM
N846RD	04	PA-46-500TP Meridian	4697186	Richard Dietrich, Cleveland Heights, Oh.	
N846YT	81	Conquest II	441-0218	True Oil Co. Casper, Wy.	N41TA
N847BA	81	King Air 200	BB-847	Beech Transportation Inc. Eden Prairie, Mn.	OH-BIF
N847TS	81	King Air 200	BB-864	King Aviation LLC. Dallas, Tx.	N92TC
N847YT	82	Conquest 1	425-0114	True Oil Co. Casper, Wy.	N68803
N848CE	76	Rockwell 690A	11303	CTS Aviation Inc. Climax, Mi.	N81409
N848NA	81	King Air 200	BB-848	BBKR LLC. Las Vegas, Nv.	RP-C267
N848PF	85	King Air B200	BB-1225	Peoples First Courier Inc. Panama City, Fl.	N40FQ
Reg	Yr	Type	c/n	Owner/Operator	Prev Regn

Reg	Yr	Type	c/n	Owner/Operator	Prev Regn
N850AT	82	King Air B200	BB-989	Mallard Aviation LLC. Lafayette, La.	
N850BK	81	King Air B200	BB-896	Honeywell International Inc. Morristown, NJ.	N367EA
N850D	92	King Air 350	FL-70	L E Bell Construction Co. Heflin, Al.	N350KC
N850MS	93	King Air 350	FL-99	State of Mississippi, Jackson, Ms.	N350MS
N851BC	82	SA-227AT Merlin 4C	AT-495B	IBC Airways Inc. Miami, Fl.	(N9U)
N851KA	79	King Air C90	LJ-851	Beech Transportation Inc. Eden Prairie, Mn.	N4B
N851LC	04	PA-46-500TP Meridian	4697201	New Piper Aircraft Inc. Vero Beach, Fl.	
N851RM	00	Pilatus PC-12/45	360	Aldridge Aircraft LLC. Santa Rosa, Ca.	HB-FSL
N852AL	98	Pilatus PC-12/45	213	Air Methods Corp/St Charles Medical Center Inc. Bend, Or.	N213WA
N853AL	97	Pilatus PC-12	168	Air Methods Corp/St Charles Medical Center Inc. Bend, Or.	N168WA
N854AL	01	Pilatus PC-12/45	397	Air Methods Corp/Cascade Health Services, Oklahoma City, Ok.	N397WA
N855JL	81	PA-31T Cheyenne 1	8104045	Capsonic Automotive Inc. Elgin, Il.	N514M
N855RA	86	King Air 300	FA-106	RA Aviation Corp. Gulfport, Ms.	N810CM
N857C	83	Conquest 1	425-0156	V2 Air LLC. Monterey, Ca.	(N156CC)
N857GA	79	King Air 200T	BT-11	Intermap Technologies Corp. Ottawa, ON. Canada. (was BB-573)	JA8815
N857MA	77	Mitsubishi MU-2N	697SA	Freedom Aviation Inc. Salina, Ks.	
N859CC	78	King Air 200	BB-389	Cirrus Airplane Leasing LLC. Brookfield, Wi.	(OY-FCT)
N859GA	80	King Air 200T	BT-12	Global Aircraft Leasing Inc. Griffin, Ga, (was BB-501).	JA8816
N859Q	68	Mitsubishi MU-2D	113	Leon County School Board, Tallahassee, Fl.	
N860H	82	King Air B200	BB-1067	State of Ohio, Columbus, Oh.	N47MM
N860MA	77	MU-2 Marquise	700SA	Professional Aviation Sales & Service, Millington, Tn.	
N860MH	77	King Air E90	LW-210	Phantom Leasing Inc. Griffith, In.	N717TM
N861PP	03	Pilatus PC-12/45	510	PPC Excursions Inc. Harrisburg, Pa.	HB-FRN
N862DD	77	King Air 200	BB-298	Drake & Drake Inc. Gravois Mills, Mo.	N5110
N865PT	00	King Air B200	BB-1709	Chilmark Air Services Inc. Short Hills, NJ.	
N866A	67	King Air A90	LJ-201	Fayard Enterprises Inc. Louisburg, NC.	(D-ILNY)
N866D	75	Mitsubishi MU-2L	656	River City Aviation Inc. West Memphis, Ar.	N666D
N867MA	80	King Air F90	LA-65	Kenair Inc. West Palm Beach, Fl.	C-GMTI
N867P	01	King Air C90B	LJ-1666	MTR Gaming Group Inc. Chester, WV.	
N868MA	78	Mitsubishi MU-2N	708SA	Klaas Air LLC. Conway, Ak.	N15UD
N869D	71	Mitsubishi MU-2G	540	Turbine Aircraft Parts Inc. San Angelo, Tx.	(PT-...)
N869P	77	Mitsubishi MU-2L	692	Airdirect LLC. Birmingham, Al.	N623DC
N870C	03	PA-46-500TP Meridian	4697159	Gardner Equipment Leasing LLC. Houston, Tx.	
N870MA	72	King Air A100	B-109	National Airplane Sales & Leasing, Bluffton, Oh.	N78MK
N871KS	91	King Air C90A	LJ-1277	Kansas State University, Salina, Ks.	N8012U
N872BA	81	King Air B200	BB-872	Chickasaw Nation, Ada, Ok.	D-IOAN
N872CA	83	King Air B200	BB-1114	Capital Aerolease, Bethesda, Md.	N9768S
N872S	69	SA-26AT Merlin 2B	T26-123	Skyway Enterprises Inc. Kissimmee, Fl.	N872D
N873CA	85	King Air 300LW	FA-79	Culver Aviation LLC. Prairie du Sac, Wi.	N828CA
N873K	68	King Air B90	LJ-344	Jose Gonzalez, Dorado, PR.	
N875DM	90	King Air B200	BB-1354	Adcap LLC. Wilmington, De.	N15JA
N875SH	03	PA-46-500TP Meridian	4697174	James Hall, Charlottesville, Va.	
N876L	68	King Air B90	LJ-342	Western Aircraft Leasing LLC. Redding, Ca.	XA-MIM
N877AQ	65	King Air 90	LJ-41	Dodson International Parts Inc. Ottawa, Ks.	N877AG
N877RC	82	King Air B200	BB-978	Kelleher Construction Inc. Burnsville, Mn.	N877RF
N877SA	00	King Air 350	FL-296	Sparks Corp LLC. Memphis, Tn.	N383AS
N877WA	98	King Air 350	FL-203	Abrams Holding Inc. Houston, Tx.	N877W
N878JL	83	Conquest II	441-0293	Executive Turbine Sales Inc. Sarasota, Fl.	N293DR
N878K	98	King Air C90B	LJ-1513	WFHCO Equipment Corp. Little Rock, Ar.	N600CF
N878RA	75	King Air 200	BB-34	Ryan Aircraft LLC. Wichita, Ks.	N87BP
N879C	86	King Air 200	BB-1249	McElroy Metal Mill Inc. Bossier City, La.	N2512R
N879SW	79	PA-31T Cheyenne 1	7904056	Cartex Production Inc. Paso Robles, Ca.	
N880AC	82	MU-2 Marquise	1559SA	Lincoln Air Inc. Gettsburg, Pa.	HB-LQN
N880H	73	King Air C90	LJ-596	State of Ohio, Columbus, Oh.	N2896W
N880SW	80	PA-31T Cheyenne II	8020086	Apple Air LLC. Great Falls, Va.	
N880TC	82	PA-42 Cheyenne III	8001071	PeeJay Ventures Inc. Miami, Fl.	N108SB
N881CS	81	King Air B200	BB-881	Huntleigh/McGehee Inc. Scottsdale, Az.	VH-USD
N881L	79	PA-31T Cheyenne II	7920090	Hanson Flight LLC. Roswell, NM.	N801L
N882AC	77	Rockwell 690B	11375	Restrepo Aircraft Corp. Pompano Beach, Fl.	N412AC
N883BB	81	King Air B200	BB-883	Oregon 883 LLC. Roseburg, Or.	TC-YPI
N883CA	03	TBM 700C	294	N777FX Aircraft LLC. San Diego, Ca.	
N883CR	92	TBM 700	83	Fourth LLC. Muskogee, Ok.	N883CA
N884D	81	Gulfstream 840	11696	Aerosales & Services Inc. Austin, Tx.	N88PD
N884PG	76	King Air 200	BB-91	Aviation Management & Construction, Reno, Nv.	N9CJ
N885RA	72	Rockwell 690	11012	Sooner Air Charter Inc. Norman, Ok.	N921HB

Reg	Yr	Type	c/n	Owner/Operator	Prev Regn
☐ N886AC	00	King Air 350	FL-284	Ariel Corp. Mount Vernon, Oh.	N4484A
☐ N887FB	88	King Air B200	BB-1311	FB Air Holding Inc. Naples, Fl.	N888CS
☐ N887JC	89	King Air B200	BB-1345	JohnJr LLC. Westerville, Oh.	N715JH
☐ N888AH	79	PA-31T Cheyenne 1	7904038	Dialysis Clinic Inc. Nashville, Tn.	(N528KC)
☐ N888AS	87	King Air 300LW	FA-136	San Tomo Partners, Stockton, Ca.	(N82HR)
☐ N888AY	84	SA-227TT Merlin 3C	TT-489	Avalon Air Corp. Concord, NH.	N655PE
☐ N888CG	95	Pilatus PC-12	127	UDP Holding Co. Rocksprings, Tx.	N33JQ
☐ N888CV	78	PA-31T Cheyenne II	7820025	M D Aviation Ltd. Rockaway, NJ.	N888SV
☐ N888DC	79	King Air 200	BB-454	South Atlantic Developers LLC. Hinesville, Ga.	
☐ N888DS	69	Mitsubishi MU-2F	159	Dixie Continental Charter Group, Dover, De.	N30MA
☐ N888ET	77	King Air 200	BB-258	JBQ Inc. San Francisco, Ca.	N40PS
☐ N888EX	77	King Air 200	BB-240	Major Airline LLC/Major Saver Fundraising Inc. Lees Summit.	N888EM
☐ N888FM	04	King Air 350	FL-418	SBL Services/Maines Paper & Food Service Inc. Conklin, NY.	
☐ N888FV	99	King Air B200	BB-1682	Raytheon Aircraft Co. Wichita, Ks.	N888FM
☐ N888JM	77	PA-31T Cheyenne II	7720066	Magna-Tech Manufacturing Corp. Muncie, In.	N499EH
☐ N888JS	85	Conquest 1	425-0215	BPR Management Corp. Denver, Co.	N1225D
☐ N888LG	81	PA-31T Cheyenne II	8120035	JLCA Partners LLC. Long Beach, Ca.	N888LB
☐ N888MA	75	King Air C90	LJ-656	Makarion Enterprises Inc. Chino, Ca.	N15GA
☐ N888PH	79	PA-31T Cheyenne 1	7904050	Tax Awareness Planning Inc. Sugarland, Tx.	N3WE
☐ N888RH	79	MU-2 Marquise	737SA	EPPS Air Service Inc. Atlanta, Ga.	N315MA
☐ N888SE	82	MU-2 Marquise	1549SA	EPPS Air Service Inc. Atlanta, Ga.	N475MA
☐ N888TF	01	TBM 700B	178	TBM Leasing Inc. Maitland, Fl.	N277GM
☐ N888TR	75	King Air 200	BB-50	Twin County Aviation LLC. Galax, Va.	N500FE
☐ N888WG	04	Pilatus PC-12/45	587	Pilatus Business Aircraft Ltd. Jeffco Airport, Mo.	HB-FQZ
☐ N888WW	80	MU-2 Marquise	791SA	TVPX Inc. Concord, Ma.	(N725SG)
☐ N888ZX	83	King Air B200	BB-1140	Old Glory Inc. Tulsa, Ok.	N42KA
☐ N889DM	77	Conquest II	441-0022	Belmullet Flying Services LLC. Hartland, Wi.	N53GG
☐ N891MA	77	King Air 200	BB-238	Mexi-tile Inc. Wilmington, De.	YV-106CP
☐ N892WA	76	Rockwell 690A	11273	David Swetland, Cleveland, Oh.	I-TASA
☐ N893KB	80	MU-2 Solitaire	415SA	Select Homes Inc. Asheboro, NC.	N860SM
☐ N893MC	98	King Air 350	FL-216	Midwest Air Services Inc. Fort Worth, Tx.	N898MC
☐ N895CA	94	King Air 350	FL-114	H L Chapman Pipeline Construction Co. Leander, Tx.	N616CK
☐ N895FK	78	King Air C90	LJ-759	Cobb Aviation Services Inc. Macomb, Il.	N133E
☐ N895MA	78	Mitsubishi MU-2N	723SA	C & M Leasing Inc. Houston, Ms.	
☐ N895TT	85	King Air B200	BB-1239	Terry Corp. Jackson, Wy.	N833BK
☐ N896DR	80	PA-31T Cheyenne 1	8004050	DRC Aviation LLC. Mobile, Al.	N812CM
☐ N896FM	86	Beech 1900C	UB-48	Intel Corp. Folsom, Ca.	N810BE
☐ N896SB	73	King Air A100	B-160	Rogers Helicopters Inc. Clovis, Ca.	OY-CCS
☐ N896SC	85	Beech 1900C	UB-40	Intel Corp. Folsom, Ca.	N809BE
☐ N898CA	79	King Air 200	BB-572	Infinity KingAir LLC/Tradewind Aviation LLC. White Plains.	N119MC
☐ N898CM	80	King Air C90	LJ-898	Mike R Craig & Assocs Inc. Little Rock, Ar.	LX-FRZ
☐ N898WW	74	King Air E90	LW-103	Douglas Cayne, Portola Valley, Ca.	D-IDEA
☐ N899D	68	King Air B90	LJ-386	Sun Charter LLC. St Petersburg, Fl.	N610K
☐ N899MC	82	King Air B200	BB-998	Deer Horn Aviation LC. Midland, Tx.	N76PT
☐ N899SD	81	King Air 200	BB-776	Sunridge Nurseries Inc. Bakersfield, Ca.	N500FP
☐ N900AC	78	King Air E90	LW-282	Turbo Air Inc. Boise, Id.	N50MB
☐ N900BE	80	King Air C90	LJ-907	Chandler Aviation inc. Richmond, Va.	N900TJ
☐ N900CK	66	King Air 90	LJ-85	Cosco Aviation Services, Crestview, Fl.	N900CF
☐ N900DG	79	King Air 200	BB-455	All Day Inc. Las Vegas, Nv.	N24SX
☐ N900DN	73	King Air A100	B-170	Par Avion LLC/Sage Financial Corp/Par Avion LLC. Salem, Or.	N900DH
☐ N900DZ	74	King Air C90	LJ-618	DLJ Aviation LLC. Little Rock, Ar.	N900DG
☐ N900ET	84	Gulfstream 900	15037	Azucarera la Grecia SA. Honduras.	C-FAWG
☐ N900HS	96	Pilatus PC-12	136	H-S Air Inc. Englewood, NJ.	N79CA
☐ N900LL	81	Gulfstream 840	11687	Grace Equipment LLC. Bend, Or.	N90WE
☐ N900M	82	MU-2 Marquise	1545SA	Atwood Aviation LLC. Antioch, Tn.	N471MA
☐ N900MS	81	Conquest 1	425-0079	Quest One LLC. Hagerstown, Md.	N6846K
☐ N900MT	83	King Air C90-1	LJ-1048	Meyer-Tomatoes LLC. King City, Ca.	N777HF
☐ N900RD	77	King Air B100	BE-33	Chandler Aircraft Marketing Inc. Chandler, Tx.	(N232EB)
☐ N900RH	81	King Air 200	BB-816	Rite-Hite Corp. Milwaukee, Wi.	N510G
☐ N900RJ	66	680V Turbo Commander	1572-27	Michael Wood, McLean, Va.	(N713SP)
☐ N900TV	69	Mitsubishi MU-2F	140	Air 1st Aviation Companies Inc. Aiken, SC.	N333RK
☐ N900VA	82	King Air C90	LJ-1002	Chase Equipment Ltd. Colchester, Vt.	D-ICLE
☐ N900YH	73	Mitsubishi MU-2J	584	Styles Aviation Inc. NY.	N791MA
☐ N901BK	71	King Air C90	LJ-521	Amerieast Inc. Columbus, Ga.	N70QZ
☐ N901DM	01	PA-46-500TP Meridian	4697051	CRC Aviation Corp. Commack, NY.	

Reg	Yr	Type	c/n	Owner/Operator	Prev Regn
N901JA	76	King Air C90	LJ-694	Emerald Aviation Inc. London, Ky.	N712K
N901JS	04	King Air C90B	LJ-1726	Raytheon Aircraft Co. Wichita, Ks.	
N901MC	81	SA-226T Merlin 3B	T-369	McBee Co. Dallas, Tx.	N1009Y
N901MT	84	PA-42 Cheyenne 400LS	5527011	McVean Aviation of N Carolina, Memphis, Tn.	N86CR
N901PC	97	King Air C90B	LJ-1505	Soc Internacional de Servicios SA. Guatemala City, Guatemala	HC-BZD
N901SA	65	King Air 90	LJ-66	AB Enterprises of Oregon, Medford, Or.	N1SA
N901TM	77	King Air E90	LW-227	Azalea Aviation Inc. Mobile, Al.	N7ZP
N901TP	92	AP68TP-600 Viator	9001	Air Coulibri Inc. NYC.	I-BAML
N901TS	96	King Air C90B	LJ-1458	R H K of Kansas Inc. Topeka, Ks.	N992WS
N901WL	68	King Air B90	LJ-410	W L Paris Enterprises Inc. Louisville, Ky.	N33CS
N902LT	97	King Air C90B	LJ-1480	Western Oilfields Supply Co. Bakersfield, Ca.	
N902TS	96	King Air C90B	LJ-1459	Clary Aviation LLC. Longview, Wa.	N994WS
N902XP	86	King Air C90A	LJ-1136	A & L Enterprise LLC. Urbandale, Ia.	N359JT
N903DC	78	Conquest II	441-0061	OCAAS LLC/SkyCare, Alamogordo, NM.	N441MB
N903EH	82	BAe Jetstream 31	605	First Capital Group Inc. Albuquerque, NM.	N903FH
N903GP	79	King Air C90	LJ-861	Myers Medical Equities Inc. Paterson, NJ.	N905GP
N903MA	04	TBM 700C	308	Huse Aviation Corp. Bloomington, In.	
N903MD*	97	King Air A90	LM-98	Dynamic Avlease Inc. Bridgewater, Va	
N903WD	77	Conquest II	441-0010	Conquoot Air LLC. Sewickley, Pa.	N20HC
N904DG	84	King Air B200	BB-1176	Profile Aviation Services Inc. Hickory, NC.	N81LC
N904DJ*	72	King Air C90	LJ-561	AERS-Aircraft Engine Reconstruction Specialist, Prescott, Az	N777NW
N904FH	83	BAe Jetstream 31	613	Coca-Cola Bottling Co. Chattanooga, Tn.	N331BA
N904HB	90	King Air C90A	LJ-1256	Louisiana Dept of Transportation, Baton Rouge, La.	
N904JP	85	King Air C90A	LJ-1121	McLane Trailer Sales Inc. Poplar Bluff, Mo.	(N20LK)
N904MC	91	King Air 350	FL-44	Malco Leasing Corp. Danbury, Ct.	N90PR
N904RB	85	King Air C90A	LJ-1088	Coil Construction Management Inc. Columbia, Mo.	N124MB
N904US	79	King Air C90	LJ-856	U S Energy Services Inc/Anoka Air Charter Inc. Minneapolis.	N904JS
N905GP	81	King Air 200	BB-789	Godwin Pumps of America Inc. Bridgeport, NJ.	N70KM
N905LC	84	PA-42 Cheyenne IIIA	5501022	reported stolen 1988. (status ?).	N4115K
N905TF	72	King Air E90	LW-6	CEI Inc. Wilmington, De.	N722M
N906HF	70	King Air A90	LM-140	Vanderwall Aircraft LLC. Peachtree City, Ga.	N7194P
N908BS	01	King Air B200	BB-1781	Blue Sky Inc. Wilmington, De.	N34GN
N908K	71	King Air C90	LJ-504	MD Charter Air Inc. Pone Vedra Beach, Fl.	(N479SJ)
N909HH	84	Gulfstream 900	15035	Gramer Air-II LLC. Bloomfield Hills, Mi.	N900DS
N909P	04	PA-46-500TP Meridian	4697187	Green Plane LLC. Wisconsin Dells, Wi.	
N910AJ	81	King Air B200	BB-910	L'Eagle Air II Inc. Key West, Fl.	ZS-LJA
N910FC	81	Gulfstream 840	11682	State of Tennessee, Nashville, Tn.	N910EC
N910HG	74	PA-31T Cheyenne II	7400009	Shipman & Associates LLP. Wilmington, NC.	N910HM
N910JP	78	PA-31T Cheyenne II	7820004	APAC Enterprises LP. League City, Tx.	N33LD
N911AZ	78	King Air E90	LW-300	State of Arizona, Phoenix, Az.	(N912AZ)
N911CF	80	King Air F90	LA-13	Custom Fire Apparatus Inc. Osceola, Wi.	N132AS
N911CX	79	King Air C90	LJ-830	LJ830 LLC. Kansas City, Mo.	N45PE
N911ER	82	Conquest II	441-0249	Acadian Ambulance Services Inc. Lafayette, La.	N800BN
N911FG	78	King Air C90	LJ-774	Aerolease LLC. Fargo, ND.	N911ND
N911FN	76	King Air C90	LJ-688	Millennium Aircraft LLC. Bethany, Ok.	N195KQ
N911MN	77	King Air 200	BB-229	Presentation Sisters Inc/McKennan Hospital, Sioux Falls, SD.	N904CM
N911ND	80	King Air 200	BB-589	Jetlease LLC/Fargo Jet Center, Fargo, ND.	N553R
N911PJ	80	Conquest II	441-0146	Windriver Trees, Garfield County, Co.	N146EA
N911RL	70	King Air 100	B-55	Dale Aviation Inc. Rapid City, SD.	N4167P
N911SF	99	King Air B200	BB-1659	Penn-Aire Aviation Inc. Bonita Springs, Fl.	
N911SR	81	King Air B200	BB-988	Lynch Flying Service Inc. Billings, Mt.	N98GA
N911VJ	78	PA-42 Cheyenne III	7800002	Southern Cross Aircraft Inc. Fort Lauderdale, Fl.	N202VJ
N912JS	03	King Air B200	BB-1845	J & S Aviation Inc. Itasca, Il.	N5005V
N912NF	74	Mitsubishi MU-2J	623	North Flight Inc. Traverse City, Mi.	N22YA
N912NM	97	Pilatus PC-12	169	Air Methods Corp. Peoria, Il.	N661DT
N912SM	79	King Air 200	BB-478	St Mary's Hospital & Medical Center, Grand Junction, Co.	N789DS
N912SV	88	King Air B200	BB-1299	St Vincent's Healthcare, Billings, Mt.	(N315SA)
N913CR	78	PA-31T Cheyenne 1	7804003	Klein Aviation LLC. Perry, Ga.	N21JA
N913DC	82	Conquest II	441-0246	Rico Aviation LLC. Amarillo, Tx.	N246SP
N914CT	98	King Air B200	BB-1614	NGF Corp. Glen Cove, NY.	N2233Q
N915CD	78	King Air C90	LJ-748	Marfa Air Transportation LLC. Houston, Tx.	N974GA
N915MP	00	King Air C90B	LJ-1637	Multi Plastics Inc. Lewis Center, Oh.	N290SA
N915RF	76	Mitsubishi MU-2L	677	Air 1st Aviation Companies Inc. Aiken, SC.	N2ND
N916AS	82	Conquest II	441-0243	JLS Group LLC. Milford, De.	N441HA
N916RT	82	Cheyenne II-XL	8166041	Newstone Aire LLC/Tiffin Aire Inc. Tiffin, Oh.	C-GFLL

396

Reg	Yr Type	c/n	Owner/Operator	Prev Regn
☐ N917F	81 PA-31T Cheyenne 1	8104030	917F LLC/High Air Inc. Plano, Tx.	N71LA
☐ N917WA	85 King Air 300	FA-77	CajunFlight LLC. Rochester, NY.	N477JW
☐ N918FM	79 PA-31T Cheyenne 1	7904025	Fenton Motor Group, McAlester, Ok.	N531SW
☐ N918SA	80 King Air C90	LJ-918	Mid South Air LLC. Rogers, Ar.	(N950HS)
☐ N918TC	81 King Air B200	BB-918	Blue Sky Ventures LLC. Ogden, Ut.	ZS-NCH
☐ N918VS	76 King Air E90	LW-200	76PW LLC. Tulsa, Ok.	N913VS
☐ N919AG	68 King Air B90	LJ-432	Aircraft Services Group LC. Derry, NH.	N345LL
☐ N919CK	84 SA-227AT Merlin 4C	AT-585	Extant Aircraft Corp. Childress, Tx.	(F-....)
☐ N919CL	87 King Air C90A	LJ-1160	MGKR Enterprises LLC. Lufkin, Tx.	N6031W
☐ N919RE	80 King Air 200	BB-824	Evernham Motorsports LLC. Concord, NH.	N824TT
☐ N919WM	80 King Air 200	BB-680	Westling Manufacturing Co. Princeton, Mn.	N675PG
☐ N920C	85 King Air 300	FA-54	Air Travel Services Inc. Nashville, Tn.	N663AC
☐ N920S	71 Mitsubishi MU-2G	534	Turbine Aircraft Marketing Inc. San Angelo, Tx.	(N78V)
☐ N920WJ	80 Gulfstream 840	11621	McDonnell Aerospace Group Inc. Albuquerque, NM.	(N23TX)
☐ N921AZ	88 King Air B200	BB-1287	Department of Public Safety, Phoenix, Az.	N713DH
☐ N921BS	94 King Air 350	FL-110	Old Dominion Aviation LLC. Hickory, NC.	N721BS
☐ N921SA	72 King Air A100	B-101	SHA Aviation LLC. Boca Raton, Fl.	(N101UJ)
☐ N921ST	74 Rockwell 690A	11200	AC Properties LLC. Portland, Or.	
☐ N922AA	82 King Air C90-1	LJ-1022	Pegasus Air Services LLC. Traverse City, Mi.	PT-OAB
☐ N922FM	72 Mitsubishi MU-2F	216	Oakton International Corp. Laporte, In.	N922ST
☐ N922HP	78 Conquest II	441-0027	Home Air Inc/Home Place Inc. Gainesville, Ga.	N900HA
☐ N922KV	81 Conquest 1	425-0052	Central Coast AG Rentals LLC. Salinas, Ca.	N425SG
☐ N922MM*	04 King Air B200	BB-1866	Medico Inc. Ridgeland, Ms.	
☐ N922RG	01 Pilatus PC-12/45	409	Riversville Aircraft Corp. Greenwich, Ct. (status ?).	HB-FQW
☐ N923AS*	79 King Air 200	BB-541	Pacific Aircraft Trading LLC. Bakersfield, Ca.	N113GW
☐ N923CR	84 King Air C90A	LJ-1074	Douglas Peacock Trust, Concord, Oh.	N6583K
☐ N923FP	98 King Air B200	BB-1605	FMP Enterprises LLC. Yakima, Wa.	N2245P
☐ N924AC	79 King Air/Catpass 250	BB-483	Gulf Air LLC. Spring Hill, Fl.	N250FN
☐ N924JD	03 King Air B200	BB-1849	Wichita Air Services Leasing LLC. Wichita, Ks.	N6109A
☐ N924JP*	03 TBM 700	277	PROMAG Retail Services LLC. Danville, Ca.	
☐ N924PC	72 Rockwell 690	11041	United CCM Corp. San Antonio, Tx. (status ?).	(N54MH)
☐ N925B	82 King Air B200	BB-1050	Atlantic Coast Leasing Corp. Wilmington, De.	(N19KA)
☐ N925HW	01 Pilatus PC-12/45	444	Screening Services International Inc. Slaughter, La.	HB-FSB
☐ N925MM	80 King Air C90	LJ-925	TCAS Enterprises LLC. Colleyville, Tx.	N925BC
☐ N925TK	92 P-180 Avanti	1021	TK Constructors Inc. Muncie, IN.	D-IPIA
☐ N925TT	80 King Air 200	BB-746	Aspen Base Operation Inc. Aspen, Co.	C-FMPE
☐ N925X	63 King Air 90	LJ-1	Avionics Research Corp. Madison, Ms.	N26CH
☐ N926ES	81 Conquest 1	425-0029	Fullers White Mountain Motors Inc. Show Low, Az.	N926FS
☐ N926FS	81 Conquest 1	425-0093	J H Jet LLC. Wilson, Wy.	N6848R
☐ N926K	80 PA-31T Cheyenne 1	8004046	Cato Enterprises Inc. Lynn Haven, Fl.	PT-WNZ
☐ N926LD	78 PA-31T Cheyenne II	7820047	North Dakota State University, Fargo, ND.	N290T
☐ N926PR	87 King Air 300	FA-127	FYK Corp. Jefferson, In.	N45BT
☐ N926S	69 King Air B90	LJ-447	Hale O'Lele Corp. Waialua, Hi.	C-GSUN
☐ N926SC	80 Gulfstream 840	11622	S E Cone Jr. Hobbs, NM.	N49BB
☐ N927BG*	04 King Air B200	BB-1854	Dream Aviation LLC. Brandon, Ms.	N6194S
☐ N927JC	80 King Air 200	BB-595	Nick Corp. Boxford, Ma.	N528JJ
☐ N927JJ	91 King Air C90A	LJ-1263	Orange & White LLC/Venture Aviation Group, Greenville, SC.	N230JS
☐ N928KG	00 King Air C90B	LJ-1632	Stoney Point Group Inc. Asheville, NC.	N608P
☐ N928US	00 King Air C90B	LJ-1604	Union Springs Aviation LLC. Cincinnati, Oh.	N925BS
☐ N929BG	04 King Air 350	FL-408	B Gentry Acquisitions LLC. Houston, Tx.	N6108A
☐ N929BW	98 King Air B200	BB-1630	Rieke Corp. Auburn, In.	
☐ N929DM	78 King Air 200	BB-398	Cindy Air LLC/Donovan Industries Inc. Tampa, Fl.	N429DM
☐ N929FD	99 King Air C90B	LJ-1585	Faust Distributing Co. Houston, Tx.	(N233SA)
☐ N929SG	81 King Air 200	BB-834	Sierra Gulf Equipment LLC. Midland, Tx.	(N68MD)
☐ N930CA	04 TBM 700C	309	Columbia Aircraft Sales Inc. Groton, Ct.	
☐ N930K	67 King Air A90	LJ-294	Opening Statement LLC. Oxford, Ms.	
☐ N930MC	96 King Air C90B	LJ-1463	Corporate Flights LLC. South Bend, In.	N771SQ
☐ N930SP	81 King Air B200	BB-930	Arkansas State Police, Little Rock, Ar.	F-GHMY
☐ N931GG	99 King Air C90B	LJ-1572	Bay Area/Diablo Petroleum Co. Salinas, Ca.	N33LA
☐ N931WC	90 King Air C90A	LJ-1231	M G W Aviation Inc. Columbia, Tn.	N931AJ
☐ N932AK	84 PA-42 Cheyenne IIIA	5501023	MT Aviation LLC/John Tisdel Distributing Inc. Mason, Oh.	N449CA
☐ N933CL	90 King Air 350	FL-19	Createc Lewis Flight Services Inc. Indianapolis, In.	(N573P)
☐ N933DG	83 PA-42 Cheyenne III	8001106	J B Air Inc. Manhattan, Ks.	N42KA
☐ N933RT	82 King Air B200	BB-955	Phelps-Tointon Inc. Greeley, Co.	G-WILK
☐ N933SE	00 Pilatus PC-12/45	375	Austin Encino Ltd. San Antonio, Tx.	N375PC
Reg	*Yr Type*	*c/n*	*Owner/Operator*	*Prev Regn*

Reg	Yr	Type	c/n	Owner/Operator	Prev Regn
N934DC	77	King Air E90	LW-202	Dixie Capital Corp. Richmond, Va.	N127
N934SH	77	King Air 200	BB-252	J & B Air Service LLC. Dalton, Ga.	N475U
N935AJ	81	King Air B200	BB-935	H & P LLC. Waverly, Al.	N500CY
N937D	81	PA-42 Cheyenne III	8001055	Red Baron Enterprises Inc. Dover, De.	N93BD
N938JW	01	PA-46-500TP Meridian	4697023	Wessman Aircraft Sales & Leasing Co. Aurora, Ca.	
N938P	90	King Air C90A	LJ-1250	Account Control Technology Inc. Canoga Park, Ca.	F-GTRM
N939C	69	SA-26AT Merlin 2B	T26-152	Vaero Inc. Blacksburg, Va.	N4ER
N939JB	79	PA-31T Cheyenne 1	7904039	RidgeAire Inc. Jacksonville, Tx.	HC-BNF
N939K	68	King Air B90	LJ-349	Pacific Coast Enterprises LLC. Las Vegas, Nv.	
N940AC	80	Gulfstream 840	11629	Dr Stephen Ritland, Flagstaff, Az.	VH-NCM
N940HC	88	King Air B200	BB-1303	General Greene Investments Co. Greensboro, NC.	N1932H
N940MA	74	Mitsubishi MU-2J	615	Intercontinental Jet Inc. Tulsa, Ok.	N349MA
N940U	69	680W Turbo Commander	1843-42	University of Oklahoma, Norman, Ok.	(YV-723P)
N941MA	79	MU-2 Marquise	744SA	EPPS Air Service Inc. Atlanta, Ga.	
N941S	79	MU-2 Marquise	738SA	HHK Safaris Inc. Wilmington, De.	N916MA
N942CE	00	King Air B200	BB-1731	Corporate Eagle Capital LLC. Waterford, Mi.	(N948CL)
N942CF	79	King Air 200	BB-494	Quest Diagnostics Inc. Reading, Pa.	N942CE
N942ST	79	MU-2 Marquise	745SA	Bankair Inc. West Columbia, SC.	N942MA
N944BT	02	Pilatus PC-12/45	468	Cumulus Ltd. Salem, Or.	HB-FQA
N944CA	01	TBM 700B	206	Chesapeake Leasing Inc. Arlington, Va.	(D-FAJS)
N944CF	78	King Air 200	BB-326	S S T Tire Service Inc. Port St Lucie, Fl.	N944CE
N944K	69	King Air B90	LJ-467	Carmine Labriola Inc. Scarsdale, NY.	
N944LS	80	King Air 200	BB-604	Mid-America AG Network Inc. Wichita, Ks.	N944CC
N944RS	76	King Air E90	LW-177	Troy Fraser, Big Spring, Tx.	N2177L
N945WS	72	King Air A100	B-94	Golden Wings Aviation Inc. Uniontown, Pa.	N12AQ
N946CE	00	King Air B200	BB-1728	Corporate Eagle Capital LLC. Waterford, Mi.	
N946JJ	95	Pilatus PC-12	115	Betten Equipment Leasing Inc. Muskegon, Mi.	N398CA
N948CE	00	King Air B200	BB-1736	Corporate Eagle Capital LLC. Waterford, Mi.	N942CE
N948HB*	80	King Air B100	BE-98	HB Air LLC/Helfrich Brothers Boiler Works, Lawrence, Ma.	
N949SW	78	King Air B100	BE-34	960PC LLC. Aurora, Il.	N203KA
N950KM	04	Pilatus PC-12/45	540	Wings Over Oregon LLC. Eugene, Or.	HB-FSN
N950M	74	Rockwell 690A	11173	State of Indiana, Indianapolis, In.	N501MQ
N950MA	75	Mitsubishi MU-2L	671	Intercontinental Jet Inc. Tulsa, Ok.	N4203C
N950TA	90	PA-42 Cheyenne IIIA	5501050	McNeil & Co. Cortland, NY.	JA8873
N951K	70	King Air 100	B-17	W H Wheeler Jr. Tyler, Tx.	
N951TB	04	PA-46-500TP Meridian	4697175	Moss Inc. Grand Junction, Co.	
N953PC	04	King Air 350	FL-411	Pacific Coast Jet Charter Inc. Rancho Cordova, Ca.	N36811
N954BL	02	King Air C90B	LJ-1681	Sarah & Clint LLC. Hays, Ks.	N4481P
N955RA	83	King Air F90	LA-201	Remington Products Co. Wadsworth, Oh.	N653LP
N956PC	00	Pilatus PC-12/45	323	Brent Brown Enterprises LLC. Provo, Ut.	HB-FRF
N957CB	98	King Air B200	BB-1624	First National Bank & Trust Co. McAlester, Ok.	N1624B
N957JF	80	King Air C90	LJ-906	Justice Bedding Co. Lebanon, Mo.	N5371
N958JH	85	King Air C90A	LJ-1108	Jim Hankins Air Service Inc. Jackson, Ms.	N438SP
N959CM	81	King Air C90	LJ-971	Clark Mason PA. Little Rock, Ar.	N971CF
N959MC	79	King Air C90	LJ-821	Midwest Corporate Aviation Inc. Wichita, Ks.	N821CT
N960GK	82	King Air B200	BB-960	White Industries Inc. Bates City, Mo.	(NZ1883)
N960V	80	King Air F90	LA-31	Executive Beechcraft STL Inc. Chesterfield, Mo.	N6675W
N961LL	99	King Air 350	FL-264	State of Illinois, Springfield, Il.	N2344H
N962TT	81	King Air C90	LJ-962	W W Flying Club Inc. Brookhaven, Mn.	TC-MCK
N963BP	68	SA-26AT Merlin 2B	T26-114	Royal Sons Inc. Clearwater, Fl.	N1AQ
N963KA	77	King Air E90	LW-242	FWF Inc. Seattle, Wa.	N95KA
N964GB	82	King Air C90	LJ-1007	N964GB Inc. Daytona Beach, Fl.	N68PC
N964LB	91	King Air 350	FL-59	The Bergquist Co. Chanhassen, Mn.	N350JJ
N965LG	77	King Air E90	LW-204	Gulf Shore Air LLC. Williamstown, Ma.	N965LC
N965SB	01	PA-46-500TP Meridian	4697005	Dettmer Equipment Leasing LLC. Fort Wayne, In.	
N967JG*	90	King Air 300LW	FA-214	J & J Black Diamond LLC. Vail, Co.	N393CF
N968MB	99	King Air B200	BB-1667	Gwinett Aviation Inc. Buford, Ga.	N600TA
N968T	79	King Air 200	BB-570	Rubloff King LLC. Rockford, Il.	(N919LN)
N969CL	78	King Air E90	LW-252	Ed's Flying Service Inc. Alamagordo, NM.	N1975G
N969MA	81	King Air B200	BB-894	Universal Air LLC. Columbia, SC.	(N894MA)
N969MB	00	King Air 350	FL-290	Clear Sky Aviation LLC. Loveland, Co.	(N290BT)
N969WB	82	King Air B200	BB-969	West Coast Charters LLC. Santa Ana, Ca.	N48N
N970M	70	SA-226T Merlin 3	T-205	Madan Construction Co. Michigan City, In.	N20GC
N970NA	98	Pilatus PC-12/45	226	Native Air Services Inc. Mesa, Az.	N308NA
N970P	97	King Air C90B	LJ-1487	Prism Aviation LC. Wilkesboro, NC.	
Reg	Yr	Type	c/n	Owner/Operator	Prev Regn

Reg	Yr	Type	c/n	Owner/Operator	Prev Regn
☐ N970PS	80 PA-31T Cheyenne II		8020023	Laurel Cheyennes Aircraft Sales LLC. Johnstown, Pa.	N611LM
☐ N971LL	00 King Air 350		FL-267	State of Illinois, Springfield, Il.	N4167H
☐ N971P	99 King Air C90B		LJ-1575	Hughes Venture Group Inc. Princeton, Ky.	
☐ N971SC	93 King Air C90B		LJ-1343	SCANA Services Inc. Columbia, SC.	N8208C
☐ N973BB	81 MU-2 Marquise		1509SA	Romeo Aviation Inc. Austria.	N973MA
☐ N973GA	76 King Air C90		LJ-675	Rick Aviation Inc. Newport News, Va.	ZS-ODV
☐ N975SC	81 King Air 200		BB-806	Max Bowen, Vinita, Ok.	EC-ESV
☐ N975TB	92 TBM 700		75	Stuart Shelk Jr. Powell Butte, Or.	N79RA
☐ N976JT	76 King Air C90		LJ-699	Tri-State Aero Inc. Evansville, In.	
☐ N976KC	80 King Air 200		BB-601	Century A/C King Air Inc. Wilmington, De.	N6687H
☐ N977AA	72 King Air C90		LJ-555	Maritime Sales & Leasing Inc. Newnan, Ga.	N108JD
☐ N977DG*	75 Rockwell 690A		11237	Adonia Aire LP/TX OK Air LLC. Denton, Tx.	N57237
☐ N977FC	77 King Air C90		LJ-733	Baru Air SA. Panama City, Panama.	N18383
☐ N977JC	80 Gulfstream 840		11641	Ace Inc. Winston-Salem, NC.	N850GA
☐ N977LX	76 King Air 200		BB-141	Lima Xray LLC. Savoy, Il.	
☐ N977MP	83 Conquest II		441-0310	Martin's Famous Pastry Shoppe Inc. Chambersburg, Pa.	N444KE
☐ N977SB	72 King Air E90		LW-10	Glideco Leasing Inc. Fort Worth, Tx.	(N596PC)
☐ N977XL	97 Pilatus PC-12/45		189	Carter Enterprises Inc. Little Compton, RI.	HB-FSX
☐ N977XT	81 PA-42 Cheyenne III		8001008	R Y Timber Inc. Boise, Id.	N808CA
☐ N980AK	80 Gulfstream 840		11636	Universal Pacific Investments Corp. Stateline, Nv.	N7649J
☐ N980BH	80 Gulfstream 980		95002	Commander 980BH LC. Rio Grande City, Tx.	(N905BL)
☐ N980CA	81 PA-31T Cheyenne 1		8104010	TLH Enterprises Inc. Corsicana, Tx.	
☐ N980DT	81 Gulfstream 980		95048	Detroit Tool & Engineering Co. Lebanon, Mo.	N9800S
☐ N980EA	80 Gulfstream 980		95031	Eagle Air Inc. Memphis, Tn. (now XC-HFW ?).	HP-1132P
☐ N980EC	80 Gulfstream 980		95011	CPI-Airservice GmbH/Carlos de Pilar Group, Munich, Germany.	N9764S
☐ N980GB	97 King Air B200		BB-1594	Robert Gentry, Ruidoso, NM.	N2132W
☐ N980GM	80 Gulfstream 980		95034	Viztek Inc. St Simons, Ga.	N980WM
☐ N980GR	81 Gulfstream 980		95049	Genesis Aircraft Marketing LLC. Bethany, Ok.	N3982C
☐ N980GZ	81 Gulfstream 980		95063	Alken-Ziegler Inc. Kalkaska, Mi.	N980GM
☐ N980HB	80 Gulfstream 980		95006	Holding & Barnes Group/HBC Aviation Inc. Southend, UK.	N171CT
☐ N980MD	80 Gulfstream 980		95030	Air Operations International, Charlotte, NC.	N980AB
☐ N980SA	80 Gulfstream 980		95012	Amstar Aviation, Dover, De.	YV-129P
☐ N981AR	98 King Air 350		FL-199	Arvinmeritor Inc. Troy, Mi.	
☐ N981LE	80 King Air 200		BB-602	Aero Charter Services Inc. San Bernardino, Ca.	N981LL
☐ N981LL	99 King Air 350		FL-265	State of Illinois, Springfield, Il.	N3265T
☐ N982GA	76 King Air 200		BB-1594	M & M Aviation Inc. Pompton Lakes, NJ.	D-IAHK
☐ N982SB	98 King Air C90B		LJ-1518	Foster Hospitality Group LLC. Springfield, Mo.	
☐ N982SS	98 King Air C90B		LJ-1523	Futrell Assocaites LLC. Raleigh, NC.	
☐ N982TM	77 King Air 200		BB-226	Merlin Aviation LLC. St Louis, Mo.	N717SP
☐ N983AR	99 King Air 350		FL-242	Arvinmeritor Inc. Troy, Mi.	
☐ N983K	66 King Air A90		LJ-169	JR's Sky Inc. Newton, NJ.	N903K
☐ N983TM	94 King Air 350		FL-94	Instrumental Technologies Inc. Warsaw, In.	N861CC
☐ N984AA	68 King Air B90		LJ-429	Active Aero Charter, Detroit-Willow Run, Mi.	N811AA
☐ N984MA	80 King Air C90		LJ-883	Montgomery Aviation Corp. Montgomery, Al.	(N527JD)
☐ N984RE	80 MU-2 Marquise		787SA	EPPS Air Service Inc. Atlanta, Ga.	N267PC
☐ N987B	80 King Air B100		BE-81	High Performance Aircraft Inc. El Cajon, Ca.	(N3737G)
☐ N987GM	73 King Air E90		LW-65	Air Methods Corp/Flagstaff Medical Center Inc. Flagstaff, Az	N3065W
☐ N987MA	68 Mitsubishi MU-2F		124	Fast Air Brokerage Inc. Miami, Fl.	N18UT
☐ N988AE	80 Conquest II		441-0175	AirEvac Services Inc. Lafayette, La.	N2723A
☐ N988C	03 TBM 700C		282	Derners of Milford Inc. Milford, Ia.	
☐ N988CC	79 King Air 200		BB-490	Jet Texas Assocs LLC. Georgetown, Tx.	N908RC
☐ N988JR	78 King Air B100		BE-46	James River Coal Service Co. Richmond, Va.	N146BT
☐ N988ME	92 King Air 350		FL-77	Flight Investors LP. Hagerstown, Md.	N4000K
☐ N988SC	78 King Air 200		BB-310	Trust Aviation Inc. Miami, Fl.	N100KM
☐ N988SL	69 King Air B90		LJ-438	D N F Inc. Grand Rapids, Mi.	N900LS
☐ N988XJ	99 King Air C90B		LJ-1566	Banana Trading Corp. Guatemala City, Guatemala.	
☐ N989GM	74 King Air E90		LW-109	Air Methods Corp/Flagstaff Medical Center Inc. Flagstaff, Az	N388SC
☐ N989LA	88 King Air B200		BB-1310	Louisiana Aircraft LLC. Oklahoma City, Ok.	N16TF
☐ N990BM	80 King Air F90		LA-70	Preakness Aviation LLC. Rancho Santa Fe, Ca.	N3687S
☐ N990CB	94 King Air C90B		LJ-1362	Fremont LLC. Springfield, Mo.	
☐ N990DA	78 King Air C90		LJ-753	Duncan Aviation Inc. Lincoln, Ne.	N601SC
☐ N990DP	01 PA-46-500TP Meridian		4697121	DDK Enterprises LLC. Fayetteville, NC.	
☐ N990F	82 King Air F90		LA-164	Air Twerps Inc. Wilmington, De.	(F-GFDM)
☐ N990JC	82 King Air B200		BB-990	Executive Aviation Group Inc. Greenville, SC.	N990RC
☐ N990KB	83 King Air C90-1		LJ-1046	Elemental Leasing LLC. Glendale, Az.	N90PU

Reg	Yr	Type	c/n	Owner/Operator	Prev Regn
N990LR	78	PA-31T Cheyenne II	7820060	SMM Aviation Inc. Pascagoula, Ms.	XA-RMT
N990SA	67	King Air A90	LJ-261	Summit Aviation Inc. Dallas, Tx.	N5115D
N991GC	84	King Air F90-1	LA-224	Cumberland Corp. Kalispell, Mt.	N29GB
N991LL	96	King Air 350	FL-142	State of Illinois, Springfield, Il.	N1072S
N991SA	03	King Air C90B	LJ-1691	Westrade Air Services LLC. Houston, Tx.	
N991SU	77	King Air 200	BB-253	Iowa State University, Ames, Ia.	N999CY
N992C	85	King Air C90	LJ-1122	Illinois Data Mart Inc. DuPage, Il.	N7244J
N992TJ	82	King Air B200	BB-992	Carolina Turbine Sales Inc. Tyler, Tx.	N340TT
N992TT	80	PA-31T Cheyenne 1	8004019	Cellular Partners Inc. Hilton Head, SC.	D-ICGD
N993CB	98	King Air C90B	LJ-1550	Tri Counties Bank, Chico, Ca.	N261GB
N993RC	85	King Air C90A	LJ-1089	Matthew Hanna, Brashear, Tx.	HB-GHW
N994DF	91	TBM 700	22	Avex Inc. Camarillo, Ca.	D-FFBU
N995HP	83	Gulfstream 900	15026	Moore Enterprises Leasing Inc. Indianapolis, In.	N120EK
N995MS	81	King Air B200	BB-931	CAM Aviation Inc. Freeport, Bahamas.	N6789
N996AB	77	Rockwell 690B	11425	Nucor Inc. Riverton, Wy.	ZP-TWV
N996LM	76	King Air 200	BB-157	Lockheed Martin Vought Systems Corp. Grand Prairie, Tx.	N93LV
N997JM	02	TBM 700C	244	Blackbrook Aviation Inc. Wilmington, De.	LX-JFG
N997ME	82	King Air B100	BE-135	S Robert Davis, Charlotte, NC.	N135AR
N997RC	72	King Air U-21J	B-97	Victor One Four One LLC. Lincoln, Ma.	70-15910
N998JB	96	Pilatus PC-12/45	148	Sherman Aircraft Sales Inc. West Palm Beach, Fl.	N2JB
N998LM	81	PA-31T Cheyenne II	8120006	Lightning Master Corp. Clearwater, Fl.	(N101TR)
N998P	98	King Air C90B	LJ-1526	Ozark Aircraft Sales Inc. Kansas City, Mo.	
N998SR	98	King Air B200	BB-1632	Sylco Inc. Advance, NC.	
N999DT	76	King Air 200	BB-138	Arkansas Bolt Co. Little Rock, Ar.	N925BQ
N999EG	81	King Air B200	BB-908	Transportation Holdings LLC. Owings Mills, Md.	N200TJ
N999EP	96	Pilatus PC-12	135	Pacific Oak Development Inc. Sacramento, Ca.	N29CA
N999ES	74	King Air C90	LJ-612	Atlantic Aero Inc. Greensboro, NC.	N3112W
N999ET	81	MU-2 Marquise	1505SA	Orion Aviation Inc. Plymouth, Wi.	N901BF
N999FG	79	Rockwell 690B	11535	SeaSpray Group LLC. Raleigh, NC.	N81709
N999G	73	King Air A100	B-144	Corporate Jets Inc. Allegheny County, Pa.	N999TB
N999GA	81	King Air B200	BB-929	Badger Airlines Inc. Milwaukee, Wi.	N81AJ
N999MG	91	King Air 350	FL-65	Raytheon Aerospace Co. Madison, Ms.	N999MC
N999MM	80	SA-226T Merlin 3B	T-309	Merlin 999 Inc. Miami, Fl.	N5668M
N999MX	82	SA-227AT Merlin 4C	AT-501	Vision Air Ltd. Nassau, Bahamas.	N3051H
N999NG	01	PA-46-500TP Meridian	4697022	Gold Aero Aviation LLC. Burbank, Ca.	
N999RC	83	King Air F90-1	LA-208	Romeo Charlie Inc. Naples, Fl.	N901SA
N999RW	01	PA-46-500TP Meridian	4697037	RHW Enterprises Inc. Colorado Springs, Co.	
N999SE	80	King Air E90	LW-344	Sawdust Airlines Inc. Montoursville, Pa.	N888RT
N999SF	72	King Air E90	LW-5	ForSee Aviation LLC. Dalton, Ga.	N999SE
N999TA	70	Mitsubishi MU-2G	514	Air Cargo Express Inc. Fort Wayne, In.	N514WG
N999UP	82	MU-2 Marquise	1557SA	JPS Airtransport LLC. Bristol, NH.	N988RR
N999VB	80	King Air 200	BB-645	Vaughan & Bushnell Manufacturing Co. Hebron, Il.	N80GB
N1007B	80	SA-226T Merlin 3B	T-327	Swearingen Aviation Corp. San Antonio, Tx.	
N1010V	81	SA-226T Merlin 3B	T-372	Aviation Business Machines, Hillsboro, Or.	
N1014V	80	SA-226T Merlin 3B	T-321	Telese Properties Inc. Tampa, Fl.	
N1031Y	96	King Air C90B	LJ-1431	H R A Marine Inc. Yorklyn, De.	
N1039Y	70	SA-26AT Merlin 2B	T26-180E	Sheila DeForest, Pitt Meadows, Canada.	A2-KAM
N1056B	03	Pilatus PC-12/45	499	Jeffrey Arrowsmith, Saluda, Va.	HB-FRF
N1057L	96	King Air C90B	LJ-1457	Petro Air LLC. Monroe, La.	
N1068K	96	King Air C90B	LJ-1448	McClatchy Newspapers Inc. Sacramento, Ca.	
N1070F	96	King Air C90B	LJ-1440	DRP Aircraft Inc. Warren, Mi.	
N1074G	96	King Air B200	BB-1534	Armstrong Family Trust, Scottsdale, Az.	
N1079D	96	King Air C90B	LJ-1462	Don Oppliger Trucking Inc/Jamie & Mary LLC. Clovis, NM.	
N1083S	96	King Air C90B	LJ-1443	Scenic Aviation Inc. Blanding, Ut.	
N1084N	96	King Air C90B	LJ-1444	Greenwolf Air LLC. Middleburg, Va.	
N1089L	96	King Air C90B	LJ-1439	Ron Anderson Chevrolet Oldsmobile, Fernandina, Fl.	
N1092H	96	King Air C90B	LJ-1454	Stanhope-Seta UK Ltd. Blackbushe, UK.	
N1093Z	97	King Air B200	BB-1593	Atlantic Aircraft Inc. Kingshill, USVI.	
N1095W	96	King Air C90B	LJ-1456	George Stieren, San Antonio, Tx.	
N1100A	70	King Air 100	B-41	Aviation Enterprises LLC. Westlake Village, Ca.	N93BC
N1100M	73	King Air E90	LW-25	Carolina Beach Fishing LLC. Denver, NC.	N4406W
N1102K	97	King Air C90B	LJ-1465	Rough Brothers Inc. Cincinnati, Oh.	
N1103G	97	King Air C90B	LJ-1475	Kenworth Inc. Birmingham, Al.	(N900KW)
N1104X	97	King Air B200	BB-1585	Raytheon Aircraft Co. Wichita, Ks.	(N257YA)
N1107W	97	King Air C90B	LJ-1477	W A S S Aviation LLC. St Robert, Mo.	

Reg	Yr	Type	c/n	Owner/Operator	Prev Regn
N1110K	97	King Air C90B	LJ-1486	Peach Air Corp. Coral Gable, Fl.	
N1114K	97	King Air B200	BB-1559	June & John Rogers/Sky Trek Aviation, Modesto, Ca.	
N1114Z	98	King Air C90B	LJ-1514	Baffin Aviation Inc. Scottsdale, Az.	
N1118G	97	King Air B200	BB-1576	Southern Farm Bureau Casulaty Insurance Co. Ridgeland, Ms.	
N1126J	97	King Air C90B	LJ-1483	Whitcombe Leasing LLC. Carlisle, Pa.	
N1130J	97	King Air C90B	LJ-1467	B/W Air, Elkhart Lake, WI.	
N1135G	97	King Air C90B	LJ-1488	Park Aviation Group Inc. Stuart, Fl.	
N1154S	66	King Air 90	LJ-108	Hellenic Aviation Inc. Sarasota, Fl.	
N1162V	80	King Air 200	BB-711	Pre-Paid Legal Services Inc. Ada, Ok.	F-GILJ
N1164F	82	MU-2 Marquise	1562SA	EPPS Air Service Inc. Atlanta, Ga.	D-ICDG
N1183G	79	PA-31T Cheyenne II	7920086	C A R Lease Corp. Brentwood, Tn.	OE-FMR
N1194C	80	King Air 200	BB-679	Executive Aviation Services Inc. Rogers, Ar.	N256PL
N1194V	83	Cheyenne T-1040	8375001	Vegas Jet LLC. Las Vegas, Nv.	5Y-JJB
N1205S	79	King Air E90	LW-319	Standridge Color Corp. Social Circle, Ga.	N2065K
N1207S	68	SA-26T Merlin 2A	T26-24	Henry Wurst Inc. Apex, NC.	
N1208S	68	SA-26T Merlin 2A	T26-25	South Jersey Airways Inc. Atlantic City, NJ.	
N1210S	68	SA-26T Merlin 2A	T26-27	Wepco Inc/Ridgley Aviation, Tyler, Tx.	
N1210Z	85	Conquest II	441-0339	Nevada Conquest Aviation LP. Carson City, Nv.	(N441CP)
N1211C	84	Conquest II	441-0340	Southern Rainbow Air Inc. Miami, Fl.	
N1212C	85	Conquest II	441-0346	Bil Mar Foods Inc. Muskegon, Mi.	
N1212K	85	Conquest II	441-0347	Pioneer Nursey, Visalia, Ca.	
N1221S	68	SA-26AT Merlin 2B	T26-109	Richard Weiner MD. Dallas, Tx.	
N1222B	82	Conquest 1	425-0060	Reid Dennis, Woodside, Ca.	N68436
N1222G	84	Conquest 1	425-0196	Rosemary Medders, Wichita Falls, Tx.	(N196TM)
N1223B	85	Conquest 1	425-0201	Conquest Technology Associates LLC. Palo Alto, Ca.	(N888TP)
N1223P	84	Conquest 1	425-0204	Gottschalks Inc. Fresno, Ca.	
N1224J	84	Conquest 1	425-0208	Lark Aviation Inc. Laguna Hills, Ca.	
N1224T	84	Conquest 1	425-0212	Grass Valley Group Inc. Grass Valley, Ca.	
N1227J	85	Conquest 1	425-0229	Prairie Dog Aviation LC. Wichita, Ks.	
N1240S	83	King Air B200C	BL-64	Windsong Aviation LLC. Wilmington, De.	N124JS
N1244J	00	King Air 350	FL-335	Air LLC. Huntingburg, In.	N385AS
N1250	86	King Air 300	FA-88	Alliance Laundry Systems LLC. Ripon, Wi.	N7255X
N1253W	01	King Air 350	FL-330	Worthington Industries Inc. Columbus, Oh.	N350KA
N1262K	85	Conquest 1	425-0234	MAC Aviation LLC. Prior Lake, Mn.	
N1290A	65	King Air 90	LJ-30	Turbine Power Inc. Bridgewater, Va.	N538M
N1310T	74	King Air C90	LJ-617	Key Aviation Inc. Cambellsville, Ky.	N65GH
N1347Z	72	King Air A100	B-114	Westernair of Albuquerque Inc. Albuquerque, NM.	XC-FIX
N1362N	76	King Air B100	B-230	MKM Aviation of Delaware LLC. Rogers, Ar.	D-IKUL
N1380	81	Cheyenne II-XL	8166008	American Trust & Savings Bank, Dubuque, Ia.	N35CA
N1421Z	98	TBM 700	140	Allied Air Services LLC. Dover, De.	(N709DM)
N1509G	88	King Air B200	BB-1308	New York State Power Authority, White Plains, NY.	
N1515H	84	PA-42 Cheyenne 400LS	5527019	Grant Equipment Leasing Inc. Dahlonega, Ga.	
N1517H	88	King Air 300	FA-167	World Color Press Inc. NYC.	
N1525C	92	King Air 350	FL-88	Cretex Companies Inc. Elk River, Mn.	N8288W
N1544V	94	King Air C90B	LJ-1366	ElanAir Inc/Heritage Flight, Burlington, Vt.	
N1546	77	King Air C-12C	BC-58	U S Customs Service, Oklahoma City, Ok.	77-22947
N1547	77	King Air C-12C	BC-50	U S Customs Service, Oklahoma City, Ok.	77-22939
N1547V	88	King Air B200	BB-1307	State of South Dakota, Pierre, SD.	
N1548K	89	King Air 300	FA-179	Chris Aviation Group LLC. Troy, Mi.	
N1549	77	King Air C-12C	BC-45	U S Customs Service, Oklahoma City, Ok.	77-22934
N1551	76	King Air C-12C	BC-39	U S Customs Service, Oklahoma City, Ok.	76-22562
N1551A	90	King Air 350	FL-24	Oso Rio LLC. Houston, Tx. (status ?).	N2SM
N1551C	94	King Air C90B	LJ-1365	ElanAir Inc/Heritage Flight, Burlington, Vt.	
N1551H	89	King Air C90A	LJ-1211	BancFirst, Oklahoma City, Ok.	
N1552G	89	King Air C90A	LJ-1206	TIMMCO Holdings LLC. Edenton, NC.	
N1553	76	King Air C-12C	BC-30	U S Customs Service, Oklahoma City, Ok.	76-22254
N1553D	89	King Air C90A	LJ-1210	MFM Aviation Inc. Houston, Tx.	
N1553G	89	King Air C90A	LJ-1214	Avera Health, Sioux Falls, SD.	
N1553M	89	King Air B200	BB-1328	Texas A & M University, College Station, Tx.	
N1553N	90	King Air C90A	LJ-1238	GEM Aviation Inc. Weddington, NC.	
N1554	76	King Air JC-12C	BC-21	U S Customs Service, Oklahoma City, Ok.	76-22545
N1556S	90	2000 Starship	NC-6	Woodland Aviation Inc. Woodland, Ca.	
N1558	73	King Air C-12C	BC-20	U S Customs Service, Oklahoma City, Ok.	73-22260
N1558H	94	King Air 350	FL-119	Tesina Trading & Investments Ltd. Cyprus.	
N1559	73	King Air C-12C	BC-16	U S Customs Service, Oklahoma City, Ok.	73-22260
Reg	Yr	Type	c/n	Owner/Operator	Prev Regn

Reg	Yr	Type	c/n	Owner/Operator	Prev Regn
N1559G	94	King Air B200	BB-1480	Horton Transportation Inc. Minneapolis, Mn.	
N1560	73	King Air C-12C	BC-9	U S Customs Service, Oklahoma City, Ok.	73-22261
N1560T	94	King Air C90B	LJ-1357	Black Oak Leasing LLC. La Crosse, Wi.	
N1562H	97	King Air 350	FL-189	La Babia LLC. Wilmington, De.	
N1564W	90	King Air C90A	LJ-1234	V J Coleman & Son, Ackerly, Tx.	
N1567G	89	King Air C90A	LJ-1217	Joseph Honeycutt, Statesville, NC.	
N1568D	89	Beech 1900C-1	UC-76	Dow Chemical Co. Midland, Mi.	
N1568E	94	King Air B200	BB-1488	Roquette America Inc. Keokuk, Ia.	
N1568X	94	King Air C90B	LJ-1368	CBEL Aviation Inc/Cherokee Brick & Tile Co. Macon, Ga.	
N1650	98	King Air B200	BB-1618	Cox Communications Inc. Atlanta, Ga.	N2225Y
N1655M	99	King Air B200	BB-1655	Michigan Aeronautics Commission, Lansing, Mi.	
N1660W	78	King Air 200	BB-390	Central Flying Service Inc. Little Rock, Ar.	(N202MM)
N1667J	99	King Air B300C	FM-10	Clayton Aircraft, Tampa, Fl.	N2328Q
N1685S	02	King Air C90B	LJ-1685	Lakeshore Leasing Ltd. Grosse Pointe Shores, Mi.	
N1727S	81	MU-2 Marquise	1504SA	Bobby Hamilton Inc. Mount Juliet, Tn.	N541NC
N1777X	84	Conquest 1	425-0222	Quest Aviation LLC. Lake in the Hills, Il.	N1226B
N1790M	80	MU-2 Marquise	756SA	Air 1st Aviation Companies Inc. Aiken, SC.	N179CM
N1801B	74	King Air C90	LJ-634	Riddell Flying Service Inc. Helena, Ar. (status ?).	N19R
N1807H	81	King Air B100	BE-119	Agrilogic Inc. College Station, Tx.	
N1836H	81	King Air C90	LJ-990	Pacjets Ltd. Baraboo, Wi.	
N1840S	78	King Air E90	LW-263	Paul Flowers Jr. Dothan, Al.	N184JS
N1843S	83	Conquest II	441-0317	M & M Aviation LLC/Westwood Partners LC. Billings, Mt.	N1208J
N1845	01	King Air 350	FL-327	National City Bank, Highland Heights, Oh.	N5027X
N1848S	96	King Air C90B	LJ-1455	HCB Aircraft Inc. Tyler, Tx.	N1085V
N1850X	82	King Air B200	BB-946	Wings to Go Leasing Co. Doylestown, Pa.	
N1857F	82	King Air F90	LA-167	Cariva Inc. Perryton, Tx.	
N1860N	81	King Air B200	BB-907	Bur-Con LLC. Peoria, Il.	(N440KC)
N1865A	99	Beech 1900D	UE-361	Wachovia Bank of Georgia NA. Atlanta, Ga.	
N1875C	00	King Air C90B	LJ-1626	Gottemoeller Corp. Fort Loramie, Oh.	N369RC
N1880C	02	King Air 350	FL-360	Clarkson Construction Co. Kansas City, Mo.	N5030D
N1883M	99	Beech 1900D	UE-354	Meijer Inc. Grand Rapids, Mi.	N30414
N1891S	84	King Air B200	BB-1153	SAN LLC. Knoxville, Tn.	N73MP
N1900C	88	Beech 1900C-1	UC-43	Raytheon Aircraft Credit Corp. Wichita, Ks.	N43GP
N1907W	70	SA-26AT Merlin 2B	T26-176	Minter Corp. St Simons Island, Ga.	N777PE
N1925P	83	King Air B200	BB-1094	Pella Corp. Pella, Ia.	N35EC
N1926A	81	King Air B200	BB-922	Arch Air 1 LLC. Philadelphia, Pa.	N80BT
N1928H	68	680W Turbo Commander	1789-19	Reed Kent Nixon, Aurora, Or.	(N260RC)
N1930P	79	MU-2 Solitaire	399SA	Superior Builders, St Joseph, Mi.	N9052Y
N1968W	01	PA-46-500TP Meridian	4697115	N1968 LLC. Hamel, Mn.	N715MA
N1976J	75	PA-31T Cheyenne II	7520005	Lock Haven Aircraft Sales Inc. Lock Haven, Pa.	
N1978P	71	Mitsubishi MU-2F	212	International Aircraft Recovery, Fort Pierce, Fl.	YV-1978P
N1981S	81	Gulfstream 980	95047	Air Operations International, Charlotte, NC.	TG-...
N1999G	68	King Air B90	LJ-319	Fayard Enterprises Inc. Louisberg, NC.	N845K
N2000E	66	King Air A90	LJ-172	Core Investments Inc. Fort Lauderdale, Fl.	
N2025M	78	King Air 200	BB-384	Water Soft Inc. Saxonburg, Pa.	
N2050A	79	King Air C90	LJ-813	Beech Transportation Inc. Eden Prairie, Mn.	N517PC
N2057C	79	King Air C90	LJ-827	King Cotton AG Inc. Corcoran, Ca.	
N2057N	79	King Air C90	LJ-815	Carolina Windsor LLC. Johnston, SC.	
N2057S	79	King Air 200	BB-425	Whayne Supply Co. Louisville, Ky.	
N2062A	79	King Air E90	LW-317	Lenders Mortgage Co. Parsippany, NJ.	
N2097W	98	King Air C90B	LJ-1507	Rebsamen Insurance Inc. Little Rock, Ar.	
N2100T	70	Mitsubishi MU-2F	182	Ranger Aviation Enterprises, Sonora, Tx.	N105MA
N2141B	78	Rockwell 690B	11484	Amhurst Development Inc. Lewes, De.	G-BLPT
N2155B	72	Rockwell 690	11046	C P Annie Productions Inc. Tulsa, Ok.	
N2164L	80	King Air F90	LA-79	Transport Aircraft Inc. Trenton, NJ.	XB-DQP
N2178A	99	King Air C90B	LJ-1542	Carolina Turbine Sales Inc. Tyler, Tx.	
N2178F	98	King Air C90B	LJ-1508	Deer Horn Aviation LC. Midland, Tx.	
N2186L	76	King Air E90	LW-186	Gold Coast Logistics LLC. St Simons Island, Ga.	
N2192L	76	King Air E90	LW-192	Siller Brothers Inc. Yuba City, Ca.	
N2222C	04	Pilatus PC-12/45	542	Air Option Corp. Miami, Fl.	N542PB
N2225H	70	King Air 100	B-34	Integrity Air LLC. Traverse City, Mi.	HI-663CA
N2247R	84	PA-42 Cheyenne IIIA	5501005	DoJ/U S Marshals Service, Oklahoma City, Ok.	N5381X
N2274L	77	King Air E90	LW-213	Press Forge Co. Paramount, Ca.	
N2291F	98	King Air C90B	LJ-1521	Custom Aviation LLC. Spokane, Wa.	
N2297C	97	King Air C90B	LJ-1497	Raviator Inc. Dallas, Tx.	
Reg	Yr	Type	c/n	Owner/Operator	Prev Regn

Reg	Yr	Type	c/n	Owner/Operator	Prev Regn
N2299W	98	King Air B200	BB-1626	Spiral Recycling Inc. Chandler, Az.	
N2303P	69	SA-26AT Merlin 2B	T26-167E	International Aviation Investors Inc. Lewisburg, WV.	D-IBMD
N2310K	98	King Air C90B	LJ-1510	Jim's Supply Co. Bakersfield, Ca.	
N2315A	97	King Air 350	FL-171	Pizzagalli Construction Co. Burlington, Vt.	
N2315L	98	King Air C90B	LJ-1515	C & K Market Inc. Brookings, Or.	
N2325Y	98	King Air 350	FL-201	NFC Marketing Associates, Dallas, Tx.	
N2326J	98	King Air B200	BB-1606	MJHR LLC. Portland, Tx.	N2326J
N2328E	98	King Air B200	BB-1608	Grouper LLC. Bozeman, Mt.	
N2338V	80	PA-31T Cheyenne II	8020049	REMC Leasing LLC. Bismarck, ND.	
N2341S	99	King Air 350	FL-241	Specsavers Aviation Ltd. Guernsey, C.I.	
N2348W	79	PA-31T Cheyenne 1	7904057	Black Knight Air Inc. Farmington, Mo.	
N2354Y	98	King Air C90B	LJ-1532	Utah Aeronautical Operations, Salt Lake City, Ut.	
N2356X	81	PA-31T Cheyenne 1	8104003	Pegasus II LLC. Wilmington, De.	
N2369V	80	PA-31T Cheyenne 1	8004035	Elsea Inc. Circleville, Oh.	
N2403X	81	PA-31T Cheyenne 1	8104014	W S Equipment Inc. Dover, De.	
N2415W	80	PA-31T Cheyenne 1	8004010	U S Nameplate Co. Naples, Fl.	
N2434V	84	PA-31T Cheyenne 1A	1104011	Franed Corp. Akron, Oh.	
N2434W	84	PA-31T Cheyenne 1A	1104006	P J Nanavati, Springfield, Il.	
N2435Y	81	PA-31T Cheyenne 1	8104049	Gas Cylinder Technologies, Lakeshore, ON. Canada.	
N2441K	78	Conquest II	441-0053	Golden Eagle Sales LLC. Overland Park, Ks.	N42MJ
N2458W	80	PA-31T Cheyenne 1	8004017	Richard Karl, Tampa, Fl.	
N2467V	80	PA-31T Cheyenne II	8020068	Harold Levy, NYC.	
N2469V	80	PA-31T Cheyenne II	8020070	Casey-Fogli Concrete Contractors Inc. Belmont, Ca.	
N2480X	81	PA-31T Cheyenne 1	8104026	Jane Air Inc. Wilmington, De.	
N2519X	81	PA-31T Cheyenne 1	8104035	G & B Oil Co. Elkin, NC.	
N2522V	80	PA-31T Cheyenne II	8020078	Weaver Aircraft Leasing Inc. Galesburg, Il.	
N2535B	98	King Air 350	FL-224	Omega Air Inc. Long Beach, Ca.	N2217C
N2552Y	82	PA-31T Cheyenne 1	8104061	Continental Fire Sprinkler Co. Omaha, Ne.	
N2556R	80	PA-31T Cheyenne 1	8004003	Henderson Group Inc. Goodland, Tx.	
N2587R	80	PA-31T Cheyenne 1	8004004	Dabingee Services Inc. Malta, NY.	
N2722D	80	Conquest 1	441-0168	USA Gasoline Corp. Agoura, Ca.	N2722D
N2722Y	79	Conquest II	441-0173	AIA Inc/Reed Taylor, Lewiston, Id.	
N2723X	80	Conquest II	441-0180	Eagle Aviation Inc. West Columbia, SC.	(N33AR)
N2725N	80	Conquest II	441-0190	Aqua Ventures Inc. Beaver Dam, Wi.	
N2748X	86	King Air B200	BB-1258	Bonneville Power Administration, Vancouver, Wa.	
N2755B	68	680W Turbo Commander	1762-8	Boyce Aviation Inc. New Port Richey, Fl.	
N2789A	92	King Air B300C	FM-7	Clayton Aircraft, Tampa, Fl.	N82324
N2820B	98	Beech 1900D	UE-331	Raytheon Aircraft Co. Wichita, Ks.	(N534M)
N2830S	78	King Air B100	BE-48	DeJarnette Enterprises Inc. Lee's Summit, Mo.	N5009M
N2883	76	King Air 200	BB-144	Maxair Inc. Appleton, Wi.	N28S
N3002S	66	King Air 90	LJ-103	Godwin Aircraft Inc. Memphis, Tn.	
N3015Q	95	King Air B200	BB-1493	Delta United Specialities Inc. Memphis, Tn.	
N3025Z	87	King Air 300	FA-120	Costa Nursey Farms Inc. Coral Gables, Fl.	
N3026H	94	King Air B200	BB-1494	Midwest Air Services Inc. Fort Worth, Tx.	
N3030G	85	King Air C90A	LJ-1117	4079 Hotel Ltd. Toledo, Oh.	N3030C
N3035P	98	King Air C90B	LJ-1535	ARB Inc. Lake Forest, Ca.	LV-ZNS
N3035T	97	King Air C90B	LJ-1482	Hartman Air LC. Harrisburg, Va.	
N3051K	94	King Air B200	BB-1495	Operation Bass Inc. Minneapolis, Mn.	
N3066W	98	King Air C90B	LJ-1536	Ruggles Group LLC. Citrus Heights, Ca.	
N3068Z	99	King Air C90B	LJ-1544	Constructora Nacional SA. Guatemala City, Guatemala.	
N3078W	99	King Air 350	FL-248	Ortho-Sport Inc. Forest Park, Il.	
N3080F	99	King Air 350	FL-249	Equipment Management Systems LLC. Jackson, Ms.	
N3084K	88	King Air 300	FA-160	The Durham Co. Lebanon, Mo.	
N3096P	04	PA-46-500TP Meridian	4697178	SB Meridian LLC. Heber, Ca.	
N3100K	69	King Air 100	B-1	Bushnell Aviation Inc. Baton Rouge, La.	N3400K
N3103A	04	PA-46-500TP Meridian	4697190	Aviation Sales Inc. Englewood, Co.	
N3115K	00	King Air 350	FL-315	FL350 Inc. Hato Rey, PR.	
N3115M	04	PA-46-500TP Meridian	4697198	New Piper Aircraft Inc. Vero Beach, Fl.	
N3117N	99	King Air B200	BB-1670	WFBNW NA. Salt Lake City, Ut. (trustor ?).	
N3120U	94	King Air C90B	LJ-1382	Virgin Islands Telephone Corp. St Croix, USVI.	
N3122Z	88	King Air 300	FA-162	Anheuser-Busch Companies Inc. St Louis, Mo.	
N3128K	00	King Air 350	FL-299	CNL Group Services Inc. Orlando, Fl.	
N3143T	99	King Air C90B	LJ-1543	Lark Builders Inc. Vidalia, Ga.	
N3160P	99	King Air C90B	LJ-1560	Legacy Air LLC. Missoula, Mt.	
N3181	80	King Air 200	BB-637	Northeast Aviation X LLC. Wilmington, De.	(N409P)
Reg	Yr	Type	c/n	Owner/Operator	Prev Regn

Reg	Yr	Type	c/n	Owner/Operator	Prev Regn
N3190S	88 King Air C90A		LJ-1190	SIF Aircraft Inc. Malvern, Pa.	
N3195Q	00 King Air C90B		LJ-1595	Western Aviation LLC. Yuba, Az.	
N3196K	94 King Air C90B		LJ-1384	Tampa Armature Works Inc. Tampa, Fl.	
N3203P	70 681 Turbo Commander		6019	Marsh Aviation International, Mesa, Az.	C-GFAE
N3216K	95 King Air C90B		LJ-1392	Casa Fuerte LLC. Lakeway, Tx.	
N3216U	95 King Air C90B		LJ-1397	Cemco Inc. Albuquerque, NM.	
N3218P	95 King Air C90B		LJ-1411	Carlyle Aviation LLC. Atlanta, Ga.	N3218P
N3220L	95 King Air C90B		LJ-1420	Pee Dee Aviation LLC. Florence, SC.	
N3222K	01 King Air 350		FL-322	Beechcraft Vertrieb & Service GmbH. Augsburg, Germany.	
N3223H	95 King Air B200		LJ-1425	Georgia Aviation & Technical College, Eastman, Ga.	(N54TF)
N3237S	88 King Air 300		FA-163	Cheds Investments Inc. Charlotte, NC.	
N3242Z	96 King Air C90B		LJ-1428	Cardinal Aviation Co/Greer Industries Inc. Morgantown, WV.	
N3246S	99 King Air C90B		LJ-1576	Watson & Hollis Investments Inc. Wilmington, De.	
N3250V	96 King Air B200		BB-1523	Standard Air News Inc. Fort Stockton, Tx.	
N3251Q	96 King Air C90B		LJ-1429	Crowley Management Services Inc. City of Industry, Ca.	
N3253Q	00 King Air 350		FL-293	Diamond Air Charter Inc. Winnetka, Il.	
N3254A	99 King Air 350		FL-254	86BP Inc. Miami Shores, Fl.	
N3262R	99 King Air C90B		LJ-1562	Scarab Enterprise LLC. Monterey, Ca.	
N3263C	96 King Air C90B		LJ-1432	Collins Timber LLC. Portland, Or.	
N3263N	99 King Air C90B		LJ-1563	Michael Guthrie, Jackson, Ms.	
N3270V	96 King Air C90B		LJ-1451	Obra Homes Inc. McAllen, Tx.	
N3321M	00 King Air C90B		LJ-1621	Hawk Equipment LLC. Minneapolis, Mn.	
N3325H	02 PA-46-500TP Meridian		4697133	Airport Vault LLC. Santa Clarita, Ca.	N104ET
N3330S	81 Conquest II		441-0205	Lario Oil & Gas Co. Wichita, Ks.	(N2727X)
N3606T	70 King Air 100		B-30	Sunshine Aero Industries Inc. Crestview, Fl.	N360BT
N3620M	91 King Air B200		BB-1396	MBC Air LLC/Elliott Aviation Flight Services, Des Moines.	N362EA
N3663B	80 King Air B100		BE-94	ATS LLC. Bogart, Ga.	
N3663M	80 King Air 200		BB-686	Shamrock Equipment Co. Midland, Tx.	
N3688P	80 King Air C90		LJ-915	Central Virginia Aircraft Sales Inc. Lynchburg, Va.	
N3690F	80 King Air C90		LJ-921	Davis Aero LLC. Memphis, Tn.	
N3695W	80 King Air C90		LJ-924	Barnett Investments Inc. LaVerne, Ca.	
N3697F	80 King Air 200C		BL-14	Columbia Helicopters Inc. Aurora, Or.	
N3700M	80 King Air E90		LW-340	Boeing Co. Philadelphia, Pa.	
N3710A	81 King Air 200		BB-760	MJL Properties LLC/Meredith McCullar Realty Co. Memphis, Tn.	
N3722Y	04 King Air 350		FL-422	Raytheon Aircraft Co. Wichita, Ks.	
N3723Q	04 King Air 350		FL-423	Raytheon Aircraft Co. Wichita, Ks.	
N3724Q	04 King Air 350		FL-424	Raytheon Aircraft Co. Wichita, Ks.	
N3726E	04 King Air 350		FL-426	Raytheon Aircraft Co. Wichita, Ks.	
N3727Q	04 King Air 350		FL-427	Raytheon Aircraft Co. Wichita, Ks.	
N3732K	04 King Air B200		BB-1892	Raytheon Aircraft Co. Wichita, Ks.	
N3739C	91 King Air 350		FL-72	Bee Line Inc. Portland, Or.	N24FT
N3805E	81 King Air C90		LJ-943	Mad Air LLC. Huntsville, Ar.	
N3809C	81 King Air F90		LA-112	Republic Refrigeration Inc. Monroe, NC.	
N3817H	81 King Air C90		LJ-938	James Jr Co. New Canaan, Ct.	
N3818C	76 King Air E90		LW-196	Midwestern Restaurants Inc. Roseburg, Or.	N3813C
N3821S	81 King Air E90		LW-346	D K Leasing, Dallas, Tx.	
N3824V	81 King Air F90		LA-110	Deutsch Engineered Connecting Device, Hemet, Ca.	
N3867N	70 681 Turbo Commander		6010	Sierra American Corp. Dallas, Tx.	XB-PAO
N3929G	73 King Air E90		LW-55	Gale Investments Ltd. San Antonio, Tx.	XB-IEI
N3951F	75 PA-31T Cheyenne II		7520010	Barron Thomas Aviation Inc. Las Vegas, NM.	XA-JOF
N4000	77 King Air 200		BB-247	MCM Construction Inc. North Highlands, Ca.	N18347
N4009L	96 King Air B300C		FM-9	Stevens Express Leasing Inc. Memphis, Tn.	N10024
N4019	73 SA-226AT Merlin III		AT-014	Orix Financial Services Inc. Kennesaw, Ga.	C-GSDR
N4042J	81 King Air B200		BB-874	Stevens Express Leasing Inc. Memphis, Tn.	N200GK
N4051X	69 SA-26AT Merlin 2B		T26-124	Rick Fowler/Western Aviators, Grand Junction, Co.	
N4053H	01 King Air B200		BB-1774	Trustmark Corp. Jackson, Ms.	
N4065D	75 Mitsubishi MU-2L		660	Intercontinental Jet Inc. Tulsa, Ok.	TF-FHL
N4100B	68 680W Turbo Commander		1803-25	Mid-State Drainage Products Inc. Port Gibson, Ms.	N5079E
N4100L	81 PA-42 Cheyenne III		8001061	Condor LC. Coon Rapids, Ia.	
N4116Q	84 PA-42 Cheyenne IIIA		5501012	Ned Good, Pasadena, Ca.	
N4116W	75 PA-31T Cheyenne II		7520032	Pace Aviation Ltd. Reno, Nv.	F-BXLC
N4146S	75 King Air C90		LJ-646	Barney Cam, Keystone Heights, Fl.	
N4152G	79 Conquest II		441-0105	Heizer Aviation Inc. St Louis, Mo.	(N11MM)
N4170N	00 King Air 350		FL-270	Mercury Research & Surveying, Dover, De.	
N4174V	01 PA-46-500TP Meridian		4697014	GLR Aviation Inc. Milwaukee, Wi.	(OY-NEW)

Reg	Yr	Type	c/n	Owner/Operator	Prev Regn
N4180A	02	PA-46-500TP Meridian	4697151	North Park Transportation Co. Billigs, Mt.	
N4185L	01	PA-46-500TP Meridian	4697025	WDW Aviation Leasing Inc. Knoxville, Tn.	
N4195S	01	King Air B200	BB-1795	A I I Services Inc. Overland Park, Ks.	
N4200A	70	King Air 100	B-64	Red Stripe Air LLC. Odessa, Tx.	
N4209S	74	SA-226T Merlin 3	T-245	Jones Aviation Inc. Lexington, Ky.	RP-C1261
N4216S	77	King Air E90	LW-211	Tica Investment Corp. San Diego, Ca.	N88RG
N4262X	69	SA-26AT Merlin 2B	T26-153	Latham Aviation Inc. Pelham, Al.	
N4270Y	01	King Air B200	BB-1770	West Coast Surgery Centers Management LLC. Long Beach.	(N4SQ)
N4276Z	81	Conquest 1	425-0103	Complease LLC. Blaine, Mt.	C-GINT
N4288S	76	King Air 200	BB-188	Porta Kamp Manufacturing/P-K Interests Inc. Bellville, Tx.	
N4298S	77	King Air 200	BB-198	Corporate Air Inc. Billings, Mt.	
N4298X	00	King Air C90B	LJ-1598	Great Texas Foods Inc. Nacogdoces, Tx.	
N4368Y	00	King Air C90B	LJ-1599	Arkwest Aviation LLC. Danville, Ar.	
N4380Y	00	King Air 350	FL-280	Citrus World Inc. Lake Wales, Fl.	
N4392K	01	King Air C90B	LJ-1642	Corporacion de Occidente SA. Guatemala City, Guatemala.	N4392K
N4392W	74	King Air A100	B-192	MTW Aerospace Inc. Montgomery, Al.	
N4415F	02	King Air C90B	LJ-1675	Blue Star Properties LLC. Winston-Salem, NC.	
N4415L	79	King Air B100	BE-67	Idaho State University, Pocatello, Id.	90-0060
N4420F	82	Conquest 1	425-0053	Thane Hawkins Aviation Inc. White Bear Lake, Mn.	(D-IFLY)
N4441T	80	Conquest II	441-0133	E W Marine Inc. Elkhart, In.	N332S
N4447W	74	King Air C90	LJ-627	St Jon Aircraft LLC. Hanford, Ca.	
N4449Q	80	King Air C90	LJ-895	Warren Oil Co/Air-Care Inc. Rocky Mount, NC.	YV-355CP
N4456A	02	King Air B200C	BL-143	Aviation Specialities Inc. Washington, DC.	
N4465F	01	King Air C90B	LJ-1665	Shelor Investments LLC. Christiansburg, Va.	(N904GM)
N4466A	03	King Air B300C	FM-11	Aviation Specialities Inc. Beltsville, Md.	N6195A
N4471M	02	King Air C90B	LJ-1671	Citrus One Inc. Yuma, Az.	
N4476Y	02	King Air B200	BB-1806	Raytheon Aircraft Co. Wichita, Ks.	
N4488L	95	King Air B200	LJ-1423	Heart of America Management Co. Moline, Il.	N3253Q
N4489A	02	King Air B200C	BL-145	Aviation Specialities Inc. Washington, DC.	
N4490M	79	King Air B100	BE-64	SkyLife Aviation LLC. St Louis, Mo.	(N497SL)
N4495N	72	King Air E90	LW-14	Super Sport Aircraft Leasing LLC. Nashua, NH.	YV-72CP
N4600K	84	King Air 300	FA-21	H-B Services Inc. Oklahoma City, Ok.	N4000K
N4622E	68	680W Turbo Commander	1723-3	Montana Department of Highways, Helena, Mt. (was 1723-94).	
N4679K	72	SA-226AT Merlin 4	AT-006	Hurley Aircraft, Yukon, Ok.	XC-UTF/TP
N4679M	78	King Air 200	BB-343	Raytheon Aircraft Co. Wichita, Ks.	
N4717V	74	Rockwell 690A	11220	Cloud Splitter LLC. Columbia, Ca.	YV-236P
N4757S	00	PA-46-500TP Meridian	4697006	Bombay Glass Corp. Depoe Bay, Or.	
N4764A	88	King Air C90A	LJ-1161	M & I First National Leasing Corp. Milwaukee, Wi.	N476JA
N4774M	78	King Air C90	LJ-771	Edgington Transport LLC. Livermore, Ca.	
N4776M	78	King Air C90	LJ-776	Zavala Airlines LLC. Dallas, Tx.	
N4799M	78	King Air 200	BB-373	Security Investments Inc. Oshkosh, Wi.	
N4920Y	00	TBM 700B	169	SOCATA Aircraft, Pembroke Pines, Fl.	
N4925T	04	King Air B200	BB-1870	King Air LLC. Spokane, Wa.	N6170G
N4947M	78	King Air C90	LJ-780	Executive Beechcraft Inc. Kansas City, Mo.	
N4948W	65	King Air 90	LJ-31	Stewart-Davis International Inc. N Hollywood, Ca.	(N505M)
N4950C	74	King Air C90	LJ-629	SkiAir LLC. Republic, Mo.	YV-39CP
N5007	78	PA-31T Cheyenne II	7820061	Empire Airlines Inc. Lebanon, Mo.	N303KL
N5021S	03	King Air B200	BB-1821	Aledo Enterprises LLC. Grand Prairie, Tx.	
N5024W	00	King Air C90B	LJ-1618	Noble King Corp. Klamath Falls, Or.	
N5025R	01	King Air C90B	LJ-1625	White Oak Holdings LLC. Rutherfordton, NC.	
N5037W	00	King Air C90B	LJ-1630	Lazy P Aviation LLC. Windsor, Ca.	
N5063K	01	King Air B200	BB-1763	Dairy Air LLC. Jerome, Id.	
N5067L	01	King Air C90B	LJ-1667	SRS Aviation LLC. Charleston, SC.	
N5078Q	04	King Air B200	BB-1868	Mayesair LLC. Dallas, Tx.	
N5092S	02	King Air B200	BB-1802	Bonita Packing Co. Santa Maria, Ca.	
N5106F	02	King Air B200CT	BN-6	Raytheon Aircraft Co. Wichita, Ks.	
N5107Z	02	King Air B200CT	BN-7	Raytheon Aircraft Co. Wichita, Ks.	
N5109V	04	King Air B200	BB-1869	Aviaservice CA. Caracas, Venezuela.	
N5111U	66	King Air A90	LJ-154	Aircraft Aloft LP/R Zadow & C Lingenfelser, Las Vegas, Nv.	N5111
N5115H	04	King Air C90	LJ-1705	Sadler LLC. Lexington, Ky.	
N5124	95	SAAB 2000	027	General Motors Corp. Detroit, Mi.	SE-027
N5128X	04	King Air 350	FL-428	Raytheon Aircraft Co. Wichita, Ks.	
N5136V	76	PA-31T Cheyenne II	7620037	Field Tech Avionics Inst. Fort Worth, Tx.	C-GFIN
N5139A	02	King Air B200C	BL-144	Aviation Specialities Inc. Washington, DC.	
N5153V	01	King Air C90B	LJ-1653	Spartan Aviation Industries Inc. Tulsa, Ok.	

Reg	Yr	Type	c/n	Owner/Operator	Prev Regn
☐ N5155A	02	King Air B200C	BL-146	Aviation Specialities Inc. Washington, DC.	
☐ N5215U	01	PA-46-500TP Meridian	4697068	Papillon Air LLC. Los Angeles, Ca.	
☐ N5245F	66	King Air 90	LJ-92	Marcelo Demaria Inc. Dover, De.	XC-FUR
☐ N5256S	99	King Air 350	FL-260	Triple AAA Water Co. Fullerton, Ca.	(VH-...)
☐ N5317M	73	SA-226T Merlin 3	T-236	Aircraft R Us Corp. San Diego, Ca.	
☐ N5319K	01	PA-46-500TP Meridian	4697076	Perkin Holding Co. Rocky Mount, Mo.	
☐ N5320N	03	PA-46-500TP Meridian	4697153	J S Heck, Bozeman, Mt.	
☐ N5322D	01	PA-46-500TP Meridian	4697074	Air Falcon LLC. Pinellas Park, Fl.	
☐ N5322M	01	PA-46-500TP Meridian	4697021	Blue Devil Flight LLC. New Castle, De.	(N555SZ)
☐ N5325P	01	PA-46-500TP Meridian	4697085	Diamond Resorts West LLC. Wilmington, De.	
☐ N5326C	01	PA-46-500TP Meridian	4697079	Estate Leasing Inc/Precision Dynamics Inc. Chandler, Az.	
☐ N5329Q	01	PA-46-500TP Meridian	4697097	Steven Buchanan, Captiva, Fl.	
☐ N5333N	01	PA-46-500TP Meridian	4697084	AvantAir Inc. Stewart, NY.	
☐ N5335R	01	PA-46-500TP Meridian	4697100	Richard Rockefeller, Falmouth, Me.	
☐ N5337N	01	PA-46-500TP Meridian	4697102	Steven Kanig, Albuquerque, NM.	
☐ N5338M	01	PA-46-500TP Meridian	4697103	Southeastern Aviation Services LLC. Asheville, NC.	N803JH
☐ N5339G	01	PA-46-500TP Meridian	4697095	Klarity LLC. Great Falls, Mt.	
☐ N5339V	01	PA-46-500TP Meridian	4697110	Newton Rogers LLC. Wichita, Ks.	
☐ N5341C	02	PA-46-500TP Meridian	4697142	Skyridge Leasing LLC. Portland, Or.	
☐ N5347V	02	PA-46-500TP Meridian	4697126	Carter-Tate Leasing LLC. Savannah, Ga.	
☐ N5353V	02	PA-46-500TP Meridian	4697141	Emergency Deal Transport LLC. Salt Lake City, Ut.	
☐ N5355S	03	PA-46-500TP Meridian	4697136	Ramsey Pontiac Corp. Des Moines, Ia.	
☐ N5356M	80	Gulfstream 980	95036	Mavax Ltd. Chesapeake, Va.	D-IOEB
☐ N5358J	02	PA-46-500TP Meridian	4697140	Clifford Davis, Newport Beach, Ca.	
☐ N5361A	02	PA-46-500TP Meridian	4697144	AirJules LLC. Wilmington, De.	
☐ N5365D	03	PA-46-500TP Meridian	4697161	Collect Air LLC. Denver, Co.	
☐ N5431M	02	King Air C90B	LJ-1673	Jerry Nutt DDS. Destin, Fl.	N3251H
☐ N5441M	77	SA-226T Merlin 3A	T-283	Worldwide Aircraft Services Inc. Springfield, Mo.	SE-GXV
☐ N5450J	82	Gulfstream 1000	96024	Gallo Air Inc. Dover, De.	YV-484CP
☐ N5462G	73	King Air E90	LW-69	Northwest Aircraft Leasing Corp. Wilmington, De.	N769AM
☐ N5552U	90	King Air B200	BB-1361	Mission Q-Sub Inc. Las Vegas, Nv.	
☐ N5559X	90	King Air B200	BB-1372	Los Angeles Police Department, Van Nuys, Ca.	
☐ N5626Y	91	King Air 350	FL-43	Land Trends Inc. New Lenox, Il.	
☐ N5639K	90	King Air C90A	LJ-1239	Chirgwin Aviation LLC. Clackamas, Or.	
☐ N5641K	90	King Air C90A	LJ-1241	R & M Leasing Inc. DeKalb, Il.	
☐ N5644E	90	King Air C90A	LJ-1244	Susan Binette, Medford, Or.	
☐ N5655K	90	King Air 350	FL-12	Crescent Electric Supply Co. East Dubuque, Il.	(N491CE)
☐ N5682P	90	King Air B200	BB-1358	Southland Airways LLC. Birmingham, Al.	
☐ N5727	70	King Air 100	B-48	Vintage Props & Jets Inc. New Smyrna Beach, Fl.	N572
☐ N5878K	80	Gulfstream 840	11626	Great Marbach Airlines Inc. Boca Raton, Fl.	
☐ N5888K	92	King Air B300C	FM-6	Freelance Air Inc. Atlanta, Ga.	N80605
☐ N5900K	80	Gulfstream 840	11648	Erwin Industries Inc. Hillsboro, Or.	
☐ N5904A	04	Pilatus PC-12/45	583	Swiss Angel LLC. Miami, Fl.	HB-FQT
☐ N5914K	81	Gulfstream 840	11662	Safeguards International Inc. Charlotte, NC.	OY-SVG
☐ N5955K	81	Gulfstream 840	11703	Security Group Inc. Fort Pierce, Fl.	
☐ N5956K	81	Gulfstream 840	11719	Leo Sullivan, O'Fallon, Il.	PT-LRQ
☐ N6028Y	04	King Air C90B	LJ-1728	Raytheon Aircraft Co. Wichita, Ks.	
☐ N6045S	79	King Air B100	BE-65	Brewster Aviation LLC/Couri & Co LLC. Ridgefield, Ct.	
☐ N6069A	78	King Air 200	BB-357	Nelson Siemon, Conover, NC.	N500DE
☐ N6077X	02	King Air C90B	LJ-1677	Alper LP. Las Vegas, Nv.	(N444ES)
☐ N6080A	78	PA-31T Cheyenne II	7820077	Coker Aircraft Sales Inc. Memphis, Tn.	
☐ N6103K	93	King Air 350	FL-103	Grimmway Enterprises Inc. Bakersfield, Ca.	(N350TT)
☐ N6107A	78	PA-31T Cheyenne II	7820087	Barrwood Equipment Corp. Concord, NH.	
☐ N6111V	04	King Air C90B	LJ-1711	Airplane 421 LLC. Yuma, Az.	
☐ N6112G	04	King Air 350	FL-412	Previti Brothers Charter Services, Ontario, Ca.	
☐ N6113X	04	King Air 350	FL-403	Bemis Manufacturing Co. Sheboygan Falls, Mi.	
☐ N6116N	04	King Air 350	FL-416	D C Interests LLC/Geneva Holdings LLC. Phoenix, Az.	
☐ N6117C	04	King Air 350	FL-417	Raytheon Aircraft Co. Wichita, Ks.	
☐ N6129Q	04	King Air 350	FL-429	Raytheon Aircraft Co. Wichita, Ks.	
☐ N6131Q	04	King Air 350	FL-431	Raytheon Aircraft Co. Wichita, Ks.	
☐ N6137	65	King Air 90	LJ-47	Turbine Power Inc. Bridgewater, Va.	N613M
☐ N6152L	04	King Air B200	BB-1852	Horizon Group Inc. Boca Raton, Fl.	
☐ N6154F	99	Pilatus PC-12/45	246	Freelance Air Inc. Atlanta, Ga.	N651CA
☐ N6165Y	04	King Air 350	FL-405	Silver Air LLC. Hicksville, NY.	
☐ N6171N	03	King Air 350	FL-371	Maverick Tube Corp. Chesterfield, Mo.	
Reg	Yr	Type	c/n	Owner/Operator	Prev Regn

Reg	Yr Type	c/n	Owner/Operator	Prev Regn
N6172B	03 King Air 350	FL-372	Hawker Pacific P/L. Milperra, NSW, Australia.	
N6173C	82 King Air C90-1	LJ-1014	Midwest Equipment of Morris Inc. Morris, Mn.	
N6175A	79 PA-31T Cheyenne II	7920011	Randall Manufacturing Co. Newark, NJ.	C-GHXG
N6175U	04 King Air B200	BB-1875	Hawker Pacific P/L. Milperra, NSW, Australia.	
N6182A	94 King Air B200	BB-1484	Colleen Corp. Philadelphia, Pa.	N200KA
N6188N	04 King Air B200	BB-1888	Raytheon Aircraft Co. Wichita, Ks.	
N6190F	04 King Air B200	BB-1890	Raytheon Aircraft Co. Wichita, Ks.	
N6190S	04 King Air C90B	LJ-1702	Justice Aviation LLC. Lexington, Ky.	
N6191H	04 King Air B200	BB-1891	Raytheon Aircraft Co. Wichita, Ks.	
N6192A	79 PA-31T Cheyenne 1	7904009	Cianbro Corp. Pittsfield, Me.	
N6192C	04 King Air 350	FL-392	Coin Builders Aviation Inc. Mosinee-Central, Wi.	
N6194V	04 King Air B200	BB-1874	Corporate Aircraft SA. Roveredo, Switzerland.	
N6194X	04 King Air B200	BB-1894	Raytheon Aircraft Co. Wichita, Ks.	
N6198N	04 King Air 350	FL-398	Archer Daniels Midland Co. Decatur, Il.	
N6203T	04 King Air B200	BB-1863	Lider Taxi Aereo SA. Belo Horizonte, MG, Brazil.	
N6207F	82 King Air C90-1	LJ-1017	Roche Fruit Co & J L Smith Co. Yakima, Wa.	
N6228Q	67 King Air A90	LJ-280	Cumberland Board of Vocational Education, Bridgeton, NJ.	N46G
N6271C	82 King Air B200	BB-1036	University of Texas, Austin, Tx.	
N6280E	82 King Air C90-1	LJ-1015	Dodson International Parts Inc. Ottawa, Ks.	
N6300F*	04 King Air B200	BB-1865	GOMACO Corp/Godbersen Smith Construction Co. Ida Grove, Ia.	N6165Q
N6308F	82 King Air B200	BB-1014	State of Texas, Austin, Tx.	
N6335F	82 King Air F90	LA-190	Dewane Investments LLC. Glendale, Az.	
N6356C	83 King Air C90-1	LJ-1052	Medical University of South Carolina, Charleston, SC.	
N6412Q	83 Conquest II	441-0319	Cessna 441-319 Inc. Las Vegas, Nv.	XC-AA10
N6451D	82 King Air B200	BB-1009	U S Department of Energy, Las Vegas, Nv.	
N6492C	83 King Air C90-1	LJ-1050	U S Auto Holdings Inc. Nashville, Tn.	
N6507B	79 King Air 200	BB-498	U S Customs Service, Oklahoma City, Ok.	N23707
N6509F	79 King Air 200	BB-493	HAB Enterprises, Oklahoma City, Ok.	N6040W
N6531N	82 King Air B200	BB-1081	Bering Marine Corp. Seattle, Wa.	
N6563K	82 King Air C90-1	LJ-1032	Beech Transportation Inc. Eden Prairie, Mn.	
N6569L	74 Mitsubishi MU-2L	645	International Jet Inc. Tulsa, Ok.	YV-11CP
N6571S	76 King Air E90	LW-171	Sky King LLC. Indianapolis, In.	
N6590Y	90 Reims/Cessna F406	F406-0052	Gussic Ventures LLC. Anchorage, Ak.	
N6591R	90 Reims/Cessna F406	F406-0054	Gussic Ventures LLC. Anchorage, Ak.	
N6604L	83 King Air B200	BB-1121	Cubic Corp. San Diego, Ca.	
N6630C	79 King Air 200	BB-565	Vader Air Corp. Ballston Spa, NY.	N920C
N6642B	84 King Air 350	FA-1	Raytheon Aircraft Co. Wichita, Ks.	
N6644J	82 King Air B200	BB-1031	Norplane LLC. New Orleans, La.	
N6646R	79 King Air C90	LJ-836	El Aero Services Inc. Elko, Nv.	
N6672N	80 King Air C90	LJ-875	Corporate Flight inc/Lawrence Printing Co. Greenwood, Ms.	
N6681S	79 King Air C90	LJ-850	Reliance Well Service Inc. Magnolia, Ar.	
N6683W	83 King Air B200	BB-1154	Red Tail LLC. Lake Osweego, Or.	
N6684B	80 King Air 200	BB-631	Pacific Coast Enterprises LLC. Las Vegas, Nv.	
N6689D	80 King Air 200	BB-623	Auman Aviation LLC. Greensboro, NC.	
N6692D	84 King Air C90A	LJ-1072	M & J Leasing LLC. Cameron, Wi.	
N6720Y	03 TBM 700C	265	Robert Felland, Three Lakes, Wi.	(N700EV)
N6723Y	82 King Air C90-1	LJ-1013	R Thomas Development Inc. Lodi, Ca.	(SE-...)
N6728H	85 King Air B200	BB-1193	Golden Corral Corp. Raleigh, NC.	(N78GC)
N6749E	80 King Air F90	LA-43	Tax Management Associates Inc. Charlotte, NC.	
N6754H	80 King Air C90	LJ-891	ACSS-Aviation Communication & Surveilance, Phoenix, Az.	(N450MT)
N6756P	80 King Air B100	BE-92	Permian Tank & Manufacturing Inc. Odessa, Tx.	
N6763K	84 King Air C90A	LJ-1064	Tri Star Aviation Inc. Fulton, Ms.	
N6767M	83 Gulfstream 1000	96064	P A Bergner & Co. Peoria, Il.	OY-BPF
N6772P	81 Conquest 1	425-0022	Dave & Rick Good Partnership, Delphos, Oh.	
N6774Z	81 Conquest 1	425-0048	Ricarda Corp. Beatrice, Ne.	(N425E)
N6789	97 King Air 350	FL-181	Olivebus Corp. Greenwich, Ct.	N2281S
N6812W	85 King Air 300	FA-38	Diversified Energy Inc. Knoxville, Tn.	
N6832M	83 Conquest II	441-0282	Firemans Fund Insurance Companies,	
N6840T	83 Conquest II	441-0299	Citation Oil & Gas Corp. Houston, Tx.	
N6844D	81 Conquest 1	425-0062	Financial Flyers II LLC. Petaluma, Ca.	
N6846S	81 Conquest 1	425-0081	Silver Skies LLC. Silver City, NM.	
N6851G	82 Conquest 1	425-0112	Jack Bowles, Oklahoma City, Ok.	
N6851T	81 Conquest II	441-0211	Ward Leasing Co. Stamford, Ct.	
N6851X	81 Conquest II	441-0212	Superior Aviation Inc. Ford Airport, Mi.	
N6853T	81 Conquest II	441-0220	Escape Air Service Inc. Wilmington, De.	
Reg	**Yr Type**	**c/n**	**Owner/Operator**	**Prev Regn**

Reg	Yr Type	c/n	Owner/Operator	Prev Regn
☐ N6855P	82 Conquest II	441-0233	Bear Claw Aviation Inc. Los Angeles, Ca.	
☐ N6860C	83 Conquest II	441-0304	New Mexico State University, Las Cruces, NM.	YV-34CP
☐ N6873Q	83 Conquest 1	425-0173	Sunrise Aviation Inc. Wichita, Ks.	N16P
☐ N6881S	69 King Air B90	LJ-450	Dodson International Parts Inc. Ottawa, Ks.	N979LX
☐ N6885P	82 Conquest 1	425-0143	Walter Hartman, Camarillo, Ca.	
☐ N6885S	82 Conquest 1	425-0144	State of Texas, Austin, Tx.	
☐ N6886U	83 Conquest 1	425-0154	Tomarce Inc. Danville, Il.	
☐ N6900K	78 Rockwell 690B	11441	Hartford Holding Corp. Naples, Fl.	ZS-KOG
☐ N7000B	66 King Air A90	LM-1	Turbine Power Inc. Bridgewater, Va.	66-18000
☐ N7007G	66 King Air A90	LM-2	Turbine Power Inc. Bridgewater, Va.	66-18001
☐ N7010L	66 King Air A90	LM-7	Turbine Power Inc. Bridgewater, Va.	66-18006
☐ N7018F	66 King Air A90	LM-13	Turbine Power Inc. Bridgewater, Va.	66-18013
☐ N7031K	82 Gulfstream 1000	96009	Eagle Air Inc. Memphis, Tn.	HK-3271
☐ N7043G	66 King Air A90	LM-37	Dynamic AvLease Inc. Bridgewater, Va.	66-18036
☐ N7057A	81 Gulfstream 840	11664	MaLeCo, Salem, Or.	G-RNCO
☐ N7069A	77 King Air C-12A	BC-54	U S Customs Service, Oklahoma City, Ok.	77-22943
☐ N7071N	66 King Air A90	LM-59	Dynamic AvLease Inc. Bridgewater, Va.	66-18058
☐ N7074G	73 King Air C-12C	BC-17	U S Customs Service, Oklahoma City, Ok	73-22266
☐ N7079S	67 King Air A90	LM-70	Dynamic AvLease Inc. Bridgewater, Va.	67-18069
☐ N7081L	67 King Alr A90	LM-72	Alaska Aircraft Finance LLC. Anchorage, Ak.	67-18071
☐ N7089Q	67 King Air A90	LM-77	Alaska Aircraft Finance LLC. Anchorage, Ak.	67-18076
☐ N7092K	67 King Air A90	LM-83	Alaska Aircraft Finance LLC. Anchorage, Ak.	67-18083
☐ N7101L	80 Gulfstream 980	95027	Southwest Jet Inc. Belton, Mo.	N83SA
☐ N7139B	81 PA-42 Cheyenne III	8001042	Fly-Biz LLC. Zeeland, Mi.	N54568
☐ N7155P	66 King Air A90	LM-107	Dynamic AvLease Inc. Bridgewater, Va.	67-18111
☐ N7157K	66 King Air A90	LM-115	Turbine Power Inc. Bridgewater, Va.	66-18119
☐ N7165Y	66 King Air A90	LM-120	Alaska Aircraft Finance LLC. Anchorage, Ak.	66-18124
☐ N7166P	79 King Air 200	BB-482	Manker Aerial Mapping Inc. Oklahoma City, Ok.	N6017
☐ N7194Y	81 Cheyenne II-XL	8166064	Pan American Trading Co. Miami, Fl.	HC-BUS
☐ N7198S	70 King Air A90	LU-1	Dynamic AvLease Inc. Bridgewater, Va.	70-15875
☐ N7199J	70 King Air A90	LU-8	Dynamic AvLease Inc. Bridgewater, Va.	70-15882
☐ N7199L	70 King Air A90	LU-9	Dynamic AvLease Inc. Bridgewater, Va.	70-15883
☐ N7199S	70 King Air A90	LU-11	Dynamic AvLease Inc. Bridgewater, Va.	70-15885
☐ N7202Y	84 King Air 300	FA-12	McDonnell Douglas Corp. St Louis, Mo.	
☐ N7206E	85 King Air F90-1	LA-234	Stroeh Corporate Ventures Ltd. Incline Village, Nv.	
☐ N7218Y	85 King Air 300	FA-37	Baker Hughes Oilfield Operations, Houston, Tx.	
☐ N7223X	85 King Air C90A	LJ-1104	Gem City Properties LLC. Laramie, Wy.	
☐ N7228T	84 King Air 300	FA-20	Lonnie Pilgrim, Pittsburg, Tx.	
☐ N7230H	85 King Air C90A	LJ-1113	Frontier Spinning Mills LLC. Sanford, NC.	
☐ N7231P	85 King Air 300	FA-56	Genesis Financial Data Services, Colorado Springs, Co.	
☐ N7233R	83 King Air B200C	BL-69	U S Department of Energy, Albuquerque, NM.	N2811B
☐ N7247Y	73 King Air C-12C	BC-3	U S Customs Service, Oklahoma City, Ok.	73-22252
☐ N7250L	85 King Air 300	FA-81	King Three LLC. Baltimore, Md.	(N125JD)
☐ N7250T	85 King Air B200	BB-1237	Puget Sound Energy, Bellevue, Wa.	
☐ N7256K	85 King Air B200	BB-1241	State of Texas, Austin, Tx.	
☐ N7285Y	92 King Air B300C	FM-5	Lindsey Aviation Services, Haslet, Tx.	N56016
☐ N7308B	77 King Air C-12C	BC-57	California Highway Patrol, Sacramento, Ca.	N118CA
☐ N7377	66 King Air A90	LJ-115	Godwin Aircraft Inc. Memphis, Tn.	N30KS
☐ N7586Z	85 King Air 300	FA-71	Wisconsin Public Service Corp. Green Bay, Wi.	ZS-LOI
☐ N7603	60 SA-26AT Merlin 2B	T26-112	TRH Inc/Robo Aviation, Fayetteville, Tn.	N1222S
☐ N7610U	65 680V Turbo Commander	1548-10	Crystal Creek Ltd. New Orleans, La.	C-FHAP
☐ N7644R	68 King Air B90	LJ-335	Dynamic AvLease Inc. Bridgewater, Va.	
☐ N7896G	84 Gulfstream 1000	96070	Golf Commander LLC. Perrysburg, Oh.	N67GA
☐ N7931D	83 King Air C90-1	LJ-1049	ACC III LLC-Cen/Cal Inc. Clovis, Ca.	
☐ N8001V	91 King Air C90A	LJ-1265	Rockwood LLC. Hobe Sound, Fl.	
☐ N8017M	92 King Air B200	BB-1438	Tucson Aeroservice Center Inc. Marana, Az.	
☐ N8021P	91 King Air C90A	LJ-1269	Contractors Material Co. Jackson, Ms.	
☐ N8061Q	69 680W Turbo Commander	1833-38	Irene C G Bitencourt, Caracas, Venezuela.	PT-KYY
☐ N8080Q	91 King Air 350	FL-54	Carolina Turbine Sales Inc. Tyler, Tx.	
☐ N8083A	79 MU-2 Marquise	739SA	EPPS Air Service Inc. Atlanta, Ga.	N707EZ
☐ N8096U	93 King Air C90B	LJ-1326	Alfalfa Aviation LLC. San Jose, Ca.	
☐ N8099G	91 King Air C90A	LJ-1274	Miles Aircraft LLC. Greensboro, NC.	
☐ N8116N	91 King Air 350	FL-58	Hardy Boys Motorsports Inc. Dallas, Ga.	
☐ N8118R	75 King Air E90	LW-118	Kopp Clay Co. Malvern, Oh.	
☐ N8131F	76 PA-31T Cheyenne II	7620042	Scenic Airlines Inc. Las Vegas, Nv.	F-GAJC
Reg	Yr Type	c/n	Owner/Operator	Prev Regn

Reg	Yr	Type	c/n	Owner/Operator	Prev Regn
☐ N8156Z	93	King Air C90B	LJ-1333	Hale-Whit Air LLC. Tulsa, Ok.	
☐ N8170J	80	King Air/Catpass 250	BB-728	N75MJ LLC. Shreveport, La.	C-GTGA
☐ N8210C	93	King Air C90B	LJ-1347	Choctaw Nation of Oklahoma, Durant, Ok.	
☐ N8220V	93	King Air C90B	LJ-1344	Harvest Moon Aviation Corp. Wilmington, De.	
☐ N8244L	92	2000A Starship	NC-29	Allen Investments Aviation & Marine, Wilmington, De.	(N121GV)
☐ N8259Q	93	King Air C90B	LJ-1332	Craig Aviation LLC. Tempe, Az.	
☐ N8287E	94	King Air C90B	LJ-1356	Vincent Zaninovich & Sons Inc. Richgrove, Ca.	
☐ N8302N	93	King Air 350	FL-98	North Pole Investments Inc. Miami, Fl.	HK-4043X
☐ N8421E	01	Pilatus PC-12/45	430	Viaplanes Ltd. Pryor, Ok.	HB-FRS
☐ N8484T	74	Mitsubishi MU-2J	617	Turbine Aircraft Marketing Inc. San Angelo, Tx.	EI-AWY
☐ N8514B	76	King Air B100	BE-6	Central Aviation LLC. Dublin, Oh.	HB-GEP
☐ N8535	73	Rockwell 690A	11131	Edward Edwards, Pensacola, Fl.	N57099
☐ N8838T	77	Conquest II	441-0003	F M Roberts, Miami, Fl.	N2899P
☐ N8887B	87	King Air C90A	LJ-1148	St Croix Acceptance Corp. St Croix, Wi.	N120RL
☐ N8897Y	81	SA-227AT Merlin 4C	AT-492	Career Aviation Academy, Oakdale, Ca.	C-FJTA
☐ N8970N	79	Conquest II	441-0092	Martin Wagner, Wischstauden, Germany.	
☐ N9008U	73	King Air C-12C	BD-5	Air Serv International Inc. Warrenton, Va.	73-1209
☐ N9029R	75	King Air E90	LW-132	Dairyland Power Corp. La Crosse, Wi.	
☐ N9032H	68	SA-26T Merlin 2A	T26-7	Napier Air Service Inc. Dothan, Al.	C-GGFJ
☐ N9059S	76	King Air E90	LW-159	State of New Mexico, Santa Fe, NM.	
☐ N9076S	77	King Air C90	LJ-715	Cadogan Properties Inc. Baton Rouge, La.	
☐ N9081R	79	King Air C90	LJ-859	Boulais Aviation Inc. Glendale, Az.	HR-AHJ
☐ N9085U	85	PA-42 Cheyenne IIIA	5501034	U S Customs Service, Oklahoma City, Ok.	
☐ N9091J	85	PA-42 Cheyenne IIIA	5501035	U S Customs Service, Oklahoma City, Ok.	
☐ N9116Q	86	PA-42 Cheyenne IIIA	5501037	U S Customs Service, Oklahoma City, Ok.	
☐ N9142B	86	PA-42 Cheyenne IIIA	5501038	U S Customs Service, Oklahoma City, Ok.	
☐ N9150T	84	PA-42 Cheyenne IIIA	5501024	U S Customs Service, Oklahoma City, Ok.	N41182
☐ N9159Y	84	PA-42 Cheyenne IIIA	5501028	Southern Arkansas University Tech, East Camden, Ar.	
☐ N9175N	73	Rockwell 690A	11071	Mark Todd LLC. Mesa, Az.	
☐ N9183C	83	PA-31T Cheyenne 1A	8304001	Peco Foods Inc. Gordo, Al.	
☐ N9223N	72	Rockwell 690	11023	BRS Services Inc. Reno, Nv.	
☐ N9233T	85	PA-42 Cheyenne IIIA	5501032	White Industries Inc. Bates City, Mo.	
☐ N9266Y	84	PA-31T Cheyenne 1A	1104008	Mad River Enterprises Inc. Lenox, Ma.	
☐ N9268Y	84	PA-31T Cheyenne 1A	1104009	David King, Wake Forest, NC.	
☐ N9279A	86	PA-42 Cheyenne IIIA	5501036	U S Customs Service, Oklahoma City, Ok.	
☐ N9331M	90	Beech 1900C-1	UC-139	Omicron Transportation Inc. Reading, Pa.	N1128M
☐ N9426	68	King Air B90	LJ-421	Ottumwa Flying Service Inc. Ottumwa, Ia.	
☐ N9442Q	72	King Air C90	LJ-542	Viking Construction Inc. Hayden, Id.	
☐ N9450Q	72	King Air C90	LJ-550	Dr Bob Fischer, Hibbing, Mn.	XB-FRW
☐ N9683N	82	Conquest II	441-0255	CPC Aviation LLC/Henry Production Co. Lafayette, La.	N68587
☐ N9756S	80	Gulfstream 980	95003	Eagle Air Inc. Memphis, Tn.	N501NB
☐ N9767S	80	Gulfstream 980	95014	3MD Charter, Portland, Or.	(N321MD)
☐ N9812S	81	Gulfstream 980	95060	Aerographics Inc. Manassas, Va.	
☐ N9838Z	68	King Air B90	LJ-435	Skydive Suffolk Aviation LLC. Suffolk, Va.	D-IHCH
☐ N9872C	76	King Air C90	LJ-698	Twin Poplar Corp. Irvine, Ca.	(N497P)
☐ N9898	98	King Air B200	BB-1627	Southern Electric Service Co. Greensboro, NC.	N744TA
☐ N9900	76	SA-226T Merlin 3A	T-266	Flex Aviation LLC. Roanoke, Tx.	(N97FT)
☐ N9901	66	King Air 90	LJ-93	Great Oaks Joint Vocational School District, Cincinnati, Oh.	N48A
☐ N9902S	82	Gulfstream 1000	96002	Hodge Electronics Inc. South Miami, Fl.	
☐ N9933N	79	King Air B100	BE-56	CMH Aviation Inc. Columbus-Bolton, Oh.	N251DA
☐ N9942S	82	Gulfstream 1000	96022	Jerry Harvey, West Palm Beach, Fl.	
☐ N9945S	82	Gulfstream 1000	96025	Zuleta Services & Trading Co. Boca Raton, Fl.	
☐ N9948S	82	Gulfstream 1000	96028	Air Operations International, Charlotte, NC.	
☐ N9966S	82	Gulfstream 1000	96046	Franks Petroleum Inc. Shreveport, La. (status ?).	
☐ N9968S	82	Gulfstream 1000	96048	Eagle Air Inc. Memphis, Tn.	
☐ N9973S	82	Gulfstream 1000	96053	Ram-Air International Inc. Miami, Fl.	
☐ N9998P	73	King Air C-12C	BC-8	Luis Horacio Hernandez Perez, Bogota, Colombia.	N999SP
☐ N11692	78	King Air C90	LJ-772	Seven Bar Flying Service Inc. Albuquerque, NM.	F-GFBO
☐ N12244	84	Conquest 1	425-0213	D L S Inc. Fort Payne, Al.	
☐ N12268	85	Conquest 1	425-0227	Sharpline Converting Inc. Wichita, Ks.	
☐ N13622	78	Rockwell 690B	11469	Kenneth Vadnais, Santa Barbara, Ca.	F-GCMJ
☐ N14886	79	PA-31T Cheyenne 1	7904036	Cianbro Corp. Pittsfield, Me.	N149CC
☐ N15234	89	King Air C90A	LJ-1194	Erickson Oil Products Inc. Hudson, Wi.	
☐ N15613	89	King Air 300	FA-193	Spencer Aviation Inc. Rockford, Il.	
☐ N17573	77	King Air C90	LJ-714	Elliott Farms Ltd. Cutler, Ca.	
Reg	Yr	Type	c/n	Owner/Operator	Prev Regn

Reg	Yr	Type	c/n	Owner/Operator	Prev Regn
N17792	78	King Air B100	BE-41	Bell Processing Inc. Wichita Falls, Tx	
N18343	77	King Air E90	LW-243	Owens Valley Board of Trustees, Bishop, Ca.	
N18471	82	King Air F90	LA-161	Polygon LLC. White Plains, NY.	
N18481	82	Conquest 1	425-0105	Green Wing Aviation Inc. Louisiana, Mo.	(N7711B)
N20564	79	King Air E90	LW-314	Falco Holdings Ltd. Helena, Mt.	(N404RW
N20880	70	King Air 100	B-63	Tony Frost & Gregory Behrens, Red Rock, Az.	F-GGFE
N22071	76	King Air 200	BB-111	Air Serv International Inc. Warrenton, Va.	N633EB
N23243	79	PA-31T Cheyenne 1	7904017	Rust Aviation LLC. Charlevoix, Mi.	
N23250	79	PA-31T Cheyenne 1	7904018	La Stella Corp. Pueblo, Co.	
N23334	79	PA-31T Cheyenne 1	7904024	Flight One Inc. Dunn, NC.	TG-LIA
N23404	77	King Air A100	B-234	National Airplane Sales & Leasing, Bluffton, Oh.	
N23426	79	PA-31T Cheyenne 1	7904035	Selland Pontiac-GMC Inc. Moorhead, Mn.	
N23605	77	King Air A100	B-236	Edgar Artecona, Alvarado, Tx.	
N23646	79	PA-31T Cheyenne II	7920078	Charlie Delta LLC. Denver, Co.	(PH-BAM
N23718	79	PA-31T Cheyenne II	7920087	James Hodge Ford Lincoln Inc. Muskogee, Ok.	
N24203	78	King Air B100	BE-40	Corvus Air LLC. Steamboat Springs, Co.	
N25677	75	SA-226T Merlin 3A	T-254	Kolar Aviation Inc. Hudson, Oh.	N58018
N27856	76	PA-31T Cheyenne II	7620041	Merritt de Jong Jr. Newburgh, In.	D-IEEA
N29997	87	King Air B200	BB-1268	Wallace Westwind Inc. Las Cruces, NM.	
N30025	04	King Air C90B	LJ-1725	Raytheon Aircraft Co. Wichita, Ks.	
N30397	03	PA-46-500TP Meridian	4697167	Larry Teuber, Rapid City, SD.	
N30854	74	Rockwell 690A	11229	Cornerstone Financial Enterprises, Van Nuys, Ca.	LV-LTO
N30983	04	PA-46-500TP Meridian	4697189	Charles Schoenberger, Alamo, Ca.	
N31094	99	King Air B200	BB-1676	Parques Industriales Amista SA/AeroMaquila Inc. Del Rio, Tx.	
N32217	04	King Air C90B	LJ-1717	Bimco Properties Inc. Panama City, Panama.	
N32229	65	King Air 90	LJ-49	Aero Trans Inc. Wilmington, De.	C-GNUX
N32238	00	King Air C90B	LJ-1580	Sun Aviation Inc. Wichita, Ks.	
N36579	04	King Air B200	BB-1879	Aerolineas Ejecutivas SA. Toluca.	
N36585	04	King Air B200	BB-1885	Specialised Aircraft Services Inc. Wichita, Ks.	
N36635	04	King Air 350	FL-435	Raytheon Aircraft Co. Wichita, Ks.	
N36715	04	King Air 350	FL-415	Hawker Pacific P/L. Yagoona, NSW, Australia.	
N36719	04	King Air C90B	LJ-1719	Piedmont Hawthorne Aviation Inc. Winston-Salem, NC.	
N36739	04	King Air B200	BB-1889	Raytheon Aircraft Co. Wichita, Ks.	
N36805	87	King Air C90A	LJ-1157	HUSCO International Inc. Waukesha, Wi.	
N36813	04	King Air 350	FL-413	Luther Aircraft LLC. Brookfield, Wi.	
N36893	04	King Air B200	BB-1893	Raytheon Aircraft Co. Wichita, Ks.	N.....
N36919	04	King Air 350	FL-419	Raytheon Aircraft Co. Wichita, Ks.	
N36929	04	King Air C90B	LJ-1729	Raytheon Aircraft Co. Wichita, Ks.	
N36948	04	King Air B200C	BL-148	Raytheon Aircraft Co. Wichita, Ks.	
N36949	04	King Air B200C	BL-149	Raytheon Aircraft Co. Wichita, Ks.	
N36987	04	King Air B200	BB-1887	Raytheon Aircraft Co. Wichita, Ks.	
N37025	04	King Air 350	FL-425	Raytheon Aircraft Co. Wichita, Ks.	
N37222	04	King Air C90B	LJ-1722	Capital Holdings 118 LLC. NYC.	
N37390	90	King Air 350	FL-11	McEagle Aviation of Delaware LLC. O'Fallon, Mo.	N3739C
N37990	81	King Air F90	LA-101	IIIB LLC. Oskaloosa, Ia.	
N38280	81	King Air C90	LJ-953	O B Aircraft LLC. Tampa, Fl.	
N38381	81	King Air B200	BB-934	Wheels of Africa, Rand, RSA.	
N40191	99	Pilatus PC-12/45	248	Tejas Aviation Management, Fort Worth, Tx.	N652CA
N40593	97	King Air 350	FL-162	Lindsey Aviation Services, Haslet, Tx.	N1112Z
N41198	85	PA-42 Cheyenne 400LS	5527030	Aircraft Guaranty Corp. Germany.	
N41462	81	Gulfstream 840	11672	Emerson Electric Co. St Louis, Mo.	VP-BLK
N43866	80	MU-2 Marquise	757SA	Moro Aircraft Leasing Inc. Fairbanks, Ak.	(N21MU'
N44776	80	Conquest II	441-0121	P M Inc. Plano, Tx.	N44776
N44882	81	King Air F90	LA-102	Spirol International Corp. Danielson, Ct.	YV-399C
N45818	73	SA-226T Merlin 3	T-235	U S Department of Justice, El Paso, Tx.	XC-UTE/
N50525	66	King Air A90	LJ-159	Wildcat Flying LLC. Larned, Ks.	86-0092
N50655	67	680V Turbo Commander	1714-88	Roger MacWilliamson, Hollister, Ca.	XB-CED
N50847	03	King Air C90	LJ-1697	Raytheon Aircraft Co. Wichita, Ks.	
N51488	03	King Air B200CT	BN-8	Raytheon Aircraft Co. Wichita, Ks.	
N53235	01	PA-46-500TP Meridian	4697083	Travel Equipment LLC. San Francisco, Ca.	
N53238	01	PA-46-500TP Meridian	4697086	Diederich Insurance Consulting Inc. Carbondale, Il.	
N53362	01	PA-46-500TP Meridian	4697109	Bonaparte Films LLC. Washington, DC.	
N53369	01	PA-46-500TP Meridian	4697088	Maverick Country Stores Inc. Afton, Wy.	
N53401	02	PA-46-500TP Meridian	4697143	Preferred Aviation & Marine Services LLC. Plymouth, Mn.	
N53516	02	PA-46-500TP Meridian	4697132	Delta Aircraft Holdings LLC. Wilmington, De.	
Reg	**Yr**	**Type**	**c/n**	**Owner/Operator**	**Prev Regn**

Reg	Yr	Type	c/n	Owner/Operator	Prev Regn
N53667	03	PA-46-500TP Meridian	4697158	Willson Consulting LLC. Naples, Fl.	
N54026	85	DHC 7-103	106	U S Department of Energy, Albuquerque, NM.	
N54163	68	680W Turbo Commander	1774-12	Sacramento Maintenance & Management Services, Sacramento.	N5416
N54199	03	PA-46-500TP Meridian	4697164	Distributors Real Estate Inc. Schofield, Wi.	
N57092	74	Rockwell 690A	11160	LaMair Aviation Corp. Wilmington, De.	
N57096	73	Rockwell 690A	11120	Commander N W Leasing, Anchorage, Ak.	
N57112	75	Rockwell 690A	11263	Hogan Manufacturing Inc. Escalon, Ca.	
N57113	73	Rockwell 690A	11113	Gaven Industries Inc. Pittsburgh, Pa.	
N57133	73	Rockwell 690A	11133	Corporate Air Inc. Billings, Mt.	(N47EC)
N57175	72	Rockwell 690	11004	Aero-Metric Engineering Inc. Sheboygan, Wi.	N37546
N57292	75	Rockwell 690A	11270	World Jet Inc. Fort Lauderdale, Fl.	
N58280	75	King Air 200	BB-61	TIPS Air Inc. San Antonio, Tx.	C-GSEP
N60383	95	King Air B200	BB-1504	Tuscon Aeroservice Center Inc. Marana, Az.	VH-HPW
N61228	82	King Air F90	LA-169	DA/PRO Rubber Inc. Tulsa, Ok.	
N61369	02	King Air B200	BB-1809	Raytheon Aircraft Co. Wichita, Ks.	
N61383	82	King Air C90A	LJ-1009	LWCR Transportation Inc. Minot, ND.	(N155RG)
N61698	03	King Air C90B	LJ-1698	Michael Wayne Investment Co. Virginia Beach, Va.	
N62366	73	Rockwell 690A	11141	Ron Air Inc. Las Vegas, Nv.	HB-GFQ
N62525	76	King Air C90	LJ-691	Talley Farms Inc. Arroyo Grande, Ca.	JA8839
N62569	82	King Air B200	BB-1028	State of Texas, Austin, Tx.	
N63200	81	King Air C90	LJ-989	Releco Ltd. High Point, NC.	(YV-442CP)
N63593	79	King Air 200	BB-552	James Latta, Fayetteville, Ar.	G-BGRD
N63686	82	King Air B200	BB-1085	Cottonwood Investment Group LLC. Sleepy Eye, Mn.	
N63791	83	King Air B200	BB-1100	Bonneville Power Administration, Vancouver, Wa.	
N66000	78	King Air C-12C	BC-66	Department of the Army, Berryville, Va.	78-23130
N66804	80	King Air B100	BE-82	M L Rhodes Ltd. Edinberg, Tx.	(N200JL)
N66820	79	King Air B100	BE-68	Bayport Air Co. Mobile, Al.	N6052C
N67511	80	King Air C90	LJ-888	Midwest Flight LLC. Tecumseh, Mi.	(N111GF)
N67726	81	Conquest 1	425-0030	J & L Oil Inc. Vernon Hills, Il.	
N68734	84	Conquest 1	425-0182	Seanaire Inc. Midland Park, NJ.	
N68865	83	Conquest 1	425-0160	State of Texas, Austin, Tx.	
N69084	82	King Air F90	LA-157	MRS Management Inc. Rapid City, SD.	
N69301	84	King Air C90A	LJ-1079	Flying Mountains LLC. Steamboat Springs, Co.	
N70088	66	King Air A90	LM-6	Turbine Power Inc. Bridgewater, Va.	66-18005
N70135	66	King Air A90	LM-9	Turbine Power Inc. Bridgewater, Va.	66-18008
N70264	66	King Air A90	LM-17	Downstown Airport Inc. Vineland, NJ.	66-18016
N70766	67	King Air A90	LM-64	PACTEC, Redlands, Ca.	67-18063
N70841	67	King Air A90	LM-73	Grant Aviation Inc. Anchorage, Ak.	67-18072
N70950	67	King Air A90	LM-86	Messenger Air Ltd. Bluffton, Oh.	67-18088
N71562	01	PA-46-500TP Meridian	4697081	FICorp Inc. Las Vegas, Nv.	
N72470	73	King Air C-12C	BC-4	U S Customs Service, Oklahoma City, Ok.	73-22253
N72472	73	King Air C-12C	BC-11	U S Customs Service, Oklahoma City, Ok.	73-22263
N72476	76	King Air C-12C	BC-26	U S Customs Service, Oklahoma City, Ok.	76-22550
N75368	65	King Air 90	LJ-75	Bruffey Flying Inc. Rome, Ga.	C-GJBE
N81432	85	Gulfstream 1000B	96207	Thomas Bijou, Plano, Tx.	N229GA
N81448	76	Rockwell 690A	11327	Lakin Law Firm, Wood River, Il.	
N81703	78	Rockwell 690B	11438	Frasca International Inc. Champaign, Il.	
N81831	78	Rockwell 690B	11447	Perryton Service Co. Perryton, Tx.	
N82094	77	PA-31T Cheyenne II	7720014	Jack Wall Aircraft Sales Inc. Memphis, Tn.	
N82156	77	PA-31T Cheyenne II	7720045	Rivett Group LLC. Aberdeen, SD.	
N82161	77	PA-31T Cheyenne II	7720049	Imperial Air LP. McAllen, Tx.	
N82290	78	PA-31T Cheyenne II	7820058	Clipper Export & Import Corp. Miami, Fl.	
N87699	81	King Air B200	BB-887	Sky King LLC. Manassas, Va.	YV-2222P
N88598	78	Conquest II	441-0060	Aircraft Sales Ltd. Santa Ana, Ca.	N441CF
N88692	83	Conquest II	441-0290	Jim Jacobs, Great Barrington, Ma.	
N88727	82	Conquest II	441-0267	Conquest Flight Group LLC/Flex Flight LLC. Parker, Co.	
N88823	78	Conquest II	441-0064	Carasali-Paganetti LLC. Reno, Nv.	
N88834	82	Conquest II	441-0269	Victory Van Lines Inc/Jennair Aviation Inc. Staten Island.	N88834
N91384	73	Rockwell 690A	11118	Airbourne Data Inc. Dover, De.	SE-FLN
N91575	85	Gulfstream 1000B	96205	Eagle Creek Aviation Services Inc. Indianapolis, In.	N5852K
N96954	80	SA-226T Merlin 3B	T-311	Woodstead Enterprises LLC. The Woodlnds, Tx.	N27563
Military					
161187	61	King Air UC-12B	BJ-3	U.S. Marine Corps.	
161188	61	King Air UC-12B	BJ-4	U.S. Navy.	
161190	61	King Air UC-12B	BJ-6	U.S. Navy.	
Reg	Yr	Type	c/n	Owner/Operator	Prev Regn

Reg	Yr	Type	c/n	Owner/Operator	Prev Regn
☐ 161191	61	King Air UC-12B	BJ-7	U.S. Navy, Code 7E, NAS Jacksonville, Fl.	
☐ 161192	61	King Air UC-12B	BJ-8	U.S. Marine Corps. Code 5Y, MCAS Yuma, Az.	
☐ 161193	61	King Air UC-12B	BJ-9	U.S. Navy.	
☐ 161194	61	King Air UC-12B	BJ-10	U.S. Navy.	
☐ 161195	61	King Air UC-12B	BJ-11	U.S. Navy, Code 8F, NAS Guantanamo Bay, Cuba.	
☐ 161196	61	King Air UC-12B	BJ-12	U.S. Navy, Code 8N, NAS El Centro, Ca.	
☐ 161197	61	King Air UC-12B	BJ-13	U.S. Navy.	
☐ 161200		King Air UC-12B	BJ-16	U.S. Navy.	
☐ 161201		King Air UC-12B	BJ-17	U.S. Navy.	
☐ 161203		King Air UC-12B	BJ-19	U.S. Navy, Code 7C, NAS Norfolk, Va.	
☐ 161204		King Air UC-12B	BJ-20	U.S. Navy.	
☐ 161205		King Air UC-12B	BJ-21	U.S. Navy.	
☐ 161206		King Air UC-12B	BJ-22	U.S. Navy, Code 7G, NAS Whidbey Island, Wa.	
☐ 161306		King Air UC-12B	BJ-23	U.S. Navy.	
☐ 161307		King Air UC-12B	BJ-24	U.S. Navy.	
☐ 161308		King Air UC-12B	BJ-25	U.S. Navy, Code 5Y, Yuma, Az.	
☐ 161309		King Air UC-12B	BJ-26	U.S. Navy.	
☐ 161310		King Air UC-12B	BJ-27	U.S. Navy.	
☐ 161312		King Air UC-12B	BJ-29	U.S. Navy.	
☐ 161313		King Air UC-12B	BJ-30	U.S. Navy.	
☐ 161315		King Air UC-12B	BJ-32	U.S. Navy.	
☐ 161316		King Air UC-12B	BJ-33	U.S. Navy.	
☐ 161317		King Air UC-12B	BJ-34	U.S. Marine Corps.	
☐ 161318		King Air UC-12B	BJ-35	U.S. Navy.	
☐ 161319		King Air UC-12B	BJ-36	U.S. Navy.	
☐ 161320		King Air UC-12B	BJ-37	U.S. Navy.	
☐ 161322		King Air UC-12B	BJ-39	U.S. Navy, Code 7X, NAS New Orleans, La.	
☐ 161323		King Air UC-12B	BJ-40	U.S. Navy, Code RW, VRC-30, NAS North Island, Ca.	
☐ 161324		King Air UC-12B	BJ-41	U.S. Navy.	
☐ 161325		King Air UC-12B	BJ-42	U.S. Marine Corps. Code 5D, MCAS New River, NC.	
☐ 161326		King Air UC-12B	BJ-43	U.S. Army, Code 7G, NAS Whidbey Island, Wa.	
☐ 161497		King Air UC-12B	BJ-45	U.S. Navy.	
☐ 161498		King Air UC-12B	BJ-46	U.S. Navy.	
☐ 161500		King Air UC-12B	BJ-48	U.S. Navy, Code 7E, NAS Jacksonville, Fl.	
☐ 161501		King Air UC-12B	BJ-49	U.S. Navy.	
☐ 161502		King Air UC-12B	BJ-50	U.S. Navy.	
☐ 161503		King Air UC-12B	BJ-51	U.S. Navy, Code 7D, NAF Fort Worth, Fort Worth JRB. Tx.	
☐ 161504		King Air UC-12B	BJ-52	U.S. Navy, Code 7B, NAS Atlanta, Ga.	
☐ 161505		King Air UC-12B	BJ-53	U.S. Navy.	
☐ 161506		King Air UC-12B	BJ-54	U.S. Navy, Code 7N, NAF Washington, Andrews AFB. Md.	
☐ 161507		King Air UC-12B	BJ-55	U.S. Marine Corps. Code 5D, MCAS New River, NC.	
☐ 161508		King Air UC-12B	BJ-56	U.S. Navy.	
☐ 161510		King Air UC-12B	BJ-58	U.S. Navy.	
☐ 161511		King Air UC-12B	BJ-59	U.S. Navy.	
☐ 161512		King Air UC-12B	BJ-60	U.S. Navy.	
☐ 161513		King Air UC-12B	BJ-61	U.S. Navy.	
☐ 161514		King Air UC-12B	BJ-62	U.S. Marine Corps.	
☐ 161515		King Air UC-12B	BJ-63	U.S. Navy, Code 5B, MCAS Beaufort, SC.	
☐ 161517		King Air UC-12B	BJ-65	U.S. Navy.	
☐ 161518		King Air UC-12B	BJ-66	U.S. Navy.	
☐ 163553		King Air UC-12F	BU-1	U.S. Navy, Code 8A, NAS Misawa, Japan.	
☐ 163554		King Air UC-12F	BU-2	U.S. Navy, Code 8A, NAF Atsugi, Japan.	
☐ 163555		King Air UC-12F	BU-3	U.S. Navy, Code 8A, NAF Atsugi, Japan.	
☐ 163556		King Air UC-12F	BU-4	U.S. Navy, Code 8A, NAF Atsugi, Japan.	
☐ 163557		King Air UC-12F	BU-5	U.S. Navy, Japan.	
☐ 163558		King Air UC-12F	BU-6	U.S. Navy. Iwakuni, Japan.	
☐ 163559		King Air UC-12F	BU-7	U.S. Navy, Iwakuni, Japan.	
☐ 163560		King Air UC-12F	BU-8	U.S. Navy, Okinawa, Japan.	
☐ 163561		King Air UC-12F	BU-9	U.S. Navy, Okinawa, Japan.	
☐ 163562		King Air UC-12F	BU-10	U.S. Navy, Japan.	
☐ 163563		King Air UC-12F	BU-11	U.S. Navy, Pacific Missile Range Facility, Barking Sands, Hi	
☐ 163564		King Air UC-12F	BU-12	U.S. Navy, VRC-30, NAS N Island, Ca.	
☐ 163836		King Air UC-12M	BV-1	U.S. Navy.	
☐ 163837		King Air UC-12M	BV-2	U.S. Navy.	
☐ 163838		King Air UC-12M	BV-3	U.S. Navy.	

Reg	Yr Type	c/n	Owner/Operator	Prev Regn
☐ 163839	King Air UC-12M	BV-4	U.S. Navy, NS Rota, Spain.	
☐ 163840	King Air UC-12M	BV-5	U.S. Navy.	
☐ 163841	King Air UC-12M	BV-6	U.S. Navy.	
☐ 163842	King Air UC-12M	BV-7	U.S. Navy, NS Rota, Spain.	
☐ 163843	King Air UC-12M	BV-8	U.S. Navy.	
☐ 163844	King Air UC-12M	BV-9	U.S. Navy.	
☐ 163845	King Air UC-12M	BV-10	U.S. Navy.	
☐ 163846	King Air UC-12M	BV-11	U.S. Navy, Code 8E, NAS Roosevelt Roads, PR.	
☐ 163847	King Air UC-12M	BV-12	U.S. Navy.	
☐ 66-15361	66 King Air A90	LJ-153	VC-6A, U S Army, White Sands Missile Range, Holloman AFB. NM	N901R
☐ 70-15908	72 King Air U-21J	B-95	U S Navy, Test Pilot School, NAS Patuxent River, Md.	
☐ 73-1208	73 King Air C-12C	BD-4	U S Army.	
☐ 73-1214	73 King Air C-12C	BD-10	USAF, U S Embassy Flight, Bangkok, Thailand.	
☐ 73-1215	73 King Air C-12C	BD-11	USAF, 412th Logistics Group, Edwards AFB. Ca.	
☐ 73-1217	73 King Air C-12C	BD-13	USAF, U S Embassy Flight, Manila, Philippines.	
☐ 73-1218	73 King Air C-12C	BD-14	USAF.	
☐ 73-22262	73 King Air C-12C	BC-10	U S Army, AEESB, NAS Lakehurst, NJ.	73-22262
☐ 76-0158	76 King Air C-12C	BD-15	USAF, Edwards AFB. Md.	
☐ 76-0160	76 King Air C-12C	BD-17	USAF, U S Embassy Flight, Riyadh, Saudi Arabia.	
☐ 76-0161	76 King Air C-12C	BD-18	USAF, Edwards AFB. Ca.	
☐ 76-0162	76 King Air C-12C	BD-19	USAF.	
☐ 76-0163	76 King Air C-12C	BD-20	USAF, U S Embassy Flight, Canberra, Australia.	
☐ 76-0164	76 King Air C-12C	BD-21	USAF, Military Training Mission, Dhahran, Saudi Arabia.	
☐ 76-0166	76 King Air C-12C	BD-23	USAF, 418th FLTS,	
☐ 76-0168	76 King Air C-12C	BD-25	USAF, U S Embassy Flight, Bogota, Colombia.	
☐ 76-0171	76 King Air C-12C	BD-28	USAF.	
☐ 76-0172	76 King Air C-12C	BD-29	USAF.	
☐ 76-22551	76 King Air C-12C	BC-27	Flight Safety Inc.	
☐ 76-22555	76 King Air C-12C	BC-31	U S Army. Flight Safety International,	
☐ 76-22559	76 King Air C-12C	BC-36	U S Army, Flight Safety International,	
☐ 76-22561	76 King Air C-12C	BC-38	U S Army, Flight Safety International,	
☐ 76-22563	76 King Air C-12C	BC-40	U S Army, Fixed Wing Training Site, Clarksburg, WV.	(N7066D)
☐ 76-3239	76 King Air C-12C	BD-24	USAF.	76-0167
☐ 77-22932	77 King Air C-12C	BC-43	U S Army, Flight Safety International,	
☐ 77-22935	77 King Air C-12C	BC-46	U S Army, Flight Safety International,	
☐ 77-22941	77 King Air C-12A	BC-52	U S Army, Flight Safety International,	
☐ 77-22942	77 King Air C-12C	BC-53	U S Army.	
☐ 77-22944	77 King Air C-12C	BC-55	U S Army, Flight Safety International,	
☐ 77-22949	77 King Air C-12C	BC-60	U S Army, Flight Safety International,	
☐ 78-23128	78 King Air C-12C	BC-64	U S Army.	
☐ 78-23132	78 King Air C-12C	BC-68	U S Navy.	
☐ 78-23133	78 King Air JC-12C	BC-69	U S Navy.	
☐ 78-23135	78 King Air C-12C	BC-71	U S Army, Tuzla, Bosnia.	
☐ 78-23140	78 King Air JC-12D	BP-1	U S Army.	
☐ 78-23141	78 King Air RC-12D	GR-6	U S Army, B/304th MIB (Training), Libby AAF, Az. (was BP-2).	
☐ 78-23142	78 King Air RC-12D	GR-7	U S Army, 3rd MIB (AE), Camp Humphries, S Korea. (was BP-3).	
☐ 78-23143	78 King Air RC-12D	GR-8	U S Army. (was BP-4).	
☐ 78-23144	78 King Air RC-12D	GR-9	U S Army, 3rd MIB (AE), Camp Humphries, S Korea. (was BP-5)	
☐ 80-23371	78 King Air RC-12D	GR-2	U S Army, 3rd MIB (AE), Camp Humphries, S Korea. (was BP-12)	
☐ 80-23372	80 King Air RC-12G	FC-3	U S Army. (was BP-13)..	
☐ 80-23373	80 King Air RC-12D	GR-4	U S Army, B/1st MIB (AE), Wiesbaden, Germany. (was BP-14).	
☐ 80-23374	80 King Air RC-12D	GR-12	U S Army, 304th MIB (Training), Libby AAF, Az. (was BP-15).	
☐ 80-23375	80 King Air RC-12D	GR-5	U S Army. (was BP-16).	
☐ 80-23376	80 King Air RC-12D	GR-11	U S Army, B/15th MIB (AE), Robert Gray AAF, Tx. (was BP-17).	
☐ 80-23377	80 King Air RC-12D	GR-3	U S Army. (was BP-18).	
☐ 80-23378	80 King Air RC-12D	GR-13	U S Army, White Sands Missile Range, Holloman AFB. NM.	
☐ 80-23379	80 King Air RC-12G	FC-1	U S Army. (was BP-20).	
☐ 80-23380	80 King Air RC-12G	FC-2	U S Army. (was BP-21).	
☐ 81-23541	81 King Air RC-12D	BP-22	U S Army, USAARL,	
☐ 81-23542	81 King Air RC-12D	GR-1	U S Army. (was BP-23).	
☐ 81-23543	81 King Air C-12D	BP-24	U S Army.	
☐ 81-23544	81 King Air C-12D	BP-25	U S Army.	
☐ 81-23545	81 King Air C-12D	BP-26	U S Army.	
☐ 81-23546	81 King Air C-12D	BP-27	U S Army, OSACOM, Det 6, CT ARNG, Windsor Locks, Ct.	
☐ 82-23780	82 King Air C-12D	BP-28	U S Army, OSACOM, Det 14, ME ARNG, Bangor, Me.	

Reg	Yr	Type	c/n	Owner/Operator	Prev Regn
☐ 82-23781	82 King Air C-12D		BP-29	U S Army, OSACOM, Hickam AFB. Hi.	
☐ 82-23782	82 King Air C-12D		BP-30	U S Army, OSACOM, Robert Gray AAF, Tx.	
☐ 82-23783	82 King Air C-12D		BP-31	U S Army, OSACOM, Det 23, RI ARNG, Quonset State Airport.	
☐ 82-23784	82 King Air C-12D		BP-32	U S Army, Flight Safety International,	
☐ 82-23785	82 King Air C-12D		BP-33	U S Army, Flight Safety International,	
☐ 83-0494	83 King Air C-12D		BP-40	USAF, U S Embassy Flight, Abidjan, Ivory Coast.	
☐ 83-0495	83 King Air C-12D		BP-41	USAF, U S Embassy Flight, Budapest, Hungary.	
☐ 83-0496	83 King Air C-12D		BP-42	USAF, U S Embassy Flight, Nairobi, Kenya.	
☐ 83-0497	83 King Air C-12D		BP-43	USAF, U S Embassy Flight, Buenos Aires, Argentina.	
☐ 83-0498	83 King Air C-12D		BP-44	USAF.	
☐ 83-0499	83 King Air C-12D		BP-45	USAF, U S Embassy Flight, La Paz, Bolivia.	
☐ 83-24145	83 King Air C-12D		BP-34	U S Army, OSACOM, Det 19, NJ ARNG, West Trenton, NJ.	
☐ 83-24146	83 King Air C-12D		BP-35	U S Army, OSACOM, Det 15, MI ARNG, Grand Ledge-Abrams, Mi.	
☐ 83-24147	83 King Air C-12D		BP-36	U S Army.	
☐ 83-24148	83 King Air C-12D		BP-37	U S Army, OSACOM, Gray AAF, Wa.	
☐ 83-24149	83 King Air C-12D		BP-38	U S Army.	
☐ 83-24150	83 King Air C-12D		BP-39	U S Army, Flight Safety International,	
☐ 83-24313	83 King Air RC-12H		GR-14	U S Army, B/3rd MIB (AE), Camp Humphreys, South Korea.	
☐ 83-24314	83 King Air RC-12H		GR-15	U S Army, B/3rd MIB (AE), Camp Humphreys, South Korea.	
☐ 83-24315	83 King Air RC-12H		GR-16	U S Army, B/3rd MIB (AE), Camp Humphreys, South Korea.	
☐ 83-24316	83 King Air RC-12D		GR-17	U S Army, B/3rd MIB (AE), Camp Humphreys, South Korea.	
☐ 83-24317	83 King Air RC-12H		GR-18	U S Army, B/3rd MIB (AE), Camp Humphreys, South Korea.	
☐ 83-24318	83 King Air RC-12H		GR-19	U S Army, B/3rd MIB (AE), Camp Humphreys, South Korea.	
☐ 84-0143	84 King Air C-12F		BL-73	U S Army.	
☐ 84-0144	84 King Air C-12F		BL-74	U S Army, Heidelberg, Germany.	N5801D
☐ 84-0145	84 King Air C-12F		BL-75	U S Army, OSACOM, Elmendorf AFB. Ak.	
☐ 84-0146	84 King Air C-12F		BL-76	U S Army, 204th MIB (AR), Biggs AAF, Tx.	
☐ 84-0147	84 King Air C-12F		BL-77	USAF, 3rd Wing, Elmendorf AFB. Ak	
☐ 84-0148	84 King Air C-12F		BL-78	USAF, 3rd Wing, Elmendorf AFB. Ak.	
☐ 84-0149	84 King Air C-12F		BL-79	U S Army, OSACOM, Elmendorf AFB. Ak.	
☐ 84-0150	84 King Air C-12F		BL-80	U S Army, OSACOM, Det 42, ND ARNG, Bismarck, ND.	
☐ 84-0151	84 King Air C-12F		BL-81	U S Army.	
☐ 84-0152	84 King Air C-12F		BL-82	U S Army, Heidelberg, Germany.	
☐ 84-0153	84 King Air C-12F		BL-83	U S Army, Heidelberg, Germany.	N58009
☐ 84-0154	84 King Air C-12F		BL-84	U S Army, Heidelberg, Germany.	
☐ 84-0155	84 King Air C-12F		BL-85	U S Army, Heidelberg, Germany.	
☐ 84-0156	84 King Air C-12U		BL-86	U S Army, Heidelberg, Germany.	
☐ 84-0157	84 King Air C-12U		BL-87	U S Army, Heidelberg, Germany.	
☐ 84-0158	84 King Air C-12U		BL-88	U S Army, HQ USEUCOM, Stuttgart, Germany.	
☐ 84-0159	84 King Air C-12F		BL-89	U S Army, OSACOM, Det 43, NE ARNG, Lincoln, Ne.	
☐ 84-0160	84 King Air C-12U		BL-90	U S Army, HQ USEUCOM, Stuttgart, Germany.	
☐ 84-0161	84 King Air C-12U		BL-91	U S Army, 6th Aviation Co. Vicenza, Italy.	
☐ 84-0162	84 King Air C-12U		BL-92	U S Army, 6th Aviation Co. Vicenza, Italy.	
☐ 84-0163	84 King Air C-12U		BL-93	U S Army, 204th MIB (AR), Biggs AAF, Tx.	
☐ 84-0164	84 King Air C-12F		BL-94	U S Army.	
☐ 84-0165	84 King Air C-12U		BL-95	U S Army.	
☐ 84-0166	84 King Air C-12F		BL-96	U S Army, A/6-52nd AVN, (TA), Seoul, South Korea.	
☐ 84-0167	84 King Air C-12F		BL-97	U S Army, A/6-52nd AVN, (TA), Seoul, South Korea.	
☐ 84-0168	84 King Air C-12F		BL-98	U S Army, A/6-52nd AVN, (TA), Seoul, South Korea.	
☐ 84-0170	84 King Air C-12F		BL-100	U S Army, A/6-52nd AVN, (TA), Seoul, South Korea.	
☐ 84-0171	84 King Air C-12F		BL-101	U S Army, OSACOM, Det 37, KS ARNG, Topeka, Ks.	
☐ 84-0172	84 King Air C-12F		BL-102	U S Army.	
☐ 84-0173	84 King Air C-12F		BL-103	U S Army, OSACOM, Det 46, OK ARNG, Norman, Ok.	
☐ 84-0174	84 King Air C-12F		BL-104	U S Army, OSACOM, Gray AAF, Wa.	
☐ 84-0175	84 King Air C-12F		BL-105	U S Army, OSACOM, Gray AAF, Wa.	84-0175
☐ 84-0176	84 King Air C-12F		BL-106	U S Army.	N5819T
☐ 84-0177	84 King Air C-12F		BL-107	U S Army, Det A C/2-228th AVN, USAR, MacDill AFB. Fl.	
☐ 84-0178	84 King Air C-12F		BL-108	U S Army.	
☐ 84-0179	84 King Air C-12F		BL-109	U S Army.	
☐ 84-0180	84 King Air C-12U		BL-110	U S Army, HQ USEUCOM, Stuttgart, Germany.	
☐ 84-0181	84 King Air C-12F		BL-111	U S Army, 204th MIB (AR), Biggs AAF, Tx.	
☐ 84-0182	84 King Air C-12F		BL-112	U S Army, OSACOM, Det 10, IN ARNG, Indianapolis, In.	
☐ 84-0484	84 King Air C-12F		BL-118	U S Army, OSACOM, Det 48, SD ARNG, Rapid City, SD.	
☐ 84-0485	84 King Air C-12F		BL-119	U S Army, OSACOM, Det 11, KY ARNG, Frankfort, Ky.	
☐ 84-0486	84 King Air C-12F		BL-120	U S Army, OSACOM, Det 47, OR ARNG, Salem, Or.	

Reg	Yr Type	c/n	Owner/Operator	Prev Regn

414

Reg	Yr Type	c/n	Owner/Operator	Prev Regn
☐ 84-0487	84 King Air C-12F	BL-121	U S Army, OSACOM, Det 53, WY ARNG, Cheyenne, Wy.	
☐ 84-0488	84 King Air C-12F	BL-122	U S Army, OSACOM, Elmendorf AFB. Ak.	
☐ 84-0489	84 King Air C-12F	BL-123	U S Army, OSACOM, Det 45, NV ARNG, Reno, Nv.	
☐ 84-24375	84 King Air C-12D	BP-46	U S Army, Det A C/2-228th AVN, USAR, MacDill AFB. Fl.	
☐ 84-24376	84 King Air C-12D	BP-47	U S Army.	
☐ 84-24377	84 King Air C-12D	BP-48	U S Army.	
☐ 84-24378	84 King Air C-12D	BP-49	U S Army.	
☐ 84-24379	84 King Air C-12D	BP-50	U S Army, ARCENT, Dhahran, Saudi Arabia.	
☐ 84-24380	84 King Air C-12D	BP-51	U S Army, Det B C/2-228th Aviation (USAR), Sherman AAF, Ks.	
☐ 85-0147	85 King Air RC-12K	FE-1	U S Army, B/1st MIB (AE), Wiesbaden, Germany.	
☐ 85-0148	85 King Air RC-12K	FE-2	U S Army, B/1st MIB (AE), Wiesbaden, Germany.	
☐ 85-0149	85 King Air RC-12N	FE-3	U S Army, B/1st MIB (AE), Wiesbaden, Germany.	
☐ 85-0150	85 King Air RC-12K	FE-4	U S Army, B/1st MIB (AE), Wiesbaden, Germany.	
☐ 85-0152	85 King Air RC-12K	FE-6	U S Army, B/1st MIB (AE), Wiesbaden, Germany.	
☐ 85-0153	85 King Air RC-12K	FE-7	U S Army, B/1st MIB (AR), Wiesbaden, Germany.	
☐ 85-0155	85 King Air RC-12K	FE-9	U S Army, B/1st MIB (AR), Wiesbaden, Germany.	
☐ 85-1262	85 King Air C-12F	BP-53	U S Army, OSACOM, Det 25, TN ARNG, Smyrna, Tn.	
☐ 85-1263	85 King Air C-12F	BP-54	U S Army, OSACOM, Det 56, PR ARNG, San Juan, PR.	
☐ 85-1264	85 King Air C-12F	BP-55	U S Army, OSACOM, Davison AAF, Va.	
☐ 85-1265	85 King Air C-12F	BP-56	U S Army, OSACOM,	
☐ 85-1266	85 King Air C-12F	BP-57	U S Army, OSACOM, Davison AAF, Va.	
☐ 85-1267	85 King Air C-12F	BP-58	U S Army, OSACOM, Davison AAF, Va.	
☐ 85-1268	85 King Air C-12F	BP-59	U S Army, OSACOM, Davison AAF, Va.	
☐ 85-1270	85 King Air C-12F	BP-61	U S Army, OSACOM,	
☐ 85-1271	85 King Air C-12F	BP-62	U S Army, OSACOM, Det 59, UT ARNG, Salt Lake City No 2, Ut	
☐ 85-1272	85 King Air C-12F	BP-63	U S Army, OSACOM, Det 35, ID ARNG, Gowen Field-Boise, Id.	
☐ 86-0078	86 King Air C-12J	UD-1	USAF, 51st Fighter Wing, Osan AB. South Korea.	
☐ 86-0079	86 King Air C-12J	UD-2	USAF, HQ USEUCOM, Stuttgart, Germany.	
☐ 86-0080	86 King Air C-12J	UD-3	USAF, 46th Test Wing, Eglin AFB, Fl.	
☐ 86-0081	86 King Air C-12J	UD-4	USAF, 3rd Wing, Elmendorf AFB, Ak.	
☐ 86-0082	86 King Air C-12J	UD-5	U S Army, 78th Aviation Btn. NAF Atsugi, Japan.	
☐ 86-0083	86 King Air C-12J	UD-6	USAF, 51st Fighter Wing, Osan AB. South Korea.	
☐ 86-0084	86 King Air C-12F	BP-64	U S Army, OSACOM, Det 26, VA ARNG, Richmond-Byrd Field, Va.	
☐ 86-0085	86 King Air C-12F	BP-65	U S Army, OSACOM, Det 20, NY ARNG, Albany County, NY.	
☐ 86-0086	86 King Air C-12F	BP-66	U S Army, OSACOM, Det 32, CA ARNG, Mather AFB, Ca.	
☐ 86-0087	86 King Air C-12F	BP-67	U S Army, OSACOM, Det 22. PA ARNG, Fort Iniantown Gap, Pa.	
☐ 86-0088	86 King Air C-12F	BP-68	U S Army, OSACOM, Det 8, FL ARNG, St Augustine, Fl.	
☐ 86-0089	86 King Air C-12F	BP-69	U S Army, OSACOM, Det 36, IL ARNG, Decatur, Il.	
☐ 87-0160	87 King Air C-12F	BP-70	U S Army, OSACOM, Det 49, TX ARNG, Austin-Mueller Field, Tx.	
☐ 87-0161	87 King Air C-12F	BP-71	U S Army, OSACOM, Det 5, AL ARNG), Montgomery-Dannelly, Al.	
☐ 88-0325	88 King Air RC-12N	FE-10	U S Army, B/224th Military Intelligence Btn. Hunter AAF, Ga.	
☐ 88-0326	88 King Air RC-12N	FE-11	U S Army, B/224th Military Intelligence Btn. Hunter AAF, Ga.	
☐ 88-0327	88 King Air RC-12N	FE-12	U S Army, B/224th Military Intelligence Btn. Hunter AAF, Ga.	
☐ 89-0267	89 King Air RC-12N	FE-13	U S Army, B/224th Military Intelligence Btn. Hunter AAF, Ga.	
☐ 89-0268	89 King Air RC-12N	FE-14	U S Army, B/224th Military Intelligence Btn. Hunter AAF, Ga.	
☐ 89-0269	89 King Air RC-12N	FE-15	U S Army, B/224th Military Intelligence Btn. Hunter AAF, Ga.	
☐ 89-0270	89 King Air RC-12N	FE-16	U S Army, B/224th Military Intelligence Btn. Hunter AAF, Ga.	
☐ 89-0271	89 King Air RC-12N	FE-17	U S Army, B/224th Military Intelligence Btn. Hunter AAF, Ga.	
☐ 89-0273	89 King Air RC-12N	FE-19	U S Army, B/304th Military Intelliegnce Btn. Libby AAF, Az.	
☐ 89-0274	89 King Air RC-12N	FE-20	U S Army, B/304th Military Intelligence Btn. Libby AAF, Az.	
☐ 89-0275	89 King Air RC-12N	FE-21	U S Army, B/224th Military Intelligence Btn. Hunter AAF, Ga.	
☐ 89-0276	89 King Air RC-12N	FE-22	U S Army, B/224th Military Intelligence Btn. Hunter AAF, Ga.	
☐ 91-0516	91 King Air RC-12K	FE-23	U S Army, B/304th Military Intelligence Btn. Libby AAF, Az.	
☐ 91-0517	91 King Air RC-12K	FE-24	U S Army, B/304th Military Intelligence Btn. Libby AAF, Az.	
☐ 91-0518	91 King Air RC-12P	FE-25	U S Army.	
☐ 92-13120	92 King Air RC-12P	FE-26	U S Army.	
☐ 92-13121	92 King Air RC-12P	FE-27	U S Army.	
☐ 92-13122	92 King Air RC-12P	FE-28	U S Army.	
☐ 92-13123	92 King Air RC-12P	FE-29	U S Army.	
☐ 92-13124	92 King Air RC-12P	FE-30	U S Army.	
☐ 92-13125	92 King Air RC-12P	FE-31	U S Army.	
☐ 92-3327	92 King Air C-12F	BW-1	U S Army.	N2843B
☐ 92-3328	92 King Air C-12F	BW-2	U S Army.	N2844B
☐ 92-3329	92 King Air C-12F	BW-3	U S Army.	N2845B
☐ 93-0697	93 King Air RC-12P	FE-32	U S Army.	
Reg	**Yr Type**	**c/n**	**Owner/Operator**	**Prev Regn**

☐ 93-0698	93 King Air RC-12P	FE-33	U S Army.	
☐ 93-0699	93 King Air RC-12P	FE-34	U S Army.	
☐ 93-0700	93 King Air RC-12P	FE-35	U S Army.	
☐ 93-0701	93 King Air RC-12P	FE-36	U S Army.	
☐ 94-0315	94 King Air C-12R	BW-4	U S Army, Heidelberg, Germany.	
☐ 94-0316	94 King Air C-12R	BW-5	U S Army, Heidelberg, Germany.	
☐ 94-0317	94 King Air C-12R	BW-6	U S Army, Heidelberg, Germany.	
☐ 94-0318	94 King Air C-12R	BW-7	U S Army, Heidelberg, Germany.	
☐ 94-0319	94 King Air C-12R	BW-8	U S Army, Heidelberg, Germany.	
☐ 94-0320	94 King Air C-12R	BW-9	U S Army, B/2-228th AVN, USAR, McCoy AAF, Wi.	
☐ 94-0321	94 King Air C-12R	BW-10	U S Army, B/2-228th AVN, USAR, McCoy AAF, Wi.	
☐ 94-0322	94 King Air C-12R	BW-11	U S Army, OSACOM, Det 16, MS ARNG, Jackson, Ms.	
☐ 94-0323	94 King Air C-12R	BW-12	U S Army, OSACOM, Det 44, NM ARNG, Santa Fe, NM.	
☐ 94-0324	94 King Air C-12R	BW-13	U S Army, OSACOM, Det 31, AZ ARNG, Phoenix, Az.	
☐ 94-0325	94 King Air C-12R	BW-14	U S Army, OSACOM, Gray AAF, Wa.	
☐ 94-0326	94 King Air C-12R	BW-15	U S Army, OSACOM, Det 41, MT ARNG, Helena, Mt.	
☐ 95-0088	95 King Air C-12R	BW-16	U S Army, Heidelberg, Germany.	
☐ 95-0089	95 King Air C-12R	BW-17	U S Army, A/2-228th AVN, USAR, Willow Grove JRB, Pa.	
☐ 95-0090	95 King Air C-12R	BW-18	U S Army, A/2-228th AVN, USAR, Willow Grove JRB, Pa.	
☐ 06 0001	95 King Air C-12R	BW-19	U S Army.	
☐ 95-0092	95 King Air C-12R	BW-20	U S Army, D/1-228th AVN, USAR, Los Alamitos, Ca.	
☐ 95-0093	95 King Air C-12R	BW-21	U S Army, D/1-228th AVN, USAR, Los Alamitos, Ca.	
☐ 95-0094	95 King Air C-12R	BW-22	U S Army, D/1-228th AVN, USAR, Los Alamitos, Ca.	
☐ 95-0095	95 King Air C-12R	BW-23	U S Army, D/1-228th AVN, USAR, Los Alamitos, Ca.	
☐ 95-0096	95 King Air C-12R	BW-24	U S Army, D/1-228th AVN, USAR, Los Alamitos, Ca.	
☐ 95-0097	95 King Air C-12R	BW-25	U S Army, B/2 228th AVN, USAR, McCoy AAF, Wi.	
☐ 95-0098	95 King Air C-21R	BW-26	U S Army, B/2-228th Aviation, Cairns AAF, Al.	
☐ 95-0099	95 King Air C-12R	BW-27	U S Army, D/1-228th AVN, USAR, Los Alamitos, Ca.	
☐ 95-0100	95 King Air C-12R	BW-28	U S Army, D/1-228th AVN, USAR, Los Alamitos, Ca.	
☐ 95-0101	98 King Air C-21R	BW-29	U S Army, A/2-228th AVN, USAR, Willow Grove JRB, Pa.	
☐ 96-0112	96 Beech C-12J	UE-256	U S Army, CBCDOM Flight Det. Phillips AAF, Md.	N10931

OB = PERU

Total 31

Civil

☐ OB-1146	78 SA-226AT Merlin 4A	AT-064E	Empresa Minera del Hierro,	OB-M-114
☐ OB-1228	81 PA-31T Cheyenne II	8120048	Aerovias SA. Satipo.	OB-M-122
☐ OB-1297	68 King Air B90	LJ-326	Aero Condor SA. Lima.	OB-T-129
☐ OB-1308	79 PA-31T Cheyenne II	7920075	Videma SA-Compania de Taxi Aereo, Trujillo.	OB-S-130
☐ OB-1364	68 King Air B90	LJ-330	Aero Condor SA. Lima. (status ?).	N66MS
☐ OB-1365	81 PA-42 Cheyenne III	8001018	ATSA-Aero Transporte SA. Lima.	N19CD
☐ OB-1468	77 King Air 200	BB-193	TAS-Taxi Aereo Selva SRL. Lima.	N131MB
☐ OB-1509	75 King Air 200	BB-20	TAMSA-Transportes Aereos Maranon SA. Tarapoto. (status ?).	N9023R
☐ OB-1558	68 King Air B90	LJ-405	SAOSA-Servicios Aereos del Oriente SA. Pucallpa.	N68RT
☐ OB-1567	67 King Air A90	LJ-228	Air Atlantic SRL. Lima.	N946K
☐ OB-1593	69 King Air B90	LJ-477	Aero Condor SA. Lima.	N7777
☐ OB-1594	68 King Air B90	LJ-322	Aero Condor SA. Lima.	N45SC
☐ OB-1595	68 King Air B90	LJ-400	TATSA-Transporte Aereo Taxi SA. Lima.	N501PP
☐ OB-1629	81 PA-42 Cheyenne III	8001067	Aero Transporte CA. Lima.	N183CC
☐ OB-1630	81 PA-42 Cheyenne III	8001022	Aero Transporte CA. Lima.	N145CA
☐ OB-1633	78 PA-42 Cheyenne III	7801003	Aero Transporte CA. Lima.	N134KM
☐ OB-1687	81 PA-42 Cheyenne III	8001016	Aero Transporte CA. Lima.	N69PC
☐ OB-1700	77 King Air/Catpass 250	BB-214	Aero Condor SA. Lima.	N26LE
☐ OB-1714	81 PA-42 Cheyenne III	8001013	Servicios Aereos AQP SA. Lima.	(N827KR)
☐ OB-932	69 King Air B90	LJ-465	Aero Condor SA. Lima. (status ?).	OB-T-932

Military

☐ AE-571	83 King Air B200CT	BN-2	Peruvian Navy, Esc 11, Lima-Callao. (was BL-58).	N6904Q
☐ AE-572	83 King Air B200CT	BN-3	Peruvian Navy, Esc 11, Lima-Callao. (was BL-59).	N2856B
☐ AE-573	83 King Air B200CT	BN-4	Peruvian Navy, Esc 11, Lima-Callao. (was BL-60).	N2790B
☐ AE-574	83 King Air B200T	BT-25	Peruvian Navy, Esc 11, Lima-Callao. (was BB-1096).	N2795B
☐ AE-575	83 King Air B200T	BT-26	Peruvian Navy, Esc 11, Lima-Callao. (was BB-1098).	N2826B
☐ EP-821	PA-31T Cheyenne	...	Peruvian Army, Lima.	
☐ EP-825	90 King Air 350	FL-21	Peruvian Army, Lima.	N666RH
☐ FAP-18	85 King Air 300	FA-41	FAP, Las Palmas-Lima.	HK-3495
☐ FAP-708	Rockwell 690	...	Fuerza del Peru, Lima.	
☐ PNP-218	Rockwell 690	...	Policia Nacional del Peru, Lima.	N50ST

Reg	Yr	Type	c/n	Owner/Operator	Prev Regn

Reg	Yr Type	c/n	Owner/Operator	Prev Regn
☐ PNP-230	73 King Air E90	LW-36	Policia Nacional del Peru, Lima.	OB-1598

OE = AUSTRIA — Total 18

Civil

Reg	Yr Type	c/n	Owner/Operator	Prev Regn
☐ OE-BBB	79 King Air 200	BB-526	Federal Office for Meteorogy & Survey, Vienna.	
☐ OE-EKD	96 Pilatus PC-12	142	Durst Aircraft Rental GmbH. Vienna.	HB-FRD
☐ OE-EPC	03 Pilatus PC-12/45	536	Diamond Flight Operations, Neustadt.	(D-FAPC)
☐ OE-ESK	03 TBM 700C	279	Aero-Charter Krifka GmbH. Wels.	
☐ OE-FDS	77 PA-31T Cheyenne II	7720056	Braunegg Lufttaxi GmbH. Vienna.	(N82169)
☐ OE-FHL	85 King Air C90A	LJ-1115	Airlink Luftverkehrs GmbH. Salzburg.	D-IBPE
☐ OE-FHM	91 King Air C90A	LJ-1284	EUROP STAR Aircraft GmbH. Villach.	N25GA
☐ OE-FKG	80 PA-31T Cheyenne II	8020036	Airlink Luftverkehrs GmbH. Salzburg.	N30DJ
☐ OE-FKH	81 PA-31T Cheyenne 1	8104029	Airlink Luftverkehrs GmbH. Salzburg.	N803CA
☐ OE-FME	93 King Air 300LW	FA-228	Airlink Luftverkehrs GmbH. Salzburg.	(D-CAIR)
☐ OE-FMG	90 King Air C90A	LJ-1236	ABC Bedarfsflug GmbH/Fly Tyrol, Innsbruck.	D-IPEL
☐ OE-FMO	81 PA-31T Cheyenne II	8120058	Cx OE- 12/04 to ?	N3GF
☐ OE-FOW	80 SA-226T Merlin 3B	T-318	Charter-Air GmbH. Innsbruck.	D-IBBD
☐ OE-FRF	81 King Air B200	BB-933	OMNI Aviacao & Tecnologia Ltda. Cascais-Tires, Portugal.	D-IAWS
☐ OE-FRS	85 King Air C90A	LJ-1124	INTER-AVIA Flugbetrieb GmbH. Vienna.	N90EP
☐ OE-FSO	91 King Air 300	FA-215	Wilhelm Schwarzmueller GmbH. Schaerding.	N8017G
☐ OE-GBB	96 Dornier 328-100	3078	Tyrolean Jet Service GmbH. Vienna.	D-C...
☐ OE-KGB	01 PA-46-500TP Meridian	4697035	TITANEN Air Flugzeug GmbH. Vienna.	N77Y

OH = FINLAND — Total 13

Civil

Reg	Yr Type	c/n	Owner/Operator	Prev Regn
☐ OH-ACN	76 Rockwell 690A	11301	Konekorhonen OY. Tikkakoski.	(N81405)
☐ OH-ADA	74 SA-226T Merlin 3	T-248	Airfix Aviation, Helsinki.	N120TT
☐ OH-BAX	81 King Air C90	LJ-984	Aerial OY/Scanwings OY. Helsinki.	LN-FOD
☐ OH-BCX	78 King Air C90	LJ-770	Airfix Aviation/Nordic Air Ambulance, Helsinki.	N88CG
☐ OH-BEX	81 King Air C90	LJ-978	Scanwings OY. Helsinki.	N725KR
☐ OH-BKA	70 King Air 100	B-39	Airwings OY/Deltacraft OY. Turku.	HB-GEN
☐ OH-BSA	89 King Air 300	FA-205	Finnair Aviation Institute, Pori.	N5672A
☐ OH-BSB	89 King Air 300	FA-206	Finnair Aviation Institute, Pori.	N5672J
☐ OH-KJJ	03 TBM 700C	258	Fortel Kiinteistoet OY. Oulu.	
☐ OH-PAY	88 PA-42 Cheyenne 400LS	5527040	Airecon/Juris Economica OY. Helsinki.	JA8870
☐ OH-STA	81 MU-2 Marquise	1515SA	Finnish Commuter Airlines OY. Seinajoki.	(F-HASI)
☐ OH-UTI	74 Rockwell 690A	11204	Savair KY. Helsinki.	SE-GSR
☐ OH-WBA	78 Mitsubishi MU-2N	718SA	Westbird Aviation OY. Seinajoki.	N150BA

OK = CZECH REPUBLIC / CZECHIA — Total 7

Civil

Reg	Yr Type	c/n	Owner/Operator	Prev Regn
☐ OK-...	79 King Air C90	LJ-837	LD Aviation Prague Sro. Prague.	N364D
☐ OK-EMA	00 Ibis Ae 270P Spirit	001	IBIS Aerospace Ltd. Prague. (Ff 25 Jul 00).	
☐ OK-EVA	04 Ibis Ae 270P Spirit	007	IBIS Aerospace Ltd. Prague.	
☐ OK-GTJ	92 King Air 300LW	FA-223	Time Air s r o, Prague.	D-IHHB
☐ OK-INA	03 Ibis Ae 270P Spirit	006	IBIS Aerospace Ltd. Prague.	
☐ OK-LIB	03 Ibis Ae 270P Spirit	005	IBIS Aerospace Ltd. Prague.	
☐ OK-SAR	02 Ibis Ae 270P Spirit	003	IBIS Aerospace Ltd. Prague.	

OM = SLOVAKIA — Total 2

Civil

Reg	Yr Type	c/n	Owner/Operator	Prev Regn
☐ OM-VIP	79 PA-31T Cheyenne II	7920002	VIP Air, Bratislava.	D-IXXX
☐ OM-VKE	89 King Air C90A	LJ-1222	Cassovia Air AS. Kosice.	OK-VKE

OO = BELGIUM — Total 11

Civil

Reg	Yr Type	c/n	Owner/Operator	Prev Regn
☐ OO-IAL*	81 King Air F90	LA-100	ASL-Air Service Liege NV. Maastricht, Holland.	D-IWAL
☐ OO-LAC	80 King Air B200C	BL-16	Sky-Service BV. Wevelgem.	F-GLTX
☐ OO-LET	94 King Air B200	BB-1473	ASL-Air Service Liege NV. Maastricht, Holland.	N8210X
☐ OO-LMO	89 Reims/Cessna F406	F406-0034	Lucorp BVBA/Air Limo. Liege.	(D-ILIM)
☐ OO-ROB	77 Rockwell 690B	11409	Robsa International NV. Essen.	N81646
☐ OO-SDU	03 King Air 350	FL-368	Bongrain Benelux SA. Breda, Holland.	N6068V
☐ OO-SDU*	King Air 350	...	Corporation Aircraft France SA.	
☐ OO-SKL	89 King Air B200	BB-1348	Sky-Service BV. Wevelgem.	D2-EST
☐ OO-SKM	91 King Air B200	BB-1407	Sky-Service BV. Wevelgem.	D2-ESQ
☐ OO-SXB	81 Xingu 121A	121040	Airventure BV. Antwerp.	PT-MBH
☐ OO-VHV	79 King Air E90	LW-316	Brachot-Hermant NV/Sky Service BV. Wevelgem.	N77WZ

Reg	Yr Type	c/n	Owner/Operator	Prev Regn

OY = DENMARK

Civil

Reg	Yr Type	c/n	Owner/Operator	Prev Regn
☐ OY-BHU	79 PA-31T Cheyenne 1	7904004	A/S Kongedybet, Copenhagen.	N131SW
☐ OY-BVB	79 King Air 200	BB-419	Aviation Assistance A/S. Roskilde.	N256EN
☐ OY-BVS	68 King Air B90	LJ-418	Danish Air Transport A/S. Vamdrup.	(SE-LEN)
☐ OY-BVW	80 King Air 200	BB-705	Skandinavisk Motor A/S-Volkswagen, Brondby.	D-IBAB
☐ OY-CBP	77 King Air 200	BB-235	Aviation Assistance A/S-UN, Islamabad, Pakistan.	(N777MW
☐ OY-EEF	97 King Air B200	BB-1548	Thrane & Thrane A/S. Roskilde.	
☐ OY-GEB	81 King Air 200C	BL-40	Aviation Assistance A/S. Roskilde.	VH-NSR
☐ OY-GEU	89 King Air 1300	BB-1341	United Nations,	VT-SAD
☐ OY-GEW	89 King Air 1300	BB-1342	ICRC/SAviation Assistance A/S. Roskilde.	VT-SAE
☐ OY-GMA	89 King Air 1300	BB-1340	Aviation Assistance A/S-UN, Islamabad, Pakistan.	(N132AZ)
☐ OY-GRB	81 King Air 200	BB-845	Aviation Assistance A/S-UN, Kabul, Afghanistan.	N486DC
☐ OY-GSA	01 Pilatus PC-12/45	421	Widex ApS. Roskilde.	HB-FRN
☐ OY-JAR	80 King Air 200C	BL-13	Aviation Assistance A/S. Roskilde.	PH-ILG
☐ OY-JRN	78 King Air 200	BB-364	Ikaros Fly ApS. Roskilde.	F-GHYV
☐ OY-JRO	68 King Air B90	LJ-327	Danish Air Transport A/S. Vamdrup.	(N507M)
☐ OY-JVL	00 King Air 350	FL-273	Eurojet Italia SRL. Milan, Italy.	N4473E
☐ OY-LAW	02 PA-46-500TP Meridian	4697138	Gefa GmbH/Air Alfa Aircraft Sales, Odense.	
☐ OY-LDA	02 PA-46-500TP Meridian	4697147	L Damsgaard Andersen,	
☐ OY-LLL	04 King Air B200	BB-1861	Lohfert & Lohfert A/S. Roskilde.	N50478
☐ OY-LMM	01 PA-46-500TP Meridian	4697108	Air Alpha Aircraft Sales A/S. Odense.	N480M
☐ OY-LSA	00 King Air C90B	LJ-1610	Peter Trane, Charlottenlund.	N44406
☐ OY-MEN	98 King Air 350	FL-229	Aviation Assistance A/S. Roskilde.	N9WV
☐ OY-NUK	80 King Air 200	BB-634	Air Greenland A/S. Nuuk.	N101CP
☐ OY-PBG	87 Reims/Cessna F406	F406-0015	BenAir Norway A/S. Oslo-Gardermoen, Norway.	(LN-PBH
☐ OY-PCL	99 King Air B200	BB-1675	Air Greenland A/S. Nuuk.	N2355Z
☐ OY-SBU	78 King Air C90	LJ-768	Danish Air Transport A/S. Vamdrup.	LN-KCG

PH = NETHERLANDS

Civil

Reg	Yr Type	c/n	Owner/Operator	Prev Regn
☐ PH-ATM	76 King Air/Catpass 250	BB-123	Tulip Air BV. Rotterdam. (status ?).	N120DA
☐ PH-BOA	81 MU-2 Marquise	1507SA	Quick Airways BV. Groningen-Eelde.	N888FS
☐ PH-CLE	88 Reims/Cessna F406	F406-0032	Lucorp BVBA/Air Limo, Liege, Belgium.	LN-TWH
☐ PH-CLZ	04 TBM 700C	299	Alibrent BV.	F-OIKL
☐ PH-DDB	77 King Air/Catpass 250	BB-221	Maglione SRL. Melfi, Italy.	SE-KYL
☐ PH-DIX	00 Pilatus PC-12/45	309	Din Air BV. Eindhoven.	HB-FRG
☐ PH-DYB	78 SA-226T Merlin 3B	T-294	Dynamic Airlines, Rotterdam.	N15KR
☐ PH-ECC	94 Pilatus PC-12	107	Elas Professional Services Network BV. Budel.	N62JT
☐ PH-ECF	82 King Air B200	BB-956	J Sprengers Den Helder Beheer BV. Den Helder.	D-IAMK
☐ PH-HUB	97 TBM 700	127	Flying Thorn BV. Eindhoven.	F-OHBV
☐ PH-JFS	02 Pilatus PC-12/45	477	Eurofilters Holding BV. Overpelt.	HB-FPD
☐ PH-JOE	83 Conquest 1	425-0168	Westerheide Management & Consultancy BV. Arnhem.	G-BJYC
☐ PH-MJM	89 Reims/Cessna F406	F406-0037	Tulip Air BV. Rotterdam.	5Y-BIS
☐ PH-MNZ	92 Dornier 228-212	8206	Kustwacht-Dutch Coastguard/Martinair Holland NV. Amsterdam.	D-CDIV
☐ PH-SBK	76 King Air 200	BB-180	Nationale Luchtvaartschool BV. Maastricht.	G-BHVX
☐ PH-SVY	80 PA-31T Cheyenne II	8020041	Slagboom en Peeters Luchtfotografie, Teuge.	N198AA
☐ PH-TCN	04 P-180 Avanti	1089	Plano di Volo/Van Gelder BV-Strovast, Rotterdam.	
☐ PH-XII	04 Pilatus PC-12/45	550	De Hondert Margen BV/Air Services UK Ltd. Rotterdam.	HB-...

Military

Reg	Yr Type	c/n	Owner/Operator	Prev Regn
☐ U-01	81 Fokker 60UTA-N	20321	RNAF, 334 Squadron, Eindhoven. 'Marinus Van Meel'	PH-UTL
☐ U-02	95 Fokker 60UTA-N	20324	RNAF, 334 Squadron, Eindhoven. 'Willem Versteegh'	PH-UTN
☐ U-03	95 Fokker 60UTA-N	20327	RNAF, 334 Squadron, Eindhoven. 'Jan Borghouts'	PH-UTP
☐ U-04	95 Fokker 60UTA-N	20329	RNAF, 334 Squadron, Eindhoven. 'Jules Zegers'	PH-UTR
☐ U-05	96 Fokker 50	20253	RNAF, 334 Squadron, Eindhoven. 'Fons Aler'	PH-KXO
☐ U-06	96 Fokker 50	20287	RNAF, 334 Squadron, Eindhoven. 'Robbie Wijting'	PH-MXI

PJ = NETHERLANDS ANTILLES

Civil

Reg	Yr Type	c/n	Owner/Operator	Prev Regn
☐ PJ-...	83 Gulfstream 1000	96065	Zunoca Freezone NV. Curacao.	N46GA
☐ PJ-CEB	76 Rockwell 690A	11292	CEB Investments BV. Curacao.	HB-GEH
☐ PJ-NAF	82 Gulfstream 1000	96008	Jarbol Avia, Curacao.	N9917S

Reg	Yr Type	c/n	Owner/Operator	Prev Regn

PK = INDONESIA Total 21

Civil

Reg	Yr Type	c/n	Owner/Operator	Prev Regn
☐ PK-AHA	96 TBM 700	119	Directorate of Civil Aviation, Jakarta.	F-OHBQ
☐ PK-AHC	96 TBM 700	120	Directorate of Civil Aviation, Jakarta.	F-OHBR
☐ PK-CAK	93 King Air B200C	BL-140	Directorate of Civil Aviation, Jakarta.	N82410
☐ PK-CAL	96 TBM 700	114	Directorate of Civil Aviation, Jakarta.	F-OHBS
☐ PK-CAM	96 TBM 700	121	Directorate of Civil Aviation, Jakarta.	F-OBHT
☐ PK-CDM	67 Gulfstream 1	177	Citra Aviation PT. Jakarta.	PK-CTE
☐ PK-DYR	78 PA-31T Cheyenne II	7820054	Deraya Air Taxi PT. Jakarta.	VH-MWT
☐ PK-ODR	80 Gulfstream 980	95019	Airfast Indonesia PT. Jakarta. (status ?).	N9772S
☐ PK-RGI	00 King Air B200	BB-1732	Eastindo, Jakarta.	N23268
☐ PK-RJA	68 Gulfstream 1	191	Pos Ekspres Prima, Jakarta. 'Anugerah II'	VH-JPJ
☐ PK-RJR	90 King Air 350	FL-30	Pos Ekspres Prima, Jakarta.	PK-TDR
☐ PK-TRA	76 King Air 200	BB-113	Indonesia Air Transport, Jakarta.	
☐ PK-TRO	64 Gulfstream 1	130	Indonesia Air Transport, Jakarta.	N3416
☐ PK-TRW	96 Beech 1900D	UE-177	Mobil Oil/Indonesian Air Transport, Jakarta.	N3237H
☐ PK-TRX	96 Beech 1900D	UE-186	Mobil Oil/Indonesian Air Transport, Jakarta.	N3233J
☐ PK-VKA	80 King Air 200	BB-732	PENAS, Jakarta.	N3716D
☐ PK-VKB	81 King Air 200	BB-794	PENAS, Jakarta.	N3720U
☐ PK-VKY	67 King Air A90	LJ-197	PENAS, Jakarta.	N2510L
☐ PK-VKZ	67 King Air A90	LJ-189	PENAS, Jakarta.	N123KA

Military

Reg	Type	c/n	Owner/Operator	Prev Regn
☐ P-2033	King Air B200	...	Indonesian Police, Jakarta.	
☐ P-2066	King Air B200	...	Indonesian Police, Jakarta.	

PP = BRAZIL Total 306

Civil

Reg	Yr Type	c/n	Owner/Operator	Prev Regn
☐ PP-BAF	01 King Air C90B	LJ-1646	SERMO Servicios de Mao Obra SC Ltda. Sao Paulo, SP.	N4446D
☐ PP-CBD	84 King Air B200	BB-1062	Rio Real Empreendimentos Ltda. Belo Horizonte, MG.	N985GA
☐ PP-CSE	85 King Air F90-1	LA-228	Covre Factoring Fomento Com Ltda.	N80WP
☐ PP-EHE	74 King Air C90	LJ-638	Caixego Caixa Econom do Estado Goias, Goiania, GO.	PT-KFV
☐ PP-EJG	91 King Air B200	BB-1410	State Government of Goias, Goiania, GO.	
☐ PP-EJO	85 King Air 300	FA-31	Governor do Estado do Minas Gerais, Belo Horizonte, MG.	PT-LNJ
☐ PP-EOP	76 King Air 200	BB-137	State Government of Roraima, Boa Vista, RR.	PP-IKN
☐ PP-EPB	81 PA-42 Cheyenne III	8001035	State Government of Paraiba, Joao Pessoa, PB.	PT-OSX
☐ PP-EPD	86 King Air 300	FA-92	State Government of Amazonas, Manaus, AM.	PT-OSZ
☐ PP-EPS	96 King Air C90B	LJ-1442	State Government of Bahia, Salvador, BA.	PT-WNI
☐ PP-ERG	98 King Air B200	BB-1603	State Government of Rio Grande do Sol, Porte Alegre, RS.	PT-WRN
☐ PP-ETR	99 King Air C90B	LJ-1578	Para Governor do Estado,	N3178R
☐ PP-EUE	68 King Air B90	LJ-409	State Government of Parana, Curitiba, PR.	
☐ PP-FOY	73 King Air A100	B-142	Departamento de Policia Federal MJ, Brasilia, DF.	
☐ PP-FPP	73 King Air E90	LW-56	Departamento de Policia Federal MJ, Brasilia, DF. (status ?)	PT-FGA
☐ PP-JSC	00 King Air 350	FL-289	Sucocitrico Cutrale Ltda. Araraquara, SP.	N3189T
☐ PP-LCB	78 King Air C-12C	BC-65	Casa Bahia Comercial Ltda. Sao Paulo, SP.	N638B
☐ PP-LCQ	78 PA-31T Cheyenne II	7820046	MEDASA-Med Neto Dist de Alcool SA. Recife, PE.	N688CA
☐ PR-AEF	03 King Air 350	FL-377		N6177F
☐ PR-APJ	00 King Air B200	BB-1755		N5055Q
☐ PR-BLP	85 King Air B200	BB-1199	Aircraft Sales of Brazil, Sao Paulo, SP.	N7203R
☐ PR-CCF	00 King Air C90B	LJ-1608	Itapemirim Taxi Aereo Ltda. Itapemirim, ES.	N4408U
☐ PR-EDF	01 King Air 350	FL-335	Lider Taxi Aereo SA. Belo Horizonte, MG.	N5135N
☐ PR-EDP	01 King Air C90B	LJ-1672	Lider Taxi Aereo SA. Belo Horizonte, MG.	N5027R
☐ PR-FKY	03 King Air C90B	LJ-1701	Lider Taxi Aereo SA. Belo Horizonte, MG.	N5134S
☐ PR-HRM	76 PA-31T Cheyenne II	7620053		C-GHRM
☐ PR-JQM	02 King Air C90B	LJ-1684	Lider Taxi Aereo SA. Belo Horizonte, MG.	N5084J
☐ PR-LIA	01 King Air B200	BB-1798		N577P
☐ PR-MLZ	01 King Air C90B	LJ-1644	Magazine Luiza SA. Franca, SP.	N90XP
☐ PR-MZP	92 King Air C90B	LJ-1311	Newberry Enterprises Inc. Georgetown, Grand Cayman.	N489JS
☐ PR-RFB	99 King Air C90B	LJ-1546		N3071H
☐ PR-RMA	03 King Air C90B	LJ-1693		N6193J
☐ PR-TIN	00 King Air C90B	LJ-1628		N3228M
☐ PR-TLL	77 King Air C90	LJ-713		N114J
☐ PR-USA	02 King Air C90B	LJ-1679	Lider Taxi Aereo SA. Belo Horizonte, MG.	N4479M
☐ PR-XIB	01 King Air C90B	LJ-1639	Carpa Serrana Agropecuaria Rio Pardo, Serrano, SP.	N51139
☐ PT-...	65 King Air 90	LJ-16	(status ?).	N51KA
☐ PT-...	77 Rockwell 690B	11391	EXBRA Impotacao e Exportacao Ltda. Sao Paulo, SP. (status ?)	N73MA
Reg	Yr Type	c/n	Owner/Operator	Prev Regn

Reg	Yr	Type	c/n	Owner/Operator	Prev Regn
☐ PT-...	80	Gulfstream 980	95038	(status ?).	N91SA
☐ PT-...	67	680V Turbo Commander	1703-79	(status ?)	N161XX
☐ PT-ASN	85	King Air F90-1	LA-232	Ayrton Senna Prom. e Empreend. Ltda. Sao Paulo, SP.	D-IWPF
☐ PT-BOY	69	Mitsubishi MU-2F	145	Oeste Redes Aereas SA/ORA Taxi Aereo SA. Cuiaba, MT.	N769Q
☐ PT-BZW	69	Mitsubishi MU-2F	175	CITEP-Com. e Imp. T. Posses Ltda. Sao Caet. do Sul, SP.	N890Q
☐ PT-BZY	70	Mitsubishi MU-2F	188	Franca Taxi Aereo Ltda. Sao Luiz, MA.	N109MA
☐ PT-DEU	68	King Air B90	LJ-355	Claudiomar Vic Kehrnvald e Outro, Redencao, PA.	
☐ PT-DIQ	68	King Air B90	LJ-398	Umuarama Const. Terrap. Paviment Ltda. Araguaina, TO.	
☐ PT-DKV	70	King Air 100	B-43	Saenge Eng. de Saneam. e Edif Ltda. Sao Paulo, SP.	
☐ PT-DNP	70	King Air 100	B-56	Jorge Wady Cecilio, Goiania, GO.	
☐ PT-DTL	71	Mitsubishi MU-2F	196	SETE Taxi Aereo Ltda. Goiania, GO.	N116MA
☐ PT-FCM	97	King Air C90B	LJ-1471	Jatoba Agric Pec e Ind SA. Curitiba, PR.	N1099D
☐ PT-FFN	89	King Air 300	FA-174	Braulino Basilio Maia Filho, Aracatuba, SP.	N1543H
☐ PT-FFS	97	King Air B200	BB-1578	Gianni Franco Samaja, Sao Paulo, SP.	N330DR
☐ PT-FGB	91	King Air 350	FL-42	Berneck & Cia. Curitiba, PR.	N17NC
☐ PT-FSA	98	King Air 350	FL-221	Bankboston NA/Feltin Management LLC.	N221Z
☐ PT-IBE	71	King Air C90	LJ-531	Translima Taxi Aereo Ltda. Belo Horizonte, MG. (status ?).	
☐ PT-ICD	72	Mitsubishi MU-2F	215	Bens Tur Passaagens e Repres Ltda. Goiania, GO.	N181MA
☐ PT-ICP	72	King Air C90	LJ-558	Voar Taxi Aereo Ltda, Goiania, GO.	
☐ PT-IEC	72	681B Turbo Commander	6069	BCN Leasing Arrend. Mercantil SA. Barueri, SP.	
☐ PT-IED	72	681B Turbo Commander	6070	MTP Industrial e Comercial Ltda.	
☐ PT-IGD	72	King Air E90	LW-9	Marcos Paixao de Araujo, Belo Horizonte, MG.	
☐ PT-JGA	73	Mitsubishi MU-2K	268	Maringa SA Cimento e Ferro-Liga, Sao Paulo, SP.	N314MA
☐ PT-JUB	93	King Air B200	BB-1455	RACC/	N8105Q
☐ PT-KGV	67	King Air A90	LJ-221	No Limits Taxi Aerea Ltda. Boituva, SP.	N38V
☐ PT-KME	75	PA-31T Cheyenne II	7520012	Lideranca Taxi Aereo Ltda. Brasilia, DF.	
☐ PT-KYF	61	Gulfstream 1	75	Jet Sul Taxi Aereo Ltda. Curitiba, PR.	N304K
☐ PT-LBZ	66	King Air A90	LJ-181	CAESGO-Cia Agricola of the State of Goias, Goiania, GO.	N223KD
☐ PT-LCE	81	King Air E90	LW-347	Edio Nogueira, Campinas, SP.	N3841V
☐ PT-LDA	72	Rockwell 690	11036	Representacaoes Seixas SA. Cpo. Eliseos, SP.	PT-FRC
☐ PT-LDL	72	Rockwell 690	11037	Taxi Aereo Marilia SA. Sao Paulo, SP.	PT-FRD
☐ PT-LER	81	King Air F90	LA-148	CTEEP-CiaTrans Energ Elet Paulista,	N1826P
☐ PT-LEW	72	Mitsubishi MU-2K	244	Aeronet Informatica Ltda. Imperatriz, MA. (status ?).	N400SM
☐ PT-LFX	74	Mitsubishi MU-2J	650	Redencao Taxi Aereo Ltda. Carlos Roberto Bueno, PA.	N990M
☐ PT-LHH	81	MU-2 Marquise	1508SA	AB Promocoes E P. Artist S/C Ltda. Anapolis, GO.	N618RT
☐ PT-LHJ	82	King Air C90	LJ-1010	Andre Luiz Sant Anna de Matto, Belo Horizonte, MG.	N6135Z
☐ PT-LHM	66	King Air 90	LJ-105	Aluisio Gregorio Motta Jr. Gurupi, TO.	PP-ENF
☐ PT-LHV	77	Rockwell 690B	11376	Omar Najar,	N81567
☐ PT-LHZ	75	King Air E90	LW-133	Luiz Rassi Jr. Goiania, GO.	(N52CB)
☐ PT-LIF	84	King Air F90-1	LA-223	ICAL-Industria de Calcinacao Ltda, S Jose da Lapa, MG.	N83KA
☐ PT-LIK	82	MU-2 Marquise	1546SA	Banco Cidade Leasing Arren. Merc. SA. Goiania, GO.	N472MA
☐ PT-LIR	80	MU-2 Solitaire	428SA	FRICOL-Frigorificos Colinas SA. Col. Tocantins, TO.	N124AX
☐ PT-LIS	79	MU-2 Marquise	749SA	Manuel Grzywacz Birembaum, Sao Paulo, SP.	N980MA
☐ PT-LJN	72	King Air A100	B-121	Santander Brasil Arrend. Mercantil, Barueri, SP.	PP-EGK
☐ PT-LJS	85	MU-2 Marquise	1568SA	Uniair Taxi Aereo Ltda. Vitoria, ES.	N501MA
☐ PT-LLG	80	PA-31T Cheyenne II	8020054	Pabreulandia Agropastoril BC Ltda. Barra do Garcas, MG.	LV-OGB
☐ PT-LLO	89	King Air C90A	LJ-1225	Fatty Taxi Aereo Ltda. Sao Paulo, SP.	N1564M
☐ PT-LLP	79	King Air F90	LA-7	Sao Joao Abrasivos e Minerios Ltda. Sao Joao da B Vista, SP.	N67RP
☐ PT-LLR	81	King Air C90	LJ-946	Safra Leasing SA Arrend Mercantil. Sao Paulo, SP.	N3236T
☐ PT-LLV	80	King Air C90	LJ-897	Realfort Distribuidora Ltda.	N758D
☐ PT-LMD	67	Mitsubishi MU-2B	026	Taxi Aereo Marilia SA. Sao Paulo, SP.	N482G
☐ PT-LMI	80	King Air C90	LJ-913	MACIFE-Materiais de Construcao SA. Taguatinga, DF.	N715AT
☐ PT-LNG	81	PA-31T Cheyenne II	8120061	Marialdo Rangel dos Santos, Nova Andradina, MS.	N831CM
☐ PT-LOH	68	Mitsubishi MU-2F	126	Belair Taxi Aereo Ltda. Belo Horizonte, MG.	N3917J
☐ PT-LPD	88	King Air C90A	LJ-1173	CESP-Cia Energetica de Sao Paulo, Sao Paulo, SP.	
☐ PT-LPG	87	King Air B200	BB-1271	A C Agro Mercantil SA. Paracatu, MG.	N3048U
☐ PT-LPJ	82	King Air C90-1	LJ-1026	Carlos Roberto Alves, Belo Horizonte, MG.	N6364H
☐ PT-LPL	80	King Air F90	LA-28	Construtora Jalk SA. Belo Horizonte, MG.	N90LL
☐ PT-LPS	79	King Air C90	LJ-817	Construtora Emccamp Ltda. Belo Horizonte, MG.	N3981Y
☐ PT-LQC	81	King Air F90	LA-132	Bandeirantes SA Arrend. Mercantil, Belo Horizonte, MG.	N38649
☐ PT-LQD	79	King Air C90	LJ-844	Emival Ramos Caiado Filho, Brasilia, DF.	N707CV
☐ PT-LQE	83	King Air C90-1	LJ-1056	Itapoan Taxi Aereo Ltda. Salvador, BA.	N90GH
☐ PT-LQS	81	King Air C90	LJ-966	HRO Empreend. e Agropecuaria Ltda. Sao Paulo, SP. (status ?)	N181JH
☐ PT-LRT	81	PA-31T Cheyenne II	8120040	Aerobert Emp. e Participacoes Ltda. Carapicuisa, SP.	N44TW
☐ PT-LSE	84	King Air C90A	LJ-1063	TERCAM-Terraplen. Const. Inc. Ltda. Belo Horizonte, MG.	N76DS

Reg	Yr	Type	c/n	Owner/Operator	Prev Regn
☐ PT-LSH	81	King Air F90	LA-94	Banespa SA. Sao Caef do Sul, SP.	N3735W
☐ PT-LSO	78	King Air C90	LJ-794	Lider Taxi Aereo SA. Belo Horizonte, MG.	N57JB
☐ PT-LSP	82	King Air F90	LA-197	Cia Cacique de Cafe Soluvel, Sao Paulo, SP.	YV-494CP
☐ PT-LSQ	81	MU-2 Marquise	1530SA	Complemento Taxi Aereo Ltda. Sao Paulo, SP.	N449MA
☐ PT-LTF	71	King Air C90	LJ-543	Ariba Aerotaxi Ltda. Belo Horizonte, MG.	N29791
☐ PT-LTO	81	King Air F90	LA-156	Lider Taxi Aereo SA. Belo Horizonte, MG.	N1827F
☐ PT-LTT	81	King Air F90	LA-103	Encalso Construcoes Ltda. Sao Jose do Rio Preto, SP.	N3802F
☐ PT-LUF	75	King Air C90	LJ-651	Magazine Liliani SA. Imperatriz, MA.	N7300N
☐ PT-LUJ	77	PA-31T Cheyenne II	7720039	Transjunior Transp. Comercio Ltda. Imperatriz, MA.	N1144Z
☐ PT-LUT	84	King Air F90-1	LA-215	Locadora Brasal Ltda. Brasilia, DF.	N6730S
☐ PT-LVI	79	King Air C90	LJ-834	Vigano Taxi Aereo Ltda. Belo Horizonte, MG.	N42QC
☐ PT-LVK	89	King Air C90A	LJ-1201	Itapemirim Taxi Aereo Ltda. Itapemirim, ES.	(N486JA)
☐ PT-LXI	80	King Air F90	LA-11	Jose Francisco da Cunha, Cabui Campinas, SP.	N18EH
☐ PT-LXY	82	King Air F90	LA-195	Turim Taxi Aereo e Outro,	N70132
☐ PT-LYI	71	Mitsubishi MU-2F	213	Heringer Taxi Aereo Ltda. Imperatriz, MA. (Status ?)	N100BR
☐ PT-LYK	88	King Air C90A	LJ-1188	Usina Santa Adelia SA. Jaboticabal, SP.	N1537H
☐ PT-LYM	82	King Air F90	LA-185	Carioca Christ Nielsen Eng SA. Rio de Janeiro, RJ.	N61DH
☐ PT-LYP	81	King Air F90	LA-126	Acucar e Alcool Osw. Rib. Mend. Ltda. Guaira, SP.	N3848V
☐ PT-LYT	82	King Air C90-1	LJ-1037	Passaro Azul Taxi Aereo Ltda.	N283DP
☐ PT-LYZ	81	King Air F90	LA-109	Novadata Sist. e Computadores SA. Brasilia, DF.	N3806U
☐ PT-LZA	74	King Air A100	B-200	Jet Sul Taxi Aereo Ltda. Curitiba, PR. (status ?).	PT-FOB
☐ PT-LZB	79	PA-31T Cheyenne II	7920063	Nellitex Industria Textil Ltda. Americana, SP.	N23KF
☐ PT-LZD	81	PA-42 Cheyenne III	8001038	Serafim Meneghel, Bandeirantes, PR.	LV-ONL
☐ PT-LZH	79	King Air C90	LJ-808	Antonio de Donno,	(N711WT)
☐ PT-LZR	79	PA-31T Cheyenne II	7920083	Nortox Agro Quimica SA. Arapongas, PR.	N31DC
☐ PT-LZT	84	King Air F90-1	LA-216	Agropastoril Faz Caramuru Ltda.	N390D
☐ PT-MCM	85	King Air 300	FA-52	Conserva de Estradas Ltda. Belo Horizonte, MG.	N50KA
☐ PT-MFL	82	PA-42 Cheyenne III	8001080	Fabio O Luchesi Advoc. Terras S/C. Sao Paulo, SP.	N882SW
☐ PT-MFW	83	Cheyenne II-XL	8166067	Flysul Aerotaxi Ltda. Porto Alegre, RS.	(N67ER)
☐ PT-MGZ	80	PA-31T Cheyenne II	8020058	TL Taxi Aereo Loc de Veiculos Ltda.	N236SR
☐ PT-MJD	97	King Air B200	BB-1589	John Deere SA. Horizontina,	N2288B
☐ PT-MJQ	99	King Air C90B	LJ-1564	Centrals Electr do Para SA. Belem, PA.	N3164R
☐ PT-MMB	82	King Air B200	BB-971	Malharia Diana Ltda. Timbo, SC.	N503RH
☐ PT-MMC	87	King Air 300	FA-113	Jet Sul Taxi Aereo Ltda. Curitiba, PR.	N299GS
☐ PT-MPN	78	Rockwell 690B	11465	Nome & Cia Ltda. Sarandi, PR.	CS-ASA
☐ PT-MVJ	97	King Air C90B	LJ-1498	Claudino SA LJ de Departementos, Teresina, PI.	PT-WOZ
☐ PT-OAJ	80	PA-31T Cheyenne 1	8004005	Osvaldo Raul Lunardi, Aracaju, SE.	N2594R
☐ PT-OAM	80	PA-31T Cheyenne II	8020028	Sudameris Arrend. Mercantil SA. Sao Paulo, SP.	LV-OGG
☐ PT-OBW	68	King Air B90	LJ-353	Alexandre Lacerda Biagi, Uberlandia, MG.	PT-FOA
☐ PT-OCC	81	King Air C90	LJ-960	Constructora Eferco Ltda. Belo Horizonte, MG.	N3861H
☐ PT-OCE	84	King Air F90-1	LA-217	Jose Maris Afonso, Belo Horizonte, MG.	N6756L
☐ PT-OCI	82	King Air C90	LJ-998	Rodoban Transportes Terrest. e Aereos Ltda. Uberlandia, MG.	N17EN
☐ PT-OCL	80	PA-31T Cheyenne II	8020033	Sudameris Arrend. Mercantil SA. Sao Paulo, SP.	N11WC
☐ PT-OCT	72	King Air C90	LJ-567	Oceanair Aero Taxi Ltda.	PP-IAF
☐ PT-OCY	79	King Air C90	LJ-847	Expresso Novalimense Ltda. Belo Horizonte, MG.	N317EC
☐ PT-ODA	69	King Air B90	LJ-466	Ocean Air, Rio de Janeiro, RJ.	PP-IAG
☐ PT-ODH	86	King Air C90A	LJ-1128	Macyr Meneghel Agropec. Uniao Ltda. Americana, SP.	N7248G
☐ PT-ODM	81	PA-31T Cheyenne II	8120042	Eucatur Taxi Aereo Ltda. Cascavel, PR.	N131CC
☐ PT-ODN	81	King Air F90	LA-85	EMSA/NTA-Nacional Taxi Aereo Ltda. Goiania, GO.	N3697P
☐ PT-ODO	83	King Air F90-1	LA-213	EMSA/NTA-Nacional Taxi Aereo Ltda. Goiania, GO.	N77M
☐ PT-ODR	80	PA-31T Cheyenne II	8020079	Co-operativa Centr. Oeste Catarinense, Chapeco, SC.	LV-OEU
☐ PT-OED	80	PA-31T Cheyenne II	8020029	Fausto Jorge, Vera Cruz, SP.	(N661AE)
☐ PT-OEP	82	King Air C90-1	LJ-1019	Lider Taxi Aereo SA. Belo Horizonte, MG.	N25AJ
☐ PT-OFB	83	King Air F90	LA-200	Construtora Andrade Gutierrez SA. Belo Horizonte, MG.	N6685H
☐ PT-OFC	72	King Air C90	LJ-534	Meier Transporte Coletivo Ltda.	N120JJ
☐ PT-OFD	81	King Air F90	LA-118	Agropecuaria Rica SA. Cuiaba, MT.	N715GW
☐ PT-OFF	91	King Air C90A	LJ-1264	Usina Matary SA. Recife, PE.	N5680Z
☐ PT-OFG	76	Rockwell 690A	11274	Cx PT- 7/97 to ?	N4432W
☐ PT-OFH	79	PA-31T Cheyenne II	7920034	CQB Aviones Ltda. Jundiai, SP.	N29KR
☐ PT-OFS	84	King Air F90-1	LA-225	Umuarama Const. Terrap. Paviment Ltda. Araguaina, TO.	N713DB
☐ PT-OFY	85	King Air C90A	LJ-1094	U & M Construcao Pesada Ltda. Juiz de Fora, MG.	N7215L
☐ PT-OHH	81	King Air C90	LJ-975	Joao Cesar Presotto, Guapore, RS.	N94SC
☐ PT-OHK	80	MU-2 Marquise	774SA	Economico SA. Arrend. Mercantil, S Caet do Sul, SP.	N15ZM
☐ PT-OHZ	82	King Air F90	LA-173	Colorado Auto Pecas Ltda. Goiania, GO.	N56TW
☐ PT-OIF	80	King Air F90	LA-49	SOTAN-Soc. Taxi Aereo Nordeste Ltda. Maceio, AL.	N200BM

Reg	Yr	Type	c/n	Owner/Operator	Prev Regn

Reg	Yr	Type	c/n	Owner/Operator	Prev Regn
PT-OIP	77 Mitsubishi MU-2P	354SA	Lindolfo Gontijo Lucas, Manaus, AM.		N739MA
PT-OIU	71 King Air C90	LJ-515	VDL-Fomento Marcantil Ltda.		N953K
PT-OIY	81 MU-2 Solitaire	453SA	Co-op Arrozeira Extremo Sul Ltda. Pelotas, RS.		N24FJ
PT-OIZ	88 King Air C90A	LJ-1174	ICAL Energetica Ltda. Belo Horizonte, MG.		N31398
PT-OJA	81 King Air C90	LJ-952	TAF Linhas Aereas SA. Fortaleza, CE.		N4490L
PT-OJE	81 PA-31T Cheyenne II	8120031	Ciclotron Ind. Eletronica Ltda.		N628DE
PT-OJI	79 King Air C90	LJ-812	Mina Emp Imob e Agropastoris Ltda. Goiania, GO.		N627KP
PT-OJM	81 PA-31T Cheyenne II	8120070	EPAGRI SA. Florianopolis, SC.		N826SW
PT-OJQ	88 King Air 300	FA-154	Marina Taxi Aereo Ltda. Belo Horizonte, MG.		N1563K
PT-OJU	80 King Air C90	LJ-900	Felisberto Moutinho Rodrigues Jr. Osasco, SP.		N415MA
PT-OKL	82 PA-42 Cheyenne III	8001103	Sococo SA Industrias Alimenticias, Maceio, AL.		N4114D
PT-OKQ	89 King Air C90A	LJ-1195	Empresa Limpadora Centro Ltda. Barueri, SP.		N70PA
PT-OKT	81 PA-31T Cheyenne 1	8104041	Sementes Maggi Ltda. Rondonopolis, MT.		N805CA
PT-OLF	80 PA-31T Cheyenne 1	8004039	Olga Youssef Soloviov, Londrina, PR.		N500AQ
PT-OLI	84 King Air 300	FA-26	Citrosuco Paulista SA, Sao Paulo, SP.		N984CF
PT-OLP	84 King Air F90	LA-220	Maeda Taxi Aereo Ltda. Ituverava, SP.		N6837C
PT-OLQ	80 King Air C90	LJ-884	Jose Trujillo Rodriguez, Sao Paulo-Marte, SP.		N88RB
PT-OLW	81 King Air C90	LJ-985	Antonio Eustaquin Alves, Belo Horizonte, MG.		N409ND
PT-OLX	81 King Air C90	LJ-903	Emival Eterno da C Firma, Goiania, GO.		N38589
PT-OLZ	80 PA-31T Cheyenne II	8120005	Magim Rodriguez Jr.		N57656
PT-OMZ	89 King Air C90A	LJ-1220	Companhia Ferroligas Minas Gerais Ltda. Belo Horizonte, MG.		N5520X
PT-ONE	81 King Air F90	LA-144	Rio das Pedras Empreendimentos Ltda. Brasilia, DF.		(N300BF
PT-ONJ	84 King Air C90	LJ-1078	EMSA/NTA-Nacional Taxi Aereo Ltda. Goiania, GO.		N78SR
PT-ONO	81 King Air F90	LA-92	Premier SA Partic e Administracao, Contagem, MG.		N3715T
PT-ONQ	82 King Air C90-1	LJ-1018	Gerson Neix,		N501LA
PT-ONU	81 King Air F90	LA-128	Construtora Gomes Lourenco Ltda. Campo Grande, MT.		N3867A
PT-OOS	78 Mitsubishi MU-2P	388SA	Agua Limpa Transportes Ltda. Rio Verde, GO.		N91CM
PT-OOT	82 King Air C90	LJ-995	ETA-Empresa de Taxi Aereo Ltda. Belo Horizonte, MG.		N1855H
PT-OOX	82 King Air F90	LA-162	Tecumseh do Brasil Ltda. Sao Carlos, SP.		N90BL
PT-OOY	80 King Air C90	LJ-882	Riana Taxi Aereo Ltda. Rio de Janeiro, RJ.		N181GA
PT-OPC	81 PA-31T Cheyenne II	8120010	Constr Villela e Carvalho Ltda.		(D-IIKW
PT-OPD	80 King Air C90	LJ-920	Gama Indl. e Com. de Sec. e Molh. Ltda.Apar de Goiania, GO.		N42KA
PT-OPE	81 King Air C90	LJ-940	APEC-Assoc. Prudent. Educ. e Cultura, Pres. Prudente, SP.		N82P
PT-OPF	80 PA-31T Cheyenne 1	8004038	Messias Rodrigues Talevi, Curitiba, PR.		N977CP
PT-OPH	76 PA-31T Cheyenne II	7620044	ATR-Travessia/Agroisa Agroindustrial Travessia, Recife, PE.		N92FC
PT-OPQ	80 PA-31T Cheyenne 1	8004007	Taxi Aereo Taroba Ltda. Cascavel, PR.		N2379W
PT-OPR	80 King Air C90	LJ-870	Banco Fibra SA.		N500MF
PT-OQH	72 Rockwell 690	11011	Taxi Aereo Florianopolis Ltda. Florianopolis, SC.		N9211N
PT-OQP	69 King Air 100	B-7	Rubens Correia Coimbra, Penapolis, SP.		N800M
PT-OQQ	70 681 Turbo Commander	6021	Cia de Ind. Gerais Obras e Terras, Canoas, RS.		N10RN
PT-OQS	82 King Air C90	LJ-1005	BIC Arrendamento Mercantil SA. Fortaleza, CE.		N6661J
PT-OQY	85 Gulfstream 900	15038	Santa Barbara Taxi Aereo Ltda. Maringa, PR.		N77PK
PT-ORB	92 King Air B200	BB-1435	INCOBRASA, Porto Alegre, RS.		N8050X
PT-ORG	94 King Air C90B	LJ-1308	Santa Coloma Inv e Part SC Ltda.		
PT-ORW	82 King Air C90	LJ-1004	Banco Bamerindos do Brasil SA. NYC. USA.		N45US
PT-ORZ	90 King Air C90A	LJ-1233	Usina Alt. Alegre SA. Asucar e Alcool, Pres. Prudente, SP.		N113TP
PT-OSI	81 King Air C90	LJ-936	Sermo Serv de Mao Obra S/C Ltda. Sao Paulo, SP.		N49FA
PT-OSN	90 King Air C90A	LJ-1260	Usina Nova America SA. Sao Paulo, SP.		N5618Z
PT-OSO	81 King Air C90	LJ 927	Tamandare Taxi Aereo Ltda. Teresina, PI.		N4492D
PT-O3R	81 King Air 200	BB-784	Sudameris Arrend. Mercantil SA. Sao Paulo, SP.		N789H
PT-OTA	82 King Air F90	LA-187	Fortaleza Sta Teres Emp Part Ltda. Belo Horizonte, MG.		N6416F
PT-OTG	85 King Air C90A	LJ-1096	Empresa Gontijo de Transportes Ltda. Belo Horizonte, MG.		N7216H
PT-OTI	90 King Air C90A	LJ-1237	Bompreco SA Supermercado do Nordeste, Recife, PE.		N338DF
PT-OTV	81 PA-31T Cheyenne 1	8104017	Impres. Cia Bras. de Impr.e Prop. Sao Paulo, SP.		N4494U
PT-OUF	81 King Air E90	LW-343	Macauba Citros Ltda. Curitiba, PR.		N3710Y
PT-OUJ	81 King Air F90	LA-155	Tiquara Taxi Aereo Ltda. Recife, PE.		N155GA
PT-OUL	66 King Air A90	LJ-125	Marcello Sergio R Costa e Outros, Boituva, SP.		N120JN
PT-OUO	70 King Air B90	LJ-499	Jaime Valler, Campo Grande, MS.		N44454
PT-OUX	81 King Air C90	LJ-937	Christiana Arcangeli, Sao Paulo, SP.		OY-BEK
PT-OVB	81 PA-31T Cheyenne 1	8104051	Frigorifico Vale do Itajai Ltda. Itajai, SC.		N47TW
PT-OVE	80 PA-31T Cheyenne 1	8004014	Altima Transp Rodoviarios Ltda.		N234PC
PT-OVP	66 King Air A90	LJ-152	Plasticom-Plast Ind e Com Ltda. Goiania, GO.		N8180
PT-OVW	77 Mitsubishi MU-2P	350SA	Air Bahia Taxi Aereo Ltda. Brasilia, DF.		N958M
PT-OVY	79 King Air C90	LJ-835	Chalet Agropecuaria Ltda. Corumba, MS.		N414AF
PT-OXU	72 King Air C90	LJ-535	Pif Paf SA. Industria e Comercio, Belo Horizonte, MG.		N794K

Reg	Yr	Type	c/n	Owner/Operator	Prev Regn
☐ PT-OYN	84	King Air C90A	LJ-1081	Caribbean Participaoes Ltda.	N60CW
☐ PT-OZJ	81	King Air C90	LJ-951	Confederal Vig e Transp Valeres Ltda.	N511D
☐ PT-OZK	75	King Air 200	BB-45	Constructora Lima Araujo Ltda. Maceio, AL.	N46JK
☐ PT-OZL	93	King Air C90B	LJ-1341	Acucareira Zillor Lorenzett SA.	
☐ PT-OZN	80	PA-31T Cheyenne II	8020061	Irmaos Muffato e Cia Ltda. Cascavel, PR.	N711DH
☐ PT-OZP	82	King Air F90	LA-175	Safra Leasing SA Arrend Mercantil, Sao Paulo, SP.	N415GN
☐ PT-OZR	83	King Air C90-1	LJ-1059	Vector Taxi Aereo Ltda. Sao Paulo, SP.	N6581B
☐ PT-PAC	99	King Air C90B	LJ-1555	Caseli e Cia Ltda. Varzea Grande, MT.	N3205W
☐ PT-WAC	97	King Air 350	FL-177	A C Agro Mercantil SA. Paracatu, MG.	N2029Z
☐ PT-WAE	67	King Air A90	LJ-191	Joao Carlos Soares de Matos, Florianapolis, SC.	N737K
☐ PT-WAG	75	King Air E90	LW-138	Luis Alexandre Igayara, Rio de Janeiro, RJ.	N90GD
☐ PT-WAH	90	King Air C90A	LJ-1245	Henrique Duarte Prata, Sao Paulo-Marte, SP.	N5654E
☐ PT-WBQ	69	King Air B90	LJ-460	Nelson Cintra Ribeiro, Campo Grande, MS.	N113TT
☐ PT-WCS	94	King Air C90B	LJ-1377	MM Aerotaxi Ltda. Campinas-Viracopos, SP.	N3042K
☐ PT-WDU	78	King Air C90	LJ-791	MPE-Montagens e Projetos Especiais SA. Rio de Janeiro, RJ.	N791RC
☐ PT-WEF	81	PA-31T Cheyenne 1	8104034	Wellington Brasil Zucato,	N100GY
☐ PT-WEG	81	King Air B200	BB-875	EGESA-Empreend. Gerais de Eng. SA. Belo Horizonte, MG.	N313SC
☐ PT-WET	80	King Air F90	LA-78	Auguri Constructora Participacoes Ltda. Sao Paulo, SP..	N90MH
☐ PT-WFB	80	PA-31T Cheyenne II	8020048	Odilio Balbinotti, Maringa, PR.	N42EJ
☐ PT-WFN	93	King Air C90B	LJ-1346	Ambar AG de Eventos e Edit Ltda.	LV-WDP
☐ PT-WFQ	78	PA-31T Cheyenne II	7820049	Aguil Algodeira Gulmaraes Ltda. Recife, PR.	N689AC
☐ PT-WGJ	81	PA-31T Cheyenne II	8120101	Delta Nat Bank of New York, Curitiba, PR. (was 8120066).	N152CC
☐ PT-WGS	93	King Air B200	BB-1446	BB Leasing Co Ltda. Belo Horizonte, MG.	N5685X
☐ PT-WGU	94	King Air C90B	LJ-1363	Citicorp Leasing International Inc. Porto Alegre, RS.	N1534T
☐ PT-WHA	90	King Air C90A	LJ-1253	CONTERSA - Const. Terrap. e Saleam. Ltda. Goiania, GO.	N309P
☐ PT-WHN	81	PA-31T Cheyenne 1	8104073	Irmaos Muffato e Cia Ltda. Cascavel, PR.	N9185Y
☐ PT-WHP	89	King Air C90A	LJ-1212	Leasing Bank of Boston SA. Goiania, GO.	N1551J
☐ PT-WIC	80	Gulfstream 840	11625	TAM/Banco Itamarati SA. Sao Paulo, SP.	N690HC
☐ PT-WIH	95	King Air C90B	LJ-1396	Coffee Holdings Inc. Varginha, MG.	N3218K
☐ PT-WIT	95	King Air C90SE	LJ-1394	Tecar Automavaic E A T Ltda. Goiania, GO.	N3217K
☐ PT-WIX	72	Mitsubishi MU-2F	232	Luiz Antonio Portelinha Bueno, Belem, PA.	N800HR
☐ PT-WJD	96	King Air C90B	LJ-1427	Frigorifico Independencia Ltda. Cajamar.	N3251E
☐ PT-WJF	94	King Air C90B	LJ-1386	Brasif Duty Free Shop Ltda. Rio de Janeiro, RJ.	N3165M
☐ PT-WKF	96	Pilatus PC-12	141	Flamingo Unimed AirTaxi Aereo Ltda. Sao Paulo, SP.	N141BL
☐ PT-WKX	97	King Air C90B	LJ-1494	Java Consultoria e Comercio Ltda. Rio Clara, SP.	N1135X
☐ PT-WLD	83	Gulfstream 900	15027	Plasutil Ind Com de Plasticos Ltda. Bauru, SP.	N900ST
☐ PT-WLJ	81	PA-31T Cheyenne II	8120011	Wagner Bisco e Outro,	N31FR
☐ PT-WLK	96	King Air B200	BB-1543	CEMIG-Cia Energetica de Minas Gerais, Belo Horizonte, MG.	N1082S
☐ PT-WMT	81	King Air C90	LJ-956	Industria de Madeiras Tozzo Ltda. Chapeco, SC.	N225AT
☐ PT-WMU	80	PA-31T Cheyenne 1	8004043	Lina Participacoes e Adm. Ltda. Tatui, SP.	N53WM
☐ PT-WMX	81	PA-31T Cheyenne 1	8104062	Fabrica de Pecas Elet. Delmar, Tatui, SP.	N2560Y
☐ PT-WNC	81	PA-31T Cheyenne II	8120020	Fabio da Silva Machado, Belo Horizonte, MG.	N56MC
☐ PT-WND	96	King Air 350	FL-141	Medley Industria Farmaceutica SA, Belo Horizonte, MG.	N1061Q
☐ PT-WNG	81	Cheyenne II-XL	8166049	Eicomon SA. Sao Paulo, SP.	(N57AF)
☐ PT-WNL	97	King Air 350	FL-159	Sementes Maggi Ltda. Rondonopolis, MT.	N1100N
☐ PT-WNN	97	King Air B200	BB-1558	UNIMED N N F C Trabajos Med. Ltda. Joao Pessoa.	N1108A
☐ PT-WNQ	97	King Air B200	BB-1584		N11355
☐ PT-WNS	83	MU-2 Marquise	1501SA	Dacunha SA. Sao Paulo, SP.	N43DC
☐ PT-WNW	85	King Air C90A	LJ-1092		N11755
☐ PT-WOF	82	King Air B200	BB-986	Planfoto Distr Materials Fotograficos Ltda. Sao Paulo, SP.	N986TJ
☐ PT-WOR	81	PA-31T Cheyenne II	8120030	Transportes Guadalupe Ltda. Goiania, GO.	N199RC
☐ PT-WPN	91	King Air C90A	LJ-1294	Otto Baumgart Ind. Co. SA. Sao Paulo, SP.	N19BK
☐ PT-WPV	78	King Air B100	BE-45	Icaro Taxi Aereo Ltda. Brasilia, DF.	N263DC
☐ PT-WQW	99	King Air C90B	LJ-1577	Aleksander Carlos Manic, Curitiba, PR.	N4477N
☐ PT-WRA	94	King Air C90B	LJ-1385	GRANASA, Belo Horizonte, MG.	N3198K
☐ PT-WSI	97	King Air 350	FL-169	Simarelli Dist. de Petroleo Ltda. Cuiaba, CT.	N1099E
☐ PT-WSJ	96	King Air 350	FL-152	Jet Sul Taxi Aereo Ltda. Curitiba, PR.	N1092S
☐ PT-WST	78	Mitsubishi MU-2N	711SA	SETE Taxi Aereo Ltda. Goiania, GO.	N171CA
☐ PT-WSX	87	King Air B200	BB-1266	M & M Administracao e Particip Ltda. Londrina, PR.	N204MS
☐ PT-WTN	68	King Air B90	LJ-346	C Nacife Jr & Partner, Belo Horizonte, MG.	PP-EOC
☐ PT-WTU	97	King Air C90B	LJ-1491	Laboratorio Teuto Brasileiro Ltda.	N2316H
☐ PT-WTW	98	King Air 350	FL-205	Uniair Admin Part Serv Med Urg Ltda. Porte Alegre, RS.	(PT-WZC)
☐ PT-WUG	98	King Air C90B	LJ-1511	First Security Bank NA. Sao Paulo, SP.	N2311J
☐ PT-WUT	99	King Air 350	FL-240	Soc de Ens do Triangulo Ltda.	N3078T
☐ PT-WVI	93	King Air C90B	LJ-1331	INTA-Indaia Taxi Aereo Ltda. Recife, PE.	N8089J
Reg	Yr	Type	c/n	Owner/Operator	Prev Regn

Reg	Yr Type	c/n	Owner/Operator	Prev Regn
☐ PT-WYO	91 King Air 350	FL-40	ADM Exp e Importadora SA. Vitoria, ES.	N8048U
☐ PT-WYT	78 Mitsubishi MU-2N	722SA	SETE Taxi Aereo Ltda. Goiania, GO.	N722MU
☐ PT-WZC	99 King Air C90B	LJ-1538	Uniair Admin Part Serv Med Urg Ltda. Porte Alegre, RS.	N3138B
☐ PT-XEG	84 King Air B200	BB-1190	Marca Agropecuaria Ltda. Barra do Garcas, MT.	N75GE
☐ PT-XHP	97 King Air C90B	LJ-1473	Henrique Duarte Prata, Sao Paulo-Marte, SP.	N1090X
☐ PT-XOC	82 PA-31T Cheyenne 1	8104064	Olga Intaschi Carvalho Cunha, Presidente Prudente, SP.	N502MM
☐ PT-XOU	97 King Air C90B	LJ-1501		N401TT
☐ PT-XOV	99 King Air C90B	LJ-1569		N505P

P2 = PAPUA NEW GUINEA   Total 8

Civil

Reg	Yr Type	c/n	Owner/Operator	Prev Regn
☐ P2-CAA	79 King Air 200	BB-415	Department of Civil Aviation, Port Moresby.	P2-PNH
☐ P2-HCN	81 King Air 200C	BL-22	Hevi Lift (PNG) P/L. Mount Hagen.	P2-PJV
☐ P2-KSA	96 King Air B200	BB-1527	Regional Air P/L. Madang.	N170W
☐ P2-MML	79 King Air 200	BB-579	Airlines of PNG Ltd/Misima Mines P/L. Port Moresby.	VH-AKT
☐ P2-NTJ	82 King Air C90-1	LJ-1024	New Tribes Mission, Port Moresby.	VH-FOM
☐ P2-NTR	82 King Air C90-1	LJ-1021	New Tribes Mission, Port Moresby.	VH-FDZ
☐ P2-PNG	92 King Air 350	FL-79	Government Flying Unit, Port Moresby.	N8246Q
☐ P2-SIA	81 King Air 200C	BL-39	Summer Institute of Linguistics, Ukarumpa.	VH-FDR

P4 = ARUBA   Total 2

Civil

Reg	Yr Type	c/n	Owner/Operator	Prev Regn
☐ P4-JML	61 Gulfstream 1	76	Transglobal AVV.	G-BRAL
☐ P4-SSI	97 King Air C90B	LJ-1476	Seahatch Laboratory NV. Maracaibo, Venezuela.	N1106M

RP = PHILIPPINES   Total 28

Civil

Reg	Yr Type	c/n	Owner/Operator	Prev Regn
☐ RP-C1341	66 King Air	...	Transglobal Aviation, Manila.	
☐ RP-C1502	94 King Air B200	BB-1500	Royal Duty Free Shop/AAI Island Hopper, Manila.	N3199B
☐ RP-C1728	94 King Air 350	FL-118	Philippine Long Distance Telephone Co. Manila.	N1555E
☐ RP-C1807	88 King Air C90A	LJ-1181	A Soriano Aviation Inc/Rikio Co. Manila.	N90PE
☐ RP-C1978	71 King Air 100	B-77	Development Bank of the Philippines, Manila.	PI-C197
☐ RP-C2100	91 King Air B200	BB-1405	Air Transportation Office, Manila.	N8129A
☐ RP-C2208	68 King Air B90	LJ-365	A M Areta Co. Manila.	N14VK
☐ RP-C223	75 King Air 200	BB-66	Ministry of Local Government of Philippines, Manila.	(N219D)
☐ RP-C2296	98 King Air 350	FL-196	INAEC Aviation Corp. Manila.	N2296G
☐ RP-C2638	96 King Air 350	FL-137	United Laboratories Inc.	N1067S
☐ RP-C264	80 King Air 200	BB-692	Development Bank of the Philippines, Manila.	RP-C513
☐ RP-C2850	96 King Air 350	FL-145	National Power Corp. Manila.	N1075G
☐ RP-C290	79 King Air C90	LJ-857	National Irrigation Administration, Manila.	N6064A
☐ RP-C291	79 King Air E90	LW-325	Lepanto Consolidated Mining Co.	N60575
☐ RP-C292	78 King Air E90	LW-277	Marcopper Mining Corp.	N4977M
☐ RP-C298	79 King Air E90	LW-302	Allied Banking Corp. Manila.	(N209D)
☐ RP-C3500	96 King Air 350	FL-148	PNB Financial Center, Manila.	N3268H
☐ RP-C3650	75 King Air C90	LJ-662	Orient Leaf Tobacco Co.	
☐ RP-C367	82 King Air B200	BB-963	Aboitiz Inc. Manila.	N37GA
☐ RP-C3885	96 King Air B200	BB-1532	Philippine Long Distance Telephone Co. Manila.	N3252X
☐ RP-C415	76 King Air E90	LW-190	Land Bank of the Philippines, Manila.	
☐ RP-C5129	78 King Air 200	BB-358	National Steel Corp. Manila.	
☐ RP-C5555	84 King Air B200	BB-1157	Subic Bay Medical Center Inc. Subic Bay.	N126AP
☐ RP-C755	82 King Air B200	BB-975	United Coconut Planters Bank, Manila.	(N208D)
☐ RP-C8300	92 King Air 350	FL-83		OY-CVL
☐ RP-C879	75 King Air E90	LW-145	Philippine Airlines, Manila.	N122HC
☐ RP-C8853	96 King Air B200	BB-1529	Star Borne Chartered Corp. Manila.	N3261E

Military

Reg	Yr Type	c/n	Owner/Operator	Prev Regn
☐ 11250	75 Rockwell 690A	11250	Government of Philippines, Manila.	N44WV

SE = SWEDEN   Total 28

Civil

Reg	Yr Type	c/n	Owner/Operator	Prev Regn
☐ SE-GHA	74 Mitsubishi MU-2K	283	SAAB Nyge-Aero AB. Skavsta.	N327M/
☐ SE-GHB	74 Mitsubishi MU-2K	287	SAAB Nyge-Aero AB. Skavsta.	N331M/
☐ SE-GHC	74 Mitsubishi MU-2K	289	SAAB Nyge-Aero AB. Skavsta.	N334M/
☐ SE-GHD	74 Mitsubishi MU-2K	293	SAAB Nyge-Aero AB. Skavsta.	N453M/
☐ SE-GHE	74 Mitsubishi MU-2K	294	SAAB Nyge-Aero AB. Skavsta.	N454M/
☐ SE-GHF	74 Mitsubishi MU-2K	299	SAAB Nyge-Aero AB. Skavsta.	N459M/
☐ SE-GHH	72 Mitsubishi MU-2F	222	SAAB Nyge-Aero AB. Skavsta.	N9PN

Reg	Yr Type	c/n	Owner/Operator	Prev Regn

Reg	Yr Type	c/n	Owner/Operator	Prev Regn
SE-IIB	77 King Air C90	LJ-723	Varmforzinkning AB. Smilandsstehar.	OY-ASI
SE-INI	80 King Air 200	BB-687	SOS Flygambulans AB. Goteborg.	EI-BIP
SE-IOV	75 Mitsubishi MU-2M	337	SAAB Nyge-Aero AB. Skavsta.	N522MA
SE-IOZ	75 Mitsubishi MU-2M	320	SAAB Nyge-Aero AB. Skavsta.	N641KE
SE-IUA	76 Mitsubishi MU-2M	345	SAAB Nyge-Aero AB. Skavsta.	N730MP
SE-IUX	80 King Air 200	BB-675	SOS Flygambulans AB. Goteborg.	N26AD
SE-IXC	85 King Air B200	BB-1210	SOS Flygambulans AB. Goteborg.	N7213J
SE-KDK	81 King Air B200	BB-909	Bromma Air Maintenace AB. Stockholm-Bromma.	N171M
SE-KFP	88 King Air B200C	BL-132	SOS Flygambulans AB. Goteborg.	
SE-KOL	89 King Air 300LW	FA-189	Waltair i Linkoeping AB. Norrkoeping.	N8208B
SE-LDL	75 King Air A100	B-213	Stanson Air AB. Stockholm-Bromma.	F-GFEV
SE-LKY	86 King Air B200C	BL-127	NEX Time Jet AB/Nextjet, Stockholm.	D2-ESO
SE-LLU	97 King Air 350	FL-175	A J Produkter i Hyltebruk AB. Hyltebruk.	N1071S
SE-LTL	80 King Air 200	BB-582	Nordkalottflyg AB. Lulea.	LN-MOA
SE-LTM	01 PA-46-500TP Meridian	4697090	Sectra AB. Linkoping.	N189DB
SE-LUB	78 PA-31T Cheyenne II	7820051	Foersaeljnings AB Balticum, Kristianstad.	OE-FBO
Military				
100001	89 SAAB 340B/Tp 100	170	Swedish Air Force, Stockholm. (Code 001 of F16).	SE-F70
100006	98 SAAB 340B/Tp 100	431	Swedish Air Force, Stockholm. (Code 006 of F16).	SE-B31
101002	79 King Air 200	BB-459	(stored Malmen pending sale 9/04).	OY-BVC
101003	80 King Air 200	BB-619	(stored Malmen pending sale 9/04).	LN-MOD
101004	81 King Air B200	BB-932	Swedish Air Force, Stockholm. (Code 014 of F7).	SE-KKM

SP = POLAND
Total   4

Civil

SP-FNS	96 King Air 350	FL-134	Prokom Investments SA/White Eagle Aviation, Gdynia.	N3252V
SP-KKH	81 PA-31T Cheyenne II	8120041	Transport Handel Uslugi Maria Komoro, Sztum.	N220SC
SP-MXH	04 P-180 Avanti	1079	Polskie Pogotowie Ratunkowe, Szczecin.	
SP-NEB	91 King Air C90A	LJ-1285	KGHM Polska Miedz SA ZH.	(F-GULM)

ST = SUDAN
Total   3

Civil

ST-ANH	79 King Air C90	LJ-823	Sudan Airways Co. Khartoum.	N580C
ST-HAL	00 King Air B200	BB-1695	Hala Air, Khartoum.	A6-SSA
ST-SFS	79 King Air 200	BB-539	Sudan Airways Co. Khartoum.	N555SK

SU = EGYPT
Total   6

Civil

SU-...	01 King Air B200	BB-1765	Ceramica Cleopatra Co. Cairo.	N540MA
SU-BAX	78 King Air 200	BB-353	Government of Egypt, Cairo.	SU-AYD
SU-BMW	97 King Air 350	FL-173	Alkan Air, Cairo.	N350KA
SU-BNJ	99 King Air B200	BB-1664	Egyptian Air Ambulance, Cairo.	N3064J
SU-ZAA	94 King Air C90B	LJ-1353	Nuclear Materials Authority, Cairo.	N8292Y
SU-ZBA	96 King Air B200	BB-1518	Orca Air, Sharm El Sheikh.	N3218V

SX = GREECE
Total   15

Civil

SX-APJ	78 King Air 200	BB-401	Aviator Ltd. Athens.	OY-JAO
SX-AVA	80 PA-31T Cheyenne II	8020026	3D General Aviation Applications, Thessaloniki.	N155DS
SX-AVB	80 PA-31T Cheyenne II	8020027	3D Avionics, Thessaloniki.	(N248WW)
SX-AVC	80 PA-31T Cheyenne II	8020038	3D Avionics, Thessaloniki.	N300HP
SX-BGO	80 King Air C90	LJ-874	Life Line Aviation Ltd. Athens.	D-IFUN
SX-BGT	75 SA-226AT Merlin 4A	AT-038	Mediterranean Air Freight, Madrid, Spain.	EC-FUX
SX-BKY	93 King Air C90B	LJ-1334	Air Intersalonika, Thessalonika.	D-IIKY
SX-ECG	78 King Air 200	BB-372	Civil Aviation Authority, Athens.	N4937M
Military				
401	76 King Air C-12C	BC-34	Aeroporias Stratu-Army Aviation, Megara.	
402	00 King Air B200	BB-1733	Greek Army,	N3156L
403	00 King Air B200	BB-1744	Greek Army,	N3157F
AC-21	00 Reims/Cessna F406	F406-0087	Hellenic Coast Guard,	F-GJJK
AC-22	00 Reims/Cessna F406	F406-0088	Hellenic Coast Guard,	F-GJJN
AC-23	00 Reims/Cessna F406	F406-0089	Hellenic Coast Guard,	F-GJJO
AC-24	01 Reims/Cessna F406	...	Hellenic Coast Guard,	

S2 = BANGLADESH
Total   2

Civil

S2-AED	04 Pilatus PC-12/45	538	Lions Air AG. Dhaka.	HB-FPP

Reg	Yr Type	c/n	Owner/Operator	Prev Regn

☐ S3-BHN	84 PA-31T Cheyenne 1A	1104007	Government of Bangladesh, Dacca.	N2436W

S5 = SLOVENIA *Total 3*

Civil

☐ S5-CAE	80 Conquest II	441-0150	Smelt Air/GIO Business Aviation, Ljubljana.	SL-CAE
☐ S5-CEC	99 King Air B200	BB-1662	Eurocity doo, Ljubljana.	N3262P
☐ S5-CMO	94 King Air C90B	LJ-1360	Alfa Histria/Kondorair, Portoroz.	N1560U

S7 = SEYCHELLES *Total 3*

Civil

☐ S7-AAI	90 Reims/Cessna F406	F406-0051	Islands Development Co. Mahe.	(9V-...)
☐ S7-IDC	98 Beech 1900D	UE-212	Islands Development Co. Mahe.	N3217U
☐ S7-SMB	89 King Air B200	BB-1316	Seychelles Marketing Board, Mahe.	ZS-MFB

S9 = SAO TOME & PRINCIPE *Total 4*

Civil

☐ S9-BAA	98 King Air 350	FL-220	Golfo International Air Services SA/SAL Express. Sao Tome,	N3120X
☐ S9-CAM	97 King Air 350	FL-163	SONANGOL Aeronautica - Helipetrol, Luanda, Angola.	N1057Q
☐ S9-CAN	00 King Air 350	FL-294	SONAIR/Golfo International Air Services SA. Sao Tome.	N3214J
☐ S9-TAP	93 King Air 350	FL-102	SAL-Sociedade de Aviacao Ligeira SA. Luanda, Angola.	D2-ECW

TC = TURKEY *Total 18*

Civil

☐ TC-AUT	74 King Air C90	LJ-622	Anadolu University Air Taxi, Eskisehir.	N104TT
☐ TC-AUV	73 King Air C90	LJ-587	Anadolu University Air Taxi, Eskisehir.	N61KA
☐ TC-DBZ	77 King Air C90	LJ-703	Top Air, Istanbul.	(F-GKSR)
☐ TC-FAH	85 PA-42 Cheyenne IIIA	5501033	THK-Turk Hava Kurumu, Ankara.	
☐ TC-FIR	82 King Air B200	BB-1082	Firat Aviation, Istanbul.	(N807BC)
☐ TC-MSS	91 King Air C90A	LJ-1276	Emi Air, Istanbul.	N8065R
☐ TC-OPM	99 King Air B200	BB-1701	Ozel Aviation, Istanbul.	N4301Y
☐ TC-OZD	94 King Air B200	BB-1496	Ozek Air, Bursa.	N3047L
☐ TC-OZY	96 King Air B200	BB-1545	Metro Air, Istanbul.	N1070E
☐ TC-THK	85 PA-42 Cheyenne IIIA	5501031	THK-Turk Hava Kurumu, Ankara.	TC-FAG
☐ TC-UPS	75 SA-226AT Merlin 4A	AT-044	Uensped Paket Servisi, Istanbul. `Beril'	C-GGPT

Military

☐ 10010	91 King Air B200	BB-1409	Turkish Air Force,	
☐ 10011	91 King Air B200	BB-1411	Turkish Air Force,	
☐ 10012	91 King Air B200	BB-1413	Turkish Air Force,	
☐ 10013	91 King Air B200	BB-1414	Turkish Air Force,	
☐ 10014	91 King Air B200	BB-1415	Turkish Air Force,	
☐ 4005	92 King Air B200	BB-1434	Turkish Air Force,	N81148
☐ 4006	90 King Air B200	BB-1375	Turkish Air Force,	M-1375

TF = ICELAND *Total 4*

Civil

☐ TF-...	74 King Air E90	LW-116	Holdur HF. Reykyavik.	F-BVRS
☐ TF-FMS	85 King Air B200	BB-1221	Directorate of Civil Aviation, Reykyavik.	TF-UUU
☐ TF-ORD	91 Reims/Cessna F406	F406-0047	Eagle Air-Lysing hf/Ernir hf, Reykyavik.	D-IAAD
☐ TF-ORF	78 Conquest II	441-0057	Lysing Hf/Ernir Air Ehf, Reykjavik.	N441AK

TG = GUATEMALA *Total 18*

Civil

☐ TG-...	02 King Air B200	BB-1808	Beechcraft de Guatemala SA. Guatemala City.	N4488N
☐ TG-...	01 King Air B200	BB-1794		N4484F
☐ TG-BAQ	95 King Air C90B	LJ-1399	Credomatic de Guatemala SA. Guatemala City.	TG-BAC
☐ TG-CCA	94 King Air C90B	LJ-1364	Transportes Aereos de Terr CA. Guatemala City.	
☐ TG-CFA	82 King Air F90	LA-181	Guatemalan Air Force,	HK-2888P
☐ TG-COB	81 PA-31T Cheyenne II	8120003	COBIGUA, Guatemala City.	N57KW
☐ TG-CPG	King Air	...	noted Fort Lauderdale Executive 6/02.	
☐ TG-EAB	80 PA-31T Cheyenne II	8020045	Compania de Jarabes y Bebidas La Mariposo SA. Guatemala City	N75CA
☐ TG-GMI	70 681 Turbo Commander	6032	Multillantas SA. Guatemala City.	N75GM
☐ TG-HCR	80 PA-31T Cheyenne II	8020032	Hotel Caimo Real, Guatemala City.	N803SW
☐ TG-HYD	94 King Air B200	BB-1479	Aldan SA. Guatemala City.	N8155L
☐ TG-LIA	81 PA-31T Cheyenne II	8120043	Aldan SA. Guatemala City.	N40H
☐ TG-OIL	80 PA-31T Cheyenne II	8020003	FUMASA-Fumigadres Aereo SA. Guatemala City.	N985CA
☐ TG-SAQ	94 King Air C90B	LJ-1373	Manuel Antonio Sanchez, Guatemala City.	TG-RWC

Reg	Yr Type	c/n	Owner/Operator	Prev Regn

Reg	Yr Type	c/n	Owner/Operator	Prev Regn
☐ TG-VAL	81 PA-31T Cheyenne II	8120045	Valores Aereos SA. Guatemala City.	N2441Y
☐ TG-VAS	78 King Air C90	LJ-782	Industria Oliaginosa de Escuintla, Guatemala City.	
☐ TG-WIZ	70 681 Turbo Commander	6022	Richard Stader Cater, Guatemala City.	C-GBIT

Military

☐ TG-MDN-P	86 King Air 300	FA-105	FAG/Guatemala Air Force, Guatemala City.	TG-MDN

TI = COSTA RICA
Total 11

Civil

☐ TI-...	72 Rockwell 690	11022	Omori Naka, San Jose.	N98MR
☐ TI-...	00 King Air C90B	LJ-1627	Raytheon Aircraft Co. Wichita, Ks.	N5027V
☐ TI-....	97 King Air C90B	LJ-1468		N1134G
☐ TI-AWM	80 King Air F90	LA-76	Multiservicios del Sur SA. San Jose.	N781VC
☐ TI-AWN	75 PA-31T Cheyenne II	7520043	Carena de la Sur Ltda.	N29KL
☐ TI-AXM	Rockwell 690	...		
☐ TI-AXU	73 Rockwell 690A	11139		N7EV
☐ TI-GEV	78 King Air E90	LW-268	Aires de Pavas SA. Pavas.	N23681
☐ TI-MEL	81 Gulfstream 980	95056	Tecno Agricola SA. San Jose.	N980BM
☐ TI-SFC	75 King Air E90	LW-141		N382TW
☐ TI-TCT	75 King Air 200	BB-87	Teletica Canal 7 Television, San Jose.	N87GA

TJ = CAMEROON
Total 3

Civil

☐ TJ-AHZ	77 Conquest II	441-0001	SEBC, Douala. (stored Geneva since 10/01).	N983SM
☐ TJ-AIM	81 Cheyenne II-XL	8166061	Societe SFID, Douala.	N983GA
☐ TJ-MJP	79 King Air E90	LW-321	SFID-Ste Forestiere Ind de la Doume, Douala.	EI-BHL

TN = CONGO BRAZZAVILLE
Total 1

Civil

☐ TN-AFG	79 King Air E90	LW-326	Congolaise Industrielle des Bois, Brazzaville.	D-IHCE

TR = GABON
Total 3

Civil

☐ TR-LDM	85 King Air B200	BB-1220	COMILOG-Cie Miniere de l'Ogoue, Moanda.	N93GA
☐ TR-LEQ	86 Reims/Cessna F406	F406-0007	Cie Equatoriale des Bois/Air Service Gabon, Libreville.	LX-LMS

Military

☐ TR-KJD	95 ATR 42F-300	131	Government of Gabon, Libreville.	(TR-KGP)

TU = IVORY COAST
Total 3

Civil

☐ TU-TDM	59 Gulfstream 1	20	Air Inter Ivoire, Abidjan.	TJ-WIN
☐ TU-TJL	77 PA-31T Cheyenne II	7720033	Air Inter Ivoire, Abidjan.	N82152
☐ TU-TOG	76 SA-226AT Merlin 4A	AT-051	Air Continental, Abidjan. (was TC-226).	C-FJTC

TZ = MALI
Total 1

Civil

☐ TZ-ZBC	75 King Air/Catpass 250	BB-86	SAS-Sahel Aviation Service, Bamako.	5Y-NDY

UN = KAZAKHSTAN
Total 1

Civil

☐ UN-......	84 PA-31T Cheyenne 1A	1104010		(N234PC)

VH = AUSTRALIA
Total 169

Civil

☐ VH-AAG	73 Rockwell 690A	11101	General Aviation Maintenance P/L. Essendon, VIC.	N57101
☐ VH-AMR	02 King Air B200	BB-1812	RFDS/Ambulance Service of NSW, Sydney, NSW.	VH-MSB
☐ VH-AMS	02 King Air B200	BB-1814	RFDS/Ambulance Service of NSW, Sydney, NSW.	VH-MVW
☐ VH-ATF	74 Rockwell 690A	11158	Jalgrid P/L. Maroochydore, QLD.	N57158
☐ VH-AYC	97 King Air B200	BB-1575	A C Airways P/L-Air Center Albury, Albury, NSW.	N501P
☐ VH-AZW	77 Conquest II	441-0026	Network Aviation Australia, Perth, WA.	VH-FWA
☐ VH-BRF	85 King Air B200C	BL-125	Provo Air Center Ltd. Providenciales.	VH-AMM
☐ VH-BUW	81 PA-42 Cheyenne III	8001047	Specialised Container Transport, Melbourne, VIC.	VH-ISW
☐ VH-CBZ	81 King Air B200C	BL-38	Curtain Niugini Purchasing P/L. Townsville, QLD.	P2-CCB
☐ VH-CLT	74 Rockwell 690A	11152	Tasmanian Seafoods P/L. Smithton, Tasmania.	VH-NMT
☐ VH-CWE	79 King Air 200	BB-470	Australasian Jet P/L. Essendon, VIC.	VH-NIA
☐ VH-CWO	84 King Air B200C	BL-84	Royal Flying Doctor Service, Port Hedland, WA.	N43CE
☐ VH-DYN	80 King Air 200	BB-690	Sabstall P/L. Toowoomba, QLD.	VH-SKN
☐ VH-EEN	83 SA-227AT Merlin 4C	AT-563	Pel-Air Aviation P/L. Mascot, NSW.	N563UP
☐ VH-EEO	83 SA-227AT Merlin 4C	AT-564	Pel-Air Aviation P/L. Sydney, NSW.	N564UP

Reg	Yr Type	c/n	Owner/Operator	Prev Regn

Reg	Yr	Type	c/n	Owner/Operator	Prev Regn
☐ VH-EEP	83 SA-227AT Merlin 4C	AT-567	Pel-Air Aviation P/L. Mascot, NSW.	N565UP
☐ VH-FDA	82 King Air B200C	BL-55	Royal Flying Doctor Service, Townsville. 'RFDS Townsville'	VH-NSD
☐ VH-FDB	81 King Air 200C	BL-26	Royal Flying Doctor Service, Cairns, QLD. 'Alan Earnshaw'	VH-WLH
☐ VH-FDC	01 Pilatus PC-12/45	426	Royal Flying Doctor Service, Mount Isa, QLD. 'RFDS Mt Isa'	HB-F..
☐ VH-FDD	99 King Air B200	BB-1697	Royal Flying Doctor Service, Mount Isa, QLD. 'RFDS Mt Isa'	N40483
☐ VH-FDE	00 Pilatus PC-12/45	332	Royal Flying Doctor Service, Port Augusta, SA.	HB-F..
☐ VH-FDF	99 King Air B200	BB-1696	Royal Flying Doctor Service, Cairns, QLD. 'RFDS Cairns'	N40481
☐ VH-FDG	84 King Air B200	BB-1172	Royal Flying Doctor Service, Derby, WA. 'Alec McLaughlan'	G-OJGA
☐ VH-FDI	82 King Air B200	BB-1037	Royal Flying Doctor Service, Brisbane. 'RFDS Brisbane'	VH-DAX
☐ VH-FDK	02 Pilatus PC-12/45	466	Royal Flying Doctor Service, Adelaide, SA.	HB-FSZ
☐ VH-FDM	01 Pilatus PC-12/45	428	Royal Flying Doctor Service, Charleville. 'RFDS Charleville'	HB-F..
☐ VH-FDO	82 King Air B200	BB-1056	Royal Flying Doctor Service, Rockhampton. 'RFDS Rockhampton'	VH-RFX
☐ VH-FDP	01 Pilatus PC-12/45	434	Royal Flying Doctor Service, Cairns, QLD. 'RFDS Cairns'	HB-F..
☐ VH-FDR	04 King Air B200	BB-1881	Royal Flying Doctor Service, Brisbane, QLD.	N36801
☐ VH-FDS	83 King Air 200C	BL-68	Royal Flying Doctor Service, Bundaberg. 'Marjorie Loveday'	N83GA
☐ VH-FDT	79 King Air C90	LJ-842	Royal Flying Doctor Service, Derby. (status ?).	N6052F
☐ VH-FDW	04 King Air B200	BB-1880	Royal Flying Doctor Service, Brisbane, QLD.	N6180Q
☐ VH-FDZ	04 King Air B200	BB-1882	Royal Flying Doctor Service, Brisbane, QLD.	N37082
☐ VH-FGR	01 Pilatus PC-12/45	438	Royal Flying Doctor Service, Adelaide-West Beach, SA.	HB-FRW
☐ VH-FGS	01 Pilatus PC-12/45	440	Royal Flying Doctor Service, Adelaide-West Beach, SA.	HB-FRX
☐ VH-FGT	01 Pilatus PC-12/45	442	Royal Flying Doctor Service, Adelaide-West Beach, SA.	HB-FRY
☐ VH-FII	80 King Air 200	BB-653	Pearl Aviation/Air Services Australia P/L. Brisbane, QLD.	VH-MXK
☐ VH-FIX	93 King Air 350	FL-90	Pearl Aviation/Air Services Australia P/L. Brisbane, QLD.	D-CKRA
☐ VH-FMC	95 Pilatus PC-12	109	Royal Flying Doctor Service, Port Augusta, SA.	
☐ VH-FMF	95 Pilatus PC-12	110	Royal Flying Doctor Service, Port Augusta, SA.	
☐ VH-FMP	95 Pilatus PC-12	122	Royal Flying Doctor Service, Alice Springs, NT.	HB-FQ.
☐ VH-FMQ	79 Conquest II	441-0109	Skippers Aviation P/L. Perth, WA.	(N26226)
☐ VH-FMW	95 Pilatus PC-12	123	Royal Flying Doctor Service, Alice Springs, NT.	HB-FQ.
☐ VH-FMZ	96 Pilatus PC-12	138	Royal Flying Doctor Service, Alice Springs, NT.	HB-F..
☐ VH-HLJ	82 King Air/Catpass 250	BB-945	Trailfinders P/L-Hinterland Aviation P/L. Cairns, QLD.	RP-C1577
☐ VH-HMZ	77 Conquest II	441-0017	Scotts Agencies P/L. Mount Gambier, SA.	N500UW
☐ VH-HWO	99 King Air B200	BB-1641	Royal Flying Doctor Service, Perth-Jandakot, WA.	N23355
☐ VH-ICA	02 TBM 700C	205	Austcom P/L. Melbourne, VIC.	N778C
☐ VH-ITA	79 King Air 200T	BT-6	AeroRescue P/L. Darwin, NT. (was BB-489.)	JA8811
☐ VH-ITH	78 King Air 200	BB-344	Interair P/L. Essendon, VIC.	N6297S
☐ VH-IWO	98 King Air B200	BB-1639	Royal Flying Doctor Service, Kalgoorlie, WA.	N23352
☐ VH-JES	70 Mitsubishi MU-2G	516	Interair P/L. Essendon, VIC.	VH-AUI
☐ VH-JET	96 King Air C90B	LJ-1464	Leppington Pastoral Co P/L. Camden, NSW.	N2040E
☐ VH-JJR	82 King Air B200	BB-1019	Robert Woolf, Bankstown, NSW.	VH-ARZ
☐ VH-JLK	96 Pilatus PC-12	126	Acestar Holdings P/L. Perth, WA.	Z-KEN
☐ VH-JMU	02 Pilatus PC-12/45	445	Jeffrey McCloy, Gateshead, NSW.	HB-FPN
☐ VH-JVN	89 Reims/Cessna F406	F406-0033	Air Charter Australia P/L. Adelaide, SA.	VH-RCB
☐ VH-KCH	83 King Air B200	BB-1125	Airflite P/L. Jandakot, WA.	A32-001
☐ VH-KFG	78 King Air C90	LJ-777	Karratha Flying Services P/L. Karratha, WA.	N9AN
☐ VH-KFN	81 King Air 200C	BL-31	Royal Flying Doctor Service, Port Hedland, WA. 'John Uhrig'	N200LG
☐ VH-KFT	93 TBM 700	92	Melbourne Air Holdings P/L. Essendon, VIC.	F-OHBP
☐ VH-KJD	98 King Air 350	FL-194	Driscoll Investments P/L-Executive Air, Brisbane, QLD.	N2314S
☐ VH-KOH	70 Mitsubishi MU-2G	521	William Funnell, Taupo, New Zealand.	VH-WYY
☐ VH-KUZ	80 Conquest II	441-0138	Anindilyakwa Air P/L. Darwin, NT.	N311RR
☐ VH-KWO	01 Pilatus PC-12/45	363	Royal Flying Doctor Service, Perth-Jandakot, WA.	
☐ VH-LAB	82 King Air B200T	BT-23	Flinders University/NSW Rural Fire Service, Bankstown, NSW.	N312D
☐ VH-LBA	78 Conquest II	441-0042	Skippers Aviation P/L. Perth, WA.	N46MR
☐ VH-LBC	82 Conquest II	441-0236	Skippers Aviation P/L. Perth, WA.	VH-TFG
☐ VH-LBD	83 Conquest II	441-0296	Aero Australia P/L. Gisborne, VIC.	N6838K
☐ VH-LBX	78 Conquest II	441-0091	Skippers Aviation P/L. Perth, WA.	VH-AZY
☐ VH-LBY	77 Conquest II	441-0023	Skippers Aviation P/L. Perth, WA.	VH-TFW
☐ VH-LBZ	77 Conquest II	441-0038	Skippers Aviation P/L. Perth, WA.	VH-HWD
☐ VH-LEM	79 Conquest II	441-0081	Fugro Spatial Soulutions P/L. Perth, WA.	N4490C
☐ VH-LKB	77 King Air 200	BB-259	Australasian Jet P/L. Essendon, VIC.	VH-APA
☐ VH-LKF	80 King Air 200	BB-660	Pearl Aviation Australia P/L. Darwin, NT.	N200TK
☐ VH-LWO	99 King Air B200	BB-1643	Royal Flying Doctor Service, Perth-Jandakot, WA.	N23356
☐ VH-LYG	82 King Air C90-1	LJ-1020	Michael Heine, Melbourne, VIC.	VH-LJG
☐ VH-MSH	01 King Air B200	BB-1787	RFDS/Ambulance Service of NSW, Sydney, NSW.	N44857
☐ VH-MSM	93 King Air B200	BB-1464	RFDS/Tasmania Ambulance Service, Launceston, Tasmania.	N133LC
☐ VH-MSU	82 King Air 200C	BL-48	Royal Flying Doctor Service, Launceston. 'Philip H Bushell'	N1860B

Reg	Yr	Type	c/n	Owner/Operator	Prev Regn
☐ VH-MSZ	81 King Air B200		BB-866	Royal Flying Doctor Service, Broken Hill, NSW. 'Fred Mckay'	ZK-PBG
☐ VH-MVJ	03 King Air B200		BB-1842	RFDS/Air Ambulance Service of NSW, Sydney, NSW.	N50152
☐ VH-MVL	89 King Air B200		BB-1333	Royal Flying Doctor Service, Broken Hill, NSW.	N1101W
☐ VH-MVS	02 King Air B200		BB-1813	RFDS/Ambulance Service of NSW, Sydney, NSW.	N61913
☐ VH-MVY	89 King Air B200		BB-1324	Royal Flying Doctor Service, Dubbo. 'Flying Doctor Society'	N7087N
☐ VH-MWO	01 Pilatus PC-12/45		379	Royal Flying Doctor Service, Meekatharra, WA.	HB-F..
☐ VH-MWQ	91 King Air B200		BB-1416	RFDS/Air Ambulance Victoria, Essendon, VIC.	VH-MSH
☐ VH-MWU	92 King Air B200		BB-1418	RFDS/Air Ambulance Victoria, Essendon, VIC.	N131GA
☐ VH-MWX	92 King Air B200		BB-1424	RFDS/Air Ambulance Victoria, Essendon, VIC.	N8236K
☐ VH-MWZ	92 King Air B200		BB-1430	RFDS/Air Ambulance Victoria, Essendon, VIC.	VH-MSM
☐ VH-MYO	94 King Air B200		BB-1472	Airking P/L. Bankstown, NSW.	
☐ VH-NAX	79 Conquest II		441-0106	Network Aviation Australia, Perth, WA.	(N441AF)
☐ VH-NBT	71 681B Turbo Commander		6047	General Aviation Maintenance P/L. Essendon, VIC.	(VH-UJN)
☐ VH-NMA	81 PA-42 Cheyenne III		8001066	Australasian Jet P/L. Essendon, VIC.	(N142AF)
☐ VH-NSN	96 King Air B200		BB-1552	Sundown Pastoral P/L. Broadbeach Waters, QLD.	ZS-NZN
☐ VH-NTE	79 King Air 200		BB-529	Pearl Aviation/NT Aerial Medical Service, Darwin, NT.	VH-SWP
☐ VH-NTG	80 King Air 200C		BL-9	Pearl Aviation/NT Aerial Medical Service, Darwin, NT.	VH-KZL
☐ VH-NTH	80 King Air 200C		BL-12	Pearl Aviation/NT Aerial Medical Service, Darwin, NT.	VH-SWO
☐ VH-NTS	81 King Air 200C		BL-30	Pearl Aviation/NT Aerial Medical Service, Darwin, NT.	VH-TNQ
☐ VH-NWO	01 Pilatus PC-12/45		396	Royal Flying Doctor Service, Meekatharra, WA.	HB-FQQ
☐ VH-NYC	72 Rockwell 690		11026	General Aviation Maintenance P/L. Essendon, VIC.	N9226N
☐ VH-OAA	79 Conquest II		441-0102	O'Connor's Air Services P/L. Mount Gambier, SA.	N4246Z
☐ VH-OCS	77 Conquest II		441-0030	Air Charter Australia P/L. Adelaide, SA.	N441MM
☐ VH-OPM	79 Conquest II		441-0088	Warrnambool Bus & Motor Co P/L. Warrnambool, VIC.	VH-EVP
☐ VH-OWN	81 King Air B200		BB-936	Hawker Pacific P/L. Milperra, NSW.	N200NS
☐ VH-OXF	02 King Air 350		FL-361	Gambamara Industries P/L-Five Star Aviation P/L. Coolangatta	VH-KDX
☐ VH-OYA	78 King Air 200		BB-365	Pearl Aviation/RAAF ARDU, Edinburgh, SA.	P2-SML
☐ VH-OYD	82 King Air B200		BB-1041	Pearl Aviation Australia P/L. Darwin, NT.	N200BK
☐ VH-OYE	78 King Air 200		BB-355	Pearl Aviation Australia P/L. Darwin, NT.	VH-SMB
☐ VH-OYH	76 King Air 200		BB-148	Pearl Aviation Australia P/L. Darwin, NT.	VH-WNH
☐ VH-OYK	81 King Air 200C		BL-41	Pearl Aviation Australia P/L. Darwin, NT.	VH-HEO
☐ VH-PCE	04 Pilatus PC-12/45		551	Pilatus Australia P/L. Canberra, ACT.	HB-...
☐ VH-PCV	76 Rockwell 690A		11283	Asia-Pacific Airlines/Commander Land & Air Invs. Sydney.	N57228
☐ VH-PFK	00 King Air C90B		LJ-1586	ST Aerospace Engineers P/L. Singapore.	N15GZ
☐ VH-PIL	98 Pilatus PC-12/45		231	Pegasus Air P/L. Sydney, NSW.	HB-FRB
☐ VH-PSK	90 King Air 350		FL-29	Queensland Police Service, Brisbane, QLD.	ZS-NAV
☐ VH-RCI	83 SA-227TT Merlin 3C		TT-474	Hurlad P/L-Rich Air, Melbourne, VIC.	N75SC
☐ VH-SAM	75 King Air C90		LJ-655	Rotor-Lift P/L. Hobart, Tasmania.	VH-NQH
☐ VH-SBM	82 King Air B200		BB-964	Barminco Ltd. Perth, WA.	VH-HTU
☐ VH-SGQ	96 King Air 350		FL-150	Queensland Government Air Wing, Brisbane, QLD.	N10691
☐ VH-SGT	75 King Air 200		BB-73	Network Aviation Australia, Perth, WA.	
☐ VH-SGV	80 King Air 200		BB-718	Great Western Aviation P/L. Hamilton, QLD.	N6728N
☐ VH-SKU	76 King Air 200		BB-165	D J & S J Barnard P/L-Skytrans, Cairns, QLD.	VH-XRF
☐ VH-SMO	80 Conquest II		441-0132	Maroomba Airlines, Perth, WA.	VH-ANJ
☐ VH-SMT	76 King Air 200		BB-162	Maroomba Airlines, Perth, WA.	RP-C22
☐ VH-SMZ	94 King Air B200		BB-1490	Maroomba Airlines, Perth, WA.	(N769WT)
☐ VH-SQH	77 King Air C90		LJ-730	Aviation Australia P/L. Eagle Farm, QLD.	N730WB
☐ VH-SSD	71 SA-226T Merlin 3		T-213	Winrye Aviation P/L. (stored Bankstown).	N174SP
☐ VH-SSL	71 SA-226T Merlin 3		T-210	Aviation Centre P/L. Bankstown, NSW.	N173SP
☐ VH-SSM	70 SA-226T Merlin 3		T-204	Winrye Aviation P/L. Sydney-Bankstown, NSW.	VH-EGC
☐ VH-TAZ	77 Conquest II		441-0005	Tasair P/L. Hobart, Tasmania.	N441RZ
☐ VH-TFB	82 Conquest II		441-0260	John Lewis, Beverly Hills, NSW.	N68597
☐ VH-TLX	79 King Air 200		BB-550	Pearl Aviation Australia P/L. Darwin, NT.	P2-MBM
☐ VH-TPM	01 PA-46-500TP Meridian		4697089	SGE International P/L. Ringwood, VIC.	
☐ VH-TSS	78 Rockwell 690B		11463	General Aviation Maintenance P/L. Essendon, VIC.	N101RG
☐ VH-UJG	73 Rockwell 690		11062	General Aviation Maintenance P/L. Essendon, VIC.	VH-NEY
☐ VH-URU	83 King Air B200		BB-1150	Heathgate Resources P/L. Adalaide, SA.	N103BG
☐ VH-UZA	82 SA-227AT Merlin 4C		AT-502	Jetcraft Aviation P/L. Brisbane, QLD.	VH-UUA
☐ VH-UZI	83 SA-227AT Merlin 4C		AT-570	Jetcraft Aviation P/L. Brisbane, QLD.	N570UP
☐ VH-VED	83 Conquest II		441-0272	Vee H Aviation P/L. Canberra, ACT.	N394G
☐ VH-VEM	80 Conquest II		441-0174	Vee H Aviation P/L-Corporate Air/Andrew Major, Canberra, ACT	VH-IJQ
☐ VH-VEZ	80 Conquest II		441-0182	Vee H Aviation P/L-Corporate Air, Canberra, ACT.	VH-AZB
☐ VH-VWO	01 Pilatus PC-12/45		400	Royal Flying Doctor Service, Kalgoorlie, WA.	HB-FQR
☐ VH-WCE	81 PA-42 Cheyenne III		8001033	Australasian Jet P/L. Essendon, VIC.	N582SW
☐ VH-WHP	04 King Air 350		FL-389	Hawker Pacific P/L. Milperra, NSW.	N6089N

Reg	Yr Type	c/n	Owner/Operator	Prev Regn
☐ VH-XDB	79 King Air 200	BB-533	Network Aviation Australia, Perth, WA.	N87RK
☐ VH-XMD	77 Conquest II	441-0025	Ross Aviation P/L-Rossair Charter, Adelaide, SA.	N441HD
☐ VH-XMG	79 Conquest II	441-0130	Central Air Services P/L. Cootamundra, NSW.	VH-KDN
☐ VH-XMJ	80 Conquest II	441-0113	Ross Aviation P/L-Rossair Charter, Adelaide, SA.	N990AR
☐ VH-YDN	00 Pilatus PC-12/45	301	Northern Territory Police Air Wing, Darwin, NT.	HB-F..
☐ VH-YDO	95 Pilatus PC-12	102	Northern Territory Police Air Wing, Darwin. (was s/n P-04).	VH-NGC
☐ VH-YFD	80 Conquest II	441-0157	Peter Campbell, Paradise Point, QLD.	(ZS-SMA)
☐ VH-ZEK	82 King Air B200	BB-1083	Silver Linings Aviation P/L. Sydney, NSW.	N969
☐ VH-ZGQ	93 King Air C90B	LJ-1345	West Wing Aviation P/L. Mount Isa, QLD.	VH-ZGO
☐ VH-ZOS	76 King Air 200	BB-145	Pagan Air Services P/L. Melbourne, VIC.	N88CP
☐ VH-ZWO	02 Pilatus PC-12/45	467	Royal Flying Doctor Service, Perth-Jandakot, WA.	HB-FQM
☐ VH-ZZE	95 Reims/Cessna F406	F406-0076	Surveillance Australia P/L. Cairns, QLD.	F-WZDX
☐ VH-ZZF	95 Reims/Cessna F406	F406-0078	Surveillance Australia P/L. Broome, WA.	VH-BPH
☐ VH-ZZG	96 Reims/Cessna F406	F406-0079	Surveillance Australia P/L. Darwin, NT.	F-WZDZ
Military				
☐ A32-339	01 King Air 350	FL-339	RAAF, 32 Sqn. East Sale, VIC.	VH-DHP
☐ A32-343	02 King Air 350	FL-343	RAAF, 32 Sqn. East Sale, VIC.	VH-JIIP
☐ A32-346	02 King Air 350	FL-346	RAAF, 32 Sqn. East Sale, VIC.	VH-UHP
☐ A32-348	02 King Air 350	FL-348	RAAF, 32 Sqn. East Sale, VIC.	VH-VHP
☐ A32-349	02 King Air 350	FL-349	RAAF, 32 Sqn. East Sale, VIC.	VH-WHP
☐ A32-350	02 King Air 350	FL-350	RAAF, 32 Sqn. East Sale, VIC.	VH-XHP
☐ A32-351	02 King Air 350	FL-351	RAAF, 32 Sqn. East Sale, VIC.	VH-YHP
☐ VH-HPP	90 King Air B200C	BL-137	Australian Army, 173 Squadron, Oakey, QLD.	ZS-NSD
☐ VH-HPX	95 King Air B200	BB-1505	Australian Army, 173 Squadron, Oakey, QLD.	N3197L
☐ VH-HPZ	92 King Air B200C	BL-138	Australian Army, 173 Squadron, Oakey, QLD.	VH-AJM

VN = VIETNAM
Total 1

Civil

☐ VN-B594	89 King Air B200	BB-1329	VASCO-Vietnam Air Services Co.	VH-SWC

VP-B = BERMUDA
Total 9

Civil

☐ VP-BBB	01 Pilatus PC-12/45	407	Flying VP-BBB Ltd.	
☐ VP-BCT	85 Gulfstream 1000	96208		N695BE
☐ VP-BJT	81 Conquest 1	425-0027	Rig Design Services Group Ltd. Booker, UK.	VP-BNM
☐ VP-BKD	01 Pilatus PC-12/45	369		N94PP
☐ VP-BKW	79 King Air C90	LJ-805	David J Sewell, Ibadan, Nigeria.	VR-BKW
☐ VP-BLS	97 Pilatus PC-12	176	Bruno Schroder, Fairoaks, UK.	(N176BS)
☐ VP-BMK	89 King Air 300	FA-202	Mike-Fly Ltd. Triengen.	HB-GIP
☐ VP-BMZ	84 Gulfstream 900	15033	Aviatica Trading Co/Marlborough Fine Arts Ltd. Fairoaks, UK.	VR-BMZ
☐ VP-BYR	85 King Air B200	BB-1202	IAL Leasing Ltd. Hamilton.	G-REBK

VP-C = CAYMAN ISLANDS
Total 2

Civil

☐ VP-CAY	82 Gulfstream 900	15011		VR-CAY
☐ VP-CLA	85 King Air F90-1	LA-231	Claessens International Ltd. Farnborough, UK.	N27PA

VQ-T = TURKS & CAICOS ISLANDS
Total 2

Civil

☐ VQ-T..	89 King Air B200C	BL-131	Air Turks & Caicos (2003) Ltd. Providenciales.	VH-AMB
☐ VQ-T..	90 King Air B200C	BL-133	Air Turks & Caicos (2003) Ltd. Providenciales.	VH-BRQ

VT = INDIA
Total 59

Civil

☐ VT-...	01 King Air B200	BB-1788		N314FH
☐ VT-AJV	87 King Air C90A	LJ-1159	Orient Flying School, Chennai.	N425SV
☐ VT-ASB	88 Reims/Cessna F406	F406-0031	Century Textiles & Industries Ltd. Mumbai.	D-IBOM
☐ VT-BAL	97 King Air B200	BB-1563	Bajaj Auto Ltd. Delhi.	N204JT
☐ VT-BHL	94 King Air 350	FL-105	Bharat Hotels Ltd. Srinigar.	VT-MNM
☐ VT-BSA	94 King Air B200	BB-1485	Border Security Force, Delhi.	N1509X
☐ VT-CIL	93 King Air B200	BB-1469	Coal India Ltd.	N82378
☐ VT-DAR	99 Pilatus PC-12/45	251	Deccan Aviation P/L. Jakkur-Bangalore.	ZS-SRL
☐ VT-DAV	99 Pilatus PC-12/45	252	Deccan Aviation P/L. Jakkur-Bangalore.	ZS-SRM
☐ VT-DEJ	95 King Air C90B	LJ-1404	Lakshmi Machine Works Ltd. Coimbatore.	N3106P
☐ VT-EBB	94 King Air B200	BB-1486	National Remote Sensing Agency, Hyderabad.	N1542Z
☐ VT-EFB	77 King Air C90	LJ-706	India Metals & Ferro Alloys Ltd. Orissa.	N23856
☐ VT-EFG	77 King Air C90	LJ-719	Government of Bihar, Patna.	N23917

Reg	Yr Type	c/n	Owner/Operator	Prev Regn

Reg	Yr Type	c/n	Owner/Operator	Prev Regn
☐ VT-EGR	81 King Air C90	LJ-967	Government of Maharashtra, Bombay-Juhu.	N3832X
☐ VT-EHB	82 King Air B200	BB-972	Government of Orissa, Cuttack.	N18409
☐ VT-EHY	82 King Air C90	LJ-1008	Government of Punjab, Chandigarh.	N1842A
☐ VT-EID	82 King Air B200C	BL-56	Government of Madhya Pradesh, Bhopal.	N1844C
☐ VT-EJZ	85 King Air C90A	LJ-1100	Government of Haryana, Ambala.	N7219K
☐ VT-EMI	86 King Air C90A	LJ-1135	Indira Gandhi Rashtriya Uran Academy,	N2602M
☐ VT-EMJ	86 King Air C90A	LJ-1137	Indira Gandhi Rashtriya Uran Academy,	N6690N
☐ VT-ENL	86 King Air B200	BB-1248	Aviation Research Centre, Cuttack, Orissa.	N7256G
☐ VT-ENM	85 King Air B200	BB-1236	Aviation Research Centre, Cuttack, Orissa.	N72473
☐ VT-EPA	86 King Air B200	BB-1254	Aviation Research Centre, Cuttack, Orissa.	N2646K
☐ VT-EPY	87 King Air B200	BB-1277	Government of Maharashtra, Bombay-Juhu.	N7241L
☐ VT-EQK	88 King Air B200	BB-1288	National Remote Sensing Agency, Hyderabad.	N30850
☐ VT-EQN	88 King Air C90A	LJ-1167	Government of Rajasthan, Jaipur.	N31174
☐ VT-EQO	87 King Air C90A	LJ-1153	Government of Uttaranchal, Dehradoon.	N70491
☐ VT-GUJ	99 King Air B200	BB-1687	Gujarat Agro-Industries Ltd. Ahmebad.	N3117V
☐ VT-HYA	94 King Air C90B	LJ-1376	Government of Haryana, Nissar.	N15542
☐ VT-JIL	99 King Air C90B	LJ-1573	Jaypee Ventures Ltd. Delhi.	N3203L
☐ VT-JNK	97 King Air 350	FL-160	Government of Jammu & Kashmir.	N1100A
☐ VT-JPK	91 King Air C90A	LJ-1278	Aerial Services P/L. Juhu.	N851GA
☐ VT-JRD	97 King Air C90B	LJ-1485	Tata Iron & Steel Co. Jamshedpur.	N886AT
☐ VT-JVL	02 King Air B200	BB-1815	Jay Pee Ventures Ltd. New Delhi.	N5015M
☐ VT-KDA	00 Beech 1900D	UE-284	Reliance Travel & Transport Ltd. Mumbai.	N1129B
☐ VT-LNT	93 King Air B200	BB-1468	Larsen & Toubro Ltd. Mumbai.	N8230E
☐ VT-MGJ	98 King Air 350	FL-192	Government of Maharashtra, Mumbai.	N2192V
☐ VT-MPG	93 King Air B200	BB-1445	Government of Chattisgarh, Raipur.	N8121M
☐ VT-MPT	01 King Air B200	BB-1775	Government of Madhya Pradesh, Bhopal.	N5075E
☐ VT-NEI	85 King Air C90A	LJ-1116	National Energy Processing Co/NEPC Airlines, Madras.	N25AE
☐ VT-NKF	95 King Air C90B	LJ-1402	Bajaj Tempo Ltd. Akurdi.	N3234K
☐ VT-PPC	94 King Air C90B	LJ-1371	Finolex Cables Ltd. Pune.	N696WW
☐ VT-RAM	78 King Air C90	LJ-790	Lake Palace Hotels & Motels Ltd. Udaipur.	VT-EFZ
☐ VT-RLL	94 King Air C90B	LJ-1369	Vidyut Travel Services Ltd. Delhi.	N3222K
☐ VT-RSB	89 King Air B200	BB-1317	Hiadalco Industries Ltd/Birla Co. Mumbai.	N591EB
☐ VT-SAZ	03 King Air B200	BB-1831	Steel Authority of India, Delhi.	N61831
☐ VT-SDJ	97 King Air B200	BB-1567	Sundaram Fiance Ltd/Jinda Steel & Power Ltd. New Delhi.	VT-CSK
☐ VT-SFL	97 King Air C90B	LJ-1496	TVS/Sundram Fasteners Ltd. Chennai.	N101SQ
☐ VT-SLK	91 King Air C90A	LJ-1270	Kirloskar Oil Engines Ltd. Pune.	N324AB
☐ VT-SRC	93 King Air B200C	BL-139	SRC Aviation Pte Ltd.	N65LW
☐ VT-TAS	02 Pilatus PC-12/45	472	Tata Iron & Steel Co. Jamshedpur.	HB-FQO
☐ VT-TIS	95 King Air C90B	LJ-1393	Tata Iron & Steel Co. Jamshedpur.	N3217M
☐ VT-TVS	97 King Air B200	BB-1572	TVS Motor Co. Chennai.	N149SR
☐ VT-UBA	77 King Air C90	LJ-711	McDowell & Co. Bangalore.	VT-EFE
☐ VT-UPA	94 King Air 300LW	FA-230	Government of Uttar Pradesh, Lucknow.	N80679
☐ VT-UPG	03 King Air B200	BB-1818	Government of Uttar Pradesh, Lucknow.	N5018F
☐ VT-UPZ	95 King Air C90B	LJ-1400	Government of Uttar Pradesh, Lucknow.	N3239K
☐ VT-VHL	87 King Air B200	BB-1267	Venkateshwara Hatcheries Group, Pun, Maharashtra.	N67GA
☐ VT-VIL	94 King Air C90B	LJ-1374	Videcon India Ltd.	N15116

V3 = BELIZE   Total   1

Military

☐ BDF-06	67 King Air A90	LJ-270	Belize Defence Force,	YV-....

V5 = NAMIBIA   Total   10

Civil

☐ V5-CCH	78 PA-31T Cheyenne II	7820085	Steel Construction/Corporate Charters CC. Windhoek.	N12HF
☐ V5-DHL	91 Reims/Cessna F406	F406-0062	DHL/Westair Wings Charters P/L. Windhoek.	N744C
☐ V5-EEZ	85 Reims/Cessna F406	F406-0004	Government of Namibia, Windhoek.	F-WIVD
☐ V5-LYZ	81 Conquest 1	425-0021	Eerste Nas Ontwkoop of South West Africa,	ZS-LYZ
☐ V5-MAC	79 Rockwell 690B	11557	Desert Air,	N75WA
☐ V5-MAD	86 Reims/Cessna F406	F406-0013	Westair Wings Charters P/L. Windhoek.	ZS-MAD
☐ V5-MDA	90 Reims/Cessna F406	F406-0058	Westair Wings Charters P/L. Windhoek.	ZS-OXE
☐ V5-MGF	78 Rockwell 690A	11432	Ango Wings, Windhoek.	ZS-JRC
☐ V5-MJW	81 Conquest 1	425-0077	Eros Air P/L. Windhoek.	ZS-MJW
☐ V5-WAK	91 Reims/Cessna F406	F406-0048	DHL/Westair Wings Charters P/L. Windhoek.	G-FLYN

Civil

Reg	Yr	Type	c/n	Owner/Operator	Prev Regn
☐ XA-...	65	Gulfstream 1	161		N925GC
☐ XA-...	77	PA-31T Cheyenne II	7720055		N2157A
☐ XA-...	00	King Air C90B	LJ-1624	Aerolineas Ejecutivas SA. Toluca.	N4324K
☐ XA-...	97	King Air C90B	LJ-1499	Marcelo de Los Santos Y Cia. San Luis Potosi.	N862CC
☐ XA-...	02	King Air B200	BB-1803	Aerolineas Ejecutivas SA. Toluca.	N5093G
☐ XA-...	02	King Air 350	FL-341		N4471J
☐ XA-...	01	Pilatus PC-12/45	405		N405PB
☐ XA-...	98	King Air C90B	LJ-1533		N628VK
☐ XA-...	67	King Air A90	LJ-200		N243D
☐ XA-...	76	King Air 200	BB-114		N25KW
☐ XA-...	84	PA-42 Cheyenne III	5501008		N777YP
☐ XA-...	99	King Air 350	FL-271		(N788MB)
☐ XA-...	04	King Air B200	BB-1859	Aerolineas Ejecutivas SA. Toluca.	N61592
☐ XA-...	67	King Air A90	LJ-287	Ruben Sanchez Martinez, Mig Hidalgo.	N502W
☐ XA-...	02	Pilatus PC-12/45	461		N461PC
☐ XA-...	99	King Air B200	BB-1661		N2361C
☐ XA-...	99	King Air B200	BB-1681		N2301K
☐ XA-...	8?	King Air F90	LA-168		N43LA
☐ XA-...	00	Pilatus PC-12/45	333		N333PA
☐ XA-...	01	King Air B200	BB-1752	Aerolineas Ejecutivas SA. Toluca.	N5152G
☐ XA-...	03	Pilatus PC-12/45	493		N493PB
☐ XA-...	78	Rockwell 690B	11503		N222EA
☐ XA-...	96	Pilatus PC-12	143		N6DQ
☐ XA-...	03	Pilatus PC-12/45	512		N512PB
☐ XA-...	03	Pilatus PC-12/45	504		N504PB
☐ XA-...	73	King Air A100	B-158		N62NC
☐ XA-...	79	King Air 200	BB-610		N200VJ
☐ XA-...	73	King Air C90	LJ-584	Ecoturistica de Xcalak SA. Chetumal, Quintana Roo.	N73LK
☐ XA-...	81	King Air F90	LA-147		N722DR
☐ XA-...	81	Cheyenne II-XL	8166025	Aviasur del Caribe,	N53WA
☐ XA-...	79	PA-31T Cheyenne II	7920041	Mexhaga SA. Saltillo.	N66WJ
☐ XA-...	77	King Air 200	BB-225		N917BT
☐ XA-...	76	PA-31T Cheyenne II	7620049		N37RL
☐ XA-...	85	Gulfstream 1000	96075		N6151W
☐ XA-...	74	Rockwell 690A	11145		N102JK
☐ XA-...	77	SA-226T Merlin 3A	T-282		N956DS
☐ XA-...	03	King Air B200	BB-1838	Aerolineas Ejecutivas SA. Toluca.	N5138Q
☐ XA-...	68	King Air B90	LJ-399		N551AT
☐ XA-...	69	SA-26AT Merlin 2B	T26-158		M4260X
☐ XA-...	74	Rockwell 690A	11185		N690JB
☐ XA-...	72	King Air C90	LJ-548		N800PW
☐ XA-...	78	PA-31T Cheyenne II	7820032		N700PT
☐ XA-ABH	78	Rockwell 690B	11454	Aerotaxi Paba SA. Culiacan, Sinaloa.	N81737
☐ XA-ALT	89	King Air 300	FA-176	Aerovics SA. Toluca.	N1570H
☐ XA-ASR	78	King Air 200	BB-395	Tomas Gonzales Sada y Pablo GL. Garza Garcia, NL.	XB-BRD
☐ XA-CAB	04	King Air B200	...	noted Houston 5/04.	
☐ XA-CHM	85	Gulfstream 900	15040	Chilchota Taxi Aereo SA. Coahuila. (status ?).	N4NT
☐ XA-DER	73	Rockwell 690	11060	Aerotaxis del Itsmo SA. Cuernavaca, Morelos.	N.....
☐ XA-EGE		King Air C90B	...	noted 5/01.	
☐ XA-FCV	99	King Air 350	FL-251	Aerolineas Ejecutivas SA. Toluca.	N3151H
☐ XA-GEC	82	King Air B200	BB-1086	Servicios Estatales Aeroportuarios, Guadalupe.	N200JM
☐ XA-GEM	75	Rockwell 690A	11267	Transportes Aereos Virva SA. Mexico City.	N57035
☐ XA-GSA	99	King Air C90B	LJ-1551	Aerolineas Ejecutivas SA. Toluca.	N3111K
☐ XA-JAG	00	King Air C90B	LJ-1623	Aerolineas Ejecutivas SA. Toluca.	N5023T
☐ XA-KUU	72	Rockwell 690	11042	Commander Mexicana SA. Mexico City.	XC-FUJ
☐ XA-LEK	81	Gulfstream 980	95042	Aerotux SA.	N9794S
☐ XA-LGT	80	King Air F90	LA-45	Aero Rentas de Coahuila SA. Coahuila.	N748GM
☐ XA-MYR	61	Gulfstream 1	71		F-GFIB
☐ XA-NTC	77	Rockwell 690B	11370	Aerotaxi del Cabo SA.	XB-NTC
☐ XA-PGT	76	PA-31T Cheyenne II	7620034	Aereo Rentas de Coahuila SA. Saltillo.	N7276C
☐ XA-PUY	72	Rockwell 690	11018	Aerovallarta SA. Quetzalcoatl.	N63PG
☐ XA-RCG	00	King Air 350	FL-277	Aerolineas Ejecutivas SA. Toluca.	N4477Q

Reg	Yr Type	c/n	Owner/Operator	Prev Regn

Reg	Yr	Type	c/n	Owner/Operator	Prev Regn
☐ XA-RFN	90	King Air C90A	LJ-1246	Aerotransportes Rafilher SA. San Luis Potosi.	
☐ XA-RJB	65	Gulfstream 1	159	Aerolineas Damojh SA. Guadalajara.	G-BNKN
☐ XA-RLK	64	Gulfstream 1	138	Aero Guadalajara SA/Aerolineas Damojh SA. Guadalajara.	N126K
☐ XA-RMX	81	King Air 200	BB-814	Aerogisa SA. Saltillo.	N6VW
☐ XA-RNL	80	MU-2 Marquise	777SA	Servicios Aereos Interestatales SA. Del Norte, NL.	XB-DJX
☐ XA-RWR	79	PA-31T Cheyenne II	7920047	Aerolineas Comerciales SA. Michoacan.	N79CA
☐ XA-RXT	91	King Air C90A	LJ-1280	Aereo Servicios Saltillo SA. Saltillo.	
☐ XA-SAW	81	King Air F90	LA-95	Aero Quimmco SA. Monterrey.	XB-CGP
☐ XA-SFD	79	Rockwell 690B	11534	Aerolineas Villaverde SA. Cordoba.	XB-BGH
☐ XA-SHP	71	681B Turbo Commander	6063	GBM Aereo SA. Cuidad Acuna, Coahuila.	XB-HUL
☐ XA-TBT	64	Gulfstream 1	136	Industrial Minera Mexico SA.	XB-GAW
☐ XA-TJD	66	King Air A90	LM-16	Aeromover SA. San Luis Potosi.	N823SB
☐ XA-TJH	81	PA-42 Cheyenne III	8001039	Aerosan SA.	D-ICMC
☐ XA-TJN		King Air B200	...	noted Dallas 6/04.	
☐ XA-TLW	82	Conquest II	441-0237	Servicios Aereos de Chihuahua SA.	N700JG
☐ XA-TMP	80	King Air F90	LA-44	Aero Laguna SA. Torreon, Coah.	N244J
☐ XA-TOR	81	Gulfstream 840	11661	XABRE Aerolineas SA. Toluca.	N840DC
☐ XA-TTR	98	King Air C90B	LJ-1524		N78XJ
☐ XA-TTU	60	Gulfstream 1	58		XB-FLL
☐ XA-VIP	91	PA-42 Cheyenne IIIA	5501058	VIP Empresarial SA. Tamps.	N985TA
☐ XA-YAS	97	King Air C90B	LJ-1479	Aerolineas Ejecutivas SA. Toluca.	N1119U
☐ XB-...	69	680W Turbo Commander	1834-39		N200QT
☐ XB-...	73	Mitsubishi MU-2K	273	Hugo Alvarez, Puebla.	N46MK
☐ XB-...	70	681 Turbo Commander	6040	Salvador Navarro Diaz Barreiro,	N9097N
☐ XB-...	78	PA-31T Cheyenne II	7820012	Marcelo Villareal Cantu, Monterrey, NL.	N781SW
☐ XB-...	72	King Air C90	LJ-536	Jose Luis Calzada, Mexico City.	N31WB
☐ XB-...	90	PA-42 Cheyenne IIIA	5501048	Transportadora Egoba SA.	N948TA
☐ XB-ACO	81	Gulfstream 980	95051	Procurad General de la Republica, Mexico City.	XC-HGG
☐ XB-AHK	00	King Air C90B	LJ-1593	Aerolineas Ejecutivas SA. Toluca.	N44693
☐ XB-BED	74	Rockwell 690A	11188	Estacion Cuauhtemoc SPR.	XA-FIZ
☐ XB-CIO	68	King Air B90	LJ-387	Representaciones Cristaleria y Peltre de Zamora. (status ?).	N824K
☐ XB-DJN	70	681 Turbo Commander	6023	Gonzalez Trejo Alejandro, Mexico City.	XA-CAG
☐ XB-DMT	77	Rockwell 690B	11360	Carrillo Caraza Rene, Culiacan, Sinalao.	N100WC
☐ XB-DSH	80	Gulfstream 840	11631		XC-TXA
☐ XB-DTD	67	680W Turbo Commander	1788-18	Fernando Nunez Chavez, Durango.	XA-DII
☐ XB-DTW	80	Gulfstream 840	11650	Dulce V Gonzalez Garduno, Mexico City.	XA-JPA
☐ XB-DZP	77	Rockwell 690B	11410	P R I. Toluca.	XC-SPP
☐ XB-ECT	82	Gulfstream 1000	96004	Francisco Lira Ortega, Ensenada, Baja California.	XA-LUV
☐ XB-EFZ	80	SA-226T Merlin 3B	T-328	Dist Int Productos Agricolas SA. Celaya.	N23X
☐ XB-EIH	74	Rockwell 690A	11214	Compras y Comisiones SA. Leon.	N57214
☐ XB-EWO	82	Conquest II	441-0235	Parson Meikle Joseph Richard, Nva Casas Grandes, Chihuahua.	N333GE
☐ XB-FKC	77	Rockwell 690B	11406	Constructadora y Edificado Comal. Toluca.	XC-SPI
☐ XB-FMS	82	Conquest 1	425-0051	Arturo Armendariz Chaparr, Chihuahua.	XA-RLN
☐ XB-FMV	67	Mitsubishi MU-2B	034	Christian Esquino,	N28HR
☐ XB-FND	80	Conquest II	441-0155	Doroteo Couret Nolasco, Los Mochis, Sinalao.	XB-BON
☐ XB-FQC	74	Rockwell 690A	11144	Lin. de Producc. SA. Toluca.	XA-RAO
☐ XB-FSG	83	Cheyenne II-XL	8166047	Grupo Fralvar de Mexico SA. Mexico City.	N457SR
☐ XB-FXK	81	Conquest 1	425-0091	Jose Luis Franco Alvarez, Mexico City.	N68478
☐ XB-FXU	79	PA-31T Cheyenne 1	7904053	Krum SA. Del Norte, NL.	N2379R
☐ XB-FYD	73	Rockwell 690	11065	Gabriela Ortega Larraury, Del Norte, NL.	XB-CZX
☐ XB-GBN	77	Conquest II	441-0021	Malva Inmobiliara SA. Queretaro.	XA-SKJ
☐ XB-GCU	78	Rockwell 690B	11460	Fausto Bermudez Hernandez, Toluca.	N42DK
☐ XB-GDS	77	Rockwell 690B	11371	Pascual Oyarvide Sanchez, Ciudad Valles, SLP.	XA-RMG
☐ XB-GJL	73	Rockwell 690	11074	Manuel Vargas Ramirez, San Luis Rio Col, Baja California.	XB-AEL
☐ XB-GMT	81	Gulfstream 840	11677	Vazquez Garcia Miguel Angel, Puebla, Chihuahua.	XB-GCV
☐ XB-GQI	80	PA-31T Cheyenne 1	8004056	Rocha Fuentes Jorge Miguel, Del Norte, NL.	N8TH
☐ XB-GTP	65	King Air 90	LJ-63		XA-MUR
☐ XB-GVI	80	PA-31T Cheyenne II	8020008	Rodriguez Gracia Juan Gerardo, Del Norte, NL.	N165CA
☐ XB-GXH		PA-42 Cheyenne	...		
☐ XB-HCL	68	King Air B90	LJ-388	Pascual Oyarvide Sanchez, Ciudad Valles, SLP.	N93EJ
☐ XB-HDY	79	King Air 200	BB-423	Rafael Rodriguez Vale, Mexico City.	N120RJ
☐ XB-HGG	75	Rockwell 690A	11257	A M Quadrini di Palma,	XC-BAP
☐ XB-HHA	84	King Air 300	FA-14	ALFACC SA.	N450AC
☐ XB-HMI	99	King Air C90B	LJ-1549	G Morfin Villalpando,	N3076U
☐ XB-HNA	79	PA-31T Cheyenne II	7920012	Constructora Brisa SA. Jalapa.	XB-RTG

Reg	Yr	Type	c/n	Owner/Operator	Prev Regn

433

Reg	Yr	Type	c/n	Owner/Operator	Prev Regn
☐ XB-HOV	69	Mitsubishi MU-2F	156	Armando Alanis Rodriguez, Del Norte, NL.	N869Q
☐ XB-HSE	74	Rockwell 690A	11225	TRC	XA-EOC
☐ XB-IMT		King Air B200	...	noted Opa Locka 7/04.	
☐ XB-JLA	80	King Air E90	LW-333	Jose Lorca Avalos, San Luis Potosi.	N90BE
☐ XB-JNC	83	PA-42 Cheyenne III	8001104	Industrias de Construcciones de Mexico SA.	N334FP
☐ XB-JRF	82	King Air F90	LA-186	J M Rocha Fuentes,	N600SF
☐ XB-KLY	79	Rockwell 690B	11563	Eduardo de la Vega Canelo, Culiacan.	N140CA
☐ XB-LIJ	76	Mitsubishi MU-2M	341	Dirigir SA. Monterrey, NL.	N726MA
☐ XB-MCB		King Air B200	...	noted Houston-Hobby 7/02.	
☐ XB-NEB	73	Mitsubishi MU-2J	583	Administracion Central SA.	N287MA
☐ XB-NUG	74	Mitsubishi MU-2J	619	Conductores Monterrey SA. Del Norte, NL.	N469MA
☐ XB-PSG	84	PA-42 Cheyenne IIIA	5501019	Prisciliano Siller Garcia, Del Norte, NL.	N819PC
☐ XB-REA	70	King Air 100	B-68	Negro Mex SA. (status ?).	XA-DEA
☐ XB-RLM	79	PA-31T Cheyenne II	7920023	Pavimentos de la Laguna SA.	N793SW
☐ XB-RZH		King Air B200	...	noted 3/02.	
☐ XB-TFS	74	King Air 200	BB-8	Transportadora de Sal SA. Tijuana, Baja California.	N923WS
☐ XB-WUI	69	King Air 100	B-4		N925BD
☐ XB-XOI	70	Mitsubishi MU-2F	189	Roberto A Mariscal Saenz, Toluca.	N110MA
☐ XB-ZRH	89	King Air 300	FA-203		N369MK
☐ XC-...	80	PA-31T Cheyenne II	0020019	State Government of Queretaro.	N85CM
☐ XC-AA12		Conquest II	...	Prourad General de la Republica, Mexico City.	
☐ XC-AA16	85	Gulfstream 1000	96084	Procurad General de la Republica, Mexico City.	XC-HGW
☐ XC-AA19	83	Gulfstream 1000	96056	Procurad General de la Republica, Mexico City.	XC-HFV
☐ XC-AA20	85	Gulfstream 1000	96091	Governor of the State of Oaxaca, Xoxocotlan.	XC-HGX
☐ XC-AA23	82	Gulfstream 1000	96001	Estado Mayor Presidencial. Mexico City.	XC-UTR
☐ XC-AA27	81	Gulfstream 840	11652	Governor of the State of Sonora, Hermosillo.	XC-HGJ
☐ XC-AA36	81	Gulfstream 840	11678	Governor of the State of Vera Cruz, Jalapa.	XC-HHY
☐ XC-AA38	75	King Air 200	BB-48	Procurad General de la Republica, Mexico City.	XB-EDZ
☐ XC-AA38		King Air B200	...	Procurad General de la Republica, Mexico City.	
☐ XC-AA40		Gulfstream 840	...	Governor of the State of Tamaulipas, Ciudad Victoria.	XC-HHK
☐ XC-AA41		Conquest II	...	Procurad General de la Republica, Mexico City.	
☐ XC-AA46	86	King Air 300LW	FA-95	Procurad General de la Republica, Mexico City.	HK-3536
☐ XC-AA49	85	King Air 300	FA-83	PGR/Mexican Drug Enforcement Agency, Mexico City.	XC-HGV
☐ XC-AA50	83	King Air 200	BB-1108	PGR/Mexican Drug Enforcement Agency, Mexico City.	XC-JAI
☐ XC-AA53	67	Gulfstream 1	179	Procurad General de la Republica, Mexico City.	HK-3622
☐ XC-AA56	81	Gulfstream 840	11695	State Government of Baja California Norte.	XB-JIO
☐ XC-AA57	63	Gulfstream 1	103	PGR/Mexican Drug Enforcement Agency, Mexico City.	PT-...
☐ XC-AA62	81	Gulfstream 980	95068	Procurad General de la Republica, Mexico City.	HK-3409W
☐ XC-AA67	80	Gulfstream 980	95000	Procurad General de la Republica, Mexico City.	YV-
☐ XC-AA71	80	Conquest II	441-0189	Procurad General de la Republica, Mexico City.	HK-3595
☐ XC-AA80	86	King Air 300	FA-74	Procurad General de la Republica, Mexico City.	HK-3519
☐ XC-AA85	77	Rockwell 690B	11382	Secretaria de Gobernacion, Mexico City.	XC-JBP
☐ XC-AA98	81	Gulfstream 980	95045	Procurad General de la Republica, Mexico City.	HK-....
☐ XC-AGS	86	King Air C90A	LJ-1132	Governor of the State of Aguascalientes.	XA-GSM
☐ XC-ALO	80	Gulfstream 840	11606	Governor of the State of Guerrero, Chilpancingo.	N5833N
☐ XC-BAD	81	Gulfstream 840	11659	Procurad General de la Republica, Zacatecas.	N402AB
☐ XC-BCN	79	King Air 200	BB-435	Governor of the State of Baja California Norte.	XC-GOL
☐ XC-CHI	97	King Air 300	FL-166	Governor of the State of Chihuahua.	N166FL
☐ XC-DIJ	76	King Air 200	BB-100	Procurad General de la Republica, Mexico City.	N75KA
☐ XC-ENL	81	Gulfstream 980	95052	Governor of the State of Nuevo Leon, Monterrey.	HK-2738W
☐ XC-FIW	72	King Air A100	B-110	Secretariat of Communications & Transport, Mexico City.	
☐ XC-FOC	72	King Air C90	LJ-553	CIAAC-Centro Int de Adto de Aviacion Civil, Mexico City.	
☐ XC-FUY	73	King Air E90	LW-33	Direccion General de Aduanas, Monterrey.	
☐ XC-GAS	79	Rockwell 690B	11556	Direccion General de Carreteras Federales, Mexico City.	
☐ XC-GON	81	Conquest II	441-0224	Secretaria de Hacienda y Credito Publico, Mexico City.	N6854B
☐ XC-GOO	81	Conquest II	441-0208	Secretaria de Hacienda y Credito Publico, Mexico City.	N2728F
☐ XC-HAB	81	Gulfstream 840	11688	Banco Nacional de Credito Rural SA. Mexico City.	(N5940K)
☐ XC-HFA	73	SA-226T Merlin 3	T-238	Governor of the State of Tamaulipas, Ciudad Victoria.	N130PC
☐ XC-HFN	82	Gulfstream 1000	96043	Governor of the State of Chihuahua.	N9963S
☐ XC-HGH	81	Gulfstream 980	95072	Procurad General de la Republica, Mexico City.	HK-3492
☐ XC-HGI	87	King Air 300	FA-114	Governor of the State of Guerrero, Chilpancingo.	XA-PIE
☐ XC-HHH	80	Gulfstream 840	11649	Procurad General de la Republica, Mexico City.	HK-3448
☐ XC-HHS	78	Rockwell 690B	11450	Governor of the State of Sinalao, Culiacan.	N81729
☐ XC-HHU	83	Conquest II	441-0275	Comision Nacional de Agua, Mexico City.	N95863
☐ XC-HMO	79	Rockwell 690B	11560	Governor of the State of Sonora, Hermosillo.	(N690RB)

Reg	Yr	Type	c/n	Owner/Operator	Prev Regn
☐ XC-JAL	77	Rockwell 690B	11417	Governor of the State of Jalisco, Guadalajara.	N81662
☐ XC-JCT	76	Rockwell 690A	11331	Fondo Nat. Fomento Al Turismo, Baja California Sur.	XB-ECX
☐ XC-JDB		Gulfstream 900	15009	Policia Federal Preventiva, Mexico City.	XC-AA39
☐ XC-LIE	64	Gulfstream 1	148		C-FWAM
☐ XC-MLM	83	Gulfstream 900	15028	Governor of the State of Michoacan,	N5916N
☐ XC-NAY	73	Rockwell 690A	11115	Governor of the State of Nayarit, Tepic.	XB-XUC
☐ XC-OAX	81	Gulfstream 840	11656	Governor of the State of Oaxaca, Xoxocotlan.	(N5908K)
☐ XC-ONA	67	King Air A90	LJ-293	Cia S N P SA. Mexico City.	N793K
☐ XC-PFB		Gulfstream 980	95018	Policia Federal Preventiva, Mexico City.	N123LA
☐ XC-PPF	81	Gulfstream 980	95061	Policia Federal Preventiva, Mexico City.	XC-AA15
☐ XC-RAM	72	Rockwell 690	11021	Secretaria de Hacienda y Credito Publico, Mexico City.	
☐ XC-SAH	78	Rockwell 690B	11516	S.A.H.O.P. Mexico City.	
☐ XC-STA	78	Rockwell 690B	11447	TAF-Transporte Aereo Federal, Mexico City.	N81723
☐ XC-TAB	78	Rockwell 690B	11504	Governor of the State of Tabasco, Villahermosa.	N106SA
☐ XC-UAT	76	PA-31T Cheyenne II	7620046	Universidad Autonoma de Tamaulipas, Victoria.	N5432V
☐ XC-VES	78	Rockwell 690B	11481	Governor of the State of Coahuila, Ramos Arizpe.	N126SA
☐ XC-VNC		Gulfstream 1	...	Procurad de la Republica, Mexico City.	
Military					
☐ 2206		Mitsubishi MU-2B	...	noted stored Santa Lucia 3/03.	
☐ 3932	78	Rockwell 690B	11494	Mexican Air Force, Mexico City.	ETE-1332
☐ 3971		King Air B200	...	UETAAM, Mexico City. (noted 3/03).	
☐ 5201	88	King Air C90A	LJ-1166	Government of Mexico,	2201
☐ 5202	88	King Air C90A	LJ-1168	Government of Mexico,	2202
☐ 5203	88	King Air C90A	LJ-1171	Government of Mexico,	2203
☐ 5204	88	King Air C90A	LJ-1175	Government of Mexico,	2204
☐ 5205	88	King Air C90A	LJ-1176	Government of Mexico,	2205
☐ 5206		King Air C90	...	noted stored Santa Lucia 3/03.	
☐ ETE-1318	82	Gulfstream 1000	96041	Mexican Air Force, Mexico City.	HK-2912P
☐ ETE-1357		Mitsubishi MU-2B	...	noted stored Santa Lucia 3/03.	
☐ MT-214	82	Gulfstream 1000	96040	Mexican Navy, Mexico City.	N900JP
☐ MT-218	82	Gulfstream 1000	96013	Mexican Navy, Mexico City.	XC-HHZ
☐ MT-219	80	Gulfstream 980	95040	Mexican Navy, Mexico City.	XB-AOC
☐ MT-221	81	Gulfstream 980	95046	Mexican Navy, Mexico City.	XB-DSA
☐ MT-222	81	Gulfstream 980	95082	Mexican Navy, Mexico City.	HK-3453
☐ MT-224	79	Conquest II	441-0101	Mexican Navy, Mexico City.	N412PW
☐ MU-1550	72	Mitsubishi MU-2J	566	Mexican Navy, Mexico City.	N210MA

XT = BURKINA FASO
Total 2

Civil

Reg	Yr	Type	c/n	Owner/Operator	Prev Regn
☐ XT-MBA	80	King Air 200	BB-698	Government of Burkina Faso/Air Burkina, Ouagadougou.	N440CF

Military

| ☐ XT-MAX | 80 | King Air 200 | BB-742 | Government of Burkina Faso/Air Burkina, Ouagadougou. | G-BPWJ |

YR = ROMANIA
Total 3

Civil

☐ YR-CAA	92	King Air 350	FL-73	Civil Aviation Directorate, Bucharest.	(G-CCCB)
☐ YR-RLA	93	Beech 1900D	UE-69	LAR Romanian Airlines, Bucharest.	YR-AAK
☐ YR-RLB	93	Beech 1900D	UE-73	LAR Romanian Airlines, Bucharest.	YR-AAL

YS = EL SALVADOR
Total 1

Civil

| ☐ YS-111N | 00 | King Air B200 | BB-1707 | Corporacion CentroAmericana de Servicios de Navegacion Aerea | N205TS |

YU = YUGOSLAVIA
Total 4

Civil

☐ YU-BMM	80	PA-31T Cheyenne II	8020021	Government Flight Inspection, Belgrade.	(D-IOOO)
☐ YU-BPF	80	PA-31T Cheyenne II	8020006	JAT General Aviation, Belgrade.	N801CM
☐ YU-BPG	80	PA-31T Cheyenne II	8020012	JAT General Aviation, Belgrade.	N2328W
☐ YU-BPH	80	PA-31T Cheyenne II	8020063	JAT General Aviation, Belgrade.	N2389V

YV = VENEZUELA
Total 245

Civil

☐ YV-...	82	SA-227TT Merlin 300	TT-447	Inversiones AGAP CA. Nueva Esparta.	HK-3980X
☐ YV-...	77	King Air 200	BB-265	Servicios Tecnicos Maracaibo.	YV-141CP
☐ YV-...	82	Gulfstream 840	11725		N66RA
☐ YV-...	82	Gulfstream 900	15012		YV-903P
☐ YV-...	81	Gulfstream 840	11694		N101KJ

Reg	Yr Type	c/n	Owner/Operator	Prev Regn

Reg	Yr	Type	c/n	Owner/Operator	Prev Regn
YV-...	82	SA-227AT Merlin 4C	AT-532	Air Trans CA. Caracas.	N3110B
YV-...	79	Conquest II	441-0097	Dr Pedro Binaggia, Caracas.	N434AE
YV-...	84	Gulfstream 900	15034		N900DJ
YV-...	82	SA-227TT Merlin 4C	TT-465	Servicios Aeronauticos de Oriente CA.	N696CP
YV-...	70	SA-26AT Merlin 2B	T26-175		N499SP
YV-...	80	Gulfstream 840	11632	Caraven SA. Caracas.	N711QP
YV-....	69	SA-26AT Merlin 2B	T26-142	Victor Moucado,	N226HA
YV-....	75	King Air 200	BB-78		N694FC
YV-....	67	King Air A90	LJ-195	Hector Enrique Acosta, Caracas.	N98DD
YV-....	68	King Air B90	LJ-396		N70SM
YV-....	69	Mitsubishi MU-2F	165		YV-1067P
YV-....	76	King Air C-12C	BC-37	Mario Gonzales Restrepo,	(N555FB)
YV-....	84	SA-227TT Merlin 3C	TT-507		N507TT
YV-....	66	King Air A90	LJ-147	Avioicaro, Caracas.	N198BC
YV-....	77	King Air 200	BB-279		N279CA
YV-....	79	PA-31T Cheyenne 1	7904013		N104RF
YV-....	77	King Air C-12A	BC-51		N48JA
YV-....	75	King Air 200	BB-31	Julio Gonzales, Caracas.	N7RW
YV-....	83	Gulfstream 900	15032		N900HV
YV-.,,,	67	King Air A90	LJ-222		(N901AS)
YV-....	78	Rockwell 690B	11472		N699CP
YV-....	75	Rockwell 690A	11228	Clover Internacional CA. Caracas.	N690HV
YV-....	66	King Air A90	LJ-151		N28AB
YV-....	75	King Air 200	BB-67		N78DV
YV-....	71	681 Turbo Commander	6044	Hector D P Peraza,	N529JC
YV-....	67	King Air A90	LJ-240		N360D
YV-....	63	Gulfstream 1	106		C-FAWG
YV-....	70	King Air B90	LJ-495		N71WH
YV-....	77	King Air A100	B-237		N43FC
YV-....	81	King Air 200	BB-779		N811CB
YV-....	66	King Air A90	LJ-124		N6238N
YV-....	78	King Air 200	BB-346	Hector Rafael Hernandez, Caracas.	N747MB
YV-....	01	King Air C90B	LJ-1659		N4409U
YV-....	68	King Air B90	LJ-383	Pablo Rafael Vero, Valencia Carabobo.	N388MC
YV-....	78	King Air 200	BB-391		N1969C
YV-....	77	King Air A100	B-231		N3EP
YV-....	75	King Air 200	BB-51		5Y-BIR
YV-....	74	King Air 200	BB-17		N900CV
YV-....	76	King Air 200	BB-167		N300DK
YV-....	73	King Air A100	B-161	Violeta Aviles Pernia, Charallave Miranda.	N62526
YV-....	68	King Air B90	LJ-357	(status ?).	N887KU
YV-....	66	King Air A90	LJ-130	Fabio Palmerini Munerato, Caracas.	N70UA
YV-....	67	King Air A90	LJ-266		N55LH
YV-....	84	PA-42 Cheyenne 400LS	5527009		N941AA
YV-....	00	King Air B200	BB-1706	Aeroservicios Catatumbo SA. Maracaibo.	N3206M
YV-....	79	PA-31T Cheyenne II	7920021		N20PJ
YV-....	66	Gulfstream 1	173	Maria de Jesus Morano, Barcelona.	N173BT
YV-....	76	King Air 200	BB-107	Daniel B Alejando, Caracas.	N115TT
YV-....	79	PA-31T Cheyenne II	7920053		N731PC
YV-01P	75	Rockwell 690A	11264	Juan Otaola Pevan,	YV-T-JOP
YV-04CP	70	King Air 100	B-73		(N73PD)
YV-04P	71	King Air 100	B-83		YV-T-ETM
YV-07CP	76	Rockwell 690A	11325	Gustavo Jimenez Pocaterra,	N81422
YV-1000CP	91	King Air C90A	LJ-1273		YV-2282P
YV-1013P	80	King Air F90	LA-16	L F Mendoza Aristeguieta, Caracas.	YV-2289P
YV-1050P	78	Rockwell 690B	11443		N104RG
YV-1051P	80	King Air 200	BB-656		YV-2576P
YV-105CP	81	Gulfstream 840	11685	(reported stolen ?)	N840BC
YV-1074CP	00	King Air C90B	LJ-1605		N4005J
YV-109CP	75	Rockwell 690A	11244		YV-02P
YV-112CP	91	King Air 350	FL-55		N5692L
YV-116CP	77	Rockwell 690B	11377		
YV-118CP	77	King Air E90	LW-234	Aerotecnica SA. Caracas.	
YV-121CP	91	King Air B200	BB-1398	(reported stolen ?).	
YV-124CP	77	PA-31T Cheyenne II	7720047	Agropecuaria Garza CA.	

Reg	Yr	Type	c/n	Owner/Operator	Prev Regn
YV-127CP	77	King Air B100	BE-28		YV-1276P
YV-1300P	77	King Air 200	BB-282	(reported stolen ?).	YV-131CP
YV-1402P	78	PA-31T Cheyenne II	7820067		N331PC
YV-1405P	67	680V Turbo Commander	1719-90	Silvio Guedes,	YV-O-CVG-
YV-143CP	77	Rockwell 690B	11378		N25PF
YV-144CP	77	Mitsubishi MU-2N	702SA		N862MA
YV-1500P	78	King Air E90	LW-270	Police Air Wing, Caracas.	
YV-152CP	77	King Air C90	LJ-739	Aero Ejecutivos CA. Caracas.	
YV-158CP	78	King Air C90	LJ-742		
YV-167CP	78	King Air C90	LJ-751	Artico SA.	
YV-170CP	80	Gulfstream 840	11603		N5NK
YV-172CP	78	King Air C90	LJ-756		
YV-188CP	78	Rockwell 690B	11461		(N81763)
YV-192CP	76	Rockwell 690A	11288	F Bermudez Motors CA. Caracas.	YV-757P
YV-1947P	68	King Air B90	LJ-370	Luis Alberto Martinez,	YV-40CP
YV-194CP	78	PA-31T Cheyenne II	7820052		N6002A
YV-1990P	75	PA-31T Cheyenne II	7520027		YV-08CP
YV-2034P	75	King Air C90	LJ-659		YV-410CP
YV-204CP	78	Rockwell 690B	11466		(N81769)
YV-212CP	84	Gulfstream 840	11735		N888KN
YV-218CP	78	Rockwell 690B	11483	MUTACA-Multitransporte Aereo CA. Caracas.	(N81806)
YV-223CP	78	King Air C90	LJ-789	Trafi CA.	N2016L
YV-225CP	78	Conquest II	441-0067	Servicios Aereos Tampa C.A.	(N88726)
YV-2263P	83	Conquest 1	425-0162		
YV-227CP	78	Rockwell 690B	11464	Arrendaven CA. Caracas.	N81766
YV-2280P	68	680W Turbo Commander	1804-26	John S Calcurian,	YV-O-INOS-
YV-229CP	78	Rockwell 690B	11502		(N81842)
YV-2317P	75	Rockwell 690A	11239	Benjamin Guillermo, Miami, Fl. USA.	N57217
YV-2323P	83	King Air B200C	BL-66		
YV-2331P	78	PA-31T Cheyenne II	7820070	Boscolo Smeraldo Smeraldi, Caracas.	N6033A
YV-2346P	81	Gulfstream 840	11671		YV-439CP
YV-2350P	81	King Air B200	BB-906	Manuel Espinoza,	YV-437CP
YV-2365P	78	PA-31T Cheyenne II	7820037		N24E
YV-2383P	70	681 Turbo Commander	6005		N35WA
YV-238CP	79	King Air 200	BB-440		
YV-2390P	78	Conquest II	441-0063	Inversiones Salvador Salvatierra SA. Caracas.	YV-176CP
YV-2401P	88	King Air 300	FA-158	Inversiones Alas Bajas CA. Caracas.	N750HL
YV-2404P	70	681 Turbo Commander	6029		N9074N
YV-2422P	79	Rockwell 690B	11515		N515WC
YV-242CP	80	SA-226T Merlin 3B	T-357	Transportes 242 CA. Caracas.	N30042
YV-2436P	68	680W Turbo Commander	1814-31	Diego Levine, Maracaibo.	N71AF
YV-243CP	78	Rockwell 690B	11488		N70AC
YV-2451P	77	PA-31T Cheyenne II	7720050	L Rosalen Hernandez, La Carlota.	YV-153CP
YV-246CP	75	Rockwell 690A	11278	Transportes 246 CA. Caracas.	N57176
YV-2475P	71	681B Turbo Commander	6052		N105SS
YV-2484P	76	King Air 200	BB-160		YV-665CP
YV-2488P	74	Rockwell 690A	11190	Transporte Lehmacorp CA. Caracas.	N8KG
YV-2501P	70	681 Turbo Commander	6024	Julio Borges, Caracas.	N22WK
YV-2505P	82	Gulfstream 840	11726	Inversiones Puerta Plata CA. Caracas.	YV-505CP
YV-251CP	79	PA-31T Cheyenne II	7920042	Multiservicios NISA CA.	
YV-2566P	80	Gulfstream 980	95009	Dr V G Ramirez,	ZS-KZW
YV-257CP	79	King Air 200	BB-517	Inversiones Rizo CA. (status ?).	
YV-2584P	78	King Air 200	BB-316	Tocars SA. Caracas. (status ?).	YV-168CP
YV-258CP	70	King Air B90	LJ-488	Molinpast CA. La Carlota.	YV-2229P
YV-2593P	75	Rockwell 690A	11253	C Acosta, Caracas.	YV-31CP
YV-2604P	77	Mitsubishi MU-2P	348SA		N500GK
YV-262CP	84	SA-227TT Merlin 300	TT-521		D-IOOO
YV-263CP	79	King Air C90	LJ-865	Vinccler CA.	
YV-2663P	00	King Air 350	FL-313	Aviaservice CA. Caracas.	N3103L
YV-2710P	80	King Air 200	BB-632		YV-1873P
YV-2772P	79	Rockwell 690B	11547	Inversiones 12-6-86 CA. Caracas.	YV-670CP
YV-290CP	80	King Air E90	LA-35	C A de Edificaciones - Resid D Paulo.	
YV-292CP	82	SA-227TT Merlin 3C	TT-459A		OY-BPK
YV-326P	76	King Air E90	LW-172	G Bracho,	
YV-32P	89	King Air C90A	LJ-1191	Aviaservice CA. Caracas.	
Reg	Yr	Type	c/n	Owner/Operator	Prev Regn

Reg	Yr	Type	c/n	Owner/Operator	Prev Regn
❏ YV-335CP	80	King Air 200	BB-598		
❏ YV-344P	67	680V Turbo Commander	1718-89		YV-340CP
❏ YV-394CP	80	Gulfstream 840	11637	Construcciones Humboldt SA. Caracas.	(N5889K)
❏ YV-39CP	80	Gulfstream 840	11618		N118SA
❏ YV-401CP	81	King Air 200	BB-796	MUTACA-Multitransporte Aereo CA. Caracas.	
❏ YV-403CP	81	King Air 200C	BL-23	Ministry of National Defence, Caracas.	
❏ YV-407CP	81	Gulfstream 980	95067	(reported stolen ?).	(N9819S)
❏ YV-42CP	80	King Air 350	FL-32	PDVSA Petroleo SA. Caracas.	YV-350CP
❏ YV-436CP	81	King Air C90	LJ-973	Transportes Guyanes SA.	
❏ YV-454CP	77	Rockwell 690B	11405	Transporte 454 SA. Caracas.	N5387V
❏ YV-465CP	72	King Air C90	LJ-556	(status ?)	YV-818P
❏ YV-467CP	74	King Air E90	LW-94	SERVIVENSA-Servicios Avensa SA. Caracas.	N98ME
❏ YV-472CP	83	SA-227TT Merlin 300	TT-471	Transporte Lux CA.	D-IISA
❏ YV-488CP	82	King Air B200	BB-1020		
❏ YV-492CP	82	Gulfstream 900	15006	(reported stolen ?)	N5852N
❏ YV-505CP	82	Gulfstream 840	11723	(reported stolen ?).	YV-45CP
❏ YV-516CP	79	King Air E90	LW-322	Servicios Avensa SA.	N600FC
❏ YV-521CP	83	Gulfstream 900	15022		D-ILAS
❏ YV-533P	81	Conquest II	441-0227	Jesus Romero,	N6854T
❏ YV-536P	68	680W Turbo Commander	1813-30		YV-T-VTY
❏ YV-53CP	83	Gulfstream 1000	96067		HK-3271
❏ YV-548CP	84	Conquest 1	425-0189	Transporte Lucania CA. Valencia.	N969ME
❏ YV-56CP	80	Gulfstream 980	95017	Inversiones 301 CA. Caracas.	N9770S
❏ YV-581CP	80	Gulfstream 980	95007	Inversiones Torgo CA.	(N123RC)
❏ YV-601P	81	Gulfstream 840	11698		YV-485CP
❏ YV-612CP	83	SA-227TT Merlin 3C	TT-468		VH-JCB
❏ YV-622CP	83	King Air F90-1	LA-207		N2DF
❏ YV-627C	66	Gulfstream 1	170	TAAN-Transporte Aereo Andino SA. Caracas.	YV-620CP
❏ YV-628C	66	Gulfstream 1	171	TAAN-Transporte Aereo Andino SA. Caracas.	YV-621CP
❏ YV-639CP	00	King Air B200	BB-1712	Aviaservice CA. Caracas.	N3212E
❏ YV-63CP	77	Rockwell 690B	11390		YV-991P
❏ YV-652CP	84	SA-227TT Merlin 3C	TT-515	Transporte La Sierpe CA. Caracas. (status ?).	N352SM
❏ YV-655CP	79	PA-31T Cheyenne II	7920018		N100KR
❏ YV-660CP	95	King Air C90B	LJ-1401		N3270K
❏ YV-663CP	77	Rockwell 690B	11358	MUTACA-Multitransporte Aereo CA. Caracas.	N810GF
❏ YV-690P	79	Rockwell 690B	11532	Oficina Tecnica Vemef CA. Caracas.	YV-281CP
❏ YV-693CP	77	SA-226T Merlin 3A	T-287		YV-180CP
❏ YV-69CP	75	Rockwell 690A	11245		N236SC
❏ YV-702CP	82	King Air F90	LA-174	Consorcio Industrial de Zulia, Caracas.	N90LL
❏ YV-703CP	78	PA-31T Cheyenne II	7820008	Jose Manuel Aguilera,	N14MR
❏ YV-706P	77	King Air E90	LW-208	DIM-Direccion Intelligence Militar, Caracas.	
❏ YV-710CP	79	SA-226T Merlin 3B	T-301	Aero Halcon 710 CA. Caracas.	N175WB
❏ YV-733P	74	Rockwell 690A	11207	Luis Enriquez Nunez,	YV-E-DPK
❏ YV-740CP	82	SA-227TT Merlin 3C	TT-456		N3019U
❏ YV-744CP	66	680T Turbo Commander	1685-66		YV-2435P
❏ YV-770CP	81	SA-226T Merlin 3B	T-384		YV-2395P
❏ YV-773CP	81	Gulfstream 840	11666	Margarita Aviacion Internacional CA. Margarita.	YV-626CP
❏ YV-775CP	77	Rockwell 690B	11366		N777RD
❏ YV-787CP	81	Gulfstream 980	95084		N980JC
❏ YV-797CP	78	Rockwell 690B	11468		N2AC
❏ YV-801CP	70	King Air 100	B-16		N925K
❏ YV-808CP	82	SA-227TT Merlin 3C	TT-435	Aero Centro de Servicios CA. Caracas.	N92RC
❏ YV-818P	76	Rockwell 690A	11285		YV-80CP
❏ YV-820CP	68	680W Turbo Commander	1775-13	Executive Air CA. Caracas.	N9RN
❏ YV-822CP	83	Gulfstream 900	15030		XA-EMO
❏ YV-834CP	73	Rockwell 690A	11114	Servicios Aeronauticos 4 CA. Maracaibo.	N57114
❏ YV-839CP	93	King Air C90B	LJ-1329		N8016Q
❏ YV-843P	67	680V Turbo Commander	1689-69		YV-843P
❏ YV-854CP	73	Rockwell 690	11061	Inversiones Regionales 001 CA. Caracas.	N853CP
❏ YV-877CP	92	King Air B300C	FM-8	PDVSA Petroleo SA. Caracas.	N55684
❏ YV-87CP	81	Gulfstream 840	11654	Aero Williams CA. Caracas.	N1NT
❏ YV-880CP	82	Gulfstream 900	15017	DCA-Directorate of Civil Aeronautics, Caracas.	N5880N
❏ YV-886CP	82	King Air F90	LA-179	Banco Fomento Region de los Andes,	YV-486CP
❏ YV-893CP	81	Gulfstream 980	95058	Aeropetrol CA. Caracas.	N243AR
❏ YV-903P	79	King Air B100	BE-61		YV-309CP
Reg	Yr	Type	c/n	Owner/Operator	Prev Regn

Reg	Yr	Type	c/n	Owner/Operator	Prev Regn
☐ YV-907CP	74	Rockwell 690A	11180		YV-900P
☐ YV-910CP	98	King Air 350	FL-206	Wyngs Aviation CA. Caracas.	N23227
☐ YV-918CP	78	Rockwell 690B	11490	Transporte Turbo Commander CA.	YV-2096P
☐ YV-946CP	79	King Air 200	BB-540	Wyngs Aviation CA. Caracas.	N964CF
☐ YV-949CP	99	King Air B200	BB-1671		N3171H
☐ YV-950CP	76	Rockwell 690A	11329		YV-86CP
☐ YV-95CP	77	King Air B100	BE-19	Banco Nacional de Venezuela, Caracas.	
☐ YV-972CP	78	King Air C90	LJ-786	Inversiones Angaz CA.	N973AC
☐ YV-980CP	80	Gulfstream 980	95028		N980CF
☐ YV-980P	76	Rockwell 690A	11318		YV-98CP
☐ YV-990CP	87	Reims/Cessna F406	F406-0022		YV-525C
☐ YV-991CP		PA-42 Cheyenne	...		
☐ YV-998C	79	Rockwell 690B	11546		YV-416CP
☐ YV-O-BDA-3	76	Mitsubishi MU-2L	685	Agricultural Development State Bank,	N845MA
☐ YV-O-CBL-5	80	King Air C90	LJ-889	State Government Ciudad Bolivar.	YV-354CP
☐ YV-O-CVG-14		680V Turbo Commander	...	Corporacion Venezolana de Guyana, Puerto Ordaz.	
☐ YV-O-FDU	78	Rockwell 690B	11500	Fondo Nacional Desarrollos Urbanos, Caracas.	(N81833)
☐ YV-O-GPA-1	74	Rockwell 690A	11198	Gabriel Matheus, Caracas.	N707MP
☐ YV-O-KWH-3	81	Gulfstream 840	11657	CADAFE-CA de Administraciones y Fomento Electrico, Caracas.	(N5909K)
☐ YV-O-MAC-2	79	PA-31T Cheyenne 1	7904040	Ministry of Agriculture, Caracas.	YV-239CP
☐ YV-O-MAR-1	76	Rockwell 690A	11323		YV-2437P
☐ YV-O-MIF-2	78	Rockwell 690B	11430	Ministry of Transport & Communications, Caracas.	YV-O-MTC-
☐ YV-O-MTC-1	82	Gulfstream 1000	96016	Ministry of Transport & Communications, Caracas.	(YV-477CP)
☐ YV-O-MTC-5	76	Rockwell 690A	11281	Ministry of Transport & Communications, Caracas.	N57183
☐ YV-O-PTJ-2	83	King Air B200	BB-1092		YV-2352P
☐ YV-O-SATA-177		King Air 200	BB-223	Sistema Autonomo de Transporte y Servicio, Miranda.	YV-O-FMO-
☐ YV-O-SATA-277		King Air 200	BB-261	Sistema Autonomo de Transporte y Servicio, Miranda.	YV-791CP
☐ YV-O-SATA-377		King Air 200	BB-273	Sistema Autonomo de Transporte y Servicio, Miranda.	YV-O-FMO-
☐ YV-O-SATA-480		King Air 200	BB-701	Sistema Autonomo de Transporte y Servicio, Miranda.	YV-O-MAC-
☐ YV-O-SATA-580		King Air 200	BB-731	Sistema Autonomo de Transporte y Servicio, Miranda.	YV-O-BIV-1
☐ YV-O-SATA-776		King Air E90	LW-189	Sistema Autonomo de Transporte y Servicio, Miranda.	YV-O-INV-3
☐ YV-O-SID-2	73	King Air A100	B-155	Siderurgica del Orinoco CA. Caracas.	

Military

☐ 2540		King Air B200	...	noted La Carlotta 3/03.	
☐ 2840	79	King Air 200	BB-520	FAV, Caracas.	
☐ 3150	79	King Air 200	BB-522	FAV, Caracas.	
☐ 3240	81	King Air 200C	BL-19	FAV, Caracas.	
☐ 3280	81	King Air 200C	BL-18	FAV, Caracas.	
☐ ARV-0201	78	King Air E90	LW-264	Venezuelan Navy, Caracas.	TR-0201
☐ EV-7702	77	King Air E90	LW-229	Venezuelan Army, Caracas.	
☐ EV-7910	79	King Air 200	BB-495	Venezuelan Army, Caracas.	
☐ GN-7593	75	King Air E90	LW-154	Venezuelan National Guard, Caracas.	N211DG
☐ GN-7839	78	King Air E90	LW-260	Venezuelan National Guard, Caracas.	
☐ GN-8270	82	King Air B200C	BL-51	Venezuelan National Guard, Caracas.	
☐ GN-8274		King Air 200	...	Venezuelan National Guard, Caracas.	
☐ GN-8595	82	King Air B200	BB-980	Venezuelan National Guard, Caracas.	YV-466CP

Z = ZIMBABWE — Total 11

Civil

Reg	Yr	Type	c/n	Owner/Operator	Prev Regn
☐ Z-AHL	77	King Air E90	LW-205		Z-DJF
☐ Z-APG	82	King Air B200	BB-1046	Medical Air Rescue Service P/L. Harare.	ZS-APG
☐ Z-DDD	92	Reims/Cessna F406	F406-0069	Government/Falcon Air, Harare.	F-GIQD
☐ Z-DDE	92	Reims/Cessna F406	F406-0068	Governmen/Falcon Air, Harare.	F-GIQC
☐ Z-DDF	93	Reims/Cessna F406	F406-0071	Governmen/Falcon Air, Harare.	F-GIQE
☐ Z-DDG	92	Reims/Cessna F406	F406-0067	Government/Falcon Air, Harare.	F-GEUG
☐ Z-LCS	79	King Air C90	LJ-848	EGAS Flight Academy of Zimbabwe, Harare.	TR-LCS
☐ Z-MRS	77	King Air 200	BB-286	Medical Air Rescue Service P/L. Harare.	ZS-XGD
☐ Z-WRD	76	King Air C90	LJ-687	Delta Corp. Harare.	N127P
☐ Z-WSG	81	King Air 200	BB-748	Medical Air Rescue Service P/L. Harare.	N154BB
☐ Z-ZLT	85	King Air B200	BB-1196	Zimbabwe Leaf Tobacco Co Ltd. Harare.	N101EC

ZK = NEW ZEALAND — Total 10

Civil

Reg	Yr	Type	c/n	Owner/Operator	Prev Regn
☐ ZK-NFD	80	Conquest II	441-0141	Garden City Helicopters, Christchurch.	VH-CFD
☐ ZK-POD	77	PA-31T Cheyenne II	7720009	Cx ZK- 4/01 to ?	ZK-MPI
☐ ZK-PVB	76	Rockwell 690A	11321	NZAM Consulting Ltd. Albany.	VH-DLK

Reg	Yr Type	c/n	Owner/Operator	Prev Regn
☐ ZK-VAA	86 Reims/Cessna F406	F406-0012	Vincent Aviation Ltd. Wellington.	ZK-CII
☐ ZK-VAF	91 Reims/Cessna F406	F406-0057	Vincent Aviation Ltd. Wellington.	F-ODYZ

Military

☐ NZ1881	82 King Air B200	BB-1054	RNZAF, 42 Squadron, Ohakea.	ZK-KAB
☐ NZ1882	82 King Air B200	BB-1008	RNZAF, 42 Squadron, Ohakea.	ZK-KAC
☐ NZ1883	82 King Air B200	BB-1087	RNZAF, 42 Squadron, Ohakea.	ZK-KAD
☐ NZ1884	84 King Air B200	BB-1178	RNZAF, 42 Squadron, Ohakea.	ZK-KAF
☐ NZ1885	82 King Air B200	BB-968	RNZAF, 42 Squadron, Ohakea.	ZK-KAG

ZP = PARAGUAY   Total   14

Civil

☐ ZP-...	80 Gulfstream 980	95035	Jesus Gutierrez, Asuncion.	N200JN
☐ ZP-...	81 Gulfstream 980	95053		N73DQ
☐ ZP-...	85 Conquest 1	425-0223		N1226G
☐ ZP-...	82 SA-227TT Merlin 4C	TT-462A		N453CP
☐ ZP-...	83 Gulfstream 900	15021	Carlos Alberto Matiauda, Asuncion.	N908TN
☐ ZP-TJW	78 King Air E90	LW-284	GOYA S A C A. Asuncion.	N200WB
☐ ZP-TTU	80 Gulfstream 980	95021	Roberto Barchini,	ZP-PTU
☐ ZP-TWY	85 Gulfstream 1000	96095	Aero Commercial SRL. Asuncion.	N73DC
☐ ZP-TWZ	82 Gulfstream 900	15005	(status ?).	N5841N
☐ ZP-TXF	85 Gulfstream 1000	96079	Aero Commercial SRL. Asuncion.	N169CR
☐ ZP-TXG	85 Gulfstream 1000B	96203	Aero Commercial SRL. Asuncion.	N64JT
☐ ZP-TYI	80 PA-31T Cheyenne II	8020066	Itaipu Binacional, Asuncion.	N555HP
☐ ZP-TYZ	Cheyenne PA-42	...	G Saba, Asuncion.	
☐ ZP-TZW	78 King Air E90	LW-261		N4283R

ZS = SOUTH AFRICA   Total 186

Civil

☐ ZS-...	82 King Air F90	LA-160		N982SA
☐ ZS-...	84 King Air B200	BB-1189	Naturelink Airlines P/L. Pretoria.	VH-KBH
☐ ZS-...	91 King Air B200	BB-1401	Naturelink Airlines P/L. Pretoria.	VH-YDH
☐ ZS-...	93 King Air B200	BB-1463	Naturelink Airlines P/L. Pretoria.	VH-YEH
☐ ZS-...	04 King Air B200	BB-1860	NAC P/L. Rand.	N6200G
☐ ZS-ABM	85 SAAB 340A	036	Anglo American Corp. Johannesburg.	N77M
☐ ZS-ACS	82 King Air B200	BB-961	Naturelink Charters P/L. Wonderboom.	A2-AHA
☐ ZS-AGI	02 Pilatus PC-12/45	471	Majuba Aviation P/L. Laneria.	HB-FQN
☐ ZS-ALE	80 King Air 200	BB-643	Superstrike Investments 29 P/L. Bryanston.	ZS-OWH
☐ ZS-ALX	62 Gulfstream 1	86	Tramon Air CC. Lanseria.	N10TB
☐ ZS-AMS	98 Pilatus PC-12/45	203	Civair, Johannesburg. 'Amanda'	(ZS-SWV)
☐ ZS-BEB	97 Pilatus PC-12/45	180	The SARX Partnership, Lanseria.	HB-FSP
☐ ZS-CBL	00 King Air B200	BB-1742	C & L Air P/L. Makwassie.	N4288L
☐ ZS-COH	02 Pilatus PC-12	436	The Pilatus Partnership, Lanseria.	HB-...
☐ ZS-COP	89 King Air C90A	LJ-1204	South African Police, Wonderboom.	N1552D
☐ ZS-CPM	82 King Air C90-1	LJ-1034	CPM Air Charter P/L. Capetown.	(N98RF)
☐ ZS-CPX	81 Conquest 1	425-0071	ONZ Partnership, Lanseria.	N6845R
☐ ZS-CVH	81 King Air 200C	BL-32	Hands On Aviation P/L. Lanseria.	C9-ASX
☐ ZS-DAT	98 Pilatus PC-12/45	242	Hands On Aviation P/L. Lanseria.	HB-FR.
☐ ZS-DCG	01 PA-46-500TP Meridian	4697055	Placo P/L. Rand.	N53283
☐ ZS-DER	04 Pilatus PC-12/45	554	Blue Nightingale Trading 129 P/L. Nigel.	HB-...
☐ ZS-DJA	98 King Air B200	BB-1607	Dennis Jankelow & Assocs Aviation P/L. Lanseria.	N724TA
☐ ZS-DMM	97 Pilatus PC-12/45	190	Inyoni Partnership, Nelspruit.	HB-FQG
☐ ZS-DSL	79 King Air 200	BB-531	Executive Turbine Aircraft Hire P/L. Lanseria.	(PH-SKS)
☐ ZS-FDR	85 King Air B200	BB-1234	Federal Air P/L. Durban.	N971LE
☐ ZS-INN	71 King Air C90	LJ-523	Executive Turbine CC. Lanseria.	V5-INN
☐ ZS-IRJ	66 King Air A90	LJ-161	Fly In SA P/L. Lanseria.	ZS-MAN
☐ ZS-JIS	68 Gulfstream 1	193	Tramon Air CC. Lanseria.	PK-TRN
☐ ZS-JMA	79 Conquest II	441-0095	Spring Lights 1 P/L. Grand Central.	VH-JFD
☐ ZS-JRA	75 Rockwell 690A	11284	South African Weather Service, Pretoria.	N57273
☐ ZS-JRB	75 Rockwell 690A	11248	South African Weather Service, Pretoria.	N122K
☐ ZS-JRH	77 Rockwell 690B	11421	Trevor Lombard Aviation, Port Elizabeth.	N81672
☐ ZS-KAA	77 King Air 200	BB-222	United Nations, Kabul, Afghanistan.	F-ODZL
☐ ZS-KAL	03 Pilatus PC-12/45	508	Fireblade Investments Ltd. Lanseria.	HB-F..
☐ ZS-KGW	78 King Air 200	BB-381	500E Toerusting P/L. Pretoria.	N4848M
☐ ZS-KLZ	80 King Air F90	LA-69	Venture Otto S.A. P/L. Menlo Park.	N6727C
☐ ZS-KMA	81 King Air C90	LJ-930	Rossair Executive Air Charter P/L. Lanseria.	N3717J
☐ ZS-KSU	81 Conquest 1	425-0115	Cargo Carriers P/L. Johannesburg.	N68807

Reg	Yr Type	c/n	Owner/Operator	Prev Regn

Reg	Yr	Type	c/n	Owner/Operator	Prev Regn
ZS-KZI	81	King Air C90	LJ-959	International Air Partnership, Port Elizabeth.	(D-IFIP)
ZS-KZU	79	King Air 200	BB-416	Mic-Dav Air P/L. Lanseria.	N396DP
ZS-KZY	82	Gulfstream 1000	96051	ESCOM-Electricity Supply Commission, Johannesburg.	N9971S
ZS-KZZ	82	Gulfstream 1000	96052	Investec Bank Ltd. Johannesburg.	N9972S
ZS-LAW	81	King Air B200	BB-889	Swiftflite Charter CC. Lanseria.	N3538K
ZS-LBC	81	King Air F90	LA-122	B C Smither, Bryanston.	N3723N
ZS-LBD	81	King Air 200	BB-837	Maxitrade 33 General Trading, Lanseria.	A2-LBD
ZS-LFL	82	King Air C90-1	LJ-1033	Inter Air P/L-Theaco Road & Earthworks P/L. Vanderbijlpark.	N6717T
ZS-LFM	82	King Air B200	BB-954	East Coast Airways P/L-G U D Filters P/L. Durban.	N1839S
ZS-LFU	82	King Air B200	BB-1018	Invicta Bearings P/L. Capetown.	3D-LKK
ZS-LFW	82	King Air B200	BB-999	King Air Services Partnership, Lanseria.	9Q-CPV
ZS-LIN	83	King Air C90-1	LJ-1053	Domberg Airways, Magaliessig.	N6891L
ZS-LNR	85	King Air B200	BB-1222	De Beers Consolidated Mines Ltd. Lanseria.	(N50FC)
ZS-LRM	73	Commander 690A	11105	Commander Partnership, Lanseria.	A2-AIH
ZS-LSY	81	Cheyenne II-XL	8166031	Hendrik Casper Investments CC. Farrarmere.	V5-LSY
ZS-LTD	80	King Air F90	LA-63	C Troskie Vliegtuie, Cookhouse.	N3686W
ZS-LTE	80	King Air 200	BB-607	Sparg Aviation Services CC. Lanseria.	N6725L
ZS-LTF	74	King Air C90	LJ-613	Davy Foods P/L. Durban.	N3053W
ZS-LTG	86	King Air B200	BB-1251	De Beers Consolidated Mines Ltd. Lanseria.	N2610Y
ZS-LTZ	80	King Air C90	LJ-919	Dakota Logistics P/L. Edenvale.	N18MB
ZS-LWD	81	King Air 200	BB-756	Mastermind Tobacco SA P/L. East London.	5Y-BWD
ZS-LWM	78	King Air/Catpass 250	BB-341	Pro-Med Construction CC. Krugersdorp.	C-FBWX
ZS-LYA	75	King Air 200	BB-26	Associated Equipment Co P/L. Springfield.	N57FM
ZS-LZR	85	King Air C90A	LJ-1118	Crystal Air P/L. Bophuthatswana.	N937BC
ZS-MBZ	78	King Air C90	LJ-795	NAC P/L. Rand.	N551GA
ZS-MCA	72	King Air C90	LJ-551	500E Toerusting P/L. Pretoria.	ZS-XAC
ZS-MCC	85	King Air B200	BB-1195	John McCormick Family Trust, Clubview.	N61AJ
ZS-MES	82	King Air B200	BB-1038	Aircraft Africa Contracts Co P/L. Lanseria.	N223MH
ZS-MFC	79	King Air 200	BB-525	Sparg Aviation Services CC. Lanseria.	N200L
ZS-MGF	74	Mitsubishi MU-2J	622	MU-2 Aircraft Investment CC. Lanseria.	(3D-AFH)
ZS-MHM	80	King Air F90	LA-47	Tony Milligan Group P/L. Ladysmith.	N984GA
ZS-MIM	81	King Air 200	BB-846	Angolan Aircraft CC. Lanseria.	5Y-BKA
ZS-MIN	81	King Air B200	BB-941	Rossair Executive Air Charter P/L. Lanseria.	N36801
ZS-MKI	85	King Air C90A	LJ-1099	SPH Group P/L. Capetown.	Z-MKI
ZS-MMV	89	King Air B200	BB-1318	De Beers Consolidated Mines Ltd. Lanseria.	N1557U
ZS-MNC	75	King Air C90	LJ-671	Container World P/L. Musgrave.	N99LM
ZS-MSF	03	Pilatus PC-12/45	506	Execujet Aircraft Sales P/L. Lanseria.	HB-
ZS-MSK	80	King Air 200	BB-597	Angolan Aircraft CC. Lanseria.	5Y-BJC
ZS-MUM	68	King Air B90	LJ-408	Civair Helicopters CC. Capetown.	N481SA
ZS-MVW	81	Conquest 1	425-0041	Algary Airlines P/L. Kensington.	N326L
ZS-NAW	82	King Air B200	BB-1027	Aircraft Africa Contracts Co P/L. Lanseria.	N40AB
ZS-NAX	80	King Air 200C	BL-8	Rossair Executive Air Charter P/L. Lanseria	5Y-NAX
ZS-NBJ	82	King Air B200	BB-1070	NBJ Partnership, Maroelana.	SE-KND
ZS-NBO	80	King Air 200	BB-706	Smith Mining Equipment P/L. Kempton Park.	N25WD
ZS-NDH	74	King Air C90	LJ-619	Dodson International Parts Inc. Ottawa, Ks. USA.	5Y-MAL
ZS-NFO	80	King Air F90	LA-51	NAC P/L. Rand.	N901NB
ZS-NHW	64	Gulfstream 1	141	Airquarius Air Charter P/L. Lanseria.	N800PA
ZS-NHX	78	King Air 200	BB-386	Vaal Mac Investments P/L. Vanderbijl Park.	N310GA
ZS-NJM	83	King Air B200	BB-1152	Executive Aircraft Turbine Hire P/L. Lanseria.	ZS-NJM
ZS-NKC	93	King Air B200	BB-1474	Metcash Aviation Services P/L. Lanseria.	N82010
ZS-NKE	93	King Air B200	BB-1475	Maizecor Meulers P/L. Silverton.	N8226M
ZS-NNA	86	Reims/Cessna F406	F406-0005	Out of the Blue Air Safaris P/L. Lanseria.	5R-MSK
ZS-NOW	92	King Air B200	BB-1427	Aviation Africa Partnership, Isando.	N8003U
ZS-NRR	77	King Air 200	BB-288	Permanne Investments P/L. Linkhills.	5Y-HHG
ZS-NTL	75	King Air 200	BB-85	Balmair Aviation P/L. Virginia.	V5-CIC
ZS-NTT	78	King Air 200	BB-350	Gideon Air P/L. Middelburg.	N125MS
ZS-NUC	78	King Air 200	BB-407	Soaring Eagle Charter P/L-Freebird Aviation, Saxonwold.	F-GFTT
ZS-NUF	79	King Air 200C	BL-4	Rossair Executive Air Charter P/L. Lanseria.	V5-AAL
ZS-NVP	89	King Air B200	BB-1325	Rodo Investments P/L. Lanseria.	OY-LKH
ZS-NWC	74	King Air C90	LJ-625	J Robbertse Vervoer P/L. Hercules.	N50AB
ZS-NWK	75	King Air 200	BB-52	ZS-NWK P/L. Umhlanga Rocks.	N400AJ
ZS-NXI	77	King Air E90	LW-224	Phillips & Franks Second Hand Dealers CC. Boksburg.	D-IATA
ZS-NXT	95	King Air B200	BB-1502	Assmang, Northern Cape.	N1515E
ZS-NYE	77	King Air E90	LW-222	Master Drilling P/L. Fochville.	VH-MTG
ZS-NYI	89	Reims/Cessna F406	F406-0030	COMAV/Air Namibia, Windhoek, Namibia.	5Y-MMJ

Reg	Yr	Type	c/n	Owner/Operator	Prev Regn
☐ ZS-NYK	96	BAe Jetstream 41	41095	Government of Kwazulu, Ulundi.	
☐ ZS-NYM	96	Pilatus PC-12	147	NYM Partnership, Bryanston.	(ZS-FDS)
☐ ZS-NZJ	80	King Air 200	BB-630	Out of the Blue Air Safaris P/L. Lanseria.	N630VB
☐ ZS-OAE	75	King Air E90	LW-151	King Air Services Partnership, Lanseria.	TR-LVH
☐ ZS-OAK	77	King Air 200	BB-197	Superstrike Investments 29 P/L. Bryanston.	(N12154)
☐ ZS-OBB	96	King Air B200	BB-1522	Fourie's Poultry Farm P/L. Potchefstrom.	N3272E
☐ ZS-OCI	76	King Air 200	BB-121	Manta Air P/L. Lanseria.	TR-LDX
☐ ZS-ODI	96	King Air B200	BB-1542	L J Investments CC. Pinegowrie.	N202JT
☐ ZS-OEB	79	King Air 200T	BT-7	NAC P/L. Rand. (was BB-510).	(N853GA)
☐ ZS-OED	83	King Air B200	BB-1149	Orion Air Charter, Randjiesfontein.	N200HF
☐ ZS-OEE	88	Reims/Cessna F406	F406-0023	Fugro Airborne Surveys P/L.	V5-...
☐ ZS-OFB	98	Pilatus PC-12/45	205	PC-XII Serial No 205 P/L. Benmore.	HB-F..
☐ ZS-OFD	98	Pilatus PC-12/45	208	Hydro Holdings P/L. Wonderboom.	HB-F..
☐ ZS-OGY	89	Reims/Cessna F406	F406-0035	COMAV/Air Namibia, Windhoek, Namibia. 'Oshakati'	S7-IDO
☐ ZS-OHB	68	King Air B90	LJ-431	Aircraft Africa Contracts Co P/L. Lanseria.	9Q-CVT
☐ ZS-OHR	75	King Air C90	LJ-669	Peter Vichos Trust, North Riding.	N971GA
☐ ZS-ONB	75	Mitsubishi MU-2L	674	Saratoga Air Services CC. Lanseria.	N299HT
☐ ZS-ONC	78	Mitsubishi MU-2N	727SA	Spring Lights 1 P/L. Lanseria.	N21MU
☐ ZS-ONR	95	Pilatus PC-12	108	Fireblade Investments Ltd. Lanseria.	N667JJ
☐ 7S-ONZ	81	Conquest 1	425-0075	C E Puckrin/Springgrove Air, Groenkloof.	ZS-PNP
☐ ZS-OOE	59	Gulfstream 1	5	Merate Aviation P/L. Randburg	F-GFGT
☐ ZS-OSB	78	King Air 200	BB-327	Trans African Aviation Sales P/L. Lanseria.	N327CM
☐ ZS-OSH	88	King Air 1300	BB-1296	Rossair Contracts P/L. Lanseria.	PH-DUS
☐ ZS-OTK	82	King Air C90A	LJ-1193	Merlin Aviation CC. Lanseria.	D2-ETJ
☐ ZS-OTL		Cheyenne T-1040	8275011	M Pohl, Duiwelskloof.	N2VZ
☐ ZS-OTP	80	King Air 200	BB-683	N J Fronemann, Lanseria.	N2877K
☐ ZS-OTS	83	King Air B200	BB-1113	SPH Group P/L. Capetown.	N745RL
☐ ZS-OTT	89	Reims/Cessna F406	F406-0040	COMAV/Air Namibia, Windhoek, Namibia. 'Swakop'	5Y-HHJ
☐ ZS-OUI	80	King Air/Catpass 250	BB-688	Skyeinvest Administration P/L. Wynberg.	5R-MGH
☐ ZS-OUO	01	PA-46-500TP Meridian	4697116	C D Wood, Orange Grove.	
☐ ZS-OUP	82	Cheyenne T-1040	8275002	Flying Colours Aviation P/L. Port Elizabeth.	5Y-UAL
☐ ZS-OUS	70	King Air 100	B-57	Lazercor 4 P/L. Port Elizaebth.	N190CA
☐ ZS-OUT	81	King Air 200	BB-764	JVS Air P/L. Lanseria.	LV-ONH
☐ ZS-OVX	86	King Air B200	BB-1253	N J Fronemann, Lanseria.	A2-AEO
☐ ZS-OYP	80	King Air 200	BB-594	Dezzo Trading 213 P/L. Durban.	N760BM
☐ ZS-PAM	81	King Air 200	BB-813	Balm Air/L Sparg & R Reid, Lanseria.	VH-IBF
☐ ZS-PAN	89	King Air B200	BB-1344	Pannar Air P/L. Greytown.	N21PS
☐ ZS-PAZ	84	King Air 300	FA-25	Naturelink K-A 300 Partnership, Sinoville.	N856GA
☐ ZS-PBH	70	King Air 100	B-9	Warne Aviation P/L. Lanseria.	3C-PBH
☐ ZS-PBL	79	King Air 1300	BB-468	Balmair Aviation P/L. Virginia.	N468SM
☐ ZS-PBS	81	PA-31T Cheyenne II	8120054	Semri Proprietary P/L. Louis Truchardt.	(N151CC)
☐ ZS-PBT	84	Cheyenne II-XL	1166004	Partnership EC II/Naturelink Airlines P/L. Wonderboom.	N90SC
☐ ZS-PCH	04	King Air B200	BB-1856	C & L Air P/L. Makwassie.	N61956
☐ ZS-PDZ	03	Pilatus PC-12/45	525	Cx ZS- 11/04 to ?	HB-FSA
☐ ZS-PEA	81	King Air 200C	BL-29	N500PH Aviation P/L. Durban.	N500PH
☐ ZS-PEI	01	King Air B200	BB-1789	Eurocoal P/L. Middleburg.	N4470B
☐ ZS-PEZ	96	King Air B200	BB-1528	Beltronixs P/L. Port Elizabeth.	N528SA
☐ ZS-PFA	68	King Air B90	LJ-395	Cenitor Management Holdings CC. Honeydew.	N81PG
☐ ZS-PFD	77	Rockwell 690B	11422	Emcom Africa P/L. Durban.	N310GA
☐ ZS-PGB	01	King Air B200	BB-1764	Vibramech P/L. Luipaardsvlei.	N4064Z
☐ ZS-PGW	81	King Air F90	LA-120	Desert Charm Trading 19 P/L. Sun Land.	N879PC
☐ ZS-PGX	04	Pilatus PC-12/45	560	S African Red Cross Air Mercy Service, Cape Town.	HB-...
☐ ZS-PHI	65	Gulfstream 1	164	Acas de Mocambique. 'Kruger Mpumalanga'	N290AS
☐ ZS-PHJ	64	Gulfstream 1	134	Nelair Aviation Services P/L. Nelspruit.	3D-DUE
☐ ZS-PHK	59	Gulfstream 1	25	Nelair Aviation Services P/L. Nelspruit.	3D-DLN
☐ ZS-PJR*	86	King Air 300	FA-89		N505BC
☐ ZS-PKM	78	King Air 200	BB-382	D S Avnit, Lanseria.	(N700E)
☐ ZS-PMM	99	King Air B200	BB-1654	Tresso Trading 693 P/L. Capetown.	N202DJ
☐ ZS-PPG	97	King Air B200	BB-1562	Pick N' Pay (Gabriel Road) P/L. Capetown.	N203JT
☐ ZS-PUF	81	King Air 200	BB-867	Sheltan Rail Trust, Port Elizabeth.	N24AR
☐ ZS-PZU	78	King Air 200	BB-315	Crucial Trade 101 P/L. Knysna.	ZS-TAB
☐ ZS-RAF	99	King Air B200	BB-1673	R A Foster, Lanseria.	N3173Y
☐ ZS-SDO	99	Pilatus PC-12/45	282	ZS-SDO Aircraft P/L. Bedfordview.	(ZS-SDP)
☐ ZS-SDP	99	Pilatus PC-12/45	286	Vengio Twelve P/L. Capetown.	(ZS-SDO)
☐ ZS-SLL	81	Gulfstream 840	11679	Vrede Textiles P/L. Dassenberg.	N840VB

Reg	Yr Type	c/n	Owner/Operator	Prev Regn
☐ ZS-SMC	94 King Air B200	BB-1489	AAA Investments P/L. Grahamstown.	N1563M
☐ ZS-SMY	95 Pilatus PC-12	113	Chrome Loads P/L. Rustenburg.	N562GA
☐ ZS-SOL	83 King Air B200	BB-1138	Bunker Hills Investments P/L. Lanseria.	(N138AJ)
☐ ZS-SRH	00 Pilatus PC-12/45	313	Tresso Trading 107 P/L. Capetown.	HB-F..
☐ ZS-SRR	00 Pilatus PC-12/45	319	November Whisky Zulu CC. Ermelo.	HB-F..
☐ ZS-TBM*	02 TBM 700C2	245	Naturelink Charters P/L. Wonderboom.	N700WH
☐ ZS-TIP	02 King Air B200	BB-1805	RVR Shelf 20 P/L. Standerton.	N4205G
☐ ZS-TLA	01 Pilatus PC-12/45	383	Hernic Exploration P/L. Brits.	
☐ ZS-TMA	80 Conquest II	441-0159	JVS Air P/L. Lanseria.	ZS-PMA
☐ ZS-TNY	81 King Air B200	BB-914	Ferox Investments P/L. Lanseria.	5X-INS
☐ ZS-TOB	95 King Air B200	BB-1515	Leonard Dingler P/L. Benoni.	N3235Z
☐ ZS-ZEN	95 Pilatus PC-12/45	125	Prostart Holdings 32 P/L. Lanseria.	N695WF
☐ ZS-ZXX	82 King Air B200	BB-1077	Matetsi Trust P/L. Parys.	(ZS-OGB)
Military				
☐ 651	82 King Air B200C	BL-45	SAAF, 41 Squadron, Waterkloof AFB.	ZS-LXS
☐ 652	81 King Air 200C	BL-34	SAAF, 41 Squadron, Waterkloof AFB.	ZS-LAY
☐ 653	87 King Air 300	FA-118	SAAF, 41 Squadron, Waterkloof AFB.	ZS-MHK
☐ 654	83 King Air B200C	BL-70	SAAF, 41 Squadron, Waterkloof AFB.	ZS-LNT
☐ 8030	97 Pilatus PC-12	145	SAAF, 41 Squadron, Waterkloof AFB.	HB-FRG

3A = MONACO
Total 4

Civil

Reg	Yr Type	c/n	Owner/Operator	Prev Regn
☐ 3A-...	79 PA-31T Cheyenne II	7920049		F-GFVO
☐ 3A-MIO	79 PA-31T Cheyenne II	7920001	Ljiljana Hennessy, Monaco.	I-NANE
☐ 3A-MON	81 King Air F90	LA-129		F-GKKK
☐ 3A-MSI	79 PA-31T Cheyenne 1	7904026	S Orlando, Cannes, France.	EX-EIM

3B = MAURITIUS
Total 2

Civil

Reg	Yr Type	c/n	Owner/Operator	Prev Regn
☐ 3B-NBC	95 Beech 1900D	UE-157	Noto Ltd. Port Louis.	N3217P
☐ 3B-SKY	90 King Air B200	BB-1363	Unitex Finance Holding (Mauritius) Ltd. Port Louis.	N5503K

3D = SWAZILAND
Total 1

Civil

Reg	Yr Type	c/n	Owner/Operator	Prev Regn
☐ 3D-TRE	60 Gulfstream 1	42	Gabon Express, Libreville, Gabon.	ZS-OCA

4R = SRI LANKA
Total 2

Military

Reg	Yr Type	c/n	Owner/Operator	Prev Regn
☐ CR-841	84 King Air B200T	BT-30	4R-HVE, Sri Lankan Air Force, Colombo. (was BB-1185).	N6923L
☐ CR-843	88 King Air 1300	BB-1314	HISAR, 8 Light Transport Sqn. Ratmalana.	N4277E

4X = ISRAEL
Total 29

Civil

Reg	Yr Type	c/n	Owner/Operator	Prev Regn
☐ 4X-CBF	81 PA-42 Cheyenne III	8001064	Z Danenberg, Sde Dov.	N932BF
☐ 4X-CBL	80 PA-31T Cheyenne II	8020080	Nesika Co Ltd. Herzlia.	N809SW
☐ 4X-CIC	82 PA-42 Cheyenne III	8001073	Moonair Aviation Ltd. Sde Dov.	N321CF
☐ 4X-CIE	79 PA-31T Cheyenne II	7920030	Ariel House Transportation Co. Sde Dov.	(N288SB)
☐ 4X-CIZ	76 SA-226T Merlin 3B	T-271	Fast Link Ltd. Netanya.	N707PK
☐ 4X-DZK	78 King Air 200	BB-306	Y Paposhado, Herzlia.	N306SS
☐ 4X-DZT	71 King Air C90	LJ-513	Chim-Nir Aviation Services Ltd. Herzlia.	N913K
Military				
☐ 4X-...	03 King Air B200	BB-1819	IDFAF, Tel Aviv.	N5019H
☐ 4X-...	03 King Air B200CT	BN-9	IDFAF, Tel Aviv.	N50969
☐ 4X-...	02 King Air B200	BB-1804	IDFAF, Tel Aviv.	N5104B
☐ 4X-...	02 King Air B200	BB-1811	848, IDFAF, Tel Aviv.	N51161
☐ 501	90 King Air B200	BB-1385	4X-FEA, IDFAF, Tel Aviv.	
☐ 504	90 King Air B200	BB-1386	4X-FEB, IDFAF, Tel Aviv.	N2872K
☐ 507	90 King Air B200	BB-1387	4X-FEC, IDFAF, Tel Aviv.	N2876B
☐ 510	90 King Air B200	BB-1388	4X-FED, IDFAF, Tel Aviv.	N2878B
☐ 6..	02 King Air B200T	BT-46	IDFAF, Tel Aviv.	N61346
☐ 622	00 King Air B200T	BT-39	IDFAF, Tel Aviv. (was BB-1684).	N32268
☐ 625	00 King Air B200T	BT-40	IDFAF, Tel Aviv. (was BB-1717).	N44717
☐ 629	00 King Air B200	BT-41	IDFAF, Tel Aviv. (was BB-1721).	N44721
☐ 633	00 King Air B200T	BT-42	IDFAF, Tel Aviv. (was BB-1724).	N44724
☐ 636	00 King Air B200	BT-43	IDFAF, Tel Aviv. (was BB-1727).	N42327
☐ 703	01 King Air B200CT	BN-5	IDFAF, Tel Aviv.	N5005M
☐ 974	82 King Air RC-12D	BP-7	4X-FSA, IDFAF, Tel Aviv.	82-23638

Reg	Yr Type	c/n	Owner/Operator	Prev Regn

☐ 977	82 King Air RC-12D	BP-8	4X-FSB, IDFAF, Tel Aviv.		82-23639
☐ 980	82 King Air RC-12D	BP-9	4X-FSC, IDFAF, Tel Aviv.		82-23640
☐ 982	82 King Air RC-12D	BP-10	4X-FSD, IDFAF, Tel Aviv.		82-23641
☐ 985	82 King Air RC-12D	BP-11	4X-FSE, IDFAF, Tel Aviv.		82-23642
☐ 987	King Air B200	FG-1	4X-FSF, IDFAF, Tel Aviv.		
☐ 990	King Air B200	FG-2	4X-FSG, IDFAF, Tel Aviv.		

5A = LIBYA
Total 4

Civil

☐ 5A-DDT	79 King Air 200C	BL-1	Libyan Air Ambulance/Ministry of Health, Tripoli.		(F-GBLT)
☐ 5A-DDY	80 King Air 200C	BL-6	Libyan Air Ambulance/Ministry of Health, Tripoli.		
☐ 5A-DHZ	80 SA-226T Merlin 3B	T-345	Air Jamahiriya, Tripoli.		OO-HSC
☐ 5A-DJX	81 SA-226T Merlin 3B	T-388	Air Jamahiriya, Tripoli.		OO-XSC

5B = CYPRUS
Total 2

Civil

☐ 5B-CJL	81 King Air C90	LJ-979	Dateline Overseas Ltd.		(D-IAAK)
☐ 5B-CKJ	00 King Air B200	BB-1729			N728AM

5H = TANZANIA
Total 5

Civil

☐ 5H-EXC	98 Pilatus PC-12/45	220	Coastal Tours & Travels Ltd. Dar-Es-Salaam,		ZS-EXC
☐ 5H-SRP	00 Pilatus PC-12/45	317	Coastal Tours & Travels Ltd. Dar-Es-Salaam.		ZS-SRP
☐ 5H-TZE	90 Reims/Cessna F406	F406-0046	Tanzanair, Dar es Salaam.		OY-PED
☐ 5H-WOW	91 Reims/Cessna F406	F406-0060	Air Excel Ltd. Arusha.		PH-GUG

Military

☐ JW9027	74 King Air A100	B-197	Tanzanian Air Force,		5X-UWT

5N = NIGERIA
Total 15

Civil

☐ 5N-AMU	81 King Air 200	BB-809	Dumez (Nigeria) Ltd. Lagos.		F-GCVQ
☐ 5N-AMW	81 Conquest 1	425-0067	Air Logistics/Airlog,		N6844V
☐ 5N-AMZ	78 King Air C90	LJ-755	Dumez (Nigeria) Ltd. Lagos.		N9085S
☐ 5N-ATR	85 Conquest II	441-0353	Julius Berger Nigeria Ltd.		N321AR
☐ 5N-AUT	75 PA-31T Cheyenne II	7520016	Seven Up Bottling Co Ltd. (status) ?		N101T
☐ 5N-BHL	78 King Air 200	BB-387	Bristow Helicopters (Nigeria) Ltd. Lagos.		G-BFOL
☐ 5N-IHS	80 King Air 200	BB-663			5N-AMT
☐ 5N-MAG	96 King Air 350	FL-153			N1083N
☐ 5N-MGV	DHC 8-102	024	Mobil Producing (Nigeria) Ltd. Lagos.		C-GMOK
☐ 5N-MPA	95 Beech 1900D	UE-149	Mobil Producing (Nigeria) Ltd. Lagos.		N3217L
☐ 5N-MPB	99 King Air 350	FL-238	Mobil Producing (Nigeria) Ltd. Lagos.		N2341R
☐ 5N-MPN	94 Beech 1900D	UE-77	Mobil Producing (Nigeria) Ltd. Lagos.		(N280KA)
☐ 5N-MPS	87 Dornier 228-201	8146	NEPA-National Electric Power Authority,		D-CALO
☐ 5N-SPC	97 Dornier 328-110	3083	Shell Petroleum Ltd. Lagos.		D-CDXO
☐ 5N-SPD	97 Dornier 328-110	3086	Shell Petroleum Ltd. Lagos.		D-CDXH

5R = MADAGASCAR
Total 1

Civil

☐ 5R-MIM	77 PA-31T Cheyenne II	7720059	Lycee Professionel St Exupery, Ivato.		N48AR

5T = MAURITANIA
Total 2

Military

☐ 5T-MAB	81 PA-31T Cheyenne II	8120024	Mauritanian Air Force, Nouakchott.		N2470X
☐ 5T-MAC	81 PA-31T Cheyenne II	8120026	Mauritanian Air Force, Nouakchott.		N2483X

5U = NIGER
Total 2

Civil

☐ 5U-ABY	78 King Air 200	BB-431	Nigeravia, Niamey.		F-GILH
☐ 5U-ACC	79 PA-31T Cheyenne II	7920056	SIM International, Niamey.		5T-TJY

5V = TOGO
Total 3

Civil

☐ 5V-TTD	69 King Air B90	LJ-453	PEFACO Ltd. Lome.		(D-IAMX)

Military

☐ 5V-MCG	81 King Air B200	BB-857	Government of Togo, Lome.		N57AC
☐ 5V-MCH	81 King Air B200	BB-858	Government of Togo, Lome.		N10AC

5X = UGANDA

Total 1

Civil

Reg	Yr Type	c/n	Owner/Operator	Prev Regn
☐ 5X-...	99 King Air B200	BB-1650		N771TP

5Y = KENYA

Total 32

Civil

Reg	Yr Type	c/n	Owner/Operator	Prev Regn
☐ 5Y-...	68 Gulfstream 1	190	Skyways Kenya Ltd. Nairobi. (status ?).	N190LE
☐ 5Y-...	80 Conquest II	441-0164		ZS-SMA
☐ 5Y-BIX	90 Reims/Cessna F406	F406-0055	East African Air Charters Ltd. Nairobi.	N65912
☐ 5Y-BKN	87 Reims/Cessna F406	F406-0021		PH-FWG
☐ 5Y-BKT	77 King Air 200	BB-256	Queensway Air Services (K) Ltd. Nairobi.	(5Y-NTM)
☐ 5Y-BLA	80 King Air 200C	BL-10		C-FAMB
☐ 5Y-BLR	60 Gulfstream 1	34	Skyways Kenya Ltd. Nairobi.	N34LE
☐ 5Y-BMA	76 King Air 200	BB-155	Skylink Aeromangement (K) Inc. Nairobi.	OY-GEH
☐ 5Y-BMC	77 King Air 200	BB-211	Skylink Aeromangement (K) Inc. Nairobi.	OY-BTR
☐ 5Y-BMR	61 Gulfstream 1	81	Skyways Kenya Ltd. Nairobi.	I-TASO
☐ 5Y-BMS	68 Gulfstream 1	194	Sincereways Kenya Ltd. Nairobi.	(FAV-8595)
☐ 5Y-BMY	78 Rockwell 690B	11474		5H-MTY
☐ 5Y-BVI	89 Beech 1900C-1	UC-55	Aviation Assistance A/S-UN, Nairobi.	OY-BVI
☐ 5Y-DDE	78 King Air 200	BB-379	IBIS Aviation Ltd. Nairobi.	G-ONEX
☐ 5Y-EKO	79 King Air 200C	BL-2	Air Bridge, Nairobi.	OY-BVE
☐ 5Y-HHA	82 King Air B200	BB-988	Blue Bird Aviation Ltd. Nairobi.	PH-LMC
☐ 5Y-HHE	79 King Air 200	BB-547	Blue Bird Aviation Ltd. Nairobi.	ZS-NIP
☐ 5Y-HHK	80 King Air 200	BB-696	Blue Bird Aviation Ltd. Nairobi.	5Y-TWB
☐ 5Y-JAI	79 King Air 200	BB-557	Capital Airlines Ltd. Nairobi.	OY-PAM
☐ 5Y-JET	60 Gulfstream 1	44	JetPet, Nairobi.	F-GFGV
☐ 5Y-JJZ	83 King Air B200	BB-1127	Cerere AG. Nairobi.	G-BMNF
☐ 5Y-JKB	75 King Air 200	BB-72	AD Aviation (Aircharters) Ltd. Nairobi. (status ?).	ZS-KJB
☐ 5Y-LRS	81 King Air 200C	BL-20	Mercedes-Benz of South Africa P/L. Wonderboom, RSA.	ZS-LRS
☐ 5Y-MAF	99 Pilatus PC-12/45	243	Mission Aviation Fellowship, Nairobi.	HB-FRN
☐ 5Y-MKM	89 Reims/Cessna F406	F406-0044		(LN-TED)
☐ 5Y-SJB	79 King Air/Catpass 250	BB-467	East African Coffee Co. Nairobi.	5H-MUN
☐ 5Y-SMB	78 King Air 200	BB-309		OY-PEB
☐ 5Y-TAL	86 Reims/Cessna F406	F406-0009	Trackmark Ltd. Nairobi.	PH-FWB
☐ 5Y-TWA	81 King Air 200	BB-803	Transworld Safaris (K) Ltd. Nairobi.	G-WPLC
☐ 5Y-TWC	81 King Air B200C	BL-37	Transworld Safaris (K) Ltd. Nairobi.	G-IFTB
☐ 5Y-XXX	58 Gulfstream 1	1	East African Air Charters Ltd. Nairobi.	ZS-NVG
☐ 5Y-ZBA	00 King Air B200	BB-1714	ZB Air, Nairobi.	N3214D

6O = SOMALIA

Total 1

Civil

Reg	Yr Type	c/n	Owner/Operator	Prev Regn
☐ 6O-SBV	83 SA-227TT Merlin 3C	TT-477	Murri Brothers, Mogadishu.	N3059Y

6V = SENEGAL

Total 2

Civil

Reg	Yr Type	c/n	Owner/Operator	Prev Regn
☐ 6V-AGO	76 PA-31T Cheyenne II	7620057	Eagle International Air Space, Dakar.	F-GDAL
☐ 6V-AGS	75 King Air 200	BB-28	Senegalair, Dakar.	F-GKPL

6Y = JAMAICA

Total 1

Civil

Reg	Yr Type	c/n	Owner/Operator	Prev Regn
☐ 6Y-JDB	77 Mitsubishi MU-2P	353SA	Aircraft & Engines Ltd. Grand Turk, Turks & Caicos Island.	6Y-JDB

7Q = MALAWI

Total 1

Civil

Reg	Yr Type	c/n	Owner/Operator	Prev Regn
☐ 7Q-YST	88 King Air 300	FA-139	Stancom Aviation, Lilongwe.	ZS-MLL

7T = ALGERIA

Total 14

Civil

Reg	Yr Type	c/n	Owner/Operator	Prev Regn
☐ 7T-VBE	93 King Air B200	BB-1453	National Institute of Cartography, Algiers.	N8153H
☐ 7T-VCV	72 King Air A100	B-93	ENESA/Air Algerie, Algiers.	N9369Q
☐ 7T-VRF	73 King Air A100	B-147	ENESA/Air Algerie, Algiers.	N1828W

Military

Reg	Yr Type	c/n	Owner/Operator	Prev Regn
☐ 7T-VRG	76 King Air 200	BB-184	Ministry of Defence, Boufarik.	
☐ 7T-VRH	76 King Air 200	BB-175	Ministry of Defence, Boufarik.	
☐ 7T-VRI	76 King Air 200	BB-171	Ministry of Defence, Boufarik.	
☐ 7T-VRO	81 King Air 200	BB-807	Ministry of Defence, Boufarik.	
☐ 7T-VRS	81 King Air 200	BB-759	Ministry of Defence, Boufarik.	F-GCTC

Reg	Yr Type	c/n	Owner/Operator	Prev Regn

Reg	Yr Type	c/n	Owner/Operator	Prev Regn
☐ 7T-VRT	81 King Air 200	BB-775	Ministry of Defence, Boufarik.	F-GCTD
☐ 7T-WCF	94 King Air C90B	LJ-1359	Ministry of Defence, Algiers.	N8280K
☐ 7T-WCG	94 King Air C90B	LJ-1379	Ministry of Defence, Algiers.	N3122K
☐ 7T-WCH	94 King Air C90B	LJ-1380	Ministry of Defence, Algiers.	N3128K
☐ 7T-WRY	81 King Air 200T	BT-20	Ministry of Defence, Boufarik. (was BB-871).	7T-VRY
☐ 7T-WRZ	81 King Air 200T	BT-21	Ministry of Defence, Boufarik. (was BB-895).	7T-VRZ

9A = CROATIA
Total 1

Military
☐ 014	PA-31T Cheyenne	...	Croatian Air Force, 27ETZ-Transport Aircraft Squadron,	

9G = GHANA
Total 1

Civil
☐ 9G-AGF	95 Beech 1900D	UE-136	Ashanti Ghana/Ashanti Goldfields Corp. Accra.	N3212K

9H = MALTA
Total 1

Civil
☐ 9H-ADV	00 King Air 350	FL-279	AWAIG Ltd. Luqa.	N3179Q

9J = ZAMBIA
Total 10

Civil
☐ 9J-...	74 King Air F90	LW-87		ZS-OGT
☐ 9J-AAV	70 King Air B90	LJ-486	ZESCO Ltd-Zambia Electricity Supply Co Ltd. Lusaka.	A2-J7T
☐ 9J-AFJ	89 Beech 1900C-1	UC-48	Roan Air Ltd/Mines Air Services Ltd. Lusaka.	N31559
☐ 9J-DCF	73 King Air C90	LJ-575	Zambia Skyways Ltd. Lusaka.	N12RF
☐ 9J-MAS	98 Beech 1900D	UE-323	Roan Air Ltd. Lusaka.	N23047
☐ 9J-MBO	98 Beech 1900D	UE-319	Roan Air Ltd. Lusaka. 'Kaingo'	N23004
☐ 9J-MED	King Air B200	...		
☐ 9J-TAF	70 King Air C90	LJ-485	TIAF, Lusaka.	ZS-AAU
☐ 9J-YVZ	68 King Air B90	LJ-338	Eastern Safaris Ltd. Lusaka.	ZS-LWZ

Military
☐ AF602	70 BAe HS 748-2A	1688	Zambian Air Force,	

9L = SIERRA LEONE
Total 1

Civil
☐ 9L-LDA	67 King Air A90	LJ-281		XU-999

9M = MALAYSIA
Total 10

Civil
☐ 9M-...	93 TBM 700	69		F-OHBL
☐ 9M-ASH	King Air B200	...		
☐ 9M-DSL	94 King Air 350	FL-122	Rimbaka Forestry Corp Sdn Bhd.	VH-OXE
☐ 9M-JPD	79 King Air 200T	BT-10	Directorate of Civil Aviation, Kuala Lumpur. (was BB-563).	N6065D
☐ 9M-KNS	77 King Air 200	BB-294	Penerbangan Sabah/Sabah Air Pte Ltd. Kota Kinabalu.	N18494
☐ 9M-TDM	86 PA-42 Cheyenne 400LS	5527032	TDM Helling Sdn Bhd. Kuala Lumpur.	N425D

Military
☐ M41-01	93 King Air 200T	BT-35	Royal Malaysian Air Force, 16 Sku, Subang. (was BB-1448).	N15509
☐ M41-02	93 King Air 200T	BT-36	Royal Malaysian Air Force, 16 Sku, Subang. (was BB-1451).	N80024
☐ M41-03	93 King Air 200T	BT-37	Royal Malaysian Air Force, 16 Sku, Subang. (was BB-1454).	N80027
☐ M41-04	93 King Air 200T	BT-38	Royal Malaysian Air Force, 16 Sku, Subang. (was BB-1457).	N80048

9Q = CONGO KINSHASA
Total 11

Civil
☐ 9Q-CBD	60 Gulfstream 1	35	CAA-Compagnie Africaine d'Aviation, Kinshasa.	N86MA
☐ 9Q-CBJ	66 Gulfstream 1	155	CAA-Compagnie Africaine d'Aviation, Kinshasa.	G-BMOW
☐ 9Q-CBU	71 681B Turbo Commander	6045		N9107N
☐ 9Q-CBY	60 Gulfstream 1	33	CAA-Compagnie Africaine d'Aviation, Kinshasa.	N23AH
☐ 9Q-CCG	74 King Air E90	LW-110	Inga Shaba, Kinshasa.	N8PC
☐ 9Q-CEM	72 King Air A100	B-105	Air Tropiques/Mimo,	ZS-TBS
☐ 9Q-CGL	70 681 Turbo Commander	6030	Cie Ciments Lacs,	D-IGAD
☐ 9Q-CKM	68 King Air B90	LJ-402	Fontshi Aviation Service, Kinshasa. 'Tshihuka'	ZS-IBE
☐ 9Q-CKZ	70 King Air B90	LJ-494	Shabair SPRL. Lumbumbashi.	(N15LM)
☐ 9Q-CRF	70 King Air 100	B-33	Forrest Air Co. Lumbumbashi.	N883K
☐ 9Q-CTG	80 King Air 200	BB-629	SCIBE Airlift, Kinshasa.	

Denotes reserved registration

Total Props	9903

Totals by Type Biz Turboprops

Type	Qty	Type	Qty	Type	Qty
2000 Starship	2	King Air 350C	1	MU-2 Marquise	108
2000A Starship	4	King Air 90	65	MU-2 Solitaire	45
680T Turbo Commander	7	King Air A100	130	P-180 Avanti	82
680V Turbo Commander	35	King Air A90	188	PA-31T Cheyenne	3
680W Turbo Commander	33	King Air B100	128	PA-31T Cheyenne 1	185
681 Turbo Commander	29	King Air B200	977	PA-31T Cheyenne 1A	17
681B Turbo Commander	17	King Air B200C	47	PA-31T Cheyenne II	412
AP68TP-600 Viator	1	King Air B200CT	9	PA-42 Cheyenne	2
ATR 42-320	1	King Air B200S	6	PA-42 Cheyenne 400LS	41
ATR 42-400MP	2	King Air B200T	15	PA-42 Cheyenne III	83
ATR 42F-300	1	King Air B300C	11	PA-42 Cheyenne IIIA	59
BAe HS 748-2A	3	King Air B90	138	PA-46 Turbo Malibu	2
BAe Jetstream 31	6	King Air C-12A	3	PA-46-400TP Meridian	4
BAe Jetstream 41	7	King Air C-12C	91	PA-46-500TP Meridian	193
Beech 1900C	9	King Air C-12D	29	PC-12 Spectre	1
Beech 1900C-1	11	King Air C-12F	57	Pilatus PC-12	75
Dccoh 1000D	29	King Air C-12J	6	Pilatus PC-12/45	421
Beech C-12J	1	King Air C-12L	3	Pilatus PC-12M	I
CASA 212-200	2	King Air C-12R	24	Pilatus PC-12M Eagle	1
CASA 212-300	1	King Air C-12U	9	Reims/Cessna F406	85
Cheyenne II-XL	77	King Air C-21R	2	Rockwell 690	64
Cheyenne PA-42	1	King Air C90	450	Rockwell 690A	201
Cheyenne T-1040	11	King Air C90-1	41	Rockwell 690AT	1
Conquest 1	216	King Air C90A	220	Rockwell 690B	196
Conquest II	326	King Air C90B	411	SA-226AT Merlin 4	12
DHC 6-300	3	King Air C90SE	2	SA-226AT Merlin 4A	30
DHC 7-103	1	King Air E90	307	SA-226T Merlin 3	32
DHC 8-102	1	King Air F90	195	SA-226T Merlin 3A	36
DHC 8-202	4	King Air F90-1	30	SA-226T Merlin 3B	63
Dornier 228-100	1	King Air JC-12C	2	SA-227AT Merlin 4C	43
Dornier 228-201	1	King Air JC-12D	1	SA-227TT Merlin 300	6
Dornier 228-212	4	King Air LC-90	5	SA-227TT Merlin 3C	26
Dornier 328-100	5	King Air RC-12D	19	SA-227TT Merlin 4C	2
Dornier 328-110	2	King Air RC-12G	3	SA-26AT Merlin 2B	58
Fairchild F-27F	3	King Air RC-12H	5	SA-26T Merlin 2A	13
Fokker 50	2	King Air RC-12K	8	SAAB 2000	5
Fokker 60UTA-N	4	King Air RC-12N	13	SAAB 340A	4
Fokker F 27-200	1	King Air RC-12P	12	SAAB 340B/Tp 100	2
Gulfstream 1	98	King Air TC90	26	SAAB 340B-SAR	2
Gulfstream 1000	98	King Air U-21J	5	TBM 700	114
Gulfstream 1000B	9	King Air UC-12B	53	TBM 700A	2
Gulfstream 1C	2	King Air UC-12F	12	TBM 700B	99
Gulfstream 840	111	King Air UC-12M	12	TBM 700C	72
Gulfstream 900	39	King Air UC-90	1	TBM 700C2	1
Gulfstream 980	78	King Air/Catpass 250	34	Xingu 121A	1
Ibis Ae 270P Spirit	5	Mitsubishi LR-1	13		
Jetcruzer 500	1	Mitsubishi MU-2B	12		
King Air	3	Mitsubishi MU-2D	4		
King Air 100	80	Mitsubishi MU-2E	5		
King Air 1300	15	Mitsubishi MU-2F	53		
King Air 200	747	Mitsubishi MU-2G	13		
King Air 200C	36	Mitsubishi MU-2J	58		
King Air 200T	24	Mitsubishi MU-2K	45		
King Air 300	216	Mitsubishi MU-2L	31		
King Air 300LW	21	Mitsubishi MU-2M	19		
King Air 350	425	Mitsubishi MU-2N	28		
King Air 350 (LR-2)	5	Mitsubishi MU-2P	34		

Business TurboProps - Written Off /Withdrawn From Use

C = CANADA

Civil

Reg	Yr	Type	c/n	Owner/Operator	Prev Regn
☐ C-FCAS	1965	King Air 90	LJ-23	W/o Sherrington, Canada. 1 May 79.	
☐ C-FCAU	1965	King Air 90	LJ-24	W/o Nr Quebec City, PQ. Canada. 30 Aug 85.	
☐ C-FCAV	1981	PA-42 Cheyenne III	8001006	Wfu. Last located Kamloops, BC. Canada.	N131RC
☐ C-FCGJ	1967	King Air A90	LJ-231	Wfu. Cx C- 4/91.	
☐ C-FCGX	1977	King Air/Catpass 250	BB-250	Wfu. Cx C- 6/04. Last located at Kamloops, BC. Canada.	N1008J
☐ C-FFEO	1967	680V Turbo Command	1693-72	W/o hangar fire Hamilton, ON. Canada. 15 Feb 93.	
☐ C-FFYC	1969	SA-26T Merlin 2A	T26-36	W/o N E of Thompson, MT. Canada. 31 May 94.	N739G
☐ C-FHBW	1968	King Air B90	LJ-336	Wfu. Located Aircraft Training School, Copenhagen, Denmark.	
☐ C-FHYX	1970	SA-26AT Merlin 2B	T26-174	W/o ground fire, Canada. Oct 73.	
☐ C-FKAL	1996	Pilatus PC-12	151	W/o Clarenville, NF. Canada. 18 May 98.	N151PB
☐ C-FKIJ	1970	King Air 100	B-52	Wfu. Last located Kamloops, BC. Canada.	N8NP
☐ C-FMAI	1973	King Air A100	B-145	Wfu. Last located Montgomery, Al. USA.	N380W
☐ C-FMAR	1959	Gulfstream 1	3	Wfu. Parts at Montreal, PQ. Canada.	N703G
☐ C-FQMS	1967	Mitsubishi MU-2B	009	W/o Athabaska, Canada. 7 Apr 80.	HB-LEB
☐ C-FRCL	1965	King Air 90	LJ-33	W/o Canada. 26 Aug 76.	N420G
☐ C-FSSU	1980	King Air 200	BB-633	W/o hangar fire Quebec City, PQ. Canada. 10 Jan 93.	N650TJ
☐ C-FUAC	1965	King Air 90	LJ-3	Wfu. Located Vincennes University, In. USA.	
☐ C-FVMH	1967	King Air A90	LJ-225	Wfu. Cx C- 8/91.	
☐ C-GAMJ	1978	PA-31T Cheyenne II	7820063	W/o Haul Beach, NT. Canada. 17 Apr 89.	N82298
☐ C-GAPT	1975	PA-31T Cheyenne II	7620004	W/o Toronto, ON. Canada. 17 Oct 84.	
☐ C-GBMI	1981	Conquest 1	425-0031	W/o La Rouche, PQ. Canada. 20 Nov 88.	N355MA
☐ C-GBTI	1974	King Air E90	LW-111	Wfu. Parts at Griffin, Ga. USA.	N11GE
☐ C-GBTI	1968	King Air B90	LJ-352	W/o Fort Frances, ON. Canada. 6 May 91.	VR-BHT
☐ C-GBTS	1979	King Air B100	BE-73	W/o Muskoka, ON. Canada. 13 Apr 99.	N54CK
☐ C-GCEV	1976	King Air 200	BB-153	W/o Sept-Iles Airport, PQ. Canada. 28 Jan 97.	N502AB
☐ C-GCSL	1976	King Air 200	BB-118	W/o Quebec City, PQ. Canada. 10 Jan 93.	
☐ C-GDOM	1968	King Air B90	LJ-368	W/o Fort Simpson, Canada. 16 Oct 88.	N1100D
☐ C-GDSD	1975	SA-226T Merlin 3A	T-251	Wfu. Cx C- 12/92.	N711RD
☐ C-GFRU	1976	Mitsubishi MU-2M	343	W/o Kelowna, BC. Canada. 18 Jan 82.	N728MA
☐ C-GHSI	1975	PA-31T Cheyenne II	7520025	Wfu. Cx C- 11/95.	
☐ C-GJNH	1966	680V Turbo Command	1587-38	Wfu. Cx C- 2/83.	N251B
☐ C-GJPD	1979	PA-31T Cheyenne II	7920070	W/o hangar fire Quebec City, PQ. Canada. 10 Jan 93.	
☐ C-GJUL	1975	King Air A100	B-218	W/o Chapleau, ON. Canada. 29 Nov 88.	N80MD
☐ C-GJWW	1973	SA-226AT Merlin 4	AT-013	Wfu. Cx C- 8/88. Parts at Griffin, Ga. USA.	N720R
☐ C-GKFG	1959	Gulfstream 1	22	Wfu. Cx C- 2/97.	N8BG
☐ C-GKRL	1981	King Air B200	BB-878	W/o Fort McMurray, Canada. 10 Dec 87.	G-BIPP
☐ C-GLOW	1974	Mitsubishi MU-2J	624	W/o Edmonton, AB. Canada. 6 Dec 81.	N474MA
☐ C-GNAK	1965	Gulfstream 1	154	W/o Linneas, Ne. USA. 19 Jul 00.	G-BNKO
☐ C-GODI	1974	Mitsubishi MU-2J	649	W/o Portage la Prairie, MT. Canada. 28 May 77.	N530MA
☐ C-GPIP	1977	PA-31T Cheyenne II	7720026	Wfu. Cx C- 1/93. Located Nr Lake City Airport, Fl. USA.	N82118
☐ C-GPPN	1968	King Air B90	LJ-389	W/o Hudson's Bay, Canada. 22 Dec 84.	N745JB
☐ C-GPTG	1968	Gulfstream 1	189	Wfu. Cx C- 3/01.	N776G
☐ C-GPWR	1970	SA-26AT Merlin 2B	T26-160	Wfu. Parts at White Industries, Bates City, Mo. USA.	N38MJ
☐ C-GQDD	1968	King Air B90	LJ-328	Wfu. Cx C- 5/87. Parts at Dodson's, Ottawa, Ks. USA.	N730K
☐ C-GSID	1975	PA-31T Cheyenne II	7520042	W/o Kirkland Lake, ON. Canada. 18 Oct 87.	(N118L)
☐ C-GSWB	1977	PA-31T Cheyenne II	7720013	W/o Montreal, PQ. Canada. 12 Nov 93.	N82092
☐ C-GTDL	1973	Gulfstream 1	110	Wfu. Cx C- 5/86.	N533CS
☐ C-GTHN	1968	SA-26T Merlin 2A	T26-16	W/o Whale Cove, NT. Canada. 29 Jun 96.	N748G
☐ C-GVCE	1972	King Air A100	B-135	W/o Calgary, AB. Canada. 21 Nov 84.	N4GT
☐ C-GVCY	1971	SA-226AT Merlin 4	AT-003	Wfu. Cx C- 5/94. Parts at Dodson's, Ottawa, Ks. USA.	N5295M
☐ C-GWCY	1968	King Air B90	LJ-345	W/o Lynn Lake, Canada. Oct 81.	N550TS
☐ C-GWFM	1975	PA-31T Cheyenne II	7520041	Wfu. Cx C- 8/93.	N54972
☐ C-GWGP	1968	Mitsubishi MU-2D	109	Wfu.	N1AN
☐ C-GWSP	1973	SA-226AT Merlin 4	AT-010	Wfu. Cx C- 10/03.	N603L
☐ C-GYMR	1970	SA-26AT Merlin 2B	T26-177	W/o Fort Good Hope, NT. Canada. 12 Oct 88.	N83RS
☐ C-GYQT	1974	King Air A100	B-189	W/o Big Trout Lake, ON. Canada. 21 Feb 95.	N22220

CN = MOROCCO

Civil

Reg	Yr	Type	c/n	Owner/Operator	Prev Regn
☐ CN-CDE	1979	King Air 200	BB-567	W/o Casablanca, Morocco. 3 Nov 86.	

Reg	Yr	Type	c/n	Owner/Operator	Prev Regn

Military

Reg	Yr	Type	c/n	Owner/Operator	Prev Regn
☐ CNA-NA	1974	King Air A100	B-180	W/o Morocco. Oct 78.	

CP = BOLIVIA

Civil

Reg	Yr	Type	c/n	Owner/Operator	Prev Regn
☐ CP-1016	1973	Rockwell 690	11053	W/o La Paz, Bolivia. 9 Aug 93.	
☐ CP-1017	1972	Rockwell 690	11054	W/o Callao, Peru. 13 Feb 74.	
☐ CP-1106	1974	Rockwell 690A	11193	Wfu.	
☐ CP-1849	1982	King Air B200C	BL-52	W/o Santa Cruz, Bolivia. 14 Mar 84.	N6872X
☐ CP-2287	1967	King Air A90	LJ-232	W/o Robore, Bolivia. 12 Apr 96.	N707EB
☐ CP-894	1970	681 Turbo Commande	6015	W/o Santa Cruz, Bolivia. 18 Jun 71.	N9066N

Military

Reg	Yr	Type	c/n	Owner/Operator	Prev Regn
☐ EB-002	1981	King Air 200C	BL-33	W/o 6 Dec 95.	FAB-002
☐ EB-003	1980	King Air C90	LJ-905	W/o 27 Nov 95.	YV-164CP
☐ FAB 006	1968	King Air B90	LJ-413	W/o La Paz, Bolivia. 26 Apr 79.	FAB 001
☐ FAB 023	1979	Rockwell 690B	11562	Wfu. Located La Paz, Bolivia.	HK-2996P

D = GERMANY

Civil

Reg	Yr	Type	c/n	Owner/Operator	Prev Regn
☐ D-CFMC	1986	King Air 300	FA-104	W/o Eichberg, Blumberg, Germany. 24 Oct 00.	(N494MA)
☐ D-IAAE	1978	Conquest II	441-0047	W/o Mount Orsa, Italy. 11 Jun 82.	(N36990)
☐ U-IAAY	1980	Conquest II	441-0144	W/o 6 Nov 80.	(N2627N)
☐ D-IAKS	1978	PA-31T Cheyenne II	7820048	W/o Borkum Island, Germany. 23 Jul 83.	OE-ΓOΓ
☐ D-IBAA	1983	Conquest 1	425-0163	W/o Hannover, Germany 24 Jan 96.	N66218
☐ D-IBAF	1976	King Air 200	BB-93	W/o Bourgas, Bulgaria. 27 Jul 77.	OE-FMC
☐ D-IBAR	1981	Gulfstream 980	95054	W/o Paderborn, Germany. 30 Jan 85.	(N9806S)
☐ D-ICBC	1993	King Air 300	FA-227	W/o St Moritz-Samedan, Switzerland. 14 Feb 02.	(SP-FNH)
☐ D-ICEK	1981	Conquest 1	425-0055	W/o Aichstetten, Germany. 10 Dec 92.	N425VC
☐ D-IDDI	1979	PA-31T Cheyenne II	7920014	W/o Cologne, Germany. 5 Feb 93.	N792SW
☐ D-IEFW	1986	Conquest 1	425-0228	W/o Lake Constance, Switzerland. 24 Jan 94.	N1227A
☐ D-IEGA	1981	Conquest II	441-0193	W/o Ascheberg, Germany. 2 Apr 00.	OE-FRZ
☐ D-IEWK	1976	SA-226AT Merlin 4A	AT-042	W/o Munich, Germany. 5 Feb 87.	OE-FTA
☐ D-IFSH	1982	PA-42 Cheyenne III	8001101	W/o Zurich, Switzerland. 28 Oct 03.	4X-CIM
☐ D-IGSW	1980	King Air 200	BB-669	W/o Keller Joch Mountain, Austria. 22 Nov 90.	N80GA
☐ D-IHAN	1979	MU-2 Solitaire	396SA	W/o Steinhausen, Germany. 9 Aug 79.	N788MA
☐ D-IHNA	1981	King Air C90	LJ-926	W/o Mindelheim, Germany. 27 May 94.	(D-IBBI)
☐ D-IHVI	1980	PA-31T Cheyenne II	8020007	W/o Southend, UK. 13 Mar 86.	N2529R
☐ D-IIWB	1980	PA-31T Cheyenne II	8020030	Wfu. Cx D- 2/96. Parts at Griffin, Ga. USA.	N37CA
☐ D-IKKS	1981	PA-31T Cheyenne II	8120034	W/o Concord, Ca. USA. 14 Jul 84.	F-GDCR
☐ D-IKOC	1978	Rockwell 690B	11498	W/o Paris, France. 21 Feb 81.	N131SA
☐ D-IKWP	1980	PA-31T Cheyenne 1	8004049	W/o Blieskastel, Germany. 10 Dec 88.	N5GW
☐ D-ILHA	1971	King Air C90	LJ-509	Wfu. Iinstructional airframe, Hamburg, Germany.	
☐ D-ILMA	1965	King Air 90	LJ-48	W/o Greven, Germany. 13 Aug 69.	
☐ D-ILNI	1966	King Air A90	LJ-116	W/o Milan, Italy. 21 Sep 67.	
☐ D-ILNU	1966	King Air A90	LJ-178	W/o Bremen, Germany. 16 Feb 67.	N798K
☐ D-ILRA	1980	PA-31T Cheyenne II	8020009	W/o Munich, Germany. 11 Aug 87.	N24HE
☐ D-ILSE	1969	SA-26AT Merlin 2B	T26-163E	W/o Stuttgart, Germany. 10 Apr 73.	F-BKML
☐ D-ILTU	1968	King Air B90	LJ-359	W/o Frankfurt, Germany. 22 Jan 71.	N7077N
☐ D-IMAY	1985	PA-42 Cheyenne 400L	5527024	W/o Nuremberg, Germany. 5 May 01.	(N400TM)
☐ D-IMON	1968	680W Turbo Comman	1819-33	W/o Lake Walchensee, Germany. 27 Dec 78.	
☐ D-IMTT	1978	PA-31T Cheyenne II	7820041	Wfu. Parts at Dodson's, Ottawa, Ks. USA.	N82WC
☐ D-IMWH	1981	King Air Γ90	LA-114	W/o Dusseldorf, Germany. 6 Dec 87.	N313BH
☐ D-INIX	1972	Rockwell 690	11013	W/o Greenland. 21 Jun 72.	N9213N
☐ D-IOET	1973	Rockwell 690A	11142	W/o Luton, UK. 1 Dec 81.	
☐ D-IOFC	1978	PA-31T Cheyenne 1	7804011	W/o Borgo Ticino, Italy. 25 Mar 84.	
☐ D-IXIE	1981	King Air F90	LA-96	Wfu. Located Orleans, France.	N96NA

D2 = ANGOLA

Civil

Reg	Yr	Type	c/n	Owner/Operator	Prev Regn
☐ D2-ECH	1978	King Air 200	BB-345	W/o Cafunfo, Angola. 28 Jan 95.	F-GHCT
☐ D2-ECL	1975	King Air 200	BB-44	W/o Luanda, Angola. 28 May 97.	F-GHAL

EC = SPAIN

Civil

Reg	Yr	Type	c/n	Owner/Operator	Prev Regn
☐ EC-COI	1975	King Air C90	LJ-663	Wfu. Located Toledo-Ocana, Spain.	E22-7
☐ EC-COJ	1975	King Air C90	LJ-664	W/o Salamanca, Spain. 4 Oct 83.	E 22-8
☐ EC-DXG	1967	680V Turbo Command	1711-86	Wfu. Loacted Globalia Training Centre, Llucmajor, Mallorca.	N535SM
Reg	**Yr**	**Type**	**c/n**	**Owner/Operator**	**Prev Regn**

Reg	Yr	Type	c/n	Owner/Operator	Prev Regn
☐ EC-EFH	1973	Rockwell 690A	11130	Wfu.	N111VS
☐ EC-ERQ	1977	King Air 200	BB-218	W/o Banjul, Gambia. 9 Oct 97.	EC-351
☐ EC-ETH	1983	Conquest 1	425-0151	W/o Nr Malaga, Spain. 4 Sep 92.	N81798
☐ EC-EXQ	1964	Gulfstream 1	142	Wfu. Located Madrid-Barajas, Spain.	EC-461
☐ EC-EXS	1961	Gulfstream 1	64	Wfu. Located Madrid-Barajas, Spain.	EC-460
☐ EC-FFE	1976	Rockwell 690A	11344	W/o Warsaw-Okecie, Poland. 29 Nov 95.	N900FT
☐ EC-GDV	1976	SA-226AT Merlin 4A	AT-043	W/o Mediterranean Sea 10 Oct 01.	EC-975

Military

Reg	Yr	Type	c/n	Owner/Operator	Prev Regn
☐ E 22-02	1974	King Air C90	LJ-621	W/o Paria, Spain. 18 Feb 04.	EC-CHA
☐ E22-5	1974	King Air C90	LJ-623	W/o Salamanca, Spain. 1 Oct 80.	EC-CHB

EI = EIRE

Civil

Reg	Yr	Type	c/n	Owner/Operator	Prev Regn
☐ EI-BGL	1978	Rockwell 690B	11507	W/o UK. 13 Nov 84.	N81850

EP = IRAN

Civil

Reg	Yr	Type	c/n	Owner/Operator	Prev Regn
☐ EP-AHN	1974	Rockwell 690A	11147	W/o.	
☐ EP-AKA	1972	681B Turbo Command	6065	Wfu. Located Aerospace Exhibition Centre, Tehran, Iran.	
☐ EP-AKB	1972	681B Turbo Command	6067	Wfu. Located Aerospace Exhibition Centre, Tehran, Iran.	

Military

Reg	Yr	Type	c/n	Owner/Operator	Prev Regn
☐ 5-59	1970	681 Turbo Commande	6009	Wfu. Located Tehran-Mehrabad.	N9059N
☐ IIN 501	1972	Rockwell 690	11049	W/o.	

F = FRANCE

Civil

Reg	Yr	Type	c/n	Owner/Operator	Prev Regn
☐ F-BNMC	1967	King Air A90	LJ-149	W/o Nr Marseilles, France. 28 Aug 97.	
☐ F-BSTM	1966	680V Turbo Command	1540-6	Wfu. Located Pelegry-Perpignan Museum, France.	F-WSTM
☐ F-BTDP	1972	King Air C90	LJ-560	W/o 17 Dec 74.	
☐ F-BTEE	1976	PA-31T Cheyenne II	7620045	Wfu. CoA expiry 16 Dec 92. Cx F- 10/00.	F-ODEE
☐ F-BUTS	1973	King Air E90	LW-68	Wfu. Cx F- 9/03.	
☐ F-BUTV	1973	King Air C90	LJ-602	W/o. Destroyed by fire, France. 28 Jul 92.	
☐ F-BVET	1975	King Air 200	BB-21	Wfu. Cx F- 10/03.	
☐ F-BVRP	1975	King Air 200	BB-38	W/o Baiuyan, China. 4 Apr 83.	
☐ F-BVVM	1965	King Air 90	LJ-26	Wfu. Cx F- 4/94.	D-ILGK
☐ F-BXAR	1975	King Air C90	LJ-658	W/o Ca. USA. Jan 79.	
☐ F-BXSF	1965	King Air 90	LJ-29	Wfu. Cx F- 3/93. Parts at Dodson's. Ottawa, Ks. USA.	D-ILMI
☐ F-GABV	1974	King Air E90	LW-102	W/o Alencon/Mount des Avaloirs, France. 1 May 98.	(F-GRCV)
☐ F-GAMP	1977	PA-31T Cheyenne II	7720029	Wfu. CoA expiry 23 Apr 93. Cx F- 10/00.	(N82122)
☐ F-GBDZ	1978	King Air E90	LW-295	W/o Paris, France. 15 Dec 82.	
☐ F-GBRD	1974	King Air E90	LW-91	W/o Barcelonette, France. 2 Nov 86.	N75DA
☐ F-GBRP	1978	King Air 200	BB-368	W/o Ribeauville, France. 17 Oct 80.	
☐ F-GCCC	1979	King Air 200	BB-504	W/o Bergamo, Italy. 26 Mar 84.	
☐ F-GCFH	1966	King Air A90	LJ-127	Wfu. Cx F- 8/96.	N72RD
☐ F-GCJS	1979	Mitsubishi MU-2P	406SA	Wfu. Cx F- 2/00.	N967MA
☐ F-GDHS	1981	MU-2 Marquise	1532SA	W/o Macey/Troyes, France. 21 May 91.	F-WDHS
☐ F-GDHV	1980	MU-2 Marquise	779SA	W/o Papeete, Tahiti. 27 May 94.	D-IFTG
☐ F-GDLE	1977	King Air 200	BB-230	W/o Moulins, France. 24 Nov 01.	G-BEHR
☐ F-GDMM	1965	King Air 90	LJ-54	Wfu. Cx F- 9/92.	N66WC
☐ F-GDPJ	1975	PA-31T Cheyenne II	7620006	W/o Paris, France. 12 Dec 84.	C-GDOW
☐ F-GDRT	1965	King Air 90	LJ-4	Wfu. CoA expiry 8/88, Cx F- 8/96.	TR-LBB
☐ F-GEBK	1976	SA-226T Merlin 3A	T-272	W/o Apr 85.	N49MJ
☐ F-GEDV	1966	King Air A90	LJ-150	Wfu. Last located Pointoise, France.	D-ICPD
☐ F-GEFR	1975	King Air A100	B-220	W/o Lille, France. 28 Aug 86.	N700K
☐ F-GEJY	1972	SA-226T Merlin 3	T-222	Wfu. Located La Roche-Sur-Yon, France.	N5306M
☐ F-GEPE	1977	PA-31T Cheyenne II	7720031	Wfu. Instructional airframe Bodo, Norway.	HB-LIW
☐ F-GERA	1977	Mitsubishi MU-2N	701SA	W/o St Just, France. 16 Apr 88.	N468DB
☐ F-GERN	1979	King Air C90A	LJ-854	W/o St Broladre, France. 30 Dec 93.	N712D
☐ F-GFBF	1976	PA-31T Cheyenne II	7620054	Wfu. Cx F- 12/99.	N39518
☐ F-GFCQ	1964	Gulfstream 1	140	Wfu. Cx F- 4/98.	N92SA
☐ F-GFHR	1982	Conquest II	441-0252	W/o Saclay, France. 17 Nov 88.	N441CG
☐ F-GFIC	1960	Gulfstream 1	49	Wfu. Cx F- 4/98.	N456
☐ F-GFJF	1967	King Air A90	LJ-262	Wfu. CoA expiry 1/89, Cx F- 8/96.	N111ME
☐ F-GFLD	1977	King Air C90	LJ-741	Wfu.	HB-GGW
☐ F-GFMS	1979	SA-226T Merlin 3B	T-296	W/o Vannes, France. 7 Nov 87.	N245DA
☐ F-GGAM	1965	King Air 90	LJ-32	Wfu. Cx F- 15 May 98.	F-BTOK

Reg	Yr	Type	c/n	Owner/Operator	Prev Regn

Reg	Yr	Type	c/n	Owner/Operator	Prev Regn
☐ F-GGRZ	1979	MU-2 Solitaire	395SA	W/o 9 May 91.	N787MA
☐ F-GHBE	1979	King Air 200	BB-500	W/o 8 Feb 91.	N13HC
☐ F-GHFM	1977	King Air 200	BB-213	Wfu. Cx F- 4/96.	C-GBWC
☐ F-GHLD	1977	King Air/Catpass 250	BB-233	W/o Libreville, Gabon. 17 Dec 98.	N50JD
☐ F-GIAL	1981	King Air 200	BB-844	W/o Caen-Carpiquet, France. 9 Sep 99. (parts at Dodsons)..	SE-IGV
☐ F-GIIX	1964	Gulfstream 1	128	W/o Lyon-Satolas, France. 28 Jun 94.	G-BMSR
☐ F-GIML	1976	King Air E90	LW-180	W/o Reims-Prunay, France. 14 Nov 00.	N2180L
☐ F-GJCN	1980	King Air E90	LW-335	W/o 18 Aug 81.	
☐ F-GJGC	1963	Gulfstream 1	111	Wfu. Located Marseille-Marignane, France.	N3630
☐ F-GJLH	1990	Reims/Cessna F406	F406-0056	W/o Strasbourg, France. Sep 93.	
☐ F-GJPL	1981	PA-31T Cheyenne II	8120029	W/o Azores, Atlantic Ocean. 5 Jun 90.	(D-IKHK)
☐ F-GLBC	1991	TBM 700	18	W/o France 15 Nov 91.	
☐ F-GLRA	1985	King Air C90A	LJ-1105	W/o Saumur, France. 19 Oct 94. Cx F- 10/95,	N72233
☐ F-GNGU	1963	Gulfstream 1	101	Wfu. Cx F- 4/98.	4X-ARV
☐ F-ODUK	1982	Conquest II	441-0270	W/o Faaa, Tahiti, French Polynesia. 4 Dec 90.	N441AC
☐ F-OHJL	1998	King Air B200	BB-1592	W/o Nr Faaa-Tahiti, French Polynesia. 16 Apr 04.	N6148X

G = GREAT BRITAIN

Civil

Reg	Yr	Type	c/n	Owner/Operator	Prev Regn
☐ G-ASXT	1964	Gulfstream 1	135	Wfu. Cx G- 4/89. Located Denver, Co. USA..	N755G
☐ G-BARX	1973	King Air A100	B-141	W/o Sturgate, UK. 12 Jan 77.	
☐ G-BGHR	1979	King Air 200	BB-508	W/o Tremblay, France. 25 Sep 79	
☐ G-BHUL	1974	King Air E90	LW-83	W/o Goodwood, UK. 22 Apr 85.	N99855
☐ G-BKID	1973	King Air C90	LJ-604	W/o Copenhagen, Denmark. 26 Dec 83.	N1GV
☐ G-BNAT	1974	King Air C90	LJ-614	W/o East Midlands, UK. 25 Jan 88.	G-OMET
☐ G-BNCE	1959	Gulfstream 1	9	Wfu. Located Dundee, Scotland.	N436M
☐ G-BOBX	1961	Gulfstream 1	77	Wfu.	9Q-CFK
☐ G-MDJI	1983	King Air B200	BB-1162	W/o Ottley Chevin Hill, UK. 19 Oct 87.	N71CS
☐ G-MOXY	1980	Conquest II	441-0154	W/o Blackbushe, UK. 26 Apr 87.	G-BHLN
☐ G-TWIG	1986	Reims/Cessna F406	F406-0014	W/o 37nm NW of Inverness, Scotland. 22 Oct 04.	PH-FWD
☐ G-WSJE	1979	King Air 200	BB-484	W/o Southend, UK. 12 Sep 87.	N84KA

HB = SWITZERLAND

Civil

Reg	Yr	Type	c/n	Owner/Operator	Prev Regn
☐ HB-...		King Air 200	...	W/o Kracow, Poland. 27 Aug 95.	
☐ HB-FOA	1991	Pilatus PC-12	P-01	Wfu. Cx HB- 31 Dec 96. Preserved at Pilatus HQ.	
☐ HB-FOJ	1996	Pilatus PC-12/45	158	W/o Brno, Czech Republic. 26 May 98.	
☐ HB-GDV	1968	King Air B90	LJ-433	W/o Kleinober, Austria. 24 Jan 86.	
☐ HB-LHT	1975	PA-31T Cheyenne II	7520003	W/o Shannon, Ireland. 12 Nov 76.	N66841
☐ HB-LLP	1980	MU-2 Marquise	767SA	W/o Basel, Switzerland. 3 Sep 94.	N251MA
☐ HB-LLS	1981	Conquest 1	425-0040	W/o Berne, Switzerland. 3 Mar 86.	N6775J

HI = DOMINICAN REPUBLIC

Civil

Reg	Yr	Type	c/n	Owner/Operator	Prev Regn
☐ HI-578SP	1989	King Air 300	FA-180	W/o Guatemala 21 Jan 90.	N1568E

HC = ECUADOR

Military

Reg	Yr	Type	c/n	Owner/Operator	Prev Regn
☐ FAE-723	1980	King Air 200	BB-723	W/o Huey Rapingo Mountain, Ecuador 24 May 81.	HC-BHG

HK = COLOMBIA

Civil

Reg	Yr	Type	c/n	Owner/Operator	Prev Regn
☐ HK-1771G	1974	Rockwell 690A	11217	Wfu. Located Bogota, Colombia.	N9227N
☐ HK-1805	1968	King Air B90	LJ-329	Wfu. Parts at Dodson's, Ottawa, Ks. USA.	N303X
☐ HK-1844P	1973	Rockwell 690	11056	Wfu. Located Charallave, Colombia.	HK-1844W
☐ HK-2217	1971	681B Turbo Command	6053	W/o Medellin, Colombia. 13 Mar 86.	HK-2217W
☐ HK-2245P	1976	Mitsubishi MU-2L	684	Wfu. Cx USA 8/95 as N600TN.	HK-2245W
☐ HK-2415	1973	Rockwell 690A	11100	W/o Bolivar Quay, Colombia. 8 Sep 91. (was s/n 11070).	N9200N
☐ HK-2438W	1979	SA-226T Merlin 3B	T-305	Wfu. Located at Catam AB. Bogota, Colombia.	N5658M
☐ HK-2451P	1980	PA-31T Cheyenne II	8020040	Wfu. Cx HK- 5/00.	
☐ HK-2478P	1980	Gulfstream 840	11609	W/o Riofrio, Venezuela. 15 Jun 90.	HK-2478W
☐ HK-2489	1978	King Air 200	BB-393	W/o Bogota, Colombia. 28 Oct 85.	N2014K
☐ HK-2532G	1967	Mitsubishi MU-2B	010	Wfu.	N4MA
☐ HK-2599P	1980	Gulfstream 840	11642	Wfu. Cx HK- 5/00.	HK-2599W
☐ HK-2674P	1981	PA-31T Cheyenne II	8120047	Wfu. Located Bogota, Colombia.	
☐ HK-2873W	1962	King Air C90	LJ-994	Wfu. Located Madrid AB. Colombia.	HK-2873
☐ HK-2907P	1981	Cheyenne II-XL	8166059	W/o Bocono, Venezuela. 13 Feb 00.	(N620AD)

Reg	Yr	Type	c/n	Owner/Operator	Prev Regn

Reg	Yr	Type	c/n	Owner/Operator	Prev Regn
☐ HK-3236P	1971	681B Turbo Command	6046	Wfu. Located Medellin, Colombia.	HK-3236X
☐ HK-3278	1984	Gulfstream 1000	96073	W/o Caqueta, Venezuela. 21 Mar 90.	N85DJ
☐ HK-3315X	1959	Gulfstream 1	24	W/o Nr Ibague, Colombia. 5 Feb 90.	N713US
☐ HK-3316X	1960	Gulfstream 1	59	W/o Monteira, Colombia. 2 May 90.	N11CZ
☐ HK-3330X	1962	Gulfstream 1	90	Wfu. Parts at Dodson's, Ottawa, Ks. USA.	N41JK
☐ HK-3337	1985	Conquest II	441-0354	Wfu. Located Bogota, Colombia.	HK-3337W
☐ HK-3412W	1980	Gulfstream 980	95010	Wfu. Located Bogota, Colombia.	HK-3412
☐ HK-3614	1980	Conquest II	441-0178	Wfu. Cx HK- 5/00.	N446WS
Military					
☐ FAC-5600	1982	Gulfstream 1000	96044	Wfu. Located El Dorado AB. Colombia.	HK-2908

HL = KOREA

Civil

☐ HL5204	1991	PA-42 Cheyenne 400L	5527043	W/o Cheju, South Korea. 20 Mar 91.	N9226B
☐ HL5223	1971	681B Turbo Command	6057	W/o South Korea. 13 Sep 74.	N9130N

HS = THAILAND

Civil

☐ HS-TFB	1966	680T Turbo Command	1573-28	W/o Bangkok, Thailand. 22 Jul 84.	N80SS
Military					
☐ 21-111	1977	SA-226AT Merlin 4A	AT-062E	W/o Thailand. 6 Nov 78.	
☐ 29-999	1978	SA-226AT Merlin 4A	AT-065	W/o Thailand. 20 Sep 82.	N5442M
☐ 348	1980	SA-226T Merlin 3B	T-348	Wfu.	N1009G

I = ITALY

Civil

☐ I-....	1978	PA-31T Cheyenne II	7820059	Wfu. (status ?).	N11BC
☐ I-CODE	1981	PA-31T Cheyenne II	8120023	W/o Malindi, Kenya. 30 Dec 86.	N2468X
☐ I-FRUT	1979	MU-2 Solitaire	413SA	Wfu. Located Rotterdam, Holland.	N994MA
☐ I-IDMA	1980	MU-2 Marquise	769SA	W/o Sardinia. 24 Oct 89.	N57MS
☐ I-KWYR	1980	King Air C90	LJ-873	W/o Rome, Italy. 10 Feb 89.	N44TG
☐ I-MDDD	1964	Gulfstream 1	143	Wfu. CoA expiry 26 Sep 91.	N914P
☐ I-MGGG	1960	Gulfstream 1	51	Wfu. Located Geneva, Switzerland.	N90PM
☐ I-MLWT	1967	680T Turbo Command	1694-73	Wfu. CoA expiry 8 Nov 89.	N999WT
☐ I-PJAR	1987	P-180 Avanti	1002	Wfu. CoA expiry 3 Jun 95.	
☐ I-PJAV	1987	P-180 Avanti	1001	Wfu. CoA expiry 7 Dec 90.	
☐ I-RWWW	1977	King Air E90	LW-220	Wfu. CoA expiry 8 Apr 90.	N17619
☐ I-TASB	1963	Gulfstream 1	105	Wfu. Located Bacong, Negros Oriental, Philippines.	N702G
☐ I-TASE	1975	Rockwell 690A	11260	Wfu. CoA expiry 9 Oct 95. Last located Bergamo, Italy.	N324BT
☐ I-TELM	1979	Rockwell 690B	11506	Wfu. CoA expiry 2 Mar 87.	D-IKAH

JA = JAPAN

Civil

☐ JA8604	1981	Gulfstream 980	95044	W/o 24 Mar 03.	N65664
☐ JA8620	1963	Mitsubishi MU-2A	001	Wfu.	
☐ JA8625	1963	Mitsubishi MU-2A	002	Wfu. Displayed at Osaka, Japan as 'KA1969'.	
☐ JA8626	1963	Mitsubishi MU-2A	003	Wfu. Displayed at Aerospace Museum Nagoya, Japan.	
☐ JA8627	1963	Mitsubishi MU-2B	004	Wfu. Cx JA 9/97.	
☐ JA8628	1963	Mitsubishi MU-2B	005	Wfu. Displayed at Tokyo-Narita, Japan.	
☐ JA8737	1970	Mitsubishi MU-2G	501	Wfu.	
☐ JA8753	1970	Mitsubishi MU-2G	504	W/o Japan. 11 Mar 81.	
☐ JA8767	1970	Mitsubishi MU-2G	520	Wfu. Cx JA 12/85.	
☐ JA8770	1971	Mitsubishi MU-2F	195	Wfu. Displayed at Senda, Japan.	
☐ JA8783	1971	Mitsubishi MU-2G	546	Wfu. Cx JA 4/86.	
☐ JA8825	1981	King Air 200T	BT-19	W/o Fukuoka, Japan. 17 Feb 87. (was BB-823).	N3718N
☐ JA8896	1992	TBM 700	68	W/o Obihiro Airport, Japan. 26 Apr 96.	F-OHBI
Military					
☐ 03-3207	1969	Mitsubishi MU-2S	907	W/o Japan. 2 Sep 70.	
☐ 03-3208	1970	Mitsubishi MU-2S	908	Wfu. (was s/n 186).	
☐ 13-3209	1971	Mitsubishi MU-2S	909	Wfu. Displayed at JASDF Hamamatsu, Japan. (was s/n 200).	
☐ 13-3210	1971	Mitsubishi MU-2S	910	Wfu. (was s/n 201).	
☐ 13-3211	1971	Mitsubishi MU-2S	911	Wfu. (was s/n 202).	
☐ 13-3212	1971	Mitsubishi MU-2S	912	Wfu. (was s/n 204).	
☐ 22-001	1967	Mitsubishi MU-2C	801	W/o Japan. 10 May 71. (was s/n 036).	
☐ 22002	1971	Mitsubishi LR-1	802	W/o Niikappu-tyo, Hokkaido, Japan. 14 Jun 77. (was s/n 203).	
☐ 22004	1972	Mitsubishi LR-1	804	Wfu. Located Mitsu-Seiki in Ichinomiya-cho, Hyogo.	
☐ 22005	1973	Mitsubishi LR-1	805	Wfu. (was s/n 275).	
Reg	*Yr*	*Type*	*c/n*	*Owner/Operator*	*Prev Regn*

Reg	Yr	Type	c/n	Owner/Operator	Prev Regn
❑ 22006	1974	Mitsubishi LR-1	806	Wfu. (was s/n 317).	
❑ 22011	1980	Mitsubishi LR-1	811	W/o Japan. 10 Aug 81. (was s/n 421).	
❑ 22012	1980	Mitsubishi LR-1	812	W/o 27km E of Miyako-jima, Japan. 7 Feb 90. (was s/n 422).	
❑ 23050	1990	King Air 350	FL-15	Wfu.Training airframe at JGSDF Utsunomiya Flying School.	N25KB
❑ 23-3213	1972	Mitsubishi MU-2F	913	Wfu. (was s/n 225).	
❑ 23-3214	1972	Mitsubishi MU-2E	914	Wfu. (was s/n 227).	
❑ 33-3215	1972	Mitsubishi MU-2E	915	Wfu. (was s/n 234).	
❑ 33-3216	1972	Mitsubishi MU-2E	916	Wfu. (was s/n 235).	
❑ 33-3217	1973	Mitsubishi MU-2E	917	Wfu. (was s/n 278).	
❑ 43-3218	1973	Mitsubishi MU-2E	918	Wfu. (was s/n 279).	
❑ 53-3219	1974	Mitsubishi MU-2E	919	W/o SW of Hamamatsu, Japan. 19 Oct 94. (was s/n 318).	
❑ 53-3271	1974	Mitsubishi MU-2J	951	Wfu. (was s/n 654).	
❑ 63-3220	1976	Mitsubishi MU-2E	920	Wfu. (was s/n 335).	
❑ 63-3221	1976	Mitsubishi MU-2E	921	Wfu. (was s/n 336).	
❑ 6801	1973	King Air TC90	LJ-597	Wfu. Gate Guardian.	N1845W
❑ 6802	1973	King Air TC90	LJ-598	Wfu. Located Tokushima AB.	N1846W
❑ 6803	1973	King Air TC90	LJ-599	Wfu. Located Hachinohe AB.	N1847W
❑ 6804	1975	King Air TC90	LJ-642	Wfu.	N7312R
❑ 6805	1975	King Air TC90	LJ-670	Wfu.	N9395
❑ 6806	1978	King Air TC90	LJ-778	Wfu.	N23780
❑ 6807	1979	King Air TC90	LJ-855	Wfu. Gate Guardian.	N6062X
❑ 73-3201	1968	Mitsubishi MU-2S	901	Wfu. Displayed at Kissa Hikojo tearooms, Hamamatsu.	
❑ 73-3202	1968	Mitsubishi MU-2S	902	Wfu. (was s/n 128).	
❑ 73-3222	1977	Mitsubishi MU-2E	922	Wfu. (was s/n 360).	
❑ 73-3272	1978	Mitsubishi MU-2J	952	Wfu. (was s/n 715).	
❑ 83-3203	1969	Mitsubishi MU-2S	903	Wfu. (was s/n 147).	
❑ 83-3204	1969	Mitsubishi MU-2S	904	Wfu. (was s/n 148).	
❑ 83-3273	1978	Mitsubishi MU-2J	953	Wfu. (was s/n 716).	
❑ 93-3205	1969	Mitsubishi MU-2S	905	W/o Japan. 11 Apr 73.	
❑ 93-3206	1969	Mitsubishi MU-2S	906	Wfu. (was s/n 176).	
❑ 93-3274	1978	Mitsubishi MU-2J	954	Wfu. (was s/n 717).	

LN = NORWAY

Civil

Reg	Yr	Type	c/n	Owner/Operator	Prev Regn
❑ LN-KCR	1978	King Air C90	LJ-793	W/o Skien, Norway. 2 Apr 87.	
❑ LN-MAH	1977	Conquest II	441-0002	Wfu. Parts at Dodson's, Ottawa, Ks. USA.	SE-IBI
❑ LN-PAG	1976	King Air 200	BB-119	Wfu. Cx LN- 7/92.	OY-AUJ
❑ LN-TSA	1978	King Air 200	BB-308	W/o Nr Gello, Norway. 19 March 93.	N98WP
❑ LN-VIP	1967	King Air A90	LJ-271	W/o Bodo, Norway. 28 Jun 68.	
❑ LN-VIP	1982	Conquest II	441-0279	W/o 11 Oct 85.	G-BJYB

LV = ARGENTINA

Civil

Reg	Yr	Type	c/n	Owner/Operator	Prev Regn
❑ LV-LDB	1972	681B Turbo Command	6064	Wfu.	LQ-LDB
❑ LV-LTA	1974	Rockwell 690A	11197	W/o Argentina. 26 Oct 75.	LV-PTI
❑ LV-MAV	1977	Rockwell 690B	11397	W/o Argentina. 12 Sep 84.	LV-PVM
❑ LV-MBR	1975	Rockwell 690A	11266	W/o Buenos Aires, Argentina. 14 Sep 80.	LV-PUV
❑ LV-MOC	1979	PA-31T Cheyenne II	7920031	W/o Buenos Aires, Argentina. 4 May 80.	LV-P..
❑ LV-MOP	1979	MU-2 Marquise	742SA	W/o en route Neuquen-Bahia Blanca, Argentina. 4 May 95.	LV-PBY
❑ LV-MYY	1979	PA-31T Cheyenne II	7920080	W/o Buenos Aires, Argentina. 1 Feb 80.	LV-P..
❑ LV-OEV	1980	Gulfstream 840	11628	W/o 26 Aug 81.	LV-PHJ
❑ LV-PAC	1978	PA-31T Cheyenne II	7820065	W/n Lima, Peru. 14 Jul 78.	
❑ LV-WLW	1973	SA-226T Merlin 3	T-230	W/o Ushaia, Argentina. 4 Apr 96.	N789D

Military

Reg	Yr	Type	c/n	Owner/Operator	Prev Regn
❑ 4-G-46/074	1979	King Air 200	BB-543	W/o Tierra del Fuego, Argentina. 15 May 86.	
❑ AE-177	1977	SA-226T Merlin 3A	T-277	W/o Argentina. 1982.	N5395M
❑ GN-705	1980	PA-31T Cheyenne II	8020092	W/o San Manual, General Villegas, Argentina. 6 Oct 95.	LV-OIF

LX = LUXEMBOURG

Civil

Reg	Yr	Type	c/n	Owner/Operator	Prev Regn
❑ LX-KTY	1968	King Air B90	LJ-339	W/o Nouadhibou Airport, Mauretania 3 Feb 04.	(F-GKTY)

N = USA

Civil

Reg	Yr	Type	c/n	Owner/Operator	Prev Regn
❑ N1KA	1978	King Air 200	BB-411	W/o Mar 80.	
❑ N1MU	1973	Mitsubishi MU-2J	578	Wfu. Cx USA 12/02.	N578EH
❑ N1NR	1972	Rockwell 690	11024	W/o Wellsburg, WV. USA. 14 Aug 72.	
Reg	Yr	Type	c/n	Owner/Operator	Prev Regn

Reg	Yr	Type	c/n	Owner/Operator	Prev Regn
☐ N1PT	1971	King Air C90	LJ-505	Wfu. Parts at Dodson's, Ottawa, Ks. USA.	N886K
☐ N1VY	1972	Mitsubishi MU-2J	567	W/o Hilton Head, SC. USA. 1 Aug 01.	N1VN
☐ N2CJ	1978	Mitsubishi MU-2N	726SA	W/o Santa Barbara, Ca. USA. 28 Jun 91.	N898MA
☐ N2EP	1967	King Air A90	LJ-284	W/o Crestview, Fl. USA. 13 Nov 90.	
☐ N2GG	1969	King Air B90	LJ-462	W/o Joliet, Il. USA. 15 Feb 75.	N821K
☐ N2GT	1977	Mitsubishi MU-2P	367SA	Wfu. Cx USA 11/97.	N67GT
☐ N2MF	1966	King Air 90	LJ-96	W/o Houston, Tx. USA. 19 Mar 78.	N3PC
☐ N3ED	1968	Mitsubishi MU-2D	101	W/o Riverton, Wy. USA. 17 Jun 81.	N75MD
☐ N3GS	1978	King Air B100	BE-36	Wfu. Cx USA 4/93. Parts at Griffin, Ga. USA.	N200TV
☐ N3MU	1969	Mitsubishi MU-2F	143	Wfu. Parts at White Industries, Bates City, Mo. USA.	N700MA
☐ N3RB	1971	SA-226T Merlin 3	T-214	W/o S of Grand Isle, La. USA. 17 Sep 85.	N7090
☐ N4BC	1970	SA-226T Merlin 3	T-205E	Wfu.	N1226S
☐ N4GN	1973	King Air E90	LW-38	W/o New York City, USA. 10 Mar 80.	N5000T
☐ N4NA	1965	Gulfstream 1	151	Wfu. Located Pima Air & Space Museum, Az. USA.	NASA4
☐ N4TN	1968	Mitsubishi MU-2D	115	Wfu.	N102MA
☐ N4TS	1972	King Air C90	LJ-541	W/o Ossian, In. USA. 24 Oct 83.	N9314Q
☐ N4UB	1990	2000 Starship	NC-4	Wfu. Last located 10/04 at Marana, Az. USA.	N75WD
☐ N5AP	1973	Mitsubishi MU-2J	604	Wfu. Cx USA 8/01.	N300WT
☐ N5ER	1968	680W Turbo Comman	1760-6	Wfu.	N177DC
☐ N5LN	1980	MU-2 Marquise	799SA	W/o Nr Rock, Ks. USA. 4 Nov 98.	N928VF
☐ N5NP	1970	681 Turbo Commande	6042	W/o Greenup, Ky. USA. 8 Mar 78.	N5NR
☐ N5NQ	1977	Mitsubishi MU-2P	356SA	Wfu.	N5NC
☐ N5NW	1973	Mitsubishi MU-2J	597	W/o Searcy, Ar. USA. 23 Jan 79.	N5MW
☐ N5WU	1974	King Air C90	LJ-635	W/o Newton, WV. USA. 16 Feb 98.	N5GC
☐ N6JM	1979	PA-31T Cheyenne 1	7904011	W/o Baker, Nv. USA. 8 Aug 98.	N96MM
☐ N6PE	1981	King Air B200	BB-856	W/o Nr Tulsa, Ok. USA. 8 Dec 04.	N1802H
☐ N7GA	1972	King Air A100	B-119	W/o Williamstown, Ms. USA. 4 Aug 94.	OH-BKC
☐ N8CC	1972	Mitsubishi MU-2J	569	W/o Bartlett, Tx. USA. 6 Jun 86. Cx USA 9/93.	N213MA
☐ N8VB	1959	Gulfstream 1	12	Wfu. Parts at Dodson's, Ottawa, Ks. USA.	(XA-TBT)
☐ N9JS	1969	Mitsubishi MU-2F	178	W/o Alpena, Mi. USA. 22 Apr 81.	N711SH
☐ N9PU	1980	King Air F90	LA-57	W/o Ruidoso, NM. USA. 9 Dec 89.	HP-80SF
☐ N9TW	1968	King Air B90	LJ-379	Wfu. Cx USA 5/01.	N73LC
☐ N10DA	1972	Mitsubishi MU-2J	551	Wfu. Cx USA 7/01.	N3330K
☐ N10TN	1970	681 Turbo Commande	6037	Wfu.	N9090N
☐ N11LG	1973	Mitsubishi MU-2J	595	Wfu. Cx USA 2/94.	N299MA
☐ N11SS	1970	Mitsubishi MU-2G	518	W/o Hawesville, Ky. USA. 19 Jan 79.	N144MA
☐ N11WU	1972	Mitsubishi MU-2J	565	Wfu. Cx USA 3/94.	N11WF
☐ N12AB	1965	King Air 90	LJ-45	Wfu.	HB-GBK
☐ N12EW	1974	Mitsubishi MU-2K	316	Wfu. Cx USA 10/94. Parts at White Industries, Mo. USA.	N77SS
☐ N12GW	1959	Gulfstream 1	19	Wfu.	PK-WWG
☐ N12KA	1973	King Air E90	LW-41	W/o Bloomington, Il. USA. 21 Jul 02.	N2AS
☐ N12KV	1967	680V Turbo Command	1675-58	Wfu.	N12KW
☐ N13RR	1976	Mitsubishi MU-2L	682	Wfu. Cx USA 3/04.	N13PR
☐ N13TV	1973	Rockwell 690A	11148	Wfu. Cx USA 1/01.	(N2KC)
☐ N14TK	1967	King Air A90	LJ-255	Wfu. Parts at White Industries, Bates City, Mo. USA.	N5113
☐ N14VR	1991	2000 Starship	NC-22	Wfu. Last located 10/04 at Marana, Az. USA.	N14VP
☐ N15NG	1980	King Air 200	BB-666	Wfu. Cx USA 3/04.	N15NA
☐ N15SS	1978	PA-31T Cheyenne II	7820068	W/o Madison, In. USA. 30 Nov 81.	N6027A
☐ N16CG	1980	MU-2 Solitaire	418SA	W/o The Woodlands, Tx. USA 1 May 01.	YV-11CP
☐ N17AE	1980	King Air F90	LA-80	W/o Nashville, TN. USA. 24 Jan 01.	N614RG
☐ N17CA	1964	Gulfstream 1C	123	Wfu. Located Detroit-Willow Run, Mi. USA.	N2602M
☐ N17JJ	1973	SA-26AT Merlin 2B	T26-166	Wfu. Cx USA 6/01.	N23X
☐ N18LP	1967	King Air A90	LJ-278	Wfu. Cx USA 9/98. Parts at Dodsons, Ks. USA.	N741L
☐ N18SE	1969	SA-26AT Merlin 2B	T26-134	Wfu.	N1UA
☐ N18WP	1974	Mitsubishi MU-2J	648	Wfu.	N529MA
☐ N20FD	1989	King Air C90A	LJ-1213	Wfu. Cx USA 5/99.	N1559T
☐ N20HF	1960	Gulfstream 1	47	Wfu.	N20CC
☐ N20PT	1969	SA-26AT Merlin 2B	T26-128	W/o Winchester, Va. USA. 18 Mar 94.	C-FBVI
☐ N21LF	1982	Lear Fan	E003	Wfu. Located Frontiers of Flight Museum, Dallas, USA.	(N327ML)
☐ N21MK	1967	Mitsubishi MU-2B	032	Wfu. Cx USA 12/94.	N707EB
☐ N21PC	1974	Mitsubishi MU-2K	295	Wfu. Cx USA 9/95.	N455MA
☐ N21VM	1971	Mitsubishi MU-2G	535	Wfu.	N159RS
☐ N22CN	1979	PA-31T Cheyenne 1	7904049	W/o Nr Glendive, Mt. USA. 30 Nov 94.	N2368R
☐ N22EQ	1971	Mitsubishi MU-2F	192	Wfu. Cx USA 6/95.	N22LC
☐ N22TE	1972	King Air A100	B-115	Wfu. Parts at White Industries, Bates City, Mo. USA.	N22T
☐ N23CD	1969	Mitsubishi MU-2F	142	W/o El Paso, Tx. USA. 17 Oct 85.	N209MA
Reg	*Yr*	*Type*	*c/n*	*Owner/Operator*	*Prev Regn*

Reg	Yr	Type	c/n	Owner/Operator	Prev Regn
☐ N23FL	1993	2000A Starship	NC-32	Wfu. Last located 10/04 at Marana, Az. USA.	N23FH
☐ N23LS	1977	Rockwell 690B	11372	W/o.	N81557
☐ N23UG	1963	Gulfstream 1	108	Wfu.	N1707Z
☐ N24CV	1996	King Air B200	BB-1524	W/o Pacific Ocean off San Diego, Ca. USA. 24 May 00.	N1024A
☐ N25ST	1971	King Air C90	LJ-507	W/o Gold Beach, Or. USA. 21 Aug 89.	N5PT
☐ N26CA	1978	PA-31 Cheyenne II	7820062	Wfu.	(N82295)
☐ N26JB	1969	SA-26AT Merlin 2B	T26-163	W/o Colorado, USA. 13 Feb 92.	N111SE
☐ N26RA	1995	2000A Starship	NC-53	Wfu. Last located 10/04 at Marana, Az. USA.	N6MF
☐ N26RT	1971	SA-226T Merlin 3	T-216	W/o Helsinki, Finland. 24 Feb 89.	N50PK
☐ N27GP	1967	Mitsubishi MU-2B	027	W/o Schellville, Ca. USA. 13 Jul 82.	N57907
☐ N27MT		Rockwell 690B	11533	W/o Springfield, Mo. USA. 8 Oct 94.	N376RF
☐ N27RA	1985	Beech 1900C	UB-37	W/o 125nm NW of Las Vegas, Nv. USA. 16 Mar 04.	N7214K
☐ N28AD	1976	Rockwell 690A	11291	W/o Shepahua, Peru. 17 May 93.	
☐ N28CG	1960	Gulfstream 1	50	Wfu.	N820CE
☐ N28SE	1967	King Air A90	LJ-239	W/o Apalachicola, Fl. USA. 30 Jun 85.	N28S
☐ N29AA	1966	King Air 90	LJ-110	Wfu.	N695V
☐ N30EM	1982	King Air B200	BB-958	W/o Rangeley, Me. USA. 22 Dec 00.	N82AJ
☐ N30LH	1994	2000A Starship	NC-47	Wfu. Last located 10/04 at Marana, Az. USA.	N64GQ
☐ N30LT	2001	TBM 700B	201	W/o Nr Oxford-Kidlington, UK. 6 Dec 03.	
☐ N30PC	1980	King Air 200	BB-702	W/o Pensacola, Fl. USA. 10 Apr 89.	
☐ N30SA	1979	King Air A100	B-246	W/o Charlotte, NC. USA. 11 Dec 97. (parts at Dodsons).	N20FS
☐ N30SG	1968	SA-26T Merlin 2A	T26-28	Wfu. Parts at White Industries, Bates City, Mo. USA.	N1212S
☐ N31CL	1967	Mitsubishi MU-2B	015	Wfu. Cx USA 4/96.	N707EB
☐ N31XL	1981	Cheyenne II-XL	8166003	W/o Jackson, Tn. USA. 3 Jun 01.	
☐ N32DF	1966	680V Turbo Command	1624-53	Wfu.	N1010M
☐ N32HG	1976	King Air 200	BB-146	W/o New Castle, De. USA. 16 Jun 92.	N32CL
☐ N32RL	1981	King Air B100	BE-117	W/o Gold Beach, Or. USA. 30 Sep 87.	
☐ N33BJ	1977	PA-31T Cheyenne II	7720061	Wfu.	
☐ N33SE	1970	SA-26AT Merlin 2B	T26-170	Wfu. Cx USA 8/95.	N19SE
☐ N33TF	1964	Gulfstream 1	133	Wfu. Parts at White Industries, Bates City, Mo. USA..	TU-VAC
☐ N34F	1966	King Air A90	LJ-119	W/o 10 Mar 77. Parts at White Industries, Bates City, Mo.	N25CA
☐ N34SM	1976	SA-226T Merlin 3A	T-263	W/o San Antonio, Tx. USA. 3 Feb 77.	N5377M
☐ N35GT	1976	PA-31T Cheyenne II	7620030	Wfu. Parts at White Industries, Bates City, Mo. USA.	N300CM
☐ N36CA	1979	PA-31T Cheyenne II	7920013	W/o Riviera, Az. USA. 8 Feb 84.	
☐ N38B	1972	King Air 200	BB-1	Wfu. Cx USA 3/95.	
☐ N38GP	1965	King Air 90	LJ-46	Wfu. Last located Deland, Fl. USA.	C-GZIZ
☐ N39BC	1967	Mitsubishi MU-2B	020	Wfu. Parts at White Industries, Bates City, Mo. USA.	N3552X
☐ N39TU	1991	2000 Starship	NC-23	Wfu. Located Pima Museum, Tucson, Az. USA.	N39TW
☐ N39YV	1975	King Air/Catpass 250	BB-39	W/o Pasadena, Ca. USA. 12 May 89.	N63JR
☐ N40MP	1973	Rockwell 690A	11116	W/o Kingston, Ut. USA. 12 Nov 74.	
☐ N40PP	1970	Mitsubishi MU-2G	515	Wfu.	N155WC
☐ N40RM	1966	King Air A90	LJ-155	Wfu.	N7HU
☐ N41BE	1979	King Air A100	B-245	W/o Eveleth, Mn. USA. 25 Oct 02.	N41BP
☐ N41DZ	1968	King Air B90	LJ-412	Wfu. Cx USA 12/98.	(N56K)
☐ N41KA	1976	King Air B100	BE-1	Wfu. Cx USA 8/87. (was B-205).	
☐ N41VC	1967	King Air A90	LJ-242	W/o Alice, Tx. USA. 12 Aug 97.	N812PS
☐ N42CA	1964	Gulfstream 1	137	Wfu. Dismantled at Detroit Willow Run, Mi. Cx USA 4/95.	(N811CC)
☐ N43DT	1965	King Air 90	LJ-6	Wfu. Cx USA 6/95. Parts at White Industries, Mo. USA.	C-GSFC
☐ N43GT	1975	King Air C90	LJ-652	W/o Chamblee, Ga. USA. 1 Oct 89.	N4072S
☐ N44MR	1973	Mitsubishi MU-2J	611	W/o Port Aransas, Tx. USA. 30 Nov 80. (parts at White Inds.)	N344MA
☐ N44UE	1973	King Air A100	B-140	W/o Atlanta, Ga. USA. 18 Jan 90. (parts at White Inds.).	N44UF
☐ N45BS	1972	Mitsubishi MU-2J	558	W/o Carolina, PR. 15 Apr 02.	(N558BK)
☐ N45EV	1971	Mitsubishi MU-2F	211	Wfu. Cx USA 6/95.	N123GS
☐ N45Q	1980	Gulfstream 840	11623	W/o Deadhorse, Al. USA.12 Oct 90.	N11EX
☐ N45QC	1966	680T Turbo Command	1542-7	Wfu.	N45Q
☐ N45RM	1976	King Air E90	LW-174	W/o Nr Yurimaguas, Peru. 1 Jul 92.	N21KE
☐ N46WA	1965	King Air 90	LJ-65	W/o Golfe du Lion-Marseilles, France. 13 Jan 94.	N981LE
☐ N47CC	1978	PA-31T Cheyenne II	7820016	W/o Richlands, Va. USA. 29 Jul 81.	N82218
☐ N47CP	1981	PA-31T Cheyenne II	8120039	Wfu. Cx USA 8/90.	N2589X
☐ N47R	1961	Gulfstream 1	69	Wfu. Located Pratt Community College, Ks. USA.	N47
☐ N47WM	1979	King Air E90	LW-307	W/o NW Kingston, ON. Canada. 20 Jan 95.	N300EH
☐ N48FL	1994	2000A Starship	NC-40	Wfu. Last located 10/04 at Marana, Az. USA.	N8300S
☐ N50ES	1966	King Air 90	LJ-111	Wfu. Cx USA 5/96.	N27LR
☐ N50JJ	1967	King Air A90	LJ-290	Wfu. Last located Montgomery, Al. USA.	N50JP
☐ N50KW	1980	MU-2 Marquise	784SA	W/o Columbia, SC. USA. 19 Jan 96.	N785MA
☐ N50LT	1977	King Air 200	BB-284	Wfu. Cx USA 9/97.	N25MK
Reg	**Yr**	**Type**	**c/n**	**Owner/Operator**	**Prev Regn**

Reg	Yr	Type	c/n	Owner/Operator	Prev Regn
N50PC	1970	King Air 100	B-19	W/o Birmingham, Al. USA. 1 Dec 74.	
N50VS	1978	Mitsubishi MU-2P	379SA	W/o Mansfield, Oh. USA. 2 Jan 89.	(N500V)
N53AD	1980	MU-2 Marquise	776SA	W/o Saratoga, Wy. USA. 5 Nov 81.	N262MA
N53LG	1979	Rockwell 690B	11523	W/o Nr Homerville, Ga. USA. 27 Mar 03.	N333PA
N55MG	1967	King Air A90	LJ-303	W/o Charleston, SC. USA. 26 Nov 77.	N55MP
N55MU	1993	2000A Starship	NC-30	Wfu. Last located 10/04 at Marana, Az. USA.	N55MP
N55PC	1969	Mitsubishi MU-2F	146	Wfu. Cx USA 9/93.	(N78HC)
N55ZM	1968	SA-26T Merlin 2A	T26-11	Wfu.	N55JM
N56KA	1973	King Air E90	LW-46	Wfu. Cx USA 1/95. Parts at Dodson's, Ottawa, Ks. USA.	
N57MM	1966	King Air A90	LJ-126	Wfu. Parts at White Industries, Bates City, Mo. USA.	N570M
N57V	1967	King Air A90	LJ-268	W/o Washington, DC. USA. 25 Jan 75.	N573M
N58FS	1969	SA-26AT Merlin 2B	T26-120	Wfu.	N74YC
N59MD	1980	Conquest II	441-0177	W/o Derry, Pa. USA. 11 Nov 85.	
N60AW	1980	PA-31T Cheyenne II	8020051	W/o Big Bear Lake, Ca. USA. 17 Feb 92.	N2343V
N60BN	1969	Mitsubishi MU-2F	163	Wfu.	N6TN
N60BT	1977	Mitsubishi MU-2P	358SA	W/o Edgartown, Ma. USA. 6 Oct 2000.	C-GIRO
N60KG	1970	Mitsubishi MU-2G	511	Wfu. Cx USA 5/99.	N60KC
N62BC	1976	PA-31T Cheyenne II	7620043	Wfu.	N52BC
N63XL	1981	Cheyenne II-XL	8166037	W/o Colorado Springs, Co. USA. 15 Sep 89.	D-IESW
N64MD	1979	MU-2 Marquise	747SA	W/o Rapid City, SD. USA. 9 Feb 90.	N777ST
N65CE	1960	Gulfstream 1	45	Wfu. Located Des Moines Central Campus Aviation Laboratory.	N329CT
N65TD	1970	King Air 100	B-50	W/o Windsor, Ma. USA. 10 Dec 86.	N166TR
N66CA	1979	PA-31T Cheyenne 1	7904055	W/o Mexico. 21 Apr 83.	
N66KS	1971	SA-226T Merlin 3	T-209	W/o Bahamas. 9 Sep 86.	N400SU
N66LM	1983	Conquest 1	425-0137	W/o Lakeland, Fl. USA. 11 Feb 92.	N6884L
N66U	1974	Mitsubishi MU-2K	309	W/o Hayden, Co. USA. 12 Sep 82.	N44RF
N68KA	1981	King Air B200	BB-793	Wfu. Impounded by Mexican Government in 1986.	
N68TG	1961	Gulfstream 1	68	W/o Tri Cities Airport, Bristol, Tn. USA. 15 Jul 83.	N7ZA
N69BS	1991	TBM 700	10	W/o Spearfish, SD. USA. 4 Aug 98.	N19AP
N69QJ	1973	Mitsubishi MU-2K	254	W/o Morristown, Tn. USA. 13 Nov 75.	N616AF
N69TM	1976	Rockwell 690A	11322	W/o Nr Cashion, OK. USA. 12 Feb 95.	N4601L
N70QR	1964	Gulfstream 1	144	Wfu. Cx USA 3/91.	N70CR
N71CJ	1963	Gulfstream 1	107	Wfu. Last located Houston-Hobby, Tx. USA.	N71CR
N71CR	1965	Gulfstream 1	163	W/o Addison, Tx. USA. 11 Jul 75.	N618M
N72B	1979	MU-2 Marquise	735SA	W/o Jefferson, Ga. USA. 24 Mar 83.	N913MA
N72BS	1972	King Air A100	B-113	W/o Milville, NJ. USA. 2 Feb 85.	N9439Q
N72VF	1975	Rockwell 690A	11242	W/o Yakima, Wa. USA. 12 Dec 97.	N72VT
N74CC	1974	King Air C90	LJ-620	W/o Somerset, Ky. USA. 18 Jan 00.	
N74EJ	1978	King Air 200	BB-340	W/o Dalton, Ga. USA. 14 Aug 97.	(N74PF)
N74FB	1980	MU-2 Marquise	770SA	W/o Indianapolis, In. USA. 11 Sep 92.	N378RM
N74MA	1969	King Air B90	LJ-479	Wfu. Cx USA 10/02.	(N502M)
N74NL	1977	PA-31T Cheyenne II	7720010	W/o Lake County, In. USA. 30 Dec 86.	N2YP
N74TD	1992	2000A Starship	NC-27	Wfu. Evergreen Aviation Museum, McMinnville, Or.	N74TF
N75CF	1977	King Air E90	LW-212	W/o Beaufort, SC. USA. 19 Dec 99.	
N75GC	1977	King Air C90	LJ-727	W/o Marathon, Fl. USA. 31 Jan 04.	N888BK
N76BT	1966	680V Turbo Command	1567-23	Wfu. Cx USA 6/02.	N76D
N76GM	1970	King Air B90	LJ-498	W/o Longmont, Co. USA. 23 Jan 97. (Parts at Dodsons, Ks.).	N100CQ
N76ST	1967	SA-26T Merlin 2A	T26-4	Wfu. Parts at Dodson's, Ottawa, Ks. USA.	N700SC
N77PR	1977	PA-31T Cheyenne II	7720006	Wfu. Cx USA 1/94.	N77CG
N77TM	1968	Mitsubishi MU-2D	116	Wfu. Lake City, Fl. USA.	N862Q
N78D	1966	680V Turbo Command	1580-33	W/o New Orleans, La. USA. 5 Dec 71.	
N78L	1973	King Air A100	B-167	W/o Brookville, Fl. USA. 8 Nov 86.	N65HC
N79BJ	1966	680V Turbo Command	1610-46	Wfu. Located Area Technical School, Atlanta, Ga. USA.	N79D
N80GP	1966	King Air A90	LJ-137	W/o Wheeling, WV. USA. 13 Nov 97.	N24PR
N80RD	1968	Gulfstream 1	198	W/o Houston, Tx. USA. 23 Aug 90.	N100C
N81MD	1974	King Air A100	B-203	W/o Lagos, Nigeria. 11 Aug 78.	N7373R
N81SM	1981	PA-42 Cheyenne III	8001007	W/o Horseshoe Bay, Tx. USA. 7 Feb 87. Cx USA 9/95.	N51SM
N81TR	1981	Gulfstream 840	11690	W/o Nr Denver, Co. USA. 23 Dec 92.	N5942K
N82	1988	King Air 300	FF-17	W/o Nr Winchester Regional Airport, Va. USA. 26 Oct 93.	
N82MA	1975	Mitsubishi MU-2L	665	W/o Nashville, Tn. USA. 6 Sep 90.	SX-AGQ
N83MC	1973	Rockwell 690A	11124	Wfu. Cx USA 9/91.	(N83RV)
N85BK	1981	King Air 200	BB-734	W/o Morlan, Ga. USA. 4 Dec 03. (parts at AAR, Griffin, Ga).	N85BC
N85NL	1966	King Air 90	LJ-90	Wfu. Parts at Dodson's, Ottawa, Ks. USA.	N65NL
N86SD	1980	MU-2 Marquise	765SA	W/o Dubuque, Ia. USA 19 Apr 93.	N984MA
N87YB	1969	SA-26AT Merlin 2B	T26-130	Wfu. Cx USA 3/98.	N87Y
N88CA	1980	PA-31T Cheyenne II	8020081	Wfu. Cx USA 6/97.	C-GCNO

Reg	Yr	Type	c/n	Owner/Operator	Prev Regn
N88CR	1971	King Air C90	LJ-514	W/o Houston, Tx. USA. 16 Jan 79.	N111HR
N88LB	1974	PA-31T Cheyenne II	7400004	Wfu. Parts at White Industries, Bates City, Mo. USA.	N61DP
N88TW	1980	King Air F90	LA-29	Wfu. Cx USA 4/01.	N667HE
N88WZ	1967	680V Turbo Command	1713-87	Wfu.	N1123V
N89CR	1972	Mitsubishi MU-2F	233	Wfu. Cx USA 7/99.	N5NE
N89DA	1967	680V Turbo Command	1702-78	W/o Damphries, Jamaica. 15 Nov 82.	N89D
N89JR	1967	King Air A90	LJ-185	Wfu.	N769
N90AF	1973	King Air E90	LW-29	W/o Cuzco, Peru. 26 Sep 93.	N1739W
N90BB	1976	PA-31T Cheyenne II	7620027	Wfu. Parts at White Industries, Bates City, Mo. USA.	N82013
N90DA	1972	King Air E90	LW-22	Wfu. Cx USA 10/03.	(0B-1602)
N90JR	1967	King Air A90	LJ-211	Wfu. Cx USA 5/96. Parts at Dodson's, Ottawa, Ks. USA.	(D-ILKC)
N90NY	1965	King Air 90	LJ-73	Wfu. Parts at White Industries, Bates City, Mo. USA.	N6GT
N90RG	1972	King Air C90	LJ-546	W/o Pontiac, Mi. USA. 6 Aug 92.	N45BE
N90SJ	1966	King Air A90	LJ-177	Wfu. Parts at White Industries, Bates City, Mo. USA.	N31NC
N91G	1960	Gulfstream 1	37	W/o Houston, Tx. USA. 24 Sep 78.	N20S
N91TW	1978	PA-31T Cheyenne II	7820078	W/o Delta, Ut. USA. 17 Jan 82.	
N92JR	1967	Mitsubishi MU-2B	006	W/o Miami, Fl. USA. 13 May 81. (parts at White Inds.).	C-GMUA
N93NB	1982	King Air B200	BB-970	Wfu. Cx USA 1/97.	N124CS
N93UM	1971	Mitsubishi MU-2G	537	Wfu.	N161MA
N94HD	1968	680W Turbo Comman	1811-28	W/o Lucerne, Ca. USA. 11 Nov 78.	N94HC
N94U	1981	King Air F90	LA-124	W/o Lynchburg, Va. USA. 24 Nov 00.	N13
N95MJ	1984	MU-2 Marquise	1564SA	W/o Egelsbach, Germany. 11 Jan 99.	N5PC
N95UF	1966	King Air 90	LJ-78	Wfu. Last located at Deland, Fl. USA.	N730K
N96JP	1972	Mitsubishi MU-2J	556	W/o Casper, Wy. USA. 6 Apr 93. Cx USA 7/94.	N33RH
N96JS	1976	PA-31T Cheyenne II	7620021	Wfu. Parts at White Industries, Bates City, Mo. USA.	N131RG
N96MA	1967	Mitsubishi MU-2B	011	Wfu.	N96MA
N96WF	1996	Pilatus PC-12	139	Wfu. Cx USA 8/03.	HB-FRA
N98AL	1968	Mitsubishi MU-2D	105	Wfu. Cx USA 2/96.	N2RA
N98MK	1962	Gulfstream 1	98	Wfu. Parts at White Industries, Bates City, Mo. USA.	N29AY
N100BE	1975	King Air A100	B-221	W/o Colorado Springs, Co. USA. 21 Dec 97.	HZ-AFE
N100CT	1966	680V Turbo Command	1618-50	W/o Bridgeport, Ct. USA. 3 Sep 84.	N4693E
N100HC	1976	King Air 200	BB-98	W/o Greenville, Tx. USA. 12 Aug 85.	
N100LB	1977	PA-31T Cheyenne II	7720021	Wfu. Parts at White Industries, Bates City, Mo. USA.	(N234C)
N100NL	1969	SA-26AT Merlin 2B	T26-168	W/o Hot Springs, Va. USA. 16 Oct 71.	N20DE
N100NX	1967	SA-26T Merlin 2A	T26-3	Wfu. Parts at White Industries, Bates City, Mo. USA.	N100MX
N100RN	1978	PA-31T Cheyenne II	7820091	W/o Utica, Wi. USA. 23 Feb 85.	N6121A
N100SW	1971	Mitsubishi MU-2G	539	W/o between Miami & Atlanta, USA. 1 Apr 77. Cx USA 6/95.	N163MA
N100TN	1975	PA-31T Cheyenne II	7520013	Wfu.	
N101FB	1974	PA-31T Cheyenne II	7400007	Wfu. Parts at White Industries, Bates City, Mo. USA..	(N66836)
N101GA	1965	King Air 90	LJ-11	W/o Royal, Ar. USA. 3 Jan 95.	N2JJ
N101LR	1978	King Air C90	LJ-802	W/o Quito, Ecuador. 15 Sep 81.	
N101XC	1967	King Air A90	LJ-219	Wfu. Parts at White Industries, Bates City, Mo. USA.	N52C
N102JC	1997	Jetcruzer 500	001	Wfu. Cx USA 1/98.	
N102RB	1972	King Air E90	LW-19	W/o Nr Otuzco, Julcan, Peru. 18 Mar 93.	N1716W
N104BR	1976	SA-226T Merlin 3A	T-269	W/o DuPage, Il. USA. 28 Aug 01.	N5039F
N105FL	1989	King Air C90A	LJ-1215	W/o St Augustine, Fl. USA. 9 Apr 92.	
N105MA	1968	Mitsubishi MU-2F	123	Wfu. Cx USA 9/93.	C-FHTL
N106DP	1973	Mitsubishi MU-2J	571	Wfu. Cx USA 7/94.	N5HE
N106EC	1968	SA-26T Merlin 2A	T26-34	Wfu. Parts at White Industries, Bates City, Mo. USA.	N96D
N106MA	1970	Mitsubishi MU-2F	184	W/o Lake Texoma, Tx. USA. 7 May 91.	
N107DC	1968	680W Turbo Comman	1777-15	Wfu. Parts at Dodson's, Ottawa, Ks. USA.	N24099
N107MA	1970	Mitsubishi MU-2F	185	Wfu. Cx USA 10/95.	
N108SC	1971	Mitsubishi MU-2G	545	W/o Alamogordo, NM. 25 Jun 92.	N169MA
N109P	1963	Gulfstream 1	109	Wfu. Cx USA 12/98.	N307AT
N109TW	1971	Mitsubishi MU-2G	543	W/o Pago Pago, American Samoa. 22 Nov 81.	YV-1049P
N110JK	1983	Cheyenne T-1040	8375005	Wfu. Cx USA 6/01.	PJ-WIG
N110LT	1977	King Air C90	LJ-729	W/o Burlington, NC. USA. 13 Feb 90.	
N110SL	1968	King Air B90	LJ-364	Wfu. Cx USA 8/98. Parts at Griffin, Ga. USA.	N555TB
N111FL	1974	Rockwell 690A	11163	W/o Taos, NM. 29 Mar 92.	N9769S
N111LA	1976	Rockwell 690A	11324	Wfu. Cx USA 7/92.	N81441
N111PT	1968	SA-26T Merlin 2A	T26-15	Wfu.	N341T
N111QL	1976	Rockwell 690A	11312	W/o Nacogdoches, Tx. USA. 17 Sep 83.	N1QL
N111RC	1981	Conquest II	441-0188	Wfu. Cx USA 3/04.	N441GP
N111WE	1966	680V Turbo Command	1593-41	Wfu.	N688NA
N112SK	1974	Mitsubishi MU-2J	651	W/o Robert Lee, Tx. USA. 1 Dec 84.	N55KV
N113TC	1965	King Air 90	LJ-22	W/o Knoxville, Tn. USA. 16 Jul 74.	N9502Q

Reg	Yr	Type	c/n	Owner/Operator	Prev Regn
N114CM	1977	King Air C90	LJ-709	W/o Jackson, Wy. USA. 16 Jun 86.	N33TW
N114K	1975	King Air E90	LW-122	W/o Mineral Wells, Tx. USA. 26 Oct 81.	VH-DDG
N117EA	1980	Conquest II	441-0191	W/o ground fire, Pa. USA. 30 Nov 86.	C-GGMK
N118LT	1960	Gulfstream 1	55	Wfu.	N9446E
N119WM	1980	King Air 200	BB-662	W/o Salt Lake City, Ut. USA. 3 Mar 97.	N117WM
N121BE	1980	PA-31T Cheyenne 1	8004036	W/o Great Falls, Mt. USA. 19 May 98.	N657DC
N121MA	1971	Mitsubishi MU-2F	206	Wfu.	
N122G	1967	Mitsubishi MU-2B	033	Wfu.	N3563X
N123AX	1972	Mitsubishi MU-2F	220	Wfu. Cx USA 10/94. Parts at White Industries, Mo. USA.	N123UA
N123VC	1971	Mitsubishi MU-2F	214	Wfu. Located Technical School Vasteras-Hasslo, Sweden.	N129MA
N125AB	1981	MU-2 Marquise	1531SA	Wfu. Cx USA 4/94.	N450MA
N126AB	1969	Mitsubishi MU-2F	139	Wfu. Cx USA 8/01.	LV-WME
N129D	1972	King Air A100	B-134	W/o Dieques, PR. USA. 17 Aug 83.	N84B
N129GP	1967	King Air A90	LJ-216	W/o Endicott, NY. USA. 16 Apr 67.	
N131AF	1978	PA-31T Cheyenne II	7820005	Wfu. Parts at White Industries, Bates City, Mo. USA.	N5MC
N132MA	1970	Mitsubishi MU-2G	503	W/o Atlantic City, NJ. USA. 16 Apr 72.	JA8739
N133MA	1970	Mitsubishi MU-2G	506	W/o Rollinsville, Co. USA. 26 Dec 75.	
N135SP	1968	SA-26AT Merlin 2B	T26-111	Wfu. Located Long Beach, Ca. USA.	VH-CAH
N136JC		Jetcruzer 500	003	Wfu. Cx USA 3/02.	
N142LM	1965	King Air 90	LJ-28	Wfu.	N142L
N148CP	1976	King Air 200	BB-129	W/o Hampton, NY. USA. 9 Jun 85.	N143CP
N149JA	1979	MU-2 Solitaire	402SA	Wfu. Cx USA 5/95. Parts at White Industries, Mo. USA.	N963MA
N151BU	1966	King Air A90	LJ-183	Wfu. Cx USA 9/99.	C-FPCB
N152BK	1982	MU-2 Marquise	1537SA	W/o Lewiston, Id. USA. 11 Feb 00.	OY-BHY
N154MF	1967	Mitsubishi MU-2B	024	Wfu.	N111FN
N154RH	1964	Gulfstream 1	132	Wfu. Cx USA 9/03.	N154NS
N155BM	2001	PA-46-500TP Meridia	4697053	W/o Daytona Beach, Fl. USA. 17 Dec 03.	N61PK
N155S	1965	King Air 90	LJ-14	Wfu. Stevenson Aviation & Aerospace Training, Winnipeg, MT.	D-ILTI
N161RS	1980	SA-226T Merlin 3B	T-341	Wfu. Parts at White Industries, Bates City, Mo. USA.	N61RS
N163D	1967	680V Turbo Command	1701-77	Wfu.	N11CK
N165MA	1971	Mitsubishi MU-2G	541	W/o Lookout Mountain, Ga. USA. 20 Apr 82.	N165MA
N171TE	1966	King Air B90	LJ-180	W/o N of Haiti. 29 Nov 98.	N610W
N176CC	1976	PA-31T Cheyenne II	7620024	W/o Lamar, Co. USA. 2 Jun 78.	N82009
N177MF	1970	SA-26AT Merlin 2B	T26-179	W/o Albany, Ky. USA. 3 Dec 80.	ZS-RTZ
N178MA	1972	Mitsubishi MU-2J	554	W/o Raton, NM. USA. 25 Aug 78.	N178MA
N180B	1973	King Air C90	LJ-569	Wfu. Parts at White Industries, Bates City, Mo. USA.	
N181CE	1993	2000A Starship	NC-31	Wfu. Last located 10/04 at Marana, Az. USA.	N1558S
N181LL	1976	King Air B90	LJ-440	Wfu. Cx USA 4/91.	N19HS
N181TG	1967	Gulfstream 1	181	W/o Nashville, Tn. USA. 1 Jun 85.	N25WL
N182	1972	Rockwell 690	11048	W/o Canton, Md. USA. 15 Jan 80.	N1NR
N184MA	1972	Mitsubishi MU-2F	218	W/o Fort Lauderdale, Fl. USA. 20 Jun 87.	
N187AF	1970	Mitsubishi MU-2F	187	W/o Cerillos, NM. USA. 10 Jun 01.	OY-DLM
N191DM	1966	King Air 90	LJ-100	Wfu. Cx USA 3/93. Parts at White Industries, Mo. USA.	N1NL
N191SA	1960	Gulfstream 1	61	Wfu. Parts at Dodson's, Ottawa, Ks. USA.	N734HR
N193GA	1974	King Air 200	BB-12	Wfu. Parts at Lake City, Fl. USA.	VH-NIH
N195B	1976	King Air E90	LW-195	Wfu. Parts at Dodson's, Ottawa, Ks. USA.	N195WF
N199TA	1968	SA-26AT Merlin 2B	T26-110	W/o Del Rio, Tx. USA. 19 Jun 85.	N20TA
N200BE	1981	King Air 200	BB-832	W/o Rupert, WV. USA. 13 Jun 04.	N45BR
N200BR	1971	Mitsubishi MU-2F	205	W/o Provo, Ut. USA. 21 Dec 79.	N120MA
N200CM	1977	PA-31T Cheyenne II	7720004	Wfu. Parts at White Industries, Bates City, Mo. USA.	(N82073)
N200FD	1975	PA-31T Cheyenne II	7520040	W/o Lawrence, Ma. USA. 20 Mar 87.	N54971
N200HL	1968	Mitsubishi MU-2D	120	W/o New Orleans, La. USA. 20 Sep 74.	N284MA
N200MB	1979	King Air B100	BE-71	Wfu. Cx USA 3/93. Parts at White Industries, Mo. USA.	N66480
N200MR	1977	King Air 200	BB-219	Wfu. Parts at White Industries, Bates City, Mo. USA.	N884CA
N200PR	1983	Gulfstream 900	15029	W/o Price, Ut. USA. 7 May 86.	N36GA
N200RS	1985	PA-31T Cheyenne II	7520011	W/o St Louis, Mo. USA. 18 Jan 88.	N66844
N202JP	1975	PA-31T Cheyenne II	7520018	Wfu. Parts at White Industries, Bates City, Mo. USA.	N300WT
N204AJ	1970	King Air 100	B-10	W/o Houston, Tx. USA. 16 Sep 89.	N400BE
N206RF	1991	2000 Starship	NC-21	Wfu. Last located 10/04 at Marana, Az. USA.	N206R
N208MA	1967	Mitsubishi MU-2B	016	W/o Hays, Ks. USA. 3 Aug 79.	(N232LJ)
N208MS	1978	King Air 200	BB-400	W/o North Adams, Ma. USA. 6 Oct 99.	N999BT
N211X	1967	King Air A90	LJ-279	Wfu. Cx USA 9/91.	
N212CM	1966	680V Turbo Command	1626-54	Wfu.	N212CW
N212MA	1973	Mitsubishi MU-2K	262	Wfu. Cx USA 5/95.	N282MA
N213GA	1960	Gulfstream 1	48	Wfu.	G-AWYF
N214JB	1990	2000 Starship	NC-14	Wfu. Located Southern Museum of Flight, Birmingham, Al. USA.	N5674B

Reg	Yr	Type	c/n	Owner/Operator	Prev Regn
☐ N217SB	1973	Mitsubishi MU-2J	586	Wfu. Cx USA 6/01.	N21AU
☐ N218CS	1982	Cheyenne T-1040	8275016	W/o Stebbins, Ak. USA. 7 Apr 97.	C-GKIF
☐ N220CS	1982	Cheyenne T-1040	8275013	W/o Nuiqsut, Ak. USA. 18 Sep 00.	C-GBDJ
☐ N220F	1981	King Air C90	LJ-981	W/o East Greenwich, RI. USA. 27 Nov 85.	
☐ N220MA	1981	MU-2 Solitaire	441SA	W/o Concord, NH. USA. 9 Jul 92.	N234BC
☐ N221AP	1959	Gulfstream 1	6	Wfu. Cx USA 8/97.	S9-NAU
☐ N221CH	1969	King Air E90	LJ-436	W/o Tucumcari, NM. 15 May 01.	N309L
☐ N221MJ	1971	King Air C90	LJ-512	W/o Charleston, WV. USA. 4 Nov 75.	N659H
☐ N221NC	1968	King Air B90	LJ-393	W/o Creede, Co. USA. 25 Jun 99.	(F-GSJL)
☐ N225MS	1979	King Air 200	BB-496	Wfu. Cx USA 6/95 as stolen.	N180S
☐ N226AT	1971	SA-226AT Merlin 4	AT-003E	Wfu.	N226TC
☐ N227	1970	Mitsubishi MU-2G	510	Wfu. Cx USA 11/00.	N137MA
☐ N230E	1960	Gulfstream 1	36	Wfu. Last located El Mirage, Ca. USA.	N130A
☐ N230TW	1969	King Air B90	LJ-445	W/o Nr Fort Drum, Fl. 5 Jan 94.	N70CS
☐ N231RL	1981	King Air 200	BB-868	Wfu. Cx USA 3/97.	N3872K
☐ N233MA	1973	Mitsubishi MU-2K	251	W/o McCleod, Tx. USA. 2 Sep 81.	
☐ N234K	1976	PA-31T Cheyenne II	7620017	Wfu.	N57526
☐ N234MA	1973	Mitsubishi MU-2K	252	W/o Jacksboro, Tx. USA. 26 Nov 79.	
☐ N234MM	1963	Gulfstream 1	121	Wfu. Displayed at Disney-MGM Studio Theme Park, Orlando, Fl.	N732G
☐ N239P	1969	SA-26AT Merlin 2B	T26-147	W/o Willoughby, Oh. USA. 29 Jan 70.	
☐ N241DT	1973	SA-226T Merlin 3	T-242	W/o Santa Fe, NM. USA. 25 May 93.	N770U
☐ N241FW	1982	Conquest II	441-0241	W/o Chicago, Il. USA. 23 Nov 86.	(N6856S)
☐ N242DA	1970	King Air B90	LJ-484	Wfu. Parts at Dodsons, Ottawa, Ks. USA.	ZS-KLW
☐ N242DA	1965	King Air 90	LJ-20	Wfu. Parts at Dodson's, Ottawa, Ks. USA.	C-FMLC
☐ N242TC	1974	Rockwell 690A	11219	Wfu. Cx USA 12/02.	N50MP
☐ N245CA	1961	Gulfstream 1C	83	Wfu. Located Detroit-Willow Run, Mi. USA.	N117GA
☐ N245MA	1973	Mitsubishi MU-2J	576	Wfu.	
☐ N250TJ	1981	PA-42 Cheyenne III	8001024	W/o Grand Junction, Co. USA. 31 Oct 92.	C-GRCY
☐ N251M	1967	Mitsubishi MU-2B	013	W/o Gardner, Ks. USA. 9 Apr 79.	N3545X
☐ N253TA	1991	2000 Starship	NC-10	Wfu. Last located 10/04 at Marana, Az. USA.	N1563Z
☐ N254PW	1976	Rockwell 690A	11275	W/o Cadillac, Mi. USA. 10 Oct 85.	N952HE
☐ N254TP	1973	Mitsubishi MU-2J	575	Wfu.	N7PW
☐ N255C	1971	Mitsubishi MU-2G	536	Wfu.	N58BC
☐ N256TM	1976	King Air 200	BB-96	W/o New Orleans, La. USA. 18 Apr 77.	
☐ N257CG	2000	King Air B200	BB-1739	W/o Leominster, Ma. USA. 4 Apr 03.	N612TA
☐ N261PL	1969	SA-26AT Merlin 2B	T26-121	Wfu.	N4252X
☐ N269M	1985	Gulfstream 1000	96098	W/o Boca Raton, Fl. USA. 22 Jan 98.	N699GN
☐ N269TA	1981	King Air 200	BB-749	Wfu. (aircraft stolen, de-registered 10/99).	N12KW
☐ N270TC	1979	King Air C90	LJ-858	W/o Ronkonkoma, NY. 18 May 01.	F-GHFS
☐ N271MA	1980	MU-2 Marquise	797SA	W/o Chicago, Il. USA. 16 Nov 88.	
☐ N274MA	1980	MU-2 Marquise	786SA	W/o Tulsa, Ok. USA. 22 Feb 91.	
☐ N275CA	1978	PA-31T Cheyenne II	7820089	Wfu.	XA-JGS
☐ N275DP	1965	King Air 90	LJ-34	Wfu. Smithsonian 'Business Wings' exhibit 6/98-6/99.	N200SW
☐ N275MA	1973	Mitsubishi MU-2K	255	W/o West Point, Va. USA. 5 Jan 85. (parts at White Inds.).	
☐ N278DU	1967	King Air A90	LJ-243	W/o Denver, Co. USA. 10 Jul 78.	N578DU
☐ N287MN	1975	PA-31T Cheyenne II	7520004	Wfu. Parts at White Industries, Bates City, Mo. USA.	
☐ N289MA	1973	Mitsubishi MU-2J	585	Wfu. Cx USA 10/94. Parts at White Industries, Mo. USA.	
☐ N295X	1967	King Air A90	LJ-244	W/o Racine, Wi. USA. 1 May 72.	
☐ N296A	1967	King Air A90	LJ-208	Wfu. Located Chenault Air Park, Lake Charles, La. USA.	N29SA
☐ N296MA	1973	Mitsubishi MU-2J	592	W/o Coral Sea, Australia. 9 Dec 88.	
☐ N298MA	1973	Mitsubishi MU-2J	594	Wfu. Cx USA 6/01.	
☐ N299F	1973	Rockwell 690A	11112	W/o Calumet, Ok. USA. 27 May 78	N57112
☐ N300BD	1971	Mitsubishi MU-2G	547	Wfu.	N171MA
☐ N300CP	1977	Rockwell 690B	11374	W/o South of Susanville, Ca. USA. 31 Dec 92.	N81562
☐ N300CW	1980	MU-2 Marquise	795SA	W/o Putnam, Tx. USA. 14 Feb 90.	N287MA
☐ N300HG	1966	King Air 90	LJ-94	Wfu. Parts at White Industries, Bates City, Mo. USA.	N300HC
☐ N300KQ	1967	680V Turbo Command	1709-84	Wfu.	N300KC
☐ N300MA	1973	Mitsubishi MU-2J	596	W/o Easton, Md. USA. 8 Feb 76.	
☐ N300MC	1960	Gulfstream 1	32	Wfu. Cx USA 12/88.	N297X
☐ N300SP	1976	King Air E90	LW-166	W/o Flagstaff, Az. USA. 31 Jan 96.	N26902
☐ N300WC	1992	TBM 700	82	W/o Englewood, Co. USA. 26 Mar 01.	
☐ N301DK	1968	King Air B90	LJ-372	W/o Dillinghan Airport, Mouleia, HI. USA. 22 May 99.	N301TS
☐ N301KS	1985	King Air 300	FA-61	W/o Daytona Beach, Fl. USA. 14 Apr 04.	N7234E
☐ N302WB	1972	Rockwell 690	11003	W/o Soto La Marina, Mexico. 16 Sep 03.	N72TT
☐ N302X	1967	Mitsubishi MU-2B	030	Wfu.	N3561X
☐ N303CA	1981	MU-2 Marquise	1518SA	W/o Rifle, Co. USA. 5 Mar 92.	N678KM
Reg	*Yr*	*Type*	*c/n*	*Owner/Operator*	*Prev Regn*

Reg	Yr	Type	c/n	Owner/Operator	Prev Regn
☐ N303MC	1981	Conquest 1	425-0034	W/o London, Ky. USA. 18 Jan 94.	N6773E
☐ N304L	1968	Mitsubishi MU-2F	137	W/o March Harbour, Bahamas. 21 Apr 79.	N304LA
☐ N304M	1968	SA-26T Merlin 2A	T26-8	Wfu.	
☐ N307MA	1967	Mitsubishi MU-2B	007	W/o Las Vegas, Nv. USA. 28 Apr 80.	(D-IHFS)
☐ N308PS	1974	King Air E90	LW-92	W/o Locust Grove, Ar. USA. 18 Nov 88.	N300PS
☐ N309MA	1973	Mitsubishi MU-2J	602	W/o Smyrna, Tn. USA. 21 Sep 95.	
☐ N313BB	1970	Mitsubishi MU-2G	529	Wfu. Cx USA 4/94.	N3MP
☐ N313PC	1971	Mitsubishi MU-2G	531	Wfu.	N155MA
☐ N318DH	1982	SA-227AT Merlin 4C	AT-469	W/o Beaver island, Mi. USA. 8 Feb 01.	C-GCAU
☐ N319JG	1976	PA-31T Cheyenne II	7620056	Wfu.	N110DE
☐ N320MA	1973	Mitsubishi MU-2K	274	Wfu.	(N10GE)
☐ N321MA	1973	Mitsubishi MU-2K	276	W/o Double Springs, Al. USA. 4 Apr 77.	
☐ N321MG	1973	Rockwell 690	11069	Wfu. Last located Malindi, Kenya.	(5Y-NCF)
☐ N321MK	1991	2000 Starship	NC-20	Wfu. Last located 10/04 at Marana, Az. USA.	N8168S
☐ N321ST	1974	Mitsubishi MU-2K	307	W/o Campbell Lake, Canada. 8 Sep 91.	N200TM
☐ N328CA	1963	Gulfstream 1C	116	Wfu.	N159AN
☐ N330CB	1965	King Air 90	LJ-27	Wfu.	N400PQ
☐ N332K	1966	King Air 90	LJ-79	W/o Laredo, Tx. USA. 3 Sep 79.	N33JC
☐ N333BR	1968	Mitsubishi MU-2D	119	Wfu.	(N101ES)
☐ N333CA	1973	Rockwell 690A	11117	W/o Oklahoma City, Ok. USA. 22 Aug 73.	
☐ N333CS	1965	King Air 90	LJ-44	Wfu. Parts at White Industries, Bates City, Mo. USA.	XB-YAZ
☐ N333LM	1979	PA-31T Cheyenne II	7920052	W/o Malvern, Ar. USA. 29 May 96.	N333MZ
☐ N333MA	1974	Mitsubishi MU-2K	288	W/o Gander, Canada. 24 Mar 74.	
☐ N334DP	1984	King Air B200	BB-1188	W/o Fort Atkinson, Wi. USA. 16 Nov 87.	N334D
☐ N336SA	1980	SA-226T Merlin 3B	T-336	W/o Tx. USA. 19 Jan 82.	
☐ N338AS	1970	King Air B90	LJ-493	W/o West Palm Beach, Fl. USA. 3 Sep 99.	LV-WMD
☐ N339MA	1973	Mitsubishi MU-2J	607	Wfu.	(N200MK)
☐ N339W	1992	TBM 700	39	W/o Lake Tahow, Nv. USA. 29 Aug 92.	
☐ N340X	1968	SA-26T Merlin 2A	T26-17	Wfu. Parts at White Industries, Bates City, Mo. USA.	
☐ N345CA	1969	680W Turbo Comman	1842-41	Wfu. Parts at White Industries, Bates City, Mo. USA.	N39480
☐ N345RD	1992	TBM 700	76	W/o Truckee, Ca. USA. 13 Mar 98.	
☐ N346K	1974	Mitsubishi MU-2K	292	Wfu.	N452MA
☐ N346MA	1973	Mitsubishi MU-2J	613	W/o Houston, Tx. USA. 14 Feb 80.	
☐ N360LL	1975	PA-31T Cheyenne II	7520036	W/o Nr Denver, Co. USA. 24 Jan 03.	HC-BXZ
☐ N363N	1967	King Air A90	LJ-236	Wfu. Parts at White Industries, Bates City, Mo. USA.	
☐ N371BG	1959	Gulfstream 1	4	Wfu.	N89DE
☐ N375A	1967	680V Turbo Command	1692-71	Wfu.	
☐ N385GA	1974	King Air 200	BB-15	Wfu. Cx USA 1/97.	ZS-MNF
☐ N386TM	1978	Mitsubishi MU-2P	386SA	W/o San Antonio, Tx. USA. 21 Jan 2000.	N999BE
☐ N388MC	1969	King Air B90	LJ-442	W/o Yazoo City, Ms. USA. 10 Jan 78.	(N745LP)
☐ N398DE	1986	King Air 300	FA-109	Wfu. Cx USA 12/00.	N364C
☐ N399T	1966	680T Turbo Command	1532-2	W/o Olathe, Ks. USA. 31 Jan 75.	HB-GEK
☐ N400AM	1968	King Air B90	LJ-354	W/o Burlington, Co. USA. 10 Sep 83.	(N506M)
☐ N400BG	1978	Conquest II	441-0069	W/o Dallas, Tx. USA. 1 Oct 85.	N441SE
☐ N400FA	1983	SA-227AT Merlin 4C	AT-557	Wfu.	
☐ N400KK	1968	Mitsubishi MU-2D	118	Wfu.	N100KK
☐ N400N	1974	Rockwell 690A	11156	W/o Kelso, Wa. USA. 1 Dec 90.	N57077
☐ N400NL	1960	Gulfstream 1	62	Wfu.	N205M
☐ N400PT	1983	PA-42 Cheyenne 400L	5527001	Wfu. Cx USA 6/98. (was 8427001).	
☐ N400TR	1969	Mitsubishi MU-2F	161	Wfu. Cx USA 7/99.	N11LQ
☐ N401AS	1991	2000 Starship	NC-19	Wfu. Last located 10/04 at Marana, Az. USA.	N8025L
☐ N409ET	1974	Rockwell 690A	11213	Wfu.	N925MC
☐ N410W	1965	King Air 90	LJ-39	Wfu. Partsat White Industries, Bates City, Mo. USA.	N410WA
☐ N411X	1969	SA-26AT Merlin 2B	T26-126	W/o Nashville, Tn. USA. 28 Mar 72.	
☐ N418CD	1976	Mitsubishi MU-2M	344	Wfu. Cx USA 10/94. Parts at White Indusries, Mo. USA.	N729MA
☐ N425AC	1980	Conquest 1	425-0009	W/o Natchez, Ms. USA. 18 Nov 81.	(N98896)
☐ N425BN	1981	Conquest 1	425-0057	W/o Las Vegas, Nv. USA. 11 Jan 92.	N67761
☐ N425EW	1983	Conquest 1	425-0150	W/o Nr MacArthur Airport, NY. 16 Dec 96.	(N68854)
☐ N425K	1968	King Air B90	LJ-318	Wfu. Located Middle Georgia Technical Institute, W-Robins.	
☐ N425SC	1982	Conquest 1	425-0126	W/o Granby, Co. USA. 11 Jan 86.	N607DD
☐ N430C	1967	King Air A90	LJ-273	Wfu. Parts at Dodson's, Ottawa, Ks. USA.	N585S
☐ N431G	1960	Gulfstream 1	29	Wfu. Located Toronto-Pearson, ON. Canada.	N222SE
☐ N439AF	1982	SA-227AT Merlin 4C	AT-439	Wfu. Cx USA 5/04.	N555GB
☐ N440D	1967	King Air A90	LJ-235	Wfu. Cx USA 5/99.	N7SD
☐ N440MA	1981	MU-2 Marquise	1524SA	W/o Scottsdale, Az. USA. 27 Jan 83.	
☐ N441AW	1981	Conquest II	441-0199	W/o Rio Grande, PR. USA. 5 Jan 02.	N441JG

Reg	Yr	Type	c/n	Owner/Operator	Prev Regn
N441CC	1975	Conquest II	441-679	Wfu.	N7185C
N441CC	1977	Conquest II	679	Wfu.	
N441CD	1980	Conquest II	441-0131	W/o West Columbia, SC. USA. 15 Jan 86,	(N2625Y)
N441CM	1980	Conquest II	441-0169	W/o Marble Falls, Tx. USA. 24 Dec 84.	N441CN
N441KM	1981	Conquest II	441-0196	W/o St Louis, Mo. USA. 22 Nov 94. (parts at White Inds.).	N992TE
N441MS	1978	Conquest II	441-0056	W/o Lakeland Linder Airport, Fl. USA. 2 Jan 97.	C-GDBB
N441NC	1979	Conquest II	441-0099	W/o Virginia, USA. 11 Jan 80.	N4106G
N441W	1980	Conquest II	441-0181	W/o Birmingham, Al. USA. 10 Dec 03.	N81WS
N441W	1978	Conquest II	441-0052	W/o Walkers Cay, Fl. USA. 20 Apr 96.	N441GM
N442TC	1968	King Air B90	LJ-332	Wfu. Parts at White Industries, Bates City, Mo. USA.	N440TC
N444AR	1972	Mitsubishi MU-2J	555	W/o Eagle, Co. USA. 18 Nov 81.	N444NR
N444GB	1966	680V Turbo Command	1565-21	W/o Keflavik, Iceland. 5 Aug 90.	(N444GP)
N444JV	1981	Conquest 1	425-0013	W/o San Jose, Ca. USA. 6 Mar 02.	(N117EE)
N444JW	1977	PA-31T Cheyenne II	7720015	W/o San Angelo, Tx. USA. 3 Dec 79. (parts at Dodson's).	N775SW
N444LM	1978	SA-226T Merlin 3B	T-295	W/o Livermore, Ca. USA. 3 May 85.	N4444F
N444PA	1977	Mitsubishi MU-2N	691SA	W/o Patterson, La. USA. 20 Oct 83.	N851MA
N444SR	1968	King Air B90	LJ-416	W/o Seal Beach, Ca. USA. 17 Feb 85.	N869K
N447AB	1972	Mitsubishi MU-2F	223	Wfu. Cx USA 7/94. Parts at Dodson's, Ottawa, Ks. USA.	N189MA
N451ES	2001	Pilatus PC-12/45	425	W/o Westphalia, Mo. USA. 14 Sep 02.	HB-FRO
N456L	1976	King Air 200	BB-112	W/o Denver, Co. USA. 27 Mar 80.	
N466MA	1981	MU-2 Marquise	1540SA	W/o Burlington, Ct. USA. 19 Apr 84.	
N468MA	1974	Mitsubishi MU-2J	618	Wfu. Cx USA 7/94. Parts at Dodson's, Ottawa, Ks. USA.	9Q-CAA
N469JK	1967	King Air A90	LJ-274	Wfu. Parts at Lake City, Fl. USA.	N30AA
N473FW	1973	Mitsubishi MU-2K	269	Wfu. Cx USA 10/94. Parts at White Industries, Mo. USA.	(N473W)
N473MA	1982	MU-2 Marquise	1547SA	W/o North Adams, Ma. USA. 18 Mar 83.	
N474H	1969	King Air B90	LJ-474	Wfu. Parts at White Industries, Bates City, Mo. USA.	N14RA
N474U	1969	SA-26AT Merlin 2B	T26-133	Wfu. Cx USA 11/99. Parts at Lake City, Fl. USA.	N401NW
N480CA	1980	PA-31T Cheyenne 1	8004051	W/o Toussus Le Noble, France. 2 Jan 04.	
N480K	1969	King Air B90	LJ-480	W/o Nr Bahamas. 27 Dec 71.	N480K
N483D	1967	King Air A90	LJ-212	Wfu. Cx USA 9/92.	N483G
N500AK	1984	SA-227TT Merlin 300	TT-527	W/o Sullivan County, Tn. USA 1 Apr 93.	N40EF
N500CP	1992	2000A Starship	NC-25	Wfu. Last located Orange County SNA, USA.	N1553Y
N500GL	1973	Mitsubishi MU-2J	579	W/o Lajitas, Tx. USA. 19 Apr 81.	N441FS
N500JP	1970	681 Turbo Commande	6003	W/o Winnemucca, Nv. USA. 27 Jan 81.	C-FFDB
N500ML	1980	King Air B100	BE-78	W/o Jackson, Ms. USA. 13 Nov 97.	N3UL
N500QX	1968	Mitsubishi MU-2F	133	Wfu. Cx USA 7/04.	N488GB
N500X	1968	Mitsubishi MU-2D	114	Wfu. Located Bush Field Airport, Augusta, Ga. USA.	N908108
N500X	1967	King Air A90	LJ-199	W/o Galveston, Tx. USA. 26 Nov 69.	
N501FS	1969	SA-26AT Merlin 2B	T26-146	W/o St George, Ak. USA. 7 Jul 98,	N7WY
N501M	1966	King Air A90	LJ-175	Wfu. Parts at White Industries, Bates City, Mo. USA.	N50RM
N501RH	1981	King Air 200	BB-805	W/o Martinsville, Va. USA. 24 Oct 04.	N3812S
N504W	1968	SA-26AT Merlin 2B	T26-104	Wfu.	
N505SA	1967	Mitsubishi MU-2B	008	Wfu.	N224FW
N508GW	1968	SA-26T Merlin 2A	T26-35	Wfu. Instructional airframe Northrop University, Ca. USA.	N500DM
N511BF	1966	King Air A90	LJ-179	W/o Fentress, Tx. USA. 17 Oct 03.	N711CF
N512DM	1969	Mitsubishi MU-2F	155	Wfu. Cx USA 6/95.	N513DM
N513DC	1981	MU-2 Marquise	1513SA	W/o Eola, Il. USA. 5 Mar 86.	N275CA
N513NA	1970	Mitsubishi MU-2G	513	Wfu. Cx USA 6/95.	VH-UZD
N515AC	1990	2000 Starship	NC-16	Wfu. Last located Wichita BEC, Ks. USA.	N80KK
N515JS	1995	2000A Starship	NC-52	Wfu. Last located 10/04 at Marana, Az. USA.	N1564Q
N515WB	1977	PA-31T Cheyenne II	7720023	W/o Nr Columbus, Oh. USA. ? Dec 93,	C-GGMD
N518DM	1967	King Air A90	LJ-251	W/o Marine City, Mi. USA. 31 Jul 99.	N516DM
N522RF	2001	PA-46-500TP Meridia	4697119	W/o Albuquerque, NM. USA. 7 Mar 03.	
N525MA	1976	Mitsubishi MU-2M	340	Wfu. Cx USA 11/94.	(N912DM)
N529N	1966	King Air 90	LJ-112	W/o Green Castle, Mo. USA. 11 Mar 66.	
N529V	1970	King Air B90	LJ-487	Wfu. Parts at White Industries, Bates City, Mo. USA.	N529M
N530N	1966	King Air A90	LJ-141	W/o USA. 1 May 93.	
N531MA	1968	Mitsubishi MU-2F	130	W/o Burlington, Vt. USA. 18 Feb 76.	N1173Z
N538EA	1981	MU-2 Marquise	1538SA	W/o Englewood, Co. USA. 10 Dec 04.	N538MC
N539MA	1972	Mitsubishi MU-2J	552	Wfu. Cx USA 8/02.	N246W
N539SA	1983	SA-227AT Merlin 4C	AT-539	Wfu. Cx USA 5/86.	
N541F	1966	680V Turbo Command	1609-45	W/o Fort Lauderdale, Fl. USA. 3 Nov 90.	C-GPRO
N541W	1966	680T Turbo Command	1554-13	W/o Pompano Beach, Fl. USA. 3 Oct 70.	N5419
N542TW	1981	PA-42 Cheyenne III	8001052	W/o Charlotte, NC. USA. 28 Jun 85.	
N549LK	1967	Mitsubishi MU-2B	022	W/o Northfield, Oh. USA. 13 Oct 70.	N3554X
N550MA	1969	Mitsubishi MU-2F	169	Wfu. Cx USA 6/95.	N883Q

Reg	Yr	Type	c/n	Owner/Operator	Prev Regn
N551TR	1982	King Air B200	BB-1033	W/o 29 Jun 86.	N551TP
N555AM	1970	SA-226T Merlin 3	T-201	W/o Cameron, La. USA. 10 Jun 81.	N555DB
N555CH	1970	Mitsubishi MU-2G	508	Wfu. Cx USA 12/94.	N950MA
N555KG	1993	2000A Starship	NC-36	Wfu. Last located 10/04 at Marana, Az. USA.	XA-TNR
N558M	1974	Mitsubishi MU-2J	639	Wfu. Cx USA 7/94.	N550M
N561AF	1972	Mitsubishi MU-2J	561	Wfu. Cx USA 3/04.	VH-JMZ
N568H	1972	Rockwell 690	11027	W/o Los Angeles, Ca. USA. 26 Oct 76.	
N568UP	1983	SA-227AT Merlin 4C	AT-568	W/o London, Ky. USA. 31 Jan 85.	N568SA
N569H	1972	Rockwell 690	11029	Wfu. Located Technical School near Tara Field, Va. USA.	
N570AB	1975	PA-31T Cheyenne II	7520038	Wfu. Cx USA 6/89.	N54970
N571L	1966	King Air A90	LJ-135	Wfu. Parts at White Industries, Bates City, Mo. USA.	N571M
N575HC	1973	King Air E90	LW-67	W/o Pine Bluff, Ar. USA. 19 May 85.	N575HW
N577KA	1972	SA-226AT Merlin 4	AT-008	W/o Billings, Mt. USA. 7 May 86.	TR-LZS
N580BC	1961	Gulfstream 1	63	Wfu. Last located El Mirage, Ca. USA. Cx USA 7/03.	N144NK
N590DL	1975	PA-31T Cheyenne II	7520031	Wfu. Located Calgary Springbank Airport, AB. Canada.	SE-GLA
N600BV	1977	King Air 200	BB-254	W/o Madeira Island, Portugal. 12 Sep 03.	N600BW
N600CM	1977	PA-31T Cheyenne II	7720024	W/o Flat Rock, NC. USA. 23 Aug 85.	(N82116)
N600TB	1973	Mitsubishi MU-2K	258	Wfu. Cx USA 6/95.	N278MA
N600WR	1976	PA-31T Cheyenne II	7620038	Wfu. Parts at Dodson's, Ottawa, Ks. USA.	N82028
N601G	1966	680T Turbo Command	1605-44	W/o Alphaha, Ga. USA. 8 Aug 76.	N6537V
N602PA	1966	680T Turbo Command	1534-3	Wfu. Cx USA 10/84.	N441LM
N602RM	1979	PA-31T Cheyenne II	7920081	W/o Deerfield, Va. USA. 1 Jul 99.	N600RM
N607DD	1975	PA-31T Cheyenne II	7520028	Wfu. Parts at White Industries, Bates City, Mo. USA.	VH-HMA
N611VP	1966	King Air A90	LJ-171	W/o Narssarsuaq, Greenland. May 88.	N755K
N616AS	1966	King Air A90	LJ-160	W/o West Jordan, Ut. USA. 19 Apr 97.	N42CG
N616E	1967	680V Turbo Command	1707-82	Wfu. Cx USA 8/00.	N616MC
N616F	1966	King Air A90	LJ-165	W/o Lake Point, Ut. USA. 14 Jan 01.	N6HF
N617MS	1981	King Air 200C	BL-35	W/o Madisonville, Ky. USA. 24 Jun 87.	N26732
N618B	1975	Rockwell 690	11232	Wfu. Cx USA 1/94. Parts at White Industries, Mo. USA.	N618
N618BB	1971	Mitsubishi MU-2G	533	Wfu. Cx USA 1/97.	C-FKCL
N626BL	1980	Lear Fan	E001	Wfu. Located Museum of Flight, Seattle, Wa. USA.	
N631DS	1994	2000A Starship	NC-44	Wfu. Last located 10/04 at Marana, Az. USA.	N1863Q
N631PT	1977	PA-31T Cheyenne II	7720001	W/o Harrisburg, Pa. USA. 24 Feb 77.	(N82065)
N631SR	1977	King Air 200	BB-244	W/o King Cove, Ak. USA. 15 Jul 81.	
N636SW	1974	Mitsubishi MU-2J	636	Wfu. Cx USA 10/94. Parts at White Industries, Mo. USA.	N20PS
N638LD	1991	2000 Starship	NC-18	Wfu. Last located 4/03 at Marana, Az. USA.	N8246S
N638MA	1974	Mitsubishi MU-2J	638	Wfu. Cx USA 4/94.	N8LC
N641SE	1994	2000A Starship	NC-46	Wfu. Last located 10/04 at Marana, Az. USA.	N312KJ
N642WM	1969	SA-26AT Merlin 2B	T26-125	Wfu. Parts at Lake City, Fl. USA.	N393W
N648KA	1980	King Air 200	BB-648	W/o Bay View, Tx. USA. 10 Dec 04.	N17DW
N656A	1967	King Air A90	LJ-304	Wfu. Parts at White Industries, Bates City, Mo. USA.	
N660NR	2000	Pilatus PC-12/45	356	W/o Sea of Okhotsk, Western Pacific. 8 Jul 01.	HB-FSH
N660RB	1976	Rockwell 690A	11305	W/o Little Rock, Ar. USA. 17 May 88.	C-GIAB
N662DM	1972	Rockwell 690	11015	W/o Bridgeport, Ct. USA. 21 Jun 87.	N412FS
N666HB	1974	Mitsubishi MU-2K	281	Wfu. Cx USA 4/94.	N111PM
N666RK	1968	Mitsubishi MU-2D	110	Wfu.	N857Q
N666SE	1969	SA-26AT Merlin 2B	T26-154E	Wfu. Parts at White Industries, Bates City, Mo. USA.	N90874
N677WA	1978	Rockwell 690B	11473	Wfu.	5H-TAA
N680X	1968	680W Turbo Comman	1778-16	Wfu.	C-GPNV
N686N	1964	680T Turbo Command	1473-1	Wfu. Cx USA 7/92.	(N48AD)
N688DC	1966	680T Turbo Command	1612-47	Wfu.	
N688SH	1966	680T Turbo Command	1597-42	Wfu. Cx USA 2/99.	N676MB
N690JC	1978	Rockwell 690B	11479	W/o Konowa, Ok. 25 Jun 92.	N51MF
N690JM	1973	Rockwell 690	11072	W/o Temecula, Ca. USA. 14 Oct 01.	RP-C1956
N690JP	1976	King Air C90	LJ-690	W/o Dallas, Tx. USA. 9 Oct 01.	N80TB
N690TB	1973	Rockwell 690A	11109	W/o Bishop, Ca. USA. 11 Aug 02.	N920AU
N690X	1969	SA-26AT Merlin 2B	T26-141	Wfu. Cx USA 6/91.	C-GHWM
N693PA	1977	Mitsubishi MU-2N	693SA	W/o Malad City, Id. USA. 15 Jan 96.	F-GHDS
N693PG	1971	SA-226T Merlin 3	T-207	W/o Chico, Ca. USA. 18 Sep 95.	N500QP
N696JB	1970	King Air 100	B-13	W/o Garner, Tx. USA. 28 Mar 90.	N100BW
N698X	1969	SA-26AT Merlin 2B	T26-137	W/o Jacksonville, Fl. USA. 27 Nov 03.	(N192GK)
N700AR	1991	TBM 700	23	W/o Moulins, France. 13 May 02.	F-GLBR
N700CM	1978	PA-31T Cheyenne II	7820007	W/o Jacksonville, Fl. USA. 9 Jan 86.	
N700FN	1968	Mitsubishi MU-2F	127	Wfu.	N700DM
N700JW	1960	Gulfstream 1	53	Wfu. Cx USA 6/94. Parts at White Industries, Mo. USA.	(N701JW)
N700PP	1992	TBM 700	59	W/o Leesburg, Va. USA. 1 Mar 03.	
Reg	Yr	Type	c/n	Owner/Operator	Prev Regn

Reg	Yr	Type	c/n	Owner/Operator	Prev Regn
N700R	1978	Rockwell 690B	11434	W/o hangar fire Pekin, Il.. USA. 25 Dec 85.	N113SA
N700SP	1972	King Air A100	B-92	W/o Hilton Head Island, SC. USA. 26 Apr 75.	N6739
N700SR	1974	Rockwell 690A	11164	W/o Cortez, Co. USA. 3 Jan 04.	N57152
N701DM	1969	Mitsubishi MU-2F	149	W/o Nr San Diego, Ca. USA. 28 Feb 89.	N8527Z
N701K	1979	MU-2 Solitaire	410SA	W/o Perry Sound, ON. Canada. 24 May 99.	N329WM
N702FN	1973	Mitsubishi MU-2K	249	Wfu. Cx USA 8/94.	N702DM
N705G	1965	Gulfstream 1	152	Wfu.	OB-M-1235
N705QD	2001	TBM 700B	231	W/o Mobile, Al. USA. 24 Apr 03.	
N707BP	1976	Rockwell 690A	11326	Wfu. Cx USA 3/94.	N10VG
N707CE	1967	King Air A90	LJ-314	W/o Algeria. 29 May 90.	N971EL
N707WC	1967	King Air A90	LJ-188	W/o Cleveland, Oh. USA. 18 Oct 68.	N703K
N708G	1959	Gulfstream 1	8	Wfu. Located South of Houston-Hobby, Tx. USA.	
N709K	1966	King Air 90	LJ-97	Wfu. Parts at White Industries, Bates City, Mo. USA.	(N504M)
N710CA	1975	Mitsubishi MU-2L	669	Wfu.	TF-JMC
N711AH	1968	SA-26T Merlin 2A	T26-14	Wfu.	N952HE
N711AH	1970	Mitsubishi MU-2G	523	W/o Glenwood Springs, Co. USA. 2 Mar 74.	N711
N711FC	1971	King Air C90	LJ-516	W/o Columbia, SC. USA. 20 Dec 73.	N555RH
N711LL	1969	Mitsubishi MU-2F	180	Wfu. Cx USA 6/95.	N180SB
N711TB	1978	PA-31T Cheyenne II	7820031	Wfu. Parts at White Industries, Bates City, Mo. USA.	N82238
N711TT	1977	Rockwell 690B	11362	W/o Albuquerque, NM. USA. 8 Oct 87.	N81537
N713GB	1971	Mitsubishi MU-2G	538	Wfu.	N77RZ
N713SP	1968	680W Turbo Comman	1805-27	W/o Alexandria, La. USA. 4 Oct 79.	N5082E
N715G	1963	Gulfstream 1	118	Wfu.	
N715RA	1960	Gulfstream 1	31	Wfu.	C-FJFC
N716RA	1960	Gulfstream 1	43	Wfu. Cx USA 1/91.	N39289
N718RA	1966	Gulfstream 1	174	Wfu.	N7004B
N720K	1965	King Air 90	LJ-37	Wfu. Last located Deland, Fl. USA.	
N720X	1961	Gulfstream 1	73	W/o Arizona Desert, USA. Feb 87.	N207M
N721DM	1974	Mitsubishi MU-2K	312	Wfu. Parts at White Industries, Bates City, Mo. USA.	N444RG
N721K	1965	King Air 90	LJ-43	Wfu. Cx USA 2/96. Parts at Dodson's, Ottawa, Ks. USA.	
N721RA	1961	Gulfstream 1	65	Wfu. Cx USA 11/88.	N641B
N722DM	1972	Mitsubishi MU-2K	245	Wfu.	N180SB
N722RA	1966	Gulfstream 1	168	Wfu. Cx USA 11/88.	N209T
N723RA	1959	Gulfstream 1	14	Wfu. Cx USA 11/88.	N1607Z
N724FN	1974	Mitsubishi MU-2K	300	Wfu. Cx USA 11/96.	N724DM
N724N	1966	King Air 90	LJ-82	W/o Leeville, La. USA. 22 Dec 79.	
N724RA	1963	Gulfstream 1	114	Wfu. Cx USA 1/89.	VH-WPA
N725MA	1973	Mitsubishi MU-2J	582	Wfu. Cx USA 6/01.	N155BA
N727DM	1972	Mitsubishi MU-2K	242	Wfu. Cx USA 3/94.	N211BA
N727MA	1976	Mitsubishi MU-2M	342	Wfu.	
N729FN	1974	Mitsubishi MU-2K	296	Wfu.	N729DM
N730SF	1973	Mitsubishi MU-2K	246	Wfu.	N228MA
N735K	1965	King Air 90	LJ-35	Wfu. Located S Seattle Community College, Wa. USA.	
N737EF	1968	SA-26T Merlin 2A	T26-22	Wfu. Cx USA 3/93. Parts at White Industries, Mo. USA.	N999DT
N741P	1977	PA-31T Cheyenne II	7720025	Wfu. Parts at White Industries, Bates City, Mo. USA.	(N710MA)
N741P	1975	PA-31T Cheyenne II	7520020	W/o Jamaica. Oct 81.	N55SM
N742FN	1975	Mitsubishi MU-2L	670	W/o Edwards AFB, Ca. USA. 18 May 92.	N742DM
N743G	1961	Gulfstream 1	72	Wfu.	C-FNOC
N743K	1967	King Air A90	LJ-187	Wfu. Parts at White Industries, Bates City, Mo. USA.	N610K
N746G	1960	Gulfstream 1	46	Wfu.	
N747DN	2001	PA-46-500TP Meridia	4697038	Wfu. Cx USA 4/02.	
N747K	1965	King Air 90	LJ-51	Wfu. Cx USA 2/92. Parts at White Industries, Mo. USA.	
N747KF	1975	King Air 200	BB-70	Wfu. Cx USA 3/96.	N87JR
N750BR	1963	Gulfstream 1	99	W/o Nr Frankfurt, Germany. 13 Nov 88.	N364L
N750MA	1977	MU-2 Solitaire	365SA	W/o Fernandina Beach, Fl. USA. 19 Nov 81.	
N750Q	1967	Mitsubishi MU-2B	017	Wfu. Cx USA 4/02.	N269AA
N750QQ	1968	Mitsubishi MU-2F	125	Wfu.	N71674
N755AF	1980	MU-2 Marquise	755SA	W/o Baltimore, Md. USA. 14 May 04.	SE-KGO
N757Q	1969	Mitsubishi MU-2F	151	W/o Manning, SC. USA. 20 Nov 72.	
N758Q	1968	Mitsubishi MU-2F	134	W/o Trenton, NJ. USA. 15 Apr 69.	
N762JK	1992	TBM 700	62	Wfu. Parts at Dodsons, Ottawa, Ks. USA.	N45PM
N764Q	1969	Mitsubishi MU-2F	141	W/o Salisbury, Md. USA. 16 Jan 70.	N753Q
N765MA	1978	Mitsubishi MU-2P	372SA	W/o Bedford, NH. USA. 28 Aug 78.	
N767K	1966	King Air A90	LJ-170	Wfu. Cx USA 8/88.	
N769WT	1980	King Air B200	BB-1319	W/o hangar fire George West, Tx. USA. 6 Sep 98.	(N366EA)
N772CB	1971	681B Turbo Command	6050	W/o Calhoun, Ga. USA. 28 Mar 85.	N56MQ
Reg	Yr	Type	c/n	Owner/Operator	Prev Regn

Reg	Yr	Type	c/n	Owner/Operator	Prev Regn
N772K	1967	King Air A90	LJ-310	Wfu. Parts at Dodson's, Ottawa, Ks. USA.	
N776K	1965	King Air 90	LJ-56	Wfu. Parts at White Industries, Bates City, Mo. USA.	
N777EC	1973	King Air E90	LW-37	W/o NY State, USA. 7 Jan 79.	N1837W
N777JM	1978	PA-31T Cheyenne II	7820064	Wfu. Cx USA 5/94.	(N82301)
N777KU	1968	King Air B90	LJ-377	W/o Dodge City, Ks. USA. 17 Feb 04.	N8473N
N777KV	1977	PA-31T Cheyenne II	7720034	Wfu.	(N774KV)
N777MA	1972	Mitsubishi MU-2J	559	W/o Austin, Tx. USA. 18 Mar 77.	
N778HD	1979	PA-31T Cheyenne II	7920006	Wfu. Parts at White Industries, Bates City, Mo. USA.	
N780BF	1985	King Air 300	FA-70	W/o Cullman, Al. USA. 14 Jan 99.	(N66FB)
N784K	1968	King Air B90	LJ-427	Wfu. Located Griffin, Ga. USA.	
N786BP	1992	2000A Starship	NC-28	Wfu. Located Caloundra, NSW. Australia.	N82428
N791K	1967	King Air A90	LJ-253	W/o Portland, Me. USA. 13 Mar 73.	
N794CA	1981	PA-31T Cheyenne II	8120018	W/o Hobbs, NM. USA 4 Feb 02.	N406TM
N795K	1966	King Air 90	LJ-95	Wfu. Located College of Aeronautics, La Guardia, NY. USA.	
N799V	1977	Rockwell 690B	11407	W/o Wichita, Ks. USA. 2 Nov 91.	N81643
N800AW	1981	SA-226T Merlin 3B	T-403	W/o Pontiac, Mi. USA. 10 Jan 88.	N4464V
N800BR	1971	Mitsubishi MU-2F	199	Wfu. Parts at Dodson's, Ottawa, Ks. USA.	N3RN
N800DH	1969	Mitsubishi MU-2F	166	Wfu. Cx USA 4/94.	N322GA
N800VT	1967	King Air A90	LJ-249	Wfu. Cx USA 12/95. Parts at White Industries, Mo. USA.	N800S
N800W	1980	PA-31T Cheyenne 1	8004032	Wfu. Parts at White Industries, Bates City, Mo. USA.	C-FDDD
N801BT	1968	SA-26T Merlin 2A	T26-18	Wfu. Cx USA 12/00.	N12NA
N801C	1976	PA-31T Cheyenne II	7620048	Wfu. Parts at White Industries, Bates City, Mo. USA.	(N414VM)
N801HD	1976	PA-31T Cheyenne II	7620031	W/o Beckley, WV. USA. 24 Nov 77.	N35RR
N802AC	1968	SA-26T Merlin 2A	T26-21	Wfu.	N137RD
N803CC	1963	Gulfstream 1	112	Wfu. Cx USA 9/89.	N300PE
N803DJ	1968	SA-26AT Merlin 2B	T26-102	Wfu. Cx USA 8/02.	C-FBWU
N808W	1973	Mitsubishi MU-2J	609	W/o Patterson, La. USA. 14 Apr 85.	N508W
N814SW	1967	King Air A90	LJ-186	W/o Orange County Airport, Ca. USA. 16 Nov 96.	N881M
N816C	1965	King Air 90	LJ-42	Wfu. Parts at White Industries, Bates City, Mo. USA.	N81CC
N817SW	1981	PA-31T Cheyenne 1	8104044	Wfu. Cx USA 6/96.	
N831PC	1980	PA-31T Cheyenne II	8020001	W/o West Palm Beach, Fl. USA. 1 Jun 83.	
N845JB	1962	Gulfstream 1	87	Wfu. Cx USA 9/97.	N87CE
N847	1973	Rockwell 690A	11140	W/o Chicago, Il. USA. 23 Apr 77.	
N847CE	1974	Rockwell 690A	11223	W/o Nemacolin, Pa. USA. 12 Sep 75.	N57223
N850MA	1977	Mitsubishi MU-2L	690	Wfu. Cx USA 4/94.	(N88DW)
N854Q	1968	Mitsubishi MU-2D	107	W/o Rochester, Mn. USA. 8 Jan 77.	N3571X
N855Q	1968	Mitsubishi MU-2D	108	Wfu. Cx USA 6/97.	N3572X
N859DD	1981	King Air B200	BB-859	W/o Jasper, Al. USA. 23 Jun 87.	N4935X
N861H	1964	Gulfstream 1	147	W/o Le Centre, Mn. USA. 11 Jul 67.	N774G
N861K	1969	King Air B90	LJ-471	Wfu. Cx USA 8/87.	
N863Q	1968	Mitsubishi MU-2D	117	Wfu. Cx USA 7/97.	
N866K	1965	King Air 90	LJ-76	Wfu. Cx USA 10/93.	N100AN
N866Q	1968	Mitsubishi MU-2F	121	Wfu. Cx USA 5/95.	
N869	1976	King Air 200	BB-174	W/o Chicago-Meigs, Il. USA. 11 Nov 99.	N69DD
N873Q	1969	Mitsubishi MU-2F	160	W/o Nashville, Tn. USA. 1 Nov 79.	
N877Q	1969	Mitsubishi MU-2F	164	Wfu	
N878T	1967	King Air A90	LJ-246	W/o Big Piney, Tx. USA. 27 Feb 78.	
N880CA	1981	PA-31T Cheyenne II	8120001	Wfu. Cx USA 7/94.	
N882Q	1969	Mitsubishi MU-2F	168	W/o Cedillos, Mexico. 13 Jun 73.	
N885Q	1969	Mitsubishi MU-2F	172	Wfu. Cx USA 10/94. Parts at White Industries, Mo. USA.	
N887PE	1970	King Air 100	B-49	W/o Mayfield, Ky. USA. 15 Sep 89.	N887PL
N888DD	1967	680V Turbo Command	1679-61	Wfu. Cx USA 12/95.	N330LC
N888MA	1972	Mitsubishi MU-2J	550	W/o Neiva, Colombia. Feb 78.	N220SB
N888RJ	1971	Mitsubishi MU-2G	542	W/o New York, NY. USA. 5 Apr 77.	N166MA
N888TP	1982	MU-2 Marquise	1541SA	W/o Allentown, Pa. USA. 19 Jan 96.	N100TB
N892MA	1978	Mitsubishi MU-2N	721SA	Wfu. Cx USA 4/94.	
N895K	1965	King Air 90	LJ-25	W/o Billings, Mt. USA. 5 Aug 82.	
N898K	1967	King Air A90	LJ-198	Wfu. Cx USA 11/92.	C-GBFF
N899RW	1998	King Air B200	BB-1637	W/o Sandersville, GA. USA. 9 Aug 01.	
N900BP	1965	King Air 90	LJ-61	Wfu. Located Columbus State Community College, Oh. USA.	N3078W
N906F	1964	Gulfstream 1	146	Wfu. Located Opa Locka, Fl. USA.	4X-JUD
N908CM	1977	King Air E90	LW-233	W/o Hotham Inlet, Ak. USA. 25 Aug 80.	
N911KA	1967	King Air A90	LJ-254	W/o Selmer, Tn. USA. 22 Jan 98.	N781JT
N916PA	1979	King Air E90	LW-313	W/o Wiscassett, Mi. USA. 10 Jun 96.	N491KD
N917RG	1966	680V Turbo Command	1576-30	W/o Mazatlan, Mexico. Aug 76.	N1187Z
N919RD	1981	PA-31T Cheyenne 1	8104037	W/o Santa Fe, NM. USA. 16 Dec 99.	(N822WC)
Reg	**Yr**	**Type**	**c/n**	**Owner/Operator**	**Prev Regn**

Reg	Yr	Type	c/n	Owner/Operator	Prev Regn
☐ N920C	1977	Conquest II	441-0020	W/o Gainesville, Ga. USA. 10 Aug 92. (parts at Griffin, Ga.)	N700AB
☐ N931SW	1976	PA-31T Cheyenne II	7620013	Wfu. Parts at White Industries, Bates City, Mo. USA.	CX-BLT
☐ N932E	1966	680T Turbo Command	1588-39	W/o Kelso, Wa. USA. 11 Jul 84.	N932
☐ N936K	1972	King Air C90	LJ-539	W/o Cedar Rapids, Ia. USA. 3 Jan 73.	
☐ N940MA	1979	MU-2 Marquise	743SA	Wfu. Cx USA 6/95.	XB-PRO
☐ N941K	1972	King Air A100	B-111	W/o Muscle Shoals, Al. USA. 22 Jun 78.	
☐ N948CC	1977	King Air E90	LW-236	W/o Reno, Nv. USA. 13 Mar 02.	N48V
☐ N950	1968	SA-26T Merlin 2A	T26-30	Wfu. Cx USA 6/02.	N95D
☐ N950TT	1973	SA-226T Merlin 3	T-225	W/o Byers, Co. USA. 20 Dec 97.	C-GRTL
☐ N951HE	1968	680W Turbo Comman	1751-4	Wfu. Located Memphis Area VoTec School, Tn. USA.	N951HF
☐ N959L	1972	Mitsubishi MU-2J	570	Wfu. Cx USA 6/95.	N214MA
☐ N960M	1971	SA-226AT Merlin 4	AT-005	W/o Southern Pines, SC. USA. 14 Apr 75.	
☐ N961G	1960	Gulfstream 1	30	Wfu. Cx USA 11/91.	N901G
☐ N961JM	2002	PA-46-500TP Meridia	4697122	Wfu. Cx USA 8/04.	(OY-LAW)
☐ N962AT	1967	King Air A90	LJ-207	Wfu. Cx USA 3/03.	N383JC
☐ N962BL	1966	680V Turbo Command	1562-18	Wfu. (as C-GFAF).	C-GFAF
☐ N962MA	1979	MU-2 Solitaire	401SA	W/o New Orleans, La. USA. 23 Feb 80.	
☐ N965MA	1979	MU-2 Solitaire	404SA	Wfu. Cx USA 10/96.	
☐ N966MA	1979	MU-2 Solitaire	405SA	W/o Napa, Ca. USA. 11 Mar 2004.	N711TF
☐ N969MA	1979	MU-2 Solitaire	408SA	W/o Ramsey, Mn. USA. 6 Dec 80.	
☐ N974DC	1981	PA-31T Cheyenne II	8120027	Wfu. Cx USA 12/03.	N815SW
☐ N982MA	1974	Mitsubishi MU-2K	314	Wfu. Accident Sao Paulo, Brazil 10 Jul 98 as PT-LTC.	PT-LTC
☐ N987GM	1974	King Air E90	LW-98	W/o Tuba City, Az. USA. 31 May 89. (parts at White Inds.).	N439EE
☐ N998VB	1978	King Air C90	LJ-785	W/o Tomahawk, Wi. USA. 31 Dec 96.	N999VB
☐ N999CR	1970	King Air 100	B-12	W/o Houston, Tx. USA. 18 Mar 91. (parts at White Industries)	N152X
☐ N999FA	1975	Mitsubishi MU-2L	676	W/o Scottsdale, Az. USA. 20 Jul 96.	N90BC
☐ N999P	1993	2000A Starship	NC-43	Wfu. Last located 10/04 at Marana, Az. USA.	N200ZS
☐ N999PF	1974	SA-226T Merlin 3	T-247	Wfu. Cx USA 9/93.	N100T
☐ N999RF	1990	2000 Starship	NC-9	Wfu. Last located 10/04 at Marana, Az. USA.	N2009W
☐ N999WB	1970	Mitsubishi MU-2G	530	W/o Wayne, Il. USA. 30 Dec 97.	(N999TA)
☐ N1008U	1980	SA-226T Merlin 3B	T-351	Wfu. Cx USA 8/02.	
☐ N1011R	1979	SA-226T Merlin 3C	T-303E	W/o San Marcos, Tx., USA. 24 Mar 81.	
☐ N1127D	1967	King Air A90	LJ-223	W/o Quincy, Il. USA. 19 Nov 96.	N1127M
☐ N1154Z	1966	680V Turbo Command	1585-37	Wfu. Cx USA 2/83.	
☐ N1171Z	1966	680V Turbo Command	1557-15	Wfu.	
☐ N1176W	1974	Rockwell 690A	11184	Wfu.	N110GM
☐ N1184U	1976	King Air C-12C	BD-16	Wfu. Cx USA 12/02.	N60159
☐ N1195Z	1966	680V Turbo Command	1575-29	W/o Atlanta, Ga. USA. 9 Dec 72.	
☐ N1198S	1968	SA-26T Merlin 2A	T26-12	Wfu.	C-GRDT
☐ N1206S	1968	SA-26T Merlin 2A	T26-23	Wfu. Cx USA 9/93.	
☐ N1210Y	1984	Conquest II	441-0338	W/o Maiduguri, Nigeria. 26 Sep 87.	
☐ N1214S	1968	SA-26T Merlin 2A	T26-31	W/o Deadhorse, Ak. USA. 16 May 73.	
☐ N1224S	1984	Conquest 1	425-0211	W/o Perkasie, Pa. USA. 17 Aug 97.	
☐ N1283	1976	King Air 200	BB-90	W/o Jackson, Wy. USA. 11 Sep 88.	
☐ N1500X	1969	SA-26AT Merlin 2B	T26-127	Wfu. Cx USA 8/98.	
☐ N1550S	1990	2000 Starship	NC-5	Wfu. Cx USA 4/00.	N42SR
☐ N1552S	1990	2000 Starship	NC-12	Wfu. Last located 10/04 at Marana, Az. USA.	
☐ N1553S	1990	2000 Starship	NC-13	Wfu. Last located 10/04 at Marana, Az. USA.	
☐ N1560S	1991	2000A Starship	NC-24	Wfu. Last located 10/04 at Marana, Az. USA.	
☐ N1569S	1990	2000 Starship	NC-11	Wfu. Last located 10/04 at Marana, Az. USA.	
☐ N1865D	1983	King Air B200	BB-1119	W/o Treasure Cay, Bahamas. 15 May 96.	N1865A
☐ N1870S	1983	King Air B200	BB-1106	W/o Lake Tahoe, Nv. USA. 17 Jul 87.	N63882
☐ N1879W	1981	Cheyenne II-XL	8166065	W/o Des Moines, Ia. USA. 29 Nov 90. (parts at White Inds.).	N222XL
☐ N1910L	1976	King Air B100	BE-10	W/o Midland, Tx. USA. 26 Nov 83.	
☐ N2000S	1991	2000 Starship	NC-17	Wfu. Last located 10/04 at Marana, Az. USA.	N62KK
☐ N2000S	1986	2000 Starship	NC-1	Wfu.	
☐ N2019U	1978	King Air C90	LJ-792	W/o Nr St Mary's , Pa. USA. 14 Feb 85.	
☐ N2029N	1978	King Air C90	LJ-798	W/o Houston, Tx. USA. 30 Dec 78.	
☐ N2060M	1972	Mitsubishi MU-2J	564	Wfu.	N199MA
☐ N2079A	1980	Conquest 1	425-0001	W/o Dayton, Oh. USA. 29 May 85.	
☐ N2173Z	1967	680V Turbo Command	1704-80	Wfu. Cx USA 6/97.	C-GKFV
☐ N2176D	1967	Mitsubishi MU-2B	028	Wfu. Located Thief River Falls Technical College, Mn.	CP-1962
☐ N2181L	1976	King Air E90	LW-181	W/o Michigan City, In. USA. 7 Dec 80.	
☐ N2301N	1967	SA-26T Merlin 2A	T26-2	W/o Olive Branch, Ms. USA. 22 Nov 78.	N500BW
☐ N2336X	1981	PA-31T Cheyenne II	8120002	W/o Cody, Wy. USA. 20 May 87.	VH-IHK
☐ N2400X	1965	King Air 90	LJ-18	W/o Akutan Island, Ak. USA. 17 Apr 76.	
Reg	Yr	Type	c/n	Owner/Operator	Prev Regn

Reg	Yr	Type	c/n	Owner/Operator	Prev Regn
N2406U	1971	Mitsubishi MU-2F	197	Wfu. Cx USA 1/01.	XA-GAL
N2484B	1979	Conquest II	441-0112	W/o Calexico, Mexico. 15 Nov 87.	HP-...
N2517X	1981	Cheyenne II-XL	8166004	W/o Springfield, Ky. USA. 16 Feb 82.	
N2566W	1980	PA-31T Cheyenne II	8020035	W/o Pontiac, Mi. USA. 19 Feb 81.	(N321SS)
N2601S	1967	SA-26T Merlin 2	T26-1	Wfu.	
N2643B	1971	681B Turbo Command	6060	Wfu.	9Q-CGE
N2646W	1978	Rockwell 690B	11496	Wfu. Parts at White Industries, Bates City, Mo. USA.	D-IKOA
N2727A	1981	Conquest II	441-0201	W/o Lander, Ey. USA. 29 Aug 86.	
N2755H	1966	680T Turbo Command	1628-55	W/o Jackson, Ms. USA. 7 Jul 80.	
N2937A	1981	Gulfstream 840	11670	W/o Wooster, Oh. USA. 31 Oct 84.	ZS-KZP
N3019W	1974	King Air C90	LJ-639	W/o Nr Munson, Fl. USA. 25 Jun 99.	
N3042S	1987	2000 Starship	NC-2	Wfu.	
N3107W	1988	King Air 300	FA-150	Wfu.	
N3177W	1974	King Air E90	LW-77	W/o Nueva Palestina, Peru. 31 May 93.	
N3199A	1995	King Air B200	BB-1499	Wfu. Located Fort Lauderdale Executive, Fl. USA.	
N3234S	1987	2000 Starship	NC-3	Wfu. Cx USA 1/01.	
N3333D	1967	King Air A90	LJ-259	W/o Itaguazurenda, Bolivia. 11 Oct 96.	N3333X
N3544X	1967	Mitsubishi MU-2B	012	Wfu.	
N3550X	1967	Mitsubishi MU-2B	018	W/o Springfield, Mo. USA. 21 Dec 68.	
N3560X	1967	Mitsubishi MU-2B	029	Wfu. Cx USA 9/93. Parts at Dodsons, Ottawa, Ks. USA.	
N3668P	1980	King Air B100	BE-95	Wfu. Parts at White Industries, Bates City, Mo. USA.	
N3804F	1981	King Air C90	LJ-947	W/o Gadsen, Al. USA. 5 Nov 89.	
N3833P	1968	680W Turbo Comman	1761-7	Wfu.	C-GNYD
N3998Y	1980	PA-31T Cheyenne II	8020055	W/o Hobbs, NM. USA 31 Oct 02.	PH-TAX
N4089L	1978	Conquest 1	425-693	Wfu.	
N4202K	1973	Mitsubishi MU-2J	603	Wfu. Cx USA 7/94.	EC-EDK
N4207S	1977	King Air E90	LW-207	W/o Sitka, Al. USA. 31 Jul 77.	
N4284V	1973	Mitsubishi MU-2K	270	Wfu. Cx USA 3/95.	VH-MUO
N4425W	1975	PA-31T Cheyenne II	7620009	Wfu. Parts at White Industries, Bates City, Mo. USA.	C-GIVM
N4463W	1974	King Air C90	LJ-633	W/o Beaufort, Ga. USA. 30 Nov 87.	
N4468M	1969	SA-26AT Merlin 2B	T26-119	Wfu. Parts at White Industries, Bates City, Mo. USA.	VH-CAJ
N4470H	1966	680T Turbo Command	1550-11	Wfu. Cx USA 8/84.	CF-SVJ
N4505B	1981	PA-42 Cheyenne III	8001015	Wfu. Cx USA 12/91.	
N4527E	1966	680V Turbo Command	1622-52	Wfu. Parts at White Industries, Bates City, Mo. USA.	
N4556E	1966	680T Turbo Command	1614-48	Wfu.	
N4594V	1973	Mitsubishi MU-2K	256	Wfu.	HZ-BIN
N4682E	1966	680V Turbo Command	1630-56	Wfu. Located Cincinnati Technical College, Oh. USA.	N4682E
N5058E	1968	680W Turbo Comman	1787-17	W/o Atlanta, Ga. USA. 20 Nov 82.	
N5296M	1972	SA-226T Merlin 3	T-219	W/o Montreal, Canada. 10 Apr 73.	
N5329M	1974	SA-226T Merlin 3	T-243	W/o Bahamas. 3 Mar 77.	
N5549B	1992	2000 Starship	NC-15	Wfu. Last located 10/04 at Marana, Az. USA.	
N5589S	1969	Mitsubishi MU-2F	150	W/o Louisville, Ky. USA. 15 Dec 82.	C-FFER
N5805	1980	SA-226T Merlin 3B	T-324	Wfu. Located Hampton University, Newport News, Va. USA.	N77UU
N5860K	1980	Gulfstream 840	11608	W/o Patterson, La. USA. 13 DEc 81.	
N5889N	1982	Gulfstream 900	15019	Wfu. Cx USA 9/86.	
N5920C	1966	680T Turbo Command	1552-12	Wfu. Cx USA 6/69.	
N5926K	1981	Gulfstream 840	11674	W/o Freeport, Bahamas. 16 Oct 81.	
N5938K	1981	Gulfstream 840	11686	Wfu. Parts at White Industries, Bates City, Mo. USA.	
N5957K	1982	Gulfstream 840	11720	W/o 29 Mar 82.	
N6038A	1978	PA-31T Cheyenne II	7820072	W/o Swanton, Oh. USA. 31 Jan 92.	(N90TW)
N6040M	1979	King Air C90	LJ-840	W/o Indianapolis, In. USA. 5 Jun 79.	
N6069C	1967	King Air A90	LJ-291	Wfu. Parts at White Industries, Bates City, Mo. USA.	
N6123A	1978	PA-31T Cheyenne 1	7804004	W/o Baltimore, Md. USA. 22 Feb 79.	
N6134A	1978	PA-31T Cheyenne 1	7804006	W/o Graham, Tx. USA. 12 Nov 01.	
N6200B	1967	King Air A90	LJ-250	Wfu. CX USA 12/04.	(N66FS)
N6272C	1982	King Air C90-1	LJ-1025	W/o Nr Azores. 10 Mar 82.	
N6359U	1966	680T Turbo Command	1536-4	W/o Aspen, Co. USA. 22 Jan 70.	
N6514V	1966	680V Turbo Command	1581-34	Wfu.	
N6523V	1966	680V Turbo Command	1583-35	Wfu.	
N6540V	1966	680V Turbo Command	1571-26	Wfu. Located Portland Community College, Or. USA.	
N6591L	1990	Reims/Cessna F406	F406-0053	W/o Barrow, Ak. USA. 17 Aug 03.	
N6600A	1978	PA-31T Cheyenne 1	7804001	Wfu.	
N6649P	1983	King Air B200	BB-1133	Wfu.	
N6653Z	1959	Gulfstream 1	21	Wfu. Cx USA 11/95.	XC-BIO
N6771Y	1981	Conquest 1	425-0019	W/o Sanford, Fl. USA. 11 Feb 88.	
N6774R	1981	Conquest 1	425-0045	W/o Newburgh, NY. USA. 12 Dec 83.	
Reg	Yr	Type	c/n	Owner/Operator	Prev Regn

Reg	Yr	Type	c/n	Owner/Operator	Prev Regn
N6843S	1975	King Air E90	LW-137	W/o Cordova, Ak. USA. 29 Nov 76.	
N6846D	1981	Conquest 1	425-0078	W/o Augusta, Ga. USA. 31 Jan 90.	(N6844V)
N6857E	1982	Conquest II	441-0244	W/o Muskegon, Mi. USA. 16 Jul 86.	
N6858S	1982	Conquest II	441-0253	W/o Flagstaff, Az. USA. 21 Feb 87.	
N6886D	1983	Conquest 1	425-0152	W/o Ithaca, NY. USA. 25 Feb 84.	
N7138C	1969	King Air B90	LJ-446	Wfu. Cx USA 7/93. Parts at Dodson's, Ottawa, Ks. USA.	G-BLNA
N7388K	1990	2000 Starship	NC-7	Wfu. Last located 10/04 at Marana, Az. USA.	(N4NV)
N7400V	1975	King Air E90	LW-152	Wfu. Located Lima, Peru.	N9046G
N7500L	1969	PA-31T Cheyenne II	1	Wfu.	
N7676L		PA-42 Cheyenne III	31-5003	Wfu.	
N8000Q	1992	2000A Starship	NC-26	Wfu. Last located 10/04 at Marana, Az. USA.	
N8042N	1967	680V Turbo Command	1720-91	Wfu.	OO-SKF
N8074S	1993	2000A Starship	NC-33	Wfu. Last located 10/04 Marana, Az. USA.	
N8092D	1979	King Air 200	BB-418	Wfu. Parts at White Industries, Bates City, Mo. USA.	CX-BOR
N8119S	1993	2000A Starship	NC-34	Wfu. Last located 10/04 Marana, Az. USA.	
N8149S	1993	2000A Starship	NC-35	Wfu. Last located 4/04 Marana, Az.USA.	
N8158X	1994	2000A Starship	NC-42	Wfu. Cx USA 9/04. Located Boeing Museum of Flight,	
N8194S	1994	2000A Starship	NC-37	Wfu. Last located 10/04 at Marana, Az. USA.	
N8196Q	1994	2000A Starship	NC-48	Wfu. Last located 10/04 at Marana, Az. USA.	
N8224Q	1995	2000A Starship	NC-49	Wfu. Located Staggerwing Museum, Tullahoma, Tn. USA.	XA-TQF
N8280S	1994	2000A Starship	NC-38	Wfu. Last located 10/04 at Marana, Az. USA.	
N8282S	1994	2000A Starship	NC-39	Wfu. Last located 10/04 at Marana, Az. USA.	
N8283S	1994	2000A Starship	NC-41	Wfu. Located Kansas Aviation Museum, McConnell AFB. USA.	
N8520L	1966	King Air A90	LJ-156	Wfu. Located Philadelphia, Pa. USA.	N22
N9001N	1969	Rockwell 690	11000	W/o Rosedale, Ok. USA. 5 May 69.	
N9003N	1969	680W Turbo Comman	1828-36	Wfu.	N94490
N9004N	1969	680W Turbo Comman	1829-37	Wfu.	
N9019N	1969	680W Turbo Comman	1844-43	W/o Elkhart, In. USA. 28 Dec 71.	
N9058N	1970	681 Turbo Commande	6008	Wfu. Located Broward Community College, Pembroke Pines, Fl.	YV-06CP
N9060N	1970	681 Turbo Commande	6011	W/o Altus, Ok. USA. 25 Nov 70.	
N9066N	1972	King Air C90	LJ-557	W/o Ciudad Constitucion, Peru. 12 Jul 94.	C-GQPC
N9079S	1979	King Air F90	LA-1	Wfu. Cx USA 8/87.	
N9129N	1971	681B Turbo Command	6056	W/o Mansfield, Oh. USA. 30 Nov 96.	
N9150N	1973	Rockwell 690	11063	W/o Little America, Wy. USA. 25 Aug 84.	
N9150R	1976	King Air 200	BB-181	Wfu. Parts at White Industries, Bates City, Mo. USA.	C-GPKK
N9202N	1970	Rockwell 690	11002	W/o Bethany, Ok. USA. 26 Jun 70.	
N9789S	1980	Gulfstream 980	95037	W/o Carlsbad, NM. USA. 12 May 82.	
N9971F	1959	Gulfstream 1	17	Wfu.	C-FTPC
N9971G	1977	Conquest II	441-0006	W/o Greensboro, Al. USA. 15 Nov 77.	(N441SA)
N12117	1985	Conquest II	441-0345	Wfu. Used in development of Cessna 435 programme.	
N17530	1977	King Air 200	BB-204	W/o Valparaiso. In. USA. 19 Oct 77.	
N17690	1966	680V Turbo Command	1577-31	W/o Concord, Ca. USA. 3 Dec 85.	N17690
N18260	1981	King Air B200	BB-900	W/o Piqua, Oh. USA. 24 Aug 01.	
N23796	1977	King Air C90	LJ-737	W/o Pontiac, Il. USA. 23 Sep 77.	
N24169	1978	King Air B100	BE-38	W/o Romeo, Mi. USA. 22 Nov 91.	
N31434	1988	King Air C90A	LJ-1186	W/o Manaus, Brazil. 30 May 90.	
N36941	1977	Conquest II	441-0018	W/o Butte, Mt. USA. 1 Apr 80.	
N36962	1977	Conquest II	441-0033	W/o ground accident Mesa, Az. USA. Jan 84.	
N41054	1983	Conquest 1	425-0172	W/o Idaho Falls, Id. USA. 10 Nov 00.	N425LS
N45591	1970	Mitsubishi MU-2G	524	Wfu. Parts at White Industries, Bates City, Mo. USA.	C-FGWF
N46866	1973	Rockwell 690A	11108	Wfu. Cx USA 12/94. Parts at White Industries, Mo. USA.	HB-GFP
N53070	1969	SA-26AT Merlin 2B	T26-155	Wfu.	C-GVCO
N53328	2001	PA-46-500TP Meridia	4697098	W/o Palma, Spain. 19 Dec 02.	
N54985	1975	PA-31T Cheyenne II	7620007	Wfu. Parts at White Industries, Bates City, Mo. USA.	(N76NL)
N57169	1974	Rockwell 690A	11203	W/o Jacksonville, Fl. USA. 24 Jun 87.	
N57186	1974	Rockwell 690A	11186	W/o Independence, Ks. USA. 17 Nov 76.	
N57233	1975	Rockwell 690A	11247	W/o Columbus, Oh. USA. 1 Oct 79.	
N65103	1969	SA-26AT Merlin 2B	T26-140E	W/o Palo Alto, Ca. USA. 19 Oct 79.	D-IBMC
N66534	1962	Gulfstream 1	85	Wfu. Cx USA 11/95.	XC-BAU
N66847	1975	PA-31T Cheyenne II	7520019	Wfu. Parts at White Industries, Bates City, Mo. USA.	
N80398	1978	Mitsubishi MU-2N	712SA	Wfu. Cx USA 3/95.	VH-SSL
N81416	1976	Rockwell 690A	11306	W/o Winter Haven, Fl. USA. 14 Feb 83.	
N81470	1976	Rockwell 690A	11335	Wfu. Cx USA 1/94. Parts at White Industries, Mo. USA.	
N81502	1982	Gulfstream 1000	96000	W/o Chekotah, Ok. USA. 9 Oct 84.	
N81521	1977	Rockwell 690B	11351	W/o Burns, Or. USA. 7 Jan 81.	
N81601	1973	Mitsubishi MU-2J	577	Wfu. Cx USA 11/00.	C-FBAN
Reg	**Yr**	*Type*	*c/n*	*Owner/Operator*	*Prev Regn*

Reg	Yr	Type	c/n	Owner/Operator	Prev Regn
☐ N81628	1977	Rockwell 690B	11396	W/o White Plains, NY. USA. 22 Sep 90. (Parts at White Inds.)	
☐ N81717	1978	Rockwell 690B	11445	W/o Greenville, SC. USA. 17 Jan 84.	
☐ N82010	1976	PA-31T Cheyenne II	7620025	Wfu.	(N820YL)
☐ N82123	1977	PA-31T Cheyenne II	7720030	Wfu. Parts at White Industries, Bates City, Mo. USA.	
☐ N82139	1977	PA-31T Cheyenne II	7720040	Wfu. Parts at White Industries, Bates City, Mo. USA.	N14BW
☐ N82271	1978	PA-31T Cheyenne II	7820044	W/o Pellston, Mi. USA. 13 May 78.	
☐ N82282	1978	PA-31T Cheyenne II	7820055	W/o Elyria, Oh. USA. 27 Apr 79. (Parts at White Inds.).	
☐ N88832	1979	Conquest II	441-0071	W/o Mexico. Sep 79.	
☐ N98949	1968	King Air B90	LJ-407	W/o Charlotte, Tx. USA. 5 May 82.	D-ILTP

Military

Reg	Yr	Type	c/n	Owner/Operator	Prev Regn
☐ 02	1962	Gulfstream 1	92	Wfu.	N3NA
☐ 03	1962	Gulfstream 1	91	Wfu.	USCG 02
☐ 155722	1966	Gulfstream TC-4C	176	Wfu. Preserved Pensacola NAS. Fl. USA.	N798G
☐ 155723	1967	Gulfstream TC-4C	178	W/o Cherry Point, NC. USA. 16 Oct 75.	N778G
☐ 155724	1967	Gulfstream TC-4C	180	Wfu. At AMARC 10/94 as 4G002.	N786G
☐ 155725	1967	Gulfstream TC-4C	182	Wfu. At AMARC 5/00.	N762G
☐ 155726	1967	Gulfstream TC-4C	183	Wfu. At AMARC 5/00.	N766G
☐ 155727	1967	Gulfstream TC-4C	184	Wfu. At AMARC 10/94 as 4G004.	
☐ 155728	1967	Gulfstream TC-4C	185	Wfu. At AMARC 10/94 as 4G003.	
☐ 155729	1967	Gulfstream TC-4C	186	Wfu. At AMARC 10/94 as 4G001.	
☐ 155730	1967	Gulfstream TC-4C	187	Wfu. At AMARC 4/95 as 4G005.	
☐ 161185	1961	King Air UC-12B	BJ-1	Wfu.	
☐ 161186	1961	King Air UC-12B	BJ-2	Wfu. At AMARC 5G0011 10/98.	
☐ 161189	1961	King Air UC-12B	BJ-5	W/o Nr Penscaloa, Fl. USA. 2 Jan 82.	
☐ 161198	1961	King Air UC-12B	BJ-14	Wfu. At AMARC 5G0005 9/96.	
☐ 161199	1961	King Air UC-12B	BJ-15	Wfu. At AMARC 5G0009.	
☐ 161202	1961	King Air UC-12B	BJ-18	Wfu. At AMARC 5G0003 9/96.	
☐ 161311	1961	King Air UC-12B	BJ-28	Wfu. At AMARC 5G0001 9/96.	
☐ 161314	1961	King Air UC-12B	BJ-31	Wfu. At AMARC 5G0010.	
☐ 161321	1961	King Air UC-12B	BJ-38	Wfu. At AMARC 5G0007.	
☐ 161327	1961	King Air UC-12B	BJ-44	Wfu.	
☐ 161499	1961	King Air UC-12B	BJ-47	Wfu. At AMARC 5G0004 9/96.	
☐ 161509	1961	King Air UC-12B	BJ-57	Wfu. At AMARC 5G0008.	
☐ 161516	1961	King Air UC-12B	BJ-64	Wfu. At AMARC 5G0002 9/96.	
☐ 66-7943	1968	King Air C-6A	LJ-320	Wfu. Displayed at Wright-Patterson AFB.Oh.	N2085W
☐ 73-1210	1973	King Air C-12C	BD-6	Wfu. At AMARC as AACE005.	
☐ 73-1211	1973	King Air C-12A	BD-7	W/o Nr Nadiz, Iran. 31 Jan 79.	
☐ 73-1216	1973	King Air C-12C	BD-12	Wfu. At AMARC.	
☐ 73-22250	1973	King Air C-12C	BC-1	Wfu. Located Fort Rucker, USA.	
☐ 73-22265	1973	King Air C-12C	BC-13	Wfu. Located Dothan, Al. USA.	
☐ 76-0165	1976	King Air C-12C	BD-22	W/o 14 Aug 02.	
☐ 76-0170	1976	King Air C-12C	BD-27	Wfu. At AMARC.	
☐ 76-0173	1976	King Air C-12C	BD-30	Wfu. At AMARC.	
☐ 84-0169	1984	King Air C-12F	BL-99	W/o Nr Camp Humphreys, South Korea. 12 Aug 03.	
☐ 85-0151	1985	King Air RC-12K	FE-5	W/o Sommerhausen, Germany. 6 Nov 98.	
☐ 85-0154	1985	King Air RC-12K	FE-8	W/o Nuremberg, Germany. 26 Mar 01.	
☐ 85-1261	1985	King Air C-12F	BP-52	W/o Juneau, Al. USA. 12 Nov 92.	
☐ 85-1269	1985	King Air C-12F	BP-60	W/o Brazil. 11 Jan 1992.	
☐ 86-0402	1958	Gulfstream 1	2	Wfu.	N39PP
☐ 89-0272	1989	King Air RC-12N	FE-18	W/o Ossabaw Island, Ca. USA. 16 Apr 97.	

OB = PERU

Civil

Reg	Yr	Type	c/n	Owner/Operator	Prev Regn
☐ OB-1176	1980	PA-31T Cheyenne II	8020010	W/o Tocache, Peru. 28 Feb 90.	OB-S-1176
☐ OB-1212	1974	Rockwell 690A	11222	W/o Uchiza, Peru. 7 May 92.	OB-M-1212
☐ OB-1219	1978	Mitsubishi MU-2N	730SA	W/o Progreso, Peru. 11 Apr 91.	OB-M-1219
☐ OB-1234	1981	PA-42 Cheyenne III	8001019	W/o San Rafael, Peru. 16 Sep 98.	OB-S-1234
☐ OB-1284	1974	Mitsubishi MU-2K	282	W/o Juanjui, Peru. 14 May 92.	N3MP
☐ OB-1305	1967	King Air A90	LJ-302	W/o S E Cuzco, Peru. 11 Oct 91.	OB-T-1305
☐ OB-1361	1969	King Air B90	LJ-451	W/o Uchiza, Peru. 27 Feb 91.	N896K
☐ OB-1362	1969	King Air B90	LJ-448	W/o Tomay Kichua, Peru. 31 Jul 90.	N428DN
☐ OB-1403	1977	PA-31T Cheyenne II	7720022	W/o Chacham Peak, Peru. 16 Jan 96.	N14LW
☐ OB-1420	1974	King Air E90	LW-106	W/o Palmapampa, Peru. 8 Mar 94.	SE-IIU
☐ OB-M-1003	1978	PA-31T Cheyenne II	7820057	W/o Cuzco, Peru. 26 Feb 81.	
☐ OB-M-1031	1972	Rockwell 690	11008	W/o Peru. 14 Feb 79.	(N9208N)

Reg	Yr	Type	c/n	Owner/Operator	Prev Regn

OD = LEBANON

Military

Reg	Yr	Type	c/n	Owner/Operator	Prev Regn
☐ L-701	1974	Rockwell 690A	11157	W/o Beirut, Lebanon. 1980.	N57086

OE = AUSTRIA

Civil

Reg	Yr	Type	c/n	Owner/Operator	Prev Regn
☐ OE-EDU	1992	TBM 700	73	W/o Nr Freiburg, Germany. 1 Apr 93.	
☐ OE-EHG	1991	TBM 700	28	Wfu. Cx OE- 3/96.	
☐ OE-FCS	1984	Gulfstream 900	15036	W/o Lake Constance, Switzerland. 23 Feb 89.	N45GA
☐ OE-FEM	1990	King Air 300LW	FA-210	W/o en route Salzburg-Krems, Austria 12 May 96.	D-IDLS
☐ OE-FGK	1980	PA-31T Cheyenne II	8020052	W/o Friedrichshafen, Germany. 8 Feb 92.	N700GC
☐ OE-FPS	1981	Conquest 1	425-0024	W/o Hannover, Germany. 8 Oct 91	D-IEAT

OH = FINLAND

Civil

Reg	Yr	Type	c/n	Owner/Operator	Prev Regn
☐ OH-MIB	1971	Mitsubishi MU-2G	532	Wfu. Located Den Helder, Netherlands.	N30SA
☐ OH-PHA	1975	PA-31T Cheyenne II	7620001	Wfu. Instructional airframe Bardufoss, Norway.	OY-BSB

OO = BELGIUM

Civil

Reg	Yr	Type	c/n	Owner/Operator	Prev Regn
☐ OO-TBW	1970	Mitsubishi MU-2G	526	W/o Angouleme, France. 15 Aug 76.	SE-FGG
☐ OO-TLS	1974	King Air A100	B-188	W/o Bacau, Romania. 8 Jan 94. (parts at Griffin, Ga. USA).	5X-UWS

Military

Reg	Yr	Type	c/n	Owner/Operator	Prev Regn
☐ CF-03	1976	SA-226T Merlin 3A	T-262	W/o Lille, France. 16 Apr 80.	N5375M

OY = DENMARK

Civil

Reg	Yr	Type	c/n	Owner/Operator	Prev Regn
☐ OY-ATW	1976	SA-226T Merlin 3A	T-261	W/o Gronholt, Denmark. 26 Apr 78.	N300TA
☐ OY-AUI	1974	SA-226AT Merlin 4	AT-015	W/o Copenhagen, Denmark. 12 Nov 82.	N223JC
☐ OY-AZA	1973	King Air C90	LJ-593	W/o Copenhagen, Denmark. 15 Jan 79.	N90KA
☐ OY-BEP	1981	King Air B200C	BL-43	W/o Roodt-Syr, Luxembourg. 18 Sep 82.	EI-BKV
☐ OY-BVA	1965	King Air 90	LJ-68	Wfu. PT-6 engine test-bed at Roskilde. Cx OY- 11/03.	D-IKAO
☐ OY-CGM	1981	Conquest II	441-0229	W/o Isortoq, Greenland. 11 Nov 90.	N68548

PH = NETHERLANDS

Civil

Reg	Yr	Type	c/n	Owner/Operator	Prev Regn
☐ PH-DRX	1982	MU-2 Marquise	1555SA	W/o Eindhoven, Holland. 12 Sep 88.	N481MA

PK = INDONESIA

Civil

Reg	Yr	Type	c/n	Owner/Operator	Prev Regn
☐ PK-PJH	1976	PA-31T Cheyenne II	7620015	Wfu.	9V-BHF
☐ PK-TRB	1976	King Air 200	BB-116	Wfu.	
☐ PK-TRL	1960	Gulfstream 1	60	Wfu. CoA expiry 10 Jun 98.	C-FIOM
☐ PK-TRM	1960	Gulfstream 1	57	Wfu.	N66JD

PP = BRAZIL

Civil

Reg	Yr	Type	c/n	Owner/Operator	Prev Regn
☐ PP-EFC	1972	King Air E90	LW-15	W/o Goiania, GO, Brazil. 30 May 00.	
☐ PT-DUX	1971	SA-226T Merlin 3	T-215	W/o Sao Paulo, Brazil. 27 Sep 71.	
☐ PT-IEE	1972	681B Turbo Command	6071	W/o Sao Paulo, SP. Brazil. 16 Dec 00.	
☐ PT-LJR	1981	King Air F90	LA-93	W/o Sao Pedro da Aldeia, Brazil. 2 Oct 88.	N1187K
☐ PT-ONY	1981	King Air F90	LA-153	W/o Sao Paulo, Brazil. 3 Feb 93.	N200RA
☐ PT-OZY	1978	PA-31T Cheyenne II	7820030	W/o Nr Agua Comprida, MG, Brazil. 12 Jan 01.	N700TR
☐ PT-WHI	1979	PA-31T Cheyenne II	7920077	W/o Brazil. Oct 98.	LV-MZA

RP = PHILIPPINES

Civil

Reg	Yr	Type	c/n	Owner/Operator	Prev Regn
☐ RP-C202	1968	King Air B90	LJ-356	Wfu.	PI-C202
☐ RP-C2340	1965	King Air 90	LJ-57	Wfu. Located Manila, Philippines.	N2340M
☐ RP-C710	1970	King Air 100	B-15	W/o San Jose, Philippines. 28 Nov 96.	PI-C710
☐ RP-C775	1972	681B Turbo Command	6066	Wfu. Located Army Museum Camp Aquino, Tarlac, Luzon.	N2NR
☐ RP-C990	1967	King Air A90	LJ-247	W/o Philipppines. 28 Jul 99.	

SE = SWEDEN

Civil

Reg	Yr	Type	c/n	Owner/Operator	Prev Regn
☐ SE-FGE	1970	681 Turbo Commande	6033	W/o Mestersvig, Greenland. 23 Jul 73.	N9086N
☐ SE-FGO	1968	Mitsubishi MU-2D	102	Wfu.	HB-LED

Reg	Yr	Type	c/n	Owner/Operator	Prev Regn

Reg	Yr	Type	c/n	Owner/Operator	Prev Regn
☐ SE-GHG	1970	Mitsubishi MU-2F	191	Wfu. Cx USA 5/01.	(HA-...)
☐ SE-GLB	1984	PA-31T Cheyenne II	7400002	Wfu.	OH-PNS
☐ SE-GUU	1969	King Air B90	LJ-470	W/o Sindal, Denmark. 15 Oct 85.	N490K
☐ SE-IHX	1983	Conquest II	441-0291	W/o 24 Mar 84.	N88707
☐ SE-IOU	1974	Mitsubishi MU-2K	304	W/o Sweden. 16 Feb 86.	N410MA
☐ SE-IOX	1976	Mitsubishi MU-2M	331	W/o Sweden. 15 Mar 86.	N3982L
☐ SE-KBX	1973	Mitsubishi MU-2K	247	Wfu.	N5TQ
Military					
☐ 101001	1981	King Air 200C	BL-25	W/o Halmstad, Sweden. 24 Sep 90.	OY-CHE

SU = EGYPT

Civil

☐ SU-UAA	1995	King Air C90B	LJ-1418	W/o Inshas, Egypt. 10 Jun 00.	N3218X

SX = GREECE

Military

☐ P-9	1963	Gulfstream 1	120	Wfu. Preserved as '120' at Tatoi AFB. Greece.	

S9 = SAO TOME & PRINCIPE

Civil

☐ S9-NAA	1965	King Air 90	LJ-50	W/o 1988. Parts at White Industries, Bates City, Mo.	N75XA

TC = TURKEY

Civil

☐ TC-DHA	1990	King Air 350	FL-37	W/o Istanbul, Turkey. 5 Dec 98.	N4937M
☐ TC-LMK	1984	King Air C90A	LJ-1080	W/o Nr Bursa, Turkey. 21 Mar 00.	N6931W
☐ TC-SMA	1966	Gulfstream 1	172	Wfu. Located Geneva, Switzerland.	N712RD

TJ = CAMEROON

Civil

☐ 3C-JJP		Cheyenne T-1040	8275025	W/o N'Djamena, Chad. 14 Feb 01.	3C-JJP

TN = CONGO BRAZZAVILLE

Civil

☐ TN-ADP	1974	SA-226AT Merlin 4A	AT-025	W/o Pointe Noire, Congo Republic. 11 Mar 94.	N52LB

TR = GABON

Civil

☐ TR-LYA	1977	King Air E90	LW-247	W/o Liberville, Gabon. Apr 78.	F-GAPO

TU = IVORY COAST

Civil

☐ TU-TJE	1976	King Air 200	BB-163	W/o Bouafle, Ivory Coast. 28 Jun 96.	
Military					
☐ TU-VBB	1977	King Air 200	BB-295	W/o Touba, Ivory Coast. 21 Jun 90.	F-GAPV

VH = AUSTRALIA

Civil

☐ VH-AAV	1977	King Air 200	BB-245	W/o Sydney, Australia. 20 Feb 80.	A2-ABO
☐ VH-AAZ	1977	King Air 200	BB-241	W/o Bundaberg, QLD, Australia. 1991. Cx VH- 5/95.	N23915
☐ VH-AUP	1985	King Air B200C	BL-126	W/o Coffs Harbour, NSW. Australia. 15 May 03. (as VH-AMR).	VH-AMR
☐ VH-BBA	1980	MU-2 Marquise	782SA	W/o Leonora, WA. Australia. 16 Dec 88.	N269MA
☐ VH-BSS	1972	Rockwell 690	11044	W/o Botany Bay, NSW. Australia. 14 Jan 94.	N471SC
☐ VH-CCW	1977	PA-31T Cheyenne II	7720046	W/o Perth, Western Australia. 3 May 81.	N82175
☐ VH-CJP	1970	Mitsubishi MU-2G	505	W/o Cairns, QLD. Australia. 14 Nov 83.	HB-LEF
☐ VH-DRV	1978	PA-31T Cheyenne II	7820079	Wfu. Cx VH- 12/03.	N6109A
☐ VH-FLO	1963	Gulfstream 1	100	Wfu. Located Auckland, NZ.	N116K
☐ VH-FMN	1982	King Air 200C	BL-47	W/o Nr Mount Gambier, SA. Australia. 10 Dec 01.	N6334F
☐ VH-IAM	1970	Mitsubishi MU-2G	517	W/o Melbourne, Australia 21 Dec 94. (to N119BF for parts).	(N119BF)
☐ VH-IBC	1975	King Air 200	BB-74	W/o 1988.	N9730S
☐ VH-JWO	1970	681 Turbo Commande	6039	Wfu. Cx VH- 5/99. Located Essendon, VIC. Australia.	N420MA
☐ VH-KTE	1978	King Air 200	BB-320	W/o Adavale, Australia. 28 Aug 83.	N23786
☐ VH-LFH	1978	King Air E90	LW-255	W/o Nr Kingaroy, QLD. Australia. 25 Jul 90.	N258D
☐ VH-LQH	1975	King Air C90	LJ-644	W/o Toowoomba, QLD. Australia. 27 Nov 01.	N66CN
☐ VH-MLU	1981	MU-2 Marquise	1527SA	W/o Bargo, Australia. 24 May 83.	N445MA
☐ VH-MUA	1979	MU-2 Marquise	746SA	W/o Nr Meekatharra, WA. Australia. 26 Jan 90.	N943MA
☐ VH-NYB	1972	Rockwell 690	11039	Wfu. Cx VH- 4/94. Located Darwin, NT. Australia.	C-GICX
☐ VH-NYD	1970	681 Turbo Commande	6034	Wfu. Cx VH- 3/92. Located Darwin, NT. Australia.	N9087N

Reg	Yr	Type	c/n	Owner/Operator	Prev Regn

Reg	Yr	Type	c/n	Owner/Operator	Prev Regn
☐ VH-NYF	1970	681 Turbo Commande	6026	Wfu. Last located Moorabbin, VIC. Cx VH- 8/97.	N9024N
☐ VH-NYG	1970	681 Turbo Commande	6004	W/o Tamworth, Australia. 14 Feb 91.	N740ES
☐ VH-NYH	1970	681 Turbo Commande	6016	Wfu. Cx VH- 4/94. Located Darwin, NT. Australia.	N444JB
☐ VH-NYM	1967	Mitsubishi MU-2B	037	Wfu. Cx VH- 9/93.	VH-JWO
☐ VH-SKC	1975	King Air 200	BB-47	W/o Burketown, Queensland, Australia. 4 Sep 00.	RP-C200
☐ VH-SVQ	1977	King Air 200	BB-47	W/o Tasman Sea, Australia. 2 Oct 94.	VH-FOZ
☐ VH-SWP	1975	SA-226AT Merlin 4A	AT-033	W/o Tamworth, NSW. Australia. 9 Mar 94.	(N.....)
☐ VH-TNP	1979	PA-31T Cheyenne II	7920026	W/o Benalla, VIC. Australia. 28 Jul 04.	VH-LJK
☐ VH-TNZ	1979	PA-31T Cheyenne II	7920064	W/o hangar explosion Moorabbin, Australia. 29 Sep 88	N23477
☐ VH-UZC	1970	Mitsubishi MU-2G	519	Wfu. Cx VH- 3/92.	ZK-EKZ
☐ VH-WMU	1970	Mitsubishi MU-2G	512	W/o Bathurst, Australia. 7 Nov 90. Cx USA as N318MA 6/95.	N318MA

VP-B = BERMUDA

Civil

Reg	Yr	Type	c/n	Owner/Operator	Prev Regn
☐ VP-BBK	1996	King Air B200	BB-1519	W/o Blackbushe, UK. 23 Dec 00.	VR-BBK

VT = INDIA

Civil

Reg	Yr	Type	c/n	Owner/Operator	Prev Regn
☐ VT-EFF	1977	King Air C90	LJ-705	W/o Mainpuri, India. 30 Sep 01.	N2075L
☐ VT-EHK	1982	King Air B200	BB-985	W/o Nr Delhi Airport, India. 27 Aug 92.	N1841Z
☐ VT-EIE	1983	King Air B200C	BL-63	W/o Nr Buntar, India. 29 Jul 00.	N6921D
☐ VT-ELZ	1985	King Air F90-1	LA-233	W/o Bhilai, Madhra Pradesh, India. 3 Feb 98.	N72224
☐ VT-EOA	1987	King Air B200C	BL-129	W/o Delhi, India. 27 Aug 92.	N72401
☐ VT-EQM	1987	King Air 300	FA-128	W/o Nr Panvel, Bombay, India. 15 Jul 93.	N3029F
☐ VT-EUJ	1993	King Air B200	BB-1456	W/o Runda, Kulu Valley, India. 9 Jul 94.	N8090U
☐ VT-NEF	1980	King Air C90	LJ-890	W/o India. Feb 98.	ZS-LOL

XA = MEXICO

Civil

Reg	Yr	Type	c/n	Owner/Operator	Prev Regn
☐ XA-DIS	1973	Mitsubishi MU-2J	608	W/o El Paso, Tx. USA. 20 Nov 83.	N340MA
☐ XA-FOT	1966	King Air A90	LJ-168	W/o 15 Feb 78.	XB-BOF
☐ XA-IIW	1973	Rockwell 690	11050	Wfu.	XC-FUV
☐ XA-JUY	1973	Rockwell 690A	11170	Wfu.	XC-CAU
☐ XA-LIG	1981	King Air 200	BB-802	W/o Poza Rica, Mexico. 5 May 84.	
☐ XA-TDJ	1964	Gulfstream 1	127	Wfu. Last located Merida, Mexico.	N717JP
☐ XB-AEA	1974	Rockwell 690A	11199	W/o Oklahoma City, Ok. USA. 1 Jan 80.	
☐ XB-AQQ	1974	Mitsubishi MU-2J	632	Wfu. Cx USA 6/97.	N995MA
☐ XB-CIJ	1959	Gulfstream 1	10	Wfu.	N1623Z
☐ XB-ESO	1959	Gulfstream 1	15	Wfu.	N26KW
☐ XB-LIJ	1973	Mitsubishi MU-2K	259	W/o Beloit, Ks. USA. 1975.	N279MA
☐ XB-NUV	1972	King Air A100	B-128	W/o San Luis Potosi, Mexico. 13 Oct 76.	N196B
☐ XB-QIY	1974	King Air E90	LW-113	W/o Monterrey, Mexico. 2 Mar 81.	XA-FEX
☐ XC-AA38	1980	Gulfstream 980	95020	W/o Nr Monterrey, Mexico. 19 Oct 92.	XC-HFX
☐ XC-AA48	1978	King Air 200	BB-369	Wfu. Located Rantoul, Ks. USA.	HK-3555
☐ XC-FEL	1968	Mitsubishi MU-2D	103	Wfu. Parts at White Industries, Bates City, Mo. USA.	XB-TIM
☐ XC-GEI	1961	Gulfstream 1	66	Wfu.	N111DR
☐ XC-ICP	1966	King Air A90	LJ-176	W/o Vera Cruz, Mexico. 28 Jan 73.	N5656A
☐ XC-PGR	1978	King Air 200	BB-317	W/o Otay Mesa, Mexico. 28 Oct 79.	

Military

Reg	Yr	Type	c/n	Owner/Operator	Prev Regn
☐ MT-217	1982	Gulfstream 1000	96026	Wfu. Located Vera Cruz, Mexico.	HK-3157W

YV = VENEZUELA

Civil

Reg	Yr	Type	c/n	Owner/Operator	Prev Regn
☐ YV-121CP	1965	Gulfstream 1	150	Wfu.	N777G
☐ YV-1700P	1967	King Air A90	LJ-205	W/o Adicora, venezuela. 13 Jun 98.	N707PR
☐ YV-174CP	1977	Mitsubishi MU-2L	695	W/o Caracas, Venezuela. 4 Jun 81.	N855MA
☐ YV-215CP	1978	PA-31T Cheyenne II	7820071	W/o Caracas, Venezuela. 4 Jun 81.	
☐ YV-2200P	1974	PA-31T Cheyenne II	7400006	W/o Newtown, Bahamas. 20 Jun 90.	YV-146CP
☐ YV-2466P	1973	King Air C90	LJ-591	W/o Nr Fort Lauderdale, Fl. USA. 16 Jun 01.	N108TT
☐ YV-2816P	1968	King Air B90	LJ-378	W/o La Carlota, Caracas, Venezuela. 15 Nov 04.	N320E
☐ YV-288CP	1979	King Air F90	LA-8	W/o Caracas, Venezuela. 8 May 84.	
☐ YV-299P	1965	King Air 90	LJ-72	W/o Higuerote, Miranda, Venezuela. 31 Jan 79.	N901N
☐ YV-310CP	1980	Gulfstream 840	11645	W/o Nr Caracas, Venezuela. 27 Apr 96.	(N5897K)
☐ YV-385CP	1980	King Air 200	BB-740	W/o Nr Bimini, Bahamas. 20 Sep 99.	
☐ YV-426P	1976	King Air 200	BB-142	W/o Caracas, Venezuela. 4 Feb 82.	
☐ YV-597CP	1978	King Air 200	BB-394	W/o 12 Jan 89.	N223TC
☐ YV-726CP	1976	King Air E90	LW-182	W/o Caracas, Venezuela. 27 Mar 94.	YV-O-BIV-2
Reg	*Yr*	*Type*	*c/n*	*Owner/Operator*	*Prev Regn*

P4-PHS   Boeing 737-53A   photo by: Harald Helbig

P4-AOD   HS 125/700A   photo by: Jean-Luc Altherr

P4-AVJ   Challenger 604   photo by: Jean-Luc Altherr

C-FEMA   Citation S/II   photo by: Dick Milne

82-3007   BAe U-125A   photo by: Dick Milne

51-5057   Beechjet 400T   photo by: Dick Milne

N722A   BAe 125/800A   photo by: Thomas Niepel

N368AG   Gulfstream G-4   photo by: Thomas Niepel

D-CROB   Learjet 60   photo by: Thomas Niepel

92-0340   Jayhawk T-1A   photo by: Joe Handelman

N633CW   Challenger 601   photo by: Joe Handelman

163692   Gulfstream C-20D   photo by: Joe Handelman

HB-JEG   Falcon 200EX EASY   photo by: Jean-Luc Altherr

VP-CFL   Falcon 900B   photo by: Jean-Luc Altherr

N502XL   Citation Excel XLS   photo by: Jean-Luc Altherr

N666MX   Citation Excel   photo by: Jean-Luc Altherr

F-GVML   Global Express   photo by: Jean-Luc Altherr

ES-PVS   Learjet 60   photo by: Jean-Luc Altherr

EC-JBH   Falcon 200   photo by: Jean-Luc Altherr

N990H   Falcon 900EX   photo by: Jean-Luc Altherr

A6-RJA   Gulfstream G300MPA   photo by: Jean-Luc Altherr

SU-BNC   Gulfstream G-4SP   photo by: Harald Helbig

VP-CHW   Gulfstream G200   photo by: Harald Helbig

G-FRYL   390 Premier 1   photo by: Harald Helbig

D-ABCD   Challenger 604   photo by: Wolfgang Zilsk

D-IFIS   CitationJet   photo by: Wolfgang Zilsk

CS-DHB   Citation Bravo   photo by: Wolfgang Zilsk

N711MQ   Gulfstream G-2B   photo by: Jean-Luc Altherr

RA-10201   Gulfstream G-4SP   photo by: Jean-Luc Altherr

HB-IBH   Falcon 2000   photo by: Anton Heumann

LX-EAR   Learjet 31A   photo by: Anton Heumann

VP-BRM   Boeing BBJ-75U   photo by: Anton Heumann

VP-BEN   Global Express   photo by: Anton Heumann

OE-GKK   Citation Bravo   photo by: Anton Heumann

HB-VNO   Citation CJ-2   photo by: Anton Heumann

OE-FRR   CitationJet   photo by: Anton Heumann

N111AC   Sabreliner 40   photo by: Joe Handelman

N800RF   Learjet 25D   photo by: Joe Handelman

N707JA   Gulfstream G-3   photo by: Joe Handelman

D-FIRE   TBM 700B   photo by: Wolfgang Zilske

D-IKIM   King Air C90B   photo by: Wolfgang Zilske

LZ-YUK   King Air 200   photo by: Wolfgang Zilske

HB-FOU   Pilatus PC-12/45   photo by: Anton Heumann

HB-FOT   Pilatus PC-12/45   photo by: Anton Heumann

HB-FOO   Pilatus PC-12/45   photo by: Anton Heumann

23-3226   Mitsubishi MU-2E   photo by: Dick Milne

SP-MXH   Piaggio P-180 Avanti   photo Barry Ambrose BIZAV

S5-CAE   Conquest II   photo Barry Ambrose BIZAV

Reg	Yr	Type	c/n	Owner/Operator	Prev Regn
☐ YV-94CP	1976	Mitsubishi MU-2M	347	W/o 1982.	YV-1050P
☐ YV-994P	1976	King Air C90	LJ-693	W/o Caracas, Venezuela. 4 Feb 82.	
☐ YV-O-MAR-	1967	680V Turbo Command	1683-64	W/o Venezuela 17 Aug 78.	YV-O-MOP-8
☐ YV-O-NCE-	1976	King Air E90	LW-201	W/o Caracas, Venezuela. 13 Nov 95.	
☐ YV-O-SATA	1981	King Air 200	BB-770	W/o en route Miranda-Barinas, Venezuela 5 Apr 01.	YV-O-CPI-1
☐ YV-T-ADJ	1973	King Air E90	LW-53	W/o Pratt, Ks. USA. 10 May 73.	
Military					
☐ FAV....	1974	King Air E90	LW-81	Wfu. Located Griffin, Ga. USA.	YV-416P

ZS = SOUTH AFRICA

Civil

Reg	Yr	Type	c/n	Owner/Operator	Prev Regn
☐ ZS-IHZ	1970	King Air B90	LJ-497	W/o Capetown, South Africa. 26 Dec 92.	N9019Q
☐ ZS-JRF	1978	Rockwell 690B	11491	W/o. Cx ZS- 16 Aug 93.	(N690RC)
☐ ZS-KMT	1980	King Air 200	BB-767	W/o Johannesburg, South Africa. 13 Apr 87.	N3717T
☐ ZS-KRS	1980	Gulfstream 840	11644	W/o South Africa. 16 Sep 81.	N5896K
☐ ZS-KVB	1980	Gulfstream 980	95005	W/o Nr Sishen, South Africa 20 Jun 84.	N9758S
☐ ZS-LNV	1983	King Air B200C	BL-71	W/o Steynsburg, South Africa. 10 May 97.	(N771D)
☐ ZS-LUC	1978	PA-31T Cheyenne II	7820092	W/o Welkom, South Africa. 26 Apr 89.	N777DL
☐ ZS-MGR	1975	King Air 200	BB-19	W/o Marunga, Angola. 21 Oct 95.	N221B
☐ ZS-MSG	1979	King Air B100	BE-75	W/o Vrede, South Africa. 23 Dec 94. Cx ZS- 6/95.	N814GT
☐ ZS-MSL	1981	King Air 200	BB-815	W/o Lome-Abidjan, Ivory Coast. 26 Jun 98.	N255AV
☐ ZS-NEP	1981	King Air 200	BB-838	W/o Aminius nr Koudpan, Namibia. 28 Jun 93.	N14MF
☐ ZS-NRW	1977	King Air 200	BB-201	W/o Moz, South Africa. 28 Jun 04.	5Y-BKS
☐ ZS-NXY	1983	King Air C90-1	LJ-1058	W/o Sulkerbossstrand, South Africa. 13 Dec 96.	N6586K
☐ ZS-OFC	1998	Pilatus PC-12/45	206	W/o Nairobi, Kenya. 13 Feb 98.	HB-F..
☐ ZS-OIG	1989	Reims/Cessna F406	F406-0041	W/o Johannesburg, South Africa 3 Nov 01.	N563GA
Military					
☐ SAAF16	1975	SA-226AT Merlin 4A	AT-040	W/o Pretoria, South Africa. 14 July 82.	(SAAF14)

Z3 = MACEDONIA

Civil

Reg	Yr	Type	c/n	Owner/Operator	Prev Regn
☐ Z3-BAB	1980	King Air 200	BB-652	W/o S of Sarajevo 26 Feb 04.	(N88DA)

5H = TANZANIA

Civil

Reg	Yr	Type	c/n	Owner/Operator	Prev Regn
☐ 5H-SCB	1983	Conquest 1	425-0183	W/o Nr Dar Es Salaam, Tanzania. 12 Jun 00.	VH-EGS
☐ 5H-TZC	1988	Reims/Cessna F406	F406-0028	W/o Muyowasi Tanzania. 13 Aug 02.	N7073C
☐ 5H-TZD	1988	Reims/Cessna F406	F406-0029	W/o Mount Palapala Morogoro, Tanzania. 24 Apr 96.	PH-FWI

5N = NIGERIA

Civil

Reg	Yr	Type	c/n	Owner/Operator	Prev Regn
☐ 5N-ATU	1966	King Air A90	LJ-136	Wfu. Located at Gamston, UK.	F-BFRE

5Y = KENYA

Civil

Reg	Yr	Type	c/n	Owner/Operator	Prev Regn
☐ 5Y-BIW	1981	King Air 200	BB-782	Wfu. Parts at Nairobi-Wilson, Kenya.	G-THUR
☐ 5Y-BLF	1964	Gulfstream 1	131	Wfu. Located Nairobi-Wilson, Kenya.	C-FRTT
☐ 5Y-EMJ	1965	Gulfstream 1	158	W/o Busia, Kenya. 24 Jan 03.	5Y-MIA
☐ 5Y-ING	1988	Reims/Cessna F406	F406-0024	W/o 12 Jun 95 Nairobi, Kenya.	PH-PEL
☐ 5Y-JJG	1985	Reims/Cessna F406	F406-0003	W/o Nairobi, Kenya. 8 Aug 94.	PH-ALK
☐ 5Y-NAL	1989	Reims/Cessna F406	F406-0038	W/o Mar 94.	PH-ALX
☐ 5Y-NBB	1971	King Air C90	LJ-528	Wfu. Located Nairobi-Wilson, Kenya.	N883AV
☐ 5Y-TNT	1971	SA-226T Merlin 3	T-211	W/o Nairobi-Wilson, Kenya. 1 Oct 92.	TN-ADO

6O = SOMALIA

Civil

Reg	Yr	Type	c/n	Owner/Operator	Prev Regn
☐ 6O-SBQ	1974	Rockwell 690A	11151	Wfu. Located Mombasa, Kenya.	3D-BYZ

7Q = MALAWI

Civil

Reg	Yr	Type	c/n	Owner/Operator	Prev Regn
☐ 7Q-YMM	1980	King Air C90	LJ-880	W/o Blantyre-Chileka, Malawi. 9 Nov 90. (parts at Dodsons).	ZS-KLC

7T = ALGERIA

Civil

Reg	Yr	Type	c/n	Owner/Operator	Prev Regn
☐ 7T-VSH	1968	King Air B90	LJ-423	W/o Jan 76.	HB-GDT

Reg   *Yr*   *Type*   *c/n*   *Owner/Operator*   *Prev Regn*

9J = ZAMBIA

Civil

Reg	Yr	Type	c/n	Owner/Operator	Prev Regn
☐ 9J-GCF	1973	King Air C90	LJ-590	W/o Serenje, Zambia. 16 Aug 90.	N243L

9M = MALAYSIA

Civil

Reg	Yr	Type	c/n	Owner/Operator	Prev Regn
☐ 9M-CAM	1983	King Air B200T	BT-24	W/o Ipoh, Malaysia. 13 Dec 93.	9M-JPA

9Q = CONGO KINSHASA

Civil

Reg	Yr	Type	c/n	Owner/Operator	Prev Regn
☐ 9Q-...	1975	King Air C90	LJ-660	Wfu.	ZS-LXL
☐ 9Q-COI	1979	SA-226T Merlin 3B	T-302	W/o Zaire. 6 Oct 83.	G-IIIB

Military

Reg	Yr	Type	c/n	Owner/Operator	Prev Regn
☐ 9T-MBD	1974	Mitsubishi MU-2J	620	W/o.	N470MA

Business TurboProps
Cross-Reference by Construction Number

Aero Commander
Commander 680

C/N	Reg
1473-1	wfu
1532-2	wo
1534-3	wfu
1536-4	wo
1538-5	N722LJ
1540-6	wfu
1542-7	wfu
1544-8	C-GSVQ
1546-9	C-FAXN
1721-1	N39AS
1722-2	N93RA
1723-3	N4622E
1751-4	wfu
1752-5	N505RT
1760-6	wfu
1761-7	wfu
1762-8	N2755B
1763-9	N200DT
1519-95	N175DB
1548-10	N7610U
1550-11	wfu
1552-12	wfu
1554-13	wo
1556-14	N543S
1557-15	wfu
1558-16	N818L
1560-17	N687L
1562-18	N2755B
1563-19	FAC-542
1564-20	EC-DSA
1565-21	wo
1566-22	N292Z
1567-23	N666MN
1568-24	N666MN
1570-25	N370K
1571-26	wo
1572-27	N900RJ
1573-28	wo
1575-29	wo
1576-30	wo
1577-31	wo
1579-32	N808GU
1580-33	wo
1581-34	wfu
1583-35	wfu
1584-36	N512JD
1585-37	wfu
1587-38	wfu
1588-39	wo
1589-40	N698GN
1593-41	wfu
1597-42	wfu
1601-43	C-GFAB
1605-44	wo
1609-45	wo
1610-46	wfu
1612-47	wfu
1614-48	wfu
1616-49	N171AT
1618-50	wo
1620-51	N11HM
1622-52	wfu
1624-53	wfu
1626-54	wfu
1628-55	wo
1630-56	wfu
1632-57	HK-2285P
1675-58	wfu
1676-59	N66FV
1677-60	N677KA
1679-61	wfu
1680-62	N3CG
1682-63	LV-OFX
1683-64	wo
1684-65	D-IABC
1685-66	YV-744CP
1687-67	N680FS
1688-68	N4FB
1689-69	YV-843P
1691-70	N47HM
1692-71	wfu
1693-72	wo
1694-73	wfu
1697-74	N400LP
1698-75	N20BM
1699-76	N29DE
1701-77	wfu
1702-78	wo
1703-79	PT-....
1704-80	wfu
1705-81	N87BT
1707-82	wo
1708-83	N200TB
1709-84	wfu
1710-85	N111SK
1711-86	wfu
1713-87	wo
1714-88	N50655
1718-89	YV-344P
1719-90	YV-1405P
1720-91	wfu
1772-10	N514NA
1773-11	N11CT
1774-12	N54163
1775-13	YV-820CP
1776-14	EC-EAG
1777-15	wfu
1778-16	wfu
1787-17	wo
1788-18	XB-DTD
1789-19	N1928H
1790-20	N410TH
1791-21	N345TT
1792-22	N680JD
1793-23	N22ET
1802-24	N17JG
1803-25	N4100B
1804-26	YV-2280P
1805-27	wo
1811-28	wo
1812-29	N680KM
1813-30	YV-536P
1814-31	YV-2436P
1818-32	N5RE
1819-33	wo
1820-34	HP-1433
1821-35	N424PP
1828-36	wfu
1829-37	wfu
1833-38	N80610
1834-39	XB-...
1835-40	CP-1934
1842-41	wfu
1843-42	N940U
1844-43	wo
1848-44	EP-FSS
1849-45	EP-FIA
1850-46	EP-FIB

Commander 681

C/N	Reg
6001	N22RT
6002	N6E
6003	wo
6004	wo
6005	YV-2383P
6006	N113CT
6007	N68VH
6008	wfu
6009	wfu
6010	N3867N
6011	wo
6012	EP-AGU
6013	N70RF
6014	HK-....
6015	wo
6016	wfu
6018	N29PR
6019	N3203P
6020	C-FATR
6021	PT-OQQ
6022	TG-WIZ
6023	XB-DJN
6024	YV-2501P
6025	CP-2042
6026	wfu
6027	N548GQ
6028	N100GL
6029	YV-2404P
6030	9Q-CGL
6032	TG-GMI
6033	wo
6034	wfu
6035	HK-1977
6036	N681DC
6037	wfu
6038	N78CH
6039	wfu
6040	XB-...
6041	N25BE
6042	wo
6043	HK-2376P
6044	YV-....
6045	9Q-CBU
6046	wfu
6047	VH-NBT
6048	N676DM
6049	HC-BPY
6050	wo
6051	N12MU
6052	YV-2475P
6053	wo
6054	C-FCMJ
6055	N18KK
6056	wo
6057	wo
6058	N47CK
6059	N30BG
6060	wfu
6061	N520CS
6062	5-280
6063	XA-SHP
6064	wfu
6065	wfu
6066	wfu
6067	wfu
6068	5-281
6069	PT-IEC
6070	PT-IED
6071	wo
6072	5-282

British Aerospace
HS 748

C/N	Reg
1669	C-FAMO
1684	FAE-001
1688	AF602

Jetstream 31

C/N	Reg
605	N903EH
613	N904FH
634	G-BLKP
637	G-BRGN
715	G-IJYS
777	N443PE

Jetstream 41

C/N	Reg
41030	N680AS
41038	N514GP
41060	41060
41094	41094
41095	ZS-NYK
41102	B-HRS
41104	B-HRT

CASA
Casa 212

C/N	Reg
286	N434CA
294	N31BR
369	EB-50

Cessna
425 Conquest I

C/N	Reg
425-693	wfu
425-0001	wo
425-0002	N443H
425-0003	D-INGA
425-0004	N425AT
425-0005	N345TP
425-0006	N757H
425-0007	N67BA
425-0008	C-FKTL
425-0009	wo
425-0010	N425PL
425-0011	A2-AHT
425-0012	N127BB
425-0013	wo
425-0014	N425TC
425-0015	N522WD
425-0016	HB-LOE
425-0017	N794B
425-0018	N794PF
425-0019	wo
425-0020	N55AC
425-0021	V5-LYZ
425-0022	N6772P
425-0023	N707CB
425-0024	wo
425-0025	N83CH
425-0026	N540GC
425-0027	VP-BJT
425-0028	N425WB
425-0029	N926ES
425-0030	N67726
425-0031	wo
425-0032	F-GFJR
425-0033	N425GM
425-0034	wo
425-0035	N480EA
425-0036	N700WJ
425-0037	N425SF
425-0038	N425JP
425-0039	N425TX
425-0040	wo
425-0041	ZS-MVW
425-0042	N1BM
425-0043	N425JB
425-0044	N425HS
425-0045	wo
425-0046	N425BA
425-0047	N585PA
425-0048	N6774Z
425-0049	N31AD
425-0050	N37PS
425-0051	XB-FMS
425-0052	N922KV
425-0053	N4420F
425-0054	N425LC
425-0055	wo
425-0056	N502NC
425-0057	wo
425-0058	N67JE
425-0059	F-GEFZ
425-0060	N1222B
425-0061	N425SW
425-0062	N6844D
425-0063	C-GDLG
425-0064	N425XP
425-0065	N425AR
425-0066	N425DH
425-0067	5N-AMW
425-0068	N425TB
425-0069	N12NL
425-0070	N425NW
425-0071	ZS-CPX
425-0072	N425ET
425-0073	N425HB
425-0074	N10RM
425-0075	ZS-ONZ
425-0076	N14BM
425-0077	V5-MJW
425-0078	wo
425-0079	N900MS
425-0080	C-GJHF
425-0081	N6846S
425-0082	N86EA
425-0083	N425DD
425-0084	N547GC
425-0085	N71HE
425-0086	N823DB
425-0087	N616CG
425-0088	N35TK
425-0089	N73DW
425-0090	N90YA
425-0091	XB-FXK
425-0092	N425LA
425-0093	N926FS
425-0094	N105FC
425-0095	N8FR
425-0096	N425E
425-0097	N410VE
425-0098	N425DM
425-0099	N425EZ
425-0100	N425AL
425-0101	N543GC
425-0102	D-ICMF
425-0103	N4276Z
425-0104	N425PV
425-0105	N18481
425-0106	N425SX
425-0107	N425LG
425-0108	N70GM
425-0109	N818PL
425-0110	N555TP
425-0111	N77YP
425-0112	N6851G
425-0113	N425HD
425-0114	N847YT
425-0115	ZS-KSU
425-0116	N420MA
425-0117	N10FB
425-0118	HK-3036P
425-0119	N7WF
425-0120	D-IPOS
425-0121	N425D
425-0122	N751JT
425-0123	N825B
425-0124	N425JH
425-0125	N125PG
425-0126	wo
425-0127	N456FC
425-0128	N444RR
425-0129	N520RM
425-0130	N43BH
425-0131	D-ILPC
425-0132	N83GF
425-0133	N425SR
425-0134	N156GA
425-0135	N5CE
425-0136	N125SC
425-0137	wo
425-0138	N39A
425-0139	N320SS
425-0140	N15ST
425-0141	N373LP
425-0142	N101CA

c/n	Reg	c/n	Reg	c/n	Reg	c/n	Reg	c/n	Reg
425-0143	N6885P	425-0225	N225DF	441-0066	N385GH	441-0148	N441AR	441-0231	N441YA
425-0144	N6885S	425-0226	N111KU	441-0067	YV-225CP	441-0149	N419SC	441-0232	HK-3562
425-0145	N440HC	425-0227	N12268	441-0068	N3WM	441-0150	S5-CAE	441-0233	N6855P
425-0146	N146GW	425-0228	wo	441-0069	wo	441-0151	N441RJ	441-0234	N42DT
425-0147	N500WD	425-0229	N1227J	441-0070	N318AK	441-0152	HK-3620X	441-0235	XB-EWO
425-0148	N701CR	425-0230	N98EP	441-0071	wo	441-0153	N722GA	441-0236	VH-LBC
425-0149	N425LD	425-0231	N127MC	441-0072	N441TF	441-0154	wo	441-0237	XA-TLW
425-0150	wo	425-0232	N75HW	441-0073	D-IAAC	441-0155	XB-FND	441-0238	N3NC
425-0151	wo	425-0233	D-ICHS	441-0074	N441RK	441-0156	N441JC	441-0239	HK-3615
425-0152	wo	425-0234	N1262K	441-0075	LV-MMY	441-0157	VH-YFD	441-0240	N441PW
425-0153	N153JM	425-0235	JA8855	441-0076	C-GPSQ	441-0158	N3TK	441-0241	wo
425-0154	N6886V	425-0236	G-BNDY	441-0077	N441KW*	441-0159	ZS-TMA	441-0242	N441WT
425-0155	N168MA	441-0168	N2722D	441-0078	C-FWRL	441-0160	N47JR	441-0243	N916AS
425-0156	N857C	441-0343	N835MA	441-0079	VH-LEM	441-0161	N383SS	441-0244	wo
425-0157	N425PJ	**441 Conquest II**		441-0080	LV-MRT	441-0162	LN-ABU	441-0245	N441PG
425-0158	N355ES	679	wfu	441-0081	N441EE	441-0163	N38AA	441-0246	N913DC
425-0159	N813ZM	441-679	wfu	441-0082	N84LJ	441-0164	5Y-...	441-0247	N5HG
425-0160	N68865	441-0001	TJ-AHZ	441-0083	N441HT	441-0165	EI-DMG	441-0248	N441SX
425-0161	N425TW	441-0002	wfu	441-0084	C-GLGE	441-0166	N624CB	441-0249	N911ER
425-0162	YV-2263P	441-0003	N8838T	441-0085	N687AE	441-0167	N332DM	441-0250	C-GLBL
425-0163	wo	441-0004	N555JJ	441-0086	VH-OPM	441-0169	wo	441-0251	HK-3573
425-0164	N425EM	441-0005	VH-TAZ	441-0087	N441DZ	441-0170	N783ST	441-0252	wo
425-0165	N49GM	441-0006	wo	441-0088	N13NW	441-0171	N14NW	441-0253	N441X
425-0166	N425SG	441-0007	N441HH	441-0089	VH-LBX	441-0172	N441SA	441-0254	N9683N
425-0167	C-GRHD	441-0008	N441CC	441-0090	N8970N	441-0173	N2722Y	441-0255	N256DD
425-0168	PH-JOE	441-0009	N87WS	441-0091	N410MF	441-0174	VH-VEM	441-0256	N505HC
425-0169	N425HJ	441-0010	N903WD	441-0092	N441A	441-0175	N988AE	441-0257	N258VB
425-0170	N100CC	441-0011	N93HC	441-0093	ZS-JMA	441-0176	N441DK	441-0258	N441CD
425-0171	N51CU	441-0012	N441SC	441-0094	N451WS	441-0177	wo	441-0259	VH-TFB
425-0172	wo	441-0013	N442JA	441-0095	YV-...	441-0178	wfu	441-0260	HK-3512
425-0173	N6873Q	441-0014	N441ST	441-0096	N441WP	441-0179	N441EC	441-0261	N50MF
425-0174	N425KC	441-0015	N24PT	441-0097	wo	441-0180	N2723X	441-0262	N233RC
425-0175	N425WT	441-0016	HK-2390W	441-0098	N234CC	441-0181	wo	441-0263	C-GSKH
425-0176	N425TV	441-0017	VH-HMZ	441-0099	MT-224	441-0182	VH-VEZ	441-0264	C-FHSP
425-0177	C-GSFI	441-0018	wo	441-0100		441-0183	N23EA	441-0265	N441ME
425-0178	C-FVAX	441-0019	N6VP	441-0101		441-0184	N184VB	441-0266	N88727
425-0179	N333UJ	441-0020	wo	441-0102	VH-OAA	441-0185	N797RW	441-0267	HC-BXH
425-0180	N425RM	441-0021	XB-GBN	441-0103	N441MD	441-0186	N7NW	441-0268	N88834
425-0181	N24QF	441-0022	N889DM	441-0104	N273AZ	441-0187	N88GW	441-0269	wo
425-0182	N68734	441-0023	VH-LBY	441-0105	N4152G	441-0188	wfu	441-0270	HK-3456W
425-0183	wo	441-0024	N441MJ	441-0106	VH-NAX	441-0189	XC-AA71	441-0271	VH-VED
425-0184	N425SP	441-0025	VH-XMD	441-0107	N441WD	441-0190	N2725N	441-0272	HK-3009
425-0185	N425DC	441-0026	VH-AZW	441-0108	N108TJ	441-0191		441-0273	N322P
425-0186	N425FG	441-0027	N922HP	441-0109	VH-FMQ	441-0192		441-0274	XC-HHU
425-0187	N622MM	441-0028	N441DS	441-0110	HK-....	441-0193	N441VC	441-0275	HK-3596
425-0188	N188DF	441-0029	N441RB	441-0111	N59RT	441-0194	wo	441-0276	HP-...
425-0189	YV-548CP	441-0030	VH-OCS	441-0112	wo	441-0195	N441WJ	441-0277	N15DB
425-0190	C-FKTN	441-0031	PNC-204	441-0113	VH-XMJ	441-0196	N195FW	441-0278	wo
425-0191	N444KF	441-0032	N441P	441-0114	HK-2538P	441-0197	wo	441-0279	N441AE
425-0192	C-FSEA	441-0033	wo	441-0115	N441VB	441-0198	N441JK	441-0280	N689AE
425-0193	N425PC	441-0034	N441BW	441-0116	N711MB	441-0199	N447WS	441-0281	N6832M
425-0194	N577PW	441-0035	N441DR	441-0117	N441CJ	441-0200	wo	441-0282	N441EP
425-0195	N207RS	441-0036	N3AW	441-0118	N14FJ	441-0201	N423TG	441-0283	N441AB
425-0196	N1222G	441-0037	N81PN	441-0119	N22CG	441-0202	N77ML	441-0284	N707MA
425-0197	N425WL	441-0038	VH-LBZ	441-0120	C-FSKG	441-0203	N60TR	441-0285	N441MW
425-0198	N5PU	441-0039	N74BY	441-0121	N44776	441-0204	N441TA	441-0286	HK-3540E
425-0199	N425DR	441-0040	N12DT	441-0122	N441M	441-0205	N3330S	441-0287	N77R
425-0200	N425PG	441-0041	N441WL	441-0123	N441ND	441-0206	HK-3613	441-0288	N377CA
425-0201	N1223B	441-0042	VH-LBA	441-0124	N555FT	441-0207	G-FPLC	441-0289	N88692
425-0202	N788JL	441-0043	N445AE	441-0125	N48BS	441-0208	XC-GOO	441-0290	wo
425-0203	N425KD	441-0044	N441KM	441-0126	N337C	441-0209	N711GE	441-0291	N441PP
425-0204	N1223P	441-0045	N441PS	441-0127	N825SP	441-0210	N441LA	441-0292	N878JL
425-0205	N111SU	441-0046	N441CA	441-0128	N128EZ	441-0211	N6851T	441-0293	N456GT
425-0206	N425CL	441-0047	wo	441-0129	N420DB	441-0212	N6851X	441-0294	N181MD
425-0207	N425NC	441-0048	N441CT	441-0130	VH-XMG	441-0213	N716CC	441-0295	VH-LBD
425-0208	N1224J	441-0049	N441EB	441-0131	wo	441-0214	N441EW	441-0296	N441MT
425-0209	D-IDAX	441-0050	N83A	441-0132	VH-SMO	441-0215	N665TM	441-0297	C-GCYB
425-0210	N425BS	441-0051	N725SV	441-0133	N4441T	441-0216	C-FNWC	441-0298	N6840T
425-0211	wo	441-0052	wo	441-0134	N441SM	441-0217	N441BB	441-0299	N441DB
425-0212	N1224T	441-0053	N2441K	441-0135	N502BR	441-0218	N553AM	441-0300	N441SB
425-0213	N12244	441-0054	N454EA	441-0136	N207SS	441-0219	N6853T	441-0301	N500RJ
425-0214	N214LA	441-0055	N477B	441-0137	N441JA	441-0220	N441RS	441-0302	N441JR
425-0215	N888JS	441-0056	wo	441-0138	VH-KUZ	441-0221	N533M	441-0303	N6860C
425-0216	N216BJ	441-0057	TF-ORF	441-0139	C-FSKC	441-0222	N92JQ	441-0304	N441CX
425-0217	N425TM	441-0058	C-GPSP	441-0140	N604RR	441-0223	XC-GON	441-0305	N66BZ
425-0218	N425N	441-0059	HK-3401	441-0141	ZK-NFD	441-0224	N441VH	441-0306	N2NC
425-0219	N232GM	441-0060	N88598	441-0142	N142WJ	441-0225	N441AD	441-0307	N33DE
425-0220	N425AD	441-0061	N903DC	441-0143	N26PK	441-0226	YV-533P	441-0308	HK-3568
425-0221	C-GNEP	441-0062	N441KP	441-0144	wo	441-0227	wo	441-0309	N977MP
425-0222	N1777X	441-0063	YV-2390P	441-0145	N441BH	441-0228	N88QT	441-0310	N832AD
425-0223	ZP-...	441-0064	N88823	441-0146	N911PJ	441-0229	wo	441-0311	N331MP
425-0224	N425NP	441-0065	N777XW	441-0147	N564AC	441-0230	N441G	441-0312	N331MP

441-0313	N443DW
441-0314	C-GCIL
441-0315	N316CA*
441-0316	C-FSFI
441-0317	N1843S
441-0318	N300NK
441-0319	N6412Q
441-0320	HK-3550
441-0321	N441PJ
441-0322	N441BL
441-0323	N441S
441-0324	HK-3611
441-0325	N441DN
441-0326	N326RS
441-0327	N441AG
441-0328	HP-...
441-0329	N77SA
441-0330	N441HS
441-0331	N68HS
441-0332	HP-1189
441-0333	HK-3418
441-0334	N444AK
441-0335	HK-3497
441-0336	N441HK
441-0337	N337KC
441-0338	wo
441-0339	N1210Z
441-0340	N1211C
441-0341	N441DD
441-0342	N441LS
441-0344	N441UC
441-0345	wfu
441-0346	N1212C
441-0347	N1212K
441-0348	HK-3529
441-0349	N274GC
441-0350	AP-BCY
441-0351	N441PZ
441-0352	AP-BCQ
441-0353	5N-ATR
441-0354	wfu
441-0355	D-ILYS
441-0356	HK-3532
441-0357	D-IOHL
441-0358	D-IJLF
441-0359	N123ME
441-0360	N731BH
441-0361	N592Q
441-0362	C-GSSK

Reims/Cessna 406

F406-00..	98-1004
F406-01	F-ZBFA
F406-0001	N17CK
F406-0002	D2-ECN
F406-0003	wo
F406-0004	V5-EEZ
F406-0005	ZS-NNA
F406-0006	F-ZBEP
F406-0007	TR-LEQ
F406-0008	F-MABM
F406-0009	5Y-TAL
F406-0010	F-MABN
F406-0011	D2-ECO
F406-0012	ZK-VAA
F406-0013	V5-MAD
F406-0014	wo
F406-0015	OY-PBG
F406-0016	D2-ECP
F406-0017	F-ZBES
F406-0018	G-LEAF
F406-0019	D2-ECQ
F406-0020	G-TURF
F406-0021	5Y-BKN
F406-0022	YV-990CP
F406-0023	ZS-OEE
F406-0024	wo
F406-0025	F-ZBAB
F406-0026	F-OGOG
F406-0027	D-ISHY
F406-0028	wo
F406-0029	wo
F406-0030	ZS-NYI
F406-0031	VT-ASB
F406-0032	PH-CLE
F406-0033	VH-JVN
F406-0034	OO-LMO
F406-0035	ZS-OGY
F406-0036	G-MAFA
F406-0037	PH-MJM
F406-0038	wo
F406-0039	F-ZBBB
F406-0040	ZS-OTT
F406-0041	wo
F406-0042	F-ZBCE
F406-0043	D-INUS
F406-0044	5Y-MKM
F406-0045	G-FIND
F406-0046	5H-TZE
F406-0047	TF-ORD
F406-0048	V5-WAK
F406-0049	N406GV
F406-0050	N406P
F406-0051	S7-AAI
F406-0052	N6590Y
F406-0053	wo
F406-0054	N6591R
F406-0055	5Y-BIX
F406-0056	wo
F406-0057	ZK-VAF
F406-0058	V5-MDA
F406-0059	AP-BFK
F406-0060	5H-WOW
F406-0061	F-GRAI
F406-0062	V5-DHL
F406-0063	N406SD
F406-0064	G-SFPA
F406-0065	G-SFPB
F406-0066	F-ZBCG
F406-0067	Z-DDG
F406-0068	Z-DDE
F406-0069	Z-DDD
F406-0070	F-ZBCI
F406-0071	Z-DDF
F406-0072	F-....
F406-0073	F-WQFA
F406-0074	F-ZBCJ
F406-0075	F-ZBCH
F406-0076	VH-ZZE
F406-0077	F-ZBCF
F406-0078	VH-ZZF
F406-0079	VH-ZZG
F406-0080	G-MAFB
F406-0081	98-1001
F406-0082	98-1002
F406-0083	98-1003
F406-0084	98-1005
F406-0085	98-1006
F406-0086	F-ZBGA
F406-0087	AC-21
F406-0088	AC-22
F406-0089	AC-23
F406-0090	F-ZBGB
F406-0091	F-OSPJ

De Havilland

DHC-6

437	N143Z
596	N16NG
782	AP-BBR

DHC-7

106	N54026

DHC-8

024	5N-MGV
391	HK-....
435	N759A
440	N724A
441	N725A

Dornier

228

7028	A40-CQ
8146	5N-MPS
8206	PH-MNZ
8226	1112
8227	1113
8228	1114

328

3019	N328DC
3024	N28CG
3027	N653PC
3034	N38CG
3078	OE-GBB
3083	5N-SPC
3086	5N-SPD

Embraer

Xingu 121A

121040	OO-SXB

Fokker

F27

16	N235KT
35	N432NA
97	N366SB
10281	J 752
20253	U-05
20287	U-06
20321	U-01
20324	U-02
20327	U-03
20329	U-04

Gulfstream

Gulfstream 1

1	5Y-XXX
2	wfu
3	wfu
4	wfu
5	ZS-OOE
6	wfu
7	N99EL
8	wfu
9	wfu
10	wfu
11	N7SL
12	wfu
14	wfu
15	wfu
16	N615C
17	wfu
18	N48PA
19	wfu
20	TU-TDM
21	wfu
22	wfu
23	N186PA
24	wo
25	ZS-PHK
26	N185PA
27	N198PA
28	N719RA
29	wfu
30	wfu
31	wfu
32	wfu
33	9Q-CBY
34	5Y-BLR
35	9Q-CBD
36	wfu
37	wo
38	N717RS
39	EC-EVJ
40	EC-FIO
41	EC-EZO
42	3D-TRE
43	wfu
44	5Y-JET
45	wfu
46	wfu
47	wfu
48	wfu
49	wfu
50	wfu
51	wfu
52	N612DT
53	wfu
54	N164PA
55	wfu
56	N168PA
57	wfu
58	XA-TTU
59	wo
60	wfu
61	wfu
62	wfu
63	wfu
64	wfu
65	wfu
66	wfu
67	N806W
68	wo
69	wfu
70	N331H
71	XA-MYR
72	wfu
73	wo
74	N701BN
75	PT-KYF
76	P4-JML
77	wfu
78	HK-3681
79	N79HS
80	D2-EXC
81	5Y-BMR
82	N12RW
83	wfu
84	N183K
85	wfu
86	ZS-ALX
87	wfu
88	N195PA
89	N789G
90	wfu
91	wfu
92	wfu
93	N197PA
94	N8E
95	N500RN
96	N2NA
97	N184PA
98	wfu
99	wo
100	wfu
101	wfu
102	N11UN
103	XC-AA57
104	C-FHBO
105	wfu
106	YV-....
107	wfu
108	wfu
109	wfu
110	wfu
111	wfu
112	wfu
114	wfu
115	N61SB
116	wfu
117	N167PA
118	wfu
119	N165PA
120	wfu
121	wfu
122	F-GFEF
123	wfu
124	D2-EXD
125	N193PA
126	N110RB
127	wfu
128	wo
129	N129AF
130	PK-TRO
131	wfu
132	wfu
133	wfu
134	ZS-PHJ
135	wfu
136	XA-TBT
137	wfu
138	XA-RLK
139	N196PA
140	wfu
141	ZS-NHW
142	wfu
143	wfu
144	wfu
145	HK-3580W
146	wfu
147	wo
148	XC-LIE
149	N192PA
150	wfu
151	wfu
152	wfu
153	EC-EXB
154	wo
155	9Q-CBJ
156	N41LH
157	N94SA
158	wo
159	XA-RJB
160	N599TR
161	XA-...
162	C-GPTA
163	wo
164	ZS-PHI
165	N501WN
166	D2-EXB
167	N717RA
168	wfu
169	N200AE
170	YV-627C
171	YV-628C
172	wfu
173	YV-....
174	wfu
175	N173PA
176	wfu
177	PK-CDM
178	wo
179	XC-AA53
180	wfu
181	wo
182	wfu
183	wfu
184	wfu
185	wfu
186	wfu
187	wfu
188	C-FAWE
189	wfu
190	5Y-...
191	PK-RJA
192	N171PA
193	ZS-JIS
194	5Y-BMS
195	N190PA
196	N659PC
197	N520JG
198	wo
199	N183PA
200	N159GS
322	N71RD
323	HI-678CT

Gulfstream 1000

96000	wo
96001	XC-AA23
96002	N9902S
96003	HP-...
96004	XB-ECT
96005	N94PA
96006	N444WD
96007	N695AM
96008	PJ-NAF
96009	N7031K
96010	HK-3239W
96011	N695GJ
96012	N95AB
96013	MT-218
96014	N51DM

96015	N333UP
96016	YV-O-MTC-
96017	N17ZD
96018	HK-3367
96019	N200DK
96020	N93NM
96021	HK-3439
96022	N9942S
96023	HB-GHK
96024	N5450J
96025	N9945S
96026	wfu
96027	N727CC
96028	N9948S
96029	N79PH
96030	FAC-5198
96031	HP-1149P
96032	N695NC
96033	HK-3366X
96034	N700L
96035	N93MA
96036	N695GG
96037	HK-3389P
96038	N695HT
96039	HK-3060
96040	MT-214
96041	ETE-1318
96042	N303GM
96043	XC-HFN
96044	wfu
96045	HK-2909P
96046	N9966S
96047	HK-3390
96048	N9968S
96049	HK-2951
96050	N45LG
96051	ZS-KZY
96052	ZS-KZZ
96053	N9973S
96054	N71MR
96055	N695AB
96056	XC-AA19
96057	N34GA
96058	N36AG
96059	HK-3391W
96060	FAH-006
96061	HK-3218
96062	N2VA
96063	N83WA
96064	N6767M
96065	PJ-...
96066	N54GA
96067	YV-53CP
96068	N519CC
96069	HK-3961X
96070	N7896G
96071	N69GA
96072	HK-3279
96073	wo
96074	HK-3253P
96075	XA-...
96076	HK-3275
96077	HK-3192W
96078	N695GH
96079	ZP-TXF
96080	HK-....
96081	HP-...
96082	HP-...
96083	EJC-114
96084	XC-AA16
96085	N808NC
96086	HK-3193
96087	N695RC
96088	HK-3291P
96089	N45RF*
96091	XC-AA20
96092	N211AD
96093	CX-...
96094	N94EA
96095	ZP-TWY
96096	N695CT
96097	N112CE
96098	wo
96099	HK-3283W
96100	HK-3324P
96201	N115GA
96202	N27VE
96203	ZP-TXG
96204	N695MG
96205	N91575
96206	N224EZ*
96207	N81432
96208	VP-BCT
96209	N235GA
96210	N238GA

Gulfstream 840

11600	N47TT
11601	N63DL
11602	HK-....
11603	YV-170CP
11604	HK-....
11605	N125MM
11606	XC-ALO
11607	N840VM
11608	wo
11609	wo
11610	N840SE
11611	HK-3424
11612	LV-OEI
11613	LN-FWB
11614	N74EF
11615	HC-BXT
11616	N133DL
11617	N73EF
11618	YV-39CP
11619	N72TB
11620	HK-3680
11621	N920WJ
11622	N926SC
11623	wo
11624	N840CF
11625	PT-WIC
11626	N5878K
11627	N88BJ
11628	wo
11629	N940AC
11630	N106TT
11631	XB-DSH
11632	YV-...
11633	HK-2495P
11634	HC-BHU
11635	N489SC
11636	N980AK
11637	YV-394CP
11638	N840MG
11639	D-IUTA
11640	N840KB
11641	N977JC
11642	wfu
11643	N840JC
11644	wo
11645	wo
11646	N165BC
11647	N840LC
11648	N5900K
11649	XC-HHH
11650	XB-DTW
11651	HK-2601
11652	XC-AA27
11653	HK-3290P
11654	YV-87CP
11655	N406CP
11656	XC-OAX
11657	YV-O-KWH-
11658	N840JW
11659	XC-BAD
11660	N81JN
11661	XA-TOR
11662	N5914K
11663	N840BC
11664	N7057A
11665	N48BA
11666	YV-773CP
11667	11667
11668	HK-3912
11669	HC-BUD
11670	wo
11671	YV-2346P
11672	N41462
11673	HK-4065W
11674	wo
11675	N319BF
11676	N129TB
11677	XB-GMT
11678	XC-AA36
11679	ZS-SLL
11680	N777NV
11681	LN-FWA
11682	N910FC
11683	N171DR
11684	N51WF
11685	YV-105CP
11686	wfu
11687	N900LL
11688	XC-HAB
11689	N840TW
11690	wo
11691	N32PH
11692	C-FNRM
11693	N840MD
11694	YV-...
11695	XC-AA56
11696	N884D
11697	N840JK
11698	YV-601P
11699	N425MM
11700	N840SM
11701	N50WF
11702	N64PS
11703	N5955K
11709	N840LE
11719	N5956K
11720	wo
11721	HK-3700
11722	HK-3447P
11723	YV-505CP
11724	N37SB
11725	YV-...
11726	YV-2505P
11727	N840V
11728	HK-3385P
11729	N67FE
11730	N835CC
11731	N815BC
11732	N8VL
11733	11733
11734	N600BM
11735	YV-212CP

Gulfstream 900

15001	N690TP
15002	N721ML
15003	HP-...
15004	HP-...
15005	ZP-TWZ
15006	YV-492CP
15007	N337DR
15008	N6BZ
15009	XC-JDB
15010	HK-....
15011	VP-CAY
15012	YV-...
15013	N42SL
15014	N771FF
15015	N544GA
15016	N601WT
15017	YV-880CP
15018	N611
15019	wfu
15020	N600CM
15021	ZP-...
15022	YV-521CP
15023	HC-...
15024	N79SZ
15025	N29GA
15026	N995HP
15027	PT-WLD
15028	XC-MLM
15029	wo
15030	YV-822CP
15031	N471JS
15032	YV-....
15033	VP-BMZ
15034	YV-...
15035	N909HH
15036	wo
15037	N900ET
15038	PT-OQY
15039	N144JB
15040	XA-CHM
15041	N77HS
15042	C-FGWT

Gulfstream 980

95000	XC-AA67
95001	HK-...
95002	N980BH
95003	N9756S
95004	CP-2078
95005	wo
95006	N980HB
95007	YV-581CP
95008	N515AM
95009	YV-2566P
95010	wfu
95011	N980EC
95012	N980SA
95013	N519HB
95014	N9767S
95015	N655PC
95016	HK-3474
95017	YV-56CP
95018	XC-PFB
95019	PK-ODR
95020	wo
95021	ZP-TTU
95022	HK-3484
95023	N700PC
95024	N36JT
95025	N54UM
95026	HC-...
95027	N7101L
95028	YV-980CP
95029	N600MM
95030	N980MD
95031	N980EA
95032	N265EX
95033	N126M
95034	N980GM
95035	ZP-...
95036	N5356M
95037	wo
95038	PT-...
95039	D-IHSI
95040	MT-219
95041	N218MS
95042	XA-LEK
95043	HK-3461
95044	wo
95045	XC-AA98
95046	MT-221
95047	N1981S
95048	N980DT
95049	N980GR
95050	HK-3408
95051	XB-ACO
95052	XC-ENL
95053	ZP-...
95054	wo
95055	FAC-5553
95056	TI-MEL
95057	HK-3444
95058	YV-893CP
95059	HK-3819
95060	N9812S
95061	XC-PPF
95062	HK-3406
95063	N980GZ
95065	HK-3455
95066	EJC-115
95067	YV-407CP
95068	XC-AA62
95069	D-IHUC
95070	JA8600
95071	N810EC
95072	XC-HGH
95073	N200TT
95074	N357ST
95075	HK-3407
95076	N76HH
95077	N221K
95078	JA8826
95079	HK-3481
95080	HK-....
95081	N808NT
95082	MT-222
95083	HK-3450
95084	YV-787CP

Ibis

Ae 270P

001	OK-EMA
003	OK-SAR
005	OK-LIB
006	OK-INA
007	OK-EVA

Jetcruzer

500

001	wfu
002	N200JC
003	wfu

Learfan

Lear fan

E001	wfu
E003	wfu

Mitsubishi

MU-2/LR-1

001	wfu
002	wfu
003	wfu
004	wfu
005	wfu
006	wo
007	wo
008	wfu
009	wo
010	wfu
011	wfu
012	wfu
013	wo
014	N155MA
015	wfu
016	wo
017	wfu
018	wo
019	N728F
020	wfu
021	HR-...
022	wo
023	N15CC
024	wfu
025	N2GZ
026	PT-LMD
027	wo
028	wfu
029	wfu
030	wfu
031	N631BA*
032	wfu
033	wfu
034	XB-FMV
035	N36G
037	wfu
038	N706DM
101	wo
102	wo
103	wfu
104	N377NJ
105	wfu
106	N28DC

107	wo	199	wfu	297	N7DD	389SA	N400ES	522	N617BB
108	wfu	205	wo	298	N188RM	390SA	N782MA	523	wo
109	wfu	206	wfu	299	SE-GHF	391SA	N783MA	524	wfu
110	wfu	207	N122MA	300	wfu	392SA	N392P	525	C-FTML
111	N721FC	208	N111HF	301	N461MA	393SA	N82WC	526	wo
113	N859Q	209	N92TC	302	N462MA	395SA	wo	527	N527AF
114	wfu	210	N38BE	303	N728FN	396SA	wo	528	N528AF
115	wfu	211	wfu	304	wo	397SA	N777WM	529	wfu
116	wfu	212	N1978P	305	N50K	398SA	N61GJ	530	wo
117	wfu	213	PT-LYI	306	N495MA	399SA	N1930P	531	wfu
118	wfu	214	wfu	307	wo	400SA	N700WA	532	wfu
119	wfu	215	PT-ICD	308	N709FN	401SA	wo	533	wfu
120	wo	216	N922FM	309	wo	402SA	wo	534	N920S
121	wfu	217	N183MA	310	N290GC	403SA	N264KW	535	wfu
122	C6-...	218	wo	311	N311RN*	404SA	wfu	536	wfu
123	wfu	219	N185MA	312	wfu	405SA	wo	537	wfu
124	N987MA	220	wfu	313SA	N100KE	406SA	wo	538	wfu
125	wfu	221	N800BY	314	wfu	407SA	N750CA	539	wo
126	PT-LOH	222	SE-GHH	315	N99SR	408SA	wo	540	N869D
127	wfu	223	wfu	316	wfu	409SA	N78FS	541	wo
129	N555C	224	N500PS	319	N54PC	410SA	wo	542	wo
130	wo	226	N107SB	320	SE-IOZ	411SA	N400PS	543	wo
131	N755Q	228	N228WP	321SA	N5LJ	412SA	N25GM	544	N544AF
132	N756Q	229	N100CF	322	N40KC	413SA	wfu	545	wo
133	wfu	231	N346VL	323	N216CD	414SA	N73MA	546	wfu
134	wo	232	PT-WIX	324	N143JA	415SA	N893KB	547	wfu
135	N54CK	233	wfu	325	N325MA	416SA	N44AX	548	N200RX
136	N115AP	239	N303AG	326	N401JC	417SA	N61JB	549	C-FTOO
137	wo	240	N64LG	327	N375AC	418SA	wo	550	wo
138	N703DM	241	N700RX	328	N305DS	419SA	N322GB	551	wfu
139	wfu	242	wfu	329	N60AZ	420SA	D-IKKY	552	wfu
140	N900TV	243	HK-2060W	330	N261WB	423SA	N100NP	553	N755MA
141	wo	244	PT-LEW	331	wo	424SA	N157MA	554	wo
142	wo	245	wfu	332	N333TX	425SA	N575CA	555	wo
143	wfu	246	wfu	333	N12SJ	426SA	N36AT	556	wo
144	N176BJ	247	wfu	337	SE-IOV	427SA	N40AM	557	N345SA
145	PT-BOY	248	N725FN	338	N450FS	428SA	PT-LIR	558	wo
146	wfu	249	wfu	339	N800ED	429SA	N361MA	559	wo
149	wo	250	N500XX	340	wfu	430SA	N66FF	560	N776CC
150	wo	251	wo	341	wo	431SA	N171MA	561	wfu
151	wo	252	wo	342	wfu	432SA	N44VR	562	N66CY
154	N720JK	253	N430DA	343	wo	433SA	N5LC	563	N198MA
155	wfu	254	wo	344	wfu	434SA	C-FGEM	564	wfu
156	XB-HOV	255	wo	345	SE-IUA	435SA	N104JB	565	wfu
157	N711VK	256	wfu	346	N10UT	436SA	D-ISTC	566	MU-1550
158	N22MZ	257	N344KL	347	wo	437SA	N145FS	567	wo
159	N888DS	258	wfu	348SA	YV-2604P	438SA	N10VU	568	N334EB
160	wo	259	wo	349SA	N316EN	439SA	N439SA	569	wo
161	wfu	260	N444FF	350SA	PT-OVW	440SA	N219MA	570	wfu
162	N573MA	261	N281MA	351SA	N10MR	441SA	wo	571	wfu
163	wfu	262	wfu	352SA	D-IAHT	446SA	N15TR	572	N300RX
164	wfu	263	N30RR	353SA	6Y-JDB	447SA	N48NP	573	N260CB
165	YV-....	264	N261KW	354SA	PT-OIP	448SA	N68CL	574	N19GU
166	wfu	265	N121CH	355SA	N741MA	449SA	N77DK	575	wfu
167	N310MA	266	N312MA	356SA	wfu	450SA	N220N	576	wfu
168	wo	267	N59RW	357SA	N21HP	451SA	N725JT	577	wfu
169	wfu	268	PT-JGA	358SA	wo	452SA	N388NC	578	wfu
170	N58CA	269	wfu	361SA	LV-MCV	453SA	PT-OIY	579	wo
172	wfu	270	wfu	362SA	N140CP	454SA	N19GA	580	N580AF
173	N18BF	271	N708DM	363SA	N110GC	458SA	N458BB	581	N93AH
174	N52CD	272	N272MC	364SA	N547TA	459SA	N459SA	582	wfu
175	PT-BZW	273	XB-...	365SA	wo	501	wfu	583	XB-NEB
177	N12RA	274	wfu	366SA	N2RA	502	N211RV	584	N900YH
178	wo	276	wo	367SA	wfu	503	wo	585	wfu
179	N777VK	277	N3GT	368SA	N78WD	504	wo	586	wfu
180	wfu	280	N460FS	369SA	N202MC	505	wo	587	N450MA
182	N2100T	281	wfu	370SA	N370MA	506	wo	588	N37KK
183	N67SM	282	wo	371SA	N30MA	507	N134MA	589	N155AS
184	wo	283	SE-GHA	372SA	wo	508	wfu	590	N640MA
185	wfu	284	N726FN	373SA	N766MA	509	N154WC	591	N99BT
187	wo	285	N11SJ	374SA	N122CK	510	wfu	592	wo
188	PT-BZY	286	N666SP	375SA	N81MF	511	wfu	593	N400RX
189	XB-XOI	287	SE-GHB	379SA	wo	512	wo	594	wfu
190	N140CM	288	wo	380SA	N333RK	513	wfu	595	wfu
191	wfu	289	SE-GHC	381SA	N356AJ	514	N999TA	596	wo
192	wfu	290	N14YS	382SA	N772MA	515	wfu	597	wo
193	N8PC	291	N291MB	383SA	N40JJ	516	VH-JES	598	N15YS
194	N282MS	292	wfu	384SA	N774MA	517	wo	599	N22XY
195	wfu	293	SE-GHD	385SA	N808PK	518	wo	600	N113SD
196	PT-DTL	294	SE-GHE	386SA	wo	519	wfu	601	C-FROM
197	wo	295	wfu	387SA	N333WF	520	wfu	602	wo
198	N91MM	296	wfu	388SA	PT-OOS	521	VH-KOH	603	wfu

604	wfu	687	N687HB	772SA	N772DA	1504SA	N1727S	1013	N128PA
605	N621TA	688	N688RA	773SA	N350RG	1505SA	N999ET	1014	N330DM
606	C-FOUR	689SA	N112MA	774SA	PT-OHK	1506SA	N160SP	1015	N181BG
607	wfu	690	wfu	775SA	N70KC	1507SA	PH-BOA	1016	D-IGOB
608	wo	691SA	wo	776SA	wo	1508SA	PT-LHH	1017	N17PA
609	wo	692	N869P	777SA	XA-RNL	1509SA	N973BB	1018	N180AV
610	N601SD*	693SA	wo	778SA	N10HT	1510SA	N17HG	1019	N121WH
611	wo	694	N13YS	779SA	wo	1511SA	N27TJ	1020	N113SL
612	N840MA	695	wo	780SA	N321TP	1512SA	N60FL	1021	N925TK
613	wo	696	N301GM	781SA	N60KC	1513SA	wo	1022	N501PM
614	N21JA	697SA	N857MA	782SA	wo	1514SA	N14VL	1023	MM62159
615	N940MA	698SA	N187SB	783SA	C-FFSS	1515SA	OH-STA	1024	MM62160
616	N110MA	699SA	N32EC	784SA	wo	1516SA	N89SC	1025	MM62161
617	N8484T	700SA	N860MA	785SA	C-GAMC	1517SA	N727TP	1026	MM62167
618	wfu	701SA	wfu	786SA	wo	1518SA	wo	1027	MM62168
619	XB-NUG	702SA	YV-144CP	787SA	N984RE	1519SA	N33EW	1028	MM62162
620	wo	703SA	N338CM	788SA	N610CA	1520SA	N429WM	1029	MM62163
621	HK-2120P	704SA	LV-MGC	789SA	N21CJ	1521SA	C-FRWK	1030	MM62164
622	ZS-MGF	705SA	N24WC	790SA	F-GEQM	1522SA	N78PK	1031	MM62169
623	N912NF	706SA	C-FJEL	791SA	N888WW	1523SA	N65JG	1032	I-DPCR
624	wo	707SA	N707AF	792SA	N34AL	1524SA	wo	1033	I-DPCS
625	N770MA	708SA	N868MA	793SA	N425EC	1525SA	N35RR	1034	D-IZZY
626	N80JN	709SA	N105WM	794SA	N794MA	1526SA	N44MX	1035	I-FXRB
627	N770RW	710SA	N710G	795SA	wo	1527SA	wo	1036	N785JH
628	C-FROW	711SA	PT-WST	796SA	C-GGDC	1528SA	N60NB	1037	C-GJMM
629	N629MU	712SA	wfu	797SA	wo	1529SA	N132BK	1038	N122PA
630	N630HA	713SA	N89DR	798SA	N661DP	1530SA	PT-LSQ	1039	N39GK
631	N621CG*	714SA	N222FA	799SA	wo	1531SA	wfu	1040	I-BCOM
632	wfu	718SA	OH-WBA	801	wo	1532SA	wo	1041	MM62199
633	N503AA	719SA	N777LP	802	wo	1533SA	N452MA	1042	HB-LTE
634	N400SG	720SA	N3UN	803	22003	1534SA	N644EM	1043	N180HM
635	EC-GOK	721SA	wfu	804	wfu	1535SA	N454MA	1044	N395KT
636	wfu	722SA	PT-WYT	805	wfu	1536SA	N544CB	1045	I-FXRC
637	N637WG	723SA	N895MA	806	wfu	1537SA	wo	1046	N29JS
638	wfu	724SA	N223JB	807	22007	1538SA	wo	1047	MM62200
639	wfu	725SA	C-FKIO	808	22008	1539SA	N42AF	1048	N629GT
640	N490MA	726SA	wo	809	22009	1540SA	wo	1049	I-FXRE
641	N211BE	727SA	ZS-ONC	810	22010	1541SA	wo	1050	N50WG
642	N680CA	728SA	N9NB	811	wo	1542SA	N88HL	1051	N61GT
643	N375CA	729SA	N61BA	812	wo	1543SA	N469MA	1052	N102SL
644	LV-WJY	730SA	wo	813	22013	1544SA	N215MH	1053	MM62201
645	N6569L	731SA	N731CJ	814	22014	1545SA	N900M	1054	N701GT
646	N118P	732SA	N80HH	815	22015	1546SA	PT-LIK	1055	C-FSTP
647	N44KU	733SA	N142BK	816	22016	1547SA	wo	1056	D-IJET
648	wfu	734SA	N271TW	817	22017	1548SA	N8RW	1057	C-GBCI
649	wo	735SA	wo	818	22018	1549SA	N888SE	1058	MM62202
650	PT-LFX	736SA	N175CA	819	22019	1550SA	C-GZNS	1059	N103SL
651	wo	737SA	N888RH	820	22020	1551SA	N444WE	1060	I-FXRF
652SA	N533DM	738SA	N941S	901	wfu	1552SA	N246W	1061	C-GWRK
653	N45CE	739SA	N8083A	902	wfu	1553SA	N479MA	1062	N133PA
655	N535WM	740SA	N360RA	903	wfu	1554SA	N480MA	1063	C-FFST
656	N866D	741SA	N193AA	904	wfu	1555SA	wo	1064	F-GZPE
657	N740PB	742SA	wo	905	wo	1556SA	N747SY	1065	C-GFOX
658	N741FN	743SA	wfu	906	wfu	1557SA	N999UP	1066	HB-LTN
659	N6KF	744SA	N941MA	907	wfu	1558SA	N157CA	1068	N105SL
660	N4065D	745SA	N942ST	908	wfu	1559SA	N880AC	1069	N320CA
661SA	N821MA	746SA	wo	909	wfu	1560SA	N513DM	1070	N106SL
662	C-FFFG	747SA	wo	910	wfu	1561SA	N64MD	1071	MM62203
663	N823MA	748SA	N102BX	911	wfu	1562SA	N1164F	1072	C-GPIA
664	N59KS	749SA	PT-LIS	912	wfu	1563SA	N7HN	1073	N107SL
665	wo	750SA	N130MS	913	wfu	1564SA	wo	1074	N72EE
666	N207BA	751SA	N117H	914	wfu	1565SA	N100BY	1077	N304SL
667	N305CW	752SA	N37AL	915	wfu	1566SA	N468SP	1079	SP-MXH
668	N500PJ	753SA	N174MA	916	wfu	1567SA	N467MA	1080	N23RF
669	wfu	754SA	N46AK	917	wfu	1568SA	PT-LJS	1081	I-BPAE
670	wo	755SA	wo	918	wfu	1569SA	N222HH	1083	N305SL
671	N950MA	756SA	N1790M	919	wo	**Partenavia**		1084	N306SL
672	C-FTWO	757SA	N43866	920	wfu	AP68TP-600		1086	I-BPAF
673	N103RC	758SA	N261MA	921	wfu	9001	N901TP	1088	N205PA
674	ZS-ONB	759SA	N759AF	922	wfu	**Piaggio**		1089	PH-TCN
675	N68TN	760SA	N322TA	923	83-3223	P-180 Avanti		1091	N307SL
676	wo	761SA	N316PR	924	83-3224	1001	wfu	1092	N136PA
677	N915RF	762SA	N762JC	925	93-3225	1002	wfu	1093	N308SL
678	HK-2403	763SA	C-GEHS	926	23-3226	1004	N180BP	**Pilatus**	
679	N679BK	764SA	N196MA	927	23-3227	1006	N111VR	PC-12/12M/Spectre	
680	N201UV	765SA	wo	951	wfu	1007	C-FNGA	P-01	wfu
681	N361JA	766SA	N6KE	952	wfu	1008	N109MS	P-02	HB-FOB
682	wfu	767SA	wo	953	wfu	1009	C-GLEM	101	N312BC
683	C-FIFE	768SA	N331MA	954	wfu	1010	N589H	102	VH-YDO
684	wfu	769SA	wo	1501SA	PT-WNS	1011	N301SL	103	N610GH
685	YV-O-BDA-:	770SA	wo	1502SA	N71DP	1012	N416LF	104	N5WN*
686	N717PS	771SA	N221MA	1503SA	N407MA				

105	N269JP	187	C-GAWP	269	N269PB	351	N351PC	433	C-FPCZ
106	N82HR	188	N188PC	270	N360DA	352	HB-FOZ	434	VH-FDP
107	PH-ECC	189	N977XL	271	N555EW	353	C-FASR	435	N435PC
108	ZS-ONR	190	HB-FOV	272	C-GMPZ	354	N354AF	436	ZS-COH
109	VH-FMC	191	N48PG	273	N273AF	355	N5DM	437	N654JC
110	VH-FMF	192	N192PC	274	C-GMPW	356	wo	438	VH-FGR
111	N222CM	193	C-GDGD	275	C-FKPA	357	C-GZGZ	439	N439WC
112	N263AL	194	N455DK	276	N276CN	358	C-FVPC	440	VH-FGS
113	ZS-SMY	195	N37DA	277	N277PC	359	F-GVJB	441	N216TM
114	N121RF	196	C-GRJP	278	N278WC	360	N851RM	442	VH-FGT
115	N946JJ	197	N613NA	279	N167AR	361	N771KT	443	N466SA
116	N1JW	198	ZS-DMM	280	C-FWAV	362	N326PA	444	N925HW
117	N117WF	199	N199WF	281	N100YC	363	VH-KWO	445	VH-JMU
118	N802HS	200	C-GRMS	282	ZS-SDO	364	N220CL	446	N131JN
119	N432CV	201	N456V	283	C-FMPB	365	C-FMDF	447	N447PC
120	N15EK	202	C-FSRK	284	N191SP	366	HB-FOS	448	N712BC
121	HB-FOT	203	ZS-AMS	285	N88NT	367	N45PM	449	N449BY
122	VH-FMP	204	C-FKUL	286	ZS-SDP	368	HB-FOU	450	N450PC
123	VH-FMW	205	ZS-OFB	287	N287PC	369	VP-BKD	451	C-FKPX
124	N124UV	206	wo	288	N777JX	370	N78PG	452	N452MD
125	ZS-ZEN	207	C-GVKC	289	N289PB	371	N71TP	453	N453PC
126	VH-JLK	208	ZS-OFD	290	HB-FOO	372	N372GT	454	N454PS
127	N888CG	209	N108JC*	291	HB-FOP	373	N373KM	455	N455WM
128	JA8599	210	N210PT	292	N715HL	374	C-GMPP	456	N456PC
129	N412KC	211	C-FVPK	293	C-GFLA	375	N933SE	457	N327YR
130	N1TC	212	N212PB	294	GN-810	376	N376KC	458	N458DL
131	N100WG	213	N852AL	295	N295PC	377	N409DR	459	N459PC
132	N361GB	214	C-GRDC	296	C-FMPN	378	N378HH	460	N460PB
133	LV-ZSX	215	N119AF	297	N269AB	379	VH-MWO	461	XA-...
134	HB-FOG	216	N216KC	298	N64WF	380	N792SG	462	N462PC
135	N999EP	217	N124PC	299	N770G	381	HB-FPB	463	N463JT
136	N900HS	218	N218WA	300	N77ZA	382	N359CV	464	N769CM
137	N116AF	219	N219PC	301	VH-YDN	383	ZS-TLA	465	N465PC
138	VH-FMZ	220	5H-EXC	302	N302PB	384	N14RD	466	VH-FDK
139	wfu	221	N221PC	303	N303JD	385	N7ZT	467	VH-ZWO
140	N2YF	222	C-FIJV	304	N304PR*	386	HB-FOY	468	N944BT
141	PT-WKF	223	N317NA	305	N695PC	387	N387W	469	N469AF
142	OE-EKD	224	N400BW	306	N271SS	388	N388PC	470	N470AH
143	XA-...	225	N69FG	307	C-FKVL	389	N389W	471	ZS-AGI
144	N312PC	226	N970NA	308	C-GKNR	390	N12DZ	472	VT-TAS
145	8030	227	C-FYZS	309	PH-DIX	391	N391EC	473	N473PC
146	N146PC	228	N12JD	310	N166SB	392	N392WC	474	N57LT
147	ZS-NYM	229	C-FMPO	311	C-GMPY	393	N393AF	475	C-GLCE
148	N998JB	230	N230PG	312	N142LT	394	N395W	476	N476D
149	N74AX	231	VH-PIL	313	ZS-SRH	395	N395PC	477	PH-JFS
150	N150PB	232	N242JH	314	C-FMPE	396	VH-NWO	478	N26VW
151	wo	233	C-FKRB	315	C-FMPW	397	N854AL	479	A6-GAK
152	N444CM	234	C-FAJV	316	N102RR	398	N398J	480	N480WH
153	N153PB	235	N105MW	317	5H-SRP	399	C-FRPC	481	N481TL
154	N217EB	236	N299AM	318	N318MT	400	VH-VWO	482	N482WA
155	N718JP	237	C-GBJV	319	ZS-SRR	401	N401PD	483	N281WB
156	N156SB	238	C-GRBA	320	N605TQ	402	N22LP	484	N667RB
157	HB-FOI	239	C-GMPI	321	N321PL	403	N128CM	485	N485PC
158	wo	240	C-FCJV	322	N444FT	404	N420DW	486	N486PB
159	C-GBTL	241	C-FGRE	323	N956PC	405	XA-...	487	N487PC
160	N55BK	242	ZS-DAT	324	C-FKSL	406	F-GRAJ	488	N56EZ
161	N161AJ	243	5Y-MAF	325	N325MW	407	VP-BBB	489	N489JG
162	N377AC*	244	C-GEOW	326	N337TP	408	N408LB	490	HB-FPJ
163	N49LM	245	C-GKPL	327	N767JT	409	N922RG	491	C-GPAI
164	C-FMPA	246	N6154F	328	N328PA	410	N524CM	492	N492WA
165	N10PF	247	HB-FPL	329	N329NG	411	HB-FOW	493	XA-...
166	HB-FOL	248	N40191	330	N515RP	412	N412MD	494	N494PC
167	N774DK	249	N399AM	331	C-FASP	413	N629SK	495	N83AJ
168	N853AL	250	C-FKPI	332	VH-FDE	414	N226N	496	N496DT
169	N912NM	251	VT-DAR	333	XA-...	415	N415PB	497	N497PC
170	C-GBXW	252	VT-DAV	334	HB-FOX	416	C-FASF	498	EC-ISH
171	N172JS	253	N253PC	335	N335WH	417	N417KC	499	N1056B
172	N172PB	254	C-FYUT	336	N422MU	418	N507AM	500	N500NK
173	N173KS	255	N401SM	337	N601HT	419	N419WA	501	N501PB
174	N562NA	256	N141VY	338	N338PC	420	N420AF	502	N124PS
175	N118AF	257	HB-FOR	339	C-FGFL	421	OY-GSA	503	N503WS
176	VP-BLS	258	N258WC	340	N343CW	422	HB-FPC	504	XA-...
177	D-FCJA	259	N259WA	341	N58VS	423	N423WA	505	N505P
178	C-GKAY	260	N260HS	342	N2JB	424	N424PB	506	ZS-MSF
179	N818RA	261	N33JA	343	N31DX	425	wo	507	N507RC
180	ZS-BEB	262	N199CM	344	N411MV	426	VH-FDC	508	ZS-KAL
181	N601BM	263	N65TB	345	N345RF*	427	N427WA	509	N4TS
182	C-FOPD	264	N264WF	346	N377L	428	VH-FDM	510	N861PP
183	N183PC	265	N68PK	347	N347KC	429	N429PC	511	N511PB
184	C-GMPE	266	N112AF	348	N348PC	430	N8421E	512	XA-...
185	N185PB	267	N267WF	349	HB-FOQ	431	N431WC	513	HB-FPK
186	N186WF	268	C-GFIL	350	N451DM	432	N432MH	514	N156SW

Reg#	Reg	Reg#	Reg	Reg#	Reg	Reg#	Reg	Reg#	Reg
515	N515AF	598	N598HC	7904056	N879SW	8104024	N225CA	7520005	N1976J
516	N629MC	599	N599PB	7904057	N2348W	8104025	N88QM	7520006	N49NM
517	N487LM	600	N600PE	8004001	N10CS	8104026	N2480X	7520007	N522AS
518	020	603	C-GPCO	8004002	N424CM	8104027	N398SP	7520008	C-GNKP
519	N519PC	604	N604WP	8004003	N2556R	8104028	N38RE	7520009	N113RC
520	N234RG	605	HB-FQQ	8004004	N2587R	8104029	OE-FKH	7520010	N3951F
521	N521PC	606	HB-FQP	8004005	PT-OAJ	8104030	N917F	7520011	wo
522	LX-JFH	611	HB-FRL	8004006	N611RR	8104031	N90VM	7520012	PT-KME
523	N523JL	**Piper**		8004007	PT-OPQ	8104032	D-IAPA	7520013	wfu
524	N524GT	*PA-46-500TP Meridian*		8004008	N701PT	8104033	N94EG	7520014	FAC-5739
525	ZS-PDZ	4697E1	N400PT	8004009	N98GF	8104034	PT-WEF	7520015	C-FYBV
526	N269AF*	4697E3	N403MM	8004010	N2415W	8104035	N2519X	7520016	5N-AUT
527	N527PB	4697001	N401MM	8004011	D-IBIW	8104036	N633WC	7520017	N707ML
528	N528EJ	4697002	N402MM	8004012	N400LJ	8104037	wo	7520018	wfu
529	N529PS	*Cheyenne I*		8004013	N31MB	8104038	N27BF	7520019	wfu
530	N530WC	7804001	wfu	8004014	PT-OVE	8104039	N824VA	7520020	wo
531	LX-LAB	7804002	N200TS	8004015	N244AB	8104040	N711LD	7520021	C-GKPC
532	N7YR	7804003	N913CR	8004016	N75TW	8104041	PT-OKT	7520022	LV-LTV
533	N533PC	7804004	N500MY	8004017	N2458W	8104042	N5RB	7520023	N40TT
534	N353KM	7804005	N96MA	8004018	N669WB	8104043	N247LM	7520024	N431AC
535	N535MJ	7804006	wo	8004019	N992TT	8104044	wfu	7520025	wfu
536	OE-EPC	7804007	N22UC	8004020	N166WT	8104045	N855JL	7520026	N181DC
537	N537PC	7804008	wo	8004021	N49AC	8104046	N221RC	7520027	YV-1990P
538	S2-AED	7804009	N331KB	8004022	N141GA	8104047	N83MG	7520028	wfu
539	N522DJ	7804010	N7VR	8004023	N52HL	8104048	N826CM	7520029	N770MG
540	N950KM	7804011	wo	8004024	I-SASA	8104049	N2435Y	7520030	N444RC
541	N541PB	7904001	N195AA	8004025	N314DD	8104050	N515GA	7520031	wfu
542	N2222C	7904002	N119RL	8004026	N314GK	8104051	PT-OVB	7520032	N4116W
543	N543PB	7904003	N37PJ	8004027	N73BG	8104052	N408SH	7520033	I-CGAT
544	HB-FPR	7904004	OY-BHU	8004028	C-GTOL	8104053	N454CA	7520034	I-HYDR
546	N546PB	7904005	N888PH	8004029	N93CN	8104054	N555AT	7520035	N17TU
547	N547AF	7904006	N300WP	8004030	N66TW	8104055	D-ISIG	7520036	wo
548	N715TL	7904007	N231SW	8004031	N60JW	8104056	N711ER	7520037	N111RF
549	G-CCPU	7904008	C-GTMM	8004032	wfu	8104057	D-IHJK	7520038	wfu
550	PH-XII	7904009	N6192A	8004033	N826RM	8104058	N277DG	7520039	C-GJPT
551	VH-PCE	7904010	N212HH	8004034	N82TW	8104059	N819SW	7520040	wo
552	N152PC	7904011	wo	8004035	N2369V	8104060	N14PX	7520041	wfu
553	N553CA	7904012	N4RX	8004036	wo	8104061	N2552Y	7520042	wo
554	ZS-DER	7904013	YV-....	8004037	N114JR	8104062	PT-WMX	7520043	TI-AWN
555	N555PE	7904014	HB-LLK	8004038	PT-OPF	8104063	CC-PBT	7620001	wfu
556	N556HL	7904015	N131DF	8004039	PT-OLF	8104064	PT-XOC	7620002	N610P
557	N557DF*	7904016	N503WR	8004040	N219SC	8104065	N777G	7620003	LV-LZO
558	N558AF	7904017	N23243	8004041	N768MB	8104066	D-IIXX	7620004	wo
559	N559PB	7904018	N23250	8004042	N617DW	8104067	LX-ACR	7620005	I-PALS
560	ZS-PGX	7904019	N70TJ	8004043	PT-WMU	8104068	N456AC	7620006	wo
561	N561ST	7904020	N187SC	8004044	HB-LQP	8104069	CC-CBD	7620007	wfu
562	N562PB	7904021	N232DH	8004045	N20DL	8104070	CC-CWD	7620008	N584PS
563	N563TM	7904022	N165KC	8004046	N926K	8104071	N482TC	7620009	wfu
564	N724HS	7904023	N52PF	8004047	N831CH	8104072	PT-WHN	7620010	C-GXBF
565	N65AF	7904024	N23334	8004048	N169DC	8104101	N75WA	7620011	F-GFEA
566	HB-FPX	7904025	N918FM	8004049	wo	*Cheyenne 1A*		7620012	C9-JTP
567	N567FH	7904026	3A-MSI	8004050	N896DR	1104004	N90WW	7620013	wfu
568	G-CCWY	7904027	N98TG	8004051	wo	1104005	N58AM	7620014	N98AT
569	N569AF	7904028	N51FT	8004052	I-LIAT	1104006	N2434W	7620015	wfu
570	N578DC	7904029	N93SH	8004053	D-ILCE	1104007	S3-BHN	7620016	C-GTFP
571	N571PC	7904030	I-POMO	8004054	N176CS	1104008	N9266Y	7620017	wfu
572	N572PC	7904031	N54EZ	8004055	N484AS	1104009	N9268Y	7620018	N232PS
573	N666GT	7904032	N188CA	8004056	XB-GQI	1104010	UN-......	7620019	C-GMDF
574	LX-JFI	7904033	N290RS	8004057	N316WB	1104011	N2434V	7620020	F-BXSK
575	N575PC	7904034	N334CA	8104001	N181SW	1104012	N622BB	7620021	wfu
576	N576RG	7904035	N23426	8104002	CC-PNS	1104013	N65EZ	7620022	N57MR
577	N577BF	7904036	N14886	8104003	N2356X	1104014	D-ILGA	7620023	C-FMHB
578	N661WP	7904037	N200FB	8104004	N70GW	1104015	D-IHJL	7620024	wo
579	D-FAPC*	7904038	N888AH	8104005	N199MA	1104016	D-IFHZ	7620025	wfu
580	N150MX	7904039	N939JB	8104006	N37TW	1104017	N65KG	7620026	C-GXCD
581	N581PC	7904040	YV-O-MAC-	8104007	HK-....	8304001	N9183C	7620027	wfu
582	N582DT	7904041	N301TA	8104008	N38TW	8304002	N810HM	7620028	N555PM
583	N5904A	7904042	N129LC	8104009	N816CM	8304003	N26DV	7620029	C-GEBA
584	N584JV	7904043	N70TW	8104010	N980CA	*Cheyenne II*		7620030	wfu
585	N585PB	7904044	N523PD	8104011	N329KK	1	wfu	7620031	wo
586	N586PB	7904045	LV-MYX	8104012	N39TL	7400002	wfu	7620032	F-GALD
587	N888WG	7904046	N222SL	8104013	N707CV	7400003	N231PT	7620033	C-FNYM
588	N588KC	7904047	N479SW	8104014	N2403X	7400004	wfu	7620034	XA-PGT
589	N589AC	7904048	N501PT	8104015	N105MA	7400005	N10BQ	7620035	N199ND
590	N629DF	7904049	wo	8104016	N481SW	7400006	wo	7620036	C-GNDI
591	N591AF	7904050	N222GW	8104017	PT-OTV	7400007	wfu	7620037	N5136V
592	N26KH	7904051	N165SW	8104018	N801CA	7400008	N227TM	7620038	wfu
593	N593PC	7904052	N137CW	8104019	N191MA	7400009	N910HG	7620039	C-FWUT
594	N594WA	7904053	XB-FXU	8104020	N26JB	7520001	N234K	7620040	N400CM
595	N212LT	7904054	CC-PHM	8104021	N112BB	7520002	F-GFLE	7620041	N27856
596	N535BB	7904055	wo	8104022	N300SR	7520003	wo	7620042	N8131F
597	N597CH			8104023	CC-PWH	7520004	wfu	7620043	wfu

Reg	Code	Reg	Code	Reg	Code	Reg	Code	Reg	Code
7620044	PT-OPH	7720069	N411LM	7820082	N7FL	7920072	CC-CZC	8020060	N112ED
7620045	wfu	7820001	N115PC	7820083	N53TA	7920073	EC-DHF	8020061	PT-OZN
7620046	XC-UAT	7820002	C-FRJE	7820084	N100WQ	7920074	N24DD	8020062	N8CF
7620047	N111CT	7820003	N55GD	7820085	V5-CCH	7920075	OB-1308	8020063	YU-BPH
7620048	wfu	7820004	N910JP	7820086	N186GA	7920076	HK-2347	8020064	N376WS
7620049	XA-...	7820005	wfu	7820087	N6107A	7920077	wo	8020065	C-GPIM
7620050	N2FJ	7820006	N14EA	7820088	N345DF	7920078	N23646	8020066	ZP-TYI
7620051	N788BB	7820007	wo	7820089	wfu	7920079	N789CH	8020067	N42CV
7620052	N220FS*	7820008	YV-703CP	7820090	N32KW	7920080	LV-MTU	8020068	N2467V
7620053	PR-HRM	7820009	N131PC	7820091	wo	7920081	wo	8020069	CC-CZX
7620054	wfu	7820010	F-GRPS	7820092	wo	7920082	CC-...	8020070	N2469V
7620055	N55R	7820011	N250CT	7920001	3A-MIO	7920083	PT-LZR	8020071	N650RS
7620056	wfu	7820012	XB-...	7920002	OM-VIP	7920084	N189GH	8020072	N83CA
7620057	6V-AGO	7820013	N813AR	7920003	LV-MNU	7920085	wo	8020073	N100CM
7720001	wo	7820014	N18ZX	7920004	N790SD	7920086	N1183G	8020074	N62E
7720002	N771SW	7820015	F-GHTA	7920005	N817CJ	7920087	N23718	8020075	N36TW
7720003	N34HM	7820016	wo	7920006	wfu	7920088	HK-...	8020076	N29LA
7720004	wfu	7820017	HB-LRV	7920007	N22WF	7920089	N171AF	8020077	HK-2585P
7720005	N28BG	7820018	N35RT	7920008	C-GVKA	7920090	N881L	8020078	N2522V
7720006	wfu	7820019	N727SM	7920009	N723JP	7920091	N26SL	8020079	PT-ODR
7720007	N99VA	7820020	CC-PZB	7920010	D-IOTT	7920092	N108NL*	8020080	4X-CBL
7720008	N730PT	7820021	N182ME	7920011	N6175A	7920093	N99KF	8020081	wfu
7720009	ZK-POD	7820022	N484SC	7920012	XB-HNA	7920094	F-GPBF	8020082	N82PC
7720010	wo	7820023	C-GGPS	7920013	wo	8020001	wo	8020083	HB-LNL
7720011	N20WL	7820024	N155CA	7920014	wo	8020002	N333P	8020084	F-ODMM
7720012	N119EB	7820025	N888CV	7920015	N200PG	8020003	TG-OIL	8020085	N154CA
7720013	wo	7820026	N473GG	7920016	N79FB	8020004	N23WP	8020086	N880SW
7720014	N82094	7820027	LX-RST	7920017	LV-MNR	8020005	N25ND	8020087	N455MM
7720015	wo	7820028	N444BN	7920018	YV-655CP	8020006	YU-BPF	8020088	N431GW
7720016	N311LM	7820029	N427DD	7920019	N20TN	8020007	wo	8020089	N333TN
7720017	N12TW	7820030	wo	7920020	N39EH	8020008	XB-GVI	8020090	C-51
7720018	N819MK	7820031	wfu	7920021	YV-...	8020009	wo	8020091	HB-LTI
7720019	N135CL	7820032	XA-...	7920022	YV-251CP	8020010	wo	8020092	wo
7720020	N37HB	7820033	N63CA	7920023	XB-RLM	8020011	N90FS	8120001	wfu
7720021	wfu	7820034	N419R	7920024	N159DG	8020012	YU-BPG	8120002	wo
7720022	wo	7820035	CC-...	7920025	N163SA	8020013	LV-OGF	8120003	TG-COB
7720023	wo	7820036	N202HC	7920026	wo	8020014	N137JT	8120004	N139CS
7720024	wo	7820037	YV-2365P	7920027	C-GLAG	8020015	HP-809	8120005	PT-OLZ
7720025	wfu	7820038	C-GVKK	7920028	N123EA	8020016	N801HL	8120006	N998LM
7720026	wfu	7820039	N233PS	7920029	N68BJ	8020017	D-IKET	8120007	N55KW
7720027	N427TA	7820040	N98TB	7920030	4X-CIE	8020018	N108UC	8120008	N778HA
7720028	N171JP	7820041	wfu	7920031	wo	8020019	XC-...	8120009	N85GC
7720029	wfu	7820042	N700RG	7920032	N88BC	8020020	N118WC	8120010	PT-OPC
7720030	wfu	7820043	N44DT	7920033	LV-MOD	8020021	YU-BMM	8120011	PT-WLJ
7720031	wfu	7820044	wo	7920034	PT-OFH	8020022	N38VT	8120012	C-FJVB
7720032	N747RE	7820045	I-CGTT	7920035	N111KV	8020023	N970PS	8120013	N60WA
7720033	TU-TJL	7820046	PP-LCQ	7920036	N160TR	8020024	N151GS	8120014	N636CR
7720034	wfu	7820047	N926LD	7920037	N53AM	8020025	N135MA	8120015	F-GKRR
7720035	N200NB	7820048	wo	7920038	N333XX	8020026	SX-AVA	8120016	N311AC
7720036	F-GGRV	7820049	PT-WFQ	7920039	N524AM	8020027	SX-AVB	8120017	CP-1678
7720037	N112BL	7820050	N250TT	7920040	N80CP	8020028	PT-OAM	8120018	wo
7720038	N77NL	7820051	SE-LUB	7920041	XA-...	8020029	PT-OED	8120019	HC-BIF
7720039	PT-LUJ	7820052	YV-194CP	7920042	C-GFAM	8020030	wfu	8120020	PT-WNC
7720040	wfu	7820053	N786AH	7920043	N47CA	8020031	N47JF	8120021	N85HB
7720041	F-ODGS	7820054	PK-DYR	7920044	N90WG	8020032	TG-HCR	8120022	N661TC
7720042	F-GJPE	7820055	wo	7920045	C-FGWA	8020033	PT-OCL	8120023	wo
7720043	N80MA	7820056	N51RD	7920046	N800EB	8020034	N97PC	8120024	5T-MAB
7720044	N23MV	7820057	wo	7920047	XA-RWR	8020035	wo	8120025	N51JK
7720045	N82156	7820058	N82290	7920048	N406RS	8020036	OE-FKG	8120026	5T-MAC
7720046	wo	7820059	wo	7920049	3A-...	8020037	F-GIII	8120027	wfu
7720047	YV-124CP	7820060	N990LR	7920050	LV-MOE	8020038	SX-AVC	8120028	CC-PCY
7720048	N521PM	7820061	N5007	7920051	N97TW	8020039	N63CM	8120029	wo
7720049	N82161	7820062	wfu	7920052	wo	8020040	wfu	8120030	PT-WOR
7720050	YV-2451P	7820063	wo	7920053	YV-...	8020041	PH-SVY	8120031	PT-QJE
7720051	N27KM	7820064	wfu	7920054	N187CP	8020042	N716WA	8120032	HK-2631G
7720052	C-GXTC	7820065	wo	7920055	N620DB	8020043	HK-3472X	8120033	D-IBSA
7720053	N613HC	7820066	D-IKEW	7920056	5U-ACC	8020044	F-GCLH	8120034	wo
7720054	N30DU	7820067	YV-1402P	7920057	N52TT	8020045	TG-EAB	8120035	N888LG
7720055	XA-...	7820068	wo	7920058	N12GR	8020046	N302TA	8120036	N33MS
7720056	OE-FDS	7820069	N155MC	7920059	N25MG	8020047	HK-2455	8120037	HK-2642P
7720057	N411DL	7820070	YV-2331P	7920060	N81WE	8020048	PT-WFB	8120038	N300PV
7720058	C-FFNV	7820071	wo	7920061	N44HT	8020049	N2338V	8120039	wo
7720059	5R-MIM	7820072	wo	7920062	N78CA	8020050	N91TS	8120040	PT-LRT
7720060	N160NA	7820073	N814W	7920063	PT-LZB	8020051	wo	8120041	SP-KKH
7720061	wfu	7820074	N274SB	7920064	wo	8020052	wo	8120042	PT-ODM
7720062	N361JC	7820075	N75TF	7920065	LV-OAP	8020053	N39K	8120043	TG-LIA
7720063	F-GFUV	7820076	N429AP	7920066	N444PC	8020054	PT-LLG	8120044	N40PD*
7720064	N211AE	7820077	N6080A	7920067	N74TW	8020055	wo	8120045	TG-VAL
7720065	LV-MDG	7820078	wo	7920068	N711RD	8020056	N314TD	8120046	N178CD
7720066	N888JM	7820079	wfu	7920069	C-FCEF	8020057	N22DT	8120047	wo
7720067	F-GHJV	7820080	N5D	7920070	wo	8020058	PT-MGZ	8120048	OB-1228
7720068	N510LC	7820081	N2DS	7920071	C-FEQB	8020059	N457TG	8120049	CC-PJH

8120050	N33MC	8166053	HK-2963	8001054	N94EW	5501053	N102AE	4697013	N465SK
8120051	HK-3043P	8166054	N444WC	8001055	N937D	5501054	B-3623	4697014	N4174V
8120052	N67JG	8166055	N85EM	8001056	HR-JFA	5501055	D-IDIA	4697015	N965SB
8120053	N87YP	8166056	D-ICGA	8001057	N158TJ	5501056	B-3624	4697016	N461BB
8120054	ZS-PBS	8166057	N774KV	8001058	N157LL	5501057	C-GSAA	4697017	N747AW
8120055	N49B	8166058	N825SW	8001059	HK-2772P	5501058	XA-VIP	4697018	N388TW
8120056	F-GGCH	8166059	wo	8001060	N631PC	5501059	B-3625	4697019	D-EPKD
8120057	N382MB	8166060	N68MT	8001061	N4100L	5501060	B-3626	4697020	N255DW
8120058	OE-FMO	8166061	TJ-AIM	8001062	HK-3000G	8301001	D-IHLA	4697021	N5322M
8120059	N18KW	8166062	N31JZ	8001063	C-GBOT	8301002	N75FL	4697022	N999NG
8120060	N31HL	8166063	N151MP	8001064	4X-CBF	*Cheyenne 400LS*		4697023	N938JW
8120061	PT-LNG	8166064	N7194Y	8001065	N395DR	5527001	wfu	4697024	N524PM
8120062	HK-4179X	8166065	wo	8001066	VH-NMA	5527002	N400VB	4697025	N4185L
8120063	N715CA	8166066	C-FWPT	8001067	OB-1629	5527003	N40FK	4697026	N184AE
8120064	F-GLRP	8166067	PT-MFW	8001068	HK-2684X	5527004	N411BG	4697027	N62LT
8120068	N43WH	8166068	N328KK	8001069	N5SY	5527005	N85SL	4697028	N264B
8120070	PT-OJM	8166069	C-GBFO	8001070	N82PG	5527006	N54DA	4697029	N529PM
8120101	PT-WGJ	8166070	CC-PTA	8001071	N880TC	5527007	N531MC	4697030	N117PW
8120102	D-INNN	8166071	N622AJ	8001072	N801JW	5527008	N408WG	4697031	N45PJ
8120103	N707WD	8166073	HK-3117W	8001073	4X-CIC	5527009	YV-...	4697032	N125WZ
8120104	N777LF	8166075	N83XL	8001074	N423KC	5527010	N105LV	4697033	N723KR
Cheyenne II-XL		8166076	N516S	8001075	HK-3693X	5527011	N901MT	4697034	N154DR
1166001	N359GP	*Cheyenne III*		8001078	N28DA	5527012	N321LH	4697035	OE-KGB
1166002	CC-PML	31-5003	wfu	8001079	N515M	5527013	N450MW	4697036	N767TP
1166003	D-IXXX	5501008	XA-...	8001080	PT-MFL	5527014	N144PL	4697037	N999RW
1166004	ZS-PBT	7800001	N420PA	8001081	N802MW	5527015	N420B	4697038	wfu
1166005	N395CA	7800002	N911VJ	8001101	wo	5527016	N500LM	4697039	N226DL
1166006	N804C	7801003	OB-1633	8001102	N760MM	5527017	N46HL	4697040	N262MM
1166007	N285KW	7801004	N48RA	8001103	PT-OKL	5527018	EC-IIP	4697041	N134G
1166008	N150TK	8001001	N51KC	8001104	XB-JNC	5527019	N1515H	4697042	N59WF
8166001	N136SP	8001002	D-IONE	8001105	N820BC	5527020	N812BJ	4697043	N301D
8166002	N431CF	8001003	N242RA	8001106	N933DG	5527021	N248DJ	4697044	N804JH
8166003	wo	8001004	N717ES	*Cheyenne IIIA*		5527022	D-IQAS	4697045	N93LL
8166004	wo	8001005	N113WC	5501003	N29TF	5527023	N722ER	4697046	N46PV
8166005	N410CA	8001006	wfu	5501004	N775CA	5527024	wo	4697047	N120WW
8166006	N282PC	8001007	wo	5501005	N2247R	5527025	N332SA	4697048	N32KE
8166007	N491MB	8001008	N977XT	5501006	N809E	5527026	JA8853	4697049	N215SD
8166008	N1380	8001009	D-IDSF	5501007	D-ICGB	5527027	N46FD	4697050	LX-FUN
8166009	N248J	8001010	N133FM	5501009	N66MF	5527028	HB-LTM	4697051	N901DM
8166010	N200XL	8001011	N619JB	5501010	N627PC	5527029	N38AF	4697052	N733P
8166011	N630MW	8001012	N528DS	5501011	C-GZRP	5527030	N41198	4697053	wo
8166012	N321LB	8001013	OB-1714	5501012	N4116Q	5527031	N431MC	4697054	N46PL
8166013	G-FCED	8001014	N373Q	5501013	N90TW	5527032	9M-TDM	4697055	ZS-DCG
8166014	N15KW	8001015	wfu	5501014	D-IFSH	5527033	HK-3451	4697056	N76MG
8166015	N192TB	8001016	OB-1687	5501015	N794A	5527034	N2UZ*	4697057	N120SL
8166016	N440S	8001017	N175AA	5501016	N313BB	5527035	JA8867	4697058	N97LL
8166017	N550MM	8001018	OB-1365	5501017	N75LS	5527036	N34ER	4697059	N84SH
8166018	N22VF	8001019	wo	5501018	N515RC	5527037	HK-3397W	4697060	C-FIPO
8166019	HK-2749P	8001020	N332SM	5501019	XB-PSG	5527038	N438GP	4697061	N633RB
8166020	N22YC	8001021	N396FW	5501020	N690E	5527039	N37KW	4697062	N801WA
8166021	N450HC	8001022	OB-1630	5501021	N141TC	5527040	OH-PAY	4697063	D-FCBE
8166022	N3RK	8001023	N69PC	5501022	N905LC	5527041	N4WE	4697064	N164ST
8166023	N88B	8001024	wo	5501023	N932AK	5527043	wo	4697065	N129EJ
8166024	N58PL	8001025	N727PC	5501024	N9150T	5527044	N313PC	4697066	N777MG
8166025	XA-...	8001026	LV-APF	5501025	D-IHVA	*Cheyenne T-1040*		4697067	N8UM
8166026	N28WN	8001027	N112BC	5501026	N690TW	8275001	N401VA	4697068	N5215U
8166027	N500PB	8001028	N48GS	5501027	N440CA	8275002	ZS-OUP	4697069	N310JM
8166028	C-FJAK	8001029	N811DA	5501028	N9159Y	8275005	N219CS	4697070	D-ESSS
8166029	N66JC	8001030	C-GPSB	5501029	D-IDBU	8275006	N311SC	4697071	N355PM
8166030	C-FCEC	8001031	N123AG	5501030	N787LB	8275007	N314SC	4697072	N135JM
8166031	ZS-LSY	8001032	N121CS	5501031	TC-THK	8275008	N223CS	4697073	N282SW
8166032	N225PT	8001033	VH-WCE	5501032	N9233T	8275011	ZS-OTL	4697074	N5322D
8166033	N67PD	8001034	N444SC	5501033	TC-FAH	8275013	wo	4697075	N711SB
8166034	N82XL	8001035	PP-EPB	5501034	N9085U	8275014	N217CS	4697076	N5319K
8166035	HK-3074P	8001036	N8RY	5501035	N9091J	8275015	HK-2926P	4697077	N19CX
8166036	N618SW	8001037	N373CA	5501036	N9279A	8275016	wo	4697078	G-DERI
8166037	wo	8001038	PT-LZD	5501037	N9116Q	8275017	N304SC	4697079	N5326C
8166038	CC-PVE	8001039	XA-TJH	5501038	N9142B	8275025	wo	4697080	N73YP
8166039	N121EH	8001040	N455JW	5501039	HK-3381G	8375001	N1194V	4697081	N71562
8166040	N824JH	8001041	N176FB	5501040	N556BR	8375005	wfu	4697082	N55ZG
8166041	N916RT	8001042	N7139B	5501041	D-IOSA	*PA-46-500TP Meridian*		4697083	N53235
8166042	N767DM	8001043	F-GXES	5501042	D-IOSB	4697003	N375RD	4697084	N5333N
8166043	N711FN	8001044	LV-WXG	5501043	D-IOSC	4697004	N250SA	4697085	N5325P
8166044	N400WS	8001045	N444LN	5501044	D-IOSD	4697005	N43VM	4697086	N53238
8166045	N600BS	8001046	N75AW	5501045	I-TREP	4697006	N4757S	4697087	N184RB
8166046	N107PC	8001047	VH-BUW	5501046	I-TREQ	4697007	N17LH	4697088	N53369
8166047	XB-FSG	8001048	D-IMIM	5501047	I-TRER	4697008	N89ST	4697089	VH-TPM
8166048	C-FGSX	8001049	N95VR	5501048	XB-...	4697009	N209KC	4697090	SE-LTM
8166049	PT-WNG	8001050	N116JP	5501049	N121LH	4697010	N333MM	4697091	C-FHVM
8166050	HB-LNX	8001051	N5PA	5501050	N950TA	4697011	N67BW	4697092	N14GV
8166051	N287CB	8001052	wo	5501051	B-3621	4697012	N520HP	4697093	N53PK
8166052	N423JB	8001053	N700VF	5501052	B-3622			4697094	N337TF

Serial	Reg.
4697095	N5339G
4697096	N455SG
4697097	N5329Q
4697098	wo
4697099	N199CP
4697100	N5335R
4697101	N530HP
4697102	N5337N
4697103	N5338M
4697104	N104BH
4697105	N429MM
4697106	N225MA
4697107	N607MA
4697108	OY-LMM
4697109	N53362
4697110	N5339V
4697111	G-RKJT
4697112	N1RQ
4697113	N26KC
4697114	C-GMYM
4697115	N1968W
4697116	ZS-OUO
4697117	N211EZ
4697118	N500SE
4697119	wo
4697120	N402GW
4697121	N990DP
4697122	wfu
4697123	N32CK
4697124	N428DC
4697125	D-EICO
4697126	N5347V
4697127	N527MA
4697128	N85TK
4697129	N395SM
4697130	N682C
4697132	N53516
4697133	N3325H
4697134	N46WE
4697135	N135FL
4697136	N5355S
4697138	OY-LAW
4697139	N562HP
4697140	N5358J
4697141	N5353V
4697142	N5341C
4697143	N53401
4697144	N5361A
4697145	N5PP
4697146	N231CM
4697147	OY-LDA
4697148	N802MM
4697149	N303JW*
4697150	N241PM
4697151	N4180A
4697152	G-DERK
4697153	N5320N
4697154	N6DM
4697155	N338DB
4697156	N248DA
4697157	N235TW
4697158	N53667
4697159	N870C
4697160	N81BL
4697161	N5365D
4697162	N501AR
4697163	N78CC
4697164	N54199
4697165	N504SR
4697166	N166PM
4697167	N30397
4697168	N341MM*
4697169	N134M
4697170	EC-IVZ
4697171	N477HC
4697172	N821J
4697173	N565C
4697174	N875SH
4697175	N951TB
4697176	N164DB
4697177	N62WM
4697178	N3096P

Serial	Reg.
4697179	N29LH
4697180	N187JD
4697181	N175WB
4697182	N152AL
4697183	N220JM
4697184	N294DR
4697185	C-GLER
4697186	N846RD
4697187	N909P
4697188	N582SE
4697189	N30983
4697190	N3103A
4697191	N28NK
4697192	N752MM
4697194	N234Z
4697195	N816BC
4697196	N27DK
4697197	N343RR*
4697198	N3115M
4697200	C-G...
4697201	N851LC
4697203	N455LG
4697209	N209ST
4697211	N777FX

Raytheon

Beech 1900C

Serial	Reg.
UB-37	wo
UB-39	N2TS
UB-40	N896SC
UB-42	N20RA
UB-43	N565M
UB-48	N896FM
UB-56	N505RH
UB-68	N521M
UB-69	N381CR
UB-72	N604RH

Beech 1900C-1

Serial	Reg.
UC-1	N640MW
UC-2	N19NG
UC-4	HZ-PC2
UC-43	N1900C
UC-48	9J-AFJ
UC-55	5Y-BVI
UC-76	N1568D
UC-78	N503RH
UC-139	N9331M
UC-169	0169
UC-170	0170

Beech 1900D

Serial	Reg.
UE-12	N45AR
UE-27	N46AR
UE-63	C-GSWX
UE-69	YR-RLA
UE-73	YR-RLB
UE-77	5N-MPN
UE-136	9G-AGF
UE-149	5N-MPA
UE-157	3B-NBC
UE-175	N61HA
UE-177	PK-TRW
UE-186	PK-TRX
UE-212	S7-IDC
UE-256	96-0112
UE-284	VT-KBA
UE-299	N305PC
UE-317	HC-BYO
UE-319	9J-MBO
UE-323	9J-MAS
UE-331	N2820B
UE-332	N535M
UE-333	N534M
UE-334	N536M
UE-353	D-CSAG
UE-354	N1883M
UE-361	N1865A
UE-368	N368DC
UE-383	N800CA
UE-394	N470MM
UE-423	A2-QLM

King Air 90/C90

Serial	Reg.
LJ-1	N925X
LU-1	N7198S
LJ-2	N812P
LJ-3	wfu
LJ-4	wfu
LJ-5	HP-....
LU-5	N92S
LJ-6	wfu
LJ-7	N46DT
LJ-8	N4RY
LU-8	N7199J
LJ-9	N613BR
LU-9	N7199L
LJ-10	N10JE
LJ-11	wo
LU-11	N7199S
LJ-12	N654C
LJ-13	C-FBPT
LJ-14	wfu
LJ-15	N37GP
LU-15	N91S
LJ-16	PT-...
LJ-17	N440TP
LJ-18	wo
LJ-19	N821U
LJ-20	wfu
LJ-21	N249PA
LJ-22	wo
LJ-23	wo
LJ-24	wo
LJ-25	wo
LJ-26	wfu
LJ-27	wfu
LJ-28	wfu
LJ-29	wfu
LJ-30	N1290A
LJ-31	N4948W
LJ-32	wfu
LJ-33	wfu
LJ-34	wfu
LJ-35	wfu
LJ-36	N3DF
LJ-37	wfu
LJ-38	N141RR
LJ-39	wfu
LJ-40	F-BTQP
LJ-41	N877AQ
LJ-42	wfu
LJ-43	wfu
LJ-44	wfu
LJ-45	wfu
LJ-46	wfu
LJ-47	N6137
LJ-48	wo
LJ-49	N32229
LJ-50	wo
LJ-51	wfu
LJ-52	N134W
LJ-53	N539DP
LJ-54	wo
LJ-55	HP-....
LJ-56	wfu
LJ-57	wfu
LJ-58	N58KA
LJ-59	N190BT
LJ-60	N1WJ
LJ-61	wfu
LJ-62	N212WP
LJ-63	XB-GTP
LJ-64	N512G
LJ-65	wo
LJ-66	N901SA
LJ-67	N777NP
LJ-68	wfu
LJ-69	N190JL
LJ-70	N516WB
LJ-71	N110EL
LJ-72	wo
LJ-73	wfu
LJ-74	N32FH
LJ-75	N75368
LJ-76	wfu
LJ-77	N58AC
LJ-78	wfu
LJ-79	wo
LJ-80	D2-ALS
LJ-81	N276VM
LJ-82	wo
LJ-83	N827T
LJ-84	C-FUFW
LJ-85	N900CK
LJ-86	N17WT
LJ-87	N98B
LJ-88	N10AY
LJ-89	N195DP
LJ-90	wfu
LJ-91	N825K
LJ-92	N5245F
LJ-93	N9901
LJ-94	wfu
LJ-95	wfu
LJ-96	wo
LJ-97	wfu
LJ-98	F-GBPB
LJ-99	N292A
LJ-100	wfu
LJ-101	N333G
LJ-102	N787K
LJ-103	N3002S
LJ-104	N814G
LJ-105	PT-LHM
LJ-106	N411RS
LJ-107	N311SR
LJ-108	N1154S
LJ-109	N48XP
LJ-110	wfu
LJ-111	wfu
LJ-112	wo
LJ-113	N105K
LJ-114	N114CW
LJ-115	N7377
LJ-116	wo
LJ-116A	N88SP
LJ-117	N115PA
LJ-118	C-FCGE
LJ-119	wo
LJ-120	N601TA
LJ-121	F-GVRM
LJ-122	HR-IAH
LJ-123	N812AC
LJ-124	YV-....
LJ-125	PT-OUL
LJ-126	wfu
LJ-127	wfu
LJ-128	F-BOSY
LJ-129	N129LA
LJ-130	YV-....
LJ-131	N80DG
LJ-132	N290CC
LJ-133	N90FA
LJ-134	C-GLRR
LJ-135	wfu
LJ-136	wfu
LJ-137	wo
LJ-138	N100UE
LJ-139	N100WB
LJ-140	N437CF
LJ-141	wo
LJ-142	N181NK
LJ-143	N751PC
LJ-144	N331AM
LJ-145	N45PR
LJ-146	N77DA
LJ-147	YV-....
LJ-148	N671LL
LJ-149	wo
LJ-150	wfu
LJ-151	YV-....
LJ-152	PT-OVP
LJ-153	66-15361
LJ-154	N5111U
LJ-155	wfu
LJ-156	wfu
LJ-157	N90GN
LJ-158	N503M
LJ-159	N50525
LJ-160	wo
LJ-161	ZS-IRJ
LJ-162	N198KA
LJ-163	N20BL
LJ-164	N17SA
LJ-165	wo
LJ-166	N777AT
LJ-167	N290RD
LJ-168	wo
LJ-169	N983K
LJ-170	wfu
LJ-171	wo
LJ-172	N2000E
LJ-173	N623R
LJ-174	N93RY
LJ-175	wfu
LJ-176	wo
LJ-177	wfu
LJ-178	wo
LJ-178A	N798K
LJ-179	wo
LJ-180	wo
LJ-181	PT-LBZ
LJ-182	N92WG
LJ-183	wfu
LJ-184	N566CA
LJ-185	wfu
LJ-186	wo
LJ-187	wfu
LJ-188	wo
LJ-189	PK-VKZ
LJ-190	N216LJ
LJ-191	PT-WAE
LJ-192	N15CT
LJ-193	N600BF
LJ-194	N55FY
LJ-195	YV-....
LJ-196	N348AC
LJ-197	PK-VKY
LJ-198	wfu
LJ-199	wo
LJ-200	XA-...
LJ-201	N866A
LJ-202	N464G
LJ-203	C-FCGH
LJ-204	N52EL
LJ-205	wo
LJ-206	F-GHDO
LJ-207	wfu
LJ-208	wfu
LJ-209	N54WW
LJ-210	HK-...
LJ-211	wfu
LJ-212	wfu
LJ-213	N250U
LJ-214	N412MA
LJ-215	N127HT
LJ-216	wo
LJ-217	CN-...
LJ-218	N801KM
LJ-219	wo
LJ-220	C-FCGI
LJ-221	PT-KGV
LJ-222	YV-....
LJ-223	wo
LJ-224	N464AB
LJ-225	wo
LJ-226	N271WN
LJ-227	CC-COT
LJ-228	OB-1567
LJ-229	N435A
LJ-230	N77SS
LJ-231	wfu
LJ-232	wo
LJ-233	N700MB
LJ-234	N212D
LJ-235	wfu
LJ-236	wfu
LJ-237	N66GS
LJ-238	N6KZ
LJ-239	wo

LJ-240	YV-....	LJ-322	OB-1594	LJ-404	N90NM	LJ-486	9J-AAV	LJ-570	N240RE
LJ-241	N22BB	LJ-323	LV-VHR	LJ-405	OB-1558	LJ-487	wfu	LJ-571	N183SA
LJ-242	wo	LJ-324	D2-EQC	LJ-406	N226JW	LJ-488	YV-258CP	LJ-572	N35TV
LJ-243	wo	LJ-325	C-FJHP	LJ-407	wo	LJ-489	LV-ZXZ	LJ-573	N90LB
LJ-244	wo	LJ-326	OB-1297	LJ-408	ZS-MUM	LJ-490	N81AT	LJ-574	N318F
LJ-245	N42CQ	LJ-327	OY-JRO	LJ-409	PP-EUE	LJ-491	N88RP	LJ-575	9J-DCF
LJ-246	wo	LJ-328	wfu	LJ-410	N901WL	LJ-492	N492PA	LJ-576	N3GC
LJ-247	wo	LJ-329	wfu	LJ-411	N14V	LJ-493	wo	LJ-577	EC-HMA
LJ-248	HK-....	LJ-330	OB-1364	LJ-412	wfu	LJ-494	9Q-CKZ	LJ-578	N71KA
LJ-249	wfu	LJ-331	F-GEXK	LJ-413	wo	LJ-495	YV-....	LJ-579	F-BVTB
LJ-250	wfu	LJ-332	wfu	LJ-414	N57MA	LJ-496	N579PS	LJ-580	N580RA
LJ-251	wo	LJ-333	LV-WRM	LJ-415	N87MM	LJ-497	wo	LJ-581	N717X
LJ-252	N33SB	LJ-334	N621TB	LJ-416	wo	LJ-498	wo	LJ-582	N66KA
LJ-253	wo	LJ-335	N7644R	LJ-417	N44RG	LJ-499	PT-OUO	LJ-583	N200TG
LJ-254	wo	LJ-336	wfu	LJ-418	OY-BVS	LJ-500	C-GCFL	LJ-584	XA-...
LJ-255	wfu	LJ-337	C-GHVR	LJ-419	N11TN	LJ-501	N43WA	LJ-585	N14CP
LJ-256	N256TA	LJ-338	9J-YVZ	LJ-420	N642DH	LJ-502	N88HM	LJ-586	N60KA
LJ-257	N299D	LJ-339	wo	LJ-421	N9426	LJ-503	N193A	LJ-587	TC-AUV
LJ-258	N123V	LJ-340	N240K	LJ-422	C-GSFM	LJ-504	N908K	LJ-588	N711BN
LJ-259	wo	LJ-341	N83FM	LJ-423	wo	LJ-505	wfu	LJ-589	N59KA
LJ-260	N96AG	LJ-342	N876L	LJ-424	N638D	LJ-506	N30HF	LJ-590	wo
LJ-261	N990SA	LJ-343	N57AG	LJ-425	N767LD	LJ-507	wo	LJ-591	wo
LJ-262	wfu	LJ-344	N873K	LJ-426	N761K	LJ-508	N708DG	LJ-592	N90EL
LJ-263	N526RR	LJ-345	wo	LJ-427	wfu	LJ-509	wfu	LJ-593	wo
LJ-264	N86MG	LJ-346	PT-WTN	LJ-428	LV-VHO	LJ-510	F-GHBB	LJ-594	N90ZH
LJ-265	N10YP	LJ-347	F-GFHQ	LJ-429	N984AA	LJ-511	N1UV	LJ-595	N767MC
LJ-266	YV-....	LJ-348	C-GTMA	LJ-430	N41WC	LJ-512	wo	LJ-596	N880H
LJ-267	N416MR	LJ-349	N939K	LJ-431	ZS-OHB	LJ-513	4X-DZT	LJ-597	wfu
LJ-268	wo	LJ-350	N7BF	LJ-432	N919AG	LJ-514	wo	LJ-598	wfu
LJ-269	N507W	LJ-351	N90LG	LJ-433	wo	LJ-515	PT-OIU	LJ-599	wfu
LJ-270	BDF-06	LJ-352	wo	LJ-434	F-GFIR	LJ-516	wo	LJ-600	N73MC
LJ-271	wo	LJ-353	PT-OBW	LJ-435	N9838Z	LJ-517	N738R	LJ-601	N611AY
LJ-272	N5Y	LJ-354	wo	LJ-436	wo	LJ-518	F-ZBBF	LJ-602	wo
LJ-273	wfu	LJ-355	PT-DEU	LJ-437	N90DN	LJ-519	N290PA	LJ-603	42-..
LJ-274	wfu	LJ-356	wfu	LJ-438	N988SL	LJ-520	HP-....	LJ-604	wo
LJ-275	N457CP	LJ-357	YV-....	LJ-439	wo	LJ-521	N901BK	LJ-605	42-...
LJ-276	N90VP	LJ-358	N61HT	LJ-440	wfu	LJ-522	F-BXAP	LJ-606	N64KA
LJ-277	N623BB	LJ-359	wo	LJ-441	CC-CVZ	LJ-523	ZS-INN	LJ-607	C-GKBB
LJ-278	wfu	LJ-360	N125A	LJ-442	wo	LJ-524	N19UM	LJ-608	42-..
LJ-279	wfu	LJ-361	N587M	LJ-443	N411FT	LJ-525	N90WJ	LJ-609	C-GRSL
LJ-280	N6228Q	LJ-362	N31SN	LJ-444	N40BA	LJ-526	N54EC	LJ-610	N89TM
LJ-281	9L-LDA	LJ-363	F-GICE	LJ-445	wo	LJ-527	EC-GOY	LJ-611	N65KA
LJ-282	N623AW	LJ-364	wfu	LJ-446	wfu	LJ-528	wfu	LJ-612	N999ES
LJ-283	N773S	LJ-365	RP-C2208	LJ-447	N926S	LJ-529	N290DP	LJ-613	ZS-LTF
LJ-284	wo	LJ-366	N68CD	LJ-448	wo	LJ-530	N3KF	LJ-614	wo
LJ-285	N98HB	LJ-367	N321DZ	LJ-449	LV-JJW	LJ-531	PT-IBE	LJ-615	N444PS
LJ-286	N43JT	LJ-368	wo	LJ-450	N6881S	LJ-532	N575C	LJ-616	I-LIPO
LJ-287	XA-...	LJ-369	N129RW*	LJ-451	wo	LJ-533	N75RS	LJ-617	N1310T
LJ-288	N270M	LJ-370	YV-1947P	LJ-452	N452TT	LJ-534	PT-OFC	LJ-618	N900DZ
LJ-289	N5WG	LJ-371	N718K	LJ-453	5V-TTD	LJ-535	PT-OXU	LJ-619	ZS-NDH
LJ-290	wfu	LJ-372	wo	LJ-454	N105RG	LJ-536	XB-...	LJ-620	wo
LJ-291	wfu	LJ-373	N275LE	LJ-455	N444WG	LJ-537	N133LA	LJ-621	wo
LJ-292	LV-ZTO	LJ-374	N54CF	LJ-456	F-GIFC	LJ-538	N65TA	LJ-622	TC-AUT
LJ-293	XC-ONA	LJ-375	N101BS	LJ-457	N299MS	LJ-539	wo	LJ-623	wo
LJ-294	N930K	LJ-376	C-FMKD	LJ-458	HK-853W	LJ-540	N123SK	LJ-624	42-..
LJ-295	N57EM	LJ-377	wo	LJ-459	N9HW	LJ-541	wo	LJ-625	ZS-NWC
LJ-296	HP-....	LJ-378	wo	LJ-460	PT-WBQ	LJ-542	N9442Q	LJ-626	N501MS
LJ-297	N140PA	LJ-379	wfu	LJ-461	N90WL	LJ-543	PT-LTF	LJ-627	N4447W
LJ-298	N615AA	LJ-380	N66AD	LJ-462	wo	LJ-544	F-GHFE	LJ-628	N800RP
LJ-299	N312VF	LJ-381	N49GN	LJ-463	N43MB	LJ-545	F-GHBD	LJ-629	N4950C
LJ-300	N70VM	LJ-382	EC-GIJ	LJ-464	N36DD	LJ-546	wo	LJ-630	N21SP
LJ-301	N11FL	LJ-383	YV-....	LJ-465	OB-932	LJ-547	XA-....	LJ-631	C-FLTC
LJ-302	wo	LJ-384	N563MC	LJ-466	PT-ODA	LJ-548	N531CS	LJ-632	N71EN
LJ-303	wo	LJ-385	N130DM	LJ-467	N944K	LJ-549	N9450Q	LJ-633	wo
LJ-304	wfu	LJ-386	N899D	LJ-468	C-FNCN	LJ-550	ZS-MCA	LJ-634	N1801B
LJ-305	N525JK	LJ-387	XB-CIO	LJ-469	N90GB	LJ-551	N53EC	LJ-635	wo
LJ-306	N124SA	LJ-388	XB-HCL	LJ-470	wo	LJ-552	XC-FOC	LJ-636	N66TL
LJ-307	N66RE	LJ-389	wo	LJ-471	wfu	LJ-553	N697MP	LJ-637	F-GCLD
LJ-308	N577DC	LJ-390	N701AT	LJ-472	N148Z	LJ-554	N977AA	LJ-638	PP-EHE
LJ-309	C-FHWI	LJ-391	N55MG	LJ-473	N90CB	LJ-555	YV-465CP	LJ-639	wo
LJ-310	wfu	LJ-392	N392TW	LJ-474	wfu	LJ-556	wo	LJ-640	N750RC
LJ-311	N711DB	LJ-393	wo	LJ-475	N32BA	LJ-557	PT-ICP	LJ-641	D-IKIW
LJ-312	N45TT	LJ-394	N394AL	LJ-476	N10TM	LJ-558	wo	LJ-642	wfu
LJ-313	C-FCGN	LJ-395	ZS-PFA	LJ-477	OB-1593	LJ-559	N904DJ*	LJ-643	N96AH
LJ-314	wo	LJ-396	YV-....	LJ-478	N7TW	LJ-560	D-IIHA	LJ-644	wo
LJ-315	N34HA	LJ-397	A6-...	LJ-479	wfu	LJ-561	N139B	LJ-645	N90CT
LJ-316	N758K	LJ-398	PT-DIQ	LJ-480	N2UV	LJ-562	N777GF	LJ-646	N4146S
LJ-317	N46AX	LJ-399	XA-...	LJ-481	N670AT	LJ-563	N45RL	LJ-647	D-IDAK
LJ-318	wfu	LJ-400	OB-1595	LJ-482	F-BRNO	LJ-564	N67PL	LJ-648	F-BXSL
LJ-319	N1999G	LJ-401	N590SA	LJ-483	N83TC	LJ-565	PT-OCT	LJ-649	N102AJ
LJ-320	wfu	LJ-402	9Q-CKM	LJ-484	wfu	LJ-566	N108KU	LJ-650	N103BL
LJ-321	N223CH	LJ-403	N603PA	LJ-485	9J-TAF	LJ-567	wfu	LJ-651	PT-LUF
						LJ-568	N108KU		
						LJ-569	wfu		

Reg	Code	Reg	Code	Reg	Code	Reg	Code	Reg	Code
LJ-652	wo	LJ-734	N284PM	LJ-816	N416BK	LJ-898	N898CM	LJ-980	6811
LJ-653	N586TC	LJ-735	N819MH	LJ-817	PT-LPS	LJ-899	N813JB	LJ-981	wo
LJ-654	N152WW	LJ-736	N635AF	LJ-818	N77NB	LJ-900	PT-OJU	LJ-982	N102FK*
LJ-655	VH-SAM	LJ-737	wo	LJ-819	G-RACI	LJ-901	N93LP	LJ-983	N391BT
LJ-656	N888MA	LJ-738	N20WP	LJ-820	N100KB	LJ-902	N21	LJ-984	OH-BAX
LJ-657	C-GTWW	LJ-739	YV-152CP	LJ-821	N959MC	LJ-903	N45SA	LJ-985	PT-OLW
LJ-658	wo	LJ-740	N502SE	LJ-822	F-GBLU	LJ-904	N94HB	LJ-986	HC-...
LJ-659	YV-2034P	LJ-741	wfu	LJ-823	ST-ANH	LJ-905	wo	LJ-987	N390L
LJ-660	wfu	LJ-742	YV-158CP	LJ-824	N1MT	LJ-906	N957JF	LJ-988	A2-DBH
LJ-661	N88SD	LJ-743	N620WE	LJ-825	N601DM	LJ-907	N900BE	LJ-989	N63200
LJ-662	RP-C3650	LJ-744	N91TJ	LJ-826	N701XP	LJ-908	N38TR	LJ-990	N1836H
LJ-663	wfu	LJ-745	N37CN	LJ-827	N2057C	LJ-909	N19	LJ-991	N19LW
LJ-664	wo	LJ-746	N322R	LJ-828	F-GNMP	LJ-910	N211PC	LJ-992	N305TT
LJ-665	N665JK	LJ-747	N8MG	LJ-829	N98AR*	LJ-911	N84TP	LJ-993	N81NA
LJ-666	E 22-01	LJ-748	N915CD	LJ-830	N911CX	LJ-912	N20	LJ-994	wfu
LJ-667	F-GOJD	LJ-749	N90EJ	LJ-831	HK-3429W	LJ-913	PT-LMI	LJ-995	PT-OOT
LJ-668	N668WJ	LJ-750	N10MD	LJ-832	N512RR	LJ-914	N402EM	LJ-996	N502MS
LJ-669	ZS-OHR	LJ-751	YV-167CP	LJ-833	N85TB	LJ-915	N3688P	LJ-997	N503CB
LJ-670	wfu	LJ-752	FAC-5570	LJ-834	PT-LVI	LJ-916	6808	LJ-998	PT-OCI
LJ-671	ZS-MNC	LJ-753	N990DA	LJ-835	PT-OVY	LJ-917	6809	LJ-999	N333TL
LJ-672	N717JG	LJ-754	N754TW	LJ-836	N6646R	LJ-918	N918SA	LJ-1000	N403EM
LJ-673	N660GW	LJ-755	5N-AMZ	LJ-837	OK-...	LJ-919	ZS-LTZ	LJ-1001	N91LW
LJ-674	N332DE	LJ-756	YV-172CP	LJ-838	N445CR	LJ-920	PT-OPD	LJ-1002	N900VA
LJ-675	N973GA	LJ-757	N104LC	LJ-839	N299K	LJ-921	N3690F	LJ-1003	N747SF
LJ-676	N1DK	LJ-758	N157CB	LJ-840	wo	LJ-922	CN-TAX	LJ-1004	PT-ORW
LJ-677	N555CK	LJ-759	N895FK	LJ-841	N249CP	LJ-923	N30GK	LJ-1005	PT-OOS
LJ-678	N150VE	LJ-760	F-GHEM	LJ-842	VH-FDT	LJ-924	N3695W	LJ-1006	N175AZ
LJ-679	N90MU	LJ-761	N410MC	LJ-843	N404SC	LJ-925	N925MM	LJ-1007	N964GB
LJ-680	C-FNED	LJ-762	N350WA	LJ-844	PT-LQD	LJ-926	wo	LJ-1008	VT-EHY
LJ-681	N90PW	LJ-763	N9VC	LJ-845	N28KP	LJ-927	PT-OSO	LJ-1009	N61383
LJ-682	N682KA	LJ-764	N775DM	LJ-846	N29TB	LJ-928	N132AS	LJ-1010	PT-LHJ
LJ-683	N269SC	LJ-765	N191A	LJ-847	PT-OCY	LJ-929	C-GCFB	LJ-1011	N278SW
LJ-684	F-BXPY	LJ-766	N642TD	LJ-848	Z-LCS	LJ-930	ZS-KMA	LJ-1012	N278AB
LJ-685	C-FHLP	LJ-767	N85DR	LJ-849	C-GCFZ	LJ-931	D-IBMC	LJ-1013	N6723Y
LJ-686	N400BX	LJ-768	OY-SBU	LJ-850	N6681S	LJ-932	N34CE	LJ-1014	N6173C
LJ-687	Z-WRD	LJ-769	N24GJ	LJ-851	N851KA	LJ-933	N3AT	LJ-1015	N6280E
LJ-688	N911FN	LJ-770	OH-BCX	LJ-852	N90LF	LJ-934	N369GA	LJ-1016	N790A
LJ-689	N689EB	LJ-771	N4774M	LJ-853	N400RV	LJ-935	N600FE	LJ-1017	N6207F
LJ-690	wo	LJ-772	N11692	LJ-854	wo	LJ-936	PT-OSI	LJ-1018	PT-ONQ
LJ-691	N62525	LJ-773	N728DS	LJ-855	wfu	LJ-937	PT-OUX	LJ-1019	PT-OEP
LJ-692	N711KP	LJ-774	N911FG	LJ-856	N904US	LJ-938	N3817H	LJ-1020	VH-LYG
LJ-693	wo	LJ-775	N386GA	LJ-857	RP-C290	LJ-939	N94CD	LJ-1021	P2-NTR
LJ-694	N901JA	LJ-776	N4776M	LJ-858	wo	LJ-940	PT-OPE	LJ-1022	N922AA
LJ-695	N695JJ	LJ-777	VH-KFG	LJ-859	N9081R	LJ-941	F-GEOU	LJ-1023	N32MA
LJ-696	N644SP	LJ-778	wfu	LJ-860	F-GBPZ	LJ-942	D-IKES	LJ-1024	P2-NTJ
LJ-697	N90AW	LJ-779	N117MF	LJ-861	N903GP	LJ-943	N3805E	LJ-1025	wo
LJ-698	N9872C	LJ-780	N4947M	LJ-862	N380SC	LJ-944	N9DA	LJ-1026	PT-LPJ
LJ-699	N976JT	LJ-781	N495NM	LJ-863	N777EB	LJ-945	N88GL	LJ-1027	N83P
LJ-700	N700CP	LJ-782	TG-VAS	LJ-864	N773PW	LJ-946	PT-LLR	LJ-1028	G-BKFY
LJ-701	N90MV	LJ-783	N197CC	LJ-865	YV-263CP	LJ-947	wo	LJ-1029	N28TM
LJ-702	N44HP	LJ-784	N62SK	LJ-866	N844C	LJ-948	N205MS	LJ-1030	N357HP
LJ-703	TC-DBZ	LJ-785	wo	LJ-867	LX-APB	LJ-949	N269JG	LJ-1031	N1GF
LJ-704	N296AS	LJ-786	YV-972CP	LJ-868	N139SC	LJ-950	N401EM	LJ-1032	N6563K
LJ-705	wo	LJ-787	N787TT	LJ-869	N732WJ	LJ-951	PT-OZJ	LJ-1033	ZS-LFL
LJ-706	VT-EFB	LJ-788	N107SC	LJ-870	PT-OPR	LJ-952	PT-OJA	LJ-1034	ZS-CPM
LJ-707	N122K	LJ-789	YV-223CP	LJ-871	N290AJ	LJ-953	N38280	LJ-1035	N396CA
LJ-708	N500KR	LJ-790	VT-RAM	LJ-872	N555MS	LJ-954	C9-ASK	LJ-1036	N11SN
LJ-709	wo	LJ-791	PT-WDU	LJ-873	wo	LJ-955	F-GIZB	LJ-1037	PT-LYT
LJ-710	F-GJRK	LJ-792	wo	LJ-874	SX-BGO	LJ-956	PT-WMT	LJ-1038	9102
LJ-711	VT-UBA	LJ-793	wo	LJ-875	N6672N	LJ-957	HK-2596	LJ-1039	N404JP
LJ-712	N70AB	LJ-794	PT-LSO	LJ-876	N153PM	LJ-958	N11FT	LJ-1040	N115KU
LJ-713	PR-TLL	LJ-795	ZS-MBZ	LJ-877	N300VA	LJ-959	ZS-KZI	LJ-1041	N541AA
LJ-714	N17573	LJ-796	N100V	LJ-878	N440KF	LJ-960	PT-OCC	LJ-1042	6812
LJ-715	N9076S	LJ-797	N797CF	LJ-879	N725AR	LJ-961	N16KM	LJ-1043	6813
LJ-716	N25DL	LJ-798	wo	LJ-880	wo	LJ-962	N962TT	LJ-1044	6814
LJ-717	F-GFHC	LJ-799	N799GK	LJ-881	N32CM	LJ-963	PT-OLX	LJ-1045	N84P
LJ-718	N90BP	LJ-800	N60KW	LJ-882	PT-OOY	LJ-964	N595RC	LJ-1046	N990KB
LJ-719	VT-EFG	LJ-801	N808SW	LJ-883	N984MA	LJ-965	N205ST	LJ-1047	6815
LJ-720	N720RD	LJ-802	wo	LJ-884	PT-OLQ	LJ-966	PT-LQS	LJ-1048	N900MT
LJ-721	N596CU	LJ-803	N469B	LJ-885	N123LL	LJ-967	VT-EGR	LJ-1049	N7931D
LJ-722	N38RP	LJ-804	N427DM	LJ-886	C-GCFM	LJ-968	N277SW	LJ-1050	N6492C
LJ-723	SE-IIB	LJ-805	VP-BKW	LJ-887	N751KC	LJ-969	N77HE	LJ-1051	N111KA
LJ-724	N5TA	LJ-806	N611DD	LJ-888	N67511	LJ-970	N121P	LJ-1052	N6356C
LJ-725	D-IHDE	LJ-807	N802DG	LJ-889	YV-O-CBL-!	LJ-971	N959CM	LJ-1053	ZS-LIN
LJ-726	N387GA	LJ-808	PT-LZH	LJ-890	wo	LJ-972	HB-GJH	LJ-1054	N167BB
LJ-727	wo	LJ-809	N549BR	LJ-891	N6754H	LJ-973	YV-436CP	LJ-1055	N771PA
LJ-728	N291CC	LJ-810	N811GA	LJ-892	HK-3277P	LJ-974	N55MN	LJ-1056	PT-LQE
LJ-729	wo	LJ-811	N330V	LJ-893	N16	LJ-975	PT-OHH	LJ-1057	N47SW
LJ-730	VH-SQH	LJ-812	PT-OJI	LJ-894	F-GCGA	LJ-976	6810	LJ-1058	wo
LJ-731	N731KA	LJ-813	N2050A	LJ-895	N4449Q	LJ-977	D-IFHI	LJ-1059	PT-OZR
LJ-732	N56DL	LJ-814	N96DQ	LJ-896	N17	LJ-978	OH-BEX	LJ-1060	6816
LJ-733	N977FC	LJ-815	N2057N	LJ-897	PT-LLV	LJ-979	5B-CJL	LJ-1061	6817

Reg	Code	Reg	Code	Reg	Code	Reg	Code	Reg	Code
LJ-1062	6818	LJ-1144	JA8847	LJ-1226	F-GULM	LJ-1308	PT-ORG	LJ-1390	N75PG
LJ-1063	PT-LSE	LJ-1145	JA8848	LJ-1227	N89KA	LJ-1309	C-GMBH	LJ-1391	F-GPLK
LJ-1064	N6763K	LJ-1146	6822	LJ-1228	N681EV	LJ-1310	C-GMBW	LJ-1392	N3216K
LJ-1065	N722KR	LJ-1147	N475JA	LJ-1229	N94MG	LJ-1311	PR-MZP	LJ-1393	VT-TIS
LJ-1066	N300FN	LJ-1148	N8887B	LJ-1230	C-FGXT	LJ-1312	N490J	LJ-1394	PT-WIT
LJ-1067	N200TR	LJ-1149	JA8850	LJ-1231	N931WC	LJ-1313	C-GMBX	LJ-1395	LV-WMG
LJ-1068	N613RF	LJ-1150	JA8851	LJ-1232	N91KA	LJ-1314	N198PP	LJ-1396	PT-WIH
LJ-1069	G-BMKD	LJ-1151	C-FGXX	LJ-1233	PT-ORZ	LJ-1315	D-IHSW	LJ-1397	N3216U
LJ-1070	N210EC	LJ-1152	N252RC	LJ-1234	N1564W	LJ-1316	N49LL	LJ-1398	N441CG
LJ-1071	N68AJ	LJ-1153	VT-EQO	LJ-1235	N92FC	LJ-1317	C-GMBY	LJ-1399	TG-BAQ
LJ-1072	N6692D	LJ-1154	N67CL	LJ-1236	OE-FMG	LJ-1318	N17KK	LJ-1400	VT-UPZ
LJ-1073	N120TT	LJ-1155	N32MT	LJ-1237	PT-OTI	LJ-1319	C-GMBZ	LJ-1401	YV-660CP
LJ-1074	N923CR	LJ-1156	N817DP	LJ-1238	N1553N	LJ-1320	N65GP	LJ-1402	VT-NKF
LJ-1075	N129RP*	LJ-1157	N36805	LJ-1239	N5639K	LJ-1321	F-GYGL	LJ-1403	N275FA
LJ-1076	N86JG	LJ-1158	D-IHKM	LJ-1240	N691AS	LJ-1322	N530CH	LJ-1404	VT-DEJ
LJ-1077	D-IGKN	LJ-1159	VT-AJV	LJ-1241	N5641X	LJ-1323	D-IUDE	LJ-1405	N59MS
LJ-1078	PT-ONJ	LJ-1160	N919CL	LJ-1242	N88PD	LJ-1324	D-IKIM	LJ-1406	N207P
LJ-1079	N69301	LJ-1161	N4764A	LJ-1243	HS-SLB	LJ-1325	D-IHMV	LJ-1407	HB-GJF
LJ-1080	wo	LJ-1162	C-FGXH	LJ-1244	N5644E	LJ-1326	N8096U	LJ-1408	N587PB
LJ-1081	PT-OYN	LJ-1163	HI-776SP	LJ-1245	PT-WAH	LJ-1327	D-IHHE	LJ-1409	F-GKSP
LJ-1082	N686GW	LJ-1164	N104AJ	LJ-1246	XA-RFN	LJ-1328	F-GNEE	LJ-1410	N90CN
LJ-1083	6819	LJ-1165	N39FB	LJ-1247	D-IAAH	LJ-1329	YV-839CP	LJ-1411	N3218P
LJ-1084	6820	LJ-1166	5201	LJ-1248	9302	LJ-1330	N555VW	LJ-1412	N422PM
LJ-1085	N360MP	LJ-1167	VT-EQN	LJ-1249	9303	LJ-1331	PT-WVI	LJ-1413	N573P*
LJ-1086	N105TC	LJ-1168	5202	LJ-1250	N938P	LJ-1332	N82590	LJ-1414	N344DP
LJ-1087	N377P	LJ-1169	N585R	LJ-1251	N87HB	LJ-1333	N8156Z	LJ-1415	N30CN
LJ-1088	N904RB	LJ-1170	N581B	LJ-1252	N72TG	LJ-1334	SX-BKY	LJ-1416	LV-WPB
LJ-1089	N993RC	LJ-1171	5203	LJ-1253	PT-WHA	LJ-1335	6823	LJ-1417	N387AS
LJ-1090	D-ILGI	LJ-1172	N32JP	LJ-1254	N779VF	LJ-1336	6824	LJ-1418	wo
LJ-1091	N179D	LJ-1173	PT-LPD	LJ-1255	N595TM	LJ-1337	6825	LJ-1419	N257CQ
LJ-1092	PT-WNN	LJ-1174	PT-OIZ	LJ-1256	N904HB	LJ-1338	6826	LJ-1420	N3220L
LJ-1093	F-GLLA	LJ-1175	5204	LJ-1257	N155A	LJ-1339	6827	LJ-1421	N61GN
LJ-1094	PT-OFY	LJ-1176	5205	LJ-1258	N40MH	LJ-1340	D-IIWB	LJ-1422	N511KV
LJ-1095	N617KM	LJ-1177	C-FGXZ	LJ-1259	N702DK	LJ-1341	PT-OZL	LJ-1423	N4488L
LJ-1096	PT-OTG	LJ-1178	C-FGXJ	LJ-1260	PT-OSN	LJ-1342	C-FTPE	LJ-1424	D-IHBP
LJ-1097	N114DB	LJ-1179	C-FGXE	LJ-1261	LX-LLM	LJ-1343	N971SC	LJ-1425	N3223H
LJ-1098	F-HJCM	LJ-1180	LV-ROC	LJ-1262	N700RF	LJ-1344	N8220V	LJ-1426	N724KH
LJ-1099	ZS-MKI	LJ-1181	RP-C1807	LJ-1263	N927JJ	LJ-1345	VH-ZGQ	LJ-1427	PT-WJD
LJ-1100	VT-EJZ	LJ-1182	9301	LJ-1264	PT-OFF	LJ-1346	PT-WFN	LJ-1428	N3242Z
LJ-1101	D-IFMI	LJ-1183	N779JM	LJ-1265	N8001V	LJ-1347	N8210C	LJ-1429	N32510
LJ-1102	N109DT	LJ-1184	N149CM	LJ-1266	N421HV	LJ-1348	N451A	LJ-1430	N178JM
LJ-1103	N8GT	LJ-1185	N50VP	LJ-1267	D-IEBE	LJ-1349	N491JV	LJ-1431	N1031Y
LJ-1104	N7223X	LJ-1186	wo	LJ-1268	N555AL	LJ-1350	JA007C	LJ-1432	N3263C
LJ-1105	wo	LJ-1187	N524TS	LJ-1269	N8021P	LJ-1351	N424EM	LJ-1433	N100RU
LJ-1106	N222WJ	LJ-1188	PT-LYK	LJ-1270	VT-SLK	LJ-1352	N426EM	LJ-1434	N313DW
LJ-1107	N101BU	LJ-1189	C-FGXL	LJ-1271	N242NS	LJ-1353	SU-ZAA	LJ-1435	N16KW
LJ-1108	N958JH	LJ-1190	N3190S	LJ-1272	N770AJ	LJ-1354	LV-WJE	LJ-1436	N828FC
LJ-1109	N95PC	LJ-1191	YV-32P	LJ-1273	YV-1000CP	LJ-1355	D-ISIX	LJ-1437	N90PR
LJ-1110	6821	LJ-1192	C-FGXQ	LJ-1274	N8099G	LJ-1356	N8287E	LJ-1438	N389AS
LJ-1111	N96FA	LJ-1193	ZS-OTK	LJ-1275	N275LA	LJ-1357	N1560T	LJ-1439	N1089L
LJ-1112	N37XX	LJ-1194	N15234	LJ-1276	TC-MSS	LJ-1358	N94TK	LJ-1440	N1070F
LJ-1113	N7230H	LJ-1195	PT-OKQ	LJ-1277	N871KS	LJ-1359	7T-WCF	LJ-1441	D-IKMS
LJ-1114	N55WF	LJ-1196	N119SA	LJ-1278	VT-JPK	LJ-1360	S5-CMO	LJ-1442	PP-EPS
LJ-1115	OE-FHL	LJ-1197	N779MJ	LJ-1279	N71VG	LJ-1361	F-HHAM	LJ-1443	N1083S
LJ-1116	VT-NEI	LJ-1198	N611CF	LJ-1280	XA-RXT	LJ-1362	N990CB	LJ-1444	N1084N
LJ-1117	N3030G	LJ-1199	N717RD	LJ-1281	9304	LJ-1363	PT-WGU	LJ-1445	N90CH
LJ-1118	ZS-LZR	LJ-1200	C-FGXO	LJ-1282	9305	LJ-1364	TG-CCA	LJ-1446	N446AS
LJ-1119	N261GB	LJ-1201	PT-LVK	LJ-1283	N700GM	LJ-1365	N1551C	LJ-1447	N569GR
LJ-1120	D-IIKM	LJ-1202	N417VN	LJ-1284	OE-FHM	LJ-1366	N1544V	LJ-1448	N1068K
LJ-1121	N904JP	LJ-1203	N485AT	LJ-1285	SP-NEB	LJ-1367	N111MU	LJ-1449	N72PK
LJ-1122	N992C	LJ-1204	ZS-COP	LJ-1286	N800PG	LJ-1368	N1568X	LJ-1450	D-IWID
LJ-1123	N621TD	LJ-1205	N169DR	LJ-1287	N718MB	LJ-1369	VT-VIL	LJ-1451	N3270V
LJ-1124	OE-FRS	LJ-1206	N1552G	LJ-1288	N27BM	LJ-1370	D-IHAH	LJ-1452	N22FS
LJ-1125	N299VM	LJ-1207	C-FGXS	LJ-1289	N1NP	LJ-1371	VT-PPC	LJ-1453	N25HB
LJ-1126	N497P	LJ-1208	N427RB	LJ-1290	JA8882	LJ-1372	N454P	LJ-1454	N1092H
LJ-1127	N814CP	LJ-1209	N53TJ	LJ-1291	JA8883	LJ-1373	TG-SAQ	LJ-1455	N1848S
LJ-1128	PT-ODH	LJ-1210	N1553D	LJ-1292	JA8884	LJ-1374	VT-VIL	LJ-1456	N1095W
LJ-1129	N506F	LJ-1211	N1551H	LJ-1293	N214P	LJ-1375	N35HC	LJ-1457	N1057L
LJ-1130	N518TS	LJ-1212	PT-WHP	LJ-1294	PT-WPN	LJ-1376	VT-HYA	LJ-1458	N901TS
LJ-1131	N811R	LJ-1213	wfu	LJ-1295	N191WB	LJ-1377	PT-WCS	LJ-1459	N902TS
LJ-1132	XC-AGS	LJ-1214	N1553G	LJ-1296	F-GLRZ	LJ-1378	N555HJ*	LJ-1460	N99MN
LJ-1133	N77WM	LJ-1215	wo	LJ-1297	N779DD	LJ-1379	7T-WCG	LJ-1461	N83LS
LJ-1134	N303CA	LJ-1216	D-IEAH	LJ-1298	N190SS	LJ-1380	7T-WCH	LJ-1462	N1079D
LJ-1135	VT-EMI	LJ-1217	N1567G	LJ-1299	F-GNMA	LJ-1381	N381SC	LJ-1463	N930MC
LJ-1136	N902XP	LJ-1218	N224CC	LJ-1300	C-GMBC	LJ-1382	N3120U	LJ-1464	VH-JET
LJ-1137	VT-EMJ	LJ-1219	N155RG	LJ-1301	C-GMBD	LJ-1383	N90WP	LJ-1465	N1102K
LJ-1138	D-ITCH	LJ-1220	PT-OMZ	LJ-1302	N322TC	LJ-1384	N3196K	LJ-1466	LV-....
LJ-1139	C-FGXG	LJ-1221	N407GW	LJ-1303	F-GMPM	LJ-1385	PT-WRA	LJ-1467	N1130J
LJ-1140	C-FGXU	LJ-1222	OM-VKE	LJ-1304	C-GMBG	LJ-1386	PT-WJF	LJ-1468	TI-....
LJ-1141	JA8844	LJ-1223	N90MT	LJ-1305	C-GPNB	LJ-1387	N500EQ	LJ-1469	N97KA
LJ-1142	JA8845	LJ-1224	N123AT	LJ-1306	N65CL	LJ-1388	N580AC	LJ-1470	JA881C
LJ-1143	JA8846	LJ-1225	PT-LLO	LJ-1307	D-IBDH	LJ-1389	N200U	LJ-1471	PT-FCM

LJ-1472	N100JD	LJ-1554	N90RK	LJ-1636	6832	LJ-1718	N720AF	LW-21	N121B
LJ-1473	PT-XHP	LJ-1555	PT-PAC	LJ-1637	N915MP	LJ-1719	N36719	LW-22	wfu
LJ-1474	N478CR	LJ-1556	CC-CVT	LJ-1638	6833	LJ-1720	N22HD	LW-23	N345V
LJ-1475	N1103G	LJ-1557	N540GA	LJ-1639	PR-XIB	LJ-1721	N145AF*	LW-24	N95LB
LJ-1476	P4-SSI	LJ-1558	N543GA	LJ-1640	N40XJ	LJ-1722	N37222	LW-25	N1100M
LJ-1477	N1107W	LJ-1559	N547GA	LJ-1641	N770VF	LJ-1723	N546C	LW-26	00923
LJ-1478	N200HV	LJ-1560	N3160P	LJ-1642	N4392K	LJ-1724	N79PE	LW-27	N379VM
LJ-1479	XA-YAS	LJ-1561	N100SM	LJ-1643	N643EA	LJ-1725	N30025	LW-28	CP-....
LJ-1480	N902LT	LJ-1562	N3262R	LJ-1644	PR-MLZ	LJ-1726	N901JS	LW-29	wo
LJ-1481	N110PM	LJ-1563	N3263N	LJ-1645	N345BH	LJ-1727	N713US	LW-30	N20WS
LJ-1482	N3035T	LJ-1564	PT-MJQ	LJ-1646	PP-BAF	LJ-1728	N6028Y	LW-31	N90WT
LJ-1483	N1126J	LJ-1565	G-ERAD	LJ-1647	N169P	LJ-1729	N36929	LW-32	N291MM
LJ-1484	N24YC	LJ-1566	N988XJ	LJ-1648	HP-1500	LJ-1732	N501P	LW-33	XC-FUY
LJ-1485	VT-JRD	LJ-1567	JA01KA	LJ-1649	N490W	King Air A90		LW-34	N690G
LJ-1486	N1110K	LJ-1568	N568SA	LJ-1650	N831E	LM-1	N7000B	LW-35	N14NM
LJ-1487	N970P	LJ-1569	PT-XOV	LJ-1651	N70VR	LM-2	N7007G	LW-36	PNP-230
LJ-1488	N1135G	LJ-1570	N214KF	LJ-1652	N722JB	LM-5	N87E	LW-37	wo
LJ-1489	LV-YBP	LJ-1571	D-IDIX	LJ-1653	N5153V	LM-6	N70088	LW-38	wo
LJ-1490	N720AM	LJ-1572	N931GG	LJ-1654	N545C	LM-7	N7010L	LW-39	HK-3907
LJ-1491	PT-WTU	LJ-1573	VT-JIL	LJ-1655	N387GC	LM-9	N70135	LW-40	N523CJ
LJ-1492	N97CV	LJ-1574	N406RL	LJ-1656	N656BA	LM-11	N611ND	LW-41	wo
LJ-1493	N98WP	LJ-1575	N971P	LJ-1657	N777YN	LM-13	N7018F	LW-42	N52KA
LJ-1494	PT-WKX	LJ-1576	N3246S	LJ-1658	N4YF	LM-14	N67X	LW-43	N600CX
LJ-1495	N495TM	LJ-1577	PT-WQW	LJ-1659	YV-....	LM-15	N76Q	LW-44	N666DC
LJ-1496	VT-SFL	LJ-1578	PP-ETR	LJ-1660	F-GTCR	LM-16	XA-TJD	LW-45	N200RM
LJ-1497	N2297C	LJ-1579	N775D	LJ-1661	N199CG	LM-17	N70264	LW-46	wfu
LJ-1498	PT-MVJ	LJ-1580	N32238	LJ-1662	N552E	LM-22	CS-DCP	LW-47	F-ASFA
LJ-1499	XA-...	LJ-1581	N326PT	LJ-1663	N588SD	LM-24	N67K	LW-48	N70MV
LJ-1500	N18XJ	LJ-1582	N46AE	LJ-1664	N789KP	LM-31	N32P	LW-49	N12LA
LJ-1501	PT-XOU	LJ-1583	F-HADR	LJ-1665	N4465F	LM-32	N64C*	LW-50	N150TW
LJ-1502	N98KS	LJ-1584	6828	LJ-1666	N867P	LM-34	N65JA	LW-51	N35CM
LJ-1503	N128SB	LJ-1585	N929FD	LJ-1667	N5067L	LM-37	N7043G	LW-52	N181Z
LJ-1504	N333BM	LJ-1586	VH-PFK	LJ-1668	N9DC	LM-48	N37H	LW-53	wo
LJ-1505	N901PC	LJ-1587	N617MM	LJ-1669	N126MM	LM-51	N70U	LW-54	N77JX
LJ-1506	N54AM	LJ-1588	N588SA	LJ-1670	N70CM	LM-59	N7071N	LW-55	N3929G
LJ-1507	N2097W	LJ-1589	N439PW	LJ-1671	N4471M	LM-64	N70766	LW-56	PP-FPP
LJ-1508	N2178F	LJ-1590	N13GZ	LJ-1672	PR-EDP	LM-68	N117CP	LW-57	N88TR
LJ-1509	N769GR	LJ-1591	JA21EG	LJ-1673	N5431M	LM-70	N7079S	LW-58	N350AT
LJ-1510	N2310K	LJ-1592	6829	LJ-1674	N821CS	LM-72	N7081L	LW-59	N290KA
LJ-1511	PT-WUG	LJ-1593	XB-AHK	LJ-1675	N4415F	LM-73	N70841	LW-60	N90PH
LJ-1512	N38XJ	LJ-1594	N590GM	LJ-1676	N771JB	LM-77	N7089Q	LW-61	N129C
LJ-1513	N878K	LJ-1595	N3195Q	LJ-1677	N6077X	LM-79	N80Y	LW-62	N14C
LJ-1514	N1114Z	LJ-1596	6830	LJ-1678	N53PB	LM-80	N518NA	LW-63	N93A
LJ-1515	N2315L	LJ-1597	N597P	LJ-1679	PR-USA	LM-83	N7092K	LW-64	N47LC
LJ-1516	N60VP	LJ-1598	N4298X	LJ-1680	N74B	LM-86	N70950	LW-65	N987GM
LJ-1517	N90KS	LJ-1599	N4368Y	LJ-1681	N954BL	LM-87	N65U*	LW-66	N554CF
LJ-1518	N982SB	LJ-1600	N812LP	LJ-1682	N21LE	LM-89	N41J	LW-67	wo
LJ-1519	N500VA	LJ-1601	N801BS	LJ-1683	N683GW	LM-92	N61Q	LW-68	wfu
LJ-1520	N55EP	LJ-1602	N807RS	LJ-1684	PR-JQM	LM-98	N903MD*	LW-69	N5462G
LJ-1521	N2291F	LJ-1603	N298D	LJ-1685	N1685S	LM-103	N75V	LW-70	LV-WZR
LJ-1522	N98BK	LJ-1604	N928US	LJ-1686	N272EA	LM-105	N38V	LW-71	N121EG
LJ-1523	N982SS	LJ-1605	YV-1074CP	LJ-1687	N437JB	LM-106	N39Q	LW-72	N81MP
LJ-1524	XA-TTR	LJ-1606	D-ITOP	LJ-1688	N629JG	LM-107	N7155P	LW-73	N743JA
LJ-1525	N88XJ	LJ-1607	N73PG	LJ-1689	N557P	LM-113	N65V*	LW-74	N71BX
LJ-1526	N998P	LJ-1608	PR-CCF	LJ-1690	JA....	LM-115	N7157K	LW-75	N75LW
LJ-1527	N488XJ	LJ-1609	N609SA	LJ-1691	N991SA	LM-120	N7165Y	LW-76	N176TW
LJ-1528	N20FD	LJ-1610	OY-LSA	LJ-1692	N692W	LM-124	N89F	LW-77	wo
LJ-1529	N66CK	LJ-1611	N322MR	LJ-1693	PR-RMA	LM-126	LX-RAD	LW-78	N15WN
LJ-1530	N588XJ	LJ-1612	N724DR	LJ-1694	N694CT	LM-130	N87V	LW-79	N60BA
LJ-1531	N150GW	LJ-1613	N549GA	LJ-1695	N124LL	LM-136	N410SP	LW-80	N20LH
LJ-1532	N2354Y	LJ-1614	N614SA	LJ-1696	N93QR	LM-140	N906HF	LW-81	wfu
LJ-1533	XA-...	LJ-1615	N700KB	LJ-1697	N50847	King Air E90		LW-82	N820RD
LJ-1534	N291DF	LJ-1616	N24DS	LJ-1698	N61698	LW-1	N190RM	LW-83	wo
LJ-1535	N3035P	LJ-1617	LV-...	LJ-1699	N456PP	LW-2	N412SR	LW-84	N111JA
LJ-1536	N3066W	LJ-1618	N5024W	LJ-1700	N550SW	LW-3	F-GJAD	LW-85	N42PC
LJ-1537	N299RP	LJ-1619	N67CC	LJ-1701	PR-FKY	LW-4	N77WF	LW-86	F-GFDJ
LJ-1538	PT-WZC	LJ-1620	N543HC	LJ-1702	N6190S	LW-5	N999SF	LW-87	9J-...
LJ-1539	LX-PBL	LJ-1621	N3321M	LJ-1703	N45PF*	LW-6	N905TF	LW-88	N29M
LJ-1540	N600FL	LJ-1622	D-IDCV	LJ-1704	N794P	LW-7	N51DN	LW-89	N98HF
LJ-1541	N438CA	LJ-1623	XA-JAG	LJ-1705	N5115H	LW-8	N132HS	LW-90	HK-....
LJ-1542	N2178A	LJ-1624	XA-...	LJ-1706	N648JG	LW-9	PT-IGD	LW-91	wo
LJ-1543	N3143T	LJ-1625	N5025R	LJ-1707	N495Y	LW-10	N977SB	LW-92	wo
LJ-1544	N3068Z	LJ-1626	N1875C	LJ-1708	N170S*	LW-11	N11DT	LW-93	N352GR
LJ-1545	N786RM	LJ-1627	TI-...	LJ-1709	N744P	LW-12	N12GJ	LW-94	YV-467CP
LJ-1546	PR-RFB	LJ-1628	PR-TIN	LJ-1710	N785JP	LW-13	N383AA	LW-95	N567GJ
LJ-1547	N399WS	LJ-1629	N229J*	LJ-1711	N6111V	LW-14	N4495N	LW-96	N214SC
LJ-1548	N574P	LJ-1630	N5037W	LJ-1712	N785P	LW-15	wo	LW-97	F-GESJ
LJ-1549	XB-HMI	LJ-1631	N86LD	LJ-1713	N713EA	LW-16	N43WS	LW-98	wo
LJ-1550	N993CB	LJ-1632	N928KG	LJ-1714	N422AS*	LW-17	N259SC	LW-99	N31WP
LJ-1551	XA-GSA	LJ-1633	N266RD	LJ-1715	N508CB	LW-18	N22ER	LW-100	N28MS
LJ-1552	LQ-ZRB	LJ-1634	6831	LJ-1716	D-I...	LW-19	wo	LW-101	N70SW
LJ-1553	N394B	LJ-1635	N771PD	LJ-1717	N32217	LW-20	N87CH	LW-102	wo

Reg		Reg		Reg	
LW-103	N898WW	LW-185	N600AC	LW-267	N20S
LW-104	N123MH	LW-186	N2186L	LW-268	TI-GEV
LW-105	N111FV	LW-187	N816RL	LW-269	N288CR
LW-106	wo	LW-188	N68PM	LW-270	YV-1500P
LW-107	N44MV	LW-189	YV-O-SATA	LW-271	N727MT
LW-108	N37HC	LW-190	RP-C415	LW-272	N62BL
LW-109	N989GM	LW-191	N258JC	LW-273	N273NA
LW-110	9Q-CCG	LW-192	N2192L	LW-274	N274KA
LW-111	wfu	LW-193	N46RP	LW-275	N47BH
LW-112	N67PS	LW-194	N117FH	LW-276	N7TD
LW-113	wo	LW-195	wfu	LW-277	RP-C292
LW-114	N700DH	LW-196	N3818C	LW-278	F-GHUV
LW-115	N76SK	LW-197	N228RA	LW-279	N390PS
LW-116	TF-...	LW-198	G-WELL	LW-280	N41WE
LW-117	N10XJ	LW-199	F-GALZ	LW-281	N31A
LW-118	N8118R	LW-200	N918VS	LW-282	N900AC
LW-119	N152D	LW-201	wo	LW-283	N48TA
LW-120	N99AC	LW-202	N934DC	LW-284	ZP-TJW
LW-121	N515BC	LW-203	N203RD	LW-285	N777KA
LW-122	wo	LW-204	N965LG	LW-286	N155LS
LW-123	N500MS	LW-205	Z-AHL	LW-287	C-FNCB
LW-124	N90BF	LW-206	N290MC	LW-288	N700DD
LW-125	N504CB	LW-207	wo	LW-289	N83WE
LW-126	N103AP	LW-208	YV-706P	LW-290	N60MH
LW-127	N71WB	LW-209	N282DB	LW-291	N824AC
LW-128	N50EB	LW-210	N860MH	LW-292	N92DV
LW-129	LV-WFP	LW-211	N4216S	LW-293	N12AX
LW-130	N47AW	LW-212	wo	LW-294	N677J
LW-131	N98PM	LW-213	N2274L	LW-295	wo
LW-132	N9029R	LW-214	N14SB	LW-296	F-GETJ
LW-133	PT-LHZ	LW-215	N56HT	LW-297	LX-LTX
LW-134	N55HC	LW-216	N439WA	LW-298	N44GK
LW-135	LV-...	LW-217	N16LH	LW-299	N127EC
LW-136	G-ORTH	LW-218	N700WD	LW-300	N911AZ
LW-137	wo	LW-219	N83FE	LW-301	N618RD
LW-138	PT-WAG	LW-220	wfu	LW-302	RP-C298
LW-139	N249WM	LW-221	N429DM	LW-303	N79CT
LW-140	N1UC	LW-222	ZS-NYE	LW-304	F-GMRN
LW-141	TI-SFC	LW-223	N333LE	LW-305	N111TC
LW-142	N7WU	LW-224	ZS-NXI	LW-306	N67V
LW-143	N300MT	LW-225	N181CG	LW-307	wo
LW-144	N812KB	LW-226	N711TZ	LW-308	N132DD
LW-145	RP-C879	LW-227	N901TM	LW-309	N160TT
LW-146	N41HH	LW-228	N692M	LW-310	N10WG
LW-147	N28M	LW-229	EV-7702	LW-311	N282TC
LW-148	N300CH	LW-230	N48TE	LW-312	N510ME
LW-149	N177MK	LW-231	N304LG	LW-313	wo
LW-150	N100EC	LW-232	N448CP	LW-314	N20564
LW-151	ZS-OAE	LW-233	wo	LW-315	N666ZT
LW-152	wfu	LW-234	YV-118CP	LW-316	OO-VHV
LW-153	CC-DSN	LW-235	N776DC	LW-317	N2062A
LW-154	GN-7593	LW-236	wo	LW-318	N443CL
LW-155	N505MW	LW-237	N17NM	LW-319	N1205S
LW-156	N414GN	LW-238	N25TG	LW-320	N366GW
LW-157	N199TT	LW-239	G-SFSG	LW-321	TJ-MJP
LW-158	N75JP	LW-240	HP-5000H	LW-322	YV-516CP
LW-159	N9059S	LW-241	N30KC	LW-323	N323HA
LW-160	N53CE	LW-242	N963KA	LW-324	N351GR
LW-161	F-BXON	LW-243	N18343	LW-325	RP-C291
LW-162	N369CD	LW-244	N611R	LW-326	TN-AFG
LW-163	N34MF	LW-245	N3LS	LW-327	N788SW
LW-164	N200RE	LW-246	N711HV	LW-328	F-GJPD
LW-165	N701X	LW-247	wo	LW-329	N652L
LW-166	wo	LW-248	N555FW	LW-330	LV-OBB
LW-167	N213RW	LW-249	N521LB	LW-331	N54PT
LW-168	N220PB	LW-250	N321DM	LW-332	N636GW
LW-169	N17SE	LW-251	F-GJCR	LW-333	XB-JLA
LW-170	N555TT	LW-252	N969CL	LW-334	N22TL
LW-171	N6571S	LW-253	N43PC	LW-335	wo
LW-172	YV-326P	LW-254	N48W	LW-336	N21NM
LW-173	N707TL	LW-255	wo	LW-337	N290K
LW-174	wo	LW-256	N63BV	LW-338	N50RV
LW-175	F-HAAA	LW-257	N355JS	LW-339	N339KA
LW-176	N662JS	LW-258	N203PC	LW-340	N3700M
LW-177	N944RS	LW-259	LV-WHV	LW-341	N341MH
LW-178	HC-DAC	LW-260	GN-7839	LW-342	N90XS*
LW-179	N676J	LW-261	ZP-TZW	LW-343	PT-OUF
LW-180	wo	LW-262	N790RB	LW-344	N999SE
LW-181	wo	LW-263	N1840S	LW-345	N336JM
LW-182	wo	LW-264	ARV-0201	LW-346	N3821S
LW-183	HK-2491	LW-265	N362D	LW-347	PT-LCE
LW-184	N4MR	LW-266	N702XP		

King Air F90

Reg		Reg	
LA-1	wfu	LA-82	N501TD
LA-2	N49CH	LA-83	N186DD
LA-3	N1MA	LA-84	HK-....
LA-4	N502SP	LA-85	PT-ODN
LA-5	N602EB	LA-86	N242LF
LA-6	N111AA	LA-87	N696RA
LA-7	PT-LLP	LA-88	N6VJ
LA-8	wo	LA-89	LV-ZPY
LA-9	N300TA	LA-90	N236JS
LA-10	N325WR	LA-91	N333WT
LA-11	PT-LXI	LA-92	PT-ONO
LA-12	N19RK	LA-93	wo
LA-13	N911CF	LA-94	PT-LSH
LA-14	N581RJ	LA-95	XA-SAW
LA-15	N124BK	LA-96	wfu
LA-16	YV-1013P	LA-97	N58EZ
LA-17	N117TJ	LA-98	N103CB
LA-18	N84JL	LA-99	N803HC
LA-19	F-GETI	LA-100	OO-IAL*
LA-20	N90ET	LA-101	N37990
LA-21	N66LP	LA-102	N44882
LA-22	F-GHIV	LA-103	PT-LTT
LA-23	N27WH	LA-104	N90NA
LA-24	N93KA	LA-105	N188BF
LA-25	N128JP	LA-106	N173PL
LA-26	N96TT	LA-107	N188JB
LA-27	N246CA	LA-108	N411RJ
LA-28	PT-LPL	LA-109	PT-LYZ
LA-29	wfu	LA-110	N3824V
LA-30	N199BC	LA-111	N632RR
LA-31	N960V	LA-112	N3809C
LA-32	N123CH	LA-113	C-GKSC
LA-33	N49PH	LA-114	wo
LA-34	N57TM	LA-115	F-GCTR
LA-35	YV-290CP	LA-116	N197AS
LA-36	N102WK	LA-117	N120RC
LA-37	N30GT	LA-118	PT-OFD
LA-38	N65MT	LA-119	N800BK
LA-39	N703JT	LA-120	ZS-PGW
LA-40	N66BS	LA-121	N182CA
LA-41	N311DS	LA-122	ZS-LBC
LA-42	N190FD	LA-123	N513KL
LA-43	N6749E	LA-124	wo
LA-44	XA-TMP	LA-125	N145MR
LA-45	XA-LGT	LA-126	PT-LYP
LA-46	N208RC	LA-127	N812CP
LA-47	ZS-MHM	LA-128	PT-ONU
LA-48	N30NH	LA-129	3A-MON
LA-49	PT-OIF	LA-130	N81SD
LA-50	HB-GHD	LA-131	N210AJ
LA-51	ZS-NFO	LA-132	PT-LQC
LA-52	N769D	LA-133	N31TL
LA-53	N5AH*	LA-134	N90BD
LA-54	N540WJ	LA-135	N422Z
LA-55	N311GC	LA-136	N93BJ
LA-56	N68DK	LA-137	N488FT
LA-57	wo	LA-138	N15
LA-58	N59EK	LA-139	N94JD
LA-59	N146FL	LA-140	N607DK
LA-60	N41WL	LA-141	F-GDAK
LA-61	N189JR	LA-142	N50AW
LA-62	F-GIFK	LA-143	N69AD
LA-63	ZS-LTD	LA-144	PT-ONE
LA-64	N322GK	LA-145	N18
LA-65	N867MA	LA-146	N90RT
LA-66	N90TP	LA-147	XA-...
LA-67	N416P	LA-148	PT-LER
LA-68	N77PV	LA-149	N44PA
LA-69	ZS-KLZ	LA-150	N80M
LA-70	N990BM	LA-151	HK-3935W
LA-71	N541MM	LA-152	N152WE
LA-72	N770SD	LA-153	wo
LA-73	N81GC	LA-154	N90SB
LA-74	N79EC	LA-155	PT-OUJ
LA-75	N600WM	LA-156	PT-LTO
LA-76	TI-AWM	LA-157	N69084
LA-77	N277SP	LA-158	N580PA
LA-78	PT-WET	LA-159	N222AG
LA-79	N2164L	LA-160	ZS-...
LA-80	wo	LA-161	N18471
LA-81	C-FCDF	LA-162	PT-OOX
		LA-163	N85PJ

c/n	Reg'n	c/n	Reg'n	c/n	Reg'n	c/n	Reg'n	c/n	Reg'n
LA-164	N990F	B-9	ZS-PBH	B-91	F-GHHV	B-173	HP-1336AP	BE-8	N45LU
LA-165	N300DM	B-10	wo	B-92	wo	B-174	C-FTMA	BE-9	N236CP
LA-166	F-GFVN	B-11	N100KA	B-93	7T-VCV	B-175	C-GJHW	BE-10	wo
LA-167	N1857F	B-12	wo	B-94	N945WS	B-176	N110VU*	BE-11	N78DA
LA-168	XA-...	B-13	wo	B-95	70-15908	B-177	N30GC	BE-12	N400AC
LA-169	N61228	B-14	C-GJKS	B-96	N116RJ	B-178	N764K	BE-13	N93SF
LA-170	N314P	B-15	wo	B-97	N997RC	B-179	N127Z	BE-14	N68DA
LA-171	N46JX	B-16	YV-801CP	B-98	N324EC	B-180	wo	BE-15	C-GDFJ
LA-172	N68AM	B-17	N951K	B-99	N921SA	B-181	CNA-NB	BE-16	C-GDFZ
LA-173	PT-OHZ	B-18	N503AB	B-100	N799DD	B-182	CNA-NC	BE-17	C-FASN
LA-174	YV-702CP	B-19	wo	B-101	C-FDOR	B-183	CNA-ND	BE-18	N93AJ
LA-175	PT-OZP	B-20	N195MA	B-102	C-GAIK	B-184	C-FGNL	BE-19	YV-95CP
LA-176	N517AB	B-21	N360C	B-103	9Q-CEM	B-185	N220KW	BE-20	N443TC
LA-177	N127DC	B-22	N577D	B-104	C-FDOS	B-186	CNA-NE	BE-21	N60TJ
LA-178	N178LA	B-23	N701RJ	B-105	C-GNAJ	B-187	CNA-NF	BE-22	N86TR
LA-179	YV-886CP	B-24	C-GNAA	B-106	C-GNAR	B-188	wo	BE-23	N93D
LA-180	N357CC	B-25	N136JH	B-107	N870MA	B-189	wo	BE-24	N234TK
LA-181	TG-CFA	B-26	N696JB	B-108	XC-FIW	B-190	C-GNAR	BE-25	N125VH
LA-182	N424CP	B-27	C-GWWA	B-109	wo	B-191	C-GJBQ	BE-26	C-GPRU
LA-183	N90TD	B-28	C-FWYO	B-110	C-FDOU	B-192	N4392W	BE-27	N87JE
LA-184	C-FCLH	B-29	N830EM	B-111	wo	B-193	C-FAIP	BE-28	YV-127CP
LA-185	PT-LYM	B-30	N3606T	B-112	N1347Z	B-194	C-GHOC	BE-29	D-IZAC
LA-186	XB-JRF	B-31	N711GM	B-113	wfu	B-195	EC-CHE	BE-30	N111YF
LA-187	PT-OTA	B-32	N122U	B-114	N601LM	B-196	F-GJJJ	BE-31	C-FAFS
LA-188	N41AK	B-33	9Q-CRF	B-115	C-FDOV	B-197	JW9027	BE-32	N1PN
LA-189	N107AJ	B-34	N2225H	B-116	N18AH	B-198	C-GAPK	BE-33	N900RD
LA-190	N6335F	B-35	C-GTLS	B-117	wo	B-199	F-GEXV	BE-34	N949SW
LA-191	N822BA	B-36	C-GXRX	B-118	C-FDOY	B-200	PT-LZA	BE-35	N364BC
LA-192	D-ITLL	B-37	N524SC	B-119	PT-LJN	B-201	C-GAVI	BE-36	wfu
LA-193	N604DK	B-38	C-FQOV	B-120	C-FXAJ	B-202	N45MF	BE-37	N49SS
LA-194	N27SE	B-39	OH-BKA	B-121	C-GJJE	B-203	wo	BE-38	wo
LA-195	PT-LXY	B-40	C-FMXY	B-122	C-GILM	B-204	C-FBGS	BE-39	C-FSIK
LA-196	N766RB	B-41	N1100A	B-123	C-FWRM	B-205	N86BM	BE-40	N24203
LA-197	PT-LSP	B-42	C-FAFD	B-124	C-GASI	B-206	C-FHGG	BE-41	N17792
LA-198	HK-...	B-43	PT-DKV	B-125	N170AS	B-207	N208SR	BE-42	N87NW
LA-199	N5NW	B-44	N440SM	B-126	wo	B-208	N14CF	BE-43	N487JH
LA-200	PT-OFB	B-45	C-GPCB	B-127	F-GEJV	B-209	N75GR	BE-44	C-FPBC
LA-201	N955RA	B-46	N770RL	B-128	N467BW	B-210	C-GNEX	BE-45	PT-WPV
LA-202	N840SB	B-47	C-FWYN	B-129	C-FLRB	B-211	N115DT	BE-46	N988JR
LA-203	N399TW*	B-48	N5727	B-130	C-GXHP	B-212	SE-LDL	BE-47	N49E
LA-204	N75MS	B-49	wo	B-131	N22BJ	B-213	N46BE	BE-48	N2830S
LA-205	N205SM	B-50	wo	B-132	wo	B-214	C-GPBA	BE-49	C-GGKJ
LA-206	N131SP	B-51	C-FWPN	B-133	wo	B-215	N28C	BE-50	N136MB
LA-207	YV-622CP	B-52	wfu	B-134	N700AT	B-216	N730EJ	BE-51	N100TW
LA-208	N999RC	B-53	N153JA	B-135	N629SC	B-217	wo	BE-52	N771CW
LA-209	N444KK	B-54	N776L	B-136	N700NC	B-218	331	BE-53	N53TD
LA-210	N415HS	B-55	N911RL	B-137	N247B	B-219	wo	BE-54	N241CW
LA-211	N808TC	B-56	PT-DNP	B-138	wo	B-220	wo	BE-55	N813BL
LA-212	A2-AHV	B-57	ZS-OUS	B-139	wo	B-221	N232AL	BE-56	N9933S
LA-213	PT-ODO	B-58	N750FC	B-140	PP-FOY	B-222	N223LH	BE-57	N75AP
LA-214	N773	B-59	C-FMWM	B-141	C-GZUZ	B-223	C-FPLG	BE-58	N564CA
LA-215	PT-LUT	B-60	N54JW	B-142	N999G	B-224	N601PC	BE-59	N777DQ
LA-216	PT-LZT	B-61	C-GSYN	B-143	wfu	B-225	N91RK	BE-60	N650JT
LA-217	PT-OCE	B-62	C-GKBQ	B-144	N200AJ	B-226	N227BC	BE-61	YV-903P
LA-218	N299KP	B-63	N20880	B-145	7T-VRF	B-227	F-GKEL	BE-62	N350TC
LA-219	N18CM	B-64	N4200A	B-146	C-GJLP	B-228	C-GMAG	BE-63	N27CS
LA-220	PT-OLP	B-65	N102LF	B-147	C-FLTS	B-229	N1362N	BE-64	N4490M
LA-221	HK-3505	B-66	N525ZS	B-148	F-GGLV	B-230	YV-....	BE-65	N6045S
LA-222	N711L	B-67	C-FWPG	B-149	C-FPAJ	B-231	C-GKAJ	BE-66	N37PC
LA-223	PT-LIF	B-68	XB-REA	B-150	C-GISH	B-232	N711RE	BE-67	N4415L
LA-224	N991GC	B-69	N207SB	B-151	C-GYQK	B-233	N23404	BE-68	N66820
LA-225	PT-OFS	B-70	N77PF	B-152	N46JK	B-234	C-GJLJ	BE-69	N794CE
LA-226	N16WG	B-71	N431R	B-153	YV-0-SID-2	B-235	N23605	BE-70	N120MG
LA-227	D-ISTB	B-72	C-GTLF	B-154	C-GDPI	B-236	YV-....	BE-71	wfu
LA-228	PP-CSE	B-73	YV-04CP	B-155	C-GUPP	B-237	N1TR	BE-72	C-FAFE
LA-229	D-IRIS	B-74	N74JV	B-156	XA-...	B-238	C-FSKA	BE-73	wo
LA-230	N393CE	B-75	N75LA	B-157	C-GLPG	B-239	N87CA	BE-74	N88FA
LA-231	VP-CLA	B-76	C-GWWQ	B-158	N896SB	B-240	N777GS	BE-75	wo
LA-232	PT-ASN	B-77	RP-C1978	B-159	YV-....	B-241	IGM-240	BE-76	N301TS
LA-233	wo	B-78	N626SA	B-160	N224LB	B-242	C-FLRD	BE-77	N580S
LA-234	N7206E	B-79	CC-CLY	B-161	C-FASB	B-243	N842DS	BE-78	wfu
LA-235	N722PT	B-80	N424SW	B-162	C-FGIN	B-244	wo	BE-79	N500KD
LA-236	N234CW	B-81	N707SS	B-163	C-G...	B-245	wo	BE-80	N93WT
King Air 100		B-82	LV-WDO	B-164	C-FAMU	B-246	wo	BE-81	N987B
B-1	N3100K	B-83	YV-04P	B-165	wo	B-247	C-GFKS	BE-82	N66804
B-2	N11JJ	B-84	C-FDJQ	B-166	N715WA	**King Air B100**		BE-83	N123BL
B-3	C-FIDN	B-85	C-GKBZ	B-167	C-FAPP	BE-1	wfu	BE-84	N700BA
B-4	XB-WUI	B-86	N53MD	B-168	N900DN	BE-2	N729MS	BE-85	N222LP
B-5	N288RA	B-87	N70JL	B-169	N720C	BE-3	N150TJ	BE-86	N264PA
B-6	N122ZZ	B-88	C-GJSU	B-170	C-GIZX	BE-4	N786CB	BE-87	N19DA
B-7	PT-OQP	B-89	C-FWYF			BE-5	N220AA	BE-88	N130AT
B-8	C-FDAM	B-90	N515AS			BE-6	N8514B	BE-89	C-GKNP
						BE-7	C-GVIK		

BE-90	N770D	BB-34	N878RA	BB-116	wfu	BB-199	F-GNPD	BB-283	C-FATA
BE-91	N717D	BB-35	N35KD	BB-117	N21DE	BB-200	N2PY	BB-284	wfu
BE-92	N6756P	BB-36	N44UF	BB-118	wo	BB-201	wo	BB-285	C-FKBU
BE-93	N142JC	BB-37	F-GPDV	BB-119	wfu	BB-202	F-GEXL	BB-286	Z-MRS
BE-94	N3663B	BB-38	wo	BB-120	C-GHOP	BB-204	wo	BB-287	N498AC
BE-95	wfu	BB-39	wo	BB-121	ZS-OCI	BB-205	N6PX	BB-288	ZS-NRR
BE-96	N802RD	BB-40	N4TJ	BB-122	N122RF	BB-206	N70AJ	BB-289	N5ST
BE-97	N97WD	BB-41	N200ZC	BB-123	PH-ATM	BB-207	C-FCGW	BB-290	N290SJ
BE-98	N948HB*	BB-42	N66TJ	BB-124	N109TM	BB-208	N62DL	BB-291	N291PA
BE-99	C-GBVX	BB-43	N520MC	BB-125	N90PB	BB-209	F-GPAS	BB-292	N393JW
BE-100	N10AG	BB-44	wo	BB-126	D2-FFL	BB-210	G-FRYI	BB-293	N200BT
BE-101	N311CM	BB-45	PT-OZK	BB-127	N200JL	BB-211	5Y-BMC	BB-294	9M-KNS
BE-102	N57TJ	BB-46	N760NP	BB-128	F-BXSI	BB-212	PNC-209	BB-295	wo
BE-103	N2TX	BB-47	wo	BB-129	wo	BB-213	wfu	BB-296	N402KA
BE-104	N67BS	BB-48	XC-AA38	BB-130	N682DR	BB-214	OB-1700	BB-297	N593BJ
BE-105	N87XX	BB-49	N222KA	BB-131	N131SJ	BB-215	N750TT	BB-298	N862DD
BE-106	N568K	BB-50	N888TR	BB-132	HS-DCB	BB-216	C-FAKN	BB-299	N200FV
BE-107	C-GPJL	BB-51	YV-....	BB-133	N717HT	BB-217	C-FCGM	BB-300	HP-....
BE-108	N108EB	BB-52	ZS-NWK	BB-134	N200EC	BB-218	wo	BB-301	C-FCGU
BE-109	N105VY	BB-53	N280RA	BB-135	HK-4236	BB-219	wfu	BB-302	G-OWAX
BE-110	N702JL	BB-54	4-G-41/069	BB-136	N277JB	BB-220	N800HA	BB-303	LX-JDP
BE-111	N118NL	BB-55	N200BC	BB-137	PP-EOP	BB-221	PH-DDB	BB-304	N103PM
BE-112	N727RS	BB-56	N44US	BB-138	N999DT	BB-222	ZS-KAA	BB-305	N11AB
BE-113	N88TL	BB-57	C-FAFT	BB-139	N810JB	BB-223	YV-O-SATA	BB-306	4X-DZK
BE-114	N125D	BB-58	N60PD	BB-140	C-GPCP	BB-224	N750KC	BB-307	HB-GPG
BE-115	C-FXRJ	BB-59	N500KS	BB-141	N977LX	BB-225	XA-...	BB-308	wo
BE-116	N116DG	BB-60	HK-4108X	BB-142	wo	BB-226	N982TM	BB-309	5Y-SMB
BE-117	wo	BB-61	N58280	BB-143	N200CJ	BB-227	N335S	BB-310	N988SC
BE-118	N101SN	BB-62	N500GN	BB-144	N2883	BB-228	N703HT	BB-311	HP-1512
BE-119	N1807H	BB-63	HK-3705	BB-145	VH-ZOS	BB-229	N911MN	BB-312	N127GA
BE-120	N110CE	BB-64	N56CD*	BB-146	wo	BB-230	wo	BB-313	N30SE
BE-121	C-FAFZ	BB-65	N440ST	BB-147	N771HC	BB-231	C-FZVX	BB-314	N767WF
BE-122	N74RR	BB-66	RP-C223	BB-148	VH-OYH	BB-232	N162PA	BB-315	ZS-PZU
BE-123	N827RM	BB-67	YV-....	BB-149	N982GA	BB-233	wo	BB-316	YV-2584P
BE-124	N150YA	BB-68	C-GMWR	BB-150	N107FL	BB-234	N80PA	BB-317	wo
BE-125	N350TJ	BB-69	N812DP	BB-151	N528WG	BB-235	OY-CBP	BB-318	N49KC
BE-126	N123WH	BB-70	wfu	BB-152	N152TW	BB-236	C-FCGC	BB-319	N6HU
BE-127	N686AC	BB-71	4-G-42/069	BB-153	wo	BB-237	HP-....	BB-320	wo
BE-128	N137D	BB-72	5Y-JKB	BB-154	N44KT	BB-238	N891MA	BB-321	N261AC
BE-129	C-GSWF	BB-73	VH-SGT	BB-155	5Y-BMA	BB-239	F-GSIN	BB-322	N710NC
BE-130	N339JG	BB-74	wo	BB-156	N69CD	BB-240	N888EX	BB-323	N811VT
BE-131	C-GSWG	BB-75	HK-3936	BB-157	N996LM	BB-241	wo	BB-324	N701NC
BE-132	N150YR	BB-76	C-GPCD	BB-158	N81PF	BB-242	N200RW	BB-325	N65EB
BE-133	N531CB	BB-77	C-GWUY	BB-159	C-FCGT	BB-243	N43AJ	BB-326	N944CF
BE-134	C-FOGP	BB-78	YV-....	BB-160	YV-2484P	BB-244	wo	BB-327	ZS-OSB
BE-135	N997ME	BB-79	N155QS	BB-161	N114SB	BB-245	wo	BB-328	N795PA
BE-136	N221TC	BB-80	F-GGMS	BB-162	VH-SMT	BB-246	N200VA	BB-329	N53CK
BE-137	N444RK	BB-81	N200FM	BB-163	wo	BB-247	N4000	BB-330	HP-....
Super King Air 200		BB-82	LZ-YUK	BB-164	HP-...	BB-248	HK-3822	BB-331	N87LP
BB-1	wfu	BB-83	N283KA	BB-165	VH-SKU	BB-249	C-GOJG	BB-332	N3DE
BB-2	C-GARO	BB-84	C-GFSB	BB-166	N84CA	BB-250	wfu	BB-333	HK-3941W
BB-3	N24SP	BB-85	ZS-NTL	BB-167	YV-...	BB-251	F-GKCV	BB-334	D2-EBG
BB-4	N397SA	BB-86	TZ-ZBC	BB-168	C-FOGY	BB-252	N934SH	BB-335	N327RB
BB-5	N399SA	BB-87	TI-TCT	BB-169	N725MC	BB-253	N991SU	BB-336	N311AV
BB-6	N300TR	BB-88	N35	BB-170	C-GPEA	BB-254	wo	BB-337	N400KW
BB-7	C-FBCN	BB-89	N200WZ	BB-171	7T-VRI	BB-255	HB-GJM	BB-338	N689BV
BB-8	XB-TFS	BB-90	wo	BB-172	N94KC	BB-256	5Y-BKT	BB-339	N545LC
BB-9	N200EZ	BB-91	N884PG	BB-173	N173RC	BB-257	N257NA	BB-340	wo
BB-10	N660M	BB-92	N192SA	BB-174	wo	BB-258	N888ET	BB-341	ZS-LWM
BB-11	FAB 0..	BB-93	wo	BB-175	7T-VRH	BB-259	VH-LAB	BB-342	O342
BB-12	wfu	BB-94	N17HM	BB-176	N67GA	BB-260	N18CJ	BB-343	N4679M
BB-13	F-GIJB	BB-95	A2-AHZ	BB-177	N456CS	BB-261	YV-O-SATA	BB-344	VH-ITH
BB-14	C-GWWN	BB-96	wo	BB-178	N36CP	BB-262	EC-HHO	BB-345	wo
BB-15	wfu	BB-97	N65RT	BB-179	N424BS	BB-263	N2U	BB-346	YV-....
BB-16	N711CR	BB-98	wo	BB-180	PH-SBK	BB-264	C-FZNQ	BB-347	C-GJLI
BB-17	YV-....	BB-99	C-FSKQ	BB-181	wfu	BB-265	YV-...	BB-348	N28J
BB-18	N846CM	BB-100	XC-DIJ	BB-182	EC-GBB	BB-266	N266EB	BB-349	F-GHLB
BB-19	wo	BB-101	D2-EXW	BB-183	N175SA	BB-267	N8BG	BB-350	ZS-NTT
BB-20	OB-1509	BB-102	N200AF	BB-184	7T-VRG	BB-268	C-GTUC	BB-351	G-CEGR
BB-21	wfu	BB-103	N201CH	BB-185	N503F	BB-269	D-IICE	BB-352	HK-3922P
BB-22	N73MW	BB-104	N40RA	BB-187	N630DB	BB-271	N131TC	BB-353	SU-BAX
BB-23	N153ML	BB-105	C-FKJI	BB-188	N4288S	BB-272	N302MB	BB-354	N221BG
BB-24	C-FCGB	BB-106	N52SF	BB-189	N56CC	BB-273	YV-O-SATA	BB-355	VH-OYE
BB-25	N601CF	BB-107	YV-....	BB-190	C-FCGL	BB-274	N8AM	BB-356	N28KC
BB-26	ZS-LYA	BB-108	G-OMNH	BB-191	N200TP	BB-275	C-GQNJ	BB-357	N6069A
BB-27	C-GFOL	BB-109	N244JP	BB-192	F-GLIF	BB-276	D-IMON	BB-358	RP-C5129
BB-28	6V-AGS	BB-110	N110BM	BB-193	OB-1468	BB-277	N593DJ	BB-359	N351MA
BB-29	C-GKBN	BB-111	N22071	BB-194	HB-GIL	BB-278	AP-CAA	BB-360	N18KA
BB-30	G-HAMA	BB-112	wo	BB-195	N5LE	BB-279	YV-....	BB-361	N1HX
BB-31	YV-....	BB-113	PK-TRA	BB-196	HK-3995X	BB-280	N280TT	BB-362	HP-....
BB-32	N160SF	BB-114	XA-...	BB-197	ZS-OAK	BB-281	N4AT	BB-363	N642TF
BB-33	HP-....	BB-115	N700KW	BB-198	N4298S	BB-282	YV-1300P	BB-364	OY-JRN

BB-365	VH-OYA	BB-448	N411BL	BB-534	N12CF	BB-621	N210CM	BB-707	N715RD
BB-366	EC-IUV	BB-449	B-13152	BB-535	C-GOGT	BB-622	F-GHSV	BB-708	N313EE
BB-367	N367RA	BB-450	HK-3923X	BB-536	N777AW	BB-623	N6689D	BB-709	N71VT
BB-368	wo	BB-451	HB-GJI	BB-537	N5MK	BB-624	N444EG	BB-710	C-GXHW
BB-369	wfu	BB-452	N500PV	BB-538	N477JM	BB-625	G-WVIP	BB-711	N1162V
BB-370	N80RT	BB-453	N23TC	BB-539	ST-SFS	BB-626	C9-ENH	BB-712	N411RA
BB-371	N151EL	BB-454	N888DC	BB-540	YV-946CP	BB-628	N711TN	BB-713	CN-CDN
BB-372	SX-ECG	BB-455	N900DG	BB-541	N923AS*	BB-629	9Q-CTG	BB-714	N500CR
BB-373	N4799M	BB-456	G-PFFN	BB-542	N542KA	BB-630	ZS-NZJ	BB-715	N140GA
BB-374	N111UT	BB-457	N15KA	BB-543	wo	BB-631	N6684B	BB-716	N765TC
BB-375	N23ST	BB-458	ANE-234	BB-544	N711VM	BB-632	YV-2710P	BB-717	N77CA
BB-376	N376RC	BB-459	101002	BB-545	D-ILIN	BB-633	wo	BB-718	VH-SGV
BB-377	N52GT	BB-460	4-F-43/074	BB-546	4-G-47/074	BB-634	OY-NUK	BB-719	N372JB
BB-378	N378SF	BB-461	N277RS	BB-547	5Y-HHE	BB-635	N30PH	BB-720	N208SW
BB-379	5Y-DDE	BB-462	N220TT	BB-548	N706DG	BB-636	N127TA	BB-721	N8EF
BB-380	N323RR	BB-463	N463DP	BB-549	4-G-48/074	BB-637	N3181	BB-722	F-HAAG
BB-381	ZS-AGW	BB-464	N561SS	BB-550	VH-TLX	BB-638	N220JB	BB-723	wo
BB-382	ZS-PKM	BB-465	N31WC	BB-552	N63593	BB-639	LV-WOS	BB-724	N804
BB-383	C-GZYO	BB-466	N206P	BB-553	N326RT	BB-640	CS-DDU	BB-725	N725RA
BB-384	N2025M	BB-467	5Y-SJB	BB-554	N5PX	BB-641	N641TS	BB-726	G-CEGP
BB-385	N381R	BB-468	ZS-PBL	BB-555	EC-GHZ	BB-642	N10BY	BB-727	N522TG
BB-386	ZS-NHX	BB-470	VH-CWE	BB-556	N79GA	BB-643	ZS-ALE	BB-728	N8170J
BB-387	5N-BHL	BB-471	LV-RTC	BB-557	5Y-JAI	BB-644	N750HG	BB-729	LV-WPM
BB-388	N26BE	BB-472	N305JS	BB-558	LV-WGP	BB-645	N999VB	BB-730	N108AL
BB-389	N859CC	BB-473	N746KF	BB-559	N795CA	BB-646	N646DR	BB-731	YV-O-SAT
BB-390	N1660W	BB-474	C-GCFF	BB-560	F-GTEF	BB-648	wo	BB-732	PK-VKA
BB-391	YV-....	BB-475	N121LB	BB-561	F-GULJ	BB-649	N649JC	BB-733	N444AD
BB-392	N392KC	BB-476	N203BS	BB-562	N120FS	BB-650	N740GL	BB-734	wo
BB-393	wo	BB-477	N57GA	BB-564	N42LJ	BB-651	N141CT	BB-735	N507BE
BB-394	wo	BB-478	N912SM	BB-565	N6630C	BB-652	wo	BB-736	N45CF
BB-395	XA-ASR	BB-479	C-GNBB	BB-566	N300HB	BB-653	VH-FII	BB-737	N703X
BB-396	N326AJ	BB-480	D2-EMX	BB-567	wo	BB-654	N93ZC	BB-738	N520DD
BB-397	F-GOCF	BB-481	HR-ANL	BB-568	G-BGRE	BB-655	N655BA	BB-739	N81RZ
BB-398	N929DM	BB-482	N7166P	BB-569	N40HE	BB-656	YV-1051P	BB-740	wo
BB-399	N399BM	BB-483	N924AC	BB-570	N968T	BB-657	N301PS	BB-741	N75AH
BB-400	wo	BB-484	wo	BB-571	N769MB	BB-658	N747HN	BB-742	XT-MAX
BB-401	SX-APJ	BB-485	N485K	BB-572	N898CA	BB-659	N77QX	BB-743	N28VU
BB-402	N318W	BB-486	N56DA	BB-574	C-GZRX	BB-660	VH-LKF	BB-744	F-GGLA
BB-403	C-FGFZ	BB-487	G-KVIP	BB-575	D-IFUN	BB-661	N777SS	BB-745	N428P
BB-404	N315MS	BB-488	4-G-45/074	BB-576	N81WU	BB-662	wo	BB-746	N925TT
BB-405	N367LF*	BB-490	N988CC	BB-577	CN-CDF	BB-663	5N-IHS	BB-747	N63SK
BB-406	F-GHOC	BB-491	N622KM	BB-578	N130CT	BB-664	N280SC	BB-748	Z-WSG
BB-407	ZS-NUC	BB-492	N64DC	BB-579	P2-MML	BB-666	wfu	BB-749	wfu
BB-409	N222LA	BB-493	N6509F	BB-580	ANE-233	BB-667	C-FWWQ	BB-750	N81TF
BB-410	N200PL	BB-494	N942CF	BB-581	N12NG	BB-668	N196PP	BB-751	N92JR
BB-411	wo	BB-495	EV-7910	BB-582	SE-LTL	BB-669	wo	BB-752	N616GB
BB-412	N316MS	BB-496	wfu	BB-583	N777AQ	BB-670	N7VA	BB-753	F-GERS
BB-413	N456PF	BB-497	N72MM	BB-584	LN-MOB	BB-671	C-GFSG	BB-754	N244JS
BB-414	N600DM	BB-498	N6507B	BB-585	N143DE	BB-672	240	BB-755	N711AW
BB-415	P2-CAA	BB-499	N499TT	BB-586	N653TB	BB-673	N503RM*	BB-756	ZS-LWD
BB-416	ZS-KZU	BB-500	wo	BB-587	N200BH	BB-674	N51EE	BB-757	C-GBBS
BB-417	N201KA	BB-501	N175GM	BB-588	N578BM	BB-675	SE-IUX	BB-758	N20RE
BB-418	wfu	BB-502	N275X	BB-589	N911ND	BB-676	F-GHVV	BB-759	7T-VRS
BB-419	OY-BVB	BB-503	N503WJ	BB-590	N524FS	BB-677	N721RD	BB-760	N3710A
BB-420	N420TA	BB-504	wo	BB-592	N432FA	BB-678	N811FA	BB-761	N78CT
BB-421	A2-AEZ	BB-505	C-GKBP	BB-593	N711KB	BB-679	N1194C	BB-762	N762KA
BB-422	N501EB	BB-506	N8SV	BB-594	ZS-OYP	BB-680	N919WM	BB-763	N56KA
BB-423	XB-HDY	BB-507	N507K	BB-595	N927JC	BB-681	F-GGPR	BB-764	ZS-OUT
BB-424	N470TC	BB-508	wo	BB-596	N72SE	BB-682	N425AP	BB-765	N765WA
BB-425	N2057S	BB-509	N72RL	BB-597	ZS-MSK	BB-683	ZS-OTP	BB-766	N52GP
BB-426	N70RD	BB-511	N202AJ	BB-598	YV-335CP	BB-684	G-ROWN	BB-767	wo
BB-427	N101GQ	BB-512	N512KA	BB-599	N48CR	BB-685	N29HF	BB-768	N413DM
BB-428	N106PA	BB-513	C-GMOC	BB-600	N500W	BB-686	N3663M	BB-769	N623VP
BB-429	N409RA	BB-514	N335TA	BB-601	N976KC	BB-687	SE-INI	BB-770	wo
BB-430	N1YS	BB-515	F-GKII	BB-602	N981LE	BB-688	ZS-OUI	BB-771	ANE-231
BB-431	5U-ABY	BB-516	N281JH	BB-603	N70RB	BB-689	N364EA	BB-772	N111PV
BB-432	N200AU	BB-517	YV-237CP	BB-604	N944LS	BB-690	VH-DYN	BB-773	N500CS
BB-433	N94FG	BB-518	N83GA	BB-605	N485R	BB-691	N84CQ	BB-774	N8NX
BB-434	N50AJ	BB-519	N721SW	BB-606	LV-WIO	BB-692	RP-C264	BB-775	7T-VRT
BB-435	XC-BCN	BB-520	2840	BB-607	ZS-LTE	BB-693	C-GXHN	BB-776	N899SD
BB-436	N382ME	BB-521	N200QN	BB-608	N284K	BB-694	EJC-117	BB-777	I-PIAH
BB-437	N503P	BB-522	3150	BB-610	XA-...	BB-696	5Y-HHK	BB-778	N266RH
BB-438	N438HT	BB-523	N500DW	BB-611	N25MR	BB-697	N5UN	BB-779	YV-....
BB-439	F-GGLN	BB-524	N524MR	BB-612	N506GT	BB-698	XT-MBA	BB-780	N780RC
BB-440	YV-238CP	BB-525	ZS-MFC	BB-613	N613CS	BB-699	LV-OFT	BB-781	N37NC
BB-441	N79CF	BB-526	OE-BBB	BB-614	A2-KAS	BB-700	N440WA	BB-782	wfu
BB-442	N442KA	BB-527	C-FIFO	BB-615	N383JP	BB-701	YV-O-SATA	BB-783	N25KA
BB-443	N700Z	BB-528	N700BE	BB-616	F-GGMV	BB-702	wo	BB-784	PT-OSR
BB-444	N444EB	BB-529	VH-NTE	BB-617	HP-960P	BB-703	HC-...	BB-785	N85FC
BB-445	N790RM	BB-530	ZS-DSL	BB-618	N269BW	BB-704	A2-AJK	BB-786	N120P
BB-446	N232JS	BB-532	N37CB	BB-619	101003	BB-705	OY-BVW	BB-787	C-FZVW
BB-447	N356GA	BB-533	VH-XDB	BB-620	D2-FEI	BB-706	ZS-NBO	BB-788	N551JL

BB-789	N905GP	BB-874	N4042J	BB-957	N800TT	BB-1040	N47DG	BB-1129	CS-DDF
BB-790	N64GA	BB-875	PT-WEG	BB-958	wo	BB-1041	VH-OYD	BB-1130	N200QS
BB-791	N791EB	BB-876	F-ZBFK/96	BB-959	N469TA	BB-1042	N142EB	BB-1131	HP-1180
BB-792	N110G	BB-877	N508MV	BB-960	N960GK	BB-1043	N277JJ	BB-1132	N127MJ
BB-793	wfu	BB-878	wo	BB-961	ZS-ACS	BB-1044	G-BPPM	BB-1133	wfu
BB-794	PK-VKB	BB-879	N4PT	BB-962	N437WF	BB-1045	N810K	BB-1134	N27RC
BB-795	N825RT	BB-880	N53KA	BB-963	RP-C367	BB-1046	Z-APG	BB-1135	N74GS
BB-796	YV-401CP	BB-881	N881CS	BB-964	VH-SBM	BB-1047	N147NA	BB-1136	LN-VIZ
BB-797	G-BVMA	BB-882	N56AP	BB-965	N300AJ	BB-1048	G-FPLB	BB-1137	N333AP
BB-799	N269LS	BB-883	N883BB	BB-966	G-BYCP	BB-1049	HK-4256	BB-1138	ZS-SOL
BB-800	N1TX	BB-884	N49JG	BB-967	N75ZT	BB-1050	N925B	BB-1139	N690SC
BB-801	N244CH	BB-885	N146MH	BB-968	NZ1885	BB-1051	D-ICIR	BB-1140	N888ZX
BB-802	wo	BB-886	N146MD	BB-969	N969WB	BB-1053	N132N	BB-1141	N500LP
BB-803	5Y-TWA	BB-887	N87699	BB-970	wfu	BB-1054	NZ1881	BB-1142	N68MY
BB-804	N174WB	BB-888	N70CU	BB-971	PT-MMB	BB-1055	N6UD	BB-1143	N23WS
BB-805	wo	BB-889	ZS-LAW	BB-972	VT-EHB	BB-1056	VH-FDO	BB-1144	LN-TWL
BB-806	N975SC	BB-890	N100PY	BB-973	C-FEVC	BB-1057	N220TB	BB-1145	N566TC
BB-807	7T-VRO	BB-891	C-GHDP	BB-974	HK-3507	BB-1058	C-FWXB	BB-1146	N194TR
BB-808	N53RT	BB-892	N81LT	BB-975	RP-C755	BB-1059	N818PF	BB-1147	N647JM
BB-809	5N-AMU	BB-893	N762NB	BB-976	N83PH	BB-1060	D2-FEG	BB-1148	N525SK
BB-810	N14TF	BB-894	N969MA	BB-977	N607KW	BB-1061	N50DY	BB-1149	ZS-OED
BB-811	AEE-101	BB-896	N850BK	BB-978	N877RC	BB-1062	PP-CBD	BB-1150	VH-URU
BB-812	C-GJFY	BB-897	D-IEFB	BB-979	N22TP	BB-1063	HR-ASY	BB-1151	N151WT
BB-813	ZS-PAM	BB-898	N911SR	BB-980	GN-8595	BB-1064	N824S	BB-1152	ZS-NJM
BB-814	XA-RMX	BB-899	N1KA	BB-981	N404FA	BB-1065	N234KW	BB-1153	N1891S
BB-815	wo	BB-900	wo	BB-982	N800PK	BB-1066	N50KG	BB-1154	N6683W
BB-816	N900RH	BB-901	N26UT	BB-983	D-ISAZ	BB-1067	N860H	BB-1155	N200UW
BB-817	N56RT	BB-902	N65TW	BB-984	HI-701SP	BB-1068	HK-3554	BB-1156	N504GF
BB-818	N145JP	BB-903	A2-BHM	BB-985	wo	BB-1069	N828FM	BB-1157	RP-C5555
BB-819	N500KA	BB-904	N430MC	BB-986	PT-WOF	BB-1070	ZS-NBJ	BB-1158	N66LM
BB-820	N369TA	BB-905	N185DH	BB-987	N200HD	BB-1071	N14HG	BB-1159	N552TT
BB-821	G-CLOW	BB-906	YV-2350P	BB-988	5Y-HHA	BB-1072	CNA-NG	BB-1160	N444KA
BB-822	N250TM	BB-907	N1860N	BB-989	N850AT	BB-1073	CNA-NH	BB-1161	N27CV
BB-824	N919RE	BB-908	N999EG	BB-990	N990JC	BB-1074	N74LV	BB-1162	wo
BB-825	N825KA	BB-909	SE-KDK	BB-992	N992TJ	BB-1075	N75LV	BB-1163	N200EW
BB-826	N800CG	BB-910	N910AJ	BB-993	N32LJ	BB-1076	C9-PMZ	BB-1164	N801NA
BB-827	N20AE	BB-911	N265EJ	BB-994	N99LL	BB-1077	ZS-ZXX	BB-1165	1165
BB-828	C-GJJT	BB-912	C-GFSH	BB-995	N454DC	BB-1078	N129TT	BB-1166	N97SZ
BB-829	LN-NOA	BB-913	N9WR	BB-996	N247JM	BB-1079	N200NA	BB-1167	N35GR
BB-830	N88MT	BB-914	ZS-TNY	BB-997	N7NA	BB-1080	N720MP	BB-1168	N844MP
BB-831	F-OHCP	BB-915	N333RD	BB-998	N899MC	BB-1081	N6531N	BB-1169	N40BC
BB-832	wo	BB-916	N770HM	BB-999	ZS-LFW	BB-1082	TC-FIR	BB-1170	N55PC
BB-833	N833RL	BB-917	N95TT	BB-1000	N580BK	BB-1083	VH-ZEK	BB-1171	N786DG
BB-834	N929SG	BB-918	N918TC	BB-1001	N772AF	BB-1084	N569SC	BB-1172	VH-FDG
BB-835	N84PA	BB-919	N505AM	BB-1002	N282CT	BB-1085	N63686	BB-1173	N3PX
BB-836	D2-EBF	BB-920	F-GPAC	BB-1003	N58GA	BB-1086	XA-GEC	BB-1174	N200MP
BB-837	ZS-LBD	BB-921	D-IKOB	BB-1004	N104CX	BB-1087	NZ1883	BB-1175	N515CR
BB-838	wo	BB-922	N1926A	BB-1005	D-ICKM	BB-1088	N68FA	BB-1176	N904DG
BB-839	N21FG	BB-923	N316JP	BB-1006	CN-TPH	BB-1089	N87SA	BB-1177	N608JR
BB-840	N712GJ	BB-924	N107MG	BB-1007	N514MA	BB-1090	N49SK	BB-1178	NZ1884
BB-841	N366EA	BB-925	N282SJ	BB-1008	NZ1882	BB-1091	N529NA	BB-1179	N204WB
BB-842	N204JS	BB-926	N203LG	BB-1009	N6451D	BB-1092	YV-O-PTJ-2	BB-1180	N221SP
BB-843	N211CP	BB-927	927	BB-1010	N702MA	BB-1094	N1925P	BB-1181	F-GJBS
BB-844	wfu	BB-928	N627FB	BB-1011	N843BC	BB-1095	N200DA	BB-1182	N416CS
BB-845	OY-GRB	BB-929	N999GA	BB-1012	N200MJ	BB-1099	N60AA	BB-1183	N91HT
BB-846	ZS-MIM	BB-930	N930SP	BB-1013	N628DS	BB-1100	N63791	BB-1184	N93NP
BB-847	N847BA	BB-931	N995MS	BB-1014	N6308F	BB-1101	N395AM	BB-1186	N186EB
BB-848	N848NA	BB-932	101004	BB-1015	N216RP	BB-1102	F-ZBFJ/98	BB-1187	N200SV
BB-849	N711MZ	BB-933	OE-FRF	BB-1016	N786SR	BB-1103	N361EA	BB-1188	wo
BB-850	N3CR	BB-934	N38381	BB-1017	N385MC	BB-1104	N1620	BB-1189	ZS-...
BB-851	N208F	BB-935	N935AJ	BB-1018	ZS-LFU	BB-1106	wo	BB-1190	PT-XEG
BB-852	N46BR	BB-936	VH-OWN	BB-1019	VH-JJR	BB-1107	N456ES	BB-1191	N177CN
BB-853	C-GADI	BB-937	D2-ERK	BB-1020	YV-488CP	BB-1108	XC-AA50	BB-1192	N61AP
BB-854	HK-3214	BB-938	N132K	BB-1021	N678SS	BB-1109	F-GLLH	BB-1193	N6728H
BB-855	N199MH	BB-939	N125KW	BB-1022	C-FDGP	BB-1110	F-GSEB	BB-1194	N585CE
BB-856	wo	BB-940	C-FZPW	BB-1023	N125NC	BB-1111	N83KA	BB-1195	ZS-MCC
BB-857	5V-MCG	BB-941	ZS-MIN	BB-1024	N83RZ	BB-1112	N311MP	BB-1196	Z-ZLT
BB-858	5V-MCH	BB-942	N4OL	BB-1025	N22F	BB-1113	ZS-OTS	BB-1197	N347D
BB-859	wo	BB-943	N280YR	BB-1026	D2-FFK	BB-1114	N872CA	BB-1198	N198DM
BB-860	N84PC	BB-944	G-FPLA	BB-1027	ZS-NAW	BB-1115	C-FLRM	BB-1199	PR-BLP
BB-861	N727BW	BB-945	VH-HLJ	BB-1028	N62569	BB-1116	F-GDJS	BB-1200	N100LA*
BB-862	N207DB	BB-946	N1850X	BB-1029	N176M	BB-1118	N586UC	BB-1201	N53GA
BB-863	N80WM	BB-947	N500WF	BB-1030	N843FC	BB-1119	wo	BB-1202	VP-BYR
BB-864	N847TS	BB-948	N25CS	BB-1031	N6644J	BB-1120	N120NA	BB-1203	N177LA
BB-865	N32SV	BB-949	N567JD	BB-1032	F-GJMJ	BB-1121	N6604L	BB-1204	B-3551
BB-866	VH-MSZ	BB-950	N8NA	BB-1033	wo	BB-1122	N87CF	BB-1205	B-3552
BB-867	ZS-PUF	BB-951	LX-ALX	BB-1034	N185MV	BB-1123	N74ML	BB-1206	B-3553
BB-868	wfu	BB-952	N185XP	BB-1035	N712GK	BB-1124	I-ASMI	BB-1207	N3ZC
BB-869	N31FM	BB-953	N24GN	BB-1036	N6271C	BB-1125	VH-KCH	BB-1208	N200SE
BB-870	LV-WEW	BB-954	ZS-LFM	BB-1037	VH-FDI	BB-1126	C-GWXH	BB-1209	N126SP
BB-872	N872BA	BB-955	N933RT	BB-1038	ZS-MES	BB-1127	5Y-JJZ	BB-1210	SE-IXC
BB-873	N525JA	BB-956	PH-ECF	BB-1039	N124GA	BB-1128	C-GGGQ	BB-1211	N10EC

BB-1212	N54FB	BB-1296	ZS-OSH	BB-1379	F-ZBMB/97	BB-1466	LN-MOH	BB-1548	OY-EEF
BB-1213	N109MD	BB-1297	N23WJ	BB-1380	N200NR	BB-1467	N95GA	BB-1549	G-MAMD
BB-1214	N200GS	BB-1298	N36GS	BB-1381	N300ET	BB-1468	VT-LNT	BB-1550	N42SC
BB-1215	N200KP	BB-1299	N912SV	BB-1382	N97WC	BB-1469	VT-CIL	BB-1551	N151CF
BB-1216	N155AV	BB-1300	N313ES	BB-1383	C-GXHG	BB-1470	LN-MOI	BB-1552	VH-NSN
BB-1217	N697P	BB-1302	C-GXHS	BB-1384	C-GACN	BB-1471	N5TW	BB-1553	N200ZK
BB-1218	N740P	BB-1303	N940HC	BB-1385	501	BB-1472	VH-MYO	BB-1554	N38WV
BB-1219	N301HC	BB-1304	C-FPQQ	BB-1386	504	BB-1473	OO-LET	BB-1555	N98DA
BB-1220	TR-LDM	BB-1305	C-GXHR	BB-1387	507	BB-1474	ZS-NKC	BB-1556	N556BA
BB-1221	TF-FMS	BB-1306	N501HC	BB-1388	510	BB-1475	ZS-NKE	BB-1557	G-SPOR
BB-1222	ZS-LNR	BB-1307	N1547V	BB-1389	N277GE	BB-1476	N109GE	BB-1558	PT-WNN
BB-1223	N586BC	BB-1308	N1509G	BB-1390	F-GMGB	BB-1477	N200PU	BB-1559	N1114K
BB-1224	C-FWXI	BB-1309	C-GACA	BB-1391	D2-ESP	BB-1478	EC-J..	BB-1560	N30VP
BB-1225	N848PF	BB-1310	N989LA	BB-1392	HK-3704X	BB-1479	TG-HYD	BB-1561	N200HW
BB-1226	N225WL	BB-1311	N887FB	BB-1393	N200ZT	BB-1480	N1559G	BB-1562	ZS-PPG
BB-1227	HK-3432	BB-1312	N312JC	BB-1394	N625N	BB-1481	N200RS	BB-1563	VT-BAL
BB-1228	N85GA	BB-1313	N312SB	BB-1395	N132MC	BB-1482	N62FB	BB-1564	G-IMGL
BB-1229	D-IBAD	BB-1314	CR-843	BB-1396	N3620M	BB-1483	N572P	BB-1565	D-IAJK
BB-1230	N224P	BB-1315	HS-DCF	BB-1397	N77HD	BB-1484	N6182A	BB-1566	LV-WYC
BB-1231	N360EA	BB-1316	S7-SMB	BB-1398	YV-121CP	BB-1485	VT-BSA	BB-1567	VT-SDJ
BB-1232	C-GBYN	BB-1317	VT-RSB	BB-1399	F-GJFE	BB-1486	VT-EBB	BB-1568	D-ILLF
BB-1233	N74AW	BB-1318	ZS-MMV	BB-1400	D-ICHG	BB-1487	N133K	BB-1569	HB-GPH
BB-1234	ZS-FDR	BB-1319	wo	BB-1401	ZS-...	BB-1488	N1568E	BB-1570	G-ORJA
BB-1235	N95CT	BB-1320	N825ST	BB-1402	N791DC	BB-1489	ZS-SMC	BB-1571	N80BC
BB-1236	VT-ENM	BB-1321	N133GA	BB-1403	N33BK	BB-1490	VH-SMZ	BB-1572	VT-TVS
BB-1237	N7250T	BB-1322	N96GP	BB-1404	N793DC	BB-1491	N700NA	BB-1573	N690L
BB-1238	N212JB	BB-1323	N4KU	BB-1405	RP-C2100	BB-1492	N44NL	BB-1574	N429PL
BB-1239	N895TT	BB-1324	VH-MVY	BB-1406	N212GA	BB-1493	N3015Q	BB-1575	VH-AYC
BB-1240	N200TK	BB-1325	ZS-NVP	BB-1407	OO-SKM	BB-1494	N3026H	BB-1576	N1118G
BB-1241	N7256K	BB-1326	N62WC	BB-1408	N764CA	BB-1495	N3051K	BB-1577	N33AR
BB-1242	N242NA	BB-1327	N67SD	BB-1409	10010	BB-1496	TC-OZD	BB-1578	PT-FFS
BB-1243	N200HX	BB-1328	N1553M	BB-1410	PP-EJG	BB-1497	N18AF	BB-1579	C-GYSC
BB-1244	F-OINC	BB-1329	VN-B594	BB-1411	10011	BB-1498	N777AJ	BB-1580	N345WK
BB-1245	N776RM	BB-1330	N92WC	BB-1412	N38VV	BB-1499	wfu	BB-1581	N613TA
BB-1246	N207CM	BB-1331	N88JH	BB-1413	10012	BB-1500	RP-C1502	BB-1582	N43TL
BB-1247	N48CS	BB-1332	N444BK	BB-1414	10013	BB-1501	N145AJ	BB-1583	N400GW
BB-1248	VT-ENL	BB-1333	VH-MVL	BB-1415	10014	BB-1502	ZS-NXT	BB-1584	PT-WNQ
BB-1249	N879C	BB-1334	LN-MOJ	BB-1416	VH-MWQ	BB-1503	N363D	BB-1585	N1104X
BB-1250	N363CA	BB-1335	N335KW	BB-1417	N203TW	BB-1504	N60383	BB-1586	N97WE
BB-1251	ZS-LTG	BB-1336	N89UA	BB-1418	VH-MWU	BB-1505	VH-HPX	BB-1587	N123ML
BB-1252	N634TT	BB-1337	N330CS	BB-1419	C-GNAX	BB-1506	N95AN	BB-1588	LV-YCS
BB-1253	ZS-OVX	BB-1338	C-GXHD	BB-1420	N212LW	BB-1507	C-GBBG	BB-1589	PT-MJD
BB-1254	VT-EPA	BB-1339	C-GNAM	BB-1421	N715CQ	BB-1508	N288KM	BB-1590	LN-MOT
BB-1255	N152RP	BB-1340	OY-GMA	BB-1422	N125TS	BB-1509	N716TA	BB-1591	D-IPSY
BB-1256	N230DC	BB-1341	OY-GEU	BB-1423	N351SA	BB-1510	N208TS	BB-1592	wo
BB-1257	N606AJ	BB-1342	OY-GEW	BB-1424	VH-MWX	BB-1511	N56AY	BB-1593	N1093Z
BB-1258	N2748X	BB-1343	C-GXHF	BB-1425	N292SN	BB-1512	D2-EDD	BB-1594	N980GB
BB-1259	N800MG	BB-1344	ZS-PAN	BB-1427	ZS-NOW	BB-1513	N415RB	BB-1595	D-IATM
BB-1260	N2PX	BB-1345	N887JC	BB-1428	N660MW	BB-1514	N31SV	BB-1596	N82PK
BB-1261	N717DC	BB-1346	N800KT	BB-1429	N80BT	BB-1515	ZS-TOB	BB-1597	N718RJ
BB-1262	N800NR	BB-1347	F-GJFC	BB-1430	VH-MWZ	BB-1516	N207HB	BB-1598	N523GM
BB-1263	N20DH	BB-1348	OO-SKL	BB-1431	JA8705	BB-1517	D-IANA	BB-1599	C-FGWD
BB-1264	D-IAKK	BB-1349	D-IBFS	BB-1432	N43TA	BB-1518	SU-ZBA	BB-1600	N480TC
BB-1265	PT-WSX	BB-1350	A7-AHK	BB-1433	G-FPLD	BB-1519	wo	BB-1601	C-GLLS
BB-1266	VT-VHL	BB-1351	N514TB	BB-1434	4005	BB-1520	N411CC	BB-1602	N203HC
BB-1267	N29997	BB-1352	OB-2	BB-1435	PT-ORB	BB-1521	LV-WOR	BB-1603	PP-ERG
BB-1268	N412SH	BB-1353	A2-AGO	BB-1436	93303	BB-1522	ZS-OBB	BB-1604	JA01EP
BB-1269	F-GJFA	BB-1354	N875DM	BB-1437	N34LT	BB-1523	N3250V	BB-1605	N923FP
BB-1270	PT-LPG	BB-1355	N480BR	BB-1438	N8017M	BB-1524	wo	BB-1606	N2326J
BB-1271	N37GA	BB-1356	N161RC	BB-1439	N38JV	BB-1525	N260G	BB-1607	ZS-DJA
BB-1272	N466MW	BB-1357	N299MK	BB-1440	N655JG	BB-1526	C-FSAT	BB-1608	N2328E
BB-1273	N713RH	BB-1358	N5682P	BB-1441	93304	BB-1527	P2-KSA	BB-1609	N60AJ
BB-1274	N450WH	BB-1359	N90GA	BB-1442	N128VT	BB-1528	ZS-PEZ	BB-1610	C-FSAO
BB-1275	N14NG	BB-1360	N326KW	BB-1443	93305	BB-1529	RP-C8853	BB-1611	HP-1515
BB-1276	VT-EPY	BB-1361	N5552U	BB-1444	N7PA	BB-1530	336	BB-1612	N200ND
BB-1277	N533P	BB-1362	D2-ECX	BB-1445	VT-MPG	BB-1531	N16GF	BB-1613	N209CM
BB-1278	N300TP	BB-1363	3B-SKY	BB-1446	PT-WGS	BB-1532	RP-C3885	BB-1614	N914CT
BB-1279	D-IBAR	BB-1364	N660PB	BB-1447	N70MN	BB-1533	N114HB	BB-1615	EJC-118
BB-1280	C-FAMB	BB-1365	N711VV	BB-1449	LN-MOC	BB-1534	N1074G	BB-1616	LV-YTB
BB-1281	N200RR	BB-1366	N777VG	BB-1450	N213DB	BB-1535	D-IBFT	BB-1617	N688LL
BB-1282	N113US	BB-1367	N55HL	BB-1452	HK-...	BB-1536	N96CE	BB-1618	N1650
BB-1283	D-IBMP	BB-1368	CC-...	BB-1453	7T-VBE	BB-1537	LN-MON	BB-1619	N240AJ
BB-1284	N32WC	BB-1369	D-IKLN	BB-1455	PT-JUB	BB-1538	N363EA	BB-1620	N800BS
BB-1285	N511AS	BB-1370	N79JS	BB-1456	wo	BB-1539	N220AJ	BB-1621	N698P
BB-1286	N921AZ	BB-1371	D2-EOJ	BB-1458	N511RZ	BB-1540	N89WA	BB-1622	N257YA
BB-1287	VT-EQK	BB-1372	N5559X	BB-1459	LN-MOD	BB-1541	N20LB	BB-1623	N603TA
BB-1288	G-VSBC	BB-1373	N25GK	BB-1460	LN-MOE	BB-1542	ZS-ODI	BB-1624	N957CB
BB-1290	N40PT	BB-1374	N784LB	BB-1461	LN-MOF	BB-1543	PT-WLK	BB-1625	N77CV
BB-1291	N333TP	BB-1375	4006	BB-1462	D-IWSH	BB-1544	F-OHJK	BB-1626	N2299W
BB-1292	N122TP	BB-1376	HK-3990X	BB-1463	ZS-...	BB-1545	TC-OZY	BB-1627	N9898
BB-1293	N401HC	BB-1377	F-GNEG	BB-1464	VH-MSM	BB-1546	N770U	BB-1628	N808DS
BB-1294	N295CP	BB-1378	N618	BB-1465	LN-MOG	BB-1547	LN-SUZ	BB-1629	N300FL

BB-1630	N929BW	BB-1713	N96AM	BB-1799	N211HV	BB-1882	VH-FDZ	BL-74	84-0144
BB-1631	N670TA	BB-1714	5Y-ZBA	BB-1800	N600RL	BB-1884	N625GA	BL-75	84-0145
BB-1632	N998SR	BB-1715	N607TA	BB-1801	N602MJ	BB-1885	N36585	BL-76	84-0146
BB-1633	D-IEDI	BB-1716	D-IBFE	BB-1802	N5092S	BB-1886	N509FP	BL-77	84-0147
BB-1634	N567US	BB-1718	N13LY	BB-1803	XA-...	BB-1887	N36987	BL-78	84-0148
BB-1635	N831TM	BB-1719	N45SQ	BB-1804	4X-...	BB-1889	N36739	BL-79	84-0149
BB-1636	N771MG	BB-1720	N208CW	BB-1805	ZS-TIP	BB-1890	N6190F	BL-80	84-0150
BB-1637	wo	BB-1722	N773TP	BB-1806	N4476Y	BB-1891	N6191H	BL-81	84-0151
BB-1638	N777AG	BB-1723	N521DG	BB-1807	N433HC	BB-1892	N3732K	BL-82	84-0152
BB-1639	VH-IWO	BB-1725	N609TA	BB-1808	TG-...	BB-1893	N36893	BL-83	84-0153
BB-1640	N25WC	BB-1726	N515CK	BB-1809	N61369	BB-1894	N6194X	BL-84	84-0154
BB-1641	VH-HWO	BB-1728	N946CE	BB-1811	4X-...	Super King Air 200C		BL-85	84-0155
BB-1642	N717LW	BB-1729	5B-CKJ	BB-1812	VH-AMR	BL-1	5A-DDT	BL-86	84-0156
BB-1643	VH-LWO	BB-1730	N611TA	BB-1813	VH-MVS	BL-2	5Y-EKO	BL-87	84-0157
BB-1644	PNC-0225	BB-1731	N942CE	BB-1814	VH-AMS	BL-3	N39PH	BL-88	84-0158
BB-1645	N777HF	BB-1732	PK-RGI	BB-1815	VT-JVL	BL-4	ZS-NUF	BL-89	84-0159
BB-1646	N399CW	BB-1733	402	BB-1816	N444LP	BL-5	N514RD	BL-90	84-0160
BB-1647	N467BC	BB-1734	G-MOUN	BB-1817	LV-...	BL-6	5A-DDY	BL-91	84-0161
BB-1648	N788TA	BB-1735	N612TA	BB-1818	VT-UPG	BL-7	HB-GJD	BL-92	84-0162
BB-1649	N154DF	BB-1736	N948CE	BB-1819	4X-...	BL-8	ZS-NAX	BL-93	84-0163
BB-1650	5X-...	BB-1737	N263SP	BB-1820	N47RM	BL-9	VH-NTG	BL-94	84-0164
BB-1651	N74RG	BB-1738	N507SC	BB-1821	N5021S	BL-10	5Y-BLA	BL-95	84-0165
BB-1652	LV-ZRG	BB-1739	wo	BB-1822	N203RC	BL-11	F-GRSO	BL-96	84-0166
BB-1653	N345DG	BB-1740	N170SE	BB-1823	N299AL	BL-12	VH-NTH	BL-97	84-0167
BB-1654	ZS-PMM	BB-1741	D-IIAH	BB-1824	N277WC	BL-13	OY-JAR	BL-98	84-0168
BB-1655	N1655M	BB-1742	ZS-CBL	BB-1825	I-MTOP	BL-14	N3697T	BL-99	wo
BB-1656	N706TA	BB-1743	N60AR	BB-1826	N205SP	BL-15	N215AA	BL-100	84-0170
BB-1657	N300PU	BB-1744	403	BB-1827	N667CC	BL-16	OO-LAC	BL-101	84-0171
BB-1658	N840CP	BB-1745	N615TA	BB-1828	N401SK	BL-17	N76HM	BL-102	84-0172
BB-1659	N911SF	BB-1746	N510GS	BB-1829	G-RAFJ	BL-18	3280	BL-103	84-0173
BB-1660	N40PJ	BB-1747	G-SGEC	BB-1830	G-RAFK	BL-19	3240	BL-104	84-0174
BB-1661	XA-...	BB-1748	C-GSAE	BB-1831	VT-SAZ	BL-20	5Y-LRS	BL-105	84-0175
BB-1662	S5-CEC	BB-1749	N616TA	BB-1832	G-RAFL	BL-21	C9-ASV	BL-106	84-0176
BB-1663	N46BM	BB-1750	N726CB	BB-1833	G-RAFM	BL-22	P2-HCN	BL-107	84-0177
BB-1664	SU-BNJ	BB-1751	N617TA	BB-1834	N399AE	BL-23	YV-403CP	BL-108	84-0178
BB-1665	N111MD	BB-1752	XA-...	BB-1835	G-RAFN	BL-25	wo	BL-109	84-0179
BB-1666	N401CG	BB-1753	N520DG	BB-1836	G-RAFO	BL-26	VH-FDB	BL-110	84-0180
BB-1667	N968MB	BB-1754	N618TA	BB-1837	G-RAFP	BL-27	N44MR	BL-111	84-0181
BB-1668	N6WU	BB-1755	PR-APJ	BB-1838	XA-...	BL-28	FAB 018	BL-112	84-0182
BB-1669	N115CT	BB-1756	N264SP	BB-1839	N712RH	BL-29	ZS-PEA	BL-118	84-0484
BB-1670	N3117N	BB-1757	N261BC	BB-1840	EC-IUX	BL-30	VH-NTS	BL-119	84-0485
BB-1671	YV-949CP	BB-1758	N619TA	BB-1841	N69LS	BL-31	VH-KFN	BL-120	84-0486
BB-1672	D-IVIP	BB-1759	N1Z	BB-1842	VH-MVJ	BL-32	ZS-CVH	BL-121	84-0487
BB-1673	ZS-RAF	BB-1760	N311G	BB-1843	N356CC	BL-33	wo	BL-122	84-0488
BB-1674	N404PT	BB-1761	N459DF	BB-1844	N99ML	BL-34	652	BL-123	84-0489
BB-1675	OY-PCL	BB-1762	N415TM	BB-1845	N912JS	BL-35	wo	BL-124	N149Z
BB-1676	N31094	BB-1763	N5063K	BB-1846	N10CW	BL-36	N111NS	BL-125	VH-BRF
B3-1677	N200HK	BB-1764	ZS-PGB	BB-1847	N635SF	BL-37	5Y-TWC	BL-126	wo
BB-1678	HS-ADS	BB-1765	SU-...	BB-1848	N215HC	BL-38	VH-CBZ	BL-127	SE-LKY
BB-1679	N55MP	BB-1766	N315N	BB-1849	N924JD	BL-39	P2-SIA	BL-128	N361TD
BB-1680	N604TA	BB-1767	N111JW*	BB-1850	N299AK	BL-40	OY-GEB	BL-129	wo
BB-1681	XA-...	BB-1768	N637WM	BB-1851	C6-...	BL-41	VH-OYK	BL-130	C-GWXM
BB-1682	N888FV	BB-1769	N80VP	BB-1852	N6152L	BL-42	C-GIND	BL-131	VQ-T..
BB-1683	N511SD	BB-1770	N4270Y	BB-1853	N45RR*	BL-43	wo	BL-132	SE-KFP
BB-1684	N808WD	BB-1771	N818AG	BB-1854	N927BG*	BL-44	C-GDPB	BL-133	VQ-T..
BB-1685	N52SZ	BB-1772	N28VM	BB-1855	N214TP	BL-45	651	BL-134	N134WJ
BB-1686	VT-GUJ	BB-1773	N777SW	BB-1856	ZS-PCH	BL-46	N312ME	BL-135	D2-ECY
BB-1687	N42LW	BB-1774	N4053H	BB-1857	N788SF	BL-47	wo	BL-136	N136AJ
BB-1688	N203TS	BB-1775	VT-MPT	BB-1858	N200HF	BL-48	VH-MSU	BL-137	VH-HPP
BB-1689	LV-ZYB	BB-1776	N23EH	BB-1859	XA-...	BL-49	D-ICWM	BL-138	VH-HPZ
BB-1690	N200NW	BB-1777	N33LA	BB-1860	ZS-...	BL-50	N58AS	BL-139	VT-SRC
BB-1691	LN-MOO	BB-1778	N1LF	BB-1861	OY-LLL	BL-51	GN-8270	BL-140	PK-CAK
BB-1692	N771SC	BB-1779	N282JD	BB-1862	N225WC	BL-52	wo	BL-141	G-ZAPT
BB-1693	N317RT	BB-1780	N46TF	BB-1863	N6203T	BL-53	N157A	BL-142	N524GM
BB-1694	ST-HAL	BB-1781	N908BS	BB-1864	N766LF*	BL-54	N654BA	BL-143	N4456A
BB-1695	VH-FDF	BB-1782	N4NU	BB-1865	N6300F*	BL-55	VH-FDA	BL-144	N5139A
BB-1696	VH-FDD	BB-1783	N360X	BB-1866	N922MM*	BL-56	VT-EID	BL-145	N4489A
BB-1697	F-....	BB-1784	N710JB	BB-1867	N119AR	BL-57	CNA-NI	BL-146	N5155A
BB-1698	N703RM	BB-1785	N101SG	BB-1868	N5078O	BL-61	N661BA	BL-148	N36948
BB-1699	N403J	BB-1786	N626TA	BB-1869	N5109V	BL-62	N662BA	BL-149	N36949
BB-1700	TC-OPM	BB-1787	VH-MSH	BB-1870	N4925T	BL-63	wo	Super King Air 200T	
BB-1701	N677JE	BB-1788	VT-...	BB-1871	N432LM*	BL-64	N1240S	BT-1	F-GALN
BB-1702	LV-ZTV	BB-1789	ZS-PEI	BB-1872	N510UF	BL-65	N399AS	BT-2	F-GALP
BB-1703	N68MN	BB-1790	C-GSAV	BB-1873	N267CB*	BL-66	YV-2323P	BT-3	N2UW
BB-1704	N418J	BB-1791	N252CP	BB-1874	N6194V	BL-67	N70LG	BT-4	AU-871
BB-1705	YV-....	BB-1792	EC-ILE	BB-1875	N6175U	BL-68	VH-FDS	BT-5	A2-MXI
BB-1706	YS-111N	BB-1793	N404J	BB-1876	N716AV	BL-69	N7233P	BT-6	VH-ITA
BB-1707	N605TA	BB-1794	TG-...	BB-1877	LV-...	BL-70	654	BT-7	ZS-OEB
BB-1708	N865PT	BB-1795	N4195S	BB-1878	N750MD*	BL-71	wo	BT-8	D2-...
BB-1709	N68FB	BB-1796	CC-CPB	BB-1879	N36579	BL-72	VH-CWO	BT-9	N120RL
BB-1710	N44KA*	BB-1797	N424RA	BB-1880	VH-FDW	BL-73	84-0143	BT-10	9M-JPD
BB-1711	YV-639CP	BB-1798	PR-LIA	BB-1881	VH-FDR			BT-11	N857GA
BB-1712	YV-639CP								

Ser	Reg	Ser	Reg	Ser	Reg	Ser	Reg	Ser	Reg
BT-12	N859GA	FA-35	N312DB	FA-117	N80BZ	FA-201	N300PH	FL-19	N933CL
BT-13	JA8817	FA-36	N206K	FA-118	653	FA-202	VP-BMK	FL-20	N99U*
BT-14	JA8818	FA-37	N7218Y	FA-119	N118GW	FA-203	XB-ZRH	FL-21	EP-825
BT-15	JA8819	FA-38	N6812W	FA-120	N3025Z	FA-204	D-IBNK	FL-22	N350AJ
BT-16	JA8820	FA-39	C-GHOG	FA-121	N268CB	FA-205	OH-BSA	FL-23	N391RR
BT-17	JA8824	FA-40	N52C	FA-122	N88RY	FA-206	OH-BSB	FL-24	N1551A
BT-18	D2-FMD	FA-41	FAP-18	FA-123	HP-1457	FA-207	CNA-NX	FL-25	N768WT
BT-19	wo	FA-42	N72DK	FA-124	N500FC	FA-208	CNA-NY	FL-26	C-GNLA
BT-20	7T-WRY	FA-43	N827CC	FA-125	N401BL	FA-209	HP-1182	FL-27	N357BB
BT-21	7T-WRZ	FA-44	N20KW	FA-127	N926PR	FA-210	wo	FL-28	N300KA
BT-22	JA8829	FA-45	N223JR	FA-128	wo	FA-211	N822VK	FL-29	VH-PSK
BT-23	VH-LAB	FA-46	N123AF	FA-130	N3AH	FA-212	N54YC	FL-30	PK-RJR
BT-24	wo	FA-47	HK-3556P	FA-131	N87YQ	FA-213	N83RH	FL-31	N126DS
BT-25	AE-574	FA-48	N271BC	FA-132	N184D	FA-214	N967JG*	FL-32	YV-42CP
BT-26	AE-575	FA-49	N312DE	FA-133	N53PE	FA-215	OE-FSO	FL-33	N15WS
BT-27	D-CACB	FA-50	N214EC	FA-134	N38RY	FA-216	N160AB	FL-34	N57SC
BT-28	JA8833	FA-51	N20NK	FA-135	N540CB	FA-217	D-IEBM	FL-35	N470SC
BT-29	N120PR	FA-52	PT-MCM	FA-136	N888AS	FA-218	N193FS	FL-36	N96KA
BT-30	CR-841	FA-53	N736P	FA-137	C-FTLB	FA-219	JA8881	FL-37	wo
BT-31	JA8854	FA-54	N920C	FA-138	N541SC	FA-220	HB-GPI	FL-38	N600CB
BT-32	JA8860	FA-55	N333WC	FA-139	70-YST	FA-221	LV-WLT	FL-39	N395MB
BT-33	HP-1316	FA-56	N7231P	FA-140	N792JM	FA-222	LV-WMA	FL-40	PT-WYO
BT-34	F-GMLT	FA-57	N75ME	FA-141	N632DS	FA-223	OK-GTJ	FL-41	N350VM
BT-35	M41-01	FA-58	N7RC	FA-142	N304JS	FA-224	D-IFFB	FL-42	PT-FGB
BT-36	M41-02	FA-59	N528AM	FA-143	N600KA	FA-225	D-IBAB	FL-43	N5626Y
BT-37	M41-03	FA-60	HK-3659	FA-144	N333DV	FA-226	F-GPRH	FL-44	N904MC
BT-38	M41-04	FA-61	wo	FA-145	N149CC*	FA-227	wo	FL-45	N111SF
BT-39	622	FA-62	N103AL	FA-146	F-GICA	FA-228	OE-FME	FL-46	D-CCBW
BT-40	625	FA-63	N35LW	FA-147	N11GS	FA-229	LV-WIP	FL-47	N350P
BT-41	629	FA-64	N103CW	FA-148	N30FE	*FA-230*	*VT-UPA*	FL-48	N555ZA
BT-42	633	FA-65	N555DX	FA-149	N92DN	*Super King Air 300*		FL-49	N350EB
BT-43	636	FA-66	N29EC	FA-150	wfu	FF-1	N66	FL-50	N300TM
BT-46	*6...*	FA-67	N79TE	FA-151	N1MW	FF-2	N67	FL-51	N75WD
Super King Air B200		FA-68	N300SE	FA-152	N20EW	FF-3	N68	FL-52	B-00135
FG-1	987	FA-69	N531MB	FA-153	N24BL	FF-4	N69	FL-53	HS-SLA
FG-2	*990*	FA-70	wo	FA-154	PT-OJQ	FF-5	N70	FL-54	N8080Q
Super King Air B200CT		FA-71	N7586Z	FA-155	N408C	FF-6	N71	FL-55	YV-112CP
BN-1	CC-DIV	FA-72	N72GA	FA-156	N397WM	FF-7	N72	FL-56	N351GC
BN-2	AE-571	FA-73	N699MW	FA-157	N350DW	FF-8	N73	FL-57	N15WD
BN-3	AE-572	FA-74	XC-AA80	FA-158	YV-2401P	FF-9	N74	FL-58	N8116N
BN-4	AE-573	FA-75	ANE-232	FA-159	HK-3433X	FF-10	N75	FL-59	N964LB
BN-5	703	FA-76	N1BK	FA-160	N3084K	FF-11	N76	FL-60	N224CR
BN-6	N5106F	FA-77	N917WA	FA-161	N221MM	FF-12	N77	FL-61	N57KE
BN-7	N5107Z	FA-78	N740PC	FA-162	N3122Z	FF-13	N78	FL-62	C-FPWR
BN-8	N51488	FA-79	N873CA	FA-163	N3237S	FF-14	N79	FL-63	N350DR
BN-9	*4X-...*	FA-80	N300HH	FA-164	N90WE	FF-15	N80	FL-64	D-CAMM
Super King Air 300		FA-81	N7250L	FA-165	N4NF	FF-16	N81	FL-65	N999MG
FA-1	N6642B	FA-82	N15PX	FA-166	N166SA	FF-17	wo	FL-66	N199Y
FA-2	N251LL	FA-83	XC-AA49	FA-167	N1517K	FF-18	N83	FL-67	N350TR
FA-3	N135MK	FA-84	N22BD	FA-168	N300TN	*FF-19*	*N84*	FL-68	N593MA
FA-4	N111SS	FA-85	N112AB	FA-169	HK-3860	*Super King Air B300C*		FL-69	N273TA
FA-5	N200WB	FA-86	HK-3547	FA-170	HB-GHV	FM-1	F-GOAE	FL-70	N850D
FA-6	N821TB	FA-87	N301CG	FA-171	N300PP	FM-2	HP-2888	FL-71	N38H
FA-7	N800RE	FA-88	N1250	FA-172	N28GC	FM-3	N430JT	FL-72	N3739C
FA-8	N826MA	FA-89	ZS-PJR*	FA-173	N325WP	FM-4	N173S	FL-73	YR-CAA
FA-9	N302NC	FA-90	N544PS	FA-174	PT-FFN	FM-5	N7285Y	FL-74	N317P
FA-10	HK-3828	FA-91	N300MC	FA-175	F-GOOO	FM-6	N5888K	FL-75	D-COLA
FA-11	N132CC	FA-92	PP-EPD	FA-176	XA-ALT	FM-7	N2789A	FL-76	D-CFMA
FA-12	N7202Y	FA-93	N93GA	FA-177	N300RC	FM-8	YV-877CP	FL-77	N988ME
FA-13	N300PR	FA-94	LX-SEA	FA-178	N313BA	FM-9	N4009L	FL-78	N598AC
FA-14	XB-HHA	FA-95	XC-AA46	FA-179	N1548K	FM-10	N1667J	FL-79	P2-PNG
FA-15	N505WR	FA-96	HK-3534	FA-180	wo	*FM-11*	*N4466A*	FL-80	F-GTEM
FA-16	N846BE	FA-97	N97EB	FA-181	N456Q	*Super King Air 350*		FL-81	N507EB
FA-17	N58ES	FA-98	N306M	FA-182	C-FWWK	FL-1	N10TX	FL-82	N4YS
FA-18	N63LP	FA-99	HK-...	FA-183	N19NC	FL-2	N400AL	FL-83	RP-C8300
FA-19	N102PG	FA-100	HK-3648	FA-184	D-IBER	FL-3	N92TW	FL-84	N614ML
FA-20	N7228T	FA-101	HK-3654	FA-185	N341DB	FL-4	N10K	FL-85	HC-...
FA-21	N4600K	FA-102	N195AL	FA-186	N404EW	FL-5	N450LM	FL-86	N27GE
FA-22	HK-...	FA-103	N827DL	FA-187	N350BF	FL-6	N350BS	FL-87	C-FMHD
FA-23	N141SM	FA-104	wo	FA-188	N815D	FL-7	N711VN	FL-88	N1525C
FA-24	N124CM	FA-105	TG-MDN-P	FA-189	SE-KOL	FL-8	N770JH	FL-89	N490TN
FA-25	ZS-PAZ	FA-106	N855RA	FA-190	N100AQ	FL-9	N1SC*	FL-90	VH-FIX
FA-26	PT-OLI	FA-107	N538AM	FA-191	N801AR	FL-10	N350FH	FL-91	N227KM
FA-27	N203RR	FA-108	N494MA	FA-192	D-C...	FL-11	N37390	FL-92	N141DA
FA-28	N401NS	FA-109	wfu	FA-193	N15613	FL-12	N5655K	FL-93	N188MC
FA-29	N300HV	FA-110	N313KY	FA-194	N811LC	FL-13	C-GJLK	FL-94	N983TM
FA-30	N642JL	FA-111	N305SA	FA-195	N195AE	FL-14	N350MR	FL-95	C6-...
FA-31	PP-EJO	FA-112	N300SV	FA-196	N825JG	FL-15	wfu	FL-96	N19GD
FA-32	N100BZ	FA-113	PT-MMC	FA-197	N416DY	FL-16	N350GA	FL-97	D-CFMB
FA-33	N311RF	FA-114	XC-HGI	FA-198	N603WM	FL-17	C-GEAS	FL-98	N8302N
FA-34	N100FL	FA-115	N300CW	FA-199	N30MC	FL-18	N688JB	FL-99	N850MS
		FA-116	N240S	FA-200	N61KA			FL-100	C-FABR

Serial	Reg	Serial	Reg	Serial	Reg	Serial	Reg
FL-101	D-CADN	FL-183	F-GNOE	FL-265	N981LL	FL-347	N350TL
FL-102	S9-TAP	FL-184	N800BJ	FL-266	23053	FL-348	A32-348
FL-103	N6103K	FL-185	N2SM	FL-267	N971LL	FL-349	A32-349
FL-104	N733NM	FL-186	23052	FL-268	N49CL	FL-350	A32-350
FL-105	VT-BHL	FL-187	N819EE	FL-269	C-GOGS	FL-351	A32-351
FL-106	N223P	FL-188	JA862A	FL-270	N4170N	FL-352	N675PC
FL-107	N344L	FL-189	N1562H	FL-271	XA-...	FL-353	C-GMEH
FL-108	B-13153	FL-190	LV-YLC	FL-272	C-GOIC	FL-354	C-FNIL
FL-109	N434BW	FL-191	JA863A	FL-273	OY-JVL	FL-355	N685BC
FL-110	N921BS	FL-192	VT-MGJ	FL-274	N64GG	FL-356	N455SE
FL-111	B-3581	FL-193	JA864A	FL-275	N275BT	FL-357	F-GKYY
FL-112	N405J	FL-194	VH-KJD	FL-276	D-CLOG	FL-359	N359MB
FL-113	B-3582	FL-195	JA865A	FL-277	XA-RCG	FL-360	N1880C
FL-114	N895CA	FL-196	RP-C2296	FL-278	N350BW	FL-361	VH-OXF
FL-115	N5XM	FL-197	N82WU	FL-279	9H-ADV	FL-362	N300R
FL-116	N711RJ	FL-198	N221G	FL-280	N4380Y	FL-363	N700U
FL-117	N43BG	FL-199	N981AR	FL-281	N552TP	FL-364	N447TF
FL-118	RP-C1728	FL-200	N76PM	FL-282	N350WP	FL-365	N350RR
FL-119	N1558H	FL-201	N2325Y	FL-283	N350NY	FL-366	N366SL
FL-120	F-GPGH	FL-202	N350TF	FL-284	N886AC	FL-367	N160AC
FL-121	N1PD	FL-203	N877WA	FL-285	C-GRJZ	FL-368	OO-SDU
FL-122	9M-DSL	FL-204	N204W	FL-286	G-BZNE	FL-369	N103BE*
FL-123	N350BD	FL-205	PT-WTW	FL-287	N555WQ	FL-370	N74TF
FL-124	D-CKWM	FL-206	YV-910CP	FL-288	N721NB	FL-371	N6171N
FL-125	N32KC	FL-207	N717VL	FL-289	PP-JSC	FL-372	N6172B
FL-126	N124EB	FL-208	C-FJOL	FL-290	N969MB	FL-373	N357RL
FL-127	C-GPPC	FL-209	N454LF	FL-291	N701FC	FL-374	CN-...
FL-128	EC-GSQ	FL-210	N111M	FL-292	JA868A	FL-375	N657PP
FL-129	N46FL	FL-211	N11TE	FL-293	N3253Q	FL-376	JA376N
FL-130	D-CSKY	FL-212	N350AB	FL-294	S9-CAN	FL-377	PR-AEF
FL-131	801	FL-213	N350JB	FL-295	JA869A	FL-378	N225CM
FL-132	802	FL-214	N350CS	FL-296	N877SA	FL-379	N790P
FL-133	N97DR	FL-215	N160SM	FL-297	JA870A	FL-381	N818WV
FL-134	SP-FNS	FL-216	N893MC	FL-298	N151E	FL-382	JA....
FL-135	N283CB*	FL-217	N350BG	FL-299	N3128K	FL-383	N500VL
FL-136	N189MC	FL-218	JA866A	FL-300	N18RN*	FL-384	N455SC
FL-137	RP-C2638	FL-219	N276JB	FL-301	F-GOSB	FL-385	C-GEJE
FL-138	N311GM	FL-220	S9-BAA	FL-302	N42EL	FL-386	N789LL
FL-139	N60CM	FL-221	PT-FSA	FL-303	N551TP	FL-387	N141CE
FL-140	N806JW	FL-222	JA867A	FL-304	N60YP	FL-388	N15EW
FL-141	PT-WND	FL-223	N1WV	FL-305	N351MP	FL-389	VH-WHP
FL-142	N991LL	FL-224	N2535B	FL-306	N525DF	FL-390	N823SD
FL-143	N789SB	FL-225	N57TX	FL-307	23054	FL-391	N142CE
FL-144	N394S	FL-226	N226K	FL-308	N825TS	FL-392	N6192C
FL-145	RP-C2850	FL-227	N823EB	FL-309	N1244J	FL-393	N350HA
FL-146	2011	FL-228	N124DA	FL-310	LV-ZXX	FL-394	N246SD
FL-147	2012	FL-229	OY-MEN	FL-311	D-CUNO	FL-395	HP-...
FL-148	RP-C3500	FL-230	N579MC	FL-312	N350JR	FL-396	N351CB
FL-149	N726T	FL-231	N103RN	FL-313	YV-2663P	FL-397	N220CG
FL-150	VH-SGQ	FL-232	N816DC	FL-314	N350J	FL-398	N6198N
FL-151	HS-ITD	FL-233	N700PG	FL-315	N3115K	FL-399	N504TF
FL-152	PT-WSJ	FL-234	C-FDTC	FL-316	N200VC	FL-400	N40GZ*
FL-153	5N-MAG	FL-235	N325JM	FL-317	C-FPCP	FL-401	N319EE
FL-154	N57VA	FL-236	C-GTEM	FL-318	B-3583	FL-402	N402JL
FL-155	N253AS	FL-237	N115GB	FL-319	N350TV	FL-403	N6113X
FL-156	N350KG	FL-238	5N-MPB	FL-320	N355DM	FL-404	HB-GJS
FL-157	N350LL	FL-239	N655SC	FL-321	N748SB	FL-405	N6165Y
FL-158	N10UN	FL-240	PT-WUT	FL-322	N3222K	FL-406	N828AJ
FL-159	PT-WNL	FL-241	N2341S	FL-323	N350KS	FL-407	N160MW
FL-160	VT-JNK	FL-242	N983AR	FL-324	N793WB	FL-408	N929BG
FL-161	N141K	FL-243	N333M	FL-325	N450DW	FL-409	N409LV*
FL-162	N40593	FL-244	N171CP	FL-326	N350MS	FL-410	D-C...
FL-163	S9-CAM	FL-245	N328AJ	FL-327	N1845	FL-411	N953PC
FL-164	N312RL	FL-246	N87YC	FL-328	EC-IBK	FL-412	N6112G
FL-165	N53TM	FL-247	N516BA	FL-329	N668K	FL-413	N36813
FL-166	XC-CHI	FL-248	N3078W	FL-330	N1253W	FL-414	N19GR
FL-167	N222PV	FL-249	N3080F	FL-331	23055	FL-415	N36715
FL-168	N108NT	FL-250	N81PA	FL-332	N133NL	FL-416	N6116N
FL-169	PT-WSI	FL-251	XA-FCV	FL-333	N390MD	FL-417	N6117C
FL-170	CN-RLE	FL-252	N525BC	FL-334	N350D	FL-418	N888FM
FL-171	N2315A	FL-253	N88WV	FL-335	PR-EDF	FL-419	N36919
FL-172	N511D	FL-254	N3254A	FL-336	N360CB	FL-420	LV-...
FL-173	SU-BMW	FL-255	D-COEB	FL-337	N707FA	FL-421	N350FW
FL-174	C-GFSA	FL-256	N350WD	FL-338	N802BS	FL-422	N3722Y
FL-175	SE-LLU	FL-257	N351DD*	FL-339	A32-339	FL-423	N3723Q
FL-176	23051	FL-258	N583AT	FL-340	HB-GJR	FL-424	N3724Q
FL-177	PT-WAC	FL-259	N327R	FL-341	XA-...	FL-425	N37025
FL-178	N675BC	FL-260	N5256S	FL-342	N512DC	FL-426	N3726E
FL-179	N350S	FL-261	N506MV	FL-343	A32-343	FL-427	N37270
FL-180	JA861A	FL-262	N771HM	FL-344	N72RE	FL-428	N5128X
FL-181	N6789	FL-263	N823SE	FL-345	JA353N	FL-429	N6129Q
FL-182	N128MG	FL-264	N961LL	FL-346	A32-346	FL-430	N631ME

Serial	Reg
FL-431	N6131Q
FL-432	N536BW
FL-435	N36635

Super King Air 350C

Serial	Reg
FN-1	T-721

King Air C-12C

Serial	Reg	Serial	Reg
BC-1	wfu	BD-1	N11
BC-2	N783MC	BD-2	N49R
BC-3	N7247Y	BD-3	N311KB
BC-4	N72470	BD-4	73-1208
BC-5	N540SP	BD-5	N9008U
BC-6	N34QP	BD-6	wfu
BC-7	N40R	BD-7	wo
BC-8	N9998P	BD-8	N12
BC-9	N1560	BD-9	N121CA
BC-10	73-22262	BD-10	73-1214
BC-11	N72472	BD-11	73-1215
BC-12	N48A	BD-12	wfu
BC-13	wfu	BD-13	73-1217
BC-14	N381PD	BD-14	73-1218
BC-15	N222DM	BD-15	76-0158
BC-16	N1559	BD-16	wfu
BC-17	N7074G	BD-17	76-0160
BC-18	N505FK	BD-18	76-0161
BC-19	N634B	BD-19	76-0162
BC-20	N1558	BD-20	76-0163
BC-21	N1554	BD-21	76-0164
BC-22	N703JR	BD-22	wo
BC-23	N369SA	BD-23	76-0166
BC-24	N145MJ	BD-24	76-3239
BC-25	N200NY	BD-25	76-0168
BC-26	N72476	BD-26	N49K
BC-27	76-22551	BD-27	wfu
BC-28	N213UV	BD-28	76-0171
BC-29	N612SA	BD-29	76-0172
BC-30	N1553	BD-30	wfu
BC-31	76-22555		
BC-32	N2MP		
BC-33	N225LH		
BC-34	401		
BC-35	N283B		
BC-36	76-22559		
BC-37	YV-....		
BC-38	76-22561		
BC-39	N1551		
BC-40	76-22563		
BC-41	N101CS		
BC-42	N1SP		
BC-43	77-22932		
BC-44	N258AG		
BC-45	N1549		
BC-46	77-22935		

BC-47	N103BN
BC-48	N45A
BC-49	N635B
BC-50	N1547
BC-51	YV-....
BC-52	77-22941
BC-53	77-22942
BC-54	N7069A
BC-55	77-22944
BC-56	N771AK
BC-57	N7308B
BC-58	N1546
BC-59	N229EM
BC-60	77-22949
BC-61	N636B
BC-62	N637B
BC-63	HP-....
BC-64	78-23128
BC-65	PP-LCB
BC-66	N66000
BC-67	N639B
BC-68	78-23132
BC-69	78-23133
BC-70	N321F
BC-71	78-23135
BC-72	N30W
BC-73	N200ET
BC-74	N121TD
BC-75	N700TG

King Air C-12D/F

BP-1	78-23140
BP-7	974
BP-8	977
BP-9	980
BP-10	982
BP-11	985
BP-22	81-23541
BP-24	81-23543
BP-25	81-23544
BP-26	81-23545
BP-27	81-23546
BP-28	82-23780
BP-29	82-23781
BP-30	82-23782
BP-31	82-23783
BP-32	82-23784
BP-33	82-23785
BP-34	83-24145
BP-35	83-24146
BP-36	83-24147
BP-37	83-24148
BP-38	83-24149
BP-39	83-24150
BP-40	83-0494
BP-41	83-0495
BP-42	83-0496
BP-43	83-0497
BP-44	83-0498
BP-45	83-0499
BP-46	84-24375
BP-47	84-24376
BP-48	84-24377
BP-49	84-24378
BP-50	84-24379
BP-51	84-24380
BP-52	wo
BP-53	85-1262
BP-54	85-1263
BP-55	85-1264
BP-56	85-1265
BP-57	85-1266
BP-58	85-1267
BP-59	85-1268
BP-60	wo
BP-61	85-1270
BP-62	85-1271
BP-63	85-1272
BP-64	86-0084
BP-65	86-0085
BP-66	86-0086
BP-67	86-0087
BP-68	86-0088
BP-69	86-0089
BP-70	87-0160
BP-71	87-0161

King Air C-12J

UD-1	86-0078
UD-2	86-0079
UD-3	86-0080
UD-4	86-0081
UD-5	86-0082
UD-6	86-0083

King Air C-12R

BW-1	92-3327
BW-2	92-3328
BW-3	92-3329
BW-4	94-0315
BW-5	94-0316
BW-6	94-0317
BW-7	94-0318
BW-8	94-0319
BW-9	94-0320
BW-10	94-0321
BW-11	94-0322
BW-12	94-0323
BW-13	94-0324
BW-14	94-0325
BW-15	94-0326
BW-16	95-0088
BW-17	95-0089
BW-18	95-0090
BW-19	95-0091
BW-20	95-0092
BW-21	95-0093
BW-22	95-0094
BW-23	95-0095
BW-24	95-0096
BW-25	95-0097
BW-26	95-0098
BW-27	95-0099
BW-28	95-0100
BW-29	95-0101

King Air RC-12D/H

GR-1	81-23542
GR-2	80-23371
GR-3	80-23377
GR-4	80-23373
GR-5	80-23375
GR-6	78-23141
GR-7	78-23142
GR-8	78-23143
GR-9	78-23144
GR-10	N321P
GR-11	80-23376
GR-12	80-23374
GR-13	80-23378
GR-14	83-24313
GR-15	83-24314
GR-16	83-24315
GR-17	83-24316
GR-18	83-24317
GR-19	83-24318

King Air RC-12G

FC-1	80-23379
FC-2	80-23380
FC-3	80-23372

King Air RC-12K/N/P

FE-1	85-0147
FE-2	85-0148
FE-3	85-0149
FE-4	85-0150
FE-5	wo
FE-6	85-0152
FE-7	85-0153
FE-8	wo
FE-9	85-0155
FE-10	88-0325
FE-11	88-0326
FE-12	88-0327
FE-13	89-0267
FE-14	89-0268
FE-15	89-0269
FE-16	89-0270
FE-17	89-0271
FE-18	wo
FE-19	89-0273
FE-20	89-0274
FE-21	89-0275
FE-22	89-0276
FE-23	91-0516
FE-24	91-0517
FE-25	91-0518
FE-26	92-13120
FE-27	92-13121
FE-28	92-13122
FE-29	92-13123
FE-30	92-13124
FE-31	92-13125
FE-32	93-0697
FE-33	93-0698
FE-34	93-0699
FE-35	93-0700
FE-36	93-0701

King Air UC-12B

BJ-1	wfu
BJ-2	wfu
BJ-3	161187
BJ-4	161188
BJ-5	wo
BJ-6	161190
BJ-7	161191
BJ-8	161192
BJ-9	161193
BJ-10	161194
BJ-11	161195
BJ-12	161196
BJ-13	161197
BJ-14	wfu
BJ-15	wfu
BJ-16	161200
BJ-17	161201
BJ-18	wfu
BJ-19	161203
BJ-20	161204
BJ-21	161205
BJ-22	161206
BJ-23	161306
BJ-24	161307
BJ-25	161308
BJ-26	161309
BJ-27	161310
BJ-28	wfu
BJ-29	161312
BJ-30	161313
BJ-31	wfu
BJ-32	161315
BJ-33	161316
BJ-34	161317
BJ-35	161318
BJ-36	161319
BJ-37	161320
BJ-38	wfu
BJ-39	161322
BJ-40	161323
BJ-41	161324
BJ-42	161325
BJ-43	161326
BJ-44	wfu
BJ-45	161497
BJ-46	161498
BJ-47	wfu
BJ-48	161500
BJ-49	161501
BJ-50	161502
BJ-51	161503
BJ-52	161504
BJ-53	161505
BJ-54	161506
BJ-55	161507
BJ-56	161508
BJ-57	wfu
BJ-58	161510
BJ-59	161511
BJ-60	161512
BJ-61	161513
BJ-62	161514
BJ-63	161515
BJ-64	wfu
BJ-65	161517
BJ-66	161518

King Air UC-12F

BU-1	163553
BU-2	163554
BU-3	163555
BU-4	163556
BU-5	163557
BU-6	163558
BU-7	163559
BU-8	163560
BU-9	163561
BU-10	163562
BU-11	163563
BU-12	163564

King Air UC-12M

BV-1	163836
BV-2	163837
BV-3	163838
BV-4	163839
BV-5	163840
BV-6	163841
BV-7	163842
BV-8	163843
BV-9	163844
BV-10	163845
BV-11	163846
BV-12	163847

Starship

NC-1	wfu
NC-2	wfu
NC-3	wfu
NC-4	wfu
NC-5	wfu
NC-6	N1556S
NC-7	wfu
NC-8	N10TQ
NC-9	wfu
NC-10	wfu
NC-11	wfu
NC-12	wfu
NC-13	wfu
NC-14	wfu
NC-15	wfu
NC-16	wfu
NC-17	wfu
NC-18	wfu
NC-19	wfu
NC-20	wfu
NC-21	wfu
NC-22	wfu
NC-23	wfu
NC-24	wfu
NC-25	wfu
NC-26	wfu
NC-27	wfu
NC-28	wfu
NC-29	N8244L
NC-30	wfu
NC-31	wfu
NC-32	wfu
NC-33	wfu
NC-34	wfu
NC-35	wfu
NC-36	wfu
NC-37	wfu
NC-38	wfu
NC-39	wfu
NC-40	wfu
NC-41	wfu
NC-42	wfu
NC-43	wfu
NC-44	wfu
NC-45	N45FL
NC-46	wfu
NC-47	wfu
NC-48	wfu
NC-49	wfu
NC-50	N500CP*
NC-51	N514RS
NC-52	wfu
NC-53	wfu

Rockwell

Commander

11000	wo
11001	N41T
11002	wo
11003	wo
11004	N57175
11005	HK-2055
11006	HZ-SS1
11007	EC-EIL
11008	wo
11009	N25BD
11010	N690RA
11011	PT-OOH
11012	N885RA
11013	wo
11014	HK-1982
11015	wo
11016	N428SJ
11017	N690WC
11018	XA-PUY
11019	LV-LEY
11020	C-GZON
11021	XC-RAM
11022	TI-...
11023	N9223N
11024	wo
11025	C-FZRQ
11026	VH-NYC
11027	wo
11028	N2DB
11029	wfu
11030	N399GM
11031	N690GK
11032	C-GFPP
11033	HK-2281
11034	N690TR
11035	C-GJFO
11036	PT-LDA
11037	PT-LDL
11038	N33WG
11039	wfu
11040	C-FAKP
11041	N924PC
11042	XA-KUU
11043	N71VE
11044	wo
11045	EP-AGV
11046	N2155B
11047	EP-AGW
11048	wo
11049	wo
11050	wfu
11051	N567R
11052	N780BP
11053	wo
11054	wo
11055	CP-2182
11056	wfu
11057	C-GWEW
11058	EC-HNH
11059	HK-3465P
11060	XA-DER
11061	YV-854CP
11062	VH-UJG
11063	wo
11064	N83G
11065	XB-FYD
11066	N68TD
11067	FAB 028
11068	C-GGOO
11069	wfu
11071	N9175N
11072	wo
11073	HP-....
11074	XB-GJL
11075	EP-AKI

11076	501	11178	N57EC	11260	wfu	11342	N76WA	11429	N771BA
11077	4-901	11179	N375AA	11261	LV-LTU	11343	N706KC	11430	YV-O-MIF-
11078	4-902	11180	YV-907CP	11262	N690DS	11344	wo	11431	N690HS
11079	4-903	11181	6-3201	11263	N57112	11350	N690RD	11432	V5-MGF
11100	wo	11182	EP-AHM	11264	YV-01P	11351	wo	11433	N690XY
11101	VH-AAG	11183	5-2505	11265	I-MAGJ	11352	N721TB	11434	wo
11102	HP-....	11184	wfu	11266	wo	11353	N690JT	11435	N600WS
11103	N690CE	11185	XA-...	11267	XA-GEM	11354	HP-1415	11436	N751BR
11104	C-GAAL	11186	wo	11268	LV-LZM	11355	N303G	11437	N167R
11105	ZS-LRM	11187	N449LC	11269	N4PZ	11356	N711PB	11438	N81703
11106	C-FCZZ	11188	XB-BED	11270	N57292	11357	N690GF	11439	N364WA
11107	CP-...	11189	N737E	11271	N690RE	11358	YV-663CP	11440	N20ME
11108	wfu	11190	YV-2488P	11272	N90AT	11359	N690NA	11441	N6900K
11109	wo	11191	N440CC	11273	N892WA	11360	XB-DMT	11442	LV-MDN
11110	HK-3597	11192	C-GDCL	11274	PT-OFG	11361	N690BH	11443	YV-1050P
11111	N801EB	11193	wfu	11275	wo	11362	wo	11444	N318WA
11112	wo	11194	N690WS	11276	N118CR	11363	N690GS	11445	wo
11113	N57113	11195	N55JS	11277	N690AS	11364	HK-2291X	11446	N137BW
11114	YV-834CP	11196	N52PY	11278	YV-246CP	11365	HK-3561	11447	XC-STA
11115	XC-NAY	11197	wo	11279	C-GEOS	11366	YV-775CP	11448	N246MC
11116	wo	11198	YV-O-GPA-	11280	N699SB	11367	LN-FAH	11449	N28TC
11117	wo	11199	wo	11281	YV-O-MTC-	11368	HP-77PE	11450	XC-HHS
11118	N91384	11200	N921ST	11282	N20EB	11369	N1VQ	11451	N690CP
11119	N690AH	11201	N24CC	11283	VH-PCV	11370	XA-NTC	11452	CS-ASG
11120	N57096	11202	N690AT	11284	ZS-JRA	11371	XB-GDS	11453	HK-2218W
11121	LN-ACE	11203	wo	11285	YV-818P	11372	wo	11454	XA-ABH
11122	HK-3147X	11204	OH-UTI	11286	N286AF	11373	N279DD	11455	N206BN
11123	N112EF	11205	N690HB	11287	N690SD	11374	wo	11456	N267R
11124	wfu	11206	N74GB	11288	YV-192CP	11375	N882AC	11457	N615SB
11125	N690EM	11207	YV-733P	11289	N95JM	11376	PT-LHV	11458	N98AJ
11126	N132JH	11208	N76EC	11290	N290PF	11377	YV-116CP	11459	N40WG
11127	N17HF	11209	N107JJ	11291	wo	11378	YV-143CP	11460	XB-GCU
11128	HK-2282P	11210	N70MD	11292	PJ-CEB	11379	N690CC	11461	YV-188CP
11129	N37BW	11211	D-IBAG	11293	6-3202	11380	wo	11462	N225MM
11130	wfu	11212	EC-EIH	11294	5-4035	11381	N46HA	11463	VH-TSS
11131	N8535	11213	wfu	11295	5-4036	11382	XC-AA85	11464	YV-227CP
11132	D2-EAA	11214	XB-EIH	11296	HK-2414P	11383	N45AZ	11465	PT-MPN
11133	N57133	11215	N32GA	11297	N208CL	11384	N690AX	11466	YV-204CP
11134	C-GHWF	11216	HK-1770G	11298	N690HF	11385	N690TC	11467	N690HT
11135	N744JD	11217	wfu	11299	N121JW	11386	HK-...	11468	YV-797CP
11136	N318TK	11218	N75U	11300	N80TB	11387	N44NC	11469	N13622
11137	N331RC	11219	wfu	11301	OH-ACN	11388	N690ES	11470	N744CH
11138	N690RK	11220	N4717V	11302	HR-...	11389	N700PQ	11471	N3TJ
11139	TI-AXU	11221	HK-3514	11303	N848CE	11390	YV-63CP	11472	YV-...
11140	wo	11222	wo	11304	N823SB	11391	PT-...	11473	wfu
11141	N62366	11223	wo	11305	wo	11392	N460K	11474	5Y-BMY
11142	wo	11224	N200JQ	11306	wo	11393	N690FD	11475	N690LS
11143	EP-AHL	11225	XB-HSE	11307	N690TD	11394	N531GK	11476	N330ES
11144	XB-FOC	11226	N690DB	11308	N99WC	11395	CP-2266	11477	N690CB
11145	XA-...	11227	N50DX	11309	N690EH	11396	wo	11478	N36JF
11146	N690SG	11228	YV-....	11310	N690RC	11397	wo	11479	wo
11147	wo	11229	N30854	11311	N690BM	11398	LV-MAW	11480	N690JK
11148	wfu	11230	LV-LTY	11312	wo	11399	N302WC	11481	XC-VES
11149	N57RS	11231	N115AB	11313	N245CF	11400	N25CE	11482	HS-TFG
11150	N333HC	11232	wfu	11314	HK-3656	11401	N78NA	11483	YV-216AP
11151	wfu	11233	N67TC	11315	N34RT	11402	N345CM	11484	N2141B
11152	VH-CLT	11234	N693VM	11316	N362SH	11403	N11HY	11485	N173DB
11153	N53RF	11235	N1KG	11317	N615DP	11404	N205BN	11486	N94AC
11154	N31DV	11236	LV-LRH	11318	YV-980P	11405	YV-454CP	11487	N690TH*
11155	N690AR	11237	N977DG*	11319	N690GZ	11406	XB-FKC	11488	YV-243CP
11156	wo	11238	LV-LTB	11320	N98PJ	11407	wo	11489	HK-2551P
11157	wo	11239	YV-2317P	11321	ZK-PVB	11408	N79BE	11490	YV-918CP
11158	VH-ATF	11240	F-BXAS	11322	wo	11409	OO-ROB	11491	wo
11159	N690HM	11241	LV-LTC	11323	YV-O-MAR-	11410	XB-DZP	11492	N643JW
11160	N57092	11242	wo	11324	wfu	11411	N690GG	11493	N690RP
11161	N291RB	11243	N677WA	11325	YV-07CP	11412	LV-MBY	11494	3932
11162	N777TE	11244	YV-109CP	11326	wfu	11413	N502DT	11495	N130TT
11163	wo	11245	YV-69CP	11327	N81448	11414	N93ME	11496	wfu
11164	wo	11246	LV-LZL	11328	EC-DXA	11415	N730SS	11497	N81831
11165	HK-3466	11247	wo	11329	YV-950CP	11416	N108SA	11498	wo
11166	N78BA	11248	ZS-JRB	11330	N112EM	11417	XC-JAL	11499	N499WC
11167	N85AB	11249	N723AC	11331	XC-JCT	11418	N555MT	11500	YV-O-FDU
11168	N690CF	11250	11250	11332	N32PP	11419	LV-BNA	11501	N12DE
11169	N38WA	11251	N251ES	11333	5-4037	11420	N60DB	11502	YV-229CP
11170	wfu	11252	N690PT	11334	5-4038	11421	ZS-JRH	11503	XA-...
11171	N690JJ	11253	YV-2593P	11335	wfu	11422	ZS-PFD	11504	XC-TAB
11172	N60B	11254	N24GT	11336	N3WU	11423	N690MG	11505	N36SW
11173	N950M	11255	HK-3314W	11337	N690SM	11424	N38LM	11506	wfu
11174	N66GW	11256	EP-KCD	11338	N222ME	11425	N996AB	11507	wo
11175	N722EJ	11257	XB-HGG	11339	N32WS	11426	N9KG	11508	N690BK
11176	N690WD	11258	LV-LTX	11340	81491	11427	N55WJ	11509	N78TT
11177	N15CD	11259	N425RR	11341	N20BP	11428	N91CT	11510	N1JG

11511	N87WZ	4	N700DE	106	F-ZVMN	188	N704QD	272	N272MA
11512	N400DS	5	N731TM	107	N701LT	190	N700VD	273	N703CA
11513	N690BA	6	N157JB	108	N555HP	191	N706AV	274	N582C
11514	N20MA	7	N138JM	109	N700CS	192	N71EE	275	N702AR
11515	YV-2422P	8	N56WF	110	F-RAXP	193	N700S	276	N700GT
11516	XC-SAH	9	N5HT	111	F-RAXM	194	N19SG	277	N924JP*
11517	N517HP	10	wo	112	N702H	195	HB-KFR	278	N700HY
11518	N25RZ	11	N700BS	113	N700CC	196	N843BH	279	OE-ESK
11519	N425DT	12	EC-FPF	114	PK-CAL	197	N707AV	280	N785MA
11520	N47EP	13	N700MV	115	F-MABQ	198	N700ER	281	N700HL
11521	N7KS	14	N700MX	116	N700ZZ	199	LX-JFD	282	N988C
11522	N84GU	15	N700PU	117	F-RAXN	200	N275CA	283	N700SY
11523	wo	16	N283BS	118	N700VX	201	wo	284	N700EG
11524	N22CK	17	N717Y	119	PK-AHA	202	N724RN	285	N90CP*
11525	HK-3379W	18	wo	120	PK-AHC	203	N700BN	286	N9EE
11526	N691PA	19	C-GBTS	121	PK-CAM	204	N700HN	287	N700EV
11527	N690AC	20	N50ST	122	N461LM	205	VH-ICA	288	D-FKAI
11528	N15SF	21	N708EF	123	N700CF	206	N944CA	289	N700GQ
11529	N690JH	22	N994DF	124	N701MK	207	N356F	290	N700GV
11530	N489GA	23	wo	125	F-RAXO	208	LX-JFE	291	N700EJ
11531	N244MP	24	D-FTAN	126	N701QD	209	N700EL	292	N262J
11532	YV-690P	25	N751J*	127	PH-HUB	210	N700KH	293	N693MA
11533	wo	26	N700SF	128	N63TP	211	N700PW	294	N883CA
11534	XA-SFD	27	N700TJ	129	N703QD	212	LX-JFF	295	N700DZ
11535	N999FG	28	wfu	130	D-FSJP	213	N559CA	296	N700KV
11536	N260WE	29	N708PW	131	F-RAXQ	214	N700WE	297	N700HM
11537	N434CC	30	N715MC	132	N700AN	215	N700PV	298	N700BQ
11538	N777EL	31	N829BC	133	N98NF	216	N702AA	299	PH-CLZ
11539	N729CC	32	F-GLBZ	134	N700DT	217	N700ND	300	N300AZ
11540	N67CG	33	F-RAXA	135	N88U	218	HB-KOL	301	N700CZ
11541	N270DP	34	N8EG	136	F-MABR	219	F-GMLV	302	D-FBFT
11542	N690CH	35	F-RAXB	137	D-FIRE	220	N2WF	303	N210CL
11543	N480K	38	JA8894	138	N198X	221	N700CV	304	N700EK
11544	N690LL	39	wo	139	F-MABS	222	N700YN	305	N700KD*
11545	N32BW	46	N701ES	140	N1421Z	223	C-GITC	306	N557CA
11546	YV-998C	49	N722SR	141	N500FF	224	N9LE	307	N700EZ
11547	YV-2772P	50	N84HS	142	D-FNRE	225	I-AESW	308	N903MA
11548	N29KG	52	N700PK	143	N724DM	226	N226PB	309	N930CA
11549	N444NR	53	N700BF	144	N144JT	227	N700TL	310	N716MA
11550	N690SS	57	N57SL	145	F-GTJM	228	N700KP	311	N700TK
11551	N253JM	59	wo	146	F-RAXR	229	N123ZC	313	N700HD
11552	N37RR	60	N700HK	147	F-RAXS	230	N324JS	314	N702MB
11553	N586DV	61	N661DW	148	N790TB	231	wo	316	N820SM
11554	N107GL	62	wfu	149	N800GS	232	EI-TBM	317	N700ZA
11555	N692T	63	LX-JFA	150	N241TL	233	N700VA	318	N12MA
11556	XC-GAS	67	N62LM	151	N70LT	234	N711PM	319	N319TB
11557	V5-MAC	68	wo	152	N767HP	235	N335MA	320	N700BD
11558	LV-MYA	69	9M-...	153	N4MD	236	N700CT	321	N700ZB
11559	N40SM	70	F-RAXC	154	N435DM	237	N700VB	322	N700ZP
11560	XC-HMO	71	N838RA	155	N321CW	238	N459CA	**Swearingen**	
11561	N690WP	72	N700VM	156	F-MABT	239	N115KC	*Merlin 2A*	
11562	wfu	73	wo	157	D-FALF	240	N811SW	T26-1	wfu
11563	XB-KLY	74	D-FBFS	158	N700KM	241	N700GJ	T26-2	wo
11564	CP-2224	75	N975TB	159	F-MABU	242	N827VG	T26-3	wfu
11565	HP-...	76	wo	160	F-MABV	243	N217DH	T26-4	wfu
11566	N186E	77	F-RAXD	161	N18SR	244	N997JM	T26-5	N201SM
SAAB		78	F-RAXE	162	D-FGYY	245	ZS-TBM*	T26-6	N600P
SAAB 2000		80	F-RAXF	163	N700VJ	246	N700GN	T26-7	N9032H
020	N511RH	82	wo	164	N164PG	247	N15SB	T26-8	wfu
027	N5124	83	N883CR	165	N702QD	248	N220MA	T26-9	N400DG
030	N509RH	84	N228CX	166	F-GZRB	249	N700PX	T26-11	wfu
051	JA003G	85	N650DM*	167	N788RB	250	N700AD	T26-12	wfu
054	JA004G	86	N700LL	168	N709MC	251	N700MK	T26-14	wfu
SAAB 340		87	N700ZR	169	N4920Y	252	N700AQ	T26-15	wfu
022	N340SS	88	N700KL	170	N58HP	253	N700RK	T26-16	wo
029	N184K	89	N5BR	171	D-FBOY	254	N700AZ	T26-17	wfu
036	ZS-ABM	90	N57HQ	172	N700WS	255	N700GE	T26-18	wfu
050	N44KS	91	N700WT	173	N22WZ	256	N700TB	T26-19	C-FSVC
170	100001	92	VH-KFT	174	N700QD	257	N700SL	T26-20	C-GLKA
385	JA8951	93	F-RAXL	175	N700WK	258	OH-KJJ	T26-21	wfu
405	JA8952	94	F-RAXG	176	N700CB	259	N459MA	T26-22	wfu
431	100006	95	F-RAXH	177	N702GS	260	N700XS	T26-23	wfu
Socata		96	N767CW	178	N888TF	261	N181PC	T26-24	N1207S
TBM 700		97	N300AE	179	N701AV	262	N700BK	T26-25	N1208S
01	F-WTBM	98	N700SP	180	N700VP	263	N263CW	T26-26	N269PM
1	N755PG	99	F-MABO	181	N721SR	264	N700JD	T26-27	N1210S
02	F-WKPG	100	F-MABP	182	N702AV	265	N6720Y	T26-28	wfu
2	N702BM	101	N755DM	183	N770DC	266	N700CL	T26-29	N187Z
03	F-WKDL	102	N88WF	184	N527TS	267	N700FT	T26-30	wfu
3	HB-KEI	103	F-RAXI	185	N700AU	268	N700PT	T26-31	wo
		104	F-RAXJ	186	D-FIVE	270	N700LF	T26-32	C-FANF
		105	F-RAXK	187	N769JS	271	N700DQ		

T26-33	N121KB	T26-171E	C-GRBF	T-270	N226SR	T-388	5A-DJB	AT-040	wo
T26-34	wfu	T26-172	N742GR	T-271	4X-CIZ	T-391	N391GM	AT-041	EC-GBI
T26-35	wfu	T26-172E	C-FCAW	T-272	wo	T-394	N59EZ	AT-042	wo
T26-36	wo	T26-173	N22NR	T-273	N463DC	T-397	N38TA	AT-043	wo
Merlin 2B		T26-174	wo	T-274	C-FAMF	T-400	N350MC	AT-044	TC-UPS
T26-100	N333F	T26-175	YV-...	T-275	AE-176	T-403	wo	AT-051	TU-TOG
T26-101	N669SP	T26-176	N1907W	T-276	N132CW	T-405	N120TM	AT-057	N31AT
T26-102	wfu	T26-177	wo	T-277	wo	T-407	N111AB	AT-058	I-NARW
T26-103	N171PC	T26-178	N717PD	T-278	N303MA	T-410	N299EC	AT-062	EC-GFK
T26-104	wfu	T26-179	wo	T-279	N34SM	T-414	N379JG	AT-062E	wo
T26-105	N345T	T26-180E	N1039Y	T-280	AE-178	T-417	N12MF	AT-063	AE-181
T26-106	N370X	**Merlin 3/3A/3B**		T-281	AE-179	**Merlin 3C**		AT-064	AE-182
T26-107	N158CA	T-201	wo	T-282	XA-...	T-303E	wo	AT-064E	OB-1146
T26-108	N480BC	T-202	N103PA	T-283	N5441M	TT-421	N75X	AT-065	wo
T26-109	N1221S	T-203	N97AB	T-284	N154L	TT-424	N266M	AT-066	C-FTIX
T26-110	wo	T-204	VH-SSM	T-285	N636SP	TT-426A	N2GL	AT-067	N120SC
T26-111	wfu	T-205	N970M	T-286	N226DD	TT-428A	N444LB	AT-068	N836MA
T26-112	N7603	T-205E	wfu	T-287	YV-693CP	TT-431	N431S	AT-069	C-GDEF
T26-113	HP-1136AP	T-206	N46NA	T-288	HP-1069	TT-433	N123LH	AT-071	60501
T26-114	N963BP	T-207	wo	T-289	N104TA	TT-435	YV-808CP	AT-071E	AE-180
T26-115	N50KV	T-208	N269DE	T-290	N75RM	TT-438	N53DA	AT-072	60502
T26-116	N96RL	T-209	wo	T-291	N800LD	TT-441	N125RG	AT-073	60503
T26-117	N802DJ	T-210	VH-SSL	T-292	N262SA	TT-444	N227TT	AT-074	EC-HBF
T26-118	N12WC	T-211	wo	T-293	F-GGVG	TT-447	YV-...	**Merlin 4C**	
T26-119	wfu	T-212	N222MV	T-294	PH-DYB	TT-450	N99JW	AT-423	F-GHVF
T26-120	wfu	T-213	VH-SSD	T-295	wo	TT-453	N31JV	AT-427	N629TG
T26-121	wfu	T-214	wo	T-296	wo	TT-456	YV-740CP	AT-434	HZ-SN8
T26-122	C-GBZM	T-215	wo	T-297	N111CZ	TT-459A	YV-292CP	AT-439	wo
T26-123	N872S	T-216	wo	T-298	F-GLPT	TT-462A	ZP-...	AT-440B	D-CBIN
T26-124	N4051X	T-217	N224HR	T-299	N512FS	TT-465	YV-...	AT-446	N573G
T26-125	wfu	T-218	N75MX	T-300	N699RK*	TT-468	YV-612CP	AT-452	N45MW
T26-126	wo	T-219	wo	T-301	YV-710CP	TT-471	YV-472CP	AT-454	N807M
T26-127	wfu	T-220	N14TP	T-302	wo	TT-474	VH-RCI	AT-461	N120FA
T26-128	wo	T-221	N22EQ	T-303	N96VC	TT-477	6O-SBV	AT-464	N313D
T26-129	N100SN	T-222	wfu	T-304	N48HH	TT-480	N81WS	AT-469	wo
T26-130	wfu	T-223	N263CM	T-305	wfu	TT-483A	N795TB	AT-492	N8897Y
T26-131	N1YC	T-224	N550BE	T-306	N226FC	TT-486A	N1MN	AT-493	D-CNAY
T26-132	N72CF	T-225	wo	T-307	N307PA	TT-489	N888AY	AT-495B	N851BC
T26-133	wfu	T-226	N70FC	T-308	N50MT	TT-507	YV-....	AT-501	N999MX
T26-134	wo	T-227	N555AM	T-309	N999MM	TT-512A	D-IBHL	AT-502	VH-UZA
T26-135	N213SC	T-228	N290TA	T-310	N49H	TT-515	YV-652CP	AT-506	N370AE
T26-136	N137CP	T-229	N78CS	T-311	N96954	TT-518	N213PA	AT-511	D-CCCC
T26-137	wo	T-230	wo	T-312	N84GA	TT-521	YV-262CP	AT-532	YV-...
T26-138	N73HC	T-231	N46SA	T-313	N326MS	TT-527	wo	AT-539	wfu
T26-139	N469BL	T-232	LV-WIR	T-314	N814SS	TT-529	D-IMWK	AT-544	N544UP
T26-140	N321PH	T-233	N300PT	T-315	N50LG	TT-534	N90GT	AT-548	N548UP
T26-140E	wo	T-234	N101MC	T-316	N616PS	TT-536	N17VV	AT-549	N471CD
T26-141	wfu	T-235	N45818	T-317	N22DW	TT-541	N112CS	AT-556	N556UP
T26-142	YV-....	T-236	N5317M	T-318	OE-FOW	**Merlin 4**		AT-557	wfu
T26-143	LV-RZB	T-237	N633ST	T-319	N601JT	AT-002	C-GTMW	AT-560	N560UP
T26-144	N558AC	T-238	XC-HFA	T-320	HK-2479W	AT-003	wfu	AT-561	N561UP
T26-145	N34UA	T-239	C-GPRO	T-321	N1014V	AT-003E	wfu	AT-563	VH-EEN
T26-146	wo	T-240	N240NM	T-322	D-IDEA	AT-004	N55CE	AT-564	VH-EEO
T26-147	wo	T-241	N23AE	T-323	N329HS	AT-005	wo	AT-566	N566UP
T26-148	N200MH	T-242	wo	T-324	wfu	AT-006	N4679K	AT-567	VH-EEP
T26-149	EC-GJZ	T-243	wo	T-325	N100CE	AT-007	HZ-SN6	AT-568	wo
T26-149E	N846BB	T-244	N244SA	T-326	N300AL	AT-008	wo	AT-569	N569UP
T26-150	N457G	T-245	N4209S	T-327	N1007B	AT-009	N479VK	AT-570	VH-UZI
T26-151	N396PS	T-246	N43CB	T-328	XB-EFZ	AT-010	wfu	AT-577	N120JM
T26-152	N939C	T-247	wfu	T-329	N405SA	AT-011	N750AA	AT-585	N919CK
T26-153	N4262X	T-248	OH-ADA	T-330	N113GS	AT-012	F-GERP	AT-591	N505FS
T26-154	N20KV	T-249	N777HZ	T-331	N331GM	AT-013	wfu	AT-602B	N240DH
T26-154E	wfu	T-250	N125WG*	T-332	N46KC	AT-014	N4019	AT-607B	N241DH
T26-155	wfu	T-251	wfu	T-336	wo	AT-015	wo	AT-608B	N242DH
T26-156	N30HS	T-252	N600DL	T-339	N15CN	AT-016	JA8828	AT-609B	N243DH
T26-157	N20EF	T-253	HK-....	T-341	wfu	AT-017	C-GPCL	AT-618B	N244DH
T26-158	XA-...	T-254	N25677	T-342	LN-SFT	AT-018	N427SP	AT-624B	N245DH
T26-158E	N8KT	T-255	D-INWK	T-345	5A-DHZ	AT-020	I-NARB	AT-625B	N246DH
T26-159	N66MD	T-256	N699KM	T-348	wfu	AT-025	wo	AT-626B	N247DH
T26-160	wfu	T-257	N39MS	T-351	wfu	AT-027	N582JF	AT-630B	N248DH
T26-161	N669HS	T-258	N772SL	T-354	N200SN	AT-028	C-GWSL	AT-631B	N249DH
T26-162	N30TF	T-259	LX-NOP	T-357	YV-242CP	AT-029	N78CP	AT-695B	N762VM
T26-163	wo	T-260	LX-RSO	T-360	N387CC	AT-030	N69ST		
T26-163E	wo	T-261	wo	T-363	N779M	AT-031	F-GMTO		
T26-164	N36PE	T-262	wo	T-366	N500SX	AT-032	N44GL		
T26-165	N160EA	T-263	wo	T-369	N901MC	AT-033	wo		
T26-166	wfu	T-264	F-GZJM	T-372	N1010V	AT-034	N54GP		
T26-167	N400DC	T-265	LX-NRJ	T-375	N800MM	AT-035	I-NARC		
T26-167E	N2303P	T-266	N9900	T-378	N98UC	AT-036	LV-WNC		
T26-168	wo	T-267	LX-PIX	T-381	N95AC	AT-037	N202WS		
T26-169	N22GW	T-268	N502WC	T-384	YV-770CP	AT-038	SX-BGT		
T26-170	wfu	T-269	wo	T-387	N36LC	AT-039	N727DP